ALSO BY PENELOPE LEACH

Your Baby & Child: From Birth to Age Five (1978)

Babyhood (1974, 1983)

THESE ARE BORZOI BOOKS
PUBLISHED IN NEW YORK
BY ALFRED A. KNOPF

THE CHILD CARE ENCYCLOPEDIA

Penelope Leach

THE CHILD CARE
ENCYCLOPEDIA

*A Parents' Guide to the Physical
and Emotional Well-Being of Children
from Birth Through Adolescence*

ALFRED A. KNOPF   NEW YORK   1984

THIS IS A BORZOI BOOK
PUBLISHED BY ALFRED A. KNOPF, INC.

Library of Congress Cataloging in Publication Data
Leach, Penelope.
The child care encyclopedia.
1. Child rearing—Dictionaries. I. Title.
HQ769.L326   1984   649'.1'0321   83–48013
ISBN 0-394-52532-9

Manufactured in the United States of America
First American Edition

*To the doctors, nurses and supporting staff of the
James Wigg Practice, Kentish Town Health Centre,
who make parent/professional teamwork in child care
a daily reality rather than just an ideal.*

This book touches on many matters which fall within the province of the general practitioner. I have naturally been concerned that information and advice concerning diagnosis and treatment should be not only accurate in content but also acceptable in tone to members of the medical profession. I am therefore extremely grateful to Dr. Michael Modell, FRCGP, MRCP, DCH, and to Dr. Alia Antoon, DCH, for their kindness, time and care in reading and commenting on the relevant portions of the manuscript.

I must stress, however, that responsibility for the opinions and interpretations presented here remains my own.

Penelope Leach
1983

Contents

What this book is for and how to use it

Since the publication of *Your Baby and Child* many kind users have written to ask for "something similar which deals with older children as well." At first I thought the commission was impossible because as children grow older more and more of their important experiences are linked not to home and parents but to school, community and friends. Every person, every family and every environment is not only unique in itself but unique in its combinations and effects, so that to write about eleven-year-olds as if they were all the same is even dicier than generalizing about "toddlers."

But as the letters went on arriving I began to see that while all the *people* in families are, of course, unique, the *issues which concern them* are not. Despite the vast differences between a single-parent family and a partnership, both have to serve meals, cope with measles, choose schools and make decisions about when to call the doctor. A family with just one six-month-old baby faces different risks from a family with three schoolchildren. Yet both must give thought to their children's safety and cope with any accidents that do occur. Money, employment, housing and the availability of relations and friends all affect family life. But both the most and the least privileged families have to decide how to allocate among their various members whatever resources are available. Finally, however much one family may differ from another, parents all share one overriding concern: we want our children to be healthy and happy. We all strive to keep them so and when things go wrong we want to be sure that we have thought of everything that might improve the situation. Every baby, toddler, child and adolescent is a unique person, yet each has to follow the same broad and winding path from birth to maturity. Every parent is a unique person, too, yet each will meet some of a range of similar experiences and issues, problems and pleasures, as his or her children grow. This book does not therefore try to follow a "typical" or "average" child through all the years he or she spends within the family but rather tries to pool those common experiences and concerns and set out those issues and problems so that individual parents can use them in their own thinking and coping, in any way which fits their particular circumstances.

The entries in this book are all arranged in alphabetical order. There is a contents page but no index. You simply look up the topic that you want, knowing that **Allergy** will come before **Anxiety** and that both will come before **Hospital** or **Play** or **Sleep**.

Wherever it makes sense that way, the material within each entry is arranged alphabetically, too. If you look up **Accidents**, for example, you will find that Burns comes before Head injuries and Sprains come before Wounds. Sometimes, though, this is not a sensible way to organize the material and you will find an age-ordering instead. **Eating**, for example, begins with babies and has a fair amount to say about weaning, feeding problems and toddlers before it goes on to discuss family eating.

Whatever topic you want to look up, you have to choose a word to look under just as I have had to choose a word to write under. I hope we shall usually have chosen the same words so that you will find what you want at the first try. Where several names were obviously possible I have only written under one of them, but you will find yourself directed from yours to mine. If you look up **Height**, for example, it will say "*see* **Growth**." If you look up **Enuresis** it will say "*see* **Bedwetting**." If the word you look up simply does not appear, try thinking of other common names for the same subject; one of them will be there—I hope.

Sometimes when you look up a topic you will find the material you were looking for but you will also find the suggestion that you "*see also* . . ." the material under another heading. This simply means that there is more discussion on the same, or a closely related topic in another article. Electric shock, for example, is described and discussed under **Accidents** /Electric shock but it suggests that you see also **Safety**/Electricity because if you are interested in how to cope with electric shock it's a reasonable guess that you might be interested in how to prevent it, too.

Although many of the entries are designed to help with immediate problems, many more are meant to contribute to the kind of thinking and family discussion which will help to avoid problems. I hope that you will look things up whenever they seem interesting to you rather than only when you are frantic. **Eating**, for example, is an interesting subject for everyone and some of the material under that heading might help you to avoid the need to look up entries on feeding problems or overweight or Anorexia Nervosa. Every child has to learn to behave, at every successive age-stage, in ways which his or her parents—and other people—find acceptable. Don't wait until your child is accused of theft or bullying, or stays out until 2 a.m. for the third night in a row, to look at **Discipline, Self-discipline and Learning How to Behave**. It raises issues which are more usefully discussed from earliest childhood. Hopefully there will be many periods during which there are no problems within the family. You may still find entries like **Play** are useful and fun, that entries like **Pets** or **Pocket Money** contribute to family discussions, or that some of the material in **School** or **Adolescence** helps you to think ahead.

The whole book is aimed at supporting you in helping your children to grow from wherever they are now towards being healthy, happy adults. As they reach middle childhood—and particularly once they pass puberty—you may find that there are entries which you would like them to read for themselves. **Safety**/On wheels, for example, might help if you have reached a stalemate over bicycles, motorcycles or cars, while many of the issues discussed under **Adolescence** might provide a useful starting point for discussion, whether or not you agree with what is written.

THE CHILD CARE
ENCYCLOPEDIA

Abdominal Pain *see also* **Pain and Pain Control; Hospital**/Surgery: Appendectomy

Abdominal pain (or "stomachache" or "tummyache" as your child may call it) may be your first warning of a real emergency or it may mean nothing important at all. Experience as a parent and knowledge of your own child will help you to draw the fine line between unnecessary midnight calls on your doctor and neglect of the pain which does turn out to be due to appendicitis. . . . In the meantime, or with any child who is not your own, play safe. The abdominal cavity runs from the chest (from which it is separated by the muscular wall called the diaphragm) to the pelvis. It contains all the organs concerned with digestion and excretion, not just the stomach but also the liver, gallbladder, pancreas, spleen, kidneys and bladder. It contains yards and yards of large and small intestine and, in females, it contains the uterus (womb), ovaries and fallopian tubes. With so many vital organs and processes grouped together it is often difficult for the victim to say exactly where the pain is and impossible for anyone but a skilled doctor to judge whether or not something is seriously amiss. You certainly need medical advice if:

Abdominal pain is accompanied by other signs of illness such as fever, loss of appetite/energy/interest, poor color, vomiting and/or diarrhea.

Pain is the only symptom but is severe enough to take the child's whole attention so that she cannot play, watch television, listen to or read a book.

Pain, even if less severe, lasts for more than a few hours at a level which keeps interrupting the child's activities; although she tries to go on with her ordinary life she cannot do so for more than a few minutes at a time.

● When you have to assess abdominal pain in your child, don't let your judgment be swayed by old wives' tales. For example, eating underripe fruit or too much ice cream, eating too fast or drinking while eating are *not* likely causes for the pain. If a child has eaten so unwisely that she really does "make herself sick" she certainly needs a doctor rather than cries of "I told you so . . . ." It is more likely that she is suffering from some form of food poisoning than from sheer gluttony. "Chills in the stomach" and "colds in the kidneys" are folk ailments rather than real diagnoses, while ordinary constipation does not cause pain.

● Be very cautious about the home treatment of abdominal pain. Most pain relievers, for example, irritate the stomach lining. If the stomach itself is the site of the pain, they may make matters worse. If the pain stems from elsewhere the drugs may simply add stomach discomfort to the child's distress. Antacids and "stomach medicines" should not be given without a doctor's approval either. They will probably have no effect at all but they might mask and confuse other symptoms. Laxatives and enemas should *never* be given to a child with abdominal pain. If the pain were due to blockage or muscle spasm somewhere in the intestine, the increased intestinal activity caused by the medicine could be disastrous. If you feel that you must do *something* for the pain, go to the doctor's office or the telephone rather than to the medicine cabinet.

Babies and abdominal pain

Since your baby cannot tell you that her stomach hurts you will probably deduce it from the fact that she screams and draws her bent legs up. Remember that babies do this when they are crying from anger, too, and that a baby who cries hard for a long time may make her stomach uncomfortable by swallowing a lot of air. Unless she seems ill, it is worth trying to comfort her with your cheerful presence and cuddling before declaring an emergency.

If nothing you can do will comfort her, she probably does need help. Some babies cry more than others, but healthy ones seldom continue to cry while being held by loved adults. Refusal to be comforted is therefore a worrying symptom.

Colic

A few babies between about three and sixteen weeks of age suffer from what is usually described as "three-month" or "evening" colic. Each day, usually after an early evening feeding, she is unable to play or settle down peacefully to sleep because of what appear to be recurrent bouts of abdominal pain. Left in her crib she screams piteously; picked up she stops but starts again as you hold her. Offered more milk she sucks hard for a moment or two but then stops to yell once more. Everything you do for her seems to help a little for a little while but nothing relieves her completely or for long, until the episode is over for the day as suddenly as it began.

A severe attack of this kind of colic mimics an abdominal emergency so that you will probably call the doctor and find it difficult to believe him when he tells you that there is nothing at all the matter with the baby. You may even feel that he is implying that the whole upset was somehow your fault; that you failed to bring up the baby's wind or that you were tense and hurried when you fed her or tired at the end of a long day and distracted by the return home of other members of the family. Accept his basic reassurance for the moment, but if the pattern of distress is repeated on the next two evenings, seek an appointment at which you can discuss the colic peacefully with him. Evening colic is not an illness; it does not suggest that there is anything wrong with the baby. But it is an exceedingly distressing phenomenon both for her and for you. It is thought to be due to immaturity of the digestive system resulting in extra activity and muscular spasm in the baby's intestines. Although she will certainly "grow out of it" during this first quarter year you are entitled to help and support while she does so. Some doctors prescribe a particular drug which reduces the mobility and muscular spasms of the colon. If this medicine, given half an hour before the feeding which precedes regular colic, is going to work for your baby, it will do so almost like magic, ending the whole problem. If it does not work, your doctor may feel that the baby is not suffering from evening colic after all. He may want to double-check for signs of illness and to discuss in detail her overall care and feeding.

• No other medicine is generally thought to be helpful in true evening colic. If your doctor does not wish to prescribe for your baby's colic, or if prescribed medicine does not help, don't dose her with anything else without his specific instructions. Particularly avoid over-the-counter remedies for colic. In some countries some of these contain undesirable sedatives including alcohol.

Small children and abdominal pain

Very small children find it even more difficult than the rest of us to localize pain. Yours may tell you that her tummy hurts when she has a middle-ear infection. Some common infections, such as tonsillitis, can produce genuine abdominal pain in the very young by affecting glands around the wall of the stomach. The child's attention may be focused on her abdomen even though the site of infection is in her throat which, in an older child, would be very painful. To make confusion worse, many small children cannot distinguish (or at least cannot report the difference) between abdominal pain and nausea. Your child may complain of tummyache when she is about to vomit.

With children in this age group it is therefore doubly important to avoid home diagnosis in favor of immediate consultation with your doctor.

Mild but long-lasting abdominal pain

If a "stomachache" is not severe enough to distress your child or worry you but nevertheless continues to be mentioned over several days, it is worth making an appointment for her to see the doctor because there are a variety of disorders which can present themselves in this way. She may have a mild urinary infection even if there are no obvious symptoms such as acute pain when she passes water. An older girl may have pre-menstrual pain even if she has not yet had her first period (*see* **Adolescence**/Menstruation); her body may be reacting to the hormonal preliminaries. Some mild food allergies show themselves in this way (*see* **Allergy**) and so do various forms of digestive difficulty including the excessive intestinal activity which is usually labelled the "irritable bowel syndrome."

Recurrent abdominal pain

Some children suffer from recurrent bouts of abdominal pain which, after proper examination and investigation by a doctor, turn out to have no abnormal *physical* cause but to be associated with stress and anxiety in the child. In some sufferers pain is the only symptom; in others the pain is associated with vomiting and occasionally with fever as well.

The causes of this kind of pain are not completely understood and probably vary from child to child. The following factors may contribute:

Small children tend to have a lot of attention focused on stomach and bowels especially if there are eating/toilet training battles going on. If she has anxious attention focused on the workings of her "insides," the child may become unusually aware of the wave-like movements of her intestines which normally stay beneath the level of consciousness but which she may feel as pain.

Emotion always affects digestion, with stress and anxiety actually increasing the blood supply and the strength of the peristaltic waves. A "strung-up" child therefore receives stronger signals from her stomach and bowels and may notice them as pain.

The reason for stress/abdominal pain may be specific to the child's life. Some, for example, always have the pain on Monday mornings during the school year but not on vacations; others have their regular outings with a separated parent ruined by the pain. A few react in this way to any socially stressful occasion so that they can go out for a snack quite happily but always have pain before a more formal party.

The reason for stress/abdominal pain may lie in the child's personality. A significantly large number of such children have exceedingly high standards of behavior and performance, being "good students," "highly responsible children" and "a child any parent would be proud of." Often the parents are indeed proud and the family is apparently happy. But the stress of successfully meeting such high expectations may take a toll on the child which neither she nor her parents fully realize.

Help with recurrent abdominal pain

Obviously a doctor must see the child and only when physical causes for the pain have been excluded can the diagnosis be made. When it is made though, the child will need:

An authoritative assurance from the doctor that there is nothing physically wrong with her body. This is vital. Pain is a worrying symptom (it is meant to be; it could not operate as a bodily warning system if it did not worry its victims) and a child is just as capable as an adult of brooding secretly about horrors like cancer. . . .

An equally authoritative explanation of the probable mechanism by which the pain is produced. The more convinced the child can be that she is noticing peristaltic waves which go on all the time in everyone but which most people do not feel, the easier it will become for her to ignore them.

A direct and genuine acknowledgment from doctor and parents that the pain is real, in the sense that they believe that she feels it and that it is unpleasant. All too often pain of non-physical origin gets labelled "imaginary," as if the poor victim was inventing a story to get sympathy and attention. She is not and she must be sure that nobody thinks she is.

Every possible attempt to lower the tensions she is under. How this is done must obviously depend on her exact circumstances. You cannot send a new baby back because he is causing stress in an older child's life, but you may be able to help her accept him and believe that she still has your secure love and care. A child cannot stop going to school because she finds it stressful, but she may need help from the teacher, help with a too difficult trip, rescue from a subtle playground bully or even a different school. You may not want her to give up all social life just because the prospect of a party makes her throw up, but you might be able and willing to arrange more informal get-togethers with her real friends and let her off the birthday parties for a while. The point, of course, is that once you dissect the occasions which your child finds very stressful, you can usually find a way of helping her to cope rather than to opt out.

● Once you know that your child is liable to recurrent abdominal pain of non-physical origin, you obviously will not consult a doctor every time it occurs. Do be watchful, though, because such a child is not immune from physical causes. If you are too quick to assume that every stomachache is "her nerves again," you may be dangerously slow to recognize the pain which is actually due to appendicitis. Every episode must be considered on its merits and, for a child with a pattern of recurrent pain, a pain which is different from usual should make you suspicious.

Abrasions *see* **Accidents**/Cuts and scrapes, grazes and puncture wounds.
Abscess *see* **Infection**/Types of infection: Localized infection.
Accident-prone children *see* **Depression**/In children before puberty; **Hyperactive Children**.

Accidents *see also* **Safety**

Although many accidents are preventable many are not. Everyone will experience minor hurts in the course of everyday life; most people will occasionally experience something more serious. A child who is so well protected that he or she never has *any* kind of accident is probably overprotected, deprived of a rightful ration of adventurous endeavor. It is important to believe this because if you are overwhelmed with guilt every time one of your children is hurt, you will not be competent to judge the seriousness of the situation, to give sensible first aid or to offer appropriate comfort. All these things need calm common sense.

Calm is particularly important when a baby or very small child is hurt. Such a child does not have the experience or memory to measure the pain, shock, surprise and anger he is feeling. He feels the pain and reacts to it, but he will take his cue as to the *importance* of that pain from your reaction. If you are frightened for him, he will be frightened for himself. If your sympathy is tempered by quiet assurance that the whole matter is trivial, he will stay calmer this time and gradually learn that the pain of a banged knee is something which can be quickly shrugged off.

At around four to six or seven, many children go through a phase during which they are disproportionately alarmed by minor accidents. Such a child, newly conscious of his or her own body and its importance as "my own self," may be fearful not so much of pain but of actual bodily *damage*. There may be fantasies of being "broken" or "spoiled." During such a phase a child may be unable to forget about an injury while he can actually see blood or grazed skin. A Band-Aid is often needed to restore morale even when the actual injury is too minor to require any treatment. You may also be able to give the child some direct and general reassurance by explaining the body's self-healing powers ("When that scab falls off in a day or two there'll be nice new skin underneath and you won't even be able to see where it happened"). Try to avoid alarming statements like "That's going to leave a nasty scar" or "I think your poor arm is broken."

In some communities, slightly older boys still suffer from the kind of sex discrimination which says that "boys don't cry" and labels them "sissy" if they do. In public you will have to help your son to behave as *he wants* to behave—he will not thank you for fussing over him in front of his friends—but in private don't encourage phony ideas about "manliness."

Older children—certainly by adolescence—need to be able to cope with minor accidents, whether to themselves or to other people. Try to share with them the "hunch" which makes you take the four-year-old to a hospital for this head injury when you did not do so when he banged his head last week. Try also to let them decide whether their own strains need resting and be the ones who dress your minor cuts. This kind of competence is both practically useful and psychologically important. In a couple of years they will want to go off on camping trips and so forth without adults and they will need to be able to cope. They are far more likely to *feel* able to cope if "squeamishness" has never been expected of them.

Coping with minor injuries

Most everyday cuts, scrapes and bumps do not need any medical treatment at all. Bodies are efficient at healing themselves and can often do so best if they are not interfered with. Antiseptic creams, for example, are usually worse than useless. They are useless because the chemicals they contain are not powerful enough to kill any harmful bacteria which might be around the wound; chemicals which were that powerful would damage the healthy tissue, too. And they are worse than useless because they can prevent the formation of a scab which is the body's own, highly efficient, wound dressing.

But even if an injury does not require medical treatment, there may be something which you can do to make the sufferer more comfortable during the healing process. Wounds can be protected so that clothes do not rub them, for example. And you may be able to provide psychological comfort, too: a child who has hurt himself often feels better if somebody appears to be doing something about it.

While you are doing that "something"—even if it is only putting a scrape under running water to remove the visible dirt—you can be doing the most important thing of all: making sure that the injury really *is* trivial. If a wound is going to need medical attention, it is far better that the attention should be sought immediately. If a cut needs stitching, for example, it must be done that same day. If you wait until the next day to decide that it is gaping open and will not close on its own, the edges of the wound will have begun to heal and stitching will no longer be possible.

For minor injuries, then, the questions are: Is there anything to be done to make the child more comfortable? And: am I sure that there is nothing seriously wrong here?

Coping with multiple minor injuries

Some injuries which would be trivial if they occurred singly can be quite serious if they occur all at once. A few pricks on a hand, for example, are nothing more than a painful nuisance, but pricks all over, following a fall into a prickly patch by a child wearing only a pair of shorts can be a very different matter. In the same way, a small bruise is trivial, but bruising over a large area of the body can be extremely serious. It is important, then, to consider how much of the child's body is affected and not to assume that a bruise is a bruise is a bruise.

Coping with more serious injuries

First aid should be exactly what the term suggests: the help that you give *first* before getting the injured child to professional help. That first aid should consist only of things that you do to try to ensure that the child's injuries and his general condition do not *worsen* in the meantime. If he has a deep and obviously dirty wound, for example, it is cruel interference to clean, disinfect and bandage it before you leave for the hospital. The moment you get him there, the staff will take off all your careful handiwork and do it all again, better. He suffers the whole process twice and a delay in the bargain. Lay a clean linen or cotton handkerchief over the wound so that he need not look at it, and leave it all to them. In the same way, once you are certain that he is hurt badly enough to require a doctor's attention, it is not your business to try to discover exactly what his injuries are. If he has *either* fractured his collar bone *or* dislocated his shoulder, your attempts to discover which—by making him wiggle his fingers, bend his elbow and so on—are pointless torment. What does it matter whether you know what is wrong? You know that something is. Diagnosis is for the professionals.

Occasionally first aid will actually save a life. You will find such dramatic events fully written out below. More often, first aid will ensure that a child reaches the hospital in better shape than he would have done without it. Those events are also fully written out.

In all other circumstances your job is confined to recognizing that an injury is, or may be, serious, and getting the child to professional help as quickly and as comfortably as possible.

If a child is unconscious or semiconscious

The **"recovery position"** will ease the job of his heart and lungs, ensure that his tongue cannot drop back so as to obstruct his breathing and guard him against breathing in any blood or vomit. When you have carried out any other appropriate first aid measures, put him in this position while you wait for the ambulance or other help. If you have to go in search of help, this is the safest way to leave him.

● Although the "recovery position" is ideal for the child's general condition you will have to adapt it to any obvious injuries. Above all, use your best judgment about moving him into it if there is any likelihood of damage to his spine (*see below* Head injuries).

Lay him on his tummy with his head well turned to one side. It should be turned far enough for his ear to be flat on the ground.

Gently bend the arm which he is facing, at the elbow. The hand should lie at about the level of his face.

Gently bend the leg on the same side, drawing it up until the foot is about level with the opposite thigh.

If a child seems to be dead

Mouth-to-mouth resuscitation, possibly with heart massage, might revive him when nothing else will do so. Even when these measures do not restart spontaneous breathing and heartbeat, they can mechanically ensure that the heart goes on circulating blood and that the lungs go on oxygenating that blood. In this way the child's brain can be protected by minimal supplies of oxygen until expert help arrives to try full-scale resuscitation.

These techniques need to be taught and demonstrated. If you ever need to use them, on your own child or on somebody else's, you will have no time to try to follow instructions and diagrams from a book which you will not have with you, in any case.

Try to learn them before your first child passes babyhood. Your nearest Red Cross or hospital will give CPR courses.

Try to have them taught to your own children before they are old enough to go adventuring without adults.

● If all parents both learned, and ensured that their children learned, these life-saving techniques, almost the whole population could become proficient within two generations. There is no doubt that some lives would be saved.

Bites and stings

Animal bites

In theory, every animal bite should be seen by a doctor; in practice, the small superficial wound made by a guinea pig or other small mammal requires no treatment other than washing. Bites from larger animals such as dogs and cats are a different matter:

If a dog bite makes a puncture wound

Immediate medical attention is important. That dog's tooth makes a hole which is very likely to carry harmful bacteria, including tetanus (*see below* Cuts and scrapes, grazes and puncture wounds).

If more than one tooth bit deeply

The wound will probably be ragged as well as liable to infection or serious bleeding; it will need careful dressing (and perhaps stitching) if a bad scar is to be avoided. Such a bite will also have bruised the tissues as a dog's teeth are not as sharp as a nail or knife. It will be painful. A child who has been attacked will probably also be very frightened.

First aid for animal bites

Speak extremely sharply, with downright amazement in your voice, to the animal. You want to convey to the bitten child that this attack was an extraordinary happening and not at all what he need expect from other animals. Run plenty of cold water into and over the wound. Cover with a sterile gauze dressing. To control bleeding, place direct pressure on the wound. Take the child to the doctor or hospital.

If there is rabies in your area

Animal bites have to be taken even more seriously, especially bites from bats, raccoons, and opossum. If this is a risk your family has to live with, or if you are going to travel to an area where rabies is prevalent, you must understand it (*see* **Rabies**).

Action after an animal bite

An animal which is liable to bite is not fit to be around children (*see* **Safety**/In the home: Safety and pets). Unless the attack was seriously provoked or more or less accidental, you may want to take action, whether the animal belongs to you or to someone else.

The bitten child may be nervous of animals after the accident (*see* **Anxiety, Fears and Phobias**). He should certainly not be expected to socialize with that same animal without concentrated adult supervision, but the more he can understand why things went wrong and therefore understand that all other animals need not be tarred with the same brush, the better.

Insect bites

Whether it is a mosquito or a flea which bites your child the local skin reaction will be similar: some swelling, some redness and some itching. Swelling is most dramatic where the skin is loose and/or richly supplied with blood vessels. A single mosquito bite near the eye, for example, can swell so that the eye is almost closed.

Prevention is the best treatment. Long-sleeved T-shirts and trousers will do something to protect a child. If he is playing in long grass or a haybarn, socks will help too. Even an insect repellent, applied and renewed according to the instructions, will do something to protect him.

If you want peaceful nights on a vacation in a mosquito-prone area and season, take large pieces of fine gauze and thumbtacks in your luggage. If insect screens are not provided they are easy to improvise.

First aid for insect bites   Cold water compresses will often reduce both swelling and itching. Calamine lotion will reduce itching at least for a few minutes (perhaps for long enough for the child to get back to sleep). An anti-histamine cream, sold for the purpose, may also help but should be used only occasionally and over small skin areas.

Insect stings   Bee and wasp stings can be painful and usually frighten a child even more than the pain merits because she feels "attacked." Many children are frightened of these flying, buzzing insects anyway, even if they have never been stung.

First aid for insect stings   Calm the child, explaining that the pain she feels is the very worst that she is going to feel. You will probably be able to see the location of the sting as a tiny puncture with a very small raised red circle around it. If you see the stinger in that central hole, quickly remove it. The sac should not be squeezed, rubbed, scratched or grasped because these manipulations cause release of more venom. Scraping the stinger with tweezers or a fingernail minimizes venom flow from the sac. Prompt application of ice packs to the stinger site will slow down absorption and relieve the itching, swelling and pain. After removing the stinger, wash the area with soap and water. Zinc oxide or calamine lotion may be applied to reduce the oozing and control some of the itching.

Larger insects—such as the hornet—can inflict a sting which is acutely painful for an hour or more. Of course you will be sorry for the child, but you need not worry about her as long as the reaction to the sting is purely a local skin reaction.

Stings requiring medical help   A sting in the mouth of an unfortunate child who bites a wasp along with her bread and jam *can* cause enough swelling to obstruct breathing. With a baby or very young child it is probably wise to seek medical help for any sting in the mouth. With an older child who can cooperate by sucking an ice cube (or ice cream) and opening her mouth to let you see what is happening, you can probably wait and see. If there is scarcely any swelling after twenty minutes, there will not be. If swelling is still increasing after twenty minutes, seek help.

A few children are allergic to the stings of bees, wasps and hornets. If yours is one, you will know at once because her reaction to the sting will not just be a local skin reaction but also a generalized reaction which makes her feel ill, short of breath and shocked. This is an emergency. Take her as fast as possible to the very nearest source of medical help, preferably getting someone to telephone ahead to say that you are bringing in a child with possible *anaphylactic shock*.

Once the shock has been successfully treated, the child will need further long-term treatment to deal with the allergy by hyposensitization (*see* **Allergy**/Principles of diagnosis and treatment in allergic conditions: Injection treatment for allergy). This is a must because after one such episode the child's reaction to a further sting will be even more severe and could be life-threatening.

If a child receives multiple stings—because she poked a wasps' nest, for example—she may become shocked not because she is allergic but because the local pain and the fear is too much for her. Treat her for shock (*see below* Shock). Wrap the stung area (or her whole body if necessary) in a cold wet cloth or sheet and take her to the hospital. She is in no danger but can be made much less uncomfortable.

Venomous creatures: snakes, spiders, scorpions, jellyfish. Also ticks

The bite or sting of a venomous creature is a very different matter from an "ordinary" insect sting because instead of injecting a substance that merely affects the skin locally, it injects a poison which may affect the child's whole system.

There are many venomous creatures in the United States, but your chances of encountering them obviously depend on where you live and on where and how you travel. Make sure that you are not only aware of any such hazards in your home area but that you also inform yourself about likely hazards in new locations. It is best not to rely on travel guides for this. They may assume that your vacation trip will follow tourist paths when in fact you mean to backpack into the mountains. Consult local people about wildlife that might be hazardous. The more you know about these creatures' habits, the easier it is to avoid an unfortunate encounter. Most snakes, for example, are extremely shy of people. If you move slowly through their habitats and look where you are putting your feet, they will have moved away before you can tread on them. Scorpions tend to seek warmth and shelter in the coldest part of the night. Most stings occur because the victim puts on a shoe or wriggles into a sleeping bag that a scorpion is already occupying. If everyone makes a habit of shaking out their clothing before putting it on, such an accident is unlikely.

If you are making a trip to an area where you will be sharing the environment with venomous creatures, it is also wise to consult a local doctor or hospital about first aid for anyone who is bitten or stung. The advice given below is certainly harmless and will be adequate for most situations. But there are a few creatures whose venom is so quickly lethal that more heroic/specific measures may be needed, especially if the accident occurs when some hours of travel separate the party from skilled help.

Snakes

There are five families of poisonous snakes in the world and four of these can be found in parts of the United States: rattlesnakes, copperheads, cottonmouths, and coral snakes. Snake identification is far more difficult than most books imply, especially as neither you nor the victim may ever see more than a whiplike movement as the snake makes its escape. Don't try to find the snake which has bitten someone and don't try to kill it, either. Immediate first aid is the same for all snakebites; a search will waste precious time and a successful search will risk someone else's getting bitten. If a snake should be killed—or found dead—don't handle it, even if it has been beheaded. Reflex movements can result in a "bite" from a snake, or snake's head, which has been dead, or separated from the body, for as much as an hour.

The bite will leave one or two punctures—fang marks. If the fangs have left marks you must, of course, assume that venom has been injected, but even while you move into action you can comfort yourself a little with the realization that the snake's venom sacs may already have been empty or that the venom may have been deposited on the skin rather than through it. By no means every bite by even a highly venomous species of snake leads to a serious reaction.

First aid for snakebite   Lay the child down immediately and calm him as much as you can —especially by appearing calm and competent yourself. Snakebite victims are usually terrified (*see* **Anxiety, Fears and Phobias**) and intense fear and horror make it much more likely that shock will develop (*see below*: Shock).

Persuade a child who is old enough and calm enough to cooperate, to keep the affected limb absolutely still. Any venom is injected into the tissues rather than directly into the bloodstream. The less the limb is moved, the more slowly it will spread. If the child will not or cannot cooperate, immobilize the limb by splinting one leg to the other or the bitten arm to his body, using belts or whatever you have with you. If you think that further action and concealment will help the child to keep calm, wash the bite area (or wipe it, using your saliva) and then cover it with the dry dressing you should be carrying with you.

Get the bitten child to the nearest hospital by the quickest possible means but don't let the journey involve walking or any movement of the limb. Travel by ambulance is ideal, but if your own car will be quicker it is best to use that, provided that the child can be carried to it.

If the bitten limb swells and/or begins to look bruised, some venom was certainly injected. If the victim feels sick or dizzy, sweats or loses consciousness, he is probably badly affected although some of these systemic reactions may be due to shock. If retching and/or vomiting occur, remember to keep the child lying on his side so that no vomit can be inhaled.

● Unless you have been specifically advised otherwise by a local hospital or doctor, *don't do anything other than the above*. Don't cut or suck the puncture wounds; don't apply ice (even if you happen to be carrying some); don't put a tourniquet above the wound to prevent the spread of venom. All these measures are recommended in some older first aid books but all have been shown to be more dangerous than they are helpful. Your job is to keep the child calm and the limb still and to reach medical help.

Spiders   Although most spiders are venomous, very few species attack humans and only two which are found in the United States are at all dangerous to life or health. The black widow (*Latrodectus mactans*) is a small black spider which characteristically has a red or yellow "hourglass shaped" marking on its abdomen. The brown recluse (*Loxosceles reclusa*) is a light brown color and has a dark brown violin-shaped marking on its thorax.

A child who is bitten by a spider should be treated exactly as if he had been bitten by a snake (*see above*).

Scorpions
There are about 40 species of scorpion in the United States. Almost all are found principally in the southwest, especially in Arizona. Only one, *Centuroides sculpturus*, is venomous enough to be a potential threat to life.

Scorpions do not bite (as snakes and spiders bite) they sting. The sting of a non-lethal species can be agonizingly painful and can produce immediate local inflammation and swelling. The sting of *Centuroides sculpturus*, on the other hand, produces no visible local signs so that the site often cannot be identified. The victim complains of pain and of abnormal sensation in the general area, but that is all. In general, then, less-serious scorpion-stings tend to appear worse than the one type that could actually kill.

Although the immediate appearance of local signs around an obvious sting suggests that the victim will recover after a few hours' pain, it is best to treat all scorpion stings exactly as advised for snakebite (*see above*).

Jellyfish
There are many species of jellyfish (*Coelenterates*) in American waters. They vary in their appearance and mobility, but all possess stinging capsules (nematocysts) which they use to hold or incapacitate their prey. Some have stinging capsules which cling to the victim by means of sticky mucus or a coiled springlike structure. Others have needle-shaped stinging capsules that inject a dose of venom through the victim's skin.

Jellyfish stings can produce a wide variety of reactions, both toxic and allergic. Very few are fatal, although some, such as the Portuguese Man-of-War, may indirectly cause death because the pain of the sting is severe enough to cause the victim to lose consciousness and drown. Acute allergic reactions also cause a few fatalities (*see* **Allergy/ Anaphylactic shock**). Jellyfish stings present more of a problem than do the bites and stings of other venomous creatures because, unlike the land-based creatures which are shy and anxious to avoid contact with people, jellyfish swim mindlessly in the water and frequently ground themselves on beaches where, even after some hours drying in the sun, they may still sting the unwary walker. You cannot hope to avoid jellyfish simply by looking out for them: many are almost invisible either in water or on sand. If many are known to be present—especially if these include Portuguese Men-of-War—do not swim and do not venture near the water's edge.

First aid for jellyfish stings
If there are jellyfish tentacles sticking to the skin, they will go on discharging their poison into the victim. Inspect the painful area carefully and pull off any tentacles, using a towel or a stick rather than your bare hands.

● Don't rub with sand or irrigate with fresh water, as some books suggest. Either procedure may cause more of the poison-sacs to fire. If you have alcohol with you, pour that over the place. It will act to fix the nematocysts so that they do not fire their poison.

If the pain is intense, the victim feels shocked and ill and/or a skin rash begins to develop, take him immediately to the nearest hospital.

If the victim complains only of more moderate pain, and there are no other physical signs, home-based first aid may be adequate. A paste of baking soda and water applied to the wound relieves most of the pain immediately. Scraping it away an hour or so later, using a blunt spoon or similar object, finally removes any remaining tentacles.

Failing baking soda, a mixture of dilute ammonia, lemon juice, meat tenderizer and sugar will inactivate remaining tentacles and relieve the pain.

● If you are far from home and cannot get help from a house on the beach, these home-mixtures will not be available. Take the victim to hospital even if he seems to be in no danger from the sting. The pain will almost certainly require some kind of relief.

Ticks

Although ticks are not venomous, ixodid ticks can transmit a serious disease called Rocky Mountain Spotted Fever. This disease used to be thought to be confined to a few Western states but it has now been found in many areas of the U.S., especially along the Atlantic seaboard.

If a tick attaches itself to you or your child, you will have no way of telling whether or not it is an ixodid tick and, if it is, whether or not it is carrying the infective organism, Ricksettsia ricketsii. Play safe; assume that any tick is dangerous.

First aid for ticks

Immediate removal of the whole tick makes the risk of infection negligible. But if you grasp the tick's body and attempt to pull it off the victim's skin the body will probably come away leaving the buried head behind; the risk of infection will then be considerable.

Grasp the tick gently and turn it *counter-clockwise*. It may then loosen its hold and come away completely.

If this is unsuccessful, try touching the tick with a very hot object, such as a match which has been allowed to burn for a moment and has then been blown out. The tick may now "let go" and fall off.

If neither of these maneuvers works and the tick either remains attached to the victim or comes away leaving its head still in the skin, go immediately to the nearest emergency room.

Blisters

Most blisters are caused by friction, as from an ill-fitting shoe. At the center of the rubbed area the outer layer of skin separates from the inner layer, which exudes fluid. The result is a fluid-filled "bubble." If a blister bursts, the raw patch underneath will be extremely sore and it will also be liable to infection. If you are shown a blister while it is still intact, do all that you can to preserve it. Over a few days the fluid will be re-absorbed and new skin will grow over the raw patch under the blister. The blister skin, which has no blood supply, will dry up and fall off.

Dressing an intact blister

The most effective protection is given by a ring-shaped corn or callus pad with an ordinary adhesive dressing over the top. Make sure the circle is high enough to keep the center of the adhesive dressing from touching the top of the blister.

Dressing a broken blister Don't remove the blister skin even if it is broken: its remains will offer at least some protection. Dress the raw area with a non-adhesive dressing such as Vaseline gauze.

● Burn or scald blisters require special attention; *see below.*

Bruises

A bruise is the visible result of blood vessels under the skin being crushed or broken. Blood escapes into the tissues. The area looks red at first, then bluish-black. As the escaped blood is broken down and reabsorbed the area may look greenish-yellow.

Trivial bruises These are a normal part of life and require no treatment. If the bump is on a part of the body with an extensive nerve supply and loose skin (such as the back of the hand), it may be very painful at the time and the subsequent swelling may be painful, too. If the child is in a fuss it may be worth giving him or her a piece of gauze or a handkerchief soaked in very cold water or wrapped around ice to hold over the area for a few minutes. The cooling will help the tiny blood vessels to close up more quickly and may therefore lessen the bruising.

Extensive bruising If a child has a bad fall, say off a bicycle, so that she bruises a large area of shoulder, hip, thigh and knee, she will certainly be extremely sore and may need treating for shock (*see below*). The point is that although there is no visible bleeding from such an injury, the child is losing blood from her circulation into the tissues. In an extreme case she may be in a state similar to that following internal hemorrhage (*see below* Shock: Causes of major shock). After such a fall you will probably have her checked over at the hospital anyway. But if she appears, and says she feels, all right, encourage her to be quiet and keep an eye on her for a few hours anyway.

"Black eyes" A blow around the eyebrow, nose or cheekbone may lead to dramatic swelling and a fearsome-looking "black eye." The eye itself is seldom damaged as it is set back in a bony socket for protection. But if you are not sure where the blow landed and are therefore worried about damage to the eye itself, get the victim to a doctor quickly. Once the eye has been closed by swelling it will be difficult for him to determine its condition.

The bruising of a black eye sometimes travels downwards before all the escaped blood is reabsorbed so that the swelling is progressively lower down the face. Although this looks odd it is harmless.

"Blackened" nails If a finger is caught in a door or the vacuum cleaner is dropped on a toe, the nail may turn black from bruising in the tissues beneath it. Such an injury is agonizingly painful because, unlike skin, the nail will not stretch to allow swelling. The bruise causes great pressure.

Although such an injury will heal of its own accord, the pain and the disability caused in either hand or foot may make a trip to the hospital worthwhile *if you can get there quickly*. A doctor can drill a tiny hole through the nail and thus let out the blood and relieve that pressure. He cannot do this effectively once the blood has coagulated.

Worries about "excessive" bruising

If your child always seems to be covered with bruises for which you cannot account, you may worry in case he might have a "bleeding disease." By all means confide this worry to your doctor, but think, in the meantime, whether there is any other evidence to suggest that the child bleeds excessively. Does a small cut go on oozing? Do his gums bleed if he brushes his teeth adequately? Does a thorn-prick bleed more than one drop? If the answers are all negative, blood disorder is most unlikely.

You may also worry in case the child is being physically bullied, at school or at play, or even in case he is being abused by an adult. Bruises on the legs and arms are likely to be accidentally self-inflicted. Bruises on the body are the ones which might feed your suspicions.

A child who is being hurt deliberately by other people will be frightened, however anxious he may be to conceal the fact. You can probably get a clue by asking him calmly, "How on earth did you get like this?"

Do remember, though, that fair-skinned children do produce visible bruises where older children whose skins are tougher, or children whose skins are darker, do not. The legs of a healthy, happy, active blonde nine-year-old may almost always be a rainbow of new and old bruises.

Burns and scalds

Burns and scalds are almost always worse than they look because they do not merely affect the skin which you can see. The heat penetrates below the skin and damages the blood vessels. These react by widening (dilating) and letting the clear colorless part of the blood ooze out through their walls. In a minor burn this fluid will puff up the dead skin at the center and make a blister. In a more serious burn which has removed the skin altogether you will see the fluid "weeping" from the raw area. The fluid you can see may be only a small part of what is being lost into the tissues from deeper-lying blood vessels.

This fluid loss is a kind of bleeding. Only the clear part of the blood is being lost, but its loss is nevertheless reducing the total volume of fluid available to the circulation. This is why burns and scalds so often lead to shock (*see below*) and why intravenous fluid replacement is such a vital and urgent part of the hospital treatment of burns.

Any burn which destroys the full thickness of the skin (third degree) may require skin to be grafted over it before the wound can heal. Even the smallest burn of this type requires immediate medical attention. Otherwise, use the *area* of a burn or scald as a rough guide to its seriousness. Any burn or scald which covers an area of skin more than half an inch square should be seen by a doctor. If the area is the size of your hand, the matter is potentially dangerous; the child should be taken rapidly to the hospital. If the area involved is as much as a quarter of his skin area it is likely to be disastrous, even with immediate and expert medical attention.

Don't indulge in wishful thinking if your child is burned or scalded. If she empties the coffeepot down her front and the skin only looks red, it is a tremendous temptation to let yourself believe that "it wasn't actually boiling; she's got away with it." The process of fluid leakage beneath that reddened skin can be slow but deadly. Get her to the hospital *now*.

Immediate treatment for all burns

Whether the burn is a tiny one on a finger or a serious one caused by a pan of boiling oil, your first job is to arrest the burning before any further damage is done. You do this by removing clothes that are soaked in scalding fluid and then by cooling the burned area itself under cold running water. This cooling will stop the heat from penetrating to deeper blood vessels, help the blood vessels which are already affected to close up again and stop oozing, and lessen the pain.

Home treatment for tiny burns

If you have quickly put your child's burned finger under the cold tap, two minutes' cooling may have reduced the pain and allowed you to see that there is nothing more than a red patch, a blister or possibly a small raw place. Pat it dry. Do not put *any* kind of grease or ointment on it, not even one which says it is for the treatment of burns. If it needs medication it needs a doctor.

Most burns will need some protection from life while they heal, but it is important not to put on either a dressing which might stick to the edges of the burned area *or* anything fluffy, like absorbent cotton, which might leave fibers in it. Use a non-adhesive dressing or a piece of sterile gauze. The burn will heal more quickly if the dressing is left undisturbed for a day or two and kept dry.

First aid for larger burns

Larger burns may be caused by taking hold of very hot cooking utensils or by splashes of boiling oil or accidents with pots and so forth. They should all be treated exactly like a small one except that as soon as you have cooled the area for five minutes it should be loosely wrapped in a clean, non-fluffy cloth—such as a handkerchief or sheet—and the child taken rapidly to the hospital.

A really large burn, such as might be caused by the child getting into a dangerously hot bath, or tipping a boiling pan down himself or catching his clothes afire is a case where your first aid may make a major contribution to his eventual recovery. Your exact actions will have to be dictated by the exact circumstances, but these are the principles:

First, stop further burning. Heat will be trapped in layers of hot-soaked clothing. Remove them, but go carefully as you reach the layer next to his skin and *don't pull off anything which is sticking to him*.

Flaming clothes will be burning him. The flames must be smothered, but remember heat and flame *rise*. If you throw him down on the flames they will lap all around him. If you leave him standing they will rise towards his face and hair. If he rushes around in panic he will fan them. Grab him; throw him down with the flames uppermost. Smother them with anything you can grab such as a rug or towel; if there is nothing else, use your own body. Lie flat on him, fast, and the flames will go out before they can burn you.

Smouldering clothes will burn him more if you press them against him, pull them off, grasping non-burning areas.

Chemicals will go on burning as long as they are touching him. Take off clothes soaked in them.

Now, stop the burning from penetrating further. The heat of the burned skin will go on penetrating until you cool it, just as it does in a small burn. Use whatever is practical for the area burned—a running tap, a hosepipe, a shower or a cold bath. But remember, cooling which does not begin within five minutes of the accident is useless.

Protect burns during transport to the hospital. Burns are very liable to infection, even from air-borne bacteria. Burned skin is also easily damaged by friction. To guard against both, cover the whole area with a clean, non-fluffy cloth, such as a handkerchief or sheet. Newly ironed items of this kind will have inner folds which are more or less sterile. If you have nothing else which is suitable, you can use plastic food wrap.

Protect the child from shock (*see below*). Keep him lying down and keep him as calm and quiet as you possibly can, both until transport arrives and during the trip. If he is wrapped in a clean sheet, cover that with a light blanket for warmth, but do not use hot water bottles. Do not give him anything to eat or drink.

Choking

If food or drink or any foreign object or irritating substance gets into the airway rather than the esophagus (food passage) a powerful reflex tightens the muscles of the airway at about the level of the larynx (voice box) and causes coughing. The closed-off airway prevents the foreign material from travelling further down to the lungs while the coughing expels it back up into the mouth. The reflex is normally highly efficient, operating as soon after birth as breathing is established and working night and day, whether we are asleep or awake. Difficulties and dangers are therefore the exception rather than the rule.

Choking and breathlessness

The spasm of the muscles which blocks the air passage to further invasion by foreign material also blocks breathing. Usually this does not matter because the first violent bout of coughing, triggered by the spasm and powered by air already in the lungs when it began, serves to dislodge the foreign material.

If that coughing bout does not clear the obstruction, the victim will have difficulty in taking in air for another effective bout. He may become short of oxygen—even to the extent of looking bluish-gray in color—not because the foreign material is completely blocking his air passage but because the muscle spasm is doing so.

To make matters worse, those same muscles may actually be clamped around the foreign material, making it more difficult to dislodge.

Breathlessness leads to panic; panic makes breathlessness worse

An older child or an adult who understands this reflex mechanism can help himself by deliberately relaxing and taking slow, gentle breaths rather than fighting for great gasps. A younger child or a person who believes that his air passage is totally obstructed will panic as soon as he feels short of oxygen. Panic will both increase the muscle spasm and increase his body's demand for oxygen.

Take action before breathlessness begins

As soon as you can see that the first bout of coughing has not brought up the foreign material:

Strike the victim several times between the shoulder blades. If that does not immediately clear the air passage and allow the victim a complete breath, use gravity to help:

Position the victim with his head and shoulders below his legs. A baby can be held upside down; a child can be slung head down over your knee; an adult can be persuaded face down over a table or bed.

Repeat the blows between the shoulder blades with the victim in this position.

Complete obstruction of breathing

Very occasionally the air passage is completely blocked by a foreign body rather than closed by muscle spasm. In an adult the fatal object is usually a too large piece of ill-chewed meat. In a child it is more likely to be an object, such as a marble, which unfortunately exactly fits the air passage.

If such a thing should occur, you will distinguish it from ordinary choking because, after perhaps one strangled gasp, the victim will not breathe at all. He will look totally terrified but make no sound; his eyes will bulge and his face will be suffused with red and then turn bluish. He will collapse. In adults eating in restaurants, bystanders often think the victim has had a stroke.

What to do

This is a grade-one emergency. The most urgent thing is to *get expert help*. Sending for an ambulance/doctor takes priority over anything else. But while waiting for help or transporting the victim to it, try:

Looking down his throat in case you can pull out the obstruction. You may be able to grip a piece of meat even if that marble is hopeless. (If you can see nothing, don't poke about blindly.)

Getting him into a head-down position and banging him repeatedly between the shoulder blades. With an older child or adult, use your clenched fist rather than your open hand to deliver real jolts. If the object is lodged high up in the throat (if you can see, but not grip, it, for example) this is very likely to dislodge it. But it is risky. If the object is lower down, your blows could shift it downwards, towards the lung, instead of up and out.

The "Heimlich maneuver" in which pressure on the diaphragm, just below the breastbone, is used to compress the air in the lungs and create an expulsive force through the whole respiratory system. With an older child, or adult, get him into a sitting or standing position, put your arms around him and use your fists to press inwards and upwards. With a baby or very young child, use one arm to support him and use just two fingers of the other hand to press on the diaphragm. This maneuver has saved many lives, but it too is risky. Over-enthusiastic thrusts may damage internal organs such as the liver.

Some other kinds of choking are less obvious and dramatic but can nevertheless be serious:

Inhaling small foreign objects

A small foreign body may get past that reflex defense, and lodge either in one of the smaller air passages or in the lung itself. Suspect this if your child has a violent fit of choking and then recovers without any foreign body appearing. Suspect it also if he has an intermittent cough, an unusual wheezy sound to his breathing or pain in his throat.

He should be taken to the hospital. Foreign bodies in the air passages or lungs can cause serious trouble later.

Inhaling liquids or body fluids

Although almost every child will "breathe" some water while swimming, from time to time, a child who is thought to have taken a lot of water into the lungs should always be observed in the hospital, even if he seems quite unaffected (*see below* Drowning).

It is dangerous for him to take fluids such as milk, or his own blood or vomit into his lungs. A baby should never be left lying with a bottle to suck. A child with a nosebleed should sit leaning forward so that blood does not trickle down his throat. A child who is vomiting should be held well forward over a toilet or basin. Anyone who is unconscious (or drunk or drugged) should be put in the "recovery position" (*see above*) so that vomit, etc. run out of the mouth.

Precautions against all forms of choking

Don't leave babies to suck alone or young children to eat or drink anything alone. Be there to bang backs if necessary.

Don't allow "foods" which might be inhaled easily. Peanuts are the worst offenders as they set up serious inflammation if they "go the wrong way."

Don't let children "throw" food into their mouths—even for a joke or a game—and don't let them pour chips, nuts or tiny sweets out of the packet into their upturned mouths.

Don't let children suck sweets in bed. Quite apart from the effect on their teeth, they may fall asleep and choke on what remains. It is best if no child ever eats anything while lying down.

Don't let them eat while rushing around and playing active games. A sudden push can lead to something "going the wrong way," especially if the child is panting.

Guard babies and young children against things which might block throats, not only objects like marbles, but also bits of larger toys like the insecurely fastened wheels of a model car. . . .

Don't let a child hold his nose when taking nasty medicine, etc. If he is trying to breathe through his mouth while swallowing the dose he is the more likely to choke.

Don't try to give food or drink to a child who is sleepy, semiconscious, unconscious or shocked. Be very careful about trying to give anything (such as coffee) to an older person who is drunk. Under all these circumstances, the choking-coughing reflex may be inefficient.

Don't force food into the mouth of a protesting child. Quite apart from the poor psychology involved, he is very likely to gag and choke.

Cuts and scrapes, grazes and puncture wounds

The principles for coping with all very minor cuts and scrapes are the same:

Interfere as little as possible. If you are not shown a bloody knee or cut finger until an hour after it happened, let it alone. Healing will already have started and "first aid" will undo it.

Avoid "antiseptics" and airtight dressings whenever you can. Antiseptic creams are largely ineffective in killing the thousands of bacteria which colonize every square inch of skin. Their greasiness can prevent the formation of the hard scab which is the body's natural protection for wounds. In combination with an airtight dressing, such a cream can actually keep a wound open (and subject to infection) for a long time.

Take action only to keep the child comfortable. That may mean an adhesive dressing (applied so that air can still get to the wound) to protect it from clothing, etc. Or it may mean applying such a dressing simply to conceal blood from a child who is frightened by it.

For quick healing, keep wounds dry. A scraped elbow will heal far more quickly if the child does not soak in a hot bath that same day.

Deeper cuts may require more attention. Their seriousness does not only depend on depth and size, however, but on the implement which made them and their exact place on the body.

Deep cuts on fingers, etc.

These are usually made by a very sharp but thin implement such as a knife or razor blade. They may be deep and they may bleed copiously, but the bleeding is easy to stop and healing is quick and neat because the skin edges and the cut tissues underneath are neatly aligned.

Put the cut under gently running cold water while you fetch some sterile gauze and an adhesive dressing. Wrap gauze around the finger and apply pressure with your own. If the bleeding takes more than a minute to control you can speed up matters by holding the child's hand above his heart level while you press (*see below* Wounds and bleeding).

As soon as bleeding slows, apply the adhesive dressing. If you place it tightly around the finger, remember to loosen it within five minutes. If you place it firmly but not tightly and the wound bleeds through, add another dressing on top. Don't interfere again for an hour or so. By that time the blood will have clotted and the edges of the wound will already have begun to knit together so you can take off the bloody dressing, put on a clean, dry one to protect it and forget the whole matter (but keep an eye out for infection, *see below*).

Deep cuts into taut skin

Where skin is taut, as on the palm of the hand or over the ankle, quite a small deep cut can be tiresome because the edges gape open. The bleeding takes longer to stop and, if it heals with the edges set apart, a comparatively large scar will be left.

Sometimes you can apply adhesive tape (over gauze) in such a way that the edges of the wound are pulled together by the dressing. You can buy special "butterfly" adhesive tape, ready-made for this. Stick one end on one side of the cut, close the edges together and stick down the other end.

If this does not work, you have a choice between accepting a slow-healing wound leaving a scar and taking the child to have the wound stitched shut. You will have to weigh the importance of a scar against the importance of the unpleasantness of the medical procedure.

Deep cuts in awkward places

A cut on a knuckle or other joint may not gape at the time but may be delayed in healing because movement continually reopens it. It may be worthwhile to place a piece of non-adhesive gauze over the actual cut and then bandage the finger in the straight position which keeps the wound closed. Even twenty-four hours will probably allow enough healing to prevent the wound from reopening.

Cuts which raise skin flaps

If a child "slices" a finger so that there is a flap of skin or of skin and tissue, you can treat it exactly as you treat a simple cut, but make sure that when you dress it you replace the flap exactly. It may heal completely in that position. If the blood supply to the cut flap does not reestablish itself, the flap will eventually dry up and fall off, but it is still the best "dressing" for the healing wound.

Jagged and dirty cuts

Such a cut tends to leave a nasty scar and is, of course, very liable to infection. If it is shallow and in a place where scarring does not matter very much (such as on the knee of a nine-year-old!) you may be able to deal with it by running it under plenty of cold water and then dressing it, doing your best to bring skin edges together. But if it is at all deep and/or in a noticeable place, take the child to the doctor or hospital.

Cuts on the head or face

The skin which covers the skull is tightly stretched and copiously supplied with blood vessels. Bleeding, even from a minor cut, is usually free and difficult to stop because skin edges cannot be pulled together.

Facial skin is soft and scars on the face matter. It is usually sensible to show such a cut to a doctor. Even quite trivial ones will often be stitched (*see* **Hospital**/Procedures; Suturing wounds).

Cuts with foreign bodies

If a cut, anywhere on the body, has glass or any other foreign body in it, *don't interfere*. Don't, on any account, try to remove it. Take the child straight to a hospital.

Grazes with grit

The exception may be a graze which has grit or gravel in it. You can cope with this at home *if the surface skin has been completely removed.*

The graze will be extremely painful. Don't try to dab the dirt out (you are likely to push some into the damaged tissue as well as causing the victim to protest); instead, try running cold tap water over it, gently at first, then harder as the child gets used to it. If one or two pieces of grit refuse to wash off, you (or better still the child herself) may be able to encourage them with a tiny piece of gauze used in the running water.

If the surface skin has not been completely removed so that there is dirt and grit trapped in pockets of skin, the graze should be professionally cleaned. If it is not, infection is very likely. If the graze is on some visible part of the body such as the face or elbow, professional cleaning is even more important. Without it, that dirt may actually stain the tissues so that when it has healed, the scar is an ugly and noticeable color.

Puncture wounds Can be dangerous when they look trivial. It can be quite difficult to decide whether or not such a wound requires hospital treatment. Many authorities say that *all* puncture wounds should receive medical attention but, if cornered, would agree that to bother a doctor with a needle run into a finger or a rose thorn into the foot would be absurd. The decisions, in every case, will be yours but the relevant facts are these:

Danger of infection in puncture wounds A puncture wound is made by a sharp object of very small diameter driving deeply into the tissues. Because it penetrates deeply, any dirt will be carried far in. Because its diameter is small, the entry hole is small. You cannot clean the bottom of the wound and it will heal very readily. If the entry wound heals with dirt trapped far beneath it, infection is very likely.

A deep hole made by a dirty object (such as the wound made when a child steps on a nail with bare feet) should always be shown to a doctor. A tiny hole made by a comparatively clean object (such as that needle in the finger) need not be. In between these extremes you must judge dirt and depth. A thumbtack, for example, may penetrate the sole of your child's shoe, but if you compare the depth of the spike and the sole you will find that the wound cannot be very deep.

If you decide that a puncture wound is not serious enough to require medical attention, *try to make it bleed*. If you or the child can squeeze the puncture and get several drops of blood out, dirt will probably be carried out, too. If squeezing does not work, the child can suck the puncture.

This is one kind of wound which you do not want to heal very quickly. Soak it well in warm water and bathe it again the next day.

Danger of tetanus from puncture wounds If your child is fully immunized against tetanus and/or has had a booster injection within the last ten years (*see* **Immunization**), you need not worry about this. If not, you should realize that tetanus toxins (poisons) are produced by tetanus bacteria which live in soil—especially soil contaminated by animal droppings. There may be such bacteria on a rusty nail in the garden. If any get into a puncture wound and the wound closes over, they are especially liable to cause trouble as these bacteria flourish in an environment with little or no oxygen. The moral is: Keep that tetanus protection up-to-date. Otherwise you really will have to worry about puncture wounds because while tetanus is far less likely than other kinds of infection, it is deadly serious (*see also* **Tetanus**).

Dislocations

In theory, any part of the body where the bones of the skeleton are jointed so as to allow movement can become dislocated. At the hip, for example, the top of the thigh bone ends in a "ball" which fits into and rotates within a "socket" of bone at the base of the pelvis. If the "ball" were displaced from the "socket," the joint would be dislocated.

In practice, dislocations are rare without accompanying fractures because in most of the body's joints the muscles and ligaments which hold them in place are both stronger and more resilient than the bones themselves. If those muscles and ligaments are torn so badly that the joint no longer functions, one of the associated bones is almost certain to be broken. At the wrist, for example, a dislocation happens because the main bone above it (the radius) is fractured. This is called a Colles fracture. A dislocation of the ankle joint goes similarly with a fracture of one of the associated bones and is called a Potts fracture.

Obviously, then, there is no point in trying to establish whether your child has fractured or dislocated these parts of the body. If he has done the one he has probably done the other, too. And the less you interfere with the injury, the better (*see below* Fractures). There are two exceptions:

Dislocated shoulder

The shoulder joint is an exceptionally mobile one, designed to allow us to windmill our arms. The "ball" at the top of the arm bone (the humerus) can rather easily be displaced from its shallow socket, especially if the arm receives a lot of weight while stretched above the head. A child who falls from a height and instinctively throws up his arms to protect his head may dislocate his shoulder.

Although you may not be certain that this is a dislocation rather than a fracture, it is important to move fast if circumstances and the child's behavior make you even suspect it. The displaced parts of the joint press on nerves and overstretch ligaments and muscles at every movement.

The child will be in excruciating pain; there will be no question of waiting half an hour to see if he starts to use the arm again spontaneously. He will obviously require immediate medical help.

Tissues surrounding a dislocated joint quickly swell, making the otherwise simple job of realigning the joint extremely difficult. The faster you can get the child to a hospital the easier it will be and the less the likelihood of long-term after-effects.

Look at the position in which the (probably screaming) child instinctively nurses the arm. He will probably be holding it across his chest.

Support the arm in that position with a big sling around his neck.

Either send for an ambulance or drive him to a hospital.

Dislocated jaw

Sometimes the lower jaw slips forwards and downwards, usually during an extra-deep yawn. A blow to the jaw seldom dislocates it; it pushes the lower jaw upwards and is more likely to fracture it.

The extreme and completely unexpected pain will probably make the child yell. Yelling sometimes causes the jaw to click back into place of its own accord.

If the child can now open and close his mouth without pain all will be well and you can regard the incident as closed.

If it does not click back immediately, take him to a hospital so that it can be manipulated back into place before much swelling takes place.

Do not underestimate a dislocation

Although we tend to think of a fracture as "worse," a dislocation is usually more painful at the time *and* more painful for longer, afterwards. Torn ligaments and bruised tissues take a long time to heal. The joint may have to be immobilized in plaster for several weeks and the child will be far more miserable than he would be after a greenstick or simple fracture.

A bad dislocation can leave the joint liable to further dislocations because the holding ligaments and muscles do not heal back to quite their original strength and elasticity. It is therefore especially important to follow scrupulously any advice concerning later exercises or hospital physiotherapy.

Drowning

Water can kill in a number of ways. The popular image of drowning is of a victim submerged in water, drawing water into his lungs instead of air and therefore suffocating. But that unfortunate swimmer can drown without ever taking any water into his lungs at all. If he is trapped (by a rock or a wreck or a heavy growth of weed) several feet below the surface, the pressure will be too great for his diaphragm to expand and contract. He will not "breathe" any water. He will die simply for lack of air.

Many water deaths are not due to interference with the air supply at all but to the kind of deep chilling which cools vital organs beyond their tolerance (hypothermia).

In many "drowning" accidents, these disastrous things happen in sequence. A child who drifts out to sea on an air-mattress, for example, becomes increasingly chilled to a point where the onset of hypothermia makes him mentally confused and clouds his judgment. Eventually he rolls off the air-mattress in the mistaken idea that he can swim to safety. His attempts to swim increase his body's oxygen demand; the hypothermia deepens and as he fights the water so some is breathed into his lungs. Unless rescue comes he will become unconscious from a combination of suffocation and hypothermia and then he will drown.

Gloomy though it all is, it is worth understanding what happens in common water accidents because the right action at the right time can save both life and health. Start by dismissing a couple of exceedingly dangerous old wives' tales.

"Human beings float." It is true that a human body, inert in water, will remain partially on the surface, but this does not mean that the victim will float in a position which enables him to breathe. He will float with his face and most of his head and his legs from the hips down submerged. Only the upper half of his back will remain above the water. The smaller a child the more certain it is that the head will be fully submerged. Babies' heads are large and heavy relative to the rest of their bodies.

"People do not drown until they have sunk three times." This is total nonsense. A victim bobbing to the surface after being temporarily trapped under water will only take water into his lungs as he emerges, but he will then take in more with every attempted "breath" unless he knows how to float with his head up. If your child falls into deep water (perhaps off a dock), he will sink deeply and then come back to the surface. You need to get him out the moment he appears. If you do so you will have saved him. If you wait while he bobs around you may be too late.

Babies, small children and shallow water   A baby or toddler can drown by falling face down in a bath, paddling pool or stream. With no experience or intention of putting his face in water, he takes a huge breath to scream his shock and outrage. The breath is water not air; that single inpouring of water into the lungs can be disastrous.

Snatch him up and turn him upside down. If he is furious and screaming all is well. If he is choking and gasping, empty all the water that will come out of him and take him immediately to a hospital (*see below*).

All ages in deep water

When a child is completely immersed in water, by accident, his fate will depend on the exact circumstances. A swimmer who gets into trouble due to a strong ocean current or to cramp, for example, may nevertheless be able to keep his head above water for quite a long period. But even the strongest swimmer may not be able to help himself if the boom of a sailboat knocked him unconscious as well as overboard, or if the water is so cold that hypothermia rapidly begins to affect him. A non-swimmer or a child who finds himself in rough sea when he is accustomed to a swimming pool, may worsen his own situation with panic-stricken thrashing which exhausts him and makes it impossible for him to coordinate in-breaths with moments when his nose and mouth are above water.

If he is still obviously breathing, whether he is fully or partly conscious, or unconscious, he will probably be all right, provided he receives the correct care:

Empty all the water out of him that will come. Hold a small child upside down; lay a heavier one on his front and then lift his lower body. Remember that he may vomit water from his stomach as well as drain it from his lungs: keep his head well turned to one side so that he does not breathe vomited water in again.

Arrest hypothermia by removing soaked clothing, replacing it with your own and protecting him from the chill wind.

Get him to a hospital if any water at all was coughed, choked, vomited or drained out of him.

If he does not seem to be breathing, don't be too quick to despair even if you cannot feel a heartbeat either. People used to think that drowning victims should not be resuscitated if they had been without oxygen for more than a few minutes. It was believed that while such a person might have his heart and breathing restarted, he was likely to remain "a vegetable" because his brain would have been permanently damaged by oxygen starvation. Recent research has shown that there is a *diving response* to sudden immersion which, by a complicated set of physiological responses, puts the heart into extremely "low gear" and concentrates the little blood it continues to pump on that vital brain. There are reliable reports of full recovery following long periods of complete immersion. Your child's chances are better if the water was very cold as the oxygen requirements of a cooled brain are reduced.

He needs mouth-to-mouth resuscitation and perhaps heart massage. If you are competent to do this yourself, start as soon as you reach a boat or dry land. If you have never done it before nor been taught how to do it, don't waste time trying to remember the words and diagrams in a book. There is real skill involved. *Send for help.* In the meantime follow the suggestions above to get water out of him and reduce chilling. He may even start breathing again spontaneously.

Why fresh water is more dangerous than sea water

Water in the lungs does not only prevent vital oxygen from reaching the circulation, it is also dangerous to that circulation. Fresh water is rapidly absorbed. It dilutes the blood and breaks down the red blood cells which release a sudden load of potassium. Heart failure is often the result. A child who appears dead following immersion in fresh water cannot usually be revived.

In sea-water drowning, a high concentration of calcium and magnesium may enter the bloodstream and stop the heart. The child appears dead, but if artificial respiration and heart massage are successfully carried out the salts may be dispersed around the circulation and diluted to a point where the heart can start again spontaneously.

Polluted or "hygienized" water is dangerous, too

Even a little water in the lungs can be dangerous so that any child who is thought to have breathed some in should always be taken to a hospital. If you are tempted to ignore this precaution because your child was quickly fished out of that swimming pool or pond, remember that polluted water or extra-clean water loaded with chemicals can both irritate the lungs and cause peculiarly unpleasant types of pneumonia. He may seem perfectly all right now that he has stopped choking, but will he be perfectly all right in twelve hours' time? Let a doctor decide.

Electric shock

The severity of an electric shock varies with an enormous number of factors; a victim who happens to be wearing rubber-soled shoes and standing on a dry floor, for example, may receive a trivial shock from a source which might have killed him if he had been standing in a puddle. To understand the risks, *see* **Safety**/In the home: Safe use of electricity.

If a child receives a momentary shock, by touching a live wire for example, the whole incident will be over before you have realized what is happening. He may suffer from minor shock (*see below* Shock) in which case he will need treating and comforting accordingly, but he is most unlikely to be seriously affected.

Electrical burns

Are a different matter. If a child touches a piece of wire which is acting as a short circuit, it will probably burn his fingers. The burn may look trivial because the action of the electric current closes up the superficial blood vessels so that you may only be able to see a tiny bluish mark. Do not be deceived. There may be amazingly extensive damage to deeper tissues.

All electrical burns should be treated by a doctor.

Continuing electric shock

Very occasionally a child can neither let go of, nor be thrown free from, a wire or appliance which is sending current through him. A.C. current tends to cause muscles to contract and may clench the hand around a faulty appliance; even with D.C. current, a child can become entangled in a live wire and thus continue to receive current.

Stop the current immediately. If there is a wall socket, switch it off or pull out the plug. If there is no socket, switch off all the mains if you can do so really quickly. If you cannot switch off in a hurry:

Move the child from the source of current but don't try to do so with your bare hands: he will be "live" and you will receive the shock, too. Use the nearest *poor conductor of electricity* you can grab: a wooden chair, a cushion, a rubber door mat, to push him clear.

The child may not be badly affected. If the current was passing only through his hand, for example, he will probably need to be treated for minor shock (*see below* Shock), but provided he is fully conscious and has not been burned, you need not worry.

Electric shock can stop both heartbeat and breathing by its effect on the nervous system. If the child is unconscious, he must be rushed to a hospital.

If he appears dead, complete recovery is still possible provided resuscitation starts soon enough and goes on until the victim can receive hospital help. If you are competent to give mouth-to-mouth resuscitation and, probably, heart massage, start immediately. If you are not, get the nearest competent helper by the fastest possible means.

Foreign bodies inserted on purpose

Small children enjoy fitting objects into holes and make no exception for the "holes" in their own bodies. Beads, buttons, fragments of food or toilet paper are often pushed experimentally into ears, noses or vaginas.

Obviously if you see this happen and can see the protruding object, you will remove it. Blunt-ended tweezers may help. If you see it happen but the foreign body is not protruding, you will have to judge whether to try to remove it yourself or to take the child to a doctor. Your judgment must be based on the shape and consistency of the object and on how far in the child has pushed it. A soft, irregularly shaped object such as a piece of apple is easy to grasp with those tweezers. If it is visible in the nostril or ear, you can safely have a try. But a hard round object such as a bead is extremely difficult to get hold of without special forceps. Even if you see it clearly, removal is better left to an expert.

The point is, of course, that while such objects do no immediate harm sitting in the outer passage of the ear or in a nostril, clumsy attempts to get them out can push them further in with disastrous results. If a bead is pushed all the way into the ear, for example, it will end up pressing on the delicate eardrum, possibly even perforating it and damaging the middle ear. Pushed all the way up a nostril, that same bead could exit into the child's air passage and cause serious choking.

If you are taking a child to the doctor or to your emergency room for removal of a foreign body, do remember not to give him anything to eat or drink in the meanwhile. He may need a general anesthetic and the more recently he has had a meal or a snack the longer you will have to wait before it is safe to anesthetize him.

Most foreign bodies are inserted when the child is alone—often because he is lonely and bored in his crib or bed. You may not discover what has happened for days; indeed you may never know.

An object made of an inert mineral substance, such as hard plastic, will set up no reaction in the ear, nose or vagina. It may simply stay there, unsuspected, until perhaps you notice that the child is not breathing with one side of his nose or is not hearing well with one ear. Many such objects probably remain indefinitely until the body's natural secretions eventually carry them out.

An organic foreign body, such as a piece of food, is a different matter. In the nose it will set up an inflammatory reaction leading to a one-sided discharge of thick, purulent pus. In the ear it will eventually decompose, leading to visible discharge. In the vagina it will similarly produce a smelly white discharge. In all such instances you should suspect a foreign body but leave a doctor to investigate.

Foreign bodies in the eye

When dust or a tiny insect gets onto the eyeball or under the eyelid the eye's natural reaction is to water and thus wash out the particle. Try to teach children not to rub the affected eye (which tends to wedge in the particle more firmly) but to concentrate on blinking instead. Younger children may find that permission to rub the *other* eye makes it easier to leave the affected one alone; rubbing the other one will actually help by increasing the tear flow of both.

Watering and blinking will usually move the particle to the outer edge of the eye. If you turn down the lower lid you may be able to see it and remove it, very gently, with a tissue. If the discomfort is under the upper lid, grasping the eyelashes and lifting the lid a little may release the particle and enable it to float down.

Even after a foreign body has been removed, the eye may still be uncomfortable; indeed the child may still insist that there is something in it. This is usually because the eyeball has been very slightly scratched. Such tiny scratches settle down with amazing speed. An older child will understand that the foreign body *is* out and that if she leaves the eye alone the discomfort will vanish within an hour or so. A younger child may go on fiddling with it, searching for the speck he is sure is still there. If distraction does not work, try covering the eye with a pad of gauze or a folded handkerchief, held on with a piece of bandage. If the eye, thus protected, remains uncomfortable for more than an hour, take the child to the doctor.

Foreign bodies on the pupil

Although eyes are surprisingly tough, a speck which is actually lodged on the pupil, remaining despite the eye's watering, should neither be left there nor be removed by anyone but an expert. Cover the eye as above so that there is no chance of the child rubbing it and thus pushing the speck into the pupil. Take her straight to your doctor or to your nearest emergency room.

Penetrating injuries to the eye

Horrible eye injuries can be caused by arrows or darts or by a stick or pencil on which a child falls. Any such injury should at once be covered by a sterile, or at least a clean, pad (sterile gauze is ideal but the inner folds of any linen which has been ironed will do) and the child rushed to a hospital. If you live in a big city which has a specialist eye hospital, you will save precious time by going directly there.

Less serious penetrating injuries can be caused by thorny branches whipping across the child's face or even by particularly sharp pieces of grit blown off a building site or thrown in a sandpit. Look at the eye carefully in good light. If you can *see* a scratch it is serious enough to need medical attention. Protect it with a pad and take the child to a hospital.

Liquids in
the eye
Many household cleaners, solvents, etc. can damage the eye. If a child splashes something into his eyes and screams with pain, don't wait to discover exactly what the liquid was. You can do no harm by getting rid of it (even if it was something painful but fairly harmless like shampoo) and, if it was something like bleach, quick action may save his sight.

You need running water from the cold tap. You need lots of it, immediately, however much the child struggles and however fantastic the flood on your bathroom floor. With his cooperation, by persuasion or by force if necessary, position the child so that you can run water from the cold tap directly through the affected eye. Make sure his head is turned so that the unaffected eye is uppermost. If you do not, you will wash the damaging liquid into that one, too.

Irrigate the affected eye really thoroughly, turning the child's head a little and parting the lids so that every millimeter of the eyeball and every fold of the lids are rinsed again and again. If you have someone else to help you, get him to check on the irritant substance. If it turns out to be harmless, you can stop the water treatment. If it turns out to be acid or corrosive, or if you are not sure whether it is really dangerous or not, get your helper to telephone your doctor or hospital to ask for advice. However dangerous the substance, ten minutes' really thorough irrigation will have done all the good it can. Take child (and substance) to a hospital.

Foreign bodies which are swallowed

Foreign bodies which are *successfully* swallowed seldom present serious problems. If a coin or a button reaches the stomach, it will almost always safely negotiate the rest of its journey and eventually appear in the feces. If you know that a child has swallowed a foreign body, by all means contact your doctor and discuss it with him. There are a few traps for the unwary such as ink cartridges which, while unlikely to cause mechanical damage, can leak and thus poison the child.

Dangerous swallowed foreign bodies are those which the child does indeed swallow but cannot "get down." Fish bones, open safety pins and irregularly shaped, sharp parts of toys will all tend to "get stuck," causing acute pain on swallowing. Expert help will be needed both to locate the foreign body and to remove it. Since the child will almost certainly need a general anesthetic, don't give him lumps of bread or drinks in an attempt to push or wash it down. Take him directly to the nearest hospital.

Foreign bodies which are inhaled

We all inhale foreign bodies quite frequently, walking or cycling through a cloud of flies or taking a rash sniff at something. Usually such particles are trapped in our noses and expelled by the normal mucus flow. If they get further they will provoke coughing and usually be successfully expelled. But a foreign body which penetrates even further still, into the tracheobronchial tree, is a different matter. An organic foreign body, such as that fly, will set up a violent inflammatory reaction so that the victim coughs up purulent material and rapidly becomes extremely ill. A mineral foreign body will set up much less reaction and may, indeed, go unsuspected. A very sudden persistent cough, breathlessness and/or wheezing in a child who is otherwise well should make you suspect a foreign body of this kind.

A child who has inhaled a foreign body will have to have it removed in the hospital, and the sooner it is removed the less likely it is that he will be really ill. Always consult a doctor if your child suddenly develops a cough and/or if an episode of choking shades into a cough.

Fractures

Although a simple definition of a fracture would be "a broken bone," fractures range from minute quick-healing cracks to shattered bones requiring major reconstructive surgery. Serious fractures are rare in young children, whose bones are still pliable and can absorb a lot of stress by bending (*see below* Greenstick fractures), but you cannot predict the probable seriousness or likelihood of a fracture from the nature of the accident. A child can fall many feet off a roof or take a terrifying tumble off a fast-moving bicycle without fracturing anything, but she can trip down one step, fall with her arm in a particular position and fracture it.

When your child has obviously hurt herself, do remember that your job is to get her to professional help as quickly, as comfortably and in as good a general condition as you can manage. If her wrist is swollen and painful, it is not your job to find out whether it is actually fractured or simply sprained. What is the point of wiggling it to try to decide? The wiggling will hurt; if there is a fracture the movement may make it worse and whatever the results she will need to see a doctor. Non-interference is the best policy whenever you are dealing with even the possibility of a fracture. If a trip to the hospital is something you want to avoid if you possibly can, concentrate on comforting and then trying gently to distract the child. Don't particularly encourage her to move or use the hurt limb; just wait and see whether she begins to do so spontaneously. A child who moves and behaves entirely normally within half an hour of an accident has not fractured anything. A child who does not needs medical advice.

When you have to deal with a fracture which is horribly obvious from the weird shape or position of the limb and from the child's acute pain and shock, remember that the damage done to bone, ligaments and muscles as they were forced into that position has already been done but that any further movement—even movement to put it back into its usual position —may do further damage.

Leave it to the professionals. If possible, send for an ambulance and keep the child still while you wait for it to come. Concentrate on comforting her and treating her for shock (*see below*) and let ambulance personnel work out the best way to move her. If you are miles from a telephone and have to transport the child yourself, *try to keep the damaged part from moving*. If an obviously broken arm is dangling at her side, for example, you can use scarves, tights, or whatever you have with you to tie it to her body, placing the ties well above and below the injury. If the arm is being held in a bent position across her body, you can fix it there with a sling around her neck. In theory a broken leg can be similarly supported by being tied to the uninjured one, but in practice it will still be exceedingly difficult to move her singlehandedly without acute pain and further damage. You would probably be better advised to find somebody who will help you or send for help. If it seems at all possible to you that a child has damaged her spine, including her neck, *moving her could kill or cripple her* by injuring the spinal cord. Do what you can to make her comfortable and treat her for shock where she is, but don't try to move her. Find some way to summon professional help.

A child with a greenstick or simple fracture (*see below*) will usually be allowed home as soon as it has been X-rayed, seen by a doctor and put into a plaster cast. Remember that:

Fractures are not usually acutely painful once they have been treated. The child may have a bad night due to a combination of pain and exhaustion following minor shock and the stress of her time at the hospital, but if she continues to complain of pain for more than twenty-four hours you should consider having her checked again at the hospital. Sometimes, for example, an injured limb continues to swell after treatment so that the cast itself becomes painfully tight.

Wearing a cast is tiring and can strain other muscles. A child who is trying to do everything one-handedly will probably become irritable and frustrated; one who is walking on crutches or with a "walking cast" will be putting a lot of strain on the good leg and may become very tired and achy by the end of the day. The trick is to let her use her energy and effort on the things she really must do (like going to school) and the things she really wants to do (like having her birthday treat all the same), but to let her off some of the routine things (like making her bed or running her own errands) in between.

Mended bones and ligaments take time to regain full strength and disused muscles become slack. When that cast is finally removed, do listen carefully to the doctor's advice about when the child should return to active sports or about any exercises which she should do either with you or in the hospital physiotherapy department. Once the drama of a fracture is over it is easy to stop bothering. Don't. If she does not give ligaments time to strengthen she may strain them and leave herself with a permanent weakness. If she demands too much of muscles which have not been used at all for several weeks she is likely to injure herself all over again.

You may hear various types of fracture mentioned in the hospital:

Greenstick fractures   The bone has bent and cracked like a green twig rather than snapping like a dry one. The fracture should heal easily and completely because the damaged part of the bone is held in place by the undamaged part and neither the blood nor the nerve supply has been completely cut off.

Simple fractures

The bone has broken completely but the broken ends are still perfectly aligned with each other. A cast will ensure that the ends do not move apart and the bone should knit together again easily.

More serious closed fractures

Sometimes the force which fractures a bone moves the broken ends out of alignment. This is far more serious than a simple fracture not only because the limb will have to be "set" (i.e., have the bone ends manipulated back into the proper position for healing), but also because those broken ends have already moved inside the limb and will have damaged nerves, muscles and blood vessels. If a major blood vessel was cut there may be enough internal bleeding to cause severe shock (*see below*) and there will almost inevitably be severe pain which will increase her shock reaction.

Comminuted fractures are those in which a bone is not merely broken and displaced but broken in two or more places or actually shattered. Open surgery will be required to reconstruct the bone. Pins may be used to hold it together while healing takes place.

Impacted fractures are those in which the broken ends of a bone have been rammed into one another. Surgery will again be required.

Compound fractures

Are fractures which are associated with an external wound. Sometimes the broken ends of the bone have moved so far that they have pierced the skin. Sometimes something has gone through the skin and flesh to fracture the bone. Whichever it is, a compound fracture is almost always more serious than a closed one because the bone is exposed to infection and the child may lose a lot of blood.

Head injuries

Every baby and small child gets a nasty bump on the head at some time or another. The younger the child, the larger and heavier his head in relation to the rest of him so the more likely it is that when he falls, his head will suffer. Older children often have better acceleration than brakes: they run into each other and into doors. Later still, contact sports, like football, take their toll, as do missiles like baseballs or even rocks. Finally, of course, even the most sensible teenager can fall off a bicycle or stand up under a beam which recent growth has suddenly made too low for him.

Bumps on the head often *look* serious. Parents know that they *can be* serious and therefore they cause a tremendous amount of worry. The worry is almost always unnecessary because there is no mystery about head injuries. If you know what to look for, you will always be able to tell whether your child needs help or not. If he seems all right and goes on seeming all right, he is all right.

Why bumps on the head often look serious even when they are not

The skin covering the head (the scalp) has a rich supply of blood vessels and is comparatively tightly stretched over a structure (the skull) with little "give" in it.

Even a tiny cut or graze tends to bleed profusely so that your child may rush in with blood trickling down his face. Cuts tend to go on bleeding, too, because even the smallest nick in that stretched skin gapes open.

While simple pressure, even through the hair, may stop such bleeding, a cut which would need no treatment if it were elsewhere on the body may need a stitch to hold the edges together.

Even if the scalp is not actually cut, bangs on the head, especially on the forehead, tend to make dramatically large and swollen bruises. If your one-year-old has a lump the size of a goose's egg it is hard to believe that the blow which caused it was unimportant.

Falls on the head are frightening. Your child may seem shocked (*see below*) after a bang which would scarcely have bothered him if he had taken it on the knee.

Why bumps on the head can be dangerous

The bony skull, covered by scalp and hair, protects the brain. Cuts and bumps on the scalp are no more dangerous than similar injuries elsewhere. Cracks or fractures in the skull are no more dangerous than similar injuries to other bones. What matters is what, if anything, has happened to the brain beneath.

There are three main ways in which the brain can be damaged by a blow on the head:

"Concussion." This loosely used term means that the brain has been jarred and shaken in such a way that part of it has knocked against the inside of the skull. Such a child may lose consciousness (be "knocked out") either momentarily or for hours. The seriousness of a concussion depends on the exact area of the brain involved, but, as we shall see, any child who is obviously concussed should be seen by a doctor.

Concussion with bleeding inside the skull. If some of the tiny blood vessels between the brain and the skull are damaged, they will bleed. Such bleeding can be inside (subdural) or outside (extradural) the brain's covering membrane. Because the free blood is trapped inside the rigid skull it can form a clot which presses into the brain. The clot will almost certainly have to be surgically removed.

Since this kind of bleeding does not produce recognizable symptoms until clotting *has* taken place, a child who has sustained a heavy blow on the head will often be kept in the hospital for twenty-four hours' "observation."

Skull fractures. Hairline fractures of the skull are common. Braced by the structure of the skull, such fractures heal themselves and are unimportant. If your child bumps his head, has an X-ray and is found to have fractured his skull, the fracture does not, in itself, mean that the head injury was serious.

But very occasionally there is a "depressed fracture." This means that a piece of the skull bone has been pushed inwards. Like a blood clot, a depressed skull fracture can put pressure on the brain. The bone will almost certainly have to be lifted back into line surgically.

Concussion and unconsciousness

Concussion does not always lead to unconsciousness, but a child who is unconscious after a bang on the head is always concussed.

Do not move him unless he is in a really dangerous place such as a room which is on fire. Until he regains consciousness you have no way of knowing which parts of him are damaged (*see above* Fractures).

Do not try to wake him up.

Do not try to give him anything to drink.

Guard his breathing by loosening any clothing which may have pulled tight around his neck and by making sure that neither blood nor vomit gets into his windpipe. If he has fallen on his back and *is* bleeding from the nose or showing signs of vomiting, you will have a difficult judgment to make. To protect that vital breathing you should turn him onto his front so that secretions run out of his mouth. But if his spine—at any level from the neck downwards—should be damaged, turning him over could do further harm.

Send for an ambulance.

If he comes around while you are waiting, keep him lying down but reassure him (and yourself as you begin to see that it is so) that he is not seriously hurt but must stay lying down until a doctor has checked him over. Remember that he will be confused and frightened because he will not remember how he came to be lying where he finds himself and that fear and anxiety increase shock (*see below* Shock).

The child who has been unconscious   Often a concussed child is momentarily "knocked out" but "comes around" within seconds of the blow. If you see him lying unconscious but he is awake by the time you reach him, lay him down, treat him for shock and send for an ambulance.

If you are not sure whether he was unconscious or not, ask him exactly what happened to him. If he cannot remember falling down or cannot remember getting up again and coming towards you, he almost certainly was unconscious and should be treated as above.

Bleeding or discharge from the ears   Blood or clear fluid coming from within the ear does suggest quite serious head injury. The child should be treated as if he had been unconscious.

Bleeding from the nose or mouth can be due to direct local injury but can also be a sign of serious head injury. If you can see blood but cannot see a cut lip or bruised nose, play it safe and treat him as if he had been knocked unconscious.

If none of the above signs are present but the child seems shocked and dazed, you can take time to comfort and observe him before sending for medical help. If a quick cuddle is enough to make him feel better enough to get on with life, let him. If he is more distressed than that or obviously "feels funny," lay him down on the sofa and chat to him while you **watch for any change in his level of consciousness, any peculiarity in his behavior or any new physical symptoms.** After about twenty minutes' rest he will probably be perfectly recovered. After this time:

You need medical advice if: He is still very pale or grayish; his breathing seems noisy although he is not crying; he complains of feeling giddy or "odd"; he seems "odd" or irrational or unable to recognize or respond to you as he usually does; he seems unable to see clearly, makes odd noises or (assuming that he is of talking age) he talks nonsense or his speech is slurred.

You would be wise to consult your doctor, at least by telephone, if he vomits or complains of headache. Vomiting can be a simple reaction to the shock of the bump while a young child may confuse headache with the pain of the actual bruise, but since these symptoms can also be signs of concussion it is best to play safe.

If none of these symptoms appear and the child wants to get up and get going, let him. The chance that the bang on his head has affected his brain is now very remote indeed. It is still remotely possible, however, that there might be a slow seepage of blood between skull and brain or that a skull fracture is causing pressure. These traumas are rare and usually show up immediately as an obvious "concussion," but they can show up over the twelve or so hours after the accident: bleeding, for example, may produce no symptoms of disturbance until the blood clots and presses inwards.

Keeping a watchful eye for later effects of head injury

You need not limit the child's ordinary activities in any way but, preferably without his being aware of any anxiety, you should be alert for the later development of any of the above signs of concussion, as well as for unusual clumsiness, irritability, jumpiness or any behavior which makes you feel uneasy. As long as he seems entirely normal and ordinary, all is well.

If he drops off to sleep after the accident his body is probably using the best possible means of getting over the shock. Let him sleep but look in from time to time to make sure that his color and breathing seem just as usual. If you have any reason to think that sleep may be turning into unconsciousness, try waking him up. He may be cross at being disturbed but too bad. You want to be sure that he is normally wakeable.

If you cannot decide whether he seems ordinary or not, call the doctor. He may see the child immediately or he may advise you to wake him a couple of times in the night to check his level of consciousness and to stay in touch by telephone. But once you have told your doctor about a possibly serious head injury you can be quite sure that he will play it super-safe so if he says "don't worry," don't. And if he admits the child to the hospital for twenty-four hours' observation, don't assume that the child is seriously affected. Such a medical watch is only a precaution which is usually unnecessary but can be life-saving.

● If an adolescent has been drinking or taking other drugs at the time of a head injury it can be extremely difficult to distinguish between the signs of intoxication and concussion. Tragedies sometimes occur when adults, who are assumed to be only drunk, are left in a police cell to "sober up" and are later found to have been concussed as well. Hospitals find it difficult, too, but the responsibility is better left to them.

Poisoning

(*see also* **Safety**/In the home: Safety from household poisons; Safety with medicines)

If a child takes something poisonous, he must be treated *quickly*. While some substances—caustic soda, for example—do damage even as they are swallowed, most do no harm until they have been in the child's stomach for long enough for the chemicals to start being absorbed into his bloodstream. If he has a handful of berries or pills in his stomach and you can get them up again more or less intact, he will come to no harm.

But although speed is vital, do slow down enough to think when you find your child in suspicious circumstances. Has he *really* swallowed those aspirins or are they clutched in his hand, scattered on the floor or neatly mailed into the toilet? Treatment for poisoning is terrifying and horrible for a child (induced violent vomiting and/or stomach pumping). Once you rush him to the hospital saying that he has taken something poisonous, the staff will have to take your word for it and proceed. It would be tragic if panic had led you to put him through that for nothing.

Poisonous substances

A long list of different chemicals which are variously dangerous if consumed in different quantities will probably not help you or the child on the day a poisoning drama strikes. Many substances are poorly labelled so that you will not be able to tell whether or not there is something lethal in that furniture polish. Although a poison center will be able to tell from the brand name alone, centers in many countries will only advise doctors so you have to seek medical aid before you can be sure whether your child is in danger or not. Finally, it is usually extremely difficult to tell *how much* of a suspicious or downright lethal substance a child has consumed. Perhaps that bottle of liquid was full, but how much has soaked into his jersey and the carpet? As for those pills, do you really know how many there were? And can you estimate how many have been ground to powdery bits in his hand?

Unless you live in a country with superb labelling and a poison control center which will directly answer parents' queries (as in the United States), it is best to play safe and assume that *any* of the following substances, in *any* quantity, may poison your child.

Pills, capsules and medicines

Whether prescribed or bought over the counter and whether intended originally for the child or an adult. The commonest causes of serious or fatal poisoning are tricyclic antidepressants, iron, paracetamol and aspirin, but you must include vitamins, contraceptive pills, travel sickness remedies and antihistamines as well as liquids like cough mixtures.

Chemicals

□ Home: including polishes, toilet cleaners, deodorizers, etc.
□ Garden: *especially* weedkillers, insecticides and fungicides.
□ Garage: not forgetting gas, oil, kerosene.

Berries

Unless you know what they are and that they are harmless.

Wild fungi

Unless you can see that they are genuine mushrooms or other edibles.

Tobacco

One whole cigarette, actually swallowed, could kill a one-year-old.

Alcohol

A good swig of neat spirits (rather than wine, beer, etc.) could kill a toddler.

Coping with poisoning

More and more authorities are coming to believe that stomach pumping (*see* **Hospital**/Procedures) is unnecessarily barbarous in many cases of possible poisoning; hospitals increasingly induce vomiting instead. If vomiting is the treatment of choice and speed is important, it may be sensible for you to get on with it without waiting until you can reach the hospital. In the United States this would certainly be the accepted advice to parents. In Britain and some other European countries you would be wise to ask your own doctor for his opinion *before it ever happens*.

Making the child vomit

If you are going to make a child vomit, you must get both the circumstances and the method right.

Don't induce vomiting if the suspicious substance is any kind of cleaner, polish, bleach, disinfectant, or petroleum product. In fact, avoid inducing vomiting for anything in the "chemicals" group. This is because some (though not all) such products either burn the mouth and throat when swallowed and will do so again coming up, or give out poisonous fumes which will be further inhaled during vomiting.

Do induce vomiting if the suspicious substance is a pill or medicine, a berry or fungus, tobacco or alcohol.

Don't try to make him sick with old-fashioned emetics such as salt and water or mustard and water. They are dangerous in themselves.

Don't rely on mechanical vomiting. You can make a child retch by boldly putting a finger to the back of his throat and wiggling it. If his retching produces a vomit containing the aspirin tablets he has just eaten, fine. But the retching may produce nothing at all or nothing useful.

If your doctor agrees, use ipecac syrup. This is a reliable and effective emetic which really does "empty" the stomach. Indeed some research suggests that it removes just as much of the stomach contents as a mechanical stomach pumping; 2 tsp of the syrup for a one-year-old, rising to 4 tsp for a three-year-old, *followed by a glass of water*, will produce vomiting within twenty minutes. Use the twenty minutes to telephone your doctor or to start for the hospital. Take a plastic bag for the vomit: the hospital staff will need to see what came up.

Summary of first aid for poisoning

☐ Remove substance remaining in child's mouth, hands, etc.
☐ Check that some really has been swallowed.
☐ Give ipecac syrup if substance is appropriate.
☐ Telephone doctor/hospital; tell them you are bringing child and what it is that he has taken so that they can use the intervening time to check with a poison center.
☐ Collect container and any scattered contents.
☐ Take child and container (plus vomit bag if appropriate) to a hospital as fast as possible.
☐ If you are driving, strap child in sitting-up position or lay him on his side, in case he vomits and breathes it in.

Older children and poisonous substances

Accidental poisoning is, of course, much rarer in older children and it is usually easier to deal with sensibly because the child herself can tell you or show you *what* she has taken, and *how much*. She might eat one poisonous berry, mistaking it for a fruit but she is unlikely to eat a handful because it will not taste good. In most such cases, call your doctor, hospital or poison center and take their advice.

Occasional tragedies happen when a child takes a swig out of a lemonade bottle which is being used as a container for weedkiller or turpentine. . . . Of course this should never happen, but it does.

There are a few substances which are exceedingly dangerous even if only a tiny drop is swallowed. If you cannot remember exactly what that liquid is in the lemonade bottle, you *must* rush child and bottle to a hospital.

- For non-accidental poisoning *see* **Suicide**.

Shock

Shock is a complicated condition whose basic cause is a sudden fall in blood pressure which reduces the efficiency with which the heart can pump blood through the circulation and therefore reduces the supply available to the brain.

The severity of shock depends on the cause and duration of that fall in pressure. When a child has a nasty fright or faints (*see* **Fainting**) reflex activity dilates the blood vessels to the internal organs so that the pressure within all the blood vessels is reduced. That child is momentarily in a state of shock, but as she recovers from her start of fear or comes round from her faint, her blood pressure will return to normal and all will be well. When a child is severely injured, however, the fall in blood pressure which puts her into a state of shock will not be so simply reversible because something other than reflex activity is causing it (*see below* Major shock).

Causes of minor shock

The cause may be entirely emotional: a reaction to bad news, to finding a pet dead or to seeing a bloody accident.

Often the cause is a mixture of emotion and physical distress; the child may get slightly hurt in particularly frightening circumstances.

Continuing pain and fear increase and lengthen any shock reaction so that a minor burn may lead to more shock than a comparable, but less painful, cut, and waiting to hear the worst may lead to more shock than bad news which is cut and dried.

Symptoms of minor shock

The victim's skin is pale, cold and clammy because, with the fall in blood pressure, the blood vessels supplying the skin close up as much as possible so that all possible blood is pumped to the vital organs.

She may shiver, tremble, feel giddy or faint; she may cry or vomit. Because its blood supply has been temporarily reduced, the brain's control over the body is disrupted.

Coping with minor shock

The child may recover so rapidly that you have no time to do anything and therefore no need to exercise your first aid talents, either. If not:

Lay her down on her side. Lying down assists the action of the heart and uses gravity to help ensure a maximal share of blood for the brain. Lying on her side ensures that if she should vomit it will run harmlessly out of her mouth rather than being inhaled.

Comfort and reassure her in whatever way is appropriate to the cause of the shock. Remember that pain and fear create a vicious circle.

Cover her with a light blanket, coat or whatever you have to preserve her body warmth.

Do not warm her artificially with hot water bottles, etc. If you do so, her skin color may improve because the warmth will force the blood vessels beneath to reopen. But although she will *look* better her condition will actually be worse because that extra blood will be being supplied at the expense of the brain and other vital organs.

Do not give anything to drink. Neither that old standby "hot sweet tea" nor alcohol is at all a good idea. The tea (or other sugary drink) cannot be absorbed from the stomach while she is in shock and is therefore likely to be vomited. If alcohol is absorbed, its effects on her central nervous system will actually delay its return to normal.

If the shock condition really is minor these measures will produce clear improvement within five minutes—perhaps less. You will see her color return to normal and her skin will dry and rewarm: tension and shakiness will relax. She may drop off to sleep or get up and get on with life. Even if the cause of the shock reaction still exists as pain, grief or horror remembered, she will no longer appear *ill*.

If there is no improvement within five minutes or recovery is not complete within half an hour, reconsider the cause of the shock; it may have been more serious than you believed. Call your doctor.

Causes of major shock   Blood pressure can be seriously lowered by:

Heavy bleeding, whether this is sudden—as from a severed artery or hemorrhage from the womb—or more insidious, as when less dramatic bleeding is allowed to continue for so long that the blood loss eventually reaches a critical level.

Internal bleeding following injuries to internal organs, such as a crushed liver or lung damaged by broken ribs, or following abdominal crises such as a ruptured appendix.

Bleeding within the tissues such as may occasionally occur around the jagged ends of a badly fractured bone or within a very large area of deep bruising (*see above*).

Loss of plasma from the circulation, as in extensive burns (*see above*).

Loss of other body fluids leading to dehydration. If violent or long-continued diarrhea and/or vomiting reduces the fluid available to the body too far, the volume available within the circulation will eventually drop, too (*see* **Diarrhea, Gastroenteritis and Food Poisoning**).

Serious shock can also be caused, without loss of fluid from the circulation or the body tissues, by overwhelming systemic illnesses such as septicemia, or if the brain's control over the circulation is disrupted.

Damage to the brain or central nervous system (*see above* Head injuries) can deprive the brain of blood or, through disruption of respiration, deprive it of oxygen even when an adequate supply of blood is still being pumped by the heart.

Symptoms of major shock
First symptoms will be similar to those of minor shock (*see above*) but may be more pronounced so that the victim is not only pale and clammy but covered in cold sweat; not only shaky and dizzy but collapsed and irrational.

Coping with major shock
Give first aid for obvious injuries such as stopping heavy bleeding or cooling burns.

If injuries are clearly serious, send for help. While waiting, treat exactly as outlined in coping with minor shock.

If injuries are not clear, treat exactly as you would treat for minor shock and wait a few minutes for signs of improvement.

If the shock condition is serious in itself you will see no improvement and must send urgently for help. These measures cannot reverse major shock because the failure of blood supply to the brain is due either to a shortage of blood or fluid or to failure of control in the circulation. Instead of recovery you will see progressive symptoms which, without prompt hospital help, may be fatal. For example:

Because the circulation is short of blood volume, the heart beats faster and the pulse races.

Because the heart is working harder and harder to pump less than the optimum amount of blood, it pumps less and less efficiently.

Because the heart pumps less efficiently, less and less blood reaches the brain whose control circuits become increasingly disrupted.

Eventually this vicious circle affects breathing. The victim may breathe very rapidly yet be unable to get enough oxygen so that she suffers from what is termed "air hunger" and begins to gasp in uncoordinated breaths.

If you do not see immediate improvement in a shocked child, send for help before you begin to see her condition worsen in this way.

While you are waiting for the ambulance or doctor, continue to treat her as for minor shock. Your first aid will not produce recovery but will do all that can be done to prevent her condition from worsening until the cause can be treated and the shock condition reversed.

Sports injuries

Few sports activities are more dangerous than other kinds of active physical exercise and few injuries received during sports are special; a fracture is a fracture whether it happens while kicking a football or climbing a tree. Nevertheless, there are some particular risks of particular types of injury which the parents of sports-mad children may want to consider.

Sports and athletics are becoming increasingly popular with more and more people practicing them and even more watching them do so. There is big money involved at the top for participants, backers, sponsors and associated industries. At the bottom, even at primary school level, there are high rewards in terms of self-esteem and status within the peer group. Children and young people tend to push themselves towards higher and higher levels of performance and competition and to be pushed, too. There are not only individual aspirations involved but also those of team mates, coaches and club supporters. Physical courage is part of the ethos of most sports and certainly a requirement for any form of athletic training at any level. If a child's own desire to succeed is bolstered by pressures to succeed for other people's honor and glory, he may train, practice and compete when he is not fit to do so. A line has to be drawn between courage and folly; the child's well-being in the long run has to be balanced against the team's well-being in tomorrow's game. Few youngsters will be able to exercise that kind of judgment for themselves when their competitive spirit is aroused. They need parents to do it for them.

General health and sports injuries

A child who has gone through all the appropriate training and reached an appropriate level of fitness for his sporting-activities (*see* **Safety**) will nevertheless risk injury if he participates when unwell. A heavy head cold, for example, partially obstructs breathing. The deliberate respiratory stress incurred in a training session can easily become respiratory distress. Fever, whatever the underlying cause, means that heavy physical activity will make him liable to heat exhaustion (*see below* Sunburn and heat illness) as well as to hypothermia if his sport involves water (*see above* Drowning). Some girls may be more liable to accidental injury at the time of their menstrual periods (*see* **Adolescence**/Menstruation), while both sexes will be vulnerable immediately after minor infections during which muscles have lost their full tone.

Overuse syndromes in sports

By definition, training for or participating in a sport involves repeated exercises affecting particular bones, tendons and muscle groups. They are stressed so that they build the strength to meet the demands of the chosen activity. But *too* many repetitions of the same movement or the slightest *change* in that movement (such as running in different training shoes or on a harder surface) can cause a minute amount of damage. The vital point in all these syndromes is that the very first symptoms are mild indicators of a very minor injury. Because the injury is mild, rest will quickly allow it to heal. But because the symptoms are minor, the child can easily override them and will often be encouraged to do so by overenthusiastic coaches and colleagues who attribute the warning pain to "a muscle strain" and suggest that the victim "work it off."

The most dramatic example of an overuse syndrome is a stress fracture. The affected bone (often the upper leg bone, the femur, in children or the lower leg bone, the fibula, in older joggers and runners) develops a minute crack rather as an airplane wing can eventually develop the minute cracks of metal fatigue. There is pain on exercise but no loss of function and, for the moment, the pain stops when exercise stops. If the exercise is avoided for a few days that bone crack (unlike the airplane wing) will heal itself. But if it continues, the crack will very gradually spread, the pain will increase and, eventually, that crack can turn into a full fracture.

Unfortunately an *early* stress fracture is almost impossible to see on a conventional X-ray. Only four to six weeks after the injury will a visible area of denser bony growth confirm such damage. The absence of early X-ray findings makes it even more likely that the child will try to dismiss his pain as "only a strain" and struggle to go on with his activities.

A stress fracture which is allowed to develop into a full fracture is an obvious disaster, but there are less dramatic examples which are equally important. Symptoms in the Achilles tendon, linking heel with ankle, for example, are often attributed to tight football shoes or hard ground conditions and therefore ignored. Yet acute inflammation or an incomplete rupture of this tendon can produce chronic pain and disability if it is left untreated and especially if it is abused by further exercise of the causative kind.

Guarding your child against the overuse syndromes takes a great deal of tact. If every time your child limps home you try to insist on a week's rest you will simply earn the label "fussy mother" and he will first try to conceal pain from you and then eventually defy you. Yet if you do not react to that limp, leaving it entirely to the child to decide whether or not he is fit to train tomorrow or compete on Saturday, you leave him to the mercies of peers and coaches who may be as concerned with their team's reputation as with your child's well-being. Some children, at some stages in their sporting lives, may actually *want* you to forbid their participation because by doing so you allow them to take time off without having to admit to personal "weakness." You may find the following ideas helpful:

Make sure you are acquainted with your child's coach, whether he is a professional or simply an enthusiastic schoolteacher or father-helping-out-with-the-kids. You need to know how concerned he is for his young sportsmen's well-being and how he balances that against "his" competitive successes. You also need to know how he handles the youngsters. If he is a "macho" type who bullies them, your child is the more liable to be pushed beyond his limits. If he puts as high a premium on courage as on skill and tends to deride anyone who claims to be injured, that child will obviously find it the more difficult to draw a well-placed line between courage and folly.

Make it clear to your child that you are among his sporting supporters but that your parenting comes first and therefore that his long-term health will always matter more to you than his short-term successes. Make it clear that you take his courage for granted and know something of the pain and discomfort which is a necessary part of all sports and athletics training, so that he will realize that any attempts to call a halt when he is injured are not simply attempts to save him pain but rather to save him the risk of disability.

Refuse to indulge in amateur sportsmedicine yourself. Don't buy or apply support bandages and liniments. Explain that a wrongly applied bandage or a bandage applied to support muscles when an underlying bone or tendon is damaged can do more harm than good. Explain also that any injury which requires treatment requires diagnosis first and that diagnosis can only be made by a doctor.

Use the child's doctor as the arbiter between you and the child whenever questions of fitness for sports cause trouble between you. The doctor may not be able to diagnose accurately an early stress condition, but he will certainly play safe by insisting on rest unless he is sure there is no risk in continued exercise. Remember that a doctor's edict will be far easier for your child to abide by than an edict from you. No self-respecting young-ster will go into the locker rooms saying, "My mom says I'm not to. . . ." "The doctor won't let me . . ." is far more socially acceptable.

Sprains and strains

People often use these terms interchangeably which is unfortunate as they differ in their nature, their usual severity and their recommended treatment.

Sprains A sprain properly refers to an injury caused by bending or twisting a joint suddenly and/or beyond its normal limits. The ligaments which support the joint are overstretched or torn. There may be extensive damage to the surrounding tissue and blood vessels. Such an injury is excruciatingly painful. There will be rapid swelling of the joint area which may also appear bruised. Occasionally, especially when it is the wrist which is sprained, the damage to the ligaments allows a partial dislocation of the joint. This complication is called a subluxation. It is almost impossible to tell a severe sprain from a fracture without the help of an X-ray, so it is best not to try:

First aid Treat a suspected sprain exactly as you would treat a suspected greenstick
for sprains fracture (*see above* Fractures).

Hospital The affected joint will probably be X-rayed both to exclude the possibility
treatment of a fracture and to enable the doctor to get some idea of the severity of the
for sprains damage done to the ligaments. Once he has this information, the sprain will probably be bandaged in such a way that support from the bandage provides some of the support to the joint which is normally given by the ligaments that have been damaged. Sometimes, especially if an ankle is severely sprained, plaster of Paris will be used to immobilize the joint.

After a sprain listen carefully to the doctor's instructions about what the child may/must do with the affected joint during the next days and weeks. A period of rest will be needed to give the ligaments time to heal, but too long a period of immobility may lead to a stiff joint. Any suggested exercises should be performed conscientiously. Pain may be more severe and last longer than in a simple fracture.

Strains A strain properly refers to overstretching or tearing of some of the fibers of a muscle or group of muscles, due to sudden or unusual movement. Sudden, awkward lifting, for example, can strain muscles low in the back, while strained muscles in the calves are common when active games are played on a slippery surface.

Because muscles occur in dense groups, these injuries are seldom serious. The affected muscle will heal itself and other muscles will support it and do its work during the recovery period. There is no risk of loss of function as there is when a joint is sprained. Very occasionally, though, a whole group of muscles may be torn to produce a much more dramatic injury. If a person grabs for a heavy, falling object, for example, the biceps can tear, leaving a visible "hole" in the upper arm which rapidly turns blue from bleeding under the skin. This rare kind of strain requires immediate hospital treatment.

First aid for mild strains   No real treatment is required. The victim will be more comfortable if he avoids stressing the damaged muscle, but he should not be encouraged to rest completely as gentle exercise will prevent stiffness and speed recovery. Strained muscles tend to be most painful first thing in the morning just because they have been at rest; the day's mobility relieves pain and stiffness.

Home treatment for strains often includes liniments rubbed into the surrounding skin. The logic for this kind of treatment is that the liniments increase the blood supply to the muscle and thus relieve pain and aid healing. In fact, especially with a deep-seated muscle, it is unlikely that the liniment can have any effect at all. The rubbing may, however, increase the blood supply as can a hot bath.

After a strain repeating the exercise which caused the strain in the first place will certainly be painful and may delay healing, so while some exercise is desirable, some limits may be desirable also. A calf strain caused during football, for example, probably ought to mean no football for a few days or until the pain has gone. Putting a support bandage on so as to enable the victim to play despite a strain is a poor idea: it is better to allow the muscle to regain its true strength rather than to provide it with artificial support.

Sunburn and heat illness

Although these things often come together to ruin a family vacation or bedevil a move to a new and hotter area, they need not be linked at all.

Sunburn is caused only by the sun's particular radiation or by "sunlamps" which are designed to mimic it. No other heat source will cause sunburn but the sun may burn even when the victim feels cool. A sunny day's sailing, for example, may lead to serious sunburn. The cool sea breeze prevents the victim from feeling hot and may indeed make it more comfortable to be in the sun than in the shade. Yet she is being doubly exposed to those rays because they are not only beating down on her but also reflecting back off the water to burn unlikely and agonizing places like the backs of her knees.

Heat illness, on the other hand, is caused by hot conditions irrespective of the source of the heat. The heat of the sun may cause it (with or without causing sunburn as well) but so may the heat from an indoor blast furnace. A long afternoon's tennis on a hot cloudy day can precipitate heat illness even though the cloud layer prevents sunburn. Without those clouds sunburn would have been a risk but heat illness would have been less likely because the victim would have found it impossible to play on in the direct sun.

Sunburn Is far easier to prevent than to treat (*see* **Safety**/On vacation). Everyone knows that unaccustomed skin should be only gradually exposed to the sun so that it can build up protective pigment ahead of the burning point. Almost everyone hurries the process in search of that tan and many pay in soreness and eventually by losing the tan in peeling. Older people may choose to risk agony for the sake of beauty but babies and young children are entitled to protection:

Choose suntan oils or lotions carefully. Most now state their "protection factor"; the higher the number, the greater the screening effect. A young child may need a factor of six or eight, but even this will protect her only if it is applied to *all* exposed skin and renewed frequently.

Remember that sunburn does not hurt at the time but only some hours after exposure. Don't ration your child's sunbathing time according to whether or not her skin feels uncomfortable *now*. It may be agonizing later.

Remember that your position relative to the sun changes as the day goes on. If you put a baby to sleep in the shade or under a sun umbrella, make sure that the spot will stay shady until she gets up again.

First aid for sunburn **If the skin is red and sore to the touch,** cool it. Don't try a cold shower or bath: the superheated skin will over-react and she will be shivery and miserable. Use tepid water and let it cool her by evaporation. Cover with moisturizer or an "after-sun" product.

Cover the sunburned area with the lightest, softest, smoothest fabric you can find. Even the seams on her T-shirt may be painful. At bedtime, make sure that her bed-sheet is tightly stretched so that the skin is not irritated by wrinkles.

Keep her in the shade. Even a brief touch of sun will hurt very much and increase the burn. If you cannot keep her in the shade while staying around the beach you may have to reorganize your day and make an inland expedition by car.

If she is miserable a couple of hours later take her temperature. There may be some heat illness associated with the sunburn (*see below*).

If the skin blisters find a doctor. Many parents treat sunburn blisters themselves, using products such as calamine lotion. Although you may get away with it this is risky. If the blisters burst infection is likely and acute pain is certain. There will be superficial scars, too.

Heat illness This is much rarer and much more serious than simple sunburn. It is most likely to occur when an *unaccustomed* individual meets some combination of the following conditions:
□ Very high air temperatures, especially if they are caused by radiant heat such as the sun, fire, etc.

□ High humidity so that as well as being extremely hot the air is "muggy" or "stuffy."
□ Active exercise.
□ Copious sweating which is not adequately replaced by drinking.
□ Copious sweating without an adequate intake of salt.

● For the individual on vacation, being even slightly unwell, perhaps with a low-grade fever, much increases the risk of heat illness. The child is anxious to waste no time and therefore does not give in to the illness. She exercises vigorously but probably is not very hungry and therefore misses the salt which would be present in her normal meals. If a child is unwell on vacation, try to persuade her that it is better to lose one day in rest than several in real illness. If a day in her room seems unnecessary, try at least to arrange for a cool quiet day rather than a hot rambunctious one.

The severity of heat illness ranges from passing faintness and feelings of exhaustion to life-threatening collapse:

Heat syncope

This is simple fainting provoked by some of the above conditions. The child "passes out" or collapses to the ground feeling dizzy. She rapidly comes around once she is lying down, but even if she feels perfectly all right she should lie in cool conditions for a while.

Heat exhaustion

This is a generic term used to describe collapse in and due to hot conditions which lasts longer than momentary heat syncope.

The victim feels faint, dizzy and peculiar because the vital salt and water balance of the body is upset and this affects the efficient working of the heart and the supply of blood to the brain (*see above* Shock). The specific cause may be shortage of water or shortage of salt or a mixture of the two. Either or both will be related to inadequate replacement of what is lost through heavy sweating. Lack of water may simply be caused by the victim failing to drink enough extra fluids to compensate for her sweat loss. Children on vacation in foreign countries, for example, are sometimes sensibly forbidden to drink the water from hotel taps, yet are less sensibly limited in the number of drinks they are allowed to purchase from the bar or café. Economizing on drinks is a very false economy indeed.

Shortage of salt is unlikely if the victim has been eating normally, but is possible if she has not wanted much food. It is also possible if heavy sweat loss has made her so thirsty that she *has* drunk a great deal of pure water. She may then have diluted the salt concentration of her body fluids too far.

Anyone who is "taken ill" in hot conditions should be made to lie down in a cool, shady, well-ventilated place and, as a first aid measure, should be given cool drinks containing a pinch of salt per glass.

If the victim does not feel very much better within half an hour and/or is not completely recovered and eager to get up and get on with life after, say, three hours at rest and two pints of drink, she should be seen by a doctor.

If there is any loss of consciousness, vomiting or fever a doctor should be sent for immediately, heat exhaustion may be turning into heat stroke.

Heat stroke True heat stroke implies that the body has been subjected to such a heat load that its internal heat-regulating mechanism has been temporarily disrupted. Simply removing her from the heat stress will not cure the condition.

The first signs will be similar to those of heat exhaustion: the child will feel dizzy, sick and "peculiar." But in addition she will shoot a sudden high fever and may rapidly become confused and delirious.

Heat stroke is a grade-one emergency. The child must immediately be admitted to a hospital where she can be cooled under controlled conditions and be treated for shock (*see above*) as well as having the fluid/salt balance of her body investigated and corrected.

Wounds and bleeding

Any wound which breaks the skin damages some blood vessels and therefore causes some bleeding. Some children (and adults!) are alarmed by the sight of blood. It may help if they realize that the bleeding from a cut helps to carry any dirt out of the wound and some is therefore highly desirable.

Bleeding from most wounds is trivial. It stops of its own accord as air reaches the broken edges of the little blood vessels. The blood clots and seals them.

Bleeding which shows no sign of stopping on its own is almost always easily stopped simply by pressing on the wound through a piece of gauze, a handkerchief or whatever. The pressure holds back the flow of blood to the cut edges of the blood vessels, thus enabling clotting to take place. Even a cut which has been dripping all over the floor will stop in three minutes if you just hold onto it.

Bleeding does not become dangerous in itself until a *very great deal of blood has been lost*. A baby or small child can lose a quarter of a pint, an older child half a pint, without danger. And half a pint of blood is a tremendous amount. If you need convincing, spill half a pint of something (preferably red to help your imagination along) into the sink and you will see.

Bleeding from a wound is only ever uncontrollable in this simple way if a large vein or an artery has been cut. Blood from a cut vein is comparatively deep red in color because most of its oxygen has already been distributed. It pours steadily from the cut. Blood from an artery has been released before it has lost its oxygen and it is therefore a much brighter red. Because arterial blood is being pumped directly by the heart, it tends to spurt rhythmically from the wound, in time with the child's heartbeat. Don't worry if you cannot tell the two apart (in a really serious wound both may be present). First aid is the same for both.

First aid for severe bleeding **Check that there is nothing (such as a piece of glass) sticking into the wound.** Grab the cleanest piece of material that is close by and press hard on the wound through it. (In a real emergency use your bare hands rather than wasting time.) If the wound is on a limb, elevate it so that it is above heart level. This will, in itself, slightly reduce the pressure of the bleeding.

If the pressure slows or stops the bleeding, keep it up while you think what to do next. Can you send, telephone or yell for help while keeping pressure on the wound? If not, bind some piece of your clothing *tightly* around it so that your hand pressure is replaced by a "pressure bandage."

If simple pressure does not slow or stop the bleeding, push against the wound in such a way that it is squeezed between your hand and the nearest underlying bone. With a hand or arm wound, you will be able to compress the cut brachial artery between your hand and the arm bone. With a wound in an awkward (though improbable) place, like the groin, you may have to use your fist to press up against the pelvic girdle. Once you have found the right angle and controlled the bleeding, don't let go. A renewed gush may make it difficult to locate the right place again. I cannot tell you how to get help while maintaining this kind of pressure because it depends on your circumstances. But this is certainly a time to yell for help if there is anyone to hear. If you are completely alone, try to improvise a way of keeping pressure against that bone. A rolled-up belt bandaged on with your tights or even the bowl of a wooden spoon tied on with the child's sock may work for long enough to let you telephone or get to a window from which your shouts can be heard.

Once you have improvised a pressure bandage, don't remove it even if blood soaks through; there may be *some* clotting and you will disturb it. Add more layers over the top.

Do remember that even if these heroic measures work like magic, the bleeding stops and, on inspection, you decide that perhaps the wound is not as bad as you had thought, you must take the child straight to the doctor or hospital. Your fingers, not to mention your handkerchief or his socks, may well have put dirt into a wound which you know has penetrated to large blood vessels. Infection is likely and would, in these circumstances, be serious.

● *Tourniquets.* Many older first aid books still recommend a tourniquet to control life-threatening bleeding especially from a cut artery. A tourniquet is a strap, belt or bandage which is put around the limb between the wound and the heart and is then tightened by having a stick or rod put through and twisted. Although a tourniquet will certainly stop bleeding from a wound it does so by preventing *any* blood flow rather than by preventing blood from escaping from the cut vessel. If you put a tourniquet around a child's arm to control bleeding from a cut wrist, you will be simultaneously depriving her whole hand of its blood supply. Such a tourniquet is both dangerous and agonizingly painful. Direct pressure on the wound is safer, more comfortable and usually just as effective. Consider using a tourniquet only in the very rare case of life-threatening bleeding from a wound on which you dare not press because it has a piece of glass or a knife sticking out of it.

Wounds and infection
(*see also* **Infection**/Types of infection: Localized infection)

Bacteria are everywhere in their millions. Some are beneficial; most are harmless; a few are not. You cannot sterilize a wound (although a doctor can). All you can do is to *clean* it (thus removing dirt which is liable to be bacteria-laden) and avoid introducing extra bacteria (which is the point of using sterile dressings and so forth).

Any wound, major or minor, can become infected. Surgical wounds in hospitals, made and treated under the best possible circumstances, sometimes become so. Infection in a minor wound does *not* mean that you were careless and should feel guilty. Being too "germ-conscious" will not improve your first aid and it may easily make your children over-anxious.

Infection in any wound should always be shown to a doctor, but if the wound was a trivial one the infection will usually be trivial, too. A grazed knee, for example, takes the protective skin off a comparatively large area, leaving it open to infection by bacteria on that dirty road, from your child's own skin or from the air in your bathroom. But because the wound is open and shallow, the infection will start off at a superficial level. It will only become serious if you neglect it and are very unfortunate.

Recognizing infection early

The early signs of infection in any wound are pain, redness/heat and swelling.

A simple cut should not be painful after about twelve hours and should certainly not become increasingly painful after this time. If it does, inspect it carefully and you will probably see some of the other signs.

A scrape or graze, especially one which is associated with bruising, may "stiffen up" and become more painful while as the bruise develops it may become more red and swollen. In such a case, consider the broken skin area itself. If the scab is yellowish (and especially if there is pus oozing at the edges) there is certainly some local infection although it may be entirely trivial. Show it to your doctor in case.

Later signs of infection

Sometimes a deeper wound appears to heal cleanly but is infected at a deeper level. This is both more serious and more difficult to spot at an early stage.

Suspect it if a wound which your child has forgotten about suddenly bothers him again. Be certain enough to make an immediate medical appointment if the pain is a continuous throbbing rather than a soreness to touch; if the area is hot to touch; if the surrounding skin is red and/or shiny looking; if there is pus seeping through the almost-healed place.

If there should be red streaks running up the child's limb from the wound area and/or he should have a temperature and/or the glands in the armpit or groin of the affected arm or leg are swollen or painful, then infection has spread from the locality of the wound into the bloodstream. Call your doctor immediately. He will either see you right away or refer you to the emergency room..

Acne *see* **Adolescence**/Problems with appearance and body image.
Addiction *see* **Habits.**

Adenoids

A child's adenoids are a pair of bodies of lymphoid tissue which lie to either side of the back of the throat behind the entrance to the nasal passageways. Unlike the tonsils, they cannot be seen without a mirror but in early childhood the adenoids are large in relation to the size of the passages to the nose and to the eustachian tubes which drain the middle ear (*see* **Ears and Hearing; Ear Disorders and Deafness**). The adenoids play a useful role in trapping and destroying bacteria and viruses but when they are fighting infection in this way, they swell. Swollen adenoids in a small child can partially block the nose so that he breathes through his mouth habitually. More seriously, they may partially block the eustachian tubes so that infected material cannot drain freely from the middle ear and chronic infection may set in. It is usually because of a risk to hearing that removal of the adenoids is recommended (*see* **Hospital**/Surgery: Tonsillectomy and Adenoidectomy; Myringotomy).

Adolescence

"Adolescence" and "puberty" are confused and confusing terms, difficult to relate exactly to each other and often impossible to relate exactly to your own child. Loosely, puberty refers to the physical changes which transform that child into a sexually mature "adult," while adolescence refers to the social, emotional and psychological changes which accompany the physical ones and which will only be completed when the quotation marks can be taken off that word "adult." So puberty can be seen as being about physical growing up and adolescence as being about all the other kinds. Exactly how they mesh together for the individual depends both on his or her personal timetable and on the expectations of his or her family, community and society. Much adolescent conflict and difficulty is due to these two related aspects of the individual's life getting out of step.

Puberty

Puberty is not an event but a process. It begins when the pituitary gland, controlled by the brain, begins to release into the bloodstream increased quantities of the stimulating hormones called gonadotropins. Follicle-stimulating hormone (FSH) stimulates the development of egg-containing follicles within girls' ovaries and sperm-producing tubules in boys' testes. Luteinizing hormone (LH) stimulates the production of estrogen by cells within the follicles in girls and the production of androgen by cells within the testes in boys.

At the beginning of the pubertal process extra gonadotropins are released only during sleep. The resulting extra stimulation is very slight and it takes time for the increase in circulating levels of estrogen and androgen to bring about bodily changes. Later in puberty, as in adult life, the stimulating hormones circulate day and night, and estrogen and androgen levels are maintained at a sexually mature and fertile level.

Boys and puberty   During roughly the first year of increased hormonal stimulation the boy's testes (balls) enlarge but his penis and the rest of his body remain outwardly unchanged.

Once the testes have matured sufficiently for sperm production to begin, their continuing growth is accompanied by rapid growth of the penis and by the first appearance of pubic and/or underarm hair. Around the midpoint of the pubertal process the hair increases, coarsens and becomes curly and once this stage has been reached the voice will deepen ("break") and some facial hair may begin to appear.

It should be noted that a boy's testes produce enough androgen to stimulate the development of these secondary sexual characteristics well before they produce the even greater quantity necessary to stimulate the pubertal growth spurt. Boys therefore often have to accept the sexual changes of manhood without the extra height which would make them feel "grown-up." Many find this difficult. On the other hand, as long as a boy is only in the early stages of sexual maturation he can be fully assured that the often longed-for physical spurt is still to come (see **Growth**).

Girls and puberty   A girl's ovaries respond to the early increase in stimulating gonadotropins just as a boy's testes do, but because those ovaries are invisible, the first outward sign of a girl's sexual development will be early breast development. In most girls this is very gradual indeed. First the areolae around the nipples become more protuberant, then some breast tissue becomes visible beneath them and then, very slowly, the breasts fill out. Although breasts may be large and shapeless in mid-puberty, girls can be assured that greater shapeliness and elegance will certainly follow.

● In both sexes early breast development sometimes produces small lumps beneath the areolae. Although any worried adolescent is entitled to authoritative reassurance from a doctor, you may be able to prevent worry by assuring him or her that the lumps are not "growths," but irregularly growing glandular tissue which will soon smooth out.

In most girls the appearance of first pubic hairs follows some breast development with underarm hair close behind. Simultaneous or reversed orders are not unusual, however.

A notable and important difference between pubertal girls and boys is that in girls, hormonal levels high enough to stimulate sexual development are more than adequate to stimulate the overall growth spurt. A girl will be growing rapidly before any secondary sexual characteristics are apparent, and her growth will have peaked and be slowing before she reaches her menarche and has her first menstrual period (see **Growth**).

Worries about puberty   Different societies have different ways of initiating children into adult society; an individual child's reactions to the physical changes in his or her body will, of course, be largely dictated by the attitudes with which he or she has grown up thus far. Some worries are common enough in most Western societies to merit mention:

Problems between the sexes, within families, school classes or other peer groups, are often caused by the differing growth rates of boys and girls. Most girls begin their pubertal growth spurt at around nine to ten years; most boys grow at child rates until eleven to twelve. Girls tend therefore to be bigger than boys during these critical years and their visible breast development adds to their more mature appearance. It is not until around fourteen to fifteen that the boys begin to catch up.

This difference in apparent maturity has obvious effects on friendship patterns and so forth, but it can also have less obvious effects on boys' morale. In some social groups boys in their early teens use exaggerated physical showing off (whether of a socially acceptable kind such as sports or a less acceptable kind such as gang warfare) to try to assert themselves over those girls. Within a family, friendship, or even tolerance, between a mature-seeming eleven-year-old girl and her still childish-looking thirteen-year-old brother often becomes impossible. Unfairly, it is usually the boy who is judged to be at fault.

Problems of early or late puberty. Most young adolescents rely heavily on the support of their friends while they fight their way from childhood. The child who must undergo conspicuous physical changes before most of his or her friends, or who gets left behind as others develop, tends to feel isolated. On the whole, boys find it easier to accept early physical growth than delay. To be the tallest in the class is usually a plus, whereas to be a boy among young men is a minus. Nevertheless, it can be very uncomfortable to tower over friends and to be unable to trust one's voice not to break suddenly while answering a teacher.

For most girls early growth in height is embarrassing and alarming. Not only is she suddenly taller than her friends, she is also dramatically taller than boys of the same age and liable to feel that she will go on towering over them so that notions of romance are laughable. Early breast development can also be embarrassing, making the girl feel clumsy and heavy rather than elegant and sexy. Girls who remain child-sized and child-shaped while friends are changing may be equally distressed, especially as they tend to find themselves excluded from female conclaves which "you wouldn't understand. . . ."

Parents can help a little by:

Making sure children understand the wide age-range of normal development so that while they may still wish that they themselves were quicker or slower developers, they are at least spared worries about whether or not they are "abnormal."

Making sure each sex understands the relationship of physical growth to sexual development so that boys who are still small despite marked secondary sexual characteristics realize that they will still make up many inches while girls who are tall but undeveloped realize that secondary sexual characteristics will appear without a great deal of further growth.

Being careful to treat both sexes according to the maturity of their behavior rather than their bodies so that the fast developer is not pitchforked into premature adulthood and the slower developer is not held back.

Helping the child to like his or her body even while it refuses to be "just like everybody else's." A little flattery for a suddenly tall son who can carry the suitcases or for a suddenly developed daughter who can lend a sweater can be extremely helpful.

Consulting with the school on behalf of any child whose development is seriously out of step with his or her peers. Very occasionally a particularly bright child will have spent childhood in a class of children a year or more older and will, as they enter puberty, find a genuine gap opening up between them. If such a child is not only younger than the others but also a slower-than-average developer, he or she may face years of feeling "out of it." A step sideways within the school may need to be considered as a last resort which, while it may cause immediate misery, may be better than social isolation.

Menstruation

Ninety-five percent of girls menstruate for the first time between the ages of ten and sixteen. Of the remainder, most will menstruate spontaneously between sixteen and eighteen but very few will do so thereafter. Around sixteen is therefore a sensible time to seek medical advice if menstruation has not yet occurred.

Menstruation cannot occur until a girl's ovaries are active; once they are active there will be signs of breast development and bodily hair. The menarche is usually considered medically late only if there are no signs of such secondary sexual characteristics by the age of sixteen. If a girl is well developed—and especially if she has been developing over the past year or more—the doctor will probably simply reassure her that puberty is proceeding normally and that her first period will appear in its own good time. If she remains child-sized and child-shaped, simple medical tests can be taken to assess her hormone output.

Although menstruation occurs after other pubertal changes, it tends to be the change which has most psychological significance for a girl. Full and early information about what will happen to her and why is obviously vital, but so is the manner in which that information is given. Value-laden euphemisms such as "the curse" or "being unwell" are best avoided, while possible difficulties such as pre-menstrual tension or menstrual discomfort (*see below*) should be left to the girl herself to raise if she wishes. These things are by no means inevitable and expecting them certainly makes them more likely to occur.

Girls tend to find the menarche more difficult to handle than the other changes of puberty because a period is sudden while they are gradual. Breasts change and grow almost imperceptibly but vaginal bleeding just happens. Many girls, even those who accept the menarche quite comfortably, also find the constancy and inevitability of the menstrual cycle hard to accept. Once it begins it will go on, whether she wills it or not. Her body controls her self. By menstruating regularly it states a sexual maturity which may be out of step with her feelings. By not menstruating regularly it states a sexual immaturity which may be similarly inappropriate. While some girls will menstruate for the first time at exactly the right emotional moment, most will face conflict, unless you can spot the likely direction of anxiety and deal with it, in leisurely discussions, well in advance.

The girl who is likely to menstruate before she feels ready needs to be reminded that it takes more than a period to make a grown-up; that people grow into their bodies and bodily functioning and that biological processes take time to settle down. It may comfort her to know that early periods are often irregular and that early cycles seldom include ovulation so that the menarche does not, in itself, imply even a bodily readiness for conception. She can also be reminded that even primary school lavatories usually contain sanitary napkin dispensers because some girls menstruate while they are still quite definitely children.

The girl who is waiting impatiently for her menarche can be told, with equal truth, that she can merit the term "grown-up" by means other than menstruating; that other secondary sexual characteristics will develop first and allow her to see her own maturity and that there is no secret society of menstruating women from which she will be excluded until it happens to her.

In either case the most important message is probably the one which emphasizes that menstruation is only a physical process which in no way overrides the social, emotional or psychological aspects of growing up. If this easy and matter-of-fact acceptance is your aim, it is probably best not to appear emotionally involved yourself in your daughter's menarche. Regrets for the "little girl who is gone forever" or bottles of champagne to celebrate the "advent of a new woman" will tend to over-emphasize the significance of the whole matter.

Practicalities of periods However accepting and matter-of-fact your daughter's attitudes to menstruation, having a period is a bore. The easier the practical aspects of coping, the more lightly she will be able to take it.

How much you will be involved in this very private aspect of her life will probably depend partly on her age at menarche. At twelve she may rely heavily on your advice and support. At fifteen she may "know all about it" and have many friends whom she has seen coping. Whatever her age, though, it is worth giving some thought to basic questions like whether she should use sanitary pads or tampons.

Pads versus tampons. While ready-made sanitary pads would seem heaven-sent to the many women in the world who have to manage without, they are nevertheless awkward and unreliable things. Even the best (and most expensive), specially shaped, waterproof backed, keep-dry lined and soluble, can show under tight clothes, leak onto white jeans, chafe and stop up toilets. Furthermore, they are embarrassingly bulky to carry to school or through a gauntlet of curious small boys from bedroom to bathroom at home; and, however regularly they are changed, they smell.

Why are so many young girls condemned to use pads when tampons are so much more convenient and efficient? Some mothers unthinkingly assume that tampons are only for the married or sexually active, while some may actually fear that using a tampon will "break a girl's hymen" so that she is no longer "a virgin." Some girls are simply nervous at the idea of "putting something up there." While no girl who is reluctant to use a tampon should be pushed into doing so until she feels ready, some of the following points may help:

An "intact hymen" very seldom covers the vaginal opening. In many, the hymen is merely a fringe of thin tissue lying around the edge of the opening; in others, the opening is partly covered. But in all, the hymen is stretchy and perfectly capable of accommodating a tampon. A girl with a hymen tight enough to make insertion of a tampon at all difficult may, in fact, do herself future good if she gently persists. A tight hymen can mean painful first intercourse. Since our society does not insist on blood-stained sheets to prove the virginity of brides on their wedding nights, this is something to be avoided if possible.

If a girl wants to use a tampon but does find any difficulty in inserting it, a tiny quantity of a sterile lubricant such as KY Jelly, placed on the end of the tampon or around the vaginal opening, can make all the difference.

There is no way in which an inserted tampon can "go in the wrong place" or "get lost." A girl who is so ignorant of her own sexual anatomy that she has this fear needs proper information. The vaginal passage is completely closed by the cervix (neck of the womb) at its upper end. Once a tampon is in place there is nowhere it can go but out again.

Tampons cannot dam up the menstrual flow and thus increase cramps.

The only "risk" in tampon use comes from their very comfort and efficiency: if a girl inserts one at the end of her period when the flow is light, she may forget that it is there. Left for days on end, tampons can give rise to odor, vaginal discharge and/or actual infection.

● A handful of reports of sudden illness associated with the use of "scented" or "deodorized" tampons suggests that these should be avoided. Such refinements are completely unnecessary.

Storage and accessibility of sanitary protection. Most girls are extremely shy about their early periods. Some may feel so private about them that their mothers are sworn to secrecy even within the family. Others may choose to tell friends yet dread brothers or sisters knowing when they are menstruating. Indeed, a very common anxiety in a girl's early adolescence is that somehow "everyone can tell."

While this emotional reaction usually settles rapidly, a girl's desire for privacy should certainly be accepted and catered to. You therefore need to work out where her sanitary protection can be stored so that it is easily available to her when she goes to the toilet and discovers that one of those unpredictable periods has begun. A bathroom drawer or place in the medicine cabinet is usually an easy answer. She will also need a way of carrying emergency protection with her when she is out and about. A tampon or two can easily fit into a special pocket of her purse. Pads may need a "make-up bag" which will camouflage them from all but the most rudely inquisitive.

Stained bedding and clothing. Stained night-things are very common at the beginning of a period. Adolescents should have their own bedrooms if this can possibly be managed but if your daughter must share, she may be grateful for a private arrangement with you such that she can pull the bedding up, knowing that you will change the linen later.

Some girls find that underwear gets stained however regularly they change pads or tampons. Changing for sports then becomes acutely embarrassing. Dark-colored underpants are a relief to many. Others prefer to wear a second pair for double security. On camping trips or at other times when laundry will be difficult and/or public, disposable underpants can be a worthwhile investment.

Odor. Menstrual debris does not develop an unpleasant odor until it has contact with the air. Tampons, changed before they permit leakage, virtually do away with this problem. Pads, on the other hand, can smell. Frequent changing and a quick wash with soap and water at each change is the only solution. Girls should not be encouraged to be oversensitive about odor during their periods. The connotations of "dirt" are psychologically unfortunate and the girl who decides she has a "problem" may be tempted by "feminine hygiene" products which are ineffective or downright dangerous (*see below* Problems with appearance and body image: Body odor).

Menstrual difficulties

Irregular menstruation is very common, especially during the first year after the menarche. Many girls menstruate once and then do not do so again for months. Others menstruate several times in the first year but with no discernible pattern. Ensure that your daughter has sanitary protection (*see above*) available both at home and at school and make it clear that there is no cause for concern.

Regular menstruation which suddenly stops is termed "secondary amenorrhea" ("primary amenorrhea" being absence of menarche). Secondary amenorrhea is caused by some disturbance in the balance between the ovaries, the pituitary gland and the hypothalamus. While, of course, the obvious reason is pregnancy (which certainly should be excluded if it is a possibility), such an imbalance is often caused by a radical change of environment (such as starting boarding school) or by a major emotional upset (such as bereavement or other serious trouble at home). The girl can be reassured that her periods will return when she has settled down. It is reasonable to wait for at least six months before seeking medical advice to exclude the faint possibility of glandular abnormality.

Parents should be alert, however, if the girl concerned has recently lost a great deal of weight. If she has been dieting, secondary amenorrhea suggests that she has lost too much weight too rapidly. If she has lost weight but does not admit that she is dieting, the amenorrhea may suggest that she is suffering from anorexia nervosa (*see* **Eating Disorders**).

Pre-menstrual tension and dysmenorrhea are both unusual during early cycles. The water retention, irritability and depression of pre-menstrual tension and the heavy aching and/or sharp cramps of dysmenorrhea both appear to be linked not just to menstruation but to menstrual cycles in which ovulation (shedding of an ovum) takes place. Many girls, just past the menarche, do not ovulate. They may have periods regularly for a year or more before ovulation becomes regular also.

You can therefore confidently expect your daughter's early periods to be trouble-free and, if you do have this confidence, you will certainly help to ensure that they are. While pre-menstrual tension and period pains are real and have a real physiological basis, they are equally certainly affected by expectations and emotions. If your young daughter assumes that her periods will be unpleasant she is far more likely to experience them as such. If you, the person closest to her, assume that she will take them in her unbroken stride, she is far more likely to be able to do so. It is often said that menstrual difficulties "run in the family." While there may be some inherited tendency, a passing-on of attitudes and example from mother to daughter is a real factor. If you are a sufferer yourself, your young daughter will, of course, know that you are. But do be sure that she also knows that yours is a medical problem, for which you are receiving treatment. Don't let her assume that it is part of "women's lot" and therefore of her inevitable inheritance.

If there does come a time when your daughter clearly has cyclical discomfort (whether it is headaches before menstruation or cramps during it), do try to react to the symptoms exactly as you would react if they occurred in a pre-adolescent. If the headache is a bad one it probably merits a simple analgesic such as aspirin or paracetamol. If the cramps are making her miserable a hot bath or a hot water bottle to take to bed may help. But don't let the fact that the headache or the cramps are part of menstruation lead you to assume (or let her assume) that she is going to be "off-color" for hours or days; that she should stay home from school or skip that outing. Above all, don't expect (or let her expect) the same discomfort to occur next month. If she can take each period calmly, as it comes, she will give her body every chance of adapting comfortably.

Disruptive menstrual difficulties are rare but merit proper attention. Pre-menstrual discomfort may take the physical form of water retention so that she not only feels "bloated" but actually cannot fasten her jeans. Some find that restricting salt intake during the immediate pre-menstrual week prevents this. But if a teenager is to keep a careful eye on her diary and concentrate on what she eats for a week in each month, she had better do it with medical advice. If salt restriction does not work, her doctor might try her on a mild diuretic (drug to increase excretion of water).

Pre-menstrual trouble may seem entirely emotional. During the pre-menstrual week, everything is "too much." Parents are bossy, siblings are acutely irritating, friends are hurtful, work impossible. . . . Parents can help by taking a little extra trouble not to pick fights during this time and perhaps by being a little more than usually tolerant when their daughter picks fights with them. You *may* also be able to help simply by reminding your tear-soaked daughter that she *is* in a pre-menstrual phase. Be careful, though; "You must be going to have your period" can be as unhelpful and more maddening than "I don't know what's the matter with you." Choose a different time to discuss the whole matter. If she agrees that things do get on top of her and that rampant hormones do seem to be the reason, suggest that she keep a note of her cycle dates and learn to *go easy on herself*. She, after all, is the one who has to learn to manage her cyclical self.

Menstrual pains can range from a constant dull, heavy ache to intermittent but violent abdominal cramps. Every year thousands of girls are admitted to the hospital because even a doctor is hard put to distinguish between really severe period pains and an abdominal emergency.

That dull, heavy aching (which is often felt most in the back) is certainly helped by simple analgesics and is equally certainly made worse by standing still for long periods.

Cramping pains are rather different. The uterus has to get rid of the debris of the rich lining it has been laying down to receive the ovum if it should be fertilized. Contractions of uterine muscles help this process but, it seems, sometimes become uncoordinated so that the muscular cramps actually dam up debris. During painful cramps a girl sometimes feels that she is "getting rid of something" and it may be that there will be visible "clots" in the menstrual flow. Heat can help by encouraging relaxation of the muscles, but lying down with a hot water bottle is not always the best treatment. Many girls find that active exercise, however disinclined they may feel for it at the beginning, increases the flow and relieves the cramping pains.

If the quality of a girl's life is being reduced by periodic discomfort, do encourage her to see her doctor and do make sure that he is not one who subscribes to the "women's lot" school of thought.

All menstrual troubles are basically side effects from the natural ebb and flow of the balance of hormones in the body, with estrogen peaking at the time of ovulation and giving place to progesterone dominance at the time of menstruation. Often a doctor will not want to tamper with this balance in a very young woman, preferring to give her body time to adjust itself. But he can still help with prescription analgesics and, above all, with reassurance that, should the troubles continue, various treatments are available and can be tried when she is a little older.

Hormone treatment will take one of two forms. In a girl who would welcome contraception, birth control pills can be prescribed and, by preventing ovulation, they will banish most menstrual troubles, too. In a girl who does not want to go "on the Pill," artificial progestogen can be given which has no effect on ovulation but markedly reduces the intensity of uterine contractions during menstruation. As an alternative to the direct administration of hormones, some doctors prescribe "prostaglandin antagonists" (such as Maltrin) that indirectly affect the body's hormone balance.

Adolescents and the adult world
(*see also* **Discipline, Self-discipline and Learning How to Behave**)

Adolescents are people: the children they were and the adults they will become. To get from one state to another most must live through personal turmoil and therefore will create social tumult from time to time. Unfortunately, the adult world makes "adolescent difficulty" into a self-fulfilling prophecy. We expect adolescents to make trouble and by treating them accordingly we often create the very problems of which we then complain. We give children a bad name ("teenagers") and hang them.

Most of these prejudices and labels are as foolish as they are damaging. A "teenager" is not a single entity to be grouped and categorized with others, but a person who is growing and changing. That person may be male or female; thirteen, fifteen or nineteen; sexually mature or immature; active or inactive; ambitious, clever and hardworking or apathetic, unintelligent and lazy. He or she may feel happy, loving and well-liked or miserable, angry and rejected. Furthermore, whatever he or she is like *now*, everything will change (for better or worse) tomorrow or next year. However changeable and therefore unpredictable and difficult an adolescent may be, parents, and other close adults, need to hang onto the fact that *this stage of life is part of a continuum of development.* This is the same person whom you nurtured as a baby and enjoyed as a child and with whom you will one day share family history. If all the adolescent years are seen as part of continuing development there will be no temptation to label and dismiss him as "a hopeless rebel" or to label and abandon her because "she's impossible to understand." The less he or she is labelled, dismissed or abandoned the more easily and steadily will the maturing take place.

Unfortunately, rich societies make few arrangements to suit growing adolescents. They insist, for example, that children remain home-and-education-based long after growth and sexual maturity have made them capable of working for money and starting families of their own. An extended period of education is fine in principle but often disastrous in practice. Many adolescents experience their last year or two of schooling as a compulsory irrelevancy with no bearing on the future. Many foresee a future of long-term unemployment that clearly states "society has no real place for you." Even within their own homes many adolescents find that they no longer have a child's role as receiver of adult care yet are still not accepted into equality with those adults. If schoolwork does not feel creative or useful and a youngster is unsure of his or her role at home, what is left? Sports and hobbies involve some; community projects involve a few. But there is a vast reservoir of creative energy left untapped within many communities because young people are not trusted to contribute. This matters not only because it is a waste but because it is our refusal to find interesting, creative and useful things for them to do which drives so many young people into doing things of which we disapprove or into doing the "nothing much" which we also dislike. It is our refusal to like them, love them, share with them which drives many to reject adults altogether and rely exclusively on each other's company. It is our refusal to trust them to be kind, sensible or responsible which makes them doubt their own goodness as people so that they sometimes act out the anti-social roles we seem to expect of them. Adolescents have to change in order to grow; adults have to try to follow the changes and provide for each piece of new growth. The more parents can understand why many of their number find this difficult the more likely it is that they will be able to tailor and retailor their own child's world so that it always fits.

Friends versus family

In the course of adolescence your son or daughter has to separate off from you so as to be free to become an autonomous adult individual. You gave him or her most childhood values and opinions so your values and opinions have to be challenged. To continue to hold them would be to continue to be a child. The adolescent may come back to them, or to some of them, but can only do so maturely if they have been well-considered first. Your adolescent is standing back from you in this way at roughly the same time as his or her friends. Agreeing that their values must change is easy, but deciding on new values is far more difficult. In order to shield themselves (and each other) from solitary personal indecision, they establish a kind of security with each other. The peer group agrees, so to speak, on norms for behavior, dress, speech, entertainment, sexual behavior and reactions to parents and other authority figures. Once these things are agreed upon, everyone who wants acceptance within that particular group must conform. Lack of conformity may be dealt with harshly because the non-conformist throws doubt on the correctness of the group's decisions and it was to protect themselves from such doubt that they grouped together in the first place. Peer-group relationships then are vitally important to most young adolescents and conformity to even quite minor conventions may truly matter to them. Parents may not share, but must accept, these feelings.

It is parents' inability to share which causes much of the trouble between the generations because many devoted parents are hurt by their exclusion. You can be very lonely for the child who, having been your faithful companion for many years, would suddenly rather be with anyone but you. Hurt adult feelings lie behind much of the criticism and nagging of which adolescents complain; nagging about "unsuitable friends," for example. As a parent you may find it very hard to stay friendly when your child rejects your carefully considered and mature advice and telephones another young idiot for advice instead. But for the moment, your child does not want to do what *you* think sensible but what his or her peers advise. Their opinion matters much more than yours and probably more than the quality of the advice, too.

Secrets make for adult hurt, too. Parents have usually been accustomed to keep secrets (or to "keep adult matters private") from their children. Now it is those children who keep them in the dark. Sometimes it helps to realize just how trivial most of those vital secrets are: snippets of gossip about who likes whom, items which you really do not need or even want to know. But their point is that you should not know, so every temptation to pry should be resisted. There is no quicker way to make your adolescent lie to you than to insist on being told of private matters. And there is no faster way to ruin the relationship between you than to invade privacy by picking up telephone extensions, going through pockets or reading letters and diaries.

The less critical you can be of your child's friends the better; they need each other and if yours knows that you accept this and are prepared to tolerate even the unexpected arrivals who strip the cookie tin, he or she will probably do you the honor of letting you meet them and hearing at least some of their news. Then, if something goes really wrong and you foresee physical or moral danger, you will be in an excellent position to muster and use your still-powerful influence. Don't waste it on trying to stop your daughter from going out with that boy with pink hair: you may need it later on when she meets a known drug pusher or the much older father of two. Don't waste that precious influence trying to be clever at the expense of your son's football friends either; he may move on into a group which invests its machismo in fast cars and bolsters its driving courage with alcohol.

If you can save your criticisms and, more especially, your vetoes, for the very occasional issues which are truly important, you will not often be defied, at least in the early stages of adolescence. However much he or she may bluster, your child knows that home is still an important haven and that he or she is more comfortable when you approve. When large issues do arise you will often find that your viewpoint has backing from the local community and/or the law and that you can use these impersonal forces as allies. In Britain, for example, sexual intercourse with a girl under sixteen is illegal. While it would be naive to suggest that the law alone would prevent a couple from having sex once their relationship had reached that point, the existence of that law may subtly act to prevent it from doing so. A girl of fourteen or fifteen may unthinkingly accept that she is "too young," however strong her sexual feelings. Boys may similarly accept that "young girls don't" or that wise young men don't let them; they may unconsciously keep relationships with them on a low sexual note.

Liquor laws, provided that you do not openly flout them yourselves, may be similarly useful. A British youngster will probably not refuse a drink in a pub just because he or she is under age but may not expect to join a group whose life is pub-based until he or she is older. In the United States, where the age limits are higher and the laws more strictly enforced, youngsters will tend to avoid bars because of the embarrassment of having their ages queried.

The point is not that good little teenagers will refrain from doing things they want to do because those things are against the law; it is that the laws may prevent them from wanting to do those things quite so early in adolescence. It is not a question of individual virtue but of group expectation. Where an individual boy or girl does *not* want to do something which the group expects he or she may be able to use this kind of external social control as a face-saver. It is far easier for a youngster to refuse to join some piece of idiocy "because I don't want to lose my license" or because "It's all very well for you, but they'll do me in if I'm caught at my age" than to admit to being scared, disapproving or in any way out of tune with the group. If you are sensitive to your adolescent's feelings and known to be generally easy going, you may even be asked to use an external veto from time to time. Your daughter asks you if she can go on a camping trip with a mixed group of new friends. Does she really want to go or is she pleased to have been asked but alarmed at the prospect? If it is the latter she may be delighted to have you say that she is too young. She can raise Cain at home about your injustice and exact plenty of sympathy from her friends because of your unreasonableness, but she will not actually have to make that trip. If you are not sure what response an adolescent is asking of you under circumstances of this kind, try something like: "I'm not at all sure. I'll think about it but I'm probably going to say no." His or her face will give you some clues.

The desire for acceptance by, and integration into, group life pushes many youngsters into activities and situations for which they know they are not ready. Parents who try to protect them with cries of "You don't have to do it just because they do," will only increase that feeling of group loyalty and leave the child to face the dilemma alone. Parents who understand and accept the need for group conformity and who realize that only the maturity of later adolescence or adulthood will enable the individual to stand on solitary principle, can subtly offer a great deal of help. If your child consistently finds that kind of help available, you may reach the delightful stage at which you can simply ask: "Would you like to say that your ogre-father absolutely forbids it?"

If many parents' feelings are hurt when their adolescents reject them in favor of friends of the same age, even more are hurt when adolescents strike up close and confidential relationships with other adults. Your child spends more and more time in another home and gradually it becomes clear that he or she does so not just to spend time with the son or daughter but also to spend time with one or other of the parents. Why will he talk to them when he has rejected you? Why will she take their advice, quoting their every opinion as gospel, when she shrugs off everything you say? The basic answer is that those adults are more acceptable *just because they are not you*. Their values, judgments and viewpoints are different from yours and, above all, the adolescent has sought them out independently rather than having them thrust upon him or her.

Such relationships with other parents, with teachers, athletic coaches or any other caring adults, can be truly valuable to an adolescent. If you find yourself resenting them, remind yourself that the child is trying to grow up, needs knowledge and experience of adult thinking and behavior and is better off getting it outside the family than not getting it at all. Remember also that such an adult confidant is no more likely to treat your adolescent irresponsibly than you would be if you were similarly placed with somebody else's child. It may be that eventually you will be so placed.

Adult communities tend to reject people at this age-stage of life. They shut them out and thus throw them, even more than the adolescents themselves wish, onto their own and each other's resources. The more they can all communicate with any and all available adults, the better.

The long road to independence

When your child enters adolescence he or she is still a dependent child; by the time it ends that child will be transformed into an adult who is no longer dependent on you for anything but the warm support and the friendly caring which all human beings can expect from those who love them. That adolescent road from dependence to independence is long and if the journey is not also to be infernally bumpy it needs to be kept smooth. It is usually smoothest if changes in the limits, expectations and permissions laid down by parents are closely matched to changes in the competence of the child rather than being geared to outside factors. A birthday, for example, may seem an obvious marker for a new privilege, but it is not the right moment for that privilege unless it happens to coincide with what is happening inside that person. Leaving school may seem to qualify him or her for new freedoms but they will neither be welcome nor well used if the change in his or her way of life does not match up with changes in thinking, feeling and coping. Sudden "freedom" can feel like a terrifying rejection: an end of caring. Equally it can be experienced as an intoxicating loss of control. To feel truly free, the adolescent has to feel able to move at his or her own pace, backed by parents who are neither pushing him or her out nor holding on. Some parents achieve this balancing act quite unconsciously, tuned to their children so that they can feel the right moments without having to think about them. Most will sometimes make a wrong decision and will need to think and rethink independence issues as they come up.

The following examples will not all be relevant to any family but some will probably be relevant to most.

Money   A child is fed, clothed, housed, transported, entertained and "treated" at his family's expense (*see* **Pocket Money**). An adult earns all these things for himself through paid work or grant qualifications. During the in-between period of adolescence, money and the goods and services it buys can be both a real facilitator and a symbolic indicator of every degree of independence.

Parents often ask "How much money should he have now that he is thirteen or fifteen or seventeen?" but such a question begs the real issues. The important point is not how much money a child should have or the age at which he should have it but the *amount of choice and responsibility he is allowed in using what he has*. This needs careful thought and gradual alteration to suit his stage of life whether you are able and willing to provide a lot of money or only token sums.

The first step up from a child's pocket money is usually a weekly "allowance" (*see also* **Pocket Money**). You may decide that it is time your child was responsible for all his out-of-pocket expenses incurred outside the home and therefore add up his necessary expenditure on things like fares and school lunches and then add a reasonable-seeming sum for spending money.

As long as your child is prepared to treat that "allowance" exactly as he treated his pocket money in the days when you simply handed out the school money as a separate transaction, all will be well. The spending money gives him a little choice over what sweets/magazines/movie tickets he buys and that may be enough for now. But this kind of allowance is seldom satisfactory for long because soon he will want to exercise more choice than can fall within the scope of the spending money. As soon as he wants to save up for extra clothes, tickets to a pop concert or even a present for you, he will start to count on the necessaries-money, walking to school to save the bus fare or buying chips instead of a proper meal. If you are prepared to let him make this kind of decision for himself, fine, but probably you will feel that lunch money is for lunch rather than nonsense.

This is the time for the next step up, only this time, instead of adding up *necessary* expenditure and then adding spending money you add up *regular expenditure that you want him to make* and then add the extra. Just as an adult must set aside money for things like rent and quarterly bills and treat only the money which remains as disposable income, so the adolescent must set aside the money you insist he spend on what you intend it for and treat only the remainder as his to spend as he pleases. Think carefully about the expenditure which you are keeping in your own power. This may be the time for him to take over responsibility for other personal expenditures such as haircuts and toiletries, but are these items to be within your or his area of decision-making? May he go without a haircut for weeks in order to use the money for something else or not? May he go without deodorant (or use yours) or do you insist that he keep his own supply? He must know exactly what money is his to dispose of as he likes.

At this stage major expenditure is still in your hands. Your adolescent must accept not only your running of the household but your control over his clothes, sports equipment, vacations, etc. Gradually he will come to resent this, not simply because he cannot have this, that or the other unless you give him the money, but because your priorities in spending money on him become different from his own. You may, for example, plan a family vacation in which he is included. He may not want to come with you, but even if he still feels that he would enjoy the trip, there may be things which are far more important to him and which he knows that he could buy with his share of the vacation cost.

This is the time to give him some choice over what is spent on him. You may insist that he come on that vacation because his presence is important to the rest of the family, but you should certainly not insist on buying him an expensive winter overcoat if he would rather have a cheap duffel coat and the balance of the money for other things. Clothing should certainly now become entirely his business whether he is a person who yearns for expensive and fashionable clothes or one who does not care. Work out what you have been spending on his clothes and hand it over. If he goes to school "unsuitably dressed," let the school authorities deal with the matter. If he gets wet and cold, let him revise his own priorities. If you get really sorry for him you can always buy a glorious/necessary garment for his birthday.

Once an adolescent handles all his money he should have a bank account, a proper current one, not simply a savings account. Nowadays almost everybody is paid by check rather than in cash and it is important that he learns to handle the form-filling as well as keep track of whether or not he has credit.

Older adolescents will probably want to make major purchases which will actually alter their way of life, such as motorbikes or cars, guitars or stereo equipment or fashionable hairdos with built-in weekly maintenance costs. If your adolescent can see that the *family* budget simply will not afford such things he is unlikely to fuss. It is when the family budget appears ample but his own is still strictly limited that he is likely to be bitter. Once again the real question is not how much money he may have but whether or not he may spend what there is in the way he chooses. How can your son accept with pleasure an expensive birthday gift he did not want when what he *does* want is money towards that car? How can your daughter be properly grateful for having her bedroom redecorated when it is her hair that she wants to make over? Money is being spent on them, but it is being spent at your discretion and for your pleasure rather than at their discretion and for their pleasure.

When you refuse a heart's desire of this kind, do make sure that your reasons are valid and that you and your child both clearly understand them. For example:

Is there enough money for him to have what he wants? He may feel that you are far more comfortably off than is really the case. Purchases he notices may be being made on credit/be necessary to your job/be forced on you in order to fulfill the terms of your mortgage. He is entitled, now, to some understanding of the family's finances.

If there is enough money, are you refusing because you disapprove of the proposed purchase? Sometimes it seems easier to dismiss a boy's desire for a motorbike with "Do you think I'm made of money?" than to discuss your real objections which have probably to do with his safety. Make the effort of honesty. It will be far better for your relationship to be considered overprotective than to be thought mean or lacking in understanding (*see* **Safety**/On wheels).

Is there enough money for the purchase but not for its maintenance? With a vehicle, or even some kinds of hairdo, maintenance can be a major expense and one for which adolescents often do not allow. Your son's mind may be so fixed on the old car which he could buy for a few dollars that he is forgetting licensing and insurance let alone fuel costs. Your daughter may be seeing herself with short, curly bleached hair and forgetting that it will rapidly grow long, straight and dark at the roots. Do explain and discuss the sums involved. Perhaps he or she wants whatever it is enough to set aside money for maintenance instead of something else. Provided he or she can stay within budget the choice should be available.

Are you perhaps refusing this heart's desire on principle? Many people believe that adolescents are overinterested and overindulged in worldly goods and think about nothing but getting their hands on the latest fashion in electronic gadgets, new sounds or new looks. If you feel like this and therefore feel inclined to say "no" to anything which is neither necessary nor edifying, your adolescent has the right to know because you are using hard cash to control his or her lifestyle. Money is a powerful weapon in our society, so until your child can earn his or her economic freedom you may well succeed. But if you are going to use that power, do it openly. You might even convince him or her that you are right and you will certainly provide an interesting adult viewpoint for thought and discussion instead of just another excuse for moaning about the frightfulness of parents.

Part-time jobs   In many families, money issues become confused with the related but separate issue of whether or not adolescents should take part-time jobs while still at school. In some societies and communities this is taken for granted. Adolescents—and indeed children—are expected to look for work before or after school and on weekends and vacations, too. In others, such jobs are not expected and in the present economic climate may be exceedingly scarce. Whatever the position in your area, the question of whether or not you want, or will allow, your adolescent to take a part-time job needs consideration as does the effect that such a job will have on his or her position at school and at home.

A child who gets up at 6 a.m. and does a couple of hours' work before school will end up working a longer day than most adults. If she also does a few hours' work on a Saturday she will work a longer week, too, with fewer leisure hours than most unions would allow. It is possible that her concentration in school, her homework and her social life will all suffer. On the other hand, it is possible that the work itself, together with the money it earns her, will provide a new stimulus and lead to important feelings of success. If you forbid her to work you may be depriving her not only of money but of the right to make the effort for it. As soon as the issue comes up, think your priorities through; make sure that she understands them and try to act upon them consistently. The following points may be relevant:

Is academic success important to her? If it is, your message must surely be "schoolwork takes priority." But if you want her to understand that you mean that it takes priority over other kinds of *work* rather than over leisure and pleasure, you may have to go further and explain that schoolwork *is* work, just as your job is work, and that you will therefore try to see that she does not suffer by comparison with less academic friends whose work earns them money.

If you have prevented her from taking a *paid* part-time job on these grounds, do also be very sure that you do not use her as *unpaid* labor yourself. If she is to spend the time after school at home because she is to work for her exams, don't constantly use her as a babysitter, gardener or cook.

Is job experience more important than schoolwork? It may be if she is less academically inclined, knows what job she wants after she leaves school and can find work during her school life which gives her some experience of it. If that is the case, do accept that she is no longer living just as a schoolgirl, but more as a part-time apprentice. You may have to explain what is happening to the school, especially if teachers complain of skimped work. And you must not expect her to drop the part-time job every time it would suit you to take her away for a weekend . . . she may lose the job or her reputation for reliability.

Is the extra money badly needed? If the family as a whole is short of money, being able to make a contribution, via a part-time job, may be very valuable to the adolescent. Whether she contributes by using the money she earns to provide her own "allowance" or by actually putting money into the family budget, do make sure that you acknowledge her contribution by treating her as a co-worker. What this means, in detail, will obviously vary from family to family, but if she is mature enough to contribute in this way she is probably mature enough to organize her own comings and goings; to be entitled to a meal at a time which suits her schedule and to be allowed to sleep late on Sundays without criticism.

Do you need to employ her at home? People who live together in a family group should, of course, all contribute to the smooth and comfortable running of their home. Adults do not expect to be paid for making their beds or doing other chores and neither should adolescents. But running a business from home and expecting your adolescent to help in it is different. You run the business to make money. If you did not have the adolescent's labor you might have to employ somebody else. Furthermore, by using her labor in this way you deprive her of the chance either of taking a part-time job or of opting for schoolwork or leisure time. It would seem fair that either she should be paid as you would pay another adolescent working for you after school, *or* that it should be reckoned that she is making a financial contribution to the family just as she would be if she was working for somebody else and putting her earnings in the family kitty. If you can make an arrangement of this kind, you may find that your adolescent is *more* contented than her friends who feel that they have no role to play in the family.

Do you need her to run the home while you work? Your adolescent's competence may be the crucial factor which enables you to hold a full-time job despite the presence of younger schoolchildren. But if she is expected to provide tea and sympathy for them and perhaps to complete the day's domestic chores and prepare an evening meal, do acknowledge that, in enabling you to do a full-time paid job, she is doing a part-time one herself. She is in exactly the same position as the adolescent who works in a family business.

While it can be very valuable for an older adolescent to feel that he or she is a necessary part of the home set-up, don't let yourself slip into dependence either on your child's earnings or labor. There will come a time when he or she wants (and needs) either to leave home altogether or to transfer to "boarder" status while attending college or serving an apprenticeship. It is one thing for the adolescent to feel needed; quite another to know that his or her presence is literally indispensable. When he or she leaves school and finds a job, you must not ask, even silently and with your eyes, "Who is to look after the little ones until I get home from work?" That must not be the adolescent's problem because it is yours. You need to have foreseen both question and answer in advance. Leaving home is difficult enough for many youngsters without that kind of added stress.

Self-care   An adolescent will not have achieved full adulthood until he or she can take reasonable care of his or her own needs. Only when self-care is perfected can the youngster ever begin to be ready for the responsibilities of caring for others which are an integral part of adult life.

Learning to take care of oneself means different things to different people. To many families with adolescents it will mean becoming proficient at a variety of domestic chores and ceasing to expect adults to pick up discarded clothes. To others it will mean "being sensible about money" while others again will see it in terms of adequate meals and sleep.

While every child should of course, learn to iron, to cook, to budget and to keep his or her health and energy at a reasonable level, many of these specifics are extremely difficult to practice in a family setting. You pick up his clothes because you dislike the sight of the littered bathroom. The adolescent knows that you will and furthermore never gets the chance to find out whether he minds his own litter because the picking up is always done before he next goes into the bathroom. If he picks them up himself, he does so *for you* rather than for himself. In rather the same way your daughter eats meals which she has perhaps helped to buy and prepare but for which she is not basically responsible. How can she tell whether she would have remembered to buy milk and bread and cat food had it all been up to her?

Where natural opportunities occur within the family, practice can be useful. Your adolescent may, for example, take over domestically while you are in the hospital or on a trip. But artificially created practice (such as a rotation for Sunday cooking) seldom does much for an adolescent's self-care. These arranged experiences are temporary whereas looking after oneself is permanent. And they take place in a setting which somebody else has arranged and for which somebody else is responsible. Self-care will only really be practiced when the youngster is away from you.

For most adolescents living away from home is a vitally important part of final growing up. But if it is to be a success experience, you need to be sure that your child has acquired more far-reaching competence than domestic skills. It really does not matter very much if your daughter cannot iron a blouse to her own standards. It will not take her more than a single evening to teach herself once there is no one else to help. But it does matter very much if she cannot keep herself basically safe and healthy; cannot find her way around a new community and its services and personnel; cannot communicate with other people, adults as well as peers, sufficiently to make herself a friendly place in a new community.

Make sure basic health principles are understood. Before an adolescent leaves home for the first time she should certainly be fully in charge of any medication which she takes regularly or frequently. A diabetic, for example, must understand not only her own daily insulin/carbohydrate balance but also what to do if it should go wrong. Be careful. You may always have nursed her through the times when her insulin needs changed because of fever, or vomiting. Can she confidently do it for herself?

If your son is subject to migraine, does he *understand* his medication or has he always swallowed the pills as you offered them, never troubling to grasp which was for what?

Does she understand both the use and the dangers of any headache remedies, laxatives and so forth which she is accustomed to having available? Will he know if a minor injury is infected and what to do about it? Will he make sensible decisions about whether or not he should go to work when unwell? Does he, for example, know how to take and then assess his own temperature and will it occur to him to do so if he feels "peculiar"?

Have you and she discussed more dramatic dangers to health so that she is unlikely, for example, to experiment dangerously with drugs, including alcohol? Has he actually taken in your lectures on contraception and venereal disease so that he will behave responsibly both to himself and to other people?

Make sure he or she can cope with food for one. (*See also* **Eating**.) Few adolescents leaving home for the first time are going to eat what most adults would regard as a "healthy diet," but yours ought at least to understand the amount of money he will need for fuel-food and some of the dietary safety measures which will help to ensure that living on junk foods does not make him inefficient or ill. It is more important that it should occur to him to buy and drink milk and orange juice than that he should be able to cook a roast to perfection.

An adolescent who is constantly fighting obesity needs some extra help. Girls especially should be aware of the dangers of starvation. All too often, once on their own, just not eating seems much easier than following a reducing diet. Adolescents who are lonely may eat for comfort if money allows. You may not be able to prevent this at long range, but you can at least make sure that they know which nibbling foods contain fewest calories and that they are aware of the dietary chaos to which bingeing can lead (*see* **Eating Disorders**).

Make sure the adolescent is competent to negotiate with the adult world. The adolescent who knows where to go for help and is able to ask for that help in a way which adults find appealing, is off to a head start. Those who hate using the telephone, are terrified of anyone in uniform and have never learned to turn on appropriate charm, will find themselves at a major disadvantage. In this area, advance practice really can help. While your adolescent is still living at home she can make her own appointments with the dentist—and then put them off herself, too, instead of getting around you to do that bit for her. She can be encouraged to do her own "asking" at school from an early age (why send a note when she can talk?) and she can not only shop but also return her own unsatisfactory goods and fight for refunds. If she wants to visit a friend in the hospital, let her go by herself and brave the dragon head nurse and let it sometimes be she who tries to persuade the television repairman into coming to the house on Christmas Eve . . . . The point, of course, is that she will not always succeed; but she will fail while it scarcely matters (as you are still behind her) and she will learn, almost unconsciously, how to cope.

Make sure that your adolescent knows what services there are, what they are for and how to find them. Practice in guessing what heading will be used in a telephone directory is useful. Familiarity with "Yellow Pages" may enable her to cope with all kinds of unexpected eventualities like locking herself out of that new apartment, while knowledge of her rights as a very new citizen and the location of those whose job it is to ensure these for her, is vital.

Adolescents newly away from home need safety nets. If yours first goes to college or to a residential training establishment of some kind, he will have a built-in safety net provided by the institution and the adults who run it. They will not produce aspirin for his headache, clean shirts for his dates or a morning call to get him up in time, but they will (or should) notice if he is really ill, make themselves available to him if he needs help or step in if he is in serious trouble.

If your adolescent is going into a completely independent and unprotected environment—into a studio in a strange town which just happens to have a job for him, for example—you may need to provide a safety net yourself. For example, if he still likes your company you could:

Settle him in. Go to his new town with him, help him to find a place to live and scratch together the things he needs to make it tolerable. You can explore the town together and identify some of the places he will need to know. The fact that you have been there and do therefore know the environment may make it much easier for him to keep in touch with you by letter and telephone.

Arrange emergency communications. Without suggesting regular telephone calls (which might spoil his feeling of self-reliance), make sure that he has an actual fund of telephone coins salted away somewhere. Although he can reverse the charges he will be able to telephone without feeling nearly so feeble and childish if he has the means to do so directly. A couple of pre-stamped pre-addressed envelopes may mean that he writes you when he needs to, even though he has run out of stationery.

Arrange emergency money. He is extremely likely to run out of money during the early weeks/months of independent life. He may simply mismanage his budget, but he may have the ill luck to discover that he is paid in arrears and/or has to pay his rent in advance. A sum of money lodged in a deposit account at the bank or post office will see him through and also ensure that he can (and knows that he can) get home for a weekend if he suddenly needs a rest from all this adulthood.

Keep home available. Few adolescents leave their parents' home and settle at once into their own "home." While yours may immediately acquire an apartment and make it into her home, she is more likely to spend quite a while feeling that her "digs" are temporary and that a large chunk of herself (not to mention many of her possessions) are still with you.

Try to keep her place, especially her room or share of a room, intact during this stage. She may not come back to it as often as you would like, but knowing that it is still there is important. Sometimes a younger child is given the adolescent's room the moment she departs for her first term at college or month in a job. However welcome she is to the living room sofa, she is bound to feel that her place has closed behind her, that she has not just left but been thrown out.

Problems with appearance and body image

Most adolescents are deeply concerned with their own looks, but although their concern may sometimes seem like mere vanity or slavish following of fashion, it is an important part of the search for self which is the prime task of this age-stage. An adolescent's appearance is the outward and visible-to-others sign of the inner self which he or she is trying to identify and confirm. The "look" for which a youngster strives will change whenever the image of self he or she wants other people to see changes. Furthermore, the self an adolescent sees mirrored in other people's reactions to his or her appearance may lead either to a confirmation or to a rejection of that particular style. At one time, for example, a girl may seek the protective camouflage of her social group's "uniform" to such an extent that she cannot decide what particular garments to wear to a particular occasion until she has spent half an hour on the telephone finding out exactly what others will be wearing. At another time, though, a boy may want, above all, to assert his difference from everyone else. The "gear" expensively collected during previous months will be abandoned and he may struggle to start a beard. If someone she cares about tells your daughter that she looks sexy in a particular outfit it may be worn constantly or never again, depending on whether sexy was what she wanted to look. If his aunt tells your son that he spoils his good looks by wearing those scruffy jeans he may abandon or hang onto them depending on how he is feeling about elderly ladies considering him good looking!

In a family, these concerns are often derided. Children seldom care deeply about their appearances; middle-aged parents have become accustomed to theirs. Caught between these two comparatively unconcerned and un-fashion-conscious groups, the wretched adolescent may be misunderstood and mocked. There may be rows over the cost of fashionable clothes; rows over pierced ears, male jewelry, unsuitable hairstyles and shoes. There may be shocked reactions to rude messages on sweatshirts or underpants. Worst of all, there may be a general attitude of "What does it matter?" "What's wrong with those jeans anyway?" "What are you fussing about, they're only spots, you'll grow out of it. . . ." "Why do you want to change your hair color anyway? It's perfectly nice the way it is."

While parents control the purse strings (*see above* Money) they have the right to limit what the adolescent can spend on his or her appearance. While they control general health and well-being (*see above* Self-care) they have a right to guard against dangerous extremes. But none of this gives them the right either to tell a youngster what he or she should look like or to try to persuade him or her that appearances do not matter. When you try to tell your adolescent what to look like it feels as if you are trying to tell him or her *what and who to be*. When you refuse to care what he or she looks like you are, to some extent at least, implying that *you do not care what he or she is or wants to be.*

While the fashions in clothes and other gear which your adolescent wants to adopt or avoid will vary from place to place and from time to time, there are some problems with appearance which are common during the adolescent years and which, because they affect his or her own body image and sense of self, always merit the greatest possible understanding, support and help.

Acne   The blackheads and whiteheads, pimples and pustules of acne can leave permanent scars on a teenager's skin and, in an extreme instance, on the personality, too. Few things erode tenuous social confidence more than a continuous crop of spots. A boy who is wondering whether any pretty girl will ever want to go out with him will be quite sure that none ever will if he feels that instead of gazing into his romantic eyes she will be mesmerized by his disgusting pustules. A girl who half longs for and half dreads that disco, will have the balance tipped towards terror if she finds a crop of spots.

Acne cannot, at the moment, be completely prevented or completely cured. But acne can be controlled. The more thoroughly it is understood, the easier it will be to cope with it in the individual circumstances of your family.

What acne is   Skin contains sebaceous glands which, like many other glands, are stimulated into activity by the changes of puberty. These glands secrete an oily substance (sebum). Most of the sebum reaches the skin's surface via the hair follicles and produces nothing worse than oily skin, or hair which gets so greasy that it needs shampooing every couple of days. In acne, though, the sebum does not flow freely, but backs up in the hair follicles. Why this should happen to most, but not all, people is not known. Nor do we know why most sufferers have only a few, or occasional, dammed-up follicles while a wretched few have hundreds of these minute blockages, not only on the face but on the chest and shoulders, too.

Blackheads and whiteheads. When sebum is trapped in a hair follicle it thickens. A whitehead is simply an accumulation of this thickened sebum. A blackhead is not black because of "dirt in the pores"; it is also only a collection of thickened sebum but the sebum is dark because it happens to contain particles of the skin pigment (melanin). Dark-skinned people tend to mind whiteheads more than blackheads; fair skins look worse with blackheads, but neither has any connection whatsoever with dirt.

Pimples and pustules. The hair follicles, along which oily sebum should flow, contain bacteria. When the sebum accumulates, the enzymes in those bacteria break the sebum down into free fatty acids which irritate and weaken the hair-follicle walls. With sebum still flowing into the follicle, behind the blockage, this irritation eventually causes the walls of the follicle to rupture so that bacteria and sebum are released into the surrounding tissues. When this happens, there is inflammation and the typical pimples of acne form. Pustules are the next stage and, if the bacteria and inflammation are deep below the skin's surface, cysts and boils may form, too.

What acne is not Old wives' tales about acne are numerous. For example:
  □ Blackheads are black because they are dirty.
  □ Blackheads and whiteheads form because the sufferer does not wash his/her face properly so that oil and old cosmetics "plug the pores."
  □ Yellow-headed pustules contain pus because the sufferer has picked at pimples or squeezed blackheads with dirty fingers.
  This is all nonsense. More importantly it is all insulting nonsense, apparently designed to make the wretched teenager believe that the acne which is driving him or her into depression anyway is due to dirty habits.

  Acne lesions come from inside the skin's structure and therefore cannot be prevented or cured by external washing (but *see below*). Advertisers have helped the cosmetics industry to make millions by suggesting that their products will produce "deep down cleanliness" or "penetrate the pores to float out the dirt you cannot see" or "steam your skin really clean all through." Resist such claims. Cleansing, whatever product is used, does not go beneath the skin's surface. Furthermore, despite popular belief to the contrary, the skin's pores cannot be opened and closed at will.

  On a par with the "dirt theory" is the equally insulting and inaccurate belief that acne afflicts only adolescents who eat junk foods (especially fried foods and chocolate), go short of sleep or are involved in sexual activity. While the hormones which affect sexual *development* certainly have a bearing on acne (*see above*) neither sexual activity nor sexual inactivity, nor the in-betweens such as masturbation and heavy petting, have anything to do with acne either way. While adequate sleep may be a good thing in itself, plenty will not improve acne nor will exhaustion make it worse.

Prevention and control of mild acne

Acne begins with plugged hair follicles so, while they cannot be un-plugged from outside, anything which helps them keep themselves clear will help prevent or control acne.

Washing with soap. Removes the grease from oily skin as well as ensuring that clogged make-up or dust is not making matters worse. Ordinary toilet soap is perfectly adequate, although if the skin is ex-tremely oily a soap containing tar and/or sulphur may be beneficially drying.

Using sunshine. The ultra-violet rays in sunshine definitely discourage acne which may clear altogether during a sunny vacation. If so, using a sunlamp will help, too.

Shampooing hair and adjusting hairstyles. Acne is often worst on the forehead where the skin is covered by bangs which are allowed to become greasy. Keeping hair free of grease may help and so may keeping it off the forehead. If hair is worn in a style which covers this area, face-washing must get right underneath it.

Removing blackheads and whiteheads. If a blackhead is visible then a hair follicle is blocked and liable to become the site of an acne pimple-pustule. Removing blackheads therefore makes sense *provided it is done properly*. Obviously squeezing it out with dirty fingernails is liable to introduce infection and to leave a nasty mark, too. Either the pads of clean fingers should be used to squeeze *gently* or a special blackhead extractor should be used.

Choosing cosmetics carefully. "Medicated" cosmetics will not help acne because the anti-bacterial chemicals they contain cannot penetrate into the follicles. Heavy, clogging cosmetics should be reserved for special occasions and for covering blemishes. Everyday cosmetics should be those intended for oily skin.

Coping with pustules and scabs. Help your adolescent to resist attempts to squeeze those painful red bumps which come before a pustule. Persistent efforts may produce a tiny bit of pus, but if there was no visible head he or she will have forced it up through skin which was still intact and made a tiny wound. *Many of these lumps will disperse by themselves* if left alone. If a yellow head does appear he or she should squeeze it as antiseptically as possible or more infection may be introduced from bacteria on the skin.

For *open* acne sores a "medicated" soap or astringent skin lotion may just be worth using. It will not cure the places but it may help prevent them from becoming secondarily infected by bacteria from outside.

Medical help for severe acne

Unless these simple measures keep the skin almost completely clear almost all the time, medical advice is needed. There is no reason for an adolescent to be left to suffer and if he or she is thus left, the acne lesions may leave scars. Medical treatment at present takes two main forms:

Attempts to reduce secretion of sebum. Drugs are becoming available which actually block the production of sebum by the sebaceous glands. Some of these are not yet available for general prescription and some have side effects which might make a doctor reluctant to prescribe them except in an extremely severe case of acne.

Girls are more fortunate in this respect than boys. Low progesterone birth control pills markedly reduce sebum production. If a girl is considering "going on the Pill" anyway, her acne may clear up as a side effect. If not, severe acne may be a reason for considering this treatment, especially if, like many girls, her acne tends to flare up with each menstrual period.

Attempts to reduce bacterial action within the hair follicle. Certain antibiotics (notably tetracycline) can inhibit the growth of bacteria within the hair follicle and thus prevent that cycle of sebum-bacterial-breakdown-inflammation-follicle-rupture-pustules.

Tetracycline works best for this purpose if it is taken in a low dosage over a long period and if the drug is taken on an empty stomach and without the calcium-containing drinks (such as milk) which may prevent it from being absorbed. Provided it is given under medical supervision and followed patiently without expectation of instant miracles, such long-term antibiotic treatment is both safe and usually effective.

Body odor   The skin contains two types of sweat-producing glands. The eccrine glands are widely distributed over the body with a slight concentration in the palms, soles and forehead. Active in everyone, whatever his or her age, these glands produce watery sweat in response to heat and/or stress. The sweat moistens the skin and cools it by evaporation. Eccrine sweat alone seldom causes an unpleasant smell unless personal hygiene is very poor. The apocrine glands are a different matter. These are concentrated mainly in the underarm area and they become active only during puberty, when underarm hair begins to grow. Their activity diminishes as adult age increases. The activity of the apocrine glands may usher in a body-odor problem because although their sweat is odorless in itself, it develops an unpleasant smell when it is acted upon by the bacteria which are on everybody's skin. These bacteria concentrate and flourish in warm, moist areas such as the underarms and it is from such areas that sweat can least easily evaporate.

Dealing with underarm odor. Frequent washing with ordinary soap and water is the most effective way of keeping skin bacteria to reasonable numbers and of removing the sweat on which they act. A combined anti-perspirant/deodorant will reduce the amount of sweat secreted under the arms and do something to mask or diminish the smell. Removing underarm hair makes it easier to keep the bacterial population down and easier to wash effectively.

Clothing which permits easy evaporation (especially during hot, humid weather and/or active exercise) also helps, so sufferers should settle for vest-shaped sports shirts which leave the underarm area naked, and for loose armholes wherever possible on other clothes. Some fabrics, usually man-made ones or fabrics with special finishes, become smelly far more quickly than others. The adolescent may have to experiment and reject a type of shirt which always leaves him embarrassed by the end of the day.

Any clothing which is allowed to become contaminated with sweat + bacteria and is then worn again without being washed is bound to become smelly. Adolescents often do not realize that washing clothing is just as important as washing themselves. Both sexes can be helped with under-arm odor if they are liberally supplied with shirts, T-shirts, blouses, etc., so that they are able to change frequently—certainly every day and perhaps twice a day.

Girls may find that clothes requiring expensive dry cleaning are more practical if they wear dress shields to absorb the sweat and protect the outer clothes from contact. Boys may find that a cotton undershirt (which will absorb sweat) will similarly prevent sweat from reaching sweaters and jackets.

If a wardrobe has a slightly stale, unpleasant smell when first opened, the adolescent can be sure that clothes are contributing to the body-odor problem.

Dealing with odor in the genital area. This is more often a problem for girls than for boys. Unpleasant odor is usually associated either with menstruation or with a discharge from the vagina. Normal vaginal discharge, like menstrual blood, does not smell unpleasant until it is exposed to the air. Frequent washing and clean underwear should therefore deal with any odor (*see above* Menstruation). A vaginal discharge caused by infection or by a forgotten tampon may smell very nasty indeed. The presence of an offensive discharge between menstrual periods should mean a visit to the doctor.

Girls are often hypersensitive about odor from the vaginal area, confus-ing the slight, distinctive odor which is natural to it with abnormal body odor. While you must, of course, be honest with your daughter if you agree that she smells (a best friend may not tell her but it would be cruel of you not to do so), do try to dissuade her from "feminine deodorants," "deodorant towelettes" and so forth. Not only are these unnecessary if she keeps herself normally clean, they may also cause rashes and other allergic reactions. Don't allow a male advertising world to convince her that she needs special deodorants for her femaleness.

Dealing with foot odor. It is usually boys who suffer from smelly feet and they themselves usually do not suffer as much as those who must share bedrooms and locker rooms with them.

Feet smell unpleasant only if sweat is allowed to become colonized by bacteria and is then trapped for hours inside man-made-fiber socks and plastic shoes and, even when these are removed, *is not washed off.* The answers, then, are washing, cotton and/or wool socks, and leather or canvas rather than "waterproof" plastic shoes. Clean socks every day should be as much a routine as clean underpants. Shoes which are not being worn should ideally be stored in an airy place.

A boy who really does follow a sensible routine of foot hygiene but still has trouble may find that his shoes (especially if they have absorbent insoles) are permanently smelly and therefore undermining all his efforts. He will have to start again with new ones.

Dealing with sweaty palms. Sweaty hands do not smell but may never-theless be acutely embarrassing in all kinds of social situations where hands are shaken and/or held. Excessive palm sweat is almost always caused by nervous excitement (although heat will not help) and therefore it bedevils adolescents on just those occasions when they want to be at their best.

Keeping cool, calm and collected will certainly help when it is possible. Apart from this, running the hands under cold water may help a little as may an astringent. "Clean-up pads" come ready-moistened with astringent lotion and packed in pocket-sized packets so they can be kept usefully available. If sweaty palms are really reducing the quality of an adolescent's life it is worth consulting a doctor. Various topical (skin) preparations help some people.

Deformities, real and imagined Adolescents need to be able to accept themselves, even like themselves, warts and all. Sometimes the warts (or sticking-out ears or over-large noses) come to assume enormous importance. It is as if the youngster has picked out one particular physical characteristic and used it as a peg on which to hang all his or her anxieties and discontents about him/herself. Parents need to tread warily.

Is the anxiety genuine or a put-on? Sometimes a youngster will say, casually, "With a nose the size of mine, I can't wear sunglasses." If she was asking you only to reassure her that her nose is entirely normal, instant sympathy may create a real problem. If in doubt, try feeding the line back: "Your nose looks OK to me, what's supposed to be wrong with it?"

If the anxiety is genuine, can you see a reality base for it? Of course this is a subjective judgment, but, at least at the extremes, you will probably know whether the feature complained of comes within normal limits or not. Large breasts, for example, are perfectly normal; the tormented possessor, aged fifteen, may be exceedingly proud of her lavish endowment in a year or two and should certainly not be encouraged to feel that a doctor could redesign her to fit her currently desired self-image. You may be able to help with better-fitting bras or better-chosen clothes but the best help you can offer will probably be warm acceptance of her new sexuality. On the other hand, markedly protruding teeth are not accepted as normal or attractive and it would, perhaps, have been kinder to have them dealt with by an orthodontist while she was still at an age when many of her friends wore braces. If you can honestly see why her teeth distress her, by all means facilitate her in seeking professional advice.

If the anxiety is both genuine and reality-based, is action practically possible? If your child has some real deformity (such as a poorly repaired harelip) your reaction to adolescent distress needs to be based on hard and up-to-date information. Could an unsightly scar be improved by plastic surgery? If so, could the surgery be appropriately performed at his or her current age or must it wait until growth is complete? What would surgical intervention mean in terms of discomfort and disruption of life? Could it be done at any time or would there be a wait of months/years for non-urgent surgery?

The point here is that if nothing can be done, you have to help your child towards acceptance, not by denying the existence of the problem but by helping him or her to see that it need not permeate all of life. If, on the other hand, action is practically possible, you have to give him or her the facts on which to decide whether or not to take any. If action involves plastic surgery, it is usually important to see to it that he or she receives expert counselling first. All too often a youngster half-believes that the surgery will transform him or her not just into a person without that blemish but into somebody beautiful.

Young people may be worried by a number of other more minor "imperfections." Too much adult attention to these "problems" will tend to heighten their importance in the child's eyes while refusal to consider them at all will seem uncaring. Some, girls especially, can easily come to feel that their mothers do not want them to be beautiful. If the mother is seen to spend some time, money and attention on her own appearance yet will spend none on her daughter's, problems of sexual jealousy between the generations can be much exacerbated. Mothers perhaps need to ask themselves: "Would *I* want to put up with that for myself?" If the answer is "no," the girl is probably entitled to some consideration.

Birthmarks, scars, etc. Many such marks can either be removed, or can be made much less noticeable, by surgical and related techniques such as dermabrasion. Others can be better disguised by special creams containing masking agents than by cosmetic cover creams. If your child has any problem of this kind *and expresses worry over it*, do facilitate him or her in making an appointment with a dermatologist (see **Birthmarks**).

Moles come in all shapes, sizes, places and degrees of pigmentation. Most can be surgically removed under local anesthesia although some degree of scarring will be left. A mole which suddenly grows and/or darkens should, in any case, be seen by a doctor to ensure that it *is* just a simple mole. The possibility of having it removed can be discussed at the same appointment.

Problems with hair: "Excess hair" The amount of facial and body hair is almost entirely a hereditary matter. While there are a few hormonal disorders which can cause sudden excess growth, the normal hormonal changes of adolescence are usually responsible for the increase. Boys will seldom be concerned by their hairiness but girls may be very bothered indeed by facial hair and/or by thick, dark hair on the arms and legs.

Many women remove hair from the legs using either a razor or a chemical depilatory. A few remove it (or have it removed) by waxing, which pulls the hairs out at root level. Single hairs (such as those which may sprout on the chin, from a mole or around the nipples) are often simply pulled out with tweezers. But if a girl has a real problem with excess hair, none of these solutions may be very satisfactory. If, for example, she is bothered by a luxuriant growth of conspicuously dark hair on her arms and upper legs, shaving will produce an uncomfortable stubbly feeling; it will take a considerable amount of time at frequent intervals and thus continually remind her of "the problem" and, when she leaves it one day too long, the stubbly hairs may be more conspicuous than the full growth. Using a chemical depilatory will keep the regrowth softer (since the ends of the hairs are not chopped off) but otherwise will be similar. To embark on such a program in the early teens seems sad. It may be better to find a way in which she can come to accept the hairiness.

If she cannot accept it and would rather swelter in long sleeves and tights in summer than reveal her hairy limbs, it may be helpful if you suggest bleaching, which makes even luxuriant hair far less conspicuous. It also has the advantage that it can be done at home, can be used in conjunction with any other temporary method of removal (from the lower legs in summer, for example) and that used repeatedly, it tends actually to weaken and reduce the growth.

Home bleach can be made by mixing six percent hydrogen peroxide (called 20-volume peroxide) with twenty drops of ammonia to each ounce. A small amount should be made up and applied to ensure that the skin is not oversensitive to it. If all is well, a fresh solution should be made up and applied immediately (peroxide action begins as soon as the ammonia is added). It should be left on for about half an hour and then thoroughly washed off.

Facial hair Probably cannot be simply accepted and may therefore be best removed by the only permanent method: electrolysis. This involves the insertion of a tiny needle into the follicle of each individual hair which is then destroyed by an electric current. It must be carried out by a trained expert (home kits are neither satisfactory nor safe as inexpert use can scar surrounding tissue) and it is therefore expensive as well as time-consuming. Nevertheless, if a young girl has a dark mustache, she will have it forever if nothing is done; so, like straightening crooked teeth, it may be worth doing. Check with your doctor for the name of a reputable electrolysist.

Scalp hair Hairs grow for two to six years and then "rest" for a few months during which time they are easily removed by brush or comb, and at the end of which time they will, in any case, be pushed out by the growth of a new hair. The loss of up to one hundred separate hairs in a day is nothing to worry about. Hair will only thin if loss exceeds regrowth. The normal rate of regrowth is such that it takes about two and a half months for scalp hair to grow one inch. Hormonal changes can lead to the scalp hair thinning. This sometimes happens in pregnancy or, occasionally, when a girl starts taking birth control pills.

Bald spots on the scalp may be due to ringworm (*see* **Ringworm**) or, rarely, to a little understood disease called alopecia areata. The cause of this disorder is not known, but spontaneous regrowth almost always occurs and certain medical treatments can hasten it.

The commonest cause of bald spots is, however, known as traction alopecia and is the result of continuous pulling on the hair, as when it is always worn tightly plaited. Usually hair growth will recover when the style is changed and the traction stopped, but occasionally some permanent damage to growth in the affected areas does occur. Rarely, pulling out the hair as a nervous habit can cause traction alopecia.

Generalized hair loss. Some individuals have a tendency to hair loss and will find their hair thinning after feverish illnesses or whenever their general health has been poor. The hair can be protected, to some extent, by minimizing the amount of manipulation to which it is subjected. Thorough brushing, for example, does not encourage growth but merely removes needed hairs which might have remained a little longer. Very frequent shampooing, chemical bleaches and perms and the use of hot rollers should all be discouraged. If fashion allows, a short style will both appear thicker and require less handling than a longer one.

Constant changes of color, involving the use of harsh chemicals, may dry out and damage the hair so that it breaks off close to the scalp. The roots are still present but the appearance is of hair loss. Although such hair will regrow, a different regime will be needed.

Glasses and contact lenses   If a child is becoming near-sighted, sight correction often becomes necessary when the growth spurt around puberty suddenly increases the myopia. He or she therefore faces a new image of self as an eyeglass-wearer just at the time in life when self-image becomes so vital.

In the past, having to wear glasses seemed traumatic to many youngsters. Now, however, your child may feel easier about it. Many people wear non-prescription tinted lenses simply because they like the look of them. Glasses have become virtually a fashion accessory.

If your child can accept glasses, do not make a drama out of it. Instead, devote yourself to helping him or her to find the frames which really suit and, perhaps, the special frames which will glamourize her for parties or him for active sports. If the very idea of wearing glasses fills the child with horror, you may want to consider contact lenses instead.

Contact lenses suit some people but not everyone. Your ophthalmologist and optician will, between them, advise on the medical suitability of various types of lens but it is up to you and your child to consider other issues. On some people, for example, contact lenses, however well they are tolerated, produce a somewhat watery appearance in the eyes which, together with the constant blinking which is necessary for contact lens wear, makes them quite conspicuous.

Daily wear lenses require careful attention to nightly hygiene and to safe overnight storage. This can be tedious and quite difficult for a youngster to manage if he or she frequently sleeps the night at friends' houses, goes camping and so forth.

Lenses are easily lost and expensive to replace. Furthermore, the prescription needed by a young teenager is likely to change quite rapidly so that expensive new lenses will be needed.

Not all types of lens can safely be worn for all sports.

Extended wear lenses, which do not have to be removed each night, require less care and are less readily lost. When they were introduced it did seem that they might be the ideal answer for youngsters who, once comfortable with them, would be able to forget their nearsightedness for long periods. Such lenses are proving to have some problems, however, and your specialist may advise you against them.

Attempts to "improve" appearance   Sometimes a youngster wishes to make some dramatic change in his or her appearance which parents consider the very opposite of "an improvement." Quell any instinctive screams of indignation with the realization that you are honored to have been consulted in advance. You are at least being given the opportunity to voice your opinions; do so gently or the next dramatic change will take place with the support of friends only.

How permanent is the change and what is the timing? If your son means to have his head shaved, he (and you) will only have to live with it for a few months. If you hate the idea you could point out that in order to get back to having a hairstyle he will have to live through the equivalent of a crew cut (which may, or may not, strike him as a horrendous notion). Otherwise it is probably not worth a row.

If your daughter means to have her hair bleached and then dyed in stripes, much the same applies except that if she has a summer job lined up which you know she will be banned from if she "looks like that," you might possibly persuade her to wait (if she wants the job). Money is a consideration. Keeping the style will cost her a lot. Having the whole lot dyed in order to conceal the stripes while they grow out will cost a lot, too.

If the change is permanent, will he/she be able to live with it forever? Pierced ears are permanent but their purpose—the wearing of earrings —need not be. You may dislike the idea of your son wearing one earring now, but even the most conservative later employer is unlikely to hold against him such inconspicuous evidence of youthful fashion conscious- ness as one hole.

Tattooing, on the other hand, is both truly permanent and something which your child is most unlikely to want to live with later. In some places tattooists are forbidden by law to work on minors. If age or place deprives you of legal support, at least make sure that your child does really know:

That tattooing hurts and that if the tattooist is more concerned with artistry than hygiene, can be dangerous.

That while a small tattoo can later be surgically removed there will be a scar.

That larger areas cannot be dealt with surgically. There are techniques for fading them or for smudging out the actual picture/message, but none remove the tattoo completely.

That removal techniques of which he/she may have heard (such as superficial dermabrasion) rely on causing inflammation in the skin of the tattooed area, thus persuading the dye to move up towards the surface. They do not always work and they often leave the skin either hairless or a different color from the rest.

Sex

Parents will have passed on their own attitudes to sexual matters long before their children reach puberty and become able to *feel* the issues which as children they could only *think about*. Nevertheless, it is during adolescence that the formal and informal "sex education" of school and home is likely to face some acid tests. Some facts and factually based opinions may be useful to parents facing new problems, unexpected questions or just the reality of sexually alive and active children.

Masturbation   Is a normal activity, widely practiced in childhood (*see* **Habits**) and almost universal in adolescence. Those who find it shocking usually have a puritanical belief that anything which is done entirely for selfish pleasure must be wrong and/or a fear of the strength of feelings and fantasies which combine to produce the complete loss of control which is implicit in orgasm (climax). Every adolescent has a right to specific assurances that:

Masturbation cannot damage penis or vagina.

Masturbation does not lead to insanity, blindness, illness or indeed to mental or physical damage of any kind whatsoever.

The feeling of weakness which follows orgasm is a normal resting reaction of the body after any form of sexual gratification. It is in no sense a sign that masturbation is "weakening."

That "having sex with oneself" does not suggest homosexual leanings even when the accompanying fantasies are of a same-sex partner.

But this kind of assurance must be tactfully given, preferably in bits and pieces as "right moments" arise over a long period of childhood. To deliver a prepared lecture on the harmlessness of masturbation would be to invade the privacy of your fourteen-year-old son or daughter.

Homosexuality   At one time or another adolescents of both sexes will probably wonder whether they are homosexual. Each of us is bisexual, to some extent, both biologically and socially. Our eventual sexual direction is never absolute but always a question of which way the balance tips. The ambiguity is especially bothering to young adolescents because they are at a stage of life during which they are both trying to find their own inner balance and being expected to make and state an outward sexual choice.

Despite strong public stands by organizations of male and female homosexuals and by other sympathetic groups, claiming that homosexuality is normal, most adolescents can only recognize it as normal in people other than themselves. To wonder whether he or she is homosexually inclined is to worry about it, although the worry is usually more acute for boys than for girls. Many pubertal girls have passionate "crushes" on older girls or women, yet most remain convinced that one day it will be males who engage their romantic attention. It may be that the prospect of childbirth—often made conscious at the menarche—makes it easier for them to take eventual heterosexual relationships for granted. In the meanwhile, most societies are kinder to females than to males in this respect. Close and exclusive friendships between girls are easily accepted and physical expressions of such friendship, such as holding hands or kissing, pass without the ribald comment which is aroused by similar behavior between boys. In many families and communities this difference in values for boy and girl begins in infancy. Girls may dress in trousers, play with trains and be admired as "tomboys." Boys, on the other hand, may never wear dresses, are seldom offered dolls and quickly learn to dread being called "sissy."

Nobody really knows why some adults prefer to have sexual relations with their own rather than the opposite sex. What we do know, however, is that the preference can neither be changed at will nor prevented by exhortation in adolescence. Parental coercion will never make a heterosexual but may easily make a permanent breach within the family. Most adolescents will worry about possible homosexuality; most will become heterosexual adults. Parents should concentrate on helping with the anxiety and leave the adolescent's personal and private development to see to the eventual outcome.

Avoid sexual labelling. Caring activities, tender emotions and artistic interests are not signs of homosexuality. Don't try to make your son behave as a "man's man." He must become his own man. Close friendships between girls are not signs of lesbianism. Don't try to make your daughter behave as a flirt. She must be herself.

Avoid sexual teasing. Boys grow and develop later than girls and, in early adolescence, often feel disadvantaged in dawning sexual battles. Don't tease your son about his "little girlfriend" when he is clearly unready for any such relationship. You may make him wonder if he ever will be ready. Many boys devote much of the energy of the mid-teens to sports and other activities rather than to sexual ones. Don't tease your sixteen-year-old for never having had a date. If you suggest that he is in some way peculiar you may increase his tendency to believe that he is.

Accept hero worship. Adolescents often worship from afar. The object of worship is often a member of the same sex and, for a boy, will often be a sports hero. Only your own hang-ups will make you prefer your son to cover his wall with pin-ups rather than action photos, or your daughter to blush for the school's leading actor rather than his female co-star.

Stay calm about mutual masturbation or homosexual approaches. Many of the close same-sex friendships of early adolescence have, at some time, an element of sexual experimentation. Probably you will never know about this but, if you do, remember that such a relationship does not suggest that your son "is homosexual," that he may well fear that it does suggest this and that if he has problems in this area a shocked reaction from you can do only harm.

Many boys receive homosexual approaches from adults at some time in their lives (*see* **Safety**/From "strangers"). Again, if such an incident comes to your notice, do underplay your reaction. If you express complete horror, your son may feel that he has been befouled, rather than annoyed. If he partly enjoyed the experience he will also feel extremely guilty.

Wet dreams (nocturnal emissions) Once a boy's testes are producing sperm (*see above* Puberty) he may (or may not) have dreams from which he is suddenly awakened by orgasm and ejaculation. These wet dreams are entirely normal and in no way under the boy's control. Their absence, however, does not suggest abnormality. Most boys have some; some boys have many more than others.

While the orgasm is intensely pleasurable, a wet dream can be worrying. If the boy does not know in advance that it is likely, he may confuse ejaculation with bedwetting or believe that his masturbation has got out of his control so that he is "doing it in his sleep." He may also worry about the nature of the dream which caused the emission; it may be overtly heterosexual but it may be homosexual and/or sadistic or masochistic in content. Finally, of course, he may worry about practicalities such as how to cope with wet pajamas and sheets. Like his menstruating sister he needs an easy and private way to cope.

Sexual activity between adolescents

Western media suggest that we live in an age of complete sexual freedom; their more sensational headlines suggest that freedom has become anarchy and back the claim by drawing attention to increases in schoolgirl pregnancies and adolescent venereal disease. Things are not quite as they are made to appear. While many adolescents do have sexual relationships with each other, many do not, at least until they are approaching adulthood. Of those who do have earlier sexual relationships, many conduct meaningful affairs in a responsible way rather than using promiscuous sex for passing entertainment.

Adults always have been, and probably always will be, quick to indict the sexual behavior of the young because adolescent sexuality frightens them and affects relationships within families in ways which they dare not recognize, let alone accept. The sheer strength of adolescent sexual feeling, for example, is something most adults choose to ignore. Good sex education may deal with "love" as well as with "the facts of life" but it seldom deals with lust; with the fact that the adolescent will *want* sex. You can accept the existence of a feeling without necessarily encouraging its expression and it is better if you do.

In families which lack this kind of understanding and acceptance the effect which adolescent sexuality has on family relationships can be devastating. Many fathers and sons who continually pick on each other, for example, are interacting as herd bulls behave with immature rivals. If a father can recognize this elemental reaction in himself he will probably be able to find more appropriate ways of acknowledging his son's maturity. If he cannot recognize it he may eventually find himself behaving like a bull to a point where he throws that son right out of the family herd. Mothers and daughters often find themselves in similarly difficult new squabbles. Many, for example, quarrel ceaselessly about the daughter's clothes, hair, make-up and general appearance. If the mother who always wants her daughter to dress less conspicuously, less "sexily," can acknowledge to herself that she is partly trying to keep out new sexual competition, she may be able to accept her daughter's right to present whatever image of herself she pleases. Sometimes father-daughter and mother-son relationships need some thought, too. It is all too easy for an adult to behave seductively to an adolescent child, telling him or herself that "there's nothing wrong with being cozy together/undressing together/flirting together: he/she is my *baby*." The adolescent is not a baby any more.

Even the closest and easiest relationships between parents and adolescents need monitoring a little. Fathers and mothers who find a new lease on life and fun in the activities of their growing children must ask themselves whether they are really watching and facilitating the adolescent's life or whether perhaps they are trying to live their own again through him or her. A close, confidant relationship can all too easily become an invasion of privacy. "Tell me all about it, darling" must mean no more than "I'm interested in anything you care to say."

Sexual customs and mores vary widely from place to place and from group to group and, of course, parental reactions vary, too. But whatever sexual behavior you think you are seeing in your adolescent and/or his or her peer group, do remember that the group will itself have sexual customs and mores. If you can come to understand what these are, you may find them both comforting and surprising. Parents often look at their children's public behavior now, in the eighties, and wrongly assume that it suggests the same private behavior which it would have suggested when they were young. In the fifties and sixties, for example, couples did not go away on vacation alone together unless they were also sleeping together. Furthermore, "sleeping together" in the same bed or tent was a euphemism for sexual intercourse. Today, the girl who tells you that she and her boyfriend are going camping together may neither be announcing that she has made love with him nor that she intends to do so. The son whom you disturb in bed with a girl may still be a virgin and intending to remain so for the moment. Things have changed, but often the change is towards a greater freedom to be close with members of the opposite sex and therefore to make more informed choices of sexual partners.

Difficulties of very early sexual activity
The difference in the rates at which girls and boys mature means that girls are often looking for romantic/sexual contacts long before their male peers are ready for them. "Dating" (or whatever less dated word is current in your children's community) has tremendous social significance for girls and the higher the standing of the boy who asks her out, the greater her social prestige. This combination of circumstances often means that a very young adolescent girl maneuvers invitations from considerably older boys. They, if they are prepared to play the "dating" game at all, seldom understand that their company is really wanted for public show rather than sexual action. Those who do understand it not unnaturally often resent it. Where such a relationship continues at all (and usually it will not) the girl often finds that the romantic element is on her side only; that there is little mutual friendship between them and that the boy's drive towards sexual contact is far stronger and more immediate than her own. If she wants to hold onto the relationship, she may find herself "paying" with sex for the boy's public company and trying to pretend to herself that the sexual contact proves that he loves her. Boys in this situation are often genuinely confused. If a girl clearly wants to dance the slow dances with him at the disco and clearly wants him to leave his male friends and pay attention to her, does she not also want to be kissed and fondled? If she wants to be kissed and fondled and if she will come with him to the car or private corner, does she not also feel the overwhelming lust which he comes to feel? If she does not share the lust, why does she insist on the evenings which build up to it? If she does share the lust why does she later seek assurances that the relationship is more than a passing and casual thing-of-the-moment?

The more both girls and boys can understand of each other's psychology and sexuality the less likely they will be to get into these painful muddles. In the meantime, young girls who go out with boys in their *own* age group are likely to have to "do the chasing," but will be doing so with boys who, because they are themselves still anxious about sexual activity, are unlikely to allow matters to go further than either of them truly wants. Eventually a boy will cease simply to be overwhelmingly interested in sex and his body's reactions to sexy sights and feelings; he will become interested in girls as people, and in one girl in particular. Then and only then will he be ready to share the kind of romantic closeness which his girl-peer has been dreaming of for so long. Then and only then do the two of them stand a chance of making a sexual relationship which is part of a whole relationship; of loving each other for however long or short a time.

Contraception   With efficient contraceptives more or less freely available, teenage pregnancies should be a tragedy of the past; instead they are on the increase. Unthinking adults tend to blame this on youthful irresponsibility. In fact, it is far more difficult for very young people to guard against unwanted pregnancies than it is for their more settled elders. Many youngsters, properly educated in the vital importance of using contraceptives whenever, wherever and with whomever they have sex, nevertheless get "caught" because intercourse takes place without either of them having intended it. If you really want to ensure that your adolescent neither causes nor experiences an unwanted pregnancy, you will need to be extremely hard-headed in your thinking and frank in your advice.

Girls who have full intercourse very early in adolescence are peculiarly at risk because they do not give themselves time to think about their own sexuality or contemplate the possibility/likelihood of having sex and realize that it is time to take precautions. Girls whose early sexual contacts are confined to fondling and foreplay are far more likely to make positive decisions. They decide that now, or with this partner, they may go farther and they therefore realize that the time has come to seek advice. It is best if a girl has "boyfriends" before she has a lover.

First times are risky because even a girl who realized in advance that intercourse was possible may well feel uneasy about preparing herself for something which might never happen. In rather the same way, blind dates and mixed-sex trips are risky because most girls will not want to admit to themselves that they might consider having intercourse if the right fellow turned up, but may still do so, unprepared, if he does.

Many parents believe that for just these reasons all girls should use the contraceptive pill "from the beginning." But what is the beginning? To suggest that a thirteen-year-old should "go on the Pill" may be to suggest that you not only expect but even recommend sexual activity. She may be bitterly hurt by what strikes her as a lack of caring. She may be shattered at your lack of trust. She may even be disgusted because she is so far from visualizing herself as an active sexual partner that she cannot bear to realize that you are ready to see her in that role.

There are physiological arguments against putting girls on the Pill early, too. Many authorities believe that it is dangerous to tamper with a newly established—or perhaps not yet fully established—hormonal balance. Many also believe that the number of years a woman spends on the Pill should be limited and therefore that it should be saved for the years when she is fully sexually active.

Other reasonably efficient methods of female contraception are also either contraindicated or difficult for the very young to manage. A very young girl—even if she is not actually a virgin—is most unlikely to be suitable for an intrauterine device. She could, of course, be fitted with a diaphragm to use with a spermicidal cream or jelly, but the chances of her having it with her when she comes to need it are negligible.

Responsibility for avoiding very early pregnancies has to lie with boys, and therefore with their parents, even though the dread of pregnancy is so much more real to girls and their parents. If boys were taught that they must use a condom whenever they had intercourse until or unless other contraceptive arrangements had actually been discussed between them and their regular partners, pregnancies *and* venereal disease would both be much reduced. Condoms are easily purchased and easily carried. A boy can become adept at using one by practicing while masturbating. If he cannot cope with the thought or the reality of using a condom he certainly is not mature enough to cope with a real sexual partner.

In some communities adolescent males have "stopped bothering" about condoms because "all the girls are on the Pill." Many girls feel pressurized by this attitude and some find themselves in situations where they have to rely on the boy withdrawing. This technique, especially used by the young and overexcited, does almost nothing to reduce the chance of her becoming pregnant while doing a great deal to reduce the chances of intercourse being satisfactory for either.

Both sexes should be taught that whatever the circumstances, *protection against pregnancy must be discussed in advance* of intercourse and that if neither partner has contraceptives available it cannot take place. If one or the other feels that no second chance will ever present itself ("he'll never ask me out again if I say no"; "it's only the moon and the drink that have made her say yes . . .") the relationship was not ready for sex.

Once a girl has become sexually active, the Pill, properly prescribed and supervised, may be right for her. Try not to pressure her either way.

Don't pressure her to take the Pill just because she has had sexual intercourse once or twice. She may have been experimenting and have decided now that she is not ready to make sex part of her life. She may feel that the Pill is a sort of punishment or stigma. Don't pressure her to go on with it if she has been taking it during an early affair which has ended. She may feel that the affair was Love and that going on holding herself in readiness for intercourse with an unknown someone else cheapens it.

Make it clear to her that you are not against the Pill for adolescents so that if and when she wants to seek a prescription for it, she can do so openly, whether or not she consults or tells you first. If she must do it all in secret she may feel unable to go to the regular family doctor, find it difficult to keep follow-up appointments or even forget to take the pills on schedule because she has to keep the packet so carefully hidden.

Occasionally a girl who has had unprotected intercourse will at once take a parent into her confidence. If her cycles are still irregular or if they are regular and the intercourse took place more than a week after a period ended, it may be worthwhile to suggest that she see her doctor and consult him about the possibility of the "morning after" pill. This is not a magic single dose but a short course of high-dose hormones with very unpleasant side effects. Such treatment is in no way a sensible alternative to contraception but will ensure that there is no pregnancy this time.

If your doctor prefers not to prescribe these hormones he may be willing to assure the girl that if she should find herself pregnant he will discuss the question of a termination with her. If not, she can consult with Planned Parenthood. A counsellor will explain to her exactly when and how she can find out whether she is pregnant and exactly what her options are if she is. A girl who is afraid she may be pregnant should always seek advice immediately. Modern, do-it-yourself pregnancy tests, available from drugstores, can give very early warning.

Many girls who have come through a false-alarm pregnancy scare spontaneously seek contraceptive advice. If your daughter, having confided the fright to you, does not, discuss it with her. If she has been living and loving in the cloud-cuckoo land of "it couldn't happen to me" it may be appropriate to remind her of the realities. But be tactful, even now. That sexual episode may still have been something she wants to forget rather than something she wants to repeat, safely. Try to let her work out her feelings with you, rather than telling her what she must do.

Venereal disease   Sexually transmitted diseases are something of which every adolescent should be aware before he or she has any such activity. VD is increasingly prevalent in the Western world. Gonorrhea, for example, is the second most common communicable disease in the United States and the United Kingdom; having declined after the Second World War, it has been steadily increasing since the 1960s. Many people still try to believe that only prostitutes, promiscuous people, homosexuals or any group but their own get VD. They are wrong. *Anyone* who is sexually active is at risk and that includes people who are currently involved with their very first sexual partner if that partner has ever had sex with anybody else. It has even recently been shown to be possible to be infected with some venereal diseases without direct sexual contact although the adolescent who maintains that he or she "must have caught it off a toilet seat" is almost certainly indulging in wishful thinking.

Non-specific urethritis (NSU) is the commonest venereal disease among British youngsters. Gonorrhea is also common and is the disease discussed here. Syphilis is rarer though more destructive. Others, such as genital herpes, are seen occasionally and appear to be on the increase. An adolescent should not need to know *which* venereal disease he or she may have caught; the faintest suspicion of any should take him or her to a doctor.

The gonococcus bacterium requires moist mucosa to live on: dry it out or expose it to air and it dies. Although it is possible to infect oneself by using a freshly infected towel, the bacteria almost always pass from genitals to genitals or from genitals to mouth or, rarely, from mouth to mouth.

Boys will usually develop a discharge from the penis and/or pain on urination within 3–7 days of sexual contact with an infected person. But some may harbor the gonococcus for up to six weeks without symptoms, while about ten percent of infected boys never have symptoms at all but remain infectious to all their sexual partners thereafter.

Girls *may* develop a thick vaginal discharge and/or inflammation of the vulva within a week to a year of contact with an infected person. But *eighty percent* of all girls infected with gonorrhea remain symptom-free but infectious to later sexual partners.

It is this ability of the gonococcus to remain infectious without causing symptoms to the carrier which makes it so difficult to control or eradicate. The use of a condom protects both partners. Apart from this precaution the only hope lies in persuading everyone to seek medical help immediately if they have genital symptoms and, if they are found to have a venereal disease, to follow the whole course of prescribed treatment and to *cooperate fully in tracing every single other person who might possibly have been infected by them*. If the many boys and men and the few girls and women who have symptoms really did report all their sexual contacts (many of whom will have no symptoms themselves and will therefore be blissfully unaware that they are carriers) gonorrhea—and other venereal diseases—could be controlled. Some authorities work extremely hard to make this kind of follow-up complete (and confidential) but at the moment they are failing. Adolescents should understand that, while it is unrealistic to think of venereal diseases as being confined to the sexually promiscuous, sex which takes place once only with a partner who cannot later be traced certainly helps to keep venereal disease on the increase.

Aggression *see* **Discipline, Self-discipline and Learning How to Behave**/Some common issues in discipline: Violence. *See also* **Jealousy**; **Tantrums**.

Air pollution *see* **Pollution**.

Alcohol *see* **Habits**/Which easily lead to addiction. *See also* **Adolescence**/Friends versus family.

Allergic rhinitis *see* **Allergy**/Hay fever.

Allergy

Allergy is a complicated subject: it is complex for medical scientists because the biochemistry involved in allergic reactions is by no means fully understood. It is even more complex for the rest of us because even basic biochemistry is difficult to grasp; and it is complex for sufferers and their parents because the actual symptoms and illnesses associated with allergy are so many and so varied. Parents who have to cope with a child's acute attacks of asthma may find it hard to believe that it bears any relation to their own mild hay fever or to another child's occasional rash. But all these, and many other disorders, are likely to share a common basis as allergic reactions and they are therefore likely to share a family basis, too. There is a strong inherited tendency in allergy.

What allergy is

The common basis for all allergic disorders lies in the hypersensitivity of the victim's immune system to proteins (antigens) in the microorganisms which are all around us (*see* **Immune Response**).

Everything we touch, eat or breathe teems with microorganisms. A tiny proportion of them present a definite threat to the human body; the rest do not. When a normal (non-allergic) person breathes room air which is teeming with cold viruses, for example, his immune system will start to produce protective antibodies against them. But when that same person breathes room air which is loaded with house dust or pollen, his immune system will not react: it "knows," so to speak, that the antigens in these substances present no threat. The immune system of the allergic person is not only jolted into producing antibodies by antigens which are a threat to everybody but also by microorganisms which are harmless. He may react as strongly to that dust or pollen as does the normal person to cold viruses, or be as ill after drinking fresh cow's milk as the normal person would be after drinking milk which was heavily contaminated with harmful bacteria (*see* **Diarrhea**, **Gastroenteritis and Food Poisoning**). A person who has "an allergy" or a strong allergic tendency is therefore distinguished from others by his abnormal bodily response to antigens which cause no response in other people.

About one in every five children develops allergies very readily. Most of them can be shown to produce an excessive amount of one particular antibody which is known as igE. People who are known to produce excess igE are known as "atopic." Any antigen (protein foreign to the body) which produces an allergic response in an individual is, for him, an "allergen." Even though we usually associate the word "protein" with food and eating, it is important to remember that, biochemically speaking, protein need not be food at all but can be a component in pollen, in animal fur and shed skin cells or in the microscopic house mites which teem in the dust of even the cleanest houses. Those proteins do not have to be eaten to affect the body, either. They can be taken in as the victim breathes or can affect him by skin contact alone.

Allergic responses—the symptoms which the victim suffers—are the result of *an interaction between a particular allergen and the antibodies which he has manufactured against it*. First exposure to a substance may lead to the manufacture of antibodies but it will not lead to allergic symptoms. They will only appear when he is exposed again to the same substance and this time his body has antibodies ready to do battle. It is vitally important that parents understand this. Allergic reactions to common drugs, such as aspirin or penicillin, can be very serious indeed. A child may have one dose without apparent ill effects yet manufacture antibodies in such numbers that a second dose makes him dangerously ill. In the same way a first bee sting may seem to have only normal effects on a child who will overreact disastrously when venom in a second sting interacts with the antibodies his body made ready on that first occasion.

Parents who are unaware of this two-stage development in allergic reactions are sometimes slow to recognize food allergies in young children. A toddler may, for example, be given his first portion of strawberries and eat them with no apparent effects other than pleasure. When he is given strawberries again he becomes very unwell. Even if they know that "not all children can tolerate strawberries" his parents may be inclined to say "It can't be the strawberries, he had them last week and there was no trouble." Last week his body had not met strawberries and therefore had made no antibodies against them. This week is different.

In most allergy-prone individuals allergic symptoms depend not only on the *presence* of a particular allergen and antibodies which he has manufactured to it, but also on the *"dose."* Some children, for example, manufacture a low level of antibodies against animals during occasional and passing contacts with various neighbors' pets. They have no symptoms; nobody is aware of the allergy until a dog is brought into the family and the child faces massive exposure. In rather the same way a person can be subclinically allergic to, say, a particular mold spore but remain unaware of it until he spends a day helping a friend to clean out a vegetable store. In some instances there need be no sudden massive exposure to the allergen but only a slow build-up over months and years. A few adults, for example, gradually develop hay fever in adult life. They have, in fact, been pollen-sensitive all their lives but only after years of low-level reaction does their antibody level become high enough for a reaction to be touched off by the next walk through a flower garden.

Allergic symptoms

When an allergen meets its antibodies a local reaction is set in process. Various chemical substances (such as histamines) are released and cause the dilation of small blood vessels. Fluid leaks through the walls of the distended vessels, causing swelling. There may be a spasm of smooth muscles—as in the air passages—and an outpouring of mucus secretions.

While this local inflammatory reaction is always similar, the resulting symptoms will obviously depend partly upon its location in the body. If allergen and antibodies interact in the nasal passageways, for example, the typical symptoms of hay fever will result. If the interaction is lower down, in the bronchi, the result may be the wheezy obstructed breathing of asthma. If the allergen is eaten and meets antibodies in the gastro-intestinal tract, the symptoms may be vomiting, cramps and diarrhea. If the allergen gets into the bloodstream (by being eaten or injected) it may cause symptoms wherever it meets antibodies—producing both digestive disturbance and the skin reactions typical of atopic eczema, for example.

But the geography of the meeting place between allergen and antibody cannot provide sufficient explanation for the exact nature of allergic symptoms. Other factors such as the following clearly play a part in dictating the exact nature of the susceptible individual's sufferings.

Age: The natural history of allergic individuals suggests an age-related pattern. An infant will be most likely to suffer from atopic eczema accompanied, perhaps, by specific skin reactions to identifiable foods, such as hives in reaction to oranges.

Early in childhood the eczema tends to improve but asthma often begins now and may worsen until adolescence.

During adolescence, the asthma may gradually lessen but hay fever, if he has not previously suffered from it, may start now and remain with him into adult life.

During his adult life hay fever also tends to improve, first becoming more spasmodic and often finally disappearing altogether.

Concentration of allergens: A susceptible individual may manufacture some antibodies to certain allergens but experience no resulting symptoms until circumstances change to provide an overwhelming dose of the offending substance. An infant may, for example, be sensitive to cow's milk protein yet remain symptom-free through the early period of mixed feeding when although there is cow's milk in her cereals, she is still receiving her liquid milk from the breast. As soon as she is weaned onto a cow's milk product, she suffers from violent symptoms. Any major environmental change which brings the individual into contact with new antigens may provoke or show up a previously unsuspected allergy.

Infections: The exact nature of the relationship between allergies and infections is little understood. A child who is liable to asthma is very likely to have an attack (or an exacerbation) each time he has a cold. Is he allergic to the infecting organisms which cause colds? Does his cold sensitize him to allergic reactions? Do the symptoms of the cold exacerbate the symptoms of the allergy? Whatever the exact relationship, those who must cope with allergies learn to expect their symptoms to increase at these times.

Stress: Tension and high emotion—pleasant or unpleasant—also play a clear but little understood part in provoking or exacerbating allergic symptoms. A child may have an attack of eczema, asthma or hives whenever she is excited about a birthday treat or miserable about a family row. An adolescent may always have to face examinations with the added stress of acute hay fever. Longer-lasting stressful situations (such as the birth of a sibling or moving) often usher in a period of the sufferer's life when allergic symptoms are much worsened.

This is a difficult area for parents to handle (*see below*) because attempts to shield an allergic child from stress may lead to her being treated like an invalid. Such treatment leads to a different (but often equally unfortunate) kind of stress as she reacts to feeling "different" from other children and/or fights for independence.

Principles of diagnosis and treatment in allergic conditions

We do not yet know how to "instruct" a human body to stop making antibodies to any but "genuinely harmful" substances. There is therefore no overall cure for allergic tendencies. Diagnosis and treatment both have to be devoted to control of allergic symptoms.

Many mild allergies diagnose themselves: slight hay fever, occurring always and only when the pollen count is high, is an obvious example. Many more cure themselves without ever being diagnosed. Hives, for example, will commonly vanish without trace long before the victim can see a doctor. If a variety of these minor troubles occur frequently, a doctor may offer medication to relieve the symptoms, but he is unlikely even to try to trace the responsible allergens. They could be a handful among hundreds and thousands of possibilities. The search would certainly cause the victim more trouble and discomfort than does that occasional runny nose in early summer or that quickly passing itchy rash.

In more serious situations, your doctor will rely on some combination of the following:

Avoidance of allergens   Some very serious allergic reactions can only be effectively dealt with by avoiding the allergen. Common examples are allergic reactions to particular drugs or foods (but *see below*). If a child has an allergic reaction to penicillin, further administration of the drug could even be fatal. Your doctor will emphasize to you (and to her) that she must never have it again. He will note the allergy in her medical records and stress it whenever he refers her to another doctor or a hospital. Strange doctors will always ask whether the new patient is sensitive to this drug. Sometimes it will be suggested that she wear a Medic-Alert bracelet so that her allergy will become known to anyone who treats her in an emergency situation when she might be unconscious.

A few less serious allergic reactions can also be dealt with by avoidance of the allergen. A person who is specifically allergic to horsehair, for example, may only discover the allergy on a rare visit to stables. She may subsequently be easily able to avoid contact with horses and with horsehair used in antique upholstery and so forth.

But these two examples should make it clear that for avoidance to be effective, the victim has both to know what specific allergen affects her and to be able to identify and avoid it in the environment. Sometimes one or the other is impossible.

Injection treatment for allergy

This form of treatment, properly called "hyposensitization" or "desensitization," may be appropriate if a specific allergen can be recognized in the environment but cannot certainly be avoided. A dramatic example is that of allergy to the stings of wasps and bees. Once the sting of one of these insects has caused a serious allergic reaction, a further sting could make the victim dangerously, even fatally, ill. The insects can be readily recognized but they cannot certainly be avoided.

A doctor will commonly start hyposensitization as soon as the victim has recovered from the effects of the sting which demonstrated her sensitivity. He knows that an insect sting was responsible but he must establish exactly which antigen in the venom provoked the symptoms. He does this by preparing extremely dilute solutions of the possible substances and then scratching through them into the child's skin. The allergen will cause a red weal at the scratch site. Antigens to which she is not sensitive will cause no such skin reaction.

Once the exact allergen has been identified, it is made up in solutions of varying strengths for a series of injections. The aim is to provoke the child's body, bit by bit, into producing a special *extra* antibody which, next time she is stung, will bind itself to the allergen and prevent it from interacting with her allergic antibodies. Injections begin with a very dilute solution and then continue (usually at weekly intervals) to inject the maximum amount which her body can tolerate without allergic symptoms. Usually a concentration which produces skin weals without a generalized reaction is enough to provoke useful antibody formation without being enough to be dangerous.

Once protective levels have been reached, regular injections will no longer be needed but skin tests will be repeated at intervals and a maintenance dose given whenever these show that her protection is fading.

Symptomatic treatment for allergy

While both avoidance and desensitization may be life-saving in a few cases of allergy, they are impractical in the vast majority.

Most allergic individuals produce antibodies against a wide range of extremely common antigens. If your child is sensitive to the mites in house dust, to mold spores, to pollens, and to animal hairs, she cannot avoid all allergens while continuing to live in a normal environment. Since desensitization has to be specific, provoking the production of a special antibody to each separate allergen, attempting such treatment would condemn her to literally years of skin testing and injections. The treatment would almost certainly be more uncomfortable and life-disrupting for her than is her hypersensitivity.

Under these circumstances, the doctor will probably rely heavily on treating the symptoms as and when they appear. Anti-histamines, for example, counteract the effects of the histamine released during the allergic process, while a variety of ointments, nasal and eye drops may be used to quell local inflammations.

Some allergic sufferers take anti-histamines on a preventative basis: perhaps all through the "hay-fever season" or whenever public bulletins warn of a rise in the pollen count. But for many, anti-histamines in effective doses produce undesirable side effects such as sleepiness. The newer disodium cromoglycate appears actually to prevent certain processes in the allergic reaction and has few common side effects. It is not taken by mouth but by inhalation.

Combining treatment approaches in allergy

Many allergic children have at least one period in their lives when no single treatment approach is adequate. The doctor must use every method at his disposal, in combination or in sequence, to keep her allergic attacks as few and as mild as possible while guarding her health and growth and allowing her to feel that she leads a normal life.

Attacks of allergic asthma, for example, may be brought on by a wide variety of antigens which are common in her environment and may be exacerbated by physical and emotional factors. No single approach will help very much and even a combined approach cannot completely protect her, but if every known factor is attacked energetically her asthma may be kept under reasonable control. Some allergens may be avoidable or at least her contact with them may be minimized. House dust, for example, may be reduced by taking special precautions in her bedroom (*see below*). Desensitization to one or two particular allergens—such as animals —may reduce the level of allergic insult to which she is subjected. Medication—both preventative and symptomatic—may reduce the number and severity of her attacks of asthma while early and energetic treatment of any infections will minimize their part in the disorder. Finally, the doctor will probably want to discuss environmental and emotional factors in her life with a view to helping you to achieve the best possible balance between treating her as an invalid and treating her as a normal child who is almost constantly ill.

Coping with allergic disorders

While medical treatment may be able to do a great deal for your child, most of the management of her hypersensitivity will fall to the family and, as she grows up, to her. The "coping" involved may be no more than providing many tissues and a few nose drops during occasional hay fever, but it may sometimes be the pivot around which family life must revolve. Different symptom complexes produce different-seeming illnesses and the notes that follow deal with the common allergic disorders in turn. But if you are the parent of an atopic child, do remember that today's problems arise from the same kind of hypersensitivity which produced last year's, and that it will probably produce problems that are different again as she gets older. If that strikes you as unduly or unkindly pessimistic, remember also that on the whole the symptoms produced by allergic responses do become milder with age.

Asthma

Not every specialist believes that asthma is mainly an allergic disorder; some believe that it is a disorder in its own right and that asthmatic children commonly have other allergic disorders, simultaneously or in sequence, together with a family history of allergy, only because the asthma makes them prone to allergy. Most, however, see asthma as at least primarily allergic even though its nature makes demonstration of the exact relationship between allergen and antibody difficult.

Asthma affects the bronchial tree. When it is stimulated by contact with an allergen or by another predisposing factor, there is an outpouring of mucus and spasm of the smooth muscles. In combination these reactions partially block the airway so that the victim must fight to get sufficient air in and out of his lungs. Breathlessness is terrifying and, of course, terror increases the need for oxygen and therefore creates a vicious circle. A child who has experienced (and a parent who has seen) an acute attack of asthma is likely to dread the next: terror of that terror may quickly become a factor in increasing the frequency of attacks.

Since asthma affects breathing, it is also likely to be brought on by anything which requires extra respiratory effort. An attack may therefore accompany strenuous exercise, disciplined singing or any kind of prolonged excitement.

Since asthma involves an outpouring of mucus within the bronchi, it is also often precipitated by upper respiratory infection. If asthmatic mucus should become infected it may precipitate such an infection.

Asthma is therefore intimately connected with the victim's daily life and activities, and has both emotional stress and physical illness intimately connected with it. Nevertheless, it need not be as devastating as many parents, newly faced with the diagnosis, may fear:

Nearly twenty percent of all children have one or two "asthmatic episodes" but only five percent have the recurrent and/or severe attacks which constitute "diagnosed asthma." It is a mistake to anticipate a ruined childhood on the basis of a first, or even a second, attack especially as your worry and your anxious concern next time the child has a cough, may make a further attack more likely.

Asthma can occur at any age but usually begins in middle childhood. If it does begin at that stage in your child's life he has an excellent chance of being symptom-free by the time he reaches puberty. Children whose asthma begins much younger, perhaps especially those who start to suffer from it during infancy, may be slower to grow out of it. It may comfort you to know that:

Seventy percent of all asthma sufferers will be free of symptoms by the time they are adult, even though some of these will continue to suffer from hay fever or other allergic complaints.

Diagnosis of asthma

Wheezing is very common in young children whose airways are small and particularly liable to partial obstruction in a number of respiratory conditions. Many doctors will use the term "wheezy bronchitis" for any wheezing child with symptoms suggesting upper respiratory infection. In fact, virus infection is the commonest factor precipitating attacks in asthmatic children under about five years. As long as the infection is treated, it does not matter what this first episode is called because it may well be a "once-only" (*see also* **Chest Infections**/Bronchitis).

Early suspicion of asthma will be aroused by combinations of the following:
☐ A family history of allergic disorders.
☐ Clear-cut allergic disorder (such as eczema) in the child.
☐ Frequent (three or more in one year) wheezy illnesses.
☐ Night-time cough continuing well after the child recovers.
☐ Negative laboratory findings eliminating other causes of wheezing.
☐ Bronchoconstriction (showing as breathlessness but measured on a Wright peak-flow meter) after exercise.
☐ High serum immunoglobin E levels (demonstrated by a blood test).

Children with chronic asthmatic disease will have persistent wheezing, due to some degree of permanent airway obstruction.

Management of asthma

Partnership between parents and a trusted doctor is essential if the asthmatic child is to be helped to grow normally (both physically and psychologically) through his disability and therefore into normal adolescence. While consultation with a distant specialist may well be desirable at some point, the readily available support of a nearby doctor or unit specializing in asthma is vital. The asthmatic child will require that combined treatment approach (*see above*) but in addition, he and his parents may require careful education in the use of special drugs, training in simple physiotherapy techniques, assurance of immediate help in crisis and, always, careful follow-up to ensure that instructions are being followed and that the child is therefore suffering as little as possible from his tendency to asthma.

Avoidance of allergens in asthma

While a few patients overreact to single allergens which can be avoided (*see below*), most overreact to many common ones. Avoidance therefore is concentrated on removing as many as possible of the most obvious. The most obvious of all is the house mite in house dust. It may be that this common allergen partly explains the high incidence of asthma attacks during the night, when the child spends many hours in one room under dust-trapping bedding. Bedroom dust can be much reduced, though not eliminated.

Mattresses and pillows should either be made of (fire-resistant) plastic foam or be sealed into plastic covers. Blankets should be banished and replaced by continental quilts of man-made fibers. Curtains, cushions, carpets and rugs should all be kept to a minimum and those left should be of cotton or man-made fiber for frequent washing.

Ideally all "dust traps" (such as shelves full of books) should be removed from the room, but unless a "playroom" can be provided, the psychological harm may outstrip the physical benefit. Sometimes less dust-trapping objects can be used to make the child's room personal and homely. Posters and so forth can be kept comparatively dust-free.

The child's bedroom should be closed off when housework is done elsewhere in the home. In the room itself furniture, etc. should be washed rather than dusted. Vacuuming removes dust but may be counterproductive if an overfull bag is itself spraying dust.

Pet animals and their dander are also the source of a very common allergen but, since such pets may be important both to the child and to his family, their banishment should at least await demonstration that it is a real factor in his case. Skin or bronchial challenge testing may be carried out or the pet may be sent elsewhere for a few weeks in order to see whether the child is less wheezy and/or has fewer asthmatic episodes in its absence.

Allergy to pets causes real heartbreak to some asthmatic children. It is sometimes worth searching for a compromise. Certain dogs, for example, can be retrained to occupy a kennel. A beloved cat may be allowed only into the kitchen. The child's own gerbils may stay if their intimate care is undertaken by someone else. . . . If all else fails, a non-furry creature such as a fish may do something to comfort the deprived pet owner (*see* **Pets**).

In some children, whose asthma is seasonal, other kinds of avoidance may be helpful. At one extreme, the installation of air conditioning may work wonders for pollen sensitivity in spring and summer. At the other extreme, changing from an annual lakeside holiday to a seaside one may prevent his most serious attacks.

Avoidance of precipitating factors such as exercise is only desirable in a very small minority of severe cases, as the psychological and social harm done may counterbalance the reduction in attacks. If he cannot tolerate the normal exercise for his age group, the matter is often better dealt with by drugs (*see below*).

Desensitization in asthma

Although some doctors enthusiastically undertake injection treatment in asthmatic children, most find that lasting benefit is exceptional. Serial injections also much increase the unpleasantness of the disorder for the child himself; indeed, "injection phobia" is thought, by some doctors, to explain the apparent reluctance of some families to seek help when the asthmatic child has an attack.

Physiotherapy in asthma

With the help of a skilled physiotherapist, child and parents can learn techniques and exercises which help both overall and during attacks. Muscle tone and posture can both be improved; relaxed breathing can help breathlessness while, after an acute attack, postural drainage can clear plugs of mucus and thus speed recovery (*see* **Chest Infections/** Chest infections with pain: Physiotherapy in chest infections).

Medication for asthma

There are now many helpful drugs available both for the prevention of asthmatic attacks and for the treatment of acute ones. While some are given by mouth or injection, many have to be administered by inhalation. These may be in powder form for use with a "spin-haler" or in liquid, either pre-packed in a measured dose aerosol or for use with a special spray that produces mist. Improved methods of delivering the right dose of the drug to exactly the right place in the respiratory tract are vitally important. Recent improvements have made possible the home use of certain drugs which were formerly for hospital use only. Others can now be safely administered to very small children by their parents where previously they could only be given by medical personnel. Your child's drug regime will, of course, be prescribed by his doctor. It may include medication to be given to him daily, medication for him to learn to take himself before energetic exercise, medication for him to take or be given under particular circumstances likely to provoke an attack, as well as medication to deal with an attack.

Effective relief when he has difficulty in breathing—especially when an attack wakes him in the night—is vital to your child's ability to live with his asthma. If he is allowed to become panic-stricken by air hunger the panic will increase the breathlessness in a vicious circle. Thereafter his fear of his own fear may contribute to sleeping difficulties and, indeed, to all kinds of difficulties over becoming appropriately independent for his age. If your child ever has an attack during which you cannot give him instant relief by following the doctor's latest instructions, do not hesitate to send for medical help whatever the time of night. Afterwards, do discuss with your doctor the drugs you have available for emergency use at home in case he can prescribe something more effective. Finally, do remember that anyone who babysits for you at night must understand these emergency drugs and how they should be used. A child who is liable to night-time asthma attacks probably should not be left with an adolescent sibling or babysitter, unless he or she is unusually calm and competent. A panic-stricken, breathless child is an alarming sight and an alarmed attendant will certainly make him worse.

Helping the asthmatic child to feel "ordinary"

Many children who are liable to asthma can and should be treated exactly as if they were liable to some mild, recurrent illness like tonsillitis. Nursed during attacks, they and their families can forget the asthma in between them and the children will be less scarred by it for being able to do so.

A less fortunate child may not be able to be treated so casually. If he is somewhat wheezy all the time, extremely breathless after exercise, and easily provoked by environmental factors into full-blown asthma attacks, he must be helped to avoid them. Chronic asthma can do permanent damage to the respiratory system. But unless your doctor persuades you that your asthmatic child is, for the moment at least, an invalid, do not treat him as one. With the aid of prescribed medication and so forth he should do and expect to do everything which his friends do, except when he is ill. "Everything" must include the things he does not actually enjoy—like his homework—as well as the things he does want to do like swim or play football.

Within that normal life you may find that you can cushion the asthmatic child enough to reduce the number of his asthma attacks but not so much as to spoil his feeling of being just like everybody else. For example:

Physical stress can be reduced by arranging a car ride home on swimming days rather than forbidding the swimming. In the same way once you know that lack of sleep tends to precipitate attacks you may be able to arrange for him to sleep late on some mornings rather than being forced to accept a "baby's bedtime." The trick is to define the physical stress and then to find a way of relieving it without making him feel overprotected and "different."

If excitement precipitates attacks, try new kinds of "treats." He may always miss birthday parties because he becomes ill at the last moment, but he may be able to take a trip to the movies or an expedition to a museum in his stride.

If anger and frustration make him ill, teach him to talk it out. If he can shout and weep he is far less likely to become breathless than he is if he bottles up all that emotion.

Although you cannot interfere in his relationships with outsiders, you may be able to educate family members into realizing that "unpleasant atmospheres" or "the silent treatment" are peculiarly bad for this particular child. If they must quarrel with him it should be openly and fast so that the matter is quickly resolved and forgotten. Trouble with his friends is outside your control, but teachers should understand that while he should certainly be punished if he deserves it, just like any other child, punishments which keep him in suspense or single him out for public ridicule, should be avoided.

Major emotional disasters, such as the death or departure of a parent, are very likely to increase the severity of the child's asthma but, since they would cause distress in any child, you would of course avoid them if possible. If you cannot, try to remember that the asthmatic child's distress shows itself in a particularly dramatic, physical way but is no more (or less) real than the distress of the child who remains healthy while grieving. Every sad child needs special consideration, but if you give the asthmatic child extra-special consideration you make it clear to him that the disorder gives him power. You will be inviting him to use his asthma as a blackmail weapon.

Eczema (atopic or "infantile")

Although there are many types of eczema, this allergic type is the most common; it is also one of the commonest manifestations of allergy in an atopic child.

An atopic child who is going to have eczema will often show the first signs at around three months of age and will commonly have the disorder in its most active form during his first two years. It usually diminishes during the pre-school period and dies down or vanishes altogether during early childhood. Some older people retain one or two eczematous patches, which become active from time to time, but full-blown eczema in later life is usually clinically different.

Recognizing eczema

Eczema usually starts with bright red, scaly and wildly itchy patches on the cheeks. In many cases, that is all there is to it.

In some babies, however, the eczema spreads. Gradually, patches of red, inflamed skin, with small raised spots and a slightly swollen appearance, may appear on other parts of the body. Moist skin creases (such as those in the groin or behind the knees) are particularly vulnerable. When the eczema is very active, acute inflammation makes the patches moist and the skin fragile.

The main problem with eczema is that the affected skin is tremendously itchy. The infant scratches and scratches and, because that skin is already fragile, often lays its surface open. He then has soreness as well as itch to contend with. All too often those open places become infected and then there may be real pain. Altogether, eczema is a miserable affliction for a baby and therefore a miserable one for his parents. A cycle of itch-scratch-cry may cease only when the baby is completely distracted by outside events. But because that cycle delays his sleeping and frequently wakes him during the night or nap, parents become less and less able to offer that distraction.

Looking for allergens in eczema

While there is no cure for eczema, your doctor may be able to help you to identify a particular allergen which has led to its first appearance in your baby. Sometimes, for example, eczema first appears when a baby starts on solid foods. One of these could be responsible and he will help you to carry out your own experiments at home, going back to milk only, perhaps, for a few days and then adding in solid foods, one at a time, to try to discover which (if any) food leads to a flare-up of the eczema. Milk itself (*see below* Gastrointestinal allergies) could be a causative factor. If eczema starts when a baby first has cow's milk formula in addition to, or instead of, breast milk, going back to breast milk may deal with it. Some babies can tolerate an ordinary mixed weaning diet (which, of course, includes cow's milk in made-up dishes) provided their liquid milk comes from the breast. If breast-feeding is impossible and investigation suggests a connection between cow's milk and the eczema, a non-cow's milk formula may be recommended. A child who is hypersensitive to cow's milk will usually be similarly affected by goat's milk but an artificial "milk," based on soy flour, is well tolerated by many.

Apart from new, or newly increased, food proteins, a search for specific allergens in infantile eczema is seldom useful. The baby may indeed be hypersensitive to many substances (as will probably be demonstrated if he should be subjected to extensive skin testing), but these reactions, while demonstrating that he is very liable to allergy, seldom help in immediate treatment.

Medical management of eczema

There are many skin applications and a few oral drugs which may be used to control the symptoms of eczema. It is important to realize that no one regime will be appropriate over a long period because it is in the nature of eczema to flare and die down and to do so not only over time but also in patches of varying severity over the body. Whatever ointments, drugs or instructions you are given, you must be absolutely sure that you understand them fully. Regular and frequent contact with your doctor (or practical nurse) will be essential.

For example, a coal-tar preparation might be prescribed and, if it is, you might be instructed to use an occlusive (waterproof, usually plastic) covering over it. But a corticosteroid cream (such as hydrocortisone) might be prescribed and, if it is, it must not be used under an occlusive dressing because, while reducing the inflammation of the skin, it also reduces its resistance to infection. If the affected area is closed off from the air, a crop of boils, thrush or some other secondary infection is very likely.

If you are told to use a corticosteroid preparation, you must be sure that you know how much to apply and over how big a skin area. Some of the active drug is absorbed into the bloodstream from the skin. The dose applied is therefore just as important as the dose of an oral drug which you give your child.

You also have to control your enthusiasm for these highly effective preparations lest you apply them, without prior consultation with your doctor, to newly affected skin. A corticosteroid preparation combined with an antibiotic might well be prescribed for areas where infection is likely, such as the diaper area. If a new "sore place" appears on your child's skin you may be tempted to use the same cream there. But you could be making a disastrous mistake. If that new patch is, in fact, a minor infection (such as a cold sore, a boil or impetigo), the use of a combined corticosteroid and antibiotic may cause it to spread disastrously.

Oral drugs, such as anti-histamines, may be prescribed both to control itching (by counteracting that allergic release of histamine) and, by their useful side effect of drowsiness, to help the child sleep. Different anti-histamines and different dosages affect individual children differently. You should keep your doctor in touch with your child's response.

Family management of eczema

There are some practical things which you can do to minimize itching, scratching, skin damage and misery.

Avoid washing with soap and water. It often seems to make affected skin worse, probably by the drying effect of the soap. Use mineral oil or baby lotion instead.

Avoid rough, scratchy or heavy clothes. A big sweater with a high neck will probably ensure a miserable morning. Several layers of thin, silky, roomy garments are far more comfortable. The baby may be most comfortable wearing nothing—or almost nothing. A room warm enough for naked play may save the day.

Keep his nails very short and as clean as possible. You cannot stop him from scratching, but you can ensure that he is rubbing the skin rather than cutting it open.

Don't (unless your doctor convinces you that it is absolutely necessary, perhaps because such a large skin area is badly infected) use physical restraint to stop the child from scratching. Mittens or, worse, splints which prevent him from getting his hand to the itch, are positively cruel. If you really *must* prevent him from touching a particular place, try to use the restraint of your own presence and distraction, gently removing his hand when it strays.

Try to accept that a child who is badly affected by infantile eczema is bound to need a great deal of extra entertainment and attention. He *cannot* give you the peaceful nap-times and nights to which you were looking forward. He *cannot* entertain himself.

Parents who can come to see the eczema as a challenge may actually be able to get some satisfaction out of each day passed in comparative pleasure; each night got through without loss of temper; each week which passes without any inflamed skin being scratched through. But parents who resent the normal demands of a small baby and/or are already overcommitted to outside work and so forth, may find the demands of the baby with eczema close to intolerable. Most parents will probably find themselves somewhere between these extremes. The following notes might help:

Eczema which is atrocious today may have subsided somewhat tomorrow. It is an affliction which comes and goes, so that you can always hope for improvement.

Eczema which truly is making everybody's life impossible can probably be lessened by a new medical regime. Call your doctor before you reach your breaking point. The simple fact that he is willing to try a different cream or ointment may give flagging morale a boost.

There is no shame in reaching your breaking point under these circumstances. Occasionally a doctor will arrange hospital admission for a badly affected baby largely to give the rest of the family some rest. Short of that, don't feel that you yourself have to attend to him night and day. Try to arrange for extra help some of the time and use it for the baby so that you can turn your attention to yourself (for sleeping, studying or whatever you are missing most) or to other children. Their health and good humor may remind you that the eczema will pass; that living with your currently afflicted and impossible infant will one day be easy and fun.

Nobody can remain patient and entertaining if his sleep is always broken (*see* **Sleep**). Try to take turns with your partner or even to import somebody one or two nights a week. If you are taking turns, try a whole night on and a whole night off rather than "you go this time and I'll go next." The cries of distress may be so frequent that the latter is no help at all.

Distraction is a key. You are the key to the distraction of a small baby. The more you can free yourself to carry him, talk to him and play with him when he is awake, the less stressed you will feel. But other things —especially as he gets older—can distract him, too. You may be able to find a parent-and-baby club whose meetings entertain him while giving you a breather. If you explain what is going on to your doctor, you may eventually be given priority for a playgroup place. Even taking your frantic baby to some busy public place, such as a department store, may distract him without his entertainment demanding much of you.

Eczema on visible places like the face may reduce your pride in your baby and may even make you feel that "everybody is looking." Emphasize to friends and acquaintances that it is not "catching" (at some stages, eczema can look rather like the rash of an infectious disease) and try to enlist their sympathy for the child. That horrid woman who looks disapprovingly at him, crying and scratching in his carriage at the supermarket, may react quite differently when she is encouraged to show him something interesting and he immediately cheers up.

Remember that this baby's experience of his own body is extremely unpleasant. Any bodily pleasure that you can give him is important and you will probably find that it makes you feel better, too. Don't let his ointments and dressings make you treat him as untouchable. Play physical games with him and cuddle him as you would any other baby. If it starts him itching again, never mind. He was going to itch again in a minute anyway. Take a real pride in the way you look after his skin (the more careful and thorough you are in applying his various prescriptions, the fewer acute exacerbations he will have) and try to convey to the baby that you are handling him with love.

Most honest parents admit that they had moments when they "could have been a baby-batterer." As parents of a baby with severe eczema you have more provocation than most.

If you ever feel that your patience has gone and that your temper might snap into physical action, do ask for help immediately. In many cities there are now telephone "help services" for parents. A cry for help from the parents of a child with eczema would be especially readily understood and acted upon.

Gastrointestinal allergies

If your child reacts badly to a particular food, do not assume that she is allergic to it. The food may have been contaminated with bacteria which have given her "food poisoning" (see **Diarrhea, Gastroenteritis and Food Poisoning**) or it may have contained additives she could not tolerate (see **Eating**/Common sense about family eating: Food additives). Lack of certain enzymes in her digestive system can make her intolerant of particular food constituents, such as lactose, while a few foods produce symptoms similar to those of gastrointestinal allergy but by a different mechanism. Strawberries, for example, contain substances which directly release histamine. The child may react as if there was an allergen in the strawberries to which she had manufactured antibodies.

Nevertheless, there are some children who are actually allergic to certain food proteins. Much the most important, in a Western diet, is allergy to cow's milk protein.

It is only in recent years that this sort of intolerance has been recognized as a true allergic response, and experts still hotly dispute the number of children affected and the importance of the condition. Some doctors —especially in the United States—believe that it is widespread and that a degree of intolerance which is too slight to be demonstrated by clinical tests and whose existence cannot therefore be proved (see below), may nevertheless be responsible for a wide range of behavioral and other difficulties. British authorities tend to be more cautious.

While a proper clinical diagnosis of gastrointestinal allergy may be vital to the well-being of a baby who is not thriving, a vague diagnosis of "milk intolerance," unbacked by clinical signs or positive tests, should not be used as a universal explanation for infant difficulties. Withdrawing milk and substituting a variety of more or less extreme diets and dietary restrictions sometimes appears to lessen toddler tantrums or even to improve a seven-year-old's behavior at school. But it may be doing so by subtle psychological mechanisms which have nothing to do with relieving her digestion of a substance against which she had manufactured antibodies. Such a child may, for example, receive a great deal of extra parental attention during dietary experiments; it may be this attention which changes her behavior. The attention may indeed be good for her, but if it is attention she needs it is a pity that it should be focused on her stomach and bowels.

Breast-feeding and food allergies

Gastrointestinal allergies are very rare in babies who are fed nothing but breast milk during their early months and who continue to take their liquid milk from the breast when mixed feeding begins. Breast milk seems to reduce allergic tendencies in two ways:

The actual breast milk protects against the formation of food allergies. This is because it contains immunoglobins of the IgA class which are often deficient in the immune systems of very young babies. These IgAs are thought to provide a sort of "protective lining" for the intestinal mucosa which reduces the likelihood of adverse reaction and antibody formation to food proteins.

Being given breast milk protects the baby against being given any other kind. If she does not meet cow's or goat's milk protein, soy protein or the gluten of wheat flour which is so often present in baby cereals, she cannot manufacture antibodies against them.

Eventually, of course, every baby must meet "foreign" proteins in her diet, but if she does not do so until her own immune system is likely to be able to protect her, and even then does so with the added protection of continuing breast-feeding, the chances of her tolerating all of them easily are much enhanced. Every baby should be breast-fed if possible. For babies who are obviously at high risk of allergy (such as the children of atopic parents) the definition of "possible" should perhaps be stretched to your personal limit (*see also* **Eating**/Types of foods for babies).

Looking for allergens in foods

Dietary proteins are absorbed through the intestinal wall. If a baby has developed antibodies to a particular protein it will cause clinical signs such as vomiting and diarrhea, and it will eventually alter the mucosa of the small intestine. This can be demonstrated if tiny fragments are taken by biopsy and examined under a microscope. Any baby with acute gastrointestinal symptoms should be seen urgently by a doctor. It is when a baby has very mild but chronic digestive symptoms that parents may find themselves reluctant to embark on medical tests, yet wondering whether they are feeding her something to which she is allergic.

The probability is highest if you or other close relations are atopic; if the baby herself has other allergic symptoms such as eczema; if she was never breast-fed and is now being put on a mixed diet or if she was breast-fed but is now being weaned. However mild her present digestive symptoms, do seek medical advice quickly if you still have breast milk available to her. If she has developed a gastrointestinal allergy—even if it is not to cow's milk protein itself—reintroducing breast-feeding may lessen her symptoms (*see above*), even though it cannot unmake antibodies which she has already made.

If both the baby's history and symptoms strongly suggest an intestinal allergy, your doctor may want to proceed immediately to a biopsy so as to clinch the diagnosis and exclude other forms of food intolerance. If the baby's symptoms are mild, however, he may prefer to explore the possibility and identity of a food allergen by the use of "elimination diets." Such diets simply eliminate suspect foodstuffs from the baby's diet, one by one and for stated periods, so that parents and doctor can see whether her digestion and other symptoms are better when she is without one or more of them. The item first excluded is usually cow's milk. A child who is allergic to cow's milk protein is very likely to react in the same way to goat's milk and either a return to breast milk or a soya-based formula will probably be recommended. For an elimination diet to work as a diagnostic test as well as an allergen avoider, *all* milk must be excluded. This means that you will have to guard the baby from licks of her brother's ice cream, from rusks containing milk protein and from a vast range of commercial babyfoods.

If a milk-free diet produces dramatic improvement, the doctor will probably regard the diagnosis as made and the treatment as obvious (*see below*). If it does not produce improvement but he still regards intestinal allergy as likely, other food proteins may have to be excluded one by one.

Living with elimination diets

Sometimes elimination diets produce quick, clear and excellent results. Sometimes they do not. If you find yourself embarking on an elimination program either with a baby or an older child, do bear the following points in mind:

A child must eat adequately. If your baby is to have nothing but soya formula, do ensure that you understand its comparative calorie value and that she drinks enough to meet her probable needs. She may not like the taste. If your child is to eliminate milk, dairy produce and eggs, do ensure that school alternatives are adequate and/or that you yourself offer adequate replacements for long-established high-calorie habits like that milky drink at bedtime or that breakfast egg. Orange juice and toast may leave her hungry or even undernourished.

Diets can be psychologically damaging. The baby who does not like soya milk is being deprived of feeding pleasure and you are being deprived of your pleasure in that pleasure. The toddler who may have no chocolate is deprived of something she may clearly associate with people being pleased with her and/or with "treats"; she may think she is being punished. The child who may have no gluten (wheat protein) probably cannot eat at the homes of friends or in school or in a restaurant. Her diet makes her feel different and may actually isolate her socially.

Elimination diets prove nothing without food challenges. No elimination diet, however effective it seems to be in improving symptoms, can *prove* that your child suffers from a particular gastrointestinal allergy or other intolerance. An apparent improvement may be due to chance, to extra attention or to natural maturation. Or the original disorder may have been due to a naturally passing infective illness like gastroenteritis.

If eliminating a particular food brings relief of symptoms, the child's body should subsequently be "challenged" with that foodstuff to see whether the symptoms recur immediately, within hours or within days. If they do recur, the food is then withdrawn again. If the symptoms are again relieved, the point is made. But even so, many doctors will wish to repeat the challenge (unless biopsy is undertaken and demonstrates a difference in the intestinal mucosa with, and without, that foodstuff). An apparent recurrence of symptoms on first challenge can be due to another illness.

Elimination diets are extremely fashionable, especially in the United States, where it is estimated that about one-third of all bottle-fed babies receive soya milk instead of cow's milk formula. There is, perhaps, a generalized feeling in American society that much ill health is caused by eating too much and eating food which is too "rich." The corollary can easily be that a diet which rigidly excludes certain items will do no harm and may do some good. A toddler, with mild but persistent diarrhea, may be put on such a diet when in truth she requires no treatment other than simple tests to ensure that the diarrhea is not due to infection. Elimination diets can only properly be used to diagnose and treat the highly specific results of sensitivity to highly specific food proteins. If they are used as a cure-all, as a hunch or because they are "healthier anyway," they are wrongly used.

Even a proven need for such a diet will have a natural end. In gastrointestinal allergy (and in many cases of proven intestinal intolerance) the child, however severely she is affected in infancy, will almost always become able to cope with the offending dietary item as she grows up. Do treat even the most clearly necessary dietary restrictions as temporary and do make sure, with your doctor's help, that periodic food challenges are offered to the child so that her dawning ability to cope is discovered as soon as possible. While there are adults who are made uncomfortable by a high intake of milk, there are very few who cannot tolerate the quantities used either in home or in commercial cooking.

Hay fever (allergic rhinitis)

Hay fever is a misnomer as the disorder is neither a fever nor connected especially with hay. Nevertheless, it is under this name that most people classify all the various allergic symptoms which are confined to the nasal passages and the eyes and are properly named allergic rhinitis. The classic symptoms are a "blocked" or "stuffy" nose, sneezing and nasal discharge. Sometimes there is obvious inflammation of the eyes (conjunctivitis) but often the eyes simply itch so that the child rubs them and may, or may not, thus make them red. If the eyes are much involved, the child may have "bags" under them so that he looks perpetually tired.

Allergic rhinitis can occur at any age and seems to be self-limiting so that whenever it begins, it seldom persists for more than ten to fifteen years. It can be seasonal or perennial (depending on the allergens, *see below*). While it can be associated with any other sign of allergy, it seems particularly associated with asthma but in a way which means that asthma and allergic rhinitis are seldom both active at the same time. A child sufferer from allergic rhinitis may (but may not) go on to experience asthma. An asthma sufferer may (but may not) have allergic rhinitis in adult life once he is free of the asthma.

While allergic rhinitis is regarded as a trivial nuisance (and even sometimes scornfully termed "psychosomatic"), it is directly responsible for many days lost at school and at work and for much discomfort. It deserves energetic treatment which can often be highly successful.

Recognizing allergic rhinitis

Hay fever is often missed in children because they themselves tend to be very tolerant of the symptoms while their parents seem ready to accept that their child "is always having colds" or "suffers from congestion."

Although your child may look as if he has a cold you can distinguish the one from the other. In a cold the nose is "blocked" by a thick discharge. In rhinitis it is "blocked" by swelling of the nasal passageways. When your child's nose runs in a cold, you can see that the discharge is thick and white or yellowy but when it runs in rhinitis it is watery. When you stop to think about it, that watery discharge could not block the passageways and his feeling that he "can't blow" has to be due to swelling. Eyes do not always itch in hay fever but they very seldom do so in a cold. If your child keeps rubbing his eyes, hay fever is more likely than infection.

Seasonal allergic rhinitis

Although children's colds often seem to run into one another so that it is impossible to remember when the last one ended and this one began, if you think carefully you may find that a long-continued "cold" always seems to occur at a particular time of year. Pollen allergy (true "hay fever") is probably the most common and this will produce symptoms in spring and early summer. Allergy to molds and spores is also quite common. This will lead to symptoms in the early autumn, when plants are dying down and vegetables are brought in for storage. Many of the children whose parents remark suspiciously that they "always have a cold when it's time to go back to school after the summer vacation" suffer from this type of allergy.

Perennial allergic rhinitis

As the name suggests, this type tends to persist (either continuously or on and off) all the year round. While it may be due, or mainly due, to a particular allergen such as the house mite in dust, it is often due to multiple allergens.

Treatment for allergic rhinitis

Seasonal allergic rhinitis, which may be due to a few identifiable allergens, may merit desensitization, but finding the allergen is not always easy—especially in children—nor always worthwhile. In young children, for example, skin-prick tests may yield negative results even though the mucosa of the nasal passages is hypersensitive to the allergen being tested. Pinprick tests are not popular with many children and neither are the injections to which successful testing will lead. Treatment designed to reduce the allergic response at mucosal level and/or to reduce exposure to the allergen may be more appropriate.

Disodium cromoglycate, administered as a powder to be sniffed up the nose, is often effective, and can be used during a period of high risk, to prevent symptoms, too. Don't use it without your doctor's advice.

Topical steroids are also highly effective in reducing the whole inflammatory picture, but applied to the nose they will have no effect on the eyes so that eye drops may be needed as well. This use of steroids is considered remarkably safe with almost no absorption of the drug. The only side effect which is at all likely is occasional nose-bleeding (*see* **Nosebleeds**).

Decongestant nose drops (both prescription and over-the-counter) are widely used, but their effect is fleeting and use over long periods can actually damage the nasal mucosa. While they may be valuable in providing short-term relief from the feeling of nasal obstruction, they should probably be reserved for occasional "emergencies." Such drops can, for example, make it possible for a child to breathe normally through a movie or allow an adolescent to enjoy a party.

The commonest oral drugs prescribed for hay fever are anti-histamines. Their effect is limited in many people or the effective dose rendered unsuitable by the side effect of drowsiness. But if symptoms (such as a cough caused by the discharge dripping down the throat) are bothersome at night, these drugs may serve a double purpose of symptom relief and sleep inducement.

Avoiding allergens in hay fever Exposure to the allergens responsible for seasonal rhinitis can often be reduced by quite simple measures which need not adversely affect the sufferer's life. For example, by listening to the broadcast pollen count he may be able to time his use of preventative medication and avoid ill-timed country walks. . . . If autumn is his worst time, heavy exposure to mold spores can be avoided by abandoning gardening and leaf-raking and passing over chores like potato storage. Sleeping with bedroom windows closed will also help, while air filtration will help even more. Few families can afford to install air conditioning for the special benefit of a hay-fever sufferer. But those with atopic children might take the existence of an air-conditioning system as a major point in favor of a new house or apartment when they are moving anyway.

In perennial rhinitis the sufferer probably overreacts to a wide variety of allergens. Measures to cut down exposure to the obvious ones such as house dust (*see above* Asthma) will be worthwhile.

Whether rhinitis is seasonal or perennial, any sudden flare-up, with streaming nose, constant sneezing, swelling and watering of the eyes, should lead to some careful thinking back over the day. Such a flare-up often results from massive exposure to an allergen which is constantly present at a lower level. Hours spent waiting for the attention of a veterinary surgeon, for example, may lead to such a flare-up in a patient who had not previously suspected that he was allergic to the family cat. A day spent cleaning up autumn leaves and garden debris may provoke a similar reaction in someone who had not realized that mold spores were part of his trouble.

Urticaria

This is a general term for any allergic reaction which shows itself in the skin. The actual meeting between allergen and antibody may take place locally, or the skin may react to problems elsewhere in the body.

Urticaria (hives, for example) often appears and vanishes again within an hour or two. Nobody has the chance to find out what has caused it and, while the white weals on reddened skin may look dramatic and the itching may be intense, the whole matter is trivial.

Calamine lotion may be effective in relieving itching. If the weals are extensive, a lukewarm bath containing half a cup of sodium bicarbonate will be even more effective and far more enjoyable.

Long-lasting or recurrent urticaria

Occasionally a child (usually one who shows other signs of being highly allergic) has an episode of urticaria in which as fast as one set of weals die down, others come up. She may be swollen and itchy for days at a time. Another child may have very frequent episodes. In either instance the doctor may want to try to hunt down specific allergens. Often this is a food or a drug which, once identified, can be avoided. But sometimes the group of allergens responsible may be the inhaled ones which often cause asthma or hay fever. If pollens and dusts are causing urticaria as well as other allergic symptoms, the urticaria may be a factor in the decision to pursue active treatment.

Papular urticaria

Usually presents itself as weals together with spots and little blisters. They are usually distributed over the buttocks and legs. Secondary infection following scratching is common. This form of urticaria is usually a reaction either to insect bites or to mite bites. Its allergic nature is demonstrated by the fact that while other family members may be bitten (as by midges at a picnic, for example), only one individual develops this extreme reaction. A hydrocortisone cream and/or anti-histamines by mouth are often prescribed.

Affected individuals may benefit from wearing close-fitting clothing when insects are active in the evening and from using an insect-repellent product. Pets should also be carefully checked for parasites and the child should avoid places (such as hay barns) where mites abound.

Angioneurotic edema (Giant hives)

This is a less common but far more dramatic form of urticaria in which a single large area of skin and underlying tissue suddenly puffs up into an enormous white weal. Common sites include the area around an eye, lip, throat or penis. The swelling goes down in a few hours and the allergen is seldom discovered.

Very occasionally this sudden swelling involves the soft tissues of the throat and may then cause difficulty in breathing. For this reason it is wise to consult a doctor for angioneurotic edema, although in practice the drama will often be over before he can see it. Any actual (as opposed to anticipated) difficulty in breathing should, of course, mean an immediate trip to the nearest hospital.

Anal fissure *see* **Constipation**. *See also* **Soiling**.
Anesthesia *see* **Hospital**/Surgery.
Angioneurotic edema *see* **Allergy**/Urticaria.
Animal bites *see* **Accidents**/Bites and Stings.
Anorexia nervosa *see* **Eating disorders**.
Antibiotics *see* **Infection**/Treatment of: Antibiotics and sulphonamides; Types of: The pros and cons of antibiotics in undiagnosed infection.
Antibodies *see* **Immune Response; Immunization; Infection**. *See also* **Allergy**.
Anti-toxin *see* **Tetanus**.

Anxiety, Fears and Phobias *see also* **School**/School phobia

Anxiety and fears

Although anxiety and fear are unpleasant feelings, they are necessary ones. Feeling afraid warns the individual of possible danger just as feeling pain warns her of possible bodily damage (*see* **Pain and Pain Control**). But, just as a child can receive inaccurate and/or excessive pain signals, so she can receive inappropriate anxiety and fear signals. Parents cannot hope, and should not try, to rear children who never experience these horrible feelings, but they can do a great deal to ensure that children are well equipped to interpret, understand and cope with them.

Unfortunately our society tends to admire tough, adventurous, "fearless" children and therefore many parents try to "teach" these qualities by teasing and pressing children who are anxious, and by laughing or scoffing at their fears. Nothing could be more likely to produce an anxious and fearful child. A better understanding of the roots of anxiety and fear may lead to the gentler handling which may truly produce a secure and confident person.

The roots of fear Adults' basic anxieties and fears are often difficult to see and understand because we all learn to cover them up, to hide from them and even to hide them from ourselves. Babies and young children have had neither the time nor the experience to develop such defenses. Their fears and anxieties are right there on the surface for all to see.

The "basic fear" is, of course, the fear of being attacked, hurt, killed. Every baby has a strong will to live and reacts with fear to any life threat. Parents, knowing that nothing would ever be permitted to threaten their beloved baby and that they themselves would lay down their lives for her, often do not allow for the instinctive nature of her basic fears or for the fact that she cannot know that her world is a safe place. When your baby jumps, screams, pales and shakes because you have dropped a saucepan lid close beside her, remind yourself that she cannot know the harmless source of the sound. Remind yourself, if you like, that back in more primitive times the sound might have been that of a hungry tiger leaping through the brush. When she reacts with panic to being put down in her crib a little carelessly, so that her head falls back before her spine is fully supported by the mattress, remind yourself that her ancestors were more physically developed than she is and were carried on the backs of mothers far hairier than you. Her panicky clutching would, in those times, have enabled her to save herself, by grabbing handfuls of hair, from a fall which might otherwise have killed her. Notice, too, that while she always reacts to pain with displeasure—snatching away the part that is pricked by the doctor's needle, for example—she only sometimes reacts to pain with fear as well. She does so if the pain occurs in a violent context. If you accidentally bang her head on the door frame as you carry her through, she will howl from fear as well as pain. If you are unlucky enough to touch her hand with a cigarette she will probably protest only briefly.

While even the youngest baby is programmed to react with instinctive fear to any obvious threat, older babies and young children need a much broader fear reaction to protect them from the vast variety of threatening situations which they may meet as they grow up. This broader reaction is an *instinctive fear of what is strange*. When your toddler reacts with terror to her first meeting with a tortoise, it is not because she thinks that the tortoise will hurt her but because she does not, cannot, know whether it will do so or not. If you feel impatient, because you know the tortoise is harmless, remind yourself that one day she might meet a poisonous snake and save her own life by reacting to it in just the way that she is now reacting to the new pet.

Part of parents' irritation with young children's fears is often due to their own feelings being hurt by the child's reaction. You would not have taken her near that tortoise if it was going to hurt her, would you? Of course you would not, but a child dare not rely totally on the judgment and protection of adults because, after all, you are not always with her now and certainly will not be with her every minute as she grows up. She needs her personal fear of the strange to protect herself independently of her protectors. But how much she needs it does depend on how protected she feels. The more secure a child is in the total protection of her parents, the less fearful she will need to be.

The roots of anxiety   A baby's survival absolutely depends on adult care twenty-four hours a day. That care usually depends on there being love between baby and adult; it is to ensure that love that the baby is born with behaviors which seem loving and rewarding to her parents (such as those early smiles) even before she has learned to tell one person from another. Once she does know her "special people" (whether they are, in fact, her natural parents or other caretakers) the love relationship which she has with them becomes the most important emotional factor in her life and remains so for many years. *Basic anxiety is anxiety over separation from those loved people and therefore loss of their care and protection* and/or anxiety over loss of their love which might lead to withdrawal of that care and protection. The more certain she is of continuing love and care the less fearful she will be, but when anything happens to shake her confidence, fear will flood to the surface because without you, without your loving care, she cannot survive. You will see this difference from very early on when you watch your baby react to strange, potentially alarming events. When she is securely held in your arms she may be able to regard that strange tortoise with calm puzzlement or tolerate nearby thunderclaps. She will look at your face to see if you are afraid and, if you are not, she will trust herself to your protection. But when she is alone—or with strangers—she is far more likely to be afraid; and if she is with you physically but separated from you emotionally by a quarrel, she may be afraid, too. This is why irritated reactions to childish fears always work against fearlessness. Your irritation makes her feel less secure in your love and therefore opens her to fear.

Fear of separation and loss of love remain the childish basis for most anxiety all through our lives. When you misread a street map and find yourself quite unimportantly lost in a strange city, it is that infantile fear of losing parents which makes your heart pound and your hands go clammy. When you cannot sleep because your partner is out of town overnight, or cannot settle down to work because your five-year-old has gone for the first time to all-day school, it is that same basic fear of separation from loved people which is acting upon you. Part of the desolation of bereavement is the infant-you feeling deserted and helpless. As adults, our physical survival does not depend on care by the people we love; we *can* survive without our partners, our children, our aged relations, but separations still remind us of a time when we could not (*see* **Death**).

If it seems to you fanciful to say that we are all more or less bedevilled by remaining fragments of baby separation fears, think about the word "good-bye." Can you say it without a quaver, or do you, like most people, avoid the echoing sadness of the word with slang alternatives like "bye-bye," "ciao" or "see you" or "cheerio." Ask yourself also how many adults you know who can leave a party or other social occasion without endlessly hovering over the coats and on the doorstep, spinning out the farewells, repeating the plans for further meetings and promising, again and again, to "see you again soon" or "speak to you on the phone tomorrow." Is there not a marked similarity with the toddler who puts off the nightly bedtime parting with cries for yet another drink of water, trip to the bathroom or just one more kiss?

The more secure we were in our love relationships as children, the more we were allowed to feel dependent on and cared for by our "special people," the less prone we shall be to this kind of anxiety and to fears of the threatening or the strange. Clearly, then, if we want to give our children security and confidence so that they grow up prone to as little anxiety and as few fears as possible, we shall not do it by scoffing, pushing and bullying, but by understanding, reassuring and loving. Above all, perhaps, we need to recognize the stages in a child's life at which she will be particularly prone to particular kinds of anxiety and fear so that we offer appropriate support at the right moments. The key is the developing child's competence: her ability to manage for herself and her confidence that she can do so. At birth she can manage nothing and will die without your constant care. As an adult she can manage everything, including the care and support of a child of her own. It is the stages inbetween which concern us here.

Babies and anxiety   Human babies are extremely helpless, physically, compared with most other mammals but they have an in-built drive to mature, to grow up and to become competent. Your baby will "manage" everything that she can manage just as soon as she is physically and mentally ready to do so. Nothing whatsoever is to be gained from hurrying her and there is much to be lost.

If she wants lots of physical holding and cuddling and is frightened by being put on the floor to "kick", follow her cues. Putting her on the floor, protesting, will not speed up her physical development; it may actually hold it back. Cuddling her is not overprotecting her; it is giving her what she is telling you she needs and therefore giving her the context in which, at this stage, this particular baby will develop fastest.

When she reaches a phase in which she is reluctant to let you out of her sight, be with her as much as you possibly can and make sure that when you cannot be there she has an alternative beloved person on whom to depend. You cannot teach her not to need you so much by depriving her of you, because her need is real. She will learn for herself that she can manage short periods without you when, and only when, the love relationship between you is so solid that it can serve her as a foundation to be taken for granted while she attends to other matters.

When it becomes clear that particular situations make her anxious and afraid, don't assume that surviving them will prove to her that "there's nothing to be afraid of." Instead, help her to find ways in which her anxiety can be kept at a tolerable level. Fear of being alone, in the dark, at night, for example, is very common towards the end of the first year. Of course, if you firmly close the door and leave her, she will eventually go to sleep. But far from teaching her that it is safe and comfortable to be left each night you will be teaching her exactly the opposite:

If it is your departure which makes her anxious, concentrate on helping her to feel that you are still available. Instead of closing the door and ignoring her cries, leave it ajar and pop back to reassure her from time to time or call to her in a friendly way as you get the supper.

If the darkness makes her room strange and therefore scary, leave a light on. A low wattage bulb uses very little electricity. When she is a little older she can have a bedside light to turn on and off herself so that *she has control over the darkness.*

If there are comfort rituals or objects which help her to be happy in her crib encourage them (*see* **Habits**/Comfort habits). A pacifier may give her something pleasant to do which masks her sadness; a special "cuddly" may "stand in" for you so that as long as she has that, she is able to let you go.

The point of all this is, of course, that *the less anxiety and fear your baby feels* the more confident and fearless she will be able to be. She learns to be these desirable things *through feeling safe.*

Toddlers' | Toddlers are particularly prone to anxiety and fears both because it is at
anxiety | this stage that many parents begin to demand tough, adventurous,
(see also | independent behavior and because their own developmental stage is an
Tantrums*)* | anxious-making one. Your toddler is at an emotional crossroads. He has

reached a point where, in order to grow towards the comparative independence and autonomy of childhood, he has to assert his own individuality and start to take charge of himself and his own life. Yet he is still very immature and totally dependent upon your love, support and approval; the dependence of babyhood still feels far easier to him. Every time he allows you absolutely to control the details of his daily life, the independent bit of him protests: "Go 'way; let me. . . ." But every time he protests and rejects you, he becomes anxious lest you take him at his word; if you do indeed "go 'way" that toddler turns instantly back into a baby, weeping bitterly because you have left the room without him.

Parents have a difficult, but infinitely satisfactory, job to do in holding the balance between these overriding toddler emotions. If you can give your toddler *all the personal independence he can take without fear*, plus *all the love and protection he can take without frustration*, you will be doing a textbook job of sensitive parenting. Nobody can do that all the time, but most of the time will produce both a secure and independent child and an enjoyable daily life for all of you.

If your toddler is feeling generally anxious—either because you are pressing him to be more "grown up" than he can easily be or because he is pressing himself—you will probably see overall signs like the following:

He will be extra-clingy, choosing to follow you wherever you go rather than stay alone in a room to play; choosing to hold your hand or ride in the stroller rather than run ahead; choosing to sit on your lap or leaning against you rather than separately on the floor.

He may seem unusually "good" because he is feeling extra-dependent on you and, therefore, whenever he can remember how you like him to behave (which will not, of course, be all the time) he will do so.

He will not enjoy new places or people because he dare not leave you to explore.

He may have new (or extra) difficulty in going to sleep, adding to his bedtime rituals, taking more and more comforting toys into bed with him and thinking up fresh ways to persuade you to return for another goodnight.

He may enter a phase of nightmares (*see* **Sleep**).

He may lose enthusiasm for food and/or for feeding himself, preferring the more babyish items in his meals (including a bottle unless this has long been abandoned) and demanding that you feed him with a spoon even though he is competent to do so himself.

A toddler who is behaving in these ways is usually feeling anxious about your love and protection and therefore anxious about his own ability to manage what he has to manage. There are some obvious measures you can take and avoid:

A large extra measure of loving attention may work wonders. It may, for example, be a good time to take a week's vacation from work so that you can be with him and he need not make the effort which may be involved in his usual day-care arrangements. If he is at home with you anyway, it may be a good time to embark on projects he can share with you rather than being busy with your own affairs and therefore anxious that he should occupy himself. It certainly will not be a good time to arrange many social engagements for him to keep without you.

New demands will certainly make matters worse, so if you were contemplating a fresh effort at toilet training/getting him off his bottle/insisting that he dress himself or tidy his own toys, go easy for a while.

Rows with you will make matters much worse and the very worst kind of row will be the kind which suggests to him that you love him less than you once did. Don't, please don't, let yourself use, even in anger, phrases like "I'm fed up to the teeth with looking after you all day . . ." or "It's no good coming to me for love when you're so naughty. . . ." A toddler who is already feeling anxious about you may take you far more literally than you intend. He may actually *believe* that you do not love him and do not like caring for him.

Feeling competent will help, feeling helpless will increase his anxiety.
Lots of praise for things he does easily and well will help him to feel that
he is "on top" of his life, but taking over tasks in the middle because he is
slow, or refusing to let him have a go because "you're too little" will have
the opposite effect.

Try, above all, not to use your superior strength and power to force him
to do as you wish. If you reinforce the command to "hurry up" by
scooping him up and carrying him when he meant to walk, you really do
make him feel helpless.

Toddler fears   Almost every toddler will have one or two specific fears at any moment in
his or her life, but toddlers who are feeling generally anxious may have
their lives dominated by many fears all operating at the same time.

The commonest fears among Western children up to the age of three-
and-a-half are, in order: fear of dogs, darkness and its associated bogeys
and ghosts, snakes and some insects, emergency sounds such as fire or
ambulance sirens, and assorted varieties of people such as uniformed
policemen or nuns in long habits. In addition to these feared objects,
children also commonly fear some of the things adults do to them or force
them to do. Being pushed high on swings heads this list, followed equally
by submersion in deep water (whether in a swimming pool, lake or
ocean), fairground rides and boat rides, and a variety of games which
combine chasing with surprise—such as some kinds of "hide and seek."

Most of these fears arise unexpectedly and pass as suddenly as they
began. If you will allow him to, your toddler will deal with them for
himself by avoiding the things or the situations which frighten him. If you
will let him steer well away from that dog, run to your arms when the
ambulance passes and keep off those swings, the fear will pass as he
enters a less anxious phase. If you try to force him to "face it," to "find out
for himself that there's nothing to be frightened of" or to "stop being such
a baby," that fear may harden into a phobia (*see below*) and his general
anxiety level will rise.

**Try to treat your toddler's fears with the same tolerant helpfulness you
would offer to an adult.** If you knew an adult friend was afraid of snakes,
you would not expect her to come with you into the reptile house at the
zoo, nor tease her for preferring to wait outside. Why must the toddler
come in? If you knew she was afraid of heights you would yourself climb
the ladder to retrieve her scarf from that tree; why must the toddler get
down from the jungle gym without help?

Every time you make your toddler experience his fear, you strengthen
it. But every time you enable him to meet or do something without feeling
afraid, you strengthen *him*. If you do not force him into that reptile house
today, he may see a grass snake in the pet shop window next week and
find it interesting instead of alarming. If you help him down from that
jungle gym today he may find that jumping the last rungs was fun and
want to climb a little way tomorrow. If you let him lead along a path which
never takes him over the edge into fear, his fears will gradually recede.

**Try to be clear, then, that there is a difference between "fearlessness"
and "bravery."** A fearless child is simply one who is unafraid. He is
someone to be proud of because he will be a child who is confident in your

loving care and therefore confident of his ability to cope with life. But a brave child is one who does, or puts up with, things, even though they frighten or hurt him. When we say to a toddler, "Oh come on, get in the water; you're not really scared; you like it really," we *pretend* that we want him to be fearless when what we are really demanding of him is that he should be brave.

Sometimes we need to demand bravery of a child—perhaps because he must have a dental filling or a painful dressing—but when we do, we should be honest about it. The message is not "It won't hurt," but "It will hurt but it will soon be over and I have to ask you to put up with it because it is necessary." Most of the time we should not demand bravery because every time we do, we expose the child to fear and reduce his fearlessness. A toddler who is continually pushed in this way may have so much of his time and emotional energy taken up by meeting your demands for bravery that he has none left for being the tough, adventurous child you so much want. Let him find fearlessness for himself; build his own courage out of confidence and find it tested only rarely and when it is necessary.

Pre-school children's anxiety and fears

If your toddler emerges into a child who is sure that you are on his side, loving and lovable, he will also be sure of himself, and feel loving and lovable. He will be all set for what can be an enthrallingly happy couple of years spent increasingly turning his attention and affection outside the family and onto new adults and peers. Cries of "my teacher says . . ." and "my friend wants me to . . ." are a vote of confidence in you as parents.

Where a pre-school child is beset by much anxiety and many fears, it is usually because of the outside demands made upon him rather than because of his internal conflicts. Points to watch are:

That nobody should hurry him or her into any new growing-up experience. Try not to push the playgroup or nursery school to admit her early "because she is so bright." She can go on being bright at home or within the parent-and-toddler group. She will still be bright when she is emotionally ready for that next step. Try not to let him be pushed into "big school" at four just because it has places in its brand-new kindergarten class. Let him enjoy being "one of the big ones" in playgroup or nursery school before he must face being a very *very* little one all over again. Try not to push for lessons in dancing or drama, piano or swimming just because other children go. If your child dreams of being a ballerina or an actor, fine, try those Saturday mornings. But if he or she has no view on the matter, don't fill every moment with formal learning even if it is not of the academic kind. A child in this age period has a lot of life-learning still to do and all the time in the world for acquiring special skills.

Anxiety when starting school

Starting school is a very big step for most children and an enormous one for some. You should almost expect an upsurge of anxiety in your child because, however capable you have helped him to feel so far, he is almost certain to wonder whether he can cope without you in this new big group with its vast noisy buildings, countless children, many so much larger than he, and all these strange adults with apparently limitless authority and power (*see also* **School**/Going to "big school"; Starting school).

Steady (almost boring) home support and home routines will see most children through. But where there are real problems over going to school or fears of events within it, you must now work with the teacher because you do not have the actual power to influence what happens to him, minute by minute and day by day when you are not there. Remember that:

Fear creates fear so that even if he overcomes his anxiety and goes into school each morning, the fact that he does so *feeling anxious* is likely to make a vicious circle. If he feels sick and shaky every Monday morning, those horrible feelings will become linked in his mind with school and he will come to dread the feelings as much as the school. He may even go on having the anxiety symptoms after he has actually come to enjoy the business of being at school. So, as before, the important consideration is that anxiety should be avoided if it possibly can be. Your aim is not just to get him there but to get him there feeling happy.

Older children and anxieties at school

As children become older and more involved in group life with others the same age, they have to find ways of concealing anxiety and fear which would be unacceptable within the group, and of coping, privately, with their own feelings. Parents sometimes have to strike a difficult balance between interference and neglect; between allowing the child her rightful autonomy and leaving her to cope when she cannot easily do so. If, for example, a child who has always loved acting refuses to join the drama club or have anything to do with school productions, you may deduce that she is anxious at the idea of performing publicly in that setting. If she seems to pick her friends always from among children who are shy, anxious to please and not very popular, you may deduce that she is "playing safe" and avoiding the risks of friendship with children who might reject her. If she always aims to arrive at school just before lessons begin and to come home the moment they end, it may be clear to you that the liberty of the school playground frightens her, while the gradual development of a "weak ankle" which keeps her off physical education and team games, may tell you something of her feelings about these activities. If a child is finding it necessary to limit her own life and experiences, do herself out of treats and generally reduce the richness of her life because of anxiety, she needs some help. If she does not get it she may project an image of herself at school which others come to believe. She may find herself valued far below her potential and suffer for it later. But if she is enjoying the life she is making for herself, if she is lively and interested and involved, it may be *your anxiety for her* which is the real issue. You may want her to shine more brightly than she feels she can. Once again, honest discussion with her teachers should give you some clues.

Handling other common fears

Older children, like adults, learn to avoid situations which make them uncomfortably anxious and to handle specific fears. Some of the "odd" behavior you may observe in your child are coping devices of this kind. The child who, for example, "prefers" to walk home the long way may, in fact, be afraid of the park he must cross on the shorter route or may have made a semiconscious pact with himself always to count that particular set of paving stones on the way home in order to ward off evil. The child who starts singing as she leaves the living room and sings loudly until she reaches her bedroom is probably frightened of a particular bogey on the stairs. The one who always seems unreasonably relieved to see you when you get home may live in terror of your being murdered on the train. . . . Parents cannot protect their growing children from this mixture of rational and irrational fear (she *might* get assaulted; you *might* be murdered; the paving stones and the singing will not avert disaster but do avert the discomfort of anxiety), but they can be sensitive to it and help to keep it within bounds. Like a younger child, this one will be less anxious overall, the less anxiety and fear she experiences in her everyday life. But, unlike a younger child, she will not want to admit to you (or even perhaps to herself) that she is afraid. Tactfully, then, you have to notice the obvious sources of anxiety, the obvious fears, and offer her more effective ways out than her own chants and charms. If you know that leaving the warm, bright living room and facing the dark lonely stairs makes your hulking twelve-year-old feel anxious, you could just happen to have left on the stair light or be going up to the bathroom yourself at the relevant moment. And if you know that about your child, you can reasonably deduce that being left alone in the house after dark will alarm her. You can see to it that if she feels too old for a "babysitter" when you go out, she has a friend to spend the night with her instead.

Adolescent anxiety and fear

Like toddlers, adolescents *have* to achieve a dramatic spurt in growing up yet seldom feel entirely safe in doing so. At this stage most of her anxiety will be focused on the kind of person she feels herself to be/wants to be/will be when she is fully adult. Most of her fears will be of various kinds of failure, whether failure to attract the opposite sex, failure to pass her examinations, failure to "stand up to" you or failure to be as beautiful and as popular as she would like to be. She has to work it all out for herself but she does not have to do it by herself (*see* **Adolescence**).

As well as offering her steadfast and unalterable love and support of the kind which sincerely means that you love and will help her now and would go on loving and helping her *whatever she did*, keep an eye out for high levels and degrees of anxiety and fear which may actually damage her ability to move into adult life.

Free-floating anxiety

This is the term used to describe anxious feelings which have no particular focus. The victim does not know what she is worried *about*; all she knows is that her heart pounds, her hands feel clammy, she feels shaky, perhaps nauseated, restless, disturbed and plagued by feelings of forboding and dread. When she wakes up in the morning she feels as if something terrible has happened or something terrifying has got to be faced. Yet thinking over the prospect of a perfectly ordinary, even potentially pleasant, day ahead brings no relief. Indeed, finding no reasonable explanation for her feelings may bring fear of the feelings themselves. "What is the *matter* with me?" she asks herself.

This kind of anxiety is a major component of many emotional disturbances and illnesses. An adolescent who remains in such a state for more than a few days or who is subject to recurrent "panic attacks" with no obvious cause, needs help from her doctor. It is to be hoped that he will not simply offer her tranquillizers to "calm her down" but will help her, either himself or by referring her to a psychiatrist, *to work out what she is really feeling anxious about*. Until she can recognize the source of those feelings, they will paralyze her and produce the same old circle of anxiety, fear of anxiety, more anxiety. Helping her to see, for example, that her imminent departure for college has touched off old separation anxieties which date back to her nursery school days or earlier will not automatically cure the anxiety but will make it possible for her to think it through and look for ways of coping better. Perhaps she is not ready to leave home so finally: perhaps her childhood room should remain available to her and plans be made for her to return on weekends until college life becomes her life. Perhaps she *is* ready but is worried that you will be lonely without her. Perhaps a seemingly commonsense suggestion by you, that she should start taking the contraceptive pill before she starts her college life, has made her feel pressured towards sexual activity for which she is not emotionally ready.

An anxious adolescent who can pinpoint the source of his or her feelings will no longer feel so hopeless and helpless because he or she will be on the way towards coping with them. Feeling able to cope will, in itself, reduce his or her anxiety level and produce a benevolent circle of confidence—competence—more confidence.

Coping with the physical effects of anxiety

People of all ages vary in the extent to which anxiety-inducing situations affect them physically. Just as pain is supposed to warn the victim of physical damage but may "misfire" so that a trivial injury hurts more than a serious one, so anxiety is supposed to prepare the body for "fight or flight," but may produce an overreaction which actually reduces competence. The adolescent who goes into an examination or onto a concert platform with no anxiety or "nerves" at all, probably will not give her best possible performance. A little extra adrenaline would produce extra effort, extra brilliance. But the adolescent who faces such a test with her hands shaking, her stomach churning, her skin clammy and her head full of the sound of her own pounding heart, will not give her best performance either. Her anxiety reaction has gone over the top and become destructive rather than useful.

Of course the way that people face challenges and stresses is intimately concerned with their basic self-confidence, as well as with their past experiences of success and failure, of ability or inability to cope. But, in the here-and-now, a great deal can often be done to bring stress reactions down to somewhere near the optimum level. Practice, for example, may be valuable, but it is important that it be the right *kind* of practice. A child who always does poorly in examinations because of acute anxiety will not learn to stay calmer by practicing having "exam nerves"—in this as in every other area, fear breeds fear. She will only learn to stay calmer by practicing *not* having "exam nerves." She may therefore benefit from being encouraged to practice writing her answers at home, rather than within the formality of an examination room; from practicing "writing to time" when there is nothing at stake but ordinary homework, or from practicing "mock exams" in which everything is as it will be on the big day except that the questions are easy and success more likely.

Parents cannot, of course, arrange this kind of help on their own, but any school, music teacher or athletic coach should be happy to cooperate on behalf of any child whose test performance does not measure up to his or her year-round standards. Under some circumstances it may also be sensible to consult the doctor. He may consider that the adolescent could benefit from a psychologist's help (*see below* Phobias).

Phobias

The line between an "ordinary" fear and a phobia is blurred but important. Where a fear is usually firmly attached to its object, so that the victim only feels afraid when she has to face the thing she fears, a phobia has an existence of its own in the victim's mind and imagination. A child with a phobia of dogs, for example, is not only frightened when she meets a dog, she is also frightened when she sees one, hears about one, thinks about one. She does not only leave the park if she sees a dog, she keeps out of the park in case there might be one there. She may not be able to look at books for fear of the fear feelings which will consume her if there is a picture of a dog; even the television advertisements may become a source of terror because of the dog-food slots.

Although phobias are common and usually insignificant in toddlers and very young children—yielding, like other fears, to a lessening of general anxiety—phobias in older people are more important. Since fear breeds fear, phobias tend to fuel themselves. The victim experiences horrible anxiety, becomes terrified of experiencing it again and therefore becomes increasingly anxious and liable to fear. Many phobias also spread and generalize themselves. That example of a phobia of dogs, for example, would, if it was left unchecked, gradually tend to confine the victim to her home, the only place where she can be quite sure no dogs will be. It is easy to see how this situation could lead to her becoming phobic of the outside world.

Behavioral psychologists have developed sophisticated techniques for dealing with phobias by a method which is known as "de-sensitization." Very briefly, the method involves first finding the "psychological distance" from which the patient can view the feared object (let us stay with dogs) *without feeling afraid*. If the sight of a dog in the far distance evokes any fear at all, even greater distance will be tried, by using a picture of a dog instead of a real one or even by using a cartoon of a puppy instead of a real picture of an adult dog. Once any kind of contact with any kind of dog stimulus can be tolerated without fear, the process of de-sensitization can be started. Day by day the psychologist increases the contact between patient and dog, making it closer and more realistic but *never allowing it to evoke anxiety*. However minute the progressive steps, the repeated experience of dogs-without-fear gradually teaches the patient not to associate dogs with fear and therefore not to be afraid. A person thus treated does not have to come to be a dog lover. She may always prefer not to own or even to pet dogs. But she will eventually come to be able to tolerate/ignore them so that their existence (in reality and in her mind) no longer dictates or limits her lifestyle.

● Parents often attempt a sort of do-it-yourself desensitization with phobic young children. "If only she would touch that sweet puppy," they say "she'd soon find out how warm and cuddly and gentle he is." Be careful. If your attempts frighten your child, you will make matters worse. If a phobia is ruining a life, expert help is needed.

Appendix

The appendix is a very small dead-end tube leading off the large intestine. It is rich in lymphoid tissue and may play some part in the production of antibodies (*see* **Immune Response**). However, it is not a necessary organ and seldom becomes of interest to the individual unless it becomes inflamed (*see* **Hospital**/Surgery: Appendectomy).

Appetite *see* **Eating**. *See also* **Eating disorders**.

Asphyxia *see* **Accidents**/Choking; Drowning. *See also* **Safety**/In the home: From general household hazards.

Asthma *see* **Allergy**. *See also* **Chest Infections**.

Astigmatism *see* **Eyes and Seeing; Eye Disorders and Blindness**/Faults in vision.

Athlete's foot *see* **Ringworm and Athlete's Foot**.

Audiometry *see* **Ears and Hearing; Ear Disorders and Deafness**. *See also* **Language**/Three to six months: Watching out for deafness; **Medical Specialities**.

Baby Alarms

A microphone placed near your baby and a speaker placed near you ensure that you will hear him if he cries or calls. Available systems range from inexpensive ones, which involve trailing wires through the house, to more luxurious built-in systems with outlets in every room. You may prefer the first type because you can put the microphone beside the carriage at the far end of the garden or take the whole thing with you when you go camping or to friends' houses.

Many families never have this kind of alarm system but those who have ever had one are seldom prepared to go back to life without it. If you know that you will hear your baby if he needs you, you can forget about him until he does. If you know the music will not drown a nightmare, you can turn the stereo as loud as you please. If you know that the wire joins the two of you, you can use any room as a nursery instead of having your arrangements constrained by the need to keep him close to where you sleep. By turning the volume control on that speaker up, you can even ensure that the smallest cry will blast a possibly neglectful or slightly deaf babysitter out of her chair.

Many baby alarms have a "talk back" facility so that by pressing a button you can speak to him. Most babies are terrified by such a disembodied (and usually slightly distorted) voice so you probably will not use it while he is very young. It may, however, become very useful at the later stage when he calls endlessly for the drinks of water which are really requests for reassurance that you are still there.

While you will not want to "listen in" to older children's private lives, a baby alarm which is left, wired in but switched off, can be useful all over again during later illness. You can agree with your eight-year-old that you will switch it on when you go to bed so that she need only call gently if she needs you during the night. You can agree to leave it switched on while she tries to have an afternoon nap so that you can be sure to hear her when she wakes or gives up. It may even enable you to sink happily into your own bed when the possibility of recurring croup or a soaring fever would otherwise force you to stay awake and on alert.

Baby Bouncers *see also* **Play**

"Baby bouncer" is a generic term for any contraption of seat and harness in which a baby can be suspended, on strong elastic cords, from the top of a doorframe or from a ceiling hook.

Most of the available ones have broad canvas straps which you buckle around the baby's waist and between her legs before hooking her onto those cords. The very best (originally made in France) consists of an actual canvas chair on elastic cords. It is very quick and easy to put a baby in and out of this type; furthermore it has a high back for good head support and a small "tray" in front so that the baby has a place for some toys.

Whatever type of bouncer you are using, the idea is not that *you* should bounce or swing the baby but that she should do it for herself. You adjust the length of those elastic cords so that as she sits, her toes just touch the floor. Small whole-body movements move the whole bouncer; pushes with her toes produce up-and-down movements. Eventually, *in her own time*, she discovers that she can push down deliberately and set herself rhythmically bouncing; later on that she can twirl around and "dance," too.

Baby bouncers give most babies tremendous pleasure because they free them to enjoy kinds of movement and degrees of power over their bodies which are not yet mature enough to achieve without that elastic aid. They also suspend the baby in an upright position from which she can see everything which is going on around her *and* change her own view by turning herself around. Successfully used, this gadget may keep her safe, active, busily occupied and in social contact with you as you get on with life, for longer periods than any other.

A couple of years ago, when the fashion for bouncers was at its peak, considerable anxiety was expressed about them in the medical and child-care press. It was thought, for example, that lengthy use might put a strain on very young backs or that mothers might leave babies confined in them for hours. Like any other gadget a bouncer needs to be used sensibly and, like any other plaything, it is intended to give pleasure and therefore should not be used at all if, after two or three experiments, your baby does not like it. You may like to check through the following points:

Type of bouncer and age of baby A bouncer whose seat provides support for the back and for the head and neck can be used safely (for a baby who enjoys free physical play) from about three months of age. But a bouncer which requires her to keep her own back and neck straight, suspending her from the crotch and waist with no support at all above that level, should seldom be used before six months and even then should not be used for long periods at a time. In the first type a baby who is tired can simply stop moving, relax, even drop off to sleep as she might in a comfortable stroller. In the second type she must exercise control over her muscles all the time.

Placing of the bouncer and safety

Some expensive bouncers come with their own stands. These are not recommended as they take up a lot of space and do not give enough height for older babies who, as they get heavier, need a long length of elastic for satisfactory (and now energetic) bouncing.

Some come with a clamp intended to fix the elastic cords to the top of a door frame. These are not recommended either because door frames are not standard and there have been accidents when clamps have failed or been improperly fixed. If you want to hang a bouncer from a doorframe it is better to use hefty screw-in hooks to hang it from. But a doorframe is only occasionally the best place for a bouncer because, ideally, the baby wants to bounce in a position from which she can see lots of people and interesting activities. If she is stuck in the doorway (unless it links kitchen and living room, for example) most of what goes on will be around the corner and out of her view.

If you can bear to deface your ceiling, hooks screwed right into a rafter in the middle of your most used room are usually the best. Those same hooks may stay in use all through her early childhood, for other gymnastics (*see* **Play**/"Messy" and energetic play for private homes).

The elastic cords are carefully tested for strength but they, together with the clips which attach them to seat and ceiling hook, must be regularly inspected for wear. The easiest way to ensure daily safety is to put your own weight on the cords as you hang them up. If they will hold you for a moment they will certainly hold your baby for as long as she cares to play.

Using a bouncer

Any piece of equipment which holds a baby safely out of the way can be misused: yours can be imprisoned in her carriage or highchair just as effectively as in her bouncer. While she is happy in it, you can indeed get on with otherwise dangerous jobs or take your eyes off her while you talk on the telephone, but obviously as soon as she is bored she should be taken out.

Some babies—especially in their first few months—are frightened by the very point of the bouncer: the ease with which it moves in space in response to their movements. If yours feels like this, don't persist now but don't decide that you have wasted the money either. She may love it in a couple of months, especially when she is at the almost-sitting, almost-crawling stage when she yearns to be more active than she can yet manage to be without help. She may take to her bouncer at six to eight months and use it frequently well into the toddler period.

A baby who does love her bouncer will probably take particular pleasure in using it outside. If you can find a convenient tree branch or have a jungle gym in your garden, hang it there sometimes (perhaps when you are working or sitting in the garden) and let her bounce in sunbeams and tree dapple.

● Don't confuse this kind of bouncer with the kind of canvas cradle-on-a-frame which is intended to provide babies too young to sit up with a very gentle springing motion as they kick. Although some young babies are comfortable in them, these are seldom worth buying because they last for only a few weeks before the baby prefers to do her kicking on the floor.

Babyfoods *see* **Eating**/Types of food for babies.

Babysitters *see also* **Working Mothers**

A baby or young child must have someone available to care for him at any moment in every twenty-four hours, and that is a commitment which no single person (no, not even his mother) should be expected to fulfill for long. If you happen to live within a large family or other group, you may be able to come and go more or less as you please, knowing that there will always be somebody around to "keep an eye on" the baby. But there are few families like that today. If you and your partner are in sole charge of that baby (or more especially if you are his only parent), it is important to get a babysitting system organized before your beloved child begins to feel like your jailer.

Choosing a babysitter   The ideal person is not really a babysitter at all but an occasional mother-substitute who may, perhaps, be the baby's grandmother. If you are fortunate enough to have a willing one available, cultivate her. She can not only "sit with" the sleeping baby while you go out in the evening, but also play with him or take him out while you pursue your own daytime interests or simply enjoy the luxury of being in your own home with nobody saying "Mom." If your baby does become accustomed to this sort of arrangement he will also have invaluable insurance against the dread day when you have to enter the hospital or spend a few days away coping with a family bereavement. Although he will be upset by your absence he will be far less upset than he would be if he were cared for by someone whom he scarcely knows or by someone who had never before offered him personal and intimate care (*see* **Anxiety, Fears and Phobias**).

If you have no willing relatives nearby you may be able to share this kind of extended babysitting with another family. It is truly idiotic that several sets of neighbor-parents should each feel trapped by their children when, with a little cooperation, all could offer each other a modicum of freedom while keeping all the children happy and secure. The trick is to be honest with yourself as well as with the other involved parents. If you have a big garden, for example, and the others have none, you are likely to find that you are the one with four toddlers around on summer afternoons. Do you mind? If you do, say so *before* you begin to feel put-upon. But perhaps you will not mind. Perhaps your own child enjoys the daytime company while you want, above all, to be freed to go out in the evening or to be relieved of the nursery school transport round.

Sometimes you will be offered daytime (as well as evening) babysitting by an adolescent who either "adopts" your family or finds it a pleasant way to earn pocket money. Be very sure that you do not ask (or allow her to volunteer) for more than she is capable of doing. She may long to take your baby for walks but be quite oblivious to the sun in his eyes, unreliable strange dogs or unevenly loaded carriages. She may love your baby when he smiles or sleeps but find him revolting when he cries or smells. She may mean to be one hundred percent responsible ninety-nine percent of the time but be quite unable to resist joining her gang when it passes your garden or slipping out to meet her boyfriend "just for a minute." Running risks of this kind is not fair to the baby, to you *or to the adolescent.* So, if she thinks she wants to replace you for short periods of that baby's life, let her do so first under your supervision so that you all have the opportunity to see how she gets on and to be sure that she really knows what she is taking on.

Daytime babysitting Anyone who is going to care for your baby or young child during his waking hours needs to know him well. Because his memory is so short and he is changing so rapidly, that means that she needs to see him frequently. Even a devoted relation will seem like a stranger to a baby who only sees her every few weeks, while the one who coped so beautifully with him when he was carriage- or chair-bound may be quite unable to keep him safe and happy once he is crawling. If you plan on daytime relief, make sure that baby and sitter meet frequently, even if you actually want to leave them together only on rare occasions.

• A complete stranger, however well trained, can never offer satisfactory care to a baby or young child. If you find yourself tempted by the nurseries offered by some hospital outpatient departments, large stores or adult education institutes, acknowledge your own desire for occasional freedom from childcare and *make proper arrangements.*

Evening babysitting If your child normally sleeps soundly, an evening babysitter will not usually have to offer him any personal service. She is there *in case something goes wrong.* Since the child *could* become ill or have a nightmare, the ideal person is still somebody whom he knows and trusts. But since he probably will not wake up, you may feel that it is legitimate to gamble a little. A complete stranger (hired, perhaps, from an agency) will obviously terrify him if he should wake, but a friendly acquaintance or regular sitter who always comes in if you go out may be acceptable. These are some of the points other parents have found important:

Don't leave a mere acquaintance to put the child to bed. He will not settle down. Put him to bed before you go out even if that means that you put him to bed a little earlier than usual.

If the child is old enough to understand, warn him that you will be out. Although he may still be amazed when Mrs. Jones comes in instead of Mommy, he will then remember what you said and, hopefully, settle down again to her assurances that you will be home soon. If you do not warn him and he does wake, he may be reluctant to settle down to sleep on subsequent nights in case you slip away.

If the child is not old enough to understand, try to leave a telephone number. If you have no telephone in your house this is obviously impossible: the sitter cannot leave the child to call you. But if you do have a telephone you can be reached, if you are needed, almost anywhere. The management of a theater or concert hall will fetch you out if you leave your seat numbers with the sitter. A cinema will flash a message on the screen for you if the sitter convinces the management that it is an emergency. Even a bar will relay a message. Of course, leaving a number means that you cannot spend a completely spontaneous evening, wandering along the river or calling on various friends to see who feels like going out for a drink, but it does not limit you to spending the evening in another private house.

Be absolutely certain that the sitter will not leave the house however late you may be. You may have every intention of being home by midnight but you could have a flat tire or an accident . . . you must be sure that your sitter will stay until you reappear and that she has no commitments (such as her own children once her husband departs for an early-morning shift) which could "force" her to leave. It is often sensible to arrange for her to sleep in your house if you should be very late, but do make sure that she does so within easy earshot of the baby (*see* **Baby Alarms**); remember that her ear may not be quite so tuned to infant cries as is yours.

Don't leave a child to care for a child. Only you can decide at what age your own older child is capable of babysitting for the younger one, but remember that *if there is a real emergency, a ten-, twelve- or fourteen-year-old may be just as frightened as the baby.* After all, you are not only guarding him against the emotional horrors of waking alone from a nightmare but from the practical horrors of fire or intruders, too. It may be that both baby and child need the security of an adult in the house.

Babytalk *see* **Language**.
Bacteria *see* **Infection**. *See also* individual conditions.
Bad breath *see* **Teeth**/Some dental problems of adolescence.
Bad language *see* **Language**/Pre-school years: Nonsense and "naughty nonsense." *See also*
   Discipline, Self-Discipline and Learning How to Behave.
Baldness *see* **Ringworm**. *See also* **Adolescence**/Problems with appearance and body image.

Bedwetting (Enuresis)

Staying dry during sleep is not a learned skill but a physiological development. Babies pass water involuntarily whether they are awake or asleep; older people's urination is a voluntary matter and therefore never takes place during normal sleep. In between those two stages, beds stop being wetted not because the child is "trained" but because he matures to a point where he can concentrate his urine sufficiently for his bladder to hold a full night's complement comfortably *and* to a point where if his bladder is too full for comfort it will cause an awakening rather than a flood.

Children mature at different rates and the rate at which they become dry at night is no exception. There are some who sleep and stay dry all night by their first birthday (even though they wet their diapers involuntarily, like any other baby, during the day). But there are equally normal children who are not reliably dry at night when they are five, even though they use the toilet, like any other child, all day.

Sometimes parents unwittingly turn normal but slow development of dryness into a bedwetting problem, by being too quick to label their child "enuretic." A rough idea of the age-stages at which most children become dry at night may help:

During the first year. Every human infant wets himself and his bed.

During the second year. Some girls and a few boys begin to stay dry during day-time naps and may have *occasional* dry nights.

During the third year. Dry nights become more frequent and parents begin to see that a "full" bladder sometimes awakens the child; she will call at 5 or 6 a.m. asking to go to the toilet.

As this year advances, many toddlers stay dry for *most* of the night but not for quite all of it. If you get your child up especially early in the morning, she is more likely to be dry than she is if the day starts at its later, normal time.

By the end of this year quite a lot of girls will have become reliably dry at night. Boys tend to be behind girls. They will probably have swapped from occasional dry nights to occasional wet ones by their third birthday.

During the fourth year. The majority of children will become reliably dry at night. There will be more boys than girls among those who still wet their beds frequently.

At around the fifth birthday. A child who still wets his bed may be just about to start staying dry or he may scarcely have started on the road towards dryness. It is important to work out which is the case for your child. If he is *becoming dry*, he will almost certainly get there on his own, and action from you may interrupt the process. If he is not already on his way, he could probably do with some help (*see below*).

Signs of progress towards dryness include even occasional dry nights; occasional awakenings and requests for the pot or toilet; and a bed which stays dry for at least some hours of each night.

The child who has scarcely started towards dryness will not only wet his bed every night, he will wet it (as you will be able to see from the state of his bedding) several times during each night. If you go to him two or three hours after he fell asleep, you will probably find that he is already wet.

Handling normal bedwetting   Every child should be given every chance to mature into night-time dryness at his own pace. Attempts to hurry the process once it has begun often backfire. Restricting the nearly dry four-year-old's evening drink, or waking him to pee at your bedtime, may serve only to focus his attention on the matter. If he realizes how much you care and becomes anxious about wetting, a problem may be created where none need have been. For the child who is *not* nearly dry, such measures are useless. What is the point of "lifting" a child at 11 p.m. when he was already wet at 9 p.m.?

Unfortunately, "leave the whole matter alone" is advice which is more easily given than taken. A child who is too big, or who feels himself too grown up, for night-time diapers and plastic pants does not just make a wet patch on his sheet, he makes a flood. Parents do not just have to "cope with the laundry," as some authorities say. They may have daily pajamas and sheets *and* soaking blankets, pillows and (when the plastic sheet wrinkles) a wet mattress too. Anything that will help you cope will help him:

Encase the mattress and pillow in waterproof material, either by sewing or by glueing it, like a large parcel. This will ensure that they do not get wet and smelly, or ruined for the future.

A washable duvet or continental quilt can be put straight into a washing machine without even removing the cover. This saves time both on unmaking and remaking the bed.

A tumble dryer means that one set of bedding will do because the whole lot can be washed, dried and ready between morning and evening.

If you simply cannot afford these aids, an alternative approach is to acquire as many sets of sheets and blankets as you can— perhaps searching rummage sales—and let the wet ones accumulate for several days in a plastic sack for a weekly wash in the large machine at the local launderette.

While coping as matter-of-factly as you can with the practicalities of wet beds it is also important to remember that:

Your child cannot help wetting. He urinates in his sleep and, by definition, what we do in sleep is outside our conscious control. Although you will sometimes make it obvious that you are fed up with the washing, you have to try to make it clear that you are not fed up with him.

He will not like waking up wet. A soaking bed is both cold and uncomfortable and, eventually, shaming, too. Far from needing scolding, he needs your casual sympathy and, above all, your confidence that one day soon he will stay dry.

He will smell if he is not washed and, as he gets older, outsiders will notice and other children will tease him. If he can have a daily bath or shower he should have it in the morning as long as the bedwetting continues. If that is impossible a thorough morning wash is vital.

His room will smell if urine-soaked items are left to dry there. The wrinkled noses of visiting friends or brothers and sisters can quickly make him feel an outcast.

If you can stay calm, your child may stay calm, too. If neither of you is anxious about his wetting, he may grow out of it without ever thinking of himself (or being thought of) as a "bedwetter." About ten percent of all little boys—everywhere in the world where studies have been done—wet their beds frequently between the ages of five and seven. The numbers drop by half during the next couple of years.

If you cannot stay calm and/or your child is beginning to worry about his wet beds, trying to conceal his bedding, refusing to stay overnight with friends and generally feeling himself at a social disadvantage, you would probably be wise to seek help (*see below*).

There are two kinds of enuresis:

What enuresis is and why it happens

Primary enuresis simply means that a child has never developed night-time dryness. The word could be used of any two-year-old but it is usually reserved for children who could be expected to have become dry. You may despair when your child is four (perhaps because he shows absolutely no signs of progress) or when he is five (perhaps because he is worrying). Some doctors refuse to use the term for anyone under about seven.

Secondary enuresis is different. The term means that a child who *has been* reliably dry, for months or even years, has started to wet his bed. This is occasionally the result of physical illness, often the result of anxiety and stress. Since secondary enuresis is very upsetting for the child, as well as his parents, advice should usually be sought immediately (*see below*).

The causes of primary enuresis are seldom direct and clear-cut. Most of the popular explanations contain a little truth, a little nonsense and a big question mark:

Enuresis "runs in families" but not, as far as we know, as a matter of direct inheritance. There seem to be two familial factors. Parents who were themselves late in becoming dry may have children who also reach this stage late. But if stress does not introduce emotional problems, such a child will still become dry spontaneously. He has not inherited enuresis but developmental delay in becoming dry. Parents who were enuretic may also unwittingly toilet train their children as they were trained, or otherwise subject the next generation to the same stresses they experienced. The child is not suffering from his genes but from a repeating pattern of child care.

Enuresis is caused by emotional/psychiatric problems. Certainly wet beds are often associated with emotional stress, but the cause-and-effect relationship is usually direct only in secondary enuresis where the child suddenly *starts* to wet after months or years of being reliably dry every night. In that situation advice should certainly be sought immediately unless the cause of the stress (such as a new baby/caretaker/school) is obvious and the parents can see how to soften it.

In other enuretic children it is thought that emotional stress *at the time when dryness should have been expected to develop* may prevent it from emerging. The child who was acutely ill, or separated from his parents, or otherwise traumatized at two or three, may fail to become dry during the subsequent year or two. But when he reaches a clinic at five or six, it is not current emotional stress which is causing his problems but the interruption to development caused much earlier, plus the stress of still being wet. Many of the enuretic children who show signs of emotional disturbance are disturbed by the effects of their wetting rather than wet because they are disturbed.

It remains true that for any group of children studied after referral to a clinic dealing with enuresis, a higher than expected number will be found to come from unhappy or disturbed family backgrounds. While it is too easy to say "he wets his bed because his Dad left," either failing to become dry *or* starting to wet may be part of a complex of reactions to anxiety-provoking situations. Where this is the case, parents will usually be able to see other signs of anxiety as well as the enuresis. They will be dealing with an unhappy and worried child whose unhappiness will be increased by the wetting, but whose wetting will seldom cease immediately even if circumstances can be improved.

Enuresis is often caused by "kidney trouble." While it is true that urinary infections are about five times more frequent in enuretic than in dry children, it does not seem likely that the infection often causes the wetting; curing the infection seldom ends the enuresis. Some doctors believe that the cause-and-effect relationship is the other way around: enuretic children being more liable to urinary infection, perhaps because instead of voiding into a receptacle they flood their beds and then lie with the urine pooled both around them and in the urethra. There are, however, certain medical conditions which do directly cause enuresis. Sickle-cell anemia and diabetes mellitus, for example, are two quite different conditions each of which causes an excessive output of unconcentrated urine and thus leads directly to wet beds. Certain congenital abnormalities, such as the invisible form of spina bifida (spina bifida occulta) make continence impossible, while some rare neurological problems cause enuresis only when the child begins a growth spurt. He may therefore become dry at night as a small child but develop what looks like secondary enuresis later on.

Enuretic children sleep more deeply than others. Although many parents believe this, there is no evidence to prove it nor has it been possible to distinguish between enuretic and dry children on the basis of their sleep rhythms and patterns (*see* **Sleep**).

Enuretic children have an unusually small bladder capacity. The question at issue here is not the actual *capacity* of the bladder but the volume of urine in the bladder which makes it necessary for the child to urinate. Research has shown that some enuretic children do feel the urge after drinking less than other children. Most authorities believe that this reflects only the general anxiety about bladder-emptying which most bedwetters come to feel. Certainly restricting fluids does not help.

Seeking help for a child who still wets his bed

Bedwetting becomes a serious problem as soon as you or your child feel that it is a real problem. When that will be depends not only on how calm you can be about his slow development, but also on whether there are *any* signs of progress and whether there are any other signs that suggest unhappiness or insecurity. A child who wets his bed every night *and* is having a lot of nightmares, is reluctant to separate from you and hates school, is rather unlikely to become dry spontaneously until life is easier for him. Similarly, the child who has just started to wet his bed, after a year of reliable dryness, may not only be upset about something in his waking life but also be exceedingly upset about his wetness.

As a rough and ready rule of thumb, then:

Don't hurry if your child is under five and you are both calm about his wet beds.

Seek help as early as four if bedwetting is new or part of general unhappiness.

Seek help by the time he is five even if he is neither worried by his wetness nor apparently anxious about anything else. If his wet beds are not worrying him yet, they soon will because he will become increasingly aware that "most children my age don't. . . ."

Delay after five only if you can see that dryness is around the corner. If his fifth birthday is coming up but the wet beds are getting rarer, you can afford to wait and see unless you are at the end of your tether or he is actually asking for help.

What kind of help and from whom? Many health professionals, including family doctors, pediatricians, community nurses, psychologists and psychiatrists, work successfully to help enuretic children and their families. The particular professional background of the person you choose to consult probably does not matter as much as his interest in enuresis. Those who are genuinely interested report high success rates for a variety of treatment approaches; those who are less personally involved report far less satisfactory results. Start, then, with whoever is most easily accessible to you—probably the child's own doctor—but do not allow yourself to be fobbed off with a "Don't worry, he'll grow out of it." If you were not already worried you would not be there; furthermore, enuresis and worry go together and nobody can stop worrying on command. Most large children's hospitals, and many other hospitals, too, have enuresis clinics; in these you will certainly find professionals who are making a study of bedwetting and its problems.

Your doctor, or other professional, will probably want to explore with you all the "causes" for enuresis outlined above. He will want to exclude physical problems, for example, and to get the fullest possible picture of any difficulties at home or at school which may be contributing. If he feels that the child's bedwetting is only part of a complex pattern of distress, he may want to refer you to a psychiatrist for advice and help. If, on the other hand, he is reasonably sure that any emotional distress is secondary to the bedwetting, he may see whether he can help the child to become dry at night by counselling you and supporting and motivating him. Even where parents have truly tried to avoid scolding or punishing a child for wetting his bed and believe that the child scarcely worries about it, there is often a vicious circle of shame and anguish which can be broken by an outsider whom the child believes in because he is "the doctor."

Everyone has his own way of working in this situation but he may, for example, go over your behavior with you in detail and point out subtle ways in which your concern, even anger, is being conveyed to the child. Perhaps you do not scold for wet beds, but do you greet a dry one with remarks like, "There you are you see; you can do it if you try!"? Perhaps you do not punish directly, but does the child get nice new pajamas when he needs them or must he wear outgrown and washed-out ones because "it's not worth buying new"? Perhaps you do not mean to shame him, but do you check up on his washing with a good sniff when he comes down to breakfast? The professional will explain to the child, as a matter of medical fact, that his wet beds are not his fault; that many children take a long time to get dry but that *he will do so*. He may offer the child a chart on which he himself is to stick a star or draw a picture whenever he wakes in a dry bed so as to make a record to show next time he visits. Above all, he will offer the child a firm series of appointments—perhaps as often as every two weeks—and make it clear that he will not stop seeing him regularly until the problem is over.

With a child of, say, seven or older, who is desperate to get dry as soon as possible, or with a child who has not improved after some months of this kind of support, more direct treatment may be suggested.

Drugs for bedwetting Some doctors use certain anti-depressant drugs in the treatment of enuresis. Imipramine ("Tofranil"), for example, is both an anti-depressant and a smooth-muscle relaxant and it has proved helpful to some children in some reported series. It is, however, potentially highly toxic. Many doctors prefer not to prescribe it for children and regard it as a dangerous drug to have in a house where there are children, as it has been responsible for many cases of accidental poisoning.

Enuresis alarms The buzzer alarm is a method by which some children can train themselves to wake up when they need to urinate rather than staying asleep and wetting their beds.

Success rates as high as eighty percent have been reported over periods of use ranging from a few weeks to about six months. One relapse is common but is usually quickly dealt with by a short period of further use and thereafter there is normally no further wetting. Some professionals report much lower success rates, but studies comparing the subjects and methods of successful and less successful use suggest that the following points may all be important:

The knowledge, enthusiasm and supportive follow-up of the professional. People who are really interested in enuresis, who use the buzzer carefully as an adjunct to counselling and support and who see patients using the buzzer at frequent intervals, are commonly successful with it. Those who use the buzzer instead of personal attention are not.

The understanding and enthusiasm of both parent and child. Where the operating mechanism is not fully understood, home conditions make its installation difficult and/or no adult is prepared to take the considerable trouble required in the early stages, success is unlikely. Where the child fears or resents the buzzer success is impossible.

The (comparative) freedom of the child from associated difficulties. Where enuresis is part of a widespread distress syndrome, the demands made by the buzzer may actually cause stress rather than helping to relieve it. Left to himself, the older child will abandon it as "useless." If it is forced on a younger child by a parent who was intended to "help" him manage it, the buzzer simply becomes part of the pressures which he is already experiencing as intolerable. His "failure" to become dry, even with the buzzer, then tends to fuel parental resentment.

A loud enough and/or correctly placed buzzer. The workings of the system are briefly explained below. The commonest cause of failure is due to the actual sound failing to awaken the child and/or parent. An amplifier and/or extension into the parent's room is often required.

How enuresis alarms work. Although several different models are available and you should be given a careful explanation, demonstration and practice session before you take one home, the principles of all are similar. They are given here for use either as a reminder or for those who do not, in fact, receive proper tuition.

The system consists of two mats which, when moisture closes the circuit between them, cause an alarm buzzer to sound.

The child's bed is made up with a waterproof sheet directly over the mattress, one buzzer mat on top of it, a flannelette drawsheet on top of the first buzzer mat and the second buzzer mat on top of the flannelette sheet. On top of that the child can have his ordinary cotton sheet so that the bed looks and feels normal, but it is best if he sleeps without pajama trousers.

● It is important that the drawsheet separating the two mats should be flannelette rather than thin cotton. Cotton can become sufficiently dampened by sweat to cause "false alarms."

Wired to the mats is a lead which goes to a box containing the buzzer, an "on-off" switch and, sometimes, a volume control. This must be placed so that the child cannot reach to switch it off without getting out of bed and so that the buzzer unfailingly wakes him up.

The child sets the alarm before getting into bed. If and when he starts to urinate in his sleep, the first few drops close the circuit, set off the buzzer, wake him and stop the urination. As soon as he wakes he has to get out of bed and switch the alarm off to stop the noise. He then finishes urinating (in a pot in his room or in the toilet) and resets the alarm before getting back into bed.

● At five or six few children can manage all this alone. A parent must either sleep in his room with him or have an extension buzzer in her own room so that she, too, is awoken and can go and supervise the procedure, check that the alarm is reset and resettle the child.

When all goes well, the buzzer alarm acts instead of the body's own awakening response to a bladder which needs emptying. It wakes the child because he is urinating and, over many weeks, his body takes over the awakening itself so that he begins to wake up before urination has begun and the alarm has sounded. Interestingly, while the child may wake up and use the toilet or potty several times each night for a while, the awakenings gradually tail off until he is sleeping through the night as well as waking dry.

● Since the alarm cannot sound until some urine has been released, there may be a patch the size of a saucer at each awakening. Dry sheets must be put on each time both to prevent "false alarms" and because a dry bed in the morning is the biggest psychological boost the child can have.

Behavior problems see **Anxiety, Fears and Phobias; Depression; Hyperactive Children; Tantrums.** See also specific problem areas in **Adolescence; Discipline, Self-discipline and Learning How to Behave; Habits; Jealousy; School.**
Bereavement see **Death.** See also **Suicide.**
Bilingual families see **Language**/Bringing up bilingual babies.

Birthmarks

Many babies are marked at birth, either by instruments used during delivery or by the pressures and stresses of the birth process itself. Any such marks will vanish within a few days. Do ask the doctor who examines your newborn about any which you have noticed. He can almost certainly reassure you that they are temporary.

True birthmarks will not vanish so quickly; indeed some may not even be visible immediately after birth but show themselves later. The commonest types are described below, but do be sure that you check on their identity with the examining doctor.

"Stork's beak" mark
This is the commonest type of birthmark. It consists of flat red patches which may be on the eyelids and/or above the bridge of the nose or the nape of the neck. The name comes from the idea that these are the places which the stork would have gripped with his beak when delivering the baby to his mother.

The marks on the face almost always vanish completely in the first year although they may show up for a while longer when the baby cries. Marks on the nape of the neck sometimes remain for life but are almost always covered by the hair.

"Strawberry" mark
Is so called because it is a reddish area which is slightly raised and soft. A strawberry mark may not be visible at birth but may appear during the first few days of life.

A strawberry mark may start as small as a pinprick but it will get steadily larger during the first six to nine months. If the mark is on your baby's face it is difficult to ignore it and you may find yourself bitterly resenting it. But *it will go away*. Signs that it is beginning to vanish are pale areas in the middle which eventually spread together so that only a red rim remains. Then the rim vanishes and the skin is left with no sign that the mark ever existed.

● Unlike most birthmarks, the skin covering strawberry marks is somewhat fragile. A hard knock can cause blood to ooze and, although the bleeding can always be easily stopped with light pressure, that surface damage may leave a slight scar which will be visible after the birthmark has vanished. If your child has a strawberry mark in a particularly vulnerable place, you may like to consult your doctor about covering it for protection.

● The *very* rare strawberry mark which does not vanish of its own accord can be removed by plastic surgery. But, because the removal will leave a scar and the scar will grow, it is seldom recommended before the child is around seven (*see* **Hospital**/Surgery: Plastic surgery).

"Port wine stain"
This very rare type of birthmark consists of a dark red or purple mark which, while it is flat, may have a slightly knobbly surface.

An extensive port-wine stain on the face can be very disfiguring and unfortunately will not go away. Plastic surgery, although still sometimes attempted, is seldom satisfactory. Excellent covering creams are now available, however, and these are specially blended for each patient so that the skin tone is exactly matched. It is usually sensible to face the misfortune and have the cream prescribed from babyhood. A child who has always had it used will both accept it and learn to apply it for himself from an early age. By the time he is old enough for playgroup or school he may take it as much for granted as putting on his clothes.

Birthweight *see* **Growth**.
Black eye *see* **Accidents**/Bruises.
Bleeding *see* **Accidents**/Wounds and bleeding. *See also* **Adolescence**/Menstruation.
Blepharitis *see* **Eyes and Seeing; Eye Disorders and Blindness**.
Blisters *see* **Accidents**.
Blood donors *see* **Blood Groups**.

Blood Groups

Most human blood contains antigens in the red blood cells and antibodies in the plasma (*see* **Immune Response**). An individual cannot have corresponding antigens and antibodies in his blood because if he did they would interact: the red blood cells would clump together (agglutinate) and block his blood vessels instead of flowing through them. This is exactly what may happen if an individual is given a blood transfusion from an unsuitable donor. If the donated blood contains antigens to which he has antibodies it will not boost his circulation but may actually destroy it.

Modern surgery depends upon the ready availability of donated blood while transplant surgery depends on more and more accurate "typing" both of blood and tissue. Everyone should know his own blood group and understand what it means both in terms of what blood he can give and be given. Everyone who is able to give blood should do so while he has it to spare, against the day when his life depends on somebody else having done so.

The entire human race can be divided into four main blood groups (there are many, less vital, subdivisions) which are described in terms of the antigens contained in the red cells. These are referred to as ABO and the four possibilities are:

□ Blood group O in which there are no antigens (45 percent of the population).
□ Blood group A in which there are "A" antigens (40 percent of the population).
□ Blood group B in which there are "B" antigens (10 percent of the population).
□ Blood group AB which has both "A" and "B" antigens (5 percent of the population).

Once the blood group is known in terms of the antigens in the red cells, the presence or absence of particular antibodies in the plasma can be deduced:

□ Since "O" blood contains no antigens it may contain both "a" and "b" antibodies.

□ Since "A" blood contains "A" antigens it cannot have "a" antibodies but will have "b."

□ Since "B" blood contains "B" antigens it cannot have "b" antibodies but will have "a."

□ Since "AB" blood contains both "A" and "B" antigens it cannot contain any antibodies.

Who can give blood to, or receive it from, whom?

If a patient's blood plasma contains antibodies, he must not be given a transfusion of whole blood which contains a matching antigen in its red cells. Even a small transfusion will stimulate those antibodies to attack the "foreign" protein and cause the blood to agglutinate. Furthermore, since those antibodies are natural to him and continually being produced, there are always more available. The disastrous reaction will not be temporary.

The patient's own antigens are less important. Even if he is given blood which contains matching antibodies those transfused antibodies will not attack his red blood cells and cause agglutination. This is because the relatively small volume of transfused plasma does not contain enough antibodies to effectively attack the vast numbers of red cells in his circulation, and because those antibodies are not natural to him, no more will be produced. As the transfused blood becomes diluted by the patient's own, any slight and temporary reaction will die away. Basically, then, it does not matter what antibodies are given or received in a transfusion (which is why plasma rather than whole blood is often used), but it matters very much indeed what antigens are given or received.

Logically, then,

People with group "O" blood can give blood to anyone. They have no antigens which recipients' antibodies could attack and their antibodies, "a" and "b," will do no harm. Such people are known as "universal donors" and their blood is invaluable to the blood banks. But,

People with group "O" blood cannot receive blood from any but a group "O" donor. Their blood contains both "a" and "b" antibodies which will attack either "A" or "B" antigens so only blood containing no antigens at all is safe for them. This is yet another reason why plentiful supplies of "O" blood are essential to the blood banks. Contrariwise,

People with group "AB" blood can receive blood from anyone. Their blood contains no antibodies and therefore cannot react against donor blood whatever antigens it contains. Such people are known as *universal recipients* and although their blood group is rare there is no special need for it in the blood banks. But,

People with "AB" blood can give blood only to other "AB" individuals. Recipients of any other blood group will have antibodies which will react against either the "A" or the "B" antigens. This is yet another reason why "AB" blood is not especially useful to the blood banks: it is unusable for ninety-five percent of the population while the remaining five percent can be given any blood which happens to be available.

In between these extremes, people with group "A" blood can donate to people with "A" or "AB" blood since neither will contain "a" antibodies and can receive blood from people with "A" or "O" blood since neither will contain the "B" antigens their own "b" antibodies would attack.

People with group "B" blood can donate to people with "B" or "AB" blood since neither will contain "b" antibodies and can receive blood from people with "B" or "O" blood since neither will contain the "A" antigens their own "a" antibodies would attack. In emergency situations (such as war or local disaster) when supplies of "O" blood may run short, supplies of both these groups may be critical. With only ten percent of the population belonging to group "B" this group, above all, requires regular donors.

The rhesus factor

Whatever a person's ABO blood group, her blood will also either contain the rhesus factor (she is "rhesus positive") or have no rhesus factor (she is "rhesus negative"). If rhesus positive blood is transfused into a rhesus negative patient, her blood plasma will produce antibodies against it and, once again, the transfusion will result in disaster. There is considerable racial variation in the number of people whose blood lacks the rhesus factor. For example, about fifteen percent of British women are rhesus negative but only about one percent of African women.

Hemolytic disease of the newborn

If a woman with rhesus negative blood has a baby with a man whose blood is wholly rhesus positive, the baby's blood will be positive, too. If the father is half positive there is a fifty-fifty chance that the baby's blood will be positive.

If that baby's blood is rhesus positive there is a chance (no more than that) that during delivery heavy pressure on the placenta will squeeze some of those rhesus positive blood cells into the mother's circulation. If this happens her rhesus negative blood will be stimulated to produce antibodies against that "foreign" rhesus factor. The present baby, now safely out in the big world, is unaffected; the mother is unaffected, but her blood now contains rhesus antibodies. If she carries a subsequent fetus with rhesus positive blood, those antibodies, carried continually around the baby's circulation via the placenta, will attack his rhesus positive red cells. He may die in the womb or he may be born suffering from severe anemia and from the acute jaundice caused by the heavy load his liver has had to carry in breaking down his vanquished red cells.

• A mother can be stimulated to produce rhesus antibodies by an abortion or a miscarriage as well as by a first live birth. This is why even first-time pregnant women are tested early in pregnancy for the presence of antibodies.

Severe hemolytic disease of the newborn is now a rarity because, provided a woman receives modern ante-natal and post-natal care, the problem can be averted. As soon as a rhesus negative mother delivers a rhesus positive baby, her blood is tested for the presence of red cells from the child. If any are found, she is given an injection of rhesus antibodies prepared from the blood of another person. These antibodies destroy the "foreign" rhesus positive cells before their presence can stimulate her to produce her own antibodies. Because the injected antibodies are not her own, they quickly die out once their job is done. Because her own immune system has not been stimulated (*see* **Immune Response**) she is left as she was when the first baby was conceived: a rhesus negative woman whose blood contains no antibodies to the rhesus factor and will not therefore attack the blood of her next rhesus positive child.

If you have a
rhesus negative
child

It is important that he or she should come to understand information such as the above well before there is any likelihood of a partnership/pregnancy.

A rhesus negative girl, pregnant with her first child, must tell her doctor of any previous abortion/miscarriage so as to ensure that he will arrange for her blood to be tested for rhesus antibodies which may otherwise damage even a first baby. She must be brought up to accept that unless she happens to marry a rhesus negative man, her children must be delivered where there are sophisticated medical facilities. She cannot afford to have her babies delivered where blood testing and, if necessary, immediate injection of rhesus antibody (called anti-D Immunoglobin) is not available nor where expert care for an affected newborn might be lacking.

A rhesus negative boy should know that he is negative both because it makes him an invaluable blood donor and difficult recipient, and because it will eventually be information of importance to his partner.

Blood poisoning *see* **Accidents**/Wounds and infection. *See also* **Infection**/Types of infection: Localized infection which is spreading.
Blood tests *see* **Hospital**/Procedures.
Blood transfusions *see* **Hospital**/Procedures. *See also* **Blood Groups**.
Body odor *see* **Adolescence**/Problems with appearance and body image.
Boils *see* **Infection**/Types of infection: Localized infection.
Bottle-feeding *see* **Eating**/Types of foods for babies. *See also* **Infection**/Preventing infection.
Botulism *see* **Diarrhea, Gastroenteritis and Food Poisoning**.
Bowel movements *see* **Constipation; Diarrhea, Gastroenteritis and Food Poisoning; Soiling; Toilet Training**.
Breast-feeding *see* **Eating**/Types of foods for babies. *See also* **Allergy**/Gastrointestinal allergies.
Breath-holding *see* **Convulsions, Seizures and "Fits."** *See also* **Tantrums**.
Bribery *see* **Discipline, Self-discipline and Learning How to Behave**/Some common disciplinary techniques.
Broken bones *see* **Accidents**/Fractures.
Bronchiolitis *see* **Chest Infections**.
Bronchitis *see* **Chest Infections**.
Bruises *see* **Accidents**.
Bullying *see* **School**/Problems over going to school. *See also* **Safety**/From "strangers"; **Suicide; Tantrums**/Triggers for tantrums.
Burns and scalds *see* **Accidents**. *See also* **Safety**/In the home.
Carbohydrates *see* **Eating**/Types of food.
Cheating *see* **Discipline, Self-discipline and Learning How to Behave**. *See also* **School**/Potential problems in school: Attitude to cheating.

Chest Infections

The upper respiratory tract includes the nose, throat and larynx (*see* **Colds; Coughs; Croup and Laryngitis**). The lower respiratory tract includes the bronchi, which are the main air passages leading down from throat to lungs, the bronchioles which are the small air passages networked through the lungs, and the alveoli which are the minute air sacs at the end of each bronchiole through whose walls oxygen passes into the bloodstream. Specific infections of these parts of the lower respiratory tract are known as bronchitis, bronchiolitis and pneumonia. They are here dealt with as a group, rather than as separate illnesses, because a parent will seldom be able to distinguish one from the other or even be certain when a child has a chest (lower respiratory) infection rather than an upper respiratory one.

Chest infections can be caused by a downward spread of cold viruses or bacteria from an infected throat. Many, however, are secondary infections following from one of the many illnesses which affect the respiratory tract. Measles, for example, is sometimes followed by pneumonia. It is not necessarily that the measles virus spreads to the lungs; it may be that the virus can do sufficient damage to make it easy for further micro-organisms to establish themselves. Children with chronic conditions affecting the respiratory system (*see* **Allergy**/Asthma, for example) may be unusually susceptible to chest infections.

Whatever specific infection you have to deal with in your child, do remember that:

There is no evidence that a "neglected cold" leads to pneumonia. Cold viruses will penetrate down into the chest if, and only if, the body fails to vanquish them at upper respiratory level. Keeping the child's feet dry has no bearing upon this matter.

Pneumonia is not the bogey illness which it was in the pre-antibiotic era. Your child may be sicker with bronchitis than with "a touch of pneumonia" and he may be sicker still with bronchiolitis, which sounds less alarming simply because few people have ever heard of it.

Bronchitis

Infection has caused inflammation and extra secretion of mucus in the bronchi which must carry air from the trachea to the lungs. The child who develops bronchitis was usually already suffering from a cold or other upper respiratory infection. The very first sign may therefore be that he begins to seem worse when you expected him to be getting better. Other signs of bronchitis include:

A "bubbly sounding" cough (perhaps replacing a dry one). If the child is old enough to cough up mucus rather than swallow it, it may be thick and yellowish-green. If he swallows the mucus he may now swallow so much that he vomits.

A rise in temperature. Bronchitis does not usually bring a very high fever, but is often heralded by some fever when the child's temperature had been normal with the preceding illness or with recovery from it.

Lack of appetite, lethargy and a general feeling of "being unwell." The child may not seem *very* ill but will seem sicker than before.

Wheezy breathing, even when he is not coughing, due to the mucus in the passages vibrating as he forces air in and out.

"Wheezy bronchitis" Is a term which, loosely used, causes much misunderstanding. Parents who hear a doctor use it of their child sometimes assume that the child has asthma and become unnecessarily alarmed.

Wheezy-sounding breathing is to be expected in a child with bronchitis, if he does not wheeze it is only because the secretions are not very copious and/or he has temporarily cleared them by coughing.

Recurrent wheezy bronchitis is a different problem. A baby who has several episodes, especially if his breathing sounds wheezy even during the periods between bouts of illness, needs careful assessment by a doctor. He may or may not have a tendency to be asthmatic, but the condition will not be diagnosed on the basis of wheeziness alone (*see* **Allergy**/Asthma).

Bronchiolitis

Infection has reached the bronchioles—the network of tiny air passages inside the lungs. In a severe case, the bronchioles swell and fill with mucus so that air which travels down the bronchi as the child breathes cannot get around the lung.

This potentially serious but unusual form of chest infection usually affects babies between about two and six months among whom it may occur in epidemics during the adult cold and flu season.

An affected baby will probably already have had signs of a "bad cold." Now he may wheeze, cough and fight for breath. He needs medical attention immediately.

If you should see a bluish color around his mouth or under his fingernails, you can be certain that not enough oxygen is reaching his bloodstream through those clogged bronchioles. Unless you can reach your doctor immediately, take the baby to the nearest hospital.

Pneumonia

Is an acute inflammation of the alveoli, which are the tiny air pockets at the ends of the bronchioles. Where bronchiolitis prevents oxygen from reaching the alveoli, pneumonia waterlogs them with inflammatory exudate so that even though oxygen reaches them, it cannot be passed through their delicate walls into the bloodstream.

Pneumonia can be caused by a variety of infecting microorganisms, but it can also be caused mechanically, by inhalation of irritant substances or semi-solids such as vomit.

The severity of pneumonia depends not only on the cause but also on the proportion of the lung which is affected. If both lungs are affected over a wide area ("double pneumonia") the child's breathing will obviously be worse than if the pneumonia affects only a small patch of one lung.

Curiously enough, a child may seem more dramatically ill with the "lobar" or "segmental" pneumonia which only affects one lung, than with broncho-pneumonia affecting both lungs. For example:

Lobar pneumonia usually starts suddenly, with high fever. The child seemed well this morning; tonight he seems extremely ill.

Broncho-pneumonia usually starts gradually as a worsening of existing illness. It may bring no fever.

● If you ever even *wonder* whether your child may be developing pneumonia, do not let absence of fever calm your fears. This is one instance where, while fever does mean illness, absence of fever does not mean lack of it (*see* **Nursing**/Fever).

Diagnosis of pneumonia

In a "classic case" of either kind of pneumonia your doctor may be able to diagnose it from the end of the child's bed from:

Extremely rapid breathing, far faster than one would expect from the height of the child's fever if he has one.

A grunting sound accompanying the breathing, quite different from the wheezing of bronchitis or bronchial asthma, or from the "barking" sound of the child with croup.

Flaring nostrils with each breath.

When he listens to and taps your child's chest, he may be able to identify affected patches in the lungs. He may arrange chest X-rays, either to confirm his diagnosis or to assess the extent of the pneumonia in deep areas of the lungs which are difficult to hear.

Treatment of pneumonia

The treatment given to your child will depend on his age, the type, severity and extent of the pneumonia, the certainty with which its cause can be stated and your doctor's preference. Some doctors prefer all children with pneumonia to be nursed in a hospital, largely because they believe that oxygen treatment is helpful to all, as well as necessary to many. Do not assume that your doctor's decision to have the child admitted necessarily means that he is dangerously ill. Ask.

Many doctors will give the child antibiotics in case the infection is bacterial or in case bacterial infection should overlay the viral one.

Some will take specimens of sputum before starting such treatment so that the original infecting organisms can be cultured and the treatment adapted if necessary. Young children usually swallow rather than cough up sputum. Some may therefore have to be washed from his stomach for this purpose.

If your child is to be nursed at home, the doctor will give specific advice and help with his symptoms. If vomiting is a marked feature for example, he will probably recommend frequent tiny drinks of a high calorie liquid. If chest pain is a marked feature he may give the child something to ease it. He will certainly teach you, or send a physiotherapist to teach you, the vital maneuvers which will help to clear his chest (*see below*).

Your doctor will certainly keep in close touch with you while you are nursing a child with pneumonia, but do remember that the diagnosis of pneumonia need not mean that your child is very ill. It is a technical name for a specific condition affecting the lung, but if only a small area is affected he may hardly seem ill at all and, with treatment, he may be completely recovered within the week.

Chest infections with pain

While a painful, aching chest is common whenever a child has a cough (*see* **Coughs**) acute pain *which occurs with deep breathing* usually means that the pleura (the lining of the chest wall and the lung) is inflamed so that as the lung expands with each breath, inflamed surfaces are rubbed. The more the lung is inflated, the more acute the pain. This kind of pain occurs quite commonly in pneumonia if the affected patches of lung tissue are close to the lung's surface. If the patches are deep within the structure of the lung there may be no chest pain. Chest pain in pneumonia does not, therefore, suggest that the illness is more serious; it merely gives a clue to the location of the affected parts.

Pleurisy

This is the name given to infection/inflammation of the pleura when there is no infection of the underlying lung tissue: no pneumonia. Pleurisy alone is unusual in young children. When it occurs in older children and adults it almost invariably arises from, or follows, a respiratory illness.

● The pain of pleurisy (or of involvement of the pleura in other chest infections) need not be felt in the chest, but may be sited at the side or under the ribs at the back. The pleura, after all, wraps the entire lung, not just the front surface.

Pleuritic pain can be difficult to distinguish from other causes of acute pain exacerbated by deep breathing (broken ribs, for example). Although any such pain should lead to medical consultation, whether or not the victim is obviously ill, pressure may give you a clue to distinguishing pleuritic from traumatic pain. A fractured rib, for example, is very painful if pressed; pleuritic pain is increased only by inflation of the lung.

Where pleuritic pain is associated with pneumonia, the natural tendency of the victim to breathe as shallowly as possible can delay recovery or be actually dangerous. Breathing exercises and effective coughing are an essential part of treatment (*see below* Physiotherapy). If you feel that pain is preventing your child from carrying out instructions or cooperating with you in this treatment, tell your doctor immediately. Pain relief may be important not only for humane but for therapeutic reasons.

In any form of pleurisy you should be aware that easing of the pain does not necessarily mean improvement in the condition. The affected pleura pours out fluid. This fluid lubricates the inflamed surfaces so that their rubbing together in breathing becomes much less painful. While this makes the situation more comfortable for the patient, the presence of fluid is pathological. The pain may be "cured" but, while there is still fluid collected there, the patient is not.

Physiotherapy in chest infections

Any chest infection involves the accumulation of secretions in the bronchi, bronchioles or alveoli. While antibiotics may clear infection they cannot remove secretions. To clear these out, the victim must cough them all the way back up the respiratory tract to the throat. At that level they can either be spat out or swallowed—the usual course in children.

"Postural drainage and percussion" is the technical term for tipping a child into a head-down position and thumping him. It is a mechanical means of clearing his chest when he cannot or will not cough effectively for himself. This maneuver is not only vital in established infections such as pneumonia but is also invaluable in preventing them from occurring, as with children liable to bronchial asthma. Many doctors who have overall charge of children with this kind of problem encourage parents to "tip and thump" as a regular routine. The value of the exercise cannot be overrated. Becoming skillful at doing it effectively and in a way to which a child does not object, is probably the major contribution a parent can make to his continued good health and/or his recovery.

● It would take a page of this book to describe how to do this; it will take your doctor or a physiotherapist two minutes to show you. Please ask.

● Swallowing his secretions, especially when your tipping and thumping gets a lot up all at one time, may well make your child vomit. While this is unpleasant for both of you, it is actually good for him. When he vomits, his stomach muscles compress his lungs and thus squeeze yet more mucus out.

Lung rupture and lung collapse

These extremely rare events are usually associated with chest infection although either can have a mechanical cause.

Lung rupture   If a part of the outer wall of the lung tears, air escapes and is then trapped in the space between the lung and the diaphragm and chest wall. This condition is called pneumothorax. A few individuals appear to have an inborn tendency to spontaneous rupture (spontaneous pneumothorax) and, of course, trauma can rupture a lung and lead to an air leak. Most often, though, the condition is associated with acute respiratory difficulties, such as partial or complete obstruction of the airways, as might occur in pneumonia or bronchial asthma.

As long as the rupture in the lung has not healed, a little more air will leak with every breath. Fortunately a little is also being absorbed continuously. A very small leak will, therefore, keep itself in balance while the "hole" closes. Such a leak will probably only be diagnosed by a doctor using a stethoscope.

A larger leak, leading to an increasing accumulation of air outside the lung, puts pressure on that lung and makes it increasingly difficult for it to keep on inflating. Left untreated, the lung might collapse; in an extreme case there might also be pressure on, even displacement of, the heart. Long before this, though, the patient would have extreme breathlessness and chest pain.

A large leak (or a small one in which the lung seems to be taking a long time to reseal itself) is often treated by inserting a tiny tube between the ribs and into the air pocket. The apparatus (which may be left in place for several days) gradually drains the air out.

Lung collapse   Technically called atelectasis, this situation arises if the alveoli of any part of a lung become completely emptied of air so that they collapse in upon themselves like minute balloons. The lungs are never normally deflated to this extent. Even when you breathe out as fully as possible, some air remains in each air sac.

Anything which totally obstructs some of the breathing passages and, therefore, deprives a particular group of alveoli of air for a prolonged period, can lead to collapse of that segment of the lung. Common infective causes of this rare situation include an infective plug of mucus in bronchial pneumonia or in acute asthma.

Chickenpox and Shingles (Herpes Zoster)

Chickenpox is a virus infection which attacks mainly children and young adults and in which the virus settles mainly in the skin.

Shingles is an infection by the same virus (which has probably been lying dormant in the body) affecting mainly the elderly. The virus attacks one or more sensory nerves and the skin which those nerves supply.

Individuals who are in contact with shingles may "catch" chickenpox. In theory the reverse is also true, although in practice it is rare for shingles to develop within a time period which suggests direct infection during contact with chickenpox.

An attack of chickenpox produces antibodies and lifelong immunity to that disease. The viruses, which can reemerge years later and give rise to shingles, are thought to travel during that attack of chickenpox through nerve endings in the skin, eventually coming to rest in the cell bodies of sensory nerves lying just outside the central nervous system. Here the viruses are protected from circulating antibodies and it is thought that they are therefore able to lie dormant until, years later when those antibody levels are waning, they begin to multiply and spread back down the nerve fibers to infect the skin.

Chickenpox

This is a highly infectious disease. It varies widely in the severity of its effects.

Incubation period. About twelve to sixteen days.

Route of infection. Droplet infection from nose and throat to nose and throat.

First symptoms of chickenpox   Older children and adults may feel generally unwell, with fever, headache or sore throat, for one or two days before the rash appears. Younger children (the most frequent victims) often produce the rash as the first symptom of infection.

Acute stage of chickenpox   The rash usually appears first on the chest, the abdomen and the inner thighs. During the next day or so the face, scalp and upper parts of the arms and legs are affected.

Each "spot" passes through several distinct phases so that as the rash develops there will be "spots" at different stages all present at the same time. Each flat, red patch thickens and becomes raised. It then accumulates fluid so that it becomes a tiny, delicate blister. Then the fluid within the blister thickens and becomes cloudy before drying out to form a scab. "Spots" tend to appear in batches over several days. As soon as new ones (flat red patches) stop appearing, the worst will be over.

A mild case of chickenpox

The child may be bothered only by the fact that the rash is furiously itchy. He may never feel ill at all. It is important to help him avoid scratching as the blisters are very liable to secondary infection with bacteria leading to impetigo or boils, for example. Any secondary infection will require treatment by a doctor. Scratching can also lead to scarring which, while it is usually temporary, may last for months or even years. Keeping his nails short will prevent some damage, while frequent warm baths with bicarbonate of soda added and/or calamine lotion freely available for him to dab on the most itchy places, may help his morale.

A severe case of chickenpox

Older people are usually more severely affected by chickenpox, but the viruses themselves vary in their virulence so that some families experience a far more severe form than others. In a severe case, the rash can cover almost every square inch not only of the external skin and the scalp but of mucous membranes and other hidden surfaces, too. The wretched patient may have lesions in his ears and nostrils, mouth and throat and so closely around his eyes that they are swollen and inflamed. He may have such a close-packed rash on his body that, as the vesicles burst, he feels raw all over. With such a severe rash there may also be high fever, as well as the specific discomforts (sore throat, sore mouth, earache, etc.) which go with the awkard placing of sores and scabs.

There is no specific treatment for chickenpox, however severe, but a doctor should certainly be called for a patient suffering in this way. A check must be kept on infection in the eyes and ears as well as for superficial infection of external skin.

Possible complications of chickenpox

Very occasionally chickenpox virus invades the lungs to produce a viral pneumonia (*see* **Chest Infections**) or the central nervous system to produce a viral encephalitis (*see* **Meningitis and Encephalitis**). Both complications can occur up to ten days after the first appearance of the rash. If a child who had seemed virtually recovered from chickenpox suddenly seems to have a respiratory infection or to become drowsy with a severe headache, seek medical help and do not forget to tell the doctor, should it be a different one, about the recent attack of chickenpox.

● Although a child with chickenpox continues to be infectious as long as new "spots" are appearing, he may be regarded as non-infectious as soon as the last crop has scabbed. There is no truth in the idea that the scabs themselves carry the infection.

Shingles (herpes zoster)

First symptoms of shingles

Sometimes the patient has a headache and fever for a few days prior to the appearance of diagnostic signs. Often the first diagnostic sign, in adolescents and older people, is acute pain in the area of the skin which is supplied by the affected nerve. In over fifty percent of cases this will be a patch of skin on the chest or abdomen, but in a few cases the nerve affected serves the face or head in which case the eyes may be involved. Sometimes the damage to the nerve produces loss of sensation rather than pain, but this pain, called "post-herpetic neuralgia," is the most usual and most troublesome symptom. While there is only pain, shingles is difficult to diagnose and some unfortunate patients find themselves dismissed as "making a fuss about nothing" when in fact they are in very real and severe discomfort. The appearance of the rash does not signal the end of the pain, but it does produce an immediate and sympathetic diagnosis.

The rash of shingles Shingles produces a rash exactly like that of chickenpox (*see above*) except that "spots" appear only along the course of the nerve affected by the viruses. The patient may, therefore, have a girdle of vesicles or a single patch or a stripe running up the chest.

Treatment of shingles There is no specific treatment for shingles although many local applications are tried and anything which the patient believes to be helpful may be so. A doctor should certainly be involved in pain control. The rash and the pain commonly clear within two to three weeks although pain outlasts the rash in some cases (*see* **Pain and Pain Control**).

Choking *see* **Accidents.** *See also* **Safety**/In the home.

Circumcision *see also* **Hospital**/Surgery

Surgical removal of the foreskin: the loose fold of skin covering the tip (glans) of a boy's penis.

Circumcision used to be an almost routine matter, taken for granted by a majority of Western parents and doctors. Now fashion and opinion have changed, especially in Britain and Western Europe. The procedure remains a necessary part of the ritual of certain religious groups, but most doctors will not carry it out "routinely" as it is very seldom medically necessary and does carry some small risk of infection and/or bleeding as well as some inevitable discomfort to even the youngest baby.

Some parents, especially in the United States, still prefer to have baby boys circumcised at birth. If you are undecided, you may wish to discuss some of the following points with the doctor who looks after mother and child during the birth.

Will an uncircumcised boy feel "different"? In most communities the up-to-date answer is "no" because those showers and locker rooms will contain both circumcised and uncircumcised penises. But there may still be pressing social reasons for infant circumcision in some families. If, for example, one of you is from a Jewish family, it is possible that even if you have no feeling one way or another about circumcision, older generations of the family will feel very differently. It would be sad if a grandmother found that your son's foreskin created a barrier between her and the baby.

Do the sexual partners of uncircumcised males have an increased risk of cervical cancer? Probably not. This belief was based on research showing very low rates of cervical cancer among Jewish women, partners, of course, of circumcised males. But these low rates now seem more likely to be due to racial differences in susceptibility to this form of cancer, rather than to the presence or absence of foreskins.

Does circumcision improve sexual performance by reducing penis sensitivity? Who knows? If the answer is "yes" it is perhaps surprising that couples seldom choose to use condoms to achieve the same effect.

Is circumcision an aid to hygiene? Yes, in a sense. A male whose foreskin is intact will have to wash beneath it to remove the white secretion (smegma) which can otherwise collect there. But in the same sense mouths would be more hygienic if we removed all our teeth so that no plaque could collect between them.

Is it not worth having a newborn boy circumcised in case the operation becomes necessary later on? Later circumcision is *very* rarely necessary unless too-early attempts are made to retract a foreskin which is not ready (*see below*). Although later circumcision can be very upsetting for the boy (*see* **Hospital**/Surgery), this does not seem a valid reason for doing it sooner. After all, we do not remove appendixes in infancy in case of later appendicitis.

If a baby is to be circumcised, when and how should it be done? Circumcision for religious reasons will be performed at specified times and perhaps by specified rituals. Jewish boys, for example, are circumcised on the eighth day after birth while Muslim boys are not circumcised until somewhere between their third and fifteenth years.

If there are no religious considerations, the operation is probably best carried out while the newborn baby is still under hospital care, provided that the doctor considers that his condition warrants it. In Britain, most doctors feel that a general anesthetic should be used. Being newborn does not prevent the procedure from being painful. In the United States, however, anesthesia is rarely used.

Care of an uncircumcised penis

Your baby's uncircumcised penis requires neither more, less nor different care from any other part of his body or from his sister's vulva. The foreskin and the glans of the penis are fused together at birth and they usually remain fused together for months and often for several years. The foreskin cannot therefore be retracted, pulled back or washed underneath and about the only mistake a parent can make with this organ is to try. So the penis gets washed with its owner and should otherwise be left strictly alone (except by its owner!). Eventually, perhaps when he is two but perhaps not until later, that foreskin will separate from the glans. You will probably first realize that this is happening when you see your son with an erection and notice that the foreskin has retracted itself. When, and only when, it can retract of its own accord, is it sensible to begin retracting it so as to remove any secretions from underneath, during bathing. Even then this kind of washing is not *necessary*. If your son objects, leave it or, better still, show him how to do it himself.

• If leaving your son uncircumcised is a big decision for you, do be sure that it is one you have made wholeheartedly. If a bit of you is still worried about that bit of him and you fiddle about trying to pull back a foreskin which is still fused to the penis, you are likely to make minute tears in it. If that happens scar tissue may form which fuses the foreskin to the glans so that it actually cannot retract when it is ready to do so. This is one of the commonest reasons for later circumcision becoming medically necessary (*see* **Hospital**/Surgery).

Care of a circumcised penis

A gauze dressing will be applied to the raw tip of the penis and the hospital staff will advise you on the care of the wound. There may be a few drops of blood in the hours after the operation, but any continuing bleeding should be reported to the doctor. The penis will be inflamed, but any extra swelling, heat or other signs of infection should similarly be reported. Usually, though, the little wound will heal without problems.

• Whatever his age, your baby son will be sore, especially if urine touches the raw area and stings, or when clothing rubs it as he is lifted or carried.

Meatal ulcers Lacking the protection of a foreskin, the sensitive tip of the penis sometimes gets chafed and irritated by diapers and urine. Occasionally a tiny ulcer develops on the edge of the glans and in the top of the urethra. Meatal ulcers cause acute pain whenever the baby passes urine and are stubbornly slow to heal because the urine destroys the forming scab. If your baby screams with pain when he urinates and you can see a tiny sore there, take him immediately to the doctor. He will probably prescribe an ointment to be applied on a tiny glass rod into the top of the urethra. This protects the ulcer from the urine and thus reduces pain and promotes healing.

• Don't neglect this kind of ulcer even if you are away from home and it is difficult to find a doctor. If it is neglected for several days it is just possible that scar tissue will begin to form, narrow the urethral opening and restrict the flow of urine. Immediate treatment will prevent this.

Cleft lip and cleft palate *see* **Hospital**/Surgery.

Colds

Colds cause more misery and loss of time from school or work than any other viral illness, yet no immunization is available. Why? The main reason is that while "a cold" may be all too recognizable to the sufferer, its causative virus may be one of many kinds. The group of viruses which are most commonly responsible are those called rhinoviruses; more than one hundred of these have already been identified and there are certainly more to be discovered. Even if it were possible to discover all the possible cold viruses, and to make a vaccine which included every single one, we still should not have really effective and worthwhile protection because although each virus does provoke specific antibodies, these do not seem to last very long. It may never be both practical and worthwhile to produce such a complex multi-vaccine and administer it, perhaps as often as every few months, to everyone.

Colds, therefore, have to be lived with. Your doctor can neither prevent nor cure them, so unless you are really worried about your child, there is little point in bothering him each time he has one. You only need medical advice and help if the cold does not follow its normal, expected and uncomfortable course. Like all virus infections, colds make the affected parts of the body (the upper respiratory system) especially liable to invasion by bacteria. If your child's cold leads to a "secondary infection" (*see below*) then it is worth seeking medical advice. Then, and *only* then, may the doctor want to consider giving an antibiotic.

Because the common cold is so common, old wives' tales concerning causes and cures are legion. Don't believe everything you hear and do bear in mind that the very existence of so many "cold cures" is in itself proof that no effective cure is really known. If you buy a particular medicine over the counter at your drugstore because it makes you feel that you are doing something for the victim, do make sure that you know *what* you are buying.

Symptoms of an ordinary cold
A cold is a virus infection of the nasal passages. First symptoms therefore are a "runny" nose which may also feel "stuffy" because the membranes are slightly swollen. The child sneezes because the discharge irritates the passages. He may cough as discharge runs down his throat and tickles.

Normal variants
Depending on the virulence of the virus and on the tissues which it infects, he may also have slightly red and watery eyes, a sore throat and hoarseness (laryngitis).

Degree of "illness"
The symptoms in themselves are enough to make anyone feel miserable, but, in small children in particular, there may also be slight fever, loss of appetite and lassitude. The victim does not exactly feel *ill* but he does not feel in top form either.

Course of an ordinary cold
Colds usually begin abruptly, developing, for example, from a sneeze at breakfast-time to a full-blown cold by evening. The acute phase usually lasts from three to four days. By the end of that time the body has mustered its defenses and stopped the viruses from multiplying further, but it may take several more days for the inflamed mucous membranes to get back to normal. A "runny" nose and an irritating cough (especially when the victim is lying down at night) may continue for a week to ten days.

● Unless you have reason to suspect a secondary infection (*see below*), you can assume that a child has stopped being infectious to others about four days after his cold began.

Babies with colds
Young babies can react quite severely to ordinary colds. In the first month of life an older child's "ordinary cold" may make your baby very ill indeed. If you suspect a cold and he seems unwell, don't judge his

condition by the reading on the thermometer. His temperature may be high, normal or unusually low. Whichever it is, he should be seen by his doctor. An older baby may run quite a high fever at the beginning of the infection and he may vomit and go off his feeds so that you need to watch out for dehydration (*see* **Diarrhea, Gastroenteritis and Food Poisoning** /Diarrhea in babies and toddlers).

Because a baby's breathing passages are very small, the excess mucus produced during the cold may bother him more than it bothers an older child. Above all, having a blocked-up nose (which he cannot yet blow) makes it difficult for him to suck. This may make him frantic at feeding times and at other times too, because he cannot suck his pacifier or fist or thumb when he is going to sleep. Because he has not yet acquired immunity to many of the pathogenic bacteria in his environment, a baby with a cold is rather more liable than an older child to get a secondary infection on top of it.

All in all, if your child catches his first cold in his earliest months, you would probably be sensible to consult his doctor. He will check that the illness *is* only a cold (or at least that it does not appear to be anything else) and he will check that there are no signs of secondary infection. He will also advise you on certain specific things which you can do to make the baby more comfortable. He may, for example, prescribe decongestant nose drops which you can use just before feedings (and perhaps just before you put the baby to sleep) so that he can suck more comfortably. Or he may show you how to use a nasal aspirator (a plastic dropper with a rubber suction bulb) to suck the secretions out of the baby's nose. He may advise you to put a pillow *under* the crib mattress so that the baby sleeps with his head raised a little to lessen coughing. Above all, he will tell you what signs to look out for so that you can call him immediately if the cold should begin to turn into anything more serious.

Different doctors prefer different kinds of treatment for very young babies with colds. Once you have discussed this first one with your doctor you will know how he would like you to proceed next time.

● Do not give any kind of "cold cure" to a baby without specific advice from a doctor.

● While you will not always succeed, it is worth trying to protect a young baby from colds. At least prevent cold-ridden older children from sneezing all over him or feeding him with virus-laden fingers.

Common sense about children with colds Your child will probably have around six to eight colds each year between his third and eighth birthdays. He will also have various infectious diseases, bouts of "flu" and the occasional gastric upset. If each of those colds has to be treated as an illness, he will be cooped up at home for several weeks of each year. Obviously when a particular cold *does* make him ill, he will have to be properly nursed through it, but when a cold makes him no more than uncomfortable and unattractive, you have to decide what your policy is going to be: are you going to keep him home (and stay home yourself) to protect other children from catching his cold or are you going to provide handfuls of tissues and brisk sympathy and help him get on with his normal life?

Colds are highly infectious especially to babies and very young children who have not yet built up any immunity to most of the common cold viruses. Your child will be infectious before he has full-blown symptoms, but it is the virus-laden mucus that he sprays around as he coughs and sneezes and smears around when he blows his nose or wipes it on the back of his hand, which will most readily pass on the cold. If you can teach him to keep his mucus to himself, his colds will be less of a menace.

Teach him to blow his nose by closing one nostril while blowing down the other. If he can acquire this genuinely difficult skill early, he will discover that it keeps him more comfortable than sniffing and wiping.

Make sure he uses paper tissues and throws them away at once. Washable handkerchiefs should be banned (except perhaps for top-pocket show) and used paper ones stuffed up sleeves or in pockets can carry viruses for some time and then clog up your washing machine.

Teach him to cover his nose and mouth and turn away from people or food when he coughs or sneezes.

Try (gently) to persuade him not to rub his face against people when he has a cold. You may even be able to teach him not to share lollipops and viruses with his friends.

Persuade him to wash his hands as often as possible. He cannot wash every time he blows his nose if he is blowing it every two minutes, but recent research does show that cold viruses are spread almost as rapidly by the hands (touching food, etc.) as by droplet infection.

If your child is not yet old enough for school and does not attend any kind of organized pre-school group, it will probably be fairly easy for you to keep him away from most other children when he has colds. Remember that small babies are usually the worst affected by these viruses, so take particular trouble to keep him away from health centers and so forth. If you share his care with a sitter, discuss colds with her in advance. She will probably agree that a cold is part of a child's normal life and be perfectly prepared to look after him as usual, provided he is not ill. But she may also be in charge of a small baby or of a child who, perhaps because of asthma, needs special protection.

As soon as your child attends an organized group—whether a day nursery, nursery school or playgroup—do discuss colds with the person in charge.

If you keep your child home with his colds but other mothers do not, he will miss more time than any of the other children while being fully exposed to all their viruses. That does not seem fair.

If you send your child with his colds but other mothers do not, you will be the one who is behaving unfairly.

Usually staff will have a clear view: either they will feel that colds just have to be accepted or they will feel that if children always stay away when they have colds, the infection rate within the group can be kept down. Whichever their point of view, if you abide by it you will be doing the best you can.

Schoolchildren and colds

You really do need the teachers' advice about when you should, or should not, keep your streaming child away. If they beg you not to send him, try not to even if it is difficult for you to take time off from work. At least you will know that other families are under the same pressure and that your child will not "lose out" by comparison with them or be labelled "delicate" because he is absent so much.

If they tell you that it is all right to send the child "unless he is unwell," do so. Your child's viruses will only be added to a general pool and you have nothing to feel guilty about.

If they do not seem to have a "cold policy," it would be sensible to raise the issue at a Parent-Teacher Association meeting.

Adolescents and colds

As your child grows up he will probably have a clear view of his own about whether or not he is fit for school on any particular occasion. Be thankful if he is somebody who always wants to go or at least always takes it for granted that he must. By this stage, colds do not spread so easily within the group because children have more immunity; those who do catch colds are seldom ill with them. It is simply not fair to expect your busy child to miss important lessons, sports events or after-school activities because of a mere cold.

If yours is one of the children who use every cold as an excuse for a day or two off from school he is probably not very happy there. Help him to face the fact that he is using his cold as an excuse. Using illness as an escape from unhappiness can become a habit and it is not a good one for later life. If he does not much enjoy school at the best of times, the misery of a cold may genuinely make it seem intolerable, so you need to tackle the unhappiness rather than just telling him off for ducking school.

When you really cannot decide whether or not your child is ill enough to need to stay at home, ask yourself whether you would stay home from work for a cold of the same degree.

Tips for making colds less uncomfortable

Although neither you nor anyone else can cure your child's cold, you can keep him comparatively comfortable while he lives through it.

Don't let room air become too dry. Centrally heated rooms, especially hermetically sealed and double-glazed ones, can be very dry indeed compared with rooms heated with gas or solid fuel fires, for example. Some moisture in the atmosphere reduces the swelling of the nasal membranes and therefore that "stuffy" feeling. Try to combine the warmth you want with some ventilation like an old-fashioned open window.

If hot, dry air is uncomfortable, it should not be surprising that colds often feel better when the victim is outside. Unless you live in a very extreme climate there is no reason why a cold sufferer should not go out.

If you have young children (and therefore years of colds and their disturbed nights ahead of you), consider buying a cold-air vaporizer. They are invaluable, not only in making children more comfortable when they have colds but in other upper respiratory infections too (*see* **Croup and Laryngitis**).

Encourage nose-blowing. Much of the coughing which goes on with an ordinary cold is due to mucus from the nose being sniffed up and trickling down the back of the throat. The child who gets rid of the mucus out of his nose will not cough so much. If he goes to bed with his nose clear he is much less likely to be woken (at least immediately) by coughing.

Many children resist blowing their noses when they have colds because the nostrils and upper lip become so sore. Vaseline, applied two or three times a day from the *beginning* of a cold, will protect the skin so that it never becomes sore.

Prop up the victim for sleeping. If mucus can trickle out of the nose there will be less disturbing coughing in the night. A child may like an extra pillow or two. Even a baby can have a pillow under the end of the mattress and be encouraged to sleep on his side rather than his back.

Use steam to "unclog" dried secretions. Children are often at their most miserable when they have just woken up and noses (and sometimes eyes) are blocked with mucus which has dried. For a child, a hot drink as soon as he wakes may make all the difference. The drink is pleasant and the steam, around his face and in his nose and mouth as he sips, "unblocks" him. A child too young to be trusted with a steamy drink can get the same benefit from a bath, from warm water play over the sink or just from having his face washed with a warm cloth.

Encourage quiet play if the child is "streaming." Although there is no *health* reason why a child should be kept quiet during an ordinary cold, there may be *comfort* reasons. If the cold is really streaming, violent physical exercise and rapid changes of temperature will provoke even more discharge. The child may be much more comfortable if he is encouraged to curl up with a book or watch television or play a quiet game with you.

Don't try to make the child stay any warmer than usual. Extra clothes and overheated rooms will make him more uncomfortable and do nothing to combat the virus.

Don't dose him with cold cures: there are no genuine ones. He needs no medicine at all (except possibly an aspirin for a headache and/or fever) unless he has a secondary infection in which case he should see the doctor.

Don't try to suppress his cough unless it is keeping the household awake to such an extent that you are getting desperate. In this case you should, again, see the doctor. Most cough medicines are ineffective. A medicine that did stop coughing would be a bad idea because it is coughing which prevents mucus (and therefore viruses) from penetrating further down the respiratory tract and perhaps reaching his lungs (*see* **Chest Infections**).

Don't rub his chest with liniments. They do no good and will only make him uncomfortable and/or convinced that he really is ill.

Don't push food on him if he is not hungry or withhold it from him if he is. The cold may, or may not, put him off his food for a day or two. It does not matter either way provided he has plenty to drink.

Colds and secondary infections
(*see also* **Chest Infections**)

Temporary damage done by cold viruses can provide an easy entry for bacteria to various parts of the upper respiratory tract and to the ears and sinuses. A bacterial secondary infection need not make the child very ill because his body's defensive system will get to work to combat it just as it worked to get rid of the original cold. Thick yellow or green nasal discharge, for example, is often the last you see of a cold. It does suggest bacterial infection but unless the child seems ill it requires no treatment. Suspect that the cold has progressed beyond a "simple head cold" if:

He gets worse instead of better. If he had no fever and did not feel ill for the first two or three days of the cold and now shoots a fever on day four, or if he started the cold with a fever but was better by day three and worse by day five, for example, you should be suspicious. A simple cold, however horrible, gets gradually better not gradually worse.

● A child whose cold symptoms seem to be getting worse and who seems to be becoming sicker and sicker may not have an infection which is secondary to that cold, but one of the infectious diseases of childhood which starts out by mimicking a cold. Measles often begins in this way (*see* **Measles**).

He has earache, especially with fever. If he has earache at all he should see a doctor the same day. Earache with fever should be treated as an emergency; ask for the next available appointment (*see* **Ears and Hearing; Ear Disorders and Deafness**/Ear disorders).

He has a bad headache, especially with fever. This may suggest sinusitis (*see below*).

His throat is suddenly sore, especially with fever. Any form of "tonsillitis" (*see* **Tonsils**) can follow a cold. In a very young child you may have to respond to fever and general signs of illness as he may not complain that his throat is painful.

● You cannot rely on swollen glands in the child's neck as a clue to an infected throat or a worsening cold. Glands swell when the body's lymph system is involved in fighting infection (*see* **Immune Response**). In childhood some swelling may remain from illness to illness.

His cough gets worse and/or his breathing seems affected. All the common upper and lower respiratory infections (*see* **Coughs; Croup and Laryngitis; Chest Infections**) can follow an ordinary cold, although unless he is feverish and ill the chances are that the cough which sounds "chesty" is not actually due to infection lower down than the throat.

● If you have any reason to think that your child has a secondary infection after a cold, by all means check with a doctor, but don't decide to be clever and give the child a few doses of the antibiotic you have left over from last time. You should not *have* any left over as the full course should have been given last time. But even if you have, only a doctor should decide whether an antibiotic is appropriate now and if so, which one. If it is, he will want the child to have a *full* course not just the remains of a bottle (*see* **Infection**/Types of: Infections which cause illness; Treatment of: Pros and cons of antibiotics).

Sinuses and sinusitis

The sinuses are air-filled, mucous membrane–lined spaces in the facial bones which all connect with the nasal passages.

When a child has a cold, his sinuses are almost certain to be affected; they produce extra mucus to add to the cold's general "runniness" and that mucus may drip to the back of his throat when he is lying down and produce a tickly cough. Usually the sinuses return to normal after the cold is over, but occasionally they become secondarily infected with bacteria to produce sinusitis which can be a quite severe and very unpleasant illness.

Just as the spaces between the bones of a baby's skull (the fontanelles) are slow to close up so that the whole skull is fused together, so the sinuses are slow to develop and enlarge to a point where their infection is possible. Since a child cannot have sinusitis in a sinus which he has not yet developed, the timetable is worthy of note:

Under two years: ethmoids only. The ethmoid sinuses are those to either side of the bridge of the nose and they are the only ones large enough for infection up to this age.

Acute ethmoiditis, or "infant sinusitis," is rare but requires immediate medical treatment, as without it infection can spread to the eyes or even to the brain. Suspect it if your baby or toddler, having had a cold or other upper respiratory infection, develops pain and swelling around the eyes together with fever.

By three or four: maxillary sinuses also. The maxillary sinuses are in the cheekbones.

Maxillary sinusitis can be caused not only by infection from the nasal passageways but also by infection from the root of a badly decayed tooth, so suspect it if fever and facial pain follows either a cold or an episode of acute toothache which was not treated (*see* **Teeth**/Some dental emergencies).

By ten: frontal sinuses as well. The frontal sinuses are in the forehead, just above each eyebrow. They are a common site of sinusitis but the illness is seldom serious.

Frontal sinusitis often presents itself as a headache, but unlike an "ordinary headache" (*see* **Headaches**) there is tenderness when the area is pressed. There may or may not be fever and/or swelling above the eyes.

Treatment of sinusitis after infancy

Acute sinusitis requires medical attention. Your doctor will probably give the child antibiotics to control the infection but the illness may hang on for many days. Antibiotics are slow to penetrate the sinuses. Even once it is "sterile," the thick matter can take a long time to reach the nasal passageways from which the child can get rid of it.

Sometimes, even once the acute infection is over, the pus-filled sinus fails to drain and the child continues to have uncomfortable pressure pain, especially when he bends down. Occasionally such a child may be referred to an ear, nose and throat specialist for further treatment. Some recommend a minor operation to drain and wash out the sinus, but others prefer a more conservative approach. Certainly a person who is prone to sinusitis may find that drained sinuses "refill" with the very next cold.

Cold Sores

These are caused by herpes simplex; a widespread virus which is carried by many people but produces symptoms in only a few. It is almost impossible to eradicate, so the child who has one crop of cold sores is likely to have others. However, the virus can lie dormant for years so that the child who is plagued by cold sores every few weeks for a year or two may then be free of them for the rest of her childhood.

Very occasionally, this same virus causes generalized illness, including infection of the penis and cervix. A mother whose genital tract is thus infected may have to have her baby delivered by Caesarean section to avoid the risk of her baby being infected during birth.

A typical first attack by herpes simplex

Does not take the form of cold sores but of mouth ulcers. The child—who is seldom below school age—has one or more shallow yellow ulcers on the inside of the lips or cheeks. They are surrounded by inflamed mucous membrane and are so acutely painful that she may be unable to eat or drink comfortably for several days. Fortunately, the ulcers soon clear up of their own accord. Few doctors consider that any local applications really hasten the healing although a little Vaseline applied to the area may reduce the painful friction between ulcer and teeth (*see also* **Mouth Ulcers**).

Second and later attacks by herpes simplex

Do not cause mouth ulcers but instead produce a collection of tiny itchy blisters close to the mouth which burst and become yellow and crusty. The itching quickly subsides but the sores are unsightly and may take a week or more to disappear.

Nobody knows why cold sores appear in some people and not in others, nor why they appear when they do. Most seem to appear spontaneously. A few seem to be a reaction to stress and fatigue. Some follow minor illnesses (like colds; this is how they acquired their misleading name), while some girls develop them before menstrual periods.

● Consult your doctor about a first crop of cold sores: there are local applications which speed healing. Do not use cortisone ointments (*see* **Infection**/Treatment of external infection and inflammation). Any cold sore which is not obviously clearing up within a few days should be seen again by a doctor, as secondary infection (*see*, for example, **Impetigo and Staphylococcal Infections**) is a possibility.

Constipation

Contrary to popular belief, constipation has very little to do with the frequency with which stools are passed but a great deal to do with the consistency (and therefore the ease of passing) of those stools. A very hard, dry stool, which is difficult or even painful to pass, is a constipated one even if it is the second in forty-eight hours. A soft stool which is easy to pass is not a constipated one even if it is the first in seventy-two hours.

In the past, people were convinced that a normally working bowel should "empty" every day and that if it did not, the owner would have all kinds of troubles such as headaches and bad breath. These nonsensical beliefs led parents to take a most unfortunate interest in their children's bowel movements and bred whole populations which took laxatives (*see* **Laxatives**) either as a once a week "precaution" or whenever a day had passed without a stool. Regular use of laxative chemicals spoils the natural rhythm of the bowel's action and, if continued for long, can actually spoil its muscle tone so that natural action becomes increasingly difficult. Unless your child is prescribed laxatives for an organic disease or problems with soiling (*see* **Soiling**), do not give her any, ever.

Natural bowel rhythm

Waste from digested food is passed along the small intestine by rhythmic activity of the intestinal muscle wall (peristalsis). At this stage it is in the form of a thick liquid. When it passes into the large intestine, liquid is absorbed through the intestinal wall so that as the waste moves down the colon, it solidifies. When it reaches the rectum, the rich supply of nerve endings signal readiness to pass a stool. If the signals are ignored (perhaps because this is not a convenient moment to seek a toilet), they die down. The rectum can expand enormously to accommodate more waste, but water continues to be absorbed from it. If further signals are ignored over many hours, the quantity of waste awaiting evacuation becomes greater and its consistency becomes drier.

Individuals vary widely in the frequency with which they need to pass stools. Some of this variation is certainly due to habit and some to diet (*see below*), but equally certainly the only "ideal" frequency for every individual is "whenever you feel the need to go."

Ideally, if your child has taken over full responsibility for looking after herself in the bathroom, you will not even know how often she passes a stool. The less concerned you are, the less concerned she will be and the less likely it is that there will be any problems. After all, you do not inquire how often she urinates, nor rush to the bathroom to check. She may be a child who passes a stool every day. If she is, she may find it convenient to do so at home rather than at school, where lack of time, privacy, hygiene and toilet paper can all present her with difficulties. On the other hand, she may be a child who goes less frequently and/or less regularly. Accept that, too.

All you need to do, by way of assistance, is to ensure that there is a toilet, time and privacy available for her when she needs it.

Constipation in young children

In a young child, the commonest reason for constipation is ignoring the signals for so long that the stool becomes hard and difficult to pass. At this stage the child may try to pass it but not have the time or patience to do so, abandoning the whole matter again and again so that it gets increasingly difficult. Or she may succeed in passing a stool but, because it is bulky and hard, doing so may be painful. It can even cause a minute tear in the sensitive tissue at the edge of the anus so that it really hurts and will hurt again next time a stool is passed.

If your child keeps going to the bathroom but emerging again in record time and without flushing the toilet, you may suspect that something of this kind is happening. Ask her. Explain. Encourage her to take a book or a comic into the bathroom with her and settle down to deal with the whole matter, pointing out that once she has done so, it need not be difficult again.

If the child should have an anal tear she will probably tell you "I can't, it hurts." Take her to the doctor. This is one of the rare occasions when he may prescribe a stool-softening laxative. He can also prescribe an anesthetic ointment for use while the split heals, which it will do very quickly.

Preventing constipation in all ages Make sure that everyone drinks enough fluid. Although most people do most of the time, there are occasions when we let ourselves become mildly dehydrated. If the body is short of water it will take all it can from the feces through the colon wall, thus making the eventual stool drier.

Try to provide all members of the family with a diet which contains plenty of "roughage." Highly refined and processed foods leave little residue for the bowels to work on. Fruit, raw vegetables, whole grain cereals and breads all add bulk. Still more can be added by using wheat bran along with flour in your baking or by serving a bran breakfast cereal.

Contraception *see* **Adolescence**/Sexual activity.
Convalescence *see* **Nursing**/Getting back to normal.

Convulsions, Seizures and "Fits"

The sight of someone having a "fit" arouses a kind of superstitious terror in most people. Parents are no exception. But if your child does ever have any kind of convulsion or seizure it is important to try and keep your head. The more accurate information you can give to your doctor about the circumstances and nature of the "fit," the more likely it is that he will be able to give you immediate reassurance that, while horrible, the matter is not serious. Furthermore, if you can stay fairly calm you will be able to ask him, directly, the questions that bother you later such as "Is he epileptic?" or "Is his brain damaged?" All too often parents dare not ask these questions for fear of the answer "yes," while doctors do not volunteer the information for fear of "putting ideas into" parents' heads. A conspiracy of desperate silence does nobody any good.

Febrile convulsions

By far the most common cause of convulsions in children under five is a very rapid rise in fever (*see* **Nursing**/Fever). About three percent of all children have a convulsion of this kind so it cannot even be regarded as unusual. The tendency to react to a sudden rise in fever in this way runs in families so that an affected child may have a parent who reacted similarly. On the other hand, the fact that your first child has such a convulsion during infancy does not necessarily mean that later children will, too.

If a child is liable to febrile convulsions, he will usually have his first while he is between one and three years old. It is very unusual indeed to have a first such convulsion after the third birthday. If he does have one while he is a baby or toddler, the risk of his having another diminishes steadily between three and five. Even a child who has been very liable to these convulsions will grow through the tendency by the time he is five.

Mechanism of a febrile convulsion

A sudden, sharp rise in body temperature at an age when the body's temperature-regulating mechanisms are not as efficient as they will later become "irritates" the brain whose control over consciousness and movement is temporarily disturbed. Neurons in the brain suddenly discharge their impulses and this results in the "fit" which you see (*see below*). Most febrile convulsions stop spontaneously within seconds, or at least within a minute or two, and do the brain no damage whatsoever.

Why a febrile convulsion is treated as an emergency

Even though it is extremely unlikely that a febrile convulsion will do your child any harm, any child who has such a convulsion must have immediate medical attention *just in case*.

If a major convulsion is allowed to continue for a long period such as twenty minutes or more, permanent damage to the brain is a possibility. Those neurons go on and on discharging; if they continue to do so for a long time their extreme activity may outstrip the body's ability to replenish their oxygen supply. The neurons become exhausted of oxygen and would eventually "die." Long-continuing and untreated febrile convulsions can lead to later epilepsy of the type known as "temporal lobe epilepsy" (*see below*) because the brain cells in the area known to be the focus for this kind of epilepsy happen to be particularly sensitive to oxygen starvation.

If you send immediately for medical help, the chances are very high that the "fit" will be over long before it can reach you. But if the "fit" is still going on it will immediately stop when a doctor gives an injection of anti-convulsant medication. The moment the drug takes effect the child's brain ceases to be at risk just as it ceases to be at risk if the convulsion ceases of its own accord.

Your child's first febrile convulsion

Many intelligent, level-headed parents report panic and a strong impulse to get away from the convulsing child; to seek help or to find somebody, *anybody*, to whom he can be handed over. If this is your reaction, don't add to your misery with later secret guilt. You are in a majority.

If you did not already know that your child was ill, he may begin to convulse wherever he happens to be: playing on the floor or in the garden or sitting in his highchair. If you already knew that he was feverish he may well be lying down in his crib or bed or on the sofa. Quite frequently he will have been asleep; the fever will have risen sharply during his nap and the convulsion will begin when you disturb him.

The "fit" usually has four phases, although many take place so quickly that these stages are not distinguishable from one another:

The child suddenly looks "strange" and/or terrified and may emit a guttural sound which parents often describe as "inhuman."

His whole body (or one side of it only) extends and becomes rigid, and his eyes either look glazed or roll up so that only the white is visible. It is at this stage that parents so often believe that the child is dead.

The rigidity gives way to more or less violent thrashing or jerking of his limbs and shuddering of his body. His teeth clench; foam may drool from his mouth; he may wet himself.

The movements cease; the child's body relaxes and he either "comes to," very anxious and confused, and then goes to sleep, or he drops off to sleep without ever "coming round."

What to do during a febrile convulsion   **Stay with him to prevent him from hurting himself.** If he convulses while sitting in a chair, put him on the floor; if he is on a bed or sofa, make sure he does not roll off. Wherever he is, don't try to control his thrashing limbs but concentrate on preventing them from hitting against anything, and on keeping him on his side.

Watch out for vomiting/choking. Left alone he could roll onto his back and choke on his own secretions.

Don't try to pry his teeth apart to prevent him from biting his tongue. If he bites his tongue, it will heal; if you break his teeth, they will not.

Don't try to shake him back to consciousness. His body is already receiving *too much* stimulation from his brain; violent action from you could make the whole episode more acute.

Look at your watch and wait with him for at least three minutes. If there is anyone else in the house, by all means call to them to telephone, but if you are alone with the child don't leave him to go for help yourself. The convulsion will almost certainly end during those three minutes. If the child becomes conscious, soothe and comfort him as calmly as you possibly can. He must and will sleep almost immediately. If he does not become conscious but simply relaxes into deep sleep, check that he is out of range of any immediate hazards, like an electric fire, and then leave him for just long enough to telephone for help or shout to a neighbor to do so.

If the convulsion has not ceased in three minutes you must summon help without waiting for it to end naturally. Use your judgment: can you safely leave him while you dial 911? If he is drooling or has vomited and there is a real risk of choking, can you pick him up as he is and carry him to the telephone or front door? As with other rare emergencies, like arterial bleeding, this may be a time to drop conventional behavior, open a window and simply yell for help.

If a convulsion has gone on for several minutes, the doctor will probably recommend admitting him to a hospital anyway, so it is probably quickest and easiest to get a neighbor or passing good Samaritan either to phone for an ambulance or to drive you and the child directly to the nearest emergency room.

After a convulsion

Most convulsions *will* have stopped within three minutes. If you can reach your doctor quickly, do so. Your own doctor is the best person to assess the child and to reassure you.

If the doctor will see you immediately, do what you can to cool the child without disturbing him during the trip. Open windows, remove blankets, fan him and so on.

What the doctor may want to know about a convulsion

What the child was like before the convulsion. Did you already know he was unwell? If so, since when? Did he have a fever? What was his temperature and when did you last take it? If you did not know he was unwell, can you see now, looking back, any signs of coming illness? Did he eat his last meal? Was he cheerful and active?

Did anything seem to "touch off" the convulsion?

Can you give any accurate idea of how long it lasted? Even if you did not manage to look at your watch (or cannot now remember what it said!), remembering your own actions and thoughts while the child was convulsing may give the doctor some idea as to whether the episode went on for seconds, a couple of minutes or five to ten minutes.

What the doctor may do about a convulsion

Apart from asking you for these and other details, he will examine the child. He will, of course, be looking for symptoms and signs of illness to account for the fever which led to the convulsion, but he may especially be making sure that he has not got meningitis (*see* **Meningitis and Encephalitis**). This is because meningitis, being an inflammation of the covering of the brain and spinal cord, is an illness which is particularly liable to cause convulsions and because it requires urgent (and almost always successful) treatment. If he cannot exclude the possibility of meningitis he will arrange for the child to be admitted to a hospital.

Some doctors prefer to admit all children who have had a first convulsion to a hospital, so if this is your doctor's recommendation, don't *assume* that he suspects meningitis or another serious illness.

If your doctor is happy for the child to be nursed at home, he may give him an injection of anti-convulsant/sedative medication. Don't assume that he does this because he thinks the child will otherwise convulse again. If he did think this, he would send him to a hospital. Such an injection is sometimes given simply as a precaution and to help protect the brain from further irritation while the fever is being reduced. Often, the doctor will do only what he always does when he sees your sick child: identify (if possible) the infection; judge whether or not to prescribe antibiotics or other medicines; advise you on nursing the child.

If you are left to nurse a child who has just had his first convulsion, do try to believe the doctor's assurances that it will not happen again this time. But since you will almost certainly find yourself worried to distraction, do also consider sending for your partner or a friend to share your vigil. Once the child has woken up from his natural or sedated sleep, his fever is under control and he is his normal (if unwell) self again, the horror will recede. But for now you are entitled to the reassurance of adult support if you can get it.

● If an older child happens to have seen the convulsion, do find time to explain it to him or her. When drama focuses on one child it is easy to ignore another. If you were frightened, he or she was probably downright terrified.

When the drama of a convulsion is over   If this first convulsion was due to the fever caused by a simple infection and you nurse the child at home, you may find yourself worrying about the possibility of further convulsions next time he is ill. Do make an appointment to discuss this with your doctor. If your child was admitted to a hospital, you should be given the opportunity for this kind of discussion before he is discharged, but if it is not offered, ask.

Your doctor will want to avoid further convulsions if possible, but he will not want you to live life in fear of them. Some parents get into the unfortunate habit of taking a child's temperature almost every day in case he has a fever, or even of giving doses of aspirin almost routinely, just in case. The following are some of the things your doctor may suggest. If you find yourself unable to follow his advice because of your own worry, do stay in touch with him. Some parents are offered routine follow-up appointments for several months after their child has had a febrile convulsion and they find this extremely valuable.

No action until or unless the child has a fever. You may be asked to forget the whole thing and just get on with life until or unless the child is unwell. When that happens you may be asked to take his temperature and to let the doctor know if it is above a specified level. He will probably ask you to start cooling the child immediately and to give aspirin (*see* **Nursing**/Fever).

Occasionally a doctor will suggest that, in addition to this, you should give the child an anti-convulsant drug, prescribed by him, by mouth, from the beginning of any fever. This will make a convulsion less likely if the fever catches you out by rising suddenly, perhaps while the sick child is sleeping. Some doctors do not think this is useful, though. A fever which is going to rise very sharply often does so at the very beginning of an illness so that by the time you know the child is feverish it is already too late: he has either convulsed or he is not going to. Also, if you have this medication in your medicine cabinet, you may find yourself tempted to dose the child not just when he has a fever but whenever you think he *might* be going to have one.

Investigations before deciding on any action. Sometimes a doctor will want a child who has had a convulsion to have an electroencephalogram. This painless investigation may help him to decide whether or not further convulsions are very likely.

Preventive medication. Some doctors sometimes suggest that a child (especially one who has had more than one febrile convulsion) should have anti-convulsant medication every day while he is in the susceptible age period. Such medication does inevitably have some side effects. It may, for example, slow the child down a little or make him irritable. The balance of likely benefit can only be decided by you and your doctor, because it depends on the individual child's reactions and on your own level of anxiety about the whole matter.

Breath-holding seizures (*see also* **Tantrums**)

A few babies and very small children have an extreme physiological reaction to shock or frustration. Instead of screaming with fear, pain or rage, they scream once, then draw in a huge breath as if to go on screaming, but hold it for so long that they become unconscious.

An attack of this kind can be almost as terrifying for parents as a febrile convulsion and even more damaging to family life. Some parents of breath-holders are so desperate to avoid attacks that they become quite unable to handle the child as they normally would, but overprotect and overindulge him so that he actually cannot learn more appropriate ways of coping with himself or his world (*see* **Discipline, Self-discipline and Learning How to Behave**).

If your child has one breath-holding attack you will, of course, seek immediate medical help because you will probably not be able to differentiate it for certain from a febrile or other seizure. Once you and your doctor are certain that the episode was due to breath-holding, try to believe the following points:

The child becomes unconscious because he has held his breath for long enough to starve his brain of oxygen. The loss of consciousness is a mechanical reaction rather than a sign of illness or neurological difficulty.

It is absolutely impossible for the child to hold his breath for long enough to kill himself or damage his brain; indeed, far from being dangerous, the loss of consciousness is a survival mechanism. As soon as he loses consciousness he loses the will to hold his breath and reflex breathing immediately takes over.

Even in the extremely rare case of a breath-holding attack leading to an actual convulsion, there is no risk of brain damage. The short period of oxygen starvation was enough to provoke unusual discharge from neurons in the brain and therefore to produce the convulsive movements, etc., but because the stimulus of oxygen starvation immediately ceases (where the provoking fever in a febrile convulsion does not), it lasts for moments only.

If you find it difficult to believe this reassurance, consider hunger strikers or people who martyr themselves for a cause by burning themselves to death. Would they take such lengthy and agonizing paths to death if it were physically possible to sacrifice themselves simply by refusing to breathe? Your breath-holding child *cannot do himself any lasting physical harm*, but he will do himself (and all of you) lasting psychological harm unless you can truly believe this.

Coping with breath-holding

There are two types of breath-holding attack.

Pallid
breath-holding

This is extremely rare. Following a sudden shock (which may be painful but may only be frightening) the child becomes very white, slumps limply and is unconscious for a few seconds. Blows on the head from behind, and immunizing injections carried out "while he's thinking about something else" are among the known triggers for a susceptible child.

As he matures, this reaction to shock will lessen both in frequency and severity, although the child may grow up to be a person who tends to marked physiological reactions to emotional shock (*see* **Accidents**/Shock: Minor shock. *See also* **Fainting**).

In the meantime, some acknowledgment of his "sensitivity" should be made by his family. Of course he should not be treated as "delicate," but older children should be discouraged from "jumping out" at him and some trouble should be taken to see that he knows in advance when an injection or other necessary procedure is coming up.

Cyanotic
breath-holding

This is the usual form and it affects mainly toddlers, with a bias towards those who are especially active/bright *and* especially intolerant of frustration. Any situation which might evoke a tantrum in one child may evoke breath-holding in a susceptible one (*see* **Tantrums**).

The outraged child screams, but as if even screams were not enough to express his feelings, he eventually holds his breath while his face goes from bright red to dark red and from dark red to grayish blue. At this point in an uninterrupted attack, his eyes may glaze or roll up, his body becomes stiff and then he slumps unconscious.

Obviously extremes of frustration are better avoided for any child, but, equally obviously, attempts to avoid *any* frustration will seriously distort your child-rearing. It is not only you who must frustrate him in the name of safety or "discipline," but life which must frustrate him in the name of learning. So while recognizing your child's extreme reaction to frustration and doing what you reasonably can to "walk round trouble" (*see* **Discipline, Self-discipline and Learning How to Behave**), you have to face the fact that you neither can nor should avoid situations which may lead to breath-holding attacks.

But if you cannot avoid them all, you can cut short any attack which occurs. Your child need never reach blue unconsciousness.

He will not have a breath-holding attack when there is nobody there to see so you need not worry about what happens to him when his toys make him furious in his crib in the morning.

When you see trouble brewing, keep an eye on him. Wait just long enough to see whether this time he *is* going to scream it out.

As soon as it is clear that the breath is being held, use your forefinger to hook forward the base of his tongue. He will release that breath as a reflex. If you always abort breath-holding attacks in this way, your child will probably give them up in favor of some other form of tantrum. If, on the other hand, you resort to traditional but ineffective methods (shaking, smacking, cold water, etc.) he may not. Some children, as they reach three or four, actually learn to breath-hold as a deliberate manipulation of parents so it is worth adopting the tongue method from the very beginning while the whole pattern is subconscious.

Other "fits" which do not suggest neurological disorder

Although nothing is as alarming as the sight of a child having a violent seizure or falling unconscious before you, any "fit" that puts your child out of touch with reality, and therefore out of reach of your voice and touch, can be peculiarly alarming. Many children become like this when a very high fever makes them delirious (see **Nursing**/Fever). A few lose touch with the real world during:

Masturbation
(*see also* **Habits**)

Masturbation and other forms of repetitive pleasurable self-stimulation are entirely normal and probably universal, but a few infants and young children adopt methods which look worryingly like "fits." A baby may rock repeatedly backwards and forwards, for example, thighs held together, muscles tensed and face reddening. A toddler may adopt an odd posture (perhaps involving rubbing himself against the crib bars) and he may be so tense that his muscles shudder, and so involved that he holds his breath so that his face becomes purple. While this sort of activity is going on the child is oblivious to anything which is going on around him. The episode will usually end with a sort of mini-climax, in which a moment's shaking leads to relaxation of the muscles and the child appearing to "come to himself."

However extreme your child's self-gratifying behavior, you can always assure yourself that he is not having a seizure simply by speaking to and touching him. Masturbation can always be interrupted. A seizure must run its course or be stopped by sedation.

Night terrors
(*see also* **Sleep**)

Night terrors are terrifying to parents because the child who is involved in one often has quite a long period during which he *looks* as if he is awake but he reacts quite irrationally to them. Sometimes he will look right through you, searching for the horrors he is seeing in his mind behind your reassuring face. Sometimes, if you force him to acknowledge your existence and presence, he will take you into his terror and make you part of the horror. Instead of accepting your comforting embrace he will fight to escape you, screaming piteously at you "don't, oh don't. . . ." It is definitely eerie, but eventually this curious semiconscious state will turn into real consciousness. The child will neither remember nor be harmed by the night terror. Yours are the nerves which may be left jangling long after he has dropped back into contented sleep.

Paroxysmal
vertigo

This is a very rare and ill-understood complaint which is only mentioned here because it is both singularly unpleasant for the child and singularly frightening for the parents. It is, nevertheless, entirely harmless. Only children between about one and five years are ever affected so that even if yours should be one of the few who suffer from it you can all be certain that she will grow out of it comparatively quickly.

The child suddenly experiences acute and overwhelming giddiness, which she may graphically describe as "everything going round and round and round." She may feel sick, vomit, sweat; she may clutch at the wall for support or lie pressed to the floor, desperately trying to find some feeling of solidity in a world gone mad. She behaves as if she were being forced to stay for much too long on a violent fairground ride.

The most unpleasant part of this peculiar affliction is that there is no loss of consciousness or awareness and that no drug has any effect. Attacks do not last for long. The child may like to be held closely during them, gaining some security from your supportive adult body.

Seizures and "fits" that do suggest neurological disorder

Children who are liable to seizures and "fits" that are not due to any of the above syndromes are commonly called "epileptic." That label sounds as if "epilepsy" were the name of a disease. It is not. It is simply a term used to describe people who have some disorder within the brain which makes them liable to some form of "fit." The nature of that underlying disorder may or may not be known. The "fits" themselves may always be of one type or they may vary. They may be touched off by particular triggers or they may occur for no discernible reason, and they may be of any degree of severity. If your child has a problem of this kind, do remember (and make sure that other people closely concerned with him also understand) that:

The seizures are not the disorder but only a sign that there is one.

The label "epileptic" conveys very little that is meaningful about the sufferer; to know anything about what he should or should not be allowed to do, for example, one needs details, not a stereotype.

A final "cure" for epilepsy is very rarely possible, but anti-convulsant medication can usually suppress the activity of those abnormally firing brain cells so that no actual seizures ever occur. With your help and the child's cooperation, doctors will try to achieve the best possible balance between over-sedating the child so that he has no seizures but cannot function normally, and under-sedating him so that he functions normally but still has the occasional seizure. This may involve some trial and error, but time is on your side. Seizures usually become less frequent with age; as your child gets older his medication can usually be reduced and he may eventually be able to give it up altogether.

Your help will also be needed in identifying "triggers" for your child's seizures. If, for example, they tend to be touched off by flickering television images or strobe lights, avoiding badly adjusted television sets and discos may enable medication to be reduced. If a girl's seizures are related to her menstrual periods, measures to prevent fluid and salt retention during that part of her cycle may much improve the medication's effect (see **Adolescence**/Menstruation).

If your child has seizures or "fits" that are eventually diagnosed as epilepsy, do try not to think of him as "an epileptic" but to think of him instead as a child with this particular tendency who, with good parental, medical and patient teamwork, can lead an entirely normal life. Such an optimistic outlook will very *very* seldom be proved wrong in the long term, even if there are short periods during his childhood when his activities have to be curtailed for safety reasons while his drug schedule is being adjusted.

Although seizure disorders are rare and must always be diagnosed by a medical team rather than a parent, a brief discussion of some of the least rare is given below. This is because early recognition and treatment is important, and because failure of the adult world to recognize a mild seizure disorder in a child sometimes leads to injustice and to unnecessary psychological damage.

Absence epilepsy ("petit mal")

This is a comparatively rare form of epilepsy; it never occurs in children under three and is commoner thereafter in girls than boys.

In a "simple absence," the child's awareness is suddenly shut off and as suddenly returns a mere few seconds later. There are no movements other than frequent eye-blinking. In a "complex absence" attack there may be jerky movements or lip-smacking or grimacing.

Although children with "petit mal" epilepsy are sometimes accused of "wool-gathering" or "not paying attention," any observant adult can distinguish between the two. In the epileptic attack the withdrawal of attention is sudden and total and *cannot be ended by adult stimulation.* If you speak to an "absent" child she will not hear or answer until awareness has returned, where the day-dreaming child will "come to" with a guilty start.

It is essential that teachers should know of a child's tendency to "petit mal" which is not completely controlled. Many school difficulties arise if irritated teachers call attention to the condition.

"Drop attacks"

These are similar to infantile spasms (*see below*) but affect children over two years of age. The child falls, often as if violently pushed, either forwards or backwards. Sometimes there is no forward or backward impetus but he simply collapses on the floor without warning.

The child rights himself so rapidly that parents sometimes do not realize that anything other than a normal fall has taken place. Your clue, at least a second time, may be the child's failure to throw his arms up to protect his head or face. Injuries are quite common and have sometimes led to accusations of "battering." Innocent parents' accounts of a child "just suddenly falling" can seem improbable to the inexperienced emergency room doctor.

"Grand mal" epilepsy

These generalized seizures are the kind which most people think of when they hear the word "epilepsy." They are of the type which is usual in febrile convulsions and are described under that heading (*see above*).

Infantile spasms ("Salaam spasms," West's syndrome)

These affect only infants under about two years. The baby suddenly jerks forward, flexing at hips and neck. The jerks are repeated (perhaps twenty or more times) with a few seconds between them. A cry sometimes accompanies each. Occasionally these spasms are mistaken for early efforts to sit up, or as attempts in an older baby to get from a sitting position to standing or crawling.

● A specific drug treatment is possible if, and only if, it is started within three weeks of the first spasm. Don't wait and hope.

Psychomotor attack   In this type of epilepsy the affected part of the brain is the temporal lobe which is responsible for the "storage" of memories, feelings and perception of smells. The affected child commonly feels that something terrifying is about to happen to him. Alternatively, he may remember something (always the same memory) or "smell" burning or some other (usually unpleasant) odor. His fright and confusion culminates in a momentary "absence" similar to that of "petit mal" attacks.

● Some "grand mal" seizures are also preceded by similar kinds of experience. Older patients sometimes "know" when a seizure is imminent because they experience a collection of sensations which together form their personal "aura."

Corporal punishment *see* **Discipline, Self-discipline and Learning How to Behave**/Some commmon disciplinary techniques: Punishment. *See also* **School**/Potential problems in school: Discipline in your child's school.

Cosmetic problems *see* **Adolescence**/Problems with appearance and body image. *See also* **Birthmarks**; **Hospital**/Surgery: Plastic surgery.

Coughs *see also* Chest Infections; Colds; Croup and Laryngitis; Whooping Cough

Coughs are difficult symptoms for parents to assess because, while a cough always denotes irritation in the respiratory system, the seriousness of a cough depends both on the *cause of the irritation* and on the *area of the respiratory system* which is affected. Furthermore, these two considerations interact with each other. If a child fails to swallow a crumb and coughs because it has "gone the wrong way," the matter is trivial as long as the crumb has only reached the larynx (voice box). But if he is coughing because that same innocent little crumb has got much farther down the system, the matter might be more serious (*see* **Accidents**/Choking; Foreign bodies which are inhaled).

If a child has a cough which lasts for several days without any obvious reason (such as a cold), he should certainly see a doctor, if only so that you can be reassured. If the nature or extent of a child's coughing (and the kind of breathing which accompanies it) really worries you, an emergency visit is called for. But most of the time most coughs are innocent. The following brief account of where and why they take place may save you from some nights of worry over the specter of pneumonia (*see* **Chest Infections**).

The respiratory system starts at the nose and mouth and culminates in the lungs. On the way air travels through the throat, the larynx, the trachea (windpipe) and the bronchi (major air tubes leading into the lungs). The cough reflex protects the respiratory system by closing off the route and forcibly expelling anything which should not travel down it, back up into the throat where it can be swallowed. That "anything" may indeed be almost anything. It may be that crumb; it may be dust; it may be air which, taken in through the mouth, is too cold to be allowed to reach the lungs without time to warm itself; above all, it may be mucus or pus, the products of infection anywhere in the system.

This protective coughing is vital because it ensures that irritants do not reach the bronchi and the lungs. When a child with a cold coughs, it is his cough which ensures that the infection stays at the upper respiratory level. Without it, virus-laden mucus might reach down to the bronchi and there set up the infection we call bronchitis. Anybody who is in a state where his cough reflex is likely to be depressed or absent, has to have his respiratory system artificially guarded. The child who is unconscious, for example (*see* **Accidents**/Coping with more serious injuries: If a child is unconscious), must be turned into the recovery position so that the secretions or vomit which he may not be able to cough up will trickle out of his mouth rather than down into his lungs. The hospital patient under anesthesia or in a coma will have an artificial airway inserted which can be kept clear by suction.

But while the basic function of a cough is protective and benevolent, the body does not always get it right. In some infections (*see below*) there is irritation of, say, the trachea, without any mucus being produced. The patient coughs and coughs, responding to that irritation when in fact there is nothing to be coughed up and therefore nothing to be prevented from going down. This kind of dry, irritating tickle-cough is one of the few kinds which it may sometimes be legitimate to quell with cough suppressants. In other infections (*see* **Allergy**/Asthma; **Croup and Laryngitis**; **Whooping Cough**) spasm of muscles in the respiratory passages produces coughing which is not only unproductive but so uncoordinated that it may actually interfere with breathing. Coughs of this kind will also require medical help.

Coughs with colds (see also Colds)

Most colds cause coughs, especially at night. During the day the child's nose runs and he either blows or wipes the mucus out or sniffs it back up and swallows it. At night, because he is lying down, the mucus tends to run to the back of the throat, tickle and cause him to cough. Because he is asleep, his swallowing is much reduced. The mucus is coughed into his mouth but runs back down to the throat so that he coughs yet again.

The only (partial) remedies for this kind of cough are mechanical ones designed to get the mucus out of the way. Raising the head of the mattress (or providing an older child with extra pillows) may help. Starting the night with a thoroughly cleared nose will help for a while. During a night which is being badly disturbed by constant coughing it is often worthwhile to wake the child so that he can sit up, clear his nose and start all over again more comfortably.

Coughs with thick, sticky mucus

Bacterial secondary infection (following a cold or almost any viral infection of the upper respiratory tract) may make secretions thick and sticky so that however much the child coughs he cannot "clear" himself. Under these circumstances an "expectorant cough medicine" may be useful. These medicines do not *prevent* coughing; they act to liquefy the mucus so that it can be coughed up more effectively and with less effort.

A young child should not be given such medicine without a doctor's advice. If you give one to an older child, perhaps because his colds "always go through a thick stage," do remember that most of them contain drugs which, in larger doses, act as emetics. If you give him more than is recommended or dose him too frequently, you may add to his misery by making him vomit.

Coughs with aching chests A constant ache in the chest, or pain when coughing, tends to alarm parents whose minds instantly turn to pleurisy or pneumonia (*see* **Chest Infections**). Remember that a child who is coughing frequently is forcing the muscles of the chest wall to do a lot of unusual work. Some aching is so frequent as to be almost the rule rather than the exception. *Sharp* pain when coughing requires medical advice. Otherwise pain associated with *breathing* matters more than pain with coughing. It may mean that infection has spread downwards.

Coughs with "chest colds" "Chest cold" is a term which is certainly imprecise and may be nonsensical. If your baby or young child's cough sounds "chesty" this will usually be because of his small size and anatomy. The distance from his throat to his lungs is, after all, only a matter of a few inches. His breathing passages are not only small, they are actually smaller for his overall size than are the passages of older people. If there is inflammation/mucus in his throat or larynx or trachea, causing him to cough, the sound will vibrate those tiny passages and you may well hear the sound as if it came from his chest. If he is old enough to tell you that his chest aches, your diagnosis of a "chest cold" or a "cold which has gone to his chest" may seem confirmed.

If you are concerned about him, you will, of course, consult your doctor. But do remember that a cold which has truly "settled on his chest" has stopped being "just a cold" and become a chest infection. If this has happened the child will be clearly unwell. It makes more sense to consult your doctor because the child is ill, whatever his cough sounds like, than to do so because his cough sounds "chesty" when he seems perfectly well in himself (*see* **Chest Infections**).

Coughs with exhaustion If a cough is too frequent and/or too violent it can be exhausting, whatever its underlying cause. If your child coughs so often during the *day* that his activities are interfered with and/or he seems floppy after each bout, it is better to seek medical help in finding the cause than to try to stop the cough with cough suppressant medicines.

Coughs with difficult breathing Often a child with a cold or other minor upper respiratory infection will breathe noisily. Any mucus in those small air passages will vibrate and may cause all kinds of snoring or whistling noises. If the infection has also given him a fever, his breathing may be more rapid than usual as well.

Neither noisy nor rapid breathing *on its own* suggests that a child's existing infection has become worse. Labored breathing, on the other hand, should be treated as an emergency and your doctor called, whatever the time of night.

Recognizing labored breathing Difficulty in getting enough oxygen to the lungs evokes fear and panic in everyone, whatever the cause. This is why attacks of asthma are so frightening (*see* **Allergy**/Asthma). If a child wakes up "short of breath," panics and cries, it may be up to you to deduce the problem. Equally, if he was already very unwell and is now asleep but looking worse, you may want to check that his breathing is easy. Take off his pajama top (or unbutton it) so that you can see his bare chest. The signs of labored breathing are:

□ Rapid, heaving chest movements which are not entirely rhythmical.

□ A definite sucking in of the lower end of the sternum (breastbone) with each breath.

□ A pulling in of the lower ribs at the sides, with every breath.

These last two signs are especially useful in babies and very young children. The sternum and lower ribs are attached to the diaphragm. When the diaphragm is having to exert unusual force in order to take in breath, these bones, which are still comparatively soft in a young child, are pulled inwards by its action. Although a panic-stricken crying child will, of course, breathe more rapidly than a calm one, rapid breathing, in which the air is passing in and out easily, will not produce these sucking-in movements.

● Labored breathing does mean that the child's body is having to work unusually hard to get air in and out, so it is an emergency. On the other hand, labored breathing does not mean that the child's body is going to give up the struggle; he can actually survive on far less air than he feels he needs. Try not to panic because the more frightened he senses that you are, the more frightened the child is likely to be. Fear actually puts up his need for oxygen (so that he will be even more "short of breath") while crying creates a vicious circle with breathlessness. The calmer and quieter you can help him to be, the less breathless he will feel and therefore the calmer he will stay.

Cramp *see also* **Adolescence**/Menstruation: Menstrual difficulties

The word "cramp" refers to acute pain caused by involuntary spasms of muscles. Cramp in internal abdominal muscles is sometimes referred to as "colic" while cramp in the muscles associated with laboring lungs is called a "stitch." Spasm in muscles of the neck is often referred to as a "crick in the neck."

The basic cause of cramp is failure of the circulation through a particular muscle or muscle group to keep it supplied with energy and to remove the waste product of its energy use. A build-up of this waste product, called lactic acid, is thought to be responsible for the actual pain.

Causes of cramp

Anything which drains a muscle of energy and allows lactic acid to build up within it can cause cramp. Causes, therefore, range from serious problems of circulation (such as narrowed arteries) through temporary interference with circulation (such as the pressure of the loaded uterus on major blood vessels late in pregnancy) to the most common, overuse of a muscle such that its energy demands and waste products outstrip the resupplying and flushing functions of its blood supply.

Coping with cramp

If your child gets a cramp while exercising, he must stop at once. Trying to go on running with a stitch or cramping calf muscles is idiotic. He will not, in fact, be able to continue and trying to do so will make the pain both worse and longer lasting.

The spasms will stop and the pain will ease as soon as rest allows the muscles to be flushed by the circulation. In the meantime, the pain may be very severe indeed. You may be able to help by:

Helping him to sit or lie still and breathe steadily so that his panic-stricken writhings do not prolong the agony.

Gently rubbing affected muscles so as to increase the blood flow to them.

● Cramp while swimming can be dangerous. Children who swim in deep water and/or alone *must* be taught how to tread water/float and be trained to a point where they can be relied upon to do so despite the pain of cramp (*see* **Safety**/In the home: By, in and on water).

Preventing cramp

Unless he exhausts muscles through overuse, a healthy child will not get cramp if he:

Always ensures that his muscles are "warmed up" before he makes stringent demands on them. Serious dancers, athletes and sportspeople are taught warm-up exercises; you can ensure that any child understands he must move about and get his circulation speeded up before he dashes off. Going up through the gears of a car is a useful parallel.

Avoids awkward positions which limit blood flow to a limb. Sleeping in cars, for example, quite often leads to cramp.

Avoids heavy exercise in circumstances which are likely to cut down the blood flow to important muscle groups. Swimming in icy-cold water without the precaution of wearing a wet suit or greasing the skin can be dangerous because the body seeks to preserve the warmth of the vital organs by reducing the blood flow to the skin and increasing it internally. This leaves outer muscle layers singularly liable to cramp. In rather the same way, swimming after a heavy meal can be dangerous because rather more of the blood flow than usual is concentrated on the processes of digestion. A heavy meal *and* very cold water are a lethal combination for swimmers.

● There is no reason why children, spending a precious day at the beach, should be deprived of going in the water for an hour after a sandwich lunch. Warmth and a light meal make cramping very unlikely.

Avoids demanding exercise in circumstances in which the circulation may already be affected. Playing tennis in high temperatures after a day spent sunbathing can make him very liable to cramping as a mild degree of dehydration and salt deprivation may already exist (*see* **Accidents**/Sunburn and heat illness).

Recurrent cramp

If a child wakes in the night with cramp he may have unwittingly deprived a muscle group of sufficient blood just by lying awkwardly. A single episode of this kind is no cause for concern. If he frequently develops cramp without obvious reason, it is worth having him checked by a doctor.

Crib deaths *see* **Death**/Sudden Infant Death Syndrome.

Croup and Laryngitis

Laryngitis is an inflammation of the larynx (voice box) and sometimes of the trachea below it. The inflammation is usually caused by an ordinary cold virus, though any microorganism which causes an upper respiratory infection can lead to laryngitis if it gets down that far.

Older children (and adults) with laryngitis usually only have a hoarse (or absent) voice, a tickly cough and perhaps a sore throat. Some very young children, on the other hand, are liable to a more dramatic form of laryngitis: the kind we call croup. Croup can be mild and unimportant but, especially in a baby or toddler, it can be severe.

Croup is also an inflammation of the larynx and/or trachea but, because of the very small diameter of the young child's air passageways, the swelling which accompanies the inflammation is enough to obstruct his breathing. The severity of an attack of croup depends on the degree of that swelling. Parents should know that sufficient swelling to cut off a child's air supply altogether is *extremely* rare. But they should also realize that a little swelling, just enough to make the breathing slightly labored, can increase if nothing is done to relieve it. So even the mildest case of croup requires quick, knowledgeable action.

Some children seem far more liable than others to have croup, either all on its own, or as part of their colds. Yours may be a child who never has a sign of croup. But if a child has one attack, he is quite likely to have another with a later upper respiratory infection. Furthermore, if one of your children is liable to croup another one is rather likely to be liable, too.

A first attack of croup (or any severe attack) certainly merits emergency communication with your doctor or a quick trip to your nearest hospital if you cannot easily reach him. But once you have nursed a child through one bout with medical advice, you may feel able to cope with later attacks yourself, only calling the doctor if the croup is not easily dealt with (*see below*). If yours turns out to be a croup-prone family, a cold-air vaporizer may be an extremely worthwhile purchase.

First signs of croup

Sometimes the child has a cold. Sometimes he already has some signs (such as hoarseness) which suggest that his larynx may be involved. But usually there are no warning signs of croup. It just happens, usually in the middle of the night.

In a severe case, with marked swelling, you are likely to be awoken by a loud, strange barking noise, immediately followed by terrified hoarse crying interspersed with a hacking, hard cough. The barking noise is the sound air makes as the child forces it in past those swollen vocal cords.

When you reach the child you may find him struggling between coughing, crying and breathing (still with that extraordinary sound). He will certainly look panic-stricken. He may even look a poor color: slightly gray and pale-lipped.

Immediate action for severe croup

If there is someone else in the house, get him or her to telephone the doctor while you concentrate on the child. If you are alone, start with the child and call the doctor yourself if your first measures do not produce an immediate and dramatic improvement.

The first thing your child needs is reassurance. Struggling and crying is making everything worse. Stay calm yourself and use whatever words and gestures will best calm your child. A baby, for example, will probably react best to being picked up and cuddled but some four-year-olds will react with relief and complete obedience to authoritative instructions.

Either cold, moist air or warm steam will relieve the swelling enough to improve your child's breathing.

If you have a cold-air vaporizer, turn it on and direct the stream of wet cold air at the child's face. The effect is often almost miraculous.

Failing that, pick up the child and take him straight into the bathroom:

Open the window so that he can breathe the cold night air (better still if it is raining) while you turn on the hot taps to make the whole place as steamy as possible. If you have a shower stall, take the child in there and turn on the hot water (don't let it burn either of you); the small space will steam up faster than the whole room.

If by any chance you have no hot water supply:

Take the child to the kitchen and stand with him by an open window or door while a kettle boils. As soon as it is steaming take him close enough to breathe the steam without getting scalded. Assess the effectiveness of the steam after about five minutes.

If there has been no improvement, or if he is still breathing with enough difficulty to frighten him (and you), take him with you while you make a dash for the telephone and call your doctor or an ambulance. Take the child back to the steam room while you wait for help to arrive.

If there has been a marked improvement (and there usually is), you may feel that you can wait until morning for a visit to the doctor or that you will call to tell him what is happening and to make sure that you can reach him in a hurry if the acute croup should recur.

If you are going to manage without an immediate visit to the doctor or hospital, stay in the steam room with the child while you plan how to moisten the air of his bedroom. Open windows are a "must" (if yours are sealed, at least turn off the central heating). If you have the kind of electric kettle which does *not* turn itself off as soon as it boils, you can use that to make steam in the room. Failing that, a pan on a camping stove will certainly make steam, but it will also give out a lot of heat which is particularly undesirable if the infection causing the croup has also made the child feverish. If you must use a stove, try simultaneously cooling the room with a fan or a blower-heater on its "cold" setting.

Nursing the after-effects of severe croup

If there is anyone to help you, get the air in the child's room a little moist while you and he stay in the steam room. If you are alone, get organized in your mind so that you can be quick and efficient about it.

Put the child into bed and make sure that he is well propped up either with pillows or, for a baby, with the head of the crib mattress raised.

Get your steam arrangements organized and grab anything you need for your own comfort. The child must not be left alone for the rest of the night in case his breathing becomes difficult again, especially if he cries for you.

● If you are using a stove to make steam, you will not be able to leave the room, even for a minute, in case of an accident.

If he is still wide awake and anxious, distraction may help. The less he thinks about breathing, and about that awful feeling of oxygen hunger, the less likely he is to have further difficulty. Being read a story is often the best possible distraction. For a baby, a stream of talk, nonsense rhymes or just "what we're going to do when you're better" will keep his attention on you rather than on himself.

During the next half hour you will see whether or not the emergency is now over:

The child may now drift off to sleep and wake up in the morning completely recovered.

It may become clear that, although the croup is over, the infection which caused it is making the child feverish and ill. Nurse him as you normally would and call the doctor first thing in the morning.

The croup may recur, probably soon after the child goes to sleep or if you go to sleep too and the steam dries up. If this happens, start all over again, but this time don't let a rapid improvement stop you from getting emergency help from your doctor. If you cannot reach him, either send for an ambulance or take the child to the hospital yourself in your own car (don't worry about taking him out in the cold air; it will actually help that breathing).

Although the acute croup does not recur, the child's breathing may remain somewhat affected and coughing fits or attempts to talk or suck a bottle may provoke short bursts of that croupy noise. Again, you need a doctor; call him now if it is still only midnight, first thing in the morning if it is now dawn.

Later attacks of croup

Two things will alter your life for the better if your child has a tendency to croup:

A cold-air vaporizer. Once you own one, you can use it as a precautionary measure whenever your child has a cold and you can use it instead of all that steam-room performance whenever he has an unheralded attack. Furthermore, cold-air vaporizers are a superb aid to nursing feverish children (*see* **Nursing**/Fever) even if they have not got croup.

An easy and reasonably comfortable way of bunking down in the child's room. Whether you make a divan part of that room's furnishings or keep a collapsible bed handy, it is a tremendous help if you do not have to think, and turn the household upside-down in the middle of the night whenever you have to supervise him.

● A tendency to croup does *not* imply that there is anything wrong with, or any weakness in, your child's respiratory system. By the time he is five or so he will almost certainly have outgrown croup. Literally outgrown it, because his larynx will be so much larger in relation to the rest of him that there will be room for a little swelling of those vocal cords to take place without obstructing his breathing. Once he is capable of having an ordinary attack of laryngitis, croup will be a thing of the past.

"Cuddlies" (Transitional comfort objects) *see* **Habits**/Comfort habits.

Cuts *see* **Accidents**/Cuts and scrapes, grazes and puncture wounds. *See also* **Safety**/In the home: From dangerous implements.

Day care *see* **Working Mothers**. *See also* **Babysitters**.

Day nurseries *see* **Working Mothers**. *See also* **School**/Pre-school and nursery education.

Deafness *see* **Ears and Hearing; Ear Disorders and Deafness**. *See also* **Language**/Three to six months: Watching out for deafness.

Death *see also* **Suicide**

Few children today are brought up in ignorance of what we call "the facts of life," but most are still kept in ignorance of the other end of that life cycle: death. Most parents have known bereavement and many live in fear of their own deaths or the deaths of people they love. Instead of accepting death as the one inevitable event in otherwise variegated lives, they shy away from thinking about it themselves and protect children from the very concept, until personal tragedy catches the whole family unawares.

Young children cannot anticipate tragedy and grief nor empathize with people who are thus suffering. They are therefore curious about death in exactly the same way that they are curious about other aspects of life, until they find that their parents cannot answer their questions straight-forwardly: that death is still the Great Unmentionable. While it would be idiotic to pretend that a child brought up with knowledge of the facts of death will be protected from personal tragedy, such a child will at least have a realistic context in which to suffer if she must. Furthermore, if the parents of this generation were to try to remove some of the mystery and horror which surrounds the subject, there would be a chance of a next generation reared with a greater acceptance of an end which must come to all of us. Parents could do for the whole population something of what the hospice movement is doing for the dying and their families.

Information about death, like information about sex, cannot be given in a series of staged lectures. It needs to filter into a growing child from the beginning of her life and, above all, to be a topic about which she can ask questions that will be sensibly and unemotionally answered so that she is always encouraged to go on exploring the topic in her own mind and at her own pace. Most children do ask about the following points, although few are thus answered. Some are points around which childish anxiety tends to focus when death first presents itself as a reality.

Everything that lives, dies. This is so obvious that our capacity to walk around the fact is amazing. It is not a difficult idea to get across even to the youngest child if you can be calm and accepting about it yourself. You can use plants, insects and animals as well as people. Questions like "Will I die?" and "Will you die?" obviously have to be answered factually, but the idea of death as a *natural* end to life can be comfortably linked to other facts which distance the matter from her emotionally such as:

Different living things live on different time scales. She will be interested, for example, to be told that some insects live (in the form which she is watching) for only a day, and to have the short gestation period and lifespan of tiny mammals contrasted with that of bigger creatures and people. She will both accept this as interesting information and have the knowledge available when her pet gerbil dies of old age. Furthermore, she will then work out, with your help, that people usually live not only through the aeons that seem to her to be going to pass before she is grown up, but also until their children have children of their own. . . .

That physical death is final. Whatever you wish to teach your child about a possible life after death, it is vital that every child understand that bodies (of whatever creature) never *ever* "come back to life" and never *ever* have any consciousness, any feeling, any life, remaining. Nobody who has been recently bereaved can fully accept the finality of death and no young child can truly encompass the concept of "never" or "forever." Nevertheless, it is important to work at this one while the matter can be impersonal, because when a child does face a death which matters to her, the feelings of the corpse and the horrors of its disposal are usually a main source of anxiety. None of us likes to think of a person enclosed in a coffin, and buried in the ground or consumed in the fires of the crematorium. The more sure we are, intellectually at least, that the body is over, finished with, the more easily we accept that shrouds, satin coffin linings and flowers are cosmetics for *us*, the living (and perhaps statements of our love to the world at large), rather than being for the dead.

Although some people may find the idea distasteful, many school-children want to know what happens to bodies after they are buried and find a natural "rightness" in the truthful answer:

That dead bodies disintegrate back into the natural elements that make up all living things. Even before she is taught about the "nitrogen cycle" in her science classes, your child will find it eminently sensible that plants, animals and people are fundamentally made up of particular chemicals and that, once dead, they eventually rot into those same chemicals and thus contribute to the building blocks of new generations.

That death is necessary for renewal. Even quite a young child can easily understand that if some pigeons/rabbits did not die, the city/field would soon be overrun by the baby ones she enjoys watching. *Of course* such an idea is not going to help her accept that Grandpa had to die to make room for baby Joseph, but it helps to convey the idea of a cycle of birth and death, of renewal and replacement.

● Be careful about using flowers of which your child is fond to illustrate this point. Those daffodils do not *die* to make room for later flowers: they *die down*. Next spring they will come up again. She must know that the same does not apply to dogs, rabbits or people.

That new, young creatures are needed because old ones "wear out." This too is an easy and comforting concept for quite young children. It is easy because she already knows that old *objects* wear out and are replaced, and she can see that old animals and people become stiff and tired and less competent. It is comforting because it links natural death with ageing and therefore removes it from her immediate concerns about herself and her family.

● If there are elderly people who are close to your child, she will probably ask whether Granny or Mrs. Jones will soon die. It is a logical and factual question. If you are shocked and/or answer it in a way which contradicts everything you have previously said, you will muddle her and probably shut her up, too. You do not have to answer "yes" or "no" because the truth is that you do not know. You can truthfully say something like "Well, most people live to be seventy and some live to be a hundred, so we don't have to worry about that yet. . . ."

That natural death is usually peaceful. Insofar as young children have any concept of death, it is usually a television concept of violence and pain. While nobody can deny that death *can* be like that (*see below*) a child who understands that most deaths are a drifting into oblivion may be partly protected from the very common horror of the actual *moment of death*. You may be able to illustrate this, in the course of her childhood, when she sees the butterfly stop flying, sit on the flower and simply become motionless, or when she herself feeds her pet one evening and finds him dead, rather than asleep, in his nest next morning.

That violent/accidental/premature death and suffering are things all human beings strive to prevent/avoid/put right. By building up a distinction in her mind between "natural" and "unnatural" death, you can make it clear that reverence for life is as important as acceptance of death and that people have a duty to look after themselves and other people and creatures. You can also make it clear that however hard we (or doctors, nurses and so forth) may try, we cannot always keep things alive. She will start to think along these lines as soon as she begins to bring you the baby rabbits cats have mauled, or the baby birds which have fallen from their nests. You and she together can try to save them, but she must learn that you will not always be able to.

● Once again, this kind of knowledge will not protect the child whose father dies in the hospital after a heart attack, from anger at the doctors who did not save him for her. But it will give her anger some realistic context.

When a child meets death

Sooner or later your child will face a death which means something to her personally. It may be the death of a pet, a relation she seldom sees, a neighbor who was part of her daily scene, a grandparent whom she loved or even a brother, sister or parent. While nobody can tell you how to handle your child while she is facing her personal grief, other parents, who have had to see their children through, emphasize the following points:

Don't shield the bereaved child with falsehood

"I couldn't bear to tell her that her precious guinea pig had died so I hid the body and bought another. I shall never forget the tissue of lies that began when she said how *small* he seemed this morning and which culminated in 'his' having babies a couple of weeks later."

"We said Georgie [the dog] had wandered off and we were sure he would find a lovely home. It never occurred to us that she would be frantic *in case* he got killed *and* heartbroken because he had left her when she thought he loved her."

"We told her Mrs. G had moved to another city. I wish we'd told her the truth, though, because first it was 'Why didn't she say goodbye?' then it was 'Why doesn't she send me a postcard?' and now it's 'I hate Mrs. G.' My lie has spoilt a relationship which mattered to her."

Don't use "sleep" for "death"

"I told her her brother had gone peacefully to sleep . . . that I'd been with him when he went to sleep and he was happy . . . all that. I meant it to make it all right for her but it was the worst thing I ever did. It was months before she slept herself; she panicked when her dad went to sleep in front of the television and then a friend said her cat had been put to sleep and that started it all up again. Now our doctor says to explain about the anesthetic for her operation as a 'special sleep' but there's no way I can. You wouldn't think a *word* could matter so, would you?"

Think carefully about whether a child should see the dead

"In my family it was taken for granted that you went and said 'goodbye' to a dead person so my mother assumed ours would see their grandfather and I didn't like to refuse her. But I wish I had. My son just froze up and wouldn't look. He was really shocked by the whole thing. The girl had hysterics: Mom said to kiss Grandpa and of course he was cold . . . she screamed and screamed. It was awful. I'd never do it again, never."

BUT

"I said no; that I'd rather they remembered their father the way he really was. But then, that night, my boy was crying and crying and I tried to talk to him and it turned out that he thought his Dad must have been in a horrible kind of accident or something 'cause I wouldn't let him go with me to see him . . . I took him to the funeral parlor the next day and he was calmer after that. He just glanced, that's all, but he could sort of see that he wasn't, well, you know. . . ."

Think carefully about children and funerals

"It's a dreadful service to me; of course I have no religion so perhaps I can't judge but it really sort of rubs your nose in it with the coffin there and everything, and the burial too; horrible if it's someone you love. I'd never take a child. Tell them, yes, but not make them go through it."

BUT

"They wouldn't take me to the funeral and I was really angry. It was my aunt. I loved her. I'm part of the family, aren't I? Why should I be left out? Eleven isn't too young to have the person die so how is it too young to kind of see them off?"

AND

"The funeral was horrible. Horrible. But once it was over and she was buried, well, she was really sort of gone and Mom seemed better too in a way, as if she could more sort of accept it. . . ."

Let children mourn

"He was so upset about the dog we went and got another puppy that same afternoon. I thought he'd never forgive us. He looked at us as if we were mad and he said 'that's no good to me' and I realized just what he meant. It was selfish, really. *We* didn't want to see him without a dog to play with and take for walks. But *he* wanted his beloved Wolf . . . We took that puppy back and it was nearly a year before he asked for another dog."

"They'd had months of me being taken up with nursing their grandfather, so when he finally died we packed them off to friends and they gave them a whale of a time. Only it didn't work out too well, really. I sort of forgot that he'd come to mean a lot to them. . . ."

"Sheila was the one who suffered most when her brother was killed. You see everybody expected us to be in pieces and we were sort of trying to look after each other. She got forgotten, really. Our son, but her brother. People told her to be good because we were miserable; she got pushed out when she needed us. I think we often underestimate how much brothers and sisters mean to each other."

But don't expect adult grief

"At first he was upset. I mean he cried and carried on like we all did. But then it was as if he'd forgotten all about it. I mean he got up and got dressed for school the very next day and then he was wanting to be out playing and he wanted his meals and all . . . I just couldn't understand it. To tell you the truth I thought he was heartless. But his teacher talked to me; said he was being very difficult at school and all that, and that children show their feelings in different ways from us. I tried to be kind but I was so miserable myself, I just couldn't cope. That's why he went to the Child Guidance in the end. . . ."

"She kept asking for her Grandma. No matter how many times I told her she'd gone she kept saying things about when Grandma would come back. I thought I'd go crazy. I mean she *knew* she'd gone. It was as if she just wouldn't believe it."

"He didn't really react at all when I told him about his brother. There was I, dreading it, and you'd have thought I'd told him his brother had gone on vacation. Then he was all over us and saying things like "You'd like me to come with you, wouldn't you, 'cause you like me best." Then he gave up all the things he liked doing and sort of stayed around the house being some kind of goody-goody. It was really strange. Then my Mom told me he'd said something to her about trying to make up for what he'd done, and do you know, it sort of turned out that he thought *it was his fault*. Our doctor says kids often feel that a death is somehow their fault, even if all they've ever done is quarrel and that. Anyway, of course after that we kept telling him that it was nobody's fault, things like that do sometimes happen. He's still not the boy he was though. But he's never shed a tear."

"Sarah was only two when her father died and truly I don't think she really *noticed* very much, perhaps because he worked such long hours he didn't have a lot to do with her directly. She asked for him lots of times but she accepted it quite cheerfully when I said he wouldn't be coming. She couldn't understand why I was so upset, though. That's what she minded. But I'm sure it was better for her to be with me through the rough bits than to be off with relations or something. I've seen that come awfully hard on kids. I even used her to cry on sometimes. Tough, I know, for such a little girl but we sort of came through together."

"Don't get me wrong, all three were very close to their mother; of course they were shattered; we all were. But the worst thing was that their whole world, their lives, fell apart. She'd been part of every detail so nothing could ever be the same."

From those and other experiences, recollected some time after the event by parents who have had time to get over at least the shock element of their own grief, there seem to be some pointers for us all:

That it is easy to overprotect children because we hate to see them unhappy. A new pet may insult rather than heal. Being sent away from a house of mourning may exclude rather than relieve. Being protected from adult grief, by everyone putting on "a brave face for the children's sake," may deprive them of support and of a feeling of mutual usefulness.

That it is easy to be so lost in personal grief that the child's is under-estimated. This is especially liable to happen when it is a brother or sister who dies. Parents feel themselves the principal mourners and those around them do too. The grief of brothers and sisters is often under-estimated; sometimes they are openly pushed out of the way to give the parents mourning space; occasionally, it is even assumed or implied that they will welcome the chance to be the only remaining child.

That most children will feel some guilt over any death which is signifi-cant to them. Guilt is part of even adult mourning: we all regret harsh words or quarrels, failures to spot illness or just time wasted on not being as close as we now feel. For children, the tendency is much increased because most children find it difficult to sort out feelings from actions and may believe, or half-believe, that the anger they felt on the morning of the death actually caused or contributed to it. Brothers and sisters often wish each other dead—and then find themselves apparently monstrously all-powerful. Children often feel hate towards a parent and when that parent dies, suffer torment.

That children's grief does not always show itself in ways adults approve or can even recognize. Tears, loss of appetite and disturbed sleep, almost universal in mourning adults, may be almost or completely absent in a grief-stricken child whose distress may show up in anger, behavior disturbances or a stalwart refusal to admit to feeling anything at all.

That the degree of upset caused by a death will usually be related to the upset it causes to daily life. Children are more or less dependent on adults, not only emotionally but for the patterning of their daily lives. A child who loses his mother often loses his way of life along with her, where the child who loses his father may lose only that special and vital person. Where other aspects of a bereaved child's life *can* be held steady (where, for instance, it is financially and practically possible for the remaining family to continue in the same house/school, etc.), mourning for the lost *person* can be more easily carried through because it is not confused with distress over the related disruption.

When a child is known to be dying

If healthy children think about death, sick ones are bound to do so too. Although both parents and medical staff often prefer to assume that young patients have no idea that they are likely to die soon, research workers brave enough to approach this taboo area have found that this is not always so. Should you, or anyone close to you, ever have to face this most extreme agony of parenthood, you might find some of the following points helpful:

Ruses like changing the beds around in a hospital ward do not prevent patients from knowing when another child has died. Such deaths naturally cause great anxiety, but the anxiety is made worse by the fact that nurses and doctors (naturally upset themselves) cannot permit the other children to ask questions. A conspiracy of silence may make children who are *not* critically ill unnecessarily fearful, while it may make children who *are* critically ill feel that they cannot ask questions about their own condition. It makes all the children feel that death is an unbearable subject to the adults and this can only make it the more terrifying to them.

Children undergoing treatment need hope, but that hope can be for realistic small improvements rather than for impossible cure. Sometimes when painful or unpleasant treatments are to be undertaken, adults feel that they must tell the child that they will make him better, when in fact they know that the child can never be cured. The child then asks, "When it's over can I go home/get up/go back to school?" or whatever, and senses that the answers he gets are uncomfortable falsehoods. Usually, such a child will readily accept much smaller and more realistic goals such as "You will be able to breathe much more comfortably/we shall be able to take out the tube so you can have a proper drink/your legs won't hurt so much. . . ."

Children who wonder if/suspect that, they are dying, usually try to ask somebody. But that somebody will often not be a parent, because even very young children sense the misery of their closest adults *and try to protect them*. Just as husband and wife often pass the last weeks of one of them with neither wanting to hurt the other by mentioning death, so the same sad loneliness often happens between parent and child. Such a child may try to ask the nursing or medical staff, but will often find his questions deflected, his remarks unheard and a facade of false assurance erected around him. All those who have worked in this painful area agree that *a child who wants to know should be answered*. Anyone to whom he gives a clue, be it a relation, a member of the domestic staff, a nurse or doctor, should be able to share the child's thoughts with the whole caring team and parents, so that all concerned can decide how best to communicate with him. One five-year-old, for example, said to a junior nurse, "I won't be here at Christmas." She chose to take that as meaning that the little girl hoped not to be in the hospital for Christmas and brightly replied, "No, I hope you'll be home with Mommy and Daddy by then." Later, the same child tried another nurse with the words, "I won't be having Christmas." She, too, chose to misinterpret and replied, "Oh, but you will, we have lovely Christmases here with carol singers and a tree and everything. . . ." That night her mother found her crying bitterly. Asked what hurt, she said, "My Christmas hurts." Fortunately, her mother found the strength to discuss the child's emotional state with the pediatrician. A conference was called, the earlier remarks came to light, and it was agreed that this particular child needed honest communication which would allow her to share her worry about dying just as she had always shared all her worries with her parents.

Children who do know that they are dying commonly fear:

The moment of death itself, which is often seen as a violent, painful and dramatic event. Tremendous comfort can be given by realistic assurances that there will be no pain or knowledge of the moment of death; that it will be, so to speak, a gentle and imperceptible drifting.

The separation from parents implied by death. Nothing makes children more anxious than the prospect of being separated from the people they love; of being alone and unprotected; of having to manage themselves instead of being supported. For this reason it is easier to comfort such a child with the agnostic's view of death as a complete absence of being, than with the religious person's view of death as a passing on to God or to heaven. The young child who is told that he will go to anyone, anywhere, will take the statements literally and will not want to go without Mommy. The child who can be convinced that Mommy and Daddy will be with him always (i.e., for as long as he exists at all) will be comforted.

Answering questions honestly need not always mean volunteering the whole truth

There are many situations in which, while his parents are in terror that a child may die, the prognosis is uncertain and the child himself has not considered the possibility. If there is *any* hope, however slender, that a life-threatening operation will succeed or that the new antibiotic will control an otherwise overwhelming infection, that hope needs to be fed into the child's own "will to live." In situations of this kind there can be no justification for burdening him with calculating the odds of his own survival and no possible benefit to him in sharing parents' fears. Furthermore, faced with surgery or with dramatic emergency treatment, his attention and anxiety will probably not be focused on the outcome but on the procedures themselves. What could be more calculated to increase his fear of surgery than the knowledge that he may never wake from the anesthetic?

There are other situations, too, in which a knowledge of the child's own concerns should probably dictate the kind and amount of "truth" which he is told. If, for example, he has some form of childhood cancer and his doctors are hopeful that intensive treatment will induce a remission, his parents will remain aware that the disease will probably kill him within a few years, but *his* attention will be on that disease-free period. To tell him that he "will not live to grow up" is to spoil for him what might have been several years of life. A sick nine-year-old is concerned with whether or not he will be back at school next term or able to join the family's summer vacation. He is not concerned with whether or not he will live to go to college, to marry or to give his parents grandchildren. If repeated treatment cycles are needed and periods of remission become shorter or less complete, there may come a time when he does ask "Will I ever be quite better?'' and then he may need some more truth. But in the meantime, he needs the promise of returning health, however temporary, to carry him through this bout of illness.

In a similar way, most wise doctors who specialize in the treatment of children with conditions in which slow deterioration is inevitable, agree that such a child needs to be helped to live with the here-and-now, unclouded by the dark future. Usually such a child will come to terms with each stage of a progressive illness as it occurs. At the stage when all he suffered from was muscle weakness, the idea of a wheelchair-bound future would have horrified him, but by the time he needs that wheelchair it spells liberty from the imprisonment of being scarcely able to walk; it is accepted as a friend rather than an enemy.

This ability to live in the present and therefore to accept gradual change, day by day, is one which some parents learn to share in the interests of their own survival. One put it like this:

"We had a couple of black weeks soon after his illness had been diagnosed when we were wondering how we would ever tell him that he'd have to be in a chair; that he'd never be able to be completely independent; never marry or have children. . . . But he was eight. He didn't care about all that. What he cared about was finishing the tests and getting out of the hospital and then about getting back to school. After a while, we realized he was happy, it was only we who were miserable. I even had a stage when I was almost angry with him for *being* happy. But then we learned; we learned that if what really mattered to him was going fishing, we'd better get fishing too *and* find a way he'd be able to fish as long as possible. That's the way we've played it ever since. . . .''

Sudden Infant Death Syndrome (SIDS) or crib death

In the Western world more babies who survive the first month of life will die before their first birthday of SIDS than for any other reason. Research effort is being lavished on these tragedies yet research findings—and their interpretation by the media—are often misunderstood, both by parents who suffer a crib death and by the community at large.

Crib deaths are unexpected deaths The essence of each tragedy is that, until the moment when he was found dead, nobody had any suspicion that the baby could be in danger. The cases which make the headlines are of healthy babies put to bed by their parents and found dead a few hours later. But some SIDS babies were known to be unwell (usually with "colds") prior to their deaths; some had been seen by their doctors on the previous day; a few have even died in hospital nurseries. Whether they were thought entirely well or not, whether they had been seen by health professionals or not, these babies' deaths were completely unexpected.

Not all crib deaths remain a complete mystery Investigations after the death sometimes reveal conditions which proved fatal although nobody knew of their existence. Some examples are septicemia, overwhelming gastroenteritis and a variety of rare congenital heart or kidney disorders. In a sense, these should not be regarded as crib deaths at all, but as sudden deaths which, while tragic, are not mysterious. Unfortunately they are sometimes counted in with the statistics on crib deaths. More unfortunately still, they sometimes give rise to headlines which suggest that because *this* SIDS baby died because of a heart condition, heart conditions have now been shown to be the (or a) cause of crib deaths.

Rather more often, investigations reveal conditions which are not normally serious enough to cause death but which may, nevertheless, have contributed to it. A particular virus affecting the upper respiratory tract is a common example. It is usually impossible to say whether the baby "died of the virus," died because the viral infection made SIDS more likely, or died because he was in some way especially sensitive to the virus.

Similar puzzles are presented when conditions are found which could either have caused the death or been caused by it. Inhaled milk in the lower respiratory tract is one example. Did the baby die because he deeply inhaled some of his feeding, or is the milk found in his lungs because of attempts at mouth-to-mouth resuscitation?

In the majority of crib deaths no explanation whatsoever can be found

It is with reference to this group of deaths that so many theories are propounded, ranging from undetectable cardiac abnormalities, through neurological peculiarities leading to a cessation of breathing, to subtle biochemical imbalances. From time to time one such theory receives wide publicity; allergic reactions to cow's milk protein (*see* **Allergy**/Gastrointestinal allergies) was one which became popular recently; but no single theoretical explanation for SIDS has yet stood up to careful investigation. *It is probable that there is no single explanation* but that SIDS can result from any, or any combination, of many factors.

Until or unless we learn more, we can only combat SIDS with excellent health care

We cannot prevent deaths whose cause we cannot discover, but we can try to carry, bear and rear our babies in circumstances which seem likely to give them the best possible chance of resisting or overriding anything which threatens them. Unfortunately many misleading statements about "social factors in crib deaths" have been widely broadcast and must have given rise to fearful guilt in families who have suffered SIDS, and to equally horrendous anxiety among those expecting a baby.

Many of the most misleading statements arise from a confusion between *sudden deaths for which a sufficient cause is later discovered* and the *true crib deaths which defy explanation*. It is widely believed, for example, that crib deaths are more frequent among families of lower socio-economic class. Taking the whole group of babies who die unexpectedly, this is statistically true, but taking only the unexplainable crib deaths, it is not. In the most recent careful British study, for example, the number of completely unexplained crib deaths was almost exactly equal for families from social classes I and II and for social classes IV and V. The greater overall number of unexpected infant deaths in comparatively deprived families probably simply reflects the fact that, despite our National Health Service, life and health are riskier for the poor than for the rich. Mothers may be less well nourished in pregnancy; they may make less use of ante-natal care; they may be unable to provide such good conditions for the new baby and they may possibly be slower to seek help for babies who are not thriving or are unwell.

It has also been stated that SIDS is more probable in bottle-fed than in breast-fed babies, but yet again this statement needs careful consideration. Breast-feeding is certainly better for young babies (*see* **Eating**/Types of food for babies: Breast-feeding). It offers protection against many infant ills, ranging from protection against allergy to cow's milk, through protection against the biochemical dangers of formula which are made too concentrated, to the specific protection against various kinds of infection which mothers pass to babies in their milk. A fully breast-fed baby may therefore be less likely to succumb to sudden death from a number of identifiable causes; he may even be "healthier" in a sense which makes him more resistant to any threat, but none of that suggests that breast-feeding will prevent a true crib death. In that same British study, forty-six percent of the babies who died inexplicably had been breast-fed for some period.

When you read headlines such as "Mothers who smoke risk crib death," don't leap to the conclusion that your smoking caused your recent tragedy or that you must now live in terror that your child will die. Take it instead as another reminder that anything you can do to optimize your own health in pregnancy (including giving up smoking!) will be good for the unborn baby, and that everything you can do to make sure that he is well cared for after birth will be good for him, too. But if you take care of yourself, accept all the help you can get from medical professionals and take care of him to the best of your ability, *you are doing or have done everything that can be done to guard against SIDS.*

After a family has experienced the unexpected death of a baby Whether the death was a true crib death which remains a mystery, or whether it is eventually explained, parents' torment is often increased by their own, or other people's failure to understand some of the feelings which are certain to be aroused.

Such a death is a bereavement just as tragic as the death of a much older child. The baby must be mourned as the unique individual who he was. His existence cannot be brushed aside just because it did not last for long, nor is it usually advisable to "replace" him by becoming pregnant again as quickly as possible. Parents who try to sidestep grief by immediately resuming life as it was before the birth commonly become exceedingly depressed within a few months. Those who are encouraged (often by medical advisers) to have another baby at once, often have very great difficulty in keeping the dead child and the new one separate in their minds and hearts and the "replacement child" often suffers severely as a result.

Such a death almost always leads to overwhelming parental guilt and often drives a wedge between parents because one or the other feels (rightly or wrongly) both blameworthy and blamed. Usually it is the mother who feels that her husband must hold her responsible. Occasionally, a father who happened to be in charge at the time of the death thinks that his wife must feel that if she had been there it would not have happened. Very often mothers receive a great deal of support from other family members and friends, leaving fathers to feel excluded from what is, after all, their bereavement too. Older children tend to suffer (*see above*) because they are simultaneously emotionally neglected, refused help in mourning their own loss and made to feel guilty at being still alive.

Investigations into the death should be the principal source of practical help because it is through them that a cause for the death may be discovered and that, even if no cause can be found, freedom from any responsibility for the death can be brought home to bereaved parents. If the baby did have a fulminating fatal infection or an unsuspected abnormality, they can be assured not only that they could not have known or saved him, but also that there is no mystery and therefore no realistic fear for subsequent babies. If no cause is discovered, it can be pointed out that what cannot be diagnosed cannot be prevented. What is intolerable is ignorance: the desperate questionings of 3 a.m., "Why us? What did I do? How could I have known? . . ." and the "If onlys": "If only I had woken up; if only I had gone in sooner; if only he had been in my bed. . . ."

The questions need answering, not only to lessen the agony of parents bereaved *now* but to increase our knowledge of sudden infant deaths so that one day, fewer parents need face such tragedies. Unfortunately parents do not always feel supported or helped by the immediate investigations. By law, any completely unexpected and inexplicable death must involve police inquiries and a coroner's inquest. The arrival of police often makes parents feel that they are under some sort of suspicion. In some neighborhoods police inquiries also make neighbors less than helpful. There is always a tendency for acquaintances and casual friends to shun the bereaved ("I wouldn't know what to say to her . . ."). Social isolation sometimes turns into cruel rumor-mongering because neighbors assume that the police are investigating "baby-battering."

In many communities organizations have been set up within which bereaved parents can both help each other and help research workers to help them. Such groups aim to support the recently bereaved and to discover from them what kind of "help" is most genuinely helpful. At the same time, the first hand accounts of these babies' deaths can provide clues which may, one day, help to prevent them. If your doctor does not know of such a group in your area, you can contact directly the National Foundation for Sudden Infant Death, 310 South Michigan Ave, Chicago, Ill. 60600.

Dehydration *see* **Accidents**/Shock: Causes of major shock; Sunburn and heat illness; **Diarrhea, Gastroenteritis and Food Poisoning.** *See also* **Nursing**/Nursing your child at home: Fluids.

Delirium *see* **Nursing**/Side effects of high fever. *See also* **Accidents**/Head injuries.

Dental health *see* **Teeth**.

Depression

Although we speak of being "depressed" when we are feeling sad, disappointed, lonely, discouraged and generally miserable, *clinical* depression is something very different from a passing mood. It may amount to a major psychiatric illness and one which carries with it a very real risk of suicide (*see* **Suicide**).

Authorities vary in the lines they draw between depressive *illness* and normal mood swings or appropriate reactions to real-life stresses. What follows is not a set of rules for do-it-yourself psychiatric diagnosis but an attempt to provide parents with some useful guidelines in deciding whether or not a child or adolescent needs help and, if she does, whether it should be practical and supportive or medical and psychiatric.

Normal depression

Everyday life is full of ups and downs. When disappointments and losses overweigh the balance, temporary depression is a normal reaction. A child may come home from school feeling depressed because she has been in trouble with a favorite teacher for poor work, has failed to make a team for which she tried out and has not received an invitation to a friend's party. How strongly she reacts to this collection of real but minor disasters will depend partly on her own internal and biochemical state. If she is overtired, convalescent or pre-menstrual, for example, physiology and misfortune will, so to speak, gang up on her so that, for the moment, she cannot see that she will feel better tomorrow. If, on the other hand, she is basically well and cheerful, she will probably be able to see them as separate misfortunes which she can either take action to put right or at least take comparatively lightly. In either case, a night's sleep and a new day will have lightened her mood. Even if she still regrets that poor mark, still wishes she had made the team, is still hurt at being left out of the party, she will be ready to get on with her life.

Longer-lasting situational or reactive depression

When something more serious happens—especially if it is something which alters every aspect of the child's life—depression is again a normal response. You may see it when a beloved pet dies or when a young lover defects. In either case, the larger the part played by the love object in the victim's life, the greater the likely response. You may also see it when a move takes a child away from her accustomed social setting or when separation or divorce disrupts the family. For the moment, the child cannot see how to manage herself and her life in this new and unhappy situation, and she may be quite unable to accept your assurances that she will "get over it." Nevertheless, she will. Even the depression which accompanies real bereavement seldom develops into true clinical depression. Those heartless-sounding aphorisms such as "time heals" are actually true; she will find herself adapting to a situation within which she honestly believed that she could never be happy again.

Cries of "pull yourself together" are scarcely tactful when addressed to someone who is miserable, whatever the reason, *but the person whose misery is reasonable* will in fact be able to cope actively with it in her own time. In life's normal moments of depression, action is often the quickest way to a more comfortable mood. The child may be able to make the effort to telephone the friend with whom she has quarrelled, or apologize to the person she has offended, and if she does so, she will feel better. If the misery arises from a collection of circumstances confused with physical discomforts, she may be able to comfort herself with a hot bath and an early night. Even in longer-lasting situational depression she may be able to see helpful action for herself, such as swallowing her pride and going to the party even without her accustomed escort. The point is that, however unhappy she may be, she can still see that there is, has been and will be happiness in her life, and however much of her life is involved in the misery, she can still feel that that life is under her own control. Her circumstances may be horrible but her image of herself is still intact even if it is swollen with weeping.

Clinical depression
People sometimes refer to true depressive illness as "primary depression," or "endogenous depression." Both terms refer to the fact that the mental state of the victim seems to arise "out of the blue" so that if her anguish is indeed "about" *anything* it is about some life event which seems comparatively unimportant to onlookers. But, of course, parents have to be careful in making such a judgment. If your son says that he is miserable this term because he is by far the smallest in his class of fourteen-year-olds, cannot compete with them in sports and has no real friends, the whole matter may seem trivial to you but be of overwhelming importance to him (*see* **Adolescence**/Puberty: Worries about puberty). In the same way, if your daughter goes into a Victorian-seeming decline over a lost boyfriend, your view of the importance of the lost relationship may be very different from hers. So while sudden depression, arising out of skies you had thought blue, should certainly alert you and make you think, you need other clues to suggest illness rather than unhappiness.

We do not know why some people are liable to clinical depression while others are not. There are certain life stresses which are often present in people who *are* clinically depressed (such as recent bereavement, childbirth, unemployment, chronic ill health and/or pain and so forth), but since there are millions of people who suffer these same stresses without depressive illness, the real-life events cannot actually be *causes* but must serve to "touch off" a depressive reaction in people who are already vulnerable. Those who lost, or were deprived of, parents or other vitally important caretakers during early childhood—especially those who did not fully mourn that loss—may be among those vulnerable personalities. So also may children whose real-life loss was not obvious, but who nevertheless grew up without the taken-for-granted security of a completely reliable and loving caretaker (*see* **Anxiety, Fears and Phobias**/The roots of anxiety).

The following are all accepted signs of clinical depression. Few victims, especially youthful ones, will display them all, but most will display some. You may see them suddenly or you may see them as a development of the existing unhappiness of situational depression. In either case your child will be unable to "pull herself together," act or react in ways which might make her happier, because this is an illness which is outside her control and one whose major features concern her inability to accept, far less seek, happiness.

Mood of hopeless sadness which the victim usually cannot, and does not try to, "justify" in terms of real events.

Loss of the ability to experience pleasure so that people, activities and treats which she normally finds fun suddenly seem hollow and empty.

Feelings of personal worthlessness. The victim tends to accept anything hurtful or unpleasant which happens to her as "no more than I deserve." She may actually deny previous accomplishments, denying that those excellent examination results were good or asserting that she was only included in that team, play or choir because "there wasn't anybody else." She will certainly be extremely pessimistic about the future because whatever challenges it offers she will be sure that she will deservedly fail to meet them.

This very low self-esteem is probably the principal sign of depression for which parents should be alert and it is also the symptom which makes it most difficult for the victim to pursue her normal life. She is robbed of motivation because there is no point in trying if you know you are going to fail. She may also rob herself of important personal relationships because there is no point in telephoning a friend who only speaks to you out of pity nor do you join a group in conversation when you know that you are not truly wanted. . . .

Feelings of guilt tend to follow on from feelings of worthlessness. The depressed child may feel guilty at failing to live up to other people's expectations or guilty because she can see that her state is upsetting you. Sometimes the guilt of depression becomes more generalized. She may feel as if she has committed some crime for which she deserves punishment; she may even take upon herself the crimes of the world and feel guilty because she has been well-fed all her life while the children of the developing world are starving.

Anxiety may, or may not, be an obvious feature of clinical depression (*see* **Anxiety, Fears and Phobias**/Free-floating anxiety). If it is, the victim may be over-active, unable to sit still and unable to concentrate on any task for long. If it is not, she may feel tired and lethargic: too tired to do anything; too tired even to formulate the flow of sentences which are needed for conversation. She may sit for long periods gazing sightlessly out of windows or at the television screen, and she may spend long hours in bed, unable to rouse herself in the morning to face a new day.

Physical symptoms are very common with clinical depression and may confuse you as to whether your child is physically or mentally ill. The most usual of all is probably disturbance of sleep. The child may have difficulty in falling asleep, but she is also very likely to awaken as early as 3 or 4 a.m. and be unable to get back to sleep until an hour or so before the time when she used to get up.

Headaches and backaches (*see* **Headaches**) are common, as are constipation and disturbances of the menstrual cycle. If clinical depression is left untreated for long, loss of appetite may lead to weight loss. Even in the earliest stages, pleasure in food is likely to be reduced so that even if she eats normally she is no longer enthusiastic about previous favorite foods.

Thoughts of suicide and a new and morbid interest in death in general are symptoms of depression which should always lead to an urgent response. Do not convince yourself that "she is not the type" or that "she wouldn't be so silly"; we do not know "the type" nor is self-destruction "silly" if you truly believe that you are a worthless, hopeless person, a burden on others and someone for whom there is no worthwhile future. . . . Actual threats of suicide are an emergency. Do not leave her alone in the black mists of her depression. She needs professional help.

Depression in children before puberty

Is often not recognized (indeed some authorities deny that it is possible) because it tends to take different forms from those suggested above. Some of its more usual manifestations seem the very opposite of depression and may therefore lead to the child being treated in highly inappropriate ways. For example, a depressed eight- or nine-year-old may:

Appear "hyperactive," undisciplined and unmanageable (see **Hyperactive Children).** He does not *say* that he feels unworthy of your love. He does not *say* that it is not worth trying to please you because nobody could ever be pleased with a child as wicked as him. He behaves as if he did not care for you, your feelings or your opinions, he calls down upon himself more and more disapproval and punishment and they reinforce the underlying depression and therefore the "bad behavior."

Appear "accident-prone" either in the sense of being completely careless of his own safety, so that he not only climbs the tall tree but tries to fly out of it, or in the sense of constantly damaging himself while apparently leading a normal life. If your child pays more visits to the emergency room, wears more plaster casts and adhesive dressings than any other child you know and embarrasses you with his frequent black eyes and facial bruises, ask yourself why. He may just be an active and courageous child who is being offered many challenges by his daily life. But he may be a child who cannot learn to look after himself sensibly because he does not feel either cared for or worthy of care.

With these younger children, most "behavior problems" relate directly to feelings of insecurity about love relationships with parents or other caretakers. Most, therefore, are reactions to sadness and inner pain. It does not matter whether or not you regard your troublesome child as *depressed* as long as you regard him as *troubled*. Above all:

Do not believe that he does not care about you, however often he says that he hates you or however don't-careish his behavior. He does care; the trouble is that he cannot, or dare not, let you see, or even let himself feel, that he cares. Ask yourself whether your love and support are truly unshakeable and, if they are, how you can help him towards believing it. If you cannot find and enact an answer, seek professional help from your doctor. Far from criticizing you for producing such a "difficult child" or scorning you for "not being able to cope with him," he will be thankful that you have been able to distinguish between "naughtiness" and emotional disturbance.

Desensitization *see* **Allergy.** *See also* **Anxiety, Fears and Phobias**/Phobias.

Diarrhea, Gastroenteritis and Food Poisoning

see also **Infection**/Preventing infection: Infection and home hygiene

Diarrhea

In the last stages of digestion, the walls of the intestine absorb much of the fluid from the material which is passing through it so that when a stool is eventually passed it is fairly firm and formed. The exact texture of stools varies from person to person and from day to day in the same person. But while soft, pasty stools may be entirely normal for the individual (particularly if that individual is a baby), the person who passes semi-fluid or completely liquid stools has diarrhea.

A diarrheal stool means that the intestine has not, on this occasion, absorbed the usual amount of liquid from the waste. There may be "intestinal hurry" such that the waves of contractions (peristalsis) are moving material so rapidly through the gut that it is never in contact with the intestinal wall for long enough for absorption to take place. There may be inflammation of the intestinal wall such that it is temporarily unable to absorb fluid. If the inflammation is acute, that intestinal wall may even be leaking extra fluid back the other way, from the circulation into the waste material.

Diarrhea need not mean that a person is ill. A baby may have diarrhoeal stools following a change in formula or the sudden addition of extra sugar to the diet. An older child may have diarrhea after a fruit feast while an adolescent may suffer in this way after his first wine party. An ill-judged dose of a stimulant laxative (*see* **Laxatives**) can produce intestinal hurry and diarrhea while broad-spectrum antibiotics quite often upset the normal flora of the gut and produce diarrhea as an unwanted side effect.

If a child past the toddler stage seems entirely well in every other way, the fact that he is passing very loose stools instead of stools which are normal for him is no cause for concern. Except in the youngest age groups (*see below*), diarrhea only requires consideration if there are other symptoms such as vomiting, fever, abdominal pain or cramps or if the stools are passed so frequently (and the need to pass them is so urgent) that the child's ordinary daily life is disrupted.

Diarrhea and bowel training   Children who are adjusting from diapers to using a pot, or the toilet, or those who have only recently acquired this kind of control, are often "caught out" by diarrhea. The urgent need to pass a liquid stool is a quite different feeling from the full-rectum sensation which they have learned to recognize. Such a child may soil his pants and be truly horrified by the mess. Of course he deserves every possible reassurance and an explanation which makes it clear to him that his loose stools are a temporary state of affairs. Even so, it may be kind to keep him close to home until the diarrhea stops. Even if his playgroup leader or nursery teacher is as understanding as you are yourself, his "friends" may not be.

Diarrhea and school   Some much older children will also find it difficult to attend school while they have diarrhea because some schools, in an effort to confine trips to the toilet to formal breaks, make it embarrassingly difficult for children to keep dashing out during a lesson.

Diarrhea can be inconvenient whenever circumstances make ready and instant access to a lavatory difficult. It can be tiresome, for example, on a long bus trip and it can waste precious time (and be embarrassing) during examinations. If an older child *who does not seem ill* has diarrhea at a time like this (and some children do react to stress with this "gut reaction") there may be a case for using one of the many "binding medicines" which are available over the counter.

Medicines for
diarrhea

Three types of medicine are widely available in many countries:

Kaolin mixtures. Kaolin is basically a kind of clay and these mixtures act simply by adding solidity to the diarrheal stool. The medicine does nothing to help the intestine absorb water or to slow up the passage of waste through it. It simply adds to what is going to be passed anyway so that the result is less liquid.

Antibiotic mixtures. Happily these are not available without a prescription in the US, but families may be offered them for "traveller's diarrhea" when on vacation in some Western European countries. They should not be accepted. Antibiotics are seldom indicated in diarrhea (*see below*) and never in diarrhea without associated illness. They are often contra-indicated.

Mixtures containing codeine or opium or morphine. Sometimes offered in combination with kaolin, these mixtures aim to calm down the peristalsis and thus slow up the rate at which waste is moved through the intestine so that more fluid may be absorbed during transit. They also ease any abdominal pain or crampiness which may accompany the diarrhea. Such a medicine, taken only in the recommended dosage, may be extremely useful.

● Don't give any medicine for diarrhea to children under about ten without your doctor's advice.

● Don't give these medicines, even to older children, if they have any symptoms apart from the diarrhea. If the loose stools are due to an infection, for example, it may be a mistake to encourage the body to retain them artificially.

Diarrhea in babies and toddlers

Whatever the cause of diarrhea, it has to be taken far more seriously in babies and very young children than in older people. Babies have a much greater turnover of water in their bodies than the rest of us. They need to drink more water for every pound of their body weight to maintain the fluid balance in their bodies, and they have only a very small margin to protect that balance if fluid should become scarce.

In diarrhea, fluid can become scarce. The baby drinks his ordinary bottle, but instead of most of its fluid (as well as its nutrients) being absorbed into his circulation, most of it is passed straight out again as a liquid stool. If his intestines are much inflamed as well as hurried, that liquid stool may contain not only the liquid from his bottle but extra fluid from earlier drinks leaked back through the walls. If he loses more water and salt than he can take in and absorb, he will rapidly become dehydrated. Untreated, dehydration can upset the chemistry of the baby's whole body and make him extremely ill, even if the original cause of the diarrhea was trivial. Dehydration is increasingly likely if:

The baby goes off his food. Milk is both food and drink to him so if he refuses his normal formula he must have some other liquid. Plain water, sweetened water or well-diluted fruit juice will all do equally well. It is the fluid which matters. The more liquid he will take the better, since only some of it is being absorbed. He will probably find frequent small drinks more acceptable than occasional full bottles.

The baby is feverish. Fever increases the body's need for water and therefore a net loss will occur more easily.

The baby is vomiting. If he vomits whatever liquid he is willing to drink, his body has no chance to absorb it and furthermore each episode of vomiting may lose him more fluid than he has just taken.

Preventing dehydration
If a baby or very young child has diarrhea, you know that he is losing fluid. If he does not seem unwell, you can afford to wait a bit before consulting a doctor. Let him have his ordinary feedings but offer extra drinks in between. The more often he is passing liquid stools (and the more copious they are) the more often you should offer drinks. You are trying to make sure that more goes in than comes out. Very young babies sometimes feed willingly even during a diarrheal illness which is serious and which is dehydrating them, so do not assume that as long as he will eat, he cannot be very ill. Unless you are quite certain that more fluid is going in than is coming out, take him to the doctor. An older baby who will feed readily and take extra drinks probably will not become dehydrated, but as soon as he refuses his normal feedings, contact your doctor. He must now be counted as "unwell."

While you are waiting for the doctor to see your child, keep soiled diapers (that smelly plastic bag will give the doctor some idea of the amount of fluid he has lost and enable him to take a sample for the laboratory if he wishes) and keep on offering whatever fluids he will drink. Try to get about 2 oz. of fluid per hour down a baby and about twice that amount down a toddler.

If he will not drink nearly that amount or especially if he vomits what he drinks, don't wait for that appointment. Ask your doctor to see him as an emergency. If this is impossible, take the child to your nearest hospital.

● A child under a year old should not be left for more than four hours without medical attention if he is having diarrhea and vomiting, especially if he is refusing to drink.

If you are far from medical help or if a baby suddenly shoots a high fever with diarrhea and vomiting, he may start to become dehydrated before you can summon help. The principal signs are:

Signs of dehydration
Lethargy. The baby seems floppy, sleepy or withdrawn and usually cannot be bothered to suck so that he does not seem at all thirsty.

● Don't be fooled into "leaving him in peace until the morning."

Glazed and sunken eyes. The baby's face looks drawn and ill, and it is difficult to get his full attention or to make him "sparkle."

Inelastic skin and dry-looking tongue.

Scanty urine. Sometimes the very first alerting sign of dehydration is an unexpected dry diaper. If urine is passed there will not be much of it and what there is will probably be highly concentrated, yellow and strong-smelling. His body is fighting to retain fluid so the urine will have an unusually high ratio of waste products to water.

● In acute diarrhea, stools may be so watery that they cannot be distinguished from urine and the diaper appears simply wet. Do not let this fool you into thinking that the diarrheal stools have stopped and that the baby is passing plenty of urine.

Lack of tears. A baby old enough to cry real tears may now cry dry-eyed.

Coping with dehydration Once the fluid and salt balance in a baby's body is disturbed, he needs hospital treatment because he needs to have the fluid and salt put directly into his bloodstream by intravenous transfusion (*see* **Hospital**/Procedures) while the cause of the diarrhea which started the trouble is found and dealt with. You can give some immediate first aid (especially if getting him to a hospital will take an hour or more).

Take one pint of water (boil it, if boiling is necessary, before you measure it out) and stir in one level tablespoonful of sugar (or glucose if you happen to have it) and one *pinch* (not more than a quarter of a level *tea*spoon) of salt. The resulting solution will be the nearest thing to the fluid the baby's body requires which you can produce at home.

If the baby will suck, but is vomiting, give him a single ounce at a time, as slowly as he will take it. If he vomits at once, give him another ounce immediately. If he keeps it down for more than a quarter of an hour it will probably have done some good. Give him another ounce half an hour after the first.

If the baby will not suck, whether or not he is vomiting, try to get at least a little of your mixture down him from a small spoon. Anything is better than nothing.

● Don't reverse those sugar and salt suggestions. A very little salt will help. Too much is extremely dangerous.

● If the fluid seems to provoke vomiting, stop it and concentrate on getting to the hospital at top speed. Remember that when he vomits he probably loses more fluid than you have just given him. On the other hand, if the vomiting seems to happen anyway, you may be able to time those tiny drinks so that some is absorbed before the next vomiting.

● It will help the hospital doctors to decide on immediate treatment if you can jot down the times at which the baby vomited, passed diarrheal stools or had something to drink.

Gastroenteritis

Although gastroenteritis really only means inflammation of the gastrointestinal tract (and could therefore be applied to any kind of diarrhea and to food poisoning), it is a term which is usually reserved for diarrhea with or without vomiting and/or fever, due to infection. As we shall see (*see below* Food poisoning), there are many types of bacteria which can cause gastroenteritis but these normally multiply in food to reach an infecting dose and are therefore considered as food poisoning except that infant food poisoning, due to multiplication of bacteria in milk, is referred to as gastroenteritis. In older children and adults, an illness referred to as gastroenteritis is usually due to infection by viruses.

Some viruses typically infect the gastrointestinal tract, but many others (including some of the common cold viruses) may infect either the respiratory or the gastrointestinal tract depending on how they are taken into the body and on where the victim is susceptible. A family "bug," which announced itself as your head cold, may give one child tonsillitis and another diarrhea and vomiting.

Gastroenteritis can be a severe illness with high fever, vomiting and copious diarrhea. But it can also be a twenty-four-hour affair amounting to no more than a few very loose stools and some nausea. The younger the child, the more likely it is that he will be badly affected because of dehydration.

Although a doctor should always be consulted about a baby or toddler with diarrhea associated with vomiting and/or fever, medical advice is only needed for an older child if he seems really unwell. There is little that a doctor can do to help in a mild case of gastroenteritis. He cannot find out exactly which microorganisms caused the infection because, as we have seen (see **Infection**/Types of infection: Difficulties of laboratory diagnosis of infection), culturing viruses in the laboratory is a lengthy (and expensive) business and pointless in an illness from which the patient will certainly recover long before results become available. He is very unlikely to want your child to have an antibiotic because the infection is likely to be viral and the drugs would, therefore, be useless at best and actually stressful to the already stressed bowel at worst. If the illness should turn out to be severe there will be plenty that the doctor can do to make sure that his general condition is well-maintained. But ordinary diarrhea and vomiting in a child past toddler age is a case for home nursing.

Nursing gastroenteritis Older children can become dehydrated too, although their bodies need more cause and more time than the bodies of younger children.

Make sure that your child drinks plenty from the time he begins to vomit and/or pass diarrhoeal stools. It does not matter at all if he does not want anything to eat but he should have at least a small glassful of something every hour while he is awake. Although you do not have to be absolutely rigid about it, try to see that he drinks at least two pints during any full day during which he is not eating and is passing a lot of loose stools.

If he is nauseated or actually vomiting, as well as having diarrhea, avoid fizzy drinks and milky ones. Plain water or fruit juice is usually the easiest to take. It often goes down best if it is iced. Small sips from a small glass are less nauseating and daunting than gulps from a tumbler.

Take his temperature. If you later have to call the doctor, he will be interested to know whether the temperature he finds is higher or lower than it was at the beginning of the illness.

Let him stay in bed if he feels like it (vomiting and diarrhea are exhausting so he may), but he does not have to stay there if he is well enough to feel bored.

Don't give "binding medicines" or painkillers. He may have gripey abdominal pains just before each diarrheal stool, but if he has continuous or severe pain then its relief is up to a doctor. Call the doctor anyway if:

The child seems collapsed, confused or ill in a way which, whether or not you can say why, really worries you.

Vomiting continues over more than twelve hours or happens more than four times in six hours. The doctor may give a medicine to stop the actual vomiting and this will be pleasanter for the child and make it far easier to keep his fluid intake up.

There is blood in the diarrheal stools.

There is continuous abdominal pain or intermittent pain which is severe enough to stop him in his tracks/make him cry/wake him in the night. It is just possible that some quite different kind of abdominal emergency is masquerading as gastroenteritis (*see* **Abdominal Pain**); you need a doctor to check. Furthermore, if it is "only" gastroenteritis, your doctor may give the child medicine to reduce the painful spasms of his intestine.

He goes on feeling and seeming ill for more than forty-eight hours. The diarrhea may continue for longer than this because it takes some time for an inflamed intestine to settle back to normal, but the child should be feeling a great deal better "in himself" by this time.

Several members of the family become ill at the same time. If they have all shared a particular meal, the gastroenteritis may be due to food poisoning (*see below*). The doctor may wish to notify the public health authorities so that any slip-up in food-hygiene arrangements can be identified and dealt with.

Preventing the spread of gastroenteritis

Although the virus can certainly be spread from one person to another via unwashed hands, etc., it may well also be one which can be spread by droplets from the nose and mouth. You may not be any more successful in controlling gastroenteritis than you can be in controlling ordinary colds. But where there is gastroenteritis in the family, it is worth making strenuous efforts to avoid infecting babies. Try to keep the baby apart from his suffering sibling. Take trouble over disinfecting anything touched by diarrhea or vomit. Make sure the patient uses only his own towel, facecloth, etc. and that you do not leave his mixed up with other people's. Above all, remember to wash your own hands between playing nurse and playing parent (*see* **Infection**/Preventing infection: Sterilants, disinfectants and antiseptics).

Food poisoning

While there are many water- or milk-borne microorganisms and other types of irritant, which can cause gastroenteritis, many outbreaks in Western societies (with their high standards of water and milk hygiene) are caused by bacteria in or on food. All can therefore be loosely termed "food poisoning," although it is not the food which is poisonous but the load of pathogenic microorganisms which it carries. Food does not have to be "bad" to cause illness. In fact rotten, smelly, moldy food is rather unlikely to make people ill as few will eat it, unless they are starving.

The food which is most likely to cause illness is not just food which contains bacteria (almost all foodstuffs do), nor even food which contains pathogenic bacteria in small numbers (most people will cope with these without experiencing symptoms), but food in which pathogenic bacteria have been given the opportunity to multiply and which is then eaten while these vast numbers are alive and active. A recent outbreak in the UK, for example, involved large quantities of frozen minced beef cooked and distributed by the Meals on Wheels service. Blocks of the mince were placed, still frozen, in a larger container and "cooked." The quantity was so large that the mince could not be thoroughly stirred so the center of each block was at full boiling point for a much shorter time than the outside. The cooking did not therefore sterilize the meat completely. The mince was now left in its vast pot overnight where it cooled, very slowly, to room temperature. Any bacteria which had survived the initial cooking now had an ideal environment in which to multiply. Next day the mince was merely warmed (not brought to a full boil and kept there for several minutes) so that once again a proportion of the now much greater number of bacteria survived. The mince was served into individual portions, placed in a warming table and distributed over a period of several hours. While that table would have kept boiling food at a safely high tempera-ture, it was not designed to heat food which was merely warm, so those hours provided yet another incubation period of gentle warmth. Almost everyone who ate the mince was ill.

This warning story illustrates the fact that the prevention of food poisoning is only partially under the control of individual families. We can take responsibility for the handling, storage, preparation and serving of food in our own kitchens, but many of us eat many meals, often prepared on a vast institutional scale, in school kitchens, cafeterias and restaurants. Furthermore, even the food which we do serve and eat at home has been pre-prepared for sale whether it is sold raw, processed or pre-cooked. We therefore have to depend very heavily on public health measures and on the public responsibility of the food industry. If there is a failure somewhere in this complicated chain, it is important that we work out where things went wrong. If you know that you ignored an expiration date or forgot to refrigerate Monday's casserole after cooking it on Sunday morning, you can learn by your own uncomfortable mistake. But where a product which is guaranteed "long life" ferments within that extended shelf-period, or where you know that your own handling of food which caused illness was impeccable, it is important that the authorities be told. In the meanwhile, a very few basic food-handling principles may help you to avoid food poisoning either from your own or from anyone else's kitchen.

Most bacteria are killed by high heat. Cooking food right through so that every bit of it is exposed to high heat will usually render it safe for immediate eating.

Most bacteria multiply fastest in food which is warm. If cooked food must be cooled for later eating, cool it covered (to prevent live bacteria from getting in) and fast (so that any live bacteria have a minimal chance to multiply). Keep it cold until wanted.

If it is to be eaten cold, keep it covered to prevent cross-contamination by other (perhaps raw) food, by flies, etc.

● Reject hamburgers and other "fast foods" served to you warm from "keep hot" containers.

If the food is to be reheated and eaten hot, make sure that it is made really hot again right through so that any bacteria which escaped the first cooking, or were introduced after it, are now killed.

● Don't ever *warm up* cooked food for a baby to just the temperature he likes. *Reheat*, cool rapidly and feed.

● Remember that your shopping bag in your office is at "room temperature," which is warm. Don't keep food which is to be eaten without further cooking there for hours.

● Remember that shops are at room temperature, too. Don't buy ready-to-eat foods from unrefrigerated counters.

Bacteria from raw foods, flies, unwashed hands or septic lesions can contaminate ready-to-eat foods. Poultry, for example, almost invariably carry pathogenic bacteria which will be killed by thorough cooking. But if raw chicken blood gets onto your chopping board or your hands and from there onto that liver sausage, those who eat the sausage a few hours later may suffer.

Septic cuts and so forth usually teem with bacteria. Again, if these get onto meat you are going to cook they will probably cause no harm, but if they get onto the creamy pastry you are going to serve cold this evening, they may multiply to an extent which will make people ill.

● Try not to buy cooked meats from counters which also handle raw meats, especially if the same slicer is used to slice, say, that cooked ham and raw bacon.

Milk, egg and sugar is an ideal growth medium for bacteria. Items such as commercially produced custard tarts and so forth will certainly breed pathogens if any are given the opportunity to reach them. Such items are probably safest sold from the freezer and/or in sealed wrappings. If you buy them "loose" make sure that the shop is observing proper precautions against flies and keeps its goods in refrigerator cases.

● While ice cream, being frozen, is reasonably safe, the ice cream cones sold to you from a van may not be as the melted spillage around the edge of the tub or on an ill-washed scoop may be teeming with bacteria. If you want to buy ices from such a source, choose wrapped items, preferably those which are water- rather than "cream"-based.

Salmonella food poisoning (Salmonellosis)

The most frequent food-borne disease reported in man, salmonellosis is caused by tiny gram-negative bacteria of which there are many varieties. Two of the most virulent cause typhus and paratyphoid fevers, which are not usually classed as "food poisoning" as the infection takes hold over ten days to two weeks after the infecting dose has been taken in.

The incidence of the many more rapid and less serious types of salmonellosis is difficult to estimate because, although it is a "notifiable disease," many attacks pass off so quickly that they are never reported to a doctor while even those seen by doctors are often simply labelled "diarrhea and vomiting" and the laboratory studies which would identify the bacteria are never carried out.

Features of salmonella poisoning First symptoms usually appear twelve to twenty-four hours after eating infected food. The first sign is usually fever, quickly followed by diarrhea and vomiting. The fever may remain high for several days so that the attack is a definite "illness" rather than an unpleasant episode.

A recovered victim may continue to excrete salmonellae in the feces for several months or even for longer. People who work in the food industry, or with particularly susceptible populations such as young babies in nurseries, are required to have a series of fecal specimens examined to ensure that they are clear of the infection before they return to work.

Sources of salmonellae Many animals, including those we kill for food, and rodents suffer salmonellae infection and may excrete the organisms in their feces even when they appear well, thus infecting each other during transport to slaughter and so forth. The most common sources of infection to people in Western communities are:

Meat, especially pork (many pigs are carriers), and pork products such as sausages, especially when these meats are eaten raw or undercooked.

Eggs and egg products such as liquid egg for catering.

• Duck eggs are often highly contaminated both inside and outside. If duck eggs are used at all, they should be kept apart from all other foods while in the shell and should never be used in lightly cooked dishes.

Hens' eggs are seldom contaminated inside the hen but shells may become contaminated and, *if the shell is cracked,* bacteria may penetrate. Never use cracked eggs for uncooked items such as eggnog or for lightly cooked custards, etc.

Dairy products which are safe when made (because our milk is pasteurized) but may become contaminated afterwards.

Fish, oysters and other shellfish taken from sewage-polluted water, especially dangerous when eaten raw (*see* **Pollution**).

Clostridial food poisoning

Clostridiae are *anaerobic spore-forming* bacteria. Widely distributed in nature, in soil, sewage and the bowels of man and other animals, the spores are very heat-resistant, sometimes surviving four to five hours' boiling. However, such potentially living spores do not multiply unless they find an environment which has no (or very little) oxygen.

Features of clostridial poisoning First symptoms may not appear for twenty-four hours after infected food is eaten. Fever and vomiting are unusual, the illness usually being confined to about twenty-four hours of diarrhea and colicky pain.

Sources of clostridiae Because they are so widespread, the microorganisms are often in raw meat and poultry before they reach the kitchen. Poisoning can be avoided, however, if cooking methods provide high heat (roasting or pressure cooking rather than simmering, for example) and, above all, if cooked meat which may contain spores is not left to cool slowly under conditions which prevent oxygen from reaching those spores. The most commonly traced sources of infection are:

Large rolled joints, pre-cooked for eating cold or for rewarming. By rolling the joint, you (or your butcher) ensure that any clostridiae on the outside of the meat are taken into the center where there will be no oxygen and where neither heat penetration nor cooling will be effective. Eaten immediately, such a joint will do no harm. Left even for a few hours it may teem with sufficient bacteria to make anyone who eats it ill.

• Joints, especially rolled joints, should not be larger than about 6 lb. (3 kg), should ideally be very thoroughly cooked and, *especially if preferred underdone*, should be eaten immediately after cooking. If a rare roast of rolled beef must be eaten cold, it should be cooled very rapidly, in airy conditions, and refrigerated as soon as possible.

Casseroles can also provide anaerobic conditions for clostridiae as well as often being cooked at a low temperature and in advance, for reheating.

• If you intend to prepare a casserole in advance in this way, cut-up meat is safer than meat in a piece and it is essential that it reach a full boil before being put to simmer. Frequent stirring during quick cooling will help to oxygenate the casserole as will stirring during reheating, which must again be to a high temperature.

Staphylococcal food poisoning. *See also* **Impetigo and staphylococcal infections**

A few strains of staphylococcus aureus can cause food poisoning if they get from their usual habitats (skin, nose and throat) into food. A few of these microorganisms do no harm. In order to produce enough toxin to make people ill, there must be considerable multiplication.

For multiplication to take place, temperatures must be fairly high. A normal room temperature, for example, will not produce as rapid multiplication as heat wave, or even warming oven, temperatures. No multiplication will take place in an acid environment.

Features of staphylococcal food poisoning

Symptoms appear very soon after the food is eaten—within one to six hours. The illness begins with violent vomiting; this is followed by diarrhea but the whole episode is often over within half a day. Fever is not a feature and, if present, suggests a different diagnosis.

Although usually trivial if unpleasant, small babies or otherwise susceptible individuals can actually die from dehydration and shock.

Sources of staphylococcae

Identified sources are almost always food handlers. They may have staphylococcal infections of the throat, or infected wounds on their hands. They pass on the bacteria by breathing on, or touching, the food.

Since it takes both time and special conditions for bacteria introduced in this way to multiply to danger level, infection is usually traced to pre-cooked meats and meat products (pies, sausages, ham, etc.) which have not only been infected but have then been stored without refrigeration, or kept warm for long periods.

• If in doubt about the hygienic standards of a café, roadhouse or cafeteria, short-order food, cooked at the time, is safer than the meat pie or sausage roll which may have spent hours in a warming table.

Botulism

"Classic" botulism occurs when people eat food which contains the toxin released by spores of clostridium botulinum after germination.

The toxin is a deadly poison affecting the nerves which control muscles. When it causes death, it usually does so by paralyzing the muscles which make breathing possible.

The botulinus bacillus itself is little threat to man because it is anaerobic (unable to survive in any oxygenated environment) and highly sensitive to heat. Its spores can survive for years, dormant, even in adverse conditions, and are widely distributed in soil, dust and so forth. But in dormant form they are no threat to man, either. Millions of people take the spores in with their food and excrete them again unchanged. Trouble only arises if spores are given the opportunity to germinate in food and that food, now contaminated with toxin, is eaten (but *see below*).

Spores are destroyed by sufficient heat applied over a long enough period. They cannot germinate where there is oxygen, where the environment is acid or in the presence of nitrites. The food industry, well aware of the probable presence and particular habits of these spores, takes trouble to ensure that no germination can take place in its products. Jars and cans, for example, which provide an oxygen-free vacuum, are exposed to high heat levels. Foods which are to be preserved raw, and which might provide an oxygen-free environment for spores, are subject to other precautions. A side of bacon, for example, which cannot be subjected to lethal heat and which might be anaerobic at the center of a large piece, will have nitrites added to its preserving solution.

Most outbreaks of botulinus poisoning are therefore due to inadequate home preserving. Home-canned fruit is safely acid but home-canned vegetables, blanched rather than boiled and sealed up without vinegar, just might be risky. Botulinus poisoning is very rare, but it is certainly worth making sure that you follow recipes exactly, or take expert advice, before you embark on canning your own beans, preserving your own ducks or smoking your own bacon. . . .

Infant botulism

This quite different version of botulism was only discovered in 1976 and is still ill-understood. Infants, like the rest of us, are frequently exposed to botulinus *spores* but are most unlikely to be exposed to botulinus *toxin* because, in the early months of life, they are unlikely to be fed on home-preserved meat or pickles with too little vinegar. . . . However, it has been found that a very few infants under six months (about three hundred in the world so far) can develop the symptoms of botulinus poisoning because they have eaten the spores and *germination and toxin production have taken place in their intestines*. A search for the bowel conditions which make this possible is being actively pursued. Since no child over eight months has yet been found to be affected, it is thought that it must be some peculiarity of the bacterial flora in the very young which makes germination within the body possible. It must, however, be emphasized that the fact that this *can* happen in the very young does not mean that it is at all *likely* to happen. Even though doctors in many countries are now interestedly watching for cases of infant botulism, and finding a minute handful, there are millions of babies taking in botulinus spores and excreting them, like older people, without ill effects.

Why mention such a scary and remote possibility? Because there is just one precaution which many authorities believe that parents may, even at this very early stage in our knowledge, like to take. That precaution is to avoid feeding honey to babies under about one year of age.

Honey and infant botulism

Honey quite often contains botulinus spores because bees collect nectar from plants growing in soil, and honey production cannot involve subjecting it to high heats. About ten to fifteen percent of honey samples studied so far have been shown to contain some spores.

Studies of babies known to have suffered from infant botulism have further shown that some (by no means all, but more than would be likely by chance alone) had been fed with honey during the days before they became ill, and that the type of botulinus organism which made them ill was identical with the type found in the honey they had eaten.

On the evidence so far, nobody whose baby has been eating honey need panic; nobody should even say "honey causes infant botulism." What one can say is that a few very young babies seem able to germinate botulinus spores in their intestines and therefore that it is sensible to avoid feeding any baby any food which is known to be likely to contain these spores, especially if that food is not a necessary part of the diet.

Diet *see* **Eating.** *See also* **Allergy**/Gastrointestinal allergies: Living with elimination diets. **Dieting** *see* **Eating**/Eating problems: Obesity.

Diphtheria

Diphtheria is a bacterial infection (caused by one of three strains) which starts with local infection of the nose, throat or larynx but in which the infecting bacteria then release powerful toxins (*see* **Infection**/Bacteria) that can kill by damaging vital organs such as the heart. The infection is usually passed by droplet infection from the air. Unfortunately, healthy immune people can be "carriers" of diphtheria and the organisms can survive for some time on dust or other contaminated articles.

Diphtheria has almost been conquered in Western countries by mass immunization. But we must be careful. When mass immunization began in the thirties, many parents and doctors were all too aware of the fearsome nature of the disease. They had seen it, or suffered its ravages; immunization was therefore gratefully received. Now, most people—even most doctors—have never seen a case of diphtheria. A real threat has become a theoretical one and fewer people are accepting immunization for their infants *and* ensuring that they receive the necessary boosters as they grow up (*see* **Immunization**). Occasional minor outbreaks and a few deaths each year make it clear that diphtheria *could* regain its foothold in our communities. It is up to each and every family to make sure that this does not happen.

Immunization against diphtheria Is not by use of killed or live-but-attenuated bacteria, but by use of diphtheria toxoid which is a chemically de-activated preparation of the toxins released by diphtheria bacilli. The toxoid is no longer poisonous, but it is still capable of stimulating the body to produce anti-toxins.

Schick test Is a simple skin test to determine whether or not an older child has diphtheria anti-toxins (whether, for example, an immunization has been successful) and/or what level of natural protection he has (whether, for example, a booster would be advisable).

    If he has no anti-toxins, the injection of a minute quantity of toxin into the skin produces reddening of the area. If he has circulating anti-toxins the injected toxins are neutralized and no reddened patch develops.

    ● Note that the interpretation of the Schick test is the reverse of the Mantoux test for tuberculosis (*see* **Tuberculosis**). In diphtheria, no reaction means that the individual is immune. In tuberculosis, no reaction means that the individual is not immune.

Anti-toxins in the treatment of diphtheria When diphtheria is clinically diagnosed, antibiotics which are at least partially effective against most of the infecting bacteria are given but, while these may kill or prevent the further multiplication of the bacteria, they are not effective against the toxins those bacteria have already released. Passive immunity to those toxins can be temporarily given by the administration of anti-toxins prepared from the blood of horses, stimulated to produce them by previous doses of toxoid. Anti-toxins are far safer than they used to be but some individuals are still hypersensitive to the horse serum which contains them. Furthermore, while anti-toxins may be life-saving in an individual case of diphtheria, they cannot *prevent* diphtheria. Passive immunity cannot do the job of active immunization.

Discipline, Self-discipline and Learning How to Behave

See also **School**/Discipline in your child's school.

Most of us would reject the idea of trying to give our children the kind of discipline which dictionaries define as "teaching rules and forms of behavior through continual repetition and drill. . . ." It sounds more appropriate to a military parade ground than to a family living room. We certainly want to produce disciplined children who will, eventually, be disciplined adults, but we do not want those disciplined people to be accurately defined as "those whose obedience is unquestioning. . . ." If we do not want the militaristic or dictionary versions of discipline, what is it that we want?

    When you are thinking about the kind of discipline you want to use, and encourage, within your family, it sometimes helps to abandon the word itself (because it is value-laden) and free yourself to think about the whole issue in a different way. If, for example, you stop calling it "discipline," but call it "learning how to behave," the whole business stops being something which is imposed on children and becomes something which, with our help, they do for themselves. Changing the word and the way we think about it also stops "discipline" from being a separate issue for serious discussion around the family conference table, and allows it to take its proper place as part and parcel of the rest of a child's growing up within the family. There is no reason why it should be any more difficult or any grimmer for a child to learn how to behave than it is for him to learn any of the other millions of things he learns as he grows up.

How *should* children behave?

It is difficult (although not always impossible) to teach knowledge or skills which you do not have yourself, so deciding how you want your child to behave is an important first step. Of course your answers will critically depend on who you are and where you live. One society's virtues can be insignificant in another and vices in a third. The difficulty of defining "human goodness" certainly contributes to the difficulties which the world's great powers have in understanding and communicating with each other. If you do not want a mini–cold war in your own household, make sure that you are all on an established wavelength which your child will be able to receive without too much interference and static.

But, of course, we do not have to work out exactly how we think a person should behave in every imaginable situation. As long as you are clear about the basic general principles of behavior which you want your child to learn, he will learn them as he learns a school subject. The do's and don'ts of daily life are simply examples of these principles. The behaviors which you prevent, correct or encourage are simply class exercises, homework and practice along the way. Whatever your own principles of behavior, your value system, your child will learn it and the behavior which is consistent with it, by the same sort of process. But your own strength of feeling on a range of issues will affect the priorities which you pass on to him. If, for example, you hold closely to a principle of non-violence, this will affect your "messages" on a range of issues from playground fights and acceptable kinds of punishment to the sports you encourage and even, perhaps, the television viewing you permit. If your value system is directed towards helping your child to become a good Catholic, you will be teaching him to accept the teaching of a higher authority than your own. If equality of the sexes underpins much of what you believe to be important, your belief will permeate what you teach to both sexes. You may find yourself encouraging particular kinds of behavior, not because you see them as "good" in themselves but because your daughter's insistence on playing school football makes a crack in a mold you want to see broken. The point is that you do not have to believe in particular ideals—certainly not the ideals implicit in these notes—to use this approach to discipline. The approach works whatever the content of the teaching.

How do children learn how to behave?

The most important part of any of a child's learning (whether of behavior, of geography or of competitive swimming) comes from inside himself. All human children, at every age-stage, have an in-built drive to grow up, to become more mature and more competent. That generalized human drive is, if you like, his engine. It is running; the power is there; he is ready to go.

Where that power takes the child is a social matter. He *can* learn almost anything which anybody chooses to show him as soon as he is physically or mentally ready. The direction the individual child takes will be dictated by the expectations of his community and society. In ours, for example, it is confidently expected that five- to seven-year-olds without specific handicaps will learn to read. Lo and behold, they do. In another culture, reading will not be expected of a child so young, but he will be expected to take responsible care of a baby or a herd of goats and he will do so. Sometimes it is interesting and surprising to abandon our own clear ideas about what children of different age-stages can and cannot do, and realize just how easily they can master a range of behavior and skills if these are part of their particular way of life.

Parents, of course, are the instruments through which those social expectations are passed on to a child, especially to a very young one. If society sets out the direction, parents plan the route and, at the beginning at least, do the steering.

The journey involved in learning how to behave is a long one. At the beginning, with a baby or toddler, you will have to keep a tight hold on the wheel and take the whole responsibility for avoiding potholes and taking corners safely. While you steer, your child is watching. He learns a great deal about how to behave from seeing how you behave—towards him and towards other people—but his own behavior is not yet his responsibility.

By the time he has acquired good control over his own body, fine coordination with his hands and eyes and the vital ability to understand and communicate in speech, he becomes ready for driving lessons. You still need dual control but he can try himself out. It is at this stage that it becomes easy to be so involved in the everyday bumps of temper tantrums and whining, breakages and cheek, quarrels and squabbles, that the goal of the journey becomes forgotten. Each of those bumps should teach your child something about how to behave, but each is only important as a minute example. If your days seem to be filled with attempts to keep your child out of the flower beds, you may sometimes need to remind yourself that the goal is not that he should learn only to run in particular places, or even that he should remember and obey your instructions. It is that he should learn to enjoy and protect places that give the whole family pleasure, and that he should reach a point where he does this himself because "keep out of the flower beds" has become part of his own control over himself. Sometimes you will actually watch this happen, stage by stage. After days and weeks of the ball-in-the-flower-bed and endless reminders and scoldings, there comes a day when, alone in the garden, he prepares to kick that ball but stops and shifts his position. "Oh no, Mike" you may hear him mutter to himself, "mind the poor flowers. . . ." Self-control is coming. He is beginning to know for himself how to behave. Soon he will be able to take charge of his own steering where the road is straight, with you to help him read the map at all the junctions.

The development of self-control is, of course, the point. However successful you may be in making a small child do as you tell him, he will not know how to behave until he can tell himself. Worthwhile discipline has to be self-discipline because the kind that keeps him safe and good when you are standing over him will not help when he is on his own. As he gets older, then, it is important not to be too hooked on obedience as a prime childish virtue. The only kind of obedience which is going to help him as an independent person is obedience to his own conscience; it is that conscience which is developing as he learns how to behave.

Some vital stages in learning how to behave

Babyhood A baby cannot learn how to behave "well" or "properly" until he has learned to behave in any particular fashion, *on purpose*. At the beginning of life his behaviors are either involuntary expressions of physical need (like crying from hunger) or spontaneous reactions to your behavior (like focusing on your eyes when you look at him and smiling and "talking" because you do).

You may find that you can build up habit patterns in him (so that you gradually "teach" him to last six hours at night without a feeding), but there will be no principle of behavior underlying what he does. He will not stay asleep longer because he ought, or because he knows he should not wake you up. He will not wake and cry because he wants to drive you mad, either.

Babies and Some parents, conscious of the importance of discipline, worry that even
"spoiling" quite young babies may get spoiled. They see older children and adults who are selfishly concerned only with their own gratification, giving no thought to anyone else's needs or feelings, and they dread being responsible for a person like that. "We'd better teach him that he isn't the only pebble on the beach," they agree, or, "Life is tough and she'd better start finding it out right now. . . ." Unfortunately, deliberate attempts not to spoil a baby have a nasty tendency to backfire.

In order to become either spoiled or the socialized opposite, a child has consciously to *want* things as well as unconsciously to need them. He has to be able to see himself as a being who is separate from a lot of other beings; to know that he has rights and that they have rights too, and to be able to plan deliberately to assert his rights to what he wants over their rights to withhold it. A baby can do none of these things. It is not that he is "naturally good," it is that he is not intellectually capable of being "bad." "If I make enough fuss can I make her stop doing that and come and play with me?" is not a question a baby is capable of asking himself. If he wants your attention it is because, for that moment, he needs it. If he needs it he will ask for it. What *you* may or may not want is irrelevant, not because he is a selfish, over-demanding spoiled brat but because he is not yet developmentally capable of putting himself in your shoes.

If you do find yourself deliberately withholding attention because your baby is "too demanding," be warned. The slower you are to meet the needs he expresses and the more you ration your attention to him, the more he will demand, because the more anxious he will become in case those needs are not going to be met. If you leave him to cry alone in his crib because "he has got to learn," he will not learn to play there quietly. Instead he will learn to cry hard the moment he awakens because experience of being left too long has made it impossible for him to be contented there. If his anxious demands harden your determination to resist him, the two of you will be into a vicious spiral which may create exactly what you were trying to avoid: an "unreasonably demanding," fretful, whiny baby.

The best possible foundation for later discipline is early love: love which is as mutual, as secure, as predictable and as enjoyable (for all concerned) as you can possibly make it. Why? Because at the very beginning your baby does not know that the two of you are separate. If he experiences you as warm and loving, good and need-fulfilling, he also experiences himself as all these things. This is, if you like, the very beginning of the good self-image and self-respect which are ultimately going to be his prime adult reasons for behaving "well" or "badly."

As he comes to realize his own separateness from you, that same loving care both makes him see himself as lovable and opens you to receiving love from him. By loving you he does two vital things:

He learns to behave in ways which show that he singles you out for love. All those enchanting behaviors which make it proudly clear that you are Mom are practice for the kinds of behavior we want him to learn later. He smiles at you because he loves you; he stops crying when you come because he loves you; he strokes you because he loves you; he "talks" to you because he loves you. He is practicing friendship; practicing love.

He acquires the loving feelings which will ensure that once he has the choice, he will prefer to please you. After all, everything which you are later going to show him and teach him about how to behave depends for its effectiveness on his caring about you, caring for your opinion, caring whether you approve of his behavior or not. There are going to be many moments in his childhood when this is the only factor which weighs in the balance to persuade him to do what he ought, rather than what he wants, to do. Weight the scales your way early.

The toddler years
Toddlers do a great many things which are tiresome, messy, wasteful or destructive. They try to do things which are dangerous. They seldom do anything which is positively helpful and they most particularly seem to avoid doing what they are told. No wonder these are the years during which many parents decide that lack of discipline is the root of their troubles and that the kind in which hand meets bottom is probably best. No conventional kind of "discipline" actually *works* with this age group, though. You need patience, humor and parent-upmanship to survive unscathed but, if you can muster them, your child will emerge, at two-and-a-half or three perhaps, *ready, willing and able to learn how* to behave.

Conflict within the toddler makes for conflict with you. He is no longer a baby who feels himself as part of you, using you as his controller, his helper, the mirror in which he views himself and his world. But he is not yet a child who feels himself a separate person, ready to take responsibility for himself and his own actions in relation to you. He is somewhere in between and if his in-betweenish behavior is confusing and irritating for you, it is downright painful for him. He *must* separate from you, reject your total control, develop his own likes and dislikes and pursue his own ends even when they conflict with yours. This is a developmental imperative: the essential next step in his growing up. But he still loves you with the unrivalled passion of infancy and still depends totally on your emotional support without which he cannot manage himself, let alone anything else. So any conflict in the interests of independence feels desperately dangerous to him. Emotionally, it would be far easier for him to remain a baby. You can see the conflict within him every time he yells at you to "Go 'way" and then dissolves into tears if you obey him. You can see how the seesaw of his emotional life goes up and down every time you try to push him into greater independence or hold him back from it. If you push him on, he is babyish and whiny. If you hold him back he rebels. Somehow you have to stand in the middle and keep that seesaw balanced for him.

The trick is in understanding that he cannot yet be "good" or "naughty" on purpose because he does not yet know "right" from "wrong," let alone know which is which in everyday life. But he wants to "be good" because he desperately wants you to love and approve of him. If you can keep him "good," most of the time, and above all avoid making him feel that you dislike or disapprove of him, when he reaches the stage where he can be good on purpose he will want to be so—usually.

Keeping a toddler "good" If you try to "discipline" a toddler you will be faced with a lack of comprehension which looks like defiance and every battle you join will end with love lost between you. So don't try for absolute control and don't join *moral* battles. He will be "good" if he happens to feel like doing what you want him to do and does not happen to want to do anything you would dislike. With a bit of parental cleverness you can arrange life so that most of the time he wants the same things that you want.

Suppose he has his dolls and soft toys all over the floor and you want them cleared away. If you tell him to do it he will probably refuse. If you explain that he should do it to help you, because you are so busy, because you do so many things for him, he will be completely uncomprehending and may make you feel that he doesn't care whether you are tired or busy or not. Cross, you can shout at him, punish him, threaten no ice cream for dinner; you can reduce him to a jelly of misery *but none of that will get the toys off the floor.*

But try saying, right at the beginning, "I bet you can't get all those toys put away before I've peeled these potatoes" and you turn the whole thing into a game. Now he *wants* to pick them up, so he will. He is not doing it because he is "good"; because he knows he ought or "for Mommy"; he is doing it because you have made him want to do what you wanted done.

Yes, this approach walks around trouble. But why is it wrong to steer his developmental car so that it does not keep crashing? The pay-off now is a pleasanter family life for all of you. The pay-off later is even more important.

That toddler is growing up. Soon he *will* understand your feelings and your rights; *will* remember your instructions, understand them and foresee the results of his own actions. Soon he *will* be able to behave well or badly on purpose. Which he chooses will depend largely on how he feels about you. If he reaches the next stage of growing up feeling that you are basically loving, approving and on his side, he will want, most of the time, to please you. So, with many lapses and mistakes, he will do as you wish. But if he reaches that stage feeling that you are basically hostile and disapproving, that what you want is incomprehensible and pushed upon him only by naked power, learning how to behave may be far more difficult for him. Some three- and four-year-olds feel that it is no use trying to please their parents because they never are pleased; no use minding when they are cross because they so often are; too dangerous to love them because they have so often seemed rejecting and hurtful. If the real business of learning how to behave is to take place smoothly and happily, your child must reach pre-school age wanting your approval; confident that it is easily earned; happy to cooperate with you to solve problems and absolutely sure that he loves you and that you love him.

A happy toddler is an easy toddler to "manage" and a toddler who is kept easy now will be easy to teach happily later on.

The pre-school child

If you like your child, are proud of him and really quite pleased with the job you have done as a parent so far, you will probably start showing him and teaching him how to behave as soon as he shows that he is ready to understand without ever really having to think about it. If you do think about it, try to remember the purpose of the whole process: it is not that he should accept discipline/instructions *from you* but that he should gradually come to discipline *himself*. If you are tough enough with a three-year-old you may be able to see to it that he obeys you, tells you the truth, behaves as you say and fears your displeasure. But none of that will keep him safe, honest and good when you are not there to tell him what to do. You are not going to be with him forever. By the time he is spending hours outside your company and influence, you want to be sure that you can trust him to look after himself and his behavior in all the ordinary situations he may meet.

All the following points are aimed in this one direction: at helping the child towards self-discipline or, if you prefer, towards the development of conscience. You will show him how to behave in countless different circumstances and situations, but you will be teaching him that all those different items of behavior add up to a few basic and vitally important principles. As he comes to understand those principles so he will become able to fit new events to them, and gradually you will be able to withdraw your constant control. He will apply the principles for himself because he has taken them in and made them part of himself.

Showing him how to behave

Do as you would be done by; your child will seldom give you (and other people) more consideration, cooperation and politeness than he gets from you. If you are always too busy to help with a construction kit and always ready to scream at him if he trips over your feet, he will not readily help you to set the supper table or refrain from yelling at you when the comb pulls his hair. . . .

Make sure that behaving well is nicer for him than behaving badly. It is easy to fall into the trap of buying a treat to keep a ceaselessly whining child quiet while you finish your shopping, and not buying one for the child who is happily fetching and carrying for you.

Try to keep instructions positive. "Do" usually works much better than "don't," partly because small children prefer activity to inactivity and partly because being forbidden to do things tends to arouse rebellion. "You can't eat that in the living room," makes him feel "Oh, can't I? Just watch me. . . ." "Bring your snack and eat it here with me" will probably work better.

Try to be clear. Some instructions *sound* positive but are so vague as to be meaningless. "Behave yourself," for example, really means "Don't do anything I wouldn't like." Not only is that negative, it is also an impossible instruction for him to follow because he cannot possibly work out all the things he might do which you might dislike.

Whenever there is time, tell him your reasons. Apart from emergencies (*see below*) you insult your child's intelligence if you ask for unthinking obedience and you also make it impossible for him to begin to fathom those vital basic principles of behavior. Suppose you say crossly, "Let that telephone alone" and he says "Why?"; there are all kinds of possible reasons for your instruction. Is it dangerous for him to touch? Is he likely to break it? Are you expecting a call which cannot come while he has the receiver off? Is it the tinging noise you are sick of? If you tell him why, he can add this snippet of behavior into his knowledge of how to behave. If you just say "because I say so" he learns nothing except that adults are incomprehensible.

Try to reserve a sharp "no" for emergencies. There are many occasions when his safety will depend on instant obedience to that command, with the reasons given later. If you fill his days with cries of "no," the word will not pull him up short as he approaches the road, the dog which looks unreliable or the power mower which has been left running. . . . If you reserve that word, in that tone, for occasions when you are protecting him from danger, he will come to see it as a protection word rather than as something to rebel against.

Try to keep "don't" for general rules. "Don't . . ." works well if you want to forbid a particular action indefinitely: "Don't fiddle with the car-locks" for example. It does not work for things like "Don't interrupt while I'm talking" because there are many times when you would actually want him to interrupt: when he saw smoke/heard the baby crying/needed to go to the toilet, for example. "Can you wait a minute until I've finished talking?" makes it clear that you would *rather* talk in peace but can be interrupted for legitimate reasons. Rules are extremely useful in keeping a small child safe, but they are too rigid and inflexible to be of much help in his learning how to behave.

Be consistent in your *principles* but don't worry about the details. As long as you know the kinds of behavior you think desirable and are consistent about those, it does not matter if daily life finds you allowing an activity one day and forbidding it the next. Your child is not a circus animal, learning always to respond to the same signal with the same trick. He is a human being, being taught to respond as best he can to a vast range of signals. If you let him jump on the bed today because it is wet, he feels energetic and you feel playful, he will not necessarily expect to be allowed to do it again tomorrow. The principle is that certain activities are only allowed sometimes. Unlimited sweets at Christmas will not undo all your plans about serving them only at dinner, either. The principle is that

Christmas is a special time. As to suddenly forbidding him to use the drum you gave him yourself last week, isn't your headache the reason for today's ban? Fair enough. The principle is that when people don't feel well other people have to try to adapt their behavior so as not to make things worse.

Even inconsistency between his parents will not confuse a child at this stage if it is honestly discussed in front of him so that he cannot play one off against the other. It is only if one parent cheats, by allowing what the other forbids as soon as his or her back is turned, that the child is likely to wonder who is right.

When you are wrong or genuinely find your view changed, say so. Your small child is watching your behavior and, to some extent, modelling himself on you. He knows he is not perfect so admitted imperfections in you make you a better model, not a less respectable one. If you accuse him wrongly and refuse to believe his truthful denials, you must apologize. By all the principles you are trying to teach, you were wrong. If you save your face you do so at the expense of his learning. If you forbid him to do something, perhaps without much thought, and he then persuades you that you could have allowed him to do it, say so. He has weighed up a question of how he should behave and come up with the right answer. If you do not acknowledge it, you make him feel that the rational persuasion which is an important part of your teaching is actually useless; that only power matters.

Trust him to mean well. The more a child feels that you are always standing over him, ready to instruct and correct him, the less he will bother to think for himself what he should and should not do. Within the limits of his age-stage, try to give him as much responsibility for his own behavior as he can take and then let him feel that he is trusted. If you are willing to let him go out with his friends, don't send him off with cries of "Remember to do this . . . don't do that. . . ." By letting him go at all you are letting him take charge of himself. Your exhortations will not make him take charge better; they will simply make him uneasy about whether he actually *can* manage.

When other children become important (see also **School***)*

Your child will accept the principles of behavior which you are trying to teach far more easily if they fit in with the behavior he sees and shares with friends outside his home. His peers are the society for which you are trying to prepare him. If his dawning conscience must conflict with peer-group activities and loyalties, he will have a hard job abiding by it. This is why it is so much easier to cope with "discipline" in a family which feels itself comfortably part of the neighborhood than in one which determinedly sets itself apart. If you want to rear your child within religious or cultural patterns which are foreign to the families of his school friends, you will certainly need to ensure that he has a second peer group of similar background among whom he can find support.

If, on the other hand, you simply find yourself vaguely disapproving of the value systems and behavior of many of your neighbors, tread carefully. Of course there is no reason for a child to be allowed to do everything that all his friends do, but if you ask him to be very different, especially if you present that difference as "morally superior," you invite eventual conflict between the value systems.

One way around this is to take the trouble to ensure that you offer, within your value system, genuine alternatives to replace what you force him to forgo. At its simplest, if you do not want him to play in the street with "the rough kids from the next block," whom *is* he to play with? A peer group he must have and if you forbid the obviously available one you will have to muster another. Likewise, if you see television as both a poor influence and a waste of time for children, you may control his early viewing strictly or even refuse to have a set in the house. But when he finds that he is the only child in his class who does not watch a particular program and cannot, therefore, share the fantasy games that spring from it, he will need to be aware of something very positive in his life which replaces that television. If he truly enjoys the activities of which you do approve—reading, playing music, growing things, keeping animals or whatever—he may accept that there is not time for everything, and that the way he spends his time is more fun than the way other children spend theirs. But if he does not enjoy those alternatives, he will feel that you deprive him of television only to make him "different" or, more painfully still, "better" than the other children when all he truly wants is to be one of the gang.

The young adolescent's behavior
If your fourteen-year-old suddenly appears to have forgotten how to behave, don't make the mistake of trying to teach him, all over again, as you taught him ten years before. Being surrounded by do's and don'ts, complete with patient explanation, will certainly not improve his behavior and may understandably increase his rebellious cries of "You treat me like a child."

Once a child reaches adolescence you have to accept that you have run out of time for teaching your principles of how to behave. The best that you can hope is that he will allow you to help him apply those principles to his new self and experiences. He does not leave his clothes on the floor because he has forgotten the principles of order you worked to teach him. He remembers them all right; he is just wondering whether they are his as well as yours: does he actually *mind* a mess? He does not leave them there for you to pick up, either. He leaves them there to be left there; you pick them up because you cannot stand the sight. If you can accept that he has the right to try out his own ways of doing things and can confine yourself only to insisting on your own rights, compromise is usually possible. Perhaps he can keep his room in a mess with the door firmly closed provided he does not spread the chaos to parts of the house you have to use, too (*see also* **Adolescence**/Adolescents and the adult world).

The older adolescent's behavior
The question now is not whether your child knows how to behave but whether he agrees with your views of how people should behave. Before he achieves independent adulthood he has to take out all those values and look at them again in the light of his new self and his new experiences. Some he will reject: he has an adult's right, now, to disagree with you, even on matters of fundamental principle. Many he will have to adapt to fit with the ideas and circumstances of his generation. Others he will probably settle with, for life (*see* **Adolescence**/Friends versus family).

Parents who cannot acknowledge an adolescent's right to question their values and to experiment with behavior based on different value systems, tend to condemn themselves not only to endless futile rows, but also to exclusion from the adolescent's thinking. If he believes that you are immovably certain of your own rectitude he will not bother to argue with you about anything more important than the ring around the tub. . . . Parents who can stand back a little and be interested in the journey of this near-adult who is now driving his own car, may still be able to offer considerable guidance over the more complicated bits of the route.

The trick seems to lie in two kinds of honesty:

Honesty about your real concerns. Many of the issues which cause trouble between adolescents and their parents are important and basic ones poorly disguised as matters of "discipline." What time, for example, should your daughter come home from Saturday night dates? Whatever time you set, be it 10 p.m. or 3 a.m., eventually there will be trouble. She will be late and you will be angry because she failed to do as she was told or as she promised. If you then "punish" her, perhaps by saying that she must stay in next weekend or accept an earlier curfew on the next occasion, the trouble will eventually intensify because you are not treating her as a near-adult but as a child-in-your-power. Since she is *not* genuinely in your power any more, you cannot ultimately win if she chooses to fight you. Deceit and defiance are both powerful weapons in the hands of a seventeen-year-old.

But, of course, that kind of row is not really about her willingness or otherwise to do as you say. It is about the anxiety you feel when her knowledge of how to behave in sexually charged situations is actually being put to the test. The late hour does not worry you because it deprives her of sleep but because *you* cannot sleep for wondering if she is in the back of a parked car or taking part in an orgy or being raped in the deserted streets. . . . If these are the real issues they are clearly not going to be resolved by a curfew. If she intends, or is going to slip into, a full sexual relationship at this stage in her life, she will do so as readily at 8 p.m. as in the small hours. If she cannot make sensible arrangements for her own safety on the streets coming home from a party she will not do so coming home after school either.

Open discussion about these real issues may, or may not, comfort you, depending on whether or not her attitudes turn out to be those you would prefer, but it will at least prevent endless, pointless arguments and allow you to be certain that issues which have previously only been discussed in theory have been brought to her practical attention. Surely it is better to know if she is, in fact, going to bed with her boyfriend so that instead of refusing to speak to her because she was late again you can make sure that she knows where to get advice on contraception. Surely it is better to know if her friends live in a risky area and parties go on late so that instead of being kept in the dark you can assure her that you would rather meet her, or at least provide the money for a taxi, than have her come home alone. Even if your expressions of this kind of down-to-earth concern make her bristle that you are "interfering," she will in fact see them as caring and she may remember them, at critical moments, when cries of "don't be late" have become part of meaningless adult background noise.

Honesty about your convenience. Much of the trivial-but-constant friction between older adolescents and their parents arises out of the difficulties which inevitably occur when extra adults (or near-adults) share a family house. Of course it is maddening to find the bathroom messy every morning; to cook meals for people who do not come in to eat them; to take careful telephone messages for them but never to receive one's own, or to have to rescue wet raincoats and muddy boots from the hall floor. A boarder who caused this kind of inconvenience would probably find himself without a room, but one's own, rather large, child is different. If it is recognized, from early in his drive for independence, that a child's right to live his own life is balanced by his parents' right to do the same, many of these irritations can be dealt with by agreeing on some ground rules for cooperative living. Unfortunately, many parents (perhaps especially mothers) cast themselves in a self-sacrificing role and then, after months of stored resentment, blow. Of *course* your eighteen-year-old should not expect a hot meal to await him every evening when more often than not he stays out until midnight. But equally he is bound to expect it if his mother has always maintained that "I'm cooking anyway, dear, so it makes no difference. . . ." Of *course* he has no automatic right to expect his mother to launder the shirts she picks up off the floor. But if she has always picked them up, washed and ironed them and returned them to his closet without comment, he is likely to take the service for granted as a kind of magic and be bitterly hurt when an innocent "Is my blue shirt ready, Mom?" suddenly brings down wrath upon his head. We need to do adolescents the honor of treating them as we would treat adult friends. We need to tell them when we are *beginning* to be irritated rather than when we reach the screaming point; we need to acknowledge equal rights and work out mutual compromises.

Of course this reasonable kind of approach will not always work. Your older adolescent may refuse to accept your ground rules; you may find life lived by any other rules intolerable. But at least if your disagreement is brought into the open, a compromise may be possible. You cannot live comfortably any more as a conventional family group, but could you still offer the cheap accommodation, occasional hot meals and background support he needs in his life if some degree of internal separation was arranged? Could he have a studio? Become, so to speak, a young boarder? Would everything ease if he had a dormitory room and came home only at vacation times? Could he have lodgings during the week and come home on weekends? Families often find that once the adolescent's independence is properly acknowledged and catered to, everything changes. Instead of being hurt and furious because he has been out four nights in a row, you may find yourself pleased and touched because he spent the fifth evening with the family.

If no compromise is possible it is sometimes better if the adolescent leaves home altogether. If he can no longer live within the family his energies will be better spent learning how to live outside it than in fighting it. At least if you agree to part you have a chance of remaining friends. One of the great tragedies of youth unemployment is that it condemns many youngsters who would be better away from home to remain in the only accommodation which they can afford, their parents' houses.

Some common issues in discipline

Common themes recur during many years of childhood. Often it is vitally important to tailor your reactions to "wrongdoing" to the exact level of your child's understanding. The following notes may help:

Obedience   Instant and unquestioning obedience might keep life peaceful for some parents for a few years but it cannot produce children who think for themselves and therefore can be trusted to look after themselves from an early age. Victorian parents got that obedience from their children but they also provided a degree of protection for their young which would be unheard of today. If you insist that your child does exactly as she is told at home, will she know what to do when nobody tells her outside? If she must always obey grown-ups, will she know that she must *disobey* the neighbor who orders her into his house (*see* **Safety**/From "strangers").

If you can rid yourself of the concepts of "obedience" and "disobedience" and think, instead, of the child cooperating, you may find that you can defuse the whole issue.

She may not do as you ask because she wants to do something different, like finish her game or stay until the end of the party. The problem is not her "disobedience" but a genuine conflict of interests. Dealing with it as such prevents it from being an issue of naughtiness and makes it one in which compromise may be possible. The young child may, when you think about it calmly, be able to have ten more minutes' play before the family meal begins to spoil. The older girl may be able to understand why her lateness worried you, and agree to telephone next time.

She may not do as you ask because she has not understood what you meant. You told her not to go out, but she did not realize you meant to ban the garden; she thought you meant out in the street.

She may not do as you ask because she forgot. Forgetting to do the shopping on the way home from school may be tiresome, careless, inconsiderate, but it is not deliberate disobedience.

She may not do as you ask because what you ask seems impossibly difficult and/or unreasonable. If you told her not to bring that friend home with her again and you catch the two of them together the very next day, you may have told her to behave in a way which she is actually unable to fit into *her* principles of how to behave. The problem is a friendship of which you disapprove, not a piece of disobedience.

She may sometimes fail to do what you ask because she is out to annoy you. She feels uncooperative and balky. You tell her not to touch your new book and she goes straight to it. You tell her to clear up her room and she sits and looks at the muddle until supper-time. . . . These, and only these, are examples of true "disobedience." They are deliberate attempts to provoke and almost always best handled by refusing to rise to the bait. "Fancy you going off and doing (not doing) the one thing I asked you not to do (to do) . . . you must be in a silly mood." Where is the argument she was looking forward to? While she is wondering, you can wonder why she is spoiling for a fight.

Lying   Do you worry about lying as a moral issue or as a practical one? It is important to decide, because if you wish to teach truth as a basic moral virtue so that lying is one of the ways in which it is always wrong to behave, you will probably have to tailor your own behavior (with the child and with other people) to fit. Most of us tell lies/untruths/"white lies" pretty frequently. Children hear us do it: hear us refuse an unwanted invitation on phony grounds, agree that the heat they know we enjoy is intolerable, and thank relatives warmly for gifts they have seen us reject. . . . If it is acceptable or even desirable (because we must not hurt people's feelings) for us to behave like this, why is it wrong for them? And if they are never to lie must they therefore always tell the truth, or must they learn the even more difficult lesson of finding something to say which is neither untrue nor hurtful?

Much childish lying is the denial of wrongdoing. If you want your child to confess voluntarily whenever he has done something wrong, by mistake or on purpose, you will have to show him that this is not only a virtuous but a sensible way to behave. If every confession is followed by overwhelming anger he would have to be pretty stupid to carry on with it.

If you want the child to admit to wrongdoing when he is rightly accused of it, you will have to offer in return a genuine readiness to believe him when he denies it. If you *know* he was responsible, it is kinder to tell rather than ask; if you ask whether he did it and he says "no," you are trapped into either withdrawing that trust or pretending to believe him when you do not.

A lot more lying comes into the category of careless or exaggerated or over-dramatic talk. Small children tell "tall stories" partly because their heads are full of Santa Claus and talking animals as well as parents who give presents and real rabbits who need feeding each day. There is room for both but the line between fantasy and reality takes a long time to solidify. Later on, your child may indeed make up elaborate stories which are in fact lies. But again, don't be too quick to moral outrage. If you want to entertain the family with the story of your day, don't you ever liven up the tale a bit? Ask yourself whether anything is being said which *matters*. Is this amusing gossip actually hurtful? Are you being given a worrying picture of that teacher or a wrong impression of your child's prowess? If you think you may be, try accepting the story as good entertainment but then asking, "By the way, what *exactly* did he say because I'm sure he can't really have been as nasty as that. . . ?" The child who was simply being entertaining will probably welcome some more conversation based on reality.

There are very practical reasons why people who care about each other should not lie. The story of the boy who cried "wolf" is still the best way I know of making it clear to little children that if they tell many falsehoods they may not be believed when it really matters. Told as part of your desire to care for and protect the child, it will probably leave a lasting impression. Older children who lie a great deal are usually either very frightened of parental disapproval or fighting off too many questions which they feel as intrusive. There are principles of how to behave at stake, but they have to do with your whole relationship with each other rather than specifically to do with honesty or falsehood.

Many adolescents lie to their parents simply to keep the wheels of life oiled. If your daughter knows that you do not approve of a particular boyfriend, but means to meet him at tonight's party, she may well misinform you simply to spare both of you from a row. If your son knows it would horrify you to know that he drinks alcohol with his friends, he may well tell you that he does not. It is for you to weigh the morals against a legitimate (and sometimes kindly) way for a budding adult to protect his or her own privacy. The principle at stake would seem to be one of communication rather than truth.

Stealing   Pre-school children are often very vague about property rights. Within the family there are lots of things that belong to everybody, some that belong to particular people but can be freely borrowed and some which are private possessions reserved for the owner's use. If you want a small child to get this straight and stick to it, you will have to spell it out *and* make sure that everybody (including her baby sister) respects her "private" things as she is expected to respect yours.

Outside the family there are genuine complications. It is all right to bring your painting home from playgroup but not a piece of plasticine. It is all right to keep the little ball you find in the bushes in the park but not to keep the coin you find nearby. It is fine to take leaflets from the supermarket checkout but not the sweets arranged at your level close by. . . .

It is important that your small child should not appear to steal because other people make such a song and dance about it. It may be a good case for a few rules which will tide her over while her understanding grows: "Don't bring anything away from anywhere without asking a grown-up if you may" and, perhaps "Always ask a grown-up if it is all right to keep anything you find or anything another child gives you." Try not to be especially moralistic about money because at this stage money is just treasure. She knows it is precious because she hears you talk about it and sees you swap it for nice things. But it is just like one of those tokens you put in slot machines; she has no concept of *real* money. If she takes money from your handbag, pause to ask yourself what you would have said if she had taken a lipstick. Then say the same thing about the money.

The small child who is forever pinching things—from you, from other children, from shops—may be in emotional trouble. She may be trying to take something which she does not feel she is being *given*. It will usually be love, approval or friendship of which she feels short. Sometimes, if you can use this kind of behavior as a cue to you to *offer* what she needs, the stealing will stop overnight.

Children who steal once they clearly understand not only that they should not, but also the social importance of honesty *may* be:

Stealing as a "dare"; a deliberately dangerous game with authority. There are sometimes outbreaks of pinching from shops, for example, which, while they need stamping out at once, are better dealt with as stupid, dangerous naughtiness than with moral outrage. Making the child return the goods to the shop may often bring home to him that the owner could have called the police.

Stealing something truly needed. Usually this will be a one-time thing: an object which you refused to buy (often because you thought it a waste of money), not realizing that the current school craze made it, in his terms, a truly necessary item. Obviously you cannot let him keep it, but you may feel it appropriate to discuss the matter with him and perhaps re-arrange his pocket money so that he will in future have an honest way of acquiring such items (*see* **Pocket Money**).

Stealing to buy friendship. Pinching small amounts of money to buy sweets for playground distribution is often the sign of trouble at school which jolts parents into action. Once again, while you have to deal with the stealing, the underlying problem is the more important.

Stealing (as the small child does) because he feels, in some deep-seated way, deprived of something nice. Unless you can easily see the problem *and* offer the love that fills the gap (no easy matter when you are shocked to find your child is stealing from you) you might be well-advised to seek help from your local mental health center. Staff will both help you to see the matter calmly and help you all to put the relationship on a more comfortable footing (*see* **Depression**/In children before puberty).

It is worth remembering that, for your child's own protection, you cannot take stealing lightly, however convinced you may be that his motives are sad rather than wicked. To be branded a thief at school or to find himself in juvenile court will do him no good at all.

Cheating   If your child is never to cheat you will have to teach her a far-reaching honesty which will guide her in innumerable different circumstances because there are so many kinds and degrees of cheating. You may, for example, teach a small child that it is cheating ("unfair") to use her greater size to push ahead in the line for the slide. You will certainly teach an older one that it is cheating to copy the answers to the French test from another child's paper. Hopefully, you will also make it clear, by your own example, that it is cheating, rather than clever, to ride the bus without paying the fare or to drive the car without renewing your license. But the basic idea behind your teaching about cheating has to reflect the fact that society cannot work if people are not basically honest with each other. Unfortunately, unless you are unusually scrupulous yourselves, she may learn easily that it is cheating to leave the restaurant without giving the busy waitress her tip, but have far more difficulty believing that it matters if she cheats the faceless insurance company or the tax man.

Cheating is most often an issue among schoolchildren who are in competition with each other. While of course you must make it clear to a child that copying that test paper is a kind of stealing of the other child's work and credit, you may also like to ask yourself why she needs to cheat. Is the school very competitive? Is the class working too fast for her? Is she afraid of the teachers (or you)? Would she be happier in a school where children competed only against their own previous best and where helping each other with set work was normal rather than immoral? (*See* **School**/Discipline in your child's school: Competition and shaming).

Violence   All mammals will use their natural weapons—teeth, claws, feet, strength —when they are angry and/or frightened. Human children are no exception. You are doing well if your child uses words rather than blows, *almost* always, by the time he goes to school.

Babies and toddlers cannot put themselves in other people's shoes and therefore genuinely do not realize that children they bite suffer exactly as they suffer when they are bitten. It is for this reason that "showing a child what it is like" by biting or hitting him back is useless. He will be hurt and horrified but he will not learn the intended lesson.

With this age group words alone are not, of course, enough. Every time you tell him not to bite/pull hair/hit/kick or otherwise hurt someone, you also have to prevent him physically from doing so. If the verbal message is always linked with direct intervention, he will eventually understand.

• A small child who goes through a stage of attacking others, apparently without provocation, can be very hard to cope with, especially as he and his mother tend to be increasingly unwelcome in the playground or parent-and-toddler group. You may find that you can get positive support from the other parents and prevent your child becoming a social outcast, if you set yourself *never to allow his attacks to succeed*. It may mean that for months you have to follow him around whenever he is playing near others. It will certainly mean that you have to foresee violence even before he registers his own aggressive feelings. But it can be done and, if you can make your watchful care feel to him like loving interest, and simultaneously relieve him of some of the home pressures which he may be feeling as overpowering, the stage will not last very long.

Schoolchildren. A sad but necessary part of learning how to behave is learning what to do when other people are horrible. To some extent your child will learn for himself on the basis of what he finds works. But you need a consistent view, too. Is he to hit back if a child hits him? Is he to hit if that is the only way in which he can extricate himself? Is he to hit if other children tease or torment him other than physically? Is he to learn to fight so that others will respect him? Is he to take problems with violence to a teacher or other adult or is that "telling tales"? Your ideas may be based on principles or partly on practical considerations such as your child's size or position in the neighborhood, but he does need to know what you think is right whether or not he can always do it. All too often a child tries to steer clear of a fight only to find his parents joining with others in calling him a sissy. Or a girl may come home scraped and proud of herself for "seeing those kids off" only to find her parents saying that she is too old to be such a tomboy. . . .

If you want your child, male or female, to follow as non-violent a path as possible, your example is important. If nobody in the family ever uses his physical strength to win a point or inflicts pain to clinch an argument, the child will accept a non-violent point of view and learn other techniques. But if physical punishment is taken for granted in the household and rows between adults commonly end with broken china, he will not take you seriously.

Television and violence   Many people blame television for the easy familiarity which today's children have with physical violence. Certainly most children of older generations would never have *seen* anyone shot, hit over the head with a brick, rammed by a car, raped or tortured. It is not yet clear how directly violent television programs affect children's real-life behavior, but it seems likely that newscasting and documentary reporting has more effect than fiction. Children, especially rather young ones, make little connection between reality and fantasy and tend to see those western "deaths" in terms of the "bang-bang you're dead" of their own games. But to see policemen dragging ordinary people through the streets by their heels, or young people hurling paving stones at each other in familiar streets, is a different matter. Children who are being reared *amidst* violence—those of Northern Ireland, for example—certainly do take violence for granted as the obvious way to express feelings or to make points. The young ones play the same violent games as other children but they play them as direct practice for a violent future and move easily from toy guns to real ones.

Whether you decide to censor your child's viewing or not, it is probably important that you view programs you expect to be violent with him so that you can, as you watch, make the important points. "It may look funny/serve him right but imagine what it would really be like . . ." and "James Bond may be able to go on climbing a mountain with four bullets in him, but anyone else would be screaming, vomiting, bleeding and dying. . . ." In the same, perhaps rather brutal, way, a child who sees documentary violence on television may need to be reminded that what he sees is tragedy. The simple fact that that bruised policeman has a wife who will be worried about him, or that that panic-stricken child has just seen her mother beaten, will often prevent a child from just accepting what he sees as part of the way people behave (*see also* **Television**).

Make-believe violence

Some families ban toy guns and war toys and, with the use of replicas in crimes on the increase, it may be that realistic toy weapons should be banned altogether by law. But even if you do refuse to allow your child this kind of toy you will not prevent make-believe violence. If he has no gun he will use a stick. If he may not have a toy tank he will use a car. . . . Some war toys and war games are singularly tasteless: many people, for example, must be offended by a game which gives maximum points to the player who can produce a nuclear explosion. Ban them on the grounds that you dislike them, by all means, but don't expect your child to share your views at least until he is old enough to understand the real implications of nuclear war and is therefore too old for the game.

Probably we teach children more about the horrors of war and the virtues of non-violence by allowing the toys as toys, but using the games that he plays with them as triggers for conversation about the realities. Bans tend to produce a backlash of extra interest.

"Allowable" violence

Before your child reaches his teens you will also need to decide your policy on the kinds of violence which our society does allow. Would you, for example, support your son in competitive boxing, a sport whose ultimate aim is unconsciousness of the opponent? Would you allow an air gun for vermin-shooting and if so a different weapon for shooting game? Would you see a military career as a welcome possibility? We certainly produce confusion if we express horror at the idea of shooting a deer but encourage shooting rats. Confusion is worse if nothing must be killed on purpose except people in a war. . . .

Some common disciplinary techniques

Arguing and bargaining

Sooner or later your child will catch onto the idea that if you want him to do something he does not want to do he has bargaining power. Instead of going meekly to change his shirt when told he says, "If I change my shirt 'cause you want me to, will you get my paints for me?" Although this kind of thing strikes some parents as cheeky (the child should do as he is told without argument), bargaining is a very useful form of human interchange and one in which your child needs some practice before he is old enough to join a trade union.

Of course it will be boring and time-consuming if your child tries to exact a return for every single thing you ask him to do, but learning the value of his bargaining power is part of his education. You might allow him some when your request is exceptionally boring for him and you might sometimes offer this kind of bargain too: "You really can't go out in those jeans, they're too filthy. Will you go and put on some clean ones if I get your bike out to save time?"

The same kind of approach can work well when much older children are arguing for rights you are reluctant to concede. If your adolescent argues for her right to live in a mess behind closed doors all week, a mutual clean-up on the weekends might be a fair bargain; if your son wants you to give drinks and sandwiches to the whole team on Saturday night, he might give you Sunday breakfast in bed.

Bribes and prizes

If you are shocked at the idea of bargains you will probably be even more shocked by the idea of bribes. They sound less immoral if you call them prizes.

Small children are usually perceptive about other people's goodwill and about justice. If you have to make a child do something he very much dislikes, a prize can both make it seem worth his while to cooperate and make him realize that you are trying to soften the blow. He is in the pool on a scorching afternoon and you realize a forgotten appointment. "I am sorry but we will have to go home now after all. Would it help if we stopped on the way and chose some ice cream for supper?" It is a bribe but it is also a perfectly reasonable bargain.

An actual prize sometimes makes all the difference to the child faced with real unpleasantness, such as stitches in his scalp or having a tooth out. It is not the *object* which matters: it is having something nice dangling just the other side of the nasty few minutes. Don't make the prize conditional on good behavior, though. The prize is for getting through the ordeal. He may need to make a fuss and, if he does, a conditional prize will only make the whole thing worse for him (*see* **Hospital**/Procedures).

Personally I do not believe that prizes from parents for the traditional things (like passing examinations or getting into teams) make much sense. The child wants to succeed anyway. If he succeeds he does not need your prize to give him pleasure. It is if he fails that he might need a morale boost. Sometimes you may actually be able to arrange this sort of back-to-front prize to good effect: "If you don't make the team we will at least be able to go to the beach that Saturday."

Punishment   The concept of "punishment" as something unpleasant done to a child because of something he has done wrong, really belongs with "discipline" rather than with "learning how to behave." A specific punishment may show your child what you will not put up with today, or now this minute, but it tells him nothing about the behavior you do want, now and always.

If you and your child are cooperating in this learning how to behave process, you will seldom need to think up a deliberate punishment because he will be working for your approval and your disapproval will make it clear to him when he has gone wrong. If you are not cooperating and he does not care whether you approve or not, you certainly are not going to get the cooperation back by punishing him.

Of *course* you are sometimes going to be cross. Of course you are sometimes going to lose your temper, shout, snatch away the ornament he is going to break, or the kitten he is mauling, or temporarily lock away the bike with which he was playing a dangerous game. But these are reactions rather than calculated punishments. As such they are often the most "fitting" kind. After all, if the reason for your anger is that he is endangering himself on that bike, what more obvious result, given that you care for him, than that it should vanish until he can be more sensible with it?

Calculated punishments are different. Looked at coldly, there is little to be said for any of the usual ones:

Smacking and other kinds of physical punishment. If you clip your child on the backside in a moment of anger you will be very unlucky if it does him any harm and it may do your state of mind some good. But physical punishments which are premeditated have nothing to be said for them. They do not work and because they do not produce the desired effect they have a nasty tendency to escalate.

You smack your child for touching the television after six warnings. He is hurt and angry but, because the touching was all impulse, tomorrow he forgets and does it again. Logically you must smack him again, but this time, harder. He will be even more upset but he still will not remember. The next day's naughtiness seems to you like deliberate defiance. This time, you decide, you must show him once and for all. . . .

Research has shown us several important things about smacking:

Children can never remember what they were smacked *for*. Smacking cannot therefore change behavior.

Children who are smacked are never sorry for what they did, even at the time. They are so overwhelmed by pain and indignity that the reaction is pure anger, not remorse.

Children who are smacked only fail to retaliate because they are conscious of the adult's overwhelming size and power. Smacking, therefore, cuts right across any attempt at cooperation and certainly across anything you are trying to teach about using strength gently or relying on words rather than blows.

Children who are often smacked do tend to take it out on younger or smaller ones; smacking may therefore contribute to the making of a bully.

An unexpectedly large minority of smacked children eventually suffer actual injury. Examples are "light blows" that happen to catch him off balance so that he hits his head on something; blows that accidentally land on his spine rather than his bottom and blows which hit an ear and burst its drum.

● Violently shaking a small child is always dangerous. It can cause whiplash injury to the spine and/or concussion because the brain is knocked against the inside of the skull.

Corporal punishment at school. Home-smacking at least goes on in an overall context of love and concern. The institutionalized use of violence and pain, to control or "teach" a child, is the cold assertion of superior power and something which most countries have long abandoned. Parents in countries where schools still maintain this right may like to ask themselves why children can be beaten when rapists and murderers may not. Sadly the answer is that teachers stand "in loco parentis" and therefore as long as parents maintain the right to beat their own children, some teachers will insist that they have the right to beat those same children when they are in the school's charge.

Parents who would prefer to withhold this right from their children's teachers may like to know that the European Court of Human Rights supports their viewpoint and that there are societies—including many experienced teachers—working actively and successfully to bring corporal punishment in schools to an end (*see also* **School**/Potential problems in school: Discipline in your child's school).

Confining a child to his room. This is not a very sensible kind of punishment either: If he hates being there alone, the punishment may put him off his room (or bed) as a friendly place for going to sleep. Can you afford that? He may come out. Are you prepared to lock the door? If he does not mind being there, but simply plays or reads, what will you do to punish him next time? Lock him in the bathroom? Or a closet? There is a real danger that imprisonment will escalate, just as smacking tends to do.

If there are occasions when you feel that it is important to be apart from your child (perhaps because he is throwing a semi-deliberate tantrum or because your own temper is going), it is better if *you* go away. With a small child you obviously cannot go far, in case he gets into danger, but with an older one who is driving you out of your mind you could always take your book into the bathroom and lock the door.

Shaming him. Punishments designed to make a child feel silly will never make him behave more sensibly. If you take away his shoes because he ran away from home, or make him wear a bib because he spilt his food down his clothes, you will make him *feel* stupid and babyish: incapable of the kind of behavior your punishment is meant to encourage.

In the course of developing the conscience which will keep on telling him how to behave once you have stopped, he will often be *ashamed of himself*, but you cannot induce that inward feeling by imposing shameful punishment on him.

Discovering what happens when he gets his behavior wrong. Life is full of "punishments" administered not by you but by the logical consequences of your child's own actions. The more certain you are that the behavior you are asking of him is right (practically, morally or both) the more certain you can be that you will not have to fall back on all those invented sanctions like "no television." If, for example, you are right in thinking that his new car will break if he uses it to play "crashes," there is absolutely no point in punishing him for refusing to stop the game. The car will break; he will be sad; you will be proved right. So direct is the lesson that you can well afford to be quick with comfort and glue. If you are right in thinking that his gang leadership is actually bullying, you will have no need to punish him for that either: the gang will melt away and he will not have one to play with, let alone to lead. Once again you can afford to be ready with explanations and help. If you are right in thinking that reading late in bed will make him too tired for school, you will not need to punish his disobedience by removing his bedside lamp: he will be tired the next day and that will be punishment enough. But are you right? Will he be tired? He may just fall asleep over his book when he needs to . . . maybe the reading in bed was not wrong after all, or maybe it was wrong because it wasted power by keeping the light on all night, rather than because it made him tired.

If you go on thinking of learning how to behave as a journey, involving a complicated route and difficult steering around obstructions, you will usually be able to cast yourself in a positive and helpful role rather than in a punitive one. If you can do that, you are likely to keep your child's cooperation, his desire to please, and therefore your ultimate sanction of displeasure.

Your anger is the most effective punishment of all. Parents who say that this approach to discipline is unrealistic usually assume that all this talk of "cooperation" implies constant sweetness and light and reasonableness all around. Of course it does not. Every parent gets cross (for good and poor reasons). The whole point is that the more cooperative the two of you are being in this business of learning how to behave, the more your child will mind your crossness. Use it as gently as you can. Above all, try, when you are irritated or angry, to make it clear to the child that you are fed up with his *behavior* rather than with him as a person. If you tell a small child, "For heaven's sake, go *away*," you may hurt his feelings and you certainly do not tell him what he has done to turn you against him. If you rephrase the message, "For heaven's sake, take that drum into the garden," you make it clear that it is the noise which offends.

Dislocations *see* **Accidents.**
Disobedience *see* **Discipline, Self-discipline and Learning How to Behave.** *See also* **Adolescence**/Adolescents and the adult world; Friends versus family.

Divorce, Separation and One-parent Families

The "normal family" of the television ads still consists of two parents who are married to each other and their mutual and legitimate children. But only a very small majority of today's children will be born to, reared within and launched into adulthood from such a family. A very large minority indeed will spend at least a part of childhood living in a different kind of family. For far too long those families have been ignored except to be condemned. "Broken homes" have been regarded as the cause of innumerable social ills, yet nobody has looked either at the severity of the breakage or at the kinds of glue which might repair it. Unmarried or separated parents have been encouraged to feel that because they were outside the social norm, they were also beyond the social pale. Often already shattered by emotional trauma in their personal lives, they have been left to cope with guilt and without either information or practical help. Very gradually, though, information is being accumulated from research studies. Armed with at least a few value-free facts you may be able to seek, or to offer, something more useful than a sermon or a platitude.

Interpreting the divorce statistics Divorce statistics make good shock headlines for the popular press. Currently, divorce ends about one in three marriages in the USA, Australia and the UK and almost half in South Africa.

But divorce statistics tell us very little about children. By no means does every divorce affect a child: about twenty-five percent of UK divorces, for example, are between childless couples, while some take place after children have grown up and left home. On the other hand, a great many children are affected by separations which are never formalized in the divorce court and therefore do not appear in those statistics. Even where it is known that children of dependent age are involved in a divorce, the statistics do not tell us how many children, nor how old they are now, or were when separation/proceedings began.

Figures giving the proportions of families in which one parent is absent are a little more informative, as long as it is remembered that these include families which have been single-parent from the beginning, as well as those in which one parent has died. Again, we do not have a complete breakdown by the numbers and ages of these children, but the current figures are estimated as follows:

Australia: one in six   S. Africa: one in three
Canada: one in four   UK: one in four
New Zealand: one in seven   USA: one in three

Families with an absent parent The father is the absent parent in more than ninety percent of single-parent families. Reasons range from the obvious ones such as the fact that there is no male equivalent to the unmarried mother, to less obvious ones such as the greater likelihood of early death among males.

Where there is separation/divorce, welfare workers and law courts still tend to recommend/direct that mothers should have custody, especially when young children are involved. Even when custody is not disputed, or is allocated equally to both parents, couples themselves usually take it for granted that the mother should assume daily care and control. Of course there *are* fathers coping alone, but they are still a rarity. Those who have young children usually have some female help, employed or otherwise (*see below*). Most have charge of school-age children, usually teenagers and often sons rather than daughters.

Family changes Statistics may tell us how many families were without a parent at the time
over time they were collected, but they tell us nothing about what will happen to
those families in the future. If divorce rates are rising, so are remarriage
rates. If separations are frequent, so are new partnerships. A child whose
father leaves the family may experience any combination of a complexity
of relationships with adults in the remaining years of his childhood.

His parents may join up again, temporarily or permanently. Many
couples go through several "reconciliations" before the marriage is ended
or reinstated.

He may live with only his mother, with his mother and a lover or series
of lovers, with his mother and a permanent partner or with his mother
and a stepfather. Any of those males may, or may not, function as
father-figures for him, and any of them may, or may not, also bring
children of their own partially or fully into the family. At the same time,
the absent father may move through a variety of relationships which may
or may not bring the child an extra mother-figure and/or children who are
formally or informally his stepbrothers and stepsisters. Eventually there
may be half-siblings, too.

For some children, "family" experience will not even remain linked
with male-female partnership. The child may be brought up within a
homosexual partnership, within a communal household, or by a
widowed grandmother who frees his mother to work.

Stereotypes such as "broken home" are meaningless unless we know a
child's exact situation, now, and furthermore know something about how
he perceives that situation.

Separation and divorce from a child's point of view

Recent British and American research, which has not only studied families in crisis but followed them up over a period of years, agrees on the
following "facts." They may or may not be true for your children, or the
children with whom you are concerned, but they are the nearest thing we
have to hard information.

Separation/divorce makes children miserable. Children too young to
understand what is going on commonly refuse to believe in the fact or
permanency of the separation. Older children bitterly resent it. It appears
that however poor the relationship between their parents has been,
children would prefer it to continue. Many dream of, and work for,
reconciliation. The only exceptions researchers have found are among the
few children who are physically terrified of the departing parent. They
and only they may be relieved to see him go.

These findings do not, of course, mean that a marriage which is not
working should be held together "for the children's sake," but they do
mean that separating parents cannot rely on children to agree that the
family would be better split up than constantly quarrelling.

Children tend to take guilt upon themselves. Younger children, unable
to fathom much of the reality of an adult sexual/ habitual/cooperating
relationship, tend to assume that they were the cause of the break-up. It is
difficult for a child who is, after all, the center of his own life and thinking,
to believe that he is not similarly the whole center of his parents'.

Furthermore, much of the friction which he has seen has often involved his own behavior—his noise or his discipline, his mother's spoiling or his father's neglect—so he easily sees these accumulated small issues as the cause of the crash. There may be subtler reasons for guilt, too. Young children are sexually aware creatures who, in the normal course of early development, dream of partnership with the person of the opposite sex whom they love most (the parent) and therefore dream of ousting the present partner (the other parent). The little boy who has secretly dreamed of "looking after Mommy" if only Daddy didn't get in the way, sees Daddy's departure not only as a practical disaster but as evidence of his own wicked and terrifying power: he wished him away and now he wishes he had not. The little girl whose father leaves is similarly placed: clearly her love object has left because it was wicked of her to want to get into her mother's place. The young child who is beset by this kind of guilt will be anxious, too. Because he is so wicked and has caused one parent to leave the home, will the other parent not also desert him? At its mildest, such anxiety tends to make the child cling to home and keep a too careful eye on his mother's movements. At the other extreme, it may make him feel so totally wicked and unlovable that he becomes convinced that neither parent can love him and that total abandonment is inevitable (*see* **Depression**/In children before puberty).

Older children, who have lived through the stage of longing to replace the same-sex parent and have begun, instead, to identify themselves with him or her, are liable to a different sort of guilt. The separation makes them angry: angry, very often, with that same-sex parent. Whatever explanations they are given for the ending of the marriage they tend to feel (as do others outside the relationship) that they could have done better. A boy may feel that he could have remembered to phone when he was working late or could have spared one weekend day for the family; a girl may feel that she could have held her tongue and avoided nagging. . . . But the anger itself leads to guilt and to anxiety. Guilt over lack of sympathy with the same-sex parent and anxiety because if those real feelings were known, surely the parent who has stayed with the family would leave, too (*see* **Depression**/Longer-lasting situational or reactive depression).

Children tend to be shut out by separation/divorce. Many parents become so involved in their own feelings that they cannot acknowledge children's mourning for the loss of the absent parent. Older children, interviewed later, say things like: "You'd have thought she was the only one it mattered to . . ." and "I just kept feeling: OK, but what about *me?*" To make matters worse, the parent who stays with the family is often as *emotionally* absent as the other parent is physically apart. Children feel unsupported and are aware that their own concerns are trivial, as compared with all this high adult emotion.

Split loyalties are agony. While some conflict of loyalties is probably inevitable, the children who suffer most are those for whom that conflict is made most acute. A few mothers actually try to enlist children against their fathers. Many more imply, often rather subtly, that any communication between the departed father and children is disloyalty. Some of the points made by adolescents highlight the pain:

"I couldn't bear him having to skulk on the street corner when he met us, but if he came to the house she looked all pained and long-suffering."

"I wanted to phone him, tell him things that had happened, you know? She never stopped me, never *said* anything, but if she came in and I was on the phone to him she'd sort of go out, looking peculiar. . . ."

"She'd ask me to do things, jobs around the place, and sigh because he hadn't done them before. I hated that; hated her for trying to make me feel I was better than him."

"Sometimes I'd say, 'Dad would have let me do such and such,' and she'd say, *very* politely, 'If your father had wanted to be the one to say what you should do, I think he'd have stayed around. . . .'"

"She was unhappy, OK, I know that, but she was always *sighing*: over money or how hard she was working and all that. Everything she said was sort of a dig at him. . . ."

Children *worry* about the absent parent. For young children in particular, exclusion from the warmth and safety of home and family seems a horrendous exile. The fact that a man has left voluntarily is either beyond their comprehension or makes no difference to the fact that they worry about how he will manage alone. Four- to ten-year-olds, especially, ask:

"Where will Daddy sleep?"

"Who will cook his supper?"

"Who is looking after Daddy?"

"Isn't he lonely?"

"Doesn't he miss us?"

"Has he got a television? Will he watch [the favorite program]?" Mothers who share this kind of concern, or can find the generosity to acknowledge the reality of the child's and can offer practical reassurance that *Daddy's all right*, do the child an important service. As soon as it is possible, children should see for themselves that the father's living circumstances *are* "all right."

Things which help children when parents separate

Talking helps. Children whose parents discuss what is happening with them survive the immediate shock better than those who are just told, so to speak, "He's gone and good riddance." Two recent studies show that only twenty percent of parents discuss the situation with children.

Knowing (seeing) that the mother is "all right." Children can accept grief and anger and need (*see above*) to be let in on what is happening, but they also need to know that, somewhere inside, the mother is "solid" not smashed; not finished.

Outside support helps. The more colleagues and friends are around, the less the child will feel isolated himself or concerned for the mother's loneliness.

Grandparents can help. The more "family" the child can feel he still has, the better. And if he used to spend time with Dad's Mom, why not now?

The structure of daily life going on as usual helps if the rest of the family can stay (at least for the first months) in the same house and therefore the same schools and neighborhood. The child who loses a parent *plus* his familiar daily life is lost indeed (*see below* Poverty).

Different treats and special days. It is birthdays and festivals, school sports days and holidays, which bring the absent parent and the lost family most painfully to the fore. Children survive better if these can be glorious in a new way: perhaps because the family teams up with friends or invites relatives.

Brothers and sisters. "Only" children tend to suffer most at the time of a separation/divorce. The burden of companioning the parent who stays, and of being, perhaps, her confidant or pawn, is very hard to bear alone. Where there are two or more children, they will often become very close in adversity and it may be from a brother or sister that the remaining parent finds out a particular child's immediate worries.

The children of one-parent families

Physical separation from one parent presents children with a shock situation. Adaptation can take a long time and will usually take about two years. But *children do survive*. A "broken home" need not be a recipe for disaster, a ticket to school failure or a passport into adolescent delinquency. Recent research, in America and Britain, has made it clear that where the consequences of divorce seem to have been damaging, the damage has usually been done not solely by the divorce itself but by the social circumstances in which the child was reared after it.

British researchers carefully studied that other large group of children from single-parent families: those who are illegitimate. When matched groups of illegitimate, legitimate and adopted children were studied over many years, the illegitimate children were found to compare poorly with the others on a range of measures from physical growth through school performance to social adjustment. Interestingly, the adopted children were found to be doing even better than the legitimate group. On the face of it, the results clearly indicated that it was better for illegitimate children to be adopted than to be brought up by single mothers. . . . Fortunately, the team did not accept this superficial interpretation but looked more carefully at their data to try to find out *why* the illegitimate children were so disadvantaged. The answer lay not in membership in a one-parent family but in the social/environmental circumstances of the families. The illegitimate children were living in poverty; as a group their families suffered from the lowest incomes, the worst housing and the most intractable employment problems. In stark contrast, the adoptive families, carefully selected by the adoption agencies, were a highly privileged, professional, middle-class group. The legitimate children, representing a British "norm," were far better off than the single-parent families but not as conspicuously privileged as the adoptive ones. The children's measured performance closely followed these social differentiations. In further analysis, the workers reexamined all the child-measures *allowing for* social factors such as income and housing. Immediately the picture changed: adopted children now did no better than the children of either of the other two groups nor did the single-parent children do any worse. In fact, once these social factors were allowed for, there were no differences between any of the groups of children *except on social adjustment*. Here, and only here, that middle group of legitimate children was found to have the edge over both other groups.

Whether a child's family is single-parent because he was born illegitimate or because he has lost a parent through separation, divorce or death, it seems that the social circumstances of the rest of his childhood are a key factor in what happens to him.

Poverty   Most families today find it difficult to maintain a standard of living which seems reasonable, to them even while the children have two adults to provide for them. In many families both parents work and there are therefore two incomes. In others, only one parent may work (because the mother takes time off to rear young children and/or because of unemployment, etc.), but the other parent is available to provide, "free" child care and to use her or his time to ensure that the money which is coming in is stretched as far as possible in myriad minutiae from buying inexpensive food to do-it-yourself activities around the house. A single parent loses out all the way around. She may have to accept low-paid work because of her domestic responsibilities, or hold onto a better-paid job which involves her in expensive arrangements for the children. Either way she is going to be short of both time and energy, and will have to spend money to replace both. Where a divorce settlement provides her with child support, this will seldom be adequate to cover *family* expenses (rent, mortgage rates, etc.), even if it does, in fact, cover out-of-pocket expenses such as clothing and pocket money. She may, of course, be allocated alimony by the divorce court, but a man cannot be forced to pay out money which he has not got, and even two-thirds of his income (the maximum a British court will settle) will not cover what one hundred percent of that income covered before the divorce. Everybody is going to be poorer, even before there is any question of a "second family."

Poverty, change   While a child can ride easily through a minor reduction in the family's
and instability   spending power, the total change in environment which is often involved when the family home must be sold and everything must change is a different matter. When a move and a new school are coupled with a mother who is not only miserable but working long hours, seldom home and permanently exhausted, it is not surprising if children react badly. A small child may cling and become disorientated; an older one may, so to speak, abandon home as a bad job and turn to his peer group. If a new stability, albeit a less privileged one, can be quickly arrived at, he will settle into his new life, but if everything continues to seem strange and chaotic he will survive as best he can and that survival may not be of the kind which is socially approved.

The experience of one mother who was superbly supported by her community and thus able to hold life steady for her three children may illustrate the down-to-earth needs which so often go unmet:

"Everybody was fantastic. It was little things that obviously mattered most and one way or another we sorted them all out. The little one was at playgroup and at a sitter's afterwards. No way could I afford that any more, but the group just gave her a free place which meant I could manage the sitter. All three were used to being driven about and my way of life had depended on a car. But a neighbor said car pooling was the in-thing and took the two older ones to school with hers and we took to doing our big shopping in her car on Saturdays. Weekends would have been hell, but my son's scout leader caught on to that one and enrolled him in a Saturday football team, and it was through him that we got on to the Big Brother scheme. All right, it's not the same doing things with a Big Brother as with Dad, but it's better for a twelve-year-old than hanging around the house with Mom and sisters, isn't it? It was the middle one who was terrified we'd have to move. Her whole life goes on within walking distance of here—all her friends, everything. Her teacher asked me straight out whether I could manage and when I said I didn't know, asked if I'd thought of taking in a boarder. I hadn't, but we haven't been without one since. Her rent pays a lot of the mortgage *and* she babysits, too; the children like having another adult in the house. I think it makes them feel more secure. . . ."

That mother was unusually fortunate in her friends and contacts, but this is the kind of help which is just beginning to be available to single-parent families through various charitable and self-help organizations.

Children's relationship with the absent parent

The child who is suddenly pitchforked into a single-parent family, because his other parent leaves, needs the practical structure of his daily life held steady, but he also needs the quaking structure of his emotional relationships steadied, too. Although, of course, every child, every parent and every relationship is unique, research does suggest that the following points are usually very important:

He will need to know, and see, that the end of mother-father love is not the end of father-child love. He needs to be helped over his immediate guilt (*see above*).

He needs to be told and shown that whatever his parents now feel about each other, the absent parent still loves and cares about him.

He needs to be told and shown that he can love and be loved by the absent parent without risking the love of the one at home. He will, from time to time, feel disloyal, but with help, can come to believe that his mother *wants* him still to "have" his father.

He needs to see that father often enough and regularly enough that they can stay in touch with each other's ordinary, everyday concerns. For a young child, that probably means at least once a week. If the gaps are longer, he will neither remember all his "news" nor feel it worth the effort of trying to keep his father informed of rapidly changing friendships, school successes/disasters and so forth.

He needs to be able to talk freely about his father to his mother, and vice versa. That means that neither must use him as a spy in the enemy camp nor freeze with disapproval when they hear mention of the ex-partner's new purchase, new friend or new problem. . . .

● More than half of the British children whose parents divorce lose touch with the absent one within a few months. Evidence suggests that none truly wish to do so and that lifelong emotional damage may be the result.

Parents who have left their families sometimes genuinely wonder whether it would not be better for the children (especially very young ones) simply to "forget about me." If visits cause obvious emotional upset it may seem easier on everyone simply to drop them. It seems that this is almost invariably a serious mistake, on a par with the mistake which used to be made when young children who were upset by being visited in the hospital were left unvisited because they "settled down better." We know now that these children needed *more* time with their parents, not less, and we have moved from timed visits to rooming-in or unrestricted access. In the same way, this child needs *more* time with the absent parent, not less; the upset caused by today's visit must be tolerated in the interests of next year, rather than avoided in the interest of immediate "peace."

Arrangements for "access"

The children who settle down most easily to life in a split family appear to be those who can have free access, as the spirit moves them, to the absent parent. In several studies, for example, having the two households within bicycling or walking distance of each other, and having a key to both, has been the children's answer to "What would be/is the ideal arrangement?" Of course this will be impossible for many families but it may serve as an ideal to which you can aspire. Whatever arrangements are made, the following points seem to be important:

Young children must have parents who will talk to each other, even if it is only on the doorstep or over the telephone. You cannot make pleasant plans using a three-year-old as a messenger, nor expect a five-year-old to explain for herself that she has a cold and may not swim, or that she will not be able to come over next week because of the school play. . . .

There are circumstances under which children need parents to be able to be together, even if only for short periods. A child who is ill in bed, for example, should not have to wait until he is completely better before he can see his dad. A child whose father is in the hospital should not have to cope alone or go without seeing him. A child whose father is mentally ill, or otherwise in alarmingly poor shape, still needs to see him, but needs to do so with the person who can give him security and explain what he saw to him afterwards. Ideally, even older children should be able to count on both parents seeing their great moments. You cannot play a match twice so that each of the people you most care about can see it separately.

As soon as possible, children need to visit the absent parent's home. However unsuitable it seems, unless it is very temporary, they need to be able to visualize his whereabouts (*see above*).

If the absent parent is to remain a *parent* rather than a visitor he needs a base. Conducting an intimate relationship on the basis of visits to the zoo and ice cream parlors is almost impossible. Using the family home as this base is usually a tremendous strain to all concerned (even where the resident parent will permit it). Unless or until he has a home of his own, a friend's house may be better than nothing.

Children need to meet people who are important to the absent parent. If he is sharing his home, bed and life with somebody, it is usually a mistake to conceal the fact and keep them away.

● Contrary to popular belief, children are often much happier once they know that separated parents have new lovers, provided those lovers did not cause the breakdown of the marriage. Once the divorce is accepted, the specter of either parent's loneliness is a horrific one to many children (*see above*).

Children who
refuse visits

This happens for many reasons and at all ages. Leaving the child to decide about visits himself is not usually the right answer.

Very young children may not like being separated from the mother, especially during this period of anxious clinging. The answer may be to start again with short visits at home, walks in a familiar park and so forth.

Fathers who have had little to do with their young children may not turn into skilled child managers overnight. While it may be tempting to "let him see what it's like to cope with them all day," it is not fair to the children, let alone their dad. Visits at a friend's house, where there are familiar playmates and another parent to learn from, may be the answer.

Older children, especially those who are getting used to the situation, may find routine visits a bore either because the parent does not find interesting things to do with them or because they want to be busy with their own friends and affairs. The occasional parent obviously has to find a way of life which works during visits, but the timing of the visits may have to be altered to suit the child better, too. Sometimes an after-school visit is better than a weekend day. The parent at home has to resist the temptation just to say, "Well you don't have to go out with him if you don't want to," because once they are out of touch it will be far more difficult for the child to regain a relationship which is basically important to him.

Adolescents often come to resent visits which are arranged *for* them or which make them different and take them away from their friends. Being allowed to plan for themselves often helps. So does being encouraged to include the absent parent in real everyday life, rather than treating visiting times as entirely separate. It may be the absent parent who can find the time to drive him to the sports center for those practice sessions or lend his stereo and space for that party.

Children's relationships with parents' lovers

There is little formal research on this topic: the following points come directly from involved families:

Beware of territory. Mothers with custody (and a shortage of babysitters) resent the fact that children accept women friends whom they meet when out with their fathers much more easily than they accept men friends who come to the family home. It is not sex discrimination. Fathers with custody have the same problems when women visit the home. The point is that the house "belongs to" the child and contains the ghost of the absent parent. The visitor invades privacy and may unwittingly use *"Mommy's* kitchen" or sit in *"Daddy's* chair."

Casual affairs are probably best based on the lover's ground. If and when the relationship develops to a point where it is important that he get to know the children, this can probably best be done on expeditions out with him, and by having him to the family home as a family visitor, rather than as your private one.

Beware of authority. Few children will readily accept instructions or reproofs from a comparative stranger, but most adults find it difficult to *live with* children without giving any. This is put forward by many parents as a strong reason against having a living-in partner until or unless he or she is going to become a parent-substitute or step-parent.

If you want to try out the business of living together as a potential family group, it often works best if you all go and do it somewhere new—in a rented vacation home, for example—so that nobody's territory is being invaded and everyone can work out the ground rules for cooperative living together.

Beware of manipulation. Many children work hard to influence parents' choice of partner. Techniques vary from the blatant (spiders in shoes) to the more subtle (pretend she isn't there at all). Either can be extremely off-putting. It works the other way, too. If you have a series of affairs, you may find your children making plans for next summer's vacation with the lover you are just getting tired of. . . .

If you know an affair is not likely to be permanent, but want everybody to have fun, try to make it clear to the children that they need not concern themselves overmuch one way or the other. But if you think or hope that it will be long-lasting, make that clear, too. All too often step-parents say sadly, "Her kids and I just never got on; I think we got off on the wrong foot." That usually means, "We none of us realized at the beginning that we had to try to like each other and by the time we knew it was too late."

Beware of repeated "desertions." Lovers who like children, and are trying to please you, may easily become close friends with yours, especially if the children are feeling starved for adult male (or female) company. Don't let the children come to count on the things they do together on weekends, the help he gives with homework or the glorious feasts she cooks on Fridays, unless you are pretty sure your own relationship is going to last. If you could not keep a marriage going "for the children's sake" you certainly won't want to keep an affair going for that reason, yet repeated experiences of being left by loved people will certainly not help them to get over the divorce or to feel kindly towards you.

Children's relationships with step-parents

Many children's ideas about step-parents come from fairy stories in which they are invariably wicked and cruel. Even if your child likes the future parent-substitute, you may find that once he knows there is to be an actual marriage his attitude changes. School friends may even tell him to "watch out for poisoned apples. . . ."

Children can develop extremely close and warm relationships with step-parents. Some even maintain that despite the misery at the time, they are glad there was a divorce because "I'm closer to my step-father than I ever would have been to my real father." Making it work takes a lot of tact. The following hints may also help:

A move makes a better start than having all of you move in with him (her), or vice versa: Although children survive the trauma of one parent leaving better if other aspects of life can stay the same (*see above*), making a new family grouping usually works more easily in a new environment. Everyone shares mutual territory about which nobody feels possessive, and there can be mutual ground rules for living in it from the beginning.

Room has to be left for the "real" parent. That means room in the child's life—so that his regular visiting days don't suddenly become new-family days—and psychological room, too. Be careful, for example, not to push him to call the step-parent "Mom" or "Dad" (unless he asks, or does it spontaneously), or to assume that he will do with the new "parent" the things he has been doing with the real but absent one.

Room has to be left for the old family, too. Don't expect the child to drop old family stories, in-jokes and so forth: tell them to the new person. Don't expect him to drop *anything*: try to make the new relationship completely extra-rather-than-instead.

Although their relationship is *because* of you, the step-parent and children cannot make it *through* you. Try not to stand in the middle, like a maypole around which everybody dances. Step-parent and children have to get to know one another as people rather than as your appendages. However jealous a child may seem to be of the newcomer, she will enjoy your new happiness and give him credit for it; eventually she will be ready to seek a share for herself.

Try not to expect the step-parent *or* children to accept sex-stereotyped family roles too quickly (if at all). A stepfather, for example, usually needs to go very easily on "discipline," "manners" and so forth. With adolescents he may never be permitted an authoritarian relationship but may, if he will accept it, eventually be offered friendship instead. A stepmother will probably need to hold back on personal care, however warmly she feels towards the children. She will be felt to be "stepping beyond the bounds" if she tries to plait hair or wash necks, at least until the children spontaneously hug and kiss her.

Try to arrange for the step- and natural parent to meet, especially if you have managed to keep your relationship civil since the divorce. Children need to feel that all the adults who are closely concerned with them are on the same side. It also helps if they do not feel that they can at all easily play one off against the other or have their wilder fantasies believed. . . .

Ears and Hearing; Ear Disorders and Deafness

The ears are not only the organs of hearing but also those of balance. Each ear has three main parts:

The outer ear   Is the visible ear itself (the pinna) together with the ear canal which is about one inch long and made into a dead end by the eardrum.
   The complex shape of the pinna gathers sound waves and directs them along the ear canal to vibrate the delicate membrane of the eardrum.

The middle ear   Is a tiny chamber, sealed off from the outer ear by that eardrum but connected to the back of the throat by the eustachian tube. This tube opening keeps air pressure equal on either side of the eardrum but it also provides a route up which bacteria or viruses can travel from the throat.

The inner ear   This is a complex set of structures:
The semicircular canals are fluid-filled tubules which act (rather like a spirit level) to convey information about balance and the position of the head. Disturbances of this part of the inner ear can lead to giddiness, vertigo and nausea. This may well be a factor in motion sickness.
The ossicles are structures which are adjacent to the eardrum and transmit its vibrations to the cochlea.
The cochlea contains the actual sound receptors, which translate those eardrum vibrations into nerve impulses and transmit them along the auditory nerve to the brain where they are interpreted as sounds.

Deafness

There are two main types of deafness, each of which may, of course, affect either one or both ears and be of any degree of severity.

Nerve deafness
(perceptive
deafness)   This type is due to malformation of, or damage to, the actual auditory nerve. Congenital deafness (such as that associated with fetal German measles) is of this type. It can also develop later due to certain infections or severe head injury, or gradually after years of work in an extremely noisy environment or with the degeneration of age. Nerve deafness is usually irreversible, although the individual can be helped with increasingly sophisticated hearing aids.

Conduction
deafness   Arises not because the actual hearing organ is defective but because something interferes with the transmission of sound waves from the outer ear to the cochlea. Many ear disorders can reduce the acuity of the affected ear, but with prompt treatment permanent deafness is unusual.

● It is vital that any deafness should be detected early. A totally deaf baby will make sounds, so do not wait for suspicious silence before checking that he can hear properly. Older children with even minor degrees of temporary deafness can miss a lot of what is said to them and may even be unfairly scolded for poor work at school. Make sure that ear troubles are carefully treated and schools kept informed.

Ear disorders

If a child has an earache he should be seen by a doctor on that same day. If he also seems ill, is feverish and/or has discharge from the ear, he should be seen as an emergency even if it is the middle of the night. There are many causes for earache which are not urgent (the pain may, for example, be referred from an aching tooth, inflamed sinus or the general congestion of a simple head cold), but if infection is present, immediate treatment is vital.

A baby will not, of course, be able to tell you that his ear hurts; indeed he may not be able to localize the pain himself so he may not even give you signs such as rubbing at it while he cries. This is one reason why a feverish baby should always be checked by a doctor. He will examine the eardrums and satisfy himself that infection there is not the cause of the illness.

● Don't use folk remedies for earache. However desperate you may be to do something to help the child, warmed oil in the ear is at best useless and at worst highly dangerous. If you must do something while you wait to see the doctor, give the correct dose of your chosen analgesic (*see* **Pain and Pain Control**).

Otitis media Infection of the middle ear is the commonest cause of acute earache. It usually arises because the child already has an upper respiratory infection and the bacteria or viruses from his throat, his tonsils or his sinuses find their way up the eustachian tubes.

● Teach the child to blow his nose by blocking one nostril while he blows down the other. Blowing both together increases the chance of matter being forced into the eustachian tubes.

Unfortunately infection reaches the middle ear more easily than it can drain from it. In small children, especially, the opening of the eustachian tubes into the throat is often partially obstructed by relatively large adenoids making the free drainage of matter difficult. If infection leads to inflammation and then to the formation of pus, pressure will build up against the eardrum. In the pre-antibiotic era, burst eardrums were commonplace as was the spread of this kind of infection into the mastoid bone behind the ear and thence into the covering of the brain (*see* **Meningitis and Encephalitis**). Nowadays prompt antibiotic treatment almost always controls the infection rapidly. If a lot of pus rapidly accumulates in the middle ear, the drum may burst before treatment can even be begun. The child will have discharge from the ear, sometimes referred to as "glue ear." With energetic treatment the infection can be controlled so that the drum heals cleanly.

Repeated middle-ear infections can leave the child with chronic scarring of the eardrum and/or a collection of fluid which will not drain. Sometimes his adenoids will be removed to reduce the number of infections/improve drainage (*see* **Hospital**/Surgery: Tonsillectomy and Adenoidectomy). Occasionally a surgical incision will be made in the eardrum so that the pus can be cleaned out and the drum heal cleanly (*see* **Hospital**/Surgery: Myringotomy).

Otitis externa Infection of the outer ear canal can be caused by bacteria multiplying in the normal earwax, by infected eczema, by a minute fingernail scratch which becomes infected, by a boil at the root of one of the hairs in its lining or by inflammation/infection around a foreign body which nobody knew was in the ear. Whatever the cause, otitis externa will usually be excruciatingly painful, especially when the ear is moved or the child tries to lie on that side. If the trouble is associated with eczema, the ear may not be painful, but infuriatingly itchy.

The child should be seen immediately by a doctor. Prescribed medicaments can be applied directly to the site in the form of ear drops, but the condition may nevertheless take a long and tedious time to clear up.

Mechanical blockage of the ear canal

Excess wax, especially wax which has become impacted due to unwise attempts to clean it out with cotton swabs, can block the passageway, causing hearing loss. Such wax will need to be first softened and then syringed out by a doctor.

Foreign bodies are quite often poked into the ears by bored children who then either forget the whole matter or are unwilling to admit it. Such a foreign body will interfere with the hearing of that ear and may lead to infection. If you suspect one, take the child to the doctor. If you can see a foreign body in the ear, do not try to remove it yourself. There is a real risk that you will push it not only further out of reach but also up against the eardrum which it might damage (*see also* **Accidents**/Foreign bodies inserted on purpose).

Mechanical damage to the eardrum

Although the eardrum is a very tough membrane, it can be damaged, even perforated, by a caretaker or child who pokes about in the ear with a hard object or falls on something sharp. If you even suspect such an accident, have the ear checked by a doctor. Although most perforations will heal leaving no permanent damage to the hearing, medical care is essential both to ensure that there is no damage to the middle or inner ear and to ensure that healing takes place without infection.

● Clean only the visible parts of children's ears and don't put anything into the ear canals. A child whose ears are never interfered with is less likely to poke things into his own or those of his baby sister.

Water in the ears

Water in the ear canal does no harm unless the child has otitis externa. If it feels uncomfortable after swimming, water may have become trapped behind some wax so that droplets are being pressed against the drum. Encourage the child to lie with the affected ear downwards to encourage drainage.

Occasionally water may reach the middle ear via the eustachian tubes, due, for example, to the child sneezing or laughing/choking while submerged. The child may complain of an irritating buzzing feeling. Unless it contributes to the beginning of a middle-ear infection, such water will eventually drain back harmlessly down the eustachian tube.

Dizziness/ vertigo

Dizziness and/or vertigo are signs that the sense of balance, controlled by the semicircular canals, is disturbed. Familiar to every child who has whirled around and around on his own feet or a fairground ride, it may also come on suddenly if middle-ear infection or head injury disturbs the canal's functioning. In later life a degenerative disorder known as Meniere's disease has vertigo as one of its principal and most distressing symptoms.

In a child, dizziness or vertigo due to ear disorders is usually fleeting; it passes as soon as he has lain down for a few minutes. If it does not, decongestant *nose* drops may help, by relieving nasal congestion, opening up the eustachian tubes and thus allowing the pressure within the middle ear to equalize with outside pressure.

Dizziness or vertigo lasting for an hour or more, or occurring after head injury, should be reported to a doctor.

Eating

It ought to be easy to feed a family in the affluent West. There is enough food for everyone and enough choice for all tastes. We do not have to worry about famine and starvation; we do not even have to adjust our eating to seasonal gluts and shortages or to the geographical peculiarities of our home areas. To the millions of people in the developing world who face life-and-death problems with food, we must indeed seem to have it easy.

But feeding a family remains fraught with anxiety. An abundance of food brings anxiety about people eating too much, becoming obese and prone to all the ills associated with overweight. A vast range of foods, available courtesy of the food industry, brings anxiety over choice itself: out of all the foodstuffs available, what *should* people eat? That range of foods can only be made available with the aid of high-technology farming and food-processing methods; how harmful are those chemical fertilizers, insecticides, preservatives, colorings and flavorings? Are we feeding our children poison in their TV dinners?

Bombarded as we are with information and exhortation, warnings and scare stories, opinions and prejudices about food, the simple and satisfactory business of eating to satisfy hunger and sustain life, health and growth has come to seem complicated and worrying. The following, deliberately simplistic and middle-of-the-road, approach to family eating is intended to defuse the emotional issue of food with an infusion of ordinary common sense in the hope that it may help some families to avoid the "eating problems" which currently bedevil so many over so many years.

First principles: food is fuel and eating is a pleasure

Bodies need food to fuel the processes of life itself, to keep hearts beating, blood circulating, lungs functioning, digestive systems working and nerves and muscles interacting as they should. Even an individual in a coma or deep sleep needs energy for this kind of maintenance. As soon as any kind of work is demanded of the body, further food-fuel is needed. Sitting in front of a television set takes more energy than lying in bed; sedentary work in an office takes more still while heavy manual labor or a day's active play will use up even more.

The fuel value of foods is measured by one of two systems: in calories or in joules. Either system assigns a numerical energy value to a given weight of particular foodstuffs. When we say that an ounce of this food "contains 200 calories" we mean that, eaten and digested, this food will make 200 calories worth of energy available to the body.

In our concern to feed our children foods which are "good for them" and to ensure that they are not deprived of vitamins, minerals and other vital nutrients, we sometimes forget that *the prime need is for enough fuel.* Every food contains calories and a body which is short of energy will use any food which it is given to meet immediate energy needs (*see below* Protein).

Bodies do not only need food to fuel activity. They also need it to repair and replace lost or worn-out tissue, from trimmed hair and nails to damaged organs and skin. Provided there is adequate food available, so that the body is not short of overall energy, it will select the nutrients it needs to keep itself in good shape from among those in its diet.

With adequate food available, bodies can also store some nutrients so that they are ready to cope with any unusual demands made upon them. If a well-fed athlete's sprint uses up the energy immediately available to his muscles, for example, his body will mobilize glucose from a short-term store in his liver. If heavy menstrual loss, or other hemorrhage, uses up the iron circulating in the bloodstream, iron reserves will be mobilized for the new red blood cells which are suddenly urgently needed. When stores have been depleted in this way they will be replenished gradually by the body, provided it is taking in food which is surplus to immediate energy requirements.

Babies, children and adolescents must meet all these needs from their food but *in addition they must grow*. Their bodies need not just the small quantities of particular nutrients taken up by repair and replacement of tissue, but the much larger quantities required for building it. Like adults, children's bodies will meet immediate energy needs first so that adequate growth will only take place when there is plenty to spare.

Since eating is a biological necessity, survival of the race depends on people recognizing their need for food (by feeling hungry) and enjoying meeting it. Without appetite and satisfaction, people might simply not bother with food. As it is, people can almost always be absolutely relied upon to eat enough for their bodies' needs, provided that adequate food is available to them. Even where emotional problems bedevil eating (*see below*) or physical problems make it painful, *people will not starve themselves in the midst of plenty*. Of course there are exceptions. A person so submerged in depression that she can no longer feel normal biological drives may indeed forget to eat. A political prisoner may override the hunger drive with a tremendous act of will and starve himself to death as may a disturbed adolescent, using similar will power but different motivation (*see* **Eating Disorders**/Anorexia nervosa). But there are no exceptions which apply to healthy children. If you can believe this, believe that your child will eat enough and should enjoy doing so, he is most unlikely to have "eating problems."

Types of food for babies

Young babies have to have all their food—and most of their vital water—in the composite form of milk. Just as the placenta carried nourishment to the baby from the mother while he was inside the womb, so her breasts carry the nourishment intended for him once he has emerged. For generations the milk which cows produce for calves has been used as an alternative. Now, recognizing that calves' milk and babies' milk are radically different (*see below*), we have learned to adapt it more and more in fairly successful attempts to bring it closer to what human babies need.

Breast-feeding   In Western societies breast-feeding is not taken for granted. Influential groups argue in its favor—and offer practical assistance to nursing mothers, too—and many individual mothers believe that it is "the natural way" or "a baby's birthright" and give it a try. But giving it a try is not at all the same as just accepting it. A bottle of formula is never further away than the nearest drugstore or supermarket, and it is from a bottle that most young mothers have watched relatives and friends feeding babies. If you ask a child to draw a picture of a new baby being fed, the chances are that she will draw a bottle. Many mothers who are thinking about how to feed their coming baby will have friends who tried breast-feeding and "failed," or who breast-fed for a dutiful few weeks and thankfully gave up. Some (according to recent British research) will have husbands who "don't like the idea." Others will have job or career plans which seem easier to arrange around bottle-feeding (*see* **Working Mothers**); others again will be in touch with health professionals whose support for breast-feeding is half-hearted. It all amounts to a situation in which *breast-feeding is a positive choice* rather than simply the way young babies are fed.

Quite a high proportion of mothers will make that positive decision and put their babies to the breast after birth. Some will enjoy the feeling; enjoy an "easy-to-feed" baby's obvious pleasure and be motivated to stick with it. Others will meet difficulties and discomforts and, after a few days or a few weeks, turn to that bottle. One of the facts that the ardent propagandists for breast-feeding often leave out of account is that getting started with breast-feeding is not always easy. The mother whose baby is not easy to fix on the nipple, who sleeps after a few sucks and who turns his head away when she offers and reoffers the breast, is liable to feel rejected. If he is offered a bottle and sucks it more eagerly, it is easy for her to feel that "he likes it better." If he is also one of the many babies who not only lose weight in their first days but gain slowly thereafter (*see* **Growth**) it is easy for her also to believe that the bottle would be "better for him." There are major physical sensations for the mother to cope with, too. Some revel in suckling as a sensual experience but others are surprised and alarmed by it. Some have painful uterine contractions when the baby sucks. Some get sore nipples which may even crack to produce sharp pain. Many find that the early milk supply gets out of phase with the baby's feeding so that there are times when he is obviously hungry and others when she is painfully engorged. These are all *early* difficulties. Mothers who persist almost invariably find that everything settles down to a perfect and pleasurable situation of supply and demand, and mothers who have had this experience with one child seldom opt for the bottle with a second. But a great many mothers never get through the rough beginnings to reach the calm which follows.

Every mother must make her own decision because it is she and her baby who have to live with that decision and nobody therefore has the right to over-persuade her. Healthy, happy babies can be reared on modern formulas, and a mother who is struggling to breast-feed when she does not really want to may cast a shadow over her whole relationship with her child. Every mother is nevertheless entitled to make that decision in the light of some facts, which babymilk advertisers will not stress. Product X is *not* "the perfect food for your baby." Only your own milk is that.

Some differences between human and (modified) cow's milk

The differences between the milk produced for calves and that produced for human babies are so great that it is infinitely quicker to list the similarities, which are water and the type of sugar called lactose. Everything else is different—either in type or concentration—and some of the differences (in the concentration of minerals such as sodium and potassium, for example) are so great that unmodified cow's milk is downright dangerous and so were the old-fashioned dried milks on which millions of babies were reared with unrecognized ill effects.

Cow's milk contains too much of the wrong kind of protein. Modern formulas reduce the protein concentration of a made-up feeding but can do little to alter its type. There are amino acids (*see below* Proteins) in cow's milk which are absent from human milk. It is these amino acids which are thought to be responsible for sensitizing some infants to cow's milk protein. Exposure to these in the first six months of life is thought to be responsible for many allergic disorders later on (*see* **Allergy**/Gastro-intestinal allergies).

Cow's milk also contains much more saturated fat than breast milk. Modern manufacturers get around this by replacing the butterfat with fats or oils of vegetable origin (*see below* Fats), but the fats in breast milk are thought to be better absorbed by babies and may therefore make it easier for them to absorb the fat-soluble vitamins (*see below* Vitamins and Minerals).

The exact nature of the minerals and vitamins in breast milk is still a vexed question, but iron, for example, although low in all milks, is far better absorbed from breast milk than from any other source so that breast-fed babies do not require extra iron from solid foods until later in their first year. Vitamin D is also readily absorbed from breast milk so that rickets (*see below*) is almost unknown among babies fed from the breast.

Breast milk also protects babies from various forms of infection. Few breast-fed babies get gastroenteritis, for example (*see* **Diarrhea, Gastroenteritis and Food Poisoning**), and this is not only because their milk comes uncontaminated from the breast, sidestepping the hazards of unsterilized bottles or visiting flies, but also because it contains a variety of protective and anti-infective substances, together with some passive immunities (*see* **Immune Response**). We cannot yet even begin to copy these in a formula.

Finally, while most studies of breast milk are carried out using pooled samples from many mothers, so that "breast milk" is described as if it were a single and consistent substance, there is recent evidence to suggest that any mother's milk changes substantially, not only from day to day but even within a single feeding. Many authorities now believe that these changes may help the baby to control his own intake of milk according to his appetite, enabling him, so to speak, to stop wanting to suck more milk when his body has received adequate nourishment. Babies who are entirely breast-fed are far less likely than bottle-fed babies to become fat (*see below* Obesity). This may not only be because they are protected from over-concentrated formulas and too many extras (*see below*) but also because the food they receive has an in-built appetite control.

"Babymilks"

If you decide to feed your baby on an artifical formula do consult your doctor or other health professional about which of the many products available in your community you should use. On the whole the most "natural" food (*see below* Common sense about family eating: "Natural foods") will not be the one to choose. You will want the most highly modified milk you can find: the one which produces a feeding least like cow's milk and most like breast milk. Obviously such a formula will be more expensive than dried cow's milk, with some minerals taken out and some vitamins added.

Some health professionals may advise you not to use a cow's milk formula at all but a formula based on goat's milk or based on soya flour. Although some people do believe that goat's milk is in some way "healthier," there are few differences between goat's and cow's milk which are at all likely to be important to a young and healthy baby. Soya-based milks are often prescribed for babies already thought to be allergic to cow's milk protein, but whether it is worth using such a milk in the hope of *preventing later* allergy is a matter for you and your doctor to decide. You might consider it if yours is an atopic family (*see* **Allergy**).

Whatever formula you feed to your baby, make sure that you always:

Mix the formula to exactly the recommended strength which the manufacturers will have worked out so that the resulting feeding is of similar concentration to breast milk. Over-concentrated feedings—even when the formula is highly modified—may at worst put a strain on your baby's kidneys, by overloading him with salt and other minerals, and at best will make him fat because he wants his normal quantity of milk mixture but you have packed in extra calories.

Prepare it hygienically remembering that warm milk is an ideal breeding ground for bacteria and that gastroenteritis is still dangerous to babies (*see* **Infection**/Preventing infection. *See also* **Diarrhea, Gastroenteritis and Food Poisoning**).

Avoid adding any extras such as sugar or spoonfuls of cereals. If your baby needs extra food calories, give them to him from a spoon so that you can see whether he actually wants them or not. If you hide them in his beloved bottle you do not give his appetite a chance to guide his eating.

Other "babyfoods" Once your baby has anything to eat in addition to milk you will probably use at least some special "babyfoods." Some of these are extremely useful. The cereals especially prepared for infants, for example, have added minerals and vitamins which may be good for him (*see below*). The fruits, meats, desserts and so forth have a smooth texture and consistent taste and may be good for you because they save you trouble. But do remember that all these "special" products are only *foods*; the only "special" things about them are that they are prepared in a form which is easy for your baby to eat and digest and that they are energetically advertised and sold to you as "first foods" or "weaning foods" or whatever.

Once a baby is ready for tastes of any "solid" foods he can have anything you normally serve at your table with the exception of hot spices, salty seasonings, drugs like alcohol or coffee and, perhaps, honey (*see* **Diarrhea, Gastroenteritis and Food Poisoning**/Infant botulism). If you want to feed him family food rather than babyfood, you will at first have to purée most items and sieve (to get rid of pits or very hard stalks, etc.) some others. A Baby Mouli will do both jobs at once.

If you have a freezer, you can compromise between using "babyfoods" and fiddling about making each family meal suitable for him; you can batch-prepare your own foods and freeze them in baby portions.

● Do be careful about frozen foods—commercial or your own—when they are being fed to babies (see **Infection**/Preventing infection: Infection and home hygiene); thorough defrosting, etc. is really important.

One great advantage, though, of feeding a baby on family food is that he will not be kept on specially puréed food for too long. Give him the opportunity to discover the exciting different textures of different foods during his first year. It is children who were fed exclusively on those oh-so-consistent cans and packets, month after month, who tend to gag on "lumpy foods" and insist that they cannot chew crusts even while they chew their toys and books to pieces.

● Although it is good for a baby to share family food, he needs his own milk (breast milk or formula) throughout his first year. After that he should have whole milk rather than the skimmed milk you may buy for older people.

Types of food for everyone else

With a wide range of foodstuffs available, it is natural that parents should be concerned to offer their children an ideal selection at every age and stage. Millions of words are written every year about introducing a baby to weaning foods, about a "good mixed diet" for toddlers, about "healthy eating" for children and about what we should all do to avoid too much sugar/too many refined foods/too much animal fat and so forth. Providing an adequate diet for a family does not have to be so complicated.

Human beings are omnivores; that means they can nourish themselves adequately on both animal and vegetable foods and on a vast range of combinations of these. There are essential *nutrients* (substances which human bodies need to obtain from foods), but *there are no essential foods* for anyone old enough to be weaned. So widely available are the nutrients we need that people can abandon or reject many foods and categories of foods before there is the least danger of malnutrition. People who "don't like vegetables" or "can't take milk" may present problems to harassed hostesses or busy mothers, but they present no problem to their own health. In a society where many foods are plentiful, nutrients missed in one food will always be available in another. Don't take too seriously the thousands of books or articles on diet which give you tables that suggest the foods your family "requires." Such tables will, for example, set out the numbers of calories (units of food energy) which people of different ages, weights, heights, sexes and levels of activity need each day. Within that overall food requirement you will be told how many grams of protein and milli- or micrograms of various vitamins and minerals there should be. Calories from high-protein foods are not usually counted into the day's total (because these foods are used so inefficiently for energy), so your table will probably also say what proportion of the day's calories should come from carbohydrates or from fats . . .

Nutritional tables of this type represent averages of the intakes of large groups of people; the researchers who first construct them intend them for the guidance of people who are responsible for feeding large groups. The dietician of a large residential establishment can, for example, take such a table and from it work out what he should make available, daily and over time, and how to provide needed foodstuffs most economically. But that dietician knows that the food he provides will not be shared out equally: he does not expect each of one hundred people to eat one-hundredth of the diet. He does not even expect that everything will be eaten or that nobody will ever wish there were more of one particular item. All he knows, or cares about, is that if he provides that diet, nobody need actually go unhealthily short of anything.

People are not average, they are individual. Their individual needs are not average either. If you try to provide a scaled-down version of that dietician's guide for your family, you will drive yourself mad weighing and measuring and trying to work out how much of this is in that. And all to no purpose because the nutrients your child needs today may bear no relation to what the tables say he "ought" to need, and they may bear no relation either to what he needed last week or will need next month.

Nobody can design an ideal diet for your child. Even a skilled professional dietician can make only an educated guess and even he will not be able to ensure that the child eats it. . . . So read all that literature if you want to, but remember that your only real criteria of the adequacy of your child's diet are his health, his growth (in weight *and* height), his energy and enthusiasm for life (*see* **Growth**).

In the following notes you will find the main groups of nutrients from which human diets are made up, but you will not find foods classified within these nutrient groups in the usual way. This is because real foods—and more especially manufactured or processed foods and cooked dishes—hardly ever consist of one nutrient alone. To suggest that a child should have two portions of food from "the protein group" and two from the "carbohydrate group" is to ignore the fact that his meat will bring fat with it, his bread will contain some protein and that both items will contain a variety of vitamins and minerals.

Carbohydrates   These are the substances which human bodies can most quickly and easily break down into the sugars that provide them with energy. As such they are basic nutrients without which nobody could eat healthily.

There are many forms of carbohydrate and they occur in a vast range of foodstuffs. Unfortunately they are linked, in many people's minds, with foods which are widely regarded as "empty calories" and "fattening starch." Sugar, for example, is pure carbohydrate. When a child eats sugar he takes in calories and nothing else: no other nutrients which his body might need, just energy. Our extensive use of pure refined sugar is certainly to be frowned upon (*see below*), but this does not mean that "sugar is bad for you." How can a source of calories be bad in itself? It can be well or foolishly used, but that is quite a different matter. All cereals and therefore the foods made from them, like breakfast cereals, breads and cakes, are high in carbohydrates and it is these foods which tend to be seen as "starchy" and "poor quality." But cereals and cereal products bring other valuable nutrients with them, especially when they are not highly processed or when processed foods are enriched during manufacture. Furthermore, neither the bulk of food which we need for ordinary digestion and excretion (*see* **Constipation**) nor the number of calories we need for basic fuel could easily be provided without carbohydrate-rich foods. A diet consisting *exclusively* of a refined cereal might indeed provide adequate energy without providing enough essential nutrients, but a diet rich in essential nutrients but without adequate calories would just as certainly lead to malnutrition.

Root vegetables are also high in carbohydrates but they too contain nutrients as well as energy. The humble potato, for example, is probably the best *single* food in the world. While nobody would recommend that a child be fed nothing but potatoes, a child thus fed would survive for longer, and grow better, than he would on any other single food except for unlimited quantities of milk.

Other vegetables and fruits, as well as items usually classified as "protein foods," such as milk and nuts, also contain varying amounts of various carbohydrates. It is the ready availability of energy within such foods which ensures that bodies can make the best possible use of the other nutrients they contain (*see below* Protein-sparing).

Proteins Every human being needs proteins because these are the substances out of which bodies build tissue and therefore they are needed for repair and replacement. Growing children have a particular need for proteins without which they cannot grow.

Proteins are made up of amino acids. Different foods contain various proportions of these amino acids. Meat, fish, eggs and other animal and dairy produce happen to contain all the amino acids needed for human growth and repair. These "animal proteins" have therefore come to be known, somewhat misleadingly, as "first class."

The term is misleading because it carries with it the implication that "second class proteins" (the various combinations of amino acids present in vegetable foods) are somehow inferior. They are not. If a child eats one of these vegetable foods alone, his body will not be able to use those amino acids to the full because they do not constitute "complete protein." But if he eats two or more vegetable foods together, the chances are that the amino acids in one will be complemented by those in the other so that his body can use them all. Equally, if he eats one of those vegetable foods with even a minute quantity of complete animal protein, the deficiency in the vegetable food will be balanced by the complete range in the animal food and he will again be able to use both.

When you add milk to a child's cereal, grated cheese to his baked potato, or ham to his sandwich, you do not just add a small quantity of protein-rich food to a carbohydrate-rich dish, you add the completing factor which will make that cereal, potato or bread fully usable both for energy and for growth.

Protein-sparing As we saw earlier, human bodies meet their current energy needs first, out of whatever food is available to them. Only when there is no "energy gap" do they use specific nutrients for specific purposes, such as growth. A child who is starving, whether in the immediate short-term sense of having used up his current energy reserve, or in the long-term sense of already suffering from malnutrition, will not therefore be able to use protein for growth until or unless he also takes in enough fuel-food, calories, for his immediate needs. Feed such a child a slice of lean meat and his body will break it down, metabolize it, to release energy. The process of this breakdown is extremely inefficient; he will get fewer calories from that slice of meat than he would have obtained from the same weight of bread and he will have received no benefit at all from the fact that the food you offered was animal protein. But give him the bread (or other carbohydrate-rich food) which his body can easily process for immediate energy, *and* some meat, and his body will spare that protein for repair or growth.

This is, of course, the logic of the particular combinations of foods which are traditional in different communities. A hamburger on a bun, fish and chips, or bread and cheese all "spare" their protein for the body's optimum use by simultaneously ensuring it an easy source of energy.

It is also the logic behind the high-protein reducing diet. If the dieter takes almost all his calories in the form of high-protein foods, he will be able to eat more for less weight gain, because those proteins will be processed to fill his energy gap less efficiently than would carbohydrate foods.

Worries about proteins
While a genuine shortage of protein is disastrous to growing children, it is exceedingly rare in the Western world. Many parents nevertheless worry incessantly about whether their children are getting enough, especially as many small children dislike the most obvious sources such as butcher's meat and fish. Some will always choose to buy a baby cereal which is advertised as "high protein," even if it is more expensive and less well liked than another brand. Some continue to push milk down school-children who are already fat, because they cannot believe that without that magic potion there could be enough protein in the diet. A good many create eating problems out of this anxiety because they are always pushing the child to eat "high protein" foods which he dislikes while holding back on the junk foods which he prefers. It may help to remember the following points:

"First class" or "animal" protein is no better for your child than completed protein, whether this comes from combinations of cereals, vegetables, and seeds or from tiny quantities of animal protein eaten with vegetable foods.

Meat, fish, eggs, cheese, etc. contain such high concentrations of amino acids that only tiny quantities are actually needed. The portions of these foods which we commonly serve really do reflect the wealth of our society. Nobody *needs* eight, ten or more ounces of lean meat at one meal. Most of that surplus protein will be inefficiently broken down for energy.

Sausages, fish sticks, hamburgers, canned infant foods, etc. contain animal protein padded with cereals and vegetables, but the balance of protein to carbohydrate is still entirely adequate. If your child (like many others) prefers his "meat" in this concealed form, there is nothing nutritionally wrong with it. You may find that a Junior Beef Dinner gives you rather little beef *for your money*, but it will give him plenty for his growth and health.

Cheese is a particularly highly concentrated source of animal protein. Many babies and young children are passionate about it if they are given the chance.

Milk is a beautifully balanced food containing plenty of protein, but the amino acids are in the skim not the cream. Products like yogurt are therefore rich in protein while products like butter are not.

Beans, seeds and nuts contain balances of amino acids which are almost adequate for human growth. While these foods are not always easy to use in a young child's diet (he may choke on roast peanuts and loathe soya beans), dishes which include them are almost always high-protein combinations. Even the much derided baked bean is good food.

Your child gets protein from unexpected sources. Many widely liked staple foods, such as bread and potatoes, contain low *concentrations* of amino acids but contribute substantially to the protein in your child's diet because they are items of which he eats a lot at one time.

Many of the items you may frown upon (like cakes and cookies) contain "good things" like milk and egg in their recipes. Even some junk foods (*see below*) contribute to his adequate protein intake. Potato chips, for example, contain quite large amounts of protein. In one dehydrated packetful the child gets the amino acids from, say, two whole potatoes, a "helping" he would not have managed if the water had not been removed.

Fats   Fats provide the most concentrated source of calories in a human diet. This means that even if you eat a large slice of bread with only a small quantity of butter on it, you may get more calories from the butter than from the bread. Similarly, a fat-free sponge cake will be far lower in calories than a layer cake whose recipe is otherwise identical, while a given portion of potatoes will yield about twice as many calories if it is roasted in fat rather than boiled, and about three times as many if it is made into French fries.

Fats do not contribute much more than energy to the diet. There are more nutrients in butter than in refined white sugar, but not many more. Apart from *minute* quantities of essential fatty acids and some fat-soluble vitamins (*see below*), human beings do not actually need any fats at all. Confusion about this sometimes arises because milk is a valuable food, dairy produce is regarded as "good for you" and therefore butter, cream and things which are made from them are regarded as "good," too. Apart from the calories (which may or may not be desirable), the "goodness" of milk is in the skim.

Nevertheless some fats, sensibly used, are useful. They do a great deal to make a diet enjoyable as anyone who has had to follow a totally fat-free diet on medical advice will tell you. They are an integral part of the art of cooking. Their many calories are processed by the body to release energy more slowly than do carbohydrates. Meals which contain some of their calories in the form of fat may therefore seem more satisfying for longer. They will, in fact, produce a slower, steadier and longer-lasting rise in blood-sugar than meals containing all their energy in the form of carbohydrates. While their high concentration of calories makes them a "fattening" item for someone wanting to eat a normal bulk of food without taking in too much energy, that same high concentration makes them extremely useful in the diet of the person who cannot get through enough bulky foods to meet his energy requirement. Babies, for example, simply could not hold enough skimmed milk to give them the calories they are likely to need. Formulas must contain fats whether they are the dairy fat in the cow's milk from which they were made or the vegetable oils often added to skimmed milk in modern babyfoods. Athletes would have to eat an extraordinarily bulky diet if they had to meet their very large energy requirements without any fats, while arctic explorers or deep-sea fishermen, whose environment and way of life imposes very high energy needs upon them, commonly rely on fats both to enable them to carry and to consume enough calories.

Fats, cholesterol and heart disease

People already suffering from atherosclerosis ("clogging up" of the arteries) or known to have high levels of cholesterol in their blood, and therefore thought to be especially liable to heart disease, may be put on special diets designed to minimize their intake both of cholesterol itself and of the kinds of fat which lead the body to manufacture cholesterol. Any medically prescribed diet must, of course, be carefully followed. For the rest of us, considerable confusion exists about the whole topic and it will probably continue to exist as new research produces new findings and their interpretation fuels controversy.

Fats are made up of fatty acids, just as proteins are made up of amino acids. They are commonly classified according to their degree of saturation. "Saturated" and "unsaturated" refer to the chemical composition of the fat in terms of whether or not it holds as much hydrogen as it can.

□ Saturated fats tend to increase the level of blood-cholesterol.
□ Mono-unsaturated fats seem to have no effect on blood-cholesterol.
□ Polyunsaturated fats actually lower the level of blood-cholesterol.

Most fats contain various proportions of all three classifications, but they are usually referred to by the predominant type. Guidance as to which type of fat should be classified within which group is difficult, because manufacturing processes can alter the balance within any one product (a margarine, for example), while the exact composition of the food offered to an animal intended for slaughter can alter the balance in its fat. Very approximately you can assume that:

Animal fats (including meat fat, egg yolk and dairy fats like butter and cream) are highly saturated. If you are not sure whether a particular cooking fat is of animal or vegetable origin, the fact that highly saturated fats are usually solid at room temperature, and unsaturated ones are not, may help you. This is not a certain guide, though. While some vegetable "shortenings" are made solid by hydrogenation and therefore lose their polyunsaturates while being made suitable for pastry-making, more recently developed solid margarines and cooking fats are specially treated to retain these cholesterol-lowering qualities.

Vegetable oils (except coconut oil) are low in saturated fat. Peanut and olive oil are classified as mono-unsaturated: they will not add cholesterol but they will not lower the blood levels either. Safflower, corn, soybean and cottonseed oils are classified as polyunsaturates and will lower cholesterol levels.

If you are not trying to lower blood-cholesterol levels but are simply trying to provide a sensible and healthy diet, the following points may help you both to keep cholesterol levels down and prevent unseen fat from adding unwanted calories:

Meat fat is likely to be highly saturated and therefore undesirable in large quantities. Don't make children eat the visible fat they almost all dislike, whether it is the fat of bacon or ham, chops or ill-trimmed casserole meat.

Many dishes are actually improved by ridding them of excess meat fat. If you roast or grill on a rack, much surplus fat can be drained off meats or favorite items like sausages. If you make casseroles and stocks a day ahead, the fat which solidifies on the top can be lifted off before use.

If these methods become a routine part of your cooking, there is no reason to deprive children of the meat fats which they regard as a treat, such as the crispy skin of chicken or the crackling on a roast of pork.

Dairy fats tend to be important *visible* luxuries so that to ban butter, cream and so forth would be a real deprivation. You can cut your family's consumption a long way, without anyone noticing, if you keep down their concealed use in cooking. If your family does not like poly-unsaturated margarine on its bread, for example, you could continue to use butter as a spread but use margarine for cakes, pastry and so forth. Most sauces which require milk can equally well be made with skim as with whole milk, while many dishes which are finished with cream can be made successfully using yogurt.

Many families serve a good deal of fried food whether they would admit it to a dietician or not. While food which is fried will always be higher in calories than food which is not, using a polyunsaturated vegetable oil rather than lard, margarine or butter will substantially reduce the family intake of saturated fats and slightly reduce its calories. Vegetable oils can be heated to a higher temperature than animal fats before they burn. Frying which is carried out at a high temperature tends to seal the food rapidly and thus prevent it from absorbing so much fat. Greasy, soggy fries have usually been fried too slowly while fried bread, mushrooms or potatoes, sautéed in butter, can absorb truly phenomenal amounts.

Milk is a *food* which happens to be in liquid form. While it is an excellent food, it is one which some families (especially in the United States) misuse. Instead of treating it as a food—and therefore as an integral part of, or replacement for, meals or snacks—it is treated as a *drink* to accompany meals or to quench simple thirst. If milk-drinking is a habit in your family, and you are concerned either about their intake of animal fat or their figures, encourage water or fruit juice instead.

Vitamins and minerals

A human body's use of those major groups of nutrients is largely controlled and regulated by the minute quantities of vitamins and minerals which it takes in at the same time. These essential substances act and interact at a basic biochemical level which is far more complex than most people realize. Everyone knows, for example, that children must have calcium "for healthy bones and teeth," but few realize that the use which a child's body can make of any calcium available to it is controlled by two subgroups of vitamin D. Everyone knows that vitamin A is needed to protect normal vision, but few realize that it also plays a subtle and far-reaching role in the body's growth system and in the formation and timed release of certain hormones.

There is no shame in being ignorant of the workings of these substances within our bodies. Medical science itself has by no means completed its work, either on the list of dietary elements which are essential or on their modes of action. But it is a pity if, in our ignorance, we succumb to the blandishments of industry and dose ourselves and our children with multivitamins and mineral tonics on the grounds that if a little vitamin A is good for you, more might be better, or that if plenty of vitamin C is recommended, some vitamin E might be good, too. Deficiency diseases kill and maim millions of people every year, but they do so in the developing world, where all food is short or where the only food available is an impoverished staple such as cassava or polished white rice. The point is that if people do not get enough of anything to eat they will get neither the basic food blocks nor the vitamins and trace elements which enable their bodies to use them. If they get enough food calories but without any of those extras, they will have the food blocks but will still not be able to use them to build and maintain healthy bodies. Vitamins and trace elements come with *foods* and where there is an adequate range of foods constantly available, people do not succumb to pellagra, scurvy or beri-beri.

Western adults do not therefore have to worry about a vitamin and mineral intake which will prevent disease and would be better advised not to go looking for one which will miraculously improve good health. Those who try to discover *exactly* what they should have of *everything* are asking for a crystal ball rather than for available information.

If you go to your doctor seeking an "ideal" regime of vitamins and trace elements, he cannot honestly do more than suggest that you take a "good mixed diet" (*see below*) and, should he see any clinical reason to do so, make specific tests to ensure that you have no specific deficiencies.

Take that familiar necessity, iron, as an example. Nutritional tables will tell you how much daily iron is suggested in the average diet for your nutritional group. If you decide to work out whether you are getting that much, by checking the iron content of all your foods, you may well find that your diet, *on paper*, falls short. If you run to the doctor for a prescription for iron, he will almost certainly tell you that you are not iron-deficient. If you demand to know how this can be, he will not be able to give you a straightforward and logical answer. It may be that you have excellent iron stores and therefore do not need that average recommendation which is for everyone's safety and, therefore, must cover exceptionally high needs in some. It may be that your calculations of the iron in your diet are wrong (did you remember that curry powder?). It may be that the traces of iron you are getting are in a form which your body can absorb efficiently whereas much dietary iron is simply excreted. If you were suffering from iron-deficiency anemia, your general health would be affected and your doctor would quickly diagnose, and prescribe for, the trouble. But if you are not clinically short of iron there is no possible benefit in taking extra whatever your reading of the dietary calculations may suggest. Crossly sidestepping your doctor and buying yourself an "iron tonic" over the counter will do you no good at all.

Industries exist primarily to make money. Those which manufacture, advertise and sell vitamins, minerals, tonics and other "health products" are no exception. In recent years public concern over health has peaked and industry has cashed in. There are thousands of products available and families spend millions on them every year. Before you join in, think:

No "tonic" can truly give you happiness, beauty, virility or health unless it contains something your body is actually short of. While it may be less damaging to take vitamins than tranquillizers when life seems hard, either one is a pseudo-escape from mood or misfortune which would be better faced and dealt with.

Families which dose themselves tend to produce children who expect a pill for everything. We already rely too much on drugs and too little on ourselves and each other.

Belief in these "health miracles" leads some people to ignore real symptoms which should be reported to a doctor. Men who become impotent can usually be helped, but not by vitamins. Elderly people who become senile need medical care not miracles. Children who lack energy may be physically or emotionally ill, but in neither case will a "tonic" help.

Overdosage with certain vitamins is actually dangerous. Too much vitamin A or D, for example, is at least as bad for your child as too little. Furthermore, the more bottles of such pills you have around your house, the greater the chance that a child will accidentally overdose himself with something which can be lethal, like iron (*see* **Accidents/Poisoning.** *See also* **Safety**/In the home: Safety with medicines.).

Leaving paper calculations about quantities strictly alone, there are nevertheless a very few vitamins and minerals which may be scarce *in the particular diets of particular groups of children.* Supplementation or an improvement in diet may be sensible for these, but you should always consult your doctor or other health professional if you think that this applies to a child within your family.

Vitamins and minerals for breast-fed babies

Your milk will contain everything your baby needs for the first four to six months at least, provided that:
- You are well.
- Your own diet is adequate and mixed.
- You are not a heavy smoker, drinker or regular drug user.
- You are not trying to follow a reducing diet as well as losing to your baby the extra fat your body laid down during pregnancy, in order to be able to make milk.

Iron. Breast milk contains very little and some doctors will recommend iron-drops. Others believe that that trace of iron is so well-absorbed that it is enough. Follow advice.

Vitamins A, D and C. The requirement for these vital vitamins during periods of rapid growth is so high that many doctors recommend routine supplementation for all infants.

Fluoride. Fluoride has now been conclusively shown to help strengthen teeth against decay. Fluoride passes poorly into breast milk, so even in an area where the water naturally contains an adequate amount, a supplement at this stage may be advisable (*see* **Teeth**/The formation of teeth).

Vitamins and minerals for bottle-fed babies When bottle-fed babies were given diluted and sweetened cow's milk they urgently required additional iron and vitamins A, D and C. Now every bottle-fed baby should instead be receiving a properly manufactured and carefully reconstituted formula and many of these are already fortified. It is essential that you check the *actual formula you are using* with your doctor or health professional so that you can be properly advised on whether or not your baby requires any extras. This is especially important with respect to vitamin D (*see below*), as a fully fortified formula plus a full dose of supplementary vitamin drops could, just possibly, amount to a dangerous overdose.

Fluoride. If formula is being made up with water in a high-fluoride area, the baby may not require any extra. Check.

Vitamins, minerals and weaning When your baby drinks "ordinary milk" instead of breast milk or formula he loses the perfection of the one and the fortification of the other.

Some weaning foods (such as baby cereals) are highly fortified with vitamins and minerals. These foods are extremely useful. The baby is most unlikely to eat such large quantities as to make supplementary vitamins A, D and C undesirable, but their regular consumption may well meet his needs for iron and other trace elements.

Vitamins and minerals from weaning to school age These are years of rapid growth and often of capricious appetite and "eating problems." Even where a lack of vitamins A, D and C cannot be demonstrated in the diet, many people consider that their supplementation is a valuable safety precaution which will do no child any harm and will do the few who might otherwise suffer from deficiency a great deal of good.

● Remember that overdosage of vitamins A and D is *dangerous*. Give only the recommended dose and lock away your supply.

Children who may be at risk of rickets Rickets is a disease in which the bones do not grow and harden properly. Limb bones may be deformed because they are too soft to carry the child's weight; the bones of the skull may be slow to join so that the fontanelles remain open for an unusually long time; the spine may be bent or twisted while the teeth may be soft and particularly liable to decay.

Such a "classic" case of rickets would be unusual in a Western country, but lesser degrees of the disorder are not nearly as rare as most people suppose.

Proper bone formation requires that the body receive adequate amounts of minerals such as calcium and phosphorus (which usually occur together in the same foods) *together with* quantities of vitamin D which will enable it to absorb and use those minerals. If a child has adequate intakes of both, there will be no problem. If he has very inadequate supplies of either one he will be at risk. If he has just adequate supplies of either one then other factors which can affect his body's readiness to absorb what little is available may tip the balance either way.

Calcium. The main source for most children is milk and the many dairy products and manufactured foods which contain milk. In Britain and some other Western countries, flour and therefore the bread made from it are fortified with calcium and other minerals. A scarcity of calcium in the diet is therefore unlikely. However, that diet may make it more or less easy for the body to use the calcium it takes in. For example, whole grains contain a substance called phytate which prevents the absorption of calcium by forming with it insoluble calcium phytate in the intestine.

Where whole grain flour is made into a risen bread, using yeast, some of the phytate is inactivated. But where such flour is used to make unleavened bread (such as chapattis) or where whole grains are eaten as cereals, the phytate may hold onto enough of the otherwise available calcium to render a rather low intake too low. It is thought that a high phytate intake may contribute to rickets in some communities which eat whole grain chapattis to the exclusion of all white flour or risen bread. It may possibly contribute to the risk of rickets in families who eat a vegan diet (*see below*) and whose children therefore receive no calcium from milk and dairy produce. It might do so in a health-conscious family which deliberately kept "fattening" dairy foods to a minimum and preferred whole grains to refined foods.

Vitamin D. The only concentrated dietary sources are fatty fish (sardine and tuna, for example) and fish oils. There are traces of the vitamin in dairy produce and some foods (such as margarine in Britain and margarine and milk in America) are fortified with it, but it would still be difficult to provide for a young child's needs from his diet alone.

Human bodies can produce vitamin D when bare skin is exposed to sunlight and it is through this process that most people obtain enough. But there can be difficulties:

Dark skin evolved to protect people from tropical sun and can "protect" them too well from weaker northern sun. A dark-skinned child will (all other things being equal) manufacture less vitamin D during the summer than his pale-skinned friend. When winter comes and sunshine is rare, his stores may be inadequate.

Skin cannot make vitamin D if it is not exposed to that sunshine. Regular exposure even of the face and hands may be enough, especially for a white child, but any child who is kept indoors almost all the time (perhaps because his mother has newly arrived from a society where women traditionally stay indoors) may make too little vitamin D.

The sun's rays cannot be effective through heavy atmospheric pollution. Even a fair child who spends quite a lot of time out of doors may fail to produce sufficient vitamin D if he lives in the overcrowded center of a city which is liable to smog (*see* **Pollution**/Air pollution).

A shortage of vitamin D is a more frequent cause of rickets in the Western world than is a shortage of calcium. If yours is a fair-skinned child who spends a lot of time out of doors wearing minimal clothes because there is lots of sunshine, he is most unlikely to be short of the vitamin. But since none of us can lay on sunshine on demand, and few of us can induce in our children a passion for herring, a daily supplement throughout early childhood is probably sensible.

● Too much vitamin D is exceedingly dangerous, leading to hypercalcemia in which extra bony deposits are laid down. Give only the dose prescribed by the doctor and keep tablets safely locked away.

Children who might need extra iron

Most of the children who are at all likely to run short of iron will be under medical care already. They may include premature babies (born without adequate stores from the mother), children with certain biochemical disorders leading to abnormal loss of iron, and any child who has had severe hemorrhage.

Regular bleeding without illness sometimes leads to iron deficiency. The most usual in young children is a marked tendency to nosebleeds. Older girls whose iron stores were only just adequate at the menarche occasionally become anemic during the first few months of menstruation, especially if this is extra-heavy (which is rare).

If you have any reason to think your child might need extra iron, seek a doctor's advice rather than buying over the counter. Many types of iron are quite unused by the body, being simply excreted. If your child is to benefit from a supplement it must be of a type his body can absorb.

● Overdosage of iron is dangerous and often fatal.

Children who might be in need of almost anything

The more severely the diet is restricted the more possible it is that some important vitamin or mineral will be lacking. The younger the child the more likely it is that such a lack will matter.

If you impose a severely limited diet on your child (*see below* When the diet is restricted) check it out with your doctor first. If, for example, you are vegetarian and prefer to exclude dairy produce and eggs as well as actual meat and fish, your child may need supplements of extra vitamins (such as B_{12}) which are thought only to come from animal sources.

If your child is placed on a severely limited diet by a doctor, make sure that his supervision of the child's disorder includes follow-up supervision of what he may eat. When the possibility of allergy is being investigated, for example, a child is sometimes limited to a very few items of food, but the limitation lasts for only a few weeks and therefore does no harm. But in biochemical disorders, a strict diet may be needed for years and therefore the implications for normal growth may be considerable.

If your young child puts himself on a severely limited diet the chances are high that it will include at least small quantities of a wide enough range of foods to supply his needs. But keep on with his regular supplement of vitamins A, D and C and, if you are worried, list what he takes and check it with your doctor.

If an older child puts herself on a severely limited diet, the chances are that it will not last for long. A few weeks' dieting will do her no harm. If it should last for months and lead to major weight loss, so that the total amount of food she is taking is clearly inadequate for her body's needs, consider the possibility of anorexia nervosa (*see* **Eating Disorders**).

Vitamin C:
the vitamin
from which
we might all
benefit

Although a clinical deficiency of vitamin C (scurvy) is almost unheard of in Western societies, it is possible that many people take in less than their bodies could use. Vitamin C not only protects against the effects of deficiency, it also positively contributes to a variety of healthy processes, ranging from the conversion of certain carbohydrates to energy and the metabolism of some proteins, to the formation of the connective tissue through which wounds heal. Some people believe that it also contributes to the body's defense against everyday infections.

Vitamin C cannot be stored by the body, so continual supplies are needed: any normal surplus is simply excreted. While it is widely distributed in fruits and vegetables, it is often destroyed by modern food processing, storage and cooking. If you are going to spend money on foods which you serve largely for their richness in vitamin C, you might as well ensure that what was in the food when it left the ground is still available when it reaches your family.

● A few years ago it became fashionable to take mega-doses of vitamin C on the grounds that it *might* help to ward off colds and even if it did no good it could do no harm. There is now some evidence to suggest that regular overdoses of the vitamin may predispose some people to form kidney stones.

Vitamin C is water-soluble and partly destroyed by heat. Soaking a vegetable takes some away: wash and dry or merely wipe clean when possible. Every time you boil and drain a vegetable you pour most of the vitamin C down the sink. Cook rapidly in as little water as possible and try to use that in soup or gravy. Canned vegetables will still have some vitamin C after processing but most of it will be in the canning liquid: use that if you can.

Stewing fruits and serving them in their juice preserves much of the vitamin C: the fact that the fruits are acid prevents the heat from breaking so much of the vitamin down.

Most vegetables and fruits have most of the vitamin directly under the skin. The less you peel the better. Potatoes, in particular, are an unexpectedly good source if cooked in their skins. The apples which are many children's favorite fruit and only raw food will have far more vitamin C if eaten skin and all.

Vegetables gradually lose vitamin C during storage, especially in sunlight and once cut or broken. Obviously the fresher the better, but if you have no control over harvesting, at least avoid vegetables which have been displayed in the open air; avoid buying more than you can use within a day or two and avoid chopping, etc. until you are ready to cook or eat.

Frozen vegetables and fruits are usually processed while very fresh and vitamin C is unaffected by very low temperatures. These items may therefore be better sources than "fresh" produce which has travelled the continent and been in the shop for days.

Dried and dehydrated fruits and vegetables have usually been heat-processed and will, therefore, contain little vitamin C unless, as with potatoes, the vitamin has been added at the end.

Easy extra sources of vitamin C include:
☐ Oranges and other citrus fruits and their (freshly squeezed) juices. The skin protects from light and the fact that we eat them raw protects from heat and water.
☐ Frozen juices or "whole fruit" or "natural fruit" juices are just as good.
☐ Salads—including many other vegetables than lettuce and tomatoes —are obvious sources but may be disappointingly low in the vitamin if they have been pre-prepared and are wilting.
☐ Tomatoes and (freshly prepared or commercially frozen) juice.

"Sources" of vitamin C which may mislead you include:
☐ "Fruit" drinks which are not actually made of fruit at all;
☐ Green vegetables which have been kept hot in steam tables, etc.;
☐ Processed items which may be somewhat misleadingly advertised such as "vegetable soup, full of natural goodness" and "whole-fruit jam."

Why a "mixed diet" is a good diet

When parents consult health professionals about food for a child after weaning, they are usually told that he should have a "good mixed diet." If they are brave enough to ask further what such a diet should consist of, they are likely to be told to make sure that he has meat or fish once a day, an egg or some cheese every day, plenty of green vegetables and fresh fruit, with bread, potatoes and cereal to "fill him up." There is nothing whatsoever the matter with such a diet except that very few small children want to eat it, not every parent wants to serve it and the implication is that unless it is complete, it will be inadequate. The moment it becomes clear that the child hates beef, refuses egg and will eat only peas as a "green vegetable," the wretched parents begin to feel that they are doing wrong. Quite soon they also feel that the child is doing wrong. Feeding problems are then almost inevitable (*see below* Common sense about family eating).

The real point about that "good mixed diet" is not that it is essential but that it should be easy. If you can provide a child with a wide range of foods in different combinations and permutations, meal by meal, day by day and month by month, you will never have to worry, or even think, about whether or not he is getting the "right" things to eat. A mixed diet ensures adequate nutrition in a number of ways:

Different foods provide different nutrients and therefore compensate for each other's deficiencies or excesses. At its simplest level this may mean that a low calorie main course (a salad, perhaps) is balanced by the accompanying potatoes or by the pie which follows for dessert. At a more technical level, that salad will provide plenty of vitamin C so the fact that there is none left in those well-boiled potatoes or in that processed pie-filling does not matter.

Different foods enable the body to make full use of important nutrients. Your child's body may need protein but it may also need energy food, right now. If you served that salad with cold meat, adding neither the potatoes nor the fruit pie, he would probably process the meat for its energy. By making sure that there is enough carbohydrate and/or fat to meet his energy gap, you ensure that the protein in that meat can be used to its best effect.

You cannot know exactly what nutrients your child needs at any given moment or on any given day, but by offering him a mixture you ensure that he will meet those needs for himself. Furthermore, if he always has enough of everything available, he will retain the stores of nutrients which help him to meet particular physical demands.

Different kinds of *meals* are important, too. Working out what nutrients may be missing from, or dangerous substances added to, processed or convenience foods is exceedingly difficult (*see below*). The easy way to be sure that you neither deprive a child of anything important nor feed him damaging quantities of anything is to mix your use of such foods into meals made from fresh ones. A diet made up entirely of takeout fast foods and frozen TV dinners might not be good for him, but as part of a mixture such meals will certainly do no harm.

Different kinds of *cooking* contribute to that mixture. If almost everything you serve is fried, for example, your family will consume a lot of fat (including oil) and whatever else the diet is like, it will be high in calories for its bulk, so the child may get fat. But if you use the same foods but sometimes fry, sometimes grill, sometimes roast, sometimes boil and sometimes bake them, there will be a far better balance. Similarly, if every vegetable you serve is boiled for ten minutes in plenty of water and then drained, very few of their vitamins will reach the child because they will have gone down the sink. Boil them sometimes, by all means, but if you sometimes stir-fry them or put them in a casserole and sometimes serve them raw, vitamin-rich meals will balance the rest.

When the diet is restricted

Some children refuse to eat a completely mixed diet (*see below* Eating problems) while others cannot be offered one. The more restricted your child's diet, the more you will have to think about the items you serve in order to be sure that his body can find what it needs from among them.

Important nutrients are so widely dispersed among different foods that a child who omits particular *items*—even if they add up to a lot of items—will seldom present any nutritional problem. It is when the diet excludes whole categories of types of food that difficulty can arise. For example:

A vegetarian diet presents no problem at all — Meat, fish and the products made from them are not a large enough food category to matter. There are many other sources of protein and, with dairy produce permitted in the diet, a vegetarian need not even search for combinations of vegetable proteins which always complement each other. He can eat vegetables and cereals and, with milk and cheese and egg in the diet, you can be sure that all will be well. Many people believe that a good vegetarian diet is actually healthier than an omnivorous one. Certainly many vegetarian families tend to serve more varied food than those who unthinkingly rely on meat and two vegetables.

A vegan diet can be healthy but needs some thought

Once dairy produce and eggs are eliminated as well as meat and fish, the child receives no animal protein at all and must therefore obtain all the protein he needs for adequate growth from a rich mixture of cereals, nuts, vegetables and fruits. If problems do arise, this is usually because such a diet tends to be low in calories for its bulk. The child therefore has to eat a comparatively large quantity of food in order to get the energy he needs and leave enough over for growth. On the whole, research shows that such children grow healthily but that they are lighter for their height than vegetarian or omnivorous children: they can seldom eat enough to lay down a surplus as fat.

The possibility of protein shortage during that critical first year, when the baby will not eat/digest large quantities of bulky vegetable foods, can be averted by lengthy breast-feeding. Thereafter, you may find that soya beans or products made from textured soya protein are a great help.

A diet containing no animal food is likely to be low in vitamins A, D and B_{12}. Unless supplementation is against your principles, the child should receive these vitamins throughout his early life. If it is against your principles you will need to discuss the matter with your doctor.

A fruitarian diet cannot support adequate growth

Some vegan families wish to restrict their diet even further by omitting cooked vegetable and cereal foods, relying entirely on raw fruits. Even if there is sufficient money available to buy a wide range of fruits both in and out of season, such a diet is not suitable for growing children. Fruits contain such low concentrations of proteins that impossibly large quantities would have to be consumed for a child to obtain his needs. If some nuts and seeds are permitted the proteins available to him will be increased, but his needs will still not be met because such foods are comparatively indigestible in the raw state.

Zen macro-biotic diets are unsuitable for children

Although the exact diets vary, these all share in a deliberate attempt to reduce the body's intake of foodstuffs to a bare minimum necessary for continued activity and survival. A child has to do more than survive: he also has to grow and he will not do so on brown rice alone.

● Parents whose beliefs lead them to offer an unusually restricted diet to their children should consult a health professional at the earliest possible moment, preferably as soon as the pregnancy is recognized and certainly before any attempt to wean the child from the breast is considered. Early consultation will almost always mean that the child's healthy growth can be ensured within the framework of his parents' beliefs and that professionals will take a great deal of trouble to find ways in which this can be done. It is when a child has already had his health impaired by an unsuitable diet that doctors sometimes have to suggest dietary additions which the parents find unacceptable, and it is when they are faced with a child who is suffering that such professionals may tend to seem less than respectful of the parents' convictions.

If a restricted diet is medically prescribed

The prescribing doctor or dietician should certainly work out with you the full implications. A diet designed to maintain a careful balance between carbohydrates and insulin in diabetes, for example, should present no additional problems provided you fully understand the freedom with which one carbohydrate-rich food may be interchanged with another. A diet that excludes the gluten in wheat and its flour may be rather more difficult because so many manufactured foods contain wheat flour. But again, full information should make it clear that the child still has available to him a very wide range of foods. In all such circumstances, it is important that you find and stay in contact with a professional whom you both trust and find easy to get along with. The problems presented by the diet will change as the child grows and changes, and the information you need will be extremely down-to-earth. You not only need lectures on the nature of carbohydrate metabolism: you need to know "What else can I give him for supper?" and "What shall I do about school meals?" and "Can he have his favorite breakfast cereal? . . ."

If money is very short
Remember that a diet can be restricted in the sense of excluding luxury or "treat" foods without being at all restricted in the dietary sense. Your child may yearn for iced cupcakes, bought pies, fun snacks and canned fruits, but while his morale may suffer if he cannot have them, his diet need not. Feeding a family adequately on very little money is most difficult when poverty goes (as it so often does) with lack of time and lack of decent cooking facilities. If you are living in one room and working all the hours the nursery will keep your child, you *need* the convenience of convenience foods and you cannot search the street markets for cheap foods or undertake the long, slow cooking which will turn them into highly nutritious dishes.

Perhaps the most useful point to remember is that *enough calories are the prime essential* because without them the child's body will not use the meat you can ill afford. Do remember, too, that *Western staples, like bread and potatoes, are good foods* much maligned by those with their minds on dieting rather than eating. Your child will be better off with enough of these to satisfy his appetite, together with small quantities of cheese, milk and so forth, than with small portions of "better quality" foods which leave him perpetually hungry.

Common sense about family eating

It is easy to write about food and eating in an easygoing and objective way. It is far more difficult to behave that way when faced with the realities of feeding a family. Food is not only a biological necessity and a physical pleasure, it is also highly emotional stuff; a symbol of love from the mother who prepares it; a symbol of acceptance or rejection of that love by the child who eats it or spits it out; a symbol of the unity of the family gathered around the meal table or of rejection of that unity by the adolescent who leaves a vacant place. But while it is often helpful to recognize these emotional aspects of family eating, it is vital to keep them under control: to keep the practical business of eating as separate as you can from more complex concerns. The more you can do so, the less likely it is that yours will be a family which is beset by "eating problems."

Keep eating separate from morals and ethics
Everyone has a right to his own moral and ethical convictions. If you are convinced vegetarians you will obviously feed your family a vegetarian diet and you may try to convert your omnivorous friends from their meat-eating. But when you do so, be clear that you are arguing with them

about ethics rather than about diet. They are not poisoning their children's bodies by giving them fish sticks, whatever you may think they are doing to their minds.

This kind of confusion between ethics and nutrition bedevils us at many levels and makes it difficult to see the wood of real issues for the lobbyists' trees. Confusion exists, for example about:

"Natural foods." There is a great deal to be said for foods which are "natural" in the sense that they are grown in their own time and place and sold to us with nothing added and nothing taken away. Some such foods are nutritionally superior to their processed counterparts. Rice, for example, loses its B vitamins when it is polished and gains nothing. Some foods are different in the natural form but the loss or gain is not absolute: whether you want the natural or the refined/processed form depends on what you want from that food. Flour is the obvious example. The most "natural" flour is simply ground whole wheat. It contains more B vitamins and more roughage than refined white flour, but the white provides more usable calcium. Whole wheat flour can be cooked in some very interesting ways but will not make a good sponge cake. White flour makes boring, cottony bread but will rise to the occasion of that sponge. The choice is yours; the variety is available but to state, as a matter of conviction, that one kind of flour is superior to another is idiotic.

Most of the foodstuffs which are available in "natural" as well as processed forms differ only in taste and not at all in nutritional value. Wartime dried egg, for example, contained all the nutrients of real eggs, yet nobody could be blamed for preferring the "natural" thing. Most people would similarly rather eat a real potato than a helping of dried mashed (even if it does have added vitamin C), and most of us would select a locally grown strawberry rather than a squashy bright pink thing out of a can. Since eating is meant to be pleasurable, taste is an excellent reason for buying one kind of food rather than another, provided we admit that we buy for the taste rather than because "natural food" is, in some vaguely moralistic way, "better."

Naturalness-for-its-own-sake, divorced from nutritional superiority or more enjoyable taste, makes the arguments silly. Some people will tell you, for example, that you should use only coarse brown sugar, never refined white. Why? There are plenty of arguments against using too much sugar of any kind but if you are going to use sugar, you might as well use the kind you prefer. The minute traces of minerals left in brown sugar and removed in the final refining which whitens it, make no useful contribution to diet, nor is that brown sugar any more "natural" than sugar which has been processed through just that final stage.

Sometimes the arguments about "natural" foods get confused with morals in a different way. People will try to persuade you to spend extra money to buy free-range rather than battery-produced eggs. Fine if you think they taste different; the nutrient value is the same. The persuaders are probably really thinking about the miserable lifestyle of those battery hens but if they are, they should say so. It is for you to decide whether or not to operate a personal ban on intensive farming.

Try not to let the slogans of the health food industry convince you that anything bought in their stores will be "good for you" and that anything bought in a supermarket will not. You will find manufactured goods on those shelves which are just as elaborately processed as anything in the supermarket and a great deal more expensive. If your baby *likes* "natural muesli" (and you can afford it) fine; if not, remember that it is only food and there are plenty of other enriched and nourishing cereals available.

Organically grown foods. Since there is no non-organic way to grow anything this is a pretty silly phrase, but it is usually taken to mean that the plant concerned has been grown without artificial fertilizers or insecticides or fungicides. It is supposed to taste like the food you might pick from your garden and it may. Once again, if you like the organically grown vegetables which are available to you, can afford the higher prices and the time it takes to remove those natural blemishes, fine. If none are available or you cannot, your family's diet will not be nutritionally affected in any measurable way. You may bitterly regret our society's use of highly dangerous pesticides and long to ban all such substances from your family's diet, but unless you really can grow *all* your own food you do not have that option. However many organically grown cauliflowers you buy, the family will still be eating mass-produced and imported items in all their other foods.

Some people feel very strongly about the risks which intensive methods of agriculture impose upon us all. Lists of pesticides in current use make terrifying reading and, when one realizes that some of the most dangerous are used because they make it possible for manufacturers to increase already vast profit margins, it is easy to become morally outraged. But there is another side to the story. Without methods of this kind, the world would be even shorter of food than it already is. There are already too many people on this planet for nature to provide without help from technology. If we must have a moral dimension to this argument at all, world hunger must surely be the overriding one.

Food additives. Some of the chemicals which are added to manufactured and processed foods are valuable additions to a family's diet. The fortification of flour, for example, much increases the nutrient value of the bread which is our staple food. The addition of vitamins to margarine makes some "difficult" ones easy to provide, while the vitamin C which is added to many commercially prepared "fruit drinks" makes a cheaper product nutritionally equivalent to the fresh juices which many families cannot afford. We cannot legitimately scorn all additives if we are considering nutrition rather than principle.

Many types of food additives are certainly undesirable, but even these usually have something to be said for, as well as against, them. Some of the most obviously worrying are:

Drugs given to animals to speed up growth, weight gain, egg laying . . . so that they reach marketable size faster and for less expenditure on their food, housing, etc., or so that hens come into lay or turkeys reach marketable sizes at convenient times, such as just before Christmas. The use of hormones and antibiotics, for example, is highly controversial and almost certainly damaging (*see* **Infection**/Treatment of infections: Problems in antibiotic use).

Preservatives used to increase the shelf-life of a vast range of manufactured foods. Without some preservatives modern food production would be impossible—those "sell by" dates would have to be today or tomorrow; there could be no "long-life" products and items ranging from packet soups to custards and jams could no longer be stocked weeks ahead either in shops or homes. Some items of food, such as sausages, bacon and cooked ham, which are now safe if they are handled properly, would become very risky, too. The nitrites which are added to preserve them may be risky, but they prevent the growth of some extremely dangerous food-poisoning organisms (*see* **Diarrhea, Gastroenteritis and Food Poisoning**/Botulism). The risks of food which has "gone bad" have to be balanced against the risks of the chemicals which stop it from deteriorating. There are three parties to any argument. Manufacturers, while it would clearly not be in their interests to poison us all, are primarily concerned to maximize their profits and will therefore tend to use as much of the most effective cheap preservative as their product needs, to take a good share of the market. Consumers want their food to be safe and well-preserved and as cheap as possible. Public health watchdogs want to strike a proper balance. Perhaps it should be their role to educate consumers as well as to control manufacturers. If we want food in which fewer and safer preservatives are used, we shall have to be prepared to shop more frequently, to refrigerate more food items and to pay more.

Colorings and flavorings are used in an extraordinarily wide range of foods and there is no doubt that some are dangerous. Rows blow up from time to time in one country or another when yet another such chemical is shown to cause cancer in laboratory animals or skin rashes in human consumers. Unfortunately there is seldom agreement among the experts as to the balance of risks surrounding one particular chemical. Saccharin, for example, has come under fire in the United States but is still permitted in British foods and for open sale as a sugar substitute. Too much sugar is fattening/bad for teeth and dangerous to certain groups of people such as diabetics, so some artificial sweeteners are perhaps needed. On the other hand, nobody would want to use a sweetener they knew to be dangerous: it would be better to go without the sweetness. The point is that the balance is one which should be struck with regard only to human health and welfare; it is worrying when such decisions are clearly made with an eye to the commercial world.

Many colorings and flavorings seem completely unnecessary. But are they? Would we, the consumers, really buy and eat canned strawberries if they were not dyed that rich pink color but were left the sickly cream shade they naturally become after canning? Would we pay for our orange jelly the kind of money that it would cost if it contained only the flavor of real orange juice? Would we settle for canned soups which all tended to be mud-colored whether they were called "tomato" or "mixed vegetable," and what would your children say about pale baked beans? Most natural colors and flavors *could* be intensified in such products by using concentrates of the actual foodstuff, but they would be very, very much more expensive. Part of the problem is that we have become accustomed to brightly colored food and have allowed our children to expect brilliant iced cupcakes and lurid soft drinks. Part of it is that we expect to eat cheaply foods which are out of season and/or native to quite another country and/or not really suitable for the purposes to which they are put.

Banana custard, for example, takes a lot of fresh bananas if it is to have much taste; its natural colour is grayish. If we want strongly flavored yellow custard we invite synthetics. . . . Common sense about family eating suggests some middle-of-the-road ways in which individuals can cope with the nutritional aspects of this kind of dilemma:

Concentrate on that *mixed* diet so that children do not consume daily portions of anything except basic foods. If there are antibiotics in veal, dangerous pesticides in fruits and a lot of risky colors and flavors in soft drinks, they are far less likely to harm the child who eats each occasionally, than the child who drinks the same fizzy potion twice a day for months on end.

Look carefully at the diet of a child who *is* hooked on a few particular food items to the exclusion of all else. Fizzy drinks are, perhaps, an unnecessary indulgence. You could stop buying them or try using simple soda water with fresh fruit juice. The child who eats baked beans twice a day will certainly be getting more of whatever is in those cans than the manufacturers *or* health officials expect, so, if you cannot wean him from them, it might be worth trying him with your own home-made version or at least ringing the changes among brand names.

Try, perhaps, to bring up children with some knowledge of what foods *really* look like and taste like so that without being moralistic about it you discourage the view that a cereal which is not rainbow colored must be boring. A child who has eaten locally grown asparagus with pleasure will not expect all asparagus to be bright green while a child who has been allowed to be a connoisseur of fresh apples will find many commercially produced "apple juices" and "apple pie fillings" unnaturally strong.

Leave artificial flavors and colors out of foods you prepare at home so that your gravies taste of the meat they are to accompany rather than of "stock cubes" and your coffee pudding tastes of coffee rather than of coffee-concentrate.

Where you really must have artificial aids—in icing a birthday cake, for example—use vegetable food colorings rather than artificial ones.

If you want to campaign about these issues, remember that your lobbying will be far more effective if it is directed towards strengthening the power of the public health authorities, so that they can be as free as possible of commercial or political interference, than if it takes the form of a private family ban on this, that or the other food item of which you have become suspicious. This is true of all the above issues: your local producer of battery hens and eggs is not even going to *know* if you refuse to buy his goods and he certainly is not going to care whether you do or not provided that other people go on doing so. He may care, he may even change some of his ways, if you join in a public fuss (*see also* **Pollution**).

Keep eating separate from family discipline

The more relaxed you can be about the food you serve to your family, the more pleasure and the fewer problems you are likely to have over children's eating. Of course this does not mean that children should be given anything they like to eat. A baby or toddler does not even know what he will like because he does not know what there is. Children have to be introduced to, and offered, a range of foods from which they can make a diet which they will enjoy with good appetite to the benefit of their bodies. The point is that you offer it and let them, as far as possible, select among it. You reserve the right to buy, cook and serve what you think fit, but you allow them the right to eat it or not as they think fit.

The basis of most common "eating problems" is again that we tend to confuse moral issues with nutritional ones; the pleasant need-fulfilling business of eating food with the less pleasant and entirely social business of table manners, general behavior and "doing what he is told." Your child must "learn how to behave" (*see* **Discipline, Self-discipline and Learning How to Behave**) and he must nourish his body; he will do each more easily, and with less wear and tear on you, if you keep the two endeavors entirely separate in your mind. The following examples of common mealtime rules and exhortations may help to make the point. A child should:

Eat everything which is put before him

Why? It may be more than he feels like eating; if you push him, you try to make him obey you rather than his own appetite. Success will not make him more obedient, just fatter. Failure will make a completely unnecessary row and a sadness to replace the pleasure of eating.

It may be food that he dislikes; if you push him you will certainly confirm the dislike so the more "important" the food, the more unfortunate the pressure.

Taste in food is something to be encouraged: he will broaden his tastes only if he is confident that "trying a bit" will *not* lead to a row if he then leaves it.

Do you eat food you dislike?

Food is certainly too valuable to waste, but it is no less wasteful to throw it away or feed it to the cat *after* a long wrangle than before, and it is surely more wasteful to feed it to a child who does not want it than to pass it on to the teenage sister who is always hungry.

Finish his meat course before being allowed any sweet

Why? That meat course may, or may not, have more food value than the sweet course; that depends both on what dishes you are offering and what nutrients his body needs. But certainly there is no surer way of making the sweet more desirable than the meat, than pressing him to earn the one he does want by eating what he does not.

Eat green vegetables

Why? There is nothing valuable in green vegetables that is not also available in other foods (*see above*).

Drink milk

Why? After early infancy there is no reason whatsoever why a child should drink milk if he does not like it. Admittedly it is a very convenient item for a child to like, but your convenience and his nutrition are different matters. Nutritionally he can get the same nutrients from things he may like very much, such as yogurt, cheese, puddings and so on.

These are all unnecessary no-win battles. You will not often manage to make him eat what he does not want and when you do, you should not. Trying will make nothing but misery for all. Some other common rules about family eating have rather more sense to them but still need tactful administration and separation from discipline:

Children should eat regular meals

Eating is largely patterned by habit. The child who is accustomed to three meals a day will probably feel hungry at roughly the usual times, but there is no physical necessity for one daily eating pattern rather than another, or for sticking to a pre-arranged schedule if appetite dictates otherwise. Dietetically there is nothing wrong with dividing a day's food intake into two or six parts rather than three.

Eat a good breakfast

This is a difficult one. Studies have clearly shown that children who go to school without having had any breakfast at all tend to flag by mid-morning. Energy levels and concentration may drop and, if tests are carried out, children's blood-sugar levels (a measure of immediately available calories) are found to be very low. But studies also show that there are many children (and older people, too) who cannot feel hungry within an hour of waking up.

If yours is one of these, try for a compromise rather than for daily rows over the cereals and eggs. Many children will be positively hungry by the time they have made the trip (and the effort) which gets them to school. A cheese sandwich to eat on arrival may be an unconventional "breakfast," but we are trying to think about diet not convention. . . . Some children can comfortably accept plenty to *drink* first thing in the morning even though they cannot comfortably eat. An egg beaten into milk and fruit juice is nutritionally just as good as the breakfast of juice, egg and milk you wanted him to have in the first place.

Avoid eating between meals

Obviously the child who takes in small quantities of food at frequent intervals all through the day is not going to want full-sized meals as well: if he does want them the combination will probably provide more total food than his body needs and therefore make him fat. Apart from this risk, there is nothing dietetically wrong with "little and often." Babies often thrive better on such a feeding pattern (as many exhausted parents know!); some toddlers prefer it and some sick children can keep themselves properly nourished and hydrated only on this basis.

Parents who feel morally outraged when a child begs for food between meals are usually worried about his being "greedy," and concerned that his snacks will consist of "junk foods" which will fill him up so that he is not hungry for proper, nourishing food.

Greed is a nasty word which we all associate with fat children who have sticky mouths and whiny voices. But greed can also be part of hunger and an entirely desirable anticipation of the pleasure of satisfying that hunger with food. If he is hungry, he should feel a little greedy. Greed is undesirable only if the child is not hungry but simply craving for sweets and/or trying to bully you.

Many children do get genuinely hungry between meals. It is a long time from lunch until supper, especially if the one was a school meal you disliked or a simple sandwich and the other is on the late side because both parents work long hours. Adults who feel hungry before a meal is due or ready think nothing of having a snack to keep them going. You yourself, even as you insist that your child wait until suppertime, may well have been tasting and nibbling this and that as you prepared the meal.

If you accept that your child may be hungry between meals (rather than "just greedy") and if you also accept that if he is hungry it is right that he should have something to eat, you can easily steer a path between indulging greed and satisfying appetite.

Some common-sense "snack policies"

Accept that your child is usually hungry at this particular time of day (mid-morning, perhaps, or immediately after he comes home from school) and cater to him. A planned snack remains in your hands so that it can be anything from a mini-meal to a token gesture. The child who has such a snack is unlikely to keep begging for bits and pieces.

Realize that most of your child's begging comes from a desire for particular things which he gets only between meals—sweets and potato chips, for example. Control the intake of these (especially if he is getting fat) while still allowing for real hunger, by offering those treat foods as part of *meals* and offering the simpler foods, like bread and butter, milk and apples, when he wants something in between (*see below* Common sense about junk foods; sweets).

Decide which foods any member of the family may have whenever he is hungry and keep them available. This often works well with older children who are unlikely to raid the refrigerator for food you were planning to serve tonight, if they know they can help themselves from the cookie tin, fruit bowl or milk supply.

Common sense about junk foods

Leaving sweets aside for a moment (*see below*), commercially prepared and energetically marketed snack foods cause more trouble than they need in many families. The trouble is again largely due to a confusion between nutrition and morals.

A food is usually regarded as "junk" when it contains nothing that is nutritionally useful. But be careful. That food will yield calories even if it does not bring with them any useful proteins, minerals or vitamins. "Empty" calories may not be useless to a body which only requires a quick renewal of its energy supplies. Of course, the child who eats so many of these foods that they fulfill his energy requirement completely will then not want the foods whose calories come with other nutrients; in the long run his diet would suffer. But the child who is just plain hungry, hours before lunch, may be just as well off with "empty" calories as with more complex nourishment.

By no means do all the foods which people call "junk" consist of empty calories anyway. That package of potato chips has quite a high protein content for its calorie count. That dairy ice cream may be quite as valuable to the diet as a milk pudding, while a commercially prepared hamburger, complete with all the trimmings, can be a meal in itself. These are *foods*. Most parental dislike of them has really to do with discipline rather than nutrition. Small children beg for them and make us wonder if they are getting spoiled. Schoolchildren spend money on them that was intended for bus fares or the charity collection. Adolescents go in search of them instead of coming home in time for supper. . . .

The real indictments of such foods are:

☐ That so much money is spent on glamorous packaging and advertising that they are made both more attractive and more expensive than equivalent ordinary foods.

□ That if this leads to their being eaten *as well as* "ordinary" food they may contribute to obesity.

□ That if they were eaten to the *exclusion of all fresh and raw foods*, they would probably constitute a diet which was high in fats and low in vitamins, especially vitamin C.

□ That this group of foods, probably more than any other group, tends to be loaded with artificial colorings and flavorings.

But none of this makes these foods something to be avoided at all costs, something which it is somehow morally wrong to eat. It just makes them foods which, like all other foods, should be eaten in sensible moderation well mixed in with a varied diet.

Common sense
about sweets

If people never ate sweets they would have fewer holes in their teeth (*see* **Teeth**). There is no doubt about this. From the point of view of dental health it is a great pity that any clever manufacturer ever thought of marketing refined sugar made into pretty colored, flavored shapes. But manufacturers did think, and now families have to think for themselves about how to manage the existence of sweets. You certainly cannot get rid of them. Clearing up some factual points may make a good start:

Sweets are more or less pure refined sugar. Some (real chocolate, not chocolate-flavored candy, for example) have a few nutrients in them, but basically they are calories with additives. From the dietetic point of view they can be regarded as just the same as other "junk" foods. Apart from their effect on teeth, they are neither better nor worse.

Refined sugar produces acid in the mouth and makes the ideal environment for breeding of the bacteria which are in the plaque on teeth. These bacteria are the cause of dental decay.

All **refined sugar products have this effect.** Sweets are worse for your child's teeth than cake or sweetened cereal only to the extent that the sugar clings more closely to the teeth and remains longer in the mouth. Plain cake, washed down with a glass of milk, may leave less sugar around than a sweet, but a slice of sticky cake may be just as bad as the sweet.

Bacteria do not care where sugar comes from. The sugar in a healthy apple feeds them as sugar from the bowl of sweets does. But the sugar in the apple is less concentrated and the friction it exerts as the child chews will tend to remove most of it quite quickly. Don't make the mistake, though, of banning sweets by replacing them with raisins . . . sweet and sticky, they will not improve dental health.

It follows from all this that some types of sweet will be far worse for your child's teeth than others. Caramels, for example, take a long time to chew and are well worked into the spaces between the teeth in the process. Must he have caramels? Boiled sweets take a long, long time to suck and will be creating that acid environment all the time. Must he have them? He will be better off with M+Ms or tiny jelly sweets or anything which is rapidly melted and gone.

Most human beings seem to have an in-built desire for sweet things. New babies, for example, suck harder and for longer on bottles of sugared water than they do on plain water; children doing "taste tests" usually put the sweetest tastes at the "best-liked" end of the scale, while our historical ancestors risked a great deal to rob wild bees of the only concentrated sugar then available. The chances are that your child will like sweets, but even if he is not an especially "sweet-toothed" person, he will almost certainly want sweets because:

Millions of dollars' worth of advertising is devoted each year to ensuring that he does want them. Within those advertising campaigns every trick of the trade is used, from linking sweets with sexy holidays on palm-fringed beaches, to presenting them as symbols of parental love or peer-group popularity. For the youngest age groups, sweets are made into objects which are desirable to look at and to play with as well as to eat. What self-respecting two-year-old will *not* want a dispenser shaped like his favorite television character, even if he does not particularly like the little candies it pops out?

Distributors ensure that sweets are on show everywhere, especially where young children go with adults and are bored. It is not chance which places the candy display next to the supermarket line or the train platform.

Adults use sweets as part of the emotional currency of family life. We give sweets to console disappointed children, to comfort the hurt, reward the brave and praise the successful. We buy them to convey pleasant messages like "thank you for having me" or "happy birthday." We make them an integral part of our festivities and our treats.

If you doubt that this is an important part of "the sweet problem," ask yourself whether you ever see children whining, begging and bullying for any other kind of food they particularly like. Many children have a passion for strawberries, for example, yet they do not behave over strawberries as they behave over sweets. The fruits just do not have the same emotional importance.

While the very existence of sweets may pose a problem for all of us, they need not create particular problems within your family if you find commonsense ways of handling them. Various families have managed using each of these approaches:

Putting off the time when each child became aware of sweets. You may be able to manage this for two or three years with a first child, probably not so long with a later one. Any length of time is worthwhile for the protection it gives to those first teeth.

Studiously avoiding any emotional loading. Don't give sweets to a toddler who has been "good" about something; indeed, don't give food for this reason at all. Remember the food-is-for-satisfying-appetite approach. You may have to ask other people not to bring sweets as presents and so forth, and of course you will have to make sure that sweets are not playing a part in your adult emotional life. If your child sees his father bringing home chocolates because he is late, you do not stand a chance.

Buying the first sweets which are demanded without obvious reluctance but with the same casual air you would use if he begged to try a new vegetable.

Not keeping sweets in the house—ever—but instead assuming (as you do with other foods) that whatever is bought will be eaten and that there will be no more until the next purchase. This prevents the one-sweet-every-three-minutes-all-evening which is terrible for teeth.

Choosing the least damaging kinds of sweets and giving them neither as extras nor as enormous treats but as part of meals. Try to choose meals after which the child will brush his teeth.

Remembering that for many children *buying* sweets is part of the fun of having them. If he wants to go shopping with his pocket money, suggest some other things (fun-foods and non-foods) which he could buy.

Eating problems

While a commonsense approach to family eating will hopefully prevent most "feeding problems" among those who have plenty of food available, it will not prevent them all. Feeding children is an important part of caring for their physical needs, and physical caring is all mixed up with love, so it will never be as easy to be rational about food as the cold print of a book suggests. But if you *are* worried and know that problems are therefore looming, or even if you *have* worried and have therefore allowed problems to begin, it is still worth making the effort to reverse the trend.

Babies and eating problems

Many parents worry ceaselessly about babies' refusal to eat enough or enough of the "right" things. If you are worried about your baby it is sensible to consult your doctor or clinic immediately. If your worry has any physical foundation it should be identified as soon as possible; but it cannot be emphasized too strongly that the problem is probably yours, not the baby's. If your baby is found to be gaining weight within the (wide) normal limits for his age and physical type and to be normally healthy, energetic and contented, *the food he willingly takes is adequate for him*. Try to accept authoritative reassurance before attempts to push down more food than he wants produce real trouble. Once you have seen your doctor, it may help you to go over the following points.

Most babies whose parents worry over their eating are far from thin; many of them are actually fat. A baby who is neither thin nor failing to gain weight cannot be undernourished.

Some babies who *are* at the lower end of the normal weight range or who are gaining weight rather slowly, are particularly active types. Provided your baby is well, this is a positive rather than a negative characteristic.

Many babies who are "difficult" to feed are being asked to conform to patterns for which they are not ready. Some common ones are:

"Solid" foods in addition to breast milk/formula in the first three to four months of life. Some babies will accept these additions but many will not. No baby (unless your doctor advises you otherwise) *needs* anything but milk in this period.

Feeding times which do not fit in with his own developing patterns of digestion and hunger. Making a small baby wait for feeding, for example, can lead not to increased appetite once the milk is offered, but to so much angry miserable crying that he is too tired to do more than quell his first hunger pains before he falls into exhausted sleep. Inevitably, a very small feeding makes him likely to ask for the next one early, too, and the pattern can become a vicious circle.

Attempts at early weaning and/or early introduction of a cup. Sucking is not only a small baby's natural feeding method, it is also his greatest pleasure. If he is not allowed to suck milk from breast or bottle he will sometimes refuse to drink it at all.

Later in the first year difficulties may be due to adult attempts to make the baby eat their way rather than his. Some examples include:

Not being allowed to partake in the feeding process, by holding onto his own bottle, clutching at the spoon or dabbling in the food. Tidy-feeding often feels like forced-feeding.

Not having his dawning likes and dislikes noted. If he clearly hates spinach or egg yolk, trying to force it down him may lead to a rejection of all solid foods. Sometimes it is texture rather than taste to which the baby objects. Some find the transition from creamy-smooth babyfoods to lumpy toddler-foods very difficult. A few always gag on lumps and enjoy food more if it is *either* smooth *or* finely cut up, never carelessly mashed.

Not having the variability of his appetite from meal to meal or day to day accepted.

Toddlers and eating problems

In the rich West, problems with eating in this age group are closer to the rule than the exception. The basic reason seems to be implicit in the child's stage of development and the effect which the developments have on many parents. Toddlers are still highly dependent on adults both for physical and emotional care, yet they have reached a point where that dependence begins to conflict with their drive to grow up and become independent people in their own right. The toddler tends to alternate clinging with demands that the parent should "Go 'way" or "let me." If he is pushed in the direction of independence, he hangs on ever more tightly, but if he is kept too much in the parents' power he fights for his freedom.

Natural functions such as eating, sleeping and excreting provide the toddler with perfect battlegrounds on which to work out this sort of conflict. The ground is perfect for the toddler both because it is one which no parent can completely ignore (natural functions have to be socialized) and because it is one on which no parent can actually win. You can put your toddler to bed but you cannot force him to sleep. You can put him on a potty or toilet, but you cannot force him either to perform or to tell you when he is going to. You can sit him in front of a meal but you cannot make him eat it.

Since you cannot win it is almost always best for everyone if you do not join battle. But avoiding battles does not just mean not allowing yourself to get angry, and it certainly does not mean "giving in." It means resolutely refusing to allow these no-win situations to become issues between you and your toddler. You can teach him to "do as he is told" however you like (*see* **Discipline, Self-discipline and Learning How to**

Behave), but it is disastrous to try to teach this sort of lesson in a situation where it is easily possible for him to defy you.

Unfortunately, refusing to be drawn into battle is far more easily said than done because these issues are important to daily life and therefore you will care about them. A toddler who is spoiling for a fight about something will not be slow to realize that you care, and to exploit the fact. All you have going for you is your much greater cleverness and experience. By using these you may be able to prevent your toddler from spotting the fight potential of the meal table.

Try, from the very beginning, to treat his eating as a pleasure. That means, for example, glorying in the greedy sucking of his early months, offering first tastes of solid foods but being quick to stop if he does not like them, being far more concerned with his enjoyment than his mess and being pleased to help him take over responsibility for feeding himself as soon as he wants to. If he has never been forced, as an infant, to have more than he wants, or anything he dislikes, he will not enter the toddler period with any but positive feelings about food and the business of eating it.

Encourage meal-time independence even at the expense of "manners." If your toddler eats potatoes dipped in his juice, with pleasure, don't be too quick to make him separate them or he may refuse both. If he enjoys eating fish with his fingers don't insist on a spoon or he may reject the fish. If he likes eating but hates staying in his chair until others have finished, don't keep him imprisoned for long or the next meal may not seem worth it to him. Above all, once he can feed himself, *don't feed him*. It is the "one more for mommy" or "just a bit more or you'll be hungry later" approach which so quickly tells him that you care whether he eats or not.

Don't force him to eat (or even try) anything he does not want. If you are feeding him on his own, tell him what is available and let him say (or point to) what he wants. If he is eating with the family, ask him what he wants as you serve the food, just as you would ask an adult, or let him serve himself when he is able. There may be meals or days when he selects a very unbalanced plateful—perhaps only the meat or only the potato—but pressure from you will only make problems, where his own selection will balance itself out in time. Above all, don't ever make him "buy" the items he enjoys by eating the items he does not want. You want him to feel that *he should not have food he does not want*. In this way food can remain the pleasure and privilege which it really is, rather than the miserable duty it can so easily become.

Stick to this principle even if what he wants is nothing. No basically healthy child will starve himself if offered foods which he normally eats, so if he does not want to eat today, refusal should be his right. He may be unwell (in which case he is probably better off without the meal); he may be "trying it out," in which case the less reaction he gets the better, or he may just not be hungry, in which case he will be very ready for the next meal. Be careful, though. If, when he says he does not want any lunch, you offer quite a different dish, he is bound to realize that you can be pressured into providing not just pleasant food but any particular item he happens to fancy. Equally, if having refused any lunch, he finds himself offered an extra snack "because you must be hungry," he is bound to realize that you really cared about the lunch, however casual you seemed about it at the time. If he asks for something to eat before the next mealtime, by all means give him whatever simple snack is routine in your house. But don't make an issue of it or take more trouble than usual.

If you have allowed eating to become a battleground between you and your child, you may need an actual campaign to end the war. The tactics are much the same as those outlined above, but the following points may be useful to your planning.

Start by convincing yourself that your child is healthy and adequately nourished. If just looking at him is not enough, ask the doctor to check him over and explain why you want this. You will never convince your child that there is no more mileage to be got out of mealtime battles while you remain anxious about his eating.

Ask yourself what he likes to eat and when he usually does eat. If you find yourself answering "nothing and never," then you *are* still anxious. If necessary, make yourself a list. Those odd sips of milk, cookies, bites of apple and wheedled candies cannot be adding up to nothing or he would not be adequately nourished.

If what he likes is plain bread at breakfast, ham for lunch and milk and biscuits for supper, include those items in the meals being served to the family and let him choose and eat them. No comment; no pressure; no wheedling; no spoonfeeding.

If he is obviously surprised by your new tactics, or hurt by your apparent sudden lack of concern, find a way of talking to him about it. Something along the lines of "I think we've been getting in a muddle about meals; you're quite a big boy now and it's up to you to eat what you want so I'm not going to fuss with you about it any more . . ." may be about right. Do remember, though, that if major fusses over food have recurred at regular intervals every day for months, those fusses may have accounted for the bulk of the personal attention you have been paying to him. Withdraw the fusses and he may badly miss the attention and feel that he is being in some way punished. Try to use some of the time and energy you save on caring about *what he eats* in making it clear that *you still care about him*. If a non-lunch only takes two minutes, maybe it will leave time for an extra game, a story or a walk.

Make sure that your partner and other family members are in on your new policy. A casual remark such as "Don't let Mommy see you pushing that food around" can set back the whole campaign by days.

With misery removed from the family table, let him see that the rest of you *enjoy* food. He probably will not risk it at once, but sooner or later he will ask to try the new food that his sister is greeting with such pleasure.

Older children and eating problems   Somewhere around four or five most children, even those who have had feeding problems as toddlers, begin to eat much more enthusiastically. This is a highly imitative stage so eating in company—both at school and at home—often leads children into trying items and dishes they have previously rejected. On the other hand, this is also the age when children are liable to notice and resent any dietary restrictions which set them apart from their peers, so it is a time to be tactful about sending an apple if the others all have glamorous junk foods.

Most schoolchildren are faddish about what they eat. But the truth is that most *people* follow fads whatever their ages. The difference is that, as adults, we are free to buy, cook and serve what we like, whereas children are in the hands of others.

Children's fads need seldom present a real problem if they are tactfully and sensibly handled. Perhaps the first tactful step is to stop calling them "fads" and call them dislikes instead. Handling dislikes with a minimum of trouble usually depends on accepting that the child's diet will not suffer if he leaves out certain items which you regularly serve. Suppose, for example, that he hates eggs. What does it matter? If it is breakfast which is in question he can have the bacon without the egg. If it is egg dishes at lunch or supper, it is usually easy to substitute some cheese. . . . If he is anti-vegetables he can leave those out, too. He probably eats potatoes and might eat some other vegetables as well if you gave them to him raw. But even if he eats none at all he will come to no harm. His plate may look rather empty compared to those of other family members, but if it is empty of items he dislikes, he will not mind; the problem, as usual, is yours not his.

Unless you are prepared to cook several different versions of each meal, often over a period of years, it is probably wise to couple willingness to let him leave out the items he dislikes with unwillingness to cook something different just for him. Bacon and eggs, or just eggs, or just bacon, is one thing, but bacon and eggs or baked beans on toast is quite another on a busy morning.

Obesity: the problem of eating too much

It is ironical that parents who have worried ceaselessly because their young children did not appear to eat enough often face later worries because those children become fat.

Unless you are authoritatively assured otherwise by a doctor who has carried out appropriate investigations, you must assume that any member of the family who becomes obese *has* been eating too much. Phrases like "it's her glands . . ." may sound comforting, but they are very seldom meaningful.

How much food is too much? Nobody can answer that question honestly in terms of food intake; it can be answered only in terms of the *results* of the food intake: the individual's weight or weight trend. Human beings are so variable in the efficiency with which their bodies use food-fuel and in the activities which they ask of those bodies, that a diet which is just right for one may make another lose weight and a third become obese. The right amount of food is the amount which keeps an individual's energy intake and expenditure balanced *over time*. Anyone can put on a little over a period of Christmas celebration or take off a little during an energetic summer holiday, but if the everyday diet is right, such temporary changes will soon correct themselves. On the other hand, even a few more calories than the body can use, eaten regularly over weeks and months, will gradually be laid down as body fat.

The complication of growth. Children do not only need food-fuel for their bodies' current activities but for growth, too. Where a weight which is both appropriate and stable is the ideal for adults, a weight which increases in direct ratio to growth in height is the ideal for children. But don't expect a day-to-day match. While growth curves (*see* **Growth**) are remarkably steady over long periods of time, they often have marked short-term steps in them. Some of these are caused by short-term, but acute, illnesses which slow down weight gain without affecting growth in height. But many are simply part of the child's overall growth pattern. A baby's weight may increase to a point where he looks chubby, but then a growth spurt increases his height to a point where his weight is appropriate again. A child approaching school age may suddenly grow so rapidly that for a while he looks positively thin and "leggy," but then the height increase slows, the weight increase continues and the two get back into balance. Although it is an unkind mistake to assume that every child goes through a "puppy-fat stage" near to puberty, it is true that a relative gain in weight often precedes a spurt of growth in a boy's height and that a similar kind of weight gain is a necessary trigger for a girl's menarche (*see* **Adolescence**/Puberty).

Avoiding obesity. It is much easier to avoid accumulating body fat than it is to persuade the body to use up fat that has already formed. It is also far easier to avoid the eating habits which are likely to lead to obesity than it is to change habits which are firmly entrenched. Parents who can help their children not to become overweight may save themselves and those children a lot of later misery.

Only experience of your own child, from earliest infancy onwards, will tell you whether he is a person who uses food so efficiently that he seems able to grow and gain weight on very little, or one who uses it less efficiently and/or uses up calories in greater activity, so that however much he eats he gains weight slowly. In our society it is certainly more fun to be the latter. For the former, the greatest help comes from keeping food out of the emotional arena (*see above*) so that as far as possible he grows up treating it *only* as the pleasurable satisfaction of physical need, never as anything to do with love. He is going to want sweets and ice cream, milkshakes and pies. You cannot prevent him from wanting them, but you may be able to prevent him from wanting them particularly when he is sad or lonely (to stand in for love) or when he is having a particularly nice time (to complete it) or when he has had a quarrel (to show that all is forgiven).

Coping with children's obesity

A fat adult knows that if he can reduce his calorie intake to a point where the energy he expends each day exceeds the fuel he is taking in, he will lose weight. This simple balancing act is the basis for all the thousands of "reducing diets" which are produced each year. There is no magic in "bananas and milk" or in "dieters' meals" either. Each different formula is just a different way for people to eat less while feeling satisfied and paying manufacturers for the privilege.

Children, however, should not reduce their calories so as to produce a "net energy debt." If they do there is a chance that their bodies will be deprived of the food elements they need for growth.

Unless you are working under the direct supervision of a doctor, don't try to make a growing child *lose* weight. Instead, aim to **keep his weight where it is while his height goes on increasing.**

Young children. A diet which will stop a fat child from gaining weight while his increasing height makes him slimmer will obviously be a long-term affair. Ideally, it should be one which he barely notices. If his diet becomes a focus for your concern you will find yourself coping not just with his weight but with all the emotional problems touched on above as well.

You may like to consult your doctor about a suitable diet for him, but try to use any such diet only as a general guide to types and quantities of food. There is absolutely no reason why he should stick to any diet, item by item and meal by meal. All that matters is that he should continue to get adequate nutrition while taking in fewer overall calories than before. The following hints may be helpful.

Cut down on fats. Fats like butter and margarine, cooking oils, cream and all the things which are made with, cooked in or topped by them, are the most concentrated source of calories in the diet. Often that slice of bread and butter has more calories in the butter than the bread, just as those potatoes treble their energy value when they are made into French fries.

You can cut a child's calories substantially without his noticing any difference in his food if you change his fat intake. Even the "treat" foods which are high in fats usually have an acceptable substitute, such as water ice or sherbet instead of ice cream; yogurt (if he likes it) instead of cream with his fruit; fatless sponges instead of his usual cake and dry-fried or grilled foods instead of deep-fried ones.

● Remember that full-cream milk (especially the first glass out of an unshaken bottle) contains a lot of fat but that the things you *want* from that milk (such as protein and calcium) are in the skimmed part. You may like to buy skimmed milk for him. If not, at least make sure that you pour off the top before you give it to him. Children past infancy do not need milk as a regular drink, so if two or three glassfuls each day are a family habit, see whether he would be happy to cut them out and drink water or fruit juice.

Look at his sugar intake. There is no reason why he should not go on having the sugar which he notices and which may make the difference between food he likes and food he will not, but he may be taking in a lot of calories from sugar without even noticing it. Many commercially produced soft drinks, for example, contain a lot of sugar. He might actually prefer an unsweetened fruit juice. Jams are rich in sugar; he might like yeast extract or fish paste instead. Canned fruits in syrup are sugar-rich; you can buy the same fruits without the syrup, drain off the syrup or serve your own, far less sugared, stewed fruits.

● The trick here is to consider the sugary items your child has routinely, every day, and try to substitute for them. If you do this there is no need to upset him by banning occasional sugary *treats* whether they are actual sweets or slices of birthday cake.

Look at his other snacks. If he is eating a lot of calorie-rich snacks *and* all his meals, then you may want to see whether you can convert him to less fattening nibbles. Sometimes children's casual eating is more a matter of habit and availability than actual choice. Must he always have potato chips or would he substitute an apple if there were no chips in the house?

Are bananas the only fruits he likes or simply the only fruits you buy routinely? Would he perhaps be actually pleased to find oranges instead? Does he raid the cookie tin for whatever you have put there or does he actually insist that it contain those chocolate ones . . . ?

● Trying to ban snacks altogether is usually a mistake because it makes a noticeable difference not only to the child's food intake but also to the expected routine of his day. You will avoid making your reducing drive noticeable if you manipulate the snacks instead of banning them. Sometimes a child who nibbles all day will actually eat less if you positively offer a formalized snack than if you leave him to help himself.

Look at your own shopping and cooking. With a young child in particular, what he eats is largely dictated by what is available in the house. You may be buying, as part of your routine weekly shopping, a number of high-calorie items which he would not miss if they were not there. You may not be buying low-calorie items which he would much enjoy.

In the same way, you may be cooking, because you have always cooked, meals within which a great many calories are concealed. It may be better to put a little bit of butter *on* those mashed potatoes to make them look luxurious than to beat in a much larger amount earlier on.

Adolescents. Many adolescents, especially girls, diet as part of their general desire to improve themselves and their appearance, not only in the eyes of other people but in their own eyes, too. A teenager who has actually become obese certainly needs all your support in losing weight. It is very difficult to be fat and happy in today's teenage society. A boy who has made his growth spurt, or a girl whose menstruation is established, will probably do well on an adult reducing diet, but if you are in doubt about the possible effects on growth or general health, suggest a preliminary check-up with the doctor.

If your child is facing the fact that she is fat, try to use this new decision to get slimmer as a time for education about food and eating. If she can learn, now, to eat a low-calorie diet which is sensibly balanced, there is a good chance that she will form new eating habits which will enable her to stay somewhere near her preferred weight indefinitely. If she just goes on a crash starvation diet she will not stick to it, while if she adopts one of the commercial schemes or crank ideas, she will never learn to balance ordinary food intake against her own body's energy needs. It is really sad to watch a fourteen-year-old who is trying to reduce choose a milkshake to accompany her hamburger. Fruit juice and coffee are both available, but nobody has taught her that milkshakes are among the unnecessary extras which contribute to unwanted pounds.

● Some adolescent girls begin to diet when nobody but themselves would consider them overweight. Often this kind of dieting is part of a school craze, but it is also often part of a girl's expression of general discontent with herself and with her burgeoning body. Try to be aware of these added emotional implications. Telling her not to be so foolish will not help, but offering additional ways for her to look as she wants to look, together with assurances that you consider her attractive and lovable, may help very much indeed (*see* **Eating Disorders**).

Eating Disorders

Eating is an emotionally charged activity in Western societies, so it is not surprising that it can be the focus for a large range of emotional problems. "Eating difficulties" are very common among young children (*see* **Eating/** Eating problems) but, while parents may find them overwhelming at the time, the child's own increasing maturity usually ensures that they pass within a matter of months without seriously affecting her development. Certainly it would be a mistake to assume that your faddish three-year-old or plump-from-sweets-eating nine-year-old was suffering from an eating disorder. The toddler may be rejecting food as a way of rejecting your control, the schoolgirl may be eating sweets for comfort in a world which seems hard, but with tactful handling and help from you, each will move on to a more comfortable (or at least a different) stage in which eating plays an appropriately lesser part.

Eating disorders may be rooted in similar types of conflicts to those which produce eating problems, but there the similarity ends. Eating disorders are not common. They usually affect adolescents rather than young children and, far from passing as the child's maturity increases, they suggest that her emotional development is already at least somewhat distorted. An eating disorder is a form of emotional illness. It always reduces the quality of the victim's life and may even threaten life itself. Whatever its particular form it demands swift recognition by parents and intervention by health professionals.

Two well-publicized eating disorders are described below as if they were separate entities. It is important to realise, though, that they are probably related to each other, to different forms of eating disorder and to emotional illnesses in which food is not a focus for symptoms. Many patients with anorexia nervosa, for example, share in some of the characteristics of patients suffering from clinical depression (*see* **Depression**). Anorexics who binge and purge, rather than consistently starving themselves, share some of the characteristics of patients with bulimia, while both the anorexic and the bulimic patient will sometimes enter into a state similar to the dietary chaos syndrome. The exact diagnosis on your child's chart will reflect a clinical judgment that may be highly sensitive but cannot be entirely objective. This is an area in which society's concern still far outstrips its knowledge.

Anorexia nervosa

Victims of this puzzling disorder starve themselves in the midst of plenty. They starve themselves while they lose any excess weight; they go on starving themselves while they become thin; they starve themselves while they become emaciated; a few starve themselves to death. The disorder contradicts commonsense attitudes to food and eating (*see* **Eating/**First principles) because, while trapped in it, victims' appetites no longer operate as a guide to food intake. The "natural" drive to eat to satisfy hunger and thus to satisfy bodily needs, is overridden.

Anorexia nervosa has been given a great deal of publicity in recent years and the increase in the number of reported cases suggests an "epidemic." Some studies suggest that as many as one or two in every hundred girls will suffer from it during some part of their adolescence. We do not know whether the increase in numbers is real or whether it has appeared because of people's greater readiness to recognize a condition which has always been frequent. Certainly every parent should know something about it. Your own children will, hopefully, remain unaffected, but they are quite likely to meet and be puzzled and disturbed by others who are less fortunate. Furthermore, it seems likely that the disorder is one which can sometimes be averted if a girl at risk is recognized early. Ignored until it is well established, it is extraordinarily difficult to treat.

Public understanding is not helped by the names used for this disorder. In the United States everyone uses the proper scientific term, anorexia nervosa, but literally translated, this means "loss (or absence) of appetite for nervous reasons." The name is misleading because anorexic girls have not lost their *appetites* at all. Most of them are ravenously hungry most of the time. What they have lost is the *ability to allow themselves to satisfy their appetites*. As we shall see, the distinction is of vital importance to anyone who is trying to recognize, live with or treat anorexia nervosa.

In Britain and in parts of Western Europe the disorder is popularly known as "slimmer's disease," referring to the fact that the self-starvation sometimes begins with "normal dieting." The victim (almost always female and usually adolescent) begins to reduce, often in collaboration with friends or as part of a school craze. She may or may not be fat. Like other adolescents her dieting may be motivated by a general dissatisfaction with her body or by a desire to alter the shape of one particular part of it: an over-large bottom or breasts, for example. She goes through the usual dieting difficulties at first, but unlike most of her friends, she eventually finds that she can stick to her chosen regime and even increase its severity. She loses weight and achieves her target weight, but instead of relaxing her diet so that her weight stabilizes at this new level, she goes on restricting her eating so that her weight goes on dropping.

While anorexia nervosa can begin in this way it does not always do so. Not every persistent dieter is an anorexic and not every anorexic has ever been obese.

Causes of anorexia nervosa

Nobody knows exactly why some people become anorexic when most do not. We cannot pinpoint a cause as we pinpoint the organisms which are responsible for infectious diseases or the muscle fault which leads to a hernia. Instead, we have to look at *what anorexia nervosa seems to be about*.

Most doctors and psychiatrists concerned with the disorder would probably agree that most of the following are relevant to the condition, but the exact significance of each aspect would be disputed. Remember, as you go through these points, that at no time can we answer the question "why?" Why does one girl with this, that or the other kind of difficulty become anorexic when many others, with similar difficulties, do not? Why does one girl with this, that or the other kind of conflict "choose" anorexia nervosa as a means of coping with it when others find different coping mechanisms? We do not know the answer and indeed we may never know it because there probably is no simple answer. Different life factors interact in different ways with different personalities and the end products of the interactions are different. Your daughter's anorexic illness is unique, just as she herself is a unique individual.

Anorexia nervosa is about growing up. Although a few males, children and mature women develop anorexia nervosa, a majority of victims enter the condition during the first year or two after the menarche; a few enter it at about the time of puberty and a few more after their periods have been established for some time. Early adolescence is a time of inner uncertainty and conflict for most young people (*see* **Adolescence**), but anorexia nervosa is not a way of growing through that uncertainty and conflict but of retreating from it. This is true at many levels. At the here-and-now physical level, self-starvation actually undoes many of the visible signs of maturity. The anorexic girl loses her rounded breasts and hips and calves, returning almost to the shape typical of a pre-pubertal child. She also loses her monthly periods; those regular reminders of sexual maturity which may, for her, seem a "curse."

It is about dependence. At a deeper psychological level the self-starvation undoes many of the social and psychological expectations which go with physical maturity. It de-sexes her so that she need neither compete for sexual partners nor be sought after by them. It makes her the subject of much care and concern from her parents and thus puts off inner or outer pressure on her to become more independent of them. It gives her a rich and endless source of conflict with that concerned family which effectively replaces the more usual and age-appropriate fight for freedom from parental control.

It is about control. Anorexia nervosa requires enormous self-control from its victim, who must starve herself against the full power of her body's hunger drive. Her ability to maintain this control is one of the main "rewards" she gets from the illness, but her *fear of loss of control* is also the stick which drives her. In retrospect, parents often realize that their now anorexic daughter was always an overcontrolled and compliant child. Such children tend to set themselves high ideals, work hard to achieve them and bask in the parental approval which therefore surrounds them. They tend to be highly intelligent and to be seen as "extremely sensible." It is the more of a shock when parents are forced to accept that "good" may have been "too good"; that success may have been achieved out of fear of failure and that this is a girl who dare not allow herself even a little kick over the traces lest she find herself running wild.

It is, therefore, about pleasure. Pleasure, especially sensual pleasures such as sex, eating, physical luxury and all forms of self-indulgence, seem very dangerous to the anorexic patient who often clothes her fear in rather puritanical attitudes. Once again, parents may remember sadly that this near-adult who cannot allow herself to be warm or to rest (*see below*), was a child who was never greedy, never "spoiled," never demanding of treats and possessions.

Recognizing **Anorexia nervosa** is not a disease which a person "gets" or "catches" so
anorexia that she is healthy one week and definitely and diagnosably ill the next.
nervosa Rather, it is a condition into which a person moves, often rather gradually, so that there may never be a recognizable line marking the beginning of the disorder. Nevertheless, the earliest possible recognition, whether it comes first from the patient herself or from those who are close to her, may be important. If she can recognize her own general dissatisfaction/

unhappiness and see that her "dieting" is not truly an answer to it (although it is beginning to feel like an answer to her), she may be able to abandon it. The deeper she moves into the condition the tighter the grip which it will have upon her and the more difficult it will be for her to give it up and find other ways of coping with herself.

The following signs and symptoms apply to an adolescent girl who is indisputably in an anorexic condition. If you are worried about your own daughter or she is worried about herself or a friend, you may like to ask yourself "to what extent and in what ways does she resemble this anorexic patient?" She may be like or unlike this "typical" anorexic girl in any number of irrelevant ways; it is her similarity or dissimilarity along the dimensions set out here which is crucial.

Weight loss. All anorexics lose a great deal of weight although not everyone who loses a lot of weight is anorexic. If your daughter has not lost (and is not losing) substantially, then whatever you have to worry about it is not anorexia nervosa.

Many adolescents diet to lose weight while others lose due to other forms of illness. If your daughter is losing you will need to consider her weight in relation to other factors (*see below*) because weight loss *alone* is not diagnostic of anorexia nervosa. Severe weight loss, however, whether it is due to anorexia nervosa or not, certainly requires investigation and explanation.

How much weight loss is too much? (*See* **Growth**.) As a very rough rule-of-thumb, check on a standard weight chart (as published, for example, by life insurance firms) for the average weight for a girl of her age and height and compare that figure with what she weighs now. If she is still within, say, ten percent of that average then even if she has lost a tremendous amount, her weight alone gives no cause for alarm. She may have begun to diet while genuinely obese; she may have needed to lose 40 lb. Even if she was not fat to begin with, a weight loss which leaves her within ten percent of the average is fair enough because there is normal variation of at least that amount around the average figure. You need worry only if she is still losing.

If her current weight puts her at fifteen percent less than the average, then there is reason for concern. Why is she so different from other girls of her age and height?

A current weight as much as twenty percent below the average will already be affecting her general health. If weight loss continues it will soon cause a medical emergency.

In real terms, then, you might reckon that a girl whose "expected weight" was 126 lb. should give cause for concern if her weight dropped below 112 lb. and would be becoming progressively sicker as it dropped towards 98 lb.

If the "expected weight" is 112 lb., the comparable figures would be around 98 lb. and 84 lb.

Amenorrhea. Normal menstruation requires an adequate body weight. Female anorexics do not menstruate regularly, at least until the disorder is coming to an end. Therefore if your daughter *is* menstruating normally (and is not on the Pill so that bleeding is induced) she is not, at this time, severely anorexic.

There are, of course, many reasons other than anorexia why she may not be menstruating. Worry about the possibility of self-starvation may predate the start of her periods or the weight loss may begin during the early months following the menarche when menstruation is often irregular anyway (*see* **Adolescence**/Menstruation). Furthermore, serious physical illness, emotional stress or pregnancy may account for her amenorrhea. But if menstruation was previously established and has now ceased in conjunction with major weight loss, anorexia nervosa is a likely cause.

Attitudes to weight and to eating. If your daughter is similar to the girl with anorexia nervosa in the sense that she has lost more than fifteen percent of her expected body weight and has stopped menstruating, consider her attitudes to weight which you will probably discover most easily through her attitudes to eating and to food in general. Some or all of the following will probably seem to apply to her if she is anorexic.

Observation of her eating habits suggests that she is actively avoiding weight gain, whatever she may *say* concerning her wish to replace some of the weight she has lost. She will probably avoid carbohydrate-rich and fatty foods, will take smaller portions than those around her and will often refuse snacks, treats or extras others are having. If she announces a change in food tastes it will invariably be a change which reduces her calorie intake. She may start to take coffee black, tea without sugar, or grapefruit in place of breakfast cereal. She will probably announce that she has "gone off" any high-calorie foods for which she previously had a passion. Your chocolate cake will no longer be popular.

In other words, she behaves like a dedicated dieter but can be distinguished from the "normal" dieter both by the fact that she is behaving like this when she is already far too thin, and by the fact that she pretends to agree that she needs to put on weight rather than take off more.

Weight is fascinating to her and she cannot resist talking and reading about it as well as privately thinking about it. She is obsessively interested in other people's figures and she will read diet sheets, weight charts and calorie guides endlessly, even those which are published in magazines and comics which would not normally be to her taste. She is probably an expert calorie counter. She may be truly revolted by people who seem to her obese (since they represent what she fears might happen to her if she allowed herself to eat freely) and she may make it embarrassingly clear that she finds her own emaciated shape preferable to the bulges of those around her.

Food, which she cannot allow herself, is nevertheless an obsession with her. She may spend a great deal of time cooking for others, reading recipe books and insisting on being the family expert in cake- or dessert-making. Often she will be highly possessive not only of her role as cook but also of the dishes she makes; having cooked the sweet she insists on being allowed to serve it. She may find it difficult to keep away from places where food is sold or prepared so that she wanders around supermarkets and hangs around the kitchen during the preparation of meals she is not going to eat.

Despite all this interest, the normal consumption of ordinary food may revolt her. Sometimes she will watch every mouthful taken by other family members as if asking, "Are you going to eat more? And more? And still more?" She can be an embarrassing companion at the dinner table.

Some "failures" in her control over her food intake may occur. Sometimes these take the form of occasional "binges" so that having allowed herself a sip of milk she drains the whole container and another one and then punishes herself by even greater abstinence in the following days (*see below*). Sometimes her "failures" are of a more frequent but more minor kind. She may pick with her fingers at leftover food in the refrigerator, surreptitiously lick cooking utensils or nibble tiny fragments from the cookies in the tin. This kind of nibbling is secret, not only from everyone else but from herself. She is furious if it is called to her attention.

If your daughter seems, in all the above respects, to be in a state of anorexia nervosa, you will probably also notice other signs of her determination to control and discipline her body.

Attitudes to other aspects of her physical self. Many anorexics are fitness fanatics, aspiring athletes, dancers, joggers, or simply people who take pleasure in making their bodies do their bidding. Even as your daughter's weight drops and her muscles vanish so that arms and legs are stick-like, she may actually increase the demands she puts on herself. She may, for example, insist that she is stronger than anyone else in the family and try to prove it by being the one who carries the heaviest boxes or single-handedly pushes the stuck car. Success gives her great pleasure but she earns it at an appalling price paid in pain and effort. Easy physical pleasures are anathema to her even when they are not associated with food. She will seldom lounge in the sun, choose a comfortable chair or enjoy a luxurious late sleep on a Sunday morning.

What to do if it seems likely that your daughter is in a state of anorexia nervosa

There is no known "cure" for anorexia nervosa in the sense of an accepted treatment which will certainly bring the condition to an end. Recommendations therefore cannot be absolute; they can only be ways in which an inevitably long and hard struggle can be begun. They are also a great deal easier to give than they are to carry out. If your daughter is anorexic neither you nor she is going to have an easy time and anyone who offers you a simple cure is a charlatan.

You may find some of the following suggestions helpful; but you may find that their principal use is to be angrily rejected, thus helping you to clear your mind for your own ways of proceeding.

If she is in a state of anorexia nervosa, try to face it now rather than waiting a bit and then a little longer and then a little longer still. Anorexia is exceedingly difficult for parents to face because the disorder seems so *senseless*. The girl is underweight and hungry. The food is there. Why can't she just get on and eat it? It is also hurtful: she has always been loved, nurtured, "fed" (both physically and emotionally), why does she now insist on starving herself and thus rejecting those who care? Often it is also shatteringly disappointing because parents have had every reason to see this as an "ideal daughter" and to flatter themselves that they were not facing the kinds of adolescent rebellion common in the families of her peers. Now, apparently all of a sudden, all that goodness has turned itself into a crisis and not just the kind of crisis which might lead to an abortion or to dropping out of school, but a kind which might actually kill her. No wonder parents veer wildly between furious anger and guilty despair.

It is probably even more difficult for the anorexic girl herself to face the reality of her condition. While she may be able *intellectually* to agree that her starved body and absent menses are neither normal nor desirable she *feels* that they are infinitely preferable to that norm. Sometimes the satisfaction she takes in her concave stomach, flat chest and ability to feel "full" after eating three lettuce leaves makes her appear smug and self-satisfied. It is important to remember that her feelings are rooted in fear. Her behavior is governed by her phobia of weight gain and of the total loss of control which she feels will inevitably follow the smallest relaxation of her rules. Her satisfaction is not truly over being "better than anyone else," but over avoiding being worse than anyone else.

Parents have a tendency to confuse the criteria which suggest anorexia nervosa (such as those suggested above) with criteria concerning a girl's general happiness and well-being. While the latter are obviously vitally important, they are not relevant to recognition of the disorder. Try not to let yourself beg the issue with statements like: "She's so depressed just now we can't expect her to eat" or "She'll be better once her exams are over" or "She's far too intelligent/sensible/responsible to let this go on for long." If she is truly anorexic the depression will not miraculously lift and free her, exams or no exams, and she would not have become anorexic if her intelligence and good sense could have protected her. Burying your head in the sand will buy you nothing but more misery.

Victims will almost always seize on any such excuse which is offered to them by parents because parents whose heads *are* buried in the sand offer them time. Time to lose a bit more of that dreaded weight; time in which the fearful prospect of gaining weight need not be faced.

The disorder will almost always be faced first by parents (or other close, concerned people) rather than by its victim. Once faced, it needs discussion because no "cure" can even begin until the patient can see at least some reason for change.

Early attempts to raise the subject are usually met with hostility and denial. All too often the discussion deteriorates into a hysterical shouting match in which parents find themselves expressing their own hurt and disappointment and daughters sidestep every real issue with screams of "You're all against me." Nobody can tell anyone else how to avoid that kind of no-win situation, but it sometimes helps parents to retain their calm if they can remember:

That she is the child of both of them and therefore that it is imperative that they remain in alliance with each other rather than allowing her disturbance to force a wedge between them.

That her behavior and her defensive anger are driven by fear and therefore to answer it with anger is no more appropriate than it would be to deal angrily with a child in a night terror.

That whatever charges she may lay or excuses she may produce, the facts of her weight loss, amenorrhea and attitudes to food remain abnormal.

Don't be thrown off-course by being told that it is all your fault for moving, getting divorced or whatever. Parents are always easily thrown into guilt by their growing children but the fact remains that most children survive every kind of trauma without having to take refuge in anorexia. It makes no difference what your daughter thinks caused her trouble; the trouble remains and must remain the focus of your discussion.

At this early stage, you may need to prove your points by, for example, insisting that your daughter weigh herself/look at the weight chart you used in your thinking/go over with you what she is eating/accept evidence, such as nibbled cookies and so forth, of her unsatisfied hunger. This kind of insistent talk feels highly intrusive and will no doubt be so categorized by the sufferer who hopes that she can thus shame you into "letting her alone." But someone must intrude for the sake of her health and safety. Leave her as much dignity and privacy as you can, but bolster yourself with your conviction that the situation is serious.

Usually some measure of agreement can be reached to the effect that there is a real problem. Many anorexics give in thus far rather easily because, once again, they hope that by accepting what is said to them they can be "let alone" and thus avoid having to accept food as well as words.

If your daughter quickly admits that she has "let it all go a bit far" and announces that she will "do something about it," you will have to judge the genuineness of both the acceptance and the intention. If they are genuine then she is entitled (unless she is already seriously ill) to time to attempt self-cure. Success is not impossible but it is unusual. The lower her weight and the longer the condition has lasted, the less likely it is that she will succeed alone. However, unless she is already in physical danger from her low weight, it may be important for her to "try" because finding that she cannot change (or cannot truly want to change) her behavior may eventually help her to accept advice from an outside source.

Be prepared, though, for every kind of deception. Deceit is the rule rather than the exception in anorexia nervosa and it is often the aspect of the disorder which places the heaviest strain on family relationships. Your beloved daughter will probably lie to you about what she has eaten, hide food under the pillow, pour milk down the toilet, lie about the reading on the scales, drink pints of water and avoid the bathroom for hours before she weighs herself in front of you, and earnestly discuss all manner of imaginary plans for gaining weight. She will betray you, if she has to, in other ways, too. If the plans for more sensible eating include a packed lunch at school because that would be "easier to eat," she will let you get up in the morning and make it for her and then throw it away, day after day. If the plans include letting you serve her portions at meals she will let you try but fight you every teaspoon of the way. And, wherever food has important social connotations, she will let you down. Take her to a restaurant for dinner with your boss and you can be sure that there will be some kind of fuss over the food; offer the tiniest slice of her brother's birthday cake "to wish him luck" and you can predict her refusal.

Unless you are a saint you will sometimes be angry and that does not matter; she knows how she should behave, wishes that she could and must face the reality of her failure to do so. But you may be able to stay basically on her side—which does matter—if you keep reminding yourself that she is driven not by the obstinacy and deliberate "naughtiness" which you see, but by fear and irrational panic. *That innocent cup of milk frightens her* and when she is in a state of panic she will do almost anything to walk around her fear.

If your daughter is going to manage to work her way out of the anorexic state with only the help she can get from you and from her friends, she will probably do so fairly quickly. You can certainly give her time and space to do it her own way, however much trouble the disorder is making for her and between you all, *if her weight is rising* (*see below* Recognizing recovery from anorexia nervosa).

Seeking help for anorexia nervosa

Most anorexics, especially those who have been caught within the disorder for six months or more, will eventually have to seek outside help. Seek it urgently if she begins to alternate periods of eating as little as possible with periods of "bingeing," even if the occasional overeating means that her weight is only falling a little.

Seek it more urgently still if she "binges" but manages to prevent this "indulgence" from adding any weight either by making herself vomit or by taking vast doses of laxatives. Unfortunately, many anorexics manage the improbable feat of vomiting several times each day without any member of their highly concerned family being aware of it. But keep an eye out. Vomiting and/or purgation, in association with very low weight, can quickly disturb the body's biochemistry to a dangerous extent (*see below* Bulimia).

If her weight drops to twenty percent or more below the average for her age and height, she is likely to be increasingly unwell and less and less able to make decisions or hold on to the sustained effort which would be necessary to break out of the condition. Help is therefore urgent from the physical point of view and urgent psychologically, too, as the longer she goes on with her internal battle without success the more helpless and despairing she will feel and the more she will need the prop of her anorexia.

A weight loss of thirty-five percent of the average may itself be life-threatening. This means that a girl whose expected weight is around 126 lb. may be in real and immediate danger of death if her weight drops to 91 lb. while a girl with an expected weight of 112 lb. will be in real danger around 77 lb. You may read newspaper reports of anorexic girls admitted to the hospital at body weights as low as 63 lb., but do not let these convince you that your daughter's 84 lb. is "not too bad for her condition." How bad it is depends on what a girl of her height normally weighs.

Unfortunately there is no magic which will help every anorexic and her family, as the surgeon can help everyone with an inflamed appendix. Usually the best starting point is the family doctor, especially if he has known the girl herself since childhood. If she is willing to seek help but cannot bear to approach the family doctor, perhaps because he knows you as well as her, she might be able to make a direct approach to an adolescent counselling service or even to the emergency room at the local hospital. Her own doctor will have to be brought into any decisions about treatment, however, so persuade her to let him play his proper role from the beginning if you possibly can.

What that doctor will suggest depends on his knowledge and understanding of anorexia nervosa, his view of your daughter's immediate physical condition and the facilities which are available locally.

Treatment approaches in anorexia nervosa

The treatment of anorexia nervosa has two main aims:

The restoration of a "safe" and eventually a "normal" weight and therefore of an ordinarily balanced diet.

Loss of the weight phobia and therefore psychological readjustment which will allow the victim to find alternative ways of dealing with the biological maturity which increasing weight will rekindle.

Doctors and psychiatrists vary widely in the relative emphasis which they place on these two aspects of a "cure," as well as in the methods they use to try to bring them about, but all would agree that both are essential. It is useless, for example, to ensure that the girl regains her lost weight if nothing is done to help her lose her weight phobia. As soon as she is freed from close supervision she will lose all that she has gained. On the other hand, it may be useless to take an entirely psychological approach to the disorder because the time taken to help the girl free herself of the weight phobia may be longer than her body can survive without more food.

Professionals also vary in their feelings about attempting to help anorexic girls while they continue to live at home. While nobody can doubt that a girl's home situation and relationships within her family are relevant to the disorder, some doctors believe that removal from home into a hospital setting is a necessary first step even if she is not in dire physical straits. Others believe that problems within the home are best faced as they are lived, often with all members of the family being involved in the girl's treatment. Such a doctor might only admit to a hospital a girl who was in need of physical treatment (such as intravenous feeding) and he might keep her there only until her weight had increased to a point where her life was no longer in danger.

Hospital treatment for anorexia nervosa

Hospital treatment may include any, or any combination, of the following approaches:

A "contract' between doctor and patient in which a "target weight" is agreed; the patient agrees to stay in the hospital and follow the path prescribed for her towards that target. The doctor agrees to guard her against her greatest fear: that if she starts eating normally at all she will become a glutton and obese. He guarantees that while insisting that she eat "enough," he will neither encourage nor allow her to eat "too much."

Bed-rest until an agreed amount of weight has been regained.

Sedation to make enforced rest more tolerable.

A diet designed to increase her weight at a stated weekly rate or an ordinary hospital diet to accustom her to *normal* eating.

A variety of sanctions to ensure that she does in fact eat the food; these may range from close friendly supervision by trained nursing staff to a system under which the patient earns privileges (such as permission to get up, have visitors, etc.) by eating.

Individual psychotherapy in which she has regular meetings with one psychiatrist who will talk with her and help her to come to terms with her current situation/treatment and thence with the difficulties which led to her weight phobia.

Group psychotherapy (often called ward meetings) in which all the patients (who may all be anorexics if the unit is a special one or who may include people with a wide range of emotional difficulties if the hospital is a general one) meet under the "chairmanship" of a psychiatrist, often with the nursing staff as well. Discussions may be structured by the staff or left open for patients but will be designed to enable each one to use the experiences and support of all the rest.

Occupational therapy which may mainly be intended to keep patients pleasantly occupied or which may be an integral part of overall treatment. Art or drama therapy, for example, may be used to provide the anorexic with new ways to express her feelings and fears within the safety of a controlled environment.

● It is easy for parents to feel that a hospital is not doing anything positive for their anorexic daughter. If you find yourself thinking "all they do is give her her meals, I can do that and they'd be better meals too," do remember that the hospital staff is trying to help your daughter to live with a self which must change. Such a process is inevitably long, slow and almost invisible. The "positive action" for which you long—injections, X-rays, transfusions, pills—is not appropriate to this kind of emotional illness. If you feel that she might do better at home, by all means discuss your feelings, but she did not eat those meals you provided, did she?

● Concerned parents, who may have been closely involved for many months in their daughter's struggle with anorexia, often feel desperately cut off when she is admitted to the hospital. Sometimes the sense of isolation is increased because the girl herself and/or her doctors suggest that visits should be kept down for a while. Attempts to discuss what is happening with her doctor will often be met with a polite version of "no comment." Parents are often left with the feeling that nobody thinks they matter any more and/or that "they" believe that the parents are responsible for their daughter's problems.

The psychiatrist who is treating your daughter must have her trust and therefore must guard her confidences. He cannot talk to you as well as to her unless special "family sessions" at which she too is present, are arranged. He, in this sense, "belongs to" your daughter so the answer is for you to have someone who belongs to you, too. If you discuss your feelings about the situation either with your own doctor or with a senior member of staff at the hospital, they will probably arrange for you to be seen at regular intervals by a member of staff, such as a social worker, who is connected with the treatment team but not actually treating your daughter.

Coping with anorexia nervosa at home   Whether your daughter is trying to reverse her condition without outside help, being treated as an out-patient or trying to maintain at home gains made in the hospital, much of her struggle to eat will take place at home. Obviously you should be given every opportunity to discuss your role with those who are advising you; obviously too you will wish to behave in ways which your daughter feels will be helpful. The following may, however, be useful as discussion points or food for thought.

Your daughter's inner struggle is between her hungry body's demand for food (and her knowledge of "normal" eating, health, menstruation and so forth), and her phobia of normal weight. She is convinced that were she to begin to let herself eat she would lose control and get fatter and fatter and fatter.

Your role is to reinforce the one and help combat the other. In playing this role you will largely take that internal struggle onto yourself so that your daughter tends to feel that it is you she is fighting.

It is an essential condition of progress that *she come to accept the battle as her own* (this is one important reason why she may require to get away from home into a hospital). It is important, therefore, that whenever she can discuss matters rationally she agree to (or, better still, ask for) feeding, and that all concerned remain aware that *when she eats she does so for herself and not for you*. Likewise, when she does not eat it is herself whom she attacks and when she deceives, by vomiting or hiding food, it is her own body she is depriving not her relationship with you.

This appallingly difficult role may be easier if you can remember that you will be accepted as a trustworthy ally rather than an enemy if you are seen as *a reliable controller rather than as a feeder*. Projecting her own battle onto you, she will tend to see you as someone who will produce more and more fattening and luxurious food; press it upon her; be pleased with every mouthful she eats and the more pleased the more she eats. If she does feel this about you then you *are* the enemy. She needs to feel that you are concerned only that she eat an adequate diet; that you would be as disapproving of overeating as you are of self-starvation; as angry over a refrigerator raided for a binge as over a bedtime drink hidden behind the mirror; as appalled by a gain of 14 lb. in a week (the kind of gain she may have nightmares about) as you are by a loss of yet another 2 or 3 lb.

While nobody can tell anybody else how to convey attitudes and feelings to people they love, you might find some of the following useful:

Don't serve a special diet of either fattening foods or foods she especially likes. She is not suffering from *loss of appetite*; therefore an especially delightful dish will not tempt her to eat any more than ordinary food will. On the contrary, the more delightful the food the more her hungry body will yearn for it and the more frightened she will be. Serve whatever meals are ordinary in your household and pay neither more (nor less) attention to her fads than you do to those of other family members. If she has always hated fish there is no point serving it now, but don't leave the butter out of your usual recipe because she has decided that she cannot eat butter.

Expect her to eat that food normally: make sure that your expectations work both ways so that she is "allowed" neither to eat less of one item *nor more of another*. She must have the rice, the bread or the potatoes, but at the same time she may not have more than her ordinary share of the salad.

Don't introduce special food supplements and diet drinks unless her doctor suggests it. A mug of a high-calorie beverage may be an easy way to get some food into her but she will be treating it like medicine and feel that she is being "fattened." She has to learn to treat food as food and to feel that nobody is trying to conceal extra calories in what she takes.

Discourage nibbling between meals at least until ordinary meals are being eaten. Of course little bits picked off plates or out of saucepans will increase her calorie intake and you may therefore feel that you should turn a blind eye. Don't. You have to try and help her towards normal eating patterns and normal social behavior towards food. If you would not allow the dog to steal bits and pieces or the toddler to pick chocolate off the dessert in the refrigerator, she should not do so either.

Discourage eccentric cooking and/or eating behavior. Unless she would normally cook this meal for everyone or eat that meal alone in her room, she should not do so now.

Keep realities firmly in view when she produces one wild theory after another about food and diet. She may, for example, suddenly announce that it is better for people not to drink at mealtimes. She probably hopes to reduce the feeling of fullness which eating gives her and which she dreads. Acknowledge that, by all means, but don't accept the basic premise, which is nonsense.

Keep realities about her in view, too. The established anorexic often has a genuinely distorted perception of her own size, for example. She may feel enormous when in fact she is emaciated. She may also find it genuinely difficult to perceive portions of food normally. She feels that her plateful is vast when in fact it is smaller than the plateful being eaten by her eight-year-old brother. Acknowledge the feelings but assert the reality.

Plan how you will cope with discussion about food, eating and diet together with arguments and scenes about meals and snacks and long serious conversations about plans for reform. If you do not, they can come to take up almost all a family's time and psychic energy. Obviously this is both abnormal and damaging to all concerned. Yet equally obviously these topics cannot simply be banned when they are of central and highly emotional interest. It sometimes helps to formalize them and to find some agreed authorities to whom points of argument can be referred. For example, discussions of food and progress over eating might, by agreement, be scheduled for after the evening meal and frowned on, for all members of the family including you, at other times. Arguments over food quantities and nutrients might, by agreement, be resolved by weighing and by reference to calorie tables. Your mutual goal, in terms of her regaining weight, might also be formalized so that her daily intake of calories is agreed with a lower and an upper limit, and her weekly weight is ascertained at a stated weighing.

Some people may feel that all this places abnormal stress on eating and weight and therefore contradicts the drive to normality. But limits and limited goals also provide reassuring evidence to the anorexic that she is not simply being "fattened" in an open-ended progression to obesity and loss of control. Furthermore, since these topics *are* abnormally interesting to the family, a mildly abnormal acknowledgment of the fact may be less pathological than allowing them to submerge all other topics of family concern.

Danger signals in ongoing anorexia nervosa

Anorexia nervosa is a disorder which may last for years. Its victims commonly pursue a hilly course so that your daughter may reach a plateau on which her weight is stabilized, if low, and her fear apparently underground, only to start downhill again into a valley of crisis out of which she will again have to fight her way uphill.

Hopefully, she will be in regular contact with a doctor or psychiatrist who, even during her more stable times, will monitor her progress and take from you the responsibility for her safety. But there may well be times when she is either discharged from or reluctant to pursue such medical contact and, furthermore, when she is either not weighing herself regularly or is not telling you her weight or true weight. It may help you to know some of the common signs which suggest that anorexia nervosa is getting a renewed grip:

Increase in over-activity. While physical activity is a notable feature of anorexia nervosa, with its victims maintaining "fitness programs" and a falsely inflated view of their own strength and endurance even when starvation has reduced both their energy and actual muscle bulk to very low levels, a sudden increase in this phenomenon is often a danger sign. The girl may insist on taking over heavy tasks from her healthy brother; she may walk when she could ride and run when she could walk and/or she may suddenly add a new routine of formalized exercises or jogging into her day. Such behavior is sometimes due to a sudden realization of her own increasing weakness and a typical but erroneous belief that she can overcome that weakness by sheer effort and will, by superhuman control over a body which is letting her down.

There is a kind of restlessness which may be confused with deliberate over-activity, although it is actually part of the recognized syndrome of starvation. Just as a starving animal will fight to get to its feet again and again rather than lie still and conserve its draining energy, so the anorexic approaching crisis often becomes unable to rest or relax. She may stay up later, sleep less soundly, wake earlier and be unable to sit down for long enough to complete her homework or watch a television program.

Lack of concentration goes with that kind of restlessness because nothing which the anorexic sets out to do can keep her body still or keep her mind off its compulsive thoughts about food. Many anorexics find that even school or other academic work—usually their main source of success—becomes impossible under these circumstances and the straight-A student may flunk her examinations or fail to hand in assignments to the amazement of all who know her.

Inability to make decisions. As the anorexic reaches the weight which is her personal borderline with danger, she becomes increasingly unable to cope with even the minutiae of daily life. You will probably notice this most in the difficulty she has in making even the least important decision. She may ask you whether she should have a bath, go to bed, wear that dress or go to school. . . . But even having asked you she will often be unable to decide whether or not to take your advice. If you suddenly find that you have spent a large chunk of time discussing issues which are utterly trivial and entirely your daughter's personal business anyway, be alerted. If she does not ask you what she should do she may ask herself and answer in pathetic lists and timetables to cover each day. If you find a written schedule starting "get up, clean teeth . . . etc.," worry.

Increase in sensitivity to cold. While people of very low body weight are almost always sensitive to cold, the anorexic approaching crisis often reaches a point where her body is almost incapable of keeping itself warm irrespective of the outside temperature. Her need to avoid any self-indulgence will probably prevent her from using an electric blanket or even from wearing the extra clothes which would help her to be comfort-able, but when she reaches a point where she is obviously half-frozen even when the weather and the room are warm, beware.

Other physical phenomena. A family can become so accustomed to an anorexic daughter's emaciated appearance that it is only "noticed" when a parent returns home after an absence or, perhaps, sees a photograph taken on last month's vacation. But apart from her extreme thinness, certain other physical developments, while unimportant in themselves, may suggest that her weight is actually dropping yet again.

Hair is a give-away. The hair on her head tends to become thin and lank while an extra growth of very fine new hair (laguna) may appear on her face, arms and body.

Poor circulation is common and therefore minor physical complaints such as chilblains are common, too. But if her hands and feet actually look bluish or become blue with cold and then remain a bad color for hours after she is warm again, it is likely that she is reaching a physical limit.

Frequent headaches, in a girl who has not been previously liable to them, may suggest that her body's biochemistry is becoming disturbed.

Complaints of abdominal pain (sometimes severe enough to raise questions about appendicitis or some other abdominal emergency) often arise when the body weight drops even lower than usual. It may be that the girl's digestive system tries to "close down" and therefore produces discomfort when food *is* put into it; it may be that in this state the girl is so conscious of food in her stomach that she perceives the feelings of digestion as pain. Whatever its cause, the phenomenon does suggest renewed trouble.

While the above events may arise as part of a repeating pattern of weight loss, weight gain, stability and renewed weight loss, certain others may appear as new developments in the disorder itself. If the girl is under even the most long-range and/or intermittent medical supervision, they must be brought to the attention of her doctor. If she is not, then it is urgent that help should be sought:

Vomiting and/or diarrhea. These are often self-induced, with a finger in the throat or vast doses of laxatives, by anorexics who use them as a means either of getting rid of food which has been forced on them or of food which they have "succumbed to." Such behavior is usually kept extremely secret, but if it should come to your attention, you cannot afford to respect your daughter's privacy. Serious imbalances of body chemistry can quickly follow. Of course, the new vomiting and/or di-arrhea may be due to an infection. But if it is, medical help is still urgent. A starved body cannot afford such loss of food and fluid.

Bingeing. Sudden *excesses* of eating may have been part of your daughter's anorexia from the beginning, but if they have not, their beginning is a serious development. Don't allow yourself to feel that three pints of milk and a loaf of bread, all taken in ten minutes, is a sign of returning health. It is not.

Fluid restriction. Although this is rare, some anorexics reach a point where they cannot eat less than they are eating nor lose any more weight than they have lost. They realize that by not taking in fluid they can avoid the dreaded feeling of fullness which can follow even a glass of water into a starved stomach. Limiting fluids over a day or two produces a (to them) gratifying result on the scales, but the resulting dehydration is exceedingly dangerous.

Recognizing recovery from anorexia nervosa

If your daughter is caught in anorexia for two or three or more years, she will not emerge from it as the same person. She will have changed, not only because of the disorder but also because the passing of time has changed her expectations of herself and her relationship with the outside world. If she became ill when she was fourteen and begins to recover when she is eighteen she will have "lost" her adolescence by the time it is over. You have to look for a new young woman rather than for that schoolgirl.

She will be "cured" or "over it" when, and only when, those crucial dimensions describing anorexia nervosa (*see above*) are all reversed. She will be of normal weight (say within ten percent below or above the average for her age and height), and she will menstruate with reasonable regularity. Her attitudes to food and to eating will be within normal limits for her chosen social group and what she eats will be dictated by appetite, habit and preference rather than by fear of weight gain.

Obviously such a "cure" is not one which can come about suddenly. For example, even if she regains her lost weight comparatively quickly, her menstrual periods may not return immediately and may take some months to become regular. And while *some* change in her attitudes to eating must have taken place to allow the weight gain, it may take her a long time to lose all the quirks which have come to be associated with food and to discover relaxed pleasure in eating.

It is important that people close to the recovering anorexic should not expect miracles or conformity. If she is now to be an ordinarily healthy young woman she must, above all, have the autonomy and independence which she could not use while she was ill. She must, for example, be "allowed" to choose to stay slim, to be a vegetarian or to continue to dislike sweets. If everyone around her continues to regard any food preferences or refusals as a danger signal, she may tend to find herself wondering, all over again, whether there is a conspiracy to make her fatter than anyone has ever been before.

Once she carries enough weight to be safe and healthy and once she *wants* to take responsibility for herself, hand it to her with heartfelt thanks and the hope that her newly grown-up self will find some other way of coping with the stresses ahead.

Bulimia

Bulimia is an eating disorder which is characterized by frequent and compulsive binge-eating followed by self-induced vomiting, often combined with abuse of laxatives or diuretics and with excessively severe exercise. Despite increasing public concern and clinical interest, there are not yet many careful studies of bulimic patients nor any general consensus about its nature. Most clinicians would agree that bulimia is a manifestation of emotional illness. Some view the eating-purging pattern as a learned habit, while others believe that it is a true addiction in which victims abuse food as other addicts abuse drugs or alcohol.

Part of the confusion surrounding bulimia arises from its overlap with other eating disorders on the one hand and with "normal" behavior on the other. Bingeing and purging is part of the behaviour of at least 50 percent of all anorexics during some part of their illness and it is part of the behavior of almost every patient diagnosed as suffering from the "dietary chaos syndrome." The medical establishment has tried to clarify the difference between the *syndrome of bulimia* and the *sympton of bingeing-purging* by stating that bulimia is only bulimia if the binge-purge pattern is "not due to anorexia nervosa." Where features of both disorders co-exist, anorexia nervosa is therefore the overall diagnosis.

Increasing numbers of individuals who have not been diagnosed as suffering from any emotional or psychological difficulty binge and then purge, at least occasionally. Almost half of a recent sample of adult women on reducing diets for simple obesity, for example, admitted to occasional binges and to purging afterwards in order to avoid seeing the results of their excesses on the scales. Some appear to take self-induced vomiting for granted as an obvious aid to weight-control. Some college health authorities have also described a "new social activity" amongst students, known as "pigging out." Almost 50 percent of one sample of students said that they took part in group-eating binges after which they would rid their bodies of the excess food by vomiting, taking handfuls of laxatives and forcing themselves through stringent exercise programs. The idea of self-induced vomiting is revolting to most people, but it was common practice amongst the ancient Romans as a means of increasing their capacity for rich food. Perhaps most of us behave in a rather similar way when we deliberately over-indulge at a Thanksgiving feast and then quickly set out for a long walk to rid our bodies of their bloated feelings.

Causes of bulimia Nobody knows what "causes" bulimia; what internal and external forces act or interact on an individual to make the disorder likely. As with anorexia nervosa, we have to content ourselves with some account of what bulimia seems to be about. As with anorexia nervosa, we can list various feelings and ways of dealing with them that seem to be common to the experience of bulimics, but in this disorder such an account is distorted by hindsight. Bulimia is very seldom recognized by a second party, parent or clinican, unless the bulimic girl herself has first faced the fact of her disturbance and allowed, or insisted on, its reaching the attention of others. The following points are mostly derived from clinical interviews carried out with bulimics after diagnosis. While they may seem nicely to describe a complex of emotional difficulties that could logically form the basis for this particular disorder, there is a strong element here of circular argument: "This girl suffers from bulimia and the account she gives of her own feeling-experiences clearly explains how she comes to be this way." But does it? Detach the points from the diagnosis; remove all idea of bulimia from your mind. You will probably then feel that the points this bulimic girl makes about herself could have been made by almost any young woman of less-than-optimal self-confidence. These kinds of uncertainty, unhappiness and pain are almost universal, perhaps especially among young females. Bingeing and self-induced vomiting are not universal, however obviously they may seem to follow from the diagnosed sufferer's description. The vital link between the general emotional disturbance and the actual eating disorder is still missing.

It has to do with her need for nurturance, care and love from other people. Bulimics tend to describe themselves as "sensitive," as "people pleasers," as "always seeking for approval and never quite feeling I had it," or as "never being quite sure that I was loved, unconditionally, as I needed to be loved."

It has to do with being unsure whether she is worthy of love, so that, far from being angry at people who reject or disappoint her, the bulimic maintains that she always felt that she deserved these hurts and slights and that they left her ever more anxious to please; ever more determined to perfect herself.

Because the bulimic is chronically short of comfort from other people, she tries to give nurturance to herself through food, and she usually recalls years of "eating for comfort" before the disorder became established.

But because the bulimic feels unworthy of comfort, she cannot easily accept it, even from herself. She will often date the beginning of "real trouble" from a time when, perhaps because she was under unusual emotional stress and therefore overeating constantly, she began to be obese. Physical evidence of her self-indulgence increases her feeling that nobody can be expected to love a person like her, while increased self-dislike increases her need to comfort herself with chocolates and cookies. . . .

Typically, she feels that she must "improve herself," "deal with herself" by losing that self-indulgent weight in strict dieting. She is already caught in a vicious circle. Instead of trying to deal with her emotional stress (be it due to losing a lover or going to college) by trying to give her private self the support that it needs, she tries to deal with it by punishing herself. Instead of looking at, and accepting, her emotional needs, she looks at, and rejects, her physical body.

Because food is an emotional necessity for her, she finds dieting hideously difficult, so difficult that eventually she gives in to her craving and goes on an eating-binge. Binges do not just undo her reducing, they reaffirm her despicable nature and the impossibility of becoming perfect and therefore truly lovable. Sooner or later she will use self-induced vomiting to remove the actual food from her physical body and find that she simultaneously relieves that self-disgust and feels able to control herself once more, until the next binge. . . . This intimate meshing of food with love, of eating with pleasure and of resisting or rejecting food with virtue and self-control, makes bulimia far more a "slimmer's disease" than is anorexia nervosa.

Bulimia crystallizes when bingeing becomes a compulsion rather than a (guilty) pleasure and purging becomes a (painful) pleasure rather than a punishment. Some bulimics say: "I don't throw up because I've eaten too much; I eat too much because only throwing up makes me feel good."

Recognizing the syndrome of bulimia   People who are diagnosed as suffering from bulimia are, if their own accounts are accurate, extraordinarily successful in keeping the disorder secret from other people. Most bulimics eventually seek help for themselves rather than being persuaded/forced/brought to a doctor as anorexics usually are. Just as our (scanty) information concerning the roots of bulimia comes largely from patients in therapy, so the following points concerning recognition of the disorder are largely the result of hindsight. These are some of the features shared by individuals being treated for bulimia. They are not often signs or symptoms which might alert you in advance.

The patient is female and around twenty years old. The sex-ratio appears similar to that which holds for anorexia nervosa: about nineteen to one. The age distribution for the two disorders may be more similar than it presently appears. Anorexia nervosa often begins to take a noticeable physical toll early in adolescence and is recognized as being commonest during this age period. Bulimia is usually *recognized* at the end of the teens but victims often maintain that it has been "going on for years."

She recognizes and loathes her own compulsive binge-purge behavior and, by the time she manages to seek medical help, she consciously wishes to "stop guzzling and throwing up." This is an important difference between bulimia and anorexia nervosa. Anorexics seldom recognize their own body-shape or behaviour as abnormal. Even those who seek help willingly often pay no more than lip-service to the desirabilty of change.

Her weight is a little high, or within normal limits, for her height. The disorder does not lead to the dramatic emaciation of anorexia nervosa and this aids her in avoiding detection. On the other hand the fact that even the most stringent purging cannot produce a net weight loss in the face of binge-eating means that she must live with constant struggle and chronic failure.

Her social functioning appears unimpaired and she is frequently known (and liked) as a warm, friendly, outgoing person, quite unlike the inturned, withdrawn anorexic. Bulimic patients tend to be impatient when their popularity is pointed out to them. She may say something like: "Much they know. It's not that I'm a nice person; it's just that I can't bear not to be liked. It's not that I care about them, I just want them to care about me. . . ."

Her impatience is understandable because the bulimic's normal/acceptable appearance and social behavior is not an unmixed blessing to her. Not only does it allow her to exist, often for years, caught up in the disorder, it also deprives her of sympathy when she allows chinks in her armor to show and of offers of help when she can bring herself to appeal for it. The bulimic patient may speak with bitterness of being voted "most likely to succeed" in the high school year book; of having moments of admitted depression laughed off by friends with cries of "Oh come on! Nothing upsets you," of having early attempts to get medical help shrugged off by doctors saying "Whatever diet you're on it obviously suits you! I just wouldn't worry about it," and of having an eventual description of her problems greeted with incredulity as well as disgust.

She binges regularly, one or more times a day, often at night when she can be assured of privacy. Her binge-eating is entirely separate from normal meals which she may refuse on the grounds that she is dieting.

Her binge-eating consists mainly of high-caloric "forbidden" foods with the emphasis on items which are easy to eat in large, bulky quantities. American favorites appear to include milk, ice cream, bread, cookies, pastries and candies though a sudden yearning for fried chicken may send her in search of the ten portion from a take-out counter.

Each binge may consist of 3,000–50,000 calories: food for her sister for a day or a month.

The food costs a great deal of money. If she lives independently of her family she may spend all that she can earn, borrow or even steal, on food. If she lives with her family it is hard to see how such a drain on the stores in the refrigerator and pantry goes undetected so often and for so long.

Acquiring food, quite apart from paying for it, is difficult enough to take up a great deal of her time and attention. She may use several different supermarkets so that no one check-out person sees the scope of her purchases. She may divide up her packages so that neighbors see her only with one at a time. She may even dispose of the garbage bit by bit so that nobody sees her daily milk cartons gathered together.

She cannot resist binge-eating but the food itself gives her no pleasure now. She usually eats standing up, using her fingers, ripping open packages and devouring the contents at top speed and with little consideration of what it is or of what goes with what. Sometimes she does not even know what she has eaten; sometimes she is horrified, later on, to discover that she has devoured raw an item which should have been cooked.

Binges do not leave her satisfied but depressed and disgusted. She does not feel like someone who has satisfied a need and thereby reached greater contentment. Rather, the compulsion which drove her to binge rises through the bingeing so that she is left feeling that she has done something shameful and disgusting, and left feeling desperate for the purging which will bring relief.

Purging will usually be based on self-induced vomiting. A finger down her throat rids her of the food and the bad feelings, but she may also take vast doses of laxatives to rid herself of anything which "got through" and overdoses of diuretics to reduce her feeling of bloatedness and the weight recorded on the scales. Sometimes she will add in punitive exercise, running herself to complete exhaustion and consequent self-satisfaction.

Frequent purging may produce a variety of physical ill-effects. Bathing the teeth in acidic stomach-contents eats away tooth-enamel and produces a typical distribution of decay. Repeated infection of the salivary glands may eventually give her a "chipmunk" appearance while overloading of the stomach makes her liable to abdominal pain and to various muscle strains associated with the vomiting.

Although her overall weight remains within normal limits, she is subject to violent weight swings depending on the net balance of the binge-purge cycle. Weight changes of as much as twelve pounds in a week, especially if they are combined with interference with her body's water and salt balance through purgatives and diuretics, may also produce more global physiological disturbances such as chronically irregular menstruation.

Outside interference in the binge-purge pattern cracks her composure. If her behavior is ever noted as "odd" it will probably be because circumstances prevented her from bingeing. If supplies should run short (or her private ones be lost) on a backpacking trip, for example, she will become restless and distracted and may eventually steal for herself the stores intended for the whole party or insist on walking some impossible distance for more when everyone else considers that what remains is adequate. If she is trapped in a situation where, having binged, she cannot purge herself, her reactions will be different but equally extreme. If friends should call when she has just finished eating, for example, she will make uncharacteristically rude attempts to send them away, but if she fails she will fall into depression and perhaps into comatose sleep.

Treatment approaches in bulimia

There is no standard "cure" for bulimia any more than there is such a cure for anorexia nervosa. Although every specialist develops his own ways of working with bulimic patients, most would probably agree with the following treatment aims:

First, to stop the patient from purging. This is usually the first aim because as long as she can purge, she can eat without facing the full force of the self-disgust and fear of loss of control which binge-eating induces. Only if she is prevented from purging (sometimes by hospital observation amounting to physical restraint) can she be brought to face, and find that she can live through, that anxiety. Some clinicians do not make any attempt to stop patients from bingeing at this stage. Indeed the patient is encouraged to eat as she wishes so that the clinician cannot be seen as sharing her belief that bingeing is a wicked self-indulgence demanding punishment and so that, gradually, she can discover that she can control her own intake.

Then to rid the patient of the desire to purge. This usually means that she must be offered an alternative means of coping with the anxiety which follows binge-eating. Group therapy is often chosen as a means of providing her with an external source of support and control as well as the beginnings of work on her underlying anxiety about herself in relation to other people.

When purging has ceased to be an integral part of her life, bingeing can usually be brought under control. Instead of wolfing vast quantities of food like a terrified animal, she is helped to eat ordinary quantities in a normal fashion and to consider, within the group, what eating that food really means to her.

Once bingeing has been brought under her own control, her weight concerns are realistically considered. Many bulimic patients on the early rungs of the recovery ladder are amazed to find that they gain little weight through abandoning purging because, almost without realizing it, they reduce their binge-intake. This often provides a reassuring basis for a sensible diet, worked out with the doctor.

Once bingeing and purging are both under control work on underlying problems can begin, either in group or in individual therapy. Victims of bulimia cannot simply be tasked to abandon its mechanisms: they must be helped to find alternative ways of coping. Therapeutic work will usually focus on the patient's low self-esteem and fear of loss of control and will try to help her arrive at a self-image which reflects her as a real person: neither the perfect being she strove to be nor the disgusting creature she felt herself to be.

Therapy may follow a traditionally psychotherapeutic path or may involve certain short cuts designed especially for bulimic patients. Assertiveness training, for example, may help her to retrain her reactions to other people so that her anxiety to please, and her willingness to be ill-used, give way to a more realistic and self-protective view of her own value as a person, her own rights in relation to others.

Recognizing recovery from bulimia   A person has recovered from bulimia (as from any other eating disorder) when, and only when, food and eating can stop being a focus of her attention and emotional energy so that she is free to attend to other matters.

But detaching food and eating from the emotional web in which it has been entangled does not necessarily untangle the web itself. A girl who has "got over" bingeing and purging and who now eats normally and either accepts her weight or controls it with an easy diet, no longer suffers directly from bulimia but may still suffer intensely from whatever distortion in her emotional development or perceptions made her susceptible to it in the first place. She has abandoned bulimia as a way of coping with herself but that self still has to be coped with; until she can find new and healthier coping mechanisms, she may be extremely vulnerable. Parents and friends therefore have to allow for the possibility that the recovered bulimic will actually seem far sicker than she seemed before, when all they saw was that cheerful eager-to-please facade. She will only have recovered as a person, rather than as a bulimic, when she can begin to love and trust herself and others.

Eczema *see* **Allergy**.
Electric shock *see* **Accidents**. *See also* **Safety**/In the home: Safe use of electricity.
Enemas *see* **Nursing**/Medicines: Medicines which are not to be swallowed. *See also* **Soiling**.

Enuresis *see* **Bedwetting**.

Epilepsy *see* **Convulsions, Seizures and "Fits."**

Eye drops and eye ointment *see* **Nursing**/Medicines: Medicines which are not to be swallowed. *See also* **Eyes and Seeing; Eye Disorders and Blindness**.

Eye injuries *see* **Accidents**/Bruises: "Black eyes"; Foreign bodies in the eye. *See also* **Eyes and Seeing; Eye Disorders and Blindness**.

Eyes and Seeing; Eye Disorders and Blindness

Each eye is an almost-perfect sphere embedded for protection in bony sockets in the skull. The anatomy of the eye is complicated and probably easiest to understand in terms of three layers, each of which has separate functions:

The outermost layer—the cornea. The whole eyeball is encased in this tough fibrous layer which is called the sclera. At the front of the eye it forms the transparent cornea. Reflected light must pass through the cornea which focuses it to give us vision. If injury or disease scars or clouds its transparency, vision will be affected. Modern techniques have made corneal grafting highly successful.

The middle layer—the iris. This layer of rich blood vessels has the colored part of the eye—the iris—in front, beneath the cornea. The dark spot in the center of the iris is the pupil—an opening whose size, moment by moment, is controlled by the iris which opens it to let the maximum amount of light through when lighting is poor, and closes it up to control the amount of light when lighting conditions are good.

The innermost layer—lens and retina. The reflected light allowed through the pupil by the iris travels through the jelly-like substance that fills the eyeball to meet the lens, which focuses it on the retina. In the retina, the light triggers highly specialized nerve cells which pass the light messages, now in the form of nerve impulses, along the optic nerve to the brain which then interprets them as images.

Detachment of the retina sometimes occurs spontaneously or due to injury or disease. Modern ophthalmic surgeons have developed techniques by which detached retinas can often be "welded" back into place with laser beams.

Coordination of the eyes

Human beings are fortunate in that, unlike most other animals, they have binocular vision with the two eyes working together, viewing overlapping fields and therefore giving a very wide range of vision in depth.

Six muscles per eye, attached to the bones of the face, contract and relax constantly so that our eyes move all the time that we are looking at anything, and do so far more rapidly and accurately than we could move our whole heads. Any derangement of the action of these tiny muscles means that eye coordination is less than perfect (*see below* Squint.)

Protection of the eyes

Apart from their protectively recessed position in the skull, the eyes are also protected by the eyelids—double folds of skin lined on the inside with a lubricated layer which also covers the sclera. This lubricated layer, called the conjunctiva, ensures that the surface of the eye is not scratched by dust or other particles when the eyelids blink.

Blinking is a further protection. Like a car's windshield wipers, our eyelids flick down over the eyeballs and back again to ensure that foreign bodies are moved off the eye's surface and the cornea is kept clear. Fluid for washing is constantly supplied by the tear glands which are in the bony socket above the eyeball itself. Surplus fluid drains through tiny tear ducts in the inner corners of the eye, which carry it into the nose (*see below* Watery eye).

Faults in vision

Perfect vision depends on each part of the eye being correctly shaped and functioning in proper relation to each other part. The commonest visual deficiencies, corrected by eyeglasses or contact lenses, are:

Nearsightedness (myopia)   Generally due to an unusually long eyeball whose cornea cannot focus the reflected light rays passing through it so that the image of what the child is looking at appears exactly on the retina. Instead, the image appears in front of the retina.

The child can focus clearly on objects which are close to him, using the final focusing power of the lens of his eye, but he cannot focus clearly on objects which are at a distance. His distance vision is therefore blurred.

Eyeglasses with concave lenses move the light rays back so that they do focus exactly on the retina.

Some degree of nearsightedness is very common but is often missed in early childhood. It is only when a child is old enough to read (or finds himself unable to read) distant advertisements, bus numbers and so forth, that nearsightedness becomes obvious. He himself is unlikely to be aware of mild myopia until correction by glasses reveals to him a whole new world of distant clarity. Obviously it is a pity if young children miss any of the sights of the world they are exploring, or if older ones are scolded for poor copying from a blackboard they cannot see. Parents can help to ensure that myopic children get glasses early by:

Being alert to the possibility of nearsightedness in any child and having a particularly high index of suspicion if other members of the family are myopic.

Making sure that the child's eyes are regularly tested from about three years. Although routine testing, such as that carried out at a well-baby clinic, should detect marked myopia, milder degrees are quite difficult to establish in a child too young to use the standard test equipment or, even given stimuli designed for his age group, not certain to respond reliably. A skillful optician or ophthalmologist is needed.

Watching the child for signs of difficulty with distance vision. In a young child the most usual sign is that he screws up his eyes when he is trying to see distant objects. By doing so he can actually improve his focus by compressing the cornea.

Whether or not he screws up his eyes, parents on the watch for nearsightedness can usually compare the child's ability to identify distant objects with their own. If you can see that those are sheep rather than cows (wearing your glasses, if you require them) then he should be able to recognize the sheep, too. You, and only you, will know whether he calls them cows because he cannot see them clearly or because he is confused about animals' names. In the same way, remember that when you meet him coming down the street, he should be able to recognize you at very much the moment that you can recognize him. If his face remains blank or searching until you are nearly at your meeting point, you will have to decide whether he failed to see you because of his vision or because he was thinking about something else.

Farsightedness (hypermetropia)

In children (as opposed to the elderly) this is usually due to the eyeball being unusually short so that the cornea and lens cannot prevent the focused image from falling behind the retina. Although much rarer than myopia, farsightedness is potentially more serious. Where the nearsighted child may simply ignore objects outside the immediate surroundings within which he can see clearly, the farsighted child must continually fight to see the people and objects which are of most importance to him. He may be effectively partially blind. Continual accomodation of the lens may also lead to tiredness or even pain in the eyes. Convex lenses move the light rays forward so that they do focus exactly on the retina.

Important degrees of hypermetropia are comparatively easy to spot, even in very young children. Typical signs include:

"Backing off" from faces or objects so as to see them more easily. Instead of talking to you most concentratedly and responsively when sitting on your lap, the child may respond most socially from across the room.

"Losing" things that are close to him. The child may see the toy he wants on a high shelf but be quite unable to find it among the others when held up within reach. He may similarly become confused by food on his plate and so forth.

Lack of interest in sitting-down play. The very hypermetropic child will probably be comparatively uninterested in picture books, construction kits and so forth because "seeing what he is doing" is at least effortful and may be impossible for him.

Clumsiness. A somewhat older child may be thought clumsy or "not good with his hands" because his arms are not long enough to enable him to carry out fine tasks at a distance from which he can see fine detail comfortably.

Astigmatism

Is due to irregularity in the shape of the eyeball and therefore some distortion in the normal curvature of the cornea and lens. The most usual result is that the affected individual cannot focus on both vertical and horizontal objects at the same time: if one is in focus, the other is blurred.

Astigmatism may be present with or without near- or farsightedness. It can be completely corrected by correctly prescribed glasses.

Starting to wear glasses

Few children actually *welcome* the need for glasses, but the ease with which a child accepts them is usually directly related to the benefit he feels. The child who has never before seen a movie clearly, or been able to field a ball competently, will not readily return to his myopic world. It is the child whose vision is only mildly affected—especially if the main problem is an astigmatism which does not much bother him—who may fight against wearing what is prescribed. Occasionally your optician, after consultation with an ophthalmic surgeon, will decide that if such a child really resents his glasses he need not wear them. It will probably be suggested that you bring him in for regular reassessment, especially if there is any question of the condition worsening. Usually, though, a child who needs glasses has to be helped to accept them as a necessity. A very young child will seldom mind provided his glasses can be made easily comfortable for him. A variety of types of frames can be tried with the aim of finding one which enables him to have his glasses put on and then to forget all about them. Sometimes elasticized frames are the answer.

● While vanity does not usually turn a pre-school child off his glasses, *your vanity on his behalf* may easily do so. It is important not to allow your very natural regret at the sight of him in glasses at such a young age to suggest to him that you prefer him without them.

Older children may dislike both the idea and the appearance of glasses. Boys often feel that they ruin a "macho" or "sports" image; girls that they make them less pretty. There are a variety of ways in which, depending on the child's age and exact visual difficulty, you may be able to help him:

Explode the myths about spectacles meaning "bookishness" or lack of sexual attractiveness by pointing out the many hero and heroine figures in your child's life who wear them.

Stress the advantages of better sight by playing up the new ability to catch a ball, pick a friend out of a crowd, recognize an eagle on the wing or whatever is relevant to your child's life.

Help him organize occasional wear if this is appropriate. A slightly myopic child, for example, may prefer to reserve his glasses for long-distance activities, reading the blackboard and so forth. An astigmatic child may accept their wear only for visually complex tasks. The kind of case which will readily slip into (but not out of) clothing with a suitable top pocket makes this kind of use far easier. So does the provision of an extra pair of glasses to be kept safely against the time when the others are mislaid.

If you must insist that he wears them all the time, balance firmness on the matter with real trouble taken to find glasses he likes. Constant wear *is* going to change his appearance. Once he will accept that change at all, he has the right to make it as acceptable a change as possible. Eyeglass frames are expensive, but give him the widest choice you can possibly afford and the most honest advice you can muster.

If expense is not an obstacle, special frames for special occasions may produce miracles of acceptance. For example, some boys positively like prescription goggles for sports; both sexes often welcome prescription sunglasses which can then pass as a fashion accessory, while some girls are comforted by different glasses for party wear.

● Although every child should have at least two pairs of glasses in case one gets lost or broken, buying two which are very different, with a view to the child choosing each day as he chooses his sweater, is usually a waste of money. Glasses which are worn all day and every day become comfortable and the wearer becomes accustomed to the way they sit on the nose and so forth. Changing to a different pair produces a noticeable change in comfort and focus, as well as a change in what has now become a familiar self-image. Most children will only wear that second pair when the first *is* lost or broken and will prefer the replacements to be the same.

Consider contact lenses. For most children (though by no means all adolescents) the trouble of caring for lenses and the stresses associated with putting them in and out, dropping them and so forth, overbalance their advantages over glasses. But for some, contact lenses prove trouble-free and are very much preferred, while for many others your *willingness to consider* this comparatively expensive alternative is a morale boost in itself.

● Don't offer contact lenses without checking with the child's ophthalmic surgeon. They may be unsuitable for his visual needs (*see also* **Adolescence**/Problems with appearance and body image).

● Budget not only for providing the original lenses and replacing (or insuring) any that get lost, but also for the new ones you will have to buy as his myopia alters with age and growth. He might need as many as six new prescriptions between the ages of ten and sixteen.

Squint (strabismus)

Human beings have two eyes which are set apart from each other. The two should focus together so that the image the brain receives from the left eye merges perfectly with the image it receives from the slightly different vantage point of the right. In strabismus this perfect alignment does not take place. While one eye (let's call it the "good" eye) sends the brain an image of the object the child is trying to look at, the "bad" eye is looking elsewhere and therefore sending the brain a different image. The resulting "double vision" would be quite intolerable to the child if he did not immediately deal with the situation by accepting only the image from the "good" eye. Because his brain is able to "ignore" the unwanted extra image from the squinting eye, the child can see perfectly adequately. Parents with a child with mild strabismus may therefore not realize that there is any problem. With a more obvious squint they may see the problem as merely cosmetic. In fact, *any degree of strabismus presents a real threat to the vision.*

How a squint threatens sight   Eyes only continue to see if the images they produce are accepted by the brain. If a child is allowed to go on, for months or years, using only the images he receives from his "good" eye, the "bad" eye will progressively lose its sight and eventually become blind. While people can and do manage life perfectly well with only the sight of one eye, this is a handicap, and it is also a risk in that if any accident should befall that one sighted eye the child will be left with no vision at all. *Squints must be diagnosed early and treated.*

● If you wonder how a squinting child can possibly ignore the errant half of what would otherwise be double vision, try looking through a microscope or telescope without shutting or covering the other eye. You will find that because your attention is on the eye you are using, the different and unmagnified image which is being seen by your other eye fades out of your consciousness altogether.

Recognizing strabismus

Recognizing a marked squint in a child or adult who has not been adequately treated is all too easy. One eye looks at you as she speaks; the other "looks" away to the other side of the room. But such a squint has already been neglected for far too long. The ideal is that even very mild degrees of strabismus should be recognized as soon as they begin. They may occur from birth; they may develop during the early months or years, or they may occur only when the victim is tired.

If you think that your child's eyes do not always move exactly together, if one sometimes "wanders" away from the focus of the other or takes longer to arrive at the focusing angle, seek advice from your doctor or ophthalmologist.

● Don't let terms like "wandering eye" or "lazy eye" lull you into believing that this is not a "real squint." Such a child's strabismus may or may not be serious but it definitely needs professional supervision.

Small babies can have "pseudo-strabismus." If it is a baby under six months about whom you are concerned, you may get a pleasant surprise when you ask a professional to check her eyes. Firstly, very new babies often do have trouble in holding both eyes in steady focus. Practice and strengthening muscles may enable her to gaze into your eyes without a waver by the time she is a couple of months old. Unless one eye is *fixed* so that it never moves with the other, there is no need to concern yourself until she is around three months old.

Even at this period, a slight strabismus which you think you are noticing may not be real. Small babies have relatively less white in proportion to the colored part of the eye. They also often have marked folds of skin lying vertically down the inner corner of the eye. When such a baby looks off to one side, one eye moves to the outer side of the eye, exposing a lot of white between the inner corner and the pupil and still leaving a crescent of white between the outer corner and the pupil. The other eye, moving correctly with it, moves to the inner side where the colored part tucks itself under that fold of skin so that no white can be seen; it looks as if the two eyes are misaligned.

● The more marked the folds of skin at the inner corners of your baby's eyes the more likely you are to notice this phenomenon: Oriental babies are especially prone to it.

Treatment for strabismus

There is a variety of treatments for different kinds and degrees of strabismus in different ages of child, but all are primarily directed at preserving the sight of the "bad" eye. They are only secondarily concerned with cosmetics.

To preserve that sight the child has to be prevented from using only the images from her "good" eye and her brain forced to accept images from the "bad" eye. To this end the "good eye" may be covered (with a patch or glasses with one blanked-out lens, for example). In addition, the child may be taught various exercises designed to improve the functioning of the muscles which control eye movements and, of course, glasses may be prescribed to correct any concomitant faults in her vision.

● If a mild strabismus is picked up early, while the sight of the "bad eye" is still adequate, having the "good" eye covered may not present much hardship. But if the sight of that "bad" eye is already reduced, this vital treatment may be bitterly resented. The child feels that she is being forced to see poorly when without those glasses (or that pad or whatever) she can see perfectly well. Proper treatment of strabismus can require very great patience, especially in a child who is not old enough fully to understand or cooperate.

Surgery for strabismus Sometimes the eyes fail to align properly with each other because the controlling muscles are of unequal lengths. An ophthalmic surgeon may, in one or two operations, be able to correct the' squint (*see* **Hospital** / **Surgery; Squint**).

Color blindness

Some degree of color blindness is far more common in boys (about 8%) than in girls (about 0.5%). The resulting color confusion is seldom complete, though. Mild color blindness may present no difficulty at all. The following notes will be relevant only to severely affected children.

The most usual difficulty is in distinguishing red from green and it is unfortunate that these particular colors often stand, respectively, for "danger" and "safety" in our mechanized society.

Color blindness is often not recognized before a child goes to school because many children confuse the *name labels* for colors during the pre-school years and parents may not realize that their child's confusion is visual rather than verbal. Often the color blindness is first recognized when the child is introduced to color-coded educational apparatus. Sadly, recognition may follow only after he has already been labelled "stupid" or "obstinate."

For psychological reasons early recognition of color blindness is important, and once it is demonstrated you should take care not only to tell teachers and others concerned with your child, but to keep reminding them, too. It is easy for a teacher to forget to tell a new colleague about such a minor handicap, but it is not easy for your child to forgive an adult who bawls him out for putting on the other team's red band instead of his team's green one.

During childhood it is important to allow for color blindness in all your safety-teaching and to communicate freely with the child about it so that you know in what respects he is at risk. For example, kitchen appliances often have red lights to indicate that they are on. Can the child clearly see the indicator even though he does not see it as "red"? Traffic lights use colors but they also use positional cues. Instead of teaching your child "green for go," you have to teach him the relative positions of the stop and go lights. Electrical wiring is color-coded, too, but in most countries the red-green dichotomy has been abandoned. Check up on cheap imports, though, and make sure that your child really *can* differentiate the "live" wire from the "earth" before he starts working with them.

In adult life a few careers will be closed to your child—that of airline pilot or engine driver, for example. Some other jobs will be made far more difficult for him by his color blindness and it may be a kindness to keep open discussion going. He could, for example, train as a civil engineer or as a nurse, but if he does so, he should think carefully before taking jobs within his profession which involve much use of equipment such as color-coded plans or biochemical tests.

Most color-blind adults, however, lead entirely normal lives with only their intimates ever being aware of the problem. Many become extremely skillful at deducing the colors which are difficult for them from variations in shade and hue.

Eye disorders

"Bloodshot" eyes (conjunctivitis)

When the conjunctiva (the lining inside the eyelids and over the outside of the eyeball) becomes inflamed, the white of the eye looks red and the edges and lids may be puffy and unusually pink. This kind of inflammation is called conjunctivitis whatever caused it. Common types are:

Conjunctivitis as part of another illness. In measles, for example, this kind of inflammation is usual. It may also occur with a cold or other virus infection.

"Pink eye" or infectious conjunctivitis tends to occur in epidemics, especially in schools. The child should see a doctor who will probably prescribe an antibiotic ointment or antibiotic drops which will clear the infection rapidly.

● Do not *ever* keep such ophthalmic ointments or drops from one episode of conjunctivitis for use in another. Most have a very short shelf-life and will therefore be useless another time; furthermore, the tube or dropper is very likely to have become infected. Only sterile substances must be used to treat eyes (*see* **Nursing**/Medicines: Medicines which are not to be swallowed).

Conjunctivitis due to a foreign body in the eye. Obviously the first essential is to try to find and remove the cause of the irritation (*see below*), but the child should also see the doctor because if visible irritation has been caused, infection is likely unless the eye is treated.

Foreign bodies in eyes

When a speck of dust or other foreign body gets onto the eyeball or onto the underside of the eyelid, the eye's normal reaction is to water and thus float it out again. If you can possibly persuade your child not to rub the eye (and therefore embed the foreign body more firmly), the whole matter will probably right itself. A good trick to teach a child is to rub the *other* eye. This both fulfills his need to do something about his discomfort and helps to produce the needed watering.

If watering does not work, take the child into a good light and inspect the eyeball carefully. If a speck is stuck to it, take him to your doctor or emergency room to have it removed. It is not safe either to leave it there or to try to remove it yourself. You might worsen the scratch it will have made already.

If you can see nothing adhering to the eyeball, try lifting the top lid to give anything stuck there the chance to float down; then turn down the lower lid. If you can see a speck on either lid you should be able to remove it using the corner of a handkerchief or a piece of tissue. Even if you can see nothing, these maneuvers may allow the foreign body to move into a position where it ceases to be uncomfortable.

Even after you have successfully removed a foreign body the child may continue to complain of discomfort in the eye. It may have been slightly scratched. If he has still not forgotten the discomfort after an hour or so, show the eye to a doctor (*see also* **Accidents**/Foreign bodies in the eye).

Sticky eye   An eye which is sticky with mucus is very common in the first days of life. The hospital staff will bathe the matter away and may take swabs for the laboratory to make sure there is no bacterial infection.

In later infancy such a sticky eye usually is due to infection. The baby should be seen by a doctor who will probably prescribe antibiotic ointment and will show you how to bathe the eyes to remove all crusts and stickiness. The important points are:

Use boiled cooled water and cotton swabs.

Wipe the affected eye from the inner corner outwards so that any drops of (infected) water are unlikely to reach the other, unaffected, eye.

Lay the baby with the affected eye downwards so that watering from the affected eye does not run into the other.

Repeated sticky eyes are a nuisance, but they can always be treated successfully and, however bad they may look, they never harm the eyes.

Watery eye   If one eye keeps on watering and/or is often sticky, the baby may have a blocked tear duct so that surplus tears are not carried away into the nose but accumulate and drip out of the eye.

Blocked tear ducts usually clear themselves up during the first year, so your doctor will probably advise patience. If the problem persists, an ophthalmic surgeon can open up the duct by passing a very fine probe along it while the baby is under a general anesthetic (*see* **Hospital**/Surgery: Blocked tear duct).

"Black eye"   If you are afraid that a fall or a blow to the eye may have damaged the eye itself, take the child to a doctor quickly because if you delay, swelling may close the eye and make examination impossible.

Usually, though, a "black eye" is a misnomer because the eye itself is unaffected. Bruising is to the surrounding tissues only and although the injury may look dramatic and remain visible for some days, it is not at all serious.

• If you happen to be present *and* within reach of cold water when the blow falls, an instant cold compress laid over the area may reduce the eventual swelling. The coldness reduces the dilatation and leakage from the tiny blood vessels under the skin. Once the bruise has formed, however, there is no point in this treatment. Folk remedies, such as raw steak held to the area, have no value.

Over a few days the swelling and discoloration may move downwards. The eye reopens but the child's cheek is oddly shaped.

Styes A stye is a tiny boil on the eyelid due to infection in the hair follicle of an eyelash. Some children never have styes; some have occasional ones; a few seem prone to repeated styes. A child who has several in as many months should see his doctor; some other condition, such as dandruff, may be associated with them.

Styes are not serious and never affect the sight or do real harm to the eye, but they are painful, unsightly and infectious. The child with a stye should use only his own facecloth and towel and should try not to put his hands to his eyes because he may carry infection from the stye to the other eye. Home treatment is usually adequate for styes:

Increase the blood supply to the area by applying warmth. This will help the infection to "come to a head" and clear more easily. A piece of gauze or cotton should be wrung out in hot boiled water and, as soon as it has cooled to a bearable temperature, be held over the area. If the stye is at an awkward angle or you want to avoid any chance of spreading matter from it to another part of the eye, wrap the soaked material around something like the handle of a wooden spoon so that you can touch it to the stye only.

Remove the eyelash whose root is the source of the infection. If you look carefully in a good light, you may be able to see that one particular eyelash is embedded in the stye. If you remove it, using tweezers, pus will be able to drain away, pain will be almost completely relieved and healing will be hastened.

● It is not always possible to identify the affected eyelash. If in doubt pull *very* gently. If you have the right one, it will come out extremely easily due to its infected root.

Blepharitis Is a more generalized inflammation of the edges of the eyelids. It may be associated with a sticky eye and/or with a stye, but usually the whole margin of the eye (or perhaps both) is red and sticky and there may be pus visible in the corners and crusted all around the eye each morning.

Blepharitis is often associated with dandruff or with other skin problems, especially those with an allergic component. Although one particular member of the family may seem to be susceptible, many types of blepharitis are, in fact, infectious, so care should be taken with facecloths and towels.

If blepharitis is due to infection, your doctor can treat it with antibiotic ointment. If it is not, he will advise you on a search for other causes and cures. Do not leave it untreated as, although it is not serious and will do no lasting harm, it can last for a long time and leave the child, for a period at least, lacking eyelashes and/or with scaly scarring around the edges of his eyelids.

Fainting

A faint (or syncope as it is called in medical terminology) is possible whenever the brain is starved of oxygen—usually because something interferes with an adequate supply of oxygenated blood.

Many people never faint. Some seem prone to do so. The most usual victim is an older schoolgirl or adolescent. People who faint once or twice seem liable to do so again, but whether this is because they have a tendency to inadequate perfusion of the brain with blood, or because the experience of fainting produces fear of fainting which in itself makes fainting more likely, nobody knows. Certainly fear and anxiety play a part both in causing individual faints (as when someone faints while watching a bloody accident or after an emotional shock) and in causing the "epidemics" of fainting which occasionally affect school assemblies or military parade grounds. Under these circumstances, the sight of one person fainting is often enough to start a chain reaction.

Common causes of fainting

Brains are likely to become deprived of adequate oxygen when:

Environmental conditions are stuffy and "airless" as in a crowded and ill-ventilated room: less oxygen than usual is taken in with each breath.

Environmental conditions are very hot, whether outdoors in sunshine or in overheated rooms. Under these conditions an unusually large blood flow may be diverted to the skin in the body's efforts to cool itself, slightly less is therefore available for the brain.

The individual must stand still for a long period. Standing up means that the heart must work against gravity to keep the brain well supplied with blood. When there is physical movement—as in walking about or even in fidgeting—the pumping action in the blood vessels of the legs assists the heart, but when movement is forbidden—especially when a particular posture such as "attention" must be maintained—there can be some pooling of blood in the veins of the legs so that the blood returns sluggishly through the circulation for reoxygenation and the brain may therefore gradually become deprived.

A large meal has recently been eaten so that a larger-than-normal proportion of blood flow is being used in digestion.

Preventing faints

Institutions, such as schools, could minimize fainting if they would arrange for young people to be able to sit (even if only on the floor) during assemblies and so forth. Where emphasis must be put on standing—as in parades or for inspections—arrangements should be made for frequent short breaks during which everyone is encouraged to move around freely.

If you have a child who faints several times, or who faints only once but in acutely embarrassing and alarming circumstances, her own fear of fainting may make further episodes much more likely. Every time she faints—or feels that she may be going to do so—her anxiety and therefore her proneness to fainting will be increased.

Under these circumstances it may be important to help her *not to feel faint*, even though fainting is not, in itself, at all dangerous. Her school should certainly be sympathetic to a special request that she be allowed to sit close to an open window or exit. The child herself should be encouraged to avoid "faint-prone" circumstances. She should realize, for example, that it is better to avoid extremely crowded, hot, emotionally charged situations (such as pop concerts or demonstrations) than to risk fainting in circumstances from which she cannot easily either escape or be rescued. She should, of course, be encouraged to sit in the corridor of an overcrowded train rather than stand throughout a long journey, even if her clothes do get dirty.

Coping with faints

The victim of a faint almost always gets some warning:

She will go very pale.

She may feel sick and/or dizzy or "odd."

She may break out in a cold sweat, especially on her hands and face.

At this stage, she can rescue herself (unless she is hemmed in by a crowd). If she sits down and puts her head below the level of her heart, extra blood, bearing the needed oxygen, will reach her brain and she will recover. Alternatively, if she can force herself to walk out of the overheated hall and into fresh air, the combination of movement with more environmental oxygen will probably serve the same purpose.

● It is important to emphasize these early signs to a girl who worries about fainting. Suddenly "falling unconscious" is what she dreads; if she knows that she will always have time to escape the situation, her anxiety will lessen and with it the likelihood of a faint.

If she faints completely she will fall and, by doing so, she will start her own recovery because once she is lying down sufficient blood will reach her brain. You can help by:

Persuading other people to stand back so that she gets as much air as possible. If she is in a very hot, crowded, airless place, it may be worth carrying her outside.

Loosening anything which may restrict her breathing such as a tie or tight collar.

Turning her on her side so that if she should vomit she will not breathe it in.

Unconsciousness from an ordinary faint is usually only momentary—her eyes will probably be opening by the time you reach her side—but she should remain lying down until she ceases to feel giddy or peculiar and she should then get up slowly and stay sitting in a cool airy place until she feels normal again.

Farsightedness *see* **Eyes and Seeing; Eye Disorders and Blindness**/Faults in vision.

Fat children *see* **Eating**/Eating problems: Obesity, the problem of eating too much. *See also* **Growth**.

Fats *see* **Eating**/Types of food.

Fears *see* **Anxiety, Fears and Phobias**.

Feeding *see* **Eating**/Types of food for babies; Eating problems.

Feet *see also* **Ringworm and Athlete's Foot; Warts and Verrucae**

Your child's feet are vitally important. They have got to carry her full weight throughout a long life. Pain, deformity and loss of function in the feet is one of the commonest causes of loss of mobility and independence in otherwise healthy elderly people. If you can keep your child's feet healthy *throughout their period of growth* you will have made a real, if unglamorous, contribution to her future health and happiness. Remember that ill-fitting shoes and socks can damage soft young bones without causing pain.

First shoes and socks

In cultures where everyone goes barefoot there are few deformed feet and no corns or bunions; instead there are toes squashed by cattle and soles ripped by thorns and stones. . . . You have to steer between these two extremes, recognizing that shoes are needed for protection but that feet stay strong and healthy if they are left bare as much as is safe.

Healthy feet do not need support; they provide their own support through well-developed, well-exercised muscles. Only in special circumstances, such as athletic training or sports, are shoes needed which give "proper ankle support."

Babies are best without shoes or socks until they can walk well enough to do it outside where their feet will need protection. If you think your baby's feet will get cold, use sleeping bags or sleeping suits with big, roomy feet.

• Cool feet do not suggest that a baby is chilly. Check her bare stomach or thighs instead. If they feel warm then she is warm enough.

Have first shoes fitted by a trained fitter in a specialty shop. She should measure the length and breadth of *each* foot with the child standing up, and she should only offer you a shoe which is exactly the right fitting. Never accept a "D" instead of an "E" because it happens to be the color your child prefers. And never accept "extra room for growth" either. Trained fitters are taught to make a proper growth allowance; too much is as bad as not enough.

Whenever she wears shoes she should wear socks to prevent rubbing. Endlessly rubbed places and repeated blistering can lead to the formation of calluses on the feet.

Choose socks as carefully as shoes. Nylon stretch socks are a great help to parents but they can be disastrous for children. If you buy a sock advertised for a range of sizes such as 5–7 and your child is a size 7, buy the next size up, the 8–11. If you buy cotton or wool socks, do check, after the first washing, to be sure that they have not shrunk. The best way is to buy two pairs, wash one pair and then compare them.

Take child and shoes for remeasuring at least every three months. That specialty shop should be happy to check the old shoes for you and tell you honestly if they still fit your child. If she needs new ones, remember to make a clean sweep of *all* footwear. If those shoes are now too small so will be the boots and the socks you bought at the same time. As she gets older you will need to remember sports shoes and dancing shoes as well as tights and those spangled socks she likes for parties.

Don't pass shoes down from child to child even if the size and fitting seem appropriate. Each wears a shoe to her own particular shape which cannot be the right shape for anyone else. You may be able to make an exception for Wellingtons (rubber boots) which hold their own shape.

Shoes for schoolchildren As your child gets older you may have to fight fearful battles to persuade her to accept shoes which fit, rather than shoes which look fashionable. Shoe manufacturers are gradually beginning to realize that both these ideals should be available in one pair of shoes but it can still be difficult. Some families find that the following tips help to avoid both battles *and* damaged feet:

Willingness to buy fashionable shoes for "best" in return for cooperation over wearing "sensible" shoes for school and everyday.

● Although short periods in high heels, wedgies or pointed toes will do less harm than longer periods, do keep an eye on the fit of these shoes which, little worn, may go on looking new long after they have become too small.

Willingness to spend the money for good sports shoes so that the child has properly fitted "trainers" of which she can be proud rather than ill-fitting sneakers.

Acceptance of sloppy summer casuals balanced by encouragement to abandon them in favor of bare feet whenever possible.

● A soft canvas shoe will probably do little harm unless it is so loose and "comfortable" that the child actually screws up her toes and/or shuffles to keep it on.

Special shoes for "foot problems" A generation ago many children were compelled to wear special shoes designed to correct "flat feet" or to stop them from "toeing in." Now most authorities believe that time and growth will correct most of these "problems" anyway. Almost every toddler walks flat-footedly and appears bowlegged due to diapers and a straddle-legged stance designed to help her balance. Many older children go through phases when they walk oddly, and here again there is no substitute for growth and natural muscular development. If you are really concerned about your child's feet or limbs, by all means have her checked by a doctor. He will probably suggest as much free active play, barefoot, as possible.

Toes and toenails Injuries to toes and toenails are excruciatingly painful because of the rich nerve supply. Furthermore, a fractured toe or a nail so badly bruised that it eventually comes off can leave permanent slight deformities. Do make sure that your child has shoes which offer adequate protection for her chosen activities. Mowing the lawn in open sandals, or handling iron-shod horses in bare feet, is asking for trouble.

"Ingrown" toenails, in which the outer edge of the growing nail presses increasingly into the flesh, can be very painful and can become a chronic problem. You can avoid it by always cutting toenails straight across (rather than in a curve) and by teaching her to do the same. If an ingrown toenail does develop, take the child either to the doctor or to a chiropodist. Home treatment, such as digging out the offending corner of the nail, will only deal with the problem temporarily.

Fever *see* **Nursing**/Fever. *See also* **Infection**/Types of infection: Infections which cause illness.
Fireguards *see* **Safety**/In the home.
First aid *see* **Accidents**.
Fits *see* **Convulsions, Seizures and "Fits."**
Flat feet *see* **Feet**.
Flu *see* **Influenza**.
Fluoride *see* **Teeth**. *See also* **Eating**/Types of food: Vitamins and minerals.
Food *see* **Eating**.
Food allergies *see* **Allergy**.
Food poisoning *see* **Diarrhea, Gastroenteritis and Food Poisoning**. *See also* **Infection**/ Preventing infection: Infection and home hygiene.
Food refusal *see* **Eating**/Eating problems. *See also* **Eating Disorders**.
Foreign bodies *see* **Accidents**.
Foreskin *see* **Circumcision**.
Fractures *see* **Accidents**.
Frustration *see* **Tantrums**.
Fungus infections *see* **Infection**/Fungi: Fungi as "germs." *See also* individual conditions.
Gastroenteritis *see* **Diarrhea, Gastroenteritis and Food Poisoning**. *See also* **Infection**/ Preventing infection: Infection and home hygiene.

German Measles (Rubella)

Rubella is a virus infection which usually produces an illness so brief and mild that it may never be seen by a doctor or may be wrongly diagnosed when some other disorder is causing a rash.

Rubella would be an unimportant illness, and one which would certainly not merit mass immunization, if it were not for its potentially disastrous effects in the earliest stages of fetal life. Congenital Rubella Syndrome is most likely to affect the infants of mothers who contract rubella when they are not yet even sure that they are pregnant. Sixty percent of such mothers may have babies with a variety of defects, including deafness, cataracts in the eyes and damaged heart valves. By the fourth month of pregnancy the risk has already dropped: only about five percent of such babies are likely to be affected if the mother contracts rubella.

If a woman has had rubella in childhood or before she became pregnant, then she and her fetus will be protected. Unfortunately, many women who believe that they did have the disease in childhood turn out to have no antibodies against it. Their "German measles" was wrongly diagnosed, assumed when a transient rash occurred during a rubella epidemic or simply misremembered. There are so many virus infections which can produce mild fever and rash that definite diagnosis is usually impossible.

Public health authorities now offer rubella immunization to all girls during childhood, whether or not they are thought to have had the disease. In the U.S. it is part of the routine immunization program for infants and is given at around fifteen months. Although the vaccine does no harm even when given to an individual who already has adequate antibodies of her own in the U.S. an older girl will have her blood tested for rubella antibodies and will be immunized only if the titer is low. Unfortunately, the acceptance rate is nowhere near one hundred percent and the immunization program is so recent that there are many adult women of child-bearing age who were out of school before it was available. There will continue to be a risk to fetuses as long as any girls reach puberty unimmunized. Parents, therefore, have a heavy, double responsibility in rubella.

Make sure your own daughters are immunized

Unless your doctor advises against the injection for a particular reason (allergy to the traces of antibiotics used in the manufacture of the vaccine is the most likely), every girl should be immunized before puberty or while there is no possibility that she could be pregnant or could become so in the three months after immunization.

By ensuring this you ensure the safety from rubella of *your own daughters' children*.

Make sure your family does not infect anyone else

If immunization is available in your community to anyone who requests it, making sure that you all receive the injection is the surest way. If it is not available to boys or to younger girls, one of them may become infected and pass the infection on before you know that he has rubella. Nevertheless, you can responsibly minimize that chance:

If you know there is a local epidemic of rubella, watch out for the signs (*see below*).

If you suspect rubella, have a diagnosis attempted by a doctor whether the child is "ill" or not. He will often be able to tell you if the child has *not* got rubella, even though he probably cannot categorically state that this infection is rubella.

If rubella is likely, warn any women of reproductive age who have had contact with the child in the past *three weeks* (*see below* Incubation period). Don't only warn women you know to be pregnant; it is the women who did not know, or were not sure, three weeks ago who are likely to be at greatest risk.

Isolate the infected child not only from pregnant women or even from all women who might be pregnant, but from anyone who has not definitely had the disease/been immunized. Otherwise your child may give it to another little boy who may give it to the aunt who forgot to take her contraceptive pills last weekend. . . . Isolation needs to last for only a week. Don't listen to people who say, "Oh, send him to school. The sooner they all get it the better." In this disease, every child who "gets it" will be a risk to newly pregnant women. Better immunity by injection than by infection.

Side effects of rubella immunization

There are usually no side effects in children. In adults there may be a reaction, one to two weeks after the injection, resembling a very mild form of the disease itself (*see below*).

Having rubella **Incubation period.** Up to twenty-one days (longer periods have been recorded).

Route of infection. Droplet infection from nose and throat to nose and throat.

First symptoms Possibly a mild sore throat and mildly runny nose. Always (if the victim
of rubella searches because he/she feels unwell, which is often not the case) swollen glands in the neck, directly behind the ears and at the nape of the neck.

A day or so later (but often the first and only symptom to be noticed) rash starts on the forehead and spreads down. The rash, which may itch slightly, consists of flat (unraised) small pink areas that quickly merge together so that the skin looks flushed all over. At this stage scarlet fever is sometimes wrongly diagnosed. The rash fades, often within a day. It is not unusual for these rash stages to come and go so rapidly that they are missed altogether, or that a child goes to bed one night with a rash which her parents intend to show to a doctor the next day, but which the doctor never sees because it has vanished overnight.

Treatment None, except in the very rare case of complications such as middle-ear
of rubella infection.

● Although for most families German measles is a non-illness, with the child up and around (although isolated for a week), some older girls may suffer from pain in, or even swelling of, some joints. This may last for up to two weeks and, while unpleasant, leaves no after effects. Aspirin and rest are usually helpful.

"Germs" *see* **Infection**/What "germs" are: Bacteria; Viruses; Fungi; Protozoa.
Giddiness *see* **Convulsions, Seizures and "Fits"**/Paroxysmal vertigo; **Fainting.** *See also* **Ears and Hearing; Ear Disorders and Deafness**.
Gingivitis *see* **Teeth**/Some dental problems of adolescence.
Glands *see* **Immune Response; Infection**/Types of infection. *See also* **Adolescence**/Puberty.
Grazes *see* **Accidents**/Cuts and scrapes, Grazes and puncture wounds.

Growing Pains

As far as we know, growth is never a painful process so the sharp aching pains which afflict some children's legs cannot actually be due to growth or even to a "growth spurt." However, these pains are certainly real. They afflict particular children at particular age-stages and may be acute enough to stop a child from playing or to wake him or her in the night.

Most authorities believe that these pains must be due to mild muscular strains which arise because the child is currently spending a lot of time at one particular physical activity—whether football or hopscotch—and neither rests nor changes activities often enough to allow the affected muscles to recover.

If pains of this kind really trouble your child you may prefer, for both your sakes, to have a doctor check on them. In the meanwhile reassurance, casual sympathy, a rest or hot bath are all that is required.

Growth *see also* **Adolescence**/Puberty: Worries about puberty

The rate at which any child grows and her eventual adult size, shape and proportions, are determined by a complicated mixture of genetic and environmental influences. A girl's "growth plan" is laid down in her genes, rather as a rocket's flight plan is laid down on the drawing board. All other things being equal, she will grow to that target just as the rocket will travel to its destination. But it is a long journey from fertilization of the ovum to the resulting child's menarche at exactly fourteen years one month, or final adult height of 5 ft. 3 in. or 5 ft. 7in. Like that rocket, your child needs fuel for the journey (in the form of food and care) and, like that rocket again, deviations from the planned course can be caused by environmental disturbances like serious illness or long-term emotional upset. Many of these are self-righting (*see below* The phenomenon of "catch-up growth"), but a few, such as failure of the supply of growth hormone (*see below* Children who are "too small"), may throw her growth permanently off its track.

Thinking about your child's growth

The whole of a child's body grows. You cannot measure her bones or internal organs, but you must, at least, take account of weight *and* height. A baby's weight gain alone may assure you that she is getting enough milk and not too many cereals, but this is using weight as a clue to nutrition rather than growth. Weight gain without matching height gain may mean that she is getting fat rather than large.

Even weight and height together need looking at over time. Present measurements only tell you how much she *has* grown. You also need to know how fast she has been growing (her growth rate) and the timing of growth phases such as the adolescent spurt. To say that she is "small for twelve" is meaningless; how much and how rapid growth is still to come?

Growth charts for children

Instead of a chart giving "average" heights and weights for children of particular ages, a child's growth needs to be considered against standardized centile graphs which, by extensive research and elaborate statistical techniques, are constructed to give the expected upward curves for height and weight throughout children's growing time. Very briefly, such curves are produced by weighing and measuring thousands of children, at many different age-points, and dividing the resulting measurements so that a given number of sample children are above and below a particular point at a particular age. The divisions can be as fine as you please, but the fiftieth centile will always have half the children above and below it. The twenty-fifth centile will always have three-quarters of the children above and a quarter below. The seventy-fifth centile will always have a quarter of the children above and three-quarters below, and so on. At any age, the ninety-seventh centile will represent large children (only three in every hundred will be bigger) and the third centile will represent small children (only three in every hundred will be smaller). These centile points are still static points. They cannot tell you what happened to growth in between them. Further work is done following the actual growth, week by week, of yet more children, in order to see at what rate they gained the pounds or inches that separate two age measurements.

Before you start keeping a record for either sex, decide whether you will use kilos and centimeters or pounds and inches. Metric measures are read up the left-hand sides of the charts and are the most accurate. Pounds and inches are up the right-hand sides of the charts and are quite accurate enough. You can use each chart for more than one child if you use different colors.

WEIGHT RECORD FOR GIRLS

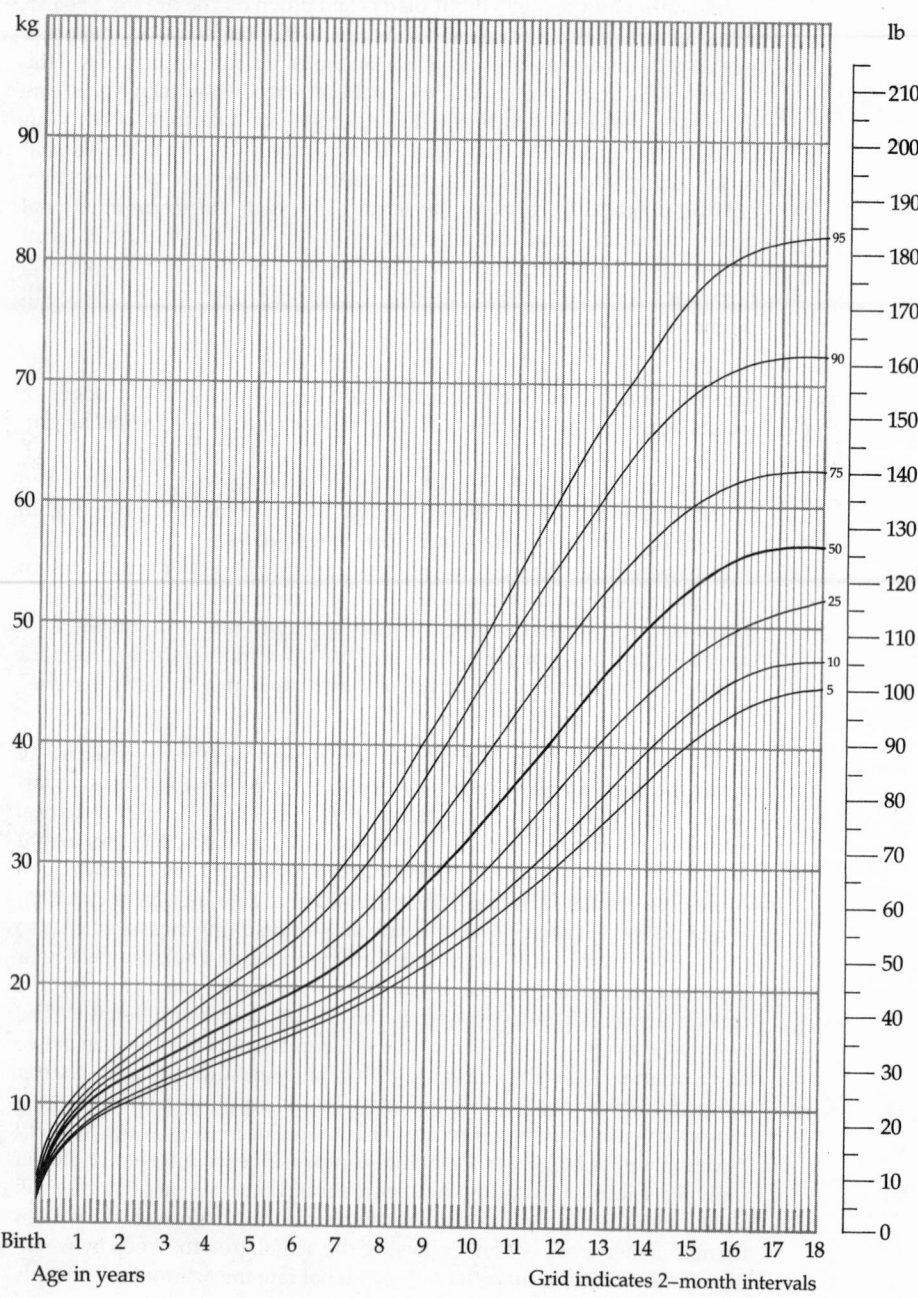

Age in years

Grid indicates 2–month intervals

Each time you want to enter a weight or height, find your child's age along the scale at the bottom of the chart and her weight or height up the side. You make your mark where a line straight up from her age meets a line straight across from her weight or height. You may find it easier to follow the lines accurately if you use two rulers or postcards.

HEIGHT RECORD FOR GIRLS

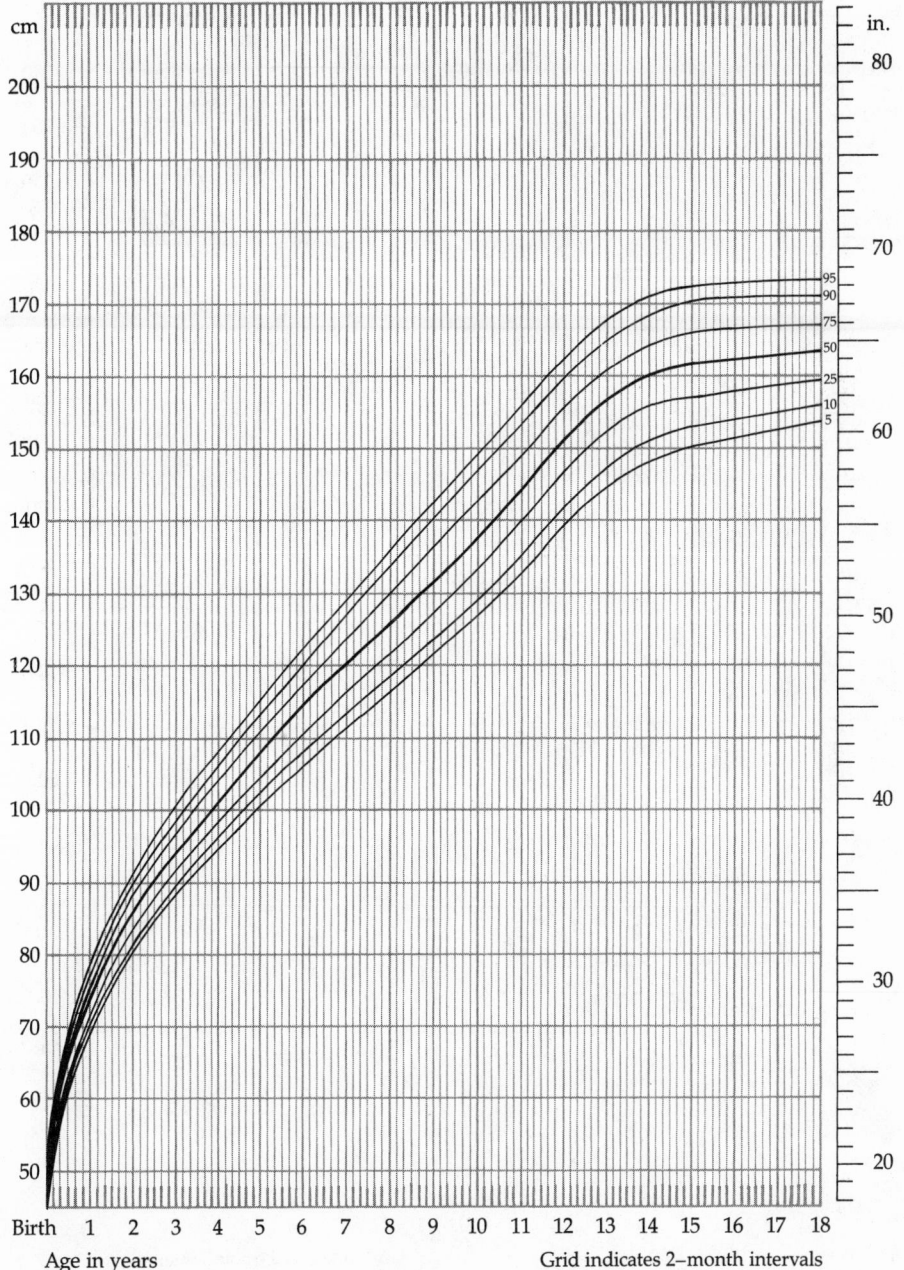

Age in years   Grid indicates 2–month intervals

Weight changes rapidly so people sometimes weigh themselves frequently, especially if they are dieting. There is no point in weighing a child very often for these records, though. If you try to record gains of less than half a kilo or one pound, your marks on the chart will not be accurate. All you are interested in is the trend over time. Three-monthly weighing would be ample.

WEIGHT RECORD FOR BOYS

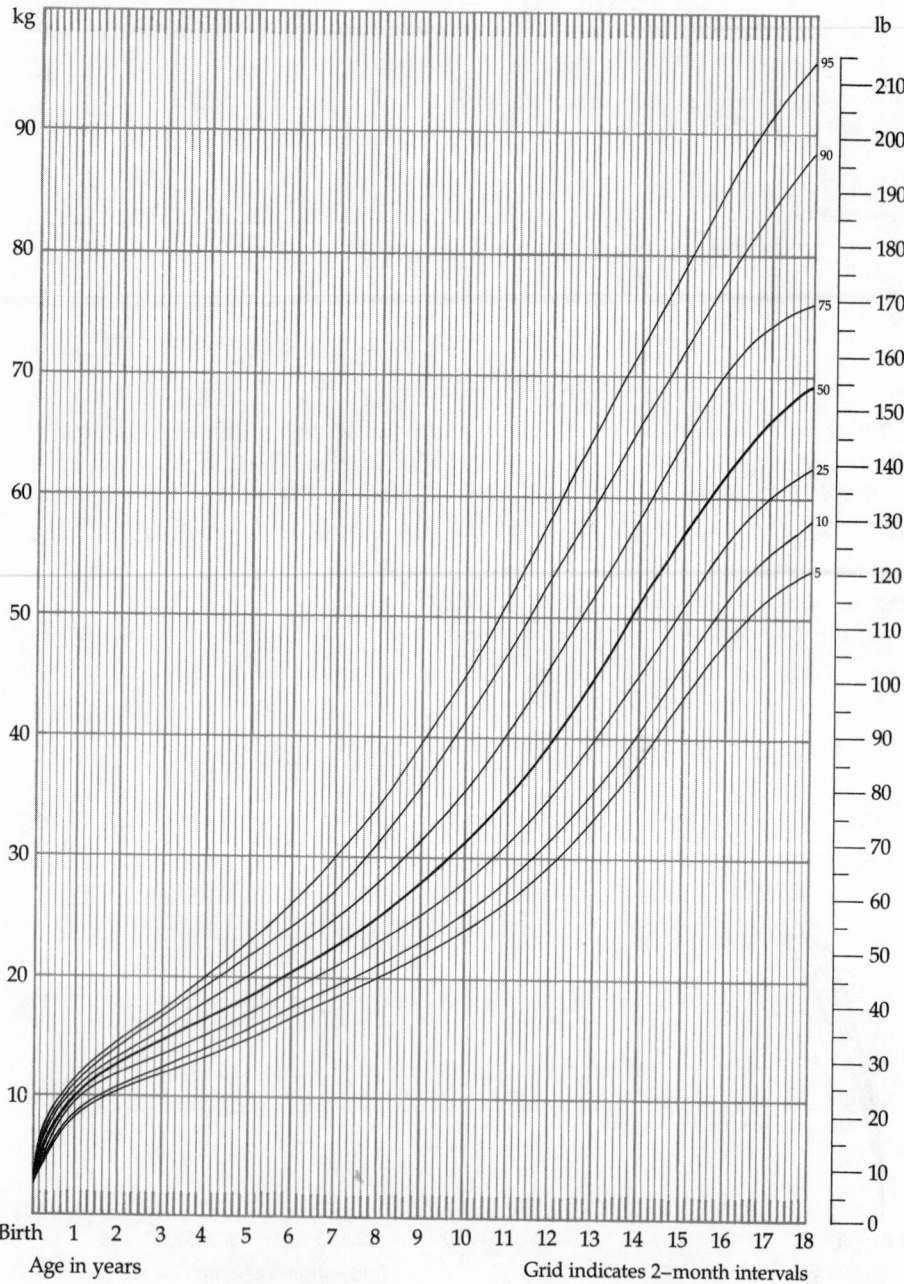

Age in years

Grid indicates 2–month intervals

Height increases even more gradually than weight and accurate measurement is more difficult, too. If you measure often you will sometimes think your child has shrunk! Three-monthly measuring would again be ample and six-monthly would be adequate. Your teenage son may enjoy being measured more often when he reaches the stage where he is growing half an inch each month.

HEIGHT RECORD FOR BOYS

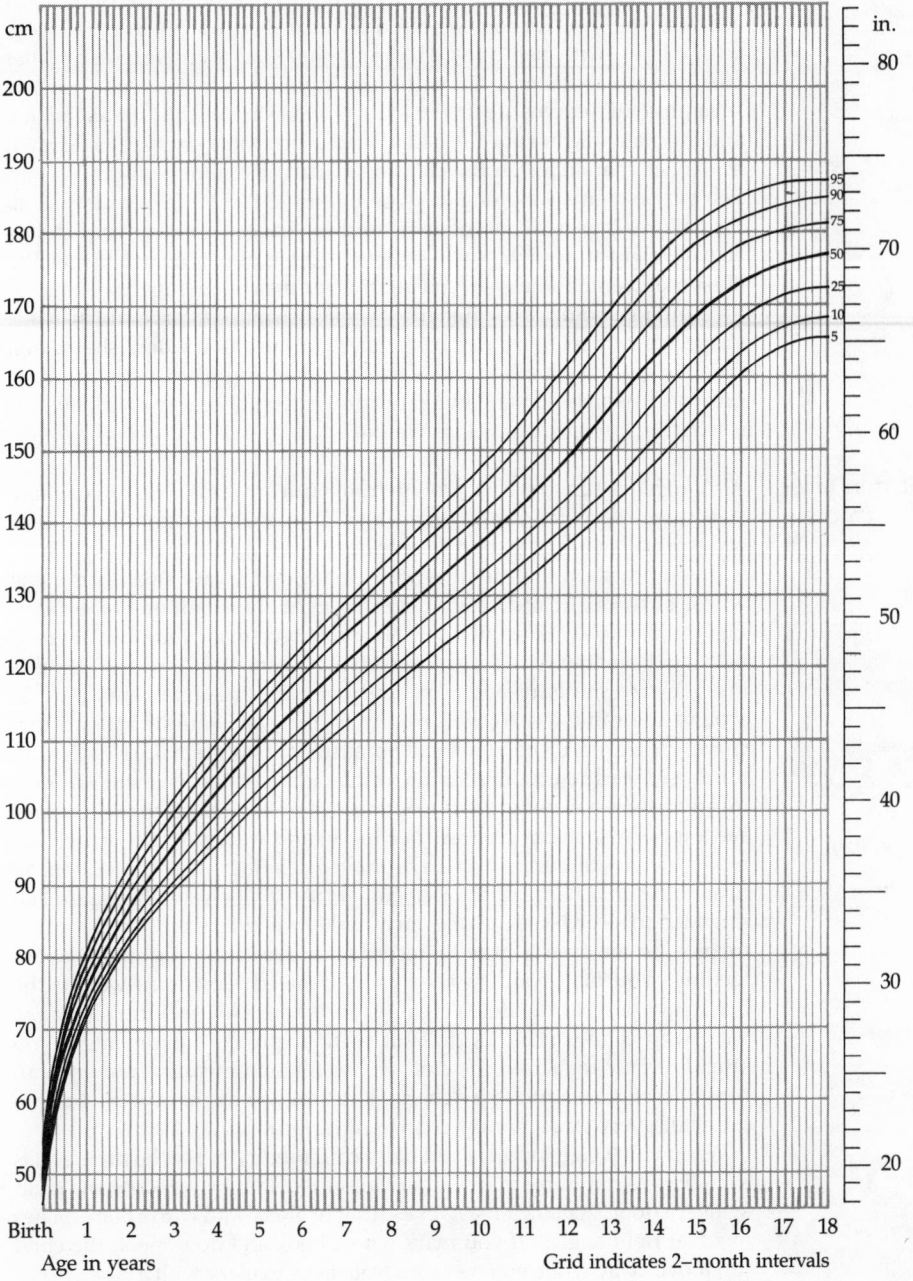

cm / in.

Age in years

Grid indicates 2–month intervals

Centile charts
for your use

The result of all that research into children's growth is put together to produce a series of curves like those on the charts overleaf. They give a background picture of normal growth. The first pair of charts show the weight increases and the height increases of girls: small girls, larger girls, big girls; girls growing at a steady rate through the middle years of childhood and girls growing rapidly towards puberty. The second pair of charts do the same for boys. The middle lines, labelled "50" are the fiftieth centile lines, with half of all children either side of it. Heavier or taller children are above this—and the seventy-fifth, ninetieth and ninety-seventh centile curves are drawn in. Lighter or shorter children are below, and the matching twenty-fifth, tenth and third centile lines are also drawn in. Notice that although the children's actual measurements vary, with two-year-old girls weighing anywhere from 22 to 33 lb., for example, all the children's growth curves are similar in shape. Whatever your child's actual weight and height now—wherever it places her, on or between the illustrated centile lines—if you record her measurements from time to time and join your marks, her growth will also make a curve which is this shape. Of course, there will be "jiggles" in the curve where she gained little weight during a hot and active summer, or put on extra during a greedy Christmas holiday, but, if her growth is proceeding normally, this is what her curve will look like over time.

Starting to use
the charts

Although it is fun to record growth from birth onwards, you can usefully start these charts for a child of any age. They are often most useful later on, especially around puberty (*see below*).

If you are starting in infancy, remember that a very small baby, one whose birthweight and length enter her right at the bottom of the chart, may be *meant* to be small. You are probably small, too, and there is nothing the matter with being a person who is smaller than most. If she is just the size she is meant to be and her early measurements put her around the third centile, her growth is likely to continue around that curve. However, if she was small because she was premature or "small-for-dates," early ejection from the womb or lack of nourishment in it may mean that she did not grow the optimum amount before birth. You may see a lot of "catch-up growth" (*see below*) and within a year or two her personal growth curve may have moved up from near the bottom to nearer the middle centiles. Remember also that these charts are not intended to record weekly, or even monthly weight gains; they are meant to provide an overall growth record, not constant reassurance about feeding. You may want to keep more detailed records as well at the beginning of a baby's life. Weighing, and more especially measuring, a baby who cannot stand is difficult without proper equipment. If you attend a clinic regularly, the staff will weigh and measure and you can copy their figures onto these charts. Later on you might take the baby to the clinic every three months or so for this purpose.

When you weigh toddlers and older children, try to use the same scales each time to minimize inaccuracy. Measure height by standing the child against a door, heels against it, eyes straight ahead and with a book on her head, at right angles. If you mark where book and door meet, the child can move away while you measure from floor to mark with a tape.

Irregularities of growth

The phenomenon of "catch-up growth"

Every child has a "natural" growth trajectory, but if the supply of fuel from the environment is inadequate, her growth may be pushed off that curve so that she does not grow as much as she could, as fast as she should. She will not *stop* growing; you will still see increases in weight and height, but she will slow up so that other children, growing more and faster, overtake her. On a growth chart the child's personal line might flatten so much that the curves beneath hers—curves which are right for naturally smaller children—cross hers in their upward paths.

Research has shown that if starvation, illness or emotional neglect are short-lived, even if they are acute, their effect on growth is temporary. As soon as conditions improve, the child grows extra-fast. A baby, born weighing only 5½ lb. because she was inadequately nourished for the last few weeks in the womb, for example, may gain almost twice as much weight each week as is expected and will go on gaining very fast until she has reached the weight she would have been if her pre-birth diet had been adequate. But she does not go on growing at that rate. If her birthweight put her around the third centile when she was genetically programmed to be a fiftieth centile baby, the rapid gain will continue until her weight curve reaches the fiftieth centile curve. Then it will slow down until she is gaining the amount which keeps her upward curve at that level.

Longer-term starvation or deprivation is a different matter. If a child's growth is slowed down for a long time, so that for months her personal curve is much flatter than the normal growth curves, a change in circumstances may indeed enable her to start a period of "catch-up growth" but it may be too late for her to catch up to her ideal and intended size. She grows at least as fast as other children, maybe faster, but the field has left her behind; her new gains are being built on to such a reduced starting point that she will always be rather small.

If your child *loses* a lot of weight, perhaps due to an acute illness coupled with pining for you from a hospital bed, you can confidently assume that "catch-up growth" will start as soon as she is home and happy and that it will put her back on track. All that her chart will show is a dip in the weight line. But if your child fails to grow and thrive over a period of months, it is important that your doctor investigate possible reasons such as malabsorption syndromes. The longer she continues to grow very slowly, the less likely it is that her growth will eventually catch itself up.

Although failure to thrive, or deliberate self-starvation (*see* **Eating Disorders**) show themselves first in failure of *weight* gain (or major and long-continued weight loss), less visible effects on *height* may be even more serious. Bodies which are short of nourishment use whatever is available to them for immediate energy (*see* **Eating**/First principles). Children grow only when there are nutrients to spare from the immediate business of staying alive. This is why no growing child, however fat, should ever be put on a diet designed to make her lose weight, but only on one which will hold her rate of weight gain down while increasing height makes her a taller, slimmer child.

Children who are "too small"

Parents sometimes become concerned about a child's height when they first see her stand beside other toddlers, or when she enters a new school class and finds herself the smallest, or when a younger brother or sister overtakes her in height. Ask yourself the question "Too small for whom?"

There is nothing wrong with being small if small is what she is meant to be. *Somebody* has to be the smallest in any group and greater size is no indication of greater health or stamina.

If she is, and always has been, healthy, she is probably a small child of small parents. Even if you have never charted her growth, you can use the centile charts to check on this, by comparing her centile position, now, with what is called a "sex-adjusted parental height":

Measure each other carefully, add your two heights together, add 4 in. if the child is a boy or subtract 4 in. for a girl and divide the resulting figure by two. If you now enter that combined height at the nineteen year point on the height chart for the child's sex, you will probably find that it falls on, or very nearly on, the same centile curve as the child's height. In other words, you will find that if, at nine years, she is of a height which puts her just below the tenth centile, the two of you together add up to "tenth-centile parents."

● That sex-adjusted parental height is also a reasonably good predictor of the child's eventual adult height.

If that sex-adjusted parental height lies on a much higher centile than hers then you are right in thinking that she is unexpectedly small. Is she growing at a normal *rate*, but doing so from a much reduced starting point caused by earlier illness or trauma? Or was her growth normal earlier on but is it now proceeding very slowly? This is a question which, failing obvious signs of illness or despair, can only be answered by growth records. If you have been keeping them, you will be able to see whether a normal upward curve has recently flattened off or whether a curve very low down the graph is proceeding normally. If you have kept no records and you take the child to a doctor because you are worried about her smallness, he will be able to tell you little until he himself has recorded all your present heights and her height gains over several months.

If a doctor finds that although your child is small, her growth rate is normal, there will be little he can do apart from reassuring you and advising on any social problems arising. Medical science cannot improve on a normal *rate* of growth. Whatever delayed her growth earlier in her life is over now.

If a doctor finds that your small child is growing very slowly or not at all, investigations may be appropriate and treatment may be possible. Apart from obvious illnesses and upsets, there are a few conditions (such as Turner's syndrome and certain thyroid deficiencies) which can interfere with growth for a long period before they produce other noticeable symptoms.

Children who, for whatever reason, lack naturally produced growth hormone, can now be given it artificially. Growth which is restarted in this way may never make up for the growing time the child has lost, but may be sufficient to turn an abnormally small person into a normal one who is not tall.

Small children
with delayed
puberty

Some children are larger than others and some children reach puberty (and therefore start their growth spurt) earlier than others. The child who is both comparatively small *and* has a comparatively late puberty may become very small indeed compared to others, and at just the time in life when comparisons with others become agonizingly important (*see* **Adolescence**/Puberty).

A girl may find herself not only yearning for the bras and tampons which signal her friends' maturity, but also shut out of their fashions and pursuits. At fourteen she may be the size and shape of most ten-year-olds. She may have to buy most of her clothes from children's shops and be bitterly aware that she looks absurd in make-up or the latest hairstyle. Because she looks like a child the adult world will tend to treat her as a child; her friends can sneak into adult movies, discos or bars; when she tries to join them she is stopped.

A boy of similar age may be equally distressed, especially if his is a social group which categorizes people by their strength, their physical toughness and their sports prowess.

Sometimes children in this situation are rejected by their peers. More often they themselves provoke dislike by trying to compensate for feelings of bodily inadequacy with self-assertive aggression. Where a child continues to mingle happily with the group it may be because other girls or boys treat the still childish one as something of a mascot. It is more comfortable to be a mascot than to be rejected, but it is important that the child be helped to see her/himself as a full person-among-young-persons rather than as a junior who is grateful for patronage.

Parents and teachers can often help a child in this situation by encouraging abilities and accomplishments which are respected by the peer group but in which small size is no disadvantage. It is no use encouraging that small teenager to improve his drawing and painting. His group will not join the art master in giving him credit. He needs something which they would all like to do well. One such boy returned to school one autumn to find himself the very last child-sized fellow in the class. He suffered on the playing fields, and provoked suffering in the locker rooms, until he was invited by the athletic director to try out for the newly formed rowing club. He became the boat's coxswain and was happy to relinquish the honor three years later when he was too big and heavy for the job. A girl in a similar situation found her own solution. She got through what might have been a sad two years on the strength of a talent for guitar-playing. She put it like this: "I felt a fool dancing at parties; like a kid at big sister's birthday party. I nearly stopped going, but someone's record player broke and somebody said I could play and I did. I don't feel a fool playing for them to sing. . . ." Folk-singing "caught on" in her group and she became a popular leader while she did her growing.

For many such children there will be no magic solutions, but all will fare better if adults grant them the maturity they feel rather than treating them as the children they still appear to be.

Ultimately, of course, small children with delayed puberty do have to accept their own biological clocks and wait for the growth spurt and the secondary sexual characteristics for which they long. Most can be helped to do so if they are assured that *they are going to grow*.

Once again, a personal record on a centile chart can be tremendously useful. The child can be shown his or her personal line on the graph and can be shown what happens to that line (or the centile lines on either side of it) when the adolescent growth spurt begins. If he or she can see that growth has always followed that curve and therefore always will, that sharp and continuing rise will be comforting even if it is still in the future. Furthermore you can point out, from the graph, that a growth spurt which starts late also finishes late. If most of his friends are already enormous, their growth is slowing while his fastest rate is still to come. If most of her friends are menstruating, their fastest growth spurt is already over and she will catch up to at least some of them. If the child would like further reassurance, it may be worth checking on probable adult height by working out your sex-adjusted parental height (*see above*). If there is not enough reassurance to be derived from looking at a height chart, a doctor can arrange for more accurate predictions of eventual adult height, using X-rays of the hand bones. From these a growth specialist can relate a child's present height to his bone age (skeletal maturity) rather than to his chronological age. If his bones are "younger" than he is, there may be even more growth still to come.

What a doctor will not, and should not, do is to go along with any desperate requests to give the child "hormone treatment" to provoke an earlier puberty. The normal adolescent growth spurt adds a predetermined number of inches to every child's height. Therefore the child's adult height depends on the height to which those inches are added. If puberty were artificially induced in a girl who was 4 ft. 3 in. tall, she would finish her growth spurt at a lower height than would be the case if the spurt starts later on when she has reached 4 ft. 7 in.

Children who are "too tall" In most communities even exceptional tallness is admired throughout childhood and continues to be admired in adolescent boys and men. It is only girls and women who are often considered "too tall."

A girl with very tall parents may indeed grow up to be a tall woman. And why not? Ideally she should be able to live with, and enjoy, this image of herself from earliest childhood. If her tallness happens to be coupled with an early adolescent growth spurt, she may have an embarrassing couple of years when she towers over her peers of both sexes. Like the "too small" child she should be shown a centile chart and made to understand that her growth will slow as others speed up and they will therefore all end up in the same league. Real worry can again be allayed by X-ray studies. They may show a degree of skeletal maturity suggesting that she is further into the growth spurt than her age implies.

Occasionally a doctor may suggest hormonally inducing an early puberty so that the growth spurt builds on a lesser height. Think carefully about such treatment. An exceptionally tall girl may have problems with her self-image, but a girl who menstruates at nine years may have problems, too.

Gum boils *see* **Teeth**/Some dental emergencies.

Habits

Habits are repetitive activities which start because they are useful or rewarding to the individual but which become semi-automatic. We all have habits; indeed most people get through the most tediously repetitive activities of daily life by carrying them out habitually. If you always put on your clothes in the same order, you never have to think about which garment to put on first; your mind is free for other matters or for drifting and dreaming.

Although most habits are harmless and some are actually useful, their very repetitiveness means that they can irritate other people and thus be a source of social stress. When a relationship begins to break down, it is often the harmless but hateful minutiae, like leaving the caps off toothpaste tubes, which become the focus for discord.

Some people are more "creatures of habit" than others. People whose calm and efficiency depends on being able to do everything in exactly the usual way and at exactly the usual time may find it difficult to adapt flexibly to unusual circumstances. If your morning's work is ruined because you could not have your habitual seat on the commuter train, rigidity may be making you rather vulnerable to stress.

Many people confuse the term "habit" with "addiction" (not least because the words are interchanged in the drug underworld of fiction), but there are some important differences. In a true addiction—whether to drugs, to gambling or to a high-risk sport like skiing—the individual develops "tolerance" to his chosen stimulus so that the dose of heroin, size of stake or steepness of mountain which satisfies him today will not do so tomorrow. He will have to seek more stimulation for the same thrill. This is quite different from an ordinary habit in which there is no conscious thrill, the original pleasure or benefit having been long buried. A true addict is probably also compulsive. Not only must he gamble for higher and higher stakes when he gambles, he cannot resist gambling even though the habit has taken his house and his car, and threatens his job and his marriage.

Almost every child or adolescent will develop "bad habits" from time to time. When you find yourself worrying over one, it can be helpful to put aside your personal irritation and ask yourself exactly what place the repetitive behavior is playing in her life and just exactly why you find it worrying. For example:

☐ Might the habit do her actual physical harm?
☐ Does it suggest to you (or to others) that she is anxious or "neurotic"?
☐ Is the habitual activity taking over her life, squashing out others?
☐ Does she herself long to give it up but find doing so impossible?
☐ Is the habit harmless to her but absolutely infuriating to you or other people?

Sometimes asking yourself that kind of question will put your worry into perspective and allow you to stop nagging the child about it. Sometimes it will show you that you do indeed have cause for concern, but about the child's life and happiness rather than specifically about her "bad habits."

Comfort habits

Thumb/finger sucking

Very young babies. Some babies are known to suck their thumbs in the womb and they go on being able to do so from birth. Others take weeks to "find" their thumbs or fingers, although they suck eagerly if helped or offered someone else's. This kind of sucking is part of an infant's exploration and learning (*see* **Play**) as well as an obviously enjoyable sensual experience and pastime. It is truly sad to discourage it.

● If you still wish she would not do it, remember that physiotherapists dealing with paralyzed babies take pains to *help* them suck their thumbs lest their disability deprive them of this important stage.

Older babies. Many (perhaps most) babies go on sucking their thumbs or fingers but gradually show that the sucking has become a relaxer and comforter rather than a pure pleasure. Unless the sucking takes almost all her waking time (*see below*), it remains a positive benefit. All other forms of comfort (your arms, the pacifier you may or may not offer, her bottle or the breast) are under someone else's control so that she can never be sure of getting them when she needs them. But her own precious thumb is hers and always available. She will probably suck it whenever she is tired, uncertain or shy. It helps her to be confident. It may enable her to let you leave her at sleep-times and to tolerate being spoken to by a stranger.

Children. Many babies give up thumb sucking spontaneously during the second year. Although parents often believe that a child would not have gone on thumb sucking if she had been allowed to go on sucking a bottle, many in fact give up both kinds of sucking at about the same time as if they had simply outgrown the need or the satisfaction.

If your child does not give it up of her own accord, don't try to make her. Nothing you can do (within the bounds of humanity) will "break the habit"; trying will cause endless friction between you and the thumb sucking will do no harm anyway. You do not have to worry lest it damage the position of her teeth until she is at least six years old (*see* **Teeth**). Even then a private thumb-sucking session when she is settling down to sleep is neither harmful nor anyone's business but her own.

Cuddlies: (transitional comfort objects)

Somewhere around his first birthday your child may adopt an old diaper, scarf or crib blanket, a teddy bear or one of his father's ties. Psychoanalysts call these beloved objects "transitional comfort objects" because children seem to use them to stand in for absent mothers as a sort of talisman of security, safety and affection.

If your child uses a cuddly, it will probably be his most emotionally important possession, the one object you must not lose, leave behind or ever, *ever* throw away. He may simply hold and finger it; he may wind it around his hand while he sucks his thumb, or he may use it in all kinds of elaborate ways with, or without, other comfort habits. Whatever he does with it, he will probably need it whenever he is to go to sleep, whenever you leave him, whenever he is overtired, upset or hurt and, above all, at any time when he is under stress and cannot have you. It must therefore go with him to the sitter or to the hospital.

Most authorities believe that cuddlies are beneficial to a young child. None believe that their use is a sign of insecurity or any other difficulty.

• The grubby look and strange smell of his cuddly is part of its benevolent nature to your child. However ashamed you may be of it, don't wash it more often than you can possibly help.

• The accidental loss of a cuddly can traumatize a whole family for weeks. As soon as your child adopts one, see whether you can find or buy another—or even two more—or, if it is a unique shawl or blanket, cut it in half before he has really learned its details and keep the other half against disaster. A new one will not smell right but is better than nothing.

Other comfort habits   Babies find a variety of rhythmical physical activities pleasing and relaxing from the early months of life. Some learn to rock themselves (and their cribs!) on hands and knees; some roll their heads from side to side; a few pull their ears or rhythmically thrust their tongues in and out. Some babies combine a habit of this kind with thumb sucking and/or using a cuddly so that the whole complex of behavior becomes their own personal comfort ritual.

If your child only falls back on these repetitive physical activities when he has got nothing else to do—as when you leave him for the night before he is sleepy, or refuse to get him up from a nap—they, like sucking, can be seen as positive behaviors and the habit will almost certainly cease when he finds other ways to entertain himself. But habits of this kind *can* suggest stress or emotional disturbance, and *can* harm the child in the sense of taking his time, energy and attention from other, more varied experiences. You may want to think rather hard about him, his relationship with you and the general satisfactions of his life if:

He prefers comfort habits to people. If he prefers to rock in a corner by himself rather than play with you, has something gone wrong between you? If he frequently needs comfort, why is that?

He will not interrupt the habit activity to respond to you. Occasionally a child uses a habit like rocking to block out the outside world, almost as a kind of self-hypnosis. Why does he need to block it out?

He often breaks off to indulge his habit in the middle of other activities. Any child can take a quick thumb-sucking, hair-twiddling rest in the middle of a game, but if you often look up to find that he has stopped crawling around with his toys and is rocking instead, then the real world is not holding his attention. He may be overwhelmed with anxiety or anger which only his comfort habit can make tolerable.

His particular habit actually causes (must cause) physical pain. The most common such habit is head-banging, in which the child typically bangs his head rhythmically against the end of his crib as he rocks on hands and knees, or against a wall or piece of furniture as he sits and sways. Some head-bangers cause bruises and grazes on their heads and appear frustrated when padding the end of the crib makes it impossible for them to actually hurt themselves.

Your child might be head-banging because he is frustrated, bored and lonely. Masses of extra loving attention and interesting play, together with a drastic reduction of the time he is expected to spend alone in his crib, may end the habit immediately. If it does not, seek professional advice quickly as habits tend to strengthen with use.

Other common and less common habits

Dirt-eating
(pica)

All exploring crawlers and toddlers occasionally put a lump of mud, piece of coal or other unsuitable object in their mouths. A very few children, usually between about two and four years, develop an actual appetite for the inedible. The habit is commoner among emotionally disturbed or mentally handicapped children than among healthy ones, although it can be related to anemia in an otherwise healthy child. If your child appears to seek out feces, earth, sticks and other "dirty" substances to eat, seek medical advice. In the meantime, guard him carefully against the high risk that he will poison himself (*see* **Safety**/In the home).

● Many people believe that pica is caused by a child having worms. This is untrue, although the child with pica is more likely than other children to become infested.

Nail-biting

Nail-biting is almost unknown in babies but may begin in a pre-school child and is extremely common in schoolchildren. It sometimes starts in direct imitation of another child, but it usually begins by chance when a long nail tempts her and she then finds biting it enjoyable.

Nail-biting is so common that it is difficult to classify it as a sign of anxiety. But the true nail-biter gives herself so much pain—not only at the time but afterwards when she must use a finger whose quick is exposed —that it is equally hard to regard it as normal. Certainly most children who bite their nails do so when they are under stress—during a difficult lesson or while waiting for an activity which makes them nervous—and can often let their nails grow when they are happy and relaxed.

Neither scolding, punishment nor supposedly "helpful" actions like painting bitter-tasting substances on the nails will help. They will only make an anxious child more anxious, and defiant as well. Appeals to vanity, backed by clear nail varnish, may help a little, but the habit will probably only cease when she is more relaxed and at ease with herself. Even then it may return whenever she feels insecure.

Nose-picking

All children pick their noses from time to time *and* eat the product. Nothing you can do will stop your child altogether because if a dried bit of mucus is tickling the inside of his nostril or obstructing his breathing, his hand will go to it quite unconsciously.

If you are tactful, you may be able to teach him *not to do it in public.* It is, after all, a question of manners rather than morals and "I don't like to see you picking your nose" is far more likely to get a three-year-old's cooperation than "you are not to pick your nose." Whose nose is it anyway?

Some children (perhaps especially those who have been nagged about it) pick their noses as a nervous habit rather than just as a quick way to get comfortable. Constant picking eventually makes scabs and scabs make the picking ever more irresistible. Looking despairingly at your six-year-old's nose, you may wonder how it can ever heal. Amazingly, it will.

You can help to prevent scabs from forming, and help them heal, by keeping the child's nails short. But don't cut his nails as a punishment or you will simply increase the emotion attached to the nose-picking business. Let him assume that you are simply cutting his nails because they need cutting (perhaps because cleaning them is otherwise so tiresome for him). Make no connection between nails and nose.

An older child may be self-conscious about visible scabs and actually enlist your help in stopping this habit. If so, as well as short nails, you can offer some Vaseline which will keep the scabbed area soft and therefore less irritating/tempting. The child may like to keep his own pot of Vaseline beside his bed to put on at night when nose-picking is most tempting.

Rituals and compulsions   Rituals serve us all as magical insurance policies against some undefined danger or ill fortune. We all use at least a few. Some people feel uncomfortable if they walk under a ladder and it is not the practical possibility of a dropped can of paint which makes them take trouble to go around. Many throw some spilled salt over a shoulder even in the most formal company and not really because they believe it will foil the devil by stinging his eyes. Almost all of us have certain ritualized actions—like kissing partners before we leave for work or looking into our children's rooms just before we go to bed—which we carry out simply because we feel uncomfortable if we do not.

Many children, especially between the ages of about seven and ten, develop rituals which are of this kind, even though they may seem especially conspicuous and silly to adults. Yours may avoid the cracks in the pavement, touch every railing, bang the other elbow if one gets knocked or chew his food a certain number of times. . . .

Rituals of this kind can be highly irritating, especially if they make a child who is already at "the dawdling stage" slower than ever to finish his meal or get ready for school. But they are not harmful nor do they suggest unusual anxiety *unless they appear to be taking over the child's life*. If you are worried, quell your irritation for a few days and watch:

Does he just run along the pavement, cracks and all, if he is in a big hurry, or will he miss the bus rather than tread on a crack?

Does he chew each mouthful in a ritualized way even if he is involved in conversation with friends or bolting a hamburger before the movie?

If his rituals are so necessary to him that he lets them get in his way, they may be turning into compulsions.

A child with a compulsion really *has* to go through his self-imposed ritual, whatever it may cost him in missed buses or ridicule. It is not just that he feels safer passing those railings if he touches each one, but that he will walk the long way around *in order to touch them*.

Compulsions are common, too, but a little more worrying than ordinary rituals, both because they may actually alter the child's life and take up time and energy better spent on other things, and because they suggest that he does not feel sufficiently in control of himself and his own life to be able to manage without these spurious external "controls." A child with a compulsion to wash his hands whenever they might be dirty, and who therefore cannot bear to play in the country where there is no washbasin to which he can keep returning, is an extreme but not uncommon example. Such a child may be having trouble with feelings of "dirtiness" perhaps to do with thoughts or dreams which shock him or with masturbation of which he is ashamed (*see below*).

If your child has a compulsion of this kind, it is often helpful to find an opportunity to talk to him, in general rather than embarrassingly personal terms, about whatever aspect of himself you think is worrying him. You might, for example, be able to introduce the subject by talking about the different ways we use the word "dirt" and the fact that earth, paint and so forth are not really "dirty" at all. You can then move on to the other meanings: the "dirty thoughts" or actions, and muse with him about the fact that to call them "dirty" is really absurd since every boy in the world shares them. . . .

Whether you can find a way to talk usefully or not, it is important to find *some* way to help such a child accept himself in a more relaxed way. If he continues for long with a compulsion like washing, he will very quickly be labelled "odd" by his peers; he may abandon games and activities which prevent him from washing so that he becomes known as the "sissy" who will not roughhouse or go fishing, and, of course, as his compulsion affects other people's view of him, their view will affect his image of himself. Your child guidance clinic may be able to help him and help you to do so.

Tics and other habit spasms

Tics are among the most irritating but least worrying of childish habits. The tic may be any repetitive gesture such as tossing the head, sniffing, rubbing a particular place on the face, or touching the nose or an ear. Other types include a variety of grimaces, blinking, screwing up the eyes and so forth.

Most tics—like other habits—start with a real purpose. The head tossing may have been effective in getting her bangs out of her eyes; the sniffing may have been part of long-continued congestion. But the habit does not stop when the hair is cut or the congestion cured, and it does not stop because you nag about it, either.

If you can manage not to make the child feel permanently "got at" and self-conscious about it, the tic will fade out on its own, but it may be replaced by some other, equally annoying, habit. Children who are liable to tics and habit spasms often have one after another and may be children who are under some kind of stress or strain. If the current habit fades during a relaxed family vacation and returns with the new school term, a visit to a separated parent or the approach of an examination, you can be fairly sure this is the case. A complete "cure" will then depend on either reducing the stress or increasing the child's ability to cope with it.

Masturbation

Small babies touch their genitals because they are there. Baby boys do so more than baby girls because there is more to get hold of. Older babies, young children, older children, adolescents and adults deliberately stimulate their genitals (masturbate) because it is exciting and enjoyable. Although most parents probably do now accept that masturbation is both universal and harmless, many still find it extraordinarily difficult to tolerate in very small children whom they would prefer to think of as innocent of sexual feelings.

Most childhood masturbation is not a "habit" but a conscious seeking for a particular kind of pleasure. Nobody has the right to try to deprive him or her of that pleasure but equally no child has the right acutely to embarrass Great Aunt Sophie. If you are clever, most masturbation can be handled as a matter of manners rather than morals.

Babies and touching

If you do not like your infant fingering himself in public, don't take his diapers off. If he is naked on the beach and discovers his penis, he can be easily distracted (*not* reproved) as long as you interrupt before he has actually started deliberately stimulating himself.

Babies and masturbation

At somewhere between a few months and one-and-a-half years, he will discover that rubbing his genitals against something hard (perhaps against the crib bars while he rocks backwards and forwards), or rubbing himself with his hand, is exciting. Some babies become abstracted, turn red in the face, pant and appear to be working themselves up to a climax. Left to themselves they eventually relax and go to sleep. If he is on his own (or was until you came in) leave him to it. Who is he harming? If you are on a crowded bus and you can't stand it, distract him as soon as he begins, perhaps using words like "not now darling."

Toddlers, pre-school children and masturbation

A toddler who has not been made to feel ashamed and furtive about masturbation will often confide to you that "I like doing that; it feels nice." This is your opportunity. Acknowledge that it does indeed feel nice to everybody, but point out that most people like to keep their genitals private from all but very close people and that playing with them is something for him to do when he is by himself. You may find the phrase "private parts" a useful one. Try to keep the whole thing on a par with what you teach him about picking his nose.

You are trying to teach him to be discreet but not to feel furtive. It follows, therefore, that if you go into his room and find him masturbating, you should ignore it. If you react with shock, even amused shock, you are contradicting that message. After all he *was* being discreet until you invaded his privacy.

● Some children discover the pleasures of masturbation much earlier than others and do it more often, or more often to your knowledge. This does *not mean that the child is "oversexed"; it does not mean that he will start other sexual interests or activities early; it does not mean that he needs circumcision/she has worms.*

Older children and masturbation

However hard you have tried not to make masturbation into a furtive activity, your child will certainly have picked up strong messages about your disapproval of it when you are around by the time he reaches school age. *Public* masturbation after, say, four or five, may well be a sign of emotional insecurity/disturbance.

Compulsive masturbation

In which the masturbation *has* become either a habit of which the child is not aware *or* a compulsion over which he has no control may suggest:

That a boy is unconsciously worried lest he lose his precious penis. Such a child will clutch himself defensively whenever he is upset, particularly if an adult is scolding him. He may sit through a scary television program stroking himself for reassurance. He may or may not have been told that mommy will "cut that off if you don't leave it alone"; equally he may or may not have been horrified to discover that there are children (girls!) without penises, and therefore worked out for himself the possibility of losing his own. Directly assure him that his equipment is his own forever, then a gentle reminder: "You don't have to hold onto it, love" from time to time may help him to be aware of the habit and to drop it.

That he is out to shock. A child who masturbates openly, and increases his tempo when he sees you have noticed, is often seriously angry with you. On an unconscious level he is feeling that you are an enemy, a killer of his pleasure. He flaunts the one pleasure which you cannot take away and which he knows you most dislike.

That the pleasure and relaxation he can get from masturbation has become compulsive because other aspects of his life are intolerable to him. Like a true addict, he must masturbate more and more, and by doing so he increasingly cuts himself off from alternative pleasures.

Under circumstances like these it is almost always best to seek professional help quickly. Public masturbation *is* taboo in our society and a child who breaks that taboo will be made to suffer for it. Don't tell him that you are taking him to see a doctor who will stop him from playing with himself. Tell him something to the effect that you think he is unhappy and worried, and that the two of you together are going to talk to someone who is very good at sorting out children's worries.

Habits which easily lead to addiction

If your child or adolescent *habitually* smokes, drinks alcohol, sniffs certain solvents or glues, or takes mind-affecting drugs, there is a real chance that she will become addicted. While it is important that parents *and children* understand and recognize the risk—because avoiding addiction is infinitely easier than shedding it—it is also important that parents do not overreact to casual social experimentation with potentially addictive substances. A cigarette behind the bleachers is more likely to turn your child green than turn her into an addict, while getting drunk at a party may turn her off alcohol for months.

The easiest way to understand why habits of this kind are more likely than habits like nail-biting or facial tics to turn into addictions is to compare them in terms of what they mean to the individual:

Addictive habits are pleasurable. The child who bites her nails gets no real pleasure at the time and the results are painful. The child who drinks alcohol, on the other hand, gets a feeling of relaxed lack of inhibition; of being more confident, wittier and generally "heightened." The fact that she may be making an idiot of herself is irrelevant. She *feels* good.

Next time this child goes to bite her nails she probably does so unconsciously and later wishes she had not. But the next time she has a drink she consciously looks forward to those pleasant feelings.

Addictive habits are usually sociable. Biting one's nails is a solitary pastime and one which peers are most unlikely to admire. Drinking alcohol or smoking pot, on the other hand, is usually part of in-group social life and, furthermore, for the child or young adolescent it usually stands as proof of readiness to join the gang.

Addictive habits directly affect body chemistry and the body may develop tolerance. Nail-biting affects fingers but it does not affect body chemistry, so the body does not come to "look forward" to the next nibble. Alcohol and other drugs do have direct physical effects and the body may become accustomed to one level of intake so that it ceases to react so markedly. At this point some tolerance has been established and, if the child is addicted to the sensations she used to get from two drinks or one pill, she is likely now to want four drinks or two pills. The addictive habits, therefore, have a built-in tendency to escalate.

The compulsion to go on with addictive habits may be increased by withdrawal symptoms. Nail-biting may be a compulsion in the sense that the child cannot stop herself from doing it even if bleeding fingertips are ruining her piano-playing and/or making her feel hideous. But at least if she manages to resist the compulsion, her body will not urge her to give in. If she is truly addicted to certain drugs, her compulsion to go on taking them may be very strongly reinforced by the fact that when she resists, or cannot get hold of them, she experiences extremely unpleasant symptoms from a body which can no longer function normally without them.

Withdrawal symptoms are usually associated in people's minds with lurid pictures of sweating, shaking, vomiting heroin addicts. In fact, many people who do not consider themselves "addicts" at all suffer from withdrawal symptoms if they run out of cigarettes in the middle of the night or cannot have their usual ration of strong coffee.

Minimizing the chances of your child developing a dangerous addiction

Nobody really knows why some children and adolescents develop addictions while others, exposed to the same subculture, do not. It does seem clear, however, that the happier your child is with herself and her growing up, the less risk there is. It is children with the most desperate need to change themselves, or prop themselves up, who seem most likely to adopt a chemical support system which may eventually destroy them. As well as taking any marked signs of insecurity, anxiety and distress in your child seriously, you may like to consider some of the following suggestions culled from parents who have, and have not, successfully steered their families around this particular hazard:

Give every child realistic information. That means ensuring that growing children understand both the compulsive nature of habits like drug-taking *and* their destructive effects. But it also means discussing with them the (sad) fact that almost everybody in our society is at least mildly addicted to something which is at least a little damaging to their health. Your child is more likely to take seriously your diatribe against heroin if you are willing to acknowledge that you cannot start the day without coffee. And she is more likely to avoid starting to smoke cigarettes herself if you can admit that you are an addict and wish that you were not than if you try to dismiss all anti-smoking propaganda as nonsense.

Try not to force your child to choose between you and her peer group. If you deeply disapprove of your child's friends and try to emphasize the distinction between her "nice" family and her chosen group, you will not persuade her to give up that group but you may edge her into a position where she keeps her peer-group activities secret from you (*see* **Adolescence**/Friends versus family). If secrets and falsehoods then come to light and there are rows, you will be inviting greater and greater rebellion; the child who might have had one drink in the bar with the others (instead of none) and come home at midnight (instead of 10 p.m.) now determinedly shocks you by coming home drunk at 3 a.m. Staying on her side and understanding that her friends are important to her gives you the best chance of being a moderating influence if one should be necessary. And it may be. Many youngsters drink or take drugs first to be "one of the gang." She may need help in finding ways of keeping her end up in such a group without getting into the habit of relying on alcohol, or she may even need help one day in extricating herself from a group whose habits she knows to be risky. If you are against her and them, yours will not be help she can accept.

Don't overreact to experiments. She may have to try the glamorous and grown-up habits she sees all around her. A true shock reaction from you is liable to hand her an irresistible weapon in any rebellion which is coming.

Differentiate honestly between types of addiction. Although most parents would prefer their children to grow up as non-smokers and only occasional social drinkers, many find that throwing too much weight against these "socially accepted" addictions lessens the force they can throw against the ones which matter even more—such as the use of hard drugs. One put it like this:

"I tell them they'd be fools to start smoking; filthy, expensive and bad for them. I tell them that their own minds and bodies can give them all the kicks they need without messing themselves up with alcohol all the time. I tell them that marijuana is illegal and I won't have it in the house whoever brings it; that I've never smoked it myself and don't want to. Then I tell them that hallucinatory drugs like LSD, and hard ones like heroin, are killers; that if they want to bump themselves off there are easier ways and that I will do *anything*, including moving to another country or getting help from the authorities, to prevent them even trying them out."

Halitosis *see* **Teeth**/Looking after teeth; Some dental problems of adolescence.
Hay fever *see* **Allergy**.

Headaches *see also* **Migraine**; **Pain and Pain Control**; **Hospital**/Procedures: Lumbar puncture

The covering of the brain itself (the meninges), the inside of the skull, the spaces within the facial bones (the sinuses), the scalp and the neck are all richly supplied with nerves and with blood vessels. Almost any stimulus to those nerves may cause pain fibers to react and send "messages" to the brain which may construe them as the pain we call headache. Many authorities believe that this kind of stimulation is going on all the time but being prevented, most of the time, from reaching conscious pain levels by the brain's own pain-control mechanisms (see **Pain and Pain Control**). It is when the control mechanisms are operating least effectively that headaches are most likely to be experienced. This does not, of course, mean that headaches are not real: the pain is certainly real and often distressing. But it does mean that headaches very seldom signal real bodily disease or damage, but are usually an overreaction by the brain to trivial stimuli. Long-continued muscular tension in the upper shoulders and neck, for example, can set up pressures which are perceived as head pain. Changes in blood pressure, dilating or restricting those large arteries, can be felt as painful. Overstimulation of the optic and auditory nerves can produce a painful spin-off effect on other nerves, while pressure changes within even healthy sinuses (see **Colds**/Sinuses and sinusitis) can produce headache.

The efficiency of the brain's own pain-control mechanisms and therefore the readiness of the brain to perceive pain are, as we have seen, associated not only with the body's general physical condition but also with mood. This seems to be peculiarly so in the case of head pain. A child is most likely to experience a headache when she is tired/stressed/anxious. The child who has very frequent headaches, or a low-level headache which seems to last for days at a time, is usually one who is depressed (see **Depression**).

Most headaches, then, are of no physical significance whatsoever, but may be of some emotional significance. Head pain which is noticed by a child who is already fed up or miserable is liable to lower her mood still further and thus prolong itself. There is, therefore, an argument for interrupting the pain with simple painkillers. This can give her mood a chance to lift so that she is protected against the return of pain when the drug wears off. On the other hand, repeated doses for a continuing headache are seldom sensible. If the headache will not lift, attention needs to be paid to the child's general mood and state. If, for example, she feels the headache as part of Monday-morning-school-miseries, a single dose of analgesic may help her get to school and through the bad patch. But if the headache recurs as part of global tension about school, it is not the pain that needs attention but the tension (see **School**/Problems over going to school).

Of course, not every headache is an overreaction to unimportant stimuli: there are serious illnesses of which headache is a symptom, while headache forms part of the picture in many minor infections. The following notes are intended to help you in your thinking about your child's headaches and to sort out the few which may signal a need for medical attention from the rest.

Headaches in babies and toddlers   These are unusual, partly because the very young either cannot communicate or cannot distinguish, the source of their pain, but also partly because they are less prone to perceiving head pain.

If a baby seems to have a headache consult a doctor. If the pain really is a headache, a cause needs to be sought; if in fact it is earache, treatment is urgent (see **Ears and Hearing**; **Ear Disorders and Deafness**/Ear disorders).

If a toddler or pre-school child has a headache, she may tell you that her eyes hurt or that her hair hurts. If the pain is sufficient to distract her from her normal activities—whether or not she has any other symptoms—consult your doctor.

Headache which is unusual for your particular child

Some people are far more headache-prone than others. A child who has rather frequent headaches will manage them and her life better if you do not overreact, but the child who suddenly produces a severe first headache, or a type of headache which surprises and frightens her, needs to be taken more seriously. If she has other symptoms you will probably be consulting your doctor anyway. If she has no other symptoms, try one period of quiet rest—lying down or sitting quietly, whichever she prefers—and then telephone your doctor for advice.

A child who is really distressed by head pain needs a doctor. The chances are against any serious cause for the pain, but she is entitled to authoritative reassurance, proper analgesia and a check-up to see whether, in fact, she is brewing an infection which is not yet producing other symptoms.

Headaches associated with menstruation

Hormonal changes and associated water retention towards the end of the menstrual cycle often lead to headaches. It is important that your daughter learn confidently to cope with her own feelings during these regularly recurring days, so if headaches are a regular feature, a consultation with her doctor is probably worthwhile. The point of the visit is not treatment for the headaches, but an opportunity for her to receive authoritative reassurance that all is well (*see* **Adolescence**/Menstruation: Menstrual difficulties).

*Headaches associated with head injury (see **Accidents**/ Head injuries)*

Any child may complain of headache after a bump on the head. Usually this is no more than the pain she feels from the actual bruise. Sometimes this trivial pain alarms her because it keeps reminding her of the fright the fall gave her. Reassurance and distraction will usually deal with the matter.

Severe headache, which prevents distraction and/or makes the child want to lie down, usually means that a medical check-up would be advisable.

Headache occurring an hour or more after the accident and after the child has gone back to her normal activities, requires medical attention because of the remote possibility that the bump has led to bleeding and pressure inside the skull.

Recurring headaches, after a head injury which was severe enough to require medical attention, should be discussed with the doctor who attended to her. Headaches of this type are often more emotional than physical in origin but can delay full recovery after a concussion.

Headaches associated with other symptoms

Many infectious diseases and viral illnesses have headache as one early symptom. If your child has a headache for which you cannot account and which you feel is unusual for her and therefore worrying, take her temperature (*see* **Nursing**/Fever). You will probably find that it is raised. The mild dehydration which often accompanies a rising fever can affect the blood vessels of the head and cause the headache. Some illnesses are famous for their continued "headachyness" (*see* **Influenza**), while some ordinary head colds lead to secondary inflammation of the sinuses, which causes its own unpleasant kind of headache (*see* **Colds**/Sinusitis). In cases of this kind, it is the general picture which is of interest rather than the headache itself.

Panic-stations headaches

If you should find yourself really worried by your child's headache, it will probably be the possibility of either meningitis or a brain tumor which is panicking you. While both these conditions do occur, it is important to remember (even at 3 a.m.!) that they are exceedingly rare and that if either does occur the child will not only have a bad headache, she will also be obviously ill. Of course, if you are worried that is reason enough to seek your doctor's help, but in the meantime the following notes may help.

Headache is not the only symptom of meningitis (*see* **Meningitis and Encephalitis**). Indeed, in the very young children who are most prone to these illnesses, headache may not even be the most notable feature. A child of any age who has meningitis will almost certainly also show some of the following signs:

☐ Unusual mood or behavior, ranging from sudden acute irritability and tearfulness to marked sleepiness and lethargy. Babies will often seem withdrawn, refusing to make eye contact with their mothers, lying gazing into space or suddenly fretfully crying.
☐ Vomiting, often sudden and not preceded by nausea.
☐ Dislike of light such that she turns away if you switch on a light, seeks a dark place to lie down or buries her head under the bedclothes.
☐ Fever—although this is often not nearly as high as people expect.
☐ Stiff neck which prevents her from putting her chin on her chest while sitting up.

The headache of a brain tumor develops as pressure builds up so that a sudden and severe headache is most unlikely to be due to a tumor. The child who really does have a brain tumor will probably gradually develop a tendency to experience head pain when she first gets moving in the morning and when she changes position or gets up suddenly after a long period of sitting still. If you should see such a pattern developing in your child, so that she complains of headache each day for several days, she should certainly see the doctor. The chances are still that the headache is of emotional origin (*see above*), but a tumor is certainly something for which your doctor will check before reassuring you both and turning his attention to whatever life stresses seem likely to be contributing to the chronic headache.

● If a child whose recurring headaches had been considered to be of emotional origin should develop an unsteady gait, or begin to use a limb awkwardly, seek medical advice immediately. These signs do suggest that there may be some untoward pressure on the brain.

Head-banging *see* **Habits**/Other comfort habits.
Head injuries *see* **Accidents.**
Hearing *see* **Ears and Hearing; Ear Disorders and Deafness**. *See also* **Language**/Three to six months: Watching out for deafness.
Heat stroke *see* **Accidents**/Sunburn and heat illness.

Height *see* **Growth**.
Hemolytic disease of the newborn *see* **Blood Groups**.
Hepatitis *see* **Jaundice**.

Hernia

A hernia (sometimes called a "rupture") is a protruding pouch of skin containing intestine which has passed through a gap in the muscular wall of the abdomen. There are two common kinds affecting babies and young children: an umbilical hernia in which the fault is close to the navel, and an inguinal hernia in the groin. In boys an inguinal hernia may involve the scrotum.

Umbilical hernias

In the fetus, the umbilical cord, with its blood vessels, comes through a gap in the abdominal muscles called the "umbilical ring." Sometimes after birth and separation of the cord stump, there is a delay in the closing of that umbilical ring in which case a portion of the intestine may bulge through.

These very common hernias, which are especially frequent among West Indian babies, vary in size and may balloon alarmingly when the baby cries, but they are harmless and self-righting. In the past, strapping was sometimes applied to hold the intestine back, but it is now thought that natural healing of the fault occurs more rapidly if it is left completely alone. The hernia will usually vanish by the time the child is two. If it does not, surgery will be considered, but is seldom required. These hernias are almost always gone by the fifth year.

● A prominent navel does not mean that a new baby has a hernia. His navel probably sticks out because he has not yet much fat covering his abdomen. By six months or so he will have acquired a layer of fat which will put his navel at the bottom of a valley rather than at the top of a mountain.

Inguinal hernias

Are less common than umbilical ones although still not unusual. They occur more often in boys than in girls. In a baby boy such a hernia may involve the scrotum and may sometimes be associated with an undescended testicle on that side (*see* **Undescended Testicle**).

During fetal development, the testicles move from inside the abdomen down an opening through the abdominal muscle wall called the inguinal canal. Usually this canal closes before birth but if it does not, a loop of intestine may later be pushed through the opening. At birth, even if the canal is open, there will seldom be any intestine in it and therefore there will be no hernia. Such a hernia can occur at any time while the inguinal canal remains open, but most usually appear in the first year of life. The swelling often vanishes when the child is lying down because in that position the loop of intestine slips back into the abdomen; if you are in doubt, consider the groin area when the child is in an upright position (*see* **Hospital**/Surgery).

Herpes simplex *see* **Cold Sores**.
Herpes zoster *see* **Chickenpox and Shingles**.
Hives *see* **Allergy**.

Hospital

If a child is hurt or ill or has some condition which needs investigation or surgical intervention, the drama surrounding those physical needs often masks all others. It is easy for frantic parents, as well as busy hospital staff, to forget that Johnny with appendicitis is still Johnny. The fact that he has a bellyache requiring expert attention does not stop him from being the child he has always been, requiring all the kinds of attention he always needs. The more parents can help the staff to deal with the person-who-is-Johnny, the more easily they will be able to cope with his body's crisis and the more "like himself" he will be when he comes home again.

If a hospital admission is planned in advance (perhaps for an elective operation like tonsillectomy (*see below*)), there is a great deal which parents can do to help it go smoothly. You may, for example, be able to choose among available hospitals and medical personnel, find out in detail what your child's life and treatment there will be like, and prepare him for it. If the admission is at short notice or as an emergency, this kind of advance planning is obviously impossible, but there will still be a great deal that you can do to minimize the child's distress.

Babies and small children in the hospital

Parents and other familiar and loved caretakers lend small children not only their security but also some part of their identity. At three months your baby literally will not know where she ends and you begin; at six months she will perceive herself-and-you as a unit and be unable to function as she usually does if she is deprived of your normal care and expected presence. At nine months she will know all too clearly and often protest if the space between you becomes too great. At eighteen months or two years she will be struggling to be a person in her own separate right, but able to maintain that vital effort only if she can voyage from a port of your making. At three or four she may be proud of her ability to manage herself in her own everyday world, yet still be thrown into incoherent panic if she must face the unfamiliar without your familiar support. She can cope with her usual routine (including, perhaps, going without you to a pre-school group and to friends' houses), but if she finds herself removed from everything and everybody she has ever known, *and* in a place which is strange and frightening, *and* faced with unpleasant, or even terrifying procedures at a time when she is in pain or feeling ill, she will be as panic-stricken as you might be if you were sent into space without warning or training.

It is hard for any adult to imagine the total dependence of babies and small children. Often those of use who are parents actually try not to imagine it, because being totally responsible for another human being's stability and happiness is a terrifyingly heavy responsibility, at the best of times. When circumstances make it impossible to protect a child from fear or pain, the burden can be almost intolerable because, if you let yourself realize her feelings, you will have to share them; to feel for her what she is feeling for herself. But if a child in the vulnerable age group must go into the hospital, the degree of her dependence has to be faced and met, just as it has to be met when parents are considering day care (*see* **Working Mothers**). *If it can possibly be managed, that child should have a parent or other familiar adult with her all the time she is in the hospital.* If she does, she will face all the strangers and the strangeness from a secure base and ride through actual discomforts better, too.

Rooming-in with your child in hospital

In Britain, the United States and other Western countries it is officially accepted that very young children do better in the hospital if they have a familiar adult with them to keep up their ordinary daily care/love/support while medical personnel deal with their physical condition. Unfortunately, official support does not mean that every consultant or head nurse approves of parents staying, nor does it mean that money has been made available for every children's unit to provide facilities for parents.

Your local hospital belongs to your community. It may be sensible to acquaint yourself with its policies and facilities before you need them. If one hospital restricts parental access to sick children, there may be another which does not. If you know which is which you may, even in an emergency, be able to pick the one that is better for you. It may be a good idea to make your position clear to your doctor, too. If he knows, from the time of your child's birth, that if she ever had to go into the hospital you would wish to go too, he can avoid, for example, referring you to a specialist who does not approve.

Within your community you may find:

A special parent-child unit with separate rooms or cubicles for each adult/child pair, plus varying extra facilities like kitchenettes and sitting rooms for the caring adults.

Wards adapted for parents and children, perhaps with some isolation cubicles equipped with adult beds as well as cribs, or with a few single rooms or side wards which are used in this way when necessary. Sometimes parents will be made very welcome in this kind of situation.

Ad hoc arrangements which usually reflect the enthusiasm of a particular nurse, or perhaps consultant, for parents staying if they wish, despite an absence of official money for facilities. There may be folding beds which can be put up beside the child's bed or even simply chaise longues and a welcome.

The trouble with ad hoc arrangements is that you do tend to get in the way of the staff. If, for example, there are no rest rooms for parents, you will have to use either those intended for the child patients or those intended for the staff. It is worth remembering that nurses who are prepared to let you stay under difficult circumstances of this kind must truly believe in your importance to your child so, even if they cannot make your stay at all comfortable, they will almost certainly ensure that it really does benefit her.

The role of a parent rooming with a child

The role the staff expect you to play will vary, not only from hospital to hospital, but from head nurse to head nurse and, of course, from child to child, too. The important thing is to *ask*, as soon after your arrival as possible, exactly what the staff would *like* you to do. If you can manage to have a conversation with the nurse in charge of the ward, you can make it clear that *you want only to help them to help your child*. You need, for example, to make it clear that you will not give the child sweets if you are told not to, give her the drink she is crying for during the hours before an operation when fluids must be banned, get her out of bed for a cuddle if you are told to keep her still and so on. You also have to make it clear (by your behavior more than words) that *you can stand what is to happen to her*. Nursing a child who is in pain from serious burns, for example, is harrowing enough for the nursing staff without having to cope with a parent who is continually in tears.

Once the staff accept that you are not going to behave in a way which makes things worse for the child (or for them), they will usually leave all her ordinary everyday care and entertainment to you, and confine themselves to actual nursing. You may like to bear in mind that this is something of a sacrifice for the staff because it means that you get the child's smiles, leaving them the tears. It often helps everyone if you can encourage your child to be friendly to the nurses.

Good children's nurses say that they learn a great deal from watching children with their parents in the hospital; you can probably learn a great deal from watching them with your child, too.

If the hospital will not let you stay

If the admission was planned in advance (say for a tonsillectomy), this should not arise. Make it clear to your doctor when the operation is first discussed that you will want to be with the child.

If your child is admitted to the hospital as an emergency, perhaps following a febrile convulsion (*see* **Convulsions, Seizures and "Fits"**) or an accident, you probably will not be able to choose where she is taken. But stay close. Nobody has the right to insist that you leave the side of a very sick or injured child at least until her condition is stable and doctors have talked to you about what they propose to do for her. If a nurse asks you to leave, just say politely that you prefer to stay "until we know more." (It is often a mistake to start off by saying that you are determined to remain indefinitely!) If you sit quietly by the bed or crib and talk sensibly to anyone who comes to examine the child, they are most unlikely to quarrel with you about leaving.

You may have to sit up on a hard chair all night, but by the next day the drama will be over; this is the time to discuss the doctors' plans for the child and your wish to stay. At the very least, they should be prepared to allow you the compromise of open access.

Open access to your child in the hospital

If a small child cannot have you with her all the time in the hospital, either because the hospital will not allow it or because you cannot manage it, open access is much better than nothing.

Taken literally, as it should be, the phrase means that you can spend as much time as you wish with your child and at whatever hours suit you. The only difference from rooming-in is that you do not actually live on the ward.

In some open-access wards, parents are positively encouraged to arrive in the morning before their children have breakfast and to stay until they are actually asleep at night. Although some small children will be appalled if they wake in the night in a shadowy ward, perhaps with another child crying and a uniformed nurse to offer comfort, a surprisingly large number either sleep right through or accept this night-time "babysitting."

If you are offered open access and your child does wake and is very upset, the nurse may allow you to sit up with her for the first night or two. She may wake, for example, during the first painful twenty-four hours after an operation, or during the acute stage of an illness when she must have drips changed and so forth. When she is a little better she may be easily able to accept that you will go home when she is asleep and come back when she wakes up in the morning.

Extended
visiting

Some hospitals offer only extra visiting time as a concession to very young patients. Although it is better to be allowed to stay with your child every afternoon and return for an hour every evening than to be confined to one or the other, even this amount of visiting is nothing like so good as rooming-in or open access.

Procedures will be carried out when you are not there so your child will have to get through them without your support and you will seldom know exactly what has been happening to her.

You will not be expected to undertake any of her care so you will lose your role as her personal person and she will have to put up with the nurses' ideas about brushing her hair or reading bedtime stories.

If you are to use every possible visiting moment you will be constantly travelling, which may be impossible and/or prohibitively expensive.

Deciding
whether you
can/should stay
with your child
in the hospital

If you are able to drop everything and everybody and devote yourself to the child who is in the hospital, fine. But can you and should you? What about other children at home? This is one of the many occasions in family life when it would be convenient to be able to divide oneself in half.

Nobody can make the decision for you, but you might find the following questions useful to your own thinking:

Can the sick child cope in the hospital without you? If the answer is not clear, try asking yourself whether you would be happy to send her alone to a residential nursery if she was well. If you genuinely think that she might enjoy staying away from home for a vacation, then she might manage in the hospital. If the idea of sending her away without her family strikes you as absurd or horrific, then she will not. A good children's ward will do its best to make life pleasant, even fun, just as that residential camp would do. But here there is the added stress of illness and the procedures associated with it.

Can children at home cope without you? Obviously this depends on your partner, extended family, social network or other possible caretakers, but it is worth remembering that even a toddler (who will miss you and be furious with you for going away) will cope better than the hospitalized child just because he is not ill and is not in a strange place.

Can you cope? People often concentrate on the needs of children in the hospital to the exclusion of their rooming-in parents. Rooming-in with a sick child can be a devastatingly boring and claustrophobic experience, especially if there are no other parents in residence and/or the child is in isolation (with you) and/or asleep most of the time. Take *things to do*. Arrange for people to *come and visit you*, and try to persuade the staff to keep you busy. Sometimes you can be enormously valuable to other children whose parents are not staying, as well as to your own.

Many hospitals assume that if anyone stays with a child it will be the mother. But things may work out better for everyone if you can all share the caring. See whether the head nurse will let your partner, your mother or your sitter stay with the child some of the time so that you can go home. If she will not, try at least to have someone the child knows well come to the hospital for an hour or two each day so that you can get out, even if it is only to walk the streets.

Older children in the hospital

If a child is to manage the experience of a hospital without your constant, or almost-constant, presence, he needs to be armed with information. If the admission is planned in advance, try to find out something about most of the following points and then pass it on to him. With a child of, say, six or eight, it is no use waiting for him to ask questions and then answering them, because he will not know what questions to ask. Worse still, he may have *mis*information (perhaps from television or tall-tale-telling friends). He will not ask because he thinks he knows, but what he knows may be horrendously wrong.

The child who must go to the hospital may need to know:

Why he needs to go to the hospital. This is not the same as knowing what is to be done to him. For example, a child can know that he is to have his tonsils removed without understanding that the operation is intended to reduce the frequency or severity of his bouts of tonsillitis.

● If that "why" is not very clearly spelled out, often again and again, many children tend to feel that the hospital experience is some kind of punishment. Adult phrases like "to make you better" are ambiguous: what kind of better?—healthier, happier or "gooder"? Missing school is often seen as "naughty" (especially by children who secretly dislike going and may have "swung the lead" from time to time) so a "cure" can easily turn into a punishment. Furthermore, many children who have been ill a good deal have heard parents grumbling about having to take time off from work and so forth so that they already feel that they are disapproved of for being unwell. Sometimes the guilt is more subtle. A child with appendicitis, for example, might be expected to accept hospitalization "to make your poor tummyache better," but he may already be seeing that tummyache as punishment for having angry thoughts about his Dad. Sometimes it is helpful to ask the child why *he* thinks he has to go into the hospital. His answer may give clues to this kind of thinking. Sometimes even the most sensitive parent will not be able to rid a child of this haunting feeling of guilt, but it will help, at least a little, if it is made clear to him that his parents wish it were not necessary and will miss him while he is away.

What is to be done to him. Many children get very confused about their bodies and where different bits are. It is important to be sure that your child knows where his tonsils are (he can look, in a mirror) or where the "middle ear" which is to be drained is (you can relate his own ear to a simple diagram). One little boy, for example, was convinced that his tonsils were in his belly (glands in his abdomen always hurt when he had tonsillitis), so he was convinced he was to have major abdominal surgery. After the event, instead of being relieved to find he was wrong, he was horrified to find that his throat was bleeding.

● For many children, any kind of surgery or medical intervention is so horrific an idea that their own fantasies about it are unbounded. If you describe that middle-ear operation, be sure to *say* that nothing will go inside his head; he may well imagine that his skull is to be cut open. If you describe that circumcision, remember to *say* that his actual penis will not be touched: he may well imagine that it is to be cut off, perhaps to turn him into a "good girl like my sister."

How it is to be done. Including anesthesia, etc. Be a bit careful what words you use here. Phrases like "they will put you to sleep" may make him remember what the vet did to that poor dog (*see below*).

● Remember that the child's view of what is horrific may not be the same as yours. You may welcome a pre-med before an anesthetic, but the fact that it is to be given by injection may worry him. Remember, too, that he will not take for granted minor discomforts that adults expect. If he knows that he will not be allowed to drink freely after the operation, for example, he will still want the drink but he will at least know that he is not being kept thirsty out of sheer brutality.

When you will be there.

What state his body will be in afterwards. He has a right to know if he is going to be in pain—and a right to know that he can have medication for it. He also needs to know if any bit of him is going to look peculiar (as a leg in a plaster cast or an arm with an intravenous drip in it will look odd to him) or if any bit of him is not going to work normally, or if there will be blood.

How (if) he can contact you, by telephone for example.

Something about ward life such as whether he will be in a big room with lots of children or a small one with just one other; whether he will be allowed his own pajamas or hospital ones; whether he will have to stay in bed or not; whether there will be ordinary toilets, or commodes, or bedpans for a while; whether there is television/a playroom/a teacher/a mobile gift cart, etc.

Obviously, if your child is admitted to the hospital as an emergency, you will not be able to give him all this information because you will not have much of it yourself. It can be a useful rule of thumb *not to leave him until you do have it*. In practice this will usually mean that you and he together go through examinations in the emergency room and wait it out while a place is found for him in a ward. You go to the ward with him and are there while he is being "settled." Sticking close, you wait until you have had sufficient opportunity to talk to the nurse in charge and to the doctor who is taking over the child's care, *and* until you have been able to pass everything you have discovered on to the child himself, before you even consider leaving him.

Adolescents in the hospital

Some hospitalized adolescents are in a similar position to full adults: subject to their fears and fantasies but free from particular age-related problems. But some are not. If your adolescent faces a planned admission, or must unexpectedly go into the hospital, it may be worth considering some of the following points:

Placement in an adult or children's ward

He may be misplaced in either. Children's wards tend to contain, and be run predominantly for, very young children. Food, meal service and "lights out" times may all be inappropriate for a fourteen- or fifteen-year-old and he may also be driven out of his mind by the demands of the young children to "read to me" and to "see what I've got." Adult wards, on the other hand, often contain many patients who are very sick and/or very elderly. Many adolescents are disturbed and depressed by what they see, hear and are told in such a setting.

Some hospitals do recognize that adolescents are usually better off if they can be nursed with their peers. There may be an adolescent unit, an "older children's ward" or at least some attempt at age-grouping within the available space. If there is not, *most* adolescents will be better off placed with children than with adults, especially if they can be helped (by you and by the staff) towards a helpful "adult" role there. It is usually more comfortable to be a "helper" (however reluctant) than a fish out of water.

Privacy

Unless your adolescent is accustomed to boarding school, camp or other forms of communal living, he or she may find the lack of general privacy on a ward very distressing, and the invasion of personal bodily privacy involved in using a bedpan or being bathed positively agonizing. There is only a limited amount which you can do to spare him or her necessary medical or nursing procedures, but you can at least make sure:

That you provide "modest" nightwear and an easy all-covering dressing gown. Girls who dislike pajamas may be happier, once they are walking around, if they have underpants to wear under a nightgown and a bed jacket to wear over the top. They may also need help from you in coping with menstruation if it occurs during the hospitalization.

That you do not tell his or her friends anything without permission. Some adolescents feel extremely private about their physical ills and would rather spend five days in the hospital visited only by their families than have their peers told intimate details and encouraged to visit them in the hospital setting.

Sexual problems

If the hospital admission involves specific attention to sexual parts, even the most sophisticated-seeming adolescent may be prey to worries and fantasies with which you, or the doctor prompted by you, may be able to help. A boy requiring late circumcision, for example, may worry that the infection under his foreskin was caused by venereal disease or by masturbation or that the doctors may think something of the kind. A girl being investigated for late menses may wonder whether an examining doctor can tell anything about her sexual life. Either sex may worry about future potency or fertility and find it difficult to ask.

- Adolescents with sexually related difficulties are often more at ease with a doctor of the same sex.

Hospital procedures

Whether your child goes to the hospital for planned investigations or surgery, or for emergency care after an accident or sudden illness, there are various procedures which you are likely to have to face together.

If he is an in-patient, he will probably be in a children's ward and senior staff, at least, will have experience with children and a special interest in them. But if he is treated in an emergency room, or even in some out-patient clinics, you cannot assume that all the staff will be especially child (or parent) orientated. In an emergency room in particular, he may be rather an unwelcome patient. Staff are often young and inexperienced so that they may be as nervous of carrying out certain procedures as you are of having them done. They are usually trying hard to impress their superiors so that any "fuss" made by the child may upset them because it seems to reflect poorly on their skill. They are often overworked and overtired—which reduces anyone's patience—and they may have life-and-death problems to cope with which rightly matter even more to them than does the less critical problem which is taking all your attention. Furthermore, some staff will be genuinely unaware of the distress which many, to them "routine," procedures can cause to a child. Of course everybody knows that pain hurts, but not everyone understands the interaction between fear and pain, or the extent to which the strangeness of the hospital setting makes a child liable to fear.

If you can see medical personnel as highly trained and caring human beings, rather than gods in whom feet of clay are intolerable, you will probably be able to work in partnership with them so that your child gets through whatever procedures are necessary with minimum trauma. Whether you find yourself beautifully supported by staff who largely relieve you of the burden of supporting your child, or completely unsupported in your solitary efforts to persuade a screaming child to keep still, there are a few techniques, hints and pieces of information which may help you all.

Supporting your child during hospital procedures

Babies, toddlers and hospital procedures

Very young children are often more upset at being separated from parents and handled by strangers than they are by the procedures those strangers carry out. If hospital staff will allow you to stay with your child whatever is done to him, do.

If he is an out-patient or emergency, staff will seldom try to dissuade you from staying close. If he is an in-patient, certain procedures may be carried out at times when you just do not happen to be in the ward. Since doctors cannot really be expected to organize their day's work around your visits, this is one good reason for living-in if possible (*see above*).

If you want to stay with your child and be the one to hold him, don't let fear that blood, needles, etc. will be too much for you, put you off. You do not have to watch what is being done to your child's body. Let the professionals get on with that while you concentrate on keeping in eye contact with the child and providing a safe focus for him-as-a-person.

Older children and hospital procedures

School-age children, or even pre-school children are usually better able to cope with strangers and may be able to make instant friends with medical personnel. A child who is an in-patient may be well able to get through routine procedures without you but will probably still manage emergency procedures better if you stay with him. Your presence can give all kinds of unspoken but nevertheless vital assurances.

You are there, so *you know what is being done to him*. Any fantasies about mad doctors and torture are kept under control, and the fact that you *accept what is done as necessary* makes it easier for him to accept it, too. If things should get bad, you will obviously be sympathetic (which the staff may be too busy to be), but just by being there while they do the unpleasant things, you make it clear that you *expect the child to put up with them*. Since he knows that you do not usually demand the impossible, this also helps him to believe (and discover) that he can manage.

You are there as a person, not as an operator, and you know the child as the medical personnel cannot. You can therefore *talk him through*, and spot extra agonies like embarrassment.

If he wants to cooperate or be "good" or "brave" you can bolster his self-esteem whatever happens. After all it *is* brave to *try* not to cry, even if the effort does not succeed. If he should feel that he has made a shaming exhibition of himself (perhaps partly because of unfortunate exhortations from the staff), you will be in a position not only to help him survive at the time but also to help him approve of himself afterwards.

Adolescents and hospital procedures

Adolescents may prefer to face unpleasant episodes on their own, especially if having you there makes them feel that they must put a good face on everything to protect your feelings. Older children and adolescents should, perhaps, have the choice, but a real choice does need to be based on real information about what is to happen to them.

The vexed question of keeping still for hospital procedures

A lot of hospital procedures either require the child to keep perfectly still or are very much easier/less uncomfortable if he can do so. There are a few tricks which can help with different children in different circumstances.

Holding babies still

If a baby is to be hurt, or even if anything which will feel strange is to be done, he will have to be held. Make sure that you hold him completely immobilized. If you half-hold him he will probably feel just restricted enough to be irritated and therefore even more inclined to wriggle than if he had not been held at all.

Depending on which part of his body is to be manipulated, wrapping the whole baby tightly in a blanket is often effective. Swaddled efficiently, you can control the whole child with one arm, leaving your other hand free either to hold the relevant part or to stroke him.

If he is not going to be hurt, or even actually touched, but is to have an X-ray or something of the kind, you may be able to keep him still without physically holding him at all. Attracting his attention will often "freeze" him for the necessary seconds.

Keeping toddlers still

It is well worth preparing for procedures which do not hurt, by actually teaching toddlers and pre-school children to keep still on command.

Games like Grandmother's Footsteps or Statues are usually very popular and can easily be evoked when needed for that X-ray.

If a toddler is to be hurt, he too will have to be held by force and may be too heavy and strong for the blanket method. Provided that the doctor can still get at the area he needs to reach, it is often easiest if you sit down yourself and stand the child between your thighs. Thrashing legs are thus isolated from the rest of him and you have both hands free for his arms.

Helping older children to keep still

Older children who *intend* to cooperate should not be held by force until or unless it becomes clear that their self-control is not up to the task. Often such a child cannot actually keep the arm that is having a needle put in it still, but can keep the rest of his body still, especially if it is up against yours. It often helps if he can sit on your lap, with one of your arms holding him against you while the other holds that arm steady.

Movement is a more or less instinctive reaction away from pain, but the energy which a child's body tells him to put into flight can often be vented in a different way. A child who is having a rectal examination, for example, can often leave the lower half of his body passively in the hands of the doctor if he is encouraged to bang his hands and arms on the couch. A child who must keep his arm still while it is stitched may manage to keep stiller if he is encouraged to shout, loudly, with each prick.

Sedation and anesthesia for hospital procedures

Doctors, and the hospitals in which they work, vary greatly in the relative importance they attach to children's distress and to the side effects or risks of sedative drugs or anesthetics. Some take great pride in making full use of such chemical aids for children, while others use the same criteria (also very variable) as they use for adult patients. In Britain, for example, some doctors use self-administered gas-and-air (exactly like that used in childbirth) for children undergoing a range of procedures from having stitches removed to having burns dressed. Others will prescribe a sedative for parents to give a child prior to procedures, such as complex kinds of X-rays, which are liable to be frightening even though they are not painful. Some use local anesthetics freely for such procedures as removal of splinters or excision of abscesses, while others reckon that in many cases the pain of injecting the local anesthetic is greater than the discomfort of the procedure itself.

Obviously you (or rather your child) are largely in the hands of your doctors. But it may sometimes be worth your while to ask, very politely, whether any extra relief can be given. In a busy emergency room, for example, it may simply not have occurred to the doctor that you would rather sit quietly with your child for half an hour while a sedative takes effect than have him dealt with now, fully awake and frightened. Remember also that the doctor who is dealing with your child in this present situation cannot know, unless you tell him, about any previous experiences which may have made that child especially sensitive. If he knew about the unpleasant treatment your child had following an accident only a month ago, he might well agree that a general anesthetic should be given this time, even if it means that the child must wait several hours until his stomach is empty.

If your child should require a *series* of procedures (such as twice-weekly dressings) and you find that he is becoming increasingly afraid of them, do make an appointment and discuss it, either with the hospital consultant or through your own doctor. Nobody wants a young child to emerge from any condition with an acute and lasting fear of hospitals and medical personnel, but the staff who actually carry out the procedure will probably not have the authority to change it on the spot if you raise the matter while they are poised and ready to proceed. You need a discussion in between appointments.

Some common hospital procedures: blood tests

A sample of your child's blood will be needed in many different circumstances ranging from diagnosis of an illness (*see* **Infection**/Infections which cause illness: When the laboratory may help in diagnosis) to establishment of his blood group in order to have cross-matched blood available to him if he should require transfusion after surgery (*see* **Blood Groups**). Always ask, though, why blood is needed. Very occasionally samples are taken "routinely." You may prefer not to have blood taken from your child unless it really is necessary.

Heel or thumb prick   If only a small quantity of blood is needed, the doctor may take it from the heel of a young baby or the thumb of an older child by "pricking" the cleaned skin with a small lancet and then squeezing out a drop or two of blood.

The "prick" hurts, of course, but this method has two great advantages: it is over so quickly that the child has no time to be afraid and, especially if he is very young, quickly forgets the whole thing; and it is not critical that he be kept absolutely still.

● If the thumb is used, be sure to tell the doctor if the child is left-handed or happens to need one particular thumb for comfort-sucking. It will need an adhesive plaster for a few hours and may be sore for a day or two.

Venepuncture (taking blood from a vein)   In older children (and adults) blood is usually taken from a vein on the inner side of the elbow, but in babies a variety of veins which come close to the surface of the skin may be used. The chosen site will depend on the size of the veins. Taking blood from the tiny veins of a small baby is a difficult task.

If a venepuncture goes smoothly at the first attempt it may scarcely bother the child, but if repeated attempts are needed it can be exceedingly traumatic. First-time success certainly requires a skilled operator and a "good vein," but a perfectly still child helps, too. Don't be surprised if the blood is taken by a technician rather than a doctor: this is a skill learned and kept up by constant practice: that technician will probably be far more expert in this particular respect than the grandest consultant.

Once a vein has been chosen, she will persuade it to stand out, either by squeezing the child's arm above the chosen spot or, in an older child, by putting a rubber strap tightly around for a few moments. She will clean the skin at the point where the needle is to go in. The needle now has to go through the skin and then be persuaded into the vein itself. If you are fortunate, these two stages will both take place as one and, once the needle is in the vein, the blood will be withdrawn without further discomfort. If you are less fortunate, the needle will go through the skin, but the vein will slip away from its point, which will then have to be moved in pursuit. It is movement of the needle under the skin which is most painful. If the vein continues to escape, the technician may withdraw the needle altogether and start again, possibly at a new site.

● Many small children are frightened by the sight of their own veins standing out. It is often best to position the child so that he cannot see or persuade an older one not to look.

● Once the needle is in the vein (ask the operator) there will be no more pain. You can safely assure the child that "it won't hurt any more," but he must keep still until the needle has been withdrawn. An older child who is interested may enjoy watching his own blood being drawn up into the syringe.

● Very occasionally an inexperienced person has real difficulty puncturing a child's vein. While she will probably seek help from someone else when she thinks the child has "had enough," you may feel entitled to ask her to do so if she wants to go on trying for longer than you consider the child can stand. If you ask whether the child may have a rest before any more is done, she will probably take the hint without taking offense.

Blood and other transfusions

Transfusions, not only of blood but of fluids to a dehydrated baby or child, or drugs to a very sick one, can be life-saving. If your child needs any kind of transfusion he will certainly be admitted as an in-patient, but the transfusion may be set up and started in the emergency room.

From the child's point of view, having a vein punctured to receive something into the bloodstream is very similar to having one punctured to take blood out. There are some differences which you may like to know:

☐ The very sharp needle with which the puncture is performed is not left in the vein. It is used to introduce a very fine plastic tube and is then withdrawn, leaving the tube to carry the transfusion.

☐ Too much movement can dislodge the tube. Veins inside the elbow are, of course, subject to a lot of arm movement so a vein on the back of the hand, wrist or forearm is a more likely choice.

☐ Whichever vein is selected, the hand/arm will be kept still (often with a splint) and the tubing will be taped to it. Your child will not be able to use that limb freely.

● Remember to tell the doctor if he is left-handed.

☐ As well as choosing a vein which is not subject to too much movement, the doctor has to find one which is large enough to carry the transfused fluid into the circulation and go on doing so for hours or even for days. In a baby, the "best vein," from both these points of view, may be one on the scalp. If a scalp vein is used, a small patch of hair will have to be shaved but this will quickly grow back. Parents watching the insertion of an intravenous needle into the scalp sometimes have the horrors because it looks as if it is going into the baby's head. It is not and, of course, it could not; there is solid skull under that scalp.

Injections into a vein If a child is going to need several doses of drugs put directly into his circulation via a vein, a transfusion set will usually be fixed up so that each subsequent dose can be "injected" into the equipment and dripped painlessly into the child. Occasionally, though, drugs will be given by direct injection into the vein, in which case, from the child's point of view, each dose will be similar to venepuncture for a blood test. Anesthetics given into a vein produce unconsciousness very rapidly and usually prevent the child from remembering the venepuncture.

Some types of X-ray are carried out following the intravenous injection of chemicals which will show up on the X-ray film and therefore enable the doctor to see, for example, the child's kidneys or other soft tissues. When an elaborate X-ray is planned for your child, do ask your doctor whether any such injection is involved. It is a pity to assure an older child that "it'll only be an X-ray and you know they don't hurt" if, in fact, there are painful preliminaries.

Other injections

You (and your child) will probably be accustomed to intra-muscular and subcutaneous injections because he will have met needles during routine immunizations, if not for any other reason. Such injections are painless, or almost so, both because they are put into ideal sites, such as the top of the buttock or upper arm, and because such a small quantity of fluid is injected.

In the hospital, you may meet some types of injection which are less quick and easy. Examples are mentioned here so that you can decide whether or not your child should be warned. If you do not warn him, he will be "good" here and now, but may be so dismayed that there is a risk of his being "needle-shy" next time he is due for a routine injection. On the other hand, if you do warn him that this one is different, fear and tension may make it worse for him. . . .

Injections into unusual sites The most common example is local anesthesia in which the drug must be placed where it will effectively deaden the nerves serving the area which would otherwise be painful. This may mean a needle passing between knuckle bones to deaden a finger, or beneath the skin of the temple to deaden the area of a face wound which is to be stitched.

The fluid has to be injected slowly so that the procedure may be rather lengthy, giving the child plenty of time to get in a panic. Furthermore, although the operator will try to keep the anesthetic moving into the tissues ahead of the needle point, so that he deadens them as he goes, he is, by definition, injecting an area which is rich in nerves; there may be considerable pain.

Injections of large volume or viscous liquids If a large volume of a thickish fluid is required, as in some forms of penicillin and in gamma globulin (*see* **Infection**/Treatment of infections which cause illness: Anti-viral drugs), the injection will be slow and comparatively painful. The fluid is pushed in gradually so as to give the tissues every opportunity to absorb it as it is given. But, inevitably, the receiving tissues become distended and this is what hurts.

● If a child goes on complaining of pain after an injection of this kind, rubbing the area (or encouraging him to do so) will speed up the dispersal of the fluid as well as give him something to do which distracts from the discomfort.

Lumbar puncture and other "needles"

Just as needles can be put into veins to take out blood as well as to put in fluids, so needles may sometimes be used to take sample fluids from various parts of a child's body.

Although it is not pleasant to think about a needle being put through your child's chest wall to remove fluid from around a lung, or through the wall of his abdomen to remove urine from his bladder, many such procedures are far worse to think about and watch than they are to experience. It may help you to remember that internal organs do not have the same kind of pain sensitivity as other body structures. Most are highly sensitive to stretching, for example, but not to being cut or punctured. If your child should have to have a procedure of this kind carried out, local anesthesia will be used to deaden the skin and underlying muscle layer, but once that injection is over the procedure will be painless although it may "feel funny."

Lumbar puncture

A lumbar puncture is performed for two purposes: to enable the doctor to measure the pressure of the spinal fluid and to enable him to take a small sample of the fluid for microscopic examination and the culture of any bacteria.

Lumbar punctures are needed relatively more often in babies and young children than in older children and adults. The very young are more liable to types of infection which may affect the brain or nervous system (*see*, for example, **Meningitis and Encephalitis**), and clinical diagnosis is much more difficult in a child too young to describe his symptoms and feelings.

Doctors and patients both vary in their views of how unpleasant lumbar puncture is and this probably reflects the fact that its unpleasantness varies. An expert operator can carry out a lumbar puncture on a relaxed child and leave him agreeing that it was "only a prick in the back." Other children find the whole procedure terrifying and are therefore far more difficult to work with. Furthermore, even the most expert operator can fail to get the needle into exactly the right place at the first attempt and further attempts can become more and more of a traumatic struggle.

A lumbar puncture will not be carried out on your child unless it is thought at least possible that he is seriously ill. That being so, it has to be accepted and got through somehow.

Some doctors very much dislike carrying out this procedure with a parent present and some experienced children's nurses maintain that if the child has to be held by force against all the will that he can muster, it is psychologically better if it is not a parent who imprisons him. You will have to decide, in consultation with medical personnel and considering your own child. Sometimes the doctor will give him a preliminary sedative which, while it will not keep him asleep throughout the lumbar puncture, may prevent him from being frightened by being taken away from you and may also mean that he remembers nothing about it later.

Whether you are to be present or not, you may find the following information helpful:

The child's physical position is critical to a successful lumbar puncture. He will be put on his side with his back parallel to the edge of the couch and then his knees will be curled up towards his chest so that his vertebrae separate. A pillow may be placed between his bent knees to keep his spine horizontal.

The spinal fluid is taken from the part of the spinal canal which carries on *below the level of the spinal cord itself*. There is, therefore, no risk of the needle going into the cord.

A local anesthetic is injected into the skin and deeper tissues first.

Once the lumbar puncture needle has been inserted and its position checked, there is no more painful manipulation: necessary pressure gauges and collecting vessels are attached to that needle.

After the procedure is over, the child will be nursed lying flat (possibly on his face for as long as he will tolerate this) for about twenty-four hours. This is to avoid the headache which can follow the removal of even a small sample of spinal fluid.

If you are with the child, persuading him to remain lying down is the most useful role you can fulfill. Picking him up, however much you/he want a cuddle, is unhelpful.

Headache, although a notorious result of lumbar puncture, only affects about half the patients on whom the procedure is performed and is severe only in about half of those. Painkilling drugs will be given if your child is one of these.

Plaster casts for fractures

If your child sustains a fracture (*see* **Accidents**) she may have the affected part encased in plaster so that the bone is held in exactly the correct position while it heals.

A serious fracture may be dealt with under general anesthesia. It may even involve surgical procedures such as "pinning" the fractured bone. A simpler fracture may not require general anesthesia so that the child watches the plaster being applied, usually in the form of a bandage, saturated in a solution which hardens as it air-dries.

Having plaster applied while conscious

In most hospitals, plastering fractures is a technician's task and not every such technician is accustomed to handling small children—especially shocked ones. There can be pain involved as the limb is moved during the procedure. There can also be fear. The child watches as her limb vanishes under layer upon layer of cold, wet material which gradually becomes stiffer and heavier until it ceases to feel like her own limb at all.

Help a small child to say a temporary farewell to her arm or leg. If you explain that it is going to be "packed up safely" so that nothing can knock it or hurt it while it gets better, you may make it easier for her to accept the cast. If you keep reminding her that the arm or leg is just as it has always been but that nobody will be able to see it again until the plaster is taken off, you may be able to help her see it as a "secret place." Don't take it for granted that she, like you, realizes that this stiff, heavy white limb is only a temporary "replacement" for her own. Some children do actually believe either that the plastered limb is an artifical replacement for their own which is somehow "lost," or that the natural limb is still there but will always have to have the plaster on it.

Coming round
from anesthesia
to discover
a plaster cast

If your child is to have a cast applied under general anesthesia, do warn her and discuss it with her in advance if circumstances allow. Sometimes parents are so concerned with the injury, and with seeing their child through the preparations for surgery, that they forget what a shock it may be if she wakes up and finds her body changed.

Whether you have managed to warn her or not, when she does come round it may be important to emphasize that:

The hurt limb is still there, under the cast.

That the cast will be removed, using some time-scale which she can understand such as "before we go on vacation" or even "when there have been six Mondays and six Tuesdays and six Wednesdays. . . ."

That when it is removed the limb will look and behave quite normally.

● This last will probably not be exactly accurate as limbs which have been in a cast usually lose both muscle bulk and tone so that they look comparatively thin and feel rather weak. But with a young child it is usually better to deal with that aspect of the matter later on, when she has adapted to having the cast and is beginning to anticipate having it off again.

● Children who attend a playgroup or go to school are often much cheered if they are reminded of the peer-group status a cast confers and of the chance of getting their friends to write on it. . . . If crutches are necessary, they, too, may be regarded with pleasure (rather like a new version of stilts) while if it is an arm which is plastered, having to have help with getting dressed, etc. may seem fun—for a while.

Stomach pumpings

If a child eats or drinks something poisonous or something which may be poisonous if enough has been taken, or deliberately takes "an overdose," the doctor may think it necessary to pump her stomach in order to remove as much as possible of the offending substance before it can be absorbed into her bloodstream (*see* **Accidents**/Poisoning). The procedure involves threading a tube up one of the child's nostrils and then working it very carefully down the throat, always making sure that it goes down her food passageway and not down her breathing passageway instead.

Most people find the placing of the tube extremely unpleasant, mainly because as soon as it touches, and moves across, the back of the throat, it makes the victim gag. Gagging and retching keep closing the throat so that working the tube further and further down is a slow business. The back of the throat is usually sprayed with a local anesthetic to reduce its sensitivity and lessen gagging. Medical personnel will try to persuade your child to keep on swallowing that tube, rather than fighting it. If she can do this, her swallowing will not only help the tube to go down but also give her something positive to do to help herself.

Once the end of the tube has completed its journey and is known to be safely in the stomach, liquid is poured down it and then suction is applied to bring that liquid—together with the poison—back out again. This siphoning procedure will be repeated until medical personnel are sure that all the poison which can be removed has been pumped out.

Gagging usually stops once the tube is in place, but the child may still be panicky because having one nostril blocked makes her feel that she cannot breathe freely. Try to help her to breathe gently and *not to fight*. If she struggles so much that she dislodges the tube she will have the whole horrible business to go through again. Even if she does not actually dislodge it, placing it by force will leave her with a very sore throat.

Suturing wounds

Suturing a wound simply means holding the edges together mechanically while it heals. Sutures may be stitches or various kinds of clips or clamps.

Some wounds have to be sutured if they are to heal cleanly, quickly and satisfactorily. A long gash, which has penetrated further than the skin into the underlying tissues and is gaping open, for example, might cause real trouble if it was not sutured. It would have to heal from the bottom up, like a hole. Before it began to heal it might be difficult to control bleeding. While it healed in this way it would be very liable to infection. After it had healed there might well be some loss of sensation and/or function in the area because severed muscles and nerves had not been given the chance to come together. There would probably be a large scar, too. A wound as serious as this will probably be dealt with like a minor operation and the child may be given a general anesthetic. If he is going to be unconscious while medical personnel deal with his wound, he will not care what they do. But with less serious wounds there may be an element of choice in treatment.

Decisions on whether or not a wound should be sutured sometimes depend partly on its position on the body. If a wound is not going to be subject to very much wound-opening movement, it may be dealt with by compromise measures. There are various types of skin closure, for example, which work on the same principles as the method recommended for home use (*see* **Accidents**/Cuts and scrapes, grazes and puncture wounds). One usual type consists of very adhesive plasters which are butterfly-shaped. One "wing" is stuck to the skin on one side of the cut; the edges are drawn together and the other "wing" is pressed to the other side so that they are held together. Another commonly used type is called a "steristrip" and has adhesive strength great enough to hold even some gaping wound edges together.

Stitches The doctor has to decide whether or not to use a local anesthetic. If he decides not to, it will not be because he is a brute but because he does not believe that the stitches will hurt much more than would the local anesthetic. This may be because the local would have to be put into a particularly uncomfortable place in order to be effective, and/or because only one or two stitches are needed, and/or because wherever the anesthetic is injected, he knows it cannot be wholly effective.

Wounds are stitched much as material is sewn. A special curved needle is threaded with a short length of suture material with a knot at the end. Holding the needle with forceps, the doctor pushes it through one edge of the cut, pulls it through so that the knot is against the skin and then pushes the needle through the other edge. When he has pulled it through so that the wound is held closed, a knot is put in that end of the suture, too, so that there is a knot at either side of the wound line.

Obviously, having the needle pushed through the skin is painful unless an anesthetic has been used and it may be felt even if one has been given, but a skilled operator can complete both sides of one stitch almost as a single movement so that the pain is very brief even though there is some fiddling about while knots are made. Most children tolerate one or two stitches well. A series of four or more is rather a different matter. Babies tend to get into a lather of despair while older children find their courage ebbing with every new needle.

● With a child who is trying to cooperate and will communicate during suturing, you may be able to offer a great deal of help by giving him constant progress reports. If he knows that you will warn him when the actual pricks are coming, for example, he may be able to relax during the in-between bits while knots are being tied or fresh needles prepared, and he may be able to avoid watching the procedure, leaving you to do so instead. If his courage is flagging you can also remind him that "that's more than half" or "only one more. . . ."

Cuts on the face Comparatively minor cuts on the face may have to be stitched. Vulnerable areas—such as the forehead—have tightly stretched skin so that cuts tend to gape and go on bleeding. Furthermore, it is of course important to minimize facial scarring.

Unfortunately the face is not the pleasantest area to have stitches put in. The child will have to lie on a couch, rather than sit on your lap, and this deprives him of some comfort and comfortable holding. Local anesthesia in this area is often rather ineffective but the skin is nevertheless highly sensitive. Having needles and forceps close to the eyes is frightening, too.

If you are faced with this situation you may like to try to be sure that the doctor attending to your child really is experienced. A combination of inexperience and a really frenzied wriggling child *could* result in nightmares and an unnecessarily untidy scar. Try confiding to the doctor that your child (perhaps already upset by the actual accident) is going to be "a bit difficult" and asking him whether he does not think that some sedation, or even an anesthetic, might be worthwhile. If he is unsure of himself (or if he is absolutely confident but sorry for you and the child) he may greet the suggestion with relief.

If he is certain that he can do a satisfactory job in the way he always intended to do it, believe him and do all you can to help.

Traction

Very occasionally a child with a serious fracture or other accidental injury must have part of her body put under traction during healing. Traction simply means that the affected part is pulled into the desired position and then held there by a system of pulleys and weights. A badly fractured thigh, for example, might require the leg to be raised on a cradle at the end of the bed with a specific weight attached to the ankle.

Being "in traction" is unpleasant for anyone. It is intensely boring to be fixed to a bed, perhaps for several weeks. It is extremely frustrating to have movement within the bed so much restricted, and a variety of minor discomforts are liable to arise, too. Bottoms get sore because patients cannot roll onto their sides; itches develop in places which cannot be reached and so forth.

For children, being in traction may also be terrifying. Always rather helpless in the ill-understood hands of the adult world, such a child is now completely helpless. Various instinctive escape routes (such as hiding under the bedclothes or running away) are physically impossible for her. Comfort rituals may be unusable because of her unnatural and imposed position. Furthermore, she may be prey to fantasies ranging from a conviction that she is being punished by this cruel confinement for some fearful private crime, to a secret belief that she has been made part of the machinery of pulleys and weights. . . .

Obviously your child's reactions will depend on her age, her maturity and her personality; obviously, too, they will depend on the kindliness of the nursing staff and the entertainment which she finds in the ward. But for most children, especially those who are too young fully to understand what is being done to them and why, and too young also to occupy themselves in reading, listening to the radio and so forth, the constant presence of a parent or other loved adult will be vitally important.

Being with a child in traction

Rooming-in may be difficult or impossible. Even if the hospital has rooms or side wards for children with their mothers, the staff are likely to want your child in the main ward so that they can see her from the nurses' station. After all, she cannot get up to fetch what she needs or go to the toilet; if she were out of sight she might get neglected.

Once any operation is over, the child is not acutely ill so you may find it difficult to justify absenting yourself and thus disrupting the lives of other family members, employers, etc. The disruption is likely to go on not for several days but for several weeks. Some kind of "open access" (*see above*) is probably your best option and, within it, some compromise.

Try to stay with her throughout her waking hours until it is clear that she has accepted her situation. With a parent's help, most children, even at three or four, once they have been in enforced residence for two or three days, will come to realize that nobody is going to do anything else which is horrible to them and that the nurses *are* friendly. During that time you will probably have been able to deal (so far as this is possible) with her fears and fantasies, too.

Once she has "settled in," help her to begin to use what the ward offers. A child confined in this way usually attracts a good deal of sympathy and attention. There may be a play-leader or teacher on the ward for part of the day and, if your child will make friends with her, this may be a time when you can leave her. There may also be older and more mobile children who will read to her or at least play their own games where she can watch them.

Help her to enjoy other visitors. With your help any but the smallest child will come to realize that, immobilized in bed, just playing with you will come to be positively boring. This is the time to enlist outside friends, child and adult, who can bring her fresh stories, jokes or gossip.

Use every trick you can think of to mark off the hours for her so that they seem to pass faster. Help her, for example, to learn the ward routine so that the arrival of the drinks cart marks off the first part of the morning or the arrival of doctors on their rounds tells her that it will soon be lunchtime. If she is old enough and a well-positioned television set is available, choosing programs, and waiting for them, can pass almost as much time as the programs themselves. Things which change as the days pass help, too. A budding pot plant will mark off the days it takes to open, while sprouting seeds grow almost visibly towards edibility.

Help her use the enforced confinement to learn something new. An active four-year-old would probably not have sat still for long enough to learn to knit or crochet, but if you teach her now, she may acquire enough skill to be proud of herself. If she is a child who enjoys being shown how to do things, you may find your hours with her less boring if you teach her, too. There are a lot of skills with which we might not bother mobile children but which those who must stay still might enjoy. The range is almost limitless: from reading to changing electric plugs.

Urine specimens

A specimen of your child's urine will commonly be needed not only if the possibility of kidney disease is being investigated, but also if the reasons for an unexplained fever or other symptoms are being sought.

If urine is to be cultured to see how many microorganisms it contains, it is obviously important that extra microorganisms should not contaminate the specimen while the child is passing it. The hospital will probably use a version of the "clean-catch" method described below. There is nothing painful about it, but babies and toddlers may resent being handled by strangers and older children may be embarrassed. In either case you may be able to help by collecting the specimen yourself, following exactly the instructions you are given.

It is worth taking a lot of trouble about this because if a satisfactory specimen cannot be obtained in this way the doctor may feel that a specimen should be taken straight from the child's bladder by supra-pubic bladder puncture (*see above* Lumbar punctures and other "needles"). Obviously it is kinder to the child to avoid this procedure if possible.

A "clean-catch" technique for babies

A baby does not know when he is going to urinate and neither do you. To get around this problem there are special plastic bags, designed for both boys and girls, which stick, with a special adhesive, around the vulva or above the scrotum. Properly applied, these bags make a tight seal to the skin so that once the genitals have been cleaned with the antiseptic provided and the bag has been applied, the urine, when eventually it arrives, will be "clean" (uncontaminated). It may be your job to watch the baby and his bag and to alert medical personnel as soon as urine is produced. The weight and wetness will quickly lead to its becoming dislodged so that the specimen is lost or contaminated.

A "clean-catch" technique for older children

The genital area has to be cleaned. You may be told to retract a boy's foreskin (if it retracts easily) and wash beneath it. For a girl, you may be told to part the labia and make sure that you swab between them.

In some cases, once cleaning is completed the child is simply asked to urinate into a sterile container, but in other cases you will be asked to have two containers ready. The beginning of the urination is discarded and only the second half caught in the container which will be used for testing. This is to ensure that any remaining microorganisms in the genital tract are washed out by the first urine so that what is caught can be regarded as representative of the urine as it was in the child's bladder.

Many schoolchildren will prefer, and be fully able, to carry out the preliminary cleansing for themselves provided you supervise. An adolescent should, of course, carry out the whole procedure for himself and may much prefer to take his instructions directly from a nurse.

X-rays

A very large number of diagnostic techniques come under the general heading of "X-rays." Some involve unpleasant preliminaries, such as the intravenous injection of contrast media (*see above*), but otherwise they are entirely painless. Because everybody knows that X-rays do not hurt, parents and hospital staff sometimes do not allow for the fact that they can frighten the very young. Familiarity with the idea of an X-ray helps a little, so do try to ensure that as soon as your child is old enough to understand about any kind of photograph he knows about this kind, too.

Helping your child in the X-ray department

If an adequate X-ray is to be taken your child will have to keep the relevant part still. He may also have to keep still in a difficult position. A chest X-ray, for example, may require him to hold his breath for a couple of seconds. An X-ray of a damaged arm may require him to keep it in a position which hurts.

Unfortunately you cannot usually *hold* your child still for an X-ray and you may not even be able to hold the rest of him for comfort while his arm is being X-rayed. Most hospitals have very strict rules which forbid anybody but the patient from being subjected to the machine's radiation (even though this is minute). Furthermore, if you were holding your child, the eventual "picture" which has to be interpreted would be confused by the mix-up between bits of you and bits of the child. He is probably, therefore, going to have to stand, sit or lie alone in front of the machine.

X-ray machinery is large and formidable. Just being near it may frighten your child. Sometimes bits of that machinery move towards and away from him as the technician adjusts distances and so forth. To a small child that movement is often the last straw that evokes panic and flight.

Try to enlist the sympathy of the operator so that the child is given time to look around. If he or she will explain a little of how it all works to a toddler or pre-school child, or show a baby the lights and their reflection in all that shiny metal, he may be able to be interested rather than afraid.

Show the child where he is going to stand or lie and which bit of the machinery is going to take "the picture." Try to get the operator to move any bits which will move later, so that the child can see, while you are still with him, that he is not going to be devoured or squashed.

Get him to practice anything he will have to do like holding his breath while you and the operator count to three.

If the child has a painful place to be X-rayed, make sure the operator knows that it is painful and ask her, in front of the child, what position she will need it in. She will have a variety of foam blocks and wedges which can be used to help keep a limb still or a child in a particular position; your aim is to get her to arrange the child to her technical satisfaction before she sends you out of the way.

Ask if you may stay in the screened cubicle used by the operators themselves. There is no reason why you should be sent right out of the room if your leaving will distress the child. If you are allowed to stay, *keep talking* to the child.

Surgery

While the full range of surgical techniques may be applied to babies and children, these brief notes on some of the more common childhood operations may be useful. They are intended to give parents a starting point for asking questions and to suggest some of the aspects of surgery which a child may find unnecessarily alarming unless he is well-prepared.

Preparations for surgery
Except in an emergency, a child will usually be admitted to the hospital at least twenty-four hours before any operation. If preliminary investigations or treatment is required he may be admitted sooner. There are several reasons for this:

Members of the surgical team will want to examine him.

The anesthetist will examine him to make sure that he is fit to receive an anesthetic. Occasionally a non-urgent operation will be delayed if a child has a respiratory infection, for example.

Nursing staff hope to "settle in" the child so that he has some familiarity with the ward and the people who will be caring for him. If he is very young, they will want to establish his level of communication, the words he uses for things he wants and so forth. This is the time to make sure that everyone realizes the importance of that rag (*see* **Habits**/Comfort habits: "Cuddlies") or those glasses.

He will have to be deprived of food and drink for a period before the operation. The risks of anesthesia when the stomach is not "empty" are very great. Hospitals usually prefer patients to be under professional care in case somebody feels that "just a little drink" does not matter, or the child helps himself.

● Although, of course, not every operation can take place first thing in the morning, this is the best time from a young child's point of view because he will then scarcely notice that he is missing meals and not being allowed a drink.

There may be specific preparations for this particular operation. Sometimes, for example, hair is shaved from an operation site, or a course of antibiotics may be started before the operation to help prevent infection afterwards.

● It is always worth asking in advance about specific preparations. Some children are more upset by non-painful procedures which they were not expecting than by the operation itself.

Anesthesia   The anesthetist is an extremely highly trained and skilled professional with a wide range of techniques at his disposal. From the child's point of view, it does not matter exactly what happens while he is unconscious. It is the "going to sleep" and the "waking up" which are important. These are some of the fears commonly expressed by toddlers and pre-school (or older) children:

"Being put to sleep" is the same as being killed. Even a child who has little understanding of the nature of death may equate anesthesia with the end of a beloved pet who was "put to sleep" by a vet.

If anesthesia is "sleep," going to sleep is dangerous. Some children specifically fear that "they" might "cut him open" while he is normally asleep at night; others fear that they might wake up in the middle of the operation or that the operation might begin before they are fully asleep.

● The words parents use to explain anesthesia are obviously critical and equally obviously have to be chosen for the individual child. Some find that "special sleep" or "magic sleep" are useful phrases. Whatever words you choose, the important thing is to make it clear to the child that anesthesia is *different* from ordinary sleep; that it occurs *only* when a doctor says it is going to and that doctors and nurses can *always tell* the difference.

Once convinced of the above, some children are terrified of the idea of being moved away from the ward while "asleep," often because they do not know where they will be taken and they therefore feel that their parents will not be able to find them.

● Depending on the child's age and condition and the hospital's policy and geography, it can be helpful if you can accompany the child to the operating theater or anesthetic induction room to show him, in advance, where it is in relation to the ward. If this is impossible, try at least to ensure that you are with the child until he is taken from the ward (he will be sleepy, *see below*) and that you are there waiting for his return.

Children are usually given premedication before an anesthetic. The drugs given will have the double effect of drying the child's respiratory tract (which will make his mouth feel dry but also lessens the chance of his choking during the anesthetic) and making him feel sleepy and don't-careish. The "pre-med" is usually given about an hour before the operation. It may be given by mouth, by injection or in the form of a small enema ("per rectum").

● The anesthetist will tell you which method he has ordered. If you are not there when he visits the child, he will have left orders with the nursing staff. Ask the senior nurse.

● If you are allowed to stay with your child once he has had his "pre-med," do encourage him to drift peacefully off to sleep. The less he fights these sedative drugs the more effective they will be, and the more effectively they work for him the less he will even realize, let alone be afraid, when he is fetched from the ward for surgery.

Recovery from anesthesia

The after-effects of anesthesia vary widely not only according to the depth of anesthesia and the length of time for which it was required, but also from child to child. Yours may recover rapidly and smoothly, but on the whole we all tend to underestimate the length of time it takes bodies to rid themselves of anesthetic drugs. Be prepared for any of the following:

In most hospitals, the child will be taken from the operating theater to a "recovery room" rather than straight back to the ward. He may be kept there until specially trained staff are satisfied that his breathing, cough reflexes, blood pressure and so forth are all back to normal.

● If you are waiting in the ward, don't assume that because your child is gone for several hours the operation has lasted for hours or has gone wrong in any way.

He may be returned to the ward looking unexpectedly (to you) ill. Anesthesia often leaves children a very bad color for a while.

Many children vomit after anesthesia. Some vomit frequently over several hours.

It is possible that he will be returned to the ward with a drain in the surgical wound, a catheter in his bladder or a drip going into a vein. Even if you have not been warned and therefore were not expecting anything of this kind, don't assume that anything has gone wrong. The surgical team aims to keep him in the best possible condition for recovery. That drip, for example, does not necessarily mean that he lost a lot of blood. It may simply be intended to ensure optimum fluids until he can drink.

While he comes round, the child may seem very distressed and/or "wild." Remember that, while there may be pain, he will overreact to *any* discomfort while he is still semiconscious. Screams need not mean agony. His state is likely to be similar to that of delirium. It will settle as his body rids itself of the anesthetic drugs.

● If staff will allow you to be with the child while he recovers, your best role is that of familiar comforter. The more you can soothe the child and persuade him to let himself sleep, the less he will know about this unpleasant period and the sooner it will be over. When he stirs or cries, tell him that you are there and that it is "all over," but then stroke him back to sleep again. Don't try to make him sit up and take notice. You may need to repeat your reassurances several times as his first "awakenings" will be brief and forgotten.

● However unpleasant this period *looks*, take comfort from the fact that the child will not remember much about it afterwards.

Even once the child is definitely awake and apparently "over" the anesthetic, he may be depressed, irritable and miserable for hours or even for a day or two.

Staff may seem brutally insistent that the child get out of bed and/or do breathing and other exercises with a physiotherapist very soon after the operation. It is vitally important that his muscle tone and efficient circulation be maintained and that, even if it hurts, he breathe deeply and cough efficiently so as to keep his respiratory tract clear of mucus.

• Your role will depend on whether staff do want to encourage activity or whether the operation was one after which they want him kept quiet. Since you are probably the person best able *either* to encourage him out of bed and into taking an interest in the other children, *or* into resting quietly while you read that favorite book aloud, do ask.

Some children, after some operations, are haunted by dressings which, they feel, may cover some horrible mutilation. Since a surgical wound is almost always less horrific than imagination suggests, your child may feel better if he has a look at his scar when the dressings are changed.

• Remember, though, that he does not have your experience of the healing process. Having discovered that his belly is still *there* after removal of his appendix, he may be convinced that the wound and stitches which he can see will remain forever. If you react favorably ("that's beautifully neat. Once those stitches are out and the skin has all healed it will hardly show . . .") he may believe you. If you happen to have a nicely inconspicuous surgical scar in the family, show it to him.

Appendectomy

Removal of the appendix, performed, as a matter of urgency, when a child has, or is thought to have, appendicitis.

The appendix is a small dead-end tube leading off the large intestine. Because it is a dead end, this tube can only discharge anything which gets into it from the intestine back the way it came and it is therefore rather liable to inflammation. Opinions about appendicitis have changed radically in recent years. It used to be thought that the appendix became inflamed when something small and hard, like a fruit pit, became wedged in it. Now it is thought that blockage of that single opening by small hard pellets of waste matter is a more frequent cause. Certainly there is no need to worry about the possibility of appendicitis just because your child swallows grape pits or a cherry stone. For many years the appendix was regarded as a completely useless, obsolete addition to the intestine. Occasionally explorers would have their appendixes removed prior to their travels in case of appendicitis while they were far from civilization. Now it is known that the walls of the appendix are rich in lymphoid tissue (*see* **Immune Response**) which might play a role in the production of antibodies. While people can manage perfectly well without their appendixes, nobody would have one removed unnecessarily.

It used to be thought that an appendix could "grumble," causing bouts of abdominal pain which then receded. Now most doctors believe that recurrent abdominal pain must have some other cause (*see below* Peritonitis). Appendicitis gets worse and worse until the appendix either bursts (causing peritonitis) or is removed.

Diagnosing appendicitis

There are many causes for abdominal pain with or without associated symptoms such as vomiting, constipation, diarrhea and fever (*see* **Abdominal Pain**). A skilled surgeon can examine the child's abdomen, assess the pain which particular maneuvers (often including a rectal examination) do or do not provoke, and make a highly educated guess as to the cause. But even he cannot always be certain of a diagnosis of appendicitis. If he is in doubt, but on balance thinks appendicitis *unlikely*, he may keep the child in the hospital for observation. All preparations for surgery (including withholding food and drink) will probably be made so that the operation can be performed immediately if the condition becomes clear. If he is in doubt but on balance considers appendicitis *likely*, he will probably operate. The risks of an unnecessary appendectomy are far less than the risks of waiting too long.

If an inflamed appendix is not removed quickly (usually within twenty-four hours of the first symptoms) it is likely to fill with pus and eventually burst. This is the situation which most often gives rise to the condition known as peritonitis, in which infected material spreads through the abdomen causing widespread inflammation and infection. Instead of the very simple operation involved in removing the appendix, the surgeon then has to repair the rupture and deal with the infection. Peritonitis, even today, is dangerous.

Removing the appendix

Appendectomy is a routine operation for the hospital even if it is a once-in-a-lifetime experience for your child. No special preparations are usually needed. Premedication and anesthesia will be given.

The appendix is removed through a small incision low down on the right of the abdomen. Many surgeons pride themselves on leaving a scar not more than a couple of inches long and below the "bikini line."

The child will probably be allowed home as soon as the stitches are removed, often about day seven.

Blocked tear (lacrimal) duct

Lacrimal ducts carry surplus tears from the eye into the nose from which they drain. When a child cries, the surplus fluid appears as external tears, but the rest of the time the ducts ensure that the eyes have enough bathing fluid but not too much.

Many newborn babies have runny or "sticky" eyes. The maternity hospital may take swabs in order to check for infection, but often the condition is simply due to debris, such as amniotic fluid or blood, getting into the eye during birth (*see* **Eyes and Seeing; Eye Disorders and Blindness**/Eye disorders).

Diagnosing a blocked tear duct

A baby who, during his first few months, has an eye which constantly runs clear fluid or which recurrently becomes "sticky," may have a blocked tear duct. The ducts usually clear themselves by six months of age so each episode of "sticky eye" will be treated symptomatically to begin with.

If there is continual running or frequent stickiness in the second half of the first year, your doctor may advise that the duct be cleared by an ophthalmic surgeon under general anesthesia.

Clearing a tear duct

Parents will often be given some choice about the timing of this very minor operation. If you feel strongly that you would prefer to wait a further three months, hoping that the tear duct will clear itself, your doctor will probably accept this. But unless you have strong reasons for waiting it is probably better to accept the earliest appointment you can be given; the whole hospital experience is likely to be more upsetting to a one-year-old than to a child of eight or nine months.

The operation only involves passing a very fine probe along the tear duct. Anesthesia is very brief; since there is no cutting involved, there should be no pain and there will be no stitches to be removed or any scarring. You may be allowed to take the baby home on the same day.

Circumcision

Circumcision is a minor operation but one which, in a child past early infancy, can cause major upset. A toddler is likely to be uncomprehendingly furious at this assault on his precious self. A four-year-old may suffer agonies (sometimes amounting almost to an identity crisis) concerning what he may see as a punishment for his sexuality or the secret sensuality of his love for his mother. Even an eight- or nine-year-old, well able to understand why the operation is needed and allowed to share in the decision to have it performed, may find the whole procedure deeply embarrassing and depressing. If a baby is left uncircumcised, the procedure is seldom needed later unless over-enthusiastic attempts have been made to retract his foreskin (*see* **Circumcision**). Some of the reasons for the operation include:

Diagnosing a need for late circumcision

Persistent or recurrent soreness/infection under the foreskin (balanitis). This can often be dealt with by a combination of drugs and improved hygiene but occasionally the frequency of the bouts, or the scarring they are causing, does make surgery necessary.

Tightness of the foreskin (phimosis) so great that the flow of urine is obstructed or slowed down.

Failure of the foreskin to roll back easily when the penis is erect. While this may go with phimosis it does occasionally occur separately. The foreskin is not tight; it can easily be retracted with the hands, but it does not retract itself as erection takes place.

Removing the foreskin

Unlike infant circumcision, the operation is always carried out under a general anesthetic. A "cuff" of foreskin is removed and the edges of the cut are stitched together (another difference from the infant procedure which requires no stitches). The patient is often allowed home later the same day, as soon as he has recovered from the anesthetic. If you are offered this "day surgery" for your child, do accept it as not having to stay in the hospital will probably much reduce his distress.

Stitches are usually removed about a week later and the soreness should be over within two weeks.

● If erection occurs in the few days following circumcision it is likely to be very painful. This can add to the distress of a very small boy who feels that his own organ is attacking him, or to that of an older boy whose erections may be a very private pleasure. Difficulty in getting to sleep after circumcision is sometimes due not only to the general upset but to the fact that the boy cannot settle down with his hand on his penis for comfort.

● While the hospital will instruct you in caring for the surgical wound, there is quite a lot you can do to make the first few days at home more comfortable. A protective "box," for example, as worn by many sportsmen, may help an older boy, a toddler's equivalent can be quickly produced if you cut a hard but hollow rubber ball in half.

● If a school-aged boy has to have this operation, do try to arrange it during the vacations and help him to keep the whole matter entirely private from his peers if he prefers. If he must return to school before the wound has healed to a point where his penis looks normal (though now circumcised) it may be a kindness to get him temporarily excused from gym or any other circumstances which demand that he strip in public.

Cleft lip

A baby's upper lip develops in two parts while she is in the womb and normally joins up before birth. If this joining fails to take place, she will be born with it still separated in the middle.

Facing a cleft lip   The first sight of their new baby with a cleft lip usually gives parents a shock which is out of proportion to the real seriousness of the condition. It looks dreadful, but it has no implications for the baby's health (unless the palate is also cleft, *see below*) and only short-term implications for her appearance. Ideally you should be shown photographs of babies whose cleft lips have been repaired, within minutes of seeing your own affected child. If nobody offers you such photographs, do ask to see some. Such babies look (and are) perfectly normal. The scars, even at the beginning, are scarcely visible. What you have to cope with is your own shock and misery—perhaps even amounting to a feeling that you cannot love a baby who looks like that—and a wait of approximately three months before surgery can put the matter right.

Repairing a   Repair of a cleft lip is usually undertaken when the baby is about three
cleft lip   months old. It should be (and almost always is) undertaken by a plastic surgeon. Some such surgeons specialize in this condition and it is certainly worthwhile to seek out such a professional if possible. The operation is not serious but it is lengthy as the finest and most careful stitching is used to bring the two parts of the lip into perfect alignment.

The baby will probably be kept in the hospital for several days as you may need help with feeding her, and with ensuring that her questing hands do not ruin the plastic surgeon's work.

Cleft palate

The "roof" of the mouth also develops in two parts and, like the upper lip, occasionally fails to close up before birth. The two conditions often, but not invariably, go together.

Facing a cleft palate

If the lip is intact, a cleft palate is not immediately obvious and therefore the shock to new parents is far less. The condition is far more serious, however. The space between the two halves of the palate means that when the baby sucks milk, it is free to go up into her nasal passages and choke her. She will not be able to feed normally.

Preparing for repair of a cleft palate

The two halves of the cleft palate cannot be finally joined together until they are of approximately the same size, and until growth within the mouth has reached a suitable point. The final operation commonly has to wait until the baby is about eighteen months old. In the meantime she has to be fed. Very early feedings may be accomplished by using a special nipple with a wide flat guard on the top which effectively prevents milk from escaping to the absent roof of the mouth. Within days, minor surgery will probably be carried out to fit a plate to the palate. This first operation serves the double purpose of blocking off that opening and encouraging the smaller half of the palate to grow relatively faster than the larger half.

These plates may need frequent changing to allow for the child's growth, to keep feeding as easy as possible for you both, and to make sure that she has the greatest possible freedom to make early sounds. If you can come to terms with this difficult period, believe that your child's difficulties really will be finally solved before she reaches kindergarten age, and work with the hospital team throughout her infancy, you will all be ideally placed to ride through the final operation when the time comes.

Repairing a cleft palate

The ease or difficulty with which the final repair of a cleft palate can be accomplished depends on all that early preparation. Being a toddler, your child is rather likely to be upset by the hospital admission, but being accustomed to hospital appointments, she may cope rather better than a child who is admitted as an emergency. The surgery itself is not dangerous but there is likely to be considerable pain and difficulty in feeding afterwards. She may be in the hospital for some days and will certainly survive better if you can be with her.

● If you know an adult whose cleft lip/palate was poorly repaired many years ago, you may find it difficult to believe that your child will ever look normal. But she will. The techniques of plastic surgery have improved and so has our knowledge of the correct timing for these operations. Once again, when you find yourself in despair, do ask for "before and after" photographs.

Hernia (inguinal)

Diagnosing an inguinal hernia

If you should notice a "swelling" low down on your baby's abdomen, in the groin area or over the scrotum, a loop of intestine may have found its way through the inguinal canal to form a hernia (*see* **Hernia**).

As we have seen, the inguinal canal usually closes up when the testicles have travelled down it to take up their permanent position in the scrotum. But sometimes the canal remains open; this is why inguinal hernias are frequently associated with undescended or retractile testicles (*see below* Undescended testicles).

The appearance of such a hernia is not an emergency in itself but it can become an emergency if that loop of intestine should become trapped outside the body and thus lose its full blood supply. If you lay the baby down, the hernia will probably vanish and this will show that the intestine has slipped back into its proper place. If laying him down does not produce this effect and the bulge remains visible, you would probably be wise to take the baby directly to your nearest emergency room.

If the hernia does vanish when the baby is lying down, make an appointment to see your doctor as soon as it is convenient. The hernia may, or may not, reappear whenever the baby is in an upright position, but as long as it continues to slip freely in and out of the abdomen there is nothing to worry about. Your doctor will probably refer you to a surgeon and the operation will be carried out as soon as it can be arranged, but not as an emergency.

Correcting an inguinal hernia

If an inguinal hernia is operated upon within days, or a few weeks, of its first appearance, the procedure is very quick and simple. All the surgeon has to do is to ensure that the testicles are in the scrotum and that the intestine is in its rightful place, and then tie the ring of muscles around the inguinal canal so that a retractile testicle can no longer go up or any intestine come down it.

If surgery is long delayed, the affected muscles may become stretched and weakened so that a far more elaborate repair is needed.

Hydrocele

A hydrocele is a collection of fluid around the testicle which makes the scrotum look enlarged and swollen. If a hydrocele is present on one side only, parents sometimes mistake it for an inguinal hernia (*see above*). Often, though, both sides of the scrotum are affected. The hydrocele is often present at birth.

A hydrocele almost always resolves itself without any treatment at all. The fluid absorbs, leaving the testicle entirely undamaged. Only in the extremely rare case of a hydrocele persisting after the first year is surgery considered.

That rarely needed surgery for hydrocele is simple in itself, but the age at which it must be carried out is unfortunate. Toddlers tend to react badly to hospital admission, while little boys are usually extremely concerned about their genitals and may react very badly to any surgical interference in that area.

Intussusception

Although this is not at all a common condition, it is mentioned here because immediate recognition and surgery are vitally important.

Acute intussusception occurs when a portion of the intestine telescopes into the portion immediately ahead of it, causing a concertina-like bowel obstruction. This rare abdominal emergency is least uncommon in babies between about three months and one year. It can usually be differentiated from other forms of "colic" by the following signs:

Diagnosing
intussusception

Excruciating pain causes the baby not only to scream and draw up his legs, but to go very pale or grayish and sometimes to become soaked in sweat so that his hair is plastered to his desperately thrashing head.

The pain occurs in distinct bouts geared to the rhythmical contractions of the bowel. As these peristaltic movements force the telescoped bowel forward, pain occurs. As the wave of intestinal movement passes, the pain stops. A baby who has had one or two bouts of pain of this intensity will commonly drop off to sleep from sheer exhaustion, but will be woken within a minute or two by the next bout.

The baby is very likely to vomit and to bleed from his rectum so that any stool he passes looks like red currant jelly. But if you suspect this emergency, don't assume that because he has not vomited or passed a "red currant jelly" stool, you must be wrong: seek medical advice immediately.

Correcting an
intussusception

If an intussusception is operated upon early, the surgery involved is comparatively simple. An incision is made through the abdominal wall and the intestine pulled back into shape. If surgery is delayed, the affected part of the intestine may be squeezed tightly for so long that lack of blood causes it to become gangrenous. The damaged part has to be removed and the operation becomes a very serious procedure.

Myringotomy (drainage of the middle ear)
(*see* **Ears and Hearing; Ear Disorders and Deafness**)

Repeated infections in the middle ear, especially if these are combined with much-enlarged adenoids, can lead to the accumulation of matter which will not drain freely down the eustachian tubes and into the throat. Matter or fluid in the middle ear immediately affects hearing, repeated infection can cause scarring which will reduce hearing permanently.

Draining the
middle ear

A tiny incision is made in the eardrum so that the middle ear can be drained from the outer ear. On its own, this is a very minor surgical procedure. Your child will be given a general anesthetic but will usually be allowed home as soon as he has recovered from it.

Sometimes a tiny plastic or metal tube (called a grommet) is left in the surgeon's incision so that any further accumulations of fluid can continue to drain out. You may have to ban swimming, and take care that no water gets into the child's ear during bathing. The grommet usually comes out by itself as healing proceeds.

Myringotomy is sometimes combined with removal of the adenoids if these are thought to have been contributing to the ear problems. In that case, of course, your child will be kept in the hospital for a few days (*see below* Tonsillectomy and adenoidectomy).

Plastic surgery

While the work of a plastic surgeon may be vital—and almost miraculous —to a child born with a cleft lip or seriously scarred in an accident, its use to correct minor blemishes and deformities is, and should be, strictly limited. Plastic surgery involves cutting; cutting makes scars and scars grow as a child grows. If your child is born with a strawberry mark on her face (see **Birthmarks**) she *will* be able to have it removed surgically if it should be one of the rare ones which does not vanish of its own accord, but you and she will both have to accept it for several years first. If she has a dark and ill-placed mole, this too can be removed one day, but that day is so far into the future that it is a pity if she has to go through most of her childhood waiting to change herself. On the whole, characteristics like sticking-out ears or "odd" noses are better accepted as part of the individuality of the individual child. If you can accept and love her as she is, she will probably be able to do so, too.

Appearance usually becomes vitally important to adolescents and at this stage plastic surgery is more likely to be satisfactory because growth is almost complete. If the blemish is real—in the sense of being not only clearly visible but also ugly to everyone who sees her—its removal may do a great deal to boost her confidence and to help her approve of her nearly grown-up self. Be cautious, though. Some adolescents pick on a particular physical characteristic and use it as a focus for discontent which is really far more deep-seated. A "nose job," however expertly performed, may cast your daughter even farther into a depression which was not really about her face but about her identity as a person (*see* **Adolescence**/Problems with appearance and body image).

If ever you contemplate seeking plastic surgery for a child of any age, do start by consulting the doctor who knows her best. In some communities there are plastic surgeons whose practice is almost entirely "cosmetic," rather than medical, and who will strive to give the patient what she says she wants without a full assessment designed to ensure that the procedure is in her best interests. The recent example of a fifteen-year-old who responded to an advertisement and had her breasts "augmented" is a salutary case in point. Nobody pointed out to her that, even if the procedure was entirely "successful," it was likely to cause difficulties if she ever wanted to breast-feed a baby.

Pyloric stenosis

The pylorus is the muscular valve which controls the flow of food and gastric juices from the stomach into the duodenum and thence into the intestines. In pyloric stenosis, the muscles thicken so that the valve does not function correctly. Food-flow is either partially or completely blocked. The condition is far commoner in boys than in girls but is also commoner in first born than in later children. If your first son has it, the chances of later boys in your family having it, too, are only a little greater than the chances for an unaffected family.

Signs of pyloric stenosis If milk is taken into the stomach but cannot reach the duodenum, there is only one place for it to go: back up again. The principal sign of pyloric stenosis, then, is vomiting. It may take place during feeding or soon afterwards. While the first episodes may seem like ordinary "spitting up," the vomiting becomes extremely forceful as the degree of obstruction increases. Milk is often ejected several feet, perhaps hitting the wall behind you. It is accurately named "projectile vomiting."

Left untreated, pyloric stenosis deprives a baby of nourishment and, more importantly, of fluid. He will therefore lose weight and become dehydrated. He will produce very little waste matter as his food is not reaching the intestine.

Recognizing pyloric stenosis early

Ideally pyloric stenosis should be recognized before the obstruction has become great enough to deprive the baby of fluid and food. You will probably distinguish between the vomiting of early pyloric stenosis and vomiting due to any other cause, such as infection, if you notice that although he vomits whenever he is fed *the baby is hungry*. He is not ill. He wants the food and this is your clue to the fact that the vomiting is mechanical.

● It takes that muscular valve a week or two to thicken enough to cause trouble, so any vomiting in the very first week or two of life is unlikely to be from this cause. On the other hand, if the pylorus is going to cause obstruction it will certainly have begun to do so by the time the baby is around six weeks. Vomiting which *begins* later must have another cause.

Diagnosis of pyloric stenosis

Your doctor or nurse can confirm your suspicions by watching the baby during a feeding. Forceful contractions of the distended stomach can be seen against the obstruction outlined under the baby's skin. Even without watching a feeding, your doctor may be able to feel the thickened muscular valve through the skin of the abdomen.

Treatment of pyloric stenosis

In some countries such babies are treated with special feedings and antispasmodic drugs in the expectation that the condition will right itself. But in most Western countries, and certainly in Britain and the United States, definitive surgery is undertaken as soon as possible. Should you have to wait a few days for surgery, dietary and drug treatment may be prescribed in the meantime.

Relieving the obstruction of pyloric stenosis

The operation is simple and quick, involving only a short general anesthetic while the surgeon makes an incision through the abdominal wall and pylorus so as to relieve the obstruction. The baby can usually be fed normally within a few hours (although he may vomit at the first couple of feedings) and normal digestion begins immediately and continues thereafter. No further problems need be anticipated.

Squint (strabismus; "cross-eyes"; "lazy eye")
(*see* **Eyes and Seeing; Eye Disorders and Blindness**)

Not all squints can be cured by surgery, but some, especially the types which are present from birth or noted in the first year, are largely due to an imbalance in the lengths of the muscles controlling the movements of the two eyes. An ophthalmic surgeon can readjust the muscles so that the eyes work together.

Although eye surgery on a baby or small child is neither pleasant to think about nor to undergo, a surgical solution is a far happier option than the long drawn-out treatments which may otherwise be needed.

● If your child is to have surgery for strabismus do make every effort to stay with him. There are several reasons why this is especially important.

Eyes may or may not "window the soul," but they are certainly very personal-feeling, even to a baby. The many eye examinations he will have to undergo will upset him more than examinations of, say, a hernia.

If he needs one operation he may well need a second later on. The less traumatic the first the more easily he will ride through the next.

Eye surgery probably means quite a lot of other procedures, such as eye drops and so forth, before and after the operation. He will tolerate these better if you are there.

He will probably have to have one or both eyes covered for a period. Busy nurses may be unable to watch him every moment so if he pulls the bandages off when left alone they may even resort to tying his hands to the sides of the crib. If you are there you can protect him from all that. Even if he is old enough to cooperate in leaving the bandages alone, being unable to see is very frightening for anyone and positively terrifying for a small child in a strange place. He needs to be able to hear you and feel your touch.

Tonsillectomy and adenoidectomy

Children under five tend to have rapidly growing tonsils and adenoids and to be prone to tonsillitis, middle-ear infections and congestion problems. A couple of generations ago it was thought that the tonsils and adenoids *caused* these childish illnesses and they were therefore removed, almost as a matter of routine, from many children. Now, both knowledge and attitudes have changed and the operations have become much less frequent.

A five-year-old who has three or four bouts of tonsillitis and several colds in one year looks rather pale, has a poor appetite and breathes through his mouth, will probably be found to have enlarged adenoids and big, wobbly tonsils which almost meet in the middle. During his illnesses, those tonsils may have white or yellowy flecks on them. It is easy to see why people believed that the tonsils were harboring the infection and that taking them out would produce a healthier child. In fact those tonsils are *reacting to* infection rather than causing it. Since it is their prime function to react to infection by instigating the production of antibodies, the child may well be better off with than without them. Some research comparing the later health of children who have, and have not, had tonsillectomies/adenoidectomies shows no significant difference in the number or severity of later infections. All tend to "grow out of" the tendency to frequent upper respiratory infections by the age of about seven, while the tonsils and adenoids shrink significantly during the early school years.

When tonsillectomy may be advisable

Some authorities believe that tonsils which have been infected again and again may have pockets of pus trapped within them which can act as a reservoir of infection which flares up to cause recurrent symptoms. Whether or not tonsils ever actually cause infection, most authorities would agree that their removal should be considered if a school-aged child has had three or four bouts of acute tonsillitis a year for at least the last two years. If a child's tonsils are removed his adenoids will probably be removed at the same time.

When adenoidectomy may be advisable

If enlarged adenoids are contributing to frequent middle-ear infections, by obstructing free drainage through the eustachian tubes (*see above* Myringotomy) their removal may be urgent.

● Mouth-breathing, snoring and so forth are not in themselves sufficient reasons for this operation because they will resolve spontaneously as the adenoids shrink during childhood.

An adenoidectomy which is undertaken to protect a child's ears and hearing may be carried out when he is only two or three years old. The tonsils will seldom be removed at the same time because they still have years of useful work ahead of them.

When tonsils and adenoids are removed

Although "T and A" is now a very safe operation, the immediate post-operative period may be very unpleasant for the child and alarming for parents.

The child's throat is naturally extremely sore (although the raw patches heal surprisingly quickly). If he vomits because of the anesthetic, there may be bleeding. If he cries because of the pain, the blood and the vomiting, he will increase all three and may get himself into a horrible vicious circle. It is as well that you should be warned because, provided that the hospital will allow you to be with the child while he recovers, and provided you do not panic, you have a vital role to play.

Keep the child as quiet and calm as you possibly can. The stiller he keeps and the more he allows himself to sleep off the anesthetic, the less likely it is that he will vomit. The less panicky he gets because of pain and blood the less there will be of either.

● A few hospitals still try to prevent parents from sitting with children while they recover from "T and A" anesthetics because they do not trust those parents not to get upset. Try to select a hospital which cooperates with parents and prove to the staff that you can help, rather than hinder, them and the child.

Undescended testicles
(for recognition of the condition *see* **Undescended Testicle**)

A testicle which has not descended by the time a boy is around three or four must be brought down into the scrotum and fixed there. The operation is not physically serious but its nature and timing are psycho-logically unfortunate. Whether your son can voice these feelings or not, he is very likely to see this interference with his sexual parts as some kind of attack on his maleness.

Some doctors and surgeons may agree to leave the operation until a little later in a boy's life, but any such decision should be reached very carefully. Early descent of the testicle is thought to optimize its chances of absolutely normal sperm production later. The abdomen is too warm for testicles which have evolved into their scrotal position largely because they function best if kept a few degrees cooler than the rest of the body. Perhaps slightly reduced sperm production in one testicle would not matter very much to your son—many men father plenty of children with only one—but there is always the slight risk of the "good" one getting damaged. . . . Furthermore, delaying the operation until, say, seven or eight, may help the boy to accept explanations about the surgery but may have left him vulnerable to feeling "different" when boys at school first compared sexual parts.

On the whole it is probably best to accept the earliest operation your medical advisers suggest and to concentrate on seeing your child through it as best you can. This is another occasion when having a parent room-in with him will certainly help.

Visiting by children

Hospitals vary in their attitudes to visiting children: some pride themselves on making them welcome, others ban them altogether or tolerate only those above a certain age.

If you are considering taking a young child to visit, say, a parent who is in the hospital, do consider the following points before you do so:

A child who wants Mommy wants her as she usually is

However much he is missing her, a mother who, because of her physical state, neither looks nor can behave as he expects, can be extremely frightening. Before you take him to visit her, go by yourself and try to consider her through his inexperienced eyes. It may be better to delay the visit if, for example:

Her color is bad, eyes puffy, hair stringy. . . . The child will look mostly at her face. Does it look worse than he has seen it first thing in the morning after she has had an especially bad night?

She has anything attached to her such as an oxygen mask, nasal tube, intravenous drip. A young child, who will inevitably feel that his mother has been "taken over" by the hospital, may have terrifying fantasies about her having become "part of those machines."

She is in pain. A young child probably will not recognize pain as pain, but he will register it as distress and be very distressed himself.

She is obviously sedated. Again the child will not recognize sedation for what it is, but will sense his mother's strange detachment from reality (which for him means himself) and may feel that she rejects him.

● The sick parent may long to see the child and be convinced that he or she can put on an act sufficient to reassure him. Use *your* judgment; the patient cannot see him/herself.

If the child saw an accident or drama, a glimpse may reassure

If the whole family was in a car crash and the father was badly hurt, children who saw him carried, covered in blood and unconscious, into the ambulance, may desperately need to glimpse him in his hospital bed just to see that he is actually alive. Under those circumstances a quick wave from the doorway of the ward may be a good compromise.

If a brother or sister got hurt or fell dramatically ill (as with a febrile convulsion, for example) in front of the child, she may be convinced that the whole thing was her fault and that everybody (especially the sick sibling) now hates her. Again, a visit may be important, even if the patient is in a bad way, but be sure that everything the child sees is carefully explained.

If a parent has elective surgery a child may feel the hospital made him/her ill

It is extremely difficult for a young child to understand why a parent who appeared perfectly well should choose to enter a hospital and have an operation which appears to make her ill. If the procedure only involves a short stay, it may be better if the absence is carefully explained but the child does not visit. If the hospital admission is for a week or more you will have to explain very carefully, using any parallels in the child's experience which you can think of. Has he, for example, ever had a tooth extracted? If so, you may be able to point out that, just as the dentist had to pull the tooth out, leaving a sore hole, because otherwise it would not stop aching, so the doctor has had to make Mom's leg sore to deal with the varicose veins which would not stop aching.

Hydrocele

A hydrocele is a collection of fluid swelling the scrotum around one or both testicles. For further discussion *see* **Hospital**/Surgery.

Hygiene *see* **Infection**/Preventing infection: Infection and home hygiene; sterilants, sterilization, disinfectants and antiseptics. *See also* **Diarrhea, Gastroenteritis and Food Poisoning; Nursing.**

Hyperactive Children (The Hyperkinetic Syndrome)

Does your child have a very short attention span so that, left to himself, he darts from one thing to another and, even given attention, finds it difficult to concentrate for more than a minute or two? Does his supply of energy seem to be inexhaustible so that he rushes around all day, finds himself physical activities even in the most unsuitable circumstances and wears out everyone except himself? Is he so impulsive that he seems to have no thought for his own safety or anyone else's, so that he is courageous to the point of recklessness and boisterous to the point of violence? If so, he may be a perfectly normal toddler or pre-school child, a somewhat anxious and unhappy school child, or a "hyperactive" child.

Which he is depends not so much on his behavior, or even on whether or not he is past the age when this kind of behavior is universal, but on what you, and other adults who are significant to him, think of that behavior.

If he is loved, accepted and "managed" without undue stress, the question of whether his behavior is "normal" will not arise. You and the rest of the family accommodate him as the individual he is and, while you may sometimes moan about the sheer hard work involved in parenthood, it will probably not occur to you that he could be altered by anything but the normal processes of socialization: his own maturing and the influences around him. But if you and the rest of the family are having your lives disrupted by this child, the havoc he wreaks, the supervision he needs, his noise, his refusal to pay attention to you or to respond to what seems to you to be ordinary discipline, you may begin to wonder whether there is something wrong which could be righted. Once you begin to wonder, the reactions of outsiders will begin to have an impact too, especially if reciprocal child-visiting arrangements break down because your neighbors do not want him in the house, sitters refuse to care for him because he is so disruptive and grandparents stop suggesting family Sundays because they find him intolerable.

Pre-school or infant schoolteachers are probably the most influential outsiders in a child's life and it is often they who first *alarm* parents about a child's over-activity. A teacher has responsibility not just for your child but for a group. She has expectations as to the limits within which all those children should behave, and she has planned activities and learning processes which the group is to undertake. There is no doubt that one child who is, for whatever reason, unable, unready or unwilling to cooperate can make her job far more difficult—even impossible. If the child's impulsive behavior includes overturning furniture onto other children's toes, bopping them over the head with toys and/or physically attacking them, she may have complaints from other parents to deal with as well as her own sense of inadequacy in not being able to hold your child's attention or peacefully pursue her group's education.

Once criticism and complaint from the school are added to your own exhaustion and stress in dealing with the very active, distractable, impulsive child at home, you may well feel that you need some help.

You can seek help and advice from your doctor or, if the child is of school age, from the school medical officer. But the help and advice you are offered will depend on where you live and on the attitudes of those you consult. Broadly speaking, in most parts of Britain, problems concerning a child's behavior and management will be regarded as social/psychological issues; but in most of the United States and in a few places in Britain, these particular problems of "hyperactivity" will be regarded as medical. The difference may be crucially important to the whole family and particularly to the child himself. They may, indeed, be important to society as a whole.

The socio-psychological approach to "hyperactivity"

All behavior results from an interaction between the child's unique self and the people who care for him in the environment they all share. A child emerges from the womb. He is already partly shaped by a combination of his genetic make-up and his experiences before and during birth. He is born to parents who already have an infinite complexity of personality, and of aspirations and expectations about him. As they meet they begin to affect each other's behavior in an endless feedback loop. Perhaps the newborn is jumpy and irritable. His parents may react to his behavior with soothing comfort, with impatience or with inept anxiety. Whatever their reaction, it will influence the handling they offer the baby, and that handling will affect the next stages of his development and, therefore, the feedback which they get from him. . . . Sometimes a child "fits" so perfectly with his parents that all seem to dance, all through his child-hood, to the same familiar melody. More often there are periods in a child's life when he seems to dance to a different rhythm. Occasionally child and parents find each other "difficult" from the beginning so that the band spends more time in discord and retuning than in music.

This sort of approach recognizes that a parent's power to *change* a child's current behavior is always limited by that child's personal growth and maturity. However strong and mutual the theme, you cannot teach a two-year-old to behave as we expect eight-year-olds to behave. But it also recognizes that the stronger that mutual theme has been and, therefore, the more confident all parties are that they both love each other and are loved, the greater will be their fundamental desire to cooperate with each other. Parents who have enjoyed a child's infancy and reached the toddler phase able to respect themselves as "good parents" and the child as a "smashing fella," will usually ride through two-year-old tantrums and teases easily. That same child, sure that he is loved and approved of by parents whom he trusts, will not usually have to put up too big a fight about growing up. The longer such a mutually beneficial circle goes on being traced and retraced the solider the base it makes for the increasing complexities and stresses offered to the growing child by the outside world. But there are vicious circles, too. Diverse forces may act to put parents and child out of step with each other. A new baby can change a mother's view of her toddler, from "healthily active" to "a pain in the neck," almost overnight, and more gradually change his confidence and his image of himself, too (*see* **Depression**/In children before puberty). A move—perhaps from the casual informality and open spaces of a rural setting to the tight scheduling and restrictions of life in a city apartment —can change a four-year-old's way of life so radically that the *joie de vivre* which formerly made his parents laugh at most of his antics turns to a sulky anxious whining which makes them notice and reprove him for every infraction of a new set of rules. The point is that anything which acts strongly on either parents or child will act also on the rest of the family—to good effect or to bad.

Seeking help if your child is "hyperactive"

If your child seems to you to be unmanageable, whether or not teachers and other adults are complaining about him, discuss the matter with your doctor. Unless he can help you directly, you will be referred, probably, to a child guidance clinic. The professional who actually talks to you will probably be a member of a team which includes medical doctors, psychiatrists, psychologists, neurologists and teachers.

She will be acutely aware that the behaviors which lead to some children being labelled "hyperactive" are normal behaviors for most children some of the time. We cannot say "This child is hyperactive: look, he threw a chair through the window and then rushed off for no reason and pushed over the baby and when I called him for supper he took ten minutes to come and then only sat up for three seconds." That could be any strong, unsupervised toddler, or any four-year-old who was having a really bad day. The professional accepts that you believe your child's behavior is at least exceptional, if not abnormal. But she has to call on all the team's knowledge of the vast variety of normal behavior in children of whom nobody is complaining, in order to assess your child's for herself. It is important not to be offended if she appears to doubt, or minimize, the incidents you report to her. She does not doubt your stress and distress, nor the accuracy of your reports, but she has to put them into a developmental context. It may help, amuse or shock you to learn that two big surveys in the United States showed that *forty-nine percent of all parents thought their children were overactive* while teachers classified *fifty percent of children as restless and unable to sit still and thirty percent as definitely hyperactive.* Figures like these make it clear that many adults would like children to behave differently from the way most of them actually do behave. Many parents and teachers obviously fall into the trap of assuming that most other children behave "better" than the ones they have to deal with and therefore that it is the "good" and "easy to manage" children who are the norm. It is not.

The team will want to discover whether the child's behavior *always* seems hyperactive or whether there are circumstances in which he does not single himself out from other children. The mother who said, "He's not hyperactive this year. He's got a good teacher," put her finger squarely on an important variable. The child's behavior will seem aberrant to adults who cannot cope with it, but you need to know whether the relevant factor is his behavior or that of the adults. Children who are wildly hyperactive at school but not at home, or vice versa, are usually reacting to an environment which they find impossibly stressful/boring. Environmental changes will usually improve the behavior.

If the professional discovers that the child's behavior is hyperactive under all circumstances, to a degree which renders his behavior quite inappropriate to his age and developmental stage, she will want, with her colleagues, to exclude the possibility that he has any medical or neurological condition which is either causing the behavior or being associated with it in his interaction with other people. Epilepsy, for example, is sometimes directly associated with hyperactive behavior (*see* **Convulsions, Seizures and "Fits"**), while some hyperactive children have associated handicaps such as mental subnormality or undiagnosed deafness. Usually, though, no physical problems are found (but *see below* The medical approach).

Many "hyperactive" children are unhappy, anxious children; the professional will want to explore both the present and past interaction between the child and yourselves and any key changes or events which may *either* have caused him to become distractable and wild *or* caused you to begin to react differently to such behavior. This kind of discussion can be very threatening to parents who probably already feel both deeply angry at the disruptive child and extremely guilty at not being able to accept, love and manage him. It sometimes helps to remember that the professional is far from seeking a place to put the blame. It is the essence of her approach that the child's behavior and yours are the music which result from your playing upon each other. It is not your fault that you are as you are; it is not the child's fault that he is as he is, nor are any of you directly responsible for all of you being as you are. She wants to see whether you can all be helped to rewrite the score so that there is music rather than discord.

There is seldom any magic in this kind of work. Very occasionally a third party can spot a flaw in the warp of family life which those who are knitted into it cannot see, and it may be possible to go back and pick up the dropped stitches. In one family, for example, the mother was deep in grief for a miscarried baby of whom the two-year-old had had no knowledge. Since she knew he could not be grieving for the baby and it never occurred to her that he could be grieving for the loss of the happy mother she had been, she reacted to his increasingly uncontrolled behavior more and more strictly. Furious that he should become so "difficult" just when she needed peace, she first took away all his most "grown-up" toys because he kept breaking them, and then confined him for hours at a time to his crib because she did not feel energetic enough to keep him safe in any other way. Over the next few months a vicious circle of depression and anger was established between them. The father, desperate for them both but seldom at home, maintained some kind of relationship with the little boy whom he found "just about manageable if you kept on the go with him all the time, but quite impossible to settle to playing on his own or even to any kind of mutual play he found at all difficult." When he was three he was sent to nursery school. A month later he was excluded as "totally disruptive and violent to the other children" and he was referred to the clinic. It did not take long for that mother to see where life had gone wrong for her child. It took longer for her to forgive herself on the grounds that life had, at that point, gone tragically wrong for her, too. It will probably take longer still for the child to regain confidence in her love and approval and become able to feel valued enough to try the next tentative stages in growing up. But a start has been made.

Much more usually, though, no specific event can be pinpointed. The interaction between child and parents may always have been off-key and successive events, changes and developments in all family members may simply have driven this child further and further into what has become a self-fulfilling prophecy of doom. Under these circumstances the whole team will be involved in offering help on several fronts at once. A counsellor may work with you for greater understanding of the child's feelings *and* for decisions about what behavior should be tolerated, even provided for, and which should be firmly controlled or banned. A place may be offered in a particular nursery or kindergarten where teachers will strive to enable your child to listen and play for long enough to discover pleasure in doing so. Child guidance clinic staff may work with you on a regular basis to help you devise and implement structured ways of playing with the child and to give you support. All concerned will try to keep it clear that *you cannot be expected to tolerate the intolerable* but that *your child cannot flourish where he is rejected.* What helps one of you will therefore help you all.

Most professionals, even in Great Britain, acknowledge that there remains a small percentage (perhaps around one percent of *children who are referred to psychiatric clinics*) whose hyperkinesis is marked, all-pervasive and unresponsive to the kinds of help outlined here. Such children may indeed be best helped within the medical model outlined below.

The medical approach to "hyperactivity"

Lack of attention, concentration and forethought, together with marked physical restlessness, impulsiveness and rashness, are occasionally symptomatic of brain damage—either congenital or accidental. Similar behavior, observed in children in whom no brain damage can be demonstrated, is assumed, in the medical model, to be due to some undiagnosable disturbance or dysfunction in the brain or in its complex biochemical feedback with the central nervous system. The assumption is attractive because:

If the child has a "disorder," parents need blame neither themselves nor the child. They are relieved of personal guilt and of much of their anger at the child and, thus relieved, they can face critical relatives, neighbors or teachers with open demands for support and assistance.

If the child is a "patient," that role can break the vicious circle his behavior was creating with his family and moods and relationships can become warmer. This is true even if the medical diagnosis does not immediately change the disruptive behavior. If a bedwetting child is found to have a kidney disorder, everyone's attitudes to him and his problem will alter even if the bed is still wet every night. In the same way, a diagnosis of minimal brain dysfunction or hyperkinetic syndrome changes the attitudes of the adult world, even if mother still gets little sleep and no relaxation, and the classroom remains in daily turmoil.

If the child is "under the doctor's care" his "condition" can be "treated," whether the treatment is unpleasant for him or not. Instead of worrying about whether they are being too harsh with him for bad behavior, parents can accept doctor's orders and sympathetically support the child through whatever is prescribed.

Medical help in "hyperactivity"

Medical treatment usually consists of the long-term administration of stimulant drugs which, while stimulating the heart rate and the whole metabolism, paradoxically exert a calming effect on the child's behavior. The drug most often prescribed for this purpose is called Ritalin. The main reported effects are:

A generally calming effect and reduction of frenetic activity. This is so marked, in at least some children, that parents and teachers maintain that they know immediately if a child forgets even a single dose of the drug.

Increased concentration and improved performance on cognitive tasks carried out in a laboratory or "test" situations. Teachers especially notice these effects but, while they hold for normal as well as hyperactive children, they do not seem to carry over from test situations to general levels of performance. Teachers expect children on the drug to get better grades and believe that they are doing better work. But when that work is looked at over time, there is usually no significant effect.

Changes in mood such that the child becomes much more open to adult suggestion/control, much less defiant and "don't careish"; much more the kind of child adults find acceptable. Unfortunately this effect, welcome though it is to those who must keep the child safe and try to love and teach him, has a less pretty side. The child may become depressed and weepy and lose his joy in life, his ebullience.

Increase in heart rate, loss of appetite and disturbance to growth. Ritalin speeds up the metabolism. In the child's everyday life, it may keep him awake if given too late in the day and cause him to lose weight because he does not feel hungry for sufficient food. In the longer term, it may slow up his growth or even permanently retard it. "Drug holidays" are often recommended for this reason, but there is evidence that parents often do not follow this advice because, having established the child on the drug, they cannot face the possibility of his returning to his former behavior patterns, even for a couple of weeks.

Implications of medical treatment for hyperactivity

A hyperkinetic child can bring intolerable stress and even danger to himself and his family and to other people. The strain of trying to keep him safe, and to protect other people and places from his impulsive outbursts or wild exploits, is appalling and often unsuccessful. He will probably both suffer and cause many accidents, and leave a trail of less important destruction in his daily wake. Although his behavior is likely to calm down as he matures (the peak of complaints is at around six; adolescents usually appear "normal" although they may still be impulsive and accident-prone), his current behavior may cut him off from most of the important experiences of childhood. He does not sit and concentrate for long enough to learn either academic or manual skills, and few other children will want to be his friends. Furthermore, the longer he continues to behave in ways which the people around him find intolerable/"mad," the more likely it is that he will come to see himself as "mad," "bad" or both. Additional emotional disorder is therefore likely.

Given that picture and given a drug which changes it, almost always, for the better, the argument for the use of Ritalin or a similar substance seems very strong indeed. But there are real problems. Perhaps they are not problems which should torment the parent who, perhaps after years of misery, is at last able to communicate with and love her child and to see him playing and learning with others. But they are certainly problems which should concern the rest of us.

Is it ethically acceptable to use drugs to force changes in behavior? Adults do not like the way the hyperactive child behaves. By giving him Ritalin they can make him behave "better," but perhaps he does not want to behave differently. Perhaps he has a right to be himself, however inconvenient that self may be for other people. Perhaps the drug forces him into a mold when in fact it is the mold rather than the child's behavior which should be broken.

Questions of this kind apply to the use of all psycho-active (mood- and behavior-modifying) drugs; they need to be considered particularly carefully when they are to be administered to people who are not free to accept or reject them. Many people decry the widespread use of anti-depressant and tranquillizing drugs such as Valium, for example. But at

least the millions of people who take these do so largely of their own
volition, because they do not want to live with the depression, anxiety
and pain which the drugs help to modify. The use of drugs to reduce
aggression or aberrant sexual drives in prisoners or mental hospital
patients is widely decried because such drugs are either given without
consent or under a forced consent which is really blackmail concerning
possible release. The use of Ritalin in children falls, perhaps, somewhere
between these two and the ethical decisions have to be made with the
greatest care *for every individual case*.

**If we argue that it is ever ethically acceptable to use drugs to change a
child's behavior, why should we stop at hyperactivity?** There are many
other kinds of childish behavior which the adult world finds distressing.
Would it be legitimate to give sleeping drugs *routinely* to the many babies
and young children whose parents are desperate for unbroken nights? It
would be as easy to argue that well-rested parents can give a child a better
life as it is to argue that the adult world can be pleasanter to children
restrained from hyperactivity, yet most of us would probably maintain
that, with the exception of occasional crises, infant wakefulness must be
lived with rather than overridden.

Is it ethically acceptable to use drugs to improve performance? Stimulant
drugs reliably improve some aspects of performance on some intellectual
tasks and while this effect was once thought to be specific to (and
therefore diagnostic of) hyperactivity, it is now clear that it is universal.
An effective chemical performance-enhancer raises ethical problems as
great as those raised by a chemical behavior-modifier. Although some
individuals have always used chemicals in attempts to "improve" their
performances, drugs which *reliably* had the desired effect have not previously been available and widely distributed. A few students sniffed
amphetamine inhalers, but as many experienced a disastrous "high" or
mistimed "low" as felt real benefit during their examinations. People
drink alcohol to make them feel happy but as often find themselves
maudlin as cheered.

If effective and specific drugs which would enhance our performances
in a variety of spheres were readily available, would we, competitive as
we are for our children or our nation if not for ourselves, really resist
them? At present society is against the idea, as the strict regulations
concerning the use of drugs in competitive sports show. Such drugs are
unfair when only a few use them but what if they were available to all?
Many people would say that fear of addiction and of side effects would
put the brakes on non- or quasi-medical drug use, but the evidence is
against them. The non-specific and unreliable drugs almost all of us use,
like alcohol, caffeine and nicotine, are highly addictive and have devastating side effects. The specific and reliable stimulants we are giving to
children have side effects which we certainly should not tolerate in a
cold-cure, let alone a food. We use all these and, if the vast drug industry,
spurred by its success and profit in this area, were actually to produce
"harmless" pink pills which would improve the home team's game,
green ones to help us through that examination and blue ones for the
performance of a Casanova, we should probably accept them all.

Most doctors would probably answer points of this kind in terms of their overriding duty to act only in the best interests of their own individual patients. Certainly the prescription of a drug like Ritalin can be legitimate under the kinds of exceptional circumstances described above. Unfortunately, experience in the United States suggests that such carefully limited use of drugs which are effective in altering behavior is exceedingly difficult to maintain, if only because it is impossible to keep such drugs entirely within the *medical* domain.

Hyperactivity, or Minimal Brain Dysfunction as it was termed until recently, is not a "disease" or "disorder" with physical signs which can be demonstrated by medical tests. It is not even a collection of symptoms described by a patient seeking relief. It is a (widely varying) collection of behaviors which *somebody else wants the doctor to change*. That doctor may decide to assume that those behaviors are symptoms of a disorder or dysfunction which is present even though he cannot demonstrate it, but his usual clinical role is already distorted by the lack of objective diagnosis and by the intervention of third parties between himself and the patient. He believes that a prescription for the drug is in that patient's best interests, because others tell him so rather than because he clinically judges that it is so. If doubts beset him and he refuses to prescribe the drug, then it may be made clear to him that he is acting against the patient's interests because, unless that child's behavior improves, he will be excluded from school/locked in his room/knocked down by a car.

In the United States, despite strenuous efforts by many doctors and medical authorities, MBD or just LD for Learning Disorder has been taken over as a diagnosis by teachers and parents often acting with each other through Parent-Teacher Associations or community groups. It has been used as a label for hundreds of thousands of children who fall foul of the adult world. The single unifying point in the thousands of descriptions given of these children is that parents and teachers find them "difficult." Far from all being the dangerously impulsive and disruptive children who might, after lengthy consideration, be prescribed drugs in Britain, many of these American patients are "restless and a poor reader" or "slow to respond to authority and unpopular with peers." While everyone must sympathize with the teacher whose classroom is continually violently disrupted, many of the teachers who attach this label to children are not seeking to have impossible behavior modified but to have less-than-perfect behavior perfected. As one put it: "OK, he's not too bad. But I just *know* he'd learn better if he was on medication. Isn't it right that he should have what will make it easy on him?"

As the effectiveness of stimulant drugs became known in the United States (and a vast advertising campaign for Ritalin, much of it aimed directly at parents and teachers, certainly played its part), children began to come home from school with notes containing messages like "John is not concentrating. Please see your physician" or "Jake is still restless in school, please arrange medication before he returns from vacation." For how long could doctors be expected to go on saying "whatever for?" against this growing tide?

The medical authorities of the United States acted to reduce the trend. They eventually banned the use of the term Minimal Brain Dysfunction as a diagnosis, recognizing that it was too vague to describe a medical entity. But doctors were still allowed to prescribe for the separate "manifestations" of MBD such as "restlessness." They acted against direct advertising, too, insisting that Ritalin and similar drugs be advertised only in "ethical" (medical) journals and pamphlets. But they were largely too late. So many families were using the drugs that every family could find out about them. They also placed these drugs on the index which restricted repeat prescriptions, so that instead of taking the same prescription back to the pharmacist for a refill, parents had to seek a new one each time. But while that may have helped to limit the use of a child's stimulants by drug-abusing older people, it did not limit their availability to the child "patients." Instead of prescribing for a month and then seeing the children again, doctors gave hundreds (in some instances, a thousand or more) pills on one prescription.

Doctors cannot be blamed, teachers cannot be blamed, parents cannot be blamed. Ritalin makes children "easier" and it is easier to be kind to less bothersome children. Ritalin makes children accept school teaching more easily and it is easier to teach children who accept the process. Everyone has the welfare of those children at heart, but whether this overwhelming American tide of drug use to modify socially unacceptable behavior is socially desirable, people must decide for themselves.

Hyperkinetic syndrome *see* **Hyperactive Children**.
Illness *see* **Infection**/Types of infection: Infections which cause illness. *See also* **Nursing** *and individual conditions*.

Immune Response

Although human bodies are well-designed both to keep out and to deal with potentially harmful microorganisms (*see* **Infection**/Defenses against infection) some do get through these early lines of defense. Their arrival in the tissues or the bloodstream stimulates the next line of defense: the immune response.

Every microorganism contains proteins. The proteins of, say, a diphtheria bacillus or a polio virus are recognized by the body as antigens. While increasing numbers of certain types of white blood cells strive to engulf the dangerous microorganisms, fragments of them, or of their toxic products, are carried by other white cells either through the bloodstream or through the lymph system to the liver, the spleen or nearby lymph nodes ("glands"). Here, plasma cells perform a "chemical analysis" on the foreign proteins (the antigens) and produce exactly corresponding proteins called antibodies. These antibodies combine with, and neutralize, the antigens and, in doing so, destroy the microorganisms.

Obviously it takes time for plasma cells both to perform their "chemical analysis" and to produce sufficient quantities of antibodies to deal with the number of invading microorganisms. If and when they have done so, the current "illness" will be over, but the role of those plasma cells continues. Plasma cells which carry a "memory" of that particular antigen-antibody will remain in the gamma-globulin fragment of the blood. It is rather as if a secret force, having produced the weapon which turned the tide of a battle, filed its blueprints and components so that the weapon could be produced instantly should the invader return. If the body is challenged again at a later date *by those same infective microorganisms*, large numbers of antibodies will be released with no delay and there will therefore be no illness. The body has "learned" how to combat those particular microorganisms. The individual has made his own active immunity to that disease.

It is important to understand that immunity is not due only to actual antibodies continuing to circulate in the bloodstream once the immediate need for them is over, but to that "memory trace" remaining in the plasma cells. It is that "memory" which explains the vital difference between the *active immunity* which an individual makes for himself and the *passive immunity* which can be passed on to him by somebody else.

Newborn infants acquire passive immunity to many virus diseases because antibodies to viral antigens are small enough to pass through the placenta from the mother's bloodstream to that of the fetus. Antibodies to bacteria (especially gram-negative bacteria) are too large for such transfusion. The placenta filters them and the infant is born without passive immunity to those diseases.

Passive immunity to diseases such as measles is, of course, extremely valuable, but, like all such immunity, it is short-lived in comparison with active immunity. The infant receives antibodies to measles antigen in his circulation from his mother's blood. But he has no "memory trace" of that antigen in his plasma cells. For a while, those ready-made antibodies will protect him if measles infection threatens, but as the level of antibodies drops, he will be less protected and, unless active immunity is provoked by immunization (*see* **Immunization**) his body may eventually have to fight the measles bacillus without the benefit of that "secret weapon."

Passive immunity can be, and often is, conferred on people without active immunity who are at some special risk. Techniques for doing this are extremely valuable but it is vital that everyone understand that passive immunity is temporary and that although it may be life-saving today, it cannot replace active immunity next year.

Confusion is still sadly common in the case of tetanus. An individual who has not received primary tetanus immunization or has not kept it up-to-date with boosters, suffers an injury which hospital staff consider susceptible to tetanus infection. He may be given anti-tetanus serum, a concentration of tetanus antibodies. If tetanus infection should threaten in this wound, those antibodies will combat it, but they will not provoke his body into producing its own antibodies. He is protected against contracting the disease this time, but he is no more immune for the future than he was before. As long as he realizes this, all will be well. He can now seek active immunization and, even if he does not, anti-tetanus serum can be given to him again on another occasion. The danger is in confusion. At the time of a further injury he will again be asked about tetanus shots and whether his immunization is up-to-date. If he has never understood the difference between active and passive immunization he may reply that he received "tetanus shots" only last year . . . (*see* **Tetanus**).

Similar confusion sometimes arises when gamma globulin, rich in antibodies, is given to a child who is exposed, for example, to measles, at an age when his passive immunity from his mother is likely to be waning, but active immunization has not been carried out. Told that this injection will "probably stop him from getting it and anyway will make the illness much milder if he does," the mother is relieved that the child stays well and puts the whole question of measles out of her mind. That child still requires his measles shot and should have it as soon as the temporary passive immunity conferred by the gamma globulin has worn off.

The message is simple but important: only having a disease or being actively immunized against it gives lasting protection by stimulating the individual's own immune response.

Immunization *see also* **Diphtheria; German Measles; Measles; Mumps; Rabies; Tetanus; Tuberculosis; Whooping Cough**

The body's immune system cannot provide perfect protection from all disease. Sometimes the "invading" microorganisms may be so numerous that plasma cells cannot produce enough antibodies quickly enough to combat them. Sometimes the bacteria or viruses multiply so rapidly that they outstrip the rate of antibody production. Sometimes those "invaders" cause so much harm within the body that the whole system is overwhelmed. But, above all, that immune system cannot, by definition, protect the body against the *beginning of the first* episode of any particular illness. It is only the presence of the antigens of those "germs" which stimulates the production of antibodies so that, in the natural course of events, the individual must suffer from the illness before he or she can generate specific protection against it.

Fortunately, during the last century, we have learned to interfere with that natural course of events and stimulate the body into producing antibodies without first experiencing active infection. This is the process called immunization.

When a person is immunized, dead or weakened strains of the bacteria or viruses responsible for causing specific diseases are injected or, in the case of polio vaccine, for example, taken by mouth. Although the "germs" in these vaccines are not capable of causing the full-blown illness for which they would be responsible in their fully active state, they still contain the antigens which will stimulate antibody production. Vaccine preparation and the schedule of administration are both vitally important. Too active a vaccine could make the recipient ill. Too weak a vaccine could fail to evoke that antibody response. In many cases ample antibody production without illness is best achieved by a series of injections given at carefully worked-out intervals.

We cannot immunize against every infecting organism, largely because some common illnesses (such as "influenza" or the "common cold") are not really individual illnesses at all but collections of symptoms which may be caused by a vast range of microorganisms which, to complicate matters further, are constantly changing (mutating). We can isolate one particular strain of flu, for example, make a vaccine and use it. But the people who receive it are still at risk from many, many other strains of flu, and even the protection which they received against that first strain may not last for very long. This is why "flu shots" are usually given only to people who are at very special risk, either because their health is already so poor and/or because their work is among the sick and/or because there is a current epidemic of a known strain.

Immunization programs are not developed only by the criteria of what is scientifically possible, but also according to social and economic criteria. Clearly, immunization against a particular disease is impossible if a safe vaccine is not technically possible. But possession of a safe vaccine may not lead to a mass immunization program. Those who administer public health programs have to ask (and answer) questions such as: "Will the cost of mass immunization be repaid, either monetarily (in terms of fewer workdays lost and lower medical costs) or in social terms such as less human misery?" Such questions can only be answered in terms of yet other questions such as: "How serious and how frequent is this disease in an unimmunized population? What degree of protection will the vaccine give to how many people and for how long? What are the risks of vaccination itself and how do those risks balance against the probable benefits for vaccinated individuals?" By building up cost-benefit equations for questions of this kind, the medical administrators must decide, for each possible vaccine and for every different population, whether mass immunization is worthwhile. An interesting example is that of immunization against smallpox, the scourge of our immediate ancestors and part of every civilized country's public health program until very recently. Some years ago, as the incidence of smallpox around the world declined, more and more exceptions to the general rule of immunization for everyone were made. Doctors exempted more and more infants on slighter grounds; countries relaxed their rules about the entry of unimmunized travellers and, eventually, the picture changed to one in which smallpox immunization was recommended only for those who actually intended to travel to and from the few remaining areas where the disease remained active. Now, smallpox has been officially eradicated and mass immunization has ceased. There remain a handful of individuals (such as those who work in laboratories handling the infecting organisms of smallpox) for whom immunization is still "worthwhile," but for the rest of us, the cost (monetary and health) of immunization now outweighs a benefit which has become infinitesimal as has the risk of infection.

Disease patterns change and are changed by our interference. The immunization program which is right for one population at one time will not necessarily be the best for other populations at other times. But individuals, wherever they live, can be sure that the program which is recommended to them by their medical personnel has been extremely carefully worked out and weighed. Those who reject or ignore such a program not only do so at their own peril but to the peril of others, too. Smallpox would not have been "eradicated" from our lives if we had not all followed the program of immunization against it, and thus gradually bred generations of people whose resistance was such that the infecting organisms could find no breeding ground. Nevertheless, while accepting the immunization program of your community, it is important to remember that, like those smallpox laboratory scientists, there will always be people whose individual needs differ from those of the population around them. When it is time for the immunization of your child, his special needs must be conveyed to, and discussed with, a doctor. If he has had febrile convulsions, for example, whooping cough immunization may carry an increased risk of side effects. It may be better to exempt him. On the other hand, if that child is to travel to certain areas of the world where whooping cough is very prevalent, or if there is currently an epidemic of the disease in his community, it may be appropriate to vaccinate him all the same. Now an individual doctor (rather than a public health authority) is weighing the balance of risks and benefits for your individual child rather than for the population of which he is a member. How likely is he to "catch" the disease? How much will it matter if he does? How probable and how serious are the side effects of vaccination likely to be? (*see* **Whooping Cough**).

Your family's immunizations

Follow your community's program, with each member's individual needs discussed with the doctor beforehand. Above all, remember that while immunization begins in infancy, these are not only "baby shots." Boosters to keep the antibody level effectively high are almost as important as those primary doses. Keeping records for every family member, after infancy, is important.

Although the timing of these immunizations will vary, your child will almost certainly receive the following:

Diphtheria, whooping cough (pertussis), tetanus

These three are usually combined into one "triple vaccine" (DPT) and given as an injection into the buttock, thigh or upper arm.

Three of these "triples" are needed to build an infant's basic immunity. Different communities space them differently, but it is usual for the first to be given in the first three months and the third late in the year. Where the third dose is given early, a booster may be recommended in the second year. Where the third dose is given later there may be no need for a booster until the child is ready to start school. A further booster, omitting pertussis, is given before the child leaves school.

The interval between injections is important but not critical. If your child is two weeks late he will not need to start the series all over again, but if you forget for several months he might have to. Consult your doctor.

Side effects are uncommon and mild. Your baby might be irritable and possibly slightly feverish twelve to twenty-four hours after an injection and there might be a red lump at the needle prick site which will soon disperse. Marked reactions should be seen by, or at least reported to, the doctor who might reduce, or leave out, the pertussis component of the next dose (but *see* **Whooping Cough**).

Polio

(Trivalent vaccine against three main strains.) This is given as drops of syrup on the same schedule as the above. There are no side effects.

Measles, mumps and German measles (rubella)

In the United States, these are also combined into a triple vaccine (MMR) which is given at around fifteen months. A single shot produces adequate lifelong immunity. Although measles is an exceedingly unpleasant disease which is dangerous to babies (*see* **Measles**), it is difficult to protect them by earlier immunization because the shot will be ineffective while there are still antibodies from the mother in his bloodstream (*see* **Immune**

Response). But if every child is protected from these three illnesses, at fifteen months, the likelihood of a younger (and not yet protected) baby being infected by an older brother or sister, is much reduced.

Mumps is a very mild illness in children but becomes potentially serious for pubertal and adult males who may suffer from orchitis: a painful and sometimes damaging inflammation of the testicles (*see* **Mumps**). By protecting children early, we reduce the likelihood of adults' being infected.

German measles is also a very mild illness in children and in non-pregnant adults, but it can, of course, disastrously damage fetuses. Once again the early immunization of all children serves the double purpose of protecting individual girls from the risk of rubella during their reproductive years and of reducing the reservoir of infection (*see* **German measles**).

The immunization programs for these three diseases vary widely from country to country. Although most include measles in the infancy schedule, many withhold mumps and rubella vaccines until children are approaching puberty, and may then selectively immunize only those who have never been infected.

Tuberculosis (BCG)

In the United States no routine immunization against tuberculosis is recommended. Children who are known to have had contact with the disease or who are thought to be especially susceptible or at risk are given a skin test. If this shows that the child has had no contact with the disease, no further action is taken. There is no immunity, but the risk of acquiring the infection is considered too small to merit the use of BCG vaccine. If the skin test is positive, though, antituberculous treatment will be instituted whether or not the infection is thought to be active.

In many other countries, skin testing and immunization of all children with negative results, using BCG vaccine, is routine. This is usually conducted through schools, just before puberty. Children with positive skin-test results are investigated for active infection, but if none is discovered no treatment is given (*see* **Tuberculosis**).

Yellow fever, cholera, typhoid fever, rabies

Immunizations will be routine in some areas of the world and required for Western children travelling to them. It is essential that public health experts be consulted before travel is undertaken to areas where diseases virtually unknown in the parent-country are endemic. Occasionally the immunization requirements will make vacation trips inadvisable as only necessity will balance the discomfort of likely side effects.

Tetanus

● Because primary immunization with tetanus toxoid is included in the triple vaccine given in infancy and early childhood (*see above*), many people forget, or never realize, that protection against this peculiarly unpleasant and dangerous disease is *not complete and lifelong* when the prescribed series of those triple injections has been completed.

A tetanus booster is required every ten years throughout life if antibody levels adequate to protect against this infection in susceptible wounds are to be maintained (*see* **Tetanus**).

Diphtheria

● While contact with a diphtheria patient is much rarer than are wounds which might be susceptible to tetanus, diphtheria still exists, as a recent small-scale epidemic in the United States and a recent death in Britain have painfully demonstrated. Theoretically, lifelong protection requires ten-yearly boosters but, because the side effects in school-age children and adults can be severe, boosters after infancy are not a routine matter. If diphtheria should make a comeback, this policy may change. Until that time, consult your doctor if an older member of the family is at special risk of contact with the disease.

Impetigo and Staphylococcal Infections

Impetigo is a superficial infection of the skin caused either by streptococci or by staphylococci. These bacteria can infect healthy skin, but infection is especially likely when skin is already damaged by eczema, etc.

At the sites of infection there is oozing of pus or the formation of pus-filled blisters which burst. The pus dries to form thick, yellowish crusts. The infection often starts around the nose or mouth but rapidly spreads to other parts of the body. It is extremely contagious; if unchecked it spreads rapidly through schools, nurseries or other institutions.

Although merely tiresome in children, who are quickly and easily treated with local and/or systemic antibiotics, impetigo, especially if caused by staphylococci, can be extremely serious in babies (*see below*).

Staphylococcal infections (*see also* **Diarrhea, Gastroenteritis and Food Poisoning**)

Apart from the strains of these bacteria which can cause food poisoning, there are many pathogenic strains, often spread by symptom-free "carriers," which cause a variety of skin infections such as boils and carbuncles. In hospitals, these bacteria cause much post-operative infection.

While boils and so forth are usually trivial infections, easily dealt with by antibiotics, various strains of staphylococci can cause serious trouble:

Bloodstream infection by staphylococci Rarely in children and adults, but more often in young babies, superficial infection with staphylococci may lead to septicemia. Infection may settle in an internal organ, such as a bone, and produce an abscess there. Or infection may settle in the lung and cause a serious form of pneumonia. This type of pneumonia is a leading cause of death among the few young adults who die from complications following influenza.

Antibiotic resistance: "hospital staph" Staphylococci in hospitals, often spread by "carriers" among the staff, are often of strains which have developed resistance to many common antibiotics as well as high levels of virulence. Infection with these microorganisms can spread through successive intakes of patients (sometimes reaching infection rates as high as forty percent in a newborns' nursery) and can prove extremely difficult to treat. Attempts have been made to reserve particular antibiotics for this purpose and to use them only on isolated patients so as to minimize the likelihood of resistance developing (*see* **Infection**/Antibiotics). Unfortunately, overcrowding in hospitals, with limited facilities for isolation, has led to the failure of this policy.

Now, strenuous attempts are being made in many hospitals to limit the invasion and spread of these bacteria. Such efforts include measures to detect "carriers" among both professional and domestic staff, avoidance of overcrowding, isolation and "barrier-nursing" of any infected patient and the establishment of "ultra-clean" areas (including newborn nurseries) where patients at special risk can be nursed.

One infection with staphylococci does not appear to lead to immunity, even from infection by the identical strain. Research is nevertheless going on to try to find artificial means of producing at least some immunity.

Infant Development and Care

Since this book concerns all dependent children in families, the nature and needs of babies and very young children are dealt with wherever they are relevant which is, of course, in a majority of its entries. Parents who are especially interested in this youngest age group may nevertheless find the following guidance useful:

Emotional development and needs

See **Anxiety, Fears and Phobias**, especially The roots of fear and The roots of anxiety, which deal with the importance of a baby's security with a loved caretaker.

This topic is further dealt with in **Working Mothers** and extended to issues such as "spoiling" in **Discipline, Self-discipline and Learning How to Behave**. Problems related to this security-insecurity dimension are dealt with under headings such as **Jealousy**/Of a new baby; **Hyperactive Children** and **Depression**.

Overall development: emotional, mental and physical

See **Play**, especially Playthings for babies, which includes a chart of pointers within the baby's development suggesting activities and social interactions which he or she is likely to enjoy. A similar approach to general development in the second and third years will be found in **School**/Pre-school and nursery education.

Physical growth

See **Growth**, which includes a chart, both for reference and use, of "expected" weight and height gains from birth to age nineteen. **Eating** /Types of food for babies, deals with breast-feeding and bottle-feeding, with the shift towards an ordinary diet and, later, with feeding problems.

Specific developments and problems

Will be found under their topic headings. **Language**, for example, deals both with the normal development of language and with such issues as stammering. **Toilet Training** includes an account of the physiological developments which must precede bladder and bowel control and of common problems. **Sleep** similarly covers both general and problem-orientated information while **Safety**/In the home, puts the safety precautions needed for babies at different age-stages into the context of their overall development.

Specific issues in early child care

Will be found by looking up the particular issue with which you are concerned. If you are thinking about whether or not a toddler should watch television, turn to **Television**; if you are worrying about how to break the news of a death or a divorce, turn to **Death** or **Divorce, Separation and One-parent Families**. If there is no entry on the topic you are looking for, the topic word should nevertheless direct you to a relevant article. Smacking, for example will take you to **Discipline, Self-discipline and Learning How to Behave**/Punishment, while thumb sucking will take you to **Habits**/Comfort habits and also to **Teeth**.

Infantile eczema *see* **Allergy**.
Infantile paralysis *see* **Immunization**/Your family's immunizations: Polio.

Infection (for further information on infections mentioned, *see* individual conditions)

It is impossible to understand (even a little) about the nature, prevention and cure of infection without understanding at least some science. Most people do not and, as a result, old wives' tales (often outdated, sometimes downright harmful) stand in for even a version of the facts.

The following is indeed only "a version," a vastly compressed and simplified account of a huge topic. But people who will follow it through may find it worthwhile. Not only will you be better able to understand what your doctor is talking about next time a member of your family is hurt or ill, you will also find that you can simultaneously increase the efficiency *and* the simplicity of your everyday hygiene, nursing and first aid. You may even save money by becoming able to ignore advertising pressures to "disinfect" your kitchen with one product and your skin with another and to "sterilize" everything from your toilet to your dustbin.

What "germs"   Everyone knows that infection is caused by germs, but what are they? The
are   organisms which can infect people are so diverse that that term is not really very useful. We need to know *what kind of germ* we are talking about.

Our world has three life-forms: animals (including us, of course), plants and protists. It has one more semi-life-form, too: the virus, which is not included in any of those categories but must certainly have an important place in any discussion of infection.

We can get rid of the animals and the vegetables because while members of either life-form can certainly harm us, neither infects us in the "germ" sense. Berry may cause vomiting, poison ivy, a rash, but in both cases chemicals, acting as poisons, are responsible, not "germs."

With animals, we must be more careful. Many species play a vital part in the *spread of infection*. The mosquito which spreads malaria from person to person and the flea which colonizes plague-carrying rats are obvious examples of these "animal vectors." But again it is not the animals themselves which infect us but the "germs" they carry. Other animals can cause damage themselves, rather than bringing us their damaging "germs," but they do so by living as parasites on or in us—like the mite which lives around hair follicles or the many varieties of worm which may inhabit the intestines. Their presence or habits cause mechanical damage; it may be invasive but it is not infective.

"Germs" are protists unless they are viruses

The group biologists classify as "protists" include bacteria, fungi, protozoa and algae. We can forget the algae which are innocent of causing infection. Bacteria, fungi and protozoa can all infect man, although, of course, bacteria are the most important in infection, especially in people in the Western world.

How protists differ from animals and plants

All living things are made up of cells and all cells (whether of an onion skin, your skin or a bacterium) have a similar chemical composition of three molecules. They all carry out similar chemical activities, collectively known as metabolism and including taking in and excreting foodstuffs, converting chemicals from foodstuffs into energy for other activities, respiration and reproduction. We usually think of "metabolism" as a characteristic of a whole creature (and do not think of a plant as having a metabolism at all), but in fact all the metabolic processes go on in each cell.

The vital difference between animals and plants and the protists is in the degree of differentiation and specialization of their cells. Animals and plants both have specialized cells grouped into tissues: stems, flowers, livers and so forth. Animals not only have specialized tissues but complex organs in which tissues of different specializations are grouped together to perform complex tasks. The heart, for example, combines muscle, nerve and connective tissue to perform the task of pumping blood.

Protists, in contrast, consist of independent, unrelated cells. Usually the whole protist organism is one single cell, but even where many are joined together (as in many algae; seaweed, for example) each cell is the same; none are specialized for different functions as in a true land plant.

The hard-to-classify virus

Whether or not a virus is a "living" thing is a philosophical question, but certainly it has very different characteristics from all other living things.

Viruses are smaller than microscopic: that is literally true. They are so small that a large majority cannot be seen through an ordinary microscope. They are only visible with the far higher magnification of an electron microscope. Until sufficiently powerful instruments were invented, nobody knew that viruses existed. Even today, when we not only have the instruments with which viruses can be examined, but know that there are still many to be discovered and identified, their size remains one (but only one) difficulty in studying them.

Viruses are not "cells" in the usual three-molecule sense. Instead they consist only of an outer coating of a protein substance which contains an inner core of nucleic acid. Each is distinct. Not being cells, viruses have no independent life processes. They do not convert chemicals to provide themselves with energy in order to keep themselves "alive." They have no metabolism of their own and therefore they cannot reproduce themselves. Their only "function" is the invasion of other cells. Once a virus has taken over a cell, it uses that cell's life functions for its own propagation.

This necessity to invade, to take over actual *cells*, is a vitally important difference between viruses and any other infecting organism—a bacterium, for example. That bacterium may exist in your intestine, taking in nutrients from your waste products and generally using *for its own life cycle* the environment provided by your body. But the virus which finds itself in your intestine must either lie dormant or must invade one of your body cells and take it over, imposing its reproductive function on the natural function of that cell, which is thereby destroyed.

This, of course, is the major reason why the identification and study of viruses were so difficult, and it is why the treatment of virus infections remains so difficult today. Scientists could not breed viruses on a petri dish filled with suitable nutrients, as they grow bacteria. They had to learn to breed them inside living cells, in white mice and chick embryos, for example. Even today, when antibiotics (*see below*) can so effectively destroy a wide range of harmful bacteria, we cannot produce a similar *kind* of anti-viral agent because the viruses we want to destroy are inside the living cells of the host we are trying to cure. Destroy the virus and you destroy the cell (but *see below*).

Bacteria

Many "germs" are bacteria but only an infinitesimal proportion of bacteria are "germs."

If it were possible to calculate the mass of all the animal life on earth, and compare it with all the bacterial life, scientists reckon that the mass of bacteria would be twenty times greater than all the rest put together. You cannot see them but they are (almost) everywhere.

One of the most widespread and unfortunate old wives' tales in daily life is that bacteria are dangerous things humans should avoid. Humans cannot nor should they wish to. The whole of life as we know it depends upon bacterial action. Bacteria process all types of once-living-now-dead matter, breaking it down into its component chemical parts. When they have done so, they have made those basic chemicals available to be used all over again by the living and the living-still-to-come. A cow dies. Its body was built from nutrients it obtained by eating grass. The grass was nourished by nutrients in the soil. By bacterial action its body will be broken down again into the chemical elements it obtained from the grass and made available in the soil so that more grass will grow to nourish another animal. . . . Without bacteria, the "life cycles" familiar to all of us from school lessons could not continue. Instead of being able to use our planet's natural organic resources knowing that once our bodies had had what they needed from them, they would be returned to replenish the natural stock, we would *use them up*, just as we use up resources such as oil, which, made into plastics or burned as gasoline, is not recycled to keep the oil wells full.

There are, of course, millions of kinds of bacteria. Some can flourish wherever there is dead organic matter to be broken down; some require more specialized living conditions. There are, for example, many types which are found in soil, but some of these seek well-oxygenated earth while others flourish where there is little oxygen, deep beneath the surface. There are several types which flourish on normal human skin. Recent research suggests that a normal adult male armpit will carry about 200 million per square centimeter while there may be as many as 500 million bacteria in every gram of scurf from the scalp. There are bacteria which flourish in animal intestines and others which concentrate where there are dead particles in water.

Bacteria which are normal inhabitants of the bodies of animals are called their "normal flora" (nothing to do with flowers!). Their presence is an integral part of the body's functioning; a sort of peaceful coexistence. The bacteria find the right environment for nourishing and reproducing themselves within the animal's body; their presence does no harm and is often positively useful. Sometimes their presence is actually essential to the animal host's life. Ruminants like cows, for example, depend upon bacterial action in their multiple-stomach system to break down the cellulose in their grass diet and release its nutrients for their use. If you were able to sterilize that cow's stomach, she would die of starvation. She has no intrinsic ability to use cellulose. Humans also have valuable normal flora in their guts. It is bacteria, for example, which, while using our eventual wastes for their own nutrition, release the chemical we call vitamin K.

Bacteria as germs

It is from among this vast and essential population of bacteria that the ones which can and do damage man come. Such bacteria are certainly "germs," but it is so easy to tar all other bacteria with the same value-laden brush that it may be better to stick to the more scientific term "pathogenic bacteria" or pathogens. A bacterium may become a pathogen in a number of ways:

It may be a member of a species which is always pathogenic to man, meaning that it is never part of "normal flora" but, should it gain entry to the body, will always cause more or less trouble (for how much trouble it may cause, *see below*).

Many of the most pathogenic species of bacteria are those which produce toxins (poisons) in the body. The tetanus bacilli, for example, need multiply only at one local site (such as a puncture wound) in the body to produce toxins which then circulate around the body to produce severe illness and often death. In contrast, most of the pathogenic bacteria which can infect wounds cause only local infection (*see below*). In order to produce an infection involving the whole body, these bacteria have to multiply enormously and penetrate into the bloodstream.

It may be a member of a pathogenic strain of an otherwise harmless species. *B. coli*, for example, is a normal and normally harmless inhabitant of the human bowel, yet there are strains of *B. coli* which are pathogenic and it is these which often cause epidemics of gastroenteritis in infants.

It may evolve from a harmless parent species. Many of the virulent intestinal infections, such as typhoid and para-typhoid, are caused by bacteria thought to have evolved from *B. coli*.

It may be a harmless inhabitant of one area of the body which is pathogenic when it reaches another. Clostridium tetani, for example, is a strain of *B. coli* and is itself a normal and harmless inhabitant of the bowel. But in deep wounds which provide the comparatively airless conditions which it requires, it is highly pathogenic.

It may be a normally harmless inhabitant of the body which behaves as a pathogen when the condition of that body "invites" virulent invasion rather than continued peaceful co-existence. Perhaps the best-known example is that of the pneumococcus, many strains of which colonize the mouth and throat. If a viral cold alters that normal environment (and lowers the body's general resistance, *see below*) the pneumococcus may behave as a virulent pathogen, invading the respiratory system and producing bronchitis.

It may be a member of a species or strain of bacteria which some people can carry, without ill effects, almost all the time, but which act as virulent pathogens in other people. All human skin, for example, is colonized by staphylococci whose strains range from harmless to highly virulent. Some "carriers" can carry the most virulent strains (often in the nostrils) without ill effects to themselves; unsuspecting and symptom-free, such a carrier is often the source of epidemics of staphylococcal infection in hospitals or among the infants in a nursery.

Viruses

All the viruses which you hear about are likely to act as germs either in animals or in plants. This is not to say that there are *no* viruses which are not germs, but that viruses are discovered only when plant or animal symptoms lead to scientific research. In general, we recognize viruses only by the diseases they cause.

Viruses as germs   Infection by viruses is rather different from infection by pathogenic bacteria, even though the resulting symptoms may be distinguishable only with laboratory help. The differences are due to differences in the nature and behavior of the two types of microorganisms.

Viruses that are not in a host cell are not active. Some are able to exist (though not to reproduce) for quite long periods without a host cell. The smallpox virus, for example, can exist for a long time in a completely dry environment. Dust from the clothing or bedding of an infected person can infect others if it is inhaled.

Most viral illnesses, however, are contracted by a route which passes virally infected cells directly from one living creature to another. The most common route of all is probably "droplet infection" by which viruses, such as those of colds, influenza and measles, are sneezed or coughed or otherwise sprayed out by one person and inhaled by another. There is probably some sense, therefore, to the belief that children will not "catch" each other's colds if they play together outside. Air currents will carry droplets away unless the two have their heads together.

Many viruses are eaten. Food which is contaminated with feces, for example, may pass on the enteroviruses that cause such illnesses as gastroenteritis (echoviruses and Coxsackie viruses) and the virus of infectious hepatitis.

Viruses seldom seem to penetrate normal skin (although the spread of verrucae, certainly viral in origin, remains a puzzle). Nor do viruses in the quiescent, perhaps dust-borne, state, appear to lodge in wounds or otherwise damaged skin. But many are transmitted *through* the skin by the bites of infected animals. Rabies is the most dramatic example, but there are also many "arthropod-borne," or arboviruses, which flourish either in blood-sucking arthropods such as mosquitoes, ticks and lice or in susceptible vertebrates bitten by those arthropods. Malaria and yellow fever, for example, are spread by mosquitoes, while several kinds of viral encephalitis are spread by ticks. In a rather similar way, serum hepatitis is passed on when injections are carried out with improperly sterilized hypodermic needles so that the virus is injected directly into the victim's bloodstream, or where even the minutest droplet of blood containing the virus gets into a cut on the skin of a new victim.

With their minute size, virus particles can also pass through the placenta to infect the fetus. German measles (rubella) virus is a grim case in point (*see* **German Measles**). Fortunately, if viruses are of a size readily to pass through the placenta (which most bacteria cannot do) virus antibodies can and do pass also (which bacterial antibodies cannot do). This is why babies are born with immunity to viral diseases much greater than their immunity to bacterial diseases (*see* **Immune Response**).

Spread of viruses within the body

Where viruses attack sheets of cells—as on the skin or mucous membranes—spread may be directly from cell to cell with the film of moisture moving over mucous membranes assisting the process.

Within the body, spread takes place along various routes depending on whether the infection is a localized or a generalized one. A generalized infection (viremia), usual in most virus diseases, means that viruses are being transported to target cells in the bloodstream or through the lymph system. Some viruses reach susceptible cells by specific routes, however. The rabies virus, for example, travels along the nerves, from the skin at the site of infection, to the brain. When chickenpox (varicella) virus causes herpes zoster (shingles), it too travels along the nerves.

Many viruses undergo their multiplication in specific types of cells within the body. We do not fully understand this viral "targeting" of specific organs, but it is certainly an important factor in any particular viral disease. For example, the viruses responsible for the familiar "infectious diseases of childhood," such as chickenpox and measles, have a preference for skin cells, hence rash is a predominant feature of these infections. Other viruses, such as poliomyelitis and certain arboviruses, have an affinity for nerve cells and the symptoms of the disease depend upon which particular kinds of nerve cells are affected. In infectious hepatitis the cells of the liver appear to be especially susceptible, hence liver damage and jaundice are the recognizable features of this infection.

Viruses and cancer

Certain viruses invade host cells but, rather than instigating reproduction of themselves within those cells, may instead "transform" them, "switching off" the mechanism by which cell division is normally controlled and thereby inducing abnormally rapid and crowded cell multiplication. This process, and therefore certain viruses known to be associated with it, has been shown to occur in various forms of cancer. Burkitt's lymphoma, for example, may be due to an arbovirus. The possibility of a viral origin of at least some forms of cancer has stimulated a tremendous spate of biomedical research. It raises the possibility of cancer control.

How invasion by virus causes disease

Where the invading virus multiplies within specific types of cells, the resulting disease can usually be simply explained in terms of the massive damage done to those host cells. If a virus establishes itself in nerve cells in the brain, for example, the resulting encephalitis or paralysis is not surprising. But in these diseases, as well as in general virus diseases such as influenza, symptoms arise which do not seem to be due to specific cell damage by the multiplying viruses. In polio, for example, while the paralysis is easily explained by the viruses' affinity for cells in the nerves which control voluntary movement, the early symptoms are much less specific. What produces the sore throat, the headache, the fever and nausea which are the typical first symptoms not only of polio but also of flu and almost every generalized virus disease? Such symptoms in a *bacterial* disease are thought to be related to the body's reaction to foreign proteins and/or to the release of bacterial toxins. Similar, though as yet ill-understood, mechanisms may be at work in viral infections. There is still an enormous amount to be learned.

Fungi

Fungi affect human beings far more as "plant germs" than as direct causers of human illness. Indeed, these fungal plant diseases have several times altered the course of human history, as in the nineteenth century when fungus wiped out the Irish potato crop, killed millions, led to the emigration of more than a million to the United States and profoundly influenced English political life. Even today, fungal diseases require constant vigilance and continual new research if acceptable crop yields are to be maintained. Several main groups of fungi can, however, directly disturb human health:

Fungi as "germs"

Dermatophytes. These fungi are not normal inhabitants of the human body but are common in nature and tend to proliferate on the skin, hair or nails of individuals who are for some reason temporarily susceptible (*see*, for example, **Ringworm and Athlete's Foot**).

Yeasts. These fungi are normal inhabitants of the human body and yeast infections arise only when the local conditions of a particular body part change so as to provide an environment which leads to their explosive multiplication. For example:

Candida albicans is the fungus that produces "thrush," which can cause inflammation overlain by the typical white patches seen especially in the vagina and the mouth. Thrush infection of the mouth is common in newborn infants who become infected during their passage through an infected vagina.

Aspergillus is very widespread in nature and therefore in dusts from hay, bird seed, animal housing and so forth. Spores can be found in the sputum of normal individuals.

The disease called aspergillosis arises when the fungi find a foothold in lungs or respiratory tracts already damaged by disease. The more serious disease known "farmer's lung" is a hypersensitive reaction to these spores (*see* **Allergy**).

"Systemic mycoses." These are fungi which "choose" internal organs as their first target. While the first attack is usually self-limiting, further invasion can, in some susceptible individuals, produce widespread systemic disease with a high mortality rate in the untreated.

Such fungus diseases are almost unknown in Britain. Some, such as "San Joaquin fever," are common in particular areas of the United States, and are a common cause of disability and death in many underdeveloped areas of the world.

Fungal food poisoning. Fungus activity is responsible for an enormous amount of food *spoilage*, but it can also be responsible for serious forms of food *poisoning* due to the release of toxins by the fungus interacting with the foodstuff.

Called mycotoxicoses, these diseases include the first-discovered "St. Anthony's Fire," now known as ergotism. This is the result of eating rye or other grain contaminated with the ergot fungus. More and more fungal toxins are being identified as serious health hazards. A fungal toxin in peanut meal (aflatoxin), for example, is being indicted as a possible factor in cancer of the liver, while many others are under suspicion as causative factors in a variety of serious human disorders.

Strenuous attempts are being made to improve harvesting and storage practices in agriculture, so as to reduce fungus attack on foodstuffs and also so as to exclude affected products from the category of "fit for human consumption." In the meantime, the eating of moldy food should certainly be avoided despite the common belief that the mold is "probably penicillin."

● Never allow children to eat foodstuffs marketed for animals, even if the pet shop's whole peanuts do appear equally suitable for people and parrots. Importation regulations and quality/hygiene checks may be dangerously inadequate.

Protozoa

Protozoa as germs

Protozoa are minute single-celled creatures that live as parasites within animal hosts. Their life cycles are invariably complex. They often involve two hosts which may be of different species so that, for example, the sporozoites of malaria can multiply only through some of their life forms while in a human host. Their further development, and the eventual production of more infective sporozoites, is dependent on their being taken into a new host, a mosquito. Thus certain species of mosquitoes are not only vectors for malaria but also a necessary part of the sporozoites' life cycle. In a similar way (although the life cycle is different), the trypanosome, which causes sleeping sickness, requires not only a human host but also a tsetse fly which first nurtures certain stages of its development and then serves as a vector to pass on the infection.

Not all protozoan infections thus require multiple hosting. Indeed, some of these parasites appear to be normal (or at least often harmless) parasites in man. Various kinds of amoebae, for example, live in the human bowel, causing no symptoms. One such is called *Entamoeba histolytica*. For reasons which are not fully understood, this amoeba, carried without knowledge or harm in many individuals, can suddenly become a virulent agent in another. Instead of floating freely in the bowels, it attaches itself to the bowel wall, feeding on the tissues and red blood cells and producing ulceration and the disease we call amoebic dysentery. In certain cases, amoebae are released into the blood circulation and are transported to various organs (including the liver and the brain) where they cause amoebic abscesses.

Amoebic dysentery can be passed on only by fecal contamination. A victim or carrier excretes the amoebae which, either directly or via flies, contaminate water, vegetables or other foods which are then eaten by a new victim within whose body the amoebae can start a new life cycle. The disease used to be thought of only as a "tropical disease," but we now know that it can (and does) occur whenever sanitary conditions, especially public health sanitation such as control of drinking water and food production, are poor. Its true incidence is difficult to assess, as many other bowel infections can produce similar symptoms and the amoebic nature of the infection can be proven only by complex laboratory identification procedures. While the disease is certainly extremely rare in Britain and, when it occurs, likely to have been brought in from abroad, some estimates put the incidence in certain areas of the USA as high as twenty percent.

Defenses against infection (*see also* **Immune Response**)

Sharing an environment with countless millions of microorganisms, human bodies have many defenses against those which are, or might become, harmful.

Resistance to infection

Microorganisms have no "intent." They do not "mean" to do an individual good or harm. Their sole "purpose" is survival and multiplication and they will therefore colonize human bodies *if and when those bodies offer a suitable environment.*

An individual may be highly resistant to a *specific* infection, perhaps because he has a high level of antibodies to that microorganism and therefore it has no chance of gaining a foothold (*see* **Immune Response** and **Immunization**). But that individual may also be resistant to infection in more general sense. He may be able to maintain an optimum balance between his own body and the various microorganisms which share it with him or with which he has contact in their mutual environment. "Perfect health" is something which we cannot even define, let alone achieve, but there is no doubt that general health and resistance to disease are related. The relationship is not easy to see at the positive pole because even when we live with someone who "never seems to get ill" and "always heals quickly" and "has an iron stomach," we cannot know what threats to health were offered and shrugged off: what would have happened to him if he had been less robust. But the relationship is easy to see at the negative pole. People who are undernourished, poorly sheltered, chronically sick, old or newly born and frail, acquire more infections than other people, and their bodies combat them less efficiently so that they suffer more from each. People who insult their bodies in particular ways—by heavy smoking, for example—do not only render themselves more liable to infection of the affected body parts, but also make it far more difficult for the body's own defenses to function efficiently when needed. If the respiratory tract is chronically irritated by the thousands of cigarettes smoked over many years, it will probably offer a hospitable environment to a variety of "germs." When germs gain a foothold, the reduced activity of the protective mucous blanket covering that respiratory tract may enable them to multiply and spread.

Sometimes attempts to improve general health and hygiene actually misfire because they upset the delicate balances between one body system and another, or between one part of the body and its microorganisms. An important example is our use and misuse of antibiotics to which we shall return (*see below*), but there are other everyday examples, too. In the vagina, the normal flora feed on shed cells from which they release sugars which ferment. The fermentation produces a slightly acid vaginal environment which discourages the growth of pathogens. When a woman uses "feminine sprays" or douches, in a misguided attempt to keep the area extra-clean or "germ-free," she upsets the balance, reduces the acidity and actually encourages exactly the kind of bacterial invasion she intended to prevent. The lesson is that under ordinary circumstances of "good health" (i.e., absence of symptoms) bodies resist infection best if they are left to do so for themselves.

Mechanical barriers against infection: skin

Skin is a tough envelope consisting of several layers of cells with an outermost layer of dead, horny ones. As long as all those layers are intact, skin cannot be penetrated by microorganisms.

But skin is not only a vital mechanical barrier to infection; it also has in-built decontamination properties. Its resident population of harmless bacteria, together with its own excretion of chemical substances (such as sebum), combines to discourage the growth *on* the skin of microorganisms which might land there.

● Removing intact skin—from an unbroken blister, for example—often increases the likelihood of infection in the exposed raw tissue. Similarly, an over-enthusiastic use of man-made decontaminants (such as disinfectants, *see below*) can remove the normal flora and secretions and leave the artificially cleaned skin more vulnerable than it would have been in its natural state.

Specialized "skin": mucous membrane

Routes from the outside world into the body, such as the nose and respiratory system, the mouth and alimentary tract, the vagina, the anus and the outer surface of the eye, all have specialized protection. The nose and respiratory tract can serve as an example.

The tract is covered by a fine mucous blanket which offers both mechanical and biological protection. First defenses are concentrated in the nose, where hairs in the mucous blanket may trap as much as ninety percent of inhaled foreign material. Trapped particles are conveyed, by the constant movement of the mucous blanket, either towards the nostrils or backwards down the throat. Particles and mucus together either drip out of the body or are swallowed for excretion via the stomach and intestines. The mucous blanket is also impregnated with various antibacterial substances (an enzyme called lysozyme, for example).

Particles which get through these nasally based barriers (which they may do when breathing is through the mouth, for example) are similarly dealt with in the trachea and the bronchi. From this area, particles are conveyed, by the moving mucus to the larynx to be coughed into the pharynx and swallowed (*see* **Colds; Coughs; Croup and Laryngitis**).

Only the minutest particles reach the end structure of the air passages, the alveoli. Here there are special cells called alveolar macrophages which can engulf and kill bacteria (*see* **Chest Infections**).

Most of the normal secretions of these body areas have self-cleansing and/or decontaminating properties. Both saliva and tears, for example, destroy some bacteria and inhibit the multiplication of others. Once again, attempts to prevent such normal secretions or to substitute artificial ones often make it more difficult for the body to care for itself. Tears are better for eyes than most "soothing" eye lotions while a running nose is usually serving a purpose which is better not halted by "nose drops to dry it up."

The second line of defense: inflammation

Whenever that first line of defense, the enclosing skin, is breached in any way, the immediate response is inflammation. The injury can be to any type of skin: the skin of your finger, the skin (mucous membrane) which lines your throat or the membrane which encases your liver.

The injury can be of any type. That finger may be cut or burned; that throat may be irritated by chemicals in dust or attacked by viruses; the liver can be invaded by bacteria. We call inflammation in different parts of the body by different names (internal ones have the suffix "itis," as in meningitis, appendicitis, laryngitis), but the process by which the body reacts to insult or injury and takes the first steps towards repairing the damage is always the same. Signs of inflammation are:

Redness (and sometimes heat). The small vessels supplying the damaged area (the arterioles) dilate so that more blood can reach the site. The minute capillaries also dilate so that the extra blood is not carried away too rapidly. The result is the red flush you see around, say, a bad graze or in a sore throat or an irritated eye.

Swelling and pain. Capillary walls become more "leaky" when dilated, so plasma (the clear part of the blood) loaded with many kinds of white blood cells (polymorphs) which travel to the area of injury ooze through the walls and accumulate in the tissue. This fluid is the exudate which you can see from that graze; it is the cause of the swelling in a sprained ankle or internal inflammation. Pain arises not only from nerve endings damaged in whatever accident caused the inflammation, but also by this swelling which causes pressure, and, probably, by substances, such as histamines, released from the cells. The functions of this exudate include:

Dilution of any irritants which may have been introduced as, for example, in an insect sting.

Concentration of a protein substance (fibrin) which helps to clot blood in an open wound, but which also produces minute "internal clots." These act as partial two-way barriers. They make it more difficult for invading bacteria to penetrate further and they also make it more difficult for the exudate to be carried away from the damaged area with the lymph flow. Obstruction of the lymph flow minimizes the risk of bacteria being carried with it, deeper into the body. It also ensures that the polymorphs (*see below*) remain in the area to perform their functions.

Concentration of polymorphs which perform elaborate scavenging tasks, engulfing bacteria, cell debris, etc., so that they can be destroyed by enzyme activity.

If tissue damage is slight and this first burst of polymorph activity succeeds in "clearing up" the area, inflammation simply resolves; blood vessels return to normal and the exudate is reabsorbed.

If tissue damage is considerable, polymorphs clear dead cells to allow healing. Continued inflammation and exudate show that their activity has not been successfully completed. When a clean wound stops oozing, or the swelling of an internal or joint injury goes down, healing will begin.

Types of infection

Localized infection

Some bacterial contamination of external wounds is very common. The bacteria which are "normal flora" for the *outside* surface of the skin are "foreign" to the polymorphs in that exudate. They must therefore be engulfed and prevented from getting further into the body via the lymph system or the bloodstream.

Pus is inflammatory exudate, packed with the dead and dying cells of polymorphs and bacteria, both being broken down by enzyme activity.

Pus from a wound certainly means that some microorganisms got in, but it also means that some, at least, are being dealt with by the white cells. A few droplets of pus from an open wound suggest the successful end to a minor battle *if other signs of inflammation have gone*. Pus oozes from a wound or dries into a scab. The tissue can then heal cleanly behind it.

If there is pus and inflammation continues, it is clear that the battle between polymorphs and bacteria is not over. It may still be successfully resolved (i.e., healing may take place without spread of infection), but "back-up troops" within the body will be being mobilized (*see below*).

● If there is visible pus in, on or coming from a wound, check whether there is still redness, heat, swelling and pain around it. If there is none, healing is under way. If there is inflammation, watch carefully to make sure it is diminishing rather than increasing. Seek medical help, even for a small injury, if inflammation increases.

Pus

Since pus contains the protein of cells "foreign" to the body, it must be ejected before healing can take place. In a superficial wound this is no problem—the pus oozes out. But in a deep or jagged wound, or when infection is internal, in an appendix, for example, it can be a problem.

When the polymorphs have controlled the bacterial enemy, destroying bacteria at least as fast as they are increasing, and preventing spread via blood or lymph, healing will commence *around* the area but cannot take place *within* the pus-laden tissues. The body has controlled the infection but cannot eliminate it. The result is an abscess.

Abscesses

There are many kinds of abscesses, ranging from the kinds which occur when pus collects just beneath the skin (boils, carbuncles, styes, etc.) through the kinds which are fairly superficial but out of reach (tooth and ear abscesses) to the internal ones like acute appendicitis. All abscesses are painful because the accumulated pocket of pus puts pressure on surrounding tissue and nerves. The less room an abscess has for expansion, the greater will be the pressure and the agony. Hence the sleepless nights of tooth and ear abscesses. Wherever the abscess, pus has to be got rid of before healing can take place. A superficial abscess, like a boil, will eventually "burst" and let out its own pus. Abscesses which are buried within body tissues or in internal organs will burst, too, if they are allowed to go on accumulating pus. But if that pus can find no direct route out of the body, the bursting of the abscess will spread it through surrounding tissues, often causing more generalized infection. This is why medical and/or surgical treatment is usually preferred.

If the root of a tooth is abscessed, for example, your dentist may refuse to take out the tooth and thus relieve the intense pain until he can be sure that your body's defenses will be able to cope with the consequent leakage of pus from the socket. He will often insist on giving a course of antibiotics to boost those defenses before the extraction (*see* **Teeth**/Some dental emergencies).

If an appendix is inflamed and therefore likely to begin to accumulate pus, its surgical removal is urgent (*see* **Hospital**/Surgery: Appendectomy). If it is permitted to build up pressure and burst, infected material will be spread through the abdomen to produce the very serious condition called peritonitis.

● When a collection of pus *can* find its own way out, it will do so. Don't be in a hurry to squeeze a hot, red, painful boil which has not yet made a "head." The body's defenses may yet deal with the infection so that the lump vanishes without ever draining pus. If it does not, forcing pus up through skin which is still intact may also force it down, breaking down the fibrin clots that prevent infection from spreading inwards.

Localized infection which is spreading

Local infection cannot always be dealt with, or even contained, by the defensive tactics of the body's general inflammatory response. The child himself may be in a state where that response is comparatively inefficient (*see above* Resistance). The infecting organism may have been introduced in great numbers, be highly virulent and/or have found an ideal site for multiplication. When infection threatens to spread, the body's next line of defenses is mobilized (*see* **Immune Response**). It is important, though, that you should recognize spreading infection early so that medical and/or surgical treatment can intervene before local trouble turns into generalized illness. Seek a medical opinion if:

Inflammation (including pain, swelling, redness, etc.) continues or increases.

Pus forms or continues to be formed after being carefully cleaned away on the first occasion that it was visible.

Inflammation spreads away from the site of the wound. This shows that "battle" is being waged in tissues other than those originally involved in the injury. The classic sign is red streaks under the skin running from the wound towards the nearest lymph nodes, but a spreading patch of dull-red skin around or near to the wound is a common sign, too.

Lymph nodes swell. If an injury is to the hand or arm and infection is spreading, the lymph nodes in the armpit will eventually swell. In a foot or leg injury it will be the lymph nodes in the groin which are affected. If the jaw or face is the site of injury, there may be swelling of lymph nodes in the angle of the jaw. Swollen lymph nodes are a clear sign that the body's immune system is involved in fighting the infection. By this stage there may be further signs of whole-body involvement such as fever.

● Although it is obviously better to prevent localized infection from spreading, don't let "blood poisoning" be a specter which haunts you. Even if infection in a small wound has given rise to enlarged lymph nodes and perhaps fever, antibiotics prescribed by your doctor will quickly resolve the infection.

Infections which cause illness   When microorganisms invade the body without an obvious wound as the entry point or an obvious injury as their site of multiplication, the body's infection can only be recognized by the symptoms which they cause. We therefore tend to feel that "being unwell" is quite different from "being hurt" but, from the point of view of the body's reactions, both conditions are similar. Some pathogenic microorganisms do eventually produce specific and recognizable symptoms (such as the various skin rashes of the infectious diseases of childhood), but most of them first produce the vague and general symptoms which might be the beginning of almost any infection and may indeed be dealt with by the body before they turn into anything "diagnosable." The very first signs of infection may, in fact, not be signs of illness at all but of the very fact that the body *is coping with a threat*. A sore throat, for example, means that something has irritated that mucous membrane. The irritation could be from dust and have nothing to do with infection by "germs." But if it is a reaction to "germs," the sore throat may never "turn into" the cold, the tonsillitis or the measles which you find yourself expecting. Local inflammatory reaction may deal with the threatened invasion and the throat will return to normal.

The more types of bacteria and viruses an individual's body has battled with, the more readily will it cope, at this quick, local level, with further contacts with them (*see* **Immune Response** and **Immunization**). Many older people, for example, quite frequently think they are going to have colds, judging by first symptoms of blocked-feeling noses and perhaps soreness at the very top of the throat. Yet most of the time the expected cold does not develop. It has been "shrugged off" by primed defenders.

Unfortunately that well protected adult can, and often does, pass on the cold he himself is not going to suffer to someone who is less well protected. When a particular infection is going around a family, some members will avoid illness altogether, some will have mild symptoms and others may have very marked ones (*see below* Preventing the spread of "infectious" illnesses). The nature of the symptoms experienced by people exposed to the same infection may vary, as well as their severity. That resistant father's body may stop the invasion of viruses within the nasal passages so that he only ever has a blocked and runny nose. The viruses he passes on may cause a middle-ear infection in one child, croup in another and a humdinger of a head cold in another.

With everyday (or at least every-year) infections, then, parents usually have to wait and see. Your child reports a stuffed-up nose and you wait and see whether it will "just go" or whether it will "develop." If it just goes, well and good; if it develops, you have to see what it develops into. On the whole your best overall indication that an infection is *not yet* being adequately dealt with by the body's own defenses is fever (*see* **Nursing/ Fever**). While an individual can be seriously, even fatally, ill, without ever having fever at all, most infections which are more than local do have fever associated with them; furthermore, while the body's normal temperature is more variable than many people believe, high fever does mean that the body is under stress, is fighting something.

Apart from the presence or absence of fever, the number of symptoms or the number of parts of the body affected is also a useful rough and ready guide to the progress of infection. A child may be nauseated (feel sick) for many reasons, many of them trivial and/or having nothing to do with infection. But if she also has diarrhea, infection is probable. If she has fever as well as nausea and diarrhea, some kind of infection which her body is having trouble eliminating, is almost certain. In the same way, a child with a headache can have (or be starting) almost anything or nothing physical or nothing diagnosable. Add in fever and it becomes likely that the headache is part of a physical illness. Add in a generalized achiness of her muscles and you can be sure that she has "got something."

Multiple infections If this all sounds very vague, that is because recognizing infections, especially early on, is a vague business. On the whole, vague and general symptoms either declare themselves by developing into more specific ones or they go away. When symptoms do develop and become more specific, it is often not the *original* infection which is responsible but the joining in of a second "germ" along a path paved by the first. A mild flu suddenly "turns into" a serious attack of bronchitis with thick sputum, yellow with pus, being coughed up. Parents may feel that they did not take the original flu seriously enough and that it is their fault that the child is now really ill. But it is nobody's "fault." Flu virus damages the lining of the bronchi and bronchioles. The body was in the process of dealing with the virus invasion, but that throat was open to further invasion by some of the many bacteria which commonly live harmlessly there (*see above*). The mild viral illness has been followed by a more serious bacterial one.

Secondary infections, following, or occurring simultaneously with, the first infection, are often much more serious than one on its own. The marked tendency of the measles virus to pave the way for bacterial infections of the middle ear, throat and bronchial tree is one excellent reason for mass immunization against measles.

Difficulties of medical diagnosis of infection Parents of an undeniably ill child often want their doctor to perform not only as a skilled diagnostician but also as a magician. They want to know "What has she got?" It is important to the parent-doctor partnership to understand that the question is often unanswerable.

Doctors, like parents, can only see symptoms. They can look for signs hidden from lay eyes (respiratory signs, for example, detectable only by a stethoscope used by a skilled ear) and they can relate to each other symptoms which lay-people tend to regard as separate (abdominal pain as part of tonsillitis, for example). By these means they can often establish *what kind* of illness the child has—an upper respiratory infection, for example—but still be unable to say what "germ" has caused it or what, if anything, is likely to follow. The most valuable result of a careful physical examination is often entirely negative. The doctor assures himself (and the parents) that the child's symptoms and signs are *not* suggestive of particular kinds of illness. He may, for example, tell you that her "lungs are clear," meaning that whatever infective organism has made her ill, she has not, at the moment, "got pneumonia."

Quite often such a physical examination reveals no signs or symptoms at all except those (such as a quickened pulse and breathing rate) which go with fever, whatever that fever's cause. Then the doctor himself has to take a wait-and-see approach unless the child is so ill (and/or the parents so frantically worried) that he considers that she should be admitted to the hospital.

Wait-and-see means that the doctor believes that the child will either produce some more symptoms (which will give him some new data to work on) or get better. It works best for parents if they know how long he plans to wait (i.e., when will he see the child again and/or how can they reach him if they get worried again) and the kind of sign or symptom he is waiting for. If those points are not volunteered, it is often worth asking the doctor what you should look out for and under what circumstances you should call him again.

Difficulties of laboratory diagnosis of infection

Wait-and-see also means that, given the present symptoms and lack of signs, the doctor does not consider that laboratory work to try to discover the infecting organism is possible or worthwhile. Again, it can help the partnership if parents understand why the doctor makes this decision.

If there are no special symptoms *the doctor and his back-up laboratory staff have no starting point.* They have no way of knowing what kind of organism they are looking for or which body system it is most likely to be in. It may seem that one could take a sample of blood, of urine, of feces and tell the lab staff to "look for pathogens." But that search would be not just difficult, expensive, time-consuming, but actually impossible. Of the hundreds of thousands of organisms which can cause trouble, many would be found because many live in the body anyway. Just finding them would tell one nothing. Each organism found would have to be counted; only an excess far above normal populations would even suggest infection. Then again one cannot just look and count. It is tempting to think of putting a drop of urine under a microscope and seeing and counting microorganisms, but it is not possible. Microorganisms have to be cultured (grown) and different kinds require different culture environments. Without some idea of what is being sought, the search cannot even begin.

If there are some special symptoms the doctor may know which body system he would be searching and therefore what kind of specimen to take, but the search may still be inappropriate.

Suppose, for example, that the ill child has upper respiratory symptoms. The doctor could take a swab from her throat or nose and ask his laboratory to make cultures from it. But the chances are high that the causative organism will be a virus not a bacterium, and virus culture is a technique which is still so new and difficult that facilities for it do not even exist in many places. He could tell the lab to culture for bacteria (on the grounds that if they found no infecting bacteria he could then assume that the illness was viral), but why should he bother? If there is a bacterial cause for the illness then an antibiotic will probably be appropriate; if it is viral then an antibiotic will not. If he thinks that an antibiotic is a reasonable prescription he will want to prescribe it now, not wait several days for cultures. If he is not going to prescribe one now, the chances are that by the time he gets the lab results which suggest that an antibiotic would have helped, the child will be better.

The pros and cons of antibiotics in undiagnosed infection

Your doctor's clinical judgment is on the line every time he has to decide whether or not to prescribe antibiotics for an ill child with indefinite symptoms. Parents tend to be unhelpful because, even when they understand that under most circumstances a laboratory hunt for a bacterium takes too long to be useful, they cannot understand why the doctor does not prescribe one *just in case* the cause of the illness is bacterial rather than viral. The answer to that is as simple as it is vital: bacteria change and evolve very readily. One of the aspects of themselves which they change most readily is their own resistance to antibiotics. If your child is given an antibiotic whenever she is ill, it will sometimes help her body deal with an infection, but all the other times it will simply encourage her normal bacteria to become antibiotic-resistant. Then, when she does suffer an invasion by bacteria (perhaps by those usually harmless residents, after she has had a virus infection) the antibiotics which should have cured her will have no effect. If your doctor does prescribe an antibiotic for your child at the beginning of a particular illness, it will probably be for one or more of the following reasons:

That her symptoms and condition make him suspect a bacterial cause. His suspicion may be based on long experience and clinical judgment so that he could only describe it by saying something like "throats that look like this, as part of this clinical picture, often are bacterial . . . ," or it may be based on harder data which he can more easily explain to you. The child may, for example, have had measles which is a viral infection. She was recovering but is now severely ill with high fever and acute ear pain. The chances are high that a bacterial secondary infection has moved in.

That an outbreak or epidemic of bacterial infection is taking place. If this child is the third member of a family, or the thirtieth member of a school, to come down with a similar symptom pattern which has been shown to be of bacterial origin in other people, the chances that there is a bacterial cause in her case are obviously high.

That previous and similar illnesses in this child have cleared up much faster when he did prescribe antibiotics than when he did not. Recurrent tonsillitis is a good example. Many children have several bouts each winter for two or three years. The infection may be bacterial or viral and, during the first few episodes, the doctor will have to use his clinical judgment to inspire guesswork. If antibiotics always "work," he will probably decide that the *probability is that this new bout is bacterial, too.* It may not be, but on balance he may feel that antibiotics should be given.

That the severity of the illness and/or condition of the child is such that every possible precaution against secondary infection must be taken even if the current infection is of viral origin. Antibiotics are often given to babies, for example, because even though their current infections may be viral, their in-built protection against secondary invasion by bacteria is very poor (*see* **Immune Response**). They might be given to a young child who was exceedingly ill with measles because that illness had reduced her general resistance to a low level. They might even be prescribed for an adolescent who, while not very ill now, faces important examinations in a week's time and therefore implores the doctor to use every tool at his disposal to "get me better."

That you will give him no peace and/or will consider him uncaring if he does not. Of course, no parent would like to admit that she bullied (or could bully) a doctor into giving treatment he considered inappropriate, and certainly no doctor would like to admit that he would allow such a thing to happen. But practicing medicine is an art as well as a science; human relations matter as well as symptoms and their relief. If the doctor must toss-up whether or not to prescribe that antibiotic (because there are insufficient clinical signs to give him clear guidance) and you are putting heavy pressure on him to do so, that pressure may, in fact, tip the balance.

When the laboratory may help in diagnosis

Different doctors have different kinds of laboratory help more or less readily available to them, as well as varying in the extent to which they like to rely on clinical judgment or have that judgment backed by evidence. Some therefore order the culture of throat swabs, or blood or urine tests (*see* **Hospital**/Procedures) much more readily than others.

Some doctors also take a great interest in public health and in the pattern of disease occurring in their own practices. They may sometimes seek a laboratory finding not only to assist in their management of this particular patient's current illness, but also to fill in another tiny piece in the jigsaw puzzle of an epidemic.

For most families, laboratory help for a patient who is being nursed at home will most commonly be sought under some of the following sets of circumstances:

Chronic ill health, whether this takes the form of "failure to thrive" in a baby or of complaints of lassitude, occasional unexplained fever and a general feeling of being "under par" in an older child. If the doctor can find no satisfactory explanation, he may order laboratory tests both to confirm or deny specific possibilities and to guide him in his general search for ways of improving the child's health. A blood test, for example, can answer many different questions. The blood may be tested specifically to check whether or not the child is anemic or suffering from a particular infection—such as glandular fever (infectious mononucleosis)—which would fit the clinical picture. A count can be made of the total number of white cells. An abnormally high number suggests that the body is fighting some kind of infection, somewhere. Certain infections stimulate the production of certain types of white cells, so a more discriminating count may give the doctor further guidance.

Recurrent illness such as repeated attacks of urinary infection. The doctor may decide that symptomatic treatment, with or without antibiotics, is no longer satisfactory. He may order a full urinalysis in order to establish just how many of which bacteria are present during an attack and which antibiotics they are sensitive to. He may also order tests of kidney function in order to ensure that there is no kidney damage, or inadequate function, which might be increasing the tendency to infection.

Epidemic or potentially epidemic illness. A few illnesses must, by law, be reported to the public health authorities. Those authorities also sometimes request all doctors to be on the alert for cases of a particular illness of which an epidemic seems likely. If your child suffers from "food poisoning" when her doctor has been thus requested to be extra-alert, he may order laboratory tests of her feces.

Special risks. Some serious illnesses are easy to diagnose through laboratory testing and worth testing for, even on suspicion, because early treatment is important. If your doctor even suspects meningitis, for example, he will order a lumbar puncture (*see* **Hospital**/Procedures) so that the spinal fluid can be examined (*see* **Meningitis and Encephalitis**).

Some conditions—heart conditions, for example—make any infection a special risk. Most doctors will make unusually heavy calls on laboratory help for such a patient.

Travelling or working in faraway places makes diseases which are rare and exotic for your home area into possibilities. Doctors will often seek laboratory help in diagnosing conditions which they seldom, if ever, meet, but which seem possible in these particular circumstances.

Treatment of infections which cause illness

Until the Second World War we could not directly treat infections in the sense of destroying "germs" which were causing illness within the body. Within two generations we have come to take such treatment for granted. Our grandparents will probably have nursed relatives dying from unchecked pneumonia, yet we no longer quite believe that people can die from simple *illness* in places where the full range of medical might is available to them. Death from accidents, from mechanical problems within the body and/or from surgical attempts to put them right, we can still accept; cancer is a special case: a kind of horror story of the modern world. But ordinary illness . . . surely there is a pill, an injection, a medicine? Surely there is a cure?

Antibiotics are the drugs which produced that miracle of forgetting, the drugs which seemed to give man control over infection. They are amazingly effective; they do cure many infections. But, as we shall see, they are not cure-alls. Virus infections remain largely untouched by modern treatments, their control being almost entirely a matter of prevention by immunization. Only some stages of some protozoan infections are directly "curable" in man; their control still has to depend on public health measures and on the control of animal vectors. Fungus infection of foodstuffs produces poisons which we still cannot "cure," so that attention must be focused on preventing such foods from being eaten in the first place. Insofar as man has defeated infection, then, he has still done more by prevention than by cure and will have to continue to do so. Public health measures may not help your family *when members are ill*, but it is those measures which ensure that they are not ill more often.

Antibiotics and sulphonamides

Sulphonamides were the first anti-bacterial chemicals to be used in medicine. Their role has been largely usurped by antibiotics, mainly because of problems of bacterial resistance to sulphonamides (*see below*).

Antibiotics are chemicals produced by bacteria and fungi which interfere with the life cycle of other bacteria and fungi. Those which interfere to *prevent the multiplication* of pathogenic microorganisms are called "bacteriostatic" drugs. They can halt the spread of infection and thus give the body's own defenses the chance to overwhelm the already present "germs," but they do not kill them. "Bactericidal" drugs actually destroy the "germs." The difference can be extremely important where the victim's own defenses are poor (due, perhaps, to immuno-suppressive drug treatment) or where infection has taken place in a part of the body which always lacks defense because (like nerve cells in the brain or the central nervous system) it is sealed off from normal blood flow.

Antibiotics may be the isolated and purified chemicals from cultured molds: ("natural antibiotics") they may be "natural antibiotics" which have been chemically modified ("semi-synthetic antibiotics"); or they may increasingly be "synthetic antibiotics" which have been, so to speak, chemically constructed from component parts. It is by tampering, in a variety of highly sophisticated ways, with these chemicals that medical scientists are able to alter and control antibiotic action. Some naturally occurring ones, for example, cannot be absorbed from the digestive tract and are therefore active only when given by injection. Some are active only against certain specific types of pathogenic bacteria. Some are very rapidly processed by the body so that frequent doses are necessary to keep up adequate blood levels. The original penicillin G, for example, had to be injected and was mainly active against pathogens of the cocci group. By isolating the penicillin molecule's nucleus, scientists made it possible to add to it other chemical groups and thus to produce the wide range of penicillins which are in use today.

Problems in antibiotic use: Bacterial resistance to antibiotics

Pathogenic bacteria can become resistant to the action of a particular antibiotic in a number of complicated ways, the most important of which is called "transformation." This process involves a population of bacteria (say in a wound) taking up fragments of genetic material (DNA) released by dead bacteria, using that "genetic information" and consequently reproducing themselves with the ability to resist that antibiotic.

For example, if there is an epidemic of dysentery, victims will have both harmless and pathogenic bacteria in their guts. Given an antibiotic, the pathogenic bacteria (along with plenty of harmless ones, *see below*) will be destroyed, but the surviving harmless inhabitants may acquire resistance to that antibiotic. This does not matter *at the time* because the resistant bacteria are not virulent pathogens. But if and when the patient's gut is invaded by another virulent strain, those bacteria will acquire antibiotic resistance from the harmless but resistant bacteria occupying the gut. The new infection will prove far more difficult to treat. Antibiotic resistance does not just affect the bacteria involved in one illness, person or epidemic, but may be passed on, via other pathogenic or harmless organisms, so that whole bacterial populations acquire it.

It was this problem of resistance which brought the extensive use of the first "magic drugs," the sulphonamides, to an end. And it is still this problem which bedevils antibiotic treatment. The chemical industry is involved in a non-stop race to evolve new antibiotics, or adaptations of existing ones, more quickly than bacteria can evolve resistance to them. Already there are some groups of bacterial infections (especially bowel infections) which respond so poorly to existing antibiotics that many doctors consider their use inadvisable. The antibiotic may not help the individual (whose "germs" are probably resistant to it) and it will certainly lead to yet more resistant strains developing via his normal bowel flora.

Fortunately some pathogens show no sign of developing resistance to commonly used and safe antibiotics. Syphilis, for example, remains sensitive to the original penicillin after almost two generations of frequent use (*see* **Adolescence**/Sex: Venereal disease).

● The more antibiotics are introduced into our bodies, the more opportunity there is for resistant bacteria to develop and the more difficult it will become to find safe antibiotics to which pathogenic bacteria are sensitive. This is why the temptation to take an antibiotic in every illness "just in case" must be avoided. It is also why the non-medical use of antibiotics (in the fattening of animals for meat, for example) is to be deplored. If we cannot use antibiotics responsibly, our grandchildren may find themselves in a world where the "miracle drugs" are no longer miraculous.

Side effects of antibiotics
Since pathogenic bacteria live and breed outside the cells of the infected patient, antibiotics can attack them without damaging the host cells. Nevertheless, there are side effects, varying from antibiotic to antibiotic and from individual to individual, but ranging from skin rashes to allergic shock reactions which can cause death.

Most minor side effects result from the fact that, while no antibiotic attacks all bacteria, many attack quite a wide range. While killing pathogens they also kill harmless bacteria of the individual's "normal flora" and by doing so they can upset the balance of various body systems. An upset in the normal flora of the bowel, for example, often leads to diarrhea in a patient taking oral antibiotics for an upper respiratory infection.

Antibiotics which are active against bacteria are inactive against fungi (and vice versa). Antibiotic treatment for a bacterial infection can therefore lead to an upsurge in resident fungi and to consequent infection by yeasts and so forth (*see above*). "Thrush" infections of the vagina, for example, are a frequent accompaniment to treatment with broad-spectrum antibiotics.

● Ill effects from an antibiotic should always be reported to a doctor and, if there is any question of allergy, carefully noted. A child who is allergic can (and must) be taught that he "must not have penicillin." This information could be vital if he should be ill when away from home.

● Children on long-term antibiotics (perhaps because of recurrent infections of the urinary tract) will inevitably be suffering some upset of body chemistry, and some likelihood of resistance to antibiotics if an acute bacterial illness should occur. You, with your doctor, must allow for this when deciding the pros and cons of prolonged antibiotic administration.

Choice of antibiotic and method of administration
As we have already seen (*see above*) a doctor who has decided to prescribe an antibiotic to a patient will usually want to begin the treatment immediately. While he may take swabs or specimens for laboratory culture, so that the treatment can be altered later if necessary, he will prescribe his "best guess" in the meantime.

That "best guess" may be easy: most bacterial tonsillitis, for example, involves a bacterium known to be sensitive to particular penicillins which are safe (except if the patient is allergic to them), comparatively cheap, and effective by mouth. Most bacterial urinary infections are associated with gram-negative bacteria and the doctor's "best guess" would therefore probably be different but equally easy.

Sometimes the choice is more difficult. If the doctor is puzzled, he may want to cover many options by prescribing a "broad-spectrum" antibiotic, one which is effective against a wide range of bacteria. If a present infection seems likely to be the continuation (or flaring up) of one which has already been treated with an antibiotic, he may think it likely that the bacteria infecting the patient now are, or have become, resistant to the first drug. He may therefore prescribe an antibiotic from a different group. In a hospital, especially, a doctor may have knowledge of particular resistances in the local bacterial population. His prescribing of antibiotics may be carefully tailored both to fit remaining bacterial sensitivities and to avoid creating yet more resistance.

Sometimes a doctor will prescribe an antibiotic which must be given by injection. This may be because the drug he wants the patient to have is only effective by this route, or because it can be given either by injection or orally but works more rapidly by this method.

Some antibiotics (especially antibiotics against fungal infections of the skin or mucous membranes) are prescribed as a cream, lotion, ointment or drops. They are not absorbed from the gut and cannot therefore be taken as tablets.

In more serious illnesses, antibiotics may be given by intravenous injection or by being added to an intravenous drip (*see* **Hospital**/ Procedures: Blood and other transfusions). This may be for maximum speed of action and/or for most effective distribution, especially to areas of the body with limited blood flow, and/or to ensure a constant level of the drug in the bloodstream rather than the highs and lows which are the inevitable result of periodic administration.

● Trust your doctor. If you do not, you should have found another long ago and should do so now. Ask why he prescribes this drug by that route, by all means, but try not to imply that it is his job to give you what you want. His job is to give your child what her body needs and it may need the injections she hates.

● Do as he says and therefore do make sure that you have understood his instructions. Does a prescription which says "every six hours" mean that the patient should be woken for the drug once in the night or does it mean "four times a day"? (*see* **Nursing**/Medicines).

● If you cannot follow the instructions exactly, do consult the prescribing doctor, at least by telephone. If a drug says "with food," for example, it may, or may not matter very much if your ill and unhungry child takes it on an empty stomach. You could try a compromise glass of milk but if that is refused or vomited, you must ask.

● Following your doctor's instructions means that *every single prescribed dose should be taken*. Stopping a medicine which a child dislikes as soon as she seems better is a temptation, but do resist it. A half-course of an antibiotic may quell the infection without eliminating it. She might quickly relapse. There is even a possibility that those pathogens will now have mutated so that they are resistant to the antibiotic which would have killed them if she had taken the full course. If you want to stop before the prescribed course of antibiotic has been given, ask your doctor first.

Anti-viral drugs Viruses live and multiply *within* living cells, using the chemistry of those cells for their own purposes. Drugs which could attack viruses would therefore have to do so by attacking the host cells. Indeed, it is difficult to see how they could avoid attacking the healthy cells of the body as well. For all practical purposes it is true to say that we have no drugs for the cure of established virus infections. Several chemicals are being developed experimentally, however. One (idoxuridine) is in use for the treatment of virus eye ulcers, cold sores (herpes simplex) and shingles (herpes zoster).

Interferon is the name given to a substance, discovered in the fifties, which is produced by cells when they are invaded by viruses. Its action is to prevent the multiplication of a virus within the cell and therefore its ability to spread to further cells.

Experimental work on the manufacture and administration of interferon raised high hopes which have not yet been realized. The substance is species-specific, so that people must have interferon manufactured by human cells. This means that it is both costly and difficult to produce. When injected, it acts for only a very short time.

Much scientific effort is now being devoted to finding substances which will stimulate the body itself to produce extra interferon.

Gamma globulin. Since viral vaccines produce antibodies and antibodies remain in the gamma-globulin fraction of the blood plasma, it seems logical to use human gamma globulin in the prevention and treatment of virus infections.

Gamma globulin used in this way cannot "cure" existing infection because antibodies act by combining with the virus and thus preventing it from penetrating a new cell. Viruses which are already within cells are therefore immune from antibody attack until they have multiplied to a point where they are ready to leave that dead or damaged cell and enter new ones. In theory, though, gamma globulin should help to protect an individual from viral infection and should slow down or limit the spread of viral infection within him.

Immunoglobulin is prepared so that it contains ten to twenty times the concentration of all the antibodies which are normally present in an adult's plasma.

Hyper-immune immunoglobulin is a similar preparation except that it is made from the blood of patients convalescing from particular viral infections and should therefore contain much higher quantities of antibody to that particular infection.

Despite some outstanding successes in protecting populations newly exposed to virus diseases against which they had no immunity, gamma globulin has proved disappointing as a means of protecting individuals. It cannot, for example, be relied upon to protect the fetus of a pregnant woman who has been in contact with German measles (rubella virus). It is, and will remain, a scarce and expensive commodity and will therefore probably continue to be used only in a limited way. Its greatest application, currently, is the protection of contacts of infectious hepatitis within closed communities such as nurseries.

Treatment of external infection and inflammation

The skin and mucous membranes are, as we have seen, the body's first line of defense against infection, a defense which is frequently breached. There are many highly effective drugs which can be applied to the skin to combat local infection, but it is unfortunate that our attitudes to these drugs tend to be less respectful and responsible than our attitudes to similar drugs taken internally. People who would not be so foolish as to give one child's "tonsillitis medicine" to another sore throat sufferer, will casually apply the cream prescribed for one to another. These casual attitudes are often reflected in the difference between the control of sales of internal and external drugs. Many countries which allow the sale of oral antibiotics only on prescription, nevertheless allow them to be freely available in creams, ointments and lotions.

Skin applications containing active drugs (as opposed to palliatives, such as softening agents for skin-chapping and so forth) should be treated with just as much respect as oral drugs. That means that before using any such application you will often need a doctor's advice, especially as skin infections are often extremely difficult to diagnose and/or to differentiate one from another.

The "base" in which the drug is contained is often as important as the active drug. Applications to be used in or on the eye, for example, *must* be sterile. The use of an antibiotic cream, intended for application elsewhere, on a stye or other eyelid infection could be disastrous. The same applies, of course, to appropriate bases for drugs applied to mucous membranes. The base for a skin antibiotic may be damaging, even poisonous, if applied to a mouth ulcer. Even where such obvious follies are avoided, bases remain important. Some infections of the skin require an application which dries up the affected skin; others require the very opposite. Some skins are allergic to some bases but not to others. Some bases are suitable for application to open wounds, some must not be applied if the skin is damaged.

The "shelf-life" of many skin applications is comparatively short. An outdated application may be useless; worse, if the shelf-life of the chemicals used to prevent it from becoming contaminated is over, the ointment may actually be harboring "germs." Even if there is an indication of shelf-life on the tube or jar (and you can understand it), the date it suggests may apply to its *unopened* shelf-life.

Many skin applications contain more than one drug or chemical. While one of these ingredients may be appropriate to the condition you are considering treating, the other(s) may be contra-indicated (*see below*, Applications for inflammations).

Some drugs are absorbed through the skin into the underlying tissues and thence into the circulation. An application which is safe for its prescribed use on a prescribed skin area, may amount to overdosage if it is applied to a larger skin area. So even where you are using the application prescribed by a doctor for this particular skin infection, it is important to check back with him before you extend that treatment. Ideally, any skin infection which is getting worse or more widespread, despite prescribed treatment, should be seen again by the doctor.

The following types of skin application may serve as examples both of the kinds of treatment available and of the treatment errors which may easily be made at home.

Applications for bacterial infections

Certain bacterial infections of the skin itself can be almost magically treated with antibiotic applications. Impetigo, for example, may clear almost overnight.

Where superficial wounds are becoming infected, antibiotic ointment or impregnated dressings may be effective in helping the body to clear up the infection and thus may promote healing. Doctors try not to prescribe for local application antibiotics which are also widely used internally, because such use on the skin increases the antibiotic-resistant population of bacteria and may act as a sensitizing dose of antibiotic to those who are allergic. For these reasons, antibiotics such as penicillin are usually avoided in favor of chlortetracycline, bacitracin and/or neomycin.

● Infections *under* the skin, even when pus is clearly going to break through, as in a boil, are unaffected by external applications of antibiotics. If an antibiotic is needed at all, it will be needed in the bloodstream (by mouth or by injection).

● Crops of pustules or patches of skin which are "weepy" *may* be due to bacterial infection but they may not. Skin infections are difficult to diagnose so this is a task for a doctor. Self-treatment (with that antibiotic wound cream, for example) could be totally inappropriate.

Infections of the eye and external ear may be bacterial and, if they are, drops containing an antibiotic such as Aureomycin may be prescribed.

● Never put anything in an eye or ear without medical advice. The cost of "getting it wrong" can be too high.

Vaginal infections are seldom bacterial (*see below*) and if they are, medical advice is certainly needed. Male genital infections must be diagnosed by a doctor. In a sexually active individual, genital symptoms may be due to a venereal disease (*see* **Adolescence**/Sex: Venereal disease), and medical treatment is urgent and essential not only for the individual's health but for everybody's.

Applications for fungal infections

Infections such as ringworm and thrush (some variety of which is the most common vaginal infection) can be very successfully treated with those antibiotics which are active against these particular micro-organisms (*see above*).

● Most antibiotics are active *either* against bacteria *or* against fungi but not both. Selecting the right drug therefore depends on the right diagnosis of the skin infection you can see.

Applications for inflammations

Many of the most annoying skin disorders are characterized by signs of inflammation such as redness, swelling, soreness or itching. Inflammation which is "inappropriate" (such as diaper rash, contact dermatitis and so forth) can often be effectively relieved by skin applications containing one of the many corticosteroid drugs. But these, perhaps above all other skin applications, should be treated with the greatest care. It must always be remembered that steroid (and derivative) applications *suppress* inflammation and that inflammation is the skin's normal first reaction to injury or infection. If infection is causing the inflammation, such a cream will *suppress the reaction but not the cause*. Indeed, the body's ability to deal with that infective cause will be much reduced because the drug has disarmed it.

● Never, ever, use a corticosteroid application on a skin inflammation which even *might be* infective. If you are dealing with what you think is an infective skin disorder, be careful not to use a combined antibiotic/steroid cream (*see below*). If you put such a cream on a patch of impetigo, for example, wanting the antibiotic effect, you may provoke a widespread and serious septic rash because the anti-inflammatory effect of the steroid will be much greater than the bactericidal effect of the antibiotic, and the skin will be unable to prevent the infection from spreading. Put such a combination on a cold sore (herpes simplex virus) and the antibiotic will, of course, be ineffective while the anti-inflammatory will allow the virus infection to lead to a nasty ulcer. Even athlete's foot may spread over a large area if treated in this way (*see* **Ringworm and Athlete's Foot**).

● Corticosteroid/antibiotic combinations can be extremely useful if they are used for skin conditions which are *primarily allergic* but where there is (or is likely to be) superimposed infection. They may be prescribed for eczema which a child has infected by scratching, or for severe diaper rash which is liable to infection every time he passes a stool (*see* **Allergy/ Eczema**).

● Because these conditions are difficult to diagnose and because cortico-steroids can do so much good when used appropriately and so much harm when used wrongly, it is best never to use them without a doctor's prescription (even if they are on open sale in your country), and *never* to use one which has been prescribed for another occasion or person.

● Even prescribed corticosteroid preparations on appropriate skin dis-orders can lead to secondary infection because they reduce the skin's natural inflammatory response and therefore provide an excellent hold for bacteria or fungi. If boils, thrush, etc. should develop, stop the treatment immediately and see your doctor.

Preventing infection

In the Western world, public health authorities do more to protect families from serious and/or epidemic infections than those families can ever do for themselves. Clean water, efficient sewage disposal, hygienic production, handling and distribution of milk and other foodstuffs, the disinfection of public places, immunization programs and the compul-sory notification of particular diseases all combine to let most of us take freedom from infection for granted, most of the time. It has not always been so and it is still not so in many parts of the world. Reasonable cooperation with such authorities is still probably the main contribution which each family can make both to its own and to every other family's health. However overburdened we may be by bureaucracy, health rules, regulations and exhortations are not appropriate ones at which to sneer or to encourage children to sneer. If they swim in that forbidden reservoir they may introduce infection which could affect thousands. If they cleverly avoid the disinfectant footbath at the swimming pool they are negating public efforts to keep down fungus diseases like athlete's foot. If they manage to skip school on the day those tuberculosis tests are given they defeat public efforts to ensure that the whole population is either naturally immune or immunized. . . . If children can be brought up to understand the purpose of regulations of this kind and, perhaps through foreign travel and television documentaries, to see something of what life is like where basic public health measures are still not realized and crippling diseases are still endemic, they may reach adolescence with a sense of responsibility both for their own health and for other people's. The adolescent who spreads venereal disease through a wide circle of contacts does not *mean* to be a public menace. He simply does not realize that it can have happened to him. The girl who serves at the cooked meat counter and does not report the septic spot on her hand does not *mean* to poison her customers. She does not take hygiene instructions seriously.

Infection and home hygiene

There are bacteria everywhere and nothing that you can do will rid your home, or even your body, of them. But those bacteria are not a constant threat. Most of them are harmless anyway. A few are pathogenic, but when they get into the body in small numbers the body's own defenses deal with them without signs of clinical illness. It is only if a large number of virulent microorganisms find a way into the body of a susceptible person that infection will take place.

Numbers are critical. There are bacteria on the surface of that table, but there will not be many and they will not be there for long because, in the absence of food, they cannot multiply. If there are crumbs on the table, bacteria may be breeding. But they will not breed for long. Either the crumbs will be wiped away or that small food source will run out. Colonies of bacteria can only establish themselves and breed in rapid millions where they have a source of food—and other facilities such as warmth and moisture—and where they are left undisturbed.

If a colony of potentially pathogenic bacteria does establish itself in the home it does theoretically present a threat to human health. But no infection will take place unless those bacteria get into a human body.

Home hygiene against infection is therefore twofold. It should aim to discourage the undisturbed growth of vast colonies of bacteria, some of which may be pathogenic. And it should aim to prevent colonies which may grow from being eaten, introduced into wounds and so forth.

Bacterial breeding grounds

Food for bacteria is living matter which is now dead. Much household "dirt" is not, in this sense, "dirty" at all. You may dislike the look of city dust on your windowsill but it probably will not breed many bacteria. Your child's room, littered with books, models, toys and spilled paint, may look "filthy," but its condition is not a threat to health. The kind of "dirt" which will breed bacteria if it is left to do so is:
□ Feces, human or animal.
□ Blood, scurf and hair, human or animal.
□ Dead rodents, insects, etc.
□ Food, human or animal.

Feces are largely made up of bacteria and, as we have seen, while most are harmless to their host, a few which are harmless to one person can behave as pathogens in another. Standard hygienic measures, such as handwashing after using the toilet, are therefore sensible. Even more important, perhaps, are measures to prevent animal feces from contaminating food or hands which will then go to the mouth. Animal "accidents" in the home require careful cleaning up and disinfection of the area (*see below*). Animal toilet trays need regular cleaning and disinfection and crawling babies and small children should, as far as possible, play where the ground is not fouled by dogs and cats.

Blood is a good growth medium for many bacteria, but it is seldom a contaminant in the home because we tend to wipe it away wherever it is shed. Sanitary pads should never be allowed to accumulate, even in a closed container. If they cannot be flushed down the toilet they should be burnt. If a wound dressing becomes blood-soaked, so that there is blood exposed to bacterial contamination from the air or from things the victim touches, it should be changed.

Scurf and other shed skin cells certainly provide a breeding ground for bacteria, but quantities are so small that there is seldom a practical problem unless one family member has a skin infection (which might be passed on), or any kind of skin inflammation (which might render their own skin liable to bacterial infection). Ideally, of course, brushes, combs, facecloths and towels should be kept for individual family members as well as being frequently washed. In practice, a good deal of sharing goes on in many families without ill effects. Animal scurf and shed hair may harbor bacteria to which human members of the family are less resistant. It is sensible to keep small children away from pets' bedding and to vacuum more than usually carefully during the molting season.

Dead rodents, insects, etc. The mouse which your cat kills, rediscovers three days later and brings into the kitchen, will teem with bacteria. Flies and other insects are not only a threat to hygiene while they are buzzing around the kitchen, inoculating food with bacteria from outside, but also when they are dead and floating in the mayonnaise.

Food. Although most of the food you buy will contain bacteria or acquire bacteria as you prepare it, large colonies will have little chance to grow if you avoid giving them ideal circumstances. If you are unfortunate enough to buy food containing really virulent microorganisms, kitchen hygiene will not help you. "Food poisoning" is by no means always the cook's fault (*see* **Diarrhea, Gastroenteritis and Food Poisoning**).

Hygienic reminders **Cold discourages bacterial growth.** A refrigerator will slow up growth; a freezer will halt it.

High temperatures kill most common bacteria. Cooking will render most food safe.

Gentle warmth—like that in the open kitchen—is ideal for many bacteria. Food standing in the open may have bacteria rapidly multiplying in it as well as being liable to acquire further bacteria from the air, from flies and so forth. Watch out for:

Frozen food which is inadequately defrosted before cooking. Heat inside a chicken or turkey, for example, may never reach bactericidal levels but only encouraging warmth.

Frozen food which is to be eaten cold. Defrosting and then reaching room temperature may provide ideal bacterial breeding conditions.

Cooked dishes or leftovers, whether frozen or not, which are to be eaten hot. If these are merely *warmed* (as is often done for babies) bacteria may find a superb breeding environment. Make sure such dishes are re-cooked or at least made boiling hot all the way through.

Milk, especially for babies (*see below*). For many bacteria, milk is a superb growth medium and milk at room temperature can produce vast colonies very rapidly. Don't leave opened milk bottles standing around the kitchen, babies' bottles waiting until they are wanted or children's milk drinks by their beds. . . .

Cross contamination in cooking. Blood from raw meat or poultry, for example, can get onto your hands and/or working surfaces and from there onto foods which are then eaten raw. Try to deal with these foods separately and wash and clean up carefully in between.

Wounds and other skin lesions. If you have a septic wound on your finger you may contaminate foods in which bacteria can actively breed until they are eaten; a bowl of whipped cream, for example. Equally, if you have a clean but open wound on your finger, bacteria from that raw meat may contaminate it, unless you wash, frequently, as you cook.

Cook's wounds should be carefully covered. If you have a septic place, a boil or whatever, use a waterproof dressing and a rubber finger while you are preparing food.

Some of the implements we use in the kitchen are positively revolting if looked at through a microscope. Some of the worst are:

Wall can openers which dip their points into the cat food and then the sardines and then the baby's dinner, but which are seldom washed.

Cloths used for drying up. They accumulate food particles suspended in warm water and often do not even dry out completely between uses. Dishwasher or air-drying is certainly more hygienic. So are paper or disposable cloths, provided they really are disposed of.

Washing-up brushes (and toilet brushes). They all tend to trap and retain solid matter between the bristles.

Babies need some special hygiene Babies are more likely than most people to be susceptible to bacterial infection because they have not been around long enough to develop wide-ranging immunity from constant low levels of exposure to various pathogens, and their bodies' own defense mechanisms are less efficient. Furthermore, if they are not breast-fed, they are fed instead with that ideal bacterial breeding substance, warm milk, and they spend considerable periods in intimate contact with their own feces. Gastroenteritis kills thousands of babies every year in less hygiene-conscious parts of the world, and it still makes many Western babies ill, too. Various forms of infected diaper rash are as common as they are uncomfortable. Sensible precautions in the early months include:

Careful washing of bottles, nipples and any equipment used to prepare

feedings with detergent and water (to remove milk traces) **followed by sterilizing** either with a chemical, sold for the purpose, or by boiling.

Careful washing and sterilizing or boiling of diapers, one-way liners or any non-disposables.

Frequent changing of soiled diapers and washing of the baby's bottom with soap and water to remove all traces of feces.

Extravagance with formula and/or solid foods so that milk which has been out of the refrigerator is never saved for another feeding, and solid foods are never reheated more than once, if at all.

Care over washing hands before preparing babyfood or at least between visits to the toilet/diaper changing and preparing babyfoods.

Washing of pacifiers which, while they provide no food for bacterial growth, may collect bacteria when dropped on the floor or in the park.

Small children need special hygiene, too   Although older babies and toddlers are rapidly developing the ability to cope with the "family germs," they expose themselves to bacterial infection more than most older people do because they naturally tend to explore things with their mouths and they are seldom held back from doing so by the revulsion which comes with age!

If anybody is going to explore the kitchen waste-bin it will be a young child. If anyone is going to smear feces around and then suck his fingers it will be a young child. If anyone is going to suck that dishcloth or the toilet brush it will be a young child. And, of course, if anybody is going to drop a piece of doughnut on the living-room floor and then discover and eat it two days later, it is going to be a young child. . . .

You cannot stop babies and toddlers from sucking objects and their fingers; indeed it is a great mistake to try. With this age group in the house you have to make doubly sure that "dirty dirt" is kept out of reach.

Sterilants, disinfectants and antiseptics   Germ-killing chemicals are the subject of massive advertising campaigns and much public confusion. There are many chemicals available and attempts to use exactly the right one for each and every purpose will lead to the spending of a great deal of unnecessary money, and probably eventually to the wrongful use of one or the other when an overstocked cupboard confuses you in a crisis. If you understand how these chemicals do and do not work, you can then choose one or two which will meet every ordinary household and first aid requirement. Whatever those advertisements may imply, neither "good hygiene" nor being a "good parent" depends on the use of miracle products.

Sterilization   Properly refers to the destruction or removal of *all* microorganisms. Although we talk of "chemical sterilants" (*see below*) the phrase is inaccurate. There will be some microorganisms (especially the spores of some bacteria and fungi) which survive almost any chemical treatment. True sterilization can be reliably carried out only by physical rather than chemical means, and even then the method of sterilization has to be matched to the material to be sterilized. Heat, as in boiling or autoclaving, for example, is used to sterilize canned foods and surgical instruments.

Filtration, in which air or liquid is forced through mesh fine enough to trap the relevant microorganisms, is used to sterilize the air in operating rooms or liquids for injection. Various forms of radiation and toxic gases are used to sterilize materials, such as plastics, which are not heat-proof.

In the home, there are very few occasions when sterilization, as opposed to disinfection, is needed.

Home "surgery." Needles for removing splinters, etc. can be sterilized by heating the tip in a match flame until it is red-hot. Tweezers, scissors, etc. can be sterilized after use around a septic wound by boiling for ten minutes in a covered pot.

Home emergencies. If you need a near-sterile pad or bandage in a hurry, choose something which has been ironed with a hot iron. The inner folds of a sheet or handkerchief, for example, will be very nearly sterile unless, of course, they were drip-dried.

Skin infections. As we shall see, normal disinfection of babies' diapers and so forth does not always kill all "germs." If a baby or child has a skin infection and you want to sterilize everything and, so to speak, start again, diapers, sheets, towels, facecloths, etc. can all be boiled. If you don't want to rely on the hot water cycle of your washing machine, an old-fashioned boiling on your stove (perhaps in a water-bath canner) will be most effective. Make sure that the water reaches a full boil and keep it there for at least ten minutes.

Disinfectants and antiseptics

These are chemicals which, used in an adequate concentration and for a sufficient time, destroy most microorganisms: bacteria, viruses, fungi, yeasts and at least some resistant spores. The term "disinfectant" is used when a chemical is applied to inanimate objects—working surfaces, drains, diapers; the term "antiseptic" is used when the chemical is applied to living skin or mucous membranes. Sometimes disinfectants and antiseptics are different concentrations or formulations of the same chemical, but do not use them interchangeably unless you are very sure of your own chemical/medical knowledge. A disinfectant used on the skin could be exceedingly dangerous. An antiseptic used down the toilet would probably be ineffective.

Disinfectant action

For a disinfectant to kill "germs," a particular concentration of the chemical must both reach the microorganisms and stay in contact with them for a particular length of time.

If you pour disinfectant down the drains it will immediately be diluted by the standing water in the pipes, and any which remains on the sides of those pipes will be washed away the moment anybody turns on a tap or flushes the toilet.

If you wipe the toilet bowl or your kitchen working surfaces with disinfectant, you may indeed use the right dilution and leave it there for the right length of time, but "germs" will be killed by most disinfectants only if you have first removed all solid matter, and any grease, by thoroughly washing it with detergent and water. Applied without prior washing, the disinfectant chemicals cannot reach the cells of the microorganisms. If thorough washing is carried out there will be very few microorganisms left for them to kill. Ordinary cleanliness must precede disinfection and, in most cases, ordinary cleanliness is quite enough.

Snags to disinfectant use
Most efficient disinfectants (chlorine-releasing hypochlorites, for example, such as Chlorox or Purex) are dangerous to people as well as to "germs." Those named here, for example, are powerful acids. If a child swallows them or gets them in her eyes, they will do serious damage. The chlorine gas they release is also dangerous if it comes into contact with other chemicals, so absentmindedly using such a disinfectant along with another toilet product (a "deodorizer," for example) can cause poisonous fumes or even an explosion. Even used carefully, such products are not without snags. They are powerful bleaches, for example, and while they may make your bath look beautifully white they will also ruin your carpet or your clothes.

Choosing and using a disinfectant
If you have a baby in the house, a hypochlorite disinfectant intended for babies' bottles (and therefore sold in a much safer and more diluted form) can safely be used to soak and store those bottles. When you change the bottle solution, the used solution can then be used to disinfect and mildly bleach diapers and so forth. You can use the same dilution of the same product occasionally to disinfect toys or pacifiers if they have fallen on dog-fouled ground, or to disinfect potties or the toilet if someone has been having diarrhea. If you want to disinfect everything you can think of, perhaps including cutlery, china and bedding, because of illness in the house, the same product will do the job safely and efficiently. You will not kill "all known germs" at this sort of concentration, but you will not kill anything else either.

While you are nursing an illness, it is sensible to disinfect thermometers between uses. Your thermometer can stand in disinfectant solution which should be changed daily.

If you have no very small children in the house you will have no prior need for bottle sterilant. You may, of course, want to use a full-strength domestic hypochlorite solution because you want its bleaching action on your laundry or your bath. But if you want a safe general disinfectant which, diluted according to the instructions, can be used for anything from disinfecting the carpet when the dog has been sick to disinfecting vomit bowls or thermometers, you may do better with a preparation such as Zephiren. Although this product is not as lethal to as wide a range of "germs" as are the hypochlorite preparations, it is quite lethal enough to common household ones and infinitely safer and easier to use. It has the great advantage of being intrinsically detergent as well as disinfectant, so you can wash things with it instead of washing first and then disinfecting. The disinfectant action is inactivated by many soaps, so if you are trying to disinfect your hands before or after dealing with a wound, for example, use your chosen product to *wash* with or make sure you rinse off your toilet soap first.

Antiseptic action
Antiseptics are also widely misused. People use antiseptic mouthwashes and gargles "for sore throats," never stopping to think that the sore throat

is probably caused by viruses and that since viruses are inside their own cells, no antiseptic can kill the viruses without destroying the cells, too. Antiseptics are also applied to wounds which, if they are clean, require none, and which, if they are infected, probably require medical attention. Antiseptics are further used, in an even vaguer fashion, for "personal hygiene" ranging from washing armpits with "antiseptic" soaps to douching vaginas. Skin does not require artificial help in holding a balance between normal and pathogenic bacteria. If it is healthy and intact, such "aids" may actually interfere with the balance. If it is not healthy and intact, it probably requires a specific chemical prescribed by a doctor.

Choosing and using an antiseptic

If the skin, damaged or undamaged, does require an antiseptic then it certainly needs to be cleaned in the ordinary sense of having dirt and grease removed. Ordinary washing with soap and water is far more effective than an antiseptic cream if either is to be used alone. If ordinary washing does not satisfy your need to "do something," wash with a suitable dilution of detergent/antiseptic: the same product suggested for general disinfection (Zephirin) is satisfactory for this and has the advantage of giving you only one product for use in all circumstances where you want to disinfect either something or someone.

The same types of antiseptic are often applied, in cream or ointment form, to wounds where people want the antiseptic action to persist for longer than a diluted liquid will remain active on the skin. Remember, though, that the cream vehicle may in itself delay wound healing by keeping the skin from the hardening effect of air. Furthermore, if an antiseptic-cream-and-dressing combination is left on a wound for too long, that cream, combined with exudate from the wound, may provide an actual growth medium for the bacteria you are trying to kill or keep out.

Preventing the spread of "infectious" illnesses
(*see also* individual conditions)

Although that phrase "infectious illness" makes most people think of the common infectious diseases of childhood, like measles or mumps, any infection can, of course, be spread from one person to another. Some infections (like those childhood ones) will always produce similar symptoms in susceptible individuals (although their severity and any complications will vary), but others will, as we have seen, produce different symptoms depending on the nature of the "germs" being passed on, the route they take into the next person's body, and the "reception" they get there. Even while you think about preventing the spread of chickenpox or the common cold around your family, remember that your baby's septic diaper rash *could* infect the cut on your finger and a trace of the resulting pus in her food *could* give her an intestinal infection.

Many illnesses are infectious to other susceptible people even before the first victim has any symptoms. There is an "incubation period" during which viruses are multiplying in her body. Their concentration is not yet great enough for her to show clinical symptoms of the disease, yet she is excreting or spraying out quite enough to infect somebody else.

Old-fashioned quarantine regulations were intended to control the spread of infection by isolating not only those who were sick but also any close contacts who might therefore be incubating the illness. As soon as one child in a family developed chickenpox, all other children in the family were sent home, too. There they were to stay until either they had suffered and recovered from the disease or the incubation period had passed and it was clear that the infection had missed them. At some times and in some communities, quarantine was taken so seriously that schools and other institutions were closed down and families lived in self-imposed purdah. Yet, little by little, it became clear that even extreme quarantine measures do little to limit the spread of most infections. In chickenpox, for example, the child is highly infectious for several days before symptoms appear. During that period she may pass the disease to her brothers, sisters and friends, and any of those children who acquire the infection will do the same. By the time that first child has diagnosable chickenpox, her contacts are only a few among, many people, networked through the community, who may be incubating the disease.

Quarantine regulations for most diseases have been relaxed in most communities as knowledge of the natural history of various infections, together with immunizations against them and treatments for them, have been developed. Every family needs to know the regulations for its own schools and so forth but, on the whole, while quarantine of the sick is still normal practice, and usually common sense, quarantine of healthy contacts is reserved for exceptionally dangerous diseases and especially vulnerable communities. If your child suffers from measles, for example, other members of her family will be allowed to pursue their ordinary lives until or unless they become sick. If she has diphtheria, on the other hand, quarantine may well be required for the whole family. If a child in a residential nursery suffers from measles she will certainly be nursed in isolation from the other children, and her close contacts, including staff, may also be separated from children who scarcely knew her.

For some diseases, "surveillance" has replaced the quarantine of healthy contacts. The family and friends of a patient are allowed to lead their normal lives during the incubation period of the disease, but they are regularly checked by a doctor so that they can be isolated and treated at the very first signs of disease.

Schools and other institutions themselves play a part in the control of a few diseases and infestations which are mild yet quick to spread in a closed community. If your child has ringworm, for example, her close contacts may be inspected and treated by the school doctor. If one child in a class is found to be infested with head lice, every child in the school may be inspected and either treated or sent home with instructions for treatment which must be carried out before they will be readmitted.

Public health measures control the spread of most common infections within the community; your own hygienic precautions minimize the hold which pathogens are likely to achieve within the house (*see above*). It is your children's own bodily defenses which will play the largest remaining part in keeping them healthy. As they grow up they will meet most of the "germs" which are common within the family/community and they will develop immunity to them. Even if you feel that your adolescent children suffer from all-too-many colds and other minor infections, you can be sure that their bodies encounter hundreds more which they are able to resist or "shake off" with only the mildest and most transient symptoms.

Infection is most likely when a susceptible individual meets a "new germ." That "new germ" may be fresh to the whole community (as when a new strain of flu sweeps through a population); new to your family (as when a vacation abroad is ruined by a "tummy bug" which causes local residents no problems); or it may simply be new to the individual, either because she has chanced to miss out on previous contacts or because she herself is newly born.

A new baby has met no "germs," so every pathogen with which she has contact is a potential threat. For a few months she will have passive immunity to virus infections passed to her across the placenta from her mother's bloodstream but, as we have seen, passive immunity is short-lived (see **Immune Response**). Against bacterial infections she does not even have that passive immunity: antibodies to bacteria are too large to pass the placental barrier. During her early months and years, that baby must meet and overcome all the infections which are common in her environment, building her own internal protection against them as she goes. Against a few specific infections we can immunize her (see **Immunization**) but against the many, many others, she must immunize herself.

In many families minor illnesses are most frequent among two- to seven-year-olds. Passive immunity has waned and the child is exposed to "germs" brought into the home by older family members and by visiting children. When she first attends a playgroup or nursery school, whole classes will pass infections back and forth among themselves. There may seldom be a day when every pupil is present. Once she is old enough for real school she will have built some immunity to some "germs," but her big new world will expose her to more which are new to her.

An apparently endless series of infections can be almost as hard on parents as on the child herself; it may comfort you a little to realize that she will "grow out of it" because her body will gradually learn to cope, shrugging off some invaders altogether and limiting the growth and spread of others. As the frequency of her illnesses begins to drop, so will the severity of most of them. A baby is often ill with an ordinary cold: a child is rarely more than uncomfortable (see **Colds**).

It is arguable that there is so little you can do to limit the spread of minor infections within the family that it is not worthwhile to try. But while it is true that a child who has a cold today may well have passed it to his sister yesterday, it is also true that he is more infectious today, with this streaming nose and cough, than he was while he was merely incubating the viruses. Some degree of exposure is probably inevitable for every family member every time one is unwell, but that need not mean that it is always sensible to allow everyone to be exposed to the limit.

Whatever infection you are considering, that question of degree of exposure will apply. The child with a cold sprays virus-laden particles around every time she coughs or sneezes. Another child is most likely to breathe them in if the two faces happen to be close together when that sneeze happens. The child with an intestinal infection excretes viruses in her liquid stools; another child is most likely to acquire the "germs" if traces of those feces get from the patient's or your hands onto the family's food. Taking the trouble not to pass on infection in the most obvious ways *may not* protect anyone, but it reduces the likelihood of spreading.

If your child has some underlying condition, such as severe asthma (*see* **Allergy**), which makes everyday infections pose a real threat to his health, he will be under a doctor's care and you will be given detailed guidance. Basically healthy children neither require nor benefit from being wrapped in cotton, but even for them there are times when one more infection can be one too many.

Protecting very young babies A simple head cold can make a young baby quite ill and, by blocking his nose, make feeding sufficiently awkward to slow up his weight gain. A superficial bacterial skin infection in an older child (impetigo, for example) may take the form of a serious bloodstream infection in a small baby. Whooping cough, fortunately less common than it was, thanks to immunization, can still kill if it strikes a baby before his own course of injections has protected him.

Protecting such a young child from infection is not as difficult as protecting older ones; you can keep him semi-isolated without his noticing, while anti-infective hygiene measures are simply an unusually careful version of normal baby care.

Keep infectious visitors away: out of the house if possible, out of the baby's room anyway.

Don't let your own children cuddle him while they are obviously infectious.

Don't take him to crowded places in winter unless it is unavoidable.

If you must nurse an older child while caring for a baby, try to put the baby's carriage in a next door room, and divide your time and attention between the two rather than having them in the same room together.

Whatever the particular infection which is in the family, washing your hands carefully before you handle the baby or his food or drink will probably help.

If it is you who is ill, the baby was almost certainly thoroughly exposed to your "germs" before you had any symptoms, so if he is going to "catch" them he will already have done so. Handing him over to someone else, and isolating yourself, will almost certainly do more harm than it can do good. It is worth taking extra care not to let him suck your streaming nose, though. Some people recommend masks as a way of cutting down a baby's exposure to parental "germs," but inexpertly used, such a mask can do more harm than good. It will not trap all viruses. Those which it has accumulated will be positively showered on the baby if he grabs at the mask as you bend over him, or if you rip it off impatiently to answer the telephone with him on your hip.

Protecting ill children and convalescents As we have seen, a secondary infection with bacteria sometimes follows viral infection and the result is usually more severe than the first illness. If a child has an upper respiratory infection which the doctor is treating as viral, don't assume that the next family member to become ill is "bound to have the same." Nursing two together may be easier for you and more cheerful for them but, unless you are sure that they both have one, clearly identified illness, it may be a mistake. For the same reason it is sensible not to hurry a child who has been ill back into his normal activities, especially if these involve school or playgroup where there will be various "germs" around. Such a child often appears to recover, goes back to school and becomes ill again within a couple of days. It is not that his original illness has recurred but that it has made him especially liable to a new one.

Remember the possible side effects of any treatment the child may have had for the first illness. If he has had a course of antibiotics for that upper respiratory infection, for example, his normal gut flora will be disturbed and he may be especially liable to intestinal infections for a while.

Sometimes a child who acquires one infection after another so that he never seems to be completely well can have a vicious circle of infection and reinfection broken if you can arrange for him to have a couple of weeks to get right back to normal. In the past such children were sometimes sent away to "convalescent homes," but we now know that stress increases the liability to infection and that institutions tend to be hotbeds for "germs." Having a vacation at home, with plenty of outdoor activity and as little time as possible in crowded places, can give the child a chance to cope with all remaining infection before he has to face any more. While it may be difficult for you to arrange to stay at home for such an extended period, it may save you many days off work in the end.

Infectious diseases see individual conditions. *See also* **Immunization; Infection**/Preventing the spread of "infectious" illnesses; **Nursing.**

Inflammation see **Infection**/Defenses against infection: The second line of defense; Treatment of external infection and inflammation. *See also* individual conditions *and* **Accidents.**

Influenza (Flu)

For many people flu is a catch-all term used to describe any otherwise indefinable illness with fever, usually headache, often head-cold symptoms and sometimes exhaustion or depression. Often an individual who is ill but in whom no specific symptoms leading to a different diagnosis emerge, is assumed to be suffering from flu.

Often he will be infected with a flu virus, even if the illness he is describing is quite different from the flu from which his neighbor is suffering. Flu viruses are specific infectious agents, but not only are there many strains in the community at any one time, there are also new strains cropping up in various parts of the world. It is the tendency of influenza viruses to develop and change which has so far foiled all attempts at controlling them. Vaccines produce antibodies but they produce them only to those known strains which could be included in the injection. The next local, national or worldwide flu epidemic is often of a strain against which those antibodies provide no protection. Given that protection against the known strains lasts only for around one year, so that annual reimmunization is necessary, it is not surprising that, at present, immunization is reserved for those individuals or groups that are especially at risk and/or whose illness during a flu epidemic would cause particular disruption. People with heart defects or chronic lung conditions may be offered immunization; doctors, nurses and ambulance drivers may be given it, either routinely or when an epidemic threatens.

In 1968 the variant known as Hong Kong flu spread rapidly across the world. In the U.S., for example, during 1968–69 more than 30 percent of the entire population was affected, with about 40,000–50,000 "extra" deaths attributable to the infection or its side effects. Yet even this did not produce enough immunity in the population to prevent a further explosive outburst of the same strain in 1969–70.

Having flu **Incubation period.** About two days.

Mode of infection. Droplet infection from nose and throat to nose and throat.

First symptoms of flu Almost always some sore throat/nasal congestion, as the infection takes place locally. These "cold" symptoms may, however, seem minor, as they often occur simultaneously with a rapid rise in temperature and severe headache. There may also be backache, restless aching limbs and attacks of shivering.

Acute phase of flu Flu usually develops very quickly so that the first day's symptoms are the most severe. In most patients the whole infection is brief, being over in three to four days. Cough is often a troublesome remaining symptom.

Convalescence from flu While most children and healthy young people will recover rapidly and be ready to return to their normal activities two to three days after the fever has gone, prolonged lassitude and/or depression is not uncommon, especially in the elderly.

Complications of flu Flu is an infection of, or via, the upper respiratory tract. Its common complications are those which arise either when the flu virus damages the lower respiratory tract (virus pneumonia, for example) or when bacterial secondary infection takes place (staphylococcal pneumonia, for example). Other common complications include sinus or middle-ear infections. Certain strains of flu can occasionally lead to central nervous system symptoms, such as meningitis (*see* **Meningitis and Encephalitis**).

● If a child has a "feverish cold" or some kind of "fluey bug," it really is not important to know whether she actually has influenza or not; whatever infection she is suffering from, symptomatic nursing (*see* **Nursing**) is all that she requires until or unless more specific symptoms develop. On the other hand, if a child seems really ill, the fact that it is "probably only the flu" should not prevent you from calling a doctor. Even though he can do nothing to cure flu, he can make sure that nothing more sinister is involved and that there are no signs of complications.

● If there appears to be a flu epidemic in your community or within a school or other institution, and you have a child for whom infection might be especially unfortunate, do consult your doctor about the possibility of immunization.

Ingrown toenails *see* **Feet.**
Injections *see* **Hospital**/Procedures. *See also* **Immunization**.
Insect stings *see* **Accidents**/Bites and stings.
Intelligence *see* **Language; Learning Difficulties and Disabilities.** *See also* **Play; School/** Children with special needs.

Intussusception

This is an acute abdominal emergency in young babies caused by the telescoping of a portion of the intestine into the portion ahead of it. *See* **Hospital**/Surgery.

Jaundice

Describes a state in which the individual's skin, the whites of her eyes and other less visible body tissues are stained a yellow color.

The yellow staining comes from a substance called bilirubin which is formed when red cells which have reached the end of their lifespan are broken down in the liver. The normal lifespan of red cells in the blood is about three months. A normal liver, working at full capacity, dissolves them when they are finished with, liberates the hemoglobin they contain, converts it into bile and passes the bile (which contains other substances also) into the intestine for excretion. If the liver is not working normally this process does not work smoothly. Broken-down and partly broken-down red cells accumulate and there is a build-up of the resulting bilirubin which, instead of being excreted, gets back into the circulation and produces the typical yellow skin and eyes.

Jaundice, therefore, always suggests malfunction in the liver but the reasons for, and the seriousness of, the malfunction are various. The most common are:

"Physiological" jaundice of the newborn
Which may affect any baby whose liver is working at less than full capacity; it is commonest in babies born prematurely. It is termed "physiological" because this type of jaundice reflects the temporary inability of the newborn baby's liver to cope efficiently with a task formerly supported by the mother's circulation. It does not suggest liver disease or abnormality and it usually clears up within a few days, with or without treatment.

Jaundice due to excessive breakdown of red cells
Such as may occur when red cells which have not completed their normal lifespan are being "attacked" by antibodies in, for example, rhesus incompatibility, or following the transfusion of ill-matched blood (*see* **Blood Groups**).

Jaundice due to obstruction of the bile flow
Such as may occur if there are deformities of the bile ducts or if there are gallstones. This last kind of obstruction, a common cause of jaundice in adults, is increasingly common among adolescents.

Jaundice due to infection
A variety of viruses can cause liver infection in babies, children, adolescents and adults. Two common types are:

Infectious (or epidemic) hepatitis, which is usually spread from person to person by fecal contamination of food or drink. Mothers with this type of hepatitis used to be separated from their babies and small children. Now we realize that although the illness is both infectious and potentially serious, this added misery is pointless. The incubation period is between fourteen and forty days so that anyone who is going to have the disease will have had countless opportunities to infect others long before she is ill herself and therefore able to appreciate the risk to her children.

Serum hepatitis, which is usually spread by the use of contaminated needles or syringes and has an incubation period which is normally about three months but can be as long as twenty months. Tragically common among people who are addicted to injectable drugs, this type is also a risk to the many other people who give or receive many injections, from the staff in kidney dialysis units to the diabetic children who must inject themselves with insulin.

There is no cross-immunity between these two types of hepatitis: in theory one wretched individual could have first one and then the other. Both, however, follow a similar illness pattern.

The first symptom is often loss of appetite which, during two or three days, is coupled with general feelings of lethargy, nausea and, sometimes, abdominal pain.

Eventually the urine becomes conspicuously dark—the color of tea without milk rather than the usual lemonade range of colors, and the **stools** become putty-colored.

On about days five to seven, yellow jaundice may appear. If it does, the diagnosis is easily confirmed, but in some instances the child or adolescent has infectious or serum hepatitis without ever "turning yellow." Under these circumstances the diagnosis can be difficult.

Once he is jaundiced, he may feel better although he looks worse. He is likely to remain visibly yellow for two to four weeks but may be well enough to start convalescing before his color is normal.

Hepatitis is always unpleasant, can be serious, requires medical attention, bed-rest in the acute phase and perhaps weeks of convalescence. Your doctor will do everything he can to minimize the possibility of any permanent damage to the liver. Bed-rest may be imposed on the victim even if he feels well enough to be up. Various types of diet may be recommended to minimize the liver's work. Alcohol is likely to be banned for quite a long period.

● Always seek medical advice if your child, whatever his age, looks yellow, whether or not you know that he is ill.

● If hepatitis is diagnosed, be prepared for a long illness and for a very miserable, and possibly depressed, child or young person. It is usually better for an adolescent if he or she can accept, from the beginning, that this illness will cancel imminent examinations or social/vacation plans in the immediate couple of months. Struggling to get going again before the liver has returned to normal is not advisable.

Jealousy

Jealousy is a painful emotion and one which, instead of stimulating healthy action, as can anger, for example, tends to paralyze the victim and feed upon itself. Within many families there will be phases when somebody suffers from the green-eyed monster, but more can be done to keep him at bay than many people realize.

Jealousy and envy

Although these two words are often used interchangeably, they are not at all the same thing. Envy is a comparatively outward-looking and simple matter of wishing that one had for oneself something which somebody else has. A child may envy his friend's bicycle; an adolescent may envy her friend's figure, yet neither child need feel jealous on that account.

Jealousy is not about wanting what someone else has but about being anxious about what one lacks. If that child *is* jealous of the friend with the bicycle it will not just be because he wants a bicycle like that for himself, but because he feels that it is a love-cycle, a symbol of some love and security which the other boy enjoys and he does not. If that girl *is* jealous of the friend with the enviable figure it will be because her physical shape represents, for the monster's victim, a kind of adolescent happiness and self-acceptance which she cannot feel for herself.

Jealousy, then, is about not loving and being loved enough and, therefore, about feeling insecure and anxious about oneself in relation to the people who are important to one. Every human being has cause for envy from time to time. Life is not "fair." But to be able to envy someone without acute pain is healthy and realistic. It is only when the envy of superficial events or objects or achievements becomes muddled up with deep-seated anxieties that there is cause for concern.

The roots of anxiety lie in infancy, in a baby's need for absolutely dependable protection and loving care (*see* **Anxiety, Fears and Phobias/** The roots of anxiety). The more securely loved, loving and lovable a baby and young child can feel himself, the less liable to jealousy, then or later, he will be. If you can rear a child who has a basic faith in your unshakeable love and who, because of it, can approve of and accept himself, you will have reared one who can say "Isn't he lucky?" without meaning "Aren't I a poor unworthy worm?" If you cannot, no amount of "treating all the children exactly alike" or "trying to give him everything he wants" will prevent him from feeling jealous because there are not enough possessions and treats in the whole world to cover the pain of basic anxiety.

Jealousy of a new baby

Many families have a second or later child when the older one is somewhere between one and three years old. At this age—especially in the second year—even the most securely loved and accepted toddler is liable to be going through an insecure patch because he is having to assert his independence of you in outward ways, while still feeling totally dependent inside. It will take him a while to discover that you do not only love and care for dependent babies who do as they are told, but also tough little children who do as they wish. When (and if) he has discovered this, he will be able to stop being so bolshy (because once he feels that there are no limits to love there is no longer any compulsion to try to discover them), and he will also be able to see himself, reflected in you, as a good and lovable person. He will not be totally insulated against jealousy; no human being's security can ever be total, but he will be very well protected.

If a new baby arrives before this vital point in an older child's personal growth he is almost certain to be made deeply anxious. An important first step in handling the situation appropriately is simply realizing that this is so. Many parents, loving their first child and looking forward to the second, find the idea of the older child being jealous almost unbearable. They are pleased and they want him to be pleased, too. Unfortunately, wishing will not make it so and to try to pretend to yourselves that the toddler looks forward to, and will love, the coming baby is often a bad mistake. Looking at it from his point of view you are asking him to put up with being supplanted as your baby, your only child, the third member of a three-person unit, and he is going to mind. However hard you try to make him feel good about it in advance (always supposing that he has any idea of your real meaning), the whole thing is going to make him feel hurt. The point is that he loves you and needs to be sure that you love him. When we love people, we want to be "enough" for them. The new baby is a usurper of love. Put the kinds of phrases you might use to break this news to a toddler alongside your husband's attempts to get you to welcome a second wife; you can see that both are doomed to failure!

Parent to toddler	Husband to wife
"We're going to have a new baby, darling, because we thought it would be so nice for you to have a little brother or sister to play with."	"I'm going to marry a second wife, darling, because I thought it would be so nice for you to have some company and help with the work."
"We love you so much we just can't wait to have another gorgeous baby."	"I love you so much I just can't wait to have another gorgeous wife."
"It'll be *our* baby; it will be part of our family, belong to all three of us and we'll all look after it together."	"She'll be *our* wife; she will be part of our family, belong to both of us and we'll both look after her together."
"Of course we won't love you any less. There's plenty of loving for everybody and we'll all love each other."	"Of course I won't love you any less; there's plenty of loving for everybody and we'll all love each other."
"I shall really need my big boy/girl now, to help me look after the tiny new baby."	"I shall really need my reliable old wife now, to help me look after this young new one."

Don't you think that you might be just as liable to hit first your husband and then that dear little wife over their heads with a frying pan as your toddler is to hit first you and then that baby with the nearest block?

Minimizing jealousy of the new baby

If you can accept that this is a truly difficult situation for him you will not fall into the trap of trying to make him share your pleasurable anticipation. The new baby is something you want and are entitled to. But it is not something your toddler wants but simply a life development he will have to put up with. Instead, hold back for a while on telling him and concentrate on making him as secure with you, and content with himself, as you possibly can. How you do this obviously depends on his age, stage and circumstances but it might include:

Resolving current conflicts quickly one way or another. If you are in the middle of a toilet training or eating battle (*see* **Toilet Training** *and* **Eating/ Eating problems**), solve them if you can do so within the next month or so, but if you know that you cannot, drop them so that the child does not feel in any way disapproved of or attacked when he comes to know of your pregnancy.

Giving him as much of you as he seems able to use. He may, of course, have this already, but if he is going *reluctantly* to a babysitter (*see* **Working Mothers**) while you do a job which you are going to have to give up in late pregnancy, it will be far better for him if you can give it up much sooner. If you work for as long as you can, stopping at home only for a couple of weeks before the birth, that toddler is going to feel that you did not love him enough to stay home with him but that you do love the new person enough to do so. All those reassuring things you have said to him in the past, about Mommies and Daddies having to work for money and so forth, will then seem to him like lies: you left him because you did not care; you stay with the baby because you do care.

Within the limits of his age-stage, finding him some other people who are important to, and fun for, him. Once the baby comes and you *are* tired, abstracted and busy, it will be far easier for him to sail through his days if he does not always even want your attention. If he is very young you may only be able to engineer Saturday outings with his father or visits to another relative's house or occasional play sessions with another toddler who lives nearby. If he is old enough, or nearly old enough, for playgroup, the leader might allow you to start settling him in immediately so that by the time the baby comes, "my group" is a grand and important aspect of his life. Don't, whatever you do, plan to start him at such a group or at a nursery school just before or just after the baby's birth. He will certainly see it as being "sent out of the way," and this will both increase his jealousy and possibly make it difficult for him to settle in (*see* **School/ Pre-school and nursery education**).

Trying to get him used to the idea that families have more than one child. Point out the brothers and sisters of his friends and try to find a toddler whom he knows who has a baby in the house. If he can come to accept the *idea*, the *actuality* will not be so likely to seem to him like a particular tragedy or punishment for which he alone has been singled out. It is in this general context that you can best introduce the positive aspects of having a brother or sister. "Somebody always there to play with," for example, is indeed an appealing notion, but if you link it directly to your own coming baby you are being unfair and misleading because that baby will not be a playmate for a long time.

Start early to get him used both to the arrangements you plan for him at the time of the birth and practical changes afterwards. If he will stay with his aunt while you are in the hospital, let him pay a few visits during these next months and make sure that they are treats. If his father will take charge of him make sure that he gets some practice, not just at the things he always does but at any aspects of the toddler's routine with which he is not familiar. Minute details—such as the exact degree of the bacon's crispness—will seem overwhelmingly important to the toddler once he is stressed by your absence. If Daddy is not normally there for breakfast he may simply not know how to cook it "so it's *nice*."

Changes after the birth may include a change of room or promotion from a crib to a real bed. If you introduce these early enough you can probably make them seem like privileges. If you introduce them just before or after the birth they will probably seem like deprivation.

If you can trust other people not to let the news out, wait to tell the toddler until you are about six months' pregnant. There are a lot of different reasons for delaying this long:

By six months a miscarriage is unlikely. The miscarriage of a baby he knew about is an extremely difficult and painful thing to try and explain to a toddler, and if he does have to know he will make it far more difficult for you to get through the days because he will keep asking about the baby.

Once he knows that a baby is coming at all it is easier for him if he can see some evidence that she is real. By six months he will be able to see the bump she makes (although he will not notice your change in shape until it is pointed out to him), and he will be able to feel her moving around and see the sharp little bumps her feet or elbows make as she kicks. Given that physical reality, you can begin to help him to think of her realistically, not as a playmate but as someone who will be helpless and wet both ends. Aim to inculcate an attitude of tolerant and amused superiority in the toddler, by telling him ruefully about the things that babies do (like throwing up on people's shoulders) and by thinking up some funny stories about the things he did when he was a tiny baby, like the time he peed on Granny's dress or bit the doctor. . . .

With only two or three months to go and all this talk going on, the toddler may be able to remember about the coming baby so that, by the time she is born, he really is expecting her. If a toddler is "told the news" when mother first has the pregnancy confirmed, and life then goes on just as usual for nearly a quarter of his life so far before anything happens, he has usually forgotten all about it.

About two weeks before the expected date, tell him your plans for the actual birth but be very careful not to make any promises you might not be able to keep. If you hope, for example, for a twenty-four-hour stay in the hospital, tell him that "Daddy [or whoever it is] will be here with you and I shall be back with the baby very soon. . . ." If you stress that you will only be away for "one bedtime, one breakfast, etc." and then either your condition or the baby's keeps you away for several days, he will be angry/sad and that will not help him to tolerate the baby when the two of you do get home.

When you go into the hospital, say good-bye whatever the time. It is better for him to face the parting he has to face than to wake up one morning and find you gone and the household in drama.

When you come home with the baby, remember that it is you, not the baby, he wants to see. Of course he has to accept the baby's existence and presence and all the care which you give her, but he does not have to accept it all at once. In the first couple of days, give him as much time as you can and discourage whoever is helping you from cries of "let's leave Mommy in peace now." It will not hurt the new baby if, just for these first days, you pay her your most wholehearted and soppy attention during her evening and nightwaking times (*see* **Play**). It may be tactful to avoid breast-feeding in front of the toddler, too, by briefing your helper to lure him subtly away to do something fascinating. When you do feed in front of him, explain that this is how new babies feed; that this is how he fed when he was tiny. If he asks to try your milk try not to look shocked; you can always let him taste off your finger so as to be sure that the baby is not getting something better than the best of milkshakes.

Later on, accept any offers of help but don't ask him to be your "big boy." He may not be feeling at all big; or rather he may be feeling that his bigness is his whole problem: if he were tiny he would get as much cuddling and loving as that beastly baby. Don't make him feel that he has to help you, now, to get your approval, or that the more he appears to "love" the baby the more you will love him. The opposite approach works better.

Offer him chances to be extra-babyish for a while. You might let him sit in the baby bath and have a sprinkle of talcum powder afterwards; you can cuddle him, pat his back and sing him a song. It may sound absurd but it is not. You want him to feel that the new baby is *not getting anything he cannot have* but only *things he has grown out of*. The sooner he can assure himself that the big bath is better or that he prefers his juice from a cup to milk out of that stupid bottle, the better.

Try to find some practical advantages to suddenly being 'the eldest" to balance the inevitable disadvantages. This may be the moment for spending money or a later bedtime. It is certainly the moment for some special expeditions with Dad (and without the baby).

His father can make all the difference to this period if he will take a full part in caring for and companioning both children. If he will do exciting things with the toddler while you cope with the baby, or cope himself while you do things with the toddler, the pull between infant and toddler needs will be much less painful. Many fathers find that they cement their relationship with the older child now. He is under stress, needs his father and turns to him because he is somewhat upset by his mother. Getting a warm response, he comes eventually to see a balance in *two* parents and *two* children.

Acknowledge jealous *feelings* while guarding against jealous *acts*. Don't ask the toddler to love the baby or ever let him feel that if you knew his real feelings you would hate him. Instead, acknowledge that she is a considerable nuisance to him just now while assuring him that one day they will be friends and companions. But don't let him hurt the baby, for his sake as well as hers. He will be dreadfully guilty, however hard you try to pretend that it was an accident. If necessary, use a cat-net to protect her against those toys thrown accidentally-on-purpose, and don't tempt him and providence by leaving him in charge of the carriage outside shops.

Work to make the toddler feel that the baby likes him. We all find it easier to like people who seem to like us; your child will find it much more possible to accept his new sister if he feels that she makes affectionate advances. Arranging it is an easy piece of parent-upmanship: if the toddler puts his face close to the baby's and smiles and makes noises, she will smile at him. Once she smiles, you can play it up a little: "He's the one she really likes," you say to the admiring visitor who had been ignoring him.

If you can reach a point when the older child says something like, "I'll keep her quiet for you, Mommy, she'll stop crying for *me*. . . ." you will know that the worst is over.

With some luck and a lot of tact, two or three months will see you through to a point where he can be amusedly patronizing about the baby most of the time. Try to get there before she becomes mobile anyway. While she lies where she is put she is only a nuisance to him in the emotional sense of taking up your time and attention. Once she crawls into games and snatches and chews his toys, she will be a major practical nuisance, too. If he can say resignedly, "Oh, isn't she *silly*" or "I s'pose she's trying to copy me again," their relationship is building. If he simply dislikes her, you are all in for a difficult couple of years.

Coping with later jealousies
Jealousy between brothers and sisters seldom ends just because the older child forgets what life as an "only" was like. Balancing the emotional needs of two or more children of different age-stages continues to need thought. If, for example, one starts at school and the other at nursery school, both in the same term, both will need your full support and you will have to share it out. There will be problems over suiting everyone in treats, expeditions and vacations; problems over nursing a sick one without neglecting the other and problems over coping fairly when one gets her own way with charm and the other fails to get it by bullying.

Remember, always, that jealousy is about feelings, not objects or events. If one child feels that you care more about the other (perhaps represented by his birthday celebration) than you do about her, the fact that you take just as much (or even a little more) trouble about her birthday when it comes around will not do a bit of good.

Remember, also, that there may be jealousy *both ways around*. While older children certainly suffer when later ones arrive, younger children are often bitterly jealous of older brothers and sisters, especially if parents go on and on emphasizing the first child's superiority in the family. Behavior which is tactful in the first six months of a baby's life can become downright insensitive in the second year.

Try not to assume that brothers and sisters love each other. Some parents continue to insist that "they're very close really," even when constant squabbles and complaints suggest otherwise. They are individual people. They may or may not get on well together. They have to tolerate and behave decently to each other but that is all. If you can avoid forcing them into each other's company, forcing them to share every friend and activity, they may eventually surprise you with their fierce loyalty.

Respect each child's individual dignity. If you can make it clear that you love each one individually and will never make them look small either to each other or to outsiders, you will not go far wrong. That means that you will never compare them with each other. There is no more point than there would be in comparing an orange with an apple. And it means that you will never hold one up as an example to the other, either. The charming manners and neat habits which come so easily to one may be truly difficult for the other to acquire: you will not help her by suggesting that she "look at your brother; he doesn't leave a mess for me to clear up."

Jock itch *see* **Ringworm and Athlete's Foot.**

Language *see also* Play

Language is the basic tool of human beings. If rising onto their hind legs, freeing their front ones to become tool-using hands, gave developing people an advantage over other animals, developing speech gave an even greater one. By using language we can communicate about things which are not physically present and about ideas which do not physically exist. We can say anything that we can do; say what we cannot do; say what no person has ever done. We can discuss possibilities, probabilities, projects and ideas which are truly "new" in the sense of being as yet outside human experience. With this vital tool, one generation can pass on its experiences to the next so that children can build onwards without having to waste time finding out everything for themselves. The saving of time and effort and the creative possibilities which all this opens up are immeasurable: they add up to what we call "culture."

Children do not have to be "taught" to speak any more than they have to be taught to walk, but they can certainly be helped to acquire and use rich and rewarding speech. A child who does acquire the "best" language of which she is capable will also make the best possible use of her intelligence. The relationship between language and intelligence, language and thinking, is two-way. People need intelligence to learn to understand and to use language fluently and meaningfully; they also need fluent and meaningful language for their intelligence to work on. If high intelligence helps us to find the words to say what we think, so the words we know help us to decide what to think. Providing an enriched verbal environment for a child is just as important to her developing intellect as is a good diet to her developing body.

Research into language is highly complicated and controversial. No attempt will be made here to review the theories or to prove and disprove them with summaries of the studies. Interested readers can find all that in many excellent specialist books. Instead, an attempt will be made to answer the question: "What can I do to help my child acquire and use language well?"

The biggest single step is a negative one: to get rid of the common notion that language means talking; that talking means using words and that therefore the whole process of language-learning is delayed until a baby is nearly a year old. Language is communication between one person and another. It starts as soon as a new person meets her mother in the first contact after birth. Actual *speech* is the formalized culmination of an ongoing process rather than the beginning of anything, so if you wait to interest yourself in your child's language until she can speak, you will have missed a great deal of the fun.

The other important step is to realize that children eventually use words because they want to, rather than because they have to, or need to. A baby gets everything she needs from the adults who care for her without words. She uses crying, other sounds, facial expressions, gestures, body language . . . her needs would go on being met even if she never learned to use words. Furthermore, as we shall see, early words have nothing to do with "need": they do not help the baby to manage her parents or her environment as a whole. Her motivation is pleasure: fun in communicating with loved people; pleasure in play, in cooperation, in sharing. This is important because you will never *ever* be able to force or stress a young child into speech. If you make her unhappy she will not talk, she will cry. Everything you do which extends her communication/speech will be pleasurable for her and therefore probably fun for you, too.

New babies' "conversations"

Every mother knows that she studies her new baby, talks to her, jiggles her about and makes faces at her. But few mothers realize that, far from being passive receivers of such attention, even the newest babies are active partners in the interplay. Careful video taped studies of mother-baby pairs have shown that, from the very beginning, these social sessions have all the qualities of "conversation" except that they do not employ words. Furthermore, most of the "conversations" are in fact started, conducted and ended by the babies rather than by the adults. Settled together after a feeding, for example, the baby focuses her eyes on the mother's. The mother smiles at her. The baby, still looking at the mother, changes her facial expression: perhaps she wrinkles her brow. The mother reacts: perhaps she says, "You're getting tired, aren't you?" The baby makes a small sound and moves her arms and again the mother answers, perhaps by making that same face back and tightening her arms in a cuddle. As long as the baby goes on gazing into the mother's eyes and interacting with her, it will take a major domestic crisis or crass interruption to make the mother break off the "conversation." It will end when the baby breaks the eye contact by closing her eyes, turning her head or simply ceasing to focus.

In these early interactions mothers imitate babies far more than babies imitate mothers. Many charming pictures of mother-baby pairs have been published with captions suggesting that the baby is copying mother's grimaces. Careful study of videotapes shows that it is usually the baby who puts her tongue out first and the mother who follows. She is mirroring the baby's actions for her, showing her what she is doing, lending gradual meaning to what may at first be randomly "social" activity. This mirroring and lending of meaning is vitally important and goes on all through early childhood. When a baby's face wrinkles into the sad expression which comes before crying, the mother will imitate the face and will probably *say*, "Oh dear . . ." in sad/sympathetic tones. Quite unthinkingly she tells the baby, "This is what that face looks like and this is the feeling-meaning it conveys."

While the very earliest "conversations" may contain few sounds from the baby, her sound-making increases rapidly so that by three to four months she is seldom silent during a social situation (except when it is the adult's turn to answer her) and uses expressive and varied voice tones. The tones are high-pitched and lilting when compared to later speech (we usually call the whole lot "cooing") and the mother adopts similar tones and rhythms in her replies. The mother who "feels silly" when she makes noises at her baby, or is told by a third party that she sounds idiotic, may like to know that *adult* speech tones will immediately silence her baby. It has been tried experimentally. Even at this very early age the baby has expectations of her conversations with mother and if she gets no answer, or an unexpected or inappropriate one, she will come to a full stop, look worried and probably cry. So coo away. As is so often the case with young babies, the thing which comes naturally and feels right *is* right.

The more concentrated one-to-one attention a young baby gets, the more readily she will "talk," and the more sensitively her communications are noticed and mirrored, the more she will vary them. Most mothers are familiar with the saying that the more an infant is *talked to* the more she will talk, but it is more accurate and useful to rephrase it in terms of being talked *with*. Chatting to your baby as you move around the room or cuddling her while you talk to her toddler-brother is fine, but the kind of talk which will increase her language capacity is the kind that involves you totally and leaves no room for anyone else or space between you.

Three to six months: "talking" about talking

By around three months, you and your baby will have fallen into a conversational rhythm such that whoever starts the interaction (perhaps by catching the other's eye and smiling) each of you will then take turns so that the sounds, smiles, expressions and movements of each of you mesh together as if you were dancing to the same tune.

By around the middle of this first year, your baby will have done a great deal of sorting out, in preparation for the recognition and use of sounds, separated from physical contact, facial expressions and gestures. At three months, for example, she will differentiate between a human voice and any other sound, so that a human "reply" keeps her "talking" where ringing a little bell whenever she pauses does not. But by six months she will differentiate between voices, knowing yours from her father's and all familiar ones from the voices of strangers. She will sort out her listening and her looking, too, so that instead of looking at *something* when she hears a human voice, she learns to search for the face of the person who spoke. Soon she will learn also to respond to stimuli which are applied only to one sense at a time. She will learn, for example, to smile because you smile, rather than smiling-and-talking because you smile-and-talk. And she will learn to babble in reply to voices which she hears from a tape recorder or unseen person, without the added cues given by looking. These are all important signs of her growing up. If she continued only to respond to the global social cues which stimulated her first social interactions, she would never be able to recognize an unheard friend across the street or talk to an unseen one on the telephone.

Watching out for deafness

While a baby is learning to make these differentiations and to sort out her sensory reactions, it is tragically easy to miss the fact that she is deaf.

Because early communication is social, and because early social stimuli are a mixture of sensory impressions, a totally deaf baby, who is neither hearing sounds from other people nor from herself, will appear to react normally to you *and* will continue, perhaps for the first half-year, to make a normal range of cooing and babbling sounds. It is only at the stage when hearing and sound-making are separated from sociable sights and feelings that her handicap will become obvious.

If she should be deaf, early recognition and expert help are important. Parents cannot assure themselves that a baby hears normally over the full range of sounds by home-testing; nor can a well-baby clinic doctor. Complete assessment of hearing requires the expertise of an audiologist and the use of techniques such as pure-tone audiology. If you have any reason to suspect that your baby's hearing is anything other than normal, or any reason (such as a family history of deafness) to worry especially about it, consult your doctor or clinic and do not be surprised or further worried if you are referred to a specialist. But if you have no reason for suspicion, it is nevertheless sensible to assure yourselves that the baby is hearing voices and ordinary everyday sounds.

"Testing" a baby will take two of you (or you and a member of the clinic staff). With the baby sitting in her chair, one adult makes the "test sounds" at about eighteen inches from her ear but from just behind her so that she cannot see the object or person. The other watches her eyes or, if she is coming up to six months, the movements of her head. If she hears the sound she will move her eyes or whole head towards it. To ensure that any movements seen do not happen by chance, it is sensible to make a second sound about eighteen inches from the other ear. As she moves or looks towards that sound it is stopped and the "test" sound is made. An abrupt change in the direction of her eye or head movements shows that she has heard it.

Suitable sounds are made by crumpling hard toilet paper, ringing a small bell, shaking a light rattle and stroking a spoon gently around the inside of a cup. Voice sounds should be tried, too, using a Psss for high tones and a gentle Oooo for low ones. Ideally, each sound should be tried for each ear but remember:

Failure to respond is usually due to distraction, boredom or tiredness. Don't panic; don't decide she *is* deaf. Try again later in the day and/or take her for a check-up.

The fact that she responds to a whisper does not mean that her hearing is perfect. Parents have made the tragic mistake of trying the quietest whisper they could manage, from just behind the baby, and then believing that if she responded to such a quiet sound she must be able to hear all other louder ones. It need not be so. A whisper uses very high frequencies. Although it is *quiet* it may nevertheless be detected by a baby who has serious hearing loss for lower frequency ranges.

Talking games and playing talk

The baby who is talking-about-talking and sorting out verbal talking from all the other kinds of communication, is the person all those nursery games like "This little piggy went to market" or "Round and round the mulberry bush" are made for. Your everyday conversations can share in the characteristics which make them perfect:

They are played in a fun context, meant to give pleasure, and they usually end in laughter.

They have rhythm which matches her rhythms and helps her to know what to expect and what will happen next.

Their rhythm usually builds into some kind of climax (the final poke in the tummy or tickle of the ribs) and that fits with the natural ending of one "paragraph" and the start of another piece of "conversation."

They have repetition which is again important in giving the baby time to foresee what is coming next and to organize her responses.

They involve only the baby and her partner. They do not require the two of them to talk about anything else than the conversation.

Six to twelve months: "talking" about other things

In the second half of her first year the baby begins to sit up and play with objects and to move around looking at things, finding things and generally experimenting with what the environment has to offer. Now she will begin to want to talk about those things rather than just talking for its own sociable sake. She learns to use her voice for more and more complex sound-making, stringing together syllables of babble and using expression and inflection until her sounds (now usually called "jargoning") really do sound like real speech, although there are still no words.

Using this newly enriched repertoire, she learns to call attention to things she has seen and to indicate things that she wants; she learns to ask questions and make exclamations; she learns, most touchingly of all, to make jokes and laugh at them herself. Listening to a child at this stage, it really does seem that language is just around the corner but that when it comes it will be fully-fledged fluent *talking* rather than the few, stilted single words with which she must begin.

Although those nursery word games will probably still be popular, a new type takes first place. These are the games in which objects come and go, get passed from one to the other or get put into boxes. She will play "peek-a-boo" in any version you please (from all of you behind the curtains, to your face covered with your hand) for minutes on end and she will punctuate each new round with sounds meaning "Where's it gone? There it is. . . ." She will play ball, too, either rolling the ball to you and fetching it when you roll it back, or simply passing it from her hand to yours. Again she will punctuate, with her version of "your turn; my turn. . . ." Just as her very earliest communications with you had all the features of proper "conversation", so these have all the features of the cooperative and problem-solving behavior for which human speech is uniquely valuable.

This is the kind of play which will now contribute most to her general language development and the more she has of it the better. But there is more specific learning going on now, too: the learning of actual words. She is not quite ready to *use* words herself, but she is ready to pick out some of the words you use and begin to understand them, to discover what they refer to and therefore to work out some of what you mean.

Learning what words mean

Babies of eight or nine months commonly become highly imitative and will imitate sounds as well as funny faces, gestures and so on. Parents sometimes spend a lot of time holding up objects and saying, "Cup. Say cup, darling. Cup, cup, come on, say cup." And sometimes the baby will respond with a passable imitation of the sound so that the parent becomes convinced that he or she is "teaching her to talk."

While such a game is harmless, provided the baby enjoys it as just another play conversation, it will not actually help her to learn language. Your conviction that it does may prevent you from offering more useful kinds of talk, or even make you irritated when she refuses to "say again" something she imitated earlier.

A baby does not learn to say words for their own sake (or yours). She learns to say words in order to communicate more, or more meaningfully, with you. That means that she will have no interest in *saying* a word until she knows what it *means* and that even once she does know what it means, she will not bother saying it until or unless she has something she wants to communicate about it. It seems to work something like this:

The baby hears a word like "cup" over and over again as the one constant sound in a large variety of sound-strings (sentences) which you utter. She hears, "I'll just get your cup"; "Let's put some in this cup"; "Would you like this cup?"; "I need a cup of coffee" . . . That one word "cup" is the sound which is common to all those utterances and it is always associated with something to drink. Over days and weeks the baby comes to see that the sound and the object always go together. When she has made the association "cup" equals what the drink is in, she will know what "cup" means.

Helping her to listen and understand words

She still cannot pick words or meanings out of a general blur of family conversation, with half-finished sentences, expressive shrugs and the television turned on. She still needs face-to-face conversation, or talk directed only at her and in a reasonably quiet room. And she still needs it from you, or from very familiar and beloved people. She must find word meanings by discovering constant sounds despite changes in expression and inflection; she cannot also cope with a stranger's voice.

When you are talking to her, it is worthwhile to remember to use the key labelling-words that she will be picking up, like that label-word "cup." If you say, "Here's your cup; I'll just pour some milk for you" you give her yet another opportunity. If you say "Here it is; I'll just pour some milk for you", you do not. So when the door needs shutting, make sure you say "I'll just shut the door" rather than "I'll just shut it" and make sure you lead a search for the dog (or "Jack" or whatever his name is) rather than "that damn animal."

Name-labels are vital for her, especially her own. At this stage she cannot possibly think of herself as "I" or "me," especially as, in English at least, the correct word for oneself depends on who is speaking. I am "me" to myself but I am "she" or "you" to you. So use her name and don't let "Does Mary want a biscuit?" embarrass you because it is "babytalk." It is her talk and she is the one doing the learning.

She will not learn name-labels for things which are not physically present, so the most useful kind of talk relates an object which is there to its name-word. The only exception is looking for things together. If you search for that dog, she may or may not know what you were both looking for to start with, but once you find him, the excitement of the successful climax to the "game" will give its name-word extra significance for her. Name-labels which you know she understands (even if she is not using them yet) will begin to mean something to her if she sees a picture of the object, so books with realistic pictures of everyday objects can begin to provide an ever-ready version of the looking-for-something game ("Where's the cup? . . . See, here it is, on the table. And down here there's a chair just like Mary's chair . . ."). Later still, such understood words will make interesting conversation or stories for her, though her father's account of his day at "the office" (which she has never seen and therefore cannot visualize) still means nothing to her.

Talent as an actress (or a ham) is very useful at this stage. Babies with outgoing, dramatizing parents sometimes learn to understand first of all the emphatic exclamations they hear excitedly repeated. "Oh dear!" she may hear as you pick her up from every tumble and "Up you come!" each time you lift her from her crib.

But as well as giving her as many interesting words as you can in easy-to-understand situations, you also need to give her the greatest possible rewards for her own speech efforts. This is where it is important to remember yet again that she is not trying to learn to *say words* but to *communicate with you*. The more you can show her that you are listening, understanding and sharing her pleasure when you get it right, the more she will be stimulated to try. If she gestures vaguely towards a kitchen counter and makes an obviously "wanting" sound, you might look where she is indicating and list for her the various things for which she might be asking. It does not matter whether or not her sound bears any relation to the "proper" name for the object you eventually find. What matters is that she communicated with you; used an "own-word" and made you understand it.

As she approaches real word use she will use more and more "own-words." Don't ever correct or pretend not to understand them. Correction will only bore her because she does not want to say the same thing again, better; she wants to say something else now. The correction will not even help because if she is using an own-word it is because it is the best she has to offer at the moment. The "proper" word will evolve when, and only when, she is ready. If you pretend not to understand her when you do, you are cheating her out of successful communication and therefore making her feel that the whole business is more difficult than it is. It will not work, either. If you refuse to hand her her bottle until she says "bottle" instead of "bah-boo," you are cutting across that vital pleasure principle in language-learning. You will make her feel frustrated and cross and you are more likely to get tears than a word.

First words　　Your child will probably understand dozens of words before it occurs to her that she can use one particular sound to refer to one particular person or object. Up to now her language has had all to do with action and relationships: with what she and her adult partner are doing and feeling.

That jargoning, which sounded so like fluent talk, was doing-feeling-talk. But now she has sorted out enough words to start trying word language for herself. She starts with name-labels and, since her language is still tied up with pleasure not need, they are labels for people or things she finds exciting, pleasurable or loving. Although some families report "No!" as a first word, most children will name the cat, a parent, a favorite food or a first pair of bright red shoes. . . .

Average ages for acquiring words are dangerous things to set out because children acquire words at widely varying ages and rates, and the words themselves, despite parents' anxiety, are poor indicators of language development since understanding matters so much more than word production. Still, most babies will have one or two labels (which may be real words or own-words but will be proper labels in the sense that they are used consistently for one and only one thing) by ten or eleven months and a dozen or so by a year. Most will be using a lot of single words and some two-word phrases (*see below*) by their second birthdays.

Later talkers   Many babies will not produce any recognizable words at all before their second birthdays, while a lot more will acquire two or three words during the second year but add no more for months. The most usual "reasons" (if you need a reason for delay which is part of normal variation) are:

That the baby is a boy. We do not actually know why the sexes differ in this respect (although recent research suggests that there are neurological differences which may explain differential rates of development in many areas) but they certainly do. Most boys speak later than most girls, although there is some overlap in the middle so that a boy who speaks early may speak sooner than a girl who speaks late.

That the baby always has to share, and compete for, attention from her special adults. It is this element of competition and distraction which sometimes delays speech in twins. If "private language" develops between them, it is usually because they are short of adult one-to-one talk rather than because they choose to talk to each other instead. Last children in large families sometimes share this disadvantage, as do babies who follow closely after a brother or sister who is therefore at his most demanding toddler stage during the baby's critical language-learning months.

That the baby is cared for by a succession of caretakers so that it is difficult for her ever to build up the easy loving familiarity which accelerates language development.

That she is cared for by very silent or non-verbal people. The child of totally deaf parents is likely to be very slow to acquire language even if her own hearing is perfect. The child of a mother who was very depressed and withdrawn over many months may similarly be slowed up unless she also has more reactive caretakers available. The child who is cared for by foreign-speaking "au pairs" or nannies may be delayed if they can neither offer adequate English nor allow her to speak in their mother tongues (*see below* Bringing up bilingual babies).

That she spends her days in group care from a very early age. Children do not learn language from each other until word talking is firmly entrenched in them. Unless a group provides a very high adult-child ratio, and an approach to care which provides each child with a mother-substitute, group membership may slow up her speech.

The second (or third) year and the importance of "motherese"

Whether your child's single label-words start to come early or late and arrive one at a time or by the dozen, they will come unless she has some major handicap such as deafness. As long as she is of an age where you think at all about her talking, it goes on being more useful to think about her interest in, and understanding of, language than about her production of it. You cannot squeeze words out of her. She is not a parrot. Nor are unmeaningful words useful language. If you are in a foreign city, will it be useful to you to learn by heart how to ask "Where is the railway station?" No, the question is useless unless you can understand the answer.

Most parents automatically adopt, at this stage, a particular form of language which has been christened "motherese." It is not babytalk in the sense of using to the child her own words or phrases. It is baby-adapted talk which, whether you use it deliberately or not, makes it easy for the child to find, recognize and understand your words.

Motherese uses short simple sentences which are highly inflected and often repeated. The actual speech is rather high-pitched and musical and contains a lot of question marks. It is used with much gesture and action, can sound *daft* to childless friends, but is both vital and natural to the mother-child pair. If your work colleagues curl their lips to hear you say: "Mary want Teddy? Want Teddy darling? Mommy will get Teddy for Mary. Here's Teddy for Mary. Yes . . . Mary's Teddy . . ." they had better visit after Mary's bedtime in the future. But maybe you can remind them that while Mary is certainly not a moron, she *is* a beginner. A piano teacher offers beginners a tuneful series of easy single notes rather than a concerto. Motherese does the same.

Through motherese, you go on offering your child a wide variety of relevant single word-labels for her to select among, and pick up when she wants to. Through her extraordinary *use* of those single words she makes them do the work of your sentences. "Up?" she pleads, holding onto your leg and gazing into your face. "Up-up," she comments happily, copying, as you lift her, the tone in which you say "Up you come." "Up!" she announces with enormous satisfaction, comfortably settled on your hip.

There can be few single words more variously communicative than those of a child who is learning to talk. Your job is to give her the pleasure of knowing her communications are succeeding and, by doing so, to provide her with a bridge from single words to phrases. When she says "Dog!" in obvious alarm as a Great Dane bounds towards you, feed back her meaning with something like "Yes, isn't it a *big* dog?"

When she does start to string words together, first in pairs and then in longer phrases, it will be descriptive or action words which she adds to those name-labels. She will not bother to say *"the* dog" because the second word adds nothing to the communication. "Big dog" is much more useful. Don't look for grammar, then; look for content and color. Every language studied contains among its earliest word combinations the phrase which translates as "hit ball." It is ungrammatical. No adult would say it, but it expresses something clearly desirable to children of every nationality.

Struggling with grammar

Between about two and about five children have to master the particular rules of the grammar of their own language. They do not acquire these by direct imitation (when did you last say "hit ball"?) because they are not interested in saying what you say but in saying what they mean. They try to ascertain grammatical rules by picking out the constants from other people's speech. The results can be comical but are almost always logical. If there are two dogs why isn't that a flock of sheeps?

Correcting own-grammar is just as futile and saddening as correcting own-words, but new motherese techniques will lead you to offer the child a correct model in your answers to her incorrect tries. The trick (which comes naturally to all but very anxious parents) is to keep her interested in communicating with you by giving her a quick and understanding response to her speech, but to keep a correct model always available for her by answering in your own adult speech. When she rushes into the kitchen saying "Baba cry. Quick . . ." you know that she means to tell you that the baby is crying and you should go to him at once. You show that you understand her language but you answer in your own, "Oh, is Billy crying? Thank you. I'll come and see to him at once." You let her tell you that she has "eated dat biccit," but you ask her whether she has "eaten that biscuit." You let her talk her way but you talk yours. As long as you both understand each other, and you both say plenty to each other, the grammar will come.

Pre-school years: talking about ideas and feelings

Three- and four-year-olds who talk all the time still have not finished with language-learning. They have learned to use words in communication, but still largely in situations where action and gesture would do, or almost do, instead. Now they have to learn to use those words for that most important purpose: communicating about things which are not in the room but in their heads and for expressing ideas which are theirs alone.

The child still needs most of all your interested listening and your interesting talk. But gradually you will find that she is picking out words and phrases which allow her to talk about increasingly abstract ideas. The more idea-words you can feed in, the sooner she will be able to use them in her thinking and her play, and the more ideas she will be able to produce. She is going to learn about ideas like weight and volume and shape. Before she can really use the idea of roundness, for example, she will need the use of the word so as to be able to label for herself the difference between round and square. She is going to notice color and begin to categorize objects by it, but before she can think and talk about color, she needs the words. She is going to need value abstracts like good and bad, pretty and ugly, but she will not be able to tell you her views until she can sort out those words, too.

As the child sorts out the characteristics of people, animals and objects, you will see a burgeoning of imaginary and dramatic play and hear it reflected in her language. She cannot pretend to be a horse until she has recognized some characteristics which differentiate horses from other things, but she cannot let you know that she is a horse until she can use words either to tell you or to express those characteristics in pretend-neighing or clip-clopping. Much of her most important language-learning will still be directly associated with her play, so that even though she has reached an age when play with other children is important, it is a pity if she no longer also gets the chance to play both alone and with you. It is by joining her games, active, constructive and imaginative, that you will most easily see where she has got to with words and what kinds of words she currently needs.

Asking "what's that?" and "why?"

Fortunately the child will reach a point where she asks you directly for the word-ideas she needs. At first, often at around three, she collects name-words by continually asking you "what's that?" It is usually a *name* she is looking for rather than an elaborate explanation, so when she points to a parcel and asks what it is, give her the simple answer "a parcel." If she actually wants to know what is inside it, she will find a different way of asking; if you volunteer information for which she has not actually asked you may muddle her.

"Why?" comes next and usually does mean that she wants something more or something different from the name. She may indeed start a why-session with a "what's that?" and go straight on to "why?":

"What's that?"

"It's thunder."

"Why?" . . .

When "why?" is unanswerable because it is not the right question, you can sometimes give the child what she *is* asking for and save yourself from cloud cuckoo land if you treat it as meaning "tell me more about it. . . ."

Desirable and less desirable talking

During these pre- and early school years you will hear her use words for many different purposes and some will probably strike you as less desirable than others. She will use them, for example, to tell *herself* what to do, scolding herself in private games, instructing herself, "careful, Sarah . . . ," but she will use them to instruct others, too. Four-year-olds can be very bossy. You will hear her boasting too and spinning fantasies about herself and her family, and you will hear her using her new words-for-ideas in smug assertions of her own "goodness" or "prettiness." Above all, you may moan that she seems never to *stop* talking. She may utter 20,000 words in a day with only 500 in her vocabulary and that is a lot of repetitions to listen to. She *must* talk; she must practice the sounds, the inflections and the effects of her words. You will find it less boring if you actually join in, rather than trying to tune her out and responding with only the occasional "Uh-huh." Keeping her talking, freely and with pleasure, is what really matters. If she is to go as far as she can in the later world of education, she needs to feel that words are always her friends and that people can always be reached by talking.

Stuttering or stammering

Her ideas are usually ahead of her vocabulary so that she still finds it difficult to express a flow of thought smoothly. When she is excited, or hurried, searching for the right word holds her up so that her talk keeps hiccuping.

Jerky and uneven speech happens to almost every pre-school child from time to time but it only rarely turns into a real stutter. It is most likely to become a "speech problem" if you react to it anxiously; correct her; try to make her speak slowly. If you can accept her talk calmly, so that it never occurs to her that it is in any way inadequate and so that she never has to *think* about how she is speaking, it will all smooth out with practice. Being calm and accepting really is important. To see why, try consciously controlling your own breathing for a minute. It at once becomes labored and peculiar. The same thing happens to speech if you insist that a child be conscious of it.

Babytalk   Children who insist on using babytalk, long after they are capable of expressing themselves in ordinary words, have usually discovered that adults find it appealing. When you suddenly decide that it is ridiculous, don't clamp down abruptly on talk you have previously seemed to welcome, or you may hurt her feelings and shut her up. Instead, vow that never again will your face soften to babytalk and that never again will you use it to her. Translate everything she says into proper English so that you put an adult version beside hers and, without further comment from you, she will drop it over a few months.

Some kinds of babytalk are positively useful, though. If a child does not know the word for something and can coin one which communicates her meaning, she is making language work for her in a creative way. One child, for example, inquired anxiously about the "bell-van" because she did not know the word for ambulance. Everybody knew what she meant and she discovered, with pleasure, that she could make meaningful words of her own. If such words pass into the family vocabulary for a while that is a compliment to her and she will learn the "proper" name while enjoying her personal one.

Nonsense and   Words are powerful; their power over other people is one of the things the
"naughty   child must discover and learn to manipulate. Along the way she may
nonsense"   discover some which evoke a particularly strong reaction from adults. If she does she will use them again and again. "Pee-pee," she shouts. If everyone shushes her she will certainly say it again and probably add in "wee-wee" and "piss-piss-piss" for good measure.

If you scold you will get into deep water. What are you scolding for? A word? Can a word be naughty? Surely not, words are just tools for her to use. If you ignore this kind of nonsense, so that the words you dislike do not have any special power, she will probably get bored with them. But you can do something more positive, too. All children love repetitive nonsense rhymes and chants. Introduce some that you *do* like and take the opportunity to start her with the sounds and rhythms of poetry, too. She may not understand all the words in *Hiawatha*, but her enjoyment of its regular beat and lovely word-sounds will help her to listen, to think and to enjoy language.

Insults   When a furious child screams that she will kill you it is easy to react with anger. But it is not fair to do so. She is using enormous self-control in sticking to words rather than physical attack, and since her anger is probably already frightening her, an angry response from you will not help. Try to acknowledge the *feeling* and help her to carry on using words to tell you more—"I'm sorry you're feeling so cross; what is it about, do you think?"

Lesser insults of the "silly old cow" variety can usually be defused if you can remember that it is a *child* who is insulting you and that you do not therefore have to be deeply offended. "If I'm a silly old cow you are a cross little calf" will probably end the whole episode in giggles.

The point, of course, is that as she grows up you *want* her to be able to use words for feelings, words for attack or defense, because words do less harm than actions and because being able to express herself verbally is her best assurance of good communication with other people all through her life. It is the teenager who finds himself silenced by the sarcasm of the schoolteacher who is liable to slash her car tires. The one who can "answer back" has far less need to be violent.

Bringing up bilingual babies

Parents often ask whether it will be a good or a bad thing to bring up their child in two languages. There is surprisingly little research on the topic, but some inferences can be drawn from what is known about speech development in general.

Very young babies start out by differentiating the sounds of human speech from all other sounds rather than the sounds of the speech of one language from those of another. They also make sounds which occur in all languages. It is impossible to tell the nationality of a baby by listening to her cooing or babbling. Differentiation between languages does not begin until the baby discovers that some sounds communicate while others do not. It is feedback from adults who pick up "English-sounding" babble and ignore "Japanese-sounding" sounds which biases a baby gradually towards the production of his family's language sounds. It follows then that any sounds, from any language, can and will be used by the baby if they do in fact communicate and are in fact fed back to her. She learns language in the communication of shared play with loved adults. Therefore, if she experiences this kind of communication in two languages from the beginning of her life, she will come to use them both. Parents who are themselves truly bilingual can therefore be assured that if they continue to use both their languages in whatever balance is natural to them, the baby will come to adopt a similar language pattern, at least until the influence of outside people strengthens. There is no reason to suppose that learning two languages in this way is any more difficult for her than learning one. She is selecting effectively communicative sounds from all the sounds she hears around her. If she learns only English, she will come to know that the dog can be "dog," "pup" or "Jack." If she learns English and French, she will discover that that same dog can also be "chien" or "Jacques." Such a child will certainly go through phases in which her two languages are intermingled, but this is no different from the phase in which the single-language child intermingles "real" words with "own" words. The child in a bilingual family will sort them out in exactly the same way.

But there are often complications which usually have to do with the nature of the parents' bilinguality. The following are the most common:

Deliberate rather than spontaneous bilinguality

If two languages are to become natural to the child, both must give her equal pleasure, feedback and reward. For this to come about the parents need not only to be equally competent in both but to use them with equal spontaneity. Often this is not the case. Italian parents, for example, may have been long resident in the U.S. and long accustomed to conduct their lives and relationships in English. Yet they may have retained complete fluency in Italian and have continued to use (and think in) that language when visiting their families and so forth. When a child is expected they may decide to give her the benefit of her mother tongue and therefore make it a matter of policy to speak to her some of the time in Italian and to encourage her to produce sounds and then words in both languages.

Under these circumstances policy is often the enemy of fluency. Because English is the language she hears most and in which she hears her parents talking to each other as well as in most of their conversations with her, English is the language in which spontaneous first words will be produced. But because they want her to produce Italian as well, her parents now begin to pressure her. When she says "Bus!" excitedly to her mother, she does not always get a rewarding "Yes, isn't it a big bus?" Sometimes her mother ignores the content of her communication and instead tells her to say "Autobus." This kind of behavior contradicts every principle of early language-learning by removing the element of pleasurably shared communication and substituting deliberate attempts to teach. Such a child is likely to become confused; not so much confused between the two languages but confused about communication/language itself. She may become a two-year-old who says very little in any language other than the tantrum language of frustration. If you do not live bilingually, you cannot successfully rear a bilingual child.

Multilingual families

Sometimes parents do not themselves share a mother tongue but communicate with each other in a third language which both are struggling to acquire. A Polish woman may marry a German man, for example, and the two of them may produce a child while they are still far from fluent in the English of their adopted country. This is a difficult situation because if the child is brought up to be bilingual in Polish and German and to acquire English later and from outside the family, one or the other parent will be unable to respond to her communications whichever language they are in. Since it is vitally important that she be understood, it is probably better to rear her in English—even if that English is not fluent—so that the family goes on learning together. Such a child may pick up peculiar phrases or idiosyncratic inflections from her parents, but these will soon right themselves when she is mixing with other children and their families. Families which have adopted this approach say that their own English rapidly improves once their child can serve as a model for them.

Families with one "foreign" parent

A more usual situation is that in which a parent of another nationality marries a native and, while using his language for daily life, retains her own for more private moments. Children in such families often seem able to acquire both languages, but do not acquire the "foreign" one as a bilingual child does but as a private language especially linked to intimacy with that parent. Others do not actually learn to *speak* the "foreign" language but nevertheless come to understand it, especially where it has been experienced as part of especially affectionate and rewarding situations such as bedtime lullabies. . . . When such a child reaches school age she may not be *aware* that she "knows French," but she may nevertheless find that language extraordinarily easy to learn.

Laryngitis *see* **Croup and Laryngitis.**
"Latch-key children" *see* **Working Mothers.**

Laxatives *see also* Constipation

Due to the mistaken belief that there is some relationship between good health and a regular daily bowel movement, these drugs are extensively misused. Their purpose is to produce a soft, formed, easy-to-pass stool but, given adequate fluids, a diet containing plenty of roughage from fruit, vegetables, whole grains and/or bran and normal health and activity, the individual's bowels will produce such stools without chemical assistance. While an occasional laxative is not harmful, regular laxatives can so upset the bowel's natural rhythm that normal evacuation becomes almost impossible.

The laxative habit

Occasional laxative use easily turns into habitual use. If a person has gone, say, three days without passing a stool and becomes concerned and takes a laxative, the medicine will lead to a large stool which leaves the rectum empty. Because it is empty, it may take several days before enough feces accumulate to give her the natural signals to go. If the original three days caused her concern, it is likely that this "pause" will lead to further anxiety. She may well take another dose of laxative and thus enter into a vicious circle.

In extreme cases, the laxative habit can lead to loss of tone in the bowel wall or even to its chronic inflammation. If the dose is built up to a point where it provokes diarrhea, there may be too much loss of fluid and of salt and, because food is hurried through the bowels, there may be loss of certain nutrients, too.

Laxatives may be desirable for a short period whenever passing a stool may be painful, or straining to pass a hard stool dangerous. Adult conditions of this kind include the post-partum period, piles, rectal surgery and so forth. Conditions which may affect children or young people include anal fissures (*see* **Constipation**), chronic constipation (*see* **Soiling**) and abdominal surgery.

A laxative may also be useful if constipation arises after an illness, due to the combination of little food and no exercise. Certain drugs, such as codeine, also tend to cause constipation.

A single dose of a laxative will do no harm if a child or young person complains that her stools have become uncomfortably hard and difficult to pass. But having taken one dose, the possibility that a thorough emptying of the rectum will lead to a delay before she next passes a stool should be explained to her. Further doses should be withheld from a child or discouraged in a teenager.

When laxatives **No laxative should ever be taken by a person with abdominal pain** (*see*
are dangerous **Abdominal Pain**), colic, nausea and/or vomiting. The sufferer may have
some acute abdominal condition. Artificial stimulation of the bowels
could make it much worse.

Learning Difficulties and Disabilities *see also* Hyperactive Children; School

In most Western societies every child has a theoretical right to the
education "best suited to his age, abilities and aptitudes." School programs would ideally be tailor-made (or custom-altered) to fit each custom-
er, and aim both to help children with special talents to use them to best
advantage, and to help those with general or specific handicaps to ·
overcome them as far as possible. In practice, of course, this is largely
impossible. An individual family finds it difficult enough to meet the
needs of two or three children, spaced a couple of years apart. A school
cannot possibly individualize its offering to every pupil. Most educational
programs are therefore necessarily set up and run to suit some theoretical
"average" child of a given age, which inevitably leaves a high proportion
of children floundering or bored, in at least some areas at some stages in
their lives. By no means are all difficulties with the learning aspects of
school due to learning disabilities. Many are due to a (usually temporary)
mismatch between the expectations of the school/class and the child's
particular stage/interests. A great many more "learning difficulties"
reflect not intellectual or cognitive problems, but emotional or social ones
which hamper the learning process. A child who is unhappy, anxious or
depressed cannot learn easily or with pleasure, whether the cause of the
upset is based within the school or at home. Sometimes apparently minor
social problems have a disproportionate effect on a child's learning. A
long journey to school (often associated with an inadequate breakfast
before leaving home) has been shown to reduce a child's day-to-day
performance and overall term grades (*see* **Eating**/Common sense about
family eating). Door-to-door transport and a substantial morning snack at
school produce major improvement under such circumstances. It has also
been shown that a teacher whom the child really dislikes (usually because
she "makes him feel small" or "doesn't like me whatever I do" or "shouts
and bangs about") is a sadly good predictor of learning difficulty for that
child in that subject. In the early stages of school life such personal
animosity between teacher and pupil can, in the course of a school year,
convince the child that he is "no good at math" and the feeling—and
consequent poor results—can be extremely hard for the next teacher to
overturn.

It is important, for all these reasons, that all the adults concerned with
an individual child should keep "learning difficulties" separate in their
minds from "school difficulties." To attach a learning-difficulty label to a
child is to *convince him that he cannot be expected, or expect himself, to perform
well in a particular subject or area.* Such a conviction can be a great relief to a
child who has genuinely been struggling to learn to read and whose best
efforts have only served to earn him the name "Thicko." But it can be
exceedingly damaging to the child who simply does not like school/this
school/this teacher, or who is not ready to read or willing to try.

Intelligence and learning difficulties

While nobody can doubt that general "intelligence" goes with the ability to learn, so that those of lower intelligence will find learning more difficult, research suggests that we are far too ready to ascribe early difficulties in school to tested IQ levels. In Britain, for example, a child whose tested IQ is found to be below eighty-five may well be considered more suitable for a special school than the community school, and one major reason is that he is thought likely to have difficulty in learning to read and write. In fact, becoming literate does not require above-normal or even normal intelligence. Given the normal opportunities, that child will probably read and write just as early and as well as peers with higher IQs. *What* he writes, later on, is more likely to be affected by his lower intellectual capacity than the sheer ability to do so. Sadly, "special schools" are often used as rag-bags for the many children who for countless different reasons do not "fit" ordinary school provision. No parent should readily accept that such a school will offer the child "the special help he needs" unless satisfied both that special help *is* needed and that the school will demonstrably provide it (*see* **School**/Children with special needs).

Specific learning difficulties

Just as hot debate rages not only about the nature but also about the very existence of the hyperkinetic syndrome (*see* **hyperactive children**), so there is ongoing debate about the nature and existence of specific learning difficulties.

Nobody doubts that some children find some kinds of learning more difficult than other kinds. Every family knows that a child may struggle with foreign languages but flourish in the science laboratories; fear and hate mathematics but excel in literary subjects. But skill in a *subject* is the end-product of the complex processes, the mental skills, required to handle it. The debate is about whether or not there are specific neurological variations or abnormalities which handicap affected individuals in acquiring those mental skills.

The brain is enormously complex, so complex that we are only just beginning to identify the structural areas which are responsible for some different human functions. Although a little is known about the interlinking of various parts of the brain and central nervous system and its biochemical controls and feedback mechanisms, we are a very long way away from a full understanding of "how the brain works." While it is reasonable to guess that a system so complicated might have parts which functioned better, or more smoothly, than other parts, and that people might vary in which functioned best, we are still a long way from being able to prove it. It can crudely be shown, for example, that an individual who has a certain part of his brain destroyed, by accident or surgery, loses certain functions, or that the individual, a part of whose brain is directly stimulated by electric current, will react in certain ways. But it cannot be shown that this individual's brain structure or biochemistry is better or worse for this, that or the other kind of mental activity.

Just as hyperkinesis or minimal brain dysfunction is deduced from behavior (it must be there even though it cannot be demonstrated), so a neurological foundation for specific learning disabilities is deduced. A medical model for a child's learning difficulties has the same advantages and disadvantages as does the medical model in hyperactivity and needs treating with similar caution. At present, though, the medical model in learning seldom includes the prescription of drugs except where the learning disability appears alongside unacceptable behavior and is therefore liable to be classified as part of MBD. It may, indeed, be through professionals working to a medical model that your child will receive highly skilled and specialized teaching rather than consignment to a special school or "slow-learners class."

Many different kinds of learning disability are postulated to account for a wide range of difficulties. The best known is usually referred to as dyslexia (congenital dyslexia; developmental dyslexia; "word blindness"), which can stand as an example.

Congenital dyslexia

Dyslexia is usually considered to be a congenital disturbance of brain function which gives rise to a variety of learning difficulties, especially relating to reading and spelling. It affects more boys than girls, but numbers are not known as referral varies so widely from place to place. A family history of similar difficulties (or of poor literacy now) is common.

Recognizing dyslexia

A child is inappropriately described as dyslexic unless he is:

Of normal, or greater than average, intelligence. A child with a low IQ would be assumed to have a general, rather than a specific, learning disability.

Normally hearing and sighted. Auditory and visual handicaps would be thought to override, or certainly confuse, a diagnosis of dyslexia.

Not demonstrably brain damaged either congenitally or accidentally.

Appropriately educated throughout his life thus far, so that he has been offered the kind of care and stimulation as well as teaching which is normal for his age in his community.

Without a "primary emotional disturbance." This last is a tricky point because, as we shall see, many children who are diagnosed as dyslexic are certainly disturbed, but may have become so because of the distress associated with the learning disability. An attempt must be made, however, to be sure that the cause and effect is indeed in that direction.

Those negative points exclude the most usual non-dyslexic causes for serious difficulty in learning to read and write. The professional then looks for certain aspects of the difficulty and, if most of them are present, regards the diagnosis as confirmed:

He is having major difficulty with reading and writing at about the age of seven. This age is singled out because while almost every five- to six-year-old has difficulties, the majority of seven-year-olds are making steady and rapid progress. Professionals point out that learning to read is a comparatively easy skill which most children, even those of below average intelligence, readily acquire. It is when others are succeeding and the averagely or highly intelligent child is failing by comparison that he should be noticed and watched with care.

He can probably read words with which he has been familiar for some time but cannot read even the simplest new word. If early teaching has been by the "look and say" method, the child may have quite a lot of words he can "read." But he recognizes them by their whole shape and cannot generalize the rote-learning.

He cannot use individual letters as the building blocks of words. Extremely affected children may actually be unable to recognize or differentiate individual letters. Moderately affected children may recognize them individually but still be unable to put them together as words. This is why the dyslexic child who can read (by shape recognition) the word "man" and the word "cat" may still be unable to read the new word "mat." Phonetic reading schemes teach children partly by means of the sounds individual letters make. But it is useless to say to the dyslexic child "What does *m* say?" It says nothing at all to him.

Since the child cannot use individual letters as building blocks, he cannot spell either. How can he work out the letters which will make a word when to him the only comprehensible words are ones which, over and over again, he sees complete?

He may be able to write words he has learned by shape recognition, but as long as the overall shape looks right he will not know if he is wrong. Reversals of letters (mirror writing) and reversal of letter order are therefore common. If he is asked to write down a word which he has not learned to recognize by shape, he may have literally no idea how to proceed. Hearing the word does not help him translate it into letters on a page, nor does he have clues such as the number of letter sounds in the word the teacher dictates. His attempts at "taking dictation" may therefore be extremely wild.

His actual letter formation, even when copying, is usually very poor. Since the individual letters are meaningless to him they have no integrity of shape and he cannot therefore learn to "make a nice *m*." If he is making any kind of *m* it will be as part of an attempt to "draw" the shape of a whole word or to copy something totally meaningless to him.

He is probably confused about "right" and "left." Although all small children have to learn which is which, most children do so through their own growing awareness of their bodies. The child learns that this is one of her hands and that it is *called* right and that everything to that side of something else is therefore right rather than left. The dyslexic child, with right-left disorientation, may be actually unable to distinguish his own right and left arms. Other signs of this disorientation include:

Difficulty in telling the time because he cannot tell whether clock-hands are pointing *to* or *past* the hour.

Difficulty with tying bows or any manual skill involving right-to-left.

Difficulty with arithmetic where, although most of us seldom give it much thought, right-left is vital. Multiplication, for example, becomes a nightmare if the numbers appear random.

He may have varying difficulties with other forms of symbolism. Plus, minus, multiply and divide signs are often confused as are the symbols for points of the compass.

He may be left-handed, mixed-handed or come from a mixed-handed family. This is by no means always the case, so nobody should fear dyslexia just because a child happens to be left-handed or be afraid of producing a dyslexic child because there is a mixture in the family. However, once dyslexia has been diagnosed, it is often found that this is a child or family in whom right-left dominance is not firmly established. The child himself, or other family members, may prefer the right hand for some activities, the left for others or may prefer to kick a ball with the right foot even though he is left-handed.

Most people are firmly one-sided for all activities—having a complete preference for either the right or the left hand, eye, foot and so forth. It is thought that one hemisphere of the brain dominates the other to produce this effect. It is possible that the brains of mixed-handed individuals fail to develop in this one-sided way but instead develop both hemispheres equally. Instead of being an advantage, as common sense might suggest, it is thought that this could lead to confusion between the functions of the two sides and therefore contribute to the symptoms of dyslexia.

Helping the dyslexic child

A fine line has to be drawn between over-readiness to diagnose an educational handicap of this kind and lateness in doing so. A child who has watched his peers easily acquire reading and writing skills which remain impossible for him, has experienced a gradual sinking of his position in class as they improved and he did not, who may even have been teased, scolded or patronized for his stupidity or punished for his refusal to try, will experience tremendous relief once both he and the adults around him understand that there is a reason for his difficulties. On the other hand, a child who might have overcome mild difficulties for himself, or whose learning problems are due to emotional causes, may actually suffer loss of motivation and a distortion of his self-image if the "dyslexic" label is attached to him. Although helping the dyslexic child is a professional matter, deciding how much emphasis should be put on his disability, and at what point in his development, is very much a job for parents.

Teaching approaches in dyslexia

The aim of any teaching program for a dyslexic child (as for a child with any other kind of handicap) should be to try both to enable him to keep up, as far as possible, with the education of his peers *and* to help him to develop any special talents or skills which come easily to him so as to ensure that there are areas of his daily life in which he can have the satisfaction of shining.

Dyslexic children have to be helped to overcome the basic hurdle of becoming literate. In our society, people who cannot read and write are seriously disadvantaged, however intelligent they may be. It is thought that some of the thousands of illiterate and semi-literate adults in highly developed countries may in fact have been dyslexic children whom nobody recognized or helped.

Remedial teaching in reading and writing (and perhaps in arithmetic, too) will certainly be needed, but the school's program for slow learners may not be helpful. The dyslexic child cannot learn to read and write by phonic methods, however slowly and individually these are taught. Instead, he has to learn by boring rote and prodigious feats of memory.

He has to learn the letters of the alphabet one by one by pure repetition.

He has to learn words by rote, too, being presented with very very simple groups of letters-which-make-words, again and again, until he knows that that is "cat" and that is "man," by memory, rather than by the mixture of memory-and-phonics which most children use.

This kind of learning has to be a "drill," with constant testing of recent learning and practice of past learning, because the dyslexic child finds this kind of remembering desperately difficult. In this respect the old-fashioned term "word blindness" is descriptive. Just learning the word "cat" will not put "cat" into his memory forever: it will only become imprinted if it is repeated endlessly.

Tricks have to be devised to tell him which is right and which is left. Reliable access to this information will help him to keep his learned letters in the right order, and the right way up, as well as helping him to decode the many other directional cues we all use. Sometimes a child has a mark (perhaps a scar or a mole) on one side of his body and not on the other, and he can be taught that that mark is the right (or left) and therefore that the other side is the opposite. Often a more readily visible mark helps: some teachers put an indelible star on the right hand or ask parents to sew a thread to every right pocket, and so on.

● Don't be trapped by shoes or boots with "Right" and "Left" written on the toes. The dyslexic child will certainly put them on the wrong feet from time to time and confuse himself further. The mark that he uses must be *part of his body* so that it can serve to replace other children's consciousness of which is their own right hand or foot.

The child has to learn to write and to spell and this may present an even more difficult problem than reading. His letter formation will be spidery and immature, and he will probably never acquire an easy and personal handwriting. His spelling will be bizarre and he will always lack the "knowledge of letters" which the rest of us use to work out how to spell a word which is unfamiliar or which we have forgotten. He will have to acquire a written vocabulary by rote/practice.

Most dyslexic children, given appropriate help early enough, can learn to read well enough to be "literate," but writing is not only technically difficult for them but remains a poor method of communicating. However large his spoken vocabulary, however vivid his imagination and high his intelligence, the dyslexic child will never, even in adult life, do justice to himself on paper. So, while he must learn to write as well as he possibly can, other methods of verbal communication must also be opened up for him. Eventually he must be "tested" and "examined" by methods which give him a reasonable chance of doing himself justice.

He can learn, even at six or seven, to use a typewriter which will eventually relieve him of the necessity to go through the mechanics of handwriting. In some schools arrangements can be made for dyslexic people to take examinations using typewriters. It is not unrealistic to expect that word processors will soon become available within schools: properly programmed, such an aid can correct the dyslexic's spelling, too.

He can learn to use a tape recorder or dictating machine. Every dyslexic should have one of these, and even the youngest should be allowed to speak their stories and essays onto them so that their ideas can flow freely. Some schools allow children to dictate their work if parents will then write it out. Others will accept a tape cassette rather than an exercise book.

Help in dyslexia at, and from, home   If a child has real problems of this kind and it is decided that he should understand as much as possible about the condition so as to realize that he is not stupid, compared with others, but faced with a much more difficult learning process, home support will be vital:

He is probably of normal or better than normal intelligence and must know it. Every effort must be made not to allow his handicap to make him feel stupid. He need not have "happy birthday" written on his party cake; menus can be read to him without comment; the whole family can leave taped messages for him and each other rather than writing notes. . . . At the same time, this sort of tact needs to be balanced with encouragement in those areas where he can shine, whether these are drama, painting or sports, and by careful provision of information in non-written form, by television, and reading aloud, for example.

His basic learning cannot be a pleasure to him so motivation is vital. Even the most skilled specialist teachers cannot make the drill of literacy truly interesting for the dyslexic child. It demands effort and concentration far beyond that which other children must give. A good relationship with that teacher is vital, but so is family support which honestly acknowledges the boredom.

He cannot compete with a normal class in reading and writing, but needs normality where he is not handicapped and the stimulus of others where he is. This often means that he is best served by membership in an ordinary school class, supplemented by attendance at a special group. Although this may involve parents in a demanding schedule of driving him from place to place, and may even involve them in moving so as to come within reach of specialists, it is worth it. Neither full-time membership in a generalized "special school" nor membership in an ordinary school with individual help sessions will be as good.

If the handicap is marked, course and career choices may need steering. It is probably better that he should be steered towards a kind of education and job which he will be able to fulfill at his true intellectual level than that he should choose as others do, but condemn himself to remaining always at a level below his true capability. Parents need to seek not only career advice but advice directly from examination boards and training establishments as to what allowances/special arrangements they may be prepared to make. One such child, for example, has made an excellent career in forestry. The authorities felt that the job would be suitable and were prepared to give every assistance to him in getting over the preliminary examination hurdles. Another fought his way into the Civil Service but, good though he is at his present lowly job, finds himself barred from promotion by examinations. The important point is that, in many jobs, it is the *getting there* which presents the worst problems. Once he can achieve a certain status and seniority, the affected individual can use a dictating machine/secretary and be scarcely affected by his handicap.

Leaving home *see* **Adolescence**/The long road to independence.

Lice

Lice are insects, about 0.08 in. long, which feed on blood and lay their eggs (nits) on hairs. The nits are tiny, white cigar-shaped objects and each one is firmly glued to an individual hair. They hatch in two to three weeks. The bites of the adult lice cause itching so your first clue to infestation in your child may be continual scratching of her head.

Infestation is becoming increasingly common among schoolchildren and, while some people believe that adult lice are more likely to move onto dirty greasy hair than onto freshly shampooed hair, it is simply not true that "only dirty neglected children get lice." Any child who plays and rough-houses with lots of others and/or uses their hairbrushes, can find herself playing hostess. If you examine her hair (as the school nurse will probably do once or twice each term) and see either dark colored moving creatures on her scalp, or the little nits on the hair shafts, try not to react with horror or you will horrify her, too.

Getting rid of head lice Some of the old standard treatments for head lice are becoming ineffective because the lice are resistant to them. Your child's school, health visitor or local pharmacist will advise you as to which chemical is currently being used in your district. It will probably be a lotion or shampoo containing the chemical malathion.

● Follow instructions very carefully and keep this poison locked away.

If an anti-lice shampoo (such as Kwell) is recommended, it will kill the living lice and make a very inhospitable environment for any nits that are about to hatch. Follow the instructions carefully: you may be advised to repeat the shampooing after an interval.

If an anti-lice lotion is recommended you will probably be instructed to comb it all through the child's hair, making sure the whole scalp is covered, to leave it on overnight and to shampoo it out in the morning. Whether you use a shampoo or a lotion, you can remove most of the nits which are sticking to the shafts of the child's hairs if you comb it through with a really fine-toothed comb. Special combs are sold for this purpose.

It is sensible to check the heads of all other family members, especially other children. You should also wash all brushes and combs—dipping them in the lotion if you wish—and you must launder the affected child's pillowcases and so forth.

- There is no point in disinfecting the entire house: lice cannot live without blood nor will they lay eggs where there are no hairs. So only objects on which there may be hairs need concern you.

- Since nits are laid close to the scalp and hairs grow about 6 in. per year, you can work out how long your child has been infested. If there are nits even one centimeter up the hair shafts, she must have been harboring them for nearly a month.

Life-saving *see* **Accidents; Safety.**
Lost child *see* **Safety**/From "strangers."
Lumbar puncture *see* **Hospital**/Procedures. *See also* **Meningitis and Encephalitis.**
Lungs and lung disorders *see* **Chest Infections.**
Lying *see* **Discipline, Self-discipline and Learning How to Behave.**
Masturbation *see* **Habits.** *See also* **Adolescence**/Sex.

Measles

Unlike some other "infectious diseases of childhood" measles is an acute and exceedingly unpleasant illness. In the Western world the infection, with its complications, still causes several hundred deaths each year. In the less-developed world it is responsible for as many as half of all childhood deaths from infection.

Measles is a virus infection. Although it is always present in the community, it tends to flare up into epidemics in alternate years.

Babies are born with some passive immunity from their mothers to this as to other common viruses. Immunization against the disease cannot be effective if it is given while passive immunity still exists, but if immunization is delayed for too long the baby will be at risk of catching the disease at just the age-stage when it is most likely to affect him severely.

Immunization
against measles

The exact timing of immunization must be discussed with your doctor or the staff of your health clinic. Discussion should take account of the following points:

It is usual to give the vaccine at fifteen months as part of the MMR. But if an epidemic is brewing in the neighborhood your doctor may advise protecting the child sooner.

Your doctor may prefer not to immunize a child who has suffered any central nervous system infection (such as meningitis) or one who is liable to febrile convulsions. But if your doctor does decide to leave your child unimmunized, it may be because he is relying on a high level of immunity within the neighborhood to make it unlikely that he will meet the disease. If an epidemic occurs, or if the child actually has contact with a measles-sufferer, check with the doctor again. He might wish to reconsider.

Immunization can sometimes produce worthwhile levels of antibody even in a child who is already incubating the disease. A doctor will therefore sometimes carry out a crisis immunization to try to protect the youngest member of a measles-ridden family.

Measles vaccine is cultured in an egg medium and therefore must not be given to a child who is allergic to eggs. It is important to mention any such allergy to any doctor who is considering immunizing your child. If a child who cannot be protected for this reason has contact with the disease, your doctor may wish to give him an injection of gamma globulin (*see* **Infection**/Treatment of infections which cause illness: Anti-viral drugs) in the hope of reducing its severity.

Measles vaccine contains live (though attenuated) measles virus and therefore causes a very mild version of the disease in some children. About thirty percent will be feverish after a week to ten days; some of those will also develop a measles-like rash. About one child in every one thousand immunized may have a convulsion as a result of this fever, but since about seven in every one thousand children who have real measles have a convulsion, immunization is still a good swap for the disease (*see* **Convulsions, Seizures and "Fits"**).

Having measles   **Incubation period.** Ten to fourteen days.

Route of infection. Droplet infection from nose and throat to nose and throat.

First symptoms   Look like a bad cold, usually with slight to moderate fever, a cough and
of measles   often with puffy, reddened and watery eyes. Unlike a normal cold, the illness worsens over the first one to three days. Inside the mouth the mucous membranes are inflamed and "Koplik's spots" may be seen, especially inside the cheeks at about the level of the molars. These spots (for which a doctor will search as they are diagnostic of an early case of measles) look like little white grains of rice, standing out against a red background.

Acute stage   Around the third day the child may become irritable and unusually
of measles   sensitive to bright light and to loud noises. He seems much sicker and his fever suddenly runs very high—often to around 104°F (40°C). It is at this stage that the child who is liable to react to high fever with convulsions is liable to have one. Convulsions, however, are not a special feature of measles but only of the high fever which this disease has in common with many others (*see* **Nursing**/Fever).

Soon after the fever reaches its height, the typical rash begins to appear, starting behind the ears and along the hairline and working down the body. The individual "spots" are quite small, red and scarcely raised. However, so many "spots" characteristically appear that they may join to produce dusky red "blotches." The rash is not itchy.

By the time the rash has spread to the chest, the worst (barring complications) of the illness is over. By the time the rash has reached the legs and feet the fever will probably be dropping. Once the rash has finished appearing the child can be expected to be recovered within a day or two. In an uncomplicated case the whole acute stage seldom lasts for more than a week, with the child at his sickest in the middle of it.

Treatment of measles   Although measles is a virus infection, the damage to the respiratory tract lays the victim open to secondary infection by pathogenic bacteria sometimes resulting, for example, in complications such as bronchopneumonia, middle-ear infection or infection of the inflamed eyes (conjunctivitis). Occasionally a doctor may give antibiotics from an early stage to prevent these possibilities. If he does not, he will certainly keep a careful eye on the child in order to start such treatment at the first signs of such secondary infection. He may advise you to sponge the eyes and mouth with prescribed antiseptics.

● The child will probably feel extremely miserable and ill and will require careful symptomatic nursing (*see* **Nursing**). You should also keep a watchful eye, especially in the very young child, for two rare but potentially serious complications.

Post-infectious encephalo-myeletis   Very occasionally, measles infection can cause inflammation within the central nervous system which will usually first show itself either in extreme drowsiness or coma, or in convulsions after the initial high fever has begun to drop. Although any very feverish child may have periods when he is delirious, hard to awaken and/or jittery and shaky when awakened, you are certainly entitled to a doctor's help in distinguishing such fever reactions from early signs of this complication.

Inflammation of the vocal cords   Swelling of this area of the throat can occasionally occur and lead to partial obstruction of the breathing, with harsh crowing sounds as the child breathes out and obvious effort (including a sucking in of the ribcage) as he breathes in. If the child appears to be having any difficulty with his breathing, seek medical help.

Convalescence from measles   Unless there have been complications, measles may be over in a week and the child completely recovered within a day or two more.

Meatal ulcers *see* **Circumcision**.

Medical Specialities

Your family's doctor   Few people think of their family doctor or general practitioner as a specialist in medicine but, while he is not a consultant with a team of less-senior doctors working under him in a hospital, he certainly is a specialist and invariably the most important one to any family. Don't make the mistake of thinking of him as less well qualified than those who undertook special training in the specialities described below; he undertook special training too, but training in how to cope with people of all ages and all their ills rather than with particular groups of people or ailments.

Different family doctors choose to practice in different settings and different ways. Yours may work with only a receptionist to help him or as part of a big health center which is almost like a mini-day-hospital. He may pride himself on being personally accessible to you at almost any time or he may rely heavily on appointment, rotation and relief systems. Like any other professional he is bound to enjoy certain aspects of his work more than other aspects and this may affect the services he offers. In Britain, for example, he may or may not undertake ante-natal care and operate his own well-baby clinic. All British family doctors (unlike those in other parts of the Western world) make at least some home visits to patients, but even in Britain the readiness with which a doctor will come to your child, rather than always asking you to take her to him, will depend largely on his own attitudes. He may feel that the personal contact and view of his patients' backgrounds which such visits give him are worth their enormous drain on his time and energy. But he may feel that they take so much time from other patients that they should be kept to an absolute minimum. In the U.S. home visits are not part of routine medical care but are still made occasionally by doctors who have a particular appreciation of the importance of family background to individual health.

However healthy your family, a doctor whom you (all) like, trust and feel easy with is absolutely essential. It is he on whom you will rely in those occasional but terrifying crises—like a first febrile convulsion (*see* **Convulsions, Seizures and "Fits"**). It is to him that you will take those embarrassingly vague questions like: "She doesn't seem quite herself . . . nothing special really, but I'm not happy about her . . . am I being silly?" And you will have to rely on him not to be irritated when two children manage, between them, to produce symptoms needing medical advice eight times in six weeks. . . .

If you have a child who is, for the moment and in some respects, less than healthy, your family doctor will be even more important to you, however grand the hospital specialist who oversees her case. A child with severe asthma (*see* **Allergy**/Asthma), for example, will certainly be under the hospital's care, but her day-to-day care and the implementation of any special treatment recommended will be between you and that doctor.

Should any of you ever develop a mysterious and/or serious condition, it is your family doctor who will diagnose it, or at least recognize the difficulty of diagnosis and steer you in the right direction for specialist help. He knows a very great deal, but not the least important thing he knows is who *will* know when he does not.

Although you cannot, so to speak, go shopping for the right doctor, you do have some choice, at least in the sense of being entitled to change doctors if you are not happy later with the one you originally selected. Do remember, though, that most family doctors feel that they can do their best work with families whom they get to know well, and with children whom they have seen through infancy and the infectious diseases of childhood before they are faced with worries about puberty or with adolescent depression. Try to see your relationship with him as two-way because how well he can fill his role as your family doctor depends at least as much on you as on him. Perhaps he "won't explain," but perhaps you did not ask him or only thought afterwards of the questions you wanted answered and were then too shy to telephone and say so? Perhaps he "won't see us when he's asked," but perhaps your requests are not always reasonable. Most of the common dissatisfactions between doctors and parents can be sorted out by sensible communication (*see* **Nursing/ Contact with the doctor**).

Your child may be referred by your doctor to a consultant or to a specialized hospital clinic which will be under the overall charge of a consultant. Occasionally you may want to ask for consultation with a specialist. The names and functions of different specialities can be somewhat confusing so the following notes on those you might meet may help:

Audiologist (audiology) A specialist in the diagnosis and management of every type and degree of deafness (*see* **Ears and Hearing; Ear Disorders and Deafness**). *See also* ENT surgeon (*below*).

Dermatologist (dermatology) Specialist in skin diseases and disorders. A dermatologist might help your doctor to manage a child with acute infantile eczema (*see* **Allergy/ Eczema**).

ENT surgeon (otolaryn- gologist; specialist in otolaryngology) Specialist in ear, nose and throat disorders: this will be the speciality to which your child will be referred if there is any question of tonsillectomy, adenoidectomy or surgery to relieve deafness caused by infection (*see* **Hospital**/Surgery: Myringotomy).

If a child is partly, or wholly deaf, his *medical* condition and needs will be the province of this speciality, but any remaining hearing difficulty will be dealt with under the supervision of an audiologist who will be responsible, for example, for prescribing hearing aids and arranging for speech training.

Gynecologist (gynecology) Specialist in female health and illness, especially concerned with the genital organs and reproductive tract.

Girls needing advice concerning delayed menarche or menstrual problems (*see* **Adolescence**/Menstruation), however, will often be referred to a "pediatric gynecologist" who will be especially experienced in handling the sensitivities of the very young.

Neurologist (neurology) Specialist in diseases/disorders/dysfunctions of the brain and nervous system.

Your child might be referred to a neurologist following a head injury (*see* **Accidents**/Head injuries); for assessment of the significance of convulsions (*see* **Convulsions, Seizures and "Fits"**) or if he developed any form of paralysis. Neurologists do not deal with "nerves" in the sense of *nervousness*. This is the province of Psychiatry (*see below*).

Obstetrician (obstetrics) Specialist in the management of childbirth. The role may overlap with that of the gynecologist (*see above*).

Oculist General term for a medical specialist in eye disorders. The term has an identical meaning to ophthalmologist (*see below*), which is the one that is more often used. Do not confuse "oculist" with optician (*see below*).

Oncologist (oncology) A specialist in the study and treatment of tumors. Although this term is obviously associated with the treatment of cancer, benign tumors, "lumps" and "growths" of all kinds are also the province of this speciality. Referral to an oncology clinic is not, in itself, reason to assume that cancer is suspected.

Ophthalmologist   A medical doctor specializing in the prevention, diagnosis, treatment
(ophthalmology: and cure of disorders of the eye. If a child is referred because of an injury
"eye doctor";   to the eye or because, for example, of recurrent infection (*see* **Eyes and**
"eye clinic"),   **Seeing; Eye Disorders and Blindness**), he will be under the care of an
ophthalmic   ophthalmologist. If he has problems with vision, his overall *medical* care
surgeon   (including any possible surgery, as for a squint) will remain the ophthalmologist's responsibility, although in simple sight problems such as nearsightedness, his *practical* management may be delegated to an optician (*see below*).

Optician   The word really means a designer/maker of optical instruments, especial-
(optics)   ly glasses.

An optician is not a medical doctor and cannot deal with, or prescribe for, eye injuries or disorders. With a bewildering variety of other qualifications, however, he may assume responsibility for prescribing and supplying a wide range of aids to vision. The important distinction between one type of optician and another is that:

A dispensing optician only makes spectacle lenses to the prescription of an ophthalmologist. He cannot test your child's sight and prescribe for him himself.

A "sight testing" or "ophthalmic" optician (also sometimes called an optometrist) can both test sight and prescribe for sight defects, as well as actually provide the spectacles. These specialists may also prescribe and supply contact lenses, and may prescribe and teach exercises to assist with certain vision problems such as squints.

● Many ophthalmic opticians or optometrists work in a commercial setting. While it is usually convenient to buy glasses for a child in the same place where his need for them was established and the prescription given and made up, you do not have to do so. When you have a child's sight tested you are paying for a professional service. You have every right to purchase the glasses elsewhere if you prefer.

Orthodontist   A dentist who specializes in preventing, or curing, crooked, overcrowded
(orthodontics)   or otherwise misaligned teeth. If your child's teeth need attention of this kind, your own dentist may be qualified to carry out the work or may refer you to an orthodontist.

Orthopedic   Specializes in abnormalities of bones, joints and their associated muscles
surgeon;   and ligaments. A *pediatric orthopedic* surgeon will be one who further
(fracture clinic)   specializes in the orthopedic problems of children, which are different from those of adults because of continuing growth.

All fractures are dealt with by this speciality. Your child may also be referred to an orthopedic surgeon following a sprain or sports injury (*see* **Accidents**).

Pediatrician
(pediatrics)

A doctor specializing in children's problems. Many pediatricians specialize further (*see above* Orthopedic). Hence, the pediatrician who supervises the care of a newborn baby will be specially trained in neo-natal medicine, while the psychiatrist (*see below*) who sees a troubled ten-year-old will be specially trained in child psychiatry.

Physiotherapist
(physiotherapy;
"physio" clinic)

A term used to cover a wide range of treatments—such as massage, heat, exercise and so forth—given to cure, or to prevent, an even wider range of illnesses and disabilities.

Physiotherapists are trained in the normal functioning of the body and in the ways in which it can be assisted in curing or strengthening itself or in overcoming and compensating for its weaknesses. The physiotherapist who makes your child do breathing exercises and tips him up while she taps his chest so that he coughs up secretions (*see* **Chest Infections/** Chest infections with pain: Physiotherapy) may be doing as much to help him over his chest infection as the doctors themselves. The one who shows another child how to exercise the muscles of a leg, wasted after weeks in plaster, is ensuring that the leg will quickly regain its normal strength and shape. The one who teaches you how to handle your asthmatic or spastic child is minimizing the risk of deformities developing because of her existing disability.

Almost all physiotherapy depends, however, on real patient cooperation. What the physiotherapist herself does *to* your child during a session cannot be as valuable as what you and the child continue to do in between sessions. Hers is a vital role, but if you do not take her advice seriously and work according to her recommendations, her skills cannot work for you as they should.

Psychiatrist
(psychiatry;
psychiatric
hospital or
clinic)

A medical doctor who specializes in the prevention, diagnosis and treatment of emotional and mental disorder.

Psychiatry is the medical branch of psychology (*see below*). Where the psychological *treatment of patients* is undertaken, the psychiatrist will normally be the senior consultant with overall responsibility for those patients.

● Referral to a psychiatrist does not mean that a person is "mad" or "crazy." The fully fledged mental disorders to which these slang terms refer (such as schizophrenia and other psychoses) form only a small part of the psychiatrist's work and occupy only a small number of beds in psychiatric hospitals and units. The larger part of psychiatric resources is devoted to the emotional upsets and neuroses to which every human being is subject (*see* **Anxiety, Fears and Phobias** and **Depression**, for examples).

Psychoanalyst
(psycho-
analysis)

Psychoanalysis stems from the pioneering work of Freud, but psychoanalytic theory and practice have developed and diversified so that one analyst may differ widely from another, both in his ideas and in his ways of working with patients. In general, though, psychoanalysis may be regarded as a process of assisted self-discovery. The patient may not be "ill" in the medical sense but will be unhappy about himself, dissatisfied with his own life and relationships and generally unable to be the person he feels he would like/ought to be.

Psychoanalysts believe that the roots of present emotional difficulties lie in unconscious conflicts. The patient can see the tangled vines which are dogging his every footstep, but he cannot see their source and therefore cannot uproot them. Through one-to-one work with the analyst (five times weekly in classical psychoanalysis but sometimes two or three times weekly in modern practice) these unconscious forces and motivations can be brought into conscious view where they can eventually be dealt with rationally; the individual's life and relationships need no longer be bedevilled by his personal past.

A psychoanalyst need not be a medical doctor, but if he is not he will work in collaboration with one, usually with a psychiatrist. He himself must have undergone one of a very few, highly demanding, training courses.

Psychoanalysis is an extremely time-consuming and therefore expensive form of therapy. It is seldom fully reimbursed under health insurance plans. Reduced fees are, however, sometimes available to individuals who seek help from recognized training institutes, where trainee analysts work with them under the supervision of experienced therapists.

● In some communities it sometimes becomes fashionable to seek psychoanalytic treatment. It cannot be too strongly emphasized that such treatment requires an enormous personal commitment which should never be entered into lightly.

It must also be emphasized that, while stringent professional rules govern the registration of psychoanalysts in Britain and the U.S., this is not true of all countries. Be careful. This kind of "treatment" given by an ill-qualified "therapist" can be highly destructive.

Psychologist
(psychology;
psychological)

Psychology as a subject deals with the study of the mind and therefore of every aspect of human behavior, emotion, thinking, learning, interacting. Some psychologists devote their professional lives to studying the structure and function of the brain and central nervous system. Others study whole populations of people, compiling, for example, the statistics from which we derive "norms" for everything from "intelligence" to voting behavior. Some work with organizations and institutions ranging from advertising agencies to prisons. Others work directly with individual patients/clients in a wide range of counselling and helping roles. Your child will have considerable indirect contact with psychologists via, for example, the assessment tests which he takes at school. He may have direct contact with a psychologist whenever he is thought to need help with emotional or learning difficulties or whenever you, his school and/or his doctor are trying to decide whether or not he does need help (*see*, for example, **Hyperactive Children**).

Psychotherapist
(psychotherapy;
psycho-
therapeutic)

The concept of psychotherapy began with Freud (*see above* Psychoanalysis). Since then, the term has been extended and diffused so that it may be used to describe almost any attempt to alleviate emotional or mental disorder or maladjustment *through talking*. At one extreme, psychoanalysis itself is a form of psychotherapy, but at the other extreme a brief series of counselling appointments may be described in the same way.

Group therapy is the term used to describe a situation in which a carefully selected group of patients meets regularly, under the leadership of a psychiatrist or psychologist, to share, discuss and, hopefully, to illuminate, each other's problems. This method enables one trained professional to attend to several patients simultaneously, but the benefits of group membership are intended to be greater than mere economy.

Child psychotherapy ("play therapy") is the term often used to describe psychotherapy with children who are not sufficiently mature to use purely verbal help. The therapist obtains many clues to the child's thinking, and to his inner reality, both by watching his play and by playing with him in the roles which he assigns to her.

A psychotherapist need not be a medical doctor but should be trained in psychotherapeutic techniques. Some medical doctors, some psychiatrists and some psychologists undertake this further training. There are also a few (pitifully few) trained lay psychotherapists.

● Anyone can talk to a child about his feelings and his problems. In this basic sense you yourselves act as psychotherapists when you try to relieve particular anxieties or find the underlying reasons for particular behavior. In this sense, also, many members of the helping professions, doctors, social workers, teachers, counsellors, may offer a child psychological support in the course of their contacts with him. Do remember, though, that psychotherapy in the professional sense is something different, and that the selection of a therapist is vitally important. If you are worried about your child, ignore advertisements by "cowboy therapists" (no properly trained psychotherapist would ever advertise for business nor, given the present shortage, ever be tempted to do so). Seek such help only through your doctor, the child's school, a psychiatric training institute or an established youth guidance clinic or similar facility.

Medicines *see* **Infection**/Treatment of infections which cause illness; **Nursing**/Medicines; **Pain and Pain Control.** *See also* **Safety**/In the home.

Meningitis and Encephalitis

Meningitis refers to inflammation of the meninges, the membrane which encases the brain and spinal cord. Encephalitis refers to inflammation of the brain itself inside the meninges.

Although this kind of inflammation can be caused by accidental injury, the usual cause is infection. Bacteria, viruses or even fungi can multiply in, say, the throat or the intestine, reach the bloodstream and attack the nervous system by that route. Some "germs" are more prone than others to behave in this way. The meningococcus, for example, seems to have a real affinity for the meninges from which it takes its name. It can cause actual epidemics of meningitis. Other bacteria are far less likely to attack the nervous system and, even where they cause meningitis in one patient, will usually cause only a simple throat or other "ordinary" infection in anyone whom that patient infects. Most of the viruses which cause the infectious diseases of childhood *can* attack the nervous system but again, some do so more readily than others. The measles virus, for example, is a more frequent cause of meningitis than is the chickenpox virus, while mumps is more likely than German measles to lead to encephalitis.

Meningitis and encephalitis are scary illnesses not only because they can threaten a child's life but also because they can leave a recovered child with a damaged brain or nervous system. Fortunately, the chances of your child ever contracting this kind of nervous system inflammation are very small and the chances of successful early treatment are very high.

Early treatment is vitally important so, far from trying to diagnose meningitis or encephalitis yourself, you should simply be quick to be suspicious and check with a doctor.

● If you ever do suspect that your child's symptoms might be those of nervous system inflammation, don't put off calling the doctor because it is 2 a.m. "and I'm bound to be wrong. . . ." The doctor himself will act on nothing more than his own suspicions; he will admit the child to the hospital for tests unless he can be quite certain that there is no nervous system involvement in the illness.

Signs which might suggest meningitis/ encephalitis

Contrary to popular belief there are no absolutely certain signs and symptoms of these illnesses which are diagnostic of all types in all age groups. Any of the following might be reasonable cause for suspicion. The more of these signs and symptoms your child shows, the more suspicious you should be:

Fever with delirium, marked sleepiness or altered consciousness. Although fever can be very high in these illnesses, it need not be. Even a low fever affects consciousness, though, when the site of inflammation is the brain or nervous system. Meningitis or encephalitis is therefore more likely in a child whose temperature is only 100°F(38°C) but who is behaving as if it were 104°F(40°C), than it is in a child whose fever really is so high that delirium is to be expected.

Acute irritability in a baby or toddler who may seem positively maddened by anything and everything, and quite impossible to comfort, cheer or calm by any of your usual methods.

● In a young baby, apathetic withdrawal, such that he will not make eye contact with you or join in any kind of social interaction, should arouse your suspicions. The apathy may alternate with irritable crying and the lack of response means that he is not comforted when you pick him up. If your baby suddenly seems *not to care* whether or not you are there and whether or not you are paying attention to him, don't assume that he has "gone off you"; seek medical advice quickly.

Acute headache in an older child. This, the most famous of all symptoms of meningitis, is actually rather an unreliable one. The very young children who are most prone to the illness often do not appear to have headache with it at all or, if they do, they do not localize the pain but react instead with general irritability and misery. Older children, who certainly will have headache with meningitis, may, of course, have head pain for many other reasons (*see* **Headaches**).

Neck stiffness. This symptom is also famous but unreliable. A child whose spinal cord is inflamed will not be able to drop his chin comfortably onto his chest. His inability to do so is certainly one sign which will increase an examining doctor's suspicions. But *most* stiff necks are caused by muscular strains or by simple throat infections.

Dislike of light which may lead the child to cry and burrow under the bedding when you open the curtains, or to beg you to switch off the light beside the bed.

A convulsion (*see* **Convulsions, Seizures and "Fits"**). Any illness in which a child suddenly shoots a high fever may lead to a febrile convulsion, but these nervous system infections may lead to convulsions even when fever is not very high, or when the victim is past the age for ordinary febrile convulsions.

Treatment of meningitis or encephalitis

If your doctor suspects meningitis or encephalitis he will immediately have the child admitted to a hospital.

A spinal tap (*see* **Hospital**/Procedures: Lumbar puncture) will probably be done at once. The pressure of the spinal fluid will be tested; it will be inspected for unusual cloudiness and a sample will be sent to the laboratory for microscopic examination and culture. The doctor who carries out the test may be able to tell you immediately whether or not any central nervous system infection is *likely*, but there may be a wait for laboratory results before you can know the exact situation.

If the child does have either meningitis or encephalitis but no bacteria are found in the spinal fluid or blood, it will be assumed to be caused by a virus and no definitive drug treatment will be possible. But be comforted. Viral versions of these illnesses are far less dangerous than bacterial ones.

If there is bacterial meningitis or encephalitis, treatment will probably be by antibiotics given into a vein for maximum and most rapid effect. The child may be nursed in isolation (where you should be encouraged to stay with him). Energetic attempts to get his fever down may include packing him in ice and/or using an electric fan on bare skin. Drugs will also be given for acute headache or to sedate him if he is very confused and afraid.

● Try not to be too alarmed by all this. Your child may be more or less unconscious (due to illness and drugs) for a day or two; he may obviously be dangerously ill yet *still* will almost certainly recover fully. As he begins to get better, don't allow the fact that he is weak and babyish to convince you that his brain is damaged. It takes time for both muscles and spirits to recover from this sort of illness. Consult the doctor in charge of him: he has seen many children recovering from nervous system illnesses and will probably know, even before formal tests are carried out, whether yours is, or is not, one of the few who is permanently damaged.

● A small child, even once he has fully recovered physically, may be extremely disturbed and clingy after this sort of illness. Try to arrange for him to have plenty of your time and attention for the first weeks at home.

Menstruation *see* **Adolescence**.

Migraine *see also* Headaches; Abdominal Pain/Recurrent

There are many types and degrees of migraine and many suggested causes and methods of relief. This is probably because migraine is not a single disorder but a more generalized tendency to periodic headaches with other associated symptoms.

The following is a brief description of a "classic" migraine, together with the most commonly accepted explanations for it. Do realize, though, that while one person may lose two working days every two weeks with attacks of this kind throughout youth and middle age, another can have occasional attacks which are much milder and over within a few hours, while yet another may be somewhat prone to ordinary headaches yet experience only two or three full-blown migraine attacks in a lifetime.

Migraine sufferers Include equal numbers of boys and girls and more usually those with a family history of similar attacks. Some children who are going to be subject to migraine suffer from recurrent abdominal pain or periodic vomiting during early or middle childhood.

Migraine can begin during infancy (although it is seldom recognized as such). Typically it begins during pre-adolescence, may peak during the adolescent years, settle into a pattern during young adulthood and gradually subside with increasing age.

The beginning of a "classic" migraine Migraine often begins with a short-lived phase known as the "aura." This is a varying sensory disturbance during which the victim may see zig-zag lines or flashes of light or lines of black dots across his visual field, may feel giddy and generally "peculiar" and may smell "phantom odors" or hear peculiar noises.

The migraine headache typically comes on after the aura is established and, once the pain begins, the aura gives way to nausea. There may or may not be vomiting.

The "classic migraine pain" is one-sided and to the front of the head; it is a throbbing pain and may be very acute. It is usually relieved a little by lying down and, intense though it is, does not usually prevent sleep. Indeed many migraine victims quickly learn that to go to sleep is the best way to survive an attack as well as offering the best chance of a quick ending to it.

Duration of a migraine Some children can sleep off even a bad attack in a few hours, emerging completely recovered. Others can rid themselves of the acute pain, yet remain pale and unwell for hours more. Yet others have attacks lasting as long as twenty-four hours.

Precipitating factors in migraine The most usual explanation is stress, but while most migraine attacks do occur when the victim has been under stress, the same people survive apparently equal amounts of stress on other occasions without having migraine. Many people believe that particular foods (such as wheat, chocolate, milk and alcohol) are associated with migraine (*see* Allergy/Gastrointestinal allergies) while others blame noise, climatic conditions and a wide range of other factors.

Possible physical basis for migraine

It is thought that the "aura" may be caused by abnormal constriction of arteries within the brain, causing lack of oxygen to the particular parts affected. The pain is thought to be due to dilatation of arteries in the scalp (and perhaps within the skull, too); some people believe that this extra pressure from the blood vessels stimulates pain fibers in the artery walls themselves.

Coping with migraine

Migraine tends to run in families and the lives of some adult sufferers are dominated by the affliction. When the child of such a family first shows signs of migraine, everyone naturally assumes that he too must face the worst that they face, both in terms of the frequency of attacks and of their severity. Difficult as it is to avoid it, it is vitally important not to jump to this conclusion. If you do, the child will come to see himself as a "sufferer," come to expect two days off from school with every headache just as you have to take two days off from work, come to see himself as different from his fellows. Attitudes and expectations affect pain (*see* **Pain and Pain Control**) and tension especially affects the severity of headaches. It is easy to create a situation in which migraine is a more severe problem than it need have been. If yours is a migrainous family, or if your child produces a definite first migraine, remember:

Although migraine runs in families, not by any means every member suffers from it. Migraine is certainly not something to expect, look out for or even mention as a possibility to a child.

Not every headache is a migraine. The child of migrainous parents is just as liable to "ordinary" kinds of headaches as any other child.

One full-blown migraine need not predict frequent attacks. Even a headache-prone child or adolescent may only very occasionally (perhaps only once or twice in a lifetime) have another classic migraine. Many migraine sufferers have attacks only a couple of times a year.

Migraine, even if frequent, need not be disabling. By no means does every sufferer follow the "classic" pattern (*see above*). Many, for example, never experience any "aura," but simply start their attacks with headache, while a few sometimes experience the aura without any head pain. Many others never vomit during their migraines and quite a few do not usually even feel sick. While most will feel a need to lie down and sleep during an attack, a great many can be rid of the episode after a two-hour nap.

Seeking medical advice for migraine

If a child has two or three really bad headaches which make him seem unwell, prevent him from getting on with life and probably only resolve completely when he has slept, you may want to consider getting a doctor's advice. In the case of a pre-adolescent, it may be better to have a preliminary talk with the doctor on your own so that the child does not hear you "making too much of" his headaches. Eventually, the doctor will probably want to see the child to exclude the rare physical causes of acute headache (*see* **Headaches**). Once he has convinced himself, you and the child that he does not have a brain tumor/need glasses, his attention will probably turn to methods of preventing the migraines and/or hastening the end of attacks.

Allergy is a possible cause of migraine and some doctors pursue this line energetically, especially if the child and/or his family have known allergic tendencies. Unfortunately, discovering the allergic trigger for migraine attacks can be a long process because the attacks themselves are so infrequent. If milk, for example, is eliminated, on a trial basis, from the child's diet, it may be many months before you can be certain that the diet has lessened the frequency of his migraine.

Stress can be either a cause or an exacerbation of migraine and some doctors take extremely detailed histories of recent attacks in order to try to identify particular stress factors. Migraine which begins, or becomes much worse, when the victim is in the twelve-to-fourteen age bracket, for example, is sometimes related to tensions over puberty, to hormonal changes associated with menstruation (*see* **Adolescence**/Puberty) and/or to stress associated with promotion to secondary school or the start of college preparatory courses.

When frequent migraines are ruining a child's life, preventative medication can help, although nobody should embark on it lightly as side effects are quite frequent. If it is thought necessary, your doctor may refer the child to a special migraine clinic where doctors, with many years' experience of the condition and the drugs, are ideally placed both to prescribe for him and to monitor his response.

Medication during attacks can certainly shorten them. "Ordinary painkillers" (*see* **Pain and Pain Control**) are often ineffective and are sometimes vomited. Your child may need a painkiller given with an anti-vomiting drug. He may also benefit from medication which acts on the constricted or dilated arteries (*see above*).

● Once you have any suspicion that a child is suffering from migraines, don't just dose him each time with larger and larger doses of whatever painkillers you have in the house. Prescribing for migraine is a specialized business.

Early treatment means shorter attacks. Once it is clear that migraine attacks are to be a regular, even if occasional, part of your child's life, he needs to be helped to learn to react quickly and effectively to them. If they lift when he lies down and goes to sleep, he should not struggle to complete the school day. Four hours' courage may turn what would have been a half-day's migraine into a much longer one. If prescribed drugs abort the attacks, he should learn always to carry a small quantity when he is away from home so that he can take them at the first sign.

● If a child starts to have migraines when he is very young, you and his teachers will, of course, have to manage them for him. But however young he is, he should learn to take charge of his migraine for himself at the first possible moment. If he feels confident that he can cope independently whenever a migraine strikes him, he will not feel unable to go to camp or stay over with friends just in case.

Milk *see* **Eating**/Types of food for babies. *See also* **Allergy**/Gastrointestinal allergies.

Minerals in diet *see* **Eating**/Types of Food: Vitamins and minerals. *See also* **Teeth**/The formation of teeth.

Minimal brain dysfunction *see* **Hyperactive Children**.

Mixed feeding *see* **Eating**/Types of food for babies.

Mother-substitutes *see* **Babysitters; Working Mothers**. *See also* **Divorce, Separation and One-parent Families**.

Motion sickness *see* **Vomiting**.

Mouth to mouth resuscitation *see* **Accidents**/Coping with more serious injuries.

Mouth Ulcers *see also* **Cold Sores**

Although a crop of painful ulcers inside the lips or cheeks of a small child can be due to infection by the herpes simplex virus and therefore suggest that he or she may be prone to later cold sores, most mouth ulcers occur singly and for reasons which we do not understand.

The ulcer may be inside the cheek, inside the lip or on the gum. Wherever it is there will be an inflamed red area with a shallow, yellowish-white ulcer in the center. It will be exceedingly painful.

Mouth ulcers clear up of their own accord in about a week to ten days but, in the meantime, they may make your child's life a misery. Food creates painful friction; fruit drinks sting; and, if the ulcer is in a place where it is constantly rubbed by the tongue or against the teeth, she may be conscious of the pain almost all the time.

You may be able to help a little by applying Vaseline to the area so as to reduce that painful friction. Your doctor may be able to help much more if he considers it appropriate to treat the ulcer with a cortisone ointment.

If your child is one of the unfortunates who gets these ulcers frequently, do mention them to your dentist as they are sometimes provoked by dental troubles. Otherwise there is little you can do except to assure her that, while many children never suffer from this kind of ulcer at all, even those who do so frequently usually seem to "grow out of" the tendency. Even if she has had several this year, she may never have one again.

Multiple minor injuries *see* **Accidents**.

Mumps

Mumps is a moderately infectious virus disease. It varies widely in its severity and effects. Most known cases are mild but unpleasant illnesses in older children and young adults. A few cases, especially in males past puberty, suffer serious complications (*see below* Possible complications in mumps). A larger group than both these put together consists of children who are infected so mildly that they acquire mumps antibodies without ever being clinically ill.

There is a safe and effective vaccine against mumps, although it is too recent for anyone yet to be sure whether its protection is lifelong. In the U.S. it is given routinely to all babies as part of the fifteen months MMR shot. In other countries the vaccine may be offered only selectively. It is males past puberty for whom protection is most important yet, by this age, most boys will already be immune to the disease either because they have suffered the illness or because they have been subclinically infected. A public health program to test boys for antibodies when they entered their teens, and to immunize those few who had none, would be extremely expensive, yet a program to immunize all such boys except those known to have had the full-blown illness involves many unnecessary injections. It may be that mumps will eventually be universally included among the routine immunizations offered in early childhood. In the meantime, it is comforting to realize that even if you do not think anyone in your family has ever had mumps, they may well be among the many who are immune following subclinical infection; even if they are not, the chance of their "catching" mumps during an epidemic is far less than the chance of their "catching" other epidemic illnesses such as measles or chickenpox.

Having mumps **Incubation period.** Two to four weeks.

Route of infection. First droplet infection from nose and throat to nose and throat, but the virus is then carried in the bloodstream to produce a generalized infection which may affect various organs and be passed on by various routes.

First symptoms
of mumps Older children and adults may feel generally unwell, with slight fever, headache and stiff neck. Younger children often miss this stage.

Acute stage
of mumps The virus tends to settle in the salivary glands, especially the parotid gland, which is located in *front* of the ear. The typical swelling of mumps—often the first sign of the disease in children—runs from in front of and below the ear down to the jawline. Swelling may extend in both directions so that the child's face is misshapen from temple to neck. Usually the first swelling is one-sided. Often the other side will swell in its turn, sometimes several days after the first.

The swelling makes eating and talking painful and the affected salivary glands cease to function properly so that the mouth tends to be very dry.

A mild case
of mumps A child with mumps may not feel ill at all, although her swollen and painful face and neck will probably bother her. Eating is virtually impossible and good nursing therefore involves offering plenty of drinks, perhaps including milkshakes and other nourishing liquids. A straw makes these easier to take.

The swelling will probably go down in three to seven days, depending whether both sides are affected together or in sequence, or whether only one side ever swells.

● *Avoid acid drinks.* Many children remember for the rest of their lives the black currant juice or lemonade offered them when they had mumps. Such drinks will stimulate the inflamed salivary glands and will cause extreme pain.

● *Avoid mockery.* Most affected children are of school age and can be really upset if their deformed faces cause rude mirth.

Possible complications of mumps

Mumps is the infectious disease most likely to cause meningitis or encephalitis (*see* **Meningitis and Encephalitis**). Some studies have suggested that as many as ten percent of children with mumps may have central nervous system symptoms. Involvement of the central nervous system can occur even before the diagnostic swelling, or it can occur later in the illness. Any high fever, drowsiness, severe headache, vomiting and/or delirium should be reported to your doctor. There are seldom any lasting ill effects.

In boys past puberty or in young men, inflammation of the testes (orchitis) occurs in about twenty percent of cases. Like the salivary gland, the testis becomes inflamed, swollen and painful. Although extremely unpleasant, orchitis very seldom affects fertility. Often the affected testis recovers completely. Even if it does not, both testes are very seldom involved.

Older girls and young women may suffer similar inflammation of the ovaries (oophoritis) indicated by abdominal pain and tenderness. This is seldom as troublesome as orchitis.

Inflammation of these kinds, caused by the mumps virus, usually responds well to anti-inflammatory drugs. Contact your doctor immediately if a mumps patient complains of pain and tenderness other than in his salivary glands.

Nailbiting *see* **Habits**.
Nearsightedness *see* **Eyes and Seeing; Eye Disorders and Blindness**/Faults in vision.
"Nerves" *see* **Anxiety, Fears and Phobias; Depression**.
New baby in the family *see* **Jealousy**.
Nightmares and night terrors *see* **Sleep**.
Nits *see* **Lice**.

Nosebleeds

Nosebleeds are common and, in a child or young person, almost always unimportant. Often the cause of the bleeding is unknown, but sometimes it starts following nose-blowing or violent sneezing. Picking the nose is more usually the result than the cause of a nosebleed. A child picks his nose if there are uncomfortable traces of dried blood there.

Whatever causes the bleeding to begin, a nosebleed in a child or young person almost always comes from a tiny vein in the nose.

First aid for nosebleeds

Sit the child up as soon as bleeding begins. This has the double effect of lowering the venous pressure (and thus making it more likely that the bleeding will stop) and preventing her from swallowing the blood which will probably make her feel sick. If she sits leaning over the washbasin, a tap can be left running so that the blood is washed away as it drips; the child need not therefore see what can seem an alarming quantity of gore.

Tell the child to breathe through her mouth and to avoid sniffing or swallowing. The idea is to avoid disturbing any clot which may be forming in the nose.

The bleeding may stop as abruptly as it began, in which case nothing further need be done except to watch and/or distract a younger child so that she does not disturb the coagulating blood in the nostril until the clot farther up has had time to become firm.

If the bleeding does not stop quickly, get the child to pinch her own nostrils firmly between thumb and finger or, if she is too young or frightened to cooperate, do it for her. Keep pressing firmly for ten minutes.

If this does not stop the bleeding, or if it starts again, repinch the nostrils, but this time apply a very cold wet cloth or, better still, a couple of ice cubes well wrapped up, to the bridge of the nose.

Persistent *Very* occasionally a nosebleed is so copious that a significant amount of
nosebleeding blood can be lost in a short time. If such an outpouring continues, or restarts after, say, fifteen minutes of the above measures, the child should be taken to the doctor or local hospital. More often, although still rarely, a gentler nosebleed continues despite first aid measures. This usually means that the affected vein is so placed that pinching the nostrils does not put effective pressure on it. A gentle dripping would take many hours to amount to dangerous blood loss, but it must nevertheless be stopped, for convenience as well as safety. Take the child to the doctor.

Repeated If a child's nose bleeds frequently—perhaps weekly or more often over a
nosebleeds period of months—the inconvenience will merit medical attention. The doctor will probably spray the inside of the nose with a chemical which both shrinks the mucosa to give him a better view and anesthetizes it. He will then look for a weak spot in a nasal vein and, if he finds one, he will probably cauterize it. The doctor's task may be easier if the child is having, or has very recently had, a nosebleed when he is first consulted. Once you have decided that one more nosebleed will be one too many, visit the doctor as soon as it occurs.

Nose-blowing *see also* **Habits**/Nose-picking

Blowing his nose is a difficult technique for a small child to learn and one which will probably seem pointless to yours, as he will have no objection to a runny nose, periodically wiped on the nearest sleeve. You will be doing well if your child can blow his own nose efficiently *and discreetly* by the time he goes to school.

You can teach him to blow his nose efficiently at an earlier age if you do not bother about discretion. Show him how to block one side of his nose with his finger and then to blow down the other. The results will not be any more revolting than a continually runny nose and, if other people are present, you can hold a tissue ready to wipe the immediate results. Once he has got the idea he will soon learn to muffle the whole performance in a tissue by himself.

If you introduce the tissue too soon, the child will probably try to snort down both nostrils at once. Not only is this inefficient, it is also undesirable as mucus may be forced into the eustachian tubes and can cause middle-ear infection (*see* **Ears and Hearing; Ear Disorders and Deafness**).

Do accustom your children to tissues from the very beginning, and encourage them to throw away each one immediately after use rather than squirrelling them up a sleeve for another time. Linen or cotton handkerchiefs are extremely unhygienic (as well as horrible to launder). They must have been directly responsible for the spread of millions of colds.

Nursery schools *see* **School**/Pre-school and nursery education.

Nursing *see also* **Accidents**; individual conditions

Nursing your child at home

Most of the nursing you will do at home is more a matter of common sense than of particular skills: it is ordinary child care writ rather larger than usual. But there are times in the lives of most families when competence and confidence in nursing a child may make a big difference. For example, going to the hospital is always upsetting for a baby or young child. The more confident you can become in nursing her through illnesses, the more likely it is that she will be able to stay at home. If the doctor can see that you are panic-stricken by her croup or her raging fever, he may send her to the hospital as much for your sake as for hers; equally, if he is not at all sure that you are capable of taking her temperature accurately or getting the right amount of medicine down her, he may send her to the hospital even though she does not really require *professional* nursing.

Almost all illnesses will get better (with or without medicine) without any special nursing, but your skill may sometimes speed up the recovery or at least make a relapse less likely. And it can almost always make being ill a less uncomfortable experience for your child.

Finally, while you may reject all the specific suggestions made here, preferring your own ways of doing things, working out how you *are* going to cope with your children when they are ill can make those deadly winters of recurrent "bugs" much less unpleasant for you.

Basic needs of sick children — A sick child needs all the things a well one needs, only she needs them adapted to her physical condition and brought into line with any instructions from the doctor. They are summarized here only because some of them are the subject of misleading myths.

Food: unless the doctor orders otherwise (for example, *see* **Diarrhea, Gastroenteritis and Food Poisoning**), the child can have anything she wants to eat and need have nothing that she does not want. All those sayings like "feed a cold and starve a fever" are nonsense unless they happen to fit in with the child's appetite.

Fluids are always more important than food and especially so if a child is vomiting and/or having diarrhea and when she is feverish. She need not eat if she does not want to, but she must drink. If she will not, cannot, or drinks and then vomits, you need a doctor's advice.

● An almost weaned baby will often drink more if she is given her bottle instead of that cup. A bottle-fed baby who will not take her ordinary formula will often take plain water or diluted juice instead. Breast-fed babies seldom refuse to suck at all (two feedings refused is certainly reason to consult a doctor) but may take less than usual at each feeding. It is sensible to offer the breast more often and to offer water or juice from a bottle in between.

Older children are often put off by a large glass of something boring. They drink three sips and then leave it to get warm and dusty by the bed. Gimmicks like a *tiny* glass, a curly straw or a jug out of which to help themselves often help. So does ringing the changes between drinks, or indulging them with frozen juice cubes or pink (strawberry jam? food coloring?) milk.

Warmth: people often believe that sick children should be "kept warm," but if your child has a fever (*see below*) this is not only nonsense but may be dangerous nonsense.

Sick children (especially babies) need to be able to use all their energy for fighting infection and getting well. So they need to be kept at a temperature which saves them from having to use any energy for keeping warm *or* getting cool. That does not mean keeping them extra-warm but keeping them, as far as is reasonably possible, at a *steady* temperature. If your home is centrally heated, most rooms are probably within a few degrees of each other anyway. If your bathroom is icy you may want to let her wash at the kitchen sink. If she is in bed, the pajamas that keep her comfortable when she is well will be right now, too. If she is up, ordinary indoor clothes will be fine. If she is in and out of bed she may need a compromise, like pajamas with a light jersey and slipper-socks.

● Children with upper respiratory infections (colds, coughs, etc.) will be far more comfortable if you can keep rooms normally warm but airy and not too dry. A space heater on and window open may seem extravagant of energy (and impossible if you have sealed windows and air conditioning) but it is probably the ideal.

The question of staying in bed

Once upon a time anyone who was sick stayed in bed, often for days at a time. Then doctors realized that lying still can cause all kinds of problems, ranging from serious ones like thromboses in adults to loss of muscle tone in anyone. They also realized that children, bored with being in bed, often use more energy leaping about there than they use if they are allowed up. The pendulum of opinion swung so that now you will only very seldom be told to keep your child in bed. But not *having* to keep her there does not mean that she may not choose and should not be allowed to stay in bed. Older children (like adults) often retreat to bed as a comfortable and private place of safety when they are ill. Younger children may feel unwell enough to welcome having at least a version of bed available to them.

A baby's ideal version of bed is probably your arms. She will welcome as much cuddling and carrying and sitting on laps as you can offer. When she cannot be cuddled by you, she can *feel* cuddled if you bring her carriage close to where you will be and settle her in that. She probably will not want to be put right away in her crib in her bedroom (but *see below* Handling and routines).

An older child's version of bed: If an older child stays in bed in her room, you will probably spend half the time running up and down stairs and she will spend the other half feeling bored and miserable. The answer is to provide her with some kind of nest in a central area. You may have an ideal sofa in your living room, but a portable nest has advantages. A bean-bag chair with a couple of pillows may do for a toddler but for a bigger child a fold-up "guest bed" is more comfortable. It can be erected anywhere you please and is just the right height for her to get in and out of freely. If she is ill enough to confine herself there, you can move bed and child to make a change of scene or to give her access to the television. If the weather is right she can even have it in the garden.

Handling and routines

Like the rest of us, children who feel unwell are usually irritable and easily frustrated. Being totally indulgent is not usually a solution. Having you at her beck and call and indulging her every whim will not actually make her feel any happier for more than a minute per treat and, by the end of a day or two, she will be bewildered by your unusual behavior and you will probably be beginning to see her as a tyrant rather than a poor little girl. Total indulgence during illness is not good in the long run either. You do not really want her to grow up believing that whenever she can persuade you that she is ill, she can do exactly as she pleases and have your undivided attention.

Of course it is no good expecting a child's most reasonable and mature behavior when she is ill because you will not get it. A happy medium between total indulgence and unrealistic expectations often means treating the child as if she were one stage younger than she really is. You will probably get it about right if you treat a primary school child as you did when she was in kindergarten; a pre-school child like a toddler; a toddler like a crawler and a crawler like a baby. A sick baby will simply need to drop her most independent veneer and have as much of you as you can offer her.

If you do agree with yourself to accept rather unusually "babyish" behavior during the illness, there will probably be some top-level demands which you will therefore want to drop until she is better. An eight-year-old might be let off the new effort of plaiting her own hair. A four-year-old might be given some help with her buttons. A two-year-old might be allowed to use fingers instead of a spoon while a one-year-old might get her bottle during the day instead of only at night. But having softened your demands in this sort of way, do ask for (or, better, behave as if you take for granted) ordinarily civil behavior at this temporary new level. That eight-year-old gets her hair plaited for her, but that does not mean that she is not expected to be pleasant about it. That four-year-old gets her buttons done up but can still say "thank you." The toddler may use her fingers but you are still entitled to be cross if she deliberately chucks the food at you.

Expecting ordinary civil behavior will usually keep a child behaving (fairly) civilly. In the same way, keeping to at least a version of her ordinary daily routines will usually keep her feeling as normal as her illness allows. She can "get up" in the morning even if it is only into fresh pajamas. She can have meals at the ordinary times even if they consist only of soup or a juice which is different from the one she has been sipping all afternoon. She can be settled for her usual naps/bedtime even if she has been resting for most of the day. Routines of this kind provide punctuation marks in the child's day and may make it easier for you to get through the time, too.

Difficulty (or renewed difficulty) over going to bed is a common sequel to a small child's illness. Using a "nest" or day-bed during the day (*see above*) helps to avoid this. If she has not been in her real bed and room during the daytime, going there at night provides a change of scene, a return to normality and a different kind of comfort (*see* **Sleep**/Varying sleep needs: Making bed a pleasant place).

Passing the time

Nothing is more boring than being a child who is ill unless it is being that bored child's mother. If the illness is brief—a very bad cold, for example —you can probably keep her happy and stay sane yourself if you resign yourself to a couple of days of reading aloud, board games or whatever the current passion may be. But if she is likely to be ill for much longer—with a bad bout of measles, for example—it is worth getting organized.

For your own sake, cancel any engagements/work plans that are coming up. The more it matters to you that she should be well enough to go to her sitter/school by next Wednesday, the more the intervening days will drag. Try to arrange for somebody either to lay in food for easy meals or, even better, to keep her company while you get out and shop. Try also to think of some things to do which will amuse you (or at least give you a sense of accomplishment) and amuse her, too. She may enjoy your practicing the guitar or yoga, but she will not enjoy your reading or talking endlessly on the telephone. Some mothers restock freezers with home-made bread, clean out junk closets or redecorate rooms while companioning sick children. If most of your usual adult company is at your workplace, try to arrange a few visits from friends, too, so that you remember there is an adult world out there.

Apart from obvious occupations for your child, like being read to or watching television, some of the following may occupy her happily enough to give you some peace:

A "being-ill" box

This is a Treasure Trove brought out whenever (but only when) the child is ill. She is allowed to know that it exists, but she never knows (unless she is ill three times in as many weeks in which case she may catch you out) exactly what is in it. If you are clever, such a box can become appropriate when a child is around eighteen months and stay much loved until she is old enough to occupy herself with a new library book. Obviously the box can contain anything you (or your child) like, but the basic idea is that it should contain a large number of items (so that just looking through it takes pleasant time) of sufficient variety that at least a few are likely to take her fancy at this particular moment. With a small child in particular, the items need not all be new—even to her—as forgotten objects, or seldom-seen old friends, will often give just as much pleasure.

Put in all the surplus objects your children acquire like the second and identical coloring book one received at his birthday party or the package of felt-tip pens this one was given when she was not yet interested in drawing.

Add all the fairground/crackerjack junk the family has acquired. "Winning" that cardboard doll gave her pleasure at the time, but in the excitement of the moment it was probably scarcely looked at.

Save for the box any pretty things which come your way such as wrapping paper which could be cut up to be used in a scrapbook; tinsel which could make a collage or headdress; little boxes, jars and other attractive packagings. You can also save things which are particularly appropriate for your own child's interests: that Sunday supplement full of photographs of cars or horses, for example.

Spice the collection with small items which you buy whenever they catch your eye and/or you are feeling generous: new plasticine, pencils, gummed paper shapes, colored drawing paper, miniature playing cards, etc. Each of these will be new to the child once, and still welcome on other occasions when there will be some other small item which is new.

If you want to make the box more elaborate, buy wholesale "tiny toys." If you look in certain publications you will find advertisements for, say, "One hundred items suitable for boys and girls from two to seven." They are intended for corner shops to sell as "pocket-money toys" at a hefty mark-up, but if you buy the collection they work out at only a few cents each. The toys are mostly junk, of course, and they may not be safely suitable for the youngest children, but the novelty of, say, ten new things all at once is irresistible to a bored, miserable child.

Add any larger toys which your normally active child will not bother with. This, for example, may be the place for that construction set to which she has never settled down because she is at a rushing-about-stage. If you leave it in her toy chest, familiarity will breed contempt and it will probably never be used, but put in the being-ill box it may transform a bad day or even a whole bout of tonsillitis.

Surprise her with any plaything she is not normally allowed. Some families, for example, will not permit battery-operated items in daily play because batteries are now so expensive. The price of a battery may be worthwhile when she is having the flu. Others ban noisy toys like mouth-organs or drums, but will willingly pay the noise price for the child's pleasure while she is ill.

If you are running a box like this, do try to remember to sort it out after each bout of illness because otherwise it will be an unattractive jumble next time it is wanted. Remember to keep it stocked, too, preferably by adding bits and pieces to it during the summer months when (hopefully) it is little used.

A "being-ill friend"   This can be any soft toy or cuddly person which does not happen to have become part of your child's permanent family. He emerges whenever she needs him because she is ill, and he goes away again to celebrate her being better. Such "friends" often become important mascots to children who are "too grown up for dolls" when they are well.

Finger or glove puppets can serve as "being-ill friends" and fill a useful role in communication, too. Your child may confide worries about injections, medicines and so forth to a puppet. A puppet on her hand may answer questions from another on yours, too. If you cannot get a direct answer to questions like "Where does it hurt?" you might like to try working through puppet-intermediaries.

Other "being-ill" toys

Possessions of yours which your child yearns for, but is not usually allowed to touch, can be lent to good effect when she is ill. Costume jewelry and discarded make-up (and a mirror to see the effect) are usually especially popular with both sexes. Sick children get tired and when yours is too tired to play she will need interesting things to look at and fiddle with. A mobile (you might make it together first) hung in a draft, the family goldfish bowl, a string of beads, a squeaky toy or fiendishly fiddly puzzle may all pass the boring minutes which sandwich bouts of your attention.

If a child is in bed, or immobilized by a plaster cast, for some time, she must have a proper play surface. A tray on her knees is better than nothing but a swing-across bed table is far better because she need not keep still. With a large plastic tablecloth (not a thin plastic sheet, of course) right over the bed, sofa or "nest," she can do almost anything she normally does. Special adaptations of play for bed include:

Sugar for sand. A large mixing bowl with a couple of pounds of sugar, spoons, little pots, etc. stands in well for sand-play as long as the child is old or ill enough not to eat it (much).

Marbles in a bowl. Provided she will not put them in her mouth, marbles whizz deliciously around and around a big salad or mixing bowl. A simple game, few can resist this one whatever their age; you may enjoy it, too.

Cars and a tray for crashes, parking arrangements, etc.

Pastry for clay. However gray it becomes you can probably bake the final result as "jam tarts"—you do not have to eat them.

"Magic" for painting. If you cannot cope with real paint while she is in bed, the kind of book in which colors appear when she paints with plain water is irresistible. It will not stunt her imagination in a few days.

"Fishing." A magnet on a string and anything safe which it will collect can be used for "fishing" over the edge of a bed or couch.

Being confined in bed is a time when a child may take to "educational" activities which she could not be bothered with while she was active. Try her with new activities that involve sitting still. She might like to try cutting out or knitting for the first time at one stage, or looking up things in an encyclopedia at another.

When she is bored and you really need to do something else, try starting her off on something and then leaving her to do the next bit until you come back:

Photograph albums can be used for various activities of this kind. A young child could be asked to find all the pictures of herself; an older one might sort last year's vacation pictures and stick them in.

Magazines can be used for all kinds of identification games. You might help a young child find all the cars and then ask her to cut them out. A slightly older child might like to design a scrapbook.

Beads: if she is old enough to handle beads you might start a necklace for her to finish.

Making books, etc. If you can cut out paper dolls she might go on and color them; if you can tell a story and write it down she might illustrate it.

Although a young child probably will not know that she cares about a muddle, most children will stay happier and feel more occupied if you can keep things sorted out, and put away what is not being used. A big cardboard box that everything can be bundled into is quicker than proper putting away, and tidier and more comfortable than having everything strewn around. Ideally, use the time when she is napping or in bed in her own room to clear up her daytime "nest" so that she can start again.

Contact with the doctor
(*see also* **Medical Specialities**/Your family's doctor)

When an illness begins   It is up to you to decide whether or not your child needs to be seen by the doctor. If you telephone, recite her symptoms and then say, "Do you think you ought to see her, Doctor X, or will she be all right?" you are putting the doctor in an impossible position. He may think, from what you have told him, that the illness is probably trivial, but how can he be sure that you have reported fully and accurately? How can he, a responsible person, risk *not* seeing a child who might later on turn out to have needed him? Such a call from a parent is tantamount to a request for an appointment and it will save everybody's time if you simply make one.

Occasionally, though, it is worth making this sort of call if an illness begins late in the day or at the beginning of a weekend or vacation. In that case, you are not making an appointment because there are no normal appointments available. Instead, you are warning the doctor that, if things should get worse, you might have to ask for out-of-hours attention. The doctor can leave a message with his answering service if he wishes, or tell you where to reach him later if you do need him.

Taking the child to the doctor's office   In Britain, parents are exceedingly fortunate in that home visits from general practitioners are still accepted as part of ordinary family medicine. But however kindly your own doctor may be about such visits, try not to abuse them. In most of Europe and all over America, home visits are rare or non-existent. There is a lot to be said for taking your child to the doctor if you can, rather than bringing the doctor to her.

Home visits inevitably use up a lot of a doctor's time and while you may resent the implication that his time is any more valuable than yours, you probably also resent having to wait for hours in his office if he has been called out by somebody else.

Facilities for examining your child are likely to be better at the office than at home.

These days many offices have facilities for performing a variety of simple diagnostic tests on the spot. Using these may enable the doctor to start treatment sooner.

On the other hand, of course, the doctor who visits your child at home will probably see her more relaxed and at ease, and will gain insight into the family background which may be useful to him on another occasion even if it is not relevant this time. He may also be able to give you better guidance about nursing her: "This room is much too hot" is more effective than "Keep her room cool, won't you?"

When a doctor examines your child

You are in a position similar to that of the nurses he works with elsewhere: your job is to help him do his job for your child efficiently.

DON'T:

Take the opportunity to tell him all your troubles or all your partner's symptoms.

DO:

Tell him, or let her tell him, or help her tell him (depending on her age and shyness) what her symptoms are. Long stories about the amount of flu in the neighborhood will not help him. He needs to know what she feels, not what you deduce that she has "caught."

Help him set up any examination he wants to make. For example, he cannot listen to the chest of a fully clothed child or of a toddler who is sitting on the floor. He cannot work without a reasonable light either.

Keep quiet while he is using a stethoscope. He cannot hear you properly if you speak to him, nor hear the child's breath sounds if she talks to you.

Give the child, however young, a good chance to answer his questions herself. If he asks "Does that hurt?" he wants the child's answer (in words or behavior or facial expression) rather than yours. If the child gives what seems to you a completely misleading answer (like "no" when she had just told you that it hurt badly) it is fair enough to point out the discrepancy. Maybe the hurting has stopped; that could be useful information.

Supervise the child so that she does not, for example, empty the doctor's case while he is writing a prescription.

Tell him the form of medicine the child prefers (*see below*** Problems of** administering medicines) **before** he has written out the prescription.

Ask for exact information/instructions.

Ask when/if/under what circumstances he will/want to see the child at the office/want a progress report by telephone.

Telephone
contact with
the doctor

Once a doctor has seen your child, telephone contact can save time and effort for all of you because the doctor will have a picture of the child's condition and a view of how the illness is likely to progress. Whether you telephone because he asked you to do so or because you are worried by new developments or slow progress, do try to have clear in your mind the changes which have taken place since he saw her.

If he is not expecting you to telephone, it is usually best to call and tell the receptionist that you would like to speak to him when it is convenient. Often she will arrange to call back later on. The point is not only to avoid interrupting him in the middle of examining another patient, but also to give him a chance to have your child's chart in front of him. Her illness may be uppermost in *your* mind, but *he* has probably seen dozens of patients since. If your doctor has a nurse practitioner who works with him, she may be able to answer your questions or relay them to the doctor and call you back to report his response. But if you should feel that you would prefer to speak directly to the doctor, you are certainly entitled to do so.

Coping with miscellaneous discomforts

Aches and pains

While a child whose illness has *acute* pain as one of its symptoms should always be seen by a doctor before any attempt is made to deal with that pain with over-the-counter remedies, many minor feverish illnesses are made miserable by headache and/or restlessly aching limbs.

If you are giving aspirin to control fever (*see below*) it will help these discomforts, too. Even if fever is not a problem, aspirin or paracetamol may make the child more comfortable. An older child or adolescent who has severe headache may find that a painkiller containing codeine is more effective. It is sensible, early in your career as a parent-nurse, to choose an over-the-counter pain remedy and check it out with your doctor (*see* **Pain and Pain Control**). If you have not done this in advance, bear the following points in mind:

A baby who is feverish enough to need medication, or in enough discomfort to need relief, should always be seen by a doctor. She cannot tell you what is wrong nor can you accurately and safely deduce anything from her behavior, other than that she is unwell.

Toddlers and pre-school children must receive doses of medicine which are correct for their *weight* rather than their *age*. It is all too easy to overdose a lightweight three-year-old by giving her the recommended amount for "children from three to five."

It is always better to use a pediatric (children's) medicine than a smaller dose of one intended for adults. Breaking tablets in halves and quarters leads to inaccuracy.

Most such medicines can be given every four hours, but that does not mean the child should have a dose every four hours indefinitely. Some containers will tell you the maximum number of doses which it is safe to give within a twenty-four-hour period, but if your child even comes close to needing that much medication, check with your doctor.

Fevers tend to rise towards evening and sick children become tired and fretful then, too. A dose in the early evening may enable her to pass a more relaxed and cheerful time and thus settle down better for the night, so try to "save" a permitted dose from earlier in the day.

Aspirin (and some other over-the-counter pain remedies) tend to inflame the lining of the stomach, especially if it is empty. Give them after a meal and always with a copious drink. If the child is eating very little, try giving the medicine with a glass of milk.

Itching   Some of the infectious diseases bring skin rashes which are intolerably itchy. A warm bath with a handful of bicarbonate of soda dissolved in the water often helps. If the child feels well enough, it may also provide a good opportunity for water-play.

Cooling lotions (such as calamine) help too, but the cool wetness and the psychological effect of doing something about the itching other than scratch, are as important as the medication. A child may scratch and moan less if she has her own supply to dab on where and when she feels the need. If you are worried about spills, measure out a "ration" into a small plastic container.

A child with a limb in a plaster cast may be tormented by itching skin inside it, where she cannot reach to scratch. A "back-scratcher" may enable her to reach down to the itchy place. If not, find a ruler or other long thin object which she can poke inside the cast.

Sore skin   Constant nose-blowing, or the inflammatory effects of infected mucus running from the nose, can make the skin miserably sore. Protect it, from the beginning of the illness. Some "barrier creams" are safe, even though the child may lick it. Check. Simple Vaseline or petroleum jelly will keep the skin lubricated. An older girl may prefer a "night cream."

High fever can lead to dry lips which then crack. Again, lubrication with petroleum jelly will prevent this, although a lipstick-shaped and flavored lip gloss may be more amusing.

If a feverish child is in bed for a few days "pressure areas" such as her shoulders, buttocks and heels may begin to feel sore. Tightly tucked sheets which are not allowed to get crumbs on them will help. So will a good quality bath powder applied to the carefully dried skin; it reduces the friction. A child who is still in diapers is often especially liable to diaper rash during fever because the body, requiring extra water, concentrates the urine more than usual. As well as keeping up her fluid intake it is sensible to apply a preventative cream (such as castor oil cream) during this time, even if you do not normally use one.

Sore throats   Whatever the cause of a sore throat it is usually most sore when it is least lubricated, and least lubricated when the child has been sleeping and breathing through her mouth. A drink on waking helps, so wake a baby with breast at the ready or bottle in hand, and wake an older child with a glass of something or the treat of "early morning tea."

Throat pastilles/lozenges may help the older child's sore throat, but if they do, it will be more because sucking produces lubricating saliva than because of the medication they contain. If buying lozenges from a drugstore gets around a family ban on sweets, fine. If there is no such ban, an occasional jelly bean to suck may be just as effective and more popular.

Medicines

Your doctor will prescribe medicines only if your sick child needs them. If she needs them at all, she needs exactly the amount and at exactly the intervals the doctor and/or the instructions on the container suggest. Never alter the quantity or dosage schedule of a drug without asking your doctor first, unless you were told, from the beginning, that she should take it "as required":

Drugs to be given "as required"

If your child has an uncomfortable symptom, the doctor may prescribe a drug to ease it and the instructions may say something like "four hourly as required." That would probably mean that she could have as much as one dose every four hours but not more. It would also mean that she did not *have* to have it at all, or go on having it once the symptom was better.

Medicines prescribed in this way might be for pain, for an irritating cough or for crampy diarrhea (*see* **Diarrhea, Gastroenteritis and Food Poisoning**).

Do make sure that you know what the medicine is *called* (even if the name means nothing to you, knowing it will enable you to discuss it, if necessary, over the telephone with the doctor), what it is *for* and *what the instructions imply*. Would he prefer her to have it regularly if taking it is no problem, or will he be more pleased if she can manage without it? If it is going to be helpful, will the help be apparent from the first dose or can no difference be expected until she has had several?

Over-the-counter medicines "as required"

As well as prescribing medicine "as required," your doctor may agree to your giving the child an over-the-counter medicine such as aspirin for fever (*see below*). If you want to give the child anything out of your medicine cabinet, make sure that you mention it to the doctor who is prescribing for her. Drugs can interact with each other in peculiar ways and there is also a risk of overdosage if he does not know exactly what she is taking. As an example, Codis is often given to older children for feverish illnesses with aches and pains. If you dose your child with Codis, and the doctor has prescribed a cough medicine which also contains codeine, she may have far too much.

With all "as required" medicines, prescribed or otherwise, be sure to ask how long you may go on with regular doses. The doctor may expect the fever to be down within twenty-four hours and suggest aspirin four hourly. But if the child is still feverish after thirty-six hours, are you to continue the aspirin, telephone him or stop?

Medicines to be given on schedule

Many drugs—especially antibiotics—work best if they are given very regularly indeed, so that the level of the drug in the child's bloodstream stays at a steady and effective level. But children—even sick ones—commonly sleep at night and parents prefer to do so, too. Your doctor may, or may not, want you to get up and wake the child to take a night-time dose. His instructions to you should make this point clear but if they do not, ask. If he says that she is to have the drug "morning and evening," for example, you can obviously give it to her when she wakes up and before she settles down for the night. But if the instructions are "four times per day," is it all right to fit four doses into waking hours or not? "Four hourly" or "six hourly" ought to mean that you are to wake her, but it is still worth checking in case you need not. Your doctor will sometimes say, "Give it to her if she wakes up, which she probably will with that cough, but don't actually wake her up for it."

It is easy to get muddled about a drug schedule, especially if you *are* allowed some leeway with it; it is even easier if you are giving one drug on schedule and another "as required."

It may be worth your while to write down the times she takes the medicine. If you do, you may like to use the same sheet to note other aspects of your nursing/her illness, such as her temperature, fluid intake or anything else which is of particular concern, in this particular illness.

Medicines to be given on a full or empty stomach
Some drugs are not well absorbed from a stomach containing a recent meal which is being digested; others can irritate the stomach unless it also contains food. When a child is ill it is not usually difficult to arrange for her to be "empty," but it may be quite impossible to give medicine "after meals" because she is not having any. Check with your doctor: he may suggest a glass (or even half a glass) of milk as a replacement for that meal.

Problems of administering medicines

Some doctors do not seem to realize just how difficult it can be to get medicine down a baby or small child. Your doctor may even seem a bit scornful if you express doubt about it. But if you cannot get the right amount down, you must tell him. A different formulation of the same drug might be easier for her to take. If all else fails he might want to give her the drug by injection. Don't use that as a threat to an uncooperative child, though. Most of them dislike injections very much indeed, but occasionally have to have them. Making them sound like a punishment for spitting out medicine is not helpful.

Very occasionally a child will vomit medicine, either because vomiting is part of her illness or because fever makes her inclined to vomit and medicine-by-force makes her retch. If this happens more than once you must tell the doctor because it is very difficult to be certain whether she will have absorbed none, some or all of the dose before vomiting.

Having said all that, some babies and small children are completely cooperative—even enthusiastic—about most medicines. Don't make any kind of drama (or bother with the next paragraphs) until you are sure you have trouble. An attitude which simply assumes that the child will take what you offer her often works beautifully.

Liquid medicines
These are usually prescribed for children in preference to pills or capsules because they are thought easier to take. Unfortunately many children dislike the synthetic fruit flavors which ill-conceal bitter drugs. Fortunate-

ly, *babies* may not connect the first pleasant taste with the nasty after-taste and may therefore accept the dose and cry afterwards . . . older children catch on quickly, though.

Giving the correct dose. Your pharmacist can give you a 5 ml plastic spoon with the medicine. If he does not, ask for one. Domestic teaspoons vary in size. Use this "standard" spoon for measuring, but not for administering, the medicine. A full spoon will almost certainly get spilled and anyway children have been known to bite these plastic spoons into lethally sharp pieces.

Measure the correct dose into a larger spoon, or make life easy for yourself by buying a special one which is like an icing syringe with a spoon instead of a nozzle. These have the great advantage that you can stand them up, with the correct dose safely in the bottom, while you organize the child.

Sit the child up (never give medicine to a child who is lying down; she might choke), put a glass (or bottle) containing some of her favorite drink beside her ready to wash away the taste. Get her to open her mouth and then pour the medicine, all at once, as far back as you can. The further back it goes the less she will taste it.

If you do use one of these special non-spill medicine containers, even a toddler may accept the medicine more easily if she is allowed to "do it herself." Schoolchildren may prefer to do it themselves, too, but may find medicine easier to take from a small glass than from any kind of spoon.

Trouble with liquids

Don't mix the medicine with a drink. It will either sink to the bottom or stick to the sides. The child will probably only drink half the "juice," and even if she empties the glass you will not know how much she has had. Effervescent tablets, such as some forms of junior aspirin, are the exception to this. They are meant to be mixed into liquids and will dissolve completely if you stir them well. You may still get stuck with a half-full glass but if the child will empty it she will have had it all.

Try concealing liquid medicine in a spoonful (no more) of something soft and strong-tasting that she really likes. Apple sauce, chocolate mousse or ice cream are good ones to try. Tell her it is medicine but does not taste nasty this way; proceed on the assumption that she will take it.

● If you pretend it is *only* apple sauce, the peculiar taste of the spoonful may put her off apple sauce as well as medicine.

Force sometimes works, is sometimes necessary and is not as psychologically unfortunate here as in most situations. The fact that you will *make* her take it makes it clear to the child that the medicine really matters. While that may not stop her from fighting you, it is not a bad attitude to implant.

Wrap a baby or toddler in a blanket so that she cannot bat the spoon out of your hand and then just sit there, with her on your lap and the medicine in your hand, and wait her out.

As soon as she opens her mouth (to cooperate, speak or yell) pop it in.

Emphasize the speed with which it was "all over" in the hope that it will not seem to her worth such a performance next time.

Bribery. With a pre-school or older child you can often strike a bargain about medicine. A sweet afterwards is traditional (if she does not feel too ill), but a new comic or the promise that you are ready for a game or a story the moment the medicine has gone, may work just as well.

Capsules or sugar-coated pills

By no means is every drug commonly prescribed for children made in either of these forms *in children's dosages*, but if the medicine you need is available in these forms they can be especially helpful to children who want to cooperate but truly find it impossible to get down the liquid without gagging. Don't use them with an uncooperative child, though. Capsules must never be opened or crushed and if you crush a sugar-coated pill there is no point to the sugar-coating.

Moisten the gelatin coating of a capsule slightly so that it is slippery and easier to swallow. Explain to the child that either the gelatin or the sugar-coating will stop her from tasting anything nasty if she gets it down quickly. Either get her to open her mouth while you pop it in, well back, for her, or let her do it herself.

Some children take these forms of medicine very efficiently and happily even as early as three years or thereabouts. If yours learns to do so, she will probably be able to take ordinary tablets similarly and then she will seldom have to face nasty-tasting liquids.

Ordinary tablets

If your child cannot just swallow a tablet with a drink, it can be crushed to a really fine powder and the powder may be easier to "cover up" than a disliked liquid. Not every doctor realizes this, so you will probably have to ask for tablets specially. It will not occur to him to prescribe tablets for a one-year-old unless you explain.

● When you crush a tablet, be extremely careful that you do not lose even a grain of powder. It is usually easiest to put it into a small plastic bag (or between two layers of foil), crush it with a wooden spoon and then tap out the powder.

Put a layer of anything strong-tasting and slippery that your child likes into the bottom of a small spoon (jam? chocolate spread?). Put the powder on top, all in one place, and cover it completely with another delicious layer. The whole spoonful should now slide down the child's throat without her ever tasting the powder at all.

If you cannot think of anything the child will manage a whole spoonful of just now, you can, for a toddler or older child, try *mixing* the powder into a tiny quantity of something with a really strong cover-up taste like yeast extract. The result of your mixing should be a pellet, certainly no larger than a pea, which she can swallow easily. The surprise of the saltiness helps to conceal the powder.

● Remember that extra salt, especially this comparatively large "dose" of salt, is not desirable for a baby.

If you are still stuck, there is one more trick you could try with an older child and a whole tablet.

Break off the tiniest piece of banana which will contain the pill. Push it in to make a "banana pill" and get the child to swallow it straight down.

● Don't try this method with a grape or cherry even though the pill will neatly replace its stone. The child might choke.

Medicines which are not to be swallowed

Sometimes your doctor will prescribe (or suggest) drugs for your child which she is not to swallow but to have applied to various parts of her body by various means. Do remember that a drug which is to be dropped up her nose, or spread on a particular patch of skin, is still a drug. You need to be just as careful to understand the instructions as to dosage and frequency, and just as careful to lock away such medicines after use, as you are with oral drugs (*see* **Infection**/Treatment of external infection and inflammation).

Ear drops   The middle ear is the most usual site of ear infections but, because it is sealed off from the outer ear passage by the eardrum, drops instilled into the ear cannot reach it. If a doctor wants medication to reach the middle ear in the form of drops, these will be instilled into the nose (*see below*).

Ear drops are sometimes given to a child with an infection in the outer ear canal. Such infections are often extremely painful, especially when the ear itself is moved. If you are giving drops for this reason you will have to get the child into position without touching the ear; if you try to hold onto her earlobe, for example, you will probably have a screaming fight on your hands.

Ear drops are also sometimes given to soften wax which has become impacted in the ear canal. Often a doctor will do this himself, but occasionally he may ask you to repeat the dose once or twice and then bring the child back to see him.

Don't put *anything* into a child's ear without specific orders from a doctor. All home remedies – such as warmed oil for earache—are at best useless and at worst dangerous.

To give ear drops to an infant   Draw up the correct number of drops into the dropper. Settle the baby on your lap with her head low and well turned to one side. Drop the drops into the uppermost ear and *keep her still*. If she turns over or sits up, the solution will simply run out again as the passage is a dead end.

Enemas (and suppositories)   Enemas are liquids injected into the rectum (back passage); suppositories are meltable solids—usually bullet-shaped—which are pushed into the rectum. The best known are intended to induce a bowel movement or to soften impacted feces so that a bowel movement is possible, but these methods can also be used to give a variety of medicines. Anesthetics are sometimes given to babies and young children in the form of enemas, to spare them the trauma of intravenous injection (*see* **Hospital**/Surgery). Other medicines may be given "per rectum" to a child who vomits if medicine is given by mouth. The drugs are absorbed into the bloodstream through the mucous membrane of the bowel instead of being absorbed from the stomach or upper intestine.

In some countries enemas and suppositories are still widely used, but in most of the Western world they are not. *Never give an enema or suppository without specific instructions from your doctor*. If he does tell you to do so, ask him to show you the best method, because this will depend both on *why* medication is being given by this route and on the age of your child. If you are told to give enemas as part of the treatment for a child who soils due to long-standing constipation, for example, you will already be dealing with an emotionally charged situation (*see* **Soiling**) and it is important that you, the doctor and the child are all aware of the implications.

Eye drops   May be prescribed by your doctor for a variety of irritations/infections. If you find them very difficult to administer, he may be willing to prescribe an eye ointment instead.

● Eye drops and ointments are sold *sterile*. Their shelf-life, once the container is opened, is often very short, so they should never be kept in the medicine cabinet for use another time. Furthermore, one batch of drops or ointment should never be used for more than one child; there is a real risk of cross-infection.

To give eye   Draw up the correct number of drops into the dropper, being careful not
drops to an   to touch the end with your (unsterile) fingers.
infant   Wrap a shawl or blanket around the baby so that her arms are tactfully confined. Settle her on your lap with her head back against your upper arm. Now put that wrist around the back of her head so that your hand can reach her face. Gently open her lids with your thumb and forefinger, poise the dropper and wait. Despite your fingers, she will blink. As she does so, drop the drops into the inner corner of the eye. If you get your timing right, the solution will land during the second that the eye is open between blinks. Release her lids and keep her lying still for a second while the solution is spread by her blinking.

● An older child can be given eye drops lying across a bed but, however much she means to cooperate, will still need your hand around her head to hold the eye open. Blinking or turning away is a protective reflex which she will not be able to control without your help.

Nose drops   Are sometimes prescribed in an attempt to reach the middle ear with medication. "Attempt" is the right word because in order to reach the middle ear the liquid you instill in her nostrils must run down to her throat and then find its way up the eustachian tubes. However, drops which do not penetrate all the way to an affected middle ear may still be useful if infected adenoids (which the nose drops will reach) are contributing to the problem. Nose drops which you can buy over the counter under the general heading of "decongestant" may be useful if a child has a badly "stuffed-up" nose because of a cold or a sinus infection. They can be invaluable to a baby who *must* breathe through her nose in order to suck her food, important to an older child who cannot settle down to sleep without sucking her thumb and occasionally useful to an adolescent who must partake in a school play or get through a party. Use them with discretion and your doctor's blessing, though. Used frequently or for more than a day or two, they can produce so much artificial "dryness" in the mucous membranes of the nasal passages that those passages produce extra secretions to compensate. The child may end up feeling even more "blocked up" than before.

To give nose drops to an infant

If the dropper is made of glass or rigid plastic, buy a separate soft rubber dropper, which cannot damage her nose.

Use the dropper provided to draw up the correct number of drops and drop them into a clean spoon. Then suck the liquid into the soft dropper.

Lie the baby over your lap with her head slightly lowered. Turn her head a little to one side with one hand and use your other hand to put the drops up her upper nostril. Hold her still for a few seconds and then turn her head a little the other way and repeat the process for the other nostril.

● Some nasal drops sting a little if the mucous membranes are inflamed. If there is a real struggle it may be kinder to have someone else to hold her head still so that you can get the whole thing over more quickly.

● With a child too big to lie across your lap, but old enough to cooperate, lying across a bed is usually the best position. Don't let her sit up too quickly after the drops are in. If she does, some of the bitter medication may run forward in her throat to reach her taste buds.

Fever

Fever means that a child's body temperature is abnormally high. It is a very common response to infection but not an infallible sign. Neither the presence, absence nor height of a fever is a reliable guide to the presence, absence or severity of any illness. Every family should own a clinical thermometer and know how to use it, but it will not be helpful to you if you do not interpret its readings sensibly. For example:

Absence of fever

Your child can be ill, even dangerously ill, without having any fever at all. Babies in particular (and newborn ones especially) sometimes have sub-normal (abnormally *low*) temperatures when, far from being well, their bodies are actually being overwhelmed by infection to such an extent that their bodies have given up fighting it. So don't ever let the fact that a child "has no fever" convince you that she is well. If she *says* she feels ill and cannot go to school and you suspect that she is ducking because she has not done her homework, take her temperature if you want to, just to be sure it is not high, but don't base your decision to send her to school on just the fact that that temperature is normal. Base it on more general criteria like her appetite, energy and general good cheer at home, if not at school.

"Slight" fever

Although "normal" is marked on clinical thermometers as a single point (*see below*) there is quite a wide range. Your child's body temperature will rise a little when she generates heat through active play; it will drop a little if she gets very cold while sitting still watching a parade; it will, in any case, tend to rise a little during the late afternoon and evening and be at its lowest in the small hours and early morning.

Because of this entirely normal variation, it is almost always a mistake to take the temperature of a child who seems entirely well, because if you do take it and you do find it a couple of points above normal, what are you going to do with that piece of information? Are you going to decide that, contrary to all appearances, she must be unwell? That would be a great mistake because the chances are that she is as she seems. If you are going to disregard that "slight fever" reading, why did you take her temperature in the first place? The point is, of course, that a "slight fever" is only one tiny piece of indefinite data to add to other pieces of data about the child's state. If you have such other data (she looks ill, feels ill, has vomited, cannot eat, does not want to play . . .) then take her temperature by all means. But if there is nothing to suggest that she is unwell, leave the thermometer in the medicine cabinet.

"Real" fever   Barring the recent consumption of a hot drink or a furtive touch of thermometer to hot water bottle or light bulb, a temperature which is a whole degree (Fahrenheit) or more above normal probably does suggest that the child is unwell. This can be useful information for decision-making. For example, her grumpiness probably is more than "teething" or "Monday-morning blues"; she probably ought not to go to nursery /school/or on that trip; you probably should keep an eye on her and take her temperature again, in a few hours, to see if it is rising or falling. But even so, the fever itself will not tell you how to handle the child. If she feels well, the fever does not mean that she must go to bed and adopt a "sick role" unless she feels like it. The fact that it is very high does not necessarily mean that what you thought was "only a cold" is something worse.

Finding out if a child is feverish

Some families rely on touching a child's forehead with the back of the adult hand to see if she feels extra-hot. Some reckon that they can tell, just by looking at her, whether their own child has a fever. While both methods used together have the advantage of being part of a general consideration of the child, they are pretty inaccurate and certainly will not provide useful information to the doctor if he is consulted.

Fever-testers   Modern technology has provided a more accurate version of that back-of-the-hand method in the form of special strips with heat-sensitive symbols. You place the fever-testing strip on the child's forehead and color-coded symbols will rapidly appear. One, for example, produces a brown N if the temperature is within a normal range; a brownish-blue NF if it is slightly above normal and a blue F for definite fever. The more sophisticated testers may show you how to interpret changing color for that F which may, for example, get less blue and more green as it gets hotter.

Testers may be useful for finding out whether a child is feverish at all (when you are making one of those difficult decisions, for instance) and for babies and toddlers who cannot be trusted with a clinical thermometer in their mouths (*see below*). But they are not as reliable as thermometers and most kinds cannot tell you the exact height of a fever; once you have discovered that an older child is feverish you may want to switch to a real thermometer.

Clinical   Consist of a glass rod with a mercury-filled bulb at one end. When this
thermometers mercury-filled bulb heats up, a thin thread of mercury is forced up the tube, which is marked off in degrees of temperature. The mercury will

stop at the level of the child's body temperature and it will stay there, even when the thermometer cools down again. The mercury will only go back down towards the bulb (so that you can start again) if it is shaken, with a flick of the wrist.

You can record a child's temperature by putting that mercury bulb anywhere you can seal the child's skin or mucous membrane around it, excluding outside air as much as possible.

The usual technique with older children and adults is to put the bulb end of the thermometer under the tongue and leave it there with the mouth closed for a whole minute or more.

Babies and toddlers obviously cannot be trusted with a breakable glass rod containing poisonous mercury in their mouths. Their temperatures used to be taken by inserting the lubricated thermometer an inch or so up the rectum (back passage) and holding it there for two minutes. Although this is still usual in many hospitals and some homes, it is seldom either necessary or desirable. A wriggling baby may get delicate membranes bruised by the thermometer. A toddler will probably be highly affronted by the procedure. Unless your doctor tells you to use this method (perhaps because he wants accurate records of a fluctuating fever), don't.

Use a fever-tester to establish that a fever is present. If the illness requires you to keep an eye on the height of the fever, you can then use a clinical thermometer under the child's arm or in her groin. Extend the arm or leg fully; put the bulb in the center, where the skin folds will come, and then fold the arm or leg across the chest or abdomen so that the bulb is completely covered but you can still hold on to the other end. By this method, the mercury may take a full two minutes to reach its full height so you will have to keep the child still.

● When reporting to a doctor, tell him where you put that thermometer. Rectal temperature will be a couple of points higher than oral, which will be higher than armpit or groin.

Reading the thermometer

You can take your time over reading it because the mercury will not slip back down the tube until it is shaken down.

Hold the thermometer at either end. You will see that it is marked off, rather like a ruler, with big dashes for whole degrees and smaller dashes for points of a degree. The marks may be Fahrenheit, Centigrade or both.

Fahrenheit markings will probably start at 94° towards the bulb end and stop at about 108° at the other end. There will be an arrow or indicator at either 98.4° or 98.6° and this is your guide to "normal." The matching Centigrade markings will be about 35° and 42° with that normal indicator at 37°.

If you turn the thermometer slowly between your fingers so that the numbers face you, a thick line of mercury will appear. Look at the end of that line furthest away from the bulb. The number that its end is opposite is your child's temperature. If it is in between two numbered whole-degree markings, you will have to count the smaller markings. In Fahrenheit, tenths of a degree are marked only in pairs, so one marking above 101°F will mean that her temperature is 101.2°F. In Centigrade, the points of a degree are marked individually so the equivalent would be about 38.5°C.

As a *very* rough rule of thumb you might want to disregard anything below 99°F or 37.2°C and regard as fever anything at or over 100°F or 37.8°C. In between is suspicious/dubious.

Looking after the thermometer

Shaking it down for reuse is an acquired skill. Hold it between thumb and finger by the non-bulb end and then flick your wrist. Practice over a bed. You will probably drop it a few times before you acquire the technique.

● Always check that the thermometer is reading well under normal before you use it. If you do not, it may not tell you what your child's temperature is now but what it was last time you measured it. The point is that the mercury cannot go *down* (without being shaken down) but only up. If it is reading 103°F (39.5°C) (from last month) when your child's present temperature is only 100°F (37.8°C), it will mislead you.

Clinical thermometers are extremely carefully tested and you can assume that they are accurate. They are easily broken, however, by being dropped on a hard surface or knocked against something. If the bulb of a thermometer is brought into contact with something *much* hotter than a human body ever could be (boiling water, for example), the column of mercury will shoot right to the top of the tube and may jam there so that it cannot be shaken down.

Keep it in its protective case where children cannot get at it and never leave it, uncased, on a bedside table or anywhere where it could get knocked off or otherwise smashed.

Stand it, bulb-end downwards, in a mild disinfectant if you are using it for more than one patient at the same time. While "germs" will not readily survive on clean glass, you could transfer virus-laden saliva directly from a child with measles to another with a cold.

Coping with fever

A lot of children run major fevers for minor reasons like the beginning of an ordinary cold. On the whole, the younger the child the higher her temperature may go without it indicating anything serious. While this is by no means an invariable rule, it is *likely* that a twelve-year-old with a temperature of 102°F (38.8°C) is sicker than her three-year-old brother whose temperature is the same.

While many children can run quite high temperatures without seeming especially affected by them, many have a sort of personal "critical level" above which the fever itself, whatever its cause, seems to make them very unwell. Unless your children are lucky enough to avoid the usual run of infections, you will learn each one's "critical level" and you may watch it change, too, as he or she gets older. It is always worthwhile to try to spot *high* fever early, and work to keep it under that critical level, because while fever itself will not harm your child, the side effects of fever which has gone "too high" are both unpleasant and alarming (*see below*).

As a very rough rule of thumb, you might expect that 103°F (39.5°C) was likely to be "too high" for a baby or toddler; that 102.4°F (39°C) might be "too high" for a pre-school child and 102°F (38.8°C) "too high" for a young schoolchild. Older children and adolescents are less liable to the side effects of high fever but will often feel very unwell indeed with temperatures of 101°F (38.3°C) or above.

If you know that a child is unwell and use a thermometer sensibly, you can usually keep the fever to reasonable levels by adapting the heroic measures suggested for reducing fever (*see below*). But quite often you will have no advance warning. Either the child's temperature will go up very rapidly, or she will return home from school, or wake up in the morning, already very feverish. A very sudden and sharp rise, such that your toddler is perfectly well at breakfast-time but has a temperature of 103°F and a bit (39.5°+C) by mid-morning, for example, is the most likely to provoke side effects. These are all due to the effect of the fever on the child's nervous system; the more sudden the rise the less chance her body has to adapt.

Side effects of high fever

High fever, especially one which is rising very rapidly, naturally affects a child's brain and central nervous system as well as the rest of her body. The most extreme effect is the kind of "fit" known as a febrile (feverish) convulsion. Only about three per cent of children are liable to those, and only between the ages of about one and three years, so you will find them dealt with separately (*see* **Convulsions, Seizures and "Fits"**). Other "nervous system effects" are common:

Shivering and trembling in high fever

Healthy bodies shiver in order to warm themselves when they are cold, but a quickly rising fever upsets the body's smooth regulation of its own temperature mechanisms. A feverish child may shiver although she *is* very hot, and may be very confused as to whether she *feels* hot or cold. A "shivery feeling" is often the first symptom of fever which a verbal child will report. Your first clues to fever in a younger child may be that she cuddles by the heater in a room which to you feels comfortably warm, or fights to rid herself of a sweater in a room which feels cool.

Once a feverish child is resting and her body is adapting, the hot-and-cold feelings usually settle down, but she may go on being definitely trembly until the fever drops a little. If you pull back the bedding you can see little movements of the thigh muscles, for example.

Nausea and vomiting in high fever

Some of the illnesses which cause fever also cause gastric upset, but fever which has nothing to do with gastric infection may make your child feel sick. Nausea can make it difficult to persuade her to drink enough fluids. For a child who is old enough, cracked ice or ice cubes to suck often serve the double purpose of helping the nausea and providing water.

Of course any child who is nauseated may vomit, but if fever upsets the vomiting center in the brain, your child may suddenly vomit without having any warning of nausea first.

Sudden vomiting is always something to watch out for in a very young child who is feverish because of the risk of her breathing vomit into her lungs. It is also a risk in much older children if their level of consciousness is affected by the fever (*see below*).

General
hypersensitivity
in high fever

The child's whole nervous system may overreact to high fever, so that her skin is hypersensitive to touch, she covers her ears at loud noises and cannot bear to be moved around. A baby may cry when you pick her up and try to cuddle her; an older child may shrink as if in pain when you try to sponge her face or brush her hair. Apart from working to get the fever down to her tolerance level, leave her as much in peace as you can. It is better just to stay quietly with her than to fuss with her pillows or insist on reading to her if she can doze.

Effects of
high fever on
consciousness

Sometimes a child with very high fever seems "off her head" or delirious. She may talk, sometimes loudly and excitedly, but although she looks awake, what she says makes no sense and, after a few attempts to answer, as in an ordinary conversation, you realize that she is not really talking to you; indeed that she is not really "with you" at all. Nursing a delirious child is rather like coping with a night terror (*see* **Sleep**/Night terrors).

A delirious child's brain is already receiving too much (inappropriate) stimulation. Apart from necessary disturbances, like your efforts to reduce the fever or a visit to the doctor, it is best if she is not stimulated any more. If she is talking in her sleep, don't try to wake her; try to soothe her into more peaceful sleep instead. If she suddenly talks irrationally in the middle of a conversation, don't ask her what on earth she means, or even let her see you looking taken aback; just pass it off and try to help her doze off. If a baby who does not yet talk suddenly detaches herself and gazes off into space, don't work to get her attention back; just let her rest quietly with you.

● Most people find nursing a delirious or otherwise irrational child decidedly "spooky". But children in this state tend to be sensitive to other people's feelings so that if you are frightened, or upset they are frightened too. Try not to face this kind of nursing alone. An adult friend or partner, to share the watches with you, can go a long way to helping you hang onto your sane adult self.

● Although children who are unwell are no longer automatically put to bed until they are better, a child with high fever, especially fever which is causing this kind of side effect, is both physically safer and better protected from unwanted extra stimulation if she is in bed. That "bed" can, of course, be her carriage or "nest" near to you, but until the fever is controlled she will be better off away from the hurly-burly of other children, television, etc.

● Nobody, not even the most sensible adolescent, should be left alone while fever is affecting consciousness. Until she is fully rational again she needs somebody there.

Reducing and controlling fever

When a body begins to get too warm, blood vessels near to the surface of the skin dilate so that they can carry as much blood as possible. This means that as the total volume of blood circulates around the body, an unusually large part of it is exposed to the cooler conditions of the body's surface. You can see this happening. As your child plays vigorously, her face will become flushed and the veins which are visible (on the insides of her wrists, for example) stand out. As body heat builds up, the sweat glands of the skin produce a thin film of moisture which cools by evaporation. If your hot and sweating child stops playing and stands around, she will rapidly cool off. If there is a breeze blowing and she stands around without a sweater, the cooling effect of rapid evaporation from her skin will be so marked that she will soon feel chilly.

Whether you are trying to reduce a fever which is "too high" or trying to control one so that it does not rise to your child's own limit of tolerance, the trick is to help her body to carry out its own cooling efficiently and to be ready with artificial aids should it fail to do so.

Whenever a child is feverish

Don't insulate her with warm pajamas and heavy bedding. The extra blood circulating through those dilated blood vessels under her skin is meant to carry coolness back into the general blood supply. If the skin surface is being kept as warm as her internal organs, it cannot do so. Her lightest nightgown, and the minimum of bedclothes under which she can feel comfortable, will give her body a better chance.

Don't keep room air too warm or too still. A child in bed always gives off heat so that the air inside the bed is warmer than the air around it. A feverish child gives off extra heat which her skin is trying to shed. As well as avoiding trapping too much heat *in* the bed, you need to ensure that, as she moves around, there is plenty of cooler air into which her fever heat can be dispersed. Try to get the temperature of the room as a whole down to around 65–68°F and to keep the air circulating. If your windows can be opened, open them at the top so that warm air (which always rises) goes out, bringing cooler air in. If your windows are sealed, try keeping the door open and using the "cold" setting of a blower-heater to keep the air moving.

Don't leave her snug and still for long at a time. If she snuggles down with even that lightweight bedding pulled well around her and her face half-buried in the pillow, for a good long nap, she will have accumulated a lot of super-warmed air by the time she awakens. Sitting up while you turn those pillows cool side up and shake out the bedclothes will help her to cool down again.

● Watch out for duvets or continental quilts. Their whole point is that they are excellent insulators which swathe the child, leaving no drafty gaps. The quilt which keeps your child snug on a winter's night may keep her far too snug when she has a fever. If she will not accept a sheet or light blanket instead, try at least to persuade her to have the quilt over her rather than rolled all around her. . . .

Make sure she drinks plenty: her body needs surplus fluid for efficient sweating/cooling as well as to prevent general dehydration.

When a child's fever is "too high"

It may not be enough just to give her body easy circumstances in which to keep itself cool; you may have to do the cooling for it. But it is still better to cool the child by the body's own methods than by the cruel and ineffective measures which used to be suggested. Putting her in a cold bath, for example, will not only distress, even shock her, it will also cause all those superficial blood vessels to close up *so as to preserve body heat*. Unless you are actually instructed to do this, by a doctor, don't. Instead:

Provide an artificial sweat layer by sponging the child with water which feels just warm to your own hand. It will still feel cool to her overheated skin but, because it is warm, those blood vessels will stay dilated and, as it evaporates, the blood they carry will cool. Concentrate your sponging on areas where you can actually see a lot of blood vessels, such as her face and neck, the insides of her wrists and arms and, unless it disturbs her too much, her groin and inner thighs.

Leave her skin wet. If you dry the moisture away there will be less evaporation to cool her.

Speed up the rate of evaporation by providing an "artificial breeze." If you have an electric fan, place it so that a stream of air passes over her. Failing that, place a fan-heater near to the bed with the setting on "cold." Even if the air current does not play directly on her skin, it will rapidly remove the warm air from around her damp body. Failing any electric gadgetry, fan her for a few minutes with a magazine or book. By the time her skin is dry, her fever should have dropped by at least half a degree.

● A very feverish child may find even this, comparatively gentle, cooling very unpleasant and may feel cold and shivery when you have finished. Don't make the mistake of providing a hot water bottle and three extra blankets or all your work may be undone.

If your child's illness is forcing her fever up against everything you can do to help her body cool itself, she may need the further help of fever-reducing medicines.

Consider aspirin or its equivalent. If you are already consulting a doctor about this illness, ask him what he recommends. If not, give the dose of soluble aspirin which is appropriate to the child's weight, along with the biggest drink you can persuade her to take. She could have this dose again, four hours later, but if her fever continues to run so high that you feel you must go on with regular doses for more than a day, a doctor should be consulted.

Don't give aspirin to a baby under six months without a doctor's advice.

Don't give aspirin to anyone with stomach pains associated with fever.

Don't persist in trying to give it if it makes her vomit; each time she vomits she is likely to lose more fluid than there was in that medicine glass, and water matters more than aspirin to her feverish body.

Getting back to normal

After most illnesses, most basically healthy children snap rapidly back to normal as soon as fever and other symptoms subside. Unless your doctor advises you otherwise, there is no need to impose any of the old rules like "twenty-four hours in bed after the fever drops" or "one full day quietly at home for every day of illness."

Illnesses do, of course, use energy and may have depleted bodily reserves, but bodies are remarkably good at meeting their own needs so the convalescent child who needs extra food or rest will probably simply eat and sleep more than usual. You can usually assume that a child who has no fever or other symptoms, is eating well, seems full of energy and enthusiasm again and wants to get on with life, is ready to do so. Sometimes, though, you may have more complicated decisions to make in convalescence:

Symptoms which outstay illness

Some illnesses recede leaving symptoms which drag on. Whooping cough, for example, may leave a cough which lasts for weeks after the child is better. Illnesses which have been treated with antibiotics sometimes leave diarrhea to remind you that even the most useful drugs can have side effects. Upper respiratory infections can leave congestion, nasal discharge and/or a cough which sounds like active illness but is not. The point is usually that the body has dealt with the original infection but the affected body parts have not yet returned to their pre-illness state. Sometimes parents keep such a child at home because they are afraid of other people thinking them irresponsible if the child returns to public life. Others reject public opinion and return her to normal, only to regret it later because she picks up a secondary infection and is ill all over again.

A happy medium probably involves having a final check made by the doctor and, if he is happy for her to be out and about, keeping an eye on her activities for a while both to try to avoid situations in which further infection is especially likely and to spot it early should it occur.

Depression after illness

Some illnesses, perhaps especially flu (*see* **Influenza**), are notorious for leaving their victims depressed. A child who is uncharacteristically irritable and/or liable to sudden tears, probably is not ready for the hurly-burly of ordinary daily life, but will feel better sooner if she can be busy and interested rather than sitting drearily around thinking how awful she feels. That old-fashioned remedy "a vacation" often works wonders, even if it only consists of a weekend. Failing that, a couple of days of traditional "convalescence," complete with tempting food and treats geared to her stage of recovery, usually helps. An older child or adolescent, puzzled and worried by her own feelings, is certainly entitled to reassurance that they are a hangover from the illness. Often knowing that there is a physical reason for misery is cheering in itself (*see* **Depression**).

Difficulty in giving up the "sick role"

Even when the illness itself was not especially depressing, it can be difficult for a child to make the switch from her ill self to her normal self, especially if being ill has brought her a lot of gratification and her everyday life is less than perfect. A small baby, for example, may have lost the recent patterning of her eating and sleeping during even a brief illness; she may go on being "demanding" and unpredictable for a while. A pre-school child may have enjoyed a few days of your (almost) undivided attention and find herself reluctant to return to her sitter or kindergarten. A schoolchild may be sure that she has lost her best friend to a rival, while an adolescent may be worried about catching up on missed assignments or training sessions. Even without special worries of this kind, anyone whose workday routine has been broken by illness, and its attendant freedom from responsibility, may feel that "getting going again" is a big effort.

If your child seems to feel like this—so that her face falls when the doctor says, "You're better, young lady; back to normal by Monday"—try to re-introduce the more enjoyable aspects of everyday life *first* so that by the time she has to face the less desirable bits she can remember the shape and point of it all. If your small child spends her mornings with a sitter but usually plays with her friend from next door in the afternoon, make sure the two of them get together the day *before* you go back to work. If your schoolchild has been missing her favorite "late-night" television program because of her illness, make sure you hand back that privilege of health as soon as you are calling her fit for school. If a full day plus all her after-school activities is going to be too much for her for a while, don't assume that she should complete the school day but miss her fun. A few days of morning school, an afternoon nap and then those activities may make a transition back to normal life which is both fairer and smoother. Many adolescents who say that they are worrying about what they have missed at school are actually missing the current gossip more than the work assignments. A few chats on the telephone will help. Having friends to visit the house at the end of the illness may then help them to change easily back into their normal independent gear.

Obesity *see* **Eating**/Eating problems: Obesity: The problem of eating too much; **Growth**.
One-parent families *see* **Divorce, Separation and One-parent Families**.
Operations *see* **Hospital**/Surgery.
"Organically grown" and "natural" foods *see* **Eating**/Common sense about family eating.
Overweight *see* **Eating**/Eating problems: Obesity: The problem of eating too much; **Growth**.
Pacifiers *see* **Habits**/Comfort habits and objects. *See also* **Teeth**/Looking after teeth.

Pain and Pain Control *see also* **Abdominal Pain; Accidents**/Shock; **Cramp; Headaches; Hospital**/Procedures: Sedation and anesthesia; **Teeth**/Some dental emergencies

Although pain is an experience which is common to every human being and almost universally detested, it is a complicated phenomenon which is still not fully understood by scientists and is seriously misunderstood by many other people. If you know at least a little about pain and its functions, you will be both better able to cope with a vast variety of childhood mishaps and behaviors, and better able to teach those children to understand and cope with their own pains and to use them properly in learning to look after themselves.

The ability to perceive pain is vitally important, so important that an individual who had no pain sensitivity would be unlikely to survive. The most primitive, and arguably the most vital, pain mechanism is the "reflex arc" which makes a child snatch his hand back from the hot stove even before he is aware of being burned. His hand gets dangerously close to the heat and pain receptors in the skin dispatch impulses along special nerve fibers. While most of these will travel to the brain (*see below*) some take a shortcut through the spinal cord and stimulate reflex muscular withdrawal of the threatened hand or finger. The speed of the reflex arc prevents or minimizes damage while the automatic muscular response ensures that the correct avoiding action is taken. A newborn baby might not "know how" to escape the needle which jabs his heel for a blood sample; the reflex arc does it for him. The drunken or unconscious individual might be too confused to respond appropriately to pain, but the reflex arc will continue to function, at least until he is deeply in coma.

The importance of those pain receptors in the skin in protecting us from injury can most clearly be seen when they are lacking. When a dentist gives a local anesthetic in the mouth, for example, he warns the patient not to drink hot liquids and to be careful not to bite the numbed parts of his mouth. But despite the warning and despite the short period of insensitivity, some minor damage is very usual. The anesthetic wears off and the patient finds that he has made a sore patch on the inside of his cheek while chewing the end of that pencil. . . . Some accidental injuries leave areas of insensitive skin and, however aware of the risk the patient may be, and however hard he tries *consciously* to protect that area from damage, he is usually unable to do so. The "dead" area on a hand may be repeatedly burned during cooking, ironing, boiler-stoking or smoking; a dead area on the face may mean that wet-shaving is impossible.

Underneath the skin, almost every area of the body is liberally supplied with special nerve fibers whose sole function is to carry to the brain impulses which that brain may bring into consciousness as pain. It is important to understand that when pain is felt, it is not the wound itself nor yet the nerves, which hurt. It is the brain which interprets the impulses it is receiving and, so to speak, tells you "that hurts." Sometimes you can prove this for yourself. If you bang your head on a low beam or stub your toe on something, there is often a noticeable delay between the damage and the onset of pain. You may have time to collapse on the floor and rub your head before it starts to hurt. You are not waiting for the knock—that has already happened—nor for the nerve fibers to send their impulses—they start to react almost instantaneously—you are waiting for your brain to sum up the whole incident as painful.

This idea that pain is not a thing-in-itself nor an integral part of injury/disorder but an interpretation by the brain, is an important one. If you accept it, you will not subscribe to the many misconceptions about pain which make sufferers miserable. When no obvious physical cause can be found for a child's pain, for example, many people say scoffingly that it is "all in the mind." But of course the pain is in his mind; *all pain is in the mind* because only the mind (brain) can give the individual a pain message. Pain which is due to a demonstrable physical cause—to appendicitis or a fractured bone, for example—is therefore no different from the pain of a tension headache or the recurrent stomachache of a child who is anxious about school (*see* **Abdominal Pain**/Recurrent abdominal pain). If he feels pain, then that pain is real. It is sometimes important to explain to a sufferer that there *is* no physical cause for his pain, but he must never be allowed to think that this message means that he is thought to be lying about being in pain, to be "making it all up." Similarly, when someone tells you that an experience you would assume to be painful does *not* hurt, that person too will usually be telling the truth. Most women experience pain in childbirth, for example, but some women, sharing the physical experience, nevertheless do not share the pain sensations. Their brains interpret similar nerve impulses differently.

Although pain is a vitally important warning system it is by no means an infallible one. The intensity of pain, for example, is not always appropriate to the degree of trouble being experienced by the body; an unimportant bang on the head may be as painful as a bang which has actually damaged the skull (*see* **Accidents**/Head injuries), while trivial and temporary distension of the bowel with gas can be as painful as a serious abdominal condition. Some life-threatening conditions are not painful at all, or at least not until the disease process is very far advanced; this is why many forms of cancer, for example, go undetected for so long. In some illnesses pain continues to be perceived long after the disease process seems clinically over (*see* **Chickenpox and Shingles**, for example) while in other conditions, such as some kinds of low back pain, pain is not felt during ill-advised activity (when it might serve the useful purpose of restraining the individual) but hours afterwards. Sometimes, too, the site at which pain is felt is misleading because the brain fails to interpret the source of its signals correctly. If you sharply hit the inner side of your elbow, for example, you will probably feel acute pain in your little finger. This is because all your brain "knows" is that it has received impulses that it perceives as painful from somewhere on the ulnar nerve, which runs from that little finger up the inner arm and then via the spinal cord to the brain. Insults to that pathway are always perceived as pain in the finger where it begins. Furthermore, your brain would continue to tell you that it was your little finger which was hurt, rather than your elbow, even if that little finger had been amputated. (This phenomenon is called "phantom pain.") Some pathways from internal organs converge in the spinal cord. Since many of these organs begin their development in one part of the embryo and later migrate to another part, trailing their original nerves with them, the confusion of "referred pain" is very common. The diaphragm, for example, which separates the heart and lungs from the liver and the stomach, first develops in the same part of the embryo as the shoulders. When the diaphragm is inflamed during pleurisy (*see* **Chest Infections**) or liver disease (*see* **Jaundice**) pain tends to be felt in the shoulder and may easily be mistaken for muscular pain.

Clearly, then, while our brains dictate the presence or absence of pain, by telling us or not telling us "that hurts," we have to interpret for ourselves the significance of perceived pain as well as deciding what, if anything, we should do about it. In the notes which follow it will be clear that "doing something about pain" is still something which medicine finds difficult. Much research is in progress and many people believe that a breakthrough may come when we understand more of the body's own means of pain control. It has been found, for example, that our brains produce chemicals called endorphins which can be described as nature's own opiate-type painkillers. They appear to be produced and circulated, at a low level, more or less all the time and may be responsible for our *not* receiving pain messages from our brains more often than we do. The level of these chemicals in the body is raised in circumstances which are only now being described; the known circumstances do, however, make sense of some previously recognized but unexplained phenomena. It is known, for example, that when somebody has chronic pain that is not extremely intense, that pain often ceases to be felt if *another* painful stimulus is applied. We all act on this idea of "counter-irritants" in our daily lives when we bang our hands on the table to distract ourselves from that stubbed toe. . . . The explanation may lie in the fact that the second painful stimulus raises the level of circulating endorphins and thus provides a raised dose of "natural painkiller" to cope with the original pain. It may even be that this partly explains the mechanism by which acupuncture can sometimes help with chronic pain. Endorphin production has also been found to increase when individuals have been given dummy pain-killers (placebos) and therefore have reason to *believe* that their pain will lessen. It may be that the much discussed "placebo effect" (often treated as a phenomenon which suggests that the pain was not "real" in the first place) results from real biochemical pain relief, but relief provided by the body for itself rather than by active chemicals in tablets.

It is to be hoped that research of this kind will produce a much clearer understanding of both pain and its relief over the next few generations, but in the meantime we can help our children to make the most of the knowledge and relief which is available.

Coping with pain

Every child will experience pain and every parent has to draw a careful line between taking it too seriously and not taking it seriously enough. Pain sensations are not only unpleasant, they are also frightening. Fear and anxiety increase sensitivity to pain, probably by making the brain likely to interpret more of its received signals as pain than it would do otherwise. If a child hurts himself and at once becomes the focus for anxious adult attention, he is bound to fear for himself and thus increase his own distress. On the other hand, pain *is* a protective signal. If that same child's pain is ignored, he is actually being prevented from learning to take due notice of his own body's signals. If his pain is not only ignored but *denied* ("it doesn't really hurt, don't make such a fuss") he may become very confused about what it is that he is actually feeling. The fine line therefore is the one which keeps him interested and in touch with his body, but confident in it and unafraid of its phenomena.

Attitudes to a child's pain   The secret seems to lie in showing your child, from the beginning of his life, that the first thing which matters is the *cause* of his pain. It is a signal from his brain about his body, to himself—a self for which you stand in when he is very young. If the signal is correctly interpreted the pain can be appropriately dealt with.

When the cause of the pain is obvious and trivial he needs acknowledgment of the unpleasant sensation ("bad luck, that is a nasty scrape") plus confident reassurance that the *damage* is not in any way serious and that the *pain will soon stop.* You can use this set of messages to fit innumerable circumstances and over all age groups. It applies, for example, to routine injections in the immunization program as well as to dressing boils or removing splinters.

When the cause of the pain is not obvious he needs to see both that you are interested in looking for the meaning of the signal and that failure to find a cause does not lead you to dismiss his discomfort. If he is complaining of pain in a watering eye, you are interested in looking for a foreign body; if it is his ankle which is hurting, you are interested to see if there is swelling or discoloration which might suggest a sprain (*see* **Accidents**). But if you can find nothing, you are still interested in helping him to feel better (*see below* Pain control).

When the cause of pain is discovered, and suggests that the pain will continue, he needs you to separate for him dislike of the sensation from fear of bodily damage. If his tummyache is diagnosed as part of tonsillitis (with inflamed glands around the abdomen) you cannot assure him that now you know the cause you also have a cure. But you can explain that cause, and explain that as the infection recedes so will the pain, and you can emphasize that it will not get worse and does not suggest anything dangerous "happening inside him." If a girl has pre-menstrual pain (*see* **Adolescence**/Menstruation) you cannot promise that it will not recur, but you can explain the mechanism and assure her that discomfort does not suggest that her newly grown-up self works less than perfectly.

When pain has no discoverable cause, you can teach him that once its signals have been attended to and found unanswerable, it is legitimate to concentrate on turning them off. This is probably the best approach to take to pains like headaches or recurrent stomachaches, for example. That headache does not mean anything sinister; it will go of its own accord eventually, but may be hastened on its way.

Extreme pain

Very acute pain, even when the cause is trivial or probably psychogenic rather than physical, is *a personal emergency*. Not only does the sensation crowd out all competing sensations, it also leads the body to declare crisis, stimulating other physical reactions such as sweating, racing pulse, nausea, pallor and feelings of faintness. A child with this sort of pain needs medical attention because the pain in itself is liable to lead to shock (*see* **Accidents**/Shock). He also needs psychological attention in the sense of needing assurance that nobody expects him to put up with *that*. Parents are likely to be quick to respond to this level of pain because it is usually associated either with an obvious accident or with an acute worsening of a condition (such as appendicitis) which was already being watched. Don't be caught out by occasional causes though. A child who is subject to migraine, and has medication for it, may have a particularly painful attack and require an injected painkiller (*see* **Migraine**). A child with a small burn or scald (which you long to minimize because nobody wants to admit that an avoidable accident was serious) may be suffering "too much" even if the injury is not dangerous.

Long-continued pain

Very few children are subject to the chronic pain which bedevils so many adults as age makes us liable to degenerative disorders of joints and so forth. There are a few conditions, though, in which pain which is not extreme will nevertheless continue over a long enough period to require special handling. Most such children will be in the hospital, but if you have such a child at home, whether with an inflamed and fluid-filled knee which takes several days to settle, or with a pleurisy which does not respond to the first antibiotic, the following points may be useful.

Long-continued pain tends to "take over" the personality so that although its intensity does not increase (and may even be diminishing) its duration gradually wears down the patient's ability to cope with it. Distress about pain–pain–more distress about pain–more pain becomes a vicious circle.

The pain is easy to *interrupt* even if it cannot be banished; the more it is interrupted the better. Almost everything (*see below* Pain control) will help for a little while, though no relief will last. The trick is to keep on interrupting that vicious cycle of pain-distress with different weapons. If you can do this, the pain will at least be confined to its base level and will never soar to panic heights.

Since pain is the brain's interpretation of nerve impulses, anything which makes the brain more likely to perceive pain will make that pain worse. Long-continuing pain will almost always be felt more in the solitude of 3 a.m. than the social caring of 3 p.m. It will be worse when the child is tired, bored, uncomfortable in other ways. It will also be worse when—perhaps in an entirely praiseworthy attempt to keep up normal standards of behavior—you are cross with him.

Pain control   Most people assume that "pain control" will mean "painkillers"—that our principal weapons against pain come from the medicine cabinet. In fact our principal weapons are in the kinds of attitudes laid out above. Whatever the victim's age and whatever the cause of his pain, each of the following will almost certainly make it worse, by encouraging his brain to force the interpretation "pain" into his consciousness.

Fear, especially fear about what has happened to him already (perhaps the accident that caused the pain and which he feels might have "broken" him), fear about what is going to happen to him (perhaps fear of the doctor or of the hospital to which he is being taken) and fear of the pain itself. Fear of the pain takes many different forms. It may be fear that it will go on forever, fear that it will get worse and worse, or fear that he will "lose control."

Other people's anxiety which feeds fear. *Don't* scream for help unless his life is actually in danger. Go and ask for it instead.

Ignorance of what *has* happened and *will* happen. In all but the youngest child in pain, ignorance also feeds fear and fantasy fears, too. An adolescent with severe abdominal pain is far better off knowing that the doctor thinks he does have appendicitis than left behind closed doors while adults mutter and he secretly imagines that his insides are bursting open.

Other people's ignorance. A person in pain needs to feel that somebody can help. Be careful about announcements like "You're a real mystery. . . ." If a diagnosis is not possible (whether he is to be rushed to the hospital for tests or left at home because "it will pass") he needs to feel that the ignorance is coupled with experience which makes it safe: "I can't tell you why your legs hurt so much, but we do know that lots of children your age get this sort of pain from time to time and that it always passes off in an hour or two. . . ."

Other people's disbelief. When a child suffers from pain whose cause is trivial, unknown and/or probably psychogenic, having it implied that he is "making it up," "swinging the lead," "playing for sympathy" or "just trying to get out of school" will almost always increase the actual pain he feels as well as his general unhappiness. It is almost as if his brain must force into his consciousness additional evidence that he is not cheating. In this sense the sufferers whose regular Monday-morning tummyaches bring pallor and vomiting with them (*see* **Abdominal Pain**/Recurrent abdominal pain) are the lucky ones because however scornfully the illness is labelled "neurotic," it clearly exists.

In most instances you will be able to do better than just avoiding making the child's pain worse: the following will actually make him feel it less.

Distraction. If people have nothing to think about but their pain, they are more conscious of that pain than they are when other stimuli are competing for conscious attention. This phenomenon is often sadly misunderstood. People will say "He's laying it on a bit thick; when I try to get on with anything else he just lies there and moans, but he cheers up the minute I pay attention to him." The implication is that he does not *have* to moan when alone if he need not moan when in company. The truth is that he does not *feel like moaning* when distraction dilutes his pain perception, but that the pain overwhelms him when there is nothing else to occupy his mind.

Of course you cannot play with a child in extreme pain with associated shock. But even he will actually suffer less if he can safely be kept in verbal or hand-holding contact with someone and be kept aware of the real world outside the nightmare of his pain. Of course a child with a bad headache may be more comfortable lying down in a quiet room, but the hope is that either the pain will wear off or he will fall asleep. If neither is the case, he too will eventually feel less pain if he is read to or listens to a play on the radio. For any child in pain, appropriate occupation matters (*see* **Nursing**/Passing the time).

Changes of position and other physical stimuli. Some of the measures we take for the comfort of people in pain are really types of distraction and ways of interrupting the pain-distress about the pain cycle (*see above*). They are nevertheless powerful weapons in your hands. There may be no single position in which your child's newly sprained ankle or newly set fracture ceases to hurt, but each new position will seem better for the moment. Whatever position (within reason) it is in, the pain he perceives will gradually increase until he changes it, and will then gradually rise again until it is again changed. Fussing with supporting pillows, changes from chair to bed and back again, cold compresses, hot water bottles and so forth are therefore not *only* ways of showing him your loving care, but also of making him hurt less overall, and hurt acutely for shorter periods.

● This is why painful injuries which are treated by immobilizing the child, especially if he must also be isolated, tend to be the most traumatic of all. A child with spinal damage, for example, newly entrapped in traction, will require all your support and a really imaginative use of those stimuli you are free to change: skin sensations from cold sponging, different things to look at and so forth. The newly burned child, with splinted limbs and in an isolation or controlled humidity room, is exposed to the full and uninterrupted force of his own pain perception. He will need more painkillers than in any other circumstances.

Non-chemical painkillers

Not all painkillers are drugs. You can sometimes kill pain, whose cause you know, just by removing that cause. Children should learn this kind of painkilling technique from early on. If they do, they will be taking an intelligent interest in their own bodies, they will be able to take sensible care of themselves at a relatively early age and they will be useful to others. Obvious examples are:

The pain of a burn which is relieved by cold water. The pain is due to continuing damage by heat under the burned surface; cold water halts it (*see* **Accidents**/Burns and scalds).

The pain of trapped pus which is relieved by releasing the pressure. The pain is due to pressure on the tissues underneath the skin. If the pus can be released the pain will stop (*see* **Infection**/Types of infection: Localized infection).

The pain of "cramp" which is relieved by massage. The pain is due to the waste products of muscular activity which have accumulated in the affected muscle because the amount of blood reaching it was not adequate to remove those wastes and reoxygenate the muscle. Massage hurries the blood supply and dispersal of wastes; the cramp stops (*see* **Cramp**).

The pain of irritation by foreign bodies which is relieved when they are removed. Whether it is dust in the eye or a splinter in the finger, pain will cease when it is gone.

Chemical painkillers for diagnosed conditions

If your child is under medical care, relieving his pain will be part of his treatment, not only for humane reasons but also because pain itself may worsen his general condition (*see above* Extreme pain). Sometimes it seems to anxious parents that hospital staff are reluctant to give effective drugs, or effective doses of drugs, for pain. While, of course, every case is different and you should discuss your child with those who are caring for him, it may help to realize that:

Drugs which have sufficient effect on the brain to reduce awareness of pain also have side effects. Morphine and pethidine, for example, the best-known narcotic pain relievers, tend to cause vomiting (which may be both agonizing and dangerous following abdominal surgery). Morphine causes constipation, which may be similarly unfortunate. Any narcotic drug may depress the cough reflex, or indeed respiration itself, and thus make the patient much less efficient at keeping his chest and upper respiratory tract clear. He may even pay for his pain relief with post-operative pneumonia. Such drugs also tend to make the child sleepy and/or uncooperative. Not only does this make him more difficult to nurse, it may also lead to his feeling more pain and needing more drugs. If a child is half-asleep, non-chemical methods of pain control are far less effective, too (*see above*).

Drugs which seem puny weapons against severe pain because you yourself use them for minor pain, may have specific effects the child needs. Aspirin, for example, is particularly effective against pain stemming from injury to joints, ligaments and so forth and it also has specific effects against inflammation. The aspirin tablets your child is given following that knee operation may actually relieve his pain far better than morphine.

If you know why your child is in pain but he is not under medical care, any use of painkilling drugs will be up to you. Remember that it is through his experiences of having such drugs used *for* him that your child will learn how to use them for himself later (*see also* **Adolescence**/The long road to independence: Self-care).

You may wish to avoid—and to teach him to avoid—the use of any drug under almost any conditions. On the other hand, you may feel that quick and readily available pain relief is a legitimate benefit of modern civilization and that a "pill for everything" is your right. Between these two extremes you may find the following points useful to think about:

Many common pains (headache, muscle strain, menstrual pain) will relieve themselves within a very short period of time. Most headaches of the "tension" variety will "go off" if the victim comes out of the crowd/ stops trying to learn his French homework/rests and relaxes. Most muscle strains of a minor kind respond almost instantaneously to rest, while most menstrual pain will stop when the flow is fully established and, in the meantime, may be relieved either by a short rest lying down *or* by exercise and a hot bath.

This argues that drugs are unnecessary in such situations and that children should be taught to adopt non-chemical means of responding to these everyday pain signals. But the argument has another side.

Pain responds better to analgesic drugs when they are taken before it has become severe or has continued for very long. If you "catch" a headache at the beginning, a single dose of analgesic will probably banish it, while if you wait for several hours until the child is miserable with it, the first dose may be ineffective.

There is a conflict here and it is one which has to be resolved in practical terms of the life demands the child faces. If, for example, the headache starts at lunch-time and he faces a test during afternoon school, with no opportunity to rest or relax, an analgesic is probably sensible. But if he comes home with a headache at the end of the day it may be reasonable to suggest that he do something quiet for a while to give it a chance to wear off. If a girl always has menstrual pain, it is a pity if she comes to associate this regular sign of maturity with pain, but it is also a pity if she associates it with two days a month of four-hourly analgesics. She should, perhaps, be encouraged to wait and see, each time, how bad the pain is going to be, before she takes anything for it. In this way she at least gives herself a chance to experience pain-and-drug-free menstruation when she can.

Acute pain which you know will end when definitive treatment is carried out, is probably best dealt with energetically from the beginning. The two commonest examples are probably toothache (when the child must get through a night before his dental emergency appointment) and earache which a doctor has diagnosed as due to middle-ear infection and for which the child is taking antibiotics which will take a day or so to start being effective. In either case, a night of extreme pain will make the child much sicker than he need have been. Exhausted, he will tolerate that dental treatment less well. Desperate with the pain in his ear, his fever will be more difficult to control and he will not get the rest which could help his body fight the infection.

● Don't let the effectiveness of a dose of analgesic fool you into putting off the definitive treatment. Getting rid of the toothache or earache does not mean that he does not need the dentist or the doctor.

Chemical pain-
relievers for
undiagnosed
conditions

If a child complains of pain which is outside the ordinary run of headaches, and minor aches and pains, and neither you nor he has any idea what may be causing that pain, be very cautious about giving analgesics.

If they kill the pain and he then needs a doctor's attention, they may "mask" the condition so that diagnosis is difficult. This is especially true of babies; they cannot tell the doctor where it was hurting before, and will not give him clues by their behavior if it is not hurting now. It is also surprisingly true of older people. Pain in the chest, for example, seems unforgettable while it is going on, but relieve it and it becomes difficult to remember *exactly* where it was and *exactly* how deep a breath it took to exacerbate it.

Whether or not they kill the pain, just giving the drugs may make you delay in seeking medical advice. A few potentially serious illnesses, such as meningitis, sometimes start with severe headache. If you give the child analgesics, wait four hours, accept that the first dose did not work and give another dose and wait for that to work, you may have delayed most of a day or night before reporting a condition which requires immediate treatment. If your frantic toddler calms down and goes to sleep on a dose of analgesic, he may wake later not just with renewed earache but with a burst eardrum.

Some painful conditions are actually made worse by the very drugs you give to relieve the pain. Aspirin, for example (*see below*), has inflammatory effects on the stomach lining and may even occasionally cause bleeding in the stomach. It may seriously exacerbate many of the disorders that give rise to "stomachache."

You may, then, like to develop a rule of thumb for yourself along some of the following lines:

If pain is so severe that you are seeking medical advice don't give painkillers meanwhile: wait for a diagnosis and doctor's recommendation/prescription.

Don't give painkillers for undiagnosed abdominal pain. If the child does not (yet) need to see a doctor, he does not (yet) need chemical pain relief.

Don't give painkillers to babies with undiagnosed pain. If a baby is in pain he does need a doctor because he cannot give you any of the information which can safely assure you that the matter is trivial.

Don't give painkillers for unusual pain. If your child is subject to headaches or to menstrual pain or has an old ankle injury which "plays up" after heavy exercise, home pain relief, on the assumption that this is the picture-as-before, may be fair enough. But if this is a new or different kind of pain from any with which the child and you are familiar, and it cannot be dealt with by non-chemical means, you need a doctor's diagnosis.

Painkillers
for home use

There are literally thousands of analgesic tablets available without a doctor's prescription. Most of them are slightly varying combinations of a very few drugs. The drug industry makes enormous profits from our readiness to believe that this one will be more effective than that. If you want to give your child only the drugs he actually needs, and to do so as cheaply and simply as possible, be wary of:

Advertising. Using the same headache remedy as that prima ballerina will not make your daughter dance better.

Copy-writing. The fact that a package *says* that these tablets are the most effective remedy for a particular kind of pain does not make it so.

Expensive additives. Many of the additives which make you believe that this product will be more effective than another actually have no effect on the pain you are trying to deal with. If you want the additives for their own sake it is usually far cheaper to provide them separately.

Expensive packaging. Quite apart from the obvious expense of colorful and eye-catching wrappings, some painkillers are promoted on the basis of their convenient-for-your-handbag packs and/or their foil-wrapped safety from exploring children. Remember that small quantities always cost more than large ones, and that if you want to carry a few with you, or give an older child a couple to put in her pocket, you can easily buy a tiny pill-box or bottle (which of course you must label; *see* **Safety**/In the home: Safety with medicines). If you want to keep *any* drug safely away from children, *a foil wrapping will not do.* Drugs need to be locked away.

The actual drugs among which you will probably choose are mentioned below. If you consider their various actions and their various side effects, you will be able to make a sensible choice among them for general use and for any more specific purposes. Buy them in the cheapest available form (which, in the United States, will not be under any brand name but under the generic name for which you can ask your pharmacist).

Before letting yourself be tempted into buying a different—and more expensive—formulation, read the small print which tells you how much of what is in each tablet and compare it with your basic supply.

Aspirin

This is a "Salicylate." The other very common salicylate is called salicylamide. Its effects and side effects are similar so the two can be considered together, but aspirin is generally the more effective of the two. When you are doing your research, you may also find aspirin referred to as acetylsalicylic acid, acid acetylsal or acetylsalicylicum.

Aspirin has three principal useful effects: it relieves mild pain, especially such pains as headache, toothache, painful muscles, ligaments and joints. It is "anti-pyretic" which means that it brings down fever (*see* **Nursing**/Fever) and it is anti-inflammatory, which is why it is often used in rheumatic/arthritic disorders and why it is doubly effective following sprains and so forth.

Used occasionally and in the recommended doses, aspirin is remarkably safe. Accidents do occur; small children do suffer accidental overdosage and people do kill themselves with the drug, but this must be set against its wide availability and against the fact that more people take more aspirin, without ill effects, than any other drug.

Side effects include ringing in the ears as a first sign that mild over-dosage has occurred, irritation of the stomach—sometimes with nausea and vomiting, eventually with bleeding.

Contra-indications include heart disease (aspirin increases the work of the heart); vomiting/diarrhea/dehydration (aspirin has to be excreted by the kidneys, the patient therefore must have plenty of fluids); inability to eat (aspirin is more likely to irritate an empty stomach and therefore should not be given to a patient who will not eat unless he can drink milk or some other "food-drink").

Paracetamol Is a breakdown product of phenacetin—previously a very commonly used pain reliever but now known to be damaging to the kidneys. Do not buy any product containing phenacetin: all its useful properties, without its dangers, are present in paracetamol. You may find it referred to as acetaminophen or panadol.

Paracetamol relieves mild pain to about the same extent as aspirin; it is therefore a suitable alternative for a child who is sensitive to aspirin. It is anti-pyretic. It has no anti-inflammatory properties and is not therefore useful in rheumatic/arthritic conditions and may be less effective than aspirin in sports injuries, strains and sprains.

Side effects are less obvious than with aspirin because paracetamol is less irritating to the stomach. Nevertheless, it is probably slightly less safe than aspirin, if taken frequently or over a long period, because it can contribute to anemia by a direct effect on the red blood cells and it can also cause kidney and/or liver damage.

Codeine Is obtained from opium and is therefore related to morphine. You may see it referred to as methylmorphine.

Codeine is a somewhat more powerful pain reliever than aspirin, although far less powerful than morphine. It is not anti-pyretic nor is it anti-inflammatory. You will often find it combined with aspirin to produce a compound with all aspirin's beneficial effects plus an increase in analgesic power.

Side effects of codeine alone include constipation which, if the drug is taken over a long period, can be severe. It is for its constipating effect that you will find it included in mixtures for the treatment of diarrhea. Although codeine does not suppress the cough reflex to as great an extent as does morphine, it does have this effect. It is for this reason that you will find it included in cough suppressant cough medicines.

Dosages Children under five should always be given pediatric ("junior") aspirin or paracetamol. If this is in liquid form, make sure you measure doses with a pharmacist's 5 ml spoon, not a domestic and variable "teaspoon" (*see* **Nursing**/Medicines). Follow the recommended doses for your child's weight.

Older children may be given adult aspirin or paracetamol in a suitable dosage which, for a six- to ten-year-old, might be one tablet at intervals of not less than four hours, amounting to not more than four doses in twenty-four hours. (If pain continues, consult a doctor.) Once a child is of near-adult weight, he can have adult doses.

- Whatever the age of your child, remember that it is his weight which is relevant to dosage. If yours is a very small six-year-old, he might still be better off with "junior" aspirin. If in doubt, ask your doctor.

Papular urticaria *see* **Allergy**/Urticaria.
Part-time jobs *see* **Adolescence**/The long road to independence; **Working Mothers**. *See also* **Pocket Money**.
Periods *see* **Adolescence**/Menstruation.
Peritonitis *see* **Hospital**/Surgery: Appendectomy.
Pertussis *see* **Whooping Cough**. *See also* **Immunization**/Your family's immunizations.

Pets *see also* **Accidents**/Bites and stings; **Rabies**; **Safety**/In the home; Safety and pets

Many families find themselves saddled with animals which give nobody any pleasure while others keep no creatures but feel a sense of loss as a result. The secret of finding the right "pet policy" for your family is to think realistically. Who in the family wants a pet? What for? Will the type of creature he or she yearns for actually fill the role envisaged? How will its needs fit in with other family commitments? Would a different kind of animal give the same pleasure for less disruption?

While children are very young—certainly while they are under school age—it is foolish to acquire any animal unless you yourselves positively want it. However much you may believe that a "house isn't a home without a pet" or that "children learn responsibility by caring for helpless creatures," *you* are actually the ones who are going to spend money, if not on the animal, then on its housing, food and so forth. And *you* are the ones who are going to do the caring, too. If you will enjoy coping with animals as well as babies, fine. Everybody may benefit. But if you will not, don't give in to your three-year-old's pleas for a rabbit. He may think he wants one and he may mean to look after it himself. But he can neither understand the care that rabbit will need nor the limitations it will have as playmate/toy.

A family pet will probably mean a dog or a cat. Don't acquire a cat because you really want a dog but do not feel you can provide the right environment. Cats are not at all like dogs and are not therefore likely to be very satisfactory as direct replacements. If you can provide decent circumstances and care for a small child you can also provide them for a dog, if you really want to. Do remember, though, that any uncaged animal will restrict the family's freedom to some extent. It is difficult to take a cat out for the day and dogs are not always welcome overnight guests.

Caged pets can usually be taken around to a friend's house for temporary care, but they are not always a suitable mix with small children. Ferrets, for example—exceedingly popular just now in the United States—are often not trustworthy with the very young, while birds, though fun for a child to watch, are too delicate for him to handle.

Children's own pets
School-aged children often genuinely want animals and can certainly learn to take care of them, although the final responsibility will, for a long time, rest with you.

If you are not an animal-loving family, your seven- or eight-year-old probably will not be offered a dog or cat. Rabbits and rodents are cheap to feed and easy to look after but they can be unexpectedly disappointing. Rabbits are misrepresented in children's stories so that new owners often expect a kind of recognition and affection which is not forthcoming. Guinea pigs have some very saddening habits—like fighting each other or eating their young—and they scratch, too. Hamsters are usually so determinedly nocturnal that they will not play, or even eat, when a child is awake. Gerbils and mice are fiendishly difficult to hold onto and do not easily survive being dropped. . . . All these creatures breed and die with a relentless speed which may be educational but may be too much either for you or for the young owner (*see* **Death**).

Temporary pets   If you live in a rural area you can sometimes arrange for a child to take temporary charge of an orphaned lamb or calf. Although there is loss implicit in such an undertaking, it is not the tragic loss of a death (often with associated guilt about lack of care or physical carelessness) but simply loss of a baby creature who is a baby no longer. The loss of the creature as a pet and companion may be more than counterbalanced by the joy of having successfully reared it to a point where it can rejoin others of its kind. If such an opportunity should present itself to your animal-mad child, do consider it carefully. A couple of months of bottle-feeding a calf, being followed everywhere, called to, butted and played with, can give a child more pleasure and education than years of cleaning out rabbit hutches.

Pets for interest   If your child's desire for animals comes from interest in other species, rather than from a yearning to love and be loved by something warm and cuddly, there are all kinds of creatures he can keep. There is real skill and care in the successful hatching of frog spawn. It is a good thing to do, too, as frogs are becoming horribly scarce in many places. Educational suppliers now sell wormeries and anteries. These viewing houses really do prevent the creatures from getting out while enabling a child to feed them and to watch everything they do.

Fish are fun to watch and easy to look after although disease and death can be uncomfortably frequent (*see* **Safety**/Safety and pets).

If you live in a reasonably warm part of the country and have a garden, tortoises are as agreeable as they are undemanding.

Pets to avoid   Obviously a young child should not be allowed to keep dangerous, or potentially dangerous, creatures. But neither should he be encouraged to keep those to whom he is dangerous. Many children rescue a fledgling bird from a cat, or find an injured baby rabbit, and at once long to put it in a cage and keep it. If you let your child do this you are betraying his undoubtedly good intentions. These young creatures will stand a chance of survival only if they are left where their parents can find and retrieve them. Some will actually die of terror (stress) if confined in human hands.

Watching wild   If wild creatures should not be touched or "kept safe," they can certainly
creatures   be watched and some can even be sufficiently "tamed" to give a child enormous pleasure. Bird tables and garden nesting boxes really help

species struggling to survive in urban or suburban surroundings, while once you have spotted a chipmunk in your garden, a nightly snack may turn him into a regular visitor.

Phobias *see* **Anxiety, Fears and Phobias.**
Pica (eating dirt) *see* **Habits.**
"Pink eye" *see* **Eyes and Seeing; Eye Disorders and Blindness**/Eye disorders: Conjunctivitis.
Plastic surgery *see* **Birthmarks; Hospital**/Surgery. *See also* **Adolescence**/Problems with appearance and body image.

Play *see also* **Nursing**/Passing the time

Parents need to take children's play seriously enough but not too seriously. If it is regarded as entirely trivial—a matter of keeping children occupied until they are old enough to do something more useful—the wherewithal for satisfactory play probably will not be provided because nobody will bother. But if play is seen as vitally important—the child's work and the principal medium through which she learns—too much self-conscious attention will probably be paid to her activities, and she will be deprived of the freedom and spontaneity which is the point of her very best play. It is sometimes helpful to remember that:

Play is enjoyment

A child plays because she wants to play. She goes on playing because she is enjoying herself and she stops when the fun runs out.

Play is therefore self-motivated

Although suggestions for particular kinds of play often come from someone else, the drive to play comes from inside the child. If you make her paddle in the sea she is not playing, until or unless she stops doing it to please you and starts doing it to please herself.

Play is self-directed

No child has to be told how to play. She uses the available ideas, materials and facilities to develop her games for herself. If there are rules they are her rules. If you make her play your way, she is not playing until or unless she chooses to make your rules her own, in order to share the activity with you. In middle childhood she will eventually choose to adopt group rules in order to share playground or organized games with others, but this is not at all the same as having rules imposed upon her.

Play and learning

Babies and young children "learn through play." This idea is central to pre-school education in the Western world, an acknowledgment of the fact that if they are offered appropriate circumstances, opportunities and materials, children will use them, without urging or direction, to find out many of the things adults want them to know. But although it is interesting to think about what your child may be discovering or practicing as she plays in various ways, it is important not to let interest tip over into interference. Manipulative play with a construction kit may look more "useful" than dashing around and around the garden, yelling. But it is just as important for the child to discover what her body feels like when cornering fast, or how much yelling the adults who share her space will stand, as it is for her to learn more "intellectual" lessons. "Learning through play" means learning everything about herself, her world and the objects and people in it. Play is the child's work, but what she earns from it is her own rounded growth at her own pace, not solutions to a set of problems which adults set for her. Parents who try to provide opportunities for their child to have fun, in any direction she seems to enjoy, will probably facilitate more learning than those whose eyes are always fixed on her "education."

Unfortunately, our societies place a high premium on recognizable achievement, and the big-business world has not been slow to cash in on parental concern with a vast industry of "educational" toys, books, records, television programs and "early learning schemes." Salesmen know that many parents will more readily spend money on such products than on toys that are "just for fun." If you happen to buy a "mailbox" at just the moment when your child is interested in different colors and shapes *and* enjoying her new ability to drop things accurately from her hand, she may genuinely enjoy it in just the way the manufacturers suggest. But if you buy that same toy at the wrong moment in her development, it may have no play value for her at all. The lack of play value will not matter to the child. She will either ignore the toy or use its packaging or component parts to suit herself. But it will matter if, irritated by her apparent inability to perform a "play task" which the manufacturers maintain is appropriate for her age, you try to make her play with it "properly." And it will matter, too, if buying that toy has made it impossible for you to buy some other play material for which she is waiting. If you provide playthings for fun, your child will educate herself. If you buy toys for education she will not always have fun.

Play, teaching and work

Children have an in-built drive to mature, to grow up and to learn to do the things they see older people doing. From her earliest months your child will be watching and listening to you, copying you, picking up ideas and suggestions from you. She will personalize this kind of learning by incorporating it into her play, and, because that play is fun and is under her own control and direction, the learning will be thorough and complete. It is a process, though, which can easily be spoiled or interrupted by too much direct teaching, especially teaching which masquerades as play. If your child is playing in a sandpit, with yogurt containers and sand pails, you can certainly show her what happens if damp sand is packed into a pail and the pail is then gently overturned. She may be delighted. She may instantly set about making her own "castles" or "jellies" or "cakes." But if you try to *teach* her to make them, insisting on an efficient technique, monitoring the amount of water, helping to overturn the mold and so forth, you will probably distress her and you will certainly spoil whatever sand-play she actually had in mind. This kind of interference, carried into many of her activities over a long period, conveys an extremely confusing message to the child. Is the activity really for her or is it for you? Is it really play or is it a duty? Eventually, the child whose play does not please you because she does not do it "right" may come to feel that she herself is not pleasing to you, that she does not live up to your expectations and is in general not "good enough for you." Teaching skills to very small children is fun and can be fun for them, too, but it is less confusing if you keep it to areas where the motivation and direction clearly *are* yours and where there is no pretense at trying to please her but an open desire to get her to please you. On that basis she may be delighted to learn to put on her own socks. . . .

As she grows older she will inevitably learn not only the difference between "play" and "work," but the difference in the value society puts on them, too. At school she will find lessons interspersed with playtimes, and discover that activities like learning to read are compulsory while activities like learning to skip are not. You cannot protect her from this skewed approach to life's activities, but you can at least make sure that every aspect of herself, and of what she does, is equally valued at home. It is sad to hear parents complaining that a three-year-old at nursery school "does nothing but play," making it clear that they already feel there is a better way for her to spend her time. It is sad to find older children being asked to earn the right to play by working, whether at homework or chores, and to see those who are playing constantly interrupted by adults who would respect their peace and privacy if they were at their desks. It is saddest of all to watch schoolchildren discovering that they can only preserve their right to play by turning that play into yet another kind of work. The child who wants to spend a lot of time with a ball must try out for the tennis team; the one who loves music or dancing must accept lessons, practice and examinations. . . . We deprive children of growing time by insisting that they have "something to show for" everything they do. We turn play into work by insisting that "if it's worth doing it's worth doing well." It is not surprising that, by puberty, many children have lost the ability to motivate and direct themselves in fun activities, giving most of their "leisure time" to the passive relaxations of television and spectator sports. It is a pity, though. Play remains a human need all through life. Everyone manages herself better if she sometimes does things just for fun, when she wants to, as she wants to, for herself and her pleasure alone. We should not have to label our play as a "hobby" or a "sport" to get it accepted, nor should we have to apologize for "just mucking about." Fun, however "purposeless," is never a waste of time. The only true waste of time is boredom.

Providing for play

While it is up to your baby or child to choose when, how and with what she plays, offering the widest and most comprehensive possible set of choices is up to you, especially while she is too young to have much experience outside her home. She cannot ask you for paint until she knows of its existence and its potential; she cannot play at being a fireman she has never seen; she cannot discover the thrill of clay or dough if there is none for her to use or know the thrilling and fearful anticipation of hide-and-seek if nobody draws her into the earliest versions of the game. Your child will play with, and within, the world she sees and experiences. So when you are thinking about providing for many different kinds of play, you have to think about the whole environment and way of life which she shares with you, and try to see it through her eyes. It is not a careful collection of toys which she needs so much as a careful inventory of the kinds of experience and activity which are obviously available to her and of the kinds which she may miss unless you take positive action. Think, for example, about *where* she lives, about the actual house or apartment which will be her first environment. Think about the *kind of community* her home is in, and its way of life which she will see and share. And think about the people there are for her to know and love. What will her life be like? What "play" is built in to it, and what needs adding on?

Life in a farm-house offers different experiences from life in a city apartment

Each may provide a rich and satisfying home for any child, yet each will automatically provide certain play experiences and tend to deprive her of others. In that city apartment, for example, she may have other children to play with under the same overall roof, a constantly changing panorama of people and traffic to watch and plenty of interesting places (from playgrounds to big shops or railway stations) to be taken to by adults. But unless you work at it, she may lack experience of her own self in wide-open spaces, of changing seasons, of animals and other living, growing things.

In that farmhouse setting she will have every opportunity to explore the natural world and her own place in it, but unless you make the effort to show her other ways of life, she may have only a very limited view of how most people live, behave and work.

Life in different kinds of family groups offers different experiences

The people in your child's household are the most vital factor in her environment; on them hinges the use which she can or cannot make of all the rest. At the beginning of her life they are also her most important playthings and partners. Will your child grow up knowing both sexes and all ages, with brothers and sisters, grandparents and aunts, cousins and relations-of-relations all sharing the interplay of their relationships with each other, and with her? Or will her basic experience be of life-with-mom so that you need to seek out more people for her to know and know about?

Different amounts and kinds of space offer different experiences

A new baby does not take up as much space as her own equipment, but as soon as she is mobile she needs safe space to explore. As she grows, the amount of space she needs for active play increases, as does her need for different kinds of space for different uses. If you know she is going to be short of space for play, possessions and privacy, you may yearn for a playroom, but if you have one you will probably find it used for anything and everything except children's play. Your child will want to spend her time where you (or whoever looks after her) spend time. The money and effort you might have spent on making a playroom will be better spent on making safe play space in the kitchen, or on adapting the living room so that daytime use for play does not make it uninhabitable by adults in the evening.

Gardens are not only rich play resources in themselves but also accommodate many kinds of play to which the insides of homes may not take kindly. If you have no real garden, you may still have outdoor space which can be made safe and useful with a little money and lots of imaginative work. A basement area, car port or balcony, for example, can each give her the freedom to play with real mud when she is a year old (yes, you will have to fetch the mud), grow string beans in pots when she is two and keep guinea pigs when she is three. . . .

"Toys"

If people are asked what parents must provide for children's play they usually answer "toys." Commercially produced toys certainly have a place in children's play and pleasure, but many of your child's most used playthings will not be ready-made for children at all but will be pieces of your adult world which you share with, lend to, or adapt for, her. When you buy things especially for your child's play, you will often find what she needs, at a price you can afford more easily, at a hardware or stationery store than from a toy counter.

● Remember that while toy manufacturers have to make their products to certain safety standards, stores which are not marketing their goods for children's use do not. Take care (*see* **Safety**/In the home).

Skillful parents can often make playthings which cost much less than the same object bought from a shop and which, designed and decorated specifically for their own children, give more pleasure as well. This book suggests comparatively little do-it-yourself toymaking because, in the author's hands, cardboard boxes and glue turn into sticky cardboard boxes. The playthings-for-making suggested here are either truly easy —requiring more imagination than craft—or items on which you could still save money over toy-shop prices if you employed somebody else to make them for your child.

● If you are skilled and do want to make toys, remember that the fact that your handiwork is on her behalf will not prevent her from resenting the time you spend on it. The most beautiful hand-made Christmas crèche will not compensate a four-year-old for many December afternoons spent in lonely boredom while you carved the donkey and stitched Mary's clothes. If the creative process cannot be truly shared (as making the festive cake can be shared) it needs to take place in adult, rather than in family, time.

Playthings for babies

Very young babies have little use for conventional "toys" despite the millions bought to celebrate their arrival. But most of them love to "play" if somebody beloved will play with them. Of course your baby will be playing with you every time you pick her up, change her diaper, feed or bathe her. But the fun of play does not have to be saved for times when you are doing practical things for her, nor reserved for times when she is distressed and you are trying to comfort her. She can play for pleasure at two months as well as two or twelve years.

Older babies want and need to explore the brand-new world in which they find themselves, but they can only explore the pieces of that world which you will offer. If you try to provide enough "real toys" to satisfy that endless curiosity, you will certainly run out of money and storage space. This is a time when you really need to offer an imaginative range of personal and household objects as well.

Towards the end of this first year, your baby will have explored so many objects, and become so competent at managing her own body and making it manipulate those objects, that she will be ready to *use* toys as well as examine them. This is a stage when you will probably want to buy her quite a lot of "real" toys, but you can save money and disappointment by making sure that your selection fits her stage and interests. She will also be especially interested in your "toys" and most interested of all in the ones you use in her care. If you will offer her the hairbrush or the facecloth, richly interesting play for her may actually get one of your jobs done—after a fashion.

Babies can neither ask for, nor go to find, playthings for themselves so they are peculiarly dependent on adults to offer them safe and interesting objects and activities. Remember that the most interesting playthings of all are loved adults and that the very best activities are shared. Whatever else she does or does not have, make sure she has plenty of *fun with you*. The following chart is designed to suggest the kinds of play and the kinds of playthings which are likely to give pleasure at various stages of development. Because every baby is unique, it contains no *age-guidance* but only *stage-guidance*. Rattles, for example, are superb playthings for babies whose hands are mostly open and who are beginning to use their eyes to look for the source of sounds. But they are useless to babies whose hands are still mostly fisted, because babies at this stage are simply not ready to enjoy deliberate holding on to anything. So if you want to decide whether or not your own baby is likely to enjoy some of the suggestions at a particular point in the right-hand columns, look first in the left-hand column and see where her behavior has got to. The suggestions that match her stage of development are the ones most likely to give pleasure.

The chart is not a prescription. Your baby does not have to do and to have everything it suggests, nor should her play activities be in any way limited by it. It is simply a series of suggestions which may give you an enjoyable jumping-off point in providing for her pleasure (and your own) at various stages. Remember that play is for fun so any activity which your baby does not enjoy is, by definition, wrong for her. She may (or may not) come to it later. Remember, above all, that fear is the enemy of play, so any object or activity which upsets or frightens your baby should be abandoned, fast.

Pointers within her development	Some activities she may enjoy and ways of providing for them	
After birth she must settle into an environment which bombards her with stimuli because it is always changing rather than being always the same as was the womb. She may be happiest without much extra stimulation over that which goes with tender loving care.	Sucking, which is, of course, a necessity, but which should quickly become luxurious pleasure. Whether she is fed from breast or bottle, try to *offer* rather than force; touch the cheek nearest to	you gently so that she turns towards the nipple; let it brush her mouth so that she herself actively takes it, rather than passively accepts it.
Her survival depends on the adults who care for her, and her first "developmental task" is to discover human faces and voices and to respond socially to them.	Being held, face to face. Looking at your face, scanning it closely, listening to your voice as you talk to her. She does not need fluffy ducks and plastic rabbits if you will give	her your smiling, talking face. Very soon she will play "conversations": watching your expression, answering with her own; listening to your voice and making her own sounds.

Pointers within her development	Some activities she may enjoy and ways of providing for them	
She is still close to the enclosed world of the womb and likely to be frightened of being exposed in wide open spaces. Nevertheless she is a highly sensual creature who must discover the pleasures of all five senses and will do so through you.	She will enjoy from the start those which mimic but extend that womb-world which was warm and soft, dark and rhythmical. As she becomes more confident of herself in this outside world, she may enjoy sensual adventures too: movement and touch, her own body in water, sucking for pleasure rather than for food. Hold her closely, face to face against your shoulder. Support her head carefully and then walk,	jiggle gently, dance a little. 　　Hold her cradled on your lap and stroke her bare skin, all over, in a range of rhythms. 　　See if you can hold her in a warm bath so securely that she is not afraid but can discover the joy of moving her limbs freely with the water's support. 　　Choose a time when she is not hungry and help her fist to her mouth and give her your own finger to explore with her mouth and to suck.
As soon as she stays awake for longer periods than you want to hold her she will be ready to start discovering her world by looking at bits of it. She cannot coordinate seeing with doing, eyes with hands, but she can learn about all kinds of things by looking alone. She still looks at your face for preference, but other things— especially complex and moving shapes—will hold her pleased attention. Her best focusing distance is still only about ten inches, so she will see fine detail best from close-up.	Looking: at as many new and different objects as you can provide. Hang things at about ten inches above her carriage and crib, making sure that they are within her eye-line as she lies in her own preferred position, which is probably curled to one side. She	can have mobiles and carriage toys but the familiar is uninteresting. She will prefer the wash dancing on the line, a balloon tied to the carriage handle and moving in the breeze. A foil plate dangling where it catches the light; a shimmery scarf tied to the crib bars. . . .
Her first social smile is on the way; it will come in response to your smiling and talking face.	Being held and talked to. Try to make sure that you give her some conversation time which is	neither part of her physical care nor interrupted by your talking to her brother. She will concentrate on you if you concentrate on her.
She probably will not be happy alone and awake for long, even with things to look at. She wants to be very close to you.	When you cannot hold and concentrate on her, she will enjoy any "activity" which keeps her with you. Carry her, sometimes, in a sling as you go about your business. Sit her in a babychair close to where	you are working and take time to show her bits of what you are doing.
She will soon find her first "playthings" which will be her own hands. She will find one with the other, by touch alone, and pull at the fingers without looking. From time to time she will catch sight of one waving in the air and look without touching.	Being awake but alone in her carriage or crib *as long as she is content.* If she is awake but "busy," don't feel you have to get her up immediately. 　　Leave her hands always free of	wrappings or mittens so that she can "find" them as soon as she is able and discover that they are there for her whenever she pleases.

Pointers within her development	Some activities she may enjoy and ways of providing for them
When her hands are open (rather than fisted) most of the time that she is awake and she plays with one with the other, she will be on the verge of making vital discoveries about the connections between seeing and doing, looking and feeling.	Holding onto things which are put into her hands; sometimes glimpsing what she is holding as her waving arms bring it into view. Gradually discovering that those hands are part of her; under her own control; that she can make them bring what they hold to where she can see it and then that she can make them bring what they hold to her mouth for sucking-exploration, too. Give her lots of *different* things to hold. Rattles are ideal because the sound they make, as she	randomly waves them, attracts her attention and makes it more likely that she will see as well as do. But novelty is important so home-made "rattles" are useful. Fill little plastic pots with things which will make different sounds (dried peas, a coin, two marbles, etc. . . .). Put a little water in a small plastic bottle for a different sound and feel. Offer things which have interesting textures even if they do not make sounds: the rubber ring from a mason jar; a piece of fur fabric; a ball she can hold but not swallow. . . .

• Seal home-made "rattles" carefully and think about the safety of anything she puts in her mouth: soon that will be everything. . . .

As her hands open her body will uncurl so that when she is awake she lies with her back flat on the mattress and both arms and legs free to move.	Learning to kick, smoothly and rhythmically, and experimenting with this new physical freedom which will lead to increasing physical control. Unwrap her and put her on a rug on the floor, or in the center of a double bed, so that she can have safe and comfortable freedom of action.	Play physical games with her like gently bicycling her legs or clapping her hands. Leave time for long baths in which the support of the water will double the power of her kicking and make her feel like a super-person.
By the time her body has uncurled her control over her own head will be much improved.	Activities which allow her to practice holding up her own head rather than always having it supported by your hand. Hold her against your shoulder with your hand poised to protect her if her head should "flop" but not interfering with her if it does not. She may rhythmically "bump" it against your shoulder	as she tenses and relaxes her muscles. When she can hold it up reliably while you are still, try walking, then jiggling and eventually dancing with her at your shoulder. Put her sometimes on her tummy, not just for sleep but for floor-play, too. She will practice lifting and turning her head.
Once she is confident when her body is free of wrappings on a large surface, she will start to roll over, first from her side to her back, then from her back to her side; then all the way over. Rolling gives her new power: power over herself and power to alter her own position, view and activities. . . .	Increasing amounts of physical freedom, until you reach a point where you unwrap her and take blankets, etc. out of her way whenever she is awake. If you want to leave her to entertain herself in her carriage or crib, visit her and take off covers, etc. so that she can choose how	she plays. Remember to relieve her of diapers, too, from time to time, so that she can see and feel her whole body. When you can see that she is trying to do something specific, like roll right over, help her to go back and forth so that she experiences some successes.

Pointers within her development	Some activities she may enjoy and ways of providing for them	
Once her head is steady and she can control her upper back, she will be ready to be propped up in a semi-sitting position.	"Sitting" where she can see you. Find lots of different places where she can be safely propped up. Her	babychair is fine, but a corner of the sofa or an armchair makes a change, provided you are close by to supervise.
When she has "found" her hands with her eyes (and learned to explore them with her mouth, too). She will be beginning the vital process of learning to get hold of things. She will not only look at things at different distances, but will actually search for something interesting to look at whenever she is awake.	Looking at things and experimenting with getting her hands to them, especially anything which she can hit, so that she both feels her hand connect and sees it swing. Hang things which she can safely hit at, within arm's reach above	crib or carriage. Try a woolly ball/soft toy, a softish balloon, a gay paper cup, a chiming ball, paper streamers, a bunch of rattly foil strips. . . . Ring the changes so that when she succeeds in her hitting she is rewarded with different feelings, sounds and movements.
Soon she will clearly realize that when she sees something interesting, she can do something about getting hold of it.	Being propped in a sitting position with interesting objects on a tray in front of her so that she can try, at her own pace, actually to get hold of them. All those rattles and things she used to have just to look at, will be interesting again for getting hold	of. Don't stick to plastic: try a pair of rolled-up socks, a soft bread roll and that furry toy rabbit. When you must sit still with her in a bus or doctor's waiting room, wear something interesting around your neck for her to work at reaching.

• Anything she can grasp will now be sucked; is it safe? It may also be wildly waved; will it hurt if she hits herself in the eye?

Once she can reach out for things and get hold of them she will be able to explore her world, object by object.	Getting, holding and exploring the widest possible variety of objects. She will not yet be interested in *doing* anything with them, just in finding out about them. Objects which swing when she gets her hands to them will frustrate her now because she will not be able to grasp them. She needs things which will keep still for her.
	    She will do her best playing with objects when she is properly supported in a babychair.
	
	More and more and *more* objects to handle, look at and mouth. Nobody can afford to buy a new toy every day, so look around and choose what you can offer. Some objects which would not be safe for her to have when she is alone are all right if you are watching. Try for differences of shape, color, weight, texture, sound . . .
	    Pots, packages, boxes, bottles—empty and full. Little
		clear plastic bottles can have colored soapy water for pretty foam when she shakes, or a single marble for a nice thud.
		    Little cloth bags which you make and fill with cornflakes for a light scrunch, lentils for shifting weight, a single potato for a heavy lump. . . .
		    Different kinds of paper for different kinds of crumple (not newsprint; the ink may be poisonous). Different kitchen utensils, small saucepans, wooden and plastic spoons and plates. . . .
		    Fruits for their shape and a surprise when she sucks them.
		    A few really big things (like an uncut loaf of bread or big soft toy or beach ball) for her to get hold of in both arms.
		    Things for careful looking. Show her a bold picture book. Make chewable books by sealing bold pictures into plastic wallets.

Pointers within her development	Some activities she may enjoy and ways of providing for them	

She will also be exploring her own body-in-that-world; finding out what she can make it do and where it ends and the outside world begins.	Probably all kinds of physical and "gymnastic" play, but with the level adjusted to her enjoyment so that she is never frightened or made to jump.
	
	All those nursery games which involve bits of her body: "This little piggy went to market," "This is the way the farmer rides"; toe-counting; tummy-tickling. Being held standing so she can
		"dance"; being gently pulled to sitting.
		    "Coming and going" games so that you hide your face and peep out/cover a toy and reveal it; bounce your face towards her and away again. . . .
		    A baby bouncer, hung so that as she sits, her toes just touch the floor and as she pushes down, she bounces. (Don't bounce her; let her adjust the activity for herself.)

She will learn to control her limbs and make them do what she wants on purpose, and she will increasingly be able to control her own position, by rolling over; getting into crawling position; sitting forward in her chair so that only the base of her spine is supported.	Any which combine physical freedom with interesting sights, sounds, feelings, objects—especially people. Physical play in lots of different circumstances: being bounced on the middle of your bed; rolling on grass; kicking in the bath, lying on	front or back on a safe floor. Being propped sitting in carriage or car seat so she is moving and looking: or near you so she can see (and join) what you are doing.

From the above stage of hand-eye coordination and physical control? Six months. Having learned a lot about objects by looking at them and a lot more by handling-and-looking, she will become ready to explore not just the objects but what they will do, their behavior and her own power over them. The direction of this kind of exploration is affected by her deep attachment to you and by her readiness to imitate you.	The beginnings of manipulative play such that she does something (like making a bell ring) by accident and then finds that she can make it happen again on purpose.
	
	"Helping" you and being shown how things work.
	    Play with objects you use in her care.
	    Find her some playthings which give her clear cause-and-effect: toys which squeak when squeezed or rattle when banged (a saucepan and spoon are as good as a drum . . .). Cars that run when pushed, balls and apples that roll, paper which tears. She will be interested, too, in discovering the basic characteristics of objects which do
		not behave similarly even if she treats them the same. The ball rolls, the block does not; the cookie crumbles, the slice of toast does not.
		    Love and imitation will meet in play with her own brush, facecloth and toothbrush, in attempts to feed herself and you, and in a passion for what she sees you use most—whether cooking pots, piano or typewriter. Let her have a go, too (whatever the activity), for the best game of all, provided it is safe for her.

She is ready to increase her competence but because she still needs you to arrange experiences for her, its level will depend on what you offer. You probably will not affect her eventual "intelligence" but you will affect her happiness. . . .	Anything that you will do *with* her which she can enjoy *either* at the simple watching level *or* at the more advanced level of discovering how it works and copying. Pull-string music-box, nesting toys, boxes to fill and empty,	block towers built and knocked down, balls run through cardboard tubes, piano or xylophone banged.

Pointers within her development	Some activities she may enjoy and ways of providing for them

She will now be learning to sit alone and to crawl, and to recognize, match and manipulate objects and soon to name them. These are vital accomplishments and, though she will achieve them all (probably by her first birthday), she may not be able to concentrate on them all at once. If she is a baby whose heart is set on getting mobile, her play with objects may not seem to become much more sophisticated for a while. If objects fascinate her, she may spend so much time and attention on them that she advances less rapidly in the physical areas. Follow her enjoyment-lead. If she is busy and happy most of the time, then the balance of activities you are offering is right for her.

Remember that these are also the months when her attachment to you is likely to reach its peak. There is both a positive and a negative side to this area of development. The positive side is that it is out of her joy in your love and company that she elaborates her communication, until eventually she shares not only your life but also your language (*see* **Language**). The negative side may be that she becomes "clingy" and shy of strangers so that there are many activities which she enjoys to the full only if you are with her.

If her concentration is on sitting/crawling she will want to practice, again and again, her latest achievement. Unfortunately, this kind of practice usually involves adult help, so although she wants the freedom of the floor whenever she is awake, she also needs a great deal of attention.

Until she can sit absolutely steadily on the floor, her richest play with objects will take place when she is sitting in her chair with objects on its tray in front of her. If objects are her main passion she may want to spend long periods like this; if they are not, "toys" may hold her attention for only a few minutes while she waits for a meal or her freedom.

Try to arrange times when there is nothing you have to do but be her partner. Sit on the floor with her and pull her into a sitting position or help her turn over to a crawling position as many times as she wants you to. When this is the kind of play she needs, nothing else will give equivalent pleasure and your wholehearted help will be more fun for both of you than attention given only reluctantly and because it is moaned for.

Once she can sit alone, even for moments only, don't expect her to be able to play with her hands: she needs them for balance. Instead, surround her with cushions or rolled quilts and let her practice, with assurance of a soft landing when she topples.

Once she can crawl, or get across the room by some combination of rolling/crawling/wriggling, offer interesting things for her to move towards: a big truck, a box with things in it, a basket to empty or an animal on wheels which she can push if she can get there. Provide some big objects on which she can vent some of the frustration of her efforts, too: cushions to pummel, big soft toys to "fight." Once she really can

crawl she will push and follow a big beach ball or car.

She likes things which she can "mail." Commercial "mailboxes" may be too difficult yet awhile but try a shoe-box with big holes cut in the lid and balls and blocks to mail in. She needs lots of boxes of every size and shape and lots of things to pile in and empty out. As usual you will hold her interest with novelty: spoons and a cookie tin? Socks and a shopping bag? Old playing cards and a freezer-box?

She likes (mild) surprises, too, so try her (from a distance at first) with a jack-in-the-box, a pop-up book, a squeaky toy. If she likes one particular object she will probably enjoy another which is the same-only-different so try a red sausage-shaped balloon to follow success with a round blue one.

She is beginning to enjoy and recognize finely detailed copies of the real world she knows, so she will probably enjoy a doll with removable clothes like her own, picture books with familiar scenes, the family photograph album and a model car or dog which she can see is like the one the family owns.

Although there is so much of the world for her to explore that she must concentrate on new things and experiences, she is also beginning to remember a repertoire of familiar and enjoyable experiences and to love repeating them. This is the time to take her, again and again, to feed those ducks or visit that cat. It may be boring for you but it is not for her.

Gradually she will build her own kinds of repeated pleasures: she will make a ritual of special bedtime games and stories, and find particular activities which she must always share with particular people.

Pointers within her development	Some activities she may enjoy and ways of providing for them	
Her curiosity and her physical abilities develop much faster than the memory or foresight which will one day make her "sensible."	Her desire to explore, both physically and by looking and touching, means that (as long as you are there) she will enormously enjoy going to new places. But she will constantly get into danger if they are unsuitable for her.	When home cannot mop up her endless curiosity, find safe places where she will be welcome like a parent-and-baby club, an under-five playground, parks, gardens and the houses of friends who also have crawlers.

Her increasing passion for you makes her both very ready to imitate you and very keen to do what she sees you doing most often.	Anything that you will demonstrate and then let her try.
	
	Play with her, demonstrating building with blocks or scribbling with crayons, and let her do it, too, *but in her own way*. This is play not teaching. If she wants to knock down the castle she watched you build, do you *really* mind?
	    If you cook, type or play the piano, she will want to, too. Find
		a safe way for her to have a go because it will give her not only pleasure but a supreme sense of grandeur, too.
		    Above all, let her share in the things you do as you care for her. Let her have a go at feeding herself, washing her face, brushing her hair and so on. What starts as pure fun will soon be useful, too.

Part of the reason for her extreme attachment to you is her increasing (and sometimes alarming) awareness that you and she are separate people. The more she can control the distance between you and assure herself that you always come together again after separations either in time or space, the more confident she will be of her own ability to manage and to enjoy being what she begins to think of as "me."	Games which involve taking turns and swapping, coming and going, hiding and finding, all enable her to control this sort of separateness and togetherness. Let her feed you bits of what you are feeding her; take turns with anything from ice cream to throwing bread to the ducks; play at rolling a ball to each other; invent versions of hide-and-seek from bobbing from behind the curtains to simply covering your face asking "Where've I gone?" and uncovering it again to "Here I am."	Recognizable personal possessions will begin to give pleasure, too. This is the time for her special mug, plate and towel. For photos of herself, with and without you. For a safety mirror with holes in the frame so that she can hold it and examine "me," and for the made-up serial story of her daily life with herself as the main character.
The more she shares with you the more elaborately she will want to communicate with you.	Any verbal activity; not just being talked to and jargoning back, but being read to, recited to, sung to, and joining in. Any game in which you use words with pleasure will please her. If you enjoy reciting Shakespeare, she will listen to the sounds and rhythms and be your best audience ever. If you have a fund of songs and rhymes she will pick them up and store them	against the time when she will surprise you by reproducing a snatch. If you are a great one for the telephone she will want to "talk," too, and perhaps will need a toy one to save the bills. Above all, though, tell her what the two of you are doing; point out to her what other people are doing; help her to tell her father what happened this afternoon. Quite soon now she will be talking, and that is one of the best games of all.

Playthings for near-toddlers and toddlers

By around a year your more-or-less-mobile and almost verbal child will be building a rich and complex play-world out of a combination of the materials you provide and her own rapidly increasing competence. Many of the playthings she already has will not only remain popular but take on a new lease of life as she makes new discoveries about them. That soft toy, which she pummelled in rage two months ago, may now become her dearest companion and bedfellow. That music-box, which you used to set going for her as part of a bedtime ritual, may now become something which she can not only work for herself but through which she can feel the glorious power of having music whenever she pleases. The books you showed her as she sat on your lap will now reveal their secrets without your help, because she can turn the pages for herself, while the stacking beakers, which she never much enjoyed for fitting-play, may prove ideal as doll's cups or sand-toys.

Most parents will nevertheless find themselves buying, making, or otherwise acquiring, a lot of new playthings during this age period because the child is so clearly ready and able to enjoy more and more different things, and because many of the toys available are so attractive to adults' eyes and memories. Choosing from the enormous range available needs some thought. You are the people who know your child best and the only ones who know her in her environment, so trust your own judgment as to what is suitable/desirable/worthwhile for her rather than anyone else's. The following general points may be useful in your thinking not only about toys for now, but also about the organization of her play-life for the next year or two.

Safety Keeping toddlers safe in a family environment is always difficult (*see* **Safety**/In the home) but ill-chosen or ill-organized playthings can make it impossible. Toxic paints, ill-fixed dolls' eyes and sharp edges are obviously dangerous to a child of any age, but there are particular dangers which are peculiar to this age group:

Watch out for the incompetence of early walking. When she first discovers that she can pull herself up to a standing position, she will try to do so using anything within reach. Don't buy, or even have around, a doll's carriage, truck or toy intended to be pushed by a child on two feet. If she grabs the handle it will tip over on her. If she should find herself standing up with it, it will run away with her. Push toys should wait until she can both get up without support and walk steadily. Even then, remember that early walking is short on brakes and steering. If you put a toddler in charge of a wheeled vehicle you ask her to control its motion as well as her own. Confine such toys to safe indoor or garden spaces, ban them from pavements and watch out for steps and stairs.

Some children do become very angry when they can get to their feet but cannot actually progress around the room. Don't try to help by buying her the kind of "walker" which sits her in a canvas sling on wheels and allows her to scoot around. Children have scooted into fires, down flights of stairs and over new babies. If you want to do *something* to help, either arrange the furniture so that she can hand herself from the support of the sofa back to the armchair to the table and around again, or buy her the kind of safety-truck which is usually called a "baby-walker" or "toddler-truck." The special design of this often-magical first birthday present ensures that the vehicle will not tip if she pulls herself up by the handle and will not run away as she lurches forward holding on to it. With years of use ahead as a brick transporter or animal truck, it may be a real best buy.

Watch out for ride-on toys with wheels rather than castors. Once she can walk well enough to manage getting on and off, your child will probably much enjoy the kind of vehicle (sometimes animal-shaped, sometimes like a tricycle without pedals) on which she can sit and propel herself with her feet. But she will use those feet to push sideways as well as along; if she does that on a wheeled vehicle it will tip over rather than swivel.

Remember that she has a short memory and little foresight. She will not remember accidents, scoldings or warnings, nor will she foresee difficulties or dangers. That means that whenever danger presents itself as she plays, you have to deal with it once and for all. If she hits her head on the toy cabinet door today, you can be quite sure she will do so again, in something between two minutes and two days, unless you lock, remove or pad it. If she bops her baby brother over the head with her largest block and blackens his eye, nothing you say or do will stop her from doing so again next time hand, block, baby and temper happen to meet; it is up to you to make sure they do not. If she finds that she can climb into a high cupboard during a game of hide-and-seek, she will not be stopped by wondering how she will get out again, and even getting stuck in that cupboard for a few minutes will not stop her from hiding in your freezer chest a day or two later. Stopping her takes a lock and/or supervision.

Supervision is the essence of toddler play which is both safe and free, but although you can (and will) develop eyes in the back of your head and a kind of instinct for the sort of silence which means danger, you cannot watch and attend to her every minute. Sooner or later she will go into a room alone while you are getting dressed, thinking her safely close by, or embark on a new activity while you are engrossed in conversation on the telephone. Supervision needs backing by:

Regular checking of all her playthings as you put them away each evening. The point is to make sure that junk objects are not deteriorating to reveal sharp rivets and so forth, that vehicle wheels have not come off leaving lethal axles, and that forbidden objects, like sharp scissors, lent for a specific purpose under your eye, have not become mixed in with her things.

Careful organization of her play-storage so that objects which she must not use without your knowledge and attention are out of reach, so that she has to ask you for them (*see below*).

Storage   Lack of storage space may limit, even more than lack of money, the playthings you can make available to your child. Poor storage can also make what she does have virtually unusable because she cannot see what is there or find all the bits of anything.

Unless you positively enjoy sorting out closets and drawers (probably weekly and certainly monthly), you may find that it is a mistake to try to store the toys of this age group in a way which banishes them from adult sight. A range of open shelves is often more efficient and it can look good, too, if trouble is taken.

You could, for example, accumulate half-gallon plastic ice-cream containers and some plastic seed trays and use them for keeping all her small toys, or toys with many separate parts. Large, heavy toys and the ones to which she is allowed to help herself at any time, can go on the lowest shelves; things you want her to have to ask for, plus the ones she uses least, can go higher up. She can be reminded of what is there, even in the boxes she cannot reach, by having one item glued on the outside of the box or a picture of it drawn with a felt-tip pen.

You may find that some playthings are best stored hanging up in bags. Drawstring bags are easy to make, either out of a pretty fabric or out of nylon "string" so that she can see what is in them. Different sizes will take anything from a collection of balls to her favorite dressing-up clothes and accessories.

Dolls and soft toys can be a problem as, if she has many, they will both take up shelf space and keep falling over. You could try the "hammock" approach. Under one of your existing shelves, fix a simple framework of wooden slats, wide enough to stick out in front of the shelf. Tack fabric to the front and back, all along its length, to a depth which fills the space before the next shelf. Her "people" can now sit in their hammock in a long row. She can see each one; she will feel that they are "comfortable," and they look friendly, too.

Until she is old enough both to have a lot of books and to be able to find the one she wants by looking only at the spine, visible in a conventional bookshelf, you may find a home version of the playgroup book-display method useful. All you need is a blank piece of wall or the back of a door or side of a cabinet. You screw pieces of wooden slats across the space at book-sized intervals and then stretch stout elastic between them. The books sit on the slats held flat by the elastic: visible and accessible.

However tidy and efficient your main toy-storage area, you will almost certainly need at least two "junk" containers, whether they are cardboard boxes (which you could, of course, paint), wicker or plastic laundry baskets or even lovely Victorian blanket chests (watch out for heavy lids which squash fingers). One is for you: a quick and easy place to save for her the hundreds of potentially interesting and useful bits and pieces which come your way from packaging, sewing leftovers and so forth. The other is a place where the child can keep the hundreds of "treasures" which she finds and cannot bear to throw away—yet.

An added bonus to this kind of toy storage is that for many children it makes the otherwise hateful business of "cleaning up" into a part of play. Sorting toys into the right boxes is (sometimes) fun. Putting books away is like doing a jigsaw puzzle if you can actually see the right-sized spaces; and opening and closing drawstring bags is fun, too. When you first set up a toy-storage or play area, try to allow for the future: for expansion in the collection of playthings and for change in the child.

For the moment she needs her playthings where she plays, which is near

you, but as she overflows that first space she will want/be able to use space which is more separate from you, perhaps in her bedroom. It is usually sensible to *start* in the living room, and make new storage upstairs later, than to begin with a "nursery" and then find that although it is never used for playing in, its shelves are overflowing.

She must have floor space now and table space later. If you can arrange for her corner to have suitable wipe-clean flooring, most of her current play will take place on it. Later on you can install a table or counter-top for craft-type play (*see below*).

She will eventually need display space for her current pictures, etc. and probably blackboard space too, so try not to design your first set of storage shelves so that they take up every available piece of wall.

She will probably need lay-out space for farms, zoos, villages, car tracks or railways. If there is nowhere she can leave an elaborate set-up over-night, she will actually be discouraged from a kind of play which is valuable to many children. If floor space is short, or the room is multi-purpose so that you know you will dislike even the most orderly versions of "toys on the floor," try to build a wide counter-top or shelf into the storage unit for lay-out purposes.

She will need somewhere that is comfortable for resting, as well as efficient/hygienic for playing. At eighteen months she probably sprawls on your lap for a rest or a story, but at three or four she will need a rug or cushions or somewhere luxurious, to cuddle dolls, look at books or just think.

Choosing toys   Bought toys are expensive, so most parents want to be sure that they get good value for the money they spend. Unfortunately, you cannot work out value for money in toys just in terms of whether the object you get is worth the money it cost. Often you will be buying an idea, a name, a patent, rather than an object which is of value in itself. An expensive board game, for example, may consist only of a piece of cardboard and a few pieces of plastic. Clearly the materials and workmanship are not worth the dollars it costs, but if that is the retail price of the game and that game is the one your child wants, it may still be a worthwhile purchase. At the other extreme you may sometimes buy an object whose materials and workmanship clearly are worth the money charged—as with some hand-crafted wooden toys, for example—but if your child does not play with the toy, but leaves it gathering dust on a shelf, it will not have been a worthwhile purchase. The point, of course, is that toys are for play and play is for fun; the true worth of a toy can only be measured in terms of the fun it gives your child.

If you look at some of the toys your child already has, note down their price and divide that by the number of minutes of play in which each has been vital, you will get a range of costs-per-minute's-play. You will probably find that on this basis large, expensive items and small, cheap ones both emerge as "better value" than many medium-priced toys. A jungle gym, for example, may cost $250 but be used by two children for at least an average of one hour per day for half of each of five successive years. That is 1824 play hours for $250, which is less than 15¢ per *hour*. A little plastic car may cost $1 and be played with for twenty minutes while it is brand new and for another five minutes the next day before it breaks or is forgotten. That is 4¢ per minute. An educational construction set may cost $10 and be played with for only two hours in total over several months. That is nearly 8¢ per minute. The point of this frivolous set of calculations is only to help you remember that when you are considering whether or not a toy is "worthwhile," you have to think in terms of the child's pleasure, of what she wants the toy for. If you are determined never to buy "junk," or always to buy "decent educational stuff that will teach her something," you may waste your money while doing her out of a lot of fun.

Sometimes you can get excellent play-value-for-money by making yourself, or having made for you, items on which retailers really do make enormous profits. Blocks are a case in point. Your child needs lots of them and will probably use them in different ways over several years, so if you can afford to buy them they are certainly worthwhile. But if you cannot, you only have to persuade your lumberyard to cut 2 in. × 2 in. timber (5 cm × 5 cm) into four inch, two inch and one inch lengths and you have your basic blocks for about one-third of a toy shop's price. You will have to sandpaper and paint or seal them, but although that is a slow and boring job, there is almost no skill involved. Rather the same applies to the dolls' clothes which most children yearn for at some point. They are usually sold in sets, at absurdly high prices, so that you are forced to buy the handbag and shoes your child will instantly lose in order to obtain the jeans her doll must have. If you can sew, you can make the jeans out of her outgrown ones, for nothing. If you can glue felt, you can make a version for almost nothing. If there is no way you can make the clothes yourself, a dressmaker will probably run them up for you for a quarter the price a shop would charge *and* add the final touches which make them "just like mine."

There are a great many large playthings which almost every child yearns for but which are outgrown within a year or two. Your child will almost certainly want a tricycle and, if she has a first one when she is only two or three, she will very likely yearn for a bigger one before she is ready to move on to a first two-wheeler (*see* **Safety**/On wheels). She may want a doll's carriage or furniture for "house play" (*see below*). You may long for her to have a slide or a garden swing or some other piece of outdoor equipment. Each of these items costs a very great deal of money if you buy it new and it seems ridiculous that, when one child has finished with it, another should not share the pleasure. Buy secondhand if you possibly can. You can usually acquire them through notices in shops, at the baby clinic or in the local paper, at rock-bottom prices; once a family has outgrown them, their space is usually urgently needed. Of course it is sad for a child who had visualized a shiny new tricycle for Christmas to be given a battered old one, but even if you pay for professional renovation it will look like new for about half the new cost.

Sometimes you can get the best play-value-for-money of all by *inventing* playthings for your child in the ways suggested in Presents (*see below*). The point here is not that you make a copy of something which is available in the shops, but that you collect, assemble or otherwise put together small cheap items which, because your idea exactly fits your child's current interests, add up to a major plaything.

When you do buy new from a shop, do check that:

She/you are not being misled by advertising. While every child should sometimes have a particular toy just because it is her heart's desire, many such yearnings will be inspired by television commercials, and the disappointment that follows its purchase will often be just as cruel as the disappointment of having that purchase refused.

Always have the box or package opened before you buy. The scenes on the box may show working models, lunar landscapes or whatever, but the contents may be lumpy, sterile plastic and pieces of cardboard. Does the toy do what the child thinks it will do? Look as she expects it to look? Is it on the scale she is imagining?

The toy is a practical plaything for her. Will she actually be able to use the toy or does it require more skill than she has, more help than you are prepared to give, more space than is available or weather you cannot expect in the next six months?

It "fits" with the child's current play. You know how your child plays, the manufacturer does not. She may yearn for that plastic model plane but, if most of her play just now involves trying to make things behave realistically, she will probably throw it through the air to make it fly, which will both break it and turn it into a lethal missile. Can you divert her to a glider which is intended to be "flown"? She may yearn for that talking doll, but it will not "talk" for long if all the dolls in your house are bathed every day. Might she settle for a doll which "wets" instead?

On the other hand, don't refuse items just because your child already has many similar toys. If she is into dolls or soft toys or Lego, her idea of "enough" will not be the same as yours because she needs new fuel for the same range of play.

She will be free to use it as she pleases. It is usually a mistake to buy toys which are so delicate/expensive/noisy/risky that you have to limit and control their use. If you are going to say "sshh" every time she bangs that drum or "careful" every time she touches the doll's house, don't bother to buy them. Don't buy battery-operated toys unless you are prepared to keep on buying batteries, either. The more successful the toy, the more it is going to cost you to keep it running/the child playing.

● When you buy playthings with many small pieces, check the availability of spares and, if possible, buy some extras from the beginning. An expensive marble-run which will only accept its own marbles can be useless in a week if they all get lost. Often the manufacturer will send you this kind of extra if you write at the time of purchase. Check the manufacturer's address with the toy shop: it is often hard to track down from the information given on the packaging.

"Messy" and energetic play for private homes

Some play materials and play experiences are basic to a child's knowledge of the raw materials of her world and of her own self within it. She must, for example, have opportunities to discover how sand and water behave,

separately and together, and what she can do with them. She must find
out the changing limits of her own physical strength and courage, by
climbing, swinging and generally having the opportunity to use herself.

Many parents associate this sort of play with nursery school or playgroup and feel that they could not provide it at home. But not every child
attends any kind of playgroup and few should attend before they are
three. These are play activities which should be available from a much
earlier stage and they can be made available under almost any home
circumstances as the following notes and suggestions hopefully make
clear. The trick is to think what it is that you are trying to offer (let's say
"water"); think what it may mean to the child and then realize that while
there are large-scale and grand ways of providing for it, there are also
modest and manageable ways. Water-play does not have to mean six
children in matching waterproof aprons pouring the lovely stuff into
measuring-jugs. It can mean your own child in Wellington boots in a
puddle.

The basic activity and why she will enjoy it	Ways of providing this kind of fun from the grand to the modest
Water. Playing in, and with, water gives your child all kinds of interesting physical experiences like being extra-buoyant and getting wet. It also gives her the chance to acquire information about the behavior of her world's most basic element. You know that if you allow water to get out of its container it will splash onto, and spread over, the floor. Your child has to find out for herself. As she plays, scooping up water and letting it go, pouring it from one container into another and so forth, she also makes countless other discoveries which she cannot put into words but we can: she finds out about volume, for example: about how much water will "fit into" a small cup and how much space that water leaves when she pours it into a bigger one. She finds out a lot of limits, too, like what happens if you go on pouring into a cup which is full. When she has water to use with other materials (sand, mud) there is a whole new range of discoveries to be made about how they behave together.	**Being in water.** If you have garden-space a *paddling pool* is obvious fun when the weather is warm enough. Filling it with warm water helps. Since you cannot leave a full pool in the garden (see **Safety**/In the home) and daily emptying is a nuisance, consider investing in a *splasher pool*. It will be about ten feet across and two feet six inches deep and will cost about the same as five ordinary paddling pools. It is a lot of money, but five paddling pools are a reasonable number for a two-child family to get through (they do eventually puncture beyond repair) so if you have the space it may be a worthwhile one-time investment. A child cannot climb over the high straight sides, so it is safe to leave it full. She can play in it (under supervision) if you put only six inches of water in, but she can actually learn to swim in it if you add more water. At the other extreme, her old *baby-bath*, filled with warm water, will give her almost as much fun as a pool, and is easy to empty and store. If you have no large water container at all, try a *home-made* wallow on a hot afternoon. All you need is a large plastic sheet with the edges rolled around garden poles or whatever you have. Turn the hose on gently and you have a large expanse of water only about one inch deep. It will leak away, but not before she has had a lot of fun sliding on her bottom and sailing Ping-Pong balls and leaves. • It will be slippery. Encourage toddlers to crawl rather than walk and place it so that others cannot hit their heads on anything if they fall. She can go in other kinds of water, too. Most *public swimming pools* have toddler sessions which she *may* enjoy but which do not cater to anything but body-in-water play, as they will not allow her to take in containers, etc. She can go in every available *puddle* if you dress her suitably and, above all, *she can play in the bath*. Baths do not always have to be for cleanliness or routine. Provided you have enough hot water and time to supervise, she can get in the bath with all her water toys simply as a pleasure activity on a boring wet Monday afternoon.

The basic activity and why she will enjoy it	Ways of providing this kind of fun from the grand to the modest

Water . . .

Playing with water. Your child need not be submerged in water to enjoy the stuff. If she wants to play with it at all today she will play on the scale which you can provide. If she can safely stand up at the *kitchen sink* you can give her small saucepans, ladles and sieves. If that is impossible try a *washing-up bowl* on newspapers on the floor, but find her small cups and pots (perhaps her own doll's tea-set) to use with it.

Sand. Dry silver sand behaves rather like water but with interesting differences and feelings. Damp sand has a new set of characteristics (like piling up and turning out). Wet sand is different again. As with water, your child will play happily with the basic material on the scale which you can provide.

If you have garden, courtyard or balcony space, a *sandpit* is an excellent investment. Try for one at least four feet square so that two children can get right in. It can be molded plastic or wood, but it must be placed where water can drain, and have a cover so that the local cats do not use it as a lavatory. A wooden one is truly easy to make yourself. You need four pieces of timber about four feet long by nine inches wide by one inch thick, plus another piece twelve inches square which you saw in half diagonally to make two corner seats which also brace the structure. Screw the four pieces of timber together at the corners to make a square. Screw the two triangular pieces across the front corners and there you are. On concrete or paving, it will drain itself. On grass or earth, put down a plastic sheet, studded with small drainage holes, first. You can cover with a sheet of hardboard or fold a sheet of heavy-duty plastic over the top (as if wrapping a parcel) and staple the corners. You will then be able to slip it on and off.

● Fill with "washed sand" or "silver sand" rather than ordinary builder's sand. The latter may contain harsh chemicals and/or stain clothes bright orange.

A *baby-bath or washing-up bowl* full of sand will occupy her almost as happily as a sandpit if you provide ordinary size spoons, pots, etc. rather than spades and buckets. You may feel that sand and water combined is for outside use only, but sand alone is not difficult to sweep up off a hard floor.

If you want to provide this kind of play indoors and cannot cope with real sand, a couple of pounds of flour, or even sugar, is fun, too. Extravagant, perhaps, but you can sweep it up and save it for next time. Once you start on this idea you may want to elaborate it: the cereal which has gone soggy, lentils or cereal oats are all superb and differing materials. She will progress from the dry material to "play-cooking" and thence to "real" pastry-making (*see below* Clay, dough, plasticine and mud and *see* Presents).

Clay, dough, plasticine and mud. Materials of this kind all behave slightly differently but all offer the child the opportunity to explore material which she can mold, pierce, roll, break apart and stick back together again. They all make her "dirty," too, and let her find out about the way her skin comes clean again under the tap.

Real clay is a difficult material for a small child to use because it is too stiff and hard. There are many easier materials on the market and they have the advantage of being brightly colored, too, but the disadvantage of being expensive, especially as the colors become mixed to muddy brown and the child wants that lovely red again next time. Home-made play-dough (*see* Presents) is an easy and cheap alternative and she can also have your real pastry scraps whenever any are available.

Not every family will happily dig up a bucket of real mud for a child to dibble in, but "helping" you to dig the garden, or even fill indoor pots with compost, will give her great pleasure and may lead to gardening-type activities (*see below* Bringing outdoors indoors).

Whether you live in the country or the town, try to let her take advantage of any opportunities for mud-play, whether they are only the occasional puddle-in-the-park or a regular part of outdoor life.

The basic activity and why she will enjoy it	Ways of providing this kind of fun from the grand to the modest

Bringing outdoors indoors. Some city and suburban children reach school age so ignorant of the living world that they truly believe that milk comes from bottles, that honey is made like jam and that fresh fruit and vegetables are the ones people forgot to put in cans. While no small child needs biology *lessons*, every child has the right to find out about the real nature of her world and her place in it. If things are not living and growing all around her, import some on which she can exercise her natural curiosity.

If you have a garden and pets (*see* **Pets**) or live in the countryside, your child's interest will lead her to find out all she needs to know. If not, you can easily ensure that some aspect of the natural world is around most of the time for her to think about:

Let her bring natural treasures in and keep them: pebbles, leaves and twigs may be used for sorting-play or just left on her ''display shelf'' (*see above*) where she may one day notice how they change as they dry out. A skeleton-leaf is interesting; so is the snap of a dried twig which only bent last week. *Watching things grow is interesting* and, for a small child, growing things to eat is the most fun of all. Try mustard and cress on damp flannel or blotting paper, or mung beans or other sprouts in a screw-top jar of water. She can see daily progress after forty-eight hours and eat them a week later. If she is remotely interested in your house plants, line an empty jam jar with a cylinder of damp blotting paper and place a bean or pea between the blotting paper and the side of the jar. She will be able to watch both the roots and the shoots, and you will not have to *teach* her that roots go down and shoots go up.

Watching creatures can be fun, too, and even if you have no room or inclination for pets she can have some. Buy a *wormery* or simply fill a glass dish with earth, find some worms to put in it and top with fine wire mesh. She will be able to watch the worms underground and, if she waters the top lightly, they will surface. An *ant farm* is best bought (from a pet shop or educational supplier) as it is difficult to make an ant-proof container yourself. It is not quite as easy to establish a flourishing colony as the instructions suggest, but if you succeed, they are fascinating to watch and the child can feed them herself. Frogs are rare in many parts of the world, so if you are going to rear *tadpoles* do it responsibly and make sure that the baby frogs are released back into the pond where you found the frogspawn. Put the spawn and pond water in a large container; add rocks and gravel. Top with more of the same water whenever possible (going to fetch some more may be a fun expedition in itself) or with rainwater when it is not (putting out a rainwater collector is fun, too). Tap water will usually kill tadpoles. Once tadpoles free themselves of the spawn and swim free, let the child feed them with tiny quantities of the fish food sold for baby fish. Raw meat leads to dead tadpoles and stinking water.

Climbing, swinging, jumping and rolling play. The raw materials for this kind of large-scale physical play are only your child's own body-in-space and her own muscles working against a vast range of forces. She will run; she will climb, even if it is only on the furniture; she will swing, even if it is only from her father's hand. A country child with lots of open space and trees and gates to climb probably needs no extra aids from you. A city child may need, and will certainly enjoy, them. You do not even have to have a garden to provide for active and enormously satisfactory physical play.

The best investment for this type of play is a *jungle gym*. A big one for the garden will cost a lot of money but will give superb play value and probably hold its resale value, too. Choose between tubular metal (which is cold and slippery when wet but needs no maintenance) and wood which is kinder but will need checking for loose joints and occasional coats of wood preservative. Don't try to make one yourself unless you are truly competent. Your child's safety depends on its solidity. If you are going to buy a frame at all, buy the biggest you can: your two-year-old will still be using it when she is ten. Put it in a sunny part of the garden where you can easily supervise it, preferably on grass rather than concrete or paving. Falls are unusual, but a soft landing makes the prospect less alarming.

You can make a wooden jungle gym a wide range of *exciting extras* for very little money.

Platforms. Measure across one of the bays. Buy a rectangle of timber one inch more than the space. Sandpaper and wood-preserve it. Mark on the underside exactly where it crosses the frame-bars and screw on stout clips which fit those bars exactly. It can now be clipped safely in place and removed again when the frame is wanted for swinging.

The basic activity and why she will enjoy it	Ways of providing this kind of fun from the grand to the modest
Climbing, swinging, jumping and rolling play....	**Swings.** Buy a rope about 1½ inches in diameter (expensive but it will last forever). Tie it to the top rail of the jungle gym and make a huge knot in the bottom. The child will swing by her arms and eventually discover that she can straddle the knot and sit while she swings. Then you can buy a circle of timber about fifteen inches in diameter, drill a hole through the middle, thread your rope through and knot it underneath to give her a "monkey swing." Try a car tire, too.

Balancing planks. If you buy, sand and wood-preserve planks of wood about eight feet long, eight inches wide and one inch thick, you can screw clips on the underside of one end so that they can be securely fastened to the frame as an extension. Your child can eventually walk up them, jump off them and slide down them.

A cover. Some jungle gyms have covers as very expensive optional extras but an old double sheet or dust cover thrown right over the whole frame makes a fantastic house or tent (*see below* "Houses").

Failing outdoor space, there are indoor jungle gyms available which are constructed to stand safely on a hard floor and to fold up when not in use. They take a lot of space even when folded, though, and they are not big and heavy enough for older children. Such a frame may not be a good investment for a single family. If you have no garden, consider instead:

A home-made climbing set. Acquire a couple of big wooden boxes or strong plastic bales, large enough for the child to get right inside. Tea chests are the easiest to find but check them carefully for sharp metal bits. Buy one or two planks, about six feet long by eight inches by one inch. Sandpaper the lot and paint it, perhaps, with brilliant colored gloss paint. The child will use this collection, separately and together, for years. She will hide in, climb on, and jump off the boxes; put them together for a train or on top of each other for a ship's bridge. The planks will be walked along on the floor and put across the boxes for a bridge. With one end on the box she has a slide, with the middle over the box she has a seesaw.

• You may help your own storage problems if you find one box which is smaller than the other so that they fit inside each other when not in use. If you cannot store the boxes, it is still worth making the plank alone. Propping one end on the sofa makes a balancing bar or slide and when she is not using it herself she will sit dolls on it or run cars down it.

Indoor swings. If you can screw two heavy-duty hooks into a ceiling joist in a room which has enough clear floor space, your child will have the potential for endless swinging play. The easiest way to provide it is with a "gym set," which you can buy from large toy suppliers. The set usually consists of a pair of ropes with special safety clips on either end. You clip one end onto your ceiling hooks and the other onto the interchangeable rope ladder, trapeze bar or swinging rings. Of course you can follow this idea using your own ropes, but those clips do make it easier and safer to make the changes.

For a brand-new experience for an older pre-school child, hang either the *elasticated rope* from her now-outgrown baby bouncer, or the kind sold by car accessory shops for fastening over roof racks. Holding onto this she can jump and feel that she is defying gravity.

If the floor beneath your hooks is hard, you may be happier if you provide her with a soft landing. A sheet of one and a half inch foam rubber will do a great deal to protect her and can be neatly rolled in an elastic band for storage. Such a "gym mat" will be a plaything in its own right, encouraging her in all kinds of adventures like turning somersaults and standing on her head.

The basic activity and why she will enjoy it	Ways of providing this kind of fun from the grand to the modest

"Houses" and other secret and private places. Children need "houses" for many different kinds of play over a number of years. "Wendy-house" games, involving dolls and domestic equipment, are only a small part of this. A house is also needed as expedition headquarters, clubhouse, camp, hospital or simply as a retreat from adults.

You can buy your child a house, ranging from a wooden one to stand in the garden to an adaptable wooden house/puppet theater/shop to stand indoors, or a house-shaped tent to be put up anywhere. But they are all expensive and, because they are always the same, a bit limiting. Some or all of the following ideas will probably serve a vast variety of purposes better:

A wigwam is cheap and self-supporting, as useful in the living room as in the garden and a good pre-school present.

An old-fashioned screen can be used across any corner. If you want to elaborate it you can cut a door and window.

A vast cardboard box of the kind that stoves, refrigerators and freezers are delivered in, makes a superb house if you can possibly find the space to store it. It will not last forever, but if you enjoy handiwork you can transform it into something a bit more permanent. Seal it all over with size and then with paint and strengthen all the joins and edges with insulating tape. Use simulated-brick wallpaper, stick on flowers, or whatever you please to decorate it, and make a small window (cutting out too much cardboard will weaken the structure). Treated like this it should stand up to months of use.

Curtained bay windows make excellent "houses" if you hang the curtains so that they draw across rather than around the bay.

Vast tablecloths over tables transform the area under the table into a hideout.

Arts and craft play. From the time she first discovers that a crayon can mark a sheet of paper, this kind of play will be important to your child. Through drawing and painting she will not only learn to manage the preliminaries to writing, she will also learn about color and shape, and express some of her views about the world and her own problems. Through cutting and sticking and trying to make things she will acquire manual dexterity as well as the pleasure which can come only through her own efforts. Through dabbling in finger painting or messing around with dough she will get tremendous sensual pleasure and, later on, when she can actually create things which satisfy her, she will discover not only the behavior of the materials she uses but also that she can control them.

This whole category of play activity can be difficult to provide for if space is very short and cleanliness important. Try to make a corner for her which has an easy-clean table at the right height, shelf space for her materials and, ideally, at least some space for her to "display" her afternoon's work.

Remember that when a child first tries out a new activity of this kind she probably does not want to draw, paint or make *anything in particular*. She is exploring the material and its potential, so if you try to make her "draw mommy" or "cut out a star" you will be interfering with her play. In the same way, coloring books, painting-by-numbers and many craft kits can set such rigid limits around the child's activity that they frustrate and bore her. Stick to open-ended activities until or unless she actually asks for something more structured.

On the whole, the younger the child the larger should be her materials—whether these are lumps of dough, sheets of paper or paintbrushes. When she is in a phase of much enjoying this kind of activity, she can easily use twenty very large sheets of paper in an afternoon and perhaps half a pint of paint (some used, the rest inextricably mixed to muddy brown). Few families can afford to cater on this scale if they are buying from an art shop. Your best sources of materials are probably educational suppliers (many of whom produce catalogues for mail-order buying). Sometimes several families can share a bulk order of a basic supply such as construction paper or powder paint. When you have nothing special available for her, your child will be better off with large sheets of shelf paper (or even newspaper) and large quantities of home-made paint than with a strictly rationed supply of typing paper and "real" poster color. Plasticine and play dough can become very expensive, too, because a freely playing child mixes the colors as part of the activity but will not happily use the resulting brownish lump for her next session. It is far cheaper to make your own. You will find some recipes under Presents (*see below*).

The basic activity and why she will enjoy it	Ways of providing this kind of fun from the grand to the modest

Imaginative and "acting" play. In a sense, all play is imaginative but, at certain stages in childhood, much of your child's play will involve *pretending* that she is somebody else or *pretending* that the objects she uses are something else. It is through this kind of play that she tries out other people's roles ("mommy"; that policeman, etc.) and strives to understand other ways of life ("going to the office," for example). It is also through these games that she may try to sort out, and come to terms with, worries and bad experiences like going to the hospital or getting "lost." The most important thing you can provide for this whole vital area of activity is a sympathetic, interested but unintrusive ear. But there are a few practical aids she may also enjoy.

There are hundreds of commercially produced "props" for imaginative play ranging from tea-sets for dolls to plastic replicas of almost everything adults use from brooms and vacuum cleaners to typewriters and record players. Although your child may enjoy a few possessions of this kind, they are likely to be status symbols rather than uniquely useful playthings because they tend to limit rather than extend the functioning of her own imagination. Take that broom as an example: if she actually wants the floor to be clean, she will probably sweep more efficiently with your handbrush than with that toy broom. If she wants to *be you*, she will certainly feel more like you if she struggles with your own big broom, or pretends that a stick is that broom, than she will with the toy one.

She needs some props for imaginative play but the best ones will be yours which you will let her use and/or old ones which you have finished with. If you can find some junk storage space (if you are lucky enough to have an attic or a cellar, for example, or even a big understairs closet) try to save for her your old shopping bag/handbag, discarded cleaning tools and cooking tools; plastic picnicware, slightly broken umbrellas (watch out for sharp bits), old hats, gloves, shoes and any accessories you do not want like hideous scarves or outdated "jewelry" (watch out for small beads). Anything which you might have sent to a rummage sale may be useful in her play, so when you have a clear-out, put yourself in her shoes before you let anything go.

Imaginative play often involves dressing in the part. Even if you have not the space to store much junk, try to assemble a "dressing-up box" not of bought costumes for specific characters ("Superman" will not fit her in another six months, anyway) but of cast-off clothes which she can use for many different characters. An old but glamorous nightgown, for example, can serve as ball gown, queen's robe or fairy dress. Father's discarded pajamas can clothe a famous baseball player or an overalled workman. Any kind of uniform (even the school gear discarded by an older brother or sister) transforms a very young wearer into a number of official characters from policeman to train conductor.

When you can see that a particular role is absorbing your child—as a doctor's role may interest her after a stay in the hospital, for example—you may be able to help her along with a specific kit, tailored to her particular age, stage and needs. You will find some ideas in Presents (*see below*).

Books. Pleasure in the written word will be almost as important to your child as enjoyable talking (*see* **Language**). She does not have to *learn to read* early, she only has to feel, from her very first months, that books are fun: that they have interesting pictures in them for her to gaze at, then identify, then name . . . that they contain stories and rhymes which you will read to her and which she can relate to those squiggly symbols through their illustrations. If she loves them at two and discovers, at four, that a book will sometimes enable you to answer her "why?" questions, she will *want* to read. When she is ready, she will do so.

Your child can enjoy books almost from birth. The more she has and the earlier she has them, the more she will take them for granted as a fun part of her life. She should be a welcome member of your local children's library from the beginning, but try to buy her books, too, so that she can turn her favorites into old friends and learn some by heart long before she can read.

She needs some with big, realistic pictures of familiar everyday objects. The two of you can look at them together and, over months of watching you turn the pages for her, she will discover how books "work"—from front to back and left to right. Cloth, board and home-made books (*see* Playthings for babies) will be valuable; she can hold and chew and "read" them for herself.

She needs you to read her stories, especially storybooks with pictures, so that she can read the illustrations while you read the words. Even when she goes to school (especially if being taught to read is boring her) she needs the pure pleasure of a book she enjoys, read aloud chapter by chapter, night by night. And even before she can read, get her some "reference books" and let her see you check up on things she wants to know like what Roman soldiers wore. . . .

Presents

Buying presents for children is fun if you have enough money. Making presents for children is fun if you have enough time and skill. But *assembling* presents for children, of the kind outlined below, is the most fun of all because with a little money and a lot of loving imagination, the child gets a gift which you can exactly fit to her interests, her age-stage and her very own preferences-of-the-moment.

Don't be prevented from assembling one of these presents by the fact that your child already has and uses one of its component parts: a big part of the point of each is the way the various objects and materials are presented together. She may have been painting for months yet still be enchanted by one of the painting sets. Do take trouble over the presentation, though. One of the sad differences between a "bought" and a "home-made" gift is often the presence or absence of a shiny new box to keep everything in. If you are going to take this much trouble over your present, it is worth taking the extra trouble to find a box everything will fit into and pretty it up with paint or wallpaper.

The suggestions outlined here are intended only to generate your own ideas: these are all 'kits' which the author's own children enjoyed and used in their play, but that does not mean that they are exactly right for yours. If you are going to do something similar, though, remember that *this kind of present assembly takes time.* If you are going to do it as cheaply as possible, it may take weeks to assemble all the bits and pieces. Decide well in advance of the child's birthday, or whatever, or you will end up buying a commercial kit after all and losing the whole point.

"Art" presents Most children love to paint. Very young ones usually enjoy finger painting most of all but seldom have *all* their favorite colors at the same time, because parents naturally want the only-slightly-muddy green used up before they buy more. These cost very little to make and will keep indefinitely in the refrigerator.

Finger paints. Combine non-toxic wallpaper paste and dry powder paint and mix with water to the consistency of thick cheese sauce.

Use bright and subtle colors (remembering your own child's favorite, however peculiar) and include black and white.

Either buy clear plastic screw-topped jars or save matching glass jars (instant coffee jars do well if you can save enough in the time you have left yourself) which you cover with sticky-backed plastic so that if they break the glass cannot shatter and splinter free. Leave a clear strip down the jar so that the paint color can be seen, or paint the screw top to match the contents.

Present with some or all or more of the following:

- □ A square of white Formica-covered board ⎫
- □ A square of glossy linoleum ⎬ She can paint,
- □ A large "mirror-tile" from ⎬ wash and reuse
  a bathroom center ⎭ all these
- □ A comb ⎫
- □ A plastic fork ⎬ for making patterns in the paint
- □ A butter curler ⎭ as a change from fingers

Folded, drippy and air painting. Even a child who has graduated from finger painting to a brush and poster paints may enjoy this kit, which is really a set of suggested activities and the wherewithal to carry them out.

Folded paintings require big sheets of paper which you present, already creased down the middle, along with an eye dropper (from the drugstore), plastic spoon and drinking straw. She drops paint, from whichever implement she chooses, onto one-half of the paper and then closes it for a "mirror image."

Drippy paintings require the same tools, but in addition, some large sheets of shiny cardboard. You can buy bright colors from an art shop. The child again drops paint however she pleases, but she then tips the card in different directions to make drip patterns.

Air paintings can be done either on the same kind of card or on Formica board or linoleum. There are several versions, requiring increasingly expensive equipment and mature skill:

Drop the paint and then blow through a straw.

Apply the paint through a plastic squeeze bottle (you can buy empty ones—intended for cosmetic refills) from Woolworth's.

Apply the paint in a fine spray from a garden hand-sprayer (you can buy a pint size from any garden shop).

These types of "paintings" require rather thin paint but are dull if the colors are not rich. Powder paint mixed to the consistency of milk will do, but liquid paint from a craft shop—which comes in amazing colors and is already exactly the right texture—is better.

Present the paint, the equipment and an example of each result so that she can see the point, all together in a box.

Printing. The process of banging a stamp onto an ink pad and then onto paper enchants most children, but the standard letter-printing sets are much too fiddly.

You can buy sets of stamps with animal shapes or funny figures, and ink pad sets, but you can give a much more elaborate and imaginative activity for less money if you make your own, or at least add to the bought set.

Make the stamps out of one-inch softwood cubes. Sandpaper them smooth and then glue all kinds of interesting shapes on to one surface of each block. Obvious ones are a curtain ring; a squiggle of string; a cross made of sponge-rubber; a big flat button with holes in it; a random array of matchsticks and a variety of shapes cut out of felt. Make the ink pads by lining flat tins with quarter-inch sponge rubber and soaking each in a different brilliant color of washable ink from an art shop.

If this present catches on, the child can elaborate it for herself by discovering that anything textured which she presses on her ink pads will transfer a pattern onto paper. She can try a make-up sponge, a chunk of bread, a grainy piece of wood . . . one day she will make "potato cuts."

To make a grand present out of this idea, take the trouble to paint the stamp-cubes in shiny colors before you glue on their printing ends. You can take the surface off your tins with steel wool, too, or paint those with enamel hobby paints.

Cutting and sticking. However much cutting and sticking your child has done, you can make a present which will thrill her if you give a really large collection and make sure that it includes some items which she has not been offered before. It is getting it all at once, like a treasure chest, which is the point, so make sure that you present everything in one box and laid out so that she can see tempting corners of this and glimpses of that as she opens it. It might include basics like:

☐ Different colors of construction paper (including black)
☐ Shiny gummed papers
☐ A glue pen
☐ Round-ended real scissors

Extras like:

☐ Colored tissue
☐ Colored foils
☐ Paper doilies
☐ Stiff colored cardboard
☐ Gummed paper shapes

Trimmings like:

☐ Sticky stars, labels, pictures and motifs
☐ Pipe cleaners
☐ Paper streamers
☐ Small balls of colored wool
☐ Scrapbook pictures

Making things Many pre-school children long to make things, things they can really use or keep, but few of them are ready for commercial kits. You can pre-prepare a kit to fit your own child's exact interests and abilities but you will need time, patience and privacy in which to do it.

Woodwork. Cut the basic shapes of boats, doll's house furniture, model village houses, or whatever, out of softwood. Balsa wood is much the easiest to work with but also much the most expensive.

Present them with strips of dowelling, sandpaper, glue, scraps of material for sails/cushions, etc. so that the child can finish and decorate them herself.

Dressing up. Cut out masks, crowns, etc. from stiff cardboard and give with paints, sticky papers, elastic, etc. for the child to finish for herself.

Dolls' clothes. Make basic dresses or skirts with elasticized necks/waists so that they will fit a variety of dolls. If you hate sewing, use felt. It needs no hemming and can even be glued.

Give to the child with a collection of pretty buttons, fringe, lace, ribbons, etc. so that she can make them as elaborate as she pleases with a minimum of effort.

Soft toys. The boring part for a child is the sewing of the basic shape. Sew this for her and then present it with a bag of foam-crumbs for stuffing and a collection of button eyes, bits of fur fabric for special ears and so forth.

Polystyrene modelling. If your child is old enough to be trusted with orange sticks or toothpicks, which are sharp, she can make elaborate people, vehicles, etc. using polystyrene balls, blocks and sheets.

Buy a selection of these polystyrene pieces from a craft shop. Present with toothpicks, dowelling, glue, paint, wool and material scraps. She can fasten the polystyrene pieces together simply by pushing a toothpick into each. She can then dress or decorate her people or other objects, or paint them to hang as mobiles or Christmas decorations.

Box modelling. Although your child will almost certainly already have "made" things out of boxes and other junk, a big collection of carefully saved and presented material, perhaps with one model already started to give her the idea, can be bliss. You might want to include:
- ☐ Stout, pretty boxes—especially shoe and chocolate boxes
- ☐ Matchboxes
- ☐ Different cardboard tubes (from toilet paper, paper towel rolls, etc.)
- ☐ A good paper glue
- ☐ Mail tags
- ☐ Stamp hinges
- ☐ Ring reinforcements
- ☐ Colored string
- ☐ Colored sticky tape

If you want to make a grand present and you can trust the child to take care of her fingers, add a small stapler which is much more effective in box-modelling than yards of sticky tape.

Play dough and play cooking

If you make dough from equal parts of plain flour and salt, mixed with just enough water to give a "pastry" texture, it will keep for a long time in the refrigerator and, because it is cheap, you will probably feel able to replace muddy colors with fresh ones.

You can color the dough either by using food coloring in the water or by mixing powder paint with the flour.

Assemble a basic present by filling matching plastic pots (such as half-gallon ice cream containers) with different colors of dough, sticking a label to match the contents on each pot.

Add extras such as cookie cutters, rolling pins, etc. and pack in a box with the plastic tablecloth you hope she will use.

Unless the idea of "playing with food" shocks you (and after all she will one day have to learn to cook) you can assemble a play-cooking set of any degree of elaboration. A really good one might include:
- ☐ Many small pots and other lidded containers (all with their printing scrubbed off) filled with flour, sugar, various cereals, chocolate bits, alphabet pasta, dried lentils, cocoa powder, etc.
- ☐ A collection of small plastic spoons, measuring scoops (like the ones which come with baby formula or soap powder), a wooden spoon and one or two plastic mixing bowls.
- ☐ As many miniatures of jam, ketchup, salad dressing and so forth as you can decently collect.
- ☐ Any more expensive extras you would like her to have, like cake-tins, an egg whisk or even a battery-operated toy food mixer.

Present the whole lot in a deep plastic tray and make it clear that washing up is part of the fun.

● For her own sake, make one rule for play cooking: "Always put the things you want to mix into one of your bowls." If she adds the contents of her chocolate bits pot to her pot of flour, she will have neither next time; if she adds water to her pot of pasta you will have a very smelly collection indeed.

Imaginative play sets

If your child is currently fascinated by doctors, nurses and hospitals, or by shops or offices, you may be able to elaborate on commercial outfits to double their play value.

Medical kits. Unless you can sew you will probably have to buy a basic uniform, but you can assemble the rest of a realistic kit more cheaply using real items than play ones. For example, your pharmacist will give (or sell for very little):

☐ Disposable syringes (without the needles, of course)
☐ Pill containers (not child-proof; you do not want her to practice getting those open)
☐ Tongue depressors.

☐ Real adhesive dressings and bandages cost no more than play ones.
☐ A pen-light can be used for inspecting throats, eyes and ears.
☐ A thermometer case (when you have broken the contents) can have a play thermometer in it and still seem real.

If you want to assemble a very grand present, or are helping your child to play out a hospital stay which is obviously still haunting her, you can buy even more medical-seeming equipment quite cheaply if you look at the ranges of disposable goods which are intended for families carrying out long-term nursing at home. There are disposable drawsheets and bedpans, for example.

If you want to present all this "medical equipment" in the equivalent of a doctor's bag, a first aid kit intended for schools or offices will be cheaper and look more realistic than a child's "doctor set."

Shops. There are plenty of miniature shops on the market, but the contents of the little containers are seldom real—which is disappointing—and only the most hideously expensive include the items which are most fun, such as scales.

You can refill commercially produced containers with your own contents and add some extras and some real samples—such as miniature jams and honeys, too. If you want to add a bakery, you can either buy doll's house bread and cakes, or bake your own flour and water and then paint them. You can buy or make marzipan fruit and vegetables to add a greengrocery department, too.

For a grand present, add a small set of working scales and a toy till with play money (or real money if she will not put it in her mouth). Add some tiny paper bags which you can charm out of your sweet shop, and a receipt pad bought from a stationery store.

Present the whole lot in a large cardboard box which you have covered in sticky-backed plastic. It will serve as the counter when it is emptied and turned upside down.

Post office or office. Many children are both fascinated and puzzled by the work they see going on behind the counters of post offices, banks and libraries and by the strange activities they hear about "at the office." An office set is easy to assemble:

Collect every one of the enormous variety of official-looking forms available to you, free, at the bank, the post office or the building society. Your child will not mind whether this is a television license application or a payment form, as long as she has lots of different ones.

Collect as many trading stamps as you can for her to use as stamps. Ask your post office for "airmail," "urgent," "first class" and "fragile" stickers.

Supply various kinds of paper, envelopes, etc. from the family supply. So far your kit is more or less free, but the present will become grander if you add some of the following:

☐ Blotting paper and real (washable) ink is a treat these days for all but the very youngest children.

☐ A telephone is a must for offices (save an old telephone book).

☐ An ink pad and date-stamp will be the pinnacle of grandeur.

Older children and playing at work

By middle childhood, imaginative acting-out play has usually given place to a great desire in the child to try out adult activities for real. Cooking a cake or a meal, digging the garden, cleaning the car or painting the ceiling, doing the shopping or bathing the baby may all be work to you, but to your child they may be among the most desirable kinds of play.

Try not to be in too much of a hurry to indict all such chores as "boring" or to label them as undesirable by offering the child money for doing them. The more activities she can try out and the more useful activities she can find fun, the better. Sometimes parents are so smitten with guilt at the sight of a twelve-year-old doing the ironing they loathe that they quite forget that she is only doing it for fun and that in this situation everyone gains. It is important, though, to be sensitive to the moments when novelty wears off, sufficient skill has been acquired and the game is turning into a chore. If she wanted to paint that fence, by all means insist that she finish it, but don't expect her to paint the one in the back as well.

If you can provide enough opportunities for children old enough to acquire the skills but still young enough to lack adolescent self-consciousness, your family may acquire a great many techniques which will benefit them when they are grown up. The child who learns to clean spark plugs as part of play-tinkering with the car will not forget how when her own car refuses to start. The one who teaches herself to type or use a computer at ten will have a flying start in that training course later on.

Older children and play

Some children continue to be able to play unselfconsciously with actual toys for far longer than others. The child who can play in this way almost certainly uses her play both to relax herself and to provide a structure for a different kind of thinking-play which is going on inside her head. Don't be in any hurry to get rid of toys and don't ever suggest, or even imply, that any child is "too old for" anything.

A child who wants to play, but cannot quite let herself, may find a way out in playing with younger children: her own brothers and sisters, neighbors or the children in the local playgroup. Don't open up this harmless piece of self-deception. If she is enjoying herself and the younger ones are having fun, too, why must she be forced to realize that she is really making clay animals for herself rather than them?

Some older children stop playing *games* with their toys but continue to value them—often for years—as friendly familiars and ornaments, that go on inhabiting the shelves in their rooms and a corner of their minds and emotions. Some elaborate collections of dolls or soldiers, model animals, guns or cars start in this way, and a few turn into new kinds of "games," acceptable to adults, such as a passion for model railways or radio-controlled cars.

Much of the best play of older children does not involve play *objects* at all, but either centers around mutual activities like cycling or fishing, or is simply the nameless and varying activity of companions exploring increasing independence. If you ask an eleven-year-old what she is going to do this afternoon, she is likely to answer, "I'm meeting Jane." The companionship *is* the activity and they will play in talk always and in action sometimes. They may look totally unoccupied to you yet be absorbed.

Some children's lives become so full of structured activities that spontaneous just-for-fun play almost ceases. Ironically, these include some of the children who seem, to adults, best occupied. They may be children whose parents and community organize for them a ceaseless round of out-of-school activities, so that every evening is taken up with swimming lessons or drama groups or one club or another. Or they may be children who spend almost every moment out of school involved in the organized sports which are so much in vogue. Many sports activities are referred to as "playing games," but in truth most are not play at all for the majority of participants. Competition ensures that they are stressful and, to some extent, destructive of social relationships. Training and practice ensure that they are often hard, and sometimes reluctant, work, while the involvement of supporters, coaches and a team ensures that the child is not free to make her own decisions about what she wants to do but is forced to perform, willy-nilly, for the sake of others' opinions.

If your child is singled out for sports activity by her school or club and wants to participate, you are most unlikely to be able to stop her and therefore you will probably want to support her. But you may at least be able to avoid giving her the feeling that you, like all those others, love her only for her prowess. She needs to be sure that, proud though you may be of her skills, you are even more proud of her as a person, and that her happiness is now, and always will be, more important to you than any of her victories.

Whatever the pattern of your older child's life, whatever its balance between school and home, school friends and home friends, group activities and solitary or paired activities, there needs to be some space left in it for sheer spontaneous, possibly pointless, fun. If we allow our older children to be driven from one achievement to the next, on an ever-tighter schedule, we cannot be surprised if they become as harassed as striving executives and ready, in adolescence, either to break away from all achievement to look for a peace of their own, or to join their ulcer-ridden elders in the nearest bar.

Playgroups *see* **School**/Pre-school and nursery education.
Pleurisy *see* **Chest Infections**.
Pneumonia *see* **Chest Infections**.

Pocket Money *see also* **Adolescence**/The long road to independence: Money

Like it or not, money is important in our society. It not only *buys* material necessities, comforts, treats and luxuries; it also *represents* psychological necessities, like aspects of our self-esteem, status, success and independence.

A child's pocket money will probably be his introduction to financial and economic life. It is worth thinking carefully not just about how much he should have, at what age, but about what you want his pocket money to be for, and to stand for, to him.

Very young children and money

Most pre-school children cannot understand money as anything but "treasure," another version of the tokens they put in slot machines, or possibly as mysterious things which can be swapped for things of obvious value like sweets or comics.

There is no real point in money for a child at this stage. If you buy for him the little Saturday treats he may later buy for himself, he will lose nothing by not having pocket money. He is not ready.

● To check on this, try giving your very young child a Saturday coin. You will probably find that:

If circumstances allow he will at once spend it, happily swapping it for that comic but being quite uninterested in either the change or the possibility that he could buy a cheaper comic *and* a lollipop.

If he cannot at once spend it he will abandon it. Although pleased with the friendly gesture of being given the money, even an hour's delay before he can turn it into something "real" means that you will find that coin dropped on the bathroom floor, forgotten.

First pocket money

However small the weekly sum you can afford, your child's pocket money can be valuable in all senses to him if:

It is money freely, pleasantly and regularly given as his right. This small sum of money is, so to speak, a non-earning child's equivalent of your wage or salary. You get it because you are you and because you do what you do. Your boss does not withhold your wage because he is angry with you or threaten to do so, or forget to give it to you. In the same way, the pocket money must be given to the child because he is himself, and there must be no way whatever (but *see below*) in which that right can be removed.

It is money which is kept entirely separate from any money he earns from "chores." If you want to pay him for mowing the lawn or cleaning the floor or the car, fine, but that should be an entirely separate negotiation. He gets his pocket money anyway, whatever he does or does not do.

It is money which he is genuinely free to spend as he pleases. If you give him a weekly sum but insist that he save half, then you are really giving him only half the pocket money stated between you. If you want him to accumulate money, perhaps in a savings account, for spending on other people's Christmas presents or whatever, give it to him separately.

Pocket money is for spending as, when and how he wishes. If he chooses to spend it immediately on sweets, that is his right unless you can educate him out of sweet-eating. If he chooses to buy plastic nonsense which will break before the day is over, that is his right (and his eventual sorrow), too. If he chooses to save up for something specific, fine, and if he chooses just to let the money accumulate in a moneybox for nothing in particular, that's fine, too. It is up to him. He may spend it, always, on presents for you. Don't worry; the freedom to give is an important one.

When a child thinks his pocket money is too little

Older children usually feel a great need to be on a financial par with their friends—just as adults like to be paid at the same rate for the job as their colleagues. But sometimes your child will completely misunderstand the financial arrangements of other families and will feel deprived when in fact he is not. If he feels that you give him far too little, check on the following:

Are the large sums given to others pocket money or necessity money? Some parents who cannot be at home at the end of the school day, for example, give their children quite large daily sums to cover the purchase of an afternoon snack and, perhaps, some entertainment. Others give their children lunch money, rather than paying for a school meal or providing a packed one. In discussion, you should be able to clarify with your child the difference between his pocket money (which is purely for fun) and their "maintenance money."

Are these large sums pocket money or an "allowance"? Some families allocate and give a weekly sum which is not just for pleasure-spending but for *all* occasional-spending. Such a child may be expected to pay his own fares, even when he is with his family; to buy his own school supplies; to buy any odd toiletries he needs and so forth. Once again, your child should be able to see the difference between this kind of money and the money he is given which is extra to the total provision made for him by you.

● If you and your child want to go onto an "allowance" system at an early stage, of course you can. Make sure, though, that the child does understand that the allowance is not just *more* money, but money for different purposes. There are also some snags:

It deprives you of the pleasure of buying for him. And the surprise purchase of minor items, like a new drawing book or felt-tip pen, some new talc and so forth, can be a great pleasure to you both.

It is difficult to stick to the "rules" when the family is together. If you all go to a movie and want a hot dog which the child cannot afford today, is he to go without or are you going to buy him one yourself even though he had the money and spent it on something else?

Are these large sums in fact "wages"? Some families regularly pay their children not just for odd chores but, for example, for Saturday help in the shop (*see* **Adolescence**/The long road to independence: Part-time jobs).

Are these large sums already partly spoken for? Some of the children whom your child considers rich will in fact be forced to put a certain sum in the savings bank, another sum in the church collection box and yet another towards the family's favorite charity. Your child should understand that only the money left over, after all that, can really be compared with his pocket money.

Is your child actually prevented, by his comparative poverty, from taking part in the life of his group? If, for example, a weekend trip to the movies or swimming pool is taken for granted by most of the kids, it is obviously sad for yours if he cannot go because he has no money for a ticket. But if you reckon to give him that kind of money, as and when he needs it and you can afford it, his actual pocket money may not be too little after all.

● Such a child may not be asking for *more money* overall but for the independence of budgeting for himself.

When you think his pocket money is too much

If your child is continually treating others to sweets or chips, buying gimmicks to take to school to show others and generally being generous to a fault, he may be trying to buy attention and popularity. Just cutting down the money he has available will not help, but you might need to ask yourself whether you are giving him money instead of your attention, and whether he might not make more genuine friendships if he was encouraged to offer the warmth and hospitality of his home.

If you think he spends his money stupidly

You cannot control how he spends his money without ruining the point of him having it, but if he does always spend it all on sweets you may like to consider the following:

Is it enough money for him to be able to buy anything other than sweets which he really wants? If you are giving him 50¢, for example, it may not seem to him worthwhile doing anything with it other than guzzle. He might spend more "sensibly" if he had rather more—enough, for example, to buy occasional additions to whatever he collects, or items for his current hobby.

Are you sure the items he buys are "stupid" *in his terms?* While some comics are certainly junk and you may disapprove of them, it can be argued that it is better that he should read comics than that he should not read at all. While small plastic toys do certainly break, they can give a great deal of pleasure in their short lives. Not all "collections" have to be formalized assemblies of stamps or butterflies; some children informally accumulate balls or dolls or toy guns and get infinite pleasure out of having every one-of-a-type. Finally, of course, many of the idiotic items children want/buy are part of mysterious school crazes parents cannot —and probably should not—understand. If yo-yos are "in" this term, a yo-yo is an essential.

Later on: money to meet commitments

Your schoolchild will eventually need to have some money available to him to meet the self-imposed commitments which are an excellent sign of responsible growing up. How, for example, can he offer to pay for that broken window if he has no money of his own? To have you say "I shall hold back your pocket money until it is paid for" is to *be punished* rather than to make retribution. How can he buy carefully thought-out and searched-for gifts if he has to ask the recipients for the money? How can he even decide to answer the current UNICEF disaster appeal with real self-sacrifice, if he has nothing to sacrifice?

Somewhere between, say, nine to eleven, every child needs to be helped towards some accumulation of money (however minute) in order to be able to do these things. It still should not be a compulsory segment of that pocket money but it might, for example, be an additional monthly sum to be put in the savings account under his own name. The extra can be given instead of an annual pocket money increase, if you prefer.

This money is the part of his "income" which he may wish to add to, or replace by, money he makes from a Saturday job.

Learning "the value of money" Whether you are rich, poor or in-between and whether you reckon that your children's needs and wishes have a high or lower priority in your family budgeting, every child does have to learn those hard lessons about money not growing on trees/having to be earned/not being able to be spent twice, and so forth. Fortunately, most children do absorb this kind of information because they hear you talking, see you shopping around for bargains, and know, almost instinctively, what *sort* of birthday presents it is worth asking for and which are totally out of reach.

Children are far more sensitive to their parents' feelings than many people realize. It is a rare ten-year-old who will ask for a racing bike when you are both out of work.

If you are afraid that your child really does not realize that the money you can earn limits what can be bought, and that what is bought today limits the money left for tomorrow, do him the honor of letting him share your worries and discussions. He may not yet realize:

The difference between salaried, weekly and hourly work. If your child is accustomed to a family in which salaries go on coming in no matter whether the earner is ill, on vacation or what, he may totally fail to understand what a strike or long period of illness can mean to his friends. If he is accustomed to your being able to organize your working hours around his needs, he may not understand that his best friends' mothers simply cannot afford not to turn up for their evening jobs because attending the school play will cost them three hours' money.

The difference between down payments and total costs. Many children whose families make all major purchases on extended credit or via credit "clubs," really believe that the down payment is the payment. The intricacies of interest may be beyond a seven-year-old, but the idea that if you borrow the money to pay for something you have to pay for the privilege as well as the something and, therefore, that it is cheaper to save up until you can buy outright, will not be.

The difference between what can be afforded and what is worthwhile. Many children, pleading to eat in an expensive restaurant, for example, will ask, "But haven't you *got* that much money?" They need gradually to learn that just possessing the cash, or having the money in the bank and a checkbook or credit card in your pocket, does not make that meal "affordable." Once again, you can put it to quite young children in simple terms: "There are seven dinners in the week and we usually spend about X on each one. If we spend Y on this one dinner there will only be a very little left for all the others. . . ."

"Hidden" expenditure like utility bills. While young children are bound to feel that electricity, water and telephone calls are freely "on tap," older children must learn about service costs. Many of the young adolescents whose parents grumble bitterly about the phone bills they run up and the lights they leave on have actually never been taught about these things. Persuade the child to make one of his phone calls from a coin box and let him see how fast he has to put in money; get him to watch the electric meter while that heater is on; eventually, show him the bills and let him help you to work it out.

Discussions of this kind can be both interesting and educational and, if you start them early enough, you may find your child applying the principles to his own expenditure ("I could buy the car but it uses up batteries so fast I'll never be able to go on affording it") and to yours, too ("Shall we sit in the cheaper seats and have ice cream as well?").

Poisoning *see* **Accidents**; **Safety**/In the home: Safety from household poisons; Safety with medicines. *See also* **Pollution**; **Suicide**.

Pollution *see also* **Allergy**; **Eating**/Common sense about family eating: Food additives

Human beings have worked to make living environments which are safer, more convenient and more productive/profitable for more and more people. But in doing so we have fouled our own nests. The self-maintaining and self-cleaning processes of our planet are stretched to their limits by the waste and by-products of our mechanized societies and vast populations. Human interference threatens the delicate balance of ecosystems upon which our survival, like that of all living things, depends. Every "technological fix," which improves some aspect of life for some group of people somewhere, tends to produce a ripple effect of disaster for another group elsewhere. Many people believe that unless we can learn to live in cooperative harmony with our natural environment, rather than raping it as the fancy or the invention takes us, we shall eventually poison the whole planet and humanity with it.

Individuals can do a great deal to increase public awareness of environmental issues and to put pressure on governments and industries for specific improvements. But even the most convinced and seasoned campaigner still has to live within the society he is trying to change. Parents, with the particular responsibility which they have for the lives of society's new individuals, have to realize that they cannot completely protect their children from the pollution brought about by earlier generations, nor prepare them to make a better future world by trying to do so. If you allow yourself to be overwhelmed by articles about air pollution, lead poisoning or chemical additives in commercially produced food, you will come to feel that you can keep your children healthy only by dropping right out of society and finding some untouched hillside retreat from which you can scratch a "natural" existence without technological aid. The truth is that only the very wealthy and eccentric can do that, and that those who do deprive themselves of the best that society can offer, as well as protecting themselves from the worst and offering it nothing.

Most of us are not rich, eccentric or escapist. We want our children to enjoy the best which their world has to offer *and* to be protected from the worst. We have to accept that their overall protection is not in the hands of individual families—except insofar as they are members of pressure groups—but in the hands of governments, industries, public health authorities and all the other giants of bureaucratic life. But if the protection against pollution which parents can give to their own children is limited, it is nevertheless real.

Air pollution   The air we breathe should ideally contain twenty percent oxygen and seventy-nine percent nitrogen, with only traces of other gases and no dirt particles. The oxygen balance of the planet as a whole is maintained by the coexistence of plant and animal life. Plants take in carbon dioxide and release oxygen; animals take in oxygen and release carbon dioxide. Urban areas, full of people and denuded of plant life, already strain that balance. Gasoline engines—especially the cars which clog city streets—burn oxygen and release carbon dioxide. Furthermore, *unburnt* gases from gasoline and diesel engines give off carbon monoxide which is lethal if a high concentration is breathed in. In the streets of Tokyo, traffic policemen carry oxygen equipment so that they can counteract subtle suffocation by carbon monoxide with a quick "breather" whenever they feel the need. In Britain, the law requires that the flue gases from factory chimneys should not contain more than thirty parts of carbon monoxide per million parts of air. But in a busy street the carbon monoxide level may easily reach three hundred parts per million. In some cities, particular combinations of landscape and climate lead to even greater hazards. In Los Angeles, for example, there are frequent "temperature inversions" which lead to polluted air being trapped over the city in the form of smog which, in the presence of sunlight, also contains the even more lethal gas, ozone.

Apart from distortions in the gaseous composition of air, city-dwellers also tend to breathe in "particulate matter" (dust, soot and ash) suspended in the atmosphere; 18,000 tons are put into the air over Manhattan each year; over St. Louis, 43,000 tons, and over Los Angeles even more, despite major improvement brought about in recent years by Clean Air legislation. Lung cancer and other lung complaints are commoner among city-dwellers—even among those who do not smoke.

Family action on air pollution   If a child spends several hours in an atmosphere containing too little oxygen relative to poisonous gases, she may feel ill. It is worth trying to avoid extreme situations, especially for babies and very young children. For example:

Try not to take a baby shopping in a packed main street in still, muggy weather with a cloudy sky; a few hours amid the trapped fumes and she (like you) may well be headachey and irritable.

● Strollers tend to put their occupants at exactly the level of vehicle exhaust pipes. She may be better off if you carry her in a sling.

Try to avoid long periods in a car stuck in crawling traffic jams or lines to get out of multi-story parking garages. Leave the city or the sports event early, if you can, so that you escape before the crowd and its exhaust fumes.

Heed warnings of local "smog" conditions. If the authorities suggest keeping children inside, or home from school, or out of particular areas, do as they say.

Theoretically, a child who spends all her time in a polluted atmosphere could be liable to mild but chronic ill effects both from that imbalance of gases and from the inflammatory effect on her lungs of those solid dirt particles. The best that you can do is to ensure that she has the cleanest possible air to breathe for as much of the time as possible. For example:

If you live in a highly polluted part of the city you may be able to enroll her at a school in a suburban area. It is the children who must both live and work in cramped backstreets, packed with traffic and overshadowed by industrial chimneys, who are most at risk.

Within the home you can do at least a little to avoid making dirty air dirtier. Whatever that air is like, living with heavy smokers will certainly make it worse for your child. If you must smoke, try not to do it in her bedroom or to "share" your cigarettes with her by smoking while she sits on your lap. If your home is on a busy street, try to organize the rooms so that she spends most of her time on the quieter side of the house. If open windows let in the stink of exhaust fumes and a lot of black specks, keep them closed and consider the possibility of air conditioning.

Try for occasional breaks: country weekends, mountain vacations or trips to the beach will all help.

Lead poisoning   Lead can accumulate in the bones of young children and it can also cause brain damage. Florid lead poisoning is rare and usually associated with the victim having chewed objects covered with lead-containing paint or picked and eaten old lead-containing plaster (see **Habits**/Other common and less common habits: Dirt-eating). Many authorities, however, now believe that lower levels of lead—insufficient to cause obvious illness —may nevertheless be damaging children. Some believe that the "safe levels" set by governments are too high; others that they are being much exceeded. Although the whole matter is still highly controversial, it may be that young children are being subtly poisoned; their intelligence reduced; their irritability increased.

The major additional source of lead in the environment comes from anti-knock additives to gasoline which produce lead-laden exhaust fumes. Some countries, including the U.S., are moving to a ban on such additives. In Britain they are still permitted as I write, although legislation to ban them is about to be passed. It remains to be seen how quickly and how effectively new laws will be enforced. As is so often the case in environmental health arguments, money is the key. A ban on lead in gasoline will make British motoring fractionally more expensive and may therefore damage the car industry.

Anything you do to give your child clean air to breathe (*see above*) will do something to protect her from lead. In addition:

Family action on lead pollution   **If you live in an old house, check for lead-containing paint/plaster.** You may believe that no child of yours would be so idiotic as to *eat the inedible*, but some children do.

● If you buy an old crib or painted toy, it is not enough to repaint it with safe paint. If the original covering might be unsafe, you must remove it first. A chewing child will soon get through a top layer.

Check water tanks and piping. Old houses still sometimes have lead-lined plumbing and this can mean running water with dangerously high lead levels, especially if the water is "soft" and therefore more liable to dissolve that lead.

Water pollution Rivers and oceans become polluted by industrial wastes from factories which discharge into them, by chemicals used in agriculture which are washed into them, and by human waste from inadequate or overtaxed sewerage systems. In the Western world you can be reasonably sure that water described as safe for drinking is safe, although it will usually have been made safe by the addition of chemicals which may, in themselves, be a kind of pollution. You may like to bear the following points in mind, though, especially when you are on vacation:

Family action **Don't let children drink from unusual water-sources unless you know**
on water **that they are pure or purified.** The old well at your vacation cottage may
pollution contain ice-cold, delicious-tasting water which generations of families lived on. But it may now be polluted by chemicals running off the nearby factory farm.

Don't let children swim in lakes, canals or rivers which are in, or downstream of, industrial areas.

Try to check on the state of beaches in your proposed vacation area before booking. Poorly treated sewage, which is not carried far enough out to sea, is not just revolting, it is also dangerous: there are bound to be some disease carriers among the tourists in the town (*see* **Infection**).

Pay attention to any warnings you are given about local seafood. Some shellfish, for example, actually concentrate in their bodies the chemicals and metals in polluted seawater.

Projectile vomiting *see* **Pyloric Stenosis.** *See also* **Hospital**/Surgery: Pyloric Stenosis.
Proteins *see* **Eating**/Types of food. *See also* **Allergy**/What allergy is: Gastrointestinal allergies.
Puberty *see* **Adolescence.**
Punishment *see* **Discipline, Self-discipline and Learning How to Behave.**
Pus *see* **Infection**/Types of infection: Localized infection. *See also* **Accidents**/Wounds and infection.

Pyloric Stenosis (Projectile Vomiting)

A condition in which the pylorus, the muscular valve controlling the flow of food from the stomach into the intestines, thickens to cause obstruction in early infancy. Over the first week or two of the baby's life milk becomes unable to leave the stomach by the normal route and is forcibly vomited. *See* **Hospital**/Surgery.

Quarantine *see* **Infection**/Preventing the spread of "infectious" illnesses. *See also* named infectious diseases.

Rabies

Rabies is a virus disease. When a rabid animal bites, viruses are introduced into the victim's bloodstream with the saliva. They then travel along the nerves towards the brain. The incubation period can be as much as a year so that the bite is both healed and completely forgotten long before there are any signs of illness. Once rabies is established, though, it is almost inevitably fatal. The victim suffers many nervous symptoms including the painful spasms of the throat when he tries to drink, or even thinks of water, which led to rabies being termed "hydrophobia." He becomes deranged and usually highly aggressive, which increases the likelihood of another victim being bitten and infected. Death usually comes during massive convulsions due to the infection having reached the brain.

Rabies mainly affects meat-eating animals and can become established in populations of wild creatures (foxes, skunks and mongooses, for example). Once this happens, any domestic carnivore, such as a dog or cat, which has contact with wild creatures, is at risk of being bitten and contracting the disease which it then brings into contact with its human environment. Humans who work with wild animals are also at direct risk. Blood-sucking (vampire) bats, for example, live off the blood of cattle in the tropics. Rabid ones infect those cattle and also attack the men who care for them.

Public health authorities fight a brave and largely successful battle against rabies and every family needs to understand something of the battle and lend them their support. In the U.S. rabies is not a disease which people constantly fear; yet the figures suggest that without the alertness of public health "watchdogs" it could rapidly become a widespread threat. There are about 7,000 cases reported among animals each year. While most of these are among wildlife (skunks in particular but also raccoons, foxes and bats), there are about 500 cases annually among domestic livestock and 400 victims among pet dogs and cats. Around 25,000 people receive preventive treatment following risky incidents with animals known to be, or thought likely to be, infected and the net result is that only 1 to 5 human cases of rabies occur each year.

Britain's island status, stringent importation restrictions and quarantine regulations have kept her free of rabies. Yet even here, many people resent those laws and regulations and dice with their good fortune by flouting them. It is not that any individual would deliberately introduce a potentially lethal disease into the U.K.—any more than he would deliberately spread it further in the U.S.—it is that individuals do not believe that the particular animals with which they are concerned *could* be infected. If you are ever tempted to smuggle a dear little puppy into the U.S. rather than submit him to vaccination and the required 30 days confinement, or if you are tempted to sidestep the expense of vaccination or to adopt a stray onto your vacation boat and take him across the six states which separate you from home, remember:

However healthy it may appear, rabies virus may be working slowly in its nervous system. It may stay healthy for months yet still become a "killer."

However convinced you are that it has never been bitten by an animal while abroad you cannot be certain. A tiny bite which only just breaks the skin is enough to introduce the virus.

However carefully you intend to restrain and observe the animal, if it is incubating rabies it will eventually escape your control as the virus affects its nervous system and alters its habit patterns, obedience and docility. It will be infectious and dangerous before you are aware that it is ill.

A rabid animal on the loose is not only a danger to the people it may bite but also to any other carnivorous animal—domestic or wild—which it may meet. Your animal may be caught and destroyed before it has infected any person, but it may already have seeded the infection among wildlife or started a chain of tragedy among the neighborhood's pets.

Countries which have rabies endemic in their wild animal populations employ a range of controls both to keep down their numbers and to prevent them from having contact with domestic pets and therefore with human beings. In some areas, for example, dogs are not allowed out unmuzzled/off leads/without human escorts. It is vitally important that the public abide by this sort of control.

If you live in, or visit, an area where there is known to be rabies, do make sure that you understand any regulations which may be in force and that you take precautions against the unlikely but disastrous possibility of your child being infected. For example:

Don't let children pet strange dogs or cats, especially those which are obviously "strays."

Don't encourage them to try to touch any wild creature even if they are passionate naturalists seriously observing wildlife. Remember that a healthy wild animal will seldom allow human handling; the skunk your child picks up is rather more likely than most to be sick. If there is rabies in the area, it *could* be rabid.

If a child is bitten by an animal which even could be rabid

Take the following precautions immediately even if the wound is no more than a pinprick:

Notice the creature. If it was a dog, you or other people may be able to catch it but don't risk getting bitten yourself. Instead, let it go but observe it carefully so that you will recognize it again, and notice where it goes so that you can later bring the authorities to the spot. The point is that doctors must proceed to treat your child as if she had been infected, but the animal must nevertheless be found and caught. They will need to establish whether or not it *was* rabid so as to protect other people and animals in the area if it was, or to relieve you if it was not.

If you are a visitor and the creature is unfamiliar to you (would you recognize a skunk?), notice it as carefully as you can so that you can describe it to a local expert. If it was not a meat eater, for example, you have nothing to worry about.

Clean the wound as thoroughly as you quickly can. If you can flood away the animal's saliva, you will at least reduce the load of virus introduced into the wound.

Get the child to expert medical attention. Local cleansing of the wound, together with immediate passive immunization against rabies, is vital. Treated immediately, your child's chances are excellent. The disease becomes unmanageable only once the viruses penetrate from the locally infected tissues into the bloodstream and from there into the nervous system.

Immunization against rabies Both passive and active immunization, for humans and for animals, are rapidly improving. Have your own pets protected. If you work with wild animals or your child plans a trip or a career involving handling them in high-risk areas, inquire about immunization for her.

Rashes *see* individually named diseases. *See also* **Allergy/**Urticaria.
Remarriage *see* **Divorce, Separation and One-parent Families**.
Resistance of "germs" to drugs *see* **Infection/**Treatment of infections.
Resistance to disease *see* **Immune System; Immunization; Infection**.
Respiratory disorders *see* **Chest Infections; Colds; Coughs; Croup and Laryngitis**.
Rhesus disease *see* **Blood Groups/**Who can give blood to, or receive it from, whom?
Rheumatic fever *see* **Scarlet Fever and "Strep" Throats**.

Ringworm and Athlete's Foot

Ringworm is a generic term for skin diseases which may be caused by any of several groups of fungi. The infecting organisms may be specific to humans, to cats and dogs or to cattle. Although they are not in themselves serious, fungal skin disorders are usually highly contagious so that bothersome epidemics easily occur in schools and other institutions. Laboratory help to identify the exact fungus responsible and therefore the exact treatment to which it will be sensitive is usually needed.

Ringworm of the scalp

Whether acquired from human, pet or cattle sources, the disease is easily passed on by direct contact, either head to head in contact sports or via infected brushes and combs.

First signs of scalp ringworm A small scaly spot appears on the scalp. It is easily missed because it is still hair-covered, but careful examination shows a few broken hairs on its surface.

Older lesions have grayish scales which may be thicker at the edges so that each patch has a distinct margin. Fungus is growing in the hair shafts, weakening each hair so that it breaks off close to the scalp.

If the infection was acquired from cattle (from rubbing posts, etc.) the patches may be inflamed. The more inflamed the patches, the more likely it is that the body will in fact eradicate the infection for itself. Treatment can, however, shorten the process by preventing the appearance of further lesions.

Treatment of scalp ringworm

Local treatments used to include many ointments and dyes together with plucking out the infected hairs. Now your doctor may prescribe a specific fungicide to be applied locally and a safe and effective antibiotic (griseofulvin) to be taken by mouth.

Most schools will exclude infected children (and may examine others for early signs) until they are clear of active infection. If the school does not exclude your child, you should probably keep her at home anyway. Apart from the risk of her spreading the fungi, she is likely to be extremely self-conscious about her "bald" patches.

After a widespread infection is over, normal regrowth of the hair takes some weeks. A change in hairstyle may help to camouflage the patches or a kerchief, scarf or baseball cap may be acceptable "headgear" in the child's social group.

Preventing the spread of scalp ringworm

Within the home the infection can usually be contained and prevented from spreading to other family members if:

The infected child scrupulously avoids any hairbrush, comb or towel but her own (and others avoid hers).

She avoids other people's pillows and they avoid hers.

She wears some form of head covering so as to minimize the likelihood of infected dead hairs and scales falling on other people.

Ringworm of the beard area

This is usually acquired by individuals in close contact with infected cattle. Leaning the face against the flank of an infected dairy cow during milking is the most common cause. This kind of ringworm often produces severe inflammation and swelling and requires medical attention.

Ringworm of the body skin

This often, though not necessarily, coexists with scalp ringworm.

First signs of ringworm on the body

As in scalp ringworm, patches of pale scaly discs on the skin may have a raised and defined edge and may, if the fungus is of animal origin, be highly inflamed.

The affected skin is extremely itchy. Scratching can lead to local secondary infection and/or to the eventual appearance of ringworm of the nails (*see below*).

"Jock itch"

Is the name given to ringworm of the groin area which, because of the moist warmth, is often especially active.

Treatment

Is similar to scalp ringworm: Local fungicide and/or griseofulvin.

Preventing the spread of ringworm of the body skin

This kind of ringworm can certainly be acquired by contact with scalp ringworm or via shower mats, towels, etc. It may also be acquired from borrowed clothing. The spread of infection within the home (and day institution) can usually be prevented if, as well as avoiding sharing towels, etc. with anyone else, the sufferer takes trouble over the clothing she wears next to her skin and where she removes it.

The easiest system for a schoolchild, for example, is to dress and undress in the empty bath or shower stall (which can easily be washed when she has finished). She removes her day clothes and replaces them immediately with freshly laundered nightclothes, the day clothes being put straight into the laundry. In the morning she repeats the process, putting on clean day clothes (underclothes at least) and putting her nightclothes into the laundry. In this way shed scales are never left on communal floors and there is no chance of a sister putting on an infected sweater by mistake.

Obviously these precautions require an adequate supply of clothing and excellent laundry facilities. It is for this reason that ringworm of the skin is more common and more difficult to control where social conditions are poor.

Ringworm of the feet (athlete's foot)

The term "athlete's foot" is used generically to include any fungus infection of the feet. It has nothing to do with athletics but is common in any population which shares communal baths, locker rooms, etc. so that many individuals' bare feet share warm humid conditions. Fungus infection can be differentiated from numerous other foot afflictions (such as excessive sweating, allergy to chemicals in shoe leather, etc.) only by laboratory study.

First signs of athlete's foot The most typical case begins with sodden, cracking and peeling skin between two toes, often the fourth and fifth. The skin is extremely itchy. Scratching removes the white sodden surface skin to reveal raw red skin underneath.

Bacterial secondary infection of these open sores is quite common and requires medical attention.

Treatment of athlete's foot Very acute cases can be treated with griseofulvin, although this drug may not (for reasons which are ill-understood) totally eradicate minor chronic infection.

There are many local fungicidal applications for the feet. Any one may be effective and, if the first has not proved effective within about ten days, an alternative should be tried. Treatment should continue for about four weeks, the time the skin will take to renew itself. If there is no bacterial secondary infection a doctor's advice is seldom needed.

Preventing the spread of athlete's foot Within the home, people with active infection should not go barefoot and should not share towels, etc. with others. Within schools and other institutions it is usual to exclude sufferers from swimming pools and locker rooms. In a day institution such measures may serve to control infection provided the sufferer does not go barefoot elsewhere (in the gymnasium, for example). In residential institutions infection and re-infection are common.

Ringworm of the nails

Ringworm may infect both toenails and fingernails, although the latter is more common and probably arises from scratching ringworm infections elsewhere on the body.

Infection in the nails progresses extremely slowly (often over years), gradually producing areas of nail which are dark, crumbly and deformed. Prevention is easier than cure: athlete's foot sufferers should try not to scratch active lesions. Cure is almost certain with griseofulvin, but the drug may have to be taken for as much as a year to eradicate the fungus from thoroughly infected nails.

Rituals *see* **Habits**.
Road safety *see* **Safety**/On the road; On wheels.
Rocking *see* **Habits**.

Roseola Infantum

Is a mild, moderately infectious virus disease which almost exclusively affects children under three. Although it is known to occur in small-scale epidemics, little is known about its actual prevalence because it may often pass undiagnosed.

Incubation period. Nine to ten days.

Route of infection. Droplet infection from nose and throat to nose and throat.

First symptoms of roseola infantum   Fever without any other signs. The fever may be high (perhaps as high as 103°–105°F [39.5°–40.5°C]) and the child therefore seems extremely unwell. There is nothing to guide the doctor in deciding the cause of the fever.

Diagnostic and final stage of roseola infantum   After three to five days the fever drops and simultaneously a rash of small, flat, separate pink spots appears on the child's chest and back, and may spread to the neck and limbs. A doctor who sees the child while the rash is present, and knows of the preceding fever, can now diagnose the disease, but the rash vanishes so rapidly that it is often not seen.

Possible complications   In a susceptible child, the sudden high fever may cause a febrile convulsion (*see* **Convulsions, Seizures and "Fits"**).

Rubella *see* **German Measles**.

Safety *see also* **Accidents**

In the home

Some of the worst accidents to babies and children take place within their own homes. The home setting can feel safe and comfortable to adults, with all their knowledge, experience, foresight and self-control, yet be a multi-death-trap to a child.

Making your home safe for children involves taking a tour around it, trying to see through their eyes, and then reorganizing any areas or objects which are obviously going to be dangerous. But it also involves taking a critical look at your own living habits. Installing a special cabinet for razors, pills and toiletries is easy; teaching yourself always to use it can be far more difficult. Start during the first pregnancy if you can. After the birth you have about six months before your child has enough physical mobility to match his vital curiosity and lead him into danger. They are unlikely to be the ideal months for installing new cabinets or habits.

Babies and very small children have to be *kept safe*, but at the same time they have to learn to *keep themselves safe*. If you are going to have more than one child, they will also have to learn to *keep each other safe* in turn. The keeping safe stage—which applies mostly to babies and toddlers—does involve a lot of physical precautions but, however good those are, it depends above all on supervision. However much foresight and ingenuity you use in child-proofing a room, a toddler will find something dangerous if he is given time. The precautions, then, are to enable you to take your eye off him for long enough to look up a telephone number; they will not allow you to make that call in private. At this stage the precautions are also a contribution to your sanity. If there are no used ashtrays on the coffee table you will not have to spend every other minute preventing the child from eating cigarette butts.

Keeping a first child safe is easier than protecting a later one. Stair gates protect your first child from tumbles. By the time he is three he can manage the stairs perfectly. But what about his little sister who has just started to crawl? She now needs those gates, but if you put them up again your son will be stuck and deeply offended if he has to ask for help as "if he were a baby." A later arrival in the family makes it even more difficult. The older children are rightly allowed to use knives and scissors, but will they remember to put them away in that safe place?

The sooner *all* the children learn to keep themselves safe the sooner you will be able to relax the necessary attitude of "Go and see what Matthew is doing and stop him." The very items which you lock away from that baby and toddler must be shown, demonstrated and used under supervision just as soon as the child is capable. It would be madness to leave table forks around a year-old baby who may put them in her mouth and then fall. But by two she can be shown that they are sharp and shown how to carry them—always pointing away from her—so that if somebody else carelessly leaves a fork around there is at least a chance that she will stick it in the floor rather than in herself. By four or five (when she will certainly be spending some time in houses where people are less safety-conscious than you) she could be quite reliable about either using potentially dangerous things safely or leaving them alone. She could even be beginning to help younger children keep safe because there is plenty of pride in being grown-up to be milked from "Careful, he's not old enough to be sensible with scissors yet."

Demonstrations are important to much older children, too. A twelve- or thirteen-year-old sometimes seems so sensible and competent that parents forget that there are still skills which he or she lacks, simply because there has been no learning experience. Keep your electric hedge trimmer locked away, by all means, but make sure your daughter has used it *with* you before you decide that she is old enough to trim the hedges for extra pocket money. Always get a babysitter for your children when you go out in the evening, but make sure your son knows what precautions to take when answering the front door late at night, *before* you decide that he is now old enough to be left in charge.

Life is a risky business. Care, foresight and supervision are important but, if you are human at all, you will have lapses and your children will, from time to time, have accidents. What matters is to try to ensure that you do not lapse over the things which really matter and therefore that those accidents are trivial.

Safety and baby equipment

Design is vital. Your baby could get his head wedged between the too-widely spaced bars of his drop-side crib, or choke on a pacifier which comes off its plastic flange.

If you are buying new, stick to items approved by the Consumer Product Safety Commission. If you are buying secondhand, try to establish the make/model number so that you can check, or consult your local Consumer Commission as to what safety points to look for.

Use is vital. If an infant seat is said to be safe until the child weighs twenty pounds, put it away before he gets there. Remember that a lot of baby equipment is for your convenience, not his, so if you use a changing table it is up to you to make sure he does not roll off. Carriages and strollers are designed to carry one child unless stated otherwise. Adding a toddler seat to the one or heavy shopping to the other could be a bad mistake.

Maintenance is vital. Carriage brakes will not work efficiently if levers are rusty and rubber pads worn. Bouncing cradles and baby bouncers will not be safe once elastic has worn or been replaced with a lighter grade.

Safety harness becomes vital. A child can rock and topple himself out of a highchair, carriage or anything else you sit him in, long before he can sit alone. Invest in a harness for each regularly used item. If the harness is permanently on that chair it will remind you to use it every time. If you use it every time, he will expect it and will neither object nor try to get out.

Safety from burns and scalds

These are usually more traumatic, for victim and parent, than any other injury of comparable severity. A small burn hurts much more than an equivalent cut. A more serious one means more pain, fear, time in the hospital and likelihood of permanent scarring than a fall downstairs with a concussion and a fractured arm. Serious burns and scalds can kill. Even if they do not, they commit the victim to weeks of agony and illness and possibly years of plastic surgery; they commit parents to dreadful guilt, too, because such accidents are far more preventable than most.

Be careful with fixed fires. Any radiant fire—wood, solid fuel, gas or electric—needs a fixed "safety-approved" guard: fine mesh to stop things being poked through, far enough from the fire to prevent the guard itself from getting too hot and with a top piece to prevent a child sticking things behind it.

Do not let children see you mistreat a fire (by poking in paper spills to get a light for a cigarette, for example) and do not let young ones watch you undo that guard until you are prepared to let them do so, too. If a fire needs regular attention, make a small ceremony of doing it properly so that children learn how before you first ask them to do it for you.

If the fire needs matches, keep them elsewhere.

Try not to keep anything interesting (mirror, ornaments, clock) above the fire. They may tempt the very young to climb up to look.

Choose portable fires carefully. Avoid radiant electric bar fires. The portable ones will not only be unguarded but will turn up in positions the child does not expect and have an electric cord she could trip over. If you need portable electric heat, use a warm air convector or a fan-heater.

Do not use kerosene heaters. Although the heat is still comparatively cheap, these have caused more—and more serious—domestic fires than any other single kind of appliance. Furthermore, the kerosene itself is both a fire risk in your home or garage and a poison. If you need a portable, non-electric space heater, bottled gas is far safer.

Your stove is a hazard. The worst and most frequent kitchen accidents occur when children reach up, grab a pan handle and tip the boiling contents over themselves. Use back burners whenever you can. Keep all pan handles turned to the back so that nothing projects over the edge.

Do not leave young children in the kitchen if anything is frying. Hot fat can spit. Hot oil is the most common cause of kitchen fires.

Check the temperature of the *outside* of the oven when it is up to roasting heat. A poorly insulated model may get hot enough to burn if a child falls against, or even touches, it.

When you open the oven door, watch out for the blast of hot damp air. It may be exactly at face level for your small companion.

If you should be considering a new stove, consider a split level, with eye-level oven and burners lined up along the back of the counter. Such an arrangement makes it easier to cook and companion the very young simultaneously.

The sooner children learn to cook safely, the better, but a child who cannot reach to stir a pan while standing on the floor should not use the burners. Ghastly accidents have occurred when children stood on stools to "help" with the fudge-making.

Watch out for matches, cigarettes and lighters. Sudden small flames and unexpected smoke rings are surprising and pretty to babies and very small children, so they have a real motive to play with those things if you leave them around. Don't. Smokers need to discipline themselves never to pick up or play with a child while holding a lit cigarette and never to leave one burning in an ashtray. If you often wear clothes without pockets, try a lighter on a string around your neck.

By school age children should be taught to handle matches safely. Teach them to take out one match and *close the box* before striking it. The match should be struck away from them. Burnt matches should never be put back in the box in case they are still hot.

Some children develop a passion for making fire and, even at seven or eight, find it really difficult to resist striking matches to burn scraps of paper or whatever. If you turn this into an organized, approved and supervised activity, you may speed up the end of the craze and lessen the chance of disaster. He can help with garden bonfires or the barbecue. He can even be given a cookie tin, a ration of matches and some twigs or dead leaves and be allowed to make mini-fires in the garden, under your eye.

Camping and power cuts can be hazardous. Deprived of electricity, whether by a power cut or because you are camping, you may have to use safety candles and various kinds of lamps. Of course children used to survive a life in which these were the sole forms of lighting. But a child who is accustomed to electric light may not.

Don't leave small children alone in a room with any form of unguarded flame. If they need a light in their sleeping quarters, invest in one of the battery-operated nightlamps.

Don't let even an older child carry candles. Most candlesticks are unsafe, and the candle-in-a-wine-bottle will almost certainly fall out at the wrong moment, or allow a drip of hot wax to fall on his hand so that he drops it. Even a row of candles down the middle of a table can be a hazard to a long-haired child leaning over homework.

Lamps are certainly safer than candles, but kerosene lamps need extremely careful supervision because if dropped or knocked over they may explode. Bottled gas lamps are safer and many are designed to be hung up, out of harm's way.

If you need to provide some general light in a dark house or trailer, try a group of safety candles in the bottom of a Pyrex basin with an inch of water. It is unlikely to get knocked over and if a child should try to pick up the whole thing a slosh of water will extinguish them.

Be sure that hot water is not scalding water. Most families have turned down their thermostats for economic reasons but if you have not, check that water from the hot tap is not hot enough to scald, and that central heating pipes and radiators do not get hot enough to burn.

Fixed showers *must* be thermostatically controlled as water which is not hot enough to scald hands at the basin can still scald the soft skin of a naked child.

Hand showers need watching, too, because a child reaching blindly through a lather of shampoo can easily turn on the hot instead of the cold or get the mixture wrong.

Hot water bottles are a risky luxury. Babies' beds should only be pre-warmed. Older children's bottles should not be filled with boiling water, must have excess air removed before they are closed and must be banned from pillow fights, otherwise they may burst.

Never put an uncovered hot water bottle into the bed of a child or adolescent who is seriously ill or sleeping after a shock or accident. If the sleep is abnormally deep he or she could be burned before being aroused by the pain.

Be careful with hot drinks and foods. Coffee and tea do not have to be boiling to scald; casserole dishes retain heat long after they reach the table, while the fruit in a tart or pie can literally skin the roof of an unwary child's mouth.

While children are very young, try never to use a tablecloth. It can be easily pulled off, complete with scalding meal. Coffeepots and teapots hold the heat of their contents far longer than a mere cup or mug. Ideally they should be left in a safe place in the kitchen rather than being brought to the table or living room.

Highchairs need to be kept well back from family meal tables and the temperature of a child's portion of food checked as automatically as the temperature of his bathwater.

Irons can be lethal. Although domestic ironing is a very usual occupation for people companioning playing toddlers, it is a hazardous one if anything distracts your attention. Irons stay hot for a long time after they have been switched off; they sit on ironing boards above head level but have tempting cords to pull. They are heavy enough to knock out a child while burning her, and those ironing boards themselves are often unstable and finger-pinching. If you are going to leave your ironing, even for a few moments to answer a doorbell, take the child with you.

Safety from dangerous implements

Babies at the sitting and crawling stage will pick up and put in their mouths anything they find lying around. Anything which it would be dangerous for them to suck must therefore count as a dangerous implement, but keeping these things out of their way is comparatively easy. Most parents cast a semiconscious eye over the room before they release such a baby on the floor.

The toddler stage is far more difficult. A toddler will actively search for interesting things, and the forbidden ones are often the most fascinating. While he is less likely to put things in his mouth, he is highly likely to fall down. If he falls while sucking a pencil, it could go through the roof of his mouth. If he falls with sharp scissors in his hand he could stab himself.

Pre-school children rightly want to learn to use (rather than just handle and explore) everything they see adults using. But if such a child is to learn to use knives safely, he needs to do it under supervision. He cannot be trusted to select a table knife rather than a carving knife for private experiments.

The difficulty for families is that of finding storage for potentially dangerous implements which allows members of each age group the right degree of access. How can these things be readily available to busy adults and older children, accessible with permission by pre-schoolers, totally out of the sight, mind and effort of toddlers and *never left around for the baby*? The following are examples of some solutions which have worked for some families:

Knives, scissors and kitchen implements kept on magnetic racks. Placed high on the kitchen wall, these are convenient for adults, unreachable by toddlers, visible, but only accessible via somebody taller, to pre-schoolers. Implements are so easy to find and replace that they are unlikely to be left lying around for the baby. Don't put them on the wall where there is nothing underneath, though. Carelessly placed, a knife can suddenly descend like a dagger. Put racks over work-tops.

Cutlery banished, because although spoons are fun, forks are not. You may need a locked drawer, or cabinet with a child-proof catch.

Special storage for sewing and other hobby materials. A child young enough to be endangered by needles and linoleum-cutting knives will ruin your creative work if she gets hold of it, so it is not much hardship to lock away such things. A blanket chest can serve as an "adult toybox" while a locked writing bureau or the "drinks cabinet" section of a built-in unit can take everything from knitting to letters you do not want chewed.

Personal pencils, pens and graphics equipment kept out of family space. Older children need a variety, but will want to protect them from ruination by the very young and so will probably cooperate in keeping them in their own desks or rooms. For general use (and inevitably to be left around, sometimes), large, non-toxic felt-tip pens will do little harm.

Tools and other hardware divided into "occasionally used" and "constantly available" categories. Obviously workshops or full-scale tool-boxes will have to be locked, but unless there are safe places for potentially lethal odd and ends such as screwdrivers, electric wire, cup hooks and thumbtacks, nobody will ever be able to find them or be able to put them away safely again. Yet another magnetic rack will take some objects in this category. Sets of plastic odds-and-ends drawers, designed to be screwed to the wall and placed high up, will take the rest.

Safety from dangerous machines Some household machinery can be dangerous to small children even when it is a responsible adult who is using it. Any implement with sharp moving parts which do not stop immediately after the "off" switch is pressed, for example, can do fearful damage even as you watch. Suppose that you are using a rotary lawn mower and your toddler suddenly rushes towards you. You may switch off even as she stumbles, but you cannot stop the blades and may not catch the child before they do.

Reserve dangerous jobs for times when small children are out of the way or for times when your partner can supervise them while you work.

Real safety from these things will only come with knowledge and understanding of them, so as soon as a child is old enough to listen and be interested, make a point of showing her how each implement works, what it is for and why it is dangerous. Let her, for example, feel the weight of that (switched-off) electric drill and then see how fast the sharp bit whirls around and how long it goes on turning after the motor stops.

Let primary school children serve as machine apprentices so that by "helping" you with varying tasks they become safely familiar, and eventually competent, with this kind of tool. Even a seven-year-old may be able (and delighted) to drill holes in the wall with that drill when you are putting up new shelving. She cannot safely do so without supervision, because young arms tire and attention wanders, but by doing it with you she will learn the safe way to do it without you later on.

Aim to have every child able to use these implements responsibly by adolescence because it is during early adolescence that a sudden desire to "get it done while they're out as a surprise" or to show off to friends who visit while you are out, may otherwise lead to disaster.

When a child shows that he or she is able to use a particular tool or implement sensibly, it is important to accept that he or she has earned the right to take any risk which may still be involved. If a chisel slips, for example, and there is a lot of blood and perhaps some stitches (*see* **Accidents**/Cuts) it is all too easy to blame the young victim and perhaps to say, "Since you can't be sensible, you can't use that anymore." But unless he or she really was being careless, it is not fair. Have you never cut yourself when using a chisel? If attention did wander, won't the accident have taught its own lesson?

Whenever you are trying to decide whether or not a particular child is safe with a particular tool or machine, ask yourself whether he or she is any more likely to come to harm than you would be if you undertook the job yourself.

● Do protect very young children from the early tool use of these older ones. Your eleven-year-old daughter may be just as safe as you are with that power mower, and allowed to use it, but she is most unlikely to match your unconscious vigilance for the sudden arrival of that toddler. If she is to do the mowing, you concentrate on keeping him well out of her way.

Safe use of
electricity

An electric shock can kill a small child and be a serious matter for an older one as well as a nasty experience for an adult. Shocks within the home are best avoided by making sure that you *understand how this vital power source works; prevent anyone from misusing it; keep appliances in good order.*

What you must know about electricity. Current is produced at power stations at extremely high voltages. It is carried by wires to your home's junction box where the voltage is reduced to the domestic standard. It is then carried, by further wires, to each of your electrical outlets.

Wires *into* that junction box, and the junction box itself, are therefore really dangerous to any amateur electrician. They should *never* be fiddled with.

The wires inside the walls of your home have two parts: the "live" wire which carries the current, and the "neutral" wire which carries it back to "ground" at the power station.

It is the nature of all electric current to go back to "ground." When you plug an appliance into a wall socket you complete a circuit, at that point, between the "live" and the "neutral" wires, allowing the current to follow its natural path back to ground but tapping it, on the way, to make it power your fire, light or washing machine. Shocks occur when:

Instead of completing the circuit between "live" and "ground" wires with an appliance, you tap the "live" current, offering yourself as the most direct route back to "ground." This is what would happen if your child poked a hairpin or other metal strip into the "live" hole of a socket. Current would flow up the wire and go to "ground" through his body and feet.

Instead of completing the circuit between "live" and "ground" with an appliance, you offer the current a "short-circuit" which you happen to be holding. This is what would happen if a child put one end of a piece of wire into the "live" hole of a socket and the other end into the "neutral" and held on to the wire. Current would not flow through his body but would take the shortest route to "ground" along that wire, not only giving him a shock but probably burning his hand, too.

You correctly plug in and switch on an appliance, but instead of the

circuit remaining complete, with current powering the appliance and running straight back along the neutral wire, the wires inside the appliance are touching its casing. If the casing was metal (a good conductor of electricity) and if the appliance had no third "ground" wire the casing would become "live" and anyone touching it would get a shock. If the appliance was made, say, of plastic (a poor conductor of electricity) you would probably get no shock. If the appliance had its own "ground" wire, any current into the casing would at once flow down the "ground" wire as the line of least resistance. Instead of the casing becoming "live" the appliance would simply blow a fuse because the current flowing down this "ground" wire would have broken the circuit between power-station "live" and "neutral."

You offer electric current an even better line of least resistance back to ground than its own "neutral" wire: water. Materials which will not conduct electricity when dry will do so when wet. If, for example, your stove is plugged into a wall socket which is in the "on" position although the stove itself is switched "off," current is being carried from that plug to the stove. You can safely touch or dust it with a dry hand or duster, but if you wash it and water seeps behind the plug into the holes of the socket, you may get a shock.

The faulty or broken wires of a live appliance accidentally touch a good conductor of electric current which is permanently embedded in the ground and therefore provides the easiest possible route to ground for the current. The most usual danger here is an electric water heater which, if faulty, may send current down the wet, metal cold-water pipes. If you then touch the pipes you will get a shock.

There are a few useful rules for avoiding shocks:

Have all complicated electrical work carried out by a qualified electrician. Don't even put plugs on new appliances yourself unless you are sure that you can follow a wiring diagram.

Make not touching wall sockets one of the few rules you insist upon with small children. But holes to poke things into are dangerously tempting, so back discipline with practical action: try to have all wall sockets with their own switches and keep them switched off, as well as switching off the appliances plugged in to them. If the actual socket is switched off no current will be flowing through it. If some sockets have no switches (or to play doubly safe while children are at the fiddly age or older ones are liable to forget the "switch off" rule) put dummy plugs into them.

Never leave a light socket without a bulb. If a bulb needs replacing, leave the dead one in place until you are ready to put in the new one. Left empty, that bulb holder is an easy thing to put a finger into. If the light switch (which may be a long way away or have no "on/off" indicator) is in the "on" position, the bulb holder will be carrying current. With no bulb filament to travel around to get back to ground, it will travel through that finger and its attached body, instead.

Try to have all appliances "grounded." This means three-core cable and three-pin plugs, but it also means harmless fusing instead of harmful shocks if things go wrong. When buying new appliances, avoid those with metal casing (or even metal trims) in favor of plastic wherever possible.

Never touch electric plugs, sockets or appliances with wet hands and teach this rule to everyone else, too. Be especially wary in places where people are obviously going to be wet. Bathrooms should have only safety-approved heaters and lights and should have no wall sockets other than special shaver sockets. Electrical appliances intended for use in wet or damp conditions are especially insulated. Never use indoor appliances in the garden even if it does suddenly occur to you that you could vacuum the patio. If children are helping with wet jobs—such as carpet shampooing or washing down walls—make sure they understand the danger of water carrying current through a wet cloth to a wet hand and that sockets are switched off or avoided.

Play safe over electric blankets and wet beds, too. Although the safety standards for electric blankets are stringent, it is better not to test them either with urine or a glass of water!

Use as few adaptors as possible. If you plug a three-way adaptor into a socket and then plug three separate appliances into the adaptor, the weight of that adaptor plus three plugs can pull the prongs of the adaptor forward just enough to expose some metal. Such overuse of one wall socket also makes it likely that it will be left switched "on." That exposed metal will therefore be "live" and so will all the adaptor outlets including the one which is empty because you have pulled out the plug of one of those appliances.

Minimize the wear on electric cords by avoiding excess lengths trailing about or keeping the excess neatly stored in a cord holder. If you can see that a cord is fraying or losing its insulation, have it replaced.

Don't buy toys which run off the mains (even if they do so via a transformer) until the child concerned is old enough to understand how the electrical system works, rather than just regarding it as magic when those cars whizz about. Transformers can go wrong: unsafe ones occasionally get imported from foreign countries and you cannot expect a child to respect your rule about never touching wall sockets if it has one exciting exception.

Try to make sure that children learn the principles of electric circuitry and the practices of changing bulbs, plugs, etc. as soon as they are interested, sensible and dextrous enough.

Safety from general household hazards Homes are designed for people old enough to have understanding and competence. Babies and toddlers have not yet acquired these and therefore cannot safely be left alone and on the loose. For them, the only worthwhile general safety tip is to take them with you as you move around the house.

The following "hazards" apply most often to children old enough to want to get on with their play while you do your own thing, but not quite mature enough to foresee the results of their own actions. They also apply, often painfully, to school-age children carried away by a game or a daydream or the victim of bad luck. For all their sakes, give some thought to dangers from:

Glass. Don't keep internal glass doors or French windows so clean that a child can think the glass is open space and try to walk or reach through it. Panes will prevent this as will grubby fingermarks; or have safety glass.

Don't have floor-length mirrors in rooms where children play and might fall, unless you use the kind made of plastic rather than glass.

Things that can pinch. Ironing boards, folding chairs, clothes dryers can all pinch, blacken nails or break fingers.

Swing doors or those which close automatically are difficult for a small child to time his entrance or exit through and dangerous if several are playing together. Hook them open or use a doorstop.

Beware of fingers on the *hinge* side of doors. It is easy to make sure that you are not shutting the door on your child's hand, but much more difficult to be sure that he hasn't got his hand out of your sight but in the hinge. Folding doors, where several leaves move together, are particularly difficult. It is usually best to open them right up, or close them completely, while children are playing.

Unexpected prisons. Pre-school children get into things with no thought of how they are to get out again; schoolchildren, under the stress of "hide-and-seek," do the same. The most dangerous hiding place in many homes is a chest freezer. Once in, the child is cold, has little air and, because of the insulation, *will not be heard.* Discarded freezers and refrigerators should not be left around in garages, either. Make sure walk-in closets can be opened from inside as well as outside. Bathrooms and lavatories should have their locks high up out of a very small child's reach, or have the kind of lock which, in emergency, can be opened from outside with a coin. Children who *feel* locked in *are* locked in because panic makes them unable to undo a lock which they can normally manage easily.

Windows. Young children fall out easily because their heads are heavy relative to their bodies and legs. Older children fall trying to rescue cats, inspect birds' nests in the gutters or signal friends below. If you have large, low windows upstairs, windowlocks prevent them from being opened more than a few inches. A cheap and invisible alternative to bars.

Steps and stairs. Falls down these are common and seldom serious, but watch out for groups of children pushing past each other, for rugs at the top of flights of stairs and for the open type which a child can fall off or through, rather than simply down.

If you have tempting bannisters, some children will not resist sliding down them, whatever you say. You may need to put uprights at intervals to ruin a really tempting run over a dangerous drop.

Steps in a garden or yard may be a fair hazard for children on foot but dangerous to children on tricycles or bikes. You might need a safety fence or curbstone until all concerned learn to use their brakes.

All falls will be made less likely if you discourage children from wearing socks without shoes. Bare feet are fine and so are shoes. Socks alone turn many modern plastic floors into skating rinks.

Plastic bags. These constitute the only real danger of suffocation in a modern home. We tend to be aware of the danger to babies and toddlers, but do remember the temptation to older children to use dry cleaner covers or your freezer bags to make space helmets, or water bombs to clonk on each other's heads. I have never seen a child killed this way, but I have seen eight-year-olds experimenting with putting plastic bags over their heads and then breathing in to make their faces look monstrous and distorted. The more clingy and filmy the plastic, the more likely it is to stick to the nose and mouth for too long.

Recent disasters have also made it clear that even non-clingy plastic bags can be dangerous. One child, for example, pulled a child's shopping bag, made of cotton-lined stiff plastic, over her head. Although it did not cling, the size of the bag made it a tight fit and the plastic outside prevented any air from getting through to her. She was found unconscious.

Safety from household poisons

Modern products for cleaning, disinfecting and polishing your house, for killing off pests and weeds, for stripping wood, de-rusting metal, glueing one thing to another and for beautifying, deodorizing or depilating yourself, are so many and various that even in a country which insists on proper content-labelling, you cannot hope to know what is in each product or how dangerous it may be. *Play safe.* Assume that any or all of these products might harm your children and act accordingly.

As with potentially dangerous implements, you have to find ways of storing these things so that different family members can have the right degree of access, ranging from *none* for the toddler to easy for you. Products which might actually kill that toddler must obviously be locked away. But if you try to keep a constantly used shed or garage locked, to protect him from that weedkiller, somebody (maybe you) will be certain to leave it open "just while I'm gardening" sooner or later. It may be better to have a locked cabinet for the lethal but rarely used products and accept a simple bolt, high on that garage door, to protect him from the undesirable but non-lethal things you need constantly. In the same way, household bleach, ammonia and so forth really must be locked away, but you simply will not keep locking that kitchen cabinet if you try to keep the detergent and the water softener in there, too. Avoid obvious places for infant exploration (like the cabinet under the sink) but find a workable compromise such as a high shelf. If young children have the run of your bedroom, banish depilatories, hair dyes and so forth to a locked cabinet in the bathroom.

As with other serious hazards, the safety of very young children must really depend on their being supervised by adults. But there are hazards to much older children in this area, even to children who are not being especially silly.

Inadequate and misleading labelling. In the U.S., manufacturers must list on the label any ingredients which are defined (under the Hazardous Substances Act) as dangerous or poisonous, together with the quantity and the immediate remedy if any should be taken. In Britain and some other countries no ingredients need be listed on products which are not intended for consumption. Instead, the label may say "Not to be taken" or "for external use only." American-type labelling is exceedingly useful *after* an accident; you can check on the danger in that sip of disinfectant and you can check on what to do about it, too. But labels can do little to *prevent* accidents because children who are going to taste the inedible are not going to read tiny, technical print and then think better of it.

To make matters worse, many products are named *as if they might be edible.* I have a jar in front of me instructing me to "nourish my face with pure heather honey." Could a child be blamed for having a taste? The bottle of floor cleaner I am currently using is covered with pictures of real lemons—quite enough to suggest a lemon drink to a child—while the printing does not help much, even for a reader, as after the brand name it simply says "fill your house with lemon freshness." I am not saying that many children would take more than a taste, or that a taste of either of these things would necessarily be a serious matter. But it might be. Teach children about these traps.

As more and more people economize by buying giant, cash-and-carry sizes of household products, the danger from having them poured into manageable containers that used to hold something else increases. *Never* use old food or drink containers for non-edible products. If labels are wrong (or become blurred and illegible) replace them with your own big bold stick-on labels. Some families put scarlet "POISON" labels on everything dangerous and teach children to steer clear of them. But this is too clever-clever for most of us because there comes that day when you are in a hurry and forget.

Unexpected dangers to skin, eyes and lungs. Even children who are far too mature and sensible to try to eat or drink inedible substances may not realize the dangers of getting certain chemicals on their skin or of spraying them near their eyes or in the air they are breathing. Many solvents, paint removers, etc. will irritate the skin if used with bare hands. A pair of rubber gloves taped to the container may remind you to set a good example, as well as reminding independent teenagers to take care. Aerosol sprays can easily be activated while pointing in the wrong direction. Hair spray will merely sting, but foaming spot-weedkiller in the eyes could be a disaster. Teach children to check the direction of *any* aerosol spray and avoid buying really dangerous products in this expensive if convenient form. Many glues and solvents give off dangerous fumes, too. Make sure that children are aware of these dangers and that they are encouraged to use these products in the garden, or with head averted and plenty of ventilation.

Adult pleasures which are child poisons. Watch out for alcohol and tobacco. Many people do not realize that a good swig of spirits can actually kill a pre-school child, while a whole cigarette, well chewed, will make a two-year-old extremely ill. While you have very small children around you have to lock away these adult vices, remembering that a drink like cherry brandy will actually taste quite nice to a toddler. You have to go on being careful for quite a long time. That cherry brandy will still taste nice to your eight-year-old who, encouraged by seeing you regard it as a treat, may make himself very ill. Even older children, perhaps dared by friends, may sneak drinks which they really must not have, on medical rather than moral or economic grounds.

Secondary school children often dislike the taste of all alcoholic drinks.

If so, don't encourage them to feel that a glass of wine makes them seem "grown up." If they don't *want* it they are better off without it, just as we all should be. But some children *do* like it or at least resent being forbidden it. If so, they will probably have the best chance of adopting a sensible and sociable attitude to alcohol later on if they are allowed a glass of whatever you drink on special occasions and are encouraged to take an intelligent interest in the whole business. That intelligent interest can include information about what *is* alcoholic (many children "don't count" beer, for example); knowledge of their country's age-related drinking laws which they should never be encouraged to break by, for example, being bought in a restaurant the glass of wine which, at fourteen, they would be allowed at home; and some understanding of alcoholism as a growing problem almost everywhere and the immorality of encouraging others to drink (*see* **Habits**/Habits which easily lead to addiction).

Safety with medicines   Considering how difficult it is to persuade many children to take the medicine prescribed for them (*see* **Nursing**/Medicines) it is extraordinary how readily most children between about one and five years will take medicines meant for other people. But take them they do. Every year, in the Western world, thousands of children have to have their stomachs pumped out (*see* **Hospital**/Procedures: Stomach pumpings); every year some of them die. Buy, *please* buy, a proper medicine cabinet with a safety lock. Nowhere else is really safe. If you use a cabinet with an ordinary lock and key, you may one day leave the key in the lock and that will be the day when you do not at once notice your toddler's long stay in the bathroom (*see* **Accidents**/Poisoning).

Use the safety cabinet for *all* medicines. Don't decide that you need not make space for the children's own multivitamins because they are harmless: a whole bottle will not be. Don't keep medicines in current use in the patient's room to remind you of regular doses. Keep a written message to yourself in the room and the medicine in the cabinet.

Iron tablets can be lethal. If you are taking daily iron, perhaps because you are pregnant, keep them locked away.

Remember that contraceptives are medicines. Don't keep your contraceptive pills beside your bed to remind you to take them. A month's supply will do neither sex any good at all. Put a message to yourself on the mirror or your toothbrush or something.

Don't carry medicines in your handbag. If you are prone to sudden headaches or have a chronic condition which means that you must carry tablets with you, ask your pharmacist for a child-proof container and then play safe by carrying only a very few tablets with you at any time.

Watch out when travelling. It is easy to relax home vigilance when you are on vacation and may be carrying a variety of remedies against all kinds of eventualities. A lockable vanity case or briefcase is probably the safest solution, provided you do not leave the key in it.

Be careful in other people's houses. If your host's children are much older than yours, these dangers may have been forgotten. Ask and/or check before your children are taken away to play.

Grandparents' houses can be especially dangerous. All too often there are sleeping pills by the bed, laxatives beside the washbasin and "heart pills" in pockets.

Guard against your own mistakes, for example:

Don't give medicines in the dark: you must check the label.

Don't keep medicine from one child or illness to another. Medical prescriptions are personal and immediate; the next child may need something different or the medicine for the first bout may have run out of shelf-life before he has a second.

Don't throw away medicines in waste-bins. Flush them down the toilet.

Don't rely on breaking adult tablets to arrive at a child's dose. Buy medicines specially formulated for children.

Don't use empty medicine containers for anything else.

Don't ever pretend that a sugar-coated pill is a sweet. It is important to your child's safety that the difference is made absolutely clear; you don't want her eating your iron tablets because she thinks they are M&M's.

Teach adolescents sense about medicines (*see* **Adolescence**/The long road to independence: Self-care). Unless you are morally opposed to taking any but life-saving medicines, you will probably want to teach and demonstrate a commonsense attitude to them from early on. This might include a careful following of doctor's orders over taking any prescribed medicines on time and for the full period, coupled with a restrained attitude to over-the-counter drugs. If children see you buying and using large numbers of patent remedies for everything from headaches and "stress," to constipation and colds, they are liable to grow up feeling that there ought to be a chemical remedy for everything which ever goes wrong for them.

But by puberty or soon after, children ought to be able to be trusted to take the right dose of a sensible remedy for a bad headache or period pain, to know how much of what to take if they are poor travellers journeying with friends and, of course, to manage any regular medication which has been prescribed for a chronic condition. Don't withdraw your supportive supervision too quickly, though. Many apparently sensible teenagers, going through a headachey time, slip into taking regular doses of Tylenol or aspirin "just in case" (*see* **Pain and Pain Control**). Many others drift into a laxative habit because they do not realize that a bowel which is overstimulated one day is likely to remain quiescent for a day or two before it acts naturally again (*see* **Laxatives**).

Safety and pets Many families feel that pets enrich a home for children (*see* **Pets**). The first choice, if circumstances allow, is usually a dog. Properly cared for and trained, most dogs will be safe around children, but keep an eye out for the following:

Jealousy. A few dogs—usually long-established pets—are bitterly jealous of a baby. If he is jealous, a dog does not have to be a German shepherd to be dangerous. There have been cases of ordinary small pet dogs seeking out the baby and savaging it to death. It is highly unlikely, but unthinkably horrible, so just be a little wary if the dog always wants attention when you are attending to the baby, tries to push her off your lap and so forth.

Reactions to teasing. Dogs vary in how much mauling they will take from a small child. Some will tolerate almost anything; some treat the child as they would a puppy (and that may mean a few reproving nips) while a few lose their tempers and snap. If you decide to keep a dog of less than certain temper while your own children are young, do spare a thought for their visitors. The dog may be even less tolerant of strange children; they will not want to come to the house if he frightens them, while other parents will find any snapping unforgivable.

Puppy-play. If you acquire a pup while your child is a baby, you may have difficulty meeting both their needs safely at the same time. Puppies will chew toys that belong to the baby as well as their own. They will bounce up, even if they knock a toddler down by doing so. They will, especially while they are teething, use their teeth playfully if anyone romps with them; even puppy teeth can hurt.

Diseases. There are various skin complaints and parasites which can be "caught" from dogs. Keep yours really clean and in tip-top health. Make sure that he is trained not to foul the garden or anywhere where children play. Be scrupulous about keeping any dishes he uses separate from those of the humans in your house and try to ensure that finger-sucking children wash their hands when the dog has been licking them.

Mention the existence of the dog to your doctor if he is ever puzzled by symptoms in the children.

Cats are not usually emotionally concerned with a baby, although they are often less tolerant than dogs of inept cuddling and may scratch if bothered. It is wise to use a cat net over the carriage to ensure that the cat cannot choose to use it as the ideal bed, with baby as a built-in hot water bottle. If the cat did lie on the baby's face, it is not very likely that the baby would be smothered as his struggles would disturb the cat. But he might be badly scratched as the frightened animal leapt away.

Small mammals, such as rabbits and guinea pigs, can be fun for a small child to watch and help you to care for, but they should not be given to a baby or toddler to hold, for both their sakes. They can inflict scratches which are both painful and unhygienic.

Fish are fun to watch, too, but they are liable to a variety of fungus diseases and therefore their tank water is definitely unsuitable for a small child to dabble in. Keep a top on the tank and don't make cleaning it out one of the jobs children help with, until they can be trusted not to suck their fingers before they have washed.

Safety by, in and on water

Babies can and do drown in water no more than a couple of inches deep. If a very small child finds his face submerged in water, he does not hold his breath—as an older person would—instead, he takes a deep breath ready to yell his fear or outrage. That breath does not get him air; it pulls water straight into his lungs.

Baths. A baby needs to be held in the water until he can sit absolutely steadily. But even when he can do this, he cannot safely be allowed to play in the bath unless an adult hovers within quick reach. If he can sit, he can probably crawl and/or pull himself to standing position. If he tries these maneuvers in the slippery bathtub, he may easily fall face down. Even a two- or three-year-old should have an adult in the room while he bathes. If he slips under water he needs fishing up again, fast.

A baby in the bath must take priority over other calls on your attention. If the telephone rings, let it ring, or take the dripping child with you.

Make sure that older children always let the water out of the bath when they have finished. Toddlers have been known to arrive, find the luke-warm, grubby, fascinating water, lean over to dabble, fall in and drown.

Paddling pools must be treated with just as much respect as baths. One small child will be happy with a small inflatable pool which you religious-ly empty and deflate after every supervised play session. If you also have older children who want a larger pool, be careful of a big version of the same because it will certainly be left full and will be a real hazard all summer. If you can find the money for a miniature version of an above-ground swimming pool, this may keep everybody safe and happy. The rigid sides are too high for a toddler to scramble over without steps (which can easily be removed when there is no adult in the garden), yet it need not be filled to a depth any greater than your children require (*see* **Play**/"Messy" and energetic play for private homes).

Ornamental pools. These permanent garden fixtures are the worst water hazard because you cannot keep an absolutely constant eye on a child, for whom the whole point of open space within the home environment is freedom. If you cannot get rid of them, you will really have to work to make them safe. A goldfish pond, for example, can have wire mesh over the surface without bothering the fish.

Swimming pools. These are taken almost for granted in many parts of the United States and, while giving tremendous pleasure, they also claim a lot of young lives.

If you are installing a pool for the first time while your family is very young, consider an above-ground pool rather than an in-ground one. It will not look so glorious but it will be a great deal safer. Four-foot vertical sides will prevent small children from slipping in and will foil unautho-rized adventures, too, provided the access steps are removed between swimming sessions.

If you already have an in-ground pool you will have to work out how to avoid both accidental and deliberate-but-forbidden dips. Fencing off the whole pool area will deal with the first, but it will have to be very securely done if it is to prevent the second. Older children, with free use of the pool, may have to have that privilege made conditional on their behaving responsibly about closing gates, etc. behind them.

Older children and water

If you live near the sea, a lake or a usable river, water activities may become central to your child's life. There are clubs catering to almost every imaginable water sport, from canoeing through sailing small boats, to wind-surfing. Highly safety-conscious, such a club will teach your child proper techniques, using well-maintained equipment, and will certainly try to instill responsible good sense and a proper respect for the elements.

But with older boys in particular, competence often brings over-confidence and a growing impatience with club rules. Life jackets or other flotation devices are abandoned because they hamper movement. Weather warnings are ignored, and the boy may eventually abandon club activities altogether because he wants to do his own thing in his own way. It can be extremely difficult for parents to combat this sort of thing because an element of personal risk is part of the fun of most water sports and your son will probably not be at all cooperative with your attempts to make his chosen pastime as safe as possible.

If he can interest himself in pitting his skill against the skill of others, he may be less inclined to pit himself against the elements. Even quite advanced competitive water sports tend to be less dangerous than, for example, solitary surfing.

If he does not want to compete, you may be able to persuade him that knowledge and skill are more admirable than the more obviously "macho" qualities of derring-do. If he must sail off that coast, perhaps he would first undertake some serious navigation studies.

If that approach gets you nowhere, he may value the varnish on his own equipment more than he is prepared to value his own skin. Some-times possession of his own wind-surfer, surf board or canoe turns an accident-waiting-to-happen into a sensible adult sportsman.

There are a lot of popular and dangerous misconceptions about people and water: teach him to disbelieve the following:

"People float." Some float better than others, depending on their natural buoyancy, which, in its turn, depends partly on how fat they are. But even the best floaters, lying passively in the water, only float with the tops of their heads above it. That does not enable them to breathe.

"Strong swimmers seldom drown." In very cold water even the strongest swimmer may collapse and drown within a couple of minutes, so a capsize in winter, even within sight of shore, may be fatal.

"Swimming keeps you warm." Wrong again. Swimming uses up more energy than it produces in heat. Unless safety is close by and the water is of summer-bathing temperature, the victim will stay in good condition longer if he holds on to something which will keep him afloat and stays still or, if there is nothing to hold on to, he moves only enough to keep himself afloat.

"Heavy clothing hampers swimming and should be taken off." With the exception of shoes, this is also bad advice. Swimming is not advisable anyway and heavy clothing, while it does not insulate as well in water as in air, does cut down heat loss and therefore the rate at which the victim becomes dangerously cold (hypothermic). Clothes should be kept on. If an accident on the water is foreseen, as when a small boat finds itself in worsening conditions, for example, all possible protective clothing should be put on.

Make sure that he does believe these:

Alcohol increases the risk of drowning. Even a moderate amount of alcohol makes the body far less able to fight off hypothermia. Many people drown during the midnight swimming parties which complete a good beach barbecue.

Nobody should swim or take part in any water sport, after drinking *or* taking drugs *or* when feverish or ill.

Even the strongest swimmer is more likely to survive with something to hold on to which will keep him afloat. Life jackets and other flotation devices are *not* "sissy" and the fact that they hamper swimming does not matter. They are there to save life, not to enable the wearer to break the freestyle record.

Any craft, from sailing boat to canoe to pedal boat, should have safety lines to hold on to if necessary.

Thin, fit young men and gangly children tend to have least body fat and to succumb to cold most quickly. A wet suit is a must in cold water. It is not brave and tough to surf off a Maine beach in April in bathing trunks only. It is simply stupid. Anyone serious enough about such a sport to want to do it outside the warmest season *must* have such a suit. Any parent with a serious water-sportsperson in the family must, for safety's sake, find a way of making sure he or she has one. Perhaps you could lend the money or provide the wet suit for a birthday present.

Safety on the road

In the U.S. more than 1100 children under fifteen (a third under five) are killed while they are out *walking*. In Britain more than 500 children under fifteen (twice as many boys as girls) are killed, and around 70,000 injured. Nearly a quarter of those are under five years. Running into the road accounts for about thirty percent of those accidents; coming out from behind a parked car accounts for another ten percent.

While every child and every set of circumstances is different, busy parents, also anxious to encourage their children's independence, may often be too quick to let a child out without an adult. Most of us are city-dwellers. We accept the constant stream of traffic and we forget, until tragedy strikes one of *our* children, just how dangerous it is. If instead of traffic, the streets around your house were surfaced with live, high-voltage electric wires, lethal at a touch, would you let your three-year-old out and trust him to stay on the pavement? If those wires were broken, for safe crossing of the street, only at controlled crossing points, would you let your six-year-old cross the road alone?

Toddlers and road safety

Toddlers are certainly not safe without an adult anywhere there is, or might be, moving traffic (watch out in parking lots). Even with an adult, most need careful watching lest they dash or stumble off the pavement. Never take a toddler walking where there is traffic without some way to hold on to him. The two of you can hold hands, but that is not very comfortable. He may be happy to hold on to the baby's carriage or to help you push his own stroller. But he will be safest if he wears a harness and reins or is pushed or carried. It may seem restrictive, but the street is not the place for him to have his freedom.

Pre-school children and road safety

By around three, a child can learn that the curb is a safety line between pedestrians and cars and, by three or four, can often be trusted to stay on the sidewalk, even to a point where, allowed to run ahead, he can be trusted to stop and wait for you at every crossing.

But traffic is unfair to even the most trustworthy child. Beware of the car which uses that sidewalk to increase the available space for a U-turn, or of the delivery truck which parks with its wheels on the sidewalk. Beware, too, of places where the sidewalk is roped off for work on the sewers and pedestrians have to go into the road to get around the hole.

Although many pre-school children are allowed, even expected, to cross roads alone, very few are competent to do so safely. Few can distinguish right from left and therefore be sure in which direction they should check for traffic. Few can judge either how far away traffic is or how fast it is moving. *Very* few can begin to anticipate unexpected driving maneuvers, such as U-turns or turns across the traffic flow. Even those who have grasped (and have available) various kinds of controlled crossing can easily be caught out by the motorist who anticipates the green light.

If you cannot trust your pre-school child to stay on the pavement, don't let him out alone. If he cannot do your errands without crossing a road, don't ask him to.

Schoolchildren and road safety

Ironically, the children who are most at risk when walking are often the ones who are usually chauffeured about by car. A child who is old enough for school is ready to learn about traffic behavior. But he cannot learn what he needs to know from inside a vehicle. He needs to cross hundreds of roads with an adult before he crosses even one by himself.

If you plan to chauffeur your child to and from school by car "until he is old enough to walk safely," make sure that you take him out and about on foot at other times, and familiarize him with the route to school, too. If you are going to walk him to school until you feel he is safe alone, use the daily trips for direct teaching.

Whenever and wherever you walk with the child, point out traffic behavior; let *him* tell *you* where and when it is safe to cross roads; go out of your way to show him various forms of controlled crossing and to point out hazards like failed traffic lights. He will learn road safety by imitation and by doing, just as he best learns other skills.

Safety codes

Such heavy reliance is placed on safety codes that, while entirely sympathetic with their intentions, the author feels it necessary to point out that no rigid set of rules can keep every child safe on every road. The British "Green Cross Code" can serve as an example:

First find a safe place to cross such as a pedestrian crossing, patrolled crossing, underpass or controlled lights. There may be no such place available, especially in a suburban-residential, rural or semi-rural area.

Stand on the sidewalk near the curb. Look all around for traffic and listen. In a busy area there may be constant streams of traffic.

If traffic is coming, let it pass. Again, there may be continuous traffic so that a child who "lets it pass" will never be able to cross.

Look all around again. When there is no traffic near, cross. How near is near?

Keep looking and listening for traffic as you cross.

Adapting this kind of code for your child

If you live in a quiet area, well-supplied with crossing places, you may be able to teach your child to observe a code like this as an absolute set of rules to be obeyed at all times. If so, make sure that you always obey it too, and that you do not adopt a, "Do what I say, not what I do" approach to rushed Saturday shopping trips.

If you live in a busy city area and your child has regular trips which he wants to make on foot—to school, to the local shops, to specific friends' houses, club premises and so forth—you can adapt the code *especially for him.*

Walk each route alone and work out:

Where he should cross: is there a pedestrian crossing if he goes on a little further? Is there a school crossing guard at particular times? Are there controlled lights . . . ?

When he should cross. For example, if he must cross a street with no traffic control at all, what markers can he use along the way to tell him that traffic is too close for safety? You need to be able to tell him, "Don't cross if there is anything closer than that church. . . ." If there is some form of control, he must get his timing right. May he cross to a central island if the pedestrian light is already on when he arrives, or is it so brief that he should wait for the next round?

How he should cross. For example, if there is a quiet street which has cars parked on both sides, you may have to teach him to hold on to the bumper of one while he edges his way out far enough to peer both ways.

What he is to do if he cannot cross. For example, if the usual crossing guard does not appear, is he to cross all the same? Walk on to a designated alternative? Wait for an adult and ask for help?

Walk each route with the child. Make a game out of teaching and testing him, with increasing independence as the reward and your concern for his safety as motivation. As he learns, he can take you; then go ahead of you (within warning calling range); then do the easiest part of the walk, meeting you halfway and so on.

Don't let him undertake any of these special trips alone until you are sure that he is no more likely to be knocked down than you are yourself. Be firm, whether he is five or nine. But be tactful, too. If he is meeting you halfway and is with a group of friends, they do not have to know that he is on trial.

Gradually generalize these special trips to overall road safety. Over months, the things he has learned for these particular walks can be applied more and more generally, until he is safe on other roads of similar difficulty and, eventually, on any road at all.

Road safety for older children in a hurry

Nothing you can do will absolutely ensure that an older child or adolescent will always cross roads sensibly. Can you honestly say that you never take a risk yourself? As with other kinds of safety teaching, once you are certain that your children have the necessary skills, knowledge and experience to keep themselves safe, you have to trust them to do so.

In the in-between stage, though, perhaps in the nine to fourteen age group, watch out for gangs of friends: six running home together tend to move as a mass, each thinking another is giving the signal to cross, and the one who is lagging thinking only of catching up. Be careful also of entrusting very young children to older ones; they may not allow for short legs and lack of concentration. Above all, if you *see* road idiocy, like games of "last across is chicken," be as tough as you know how. Maybe your devil-may-care child can be induced to pity the poor motorists.

● Whatever your child's age and circumstances, remember that, statistically, three conditions much increase his chances of being involved in a road traffic accident:

☐ *Myopia (nearsightedness)* (*see* **Eyes and Seeing; Eye Disorders and Blindness**).

☐ *Deafness,* often the temporary result of fluid in the middle ear (*see* **Ears and Hearing; Ear Disorders and Deafness**).

☐ *Stress in the family* which may distract him either in the immediate sense of not noticing that car or in the sense of making him careless of his own safety (*see* **Depression**/In children before puberty).

● Remember also that a child who has recently moved, or even entered a new school, has lost the protection of familiarity with local roads and crossings. Such a child may be under some stress as well.

Safety from "strangers"

Every family has the grim responsibility of trying to protect its children from the remote but hideous possibility of assault. While individual precautions have to be tailored to the home environment, the family's way of life and each child's age, sex and personality, there are some general points which will apply to most.

First lessons: NOT "Don't talk to strangers" No child of any age will come to harm just by talking. The child who is forbidden to speak to anyone he does not know is actually at a disadvantage in learning to keep himself safe in his community.

If he takes the message seriously it must make him feel that "outsiders" are peculiarly dangerous. This is neither true nor helpful to his eventual social integration.

An intelligent child probably will not take the message seriously for long because he will see it contradicted so often. *You* speak to strangers. You, a stranger, speak to small children if they fall down at your feet or you find one alone and crying. And you expect him to speak nicely to strange shopkeepers and people known to you but not previously to him.

If he is reluctant to speak, he cannot ask the way when he is lost or even respond civilly when asked the time.

BUT "Never go with a stranger" Whether approached over the garden gate, on the way home from school, or while playing in the park with friends, a child will almost certainly be safe if nothing a stranger can say will divert her. It is the child who can be tempted into a house by promises of sweets, into the bushes to see a phantom puppy, or into a car for a lift who is likely to be at risk.

"We must always know where you are" goes with this first lesson and, for a pre-school child, can serve to explain it, too. No two- or three-year-old will think it strange that you want to know where she is every minute of the day, because she wants to know where you are, too. So the message becomes "Never go anywhere with a stranger; in fact never go anywhere without telling us first."

As soon as you take the child to playgrounds and parks you can start on this. The child is on the swings and you are sitting on a nearby bench. If she wants to move to the sandpit she must come and tell you.

A little later she goes to the local store, and two doors up the road to her friend's house. If she says she is going to the store, it must be straight there and back. If she meets the friend and wants to go into her house, she must come and tell somebody first.

When she begins to come home from school alone, the same policy must apply. She must come straight home and tell you her plans before she goes off to play. If you are not going to be there, arrange for her to report to a neighbor.

As the child gets older, generalize and explain Teach the child that if he should ever get separated from you in a public place like a big store or the zoo, he should *stay where he last saw you.* He should not accept well-meaning offers from strangers to take him to the manager, home or the police. That would be breaking the "never go with strangers" rule. Equally, he should not try to be clever and get back to the parking lot alone. That would be breaking the "We must know where you are" rule. In the same way, teach him that if ever he should get home (from school or play) and find nobody there, he should *stay put* and not go wandering off to look for you.

Gradually introduce the idea that while most people are kind and like children, a few people are not and do not. Explain that kind people will know that children should not go anywhere without their parents knowing, so anyone who tries to persuade him to break this rule cannot be a nice person. Then act upon this the other way around. If the two of you come upon a lost or hurt child, *don't* try to persuade her to come into your house or go with you to the police. Either stay with her, giving what comfort you can, while you wait to see if a frantic adult turns up, or stay with her while another passer-by fetches the nearest policeman or official. If another child chums up with yours in the park and your child asks if she can come home with you to play, insist that she find the adult in charge of her and ask first.

Don't let worries about rape and murder blind you to less mind-boggling but more likely hazards. As children grow up, they will both want and need increasing freedom to come and go as they please, within agreed limits. Children (and adults, too) do get grabbed in the street, dragged into alleys and raped and/or killed, but the chances of such a tragedy striking anyone in your family are truly minute. If you keep on with that early teaching, and extend it so that your children do not walk alone after dark, do not go alone to deserted places of known risk, do not accompany strangers, however friendly they may seem, and do not, *ever*, get into strange vehicles, you are doing all you can to protect them from real disaster.

Sexual molestation of children before puberty

The chances of children being sexually molested in less devastating, but still deeply disturbing, circumstances are much higher. There is a great deal which you can do, both to protect them and to help them to protect themselves.

The most obvious danger is seldom the real one. A man who gets his kicks from displaying his sex organs to your child may deeply embarrass him or her but is most unlikely to do more. It is probably best to take a single such incident lightly, describing the man as "silly," "sad" or "rude," as your child's reaction suggests. If the man is hanging around next day, he may have fixed on your child's school or route home. Report the matter to the police and to the school, but try to convey irritation rather than danger to the child.

Some people (usually, though not invariably, men) do find children sexually exciting. They are most likely to approach them in stimulating circumstances. At the movies, for example, a perfectly strange man may try to use your daughter's hand, instead of his own, for masturbation. In a public urinal or locker room, a man may approach your son. The shock of an adult behaving in a way which is incomprehensible, but "wrong," will probably be less for the child if he or she already knows that some people do these "peculiar" things. Such contacts can best be avoided by children recognizing that there is safety in numbers and staying together when out without an adult. If your child reports an incident of this kind to you, do try not to overreact. If he or she feels that the information has shattered you, or if it commits him or her to being interviewed by the police and so forth, you may not be told of other, perhaps much more serious, incidents.

Most sexual molestation of children is not by strangers at all but by acquaintances, neighbors and relations. If you are to guard your child, without turning her into a recluse, you must try to keep an easy flow of communication going between you. You want to be sure that she will tell you if that eccentric neighbor, who loves children, wants to show her more than his pet rabbits.

Children do not always object to sexual contact with people they think of as friends. Sometimes the "odd things" the adult wants to do are accepted as a duty, as part of childishly doing what you are told. Sometimes they are accepted as a price to be paid for other aspects of the friendship, such as sweets. Sometimes a child finds herself drawn into it unwittingly, in a gradual slide from hugs and kisses, and then cannot see how to object without being rude. Sometimes a child sees the power which sex gives her, and uses it with precocious lack of mercy. However it happens, sexual contact with adults is at best inappropriate for a child and, at worst, may distort his or her later development. If you suspect it, put a stop to it, however difficult that may be. If the adult is a relation, it can be very difficult indeed.

How can you guard against this kind of relationship while still allowing your child to be friendly with adults outside the nuclear family? You will have to judge each contact on its merits, but remember:

Your child can probably safely visit in a household of two or more adults: a man who is tempted by children *and* a wife who connives at his sexual advances to them, is an unlikely, if possible, combination.

A man living alone may welcome your child because he is genuinely lonely and fond of children's company. But if so, he should welcome your company and that of your child's friends as well. Be a little wary of the entirely private and exclusive friendship. Be wary, here, with relations, too. If that uncle loves to babysit but will never join you for a family meal, ask yourself why.

Don't push your children into visiting people as a duty. If you think that elderly neighbor needs help, give it yourself if the child is reluctant. Don't push him or her into physical contact, even with relations, either. Kissing great aunt Marjorie may make him uneasy for reasons he barely perceives and certainly cannot explain.

Make the child's personal ownership of his or her body, and absolute right to keep it private, part of your everyday attitudes and practice. The use of the term "private parts" sometimes helps a child to realize that sex organs *are* personal and private, and that he or she can therefore expect everyone to keep them to themselves.

Don't indulge in, or permit, sexy teasing of this age group. A nine-year-old is not old enough to have (or want) a boy- or girlfriend other than as a person-friend. If you encourage even the most lighthearted talk of this kind, you will muddle the child into thinking that perhaps he or she *is* a sexual object. You will make it less likely that assailants will be frozen off by uncomprehending embarrassment.

Non-sexual assaults on children before puberty

Although sexual assault is the kind most parents have nightmares about, non-sexual kinds are much more frequent and, in some cities, a real risk to a child's happiness and health, if not to his life. Attacks are usually carried out by groups of youths or adolescent girls. They seem most often to be caused (and can therefore be largely prevented by attention to) the following:

Solitude. A child alone is an obvious butt/victim.

Conspicuous possessions. That brand-new football, large doll's carriage or shiny bike is a temptation in direct proportion to its rarity in your neighborhood. If your child is to be comfortable in his community, keep the possessions he uses in public roughly in line with what others have, or save the flashy ones for use when adults are around.

Conspicuous clothes. A child dressed in the uniform of a "posh" school often invites the semi-joking wrath of others. In some neighborhoods a skull-cap or turban has the same effect.

Personal vendettas. A child whose family becomes conspicuous in the neighborhood, often because it is "different" along some dimension such as race, color or social class, may be ceaselessly tormented whenever he or she goes out into the streets where young social life is going on. Do everything you can to help your children blend in to their peer group (*see* **Discipline, Self-discipline and Learning How to Behave**/When other children become important).

While doing all that you can to avoid trouble, teach your children that if they ever are stopped by a gang of older children, they should give up whatever it is the group wants without a struggle. A ten-year-old, however brave, stands no chance against five fifteen-year-olds. He or she could get seriously hurt; they could be in serious trouble and all for ten cents and some false pride.

Before a pre-adolescent demands full independence and starts to resent any "fussiness" from you, make sure that he or she really knows the home area, can manage him/herself within it and knows how to seek help if it is ever needed. For example:

Make sure she knows where all the local phone booths are, always carries the right change and always knows where to contact a responsible adult. You can give advice or take emergency action even if you are in an office on the other side of town.

She should know where the local police station is and where patrol police can usually be found; at road crossings, for example.

She should know how to get home from anywhere she is likely to go, by public transportation as well as on foot, and always carry enough money for fares. In cities, buses are usually far safer than subways.

She should know which strange adults to approach for help in any kind of emergency. Some help or protection can usually be obtained from uniformed officials. Make sure she knows of any park-keepers' offices and bus terminals, for example, in the locality.

Help her to make the arrangements which mean she goes around with friends rather than alone. That fishing party, for example, should assemble and disperse at somebody's house rather than on the riverbank. Two or more should go to the movies together rather than meeting in the lobby.

Try to be kind and generous about lifts and snacks for your child's social group. She is far less likely to walk home alone after dusk if she knows you will willingly pick her up (and drop off the others at their houses, too), and she is far less likely to set off alone if her friends are always welcomed when they call at her house.

Sexual molestation and assault on adolescents

After puberty, girls are at much greater risk than boys. While only a tiny minority of adult men find young children sexually attractive—those who do being as likely to fancy little boys as little girls—young but sexually mature girls attract a majority of heterosexual men, whether they can admit it or not. It may be that youths are equally attractive to many adult women but, since a forced sexual relationship that way around is physically impossible, boys have in-built protection.

Assault by strangers

The lurking male who drags a girl into the bushes on her way home and rapes her is every parent's horror. Fortunately he is an exceedingly rare hazard, even though it is his activities which make the headlines.

Most such ghastly incidents take place after dark and in lonely places, so it is probably sensible to get your daughter's overall agreement to certain commonsense precautions like not walking alone after dark and avoiding obviously risky places. But you cannot entirely guard against a hazard which is, by definition, unforeseeable. Violent rapes can and do take place in public places and in daylight. Probably the best that you can do is to teach your daughter to be as cautious for her safety as you are for your own, not forgetting to allow for the fact that you may have a car to get around in and/or a partner to go around with.

Other situations with definite rape potential include letting men into the house when there is nobody else there and accepting lifts in cars. Happily, hitch-hiking seems to be going out of fashion and many families will find that their daughters easily accept a complete ban on it. Avoiding letting men into the house is more difficult as refusing entry to somebody claiming to represent the telephone company can be embarrassing. In many areas it is sensible to teach girls to put the chain on a door before answering it, and to ask for proof of identity before letting anyone in. Better still, a "spy hole" lets her see the caller; she need not open to strangers.

Avoiding situations with rape potential comes hardest on girls with a taste for solitude. It certainly *ought* to be safely possible to sunbathe in a private glade, swim off a gloriously deserted cove or wander alone along a riverbank. But in many places it is not.

Molestation by strangers

If rape is rare, molestation and "teasing" are not. It must be the unusual adolescent girl who has not been embarrassed and/or frightened by being followed in the street, or joined by uninvited "guests" at her lunch table, movie seat or poolside lounger. As long as society treats *any* degree of predatoriness as an acceptable sign of macho-masculinity, this kind of thing will reduce girls' freedom to get on with their own lives in peace. Some girls learn to cope by meeting aggression with aggression, mockery with mockery. Others find that discretion is the better part of valor and abandon their lunch once it is clear that they cannot finish it in peace. They are probably right. Pert answers can misfire; insult the leader of a teasing group and it can turn nasty. Provoke somebody into making a grab, forcing a kiss, having a grope, and fear of the consequences can quickly provoke the group to violence to "shut her up."

Trouble with family and other known adults

Any form of sexual assault or molestation by complete strangers is merely the tip of a much larger iceberg. Many adolescent girls are used sexually, often over a long period, by people they know.

Incestuous relationships are much more common than most people want to realize. Close friends and neighbors, and neighborhood figures such as shopkeepers, watchmen and so forth, are also common assailants. In all these relationships sexual contact is often minimal at the beginning, but escalates when the assailant finds that he can get away not just with suggestive looks and words but with furtive and then less furtive fumblings. Why can such a man get away with it? The key to protecting your daughter is hidden in the complicated answer.

Such men get away with it because girls often do not tell anyone. Girls do not tell because, if and when they do, they seldom get the outright protection they deserve.

At the very beginning of such a relationship, when the thirteen- or fourteen-year-old feels that there is something odd about the way the man looks at her and the frequency with which he collides with her in doorways, it is extremely difficult for her to know *what* to tell. How many girls in this age group are confident enough in their own sexual attractions, *and* in their parents' trust and understanding, to be able to say, "I think Mr. Jones fancies me so I don't want to be around him any more"? If a child did say it many parents would be shocked and angry that their daughter was even able to consider such a thing. Others would simply laugh. Still others would even *tell* Mr. Jones (father's friend or the building's janitor), "Our girl's got a crush on you." So she apparently acquiesces and the man gets bolder. There is probably no physical violence but there is now the mental violence of blackmail and/or bribery. A kiss for a sweet, or a fuss and I'll tell your Dad you were with that boy from next door.

A girl who does tell, at this kissing, cuddling, fumbling stage, is often not believed. Parents cannot or will not believe that "a respectable married man" or "your very own uncle" would "do such a thing." Their deep-seated shock at the idea of sexual molestation of a young girl by a much older man does not take the form of fury at *him* but, all too often, of fury at *her*. She may find herself accused of "making up wicked stories." Ironically, she may also find herself subject to all kinds of new restrictions in her own life with her peers, as if *she* could no longer be trusted to "behave decently."

If proximity makes it impossible for the girl to avoid the man, or if his sexual demands go beyond what she can tolerate, she will eventually bring the matter into the open. But even a girl who has been forcibly assaulted, technically raped, within such a relationship, often finds that she is considered more sinning than sinned against. Forced to believe —often by painful physical evidence—that there has been sexual contact, parents accuse their daughters of "flaunting themselves" of "leading him on" or simply of "bringing shame on the family." The Catch 22 in which she finds herself is often that if she *really* had not wanted it, she would have told her parents sooner.

Such attitudes are even more usual if and when any attempt is made to take legal action against the man.

Even if a girl has clearly suffered physical harm, she will have to prove that she did not consent to being hurt. Sexual congress with a girl under the age of consent is technically rape, whatever the circumstances. Yet consent, or "reasonable grounds to believe" that she consented, together with evidence that she "looked older than sixteen," will mitigate the court's attitude and sentence.

In a lesser case of sexual interference, even when parents believe the girl's story, the police will seldom take her word against that of a "respectable man." She will be forced to relive every word and gesture for an audience of police officers whose attitudes seem to stem from a belief (or perhaps a wishful fantasy) that every pubescent girl is really a Lolita. No wonder most such cases are withdrawn before they ever reach a court.

Keep communication channels open. The more you talk, the more likely a child is to feel able to tell you if she is uneasy within any relationship.

Try to accept your daughter's sexuality. She may seem like a child to you, but don't allow your rightful desire to consider her a child blind you to the fact that she is physically mature and, therefore, potentially a victim to anyone who sees her as a sexual object rather than a very young person.

Be sensitive to her feelings. If she is uneasy with somebody, it really does not matter whether she has reason to be suspicious. The simple fact that she is uneasy is sufficient reason to help her avoid the man.

Be very clear in your own mind that in relationships with children, however sexually mature they may appear, responsibility always lies with the adult. Our society pretends to believe in individual freedom. If that freedom is to be meaningful, it must include freedom for young girls to make themselves as attractive as they can and want to be without fear of unwelcome attention being forced upon them. A fourteen-year-old should not have to pay for a provocative new dress by being mauled in corners at the party. Men must keep their hands off the package however prettily it is wrapped. We do not believe in helping them with purdah and veils. If your daughter knows that you are clear about this issue, she is unlikely to be afraid that you will blame *her*, however subtly, if she appeals to you for help.

Try to remain basically on her side whatever storms her adolescence may bring. Mutual trust is vital. She must know that if the chips finally fell, you would take her word rather than that of another adult, and that you would always put her happiness and her dignity before that of your boss or your brother.

Sexual molestation and assault by peers

Some sexual assaults are dates which go wrong. Some "rapes" are petting sessions which go too far. Every family has to arrive at its own policy on teenage dating and teenage sex (*see* **Adolescence**/Sex), but as well as deciding what they are going to "allow" their daughters to do, parents also have to help those daughters to avoid what they do not want to do.

Make sure your daughter understands that if she gets a young man going too fast, his brakes may fail. While it is equally important to bring up boys to understand and control their own sexuality, it is vital that girls realize that theirs is usually less direct and urgent than their partners; if they want to say "enough" they had better do so while they can still be heard.

Try to ensure that she knows what to expect of any particular occasion or group. If she knows that the midsummer barbecue always ends with a nude midnight swim and she is pleading to go, then whether she goes or not is between you all. But if she is pleading to go to that barbecue without knowing about the midnight swim, she may find herself out of her depth in more ways than one.

Safety on vacation

Wherever you stay on vacation, your accommodations will be the family's temporary home. All the safety points which apply in your real home will apply there, too, but you may need to be even more vigilant than usual because you will be without your own safety precautions, and the children will be without the protection of familiarity. While very young children will need constant supervision, freedom may be the point of the vacation for older ones. Parents need to ask themselves whether those older children, whether they are five, ten or fifteen years old, have the knowledge and experience to keep themselves safe in the vacation environment.

Some of the most obvious hazards are noted below. Obvious they may be, but they claim lives (or at least ruin vacations) for some families every year.

Beach hazards Children new to the ocean cannot be expected to understand the strength of its waves or the likelihood and power of currents or undertow. They cannot know that various states of the tide produce suddenly shelving beaches, wickedly concealed rocks or a rapidly closing escape route.

If you are in a resort, use a patrolled stretch of beach and make sure children understand the warning symbols. If you have found a deserted place, take local advice.

Be careful with inflatables. A strong on-shore breeze is your best insurance against children being carried out to sea. If in doubt, keep inflatables on a line.

Sand dunes are blissful places to play but don't let children tunnel in them. A cave-in can mean lungs full of sand, however quick the rescue.

Cliff-scrambling is fun, too, but crumbling rock is dangerous and so is getting stuck halfway up.

Water sports—simple swimming, water skiing, sailing or whatever—are all very different in the ocean from in a pool or lake. Make children prove their ability to manage these new conditions before you let them venture forth without you or an instructor.

Rural hazards Even you may not realize the depth of an urban child's ignorance of country hazards. Will he both recognize and avoid a bull? If he has never before met a snake might he try to pick it up? He may be used to finding his way around the city but will he find his way around those woods? If he makes friends with local youngsters, remember that they will be totally familiar with the environment while he is not; they may unwittingly lead him into situations he cannot cope with, especially if, understandably, he is reluctant to admit that it is all new to him.

Foreign hazards Being in a foreign country emphasizes the risks which are built-in to being in a strange environment. A foreign language, for example, means that a child will not be able to read warning notices or direction signs and will not understand the helpful remarks of local residents.

There may also be specific risks associated with the particular place. For example, Caribbean sun is very different from American sun. A warning to be careful may not be enough, although a glimpse of the flayed back of another unwary visitor may make the point for you (*see* **Accidents/** Sunburn and heat illness).

If you take children to a country where traffic drives on the "wrong" side of the road, be very sure that they can reverse the built-in drill of home before you let them wander alone.

Make sure that they understand local laws and conventions, too. In some countries you may only cross the road at a crossing; jay-walking can lead to an instant arrest. A girl in shorts may be spat on in a Middle Eastern country, or find that by crossing a Roman square alone in the evening, she has invited the attentions of every young man in sight. In many Eastern bloc countries there are rigid rules about taking photographs. Unwittingly breaking one can mean at best a ruined film, at worst a trip to the nearest police station.

Finally, of course, there may be health hazards which a child simply cannot foresee. It is up to you to make sure she knows if she should avoid drinking water from the hotel taps, eating fruit from local stalls, wading in nearby streams or putting on her shoes without first checking for scorpions.

Safety on wheels

Cars   With more and more cars on our roads, more and more children are exposed to the dangers of riding in them, as well as the danger of walking near them (*see above* On the road).

Do remember that the difference between "a little bump" and a serious accident is not measured in scratched paint or buckled metal. What really matters is whether or not anyone is hurt.

In a *majority* of accidents, no one need be hurt if everyone is using appropriate and well-fitted safety restraints.

Babies in cars   The following suggestions conform to the laws of the many states which regulate the ways in which babies and young children may be carried in cars. Do follow them voluntarily even if you are not legally obliged to do so.

Sanctioned infant seats are strapped into the car by safety belts and have a five-point harness. They must be positioned so that the baby travels facing *backwards* and thus absorbs the impact of any collision through the strongest part of his body: his back. It is legal, but ill-advised, to put the backward-facing seat in the front of the car. Although it is easier for the driver to chat to a baby travelling there, he will be far more likely to survive a serious accident if his seat is in the back of the car.

The seat sanctioned for children between about nine months and four years (or 18 lbs and 40 lbs) is similar in design and fastenings but faces forward. You can save yourself the expense of two seats if you buy the convertible type. It is installed as a backward-facing, semi-reclined seat for the new baby and then re-positioned later on in a forward-facing and upright position.

Some children object to being strapped into their seats but this is one battle which you must win. Try behaving as if seat-harness and car-ignition were linked. You will not start the car until the child is safely settled and you stop immediately an older one attempts to release himself.

● Don't, *please* don't, ever have a baby on your lap in the front passenger seat, even if you are both belted in yourself and legally within your rights. A head-on collision will put the baby through the windshield, however firmly you were holding him. In a less serious accident, his body will protect yours. If you want to be close to him, join him in the back.

Toddlers and pre-school children in cars

A young toddler can go on using that car safety seat, but when he reaches about forty pounds he should have it replaced by a safety approved child harness. Like adult seat belts these have to be bolted to the frame of the car by a garage, but they include a special cushion which sits the child at a height from which he can see out. Most children, used to seats, appreciate the new freedom of the harness and accept the change as promotion. If yours does not accept it willingly, he, too, will have to discover that no harness means no travel.

Older children in cars

When a child weighs around eighty pounds, he will be able to wear an adult-type seat belt and that means that he *could* ride in that front passenger seat, properly belted in. But he will still be much safer with a properly fitted belt *in the back*. While a seat belt makes that front seat much safer, it is still the most dangerous place in the car. If you must use it (perhaps because your family fills your vehicle), provide seat belts for all seats and at least save the "privilege" of riding in front until a child is tall enough to travel with his bottom well back on the seat and his feet flat on the floor.

Friends' cars and friends in your car

Ideally you should not let your children ride in other people's cars unless those cars have appropriate seat belts for them and you know that their use will be insisted upon. By the same token, you should not carry more children than you can belt in. Certainly, if you are going to do so you should point out the deficiency to the other child's parents.

If this is a counsel of impossible perfection, at least avoid the following traps:

Don't put anyone in the front seat without a belt.

● This is illegal in some countries; irresponsible in all.

Don't put a small child in the front seat with an *adult* belt. A belt which does not fit can in itself be extremely dangerous, not just because it may not hold the child in a crash, but because it may fit across his neck rather than his shoulder and strangle him.

Don't let anyone have a child on a lap in front.

Don't let anyone hold a baby or toddler on a lap, even in the back, unless he or she is near-adult in size and weight. Even from the back seat, such a baby can be thrown straight through the windshield if inadequately restrained.

Don't let children stand up on the floor of the back, holding on to the back of the front seats. A crash-somersault can fracture spines.

If you are determined to carry a gaggle of children—in a school car pool or as a birthday treat—they will probably be safest in the back section of a station wagon facing backwards.

Car windows, doors and locks

Don't have windows open enough for children to put out their heads or their arms. Even if you do not scrape them against another vehicle, high-speed dust in the eyes is dangerous and so is the effect of random hand signals on the cars behind you.

Child-proof locks on all doors are vital, especially at the bored fiddly toddler stage, or with a car-sick child who might try to get out before it is safe to do so. Do get into the habit of waiting until you can see all hands inside the car before you shut children in. Car doors are responsible for thousands of truly agonizing blackened fingers every year (*see* **Accidents/** Bruises: "Blackened" nails).

Car parking

Try to park so that children can get out, or be lifted out, on the sidewalk side of the road. In parking lots, let everybody out on one side so that you can keep an eye on them; other cars, with drivers who are only thinking about reversing in tight spaces, can be extremely dangerous to those too small to be easily seen.

Never leave the engine running if children stay in the car while you mail a letter or whatever. In some cars it is easy to engage "Drive" and some children would love to try. Likewise, don't leave children in a car parked on a hill with only that hand brake between them and disaster.

It is wiser never to leave the keys in the ignition when you park the car at home. Maybe your own children would not dream of having a go, but there may be others who would.

Bicycles

Almost every school-aged child *wants* a bike; some children actually need bikes to get around on. Only you can decide whether your child should have one and if so, when and for what.

First bikes for fun

Most children can balance a two-wheeler when they are around five. There is fun (and status) to be had even from riding one in the garden.

Small bikes will usually fit in a car and can be taken to parks or out into the country. When your child can safely walk along the sidewalk alone, there may be a nearby park to which he can push it.

Falls are inevitable at first so encourage jeans and jackets rather than shorts and T-shirts.

Don't allow him to ride even a few yards on the road. It is not only his incompetence which may endanger him, but the size of the bike: the driver of a large truck may totally fail to see such a minute vehicle.

Bikes in the country

If you live in a rural area, cycling may be the only way for your children to get to school or to get around on vacations. Even if they do not actually *need* bikes this urgently, they may desperately want them for the freedom and the vistas they open up.

If traffic is really sparse and the area is not very hilly, a child might manage safely, in daylight, at around eight or nine. You will need to do some advance safety planning though.

Do make sure that she is consistently safe and sensible on the roads *on foot*, before you consider letting her out on a bike.

Do buy her a bike which fits her, not one she will "grow into" unless it is the kind designed to change with the child.

Do teach her, or have her taught properly, even if she already rides a bike in your garden.

Do consult with your local police and equip both bike and child with whatever safety gear (reflective strips, etc.) is recommended.

Do have the bike checked over by a professional, even if it is brand new. Many leave the factories with tight chains, slack brakes, etc.

Do have the bike regularly "serviced" (if you cannot do it yourself).

Do have a proper luggage carrier fitted. Shoulder bags and parcels on handlebars are dangerous.

Do take her (or find someone else if you do not cycle) on several trial runs before you let her cycle on the roads alone or with her friends. Emphasize safety points like stopping, as well as signalling, before turning left, and emergency measures like turning into the shoulder.

Don't let her ride her bike after dusk. Teach her to phone if held up at school.

Don't let her ride in really bad weather conditions. When roads are wet and slippery and/or there is a wind or fog, her riding will be erratic and so will the behavior of cars.

Bikes in the city   The accident rate for adult cyclists in cities is very high; for child cyclists it is devastating. Despite the increasing popularity of the bicycle as a cheap, healthy, non-polluting form of transportation, you may feel that it is just too dangerous for a city child unless there are special cycle routes or it is an area (such as many university towns) where there are so many cyclists that motor traffic is resigned to giving them space. Most city-dwelling nine-year-olds are far safer using public transportation than their own bikes.

If your child really needs to get around the city by bicycle, or passionately wants the independence of his personal transport, make sure that he gets as much cycling practice as possible in safer areas, first. That way he will only have to worry about the traffic; control of his own vehicle will already be second nature to him.

Motorbikes   The accident statistics concerning youngsters, especially males, on
and scooters   motorbikes and scooters are truly grim. On a motorbike, your child is as unprotected as he is on a pedal-bike yet he travels at the speed of a car. Youngsters fall off bikes and later on they make dents in car fenders, but it is accidents off motorbikes which most often cause serious injury.

If your child yearns for the glamour and open-air speed of motorcycling and is determined to acquire one the moment he is old enough to take it on the road, you probably will not be able to dissuade him. After all he can back his preference for motorbikes over cars with a whole year's age difference, cheaper maintenance, cheaper insurance, fuel economy, speed through traffic and easy parking. If he is old enough for a license he will be old enough to earn the money and too old to forbid.

Use whatever influence you do have to persuade him to *learn to ride that bike*. Practice, in an off-road area, under supervision, really does reduce accident rates. Try to make sure (perhaps with well-timed birthday presents) that he wears not only an approved helmet, but also top-quality protective clothing. That leather may save him from lifelong scars.

See whether you can persuade him that, while he insists on the right to risk his own neck, he does not have the right to risk other people's. He might agree not to carry pillion passengers and you might also be able to ban his sister from riding behind her boyfriend.

Cars instead of motorbikes   If your child is immune to motorcycle *glamour* and longs only for motor transport, you may be able to persuade him to wait until he is old enough to drive a (far safer) car. Your willingness to pay for driving lessons, share the family car with him after he has passed the test, or lend him the down payment for his own may all help.

Scalds *see* **Accidents**/Burns and scalds; **Safety**/In the home.

Scarlet Fever and "Strep" Throats

One child's streptococcal sore throat can be another child's scarlet fever. The two diseases are identical except that in scarlet fever a particular toxin (erythrogenic toxin) produced by the bacteria causes a lobster red rash all over the body. People become immune to the effect of that toxin, so that a child can have repeated "strep" throats but only have scarlet fever once. That child can, of course, pass on his throat infection to another individual who may produce scarlet fever.

Although it used to be a killer disease, scarlet fever is now a very mild one. It is thought that the virulence of the streptococcus has declined. Should more virulent strains reemerge, they can be efficiently treated with penicillin. The disease is not, therefore, one to be feared and it is not thought worthy of attempts at immunization.

Incubation period. Two to four days.

Route of infection. Often by symptomless carriers who harbor the streptococci in the nose or throat. Infection may be by droplets via the throat, but it can be acquired from contaminated food or objects, and infection can also enter the body through wounds. The puerperal fever of past times was in fact a streptococcal infection of the uterus.

First symptoms of scarlet fever   Similar to any "tonsillitis": a sudden fever, sore throat and perhaps vomiting. The tonsils become enlarged and inflamed, and the tongue is furry and white with tiny red dots. The tongue then becomes bright red with the white furry substance peeling back from the tip and edges.

The rash of scarlet fever

If the individual is not immune to the toxin, the rash of scarlet fever appears a day or so after these mouth and tongue changes. The rash usually starts on the neck and spreads, over a day or two, to cover the whole body. From afar the skin looks a uniform bright red. Close examination reveals countless minute red dots. The skin may "peel" after the rash has faded.

Treatment and complications of scarlet fever

The bacteria can invade the lungs and bloodstream and many scarlet fever deaths in the past were due to resulting pneumonia or septicemia. Today these side effects are extremely rare, even in an untreated case, and can always be prevented by treatment with penicillin. An untreated patient today may experience local spread of the streptococci into the sinuses or the middle ear. Penicillin will almost always be given to any patient with a "strep" throat (with or without scarlet fever rash) to prevent this.

The "post-streptococcal" state

Certain diseases, such as rheumatic fever or acute kidney damage (nephritis), can develop one or two weeks after any acute streptococcal infection. They are thought to be due to some unusual reaction in the body to the presence of antigens to streptococci. They are now extremely rare, thanks to antibiotic treatments.

These diseases are infinitely more damaging than the original infection. The chance that an attack of "tonsillitis" is due to infection with streptococci (rather than more usual and innocent viruses) is one excellent reason why a doctor may prescribe penicillin for such an illness.

● A child with a sore throat accompanied by general signs of illness, such as fever and vomiting, should always be seen by a doctor.

● If antibiotics are prescribed in a situation like this, it is absolutely essential that the full course be given, even if the illness resolves itself in a couple of days and/or the antibiotic appears to be giving the patient diarrhea.

Scars *see* **Hospital**/Surgery: Plastic surgery. *See also* **Adolescence**/Problems with appearance and body image.

School

Pre-school and nursery education

In almost every Western country fierce argument flares and dies concerning every aspect of education for children under compulsory school age. Campaigning groups, via the media, simultaneously announce that such education is "a basic right for every child" and that many children "do better at home." They tell us that excellent and universally available pre-school groups are a necessity in societies where women-who-are-mothers expect to work outside their homes and they tell us that pre-school education is irrelevant to the issue of child care during mothers' working hours. One research study tells us that children with experience in a pre-school group acquire basic skills (like reading) more quickly once they start school, but another study tells us that pre-school attendance makes no difference either way. It is all very confusing.

The coexistence of so many conflicting theories and convictions is partly due to the fact that people seldom define their terms. What, for example, *is* pre-school education? Is it a curriculum, an experience or some of each? A sensible answer to that question depends on being able to decide what pre-school education is *for*. Is it intended to give children an academic head start in formal school, or to broaden their overall experience, or to accelerate their development, or to keep them happy? Or is it primarily intended to take some pressure off their parents? Again, sensible answers to questions of that sort would depend on knowing the actual children, parents and group leaders under discussion. What might be appropriate for a four-year-old living alone with a depressed mother in a high-rise apartment may be unnecessary for a three-year-old in jollier circumstances, and downright damaging to many two-year-olds. The truthful answer to questions such as "Is pre-school education a good thing?" has to be "It depends." Parents who are trying to decide whether or not to seek admission to a pre-school group for their own child may therefore need to shut their ears to everybody else's theories and convictions and think, in a very down-to-earth way, only about their own child, their own lives and the actual groups which are available to them. Ask yourselves, for example, why you are considering sending the child.

If going to a group is for fun only

You need to be sure that the group available is likely to meet the needs you can identify. Does it provide the kinds of activity and the personal relationships which this particular child enjoys? She might, for example:

Enjoy the company of other children. Although toddlers usually play side by side rather than actively with each other, many much enjoy watching and copying each other provided that an adult is available to help each one to control her own snatch-and-grab tendencies. Children of, say, three or four are usually very ready to enjoy playing *with* each other, and quickly discover that two together can often manage something that one alone cannot. A child who starts at "big school" with virtually no experience of other children is likely to find them surprising and rather alarming. She may, for example, always have been given the largest cakes and the winning hands. Thrown into school she discovers that she is not a princess but simply one of a crowd. Although she may pick up the new "rules" at lightning speed, her ignorance of social group life may, quite unfairly, make her unpopular.

Almost any kind of pre-school group will certainly give your child the company of others, but that does not mean that only a group can do so. If yours has brothers and sisters, playmates and neighbors, she may have all the company she needs. The same applies to all the other potential social benefits of group attendance. If a child is isolated with one depressed parent in a high-rise apartment, she may indeed benefit from contact with other, interested and interesting adults, of both sexes, as well as from extra space, new things to do, talk, music and fun. But a child can have all those things at home, too. If you and your child have a full and satisfying life, with enough people around so that neither of you is lonely or bored, the group may have little to offer her socially.

Enjoy activities you cannot provide at home. Every child needs a range of activities (*see* **Play**), including some which can seem difficult to find in a small city home. She needs to run and jump and tumble; she needs to climb and swing and balance. She needs to make a noise, too, not just the noise that goes with being physically active but the noise that goes with making rhythm and music and fun. With a lot of ingenuity and a little money, it is usually possible to provide for most of this at, or near, home, especially if you live in an area which has parks and playgrounds, or at least open spaces, nearby. But if you cannot bring yourself to make obstacle courses out of the living-room furniture on rainy days, or tramp to the nearest sandpit on fine ones, she may very much enjoy a group which emphasizes this sort of activity. Do check, though, to be sure of that emphasis. If this is your main reason for sending your child to a group it will be shattering to discover that the garden you were shown is seldom used and that a lot of the children's time is spent sitting down with colored crayons.

If a group is to "do her good" whether she likes it or not

There are probably aspects of her behavior or development which are worrying you, even though she is not aware of them. If you feel, for example, that your two- or three-year-old's slowness in learning to talk, or tendency to have tantrums, is your fault, you may also feel that somebody else will be better able to help her than you are. You may be right but you probably will not be. A child who is sent to a group because her parents are dissatisfied with her is rather likely to sense that she is being banished. She is more likely to settle down quickly and happily if you can get over the bad patch first and then send her.

Group attendance is not often the right prescription for difficulties of development at this sort of age anyway. That child who is slow in talking, for example, is most unlikely to talk more freely with a teacher whom she does not know than she does with you, and at this stage she will not learn speech directly from other children (*see* **Language**). Tantrums are usually a very direct response to parents, part of the power struggle which has to take place while a child is asserting her own progress from dependent babyhood to self-possessed childhood. She may not have any tantrums at a group because her relationship with the adults there will probably not be close enough to provoke her need to assert herself. But just being at the group and not having tantrums will not cure her of having them when she is at home. Indeed, if she does not enjoy going to the group and feels that you are making her go, getting rid of her, she may be even more inclined to let rip at home.

The point is that most of a child's important development takes place in the context of her relationship with the person or people she cares about most deeply. Arranging life so that she spends less time with those people, and more with others, is scarcely ever directly helpful to that child's developmental difficulty. But, of course, it may be very helpful to those special adults (*see below*) and if it provides them with renewed stamina it may be indirectly helpful to her.

A four- or five-year-old may be a very different matter. If circumstances have kept your older pre-school child socially isolated, she may, as we have said, truly need some practice in socializing with other people. If she is painfully shy, hates being separated from you, fights any attempts to encourage independence at meals or in the bathroom and so forth, you may be really frightened for her at the prospect of compulsory all-day schooling. Part-time attendance at a small group with sympathetic adults can certainly provide an easier start for such a child, but do make sure that it is the right kind of group. After all, if you are trying to avoid miserable tears when school begins in nine months' time, you are unlikely to do so by provoking them now. If you cannot find a gentle group at which, bit by bit, she can settle down happily, it may be better to allow her that nine months for growing up under your very gradually withdrawn wing.

If a group is to give her a head start in education

Try not to let yourselves believe that "education" is the key to getting on in life and that the more a child has of it, and the earlier she begins, the better. If you do, you will underestimate the "education" you have been giving your child since birth. She has learned a fantastic amount already and, provided she is usually busy and interested and has an adult to show her things, talk to her and listen to her ideas and questions, she will go on doing so. The education offered by most pre-school groups is no more formal than the "lessons" your child gets when you take her to the supermarket and ask her to get two red packages of cereal, or when you sit with her to watch a television program and talk about it afterwards, or when you go for a walk and "read" the advertisements, count dogs or pretend to fly.

Some groups do give four-year-olds formal lessons in reading, writing and number work. While these certainly don't do a child any harm *if she enjoys them*, it is questionable whether they actually speed up her learning of these basic skills, either. Most research suggests that if you start directly teaching a child to read when she is four, she will become proficient two to three years later, but if the formal teaching starts when she is five she will become proficient one to two years later. The point is that that child was going to read at around six to seven anyway. The starting date has more to do with how long drawn-out the process is than with her later competence.

The feeling that education is so important that young children should be pushed ahead has led to the publication of reading and number schemes designed to be used in teaching babies, as well as to powerful advertising for a vast range of "educational" toys. Few parents are foolish enough to try to force these activities on a child who is clearly bored or bewildered by them, so they probably do not often do any harm. It is a pity, though, if the rare baby who really does take enthusiastically to the written word at two makes other parents feel that their children are "backward" or "deprived." And it is a pity if pushy advertising black-mails parents into spending more than they can afford on toys which are "educational," and less than they otherwise might have done on materials which the child can use as she wishes (*see* **Play**).

If you do decide to send your child to a pre-school group because you want her exposed to as many "educational" influences as possible, do again make sure that you select the right kind of group. If your child is to settle down happily, she will need to feel that you approve of what she is doing and of the people she is doing it with. If you send her to a group which deliberately avoids any formal teaching, preferring to concentrate on free, imaginative and creative activities, and you keep asking her "Didn't you do anything but play?" you may confuse her badly.

Group attendance may be for your sake rather than hers

Some parents find it difficult to admit, even to themselves, that they *could* want to be rid of their child. But many can and do. If she is to be sent to a pre-school group largely for your convenience, do be honest with yourself. If you are not, you may select a group which does not actually meet your needs at all, however much the child comes to like it.

If what you need is some time away from the child, either to be alone to do your own thing or, perhaps, so as to give uninterrupted time to a younger baby, any group at which the child will settle happily down may give you what you need. But if you are planning to take a job or a course, your child's pre-school group will have to be one which offers child *care* as well as "education." The "as well as" may be a pipe dream. In practice it is still quite rare to find the two things provided together with equal weight given to each (*see below* Choosing a pre-school group).

Some parents feel that they and their child have got into a rut, run out of fun or simply reached a point where they are ready for new people and ideas. Others believe that their young child needs to have them around pretty well all the time, but find it boring and lonely being at home with her. You do not necessarily have to choose between being stuck in with her or being without her. You can probably find a group which you will both enjoy. If you can find a parent-run community group which really welcomes parents, not just as visitors but as an integral part of the environment of the group, you will eventually have a choice. Once you have been going there for a few weeks or months, you will either find that the child is entirely settled within the group and that you, having broken your isolation, are ready to leave her there and go and do something else, or you will find that whether or not she is fully settled, you have become involved with the group and want to include yourself in its running. As always, though, you will need to choose your group carefully. Names and stated policies can be very misleading. Some playgroups which say that they are run by parents are really run, in the day-to-day sense which matters to you, by a paid and qualified play-leader who wants no more than a biweekly stint of cleaning up from you. Some others are more genuinely run by parents, but have become "cliquey" so that it is very difficult for a new parent to break into the magic circle as more than someone who drops her child off and collects her again. A very great many are still amazed if a father tries to become involved.

Choosing a pre-school group

The provision of pre-school facilities is spotty. In some places there may be a wide range of groups, and spaces in them; in others there will be only two or three and all with waiting lists; if you are unfortunate there may be no group at all within range.

If you do have choice available, you can only pick a group which is likely to be right, for your child and for you, by going to see it. You may need to make several visits because it is important that you see the children getting on with life within it *and* that you talk to the adults who would be in charge of your child *and* that you take her on a visit so that she knows what you are talking about before you expect her to attend. The adults cannot (or certainly should not) give you their attention while they have a group of children in their charge; you cannot (or certainly should not) discuss your own child in front of her. You may need three separate visits.

Names are misleading. A group which calls itself a "playgroup" may be a nursery school in all but that name; a "nursery school" may be organized more for the convenience of working parents than the education of children, while a nearby "day-care center" offers the very best in child-centered experience. Depending on what you have decided you want from a group, you may like to look out for (or ask about) some of the following:

Overall size and internal group size
A privately run playgroup may take only six children at a time, offering one, two or three half-day sessions per week to each group. A small group may suit your child, but check that it is always the same children who attend particular sessions, otherwise she may not find it easy to make friends.

A large nursery school or center may have one hundred or more children. Check how they are split up. It may be by rigid age limits with internal promotion, as in a school, or it may be into groups of all ages. Group size may be dictated by the number of rooms available. Twenty three-year-olds are noisy enough to daunt some children, however high the adult-child ratio.

A big center may cater to children attending for only a couple of hours per day and for children who are there all day while both parents are at work. Check whether the kind of attendance you want for your child is likely to make her feel "out of it" or "abandoned." A child who must go all day and every day could find that her eventual "best friends" are there only in the mornings or even that they turn up only sometimes.

Adult-child ratio in the group
Your child will need a "special" adult who replaces you in giving her a feeling of being securely cared for. How does the group provide this? Watch out, for instance, for constantly changing "staff"; for heavy reliance on voluntary and *occasional* help from parents, and for rotation systems which can mean that your child never knows which of several adults will be there.

An ideal ratio of adults to children cannot be stated as it depends on individual personalities, availability of back-up help in emergencies and so forth. But as a general rule even the smallest group must have a minimum of two. One adult (as parents know) cannot properly cope with even three children, because if one requires intensive attention for a while, the others have nobody. Two adults, on the other hand, may be able to cope well with more than twice that number.

If there are too many children for the available adults, your child will not only get rather little "individual attention," she may also get very bored because every change of activity takes such a long time. It will take a long time, for example, for one adult to get ten children into their outdoor clothes or settled for a snack. Those who are not being seen to (or who need no help) just have to wait.

However good the adult to child ratio, watch a session in progress to ensure that the adults "on the roll" are actually available to the children. One may be continually involved in discussions with parents, other visitors, or on the telephone. There may be a lot of behind-the-scenes domestic chores going on, or even rather too much gossip between the adults themselves. The ideal, perhaps, is not to have adults constantly calling for children's attention or intervening in their activities, but to have them available, reasonably quickly, to any child who wants to talk or show, weep or cuddle.

The group's
facilities

Specially built and beautifully equipped nursery groups can look very appealing, compared to an old hall or semi-converted tenement. But try to look through your child's eyes. Will she like that long row of identical hand towels on scarlet pegs or will she feel that she cannot find her own? Will she appreciate the darling little desks or does she prefer to sit on the floor which, here, is cold, hard plastic? Just occasionally you can discover something important about the *feeling* of a group by looking carefully at its facilities. I know a group of twenty, for example, which has fifteen identical potties as well as four toilets. Why so many potties? Because children are sat upon them all together at pre-arranged intervals, rather than individually when each feels the need. Is the garden impeccably tidy with mown grass and flourishing flowers? It may not be used freely. Is the kitchen or "utility area" tucked away behind closed doors? Its activities may be a secret from the children and one which takes an adult away. Are the walls covered with tasteful pictures and posters? There may be no space for the children's own work. Within limits, a muddle can be homey and comfortable for children. After all, you cannot keep your own home looking as if no child lived there, can you?

Try to get a careful look at the toys and other equipment, too. Children do not need elaborate "educational toys" to play and learn, but anything which is provided for them should, if their play-learning is truly respected, be decently kept. Puzzles with missing pieces, trains with broken links, books with missing pages and torn covers, and wheeled vehicles without wheels should all make you wonder. Every group has to economize to some extent, but some things must be freely available to children if they are to be available at all. Exercise-book-sized pieces of paper, for example, are useless to a painting three-year-old; she will be better off with big sheets of the cheapest paper available. The same applies to tiny paintbrushes, minute pieces of clay or dough and demands that she "use up" the stub ends of crayons or the mud-colored remains in that paint pot. If, on the other hand, you should find that dressing-up clothes are not only available but clean, mended and occasionally ironed, you can be fairly sure that somebody cares.

The group's
hours and
organization

Short hours (often two and a half hours at a time) may be excellent for children just starting at a group, but they may be bothersome for you. By the time you get home from taking your child you have scarcely time to do anything useful or enjoyable before you must fetch her again.

Short hours every weekday are often easier for a child than longer hours two or three times a week. A three-year-old may find it difficult to keep track of "group days" and "home days," and may find it difficult to settle into any satisfactory routine. If this group insists that your child begin in this way, is there any likelihood of daily attendance later on?

All-day attendance may mean anything from a short "school day" such as 9:30 to 3:30, to a full adult working day with allowance for travel time: perhaps 8 to 6. Even one meal at the group makes a lot of difference to your child. She will have to face strange food, strange customs and intimate attention from strangers. Providing the meal may take a lot of adult time, too. All-day attendance (with all meals provided) means that the group is offering complete day *care* as well as "education," and you will need to find out how these are balanced. There are groups—even highly reputable and expensive ones—which still provide something closer to "safe custody" than to any kind of "education." If the adults are encouraged to see their working day as punctuated by meals, snacks, toileting and housekeeping activities, rather than by different child-activities, the intervals between these chores tend to be regarded as "just play" and to be used by those aduls for "getting ahead with the cleaning up" rather than for any kind of interaction with the children.

Money and pre-school groups

In some Western countries (such as France and Holland) almost all the pre-school education is provided by the state and is therefore free (or heavily subsidized). In this situation playgroups and children's centers can flourish in a variety which reflects the enthusiasm of educators and the preferences of parents. In the United States (and, to some extent, in Britain) most of the places available in pre-school groups are provided by private enterprise, with some provided by voluntary or community organizations and only a few run by federal or state agencies.

It is important to research the funding situations of any groups within your own community. Above all, do not assume that the most expensive facility will necessarily be the best for your child. Private-enterprise groups, whether they are single centers or parts of a state-wide chain, primarily exist to make a profit for somebody. They may do a great job for your child on the way, but doing that job is not, and cannot be, their prime purpose. If a group cannot make a profit, it will close and then it will not be able to do a good job for anybody. If such a center has unfilled places, you can be fairly sure that economies will be made so as to stretch the incoming fees more thinly over the attending children. Many unfilled places will probably eventually mean that the fees per child go up and this, in its turn may lead to a drop in the roll.

If there are both fee-paying and subsidized groups in your area, you have to be even more careful. Some of the subsidized groups have generous backing and are able to provide excellent facilities which seem amazingly cheap. Understandably such a center will be popular with parents (who wants to spend money if he need not?), but the more children it takes in, the fewer will be sent to the fee-paying center and the more financial trouble it will then be in. Remember that the real costs of good pre-school care are high and don't be too quick to condemn the fee-scale of one center as compared with the subsidized cost of another.

If you (and your child) prefer a small and informal group, you may want to involve yourself in a parent-run playgroup, perhaps one which takes only ten children or less. You need to do this with a high degree of personal commitment to making the arrangement work out. If your child is withdrawn and sent to another group, his departure alone may stop the small group from being viable. A tenth of the incoming fees is a very large cut.

Watch out, also, for a confusion of mixed funding with social class and status. Many federally funded centers are intended primarily for families with special needs. Sometimes the resulting reputation leads to their being shunned by families who would be entitled to use them. Some such centers have actually closed for lack of support while impoverished families fought for places at commercially run and poorly equipped centers. Some highly subsidized facilities, on the other hand, carry extremely high local status, perhaps because they are attached to a local university. Families who could easily afford the fees at private centers then resort to every kind of trickery to get their children admitted, thus draining resources from local fee-paying centers and leaving poorer families without any provision which they can afford.

Amid all this complexity, the most important thing to remember is that no playgroup or children's center wants unfilled places. The resources are there: if they are under used, everyone gets less value for money. If there is plenty of choice locally available and you want the very best for your child, with money no object, consider a fee-paying center with a waiting list. Whatever its fee-scale it is unlikely to be running at a loss and therefore the facilities you see now are likely to be maintained. If, on the other hand, you want the very best but the best available is beyond your means, don't hesitate to go and talk to the person in charge. Many such groups can find grant money for a certain number of free or assisted places and there is no shame whatsoever in taking advantage of this because an unfilled place is bad for the group. If the only available places, or the only places you can afford, are in groups which do not seem to you to be satisfactory, consider not only the effect of the group on your child but also your own effect on the group. Your involvement might be able to change things for the better.

Going to "big school"

Children have to go to school every day on which the school is open, from the moment they reach the legal starting age until they reach the legal leaving age. Unless he or she is ill, the child has no choice in the matter and neither do the vast majority of parents. It is possible to educate your child at home; however, you need not only qualifications but also a special kind of determination, to win the battle to do so.

Folk wisdom says that "school days are the happiest days of your life." If they prove to be so for your child, you will not need the following pages. But if school days do not prove happy, your child's whole happiness will be at risk. He has got to spend most of the waking hours of 180 days of each year in that school. It is not just a place where he goes to learn while his "real life" carries on at home. It is the place where he will have (or not have) most of his friends; where he will make (or not make) most of his meaningful relationships with non-family adults; where he will find (or fail to find) most of his sports and leisure activities. School will be central to his life. If it is not central, then his life may indeed have a vital gap in the middle which home and after-school people and activities will be hard put to fill.

Sometimes parents forget how important school is to a child because going to school quickly becomes a routine and what goes on in school is a mixture of mystery and trivia. It is the home-child parents see and know, and it is easy for them to forget that the child actually has to *live* those unseen hours. School matters.

Assigned schools and alternatives

A school is a living community of people, adults and children, and the relationships which your child makes with these people will matter to him far more than even the most extensive curriculum or most elaborate facilities. He will appreciate and use what a school has to offer only to the extent that he is happy there; he will be happy only to the extent that he feels acceptable and accepted.

Whether he is just about to start his formal education, ready for promotion from elementary school or needing a new high school placement because his family has moved, your child will be assigned to a school within the district where you live and pay school taxes. If you can accept that allocation and allow him to follow the expected subsequent route through the public school system, you may maximize his chances of all-round happiness and success.

His assigned school will be both geographically and socially close to home and this will help him to feel that his life is a complete whole rather than one sharply compartmentalized into "home" and "school." Most of the other children in his grade will live in the neighborhood and, as he makes the good friends which are so vital to his happiness, he will be able to share home experiences as well as classroom hours with them. As they all grow older, "the gang" which forms, shifts and re-forms, will probably be able to drift comfortably in and out of each other's homes and around the local swimming places or ice cream parlors, with none of the dread isolation which comes from being on vacation in a place where "the kids don't want to know me 'cause I'm different . . ."

It will probably be easier for you to play your vital part in a neighborhood school. Every schoolchild, whatever his age, needs to feel that parents are interested in what he does at school, eager to attend parent-teacher conferences, drama productions and so forth and ready to help out from time to time by chaperoning groups or decorating the place for special occasions. While parents *can* do all that in a school which is some way away from home, or in a private school which encourages parent-participation, most find it easier in a school which is part of the community in which they have chosen to live and which they feel belongs to them.

In some areas, the school to which your child is assigned will be the only one there is so that, unless you want to send your child away and can afford boarding fees, you have no choice at all. The American public education system often works best under these circumstances. No choice of school for anyone means that no child is privileged or disadvantaged in his education. Furthermore, parents and educators alike, aware that the school is the one-and-only, are often highly motivated toward making the best of it. Educators may be particularly careful to listen to parents' wishes, while parents may be more inclined to work for improvement from within the school than to criticize it from outside. So if you should find yourself in a one-school community, don't make plans to move to another district without looking at the situation closely. You may find that this is the type of school which most clearly deserves the term "neighborhood school" and that the parents of the children in it are truly your neighbors.

Most Americans live in densely populated urban areas where each school district contains several schools at each age-level. Your child will still be assigned to one—usually the one nearest to his home—but you will have at least the possibility of some choice. How much choice you can actually exercise depends upon where you live and on how wealthy you are.

Choice among
public schools

Different school districts adopt different enrollment policies and then enforce them with varying strictness. Your district may offer:

Open enrollment which allows you to enroll your child in any school in the district, subject only to particular schools' becoming overfull. If you live in an open-enrollment district, whatever educational stage your child has reached, make sure that you inform yourself about all the available schools, well in advance of promotion-time (*see below*). In this situation some schools are always more popular than others, for good or poor reasons. The more popular schools will usually be filled on a first-come-first-served basis unless the school board adopts a selection procedure (*see below*).

Alternative schools which are designed to be unlike the mainstream schools of the district. In an area where the public schools are liberal-arts oriented, an alternative school might be back-to-basics traditional. In an area where the public schools are highly structured in their curriculum, the alternative school may be more open and offer a more self-directed style of education. Alternative schools are usually over-subscribed and many screen their applicants.

Specialist schools which are usually concentrated in the big cities. These may, for example, specialize in music, dance, drama or other arts. Many are high schools. Most require student auditions or other admissions tests.

Vocational schools which were once regarded as inferior to more academic schools but are now increasingly popular. Vocational high schools commonly split their pupils' days between liberal-arts teaching and courses in auto-mechanics, secretarial skills, food service and so forth. Admission tests are not usually required although interviews are usual.

You will need to discover not only the formal enrollment policy of your school board but also the exact situation within each of the schools you might consider. Open enrollment, for example, can only mean a free choice for every family in the unlikely situation of there being enough places for every child at several equally popular schools. A policy of strict allocation, on the other hand, will often be softened for you if you happen to want to enroll your child in a school which is less popular (and therefore less full) than the one to which he has been assigned.

Added choices
within the
public system:
if you can
pay extra

Wherever you send your child to school you will have to go on paying school taxes in your home district. If you are prepared to pay more than this (although not so much as private education would cost you), you may be able to widen your choice of schools:

You may be able to request enrollment at a school in a nearby district provided that you pay a tuition fee to the second district as well as school taxes in your own. The costs can approach private school fees, so make detailed inquiries in advance.

Schools which are short of students, or of students of particular age, sex or ability groupings, sometimes advertise for students from outside their jurisdiction. In such a case, while school taxes will still be payable, you may find that the school board is generous with bussing arrangements and so forth.

You may be able to claim enrollment in another district by lodging the child with relatives during the week. Some parents try to use the address without altering the child's living arrangements, but such accommodation addresses are usually found out by school board investigations.

You may claim that your child has special needs due to handicap and that these needs cannot be met by any school in your district. Enrollment in a school with an appropriate program will usually be arranged but you may have to meet any costs involved in transporting or lodging the child (*see also below*).

Choosing to
pay for private
education

The best available school for your child may be an independent school, but that is not to say that schools in the private sector are necessarily (or even usually) better than public schools. Your task is to find one school for one child. If you search only within the independent sector, you may not only pay out unnecessary money but do so for a less excellent education than your child could have had through your tax payments. The following points are often raised by parents to explain their preference for fee-paying education *in general*. Note that each point can be argued. However comfortably you can afford to pay fees, search for the right individual school for your own child irrespective of which sector it belongs to (*see below* Choosing from the available schools).

Parents say that private schools have better discipline. This view reflects the headline stories of drug abuse and violence in a few public schools and the fact that no fee-paying school could survive for long if it allowed such behavior to emerge. However, most public schools do not suffer in this way and many are at least as assertive in their discipline as are most parochial schools. Choose your school.

Some parents appreciate *outward signs of strict discipline*, such as the dress codes which are still common only in independent schools. Note, though, that despite (or perhaps because of) the abolition of dress codes in public high schools, students are tending to dress more conservatively than a decade ago. Adult insistence on certain codes of behavior does not always promote the self-discipline which really matters.

Parents say that private schools provide a wider curriculum/"better" education. Some private schools are abysmal, many are mediocre, a few are excellent: exactly the same is true of the academic performance of public schools. A school may, for example, boast that all its small pupils learn French. But that "learning" may consist of twenty minutes twice a week from a harrassed teacher who is responsible for the subject all through the school. Or, if the French teaching is adequate, it may be given at the expense of a solid grounding in math. Be wary of any "extras" which are offered as part of the school's daily routine; paying for your child's education does not give him extra hours or energy; those extras must be instead of something else. If they are instead of meaningless and unsupervised time in the playground, fine. If they are instead of basics, or sports, or hobbies, they need careful consideration.

Parents say that private schools provide better teachers. Independent schools do not require teaching credentials but are free to hire anyone who is academically qualified in his/her own subject. This can be an advantage or a disadvantage, depending on the individuals concerned and on what you want from the school.

Do you long for your child to be taught English by a novelist who will inspire him to enjoy creative writing? Or is it more important to you that he be taught by someone who not only majored in the subject but has been taught how to teach its grammar?

Private school faculty are usually paid less than public school faculty, yet many who are qualified to teach in public schools choose to remain in the private sector in order to have more freedom in their teaching. You may therefore find many dedicated teachers among their ranks. Many also enjoy using life skills as well as academic ones, so that a physics teacher may coach the ball team or a French teacher lead the drama group. Again you will have to judge whether the result is a refreshing enthusiasm and lack of rigidity or whether it amounts to amateurism.

When you are weighing the educational standards of a private school versus your allocated school, do find out whether the private school is accredited. This is especially important at secondary level as students from unaccredited high schools may not be eligible for admission to certain colleges. Accredited independent high schools may provide easier access to higher education than do most public high schools. Many have excellent counseling programs to help students select colleges; some have close ties with particular colleges.

Parents say that private schools provide smaller classes and more personal attention. This is the private school claim which is most likely to be valid. Smaller classes do, on the whole, allow a teacher to devote more time to each pupil. At the youngest age levels it may mean more time to hear his reading; at older ages it may mean more time to read and correct his written work; as graduation approaches it may mean more time to devote to thinking about him and his future and advising him carefully about his further education or job prospects.

Parents point out that private schools tend to be smaller and more socially homogeneous. Some public schools are vast and impersonal institutions within which a child can feel lost and from which he can become alienated. Some cater to such socially divergent groups that the class-wars of adult society are waged in miniature in their classrooms. But the fact that a school can be too large and too divergent does not mean that the ideal school must be small and homogeneous. Some private schools are too small to provide good sport facilities, wide-ranging after-school activities or even modern teaching aids like language laboratories and computers. A great many are too small to provide special help for children with learning difficulties, although most will arrange such help from outside if a student requires it. As to homogeneity, do you actually want your child to be educated only with others from similar social, religious and financial backgrounds?

Many private schools are well aware that they could be charged with too much homogeneity, with snobbery, indeed. Some therefore make an effort to enroll students from a variety of ethnic and religious backgrounds, and many arrange some scholarships or easy-payment schemes for the tuition of children from middle-income families. Be careful, though. The school to which you want your child to go may offer you financial terms which you can just manage, but you may still find the hidden extras (student activities, books and other equipment, for example) too much. If sending him to this school is a struggle for you, keeping up appearances within it may be a struggle for your child, too. He may both long for the clothes and personal possessions which his friends take for granted and hate himself for feeling that way when he knows that you are depriving yourselves for his sake. As he gets older, he may feel further and further separated from the wealthier children by their trips abroad, their automobiles and their plans for graduation. Being a member of an underprivileged minority is never pleasant, even when the deprivation is at luxury level. A complete social mix is usually easier on everyone.

Collecting information about the schools available to your child

Some schools are notorious, some are famous. No school's local reputation is to be relied upon, as both overall atmosphere and academic performance can change rapidly in response to changes in faculty or student enrollment. Some schools put out elaborate glossy prospectuses, others publish only bare details, but again a school's own publicity is not to be relied upon. A school board which allocates money for glossy publications may be mean with money for new toilets; one which refuses prospectus money may lavish it on library books.

See every school for yourself during a working school day. If an admissions interview is arranged for your child during a vacation period, make sure you visit the school again during the semester. Don't just accept a guided tour of the school's newest facilities, either. Ask to visit classrooms and cloakrooms; try to see children working, playing, talking, eating. Stay alert to the way children speak to their peers and to older and younger students as well as to teachers, and try to notice teachers dealing with questions and misdemeanors. Listen, hard, whenever two teachers are talking together nearby. Although most teachers occasionally speak scathingly of children, their parents or of colleagues, a faculty which appears to loathe the younger generation as a whole should make you wonder what the day-to-day atmosphere of the school is really like.

Try to talk to other parents and students. They may not want the same things as you from a school, but if they will describe this school's strengths and weaknesses from their own point of view, you will be able to make your own assessment. If a parent tells you, for example, that the school sets far too many vacation assignments, don't shut her up by saying "Oh I'm all for vacation work myself." Instead, ask her to describe what her child had to do during the last vacation and what would have happened if he had failed to complete the work.

Try to talk also to staff at the school to which your child would be promoted from this one. If you are considering an elementary school, for example, discuss it with the junior high admissions person. Does she feel that children come well prepared? Do they seem generally happy and easy to integrate into the new setting?

Become a "school bore" among your acquaintances. Almost every local resident will have some snippet of information, some piece of gossip or second-hand opinion to add to your store. You will not believe everything you hear but the more you are told the more flesh there will be on the bones of your impressions.

Discuss with your child what he wants from any/this school. A very young child may want to go to "big school" only if he can go with his friend, or in that school bus, but older children will usually feel strongly about specific points, which should certainly be taken into account.

Now go back to the school, armed with questions for the principal. In a reasonably open school, counting on a high level of parental participation, he or she should be prepared to tell you anything you want to know about the school's internal workings, its performance in various spheres, its disciplinary policies and problems and its future plans. The trick is to ask questions which ensure specific and factual answers rather than meaningless generalities. If your research has suggested that on two days each week the lunch-break is extended to allow for a teacher-conference, ask "what do the children do during that time? Who supervises them?" If it has been suggested to you that children cannot be scheduled for active participation in both sports and music, ask "what happens if a child is keen to be on the ball team as well as studying piano?"

Write down points arising from all these researches. If you are considering several schools, it is extraordinarily easy to become confused so that, in your mind, the warm and enthusiastic librarian of one school comes to be placed in the superb library of another when, in fact, the librarian who impressed you was making the very most of rather poor facilities.

Starting school

It is in school that your child will make relationships and undertake activities which are, by definition, separate from you and from home. You cannot do it for him, but you may be able to help him do it for himself. In all a parent's dealings with a school, whatever the age of the child, there is a fine line to be tactfully drawn between interference and neglect. Sometimes one sees examples of both, when young children have just started school. One parent insists on being told every detail of the child's day, whether he wants to talk about it or not. Furthermore, if he admits that he has been writing his name or learning his colors, the parent at once wants to "help him at home," settling him down to practice so that he will "do better" in school. That parent is interfering. Another parent presses for no details and may not even listen to anything the child wants to tell. When an "open day," parents' evening or end-of-term display comes up, the parent is too busy to go. School is the teacher's business. That parent is being neglectful. The happy medium falls in the wide range in the middle. It has something to do with always being interested enough to listen, and a lot to do with always being eagerly willing to be involved when the child or the school issues any kind of invitation. But perhaps it has most of all to do with sensing when your child wants your help and support, and when he wants to live his school life without any parental involvement at all.

While probably no child can be happy for every day of every term in all the years of compulsory schooling, being happy in the first days of the early terms is a good start. If your child discovers that he can cope with his new independent life, make friends, fit in, meet the expectations of teachers and of his group, he will have a foundation on which to build the rest of his school life. A nine-year-old who has a miserable patch may be mourning a best friend who has left, or reacting against a new teacher whom he dislikes. But if he has already had the experience of being happy at school, he will have a much better chance of getting happy again quickly. He knows that children can be friends with him; that teachers can be pleasant. Giving your child a good start is worth a lot of effort.

Early days   For some children "school life" really does begin on the first day of their compulsory education. For many others it begins long before, perhaps in a gradual progression from half days at a playgroup through short days at nursery, to membership in a specially staffed and equipped pre-school class. The following suggestions apply to any child past toddlerhood who is first regularly attending a group without a parent or other known caretaker.

At this first stage, whether your child is three or five, his ability to settle into enjoying school life will probably depend very much on his feeling secure about the link between school and home life. The following are examples common to many children; any parent will be able to add others which are particularly important to a particular child:

He needs to know that by leaving you, he will not lose you. You know he will not, but does he? Sometimes a small child, sent through the door of a big building which seems packed with strangers, feels not just that *he* will never find *you* again but that *you* may not be able to find *him*. It sometimes helps to spell out:

That you know the school; know where it is in relation to everywhere else you ever go; how to telephone it (that nice lady in the office up there . . .); where to find him inside the building; which his classroom is and who his teacher.

That you (or another known and expected caretaker) will always come for him at the right time. Quite apart from the safety aspect (*see* **Safety**/On the road), most children start school more happily if they are collected, at least at the beginning, from the same place at the end of every school day. Muddly arrangements which vary from day to day can put great strain on a young child. He may ruin his afternoon by wondering whom he will see at the door, or whether you have remembered that this is the day when he finishes up at the sports field. With most small children it is worth taking endless trouble to ensure that they are never left standing waiting when others have gone. For some children, even social arrangements which involve their going home with another child are a bit upsetting. If your familiar figure waiting at the door is obviously important to your child, yet you want him to deepen his new friendships, it may be worth your while to meet him all the same on these early occasions so that you see him off to his party with assurances that you know where he will be, and that you will be there to collect him at the suggested time.

He needs to know that you approve of the school and its people. Some of the things that are said and done, both to him and to other children, will seem strange to the child who is new to group life. The more he feels that you approve of it all and trust the power figures, the teachers, the more easily he will probably accept his new environment.

Try not to criticize teachers or other children. If he is not allowed to go barefoot at home but has to take off his shoes and socks for gym, for example, you can easily make him feel all right about it by pointing out that it is different at school where the floor of the gymnasium is specially made for bare feet. If he tells you, wistfully, that the other children eat sweets at playtime, try not to say that they will get holes in their teeth. An apple for him to eat at playtime might make a happy compromise.

If the child reports something which makes you angry, do ask his teacher about it. He may have got it wrong (in which case he needs correct information). If he was right and there is a real injustice being done, it is better to explain your feelings about it to the teacher (who can do something about it) than to the child who, without her help, cannot.

He needs to know that you are on his side. While most children are more comfortable knowing that parents like, trust and approve of teachers and schoolmates, yours needs to be sure that you will not go overboard and either enter into conspiracies or "let him down" in the eyes of either.

If a teacher must know of a child's private problem, tell her privately, and don't add unnecessary details about his minor eccentricities. Perhaps she must know that he is getting help from a speech therapist, for example, but that does not mean that she also has to know that he still takes a pacifier to bed. It is important to be tactful in front of his new friends, too. However glad he is to have you at the school door, he will not be glad to be greeted by that family pet name he had hoped to keep private.

He needs to know that you trust him to manage and that you will help. There is often a fine line to be drawn here. If the child does not think that you believe he can cope with, and enjoy, his school life he is liable not to believe it himself. On the other hand, lost sneakers or forgotten messages can loom very large if he has not sorted out the lost property system or got used to being a note bearer. If he keeps getting into muddles, make it your business to know what he needs on different days so that you can tactfully remind him, and offer to help go through his bag from time to time so that those forgotten pieces of paper are found in time.

Allow for the fact that some schools are really tough on forgetful, inefficient children. Helping him keep himself sorted out is not spoiling.

If he is always in a row for having forgotten or lost something, he will not get more efficient, just more confused and miserable.

He needs to know that you are interested in what he does. Sometimes he himself will be bored by what he has to do in school. The fact that you actually want to hear the song, see his somersaults, or read his first bits of writing may make a real difference both to his feelings and to his performance.

Try to listen properly to everything he volunteers. If he cannot compete with older children (or you are not there) immediately after school, he may like to talk at bedtime. If he volunteers nothing, it is usually better not to push, except in the most general sense of "Was it a good day?" and perhaps "Did anything special happen?" But even if he is a child who gives you almost no information about school:

Try to accept every invitation to go to the school. However offhand he is about it, a young child, at least, will usually be saddened by an open day or end-of-term "do" at which he has nobody. Teachers also can be saddened and made to feel that nobody is interested in what they are trying to do.

Problems over going to school

Helping your child to take school for granted

Although it may sound brutal, it is helpful to many children to realize, from a very early age, that *school is legally compulsory*. Even at six years old, your child is capable of understanding that if all children have to go, by law, there is little point in his thinking too hard about whether he actually wants to or not. If he is unhappy at school, it will also help him to realize that, while you may be able to do a lot to make school easier for him, even including sending him to a different school if necessary (*see below* Looking for happiness in a different school), you cannot actually let him off altogether.

Occasionally, patchy attendance at a pre-school group gives a child the wrong idea about this. If he has been accustomed to staying at home the day after he has had a late night, when a treat is in store or he just doesn't feel like going to the group, it may be a great shock to him to find that he suddenly has to go whatever he is feeling like, unless he is actually ill. A few children quickly decide that illness is the key and learn to say "I can't go to school today 'cause I've got a stomachache" rather than "I don't think I'll go today." If your child goes to a pre-school group at all it is probably a good idea to make sure that he attends absolutely regularly, for whatever hours are expected, at least in the last year before he starts regular school.

Many schools do in fact allow parents a lot of latitude about sending their children. Your child's school may be prepared to accept vague "sick notes," or even more truthful notes saying that the child was "too tired" for school. But it is often a mistake for parents to accept this casual attitude to attendance. If you allow your child to feel that there is any chance whatsoever of his getting out of going, you force him to make a series of choices about something which it would, in the end, be more comfortable for him to take for granted. And, as we shall see, whatever the reason for the child not wanting to go, it will hardly ever be made better by his staying away.

Helping him want to go to school when going seems an effort

Vague unease about school, or a dispirited reluctance to face it, can often be prevented from getting worse if you spot it early. For example, the child who finds it hard starting again after a weekend, a vacation or an illness has usually got so involved with home that he has, for the moment, forgotten his involvement with school. He feels as if he is going out of a warm life into emptiness. If you can help him to remember that school is warm and full, too, he may cheer up immediately. People are usually the key:

Talking to a friend on the telephone or having one around to the house often works. Some children really need to have contact with school-friends at the end of every break.

A child who has been ill for more than a couple of days will often feel better about going back if he gets a note or a get-well card from his teacher. Most teachers are happy to do this if you let them know that the gesture would be appreciated.

"Getting ready for school" can help the child get ready in his mind as well as his schoolbag. The child who starts gloomily on his Sunday night routine may be quite cheerful by the time his clothes are laid out ready for the morning.

The actual business of going to school (especially when he does not like parting from you) is often much easier if he goes with a friend.

Softening the transition between home life and school life can sometimes help children with more serious versions of the Sunday night blues. If your child normally travels both ways alone, you may be able to make Mondays seem more tolerable by arranging to pick him up, just on that day. If he normally comes home well before your working day ends, Monday may be the very best day for you to come home early if you can. In a similar way, a child who really dreads going back to school after a long vacation or illness may feel quite differently about it if he is allowed to come home for his lunch during the first few days. Whatever the particular arrangements that you are able and willing to make (and they will, of course, depend on the school and on your other commitments) the point is to ask the child to make not one hundred percent of the effort that feels too much, but the ninety-five percent which, in comparison, feels manageable.

Helping the child who really does NOT want to go to school

A child who is really miserable or frightened about school may be reacting mainly to something in his school life or mainly to leaving his home life. The latter is the fashionable explanation but it is not always the correct one. It can be a mistake to be too "psychological" too quickly when a child is having trouble going to school. It is possible to get enmeshed in deeply emotional issues when, in fact, the problem is a simple one which can easily be dealt with.

All kinds of things about a school can put off a child (especially a young one). Sometimes parents don't ask (because they at once assume that the weeping child is deeply disturbed). Sometimes they ask but do not believe that such distress could be caused by the "trivial" trouble the child discloses. Sometimes they ask, but the child will not tell. Three recent and genuine examples cover the scope of this kind of problem:

A six-year-old boy's new teacher told him (perhaps a little sharply) that going to the toilet during lessons was not allowed. Convinced that he would never be able to "last" from before school until playtime, the child became unable to go to school at all. Once the teacher had explained that she had meant only that children were expected to go in breaks so that they were less likely to need to leave lessons, but that, of course, any child who did need to go could do so at any time, he went back happily to school.

A nine-year-old girl, newly arrived at the school, refused to go on her second Tuesday or Thursday. She had heard that "everyone has to shower after gym" and had assumed that the only showers she had seen were communal for both sexes. They were not. The child joined the gymnastics club before the end of her first term.

A thirteen-year-old girl, newly transferred from a single-sex elementary to a mixed-sex junior high school, became upset in her first week and, by the second, was showing every sign of real school phobia. She could only tell her parents that "there's a boy I don't like." It turned out that this twelve-year-old had adopted her as his "girlfriend," to her deep embarrassment. The teacher had noticed them together but had assumed the friendship was mutual. He managed to warn off the boy (gently; he had done nothing wrong) and this cheerful, sociable girl settled in at once.

Some problems which are within the school are much more difficult to deal with. Much the most usual are problems concerning the child's relationships with other people. Sometimes a child really cannot get along with a particular teacher. Although teachers usually have a considerable interest in "children," no human being, whatever his or her training and experience, can like every other human equally. There will always be some children who irritate some teachers, and vice versa. But whatever his or her feelings towards a particular child, it is part of a teacher's job to be able to treat every child fairly and decently. Very often, if a personality clash of this kind is really upsetting your child, the teacher can and will put it right, especially if you can manage to raise the matter without being offensive and therefore putting the teacher on the defensive.

There is less that you can do about problems in the relationships your child has with other children; sometimes trying to do anything is a mistake. Desperate with misery for your deeply unhappy child, you may be tempted to ask the others to "be nice to Johnny." Don't. Johnny wants them to like him and only he can make them do that. Your interference will only shame him, embarrass the others, and fuel any dislike which may be smouldering. Try not to encourage him to buy friendship either. Giving him a large bag of sweets to pass around may make you feel you are helping him; it may even make one lunch break fairly pleasant for him, but it will not help him to make friends. Children do tend to like others who are generous in sharing whatever they have, but they are very quick to notice the difference between that kind of sharing and the bringing of goodies *to* share.

If your child is friendless

A very young child may be able to use some help in making friends just in the sense of being given plenty of opportunities. At this early stage, when many friendships do still begin with parental ones, it may be helpful if you can be sociable with other parents, willing to chat at the school door or offer a cup of coffee, able to take the child to the parks or playgrounds others use.

An older child may be trying to break into a group which is already close-knit—he may have changed schools at an unusual age or moved in from another district. Sports and hobbies can sometimes help: it may be easier for him to make friendly contact in an after-school football practice than in the classroom. You may be able to do some subtle local detective work to discover whether there are classmates whose homes are nearby. Acquaintance made out of school often carries easily into it.

Your child may be behaving in a way which puts off others. If you really want him to be happy, take a hard private look at him, especially at the way he behaves when he is with other children. You may be able to see him in the school playground or walking home; you may pick up clues from what other children (including his brothers and sisters) say about or to him. Is he so over-anxious to please that he invites snubbing? Is he extremely bossy and always right? Does he cover up his uncertainty by showing off all the time or boasting about things he owns or has done? Has he characteristics which set him apart from the rest, making it more difficult for him to meld into the group? An early or late growth-spurt (*see* **Adolescence**/Puberty: Problems of early or late puberty), different color skin, different accent, physical handicap and so forth of course *should* not make his life more difficult. But, at certain ages and in certain groups they will, and he will have to find ways of overcoming them while the group learns to find him acceptable. You may have to help at least by allowing your child to adapt. If only goody-goodies go straight home after school, for example, you will either have to change rules or schools, or accept that you are asking your son to survive as a goody-goody.

If your child is actually being bullied adult interference may be necessary both for his sake and for the sake of the bullies and the school. Sometimes parents who would be at the school immediately if a child came home with bruises and torn clothes do not feel that they can take any action about more subtle bullying. But give the school a chance. Every teacher knows that children can terrorize each other without inflicting physical harm, and that once a reign of terror gets hold the whole school can be badly affected. In some recent and widely reported instances, where adolescents actually ran away or even killed themselves "because of bullying at school," the teachers at the schools concerned had had no idea what was going on. They had not even been told that the youngsters concerned were unhappy. Do give your child's school the chance to help him and the others.

School phobia (*see also* **Anxiety, Fears and Phobias**)

If a child continues to be very anxious about going to school, even when any specific worries which he can produce have been dealt with, and even when the teachers seem to like him and there appear to be children who are willing to accept him and be friends, the basic trouble may not be with the school at all but with the child's feelings about leaving home. "School phobia" is not really an appropriate name because it is not the *school* which makes him anxious but the separation from you which going to school involves.

If this is the case, you will probably find that some of the following suggestions ring true for your child:

That he dislikes other kinds of separation, too. You may not have noticed this before (especially if he is very young) because he may be a child who has always lived fairly closely within the family and has not often been expected to be away for hours on end or nights at a time. But if you consider him anew in the light of his school difficulties, you may realize that he has always preferred to have visitors rather than to go visiting, that he has always liked to know exactly where you were and what you were doing and that he has always tended to get upset if plans went awry so that you were late home and so forth.

That the acute anxiety over school was triggered by something which happened to you, not to him. Sometimes the trigger is an obviously traumatic one, such as parents' separating or one of them being away for a long time in the hospital or on business. But sometimes it is something much more trivial. A minor illness, for example, which meant that the child had to leave you in bed when he went to school. A minor depression, perhaps, such that the child was made aware that you were unhappy. An overheard row between the two of you which, rightly or wrongly, made him wonder whether all was well between you or whether his family was going to break up.

The point, usually, is that the child, already sensitive concerning your welfare and already tending to feel it necessary to keep an eye out for it, was made to wonder whether you were "all right." Once he has begun to wonder, being away at school all day becomes intolerable as he imagines all the fearful things which may have happened to you while he was gone. Will you be there when he gets home? Will he find you in a crumpled heap/pool of blood/floods of tears? Will you have "gone mad" so that you no longer know or love him? Once his imagination runs riot in this way, logical probabilities and possibilities cannot comfort him.

That the level of his anxiety varies from day to day, being highest after a break from school or when there is trouble at home, and lowest when he is settled into a school week and everything at home is running smoothly and peacefully.

That at its worst, the anxiety shows up in physical symptoms. The child may be quite unable to eat breakfast; he may be actually sick; he may have stomach pains severe enough to make him a bad color; he may have headaches or migraines; he may be trembly. If the phobia is severe, some or all of his typical physical symptoms may show up not only when he is actually faced with going to school, but also when he is made to think about, or discuss, going to school.

That fear and fear-of-fear make a vicious circle. The child who finds himself "in a state" on Monday mornings soon comes to dread those horrible feelings as well as the school which first evoked them.

Coping with school phobia

Probably you will already be in close touch with the school as you will have been trying to discover and deal with any practical aspects of school life which might have been causing the child's anxiety. But if you are not, do go and see the child's teacher immediately and enlist help for the child. Between you, it may be possible to help him cope quite quickly. But you may need further help from someone else who can act for the child as go-between with both school and home. An older child, in particular, may find it easier to manage if he has someone else to talk to. Through the school you can get help, if you need it, from the school psychological service. Through your doctor, you can get help from him or from someone he recommends. Whether you seek professional help or not, the following brief guidelines may be useful:

Don't take the easy road of allowing the child to stay at home. It is not really making it easier for him because he must, and he knows he must, go to school so that a "day off" is only a temporary reprieve from something which has to be faced. Furthermore, since going back to school after breaks is usually the most difficult of all for him, being at home today usually only means that tomorrow will seem worse.

Very occasionally a child *has* to be allowed to stay at home because his anxiety when he is taken to school reaches panic levels so that he cannot control himself and will scream, vomit or run away. But if this is the case (and it is very unusual) the child should certainly be under urgent professional care. A doctor may, for example, make a bargain with the child such that he may stay at home today and tomorrow (Thursday and Friday) but will start again and go *every* day from Monday on.

Don't let milder, but chronic, school phobia lead you into changing schools. The school the child is at may, or may not, be the best available school for him, but if he cannot make himself attend this one at all he certainly will not be able to settle happily in a new one. These are circumstances in which he certainly will take his school difficulties with him. The basic problem has to be at least recognized and partly solved before a change of school can be truly useful (*see below*, Looking for happiness in a different school).

Try to offer direct reassurances about your own safety and happiness. Although you will not want to hurt his feelings by stressing how glad you are to be rid of him on school days, you may be able to make it clear that each family member has things of his own to do during the day and is pleased to see the others at the end of it. With a young child in particular, it is often helpful to describe what you do when he is not there in such a way that it sounds both busy and (to him) boring.

If you are not safe and happy without him, don't lie. If his school phobia has flared up while you are mourning your own mother, for example, attempts to put a brave face on things "for the sake of the children" may be one of the causes of the trouble. He may be relieved if you can manage to admit that you are sad; explain that although elderly people do eventually die and their grown-up children are always sad, the sadness does not spoil your basic happiness with your family (*see* **Death**).

If you are ill, it may help to acknowledge this, too, and discuss it with him. However horrible the truth, it is seldom as terrifying to a child as the half-truth upon which his imagination is left to work.

If having him at school does leave you lonely (perhaps because he is your youngest child and you have not yet decided what you are going to do with all the rest of your adult life), it may be that he cannot be happier until you can be. Certainly going to school will be difficult for him if he can sense that you prefer having him around and that you are as relieved as he is if that thermometer records a fever and gives you both an excuse.

An older child sometimes has a much more practical basis for her emotional need to stay at home. Although this can happen to either sex, it is usually a girl who identifies with a mother who is over-stressed by a combination of young children, poor health and difficult circumstances. If your daughter really feels that you cannot manage without her, she may find leaving you very difficult. The more she wants to leave and lead a normal life, the more guilty she is liable to feel about this "disloyalty" and therefore the more determined she becomes to stay and help you.

Try to demonstrate the safety of going to school by making the pattern of family life as smooth and "boring" as you can. If the child can go to school at all, he can hopefully discover, as anxious day follows anxious day, that there is actually nothing to be anxious about. You always *are* there, safe and normal when he comes home. The evenings always follow their normal routine. The mornings are always the same kind of rush. Nothing dramatic happens.

Sometimes a change in the usual pattern is the trigger for school phobia and, if you can identify that change and go back to the pattern which preceded it, that is helpful. You may recently have decided that the children are old enough to look after themselves for a couple of hours after school so that you have turned a part-time job into a full-time one, for example. If you can manage to go back to being there when the child comes home, he may settle down again.

Experiment with different ways of getting the child to school, remembering that the less anxiety he has to feel today the less frightened of being anxious he will be tomorrow. Some children find it easiest to go to school with a friend, leaving you at home (even if you are waiting to go to work). Some find it easiest to go with another family member. Some do best if you take them and, furthermore, if you take them right into the school and pass them over, so to speak, to the teacher. For some children it is important to get up early enough to have time to face the day in prospect but for others it is easier to get up and go; the greater the rush the better as it leaves less time for dread.

Encourage the child to believe that his anxiety will pass. He sees other children rushing cheerfully into school, apparently able totally to forget their homes and families and to enjoy their own environment. He cannot, and so he feels peculiar. It will help him to know that many children go through patches of anxiety like his, that it will pass and that, as long as he keeps trying, the effort of going to school will get less and less.

School refusal   Sometimes the difference between school phobia and school refusal is only one of the child's age. A younger child who is school phobic can, if necessary, be physically forced into school. The older one who is school phobic may refuse to go, knowing full well that if he sticks to his guns there is very little anyone can do to force him. If he is forced to go, he may refuse to stay; school refusal easily turns into truancy (*see below*).

If an adolescent refuses to go to school parents are often wise to seek *medical* help as soon as possible. If a child in this age group comes to the attention of the educational authorities as a "non-attender" or as a truant, legal proceedings may be started so that the whole issue rapidly comes to be handled as one of delinquency rather than unhappiness. If parents have "medicalized" the situation right at the beginning, this unfortunate chain of events can usually be stopped before it starts.

It must, however, be said that some adolescents who refuse to go to school are not emotionally disturbed at all but simply disillusioned with an institution and an educational system which does not offer them what they feel they need. If nothing can be done through discussions with the school, changes of course and so forth, parents may have to appeal to the child's good sense to keep him on the right side of the law. Sometimes arrangements made out of school can be used as bargaining counters to keep him in school. A boy who loathes the semi-academic courses which he feels to be inappropriate for him and at which he feels a failure, will sometimes agree to maintain a legal minimum of attendance if a part-time apprenticeship, or other forward-looking arrangement, is made for him out of school hours.

Provided that you still have your child's confidence and he still has your goodwill, it is usually possible for home and school together to produce a way of life which he finds acceptable. It is when communication has broken down, between child and family and/or family and school, that things most often go seriously awry.

Truancy   In theory it is impossible for a child to truant without the school's noticing his absence and checking it out with his family. In some areas (notably in New York) schools are so aware of the danger of kidnapping that particular trouble is taken to ensure that somebody knows the whereabouts of a child who is out of school. But in practice and in some areas a truant child can fool both parents and school. He can fool his parents by leaving the home at the ordinary school time and staying away until the school day is over. He can fool the school by going in first thing in the morning and slipping out again once his presence has been marked on the register. If his actual absence is still likely to be noticed by the various teachers who expect to see him during the day he may take the deception further by forging notes concerning sickness and other excuses.

Anger is a very natural reaction to this situation. Nobody likes to be deceived and few things can make a parent feel sillier than the appearance of the truant officer with the bombshell information that the child has spent only half the required number of days in school during the semester. Be angry if you feel angry, but keep the anger between you and the child. The school authorities will tend to be upset as well because they, too, have been made to look foolish and/or uncaring.

Some adolescents truant with their parents' connivance. However sympathetic you may be to your child's feeling that he is much too old for school and that the school has nothing to offer him, don't ever imply that you do not care whether he goes or not. Not only is he likely to be called in eventually by the educational authorities, he is also extremely likely to be picked up by the police (who are alert for youngsters hanging around in public places during school hours). He is also very likely to break other laws out of sheer boredom and the difficulty of finding enough to do all day without much money to do it with. If he cannot and will not live as a school-person any longer, he must be helped to live as something else *which is positive*. Truanting is anti-authority emptiness even when it is fun (*see* **Adolescence**/The long road to independence: Part-time jobs).

But some children—young as well as old—truant, like Tom Sawyer, because blue sky or a town fête beckon and school suddenly feels like a prison. Even as adults, most of us skip, just occasionally, in order to do what we want rather than what we should. One illicit fishing trip does not make a truant.

Looking for happiness in a different school

If a child is chronically unhappy at school he is chronically unhappy altogether. School is too large a part of his life to be ignored or compensated for by home friends and activities.

Heartbreaking though it is to be the parent of such an unhappy child, and brutal though it seems to send him dragging off each morning, the decision to take him out of that school (and therefore send him to another) cannot be made lightly. The fact that your child is unhappy at his present school does not increase the choice of schools available to him (*see above*). There may be no other school available, or none which will accept him or which you can afford. Furthermore a different school may not be the best solution to his difficulties. Some parents, wealthy enough to find choice within the private sector, do move their children from school to school, always hoping that this time the child will be happier, but always disappointed because the child takes his troubles with him.

Longterm unhappiness at school usually stems not from the school but from the child himself, and it is usually rooted in difficulties in getting along with other children (*see above* If your child is friendless). If you consider the difficulties which friendly, outgoing, formerly popular children often have when a move to a new state forces them to adapt to a new group, you will realize that a solitary, inturned and unpopular child is unlikely to find his life transformed by a fresh school. Most unhappiness at school—especially if it continues through several classes—needs dealing with *within that school setting*. The child needs to be helped (professionally if necessary) to win himself a place which feels comfortable, rather than being offered an escape which may make matters worse.

There are exceptions, however, and there are districts in which school boards are sympathetic to special requests for transfers at unusual stages in a child's schooling. If you think that your unhappy child may be one of these exceptions, consider the following points and then discuss them and the child with the people who know his school-personality best; his teachers:

The child has always felt himself a failure. To be happy at school (as in any other group setting) a child needs to feel himself to be reasonably popular and reasonably successful. If he has always felt himself to be a social or academic failure, liked by no one, good at nothing, his image of himself will be poor and will get poorer as he gets older. Eventually a vicious circle is created: because nobody likes or respects him, he cannot like or respect himself; because he does not like or respect himself, he no longer expects other people to like or respect him. Once he ceases to expect liking and respect he is unlikely to get it. A concerned teacher, or new grouping within a school, can (and often does) break this sort of vicious circle so that the child suddenly "blossoms" with new confidence and interest. But sometimes the circle can be most easily broken by giving him a "fresh start." If such a new beginning is to work for him, he needs to know, in himself, that he can now leave behind the labels which have dogged him so far. He must know that he is not "a dolt" or "a bully," a "fusspot" or a "crybaby." . . . If his self-confidence allows him, now, to meet with a new school on equal terms, the move may transform his life.

The child has "outgrown" this particular school. Each society or community lays down the stages in a child's life at which he should be "promoted" from one kind of school to another. Inevitably, there are some children who require promotion either at a different time or of a different type. A child who is bored with school at the age of nine may have *become* bored because he found the demands of school, both social and academic, easy. But that bright child will not stay ahead of the game if he is forced to play by those same rules for another two to three years.

Sometimes a child develops particular interests or skills for which his school has no facilities and no respect. An exceptionally musical child, for example, may be happy in a school without particular musical facilities, provided that his interest is appreciated and at least some leeway allowed to him for making arrangements outside for tuition and practice. But if his school neither provides music nor supports his desire for it, trying only to get him out onto the sports field "like all the other boys," he may become extremely unhappy, not only with his daily life, but with the institution itself. The same kind of thing sometimes happens where a child develops a strong practical bent within a school which is only equipped for, and interested in, academic subjects. Lack of workshops is bad enough, but scorn for the use of hands as well as head can be intolerable.

In every such case, the danger is that if the child is left in the school which no longer meets his needs, he will come to feel himself at odds with the school as a whole and with all the people in it. He may try to change himself so that he fits in better, as an exceptionally bright child will often play the fool or simply stop trying. He may have the strength to fight for his own individuality and come to see himself as a rebel and a cast-out, as so many older children in school do. Or he may retreat from a situation which he can neither fully understand or control. Before any of these things happen, the child needs a change. If things can be changed within the school, well and good. But if they cannot, a change of school may be the only answer.

If you, the child, and teachers whom you all respect, agree that a different school would provide a "new start" or an important new stimulus, you may decide that you must seek it within the independent sector. If so, remember that grants may be available to you. Any school to which you are thinking of sending your child will give you details of the financial help available.

Sometimes a child who longs to escape from school, and all its associations, will ask to go to boarding school. Sometimes such a radical change of lifestyle can transform a young life for the better. But be careful. Such a child feels that he failed at the neighborhood school. He wants to get away because he feels that nobody likes him. If you, his family, send him away (even if he asks you to do so) the move may actually increase his sense of failure, isolation and lack of love.

Potential problems in school

If a child has trouble in school, the central issue will often be one of those discussed below. These notes are designed to help you act as trouble-shooter.

Discipline in your child's school

If your child is reasonably happy in a school which you trust, its particular disciplinary policies and methods are unlikely to cause you any problems. It is if he is unhappy that you are both likely to feel that anger and punishment are part of the problem and it is if you scarcely know the teachers that you are likely to make monsters out of them in your mind.

If school is going smoothly for your child it is usually a mistake to overreact if and when he is punished. He may hate being given extra work. You may both feel that writing "lines" is a complete waste of time and the child may tell you (truthfully or otherwise) that he had done nothing wrong anyway. But after all he is not meant to *enjoy* his punishments. Teachers, being human, can momentarily lose their tempers and be unreasonable. Perfect justice in a large group is not always possible. If a whole class has been rowdy and inattentive and it is your child who was finally punished for talking, it is just his bad luck if he was actually only responding civilly to another child's request to borrow a pencil. Sometimes it is also important to remember that the child you know at home may bear only a slight resemblance to the child the math teacher knows at school. The child has a right to be whoever he pleases in the different settings of his life, but that teacher can only react to the behavior he sees. If you cannot imagine your little angel as a hellion remember that the teacher may not be able to imagine him as anything else. If clashes are frequent, and *bothering the child*, you may like to arrange for a talk with the school. If clashes are frequent and *bothering the teacher*, he will probably ask to see you.

A few schools may have disciplinary policies of which you disapprove, not only for your own child, but for children in general. Some schools will inevitably contain a few teachers who, even in defiance of school policies, use methods which really upset your child. You may like to find out about policies before you decide on a particular school for him; once he is there you are contracted, so to speak, to accept the school's discipline for him. If an individual teacher uses his authority in ways which you consider wrong you may need to enlist the confidential help of the school's principal.

Corporal punishment is a case in point. Forty-four states still allow their schools to beat children. Only New Jersey and Massachusetts specifically forbid it. State statutes and school regulations hedge corporal punishment around with "controls" (use only of a paddle on the buttocks;

statement of reasons, warning notice, cooling-off period, presence of a witness, and so on) and few schools administer this kind of punishment often, or as anything but a last resort. Nevertheless you may feel that the *possibility* of physical pain being used as a method of discipline is repugnant and likely to encourage children to feel that force and violence are legitimate ways to assert themselves. Certainly the U.S. and the U.K. are both out of line with the rest of the Western world, which has long banned corporal punishment.

The arguments against retaining even a seldom-used *right* for any teacher to beat any child rest not so much on the emotional or ethical arguments against it but on the fact that corporal punishment clearly does not work.

Schools which do not retain this right are not less well-disciplined than schools which do keep a paddle. Indeed some research shows that such schools are better-disciplined, suffer less from bullying, vandalism, etc. and have fewer truants. Furthermore, schools which have recently abolished corporal punishment often seem to improve in these respects, especially where the principal and other teachers were in favor of abolishing corporal punishment rather than having the change forced upon them.

Within schools which beat children, the "final sanction" or the ability to "force them to behave" does not work either. Studies of school punishment books show that the same children are repeatedly beaten. Whatever a beating does or does not do to a child, it certainly does not seem to prevent him from committing further "offenses."

Children themselves are not always against corporal punishment and much is sometimes made of the results of surveys which show a majority of children stating that they prefer corporal to other forms of punishment. But such children, coming from schools retaining this "right," can only contrast a beating with other forms of coercion. They cannot know whether they would in fact be happier within schools which rely on getting the cooperation of pupils rather than on any assertion of direct power by the adults. Many people believe that the mere possibility of physical force being used between a teacher and a child spoils the atmosphere of a school, breeding violence between those who beat and are beaten, and destroying confidence between those who might beat and those who might be (even if they never are) beaten.

If you are against corporal punishment *in principle*, take the matter up with your school board or within the PTA.

If you are against corporal punishment for your own child, it is worth making your feelings known (and making sure they are recorded) at the admission interview. Should serious trouble and the possibility of a paddling ever arise, it is far easier for the principal to avoid that form of punishment in favor of another, than to reverse an already-stated decision.

Merits and demerits. Most schools which are trying to run themselves as places of cooperative endeavor, between teachers and children and children and children, prefer to manage without any kind of institutionalized reward or punishment. Children are expected to do their best. Effort is praiseworthy whatever its results. Lack of effort is blameworthy even if it still leaves the child well ahead.

Some schools find that merits (often little sticky stars) give stimulating pleasure to very young children and therefore use them in early academic work. Others find that demerits, which perhaps accumulate towards an automatic detention for a child who gets, say, six in a term, help to keep down minor nuisances like noisiness in corridors. Such a system does at least have the advantage that the child with four demerits has some control over his eventual punishment or otherwise. If he really does not want to be kept in, he will watch his step for the rest of the term. So while any such system can be abused, you really need to know a good deal about how it is used before you can judge it.

Competition in your child's school

Most modern educators believe that success in learning breeds success and that the rewards of feeling successful are a better stimulus to effort than the punishment of feeling shamed by failure. But there are still some schools (especially in the private sector) which encourage cut-throat competition.

If your child finds it comparatively easy to achieve excellence, he may appear to flourish in a highly competitive atmosphere, but it may still make you feel uneasy about his overall development. Excellence in math or baseball may be highly desirable in themselves, but if they are achieved at the expense of kindness, cooperation and a genuine understanding of the range of peoples' strengths and weaknesses, the price may be too high.

Watch out for the effects of homogeneously grouped elementary school classes. It is fine for your child to be one of the 3's in math provided that *he feels it is fine*. If he is one of the 1's in English and a sport star, he probably will feel this. If he is in the bottom group for everything, he may not.

Watch out for class ranking in high schools. Usually student scores are only divided into quadrants, so that nobody knows exactly how he compares with his neighbor. But sometimes the top 50 students will be listed in merit-order and, in some schools, the struggle in the top group can be painful.

Watch out for academic "pushing" in selective private schools. Some reckon that a performance which is good by national standards is still not good enough and, in the drive for exceptional excellence, make bright, hardworking children feel stupid idlers (*see below* Standardized testing).

Measuring himself against other children is part of your child's school-life; he will do it for himself even if nobody does it for him. But continually being measured *and found lacking* is bad for any child's self-image and morale. You can do a great deal to protect your child from damaging competition by treating him as a valued and valuable person (rather than an academic performer) at home. But if there is a phase in his school life during which he seems to be resignedly accepting himself as in some way "second class," talk to his teachers.

Attitude to cheating. Every child must work at answers without help from books, notes or friends before he can take tests successfully. But too much emphasis on "cheating" suggests that marks or positions matter very much, and that the boy or girl who cheats is stealing something from somebody. A healthier attitude may suggest that a child who cheats on a test is cheating *himself* of information concerning his progress. Cheating by getting help with homework can be another indicator. If homework is to contribute to education, it should not always be a test, but a way of acquiring knowledge or putting knowledge into practice. A school which bans all help with homework, and labels the child who gets help as a "cheat," is likely to be taking a very competitive attitude.

Public announcements of success and failure. A school which really cares for individuals, for their feelings as well as their accomplishments, may wish to give public recognition and feelings of success to those who are trying, in any field. But it will not wish to attract public blame and shame to any child. Western societies have long abandoned the stocks. Why then should schools continue to shame children in front of their peers?

You may like to inquire *what is done with* merits and demerits, with examination results, sports results and so forth. A school assembly can be asked to congratulate all the following who passed such-and-such an examination without also being given the list of those who did not pass. Teams can be thanked for playing well for the school without the finger being pointed at teams which did not win. As for merits and demerits: whether these are given for academic work or for other aspects of behavior, they can fulfill their role as marks of congratulation or disapproval without being made public. What possible business can it be of the whole school assembly that one particular child has pleased or displeased the adults?

Standardized testing in your child's school

American education relies heavily on the standardized testing of all students, usually in the third, fifth and eighth grades. In an increasing number of school districts basic skills tests in English and math are also given. The scores of all these tests are confidential, but they are placed in the child's record (*see below* Your child's school record) and are therefore available to future teachers and administrators.

Tests cause a great deal of heartache, largely because they are part of an "educational mystique" which is ill-understood by parents and students. It could be argued that if a child's future is partly to depend on scores of this kind *and he is to know that it does*, it would be better if the tests and their complex scoring pro-formas were actually made public so that instead of speculating wildly over the significance of a given score, families could assess it for themselves. In the U.K., where such tests are also used, children are given many practice sessions within their normal classes and are not told in advance when an actual test-session is coming up. This does seem to do away with many of the problems associated with parental pressure and student nerves.

Explain these tests to your child in a positive way. Instead of telling him that "they want to see how well you do these problems compared with all the other children of your age in the district," try telling him something like this: "All schoolchildren learn math, but of course different teachers teach it different ways so they set lots and lots of problems and let all the children have a go. Nobody will get them all right and lots of children won't even have been taught how to do all of them. You just do all the ones you can."

Make sure your child is familiar with the kinds of tests he will have to do. Everyone does better if he knows what will be expected of him and is familiar with that particular way of working. It is not usually a good idea to try and make your child "cram" for tests—to do extra learning for them—but it is usually helpful to encourage him to practice answering questions in the test format (and many teachers plan test-like activities for practice) and, for an older child, to buy SAT practice books so that he can get used to using what he already knows in that particular way. Some American college students, bright enough to be given scholarships to come to British universities for a special year's study, find themselves all at sea because they are expected to do almost all their written work in the form of essays instead of in the multiple-choice format to which many of them are accustomed. Essay-writing practice in advance would save them a lot of stress; test-practice will do the same for your fifth grader.

Make test practice fun by doing it yourself. You will probably be amazed to find that eighth grade tests are difficult for you because you are not accustomed to them. Your child's confidence will be tremendously increased when he finds that he can do them more easily, and faster, than you.

Play down the importance of test results, whatever attitude the school appears to be taking. If classroom tension appears to be building, you may need to spell out your belief that the year's work is what matters, not scores on one day's tests.

With an older child, who may be all too aware that those scores do matter, stress the fact that however he performs this time, *he will always have another chance.* He must not be allowed to feel that he has "blown it" in a way which seriously affects his future.

Prepare for the test day in just the way you would prepare for a school drama production or other "big day." It is obviously sensible for the child to have a peaceful evening (no quarrels, no babysitters, no overheard troubles) and an early night. It is obviously friendly to produce his favorite breakfast and to wish him luck. But it is *not* sensible to let him sense that you are tense about tomorrow; to let him sit up studying (it is too late anyway) or to make him feel that tomorrow's results will affect your feelings about him either for good or for ill.

If your child does his best, that should be enough. When he comes home, let him tell you about it but don't press for details or ask: "Is that all you could do?" If he seems to have the impression, later on, that he did not do well, assure him that he did fine and, if necessary, ask for a meeting with his teacher so that you can report to him that she is perfectly satisfied. If she should be inclined to take a different attitude to an unexpectedly low score, try to persuade her that, however "badly" the child did, making him feel that he failed will only make a poor score on the next round of tests more likely.

Watch out for advanced placement standardized tests in some selective schools. If your child is being educated in a school for academically high-flying children, he probably will be expected to take these tests and to do well on them. Make sure that he realizes that the tests are of an exceptionally high standard and therefore that a reasonable mark on one of them probably represents an excellent mark on the tests taken by almost every other child his age.

If a school heavily pressures children toward this kind of success, generating real tension and a feeling that the child who does not do well has let down both his teacher and himself, you may need to put your loyalty to your child ahead of your loyalty to the school. Explain to the child that these test results reflect good or bad teaching as well as learning, and that this is why some teachers get quite anxious about them.

Homework in
your child's
school

In most schools it is left to individual teachers to decide whether or not to give homework or vacation assignments to particular classes. If homework should present problems (or lack of homework prove a disappointment) for your child, seek a conference with the teacher. Remember that:

Many small children enjoy homework and, in the first grades, regard it as part of the "grownupness" of being at real school rather than kindergarten. Don't abhor your seven-year-old's assignment *on principle*; wait and see whether he looks forward to it and enjoys doing it.

Homework which is set for older children must be done if your child is to be comfortable in class. Don't encourage him to skip or skimp it. If you feel that he is being expected to do too much, talk to his teacher but see that he does what has been assigned in the meantime.

A child who is expected to do a fair amount of homework will certainly need a comfortable place and the time in which to do it. Don't encourage him to put it off (perhaps because you want him to play with his younger sister or to do some chores with you); instead, try to agree on a homework routine and then help him stick with it. Many children find it easiest if they have a snack and a chat as soon as they reach home and then go immediately to work, so that they are free to play during the evening.

An older child who is studying hard needs priority. Don't expect him to do the cleaning up after supper *or* to keep you company in front of the television if you know that he has an assignment.

Facilitate his working but don't interfere with his work. Whatever his age, work which your child is told to do at home is work which he is meant to motivate himself to do and which he is meant to manage without a teacher. Some parents take the teacher-role upon themselves and sit over their children, insisting on reading and commenting on the work. It is better to leave that to the school unless the teacher has actually asked you to help out.

A child who is doing homework late at night may be stretching his energies too thinly over too many activities, or may have misunderstood what is really expected of him. Take a careful look at his working day. Does he have a long trip to school so that he arrives home rather late? Does he have a full program of after-school activities so that he can never settle down to his homework until after supper? Does he have other commitments (such as practicing a musical instrument)? It may be that the whole school week needs replanning with and for him.

If it is the homework itself which is overfilling his evenings, is he clear about the amount of time and effort he is expected to put into it? He may be expected to give a half-hour to a math assignment but, finding it impossible to complete the work in that time, be working on until it is finished. When you have sorted out the child's views and feelings about the whole situation, seek a conference with his teacher. She should certainly be anxious to help you revise his schedule so that he has time to do everything, and to do the nothing-in-particular which is every human being's right.

Your child's
school records

A particular teacher or school can have a longterm effect on your child's personal life via the records which he, she or it keeps.

In the United States you (and your child, after his eighteenth birthday) have the right of access to these records under the Family Educational Rights and Privacy Act (1974). You can inspect and review the records. You can request corrections to them and, if these are refused, there is an appeals procedure. After an appeal, if the school is not directed to change the record, you can still insert a note into the file explaining your objection to it. Schools also have to obtain your written permission (or that of the ex-student) before any but "directory material" can be shown to anyone other than specified teachers, administrators and legal representatives.

These are important rights but they will only work for your child if you take trouble to exercise them. Remember that:

School records last for many years. If a five-year-old is described as "disruptive and unpopular with other children" that description will still be there when a high school teacher reviews the file years later. Of course she should realize that remarks made about kindergarten children cannot be applied to adolescents, but will she stop to consider the dates or will that remark just stick in her memory when she meets her new class?

They can affect not only schooling but college and job prospects. Personal references from principals are often needed in adult life. That principal, having long-forgotten this particular individual, has only his personal records on which to base her remarks about him.

Entries are often made by barely qualified people yet when they are read by others, months or years later, there is no way of assessing the competence of the writer. Your child could therefore lose out in some way because a young and inexperienced teacher disliked him, or because an acting principal, who scarcely knew him, had decided to make a lengthy and authoritative-seeming entry concerning his personality or social behavior.

They are rather likely to contain actual inaccuracies because they begin in early childhood and are based, at least in part, on what teachers learn from the child himself. Childish misunderstanding and miscommunication are common. One high school student, for example, recently discovered that her records described her as "from a broken home." When she indignantly corrected this misapprehension, her new teacher traced the item back to a statement she herself had made at the age of six. Asked about her father, she had said "Oh my daddy went away a long long time ago." He had indeed gone away: two weeks before the conversation for a four-week business trip! Since that time, he had attended many school functions, conferences and so on, but had always been assumed to be doing so as a devoted but divorced father. Nobody had meant any harm; no real harm had been done, but an important factor in her background had been misunderstood all through her elementary school life and it *might* have mattered very much indeed.

Try to ensure that teachers have accurate information. If you have rightly shared troubles with a teacher, share also the news of any improvement.

Try, whenever the school schedules confidential discussion between you and the teacher, to give her the chance to tell you what she does think of your child. If she volunteers little, try asking her a few pertinent questions such as "How do you feel he gets along with the others?" or "What is he like to teach?" or even "I hope he isn't a nuisance . . . ?" If you can get her to formulate her thoughts she will tell you the same kind of thing that she might put in the file, and you will be able to argue the matter out.

If your child is ever involved in a school row of any importance, see the principal while it is being sorted out. If there is any confusion about your child's part in it, you can ensure that the principal has your viewpoint even if you cannot insist on her sharing, or recording, it.

At critical points in your child's school life (perhaps especially when he is transferring from one school to another or from school to college or a job) don't hesitate to *ask* the principal whether there is anything on record against your child. Some principals will show you reports. Others will certainly be prepared to tell you if a report is going to say that the child is in some way unsuitable for whatever he is applying for. Sometimes she will even welcome contrary evidence, and include information from it in a report. One child, for example, was not going to be heartily recommended for a nursery nurses' course as her records did not suggest that she was especially caring or responsible. Her teacher's view was summed up in the words "She plays so little part in school life that I cannot see her contributing greatly to a caring institution." The child had been devoting all her spare time over the past two years to helping in a home for the handicapped. The principal welcomed a letter from the head of that home; heartily recommended the girl for training and expressed her sorrow that the school had known her so little.

If your child is unfortunate enough to get on poorly with his last teacher, or the one in the school who is responsible for college applications, ask for an appointment with the principal and express your anxiety honestly. If the present teacher's report *is* unflattering, the principal will certainly take extra trouble to compare her views with those of others who have known your child well.

If your relationship with a school has always been stormy or you have always felt that its view of your child was inaccurate or unfair, consider arming him with reports from other sources. Very occasionally, for example, a young child who is extremely bright dislikes school, will not work, is considered "below average" and is therefore thrust into a vicious circle of under-achievement. A report from a private psychologist might help this school to reconsider its view of him, or another school to place him where he will be better-stretched and therefore happier and better able to work. An adolescent, seeking admission to college, may realize with alarm that she has pigeonholed her life so that the school knows nothing of her many interests and activities and may therefore describe her as "narrowly studious." A letter from a community leader who knows her well may do a great deal to redress the balance.

Children with special needs

Neighborhood schools, whether elementary or secondary schools, are meant to meet the needs of *all* local children. At present many do not do so. Some children go to ordinary schools but fail to meet their full potential because they have special needs for which the school does not provide. Many others are excluded from ordinary schools because they have physical, mental or behavioral problems for which those schools do not provide. Many such children are allocated to special institutions (for the physically handicapped, the blind, the deaf and so forth) or to the one school in the community in which all the learning specialists for the entire district have been concentrated.

"Special" schools are often presented to parents as specialist establishments within which a child can be given very particular attention, teaching and treatment. The parents of a child who is deaf, for example, may be thrilled by a place in a school for the deaf because they believe it to represent her only chance of achieving the adequate speech and skill in lip-reading which will enable her to lead a comparatively normal life. Other parents, less delighted by a special placement, nevertheless accept, without question, that their child "can't keep up with an ordinary class" or is "too difficult for an ordinary school."

There are a few (a *very* few) children for whom separate education probably is appropriate. But almost all of these will be the children for whom there is little hope of an independent adult life. For any child for whom later independence seems possible, there is a very strong argument for education with "normal" children and within the ordinary community. Whatever a child's particular difficulties, she is still a child. Her difficulties give rise to special needs but in no way lessen all her other needs: the needs of every child. She needs to be a child among children, a person among people, rather than seeing herself as one in a category labelled "the blind" or "the disabled." The blind child needs Braille in order to learn to read and write, but if Braille teaching and equipment is available within the ordinary school, she can learn to be literate while using almost everything else that school has to offer "normal" pupils. If she stays in a school for the blind, will she ever discover that, in the eyes of the sighted, she is ravishingly pretty? The child with Down's Syndrome needs academic teaching which is geared to his pace and attention span but, if he has that, he too can benefit from most of the non-academic aspects of school life. If he stays in a school for the educationally subnormal, will he ever get the chance to use his musical talent and singing voice on anything more exhilarating than nursery songs? Even the child with serious physical disabilities which confine her to a wheel-chair will ultimately be better off making the (often considerable) effort to cope in a barely adapted ordinary school than in the single-story facilities of a special school. Her adult world is going to be full of mobile people and it is going to present her with endless problems of access. In an ordinary school she will learn to cope as she will have to cope later. In return for that effort, she will at least have the opportunity for the best education her community offers to anyone.

Your child's
right to
mainstream
education

Every American child, from age 3 to 21, has a right to a free and appropriate education under the least restrictive circumstances (P.L. 94-142, 1975). If you feel that the education your child is receiving is not appropriate (perhaps because she is receiving no specialist help with a learning problem) or that it is restrictive (because it is separating her from her peers) you may have to fight for her rights. If you do have to fight, you will need help both from recognized "experts" and from administrators.

If you want extra help for your child within her present school, start by trying to get her teacher and principal to agree with you as to what help she needs. Sometimes a child with dyslexia is perceived by her class teacher as lazy and inattentive rather than handicapped (*see* **Learning Difficulties and Disabilities**). Sometimes a "hyperactive" child is perceived as in need of medication rather than psychiatric help (*see* **Hyperactive Children**). Occasionally a physical problem (such as reduced hearing acuity) is not recognized in school. The first step is to agree that the child has a special need and that it is not being met.

Next, discuss with the principal the arrangements which are usually made for meeting special needs of this kind. In some communities specialist teachers can be called in when they are needed, for example. Let the tone of your discussion suggest that you are assuming that the school will help and that it, like you, will be determined that the child's needs should be met. Try not to get aggressive until, or unless, it becomes clear that no help will be forthcoming.

If necessary, offer (rather than threaten) to attend a schoolboard meeting and put the case for what is required.

If your child is already in the school, is not being "disruptive" and requires only a few hours each week of extra help, you are likely to succeed. A variety of arrangements may be made, including part-time or after-school attendance at a special facility or the payment of fees for help from a private teacher. If your child is "disruptive," pleas for help may be met by the suggestion (overt or covert) that she would be better in a different school. If she needs a kind of help which would require major expenditure, such as the employment of an extra teacher or the provision of access ramps for a wheelchair the school board may argue that it would be uneconomic and irresponsible of them to spend so much on one child and that she should therefore be moved to a school where such facilities are already available. The economic argument is the backbone of the anti-mainstream faction and can probably be combatted only at political level.

If you want a less restrictive placement for your child than the special facility which she is in or to which she is allocated you will need discussions both with her present school and with the one to which you would like her to be sent. If the former agrees that she could benefit from attendance at the neighborhood school and the latter agrees to accept her, subject to certain facilities being made available, you have a powerful case to put to the school board.

Sometimes help from parents' organizations is valuable, too. If your child would need access-ramps, extra-wide doors and so forth because she spends all day in a wheelchair, the school board may welcome parental offers to carry out, or finance, the work involved. If your child is emotionally disturbed so that she needs constant adult supervision to ensure that other children's lives are not disrupted, teachers may welcome parental offers to supervise her during lunch breaks and so forth.

If the school board will not agree to enroll your child in the neighborhood school, or insists that it cannot provide for her education there, you may be able to insist that the school district fund your child at a private school, as provided under section 504 of federal law 93–112. It is wise to find such a school—and get its agreement in principle to the child's enrollment—before you ask for this funding. Advice from the National Association of Private Schools for Exceptional Children, 8038 Inverness Ridge Road, Potomac, Md 20854 may be useful.

This kind of battle can be long and drawn out, tedious and painful. You will probably find it easier if you have the support of one or more professionals who know your child well and have accepted expertise in the field of her handicap. The fees of a private psychologist or educational counsellor may be an extremely worthwhile investment. You may also find that other families who are in, or have been in, a similar situation can be very supportive. And, should mainstreaming become a political issue in your school district, several families, working together for the benefit of all their children, will carry far more weight than you can carry alone.

Self-control *see* **Discipline, Self-discipline and Learning How to Behave**. *See also* **Tantrums**.
"Separation anxiety" and **"stranger anxiety"** *see* **Anxiety, Fears and Phobias**. *See also* **Divorce, Separation and One-parent Families**.
Sex *see* **Adolescence**. *See also* **Safety**/From "strangers."
Shingles *see* **Chickenpox and Shingles**.
Shock *see* **Accidents**. *See also* **Fainting**.
Shoes and socks *see* **Feet**.
Sibling rivalry *see* **Jealousy**.
Single parents *see* **Divorce, Separation and One-parent Families**. *See also* **Death**; **Working Mothers**.
Sinusitis *see* **Colds**.
Skin and skin disorders *see* **Adolescence**/Problems with appearance and body image: Acne; **Allergy**/Eczema; Urticaria; **Birthmarks**; **Infection**/Defenses against infection; Types of infection: Localized infection. *See also* individual conditions for rashes, etc.
Skull fracture *see* **Accidents**/Head injuries.

Sleep

Our world has a twenty-four-hour cycle of night and day and many of our bodies' biological rhythms are in tune with that timing. Late at night and in the small hours of the morning, normal body temperature, for example, reaches its lowest point whether the individual is asleep or awake:

mental agility is at its lowest, whether the individual realizes it or not, and a variety of biochemical functions reach a low ebb only to build again as morning approaches and to reach their peak around the middle of the day.

Sleep is a necessary part of this biological rhythm and the "natural" time to sleep is during that night-time trough in all activities. People who stay awake through the night (whether to work or to attend an all-night party) are deliberately overriding their body clocks and, while they can make up the hours of sleep they have missed by napping at another point in the twenty-four hours, they cannot thus put right the timing. This is why people transferred to night work, for example, often find the adaptation very difficult. Even if they manage to sleep for six or seven hours in the daytime (which may be difficult as not only is the world awake and light, but their bodies are awake and alert, too) they still find it difficult to stay awake and efficient through the night because, biological-ly, their bodies are ready to sleep.

In the modern world, jet travel has allowed us to turn night and day topsy-turvy by flying across time zones. Jet lag can seriously upset every human function from digestion to judgment. Travellers—especially those with difficult decisions to make on arrival or potentially dangerous things to do, like driving cars—have to learn to allow for it. Bodies can and do adapt, but they cannot do so in immediate response to the time stated on the watch you have put forward six hours.

Experiments concerning adaptation to different times have been car-ried out and have clearly shown that you can, so to speak, *teach your body to believe* that it is any time you care consistently to tell it. Volunteers, living in areas of the world where there is no perceptible night during summer, were given clocks which falsely recorded days twenty-one or twenty-seven hours long. For some days their bodily functions ran increasingly out of step with the clocks, but gradually they adapted to the new lengths of artificial day and night. Nevertheless, weeks after those volunteers thought that their adaptation was complete, certain biochem-ical functions, such as the release of potassium in their bodies, still clung obstinately to the twenty-four-hour clock. Within normal daily life, the twenty-four-hour clock which is true in nature has also been enshrined in our social behavior. We "close down" active life during the hours when our bodies "close down." When we want or need to behave to a different time-scale, we have both in-built and learned behaviors to overcome.

Although we still do not know exactly why human bodies need sleep—exactly what scientific function it serves apart from the common-sense function of "rest"—we do know that sleep is essential. People who are kept awake for long periods (either in traumatic circumstances or during sleep-deprivation experiments) rapidly deteriorate both physical-ly and mentally. Judgment and reasoning suffer; manual dexterity and speed of reaction suffer; eventually the individual begins to suffer from hallucinations, panic, fits of aggression. At the end of experiments, many volunteers appear floridly insane. It is the more surprising that a few hours of uninterrupted sleep invariably restore them to normal. Few people living ordinary lives ever experience clinical sleep deprivation, but a very great many parents have periods in their lives with babies and small children when they come close to it. If your baby awakens you three or four times every night over weeks or months, not only will you lose hours of sleep but also your sleep pattern will be disrupted. It is easier to make up the hours (by napping in the afternoon or going to bed early) than it is to right the pattern. If you find yourself becoming irritable, tearful, irrational, during one of these phases, try to arrange a full night's uninterrupted sleep for yourself rather than a series of short rests "while he takes the baby out."

Two types of sleep

While we sleep our brains continue to give out electrical impulses which can be measured, studied and compared in the form of tracings called electroencephalograms (EEGs).

Commonsense observation shows that an individual spends some sleeping time in what looks like "deep sleep" and some in "light sleep" during which his closed eyes move rapidly, he makes faces, his muscles twitch, he may be physically restless and he is comparatively easy to awaken. Early scientific study christened this "lighter" sleep "Rapid Eye Movement" (or REM) sleep and therefore called the other kind "Non-Rapid Eye Movement" (NREM, often called Non-Rem) sleep. But the terminology has changed again. In man REM sleep is always associated with rapid movements of the eyes, but a kind of sleep which shows similar brain activity also occurs in animals such as moles, whose rudimentary eyeballs are incapable of rapid eye movements. The two types of sleep are now usually referred to as "orthodox sleep" and "paradoxical sleep." Call them what you will, but they are *not* "deep" and "light" but qualitatively different.

When a person goes to sleep he almost always passes first into orthodox sleep in which he appears very relaxed and quiet, with only occasional large movements such as rolling over. After a period of about ninety minutes his brain activity changes, rapid eye movements and so forth begin and he enters a phase of paradoxical sleep. For the rest of the night he will alternate between the two although, if he is deliberately awakened every time a period of paradoxical sleep begins, he will, as soon as he is left in peace, spend an unusually large amount of his sleeping time in paradoxical sleep as if he needed to "catch up."

Dreaming   Most vivid, active and emotionally laden dreams take place during paradoxical sleep. Some experts believe that it is because of a "need to dream" (perhaps to discharge emotional tensions or to sort out emotional life) that people "insist" on their ration of paradoxical sleep. Dreams during this kind of sleep have been shown to occupy realistic spans of time rather than to be concentrated, as many people imagine, into lightning flashes. A person who is awoken after ten minutes of paradoxical sleep may be in the middle of a dream and may actually return to it when allowed to sleep again. These dreams carry with them a full range of emotion and of the physical effects of emotion with which we are familiar in waking life. A sexual dream, for example, may bring all the physical signs of sexual arousal and a full orgasm. An anxious or frightening dream floods the body with adrenaline and sets the heart pounding. Dreaming of competing in an athletics meet will raise the heart and breathing rate so that the dreamer may wake to the sound of his own panting. One very common form of nightmare is that in which the victim faces mortal danger but is unable to do anything to save himself because he is "paralyzed with fright." Even this described feeling has been shown to have some physical reality in paradoxical sleep because nerve impulses to particular muscle groups are selectively blocked for periods of half a minute or so and then surge through. The dreamer's legs may indeed have been "paralyzed" until the dream tension built to a point where he could escape or awaken.

Most people dream much less during orthodox sleep and when they do the dreams tend to be different. Many of them are everyday and emotion-free: clear replays of the events of the day so that, for example, the dreamer sees herself getting ready for school and walking there, or going shopping, or playing in the garden. These dreams are more like memories of reality than the imaginative roamings of paradoxical sleep. When reality or its memories are painful or frightening, it is orthodox sleep dreams which will reflect the fact so that the victim of an accident will relive it. It is this kind of sleep which is being affected when a victim dare not let himself sleep "because I shall dream about that again." It is also orthodox sleep which is interrupted by night terrors or by sleep-walking (*see below*). There is no lengthy "story-dream" but a sudden flash of fear—usually from a single thought or image such as "something in that corner"—or a sudden urge to go somewhere or search for something.

Varying sleep needs

Although every human being needs to sleep, some need to sleep more than others. The hours of sleep an individual needs tend to be longest when he is a young baby and shortest when he is elderly but, whatever his age, one individual may always need more or less sleep than his peers.

To give the actual number of hours likely to be required by a three-month-old baby, a thirty-year-old or a seventy-year-old is dangerously misleading because of this individual variation. Figures given in books are usually the average number of hours slept (or reported to be slept) by large groups of people of particular ages. Such average figures may be interesting but they should never be applied to individuals. An average figure for three-month-old babies, for example, might be as high as eighteen hours per twenty-four. But if you allowed that information to make you feel that your baby *should* sleep for that long, you might well be worried and he might well become bored with his bed. Your baby may sleep for as little as twelve to thirteen hours each day. Similarly, to believe that you yourself "ought" only to need seven hours' sleep each night might be to deprive yourself of the extra hour or two which meets your personal requirement. It might also deprive you of yet more *time in bed* which you may not need for actual sleep but may, nevertheless, need for physical rest, for privacy from demanding children and for the kind of relaxed and comfortable contemplation which helps you cope with a busy and stressful life.

Ideally everyone, baby, child and adult, should be given the opportunity for as much sleep as he or she chooses to take but without anyone even implying that he or she should *try* to sleep. But in this respect, as in many others, family life often falls short of the ideal because it is difficult to mesh a bunch of varied sleep patterns together so that both each individual and the family-as-a-whole gets what it needs. As an obvious example, take the woman who has a small baby, a young teenage son and her own mother living with her. That baby goes to sleep early in the evening and wakes her rather often in the night while insisting on an early start to his day. To fit with the baby, the mother would probably go to bed rather early herself and accept the early breakfast. But her teenage son has homework and leisure activities and does not want either to go to bed or to get up early, while the grandmother probably needs less sleep than her daughter, is somewhat lonely during the day and would like her to sit up companionably late. The problem, then, is not so much one of *hours* of sleep but of their timing, and their fitting around companionship and dependency needs. Help yourself to get it right in your family by:

Not allowing yourself to feel guilty at wanting to "get rid of" a baby or child into bed/sleep. If your day is made easier by your baby taking a midday rest in which he does not sleep but simply plays and talks to himself, what is wrong with that? Of course it would be wrong to imprison him in his crib and leave him there screaming, but if he can be happy away from you, there is no reason to feel that a rest can only be imposed on him if he actually sleeps.

In the same way, many small children are put to bed at night long before they are ready for sleep. Parents often find it necessary to pretend—even to themselves—that a 7 p.m. bedtime is somehow "right for a four-year-old" when the truth is that to be free of the demands of children in order to have a private evening is "right for adults" (or for some adults). Provided that child has had a busy and well-companioned day and has enough to occupy him in bed, there is nothing the matter with such a plan.

Not allowing yourself to feel that he "ought" to sleep. This is often the other side of the same coin. Children are sent to bed after an early supper, but instead of being allowed to play and talk until sleep overcomes them, their parents keep urging them to "go to sleep." They cannot do so on command any more than you can enforce the command, and simply delivering it, again and again, sets up a sort of anxiety about the whole situation. Unless they are unhappy or actually being destructive or getting into danger, let them be.

Not sticking to conventional routines which do not happen to suit your child/family. Most small children have at least one daytime nap until they are between two and three years old. However long or short their night's sleep, few can stay awake and active right through the day before this age. But some toddlers can. And some, offered a daytime nap, take it at the expense of their night's sleep so that their parents lose either evening peace or some of their own sleeping time. If it suits all of you to keep such a child up all day, or up until an unconventionally late hour in the evening, why not? It will certainly do him no harm because he will sleep when he needs to, and for as long as he needs to, whereas you can only sleep when he lets you.

Making bed a pleasant place from the earliest possible age. In some families, children's beds and bedrooms are places only for sleep. No attempt is made to make them warm, friendly or interesting places in which to *be*, and all enjoyable activities are carried on elsewhere. The trouble with this approach is that it minimizes the time a child of any age will willingly spend in bed when he is not ready to sleep. The opposite approach is far more likely to give you the flexibility to meet everybody's needs:

Make even a baby's crib into a special place with its own playthings and soft toys and its own luxurious comfort. Make sure it is never an isolation cell because if he cries or calls, one of you always goes to him even if it is only for a moment. The more sure he is that you will come, the less often he will need to call and the less likely he is to teach himself to climb out to get you.

Make sure that bed is never a punishment cell, either. Don't ever let him associate it with anger or punishment, by putting him in that crib to "cool off" or by sending an older child to his room "until you can behave." If you want a cooling-off period between you, let it be you who goes away for the necessary minutes.

Make promotion to a "real bed" a time when his room becomes his castle. Whether you want, and can afford, to spend money on a bunk shaped like a fire engine and all the trimmings of special linen and so forth, or can only give him a corner of the room he must share, you can make it a place which he feels is his personal space. He can gather possessions, keep special books and things he likes to look at there. He can have a light which he can turn on and off for himself, and permission to do so. He can have friendly stuffed "people," photographs of the family, baby-things (his old pacifier perhaps) which are now for private use only. He can also have the feeling of personal ownership which comes from other people respecting his space. His older sister can keep out of "his bit," even if she shares the room, and keep her hands off "his things," too. And you can studiously avoid the kind of "spring cleaning" which makes it feel different and spoils it all for him.

If, instead of being banished to his room as a punishment, a young child voluntarily retires there for comfort, you will know that you are winning and that when you desperately want an extra hour's sleep on a Sunday, it will do him no harm to stay there until later than usual.

Build on the "castle" idea so that older wakeful children do not need your company. A six-year-old who is woken by a nightmare (*see below*) must have you, but when she wakes at 4 a.m. because she has had enough sleep for the moment, she can manage life for herself in this small private world. Help her to do so by keeping rules about what can go on in the night to a minimum. If she is forbidden to get out of bed, for example, she will have to call you if she has dropped her teddy bear or needs to go to the toilet. But if she has permission and the necessary light to go by herself, you can be undisturbed.

Gradually separate "bed" time from sleep time so that even if an older child actually needs less sleep than you do, he is content to spend extra time in the privacy of his room. Ideally, you want to be able to propose an early night to an eleven-year-old without it occurring to him to protest that he is not tired. There is no deprivation for him in going to his room earlier than usual, provided that he can read or play or listen to the radio.

Adolescents will usually welcome this kind of "private time," provided they have a place which feels like home and provided that you do not come barging in saying "Why isn't your light out?" when they had planned to read for half the night. Privacy is two-way. You can have it for yourself by offering it gradually to growing children.

Nightmares

All of us dream for periods of up to several hours each night. We only remember a minute (but widely varying) fraction of our dreams; usually the portion of dream life which was going on just before we were awakened.

The dreams of paradoxical sleep are imaginative and sometimes fantastic. They can depict, or focus around, anything of which the dreamer has any knowledge or experience. A newborn baby could not, as far as we know, dream the images which richly populate the mental life of older people, because he has not yet seen those things in reality and they are therefore not available to him for thinking or dreaming about. But as he gets older he can certainly build dreams around things he has not actually seen or experienced, provided he has enough information and images (from stories and television, for example) to fuel his imagination.

With such a large amount of rich dreaming going on night after night, it is not surprising that some dreams should be frightening. People who state that they never have nightmares are not necessarily "better balanced" or "less anxious" than the rest of us. They may simply be people who do not often remember what they have dreamed.

A baby or child who has had a nightmare usually wakes with a terrified scream or, sometimes, with a gurgling shout. He wakes himself because, in paradoxical sleep, his state is already comparatively aroused and the stimulus of the dream itself eventually penetrates his consciousness. His physical state as he awakens will often reflect the "story" of his dream, so that if he was crying in that dream he may be soaked in tears; if he was struggling with enemies he may struggle into wakefulness; if he was desperately trying to call out it may be his own, eventually successful, shout which alerts you.

Reach the child who has had a nightmare quickly because whether or not he remembers what he has been dreaming, his own physical state will terrify him. He finds himself crying or shaking, feels his heart pounding, hears his own horrible cry echoing in his head. Unless you arrive instantly to soothe him, that fear will build up upon itself and, if it does, he will remember the horror of the nightmare experience even if he does not at all remember the actual dream.

Try simply soothing him. Very often he can settle back into peaceful sleep the very moment he hears your familiar voice or feels your stroking hand. Don't feel that you must "wake him up properly" or "put on the light, so that he can see there is nothing to be afraid of," unless you see that he cannot drop off again at once.

Don't always try to make him tell you about his dream. If he wants you to know what it was about, he will tell you, but if he does not, forcing him to try to remember may make the whole fantasy more real to him than it need have been.

This kind of "ordinary" nightmare (*see below*) does not seem to be much influenced by what has been happening to the child before he went to sleep—by scary television programs or stories, for example—because it reflects the child's own inner life, his fantasy world, which is only indirectly fed by reality. The frequency of nightmares—or the frequency with which they awaken the child—may, however, be increased by his being in a high overall state of anxiety; less than peaceful in his mind, so to speak. On the whole, though, you can be assured (and should assure the child himself if he is old enough) that everyone does have "bad dreams" and that for most people they come in patches. He may have a nightmare every night for weeks on end and then not again for months. If you can prevent him from becoming afraid of going to sleep "in case I have a bad dream," nightmares, quickly soothed by a beloved adult, will do no harm.

Night terrors

Night terrors do not occur during paradoxical sleep but during orthodox sleep. Instead of being part of long, complicated story dreams, as night-mares are, they are usually an extreme response to a single, brief, terrifying thought or image-in-the-mind. The flash of extreme fear catapults the dreamer out of sleep and into a state which looks like wakefulness but is not truly conscious. Your child suddenly utters an ear-splitting, mind-bending shriek. You rush to his bedside and find him sitting bolt upright, gazing into a corner of the room. He may by now be calling piteously for you, but even when you touch and speak to him he does not seem aware of your presence but only of some other "Presence" which is lodged in that corner of his mind. As you persist in trying to make contact with him, he may even make you part of the terror, cringing from you, shrieking, "No no, oh no."

Children never remember night terrors; parents almost invariably remember them with horror. A child who seems conscious but is out of touch with the real world is difficult to deal with calmly; his state seems eerie and his fear is infectious. Many a stalwart parent has found herself joining the child in gazing nervously into that corner.

Don't insist on your child becoming aware of you. After most night terrors he will settle back and go to sleep as suddenly as he "woke." Give him every chance to do so, but stay quietly beside him in case this occasion is one of the exceptions.

If he tries to get out of bed, try gently to keep him there. It is far better if he does not run, semiconscious and hysterical, around the house. He might hurt himself and will almost certainly wake himself up and be frightened to discover himself behaving so oddly in the middle of the night.

If he struggles against you, or hysteria seems to be building, offer some reassuring stimulus in the hope that you can wake him up without his ever realizing what has happened. Switching on the room light, changing his pillows around, smoothing back his hair and so forth are all everyday actions which may gently penetrate to consciousness and "bring him round." If he does thus become aware of you, try not to let him see that you have been upset or that there has been any kind of drama. "You had a bad dream" is usually the best message to give him to explain your presence and the fact that he is now awake, in the middle of the night, without knowing how he came to be.

If he does awaken completely, you may have to "put him to bed" all over again because having awoken from orthodox, rather than paradoxical, sleep, he has had a jolting kind of disturbance which it may take him some minutes to overcome. It may be worthwhile to offer a drink, a trip to the bathroom, even a lightning version of his whole bedtime ritual, to get him settled down feeling "ordinary" again.

Night terrors do seem to be influenced by things which have happened to the child in reality, although the cue for the terror is not the whole event—the "story"—but a single feeling from it. A child who is recently home after surgery, for example, may have a succession of night terrors focused, perhaps, around his own helplessness when "they" held him for an unpleasant procedure (*see* **Hospital**/Procedures). Another child may have night terrors focused around the sight of his mother who had fainted, or around his heart-stopping terror when an older child leapt out at him in the dark. If television or stories are going to cause trouble in sleep it will probably be of this kind, too. He will not dream the horror story but the horror which he felt as it was told.

Since night terrors are never remembered and are not, as far as we know, ever about incidents but about raw emotions, directly talking to the child about what has frightened him is seldom useful. It may indeed be damaging because it is scary for him to be told that he was terrified in the night when he himself has no recollection of the incident. A different kind of talking (and of action, too) may be needed, though. If you can work out what sort of fear or anxiety your child is likely to be reliving in his terrors, you may be able to open it up and look at it so that it loses its focus. You may also be able to build the child's general confidence, his security that he can manage himself in his world, to a point where his own emotions are easier for him to tolerate. In the meanwhile, don't leave a child who is currently subject to night terrors with a strange, or very young babysitter. If the stranger awakens him, terror will be added to terror. If a youngster has to cope with a true night terror, she will be terrified into needing a babysitter for herself.

Sleep-talking

While almost everyone occasionally mutters during paradoxical sleep, some people talk, loudly and fluently, almost every night. A few even carry on conversations with fantasy companions, laugh, scold and make jokes.

Sleep-talking is of no significance to the talker but may make him a very uncomfortable and frightening roommate. If one of your children is a confirmed sleep-talker, try to arrange for him to have a room to himself.

Whether or not the talker can sleep alone, do try to ensure that nobody teases him about his sleep-talking or tells him even the funniest and most innocent things that he said. Most children find it not only embarrassing, but alarming, to think that they "communicated" with somebody else without conscious intent. It is as if the child had no power over himself; was "taken over" by someone else during the night. A slightly older child may worry that he will "give away his secrets."

Sleep-walking

Some children sleep-walk frequently throughout childhood; most never do so at all; a few sleep-walk once and never again.

Sleep-walking, like night terrors, occurs always in orthodox sleep. Contrary to what many people believe, the physical activity of getting out of bed and wandering about is not part of dream action but rather a response to a sudden and unformulated need to "do something." It is, if you like, action for action's sake, just as the night terror is terror for terror's sake.

If a child is going to sleep-walk he will usually do so early in the night, often towards the end of that initial period of orthodox sleep, perhaps an hour or so after he has fallen asleep. A child who has been asleep for several hours before adults go to bed will seldom walk in his sleep later on, although you cannot rely on this (*see below*).

A sleep-walking child characteristically gets out of bed and wanders around the house with his eyes open, looking somewhat anxious and distressed but not really frightened. He does not seem to be going anywhere in particular or searching for anybody or anything in particular, although there may be troubled mutterings such as "must . . . I must . . ." or "now I got to . . . got to . . . yes got to . . ." There is an old wives' tale which suggests that it is dangerous to awaken a sleep-walking child. This is nonsense. But waking him may be exceedingly difficult; he is deaf and blind to your presence. It may also be tactless because once you have forced him back to consciousness, he has to face the peculiarity of being downstairs in the dining room in his pajamas when the last thing he remembers is going to sleep in his bed. Waking a sleep-walking child is hardly ever necessary. If you go to him and gently steer him, by taking his hand or putting yours on his shoulders, he will almost invariably allow himself to be led peaceably back to bed. If he sleeps in a high bunk, he will even climb the ladder as soon as you have positioned him at the bottom.

Sleep-walking can put a child in danger. Although sleep-walkers seem to retain some contact with reality, so that they avoid most major obstacles and so forth, children in this state have been known to fall downstairs, to climb out of upstairs windows or to let themselves out of houses. If your child sleep-walks more than once, you may need to take some precautions such that he cannot do anything which might endanger him without making enough noise to awaken you.

Sleep-walking does sometimes go with emotional disturbance either in the sense that a child who has never walked in his sleep may do so for the first time when he is very upset or at odds with his life, or in the sense that a sleep-walking child may do so more frequently under these circumstances. You may, therefore, want to use sleep-walking as the cue to a careful consideration of what is happening to the child; what anxieties may be simmering. On the other hand, you may like to comfort yourself with the fact that sleep-walking tends to run in families. If you and other relatives also had this tendency, it may not be that your sleep-walker is *especially* anxious, but that he is a child who is going to sleep-walk whenever he is the *least bit* anxious.

Smacking *see* **Discipline, Self-discipline and Learning How to Behave**/Some common disciplinary techniques: Punishment. *See also* **School**/Potential problems in school: Discipline in your child's school.
Smallpox *see* **Immunization**.
Smoking *see* **Habits**. *See also* **Pollution**.
Smothering *see* **Safety**/In the home: From general household hazards; On vacation: Seaside hazards.
Snakebite *see* **Accidents**/Bites and stings.

Soiling *see also* **Toilet Training**

For most children, bowel-control is far easier than bladder control and therefore, once basic "toilet training" is completed, soiling is a rarity while wetting is not. Of course, any young child can pass an occasional movement in his pants by mistake, especially if he is caught out by the beginning of an episode of diarrhea. But if a child whom you had thought to be "reliable" passes feces in his pants on more than a couple of occasions, don't just dismiss it as "something he will grow out of." He may need your help in doing so.

Why young children soil

Soiling seems often to be part of the power relationship between parents and child, rooted in the kinds of conflict which are common in the toddler years.

Toddlers are still deeply dependent and passionately attached to their parents, yet they have reached an age-stage in which they are also beginning to feel themselves to be separate and independent individuals. The desire to be dependent and protected clashes with the desire to be independent and autonomous. That clash produces the typical emotional lability of the two-year-old who alternates between clinging and cries of "Let me!"

If a toddler feels overpowered, bossed and bullied by his parents, he will tend to look for areas in his life in which he can assert some power of his own. If he is not allowed any such power, feeling himself controlled at every turn, he will seek for ways of asserting power directly over those controlling adults; ways of getting back at them, of wielding some power of his own and thus redressing the balance.

Parents ask toddlers to do, and not to do, a great many things and, when compliance is not forthcoming, they often use their superior size and strength to enforce obedience. The child who will not come in from the garden is carried in, despite his screams and kicks. The child who will not sit up at the table may be forced into his highchair and strapped there. But there are some things which no parent can force an unwilling child to do and among these are some of the things which are most important to them. They can sit him up at the table but they cannot make him eat. They can (perhaps) make him stay in bed but they cannot make him sleep. They can sit him on a potty or toilet but they cannot make him pass a stool.

If a toddler is spoiling for a power fight he may "choose" any or all of these areas as his arena, but he is most likely to choose one on which his attention has already been focused by obvious parental concern and anxiety. Just as the mother who is anxious about her child's eating is the mother who is most likely to have a toddler with "eating difficulties" (*see* **Eating**/Eating problems), so the mother who has been over-enthusiastic and/or premature in her efforts to toilet train her child is the one whose child is most likely to choose the toilet as his battleground.

Most of the toddlers who do put up a fight over the potty, still do not soil. If their objections take the form of refusing to sit on the potty, and their mothers accept the refusal and avoid even trying to force the issue, it usually resolves itself. But if a mother cannot take no for an answer, insisting, so to speak, that the child's stools belong to her and that she will have them, where and when she says and whether he is willing or not, she is inviting him to defy her with his body, and stressing to him the emotional importance of his feces.

The first steps towards soiling

Quite a lot of two-year-olds go through a phase when they will use the potty or toilet for urination but not for defecation. The child will sit on the potty, but will either pee or do nothing. As soon as he is allowed up, he will go to some secret place—such as under the table or behind the curtains—and there he will pass his stool, in his diaper or pants.

Sometimes the power play is even more obvious. When he is first allowed up from the potty, the child knows that his mother is keeping an eye on him, waiting to whisk him back as soon as she can see signs that he needs to pass a motion. So he waits; he waits until she is distracted and doing something else and *then* he slips away and fills his pants before she can catch him.

Coping with early soiling

To an outsider, such transparent defiance, from such a small person, is positively funny. If parents themselves can find it (privately) funny, they will be able to defuse the situation before it progresses any farther. They can choose their own words in which to convey to the child the message: "You've made it quite clear that you don't want to put your stools where we suggest. So OK. It doesn't matter. Do it in your pants (or wear your diapers) if you prefer. When you're bigger you will probably want to do it in the toilet like older people do, but there's no hurry. . . ."

If they *really* don't care, taking off the pressure will drain the emotion out of the whole performance and make it pointless for the child. The toilet arena will be closed to him and he will quickly complete his own toilet training while finding something else to fight about with them. But if they really do care, and are furiously angry inside at his defiance, and/or revolted and upset by his dirty pants and bottom, the child will know; assurances to the contrary will only make more of a muddle. So unless the child's parents can truly come to believe that they hurried the whole toilet business, and that perhaps they have been pushy in other ways too, and need to let up on him a bit and give him some extra growing space, it probably will not work.

If it does not work, more and more attention and emotion will inevitably come to be focused on "The Problem" and, while the child still may turn his attention to other ways of communicating with his parents, he may be unable to let go of what will now have become "a symptom."

Some toddlers continue their refusal to defecate in potty or toilet and go on, through the pre-school years, doing it in their pants. As the child gets older, so this behavior affects more and more of his life and that of his family. Once he passes an age at which diapers are considered even marginally appropriate, he will be unacceptable in a group and will be an unwelcome guest in many private houses, too. Even his own parents may find the prospect of having to clean him up in public toilet facilities daunting enough to limit the trips on which they are prepared to take him. His own private life with his peers will be affected, too. It is hard to be popular if you are called "smelly" and hard to feel likable if you know the name is merited.

Passing stools in inappropriate places

Sometimes such a child gives up passing his stools in his pants but still refuses to pass them in the intended places. He may take down his pants and pass his stool on the floor. Very occasionally parents try to "normalize" a child's life in this situation by putting down newspaper for him to use and trying to see that he defecates there first thing every morning so that the matter does not arise to bedevil his day in society. This kind of maneuver may indeed enable a child to go to school and so forth without others becoming aware of his peculiarity, so it might, under certain circumstances, be recommended within the context of ongoing psychiatric advice and/or treatment. But it should not replace such advice and treatment. The child who uses newspapers instead of a toilet is insisting on behaving like a dog not a child. His image of himself cannot therefore be a satisfactory one. Furthermore, the child who thus insists on flaunting his stools is offering bits of himself as gifts to the adult world and having those gifts rushed disgustedly out of sight. All concerned need help with their feelings.

Withholding stools and resulting soiling

Most pre-school and later soiling takes a related but importantly different form. Instead of insisting on putting his stools where he pleases, the child passively refuses to give them up to the parents' command, holding on to them instead in his own body.

A child who "holds on" in this way eventually becomes constipated (*see* **Constipation**). Feces accumulate in an evermore distended rectum and eventually become so dry and hard that he could not pass them if he wanted to. But because waste matter is still accumulating, it will eventually start to leak, in semi-liquid form, from above the now rock-like blockage. Instead of filling his pants occasionally, such a child will soil them, just a little bit, almost constantly.

Unwary parents may be very slow to spot that such a child has a problem. The soiled pants *could* result from inefficient wiping after a normal bowel movement. If they allow themselves to realize that such constant carelessness is unlikely, they may decide, from the liquidity of the leaking feces, that the child is suffering from diarrhea. The soiling cannot, therefore, be regarded as his fault or responsibility.

Such a child needs medical help first of all. Until his loaded rectum is cleared, normal patterns of elimination cannot be established and, if matters are left too long, the normal sensations, which indicate the need to defecate, may be lost altogether.

Sometimes, especially if the child is very young and the pattern of soiling new, clearance of the blockage will be found to right the whole matter. The withholding may have begun as a response to the pain of an anal fissure (*see* **Constipation**) and once this physical problem is overcome, and the child assured that it will not be allowed to return, it is found that there is no emotional barrier between him and the establishment of ordinary behavior.

More usually, though, psychological help and guidance will be needed to prevent the problem from recurring, and enable the child to grow through this particular anal phase to find more acceptable ways of coping with, and communicating, his feelings.

Medical treatment of withholding feces

Some doctors will vigorously clear the lower bowel with enemas, washouts and laxatives and then try to "reeducate" the child towards "normal" habits. While this approach may appear successful, especially in the older child who, consciously at least, wants to be rid of his soiling, it can be psychologically risky. If the child originally began to withhold his feces in order to keep at least that bit of him under his own control and out of his parents', he is almost certain to see the bowel wash-outs, and other unpleasant procedures as a punishment, and the successful production of his feces as yet another naked assertion of his parents' power.

Many pediatricians, especially those with a particular interest in children's psychology, now tend to take a gentler and less direct approach to the necessary clearance of the rectum. They may use dietary adjustments and perhaps mild laxatives, and they will combine these with attempts to modify the difficulties between the child and his parents. The message such a doctor will try to get across to the child might be something like this: "It is your body and I am entirely confident that it will work perfectly for you as soon as you can feel all right about it doing so. If you want to see whether going to the toilet the way other people do is nicer for you than all this fuss about dirty pants, this medicine will make the beginning easier for you because it will make the feces which have got hard because they've been in there so long, a bit softer."

Whatever your doctor's approach, it is important that you yourselves should not undertake *any* procedures which are unpleasant and embarrassing for the child. If he is to have enemas or suppositories, adults looking at and fiddling with his anus and rectum, let doctors, with whom he is not emotionally involved as he is with you, be the ones to inflict these indignities on him.

Soiling and emotional disturbance

Soiling is still a forbidden topic for many people, including many parents of child victims. When it is mentioned, it is often described as inevitably symptomatic of deep-seated and disastrous emotional disturbance. It is pointed out that, in older children, this symptom tends to go with all kinds of other, obviously emotional, problems, such as difficulty in making friends, failures in school achievement, running away, delinquent behaviors and so forth. No wonder parents find it difficult to admit, even to themselves, that their child soils.

While the *beginning* of soiling does seem usually to be based in conflict between parents and child, and on unrecognized and unmet needs in him, these conflicts are not necessarily more sinister than those of other young children which present themselves, for example, as eating or sleeping difficulties. The later associated difficulties which children who soil experience are as likely to be the *result* of their soiling as to be part of a seriously disturbed whole. Our society will not tolerate a child who stinks. In that simple statement lies the urgency of facing, and trying to deal with, the soiling the moment it becomes inappropriate to the child's age-stage. If you allow a child to go on soiling after infancy, you are rearing one whom society will not tolerate. What better recipe could there be for the creation of a child who is unhappy, isolated, sure of his own worthlessness and, eventually, anti-social?

Sudden soiling in older children

An older child who suddenly begins to soil *may* be suffering from chronic constipation. He may be as upset as you are by his inability to control leaking feces. It is certainly worth talking to him, immediately and matter-of-factly, to establish whether this is a purely temporary, physical problem which, perhaps with help from his doctor, he can quickly deal with. If this is the case, a full explanation of what has happened to him, either from the doctor or from you, is essential. Once both his anxiety and his overburdened bowel are relieved make sure that he understands that he must not allow this to happen again; that he is eating sensibly and drinking enough fluids and that he will ask for help, on another occasion, more quickly.

If the soiling is not caused by long-standing constipation and the doctor finds no sign of any other physical cause, you will have to face the fact that an older child who suddenly begins to soil for emotional reasons is "choosing" a peculiarly self-damaging symptom. It is likely to reflect a very poor valuation of himself and a very great anger at the world in general, and probably at his parents in particular. It is difficult to imagine a more extreme way for a child to shout, "I don't care . . ." (*see also* **Depression**/In children before puberty).

The child himself will not, of course, have any idea why he soils; it is no good asking him. You will probably not have any idea, either. If you all knew what each other was feeling, the problem would not have arisen. Seek professional help, through your doctor, as quickly as you can because your child, even more than a younger one, will quickly be ostracized by, or withdraw from, his fellows.

Special education *see* **School**/Children with special needs. *See also* **Hyperactive Children; Learning Difficulties and Disabilities.**

Speech *see* **Language.**

Splinters *see* **Accidents**/Cuts and scrapes, grazes and puncture wounds.

Spoiling *see* **Discipline, Self-discipline and Learning How to Behave**. *See also* **Anxiety, Fears and Phobias; Tantrums.**

Spoon feeding *see* **Eating**/Eating problems: Babies and eating problems.

Sports injuries *see* **Accidents**. *See also* **Cramp**.

Sprains *see* **Accidents**.

Squints *see* **Eyes and Seeing; Eye Disorders and Blindness.** *See also* **Hospital**/Surgery.

Stammering *see* **Language**.

Stealing *see* **Discipline, Self-discipline and Learning How to Behave**/Some common issues in discipline.

Step-parents *see* **Divorce, Separation and One-parent Families**/Children's relationships with step-parents.

Sterilizing *see* **Infection**/Preventing infection: Sterilants, disinfectants and antiseptics.

Stitch *see* **Cramp**.

Stitches/sutures *see* **Hospital**/Procedures. *See also* **Accidents**/Cuts and scrapes.

Stomachache *see* **Abdominal Pain**. *See also* **Adolescence**/Menstruation.

Stools *see* **Constipation; Diarrhea, Gastroenteritis and Food Poisoning; Toilet Training**.

Styes *see* **Eyes and Seeing; Eye Disorders and Blindness**.

Sucking *see* **Eating**/Types of food for babies; **Habits**/Comfort habits. *See also* **Teeth**.

Sudden Infant Death Syndrome *see* **Death**.

Suffocation *see* **Accidents**/Choking: **Safety**/In the home: From general household hazards.

Suicide *see also* **Adolescence; Depression**

Suicide by children and young people

Many people believe (and perhaps choose to believe) that only adults ever kill themselves on purpose. This is a dangerous delusion. Thousands of adolescents, hundreds of twelve- to fourteen-year-olds and a handful of even younger children are officially recognized as having died by their own hands each year. Concealed within "open" verdicts or verdicts of "death by misadventure," there are probably many times more suicides among the young. Few coroners will burden parents with a verdict of suicide if there is any room at all for uncertainty.

There is no uncertainty about the figures for attempted suicide among children and young people. Self-poisoning, for example, accounts for around twenty percent of all teenage admissions to acute medical wards.

Adult society chooses to believe that most of these attempted suicides are attention-seeking acts rather than "serious" attempts to die. They are now usually referred to as "parasuicide" and are often treated with scorn and anger by overworked hospital staff who see these unhappy children as selfishly taking up professional time which could be better spent on "people who are really ill." Occasionally, necessary treatment, (such as pumping the stomach of a girl who has taken "an overdose" (*see* **Hospital**/Procedures), is carried out in such a way that it is seen not as care but as punishment.

Many young people who survive suicide attempts say that they are glad to be alive after all; some say that even at the time of the act they did not actually want to be dead; they agree that they arranged matters so as to make it likely that they would be discovered in time. But this does not justify taking a suicide threat lightly or treating a child who takes poison as if she were a spoiled toddler who had thrown an especially embarrassing temper tantrum. Are we only to respond helpfully to those who are beyond help? A person who thinks about killing herself, threatens to kill herself or takes actions which she knows might kill her is *suffering*. It is up to those around her to see her pain and relieve it.

Many adolescents go through periods of acute unhappiness with, and within, themselves. The vast majority eventually find ways of coming to terms with themselves and making an adult life. But the stories of a few who killed themselves leaving notes behind, or who attempted suicide and later worked out what had led to their attempts at self-destruction, may illustrate the kind of misery for which parents should watch, and in the context of which any hint that the child is suicidal should be treated as an emergency. It is no coincidence that all these youngsters shared in feeling hopeless, helpless and angry.

Suicide by a schoolboy aged fifteen

This boy lived with his mother, his father having left the family. He had never enjoyed school and had been treated for school phobia (*see* **School**) at the time of his promotion to secondary school. During the school year which ended in his death he had been continually bullied by other boys and had confided this to his principal, his mother and the truant officer following inquiries into his frequent absences. His note said: "Day after day it's the same with no way out. I can't stop them; I ought to be able to stand up for myself but I can't. Nobody will stand up for me because nobody really cares about me and I can see why."

Suicide by a girl aged fourteen

This girl's mother had died of cancer two years previously and her father had recently remarried, making, he and his new wife honestly believed, a secure new home for her. She left a long letter which read, in part: ". . . I know you will be very unhappy and I am truly sorry because I know you tried; but although everybody said I'd feel better one day, that day just never comes. I just want to be with Mom. I can't manage without her. Nobody will do instead so I'm going where she is."

Attempted suicide by a girl aged sixteen

This girl had been at loggerheads with her parents for the past eighteen months, with trouble focusing around her sexuality. She took every pill she could find in the family bathroom after her father had found her in bed with her boyfriend and told her that he had always known she was a slut. She explained it like this: "It wasn't exactly that I wanted to be dead; I didn't think about it like that. I didn't really think much at all, I just took them. What else could I do? He was right, wasn't he? I am what he said. But there's nothing I can do about it, is there? I mean it's a bit late to call names now. Anyway, I gave him something else to think about, didn't I?"

Attempted suicide by a boy aged seventeen

This boy came from an apparently happy and devoted family and was a highly successful student who excelled in music and art. His suicide bid amazed everyone concerned. Fortunately, a concerned social worker at the hospital outmaneuvered the family's attempt to treat it as a "brainstorm" and arranged for him to see a psychiatrist. Over several lengthy conversations, it became clear that the boy was deeply dissatisfied with the self which the adults around him so appreciated. He did not want to be a sensitive musician but a tough sportsman. He did not want to be a beloved son but a sexy lover. He did not want to be the adult world's ideal teenager but his peer-group's hero. His actual suicide attempt was touched off by a particular fantasy during masturbation which had suddenly led him to decide that he was probably homosexual. But he described himself as "trapped, you see, because they like me as I am and I don't, and they don't seem to see that I'm the one who's got to *be* me. . . ."

Probably everyone who is suicidal feels hopeless, helpless and angry, but these feelings are especially likely to overwhelm those who are both vulnerable and very young. An adult who is deeply depressed may be able to remember what she felt like as a person before she entered the illness. She may, therefore, be able to accept assurances that, like other illnesses, the depression will pass and she will feel "herself" again. A thirteen- or sixteen-year-old has had no time to discover herself as an adult female and, therefore, has no such reassuring memories with which to combat a present which feels swamped in a gray mist. If she is encouraged to look forward, what is she looking forward to? An unknown which, from her present position, can only be grim.

While anyone who is clinically depressed is helpless to "snap out of it," youngsters are often realistically helpless, too, because every outward aspect of their lives is under someone else's control. An adult who is finding life in her present job or marriage intolerable can, if she can only find the psychic energy, break free and try something else. A child has no room for maneuver. She cannot choose to leave school or find herself a new family.

While every suicide is probably at least partly an act of aggression against other people, youngsters, newly emerging from the complete dependency of childhood, are particularly vulnerable to adults failing to understand or help.

Far from refusing to take seriously the threatened or attempted suicide of someone who is "scarcely more than a child," we should probably take it more seriously. Far from "punishing" those who "waste medical time" by taking pills "just to get attention," we should be grateful that their need was forced on our attention before it was finally too late to meet it.

Suicide by parents and other people important in children's lives

Suicide is not a loving act. It is always a selfish and rejecting one and usually aggressive also. The grandmother who leaves a note saying that she has killed herself because "you will all be better off without me" may see her self-destruction as loving, even self-sacrificing, but within that open message are the hidden barbs: "You made me feel a burden/in the way/not worth having."

A child whose parent commits suicide faces not only the grief which must follow any bereavement but also additional psychological burdens. Perhaps the heaviest is the burden of knowing that that parent did not love him, or at least did not love him enough to stay alive and be with him. Voluntarily to die is to desert a child in the most final way there is. When all the grieving and talking and explaining are over, that agonizing knowledge remains. The dead parent abandoned him.

The death of someone close always causes guilt, but a suicide causes more than most because that message "He/she did not care enough about me to stay alive for me" inevitably carries with it the message "If I had loved him/her more/been a better son/daughter/been more helpful, more understanding, more worthy of love, more *something*, perhaps he/she would have felt able to stay alive."

Anger at being so cruelly deserted, and guilt at having failed the dead parent, tend to interact with each other. The child finds himself angry, yet to be angry with someone so tragically dead is in itself something to be guilty about. If the anger dominates the child's feelings he may come to hate the dead parent for the misery his/her death has caused—and feel guilty for that hate. If guilt dominates his feelings he may actually come to feel that he *caused* the death by his behavior and/or by his secret aggressive feelings to the parent during life. Then he will feel angry at the injustice of feeling so guilty for something which the rational bit of him knows was not his responsibility.

When someone who is close to a child or young person commits suicide, there are hard decisions to be made which the living parent and other family members may themselves be too involved to make. Should the child (whatever his age) *know* that the death was a suicide if it could be kept from him? Should he be told why it happened, insofar as others understand it? Whatever decisions are taken, their consequences can be far-reaching so it may be wise to take them, if it is possible, with the help of a health professional who can look at the situation with enough objectivity to see beyond the family's present hell and into the child's future. A suicide within the close family is a crisis which merits psychological first aid.

Youngsters are often deeply shocked by the suicide of a friend or schoolmate. There may be personal guilt associated with it, ranging from "If I'd only known how unhappy she was . . ." to the more direct "I wouldn't have joined the ribbing if I'd known she really minded." But there is usually also a degree of personal fear: "Could I be unhappy enough to die?" and perhaps of envy, too, because the dead youngster has, in a single act, achieved the kind of concentrated attention from the adult world which many adolescents feel that they lack in life. If your adolescent should meet this experience, make sure that it is discussed and that your carefully tuned ear picks up her subtle messages. You may, for example, need to help her realize:

That she is not all-powerful and that nothing she could have done/left undone would have made any difference because her relationship was not central to the dead girl's life.

That she is not in a position to assign blame to herself, to the dead girl or to anyone else who might have contributed to that death because, as a friend or acquaintance, she simply does not know those concerned well enough to understand their relationships with each other.

That such a death is always, and above all, a waste because whatever happens to the very young, their lives are always going to change and that change is always worth working and waiting for.

Sunburn *see* **Accidents**.
Suppositories *see* **Nursing**/Medicines which are not to be swallowed: Enemas (and suppositories).
Surgery *see* **Hospital**/Surgery.
Swallowed foreign bodies *see* **Accidents**.

Swearing *see* **Language**/Pre-school years: Nonsense and "naughty" nonsense. *See also*
Discipline, Self-discipline and Learning How to Behave.
Sweets and snacks *see* **Eating**/Some commonsense policies. *See also* **Teeth.**
Talking *see* **Language.**

Tantrums *see also* **Convulsions, Seizures and "Fits"**

Temper tantrums have nothing to do with "naughtiness" and very little
to do with "temper" in the usual derogatory sense. A genuine tantrum is
a sort of emotional blown fuse caused by an overload of frustration. It is
not within the child's control at all and, while probably infuriating and
embarrassing for you, it will usually be downright terrifying for her.

Drive,
frustration and
tantrums

Human babies are born very incompetent compared with most mammals,
but they pack a truly fantastic amount of learning into their lengthy
infancy and childhood. Fortunately, a baby does not rely on you, or
anything outside herself, to provide the motivation for all this learning
and developing. Every baby seems to be born with an in-built and
self-perpetuating drive to learn, to practice and to succeed in every one of
the thousands of tiny tasks which contribute to her growing up. When
she is a schoolchild, you and her teacher may have to push and coax her
into learning her French verbs, but in infancy nobody has to push her to
learn to walk. As soon as she is physiologically ready, she will start trying
and she will go on and on trying, no matter how many times she falls and
hurts herself, until she succeeds. Any adult who found walking that
difficult would give up and send for a wheelchair. But not that baby: the
stroller may be meant to rest her legs, but it will also frustrate her drive to
walk; it may well be one tantrum-trigger.

While every baby has this kind of inner drive (and no baby could
develop fully without it) children do vary both in how easily they become
frustrated and how violently they react when they do. Where one child
will go on patiently trying to unscrew a lid, another will give up much
sooner. Where one will eventually admit defeat gracefully and move on
calmly to something else, another takes every failure to heart and gives
full voice to her despair. Of course, every child's frustration tolerance
varies, both from day to day and from stage to stage, but there is no doubt
that some are more phlegmatic, almost, one might say, philosophical,
overall, than others. When you are coping several times a day with a
tantruming child you may wish for a more placid one, but it helps to
remember that the frustrated screaming child is only frustrated because
she is trying and that, because she is trying, she will learn.

● Some of the children who have a great many tantrums and/or start
them comparatively early—perhaps in their first year rather than the
more usual second—turn out to be particularly bright: they frustrate
themselves a great deal because they can see how to do, and therefore
want to do, a great many things they are not yet physically mature
enough to do. But be careful if you are taking comfort from this fact. Some
others have a great many tantrums because some unsuspected dis-

ability—notably deafness (*see* **Ears and Hearing; Ear Disorders and Deafness**)—is loading them with a basic frustration with which they cannot cope.

Triggers for tantrums

Children frustrate themselves by setting themselves tasks they cannot perform; objects frustrate them by not behaving as they intended them to behave; but, above all, adults frustrate them, usually by trying to exercise the kind of total control which contravenes a toddler's dawning sense of personal autonomy.

Babies start out quite unable to distinguish between themselves and the people who care for them. Your baby does not know where she stops and you begin; indeed you can regain the use of your hand when she is sucking it by giving her her own hand to suck instead. Through the first year or so a baby tends to feel herself still part of you. She has no idea that you have separate feelings and activities; no concept of your adult life. You-and-she are the center of her world and she assumes that the same is true of you. But in order to grow into an independent, mature human being, that child has to discover her lonely separateness from everybody else; she has to practice being that self even when her wishes and activities clash with yours. It is during the early part of the second year that this necessary drive for personal autonomy usually becomes clear. Unfortunately, separating off from you is often a painful business for the baby because she still loves you and depends upon you totally. Every time she clashes with you she is caught between the devil of giving in and the deep blue sea of losing your support and approval. Developmentally, she must assert herself, but emotionally, it would be far easier for her to go on being a comparatively controllable baby.

Any situation in which you try directly to control your child's behavior can become a tantrum-trigger at this stage. The more "personal" she feels her behavior to be, the more likely she is to be violently frustrated by your insistence that she do it (or not do it) your way. She is liable to resent, for example, your insistence on her using a potty, eating certain foods at certain times, going to bed when she does not accept that she is tired, wearing "suitable" clothes, coming when she is called, going out when it suits you and coming home when you say it is time.

If she feels harried, bullied, pressurized and rushed she will resist and, if you use your superior strength and intelligence to defeat her, she is likely to explode into a tantrum. She does not want to wear a sweater; she feels (perhaps) that it is her body and that the clothes put onto it should (for this moment at least) be up to her. She throws the sweater on the floor and runs away. When you catch her, hold her between your knees and force that sweater over her head, she is likely to blow that fuse. She does not want to leave the supermarket and she cannot see why she should come with you just because you are in a hurry. She tries passive resistance by just going on wandering down the aisles, but when you pick her up and strap her in her stroller, her furious frustration overwhelms her. She wants to get out her blocks and neither can nor wants to understand that the afternoon's play is over. She tries to get them for herself, finds that they are too heavy, looks to you to help her as you usually do but, when you remain adamant, explodes. The tantrum is triggered by helplessness, by defeat, by feelings of being overpowered by people or circumstances.

Avoiding tantrums With some children you will not be able to avoid tantrums entirely because the degree to which any child is frustrated is not entirely within your control. But whether your child is a placid type or has a very low frustration tolerance, you can keep tantrums to a minimum by teaching yourself to feel sympathetic to these difficulties in growing from baby to child and by learning to behave tactfully in the danger areas.

Try to help her feel that she is in control of her own personal life: it is up to you what food you give her, but it can be up to her whether she eats it or not. It is up to you to take her to that potty, but it can be for her to decide whether to sit on it or not. It is your responsibility to see that she dresses adequately, but you can protect her from being cold later on just as effectively by taking the hated sweater with you as by forcing her to wear it, this minute, when she does not feel cold.

Cultivate talent as an actress. There will be many occasions when you are in a hurry but when, if you rush her, there will be trouble which will waste more time. If you can conceal your impatience and, instead of dumping her in that stroller, offer to be a horse and *pull* her home in it, you will get there faster as well as more happily.

Try not to back her into corners. Absolute orders absolutely refused spell nothing but trouble; leave her an escape route and her intact dignity, whenever you can. Often this means offering her an excuse for her own behavior ("I know you're tired so I'll help you pick it up this time . . ."). Often, too, it means distracting her: "This quarrel over touching the plugs is getting boring; let's go and. . . ." It is "walking around trouble" but why not? Trouble is trouble for both of you and tantrums teach nothing (*see* **Discipline, Self-discipline and Learning How to Behave**).

Try to treat her as politely as you treat older people. If your partner picked up your knitting and inspected it, would you scream at him while snatching it away and hiding it? Probably you would just say, "Do you like the color? You'll watch out that no stitches come off, won't you . . . ?" If your older child was washing his face, very slowly and ineffectually, would you grab the facecloth and his hair and do it for him, rather too hard? I doubt it. If your teenage daughter, trying to be helpful, spilled the dust out of your dustpan, would you shout at her and push her into another room? You would be more likely to say, "Oh, isn't it maddening when that happens? Never mind, just sweep it up again for me. . . ."

Try to cultivate the sense of humor that will let you enjoy your small child. Many quarrels stem from a kind of teasing which is your child's way of testing the water of your mood. It is sad if she *always* finds that water freezing. Running away is a very usual example. She runs away from you partly because she does not want to come home/come to bed/get dressed, but partly to see whether this is one of the days/times when you will join a chase-game or one when you will be furious. The chase-game is usually more enjoyable *for both of you* and quicker, too.

Keep an eye on the other sources of frustration in her daily life. Of course you cannot (and should not) try to protect her from everything she finds difficult because she must learn and she must experience success. But while frustrating objects can be extremely educational, objects which are too frustrating, offering her no chance of victory, contradict their own ends. For example, she may be getting furious because she cannot fit those round pegs into the square holes of that toy mailbox. It is a fact of solid geometry that round pegs will not fit into square holes and, if she is ready for fitting toys at all, it is a fact which she might as well learn. But she need not do so unaided. Help her make the discovery. If "mailing" things is her current passion and this toy is really too grown up, you could offer her an easier version such as a cardboard carton with big holes for balls and blocks . . . (*see* **Play**). The point is to distinguish between the kind and degree of frustration which will spur her onto greater efforts and eventual success and pleasure in her own achievement, and the kind which is self-defeating because she just becomes angrier and angrier, less and less competent.

The child is learning to understand objects and their behavior, so toys whose behavior she does understand but which she still cannot manage because of her physical immaturity, are an unfair additional source of frustration. She may, for instance, long to push that doll's carriage but be unable to reach the handle; long to kick that football but be too unbalanced to manage its weight; long to play the music box but be unable to turn the tiny, stiff handle. To be faced with a push toy which is too high is as maddening for her as a six foot stove would be to you; to try to play ball with a real football is as sad as it would be to try to play tennis with a baseball; to have to manipulate that little handle to make music is as frustrating for her as it would be for you to face a violin and bow rather than a piano. Children do not need rooms full of expensive toys either for their development or their pleasure, but any equipment they are to have must be appropriate for them. If she cannot have a little carriage or push-truck, a plastic "football" or a pull-string music box, she is better off with none at all until she is older.

Form and frequency of tantrums

Tantrums take many forms. Some children rush frantically around, screaming and banging into the furniture. Some throw themselves on to the floor and behave as if they were wrestling with devils. Some use any weapon which comes to hand to bang and wallop things and will hit their own heads against the wall if there is no alternative. A very few "scream themselves blue in the face" (*see* **Convulsions, Seizures and "Fits"**).

Whatever form your child's tantrums take, do realize that they are a normal phenomenon. If you are tempted to feel that yours is the only affected child, some recent survey figures from Britain may comfort you. Two research studies, carried out among large and differing samples, showed that parents admitted to frequent tantrums among sixty percent of boys and forty-five percent of girls aged twenty-one months and to very frequent tantrums in seventy percent of both sexes at three years. A further sample showed that fourteen percent of babies were having very frequent tantrums by their first birthday while fifty percent were already having at least one big one every fortnight.

Coping with tantrums

A child who is having a tantrum is lost to the conscious world. She is not open to exhortations to "stop that"; scolding will do no good because she cannot hear you. She is overwhelmed by her own flooding internal anger and she is probably terrified by it, too. She behaves as if she would like to kill everyone and destroy the world. Can she in fact know that she cannot? Over the years she has got to learn that it is safe to be angry: that feelings and words cannot physically injure people or objects. But at this stage she cannot be sure. Her anger must feel hideously dangerous.

The adult's job is to try to ensure that the child "comes round" from her tantrum to find no evidence that she is dangerous.

She must not find that she has hurt herself/hurt you/broken anything. If she does she will feel not only that she cannot control herself, but that you cannot control her either: she is truly an all-powerful monster.

If she will let you, hold her securely in your arms, safely on the floor. As her anger subsides she finds herself close to you. As she relaxes, the screams changing into sobs, she finds, often with obvious amazement, that everything is quite unchanged by the storm. The furious monster reverts to a pathetic baby who has frightened herself silly.

Some children are too big and heavy to hold safely and/or are further provoked by being physically restricted. If yours is one of these don't put a shoulder lock on her arms or keep her still by lying on her. Leave her free, but try to fend her off the walls and to remove objects she will otherwise knock over or smash. Wait for the change in note, from fury to pathos, and then try to gather her to you.

Try not to meet anger with anger. This is much easier said than done because anger is infectious. Many parents lose their tempers with a tantruming child and match her shout for shout. About fifty percent of the mothers surveyed (*see above*) admitted that they lost their tempers and punished children for having tantrums. It really is better not to. Anger and punishment while the tantrum is on will have no effect. Afterwards, they will only increase the child's feeling that the world is an angry and dangerous place, with herself one of its angriest and most dangerous occupants.

If you feel yourself losing control, it is sometimes best to remove yourself while the storm blows itself out. The risk of the child hurting herself without your protection is probably less than the risk of your hurting her if your temper goes completely.

Never, ever, let a child's tantrums affect your behavior towards her. If she had the tantrum in the first place because you would not give her something or let her do something, don't allow it afterwards. She needs comfort and the assurance of your love as she recovers, but not sweets or anything she could see as a reward, and certainly not evidence that the tantrum has served to manipulate you. She must see, from her very first outburst, that tantrums are horrible for her and have absolutely nothing to do with whether or not she gets her own way.

Unfortunately, many mothers find public tantrums horribly embarrassing and therefore are affected by the mere likelihood of the child throwing one in the street, in the store or in front of visitors. Try not to treat her with saccharine sweetness whenever there are strangers present, in the hope of averting trouble. She may not notice at two, but she will certainly realize this power by the time she is three and she would not be the intelligent human being she is if she did not then move towards the semi-voluntary tantrums typical of mishandled four-year-olds. Such children work themselves up on purpose, one eye on mother's reactions, until, if the ruse looks like failing, they reach the point of no return and genuinely lose control.

Older children and tantrums We can all lose our tempers and some of us find it difficult to find a way of releasing the extreme tension of our frustration without resorting to some violent physical action. Some people shout or stamp or bang doors; some marital rows regularly end with broken china and some battered babies are the result of this kind of episode.

If your child works herself up (*see above*) to genuine tantrums when she is of school age, try pointing out to her, very straightforwardly, that more self-control than that is expected from people of her age and that, while you know that she cannot help herself once she has got started, you also know that she could pull herself together at an earlier stage if she tried. If you do not, in fact, believe that she could stop herself, try offering (still entirely openly) some more acceptable ways for her to relieve herself of that intolerable tension. It can help if you actually encourage her to shout as loudly as she can. She may learn, with your help, to burst out of the house and race around the garden three times whenever she feels herself intolerably angry. She may even like to have a special cushion for pounding when she feels like pounding you or her baby brother. Whatever particular plans you make, the point is to acknowledge the feelings, but make it clear to her that tantrums will not do and therefore that she must find another way of dealing with them.

Teeth

The formation of teeth

Teeth before birth A baby's first (or "milk" or "baby") teeth begin to form very early in your pregnancy and go on developing until shortly before she is born.

Healthy first teeth need minerals, such as calcium and phosphorus, together with the vitamins which facilitate their proper absorption (*see* **Eating**/Types of food: Vitamins and minerals). But ensuring that the growing fetus gets what she needs is not difficult because:

That growing baby's needs are met first out of the nutrients in your bloodstream. This means that as long as your diet is providing enough of these substances to keep *you* healthy, you can be quite certain that *she* is getting all she needs. If your diet before pregnancy should contain only *just* enough of one of them so that there is not an adequate supply both for you and the fetus, it is your body which will go short, not hers. This is why babies born to women on very inadequate diets—in occupied countries during the Second World War, for example—were often amazingly healthy. Their intrauterine development was achieved at the expense of increased privation for their mothers' bodies. So if you are healthy yourself, do not worry about "drinking enough milk for the baby."

Ignore old wives' tales such as "you lose a tooth for every baby." That saying was based on the idea that a fetus somehow "drained" the calcium from her mother's teeth to form her own. It is nonsense, of course. If your pregnant body was so short of calcium that the baby's needs could be met only by breaking down some part of you to provide it, it would be your bones from which it would come, not your teeth.

Pregnant women do sometimes have dental problems but this is due to hormonal changes. They may cause swelling of the gums which consequently trap more food particles, breed more bacteria and cause extra tooth decay (*see below* Why teeth need cleaning). See your dentist early in each pregnancy and take extra trouble over dental hygiene during it.

If you stay healthy yourself you are doing all you can for her developing teeth. A severe infection during pregnancy *could* upset your body's biochemistry and prevent her teeth (as well as other aspects of her body) from developing perfectly, but there are no positive steps which you can take to produce extra-good infant teeth. Fluoride, for example, will be extremely valuable in strengthening her teeth later, but you cannot get it to her in the womb, by taking extra yourself, because almost no fluoride can pass across the placenta.

After birth: the time to think about fluoride

Even though you cannot yet see them, her first teeth are formed and waiting to emerge. It is her second (permanent) teeth which are now being formed. You can help them to develop well and to be strong and resistant to attack by caries, by feeding her in such a way that her body has adequate supplies of vitamins and minerals and by making sure that, one way or another, she has an adequate intake of fluoride.

Few people any longer doubt that an adequate intake of fluoride helps produce teeth whose enamel is comparatively hard and caries-resistant. The continuing arguments you may hear are not about that basic proposition but about the best way to ensure that every baby gets that fluoride. Some people believe that community water supplies should be fluoridated (except in areas where there is plenty in the water already); others believe that fluoridation is equivalent to "dosing people without their consent" and is therefore immoral. In between, there are people who do not object to fluoridation on principle, but who are concerned lest it lead to a few children taking in an overdose of fluoride which, far from being good for them, can actually be harmful.

In order to ensure that your own baby gets enough fluoride but not too much, you will need the advice of your own doctor and/or dentist and he will need information on the following points:

How much fluoride occurs naturally in your community's water supply. If it is rich in fluoride your child may never need a supplement and indeed may be far better off without one. Too much fluoride will produce tiny white spots on the surfaces of her teeth.

Exactly how she is fed at various ages. Very little fluoride passes into breast milk so a baby who is *exclusively* breast-fed may benefit from daily fluoride drops from birth.

If she is bottle-fed, or breast-fed with occasional supplementary bottles, her need for fluoride will depend not only on the amount which is in the water with which the bottles are made up, but also on the formula which is used. Some manufacturers add fluoride along with other minerals.

Once she is being weaned and is also drinking ordinary cow's milk, her fluoride needs will have to be reassessed. In a low fluoride area she will almost certainly benefit from daily drops or tablets; in an area with some natural fluoride in the water a small supplement may still be considered safely desirable while in a high fluoride area she may get plenty.

A time to encourage sucking

Sucking is not only a means of getting nourishment, it is also a baby's greatest pleasure. Fortunately, at this stage of life, it is to be encouraged, from the dental point of view. The more the muscles of her mouth, jaw and face are exercised, the better they will play their proper role in steering those first teeth into their proper places. Breast-feeding makes a baby work ideally hard at sucking, but bottles, fists, thumbs and pacifiers can all be useful. Do read the notes on malocclusion, though (*see below* Looking after teeth) because while sucking is excellent for teeth which have not yet emerged, it becomes progressively less desirable for teeth which are actually through.

Cutting the first teeth

Teeth are usually cut in a certain order but may do so on a widely varying time-scale. There is no advantage or disadvantage in cutting them early or late. The timing has no connection with a baby being generally "forward" or "backward" in overall development. At *least* six months on either side of the following "average ages" counts as entirely within the normal range.

The first tooth: usually a lower central incisor. The incisors are the flat teeth in the front of the mouth and they tend to appear in pairs. The very first tooth will probably be one of the lower pair and the second will probably be the one next to it. Six months is a usual time to see the first one. The second will probably appear before the next pair begin:

The third tooth: an upper central incisor. One of the top central incisors will probably be seen at about seven to eight months and its matching pair will emerge soon after to be closely followed by:

The fifth to eighth teeth: lateral incisors (the lower ones tend to appear first). With a pair of incisors in the front of either jaw the baby will next produce an incisor on either side of each. These four teeth will probably begin to emerge at around nine months.

The ninth to twelfth teeth: first molars (the lower ones tend to appear first). With four teeth along the front of each jaw the baby will now produce the first molars which are not next door to the existing teeth but one space away. You may see the first of these four at around ten months; they will probably all be in at around fourteen months.

The thirteenth to sixteenth teeth: the canines (the lower ones tend to appear first). These are the more pointed teeth which fill in the four spaces left between the lateral incisors and the first molars. They will tend to appear between sixteen and eighteen months.

The seventeenth to twentieth teeth: second molars (the lower ones tend to appear first). These are the final four which appear behind the first molars in each corner of the child's jaw. They usually come through towards the end of the second year.

● If a child does not have a complete set of twenty first teeth by the time she is three (or if she should have an extra one) it is important to show her mouth to a dentist (*see below*). It is important to her later dentition that these first ones should all be present and correctly placed. And it is important to her maturing jaw and face that the permanent teeth take up their proper positions.

Teething

Cutting teeth is probably not nearly as uncomfortable for babies as many people think. The "crankiness" which is often put down to teething may well be due to other factors in her development, such as an increasing need for company in the second half of the first year. If the fact that you think she is "teething" makes it easier for you to be sympathetic with such moods and feelings, fine. It often *is* easier to go on being patient with a grumpy baby if she is thought to have a *physical* discomfort. But don't ever let yourself believe that any physical symptoms more important than dribble are due to those teeth:

If your baby has a temperature she is unwell; if she goes off her food she is unwell; if she vomits she is probably unwell; if she keeps crying while rubbing an ear she probably has earache. All these are signs of probable illness and should be treated as such: of course, she may be teething as well. . . .

Aids to teething babies

If your baby really does seem restless and irritable when a tooth is coming through, and she has no symptoms of illness (or has been checked by her doctor), any of the following tricks may help. The chances are that the main effect is to make you feel you are doing something for her and therefore for her to feel your confidence. Still, if it makes you both feel better, where's the harm?

She may like to chew. Chewing is good for babies anyway so she cannot have too much practice. She will chew her own fingers—and yours—but she can have harder, nicer-tasting, things as well. You can offer obvious things like teething rings or other things like scrubbed carrots or hard rusks. If she is too young to hold them, hold them for her and let her really work at them.

● Watch out for choking. A toothless baby may chew a rusk until pieces are soft enough to go down her throat. A baby with one or two brand-new teeth may grate a tiny piece off that carrot and choke. Even the earliest chewing is a game for her to play when she is sitting up and has your attention (*see* **Accidents**/Choking).

She may like cool things in her mouth. Some teething rings are filled with a gel which cools and holds its low temperature if it is kept in the refrigerator between sessions. Failing that, those carrots may be more acceptable from the refrigerator.

● Don't give her ice, or even rub unwrapped ice on affected gums. It could damage the covering of the gum.

She may like to have her gums rubbed. Dip your finger in ice-cold water first for maximum effect. Unless your doctor advises it, don't rub any teething gels on her gums. Some of them contain local anesthetic agents which, while they may comfort her, are neither necessary nor desirable. A few contain aspirin-like chemicals which could overdose her. Some, which you may be offered if you are abroad on holiday, even contain alcohol. Others contain sugar, just what you do *not* want to put on an emerging tooth.

Losing first teeth and cutting permanent ones

Your child is going to lose twenty teeth and acquire twenty-eight to thirty-two. Those permanent teeth are not only more numerous than the ones they replace but also much larger and often not so white. Prepare yourself not only for that (often enchanting) gappiness, but also for a child with a decidedly mixed set.

At around six. The first permanent teeth start to emerge. They are the four molars which come in behind the existing baby teeth, without displacing any. Your child's mouth now has four new "corners."

At around seven. Those first four front incisors will be shed, one by one, and your child will have various "gaps" until the permanent ones have completed their replacement at around ten.

Eight to ten. The first and second "first" molars will gradually be shed, one by one, to be replaced by the eight permanent pre-molars. Your child will now have twenty-four teeth.

Ten to thirteen. The canines loosen, come out and are replaced, while the second permanent molars appear behind those first, six-year-old molars. By the time your child is around fifteen, this stage will be completed and she will have twenty-eight permanent teeth.

Fifteen upwards. The third permanent molars (the "wisdom teeth") may or may not appear (*see below* Some dental problems of adolescence).

Looking after teeth

The principles of looking after teeth apply as much to the first as to the permanent ones. Your child is going to have to use most of them for many years; furthermore, their presence, position and health can affect the permanent teeth you cannot yet see. Don't bank on that second (and final) set to correct the mistakes or omissions of the early years, such as:

Not cleaning the first few teeth

Of course, two or three single teeth do not need the full suggested routine, but if you read the notes on why teeth need cleaning, you will see that it is a good idea to clean the surfaces of even her very first tooth on a regular basis. Wiping them carefully with a piece of damp gauze each morning and evening will be a help.

Allowing first teeth to spend hours bathed in sweet fluids

A child who has ten teeth with holes in them at the age of four or five has almost always been allowed one of the following:

A bottle with which to suck herself to sleep, filled with milk or juice. Often it stays in her mouth for occasional sipping through the night.

A "dinky feeder" filled with juice or syrup to use instead of a pacifier.

A pacifier dipped in sugar, honey or some other sweet stickiness.

Do remember that these habits are truly pernicious for teeth *and are in your control.* Your baby may need a pacifier; fine. But if you never dip it in anything sweet she is never going to think of demanding it, any more than she can think of the joy of taking her bottle to bed. If you let these habits start she really may refuse to go to sleep without (*see below* Sugar, sweets and dental decay).

Conniving with comfort habits (see Habits) which may lead to malocclusion

Many of the kinds of comfort sucking which babies enjoy are good for them on every level *provided that they do not go on, too intensively, for too long.* Some will tend to misplace first teeth, and possibly the teeth which are to follow, if they continue for hours each day until the child is five or six.

If your baby has a pacifier that's fine if, as she reaches a year, you can gradually confine its use to the few minutes before she drops off to sleep. If she prefers her own thumb or fingers, that's fine too provided she does not suck for too long, too often. It is the child who sucks on something in a particular way, for long periods of every day, right through pre-school, who may do damage.

Not taking toddlers for dental check-ups

Most dentists prefer to meet a patient for the first time when she is two or three years old. Regular supervision will help to prevent anything from going wrong; early recognition will make any treatment easy and painless; practice will make later trips to the dentist an accepted part of life.

Letting young children care for their own teeth too soon

A child will not have the fine coordination to care for her teeth properly until she is at least five, perhaps older. If she cannot yet manage a pencil well enough to begin to write, she will not manage brush and floss. Encourage her to help, but keep the responsibility yourself.

Dentists' knowledge of the causes of decay has increased dramatically in recent years and their recommendations for home care have changed with it. If you understand modern thinking, the time you spend supervising the care of your children's teeth will be used effectively:

Why teeth need cleaning: plaque

Plaque is a thin film of sticky material which forms all over teeth all the time. On this film bacteria breed, feeding on the food we put in our mouths and releasing acid as they break down sugars (*see below*). Left undisturbed, the plaque layer gets thicker and thicker and provides a home for more and more bacteria. As they use up the oxygen in that sticky layer, the environment becomes acceptable to anaerobic bacteria and it is the gases which these release that are most often responsible for bad breath (halitosis). That sticky plaque is not only the breeding ground for all these acid-producing bacteria: it is also the glue which holds them against the tooth enamel. Over time, that acid will eat into the enamel and make the entry point for the bacteria which will then produce caries. Left undisturbed for long enough, some of that plaque will harden into the chalky white deposit called tartar, only removable with special dental tools.

Obviously that sticky layer of plaque will sometimes be disturbed by things we eat (this is the argument for crisp foods like apples). But unless steps are taken to remove it, it will certainly accumulate down the sides of the teeth, where they butt against each other, in the irregularities in molars and around the bottom where the tooth goes into the gum.

The more efficiently plaque is regularly removed, the fewer bacteria there will be in the mouth to produce acid from food, and the less "glue" there will be to hold that dangerous combination against the enamel.

How to keep plaque at bay

It takes about twenty-four hours for plaque to build up to a tooth-damaging level if the teeth were adequately cleaned the time before. Once-daily cleaning that was really thorough would be enough. Twice-daily is a better bet for families because somebody is bound to skimp sometimes. But it is certainly better for a child to clean properly once a day than to give her teeth a quick token scrub morning and evening.

It is best to get your dentist to show you how to clean your child's teeth so that you first do it correctly yourself and you then teach her correctly, too. The principles are:

As soon as she has any teeth at all, wipe each one carefully every day, with a piece of damp gauze.

As soon as she has molars and teeth with next-door neighbors, switch to a brush.

Use a softish brush with a small head. Scrub every surface of each tooth, quite gently, but quickly so that you swirl off the film. If you want to use toothpaste make sure it is a fluoride one. This is an excellent way of regularly applying fluoride to the tooth surfaces.

You have now cleaned plaque off all the outer surfaces of the teeth but not off the cracks between them or the margins where they go into the gum. *You cannot do this with a brush.*

Follow brushing by using a length of dental floss which you work gently in between each pair of teeth so that it rubs against every surface. Then bring it around the base of each tooth so that it clears that gum margin. Be gentle (with her or with yourself). Unlike the old hard brushes, dental floss should never hurt or make healthy gums bleed.

When cleaning is most important

It would be ideal for *teeth* to be thoroughly cleaned whenever food was eaten and therefore the resident bacteria were busily making acid. But it would not be ideal for *people*, few of whom are going to carry toothbrushes and dental floss with them to school, to college or to work. The most vital time to remove plaque and bacteria is before the night. If the teeth are cleaned after the last food of the evening there will not be much acid formed to attack them while the child is asleep. Cleaning them again after breakfast will give them a good start to the day, too.

But this regime, even if the cleaning is really thorough, will not prevent all caries in all children. What she eats, and when and how she eats it, will affect her teeth, too.

Sugar, sweets and dental decay

Everyone knows that sweets are "bad for the teeth" but not everyone understands exactly why this is so. The following points are designed to help you work out a sensible family policy concerning sweets and to help you avoid the waste of effort involved in trying to ban *sweets* while freely allowing all kinds of other highly sweetened foods (*see also* **Eating**/Common sense about family eating: Common sense about sweets). Sugar is "worse" for teeth than any other foodstuff because:

It feeds the acid-producing bacteria in the mouth rapidly and directly so that a sugary mouth is both acid and hospitable to bacteria.

Other foods—such as bread—are broken down much more slowly by the bacteria. This means that the bread particles may be cleansed out of the mouth by the flow of saliva before enamel-attacking acid is produced. If a particle of such a food is caught between two teeth so that saliva cannot sweep it away, it will still take time before it is broken down into the sugars which will produce acid and that is time during which the next brushing-flossing session is approaching.

Sugary foods are often sticky. The more sticky a sweet food, the more likely it is that fragments will be trapped between teeth or in their crevices; that overall stickiness will help the sugar to adhere to the plaque all over the teeth.

These points apply to every kind of sugar and all sugary foods. Bacteria do not produce acid more readily if fed on refined white sugar rather than brown, or honey rather than an apple. The only differences, in terms of dental health, are the differences in the concentration of sugar and that stickiness. A spoonful of white sugar, for example, produces a rapid burst of acid in the mouth but it is acid which can be washed away comparatively easily. An apple has less concentrated sugar and the flow of saliva caused by chewing will help to wash it away, but it may leave pieces of skin wedged between teeth. Catalogue sweet foods, then, in terms of their sugar concentration and their texture. If you do this, you will see that while sweets (always concentrated sugar and often sticky, too) are obviously dangerous, so is sticky cake or gingerbread and so, sadly, are the items some parents often offer instead of sweets. Worst offender here is probably the raisin.

But sweets may still be the worst hazards to your child's teeth for reasons which have to do with her eating habits rather than the sugar content or texture.

Every time a concentrated dose of sugar is taken into the mouth it takes about twenty minutes for the saliva to neutralize the acid and wash the mouth clean. If there are trapped particles which saliva cannot reach, acid will remain in close contact with the tooth for much longer, but twenty minutes of risk is an educated average guess. If your child eats an apple or a slice of bread and honey or a piece of cake, she is likely to eat it all and then stop. Twenty minutes afterwards her mouth will be back to normal. But if she eats a sweet she is very likely to suck it slowly. All the time she is sucking, sugar is being released and acid is being formed. She is also very likely to follow that sweet with another and then another. Indeed, she may eat several sweets every half hour for several hours, getting slowly through a quarter-pound package during a trip, for example. If she does this her teeth will be in a dangerously acid environment throughout.

Sweet *foods* are usually eaten at mealtimes. This both restricts the number of times per day that acid assaults the tooth enamel and makes it likely that a teeth-cleaning session will soon follow. Sweets, on the other hand, are most usually eaten between meals and, very usually, in circumstances where teeth-cleaning is most unlikely. Watch commuters eating them in cars and trains, children eating them on their way to and from school and whole families settling down with them at the movies or in front of television sets.

A sensible sugar policy While every family must decide for itself how seriously it will take the threat to teeth posed by sugar and sweets, and what attitude it will take to sugar on other, perhaps moral, grounds, a plan like the following would allow your child to enjoy sweets and sweet foods without posing any extra threat to her teeth at all. All you have to remember is that the shorter the time sugar remains in her mouth, and the less often it is put there, the less acid will be made and the less likely it is that it will eat into tooth enamel. So:

Give sweets and other sweet sticky foods immediately before teeth-cleaning. If your child is going to clean her teeth after supper, there is no reason why she cannot finish the meal with her favorite dessert and/or some sweets. But watch out for fool-traps like that mug of hot chocolate *after* she has cleaned her teeth and before she goes to sleep. If she likes sweetened cereal and toast and jam for breakfast, they will do no harm if she cleans afterwards.

If she has sweets and other sweet foods at other times of day, keep them to mealtimes. She is going to eat some lunch anyway. If she adds a sweet food to that sandwich and apple, or a sweet to the school's apple tart, she will not be much increasing the risk to her teeth. It is if she eats the apple tart, gives her mouth time to neutralize the acid and then starts eating sweets at 3 p.m. that she is really putting her teeth at extra risk.

If she has sweets between meals control the type. If you are being fairly liberal about sweets and sweet foods, you may find that a family ban on the very worst kinds—like caramels—is easily accepted. Chocolate will do far less harm.

Encourage her to munch and finish. If she is to be allowed three individual sweets or a tiny package, or thirty cents worth or whatever, encourage her to eat them all immediately. Try never to let her just have sweets *available*, to nibble when she pleases. Again, this is not a difficult rule to enforce: you would not let her keep a large slice of bread in her room to nibble on throughout the day, would you?

● You will obviously have to set an example here. If you nibble sweets you cannot expect her not to. Equally, if you keep a well-stocked sweet tin or a large box of chocolates lying around the house, she is bound to help herself.

Don't offer sweet alternatives to sweets. Those raisins may give you a virtuous feeling that you are avoiding giving your child those nasty commercial sweets, but they will be no less harmful to her teeth.

Try to make readily available snacks from savory foods (*see* **Eating**/ Common sense about family eating: Some common sense "snack policies"). Many of the snacks children eat *are* sweet because it is sweet foods which are attractively packaged and heavily advertised for them. But there are a range of these "high status" snacks in the savory bracket too (such as potato chips, popcorn and nuts) and it is just as quick and easy to give a child a cracker with cheese as a sweet, chocolate-covered cookie. Older children may enjoy having the week's snack foods left pre-prepared in the refrigerator so that they know there are celery sticks, tiny tomatoes and cubes of cheese readily available.

Remember that a child can "buy" a sweet indulgence by cleaning her teeth. If she wants a slice of cake for her mid-morning snack and you don't want her to have it, "You can eat and then clean or not eat and not clean" will often seem a fair bargain.

Remember that sweet drinks contain sugar. Some families are careful, or even strict, about sweets and sugary foods, yet take a nearly constant consumption of sweet drinks for granted. Don't. A constant intake of cola or its equivalent certainly will not help your child's teeth. Once again, restricting sweet drinks to mealtimes, and encouraging plain water in between, is usually the answer.

Additional protection for teeth

Fluoride

While it is important that your child take into her body the optimum amount of fluoride for healthy, decay-resistant enamel (*see above*), fluoride which is applied to the enamel itself (topical fluoride) can also strengthen teeth. This is the only dental reason for using a toothpaste when brushing. Non-fluoride toothpaste is nothing but a pleasant taste.

Your dentist may also suggest one of various methods of applying more concentrated fluoride to your child's teeth. There are various fluoride gels and paints available and he will probably have his own favored one.

Other cleaning aids

Toothpaste is useful if it contains fluoride or encourages brushing.

Electric toothbrushes can do an efficient job, provided they substitute only for the ordinary brush, not for the floss. Bought to encourage a reluctant older child, they will probably only be effective while the novelty lasts.

Mouthwashes sweeten the breath by masking the odor which is usually caused by gas-producing bacteria in neglected plaque. If you buy them at all, don't let them be used to put off necessary visits to the dentist or dental hygienist or to substitute for teeth-cleaning. They cannot remove plaque.

Fluoride mouthwashes are another way of bringing fluoride into contact with the teeth but, if your dentist wants your child to have topical fluoride on her teeth, he has more effective ways of putting it there.

Water jets and other irrigating devices. These can be effective in removing *loose* food particles, useful to a child who wears braces or to someone with extensive bridgework. They do not remove plaque though.

Toothpicks, etc. Many types now exist but none are as good, or as safe for a child to use, as dental floss.

Chewing gum does not clean teeth. Sweetened gum does the opposite.

Rinsing the mouth with water may remove harmful food debris, especially sugar, so it is better than nothing, but rinsing cannot remove plaque.

Eating crisp food might dislodge some food particles and might even break up some of the plaque layer, but it will also leave its own bits and pieces and its own bacteria-feeding sugars in the mouth. Don't rely on it. A rinse with water is certainly better; neither is adequate.

Treatment by a dentist

The more regularly a child visits a dentist the less treatment she will need—now, or in the future. Ideally, you should have a family dentist just as you have a family doctor. Someone who knows you all, and sees each child at every stage of her life, will be far better able to advise you well and treat everyone without upset than someone who sees you for the first (and perhaps the only) time because of an emergency. Unfortunately, this is not always easy. In the United States, such visits can be expensive enough to deter parents unless their children have toothache. In Britain, by no means every dentist welcomes time-consuming small children onto his already full lists.

If possible, take your child to the dentist for the first time when she is around two (unless, of course, you have had worries about her teeth even earlier). This is a "get to know you" visit. She may never sit in the chair (or only in your lap), she may not even open her mouth while the dentist is looking, but even if she does not, it will make next time easier.

Try to schedule appointments every six months after that. If you really take your child that often to the dentist, as well as looking after her teeth as outlined above and as he shows you, there is no reason why any major treatment should ever be needed. Good dentistry is almost all preventative. And that applies even to the tiny cavity which appears despite your best efforts and which he can fill so easily at this early stage.

Helping your child to tolerate dentistry
Try to remember that dentistry really has changed since you were a child. If yours becomes frightened, it is as likely to be due to her sensing your tension as to genuine pain. The high-speed drills of today neither vibrate nor take so long as the old ones did. First teeth can often have a tiny cavity filled without any need for an injection. If an injection is needed (perhaps because the dentist can see that he is likely to touch a nerve, he will not wait until the child yells to decide), the child can have a local anesthetic jelly rubbed onto the gum first, after which most injections can be given almost painlessly with the dentist putting the anesthetic in very slowly so that the tissues are numbed ahead of his advancing needle. It is not all *fun.* Few people, even today, actually enjoy fillings, but it really is not the horror it once was.

As part of his routine treatment your dentist will probably want his hygienist to clean the child's teeth so that every bit of plaque is removed. Do remember that if plaque has been left in peace to form tartar, this has to be "chipped" off down the cracks between the teeth and along the gum margin and can be unpleasant. Dental floss can save your child that discomfort.

The dentist will also keep a close eye on the child's emerging teeth and on the ones that are loosening. Occasionally a first tooth needs to be taken out because it is delaying a permanent tooth or getting in its way. If he knows your child well, the dentist will be able to advise on the kind of anesthesia she should have for an extraction. Most (especially the extraction of first teeth which have small roots and whose roots may, in any case, have begun to be reabsorbed ready for natural shedding) can be taken out with a local anesthetic and little trouble. Most dentists believe that no general anesthetic of any kind should ever be given to a patient unless there is a second professional present, to act as anesthetist. If a single-handed anesthetic should ever be suggested for your child, you might prefer to delay until there can be a second person, or to go elsewhere.

With a close eye kept on her teeth, any irregularity or misspacing can be rapidly corrected as soon as it begins. Very early orthodontic treatment is now generally accepted as saving both time and money. Your nine-year-old will not mind wearing braces now, nearly as much as she would mind later, and if it is done now she probably will not have to wear them for nearly as long.

Some dental emergencies

Toothache   Sudden excruciating toothache is usually due to a cavity in which bacteria are living, breeding and producing acid. The pain starts at the moment when that acid finally breaks through the base of the cavity and touches the nerve. Often this kind of intense pain starts when the child has been eating something sweet: the sugar produces a burst of acid from the resident bacteria.

Use a really good light and try, with the child, to identify the painful tooth. Use a toothbrush to clean out the cavity (or what look to you like the normal indentations on the tooth) really well. If you can clean it of all food particles and most of the bacteria, the pain will stop in a few minutes because no more acid will be produced to penetrate.

● Don't let the complete relief of the pain deter you from making an immediate appointment with the dentist. It will recur when she next eats.

A second type of toothache sometimes starts off less dramatically with a dull throbbing ache which comes and goes. Neglected, it may suddenly wake the child in the night. The tooth is agony to touch or bite down on. The gum, or even the side of the face, may be swollen. Decay in the tooth has killed its nerve and made an abscess. The memorable pain is the result of pressure from gas and/or pus confined inside. Nothing but opening it up to relieve the pressure will fully cure the pain.

Sometimes the tooth will "open itself up" by making a gum boil through which to discharge gas and pus. Sometimes the dentist will drill an opening. Sometimes the tooth will have to be removed. Just occasionally, if the infection is dealt with by antibiotics, the whole affair may settle so that the original cavity can be filled.

For the moment, try cleaning out the tooth as discussed above. Pain may be being made worse by foodstuff pressing through the cavity onto the nerve.

The child may be more comfortable well propped up so that the blood does not feel as if it pounds through her head quite so strongly. Aspirin, or a compound of aspirin with codeine, will help relieve the pain (*see* **Pain and Pain Control**).

If you cannot get her to the dentist within the next few hours—especially if there is visible swelling—take her to your doctor. He will prescribe antibiotics if he thinks them advisable. If she is in a great deal of pain he may even prescribe something to help her through the waiting time. Whether she sees the doctor or not, she needs the first possible appointment with the dentist.

When a tooth is knocked out

Front teeth are vulnerable, especially in toddlers who tumble and in eight- to ten-year-olds playing gang or team games. Apart from obvious safety precautions (*see* **Safety**/On wheels):

Always use a seat belt, if a child travels in the front of the car.

Always use a safety car seat or belt for a young child in the back.

Encourage your child to use a mouth guard for contact sports (these are gradually becoming more usual in junior high school games. You cannot encourage your child to do what he thinks will make him appear a "sissy," but if anyone wears protection, encourage him to do likewise).

If you can find the tooth, wipe or rinse it and put it back in its socket, pressing it in as far as it will go. Make for the nearest dentist. If you cannot bear to do this (perhaps because the mouth is also cut) either wrap the tooth in a damp tissue or, if she is old enough and calm enough, get the child to hold it in her cheek or under her tongue while you make for the nearest dentist.

A first tooth which is reimplanted in this way will usually give good service until the child's permanent replacement is almost ready to come through.

A permanent tooth will not usually survive for more than two or three years after being reimplanted. Dentists are trying to find ways of preventing the roots from reabsorbing.

When a tooth is broken

Assess whether or not the chip or fracture has exposed or penetrated the nerve. If it has the child will be in pain. Assess whether or not the tooth is now sharp or jagged enough to be dangerous to the child's lip.

If either of these is the case, treat as an emergency and make for the nearest dentist.

If there is no pain and no sharpness, make the first possible appointment with your own dentist (if much delay is suggested make sure his receptionist understands that a tooth is broken). Assure the child that the tooth can be repaired so that the final result is indistinguishable from a whole tooth. With the use of liquid quartz, a perfect result can often be achieved without the extensive drilling (and expense) of a cap.

Some dental problems of adolescence

Wisdom teeth

The third molars, way back in the jaw, do not always emerge. They may stay there, visible only to X-rays, causing no problems. Your dentist may check on their position/progress from time to time during the adolescent years.

Sometimes a wisdom tooth begins to push up but, without emerging through the gum, becomes jammed up against the root system of the second molar. This can be a very painful situation. The dentist should certainly be consulted if there is pressure pain. Neglected, that pressure may build up and cause swelling of the face and sometimes of the gum, or even the tissues at the very back of the mouth and top of the throat.

Wisdom teeth which will neither emerge nor lie dormant usually have to be removed surgically. This will be done with a general anesthetic and your child should allow for several days' discomfort and recuperation afterwards.

Sometimes a wisdom tooth begins to emerge, cannot find enough space for itself, and causes pain by pressing against the second molar. "Impacted" wisdom teeth are often removed under local anesthesia but the extraction is also often remembered with some horror. If your child is offered a general anesthetic, you may like to encourage her to accept. These teeth are large and very deep-rooted. Even once they are visible they cannot just be pulled out. The force needed to pry and lever them is very unpleasant. There will be considerable soreness afterwards.

Bleeding gums (gingivitis)

Periodontal (gum) diseases are more usual in adult life than in childhood, but mild episodes of gingivitis sometimes occur in adolescence, especially if new independence breaches old habits of dental hygiene.

In gingivitis, the margins of gum around the teeth become swollen and delicate so that they bleed when the teeth are brushed. While there may be actual infection from the bacteria in plaque which has been allowed to accumulate and work its way into those margins, the condition can be due to that plaque solidifying into deep-seated tartar which is causing inflammation. In either case, especially thorough brushing and flossing, despite the bleeding which this causes, should clear the condition within a few days. Your child should *not* avoid brushing a particular area because it bleeds, as only cleansing will cure. If gingivitis is long-lasting or recurrent, she should see the dentist. It may be that tartar has penetrated deeply and must be professionally removed.

Bad breath (halitosis)

Although bad breath can be caused by digestive upsets and, of course, by the lingering smell of garlic and other foods, the most common cause is lack of dental hygiene. If plaque accumulates so that it can provide an oxygen-free environment for anaerobic bacteria, these will join the others which are already resident in the mouth. The gas which is given off by their activity is hydrogen sulphide, the same gas which comes out of sewers. Don't let your child assume the smell is from decaying food particles: it is not, so just brushing out all particles will not deal with halitosis. It is the plaque which has to be attacked.

Television

Modern Western societies are notable for their reliance on mass facilities made available by advanced technology. Television is one such facility and the target for much worry and complaint. Is it bad for children? Does it destroy family life/conversation/individuality? Is it depriving us of the habit of reading for pleasure or of providing our own entertainment? Would families be better off if it did not exist at all? Would individual families be better off if they had no sets in their homes? While every family must pose and answer questions of this kind for itself, it is perhaps important to remember that exactly the same issues are raised by other products of high technology which are largely accepted without comment. Would our society be better off without private cars, for example? However bad the influence of television may sometimes be, it certainly does not kill as many people as cars do. Would we be better off without advertising and mass marketing? However difficult it may be to escape television culture, it would be even more difficult to get back to home production of all a family needs. Would we be better off without computers, without the thousands of facilities made possible by the microchip, without worldwide instant communication networks? Perhaps; but these things are fundamental to our society's organization and inveighing against them is not going to remove them from our lives. We have to learn to live with them and to control them so that they do not control us. The same applies to television.

You can, of course, decide that you will *not* live with television; that you will not have a set in the house. But absence of a set will not mean that you have banished the medium's influence. Other children will tell yours about the programs they see. If you will not allow them to watch on their friends' sets they will be left out of many games/fantasies/in-group jokes and "languages." And they will miss out on some information which even their teachers assume they will have. If they may watch in friends' houses you may find that, far from having more family conversation than other people, you have less because your children are always next door. Looking at the main criticisms of television made by parents during a research project, it does look as though it is better to *regard television as a facility*, and concentrate on *using it well* rather than pretending, or wishing, that it did not exist.

Common worries about children and television

Television takes up so much time that children play/talk/read/study too little. But television takes up just exactly the amount of your child's time as he spends sitting watching it. How much time that is must be up to you.

Figures for the average hours spent viewing, by children of different ages, are alarmingly high. But why do they watch for so long, so often? Could it be that, because television programs are available and can be counted upon to keep children quiet and out of mischief, other activities (especially those which will involve adults) are not provided? Would he watch all Saturday morning if you were keen to take him out or play a game or entertain his friends? Would she insist on watching right up to bedtime if her father was waiting to read the next installment of their bedtime story?

Television is all tripe. But television programs *vary*. Whatever your personal definition of "tripe" you will certainly find plenty, but you will find plenty else, too.

Selective viewing apart, the sheer volume of information made available to every one of us through this medium must never be ignored. Children who grew up before it was available labored under an ignorance which now seems incredible. Many, for example, had never seen a person of a different race or color from themselves; had never seen an environment (large city, high mountain, ocean, snowscape) foreign to their own; had never seen this planet's creatures outside the confines of a zoo or looked down a microscope or inside an operating room. Many simply did not know that there *were* people who talked differently from their neighbors; families who lived differently; people who worked at jobs not locally available. And few people, of course, had actually seen the rich or famous and shared their privileged activities, or seen the lives of the impoverished and shared their pain. If your child knows what a lighthouse is like, he probably saw one on television. If he can tell you the difference between a brown bear and a polar, that will be television, too. And if he has seen a wide range of plays and movies, most of those will have been through television because few families have the money or the facilities to take their children regularly to the movies or the theater.

Television takes over children's lives so that they all play "Batman." Children have always created subcultures for themselves so that they could share imaginative play and hero worship. They use the stimuli which adults make available to them (*see* **Play**) and create for themselves. Batman is not the worst that can be offered. The children of Northern Ireland use playgroup Lego to make guns. Ask them, "Now shall we make something nicer?" and many will reply, "When we've finished these we're going to make gasoline bombs."

Television violence makes children behave violently. Nobody knows whether this is literally true or not. The occasional murderous youth says that he copied his monstrous methods from television drama, but others maintain (without such publicity) that they copied theirs from brutal real-life adults or the sadistic sections of pornographic magazines. The truth is probably that a violent *society* produces violent people *and* screens violent "entertainment." *See also* **Discipline, Self-Discipline and Learning How to Behave**/Television and violence.

Tips from parents who use television rather than letting it use them

Keep viewing as a positive decision/activity from the beginning. That means that, from toddlerhood onwards, children are encouraged to have particular programs which they watch, which are planned for and switched on for them, but that the set is *never* switched, or left, on "to see what's on" or because "I'm bored" or as background "company."

Many families forbid young children to turn on the TV for themselves, pointing out that such a ban is no more authoritarian than forbidding children to help themselves to ice cream from the freezer.

As children get older, the positive approach to viewing is kept up by buying, and encouraging them to use, the television guides, and, when necessary, to choose between available programs. These parents seldom recommend rigid rationing of viewing-time; this only increases the likelihood of children seeing television as a constant good of which they cannot get enough. Furthermore, a "ration" contradicts the central idea of selective viewing: that the family watches television when, but only when, there is a program people genuinely want to see.

Keep viewing sociable. Very young children can get little benefit from viewing without an adult, because even the most excellent children's program cannot be geared to each child's attention span, need to play out what he has just seen, and bewilderment when he returns to find that it has moved on without him. Children who habitually watch with parents and/or older brothers and sisters take *talking about programs* for granted. Many of these families maintain that family viewing creates at least as much conversation as it quashes.

Avoid using television as a babysitter. If a child is encouraged to view because it suits you, rather than because the program suits him, the positive-viewing attitude will be lost.

Make sure the whole household follows the same line. If he knows that you watch all evening, as soon as he has gone to bed, or he finds you dozing in front of a movie you are clearly not enjoying, he will quickly adopt the same habits.

Remember that extras like video recorders may assist positive viewing. These families insist that, far from leading to even more viewing, a recorder can help selectivity because it enables the family to escape from the networks' scheduling and see the programs they want to see at times which suit them.

Temper *see* **Tantrums.** *See also* **Discipline, Self-discipline and Learning How to Behave/**
Some common issues in discipline: Violence.
Temperature *see* **Nursing**/Fever. *See also* **Infection**/Types of infection: Infections which cause illness.
Testes *see* **Adolescence**/Puberty. *See also* **Mumps; Undescended Testicle**.

Tetanus ("Lockjaw")

Tetanus is not an infectious disease in the sense of being one which can be passed from victim to victim. But it is an extremely serious illness which still kills thousands in the developing countries and is a potential threat to everyone. Its rarity is due to immunization. Carelessness in following recommended immunization programs, including later boosters, is often due to misunderstandings about the nature of the infection; this is tragic as the disease is, and is likely to remain, very much easier to prevent than to treat (*see* **Immunization; Infection**). Tetanus is caused by bacteria with two important characteristics:

They are spore-forming bacteria and, while the bacteria themselves are normally sensitive to antibiotics and to a variety of sterilization and disinfection procedures, as well as requiring particular conditions in which to live and multiply, the spores are a different matter. Tetanus spores are highly resistant to heat and to chemicals, to drying, etc. They can remain in a state one might call "suspended animation," for long periods in conditions which would provide no sustenance for the living bacteria. When and if circumstances become ideal, the spores produce active bacteria, which, in their turn, produce more spores.

The bacteria themselves are anaerobic, meaning that they flourish and multiply only under conditions where there is no, or very little, oxygen. Their normal habitats include soil and the bowel content of many animals. Living tetanus bacilli can normally be found deep in the earth of a garden or in the droppings of a horse or goat. Spores are frequent inhabitants of road dust or surface soil.

Infection by tetanus

These bacteria and their spores are harmless while they remain outside the body or if they are swallowed and thus taken into the digestive system. Your child will not "get tetanus" from sucking fingers contaminated with manure-enriched soil. But if these bacteria or their spores are introduced into a wound which happens to provide anaerobic conditions, infection may take place.

A wound which is liable to active infection by tetanus is one where there is tissue without much blood supply and therefore with very little oxygen, contaminated by the kind of "dirt" which is liable to contain tetanus organisms. Most of the world's deaths from tetanus occur where the umbilical cords of newborn babies are either cut with contaminated instruments or actually "dressed" with cow dung. That cut cord, designed to dry up and shrivel, provides both a low-oxygen environment and a route into the baby's bloodstream. While any large or deep wound incurred out of doors (on the battlefield or in road accidents, for example) carries a risk of tetanus infection, much less serious injuries of particular kinds carry the risk, too. A small but deep burn, for example, kills tissue and may provide an ideal breeding ground for tetanus organisms if it is contaminated. A deep puncture wound damages tissue to a considerable depth, yet rapidly seals itself at the surface, thus cutting off the external oxygen from the interior of the wound. If tetanus organisms were introduced by whatever made the wound (a barnyard nail, for example) and if the wound does not itself have an excellent oxygen-carrying blood supply, the risk is very real.

Tetanus bacilli merely colonize a wound, they do not themselves invade the body. They cause disease by releasing a toxin (infinitely more poisonous than strychnine) which affects the nerves and the central nervous system. Damage to the nerves leads to muscular spasms (often first affecting the jaw, hence the popular name for this disease: lockjaw). These spasms may increase to generalized convulsions and eventually to death from asphyxia.

Treatment of tetanus

In a modern hospital, a tetanus victim receives intensive nursing and supportive care, combined with muscle relaxants to banish or reduce the spasms, and, if necessary, assistance with breathing. He will be given antibiotics to halt the multiplication of bacteria in his wound. The wound itself will also be energetically treated, to remove all dead tissue and thus expose any bacteria to oxygen. Tetanus anti-toxin will be given to neutralize the effects of the poison but, while this can effectively prevent *further* nerve damage, it cannot touch toxins which have already invaded nerves.

Prevention of tetanus

Immunization against tetanus is not aimed at producing antibodies against tetanus bacteria but against the toxins they release. Tetanus toxoid is the "T" in the triple vaccine given to infants. It is highly effective, but *must be "boosted,"* at five years and about ten-yearly, if high levels of protection are to be maintained (*see* **Immunization**).

In an immunized individual, a booster of tetanus toxoid, given at the time of a risky injury, rapidly increases the level of protection. But in an unimmunized individual tetanus toxoid at the time of injury is useless. One injection cannot produce enough immunity quickly enough to be of any use on this occasion.

Until quite recently, unimmunized individuals (or those whose immunization was years out of date) were given tetanus anti-toxin to confer passive immunity to the infection in a susceptible wound. Although anti-toxin clearly saved many lives during the First World War (when toxoid was not yet available) and was used, as well as immunization with toxoid, for soldiers wounded in the Second World War, it is now discredited in many places. Despite extremely careful refinement, many individuals are hypersensitive to the horse serum from which the anti-toxin is derived.

Hospital treatment of susceptible wounds in unimmunized individuals now tends to consist of measures designed to prevent tetanus bacilli from multiplying and therefore releasing toxin, and simultaneously to prevent tetanus spores from finding the right circumstances in which to come alive. Very careful cleaning of wounds to remove all damaged tissue and thus expose tetanus organisms to the oxygen in the circulation and/or the air, or even an artificially oxygenated environment, is combined with the administration of antibiotics.

Common sense about tetanus and small wounds

If every member of your family receives the full course of primary immunization against tetanus and receives boosters at the recommended intervals, you need not add tetanus to your consideration of everyday wounds. If a wound is serious enough to require medical attention, the doctor will decide whether a tetanus booster is needed. If it does not, in itself, merit medical attention then you can rely on that basic protection while treating the wound sensibly at home.

If an unimmunized member of the family, or one who has not received a booster for more than ten years, receives a susceptible wound, medical attention should certainly be sought and the whole drama should mean that he now receives the first injection of toxoid *and will return for the rest of the series.*

A shallow wound which bleeds freely is not susceptible to tetanus.

A deeper wound which bleeds freely is unlikely to be susceptible if you can see every cut surface and can therefore be sure that oxygen from the air meets with oxygen in the blood which oozes from its deepest points.

A wound which does not meet these criteria is still not likely to be susceptible if it was made by something which is unlikely to have been in contact with soil or animal feces. Even a deep puncture wound is unlikely to be a tetanus risk if it was made, for example, by a corkscrew. But if that corkscrew was being used on a picnic in a field grazed by animals, it might be a different matter. Did it come straight out of the hamper or had the toddler been digging in the earth with it?

Wounds with dead tissue (tissue which is not being constantly suffused with oxygen-carrying blood) are susceptible to tetanus infection later on, even if there was no risk at the time that they were caused. Burns, etc. should therefore be covered, as should septic wounds in which tissue will have been destroyed by other bacteria. Even in minor wounds (cuts on the fingers, damage from ingrown toenails, etc.) it is best to remove obviously "dead" flaps of skin, provided they are not acting as complete seals for underlying damage, as does the skin of a blister, for example.

Despite popular belief, there is no particular risk of "lockjaw" if the web between thumb and first finger sustains a cut. Nor is there any particular danger attached to rust. The rusty nail in the foot is dangerous because of the outdoor circumstances in which the nail is likely to have gone rusty. If a non-stainless steel knife has gone rusty in the steam of your kitchen, its cut is no more likely to carry tetanus organisms than are any of your other kitchen implements.

The kind of everyday wound which might possibly merit medical attention because of the risk of tetanus when, without this risk, you would treat it at home, is a graze, acquired on the road or gravel drive, which has left pockets in the skin. Although such grazes are often very painful, first aid must include the kind of bathing which ensures that every "pocket" is laid open. If this is done, dirt which might carry spores is washed out and none can heal over to leave a contaminated and airtight breeding ground (*see also* **Accidents**/Cuts and scrapes, grazes and puncture wounds).

Thrush (Candidiasis)

The yeast-like organism candidiasis is a normal and harmless inhabitant of the mouth and bowel. Infection takes place only when there is some local or general reduction in the tissues' resistance to infection. The most usual causes of lowered resistance to candidiasis are:

Wide-spectrum antibiotics   By suppressing the growth of both pathogenic and harmless bacteria, antibiotics, particularly if taken over a long period, can upset the normal balance of microorganisms in various parts of the body and thus predispose to invasion by *Candida albicans* (*see* **Infection**/Treatment of infections which cause illness: Problems in antibiotic use).

Corticosteroids   Whether these drugs (such as cortisone or prednisolone) are taken by mouth or applied locally, to reduce inflammation in eczema, for example, they disturb the body's resistance in many ways and may therefore predispose to invasion by a variety of microorganisms including *Candida albicans* (*see* **Infection**/Treatment of external infection and inflammation).

Pregnancy,
diabetes and
the Pill

Yeasts thrive in acid conditions, especially when there is plenty of carbohydrate available. The epithelial cells of the vagina, normally inhospitable to yeasts, may become ideal breeding grounds during pregnancy, diabetes or the taking of estrogen-containing contraceptive pills.

● Young babies easily become infected, not because their resistance is lowered but because it has not yet been built up.

Recognizing
thrush

Infection with *Candida albicans* has a similar appearance whatever part of the body is affected. Clusters of the yeast organisms produce fluffy white patches (like the white down on the breast of a thrush, from which the popular name comes). Under the white growth is raw, inflamed skin or mucous membrane. Thrush may be itchy. Scratching alters the appearance of the lesions and may lead to secondary infection.

Common sites for infection by *Candida albicans* include:

Vagina and external female genitals. Infection produces a whitish discharge together with itching and, perhaps, sore patches on the labia.

Mouth—usually of infants but occasionally of adults following drug treatment. White fluffy patches can be seen inside the cheeks. If they are wiped away, raw patches appear underneath. A baby may be extremely reluctant to feed. The baby born to a mother with vaginal thrush may acquire the infection during the birth process.

Anus and buttocks, usually of infants. Thrush may complicate "diaper rash," especially if the baby has been receiving antibiotics for another infection. Since the organisms are normal bowel inhabitants, every soiled diaper introduces more to the area and, once the skin is infected, careful hygienic measures (frequent changing, sterilizing of diapers, etc.) will be needed (*see* **Infection**/Preventing infection: Sterilants, disinfectants and antiseptics).

Already inflamed skin being treated with corticosteroids. If anti-inflammatory ointments and creams are being used on skin already damaged by, for example, eczema, especially if the area is covered by an airtight dressing, invasion by *candida albicans* may follow. Sometimes this leads to the assumption that the treatment is not working, when in fact it has done the anti-inflammatory job for which it was applied, the continuing lesions being due to invasion by these yeasts.

Treatment
of thrush

Although a variety of local applications used to be employed and some (gentian violet, for example) were reasonably effective, an antibiotic called mycostatin is now usually prescribed. Its absorption from the gut is limited so, except in rare cases of heavy infestation of the bowel, it is seldom given by mouth. Instead, various local applications are manufactured for application to different sites. A vaginal infection may be treated with mycotatin pessaries; infection of the diaper area or other part of the skin may be treated with creams or lotions containing the antibiotic, while thrush in the mouth of an infant will often be treated with mycotatin liquid, applied in drops to the patches.

Thumb sucking *see* **Habits**/Comfort habits. *See also* **Teeth**/Looking after teeth.
Tics and other habit spasms *see* **Habits**.
Toes and toe injuries *see* **Feet**. *See also* **Accidents**/Bruises: "Blackened" nails.

Toilet Training *see also* **Bedwetting; Soiling**

In recent years most parents have come to realize that a child-paced and child-orientated approach to toilet training saves time, energy and aggravation. Parents used to look at it as a matter of *preventing a child from wetting and soiling his diapers or the floor*. This negative aim could (and often did) start from the earliest months, with "catching" movements and urine in a potty. This may have saved some washing, but had nothing whatsoever to do with "training"; it usually led to rebellion as soon as the child realized that those were *his* excreta and therefore that what he did with them was, or should be, his business. Hardly surprisingly, toilet training struggles were common and the potty often served as a focus for toddlers' struggles for independence. Now, most parents are able to look at toilet training as a matter of *helping a child to take charge of his own excretion and waste disposal as do the older members of his society*. This positive aim is with and for the child, rather than at and against him. It cannot begin until the child shows that he is ready for the responsibility and, far from contradicting his dawning desire for autonomy, it can pander to it.

If you should have remaining doubts about taking this positive approach, the following points may help to resolve them:

However hard you try, however tough you are prepared to be, you cannot *make* your child use a potty/toilet. You may be able to force him to sit on it, but only he can decide whether or not to perform. Any battle is one which you cannot win and had therefore better not join.

Your child can only cooperate in toilet training because he wants to cooperate with you, as representatives of the grown-up world. He has no other motive for becoming clean and dry. In this sense, toilet training is different from socializing other natural functions like eating. When you ask him to eat "nicely," you have going for you the fact that he wants the food. But when you ask him to pee in a potty you have nothing going for you but that desire to please. He was going to pee anyway; only you care where.

Almost every healthy child will be clean and dry before he goes to school. Turn by all means to the entries on **Bedwetting** and **Soiling**. But before you despair of your three-year-old, ask yourself how many schoolchildren you know who still wear diapers.

"Readiness" for toilet training

Your child cannot begin to take charge of his own excretion until he is aware of what he does. At one year, everyone in the household may know (from his scarlet face and happy grunts) when a movement is coming —except him. If he passes a movement, or pees, when he happens to be naked, he will squat, perform, and then go on with his play without so much as a glance at what came out of him. Until he makes this vital connection between the feeling and the product, he is not ready for "training."

Somewhere between twelve and eighteen months this awareness usually begins; there is no doubt that summer nakedness speeds it up. Now when he makes a puddle he may turn to inspect it, exclaiming with interest over it. But as long as he is only aware *after the event* he is still not ready.

Bowel training   Bowel training is infinitely easier for a child than urine training:

He probably passes only one or two movements per day while he may pee eight or ten times.

He may be quite regular in his timing whereas his urination is irregular.

Once he connects the sensations of an impending movement with what comes out, he has plenty of time to go to a potty or toilet if he wishes. Early awareness of a coming urination gives him only a couple of seconds before the flood.

The simplest way to bowel train a child is simply to point out to him, once he is aware of the feeling-product connection, that, *if he wanted to*, he could put that movement in a potty or toilet, as other people do, instead of in his diaper. If it is presented as an interesting new idea, backed by an interesting new potty or toilet seat, he will probably want to give it a try. You can repeat the suggestion next time you see that he is going to pass a movement, but if he is too busy playing to bother, drop it. The secret is to *avoid any implication that he must*. If and when he does, you can of course comment with pleasure on how grown-up he is getting, but it is a mistake to go overboard with the congratulations and an even bigger mistake to be disappointed when he uses his diaper the next time. Using that potty is not the be-all and end-all of everything. It is just something that you are absolutely confident he will do, because everyone does eventually.

● If you have no strong preference for a potty or toilet, these are some of the pros and cons of each:

Potties are portable, and can therefore be put where the child will be, where he can easily get to them himself. This can be a big advantage when urine training begins. Speed becomes important and urination is so frequent that it is irritating for the toddler if he must always be taken upstairs to the toilet.

Well-designed potties (preferably potty-chairs) are safe and comfortable. The child can sit himself down without help, and has his feet firmly on the floor, instead of being perched up on a toilet where, even with a small seat, he may feel worried.

Toilets are what older people use and therefore using one may make it clearer to the child that his new behavior is "grown-up."

A child who is used to toilets will not need you to cart his potty around and carrying a potty wherever you go can become tedious.

Whichever you choose (and both is usually the best) remember:

A potty for a boy needs a shield on the front; he will pee sitting down for quite a long time and it will not go into the potty without this aid!

● Don't use a shielded potty for a girl. Sitting down unwarily has led to lacerations of the labia which, in a few children, have actually had to be stitched.

A toilet a child will use must have a small seat and a footstool. The small seat stops him from feeling as if he is going to fall in; the footstool helps him climb up, makes him feel more safely planted when he gets there *and* gives him a physiologically efficient position in which to pass a movement.

Whichever he uses, be tactful about disposing of his movements. Many children are terrified of a toilet's flush; their size concepts are still so primitive that they may truly believe that they, too, could be flushed away. Furthermore, those feces are part of them, their body's product. When you flush their feces away you do, in a way, flush part of them away. So whether you are emptying a potty or flushing a toilet your child has used, wait until he is out of the room. When he expresses unworried interest in what happens to the movements, explain where they go and why; point out that there will always be more tomorrow, and see if he would like to flush the toilet for himself.

Urine training   Although a child's awareness of being about to pee and of producing a puddle may develop simultaneously with his awareness of bowel movements, taking charge of them is far more difficult. They happen often and unpredictably; sensation gives him only a few seconds' warning, and once he has the warning he cannot run for his potty because the only way he can delay, even that long, is to "clench his bottom" and stay rooted to the spot. You will not have to suggest to your child that he could pee in the potty instead of in his diaper because he will often do so while passing a movement, but don't take him out of diapers, and thus expose him to endless failures (and your carpets to inevitable disasters), until he can recognize the need to pee while there is still time for him to get to his potty.

Once he can wait a little, you can start in one of two ways. If it is summer and warm, so that you can leave him without pants, playing around in the garden, potty at hand, do. Encourage him to sit on the potty when he feels a pee coming and encourage him, for a change, to "water" a particular bush, too. It will all help him to bring his urination under voluntary control.

If he cannot be outside, pick a day when he happens to wake up dry from a nap and suggest that he might like to pee on his potty. If he would *not* like to sit there, or if he sits and does not pee, just leave him without diapers, making sure the potty is close by, and suggest he sits down when he feels one coming. The point here is to try to give him a success experience without too much boring waiting around. If he stayed dry all through that nap he is bound to pee soon. If he does pee in the potty be calmly congratulatory but dress him, diapers and all, as usual. If he gets absorbed in play and makes a puddle, don't make a fuss; just dress him. After a few days of occasional casual successes, take him out of diapers *when he is awake and at home.* Don't make too big a thing of this or he will feel sad and demeaned by having them back on again for naps, outings and nights. Just say that he will probably be more comfortable in pants and the potty is right there when he needs it. At this stage you need to be actually sympathetic about puddles ("Bad luck; you left it a bit late, didn't you? Let's mop it up . . ."). It *is* a puddly stage. You may find that plastic-coated trainer pants reduce the flood damage a bit.

You will now be at a halfway stage where tact, and giving the child as much choice as possible, is vital.

As long as he ever wears diapers in the day time, he will not finally realize that every full-bladder sensation means a trip to the potty or toilet. You cannot expect him to think to himself, "I'm going to pee in a minute; now let me see, am I wearing a diaper or not?" so he will not become reliably dry until those diapers become something he wears only at night.

But once half-trained, he will not like wetting himself, so it is unfair to take him to the supermarket without diapers when you know there is no toilet you could reach if it were needed.

Sometimes the best compromise is to agree with him that he doesn't need diapers in the day any more *except when you go to particular places*, and to let him choose whether or not he prefers to wear diapers for naps.

Urine training should now proceed smoothly, although not without plenty of "accidents." Do bear in mind the following points though:

If you keep reminding him to sit on the potty you ruin the whole process. However it may sometimes feel to you, you are not trying to keep the floor dry but trying to help him recognize and act on his own need to pee. If you keep reminding him, you are doing his thinking for him and you may actually delay the time when he can be fully reliable.

He cannot urinate in advance of feeling the need and will certainly not be able to do so before he is three or four years old. Sending him to the toilet before you go out "so you won't need to go later" is useless. Scolding him for a puddle in the car, because "you should have gone before we came out," is unjust.

Your skill as a lavatory-finder is important. When he does need to go he will still need to go *now*; the best parents have an almost magical ability to find a toilet at almost any time and under almost any circumstances. Learn where your local public facilities are; get into the habit of spotting that important door in any fast-food joint or service station and be charmingly ruthless about asking shopkeepers for the use of their facilities if no public ones are available. And don't, *ever*, allow a driver to refuse to stop for a child to pee, or a nursery teacher to reprove a child who needs to go during story-time instead of a break.

Help children learn the art of al fresco peeing. Unless you introduce the idea of peeing outside, at an early stage, a newly trained child may be so shy about it that he or she is actually unable to let go.

Little boys have the edge here; it is easy for them to pee behind a bush or even, in a real emergency, against the back wheel of the car or down a drain. Little girls need a bit more help as mine crossly pointed out when she asked me why I hadn't given her one of those useful things her brother had, to bring on the picnic. A girl obviously needs protection from thorns, thistles and ants. She also needs help with keeping her pants out of the way while she squats because the whole performance is ruined for her if her pants get wet all the same. If there is enough privacy, taking the pants off altogether is usually the best solution. Finally, if she finds the squatting difficult, try "holding her out" by crouching behind her with your hands holding her bent knees and your elbows cradling her hips. She may find the whole thing easier if you do.

• When you start thinking about toilet training your child you have to decide what words you are going to use. Our language is full of euphemisms for toilets and what we put in them but, while adults usually find it easy to adapt their language to the company they are in, small children will tend to accept your early labels and go on using them for years. An invented baby-name for a bowel movement may seem perfectly appropriate when your child is two, but totally fox a teacher three years later. Correct medical terminology from the beginning may seem the answer, but unfortunately classmates are liable to laugh if your four-year-old announces, "I need to urinate. . . ." Family slang may be automatically picked up by the child, but some teachers will raise an eyebrow if he announces, "I need a crap. . . ."

It may be worth your while to listen carefully both to the words local families use among themselves, and to the words small children use in your local parks and playgrounds. You are looking for that fine (and personal) line between "acceptable" and "rude."

Tonsils

The tonsils are a pair of oval bodies of lymphoid tissue situated at the top of the throat where they are often visible on either side of the uvula.

Like the nearby adenoids, the tonsils play a role in trapping and destroying bacteria and viruses which might otherwise penetrate more deeply into the body. Enlargement and redness of the tonsils (often with fever and sore throat) is called tonsillitis; it is not really a disease in itself but a sign that the tonsils are actively engaged in coping with one of a variety of "germs."

It used to be thought that enlarged tonsils were more often a focus and source of infection than a protection from it. Very young children had their tonsils surgically removed, almost as a routine. Now most doctors are reluctant to recommend removal of the tonsils as long as they are active. The operation is rarely carried out before middle childhood, if at all (*see* **Hospital**/Surgery: Tonsillectomy and adenoidectomy).

Tonsillitis *see* **Tonsils**. *See also* **Scarlet Fever and "Strep" Throats.**
Toothache *see* **Teeth**/Some dental emergencies.
Toys *see* **Play**. *See also* **Nursing**/Passing the time.
Traction *see* **Hospital**/Procedures.
Travel sickness *see* **Vomiting**.
Truancy *see* **School**/School phobia: Truancy.

Tuberculosis (TB)

Although TB is now extremely rare among the privileged families of Western societies, it is still probably the most important infectious disease in the world. There are more than twenty million active cases today. In the next year one to two million of today's victims will die of the disease and two to three million new victims will be infected.

The full story of man's fight against tuberculosis has no place in this book (it would make it even longer!), but every family should know something of what is done to protect us if only so that each can cooperate, with understanding, in vital public health measures.

Tuberculosis is caused by one of two types of bacteria: the "human" form or the "bovine" (cow) form.

The bacteria can be taken into the body either by respiration— breathing air contaminated by bacteria from a coughing TB victim—or by drinking milk from an infected cow, for example.

Entry of the tubercle bacilli to the body is by no means always followed by open disease. Whether or not an exposed person develops open infection seems to depend both on the size of the dose of bacilli and on the age and health of the infected individual. TB spreads most widely in areas where poverty and malnutrition combine with a large reservoir of infection in the human and cattle population.

• If your healthy child has passing contact with someone later shown to have active tuberculosis, the chances of her getting the disease are still very small. Medical authorities will investigate and take precautions (*see below*) *not* because they think she has, or will have, acquired it, but because the infection is so serious that even the slightest risk merits action.

The bacilli are carried in the bloodstream and can affect virtually any organ of the body, including the central nervous system. Infection of the lung is the most common form (pulmonary tuberculosis). Infection in babies and young children ranges from the widespread, overwhelming attack which so rapidly kills malnourished infants in underdeveloped countries, to the localized attack (often affecting only a small portion of lung tissue and associated glands) which is still occasionally seen in the West.

Control of tuberculosis in the Western world

Tuberculosis and poverty walk hand in hand. It is in underdeveloped countries that the disease is still rampant, and in poverty-stricken corners of affluent ones that it can still be found. Most of us in the West are primarily protected by the standards of living, especially of nutrition, which we are fortunate enough to enjoy. Specific effective control measures of the last generation have included:

Control of bovine tuberculosis

Bacilli circulate in the bloodstream of infected cows and pass into the milk. Separation of that milk, so that cream may be sold or made into butter, tends to concentrate the bacilli so that these dairy products may be even more infective than the milk itself. Cow's milk used to be a major source of infection, especially to young children. Now, all dairy cows must, by law, be tested; no cow shown to have (or ever to have had) the infection may be used in milk production. Herds must be tested regularly and, as a further precaution against this and other milk-borne infections, almost all milk sold commercially is further treated by pasteurization or sterilization.

● Wise families will not buy raw, untreated milk from farmers who are not commercial producers. However attractive you may find the idea of "milk straight from the cow," it is not worth the minute risk that the cow is less than healthy.

Development of effective drugs

Antibiotics, such as streptomycin or isoniazid, control the disease in the individual patient and, by rendering her non-infective, reduce the reservoir of infection in the community. It is these drugs which have made the safe treatment of tuberculosis possible at home, and thus removed the horrors of long confinement in sanatoria.

Diagnosis of early pulmonary TB by mass X-ray

Mass radiography now detects so few new cases of TB that the service is being brought to an end. However, there is no doubt that, by detecting cases which might have remained infectious but symptom-free for many years, the service made a major contribution to the control of tuberculosis. It has, in the best sense, "worked itself out of a job."

● In some communities, institutions and jobs, chest X-rays are still required. They should always be accepted as a measure designed to protect both the individual and the rest of the community. If any member of your family has such a chest X-ray, do make a note of the date so that the doctor or public health official will know whether or not she should be X-rayed again on another occasion.

Development of vaccine (BCG)

BCG stands for bacillus Calmette and Guérin, Calmette and Guérin being the two French scientists who devoted their lives to developing it. It is an effective vaccine which appears to give almost complete and long-lasting protection against infection. People are often confused, however, by the way it is used:

Use of BCG vaccine

Many people, even in Western communities, are immune to TB because, even without open and obvious infection, they have had contact with the disease and their bodies have manufactured their own protection against reinfection.

Unlike many infectious diseases, TB does not produce circulating antibodies which can be detected by a blood test. The body's immunity is at cellular level.

Unlike many vaccines, BCG must not be given to people who *are* immune to TB, whether they are actually suffering from the disease or have simply had sufficient contact with it to produce an immune reaction. Immune individuals react "allergically" to the attenuated bacilli in the vaccine. They may develop ulcers at the injection site and other unpleasant side effects.

The Mantoux test

Before any individual is given BCG vaccine, then, she must be tested to see whether or not she already has TB, or immunity to TB. Since it is not possible to tell with a blood test, a special skin test using the purified products of killed TB bacilli (tuberculin) is carried out. A tiny quantity of tuberculin is smeared on the upper arm and then a Heaf gun is used to make several tiny punctures carrying the tuberculin into the skin.

Individuals without tuberculosis, or immunity to tuberculosis, show no skin reaction to tuberculin.

Individuals who have tuberculosis, or had contact with it in the past and are therefore immune, have a reddened and swollen patch of skin at the site of the punctures.

● A *negative* (no reaction) Mantoux test means that the individual is not immune and can safely be given BCG vaccine.

● A *positive* (skin reaction) Mantoux test means that the individual has either TB or immunity from past contact. She must *not* be given BCG but will be the subject of further investigations.

Different countries use the Mantoux test and BCG vaccination in different ways; usage is changing as infection becomes rarer.

Mass vaccination. In some areas of the world, mass testing and vaccination are carried out and are being extended as rapidly as possible. Vaccination in earliest infancy is used to protect babies who, because the disease is endemic and conditions are poor, would be very likely to acquire active tuberculosis during childhood. A new baby can be protected with BCG without the precaution of a Mantoux test because she has had no time to acquire the infection/immunity which would make immunization dangerous.

United States. In the United States, many schoolchildren are tested (often repeatedly), but those with negative tests are not normally given BCG as the risk of contracting the infection is regarded as too small to merit immunization. The Mantoux test is therefore seen not as an indicator for immunization but as an indicator for treatment. Any child with a positive Mantoux test is subjected to a full range of tests in case active infection can be found. But even if all these tests are negative, she is likely to be prescribed anti-tuberculosis antibiotics for a period of around one year, whether or not any signs of active disease ever appear. This is to cover the small risk of a pocket of infection smouldering on within the body to flare up in later life.

Britain. In the UK, all schoolchildren are tested at around the age of twelve or thirteen and all those who are negative on the Mantoux test (which nowadays is the vast majority) are given BCG vaccine a few weeks later.

Those children who have positive reactions to the Mantoux test may be given chest X-rays and other tests to determine whether the positive result is due to present, active infection or to minor infection long since dealt with by the body.

● Amid these complexities, what parents need to know is that:
□ Children should be given at least one Mantoux test.
□ Those who are negative should accept BCG if it is offered.
□ Those who are positive *may* have contracted TB which may still be active. Any investigations or treatment offered should be accepted. On the other hand, the child may well simply have acquired immunity by having contact with TB which has done no damage and is long past. A positive Mantoux test therefore merits careful discussion with a doctor, but it does not merit panic or despair.

If a child is known to have had contact (however fleeting) with someone who is then shown to have active tuberculosis, a Mantoux test will at once be carried out unless the child has already had BCG vaccine. It sometimes happens, for example, that a member of the staff of a school is found to have the infection. All the pupils will then be tested in order to pick up, as quickly as possible, any who may have been infected. This is why some families will find that Mantoux tests are being carried out on six- or seven-year-olds at school, and why they may also hear rumors about the children "being exposed to TB." The precaution is, of course, worthwhile, but the chances of infection are very small indeed.

If you are to travel, or more especially to live for a period, in a community where tuberculosis is endemic, do consult your doctor about protection for your children in advance. Under these circumstances early Mantoux testing and, if appropriate, BCG vaccination, may be given however young the children are.

If you take your child to the doctor because of a persistent cough (see Coughs) do not be surprised if he carries out a Mantoux test—it is a normal precaution. Do not be too alarmed if the test is positive; it may, but need not, mean that the cough is due to pulmonary tuberculosis.

On the other hand, a long-continuing cough, especially if it is associated with fever (even of low grade) and/or tiredness, loss of weight and night sweating, should certainly lead to a visit to the doctor. Once again, such a complex of symptoms does not necessarily mean that the child has TB but it does mean that you must make sure she has not.

Unconsciousness *see* **Accidents**/Coping with more serious injuries; Head injuries; **Convulsions, Seizures and "Fits."** *See also* **Fainting; Nursing**/Fever; Side effects of high fever.

Undescended Testicle *see also* **Hospital**/Surgery

A baby boy's testes descend down the inguinal canal, from the abdomen into the scrotum, shortly before birth. Once they are fully descended, the canal closes behind them. About three to four percent of boys are born before this descent is complete. Most of these testes will descend spontaneously during the first year, leaving fewer than one percent of boys with an undescended testicle by their first birthdays.

It is easy for parents to confuse an undescended testicle with one which is "retractile." In early infancy the testes can be drawn up out of the scrotal sac and into a superficial "inguinal pouch," when the scrotal muscle contracts. Contraction of this muscle may take place in reaction to cool air or a cool hand. Whenever you remove your baby's warm clothes or touch his scrotum with a cold hand, his testes may "vanish," only to reappear when you stop looking for them.

The eventual positioning of the testes in the scrotum is very important to a boy's eventual fertility. A testicle which remains permanently within the abdomen cannot function. A testicle which remains in the abdomen until late in childhood will have been too warm for normal development. Even when it is eventually brought down into the cooler scrotum, it may never produce living sperm.

The doctor who examines your newborn boy will check to make sure that both testes are in the scrotum; he will skillfully persuade one which insists on retracting to descend for his warmed hand to feel. If he can establish that both are descended you can forget the whole matter although it will be checked again at your son's first school "medical."

If one testicle does appear to be undescended, the doctor will probably ask you to keep an eye open for its spontaneous descent. One day, perhaps when he is sucking his toes while you try to change his diaper, you will probably see that both testes are in the scrotal sac, clearly outlined, like little eggs, inside the delicate skin.

If you have never seen or felt that testicle by your baby's first birthday, mention it to the doctor. If it is truly undescended, rather than still retractile, the baby will probably be referred to a surgeon so that arrangements can be made for it to be brought down into the scrotum and permanently fixed there.

Although this operation used to be deferred until a boy was of school age, many authorities now consider that it should be carried out between the ages of two and four years. The earlier it is done the less chance there is of any reduction in the testicle's later efficiency.

Upper respiratory illnesses see **Colds; Coughs; Croup and Laryngitis; Hospital**/Surgery: Tonsillectomy and adenoidectomy.

Urine see **Bedwetting; Toilet Training**. See also **Diarrhea, Gastroenteritis and Food Poisoning**/Diarrhea in babies and toddlers: Signs of dehydration; **Hospital**/Procedures: Urine specimens.

Urticaria see **Allergy**.

Vaccination see **Immunization**.

Venereal disease see **Adolescence**/Sex.

Verrucae see **Warts and Verrucae**.

Violence see **Discipline, Self-discipline and Learning How to Behave**. See also **Tantrums; Television**.

Viruses see **Infection**. See also individual conditions.

Vision see **Eyes and Seeing; Eye Disorders and Blindness**.

Vitamins see **Eating**/Types of food: Vitamins and minerals.

Vomiting

Vomiting (or "being sick") is the forcible expulsion of stomach contents. Nausea (or "feeling sick") usually warns the victim of what is to happen. Retching is the name given to the repeated spasms which finally produce the vomit. If the stomach is fairly full there may be little retching; if it is more or less empty there may be more. Sometimes violent retching produces only a little foul-tasting bile. The whole business of vomiting is unpleasant and exhausting. Although the victim will feel better from her nausea once she has vomited, she may be covered in cold sweat, limp and shaky by the time she has finished.

Vomiting which is not associated with illness   Some people vomit very easily while others do so only in response to gastric illness. You will need to know your own child in order to know how seriously any particular episode should be taken. Some types of vomiting are due to "mechanical" causes rather than to infection:

Newborn babies with a fault in the muscular outlet from the stomach may vomit every feeding with great force (*see* **Hospital**/Surgery: Pyloric stenosis).

Milk-fed babies often bring up milk with air. This is not true vomiting in the sense that it does not distress the baby or suggest that anything is wrong. The usual mechanism is that the milk becomes layered, or intermixed, with air in the stomach so that when that air is burped out, milk comes up with it. You may be able to lessen the tendency by feeding the baby in a more upright position. The heavier milk then drops below the air level in the stomach and the air can therefore escape without bringing milk with it. Handling her gently after meals may help, too.

A few children bring up any surplus if they overeat. While this is much rarer than all those adult cries of "you'll make yourself sick . . ." suggest, it does occasionally happen, especially if a child drinks a great deal of fizzy liquid along with a large meal. Her uncomfortably distended stomach may then simply eject what it cannot hold.

Many children suffer from motion sickness. Whether your child gets sick only on violent fairground rides or rough seas, in cars and buses but not on trains or airplanes, or in every kind of vehicle, the mechanism is probably the same: the motion disturbs the balance mechanism of the inner ear (*see* **Ears and Hearing; Ear Disorders and Deafness**). For this reason, the single most effective preventive measure is to persuade her to keep her head supported and still. If she can actually lie down, so much the better. If she cannot, being propped up with a pillow in a corner of the car will certainly help. If she insists on looking out, trying to play, walking around on the boat or going up and down the aisle of the plane or train, she is far more likely to be sick.

Travel-sickness pills help, too, but at least partly because they tend to make her sleepy and therefore more inclined to keep still. They do have side effects, such as an unpleasantly dry mouth.

Some children vomit from excitement/nervous tension and this may be because the excitement keeps the body in a state of action readiness during which normal digestion cannot take place. Such a child may eat her supper and go to bed where she lies tossing and turning in anticipation of tomorrow's thrilling treat or dread return to school. In the morning she feels sick over her breakfast. She eventually vomits what is clearly last night's almost unaltered food.

A similar type of vomiting may go with frequent bouts of abdominal pain for which no physical cause can be found (*see* **Abdominal Pain**/Recurrent abdominal pain).

With this sort of vomiting (which may, of course, be associated with motion sickness if the excitement is about something which involves travel), care over what the child eats may be worthwhile. A light meal which is easy to digest, given before her excitement builds to a high peak, may make vomiting less likely.

Vomiting and illness   Some children vomit once or twice at the beginning of almost every infection, even if it is not the digestive system which is under attack. Your child may be sick at the beginning of a cold or whenever she has a fever. If this is not your child's usual pattern and/or she vomits several times, the likelihood is that she has some form of gastroenteritis or food poisoning (*see* **Diarrhea, Gastroenteritis and Food Poisoning**). Seek medical advice if:

She vomits repeatedly. Whatever her other symptoms, this kind of vomiting is exhausting, will prevent her from getting much nourishment even if she eats in between, and may eventually lead to dehydration.

She also has diarrhea. Losing fluid from both ends makes dehydration very likely. In a baby or small child this is a serious threat to life.

She feels ill and nauseated, even immediately after vomiting.

She has stomach pain although you may not be able to distinguish between pain and nausea in a small child who can seldom tell the difference.

She has fever, with or without diarrhea, etc. Under these circumstances fever or its absence is a valuable guide. If she has fever then there *is* infection and the vomiting is unlikely to be due to simple ejection of food she could not digest.

Vomiting and injury Very occasionally a child will vomit after an injury. If she does so more than once, a doctor should see her. She may vomit because of the shock, in which case she should be checked over to make sure that her body can now deal with the after-effects of the shock without help. She may also vomit due to head injury (even if you were not aware that the fall or other accident had affected her skull). In that case medical attention is urgent (*see* **Accidents**/Head injuries; Shock).

Vomiting and poisoning If your child eats or drinks something poisonous, it may make her sick. If it does not, it may be necessary to make her vomit, deliberately, in order to rid her body of it (*see* **Accidents**/Poisoning).

Warts and Verrucae

Warts are harmless growths on the skin due to a virus. There are many different kinds, some of which are easily passed from one child to another. The commonest of these is the plantar wart, or verruca, which develops on the soles of the feet.

The hands, knees and feet are the most usual sites for warts. They may appear in crops and will eventually vanish even without treatment. This is why there are so many old wives' tales about miracle wart cures: swinging that black cat in the churchyard probably coincided with the spontaneous disappearance of the wart it was meant to "treat."

Verrucae do spread easily wherever children go barefoot together (as in swimming pools and locker rooms) and, because they are on the sole of the foot and therefore get pressed inwards by the child's weight, do also become painful. A child with a verruca should therefore be kept out of public pools, and be forbidden to go barefoot in public places, unless the wart is covered with a special waterproof covering. Your doctor or clinic may treat the verruca gradually, by daily application of a special ointment or by soaking the area regularly in formalin. Scraping and cutting is quicker but can be painful enough to matter and usually needs repeating several times; opt for another method if you can.

Weaning *see* **Eating**/Types of food for babies.
Weight *see* **Growth**. *See also* **Eating**; **Adolescence**/Puberty; **Anorexia Nervosa**.
Wet dreams *see* **Adolescence**/Sex.
Wheezing *see* **Allergy**/Asthma; **Chest Infections**; **Croup and Laryngitis**.

Whooping Cough (Pertussis)

Whooping cough has been a serious scourge among children, and a killer disease in the youngest age groups, for at least two hundred years. Although its incidence has been much reduced by immunization, and its mortality even further reduced by antibiotics effective both against the causative bacillus and against other bacteria causing secondary infections, it is still a very serious illness and by no means one which you should allow yourself to believe has vanished.

Vaccination against whooping cough is carried out with a killed vaccine which is not one hundred percent effective (although it is very nearly so provided that the full course is given). New strains of the causative bacteria do appear from time to time and therefore fully vaccinated children do succumb to infection, even though their illnesses are usually less severe than those of completely unprotected children. Unfortunately, an attack of whooping cough in a vaccinated child is just as infectious as an attack in an unvaccinated one. Small babies, even in families which have been scrupulous in following the vaccination program, may get whooping cough from an older brother or sister before their own immunization commences or becomes effective.

While scientists work to produce more effective, safe vaccines and to ensure that all the strains active in the community are included in them, parents must do their part by ensuring that all children are immunized unless their doctors advise against the series of injections for a particular child. Recent publicity given to rare side effects of the vaccine has led to a reduction in the number of infants protected. It may therefore lead to a horrifying upsurge in the incidence of whooping cough in years to come. A recent minor epidemic has already killed more than one infant.

The risks from whooping cough immunization   Very occasionally this vaccine causes convulsions. Much more rarely still it can produce permanent brain damage. While even one such tragedy is one too many, and no affected family can possibly be expected to take an objective view, other families have to try to do so.

The numbers of injections which are followed by convulsions is about one in every 110,000. So the risk of this type of reaction to a child having the basic three injections is one in 37,000, except that the real risk is even lower since if he has no ill effects from the first dose he is even less likely to suffer from the next. The number of injections followed by persistent neurological damage one year later is about one in 310,000. Again, the three-injection child therefore has a risk rate rather less than one in

103,000. If you feel that you should avoid even this minute risk by leaving your child unimmunized, do remember that every family which refuses immunization increases the number of children likely to become infected during an epidemic, and that the more children who catch whooping cough the higher the chances of their friends catching it, too. Of those who do suffer a full-blown attack (rather than the milder form which may occur in immunized children) up to forty percent of those (rare) babies who catch it in the first six months will die. Among older babies and young children, one in each several hundred victims will die, and several more will be left with various, but permanent, forms of lung damage. In protecting your child from the risks of immunization, you may expose him to far greater risks from the disease itself.

Now that the risk of ill effects on the brain and central nervous system are recognized, whooping cough immunization is already much safer. Your doctor will not give these injections to your baby if he has any other illness at the time. He will not give them if the baby has had convulsions for any other reason. Furthermore, if the first injection should produce a convulsion or any nervous system symptoms such as fever or shakiness, he will not complete the course.

The decision whether or not to accept whooping cough immunization for your baby is yours: there is no legal requirement and nobody should pressure you either way. But if you are doubtful, do at least discuss it with your doctor. If you (or he or all of you) do decide that the baby should not have it, it is vital that your doctor realize his unprotected status. If an epidemic should approach your community, the baby can be given at least a little protection with hyperimmune gamma globulin (*see* **Infection**/Treatment of infections which cause illness: Anti-viral drugs).

Having pertussis

Incubation period. Ten to fourteen days.

Route of infection. Droplet infection spread by coughing. Bacteria invade the bronchi and the bronchioles—the air passages within the lungs.

First symptoms of whooping cough

Similar to a common cold: runny nose, slight fever, cough. This develops into the typical cough in which there are spasms of barking coughs on an outward breath, followed by the characteristic "whoop" as the child fights to breathe in again through partially closed air passages.

Acute stage of whooping cough

Coughing spasms may occur dozens of times daily and each may end with the child vomiting. Dehydration, loss of weight and exhaustion are real problems. The child may need to be given tiny quantities of food and drink immediately after a coughing fit in the hopes that he will absorb some nourishment and fluid before the next bout leads to more vomiting.

Some babies fail to take in air quickly enough at the end of a coughing fit. Instead of whooping they may turn grayish-blue and lose consciousness and/or have convulsions.

Treatment of whooping cough

Antibiotics (usually erythromycin) may be effective if given in the very early stages. Sedatives are often given to help the child sleep. Careful checks are kept on the state of his lungs and on his general state.

Excellent nursing care is essential. A baby may need to be held upright through every coughing fit and no child should be left to cough alone in the acute stages. The acute stage is usually over in about three weeks.

Convalescence from whooping cough In an uncomplicated illness, the characteristic cough will last for a further two to four weeks and the child will need this period to rebuild his strength. If there have been complications, such as pneumonia, the whole illness may last much longer. Many children will continue to cough for as long as two to three months after they have stopped "whooping."

● Very young babies, in whom the disease is most dangerous, may never develop that characteristic "whoop." The definite diagnosis, which in this case is important, may have to be made by laboratory analysis of a swab taken from far back in the throat.

● Whooping cough in an older child, especially a vaccinated one, may be a much milder illness. If your whooping child is up and about within a few days, do remember the small babies in your community and *keep him away from public places.*

● A serious attack of whooping cough is one of the lengthiest and most demanding illnesses from the nursing point of view. As soon as you know the diagnosis, do try to arrange for regular help and relief.

"Word blindness" *see* **Learning Difficulties and Disabilities**.

Working Mothers

Once upon a time, growing up meant marriage and marriage brought babies. Once babies came, men went out to work to earn money while women stayed at home to care for the children. The greater the man's skill and industry, the more money that family would have; the greater the woman's domestic skill and industry, the more comfort that money would buy. No matter how many exceptions there were, that was the generally expected pattern. If you were a rebel, you at least knew what you were rebelling against.

That expected pattern of adult life is now a horror story (or a fairy tale, depending on your point of view). Women have rebelled, with great success, against a division of labor which carried with it a devastating division of responsibility and power between the sexes. Thanks to the Women's Movement, some major battles for equality of opportunity and of reward have already been won. Few political leaders dare speak against "women's rights" even if they drag their feet on the way to making those rights into realities.

In capitalist societies with a strong work ethic, equality of opportunity and reward has to be fought for first in the job market. While women are excluded from the man's world of labor and pay, they are also excluded from decision-making and power. While they depend on male productivity for their own subsistence they are deprived of influence. But even in such industrialized societies, jobs and wages are not the whole of a human being's life. Many women, having won the right and the opportunity to work shoulder-to-shoulder with men and to bring home an equal paycheck, are discovering that in those areas of life which are traditionally unpaid (and often not regarded as "work" at all), there is another, perhaps subtler, battle still to be fought. Many, for example, find themselves expected to fit what used to be a full-time female role around the edges of what used to be exclusively a male one. They work a full and equal day yet, when it is over, domestic responsibilities are still left to them, together with civic and community responsibilities, the organiza- tion of family leisure and most of the social organization which keeps "home" running smoothly. Worse, perhaps, than the actual labor left to working women is the responsibility. Many men, for example, will attend that meeting or give that piece of help to a neighbor *if their partners suggest it*. Far fewer make it their business to know when the meeting is coming up or to keep an eye on the neighbor's needs. Many men will clean up after the meal their partners cooked, or even cook the food a partner bought. But far fewer assume that it is their business to do the thinking and the shopping which ensure that the wherewithal for a meal is in the house. Above all, when some domestic crisis demands that one or the other take a day off from work, it is usually women who are expected to do so.

While a couple live together without children, issues of this kind may be mere pinpricks or only occasional triggers for trouble. The woman still has some choice over the burdens she is prepared to accept. Most domestic chores can be pared to a minimum; couples do not have to be involved with the community or with their neighbors. There does not even *have* to be a meal, and the absence of food may lead to masculine apologies and a quick trip to the nearest takeout counter. But once there is a baby, the whole issue of two-way equality between partners, at home as well as at work, becomes much more urgent. Child care is a non-stop imperative. The battle for the rights of women-who-are-mothers has barely begun.

If society had truly recognized men and women as equal persons, all the labor (paid and unpaid, "productive" and "personal") which needed to be done would have been pooled for sharing, both according to need and choice, among all the available adults. But when it comes to a baby's need for adult attention or instant availability during every moment of each twenty-four hours, it becomes clear that this kind of social organiza- tion is still far away. There are many men who would like to take a full share in bringing up their children and who recognize that two adults can meet a child's needs while doing a job outside the home and, hopefully, having fun, too. Some strive to make such a life pattern work within their families, but strive they must. They are flying against social expectations and can expect little support. There are many forms of communal living designed to aid this kind of whole-life sharing. But against social pres- sure, few survive from generation to generation. There are nibbles at the conventional "working day" in the form of "job-sharing" and "flexi- time," but vital though these are as possible models for the future, they are far commoner in the media than in real life and more often prom- ulgated as an aid to working mothers than as a more satisfactory or equitable life for us all. There are even some attempts to give men and women equal choice in life activities. But where these are applied to people-who-are-parents, they are referred to as "role-swapping." Could there be a clearer indication of society's view of child care as still basically a female role? Or of its inability to understand the need for pooled labor? It may suit a particular couple to reverse responsibility for wage-earning and child care, but it leaves untouched the basic dilemma of being available both to a child and to a paid job. However much a man wants to share children with his partner, society (whether in the form of his friends, his colleagues or his superiors) does not expect the man-who-is-a-father to behave any differently from the man who is not. Whereas a woman who takes a day off from work because her child is ill may face disapproval from her boss, a man will face an amazement which may begin in amusement but will quickly lead to worse. Where a woman who is known to have a child to collect from a sitter at the end of the working day will usually make a punctual escape, a man may meet real obstruction. He is supposed to put his work first and not dilute that concern with inconvenient family matters. It will often be suggested to him that his refusal of overtime, or of that after-work drink, is a serious barrier to promotion. Even within the world of people who are caring for young children, fathers may find themselves less than welcome. As one put it, after first accompanying his child to playgroup: "All parents are welcome unless they are male." That old-style "woman's world" can be as difficult for a man to break into as was the "man's world" for women.

Every woman who is (or is going to be) somebody's mother has to find a personal solution to the dilemma posed by doing, or not doing, a paid job while coping with child care. Individual circumstances, ranging from partners' attitudes to personal earning power, make such an overwhelming difference that no general guidance can make sense for all. There are, however, some common problems and problematical social attitudes which you may meet.

Planning in pregnancy Of course it is sensible to try to plan ahead, but many women regret commitments made in advance once the baby is born. Try to keep some options open, for example:

Think carefully before you accept generous maternity leave and pay in exchange for a guaranteed date on which you will be back at your job. When the time comes you may not want to return. On the other hand, try not to close the door of your workplace finally behind you in your seventh month. If you want to go back later you will have a better chance if your personnel file is still open and if you have discussed possibilities, such as part-time and/or home-based work, with the firm.

Don't rely in your planning on casual offers of day care, whether from a babysitter who can "always make room" or a neighbor who is "always at home and pleased to help." Only a booked place or firm agreement, tied down to the last detail, is worth having.

Build breast-feeding into your thinking. If you want to breast-feed and are doing so happily, you probably will not want to stop. A workplace nursery might enable you to go on, but without it, breast-feeding probably means no outside work (*see* **Eating**/Types of food for babies).

Make sure you get your figures right. Many women who feel they must get back to work as soon as possible for financial reasons discover, over a few stressful months, that the net gain to the family from their working is almost nil. Make sure you allow for hidden costs like travel to and from a sitter as well as to and from work; lunch-hour shopping in comparatively expensive places and uneconomic quantities; convenience foods because you are always in a rush and even placatory treats for other children/partners/sitters, because you are always late.

Beware of people who tell you what you should do or what you will do. There are grains of truth in all those contradictory statements like "Every baby needs his mother" and "Women who are content to be 'just mothers' are traitors to their sex." But only you can sift those grains from the over-generalized rhetoric and put together something that feels true for you. "You'll never be happy at home, dedicated to your job as you are" and "Of course, you've always longed for the domestic bit . . ." are almost as damaging. Let them all wait and see.

Babies and day care Making arrangements for a baby, as opposed to an older child, can be truly agonizing. You may find yourself caught between people who suggest that you will harm your baby if you leave him for a second and people who insist that it is better for babies to be cared for by "experts." Both camps will tend to ignore two vital factors: your *own* feelings which may make it quite impossible for you to leave him happily, and the non-existence of those "experts" which, in many areas, will mean that there is nowhere to leave him.

If you are looking for somewhere to leave him, make your decisions by considering your own relationship with him in terms of his development.

Early learning seems to take place mainly through a baby's interaction with known and loved adults. A lot of recent research has shown that, right from the beginning, a baby does not only *react to* a friendly talking adult but also influences that adult: their interaction is always two-way. You may assume that your baby smiles at you because you are smiling at him, but the truth is just as likely to be that you are smiling because he smiled. You may be amazed at yourself for making silly noises at him when you intended never to use "babytalk," but most of your sounds are copies of his, and that special, high-pitched rhythmical tone you use is not idiocy but the most effective form of verbal communication with a two-month-old human. Adults believe that they provide an environment for a baby, but every baby plays a large part in shaping his environment for himself, and that includes his working to adjust your behavior to match today's needs, shaped by yesterday's interaction.

This two-way influence is probably the most important contributory factor to a baby's overall development, after the maintenance of health through adequate physical care. You and your behavior act, so to speak, as a mirror in which he can see himself and his world. He cries; you pick him up and he stops crying and gurgles at you instead. Through your facial expressions, your body movements, your voice tones and your readiness to join in the gurgling but not the crying, he learns some important things about crying and about the effects of his behavior on you. Through the day you bring him little bits of the world to consider, and you shield him from other bits; as you do so you interpret that world for him. Consciously and unconsciously you interpret larger slices of the world which are as yet far beyond his understanding. It is by watching your consistent reaction, for example, that he learns to regard the telephone ring as a sound which is alerting but not alarming.

The two-way influence of earliest infancy is the beginning of almost every kind of learning which will be important to the child later on. The early smiles and "conversations" are the prototypes of later communication and he uses from the beginning the "rules" which he will use forever (*see* **Language**). He utters and then pauses, waiting for your response, fitting his next utterance to it or ending the interaction, as he will always do, by looking away. Those first games with fingers and toes and toys are prototypes for later cooperation. He "takes turns," "shares" and waits, at three months, for the climax of "this little piggy" as he will wait at three years for the climax of a joke and at thirty-three for the punch line of a story. Because his behavior *evokes responses which are consistent*, he learns vital lessons about cause and effect and above all about his own effectiveness. As one British psychologist put it: "A baby must learn 'I see this, I do that and X happens'" (*see* **Play**/Playthings for babies). If your baby is to have the best possible opportunity for this kind of development, he therefore needs:

Consistent care. The mirror in which he sees himself and his own behavior and the behavior of his world should always give him the same image, and therefore enable him to build up expectations and cause-and-effect relationships.

A baby who is cared for within his own family will get this without anybody thinking about it, but a baby who is cared for by a lot of different people (however "expert") may not, because each new person will react and interact in different ways so that he is presented with different images. He cannot use a stranger until she becomes a familiar.

Continuous care. Babies develop extremely fast but in minute steps, each of which is clear to an adult who sees him constantly, but may be invisible to one who hardly knows him or has not seen him for days, so that the intermediate steps are in the past. Not only does he need to be cared for by the same people all the time, he also needs to see each person who is important in his life, frequently. Every grandmother knows that a month's absence from a baby can make you, for these emotional purposes, into a stranger.

Sufficient care. As well as enough physical care, he needs enough of this consistent and continuous social attention to make the best possible use of his own capacity to signal and receive signals. In a group, for example, he may always be cared for by the same people but, because he must compete with too many other babies, he may simply not get as much attention as he can use.

If your baby is to be cared for by someone outside the family for the whole day, he may not be best served by group care, even if there is a specially built nursery full of lovely equipment and trained staff available to you. Even a staff-child ratio of one to three does not assure him of this kind of care because it is not only the *number* of available staff which matters to him but *who they are* and whether they were there yesterday and will be there tomorrow. He may be better off with a replacement for you, either in his own home (if you have an otherwise unemployed relative or the money to employ someone) or in the home of a member of that much-maligned species: the babysitter.

But if he is only to be cared for outside the family for much shorter periods of a few hours at a time, that basic continuous interactive relationship will be rolling along within the family during all the hours at home, and the lack of some part of it during those group hours may not matter. Certainly, whatever the "babies need their mothers" camp may imply, you will not harm your baby either by sharing his care with someone prepared to act as "substitute mother" when you are absent, or by sharing it occasionally with someone who cannot be a complete love object to him. You may like to bear in mind the fact that demands for mothers to care for their babies *alone and constantly* are a recent phenomenon. In our own society in the past, and in many societies today, a baby's care was always shared between mothers, elder sisters, grandmothers and so forth. It is only we who, by suggesting a twenty-four hour a day, three-hundred-and-sixty-five-day-a-year commitment for mothers, have made "good mothering" seem impossible.

Job factors which help or hinder

Most working mothers, whatever the ages of their children, walk a continuous tightrope through daily life so that even the minutest slip or alteration of balance spells disaster. These are some of the (often trivial-seeming) factors which seem to make a difference to many:

Distance/travel. The basic problem is that you really need to be in two places at once. The closer together those places are, the more nearly you can achieve this miracle. The two places may be work and home, or work and sitter/nursery/school. Close in *time* matters more than distance, but means of transportation matters, too, because a ten-minute train ride exposes you to the vagaries of weather, strikes, etc. So strong is this factor that many women prefer to take a less satisfactory job nearer home. Many of us believe that jobs within local communities should be offered first to local mothers. Perhaps increasing numbers of female *employers* will adopt this attitude. Workplace nurseries can help, too.

Attitudes to you as a mother. Employers and colleagues vary wildly in their attitudes, of course, but ideally you need a job where a certain priority for your children is not just *allowed* but positively *expected*. You will not always find this in obvious places. A child development research unit may be soullessly grudging where the local bank manager positively insists that you attend every sports day "because she will be sad if you aren't there." A welcome for occasionally visiting children, and helpfulness when they telephone you, usually goes with this.

Possibility of fulfilling work obligations at home. However nice they may be about it, letting down colleagues is no fun and during a winter full of colds and tonsillitis *you* may feel that you have not earned your salary even if they do not. If you can take work home and do it, if necessary, in the middle of the night, this whole area is much more comfortable. Of course you cannot take a production line home, but many women do manage in a variety of jobs. Typing or telephoning can both be done at home as, of course, can all kinds of work involving reading, writing memos and reports, etc. Teachers can prepare and mark work even when they cannot be in school for lessons. Some women find their lives much improved when they manage to accumulate special work equipment at home for this reason. If you have a piano, your music pupils can come to you; a drawing board means you need not be late with those designs.

Emergency communications. A job at which you cannot be reached is alarming for you and may be alarming for your child or his caretakers, too. You really do need the number of a telephone which will always be answered and from which somebody will always bring you a message.

Hours and their organization. Few mothers can comfortably hold down absolutely full-time jobs, especially if they also involve travel time and your physical presence.

You may be able to manage full-time *hours* if you are able to have some flexibility (formal or informal) about when you fulfill them. Three long days and two half days, for example, may make for a much easier pattern of home life than five ordinary-length days.

Part-time work is a usual compromise but can be of dubious value. You may lose a disproportionate amount of money for the amount of time you save, and some part-time workers get passed over for promotion and plum assignments, too. Part-time work in shops and so forth may not fit well with family life because you may be needed at work just at the times when you are most needed at home—on Saturdays, for example.

If an employer really wants you (and sadly, in the present state of the job market, he may not care very much whether he has you or somebody else), he may be willing to accept a variety of easements. Various women swear by each of the following:

Full-time work for full pay but with acceptance of the principle that while the work must always be completed, when it is finished (or slack/non-existent) they do not have to be there. Work, in other words, with no time clock to punch. Formalized "flexi-hours" make this approach possible even where the job involves somebody being there to answer the telephone or deal with the public. One such scheme demands that every employee be "in" from 11 a.m. to 2 p.m. Beyond that commitment, each sets his/her own hours.

Job-sharing, such that the employer does not care which of two or three of you is there as long as one is. Sometimes two women-who-are-mothers (or two parents if the job pays enough) can work this out very satisfactorily. You might want to do mornings while your pre-school child is at nursery school; afternoons might suit your friend and colleague because her baby usually sleeps then. Either of you can stand in for the other, at work or at home, during domestic crises.

Shift work, so that however inconvenient and difficult life may be this month, it will be easier (or at least different) next. Some parents work shifts which fit together so that one is always available to the children; but they do not tend to be very available to each other. Some women —especially those with older children—do permanent night work and feel that they can leave home after a pleasant family evening, be home to see everybody off for the day, and then get enough sleep before they come home again.

Working at home and/or self-employment

For many women, bringing the demands of work and home together in one place proves a tremendous relief because it not only gets rid of most of the obvious conflict, but it also remolds life into a coherent whole so that the woman feels like a whole person instead of one who is chopped into little bits. It can improve home life, too, by making it feel like part of life instead of a retirement from it. As jobs get harder to find, more and more people, men and women, are "setting up on their own," and many believe that the days of the big central organization to which workers flock each day are numbered. We may all work at, or from, home if the micro-computer people have their way.

But not only is this not possible for everyone, some people find that they dislike it. You need to be careful before you take on home-knitting or craft assignments, for example. Some work of this kind is very poorly paid. Some people who have the opportunity for more creative freelance work find that working at home does them out of the adult company they crave, while others just find it impossible to wear a mother-hat and a worker-hat at the same time.

Work and schoolchildren

It is a myth that working outside the home becomes easier for mothers once their children are at school. In many cases it actually gets more difficult.

However hard they may be to find, day-care facilities for younger children are at least intended to cater to them while you work. Schools do not even pretend to do so, because their stated purpose is the child's education and there is therefore no compulsion on them to concern themselves with any aspect of your convenience.

School hours are short compared to full-time adult work.

School terms are interrupted, not only by half-term breaks and vacations, but also by unforeseeable extras like days when the school building is being used for election booths.

Schools demand greater or lesser participation from parents which may include daytime meetings and so forth. Children whose parents can *never* come may be at a disadvantage (*see* **School**).

Schoolchildren, especially young ones, get ill quite frequently and when they are ill they cannot go to school.

Some people believe that schools should be adapted to fit more closely into the needs of the adult working day and a large number of vacation recreation programs and after-school clubs are being tried in different areas. Other people feel that the school day and year are already quite long enough for many children, and/or that school as a place of education is diluted or disturbed if "custodial care" is intermingled with it. They would prefer to see the work world adapted to the school. Whatever is available to you, and whatever your own (and your children's) views, do make sure that proper arrangements of some kind are made. Suppose that there is a recreation program for your child for four weeks of the summer vacation, who will be with him for the other weeks? If you take your annual leave then, what will happen at Christmas? If you are fortunate enough to live in the kind of neighborhood where all the children play together and are in and out of each other's houses anyway, you may be able to leave yours with the gang, knowing that some adult will feed them and cope in a crisis. But that kind of life is sadly rare, especially in large cities. Children who are left to fend for themselves all day and every day *do* have more accidents than supervised children, *do* get into trouble with the law more often, *do* suffer from having responsibility for even younger ones imposed on them and *do* get extremely bored and lonely.

Coping with illness

If your vacation arrangements are all right, your child's illnesses may be your main problem. Various women use combinations of the following:

An occasional "babysitter" (often a retired person) who is happy to be called upon for the occasional day or two to supervise a child in his own home. Some children like some sitters; some tolerate and some detest them.

Staying at home and telling employers that they themselves are ill (thought better than allowing bosses any excuse for not employing women-who-are-mothers).

Leaving the child in bed and keeping in touch by telephone (and sometimes by visiting during lunch hour).

Taking the sick child to a relative, neighbor or one-time sitter, who does not mind having him as long as she does not have to come out.

Sending the child to school all the same hoping that he will be "all right" and knowing that if he is not, the school will not send him home if there is nobody there to look after him. (In real illness, though, this only copes with the first day. The child tends to bring a stiff note home with him at the end of it.)

Staying home from work and taking the necessary days as part of annual leave or paid vacation. That may ruin carefully laid plans for coping with the child's next vacation, though.

Staying home from work and asking to have it counted as unpaid or compassionate leave (many find that a decent boss accepts the gesture but does not withhold the money).

Obviously all these measures depend on entirely individual factors like how old/ill/unhappy the child is, and so forth. But, as a bunch, they do serve to illustrate the extreme conflict in which women-who-are-mothers-and-workers often find themselves.

Latch-key children

This emotive term is used to describe children who come home from school and let themselves in because there is nobody there to open the door. Is that really so bad?

Again, the only honest answer must be that it depends on your child and your exact circumstances. The emotive term has caught on, especially in Britain, because not having an adult at home after school often *goes with* not having enough adult attention at other times. But, of course, these two things don't have to be linked at all. If your child is at an age and stage where he himself is entirely happy to be first home, and is clearly unlikely to do anything dangerous while he is alone, it will probably be perfectly all right. You may want to try to work out a different plan if:

He is not happy about it, especially if he tends to be frightened of the dark, nervous of noises, etc. It certainly will not be good for him to come home each day to day-mares, in which his imagination fills the house with monsters (*see* **Anxiety, Fears and Phobias**).

He will be expected to look after younger children as well as himself. If those younger children would not be safe alone, it may not be fair to leave them with him routinely. He might be late; they might refuse to do what he told them, and if anything goes wrong he will feel desperately guilty.

You feel you have to put all kinds of restrictions on him to make it safe. Some children, for example, are forbidden to make themselves a cup of tea or coffee, or to turn on the heat until an adult comes home. In winter that is a pretty miserable prospect for a cold tired child.

He is not, at the moment, happy at school. Not only can a solitary return home be a depressing prospect when a child is facing a depressing day, the fact that you are not there may also mean that he never discusses his miseries with you while they are fresh in his mind (*see* **School**/Problems over going to school).

You would not, under other circumstances, want him to make the trip home alone (*see* **Safety**/On the road).

While a lot of children are, sadly, left to fend for themselves perhaps for several hours after school, the following compromises work well for many families:

The child who is expected to do homework either stays and does it at school (which many schools will allow as there are usually some staff in the building in charge of after-school activities) or goes and does it at the local public library until it is time to meet you on your return.

The child comes and collects you from work (geography permitting), which may have the advantage not only of sociability but of making it clear to your coworkers when it is time for you to go.

The child comes home alone on one or two days of the week but has after-school clubs, or dates with friends, on other days.

He goes and has a snack with a friend or neighbor and is either collected from there or leaves in time to meet you at home.

He comes home alone but has an open invitation to visit the house next door if he wishes, and an obligation to do so in any kind of crisis. ("Keeping an eye out for children" is a very valuable skill which the best neighbors develop to a high level and will share.)

He comes home alone and you telephone him as you leave work so that he can walk to meet you.

The child comes home and leaves a note to say where he is going and is then free to play (within agreed limits) with friends, until a specified time after your return.

Miscellaneous additional problems

Careful planning and arrangements may be ruined for you if your children are at different schools with different vacation breaks. One London mother of three recently enjoyed a spring term in which all the children were at school at the same time *for only two weeks*. Everything else being equal, this may be a strong argument for sending your children to the same school whenever the age-gaps make this possible. Otherwise, you can sometimes effectively get together with other parents to put pressure on local schools to cooperate over dates.

Sometimes children "old enough to manage" cannot safely and happily be left to manage together because they quarrel so. You are unlikely to be able to stop them from tormenting each other, or even to be sure what is whose fault. Brothers and sisters do not always like each other (or like each other all through childhood) and there may be a real personality clash or problem in the balance of power. Sad and infuriating though it may seem, you will probably have to make separate arrangements for each one. Children change, though. If you do arrange separate after-school "timetables," you may suddenly find them saying, "Why can't we just come straight home together?" and this time they may do so companionably.

Worms

Many types of worm can live as more-or-less damaging parasites in human intestines, but only the harmless pinworm is at all common. Pinworms look like tiny pieces of (lively) white thread and are usually discovered when a child passes a stool in which myriads are moving. It is revulsion rather than physical damage which may give him a stomach-ache; if he is so young that it is you who wipes his bottom and discovers the worms, *don't show them to him*. He will have to know about them because he will have to be treated, but he need not look. An older child who discovers pinworms will probably be horrified. Do explain that the infestation is common, can happen to anyone, is nothing to do with being "dirty" and can easily be dealt with.

Pinworms' life cycle

A child may get pinworm eggs on his fingers when he holds hands with another infested child (*see below*). When he sucks those fingers he swallows some eggs and they hatch in his intestine.

Female worms are fertilized while in his gut, but they like to emerge from the anus and lay their eggs outside the body when it is very warm. The most usual time is when the child is warmly snuggled in bed. The females return through the back passage, but the eggs remain. If the child scratches and then sucks his fingers, he will reinfest himself. If he goes to school with eggs under his fingernails, he may pass them to somebody else.

Coping with pinworms

Ask your doctor for a prescription for whichever medicine he prefers for pinworms. They are all effective but vary in dosage, taste and any mild side effects such as diarrhea.

Every member of the family must take the medicine, otherwise it may clear one child of heavy infestation but leave another who is already harboring a few worms, to reinfest him and all of you.

Dosage is by weight. Your doctor will prescribe enough for all of you but you will have to work out how much each member of the family should have. Your pharmacist will help if you ask when you pick up the medicine.

While the medicine does its job: get the child to cut his fingernails short in case there are eggs trapped there, and suggest that he sleep in close-fitting underpants for a few nights so that if he scratches, he will not pick up more eggs, suck his fingers and reinfest himself.

Wounds *see* **Accidents.**

X-ray *see* **Hospital**/Procedures. *See also* **Growth**/Irregularities of growth: Children who are "too small" or "too tall."

A NOTE ABOUT THE AUTHOR

Penelope Leach was educated at Cambridge University and the London School of Economics, where she received her Ph.D. in social psychology for a study of the effects of different kinds of upbringing and discipline on personality development. She has lectured at the London School of Economics on psychology and child development, and for four years ran a study, under the auspices of Britain's Medical Research Council, of the effects of babies on their parents. She is vice president of the Pre-School Playgroups Association and the Health Visitors' Association, has served on the committee of the Developmental Section of the British Psychological Society, and is the author of *Your Baby and Child* and *Babyhood*. She is married to an energy specialist, and they have two children.

A NOTE ON THE TYPE

The text of this book was composed in a film version of Palatino, a type face designed by the noted German typographer Hermann Zapf. Named after Giovanbattista Palatino, a writing master of Renaissance Italy, Palatino was the first of Zapf's type faces to be introduced in America. The first designs for the face were made in 1948, and the fonts for the complete face were issued between 1950 and 1952. Like all Zapf-designed type faces, Palatino is beautifully balanced and exceedingly readable.

Composed in Great Britain by
Rowland Phototypesetting Ltd, Bury St Edmunds, Suffolk
Printed and bound in the United States by
The Haddon Craftsmen, Scranton, Pennsylvania

This

NIV**TEEN STUDY BIBLE**

was given to:

_____

_____

on _____

_____

from _____

_____

Show me your ways, Lᴏʀᴅ, teach me your paths. Guide me in your truth and teach me, for you are God my Savior, and my hope is in you all day long.

Psalm 25:4–5

The
Apostles' Creed

I believe in God, the Father almighty,
> creator of heaven and earth.

I believe in Jesus Christ, his only Son, our Lord,
> who was conceived by the power of the Holy Spirit,
> born of the virgin Mary,
> suffered under Pontius Pilate,
> was crucified, died, and was buried;
> he descended to the dead.
> On the third day he rose again,
> he ascended into heaven,
> is seated at the right hand of the Father,
> and will come again to judge the living and the dead.

I believe in the Holy Spirit,
> the holy universal Church,
> the communion of saints,
> the forgiveness of sins,
> the resurrection of the body,
> and the life everlasting. Amen.

The History

Behind the Apostles' Creed

This 15th Century statement of faith transcends various denominational differences and highlights the core truths of faith that all Christians, no matter what denomination, believe in. This Creed has stood the test of time, is easy to memorize and is used in churches worldwide.

The Apostles' Creed unifies us all as believers; it helps us remember what Christians around the world believe and agree upon, and equips us to fight the questions and challenges to our faith.

We Believe...

Do you have questions
about what you believe
and why? Check out the "We Believe" feature.
Stop here for explanations of The Apostles' Creed, a foundation of
Christian truth, and the Bible passages that support it. Throughout this
Bible, each thought from the Apostles' Creed is explained, tying it with the
Scripture passage it reflects.

Here's a guide that shows where to find each feature:

Phrase from Creed	Bible Reference
I believe	John 3
in God, the Father	Psalm 103
almighty	Psalm 89
creator of heaven and earth.	Genesis 1
I believe in Jesus Christ,	Colossians 1
his only Son,	John 1
our Lord,	Romans 14
who was conceived by the power of the Holy Spirit,	Luke 1
born of the virgin Mary,	Isaiah 7
suffered under Pontius Pilate, was crucified,	Isaiah 53
died, and was buried;	Matthew 27
On the third day he rose again,	Luke 24
he ascended into heaven, is seated at the right hand of the Father,	Hebrews 9
and will come again	Mark 13
to judge the living and the dead.	Revelation 20
I believe in the Holy Spirit,	Acts 2
the holy universal Church,	1 Peter 1
the communion of saints,	Ephesians 2
the forgiveness of sins,	Jeremiah 31
the resurrection of the body,	Daniel 12
and the life everlasting. Amen.	Revelation 21

TEEN STUDY BIBLE

NIV

TEEN STUDY BIBLE

Features written by
Larry and Sue Richards

ZONDERVAN®

Table of CONTENTS

HOW TO USE this Bible

As an on-the-go teen, you're moving fast. God is moving faster! The *Teen Study Bible* will help you keep in step with all he has done, is doing, and will do in the world—and in your life. This best-selling Bible will help you discover the eternal truths of God's Word and apply them to the issues you face today. Features include:

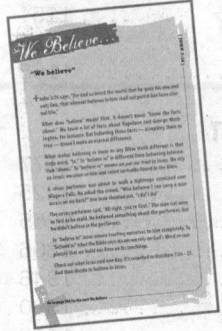

WE BELIEVE—Throughout this Bible, an exciting feature called "We Believe" lays out the foundation of the Christian faith by explaining the Apostles' Creed, statement by statement, linking each one to the Bible passage that supports it. This feature will help you remember what Christians around the world agree on and will equip you to handle the many questions you are asked and challenges you face regarding your faith.

PANORAMA—To help keep the big picture of each book of the Bible in view, this feature reminds you of the main theme from each book of the Bible as you work your way through it.

TO THE POINT—Does the Bible say anything about the problems and issues you face every day? Yes! "To the Point" shows you where and explains a passage of Scripture in the process.

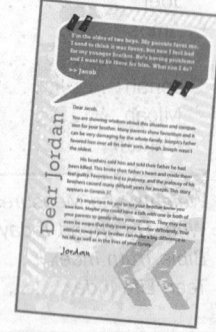

DEAR JORDAN—Are you looking for advice? Jordan willingly gives it. The questions you ask most often are answered in this advice column. The answers are based on a biblical character or situation. The characters of the Bible lived thousands of years ago. The teachings were written down thousands of years ago. But guess what! They are still relevant for today. And "Dear Jordan" shows you how.

KEY INDEXES—Help with in-depth Bible study. The Bible Truth Index is tied to the "We Believe" and "To the Point" features. The Teen Life Index is tied to the "Instant Access" and "Dear Jordan" features. And the "We Believe" index provides a guide for where each of these features can be found in your Bible.

INSTANT ACCESS—You've probably already faced lots of hard situations in your life. And you've probably wondered at times, "What do I do?!" "Instant Access" covers almost every problem and situation you can think of. It does it directly and honestly, telling you what God has to say.

BIBLE PROMISES—There are many great verses in the Bible. This feature highlights some of them for you.

BOOK INTRODUCTIONS—Provide an overview for each of the 66 books of the Bible and relates it to your life. Includes "headlines" that outline key events that happen, and a "news ticker" along the bottom that lets you know what was happening in the world when each book was written.

Q&A—If you like trivia, this feature is for you. Tests your knowledge of the Bible.

WHAT DO I READ TODAY?—If you've been wondering what to read in the Bible or where to start, there's a reading plan in the back to get you going.

Best of all, *The Teen Study Bible* contains the full text of the New International Version of the Bible. It's contemporary, it's accurate, and it's written in language you can understand.

Preface
to the NIV

The goal of the New International Version (NIV) is to enable English-speaking people from around the world to read and hear God's eternal Word in their own language. Our work as translators is motivated by our conviction that the Bible is God's Word in written form. We believe that the Bible contains the divine answer to the deepest needs of humanity, sheds unique light on our path in a dark world and sets forth the way to our eternal well-being. Out of these deep convictions, we have sought to recreate as far as possible the experience of the original audience—blending transparency to the original text with accessibility for the millions of English speakers around the world. We have prioritized accuracy, clarity and literary quality with the goal of creating a translation suitable for public and private reading, evangelism, teaching, preaching, memorizing and liturgical use. We have also sought to preserve a measure of continuity with the long tradition of translating the Scriptures into English.

The complete NIV Bible was first published in 1978. It was a completely new translation made by over a hundred scholars working directly from the best available Hebrew, Aramaic and Greek texts. The translators came from the United States, Great Britain, Canada, Australia and New Zealand, giving the translation an international scope. They were from many denominations and churches—including Anglican, Assemblies of God, Baptist, Brethren, Christian Reformed, Church of Christ, Evangelical Covenant, Evangelical Free, Lutheran, Mennonite, Methodist, Nazarene, Presbyterian, Wesleyan and others. This breadth of denominational and theological perspective helped to safeguard the translation from sectarian bias. For these reasons, and by the grace of God, the NIV has gained a wide readership in all parts of the English-speaking world.

The work of translating the Bible is never finished. As good as they are, English translations must be regularly updated so that they will continue to communicate accurately the meaning of God's Word. Updates are needed in order to reflect the latest developments in our understanding of the biblical world and its languages and to keep pace with changes in English usage. Recognizing, then, that the NIV would retain its ability to communicate God's Word accurately only if it were regularly updated, the original translators established The Committee on Bible Translation (CBT). The committee is a self-perpetuating group of biblical scholars charged with keeping abreast of advances in biblical scholarship and changes in English and issuing periodic updates to the NIV. CBT is an independent, self-governing body and has sole responsibility for the NIV text. The committee mirrors the original group of translators in its diverse international and denominational makeup and in its unifying commitment to the Bible as God's inspired Word.

In obedience to its mandate, the committee has issued periodic updates to the NIV. An initial revision was released in 1984. A more thorough revision process was completed in 2005, resulting in the separately published Today's New International Version. The updated NIV you now have in your hands builds on both the original NIV and the TNIV and represents the latest effort of the committee to articulate God's unchanging Word in the way the original authors might have said it had they been speaking in English to the global English-speaking audience today.

The first concern of the translators has continued to be the accuracy of the translation and its faithfulness to the intended meaning of the biblical writers. This has moved the translators to go beyond a formal word-for-word rendering of the original texts. Because thought patterns and syntax differ from language to language, accurate communication of the meaning of the biblical authors demands constant regard for varied contextual uses of words and idioms and for frequent modifications in sentence structures.

As an aid to the reader, sectional headings have been inserted. They are not to be regarded as part of the biblical text and are not intended for oral reading. It is the committee's hope that these headings may prove more helpful to the reader than the traditional chapter divisions, which were introduced long after the Bible was written.

For the Old Testament the standard Hebrew text, the Masoretic Text as published in the latest edition of *Biblia Hebraica*, has been used throughout. The Masoretic Text tradition contains marginal notations that offer variant readings. These have sometimes been followed instead of the text itself. Because such instances involve variants within the Masoretic tradition, they have not been indicated in the textual notes. In a few cases, words in the basic consonantal text have been divided differently than in the Masoretic Text. Such cases are usually indicated in the textual footnotes. The Dead Sea Scrolls contain biblical texts that represent an earlier stage of the transmission of the Hebrew text. They have been consulted, as have been the Samaritan Pentateuch and the ancient scribal traditions concerning deliberate textual changes. The translators also consulted the more important early versions—the Greek Septuagint, Aquila, Symmachus and Theodotion, the Latin Vulgate, the Syriac Peshitta, the Aramaic Targums and, for the Psalms, the *Juxta Hebraica* of Jerome. Readings from these versions, the Dead Sea Scrolls and the scribal traditions were occasionally followed where the Masoretic Text seemed doubtful and where accepted principles of textual criticism showed that one or more of these textual witnesses appeared to provide the correct reading. In rare cases, the committee has emended the Hebrew text where it appears to have become corrupted at an even earlier stage of its transmission. These departures from the Masoretic Text are also indicated in the textual footnotes. Sometimes the vowel indicators (which are later additions to the basic consonantal text) found in the Masoretic Text did not, in the judgment of the committee, represent the correct vowels for the original text. Accordingly, some words have been read with a different set of vowels. These instances are usually not indicated in the footnotes.

The Greek text used in translating the New Testament is an eclectic one, based on the latest editions of the Nestle-Aland/United Bible Societies' Greek New Testament. The committee has made its choices among the variant readings in accordance with widely accepted principles of New Testament textual criticism. Footnotes call attention to places where uncertainty remains.

The New Testament authors, writing in Greek, often quote the Old Testament from its ancient Greek version, the Septuagint. This is one reason why some of the Old Testament quotations in the NIV New Testament are not identical to the corresponding passages in the NIV Old Testament. Such quotations in the New Testament are indicated with the footnote "(see Septuagint)."

Other footnotes in this version are of several kinds, most of which need no explanation. Those giving alternative translations begin with "Or" and generally introduce the alternative with the last word preceding it in the text, except when it is a single-word alternative. When poetry is quoted in a footnote, a slash mark indicates a line division.

It should be noted that references to diseases, minerals, flora and fauna, architectural details, clothing, jewelry, musical instruments and other articles cannot always be identified with precision. Also, linear measurements and measures of capacity can only be approximated (see the Table of Weights and Measures). Although *Selah,* used mainly in the Psalms, is probably a musical term, its meaning is uncertain.

Since it may interrupt reading and distract the reader, this word has not been kept in the English text, but every occurrence has been signaled by a footnote.

One of the main reasons the task of Bible translation is never finished is the change in our own language, English. Although a basic core of the language remains relatively stable, many diverse and complex linguistic factors continue to bring about subtle shifts in the meanings and/or connotations of even old, well-established words and phrases. One of the shifts that creates particular challenges to writers and translators alike is the manner in which gender is presented. The original NIV (1978) was published in a time when "a man" would naturally be understood, in many contexts, to be referring to a person, whether male of female. But most English speakers today tend to hear a distinctly male connotation in this word. In recognition of this change in English, this edition of the NIV, along with almost all other recent English translations, substitutes other expressions when the original text intends to refer generically to men and women equally. Thus, for instance, the NIV (1984) rendering of 1 Corinthians 8:3, "But the man who loves God is known by God" becomes in this edition "But whoever loves God is known by God." On the other hand, "man" and "mankind," as ways of denoting the human race, are still widely used. This edition of the NIV therefore continues to use these words, along with other expressions, in this way.

A related shift in English creates a greater challenge for modern translations: the move away from using the third-person masculine singular pronouns—"he/him/his"—to refer to men and women equally. This usage does persist at a low level in some forms of English, and this revision therefore occasionally uses these pronouns in a generic sense. But the tendency, recognized in day-to-day usage and confirmed by extensive research, is away from the generic use of "he," "him" and "his." In recognition of this shift in language and in an effort to translate into the "common" English that people are actually using, this revision of the NIV generally uses other constructions when the biblical text is plainly addressed to men and women equally. The reader will frequently encounter a "they," "them" or "their" to express a generic singular idea. Thus, for instance, Mark 8:36 reads: "What good is it for someone to gain the whole world, yet forfeit their soul?" This generic use of the "indefinite" or "singular" "they/them/their" has a venerable place in English idiom and has quickly become established as standard English, spoken and written, all over the world. Where an individual emphasis is deemed to be present, "anyone" or "everyone" or some other equivalent is generally used as the antecedent of such pronouns.

Sometimes the chapter and/or verse numbering in English translations of the Old Testament differs from that found in published Hebrew texts. This is particularly the case in the Psalms, where the traditional titles are often included in the Hebrew verse numbering. Such differences are indicated in the footnotes at the bottom of the page. In the New Testament, verse numbers that marked off portions of the traditional English text not supported by the best Greek manuscripts now appear in brackets, with a footnote indicating the text that has been omitted (see, for example, Matthew 17:[21]).

Mark 16:9–20 and John 7:53–8:11, although long accorded virtually equal status with the rest of the Gospels in which they stand, have a very questionable—and confused—standing in the textual history of the New Testament, as noted in the bracketed annotations with which they are set off. A different typeface has been chosen for these passages to indicate even more clearly their uncertain status.

Basic formatting of the text, such as lining the poetry, paragraphing (both prose and poetry), setting up of (administrative-like) lists, indenting letters and lengthy prayers within narratives and the insertion of sectional headings, has been the work of the committee. However, the choice between single-column and double-column formats has been left to the publishers. Also the issuing of "red-letter" editions is a publisher's choice—one the committee does not endorse.

The committee has again been reminded that every human effort is flawed—including this revision of the NIV. We trust, however, that many will find in it an improved representation of the Word of God, through which they hear his call to faith in our Lord Jesus Christ and to service in his kingdom. We offer this version of the Bible to him in whose name and for whose glory it has been made.

The Committee on Bible Translation
September 2010

Names of the translators and editors may be secured from Biblica, Inc.™, translation sponsors of the New International Version, 1820 Jet Stream Drive, Colorado Springs, Colorado 80921–3696 U.S.A.

>>OLD TESTAMENT

GENESIS

The Name Means "Beginnings."

And the book answers some of life's biggest questions. Where did the universe come from? How can there be evil in a world that a good God created? One of the biggest questions Genesis answers is whether or not God truly cares about the people he created. That question is answered when God promises to bless Abraham and all his descendants.

Genesis is also the story of how God's promises to Abraham were passed on to the generations after him. The people you will meet in Genesis don't always do what's right, but God keeps his promises to them—just as he keeps his promises to you today.

>>**GOD CREATES SOMETHING REALLY SPECIAL**
Story in Genesis 2:3–4

>>**GOD MAKES SEVEN STUNNING PROMISES**
Read them in Genesis 12:1–3,7

>>**OLDER BROTHER CHASES YOUNGER FROM HOME**
Details in Genesis 27:1–45

>>**INNOCENT MAN DOES RIGHT, GOES TO JAIL**
Accusation reported in Genesis 39

>>**VICTIM CLEARED, PROMOTED TO RUN EGYPT**
"Impressive," Pharaoh says. See Genesis 41

preview

Genesis doesn't give a date for Creation.

Key people: Adam and Eve, Noah, Abraham

The Jews are descendants of Abraham's son, Isaac. The Arabs are descendants of Abraham's son, Ishmael.

Moses wrote Genesis, around 1400 B.C.

While Abraham lives, around 2100 B.C., Egyptians establish the first libraries. The first picture of skiing is carved on a rock in what is now Norway.

The Beginning

1 In the beginning God created the heavens and the earth. ²Now the earth was formless and empty, darkness was over the surface of the deep, and the Spirit of God was hovering over the waters.

³And God said, "Let there be light," and there was light. ⁴God saw that the light was good, and he separated the light from the darkness. ⁵God called the light "day," and the darkness he called "night." And there was evening, and there was morning—the first day.

⁶And God said, "Let there be a vault between the waters to separate water from water." ⁷So God made the vault and separated the water under the vault from the water above it. And it was so. ⁸God called the vault "sky." And there was evening, and there was morning—the second day.

⁹And God said, "Let the water under the sky be gathered to one place, and let dry ground appear." And it was so. ¹⁰God called the dry ground "land," and the gathered waters he called "seas." And God saw that it was good.

¹¹Then God said, "Let the land produce vegetation: seed-bearing plants and trees on the land that bear fruit with seed in it, according to their various kinds." And it was so. ¹²The land produced vegetation: plants bearing seed according to their kinds and trees bearing fruit with seed in it according to their kinds. And God saw that it was good. ¹³And there was evening, and there was morning—the third day.

¹⁴And God said, "Let there be lights in the vault of the sky to separate the day from the night, and let them serve as signs to mark sacred times, and days and years, ¹⁵and let them be lights in the vault of the sky to give light on the earth." And it was so.

¹⁶God made two great lights—the greater light to govern the day and the lesser light to govern the night. He also made the stars. ¹⁷God set them in the vault of the sky to give light on the earth, ¹⁸to govern the day and the night, and to separate light from darkness. And God saw that it was good. ¹⁹And there was evening, and there was morning—the fourth day.

²⁰And God said, "Let the water teem with living creatures, and let birds fly above the earth across the vault of the sky." ²¹So God created the great creatures of the sea and every living thing with which the water teems and that moves about in it, according to their kinds, and every winged bird according to its kind. And God saw that it was good. ²²God blessed them and said, "Be fruitful and increase in number and fill the water in the seas, and let the birds increase on the earth." ²³And there was evening, and there was morning—the fifth day.

²⁴And God said, "Let the land produce living creatures according to their kinds: the livestock, the creatures that move along the ground, and the wild animals, each according to its kind." And it was so. ²⁵God made the wild animals according to their kinds, the livestock according to their kinds, and all the creatures that move along the ground according to their kinds. And God saw that it was good.

²⁶Then God said, "Let us make mankind in our image, in our likeness, so that they may rule over the fish in the sea and the birds in the sky, over the livestock and all the wild animals,ᵃ and over all the creatures that move along the ground."

²⁷So God created mankind in his own image,
in the image of God he created them;
male and female he created them.

ᵃ 26 Probable reading of the original Hebrew text (see Syriac); Masoretic Text *the earth*

We Believe...

God is "the Maker of Heaven and Earth"

✛ Genesis 1 teaches that God created the universe. Life didn't "just happen" as molecules bumped into each other. How do you know? Psalm 19:1 and Romans 1:18–20 suggest that you look around. If you saw a shiny new Mustang in a junkyard, would you think it "evolved" from the junkyard parts? The universe is thousands of times more complex than a Mustang. It didn't "just happen." God designed this world—all of it:

* God created the universe from nothing.
  (Psalm 33:6,8–9)

* Creation reminds you of the greatness of your God.
  (Isaiah 40:26,28)

* You accept the evidence that God created the universe by faith.
  (Hebrews 11:3)

Isn't it great to know that the heavenly Father who loves you is the all-powerful Creator of the universe?

Go to page 1473 for the next We Believe

NOTE TO READER: If you'd like to start at the very beginning of this feature, go to page 1312.

28God blessed them and said to them, "Be fruitful and increase in number; fill the earth and subdue it. Rule over the fish in the sea and the birds in the sky and over every living creature that moves on the ground."

29Then God said, "I give you every seed-bearing plant on the face of the whole earth and every tree that has fruit with seed in it. They will be yours for food. 30And to all the beasts of the earth and all the birds in the sky and all the creatures that move along the ground—everything that has the breath of life in it—I give every green plant for food." And it was so.

31God saw all that he had made, and it was very good. And there was evening, and there was morning—the sixth day.

2 Thus the heavens and the earth were completed in all their vast array.

2By the seventh day God had finished the work he had been doing; so on the seventh day he rested from all his work. 3Then God blessed the seventh day and made it holy, because on it he rested from all the work of creating that he had done.

Adam and Eve

4This is the account of the heavens and the earth when they were created, when the LORD God made the earth and the heavens.

5Now no shrub had yet appeared on the earth*a* and no plant had yet sprung up, for the LORD God had not sent rain on the earth and there was no one to work the ground, 6but streams*b* came up from the earth and watered the whole surface of the ground. 7Then the LORD God formed a man*c* from the dust of the ground and breathed into his nostrils the breath of life, and the man became a living being.

8Now the LORD God had planted a garden in the east, in Eden; and there he put the man he had formed. 9The LORD God made all kinds of trees grow out of the ground—trees that were pleasing to the eye and good for food. In the middle of the garden were the tree of life and the tree of the knowledge of good and evil.

10A river watering the garden flowed from Eden; from there it was separated into four headwaters. 11The name of the first is the Pishon; it winds through the entire land of Havilah, where there is gold. 12(The gold of that land is good; aromatic resin*d* and onyx are also there.)

>> INSTANT ACCESS

Sometimes you don't feel very special. You say something stupid in class. You look in the mirror and see a giant zit on your face. You? Special? You bet! You're a human being, totally special to God. When God made animals he simply spoke them into existence. But when he made Adam, God personally fashioned Adam's body from clay and then breathed the gift of life into him, a human being made in the image and likeness of God (Genesis 1:27). Oh, you'll get zits. And maybe you'll say a stupid thing or two. But don't let things like that rob you of feeling special, because you are.

{Genesis 2:7}

---

a 5 Or *land*; also in verse 6   *b* 6 Or *mist*   *c* 7 The Hebrew for *man (adam)* sounds like and may be related to the Hebrew for *ground (adamah)*; it is also the name *Adam* (see verse 20).   *d* 12 Or *good; pearls*

13 The name of the second river is the Gihon; it winds through the entire land of Cush.[a] 14 The name of the third river is the Tigris; it runs along the east side of Ashur. And the fourth river is the Euphrates.

15 The LORD God took the man and put him in the Garden of Eden to work it and take care of it. 16 And the LORD God commanded the man, "You are free to eat from any tree in the garden; 17 but you must not eat from the tree of the knowledge of good and evil, for when you eat from it you will certainly die."

18 The LORD God said, "It is not good for the man to be alone. I will make a helper suitable for him."

19 Now the LORD God had formed out of the ground all the wild animals and all the birds in the sky. He brought them to the man to see what he would name them; and whatever the man called each living creature, that was its name. 20 So the man gave names to all the livestock, the birds in the sky and all the wild animals.

But for Adam[b] no suitable helper was found. 21 So the LORD God caused the man to fall into a deep sleep; and while he was sleeping, he took one of the man's ribs[c] and then closed up the place with flesh. 22 Then the LORD God made a woman from the rib[d] he had taken out of the man, and he brought her to the man.

23 The man said,

"This is now bone of my bones
    and flesh of my flesh;
she shall be called 'woman,'
    for she was taken out of man."

24 That is why a man leaves his father and mother and is united to his wife, and they become one flesh.

25 Adam and his wife were both naked, and they felt no shame.

The Fall

3 Now the serpent was more crafty than any of the wild animals the LORD God had made. He said to the woman, "Did God really say, 'You must not eat from any tree in the garden'?"

2 The woman said to the serpent, "We may eat fruit from the trees in the garden, 3 but God did say, 'You must not eat fruit from the tree that is in the middle of the garden, and you must not touch it, or you will die.'"

4 "You will not certainly die," the serpent said to the woman. 5 "For God knows that when you eat from it your eyes will be opened, and you will be like God, knowing good and evil."

6 When the woman saw that the fruit of the tree was good for food and pleasing to the eye, and also desirable for gaining wisdom, she took some and ate it. She also gave some to her husband, who was with her, and he ate it. 7 Then the eyes of both of them were opened, and they realized they were naked; so they sewed fig leaves together and made coverings for themselves.

8 Then the man and his wife heard the sound of the LORD God as he was walking in the garden in the cool of the day, and they hid from the LORD God among the trees of the garden. 9 But the LORD God called to the man, "Where are you?"

10 He answered, "I heard you in the garden, and I was afraid because I was naked; so I hid."

11 And he said, "Who told you that you were naked? Have you eaten from the tree that I commanded you not to eat from?"

12 The man said, "The woman you put here with me—she gave me some fruit from the tree, and I ate it."

13 Then the LORD God said to the woman, "What is this you have done?"

The woman said, "The serpent deceived me, and I ate."

14 So the LORD God said to the serpent, "Because you have done this,

"Cursed are you above all
        livestock
    and all wild animals!
You will crawl on your belly
    and you will eat dust
    all the days of your life.
15 And I will put enmity
    between you and the woman,

---

[a] 13 Possibly southeast Mesopotamia   [b] 20 Or the man   [c] 21 Or took part of the man's side   [d] 22 Or part

and between your offspring[a] and
hers;
he will crush[b] your head,
and you will strike his heel."

16 To the woman he said,

"I will make your pains in childbearing
very severe;
with painful labor you will give birth
to children.
Your desire will be for your husband,
and he will rule over you."

17 To Adam he said, "Because you listened to your wife and ate fruit from the
tree about which I commanded you, 'You
must not eat from it,'

"Cursed is the ground because of
you;
through painful toil you will eat food
from it
all the days of your life.
18 It will produce thorns and thistles for
you,
and you will eat the plants of the
field.
19 By the sweat of your brow
you will eat your food
until you return to the ground,
since from it you were taken;
for dust you are
and to dust you will return."

20 Adam[c] named his wife Eve,[d] because
she would become the mother of all the
living.
21 The LORD God made garments of skin
for Adam and his wife and clothed them.
22 And the LORD God said, "The man has
now become like one of us, knowing good
and evil. He must not be allowed to reach
out his hand and take also from the tree
of life and eat, and live forever." 23 So the
LORD God banished him from the Garden
of Eden to work the ground from which he
had been taken. 24 After he drove the man
out, he placed on the east side[e] of the
Garden of Eden cherubim and a flaming
sword flashing back and forth to guard
the way to the tree of life.

INSTANT ACCESS

Adam and Eve felt scared
and guilty when God
confronted them after they ate
the forbidden fruit (Genesis
3:1–13). They probably felt a
little like you do when your
mom or dad says, "Hey, why
are you kids fighting?" Or when
one of your friends says, "Why
did you tell Sarah?" Adam and
Eve acted like people do today.
When confronted with his sin,
Adam blamed Eve. And Eve in
turn blamed the serpent. Sound
familiar? Sort of like, "Mom,
he started it." Or, "Dad, it's not
my fault." But try to remember,
you're responsible for your
choices. And, as Adam and Eve
found out, the consequences of
bad choices can hurt.

{Genesis 3:12–13}

Cain and Abel

4 Adam[c] made love to his wife Eve, and
she became pregnant and gave birth
to Cain.[f] She said, "With the help of the
LORD I have brought forth[g] a man." 2 Later
she gave birth to his brother Abel.

Now Abel kept flocks, and Cain worked
the soil. 3 In the course of time Cain
brought some of the fruits of the soil as
an offering to the LORD. 4 And Abel also
brought an offering—fat portions from

---

[a] 15 Or seed   [b] 15 Or strike   [c] 20,1 Or The man   [d] 20 Eve probably means living.   [e] 24 Or placed in front
[f] 1 Cain sounds like the Hebrew for brought forth or acquired.   [g] 1 Or have acquired

> Why is resisting temptation so hard? I have no one to talk to about this. Please help me.
>
> >> David

Dear Jordan

Dear David,

Resisting temptation can be very difficult. It has been since Adam and Eve were in the Garden of Eden. This is where we first find Satan's strategies to tempt people.

Read Genesis 3:1–6. Satan begins to raise doubts about God's Word. "Did God *really* say, 'You must not eat from any tree in the garden'? … You will not certainly die." Then the serpent tells Eve, "For God knows that when you eat from it your eyes will be opened, and you will be like God, knowing good and evil."

Adam and Eve had a huge garden to enjoy. God told them not to eat the fruit of only one tree. But instead of focusing on all God had given them to enjoy, Satan focused on the one forbidden thing. He wanted Eve to believe God was keeping the best from her. Satan wants us to doubt God's motives and to see him as having too many rules. Eve looked at the beautiful fruit. She wanted it. She took it and ate it.

Teens have so many things the world says are wonderful to try. Alcohol, sex, drugs … Satan wants you to believe these are good for you. But God tells you the truth. They're not. Alcohol and drugs cause you to make bad choices. And sex is God's amazing gift to married people. This gift is spoiled when it is abused.

Temptation is difficult because the urge comes from within us. But making good choices about what you drink, where you go and who you hang out with will help you resist falling into terrible traps.

Jordan

some of the firstborn of his flock. The LORD looked with favor on Abel and his offering, [5]but on Cain and his offering he did not look with favor. So Cain was very angry, and his face was downcast.

[6]Then the LORD said to Cain, "Why are you angry? Why is your face downcast? [7]If you do what is right, will you not be accepted? But if you do not do what is right, sin is crouching at your door; it desires to have you, but you must rule over it."

[8]Now Cain said to his brother Abel, "Let's go out to the field."[a] While they were in the field, Cain attacked his brother Abel and killed him.

[9]Then the LORD said to Cain, "Where is your brother Abel?"

"I don't know," he replied. "Am I my brother's keeper?"

[10]The LORD said, "What have you done? Listen! Your brother's blood cries out to me from the ground. [11]Now you are under a curse and driven from the ground, which opened its mouth to receive your brother's blood from your hand. [12]When you work the ground, it will no longer yield its crops for you. You will be a restless wanderer on the earth."

[13]Cain said to the LORD, "My punishment is more than I can bear. [14]Today you are driving me from the land, and I will be hidden from your presence; I will be a restless wanderer on the earth, and whoever finds me will kill me."

[15]But the LORD said to him, "Not so[b]; anyone who kills Cain will suffer vengeance seven times over." Then the LORD put a mark on Cain so that no one who found him would kill him. [16]So Cain went out from the LORD's presence and lived in the land of Nod,[c] east of Eden.

[17]Cain made love to his wife, and she became pregnant and gave birth to Enoch. Cain was then building a city, and he named it after his son Enoch. [18]To Enoch was born Irad, and Irad was the father of Mehujael, and Mehujael was the father of Methushael, and Methushael was the father of Lamech.

[19]Lamech married two women, one named Adah and the other Zillah. [20]Adah gave birth to Jabal; he was the father of those who live in tents and raise livestock. [21]His brother's name was Jubal; he was the father of all who play stringed instruments and pipes. [22]Zillah also had a son, Tubal-Cain, who forged all kinds of tools out of[d] bronze and iron. Tubal-Cain's sister was Naamah.

[23]Lamech said to his wives,

"Adah and Zillah, listen to me;
    wives of Lamech, hear my words.
I have killed a man for wounding me,
    a young man for injuring me.
[24]If Cain is avenged seven times,
    then Lamech seventy-seven
        times."

[25]Adam made love to his wife again, and she gave birth to a son and named him Seth,[e] saying, "God has granted me another child in place of Abel, since Cain killed him." [26]Seth also had a son, and he named him Enosh.

At that time people began to call on[f] the name of the LORD.

From Adam to Noah

5 This is the written account of Adam's family line.

When God created mankind, he made them in the likeness of God. [2]He created them male and female and blessed them. And he named them "Mankind"[g] when they were created.

[3]When Adam had lived 130 years, he had a son in his own likeness, in his own image; and he named him Seth. [4]After Seth was born, Adam lived 800 years and had other sons and daughters. [5]Altogether, Adam lived a total of 930 years, and then he died.

[6]When Seth had lived 105 years, he became the father[h] of Enosh. [7]After he became the father of Enosh, Seth lived 807 years and had other sons and daugh-

---

[a] 8 Samaritan Pentateuch, Septuagint, Vulgate and Syriac; Masoretic Text does not have *"Let's go out to the field."*   [b] 15 Septuagint, Vulgate and Syriac; Hebrew *Very well*   [c] 16 *Nod* means *wandering* (see verses 12 and 14).   [d] 22 Or *who instructed all who work in*   [e] 25 *Seth* probably means *granted.*   [f] 26 Or *to proclaim*   [g] 2 Hebrew *adam*   [h] 6 *Father* may mean *ancestor*; also in verses 7-26.

ters. 8Altogether, Seth lived a total of 912 years, and then he died.

9When Enosh had lived 90 years, he became the father of Kenan. 10After he became the father of Kenan, Enosh lived 815 years and had other sons and daughters. 11Altogether, Enosh lived a total of 905 years, and then he died.

12When Kenan had lived 70 years, he became the father of Mahalalel. 13After he became the father of Mahalalel, Kenan lived 840 years and had other sons and daughters. 14Altogether, Kenan lived a total of 910 years, and then he died.

15When Mahalalel had lived 65 years, he became the father of Jared. 16After he became the father of Jared, Mahalalel lived 830 years and had other sons and daughters. 17Altogether, Mahalalel lived a total of 895 years, and then he died.

18When Jared had lived 162 years, he became the father of Enoch. 19After he became the father of Enoch, Jared lived 800 years and had other sons and daughters. 20Altogether, Jared lived a total of 962 years, and then he died.

21When Enoch had lived 65 years, he became the father of Methuselah. 22After he became the father of Methuselah, Enoch walked faithfully with God 300 years and had other sons and daughters. 23Altogether, Enoch lived a total of 365 years. 24Enoch walked faithfully with God; then he was no more, because God took him away.

25When Methuselah had lived 187 years, he became the father of Lamech. 26After he became the father of Lamech, Methuselah lived 782 years and had other sons and daughters. 27Altogether, Methuselah lived a total of 969 years, and then he died.

28When Lamech had lived 182 years, he had a son. 29He named him Noaha and said, "He will comfort us in the labor and painful toil of our hands caused by the ground the LORD has cursed." 30After Noah was born, Lamech lived 595 years and had other sons and daughters. 31Altogether, Lamech lived a total of 777 years, and then he died.

32After Noah was 500 years old, he became the father of Shem, Ham and Japheth.

Wickedness in the World

6 When human beings began to increase in number on the earth and daughters were born to them, 2the sons of God saw that the daughters of humans were beautiful, and they married any of them they chose. 3Then the LORD said, "My Spirit will not contend withb humans forever, for they are mortalc; their days will be a hundred and twenty years."

4The Nephilim were on the earth in those days—and also afterward—when the sons of God went to the daughters of humans and had children by them. They were the heroes of old, men of renown.

5The LORD saw how great the wickedness of the human race had become on the earth, and that every inclination of the thoughts of the human heart was only evil all the time. 6The LORD regretted that he had made human beings on the earth, and his heart was deeply troubled. 7So the LORD said, "I will wipe from the face of the earth the human race I have created—and with them the animals, the birds and the creatures that move along the ground—for I regret that I have made them." 8But Noah found favor in the eyes of the LORD.

Noah and the Flood

9This is the account of Noah and his family.

Noah was a righteous man, blameless among the people of his time, and he walked faithfully with God. 10Noah had three sons: Shem, Ham and Japheth.

11Now the earth was corrupt in God's sight and was full of violence. 12God saw how corrupt the earth had become, for all the people on earth had corrupted their ways. 13So God said to Noah, "I am going to put an end to all people, for the earth is filled with violence because of them.

a 29 Noah sounds like the Hebrew for comfort.   b 3 Or My spirit will not remain in   c 3 Or corrupt

I am surely going to destroy both them and the earth. ¹⁴So make yourself an ark of cypressᵃ wood; make rooms in it and coat it with pitch inside and out. ¹⁵This is how you are to build it: The ark is to be three hundred cubits long, fifty cubits wide and thirty cubits high.ᵇ ¹⁶Make a roof for it, leaving below the roof an opening one cubitᶜ high all around.ᵈ Put a door in the side of the ark and make lower, middle and upper decks. ¹⁷I am going to bring floodwaters on the earth to destroy all life under the heavens, every creature that has the breath of life in it. Everything on earth will perish. ¹⁸But I will establish my covenant with you, and you will enter the ark—you and your sons and your wife and your sons' wives with you. ¹⁹You are to bring into the ark two of all living creatures, male and female, to keep them alive with you. ²⁰Two of every kind of bird, of every kind of animal and of every kind of creature that moves along the ground will come to you to be kept alive. ²¹You are to take every kind of food that is to be eaten and store it away as food for you and for them."

²²Noah did everything just as God commanded him.

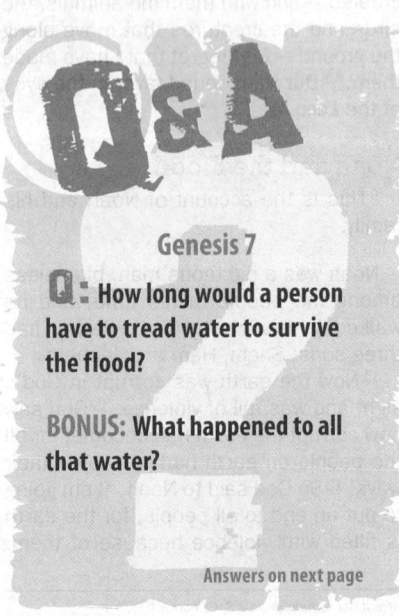

Genesis 7

Q: How long would a person have to tread water to survive the flood?

BONUS: What happened to all that water?

Answers on next page

7 The LORD then said to Noah, "Go into the ark, you and your whole family, because I have found you righteous in this generation. ²Take with you seven pairs of every kind of clean animal, a male and its mate, and one pair of every kind of unclean animal, a male and its mate, ³and also seven pairs of every kind of bird, male and female, to keep their various kinds alive throughout the earth. ⁴Seven days from now I will send rain on the earth for forty days and forty nights, and I will wipe from the face of the earth every living creature I have made."

⁵And Noah did all that the LORD commanded him.

⁶Noah was six hundred years old when the floodwaters came on the earth. ⁷And Noah and his sons and his wife and his sons' wives entered the ark to escape the waters of the flood. ⁸Pairs of clean and unclean animals, of birds and of all creatures that move along the ground, ⁹male and female, came to Noah and entered the ark, as God had commanded Noah. ¹⁰And after the seven days the floodwaters came on the earth.

¹¹In the six hundredth year of Noah's life, on the seventeenth day of the second month—on that day all the springs of the great deep burst forth, and the floodgates of the heavens were opened. ¹²And rain fell on the earth forty days and forty nights.

¹³On that very day Noah and his sons, Shem, Ham and Japheth, together with his wife and the wives of his three sons, entered the ark. ¹⁴They had with them every wild animal according to its kind, all livestock according to their kinds, every creature that moves along the ground according to its kind and every bird according to its kind, everything with wings. ¹⁵Pairs of all creatures that have the breath of life in them came to Noah and entered the ark. ¹⁶The animals going in were male and female of every living thing, as God had commanded Noah. Then the LORD shut him in.

ᵃ 14 The meaning of the Hebrew for this word is uncertain. ᵇ 15 That is, about 450 feet long, 75 feet wide and 45 feet high or about 135 meters long, 23 meters wide and 14 meters high   ᶜ 16 That is, about 18 inches or about 45 centimeters   ᵈ 16 The meaning of the Hebrew for this clause is uncertain.

17 For forty days the flood kept coming on the earth, and as the waters increased they lifted the ark high above the earth. 18 The waters rose and increased greatly on the earth, and the ark floated on the surface of the water. 19 They rose greatly on the earth, and all the high mountains under the entire heavens were covered. 20 The waters rose and covered the mountains to a depth of more than fifteen cubits.a,b 21 Every living thing that moved on land perished — birds, livestock, wild animals, all the creatures that swarm over the earth, and all mankind. 22 Everything on dry land that had the breath of life in its nostrils died. 23 Every living thing on the face of the earth was wiped out; people and animals and the creatures that move along the ground and the birds were wiped from the earth. Only Noah was left, and those with him in the ark.

24 The waters flooded the earth for a hundred and fifty days.

8 But God remembered Noah and all the wild animals and the livestock that were with him in the ark, and he sent a wind over the earth, and the waters receded. 2 Now the springs of the deep and the floodgates of the heavens had been closed, and the rain had stopped falling from the sky. 3 The water receded steadily from the earth. At the end of the hundred and fifty days the water had gone down, 4 and on the seventeenth day of the seventh month the ark came to rest on the mountains of Ararat. 5 The waters continued to recede until the tenth month, and on the first day of the tenth month the tops of the mountains became visible.

6 After forty days Noah opened a window he had made in the ark 7 and sent out a raven, and it kept flying back and forth until the water had dried up from the earth. 8 Then he sent out a dove to see if the water had receded from the surface of the ground. 9 But the dove could find nowhere to perch because there was water over all the surface of the earth; so it returned to Noah in the ark. He reached out his hand and took the dove

A: About five months (compare Genesis 7:11 and 8:4).

BONUS: Many think it fills our oceans. The weight of the waters pressed down the seabeds and thrust up the mountains.

and brought it back to himself in the ark. 10 He waited seven more days and again sent out the dove from the ark. 11 When the dove returned to him in the evening, there in its beak was a freshly plucked olive leaf! Then Noah knew that the water had receded from the earth. 12 He waited seven more days and sent the dove out again, but this time it did not return to him.

13 By the first day of the first month of Noah's six hundred and first year, the water had dried up from the earth. Noah then removed the covering from the ark and saw that the surface of the ground was dry. 14 By the twenty-seventh day of the second month the earth was completely dry.

15 Then God said to Noah, 16 "Come out of the ark, you and your wife and your sons and their wives. 17 Bring out every kind of living creature that is with you — the birds, the animals, and all the creatures that move along the ground — so they can multiply on the earth and be fruitful and increase in number on it."

18 So Noah came out, together with his sons and his wife and his sons' wives.

a 20 That is, about 23 feet or about 6.8 meters   b 20 Or rose more than fifteen cubits, and the mountains were covered

19All the animals and all the creatures that move along the ground and all the birds—everything that moves on land—came out of the ark, one kind after another.

20Then Noah built an altar to the Lord and, taking some of all the clean animals and clean birds, he sacrificed burnt offerings on it. 21The Lord smelled the pleasing aroma and said in his heart: "Never again will I curse the ground because of humans, even though*a* every inclination of the human heart is evil from childhood. And never again will I destroy all living creatures, as I have done.

22 "As long as the earth endures,
seedtime and harvest,
cold and heat,
summer and winter,
day and night
will never cease."

God's Covenant With Noah

9 Then God blessed Noah and his sons, saying to them, "Be fruitful and increase in number and fill the earth. 2The fear and dread of you will fall on all the beasts of the earth, and on all the birds in the sky, on every creature that moves along the ground, and on all the fish in the sea; they are given into your hands. 3Everything that lives and moves about will be food for you. Just as I gave you the green plants, I now give you everything.

4"But you must not eat meat that has its lifeblood still in it. 5And for your lifeblood I will surely demand an accounting. I will demand an accounting from every animal. And from each human being, too, I will demand an accounting for the life of another human being.

6"Whoever sheds human blood,
by humans shall their blood be
shed;

for in the image of God
has God made mankind.

7As for you, be fruitful and increase in number; multiply on the earth and increase upon it."

8Then God said to Noah and to his sons with him: 9"I now establish my covenant with you and with your descendants after you 10and with every living creature that was with you—the birds, the livestock and all the wild animals, all those that came out of the ark with you—every living creature on earth. 11I establish my covenant with you: Never again will all life be destroyed by the waters of a flood; never again will there be a flood to destroy the earth."

12And God said, "This is the sign of the covenant I am making between me and you and every living creature with you, a covenant for all generations to come: 13I have set my rainbow in the clouds, and it will be the sign of the covenant between me and the earth. 14Whenever I bring clouds over the earth and the rainbow appears in the clouds, 15I will remember my covenant between me and you and all living creatures of every kind. Never again will the waters become a flood to destroy all life. 16Whenever the rainbow appears in the clouds, I will see it and remember the everlasting covenant between God and all living creatures of every kind on the earth."

17So God said to Noah, "This is the sign of the covenant I have established between me and all life on the earth."

The Sons of Noah

18The sons of Noah who came out of the ark were Shem, Ham and Japheth. (Ham was the father of Canaan.) 19These were the three sons of Noah, and from them came the people who were scattered over the whole earth.

> *Never again will there be a flood to destroy the earth.*
> Genesis 9:11

---

a 21 Or *humans, for*

20Noah, a man of the soil, proceeded[a] to plant a vineyard. 21When he drank some of its wine, he became drunk and lay uncovered inside his tent. 22Ham, the father of Canaan, saw his father naked and told his two brothers outside. 23But Shem and Japheth took a garment and laid it across their shoulders; then they walked in backward and covered their father's naked body. Their faces were turned the other way so that they would not see their father naked.

24When Noah awoke from his wine and found out what his youngest son had done to him, 25he said,

"Cursed be Canaan!
    The lowest of slaves
    will he be to his brothers."

26He also said,

"Praise be to the LORD, the God of
    Shem!
    May Canaan be the slave of Shem.
27May God extend Japheth's[b] territory;
    may Japheth live in the tents of
    Shem,
    and may Canaan be the slave of
    Japheth."

28After the flood Noah lived 350 years. 29Noah lived a total of 950 years, and then he died.

The Table of Nations

10 This is the account of Shem, Ham and Japheth, Noah's sons, who themselves had sons after the flood.

The Japhethites

2The sons[c] of Japheth:
    Gomer, Magog, Madai, Javan, Tubal, Meshek and Tiras.
3The sons of Gomer:
    Ashkenaz, Riphath and Togarmah.
4The sons of Javan:
    Elishah, Tarshish, the Kittites and the Rodanites.[d] 5(From these the maritime peoples spread out into

their territories by their clans within their nations, each with its own language.)

The Hamites

6The sons of Ham:
    Cush, Egypt, Put and Canaan.
7The sons of Cush:
    Seba, Havilah, Sabtah, Raamah and Sabteka.
The sons of Raamah:
    Sheba and Dedan.

8Cush was the father[e] of Nimrod, who became a mighty warrior on the earth. 9He was a mighty hunter before the LORD; that is why it is said, "Like Nimrod, a mighty hunter before the LORD." 10The first centers of his kingdom were Babylon, Uruk, Akkad and Kalneh, in[f] Shinar.[g] 11From that land he went to Assyria, where he built Nineveh, Rehoboth Ir,[h] Calah 12and Resen, which is between Nineveh and Calah—which is the great city.

13Egypt was the father of
    the Ludites, Anamites, Lehabites, Naphtuhites, 14Pathrusites, Kasluhites (from whom the Philistines came) and Caphtorites.
15Canaan was the father of
    Sidon his firstborn,[i] and of the Hittites, 16Jebusites, Amorites, Girgashites, 17Hivites, Arkites, Sinites, 18Arvadites, Zemarites and Hamathites.

Later the Canaanite clans scattered 19and the borders of Canaan reached from Sidon toward Gerar as far as Gaza, and then toward Sodom, Gomorrah, Admah and Zeboyim, as far as Lasha.

20These are the sons of Ham by their clans and languages, in their territories and nations.

The Semites

21Sons were also born to Shem, whose older brother was[j] Japheth; Shem was the ancestor of all the sons of Eber.

---

a 20 Or soil, was the first   *b 27 Japheth sounds like the Hebrew for extend.*   *c 2 Sons may mean descendants or successors or nations; also in verses 3, 4, 6, 7, 20-23, 29 and 31.*   *d 4 Some manuscripts of the Masoretic Text and Samaritan Pentateuch (see also Septuagint and 1 Chron. 1:7); most manuscripts of the Masoretic Text Dodanites*   *e 8 Father may mean ancestor or predecessor or founder; also in verses 13, 15, 24 and 26.*   *f 10 Or Uruk and Akkad— all of them in*   *g 10 That is, Babylonia*   *h 11 Or Nineveh with its city squares*   *i 15 Or of the Sidonians, the foremost*   *j 21 Or Shem, the older brother of*

22 The sons of Shem:

Elam, Ashur, Arphaxad, Lud and Aram.

23 The sons of Aram:

Uz, Hul, Gether and Meshek.[a]

24 Arphaxad was the father of[b] Shelah, and Shelah the father of Eber.

25 Two sons were born to Eber:

One was named Peleg,[c] because in his time the earth was divided; his brother was named Joktan.

26 Joktan was the father of

Almodad, Sheleph, Hazarmaveth, Jerah, 27 Hadoram, Uzal, Diklah, 28 Obal, Abimael, Sheba, 29 Ophir, Havilah and Jobab. All these were sons of Joktan.

30 The region where they lived stretched from Mesha toward Sephar, in the eastern hill country.

31 These are the sons of Shem by their clans and languages, in their territories and nations.

32 These are the clans of Noah's sons, according to their lines of descent, within their nations. From these the nations spread out over the earth after the flood.

The Tower of Babel

11 Now the whole world had one language and a common speech. 2 As people moved eastward,[d] they found a plain in Shinar[e] and settled there.

3 They said to each other, "Come, let's make bricks and bake them thoroughly." They used brick instead of stone, and tar for mortar. 4 Then they said, "Come, let us build ourselves a city, with a tower that reaches to the heavens, so that we may make a name for ourselves; otherwise we will be scattered over the face of the whole earth."

5 But the LORD came down to see the city and the tower the people were building. 6 The LORD said, "If as one people speaking the same language they have begun to do this, then nothing they plan to do will be impossible for them. 7 Come, let us go down and confuse their language so they will not understand each other."

8 So the LORD scattered them from there over all the earth, and they stopped building the city. 9 That is why it was called Babel[f]—because there the LORD confused the language of the whole world. From there the LORD scattered them over the face of the whole earth.

From Shem to Abram

10 This is the account of Shem's family line.

Two years after the flood, when Shem was 100 years old, he became the father[g] of Arphaxad. 11 And after he became the father of Arphaxad, Shem lived 500 years and had other sons and daughters.

12 When Arphaxad had lived 35 years, he became the father of Shelah. 13 And after he became the father of Shelah, Arphaxad lived 403 years and had other sons and daughters.[h]

14 When Shelah had lived 30 years, he became the father of Eber. 15 And after he became the father of Eber, Shelah lived 403 years and had other sons and daughters.

16 When Eber had lived 34 years, he became the father of Peleg. 17 And after he became the father of Peleg, Eber lived 430 years and had other sons and daughters.

18 When Peleg had lived 30 years, he became the father of Reu. 19 And after he became the father of Reu, Peleg lived 209 years and had other sons and daughters.

20 When Reu had lived 32 years, he became the father of Serug. 21 And after he became the father of Serug, Reu lived 207 years and had other sons and daughters.

22 When Serug had lived 30 years, he became the father of Nahor. 23 And after

---

a 23 See Septuagint and 1 Chron. 1:17; Hebrew *Mash*.   b 24 Hebrew; Septuagint *father of Cainan, and Cainan was the father of*   c 25 *Peleg* means *division*.   d 2 Or *from the east; or in the east*   e 2 That is, Babylonia   f 9 That is, Babylon; *Babel* sounds like the Hebrew for *confused*.   g 10 *Father* may mean *ancestor*; also in verses 11-25.
h 12,13 Hebrew; Septuagint (see also Luke 3:35, 36 and note at Gen. 10:24) *35 years, he became the father of Cainan.* 13And after he became the father of Cainan, Arphaxad lived 430 years and had other sons and daughters, and then he died. When Cainan had lived 130 years, he became the father of Shelah. And after he became the father of Shelah, Cainan lived 330 years and had other sons and daughters

he became the father of Nahor, Serug lived 200 years and had other sons and daughters.

²⁴When Nahor had lived 29 years, he became the father of Terah. ²⁵And after he became the father of Terah, Nahor lived 119 years and had other sons and daughters.

²⁶After Terah had lived 70 years, he became the father of Abram, Nahor and Haran.

Abram's Family

²⁷This is the account of Terah's family line.

Terah became the father of Abram, Nahor and Haran. And Haran became the father of Lot. ²⁸While his father Terah was still alive, Haran died in Ur of the Chaldeans, in the land of his birth. ²⁹Abram and Nahor both married. The name of Abram's wife was Sarai, and the name of Nahor's wife was Milkah; she was the daughter of Haran, the father of both Milkah and Iskah. ³⁰Now Sarai was childless because she was not able to conceive.

³¹Terah took his son Abram, his grandson Lot son of Haran, and his daughter-in-law Sarai, the wife of his son Abram, and together they set out from Ur of the Chaldeans to go to Canaan. But when they came to Harran, they settled there.

³²Terah lived 205 years, and he died in Harran.

The Call of Abram

12 The LORD had said to Abram, "Go from your country, your people and your father's household to the land I will show you.

TO THE POINT

God Keeps His Promises

God made Abraham several promises in Genesis 12:2–3, and he has kept every one!

+ Abraham's descendants, the Jews, are still a distinct and numerous people today.

+ Abraham was wealthy and protected by the Lord throughout his long life.

+ Even after 4,000 years, three world religions—Christianity, Judaism and Islam—honor Abraham.

+ The Hitlers of history who have tried to destroy the Jews have been destroyed themselves.

+ Jesus, a descendant of Abraham, brings salvation to all who will believe.

God's Word is full of his promises to you—and you can count on him to keep every one.

² "I will make you into a great nation,
   and I will bless you;
I will make your name great,
   and you will be a blessing.ᵃ
³ I will bless those who bless you,
   and whoever curses you I will curse;
and all peoples on earth
   will be blessed through you."ᵇ

⁴ So Abram went, as the LORD had told him; and Lot went with him. Abram was seventy-five years old when he set out from Harran. ⁵ He took his wife Sarai, his nephew Lot, all the possessions they had accumulated and the people they had acquired in Harran, and they set out for the land of Canaan, and they arrived there.

⁶ Abram traveled through the land as far as the site of the great tree of Moreh at Shechem. At that time the Canaanites were in the land. ⁷ The LORD appeared to Abram and said, "To your offspringᶜ I will give this land." So he built an altar there to the LORD, who had appeared to him.

⁸ From there he went on toward the hills east of Bethel and pitched his tent, with Bethel on the west and Ai on the east. There he built an altar to the LORD and called on the name of the LORD. ⁹ Then Abram set out and continued toward the Negev.

Abram in Egypt

¹⁰ Now there was a famine in the land, and Abram went down to Egypt to live there for a while because the famine was severe. ¹¹ As he was about to enter Egypt, he said to his wife Sarai, "I know what a beautiful woman you are. ¹² When the Egyptians see you, they will say, 'This is his wife.' Then they will kill me but will let you live. ¹³ Say you are my sister, so that I will be treated well for your sake and my life will be spared because of you."

¹⁴ When Abram came to Egypt, the Egyptians saw that Sarai was a very beautiful woman. ¹⁵ And when Pharaoh's officials saw her, they praised her to Pharaoh, and she was taken into his palace. ¹⁶ He treated Abram well for her sake, and Abram acquired sheep and cattle, male and female donkeys, male and female servants, and camels.

¹⁷ But the LORD inflicted serious diseases on Pharaoh and his household because of Abram's wife Sarai. ¹⁸ So Pharaoh summoned Abram. "What have you done to me?" he said. "Why didn't you tell me she was your wife? ¹⁹ Why did you say, 'She is my sister,' so that I took her to be my wife? Now then, here is your wife. Take her and go!" ²⁰ Then Pharaoh gave orders about Abram to his men, and they sent him on his way, with his wife and everything he had.

Abram and Lot Separate

13 So Abram went up from Egypt to the Negev, with his wife and everything he had, and Lot went with him. ² Abram had become very wealthy in livestock and in silver and gold.

³ From the Negev he went from place to place until he came to Bethel, to the place between Bethel and Ai where his tent had been earlier ⁴ and where he had first built an altar. There Abram called on the name of the LORD.

⁵ Now Lot, who was moving about with Abram, also had flocks and herds and tents. ⁶ But the land could not support them while they stayed together, for their possessions were so great that they were not able to stay together. ⁷ And quarreling arose between Abram's herders and Lot's. The Canaanites and Perizzites were also living in the land at that time.

⁸ So Abram said to Lot, "Let's not have any quarreling between you and me, or between your herders and mine, for we are close relatives. ⁹ Is not the whole land before you? Let's part company. If you go to the left, I'll go to the right; if you go to the right, I'll go to the left."

¹⁰ Lot looked around and saw that the whole plain of the Jordan toward Zoar was well watered, like the garden of the LORD, like the land of Egypt. (This was before the LORD destroyed Sodom and Gomorrah.) ¹¹ So Lot chose for himself the whole plain of the Jordan and set out toward the east. The two men parted compa-

---

ᵃ 2 Or *be seen as blessed*   ᵇ 3 Or *earth / will use your name in blessings* (see 48:20)   ᶜ 7 Or *seed*

ny: [12]Abram lived in the land of Canaan, while Lot lived among the cities of the plain and pitched his tents near Sodom. [13]Now the people of Sodom were wicked and were sinning greatly against the LORD.

[14]The LORD said to Abram after Lot had parted from him, "Look around from where you are, to the north and south, to the east and west. [15]All the land that you see I will give to you and your offspring[a] forever. [16]I will make your offspring like the dust of the earth, so that if anyone could count the dust, then your offspring could be counted. [17]Go, walk through the length and breadth of the land, for I am giving it to you."

[18]So Abram went to live near the great trees of Mamre at Hebron, where he pitched his tents. There he built an altar to the LORD.

Abram Rescues Lot

14 At the time when Amraphel was king of Shinar,[b] Arioch king of Ellasar, Kedorlaomer king of Elam and Tidal king of Goyim, [2]these kings went to war against Bera king of Sodom, Birsha king of Gomorrah, Shinab king of Admah, Shemeber king of Zeboyim, and the king of Bela (that is, Zoar). [3]All these latter kings joined forces in the Valley of Siddim (that is, the Dead Sea Valley). [4]For twelve years they had been subject to Kedorlaomer, but in the thirteenth year they rebelled.

[5]In the fourteenth year, Kedorlaomer and the kings allied with him went out and defeated the Rephaites in Ashteroth Karnaim, the Zuzites in Ham, the Emites in Shaveh Kiriathaim [6]and the Horites in the hill country of Seir, as far as El Paran near the desert. [7]Then they turned back and went to En Mishpat (that is, Kadesh), and they conquered the whole territory of the Amalekites, as well as the Amorites who were living in Hazezon Tamar.

[8]Then the king of Sodom, the king of Gomorrah, the king of Admah, the king of Zeboyim and the king of Bela (that is, Zoar) marched out and drew up their battle lines in the Valley of Siddim [9]against Kedorlaomer king of Elam, Tidal king of Goyim, Amraphel king of Shinar and Arioch king of Ellasar — four kings against five. [10]Now the Valley of Siddim was full of tar pits, and when the kings of Sodom and Gomorrah fled, some of the men fell into them and the rest fled to the hills. [11]The four kings seized all the goods of Sodom and Gomorrah and all their food; then they went away. [12]They also carried off Abram's nephew Lot and his possessions, since he was living in Sodom.

[13]A man who had escaped came and reported this to Abram the Hebrew. Now Abram was living near the great trees of Mamre the Amorite, a brother[c] of Eshkol and Aner, all of whom were allied with Abram. [14]When Abram heard that his relative had been taken captive, he called out the 318 trained men born in his household and went in pursuit as far as Dan. [15]During the night Abram divided his men to attack them and he routed them, pursuing them as far as Hobah, north of Damascus. [16]He recovered all the goods and brought back his relative Lot and his possessions, together with the women and the other people.

[17]After Abram returned from defeating Kedorlaomer and the kings allied with him, the king of Sodom came out to meet him in the Valley of Shaveh (that is, the King's Valley).

[18]Then Melchizedek king of Salem brought out bread and wine. He was priest of God Most High, [19]and he blessed Abram, saying,

"Blessed be Abram by God Most High,
    Creator of heaven and earth.
[20]And praise be to God Most High,
    who delivered your enemies into
        your hand."

Then Abram gave him a tenth of everything.

[21]The king of Sodom said to Abram, "Give me the people and keep the goods for yourself."

[22]But Abram said to the king of Sodom, "With raised hand I have sworn an oath to the LORD, God Most High, Creator of heaven and earth, [23]that I will accept nothing

---

[a] 15 Or seed; also in verse 16   [b] 1 That is, Babylonia; also in verse 9   [c] 13 Or a relative; or an ally

belonging to you, not even a thread or the strap of a sandal, so that you will never be able to say, 'I made Abram rich.' 24I will accept nothing but what my men have eaten and the share that belongs to the men who went with me—to Aner, Eshkol and Mamre. Let them have their share."

The LORD's Covenant With Abram

15 After this, the word of the LORD came to Abram in a vision:

"Do not be afraid, Abram.
I am your shield,[a]
your very great reward.[b]"

2But Abram said, "Sovereign LORD, what can you give me since I remain childless and the one who will inherit[c] my estate is Eliezer of Damascus?" 3And Abram said, "You have given me no children; so a servant in my household will be my heir." 4Then the word of the LORD came to him: "This man will not be your heir, but a son who is your own flesh and blood will be your heir." 5He took him outside and said, "Look up at the sky and count the stars—if indeed you can count them." Then he said to him, "So shall your offspring[d] be."

6Abram believed the LORD, and he credited it to him as righteousness.

7He also said to him, "I am the LORD, who brought you out of Ur of the Chaldeans to give you this land to take possession of it."

8But Abram said, "Sovereign LORD, how can I know that I will gain possession of it?"

9So the LORD said to him, "Bring me a heifer, a goat and a ram, each three years old, along with a dove and a young pigeon."

10Abram brought all these to him, cut them in two and arranged the halves opposite each other; the birds, however, he did not cut in half. 11Then birds of prey came down on the carcasses, but Abram drove them away.

12As the sun was setting, Abram fell into a deep sleep, and a thick and dreadful darkness came over him. 13Then the LORD said to him, "Know for certain that for four hundred years your descendants will be strangers in a country not their own and that they will be enslaved and mistreated there. 14But I will punish the nation they serve as slaves, and afterward they will come out with great possessions. 15You, however, will go to your ancestors in peace and be buried at a good old age. 16In the fourth generation your descendants will come back here, for the sin of the Amorites has not yet reached its full measure."

17When the sun had set and darkness had fallen, a smoking firepot with a blazing torch appeared and passed between the pieces. 18On that day the LORD made a covenant with Abram and said, "To your descendants I give this land, from the Wadi[e] of Egypt to the great river, the Euphrates— 19the land of the Kenites, Kenizzites, Kadmonites, 20Hittites, Perizzites, Rephaites, 21Amorites, Canaanites, Girgashites and Jebusites."

I am your shield, your very great reward.
Genesis 15:1

Hagar and Ishmael

16 Now Sarai, Abram's wife, had borne him no children. But she had an Egyptian slave named Hagar; 2so she said to Abram, "The LORD has kept me from having children. Go, sleep with my slave; perhaps I can build a family through her."

Abram agreed to what Sarai said. 3So after Abram had been living in Canaan ten years, Sarai his wife took her Egyptian slave Hagar and gave her to her husband

---

a 1 Or sovereign   b 1 Or shield; / your reward will be very great   c 2 The meaning of the Hebrew for this phrase is uncertain.   d 5 Or seed   e 18 Or river

D o you ever feel like running away? Maybe your brothers and sisters bug you. Mom doesn't understand. Dad yells at you. Things are so bad at home you can't get your schoolwork done, and your grades have dropped so low you are afraid you might fail. But is running away the only option? In this Bible story, Hagar was so hurt by Abram's jealous wife Sarah that she ran away. But God's angel told Hagar to go back and submit. The angel added, "I will increase your descendants" (Genesis 16:10). Running away when things are tough may seem like the only way out. But usually it's hanging in there that leads to God's blessing.

{Genesis 16:6–10}

》INSTANT ACCESS

said. "Do with her whatever you think best." Then Sarai mistreated Hagar; so she fled from her.

⁷The angel of the LORD found Hagar near a spring in the desert; it was the spring that is beside the road to Shur. ⁸And he said, "Hagar, slave of Sarai, where have you come from, and where are you going?"

"I'm running away from my mistress Sarai," she answered.

⁹Then the angel of the LORD told her, "Go back to your mistress and submit to her." ¹⁰The angel added, "I will increase your descendants so much that they will be too numerous to count."

¹¹The angel of the LORD also said to her:

"You are now pregnant
    and you will give birth to a son.
You shall name him Ishmael,ᵃ
    for the LORD has heard of your
        misery.
¹²He will be a wild donkey of a man;
    his hand will be against everyone
        and everyone's hand against him,
    and he will live in hostility
        towardᵇ all his brothers."

¹³She gave this name to the LORD who spoke to her: "You are the God who sees me," for she said, "I have now seenᶜ the One who sees me." ¹⁴That is why the well was called Beer Lahai Roiᵈ; it is still there, between Kadesh and Bered.

¹⁵So Hagar bore Abram a son, and Abram gave the name Ishmael to the son she had borne. ¹⁶Abram was eighty-six years old when Hagar bore him Ishmael.

The Covenant of Circumcision

17 When Abram was ninety-nine years old, the LORD appeared to him and said, "I am God Almightyᵉ; walk before me faithfully and be blameless. ²Then I will make my covenant between me and you and will greatly increase your numbers."

³Abram fell facedown, and God said to him, ⁴"As for me, this is my covenant with you: You will be the father of many

to be his wife. ⁴He slept with Hagar, and she conceived.

When she knew she was pregnant, she began to despise her mistress. ⁵Then Sarai said to Abram, "You are responsible for the wrong I am suffering. I put my slave in your arms, and now that she knows she is pregnant, she despises me. May the LORD judge between you and me."

⁶"Your slave is in your hands," Abram

ᵃ 11 Ishmael means God hears.   ᵇ 12 Or live to the east / of well of the Living One who sees me.   ᶜ 13 Or seen the back of   ᵈ 14 Beer Lahai Roi means   ᵉ 1 Hebrew El-Shaddai

nations. [5]No longer will you be called Abram[a]; your name will be Abraham,[b] for I have made you a father of many nations. [6]I will make you very fruitful; I will make nations of you, and kings will come from you. [7]I will establish my covenant as an everlasting covenant between me and you and your descendants after you for the generations to come, to be your God and the God of your descendants after you. [8]The whole land of Canaan, where you now reside as a foreigner, I will give as an everlasting possession to you and your descendants after you; and I will be their God."

[9]Then God said to Abraham, "As for you, you must keep my covenant, you and your descendants after you for the generations to come. [10]This is my covenant with you and your descendants after you, the covenant you are to keep: Every male among you shall be circumcised. [11]You are to undergo circumcision, and it will be the sign of the covenant between me and you. [12]For the generations to come every male among you who is eight days old must be circumcised, including those born in your household or bought with money from a foreigner—those who are not your offspring. [13]Whether born in your household or bought with your money, they must be circumcised. My covenant in your flesh is to be an everlasting covenant. [14]Any uncircumcised male, who has not been circumcised in the flesh, will be cut off from his people; he has broken my covenant."

[15]God also said to Abraham, "As for Sarai your wife, you are no longer to call her Sarai; her name will be Sarah. [16]I will bless her and will surely give you a son by her. I will bless her so that she will be the mother of nations; kings of peoples will come from her."

[17]Abraham fell facedown; he laughed and said to himself, "Will a son be born to a man a hundred years old? Will Sarah bear a child at the age of ninety?" [18]And Abraham said to God, "If only Ishmael might live under your blessing!"

[19]Then God said, "Yes, but your wife Sarah will bear you a son, and you will call him Isaac.[c] I will establish my covenant with him as an everlasting covenant for his descendants after him. [20]And as for Ishmael, I have heard you: I will surely bless him; I will make him fruitful and will greatly increase his numbers. He will be the father of twelve rulers, and I will make him into a great nation. [21]But my covenant I will establish with Isaac, whom Sarah will bear to you by this time next year." [22]When he had finished speaking with Abraham, God went up from him.

[23]On that very day Abraham took his son Ishmael and all those born in his household or bought with his money, every male in his household, and circumcised them, as God told him. [24]Abraham was ninety-nine years old when he was circumcised, [25]and his son Ishmael was thirteen; [26]Abraham and his son Ishmael were both circumcised on that very day. [27]And every male in Abraham's household, including those born in his household or bought from a foreigner, was circumcised with him.

The Three Visitors

18 The Lord appeared to Abraham near the great trees of Mamre while he was sitting at the entrance to his tent in the heat of the day. [2]Abraham looked up and saw three men standing nearby. When he saw them, he hurried from the entrance of his tent to meet them and bowed low to the ground.

[3]He said, "If I have found favor in your eyes, my lord,[d] do not pass your servant by. [4]Let a little water be brought, and then you may all wash your feet and rest under this tree. [5]Let me get you something to eat, so you can be refreshed and then go on your way—now that you have come to your servant."

"Very well," they answered, "do as you say."

[6]So Abraham hurried into the tent to Sarah. "Quick," he said, "get three seahs[e] of the finest flour and knead it and bake some bread."

---

[a] 5 *Abram* means *exalted father.*   [b] 5 *Abraham* probably means *father of many.*   [c] 19 *Isaac* means *he laughs.*
[d] 3 Or *eyes, Lord*   [e] 6 That is, probably about 36 pounds or about 16 kilograms

[7] Then he ran to the herd and selected a choice, tender calf and gave it to a servant, who hurried to prepare it. [8] He then brought some curds and milk and the calf that had been prepared, and set these before them. While they ate, he stood near them under a tree.

[9] "Where is your wife Sarah?" they asked him.

"There, in the tent," he said.

[10] Then one of them said, "I will surely return to you about this time next year, and Sarah your wife will have a son."

Now Sarah was listening at the entrance to the tent, which was behind him. [11] Abraham and Sarah were already very old, and Sarah was past the age of childbearing. [12] So Sarah laughed to herself as she thought, "After I am worn out and my lord is old, will I now have this pleasure?"

[13] Then the LORD said to Abraham, "Why did Sarah laugh and say, 'Will I really have a child, now that I am old?' [14] Is anything too hard for the LORD? I will return to you at the appointed time next year, and Sarah will have a son."

[15] Sarah was afraid, so she lied and said, "I did not laugh."

But he said, "Yes, you did laugh."

Abraham Pleads for Sodom

[16] When the men got up to leave, they looked down toward Sodom, and Abraham walked along with them to see them on their way. [17] Then the LORD said, "Shall I hide from Abraham what I am about to do? [18] Abraham will surely become a great and powerful nation, and all nations on earth will be blessed through him.[a] [19] For I have chosen him, so that he will direct his children and his household after him to keep the way of the LORD by doing what is right and just, so that the LORD will bring about for Abraham what he has promised him."

[20] Then the LORD said, "The outcry against Sodom and Gomorrah is so great and their sin so grievous [21] that I will go down and see if what they have done is as bad as the outcry that has reached me. If not, I will know."

[22] The men turned away and went toward Sodom, but Abraham remained standing before the LORD.[b] [23] Then Abraham approached him and said: "Will you sweep away the righteous with the wicked? [24] What if there are fifty righteous people in the city? Will you really sweep it away and not spare[c] the place for the sake of the fifty righteous people in it? [25] Far be it from you to do such a thing— to kill the righteous with the wicked, treating the righteous and the wicked alike. Far be it from you! Will not the Judge of all the earth do right?"

[26] The LORD said, "If I find fifty righteous people in the city of Sodom, I will spare the whole place for their sake."

[27] Then Abraham spoke up again: "Now that I have been so bold as to speak to the Lord, though I am nothing but dust and ashes, [28] what if the number of the righteous is five less than fifty? Will you destroy the whole city for lack of five people?"

"If I find forty-five there," he said, "I will not destroy it."

[29] Once again he spoke to him, "What if only forty are found there?"

He said, "For the sake of forty, I will not do it."

[30] Then he said, "May the Lord not be angry, but let me speak. What if only thirty can be found there?"

He answered, "I will not do it if I find thirty there."

[31] Abraham said, "Now that I have been so bold as to speak to the Lord, what if only twenty can be found there?"

He said, "For the sake of twenty, I will not destroy it."

[32] Then he said, "May the Lord not be angry, but let me speak just once more. What if only ten can be found there?"

He answered, "For the sake of ten, I will not destroy it."

[33] When the LORD had finished speaking with Abraham, he left, and Abraham returned home.

---

[a] 18 Or will use his name in blessings (see 48:20)   [b] 22 Masoretic Text; an ancient Hebrew scribal tradition *but the LORD remained standing before Abraham*   [c] 24 Or *forgive*; also in verse 26

Sodom and Gomorrah Destroyed

19 The two angels arrived at Sodom in the evening, and Lot was sitting in the gateway of the city. When he saw them, he got up to meet them and bowed down with his face to the ground. ²"My lords," he said, "please turn aside to your servant's house. You can wash your feet and spend the night and then go on your way early in the morning."

"No," they answered, "we will spend the night in the square."

³But he insisted so strongly that they did go with him and entered his house. He prepared a meal for them, baking bread without yeast, and they ate. ⁴Before they had gone to bed, all the men from every part of the city of Sodom—both young and old—surrounded the house. ⁵They called to Lot, "Where are the men who came to you tonight? Bring them out to us so that we can have sex with them."

⁶Lot went outside to meet them and shut the door behind him ⁷and said, "No, my friends. Don't do this wicked thing. ⁸Look, I have two daughters who have never slept with a man. Let me bring them out to you, and you can do what you like with them. But don't do anything to these men, for they have come under the protection of my roof."

⁹"Get out of our way," they replied. "This fellow came here as a foreigner, and now he wants to play the judge! We'll treat you worse than them." They kept bringing pressure on Lot and moved forward to break down the door.

¹⁰But the men inside reached out and pulled Lot back into the house and shut the door. ¹¹Then they struck the men who were at the door of the house, young and old, with blindness so that they could not find the door.

¹²The two men said to Lot, "Do you have anyone else here—sons-in-law, sons or daughters, or anyone else in the city who belongs to you? Get them out of here, ¹³because we are going to destroy this place. The outcry to the LORD against

its people is so great that he has sent us to destroy it."

¹⁴So Lot went out and spoke to his sons-in-law, who were pledged to marryª his daughters. He said, "Hurry and get out of this place, because the LORD is about to destroy the city!" But his sons-in-law thought he was joking.

¹⁵With the coming of dawn, the angels urged Lot, saying, "Hurry! Take your wife and your two daughters who are here, or

---

≫ INSTANT ACCESS

Do you ever worry that God might be upset when you keep on asking for something? Abraham felt the same way. He said, "May the Lord not be angry, but let me speak just once more" (Genesis 18:32). God wasn't angry at all. For one thing, Abraham was asking God to be merciful. Abraham asked God to spare Sodom for the sake of ten righteous people. God could find only one: Lot. So he made sure Lot and his family escaped before fire destroyed the wicked city. If you know that what you're praying for honors God and is the kind of thing he wants to do, you don't need to be anxious. Your prayers are pleasing to the Lord.

{Genesis 18:32}

ª 14 Or were married to

you will be swept away when the city is punished."

¹⁶When he hesitated, the men grasped his hand and the hands of his wife and of his two daughters and led them safely out of the city, for the Lord was merciful to them. ¹⁷As soon as they had brought them out, one of them said, "Flee for your lives! Don't look back, and don't stop anywhere in the plain! Flee to the mountains or you will be swept away!"

¹⁸But Lot said to them, "No, my lords,ᵃ please! ¹⁹Yourᵇ servant has found favor in yourᵇ eyes, and youᵇ have shown great kindness to me in sparing my life. But I can't flee to the mountains; this disaster will overtake me, and I'll die. ²⁰Look, here is a town near enough to run to, and it is small. Let me flee to it—it is very small, isn't it? Then my life will be spared."

²¹He said to him, "Very well, I will grant this request too; I will not overthrow the town you speak of. ²²But flee there quickly, because I cannot do anything until you reach it." (That is why the town was called Zoar.ᶜ)

²³By the time Lot reached Zoar, the sun had risen over the land. ²⁴Then the Lord rained down burning sulfur on Sodom and Gomorrah—from the Lord out of the heavens. ²⁵Thus he overthrew those cities and the entire plain, destroying all those living in the cities—and also the vegetation in the land. ²⁶But Lot's wife looked back, and she became a pillar of salt.

²⁷Early the next morning Abraham got up and returned to the place where he had stood before the Lord. ²⁸He looked down toward Sodom and Gomorrah, toward all the land of the plain, and he saw dense smoke rising from the land, like smoke from a furnace.

²⁹So when God destroyed the cities of the plain, he remembered Abraham, and he brought Lot out of the catastrophe that overthrew the cities where Lot had lived.

Lot and His Daughters

³⁰Lot and his two daughters left Zoar and settled in the mountains, for he was afraid to stay in Zoar. He and his two daughters lived in a cave. ³¹One day the older daughter said to the younger, "Our father is old, and there is no man around here to give us children—as is the custom all over the earth. ³²Let's get our father to drink wine and then sleep with him and preserve our family line through our father."

³³That night they got their father to drink wine, and the older daughter went in and slept with him. He was not aware of it when she lay down or when she got up.

³⁴The next day the older daughter said to the younger, "Last night I slept with my father. Let's get him to drink wine again tonight, and you go in and sleep with him so we can preserve our family line through our father." ³⁵So they got their father to drink wine that night also, and the younger daughter went in and slept with him. Again he was not aware of it when she lay down or when she got up.

³⁶So both of Lot's daughters became pregnant by their father. ³⁷The older daughter had a son, and she named him Moabᵈ; he is the father of the Moabites of today. ³⁸The younger daughter also had a son, and she named him Ben-Ammiᵉ; he is the father of the Ammonitesᶠ of today.

Abraham and Abimelek

20 Now Abraham moved on from there into the region of the Negev and lived between Kadesh and Shur. For a while he stayed in Gerar, ²and there Abraham said of his wife Sarah, "She is my sister." Then Abimelek king of Gerar sent for Sarah and took her.

³But God came to Abimelek in a dream one night and said to him, "You are as good as dead because of the woman you have taken; she is a married woman."

⁴Now Abimelek had not gone near her, so he said, "Lord, will you destroy an innocent nation? ⁵Did he not say to me, 'She is my sister,' and didn't she also say, 'He is my brother'? I have done this with a clear conscience and clean hands."

⁶Then God said to him in the dream,

ᵃ 18 Or No, Lord; or No, my lord   ᵇ 19 The Hebrew is singular.   ᶜ 22 Zoar means small.   ᵈ 37 Moab sounds like the Hebrew for from father.   ᵉ 38 Ben-Ammi means son of my father's people.   ᶠ 38 Hebrew Bene-Ammon

"Yes, I know you did this with a clear conscience, and so I have kept you from sinning against me. That is why I did not let you touch her. ⁷Now return the man's wife, for he is a prophet, and he will pray for you and you will live. But if you do not return her, you may be sure that you and all who belong to you will die."

⁸Early the next morning Abimelek summoned all his officials, and when he told them all that had happened, they were very much afraid. ⁹Then Abimelek called Abraham in and said, "What have you done to us? How have I wronged you that you have brought such great guilt upon me and my kingdom? You have done things to me that should never be done." ¹⁰And Abimelek asked Abraham, "What was your reason for doing this?"

¹¹Abraham replied, "I said to myself, 'There is surely no fear of God in this place, and they will kill me because of my wife.' ¹²Besides, she really is my sister, the daughter of my father though not of my mother; and she became my wife. ¹³And when God had me wander from my father's household, I said to her, 'This is how you can show your love to me: Everywhere we go, say of me, "He is my brother." ' "

¹⁴Then Abimelek brought sheep and cattle and male and female slaves and gave them to Abraham, and he returned Sarah his wife to him. ¹⁵And Abimelek said, "My land is before you; live wherever you like."

¹⁶To Sarah he said, "I am giving your brother a thousand shekels*ᵃ* of silver. This is to cover the offense against you before all who are with you; you are completely vindicated."

¹⁷Then Abraham prayed to God, and God healed Abimelek, his wife and his female slaves so they could have children again, ¹⁸for the Lᴏʀᴅ had kept all the women in Abimelek's household from conceiving because of Abraham's wife Sarah.

The Birth of Isaac

21 Now the Lᴏʀᴅ was gracious to Sarah as he had said, and the Lᴏʀᴅ did for Sarah what he had promised.

> # ≫ INSTANT ACCESS
>
> **M**oving away and going to a new school can be pretty scary. Abraham was afraid when he moved to a new area of what we now call the Holy Land. He was so afraid that he asked his wife Sarah to lie for him. That lie got him into all sorts of trouble. Abraham was afraid of the strangers because they didn't know God. But he forgot that God knew them! If you find yourself in places where people don't know God or don't live godly lives, remember that God is there already. Read this story, and remember that wherever you go, God goes too.
>
> {Genesis 20:11}

²Sarah became pregnant and bore a son to Abraham in his old age, at the very time God had promised him. ³Abraham gave the name Isaacᵇ to the son Sarah bore him. ⁴When his son Isaac was eight days old, Abraham circumcised him, as God commanded him. ⁵Abraham was a hundred years old when his son Isaac was born to him.

⁶Sarah said, "God has brought me laughter, and everyone who hears about this will laugh with me." ⁷And she added, "Who would have said to Abraham that Sarah would nurse children? Yet I have borne him a son in his old age."

ᵃ *16 That is, about 25 pounds or about 12 kilograms*   ᵇ *3 Isaac means he laughs.*

Probably nothing hurts as much as rejection. Sometimes kids of divorced parents feel like their parents divorced them instead of each other. And sometimes a child actually *is* rejected or abandoned. Abraham didn't want to send Hagar or Ishmael away, but God told him to do what Sarah insisted. It hurt Abraham to be separated from his son. It also hurt Ishmael, who was a teenager. But God spoke to each of them to make the hurt easier to bear. At times you will feel rejected by someone you love. When that happens, try to remember this story. Whatever happens, God will be at your side.

{Genesis 21:8–18}

》》INSTANT ACCESS

Hagar and Ishmael Sent Away

8The child grew and was weaned, and on the day Isaac was weaned Abraham held a great feast. 9But Sarah saw that the son whom Hagar the Egyptian had borne to Abraham was mocking, 10and she said to Abraham, "Get rid of that slave woman and her son, for that woman's son will never share in the inheritance with my son Isaac."

11The matter distressed Abraham greatly because it concerned his son. 12But God said to him, "Do not be so distressed about the boy and your slave woman. Listen to whatever Sarah tells you, because it is through Isaac that your offspring[a] will be reckoned. 13I will make the son of the slave into a nation also, because he is your offspring."

14Early the next morning Abraham took some food and a skin of water and gave them to Hagar. He set them on her shoulders and then sent her off with the boy. She went on her way and wandered in the Desert of Beersheba.

15When the water in the skin was gone, she put the boy under one of the bushes. 16Then she went off and sat down about a bowshot away, for she thought, "I cannot watch the boy die." And as she sat there, she[b] began to sob.

17God heard the boy crying, and the angel of God called to Hagar from heaven and said to her, "What is the matter, Hagar? Do not be afraid; God has heard the boy crying as he lies there. 18Lift the boy up and take him by the hand, for I will make him into a great nation."

19Then God opened her eyes and she saw a well of water. So she went and filled the skin with water and gave the boy a drink.

20God was with the boy as he grew up. He lived in the desert and became an archer. 21While he was living in the Desert of Paran, his mother got a wife for him from Egypt.

The Treaty at Beersheba

22At that time Abimelek and Phicol the commander of his forces said to Abraham, "God is with you in everything you do. 23Now swear to me here before God that you will not deal falsely with me or my children or my descendants. Show to me and the country where you now reside as a foreigner the same kindness I have shown to you."

24Abraham said, "I swear it."

25Then Abraham complained to Abimelek about a well of water that Abimelek's servants had seized. 26But Abimelek said, "I don't know who has done this. You did not tell me, and I heard about it only today."

---

[a] 12 Or seed   [b] 16 Hebrew; Septuagint *the child*

27 So Abraham brought sheep and cattle and gave them to Abimelek, and the two men made a treaty. 28 Abraham set apart seven ewe lambs from the flock, 29 and Abimelek asked Abraham, "What is the meaning of these seven ewe lambs you have set apart by themselves?"

30 He replied, "Accept these seven lambs from my hand as a witness that I dug this well."

31 So that place was called Beersheba,[a] because the two men swore an oath there.

32 After the treaty had been made at Beersheba, Abimelek and Phicol the commander of his forces returned to the land of the Philistines. 33 Abraham planted a tamarisk tree in Beersheba, and there he called on the name of the LORD, the Eternal God. 34 And Abraham stayed in the land of the Philistines for a long time.

Abraham Tested

22 Some time later God tested Abraham. He said to him, "Abraham!"

"Here I am," he replied.

2 Then God said, "Take your son, your only son, whom you love—Isaac—and go to the region of Moriah. Sacrifice him there as a burnt offering on a mountain I will show you."

3 Early the next morning Abraham got up and loaded his donkey. He took with him two of his servants and his son Isaac. When he had cut enough wood for the burnt offering, he set out for the place God had told him about. 4 On the third day Abraham looked up and saw the place in the distance. 5 He said to his servants, "Stay here with the donkey while I and the boy go over there. We will worship and then we will come back to you."

6 Abraham took the wood for the burnt offering and placed it on his son Isaac, and he himself carried the fire and the knife. As the two of them went on together, 7 Isaac spoke up and said to his father Abraham, "Father?"

"Yes, my son?" Abraham replied.

"The fire and wood are here," Isaac said, "but where is the lamb for the burnt offering?"

8 Abraham answered, "God himself will provide the lamb for the burnt offering, my son." And the two of them went on together.

9 When they reached the place God had told him about, Abraham built an altar there and arranged the wood on it. He bound his son Isaac and laid him on the altar, on top of the wood. 10 Then he reached out his hand and took the

>> **INSTANT ACCESS**

Faith is doing right even when you don't know how God is going to work things out. Abraham had that kind of faith. God promised Abraham that his descendants would come through Isaac. But when God told Abraham to offer his son Isaac as a sacrifice, Abraham didn't hesitate. Abraham was sure that God would keep his promises even though he didn't know how God could if Isaac were dead. That's the kind of faith that will give you the courage to always do what's right. You don't have to know how God will work things out. You only need to know that, if you obey, God will keep his promises.

{Genesis 22:5}

knife to slay his son. ¹¹But the angel of the LORD called out to him from heaven, "Abraham! Abraham!"

"Here I am," he replied.

¹²"Do not lay a hand on the boy," he said. "Do not do anything to him. Now I know that you fear God, because you have not withheld from me your son, your only son."

¹³Abraham looked up and there in a thicket he saw a ram[a] caught by its horns. He went over and took the ram and sacrificed it as a burnt offering instead of his son. ¹⁴So Abraham called that place The LORD Will Provide. And to this day it is said, "On the mountain of the LORD it will be provided."

¹⁵The angel of the LORD called to Abraham from heaven a second time ¹⁶and said, "I swear by myself, declares the LORD, that because you have done this and have not withheld your son, your only son, ¹⁷I will surely bless you and make your descendants as numerous as the stars in the sky and as the sand on the seashore. Your descendants will take possession of the cities of their enemies, ¹⁸and through your offspring[b] all nations on earth will be blessed,[c] because you have obeyed me."

¹⁹Then Abraham returned to his servants, and they set off together for Beersheba. And Abraham stayed in Beersheba.

Nahor's Sons

²⁰Some time later Abraham was told, "Milkah is also a mother; she has borne sons to your brother Nahor: ²¹Uz the firstborn, Buz his brother, Kemuel (the father of Aram), ²²Kesed, Hazo, Pildash, Jidlaph and Bethuel." ²³Bethuel became the father of Rebekah. Milkah bore these eight sons to Abraham's brother Nahor. ²⁴His concubine, whose name was Reumah, also had sons: Tebah, Gaham, Tahash and Maakah.

The Death of Sarah

23 Sarah lived to be a hundred and twenty-seven years old. ²She

died at Kiriath Arba (that is, Hebron) in the land of Canaan, and Abraham went to mourn for Sarah and to weep over her. ³Then Abraham rose from beside his dead wife and spoke to the Hittites.[d] He said, ⁴"I am a foreigner and stranger among you. Sell me some property for a burial site here so I can bury my dead."

⁵The Hittites replied to Abraham, ⁶"Sir, listen to us. You are a mighty prince among us. Bury your dead in the choicest of our tombs. None of us will refuse you his tomb for burying your dead."

⁷Then Abraham rose and bowed down before the people of the land, the Hittites. ⁸He said to them, "If you are willing to let me bury my dead, then listen to me and intercede with Ephron son of Zohar on my behalf ⁹so he will sell me the cave of Machpelah, which belongs to him and is at the end of his field. Ask him to sell it to me for the full price as a burial site among you."

¹⁰Ephron the Hittite was sitting among his people and he replied to Abraham in the hearing of all the Hittites who had come to the gate of his city. ¹¹"No, my lord," he said. "Listen to me; I give[e] you the field, and I give[e] you the cave that is in it. I give[e] it to you in the presence of my people. Bury your dead."

¹²Again Abraham bowed down before the people of the land ¹³and he said to Ephron in their hearing, "Listen to me, if you will. I will pay the price of the field. Accept it from me so I can bury my dead there."

¹⁴Ephron answered Abraham, ¹⁵"Listen to me, my lord; the land is worth four hundred shekels[f] of silver, but what is that between you and me? Bury your dead."

¹⁶Abraham agreed to Ephron's terms and weighed out for him the price he had named in the hearing of the Hittites: four hundred shekels of silver, according to the weight current among the merchants.

¹⁷So Ephron's field in Machpelah near Mamre—both the field and the cave in it, and all the trees within the borders of the field—was deeded ¹⁸to Abraham as his

---

[a] 13 Many manuscripts of the Masoretic Text, Samaritan Pentateuch, Septuagint and Syriac; most manuscripts of the Masoretic Text *a ram behind him*   [b] 18 Or *seed*   [c] 18 Or *and all nations on earth will use the name of your offspring in blessings* (see 48:20)   [d] 3 Or *the descendants of Heth*; also in verses 5, 7, 10, 16, 18 and 20   [e] 11 Or *sell*   [f] 15 That is, about 10 pounds or about 4.6 kilograms

property in the presence of all the Hittites who had come to the gate of the city. 19 Afterward Abraham buried his wife Sarah in the cave in the field of Machpelah near Mamre (which is at Hebron) in the land of Canaan. 20 So the field and the cave in it were deeded to Abraham by the Hittites as a burial site.

Isaac and Rebekah

24 Abraham was now very old, and the LORD had blessed him in every way. 2 He said to the senior servant in his household, the one in charge of all that he had, "Put your hand under my thigh. 3 I want you to swear by the LORD, the God of heaven and the God of earth, that you will not get a wife for my son from the daughters of the Canaanites, among whom I am living, 4 but will go to my country and my own relatives and get a wife for my son Isaac."

5 The servant asked him, "What if the woman is unwilling to come back with me to this land? Shall I then take your son back to the country you came from?"

6 "Make sure that you do not take my son back there," Abraham said. 7 "The LORD, the God of heaven, who brought me out of my father's household and my native land and who spoke to me and promised me on oath, saying, 'To your offspring[a] I will give this land'—he will send his angel before you so that you can get a wife for my son from there. 8 If the woman is unwilling to come back with you, then you will be released from this oath of mine. Only do not take my son back there." 9 So the servant put his hand under the thigh of his master Abraham and swore an oath to him concerning this matter.

10 Then the servant left, taking with him ten of his master's camels loaded with all kinds of good things from his master. He set out for Aram Naharaim[b] and made his way to the town of Nahor. 11 He had the camels kneel down near the well outside the town; it was toward evening, the time the women go out to draw water.

12 Then he prayed, "LORD, God of my master Abraham, make me successful today, and show kindness to my master Abraham. 13 See, I am standing beside this spring, and the daughters of the townspeople are coming out to draw water. 14 May it be that when I say to a young woman, 'Please let down your jar that I may have a drink,' and she says, 'Drink, and I'll water your camels too'—let her be the one you have chosen for your servant Isaac. By this I will know that you have shown kindness to my master."

15 Before he had finished praying, Rebekah came out with her jar on her shoulder. She was the daughter of Bethuel son of Milkah, who was the wife of Abraham's brother Nahor. 16 The woman was very beautiful, a virgin; no man had ever slept with her. She went down to the spring, filled her jar and came up again.

17 The servant hurried to meet her and said, "Please give me a little water from your jar."

18 "Drink, my lord," she said, and quickly lowered the jar to her hands and gave him a drink.

19 After she had given him a drink, she said, "I'll draw water for your camels too, until they have had enough to drink." 20 So she quickly emptied her jar into the trough, ran back to the well to draw more water, and drew enough for all his camels. 21 Without saying a word, the man watched her closely to learn whether or not the LORD had made his journey successful.

22 When the camels had finished drinking, the man took out a gold nose ring weighing a beka[c] and two gold bracelets weighing ten shekels.[d] 23 Then he asked, "Whose daughter are you? Please tell me, is there room in your father's house for us to spend the night?"

24 She answered him, "I am the daughter of Bethuel, the son that Milkah bore to Nahor." 25 And she added, "We have plenty of straw and fodder, as well as room for you to spend the night."

26 Then the man bowed down and wor-

---

[a] 7 Or seed   [b] 10 That is, Northwest Mesopotamia   [c] 22 That is, about 1/5 ounce or about 5.7 grams   [d] 22 That is, about 4 ounces or about 115 grams

Choosing the person you will marry is serious business. A good choice will bring you a happy, rewarding life. A poor choice can make you miserable. That's why it's important to involve God in your dating life even when you're young. You're probably not planning to get married yet. Dating is a time for fun and for getting to know lots of kids of the opposite sex. But it's also a time when you develop attitudes that will shape your choice of a mate. Genesis 24 teaches that God will lead you if you ask his help in choosing a mate.

{Genesis 24:14}

≫ INSTANT ACCESS

shiped the LORD, ²⁷ saying, "Praise be to the LORD, the God of my master Abraham, who has not abandoned his kindness and faithfulness to my master. As for me, the LORD has led me on the journey to the house of my master's relatives."

²⁸ The young woman ran and told her mother's household about these things. ²⁹ Now Rebekah had a brother named Laban, and he hurried out to the man at the spring. ³⁰ As soon as he had seen the nose ring, and the bracelets on his sister's arms, and had heard Rebekah tell what the man said to her, he went out to the man and found him standing by the camels near the spring. ³¹ "Come, you who are blessed by the LORD," he said. "Why are you standing out here? I have

prepared the house and a place for the camels."

³² So the man went to the house, and the camels were unloaded. Straw and fodder were brought for the camels, and water for him and his men to wash their feet. ³³ Then food was set before him, but he said, "I will not eat until I have told you what I have to say."

"Then tell us," Laban said.

³⁴ So he said, "I am Abraham's servant. ³⁵ The LORD has blessed my master abundantly, and he has become wealthy. He has given him sheep and cattle, silver and gold, male and female servants, and camels and donkeys. ³⁶ My master's wife Sarah has borne him a son in her old age, and he has given him everything he owns. ³⁷ And my master made me swear an oath, and said, 'You must not get a wife for my son from the daughters of the Canaanites, in whose land I live, ³⁸ but go to my father's family and to my own clan, and get a wife for my son.'

³⁹ "Then I asked my master, 'What if the woman will not come back with me?'

⁴⁰ "He replied, 'The LORD, before whom I have walked faithfully, will send his angel with you and make your journey a success, so that you can get a wife for my son from my own clan and from my father's family. ⁴¹ You will be released from my oath if, when you go to my clan, they refuse to give her to you—then you will be released from my oath.'

⁴² "When I came to the spring today, I said, 'LORD, God of my master Abraham, if you will, please grant success to the journey on which I have come. ⁴³ See, I am standing beside this spring. If a young woman comes out to draw water and I say to her, "Please let me drink a little water from your jar," ⁴⁴ and if she says to me, "Drink, and I'll draw water for your camels too," let her be the one the LORD has chosen for my master's son.'

⁴⁵ "Before I finished praying in my heart, Rebekah came out, with her jar on her shoulder. She went down to the spring and drew water, and I said to her, 'Please give me a drink.'

⁴⁶ "She quickly lowered her jar from her shoulder and said, 'Drink, and I'll water

your camels too.' So I drank, and she watered the camels also.

⁴⁷"I asked her, 'Whose daughter are you?'

"She said, 'The daughter of Bethuel son of Nahor, whom Milkah bore to him.'

"Then I put the ring in her nose and the bracelets on her arms, ⁴⁸and I bowed down and worshiped the Lord. I praised the Lord, the God of my master Abraham, who had led me on the right road to get the granddaughter of my master's brother for his son. ⁴⁹Now if you will show kindness and faithfulness to my master, tell me; and if not, tell me, so I may know which way to turn."

⁵⁰Laban and Bethuel answered, "This is from the Lord; we can say nothing to you one way or the other. ⁵¹Here is Rebekah; take her and go, and let her become the wife of your master's son, as the Lord has directed."

⁵²When Abraham's servant heard what they said, he bowed down to the ground before the Lord. ⁵³Then the servant brought out gold and silver jewelry and articles of clothing and gave them to Rebekah; he also gave costly gifts to her brother and to her mother. ⁵⁴Then he and the men who were with him ate and drank and spent the night there.

When they got up the next morning, he said, "Send me on my way to my master." ⁵⁵But her brother and her mother replied, "Let the young woman remain with us ten days or so; then you*a* may go." ⁵⁶But he said to them, "Do not detain me, now that the Lord has granted success to my journey. Send me on my way so I may go to my master."

⁵⁷Then they said, "Let's call the young woman and ask her about it." ⁵⁸So they called Rebekah and asked her, "Will you go with this man?"

"I will go," she said.

⁵⁹So they sent their sister Rebekah on her way, along with her nurse and Abraham's servant and his men. ⁶⁰And they blessed Rebekah and said to her,

"Our sister, may you increase
  to thousands upon thousands;

may your offspring possess
  the cities of their enemies."

⁶¹Then Rebekah and her attendants got ready and mounted the camels and went back with the man. So the servant took Rebekah and left.

⁶²Now Isaac had come from Beer Lahai Roi, for he was living in the Negev. ⁶³He went out to the field one evening to meditate,*b* and as he looked up, he saw camels approaching. ⁶⁴Rebekah also looked up and saw Isaac. She got down from her camel ⁶⁵and asked the servant, "Who is that man in the field coming to meet us?"

"He is my master," the servant answered. So she took her veil and covered herself.

⁶⁶Then the servant told Isaac all he had done. ⁶⁷Isaac brought her into the tent of his mother Sarah, and he married Rebekah. So she became his wife, and he loved her; and Isaac was comforted after his mother's death.

The Death of Abraham

25 Abraham had taken another wife, whose name was Keturah. ²She bore him Zimran, Jokshan, Medan, Midian, Ishbak and Shuah. ³Jokshan was the father of Sheba and Dedan; the descendants of Dedan were the Ashurites, the Letushites and the Leummites. ⁴The sons of Midian were Ephah, Epher, Hanok, Abida and Eldaah. All these were descendants of Keturah.

⁵Abraham left everything he owned to Isaac. ⁶But while he was still living, he gave gifts to the sons of his concubines and sent them away from his son Isaac to the land of the east.

⁷Abraham lived a hundred and seventy-five years. ⁸Then Abraham breathed his last and died at a good old age, an old man and full of years; and he was gathered to his people. ⁹His sons Isaac and Ishmael buried him in the cave of Machpelah near Mamre, in the field of Ephron son of Zohar the Hittite, ¹⁰the field Abraham had bought from the Hittites.*c* There Abraham was buried with his wife Sarah.

a 55 Or she   *b* 63 The meaning of the Hebrew for this word is uncertain.   *c* 10 Or the descendants of Heth

¹¹After Abraham's death, God blessed his son Isaac, who then lived near Beer Lahai Roi.

Ishmael's Sons

¹²This is the account of the family line of Abraham's son Ishmael, whom Sarah's slave, Hagar the Egyptian, bore to Abraham.

¹³These are the names of the sons of Ishmael, listed in the order of their birth: Nebaioth the firstborn of Ishmael, Kedar, Adbeel, Mibsam, ¹⁴Mishma, Dumah, Massa, ¹⁵Hadad, Tema, Jetur, Naphish and Kedemah. ¹⁶These were the sons of Ishmael, and these are the names of the twelve tribal rulers according to their settlements and camps. ¹⁷Ishmael lived a hundred and thirty-seven years. He breathed his last and died, and he was gathered to his people. ¹⁸His descendants settled in the area from Havilah to Shur, near the eastern border of Egypt, as you go toward Ashur. And they lived in hostility toward*ᵃ* all the tribes related to them.

Jacob and Esau

¹⁹This is the account of the family line of Abraham's son Isaac.

Abraham became the father of Isaac, ²⁰and Isaac was forty years old when he married Rebekah daughter of Bethuel the Aramean from Paddan Aramᵇ and sister of Laban the Aramean.

²¹Isaac prayed to the LORD on behalf of his wife, because she was childless. The LORD answered his prayer, and his wife Rebekah became pregnant. ²²The babies jostled each other within her, and she said, "Why is this happening to me?" So she went to inquire of the LORD.

²³The LORD said to her,

"Two nations are in your womb,
    and two peoples from within you will
        be separated;
one people will be stronger than the
        other,

and the older will serve the
        younger."

²⁴When the time came for her to give birth, there were twin boys in her womb. ²⁵The first to come out was red, and his whole body was like a hairy garment; so they named him Esau.ᶜ ²⁶After this, his brother came out, with his hand grasping Esau's heel; so he was named Jacob.ᵈ Isaac was sixty years old when Rebekah gave birth to them.

²⁷The boys grew up, and Esau became a skillful hunter, a man of the open country, while Jacob was content to stay at home among the tents. ²⁸Isaac, who had a taste for wild game, loved Esau, but Rebekah loved Jacob.

²⁹Once when Jacob was cooking some stew, Esau came in from the open country, famished. ³⁰He said to Jacob, "Quick, let me have some of that red stew! I'm famished!" (That is why he was also called Edom.ᵉ)

³¹Jacob replied, "First sell me your birthright."

³²"Look, I am about to die," Esau said. "What good is the birthright to me?"

³³But Jacob said, "Swear to me first." So he swore an oath to him, selling his birthright to Jacob.

³⁴Then Jacob gave Esau some bread and some lentil stew. He ate and drank, and then got up and left.

So Esau despised his birthright.

Isaac and Abimelek

26 Now there was a famine in the land—besides the previous famine in Abraham's time—and Isaac went to Abimelek king of the Philistines in Gerar. ²The LORD appeared to Isaac and said, "Do not go down to Egypt; live in the land where I tell you to live. ³Stay in this land for a while, and I will be with you and will bless you. For to you and your descendants I will give all these lands and will confirm the oath I swore to your father Abraham. ⁴I will make your descendants as numerous as the stars in the sky and

ᵃ 18 Or *lived to the east of*   ᵇ 20 That is, Northwest Mesopotamia   ᶜ 25 *Esau* may mean *hairy.*   ᵈ 26 *Jacob* means *he grasps the heel*, a Hebrew idiom for *he deceives.*   ᵉ 30 *Edom* means *red.*

will give them all these lands, and through your offspring[a] all nations on earth will be blessed,[b] [5]because Abraham obeyed me and did everything I required of him, keeping my commands, my decrees and my instructions." [6]So Isaac stayed in Gerar.

[7]When the men of that place asked him about his wife, he said, "She is my sister," because he was afraid to say, "She is my wife." He thought, "The men of this place might kill me on account of Rebekah, because she is beautiful."

[8]When Isaac had been there a long time, Abimelek king of the Philistines looked down from a window and saw Isaac caressing his wife Rebekah. [9]So Abimelek summoned Isaac and said, "She is really your wife! Why did you say, 'She is my sister'?"

Isaac answered him, "Because I thought I might lose my life on account of her."

[10]Then Abimelek said, "What is this you have done to us? One of the men might well have slept with your wife, and you would have brought guilt upon us."

[11]So Abimelek gave orders to all the people: "Anyone who harms this man or his wife shall surely be put to death."

[12]Isaac planted crops in that land and the same year reaped a hundredfold, because the LORD blessed him. [13]The man became rich, and his wealth continued to grow until he became very wealthy. [14]He had so many flocks and herds and servants that the Philistines envied him. [15]So all the wells that his father's servants had dug in the time of his father Abraham, the Philistines stopped up, filling them with earth.

[16]Then Abimelek said to Isaac, "Move away from us; you have become too powerful for us."

[17]So Isaac moved away from there and encamped in the Valley of Gerar, where he settled. [18]Isaac reopened the wells that had been dug in the time of his father Abraham, which the Philistines had stopped up after Abraham died, and he

INSTANT ACCESS

Picture Esau, hungry after being out hunting. His brother Jacob held out a pot of stew and offered a trade: a bowlful for a birthright. As the oldest son, Esau had the right to inherit his father Isaac's possessions as well as God's promises to his grandfather Abraham. Esau looked at that stew and, without giving a second thought to God, told Jacob to take the birthright because he was famished! Foolish? You bet. Just as foolish as the choices some teens and adults make today, trading away their tomorrow for the thrills of today.

{Genesis 25:24–34}

gave them the same names his father had given them.

[19]Isaac's servants dug in the valley and discovered a well of fresh water there. [20]But the herders of Gerar quarreled with those of Isaac and said, "The water is ours!" So he named the well Esek,[c] because they disputed with him. [21]Then they dug another well, but they quarreled over that one also; so he named it Sitnah.[d] [22]He moved on from there and dug another well, and no one quarreled over it. He named it Rehoboth,[e] saying, "Now the LORD has given us room and we will flourish in the land."

[23]From there he went up to Beershe-

---

[a] 4 Or seed   [b] 4 Or and all nations on earth will use the name of your offspring in blessings (see 48:20)   [c] 20 Esek means dispute.   [d] 21 Sitnah means opposition.   [e] 22 Rehoboth means room.

ba. 24That night the Lord appeared to him and said, "I am the God of your father Abraham. Do not be afraid, for I am with you; I will bless you and will increase the number of your descendants for the sake of my servant Abraham."

25Isaac built an altar there and called on the name of the Lord. There he pitched his tent, and there his servants dug a well.

26Meanwhile, Abimelek had come to him from Gerar, with Ahuzzath his personal adviser and Phicol the commander of his forces. 27Isaac asked them, "Why have you come to me, since you were hostile to me and sent me away?"

28They answered, "We saw clearly that the Lord was with you; so we said, 'There ought to be a sworn agreement between us'—between us and you. Let us make a treaty with you 29that you will do us no harm, just as we did not harm you but always treated you well and sent you away peacefully. And now you are blessed by the Lord."

30Isaac then made a feast for them, and they ate and drank. 31Early the next morning the men swore an oath to each other. Then Isaac sent them on their way, and they went away peacefully.

32That day Isaac's servants came and told him about the well they had dug. They said, "We've found water!" 33He called it Shibah,ª and to this day the name of the town has been Beersheba.ᵇ

Jacob Takes Esau's Blessing

34When Esau was forty years old, he married Judith daughter of Beeri the Hittite, and also Basemath daughter of Elon the Hittite. 35They were a source of grief to Isaac and Rebekah.

27 When Isaac was old and his eyes were so weak that he could no longer see, he called for Esau his older son and said to him, "My son."

"Here I am," he answered.

2Isaac said, "I am now an old man and don't know the day of my death. 3Now then, get your equipment—your quiver and bow—and go out to the open country to hunt some wild game for me. 4Prepare me the kind of tasty food I like and bring it to me to eat, so that I may give you my blessing before I die."

5Now Rebekah was listening as Isaac spoke to his son Esau. When Esau left for the open country to hunt game and bring it back, 6Rebekah said to her son Jacob, "Look, I overheard your father say to your brother Esau, 7'Bring me some game and prepare me some tasty food to eat, so that I may give you my blessing in the presence of the Lord before I die.' 8Now, my son, listen carefully and do what I tell you: 9Go out to the flock and bring me two choice young goats, so I can prepare some tasty food for your father, just the way he likes it. 10Then take it to your father to eat, so that he may give you his blessing before he dies."

11Jacob said to Rebekah his mother, "But my brother Esau is a hairy man while I have smooth skin. 12What if my father touches me? I would appear to be tricking him and would bring down a curse on myself rather than a blessing."

13His mother said to him, "My son, let the curse fall on me. Just do what I say; go and get them for me."

14So he went and got them and brought them to his mother, and she prepared some tasty food, just the way his father liked it. 15Then Rebekah took the best clothes of Esau her older son, which she had in the house, and put them on her younger son Jacob. 16She also covered his hands and the smooth part of his neck with the goatskins. 17Then she handed to her son Jacob the tasty food and the bread she had made.

18He went to his father and said, "My father."

"Yes, my son," he answered. "Who is it?"

19Jacob said to his father, "I am Esau your firstborn. I have done as you told me. Please sit up and eat some of my game, so that you may give me your blessing."

20Isaac asked his son, "How did you find it so quickly, my son?"

"The Lord your God gave me success," he replied.

ª 33 *Shibah* can mean *oath* or *seven.*   ᵇ 33 *Beersheba* can mean *well of the oath* and *well of seven.*

21 Then Isaac said to Jacob, "Come near so I can touch you, my son, to know whether you really are my son Esau or not."

22 Jacob went close to his father Isaac, who touched him and said, "The voice is the voice of Jacob, but the hands are the hands of Esau." 23 He did not recognize him, for his hands were hairy like those of his brother Esau; so he proceeded to bless him. 24 "Are you really my son Esau?" he asked.

"I am," he replied.

25 Then he said, "My son, bring me some of your game to eat, so that I may give you my blessing."

Jacob brought it to him and he ate; and he brought some wine and he drank. 26 Then his father Isaac said to him, "Come here, my son, and kiss me."

27 So he went to him and kissed him. When Isaac caught the smell of his clothes, he blessed him and said,

"Ah, the smell of my son
    is like the smell of a field
    that the LORD has blessed.
28 May God give you heaven's dew
    and earth's richness—
    an abundance of grain and new
        wine.
29 May nations serve you
    and peoples bow down to you.
Be lord over your brothers,
    and may the sons of your mother
        bow down to you.
May those who curse you be cursed
    and those who bless you be
        blessed."

30 After Isaac finished blessing him, and Jacob had scarcely left his father's presence, his brother Esau came in from hunting. 31 He too prepared some tasty food and brought it to his father. Then he said to him, "My father, please sit up and eat some of my game, so that you may give me your blessing."

32 His father Isaac asked him, "Who are you?"

"I am your son," he answered, "your firstborn, Esau."

33 Isaac trembled violently and said,

INSTANT ACCESS

Are you envious of that guy in the next row? You know, the one with all the answers written on his hand? He got an A on the last test! But before you decide cheating pays off, check what happened when Jacob cheated his brother Esau out of their father's blessing. In Old Testament times a father's "blessing" was both a will and a prophecy. It guaranteed the success of the son who received it. And Jacob got that blessing—by cheating. But read verse 41 and you'll see that Jacob got more than he bargained for. Sure, some people cheat and get away with it, but usually cheating brings more negative results than you expect.

{Genesis 27:1-41}

"Who was it, then, that hunted game and brought it to me? I ate it just before you came and I blessed him—and indeed he will be blessed!"

34 When Esau heard his father's words, he burst out with a loud and bitter cry and said to his father, "Bless me—me too, my father!"

35 But he said, "Your brother came deceitfully and took your blessing."

36 Esau said, "Isn't he rightly named Jacob[a]? This is the second time he has

---

[a] 36 Jacob means he grasps the heel, a Hebrew idiom for he takes advantage of or he deceives.

taken advantage of me: He took my birthright, and now he's taken my blessing!" Then he asked, "Haven't you reserved any blessing for me?"

37 Isaac answered Esau, "I have made him lord over you and have made all his relatives his servants, and I have sustained him with grain and new wine. So what can I possibly do for you, my son?"

38 Esau said to his father, "Do you have only one blessing, my father? Bless me too, my father!" Then Esau wept aloud.

39 His father Isaac answered him,

"Your dwelling will be
    away from the earth's richness,
    away from the dew of heaven
        above.
40 You will live by the sword
    and you will serve your brother.
But when you grow restless,
    you will throw his yoke
    from off your neck."

41 Esau held a grudge against Jacob because of the blessing his father had given him. He said to himself, "The days of mourning for my father are near; then I will kill my brother Jacob."

42 When Rebekah was told what her older son Esau had said, she sent for her younger son Jacob and said to him, "Your brother Esau is planning to avenge himself by killing you. 43 Now then, my son, do what I say: Flee at once to my brother Laban in Harran. 44 Stay with him for a while until your brother's fury subsides. 45 When your brother is no longer angry with you and forgets what you did to him, I'll send word for you to come back from there. Why should I lose both of you in one day?"

46 Then Rebekah said to Isaac, "I'm disgusted with living because of these Hittite women. If Jacob takes a wife from among the women of this land, from Hittite women like these, my life will not be worth living."

28 So Isaac called for Jacob and blessed him. Then he commanded him: "Do not marry a Canaanite woman. 2 Go at once to Paddan Aram,[a] to the house of your mother's father Bethuel. Take a wife for yourself there, from among the daughters of Laban, your mother's brother. 3 May God Almighty[b] bless you and make you fruitful and increase your numbers until you become a community of peoples. 4 May he give you and your descendants the blessing given to Abraham, so that you may take possession of the land where you now reside as a foreigner, the land God gave to Abraham." 5 Then Isaac sent Jacob on his way, and he went to Paddan Aram, to Laban son of Bethuel the Aramean, the brother of Rebekah, who was the mother of Jacob and Esau.

6 Now Esau learned that Isaac had blessed Jacob and had sent him to Paddan Aram to take a wife from there, and that when he blessed him he commanded him, "Do not marry a Canaanite woman," 7 and that Jacob had obeyed his father and mother and had gone to Paddan Aram. 8 Esau then realized how displeasing the Canaanite women were to his father Isaac; 9 so he went to Ishmael and married Mahalath, the sister of Nebaioth and daughter of Ishmael son of Abraham, in addition to the wives he already had.

Jacob's Dream at Bethel

10 Jacob left Beersheba and set out for Harran. 11 When he reached a certain place, he stopped for the night because the sun had set. Taking one of the stones there, he put it under his head and lay down to sleep. 12 He had a dream in which he saw a stairway resting on the earth, with its top reaching to heaven, and the angels of God were ascending and descending on it. 13 There above it[c] stood the LORD, and he said: "I am the LORD, the God of your father Abraham and the God of Isaac. I will give you and your descendants the land on which you are lying. 14 Your descendants will be like the dust of the earth, and you will spread out to the west and to the east, to the north and to the south. All peoples on earth will be blessed through you and your offspring.[d]

a 2 That is, Northwest Mesopotamia; also in verses 5, 6 and 7   b 3 Hebrew El-Shaddai   c 13 Or There beside him
d 14 Or will use your name and the name of your offspring in blessings (see 48:20)

¹⁵I am with you and will watch over you wherever you go, and I will bring you back to this land. I will not leave you until I have done what I have promised you."

¹⁶When Jacob awoke from his sleep, he thought, "Surely the LORD is in this place, and I was not aware of it." ¹⁷He was afraid and said, "How awesome is this place! This is none other than the house of God; this is the gate of heaven."

¹⁸Early the next morning Jacob took the stone he had placed under his head and set it up as a pillar and poured oil on top of it. ¹⁹He called that place Bethel,ᵃ though the city used to be called Luz.

²⁰Then Jacob made a vow, saying, "If God will be with me and will watch over me on this journey I am taking and will give me food to eat and clothes to wear ²¹so that I return safely to my father's household, then the LORDᵇ will be my God ²²andᶜ this stone that I have set up as a pillar will be God's house, and of all that you give me I will give you a tenth."

Jacob Arrives in Paddan Aram

29 Then Jacob continued on his journey and came to the land of the eastern peoples. ²There he saw a well in the open country, with three flocks of sheep lying near it because the flocks were watered from that well. The stone over the mouth of the well was large. ³When all the flocks were gathered there, the shepherds would roll the stone away from the well's mouth and water the sheep. Then they would return the stone to its place over the mouth of the well.

⁴Jacob asked the shepherds, "My brothers, where are you from?"

"We're from Harran," they replied.

⁵He said to them, "Do you know Laban, Nahor's grandson?"

"Yes, we know him," they answered.

⁶Then Jacob asked them, "Is he well?"

"Yes, he is," they said, "and here comes his daughter Rachel with the sheep."

⁷"Look," he said, "the sun is still high; it is not time for the flocks to be gathered. Water the sheep and take them back to pasture."

⁸"We can't," they replied, "until all the flocks are gathered and the stone has been rolled away from the mouth of the well. Then we will water the sheep."

⁹While he was still talking with them, Rachel came with her father's sheep, for she was a shepherd. ¹⁰When Jacob saw Rachel daughter of his uncle Laban, and Laban's sheep, he went over and rolled the stone away from the mouth of the well and watered his uncle's sheep. ¹¹Then Jacob kissed Rachel and began to weep aloud. ¹²He had told Rachel that he was a relative of her father and a son of Rebekah. So she ran and told her father.

¹³As soon as Laban heard the news about Jacob, his sister's son, he hurried to meet him. He embraced him and kissed him and brought him to his home, and there Jacob told him all these things. ¹⁴Then Laban said to him, "You are my own flesh and blood."

Jacob Marries Leah and Rachel

After Jacob had stayed with him for a whole month, ¹⁵Laban said to him, "Just because you are a relative of mine, should you work for me for nothing? Tell me what your wages should be."

¹⁶Now Laban had two daughters; the name of the older was Leah, and the name of the younger was Rachel. ¹⁷Leah had weakᵈ eyes, but Rachel had a lovely figure and was beautiful. ¹⁸Jacob was in love with Rachel and said, "I'll work for

> *I am with you and will watch over you wherever you go.*
> **Genesis 28:15**

ᵃ 19 Bethel means house of God.   ᵇ 20,21 Or Since God . . . father's household, the LORD   ᶜ 21,22 Or household, and the LORD will be my God, ²²then   ᵈ 17 Or delicate

you seven years in return for your younger daughter Rachel."

¹⁹Laban said, "It's better that I give her to you than to some other man. Stay here with me." ²⁰So Jacob served seven years to get Rachel, but they seemed like only a few days to him because of his love for her.

²¹Then Jacob said to Laban, "Give me my wife. My time is completed, and I want to make love to her."

²²So Laban brought together all the people of the place and gave a feast. ²³But when evening came, he took his daughter Leah and brought her to Jacob, and Jacob made love to her. ²⁴And Laban gave his servant Zilpah to his daughter as her attendant.

²⁵When morning came, there was Leah! So Jacob said to Laban, "What is this you have done to me? I served you for Rachel, didn't I? Why have you deceived me?"

²⁶Laban replied, "It is not our custom here to give the younger daughter in marriage before the older one. ²⁷Finish this daughter's bridal week; then we will give you the younger one also, in return for another seven years of work."

²⁸And Jacob did so. He finished the week with Leah, and then Laban gave him his daughter Rachel to be his wife. ²⁹Laban gave his servant Bilhah to his daughter Rachel as her attendant. ³⁰Jacob made love to Rachel also, and his love for Rachel was greater than his love for Leah. And he worked for Laban another seven years.

Jacob's Children

³¹When the LORD saw that Leah was not loved, he enabled her to conceive, but Rachel remained childless. ³²Leah became pregnant and gave birth to a son. She named him Reuben,ᵃ for she said, "It is because the LORD has seen my misery. Surely my husband will love me now."

³³She conceived again, and when she gave birth to a son she said, "Because

the LORD heard that I am not loved, he gave me this one too." So she named him Simeon.ᵇ

³⁴Again she conceived, and when she gave birth to a son she said, "Now at last my husband will become attached to me, because I have borne him three sons." So he was named Levi.ᶜ

³⁵She conceived again, and when she gave birth to a son she said, "This time I will praise the LORD." So she named him Judah.ᵈ Then she stopped having children.

30 When Rachel saw that she was not bearing Jacob any children, she became jealous of her sister. So she said to Jacob, "Give me children, or I'll die!"

²Jacob became angry with her and said, "Am I in the place of God, who has kept you from having children?"

³Then she said, "Here is Bilhah, my servant. Sleep with her so that she can bear children for me and I too can build a family through her."

⁴So she gave him her servant Bilhah as a wife. Jacob slept with her, ⁵and she became pregnant and bore him a son. ⁶Then Rachel said, "God has vindicated me; he has listened to my plea and given me a son." Because of this she named him Dan.ᵉ

⁷Rachel's servant Bilhah conceived again and bore Jacob a second son. ⁸Then Rachel said, "I have had a great struggle with my sister, and I have won." So she named him Naphtali.ᶠ

⁹When Leah saw that she had stopped having children, she took her servant Zilpah and gave her to Jacob as a wife. ¹⁰Leah's servant Zilpah bore Jacob a son. ¹¹Then Leah said, "What good fortune!"ᵍ So she named him Gad.ʰ

¹²Leah's servant Zilpah bore Jacob a second son. ¹³Then Leah said, "How happy I am! The women will call me happy." So she named him Asher.ⁱ

¹⁴During wheat harvest, Reuben went out into the fields and found some

---

ᵃ 32 Reuben sounds like the Hebrew for he has seen my misery; the name means see, a son.   ᵇ 33 Simeon probably means one who hears.   ᶜ 34 Levi sounds like and may be derived from the Hebrew for attached.   ᵈ 35 Judah sounds like and may be derived from the Hebrew for praise.   ᵉ 6 Dan here means he has vindicated.   ᶠ 8 Naphtali means my struggle.   ᵍ 11 Or "A troop is coming!"   ʰ 11 Gad can mean good fortune or a troop.   ⁱ 13 Asher means happy.

mandrake plants, which he brought to his mother Leah. Rachel said to Leah, "Please give me some of your son's mandrakes."

¹⁵But she said to her, "Wasn't it enough that you took away my husband? Will you take my son's mandrakes too?"

"Very well," Rachel said, "he can sleep with you tonight in return for your son's mandrakes."

¹⁶So when Jacob came in from the fields that evening, Leah went out to meet him. "You must sleep with me," she said. "I have hired you with my son's mandrakes." So he slept with her that night.

¹⁷God listened to Leah, and she became pregnant and bore Jacob a fifth son. ¹⁸Then Leah said, "God has rewarded me for giving my servant to my husband." So she named him Issachar.ᵃ

¹⁹Leah conceived again and bore Jacob a sixth son. ²⁰Then Leah said, "God has presented me with a precious gift. This time my husband will treat me with honor, because I have borne him six sons." So she named him Zebulun.ᵇ

²¹Some time later she gave birth to a daughter and named her Dinah.

²²Then God remembered Rachel; he listened to her and enabled her to conceive. ²³She became pregnant and gave birth to a son and said, "God has taken away my disgrace." ²⁴She named him Joseph,ᶜ and said, "May the LORD add to me another son."

ᵃ *18* Issachar sounds like the Hebrew for *reward.*   ᵇ *20* Zebulun probably means *honor.*   ᶜ *24* Joseph means *may he add.*

TO THE POINT

One Man, One Woman

Jacob had four wives (Rachel, Leah, Bilhah and Zilpah). Why shouldn't people today have more than one spouse?

Bear in mind that the historical books of the Bible report that what happened in history didn't always go according to what God had in mind for his creation.

Jesus taught that God's best is for "the two" to "become one flesh" (Matthew 19:5). God wants one man and one woman to love each other completely and to grow closer through the years.

If you think it would be fun to have more than one husband or wife, read Jacob's story closely (Genesis 29:30—30:24). You'll find that there was more competition than love going on.

God's ideal of a lifetime marriage between one man and one woman is best. Choose your future husband or wife wisely. If you do, you'll find more happiness with one person than with any number of marriage partners.

Jacob's Flocks Increase

²⁵After Rachel gave birth to Joseph, Jacob said to Laban, "Send me on my way so I can go back to my own homeland. ²⁶Give me my wives and children, for whom I have served you, and I will be on my way. You know how much work I've done for you."

²⁷But Laban said to him, "If I have found favor in your eyes, please stay. I have learned by divination that the LORD has blessed me because of you." ²⁸He added, "Name your wages, and I will pay them."

²⁹Jacob said to him, "You know how I have worked for you and how your livestock has fared under my care. ³⁰The little you had before I came has increased greatly, and the LORD has blessed you wherever I have been. But now, when may I do something for my own household?"

³¹"What shall I give you?" he asked.

"Don't give me anything," Jacob replied. "But if you will do this one thing for me, I will go on tending your flocks and watching over them: ³²Let me go through all your flocks today and remove from them every speckled or spotted sheep, every dark-colored lamb and every spotted or speckled goat. They will be my wages. ³³And my honesty will testify for me in the future, whenever you check on the wages you have paid me. Any goat in my possession that is not speckled or spotted, or any lamb that is not dark-colored, will be considered stolen."

³⁴"Agreed," said Laban. "Let it be as you have said." ³⁵That same day he removed all the male goats that were streaked or spotted, and all the speckled or spotted female goats (all that had white on them) and all the dark-colored lambs, and he placed them in the care of his sons. ³⁶Then he put a three-day journey between himself and Jacob, while Jacob continued to tend the rest of Laban's flocks.

³⁷Jacob, however, took fresh-cut branches from poplar, almond and plane trees and made white stripes on them by peeling the bark and exposing the white inner wood of the branches. ³⁸Then he placed the peeled branches in all the watering troughs, so that they would be directly in front of the flocks when they came to drink. When the flocks were in heat and came to drink, ³⁹they mated in front of the branches. And they bore young that were streaked or speckled or spotted. ⁴⁰Jacob set apart the young of the flock by themselves, but made the rest face the streaked and dark-colored animals that belonged to Laban. Thus he made separate flocks for himself and did not put them with Laban's animals. ⁴¹Whenever the stronger females were in heat, Jacob would place the branches in the troughs in front of the animals so they would mate near the branches, ⁴²but if the animals were weak, he would not place them there. So the weak animals went to Laban and the strong ones to Jacob. ⁴³In this way the man grew exceedingly prosperous and came to own large flocks, and female and male servants, and camels and donkeys.

Jacob Flees From Laban

31 Jacob heard that Laban's sons were saying, "Jacob has taken everything our father owned and has gained all this wealth from what belonged to our father." ²And Jacob noticed that Laban's attitude toward him was not what it had been.

³Then the LORD said to Jacob, "Go back to the land of your fathers and to your relatives, and I will be with you."

⁴So Jacob sent word to Rachel and Leah to come out to the fields where his flocks were. ⁵He said to them, "I see that your father's attitude toward me is not what it was before, but the God of my father has been with me. ⁶You know that I've worked for your father with all my strength, ⁷yet your father has cheated me by changing my wages ten times. However, God has not allowed him to harm me. ⁸If he said, 'The speckled ones will be your wages,' then all the flocks gave birth to speckled young; and if he said, 'The streaked ones will be your wages,' then all the flocks bore streaked young. ⁹So God has taken away your father's livestock and has given them to me.

[10] "In breeding season I once had a dream in which I looked up and saw that the male goats mating with the flock were streaked, speckled or spotted. [11] The angel of God said to me in the dream, 'Jacob.' I answered, 'Here I am.' [12] And he said, 'Look up and see that all the male goats mating with the flock are streaked, speckled or spotted, for I have seen all that Laban has been doing to you. [13] I am the God of Bethel, where you anointed a pillar and where you made a vow to me. Now leave this land at once and go back to your native land.' "

[14] Then Rachel and Leah replied, "Do we still have any share in the inheritance of our father's estate? [15] Does he not regard us as foreigners? Not only has he sold us, but he has used up what was paid for us. [16] Surely all the wealth that God took away from our father belongs to us and our children. So do whatever God has told you."

[17] Then Jacob put his children and his wives on camels, [18] and he drove all his livestock ahead of him, along with all the goods he had accumulated in Paddan Aram,[a] to go to his father Isaac in the land of Canaan.

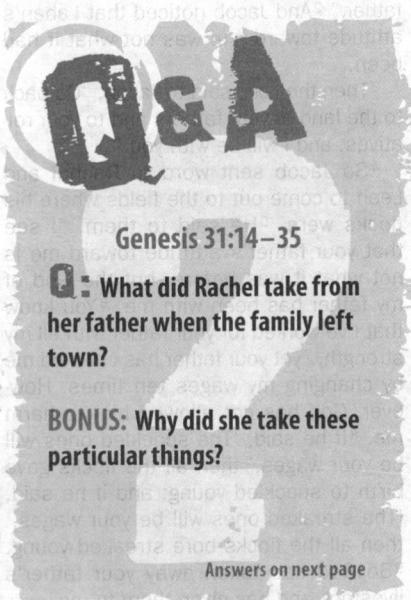

Genesis 31:14–35

Q: What did Rachel take from her father when the family left town?

BONUS: Why did she take these particular things?

Answers on next page

[19] When Laban had gone to shear his sheep, Rachel stole her father's household gods. [20] Moreover, Jacob deceived Laban the Aramean by not telling him he was running away. [21] So he fled with all he had, crossed the Euphrates River, and headed for the hill country of Gilead.

Laban Pursues Jacob

[22] On the third day Laban was told that Jacob had fled. [23] Taking his relatives with him, he pursued Jacob for seven days and caught up with him in the hill country of Gilead. [24] Then God came to Laban the Aramean in a dream at night and said to him, "Be careful not to say anything to Jacob, either good or bad."

[25] Jacob had pitched his tent in the hill country of Gilead when Laban overtook him, and Laban and his relatives camped there too. [26] Then Laban said to Jacob, "What have you done? You've deceived me, and you've carried off my daughters like captives in war. [27] Why did you run off secretly and deceive me? Why didn't you tell me, so I could send you away with joy and singing to the music of timbrels and harps? [28] You didn't even let me kiss my grandchildren and my daughters goodbye. You have done a foolish thing. [29] I have the power to harm you; but last night the God of your father said to me, 'Be careful not to say anything to Jacob, either good or bad.' [30] Now you have gone off because you longed to return to your father's household. But why did you steal my gods?"

[31] Jacob answered Laban, "I was afraid, because I thought you would take your daughters away from me by force. [32] But if you find anyone who has your gods, that person shall not live. In the presence of our relatives, see for yourself whether there is anything of yours here with me; and if so, take it." Now Jacob did not know that Rachel had stolen the gods.

[33] So Laban went into Jacob's tent and into Leah's tent and into the tent of the two female servants, but he found nothing. After he came out of Leah's tent, he entered Rachel's tent. [34] Now Rachel had

---

[a] 18 That is, Northwest Mesopotamia

taken the household gods and put them inside her camel's saddle and was sitting on them. Laban searched through everything in the tent but found nothing.

35 Rachel said to her father, "Don't be angry, my lord, that I cannot stand up in your presence; I'm having my period." So he searched but could not find the household gods.

36 Jacob was angry and took Laban to task. "What is my crime?" he asked Laban. "How have I wronged you that you hunt me down? 37 Now that you have searched through all my goods, what have you found that belongs to your household? Put it here in front of your relatives and mine, and let them judge between the two of us.

38 "I have been with you for twenty years now. Your sheep and goats have not miscarried, nor have I eaten rams from your flocks. 39 I did not bring you animals torn by wild beasts; I bore the loss myself. And you demanded payment from me for whatever was stolen by day or night. 40 This was my situation: The heat consumed me in the daytime and the cold at night, and sleep fled from my eyes. 41 It was like this for the twenty years I was in your household. I worked for you fourteen years for your two daughters and six years for your flocks, and you changed my wages ten times. 42 If the God of my father, the God of Abraham and the Fear of Isaac, had not been with me, you would surely have sent me away empty-handed. But God has seen my hardship and the toil of my hands, and last night he rebuked you."

43 Laban answered Jacob, "The women are my daughters, the children are my children, and the flocks are my flocks. All you see is mine. Yet what can I do today about these daughters of mine, or about the children they have borne? 44 Come now, let's make a covenant, you and I, and let it serve as a witness between us."

45 So Jacob took a stone and set it up as a pillar. 46 He said to his relatives, "Gather some stones." So they took

Q&A

A: Her father's household gods (Genesis 31:19).

BONUS: She wanted them for her children. The person who owned the family gods was the heir of the family fortune.

stones and piled them in a heap, and they ate there by the heap. 47 Laban called it Jegar Sahadutha, and Jacob called it Galeed.[a]

48 Laban said, "This heap is a witness between you and me today." That is why it was called Galeed. 49 It was also called Mizpah,[b] because he said, "May the LORD keep watch between you and me when we are away from each other. 50 If you mistreat my daughters or if you take any wives besides my daughters, even though no one is with us, remember that God is a witness between you and me."

51 Laban also said to Jacob, "Here is this heap, and here is this pillar I have set up between you and me. 52 This heap is a witness, and this pillar is a witness, that I will not go past this heap to your side to harm you and that you will not go past this heap and pillar to my side to harm me. 53 May the God of Abraham and the God of Nahor, the God of their father, judge between us."

So Jacob took an oath in the name of the Fear of his father Isaac. 54 He offered a sacrifice there in the hill country and

---

[a] 47 The Aramaic *Jegar Sahadutha* and the Hebrew *Galeed* both mean *witness heap*.   [b] 49 *Mizpah* means *watchtower*.

invited his relatives to a meal. After they had eaten, they spent the night there.

⁵⁵Early the next morning Laban kissed his grandchildren and his daughters and blessed them. Then he left and returned home.ᵃ

Jacob Prepares to Meet Esau

32ᵇ Jacob also went on his way, and the angels of God met him. ²When Jacob saw them, he said, "This is the camp of God!" So he named that place Mahanaim.ᶜ

³Jacob sent messengers ahead of him to his brother Esau in the land of Seir, the country of Edom. ⁴He instructed them: "This is what you are to say to my lord Esau: 'Your servant Jacob says, I have been staying with Laban and have remained there till now. ⁵I have cattle and donkeys, sheep and goats, male and female servants. Now I am sending this message to my lord, that I may find favor in your eyes.' "

⁶When the messengers returned to Jacob, they said, "We went to your brother Esau, and now he is coming to meet you, and four hundred men are with him."

⁷In great fear and distress Jacob divided the people who were with him into two groups,ᵈ and the flocks and herds and camels as well. ⁸He thought, "If Esau comes and attacks one group,ᵉ the groupᵉ that is left may escape."

⁹Then Jacob prayed, "O God of my father Abraham, God of my father Isaac, Lord, you who said to me, 'Go back to your country and your relatives, and I will make you prosper,' ¹⁰I am unworthy of all the kindness and faithfulness you have shown your servant. I had only my staff when I crossed this Jordan, but now I have become two camps. ¹¹Save me, I pray, from the hand of my brother Esau, for I am afraid he will come and attack me, and also the mothers with their children. ¹²But you have said, 'I will surely make you prosper and will make your descendants like the sand of the sea, which cannot be counted.' "

¹³He spent the night there, and from what he had with him he selected a gift for his brother Esau: ¹⁴two hundred female goats and twenty male goats, two hundred ewes and twenty rams, ¹⁵thirty female camels with their young, forty cows and ten bulls, and twenty female donkeys and ten male donkeys. ¹⁶He put them in the care of his servants, each herd by itself, and said to his servants, "Go ahead of me, and keep some space between the herds."

¹⁷He instructed the one in the lead: "When my brother Esau meets you and asks, 'Who do you belong to, and where are you going, and who owns all these animals in front of you?' ¹⁸then you are to say, 'They belong to your servant Jacob. They are a gift sent to my lord Esau, and he is coming behind us.' "

¹⁹He also instructed the second, the third and all the others who followed the herds: "You are to say the same thing to Esau when you meet him. ²⁰And be sure to say, 'Your servant Jacob is coming behind us.' " For he thought, "I will pacify him with these gifts I am sending on ahead; later, when I see him, perhaps he will receive me." ²¹So Jacob's gifts went on ahead of him, but he himself spent the night in the camp.

Jacob Wrestles With God

²²That night Jacob got up and took his two wives, his two female servants and his eleven sons and crossed the ford of the Jabbok. ²³After he had sent them across the stream, he sent over all his possessions. ²⁴So Jacob was left alone, and a man wrestled with him till daybreak. ²⁵When the man saw that he could not overpower him, he touched the socket of Jacob's hip so that his hip was wrenched as he wrestled with the man. ²⁶Then the man said, "Let me go, for it is daybreak."

But Jacob replied, "I will not let you go unless you bless me."

²⁷The man asked him, "What is your name?"

ᵃ 55 In Hebrew texts this verse (31:55) is numbered 32:1.   ᵇ In Hebrew texts 32:1-32 is numbered 32:2-33.
ᶜ 2 *Mahanaim* means *two camps*.   ᵈ 7 Or *camps*   ᵉ 8 Or *camp*

When is the last time you were terrified enough to pray hard? How did you pray? Jacob was terrified when returning to his home in Canaan. He had cheated his brother Esau 20 years before, and Esau had sworn to kill him. Would Esau still be angry? Here's how Jacob prayed when he was afraid: Jacob reminded God that he was being obedient (Genesis 32:9). Jacob remembered all the good things God had done for him (Genesis 32:10). Jacob begged God to save him (Genesis 32:11). Jacob quoted God's promises (Genesis 32:12). What a model for your prayers when you're anxious or afraid.

{Genesis 32:1–12}

INSTANT ACCESS

"Jacob," he answered.

28 Then the man said, "Your name will no longer be Jacob, but Israel,[a] because you have struggled with God and with humans and have overcome."

29 Jacob said, "Please tell me your name."

But he replied, "Why do you ask my name?" Then he blessed him there.

30 So Jacob called the place Peniel,[b] saying, "It is because I saw God face to face, and yet my life was spared."

31 The sun rose above him as he passed Peniel,[c] and he was limping because of his hip. 32 Therefore to this day the Israelites do not eat the tendon attached to the socket of the hip, because the socket of Jacob's hip was touched near the tendon.

Jacob Meets Esau

33 Jacob looked up and there was Esau, coming with his four hundred men; so he divided the children among Leah, Rachel and the two female servants. 2 He put the female servants and their children in front, Leah and her children next, and Rachel and Joseph in the rear. 3 He himself went on ahead and bowed down to the ground seven times as he approached his brother.

4 But Esau ran to meet Jacob and embraced him; he threw his arms around his neck and kissed him. And they wept. 5 Then Esau looked up and saw the women and children. "Who are these with you?" he asked.

Jacob answered, "They are the children God has graciously given your servant."

6 Then the female servants and their children approached and bowed down. 7 Next, Leah and her children came and bowed down. Last of all came Joseph and Rachel, and they too bowed down.

8 Esau asked, "What's the meaning of all these flocks and herds I met?"

"To find favor in your eyes, my lord," he said.

9 But Esau said, "I already have plenty, my brother. Keep what you have for yourself."

10 "No, please!" said Jacob. "If I have found favor in your eyes, accept this gift from me. For to see your face is like seeing the face of God, now that you have received me favorably. 11 Please accept the present that was brought to you, for God has been gracious to me and I have all I need." And because Jacob insisted, Esau accepted it.

12 Then Esau said, "Let us be on our way; I'll accompany you."

---

[a] 28 Israel probably means he struggles with God.　[b] 30 Peniel means face of God.　[c] 31 Hebrew Penuel, a variant of Peniel

¹³But Jacob said to him, "My lord knows that the children are tender and that I must care for the ewes and cows that are nursing their young. If they are driven hard just one day, all the animals will die. ¹⁴So let my lord go on ahead of his servant, while I move along slowly at the pace of the flocks and herds before me and the pace of the children, until I come to my lord in Seir."

¹⁵Esau said, "Then let me leave some of my men with you."

"But why do that?" Jacob asked. "Just let me find favor in the eyes of my lord."

¹⁶So that day Esau started on his way back to Seir. ¹⁷Jacob, however, went to Sukkoth, where he built a place for himself and made shelters for his livestock. That is why the place is called Sukkoth.ᵃ

¹⁸After Jacob came from Paddan Aram,ᵇ he arrived safely at the city of Shechem in Canaan and camped within sight of the city. ¹⁹For a hundred pieces of silver,ᶜ he bought from the sons of Hamor, the father of Shechem, the plot of ground where he pitched his tent. ²⁰There he set up an altar and called it El Elohe Israel.ᵈ

Dinah and the Shechemites

34 Now Dinah, the daughter Leah had borne to Jacob, went out to visit the women of the land. ²When Shechem son of Hamor the Hivite, the ruler of that area, saw her, he took her and raped her. ³His heart was drawn to Dinah daughter of Jacob; he loved the young woman and spoke tenderly to her. ⁴And Shechem said to his father Hamor, "Get me this girl as my wife."

⁵When Jacob heard that his daughter Dinah had been defiled, his sons were in the fields with his livestock; so he did nothing about it until they came home.

⁶Then Shechem's father Hamor went out to talk with Jacob. ⁷Meanwhile, Jacob's sons had come in from the fields as soon as they heard what had happened. They were shocked and furious, because Shechem had done an outrageous thing inᵉ Israel by sleeping with Jacob's daughter—a thing that should not be done.

⁸But Hamor said to them, "My son Shechem has his heart set on your daughter. Please give her to him as his wife. ⁹Intermarry with us; give us your daughters and take our daughters for yourselves. ¹⁰You can settle among us; the land is open to you. Live in it, tradeᶠ in it, and acquire property in it."

¹¹Then Shechem said to Dinah's father and brothers, "Let me find favor in your eyes, and I will give you whatever you ask. ¹²Make the price for the bride and the gift I am to bring as great as you like, and I'll pay whatever you ask me. Only give me the young woman as my wife."

¹³Because their sister Dinah had been defiled, Jacob's sons replied deceitfully as they spoke to Shechem and his father Hamor. ¹⁴They said to them, "We can't do such a thing; we can't give our sister to a man who is not circumcised. That would be a disgrace to us. ¹⁵We will enter into an agreement with you on one condition only: that you become like us by circumcising all your males. ¹⁶Then we will give you our daughters and take your daughters for ourselves. We'll settle among you and become one people with you. ¹⁷But if you will not agree to be circumcised, we'll take our sister and go."

¹⁸Their proposal seemed good to Hamor and his son Shechem. ¹⁹The young man, who was the most honored of all his father's family, lost no time in doing what they said, because he was delighted with Jacob's daughter. ²⁰So Hamor and his son Shechem went to the gate of their city to speak to the men of their city. ²¹"These men are friendly toward us," they said. "Let them live in our land and trade in it; the land has plenty of room for them. We can marry their daughters and they can marry ours. ²²But the men will agree to live with us as one people only on the condition that our males be circumcised, as they themselves are.

ᵃ *17 Sukkoth means shelters.*   ᵇ *18 That is, Northwest Mesopotamia*   ᶜ *19 Hebrew hundred kesitahs; a kesitah was a unit of money of unknown weight and value.*   ᵈ *20 El Elohe Israel can mean El is the God of Israel or mighty is the God of Israel.*   ᵉ *7 Or against*   ᶠ *10 Or move about freely; also in verse 21*

23 Won't their livestock, their property and all their other animals become ours? So let us agree to their terms, and they will settle among us."

24 All the men who went out of the city gate agreed with Hamor and his son Shechem, and every male in the city was circumcised.

25 Three days later, while all of them were still in pain, two of Jacob's sons, Simeon and Levi, Dinah's brothers, took their swords and attacked the unsuspecting city, killing every male. 26 They put Hamor and his son Shechem to the sword and took Dinah from Shechem's house and left. 27 The sons of Jacob came upon the dead bodies and looted the city where[a] their sister had been defiled. 28 They seized their flocks and herds and donkeys and everything else of theirs in the city and out in the fields. 29 They carried off all their wealth and all their women and children, taking as plunder everything in the houses.

30 Then Jacob said to Simeon and Levi, "You have brought trouble on me by making me obnoxious to the Canaanites and Perizzites, the people living in this land. We are few in number, and if they join forces against me and attack me, I and my household will be destroyed."

31 But they replied, "Should he have treated our sister like a prostitute?"

Jacob Returns to Bethel

35 Then God said to Jacob, "Go up to Bethel and settle there, and build an altar there to God, who appeared to you when you were fleeing from your brother Esau."

2 So Jacob said to his household and to all who were with him, "Get rid of the foreign gods you have with you, and purify yourselves and change your clothes. 3 Then come, let us go up to Bethel, where I will build an altar to God, who answered me in the day of my distress and who has been with me wherever I have gone." 4 So they gave Jacob all the foreign gods they had and the rings in their ears, and Jacob buried them under the oak at Shechem. 5 Then they set out, and the terror of God fell on the towns all around them so that no one pursued them.

6 Jacob and all the people with him came to Luz (that is, Bethel) in the land of Canaan. 7 There he built an altar, and he called the place El Bethel,[b] because it was there that God revealed himself to him when he was fleeing from his brother.

8 Now Deborah, Rebekah's nurse, died and was buried under the oak outside Bethel. So it was named Allon Bakuth.[c]

9 After Jacob returned from Paddan Aram,[d] God appeared to him again and blessed him. 10 God said to him, "Your name is Jacob,[e] but you will no longer be

---

[a] 27 Or *because*   [b] 7 *El Bethel* means *God of Bethel.*   [c] 8 *Allon Bakuth* means *oak of weeping.*   [d] 9 That is, Northwest Mesopotamia; also in verse 26   [e] 10 *Jacob* means *he grasps the heel,* a Hebrew idiom for *he deceives.*

called Jacob; your name will be Israel.*a"* So he named him Israel.

[11] And God said to him, "I am God Almighty*b*; be fruitful and increase in number. A nation and a community of nations will come from you, and kings will be among your descendants. [12] The land I gave to Abraham and Isaac I also give to you, and I will give this land to your descendants after you." [13] Then God went up from him at the place where he had talked with him.

[14] Jacob set up a stone pillar at the place where God had talked with him, and he poured out a drink offering on it; he also poured oil on it. [15] Jacob called the place where God had talked with him Bethel.*c*

The Deaths of Rachel and Isaac

[16] Then they moved on from Bethel. While they were still some distance from Ephrath, Rachel began to give birth and had great difficulty. [17] And as she was having great difficulty in childbirth, the midwife said to her, "Don't despair, for you have another son." [18] As she breathed her last—for she was dying—she named her son Ben-Oni.*d* But his father named him Benjamin.*e*

[19] So Rachel died and was buried on the way to Ephrath (that is, Bethlehem). [20] Over her tomb Jacob set up a pillar, and to this day that pillar marks Rachel's tomb.

[21] Israel moved on again and pitched his tent beyond Migdal Eder. [22] While Israel was living in that region, Reuben went in and slept with his father's concubine Bilhah, and Israel heard of it.

Jacob had twelve sons:

[23] The sons of Leah:
Reuben the firstborn of Jacob, Simeon, Levi, Judah, Issachar and Zebulun.
[24] The sons of Rachel:
Joseph and Benjamin.
[25] The sons of Rachel's servant Bilhah:
Dan and Naphtali.

[26] The sons of Leah's servant Zilpah:
Gad and Asher.

These were the sons of Jacob, who were born to him in Paddan Aram.

[27] Jacob came home to his father Isaac in Mamre, near Kiriath Arba (that is, Hebron), where Abraham and Isaac had stayed. [28] Isaac lived a hundred and eighty years. [29] Then he breathed his last and died and was gathered to his people, old and full of years. And his sons Esau and Jacob buried him.

Esau's Descendants

36 This is the account of the family line of Esau (that is, Edom).

[2] Esau took his wives from the women of Canaan: Adah daughter of Elon the Hittite, and Oholibamah daughter of Anah and granddaughter of Zibeon the Hivite— [3] also Basemath daughter of Ishmael and sister of Nebaioth.

[4] Adah bore Eliphaz to Esau, Basemath bore Reuel, [5] and Oholibamah bore Jeush, Jalam and Korah. These were the sons of Esau, who were born to him in Canaan.

[6] Esau took his wives and sons and daughters and all the members of his household, as well as his livestock and all his other animals and all the goods he had acquired in Canaan, and moved to a land some distance from his brother Jacob. [7] Their possessions were too great for them to remain together; the land where they were staying could not support them both because of their livestock. [8] So Esau (that is, Edom) settled in the hill country of Seir.

[9] This is the account of the family line of Esau the father of the Edomites in the hill country of Seir.

[10] These are the names of Esau's sons:
Eliphaz, the son of Esau's wife Adah, and Reuel, the son of Esau's wife Basemath.

---

a 10 Israel probably means *he struggles with God.*   *b 11* Hebrew *El-Shaddai*   *c 15 Bethel* means *house of God.*
d 18 Ben-Oni means *son of my trouble.*   *e 18 Benjamin* means *son of my right hand.*

11 The sons of Eliphaz:

Teman, Omar, Zepho, Gatam and Kenaz.

12 Esau's son Eliphaz also had a concubine named Timna, who bore him Amalek. These were grandsons of Esau's wife Adah.

13 The sons of Reuel:

Nahath, Zerah, Shammah and Mizzah. These were grandsons of Esau's wife Basemath.

14 The sons of Esau's wife Oholibamah daughter of Anah and granddaughter of Zibeon, whom she bore to Esau:

Jeush, Jalam and Korah.

15 These were the chiefs among Esau's descendants:

The sons of Eliphaz the firstborn of Esau:

Chiefs Teman, Omar, Zepho, Kenaz, 16 Korah,ᵃ Gatam and Amalek. These were the chiefs descended from Eliphaz in Edom; they were grandsons of Adah.

17 The sons of Esau's son Reuel:

Chiefs Nahath, Zerah, Shammah and Mizzah. These were the chiefs descended from Reuel in Edom; they were grandsons of Esau's wife Basemath.

18 The sons of Esau's wife Oholibamah:

Chiefs Jeush, Jalam and Korah. These were the chiefs descended from Esau's wife Oholibamah daughter of Anah.

19 These were the sons of Esau (that is, Edom), and these were their chiefs.

20 These were the sons of Seir the Horite, who were living in the region:

Lotan, Shobal, Zibeon, Anah, 21 Dishon, Ezer and Dishan. These sons of Seir in Edom were Horite chiefs.

22 The sons of Lotan:

Hori and Homam.ᵇ Timna was Lotan's sister.

23 The sons of Shobal:

Alvan, Manahath, Ebal, Shepho and Onam.

24 The sons of Zibeon:

Aiah and Anah. This is the Anah who discovered the hot springsᶜ in the desert while he was grazing the donkeys of his father Zibeon.

25 The children of Anah:

Dishon and Oholibamah daughter of Anah.

26 The sons of Dishonᵈ:

Hemdan, Eshban, Ithran and Keran.

27 The sons of Ezer:

Bilhan, Zaavan and Akan.

28 The sons of Dishan:

Uz and Aran.

29 These were the Horite chiefs:

Lotan, Shobal, Zibeon, Anah, 30 Dishon, Ezer and Dishan. These were the Horite chiefs, according to their divisions, in the land of Seir.

The Rulers of Edom

31 These were the kings who reigned in Edom before any Israelite king reigned:

32 Bela son of Beor became king of Edom. His city was named Dinhabah.

33 When Bela died, Jobab son of Zerah from Bozrah succeeded him as king.

34 When Jobab died, Husham from the land of the Temanites succeeded him as king.

35 When Husham died, Hadad son of Bedad, who defeated Midian in the country of Moab, succeeded him as king. His city was named Avith.

36 When Hadad died, Samlah from Masrekah succeeded him as king.

37 When Samlah died, Shaul from Rehoboth on the river succeeded him as king.

38 When Shaul died, Baal-Hanan son of Akbor succeeded him as king.

39 When Baal-Hanan son of Akbor died, Hadadᵉ succeeded him as king. His city was named Pau, and his

---

ᵃ 16 Masoretic Text; Samaritan Pentateuch (also verse 11 and 1 Chron. 1:36) does not have *Korah*. ᵇ 22 Hebrew *Hemam*, a variant of *Homam* (see 1 Chron. 1:39) ᶜ 24 Vulgate; Syriac *discovered water*; the meaning of the Hebrew for this word is uncertain. ᵈ 26 Hebrew *Dishan*, a variant of *Dishon* ᵉ 39 Many manuscripts of the Masoretic Text, Samaritan Pentateuch and Syriac (see also 1 Chron. 1:50); most manuscripts of the Masoretic Text *Hadar*

wife's name was Mehetabel daughter of Matred, the daughter of Me-Zahab.

⁴⁰These were the chiefs descended from Esau, by name, according to their clans and regions:

Timna, Alvah, Jetheth, ⁴¹Oholibamah, Elah, Pinon, ⁴²Kenaz, Teman, Mibzar, ⁴³Magdiel and Iram. These were the chiefs of Edom, according to their settlements in the land they occupied.

This is the family line of Esau, the father of the Edomites.

Joseph's Dreams

37 Jacob lived in the land where his father had stayed, the land of Canaan.

²This is the account of Jacob's family line.

Joseph, a young man of seventeen, was tending the flocks with his brothers, the sons of Bilhah and the sons of Zilpah, his father's wives, and he brought their father a bad report about them.

³Now Israel loved Joseph more than any of his other sons, because he had been born to him in his old age; and he made an ornate*ᵃ* robe for him. ⁴When his brothers saw that their father loved him more than any of them, they hated him and could not speak a kind word to him.

⁵Joseph had a dream, and when he told it to his brothers, they hated him all the more. ⁶He said to them, "Listen to this dream I had: ⁷We were binding sheaves of grain out in the field when suddenly my sheaf rose and stood upright, while your sheaves gathered around mine and bowed down to it."

⁸His brothers said to him, "Do you intend to reign over us? Will you actually rule us?" And they hated him all the more because of his dream and what he had said.

⁹Then he had another dream, and he told it to his brothers. "Listen," he said, "I had another dream, and this time the sun and moon and eleven stars were bowing down to me."

¹⁰When he told his father as well as his brothers, his father rebuked him and said, "What is this dream you had? Will your mother and I and your brothers actually come and bow down to the ground before you?" ¹¹His brothers were jealous of him, but his father kept the matter in mind.

Joseph Sold by His Brothers

¹²Now his brothers had gone to graze their father's flocks near Shechem, ¹³and Israel said to Joseph, "As you know, your brothers are grazing the flocks near Shechem. Come, I am going to send you to them."

"Very well," he replied.

¹⁴So he said to him, "Go and see if all is well with your brothers and with the flocks, and bring word back to me." Then he sent him off from the Valley of Hebron.

When Joseph arrived at Shechem, ¹⁵a man found him wandering around in the fields and asked him, "What are you looking for?"

¹⁶He replied, "I'm looking for my brothers. Can you tell me where they are grazing their flocks?"

¹⁷"They have moved on from here," the man answered. "I heard them say, 'Let's go to Dothan.'"

So Joseph went after his brothers and found them near Dothan. ¹⁸But they saw him in the distance, and before he reached them, they plotted to kill him.

¹⁹"Here comes that dreamer!" they said to each other. ²⁰"Come now, let's kill him and throw him into one of these cisterns and say that a ferocious animal devoured him. Then we'll see what comes of his dreams."

²¹When Reuben heard this, he tried to rescue him from their hands. "Let's not take his life," he said. ²²"Don't shed any blood. Throw him into this cistern here in the wilderness, but don't lay a hand on him." Reuben said this to rescue him from them and take him back to his father.

ᵃ 3 The meaning of the Hebrew for this word is uncertain; also in verses 23 and 32.

> I'm the older of two boys. My parents favor me. I used to think it was funny, but now I feel bad for my younger brother. He's having problems and I want to be there for him. What can I do?
>
> >> Jacob

Dear Jordan

Dear Jacob,

You are showing wisdom about this situation and compassion for your brother. Many parents show favoritism and it can be very damaging for the whole family. Joseph's father favored him over all his other sons, though Joseph wasn't the oldest.

His brothers sold him and told their father he had been killed. This broke their father's heart and made them feel guilty. Favoritism led to jealousy, and the jealousy of his brothers caused many difficult years for Joseph. This story appears in Genesis 37.

It's important for you to let your brother know you love him. Maybe you could have a talk with one or both of your parents to gently share your concerns. They may not even be aware that they treat your brother differently. Your attitude toward your brother can make a big difference in his life as well as in the lives of your family.

Jordan

²³So when Joseph came to his brothers, they stripped him of his robe—the ornate robe he was wearing— ²⁴and they took him and threw him into the cistern. The cistern was empty; there was no water in it.

²⁵As they sat down to eat their meal, they looked up and saw a caravan of Ishmaelites coming from Gilead. Their camels were loaded with spices, balm and myrrh, and they were on their way to take them down to Egypt.

²⁶Judah said to his brothers, "What will we gain if we kill our brother and cover up his blood? ²⁷Come, let's sell him to the Ishmaelites and not lay our hands on him; after all, he is our brother, our own flesh and blood." His brothers agreed.

²⁸So when the Midianite merchants came by, his brothers pulled Joseph up out of the cistern and sold him for twenty shekels[a] of silver to the Ishmaelites, who took him to Egypt.

²⁹When Reuben returned to the cistern and saw that Joseph was not there, he tore his clothes. ³⁰He went back to his brothers and said, "The boy isn't there! Where can I turn now?"

³¹Then they got Joseph's robe, slaughtered a goat and dipped the robe in the blood. ³²They took the ornate robe back to their father and said, "We found this. Examine it to see whether it is your son's robe."

³³He recognized it and said, "It is my son's robe! Some ferocious animal has devoured him. Joseph has surely been torn to pieces."

³⁴Then Jacob tore his clothes, put on sackcloth and mourned for his son many days. ³⁵All his sons and daughters came to comfort him, but he refused to be comforted. "No," he said, "I will continue to mourn until I join my son in the grave." So his father wept for him.

³⁶Meanwhile, the Midianites[b] sold Joseph in Egypt to Potiphar, one of Pharaoh's officials, the captain of the guard.

Judah and Tamar

38 At that time, Judah left his brothers and went down to stay with a man of Adullam named Hirah. ²There Judah met the daughter of a Canaanite man named Shua. He married her and made love to her; ³she became pregnant and gave birth to a son, who was named Er. ⁴She conceived again and gave birth to a son and named him Onan. ⁵She gave birth to still another son and named him Shelah. It was at Kezib that she gave birth to him.

⁶Judah got a wife for Er, his firstborn, and her name was Tamar. ⁷But Er, Judah's firstborn, was wicked in the LORD's sight; so the LORD put him to death.

⁸Then Judah said to Onan, "Sleep with your brother's wife and fulfill your duty to her as a brother-in-law to raise up offspring for your brother." ⁹But Onan knew that the child would not be his; so whenever he slept with his brother's wife, he spilled his semen on the ground to keep from providing offspring for his brother. ¹⁰What he did was wicked in the LORD's sight; so the LORD put him to death also.

¹¹Judah then said to his daughter-in-law Tamar, "Live as a widow in your father's household until my son Shelah grows up." For he thought, "He may die too, just like his brothers." So Tamar went to live in her father's household.

¹²After a long time Judah's wife, the daughter of Shua, died. When Judah had recovered from his grief, he went up to Timnah, to the men who were shearing his sheep, and his friend Hirah the Adullamite went with him.

¹³When Tamar was told, "Your father-in-law is on his way to Timnah to shear his sheep," ¹⁴she took off her widow's clothes, covered herself with a veil to disguise herself, and then sat down at the entrance to Enaim, which is on the road to Timnah. For she saw that, though Shelah had now grown up, she had not been given to him as his wife.

¹⁵When Judah saw her, he thought she was a prostitute, for she had covered her face. ¹⁶Not realizing that she was his daughter-in-law, he went over to her by the roadside and said, "Come now, let me sleep with you."

---

[a] 28 That is, about 8 ounces or about 230 grams   [b] 36 Samaritan Pentateuch, Septuagint, Vulgate and Syriac (see also verse 28); Masoretic Text *Medanites*

"And what will you give me to sleep with you?" she asked.

¹⁷"I'll send you a young goat from my flock," he said.

"Will you give me something as a pledge until you send it?" she asked.

¹⁸He said, "What pledge should I give you?"

"Your seal and its cord, and the staff in your hand," she answered. So he gave them to her and slept with her, and she became pregnant by him. ¹⁹After she left, she took off her veil and put on her widow's clothes again.

²⁰Meanwhile Judah sent the young goat by his friend the Adullamite in order to get his pledge back from the woman, but he did not find her. ²¹He asked the men who lived there, "Where is the shrine prostitute who was beside the road at Enaim?"

"There hasn't been any shrine prostitute here," they said.

²²So he went back to Judah and said, "I didn't find her. Besides, the men who lived there said, 'There hasn't been any shrine prostitute here.'"

²³Then Judah said, "Let her keep what she has, or we will become a laughingstock. After all, I did send her this young goat, but you didn't find her."

²⁴About three months later Judah was told, "Your daughter-in-law Tamar is guilty of prostitution, and as a result she is now pregnant."

Judah said, "Bring her out and have her burned to death!"

²⁵As she was being brought out, she sent a message to her father-in-law. "I am pregnant by the man who owns these," she said. And she added, "See if you recognize whose seal and cord and staff these are."

²⁶Judah recognized them and said, "She is more righteous than I, since I wouldn't give her to my son Shelah." And he did not sleep with her again.

²⁷When the time came for her to give birth, there were twin boys in her womb. ²⁸As she was giving birth, one of them put out his hand; so the midwife took a scarlet thread and tied it on his wrist and said, "This one came out first." ²⁹But when he drew back his hand, his brother came out, and she said, "So this is how you have broken out!" And he was named Perez.ᵃ ³⁰Then his brother, who had the scarlet thread on his wrist, came out. And he was named Zerah.ᵇ

Joseph and Potiphar's Wife

39 Now Joseph had been taken down to Egypt. Potiphar, an Egyptian who was one of Pharaoh's officials, the captain of the guard, bought him from the Ishmaelites who had taken him there.

²The Lᴏʀᴅ was with Joseph so that he prospered, and he lived in the house of his Egyptian master. ³When his master saw that the Lᴏʀᴅ was with him and that the Lᴏʀᴅ gave him success in everything he did, ⁴Joseph found favor in his eyes and became his attendant. Potiphar put him in charge of his household, and he entrusted to his care everything he owned. ⁵From the time he put him in charge of his household and of all that he owned, the Lᴏʀᴅ blessed the household of the Egyptian because of Joseph. The blessing of the Lᴏʀᴅ was on everything Potiphar had, both in the house and in the field. ⁶So Potiphar left everything he had in Joseph's care; with Joseph in charge, he did not concern himself with anything except the food he ate.

Now Joseph was well-built and handsome, ⁷and after a while his master's wife took notice of Joseph and said, "Come to bed with me!"

⁸But he refused. "With me in charge," he told her, "my master does not concern himself with anything in the house; everything he owns he has entrusted to my care. ⁹No one is greater in this house than I am. My master has withheld nothing from me except you, because you are his wife. How then could I do such a wicked thing and sin against God?" ¹⁰And though she spoke to Joseph day after day, he refused to go to bed with her or even be with her.

¹¹One day he went into the house to

ᵃ 29 *Perez* means *breaking out.*   ᵇ 30 *Zerah* can mean *scarlet* or *brightness.*

attend to his duties, and none of the household servants was inside. ¹²She caught him by his cloak and said, "Come to bed with me!" But he left his cloak in her hand and ran out of the house.

¹³When she saw that he had left his cloak in her hand and had run out of the house, ¹⁴she called her household servants. "Look," she said to them, "this Hebrew has been brought to us to make sport of us! He came in here to sleep with me, but I screamed. ¹⁵When he heard me scream for help, he left his cloak beside me and ran out of the house."

¹⁶She kept his cloak beside her until his master came home. ¹⁷Then she told him this story: "That Hebrew slave you brought us came to me to make sport of me. ¹⁸But as soon as I screamed for help, he left his cloak beside me and ran out of the house."

¹⁹When his master heard the story his wife told him, saying, "This is how your slave treated me," he burned with anger. ²⁰Joseph's master took him and put him in prison, the place where the king's prisoners were confined.

But while Joseph was there in the prison, ²¹the LORD was with him; he showed him kindness and granted him favor in the eyes of the prison warden. ²²So the warden put Joseph in charge of all those held in the prison, and he was made responsible for all that was done there. ²³The warden paid no attention to anything under Joseph's care, because the LORD was with Joseph and gave him success in whatever he did.

The Cupbearer and the Baker

40 Some time later, the cupbearer and the baker of the king of Egypt offended their master, the king of Egypt. ²Pharaoh was angry with his two officials, the chief cupbearer and the chief baker, ³and put them in custody in the house of the captain of the guard, in the same prison where Joseph was confined. ⁴The captain of the guard assigned them to Joseph, and he attended them.

After they had been in custody for some time, ⁵each of the two men—the cupbearer and the baker of the king of

Egypt, who were being held in prison—had a dream the same night, and each dream had a meaning of its own.

⁶When Joseph came to them the next morning, he saw that they were dejected. ⁷So he asked Pharaoh's officials who were in custody with him in his master's house, "Why do you look so sad today?"

⁸"We both had dreams," they answered, "but there is no one to interpret them."

Then Joseph said to them, "Do not interpretations belong to God? Tell me your dreams."

⁹So the chief cupbearer told Joseph his dream. He said to him, "In my dream I saw a vine in front of me, ¹⁰and on the vine were three branches. As soon as it

INSTANT ACCESS

Have you ever noticed that our society seems infatuated with sex? Advertisers sell everything from toothpaste to tires by appealing to society's obsession with sex. The story of Joseph can teach you two things about sex. First, the pressure to have sex before marriage isn't new. And second, you don't have to give in to the pressure. Joseph didn't. He refused to "do such a wicked thing and sin against God" (Genesis 39:9). That decision cost him a lot: his job and his freedom. But he was brave enough to handle it. Are you?

{Genesis 39:6–23}

budded, it blossomed, and its clusters ripened into grapes. [11]Pharaoh's cup was in my hand, and I took the grapes, squeezed them into Pharaoh's cup and put the cup in his hand."

[12]"This is what it means," Joseph said to him. "The three branches are three days. [13]Within three days Pharaoh will lift up your head and restore you to your position, and you will put Pharaoh's cup in his hand, just as you used to do when you were his cupbearer. [14]But when all goes well with you, remember me and show me kindness; mention me to Pharaoh and get me out of this prison. [15]I was forcibly carried off from the land of the Hebrews, and even here I have done nothing to deserve being put in a dungeon."

[16]When the chief baker saw that Joseph had given a favorable interpretation, he said to Joseph, "I too had a dream: On my head were three baskets of bread.[a] [17]In the top basket were all kinds of baked goods for Pharaoh, but the birds were eating them out of the basket on my head."

[18]"This is what it means," Joseph said. "The three baskets are three days. [19]Within three days Pharaoh will lift off your head and impale your body on a pole. And the birds will eat away your flesh."

[20]Now the third day was Pharaoh's birthday, and he gave a feast for all his officials. He lifted up the heads of the chief cupbearer and the chief baker in the presence of his officials: [21]He restored the chief cupbearer to his position, so that he once again put the cup into Pharaoh's hand— [22]but he impaled the chief baker, just as Joseph had said to them in his interpretation.

[23]The chief cupbearer, however, did not remember Joseph; he forgot him.

Pharaoh's Dreams

41 When two full years had passed, Pharaoh had a dream: He was standing by the Nile, [2]when out of the river there came up seven cows, sleek and fat, and they grazed among the reeds. [3]After them, seven other cows, ugly and gaunt, came up out of the Nile and stood beside those on the riverbank. [4]And the cows that were ugly and gaunt ate up the seven sleek, fat cows. Then Pharaoh woke up.

[5]He fell asleep again and had a second dream: Seven heads of grain, healthy and good, were growing on a single stalk. [6]After them, seven other heads of grain sprouted—thin and scorched by the east wind. [7]The thin heads of grain swallowed up the seven healthy, full heads. Then Pharaoh woke up; it had been a dream.

[8]In the morning his mind was troubled, so he sent for all the magicians and wise men of Egypt. Pharaoh told them his dreams, but no one could interpret them for him.

[9]Then the chief cupbearer said to Pharaoh, "Today I am reminded of my shortcomings. [10]Pharaoh was once angry with his servants, and he imprisoned me and the chief baker in the house of the captain of the guard. [11]Each of us had a dream the same night, and each dream had a meaning of its own. [12]Now a young Hebrew was there with us, a servant of the captain of the guard. We told him our dreams, and he interpreted them for us, giving each man the interpretation of his dream. [13]And things turned out exactly as he interpreted them to us: I was restored to my position, and the other man was impaled."

[14]So Pharaoh sent for Joseph, and he was quickly brought from the dungeon. When he had shaved and changed his clothes, he came before Pharaoh.

[15]Pharaoh said to Joseph, "I had a dream, and no one can interpret it. But I have heard it said of you that when you hear a dream you can interpret it."

[16]"I cannot do it," Joseph replied to Pharaoh, "but God will give Pharaoh the answer he desires."

[17]Then Pharaoh said to Joseph, "In my dream I was standing on the bank of the Nile, [18]when out of the river there came up seven cows, fat and sleek, and they grazed among the reeds. [19]After them, seven other cows came up—scrawny and

---

[a] 16 Or three wicker baskets

very ugly and lean. I had never seen such ugly cows in all the land of Egypt. 20 The lean, ugly cows ate up the seven fat cows that came up first. 21 But even after they ate them, no one could tell that they had done so; they looked just as ugly as before. Then I woke up.

22 "In my dream I saw seven heads of grain, full and good, growing on a single stalk. 23 After them, seven other heads sprouted—withered and thin and scorched by the east wind. 24 The thin heads of grain swallowed up the seven good heads. I told this to the magicians, but none of them could explain it to me."

25 Then Joseph said to Pharaoh, "The dreams of Pharaoh are one and the same. God has revealed to Pharaoh what he is about to do. 26 The seven good cows are seven years, and the seven good heads of grain are seven years; it is one and the same dream. 27 The seven lean, ugly cows that came up afterward are seven years, and so are the seven worthless heads of grain scorched by the east wind: They are seven years of famine.

28 "It is just as I said to Pharaoh: God has shown Pharaoh what he is about to do. 29 Seven years of great abundance are coming throughout the land of Egypt, 30 but seven years of famine will follow them. Then all the abundance in Egypt will be forgotten, and the famine will ravage the land. 31 The abundance in the land will not be remembered, because the famine that follows it will be so severe. 32 The reason the dream was given to Pharaoh in two forms is that the matter has been firmly decided by God, and God will do it soon.

33 "And now let Pharaoh look for a discerning and wise man and put him in charge of the land of Egypt. 34 Let Pharaoh appoint commissioners over the land to take a fifth of the harvest of Egypt during the seven years of abundance. 35 They should collect all the food of these good years that are coming and store up the grain under the authority of Pharaoh, to be kept in the cities for food. 36 This food should be held in reserve for the country, to be used during the seven years of famine that will come upon Egypt, so that the country may not be ruined by the famine."

37 The plan seemed good to Pharaoh and to all his officials. 38 So Pharaoh asked them, "Can we find anyone like this man, one in whom is the spirit of God[a]?"

39 Then Pharaoh said to Joseph, "Since God has made all this known to you, there is no one so discerning and wise as you. 40 You shall be in charge of my palace, and all my people are to submit to your orders. Only with respect to the throne will I be greater than you."

Joseph in Charge of Egypt

41 So Pharaoh said to Joseph, "I hereby put you in charge of the whole land of Egypt." 42 Then Pharaoh took his signet ring from his finger and put it on Joseph's finger. He dressed him in robes of fine linen and put a gold chain around his neck. 43 He had him ride in a chariot as his second-in-command,[b] and people shouted before him, "Make way[c]!" Thus he put him in charge of the whole land of Egypt.

44 Then Pharaoh said to Joseph, "I am Pharaoh, but without your word no one will lift hand or foot in all Egypt." 45 Pharaoh gave Joseph the name Zaphenath-Paneah and gave him Asenath daughter of Potiphera, priest of On,[d] to be his wife. And Joseph went throughout the land of Egypt.

46 Joseph was thirty years old when he entered the service of Pharaoh king of Egypt. And Joseph went out from Pharaoh's presence and traveled throughout Egypt. 47 During the seven years of abundance the land produced plentifully. 48 Joseph collected all the food produced in those seven years of abundance in Egypt and stored it in the cities. In each city he put the food grown in the fields surrounding it. 49 Joseph stored up huge quantities of grain, like the sand of the sea; it was so much that he stopped keeping records because it was beyond measure.

50 Before the years of famine came, two sons were born to Joseph by Asenath

---

a 38 Or of the gods   b 43 Or in the chariot of his second-in-command; or in his second chariot   c 43 Or Bow down
d 45 That is, Heliopolis; also in verse 50

School bore you to death? Mom and Dad treat you like a child? Your big brothers or friends are driving cars, and you're stuck with a bike? Life is passing you by, and you're stuck forever in the slow lane? Joseph probably felt the same way. He was sold into slavery as a young teen and jailed unfairly in his early twenties. Life was passing him by too, but he stuck it out and did his best. Genesis 41:46 says that at age 30 "he entered the service of Pharaoh king of Egypt" to become that country's second most powerful man. Age 30 may seem like forever away, but doing your best in little things is the way God prepares you for great things.

{Genesis 41:46}

INSTANT ACCESS

daughter of Potiphera, priest of On. ⁵¹Joseph named his firstborn Manasseh[a] and said, "It is because God has made me forget all my trouble and all my father's household." ⁵²The second son he named Ephraim[b] and said, "It is because God has made me fruitful in the land of my suffering."

⁵³The seven years of abundance in Egypt came to an end, ⁵⁴and the seven years of famine began, just as Joseph had said. There was famine in all the other lands, but in the whole land of Egypt there was food. ⁵⁵When all Egypt began to feel the famine, the people cried to Pharaoh for food. Then Pharaoh told all the Egyptians, "Go to Joseph and do what he tells you."

⁵⁶When the famine had spread over the whole country, Joseph opened all the storehouses and sold grain to the Egyptians, for the famine was severe throughout Egypt. ⁵⁷And all the world came to Egypt to buy grain from Joseph, because the famine was severe everywhere.

Joseph's Brothers Go to Egypt

42 When Jacob learned that there was grain in Egypt, he said to his sons, "Why do you just keep looking at each other?" ²He continued, "I have heard that there is grain in Egypt. Go down there and buy some for us, so that we may live and not die."

³Then ten of Joseph's brothers went down to buy grain from Egypt. ⁴But Jacob did not send Benjamin, Joseph's brother, with the others, because he was afraid that harm might come to him. ⁵So Israel's sons were among those who went to buy grain, for there was famine in the land of Canaan also.

⁶Now Joseph was the governor of the land, the person who sold grain to all its people. So when Joseph's brothers arrived, they bowed down to him with their faces to the ground. ⁷As soon as Joseph saw his brothers, he recognized them, but he pretended to be a stranger and spoke harshly to them. "Where do you come from?" he asked.

"From the land of Canaan," they replied, "to buy food."

⁸Although Joseph recognized his brothers, they did not recognize him. ⁹Then he remembered his dreams about them and said to them, "You are spies! You have come to see where our land is unprotected."

¹⁰"No, my lord," they answered. "Your

---

[a] 51 *Manasseh* sounds like and may be derived from the Hebrew for *forget*. [b] 52 *Ephraim* sounds like the Hebrew for *twice fruitful*.

servants have come to buy food. ¹¹We are all the sons of one man. Your servants are honest men, not spies."

¹²"No!" he said to them. "You have come to see where our land is unprotected."

¹³But they replied, "Your servants were twelve brothers, the sons of one man, who lives in the land of Canaan. The youngest is now with our father, and one is no more."

¹⁴Joseph said to them, "It is just as I told you: You are spies! ¹⁵And this is how you will be tested: As surely as Pharaoh lives, you will not leave this place unless your youngest brother comes here. ¹⁶Send one of your number to get your brother; the rest of you will be kept in prison, so that your words may be tested to see if you are telling the truth. If you are not, then as surely as Pharaoh lives, you are spies!" ¹⁷And he put them all in custody for three days.

¹⁸On the third day, Joseph said to them, "Do this and you will live, for I fear God: ¹⁹If you are honest men, let one of your brothers stay here in prison, while the rest of you go and take grain back for your starving households. ²⁰But you must bring your youngest brother to me, so that your words may be verified and that you may not die." This they proceeded to do.

²¹They said to one another, "Surely we are being punished because of our brother. We saw how distressed he was when he pleaded with us for his life, but we would not listen; that's why this distress has come on us."

²²Reuben replied, "Didn't I tell you not to sin against the boy? But you wouldn't listen! Now we must give an accounting for his blood." ²³They did not realize that Joseph could understand them, since he was using an interpreter.

²⁴He turned away from them and began to weep, but then came back and spoke to them again. He had Simeon taken from them and bound before their eyes.

²⁵Joseph gave orders to fill their bags with grain, to put each man's silver back in his sack, and to give them provisions for their journey. After this was done for

them, ²⁶they loaded their grain on their donkeys and left.

²⁷At the place where they stopped for the night one of them opened his sack to get feed for his donkey, and he saw his silver in the mouth of his sack. ²⁸"My silver has been returned," he said to his brothers. "Here it is in my sack."

Their hearts sank and they turned to each other trembling and said, "What is this that God has done to us?"

²⁹When they came to their father Jacob in the land of Canaan, they told him all that had happened to them. They said, ³⁰"The man who is lord over the land spoke harshly to us and treated us as though we were spying on the land. ³¹But we said to him, 'We are honest men; we are not spies. ³²We were twelve brothers, sons of one father. One is no more, and the youngest is now with our father in Canaan.'

³³"Then the man who is lord over the land said to us, 'This is how I will know whether you are honest men: Leave one of your brothers here with me, and take food for your starving households and go. ³⁴But bring your youngest brother to me so I will know that you are not spies but honest men. Then I will give your brother back to you, and you can trade*ᵃ* in the land.'"

³⁵As they were emptying their sacks, there in each man's sack was his pouch of silver! When they and their father saw the money pouches, they were frightened. ³⁶Their father Jacob said to them, "You have deprived me of my children. Joseph is no more and Simeon is no more, and now you want to take Benjamin. Everything is against me!"

³⁷Then Reuben said to his father, "You may put both of my sons to death if I do not bring him back to you. Entrust him to my care, and I will bring him back."

³⁸But Jacob said, "My son will not go down there with you; his brother is dead and he is the only one left. If harm comes to him on the journey you are taking, you will bring my gray head down to the grave in sorrow."

ᵃ 34 Or *move about freely*

The Second Journey to Egypt

43 Now the famine was still severe in the land. ²So when they had eaten all the grain they had brought from Egypt, their father said to them, "Go back and buy us a little more food."

³But Judah said to him, "The man warned us solemnly, 'You will not see my face again unless your brother is with you.' ⁴If you will send our brother along with us, we will go down and buy food for you. ⁵But if you will not send him, we will not go down, because the man said to us, 'You will not see my face again unless your brother is with you.'"

⁶Israel asked, "Why did you bring this trouble on me by telling the man you had another brother?"

⁷They replied, "The man questioned us closely about ourselves and our family. 'Is your father still living?' he asked us. 'Do you have another brother?' We simply answered his questions. How were we to know he would say, 'Bring your brother down here'?"

⁸Then Judah said to Israel his father, "Send the boy along with me and we will go at once, so that we and you and our children may live and not die. ⁹I myself will guarantee his safety; you can hold me personally responsible for him. If I do not bring him back to you and set him here before you, I will bear the blame before you all my life. ¹⁰As it is, if we had not delayed, we could have gone and returned twice."

¹¹Then their father Israel said to them, "If it must be, then do this: Put some of the best products of the land in your bags and take them down to the man as a gift—a little balm and a little honey, some spices and myrrh, some pistachio nuts and almonds. ¹²Take double the amount of silver with you, for you must return the silver that was put back into the mouths of your sacks. Perhaps it was a mistake. ¹³Take your brother also and go back to the man at once. ¹⁴And may God Almighty[a] grant you mercy before the man so that he will let your other brother and Benjamin come back with you. As for me, if I am bereaved, I am bereaved."

¹⁵So the men took the gifts and double the amount of silver, and Benjamin also. They hurried down to Egypt and presented themselves to Joseph. ¹⁶When Joseph saw Benjamin with them, he said to the steward of his house, "Take these men to my house, slaughter an animal and prepare a meal; they are to eat with me at noon."

¹⁷The man did as Joseph told him and took the men to Joseph's house. ¹⁸Now the men were frightened when they were taken to his house. They thought, "We were brought here because of the silver that was put back into our sacks the first time. He wants to attack us and overpower us and seize us as slaves and take our donkeys."

¹⁹So they went up to Joseph's steward and spoke to him at the entrance to the house. ²⁰"We beg your pardon, our lord," they said, "we came down here the first time to buy food. ²¹But at the place where we stopped for the night we opened our sacks and each of us found his silver—the exact weight—in the mouth of his sack. So we have brought it back with us. ²²We have also brought additional silver with us to buy food. We don't know who put our silver in our sacks."

²³"It's all right," he said. "Don't be afraid. Your God, the God of your father, has given you treasure in your sacks; I received your silver." Then he brought Simeon out to them.

²⁴The steward took the men into Joseph's house, gave them water to wash their feet and provided fodder for their donkeys. ²⁵They prepared their gifts for Joseph's arrival at noon, because they had heard that they were to eat there.

²⁶When Joseph came home, they presented to him the gifts they had brought into the house, and they bowed down before him to the ground. ²⁷He asked them how they were, and then he said, "How is your aged father you told me about? Is he still living?"

²⁸They replied, "Your servant our father

---

is still alive and well." And they bowed down, prostrating themselves before him.

²⁹As he looked about and saw his brother Benjamin, his own mother's son, he asked, "Is this your youngest brother, the one you told me about?" And he said, "God be gracious to you, my son." ³⁰Deeply moved at the sight of his brother, Joseph hurried out and looked for a place to weep. He went into his private room and wept there.

³¹After he had washed his face, he came out and, controlling himself, said, "Serve the food."

³²They served him by himself, the brothers by themselves, and the Egyptians who ate with him by themselves, because Egyptians could not eat with Hebrews, for that is detestable to Egyptians. ³³The men had been seated before him in the order of their ages, from the firstborn to the youngest; and they looked at each other in astonishment. ³⁴When portions were served to them from Joseph's table, Benjamin's portion was five times as much as anyone else's. So they feasted and drank freely with him.

A Silver Cup in a Sack

44 Now Joseph gave these instructions to the steward of his house: "Fill the men's sacks with as much food as they can carry, and put each man's silver in the mouth of his sack. ²Then put my cup, the silver one, in the mouth of the youngest one's sack, along with the silver for his grain." And he did as Joseph said.

³As morning dawned, the men were sent on their way with their donkeys. ⁴They had not gone far from the city when Joseph said to his steward, "Go after those men at once, and when you catch up with them, say to them, 'Why have you repaid good with evil? ⁵Isn't this the cup my master drinks from and also uses for divination? This is a wicked thing you have done.'"

⁶When he caught up with them, he repeated these words to them. ⁷But they said to him, "Why does my lord say such things? Far be it from your servants to do anything like that! ⁸We even brought back to you from the land of Canaan the silver we found inside the mouths of our sacks. So why would we steal silver or gold from your master's house? ⁹If any of your servants is found to have it, he will die; and the rest of us will become my lord's slaves."

¹⁰"Very well, then," he said, "let it be as you say. Whoever is found to have it will become my slave; the rest of you will be free from blame."

¹¹Each of them quickly lowered his sack to the ground and opened it. ¹²Then the steward proceeded to search, beginning with the oldest and ending with the youngest. And the cup was found in Benjamin's sack. ¹³At this, they tore their clothes. Then they all loaded their donkeys and returned to the city.

¹⁴Joseph was still in the house when Judah and his brothers came in, and they threw themselves to the ground before him. ¹⁵Joseph said to them, "What is this you have done? Don't you know that a man like me can find things out by divination?"

¹⁶"What can we say to my lord?" Judah replied. "What can we say? How can we prove our innocence? God has uncovered your servants' guilt. We are now my lord's slaves—we ourselves and the one who was found to have the cup."

¹⁷But Joseph said, "Far be it from me to do such a thing! Only the man who was found to have the cup will become my slave. The rest of you, go back to your father in peace."

¹⁸Then Judah went up to him and said: "Pardon your servant, my lord, let me speak a word to my lord. Do not be angry with your servant, though you are equal to Pharaoh himself. ¹⁹My lord asked his servants, 'Do you have a father or a brother?' ²⁰And we answered, 'We have an aged father, and there is a young son born to him in his old age. His brother is dead, and he is the only one of his mother's sons left, and his father loves him.'

²¹"Then you said to your servants, 'Bring him down to me so I can see him for myself.' ²²And we said to my lord, 'The boy cannot leave his father; if he leaves him, his father will die.' ²³But you told your servants, 'Unless your youngest brother comes down with you, you will

Participants at one church camp asked these questions about their brothers and sisters: "Why are they so mean?" "How can we keep from fighting?" Joseph knew all about that. His brothers sold him into slavery, and in all the years that followed, the brothers probably never tried to find Joseph or help him. But this chapter reminds you of something important: people can change. Years later in Egypt the very brother who suggested Joseph be sold as a slave was willing to give up his own freedom to protect his youngest brother. So don't give up. There really is hope for your siblings. And for you!

{Genesis 44:27–34}

≫ INSTANT ACCESS

not see my face again.' 24When we went back to your servant my father, we told him what my lord had said.

25 "Then our father said, 'Go back and buy a little more food.' 26But we said, 'We cannot go down. Only if our youngest brother is with us will we go. We cannot see the man's face unless our youngest brother is with us.'

27 "Your servant my father said to us, 'You know that my wife bore me two sons. 28One of them went away from me, and I said, "He has surely been torn to piec-

es." And I have not seen him since. 29If you take this one from me too and harm comes to him, you will bring my gray head down to the grave in misery.'

30 "So now, if the boy is not with us when I go back to your servant my father, and if my father, whose life is closely bound up with the boy's life, 31sees that the boy isn't there, he will die. Your servants will bring the gray head of our father down to the grave in sorrow. 32Your servant guaranteed the boy's safety to my father. I said, 'If I do not bring him back to you, I will bear the blame before you, my father, all my life!'

33 "Now then, please let your servant remain here as my lord's slave in place of the boy, and let the boy return with his brothers. 34How can I go back to my father if the boy is not with me? No! Do not let me see the misery that would come on my father."

Joseph Makes Himself Known

45 Then Joseph could no longer control himself before all his attendants, and he cried out, "Have everyone leave my presence!" So there was no one with Joseph when he made himself known to his brothers. 2And he wept so loudly that the Egyptians heard him, and Pharaoh's household heard about it.

3 Joseph said to his brothers, "I am Joseph! Is my father still living?" But his brothers were not able to answer him, because they were terrified at his presence.

4Then Joseph said to his brothers, "Come close to me." When they had done so, he said, "I am your brother Joseph, the one you sold into Egypt! 5And now, do not be distressed and do not be angry with yourselves for selling me here, because it was to save lives that God sent me ahead of you. 6For two years now there has been famine in the land, and for the next five years there will be no plowing and reaping. 7But God sent me ahead of you to preserve for you a remnant on earth and to save your lives by a great deliverance.*a*

a 7 Or save you as a great band of survivors

8 "So then, it was not you who sent me here, but God. He made me father to Pharaoh, lord of his entire household and ruler of all Egypt. 9 Now hurry back to my father and say to him, 'This is what your son Joseph says: God has made me lord of all Egypt. Come down to me; don't delay. 10 You shall live in the region of Goshen and be near me—you, your children and grandchildren, your flocks and herds, and all you have. 11 I will provide for you there, because five years of famine are still to come. Otherwise you and your household and all who belong to you will become destitute.'

12 "You can see for yourselves, and so can my brother Benjamin, that it is really I who am speaking to you. 13 Tell my father about all the honor accorded me in Egypt and about everything you have seen. And bring my father down here quickly."

14 Then he threw his arms around his brother Benjamin and wept, and Benjamin embraced him, weeping. 15 And he kissed all his brothers and wept over them. Afterward his brothers talked with him.

16 When the news reached Pharaoh's palace that Joseph's brothers had come, Pharaoh and all his officials were pleased. 17 Pharaoh said to Joseph, "Tell your brothers, 'Do this: Load your animals and return to the land of Canaan, 18 and bring your father and your families back to me. I will give you the best of the land of Egypt and you can enjoy the fat of the land.'

19 "You are also directed to tell them, 'Do this: Take some carts from Egypt for your children and your wives, and get your father and come. 20 Never mind about your belongings, because the best of all Egypt will be yours.'"

21 So the sons of Israel did this. Joseph gave them carts, as Pharaoh had commanded, and he also gave them provisions for their journey. 22 To each of them he gave new clothing, but to Benjamin he gave three hundred shekels[a] of silver and five sets of clothes. 23 And this is what he sent to his father: ten donkeys loaded with the best things of Egypt, and ten female donkeys loaded with grain and

INSTANT ACCESS

She ate my whole box of candy. So I'm taking her makeup!" It's not that you want the makeup. It's just that you're angry and you want revenge. After all, she did you wrong. You have a right to be upset. If anyone had a right to hold a grudge, it was Joseph. His own brothers sold him into slavery. Years later, when his brothers were starving, Joseph ruled Egypt, the only country that had food. What a chance to get revenge! But Joseph chose a better way. He threw his arms around his brothers and promised them the best of Egypt. When someone hurts you, try reacting like Joseph. Don't get even. Do good to them instead.

{Genesis 45:1–20}

bread and other provisions for his journey. 24 Then he sent his brothers away, and as they were leaving he said to them, "Don't quarrel on the way!"

25 So they went up out of Egypt and came to their father Jacob in the land of Canaan. 26 They told him, "Joseph is still alive! In fact, he is ruler of all Egypt." Jacob was stunned; he did not believe them. 27 But when they told him everything Joseph had said to them, and when he saw the carts Joseph had sent to

---

a 22 That is, about 7 1/2 pounds or about 3.5 kilograms

carry him back, the spirit of their father Jacob revived. 28 And Israel said, "I'm convinced! My son Joseph is still alive. I will go and see him before I die."

Jacob Goes to Egypt

46 So Israel set out with all that was his, and when he reached Beersheba, he offered sacrifices to the God of his father Isaac.

2 And God spoke to Israel in a vision at night and said, "Jacob! Jacob!"

"Here I am," he replied.

3 "I am God, the God of your father," he said. "Do not be afraid to go down to Egypt, for I will make you into a great nation there. 4 I will go down to Egypt with you, and I will surely bring you back again. And Joseph's own hand will close your eyes."

5 Then Jacob left Beersheba, and Israel's sons took their father Jacob and their children and their wives in the carts that Pharaoh had sent to transport him. 6 So Jacob and all his offspring went to Egypt, taking with them their livestock and the possessions they had acquired in Canaan. 7 Jacob brought with him to Egypt his sons and grandsons and his daughters and granddaughters—all his offspring.

8 These are the names of the sons of Israel (Jacob and his descendants) who went to Egypt:

Reuben the firstborn of Jacob.
9 The sons of Reuben:
Hanok, Pallu, Hezron and Karmi.
10 The sons of Simeon:
Jemuel, Jamin, Ohad, Jakin, Zohar and Shaul the son of a Canaanite woman.
11 The sons of Levi:
Gershon, Kohath and Merari.
12 The sons of Judah:
Er, Onan, Shelah, Perez and Zerah (but Er and Onan had died in the land of Canaan).

The sons of Perez:
Hezron and Hamul.
13 The sons of Issachar:
Tola, Puah,a Jashubb and Shimron.
14 The sons of Zebulun:
Sered, Elon and Jahleel.
15 These were the sons Leah bore to Jacob in Paddan Aram,c besides his daughter Dinah. These sons and daughters of his were thirty-three in all.

16 The sons of Gad:
Zephon,d Haggi, Shuni, Ezbon, Eri, Arodi and Areli.
17 The sons of Asher:
Imnah, Ishvah, Ishvi and Beriah.
Their sister was Serah.
The sons of Beriah:
Heber and Malkiel.
18 These were the children born to Jacob by Zilpah, whom Laban had given to his daughter Leah—sixteen in all.

19 The sons of Jacob's wife Rachel:
Joseph and Benjamin. 20 In Egypt, Manasseh and Ephraim were born to Joseph by Asenath daughter of Potiphera, priest of On.e
21 The sons of Benjamin:
Bela, Beker, Ashbel, Gera, Naaman, Ehi, Rosh, Muppim, Huppim and Ard.
22 These were the sons of Rachel who were born to Jacob—fourteen in all.

23 The son of Dan:
Hushim.
24 The sons of Naphtali:
Jahziel, Guni, Jezer and Shillem.
25 These were the sons born to Jacob by Bilhah, whom Laban had given to his daughter Rachel—seven in all.

26 All those who went to Egypt with Jacob—those who were his direct descendants, not counting his sons' wives—numbered sixty-six persons. 27 With the two sonsf who had been born to Joseph in Egypt, the members of Jacob's family, which went to Egypt, were seventyg in all.

---

a 13 Samaritan Pentateuch and Syriac (see also 1 Chron. 7:1); Masoretic Text *Puvah*   b 13 Samaritan Pentateuch and some Septuagint manuscripts (see also Num. 26:24 and 1 Chron. 7:1); Masoretic Text *Iob*   c 15 That is, Northwest Mesopotamia   d 16 Samaritan Pentateuch and Septuagint (see also Num. 26:15); Masoretic Text *Ziphion*   e 20 That is, Heliopolis   f 27 Hebrew; Septuagint *the nine children*   g 27 Hebrew (see also Exodus 1:5 and note); Septuagint (see also Acts 7:14) *seventy-five*

28 Now Jacob sent Judah ahead of him to Joseph to get directions to Goshen. When they arrived in the region of Goshen, 29 Joseph had his chariot made ready and went to Goshen to meet his father Israel. As soon as Joseph appeared before him, he threw his arms around his father[a] and wept for a long time.

30 Israel said to Joseph, "Now I am ready to die, since I have seen for myself that you are still alive."

31 Then Joseph said to his brothers and to his father's household, "I will go up and speak to Pharaoh and will say to him, 'My brothers and my father's household, who were living in the land of Canaan, have come to me. 32 The men are shepherds; they tend livestock, and they have brought along their flocks and herds and everything they own.' 33 When Pharaoh calls you in and asks, 'What is your occupation?' 34 you should answer, 'Your servants have tended livestock from our boyhood on, just as our fathers did.' Then you will be allowed to settle in the region of Goshen, for all shepherds are detestable to the Egyptians."

47 Joseph went and told Pharaoh, "My father and brothers, with their flocks and herds and everything they own, have come from the land of Canaan and are now in Goshen." 2 He chose five of his brothers and presented them before Pharaoh.

3 Pharaoh asked the brothers, "What is your occupation?"

"Your servants are shepherds," they replied to Pharaoh, "just as our fathers were." 4 They also said to him, "We have come to live here for a while, because the famine is severe in Canaan and your servants' flocks have no pasture. So now, please let your servants settle in Goshen."

5 Pharaoh said to Joseph, "Your father and your brothers have come to you, 6 and the land of Egypt is before you; settle your father and your brothers in the best part of the land. Let them live in Goshen. And if you know of any among them with special ability, put them in charge of my own livestock."

7 Then Joseph brought his father Jacob in and presented him before Pharaoh. After Jacob blessed[b] Pharaoh, 8 Pharaoh asked him, "How old are you?"

9 And Jacob said to Pharaoh, "The years of my pilgrimage are a hundred and thirty. My years have been few and difficult, and they do not equal the years of the pilgrimage of my fathers." 10 Then Jacob blessed[c] Pharaoh and went out from his presence.

11 So Joseph settled his father and his brothers in Egypt and gave them property in the best part of the land, the district of Rameses, as Pharaoh directed. 12 Joseph also provided his father and his brothers and all his father's household with food, according to the number of their children.

Joseph and the Famine

13 There was no food, however, in the whole region because the famine was severe; both Egypt and Canaan wasted away because of the famine. 14 Joseph collected all the money that was to be found in Egypt and Canaan in payment for the grain they were buying, and he brought it to Pharaoh's palace. 15 When the money of the people of Egypt and Canaan was gone, all Egypt came to Joseph and said, "Give us food. Why should we die before your eyes? Our money is all gone."

16 "Then bring your livestock," said Joseph. "I will sell you food in exchange for your livestock, since your money is gone." 17 So they brought their livestock to Joseph, and he gave them food in exchange for their horses, their sheep and goats, their cattle and donkeys. And he brought them through that year with food in exchange for all their livestock.

18 When that year was over, they came to him the following year and said, "We cannot hide from our lord the fact that since our money is gone and our livestock belongs to you, there is nothing left for our lord except our bodies and our land. 19 Why should we perish before your eyes—we and our land as well? Buy us and our land in exchange for food, and we

---

a 29 Hebrew around him   b 7 Or greeted   c 10 Or said farewell to

with our land will be in bondage to Pharaoh. Give us seed so that we may live and not die, and that the land may not become desolate."

20 So Joseph bought all the land in Egypt for Pharaoh. The Egyptians, one and all, sold their fields, because the famine was too severe for them. The land became Pharaoh's, 21 and Joseph reduced the people to servitude,[a] from one end of Egypt to the other. 22 However, he did not buy the land of the priests, because they received a regular allotment from Pharaoh and had food enough from the allotment Pharaoh gave them. That is why they did not sell their land.

23 Joseph said to the people, "Now that I have bought you and your land today for Pharaoh, here is seed for you so you can plant the ground. 24 But when the crop comes in, give a fifth of it to Pharaoh. The other four-fifths you may keep as seed for the fields and as food for yourselves and your households and your children."

25 "You have saved our lives," they said. "May we find favor in the eyes of our lord; we will be in bondage to Pharaoh."

26 So Joseph established it as a law concerning land in Egypt—still in force today—that a fifth of the produce belongs to Pharaoh. It was only the land of the priests that did not become Pharaoh's.

27 Now the Israelites settled in Egypt in the region of Goshen. They acquired property there and were fruitful and increased greatly in number.

28 Jacob lived in Egypt seventeen years, and the years of his life were a hundred and forty-seven. 29 When the time drew near for Israel to die, he called for his son Joseph and said to him, "If I have found favor in your eyes, put your hand under my thigh and promise that you will show me kindness and faithfulness. Do not bury me in Egypt, 30 but when I rest with my fathers, carry me out of Egypt and bury me where they are buried."

"I will do as you say," he said.

31 "Swear to me," he said. Then Joseph swore to him, and Israel worshiped as he leaned on the top of his staff.[b]

Manasseh and Ephraim

48 Some time later Joseph was told, "Your father is ill." So he took his two sons Manasseh and Ephraim along with him. 2 When Jacob was told, "Your son Joseph has come to you," Israel rallied his strength and sat up on the bed.

3 Jacob said to Joseph, "God Almighty[c] appeared to me at Luz in the land of Canaan, and there he blessed me 4 and said to me, 'I am going to make you fruitful and increase your numbers. I will make you a community of peoples, and I will give this land as an everlasting possession to your descendants after you.'

5 "Now then, your two sons born to you in Egypt before I came to you here will be reckoned as mine; Ephraim and Manasseh will be mine, just as Reuben and Simeon are mine. 6 Any children born to you after them will be yours; in the territory they inherit they will be reckoned under the names of their brothers. 7 As I was returning from Paddan,[d] to my sorrow Rachel died in the land of Canaan while we were still on the way, a little distance from Ephrath. So I buried her there beside the road to Ephrath" (that is, Bethlehem).

8 When Israel saw the sons of Joseph, he asked, "Who are these?"

9 "They are the sons God has given me here," Joseph said to his father.

Then Israel said, "Bring them to me so I may bless them."

10 Now Israel's eyes were failing because of old age, and he could hardly see. So Joseph brought his sons close to him, and his father kissed them and embraced them.

11 Israel said to Joseph, "I never expected to see your face again, and now God has allowed me to see your children too."

12 Then Joseph removed them from Israel's knees and bowed down with his face to the ground. 13 And Joseph took both of them, Ephraim on his right toward Israel's left hand and Manasseh on his left toward

---

[a] 21 Samaritan Pentateuch and Septuagint (see also Vulgate); Masoretic Text *and he moved the people into the cities*   [b] 31 Or *Israel bowed down at the head of his bed*   [c] 3 Hebrew *El-Shaddai*   [d] 7 That is, Northwest Mesopotamia

Israel's right hand, and brought them close to him. 14But Israel reached out his right hand and put it on Ephraim's head, though he was the younger, and crossing his arms, he put his left hand on Manasseh's head, even though Manasseh was the firstborn.

15Then he blessed Joseph and said,

"May the God before whom my fathers
    Abraham and Isaac walked
        faithfully,
the God who has been my shepherd
    all my life to this day,
16the Angel who has delivered me from
        all harm
    —may he bless these boys.
May they be called by my name
    and the names of my fathers
        Abraham and Isaac,
and may they increase greatly
    on the earth."

17When Joseph saw his father placing his right hand on Ephraim's head he was displeased; so he took hold of his father's hand to move it from Ephraim's head to Manasseh's head. 18Joseph said to him, "No, my father, this one is the firstborn; put your right hand on his head."

19But his father refused and said, "I know, my son, I know. He too will become a people, and he too will become great. Nevertheless, his younger brother will be greater than he, and his descendants will become a group of nations." 20He blessed them that day and said,

"In your[a] name will Israel pronounce
        this blessing:
    'May God make you like Ephraim
        and Manasseh.'"

So he put Ephraim ahead of Manasseh.

21Then Israel said to Joseph, "I am about to die, but God will be with you[b] and take you[b] back to the land of your[b] fathers. 22And to you I give one more ridge of land[c] than to your brothers, the ridge I took from the Amorites with my sword and my bow."

Jacob Blesses His Sons

49 Then Jacob called for his sons and said: "Gather around so I can tell you what will happen to you in days to come.

2"Assemble and listen, sons of Jacob;
    listen to your father Israel.

3"Reuben, you are my firstborn,
    my might, the first sign of my
        strength,
    excelling in honor, excelling in
        power.
4Turbulent as the waters, you will no
        longer excel,
    for you went up onto your father's
        bed,
    onto my couch and defiled it.

5"Simeon and Levi are brothers—
    their swords[d] are weapons of
        violence.
6Let me not enter their council,
    let me not join their assembly,
    for they have killed men in their anger
    and hamstrung oxen as they
        pleased.
7Cursed be their anger, so fierce,
    and their fury, so cruel!
I will scatter them in Jacob
    and disperse them in Israel.

8"Judah,[e] your brothers will praise you;
    your hand will be on the neck of
        your enemies;
    your father's sons will bow down to
        you.
9You are a lion's cub, Judah;
    you return from the prey, my son.
Like a lion he crouches and lies down,
    like a lioness—who dares to rouse
        him?
10The scepter will not depart from
        Judah,
    nor the ruler's staff from between
        his feet,[f]
    until he to whom it belongs[g] shall
        come
    and the obedience of the nations
        shall be his.

---

a 20 The Hebrew is singular.   b 21 The Hebrew is plural.   c 22 The Hebrew for *ridge of land* is identical with the place name Shechem.   d 5 The meaning of the Hebrew for this word is uncertain.   e 8 *Judah* sounds like and may be derived from the Hebrew for *praise*.   f 10 Or *from his descendants*   g 10 Or *to whom tribute belongs*; the meaning of the Hebrew for this phrase is uncertain.

¹¹He will tether his donkey to a vine,
  his colt to the choicest branch;
he will wash his garments in wine,
  his robes in the blood of grapes.
¹²His eyes will be darker than wine,
  his teeth whiter than milk.^a

¹³"Zebulun will live by the seashore
  and become a haven for ships;
  his border will extend toward Sidon.

¹⁴"Issachar is a rawboned^b donkey
  lying down among the sheep pens.^c
¹⁵When he sees how good is his resting
    place
  and how pleasant is his land,
he will bend his shoulder to the
    burden
  and submit to forced labor.

¹⁶"Dan^d will provide justice for his
    people
  as one of the tribes of Israel.
¹⁷Dan will be a snake by the roadside,
  a viper along the path,
that bites the horse's heels
  so that its rider tumbles backward.

¹⁸"I look for your deliverance, Lord.

¹⁹"Gad^e will be attacked by a band of
    raiders,
  but he will attack them at their
    heels.

²⁰"Asher's food will be rich;
  he will provide delicacies fit for a
    king.

²¹"Naphtali is a doe set free
  that bears beautiful fawns.^f

²²"Joseph is a fruitful vine,
  a fruitful vine near a spring,
  whose branches climb over a wall.^g
²³With bitterness archers attacked him;
  they shot at him with hostility.
²⁴But his bow remained steady,
  his strong arms stayed^h
    limber,
because of the hand of the Mighty
    One of Jacob,

because of the Shepherd, the Rock
    of Israel,
²⁵because of your father's God, who
    helps you,
  because of the Almighty,ⁱ who
    blesses you
with blessings of the skies above,
  blessings of the deep springs
    below,
  blessings of the breast and womb.
²⁶Your father's blessings are greater
  than the blessings of the ancient
    mountains,
  than^j the bounty of the age-old
    hills.
Let all these rest on the head of
    Joseph,
  on the brow of the prince among^k
    his brothers.

²⁷"Benjamin is a ravenous wolf;
  in the morning he devours the prey,
  in the evening he divides the
    plunder."

²⁸All these are the twelve tribes of Israel, and this is what their father said to them when he blessed them, giving each the blessing appropriate to him.

The Death of Jacob

²⁹Then he gave them these instructions: "I am about to be gathered to my people. Bury me with my fathers in the cave in the field of Ephron the Hittite, ³⁰the cave in the field of Machpelah, near Mamre in Canaan, which Abraham bought along with the field as a burial place from Ephron the Hittite. ³¹There Abraham and his wife Sarah were buried, there Isaac and his wife Rebekah were buried, and there I buried Leah. ³²The field and the cave in it were bought from the Hittites.^l"

³³When Jacob had finished giving instructions to his sons, he drew his feet up into the bed, breathed his last and was gathered to his people.

---

^a 12 Or will be dull from wine, / his teeth white from milk   ^b 14 Or strong   ^c 14 Or the campfires; or the saddlebags
^d 16 Dan here means he provides justice.   ^e 19 Gad sounds like the Hebrew for attack and also for band of raiders.
^f 21 Or free; / he utters beautiful words   ^g 22 Or Joseph is a wild colt, / a wild colt near a spring, / a wild donkey
on a terraced hill   ^h 23,24 Or archers will attack . . . will shoot . . . will remain . . . will stay   ⁱ 25 Hebrew Shaddai
^j 26 Or of my progenitors, / as great as   ^k 26 Or of the one separated from   ^l 32 Or the descendants of Heth

50 Joseph threw himself on his father and wept over him and kissed him. ²Then Joseph directed the physicians in his service to embalm his father Israel. So the physicians embalmed him, ³taking a full forty days, for that was the time required for embalming. And the Egyptians mourned for him seventy days.

⁴When the days of mourning had passed, Joseph said to Pharaoh's court, "If I have found favor in your eyes, speak to Pharaoh for me. Tell him, ⁵'My father made me swear an oath and said, "I am about to die; bury me in the tomb I dug for myself in the land of Canaan." Now let me go up and bury my father; then I will return.'"

⁶Pharaoh said, "Go up and bury your father, as he made you swear to do."

⁷So Joseph went up to bury his father. All Pharaoh's officials accompanied him—the dignitaries of his court and all the dignitaries of Egypt— ⁸besides all the members of Joseph's household and his brothers and those belonging to his father's household. Only their children and their flocks and herds were left in Goshen. ⁹Chariots and horsemenᵃ also went up with him. It was a very large company.

¹⁰When they reached the threshing floor of Atad, near the Jordan, they lamented loudly and bitterly; and there Joseph observed a seven-day period of mourning for his father. ¹¹When the Canaanites who lived there saw the mourning at the threshing floor of Atad, they said, "The Egyptians are holding a solemn ceremony of mourning." That is why that place near the Jordan is called Abel Mizraim.ᵇ

¹²So Jacob's sons did as he had commanded them: ¹³They carried him to the land of Canaan and buried him in the cave in the field of Machpelah, near Mamre, which Abraham had bought along with the field as a burial place from Ephron the Hittite. ¹⁴After burying his father, Joseph returned to Egypt, together with his brothers and all the others who had gone with him to bury his father.

Joseph Reassures His Brothers

¹⁵When Joseph's brothers saw that their father was dead, they said, "What if Joseph holds a grudge against us and pays us back for all the wrongs we did to him?" ¹⁶So they sent word to Joseph, saying, "Your father left these instructions before he died: ¹⁷'This is what you are to say to Joseph: I ask you to forgive your brothers the sins and the wrongs they committed in treating you so badly.' Now please forgive the sins of the servants of the God of your father." When their message came to him, Joseph wept.

¹⁸His brothers then came and threw themselves down before him. "We are your slaves," they said.

¹⁹But Joseph said to them, "Don't be afraid. Am I in the place of God? ²⁰You intended to harm me, but God intended it for good to accomplish what is now being done, the saving of many lives. ²¹So then, don't be afraid. I will provide for you and your children." And he reassured them and spoke kindly to them.

Genesis 50

Q: How was Jacob prepared for burial?

BONUS: Why did the Egyptians use this method?

Answers on next page

ᵃ 9 Or *charioteers* ᵇ 11 *Abel Mizraim* means *mourning of the Egyptians*.

The Death of Joseph

22 Joseph stayed in Egypt, along with all his father's family. He lived a hundred and ten years 23 and saw the third generation of Ephraim's children. Also the children of Makir son of Manasseh were placed at birth on Joseph's knees.[a]

24 Then Joseph said to his brothers, "I am about to die. But God will surely come to your aid and take you up out of this land to the land he promised on oath to Abraham, Isaac and Jacob." 25 And Joseph made the Israelites swear an oath and said, "God will surely come to your aid, and then you must carry my bones up from this place."

26 So Joseph died at the age of a hundred and ten. And after they embalmed him, he was placed in a coffin in Egypt.

A: He was embalmed (Genesis 50:2–3).

BONUS: To preserve the body. The Egyptians believed that the soul existed only as long as the body survived.

---

a 23 That is, were counted as his

EXODUS

preview

Moses, the son of a Hebrew slave, is raised as an Egyptian prince.

When Moses is 80, he delivers the Hebrew slaves. He leads them for 40 years.

Freedom!

God sets you free—not free to do anything you feel like doing—free to live a happy and meaningful life. The Israelites' road map of Exodus 20 can be your road map as well. You don't have to keep trying things in order to discover what's good and what's bad. Your map tells you.

The book of Exodus tells how God stepped in with stunning miracles to free the Israelites. Exodus contains the Ten Commandments, God's road map to the good life. Then Exodus records what happened when the Israelites followed the road map, and what happened when they chose detours.

>>**GOD REVEALS HIS REAL NAME**
See aged shepherd's report, Exodus 3:11–15

>>**MIRACLES WRECK EGYPT**
See plague story in Exodus 7–11

>>**GOD DEFINES "RIGHT" AND "WRONG"**
Absolute moral truths revealed, Exodus 20

>>**BETTER NOT MAKE GOD MAD!**
Angry God acts, report in Exodus 32

When the Exodus takes place around 1440 B.C., a library in the Hittite capital contains tablets written in eight languages. And prohibition is decreed in China.

The Israelites Oppressed

1 These are the names of the sons of Israel who went to Egypt with Jacob, each with his family: ²Reuben, Simeon, Levi and Judah; ³Issachar, Zebulun and Benjamin; ⁴Dan and Naphtali; Gad and Asher. ⁵The descendants of Jacob numbered seventy[a] in all; Joseph was already in Egypt.

⁶Now Joseph and all his brothers and all that generation died, ⁷but the Israelites were exceedingly fruitful; they multiplied greatly, increased in numbers and became so numerous that the land was filled with them.

⁸Then a new king, to whom Joseph meant nothing, came to power in Egypt. ⁹"Look," he said to his people, "the Israelites have become far too numerous for us. ¹⁰Come, we must deal shrewdly with them or they will become even more numerous and, if war breaks out, will join our enemies, fight against us and leave the country."

¹¹So they put slave masters over them to oppress them with forced labor, and they built Pithom and Rameses as store cities for Pharaoh. ¹²But the more they were oppressed, the more they multiplied and spread; so the Egyptians came to dread the Israelites ¹³and worked them ruthlessly. ¹⁴They made their lives bitter with harsh labor in brick and mortar and with all kinds of work in the fields; in all their harsh labor the Egyptians worked them ruthlessly.

¹⁵The king of Egypt said to the Hebrew midwives, whose names were Shiphrah and Puah, ¹⁶"When you are helping the Hebrew women during childbirth on the delivery stool, if you see that the baby is a boy, kill him; but if it is a girl, let her live." ¹⁷The midwives, however, feared God and did not do what the king of Egypt had told them to do; they let the boys live. ¹⁸Then the king of Egypt summoned the midwives and asked them, "Why have you done this? Why have you let the boys live?"

¹⁹The midwives answered Pharaoh, "Hebrew women are not like Egyptian women; they are vigorous and give birth before the midwives arrive."

²⁰So God was kind to the midwives and the people increased and became even more numerous. ²¹And because the midwives feared God, he gave them families of their own.

²²Then Pharaoh gave this order to all his people: "Every Hebrew boy that is born you must throw into the Nile, but let every girl live."

The Birth of Moses

2 Now a man of the tribe of Levi married a Levite woman, ²and she became pregnant and gave birth to a son. When she saw that he was a fine child, she hid him for three months. ³But when she could hide him no longer, she got a papyrus basket[b] for him and coated it with tar and pitch. Then she placed the child in it and put it among the reeds along the bank of the Nile. ⁴His sister stood at a distance to see what would happen to him.

⁵Then Pharaoh's daughter went down to the Nile to bathe, and her attendants were walking along the riverbank. She saw the basket among the reeds and sent her female slave to get it. ⁶She opened it and saw the baby. He was crying, and she felt sorry for him. "This is one of the Hebrew babies," she said.

⁷Then his sister asked Pharaoh's daughter, "Shall I go and get one of the Hebrew women to nurse the baby for you?"

⁸"Yes, go," she answered. So the girl went and got the baby's mother. ⁹Pharaoh's daughter said to her, "Take this baby and nurse him for me, and I will pay you." So the woman took the baby and nursed him. ¹⁰When the child grew older, she took him to Pharaoh's daughter and he became her son. She named him Moses,[c] saying, "I drew him out of the water."

Moses Flees to Midian

¹¹One day, after Moses had grown up, he went out to where his own people were

---

[a] 5 Masoretic Text (see also Gen. 46:27); Dead Sea Scrolls and Septuagint (see also Acts 7:14 and note at Gen. 46:27) *seventy-five*   [b] 3 The Hebrew can also mean *ark*, as in Gen. 6:14.   [c] 10 *Moses* sounds like the Hebrew for *draw out*.

and watched them at their hard labor. He saw an Egyptian beating a Hebrew, one of his own people. [12] Looking this way and that and seeing no one, he killed the Egyptian and hid him in the sand. [13] The next day he went out and saw two Hebrews fighting. He asked the one in the wrong, "Why are you hitting your fellow Hebrew?"

[14] The man said, "Who made you ruler and judge over us? Are you thinking of killing me as you killed the Egyptian?" Then Moses was afraid and thought, "What I did must have become known."

[15] When Pharaoh heard of this, he tried to kill Moses, but Moses fled from Pharaoh and went to live in Midian, where he sat down by a well. [16] Now a priest of Midian had seven daughters, and they came to draw water and fill the troughs to water their father's flock. [17] Some shepherds came along and drove them away, but Moses got up and came to their rescue and watered their flock.

[18] When the girls returned to Reuel their father, he asked them, "Why have you returned so early today?"

[19] They answered, "An Egyptian rescued us from the shepherds. He even drew water for us and watered the flock."

[20] "And where is he?" Reuel asked his daughters. "Why did you leave him? Invite him to have something to eat."

[21] Moses agreed to stay with the man, who gave his daughter Zipporah to Moses in marriage. [22] Zipporah gave birth to a son, and Moses named him Gershom,[a] saying, "I have become a foreigner in a foreign land."

[23] During that long period, the king of Egypt died. The Israelites groaned in their slavery and cried out, and their cry for help because of their slavery went up to God. [24] God heard their groaning and he remembered his covenant with Abraham, with Isaac and with Jacob. [25] So God looked on the Israelites and was concerned about them.

Moses and the Burning Bush

3 Now Moses was tending the flock of Jethro his father-in-law, the priest of Midian, and he led the flock to the far side of the wilderness and came to Horeb, the mountain of God. [2] There the angel of the LORD appeared to him in flames of fire from within a bush. Moses saw that though the bush was on fire it did not burn up. [3] So Moses thought, "I will go over and see this strange sight—why the bush does not burn up."

[4] When the LORD saw that he had gone over to look, God called to him from within the bush, "Moses! Moses!"

And Moses said, "Here I am."

[5] "Do not come any closer," God said. "Take off your sandals, for the place

---

>> INSTANT ACCESS

Do you ever feel like it's hard to be friends with other teens, especially when they ask you to do something you know is wrong? The midwives in Egypt had a similar problem. The king had ordered them to kill any boy baby born to an Israelite. No question about that being wrong, and no question that it would be dangerous to disobey. What happened? "The midwives ... feared God and did not do what the king of Egypt had told them to do" (Exodus 1:17). If you say no when someone tries to get you to do wrong, you show that you respect God and want to please him.

{Exodus 1:15–17}

---

[a] 22 *Gershom* sounds like the Hebrew for *a foreigner there.*

where you are standing is holy ground." ⁶Then he said, "I am the God of your father,ᵃ the God of Abraham, the God of Isaac and the God of Jacob." At this, Moses hid his face, because he was afraid to look at God.

⁷The Lᴏʀᴅ said, "I have indeed seen the misery of my people in Egypt. I have heard them crying out because of their slave drivers, and I am concerned about their suffering. ⁸So I have come down to rescue them from the hand of the Egyptians and to bring them up out of that land into a good and spacious land, a land flowing with milk and honey—the home of the Canaanites, Hittites, Amorites, Perizzites, Hivites and Jebusites. ⁹And now the cry of the Israelites has reached me,

and I have seen the way the Egyptians are oppressing them. ¹⁰So now, go. I am sending you to Pharaoh to bring my people the Israelites out of Egypt."

¹¹But Moses said to God, "Who am I that I should go to Pharaoh and bring the Israelites out of Egypt?"

¹²And God said, "I will be with you. And this will be the sign to you that it is I who have sent you: When you have brought the people out of Egypt, youᵇ will worship God on this mountain."

¹³Moses said to God, "Suppose I go to the Israelites and say to them, 'The God of your fathers has sent me to you,' and they ask me, 'What is his name?' Then what shall I tell them?"

¹⁴God said to Moses, "I ᴀᴍ ᴡʜᴏ I ᴀᴍ.ᶜ

ᵃ 6 Masoretic Text; Samaritan Pentateuch (see Acts 7:32) *fathers*   ᵇ 12 The Hebrew is plural.   ᶜ 14 Or *I ᴡɪʟʟ ʙᴇ ᴡʜᴀᴛ I ᴡɪʟʟ ʙᴇ*

TO THE POINT

God's Name Is "I AM"

In Exodus 3:14–15 God declares the name by which he is to be remembered forever: "I ᴀᴍ." What does "I ᴀᴍ" mean? Why is this name special?

I ᴀᴍ (the Hebrew "Yahweh") means that God is always present with you. When you were a baby, God was I ᴀᴍ, right there with you. Wherever you are today, God is I ᴀᴍ, right there with you. And when you grow old, God will still be I ᴀᴍ, right there with you.

This special name is found many times in the Old Testament. Every time you see the word Lᴏʀᴅ in small capital letters, the Hebrew text used this special name.

How wonderful to have a God who is I ᴀᴍ, always there for you!

This is what you are to say to the Israelites: 'I AM has sent me to you.'"

15 God also said to Moses, "Say to the Israelites, 'The LORD,ᵃ the God of your fathers—the God of Abraham, the God of Isaac and the God of Jacob—has sent me to you.'

"This is my name forever,
    the name you shall call me
    from generation to generation.

16 "Go, assemble the elders of Israel and say to them, 'The LORD, the God of your fathers—the God of Abraham, Isaac and Jacob—appeared to me and said: I have watched over you and have seen what has been done to you in Egypt. 17 And I have promised to bring you up out of your misery in Egypt into the land of the Canaanites, Hittites, Amorites, Perizzites, Hivites and Jebusites—a land flowing with milk and honey.'

18 "The elders of Israel will listen to you. Then you and the elders are to go to the king of Egypt and say to him, 'The LORD, the God of the Hebrews, has met with us. Let us take a three-day journey into the wilderness to offer sacrifices to the LORD our God.' 19 But I know that the king of Egypt will not let you go unless a mighty hand compels him. 20 So I will stretch out my hand and strike the Egyptians with all the wonders that I will perform among them. After that, he will let you go.

21 "And I will make the Egyptians favorably disposed toward this people, so that when you leave you will not go empty-handed. 22 Every woman is to ask her neighbor and any woman living in her house for articles of silver and gold and for clothing, which you will put on your sons and daughters. And so you will plunder the Egyptians."

Signs for Moses

4 Moses answered, "What if they do not believe me or listen to me and say, 'The LORD did not appear to you'?"

2 Then the LORD said to him, "What is that in your hand?"

"A staff," he replied.

3 The LORD said, "Throw it on the ground."

Moses threw it on the ground and it became a snake, and he ran from it. 4 Then the LORD said to him, "Reach out your hand and take it by the tail." So Moses reached out and took hold of the snake and it turned back into a staff in his hand. 5 "This," said the LORD, "is so that they may believe that the LORD, the God of their fathers—the God of Abraham, the God of Isaac and the God of Jacob—has appeared to you."

6 Then the LORD said, "Put your hand inside your cloak." So Moses put his hand into his cloak, and when he took it out, the skin was leprousᵇ—it had become as white as snow.

7 "Now put it back into your cloak," he said. So Moses put his hand back into his cloak, and when he took it out, it was restored, like the rest of his flesh.

8 Then the LORD said, "If they do not believe you or pay attention to the first sign, they may believe the second. 9 But if they do not believe these two signs or listen to you, take some water from the Nile and pour it on the dry ground. The water you take from the river will become blood on the ground."

10 Moses said to the LORD, "Pardon your servant, Lord. I have never been eloquent, neither in the past nor since you have spoken to your servant. I am slow of speech and tongue."

11 The LORD said to him, "Who gave human beings their mouths? Who makes them deaf or mute? Who gives them sight or makes them blind? Is it not I, the LORD? 12 Now go; I will help you speak and will teach you what to say."

13 But Moses said, "Pardon your servant, Lord. Please send someone else."

14 Then the LORD's anger burned against Moses and he said, "What about your brother, Aaron the Levite? I know he can speak well. He is already on his way to meet you, and he will be glad to see you. 15 You shall speak to him and put words

in his mouth; I will help both of you speak and will teach you what to do. ¹⁶He will speak to the people for you, and it will be as if he were your mouth and as if you were God to him. ¹⁷But take this staff in your hand so you can perform the signs with it."

Moses Returns to Egypt

¹⁸Then Moses went back to Jethro his father-in-law and said to him, "Let me return to my own people in Egypt to see if any of them are still alive."

Jethro said, "Go, and I wish you well."

¹⁹Now the LORD had said to Moses in Midian, "Go back to Egypt, for all those who wanted to kill you are dead." ²⁰So Moses took his wife and sons, put them on a donkey and started back to Egypt. And he took the staff of God in his hand.

²¹The LORD said to Moses, "When you return to Egypt, see that you perform before Pharaoh all the wonders I have given you the power to do. But I will harden his heart so that he will not let the people go. ²²Then say to Pharaoh, 'This is what the LORD says: Israel is my firstborn son, ²³and I told you, "Let my son go, so he may worship me." But you refused to let him go; so I will kill your firstborn son.' "

²⁴At a lodging place on the way, the LORD met Moses[a] and was about to kill him. ²⁵But Zipporah took a flint knife, cut off her son's foreskin and touched Moses' feet with it.[b] "Surely you are a bridegroom of blood to me," she said. ²⁶So the LORD let him alone. (At that time she said "bridegroom of blood," referring to circumcision.)

²⁷The LORD said to Aaron, "Go into the wilderness to meet Moses." So he met Moses at the mountain of God and kissed him. ²⁸Then Moses told Aaron everything the LORD had sent him to say, and also about all the signs he had commanded him to perform.

²⁹Moses and Aaron brought together all the elders of the Israelites, ³⁰and Aaron told them everything the LORD had said to Moses. He also performed the signs before the people, ³¹and they believed. And when they heard that the LORD was concerned about them and had seen their misery, they bowed down and worshiped.

Bricks Without Straw

5 Afterward Moses and Aaron went to Pharaoh and said, "This is what the LORD, the God of Israel, says: 'Let my people go, so that they may hold a festival to me in the wilderness.' "

²Pharaoh said, "Who is the LORD, that I should obey him and let Israel go? I do not know the LORD and I will not let Israel go." ³Then they said, "The God of the Hebrews has met with us. Now let us take a three-day journey into the wilderness to offer sacrifices to the LORD our God, or he may strike us with plagues or with the sword."

⁴But the king of Egypt said, "Moses and Aaron, why are you taking the people away from their labor? Get back to your work!" ⁵Then Pharaoh said, "Look, the people of the land are now numerous, and you are stopping them from working."

⁶That same day Pharaoh gave this order to the slave drivers and overseers in charge of the people: ⁷"You are no longer to supply the people with straw for making bricks; let them go and gather their own straw. ⁸But require them to make the same number of bricks as before; don't reduce the quota. They are lazy; that is why they are crying out, 'Let us go and sacrifice to our God.' ⁹Make the work harder for the people so that they keep working and pay no attention to lies."

¹⁰Then the slave drivers and the overseers went out and said to the people, "This is what Pharaoh says: 'I will not give you any more straw. ¹¹Go and get

> I will ... teach you what to do.
> Exodus 4:15

---

[a] 24 Hebrew *him* [b] 25 The meaning of the Hebrew for this clause is uncertain.

your own straw wherever you can find it, but your work will not be reduced at all.' " ¹²So the people scattered all over Egypt to gather stubble to use for straw. ¹³The slave drivers kept pressing them, saying, "Complete the work required of you for each day, just as when you had straw." ¹⁴And Pharaoh's slave drivers beat the Israelite overseers they had appointed, demanding, "Why haven't you met your quota of bricks yesterday or today, as before?"

¹⁵Then the Israelite overseers went and appealed to Pharaoh: "Why have you treated your servants this way? ¹⁶Your servants are given no straw, yet we are told, 'Make bricks!' Your servants are being beaten, but the fault is with your own people."

¹⁷Pharaoh said, "Lazy, that's what you are—lazy! That is why you keep saying, 'Let us go and sacrifice to the LORD.' ¹⁸Now get to work. You will not be given any straw, yet you must produce your full quota of bricks."

¹⁹The Israelite overseers realized they were in trouble when they were told, "You are not to reduce the number of bricks required of you for each day." ²⁰When they left Pharaoh, they found Moses and Aaron waiting to meet them, ²¹and they said, "May the LORD look on you and judge you! You have made us obnoxious to Pharaoh and his officials and have put a sword in their hand to kill us."

God Promises Deliverance

²²Moses returned to the LORD and said, "Why, Lord, why have you brought trouble on this people? Is this why you sent me? ²³Ever since I went to Pharaoh to speak in your name, he has brought trouble on this people, and you have not rescued your people at all."

6 Then the LORD said to Moses, "Now you will see what I will do to Pharaoh: Because of my mighty hand he will let them go; because of my mighty hand he will drive them out of his country."

²God also said to Moses, "I am the LORD. ³I appeared to Abraham, to Isaac

> **INSTANT ACCESS**
>
> Do you ever get discouraged? You study hard for a science test and still get a D? You clean your room, and your mom still finds 103 things you need to do before it passes inspection? Is it worth even trying? Does anyone care? Moses felt that way. He told Egypt's king to let God's people go, but the king just made them work harder. And that made the Israelites angry with Moses. Nothing was working out like it was supposed to. God had a word for Moses: "I will free you … I will take you as my own" (Exodus 6:6–7). If you belong to God, he's on your side. He'll bring you through discouraging times to a better tomorrow.
>
> {Exodus 5:22—6:8}

and to Jacob as God Almighty,ᵃ but by my name the LORDᵇ I did not make myself fully known to them. ⁴I also established my covenant with them to give them the land of Canaan, where they resided as foreigners. ⁵Moreover, I have heard the groaning of the Israelites, whom the Egyptians are enslaving, and I have remembered my covenant.

⁶"Therefore, say to the Israelites: 'I am the LORD, and I will bring you out from under the yoke of the Egyptians. I will free you from being slaves to them, and I will

---

ᵃ 3 Hebrew *El-Shaddai*   ᵇ 3 See note at 3:15.

redeem you with an outstretched arm and with mighty acts of judgment. [7]I will take you as my own people, and I will be your God. Then you will know that I am the LORD your God, who brought you out from under the yoke of the Egyptians. [8]And I will bring you to the land I swore with uplifted hand to give to Abraham, to Isaac and to Jacob. I will give it to you as a possession. I am the LORD.' "

[9]Moses reported this to the Israelites, but they did not listen to him because of their discouragement and harsh labor.

[10]Then the LORD said to Moses, [11]"Go, tell Pharaoh king of Egypt to let the Israelites go out of his country."

[12]But Moses said to the LORD, "If the Israelites will not listen to me, why would Pharaoh listen to me, since I speak with faltering lips[a]?"

Family Record of Moses and Aaron

[13]Now the LORD spoke to Moses and Aaron about the Israelites and Pharaoh king of Egypt, and he commanded them to bring the Israelites out of Egypt.

[14]These were the heads of their families[b]:

The sons of Reuben the firstborn son of Israel were Hanok and Pallu, Hezron and Karmi. These were the clans of Reuben.

[15]The sons of Simeon were Jemuel, Jamin, Ohad, Jakin, Zohar and Shaul the son of a Canaanite woman. These were the clans of Simeon.

[16]These were the names of the sons of Levi according to their records: Gershon, Kohath and Merari. Levi lived 137 years.

[17]The sons of Gershon, by clans, were Libni and Shimei.

[18]The sons of Kohath were Amram, Izhar, Hebron and Uzziel. Kohath lived 133 years.

[19]The sons of Merari were Mahli and Mushi.

These were the clans of Levi according to their records.

[20]Amram married his father's sister Jochebed, who bore him Aaron and Moses. Amram lived 137 years.

[21]The sons of Izhar were Korah, Nepheg and Zikri.

[22]The sons of Uzziel were Mishael, Elzaphan and Sithri.

[23]Aaron married Elisheba, daughter of Amminadab and sister of Nahshon, and she bore him Nadab and Abihu, Eleazar and Ithamar.

[24]The sons of Korah were Assir, Elkanah and Abiasaph. These were the Korahite clans.

[25]Eleazar son of Aaron married one of the daughters of Putiel, and she bore him Phinehas.

These were the heads of the Levite families, clan by clan.

[26]It was this Aaron and Moses to whom the LORD said, "Bring the Israelites out of Egypt by their divisions." [27]They were the ones who spoke to Pharaoh king of Egypt about bringing the Israelites out of Egypt—this same Moses and Aaron.

Aaron to Speak for Moses

[28]Now when the LORD spoke to Moses in Egypt, [29]he said to him, "I am the LORD. Tell Pharaoh king of Egypt everything I tell you."

[30]But Moses said to the LORD, "Since I speak with faltering lips, why would Pharaoh listen to me?"

7 Then the LORD said to Moses, "See, I have made you like God to Pharaoh, and your brother Aaron will be your prophet. [2]You are to say everything I command you, and your brother Aaron is to tell Pharaoh to let the Israelites go out of his country. [3]But I will harden Pharaoh's heart, and though I multiply my signs and wonders in Egypt, [4]he will not listen to you. Then I will lay my hand on Egypt and with mighty acts of judgment I will bring out my divisions, my people the Israelites. [5]And the Egyptians will know that I am the LORD when I stretch out my hand against Egypt and bring the Israelites out of it."

---

[a] 12 Hebrew *I am uncircumcised of lips*; also in verse 30   [b] 14 The Hebrew for *families* here and in verse 25 refers to units larger than clans.

6 Moses and Aaron did just as the Lord commanded them. 7 Moses was eighty years old and Aaron eighty-three when they spoke to Pharaoh.

Aaron's Staff Becomes a Snake

8 The Lord said to Moses and Aaron, 9 "When Pharaoh says to you, 'Perform a miracle,' then say to Aaron, 'Take your staff and throw it down before Pharaoh,' and it will become a snake."

10 So Moses and Aaron went to Pharaoh and did just as the Lord commanded. Aaron threw his staff down in front of Pharaoh and his officials, and it became a snake. 11 Pharaoh then summoned wise men and sorcerers, and the Egyptian magicians also did the same things by their secret arts: 12 Each one threw down his staff and it became a snake. But Aaron's staff swallowed up their staffs. 13 Yet Pharaoh's heart became hard and he would not listen to them, just as the Lord had said.

The Plague of Blood

14 Then the Lord said to Moses, "Pharaoh's heart is unyielding; he refuses to let the people go. 15 Go to Pharaoh in the morning as he goes out to the river. Confront him on the bank of the Nile, and take in your hand the staff that was changed into a snake. 16 Then say to him, 'The Lord, the God of the Hebrews, has sent me to say to you: Let my people go, so that they may worship me in the wilderness. But until now you have not listened. 17 This is what the Lord says: By this you will know that I am the Lord: With the staff that is in my hand I will strike the water of the Nile, and it will be changed into blood. 18 The fish in the Nile will die, and the river will stink; the Egyptians will not be able to drink its water.'"

19 The Lord said to Moses, "Tell Aaron, 'Take your staff and stretch out your hand over the waters of Egypt—over the streams and canals, over the ponds and all the reservoirs—and they will turn to blood.' Blood will be everywhere in Egypt, even in vessels[a] of wood and stone."

20 Moses and Aaron did just as the Lord had commanded. He raised his staff in the presence of Pharaoh and his officials and struck the water of the Nile, and all the water was changed into blood. 21 The fish in the Nile died, and the river smelled so bad that the Egyptians could not drink its water. Blood was everywhere in Egypt.

22 But the Egyptian magicians did the same things by their secret arts, and Pharaoh's heart became hard; he would not listen to Moses and Aaron, just as the Lord had said. 23 Instead, he turned and went into his palace, and did not take even this to heart. 24 And all the Egyptians dug along the Nile to get drinking water, because they could not drink the water of the river.

The Plague of Frogs

25 Seven days passed after the Lord struck the Nile. **8**[b] 1 Then the Lord said to Moses, "Go to Pharaoh and say to him, 'This is what the Lord says: Let my people go, so that they may worship me. 2 If you refuse to let them go, I will send a plague of frogs on your whole country. 3 The Nile will teem with frogs. They will come up into your palace and your bedroom and onto your bed, into the houses of your officials and on your people, and into your ovens and kneading troughs. 4 The frogs will come up on you and your people and all your officials.'"

5 Then the Lord said to Moses, "Tell Aaron, 'Stretch out your hand with your staff over the streams and canals and ponds, and make frogs come up on the land of Egypt.'"

6 So Aaron stretched out his hand over the waters of Egypt, and the frogs came up and covered the land. 7 But the magicians did the same things by their secret arts; they also made frogs come up on the land of Egypt.

8 Pharaoh summoned Moses and Aaron and said, "Pray to the Lord to take the frogs away from me and my people, and I will let your people go to offer sacrifices to the Lord."

9 Moses said to Pharaoh, "I leave to

---

a 19 Or even on their idols   b In Hebrew texts 8:1-4 is numbered 7:26-29, and 8:5-32 is numbered 8:1-28.

When you say, "I'll do my homework at six," do you keep your word? Or when you promise to be home at ten, are you there? True, these are little things. But they're important because they're issues of character. And character is shaped day by day, choice by choice. Egypt's king was a young man at the time of the exodus. The land of Egypt suffered plague after plague because its king kept refusing to do what he said he would. Oh, God probably won't send plagues your way if you don't keep every promise you make. But you can be sure he doesn't want you to be like Egypt's untrustworthy king.

{Exodus 8:15}

INSTANT ACCESS

you the honor of setting the time for me to pray for you and your officials and your people that you and your houses may be rid of the frogs, except for those that remain in the Nile."

¹⁰"Tomorrow," Pharaoh said.

Moses replied, "It will be as you say, so that you may know there is no one like the LORD our God. ¹¹The frogs will leave you and your houses, your officials and your people; they will remain only in the Nile."

¹²After Moses and Aaron left Phar-

aoh, Moses cried out to the LORD about the frogs he had brought on Pharaoh. ¹³And the LORD did what Moses asked. The frogs died in the houses, in the courtyards and in the fields. ¹⁴They were piled into heaps, and the land reeked of them. ¹⁵But when Pharaoh saw that there was relief, he hardened his heart and would not listen to Moses and Aaron, just as the LORD had said.

The Plague of Gnats

¹⁶Then the LORD said to Moses, "Tell Aaron, 'Stretch out your staff and strike the dust of the ground,' and throughout the land of Egypt the dust will become gnats." ¹⁷They did this, and when Aaron stretched out his hand with the staff and struck the dust of the ground, gnats came on people and animals. All the dust throughout the land of Egypt became gnats. ¹⁸But when the magicians tried to produce gnats by their secret arts, they could not.

Since the gnats were on people and animals everywhere, ¹⁹the magicians said to Pharaoh, "This is the finger of God." But Pharaoh's heart was hard and he would not listen, just as the LORD had said.

The Plague of Flies

²⁰Then the LORD said to Moses, "Get up early in the morning and confront Pharaoh as he goes to the river and say to him, 'This is what the LORD says: Let my people go, so that they may worship me. ²¹If you do not let my people go, I will send swarms of flies on you and your officials, on your people and into your houses. The houses of the Egyptians will be full of flies; even the ground will be covered with them.

²²" 'But on that day I will deal differently with the land of Goshen, where my people live; no swarms of flies will be there, so that you will know that I, the LORD, am in this land. ²³I will make a distinction^a between my people and your people. This sign will occur tomorrow.' "

²⁴And the LORD did this. Dense swarms of flies poured into Pharaoh's palace and

^a 23 Septuagint and Vulgate; Hebrew *will put a deliverance*

into the houses of his officials; throughout Egypt the land was ruined by the flies.

25 Then Pharaoh summoned Moses and Aaron and said, "Go, sacrifice to your God here in the land."

26 But Moses said, "That would not be right. The sacrifices we offer the LORD our God would be detestable to the Egyptians. And if we offer sacrifices that are detestable in their eyes, will they not stone us? 27 We must take a three-day journey into the wilderness to offer sacrifices to the LORD our God, as he commands us."

28 Pharaoh said, "I will let you go to offer sacrifices to the LORD your God in the wilderness, but you must not go very far. Now pray for me."

29 Moses answered, "As soon as I leave you, I will pray to the LORD, and tomorrow the flies will leave Pharaoh and his officials and his people. Only let Pharaoh be sure that he does not act deceitfully again by not letting the people go to offer sacrifices to the LORD."

30 Then Moses left Pharaoh and prayed to the LORD, 31 and the LORD did what Moses asked. The flies left Pharaoh and his officials and his people; not a fly remained. 32 But this time also Pharaoh hardened his heart and would not let the people go.

The Plague on Livestock

9 Then the LORD said to Moses, "Go to Pharaoh and say to him, 'This is what the LORD, the God of the Hebrews, says: "Let my people go, so that they may worship me." 2 If you refuse to let them go and continue to hold them back, 3 the hand of the LORD will bring a terrible plague on your livestock in the field—on your horses, donkeys and camels and on your cattle, sheep and goats. 4 But the LORD will make a distinction between the livestock of Israel and that of Egypt, so that no animal belonging to the Israelites will die.'"

5 The LORD set a time and said, "Tomorrow the LORD will do this in the land." 6 And the next day the LORD did it: All the livestock of the Egyptians died, but not one animal belonging to the Israelites died. 7 Pharaoh investigated and found that not even one of the animals of the Israelites had died. Yet his heart was unyielding and he would not let the people go.

The Plague of Boils

8 Then the LORD said to Moses and Aaron, "Take handfuls of soot from a furnace and have Moses toss it into the air in the presence of Pharaoh. 9 It will become fine dust over the whole land of Egypt, and festering boils will break out on people and animals throughout the land."

10 So they took soot from a furnace and stood before Pharaoh. Moses tossed it into the air, and festering boils broke out on people and animals. 11 The magicians could not stand before Moses because of the boils that were on them and on all the Egyptians. 12 But the LORD hardened Pharaoh's heart and he would not listen to Moses and Aaron, just as the LORD had said to Moses.

The Plague of Hail

13 Then the LORD said to Moses, "Get up early in the morning, confront Pharaoh and say to him, 'This is what the LORD, the God of the Hebrews, says: Let my people go, so that they may worship me, 14 or this time I will send the full force of my plagues against you and against your officials and your people, so you may know that there is no one like me in all the earth. 15 For by now I could have stretched out my hand and struck you and your people with a plague that would have wiped you off the earth. 16 But I have raised you up[a] for this very purpose, that I might show you my power and that my name might be proclaimed in all the earth. 17 You still set yourself against my people and will not let them go. 18 Therefore, at this time tomorrow I will send the worst hailstorm that has ever fallen on Egypt, from the day it was founded till now. 19 Give an order now to bring your livestock and everything you have in the field to a place of shelter, because the

---

a 16 Or *have spared you*

How do you know if someone really believes in God? *Not by what they say, but by what they do.* When Moses announced a hailstorm, the Egyptians who believed in God rushed to get their flocks and herds inside (Exodus 9:20–21). This is a pretty good test to apply to yourself as well as to others. Are you eager to obey God's commands? Do you make choices by asking yourself what's right, what will please the Lord? There's no wiser way to live your life, as the people of Egypt found out. The animals of the believing Egyptians survived. The Egyptians who didn't believe God lost all they owned.

{Exodus 9:13–21}

>> INSTANT ACCESS

flashed down to the ground. So the LORD rained hail on the land of Egypt; 24 hail fell and lightning flashed back and forth. It was the worst storm in all the land of Egypt since it had become a nation. 25 Throughout Egypt hail struck everything in the fields—both people and animals; it beat down everything growing in the fields and stripped every tree. 26 The only place it did not hail was the land of Goshen, where the Israelites were.

27 Then Pharaoh summoned Moses and Aaron. "This time I have sinned," he said to them. "The LORD is in the right, and I and my people are in the wrong. 28 Pray to the LORD, for we have had enough thunder and hail. I will let you go; you don't have to stay any longer."

29 Moses replied, "When I have gone out of the city, I will spread out my hands in prayer to the LORD. The thunder will stop and there will be no more hail, so you may know that the earth is the LORD's. 30 But I know that you and your officials still do not fear the LORD God."

31 (The flax and barley were destroyed, since the barley had headed and the flax was in bloom. 32 The wheat and spelt, however, were not destroyed, because they ripen later.)

33 Then Moses left Pharaoh and went out of the city. He spread out his hands toward the LORD; the thunder and hail stopped, and the rain no longer poured down on the land. 34 When Pharaoh saw that the rain and hail and thunder had stopped, he sinned again: He and his officials hardened their hearts. 35 So Pharaoh's heart was hard and he would not let the Israelites go, just as the LORD had said through Moses.

The Plague of Locusts

10 Then the LORD said to Moses, "Go to Pharaoh, for I have hardened his heart and the hearts of his officials so that I may perform these signs of mine among them 2 that you may tell your children and grandchildren how I dealt harshly with the Egyptians and how I performed my signs among them, and that you may know that I am the LORD."

3 So Moses and Aaron went to Pharaoh

hail will fall on every person and animal that has not been brought in and is still out in the field, and they will die.'"

20 Those officials of Pharaoh who feared the word of the LORD hurried to bring their slaves and their livestock inside. 21 But those who ignored the word of the LORD left their slaves and livestock in the field.

22 Then the LORD said to Moses, "Stretch out your hand toward the sky so that hail will fall all over Egypt—on people and animals and on everything growing in the fields of Egypt." 23 When Moses stretched out his staff toward the sky, the LORD sent thunder and hail, and lightning

and said to him, "This is what the LORD, the God of the Hebrews, says: 'How long will you refuse to humble yourself before me? Let my people go, so that they may worship me. ⁴If you refuse to let them go, I will bring locusts into your country tomorrow. ⁵They will cover the face of the ground so that it cannot be seen. They will devour what little you have left after the hail, including every tree that is growing in your fields. ⁶They will fill your houses and those of all your officials and all the Egyptians—something neither your parents nor your ancestors have ever seen from the day they settled in this land till now.'" Then Moses turned and left Pharaoh.

⁷Pharaoh's officials said to him, "How long will this man be a snare to us? Let the people go, so that they may worship the LORD their God. Do you not yet realize that Egypt is ruined?"

⁸Then Moses and Aaron were brought back to Pharaoh. "Go, worship the LORD your God," he said. "But tell me who will be going."

⁹Moses answered, "We will go with our young and our old, with our sons and our daughters, and with our flocks and herds, because we are to celebrate a festival to the LORD."

¹⁰Pharaoh said, "The LORD be with you—if I let you go, along with your women and children! Clearly you are bent on evil.ᵃ ¹¹No! Have only the men go and worship the LORD, since that's what you have been asking for." Then Moses and Aaron were driven out of Pharaoh's presence.

¹²And the LORD said to Moses, "Stretch out your hand over Egypt so that locusts swarm over the land and devour everything growing in the fields, everything left by the hail."

¹³So Moses stretched out his staff over Egypt, and the LORD made an east wind blow across the land all that day and all that night. By morning the wind had brought the locusts; ¹⁴they invaded all Egypt and settled down in every area of the country in great numbers. Never before had there been such a plague of locusts, nor will there ever be again. ¹⁵They covered all the ground until it was black. They devoured all that was left after the hail—everything growing in the fields and the fruit on the trees. Nothing green remained on tree or plant in all the land of Egypt.

¹⁶Pharaoh quickly summoned Moses and Aaron and said, "I have sinned against the LORD your God and against you. ¹⁷Now forgive my sin once more and pray to the LORD your God to take this deadly plague away from me."

¹⁸Moses then left Pharaoh and prayed to the LORD. ¹⁹And the LORD changed the wind to a very strong west wind, which caught up the locusts and carried them into the Red Sea.ᵇ Not a locust was left anywhere in Egypt. ²⁰But the LORD hardened Pharaoh's heart, and he would not let the Israelites go.

The Plague of Darkness

²¹Then the LORD said to Moses, "Stretch out your hand toward the sky so that darkness spreads over Egypt—darkness that can be felt." ²²So Moses stretched out his hand toward the sky, and total darkness covered all Egypt for three days. ²³No one could see anyone else or move about for three days. Yet all the Israelites had light in the places where they lived.

²⁴Then Pharaoh summoned Moses and said, "Go, worship the LORD. Even your women and children may go with you; only leave your flocks and herds behind."

²⁵But Moses said, "You must allow us to have sacrifices and burnt offerings to present to the LORD our God. ²⁶Our livestock too must go with us; not a hoof is to be left behind. We have to use some of them in worshiping the LORD our God, and until we get there we will not know what we are to use to worship the LORD."

²⁷But the LORD hardened Pharaoh's heart, and he was not willing to let them go. ²⁸Pharaoh said to Moses, "Get out of my sight! Make sure you do not appear

---

ᵃ 10 Or Be careful, trouble is in store for you!   ᵇ 19 Or the Sea of Reeds before me again! The day you see my face you will die."

29 "Just as you say," Moses replied. "I will never appear before you again."

The Plague on the Firstborn

11 Now the LORD had said to Moses, "I will bring one more plague on Pharaoh and on Egypt. After that, he will let you go from here, and when he does, he will drive you out completely. 2 Tell the people that men and women alike are to ask their neighbors for articles of silver and gold." 3 (The LORD made the Egyptians favorably disposed toward the people, and Moses himself was highly regarded in Egypt by Pharaoh's officials and by the people.)

4 So Moses said, "This is what the LORD says: 'About midnight I will go through-out Egypt. 5 Every firstborn son in Egypt will die, from the firstborn son of Pharaoh, who sits on the throne, to the first-born son of the female slave, who is at her hand mill, and all the firstborn of the cattle as well. 6 There will be loud wailing throughout Egypt—worse than there has ever been or ever will be again. 7 But among the Israelites not a dog will bark at any person or animal.' Then you will know that the LORD makes a distinction between Egypt and Israel. 8 All these officials of yours will come to me, bowing down before me and saying, 'Go, you and all the people who follow you!' After that I will leave." Then Moses, hot with anger, left Pharaoh.

9 The LORD had said to Moses, "Pharaoh will refuse to listen to you—so that my wonders may be multiplied in Egypt."

TO THE POINT

God Does Miracles

These chapters in Exodus tell of several miracles God performed. Certainly there had been locusts and hailstorms in Egypt before. Why then did people think these were miracles? Because Moses predicted the events and because he commanded them to end.

Exodus gives three reasons for these miracles:

- To show that God is Lord of all (Exodus 7:5).
- To show that God cares for his people (Exodus 6:7).
- To show that the gods of Egypt were powerless (Exodus 12:12).

Do you ever wonder why God doesn't do miracles every day? Does it seem like more people would believe in him if he did? Read John 9:28–34 and 11:1–53 to see if more people believed in Jesus because of his miracles. Miracles don't create faith. Faith comes when you hear what God says to you in the Bible and believe it.

10Moses and Aaron performed all these wonders before Pharaoh, but the LORD hardened Pharaoh's heart, and he would not let the Israelites go out of his country.

The Passover and the Festival of Unleavened Bread

12 The LORD said to Moses and Aaron in Egypt, 2"This month is to be for you the first month, the first month of your year. 3Tell the whole community of Israel that on the tenth day of this month each man is to take a lamb[a] for his family, one for each household. 4If any household is too small for a whole lamb, they must share one with their nearest neighbor, having taken into account the number of people there are. You are to determine the amount of lamb needed in accordance with what each person will eat. 5The animals you choose must be year-old males without defect, and you may take them from the sheep or the goats. 6Take care of them until the fourteenth day of the month, when all the members of the community of Israel must slaughter them at twilight. 7Then they are to take some of the blood and put it on the sides and tops of the doorframes of the houses where they eat the lambs. 8That same night they are to eat the meat roasted over the fire, along with bitter herbs, and bread made without yeast. 9Do not eat the meat raw or boiled in water, but roast it over a fire—with the head, legs and internal organs. 10Do not leave any of it till morning; if some is left till morning, you must burn it. 11This is how you are to eat it: with your cloak tucked into your belt, your sandals on your feet and your staff in your hand. Eat it in haste; it is the LORD's Passover.

12"On that same night I will pass through Egypt and strike down every first-born of both people and animals, and I will bring judgment on all the gods of Egypt. I am the LORD. 13The blood will be a sign for you on the houses where you are, and when I see the blood, I will pass

Some occasions are so important you celebrate them every year. Birthdays. Christmas. Easter. Did you know that God ordered the Israelites to celebrate a special holiday? He told them to celebrate every year their release from slavery. What has God done for you that's worth remembering and celebrating? Some people celebrate the day they accepted Christ as Savior, a "spiritual birthday." Some record answers to prayer and look back over that record at least once a year. God is good, and it's good to celebrate the things he does for you.

{Exodus 12:14–16}

>> INSTANT ACCESS

over you. No destructive plague will touch you when I strike Egypt.

14"This is a day you are to commemorate; for the generations to come you shall celebrate it as a festival to the LORD—a lasting ordinance. 15For seven days you are to eat bread made without yeast. On the first day remove the yeast from your houses, for whoever eats anything with yeast in it from the first day through the seventh must be cut off from Israel. 16On the first day hold a sacred assembly, and another one on the seventh day. Do no work at all on these days, ex-

---

a 3 The Hebrew word can mean lamb or kid; also in verse 4.

cept to prepare food for everyone to eat; that is all you may do.

17 "Celebrate the Festival of Unleavened Bread, because it was on this very day that I brought your divisions out of Egypt. Celebrate this day as a lasting ordinance for the generations to come. 18 In the first month you are to eat bread made without yeast, from the evening of the fourteenth day until the evening of the twenty-first day. 19 For seven days no yeast is to be found in your houses. And anyone, whether foreigner or native-born, who eats anything with yeast in it must be cut off from the community of Israel. 20 Eat nothing made with yeast. Wherever you live, you must eat unleavened bread."

21 Then Moses summoned all the elders of Israel and said to them, "Go at once and select the animals for your families and slaughter the Passover lamb. 22 Take a bunch of hyssop, dip it into the blood in the basin and put some of the blood on the top and on both sides of the doorframe. None of you shall go out of the door of your house until morning. 23 When the LORD goes through the land to strike down the Egyptians, he will see the blood on the top and sides of the doorframe and will pass over that doorway, and he will not permit the destroyer to enter your houses and strike you down.

24 "Obey these instructions as a lasting ordinance for you and your descendants. 25 When you enter the land that the LORD will give you as he promised, observe this ceremony. 26 And when your children ask you, 'What does this ceremony mean to you?' 27 then tell them, 'It is the Passover sacrifice to the LORD, who passed over the houses of the Israelites in Egypt and spared our homes when he struck down the Egyptians.'" Then the people bowed down and worshiped. 28 The Israelites did just what the LORD commanded Moses and Aaron.

29 At midnight the LORD struck down all the firstborn in Egypt, from the firstborn of Pharaoh, who sat on the throne, to the firstborn of the prisoner, who was in the dungeon, and the firstborn of all the live-

stock as well. 30 Pharaoh and all his officials and all the Egyptians got up during the night, and there was loud wailing in Egypt, for there was not a house without someone dead.

The Exodus

31 During the night Pharaoh summoned Moses and Aaron and said, "Up! Leave my people, you and the Israelites! Go, worship the LORD as you have requested. 32 Take your flocks and herds, as you have said, and go. And also bless me."

33 The Egyptians urged the people to hurry and leave the country. "For otherwise," they said, "we will all die!" 34 So the people took their dough before the yeast was added, and carried it on their shoulders in kneading troughs wrapped in clothing. 35 The Israelites did as Moses instructed and asked the Egyptians for articles of silver and gold and for clothing. 36 The LORD had made the Egyptians favorably disposed toward the people, and they gave them what they asked for; so they plundered the Egyptians.

37 The Israelites journeyed from Rameses to Sukkoth. There were about six hundred thousand men on foot, besides

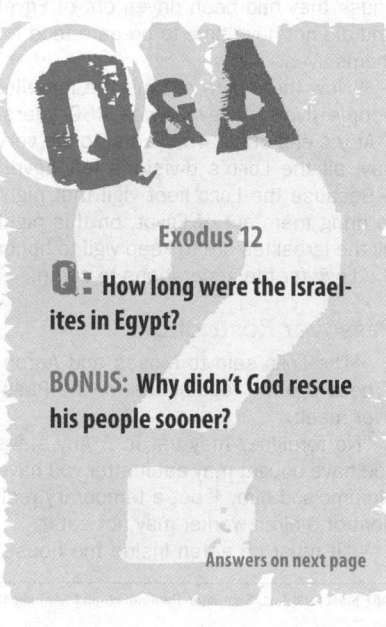

Exodus 12

Q: How long were the Israelites in Egypt?

BONUS: Why didn't God rescue his people sooner?

Answers on next page

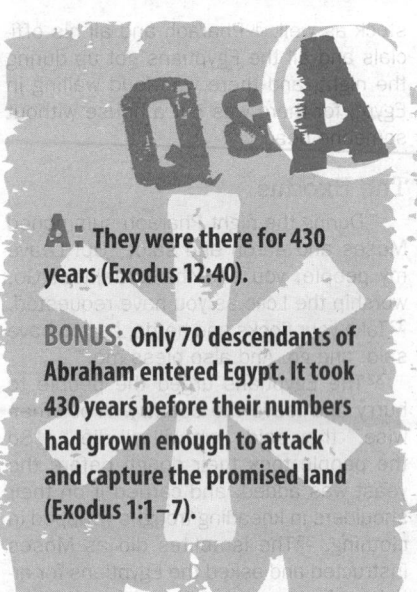

A: They were there for 430 years (Exodus 12:40).

BONUS: Only 70 descendants of Abraham entered Egypt. It took 430 years before their numbers had grown enough to attack and capture the promised land (Exodus 1:1–7).

women and children. ³⁸Many other people went up with them, and also large droves of livestock, both flocks and herds. ³⁹With the dough the Israelites had brought from Egypt, they baked loaves of unleavened bread. The dough was without yeast because they had been driven out of Egypt and did not have time to prepare food for themselves.

⁴⁰Now the length of time the Israelite people lived in Egypt*ᵃ* was 430 years. ⁴¹At the end of the 430 years, to the very day, all the Lᴏʀᴅ's divisions left Egypt. ⁴²Because the Lᴏʀᴅ kept vigil that night to bring them out of Egypt, on this night all the Israelites are to keep vigil to honor the Lᴏʀᴅ for the generations to come.

Passover Restrictions

⁴³The Lᴏʀᴅ said to Moses and Aaron, "These are the regulations for the Passover meal:

"No foreigner may eat it. ⁴⁴Any slave you have bought may eat it after you have circumcised him, ⁴⁵but a temporary resident or a hired worker may not eat it.

⁴⁶"It must be eaten inside the house; take none of the meat outside the house. Do not break any of the bones. ⁴⁷The whole community of Israel must celebrate it.

⁴⁸"A foreigner residing among you who wants to celebrate the Lᴏʀᴅ's Passover must have all the males in his household circumcised; then he may take part like one born in the land. No uncircumcised male may eat it. ⁴⁹The same law applies both to the native-born and to the foreigner residing among you."

⁵⁰All the Israelites did just what the Lᴏʀᴅ had commanded Moses and Aaron. ⁵¹And on that very day the Lᴏʀᴅ brought the Israelites out of Egypt by their divisions.

Consecration of the Firstborn

13 The Lᴏʀᴅ said to Moses, ²"Consecrate to me every firstborn male. The first offspring of every womb among the Israelites belongs to me, whether human or animal."

³Then Moses said to the people, "Commemorate this day, the day you came out of Egypt, out of the land of slavery, because the Lᴏʀᴅ brought you out of it with a mighty hand. Eat nothing containing yeast. ⁴Today, in the month of Aviv, you are leaving. ⁵When the Lᴏʀᴅ brings you into the land of the Canaanites, Hittites, Amorites, Hivites and Jebusites—the land he swore to your ancestors to give you, a land flowing with milk and honey—you are to observe this ceremony in this month: ⁶For seven days eat bread made without yeast and on the seventh day hold a festival to the Lᴏʀᴅ. ⁷Eat unleavened bread during those seven days; nothing with yeast in it is to be seen among you, nor shall any yeast be seen anywhere within your borders. ⁸On that day tell your son, 'I do this because of what the Lᴏʀᴅ did for me when I came out of Egypt.' ⁹This observance will be for you like a sign on your hand and a reminder on your forehead that this law of the Lᴏʀᴅ is to be on your lips. For the Lᴏʀᴅ brought you out of Egypt with his mighty hand. ¹⁰You must

---

ᵃ 40 Masoretic Text; Samaritan Pentateuch and Septuagint *Egypt and Canaan*

keep this ordinance at the appointed time year after year.

[11] "After the LORD brings you into the land of the Canaanites and gives it to you, as he promised on oath to you and your ancestors, [12] you are to give over to the LORD the first offspring of every womb. All the firstborn males of your livestock belong to the LORD. [13] Redeem with a lamb every firstborn donkey, but if you do not redeem it, break its neck. Redeem every firstborn among your sons.

[14] "In days to come, when your son asks you, 'What does this mean?' say to him, 'With a mighty hand the LORD brought us out of Egypt, out of the land of slavery. [15] When Pharaoh stubbornly refused to let us go, the LORD killed the firstborn of both people and animals in Egypt. This is why I sacrifice to the LORD the first male offspring of every womb and redeem each of my firstborn sons.' [16] And it will be like a sign on your hand and a symbol on your forehead that the LORD brought us out of Egypt with his mighty hand."

Crossing the Sea

[17] When Pharaoh let the people go, God did not lead them on the road through the Philistine country, though that was shorter. For God said, "If they face war, they might change their minds and return to Egypt." [18] So God led the people around by the desert road toward the Red Sea.[a] The Israelites went up out of Egypt ready for battle.

[19] Moses took the bones of Joseph with him because Joseph had made the Israelites swear an oath. He had said, "God will surely come to your aid, and then you must carry my bones up with you from this place."[b]

[20] After leaving Sukkoth they camped at Etham on the edge of the desert. [21] By day the LORD went ahead of them in a pillar of cloud to guide them on their way and by night in a pillar of fire to give them light, so that they could travel by day or night. [22] Neither the pillar of cloud by day nor the pillar of fire by night left its place in front of the people.

14 Then the LORD said to Moses, [2] "Tell the Israelites to turn back and encamp near Pi Hahiroth, between Migdol and the sea. They are to encamp by the sea, directly opposite Baal Zephon. [3] Pharaoh will think, 'The Israelites are wandering around the land in confusion, hemmed in by the desert.' [4] And I will harden Pharaoh's heart, and he will pursue them. But I will gain glory for myself through Pharaoh and all his army, and the Egyptians will know that I am the LORD." So the Israelites did this.

[5] When the king of Egypt was told that the people had fled, Pharaoh and his officials changed their minds about them and said, "What have we done? We have let the Israelites go and have lost their services!" [6] So he had his chariot made ready and took his army with him. [7] He took six hundred of the best chariots, along with all the other chariots of Egypt, with officers over all of them. [8] The LORD hardened the heart of Pharaoh king of Egypt, so that he pursued the Israelites, who were marching out boldly. [9] The Egyptians—all Pharaoh's horses and chariots, horsemen[c] and troops—pursued the Israelites and overtook them as they camped by the sea near Pi Hahiroth, opposite Baal Zephon.

[10] As Pharaoh approached, the Israelites looked up, and there were the Egyptians, marching after them. They were terrified and cried out to the LORD. [11] They said to Moses, "Was it because there were no graves in Egypt that you brought us to the desert to die? What have you done to us by bringing us out of Egypt? [12] Didn't we say to you in Egypt, 'Leave us alone; let us serve the Egyptians'? It would have been better for us to serve the Egyptians than to die in the desert!"

[13] Moses answered the people, "Do not be afraid. Stand firm and you will see the deliverance the LORD will bring you today. The Egyptians you see today you will never see again. [14] The LORD will fight for you; you need only to be still."

[15] Then the LORD said to Moses, "Why are you crying out to me? Tell the Israelites

---

[a] 18 Or the Sea of Reeds   [b] 19 See Gen. 50:25.   [c] 9 Or charioteers; also in verses 17, 18, 23, 26 and 28

to move on. [16]Raise your staff and stretch out your hand over the sea to divide the water so that the Israelites can go through the sea on dry ground. [17]I will harden the hearts of the Egyptians so that they will go in after them. And I will gain glory through Pharaoh and all his army, through his chariots and his horsemen. [18]The Egyptians will know that I am the Lord when I gain glory through Pharaoh, his chariots and his horsemen."

[19]Then the angel of God, who had been traveling in front of Israel's army, withdrew and went behind them. The pillar of cloud also moved from in front and stood behind them, [20]coming between the armies of Egypt and Israel. Throughout the night the cloud brought darkness to the one side and light to the other side; so neither went near the other all night long.

[21]Then Moses stretched out his hand over the sea, and all that night the Lord drove the sea back with a strong east wind and turned it into dry land. The waters were divided, [22]and the Israelites went through the sea on dry ground, with a wall of water on their right and on their left.

[23]The Egyptians pursued them, and all Pharaoh's horses and chariots and horsemen followed them into the sea. [24]During the last watch of the night the Lord looked down from the pillar of fire and cloud at the Egyptian army and threw it into confusion. [25]He jammed[a] the wheels of their chariots so that they had difficulty driving. And the Egyptians said, "Let's get away from the Israelites! The Lord is fighting for them against Egypt."

[26]Then the Lord said to Moses, "Stretch out your hand over the sea so that the waters may flow back over the Egyptians and their chariots and horsemen." [27]Moses stretched out his hand over the sea, and at daybreak the sea went back to its place. The Egyptians were fleeing toward[b] it, and the Lord swept them into the sea. [28]The water flowed back and covered the chariots and horsemen—the entire army of Pharaoh

that had followed the Israelites into the sea. Not one of them survived.

[29]But the Israelites went through the sea on dry ground, with a wall of water on their right and on their left. [30]That day the Lord saved Israel from the hands of the Egyptians, and Israel saw the Egyptians lying dead on the shore. [31]And when the Israelites saw the mighty hand of the Lord displayed against the Egyptians, the people feared the Lord and put their trust in him and in Moses his servant.

The Song of Moses and Miriam

15 Then Moses and the Israelites sang this song to the Lord:

"I will sing to the Lord,
　for he is highly exalted.
Both horse and driver
　he has hurled into the sea.

[2]"The Lord is my strength and my
　　defense[c];
　he has become my salvation.
He is my God, and I will praise him,
　my father's God, and I will exalt
　　him.
[3]The Lord is a warrior;
　the Lord is his name.
[4]Pharaoh's chariots and his army
　he has hurled into the sea.
The best of Pharaoh's officers
　are drowned in the Red Sea.[d]
[5]The deep waters have covered them;
　they sank to the depths like a
　　stone.
[6]Your right hand, Lord,
　was majestic in power.
Your right hand, Lord,
　shattered the enemy.

[7]"In the greatness of your majesty
　you threw down those who opposed
　　you.
You unleashed your burning anger;
　it consumed them like stubble.
[8]By the blast of your nostrils
　the waters piled up.
The surging waters stood up like a
　　wall;

---

[a] 25 See Samaritan Pentateuch, Septuagint and Syriac; Masoretic Text *removed*   [b] 27 Or *from*   [c] 2 Or *song*   [d] 4 Or *the Sea of Reeds*; also in verse 22

the deep waters congealed in the
heart of the sea.
9 The enemy boasted,
'I will pursue, I will overtake them.
I will divide the spoils;
I will gorge myself on them.
I will draw my sword
and my hand will destroy them.'
10 But you blew with your breath,
and the sea covered them.
They sank like lead
in the mighty waters.
11 Who among the gods
is like you, LORD?
Who is like you—
majestic in holiness,
awesome in glory,
working wonders?

12 "You stretch out your right hand,
and the earth swallows your
enemies.
13 In your unfailing love you will lead
the people you have redeemed.
In your strength you will guide them
to your holy dwelling.
14 The nations will hear and tremble;
anguish will grip the people of
Philistia.
15 The chiefs of Edom will be terrified,
the leaders of Moab will be seized
with trembling,
the people*a* of Canaan will
melt away;
16   terror and dread will
fall on them.
By the power of your
arm
they will be as
still as a
stone—
until your people
pass by, LORD,
until the people you
bought*b* pass by.
17 You will bring them in and
plant them
on the mountain of your
inheritance—
the place, LORD, you made for your
dwelling,

the sanctuary, Lord, your hands
established.
18 "The LORD reigns
for ever and ever."

19 When Pharaoh's horses, chariots
and horsemen*c* went into the sea, the
LORD brought the waters of the sea back
over them, but the Israelites walked
through the sea on dry ground. 20 Then
Miriam the prophet, Aaron's sister, took
a timbrel in her hand, and all the women
followed her, with timbrels and dancing.
21 Miriam sang to them:

"Sing to the LORD,
for he is highly exalted.
Both horse and driver
he has hurled into the sea."

The Waters of Marah and Elim

22 Then Moses led Israel from the
Red Sea and they went into the Desert
of Shur. For three days they traveled in
the desert without finding water. 23 When
they came to Marah, they could not drink
its water because it was bitter. (That is
why the place is called Marah.*d*) 24 So the
people grumbled against Moses, saying,
"What are we to drink?"
25 Then Moses cried out to the LORD,
and the LORD showed him a piece of
wood. He threw it into the water,
and the water became fit to
drink.
There the LORD issued
a ruling and instruction
for them and put them
to the test. 26 He said,
"If you listen carefully
to the LORD your God
and do what is right in
his eyes, if you pay at-
tention to his commands
and keep all his decrees, I
will not bring on you any of the
diseases I brought on the Egyptians, for I am the LORD, who heals you."
27 Then they came to Elim, where there
were twelve springs and seventy palm
trees, and they camped there near the
water.

> *In your unfailing love*
> *you will lead the people*
> *you have redeemed.*
> Exodus 15:13

---

a 15 Or *rulers*   *b* 16 Or *created*   *c* 19 Or *charioteers*   *d* 23 *Marah* means *bitter.*

Manna and Quail

16 The whole Israelite community set out from Elim and came to the Desert of Sin, which is between Elim and Sinai, on the fifteenth day of the second month after they had come out of Egypt. ²In the desert the whole community grumbled against Moses and Aaron. ³The Israelites said to them, "If only we had died by the LORD's hand in Egypt! There we sat around pots of meat and ate all the food we wanted, but you have brought us out into this desert to starve this entire assembly to death."

⁴Then the LORD said to Moses, "I will rain down bread from heaven for you. The people are to go out each day and gather enough for that day. In this way I will test them and see whether they will follow my instructions. ⁵On the sixth day they are to prepare what they bring in, and that is to be twice as much as they gather on the other days."

⁶So Moses and Aaron said to all the Israelites, "In the evening you will know that it was the LORD who brought you out of Egypt, ⁷and in the morning you will see the glory of the LORD, because he has heard your grumbling against him. Who are we, that you should grumble against us?" ⁸Moses also said, "You will know that it was the LORD when he gives you meat to eat in the evening and all the bread you want in the morning, because he has heard your grumbling against him. Who are we? You are not grumbling against us, but against the LORD."

⁹Then Moses told Aaron, "Say to the entire Israelite community, 'Come before the LORD, for he has heard your grumbling.'"

¹⁰While Aaron was speaking to the whole Israelite community, they looked toward the desert, and there was the glory of the LORD appearing in the cloud.

¹¹The LORD said to Moses, ¹²"I have heard the grumbling of the Israelites. Tell them, 'At twilight you will eat meat, and in the morning you will be filled with bread. Then you will know that I am the LORD your God.'"

¹³That evening quail came and covered the camp, and in the morning there was a layer of dew around the camp. ¹⁴When the dew was gone, thin flakes like frost on the ground appeared on the desert floor. ¹⁵When the Israelites saw it, they said to each other, "What is it?" For they did not know what it was.

Moses said to them, "It is the bread the LORD has given you to eat. ¹⁶This is what the LORD has commanded: 'Everyone is to gather as much as they need. Take an omer[a] for each person you have in your tent.'"

¹⁷The Israelites did as they were told; some gathered much, some little. ¹⁸And when they measured it by the omer, the one who gathered much did not have too much, and the one who gathered little did not have too little. Everyone had gathered just as much as they needed.

¹⁹Then Moses said to them, "No one is to keep any of it until morning."

²⁰However, some of them paid no attention to Moses; they kept part of it until morning, but it was full of maggots and began to smell. So Moses was angry with them.

²¹Each morning everyone gathered as much as they needed, and when the sun grew hot, it melted away. ²²On the sixth day, they gathered twice as much—two omers[b] for each person—and the leaders of the community came and reported this to Moses. ²³He said to them, "This is what the LORD commanded: 'Tomorrow is to be a day of sabbath rest, a holy sabbath to the LORD. So bake what you want to bake and boil what you want to boil. Save whatever is left and keep it until morning.'"

²⁴So they saved it until morning, as Moses commanded, and it did not stink or get maggots in it. ²⁵"Eat it today," Moses said, "because today is a sabbath to the LORD. You will not find any of it on the ground today. ²⁶Six days you are to gather it, but on the seventh day, the Sabbath, there will not be any."

²⁷Nevertheless, some of the people

---

a 16 That is, possibly about 3 pounds or about 1.4 kilograms; also in verses 18, 32, 33 and 36   *b* 22 That is, possibly about 6 pounds or about 2.8 kilograms

went out on the seventh day to gather it, but they found none. 28Then the LORD said to Moses, "How long will you[a] refuse to keep my commands and my instructions? 29Bear in mind that the LORD has given you the Sabbath; that is why on the sixth day he gives you bread for two days. Everyone is to stay where they are on the seventh day; no one is to go out." 30So the people rested on the seventh day.

31The people of Israel called the bread manna.[b] It was white like coriander seed and tasted like wafers made with honey. 32Moses said, "This is what the LORD has commanded: 'Take an omer of manna and keep it for the generations to come, so they can see the bread I gave you to eat in the wilderness when I brought you out of Egypt.'"

33So Moses said to Aaron, "Take a jar and put an omer of manna in it. Then place it before the LORD to be kept for the generations to come."

34As the LORD commanded Moses, Aaron put the manna with the tablets of the covenant law, so that it might be preserved. 35The Israelites ate manna forty years, until they came to a land that was settled; they ate manna until they reached the border of Canaan.

36(An omer is one-tenth of an ephah.)

Water From the Rock

17 The whole Israelite community set out from the Desert of Sin, traveling from place to place as the LORD commanded. They camped at Rephidim, but there was no water for the people to drink. 2So they quarreled with Moses and said, "Give us water to drink."

Moses replied, "Why do you quarrel with me? Why do you put the LORD to the test?"

3But the people were thirsty for water there, and they grumbled against Moses. They said, "Why did you bring us up out of Egypt to make us and our children and livestock die of thirst?"

4Then Moses cried out to the LORD, "What am I to do with these people? They are almost ready to stone me."

5The LORD answered Moses, "Go out in front of the people. Take with you some of the elders of Israel and take in your hand the staff with which you struck the Nile, and go. 6I will stand there before you by the rock at Horeb. Strike the rock, and water will come out of it for the people to drink." So Moses did this in the sight of the elders of Israel. 7And he called the place Massah[c] and Meribah[d] because the Israelites quarreled and because they tested the LORD saying, "Is the LORD among us or not?"

The Amalekites Defeated

8The Amalekites came and attacked the Israelites at Rephidim. 9Moses said to Joshua, "Choose some of our men and go out to fight the Amalekites. Tomorrow I will stand on top of the hill with the staff of God in my hands."

10So Joshua fought the Amalekites as Moses had ordered, and Moses, Aaron and Hur went to the top of the hill. 11As long as Moses held up his hands, the Israelites were winning, but whenever he lowered his hands, the Amalekites were winning. 12When Moses' hands grew tired, they took a stone and put it under him and he sat on it. Aaron and Hur held his hands up—one on one side, one on the other—so that his hands remained steady till sunset. 13So Joshua overcame the Amalekite army with the sword.

14Then the LORD said to Moses, "Write this on a scroll as something to be remembered and make sure that Joshua hears it, because I will completely blot out the name of Amalek from under heaven."

15Moses built an altar and called it The LORD is my Banner. 16He said, "Because hands were lifted up against[e] the throne of the LORD,[f] the LORD will be at war against the Amalekites from generation to generation."

Jethro Visits Moses

18 Now Jethro, the priest of Midian and father-in-law of Moses, heard of everything God had done for Moses and for his people Israel, and how the LORD had brought Israel out of Egypt. ²After Moses had sent away his wife Zipporah, his father-in-law Jethro received her ³and her two sons. One son was named Gershom,ᵃ for Moses said, "I have become a foreigner in a foreign land"; ⁴and the other was named Eliezer,ᵇ for he said, "My father's God was my helper; he saved me from the sword of Pharaoh."

⁵Jethro, Moses' father-in-law, together with Moses' sons and wife, came to him in the wilderness, where he was camped near the mountain of God. ⁶Jethro had sent word to him, "I, your father-in-law Jethro, am coming to you with your wife and her two sons."

⁷So Moses went out to meet his father-in-law and bowed down and kissed him. They greeted each other and then went into the tent. ⁸Moses told his father-in-law about everything the LORD had done to Pharaoh and the Egyptians for Israel's sake and about all the hardships they had met along the way and how the LORD had saved them.

⁹Jethro was delighted to hear about all the good things the LORD had done for Israel in rescuing them from the hand of the Egyptians. ¹⁰He said, "Praise be to the LORD, who rescued you from the hand of the Egyptians and of Pharaoh, and who rescued the people from the hand of the Egyptians. ¹¹Now I know that the LORD is greater than all other gods, for he did this to those who had treated Israel arrogantly." ¹²Then Jethro, Moses' father-in-law, brought a burnt offering and other sacrifices to God, and Aaron came with all the elders of Israel to eat a meal with Moses' father-in-law in the presence of God.

¹³The next day Moses took his seat to serve as judge for the people, and they stood around him from morning till evening. ¹⁴When his father-in-law saw all that Moses was doing for the people, he said, "What is this you are doing for the people? Why do you alone sit as judge, while all these people stand around you from morning till evening?"

¹⁵Moses answered him, "Because

INSTANT ACCESS

Advice is often hard to take. Dad wants to show you how to golf. Mom says she knows a better way to study. Your older brother says your shirt is out of style. Hey, whose life is it, anyway? Check out how Moses reacted when his father-in-law Jethro offered advice. Jethro started out in the worst way possible: he said, "What you are doing is not good" (Exodus 18:17). Talk about criticism! But Moses listened. He didn't get hostile. Instead he realized that Jethro was right, and he followed his advice. If one of the Bible's truly great men, Moses, can take advice without feeling attacked or getting hostile, maybe you can too.

{Exodus 18:17–19}

the people come to me to seek God's will. ¹⁶Whenever they have a dispute, it is brought to me, and I decide between the parties and inform them of God's decrees and instructions."

¹⁷Moses' father-in-law replied, "What you are doing is not good. ¹⁸You and these people who come to you will only wear yourselves out. The work is too heavy for you; you cannot handle it alone. ¹⁹Listen now to me and I will give you some advice, and may God be with you.

ᵃ 3 Gershom sounds like the Hebrew for a foreigner there.   ᵇ 4 Eliezer means my God is helper.

You must be the people's representative before God and bring their disputes to him. ²⁰Teach them his decrees and instructions, and show them the way they are to live and how they are to behave. ²¹But select capable men from all the people—men who fear God, trustworthy men who hate dishonest gain—and appoint them as officials over thousands, hundreds, fifties and tens. ²²Have them serve as judges for the people at all times, but have them bring every difficult case to you; the simple cases they can decide themselves. That will make your load lighter, because they will share it with you. ²³If you do this and God so commands, you will be able to stand the strain, and all these people will go home satisfied."

²⁴Moses listened to his father-in-law and did everything he said. ²⁵He chose capable men from all Israel and made them leaders of the people, officials over thousands, hundreds, fifties and tens. ²⁶They served as judges for the people at all times. The difficult cases they brought to Moses, but the simple ones they decided themselves.

²⁷Then Moses sent his father-in-law on his way, and Jethro returned to his own country.

At Mount Sinai

19 On the first day of the third month after the Israelites left Egypt—on that very day—they came to the Desert of Sinai. ²After they set out from Rephidim, they entered the Desert of Sinai, and Israel camped there in the desert in front of the mountain.

³Then Moses went up to God, and the LORD called to him from the mountain and said, "This is what you are to say to the descendants of Jacob and what you are to tell the people of Israel: ⁴'You yourselves have seen what I did to Egypt, and

how I carried you on eagles' wings and brought you to myself. ⁵Now if you obey me fully and keep my covenant, then out of all nations you will be my treasured possession. Although the whole earth is mine, ⁶you^a will be for me a kingdom of priests and a holy nation.' These are the words you are to speak to the Israelites."

⁷So Moses went back and summoned the elders of the people and set before them all the words the LORD had commanded him to speak. ⁸The people all responded together, "We will do everything the LORD has said." So Moses brought their answer back to the LORD.

⁹The LORD said to Moses, "I am going to come to you in a dense cloud, so that the people will hear me speaking with you and will always put their trust in you." Then Moses told the LORD what the people had said.

¹⁰And the LORD said to Moses, "Go to the people and consecrate them today and tomorrow. Have them wash their clothes ¹¹and be ready by the third day, because on that day the LORD will come down on Mount Sinai in the sight of all the people. ¹²Put limits for the people around the mountain and tell them, 'Be careful that you do not approach the mountain or touch the foot of it. Whoever touches the mountain is to be put to death. ¹³They are to be stoned or shot with arrows; not a hand is to be laid on them. No person or animal shall be permitted to live.' Only when the ram's horn sounds a long blast may they approach the mountain."

¹⁴After Moses had gone down the mountain to the people, he consecrated them, and they washed their clothes. ¹⁵Then he said to the people, "Prepare yourselves for the third day. Abstain from sexual relations."

¹⁶On the morning of the third day there was thunder and lightning, with a thick

> You will be my treasured possession.
> Exodus 19:5

---

^a 5,6 Or *possession, for the whole earth is mine.* ⁶*You*

cloud over the mountain, and a very loud trumpet blast. Everyone in the camp trembled. ¹⁷Then Moses led the people out of the camp to meet with God, and they stood at the foot of the mountain. ¹⁸Mount Sinai was covered with smoke, because the LORD descended on it in fire. The smoke billowed up from it like smoke from a furnace, and the whole mountain^a trembled violently. ¹⁹As the sound of the trumpet grew louder and louder, Moses spoke and the voice of God answered him.^b

²⁰The LORD descended to the top of Mount Sinai and called Moses to the top of the mountain. So Moses went up ²¹and the LORD said to him, "Go down and warn the people so they do not force their way through to see the LORD and many of them perish. ²²Even the priests, who approach the LORD, must consecrate themselves, or the LORD will break out against them."

²³Moses said to the LORD, "The people cannot come up Mount Sinai, because you yourself warned us, 'Put limits around the mountain and set it apart as holy.'"

²⁴The LORD replied, "Go down and bring Aaron up with you. But the priests and the people must not force their way through to come up to the LORD, or he will break out against them."

²⁵So Moses went down to the people and told them.

The Ten Commandments

20 And God spoke all these words:

²"I am the LORD your God, who brought you out of Egypt, out of the land of slavery.

³"You shall have no other gods before^c me.

⁴"You shall not make for yourself an image in the form of anything in heaven above or on the earth beneath or in the waters below. ⁵You shall not bow down to them or worship them; for I, the LORD your God, am a jealous

God, punishing the children for the sin of the parents to the third and fourth generation of those who hate me, ⁶but showing love to a thousand generations of those who love me and keep my commandments.

⁷"You shall not misuse the name of the LORD your God, for the LORD will not hold anyone guiltless who misuses his name.

⁸"Remember the Sabbath day by keeping it holy. ⁹Six days you shall labor and do all your work, ¹⁰but the seventh day is a sabbath to the LORD your God. On it you shall not do any work, neither you, nor your son or daughter, nor your male or female servant, nor your animals, nor any foreigner residing in your towns. ¹¹For in six days the LORD made the heavens and the earth, the sea, and all that is in them, but he rested on the seventh day. Therefore the LORD blessed the Sabbath day and made it holy.

¹²"Honor your father and your mother, so that you may live long in the land the LORD your God is giving you.

¹³"You shall not murder.

¹⁴"You shall not commit adultery.

¹⁵"You shall not steal.

¹⁶"You shall not give false testimony against your neighbor.

¹⁷"You shall not covet your neighbor's house. You shall not covet your neighbor's wife, or his male or female servant, his ox or donkey, or anything that belongs to your neighbor."

¹⁸When the people saw the thunder and lightning and heard the trumpet and saw the mountain in smoke, they trembled with fear. They stayed at a distance ¹⁹and said to Moses, "Speak to us yourself and we will listen. But do not have God speak to us or we will die."

²⁰Moses said to the people, "Do not

---

^a 18 Most Hebrew manuscripts; a few Hebrew manuscripts and Septuagint *and all the people*   ^b 19 Or *and God answered him with thunder*   ^c 3 Or *besides*

be afraid. God has come to test you, so that the fear of God will be with you to keep you from sinning."

²¹The people remained at a distance, while Moses approached the thick darkness where God was.

Idols and Altars

²²Then the LORD said to Moses, "Tell the Israelites this: 'You have seen for yourselves that I have spoken to you from heaven: ²³Do not make any gods to be alongside me; do not make for yourselves gods of silver or gods of gold.

²⁴" 'Make an altar of earth for me and sacrifice on it your burnt offerings and fellowship offerings, your sheep and goats and your cattle. Wherever I cause my name to be honored, I will come to you and bless you. ²⁵If you make an altar of stones for me, do not build it with dressed stones, for you will defile it if you use a tool on it. ²⁶And do not go up to my altar on steps, or your private parts may be exposed.'

21 "These are the laws you are to set before them:

Hebrew Servants

²"If you buy a Hebrew servant, he is to serve you for six years. But in the seventh year, he shall go free, without paying anything. ³If he comes alone, he is to go free alone; but if he has a wife when he comes, she is to go with him. ⁴If his master gives him a wife and she bears him sons or daughters, the woman and her children shall belong to her master, and only the man shall go free.

⁵"But if the servant declares, 'I love my master and my wife and children and do not want to go free,' ⁶then his master must take him before the judges.ᵃ He shall take him to the door or the doorpost and pierce his ear with an awl. Then he will be his servant for life.

⁷"If a man sells his daughter as a servant, she is not to go free as male servants do. ⁸If she does not please the master who has selected her for himself,ᵇ he must let her be redeemed. He has no right to sell her to foreigners, because he has broken faith with her. ⁹If he selects her for his son, he must grant her the rights of a daughter. ¹⁰If he marries another woman, he must not deprive the first one of her food, clothing and marital rights. ¹¹If he does not provide her with these three things, she is to go free, without any payment of money.

Personal Injuries

¹²"Anyone who strikes a person with a fatal blow is to be put to death. ¹³However, if it is not done intentionally, but God lets it happen, they are to flee to a place I will designate. ¹⁴But if anyone schemes and kills someone deliberately, that person is to be taken from my altar and put to death.

¹⁵"Anyone who attacksᶜ their father or mother is to be put to death.

¹⁶"Anyone who kidnaps someone is to be put to death, whether the victim has been sold or is still in the kidnapper's possession.

¹⁷"Anyone who curses their father or mother is to be put to death.

¹⁸"If people quarrel and one person hits another with a stone or with their fistᵈ and the victim does not die but is confined to bed, ¹⁹the one who struck the blow will not be held liable if the other can get up and walk around outside with a staff; however, the guilty party must pay the injured person for any loss of time and see that the victim is completely healed.

²⁰"Anyone who beats their male or female slave with a rod must be punished if the slave dies as a direct result, ²¹but they are not to be punished if the slave recovers after a day or two, since the slave is their property.

²²"If people are fighting and hit a pregnant woman and she gives birth prematurelyᵉ but there is no serious injury, the offender must be fined whatever the woman's husband demands and the court

---

ᵃ 6 Or before God   ᵇ 8 Or master so that he does not choose her   ᶜ 15 Or kills   ᵈ 18 Or with a tool   ᵉ 22 Or she has a miscarriage

allows. ²³But if there is serious injury, you are to take life for life, ²⁴eye for eye, tooth for tooth, hand for hand, foot for foot, ²⁵burn for burn, wound for wound, bruise for bruise.

²⁶"An owner who hits a male or female slave in the eye and destroys it must let the slave go free to compensate for the eye. ²⁷And an owner who knocks out the tooth of a male or female slave must let the slave go free to compensate for the tooth.

²⁸"If a bull gores a man or woman to death, the bull is to be stoned to death, and its meat must not be eaten. But the owner of the bull will not be held responsible. ²⁹If, however, the bull has had the habit of goring and the owner has been warned but has not kept it penned up and it kills a man or woman, the bull is to be stoned and its owner also is to be put to death. ³⁰However, if payment is demanded, the owner may redeem his life by the payment of whatever is demanded. ³¹This law also applies if the bull gores a son or daughter. ³²If the bull gores a male or female slave, the owner must pay thirty shekels^a of silver to the master of the slave, and the bull is to be stoned to death.

³³"If anyone uncovers a pit or digs one and fails to cover it and an ox or a donkey falls into it, ³⁴the one who opened the pit must pay the owner for the loss and take the dead animal in exchange.

³⁵"If anyone's bull injures someone else's bull and it dies, the two parties are to sell the live one and divide both the money and the dead animal equally. ³⁶However, if it was known that the bull had the habit of goring, yet the owner did not keep it penned up, the owner must pay, animal for animal, and take the dead animal in exchange.

Protection of Property

22^b "Whoever steals an ox or a sheep and slaughters it or sells it must pay back five head of cattle for the ox and four sheep for the sheep.

²"If a thief is caught breaking in at night and is struck a fatal blow, the defender is not guilty of bloodshed; ³but if it happens after sunrise, the defender is guilty of bloodshed.

"Anyone who steals must certainly make restitution, but if they have nothing, they must be sold to pay for their theft. ⁴If the stolen animal is found alive in their possession—whether ox or donkey or sheep—they must pay back double.

⁵"If anyone grazes their livestock in a field or vineyard and lets them stray and they graze in someone else's field, the offender must make restitution from the best of their own field or vineyard.

⁶"If a fire breaks out and spreads into thornbushes so that it burns shocks of grain or standing grain or the whole field, the one who started the fire must make restitution.

⁷"If anyone gives a neighbor silver or goods for safekeeping and they are stolen from the neighbor's house, the thief, if caught, must pay back double. ⁸But if the thief is not found, the owner of the house must appear before the judges, and they must^c determine whether the owner of the house has laid hands on the other person's property. ⁹In all cases of illegal possession of an ox, a donkey, a sheep, a garment, or any other lost property about which somebody says, 'This is mine,' both parties are to bring their cases before the judges.^{d} The one whom the judges declare^e guilty must pay back double to the other.

¹⁰"If anyone gives a donkey, an ox, a sheep or any other animal to their neighbor for safekeeping and it dies or is injured or is taken away while no one is looking, ¹¹the issue between them will be settled by the taking of an oath before the Lord that the neighbor did not lay hands on the other person's property. The owner is to accept this, and no restitution is required. ¹²But if the animal was stolen from the neighbor, restitution must be made to the owner. ¹³If it was torn to pieces by a wild animal, the neighbor shall bring in the remains as evidence

---

^{a} 32 That is, about 12 ounces or about 345 grams numbered 22:1-30. ^{c} 8 Or before God, and he will ^{b} In Hebrew texts 22:1 is numbered 21:37, and 22:2-31 is ^{d} 9 Or before God ^{e} 9 Or whom God declares

and shall not be required to pay for the torn animal.

14 "If anyone borrows an animal from their neighbor and it is injured or dies while the owner is not present, they must make restitution. 15 But if the owner is with the animal, the borrower will not have to pay. If the animal was hired, the money paid for the hire covers the loss.

Social Responsibility

16 "If a man seduces a virgin who is not pledged to be married and sleeps with her, he must pay the bride-price, and she shall be his wife. 17 If her father absolutely refuses to give her to him, he must still pay the bride-price for virgins.

18 "Do not allow a sorceress to live.

19 "Anyone who has sexual relations with an animal is to be put to death.

20 "Whoever sacrifices to any god other than the LORD must be destroyed.[a]

21 "Do not mistreat or oppress a foreigner, for you were foreigners in Egypt.

22 "Do not take advantage of the widow or the fatherless. 23 If you do and they cry out to me, I will certainly hear their cry. 24 My anger will be aroused, and I will kill you with the sword; your wives will become widows and your children fatherless.

25 "If you lend money to one of my people among you who is needy, do not treat it like a business deal; charge no interest. 26 If you take your neighbor's cloak as a pledge, return it by sunset, 27 because that cloak is the only covering your neighbor has. What else can they sleep in? When they cry out to me, I will hear, for I am compassionate.

28 "Do not blaspheme God[b] or curse the ruler of your people.

29 "Do not hold back offerings from your granaries or your vats.[c]

"You must give me the firstborn of your sons. 30 Do the same with your cattle and your sheep. Let them stay with their mothers for seven days, but give them to me on the eighth day.

31 "You are to be my holy people. So do not eat the meat of an animal torn by wild beasts; throw it to the dogs.

Laws of Justice and Mercy

23 "Do not spread false reports. Do not help a guilty person by being a malicious witness.

2 "Do not follow the crowd in doing wrong. When you give testimony in a lawsuit, do not pervert justice by siding with the crowd, 3 and do not show favoritism to a poor person in a lawsuit.

4 "If you come across your enemy's ox or donkey wandering off, be sure to return it. 5 If you see the donkey of someone who hates you fallen down under its load, do not leave it there; be sure you help them with it.

6 "Do not deny justice to your poor people in their lawsuits. 7 Have nothing to do with a false charge and do not put an innocent or honest person to death, for I will not acquit the guilty.

8 "Do not accept a bribe, for a bribe blinds those who see and twists the words of the innocent.

9 "Do not oppress a foreigner; you yourselves know how it feels to be foreigners, because you were foreigners in Egypt.

Sabbath Laws

10 "For six years you are to sow your fields and harvest the crops, 11 but during the seventh year let the land lie unplowed and unused. Then the poor among your people may get food from it, and the wild animals may eat what is left. Do the same with your vineyard and your olive grove.

12 "Six days do your work, but on the seventh day do not work, so that your ox and your donkey may rest, and so that the slave born in your household and the foreigner living among you may be refreshed.

13 "Be careful to do everything I have said to you. Do not invoke the names of other gods; do not let them be heard on your lips.

The Three Annual Festivals

14 "Three times a year you are to celebrate a festival to me.

15 "Celebrate the Festival of Unleavened Bread; for seven days eat bread

---

[a] 20 The Hebrew term refers to the irrevocable giving over of things or persons to the LORD, often by totally destroying them.   [b] 28 Or *Do not revile the judges*   [c] 29 The meaning of the Hebrew for this phrase is uncertain.

made without yeast, as I commanded you. Do this at the appointed time in the month of Aviv, for in that month you came out of Egypt.

"No one is to appear before me empty-handed.

16 "Celebrate the Festival of Harvest with the firstfruits of the crops you sow in your field.

"Celebrate the Festival of Ingathering at the end of the year, when you gather in your crops from the field.

17 "Three times a year all the men are to appear before the Sovereign LORD.

18 "Do not offer the blood of a sacrifice to me along with anything containing yeast.

"The fat of my festival offerings must not be kept until morning.

19 "Bring the best of the firstfruits of your soil to the house of the LORD your God.

"Do not cook a young goat in its mother's milk.

God's Angel to Prepare the Way

20 "See, I am sending an angel ahead of you to guard you along the way and to bring you to the place I have prepared. 21 Pay attention to him and listen to what he says. Do not rebel against him; he will not forgive your rebellion, since my Name is in him. 22 If you listen carefully to what he says and do all that I say, I will be an enemy to your enemies and will oppose those who oppose you. 23 My angel will go ahead of you and bring you into the land of the Amorites, Hittites, Perizzites, Canaanites, Hivites and Jebusites, and I will wipe them out. 24 Do not bow down before their gods or worship them or follow their practices. You must demolish them and break their sacred stones to pieces. 25 Worship the LORD your God, and his blessing will be on your food and water. I will take away sickness from among you, 26 and none will miscarry or be barren in your land. I will give you a full life span.

27 "I will send my terror ahead of you and throw into confusion every nation you encounter. I will make all your enemies

You find the lost term paper of a classmate who hates you — and give it back to him. You say nice things about the girl who's spreading terrible rumors about you. To most people that's crazy. They say you ought to tear up the term paper and get even with that nasty girl. But you don't, because you're following a pattern established in Exodus 23:4–5. Why does God tell you to do good to people who don't like you? Maybe because God wants you to be like *him*, not like those around you who like to hurt you. And maybe because the best way to get rid of an enemy is to make him or her a friend.

{Exodus 23:4–5}

INSTANT ACCESS

turn their backs and run. 28 I will send the hornet ahead of you to drive the Hivites, Canaanites and Hittites out of your way. 29 But I will not drive them out in a single year, because the land would become desolate and the wild animals too numerous for you. 30 Little by little I will drive them out before you, until you have increased enough to take possession of the land.

31 "I will establish your borders from the Red Sea[a] to the Mediterranean Sea,[b] and

---

[a] 31 Or the Sea of Reeds   [b] 31 Hebrew to the Sea of the Philistines

from the desert to the Euphrates River. I will give into your hands the people who live in the land, and you will drive them out before you. ³²Do not make a covenant with them or with their gods. ³³Do not let them live in your land or they will cause you to sin against me, because the worship of their gods will certainly be a snare to you."

The Covenant Confirmed

24 Then the LORD said to Moses, "Come up to the LORD, you and Aaron, Nadab and Abihu, and seventy of the elders of Israel. You are to worship at a distance, ²but Moses alone is to approach the LORD; the others must not come near. And the people may not come up with him."

³When Moses went and told the people all the LORD's words and laws, they responded with one voice, "Everything the LORD has said we will do." ⁴Moses then wrote down everything the LORD had said.

He got up early the next morning and built an altar at the foot of the mountain and set up twelve stone pillars representing the twelve tribes of Israel. ⁵Then he sent young Israelite men, and they offered burnt offerings and sacrificed young bulls as fellowship offerings to the LORD. ⁶Moses took half of the blood and put it in bowls, and the other half he splashed against the altar. ⁷Then he took the Book of the Covenant and read it to the people. They responded, "We will do everything the LORD has said; we will obey."

⁸Moses then took the blood, sprinkled it on the people and said, "This is the blood of the covenant that the LORD has made with you in accordance with all these words."

⁹Moses and Aaron, Nadab and Abihu, and the seventy elders of Israel went up ¹⁰and saw the God of Israel. Under his feet was something like a pavement made of lapis lazuli, as bright blue as the sky. ¹¹But God did not raise his hand against these leaders of the Israelites; they saw God, and they ate and drank.

¹²The LORD said to Moses, "Come up to me on the mountain and stay here, and I will give you the tablets of stone with the law and commandments I have written for their instruction."

¹³Then Moses set out with Joshua his aide, and Moses went up on the mountain of God. ¹⁴He said to the elders, "Wait here for us until we come back to you. Aaron and Hur are with you, and anyone involved in a dispute can go to them."

¹⁵When Moses went up on the mountain, the cloud covered it, ¹⁶and the glory of the LORD settled on Mount Sinai. For six days the cloud covered the mountain, and on the seventh day the LORD called to Moses from within the cloud. ¹⁷To the Israelites the glory of the LORD looked like a consuming fire on top of the mountain. ¹⁸Then Moses entered the cloud as he went on up the mountain. And he stayed on the mountain forty days and forty nights.

Offerings for the Tabernacle

25 The LORD said to Moses, ²"Tell the Israelites to bring me an offering. You are to receive the offering for me from everyone whose heart prompts them to give. ³These are the offerings you are to receive from them: gold, silver and bronze; ⁴blue, purple and scarlet yarn and fine linen; goat hair; ⁵ram skins dyed red and another type of durable leatherᵃ; acacia wood; ⁶olive oil for the light; spices for the anointing oil and for the fragrant incense; ⁷and onyx stones and other gems to be mounted on the ephod and breastpiece.

⁸"Then have them make a sanctuary for me, and I will dwell among them. ⁹Make this tabernacle and all its furnishings exactly like the pattern I will show you.

The Ark

¹⁰"Have them make an arkᵇ of acacia wood—two and a half cubits long, a cubit and a half wide, and a cubit and a half high.ᶜ ¹¹Overlay it with pure gold, both inside and out, and make a gold molding

---

ᵃ 5 Possibly the hides of large aquatic mammals   ᵇ 10 That is, a chest   ᶜ 10 That is, about 3 3/4 feet long and 2 1/4 feet wide and high or about 1.1 meters long and 68 centimeters wide and high; similarly in verse 17

around it. ¹²Cast four gold rings for it and fasten them to its four feet, with two rings on one side and two rings on the other. ¹³Then make poles of acacia wood and overlay them with gold. ¹⁴Insert the poles into the rings on the sides of the ark to carry it. ¹⁵The poles are to remain in the rings of this ark; they are not to be removed. ¹⁶Then put in the ark the tablets of the covenant law, which I will give you.

¹⁷"Make an atonement cover of pure gold—two and a half cubits long and a cubit and a half wide. ¹⁸And make two cherubim out of hammered gold at the ends of the cover. ¹⁹Make one cherub on one end and the second cherub on the other; make the cherubim of one piece with the cover, at the two ends. ²⁰The cherubim are to have their wings spread upward, overshadowing the cover with them. The cherubim are to face each other, looking toward the cover. ²¹Place the cover on top of the ark and put in the ark the tablets of the covenant law that I will give you. ²²There, above the cover between the two cherubim that are over the ark of the covenant law, I will meet with you and give you all my commands for the Israelites.

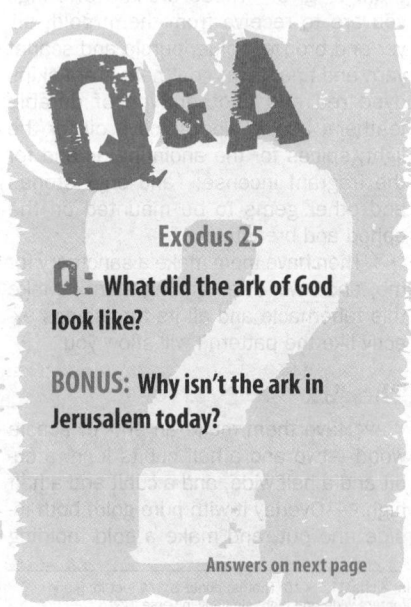

Exodus 25

Q: What did the ark of God look like?

BONUS: Why isn't the ark in Jerusalem today?

Answers on next page

The Table

²³"Make a table of acacia wood—two cubits long, a cubit wide and a cubit and a half high.ᵃ ²⁴Overlay it with pure gold and make a gold molding around it. ²⁵Also make around it a rim a handbreadthᵇ wide and put a gold molding on the rim. ²⁶Make four gold rings for the table and fasten them to the four corners, where the four legs are. ²⁷The rings are to be close to the rim to hold the poles used in carrying the table. ²⁸Make the poles of acacia wood, overlay them with gold and carry the table with them. ²⁹And make its plates and dishes of pure gold, as well as its pitchers and bowls for the pouring out of offerings. ³⁰Put the bread of the Presence on this table to be before me at all times.

The Lampstand

³¹"Make a lampstand of pure gold. Hammer out its base and shaft, and make its flowerlike cups, buds and blossoms of one piece with them. ³²Six branches are to extend from the sides of the lampstand—three on one side and three on the other. ³³Three cups shaped like almond flowers with buds and blossoms are to be on one branch, three on the next branch, and the same for all six branches extending from the lampstand. ³⁴And on the lampstand there are to be four cups shaped like almond flowers with buds and blossoms. ³⁵One bud shall be under the first pair of branches extending from the lampstand, a second bud under the second pair, and a third bud under the third pair—six branches in all. ³⁶The buds and branches shall all be of one piece with the lampstand, hammered out of pure gold.

³⁷"Then make its seven lamps and set them up on it so that they light the space in front of it. ³⁸Its wick trimmers and trays are to be of pure gold. ³⁹A talentᶜ of pure gold is to be used for the lampstand and all these accessories. ⁴⁰See that

---

ᵃ 23 That is, about 3 feet long, 1 1/2 feet wide and 2 1/4 feet high or about 90 centimeters long, 45 centimeters wide and 68 centimeters high   ᵇ 25 That is, about 3 inches or about 7.5 centimeters   ᶜ 39 That is, about 75 pounds or about 34 kilograms

you make them according to the pattern shown you on the mountain.

The Tabernacle

26 "Make the tabernacle with ten curtains of finely twisted linen and blue, purple and scarlet yarn, with cherubim woven into them by a skilled worker. ²All the curtains are to be the same size—twenty-eight cubits long and four cubits wide.ᵃ ³Join five of the curtains together, and do the same with the other five. ⁴Make loops of blue material along the edge of the end curtain in one set, and do the same with the end curtain in the other set. ⁵Make fifty loops on one curtain and fifty loops on the end curtain of the other set, with the loops opposite each other. ⁶Then make fifty gold clasps and use them to fasten the curtains together so that the tabernacle is a unit.

⁷"Make curtains of goat hair for the tent over the tabernacle—eleven altogether. ⁸All eleven curtains are to be the same size—thirty cubits long and four cubits wide.ᵇ ⁹Join five of the curtains together into one set and the other six into another set. Fold the sixth curtain double at the front of the tent. ¹⁰Make fifty loops along the edge of the end curtain in one set and also along the edge of the end curtain in the other set. ¹¹Then make fifty bronze clasps and put them in the loops to fasten the tent together as a unit. ¹²As for the additional length of the tent curtains, the half curtain that is left over is to hang down at the rear of the tabernacle. ¹³The tent curtains will be a cubitᶜ longer on both sides; what is left will hang over the sides of the tabernacle so as to cover it. ¹⁴Make for the tent a covering of ram skins dyed red, and over that a covering of the other durable leather.ᵈ

¹⁵"Make upright frames of acacia wood for the tabernacle. ¹⁶Each frame is to be ten cubits long and a cubit and a half wide,ᵉ ¹⁷with two projections set parallel to each other. Make all the frames of the tabernacle in this way. ¹⁸Make twenty frames for the south side of the tabernacle

A: **It was a small, gold-covered box topped with two gold angels (Exodus 25:10–22).**

BONUS: **It was taken to Babylon when the two tribes of Judah went into captivity (2 Chronicles 36:18) and has never been found since.**

¹⁹and make forty silver bases to go under them—two bases for each frame, one under each projection. ²⁰For the other side, the north side of the tabernacle, make twenty frames ²¹and forty silver bases—two under each frame. ²²Make six frames for the far end, that is, the west end of the tabernacle, ²³and make two frames for the corners at the far end. ²⁴At these two corners they must be double from the bottom all the way to the top and fitted into a single ring; both shall be like that. ²⁵So there will be eight frames and sixteen silver bases—two under each frame.

²⁶"Also make crossbars of acacia wood: five for the frames on one side of the tabernacle, ²⁷five for those on the other side, and five for the frames on the west, at the far end of the tabernacle. ²⁸The center crossbar is to extend from end to end at the middle of the frames. ²⁹Overlay the frames with gold and make gold rings to hold the crossbars. Also overlay the crossbars with gold.

³⁰"Set up the tabernacle according to the plan shown you on the mountain.

ᵃ 2 That is, about 42 feet long and 6 feet wide or about 13 meters long and 1.8 meters wide   ᵇ 8 That is, about 45 feet long and 6 feet wide or about 13.5 meters long and 1.8 meters wide   ᶜ 13 That is, about 18 inches or about 45 centimeters   ᵈ 14 Possibly the hides of large aquatic mammals (see 25:5)   ᵉ 16 That is, about 15 feet long and 2 1/4 feet wide or about 4.5 meters long and 68 centimeters wide

31 "Make a curtain of blue, purple and scarlet yarn and finely twisted linen, with cherubim woven into it by a skilled worker. 32 Hang it with gold hooks on four posts of acacia wood overlaid with gold and standing on four silver bases. 33 Hang the curtain from the clasps and place the ark of the covenant law behind the curtain. The curtain will separate the Holy Place from the Most Holy Place. 34 Put the atonement cover on the ark of the covenant law in the Most Holy Place. 35 Place the table outside the curtain on the north side of the tabernacle and put the lampstand opposite it on the south side.

36 "For the entrance to the tent make a curtain of blue, purple and scarlet yarn and finely twisted linen—the work of an embroiderer. 37 Make gold hooks for this curtain and five posts of acacia wood overlaid with gold. And cast five bronze bases for them.

The Altar of Burnt Offering

27 "Build an altar of acacia wood, three cubits*a* high; it is to be square, five cubits long and five cubits wide.*b* 2 Make a horn at each of the four corners, so that the horns and the altar are of one piece, and overlay the altar with bronze. 3 Make all its utensils of bronze— its pots to remove the ashes, and its shovels, sprinkling bowls, meat forks and firepans. 4 Make a grating for it, a bronze network, and make a bronze ring at each of the four corners of the network. 5 Put it under the ledge of the altar so that it is halfway up the altar. 6 Make poles of acacia wood for the altar and overlay them with bronze. 7 The poles are to be inserted into the rings so they will be on two sides of the altar when it is carried. 8 Make the altar hollow, out of boards. It is to be made just as you were shown on the mountain.

The Courtyard

9 "Make a courtyard for the tabernacle. The south side shall be a hundred cubits*c* long and is to have curtains of finely twist-ed linen, 10 with twenty posts and twenty bronze bases and with silver hooks and bands on the posts. 11 The north side shall also be a hundred cubits long and is to have curtains, with twenty posts and twenty bronze bases and with silver hooks and bands on the posts.

12 "The west end of the courtyard shall be fifty cubits*d* wide and have curtains, with ten posts and ten bases. 13 On the east end, toward the sunrise, the courtyard shall also be fifty cubits wide. 14 Curtains fifteen cubits*e* long are to be on one side of the entrance, with three posts and three bases, 15 and curtains fifteen cubits long are to be on the other side, with three posts and three bases.

16 "For the entrance to the courtyard, provide a curtain twenty cubits*f* long, of blue, purple and scarlet yarn and finely twisted linen—the work of an embroider-er—with four posts and four bases. 17 All the posts around the courtyard are to have silver bands and hooks, and bronze bases. 18 The courtyard shall be a hundred cubits long and fifty cubits wide,*g* with curtains of finely twisted linen five cubits*h* high, and with bronze bases. 19 All the other articles used in the service of the tabernacle, whatever their function, including all the tent pegs for it and those for the courtyard, are to be of bronze.

Oil for the Lampstand

20 "Command the Israelites to bring you clear oil of pressed olives for the light so that the lamps may be kept burning. 21 In the tent of meeting, outside the curtain that shields the ark of the covenant law, Aaron and his sons are to keep the lamps burning before the Lord from evening till morning. This is to be a lasting ordinance among the Israelites for the generations to come.

The Priestly Garments

28 "Have Aaron your brother brought to you from among the Israelites, along with his sons Nadab and Abihu,

---

a 1 That is, about 4 1/2 feet or about 1.4 meters   *b* 1 That is, about 7 1/2 feet or about 2.3 meters long and wide
c 9 That is, about 150 feet or about 45 meters; also in verse 11   *d* 12 That is, about 75 feet or about 23 meters;
also in verse 13   *e* 14 That is, about 23 feet or about 6.8 meters; also in verse 15   *f* 16 That is, about 30 feet
or about 9 meters   *g* 18 That is, about 150 feet long and 75 feet wide or about 45 meters long and 23 meters wide
h 18 That is, about 7 1/2 feet or about 2.3 meters

Eleazar and Ithamar, so they may serve me as priests. ²Make sacred garments for your brother Aaron to give him dignity and honor. ³Tell all the skilled workers to whom I have given wisdom in such matters that they are to make garments for Aaron, for his consecration, so he may serve me as priest. ⁴These are the garments they are to make: a breastpiece, an ephod, a robe, a woven tunic, a turban and a sash. They are to make these sacred garments for your brother Aaron and his sons, so they may serve me as priests. ⁵Have them use gold, and blue, purple and scarlet yarn, and fine linen.

The Ephod

⁶"Make the ephod of gold, and of blue, purple and scarlet yarn, and of finely twisted linen—the work of skilled hands. ⁷It is to have two shoulder pieces attached to two of its corners, so it can be fastened. ⁸Its skillfully woven waistband is to be like it—of one piece with the ephod and made with gold, and with blue, purple and scarlet yarn, and with finely twisted linen.

⁹"Take two onyx stones and engrave on them the names of the sons of Israel ¹⁰in the order of their birth—six names on one stone and the remaining six on the other. ¹¹Engrave the names of the sons of Israel on the two stones the way a gem cutter engraves a seal. Then mount the stones in gold filigree settings ¹²and fasten them on the shoulder pieces of the ephod as memorial stones for the sons of Israel. Aaron is to bear the names on his shoulders as a memorial before the LORD. ¹³Make gold filigree settings ¹⁴and two braided chains of pure gold, like a rope, and attach the chains to the settings.

The Breastpiece

¹⁵"Fashion a breastpiece for making decisions—the work of skilled hands. Make it like the ephod: of gold, and of blue, purple and scarlet yarn, and of finely twisted linen. ¹⁶It is to be square—a span*ᵃ* long and a span wide—and folded double. ¹⁷Then mount four rows of precious stones on it. The first row shall be carnelian, chrysolite and beryl; ¹⁸the second row shall be turquoise, lapis lazuli and emerald; ¹⁹the third row shall be jacinth, agate and amethyst; ²⁰the fourth row shall be topaz, onyx and jasper.*ᵇ* Mount them in gold filigree settings. ²¹There are to be twelve stones, one for each of the names of the sons of Israel, each engraved like a seal with the name of one of the twelve tribes.

²²"For the breastpiece make braided chains of pure gold, like a rope. ²³Make two gold rings for it and fasten them to two corners of the breastpiece. ²⁴Fasten the two gold chains to the rings at the corners of the breastpiece, ²⁵and the other ends of the chains to the two settings, attaching them to the shoulder pieces of the ephod at the front. ²⁶Make two gold rings and attach them to the other two corners of the breastpiece on the inside edge next to the ephod. ²⁷Make two more gold rings and attach them to the bottom of the shoulder pieces on the front of the ephod, close to the seam just above the waistband of the ephod. ²⁸The rings of the breastpiece are to be tied to the rings of the ephod with blue cord, connecting it to the waistband, so that the breastpiece will not swing out from the ephod.

²⁹"Whenever Aaron enters the Holy Place, he will bear the names of the sons of Israel over his heart on the breastpiece of decision as a continuing memorial before the LORD. ³⁰Also put the Urim and the Thummim in the breastpiece, so they may be over Aaron's heart whenever he enters the presence of the LORD. Thus Aaron will always bear the means of making decisions for the Israelites over his heart before the LORD.

Other Priestly Garments

³¹"Make the robe of the ephod entirely of blue cloth, ³²with an opening for the head in its center. There shall be a woven edge like a collar*ᶜ* around this opening, so that it will not tear. ³³Make pomegranates of blue, purple and scarlet yarn around

---

ᵃ 16 That is, about 9 inches or about 23 centimeters   *ᵇ 20* The precise identification of some of these precious stones is uncertain.   *ᶜ 32* The meaning of the Hebrew for this word is uncertain.

the hem of the robe, with gold bells between them. 34 The gold bells and the pomegranates are to alternate around the hem of the robe. 35 Aaron must wear it when he ministers. The sound of the bells will be heard when he enters the Holy Place before the LORD and when he comes out, so that he will not die.

36 "Make a plate of pure gold and engrave on it as on a seal: HOLY TO THE LORD. 37 Fasten a blue cord to it to attach it to the turban; it is to be on the front of the turban. 38 It will be on Aaron's forehead, and he will bear the guilt involved in the sacred gifts the Israelites consecrate, whatever their gifts may be. It will be on Aaron's forehead continually so that they will be acceptable to the LORD.

39 "Weave the tunic of fine linen and make the turban of fine linen. The sash is to be the work of an embroiderer. 40 Make tunics, sashes and caps for Aaron's sons to give them dignity and honor. 41 After you put these clothes on your brother Aaron and his sons, anoint and ordain them. Consecrate them so they may serve me as priests.

42 "Make linen undergarments as a covering for the body, reaching from the waist to the thigh. 43 Aaron and his sons must wear them whenever they enter the tent of meeting or approach the altar to minister in the Holy Place, so that they will not incur guilt and die.

"This is to be a lasting ordinance for Aaron and his descendants.

Consecration of the Priests

29 "This is what you are to do to consecrate them, so they may serve me as priests: Take a young bull and two rams without defect. 2 And from the finest wheat flour make round loaves without yeast, thick loaves without yeast and with olive oil mixed in, and thin loaves without yeast and brushed with olive oil. 3 Put them in a basket and present them along with the bull and the two rams. 4 Then bring Aaron and his sons to the entrance to the tent of meeting and wash them with water. 5 Take the garments and dress Aaron with the tunic, the robe of the ephod, the ephod itself and the breastpiece. Fasten the ephod on him by its skillfully woven waistband. 6 Put the turban on his head and attach the sacred emblem to the turban. 7 Take the anointing oil and anoint him by pouring it on his head. 8 Bring his sons and dress them in tunics 9 and fasten caps on them. Then tie sashes on Aaron and his sons.[a] The priesthood is theirs by a lasting ordinance.

"Then you shall ordain Aaron and his sons.

10 "Bring the bull to the front of the tent of meeting, and Aaron and his sons shall lay their hands on its head. 11 Slaughter it

---

a 9 Hebrew; Septuagint *on them*

in the Lord's presence at the entrance to the tent of meeting. ¹²Take some of the bull's blood and put it on the horns of the altar with your finger, and pour out the rest of it at the base of the altar. ¹³Then take all the fat on the internal organs, the long lobe of the liver, and both kidneys with the fat on them, and burn them on the altar. ¹⁴But burn the bull's flesh and its hide and its intestines outside the camp. It is a sin offering.ᵃ

¹⁵"Take one of the rams, and Aaron and his sons shall lay their hands on its head. ¹⁶Slaughter it and take the blood and splash it against the sides of the altar. ¹⁷Cut the ram into pieces and wash the internal organs and the legs, putting them with the head and the other pieces. ¹⁸Then burn the entire ram on the altar. It is a burnt offering to the Lord, a pleasing aroma, a food offering presented to the Lord.

¹⁹"Take the other ram, and Aaron and his sons shall lay their hands on its head. ²⁰Slaughter it, take some of its blood and put it on the lobes of the right ears of Aaron and his sons, on the thumbs of their right hands, and on the big toes of their right feet. Then splash blood against the sides of the altar. ²¹And take some blood from the altar and some of the anointing oil and sprinkle it on Aaron and his garments and on his sons and their garments. Then he and his sons and their garments will be consecrated.

²²"Take from this ram the fat, the fat tail, the fat on the internal organs, the long lobe of the liver, both kidneys with the fat on them, and the right thigh. (This is the ram for the ordination.) ²³From the basket of bread made without yeast, which is before the Lord, take one round loaf, one thick loaf with olive oil mixed in, and one thin loaf. ²⁴Put all these in the hands of Aaron and his sons and have them wave them before the Lord as a wave offering. ²⁵Then take them from their hands and burn them on the altar along with the burnt offering for a pleasing aroma to the Lord, a food offering pre-

sented to the Lord. ²⁶After you take the breast of the ram for Aaron's ordination, wave it before the Lord as a wave offering, and it will be your share.

²⁷"Consecrate those parts of the ordination ram that belong to Aaron and his sons: the breast that was waved and the thigh that was presented. ²⁸This is always to be the perpetual share from the Israelites for Aaron and his sons. It is the contribution the Israelites are to make to the Lord from their fellowship offerings.

²⁹"Aaron's sacred garments will belong to his descendants so that they can be anointed and ordained in them. ³⁰The son who succeeds him as priest and comes to the tent of meeting to minister in the Holy Place is to wear them seven days.

³¹"Take the ram for the ordination and cook the meat in a sacred place. ³²At the entrance to the tent of meeting, Aaron and his sons are to eat the meat of the ram and the bread that is in the basket. ³³They are to eat these offerings by which atonement was made for their ordination and consecration. But no one else may eat them, because they are sacred. ³⁴And if any of the meat of the ordination ram or any bread is left over till morning, burn it up. It must not be eaten, because it is sacred.

³⁵"Do for Aaron and his sons everything I have commanded you, taking seven days to ordain them. ³⁶Sacrifice a bull each day as a sin offering to make atonement. Purify the altar by making atonement for it, and anoint it to consecrate it. ³⁷For seven days make atonement for the altar and consecrate it. Then the altar will be most holy, and whatever touches it will be holy.

³⁸"This is what you are to offer on the altar regularly each day: two lambs a year old. ³⁹Offer one in the morning and the other at twilight. ⁴⁰With the first lamb offer a tenth of an ephahᵇ of the finest flour mixed with a quarter of a hinᶜ of oil from pressed olives, and a quarter of a hin of wine as a drink offering. ⁴¹Sacrifice the other lamb at twilight with the same grain

---

ᵃ 14 Or *purification offering*; also in verse 36   ᵇ 40 That is, probably about 3 1/2 pounds or about 1.6 kilograms
ᶜ 40 That is, probably about 1 quart or about 1 liter

offering and its drink offering as in the morning—a pleasing aroma, a food offering presented to the LORD.

⁴²"For the generations to come this burnt offering is to be made regularly at the entrance to the tent of meeting, before the LORD. There I will meet you and speak to you; ⁴³there also I will meet with the Israelites, and the place will be consecrated by my glory.

⁴⁴"So I will consecrate the tent of meeting and the altar and will consecrate Aaron and his sons to serve me as priests. ⁴⁵Then I will dwell among the Israelites and be their God. ⁴⁶They will know that I am the LORD their God, who brought them out of Egypt so that I might dwell among them. I am the LORD their God.

The Altar of Incense

30 "Make an altar of acacia wood for burning incense. ²It is to be square, a cubit long and a cubit wide, and two cubits high*ᵃ*—its horns of one piece with it. ³Overlay the top and all the sides and the horns with pure gold, and make a gold molding around it. ⁴Make two gold rings for the altar below the molding—two on each of the opposite sides—to hold the poles used to carry it. ⁵Make the poles of acacia wood and overlay them with gold. ⁶Put the altar in front of the curtain that shields the ark of the covenant law—before the atonement cover that is over the tablets of the covenant law—where I will meet with you.

⁷"Aaron must burn fragrant incense on the altar every morning when he tends the lamps. ⁸He must burn incense again when he lights the lamps at twilight so incense will burn regularly before the LORD for the generations to come. ⁹Do not offer on this altar any other incense or any burnt offering or grain offering, and do not pour a drink offering on it. ¹⁰Once a year Aaron shall make atonement on its horns. This annual atonement must be made with the blood of the atoning sin offering*ᵇ* for the generations to come. It is most holy to the LORD."

Atonement Money

¹¹Then the LORD said to Moses, ¹²"When you take a census of the Israelites to count them, each one must pay the LORD a ransom for his life at the time he is counted. Then no plague will come on them when you number them. ¹³Each one who crosses over to those already counted is to give a half shekel,*ᶜ* according to the sanctuary shekel, which weighs twenty gerahs. This half shekel is an offering to the LORD. ¹⁴All who cross over, those twenty years old or more, are to give an offering to the LORD. ¹⁵The rich are not to give more than a half shekel and the poor are not to give less when you make the offering to the LORD to atone for your lives. ¹⁶Receive the atonement money from the Israelites and use it for the service of the tent of meeting. It will be a memorial for the Israelites before the LORD, making atonement for your lives."

Basin for Washing

¹⁷Then the LORD said to Moses, ¹⁸"Make a bronze basin, with its bronze stand, for washing. Place it between the tent of meeting and the altar, and put water in it. ¹⁹Aaron and his sons are to wash their hands and feet with water from it. ²⁰Whenever they enter the tent of meeting, they shall wash with water so that they will not die. Also, when they approach the altar to minister by presenting a food offering to the LORD, ²¹they shall wash their hands and feet so that they will not die. This is to be a lasting ordinance for Aaron and his descendants for the generations to come."

Anointing Oil

²²Then the LORD said to Moses, ²³"Take the following fine spices: 500 shekels*ᵈ* of liquid myrrh, half as much (that is, 250 shekels) of fragrant cinnamon, 250 shekels*ᵉ* of fragrant calamus, ²⁴500 shekels of cassia—all according to the sanctuary shekel—and a hin*ᶠ* of olive oil. ²⁵Make these into a sacred anointing oil, a fra-

INSTANT ACCESS

Drew gets all A's. You don't. Courtney is a good speaker. You're not. Amber has a good voice. You can't sing a note. Kind of makes you think you'll never amount to much, doesn't it? Of course, you work harder at school than Drew. You may not be a good speaker, but you can fix just about anything on a car. This passage speaks about Bezalel. God gave him talent in all kinds of crafts—from metal work to jewelry design. Bezalel used his talent for God. Any talent you have is a gift from God. He can use your talent for his glory.

{Exodus 31:1–11}

grant blend, the work of a perfumer. It will be the sacred anointing oil. 26 Then use it to anoint the tent of meeting, the ark of the covenant law, 27 the table and all its articles, the lampstand and its accessories, the altar of incense, 28 the altar of burnt offering and all its utensils, and the basin with its stand. 29 You shall consecrate them so they will be most holy, and whatever touches them will be holy.

30 "Anoint Aaron and his sons and consecrate them so they may serve me as priests. 31 Say to the Israelites, 'This is to be my sacred anointing oil for the generations to come. 32 Do not pour it on anyone else's body and do not make any other oil using the same formula. It is sacred, and you are to consider it sacred. 33 Whoever makes perfume like it and puts it on anyone other than a priest must be cut off from their people.' "

Incense

34 Then the LORD said to Moses, "Take fragrant spices—gum resin, onycha and galbanum—and pure frankincense, all in equal amounts, 35 and make a fragrant blend of incense, the work of a perfumer. It is to be salted and pure and sacred. 36 Grind some of it to powder and place it in front of the ark of the covenant law in the tent of meeting, where I will meet with you. It shall be most holy to you. 37 Do not make any incense with this formula for yourselves; consider it holy to the LORD. 38 Whoever makes incense like it to enjoy its fragrance must be cut off from their people."

Bezalel and Oholiab

31 Then the LORD said to Moses, 2 "See, I have chosen Bezalel son of Uri, the son of Hur, of the tribe of Judah, 3 and I have filled him with the Spirit of God, with wisdom, with understanding, with knowledge and with all kinds of skills— 4 to make artistic designs for work in gold, silver and bronze, 5 to cut and set stones, to work in wood, and to engage in all kinds of crafts. 6 Moreover, I have appointed Oholiab son of Ahisamak, of the tribe of Dan, to help him. Also I have given ability to all the skilled workers to make everything I have commanded you: 7 the tent of meeting, the ark of the covenant law with the atonement cover on it, and all the other furnishings of the tent— 8 the table and its articles, the pure gold lampstand and all its accessories, the altar of incense, 9 the altar of burnt offering and all its utensils, the basin with its stand— 10 and also the woven garments, both the sacred garments for Aaron the priest and the garments for his sons when they serve as priests, 11 and the anointing oil and fragrant incense for the Holy Place. They are to make them just as I commanded you."

The Sabbath

12 Then the LORD said to Moses, 13 "Say to the Israelites, 'You must observe my

Sabbaths. This will be a sign between me and you for the generations to come, so you may know that I am the LORD, who makes you holy.

¹⁴ " 'Observe the Sabbath, because it is holy to you. Anyone who desecrates it is to be put to death; those who do any work on that day must be cut off from their people. ¹⁵For six days work is to be done, but the seventh day is a day of sabbath rest, holy to the LORD. Whoever does any work on the Sabbath day is to be put to death. ¹⁶The Israelites are to observe the Sabbath, celebrating it for the generations to come as a lasting covenant. ¹⁷It will be a sign between me and the Israelites forever, for in six days the LORD made the heavens and the earth, and on the seventh day he rested and was refreshed.' "

¹⁸When the LORD finished speaking to Moses on Mount Sinai, he gave him the two tablets of the covenant law, the tablets of stone inscribed by the finger of God.

The Golden Calf

32 When the people saw that Moses was so long in coming down from

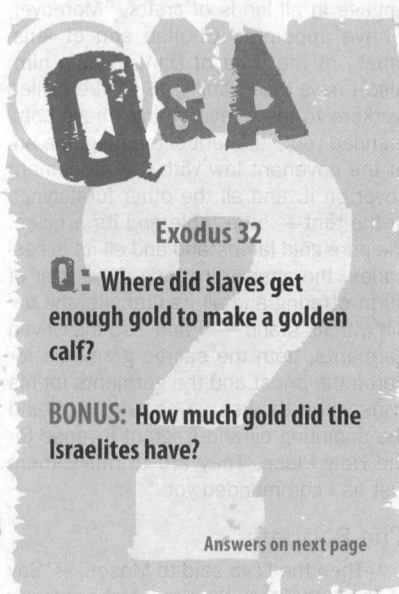

Exodus 32

Q: Where did slaves get enough gold to make a golden calf?

BONUS: How much gold did the Israelites have?

Answers on next page

the mountain, they gathered around Aaron and said, "Come, make us godsᵃ who will go before us. As for this fellow Moses who brought us up out of Egypt, we don't know what has happened to him."

²Aaron answered them, "Take off the gold earrings that your wives, your sons and your daughters are wearing, and bring them to me." ³So all the people took off their earrings and brought them to Aaron. ⁴He took what they handed him and made it into an idol cast in the shape of a calf, fashioning it with a tool. Then they said, "These are your gods,ᵇ Israel, who brought you up out of Egypt."

⁵When Aaron saw this, he built an altar in front of the calf and announced, "Tomorrow there will be a festival to the LORD." ⁶So the next day the people rose early and sacrificed burnt offerings and presented fellowship offerings. Afterward they sat down to eat and drink and got up to indulge in revelry.

⁷Then the LORD said to Moses, "Go down, because your people, whom you brought up out of Egypt, have become corrupt. ⁸They have been quick to turn away from what I commanded them and have made themselves an idol cast in the shape of a calf. They have bowed down to it and sacrificed to it and have said, 'These are your gods, Israel, who brought you up out of Egypt.'

⁹"I have seen these people," the LORD said to Moses, "and they are a stiff-necked people. ¹⁰Now leave me alone so that my anger may burn against them and that I may destroy them. Then I will make you into a great nation."

¹¹But Moses sought the favor of the LORD his God. "LORD," he said, "why should your anger burn against your people, whom you brought out of Egypt with great power and a mighty hand? ¹²Why should the Egyptians say, 'It was with evil intent that he brought them out, to kill them in the mountains and to wipe them off the face of the earth'? Turn from your fierce anger; relent and do not bring disaster on your people. ¹³Remember your

ᵃ 1 Or a god; also in verses 23 and 31   ᵇ 4 Or This is your god; also in verse 8 servants Abraham, Isaac and Israel, to whom you swore by your own self: 'I will make your descendants as numerous as the stars in the sky and I will give your descendants all this land I promised them, and it will be their inheritance forever.' " ¹⁴Then the LORD relented and did not bring on his people the disaster he had threatened.

¹⁵Moses turned and went down the mountain with the two tablets of the covenant law in his hands. They were inscribed on both sides, front and back. ¹⁶The tablets were the work of God; the writing was the writing of God, engraved on the tablets.

¹⁷When Joshua heard the noise of the people shouting, he said to Moses, "There is the sound of war in the camp."

¹⁸Moses replied:

"It is not the sound of victory,
    it is not the sound of defeat;
    it is the sound of singing that I hear."

¹⁹When Moses approached the camp and saw the calf and the dancing, his anger burned and he threw the tablets out of his hands, breaking them to pieces at the foot of the mountain. ²⁰And he took the calf the people had made and burned it in the fire; then he ground it to powder, scattered it on the water and made the Israelites drink it.

²¹He said to Aaron, "What did these people do to you, that you led them into such great sin?"

²²"Do not be angry, my lord," Aaron answered. "You know how prone these people are to evil. ²³They said to me, 'Make us gods who will go before us. As for this fellow Moses who brought us up out of Egypt, we don't know what has happened to him.' ²⁴So I told them, 'Whoever has any gold jewelry, take it off.' Then they gave me the gold, and I threw it into the fire, and out came this calf!"

²⁵Moses saw that the people were running wild and that Aaron had let them get out of control and so become a laughingstock to their enemies. ²⁶So he stood at the entrance to the camp and said, "Whoever is for the LORD, come to me." And all the Levites rallied to him.

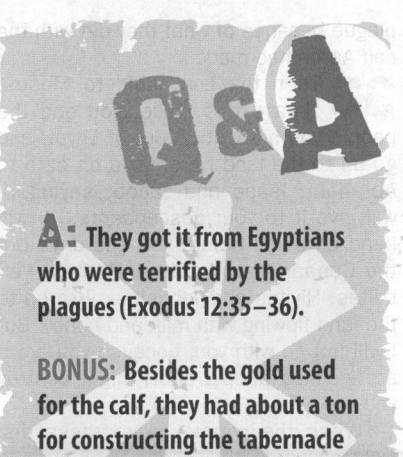

A: They got it from Egyptians who were terrified by the plagues (Exodus 12:35–36).

BONUS: Besides the gold used for the calf, they had about a ton for constructing the tabernacle (Exodus 38:21–31).

²⁷Then he said to them, "This is what the LORD, the God of Israel, says: 'Each man strap a sword to his side. Go back and forth through the camp from one end to the other, each killing his brother and friend and neighbor.' " ²⁸The Levites did as Moses commanded, and that day about three thousand of the people died. ²⁹Then Moses said, "You have been set apart to the LORD today, for you were against your own sons and brothers, and he has blessed you this day."

³⁰The next day Moses said to the people, "You have committed a great sin. But now I will go up to the LORD; perhaps I can make atonement for your sin."

³¹So Moses went back to the LORD and said, "Oh, what a great sin these people have committed! They have made themselves gods of gold. ³²But now, please forgive their sin—but if not, then blot me out of the book you have written."

³³The LORD replied to Moses, "Whoever has sinned against me I will blot out of my book. ³⁴Now go, lead the people to the place I spoke of, and my angel will go before you. However, when the time comes for me to punish, I will punish them for their sin."

³⁵And the LORD struck the people with a

plague because of what they did with the calf Aaron had made.

33 Then the LORD said to Moses, "Leave this place, you and the people you brought up out of Egypt, and go up to the land I promised on oath to Abraham, Isaac and Jacob, saying, 'I will give it to your descendants.' 2I will send an angel before you and drive out the Canaanites, Amorites, Hittites, Perizzites, Hivites and Jebusites. 3Go up to the land flowing with milk and honey. But I will not go with you, because you are a stiff-necked people and I might destroy you on the way."

4When the people heard these distressing words, they began to mourn and no one put on any ornaments. 5For the LORD had said to Moses, "Tell the Israelites, 'You are a stiff-necked people. If I were to go with you even for a moment, I might destroy you. Now take off your ornaments and I will decide what to do with you.' " 6So the Israelites stripped off their ornaments at Mount Horeb.

The Tent of Meeting

7Now Moses used to take a tent and pitch it outside the camp some distance away, calling it the "tent of meeting." Anyone inquiring of the LORD would go to the tent of meeting outside the camp. 8And whenever Moses went out to the tent, all the people rose and stood at the entrances to their tents, watching Moses until he entered the tent. 9As Moses went into the tent, the pillar of cloud would come down and stay at the entrance, while the LORD spoke with Moses. 10Whenever the people saw the pillar of cloud standing at the entrance to the tent, they all stood and worshiped, each at the entrance to their tent. 11The LORD would speak to Moses face to face, as one speaks to a friend. Then Moses would return to the camp, but his young aide Joshua son of Nun did not leave the tent.

Moses and the Glory of the LORD

12Moses said to the LORD, "You have been telling me, 'Lead these people,' but you have not let me know whom you will send with me. You have said, 'I know you by name and you have found favor with me.' 13If you are pleased with me, teach me your ways so I may know you and continue to find favor with you. Remember that this nation is your people."

14The LORD replied, "My Presence will go with you, and I will give you rest."

15Then Moses said to him, "If your Presence does not go with us, do not send us up from here. 16How will anyone know that you are pleased with me and with your people unless you go with us? What else will distinguish me and your people from all the other people on the face of the earth?"

17And the LORD said to Moses, "I will do the very thing you have asked, because I am pleased with you and I know you by name."

18Then Moses said, "Now show me your glory."

19And the LORD said, "I will cause all my goodness to pass in front of you, and I will proclaim my name, the LORD, in your presence. I will have mercy on whom I will have mercy, and I will have compassion on whom I will have compassion. 20But," he said, "you cannot see my face, for no one may see me and live."

21Then the LORD said, "There is a place near me where you may stand on a rock. 22When my glory passes by, I will put you in a cleft in the rock and cover you with my hand until I have passed by. 23Then I will remove my hand and you will see my back; but my face must not be seen."

The New Stone Tablets

34 The LORD said to Moses, "Chisel out two stone tablets like the first ones, and I will write on them the words that were on the first tablets, which you broke. 2Be ready in the morning, and then come up on Mount Sinai. Present yourself to me there on top of the mountain. 3No one is to come with you or be seen anywhere on the mountain; not even the flocks and herds may graze in front of the mountain."

4So Moses chiseled out two stone tablets like the first ones and went up Mount

Sinai early in the morning, as the LORD had commanded him; and he carried the two stone tablets in his hands. ⁵Then the LORD came down in the cloud and stood there with him and proclaimed his name, the LORD. ⁶And he passed in front of Moses, proclaiming, "The LORD, the LORD, the compassionate and gracious God, slow to anger, abounding in love and faithfulness, ⁷maintaining love to thousands, and forgiving wickedness, rebellion and sin. Yet he does not leave the guilty unpunished; he punishes the children and their children for the sin of the parents to the third and fourth generation."

⁸Moses bowed to the ground at once and worshiped. ⁹"Lord," he said, "if I have found favor in your eyes, then let the Lord go with us. Although this is a stiff-necked people, forgive our wickedness and our sin, and take us as your inheritance."

¹⁰Then the LORD said: "I am making a covenant with you. Before all your people I will do wonders never before done in any nation in all the world. The people you live among will see how awesome is the work that I, the LORD, will do for you. ¹¹Obey what I command you today. I will drive out before you the Amorites, Canaanites, Hittites, Perizzites, Hivites and Jebusites. ¹²Be careful not to make a treaty with those who live in the land where you are going, or they will be a snare among you. ¹³Break down their altars, smash their sacred stones and cut down their Asherah poles.ᵃ ¹⁴Do not worship any other god, for the LORD, whose name is Jealous, is a jealous God.

¹⁵"Be careful not to make a treaty with those who live in the land; for when they prostitute themselves to their gods and sacrifice to them, they will invite you and you will eat their sacrifices. ¹⁶And when you choose some of their daughters as wives for your sons and those daughters prostitute themselves to their gods, they will lead your sons to do the same.

¹⁷"Do not make any idols.

¹⁸"Celebrate the Festival of Unleavened Bread. For seven days eat bread made without yeast, as I commanded

you. Do this at the appointed time in the month of Aviv, for in that month you came out of Egypt.

¹⁹"The first offspring of every womb belongs to me, including all the firstborn males of your livestock, whether from herd or flock. ²⁰Redeem the firstborn donkey with a lamb, but if you do not redeem it, break its neck. Redeem all your firstborn sons.

"No one is to appear before me empty-handed.

²¹"Six days you shall labor, but on the seventh day you shall rest; even during the plowing season and harvest you must rest.

²²"Celebrate the Festival of Weeks with the firstfruits of the wheat harvest, and the Festival of Ingathering at the turn of the year.ᵇ ²³Three times a year all your men are to appear before the Sovereign LORD, the God of Israel. ²⁴I will drive out nations before you and enlarge your territory, and no one will covet your land when you go up three times each year to appear before the LORD your God.

²⁵"Do not offer the blood of a sacrifice to me along with anything containing yeast, and do not let any of the sacrifice from the Passover Festival remain until morning.

²⁶"Bring the best of the firstfruits of your soil to the house of the LORD your God.

"Do not cook a young goat in its mother's milk."

²⁷Then the LORD said to Moses, "Write down these words, for in accordance with these words I have made a covenant with you and with Israel." ²⁸Moses was there with the LORD forty days and forty nights without eating bread or drinking water. And he wrote on the tablets the words of the covenant—the Ten Commandments.

The Radiant Face of Moses

²⁹When Moses came down from Mount Sinai with the two tablets of the covenant law in his hands, he was not aware that his face was radiant because he had spoken with the LORD. ³⁰When Aaron and all

---

ᵃ 13 That is, wooden symbols of the goddess Asherah   ᵇ 22 That is, in the autumn

the Israelites saw Moses, his face was radiant, and they were afraid to come near him. [31]But Moses called to them; so Aaron and all the leaders of the community came back to him, and he spoke to them. [32]Afterward all the Israelites came near him, and he gave them all the commands the LORD had given him on Mount Sinai.

[33]When Moses finished speaking to them, he put a veil over his face. [34]But whenever he entered the LORD's presence to speak with him, he removed the veil until he came out. And when he came out and told the Israelites what he had been commanded, [35]they saw that his face was radiant. Then Moses would put the veil back over his face until he went in to speak with the LORD.

Sabbath Regulations

35 Moses assembled the whole Israelite community and said to them, "These are the things the LORD has commanded you to do: [2]For six days, work is to be done, but the seventh day shall be your holy day, a day of sabbath rest to the LORD. Whoever does any work on it is to be put to death. [3]Do not light a fire in any of your dwellings on the Sabbath day."

Materials for the Tabernacle

[4]Moses said to the whole Israelite community, "This is what the LORD has commanded: [5]From what you have, take an offering for the LORD. Everyone who is willing is to bring to the LORD an offering of gold, silver and bronze; [6]blue, purple and scarlet yarn and fine linen; goat hair; [7]ram skins dyed red and another type of durable leather[a]; acacia wood; [8]olive oil for the light; spices for the anointing oil and for the fragrant incense; [9]and onyx stones and other gems to be mounted on the ephod and breastpiece.

[10]"All who are skilled among you are to come and make everything the LORD has commanded: [11]the tabernacle with its tent and its covering, clasps, frames, crossbars, posts and bases; [12]the ark with its poles and the atonement cover and the curtain that shields it; [13]the ta-

ble with its poles and all its articles and the bread of the Presence; [14]the lampstand that is for light with its accessories, lamps and oil for the light; [15]the altar of incense with its poles, the anointing oil and the fragrant incense; the curtain for the doorway at the entrance to the tabernacle; [16]the altar of burnt offering with its bronze grating, its poles and all its utensils; the bronze basin with its stand; [17]the curtains of the courtyard with its posts and bases, and the curtain for the entrance to the courtyard; [18]the tent pegs for the tabernacle and for the court-

> Jealousy is one of those "bad" emotions, isn't it? Why then does the Bible say, "the LORD, whose name is Jealous, is a jealous God"? The Hebrew word here describes an intense love. In human beings jealousy usually is selfish. God's jealousy is different. God's jealousy is intense love, a love so strong that he wants only what is best for you. That's why God gets so upset when you sin. He loves you too much to just stand by and see you mess up your life. His intense love makes him jealous of anything in your life that pulls you away from him and the wonderful things he has planned for you.
>
> {Exodus 34:14}

≫ INSTANT ACCESS

---

[a] 7 Possibly the hides of large aquatic mammals; also in verse 23

yard, and their ropes; ¹⁹the woven garments worn for ministering in the sanctuary—both the sacred garments for Aaron the priest and the garments for his sons when they serve as priests."

²⁰Then the whole Israelite community withdrew from Moses' presence, ²¹and everyone who was willing and whose heart moved them came and brought an offering to the LORD for the work on the tent of meeting, for all its service, and for the sacred garments. ²²All who were willing, men and women alike, came and brought gold jewelry of all kinds: brooches, earrings, rings and ornaments. They all presented their gold as a wave offering to the LORD. ²³Everyone who had blue, purple or scarlet yarn or fine linen, or goat hair, ram skins dyed red or the other durable leather brought them. ²⁴Those presenting an offering of silver or bronze brought it as an offering to the LORD, and everyone who had acacia wood for any part of the work brought it. ²⁵Every skilled woman spun with her hands and brought what she had spun—blue, purple or scarlet yarn or fine linen. ²⁶And all the women who were willing and had the skill spun the goat hair. ²⁷The leaders brought onyx stones and other gems to be mounted on the ephod and breastpiece. ²⁸They also brought spices and olive oil for the light and for the anointing oil and for the fragrant incense. ²⁹All the Israelite men and women who were willing brought to the LORD freewill offerings for all the work the LORD through Moses had commanded them to do.

Bezalel and Oholiab

³⁰Then Moses said to the Israelites, "See, the LORD has chosen Bezalel son of Uri, the son of Hur, of the tribe of Judah, ³¹and he has filled him with the Spirit of God, with wisdom, with understanding, with knowledge and with all kinds of skills— ³²to make artistic designs for work in gold, silver and bronze, ³³to cut and set stones, to work in wood and to engage in all kinds of artistic crafts. ³⁴And he has given both him and Oholiab son of Ahisamak, of the tribe of Dan, the ability to teach others. ³⁵He has filled them with skill to do all kinds of work as engravers, designers, embroiderers in blue, purple and scarlet yarn and fine linen, and weavers—all of them skilled

36 workers and designers. ¹So Bezalel, Oholiab and every skilled person to whom the LORD has given skill and ability to know how to carry out all the work of constructing the sanctuary are to do the work just as the LORD has commanded."

²Then Moses summoned Bezalel and Oholiab and every skilled person to whom the LORD had given ability and who was willing to come and do the work. ³They received from Moses all the offerings the Israelites had brought to carry out the work of constructing the sanctuary. And the people continued to bring freewill offerings morning after morning. ⁴So all the skilled workers who were doing all the work on the sanctuary left what they were doing ⁵and said to Moses, "The people are bringing more than enough for doing the work the LORD commanded to be done."

⁶Then Moses gave an order and they sent this word throughout the camp: "No man or woman is to make anything else as an offering for the sanctuary." And so the people were restrained from bringing more, ⁷because what they already had was more than enough to do all the work.

The Tabernacle

⁸All those who were skilled among the workers made the tabernacle with ten curtains of finely twisted linen and blue, purple and scarlet yarn, with cherubim woven into them by expert hands. ⁹All the curtains were the same size—twenty-eight cubits long and four cubits wide.ᵃ ¹⁰They joined five of the curtains together and did the same with the other five. ¹¹Then they made loops of blue material along the edge of the end curtain in one set, and the same was done with the end curtain in the other set. ¹²They also made fifty loops on one curtain and fifty loops on

---

ᵃ 9 That is, about 42 feet long and 6 feet wide or about 13 meters long and 1.8 meters wide

the end curtain of the other set, with the loops opposite each other. ¹³Then they made fifty gold clasps and used them to fasten the two sets of curtains together so that the tabernacle was a unit.

¹⁴They made curtains of goat hair for the tent over the tabernacle—eleven altogether. ¹⁵All eleven curtains were the same size—thirty cubits long and four cubits wide.ᵃ ¹⁶They joined five of the curtains into one set and the other six into another set. ¹⁷Then they made fifty loops along the edge of the end curtain in one set and also along the edge of the end curtain in the other set. ¹⁸They made fifty bronze clasps to fasten the tent together as a unit. ¹⁹Then they made for the tent a covering of ram skins dyed red, and over that a covering of the other durable leather.ᵇ

²⁰They made upright frames of acacia wood for the tabernacle. ²¹Each frame was ten cubits long and a cubit and a half wide,ᶜ ²²with two projections set parallel to each other. They made all the frames of the tabernacle in this way. ²³They made twenty frames for the south side of the tabernacle ²⁴and made forty silver bases to go under them—two bases for each frame, one under each projection. ²⁵For the other side, the north side of the tabernacle, they made twenty frames ²⁶and forty silver bases—two under each frame. ²⁷They made six frames for the far end, that is, the west end of the tabernacle, ²⁸and two frames were made for the corners of the tabernacle at the far end. ²⁹At these two corners the frames were double from the bottom all the way to the top and fitted into a single ring; both were made alike. ³⁰So there were eight frames and sixteen silver bases—two under each frame.

³¹They also made crossbars of acacia wood: five for the frames on one side of the tabernacle, ³²five for those on the other side, and five for the frames on the west, at the far end of the tabernacle. ³³They made the center crossbar so that

it extended from end to end at the middle of the frames. ³⁴They overlaid the frames with gold and made gold rings to hold the crossbars. They also overlaid the crossbars with gold.

³⁵They made the curtain of blue, purple and scarlet yarn and finely twisted linen, with cherubim woven into it by a skilled worker. ³⁶They made four posts of acacia wood for it and overlaid them with gold. They made gold hooks for them and cast their four silver bases. ³⁷For the entrance to the tent they made a curtain of blue, purple and scarlet yarn and finely twisted linen—the work of an embroiderer; ³⁸and they made five posts with hooks for them. They overlaid the tops of the posts and their bands with gold and made their five bases of bronze.

The Ark

37 Bezalel made the ark of acacia wood—two and a half cubits long, a cubit and a half wide, and a cubit and a half high.ᵈ ²He overlaid it with pure gold, both inside and out, and made a gold molding around it. ³He cast four gold rings for it and fastened them to its four feet, with two rings on one side and two rings on the other. ⁴Then he made poles of acacia wood and overlaid them with gold. ⁵And he inserted the poles into the rings on the sides of the ark to carry it.

⁶He made the atonement cover of pure gold—two and a half cubits long and a cubit and a half wide. ⁷Then he made two cherubim out of hammered gold at the ends of the cover. ⁸He made one cherub on one end and the second cherub on the other; at the two ends he made them of one piece with the cover. ⁹The cherubim had their wings spread upward, overshadowing the cover with them. The cherubim faced each other, looking toward the cover.

The Table

¹⁰Theyᵉ made the table of acacia wood—two cubits long, a cubit wide and

---

ᵃ 15 That is, about 45 feet long and 6 feet wide or about 14 meters long and 1.8 meters wide   ᵇ 19 Possibly the hides of large aquatic mammals (see 35:7)   ᶜ 21 That is, about 15 feet long and 2 1/4 feet wide or about 4.5 meters long and 68 centimeters wide   ᵈ 1 That is, about 3 1/4 feet long and 2 1/4 feet wide and high or about 1.1 meters long and 68 centimeters wide and high; similarly in verse 6   ᵉ 10 Or He; also in verses 11-29

a cubit and a half high.[a] [11]Then they overlaid it with pure gold and made a gold molding around it. [12]They also made around it a rim a handbreadth[b] wide and put a gold molding on the rim. [13]They cast four gold rings for the table and fastened them to the four corners, where the four legs were. [14]The rings were put close to the rim to hold the poles used in carrying the table. [15]The poles for carrying the table were made of acacia wood and were overlaid with gold. [16]And they made from pure gold the articles for the table — its plates and dishes and bowls and its pitchers for the pouring out of drink offerings.

The Lampstand

[17]They made the lampstand of pure gold. They hammered out its base and shaft, and made its flowerlike cups, buds and blossoms of one piece with them. [18]Six branches extended from the sides of the lampstand — three on one side and three on the other. [19]Three cups shaped like almond flowers with buds and blossoms were on one branch, three on the next branch and the same for all six branches extending from the lampstand. [20]And on the lampstand were four cups shaped like almond flowers with buds and blossoms. [21]One bud was under the first pair of branches extending from the lampstand, a second bud under the second pair, and a third bud under the third pair — six branches in all. [22]The buds and the branches were all of one piece with the lampstand, hammered out of pure gold.

[23]They made its seven lamps, as well as its wick trimmers and trays, of pure gold. [24]They made the lampstand and all its accessories from one talent[c] of pure gold.

The Altar of Incense

[25]They made the altar of incense out of acacia wood. It was square, a cubit long and a cubit wide and two cubits high[d] —

its horns of one piece with it. [26]They overlaid the top and all the sides and the horns with pure gold, and made a gold molding around it. [27]They made two gold rings below the molding — two on each of the opposite sides — to hold the poles used to carry it. [28]They made the poles of acacia wood and overlaid them with gold.

[29]They also made the sacred anointing oil and the pure, fragrant incense — the work of a perfumer.

The Altar of Burnt Offering

38 They[e] built the altar of burnt offering of acacia wood, three cubits[f] high; it was square, five cubits long and five cubits wide.[g] [2]They made a horn at each of the four corners, so that the horns and the altar were of one piece, and they overlaid the altar with bronze. [3]They made all its utensils of bronze — its pots, shovels, sprinkling bowls, meat forks and firepans. [4]They made a grating for the altar, a bronze network, to be under its ledge, halfway up the altar. [5]They cast bronze rings to hold the poles for the four corners of the bronze grating. [6]They made the poles of acacia wood and overlaid them with bronze. [7]They inserted the poles into the rings so they would be on the sides of the altar for carrying it. They made it hollow, out of boards.

The Basin for Washing

[8]They made the bronze basin and its bronze stand from the mirrors of the women who served at the entrance to the tent of meeting.

The Courtyard

[9]Next they made the courtyard. The south side was a hundred cubits[h] long and had curtains of finely twisted linen, [10]with twenty posts and twenty bronze bases, and with silver hooks and bands on the posts. [11]The north side was also a hundred cubits long and had twenty

---

[a] 10 That is, about 3 feet long, 1 1/2 feet wide and 2 1/4 feet high or about 90 centimeters long, 45 centimeters wide and 68 centimeters high   [b] 12 That is, about 3 inches or about 7.5 centimeters   [c] 24 That is, about 75 pounds or about 34 kilograms   [d] 25 That is, about 1 1/2 feet long and wide and 3 feet high or about 45 centimeters long and wide and 90 centimeters high   [e] 1 Or He; also in verses 2-9   [f] 1 That is, about 4 1/2 feet or about 1.4 meters   [g] 1 That is, about 7 1/2 feet or about 2.3 meters long and wide   [h] 9 That is, about 150 feet or about 45 meters

posts and twenty bronze bases, with silver hooks and bands on the posts.

¹²The west end was fifty cubits*a* wide and had curtains, with ten posts and ten bases, with silver hooks and bands on the posts. ¹³The east end, toward the sunrise, was also fifty cubits wide. ¹⁴Curtains fifteen cubits*b* long were on one side of the entrance, with three posts and three bases, ¹⁵and curtains fifteen cubits long were on the other side of the entrance to the courtyard, with three posts and three bases. ¹⁶All the curtains around the courtyard were of finely twisted linen. ¹⁷The bases for the posts were bronze. The hooks and bands on the posts were silver, and their tops were overlaid with silver; so all the posts of the courtyard had silver bands.

¹⁸The curtain for the entrance to the courtyard was made of blue, purple and scarlet yarn and finely twisted linen — the work of an embroiderer. It was twenty cubits*c* long and, like the curtains of the courtyard, five cubits*d* high, ¹⁹with four posts and four bronze bases. Their hooks and bands were silver, and their tops were overlaid with silver. ²⁰All the tent pegs of the tabernacle and of the surrounding courtyard were bronze.

The Materials Used

²¹These are the amounts of the materials used for the tabernacle, the tabernacle of the covenant law, which were recorded at Moses' command by the Levites under the direction of Ithamar son of Aaron, the priest. ²²(Bezalel son of Uri, the son of Hur, of the tribe of Judah, made everything the LORD commanded Moses; ²³with him was Oholiab son of Ahisamak, of the tribe of Dan — an engraver and designer, and an embroiderer in blue, purple and scarlet yarn and fine linen.) ²⁴The total amount of the gold from the wave offering used for all the work on the sanctuary was 29 talents and 730 shekels,*e* according to the sanctuary shekel.

²⁵The silver obtained from those of the community who were counted in the census was 100 talents*f* and 1,775 shekels,*g* according to the sanctuary shekel— ²⁶one beka per person, that is, half a shekel,*h* according to the sanctuary shekel, from everyone who had crossed over to those counted, twenty years old or more, a total of 603,550 men. ²⁷The 100 talents of silver were used to cast the bases for the sanctuary and for the curtain — 100 bases from the 100 talents, one talent for each base. ²⁸They used the 1,775 shekels to make the hooks for the posts, to overlay the tops of the posts, and to make their bands.

²⁹The bronze from the wave offering was 70 talents and 2,400 shekels.*i* ³⁰They used it to make the bases for the entrance to the tent of meeting, the bronze altar with its bronze grating and all its utensils, ³¹the bases for the surrounding courtyard and those for its entrance and all the tent pegs for the tabernacle and those for the surrounding courtyard.

The Priestly Garments

39 From the blue, purple and scarlet yarn they made woven garments for ministering in the sanctuary. They also made sacred garments for Aaron, as the LORD commanded Moses.

The Ephod

²They*j* made the ephod of gold, and of blue, purple and scarlet yarn, and of finely twisted linen. ³They hammered out thin sheets of gold and cut strands to be worked into the blue, purple and scarlet yarn and fine linen — the work of skilled hands. ⁴They made shoulder pieces for the ephod, which were attached to two of its corners, so it could be fastened. ⁵Its skillfully woven waistband was like it — of one piece with the ephod and made with gold, and with blue, purple and scarlet yarn, and with finely twisted linen, as the LORD commanded Moses.

---

a 12 That is, about 75 feet or about 23 meters   *b 14* That is, about 22 feet or about 6.8 meters   *c 18* That is, about 30 feet or about 9 meters   *d 18* That is, about 7 1/2 feet or about 2.3 meters   *e 24* The weight of the gold was a little over a ton or about 1 metric ton.   *f 25* That is, about 3 3/4 tons or about 3.4 metric tons; also in verse 27   *g 25* That is, about 44 pounds or about 20 kilograms; also in verse 28   *h 26* That is, about 1/5 ounce or about 5.7 grams   *i 29* The weight of the bronze was about 2 1/2 tons or about 2.4 metric tons.   *j 2* Or *He;* also in verses 7, 8 and 22

⁶They mounted the onyx stones in gold filigree settings and engraved them like a seal with the names of the sons of Israel. ⁷Then they fastened them on the shoulder pieces of the ephod as memorial stones for the sons of Israel, as the Lord commanded Moses.

The Breastpiece

⁸They fashioned the breastpiece—the work of a skilled craftsman. They made it like the ephod: of gold, and of blue, purple and scarlet yarn, and of finely twisted linen. ⁹It was square—a span*a* long and a span wide—and folded double. ¹⁰Then they mounted four rows of precious stones on it. The first row was carnelian, chrysolite and beryl; ¹¹the second row was turquoise, lapis lazuli and emerald; ¹²the third row was jacinth, agate and amethyst; ¹³the fourth row was topaz, onyx and jasper.*b* They were mounted in gold filigree settings. ¹⁴There were twelve stones, one for each of the names of the sons of Israel, each engraved like a seal with the name of one of the twelve tribes.

¹⁵For the breastpiece they made braided chains of pure gold, like a rope. ¹⁶They made two gold filigree settings and two gold rings, and fastened the rings to two of the corners of the breastpiece. ¹⁷They fastened the two gold chains to the rings at the corners of the breastpiece, ¹⁸and the other ends of the chains to the two settings, attaching them to the shoulder pieces of the ephod at the front. ¹⁹They made two gold rings and attached them to the other two corners of the breastpiece on the inside edge next to the ephod. ²⁰Then they made two more gold rings and attached them to the bottom of the shoulder pieces on the front of the ephod, close to the seam just above the waistband of the ephod. ²¹They tied the rings of the breastpiece to the rings of the ephod with blue cord, connecting it to the waistband so that the breastpiece would not swing out from the ephod—as the Lord commanded Moses.

Other Priestly Garments

²²They made the robe of the ephod entirely of blue cloth—the work of a weaver— ²³with an opening in the center of the robe like the opening of a collar,*c* and a band around this opening, so that it would not tear. ²⁴They made pomegranates of blue, purple and scarlet yarn and finely twisted linen around the hem of the robe. ²⁵And they made bells of pure gold and attached them around the hem between the pomegranates. ²⁶The bells and pomegranates alternated around the hem of the robe to be worn for ministering, as the Lord commanded Moses.

²⁷For Aaron and his sons, they made tunics of fine linen—the work of a weaver— ²⁸and the turban of fine linen, the linen caps and the undergarments of finely twisted linen. ²⁹The sash was made of finely twisted linen and blue, purple and scarlet yarn—the work of an embroiderer—as the Lord commanded Moses.

³⁰They made the plate, the sacred emblem, out of pure gold and engraved on it, like an inscription on a seal: HOLY TO THE LORD. ³¹Then they fastened a blue cord to it to attach it to the turban, as the Lord commanded Moses.

Moses Inspects the Tabernacle

³²So all the work on the tabernacle, the tent of meeting, was completed. The Israelites did everything just as the Lord commanded Moses. ³³Then they brought the tabernacle to Moses: the tent and all its furnishings, its clasps, frames, crossbars, posts and bases; ³⁴the covering of ram skins dyed red and the covering of another durable leather*d* and the shielding curtain; ³⁵the ark of the covenant law with its poles and the atonement cover; ³⁶the table with all its articles and the bread of the Presence; ³⁷the pure gold lampstand with its row of lamps and all its accessories, and the olive oil for the light; ³⁸the gold altar, the anointing oil, the fragrant incense, and the curtain for the entrance to the tent; ³⁹the bronze altar with its

---

a 9 That is, about 9 inches or about 23 centimeters   *b* 13 The precise identification of some of these precious stones is uncertain.   *c* 23 The meaning of the Hebrew for this word is uncertain.   *d* 34 Possibly the hides of large aquatic mammals

bronze grating, its poles and all its utensils; the basin with its stand; 40the curtains of the courtyard with its posts and bases, and the curtain for the entrance to the courtyard; the ropes and tent pegs for the courtyard; all the furnishings for the tabernacle, the tent of meeting; 41and the woven garments worn for ministering in the sanctuary, both the sacred garments for Aaron the priest and the garments for his sons when serving as priests.

42The Israelites had done all the work just as the LORD had commanded Moses. 43Moses inspected the work and saw that they had done it just as the LORD had commanded. So Moses blessed them.

Setting Up the Tabernacle

40 Then the LORD said to Moses: 2"Set up the tabernacle, the tent of meeting, on the first day of the first month. 3Place the ark of the covenant law in it and shield the ark with the curtain. 4Bring in the table and set out what belongs on it. Then bring in the lampstand and set up its lamps. 5Place the gold altar of incense in front of the ark of the covenant law and put the curtain at the entrance to the tabernacle.

6"Place the altar of burnt offering in front of the entrance to the tabernacle, the tent of meeting; 7place the basin between the tent of meeting and the altar and put water in it. 8Set up the courtyard around it and put the curtain at the entrance to the courtyard.

9"Take the anointing oil and anoint the tabernacle and everything in it; consecrate it and all its furnishings, and it will be holy. 10Then anoint the altar of burnt offering and all its utensils; consecrate the altar, and it will be most holy. 11Anoint the basin and its stand and consecrate them.

12"Bring Aaron and his sons to the entrance to the tent of meeting and wash them with water. 13Then dress Aaron in the sacred garments, anoint him and consecrate him so he may serve me as priest. 14Bring his sons and dress them in tunics. 15Anoint them just as you anointed their father, so they may serve me as priests. Their anointing will be to a priest-

hood that will continue throughout their generations." 16Moses did everything just as the LORD commanded him.

17So the tabernacle was set up on the first day of the first month in the second year. 18When Moses set up the tabernacle, he put the bases in place, erected the frames, inserted the crossbars and set up the posts. 19Then he spread the tent over the tabernacle and put the covering over the tent, as the LORD commanded him.

20He took the tablets of the covenant law and placed them in the ark, attached the poles to the ark and put the atonement cover over it. 21Then he brought

>> INSTANT ACCESS

Have you ever finished a job and then stood back and looked at it with pride and satisfaction? When the Israelites finished building the tabernacle, Exodus says they did all the work "just as the LORD had commanded" and "Moses inspected the work." Can you imagine the people standing there as Moses looked over their work, proud and happy that they'd done such a good job? Life is pretty similar. You want to be able to look back at the choices you've made and feel great satisfaction. You want to watch with pride as God inspects your life and says you've lived it "just as the LORD commanded."

{Exodus 39:42–43}

the ark into the tabernacle and hung the shielding curtain and shielded the ark of the covenant law, as the LORD commanded him.

²²Moses placed the table in the tent of meeting on the north side of the tabernacle outside the curtain ²³and set out the bread on it before the LORD, as the LORD commanded him.

²⁴He placed the lampstand in the tent of meeting opposite the table on the south side of the tabernacle ²⁵and set up the lamps before the LORD, as the LORD commanded him.

²⁶Moses placed the gold altar in the tent of meeting in front of the curtain ²⁷and burned fragrant incense on it, as the LORD commanded him.

²⁸Then he put up the curtain at the entrance to the tabernacle. ²⁹He set the altar of burnt offering near the entrance to the tabernacle, the tent of meeting, and offered on it burnt offerings and grain offerings, as the LORD commanded him.

³⁰He placed the basin between the tent of meeting and the altar and put water in it for washing, ³¹and Moses and Aaron and his sons used it to wash their hands and feet. ³²They washed whenever they entered the tent of meeting or approached the altar, as the LORD commanded Moses.

³³Then Moses set up the courtyard around the tabernacle and altar and put up the curtain at the entrance to the courtyard. And so Moses finished the work.

The Glory of the LORD

³⁴Then the cloud covered the tent of meeting, and the glory of the LORD filled the tabernacle. ³⁵Moses could not enter the tent of meeting because the cloud had settled on it, and the glory of the LORD filled the tabernacle.

³⁶In all the travels of the Israelites, whenever the cloud lifted from above the tabernacle, they would set out; ³⁷but if the cloud did not lift, they did not set out—until the day it lifted. ³⁸So the cloud of the LORD was over the tabernacle by day, and fire was in the cloud by night, in the sight of all the Israelites during all their travels.

LEVITICUS

preview

The word "holy" is found 87 times in Leviticus.

"Holy" means to be set apart; show loyalty to God by keeping his commands.

The command to "love your neighbor as yourself" is found in Leviticus 19:18.

Worship.

That's what the book of Leviticus is all about. God wants you to worship him. But how do you go about it? Well, you get together with other believers and sing God's praises. You talk about what God is like and about the things he's done for you. You pray and tell God how wonderful he is. It's really quite simple.

But Leviticus will take you back to a time when worship wasn't so simple. This book is filled with rules that Israel's priests and people had to follow. It describes the required yearly religious holidays, and it lists practices that set the Hebrews apart from all the other people of the world.

>>**SILENCE A SIN?**
    Answer in Leviticus 5:1

>>**NO LOBSTER ON THIS MENU**
    See food section, Leviticus 11

>>**ONE SACRIFICE DOES IT ALL**
    Promise in Leviticus 16:15–22

>>**"ALTERNATE LIFESTYLES" CONDEMNED**
    Sexual don'ts detailed, Leviticus 18

>>**CELEBRATE!**
    National holidays listed, see Leviticus 23

The year the Israelites camp by Sinai, in Peru people are beginning to work metal. On the steppes of Asia, nomads on horseback herd cattle.

The Burnt Offering

1 The LORD called to Moses and spoke to him from the tent of meeting. He said, ² "Speak to the Israelites and say to them: 'When anyone among you brings an offering to the LORD, bring as your offering an animal from either the herd or the flock.

³ " 'If the offering is a burnt offering from the herd, you are to offer a male without defect. You must present it at the entrance to the tent of meeting so that it will be acceptable to the LORD. ⁴ You are to lay your hand on the head of the burnt offering, and it will be accepted on your behalf to make atonement for you. ⁵ You are to slaughter the young bull before the LORD, and then Aaron's sons the priests shall bring the blood and splash it against the sides of the altar at the entrance to the tent of meeting. ⁶ You are to skin the burnt offering and cut it into pieces. ⁷ The sons of Aaron the priest are to put fire on the altar and arrange wood on the fire. ⁸ Then Aaron's sons the priests shall arrange the pieces, including the head and the fat, on the wood that is burning on the altar. ⁹ You are to wash the internal organs and the legs with water, and the priest is to burn all of it on the altar. It is a burnt offering, a food offering, an aroma pleasing to the LORD.

¹⁰ " 'If the offering is a burnt offering from the flock, from either the sheep or the goats, you are to offer a male without defect. ¹¹ You are to slaughter it at the north side of the altar before the LORD, and Aaron's sons the priests shall splash its blood against the sides of the altar. ¹² You are to cut it into pieces, and the priest shall arrange them, including the head and the fat, on the wood that is burning on the altar. ¹³ You are to wash the internal organs and the legs with water, and the priest is to bring all of them and burn them on the altar. It is a burnt offering, a food offering, an aroma pleasing to the LORD.

¹⁴ " 'If the offering to the LORD is a burnt offering of birds, you are to offer a dove or a young pigeon. ¹⁵ The priest shall bring it to the altar, wring off the head and burn it on the altar; its blood shall be drained out on the side of the altar. ¹⁶ He is to remove the crop and the feathers[a] and throw them down east of the altar where the ashes are. ¹⁷ He shall tear it open by the wings, not dividing it completely, and then the priest shall burn it on the wood that is burning on the altar. It is a burnt offering, a food offering, an aroma pleasing to the LORD.

The Grain Offering

2 " 'When anyone brings a grain offering to the LORD, their offering is to be of the finest flour. They are to pour olive oil on it, put incense on it ² and take it to Aaron's sons the priests. The priest shall take a handful of the flour and oil, together with all the incense, and burn this as a memorial[b] portion on the altar, a food offering, an aroma pleasing to the LORD. ³ The rest of the grain offering belongs to Aaron and his sons; it is a most holy part of the food offerings presented to the LORD.

⁴ " 'If you bring a grain offering baked in an oven, it is to consist of the finest flour: either thick loaves made without yeast and with olive oil mixed in or thin loaves made without yeast and brushed with olive oil. ⁵ If your grain offering is prepared on a griddle, it is to be made of the finest flour mixed with oil, and without yeast. ⁶ Crumble it and pour oil on it; it is a grain offering. ⁷ If your grain offering is cooked in a pan, it is to be made of the finest flour and some olive oil. ⁸ Bring the grain offering made of these things to the LORD; present it to the priest, who shall take it to the altar. ⁹ He shall take out the memorial portion from the grain offering and burn it on the altar as a food offering, an aroma pleasing to the LORD. ¹⁰ The rest of the grain offering belongs to Aaron and his sons; it is a most holy part of the food offerings presented to the LORD.

¹¹ " 'Every grain offering you bring to the LORD must be made without yeast, for

---

[a] 16 Or crop with its contents; the meaning of the Hebrew for this word is uncertain.   [b] 2 Or representative; also in verses 9 and 16

you are not to burn any yeast or honey in a food offering presented to the LORD. ¹²You may bring them to the LORD as an offering of the firstfruits, but they are not to be offered on the altar as a pleasing aroma. ¹³Season all your grain offerings with salt. Do not leave the salt of the covenant of your God out of your grain offerings; add salt to all your offerings.

¹⁴ " 'If you bring a grain offering of firstfruits to the LORD, offer crushed heads of new grain roasted in the fire. ¹⁵Put oil and incense on it; it is a grain offering. ¹⁶The priest shall burn the memorial portion of the crushed grain and the oil, together with all the incense, as a food offering presented to the LORD.

The Fellowship Offering

3 " 'If your offering is a fellowship offering, and you offer an animal from the herd, whether male or female, you are to present before the LORD an animal without defect. ²You are to lay your hand on the head of your offering and slaughter it at the entrance to the tent of meeting. Then Aaron's sons the priests shall splash the blood against the sides of the altar. ³From the fellowship offering you are to bring a food offering to the LORD: the internal organs and all the fat that is connected to them, ⁴both kidneys with the fat on them near the loins, and the long lobe of the liver, which you will remove with the kidneys. ⁵Then Aaron's sons are to burn it on the altar on top of the burnt offering that is lying on the burning wood; it is a food offering, an aroma pleasing to the LORD.

⁶ " 'If you offer an animal from the flock as a fellowship offering to the LORD, you are to offer a male or female without defect. ⁷If you offer a lamb, you are to present it before the LORD, ⁸lay your hand on its head and slaughter it in front of the tent of meeting. Then Aaron's sons shall splash its blood against the sides of the altar. ⁹From the fellowship offering you are to bring a food offering to the LORD: its fat, the entire fat tail cut off close to the backbone, the internal organs and all the fat that is connected to them, ¹⁰both kid-

neys with the fat on them near the loins, and the long lobe of the liver, which you will remove with the kidneys. ¹¹The priest shall burn them on the altar as a food offering presented to the LORD.

¹² " 'If your offering is a goat, you are to present it before the LORD, ¹³lay your hand on its head and slaughter it in front of the tent of meeting. Then Aaron's sons shall splash its blood against the sides of the altar. ¹⁴From what you offer you are to present this food offering to the LORD: the internal organs and all the fat that is connected to them, ¹⁵both kidneys with the fat on them near the loins, and the long lobe of the liver, which you will remove with the kidneys. ¹⁶The priest shall burn them on the altar as a food offering, a pleasing aroma. All the fat is the LORD's.

¹⁷ " 'This is a lasting ordinance for the generations to come, wherever you live: You must not eat any fat or any blood.' "

The Sin Offering

4 The LORD said to Moses, ²"Say to the Israelites: 'When anyone sins unintentionally and does what is forbidden in any of the LORD's commands—

³ " 'If the anointed priest sins, bringing guilt on the people, he must bring to the LORD a young bull without defect as a sin offering[a] for the sin he has committed. ⁴He is to present the bull at the entrance to the tent of meeting before the LORD. He is to lay his hand on its head and slaughter it before the LORD. ⁵Then the anointed priest shall take some of the bull's blood and carry it into the tent of meeting. ⁶He is to dip his finger into the blood and sprinkle some of it seven times before the LORD, in front of the curtain of the sanctuary. ⁷The priest shall then put some of the blood on the horns of the altar of fragrant incense that is before the LORD in the tent of meeting. The rest of the bull's blood he shall pour out at the base of the altar of burnt offering at the entrance to the tent of meeting. ⁸He shall remove all the fat from the bull of the sin offering—all the fat that is connected to the internal organs, ⁹both kidneys with the

---

ª 3 Or *purification offering*; here and throughout this chapter

fat on them near the loins, and the long lobe of the liver, which he will remove with the kidneys— [10]just as the fat is removed from the ox[a] sacrificed as a fellowship offering. Then the priest shall burn them on the altar of burnt offering. [11]But the hide of the bull and all its flesh, as well as the head and legs, the internal organs and the intestines— [12]that is, all the rest of the bull—he must take outside the camp to a place ceremonially clean, where the ashes are thrown, and burn it there in a wood fire on the ash heap.

[13] " 'If the whole Israelite community sins unintentionally and does what is forbidden in any of the LORD's commands, even though the community is unaware of the matter, when they realize their guilt [14]and the sin they committed becomes known, the assembly must bring a young bull as a sin offering and present it before the tent of meeting. [15]The elders of the community are to lay their hands on the bull's head before the LORD, and the bull shall be slaughtered before the LORD. [16]Then the anointed priest is to take some of the bull's blood into the tent of meeting. [17]He shall dip his finger into the blood and sprinkle it before the LORD seven times in front of the curtain. [18]He is to put some of the blood on the horns of the altar that is before the LORD in the tent of meeting. The rest of the blood he shall pour out at the base of the altar of burnt offering at the entrance to the tent of meeting. [19]He shall remove all the fat from it and burn it on the altar, [20]and do with this bull just as he did with the bull for the sin offering. In this way the priest will make atonement for the community, and they will be forgiven. [21]Then he shall take the bull outside the camp and burn it as he burned the first bull. This is the sin offering for the community.

[22] " 'When a leader sins unintentionally and does what is forbidden in any of the commands of the LORD his God, when he realizes his guilt [23]and the sin he has committed becomes known, he must bring as his offering a male goat without defect. [24]He is to lay his hand on the goat's head and slaughter it at the place where the burnt offering is slaughtered before the LORD. It is a sin offering. [25]Then the priest shall take some of the blood of the sin offering with his finger and put it on the horns of the altar of burnt offering and pour out the rest of the blood at the base of the altar. [26]He shall burn all the fat on the altar as he burned the fat of the fellowship offering. In this way the priest will make atonement for the leader's sin, and he will be forgiven.

[27] " 'If any member of the community sins unintentionally and does what is forbidden in any of the LORD's commands, when they realize their guilt [28]and the sin they have committed becomes known, they must bring as their offering for the sin they committed a female goat without defect. [29]They are to lay their hand on the head of the sin offering and slaughter it at the place of the burnt offering. [30]Then the priest is to take some of the blood with his finger and put it on the horns of the altar of burnt offering and pour out the rest of the blood at the base of the altar. [31]They shall remove all the fat, just as the fat is removed from the fellowship offering, and the priest shall burn it on the altar as an aroma pleasing to the LORD. In this way the priest will make atonement for them, and they will be forgiven.

[32] " 'If someone brings a lamb as their sin offering, they are to bring a female without defect. [33]They are to lay their hand on its head and slaughter it for a sin offering at the place where the burnt offering is slaughtered. [34]Then the priest shall take some of the blood of the sin offering with his finger and put it on the horns of the altar of burnt offering and pour out the rest of the blood at the base of the altar. [35]They shall remove all the fat, just as the fat is removed from the lamb of the fellowship offering, and the priest shall burn it on the altar on top of the food offerings presented to the LORD. In this way the priest will make atonement for them for the sin they have committed, and they will be forgiven.

---

[a] 10 The Hebrew word can refer to either male or female.

5 " 'If anyone sins because they do not speak up when they hear a public charge to testify regarding something they have seen or learned about, they will be held responsible.

2 " 'If anyone becomes aware that they are guilty—if they unwittingly touch anything ceremonially unclean (whether the carcass of an unclean animal, wild or domestic, or of any unclean creature that moves along the ground) and they are unaware that they have become unclean, but then they come to realize their guilt; 3or if they touch human uncleanness (anything that would make them unclean) even though they are unaware of it, but then they learn of it and realize their guilt; 4or if anyone thoughtlessly takes an oath to do anything, whether good or evil (in any matter one might carelessly swear about) even though they are unaware of it, but then they learn of it and realize their guilt— 5when anyone becomes aware that they are guilty in any of these matters, they must confess in what way they have sinned. 6As a penalty for the sin they have committed, they must bring to the Lord a female lamb or goat from the flock as a sin offering^a; and the priest shall make atonement for them for their sin.

7 " 'Anyone who cannot afford a lamb is to bring two doves or two young pigeons to the Lord as a penalty for their sin—one for a sin offering and the other for a burnt offering. 8They are to bring them to the priest, who shall first offer the one for the sin offering. He is to wring its head from its neck, not dividing it completely, 9and is to splash some of the blood of the sin offering against the side of the altar; the rest of the blood must be drained out at the base of the altar. It is a sin offering. 10The priest shall then offer the other as a burnt offering in the prescribed way and make atonement for them for the sin they have committed, and they will be forgiven.

11 " 'If, however, they cannot afford two doves or two young pigeons, they are to bring as an offering for their sin a tenth of an ephah^b of the finest flour for a sin offering. They must not put olive oil or incense on it, because it is a sin offering. 12They are to bring it to the priest, who shall take a handful of it as a memorial^c portion and burn it on the altar on top of the food offerings presented to the Lord. It is a sin offering. 13In this way the priest will make atonement for them for any of these sins they have committed, and they will be forgiven. The rest of the offering will belong to the priest, as in the case of the grain offering.' "

The Guilt Offering

14The Lord said to Moses: 15"When anyone is unfaithful to the Lord by sinning unintentionally in regard to any of the Lord's holy things, they are to bring to the Lord as a penalty a ram from the flock, one without defect and of the proper value in silver, according to the sanctuary shekel.^d It is a guilt offering. 16They must make restitution for what they have failed to do in regard to the holy things, pay an additional penalty of a fifth of its value and give it all to the priest. The priest will make atonement for them with the ram as a guilt offering, and they will be forgiven.

17"If anyone sins and does what is forbidden in any of the Lord's commands, even though they do not know it, they are guilty and will be held responsible. 18They are to bring to the priest as a guilt offering a ram from the flock, one without defect and of the proper value. In this way the priest will make atonement for them for the wrong they have committed unintentionally, and they will be forgiven. 19It is a guilt offering; they have been guilty of^e wrongdoing against the Lord."

6^f The Lord said to Moses: 2"If anyone sins and is unfaithful to the Lord by deceiving a neighbor about something entrusted to them or left in their care or about something stolen, or if they cheat their neighbor, 3or if they find lost property and lie about it, or if they swear falsely about any such sin that people may

---

^a 6 Or purification offering; here and throughout this chapter   ^b 11 That is, probably about 3 1/2 pounds or about 1.6 kilograms   ^c 12 Or representative   ^d 15 That is, about 2/5 ounce or about 12 grams   ^e 19 Or offering; atonement has been made for their   ^f In Hebrew texts 6:1-7 is numbered 5:20-26, and 6:8-30 is numbered 6:1-23.

> I saw a girl take some makeup from another girl's backpack. I was so surprised I didn't know what to do. Was it wrong of me not to try to stop her? I feel bad.
>
> **>> Madison**

Dear Jordan

Dear Madison,

When something is stolen or damaged or someone is hurt, we need to find a way to tell someone.

God puts responsibility on us in these situations. Leviticus 5:1 tells us not only do we need to obey the law, but we also need to help others be responsible.

You said you were taken by surprise, but afterwards maybe you could have found someone to tell. If you think your classmates will give you a hard time for doing what's right, try to find a counselor or a teacher you can trust with the information. If someone stole something from me, I would appreciate a witness coming forward. I'm guessing you would too.

Jordan

commit— ⁴when they sin in any of these ways and realize their guilt, they must return what they have stolen or taken by extortion, or what was entrusted to them, or the lost property they found, ⁵or whatever it was they swore falsely about. They must make restitution in full, add a fifth of the value to it and give it all to the owner on the day they present their guilt offering. ⁶And as a penalty they must bring to the priest, that is, to the Lord, their guilt offering, a ram from the flock, one without defect and of the proper value. ⁷In this way the priest will make atonement for them before the Lord, and they will be forgiven for any of the things they did that made them guilty."

The Burnt Offering

⁸The Lord said to Moses: ⁹"Give Aaron and his sons this command: 'These are the regulations for the burnt offering: The burnt offering is to remain on the altar hearth throughout the night, till morning, and the fire must be kept burning on the altar. ¹⁰The priest shall then put on his linen clothes, with linen undergarments next to his body, and shall remove the ashes of the burnt offering that the fire has consumed on the altar and place them beside the altar. ¹¹Then he is to take off these clothes and put on others, and carry the ashes outside the camp to a place that is ceremonially clean. ¹²The fire on the altar must be kept burning; it must not go out. Every morning the priest is to add firewood and arrange the burnt offering on the fire and burn the fat of the fellowship offerings on it. ¹³The fire must be kept burning on the altar continuously; it must not go out.

The Grain Offering

¹⁴"'These are the regulations for the grain offering: Aaron's sons are to bring it before the Lord, in front of the altar. ¹⁵The priest is to take a handful of the finest flour and some olive oil, together with all the incense on the grain offering, and burn the memorialᵃ portion on the

altar as an aroma pleasing to the Lord. ¹⁶Aaron and his sons shall eat the rest of it, but it is to be eaten without yeast in the sanctuary area; they are to eat it in the courtyard of the tent of meeting. ¹⁷It must not be baked with yeast; I have given it as their share of the food offerings presented to me. Like the sin offeringᵇ and the guilt offering, it is most holy. ¹⁸Any male descendant of Aaron may eat it. For all generations to come it is his perpetual share of the food offerings presented to the Lord. Whatever touches them will become holy.ᶜ'"

¹⁹The Lord also said to Moses, ²⁰"This is the offering Aaron and his sons are to bring to the Lord on the day heᵈ is anointed: a tenth of an ephahᵉ of the finest flour as a regular grain offering, half of it in the morning and half in the evening. ²¹It must be prepared with oil on a griddle; bring it well-mixed and present the grain offering brokenᶠ in pieces as an aroma pleasing to the Lord. ²²The son who is to succeed him as anointed priest shall prepare it. It is the Lord's perpetual share and is to be burned completely. ²³Every grain offering of a priest shall be burned completely; it must not be eaten."

The Sin Offering

²⁴The Lord said to Moses, ²⁵"Say to Aaron and his sons: 'These are the regulations for the sin offering: The sin offering is to be slaughtered before the Lord in the place the burnt offering is slaughtered; it is most holy. ²⁶The priest who offers it shall eat it; it is to be eaten in the sanctuary area, in the courtyard of the tent of meeting. ²⁷Whatever touches any of the flesh will become holy, and if any of the blood is spattered on a garment, you must wash it in the sanctuary area. ²⁸The clay pot the meat is cooked in must be broken; but if it is cooked in a bronze pot, the pot is to be scoured and rinsed with water. ²⁹Any male in a priest's family may eat it; it is most holy. ³⁰But any sin offering whose blood is brought into the tent of meeting to make atonement in the

---

ᵃ 15 Or representative   ᵇ 17 Or purification offering; also in verses 25 and 30   ᶜ 18 Or Whoever touches them must be holy; similarly in verse 27   ᵈ 20 Or each   ᵉ 20 That is, probably about 3 1/2 pounds or about 1.6 kilograms   ᶠ 21 The meaning of the Hebrew for this word is uncertain.

Holy Place must not be eaten; it must be burned up.

The Guilt Offering

7 " 'These are the regulations for the guilt offering, which is most holy: ²The guilt offering is to be slaughtered in the place where the burnt offering is slaughtered, and its blood is to be splashed against the sides of the altar. ³All its fat shall be offered: the fat tail and the fat that covers the internal organs, ⁴both kidneys with the fat on them near the loins, and the long lobe of the liver, which is to be removed with the kidneys. ⁵The priest shall burn them on the altar as a food offering presented to the LORD. It is a guilt offering. ⁶Any male in a priest's family may eat it, but it must be eaten in the sanctuary area; it is most holy.

⁷ " 'The same law applies to both the sin offering[a] and the guilt offering: They belong to the priest who makes atonement with them. ⁸The priest who offers a burnt offering for anyone may keep its hide for himself. ⁹Every grain offering baked in an oven or cooked in a pan or on a griddle belongs to the priest who offers it, ¹⁰and every grain offering, whether mixed with olive oil or dry, belongs equally to all the sons of Aaron.

The Fellowship Offering

¹¹ " 'These are the regulations for the fellowship offering anyone may present to the LORD:

¹² " 'If they offer it as an expression of thankfulness, then along with this thank offering they are to offer thick loaves made without yeast and with olive oil mixed in, thin loaves made without yeast and brushed with oil, and thick loaves of the finest flour well-kneaded and with oil mixed in. ¹³Along with their fellowship offering of thanksgiving they are to present an offering with thick loaves of bread made with yeast. ¹⁴They are to bring one of each kind as an offering, a contribution to the LORD; it belongs to the priest who splashes the blood of the fellowship offering against the altar. ¹⁵The meat of their fellowship offering of thanksgiving must be eaten on the day it is offered; they must leave none of it till morning.

¹⁶ " 'If, however, their offering is the result of a vow or is a freewill offering, the sacrifice shall be eaten on the day they offer it, but anything left over may be eaten on the next day. ¹⁷Any meat of the sacrifice left over till the third day must be burned up. ¹⁸If any meat of the fellowship offering is eaten on the third day, the one who offered it will not be accepted. It will not be reckoned to their credit, for it has become impure; the person who eats any of it will be held responsible.

¹⁹ " 'Meat that touches anything ceremonially unclean must not be eaten; it must be burned up. As for other meat, anyone ceremonially clean may eat it. ²⁰But if anyone who is unclean eats any meat of the fellowship offering belonging to the LORD, they must be cut off from their people. ²¹Anyone who touches something unclean—whether human uncleanness or an unclean animal or any unclean creature that moves along the ground[b]—and then eats any of the meat of the fellowship offering belonging to the LORD must be cut off from their people.' "

Eating Fat and Blood Forbidden

²²The LORD said to Moses, ²³ "Say to the Israelites: 'Do not eat any of the fat of cattle, sheep or goats. ²⁴The fat of an animal found dead or torn by wild animals may be used for any other purpose, but you must not eat it. ²⁵Anyone who eats the fat of an animal from which a food offering may be[c] presented to the LORD must be cut off from their people. ²⁶And wherever you live, you must not eat the blood of any bird or animal. ²⁷Anyone who eats blood must be cut off from their people.' "

The Priests' Share

²⁸The LORD said to Moses, ²⁹ "Say to the Israelites: 'Anyone who brings a fellowship offering to the LORD is to bring

---

a 7 Or *purification offering*; also in verse 37   *b* 21 A few Hebrew manuscripts, Samaritan Pentateuch, Syriac and Targum (see 5:2); most Hebrew manuscripts *any unclean, detestable thing*   *c* 25 Or *offering is*

part of it as their sacrifice to the Lord. 30With their own hands they are to present the food offering to the Lord; they are to bring the fat, together with the breast, and wave the breast before the Lord as a wave offering. 31The priest shall burn the fat on the altar, but the breast belongs to Aaron and his sons. 32You are to give the right thigh of your fellowship offerings to the priest as a contribution. 33The son of Aaron who offers the blood and the fat of the fellowship offering shall have the right thigh as his share. 34From the fellowship offerings of the Israelites, I have taken the breast that is waved and the thigh that is presented and have given them to Aaron the priest and his sons as their perpetual share from the Israelites.' "

35This is the portion of the food offerings presented to the Lord that were allotted to Aaron and his sons on the day they were presented to serve the Lord as priests. 36On the day they were anointed, the Lord commanded that the Israelites give this to them as their perpetual share for the generations to come.

37These, then, are the regulations for the burnt offering, the grain offering, the sin offering, the guilt offering, the ordination offering and the fellowship offering, 38which the Lord gave Moses at Mount Sinai in the Desert of Sinai on the day he commanded the Israelites to bring their offerings to the Lord.

The Ordination of Aaron and His Sons

8 The Lord said to Moses, 2"Bring Aaron and his sons, their garments, the anointing oil, the bull for the sin offering,[a] the two rams and the basket containing bread made without yeast, 3and gather the entire assembly at the entrance to the tent of meeting." 4Moses did as the Lord commanded him, and the assembly gathered at the entrance to the tent of meeting.

5Moses said to the assembly, "This is what the Lord has commanded to be done." 6Then Moses brought Aaron and his sons forward and washed them with water. 7He put the tunic on Aaron, tied the sash around him, clothed him with the robe and put the ephod on him. He also fastened the ephod with a decorative waistband, which he tied around him. 8He placed the breastpiece on him and put the Urim and Thummim in the breastpiece. 9Then he placed the turban on Aaron's head and set the gold plate, the sacred emblem, on the front of it, as the Lord commanded Moses.

10Then Moses took the anointing oil and anointed the tabernacle and everything in it, and so consecrated them. 11He sprinkled some of the oil on the altar seven times, anointing the altar and all its utensils and the basin with its stand, to consecrate them. 12He poured some of the anointing oil on Aaron's head and anointed him to consecrate him. 13Then he brought Aaron's sons forward, put tunics on them, tied sashes around them and fastened caps on them, as the Lord commanded Moses.

14He then presented the bull for the sin offering, and Aaron and his sons laid their hands on its head. 15Moses slaughtered the bull and took some of the blood, and with his finger he put it on all the horns of the altar to purify the altar. He poured out the rest of the blood at the base of the altar. So he consecrated it to make atonement for it. 16Moses also took all the fat around the internal organs, the long lobe of the liver, and both kidneys and their fat, and burned it on the altar. 17But the bull with its hide and its flesh and its intestines he burned up outside the camp, as the Lord commanded Moses.

18He then presented the ram for the burnt offering, and Aaron and his sons laid their hands on its head. 19Then Moses slaughtered the ram and splashed the blood against the sides of the altar. 20He cut the ram into pieces and burned the head, the pieces and the fat. 21He washed the internal organs and the legs with water and burned the whole ram on the altar. It was a burnt offering, a pleas-

---

a 2 Or *purification offering*; also in verse 14

ing aroma, a food offering presented to the Lord, as the Lord commanded Moses.

²²He then presented the other ram, the ram for the ordination, and Aaron and his sons laid their hands on its head. ²³Moses slaughtered the ram and took some of its blood and put it on the lobe of Aaron's right ear, on the thumb of his right hand and on the big toe of his right foot. ²⁴Moses also brought Aaron's sons forward and put some of the blood on the lobes of their right ears, on the thumbs of their right hands and on the big toes of their right feet. Then he splashed blood against the sides of the altar. ²⁵After that, he took the fat, the fat tail, all the fat around the internal organs, the long lobe of the liver, both kidneys and their fat and the right thigh. ²⁶And from the basket of bread made without yeast, which was before the Lord, he took one thick loaf, one thick loaf with olive oil mixed in, and one thin loaf, and he put these on the fat portions and on the right thigh. ²⁷He put all these in the hands of Aaron and his sons, and they waved them before the Lord as a wave offering. ²⁸Then Moses took them from their hands and burned them on the altar on top of the burnt offering as an ordination offering, a pleasing aroma, a food offering presented to the Lord. ²⁹Moses also took the breast, which was his share of the ordination ram, and waved it before the Lord as a wave offering, as the Lord commanded Moses.

³⁰Then Moses took some of the anointing oil and some of the blood from the altar and sprinkled them on Aaron and his garments and on his sons and their garments. So he consecrated Aaron and his garments and his sons and their garments.

³¹Moses then said to Aaron and his sons, "Cook the meat at the entrance to the tent of meeting and eat it there with the bread from the basket of ordination offerings, as I was commanded: 'Aaron and his sons are to eat it.' ³²Then burn up the rest of the meat and the bread. ³³Do not leave the entrance to the tent of meeting for seven days, until the days of your ordination are completed, for your ordina-

tion will last seven days. ³⁴What has been done today was commanded by the Lord to make atonement for you. ³⁵You must stay at the entrance to the tent of meeting day and night for seven days and do what the Lord requires, so you will not die; for that is what I have been commanded."

³⁶So Aaron and his sons did everything the Lord commanded through Moses.

The Priests Begin Their Ministry

9 On the eighth day Moses summoned Aaron and his sons and the elders of Israel. ²He said to Aaron, "Take a bull calf for your sin offeringᵃ and a ram for your burnt offering, both without defect, and present them before the Lord. ³Then say to the Israelites: 'Take a male goat for a sin offering, a calf and a lamb—both a year old and without defect—for a burnt offering, ⁴and an oxᵇ and a ram for a fellowship offering to sacrifice before the Lord, together with a grain offering mixed with olive oil. For today the Lord will appear to you.'"

⁵They took the things Moses commanded to the front of the tent of meeting, and the entire assembly came near and stood before the Lord. ⁶Then Moses said, "This is what the Lord has commanded you to do, so that the glory of the Lord may appear to you."

⁷Moses said to Aaron, "Come to the altar and sacrifice your sin offering and your burnt offering and make atonement for yourself and the people; sacrifice the offering that is for the people and make atonement for them, as the Lord has commanded."

⁸So Aaron came to the altar and slaughtered the calf as a sin offering for himself. ⁹His sons brought the blood to him, and he dipped his finger into the blood and put it on the horns of the altar; the rest of the blood he poured out at the base of the altar. ¹⁰On the altar he burned the fat, the kidneys and the long lobe of the liver from the sin offering, as the Lord commanded Moses; ¹¹the flesh and the hide he burned up outside the camp.

ᵃ 2 Or *purification offering*; here and throughout this chapter also in verses 18 and 19.   ᵇ 4 The Hebrew word can refer to either male or female;

¹²Then he slaughtered the burnt offering. His sons handed him the blood, and he splashed it against the sides of the altar. ¹³They handed him the burnt offering piece by piece, including the head, and he burned them on the altar. ¹⁴He washed the internal organs and the legs and burned them on top of the burnt offering on the altar.

¹⁵Aaron then brought the offering that was for the people. He took the goat for the people's sin offering and slaughtered it and offered it for a sin offering as he did with the first one.

¹⁶He brought the burnt offering and offered it in the prescribed way. ¹⁷He also brought the grain offering, took a handful of it and burned it on the altar in addition to the morning's burnt offering.

¹⁸He slaughtered the ox and the ram as the fellowship offering for the people. His sons handed him the blood, and he splashed it against the sides of the altar. ¹⁹But the fat portions of the ox and the ram—the fat tail, the layer of fat, the kidneys and the long lobe of the liver— ²⁰these they laid on the breasts, and then Aaron burned the fat on the altar. ²¹Aaron waved the breasts and the right thigh before the Lord as a wave offering, as Moses commanded.

²²Then Aaron lifted his hands toward the people and blessed them. And having sacrificed the sin offering, the burnt offering and the fellowship offering, he stepped down.

²³Moses and Aaron then went into the tent of meeting. When they came out, they blessed the people; and the glory of the Lord appeared to all the people. ²⁴Fire came out from the presence of the Lord and consumed the burnt offering and the fat portions on the altar. And when all the people saw it, they shouted for joy and fell facedown.

The Death of Nadab and Abihu

10 Aaron's sons Nadab and Abihu took their censers, put fire in them and added incense; and they offered unauthorized fire before the Lord, contrary to his command. ²So fire came out from the presence of the Lord and consumed

» INSTANT ACCESS

Do you ever wonder about some of the shocking stories in the Bible? This is one. Aaron's sons violated God's command about offerings and were destroyed by fire. Why such a terrible penalty? Because these men were priests, responsible to teach God's decrees to others. How unthinkable that these men should show contempt for God by ignoring his commands. The greater the privileges given to you, the more responsibility you have. Christians have the wonderful privilege of knowing God personally, of drawing on God for strength, of coming to God in prayer. Let Nadab and Abihu remind you of your responsibilities because of those great privileges.

{Leviticus 10:1–11}

them, and they died before the Lord. ³Moses then said to Aaron, "This is what the Lord spoke of when he said:

"'Among those who approach me
    I will be proved holy;
in the sight of all the people
    I will be honored.'"

Aaron remained silent.

⁴Moses summoned Mishael and Elzaphan, sons of Aaron's uncle Uzziel, and said to them, "Come here; carry your cousins outside the camp, away from the

front of the sanctuary." ⁵So they came and carried them, still in their tunics, outside the camp, as Moses ordered.

⁶Then Moses said to Aaron and his sons Eleazar and Ithamar, "Do not let your hair become unkempt^a and do not tear your clothes, or you will die and the LORD will be angry with the whole community. But your relatives, all the Israelites, may mourn for those the LORD has destroyed by fire. ⁷Do not leave the entrance to the tent of meeting or you will die, because the LORD's anointing oil is on you." So they did as Moses said.

⁸Then the LORD said to Aaron, ⁹"You and your sons are not to drink wine or other fermented drink whenever you go into the tent of meeting, or you will die. This is a lasting ordinance for the generations to come, ¹⁰so that you can distinguish between the holy and the common, between the unclean and the clean, ¹¹and so you can teach the Israelites all the decrees the LORD has given them through Moses."

¹²Moses said to Aaron and his remaining sons, Eleazar and Ithamar, "Take the grain offering left over from the food offerings prepared without yeast and presented to the LORD and eat it beside the altar, for it is most holy. ¹³Eat it in the sanctuary area, because it is your share and your sons' share of the food offerings presented to the LORD; for so I have been commanded. ¹⁴But you and your sons and your daughters may eat the breast that was waved and the thigh that was presented. Eat them in a ceremonially clean place; they have been given to you and your children as your share of the Israelites' fellowship offerings. ¹⁵The thigh that was presented and the breast that was waved must be brought with the fat portions of the food offerings, to be waved before the LORD as a wave offering. This will be the perpetual share for you and your children, as the LORD has commanded."

¹⁶When Moses inquired about the goat of the sin offering^b and found that it had been burned up, he was angry with Eleazar and Ithamar, Aaron's remaining sons, and asked, ¹⁷"Why didn't you eat the sin offering in the sanctuary area? It is most holy; it was given to you to take away the guilt of the community by making atonement for them before the LORD. ¹⁸Since its blood was not taken into the Holy Place, you should have eaten the goat in the sanctuary area, as I commanded."

¹⁹Aaron replied to Moses, "Today they sacrificed their sin offering and their burnt offering before the LORD, but such things as this have happened to me. Would the LORD have been pleased if I had eaten the sin offering today?" ²⁰When Moses heard this, he was satisfied.

Clean and Unclean Food

11 The LORD said to Moses and Aaron, ²"Say to the Israelites: 'Of all the animals that live on land, these are the ones you may eat: ³You may eat any animal that has a divided hoof and that chews the cud.

⁴"'There are some that only chew the cud or only have a divided hoof, but you must not eat them. The camel, though it chews the cud, does not have a divided hoof; it is ceremonially unclean for you. ⁵The hyrax, though it chews the cud, does

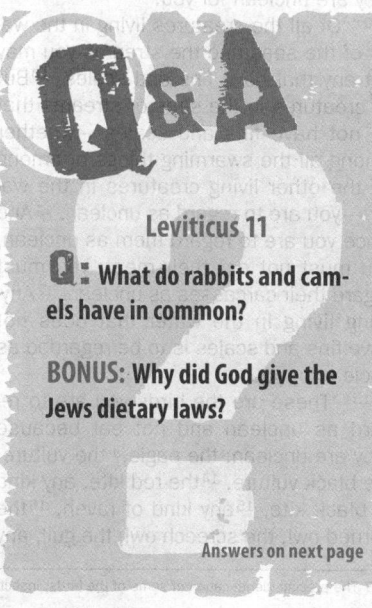

Leviticus 11

Q: What do rabbits and camels have in common?

BONUS: Why did God give the Jews dietary laws?

Answers on next page

---

^a 6 Or *Do not uncover your heads*   ^b 16 Or *purification offering; also in verses 17 and 19*

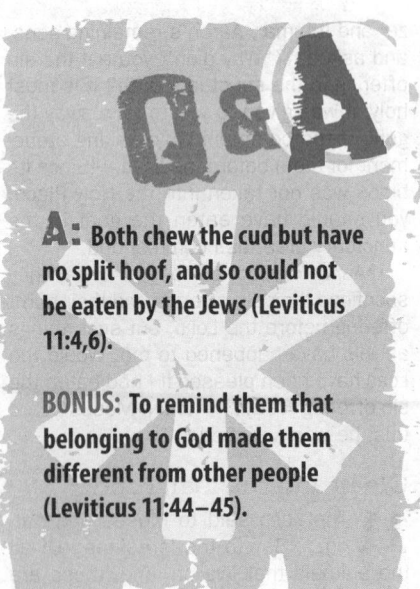

A: Both chew the cud but have no split hoof, and so could not be eaten by the Jews (Leviticus 11:4,6).

BONUS: To remind them that belonging to God made them different from other people (Leviticus 11:44–45).

not have a divided hoof; it is unclean for you. 6 The rabbit, though it chews the cud, does not have a divided hoof; it is unclean for you. 7 And the pig, though it has a divided hoof, does not chew the cud; it is unclean for you. 8 You must not eat their meat or touch their carcasses; they are unclean for you.

9 " 'Of all the creatures living in the water of the seas and the streams you may eat any that have fins and scales. 10 But all creatures in the seas or streams that do not have fins and scales — whether among all the swarming things or among all the other living creatures in the water — you are to regard as unclean. 11 And since you are to regard them as unclean, you must not eat their meat; you must regard their carcasses as unclean. 12 Anything living in the water that does not have fins and scales is to be regarded as unclean by you.

13 " 'These are the birds you are to regard as unclean and not eat because they are unclean: the eagle,[a] the vulture, the black vulture, 14 the red kite, any kind of black kite, 15 any kind of raven, 16 the horned owl, the screech owl, the gull, any kind of hawk, 17 the little owl, the cormorant, the great owl, 18 the white owl, the desert owl, the osprey, 19 the stork, any kind of heron, the hoopoe and the bat.

20 " 'All flying insects that walk on all fours are to be regarded as unclean by you. 21 There are, however, some flying insects that walk on all fours that you may eat: those that have jointed legs for hopping on the ground. 22 Of these you may eat any kind of locust, katydid, cricket or grasshopper. 23 But all other flying insects that have four legs you are to regard as unclean.

24 " 'You will make yourselves unclean by these; whoever touches their carcasses will be unclean till evening. 25 Whoever picks up one of their carcasses must wash their clothes, and they will be unclean till evening.

26 " 'Every animal that does not have a divided hoof or that does not chew the cud is unclean for you; whoever touches the carcass of any of them will be unclean. 27 Of all the animals that walk on all fours, those that walk on their paws are unclean for you; whoever touches their carcasses will be unclean till evening. 28 Anyone who picks up their carcasses must wash their clothes, and they will be unclean till evening. These animals are unclean for you.

29 " 'Of the animals that move along the ground, these are unclean for you: the weasel, the rat, any kind of great lizard, 30 the gecko, the monitor lizard, the wall lizard, the skink and the chameleon. 31 Of all those that move along the ground, these are unclean for you. Whoever touches them when they are dead will be unclean till evening. 32 When one of them dies and falls on something, that article, whatever its use, will be unclean, whether it is made of wood, cloth, hide or sackcloth. Put it in water; it will be unclean till evening, and then it will be clean. 33 If one of them falls into a clay pot, everything in it will be unclean, and you must break the pot. 34 Any food you are allowed to eat that has come into contact with water from any such pot is unclean, and any liquid that is drunk from

---

a 13 The precise identification of some of the birds, insects and animals in this chapter is uncertain.

Does the Bible say anything about complaining? My parents say I do too much of it. How can I make my feelings known?

>> Mia

Dear Jordan

Dear Mia,

There is a passage about complaining found in Philippians 2:14: "Do everything without grumbling or arguing, so that you may become blameless and pure …"

Some people seem to complain about almost everything. That's what happened when Moses was leading the Israelites to the promised land. Even though God provided them with food in the desert, they complained they were sick of it. Moses grew tired of the complaints.

Some parents feel the same way when their children complain constantly. So listen to yourself. If you have a legitimate complaint, make it. But if you find yourself complaining all the time, try to have a more positive attitude. People will listen and respond much better to someone who doesn't complain a lot. And everyone around you will feel better too.

Jordan

such a pot is unclean. 35 Anything that one of their carcasses falls on becomes unclean; an oven or cooking pot must be broken up. They are unclean, and you are to regard them as unclean. 36 A spring, however, or a cistern for collecting water remains clean, but anyone who touches one of these carcasses is unclean. 37 If a carcass falls on any seeds that are to be planted, they remain clean. 38 But if water has been put on the seed and a carcass falls on it, it is unclean for you.

39 " 'If an animal that you are allowed to eat dies, anyone who touches its carcass will be unclean till evening. 40 Anyone who eats some of its carcass must wash their clothes, and they will be unclean till evening. Anyone who picks up the carcass must wash their clothes, and they will be unclean till evening.

41 " 'Every creature that moves along the ground is to be regarded as unclean; it is not to be eaten. 42 You are not to eat any creature that moves along the ground, whether it moves on its belly or walks on all fours or on many feet; it is unclean. 43 Do not defile yourselves by any of these creatures. Do not make yourselves unclean by means of them or be made unclean by them. 44 I am the Lord your God; consecrate yourselves and be holy, because I am holy. Do not make yourselves unclean by any creature that moves along the ground. 45 I am the Lord, who brought you up out of Egypt to be your God; therefore be holy, because I am holy.

46 " 'These are the regulations concerning animals, birds, every living thing that moves about in the water and every creature that moves along the ground. 47 You must distinguish between the unclean and the clean, between living creatures that may be eaten and those that may not be eaten.' "

Purification After Childbirth

12 The Lord said to Moses, 2 "Say to the Israelites: 'A woman who becomes pregnant and gives birth to a son will be ceremonially unclean for seven days, just as she is unclean during her monthly period. 3 On the eighth day the boy is to be circumcised. 4 Then the woman must wait thirty-three days to be purified from her bleeding. She must not touch anything sacred or go to the sanctuary until the days of her purification are over. 5 If she gives birth to a daughter, for two weeks the woman will be unclean, as during her period. Then she must wait sixty-six days to be purified from her bleeding.

6 " 'When the days of her purification for a son or daughter are over, she is to bring to the priest at the entrance to the tent of meeting a year-old lamb for a burnt offering and a young pigeon or a dove for a sin offering.[a] 7 He shall offer them before the Lord to make atonement for her, and then she will be ceremonially clean from her flow of blood.

" 'These are the regulations for the woman who gives birth to a boy or a girl. 8 But if she cannot afford a lamb, she is to bring two doves or two young pigeons, one for a burnt offering and the other for a sin offering. In this way the priest will make atonement for her, and she will be clean.' "

Regulations About Defiling Skin Diseases

13 The Lord said to Moses and Aaron, 2 "When anyone has a swelling or a rash or a shiny spot on their skin that may be a defiling skin disease,[b] they must be brought to Aaron the priest or to one of his sons[c] who is a priest. 3 The priest is to examine the sore on the skin, and if the hair in the sore has turned white and the sore appears to be more than skin deep, it is a defiling skin disease. When the priest examines that person, he shall pronounce them ceremonially unclean. 4 If the shiny spot on the skin is white but does not appear to be more than skin deep and the hair in it has not turned white, the priest is to isolate the affected person for seven days. 5 On the seventh

---

[a] 6 Or *purification offering*; also in verse 8   [b] 2 The Hebrew word for *defiling skin disease*, traditionally translated "leprosy," was used for various diseases affecting the skin; here and throughout verses 3-46.   [c] 2 Or *descendants*

Do you ever feel kind of funny about putting a quarter in the church offering? Do you think maybe you should wait to give until you have a job and can give more? If you've thought that way, Leviticus 12:8 shares a good insight. In Old Testament times a mother brought a special offering to God right after the birth of a child. The best offering was a lamb, but if the family was poor, she could bring "two doves or two young pigeons," a very inexpensive offering. What counted was not how much the mother gave but the fact that she did give. How much you give is not most important. Giving even a little is a way of saying thank you to God.

{Leviticus 12:8}

» INSTANT ACCESS

again. ⁸The priest is to examine that person, and if the rash has spread in the skin, he shall pronounce them unclean; it is a defiling skin disease.

⁹"When anyone has a defiling skin disease, they must be brought to the priest. ¹⁰The priest is to examine them, and if there is a white swelling in the skin that has turned the hair white and if there is raw flesh in the swelling, ¹¹it is a chronic skin disease and the priest shall pronounce them unclean. He is not to isolate them, because they are already unclean.

¹²"If the disease breaks out all over their skin and, so far as the priest can see, it covers all the skin of the affected person from head to foot, ¹³the priest is to examine them, and if the disease has covered their whole body, he shall pronounce them clean. Since it has all turned white, they are clean. ¹⁴But whenever raw flesh appears on them, they will be unclean. ¹⁵When the priest sees the raw flesh, he shall pronounce them unclean. The raw flesh is unclean; they have a defiling disease. ¹⁶If the raw flesh changes and turns white, they must go to the priest. ¹⁷The priest is to examine them, and if the sores have turned white, the priest shall pronounce the affected person clean; then they will be clean.

¹⁸"When someone has a boil on their skin and it heals, ¹⁹and in the place where the boil was, a white swelling or reddish-white spot appears, they must present themselves to the priest. ²⁰The priest is to examine it, and if it appears to be more than skin deep and the hair in it has turned white, the priest shall pronounce that person unclean. It is a defiling skin disease that has broken out where the boil was. ²¹But if, when the priest examines it, there is no white hair in it and it is not more than skin deep and has faded, then the priest is to isolate them for seven days. ²²If it is spreading in the skin, the priest shall pronounce them unclean; it is a defiling disease. ²³But if the spot is unchanged and has not spread, it is only a scar from the boil, and the priest shall pronounce them clean.

²⁴"When someone has a burn on their

day the priest is to examine them, and if he sees that the sore is unchanged and has not spread in the skin, he is to isolate them for another seven days. ⁶On the seventh day the priest is to examine them again, and if the sore has faded and has not spread in the skin, the priest shall pronounce them clean; it is only a rash. They must wash their clothes, and they will be clean. ⁷But if the rash does spread in their skin after they have shown themselves to the priest to be pronounced clean, they must appear before the priest

skin and a reddish-white or white spot appears in the raw flesh of the burn, ²⁵the priest is to examine the spot, and if the hair in it has turned white, and it appears to be more than skin deep, it is a defiling disease that has broken out in the burn. The priest shall pronounce them unclean; it is a defiling skin disease. ²⁶But if the priest examines it and there is no white hair in the spot and if it is not more than skin deep and has faded, then the priest is to isolate them for seven days. ²⁷On the seventh day the priest is to examine that person, and if it is spreading in the skin, the priest shall pronounce them unclean; it is a defiling skin disease. ²⁸If, however, the spot is unchanged and has not spread in the skin but has faded, it is a swelling from the burn, and the priest shall pronounce them clean; it is only a scar from the burn.

²⁹"If a man or woman has a sore on their head or chin, ³⁰the priest is to examine the sore, and if it appears to be more than skin deep and the hair in it is yellow and thin, the priest shall pronounce them unclean; it is a defiling skin disease on the head or chin. ³¹But if, when the priest examines the sore, it does not seem to be more than skin deep and there is no black hair in it, then the priest is to isolate the affected person for seven days. ³²On the seventh day the priest is to examine the sore, and if it has not spread and there is no yellow hair in it and it does not appear to be more than skin deep, ³³then the man or woman must shave themselves, except for the affected area, and the priest is to keep them isolated another seven days. ³⁴On the seventh day the priest is to examine the sore, and if it has not spread in the skin and appears to be no more than skin deep, the priest shall pronounce them clean. They must wash their clothes, and they will be clean. ³⁵But if the sore does spread in the skin after they are pronounced clean, ³⁶the priest is to examine them, and if he finds that the sore has spread in the skin, he does not need to look for yellow hair; they are unclean. ³⁷If, however, the sore is un-

changed so far as the priest can see, and if black hair has grown in it, the affected person is healed. They are clean, and the priest shall pronounce them clean.

³⁸"When a man or woman has white spots on the skin, ³⁹the priest is to examine them, and if the spots are dull white, it is a harmless rash that has broken out on the skin; they are clean.

⁴⁰"A man who has lost his hair and is bald is clean. ⁴¹If he has lost his hair from the front of his scalp and has a bald forehead, he is clean. ⁴²But if he has a reddish-white sore on his bald head or forehead, it is a defiling disease breaking out on his head or forehead. ⁴³The priest is to examine him, and if the swollen sore on his head or forehead is reddish-white like a defiling skin disease, ⁴⁴the man is diseased and is unclean. The priest shall pronounce him unclean because of the sore on his head.

⁴⁵"Anyone with such a defiling disease must wear torn clothes, let their hair be unkempt,ᵃ cover the lower part of their face and cry out, 'Unclean! Unclean!' ⁴⁶As long as they have the disease they remain unclean. They must live alone; they must live outside the camp.

Regulations About Defiling Molds

⁴⁷"As for any fabric that is spoiled with a defiling mold—any woolen or linen clothing, ⁴⁸any woven or knitted material of linen or wool, any leather or anything made of leather— ⁴⁹if the affected area in the fabric, the leather, the woven or knitted material, or any leather article, is greenish or reddish, it is a defiling mold and must be shown to the priest. ⁵⁰The priest is to examine the affected area and isolate the article for seven days. ⁵¹On the seventh day he is to examine it, and if the mold has spread in the fabric, the woven or knitted material, or the leather, whatever its use, it is a persistent defiling mold; the article is unclean. ⁵²He must burn the fabric, the woven or knitted material of wool or linen, or any leather article that has been spoiled; because the

---

ᵃ 45 Or clothes, uncover their head

defiling mold is persistent, the article must be burned.

⁵³"But if, when the priest examines it, the mold has not spread in the fabric, the woven or knitted material, or the leather article, ⁵⁴he shall order that the spoiled article be washed. Then he is to isolate it for another seven days. ⁵⁵After the article has been washed, the priest is to examine it again, and if the mold has not changed its appearance, even though it has not spread, it is unclean. Burn it, no matter which side of the fabric has been spoiled. ⁵⁶If, when the priest examines it, the mold has faded after the article has been washed, he is to tear the spoiled part out of the fabric, the leather, or the woven or knitted material. ⁵⁷But if it reappears in the fabric, in the woven or knitted material, or in the leather article, it is

a spreading mold; whatever has the mold must be burned. ⁵⁸Any fabric, woven or knitted material, or any leather article that has been washed and is rid of the mold, must be washed again. Then it will be clean."

⁵⁹These are the regulations concerning defiling molds in woolen or linen clothing, woven or knitted material, or any leather article, for pronouncing them clean or unclean.

Cleansing From Defiling Skin Diseases

14 The Lord said to Moses, ²"These are the regulations for any diseased person at the time of their ceremonial cleansing, when they are brought to the priest: ³The priest is to go outside the camp and examine them. If they have

TO THE POINT

"Unclean"

In Old Testament times, people with a disease that might harm others were expected to be responsible. To avoid giving the disease to someone else, they lived alone and warned others of their condition, calling out, "Unclean!" to anyone who came near.

The word *unclean* in the Bible is used to describe several conditions that affected a person's relationship with others:

+ physical (Leviticus 13:45–46)

+ religious (Leviticus 16; Numbers 19)

+ moral (Psalm 106:34–39).

Old Testament laws of uncleanness aren't in effect today, but by reading about them you can learn responsibility and respect for others.

been healed of their defiling skin disease,[a] 4the priest shall order that two live clean birds and some cedar wood, scarlet yarn and hyssop be brought for the person to be cleansed. 5Then the priest shall order that one of the birds be killed over fresh water in a clay pot. 6He is then to take the live bird and dip it, together with the cedar wood, the scarlet yarn and the hyssop, into the blood of the bird that was killed over the fresh water. 7Seven times he shall sprinkle the one to be cleansed of the defiling disease, and then pronounce them clean. After that, he is to release the live bird in the open fields.

8"The person to be cleansed must wash their clothes, shave off all their hair and bathe with water; then they will be ceremonially clean. After this they may come into the camp, but they must stay outside their tent for seven days. 9On the seventh day they must shave off all their hair; they must shave their head, their beard, their eyebrows and the rest of their hair. They must wash their clothes and bathe themselves with water, and they will be clean.

10"On the eighth day they must bring two male lambs and one ewe lamb a year old, each without defect, along with three-tenths of an ephah[b] of the finest flour mixed with olive oil for a grain offering, and one log[c] of oil. 11The priest who pronounces them clean shall present both the one to be cleansed and their offerings before the Lord at the entrance to the tent of meeting.

12"Then the priest is to take one of the male lambs and offer it as a guilt offering, along with the log of oil; he shall wave them before the Lord as a wave offering. 13He is to slaughter the lamb in the sanctuary area where the sin offering[d] and the burnt offering are slaughtered. Like the sin offering, the guilt offering belongs to the priest; it is most holy. 14The priest is to take some of the blood of the guilt offering and put it on the lobe of the right ear of the one to be cleansed, on the

thumb of their right hand and on the big toe of their right foot. 15The priest shall then take some of the log of oil, pour it in the palm of his own left hand, 16dip his right forefinger into the oil in his palm, and with his finger sprinkle some of it before the Lord seven times. 17The priest is to put some of the oil remaining in his palm on the lobe of the right ear of the one to be cleansed, on the thumb of their right hand and on the big toe of their right foot, on top of the blood of the guilt offering. 18The rest of the oil in his palm the priest shall put on the head of the one to be cleansed and make atonement for them before the Lord.

19"Then the priest is to sacrifice the sin offering and make atonement for the one to be cleansed from their uncleanness. After that, the priest shall slaughter the burnt offering 20and offer it on the altar, together with the grain offering, and make atonement for them, and they will be clean.

21"If, however, they are poor and cannot afford these, they must take one male lamb as a guilt offering to be waved to make atonement for them, together with a tenth of an ephah[e] of the finest flour mixed with olive oil for a grain offering, a log of oil, 22and two doves or two young pigeons, such as they can afford, one for a sin offering and the other for a burnt offering.

23"On the eighth day they must bring them for their cleansing to the priest at the entrance to the tent of meeting, before the Lord. 24The priest is to take the lamb for the guilt offering, together with the log of oil, and wave them before the Lord as a wave offering. 25He shall slaughter the lamb for the guilt offering and take some of its blood and put it on the lobe of the right ear of the one to be cleansed, on the thumb of their right hand and on the big toe of their right foot. 26The priest is to pour some of the oil into the palm of his own left hand, 27and with his right forefinger sprinkle some of

---

[a] 3 The Hebrew word for *defiling skin disease*, traditionally translated "leprosy," was used for various diseases affecting the skin; also in verses 7, 32, 54 and 57.   [b] 10 That is, probably about 11 pounds or about 5 kilograms   [c] 10 That is, about 1/3 quart or about 0.3 liter; also in verses 12, 15, 21 and 24   [d] 13 Or *purification offering*; also in verses 19, 22 and 31   [e] 21 That is, probably about 3 1/2 pounds or about 1.6 kilograms

the oil from his palm seven times before the LORD. ²⁸Some of the oil in his palm he is to put on the same places he put the blood of the guilt offering—on the lobe of the right ear of the one to be cleansed, on the thumb of their right hand and on the big toe of their right foot. ²⁹The rest of the oil in his palm the priest shall put on the head of the one to be cleansed, to make atonement for them before the LORD. ³⁰Then he shall sacrifice the doves or the young pigeons, such as the person can afford, ³¹one as a sin offering and the other as a burnt offering, together with the grain offering. In this way the priest will make atonement before the LORD on behalf of the one to be cleansed."

³²These are the regulations for anyone who has a defiling skin disease and who cannot afford the regular offerings for their cleansing.

Cleansing From Defiling Molds

³³The LORD said to Moses and Aaron, ³⁴"When you enter the land of Canaan, which I am giving you as your possession, and I put a spreading mold in a house in that land, ³⁵the owner of the house must go and tell the priest, 'I have seen something that looks like a defiling mold in my house.' ³⁶The priest is to order the house to be emptied before he goes in to examine the mold, so that nothing in the house will be pronounced unclean. After this the priest is to go in and inspect the house. ³⁷He is to examine the mold on the walls, and if it has greenish or reddish depressions that appear to be deeper than the surface of the wall, ³⁸the priest shall go out the doorway of the house and close it up for seven days. ³⁹On the seventh day the priest shall return to inspect the house. If the mold has spread on the walls, ⁴⁰he is to order that the contaminated stones be torn out and thrown into an unclean place outside the town. ⁴¹He must have all the inside walls of the house scraped and the material that is scraped off dumped into an unclean place outside the town. ⁴²Then they are to take other stones to replace these and take new clay and plaster the house.

⁴³"If the defiling mold reappears in the house after the stones have been torn out and the house scraped and plastered, ⁴⁴the priest is to go and examine it and, if the mold has spread in the house, it is a persistent defiling mold; the house is unclean. ⁴⁵It must be torn down—its stones, timbers and all the plaster—and taken out of the town to an unclean place.

⁴⁶"Anyone who goes into the house while it is closed up will be unclean till evening. ⁴⁷Anyone who sleeps or eats in the house must wash their clothes.

⁴⁸"But if the priest comes to examine it and the mold has not spread after the house has been plastered, he shall pronounce the house clean, because the defiling mold is gone. ⁴⁹To purify the house he is to take two birds and some cedar wood, scarlet yarn and hyssop. ⁵⁰He shall kill one of the birds over fresh water in a clay pot. ⁵¹Then he is to take the cedar wood, the hyssop, the scarlet yarn and the live bird, dip them into the blood of the dead bird and the fresh water, and sprinkle the house seven times. ⁵²He shall purify the house with the bird's blood, the fresh water, the live bird, the cedar wood, the hyssop and the scarlet yarn. ⁵³Then he is to release the live bird in the open fields outside the town. In this way he will make atonement for the house, and it will be clean."

⁵⁴These are the regulations for any defiling skin disease, for a sore, ⁵⁵for defiling molds in fabric or in a house, ⁵⁶and for a swelling, a rash or a shiny spot, ⁵⁷to determine when something is clean or unclean.

These are the regulations for defiling skin diseases and defiling molds.

Discharges Causing Uncleanness

15 The LORD said to Moses and Aaron, ²"Speak to the Israelites and say to them: 'When any man has an unusual bodily discharge, such a discharge is unclean. ³Whether it continues flowing from his body or is blocked, it will make him unclean. This is how his discharge will bring about uncleanness:

4 " 'Any bed the man with a discharge lies on will be unclean, and anything he sits on will be unclean. 5Anyone who touches his bed must wash their clothes and bathe with water, and they will be unclean till evening. 6Whoever sits on anything that the man with a discharge sat on must wash their clothes and bathe with water, and they will be unclean till evening.

7 " 'Whoever touches the man who has a discharge must wash their clothes and bathe with water, and they will be unclean till evening.

8 " 'If the man with the discharge spits on anyone who is clean, they must wash their clothes and bathe with water, and they will be unclean till evening.

9 " 'Everything the man sits on when riding will be unclean, 10and whoever touches any of the things that were under him will be unclean till evening; whoever picks up those things must wash their clothes and bathe with water, and they will be unclean till evening.

11 " 'Anyone the man with a discharge touches without rinsing his hands with water must wash their clothes and bathe with water, and they will be unclean till evening.

12 " 'A clay pot that the man touches must be broken, and any wooden article is to be rinsed with water.

13 " 'When a man is cleansed from his discharge, he is to count off seven days for his ceremonial cleansing; he must wash his clothes and bathe himself with fresh water, and he will be clean. 14On the eighth day he must take two doves or two young pigeons and come before the Lord to the entrance to the tent of meeting and give them to the priest. 15The priest is to sacrifice them, the one for a sin offeringa and the other for a burnt offering. In this way he will make atonement before the Lord for the man because of his discharge.

16 " 'When a man has an emission of semen, he must bathe his whole body with water, and he will be unclean till evening. 17Any clothing or leather that has semen on it must be washed with water, and it will be unclean till evening. 18When a man has sexual relations with a woman and there is an emission of semen, both of them must bathe with water, and they will be unclean till evening.

19 " 'When a woman has her regular flow of blood, the impurity of her monthly period will last seven days, and anyone who touches her will be unclean till evening.

20 " 'Anything she lies on during her period will be unclean, and anything she sits on will be unclean. 21Anyone who touches her bed will be unclean; they must wash their clothes and bathe with water, and they will be unclean till evening. 22Anyone who touches anything she sits on will be unclean; they must wash their clothes and bathe with water, and they will be unclean till evening. 23Whether it is the bed or anything she was sitting on, when anyone touches it, they will be unclean till evening.

24 " 'If a man has sexual relations with her and her monthly flow touches him, he will be unclean for seven days; any bed he lies on will be unclean.

25 " 'When a woman has a discharge of blood for many days at a time other than her monthly period or has a discharge that continues beyond her period, she will be unclean as long as she has the discharge, just as in the days of her period. 26Any bed she lies on while her discharge continues will be unclean, as is her bed during her monthly period, and anything she sits on will be unclean, as during her period. 27Anyone who touches them will be unclean; they must wash their clothes and bathe with water, and they will be unclean till evening.

28 " 'When she is cleansed from her discharge, she must count off seven days, and after that she will be ceremonially clean. 29On the eighth day she must take two doves or two young pigeons and bring them to the priest at the entrance to the tent of meeting. 30The priest is to sacrifice one for a sin offering and the other for a burnt offering. In this way he will

a 15 Or purification offering; also in verse 30

make atonement for her before the LORD for the uncleanness of her discharge.

31 " 'You must keep the Israelites separate from things that make them unclean, so they will not die in their uncleanness for defiling my dwelling place,a which is among them.' "

32 These are the regulations for a man with a discharge, for anyone made unclean by an emission of semen, 33 for a woman in her monthly period, for a man or a woman with a discharge, and for a man who has sexual relations with a woman who is ceremonially unclean.

The Day of Atonement

16 The LORD spoke to Moses after the death of the two sons of Aaron who died when they approached the LORD. 2 The LORD said to Moses: "Tell your brother Aaron that he is not to come whenever he chooses into the Most Holy Place behind the curtain in front of the atonement cover on the ark, or else he will die. For I will appear in the cloud over the atonement cover.

3 "This is how Aaron is to enter the Most Holy Place: He must first bring a young bull for a sin offeringb and a ram for a burnt offering. 4 He is to put on the sacred linen tunic, with linen undergarments next to his body; he is to tie the linen sash around him and put on the linen turban. These are sacred garments; so he must bathe himself with water before he puts them on. 5 From the Israelite community he is to take two male goats for a sin offering and a ram for a burnt offering.

6 "Aaron is to offer the bull for his own sin offering to make atonement for himself and his household. 7 Then he is to take the two goats and present them before the LORD at the entrance to the tent of meeting. 8 He is to cast lots for the two goats—one lot for the LORD and the other for the scapegoat.c 9 Aaron shall bring the goat whose lot falls to the LORD and sacrifice it for a sin offering. 10 But the

goat chosen by lot as the scapegoat shall be presented alive before the LORD to be used for making atonement by sending it into the wilderness as a scapegoat.

11 "Aaron shall bring the bull for his own sin offering to make atonement for himself and his household, and he is to slaughter the bull for his own sin offering. 12 He is to take a censer full of burning coals from the altar before the LORD and two handfuls of finely ground fragrant incense and take them behind the curtain. 13 He is to put the incense on the fire before the LORD, and the smoke of the incense will conceal the atonement cover above the tablets of the covenant law, so that he will not die. 14 He is to take some of the bull's blood and with his finger sprinkle it on the front of the atonement cover; then he shall sprinkle some of it with his finger seven times before the atonement cover.

15 "He shall then slaughter the goat for the sin offering for the people and take its blood behind the curtain and do with it as he did with the bull's blood: He shall sprinkle it on the atonement cover and in front of it. 16 In this way he will make atonement for the Most Holy Place because of the uncleanness and rebellion

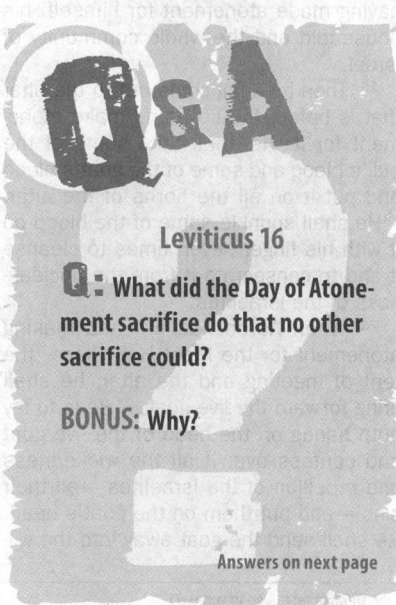

Leviticus 16

Q: What did the Day of Atonement sacrifice do that no other sacrifice could?

BONUS: Why?

Answers on next page

---

a 31 Or *my tabernacle*   b 3 Or *purification offering*; here and throughout this chapter   c 8 The meaning of the Hebrew for this word is uncertain; also in verses 10 and 26.

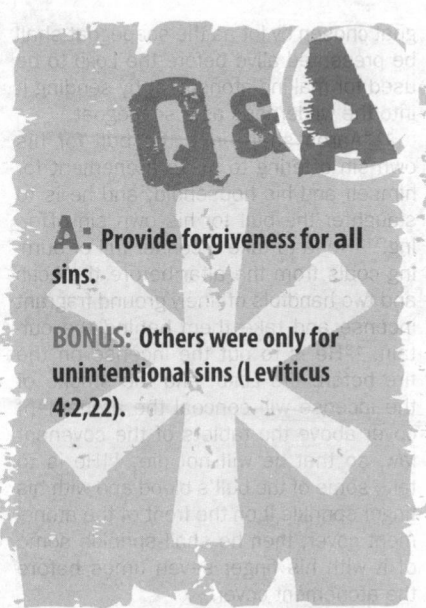

A: Provide forgiveness for all sins.

BONUS: Others were only for unintentional sins (Leviticus 4:2,22).

of the Israelites, whatever their sins have been. He is to do the same for the tent of meeting, which is among them in the midst of their uncleanness. ¹⁷No one is to be in the tent of meeting from the time Aaron goes in to make atonement in the Most Holy Place until he comes out, having made atonement for himself, his household and the whole community of Israel.

¹⁸"Then he shall come out to the altar that is before the Lord and make atonement for it. He shall take some of the bull's blood and some of the goat's blood and put it on all the horns of the altar. ¹⁹He shall sprinkle some of the blood on it with his finger seven times to cleanse it and to consecrate it from the uncleanness of the Israelites.

²⁰"When Aaron has finished making atonement for the Most Holy Place, the tent of meeting and the altar, he shall bring forward the live goat. ²¹He is to lay both hands on the head of the live goat and confess over it all the wickedness and rebellion of the Israelites—all their sins—and put them on the goat's head. He shall send the goat away into the wil-

derness in the care of someone appointed for the task. ²²The goat will carry on itself all their sins to a remote place; and the man shall release it in the wilderness.

²³"Then Aaron is to go into the tent of meeting and take off the linen garments he put on before he entered the Most Holy Place, and he is to leave them there. ²⁴He shall bathe himself with water in the sanctuary area and put on his regular garments. Then he shall come out and sacrifice the burnt offering for himself and the burnt offering for the people, to make atonement for himself and for the people. ²⁵He shall also burn the fat of the sin offering on the altar.

²⁶"The man who releases the goat as a scapegoat must wash his clothes and bathe himself with water; afterward he may come into the camp. ²⁷The bull and the goat for the sin offerings, whose blood was brought into the Most Holy Place to make atonement, must be taken outside the camp; their hides, flesh and intestines are to be burned up. ²⁸The man who burns them must wash his clothes and bathe himself with water; afterward he may come into the camp.

²⁹"This is to be a lasting ordinance for you: On the tenth day of the seventh month you must deny yourselves[a] and not do any work—whether native-born or a foreigner residing among you— ³⁰because on this day atonement will be made for you, to cleanse you. Then, before the Lord, you will be clean from all your sins. ³¹It is a day of sabbath rest, and you must deny yourselves; it is a lasting ordinance. ³²The priest who is anointed and ordained to succeed his father as high priest is to make atonement. He is to put on the sacred linen garments ³³and make atonement for the Most Holy Place, for the tent of meeting and the altar, and for the priests and all the members of the community.

³⁴"This is to be a lasting ordinance for you: Atonement is to be made once a year for all the sins of the Israelites."

And it was done, as the Lord commanded Moses.

Eating Blood Forbidden

17 The Lord said to Moses, [2]"Speak to Aaron and his sons and to all the Israelites and say to them: 'This is what the Lord has commanded: [3]Any Israelite who sacrifices an ox,[a] a lamb or a goat in the camp or outside of it [4]instead of bringing it to the entrance to the tent of meeting to present it as an offering to the Lord in front of the tabernacle of the Lord—that person shall be considered guilty of bloodshed; they have shed blood and must be cut off from their people. [5]This is so the Israelites will bring to the Lord the sacrifices they are now making in the open fields. They must bring them to the priest, that is, to the Lord, at the entrance to the tent of meeting and sacrifice them as fellowship offerings. [6]The priest is to splash the blood against the altar of the Lord at the entrance to the tent of meeting and burn the fat as an aroma pleasing to the Lord. [7]They must no longer offer any of their sacrifices to the goat idols[b] to whom they prostitute themselves. This is to be a lasting ordinance for them and for the generations to come.'

[8]"Say to them: 'Any Israelite or any foreigner residing among them who offers a burnt offering or sacrifice [9]and does not bring it to the entrance to the tent of meeting to sacrifice it to the Lord must be cut off from the people of Israel.

[10]" 'I will set my face against any Israelite or any foreigner residing among them who eats blood, and I will cut them off from the people. [11]For the life of a creature is in the blood, and I have given it to you to make atonement for yourselves on the altar; it is the blood that makes atonement for one's life.[c] [12]Therefore I say to the Israelites, "None of you may eat blood, nor may any foreigner residing among you eat blood."

[13]" 'Any Israelite or any foreigner residing among you who hunts any animal or bird that may be eaten must drain out the blood and cover it with earth, [14]because the life of every creature is its blood. That is why I have said to the Israelites, "You must not eat the blood of any creature, because the life of every creature is its blood; anyone who eats it must be cut off."

[15]" 'Anyone, whether native-born or foreigner, who eats anything found dead or torn by wild animals must wash their clothes and bathe with water, and they will be ceremonially unclean till evening; then they will be clean. [16]But if they do not wash their clothes and bathe themselves, they will be held responsible.' "

Unlawful Sexual Relations

18 The Lord said to Moses, [2]"Speak to the Israelites and say to them: 'I am the Lord your God. [3]You must not do as they do in Egypt, where you used to live, and you must not do as they do in the land of Canaan, where I am bringing you. Do not follow their practices. [4]You must obey my laws and be careful to follow my decrees. I am the Lord your God. [5]Keep my decrees and laws, for the person who obeys them will live by them. I am the Lord.

[6]" 'No one is to approach any close relative to have sexual relations. I am the Lord.

[7]" 'Do not dishonor your father by having sexual relations with your mother. She is your mother; do not have relations with her.

[8]" 'Do not have sexual relations with your father's wife; that would dishonor your father.

[9]" 'Do not have sexual relations with your sister, either your father's daughter or your mother's daughter, whether she was born in the same home or elsewhere.

[10]" 'Do not have sexual relations with your son's daughter or your daughter's daughter; that would dishonor you.

[11]" 'Do not have sexual relations with the daughter of your father's wife, born to your father; she is your sister.

[12]" 'Do not have sexual relations with your father's sister; she is your father's close relative.

[13]" 'Do not have sexual relations with your mother's sister, because she is your mother's close relative.

---

[a] 3 The Hebrew word can refer to either male or female.   [b] 7 Or the demons   [c] 11 Or atonement by the life in the blood

14 " 'Do not dishonor your father's brother by approaching his wife to have sexual relations; she is your aunt.

15 " 'Do not have sexual relations with your daughter-in-law. She is your son's wife; do not have relations with her.

16 " 'Do not have sexual relations with your brother's wife; that would dishonor your brother.

17 " 'Do not have sexual relations with both a woman and her daughter. Do not have sexual relations with either her son's daughter or her daughter's daughter; they are her close relatives. That is wickedness.

18 " 'Do not take your wife's sister as a rival wife and have sexual relations with her while your wife is living.

19 " 'Do not approach a woman to have sexual relations during the uncleanness of her monthly period.

20 " 'Do not have sexual relations with your neighbor's wife and defile yourself with her.

21 " 'Do not give any of your children to be sacrificed to Molek, for you must not profane the name of your God. I am the LORD.

22 " 'Do not have sexual relations with a man as one does with a woman; that is detestable.

23 " 'Do not have sexual relations with an animal and defile yourself with it. A woman must not present herself to an animal to have sexual relations with it; that is a perversion.

24 " 'Do not defile yourselves in any of these ways, because this is how the nations that I am going to drive out before you became defiled. 25 Even the land was defiled; so I punished it for its sin,

TO THE POINT

Only One Right Choice

"Alternative lifestyle" usually refers to making a sexual choice. The impression is that any choice is all right. It's just a matter of preference. When it comes to sex, don't kid yourself about some of those choices being morally all right:

+ It's wrong to have sex with any close relative (Leviticus 18:6–18).

+ It's wrong to have sex with animals (Leviticus 18:23).

+ It's wrong to have homosexual sex (Leviticus 18:22).

This isn't the only Bible passage that says homosexual sex is a sin. Read also Romans 1:26–27. If someone tells you homosexuality is an alternative lifestyle—meaning that it's OK—don't let those words fool you. It's an alternative all right. A sinful one.

and the land vomited out its inhabitants. ²⁶But you must keep my decrees and my laws. The native-born and the foreigners residing among you must not do any of these detestable things, ²⁷for all these things were done by the people who lived in the land before you, and the land became defiled. ²⁸And if you defile the land, it will vomit you out as it vomited out the nations that were before you.

²⁹" 'Everyone who does any of these detestable things—such persons must be cut off from their people. ³⁰Keep my requirements and do not follow any of the detestable customs that were practiced before you came and do not defile yourselves with them. I am the Lᴏʀᴅ your God.' "

Various Laws

19 The Lᴏʀᴅ said to Moses, ²"Speak to the entire assembly of Israel and say to them: 'Be holy because I, the Lᴏʀᴅ your God, am holy.

³" 'Each of you must respect your mother and father, and you must observe my Sabbaths. I am the Lᴏʀᴅ your God.

⁴" 'Do not turn to idols or make metal gods for yourselves. I am the Lᴏʀᴅ your God.

⁵" 'When you sacrifice a fellowship offering to the Lᴏʀᴅ, sacrifice it in such a way that it will be accepted on your behalf. ⁶It shall be eaten on the day you sacrifice it or on the next day; anything left over until the third day must be burned up. ⁷If any of it is eaten on the third day, it is impure and will not be accepted. ⁸Whoever eats it will be held responsible because they have desecrated what is holy to the Lᴏʀᴅ; they must be cut off from their people.

⁹" 'When you reap the harvest of your land, do not reap to the very edges of your field or gather the gleanings of your harvest. ¹⁰Do not go over your vineyard a second time or pick up the grapes that have fallen. Leave them for the poor and the foreigner. I am the Lᴏʀᴅ your God.

¹¹" 'Do not steal.

" 'Do not lie.

" 'Do not deceive one another.

¹²" 'Do not swear falsely by my name and so profane the name of your God. I am the Lᴏʀᴅ.

¹³" 'Do not defraud or rob your neighbor.

" 'Do not hold back the wages of a hired worker overnight.

¹⁴" 'Do not curse the deaf or put a stumbling block in front of the blind, but fear your God. I am the Lᴏʀᴅ.

¹⁵" 'Do not pervert justice; do not show partiality to the poor or favoritism to the great, but judge your neighbor fairly.

¹⁶" 'Do not go about spreading slander among your people.

" 'Do not do anything that endangers your neighbor's life. I am the Lᴏʀᴅ.

¹⁷" 'Do not hate a fellow Israelite in your heart. Rebuke your neighbor frankly so you will not share in their guilt.

¹⁸" 'Do not seek revenge or bear a grudge against anyone among your people, but love your neighbor as yourself. I am the Lᴏʀᴅ.

¹⁹" 'Keep my decrees.

" 'Do not mate different kinds of animals.

" 'Do not plant your field with two kinds of seed.

" 'Do not wear clothing woven of two kinds of material.

²⁰" 'If a man sleeps with a female slave who is promised to another man but who has not been ransomed or given her freedom, there must be due punishment.ᵃ Yet they are not to be put to death, because she had not been freed. ²¹The man, however, must bring a ram to the entrance to the tent of meeting for a guilt offering to the Lᴏʀᴅ. ²²With the ram of the guilt offering the priest is to make atonement for him before the Lᴏʀᴅ for the sin he has committed, and his sin will be forgiven.

²³" 'When you enter the land and plant any kind of fruit tree, regard its fruit as forbidden.ᵇ For three years you are to consider it forbiddenᵇ; it must not be eaten. ²⁴In the fourth year all its fruit will be holy, an offering of praise to the Lᴏʀᴅ. ²⁵But in the fifth year you may eat its fruit. In this

---

ᵃ 20 Or be an inquiry   ᵇ 23 Hebrew *uncircumcised*

Is it wrong to be gay or not? Some people say all gays go to you know where. Some people say that they can't help it, they were born that way. What is the truth? And how should we treat gay people?   >> Emily

Dear Emily,

There are a lot of things said on this subject so I can understand your questions. First, we know God wants you to love others as you love yourself. That means caring about all people. That doesn't mean, however, that you need to approve of the gay lifestyle or become involved in it.

God lets people make up their minds about many things. But some things he says are wrong. God does not approve of the homosexual lifestyle anywhere in the Bible. In fact, he makes it clear that it is sinful (Leviticus 18:22, 20:13, Romans 1:26–27).

When God calls something evil, we can't pretend it is right. But you can love people and pray for them. You can witness to any who will listen.

Jordan

way your harvest will be increased. I am the Lord your God.

26 " 'Do not eat any meat with the blood still in it.

" 'Do not practice divination or seek omens.

27 " 'Do not cut the hair at the sides of your head or clip off the edges of your beard.

28 " 'Do not cut your bodies for the dead or put tattoo marks on yourselves. I am the Lord.

29 " 'Do not degrade your daughter by making her a prostitute, or the land will turn to prostitution and be filled with wickedness.

30 " 'Observe my Sabbaths and have reverence for my sanctuary. I am the Lord.

31 " 'Do not turn to mediums or seek out spiritists, for you will be defiled by them. I am the Lord your God.

32 " 'Stand up in the presence of the aged, show respect for the elderly and revere your God. I am the Lord.

33 " 'When a foreigner resides among you in your land, do not mistreat them. 34 The foreigner residing among you must be treated as your native-born. Love them as yourself, for you were foreigners in Egypt. I am the Lord your God.

35 " 'Do not use dishonest standards when measuring length, weight or quantity. 36 Use honest scales and honest weights, an honest ephah[a] and an honest hin.[b] I am the Lord your God, who brought you out of Egypt.

37 " 'Keep all my decrees and all my laws and follow them. I am the Lord.' "

Punishments for Sin

20 The Lord said to Moses, 2 "Say to the Israelites: 'Any Israelite or any foreigner residing in Israel who sacrifices any of his children to Molek is to be put to death. The members of the community are to stone him. 3 I myself will set my face against him and will cut him off from his people; for by sacrificing his children to Molek, he has defiled my sanctuary and

profaned my holy name. 4 If the members of the community close their eyes when that man sacrifices one of his children to Molek and if they fail to put him to death, 5 I myself will set my face against him and his family and will cut them off from their people together with all who follow him in prostituting themselves to Molek.

6 " 'I will set my face against anyone who turns to mediums and spiritists to prostitute themselves by following them, and I will cut them off from their people.

7 " 'Consecrate yourselves and be holy, because I am the Lord your God. 8 Keep my decrees and follow them. I am the Lord, who makes you holy.

9 " 'Anyone who curses their father or mother is to be put to death. Because they have cursed their father or mother, their blood will be on their own head.

10 " 'If a man commits adultery with another man's wife—with the wife of his neighbor—both the adulterer and the adulteress are to be put to death.

11 " 'If a man has sexual relations with his father's wife, he has dishonored his father. Both the man and the woman are to be put to death; their blood will be on their own heads.

12 " 'If a man has sexual relations with his daughter-in-law, both of them are to be put to death. What they have done is a perversion; their blood will be on their own heads.

13 " 'If a man has sexual relations with a man as one does with a woman, both of them have done what is detestable. They are to be put to death; their blood will be on their own heads.

14 " 'If a man marries both a woman and her mother, it is wicked. Both he and they must be burned in the fire, so that no wickedness will be among you.

15 " 'If a man has sexual relations with an animal, he is to be put to death, and you must kill the animal.

16 " 'If a woman approaches an animal to have sexual relations with it, kill both the woman and the animal. They are to be put to death; their blood will be on their own heads.

---

[a] 36 An ephah was a dry measure having the capacity of about 3/5 of a bushel or about 22 liters. [b] 36 A hin was a liquid measure having the capacity of about 1 gallon or about 3.8 liters.

17 " 'If a man marries his sister, the daughter of either his father or his mother, and they have sexual relations, it is a disgrace. They are to be publicly removed from their people. He has dishonored his sister and will be held responsible.

18 " 'If a man has sexual relations with a woman during her monthly period, he has exposed the source of her flow, and she has also uncovered it. Both of them are to be cut off from their people.

19 " 'Do not have sexual relations with the sister of either your mother or your father, for that would dishonor a close relative; both of you would be held responsible.

20 " 'If a man has sexual relations with his aunt, he has dishonored his uncle. They will be held responsible; they will die childless.

21 " 'If a man marries his brother's wife, it is an act of impurity; he has dishonored his brother. They will be childless.

22 " 'Keep all my decrees and laws and follow them, so that the land where I am bringing you to live may not vomit you out. 23 You must not live according to the customs of the nations I am going to drive out before you. Because they did all these things, I abhorred them. 24 But I said to you, "You will possess their land; I will give it to you as an inheritance, a land flowing with milk and honey." I am the Lord your God, who has set you apart from the nations.

25 " 'You must therefore make a distinction between clean and unclean animals and between unclean and clean birds. Do not defile yourselves by any animal or bird or anything that moves along the ground—those that I have set apart as unclean for you. 26 You are to be holy to me because I, the Lord, am holy, and I have set you apart from the nations to be my own.

27 " 'A man or woman who is a medium or spiritist among you must be put to death. You are to stone them; their blood will be on their own heads.' "

Rules for Priests

21 The Lord said to Moses, "Speak to the priests, the sons of Aaron, and say to them: 'A priest must not make himself ceremonially unclean for any of his people who die, 2 except for a close relative, such as his mother or father, his son or daughter, his brother, 3 or an unmarried sister who is dependent on him since she has no husband—for her he may make himself unclean. 4 He must not make himself unclean for people related to him by marriage,[a] and so defile himself.

5 " 'Priests must not shave their heads or shave off the edges of their beards or cut their bodies. 6 They must be holy to their God and must not profane the name of their God. Because they present the food offerings to the Lord, the food of their God, they are to be holy.

[a] 4 Or unclean as a leader among his people

PANORAMA

Worship.

God wants you to worship him. This book is filled with rules that Israel's priests and people had to follow.

{LEVITICUS}

7 " 'They must not marry women defiled by prostitution or divorced from their husbands, because priests are holy to their God. 8 Regard them as holy, because they offer up the food of your God. Consider them holy, because I the LORD am holy—I who make you holy.

9 " 'If a priest's daughter defiles herself by becoming a prostitute, she disgraces her father; she must be burned in the fire.

10 " 'The high priest, the one among his brothers who has had the anointing oil poured on his head and who has been ordained to wear the priestly garments, must not let his hair become unkempt[a] or tear his clothes. 11 He must not enter a place where there is a dead body. He must not make himself unclean, even for his father or mother, 12 nor leave the sanctuary of his God or desecrate it, because he has been dedicated by the anointing oil of his God. I am the LORD.

13 " 'The woman he marries must be a virgin. 14 He must not marry a widow, a divorced woman, or a woman defiled by prostitution, but only a virgin from his own people, 15 so that he will not defile his offspring among his people. I am the LORD, who makes him holy.' "

16 The LORD said to Moses, 17 "Say to Aaron: 'For the generations to come none of your descendants who has a defect may come near to offer the food of his God. 18 No man who has any defect may come near: no man who is blind or lame, disfigured or deformed; 19 no man with a crippled foot or hand, 20 or who is a hunchback or a dwarf, or who has any eye defect, or who has festering or running sores or damaged testicles. 21 No descendant of Aaron the priest who has any defect is to come near to present the food offerings to the LORD. He has a defect; he must not come near to offer the food of his God. 22 He may eat the most holy food of his God, as well as the holy food; 23 yet because of his defect, he must not go near the curtain or approach the altar, and so desecrate my sanctuary. I am the LORD, who makes them holy.' "

24 So Moses told this to Aaron and his sons and to all the Israelites.

22 The LORD said to Moses, 2 "Tell Aaron and his sons to treat with respect the sacred offerings the Israelites consecrate to me, so they will not profane my holy name. I am the LORD.

3 "Say to them: 'For the generations to come, if any of your descendants is ceremonially unclean and yet comes near the sacred offerings that the Israelites consecrate to the LORD, that person must be cut off from my presence. I am the LORD.

4 " 'If a descendant of Aaron has a defiling skin disease[b] or a bodily discharge, he may not eat the sacred offerings until he is cleansed. He will also be unclean if he touches something defiled by a corpse or by anyone who has an emission of semen, 5 or if he touches any crawling thing that makes him unclean, or any person who makes him unclean, whatever the uncleanness may be. 6 The one who touches any such thing will be unclean till evening. He must not eat any of the sacred offerings unless he has bathed himself with water. 7 When the sun goes down, he will be clean, and after that he may eat the sacred offerings, for they are his food. 8 He must not eat anything found dead or torn by wild animals, and so become unclean through it. I am the LORD.

9 " 'The priests are to perform my service in such a way that they do not become guilty and die for treating it with contempt. I am the LORD, who makes them holy.

10 " 'No one outside a priest's family may eat the sacred offering, nor may the guest of a priest or his hired worker eat it. 11 But if a priest buys a slave with money, or if slaves are born in his household, they may eat his food. 12 If a priest's daughter marries anyone other than a priest, she may not eat any of the sacred contributions. 13 But if a priest's daughter becomes a widow or is divorced, yet has no children, and she returns to live in her father's household as in her youth, she may eat her father's food. No unauthorized person, however, may eat it.

---

a 10 Or *not uncover his head*   b 4 The Hebrew word for *defiling skin disease*, traditionally translated "leprosy," was used for various diseases affecting the skin.

14 " 'Anyone who eats a sacred offering by mistake must make restitution to the priest for the offering and add a fifth of the value to it. 15 The priests must not desecrate the sacred offerings the Israelites present to the LORD 16 by allowing them to eat the sacred offerings and so bring upon them guilt requiring payment. I am the LORD, who makes them holy.' "

Unacceptable Sacrifices

17 The LORD said to Moses, 18 "Speak to Aaron and his sons and to all the Israelites and say to them: 'If any of you— whether an Israelite or a foreigner residing in Israel—presents a gift for a burnt offering to the LORD, either to fulfill a vow or as a freewill offering, 19 you must present a male without defect from the cattle, sheep or goats in order that it may be accepted on your behalf. 20 Do not bring anything with a defect, because it will not be accepted on your behalf. 21 When anyone brings from the herd or flock a fellowship offering to the LORD to fulfill a special vow or as a freewill offering, it must be without defect or blemish to be acceptable. 22 Do not offer to the LORD the blind, the injured or the maimed, or anything with warts or festering or running sores. Do not place any of these on the altar as a food offering presented to the LORD. 23 You may, however, present as a freewill offering an ox*a* or a sheep that is deformed or stunted, but it will not be accepted in fulfillment of a vow. 24 You must not offer to the LORD an animal whose testicles are bruised, crushed, torn or cut. You must not do this in your own land, 25 and you must not accept such animals from the hand of a foreigner and offer them as the food of your God. They will not be accepted on your behalf, because they are deformed and have defects.' "

26 The LORD said to Moses, 27 "When a calf, a lamb or a goat is born, it is to remain with its mother for seven days. From the eighth day on, it will be acceptable as a food offering presented to the LORD. 28 Do not slaughter a cow or a sheep and its young on the same day.

29 "When you sacrifice a thank offering to the LORD, sacrifice it in such a way that it will be accepted on your behalf. 30 It must be eaten that same day; leave none of it till morning. I am the LORD.

31 "Keep my commands and follow them. I am the LORD. 32 Do not profane my holy name, for I must be acknowledged as holy by the Israelites. I am the LORD, who made you holy 33 and who brought you out of Egypt to be your God. I am the LORD."

The Appointed Festivals

23 The LORD said to Moses, 2 "Speak to the Israelites and say to them: 'These are my appointed festivals, the appointed festivals of the LORD, which you are to proclaim as sacred assemblies.

The Sabbath

3 " 'There are six days when you may work, but the seventh day is a day of sabbath rest, a day of sacred assembly. You are not to do any work; wherever you live, it is a sabbath to the LORD.

The Passover and the Festival of Unleavened Bread

4 " 'These are the LORD's appointed festivals, the sacred assemblies you are to proclaim at their appointed times: 5 The LORD's Passover begins at twilight on the fourteenth day of the first month. 6 On the fifteenth day of that month the LORD's Festival of Unleavened Bread begins; for seven days you must eat bread made without yeast. 7 On the first day hold a sacred assembly and do no regular work. 8 For seven days present a food offering to the LORD. And on the seventh day hold a sacred assembly and do no regular work.' "

Offering the Firstfruits

9 The LORD said to Moses, 10 "Speak to the Israelites and say to them: 'When you enter the land I am going to give you and you reap its harvest, bring to the priest a sheaf of the first grain you harvest. 11 He is to wave the sheaf before the LORD so it

---

a 23 The Hebrew word can refer to either male or female.

will be accepted on your behalf; the priest is to wave it on the day after the Sabbath. ¹²On the day you wave the sheaf, you must sacrifice as a burnt offering to the LORD a lamb a year old without defect, ¹³together with its grain offering of two-tenths of an ephah[a] of the finest flour mixed with olive oil—a food offering presented to the LORD, a pleasing aroma—and its drink offering of a quarter of a hin[b] of wine. ¹⁴You must not eat any bread, or roasted or new grain, until the very day you bring this offering to your God. This is to be a lasting ordinance for the generations to come, wherever you live.

The Festival of Weeks

¹⁵" 'From the day after the Sabbath, the day you brought the sheaf of the wave offering, count off seven full weeks. ¹⁶Count off fifty days up to the day after the seventh Sabbath, and then present an offering of new grain to the LORD. ¹⁷From wherever you live, bring two loaves made of two-tenths of an ephah of the finest flour, baked with yeast, as a wave offering of firstfruits to the LORD. ¹⁸Present with this bread seven male lambs, each a year old and without defect, one young bull and two rams. They will be a burnt offering to the LORD, together with their grain offerings and drink offerings—a food offering, an aroma pleasing to the LORD. ¹⁹Then sacrifice one male goat for a sin offering[c] and two lambs, each a year old, for a fellowship offering. ²⁰The priest is to wave the two lambs before the LORD as a wave offering, together with the bread of the firstfruits. They are a sacred offering to the LORD for the priest. ²¹On that same day you are to proclaim a sacred assembly and do no regular work. This is to be a lasting ordinance for the generations to come, wherever you live.

²²" 'When you reap the harvest of your land, do not reap to the very edges of your field or gather the gleanings of your harvest. Leave them for the poor and for the foreigner residing among you. I am the LORD your God.' "

The Festival of Trumpets

²³The LORD said to Moses, ²⁴"Say to the Israelites: 'On the first day of the seventh month you are to have a day of sabbath rest, a sacred assembly commemorated with trumpet blasts. ²⁵Do no regular work, but present a food offering to the LORD.' "

The Day of Atonement

²⁶The LORD said to Moses, ²⁷"The tenth day of this seventh month is the Day of Atonement. Hold a sacred assembly and deny yourselves,[d] and present a food offering to the LORD. ²⁸Do not do any work on that day, because it is the Day of Atonement, when atonement is made for you before the LORD your God. ²⁹Those who do not deny themselves on that day must be cut off from their people. ³⁰I will destroy from among their people anyone who does any work on that day. ³¹You shall do no work at all. This is to be a lasting ordinance for the generations to come, wherever you live. ³²It is a day of sabbath rest for you, and you must deny yourselves. From the evening of the ninth day of the month until the following evening you are to observe your sabbath."

The Festival of Tabernacles

³³The LORD said to Moses, ³⁴"Say to the Israelites: 'On the fifteenth day of the seventh month the LORD's Festival of Tabernacles begins, and it lasts for seven days. ³⁵The first day is a sacred assembly; do no regular work. ³⁶For seven days present food offerings to the LORD, and on the eighth day hold a sacred assembly and present a food offering to the LORD. It is the closing special assembly; do no regular work.

³⁷(" 'These are the LORD's appointed festivals, which you are to proclaim as sacred assemblies for bringing food offerings to the LORD—the burnt offerings and grain offerings, sacrifices and drink offerings required for each day. ³⁸These offerings are in addition to those for the LORD's Sabbaths and[e] in addition to your

---

[a] 13 That is, probably about 7 pounds or about 3.2 kilograms; also in verse 17   [b] 13 That is, about 1 quart or about 1 liter   [c] 19 Or purification offering   [d] 27 Or and fast; similarly in verses 29 and 32   [e] 38 Or These festivals are in addition to the LORD's Sabbaths, and these offerings are

gifts and whatever you have vowed and all the freewill offerings you give to the Lord.)

39 " 'So beginning with the fifteenth day of the seventh month, after you have gathered the crops of the land, celebrate the festival to the Lord for seven days; the first day is a day of sabbath rest, and the eighth day also is a day of sabbath rest. 40 On the first day you are to take branches from luxuriant trees—from palms, willows and other leafy trees—and rejoice before the Lord your God for seven days. 41 Celebrate this as a festival to the Lord for seven days each year. This is to be a lasting ordinance for the generations to come; celebrate it in the seventh month. 42 Live in temporary shelters for seven days: All native-born Israelites are to live in such shelters 43 so your descendants will know that I had the Israelites live in temporary shelters when I brought them out of Egypt. I am the Lord your God.' "

44 So Moses announced to the Israelites the appointed festivals of the Lord.

Olive Oil and Bread Set Before the Lord

24 The Lord said to Moses, 2 "Command the Israelites to bring you clear oil of pressed olives for the light so that the lamps may be kept burning continually. 3 Outside the curtain that shields the ark of the covenant law in the tent of meeting, Aaron is to tend the lamps before the Lord from evening till morning, continually. This is to be a lasting ordinance for the generations to come. 4 The lamps on the pure gold lampstand before the Lord must be tended continually.

5 "Take the finest flour and bake twelve loaves of bread, using two-tenths of an ephah[a] for each loaf. 6 Arrange them in two stacks, six in each stack, on the table of pure gold before the Lord. 7 By each stack put some pure incense as a memorial[b] portion to represent the bread and to be a food offering presented to the Lord. 8 This bread is to be set out before the Lord regularly, Sabbath after Sabbath, on behalf of the Israelites, as a lasting covenant. 9 It belongs to Aaron and his sons, who are to eat it in the sanctuary area, because it is a most holy part of their perpetual share of the food offerings presented to the Lord."

A Blasphemer Put to Death

10 Now the son of an Israelite mother and an Egyptian father went out among the Israelites, and a fight broke out in the camp between him and an Israelite. 11 The son of the Israelite woman blasphemed the Name with a curse; so they brought him to Moses. (His mother's name was Shelomith, the daughter of Dibri the Danite.) 12 They put him in custody until the will of the Lord should be made clear to them.

13 Then the Lord said to Moses: 14 "Take the blasphemer outside the camp. All those who heard him are to lay their hands on his head, and the entire assembly is to stone him. 15 Say to the Israelites: 'Anyone who curses their God will be held responsible; 16 anyone who blasphemes the name of the Lord is to be put to death. The entire assembly must stone them. Whether foreigner or native-born, when they blaspheme the Name they are to be put to death.

17 " 'Anyone who takes the life of a human being is to be put to death. 18 Anyone who takes the life of someone's animal must make restitution—life for life. 19 Anyone who injures their neighbor is to be injured in the same manner: 20 fracture for fracture, eye for eye, tooth for tooth. The one who has inflicted the injury must suffer the same injury. 21 Whoever kills an animal must make restitution, but whoever kills a human being is to be put to death. 22 You are to have the same law for the foreigner and the native-born. I am the Lord your God.' "

23 Then Moses spoke to the Israelites, and they took the blasphemer outside the camp and stoned him. The Israelites did as the Lord commanded Moses.

---

[a] 5 That is, probably about 7 pounds or about 3.2 kilograms   [b] 7 Or representative

Some people are upset by this story of a young man who was stoned because he "blasphemed the Name with a curse" (Leviticus 24:11). What they don't realize is that the word *curse* doesn't mean "swear." This man used God's name as a magic word in a curse aimed to harm the man he had fought with. Swearing certainly isn't acceptable behavior for a Christian, but cursing goes much further. That's why God required the death penalty for it.

{Leviticus 24:10–16}

The Sabbath Year

25 The LORD said to Moses at Mount Sinai, 2 "Speak to the Israelites and say to them: 'When you enter the land I am going to give you, the land itself must observe a sabbath to the LORD. 3 For six years sow your fields, and for six years prune your vineyards and gather their crops. 4 But in the seventh year the land is to have a year of sabbath rest, a sabbath to the LORD. Do not sow your fields or prune your vineyards. 5 Do not reap what grows of itself or harvest the grapes of your untended vines. The land is to have a year of rest. 6 Whatever the land yields during the sabbath year will be food for you—for yourself, your male and female servants, and the hired worker and temporary resident who live among you, 7 as well as for your livestock and the wild animals in your land. Whatever the land produces may be eaten.

The Year of Jubilee

8 " 'Count off seven sabbath years—seven times seven years—so that the seven sabbath years amount to a period of forty-nine years. 9 Then have the trumpet sounded everywhere on the tenth day of the seventh month; on the Day of Atonement sound the trumpet throughout your land. 10 Consecrate the fiftieth year and proclaim liberty throughout the land to all its inhabitants. It shall be a jubilee for you; each of you is to return to your family property and to your own clan. 11 The fiftieth year shall be a jubilee for you; do not sow and do not reap what grows of itself or harvest the untended vines. 12 For it is a jubilee and is to be holy for you; eat only what is taken directly from the fields.

13 " 'In this Year of Jubilee everyone is to return to their own property.

14 " 'If you sell land to any of your own people or buy land from them, do not take advantage of each other. 15 You are to buy from your own people on the basis of the number of years since the Jubilee. And they are to sell to you on the basis of the number of years left for harvesting crops. 16 When the years are many, you are to increase the price, and when the years are few, you are to decrease the price, because what is really being sold to you is the number of crops. 17 Do not take advantage of each other, but fear your God. I am the LORD your God.

18 " 'Follow my decrees and be careful to obey my laws, and you will live safely in the land. 19 Then the land will yield its fruit, and you will eat your fill and live there in safety. 20 You may ask, "What will we eat in the seventh year if we do not plant or harvest our crops?" 21 I will send you such a blessing in the sixth year that the land will yield enough for three years. 22 While you plant during the eighth year, you will eat from the old crop and will continue to eat from it until the harvest of the ninth year comes in.

23 " 'The land must not be sold permanently, because the land is mine and you reside in my land as foreigners and strangers. 24 Throughout the land that you hold as a possession, you must provide for the redemption of the land.

25 " 'If one of your fellow Israelites becomes poor and sells some of their property, their nearest relative is to come and redeem what they have sold. 26 If, however, there is no one to redeem it for them but later on they prosper and acquire sufficient means to redeem it themselves, 27 they are to determine the value for the years since they sold it and refund the balance to the one to whom they sold it; they can then go back to their own property. 28 But if they do not acquire the means to repay, what was sold will remain in the possession of the buyer until the Year of Jubilee. It will be returned in the Jubilee, and they can then go back to their property.

29 " 'Anyone who sells a house in a walled city retains the right of redemption a full year after its sale. During that time the seller may redeem it. 30 If it is not redeemed before a full year has passed, the house in the walled city shall belong permanently to the buyer and the buyer's descendants. It is not to be returned in the Jubilee. 31 But houses in villages without walls around them are to be considered as belonging to the open country. They can be redeemed, and they are to be returned in the Jubilee.

32 " 'The Levites always have the right to redeem their houses in the Levitical towns, which they possess. 33 So the property of the Levites is redeemable—that is, a house sold in any town they hold—and is to be returned in the Jubilee, because the houses in the towns of the Levites are their property among the Israelites. 34 But the pastureland belonging to their towns must not be sold; it is their permanent possession.

35 " 'If any of your fellow Israelites become poor and are unable to support themselves among you, help them as you would a foreigner and stranger, so they can continue to live among you. 36 Do not take interest or any profit from them, but fear your God, so that they may continue to live among you. 37 You must not lend them money at interest or sell them food at a profit. 38 I am the LORD your God, who brought you out of Egypt to give you the land of Canaan and to be your God.

39 " 'If any of your fellow Israelites become poor and sell themselves to you, do not make them work as slaves. 40 They are to be treated as hired workers or temporary residents among you; they are to work for you until the Year of Jubilee. 41 Then they and their children are to be released, and they will go back to their own clans and to the property of their ancestors. 42 Because the Israelites are my servants, whom I brought out of Egypt, they must not be sold as slaves. 43 Do not rule over them ruthlessly, but fear your God.

44 " 'Your male and female slaves are to come from the nations around you; from them you may buy slaves. 45 You may also buy some of the temporary residents living among you and members of their clans born in your country, and they will become your property. 46 You can bequeath them to your children as inherited property and can make them slaves for life, but you must not rule over your fellow Israelites ruthlessly.

47 " 'If a foreigner residing among you becomes rich and any of your fellow Israelites become poor and sell themselves to the foreigner or to a member of the foreigner's clan, 48 they retain the right of redemption after they have sold themselves. One of their relatives may redeem them: 49 An uncle or a cousin or any blood relative in their clan may redeem them. Or if they prosper, they may redeem themselves. 50 They and their buyer are to count the time from the year they sold themselves up to the Year of Jubilee. The price for their release is to be based on the rate paid to a hired worker for that number of years. 51 If many years remain, they must pay for their redemption a larger share of the price paid for them. 52 If only a few years remain until the Year of Jubilee, they are to compute that and pay for their redemption accordingly. 53 They are to be treated as workers hired from year to year; you must see to it that those to whom they owe service do not rule over them ruthlessly.

54 " 'Even if someone is not redeemed in any of these ways, they and their children are to be released in the Year of Ju-

bilee, [55]for the Israelites belong to me as servants. They are my servants, whom I brought out of Egypt. I am the LORD your God.

Reward for Obedience

26 " 'Do not make idols or set up an image or a sacred stone for yourselves, and do not place a carved stone in your land to bow down before it. I am the LORD your God.

[2]" 'Observe my Sabbaths and have reverence for my sanctuary. I am the LORD.

[3]" 'If you follow my decrees and are careful to obey my commands, [4]I will send you rain in its season, and the ground will yield its crops and the trees their fruit. [5]Your threshing will continue until grape harvest and the grape harvest will continue until planting, and you will eat all the food you want and live in safety in your land.

[6]" 'I will grant peace in the land, and you will lie down and no one will make you afraid. I will remove wild beasts from the land, and the sword will not pass through your country. [7]You will pursue your enemies, and they will fall by the sword before you. [8]Five of you will chase a hundred, and a hundred of you will chase ten thousand, and your enemies will fall by the sword before you.

[9]" 'I will look on you with favor and make you fruitful and increase your numbers, and I will keep my covenant with you. [10]You will still be eating last year's harvest when you will have to move it out to make room for the new. [11]I will put my dwelling place[a] among you, and I will not abhor you. [12]I will walk among you and be your God, and you will be my people. [13]I am the LORD your God, who brought you out of Egypt so that you would no longer be slaves to the Egyptians; I broke the bars of your yoke and enabled you to walk with heads held high.

Punishment for Disobedience

[14]" 'But if you will not listen to me and carry out all these commands, [15]and if you reject my decrees and abhor my laws and fail to carry out all my commands and so violate my covenant, [16]then I will do this to you: I will bring on you sudden terror, wasting diseases and fever that will destroy your sight and sap your strength. You will plant seed in vain, because your enemies will eat it. [17]I will set my face against you so that you will be defeated by your enemies; those who hate you will rule over you, and you will flee even when no one is pursuing you.

[18]" 'If after all this you will not listen to me, I will punish you for your sins seven times over. [19]I will break down your stubborn pride and make the sky above you like iron and the ground beneath you like bronze. [20]Your strength will be spent in vain, because your soil will not yield its crops, nor will the trees of your land yield their fruit.

[21]" 'If you remain hostile toward me and refuse to listen to me, I will multiply your afflictions seven times over, as your sins deserve. [22]I will send wild animals against you, and they will rob you of your children, destroy your cattle and make you so few in number that your roads will be deserted.

[23]" 'If in spite of these things you do not accept my correction but continue to be hostile toward me, [24]I myself will be hostile toward you and will afflict you for your sins seven times over. [25]And I will bring the sword on you to avenge the breaking of the covenant. When you withdraw into your cities, I will send a plague among you, and you will be given into enemy hands. [26]When I cut off your supply of bread, ten women will be able to bake your bread in one oven, and they will dole out the bread by weight. You will eat, but you will not be satisfied.

> *I will look on you with favor.*
> Leviticus 26:9

---

[a] 11 Or *my tabernacle*

27 " 'If in spite of this you still do not listen to me but continue to be hostile toward me, 28 then in my anger I will be hostile toward you, and I myself will punish you for your sins seven times over. 29 You will eat the flesh of your sons and the flesh of your daughters. 30 I will destroy your high places, cut down your incense altars and pile your dead bodies[a] on the lifeless forms of your idols, and I will abhor you. 31 I will turn your cities into ruins and lay waste your sanctuaries, and I will take no delight in the pleasing aroma of your offerings. 32 I myself will lay waste the land, so that your enemies who live there will be appalled. 33 I will scatter you among the nations and will draw out my sword and pursue you. Your land will be laid waste, and your cities will lie in ruins. 34 Then the land will enjoy its sabbath years all the time that it lies desolate and you are in the country of your enemies; then the land will rest and enjoy its sabbaths. 35 All the time that it lies desolate, the land will have the rest it did not have during the sabbaths you lived in it.

36 " 'As for those of you who are left, I will make their hearts so fearful in the lands of their enemies that the sound of a windblown leaf will put them to flight. They will run as though fleeing from the sword, and they will fall, even though no one is pursuing them. 37 They will stumble over one another as though fleeing from the sword, even though no one is pursuing them. So you will not be able to stand before your enemies. 38 You will perish among the nations; the land of your enemies will devour you. 39 Those of you who are left will waste away in the lands of their enemies because of their sins; also because of their ancestors' sins they will waste away.

40 " 'But if they will confess their sins and the sins of their ancestors—their unfaithfulness and their hostility toward me, 41 which made me hostile toward them so that I sent them into the land of their enemies—then when their uncircumcised hearts are humbled and they pay for their sin, 42 I will remember my covenant with

INSTANT ACCESS

Usually when you do the right thing, good things happen. But what if you make some bad choices? I mean, really bad choices. Like stealing and getting in trouble with the police. Or drinking and driving and wrecking the family car. Or going too far sexually and discovering that you're pregnant. Are you ruined for life? This Bible chapter warns that there are tragic consequences for disobeying God. But it also promises that God will not totally reject you, even for serious sins. You don't want to commit any of those serious sins. But if you do something wrong, remember God's promise. God will welcome you home and bless you again.

{Leviticus 26:42–44}

Jacob and my covenant with Isaac and my covenant with Abraham, and I will remember the land. 43 For the land will be deserted by them and will enjoy its sabbaths while it lies desolate without them. They will pay for their sins because they rejected my laws and abhorred my decrees. 44 Yet in spite of this, when they are in the land of their enemies, I will not reject them or abhor them so as to destroy them completely, breaking my

---

[a] 30 Or your funeral offerings

covenant with them. I am the LORD their God. ⁴⁵But for their sake I will remember the covenant with their ancestors whom I brought out of Egypt in the sight of the nations to be their God. I am the LORD.'"

⁴⁶These are the decrees, the laws and the regulations that the LORD established at Mount Sinai between himself and the Israelites through Moses.

Redeeming What Is the LORD's

27 The LORD said to Moses, ²"Speak to the Israelites and say to them: 'If anyone makes a special vow to dedicate a person to the LORD by giving the equivalent value, ³set the value of a male between the ages of twenty and sixty at fifty shekels*ᵃ* of silver, according to the sanctuary shekel*ᵇ*; ⁴for a female, set her value at thirty shekels*ᶜ*; ⁵for a person between the ages of five and twenty, set the value of a male at twenty shekels*ᵈ* and of a female at ten shekels*ᵉ*; ⁶for a person between one month and five years, set the value of a male at five shekels*ᶠ* of silver and that of a female at three shekels*ᵍ* of silver; ⁷for a person sixty years old or more, set the value of a male at fifteen shekels*ʰ* and of a female at ten shekels. ⁸If anyone making the vow is too poor to pay the specified amount, the person being dedicated is to be presented to the priest, who will set the value according to what the one making the vow can afford.

⁹"'If what they vowed is an animal that is acceptable as an offering to the LORD, such an animal given to the LORD becomes holy. ¹⁰They must not exchange it or substitute a good one for a bad one, or a bad one for a good one; if they should substitute one animal for another, both it and the substitute become holy. ¹¹If what they vowed is a ceremonially unclean animal—one that is not acceptable as an offering to the LORD—the animal must be presented to the priest, ¹²who will judge its quality as good or bad. Whatever value the priest then sets, that is what it will

be. ¹³If the owner wishes to redeem the animal, a fifth must be added to its value.

¹⁴"'If anyone dedicates their house as something holy to the LORD, the priest will judge its quality as good or bad. Whatever value the priest then sets, so it will remain. ¹⁵If the one who dedicates their house wishes to redeem it, they must add a fifth to its value, and the house will again become theirs.

¹⁶"'If anyone dedicates to the LORD part of their family land, its value is to be set according to the amount of seed required for it—fifty shekels of silver to a homer*ⁱ* of barley seed. ¹⁷If they dedicate a field during the Year of Jubilee, the value that has been set remains. ¹⁸But if they dedicate a field after the Jubilee, the priest will determine the value according to the number of years that remain until the next Year of Jubilee, and its set value will be reduced. ¹⁹If the one who dedicates the field wishes to redeem it, they must add a fifth to its value, and the field will again become theirs. ²⁰If, however, they do not redeem the field, or if they have sold it to someone else, it can never be redeemed. ²¹When the field is released in the Jubilee, it will become holy, like a field devoted to the LORD; it will become priestly property.

²²"'If anyone dedicates to the LORD a field they have bought, which is not part of their family land, ²³the priest will determine its value up to the Year of Jubilee, and the owner must pay its value on that day as something holy to the LORD. ²⁴In the Year of Jubilee the field will revert to the person from whom it was bought, the one whose land it was. ²⁵Every value is to be set according to the sanctuary shekel, twenty gerahs to the shekel.

²⁶"'No one, however, may dedicate the firstborn of an animal, since the firstborn already belongs to the LORD; whether an ox*ʲ* or a sheep, it is the LORD's. ²⁷If it is one of the unclean animals, it may be bought back at its set value, adding a fifth

---

ᵃ 3 That is, about 1 1/4 pounds or about 575 grams; also in verse 16   *ᵇ 3* That is, about 2/5 ounce or about 12 grams; also in verse 25   *ᶜ 4* That is, about 12 ounces or about 345 grams   *ᵈ 5* That is, about 8 ounces or about 230 grams   *ᵉ 5* That is, about 4 ounces or about 115 grams; also in verse 7   *ᶠ 6* That is, about 2 ounces or about 58 grams   *ᵍ 6* That is, about 1 1/4 ounces or about 35 grams   *ʰ 7* That is, about 6 ounces or about 175 grams   *ⁱ 16* That is, probably about 300 pounds or about 135 kilograms   *ʲ 26* The Hebrew word can refer to either male or female.

of the value to it. If it is not redeemed, it is to be sold at its set value.

28 " 'But nothing that a person owns and devotes[a] to the LORD—whether a human being or an animal or family land—may be sold or redeemed; everything so devoted is most holy to the LORD.

29 " 'No person devoted to destruction[b] may be ransomed; they are to be put to death.

30 " 'A tithe of everything from the land, whether grain from the soil or fruit from the trees, belongs to the LORD; it is holy to the LORD. 31 Whoever would redeem any of their tithe must add a fifth of the value to it. 32 Every tithe of the herd and flock—every tenth animal that passes under the shepherd's rod—will be holy to the LORD. 33 No one may pick out the good from the bad or make any substitution. If anyone does make a substitution, both the animal and its substitute become holy and cannot be redeemed.' "

34 These are the commands the LORD gave Moses at Mount Sinai for the Israelites.

---

[a] 28 The Hebrew term refers to the irrevocable giving over of things or persons to the LORD.   [b] 29 The Hebrew term refers to the irrevocable giving over of things or persons to the LORD, often by totally destroying them.

NUMBERS

Bon Voyage!

Think of life as a long trip. You have a good start, but you still have a long way to go. Along the way you have some big choices to make. A detour may take you years out of the way or even keep you from reaching your goal.

That's something the Israelites discovered. Numbers tells about their journey toward the promised land. It tells about choices they made, especially one particular choice that led to 38 years of wandering before God got them back on track. God didn't desert his people in the wilderness, and he won't desert you either. But life will be a lot better if you stay on the right road.

>>**CLOUD LEADS THE WAY**
Story in Numbers 9:15–23

>>**ISRAEL: NO, NO, WE WON'T GO!**
Scared Israelites rebel, see Numbers 14

>>**SOME PEOPLE NEVER LEARN**
Sudden deaths stun Israelites, Numbers 16

>>**SPELLS CAST AGAINST ISRAEL FAIL**
Read about them in Numbers 22–24

>>**SISTERS GET MOSES' ATTENTION**
Women challenge inheritance laws, Numbers 36

preview

The name "Numbers" comes from a census taken at Mount Sinai.

Numbers has three parts: Preparing for the journey (Numbers 1–9), detoured in the wilderness (Numbers 10–20), and back on track.

As the Israelites wander in the wilderness from 1440–1400 B.C., inscriptions are written on "oracle bones" in China. Female musicians entertain at banquets in Thebes. In Scandinavia, people are just learning to work bronze.

The Census

1 The LORD spoke to Moses in the tent of meeting in the Desert of Sinai on the first day of the second month of the second year after the Israelites came out of Egypt. He said: ² "Take a census of the whole Israelite community by their clans and families, listing every man by name, one by one. ³ You and Aaron are to count according to their divisions all the men in Israel who are twenty years old or more and able to serve in the army. ⁴ One man from each tribe, each of them the head of his family, is to help you. ⁵ These are the names of the men who are to assist you:

from Reuben, Elizur son of Shedeur;
⁶ from Simeon, Shelumiel son of Zurishaddai;
⁷ from Judah, Nahshon son of Amminadab;
⁸ from Issachar, Nethanel son of Zuar;
⁹ from Zebulun, Eliab son of Helon;
¹⁰ from the sons of Joseph:
from Ephraim, Elishama son of Ammihud;
from Manasseh, Gamaliel son of Pedahzur;
¹¹ from Benjamin, Abidan son of Gideoni;
¹² from Dan, Ahiezer son of Ammishaddai;
¹³ from Asher, Pagiel son of Okran;
¹⁴ from Gad, Eliasaph son of Deuel;
¹⁵ from Naphtali, Ahira son of Enan."

¹⁶ These were the men appointed from the community, the leaders of their ancestral tribes. They were the heads of the clans of Israel.

¹⁷ Moses and Aaron took these men whose names had been specified, ¹⁸ and they called the whole community together on the first day of the second month. The people registered their ancestry by their clans and families, and the men twenty years old or more were listed by name, one by one, ¹⁹ as the LORD commanded Moses. And so he counted them in the Desert of Sinai:

²⁰ From the descendants of Reuben the firstborn son of Israel:

All the men twenty years old or more who were able to serve in the army were listed by name, one by one, according to the records of their clans and families. ²¹ The number from the tribe of Reuben was 46,500.

²² From the descendants of Simeon:

All the men twenty years old or more who were able to serve in the army were counted and listed by name, one by one, according to the records of their clans and families. ²³ The number from the tribe of Simeon was 59,300.

²⁴ From the descendants of Gad:

All the men twenty years old or more who were able to serve in the army were listed by name, according to the records of their clans and families. ²⁵ The number from the tribe of Gad was 45,650.

²⁶ From the descendants of Judah:

All the men twenty years old or more who were able to serve in the army were listed by name, according to the records of their clans and families. ²⁷ The number from the tribe of Judah was 74,600.

²⁸ From the descendants of Issachar:

All the men twenty years old or more who were able to serve in the army were listed by name, according to the records of their clans and families. ²⁹ The number from the tribe of Issachar was 54,400.

³⁰ From the descendants of Zebulun:

All the men twenty years old or more who were able to serve in the army were listed by name, according to the records of their clans and families. ³¹ The number from the tribe of Zebulun was 57,400.

³² From the sons of Joseph:

From the descendants of Ephraim:

All the men twenty years old or more who were able to serve in the army were listed by name, according to the records of their clans and families. 33The number from the tribe of Ephraim was 40,500.

34From the descendants of Manasseh: All the men twenty years old or more who were able to serve in the army were listed by name, according to the records of their clans and families. 35The number from the tribe of Manasseh was 32,200.

36From the descendants of Benjamin: All the men twenty years old or more who were able to serve in the army were listed by name, according to the records of their clans and families. 37The number from the tribe of Benjamin was 35,400.

38From the descendants of Dan: All the men twenty years old or more who were able to serve in the army were listed by name, according to the records of their clans and families. 39The number from the tribe of Dan was 62,700.

40From the descendants of Asher: All the men twenty years old or more who were able to serve in the army were listed by name, according to the records of their clans and families. 41The number from the tribe of Asher was 41,500.

42From the descendants of Naphtali: All the men twenty years old or more who were able to serve in the army were listed by name, according to the records of their clans and families. 43The number from the tribe of Naphtali was 53,400.

44These were the men counted by Moses and Aaron and the twelve leaders of Israel, each one representing his family. 45All the Israelites twenty years old or more who were able to serve in Israel's army were counted according to

their families. 46The total number was 603,550.

47The ancestral tribe of the Levites, however, was not counted along with the others. 48The LORD had said to Moses: 49"You must not count the tribe of Levi or include them in the census of the other Israelites. 50Instead, appoint the Levites to be in charge of the tabernacle of the covenant law—over all its furnishings and everything belonging to it. They are to carry the tabernacle and all its furnishings; they are to take care of it and encamp around it. 51Whenever the tabernacle is to move, the Levites are to take it down, and whenever the tabernacle is to be set up, the Levites shall do it. Anyone else who approaches it is to be put to death. 52The Israelites are to set up their tents by divisions, each of them in their own camp under their standard. 53The Levites, however, are to set up their tents around the tabernacle of the covenant law so that my wrath will not fall on the Israelite community. The Levites are to be responsible for the care of the tabernacle of the covenant law."

54The Israelites did all this just as the LORD commanded Moses.

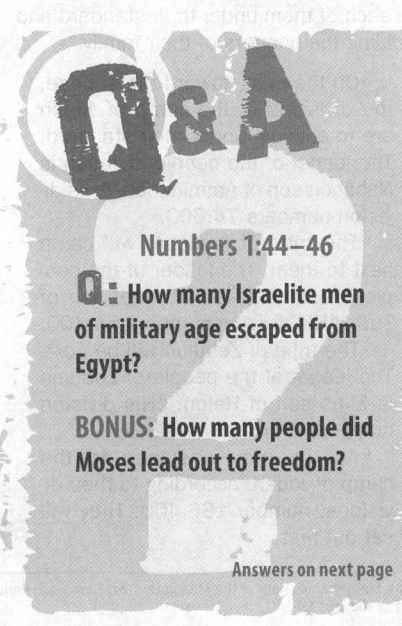

Numbers 1:44–46

Q: How many Israelite men of military age escaped from Egypt?

BONUS: How many people did Moses lead out to freedom?

Answers on next page

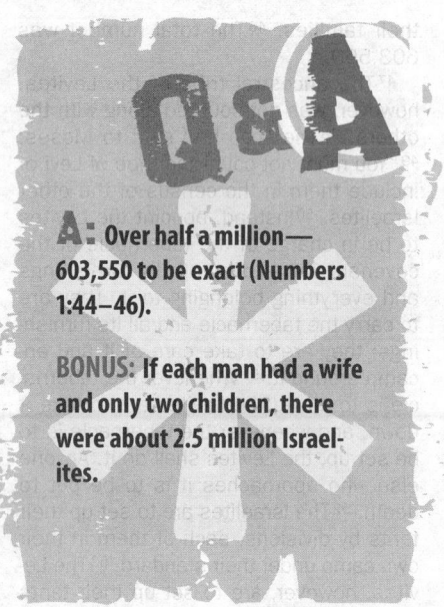

The Arrangement of the Tribal Camps

2 The LORD said to Moses and Aaron: ²"The Israelites are to camp around the tent of meeting some distance from it, each of them under their standard and holding the banners of their family."

³On the east, toward the sunrise, the divisions of the camp of Judah are to encamp under their standard. The leader of the people of Judah is Nahshon son of Amminadab. ⁴His division numbers 74,600.

⁵The tribe of Issachar will camp next to them. The leader of the people of Issachar is Nethanel son of Zuar. ⁶His division numbers 54,400.

⁷The tribe of Zebulun will be next. The leader of the people of Zebulun is Eliab son of Helon. ⁸His division numbers 57,400.

⁹All the men assigned to the camp of Judah, according to their divisions, number 186,400. They will set out first.

¹⁰On the south will be the divisions of the camp of Reuben under their standard. The leader of the people of Reuben is Elizur son of Shedeur. ¹¹His division numbers 46,500.

¹²The tribe of Simeon will camp next to them. The leader of the people of Simeon is Shelumiel son of Zurishaddai. ¹³His division numbers 59,300.

¹⁴The tribe of Gad will be next. The leader of the people of Gad is Eliasaph son of Deuel.ᵃ ¹⁵His division numbers 45,650.

¹⁶All the men assigned to the camp of Reuben, according to their divisions, number 151,450. They will set out second.

¹⁷Then the tent of meeting and the camp of the Levites will set out in the middle of the camps. They will set out in the same order as they encamp, each in their own place under their standard.

¹⁸On the west will be the divisions of the camp of Ephraim under their standard. The leader of the people of Ephraim is Elishama son of Ammihud. ¹⁹His division numbers 40,500.

²⁰The tribe of Manasseh will be next to them. The leader of the people of Manasseh is Gamaliel son of Pedahzur. ²¹His division numbers 32,200.

²²The tribe of Benjamin will be next. The leader of the people of Benjamin is Abidan son of Gideoni. ²³His division numbers 35,400.

²⁴All the men assigned to the camp of Ephraim, according to their divisions, number 108,100. They will set out third.

²⁵On the north will be the divisions of the camp of Dan under their standard. The leader of the people of Dan is Ahiezer son of Ammishaddai. ²⁶His division numbers 62,700.

²⁷The tribe of Asher will camp next to them. The leader of the people of

Asher is Pagiel son of Okran. 28His division numbers 41,500.

29The tribe of Naphtali will be next. The leader of the people of Naphtali is Ahira son of Enan. 30His division numbers 53,400.

31All the men assigned to the camp of Dan number 157,600. They will set out last, under their standards.

32These are the Israelites, counted according to their families. All the men in the camps, by their divisions, number 603,550. 33The Levites, however, were not counted along with the other Israelites, as the LORD commanded Moses.

34So the Israelites did everything the LORD commanded Moses; that is the way they encamped under their standards, and that is the way they set out, each of them with their clan and family.

The Levites

3 This is the account of the family of Aaron and Moses at the time the LORD spoke to Moses at Mount Sinai.

2The names of the sons of Aaron were Nadab the firstborn and Abihu, Eleazar and Ithamar. 3Those were the names of Aaron's sons, the anointed priests, who were ordained to serve as priests. 4Nadab and Abihu, however, died before the LORD when they made an offering with unauthorized fire before him in the Desert of Sinai. They had no sons, so Eleazar and Ithamar served as priests during the lifetime of their father Aaron.

5The LORD said to Moses, 6"Bring the tribe of Levi and present them to Aaron the priest to assist him. 7They are to perform duties for him and for the whole community at the tent of meeting by doing the work of the tabernacle. 8They are to take care of all the furnishings of the tent of meeting, fulfilling the obligations of the Israelites by doing the work of the tabernacle. 9Give the Levites to Aaron and his sons; they are the Israelites who are to be given wholly to him.a 10Appoint Aaron

and his sons to serve as priests; anyone else who approaches the sanctuary is to be put to death."

11The LORD also said to Moses, 12"I have taken the Levites from among the Israelites in place of the first male offspring of every Israelite woman. The Levites are mine, 13for all the firstborn are mine. When I struck down all the firstborn in Egypt, I set apart for myself every firstborn in Israel, whether human or animal. They are to be mine. I am the LORD."

14The LORD said to Moses in the Desert of Sinai, 15"Count the Levites by their families and clans. Count every male a month old or more." 16So Moses counted them, as he was commanded by the word of the LORD.

17These were the names of the sons of Levi:
Gershon, Kohath and Merari.

18These were the names of the Gershonite clans:
Libni and Shimei.

19The Kohathite clans:
Amram, Izhar, Hebron and Uzziel.

20The Merarite clans:
Mahli and Mushi.

These were the Levite clans, according to their families.

21To Gershon belonged the clans of the Libnites and Shimeites; these were the Gershonite clans. 22The number of all the males a month old or more who were counted was 7,500. 23The Gershonite clans were to camp on the west, behind the tabernacle. 24The leader of the families of the Gershonites was Eliasaph son of Lael. 25At the tent of meeting the Gershonites were responsible for the care of the tabernacle and tent, its coverings, the curtain at the entrance to the tent of meeting, 26the curtains of the courtyard, the curtain at the entrance to the courtyard surrounding the tabernacle and altar, and the ropes—and everything related to their use.

27To Kohath belonged the clans of the Amramites, Izharites, Hebronites and

---

a 9 Most manuscripts of the Masoretic Text; some manuscripts of the Masoretic Text, Samaritan Pentateuch and Septuagint (see also 8:16); *to me*

Uzzielites; these were the Kohathite clans. [28]The number of all the males a month old or more was 8,600.[a] The Kohathites were responsible for the care of the sanctuary. [29]The Kohathite clans were to camp on the south side of the tabernacle. [30]The leader of the families of the Kohathite clans was Elizaphan son of Uzziel. [31]They were responsible for the care of the ark, the table, the lampstand, the altars, the articles of the sanctuary used in ministering, the curtain, and everything related to their use. [32]The chief leader of the Levites was Eleazar son of Aaron, the priest. He was appointed over those who were responsible for the care of the sanctuary.

[33]To Merari belonged the clans of the Mahlites and the Mushites; these were the Merarite clans. [34]The number of all the males a month old or more who were counted was 6,200. [35]The leader of the families of the Merarite clans was Zuriel son of Abihail; they were to camp on the north side of the tabernacle. [36]The Merarites were appointed to take care of the frames of the tabernacle, its crossbars, posts, bases, all its equipment, and everything related to their use, [37]as well as the posts of the surrounding courtyard with their bases, tent pegs and ropes.

[38]Moses and Aaron and his sons were to camp to the east of the tabernacle, toward the sunrise, in front of the tent of meeting. They were responsible for the care of the sanctuary on behalf of the Israelites. Anyone else who approached the sanctuary was to be put to death.

[39]The total number of Levites counted at the Lord's command by Moses and Aaron according to their clans, including every male a month old or more, was 22,000.

[40]The Lord said to Moses, "Count all the firstborn Israelite males who are a month old or more and make a list of their names. [41]Take the Levites for me in place of all the firstborn of the Israelites, and the livestock of the Levites in place of all the firstborn of the livestock of the Israelites. I am the Lord."

[42]So Moses counted all the firstborn of the Israelites, as the Lord commanded him. [43]The total number of firstborn males a month old or more, listed by name, was 22,273.

[44]The Lord also said to Moses, [45]"Take the Levites in place of all the firstborn of Israel, and the livestock of the Levites in place of their livestock. The Levites are to be mine. I am the Lord. [46]To redeem the 273 firstborn Israelites who exceed the number of the Levites, [47]collect five shekels[b] for each one, according to the sanctuary shekel, which weighs twenty gerahs. [48]Give the money for the redemption of the additional Israelites to Aaron and his sons."

[49]So Moses collected the redemption money from those who exceeded the number redeemed by the Levites. [50]From the firstborn of the Israelites he collected silver weighing 1,365 shekels,[c] according to the sanctuary shekel. [51]Moses gave the redemption money to Aaron and his sons, as he was commanded by the word of the Lord.

The Kohathites

4 The Lord said to Moses and Aaron: [2]"Take a census of the Kohathite branch of the Levites by their clans and families. [3]Count all the men from thirty to fifty years of age who come to serve in the work at the tent of meeting.

[4]"This is the work of the Kohathites at the tent of meeting: the care of the most holy things. [5]When the camp is to move, Aaron and his sons are to go in and take down the shielding curtain and put it over the ark of the covenant law. [6]Then they are to cover the curtain with a durable leather,[d] spread a cloth of solid blue over that and put the poles in place.

[7]"Over the table of the Presence they are to spread a blue cloth and put on it

---

[a] 28 Hebrew; some Septuagint manuscripts 8,300   [b] 47 That is, about 2 ounces or about 58 grams   [c] 50 That is, about 35 pounds or about 16 kilograms   [d] 6 Possibly the hides of large aquatic mammals; also in verses 8, 10, 11, 12, 14 and 25

the plates, dishes and bowls, and the jars for drink offerings; the bread that is continually there is to remain on it. ⁸They are to spread a scarlet cloth over them, cover that with the durable leather and put the poles in place.

⁹"They are to take a blue cloth and cover the lampstand that is for light, together with its lamps, its wick trimmers and trays, and all its jars for the olive oil used to supply it. ¹⁰Then they are to wrap it and all its accessories in a covering of the durable leather and put it on a carrying frame.

¹¹"Over the gold altar they are to spread a blue cloth and cover that with the durable leather and put the poles in place.

¹²"They are to take all the articles used for ministering in the sanctuary, wrap them in a blue cloth, cover that with the durable leather and put them on a carrying frame.

¹³"They are to remove the ashes from the bronze altar and spread a purple cloth over it. ¹⁴Then they are to place on it all the utensils used for ministering at the altar, including the firepans, meat forks, shovels and sprinkling bowls. Over it they are to spread a covering of the durable leather and put the poles in place.

¹⁵"After Aaron and his sons have finished covering the holy furnishings and all the holy articles, and when the camp is ready to move, only then are the Kohathites to come and do the carrying. But they must not touch the holy things or they will die. The Kohathites are to carry those things that are in the tent of meeting.

¹⁶"Eleazar son of Aaron, the priest, is to have charge of the oil for the light, the fragrant incense, the regular grain offering and the anointing oil. He is to be in charge of the entire tabernacle and everything in it, including its holy furnishings and articles."

¹⁷The LORD said to Moses and Aaron, ¹⁸"See that the Kohathite tribal clans are not destroyed from among the Levites. ¹⁹So that they may live and not die when they come near the most holy things, do this for them: Aaron and his sons are to go into the sanctuary and assign to each

man his work and what he is to carry. ²⁰But the Kohathites must not go in to look at the holy things, even for a moment, or they will die."

The Gershonites

²¹The LORD said to Moses, ²²"Take a census also of the Gershonites by their families and clans. ²³Count all the men from thirty to fifty years of age who come to serve in the work at the tent of meeting.

²⁴"This is the service of the Gershonite clans in their carrying and their other work: ²⁵They are to carry the curtains of the tabernacle, that is, the tent of meeting, its covering and its outer covering of durable leather, the curtains for the entrance to the tent of meeting, ²⁶the curtains of the courtyard surrounding the tabernacle and altar, the curtain for the entrance to the courtyard, the ropes and all the equipment used in the service of the tent. The Gershonites are to do all that needs to be done with these things. ²⁷All their service, whether carrying or doing other work, is to be done under the direction of Aaron and his sons. You shall assign to them as their responsibility all they are to carry. ²⁸This is the service of the Gershonite clans at the tent of meeting. Their duties are to be under the direction of Ithamar son of Aaron, the priest.

The Merarites

²⁹"Count the Merarites by their clans and families. ³⁰Count all the men from thirty to fifty years of age who come to serve in the work at the tent of meeting. ³¹As part of all their service at the tent, they are to carry the frames of the tabernacle, its crossbars, posts and bases, ³²as well as the posts of the surrounding courtyard with their bases, tent pegs, ropes, all their equipment and everything related to their use. Assign to each man the specific things he is to carry. ³³This is the service of the Merarite clans as they work at the tent of meeting under the direction of Ithamar son of Aaron, the priest."

The Numbering of the Levite Clans

34 Moses, Aaron and the leaders of the community counted the Kohathites by their clans and families. 35 All the men from thirty to fifty years of age who came to serve in the work at the tent of meeting, 36 counted by clans, were 2,750. 37 This was the total of all those in the Kohathite clans who served at the tent of meeting. Moses and Aaron counted them according to the LORD's command through Moses.

38 The Gershonites were counted by their clans and families. 39 All the men from thirty to fifty years of age who came to serve in the work at the tent of meeting, 40 counted by their clans and families, were 2,630. 41 This was the total of those in the Gershonite clans who served at the tent of meeting. Moses and Aaron counted them according to the LORD's command.

42 The Merarites were counted by their clans and families. 43 All the men from thirty to fifty years of age who came to serve in the work at the tent of meeting, 44 counted by their clans, were 3,200. 45 This was the total of those in the Merarite clans. Moses and Aaron counted them according to the LORD's command through Moses.

46 So Moses, Aaron and the leaders of Israel counted all the Levites by their clans and families. 47 All the men from thirty to fifty years of age who came to do the work of serving and carrying the tent of meeting 48 numbered 8,580. 49 At the LORD's command through Moses, each was assigned his work and told what to carry.

Thus they were counted, as the LORD commanded Moses.

The Purity of the Camp

5 The LORD said to Moses, 2 "Command the Israelites to send away from the camp anyone who has a defiling skin disease[a] or a discharge of any kind, or who is ceremonially unclean because of a dead body. 3 Send away male and female alike; send them outside the camp so they will not defile their camp, where I dwell among them." 4 The Israelites did so; they sent them outside the camp. They did just as the LORD had instructed Moses.

Restitution for Wrongs

5 The LORD said to Moses, 6 "Say to the Israelites: 'Any man or woman who wrongs another in any way[b] and so is unfaithful to the LORD is guilty 7 and must confess the sin they have committed. They must make full restitution for the wrong they have done, add a fifth of the value to it and give it all to the person they have wronged. 8 But if that person has no close relative to whom restitution can be made for the wrong, the restitution belongs to the LORD and must be given to the priest, along with the ram with which atonement is made for the wrongdoer. 9 All the sacred contributions the Israelites bring to a priest will belong to him. 10 Sacred things belong to their owners, but what they give to the priest will belong to the priest.' "

The Test for an Unfaithful Wife

11 Then the LORD said to Moses, 12 "Speak to the Israelites and say to them: 'If a man's wife goes astray and is unfaithful to him 13 so that another man has sexual relations with her, and this is hidden from her husband and her impurity is undetected (since there is no witness against her and she has not been caught in the act), 14 and if feelings of jealousy come over her husband and he suspects his wife and she is impure—or if he is jealous and suspects her even though she is not impure— 15 then he is to take his wife to the priest. He must also take an offering of a tenth of an ephah[c] of barley flour on her behalf. He must not pour olive oil on it or put incense on it, because it is a grain offering for jealousy,

---

a 2 The Hebrew word for defiling skin disease, traditionally translated "leprosy," was used for various diseases affecting the skin.   b 6 Or woman who commits any wrong common to mankind   c 15 That is, probably about 3 1/2 pounds or about 1.6 kilograms

Y ou didn't mean for Keri to see the note you wrote about her. You didn't even mean what you wrote. But Keri saw the note, and she's hurt. This passage says that when you wrong another in any way (Numbers 5:6), you have to make up for it. First, admit you're guilty of doing wrong. Then make "full restitution" for the wrong, with a bonus. How? You start by telling Keri you know you did wrong. Then you tell everyone who saw the note you were wrong. You apologize to Keri in front of them and ask her to forgive you. It may be hard. It may be tough. But it's the right thing to do.

{Numbers 5:5–8}

》》INSTANT ACCESS

a reminder-offering to draw attention to wrongdoing.

16 " 'The priest shall bring her and have her stand before the LORD. 17 Then he shall take some holy water in a clay jar and put some dust from the tabernacle floor into the water. 18 After the priest has had the woman stand before the LORD, he shall loosen her hair and place in her hands the reminder-offering, the grain offering for jealousy, while he himself holds the bitter water that brings a curse. 19 Then the priest shall put the woman un-der oath and say to her, "If no other man has had sexual relations with you and you have not gone astray and become impure while married to your husband, may this bitter water that brings a curse not harm you. 20 But if you have gone astray while married to your husband and you have made yourself impure by having sexual relations with a man other than your hus-band"— 21 here the priest is to put the woman under this curse—"may the LORD cause you to become a curse[a] among your people when he makes your womb miscarry and your abdomen swell. 22 May this water that brings a curse enter your body so that your abdomen swells or your womb miscarries."

" 'Then the woman is to say, "Amen. So be it."

23 " 'The priest is to write these curs-es on a scroll and then wash them off into the bitter water. 24 He shall make the woman drink the bitter water that brings a curse, and this water that brings a curse and causes bitter suffering will enter her. 25 The priest is to take from her hands the grain offering for jealousy, wave it before the LORD and bring it to the altar. 26 The priest is then to take a handful of the grain offering as a memorial[b] offering and burn it on the altar; after that, he is to have the woman drink the water. 27 If she has made herself impure and been unfaithful to her husband, this will be the result: When she is made to drink the wa-ter that brings a curse and causes bitter suffering, it will enter her, her abdomen will swell and her womb will miscarry, and she will become a curse. 28 If, however, the woman has not made herself impure, but is clean, she will be cleared of guilt and will be able to have children.

29 " 'This, then, is the law of jealousy when a woman goes astray and makes herself impure while married to her hus-band, 30 or when feelings of jealousy come over a man because he suspects his wife. The priest is to have her stand before the LORD and is to apply this entire law to her. 31 The husband will be innocent of any

---

a 21 That is, may he cause your name to be used in cursing (see Jer. 29:22); or, may others see that you are cursed; similarly in verse 27.   b 26 Or representative

wrongdoing, but the woman will bear the consequences of her sin.' "

The Nazirite

6 The LORD said to Moses, 2 "Speak to the Israelites and say to them: 'If a man or woman wants to make a special vow, a vow of dedication to the LORD as a Nazirite, 3 they must abstain from wine and other fermented drink and must not drink vinegar made from wine or other fermented drink. They must not drink grape juice or eat grapes or raisins. 4 As long as they remain under their Nazirite vow, they must not eat anything that comes from the grapevine, not even the seeds or skins.

5 " 'During the entire period of their Nazirite vow, no razor may be used on their head. They must be holy until the period of their dedication to the LORD is over; they must let their hair grow long.

6 " 'Throughout the period of their dedication to the LORD, the Nazirite must not go near a dead body. 7 Even if their own father or mother or brother or sister dies, they must not make themselves ceremonially unclean on account of them, because the symbol of their dedication to God is on their head. 8 Throughout the period of their dedication, they are consecrated to the LORD.

9 " 'If someone dies suddenly in the Nazirite's presence, thus defiling the hair that symbolizes their dedication, they must shave their head on the seventh day—the day of their cleansing. 10 Then on the eighth day they must bring two doves or two young pigeons to the priest at the entrance to the tent of meeting. 11 The priest is to offer one as a sin offering[a] and the other as a burnt offering to make atonement for the Nazirite because they sinned by being in the presence of the dead body. That same day they are to consecrate their head again.

12 They must rededicate themselves to the LORD for the same period of dedication and must bring a year-old male lamb as a guilt offering. The previous days do not count, because they became defiled during their period of dedication.

13 " 'Now this is the law of the Nazirite when the period of their dedication is over. They are to be brought to the entrance to the tent of meeting. 14 There they are to present their offerings to the LORD: a year-old male lamb without defect for a burnt offering, a year-old ewe lamb without defect for a sin offering, a ram without defect for a fellowship offering, 15 together with their grain offerings and drink offerings, and a basket of bread made with the finest flour and without yeast—thick loaves with olive oil mixed in, and thin loaves brushed with olive oil.

16 " 'The priest is to present all these before the LORD and make the sin offering and the burnt offering. 17 He is to present the basket of unleavened bread and is to sacrifice the ram as a fellowship offering to the LORD, together with its grain offering and drink offering.

18 " 'Then at the entrance to the tent of meeting, the Nazirite must shave off the hair that symbolizes their dedication. They are to take the hair and put it in the fire that is under the sacrifice of the fellowship offering.

19 " 'After the Nazirite has shaved off the hair that symbolizes their dedication, the priest is to place in their hands a boiled shoulder of the ram, and one thick loaf and one thin loaf from the basket, both made without yeast. 20 The priest shall then wave these before the LORD as a wave offering; they are holy and belong to the priest, together with the breast that was waved and the thigh that was presented. After that, the Nazirite may drink wine.

21 " 'This is the law of the Nazirite who vows offerings to the LORD in accordance

The LORD bless you and keep you.
Numbers 6:24

---

a 11 Or *purification offering*; also in verses 14 and 16

with their dedication, in addition to whatever else they can afford. They must fulfill the vows they have made, according to the law of the Nazirite.'"

The Priestly Blessing

22 The LORD said to Moses, 23 "Tell Aaron and his sons, 'This is how you are to bless the Israelites. Say to them:

24 " ' "The LORD bless you
   and keep you;
25 the LORD make his face shine on you
   and be gracious to you;
26 the LORD turn his face toward you
   and give you peace." '

27 "So they will put my name on the Israelites, and I will bless them."

Offerings at the Dedication of the Tabernacle

7 When Moses finished setting up the tabernacle, he anointed and consecrated it and all its furnishings. He also anointed and consecrated the altar and all its utensils. 2 Then the leaders of Israel, the heads of families who were the tribal leaders in charge of those who were counted, made offerings. 3 They brought as their gifts before the LORD six covered carts and twelve oxen—an ox from each leader and a cart from every two. These they presented before the tabernacle.

4 The LORD said to Moses, 5 "Accept these from them, that they may be used in the work at the tent of meeting. Give them to the Levites as each man's work requires."

6 So Moses took the carts and oxen and gave them to the Levites. 7 He gave two carts and four oxen to the Gershonites, as their work required, 8 and he gave four carts and eight oxen to the Merarites, as their work required. They were all under the direction of Ithamar son of Aaron, the priest. 9 But Moses did not give any to the Kohathites, because they were to carry on their shoulders the holy things, for which they were responsible.

10 When the altar was anointed, the leaders brought their offerings for its dedication and presented them before the altar. 11 For the LORD had said to Moses, "Each day one leader is to bring his offering for the dedication of the altar."

12 The one who brought his offering on the first day was Nahshon son of Amminadab of the tribe of Judah.

13 His offering was one silver plate weighing a hundred and thirty shekels[a] and one silver sprinkling bowl weighing seventy shekels,[b] both according to the sanctuary shekel, each filled with the finest flour mixed with olive oil as a grain offering; 14 one gold dish weighing ten shekels,[c] filled with incense; 15 one young bull, one ram and one male lamb a year old for a burnt offering; 16 one male goat for a sin offering[d]; 17 and two oxen, five rams, five male goats and five male lambs a year old to be sacrificed as a fellowship offering. This was the offering of Nahshon son of Amminadab.

18 On the second day Nethanel son of Zuar, the leader of Issachar, brought his offering.

19 The offering he brought was one silver plate weighing a hundred and thirty shekels and one silver sprinkling bowl weighing seventy shekels, both according to the sanctuary shekel, each filled with the finest flour mixed with olive oil as a grain offering; 20 one gold dish weighing ten shekels, filled with incense; 21 one young bull, one ram and one male lamb a year old for a burnt offering; 22 one male goat for a sin offering; 23 and two oxen, five rams, five male goats and five male lambs a year old to be sacrificed as a fellowship offering. This was the offering of Nethanel son of Zuar.

24 On the third day, Eliab son of Helon, the leader of the people of Zebulun, brought his offering.

---

a 13 That is, about 3 1/4 pounds or about 1.5 kilograms; also elsewhere in this chapter   b 13 That is, about 1 3/4 pounds or about 800 grams; also elsewhere in this chapter   c 14 That is, about 4 ounces or about 115 grams; also elsewhere in this chapter   d 16 Or purification offering; also elsewhere in this chapter

25 His offering was one silver plate weighing a hundred and thirty shekels and one silver sprinkling bowl weighing seventy shekels, both according to the sanctuary shekel, each filled with the finest flour mixed with olive oil as a grain offering; 26 one gold dish weighing ten shekels, filled with incense; 27 one young bull, one ram and one male lamb a year old for a burnt offering; 28 one male goat for a sin offering; 29 and two oxen, five rams, five male goats and five male lambs a year old to be sacrificed as a fellowship offering. This was the offering of Eliab son of Helon.

30 On the fourth day Elizur son of Shedeur, the leader of the people of Reuben, brought his offering.

31 His offering was one silver plate weighing a hundred and thirty shekels and one silver sprinkling bowl weighing seventy shekels, both according to the sanctuary shekel, each filled with the finest flour mixed with olive oil as a grain offering; 32 one gold dish weighing ten shekels, filled with incense; 33 one young bull, one ram and one male lamb a year old for a burnt offering; 34 one male goat for a sin offering; 35 and two oxen, five rams, five male goats and five male lambs a year old to be sacrificed as a fellowship offering. This was the offering of Elizur son of Shedeur.

36 On the fifth day Shelumiel son of Zurishaddai, the leader of the people of Simeon, brought his offering.

37 His offering was one silver plate weighing a hundred and thirty shekels and one silver sprinkling bowl weighing seventy shekels, both according to the sanctuary shekel, each filled with the finest flour mixed with olive oil as a grain offering; 38 one gold dish weighing ten shekels, filled with incense; 39 one young bull, one ram and one male lamb a year old for a burnt offering; 40 one male goat for a sin offering; 41 and two oxen, five rams, five male goats

and five male lambs a year old to be sacrificed as a fellowship offering. This was the offering of Shelumiel son of Zurishaddai.

42 On the sixth day Eliasaph son of Deuel, the leader of the people of Gad, brought his offering.

43 His offering was one silver plate weighing a hundred and thirty shekels and one silver sprinkling bowl weighing seventy shekels, both according to the sanctuary shekel, each filled with the finest flour mixed with olive oil as a grain offering; 44 one gold dish weighing ten shekels, filled with incense; 45 one young bull, one ram and one male lamb a year old for a burnt offering; 46 one male goat for a sin offering; 47 and two oxen, five rams, five male goats and five male lambs a year old to be sacrificed as a fellowship offering. This was the offering of Eliasaph son of Deuel.

48 On the seventh day Elishama son of Ammihud, the leader of the people of Ephraim, brought his offering.

49 His offering was one silver plate weighing a hundred and thirty shekels and one silver sprinkling bowl weighing seventy shekels, both according to the sanctuary shekel, each filled with the finest flour mixed with olive oil as a grain offering; 50 one gold dish weighing ten shekels, filled with incense; 51 one young bull, one ram and one male lamb a year old for a burnt offering; 52 one male goat for a sin offering; 53 and two oxen, five rams, five male goats and five male lambs a year old to be sacrificed as a fellowship offering. This was the offering of Elishama son of Ammihud.

54 On the eighth day Gamaliel son of Pedahzur, the leader of the people of Manasseh, brought his offering.

55 His offering was one silver plate weighing a hundred and thirty shekels and one silver sprinkling bowl weighing seventy shekels, both ac-

cording to the sanctuary shekel, each filled with the finest flour mixed with olive oil as a grain offering; 56 one gold dish weighing ten shekels, filled with incense; 57 one young bull, one ram and one male lamb a year old for a burnt offering; 58 one male goat for a sin offering; 59 and two oxen, five rams, five male goats and five male lambs a year old to be sacrificed as a fellowship offering. This was the offering of Gamaliel son of Pedahzur.

60 On the ninth day Abidan son of Gideoni, the leader of the people of Benjamin, brought his offering.

61 His offering was one silver plate weighing a hundred and thirty shekels and one silver sprinkling bowl weighing seventy shekels, both according to the sanctuary shekel, each filled with the finest flour mixed with olive oil as a grain offering; 62 one gold dish weighing ten shekels, filled with incense; 63 one young bull, one ram and one male lamb a year old for a burnt offering; 64 one male goat for a sin offering; 65 and two oxen, five rams, five male goats and five male lambs a year old to be sacrificed as a fellowship offering. This was the offering of Abidan son of Gideoni.

66 On the tenth day Ahiezer son of Ammishaddai, the leader of the people of Dan, brought his offering.

67 His offering was one silver plate weighing a hundred and thirty shekels and one silver sprinkling bowl weighing seventy shekels, both according to the sanctuary shekel, each filled with the finest flour mixed with olive oil as a grain offering; 68 one gold dish weighing ten shekels, filled with incense; 69 one young bull, one ram and one male lamb a year old for a burnt offering; 70 one male goat for a sin offering; 71 and two oxen, five rams, five male goats and five male lambs a year old to be sacrificed as a fellowship offering.

This was the offering of Ahiezer son of Ammishaddai.

72 On the eleventh day Pagiel son of Okran, the leader of the people of Asher, brought his offering.

73 His offering was one silver plate weighing a hundred and thirty shekels and one silver sprinkling bowl weighing seventy shekels, both according to the sanctuary shekel, each filled with the finest flour mixed with olive oil as a grain offering; 74 one gold dish weighing ten shekels, filled with incense; 75 one young bull, one ram and one male lamb a year old for a burnt offering; 76 one male goat for a sin offering; 77 and two oxen, five rams, five male goats and five male lambs a year old to be sacrificed as a fellowship offering. This was the offering of Pagiel son of Okran.

78 On the twelfth day Ahira son of Enan, the leader of the people of Naphtali, brought his offering.

79 His offering was one silver plate weighing a hundred and thirty shekels and one silver sprinkling bowl weighing seventy shekels, both according to the sanctuary shekel, each filled with the finest flour mixed with olive oil as a grain offering; 80 one gold dish weighing ten shekels, filled with incense; 81 one young bull, one ram and one male lamb a year old for a burnt offering; 82 one male goat for a sin offering; 83 and two oxen, five rams, five male goats and five male lambs a year old to be sacrificed as a fellowship offering. This was the offering of Ahira son of Enan.

84 These were the offerings of the Israelite leaders for the dedication of the altar when it was anointed: twelve silver plates, twelve silver sprinkling bowls and twelve gold dishes. 85 Each silver plate weighed a hundred and thirty shekels, and each sprinkling bowl seventy shekels. Altogether, the silver dishes weighed two thousand four hundred shekels,[a] according to the sanctuary shekel. 86 The

---

[a] 85 That is, about 60 pounds or about 28 kilograms

twelve gold dishes filled with incense weighed ten shekels each, according to the sanctuary shekel. Altogether, the gold dishes weighed a hundred and twenty shekels.[a] 87 The total number of animals for the burnt offering came to twelve young bulls, twelve rams and twelve male lambs a year old, together with their grain offering. Twelve male goats were used for the sin offering. 88 The total number of animals for the sacrifice of the fellowship offering came to twenty-four oxen, sixty rams, sixty male goats and sixty male lambs a year old. These were the offerings for the dedication of the altar after it was anointed.

89 When Moses entered the tent of meeting to speak with the LORD, he heard the voice speaking to him from between the two cherubim above the atonement cover on the ark of the covenant law. In this way the LORD spoke to him.

Setting Up the Lamps

8 The LORD said to Moses, 2 "Speak to Aaron and say to him, 'When you set up the lamps, see that all seven light up the area in front of the lampstand.' "

3 Aaron did so; he set up the lamps so that they faced forward on the lampstand, just as the LORD commanded Moses. 4 This is how the lampstand was made: It was made of hammered gold— from its base to its blossoms. The lampstand was made exactly like the pattern the LORD had shown Moses.

The Setting Apart of the Levites

5 The LORD said to Moses: 6 "Take the Levites from among all the Israelites and make them ceremonially clean. 7 To purify them, do this: Sprinkle the water of cleansing on them; then have them shave their whole bodies and wash their clothes. And so they will purify themselves. 8 Have them take a young bull with its grain offering of the finest flour mixed with olive oil; then you are to take a second young bull for a sin offering.[b] 9 Bring the Levites to the front of the tent of meeting and

assemble the whole Israelite community. 10 You are to bring the Levites before the LORD, and the Israelites are to lay their hands on them. 11 Aaron is to present the Levites before the LORD as a wave offering from the Israelites, so that they may be ready to do the work of the LORD.

12 "Then the Levites are to lay their hands on the heads of the bulls, using one for a sin offering to the LORD and the other for a burnt offering, to make atonement for the Levites. 13 Have the Levites stand in front of Aaron and his sons and then present them as a wave offering to the LORD. 14 In this way you are to set the Levites apart from the other Israelites, and the Levites will be mine.

15 "After you have purified the Levites and presented them as a wave offering, they are to come to do their work at the tent of meeting. 16 They are the Israelites who are to be given wholly to me. I have taken them as my own in place of the firstborn, the first male offspring from every Israelite woman. 17 Every firstborn male in Israel, whether human or animal, is mine. When I struck down all the firstborn in Egypt, I set them apart for myself. 18 And I have taken the Levites in place of all the firstborn sons in Israel. 19 From among all the Israelites, I have given the Levites as gifts to Aaron and his sons to do the work at the tent of meeting on behalf of the Israelites and to make atonement for them so that no plague will strike the Israelites when they go near the sanctuary."

20 Moses, Aaron and the whole Israelite community did with the Levites just as the LORD commanded Moses. 21 The Levites purified themselves and washed their clothes. Then Aaron presented them as a wave offering before the LORD and made atonement for them to purify them. 22 After that, the Levites came to do their work at the tent of meeting under the supervision of Aaron and his sons. They did with the Levites just as the LORD commanded Moses.

23 The LORD said to Moses, 24 "This applies to the Levites: Men twenty-five years old or more shall come to take part in the

---

a 86 That is, about 3 pounds or about 1.4 kilograms   b 8 Or *purification offering*; also in verse 12

work at the tent of meeting, 25but at the age of fifty, they must retire from their regular service and work no longer. 26They may assist their brothers in performing their duties at the tent of meeting, but they themselves must not do the work. This, then, is how you are to assign the responsibilities of the Levites."

The Passover

9 The LORD spoke to Moses in the Desert of Sinai in the first month of the second year after they came out of Egypt. He said, 2"Have the Israelites celebrate the Passover at the appointed time. 3Celebrate it at the appointed time, at twilight on the fourteenth day of this month, in accordance with all its rules and regulations."

4So Moses told the Israelites to celebrate the Passover, 5and they did so in the Desert of Sinai at twilight on the fourteenth day of the first month. The Israelites did everything just as the LORD commanded Moses.

6But some of them could not celebrate the Passover on that day because they were ceremonially unclean on account of a dead body. So they came to Moses and Aaron that same day 7and said to Moses, "We have become unclean because of a dead body, but why should we be kept from presenting the LORD's offering with the other Israelites at the appointed time?"

8Moses answered them, "Wait until I find out what the LORD commands concerning you."

9Then the LORD said to Moses, 10"Tell the Israelites: 'When any of you or your descendants are unclean because of a dead body or are away on a journey, they are still to celebrate the LORD's Passover, 11but they are to do it on the fourteenth day of the second month at twilight. They are to eat the lamb, together with unleavened bread and bitter herbs. 12They must not leave any of it till morning or break any of its bones. When they celebrate the Passover, they must follow all the regulations. 13But if anyone who is ceremonially clean and not on a journey fails to celebrate the Passover, they must be cut

off from their people for not presenting the LORD's offering at the appointed time. They will bear the consequences of their sin.

14" 'A foreigner residing among you is also to celebrate the LORD's Passover in accordance with its rules and regulations. You must have the same regulations for both the foreigner and the native-born.' "

The Cloud Above the Tabernacle

15On the day the tabernacle, the tent of the covenant law, was set up, the cloud covered it. From evening till morning the cloud above the tabernacle looked like fire. 16That is how it continued to be; the cloud covered it, and at night it looked like fire. 17Whenever the cloud lifted from above the tent, the Israelites set out; wherever the cloud settled, the Israelites encamped. 18At the LORD's command the Israelites set out, and at his command they encamped. As long as the cloud stayed over the tabernacle, they remained in camp. 19When the cloud remained over the tabernacle a long time, the Israelites obeyed the LORD's order and did not set out. 20Sometimes the cloud was over the tabernacle only a few days; at the LORD's command they would encamp, and then at his command they would set out. 21Sometimes the cloud stayed only from evening till morning, and when it lifted in the morning, they set out. Whether by day or by night, whenever the cloud lifted, they set out. 22Whether the cloud stayed over the tabernacle for two days or a month or a year, the Israelites would remain in camp and not set out; but when it lifted, they would set out. 23At the LORD's command they encamped, and at the LORD's command they set out. They obeyed the LORD's order, in accordance with his command through Moses.

The Silver Trumpets

10 The LORD said to Moses: 2"Make two trumpets of hammered silver, and use them for calling the community together and for having the camps set out. 3When both are sounded, the whole community is to assemble before you at the entrance to the tent of meeting. ⁴If only one is sounded, the leaders—the heads of the clans of Israel—are to assemble before you. ⁵When a trumpet blast is sounded, the tribes camping on the east are to set out. ⁶At the sounding of a second blast, the camps on the south are to set out. The blast will be the signal for setting out. ⁷To gather the assembly, blow the trumpets, but not with the signal for setting out.

⁸"The sons of Aaron, the priests, are to blow the trumpets. This is to be a lasting ordinance for you and the generations to come. ⁹When you go into battle in your own land against an enemy who is oppressing you, sound a blast on the trumpets. Then you will be remembered by the LORD your God and rescued from your enemies. ¹⁰Also at your times of rejoicing—your appointed festivals and New Moon feasts—you are to sound the trumpets over your burnt offerings and fellowship offerings, and they will be a memorial for you before your God. I am the LORD your God."

The Israelites Leave Sinai

¹¹On the twentieth day of the second month of the second year, the cloud lifted from above the tabernacle of the covenant law. ¹²Then the Israelites set out from the Desert of Sinai and traveled from place to place until the cloud came to rest in the Desert of Paran. ¹³They set out, this first time, at the LORD's command through Moses.

¹⁴The divisions of the camp of Judah went first, under their standard. Nahshon son of Amminadab was in command. ¹⁵Nethanel son of Zuar was over the division of the tribe of Issachar, ¹⁶and Eliab son of Helon was over the division of the tribe of Zebulun. ¹⁷Then the tabernacle was taken down, and the Gershonites and Merarites, who carried it, set out.

¹⁸The divisions of the camp of Reuben went next, under their standard. Elizur son of Shedeur was in command. ¹⁹Shelumiel son of Zurishaddai was over the division of the tribe of Simeon, ²⁰and Eliasaph son of Deuel was over the division

INSTANT ACCESS

Do you ever feel like you're out there all alone? That even God isn't around? Hey, wouldn't it be great at times to have a fiery cloud floating nearby as proof that God is right there with you? And have it move to show you just where God wants you to go? Well, it won't happen. God isn't in the fiery cloud business these days. But you can still know that God is with you, for sure. Just memorize his promise: "Never will I leave you; never will I forsake you" (Deuteronomy 31:6; Hebrews 13:5). With a promise like that, you don't need a fiery cloud.

{Numbers 9:15-23}

of the tribe of Gad. ²¹Then the Kohathites set out, carrying the holy things. The tabernacle was to be set up before they arrived.

²²The divisions of the camp of Ephraim went next, under their standard. Elishama son of Ammihud was in command. ²³Gamaliel son of Pedahzur was over the division of the tribe of Manasseh, ²⁴and Abidan son of Gideoni was over the division of the tribe of Benjamin.

²⁵Finally, as the rear guard for all the units, the divisions of the camp of Dan set out under their standard. Ahiezer son of Ammishaddai was in command. ²⁶Pagiel son of Okran was over the division of the tribe of Asher, ²⁷and Ahira son of

Enan was over the division of the tribe of Naphtali. 28This was the order of march for the Israelite divisions as they set out.

29Now Moses said to Hobab son of Reuel the Midianite, Moses' father-in-law, "We are setting out for the place about which the LORD said, 'I will give it to you.' Come with us and we will treat you well, for the LORD has promised good things to Israel."

30He answered, "No, I will not go; I am going back to my own land and my own people."

31But Moses said, "Please do not leave us. You know where we should camp in the wilderness, and you can be our eyes. 32If you come with us, we will share with you whatever good things the LORD gives us."

33So they set out from the mountain of the LORD and traveled for three days. The ark of the covenant of the LORD went before them during those three days to find them a place to rest. 34The cloud of the LORD was over them by day when they set out from the camp.

35Whenever the ark set out, Moses said,

"Rise up, LORD!
    May your enemies be scattered;
    may your foes flee before you."

36Whenever it came to rest, he said,

"Return, LORD,
    to the countless thousands of
        Israel."

Fire From the LORD

11 Now the people complained about their hardships in the hearing of the LORD, and when he heard them his anger was aroused. Then fire from the LORD burned among them and consumed some of the outskirts of the camp. 2When the people cried out to Moses, he prayed to the LORD and the fire died down. 3So that place was called Taberah,a because fire from the LORD had burned among them.

Quail From the LORD

4The rabble with them began to crave other food, and again the Israelites started wailing and said, "If only we had meat to eat! 5We remember the fish we ate in Egypt at no cost—also the cucumbers, melons, leeks, onions and garlic. 6But now we have lost our appetite; we never see anything but this manna!"

7The manna was like coriander seed and looked like resin. 8The people went around gathering it, and then ground it in a hand mill or crushed it in a mortar. They cooked it in a pot or made it into loaves. And it tasted like something made with olive oil. 9When the dew settled on the camp at night, the manna also came down.

10Moses heard the people of every family wailing at the entrance to their tents. The LORD became exceedingly angry, and Moses was troubled. 11He asked the LORD, "Why have you brought this trouble on your servant? What have I done to displease you that you put the burden of all these people on me? 12Did I conceive all these people? Did I give them birth? Why do you tell me to carry them in my arms, as a nurse carries an infant, to the land you promised on oath to their ancestors? 13Where can I get meat for all these people? They keep wailing to me, 'Give us meat to eat!' 14I cannot carry all these people by myself; the burden is too heavy for me. 15If this is how you are going to treat me, please go ahead and kill me—if I have found favor in your eyes—and do not let me face my own ruin."

16The LORD said to Moses: "Bring me seventy of Israel's elders who are known to you as leaders and officials among the people. Have them come to the tent of meeting, that they may stand there with you. 17I will come down and speak with you there, and I will take some of the power of the Spirit that is on you and put it on them. They will share the burden of the people with you so that you will not have to carry it alone.

18"Tell the people: 'Consecrate yourselves in preparation for tomorrow, when you will eat meat. The LORD heard you when you wailed, "If only we had meat to eat! We were better off in Egypt!" Now the

---

a 3 *Taberah* means *burning.*

LORD will give you meat, and you will eat it. ¹⁹You will not eat it for just one day, or two days, or five, ten or twenty days, ²⁰but for a whole month—until it comes out of your nostrils and you loathe it—because you have rejected the LORD, who is among you, and have wailed before him, saying, "Why did we ever leave Egypt?" ' "

²¹But Moses said, "Here I am among six hundred thousand men on foot, and you say, 'I will give them meat to eat for a whole month!' ²²Would they have enough if flocks and herds were slaughtered for them? Would they have enough if all the fish in the sea were caught for them?"

²³The LORD answered Moses, "Is the LORD's arm too short? Now you will see whether or not what I say will come true for you."

²⁴So Moses went out and told the people what the LORD had said. He brought together seventy of their elders and had them stand around the tent. ²⁵Then the LORD came down in the cloud and spoke with him, and he took some of the power of the Spirit that was on him and put it on the seventy elders. When the Spirit rested on them, they prophesied—but did not do so again.

²⁶However, two men, whose names were Eldad and Medad, had remained in the camp. They were listed among the elders, but did not go out to the tent. Yet the Spirit also rested on them, and they prophesied in the camp. ²⁷A young man ran and told Moses, "Eldad and Medad are prophesying in the camp."

²⁸Joshua son of Nun, who had been Moses' aide since youth, spoke up and said, "Moses, my lord, stop them!"

²⁹But Moses replied, "Are you jealous for my sake? I wish that all the LORD's people were prophets and that the LORD would put his Spirit on them!" ³⁰Then Moses and the elders of Israel returned to the camp.

³¹Now a wind went out from the LORD and drove quail in from the sea. It scattered them up to two cubits[a] deep all around the camp, as far as a day's walk in any direction . ³²All that day and night and all the next day the people went out and gathered quail. No one gathered less than ten homers.[b] Then they spread them out all around the camp. ³³But while the meat was still between their teeth and before it could be consumed, the anger of the LORD burned against the people, and he struck them with a severe plague. ³⁴Therefore the place was named Kibroth Hattaavah,[c] because there they buried the people who had craved other food.

³⁵From Kibroth Hattaavah the people traveled to Hazeroth and stayed there.

Miriam and Aaron Oppose Moses

12 Miriam and Aaron began to talk against Moses because of his Cushite wife, for he had married a Cushite. ²"Has the LORD spoken only through Moses?" they asked. "Hasn't he also spoken through us?" And the LORD heard this.

³(Now Moses was a very humble man, more humble than anyone else on the face of the earth.)

⁴At once the LORD said to Moses, Aaron and Miriam, "Come out to the tent of meeting, all three of you." So the three of them went out. ⁵Then the LORD came down in a pillar of cloud; he stood at the entrance to the tent and summoned Aaron and Miriam. When the two of them stepped forward, ⁶he said, "Listen to my words:

"When there is a prophet among you,
  I, the LORD, reveal myself to them in
    visions,
  I speak to them in dreams.
⁷But this is not true of my servant
    Moses;
  he is faithful in all my house.
⁸With him I speak face to face,
  clearly and not in riddles;
  he sees the form of the LORD.
Why then were you not afraid
  to speak against my servant
    Moses?"

I t's a good thing to be an officer in your youth group or school club. Being an officer is an opportunity to help your group reach its goals. It's a way to serve God and others. Miriam and Aaron didn't see leadership that way. They were already important leaders in Israel. But they were jealous of Moses, who had the top job. They were like teens who want to be elected youth group officers so they can feel important instead of so they can contribute. It's OK to run for office, but watch your motives. And if someone else wins, try not to be jealous. Instead, get behind that person 100 percent.

{Numbers 12}

>> INSTANT ACCESS

⁹The anger of the LORD burned against them, and he left them.

¹⁰When the cloud lifted from above the tent, Miriam's skin was leprousᵃ—it became as white as snow. Aaron turned toward her and saw that she had a defiling skin disease, ¹¹and he said to Moses, "Please, my lord, I ask you not to hold against us the sin we have so foolishly committed. ¹²Do not let her be like a stillborn infant coming from its mother's womb with its flesh half eaten away."

¹³So Moses cried out to the LORD, "Please, God, heal her!"

¹⁴The LORD replied to Moses, "If her father had spit in her face, would she not have been in disgrace for seven days? Confine her outside the camp for seven days; after that she can be brought back." ¹⁵So Miriam was confined outside the camp for seven days, and the people did not move on till she was brought back.

¹⁶After that, the people left Hazeroth and encamped in the Desert of Paran.

Exploring Canaan

13 The LORD said to Moses, ²"Send some men to explore the land of Canaan, which I am giving to the Israelites. From each ancestral tribe send one of its leaders."

³So at the LORD's command Moses sent them out from the Desert of Paran. All of them were leaders of the Israelites. ⁴These are their names:

from the tribe of Reuben, Shammua son of Zakkur;
⁵from the tribe of Simeon, Shaphat son of Hori;
⁶from the tribe of Judah, Caleb son of Jephunneh;
⁷from the tribe of Issachar, Igal son of Joseph;
⁸from the tribe of Ephraim, Hoshea son of Nun;
⁹from the tribe of Benjamin, Palti son of Raphu;
¹⁰from the tribe of Zebulun, Gaddiel son of Sodi;
¹¹from the tribe of Manasseh (a tribe of Joseph), Gaddi son of Susi;
¹²from the tribe of Dan, Ammiel son of Gemalli;
¹³from the tribe of Asher, Sethur son of Michael;
¹⁴from the tribe of Naphtali, Nahbi son of Vophsi;
¹⁵from the tribe of Gad, Geuel son of Maki.

¹⁶These are the names of the men Moses sent to explore the land. (Moses gave Hoshea son of Nun the name Joshua.)

¹⁷When Moses sent them to explore Canaan, he said, "Go up through the Negev

---

ᵃ 10 The Hebrew for *leprous* was used for various diseases affecting the skin.

and on into the hill country. ¹⁸See what the land is like and whether the people who live there are strong or weak, few or many. ¹⁹What kind of land do they live in? Is it good or bad? What kind of towns do they live in? Are they unwalled or fortified? ²⁰How is the soil? Is it fertile or poor? Are there trees in it or not? Do your best to bring back some of the fruit of the land." (It was the season for the first ripe grapes.)

²¹So they went up and explored the land from the Desert of Zin as far as Rehob, toward Lebo Hamath. ²²They went up through the Negev and came to Hebron, where Ahiman, Sheshai and Talmai, the descendants of Anak, lived. (Hebron had been built seven years before Zoan in Egypt.) ²³When they reached the Valley of Eshkol,ᵃ they cut off a branch bearing a single cluster of grapes. Two of them carried it on a pole between them, along with some pomegranates and figs. ²⁴That place was called the Valley of Eshkol because of the cluster of grapes the Israelites cut off there. ²⁵At the end of forty days they returned from exploring the land.

Report on the Exploration

²⁶They came back to Moses and Aaron and the whole Israelite community at Kadesh in the Desert of Paran. There they reported to them and to the whole assembly and showed them the fruit of the land. ²⁷They gave Moses this account: "We went into the land to which you sent us, and it does flow with milk and honey! Here is its fruit. ²⁸But the people who live there are powerful, and the cities are fortified and very large. We even saw descendants of Anak there. ²⁹The Amalekites live in the Negev; the Hittites, Jebusites and Amorites live in the hill country; and the Canaanites live near the sea and along the Jordan."

³⁰Then Caleb silenced the people before Moses and said, "We should go up and take possession of the land, for we can certainly do it."

³¹But the men who had gone up with him said, "We can't attack those people; they are stronger than we are." ³²And they

INSTANT ACCESS

Are you afraid when you have to do something you've never done before? What if you make a mistake? What if you don't have all the answers or don't know what to do next? It's a real temptation to focus on the obstacles. That's what the Israelite spies did when they traveled through Canaan. Ten of the spies could only think about how strong the cities were and how big the people looked. But two of the spies, Caleb and Joshua, didn't see obstacles—they saw God. They said, "The LORD ... will lead us" (Numbers 14:8). That's the best way to approach something new. Remember that God will lead you. And then jump in.

{Numbers 13:31—14:9}

spread among the Israelites a bad report about the land they had explored. They said, "The land we explored devours those living in it. All the people we saw there are of great size. ³³We saw the Nephilim there (the descendants of Anak come from the Nephilim). We seemed like grasshoppers in our own eyes, and we looked the same to them."

The People Rebel

14 That night all the members of the community raised their voices and

---

ᵃ 23 *Eshkol* means *cluster*; also in verse 24.

wept aloud. ²All the Israelites grumbled against Moses and Aaron, and the whole assembly said to them, "If only we had died in Egypt! Or in this wilderness! ³Why is the LORD bringing us to this land only to let us fall by the sword? Our wives and children will be taken as plunder. Wouldn't it be better for us to go back to Egypt?" ⁴And they said to each other, "We should choose a leader and go back to Egypt."

⁵Then Moses and Aaron fell facedown in front of the whole Israelite assembly gathered there. ⁶Joshua son of Nun and Caleb son of Jephunneh, who were among those who had explored the land, tore their clothes ⁷and said to the entire Israelite assembly, "The land we passed through and explored is exceedingly good. ⁸If the LORD is pleased with us, he will lead us into that land, a land flowing with milk and honey, and will give it to us. ⁹Only do not rebel against the LORD. And do not be afraid of the people of the land, because we will devour them. Their protection is gone, but the LORD is with us. Do not be afraid of them."

¹⁰But the whole assembly talked about stoning them. Then the glory of the LORD appeared at the tent of meeting to all the Israelites. ¹¹The LORD said to Moses, "How long will these people treat me with contempt? How long will they refuse to believe in me, in spite of all the signs I have performed among them? ¹²I will strike them down with a plague and destroy them, but I will make you into a nation greater and stronger than they."

¹³Moses said to the LORD, "Then the Egyptians will hear about it! By your power you brought these people up from among

TO THE POINT

God Forgives, But . . .

One of life's greatest wonders is this: because God loves you he forgives, again and again. But there's something very important to remember about forgiveness: You can be forgiven for making a bad choice, but that choice still has its consequences.

That's something the Israelites learned when they rebelled against God and refused to attack Canaan (Numbers 14:1–4). God forgave them (Numbers 14:18), but he turned them back to wander in the desert. Their sin even had consequences for their children, who wandered with their parents.

You can sin and know that God will forgive you. But remember, every choice has its consequences.

them. ¹⁴And they will tell the inhabitants of this land about it. They have already heard that you, LORD, are with these people and that you, LORD, have been seen face to face, that your cloud stays over them, and that you go before them in a pillar of cloud by day and a pillar of fire by night. ¹⁵If you put all these people to death, leaving none alive, the nations who have heard this report about you will say, ¹⁶'The LORD was not able to bring these people into the land he promised them on oath, so he slaughtered them in the wilderness.'

¹⁷"Now may the Lord's strength be displayed, just as you have declared: ¹⁸'The LORD is slow to anger, abounding in love and forgiving sin and rebellion. Yet he does not leave the guilty unpunished; he punishes the children for the sin of the parents to the third and fourth generation.' ¹⁹In accordance with your great love, forgive the sin of these people, just as you have pardoned them from the time they left Egypt until now."

²⁰The LORD replied, "I have forgiven them, as you asked. ²¹Nevertheless, as surely as I live and as surely as the glory of the LORD fills the whole earth, ²²not one of those who saw my glory and the signs I performed in Egypt and in the wilderness but who disobeyed me and tested me ten times— ²³not one of them will ever see the land I promised on oath to their ancestors. No one who has treated me with contempt will ever see it. ²⁴But because my servant Caleb has a different spirit and follows me wholeheartedly, I will bring him into the land he went to, and his descendants will inherit it. ²⁵Since the Amalekites and the Canaanites are living in the valleys, turn back tomorrow and set out toward the desert along the route to the Red Sea.ᵃ"

²⁶The LORD said to Moses and Aaron: ²⁷"How long will this wicked community grumble against me? I have heard the complaints of these grumbling Israelites. ²⁸So tell them, 'As surely as I live, declares the LORD, I will do to you the very thing I heard you say: ²⁹In this wilderness your bodies will fall—every one of you twenty years old or more who was counted in the census and who has grumbled against me. ³⁰Not one of you will enter the land I swore with uplifted hand to make your home, except Caleb son of Jephunneh and Joshua son of Nun. ³¹As for your children that you said would be taken as plunder, I will bring them in to enjoy the land you have rejected. ³²But as for you, your bodies will fall in this wilderness. ³³Your children will be shepherds here for forty years, suffering for your unfaithfulness, until the last of your bodies lies in the wilderness. ³⁴For forty years—one year for each of the forty days you explored the land—you will suffer for your sins and know what it is like to have me against you.' ³⁵I, the LORD, have spoken, and I will surely do these things to this whole wicked community, which has banded together against me. They will meet their end in this wilderness; here they will die."

³⁶So the men Moses had sent to explore the land, who returned and made the whole community grumble against him by spreading a bad report about it— ³⁷these men who were responsible for spreading the bad report about the land were struck down and died of a plague before the LORD. ³⁸Of the men who went to explore the land, only Joshua son of Nun and Caleb son of Jephunneh survived.

³⁹When Moses reported this to all the Israelites, they mourned bitterly. ⁴⁰Early the next morning they set out for the highest point in the hill country, saying, "Now we are ready to go up to the land the LORD promised. Surely we have sinned!"

⁴¹But Moses said, "Why are you disobeying the LORD's command? This will not succeed! ⁴²Do not go up, because the LORD is not with you. You will be defeated by your enemies, ⁴³for the Amalekites and the Canaanites will face you there. Because you have turned away from the LORD, he will not be with you and you will fall by the sword."

⁴⁴Nevertheless, in their presumption

ᵃ 25 Or the Sea of Reeds

they went up toward the highest point in the hill country, though neither Moses nor the ark of the LORD's covenant moved from the camp. ⁴⁵Then the Amalekites and the Canaanites who lived in that hill country came down and attacked them and beat them down all the way to Hormah.

Supplementary Offerings

15 The LORD said to Moses, ²"Speak to the Israelites and say to them: 'After you enter the land I am giving you as a home ³and you present to the LORD food offerings from the herd or the flock, as an aroma pleasing to the LORD—whether burnt offerings or sacrifices, for special vows or freewill offerings or festival offerings— ⁴then the person who brings an offering shall present to the LORD a grain offering of a tenth of an ephah*ᵃ* of the finest flour mixed with a quarter of a hin*ᵇ* of olive oil. ⁵With each lamb for the burnt offering or the sacrifice, prepare a quarter of a hin of wine as a drink offering.

⁶"'With a ram prepare a grain offering of two-tenths of an ephah*ᶜ* of the finest flour mixed with a third of a hin*ᵈ* of olive oil, ⁷and a third of a hin of wine as a drink offering. Offer it as an aroma pleasing to the LORD.

⁸"'When you prepare a young bull as a burnt offering or sacrifice, for a special vow or a fellowship offering to the LORD, ⁹bring with the bull a grain offering of three-tenths of an ephah*ᵉ* of the finest flour mixed with half a hin*ᶠ* of olive oil, ¹⁰and also bring half a hin of wine as a drink offering. This will be a food offering, an aroma pleasing to the LORD. ¹¹Each bull or ram, each lamb or young goat, is to be prepared in this manner. ¹²Do this for each one, for as many as you prepare.

¹³"'Everyone who is native-born must do these things in this way when they present a food offering as an aroma pleasing to the LORD. ¹⁴For the generations to come, whenever a foreigner or anyone else living among you presents a food offering as an aroma pleasing to the LORD, they must do exactly as you do. ¹⁵The community is to have the same rules for you and for the foreigner residing among you; this is a lasting ordinance for the generations to come. You and the foreigner shall be the same before the LORD: ¹⁶The same laws and regulations will apply both to you and to the foreigner residing among you.'"

¹⁷The LORD said to Moses, ¹⁸"Speak to the Israelites and say to them: 'When you enter the land to which I am taking you ¹⁹and you eat the food of the land, present a portion as an offering to the LORD. ²⁰Present a loaf from the first of your ground meal and present it as an offering from the threshing floor. ²¹Throughout the generations to come you are to give this offering to the LORD from the first of your ground meal.

Offerings for Unintentional Sins

²²"'Now if you as a community unintentionally fail to keep any of these commands the LORD gave Moses— ²³any of the LORD's commands to you through him, from the day the LORD gave them and continuing through the generations to come— ²⁴and if this is done unintentionally without the community being aware of it, then the whole community is to offer a young bull for a burnt offering as an aroma pleasing to the LORD, along with its prescribed grain offering and drink offering, and a male goat for a sin offering.*ᵍ* ²⁵The priest is to make atonement for the whole Israelite community, and they will be forgiven, for it was not intentional and they have presented to the LORD for their wrong a food offering and a sin offering. ²⁶The whole Israelite community and the foreigners residing among them will be forgiven, because all the people were involved in the unintentional wrong.

²⁷"'But if just one person sins unintentionally, that person must bring a year-old female goat for a sin offering. ²⁸The priest is to make atonement before the

---

ᵃ 4 That is, probably about 3 1/2 pounds or about 1.6 kilograms   *ᵇ 4* That is, about 1 quart or about 1 liter; also in verse 5   *ᶜ 6* That is, probably about 7 pounds or about 3.2 kilograms   *ᵈ 6* That is, about 1 1/3 quarts or about 1.3 liters; also in verse 7   *ᵉ 9* That is, probably about 11 pounds or about 5 kilograms   *ᶠ 9* That is, about 2 quarts or about 1.9 liters; also in verse 10   *ᵍ 24* Or *purification offering*; also in verses 25 and 27

Lord for the one who erred by sinning unintentionally, and when atonement has been made, that person will be forgiven. 29 One and the same law applies to everyone who sins unintentionally, whether a native-born Israelite or a foreigner residing among you.

30 " 'But anyone who sins defiantly, whether native-born or foreigner, blasphemes the Lord and must be cut off from the people of Israel. 31 Because they have despised the Lord's word and broken his commands, they must surely be cut off; their guilt remains on them.' "

The Sabbath-Breaker Put to Death

32 While the Israelites were in the wilderness, a man was found gathering wood on the Sabbath day. 33 Those who found him gathering wood brought him to Moses and Aaron and the whole assembly, 34 and they kept him in custody, because it was not clear what should be done to him. 35 Then the Lord said to Moses, "The man must die. The whole assembly must stone him outside the camp." 36 So the assembly took him outside the camp and stoned him to death, as the Lord commanded Moses.

Tassels on Garments

37 The Lord said to Moses, 38 "Speak to the Israelites and say to them: 'Throughout the generations to come you are to make tassels on the corners of your garments, with a blue cord on each tassel. 39 You will have these tassels to look at and so you will remember all the commands of the Lord, that you may obey them and not prostitute yourselves by chasing after the lusts of your own hearts and eyes. 40 Then you will remember to obey all my commands and will be consecrated to your God. 41 I am the Lord your God, who brought you out of Egypt to be your God. I am the Lord your God.' "

Korah, Dathan and Abiram

16 Korah son of Izhar, the son of Kohath, the son of Levi, and certain

INSTANT ACCESS

Are your parents totally out of style when it comes to the clothes you like to wear? Or are they pretty stylish? It's true that teens know better what's in at school than their parents do. But there's a little more to choosing clothing than copying what your friends wear. The Israelites were told to wear tassels with a blue cord on the corners of their garments. The tassels were to remind the Israelites they were God's people. The clothing was a sign of their identity. Your clothes identify you too. Your clothes say, "This is who I am." The important thing is to be sure that your clothes say, "I'm a Christian who tries always to please God."

{Numbers 15:37–41}

Reubenites—Dathan and Abiram, sons of Eliab, and On son of Peleth—became insolent[a] 2 and rose up against Moses. With them were 250 Israelite men, well-known community leaders who had been appointed members of the council. 3 They came as a group to oppose Moses and Aaron and said to them, "You have gone too far! The whole community is holy, every one of them, and the Lord is with them. Why then do you set yourselves above the Lord's assembly?"

---

a 1 Or Peleth—took men

⁴When Moses heard this, he fell face-down. ⁵Then he said to Korah and all his followers: "In the morning the LORD will show who belongs to him and who is holy, and he will have that person come near him. The man he chooses he will cause to come near him. ⁶You, Korah, and all your followers are to do this: Take censers ⁷and tomorrow put burning coals and incense in them before the LORD. The man the LORD chooses will be the one who is holy. You Levites have gone too far!"

⁸Moses also said to Korah, "Now listen, you Levites! ⁹Isn't it enough for you that the God of Israel has separated you from the rest of the Israelite community and brought you near himself to do the work at the LORD's tabernacle and to stand before the community and minister to them? ¹⁰He has brought you and all your fellow Levites near himself, but now you are trying to get the priesthood too. ¹¹It is against the LORD that you and all your followers have banded together. Who is Aaron that you should grumble against him?"

¹²Then Moses summoned Dathan and Abiram, the sons of Eliab. But they said, "We will not come! ¹³Isn't it enough that you have brought us up out of a land flowing with milk and honey to kill us in the wilderness? And now you also want to lord it over us! ¹⁴Moreover, you haven't brought us into a land flowing with milk and honey or given us an inheritance of fields and vineyards. Do you want to treat these men like slaves*a*? No, we will not come!"

¹⁵Then Moses became very angry and said to the LORD, "Do not accept their offering. I have not taken so much as a donkey from them, nor have I wronged any of them."

¹⁶Moses said to Korah, "You and all your followers are to appear before the LORD tomorrow—you and they and Aaron. ¹⁷Each man is to take his censer and put incense in it—250 censers in all—and present it before the LORD. You and Aaron are to present your censers also." ¹⁸So each of them took his censer, put burning coals and incense in it, and stood

with Moses and Aaron at the entrance to the tent of meeting. ¹⁹When Korah had gathered all his followers in opposition to them at the entrance to the tent of meeting, the glory of the LORD appeared to the entire assembly. ²⁰The LORD said to Moses and Aaron, ²¹"Separate yourselves from this assembly so I can put an end to them at once."

²²But Moses and Aaron fell facedown and cried out, "O God, the God who gives breath to all living things, will you be angry with the entire assembly when only one man sins?"

²³Then the LORD said to Moses, ²⁴"Say to the assembly, 'Move away from the tents of Korah, Dathan and Abiram.'"

²⁵Moses got up and went to Dathan and Abiram, and the elders of Israel followed him. ²⁶He warned the assembly, "Move back from the tents of these wicked men! Do not touch anything belonging to them, or you will be swept away because of all their sins." ²⁷So they moved away from the tents of Korah, Dathan and Abiram. Dathan and Abiram had come out and were standing with their wives, children and little ones at the entrances to their tents.

²⁸Then Moses said, "This is how you will know that the LORD has sent me to do all these things and that it was not my idea: ²⁹If these men die a natural death and suffer the fate of all mankind, then the LORD has not sent me. ³⁰But if the LORD brings about something totally new, and the earth opens its mouth and swallows them, with everything that belongs to them, and they go down alive into the realm of the dead, then you will know that these men have treated the LORD with contempt."

³¹As soon as he finished saying all this, the ground under them split apart ³²and the earth opened its mouth and swallowed them and their households, and all those associated with Korah, together with their possessions. ³³They went down alive into the realm of the dead, with everything they owned; the earth closed over them, and they perished and

---

a 14 Or to deceive these men; Hebrew Will you gouge out the eyes of these men

were gone from the community. 34At their cries, all the Israelites around them fled, shouting, "The earth is going to swallow us too!"

35And fire came out from the LORD and consumed the 250 men who were offering the incense.

36The LORD said to Moses, 37"Tell Eleazar son of Aaron, the priest, to remove the censers from the charred remains and scatter the coals some distance away, for the censers are holy— 38the censers of the men who sinned at the cost of their lives. Hammer the censers into sheets to overlay the altar, for they were presented before the LORD and have become holy. Let them be a sign to the Israelites."

39So Eleazar the priest collected the bronze censers brought by those who had been burned to death, and he had them hammered out to overlay the altar, 40as the LORD directed him through Moses. This was to remind the Israelites that no one except a descendant of Aaron should come to burn incense before the LORD, or he would become like Korah and his followers.

41The next day the whole Israelite community grumbled against Moses and Aaron. "You have killed the LORD's people," they said.

42But when the assembly gathered in opposition to Moses and Aaron and turned toward the tent of meeting, suddenly the cloud covered it and the glory of the LORD appeared. 43Then Moses and Aaron went to the front of the tent of meeting, 44and the LORD said to Moses, 45"Get away from this assembly so I can put an end to them at once." And they fell facedown.

46Then Moses said to Aaron, "Take your censer and put incense in it, along with burning coals from the altar, and hurry to the assembly to make atonement for them. Wrath has come out from the LORD; the plague has started." 47So Aaron did as Moses said, and ran into the midst of the assembly. The plague had already started among the people, but Aaron offered the incense and made atonement

for them. 48He stood between the living and the dead, and the plague stopped. 49But 14,700 people died from the plague, in addition to those who had died because of Korah. 50Then Aaron returned to Moses at the entrance to the tent of meeting, for the plague had stopped.a

The Budding of Aaron's Staff

17b The LORD said to Moses, 2"Speak to the Israelites and get twelve staffs from them, one from the leader of

INSTANT ACCESS

Have you ever wondered why your mom or dad wants to meet the guy or girl you're dating? Or the kids you hang around with after school? Do you think they're just trying to annoy you? Being mean? Or is there more to it? God told the Israelites to "move away from the tents of Korah, Dathan and Abiram" when these men organized a rebellion. Then the ground opened up beneath them, and they were killed. Your parents want to know your friends in case you ever need the same warning. They don't want you in the middle of big problems or messy situations. When they say, "Stay away from there," stop a minute to listen—and obey.

{Numbers 16:23-24}

a 50 In Hebrew texts 16:36-50 is numbered 17:1-15. b In Hebrew texts 17:1-13 is numbered 17:16-28.

each of their ancestral tribes. Write the name of each man on his staff. ³On the staff of Levi write Aaron's name, for there must be one staff for the head of each ancestral tribe. ⁴Place them in the tent of meeting in front of the ark of the covenant law, where I meet with you. ⁵The staff belonging to the man I choose will sprout, and I will rid myself of this constant grumbling against you by the Israelites."

⁶So Moses spoke to the Israelites, and their leaders gave him twelve staffs, one for the leader of each of their ancestral tribes, and Aaron's staff was among them. ⁷Moses placed the staffs before the Lord in the tent of the covenant law.

⁸The next day Moses entered the tent and saw that Aaron's staff, which represented the tribe of Levi, had not only sprouted but had budded, blossomed and produced almonds. ⁹Then Moses brought out all the staffs from the Lord's presence to all the Israelites. They looked at them, and each of the leaders took his own staff.

¹⁰The Lord said to Moses, "Put back Aaron's staff in front of the ark of the covenant law, to be kept as a sign to the rebellious. This will put an end to their grumbling against me, so that they will not die." ¹¹Moses did just as the Lord commanded him.

¹²The Israelites said to Moses, "We will die! We are lost, we are all lost! ¹³Anyone who even comes near the tabernacle of the Lord will die. Are we all going to die?"

Duties of Priests and Levites

18 The Lord said to Aaron, "You, your sons and your family are to bear the responsibility for offenses connected with the sanctuary, and you and your sons alone are to bear the responsibility for offenses connected with the priesthood. ²Bring your fellow Levites from your ancestral tribe to join you and assist you when you and your sons minister before the tent of the covenant law. ³They are to be responsible to you and are to perform all the duties of the tent, but they must

not go near the furnishings of the sanctuary or the altar. Otherwise both they and you will die. ⁴They are to join you and be responsible for the care of the tent of meeting—all the work at the tent—and no one else may come near where you are.

⁵"You are to be responsible for the care of the sanctuary and the altar, so that my wrath will not fall on the Israelites again. ⁶I myself have selected your fellow Levites from among the Israelites as a gift to you, dedicated to the Lord to do the work at the tent of meeting. ⁷But only you and your sons may serve as priests in connection with everything at the altar and inside the curtain. I am giving you the service of the priesthood as a gift. Anyone else who comes near the sanctuary is to be put to death."

Offerings for Priests and Levites

⁸Then the Lord said to Aaron, "I myself have put you in charge of the offerings presented to me; all the holy offerings the Israelites give me I give to you and your sons as your portion, your perpetual share. ⁹You are to have the part of the most holy offerings that is kept from the fire. From all the gifts they bring me as most holy offerings, whether grain or sinᵃ or guilt offerings, that part belongs to you and your sons. ¹⁰Eat it as something most holy; every male shall eat it. You must regard it as holy.

¹¹"This also is yours: whatever is set aside from the gifts of all the wave offerings of the Israelites. I give this to you and your sons and daughters as your perpetual share. Everyone in your household who is ceremonially clean may eat it.

¹²"I give you all the finest olive oil and all the finest new wine and grain they give the Lord as the firstfruits of their harvest. ¹³All the land's firstfruits that they bring to the Lord will be yours. Everyone in your household who is ceremonially clean may eat it.

¹⁴"Everything in Israel that is devotedᵇ to the Lord is yours. ¹⁵The first offspring

---

ᵃ 9 Or *purification*   ᵇ 14 The Hebrew term refers to the irrevocable giving over of things or persons to the Lord.

of every womb, both human and animal, that is offered to the LORD is yours. But you must redeem every firstborn son and every firstborn male of unclean animals. ¹⁶When they are a month old, you must redeem them at the redemption price set at five shekels[a] of silver, according to the sanctuary shekel, which weighs twenty gerahs.

¹⁷"But you must not redeem the firstborn of a cow, a sheep or a goat; they are holy. Splash their blood against the altar and burn their fat as a food offering, an aroma pleasing to the LORD. ¹⁸Their meat is to be yours, just as the breast of the wave offering and the right thigh are yours. ¹⁹Whatever is set aside from the holy offerings the Israelites present to the LORD I give to you and your sons and daughters as your perpetual share. It is an everlasting covenant of salt before the LORD for both you and your offspring."

²⁰The LORD said to Aaron, "You will have no inheritance in their land, nor will you have any share among them; I am your share and your inheritance among the Israelites.

²¹"I give to the Levites all the tithes in Israel as their inheritance in return for the work they do while serving at the tent of meeting. ²²From now on the Israelites must not go near the tent of meeting, or they will bear the consequences of their sin and will die. ²³It is the Levites who are to do the work at the tent of meeting and bear the responsibility for any offenses they commit against it. This is a lasting ordinance for the generations to come. They will receive no inheritance among the Israelites. ²⁴Instead, I give to the Levites as their inheritance the tithes that the Israelites present as an offering to the LORD. That is why I said concerning them: 'They will have no inheritance among the Israelites.'"

²⁵The LORD said to Moses, ²⁶"Speak to the Levites and say to them: 'When you receive from the Israelites the tithe I give you as your inheritance, you must present a tenth of that tithe as the LORD's offering. ²⁷Your offering will be reckoned to you as grain from the threshing floor or juice from the winepress. ²⁸In this way you also will present an offering to the LORD from all the tithes you receive from the Israelites. From these tithes you must give the LORD's portion to Aaron the priest. ²⁹You must present as the LORD's portion the best and holiest part of everything given to you.'

³⁰"Say to the Levites: 'When you present the best part, it will be reckoned to you as the product of the threshing floor or the winepress. ³¹You and your households may eat the rest of it anywhere, for it is your wages for your work at the tent of meeting. ³²By presenting the best part of it you will not be guilty in this matter; then you will not defile the holy offerings of the Israelites, and you will not die.'"

The Water of Cleansing

19 The LORD said to Moses and Aaron: ²"This is a requirement of the law that the LORD has commanded: Tell the Israelites to bring you a red heifer without defect or blemish and that has never been under a yoke. ³Give it to Eleazar the priest; it is to be taken outside the camp and slaughtered in his presence. ⁴Then Eleazar the priest is to take some of its blood on his finger and sprinkle it seven times toward the front of the tent of meeting. ⁵While he watches, the heifer is to be burned—its hide, flesh, blood and intestines. ⁶The priest is to take some cedar wood, hyssop and scarlet wool and throw them onto the burning heifer. ⁷After that, the priest must wash his clothes and bathe himself with water. He may then come into the camp, but he will be ceremonially unclean till evening. ⁸The man who burns it must also wash his clothes and bathe with water, and he too will be unclean till evening.

⁹"A man who is clean shall gather up the ashes of the heifer and put them in a ceremonially clean place outside the camp. They are to be kept by the Israelite community for use in the water of cleansing; it is for purification from sin. ¹⁰The man who gathers up the ashes of the

a 16 That is, about 2 ounces or about 58 grams

heifer must also wash his clothes, and he too will be unclean till evening. This will be a lasting ordinance both for the Israelites and for the foreigners residing among them.

¹¹ "Whoever touches a human corpse will be unclean for seven days. ¹²They must purify themselves with the water on the third day and on the seventh day; then they will be clean. But if they do not purify themselves on the third and seventh days, they will not be clean. ¹³If they fail to purify themselves after touching a human corpse, they defile the Lord's tabernacle. They must be cut off from Israel. Because the water of cleansing has not been sprinkled on them, they are unclean; their uncleanness remains on them.

¹⁴ "This is the law that applies when a person dies in a tent: Anyone who enters the tent and anyone who is in it will be unclean for seven days, ¹⁵and every open container without a lid fastened on it will be unclean.

¹⁶ "Anyone out in the open who touches someone who has been killed with a sword or someone who has died a natural death, or anyone who touches a human bone or a grave, will be unclean for seven days.

¹⁷ "For the unclean person, put some ashes from the burned purification offering into a jar and pour fresh water over them. ¹⁸Then a man who is ceremonially clean is to take some hyssop, dip it in the water and sprinkle the tent and all the furnishings and the people who were there. He must also sprinkle anyone who has touched a human bone or a grave or anyone who has been killed or anyone who has died a natural death. ¹⁹The man who is clean is to sprinkle those who are unclean on the third and seventh days, and on the seventh day he is to purify them. Those who are being cleansed must wash their clothes and bathe with water, and that evening they will be clean. ²⁰But if those who are unclean do not purify themselves, they must be cut off from the community, because they have defiled the sanctuary of the Lord. The water of cleansing has not been sprinkled

on them, and they are unclean. ²¹This is a lasting ordinance for them.

"The man who sprinkles the water of cleansing must also wash his clothes, and anyone who touches the water of cleansing will be unclean till evening. ²²Anything that an unclean person touches becomes unclean, and anyone who touches it becomes unclean till evening."

Water From the Rock

20 In the first month the whole Israelite community arrived at the Desert of Zin, and they stayed at Kadesh. There Miriam died and was buried.

²Now there was no water for the community, and the people gathered in opposition to Moses and Aaron. ³They quarreled with Moses and said, "If only we had died when our brothers fell dead before the Lord! ⁴Why did you bring the Lord's community into this wilderness, that we and our livestock should die here? ⁵Why did you bring us up out of Egypt to this terrible place? It has no grain or figs, grapevines or pomegranates. And there is no water to drink!"

⁶Moses and Aaron went from the assembly to the entrance to the tent of meeting and fell facedown, and the glory of the Lord appeared to them. ⁷The Lord said to Moses, ⁸"Take the staff, and you and your brother Aaron gather the assembly together. Speak to that rock before their eyes and it will pour out its water. You will bring water out of the rock for the community so they and their livestock can drink."

⁹So Moses took the staff from the Lord's presence, just as he commanded him. ¹⁰He and Aaron gathered the assembly together in front of the rock and Moses said to them, "Listen, you rebels, must we bring you water out of this rock?" ¹¹Then Moses raised his arm and struck the rock twice with his staff. Water gushed out, and the community and their livestock drank.

¹²But the Lord said to Moses and Aaron, "Because you did not trust in me enough to honor me as holy in the sight of the Israelites, you will not bring this community into the land I give them."

¹³These were the waters of Meribah,ᵃ where the Israelites quarreled with the LORD and where he was proved holy among them.

Edom Denies Israel Passage

¹⁴Moses sent messengers from Kadesh to the king of Edom, saying:

"This is what your brother Israel says: You know about all the hardships that have come on us. ¹⁵Our ancestors went down into Egypt, and we lived there many years. The Egyptians mistreated us and our ancestors, ¹⁶but when we cried out to the LORD, he heard our cry and sent an angel and brought us out of Egypt.

"Now we are here at Kadesh, a town on the edge of your territory. ¹⁷Please let us pass through your country. We will not go through any field or vineyard, or drink water from any well. We will travel along the King's Highway and not turn to the right or to the left until we have passed through your territory."

¹⁸But Edom answered:

"You may not pass through here; if you try, we will march out and attack you with the sword."

¹⁹The Israelites replied:

"We will go along the main road, and if we or our livestock drink any of your water, we will pay for it. We only want to pass through on foot—nothing else."

²⁰Again they answered:

"You may not pass through."

Then Edom came out against them with a large and powerful army. ²¹Since Edom refused to let them go through their territory, Israel turned away from them.

The Death of Aaron

²²The whole Israelite community set out from Kadesh and came to Mount Hor.

²³At Mount Hor, near the border of Edom, the LORD said to Moses and Aaron, ²⁴"Aaron will be gathered to his people. He will not enter the land I give the Israelites, because both of you rebelled against my command at the waters of Meribah. ²⁵Get Aaron and his son Eleazar and take them up Mount Hor. ²⁶Remove Aaron's garments and put them on his son Eleazar, for Aaron will be gathered to his people; he will die there."

²⁷Moses did as the LORD commanded: They went up Mount Hor in the sight of the whole community. ²⁸Moses removed Aaron's garments and put them on his son Eleazar. And Aaron died there on top of the mountain. Then Moses and Eleazar came down from the mountain, ²⁹and when the whole community learned that Aaron had died, all the Israelites mourned for him thirty days.

Arad Destroyed

21 When the Canaanite king of Arad, who lived in the Negev, heard that Israel was coming along the road to Atharim, he attacked the Israelites and captured some of them. ²Then Israel made this vow to the LORD: "If you will deliver these people into our hands, we will totally destroyᵇ their cities." ³The LORD listened to Israel's plea and gave the Canaanites over to them. They completely destroyed them and their towns; so the place was named Hormah.ᶜ

The Bronze Snake

⁴They traveled from Mount Hor along the route to the Red Sea,ᵈ to go around Edom. But the people grew impatient on the way; ⁵they spoke against God and against Moses, and said, "Why have you brought us up out of Egypt to die in the wilderness? There is no bread! There is no water! And we detest this miserable food!"

⁶Then the LORD sent venomous snakes among them; they bit the people and many Israelites died. ⁷The people came to Moses and said, "We sinned when we spoke against the LORD and against you. Pray

---

ᵃ 13 *Meribah* means *quarreling.*   ᵇ 2 The Hebrew term refers to the irrevocable giving over of things or persons to the LORD, often by totally destroying them; also in verse 3.   ᶜ 3 *Hormah* means *destruction.*   ᵈ 4 Or *the Sea of Reeds*

that the LORD will take the snakes away from us." So Moses prayed for the people.

⁸The LORD said to Moses, "Make a snake and put it up on a pole; anyone who is bitten can look at it and live." ⁹So Moses made a bronze snake and put it up on a pole. Then when anyone was bitten by a snake and looked at the bronze snake, they lived.

The Journey to Moab

¹⁰The Israelites moved on and camped at Oboth. ¹¹Then they set out from Oboth and camped in Iye Abarim, in the wilderness that faces Moab toward the sunrise. ¹²From there they moved on and camped in the Zered Valley. ¹³They set out from there and camped alongside the Arnon, which is in the wilderness extending into Amorite territory. The Arnon is the border of Moab, between Moab and the Amorites. ¹⁴That is why the Book of the Wars of the LORD says:

> ". . . Zahab[a] in Suphah and the ravines,
>> the Arnon ¹⁵and[b] the slopes of the ravines
> that lead to the settlement of Ar
>> and lie along the border of Moab."

¹⁶From there they continued on to Beer, the well where the LORD said to Moses, "Gather the people together and I will give them water."

¹⁷Then Israel sang this song:

> "Spring up, O well!
>> Sing about it,
> ¹⁸about the well that the princes dug,
>> that the nobles of the people sank—
>> the nobles with scepters and staffs."

Then they went from the wilderness to Mattanah, ¹⁹from Mattanah to Nahaliel, from Nahaliel to Bamoth, ²⁰and from Bamoth to the valley in Moab where the top of Pisgah overlooks the wasteland.

Defeat of Sihon and Og

²¹Israel sent messengers to say to Sihon king of the Amorites:

²²"Let us pass through your country. We will not turn aside into any field or vineyard, or drink water from any well. We will travel along the King's Highway until we have passed through your territory."

²³But Sihon would not let Israel pass through his territory. He mustered his entire army and marched out into the wilderness against Israel. When he reached Jahaz, he fought with Israel. ²⁴Israel, however, put him to the sword and took over his land from the Arnon to the Jabbok, but only as far as the Ammonites, because their border was fortified. ²⁵Israel captured all the cities of the Amorites and occupied them, including Heshbon and all its surrounding settlements. ²⁶Heshbon was the city of Sihon king of the Amorites, who had fought against the former king of Moab and had taken from him all his land as far as the Arnon.

²⁷That is why the poets say:

> "Come to Heshbon and let it be rebuilt;
>> let Sihon's city be restored.

²⁸"Fire went out from Heshbon,
>> a blaze from the city of Sihon.
> It consumed Ar of Moab,
>> the citizens of Arnon's heights.

Numbers 21

Q: Why did Moses make a bronze snake?

BONUS: Who destroyed that snake, and why?

Answers on next page

---

a 14 Septuagint; Hebrew *Waheb*   b 14,15 Or *"I have been given from Suphah and the ravines / of the Arnon* ¹⁵*to*

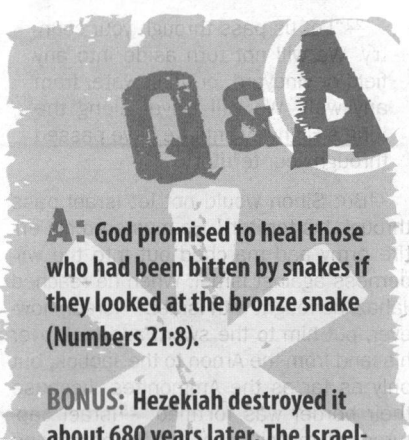

A: God promised to heal those who had been bitten by snakes if they looked at the bronze snake (Numbers 21:8).

BONUS: Hezekiah destroyed it about 680 years later. The Israelites were worshiping it as an idol (2 Kings 18:4).

29 Woe to you, Moab!
You are destroyed, people of
Chemosh!
He has given up his sons as fugitives
and his daughters as captives
to Sihon king of the Amorites.

30 "But we have overthrown them;
Heshbon's dominion has been
destroyed all the way to Dibon.
We have demolished them as far as
Nophah,
which extends to Medeba."

31 So Israel settled in the land of the Amorites.

32 After Moses had sent spies to Jazer, the Israelites captured its surrounding settlements and drove out the Amorites who were there. 33 Then they turned and went up along the road toward Bashan, and Og king of Bashan and his whole army marched out to meet them in battle at Edrei.

34 The LORD said to Moses, "Do not be afraid of him, for I have delivered him into your hands, along with his whole army and his land. Do to him what you did to Sihon king of the Amorites, who reigned in Heshbon."

35 So they struck him down, together with his sons and his whole army, leaving them no survivors. And they took possession of his land.

Balak Summons Balaam

22 Then the Israelites traveled to the plains of Moab and camped along the Jordan across from Jericho.

2 Now Balak son of Zippor saw all that Israel had done to the Amorites, 3 and Moab was terrified because there were so many people. Indeed, Moab was filled with dread because of the Israelites.

4 The Moabites said to the elders of Midian, "This horde is going to lick up everything around us, as an ox licks up the grass of the field."

So Balak son of Zippor, who was king of Moab at that time, 5 sent messengers to summon Balaam son of Beor, who was at Pethor, near the Euphrates River, in his native land. Balak said:

"A people has come out of Egypt;
they cover the face of the land and
have settled next to me. 6 Now come
and put a curse on these people, because they are too powerful for me.
Perhaps then I will be able to defeat
them and drive them out of the land.
For I know that whoever you bless
is blessed, and whoever you curse
is cursed."

7 The elders of Moab and Midian left, taking with them the fee for divination. When they came to Balaam, they told him what Balak had said.

8 "Spend the night here," Balaam said to them, "and I will report back to you with the answer the LORD gives me." So the Moabite officials stayed with him.

9 God came to Balaam and asked, "Who are these men with you?"

10 Balaam said to God, "Balak son of Zippor, king of Moab, sent me this message: 11 'A people that has come out of Egypt covers the face of the land. Now come and put a curse on them for me. Perhaps then I will be able to fight them and drive them away.'"

12 But God said to Balaam, "Do not go with them. You must not put a curse on those people, because they are blessed."

¹³The next morning Balaam got up and said to Balak's officials, "Go back to your own country, for the LORD has refused to let me go with you."

¹⁴So the Moabite officials returned to Balak and said, "Balaam refused to come with us."

¹⁵Then Balak sent other officials, more numerous and more distinguished than the first. ¹⁶They came to Balaam and said:

"This is what Balak son of Zippor says: Do not let anything keep you from coming to me, ¹⁷because I will reward you handsomely and do whatever you say. Come and put a curse on these people for me."

¹⁸But Balaam answered them, "Even if Balak gave me all the silver and gold in his palace, I could not do anything great or small to go beyond the command of the LORD my God. ¹⁹Now spend the night here so that I can find out what else the LORD will tell me."

²⁰That night God came to Balaam and said, "Since these men have come to summon you, go with them, but do only what I tell you."

Balaam's Donkey

²¹Balaam got up in the morning, saddled his donkey and went with the Moabite officials. ²²But God was very angry when he went, and the angel of the LORD stood in the road to oppose him. Balaam was riding on his donkey, and his two servants were with him. ²³When the donkey saw the angel of the LORD standing in the road with a drawn sword in his hand, it turned off the road into a field. Balaam beat it to get it back on the road.

²⁴Then the angel of the LORD stood in a narrow path through the vineyards, with walls on both sides. ²⁵When the donkey saw the angel of the LORD, it pressed close to the wall, crushing Balaam's foot against it. So he beat the donkey again.

²⁶Then the angel of the LORD moved on ahead and stood in a narrow place where there was no room to turn, either to the right or to the left. ²⁷When the donkey saw the angel of the LORD, it lay down under Balaam, and he was angry and beat it with his staff. ²⁸Then the LORD opened the donkey's mouth, and it said to Balaam, "What have I done to you to make you beat me these three times?"

²⁹Balaam answered the donkey, "You have made a fool of me! If only I had a sword in my hand, I would kill you right now."

³⁰The donkey said to Balaam, "Am I not your own donkey, which you have always ridden, to this day? Have I been in the habit of doing this to you?"

"No," he said.

³¹Then the LORD opened Balaam's eyes, and he saw the angel of the LORD standing in the road with his sword drawn. So he bowed low and fell facedown.

³²The angel of the LORD asked him, "Why have you beaten your donkey these three times? I have come here to oppose you because your path is a reckless one before me.ᵃ ³³The donkey saw me and turned away from me these three times. If it had not turned away, I would certainly have killed you by now, but I would have spared it."

Numbers 22

Q: Who rode on an animal that talked to him?

BONUS: What did that animal do to his foot?

Answers on next page

ᵃ 32 The meaning of the Hebrew for this clause is uncertain.

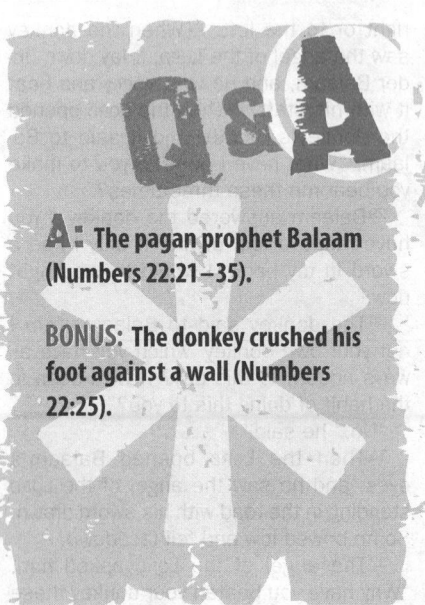

bulls and seven rams for me." ²Balak did as Balaam said, and the two of them offered a bull and a ram on each altar.

³Then Balaam said to Balak, "Stay here beside your offering while I go aside. Perhaps the LORD will come to meet with me. Whatever he reveals to me I will tell you." Then he went off to a barren height.

⁴God met with him, and Balaam said, "I have prepared seven altars, and on each altar I have offered a bull and a ram."

⁵The LORD put a word in Balaam's mouth and said, "Go back to Balak and give him this word."

⁶So he went back to him and found him standing beside his offering, with all the Moabite officials. ⁷Then Balaam spoke his message:

> "Balak brought me from Aram,
> the king of Moab from the eastern
>   mountains.
> 'Come,' he said, 'curse Jacob for me;
> come, denounce Israel.'
> ⁸How can I curse
> those whom God has not cursed?
> How can I denounce
> those whom the LORD has not
>   denounced?
> ⁹From the rocky peaks I see them,
> from the heights I view them.
> I see a people who live apart
> and do not consider themselves
>   one of the nations.
> ¹⁰Who can count the dust of Jacob
> or number even a fourth of Israel?
> Let me die the death of the righteous,
> and may my final end be like
>   theirs!"

¹¹Balak said to Balaam, "What have you done to me? I brought you to curse my enemies, but you have done nothing but bless them!"

¹²He answered, "Must I not speak what the LORD puts in my mouth?"

Balaam's Second Message

¹³Then Balak said to him, "Come with me to another place where you can see them; you will not see them all but only the outskirts of their camp. And from there, curse them for me." ¹⁴So he took him to the field of Zophim on the top of

³⁴Balaam said to the angel of the LORD, "I have sinned. I did not realize you were standing in the road to oppose me. Now if you are displeased, I will go back."

³⁵The angel of the LORD said to Balaam, "Go with the men, but speak only what I tell you." So Balaam went with Balak's officials.

³⁶When Balak heard that Balaam was coming, he went out to meet him at the Moabite town on the Arnon border, at the edge of his territory. ³⁷Balak said to Balaam, "Did I not send you an urgent summons? Why didn't you come to me? Am I really not able to reward you?"

³⁸"Well, I have come to you now," Balaam replied. "But I can't say whatever I please. I must speak only what God puts in my mouth."

³⁹Then Balaam went with Balak to Kiriath Huzoth. ⁴⁰Balak sacrificed cattle and sheep, and gave some to Balaam and the officials who were with him. ⁴¹The next morning Balak took Balaam up to Bamoth Baal, and from there he could see the outskirts of the Israelite camp.

Balaam's First Message

23 Balaam said, "Build me seven altars here, and prepare seven

Pisgah, and there he built seven altars and offered a bull and a ram on each altar.

¹⁵Balaam said to Balak, "Stay here beside your offering while I meet with him over there."

¹⁶The Lord met with Balaam and put a word in his mouth and said, "Go back to Balak and give him this word."

¹⁷So he went to him and found him standing beside his offering, with the Moabite officials. Balak asked him, "What did the Lord say?"

¹⁸Then he spoke his message:

"Arise, Balak, and listen;
  hear me, son of Zippor.
¹⁹God is not human, that he should lie,
  not a human being, that he should
    change his mind.
Does he speak and then not act?
Does he promise and not fulfill?
²⁰I have received a command to bless;
  he has blessed, and I cannot
    change it.

²¹"No misfortune is seen in Jacob,
  no misery observedᵃ in Israel.
The Lord their God is with them;
  the shout of the King is among them.
²²God brought them out of Egypt;
  they have the strength of a wild ox.
²³There is no divination againstᵇ Jacob,
  no evil omens againstᵇ Israel.
It will now be said of Jacob
  and of Israel, 'See what God has
    done!'
²⁴The people rise like a lioness;
  they rouse themselves like a lion
that does not rest till it devours its
    prey
  and drinks the blood of its victims."

²⁵Then Balak said to Balaam, "Neither curse them at all nor bless them at all!"

²⁶Balaam answered, "Did I not tell you I must do whatever the Lord says?"

Balaam's Third Message

²⁷Then Balak said to Balaam, "Come, let me take you to another place. Perhaps it will please God to let you curse them for me from there." ²⁸And Balak took Balaam to the top of Peor, overlooking the wasteland.

²⁹Balaam said, "Build me seven altars here, and prepare seven bulls and seven rams for me." ³⁰Balak did as Balaam had said, and offered a bull and a ram on each altar.

24 Now when Balaam saw that it pleased the Lord to bless Israel, he did not resort to divination as at other times, but turned his face toward the wilderness. ²When Balaam looked out and saw Israel encamped tribe by tribe, the Spirit of God came on him ³and he spoke his message:

"The prophecy of Balaam son of Beor,
  the prophecy of one whose eye
    sees clearly,
⁴the prophecy of one who hears the
    words of God,
  who sees a vision from the
    Almighty,ᶜ
  who falls prostrate, and whose eyes
    are opened:

⁵"How beautiful are your tents, Jacob,
  your dwelling places, Israel!

⁶"Like valleys they spread out,
  like gardens beside a river,
like aloes planted by the Lord,
  like cedars beside the waters.
⁷Water will flow from their buckets;
  their seed will have abundant water.

"Their king will be greater than Agag;
  their kingdom will be exalted.

⁸"God brought them out of Egypt;
  they have the strength of a wild ox.
They devour hostile nations
  and break their bones in pieces;
  with their arrows they pierce them.
⁹Like a lion they crouch and lie down,
  like a lioness—who dares to rouse
    them?

"May those who bless you be blessed
  and those who curse you be
    cursed!"

¹⁰Then Balak's anger burned against Balaam. He struck his hands together

---

ᵃ 21 Or He has not looked on Jacob's offenses / or on the wrongs found   ᵇ 23 Or in   ᶜ 4 Hebrew Shaddai; also in verse 16 and said to him, "I summoned you to curse my enemies, but you have blessed them these three times. ¹¹Now leave at once and go home! I said I would reward you handsomely, but the LORD has kept you from being rewarded."

¹²Balaam answered Balak, "Did I not tell the messengers you sent me, ¹³'Even if Balak gave me all the silver and gold in his palace, I could not do anything of my own accord, good or bad, to go beyond the command of the LORD—and I must say only what the LORD says'? ¹⁴Now I am going back to my people, but come, let me warn you of what this people will do to your people in days to come."

Balaam's Fourth Message

¹⁵Then he spoke his message:

"The prophecy of Balaam son of Beor,
    the prophecy of one whose eye
        sees clearly,
¹⁶the prophecy of one who hears the
        words of God,
    who has knowledge from the Most
        High,
    who sees a vision from the Almighty,
    who falls prostrate, and whose eyes
        are opened:

¹⁷"I see him, but not now;
    I behold him, but not near.
A star will come out of Jacob;
    a scepter will rise out of
        Israel.
He will crush the
        foreheads of
        Moab,
    the skulls*ᵃ* ofᵇ all
        the people of
        Sheth.ᶜ
¹⁸Edom will be
    conquered;
    Seir, his enemy, will
        be conquered,
    but Israel will grow
        strong.
¹⁹A ruler will come out of Jacob
    and destroy the survivors of the
        city."

Balaam's Fifth Message

²⁰Then Balaam saw Amalek and spoke his message:

"Amalek was first among the nations,
    but their end will be utter
        destruction."

Balaam's Sixth Message

²¹Then he saw the Kenites and spoke his message:

"Your dwelling place is secure,
    your nest is set in a rock;
²²yet you Kenites will be destroyed
    when Ashur takes you captive."

Balaam's Seventh Message

²³Then he spoke his message:

"Alas! Who can live when God does
    this?ᵈ
²⁴   Ships will come from the shores of
        Cyprus;
    they will subdue Ashur and Eber,
    but they too will come to ruin."

²⁵Then Balaam got up and returned home, and Balak went his own way.

Moab Seduces Israel

25 While Israel was staying in Shittim, the men began to indulge in sexual immorality with Moabite women, ²who invited them to the sacrifices to their gods. The people ate the sacrificial meal and bowed down before these gods. ³So Israel yoked themselves to the Baal of Peor. And the LORD's anger burned against them.

⁴The LORD said to Moses, "Take all the leaders of these people, kill them and expose them in broad daylight before the LORD, so that the LORD's fierce anger may turn away from Israel."

⁵So Moses said to Israel's judges, "Each of you must put to death those of

*May those who bless
you be blessed . . .*
Numbers 24:9

ᵃ *17* Samaritan Pentateuch (see also Jer. 48:45); the meaning of the word in the Masoretic Text is uncertain.
ᵇ *17* Or possibly *Moab, / batter*   ᶜ *17* Or *all the noisy boasters*   ᵈ *23* Masoretic Text; with a different word division of the Hebrew *The people from the islands will gather from the north.*

If the men had stayed in camp, it never would have happened. But they got in with a new group and did things they never would have done if they'd stuck with their families and friends. You see this every day—a teen who acts one way at your youth group or at home, and totally different when she's with the school crowd. It's not hypocrisy. She just feels a need to fit in whatever group she happens to be around. Trouble is, sin is sin no matter who we're with. God's standards don't change. Right is right, and wrong is wrong. And people of character commit to do what's right, whoever they are with.

{Numbers 25:1-3}

your people who have yoked themselves to the Baal of Peor."

6 Then an Israelite man brought into the camp a Midianite woman right before the eyes of Moses and the whole assembly of Israel while they were weeping at the entrance to the tent of meeting. 7 When Phinehas son of Eleazar, the son of Aaron, the priest, saw this, he left the assembly, took a spear in his hand 8 and followed the Israelite into the tent. He drove the spear into both of them, right through the Israelite man and into the woman's stomach. Then the plague against the Israelites was stopped; 9 but those who died in the plague numbered 24,000.

10 The LORD said to Moses, 11 "Phinehas son of Eleazar, the son of Aaron, the priest, has turned my anger away from the Israelites. Since he was as zealous for my honor among them as I am, I did not put an end to them in my zeal. 12 Therefore tell him I am making my covenant of peace with him. 13 He and his descendants will have a covenant of a lasting priesthood, because he was zealous for the honor of his God and made atonement for the Israelites."

14 The name of the Israelite who was killed with the Midianite woman was Zimri son of Salu, the leader of a Simeonite family. 15 And the name of the Midianite woman who was put to death was Kozbi daughter of Zur, a tribal chief of a Midianite family.

16 The LORD said to Moses, 17 "Treat the Midianites as enemies and kill them. 18 They treated you as enemies when they deceived you in the Peor incident involving their sister Kozbi, the daughter of a Midianite leader, the woman who was killed when the plague came as a result of that incident."

The Second Census

26 After the plague the LORD said to Moses and Eleazar son of Aaron, the priest, 2 "Take a census of the whole Israelite community by families—all those twenty years old or more who are able to serve in the army of Israel." 3 So on the plains of Moab by the Jordan across from Jericho, Moses and Eleazar the priest spoke with them and said, 4 "Take a census of the men twenty years old or more, as the LORD commanded Moses."

These were the Israelites who came out of Egypt:

5 The descendants of Reuben, the first-born son of Israel, were:
    through Hanok, the Hanokite clan;
    through Pallu, the Palluite clan;
  6 through Hezron, the Hezronite clan;
    through Karmi, the Karmite clan.
7 These were the clans of Reuben; those numbered were 43,730.
8 The son of Pallu was Eliab, 9 and the sons of Eliab were Nemuel, Dathan and

Abiram. The same Dathan and Abiram were the community officials who rebelled against Moses and Aaron and were among Korah's followers when they rebelled against the Lord. [10]The earth opened its mouth and swallowed them along with Korah, whose followers died when the fire devoured the 250 men. And they served as a warning sign. [11]The line of Korah, however, did not die out.

[12]The descendants of Simeon by their clans were:

through Nemuel, the Nemuelite clan;
through Jamin, the Jaminite clan;
through Jakin, the Jakinite clan;
[13]through Zerah, the Zerahite clan;
through Shaul, the Shaulite clan.

[14]These were the clans of Simeon; those numbered were 22,200.

[15]The descendants of Gad by their clans were:

through Zephon, the Zephonite clan;
through Haggi, the Haggite clan;
through Shuni, the Shunite clan;
[16]through Ozni, the Oznite clan;
through Eri, the Erite clan;
[17]through Arodi,[a] the Arodite clan;
through Areli, the Arelite clan.

[18]These were the clans of Gad; those numbered were 40,500.

[19]Er and Onan were sons of Judah, but they died in Canaan. [20]The descendants of Judah by their clans were:

through Shelah, the Shelanite clan;
through Perez, the Perezite clan;
through Zerah, the Zerahite clan.
[21]The descendants of Perez were:
through Hezron, the Hezronite clan;
through Hamul, the Hamulite clan.

[22]These were the clans of Judah; those numbered were 76,500.

[23]The descendants of Issachar by their clans were:

through Tola, the Tolaite clan;
through Puah, the Puite[b] clan;
[24]through Jashub, the Jashubite clan;
through Shimron, the Shimronite clan.

[25]These were the clans of Issachar; those numbered were 64,300.

[26]The descendants of Zebulun by their clans were:

through Sered, the Seredite clan;
through Elon, the Elonite clan;
through Jahleel, the Jahleelite clan.

[27]These were the clans of Zebulun; those numbered were 60,500.

[28]The descendants of Joseph by their clans through Manasseh and Ephraim were:

[29]The descendants of Manasseh:

through Makir, the Makirite clan (Makir was the father of Gilead);
through Gilead, the Gileadite clan.
[30]These were the descendants of Gilead:
through Iezer, the Iezerite clan;
through Helek, the Helekite clan;
[31]through Asriel, the Asrielite clan;
through Shechem, the Shechemite clan;
[32]through Shemida, the Shemidaite clan;
through Hepher, the Hepherite clan.
[33](Zelophehad son of Hepher had no sons; he had only daughters, whose names were Mahlah, Noah, Hoglah, Milkah and Tirzah.)

[34]These were the clans of Manasseh; those numbered were 52,700.

[35]These were the descendants of Ephraim by their clans:

through Shuthelah, the Shuthelahite clan;
through Beker, the Bekerite clan;
through Tahan, the Tahanite clan.
[36]These were the descendants of Shuthelah:
through Eran, the Eranite clan.

[37]These were the clans of Ephraim; those numbered were 32,500.

These were the descendants of Joseph by their clans.

[38]The descendants of Benjamin by their clans were:

---

a 17 Samaritan Pentateuch and Syriac (see also Gen. 46:16); Masoretic Text *Arod*   *b 23* Samaritan Pentateuch, Septuagint, Vulgate and Syriac (see also 1 Chron. 7:1); Masoretic Text *through Puvah, the Punite*

through Bela, the Belaite clan;
through Ashbel, the Ashbelite clan;
through Ahiram, the Ahiramite clan;
39 through Shupham,ᵃ the Shuphamite
clan;
through Hupham, the Huphamite
clan.
40 The descendants of Bela through Ard
and Naaman were:
through Ard,ᵇ the Ardite clan;
through Naaman, the Naamite
clan.
41 These were the clans of Benjamin;
those numbered were 45,600.

42 These were the descendants of Dan by
their clans:
through Shuham, the Shuhamite
clan.
These were the clans of Dan: 43 All of
them were Shuhamite clans; and those
numbered were 64,400.

44 The descendants of Asher by their
clans were:
through Imnah, the Imnite clan;
through Ishvi, the Ishvite clan;
through Beriah, the Beriite clan;
45 and through the descendants of Beriah:
through Heber, the Heberite clan;
through Malkiel, the Malkielite
clan.
46 (Asher had a daughter named Serah.)
47 These were the clans of Asher; those
numbered were 53,400.

48 The descendants of Naphtali by their
clans were:
through Jahzeel, the Jahzeelite clan;
through Guni, the Gunite clan;
49 through Jezer, the Jezerite clan;
through Shillem, the Shillemite clan.
50 These were the clans of Naphtali; those
numbered were 45,400.

51 The total number of the men of Israel
was 601,730.

52 The LORD said to Moses, 53 "The land
is to be allotted to them as an inheritance

based on the number of names. 54 To a
larger group give a larger inheritance,
and to a smaller group a smaller one;
each is to receive its inheritance according to the number of those listed. 55 Be
sure that the land is distributed by lot.
What each group inherits will be according to the names for its ancestral tribe.
56 Each inheritance is to be distributed by
lot among the larger and smaller groups."

57 These were the Levites who were counted by their clans:
through Gershon, the Gershonite clan;
through Kohath, the Kohathite clan;
through Merari, the Merarite clan.
58 These also were Levite clans:
the Libnite clan,
the Hebronite clan,
the Mahlite clan,
the Mushite clan,
the Korahite clan.
(Kohath was the forefather of Amram;
59 the name of Amram's wife was
Jochebed, a descendant of Levi, who
was born to the Levitesᶜ in Egypt. To
Amram she bore Aaron, Moses and
their sister Miriam. 60 Aaron was the
father of Nadab and Abihu, Eleazar
and Ithamar. 61 But Nadab and Abihu
died when they made an offering before the LORD with unauthorized fire.)

62 All the male Levites a month old or
more numbered 23,000. They were not
counted along with the other Israelites
because they received no inheritance
among them.

63 These are the ones counted by Moses and Eleazar the priest when they
counted the Israelites on the plains of
Moab by the Jordan across from Jericho. 64 Not one of them was among those
counted by Moses and Aaron the priest
when they counted the Israelites in the
Desert of Sinai. 65 For the LORD had told
those Israelites they would surely die in
the wilderness, and not one of them was
left except Caleb son of Jephunneh and
Joshua son of Nun.

ᵃ 39 A few manuscripts of the Masoretic Text, Samaritan Pentateuch, Vulgate and Syriac (see also Septuagint); most manuscripts of the Masoretic Text *Shephupham*   ᵇ 40 Samaritan Pentateuch and Vulgate (see also Septuagint); Masoretic Text does not have *through Ard*.   ᶜ 59 Or *Jochebed, a daughter of Levi, who was born to Levi*

Zelophehad's Daughters

27 The daughters of Zelophehad son of Hepher, the son of Gilead, the son of Makir, the son of Manasseh, belonged to the clans of Manasseh son of Joseph. The names of the daughters were Mahlah, Noah, Hoglah, Milkah and Tirzah. They came forward ²and stood before Moses, Eleazar the priest, the leaders and the whole assembly at the entrance to the tent of meeting and said, ³"Our father died in the wilderness. He was not among Korah's followers, who banded together against the LORD, but he died for his own sin and left no sons. ⁴Why should our father's name disappear from his clan because he had no son? Give us property among our father's relatives."

⁵So Moses brought their case before the LORD, ⁶and the LORD said to him, ⁷"What Zelophehad's daughters are saying is right. You must certainly give them property as an inheritance among their father's relatives and give their father's inheritance to them.

⁸"Say to the Israelites, 'If a man dies and leaves no son, give his inheritance to his daughter. ⁹If he has no daughter, give his inheritance to his brothers. ¹⁰If he has no brothers, give his inheritance to his father's brothers. ¹¹If his father had no brothers, give his inheritance to the nearest relative in his clan, that he may possess it. This is to have the force of law for the Israelites, as the LORD commanded Moses.'"

Joshua to Succeed Moses

¹²Then the LORD said to Moses, "Go up this mountain in the Abarim Range and see the land I have given the Israelites. ¹³After you have seen it, you too will be gathered to your people, as your brother Aaron was, ¹⁴for when the community rebelled at the waters in the Desert of Zin, both of you disobeyed my command to honor me as holy before their eyes." (These were the waters of Meribah Kadesh, in the Desert of Zin.)

¹⁵Moses said to the LORD, ¹⁶"May the LORD, the God who gives breath to all living things, appoint someone over this community ¹⁷to go out and come in before them, one who will lead them out and bring them in, so the LORD's people will not be like sheep without a shepherd."

¹⁸So the LORD said to Moses, "Take Joshua son of Nun, a man in whom is the spirit of leadership,[a] and lay your hand on him. ¹⁹Have him stand before Eleazar the priest and the entire assembly and commission him in their presence. ²⁰Give him some of your authority so the whole Israelite community will obey him. ²¹He is to stand before Eleazar the priest, who will obtain decisions for him by inquiring of the Urim before the LORD. At his command he and the entire community of the Israelites will go out, and at his command they will come in."

²²Moses did as the LORD commanded him. He took Joshua and had him stand before Eleazar the priest and the whole assembly. ²³Then he laid his hands on him and commissioned him, as the LORD instructed through Moses.

Daily Offerings

28 The LORD said to Moses, ²"Give this command to the Israelites and say to them: 'Make sure that you present to me at the appointed time my food offerings, as an aroma pleasing to me.' ³Say to them: 'This is the food offering you are to present to the LORD: two lambs a year old without defect, as a regular burnt offering each day. ⁴Offer one lamb in the morning and the other at twilight, ⁵together with a grain offering of a tenth of an ephah[b] of the finest flour mixed with a quarter of a hin[c] of oil from pressed olives. ⁶This is the regular burnt offering instituted at Mount Sinai as a pleasing aroma, a food offering presented to the LORD. ⁷The accompanying drink offering is to be a quarter of a hin of fermented drink with each lamb. Pour out the drink offering to the LORD at the sanctuary. ⁸Offer the second lamb at twilight, along with the same kind of grain offering and drink

---

a 18 Or *the Spirit*   b 5 That is, probably about 3 1/2 pounds or about 1.6 kilograms; also in verses 13, 21 and 29
c 5 That is, about 1 quart or about 1 liter; also in verses 7 and 14

Why do boys get favored over girls so much?

>> Isabella

Dear Isabella,

There are many kinds of discrimination in the world. People have experienced prejudice because of their race, nationality, religion, weight, gender and many other things. Discrimination against women is still widespread. Sometimes, even men or boys face discrimination. It is never pleasant to be a victim of discrimination. And we should never say that's just the way things are.

There's an interesting case of discrimination involving women in Numbers 27:1–8. When Zelophehad died, he had no sons to inherit his property as was the custom at that time. So his daughters went to Moses and said they should be able to inherit the land. Moses asked God what he should do. God told Moses to change the law so the daughters could inherit the property.

Even though that was not the usual pattern, God gave the daughters their father's land. God loved them and wanted the land to stay in the family. He didn't say that's not the way we do things. He made some new rules so that these women would be taken care of.

No one has to experience discrimination if we will just treat one another the way we would like to be treated. That even works with people at school.

Jordan

offering that you offer in the morning. This is a food offering, an aroma pleasing to the LORD.

Sabbath Offerings

9 " 'On the Sabbath day, make an offering of two lambs a year old without defect, together with its drink offering and a grain offering of two-tenths of an ephah[a] of the finest flour mixed with olive oil. 10 This is the burnt offering for every Sabbath, in addition to the regular burnt offering and its drink offering.

Monthly Offerings

11 " 'On the first of every month, present to the LORD a burnt offering of two young bulls, one ram and seven male lambs a year old, all without defect. 12 With each bull there is to be a grain offering of three-tenths of an ephah[b] of the finest flour mixed with oil; with the ram, a grain offering of two-tenths of an ephah of the finest flour mixed with oil; 13 and with each lamb, a grain offering of a tenth of an ephah of the finest flour mixed with oil. This is for a burnt offering, a pleasing aroma, a food offering presented to the LORD. 14 With each bull there is to be a drink offering of half a hin[c] of wine; with the ram, a third of a hin[d]; and with each lamb, a quarter of a hin. This is the monthly burnt offering to be made at each new moon during the year. 15 Besides the regular burnt offering with its drink offering, one male goat is to be presented to the LORD as a sin offering.[e]

The Passover

16 " 'On the fourteenth day of the first month the LORD's Passover is to be held. 17 On the fifteenth day of this month there is to be a festival; for seven days eat bread made without yeast. 18 On the first day hold a sacred assembly and do no regular work. 19 Present to the LORD a food offering consisting of a burnt offering of two young bulls, one ram and seven male lambs a year old, all without defect. 20 With each bull offer a grain offering of three-tenths of an ephah of the finest flour mixed with oil; with the ram, two-tenths; 21 and with each of the seven lambs, one-tenth. 22 Include one male goat as a sin offering to make atonement for you. 23 Offer these in addition to the regular morning burnt offering. 24 In this way present the food offering every day for seven days as an aroma pleasing to the LORD; it is to be offered in addition to the regular burnt offering and its drink offering. 25 On the seventh day hold a sacred assembly and do no regular work.

The Festival of Weeks

26 " 'On the day of firstfruits, when you present to the LORD an offering of new grain during the Festival of Weeks, hold a sacred assembly and do no regular work. 27 Present a burnt offering of two young bulls, one ram and seven male lambs a year old as an aroma pleasing to the LORD. 28 With each bull there is to be a grain offering of three-tenths of an ephah of the finest flour mixed with oil; with the ram, two-tenths; 29 and with each of the seven lambs, one-tenth. 30 Include one male goat to make atonement for you. 31 Offer these together with their drink offerings, in addition to the regular burnt offering and its grain offering. Be sure the animals are without defect.

The Festival of Trumpets

29 " 'On the first day of the seventh month hold a sacred assembly and do no regular work. It is a day for you to sound the trumpets. 2 As an aroma pleasing to the LORD, offer a burnt offering of one young bull, one ram and seven male lambs a year old, all without defect. 3 With the bull offer a grain offering of three-tenths of an ephah[f] of the finest flour mixed with olive oil; with the ram, two-tenths;[g] 4 and with each of the seven lambs, one-tenth.[h] 5 Include one male

---

a 9 That is, probably about 7 pounds or about 3.2 kilograms; also in verses 12, 20 and 28   b 12 That is, probably about 11 pounds or about 5 kilograms; also in verses 20 and 28   c 14 That is, about 2 quarts or about 1.9 liters   d 14 That is, about 1 1/3 quarts or about 1.3 liters   e 15 Or *purification offering*; also in verse 22   f 3 That is, probably about 11 pounds or about 5 kilograms; also in verses 9 and 14   g 3 That is, probably about 7 pounds or about 3.2 kilograms; also in verses 9 and 14   h 4 That is, probably about 3 1/2 pounds or about 1.6 kilograms; also in verses 10 and 15

goat as a sin offering[a] to make atonement for you. [6]These are in addition to the monthly and daily burnt offerings with their grain offerings and drink offerings as specified. They are food offerings presented to the LORD, a pleasing aroma.

The Day of Atonement

[7]" 'On the tenth day of this seventh month hold a sacred assembly. You must deny yourselves[b] and do no work. [8]Present as an aroma pleasing to the LORD a burnt offering of one young bull, one ram and seven male lambs a year old, all without defect. [9]With the bull offer a grain offering of three-tenths of an ephah of the finest flour mixed with oil; with the ram, two-tenths; [10]and with each of the seven lambs, one-tenth. [11]Include one male goat as a sin offering, in addition to the sin offering for atonement and the regular burnt offering with its grain offering, and their drink offerings.

The Festival of Tabernacles

[12]" 'On the fifteenth day of the seventh month, hold a sacred assembly and do no regular work. Celebrate a festival to the LORD for seven days. [13]Present as an aroma pleasing to the LORD a food offering consisting of a burnt offering of thirteen young bulls, two rams and fourteen male lambs a year old, all without defect. [14]With each of the thirteen bulls offer a grain offering of three-tenths of an ephah

of the finest flour mixed with oil; with each of the two rams, two-tenths; [15]and with each of the fourteen lambs, one-tenth. [16]Include one male goat as a sin offering, in addition to the regular burnt offering with its grain offering and drink offering.

[17]" 'On the second day offer twelve young bulls, two rams and fourteen male lambs a year old, all without defect. [18]With the bulls, rams and lambs, offer their grain offerings and drink offerings according to the number specified. [19]Include one male goat as a sin offering, in addition to the regular burnt offering with its grain offering, and their drink offerings.

[20]" 'On the third day offer eleven bulls, two rams and fourteen male lambs a year old, all without defect. [21]With the bulls, rams and lambs, offer their grain offerings and drink offerings according to the number specified. [22]Include one male goat as a sin offering, in addition to the regular burnt offering with its grain offering and drink offering.

[23]" 'On the fourth day offer ten bulls, two rams and fourteen male lambs a year old, all without defect. [24]With the bulls, rams and lambs, offer their grain offerings and drink offerings according to the number specified. [25]Include one male goat as a sin offering, in addition to the regular burnt offering with its grain offering and drink offering.

[26]" 'On the fifth day offer nine bulls, two rams and fourteen male lambs a year old,

---

[a] 5 Or *purification offering*; also elsewhere in this chapter   [b] 7 Or *must fast*

PANORAMA

Bon Voyage!

Life is a long trip. Along the way you'll have some big choices to make. Numbers tells about the Israelites' journey toward the promised land. God didn't desert them, and he won't desert you either. Life is a lot better if you stay on the right road.

{NUMBERS}

all without defect. 27With the bulls, rams and lambs, offer their grain offerings and drink offerings according to the number specified. 28Include one male goat as a sin offering, in addition to the regular burnt offering with its grain offering and drink offering.

29 " 'On the sixth day offer eight bulls, two rams and fourteen male lambs a year old, all without defect. 30With the bulls, rams and lambs, offer their grain offerings and drink offerings according to the number specified. 31Include one male goat as a sin offering, in addition to the regular burnt offering with its grain offering and drink offering.

32 " 'On the seventh day offer seven bulls, two rams and fourteen male lambs a year old, all without defect. 33With the bulls, rams and lambs, offer their grain offerings and drink offerings according to the number specified. 34Include one male goat as a sin offering, in addition to the regular burnt offering with its grain offering and drink offering.

35 " 'On the eighth day hold a closing special assembly and do no regular work. 36Present as an aroma pleasing to the LORD a food offering consisting of a burnt offering of one bull, one ram and seven male lambs a year old, all without defect. 37With the bull, the ram and the lambs, offer their grain offerings and drink offerings according to the number specified. 38Include one male goat as a sin offering, in addition to the regular burnt offering with its grain offering and drink offering.

39 " 'In addition to what you vow and your freewill offerings, offer these to the LORD at your appointed festivals: your burnt offerings, grain offerings, drink offerings and fellowship offerings.' "

40Moses told the Israelites all that the LORD commanded him.[a]

Vows

30[b] Moses said to the heads of the tribes of Israel: "This is what the LORD commands: 2When a man makes a vow to the LORD or takes an oath to ob-

ligate himself by a pledge, he must not break his word but must do everything he said.

3 "When a young woman still living in her father's household makes a vow to the LORD or obligates herself by a pledge 4and her father hears about her vow or pledge but says nothing to her, then all her vows and every pledge by which she obligated herself will stand. 5But if her father forbids her when he hears about it, none of her vows or the pledges by which she obligated herself will stand; the LORD will release her because her father has forbidden her.

6 "If she marries after she makes a vow or after her lips utter a rash promise by which she obligates herself 7and her husband hears about it but says nothing to her, then her vows or the pledges by which she obligated herself will stand. 8But if her husband forbids her when he hears about it, he nullifies the vow that obligates her or the rash promise by which she obligates herself, and the LORD will release her.

9 "Any vow or obligation taken by a widow or divorced woman will be binding on her.

10 "If a woman living with her husband makes a vow or obligates herself by a pledge under oath 11and her husband hears about it but says nothing to her and does not forbid her, then all her vows or the pledges by which she obligated herself will stand. 12But if her husband nullifies them when he hears about them, then none of the vows or pledges that came from her lips will stand. Her husband has nullified them, and the LORD will release her. 13Her husband may confirm or nullify any vow she makes or any sworn pledge to deny herself.[c] 14But if her husband says nothing to her about it from day to day, then he confirms all her vows or the pledges binding on her. He confirms them by saying nothing to her when he hears about them. 15If, however, he nullifies them some time after he hears about them, then he must bear the consequences of her wrongdoing."

---

[a] 40 In Hebrew texts this verse (29:40) is numbered 30:1.   [b] In Hebrew texts 30:1-16 is numbered 30:2-17.
[c] 13 Or to fast

Some promises are hard to keep. You say, "I'll be there. I promise." And then your mom makes you stay home. Or you say, "I'll do that tomorrow. I promise." And then you completely forget about it. Sometimes your broken promises are serious. Sometimes they're no big deal. But making a promise to God is a serious thing. When you make God a promise, whether to give regularly, to read the Bible, to witness to a particular person, whatever—be sure to do what you say.

{Numbers 30}

» INSTANT ACCESS

16 These are the regulations the LORD gave Moses concerning relationships between a man and his wife, and between a father and his young daughter still living at home.

Vengeance on the Midianites

31 The LORD said to Moses, 2 "Take vengeance on the Midianites for the Israelites. After that, you will be gathered to your people."

3 So Moses said to the people, "Arm some of your men to go to war against the Midianites so that they may carry out the LORD's vengeance on them. 4 Send into battle a thousand men from each of the tribes of Israel." 5 So twelve thousand men armed for battle, a thousand from each tribe, were supplied from the clans of Israel. 6 Moses sent them into battle, a thousand from each tribe, along with Phinehas son of Eleazar, the priest, who took with him articles from the sanctuary and the trumpets for signaling.

7 They fought against Midian, as the LORD commanded Moses, and killed every man. 8 Among their victims were Evi, Rekem, Zur, Hur and Reba—the five kings of Midian. They also killed Balaam son of Beor with the sword. 9 The Israelites captured the Midianite women and children and took all the Midianite herds, flocks and goods as plunder. 10 They burned all the towns where the Midianites had settled, as well as all their camps. 11 They took all the plunder and spoils, including the people and animals, 12 and brought the captives, spoils and plunder to Moses and Eleazar the priest and the Israelite assembly at their camp on the plains of Moab, by the Jordan across from Jericho.

13 Moses, Eleazar the priest and all the leaders of the community went to meet them outside the camp. 14 Moses was angry with the officers of the army—the commanders of thousands and commanders of hundreds—who returned from the battle.

15 "Have you allowed all the women to live?" he asked them. 16 "They were the ones who followed Balaam's advice and enticed the Israelites to be unfaithful to the LORD in the Peor incident, so that a plague struck the LORD's people. 17 Now kill all the boys. And kill every woman who has slept with a man, 18 but save for yourselves every girl who has never slept with a man.

19 "Anyone who has killed someone or touched someone who was killed must stay outside the camp seven days. On the third and seventh days you must purify yourselves and your captives. 20 Purify every garment as well as everything made of leather, goat hair or wood."

21 Then Eleazar the priest said to the soldiers who had gone into battle, "This is what is required by the law that the LORD gave Moses: 22 Gold, silver, bronze, iron, tin, lead 23 and anything else that can withstand fire must be put through the fire, and then it will be clean. But it

must also be purified with the water of cleansing. And whatever cannot withstand fire must be put through that water. 24On the seventh day wash your clothes and you will be clean. Then you may come into the camp."

Dividing the Spoils

25The LORD said to Moses, 26"You and Eleazar the priest and the family heads of the community are to count all the people and animals that were captured. 27Divide the spoils equally between the soldiers who took part in the battle and the rest of the community. 28From the soldiers who fought in the battle, set apart as tribute for the LORD one out of every five hundred, whether people, cattle, donkeys or sheep. 29Take this tribute from their half share and give it to Eleazar the priest as the LORD's part. 30From the Israelites' half, select one out of every fifty, whether people, cattle, donkeys, sheep or other animals. Give them to the Levites, who are responsible for the care of the LORD's tabernacle." 31So Moses and Eleazar the priest did as the LORD commanded Moses.

32The plunder remaining from the spoils that the soldiers took was 675,000 sheep, 3372,000 cattle, 3461,000 donkeys 35and 32,000 women who had never slept with a man.

36The half share of those who fought in the battle was:

337,500 sheep, 37of which the tribute for the LORD was 675;
3836,000 cattle, of which the tribute for the LORD was 72;
3930,500 donkeys, of which the tribute for the LORD was 61;
4016,000 people, of whom the tribute for the LORD was 32.

41Moses gave the tribute to Eleazar the priest as the LORD's part, as the LORD commanded Moses.

42The half belonging to the Israelites, which Moses set apart from that of the fighting men— 43the community's half— was 337,500 sheep, 4436,000 cattle,

4530,500 donkeys 46and 16,000 people. 47From the Israelites' half, Moses selected one out of every fifty people and animals, as the LORD commanded him, and gave them to the Levites, who were responsible for the care of the LORD's tabernacle.

48Then the officers who were over the units of the army—the commanders of thousands and commanders of hundreds—went to Moses 49and said to him, "Your servants have counted the soldiers under our command, and not one is missing. 50So we have brought as an offering to the LORD the gold articles each of us acquired—armlets, bracelets, signet rings, earrings and necklaces—to make atonement for ourselves before the LORD."

51Moses and Eleazar the priest accepted from them the gold—all the crafted articles. 52All the gold from the commanders of thousands and commanders of hundreds that Moses and Eleazar presented as a gift to the LORD weighed 16,750 shekels.a 53Each soldier had taken plunder for himself. 54Moses and Eleazar the priest accepted the gold from the commanders of thousands and commanders of hundreds and brought it into the tent of meeting as a memorial for the Israelites before the LORD.

The Transjordan Tribes

32 The Reubenites and Gadites, who had very large herds and flocks, saw that the lands of Jazer and Gilead were suitable for livestock. 2So they came to Moses and Eleazar the priest and to the leaders of the community, and said, 3"Ataroth, Dibon, Jazer, Nimrah, Heshbon, Elealeh, Sebam, Nebo and Beon— 4the land the LORD subdued before the people of Israel—are suitable for livestock, and your servants have livestock. 5If we have found favor in your eyes," they said, "let this land be given to your servants as our possession. Do not make us cross the Jordan."

6Moses said to the Gadites and Reubenites, "Should your fellow Israelites go to war while you sit here? 7Why do

---

a 52 That is, about 420 pounds or about 190 kilograms

When your youth group has a service project, do you show up? How about when your youth group visits senior citizens in a nursing home? Or delivers Christmas baskets? Can others count on you to do your share? The Israelite tribes who settled east of the Jordan River didn't just settle there and stay. First they crossed to the west side of the river and helped their fellow Israelites conquer that land. Whenever something important is accomplished, it's because everyone contributes and does his or her fair share. Your youth group needs your support.

{Numbers 32:1–24}

INSTANT ACCESS

you discourage the Israelites from crossing over into the land the LORD has given them? ⁸This is what your fathers did when I sent them from Kadesh Barnea to look over the land. ⁹After they went up to the Valley of Eshkol and viewed the land, they discouraged the Israelites from entering the land the LORD had given them. ¹⁰The LORD's anger was aroused that day and he swore this oath: ¹¹'Because they have not followed me wholeheartedly, not one of those who were twenty years old or more when they came up out of Egypt will see the land I promised on oath to Abraham, Isaac and Jacob— ¹²not one

except Caleb son of Jephunneh the Kenizzite and Joshua son of Nun, for they followed the LORD wholeheartedly.' ¹³The LORD's anger burned against Israel and he made them wander in the wilderness forty years, until the whole generation of those who had done evil in his sight was gone.

¹⁴"And here you are, a brood of sinners, standing in the place of your fathers and making the LORD even more angry with Israel. ¹⁵If you turn away from following him, he will again leave all this people in the wilderness, and you will be the cause of their destruction."

¹⁶Then they came up to him and said, "We would like to build pens here for our livestock and cities for our women and children. ¹⁷But we will arm ourselves for battleᵃ and go ahead of the Israelites until we have brought them to their place. Meanwhile our women and children will live in fortified cities, for protection from the inhabitants of the land. ¹⁸We will not return to our homes until each of the Israelites has received their inheritance. ¹⁹We will not receive any inheritance with them on the other side of the Jordan, because our inheritance has come to us on the east side of the Jordan."

²⁰Then Moses said to them, "If you will do this—if you will arm yourselves before the LORD for battle ²¹and if all of you who are armed cross over the Jordan before the LORD until he has driven his enemies out before him— ²²then when the land is subdued before the LORD, you may return and be free from your obligation to the LORD and to Israel. And this land will be your possession before the LORD.

²³"But if you fail to do this, you will be sinning against the LORD; and you may be sure that your sin will find you out. ²⁴Build cities for your women and children, and pens for your flocks, but do what you have promised."

²⁵The Gadites and Reubenites said to Moses, "We your servants will do as our lord commands. ²⁶Our children and wives, our flocks and herds will remain here in the cities of Gilead. ²⁷But your servants, every man who is armed for battle, will

---

ᵃ 17 Septuagint; Hebrew *will be quick to arm ourselves*

cross over to fight before the LORD, just as our lord says."

28 Then Moses gave orders about them to Eleazar the priest and Joshua son of Nun and to the family heads of the Israelite tribes. 29 He said to them, "If the Gadites and Reubenites, every man armed for battle, cross over the Jordan with you before the LORD, then when the land is subdued before you, you must give them the land of Gilead as their possession. 30 But if they do not cross over with you armed, they must accept their possession with you in Canaan."

31 The Gadites and Reubenites answered, "Your servants will do what the LORD has said. 32 We will cross over before the LORD into Canaan armed, but the property we inherit will be on this side of the Jordan."

33 Then Moses gave to the Gadites, the Reubenites and the half-tribe of Manasseh son of Joseph the kingdom of Sihon king of the Amorites and the kingdom of Og king of Bashan—the whole land with its cities and the territory around them.

34 The Gadites built up Dibon, Ataroth, Aroer, 35 Atroth Shophan, Jazer, Jogbehah, 36 Beth Nimrah and Beth Haran as fortified cities, and built pens for their flocks. 37 And the Reubenites rebuilt Heshbon, Elealeh and Kiriathaim, 38 as well as Nebo and Baal Meon (these names were changed) and Sibmah. They gave names to the cities they rebuilt.

39 The descendants of Makir son of Manasseh went to Gilead, captured it and drove out the Amorites who were there. 40 So Moses gave Gilead to the Makirites, the descendants of Manasseh, and they settled there. 41 Jair, a descendant of Manasseh, captured their settlements and called them Havvoth Jair.[a] 42 And Nobah captured Kenath and its surrounding settlements and called it Nobah after himself.

Stages in Israel's Journey

33 Here are the stages in the journey of the Israelites when they came out of Egypt by divisions under the leadership of Moses and Aaron. 2 At the LORD's command Moses recorded the stages in their journey. This is their journey by stages:

3 The Israelites set out from Rameses on the fifteenth day of the first month, the day after the Passover. They marched out defiantly in full view of all the Egyptians, 4 who were burying all their firstborn, whom the LORD had struck down among them; for the LORD had brought judgment on their gods.

5 The Israelites left Rameses and camped at Sukkoth.

6 They left Sukkoth and camped at Etham, on the edge of the desert.

7 They left Etham, turned back to Pi Hahiroth, to the east of Baal Zephon, and camped near Migdol.

8 They left Pi Hahiroth[b] and passed through the sea into the desert, and when they had traveled for three days in the Desert of Etham, they camped at Marah.

9 They left Marah and went to Elim, where there were twelve springs and seventy palm trees, and they camped there.

10 They left Elim and camped by the Red Sea.[c]

11 They left the Red Sea and camped in the Desert of Sin.

12 They left the Desert of Sin and camped at Dophkah.

13 They left Dophkah and camped at Alush.

14 They left Alush and camped at Rephidim, where there was no water for the people to drink.

15 They left Rephidim and camped in the Desert of Sinai.

16 They left the Desert of Sinai and camped at Kibroth Hattaavah.

17 They left Kibroth Hattaavah and camped at Hazeroth.

18 They left Hazeroth and camped at Rithmah.

19 They left Rithmah and camped at Rimmon Perez.

---

a 41 Or them the settlements of Jair   b 8 Many manuscripts of the Masoretic Text, Samaritan Pentateuch and Vulgate; most manuscripts of the Masoretic Text left from before Hahiroth   c 10 Or the Sea of Reeds; also in verse 11

20 They left Rimmon Perez and camped at Libnah.

21 They left Libnah and camped at Rissah.

22 They left Rissah and camped at Kehelathah.

23 They left Kehelathah and camped at Mount Shepher.

24 They left Mount Shepher and camped at Haradah.

25 They left Haradah and camped at Makheloth.

26 They left Makheloth and camped at Tahath.

27 They left Tahath and camped at Terah.

28 They left Terah and camped at Mithkah.

29 They left Mithkah and camped at Hashmonah.

30 They left Hashmonah and camped at Moseroth.

31 They left Moseroth and camped at Bene Jaakan.

32 They left Bene Jaakan and camped at Hor Haggidgad.

33 They left Hor Haggidgad and camped at Jotbathah.

34 They left Jotbathah and camped at Abronah.

35 They left Abronah and camped at Ezion Geber.

36 They left Ezion Geber and camped at Kadesh, in the Desert of Zin.

37 They left Kadesh and camped at Mount Hor, on the border of Edom. 38 At the LORD's command Aaron the priest went up Mount Hor, where he died on the first day of the fifth month of the fortieth year after the Israelites came out of Egypt. 39 Aaron was a hundred and twenty-three years old when he died on Mount Hor.

40 The Canaanite king of Arad, who lived in the Negev of Canaan, heard that the Israelites were coming.

41 They left Mount Hor and camped at Zalmonah.

42 They left Zalmonah and camped at Punon.

43 They left Punon and camped at Oboth.

44 They left Oboth and camped at Iye Abarim, on the border of Moab.

45 They left Iye Abarim and camped at Dibon Gad.

46 They left Dibon Gad and camped at Almon Diblathaim.

47 They left Almon Diblathaim and camped in the mountains of Abarim, near Nebo.

48 They left the mountains of Abarim and camped on the plains of Moab by the Jordan across from Jericho. 49 There on the plains of Moab they camped along the Jordan from Beth Jeshimoth to Abel Shittim.

50 On the plains of Moab by the Jordan across from Jericho the LORD said to Moses, 51 "Speak to the Israelites and say to them: 'When you cross the Jordan into Canaan, 52 drive out all the inhabitants of the land before you. Destroy all their carved images and their cast idols, and demolish all their high places. 53 Take possession of the land and settle in it, for I have given you the land to possess. 54 Distribute the land by lot, according to your clans. To a larger group give a larger inheritance, and to a smaller group a smaller one. Whatever falls to them by lot will be theirs. Distribute it according to your ancestral tribes.

55 " 'But if you do not drive out the inhabitants of the land, those you allow to remain will become barbs in your eyes and thorns in your sides. They will give you trouble in the land where you will live. 56 And then I will do to you what I plan to do to them.' "

Boundaries of Canaan

34 The LORD said to Moses, 2 "Command the Israelites and say to them: 'When you enter Canaan, the land that will be allotted to you as an inheritance is to have these boundaries:

3 " 'Your southern side will include some of the Desert of Zin along the border of Edom. Your southern boundary will start in the east from the southern end of the Dead Sea, 4 cross south of Scorpion Pass, continue on to Zin and go south of Kadesh Barnea. Then it will go to Hazar

Addar and over to Azmon, ⁵where it will turn, join the Wadi of Egypt and end at the Mediterranean Sea.

⁶ " 'Your western boundary will be the coast of the Mediterranean Sea. This will be your boundary on the west.

⁷ " 'For your northern boundary, run a line from the Mediterranean Sea to Mount Hor ⁸and from Mount Hor to Lebo Hamath. Then the boundary will go to Zedad, ⁹continue to Ziphron and end at Hazar Enan. This will be your boundary on the north.

¹⁰ " 'For your eastern boundary, run a line from Hazar Enan to Shepham. ¹¹The boundary will go down from Shepham to Riblah on the east side of Ain and continue along the slopes east of the Sea of Galilee.ᵃ ¹²Then the boundary will go down along the Jordan and end at the Dead Sea.

" 'This will be your land, with its boundaries on every side.' "

¹³Moses commanded the Israelites: "Assign this land by lot as an inheritance. The LORD has ordered that it be given to the nine and a half tribes, ¹⁴because the families of the tribe of Reuben, the tribe of Gad and the half-tribe of Manasseh have received their inheritance. ¹⁵These two and a half tribes have received their inheritance east of the Jordan across from Jericho, toward the sunrise."

¹⁶The LORD said to Moses, ¹⁷ "These are the names of the men who are to assign the land for you as an inheritance: Eleazar the priest and Joshua son of Nun. ¹⁸And appoint one leader from each tribe to help assign the land. ¹⁹These are their names:

Caleb son of Jephunneh,
 from the tribe of Judah;
²⁰Shemuel son of Ammihud,
 from the tribe of Simeon;
²¹Elidad son of Kislon,
 from the tribe of Benjamin;
²²Bukki son of Jogli,
 the leader from the tribe of Dan;
²³Hanniel son of Ephod,

the leader from the tribe of Manasseh son of Joseph;
²⁴Kemuel son of Shiphtan,
 the leader from the tribe of Ephraim son of Joseph;
²⁵Elizaphan son of Parnak,
 the leader from the tribe of Zebulun;
²⁶Paltiel son of Azzan,
 the leader from the tribe of Issachar;
²⁷Ahihud son of Shelomi,
 the leader from the tribe of Asher;
²⁸Pedahel son of Ammihud,
 the leader from the tribe of Naphtali."

²⁹These are the men the LORD commanded to assign the inheritance to the Israelites in the land of Canaan.

Towns for the Levites

35 On the plains of Moab by the Jordan across from Jericho, the LORD said to Moses, ²"Command the Israelites to give the Levites towns to live in from the inheritance the Israelites will possess. And give them pasturelands around the towns. ³Then they will have towns to live in and pasturelands for the cattle they own and all their other animals.

⁴"The pasturelands around the towns that you give the Levites will extend a thousand cubitsᵇ from the town wall. ⁵Outside the town, measure two thousand cubitsᶜ on the east side, two thousand on the south side, two thousand on the west and two thousand on the north, with the town in the center. They will have this area as pastureland for the towns.

Cities of Refuge

⁶"Six of the towns you give the Levites will be cities of refuge, to which a person who has killed someone may flee. In addition, give them forty-two other towns. ⁷In all you must give the Levites forty-eight towns, together with their pasturelands. ⁸The towns you give the Levites from the land the Israelites possess are to be given in proportion to the inheritance of

---

ᵃ 11 Hebrew *Kinnereth*   ᵇ 4 That is, about 1,500 feet or about 450 meters   ᶜ 5 That is, about 3,000 feet or about 900 meters

each tribe: Take many towns from a tribe that has many, but few from one that has few."

⁹Then the LORD said to Moses: ¹⁰"Speak to the Israelites and say to them: 'When you cross the Jordan into Canaan, ¹¹select some towns to be your cities of refuge, to which a person who has killed someone accidentally may flee. ¹²They will be places of refuge from the avenger, so that anyone accused of murder may not die before they stand trial before the assembly. ¹³These six towns you give will be your cities of refuge. ¹⁴Give three on this side of the Jordan and three in Canaan as cities of refuge. ¹⁵These six towns will be a place of refuge for Israelites and for foreigners residing among them, so that anyone who has killed another accidentally can flee there.

¹⁶" 'If anyone strikes someone a fatal blow with an iron object, that person is a murderer; the murderer is to be put to death. ¹⁷Or if anyone is holding a stone and strikes someone a fatal blow with it, that person is a murderer; the murderer is to be put to death. ¹⁸Or if anyone is holding a wooden object and strikes someone a fatal blow with it, that person is a murderer; the murderer is to be put to death. ¹⁹The avenger of blood shall put the murderer to death; when the avenger comes upon the murderer, the avenger shall put the murderer to death. ²⁰If anyone with malice aforethought shoves another or throws something at them intentionally so that they die ²¹or if out of enmity one person hits another with their fist so that the other dies, that person is to be put to death; that person is a murderer. The avenger of blood shall put the murderer to death when they meet.

²²" 'But if without enmity someone suddenly pushes another or throws something at them unintentionally ²³or, without seeing them, drops on them a stone heavy enough to kill them, and they die, then since that other person was not an enemy and no harm was intended, ²⁴the assembly must judge between the accused and the avenger of blood according to these regulations. ²⁵The assembly must protect the one accused of murder from the avenger of blood and send the accused back to the city of refuge to which they fled. The accused must stay there until the death of the high priest, who was anointed with the holy oil.

²⁶" 'But if the accused ever goes outside the limits of the city of refuge to which they fled ²⁷and the avenger of blood finds them outside the city, the avenger of blood may kill the accused without being guilty of murder. ²⁸The accused must stay in the city of refuge until the death of the high priest; only after the death of the high priest may they return to their own property.

²⁹" 'This is to have the force of law for you throughout the generations to come, wherever you live.

³⁰" 'Anyone who kills a person is to be put to death as a murderer only on the testimony of witnesses. But no one is to be put to death on the testimony of only one witness.

³¹" 'Do not accept a ransom for the life of a murderer, who deserves to die. They are to be put to death.

³²" 'Do not accept a ransom for anyone who has fled to a city of refuge and so

Q&A

Numbers 35

Q: What was a "city of refuge"?

BONUS: Who wasn't safe there?

Answers on next page

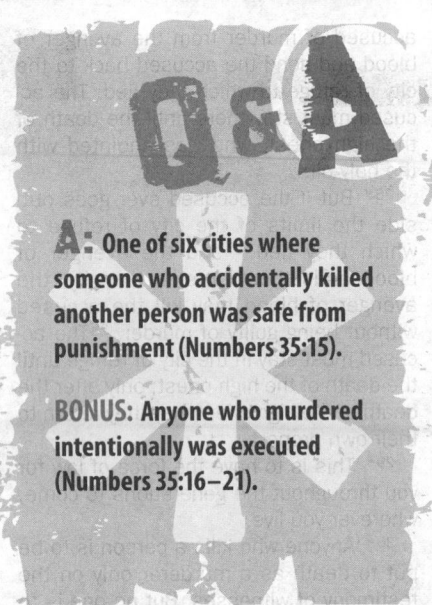

A: One of six cities where someone who accidentally killed another person was safe from punishment (Numbers 35:15).

BONUS: Anyone who murdered intentionally was executed (Numbers 35:16–21).

allow them to go back and live on their own land before the death of the high priest.

³³ "Do not pollute the land where you are. Bloodshed pollutes the land, and atonement cannot be made for the land on which blood has been shed, except by the blood of the one who shed it. ³⁴ Do not defile the land where you live and where I dwell, for I, the LORD, dwell among the Israelites.' "

Inheritance of Zelophehad's Daughters

36 The family heads of the clan of Gilead son of Makir, the son of Manasseh, who were from the clans of the descendants of Joseph, came and spoke before Moses and the leaders, the heads of the Israelite families. ² They said, "When the LORD commanded my lord to give the land as an inheritance to the Israelites by lot, he ordered you to give the inheritance of our brother Zelophehad to his daughters. ³ Now suppose they marry men from other Israelite tribes; then their inheritance will be taken from our ancestral inheritance and added to that of the tribe they marry into. And so part of the inheritance allotted to us will be taken away. ⁴ When the Year of Jubilee for the Israelites comes, their inheritance will be added to that of the tribe into which they marry, and their property will be taken from the tribal inheritance of our ancestors."

⁵ Then at the LORD's command Moses gave this order to the Israelites: "What the tribe of the descendants of Joseph is saying is right. ⁶ This is what the LORD commands for Zelophehad's daughters: They may marry anyone they please as long as they marry within their father's tribal clan. ⁷ No inheritance in Israel is to pass from one tribe to another, for every Israelite shall keep the tribal inheritance of their ancestors. ⁸ Every daughter who inherits land in any Israelite tribe must marry someone in her father's tribal clan, so that every Israelite will possess the inheritance of their ancestors. ⁹ No inheritance may pass from one tribe to another, for each Israelite tribe is to keep the land it inherits."

¹⁰ So Zelophehad's daughters did as the LORD commanded Moses. ¹¹ Zelophehad's daughters—Mahlah, Tirzah, Hoglah, Milkah and Noah—married their cousins on their father's side. ¹² They married within the clans of the descendants of Manasseh son of Joseph, and their inheritance remained in their father's tribe and clan.

¹³ These are the commands and regulations the LORD gave through Moses to the Israelites on the plains of Moab by the Jordan across from Jericho.

DEUTERONOMY

Say It!

Some things are important enough to say two or three times. Like reminding your parents you have plans for Friday night. Or reminding them that they promised to take you to the mall.

Deuteronomy means "second law." This book contains teachings Moses felt were important enough to repeat. Sort of like playing your favorite song over and over again. Deuteronomy repeats the Ten Commandments. And it reminds you that love prompted God to choose his people. And love prompted God to give them his law. Why is that important? Because rules made by someone who loves you will have your best interest at heart.

>>DOING RIGHT PAYS BIG
God rewards obedience, see Deuteronomy 6

>>RULES ARE ALL ABOUT LOVE
For the story behind the story, see Deuteronomy 11

>>MILITARY GIVEN RULES OF ENGAGEMENT
Laws limit battle damage, summary in Deuteronomy 20

>>BLESSINGS FOLLOW DOING RIGHT
Read list of rewards in Deuteronomy 28:1–14

>>TROUBLES FOLLOW DOING WRONG
Detailed warnings provided, Deuteronomy 28:15–68

>> preview

It's 1400 B.C. The Israelites are camped just outside the land God promised to give them.

Moses is 120 years old and about to die.

Deuteronomy is quoted some 80 times in the New Testament.

As the Israelites are poised to invade Canaan, a dictionary with 40,000 characters is being written in China. In Thebes workers go on strike. And Central Americans are learning to make pottery.

The Command to Leave Horeb

1 These are the words Moses spoke to all Israel in the wilderness east of the Jordan—that is, in the Arabah—opposite Suph, between Paran and Tophel, Laban, Hazeroth and Dizahab. ²(It takes eleven days to go from Horeb to Kadesh Barnea by the Mount Seir road.)

³In the fortieth year, on the first day of the eleventh month, Moses proclaimed to the Israelites all that the LORD had commanded him concerning them. ⁴This was after he had defeated Sihon king of the Amorites, who reigned in Heshbon, and at Edrei had defeated Og king of Bashan, who reigned in Ashtaroth.

⁵East of the Jordan in the territory of Moab, Moses began to expound this law, saying:

⁶The LORD our God said to us at Horeb, "You have stayed long enough at this mountain. ⁷Break camp and advance into the hill country of the Amorites; go to all the neighboring peoples in the Arabah, in the mountains, in the western foothills, in the Negev and along the coast, to the land of the Canaanites and to Lebanon, as far as the great river, the Euphrates. ⁸See, I have given you this land. Go in and take possession of the land the LORD swore he would give to your fathers—to Abraham, Isaac and Jacob—and to their descendants after them."

The Appointment of Leaders

⁹At that time I said to you, "You are too heavy a burden for me to carry alone. ¹⁰The LORD your God has increased your numbers so that today you are as numerous as the stars in the sky. ¹¹May the LORD, the God of your ancestors, increase you a thousand times and bless you as he has promised! ¹²But how can I bear your problems and your burdens and your disputes all by myself? ¹³Choose some wise, understanding and respected men from each of your tribes, and I will set them over you."

¹⁴You answered me, "What you propose to do is good."

¹⁵So I took the leading men of your tribes, wise and respected men, and appointed them to have authority over you—as commanders of thousands, of hundreds, of fifties and of tens and as tribal officials. ¹⁶And I charged your judges at that time, "Hear the disputes between your people and judge fairly, whether the case is between two Israelites or between an Israelite and a foreigner residing among you. ¹⁷Do not show partiality in judging; hear both small and great alike. Do not be afraid of anyone, for judgment belongs to God. Bring me any case too hard for you, and I will hear it." ¹⁸And at that time I told you everything you were to do.

Spies Sent Out

¹⁹Then, as the LORD our God commanded us, we set out from Horeb and went toward the hill country of the Amorites through all that vast and dreadful wilderness that you have seen, and so we reached Kadesh Barnea. ²⁰Then I said to you, "You have reached the hill country of the Amorites, which the LORD our God is giving us. ²¹See, the LORD your God has given you the land. Go up and take possession of it as the LORD, the God of your ancestors, told you. Do not be afraid; do not be discouraged."

²²Then all of you came to me and said, "Let us send men ahead to spy out the land for us and bring back a report about the route we are to take and the towns we will come to."

²³The idea seemed good to me; so I selected twelve of you, one man from each tribe. ²⁴They left and went up into the hill country, and came to the Valley of Eshkol and explored it. ²⁵Taking with them some of the fruit of the land, they brought it down to us and reported, "It is a good land that the LORD our God is giving us."

Rebellion Against the LORD

²⁶But you were unwilling to go up; you rebelled against the command of the LORD your God. ²⁷You grumbled in your tents and said, "The LORD hates us; so he brought us out of Egypt to deliver us into the hands of the Amorites to destroy us. ²⁸Where can we go? Our brothers have

made our hearts melt in fear. They say, 'The people are stronger and taller than we are; the cities are large, with walls up to the sky. We even saw the Anakites there.'"

²⁹Then I said to you, "Do not be terrified; do not be afraid of them. ³⁰The LORD your God, who is going before you, will fight for you, as he did for you in Egypt, before your very eyes, ³¹and in the wilderness. There you saw how the LORD your God carried you, as a father carries his son, all the way you went until you reached this place."

³²In spite of this, you did not trust in the LORD your God, ³³who went ahead of you on your journey, in fire by night and in a cloud by day, to search out places for you to camp and to show you the way you should go.

³⁴When the LORD heard what you said, he was angry and solemnly swore: ³⁵"No one from this evil generation shall see the good land I swore to give your ancestors, ³⁶except Caleb son of Jephunneh. He will see it, and I will give him and his descendants the land he set his feet on, because he followed the LORD wholeheartedly."

³⁷Because of you the LORD became angry with me also and said, "You shall not enter it, either. ³⁸But your assistant, Joshua son of Nun, will enter it. Encourage him, because he will lead Israel to inherit it. ³⁹And the little ones that you said would be taken captive, your children who do not yet know good from bad—they will enter the land. I will give it to them and they will take possession of it. ⁴⁰But as for you, turn around and set out toward the desert along the route to the Red Sea.ᵃ"

⁴¹Then you replied, "We have sinned against the LORD. We will go up and fight, as the LORD our God commanded us." So every one of you put on his weapons, thinking it easy to go up into the hill country.

⁴²But the LORD said to me, "Tell them, 'Do not go up and fight, because I will not be with you. You will be defeated by your enemies.'"

⁴³So I told you, but you would not listen. You rebelled against the LORD's command and in your arrogance you marched up into the hill country. ⁴⁴The Amorites who lived in those hills came out against you; they chased you like a swarm of bees and beat you down from Seir all the way to Hormah. ⁴⁵You came back and wept before the LORD, but he paid no attention to your weeping and turned a deaf ear to you. ⁴⁶And so you stayed in Kadesh many days—all the time you spent there.

Wanderings in the Wilderness

2 Then we turned back and set out toward the wilderness along the route to the Red Sea,ᵃ as the LORD had directed me. For a long time we made our way around the hill country of Seir.

²Then the LORD said to me, ³"You have made your way around this hill country long enough; now turn north. ⁴Give the people these orders: 'You are about to pass through the territory of your relatives the descendants of Esau, who live in Seir. They will be afraid of you, but be very careful. ⁵Do not provoke them to war, for I will not give you any of their land, not even enough to put your foot on. I have given Esau the hill country of Seir as his own. ⁶You are to pay them in silver for the food you eat and the water you drink.'"

⁷The LORD your God has blessed you in all the work of your hands. He has watched over your journey through this vast wilderness. These forty years the LORD your God has been with you, and you have not lacked anything.

> *The LORD your God has blessed you in all the work of your hands.*
>
> Deuteronomy 2:7

⁸So we went on past our relatives the descendants of Esau, who live in Seir. We turned from the Arabah road, which comes up from Elath and Ezion Geber, and traveled along the desert road of Moab.

⁹Then the LORD said to me, "Do not harass the Moabites or provoke them to war, for I will not give you any part of their land. I have given Ar to the descendants of Lot as a possession."

¹⁰(The Emites used to live there—a people strong and numerous, and as tall as the Anakites. ¹¹Like the Anakites, they too were considered Rephaites, but the Moabites called them Emites. ¹²Horites used to live in Seir, but the descendants of Esau drove them out. They destroyed the Horites from before them and settled in their place, just as Israel did in the land the LORD gave them as their possession.)

¹³And the LORD said, "Now get up and cross the Zered Valley." So we crossed the valley.

¹⁴Thirty-eight years passed from the time we left Kadesh Barnea until we crossed the Zered Valley. By then, that entire generation of fighting men had perished from the camp, as the LORD had sworn to them. ¹⁵The LORD's hand was against them until he had completely eliminated them from the camp.

¹⁶Now when the last of these fighting men among the people had died, ¹⁷the LORD said to me, ¹⁸"Today you are to pass by the region of Moab at Ar. ¹⁹When you come to the Ammonites, do not harass them or provoke them to war, for I will not give you possession of any land belonging to the Ammonites. I have given it as a possession to the descendants of Lot."

²⁰(That too was considered a land of the Rephaites, who used to live there; but the Ammonites called them Zamzummites. ²¹They were a people strong and numerous, and as tall as the Anakites. The LORD destroyed them from before the Ammonites, who drove them out and settled in their place. ²²The LORD had done the same for the descendants of Esau, who lived in Seir, when he destroyed the Horites from before them. They drove them out and have lived in their place to this day. ²³And as for the Avvites who lived in villages as far as Gaza, the Caphtorites coming out from Caphtorᵃ destroyed them and settled in their place.)

Defeat of Sihon King of Heshbon

²⁴"Set out now and cross the Arnon Gorge. See, I have given into your hand Sihon the Amorite, king of Heshbon, and his country. Begin to take possession of it and engage him in battle. ²⁵This very day I will begin to put the terror and fear of you on all the nations under heaven. They will hear reports of you and will tremble and be in anguish because of you."

²⁶From the Desert of Kedemoth I sent messengers to Sihon king of Heshbon offering peace and saying, ²⁷"Let us pass through your country. We will stay on the main road; we will not turn aside to the right or to the left. ²⁸Sell us food to eat and water to drink for their price in silver. Only let us pass through on foot— ²⁹as the descendants of Esau, who live in Seir, and the Moabites, who live in Ar, did for us—until we cross the Jordan into the land the LORD our God is giving us." ³⁰But Sihon king of Heshbon refused to let us pass through. For the LORD your God had made his spirit stubborn and his heart obstinate in order to give him into your hands, as he has now done.

³¹The LORD said to me, "See, I have begun to deliver Sihon and his country over to you. Now begin to conquer and possess his land."

³²When Sihon and all his army came out to meet us in battle at Jahaz, ³³the LORD our God delivered him over to us and we struck him down, together with his sons and his whole army. ³⁴At that time we took all his towns and completely destroyedᵇ them—men, women and children. We left no survivors. ³⁵But the livestock and the plunder from the towns we had captured we carried off for our-

---

ᵃ 23 That is, Crete   ᵇ 34 The Hebrew term refers to the irrevocable giving over of things or persons to the LORD, often by totally destroying them.

selves. ³⁶From Aroer on the rim of the Arnon Gorge, and from the town in the gorge, even as far as Gilead, not one town was too strong for us. The LORD our God gave us all of them. ³⁷But in accordance with the command of the LORD our God, you did not encroach on any of the land of the Ammonites, neither the land along the course of the Jabbok nor that around the towns in the hills.

Defeat of Og King of Bashan

3 Next we turned and went up along the road toward Bashan, and Og king of Bashan with his whole army marched out to meet us in battle at Edrei. ²The LORD said to me, "Do not be afraid of him, for I have delivered him into your hands, along with his whole army and his land. Do to him what you did to Sihon king of the Amorites, who reigned in Heshbon."

³So the LORD our God also gave into our hands Og king of Bashan and all his army. We struck them down, leaving no survivors. ⁴At that time we took all his cities. There was not one of the sixty cities that we did not take from them—the whole region of Argob, Og's kingdom in Bashan. ⁵All these cities were fortified with high walls and with gates and bars, and there were also a great many unwalled villages. ⁶We completely destroyedᵃ them, as we had done with Sihon king of Heshbon, destroyingᵃ every city—men, women and children. ⁷But all the livestock and the plunder from their cities we carried off for ourselves.

⁸So at that time we took from these two kings of the Amorites the territory east of the Jordan, from the Arnon Gorge as far as Mount Hermon. ⁹(Hermon is called Sirion by the Sidonians; the Amorites call it Senir.) ¹⁰We took all the towns on the plateau, and all Gilead, and all Bashan as far as Salekah and Edrei, towns of Og's kingdom in Bashan. ¹¹(Og king of Bashan was the last of the Rephaites. His bed was decorated with iron and was more than nine cubits long and four cubits wide.ᵇ It is still in Rabbah of the Ammonites.)

Division of the Land

¹²Of the land that we took over at that time, I gave the Reubenites and the Gadites the territory north of Aroer by the Arnon Gorge, including half the hill country of Gilead, together with its towns. ¹³The rest of Gilead and also all of Bashan, the kingdom of Og, I gave to the half-tribe of Manasseh. (The whole region of Argob in Bashan used to be known as a land of the Rephaites. ¹⁴Jair, a descendant of Manasseh, took the whole region of Argob as far as the border of the Geshurites and the Maakathites; it was named after him, so that to this day Bashan is called Havvoth Jair.ᶜ) ¹⁵And I gave Gilead to Makir. ¹⁶But to the Reubenites and the Gadites I gave the territory extending from Gilead down to the Arnon Gorge (the middle of the gorge being the border) and out to the Jabbok River, which is the border of the Ammonites. ¹⁷Its western border was the Jordan in the Arabah, from Kinnereth to the Sea of the Arabah (that is, the Dead Sea), below the slopes of Pisgah.

¹⁸I commanded you at that time: "The LORD your God has given you this land to take possession of it. But all your able-bodied men, armed for battle, must cross over ahead of the other Israelites. ¹⁹However, your wives, your children and your livestock (I know you have much livestock) may stay in the towns I have given you, ²⁰until the LORD gives rest to your fellow Israelites as he has to you, and they too have taken over the land that the LORD your God is giving them across the Jordan. After that, each of you may go back to the possession I have given you."

Moses Forbidden to Cross the Jordan

²¹At that time I commanded Joshua: "You have seen with your own eyes all that the LORD your God has done to these two kings. The LORD will do the same to all the kingdoms over there where you are going. ²²Do not be afraid of them; the LORD your God himself will fight for you."

ᵃ 6 The Hebrew term refers to the irrevocable giving over of things or persons to the LORD, often by totally destroying them.   ᵇ 11 That is, about 14 feet long and 6 feet wide or about 4 meters long and 1.8 meters wide   ᶜ 14 Or called the settlements of Jair

23At that time I pleaded with the LORD: 24"Sovereign LORD, you have begun to show to your servant your greatness and your strong hand. For what god is there in heaven or on earth who can do the deeds and mighty works you do? 25Let me go over and see the good land beyond the Jordan—that fine hill country and Lebanon."

26But because of you the LORD was angry with me and would not listen to me. "That is enough," the LORD said. "Do not speak to me anymore about this matter. 27Go up to the top of Pisgah and look west and north and south and east. Look at the land with your own eyes, since you are not going to cross this Jordan. 28But commission Joshua, and encourage and strengthen him, for he will lead this people across and will cause them to inherit the land that you will see." 29So we stayed in the valley near Beth Peor.

Obedience Commanded

4 Now, Israel, hear the decrees and laws I am about to teach you. Follow them so that you may live and may go in and take possession of the land the LORD, the God of your ancestors, is giving you. 2Do not add to what I command

Deuteronomy 4

Q: Why couldn't Moses enter Canaan?

BONUS: Who of the slaves who left Egypt did enter?

Answers on next page

you and do not subtract from it, but keep the commands of the LORD your God that I give you.

3You saw with your own eyes what the LORD did at Baal Peor. The LORD your God destroyed from among you everyone who followed the Baal of Peor, 4but all of you who held fast to the LORD your God are still alive today.

5See, I have taught you decrees and laws as the LORD my God commanded me, so that you may follow them in the land you are entering to take possession of it. 6Observe them carefully, for this will show your wisdom and understanding to the nations, who will hear about all these decrees and say, "Surely this great nation is a wise and understanding people." 7What other nation is so great as to have their gods near them the way the LORD our God is near us whenever we pray to him? 8And what other nation is so great as to have such righteous decrees and laws as this body of laws I am setting before you today?

9Only be careful, and watch yourselves closely so that you do not forget the things your eyes have seen or let them fade from your heart as long as you live. Teach them to your children and to their children after them. 10Remember the day you stood before the LORD your God at Horeb, when he said to me, "Assemble the people before me to hear my words so that they may learn to revere me as long as they live in the land and may teach them to their children." 11You came near and stood at the foot of the mountain while it blazed with fire to the very heavens, with black clouds and deep darkness. 12Then the LORD spoke to you out of the fire. You heard the sound of words but saw no form; there was only a voice. 13He declared to you his covenant, the Ten Commandments, which he commanded you to follow and then wrote them on two stone tablets. 14And the LORD directed me at that time to teach you the decrees and laws you are to follow in the land that you are crossing the Jordan to possess.

Idolatry Forbidden

15You saw no form of any kind the day the LORD spoke to you at Horeb out of the fire. Therefore watch yourselves very carefully, ¹⁶so that you do not become corrupt and make for yourselves an idol, an image of any shape, whether formed like a man or a woman, ¹⁷or like any animal on earth or any bird that flies in the air, ¹⁸or like any creature that moves along the ground or any fish in the waters below. ¹⁹And when you look up to the sky and see the sun, the moon and the stars — all the heavenly array — do not be enticed into bowing down to them and worshiping things the LORD your God has apportioned to all the nations under heaven. ²⁰But as for you, the LORD took you and brought you out of the iron-smelting furnace, out of Egypt, to be the people of his inheritance, as you now are.

²¹The LORD was angry with me because of you, and he solemnly swore that I would not cross the Jordan and enter the good land the LORD your God is giving you as your inheritance. ²²I will die in this land; I will not cross the Jordan; but you are about to cross over and take possession of that good land. ²³Be careful not to forget the covenant of the LORD your God that he made with you; do not make for yourselves an idol in the form of anything the LORD your God has forbidden. ²⁴For the LORD your God is a consuming fire, a jealous God.

²⁵After you have had children and grandchildren and have lived in the land a long time — if you then become corrupt and make any kind of idol, doing evil in the eyes of the LORD your God and arousing his anger, ²⁶I call the heavens and the earth as witnesses against you this day that you will quickly perish from the land that you are crossing the Jordan to possess. You will not live there long but will certainly be destroyed. ²⁷The LORD will scatter you among the peoples, and only a few of you will survive among the nations to which the LORD will drive you. ²⁸There you will worship man-made gods of wood and stone, which cannot see or hear or eat or smell. ²⁹But if from there you seek the LORD your God, you will find him if you seek him with all your heart

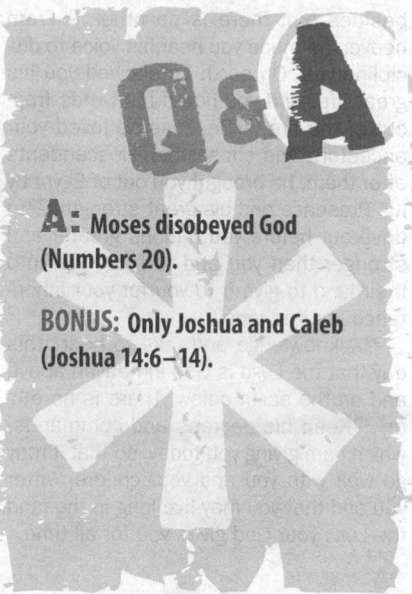

A: Moses disobeyed God (Numbers 20).

BONUS: Only Joshua and Caleb (Joshua 14:6–14).

and with all your soul. ³⁰When you are in distress and all these things have happened to you, then in later days you will return to the LORD your God and obey him. ³¹For the LORD your God is a merciful God; he will not abandon or destroy you or forget the covenant with your ancestors, which he confirmed to them by oath.

The LORD Is God

³²Ask now about the former days, long before your time, from the day God created human beings on the earth; ask from one end of the heavens to the other. Has anything so great as this ever happened, or has anything like it ever been heard of? ³³Has any other people heard the voice of God^a speaking out of fire, as you have, and lived? ³⁴Has any god ever tried to take for himself one nation out of another nation, by testings, by signs and wonders, by war, by a mighty hand and an outstretched arm, or by great and awesome deeds, like all the things the LORD your God did for you in Egypt before your very eyes?

³⁵You were shown these things so that you might know that the LORD is God;

---

^a 33 Or of a god

besides him there is no other. ³⁶From heaven he made you hear his voice to discipline you. On earth he showed you his great fire, and you heard his words from out of the fire. ³⁷Because he loved your ancestors and chose their descendants after them, he brought you out of Egypt by his Presence and his great strength, ³⁸to drive out before you nations greater and stronger than you and to bring you into their land to give it to you for your inheritance, as it is today.

³⁹Acknowledge and take to heart this day that the LORD is God in heaven above and on the earth below. There is no other. ⁴⁰Keep his decrees and commands, which I am giving you today, so that it may go well with you and your children after you and that you may live long in the land the LORD your God gives you for all time.

Cities of Refuge

⁴¹Then Moses set aside three cities east of the Jordan, ⁴²to which anyone who had killed a person could flee if they had unintentionally killed a neighbor without malice aforethought. They could flee into one of these cities and save their life. ⁴³The cities were these: Bezer in the wilderness plateau, for the Reubenites; Ramoth in Gilead, for the Gadites; and Golan in Bashan, for the Manassites.

Introduction to the Law

⁴⁴This is the law Moses set before the Israelites. ⁴⁵These are the stipulations, decrees and laws Moses gave them when they came out of Egypt ⁴⁶and were in the valley near Beth Peor east of the Jordan, in the land of Sihon king of the Amorites, who reigned in Heshbon and was defeat-

TO THE POINT

God Is Merciful

Deuteronomy 4:31 says that "the LORD your God is a merciful God." Hebrew words translated "mercy" as a love that reaches down to help people in need—even those who have done nothing to deserve help. The Greek word translated "mercy" emphasizes compassion—caring enough about another's suffering to help.

When the Bible says the Lord is merciful, it's saying that he cares when you're feeling hurt or helpless. He cares enough to help.

+ He gives you eternal life through Jesus (Ephesians 2:4–5).

+ You can pray with confidence, knowing the Lord will listen to you (Hebrews 4:16).

+ He expects you to be merciful toward others (Luke 6:36).

ed by Moses and the Israelites as they came out of Egypt. [47]They took possession of his land and the land of Og king of Bashan, the two Amorite kings east of the Jordan. [48]This land extended from Aroer on the rim of the Arnon Gorge to Mount Sirion[a] (that is, Hermon), [49]and included all the Arabah east of the Jordan, as far as the Dead Sea,[b] below the slopes of Pisgah.

The Ten Commandments

5 Moses summoned all Israel and said: Hear, Israel, the decrees and laws I declare in your hearing today. Learn them and be sure to follow them. [2]The LORD our God made a covenant with us at Horeb. [3]It was not with our ancestors[c] that the LORD made this covenant, but with us, with all of us who are alive here today. [4]The LORD spoke to you face to face out of the fire on the mountain. [5](At that time I stood between the LORD and you to declare to you the word of the LORD, because you were afraid of the fire and did not go up the mountain.) And he said:

> [6]"I am the LORD your God, who brought you out of Egypt, out of the land of slavery.
>
> [7]"You shall have no other gods before[d] me.
>
> [8]"You shall not make for yourself an image in the form of anything in heaven above or on the earth beneath or in the waters below. [9]You shall not bow down to them or worship them; for I, the LORD your God, am a jealous God, punishing the children for the sin of the parents to the third and fourth generation of those who hate me, [10]but showing love to a thousand generations of those who love me and keep my commandments.
>
> [11]"You shall not misuse the name of the LORD your God, for the LORD will not hold anyone guiltless who misuses his name.
>
> [12]"Observe the Sabbath day by keep-

ing it holy, as the LORD your God has commanded you. [13]Six days you shall labor and do all your work, [14]but the seventh day is a sabbath to the LORD your God. On it you shall not do any work, neither you, nor your son or daughter, nor your male or female servant, nor your ox, your donkey or any of your animals, nor any foreigner residing in your towns, so that your male and female servants may rest, as you do. [15]Remember that you were slaves in Egypt and that the LORD your God brought you out of there with a mighty hand and an outstretched arm. Therefore the LORD your God has commanded you to observe the Sabbath day.

> [16]"Honor your father and your mother, as the LORD your God has commanded you, so that you may live long and that it may go well with you in the land the LORD your God is giving you.
>
> [17]"You shall not murder.
>
> [18]"You shall not commit adultery.
>
> [19]"You shall not steal.
>
> [20]"You shall not give false testimony against your neighbor.
>
> [21]"You shall not covet your neighbor's wife. You shall not set your desire on your neighbor's house or land, his male or female servant, his ox or donkey, or anything that belongs to your neighbor."

[22]These are the commandments the LORD proclaimed in a loud voice to your whole assembly there on the mountain from out of the fire, the cloud and the deep darkness; and he added nothing more. Then he wrote them on two stone tablets and gave them to me.

[23]When you heard the voice out of the darkness, while the mountain was ablaze with fire, all the leaders of your tribes and your elders came to me. [24]And you said,

---

[a] 48 Syriac (see also 3:9); Hebrew *Siyon*   [b] 49 Hebrew *the Sea of the Arabah*   [c] 3 Or *not only with our parents*
[d] 7 Or *besides*

"The LORD our God has shown us his glory and his majesty, and we have heard his voice from the fire. Today we have seen that a person can live even if God speaks with them. 25 But now, why should we die? This great fire will consume us, and we will die if we hear the voice of the LORD our God any longer. 26 For what mortal has ever heard the voice of the living God speaking out of fire, as we have, and survived? 27 Go near and listen to all that the LORD our God says. Then tell us whatever the LORD our God tells you. We will listen and obey."

28 The LORD heard you when you spoke to me, and the LORD said to me, "I have heard what this people said to you. Everything they said was good. 29 Oh, that their hearts would be inclined to fear me and keep all my commands always, so that it might go well with them and their children forever!

30 "Go, tell them to return to their tents. 31 But you stay here with me so that I may give you all the commands, decrees and laws you are to teach them to follow in the land I am giving them to possess."

32 So be careful to do what the LORD your God has commanded you; do not turn aside to the right or to the left. 33 Walk in obedience to all that the LORD your God has commanded you, so that you may live and prosper and prolong your days in the land that you will possess.

Love the LORD Your God

6 These are the commands, decrees and laws the LORD your God directed me to teach you to observe in the land that you are crossing the Jordan to possess, 2 so that you, your children and their children after them may fear the LORD your God as long as you live by keeping all his decrees and commands that I give you, and so that you may enjoy long life. 3 Hear, Israel, and be careful to obey so that it may go well with you and that you may increase greatly in a land flowing with milk and honey, just as the LORD, the God of your ancestors, promised you.

4 Hear, O Israel: The LORD our God, the LORD is one.[a] 5 Love the LORD your God with all your heart and with all your soul and with all your strength. 6 These commandments that I give you today are to be on your hearts. 7 Impress them on your children. Talk about them when you sit at home and when you walk along the road, when you lie down and when you get up. 8 Tie them as symbols on your hands and bind them on your foreheads. 9 Write them on the doorframes of your houses and on your gates.

10 When the LORD your God brings you into the land he swore to your fathers, to Abraham, Isaac and Jacob, to give you— a land with large, flourishing cities you did not build, 11 houses filled with all kinds of good things you did not provide, wells you did not dig, and vineyards and olive groves you did not plant—then when you eat and are satisfied, 12 be careful that you do not forget the LORD, who brought you out of Egypt, out of the land of slavery.

13 Fear the LORD your God, serve him only and take your oaths in his name. 14 Do not follow other gods, the gods of the peoples around you; 15 for the LORD your God, who is among you, is a jealous God and his anger will burn against you, and he will destroy you from the face of the land. 16 Do not put the LORD your God to the test as you did at Massah. 17 Be sure to keep the commands of the LORD your God and the stipulations and decrees he has given you. 18 Do what is right and good in the LORD's sight, so that it may go well with you and you may go in and take over the good land the LORD promised on oath to your ancestors, 19 thrusting out all your enemies before you, as the LORD said.

20 In the future, when your son asks you, "What is the meaning of the stipulations, decrees and laws the LORD our God has commanded you?" 21 tell him: "We were slaves of Pharaoh in Egypt, but the LORD brought us out of Egypt with a mighty hand. 22 Before our eyes the LORD sent signs and wonders—great and terrible—on Egypt and Pharaoh and his whole

---

a 4 Or *The LORD our God is one LORD; or The LORD is our God, the LORD is one; or The LORD is our God, the LORD alone*

M oses told God's Old Testament people to love the Lord and live by his words. Then as they sat at home or walked along the road or stretched out to relax, they talked about those words of God that shaped their lives. This is still the best way to share your faith with others. Have an answer to prayer? Mention it to your friend when you're riding the bus to school. Do you have a different outlook on sex? Tell your friends the choice you've made, and why. You don't have to argue. All you have to do is talk naturally about the place God has in your own life.

{Deuteronomy 6:4–9}

>> INSTANT ACCESS

household. 23But he brought us out from there to bring us in and give us the land he promised on oath to our ancestors. 24The LORD commanded us to obey all these decrees and to fear the LORD our God, so that we might always prosper and be kept alive, as is the case today. 25And if we are careful to obey all this law before the LORD our God, as he has commanded us, that will be our righteousness."

Driving Out the Nations

7 When the LORD your God brings you into the land you are entering to pos-

sess and drives out before you many nations—the Hittites, Girgashites, Amorites, Canaanites, Perizzites, Hivites and Jebusites, seven nations larger and stronger than you— 2and when the LORD your God has delivered them over to you and you have defeated them, then you must destroy them totally.[a] Make no treaty with them, and show them no mercy. 3Do not intermarry with them. Do not give your daughters to their sons or take their daughters for your sons, 4for they will turn your children away from following me to serve other gods, and the LORD's anger will burn against you and will quickly destroy you. 5This is what you are to do to them: Break down their altars, smash their sacred stones, cut down their Asherah poles[b] and burn their idols in the fire. 6For you are a people holy to the LORD your God. The LORD your God has chosen you out of all the peoples on the face of the earth to be his people, his treasured possession.

7The LORD did not set his affection on you and choose you because you were more numerous than other peoples, for you were the fewest of all peoples. 8But it was because the LORD loved you and kept the oath he swore to your ancestors that he brought you out with a mighty hand and redeemed you from the land of slavery, from the power of Pharaoh king of Egypt. 9Know therefore that the LORD your God is God; he is the faithful God, keeping his covenant of love to a thousand generations of those who love him and keep his commandments. 10But

those who hate him he will repay to
    their face by destruction;
he will not be slow to repay to their
    face those who hate him.

11Therefore, take care to follow the commands, decrees and laws I give you today.

12If you pay attention to these laws and are careful to follow them, then the LORD your God will keep his covenant of love with you, as he swore to your ancestors. 13He will love you and bless

---

a 2 The Hebrew term refers to the irrevocable giving over of things or persons to the LORD, often by totally destroying them; also in verse 26.   b 5 That is, wooden symbols of the goddess Asherah; here and elsewhere in Deuteronomy

you and increase your numbers. He will bless the fruit of your womb, the crops of your land—your grain, new wine and olive oil—the calves of your herds and the lambs of your flocks in the land he swore to your ancestors to give you. ¹⁴You will be blessed more than any other people; none of your men or women will be childless, nor will any of your livestock be without young. ¹⁵The LORD will keep you free from every disease. He will not inflict on you the horrible diseases you knew in Egypt, but he will inflict them on all who hate you. ¹⁶You must destroy all the peoples the LORD your God gives over to you. Do not look on them with pity and do not serve their gods, for that will be a snare to you.

¹⁷You may say to yourselves, "These nations are stronger than we are. How can we drive them out?" ¹⁸But do not be afraid of them; remember well what the LORD your God did to Pharaoh and to all Egypt. ¹⁹You saw with your own eyes the great trials, the signs and wonders, the mighty hand and outstretched arm, with which the LORD your God brought you out. The LORD your God will do the same to all the peoples you now fear. ²⁰Moreover, the LORD your God will send the hornet among them until even the survivors who hide from you have perished. ²¹Do not be terrified by them, for the LORD your God, who is among you, is a great and awesome God. ²²The LORD your God will drive out those nations before you, little by little. You will not be allowed to eliminate them all at once, or the wild animals will multiply around you. ²³But the LORD your God will deliver them over to you, throwing them into great confusion until they are destroyed. ²⁴He will give their kings into your hand, and you will wipe out their names from under heaven. No one will be able to stand up against you; you will destroy them. ²⁵The images of their gods you are to burn in the fire. Do not covet the silver and gold on them,

and do not take it for yourselves, or you will be ensnared by it, for it is detestable to the LORD your God. ²⁶Do not bring a detestable thing into your house or you, like it, will be set apart for destruction. Regard it as vile and utterly detest it, for it is set apart for destruction.

Do Not Forget the LORD

8 Be careful to follow every command I am giving you today, so that you may live and increase and may enter and possess the land the LORD promised on oath to your ancestors. ²Remember how the LORD your God led you all the way in the wilderness these forty years, to humble and test you in order to know what was in your heart, whether or not you would keep his commands. ³He humbled you, causing you to hunger and then feeding you with manna, which neither you nor your ancestors had known, to teach you that man does not live on bread alone but on every word that comes from the mouth of the LORD. ⁴Your clothes did not wear out and your feet did not swell during these forty years. ⁵Know then in your heart that as a man disciplines his son, so the LORD your God disciplines you.

⁶Observe the commands of the LORD your God, walking in obedience to him and revering him. ⁷For the LORD your God is bringing you into a good land—a land with brooks, streams, and deep springs gushing out into the valleys and hills; ⁸a land with wheat and barley, vines and fig trees, pomegranates, olive oil and honey; ⁹a land where bread will not be scarce and you will lack nothing; a land where the rocks are iron and you can dig copper out of the hills.

¹⁰When you have eaten and are satisfied, praise the LORD your God for the good land he has given you. ¹¹Be careful that you do not forget the LORD your God, failing to observe his commands, his laws and his decrees that I am giv-

> *He is the faithful God, keeping his covenant of love to a thousand generations.*
>
> **Deuteronomy 7:9**

Y ou just got all A's on your report card, the person you like finally asked you out and your dad just said you can get a car as soon as you turn 16! God? Who needs him now? But maybe this is the time you need God most. The Bible warns that when things go well there's a danger that "then your heart will become proud and you will forget the LORD your God" (Deuteronomy 8:14). And if you forget God, you'll probably soon be in trouble. Why not write yourself a note? Remind yourself that when something really great happens, enjoy. Then stop a moment to thank God and give him credit for the good things in your life.

{Deuteronomy 8:10–18}

INSTANT ACCESS

thing your ancestors had never known, to humble and test you so that in the end it might go well with you. [17]You may say to yourself, "My power and the strength of my hands have produced this wealth for me." [18]But remember the LORD your God, for it is he who gives you the ability to produce wealth, and so confirms his covenant, which he swore to your ancestors, as it is today.

[19]If you ever forget the LORD your God and follow other gods and worship and bow down to them, I testify against you today that you will surely be destroyed. [20]Like the nations the LORD destroyed before you, so you will be destroyed for not obeying the LORD your God.

Not Because of Israel's Righteousness

9 Hear, Israel: You are now about to cross the Jordan to go in and dispossess nations greater and stronger than you, with large cities that have walls up to the sky. [2]The people are strong and tall— Anakites! You know about them and have heard it said: "Who can stand up against the Anakites?" [3]But be assured today that the LORD your God is the one who goes across ahead of you like a devouring fire. He will destroy them; he will subdue them before you. And you will drive them out and annihilate them quickly, as the LORD has promised you.

[4]After the LORD your God has driven them out before you, do not say to yourself, "The LORD has brought me here to take possession of this land because of my righteousness." No, it is on account of the wickedness of these nations that the LORD is going to drive them out before you. [5]It is not because of your righteousness or your integrity that you are going in to take possession of their land; but on account of the wickedness of these nations, the LORD your God will drive them out before you, to accomplish what he swore to your fathers, to Abraham, Isaac and Jacob. [6]Understand, then, that it is not because of your righteousness that the LORD your God is giving you this good land to possess, for you are a stiff-necked people.

ing you this day. [12]Otherwise, when you eat and are satisfied, when you build fine houses and settle down, [13]and when your herds and flocks grow large and your silver and gold increase and all you have is multiplied, [14]then your heart will become proud and you will forget the LORD your God, who brought you out of Egypt, out of the land of slavery. [15]He led you through the vast and dreadful wilderness, that thirsty and waterless land, with its venomous snakes and scorpions. He brought you water out of hard rock. [16]He gave you manna to eat in the wilderness, some-

The Golden Calf

[7] Remember this and never forget how you aroused the anger of the LORD your God in the wilderness. From the day you left Egypt until you arrived here, you have been rebellious against the LORD. [8] At Horeb you aroused the LORD's wrath so that he was angry enough to destroy you. [9] When I went up on the mountain to receive the tablets of stone, the tablets of the covenant that the LORD had made with you, I stayed on the mountain forty days and forty nights; I ate no bread and drank no water. [10] The LORD gave me two stone tablets inscribed by the finger of God. On them were all the commandments the LORD proclaimed to you on the mountain out of the fire, on the day of the assembly.

[11] At the end of the forty days and forty nights, the LORD gave me the two stone tablets, the tablets of the covenant. [12] Then the LORD told me, "Go down from here at once, because your people whom you brought out of Egypt have become corrupt. They have turned away quickly from what I commanded them and have made an idol for themselves."

[13] And the LORD said to me, "I have seen this people, and they are a stiff-necked people indeed! [14] Let me alone, so that I may destroy them and blot out their name from under heaven. And I will make you into a nation stronger and more numerous than they."

[15] So I turned and went down from the mountain while it was ablaze with fire. And the two tablets of the covenant were in my hands. [16] When I looked, I saw that you had sinned against the LORD your God; you had made for yourselves an idol cast in the shape of a calf. You had turned aside quickly from the way that the LORD had commanded you. [17] So I took the two tablets and threw them out of my hands, breaking them to pieces before your eyes.

[18] Then once again I fell prostrate before the LORD for forty days and forty nights; I ate no bread and drank no water, because of all the sin you had committed, doing what was evil in the LORD's sight

and so arousing his anger. [19] I feared the anger and wrath of the LORD, for he was angry enough with you to destroy you. But again the LORD listened to me. [20] And the LORD was angry enough with Aaron to destroy him, but at that time I prayed for Aaron too. [21] Also I took that sinful thing of yours, the calf you had made, and burned it in the fire. Then I crushed it and ground it to powder as fine as dust and threw the dust into a stream that flowed down the mountain.

[22] You also made the LORD angry at Taberah, at Massah and at Kibroth Hattaavah. [23] And when the LORD sent you out from Kadesh Barnea, he said, "Go up and take possession of the land I have given you." But you rebelled against the command of the LORD your God. You did not trust him or obey him. [24] You have been rebellious against the LORD ever since I have known you.

[25] I lay prostrate before the LORD those forty days and forty nights because the LORD had said he would destroy you. [26] I prayed to the LORD and said, "Sovereign LORD, do not destroy your people, your own inheritance that you redeemed by your great power and brought out of Egypt with a mighty hand. [27] Remember your servants Abraham, Isaac and Jacob. Overlook the stubbornness of this people, their wickedness and their sin. [28] Otherwise, the country from which you brought us will say, 'Because the LORD was not able to take them into the land he had promised them, and because he hated them, he brought them out to put them to death in the wilderness.' [29] But they are your people, your inheritance that you brought out by your great power and your outstretched arm."

Tablets Like the First Ones

10 At that time the LORD said to me, "Chisel out two stone tablets like the first ones and come up to me on the mountain. Also make a wooden ark.[a] [2] I will write on the tablets the words that were on the first tablets, which you broke. Then you are to put them in the ark."

[a] 1 That is, a chest

3So I made the ark out of acacia wood and chiseled out two stone tablets like the first ones, and I went up on the mountain with the two tablets in my hands. 4The Lord wrote on these tablets what he had written before, the Ten Commandments he had proclaimed to you on the mountain, out of the fire, on the day of the assembly. And the Lord gave them to me. 5Then I came back down the mountain and put the tablets in the ark I had made, as the Lord commanded me, and they are there now.

6(The Israelites traveled from the wells of Bene Jaakan to Moserah. There Aaron died and was buried, and Eleazar his son succeeded him as priest. 7From there they traveled to Gudgodah and on to Jotbathah, a land with streams of water. 8At that time the Lord set apart the tribe of Levi to carry the ark of the covenant of the Lord, to stand before the Lord to minister and to pronounce blessings in his name, as they still do today. 9That is why the Levites have no share or inheritance among their fellow Israelites; the Lord is their inheritance, as the Lord your God told them.)

10Now I had stayed on the mountain forty days and forty nights, as I did the first time, and the Lord listened to me at this time also. It was not his will to destroy you. 11"Go," the Lord said to me, "and lead the people on their way, so that they may enter and possess the land I swore to their ancestors to give them."

Fear the Lord

12And now, Israel, what does the Lord your God ask of you but to fear the Lord your God, to walk in obedience to him, to love him, to serve the Lord your God with all your heart and with all your soul, 13and to observe the Lord's commands and decrees that I am giving you today for your own good?

14To the Lord your God belong the heavens, even the highest heavens, the earth and everything in it. 15Yet the Lord set his affection on your ancestors and loved them, and he chose you, their descendants, above all the nations—as it is today. 16Circumcise your hearts, therefore, and do not be stiff-necked any longer. 17For the Lord your God is God of gods and Lord of lords, the great God, mighty and awesome, who shows no partiality and accepts no bribes. 18He defends the cause of the fatherless and the widow, and loves the foreigner residing among you, giving them food and clothing. 19And you are to love those who are foreigners, for you yourselves were foreigners in Egypt. 20Fear the Lord your God and serve him. Hold fast to him and take your oaths in his name. 21He is the one you praise; he is your God, who performed for you those great and awesome wonders you saw with your own eyes. 22Your ancestors who went down into Egypt were seventy in all, and now the Lord your God has made you as numerous as the stars in the sky.

Love and Obey the Lord

11 Love the Lord your God and keep his requirements, his decrees, his laws and his commands always. 2Remember today that your children were not the ones who saw and experienced the discipline of the Lord your God: his majesty, his mighty hand, his outstretched arm; 3the signs he performed and the things he did in the heart of Egypt, both to Pharaoh king of Egypt and to his whole country; 4what he did to the Egyptian army, to its horses and chariots, how he overwhelmed them with the waters of the Red Sea[a] as they were pursuing you, and how the Lord brought lasting ruin on them. 5It was not your children who saw what he did for you in the wilderness until you arrived at this place, 6and what he did to Dathan and Abiram, sons of Eliab the Reubenite, when the earth opened its mouth right in the middle of all Israel and swallowed them up with their households, their tents and every living thing that belonged to them. 7But it was your own eyes that saw all these great things the Lord has done.

8Observe therefore all the commands I

am giving you today, so that you may have the strength to go in and take over the land that you are crossing the Jordan to possess, ⁹and so that you may live long in the land the LORD swore to your ancestors to give to them and their descendants, a land flowing with milk and honey. ¹⁰The land you are entering to take over is not like the land of Egypt, from which you have come, where you planted your seed and irrigated it by foot as in a vegetable garden. ¹¹But the land you are crossing the Jordan to take possession of is a land of mountains and valleys that drinks rain from heaven. ¹²It is a land the LORD your God cares for; the eyes of the LORD your God are continually on it from the beginning of the year to its end.

¹³So if you faithfully obey the commands I am giving you today—to love the LORD your God and to serve him with all your heart and with all your soul— ¹⁴then I will send rain on your land in its season, both autumn and spring rains, so that you may gather in your grain, new wine and olive oil. ¹⁵I will provide grass in the fields for your cattle, and you will eat and be satisfied.

¹⁶Be careful, or you will be enticed to turn away and worship other gods and bow down to them. ¹⁷Then the LORD's anger will burn against you, and he will shut up the heavens so that it will not rain and the ground will yield no produce, and you will soon perish from the good land the LORD is giving you. ¹⁸Fix these words of mine in your hearts and minds; tie them as symbols on your hands and bind them on your foreheads. ¹⁹Teach them to your children, talking about them when you

TO THE POINT

Love Comes First

Don't let all the Old Testament laws confuse you. God isn't sitting in heaven keeping score of your wins and losses. And believers aren't moral athletes who make points by jumping over his hurdles. The relationship between God and the believer is one of love.

Deuteronomy 11 tells you that God's commands were given to show you what is right and good so he can bless you. That's one way God shows his love for you. Obedience is one way you show your love for God. That's why Deuteronomy 11:13 tells you that the call to obedience is a call "to love the LORD your God and to serve him with all your heart and with all your soul."

Love led God to give the law. He wants your love in return—love that expresses itself by doing what he says.

sit at home and when you walk along the road, when you lie down and when you get up. ²⁰Write them on the doorframes of your houses and on your gates, ²¹so that your days and the days of your children may be many in the land the LORD swore to give your ancestors, as many as the days that the heavens are above the earth.

²²If you carefully observe all these commands I am giving you to follow—to love the LORD your God, to walk in obedience to him and to hold fast to him—²³then the LORD will drive out all these nations before you, and you will dispossess nations larger and stronger than you. ²⁴Every place where you set your foot will be yours: Your territory will extend from the desert to Lebanon, and from the Euphrates River to the Mediterranean Sea. ²⁵No one will be able to stand against you. The LORD your God, as he promised you, will put the terror and fear of you on the whole land, wherever you go.

²⁶See, I am setting before you today a blessing and a curse— ²⁷the blessing if you obey the commands of the LORD your God that I am giving you today; ²⁸the curse if you disobey the commands of the LORD your God and turn from the way that I command you today by following other gods, which you have not known. ²⁹When the LORD your God has brought you into the land you are entering to possess, you are to proclaim on Mount Gerizim the blessings, and on Mount Ebal the curses. ³⁰As you know, these mountains are across the Jordan, westward, toward the setting sun, near the great trees of Moreh, in the territory of those Canaanites living in the Arabah in the vicinity of Gilgal. ³¹You are about to cross the Jordan to enter and take possession of the land the LORD your God is giving you. When you have taken it over and are living there, ³²be sure that you obey all the decrees and laws I am setting before you today.

The One Place of Worship

12 These are the decrees and laws you must be careful to follow in the land that the LORD, the God of your ancestors, has given you to possess—

as long as you live in the land. ²Destroy completely all the places on the high mountains, on the hills and under every spreading tree, where the nations you are dispossessing worship their gods. ³Break down their altars, smash their sacred stones and burn their Asherah poles in the fire; cut down the idols of their gods and wipe out their names from those places.

⁴You must not worship the LORD your God in their way. ⁵But you are to seek the place the LORD your God will choose from among all your tribes to put his Name there for his dwelling. To that place you must go; ⁶there bring your burnt offerings and sacrifices, your tithes and special gifts, what you have vowed to give and your freewill offerings, and the firstborn of your herds and flocks. ⁷There, in the presence of the LORD your God, you and your families shall eat and shall rejoice in everything you have put your hand to, because the LORD your God has blessed you.

⁸You are not to do as we do here today, everyone doing as they see fit, ⁹since you have not yet reached the resting place and the inheritance the LORD your God is giving you. ¹⁰But you will cross the Jordan and settle in the land the LORD your God is giving you as an inheritance, and he will give you rest from all your enemies around you so that you will live in safety. ¹¹Then to the place the LORD your God will choose as a dwelling for his Name—there you are to bring everything I command you: your burnt offerings and sacrifices, your tithes and special gifts, and all the choice possessions you have vowed to the LORD. ¹²And there rejoice before the LORD your God—you, your sons and daughters, your male and female servants, and the Levites from your towns who have no allotment or inheritance of their own. ¹³Be careful not to sacrifice your burnt offerings anywhere you please. ¹⁴Offer them only at the place the LORD will choose in one of your tribes, and there observe everything I command you.

¹⁵Nevertheless, you may slaughter your animals in any of your towns and eat as much of the meat as you want,

as if it were gazelle or deer, according to the blessing the LORD your God gives you. Both the ceremonially unclean and the clean may eat it. 16 But you must not eat the blood; pour it out on the ground like water. 17 You must not eat in your own towns the tithe of your grain and new wine and olive oil, or the firstborn of your herds and flocks, or whatever you have vowed to give, or your freewill offerings or special gifts. 18 Instead, you are to eat them in the presence of the LORD your God at the place the LORD your God will choose—you, your sons and daughters, your male and female servants, and the Levites from your towns—and you are to rejoice before the LORD your God in everything you put your hand to. 19 Be careful not to neglect the Levites as long as you live in your land.

20 When the LORD your God has enlarged your territory as he promised you, and you crave meat and say, "I would like some meat," then you may eat as much of it as you want. 21 If the place where the LORD your God chooses to put his Name is too far away from you, you may slaughter animals from the herds and flocks the LORD has given you, as I have commanded you, and in your own towns you may eat as much of them as you want. 22 Eat them as you would gazelle or deer. Both the ceremonially unclean and the clean may eat. 23 But be sure you do not eat the blood, because the blood is the life, and you must not eat the life with the meat. 24 You must not eat the blood; pour it out on the ground like water. 25 Do not eat it, so that it may go well with you and your children after you, because you will be doing what is right in the eyes of the LORD.

26 But take your consecrated things and whatever you have vowed to give, and go to the place the LORD will choose. 27 Present your burnt offerings on the altar of the LORD your God, both the meat and the blood. The blood of your sacrifices must be poured beside the altar of the LORD your God, but you may eat the meat. 28 Be careful to obey all these regulations I am giving you, so that it may always go well

with you and your children after you, because you will be doing what is good and right in the eyes of the LORD your God.

29 The LORD your God will cut off before you the nations you are about to invade and dispossess. But when you have driven them out and settled in their land, 30 and after they have been destroyed before you, be careful not to be ensnared by inquiring about their gods, saying, "How do these nations serve their gods? We will do the same." 31 You must not worship the LORD your God in their way, because in worshiping their gods, they do all kinds of detestable things the LORD hates. They even burn their sons and daughters in the fire as sacrifices to their gods.

32 See that you do all I command you; do not add to it or take away from it.[a]

Worshiping Other Gods

13[b] If a prophet, or one who foretells by dreams, appears among you and announces to you a sign or wonder, 2 and if the sign or wonder spoken of takes place, and the prophet says, "Let us follow other gods" (gods you have not known) "and let us worship them," 3 you must not listen to the words of that prophet or dreamer. The LORD your God is testing you to find out whether you love him with all your heart and with all your soul. 4 It is the LORD your God you must follow, and him you must revere. Keep his commands and obey him; serve him and hold fast to him. 5 That prophet or dreamer must be put to death for inciting rebellion against the LORD your God, who brought you out of Egypt and redeemed you from the land of slavery. That prophet or dreamer tried to turn you from the way the LORD your God commanded you to follow. You must purge the evil from among you.

6 If your very own brother, or your son or daughter, or the wife you love, or your closest friend secretly entices you, saying, "Let us go and worship other gods" (gods that neither you nor your ancestors have known, 7 gods of the peoples around you, whether near or far, from one end

---

[a] 32 In Hebrew texts this verse (12:32) is numbered 13:1. [b] In Hebrew texts 13:1-18 is numbered 13:2-19.

What if a friend asks for the answer to a test question? You shake your head no. But he whispers, "I was sick last night and couldn't study. Help me just this once." Would you still say no? What if he was a close friend? When it comes to doing wrong, the person who asks may be "your very own brother, or your son or daughter, or the wife you love, or your closest friend" (Deuteronomy 13:6). It makes no difference. This Bible passage says, "Do not yield to them or listen to them" (Deuteronomy 13:8). Acting on your convictions rather than giving in to peer pressure is tough. But it's an important part of becoming a mature adult and a mature Christian.

{Deuteronomy 13:6–11}

≫ INSTANT ACCESS

one among you will do such an evil thing again.

12 If you hear it said about one of the towns the LORD your God is giving you to live in 13 that troublemakers have arisen among you and have led the people of their town astray, saying, "Let us go and worship other gods" (gods you have not known), 14 then you must inquire, probe and investigate it thoroughly. And if it is true and it has been proved that this detestable thing has been done among you, 15 you must certainly put to the sword all who live in that town. You must destroy it completely,[a] both its people and its livestock. 16 You are to gather all the plunder of the town into the middle of the public square and completely burn the town and all its plunder as a whole burnt offering to the LORD your God. That town is to remain a ruin forever, never to be rebuilt, 17 and none of the condemned things[a] are to be found in your hands. Then the LORD will turn from his fierce anger, will show you mercy, and will have compassion on you. He will increase your numbers, as he promised on oath to your ancestors— 18 because you obey the LORD your God by keeping all his commands that I am giving you today and doing what is right in his eyes.

Clean and Unclean Food

14 You are the children of the LORD your God. Do not cut yourselves or shave the front of your heads for the dead, 2 for you are a people holy to the LORD your God. Out of all the peoples on the face of the earth, the LORD has chosen you to be his treasured possession.

3 Do not eat any detestable thing. 4 These are the animals you may eat: the ox, the sheep, the goat, 5 the deer, the gazelle, the roe deer, the wild goat, the ibex, the antelope and the mountain sheep.[b] 6 You may eat any animal that has a divided hoof and that chews the cud. 7 However, of those that chew the cud or that have a divided hoof you may not eat the camel, the rabbit or the hyrax. Although

of the land to the other), 8 do not yield to them or listen to them. Show them no pity. Do not spare them or shield them. 9 You must certainly put them to death. Your hand must be the first in putting them to death, and then the hands of all the people. 10 Stone them to death, because they tried to turn you away from the LORD your God, who brought you out of Egypt, out of the land of slavery. 11 Then all Israel will hear and be afraid, and no

---

a 15,17 The Hebrew term refers to the irrevocable giving over of things or persons to the LORD, often by totally destroying them.   b 5 The precise identification of some of the birds and animals in this chapter is uncertain.

they chew the cud, they do not have a divided hoof; they are ceremonially unclean for you. [8]The pig is also unclean; although it has a divided hoof, it does not chew the cud. You are not to eat their meat or touch their carcasses.

[9]Of all the creatures living in the water, you may eat any that has fins and scales. [10]But anything that does not have fins and scales you may not eat; for you it is unclean.

[11]You may eat any clean bird. [12]But these you may not eat: the eagle, the vulture, the black vulture, [13]the red kite, the black kite, any kind of falcon, [14]any kind of raven, [15]the horned owl, the screech owl, the gull, any kind of hawk, [16]the little owl, the great owl, the white owl, [17]the desert owl, the osprey, the cormorant, [18]the stork, any kind of heron, the hoopoe and the bat.

[19]All flying insects are unclean to you; do not eat them. [20]But any winged creature that is clean you may eat.

[21]Do not eat anything you find already dead. You may give it to the foreigner residing in any of your towns, and they may eat it, or you may sell it to any other foreigner. But you are a people holy to the LORD your God.

Do not cook a young goat in its mother's milk.

Tithes

[22]Be sure to set aside a tenth of all that your fields produce each year. [23]Eat the tithe of your grain, new wine and olive oil, and the firstborn of your herds and flocks in the presence of the LORD your God at the place he will choose as a dwelling for his Name, so that you may learn to revere the LORD your God always. [24]But if that place is too distant and you have been blessed by the LORD your God and cannot carry your tithe (because the place where the LORD will choose to put his Name is so far away), [25]then exchange your tithe for silver, and take the silver with you and go to the place the LORD your God will choose. [26]Use the silver to buy whatever you like: cattle, sheep, wine or other fermented drink, or anything you wish. Then you and your household shall eat there

in the presence of the LORD your God and rejoice. [27]And do not neglect the Levites living in your towns, for they have no allotment or inheritance of their own.

[28]At the end of every three years, bring all the tithes of that year's produce and store it in your towns, [29]so that the Levites (who have no allotment or inheritance of their own) and the foreigners, the fatherless and the widows who live in your towns may come and eat and be satisfied, and so that the LORD your God may bless you in all the work of your hands.

The Year for Canceling Debts

15 At the end of every seven years you must cancel debts. [2]This is how it is to be done: Every creditor shall cancel any loan they have made to a fellow Israelite. They shall not require payment from anyone among their own people, because the LORD's time for canceling debts has been proclaimed. [3]You may require payment from a foreigner, but you must cancel any debt your fellow Israelite owes you. [4]However, there need be no poor people among you, for in the land the LORD your God is giving you to possess as your inheritance, he will richly bless you, [5]if only you fully obey the LORD your God and are careful to follow all these commands I am giving you today. [6]For the LORD your God will bless you as he has promised, and you will lend to many nations but will borrow from none. You will rule over many nations but none will rule over you.

[7]If anyone is poor among your fellow Israelites in any of the towns of the land the LORD your God is giving you, do not be hardhearted or tightfisted toward them. [8]Rather, be openhanded and freely lend them whatever they need. [9]Be careful not to harbor this wicked thought: "The seventh year, the year for canceling debts, is near," so that you do not show ill will toward the needy among your fellow Israelites and give them nothing. They may then appeal to the LORD against you, and you will be found guilty of sin. [10]Give generously to them and do so without a grudging heart; then because of this the LORD your God will bless you in all your

INSTANT ACCESS

Do you ever wonder what happens to the money people give at church? Probably some goes to pay for the building and the pastor's salary and educational materials. But what else? In Old Testament times, ten percent of the harvest was set aside to support the temple and the priests. But every third year the tithe was kept in the village to feed "the foreigners, the fatherless and the widows who live in your towns" (Deuteronomy 14:29). Many churches show the same concern for the needy people in their communities. Helping others is a priority with God. Why not check out what your church does?

{Deuteronomy 14:28–29}

work and in everything you put your hand to. [11] There will always be poor people in the land. Therefore I command you to be openhanded toward your fellow Israelites who are poor and needy in your land.

Freeing Servants

[12] If any of your people—Hebrew men or women—sell themselves to you and serve you six years, in the seventh year you must let them go free. [13] And when you release them, do not send them away empty-handed. [14] Supply them liberally from your flock, your threshing floor and

your winepress. Give to them as the LORD your God has blessed you. [15] Remember that you were slaves in Egypt and the LORD your God redeemed you. That is why I give you this command today.

[16] But if your servant says to you, "I do not want to leave you," because he loves you and your family and is well off with you, [17] then take an awl and push it through his earlobe into the door, and he will become your servant for life. Do the same for your female servant.

[18] Do not consider it a hardship to set your servant free, because their service to you these six years has been worth twice as much as that of a hired hand. And the LORD your God will bless you in everything you do.

The Firstborn Animals

[19] Set apart for the LORD your God every firstborn male of your herds and flocks. Do not put the firstborn of your cows to work, and do not shear the firstborn of your sheep. [20] Each year you and your family are to eat them in the presence of the LORD your God at the place he will choose. [21] If an animal has a defect, is lame or blind, or has any serious flaw, you must not sacrifice it to the LORD your God. [22] You are to eat it in your own towns. Both the ceremonially unclean and the clean may eat it, as if it were gazelle or deer. [23] But you must not eat the blood; pour it out on the ground like water.

The Passover

16 Observe the month of Aviv and celebrate the Passover of the LORD your God, because in the month of Aviv he brought you out of Egypt by night. [2] Sacrifice as the Passover to the LORD your God an animal from your flock or herd at the place the LORD will choose as a dwelling for his Name. [3] Do not eat it with bread made with yeast, but for seven days eat unleavened bread, the bread of affliction, because you left Egypt in haste—so that all the days of your life you may remember the time of your departure from Egypt. [4] Let no yeast be found in your possession in all your land for seven days. Do not let any of the meat you sacrifice on the evening of the first day remain until morning.

⁵You must not sacrifice the Passover in any town the LORD your God gives you ⁶except in the place he will choose as a dwelling for his Name. There you must sacrifice the Passover in the evening, when the sun goes down, on the anniversaryᵃ of your departure from Egypt. ⁷Roast it and eat it at the place the LORD your God will choose. Then in the morning return to your tents. ⁸For six days eat unleavened bread and on the seventh day hold an assembly to the LORD your God and do no work.

The Festival of Weeks

⁹Count off seven weeks from the time you begin to put the sickle to the standing grain. ¹⁰Then celebrate the Festival of Weeks to the LORD your God by giving a freewill offering in proportion to the blessings the LORD your God has given you. ¹¹And rejoice before the LORD your God at the place he will choose as a dwelling for his Name—you, your sons and daughters, your male and female servants, the Levites in your towns, and the foreigners, the fatherless and the widows living among you. ¹²Remember that you were slaves in Egypt, and follow carefully these decrees.

The Festival of Tabernacles

¹³Celebrate the Festival of Tabernacles for seven days after you have gathered the produce of your threshing floor and your winepress. ¹⁴Be joyful at your festival—you, your sons and daughters, your male and female servants, and the Levites, the foreigners, the fatherless and the widows who live in your towns. ¹⁵For seven days celebrate the festival to the LORD your God at the place the LORD will choose. For the LORD your God will bless you in all your harvest and in all the work of your hands, and your joy will be complete.

¹⁶Three times a year all your men must appear before the LORD your God at the place he will choose: at the Festival of Unleavened Bread, the Festival of Weeks

INSTANT ACCESS

Many families plan a Christmas gift for Jesus. Some have jars for loose change, and at Christmas they count it up and give it to missions. There are many ways to make your "holidays" true "holy-days," but one of the best is to show gratitude by making a special, extra gift to the Lord. Three times a year God's people were invited to great national holidays where "no one should appear before the LORD empty-handed. Each of you must bring a gift in proportion to the way the LORD your God has blessed you." What a good reminder that God is the source of all your blessings. And what a good way to say, "Thanks!"

{Deuteronomy 16:16–17}

and the Festival of Tabernacles. No one should appear before the LORD empty-handed: ¹⁷Each of you must bring a gift in proportion to the way the LORD your God has blessed you.

Judges

¹⁸Appoint judges and officials for each of your tribes in every town the LORD your God is giving you, and they shall judge the people fairly. ¹⁹Do not pervert justice or

ᵃ 6 Or down, at the time of day

show partiality. Do not accept a bribe, for a bribe blinds the eyes of the wise and twists the words of the innocent. 20 Follow justice and justice alone, so that you may live and possess the land the LORD your God is giving you.

Worshiping Other Gods

21 Do not set up any wooden Asherah pole beside the altar you build to the LORD your God, 22 and do not erect a sacred stone, for these the LORD your God hates.

17 Do not sacrifice to the LORD your God an ox or a sheep that has any defect or flaw in it, for that would be detestable to him.

2 If a man or woman living among you in one of the towns the LORD gives you is found doing evil in the eyes of the LORD your God in violation of his covenant, 3 and contrary to my command has worshiped other gods, bowing down to them or to the sun or the moon or the stars in the sky, 4 and this has been brought to your attention, then you must investigate it thoroughly. If it is true and it has been proved that this detestable thing has been done in Israel, 5 take the man or woman who has done this evil deed to your city gate and stone that person to death. 6 On the testimony of two or three witnesses a person is to be put to death, but no one is to be put to death on the testimony of only one witness. 7 The hands of the witnesses must be the first in putting that person to death, and then the hands of all the people. You must purge the evil from among you.

Law Courts

8 If cases come before your courts that are too difficult for you to judge—whether bloodshed, lawsuits or assaults—take them to the place the LORD your God will choose. 9 Go to the Levitical priests and to the judge who is in office at that time. Inquire of them and they will give you the verdict. 10 You must act according to the decisions they give you at the place the LORD will choose. Be careful to do everything they instruct you to do. 11 Act according to whatever they teach you and the decisions they give you. Do not turn

aside from what they tell you, to the right or to the left. 12 Anyone who shows contempt for the judge or for the priest who stands ministering there to the LORD your God is to be put to death. You must purge the evil from Israel. 13 All the people will hear and be afraid, and will not be contemptuous again.

The King

14 When you enter the land the LORD your God is giving you and have taken possession of it and settled in it, and you say, "Let us set a king over us like all the nations around us," 15 be sure to appoint over you a king the LORD your God chooses. He must be from among your fellow Israelites. Do not place a foreigner over you, one who is not an Israelite. 16 The king, moreover, must not acquire great numbers of horses for himself or make the people return to Egypt to get more of them, for the LORD has told you, "You are not to go back that way again." 17 He must not take many wives, or his heart will be led astray. He must not accumulate large amounts of silver and gold.

18 When he takes the throne of his kingdom, he is to write for himself on a scroll a copy of this law, taken from that of the Levitical priests. 19 It is to be with him, and he is to read it all the days of his life so that he may learn to revere the LORD his God and follow carefully all the words of this law and these decrees 20 and not consider himself better than his fellow Israelites and turn from the law to the right or to the left. Then he and his descendants will reign a long time over his kingdom in Israel.

Offerings for Priests and Levites

18 The Levitical priests—indeed, the whole tribe of Levi—are to have no allotment or inheritance with Israel. They shall live on the food offerings presented to the LORD, for that is their inheritance. 2 They shall have no inheritance among their fellow Israelites; the LORD is their inheritance, as he promised them.

3 This is the share due the priests from the people who sacrifice a bull or a

sheep: the shoulder, the internal organs and the meat from the head. [4]You are to give them the firstfruits of your grain, new wine and olive oil, and the first wool from the shearing of your sheep, [5]for the LORD your God has chosen them and their descendants out of all your tribes to stand and minister in the LORD's name always.

[6]If a Levite moves from one of your towns anywhere in Israel where he is living, and comes in all earnestness to the place the LORD will choose, [7]he may minister in the name of the LORD his God like all his fellow Levites who serve there in the presence of the LORD. [8]He is to share equally in their benefits, even though he has received money from the sale of family possessions.

Occult Practices

[9]When you enter the land the LORD your God is giving you, do not learn to imitate the detestable ways of the nations there. [10]Let no one be found among you who sacrifices their son or daughter in the fire, who practices divination or sorcery, interprets omens, engages in witchcraft, [11]or casts spells, or who is a medium or spiritist or who consults the dead. [12]Anyone who does these things is detestable to the LORD; because of these same detestable practices the LORD your God will drive out those nations before you. [13]You must be blameless before the LORD your God.

The Prophet

[14]The nations you will dispossess listen to those who practice sorcery or divination. But as for you, the LORD your God has not permitted you to do so. [15]The LORD your God will raise up for you a prophet like me from among you, from your fellow Israelites. You must listen to him. [16]For this is what you asked of the LORD your God at Horeb on the day of the assembly when you said, "Let us not hear the voice of the LORD our God nor see this great fire anymore, or we will die."

[17]The LORD said to me: "What they say is good. [18]I will raise up for them a prophet like you from among their fellow Israelites, and I will put my words in his mouth. He will tell them everything I command

him. [19]I myself will call to account anyone who does not listen to my words that the prophet speaks in my name. [20]But a prophet who presumes to speak in my name anything I have not commanded, or a prophet who speaks in the name of other gods, is to be put to death."

[21]You may say to yourselves, "How can we know when a message has not been spoken by the LORD?" [22]If what a prophet proclaims in the name of the LORD does not take place or come true, that is a message the LORD has not spoken. That prophet has spoken presumptuously, so do not be alarmed.

Cities of Refuge

19 When the LORD your God has destroyed the nations whose land he is giving you, and when you have driven them out and settled in their towns and houses, [2]then set aside for yourselves three cities in the land the LORD your God is giving you to possess. [3]Determine the distances involved and divide into three parts the land the LORD your God is giving you as an inheritance, so that a person who kills someone may flee for refuge to one of these cities.

[4]This is the rule concerning anyone who kills a person and flees there for safety—anyone who kills a neighbor unintentionally, without malice aforethought. [5]For instance, a man may go into the forest with his neighbor to cut wood, and as he swings his ax to fell a tree, the head may fly off and hit his neighbor and kill him. That man may flee to one of these cities and save his life. [6]Otherwise, the avenger of blood might pursue him in a rage, overtake him if the distance is too great, and kill him even though he is not deserving of death, since he did it to his neighbor without malice aforethought. [7]This is why I command you to set aside for yourselves three cities.

[8]If the LORD your God enlarges your territory, as he promised on oath to your ancestors, and gives you the whole land he promised them, [9]because you carefully follow all these laws I command you today—to love the LORD your God and to walk always in obedience to him—then

My parents are so controlling they won't let me hang out with some of my friends just because they play with a Ouija board. What can I do to get control of my life?

>> Hayden

Dear Hayden,

Did you know that Ouija boards are a part of the occult? The spirit world is very real and is divided into two groups—the angels who belong to God's kingdom, and demons who don't. God has given a strong message about trying to communicate with demons. "Let no one be found among you … who practices divination or sorcery, interprets omens, engages in witchcraft, or casts spells, or who is a medium or spiritist or who consults the dead" (Deuteronomy 18:10–11).

God is spirit, and you don't need a Ouija board to talk to him. You can talk to him any time you pray. God wants you to come to him for advice. In fact, believers have the Holy Spirit of God within them. One of his jobs is to guide us in the path our heavenly Father has for us. When you go to a Ouija board, a fortune teller, tarot cards, a horoscope or palm reader, you are turning away from God to seek advice from a kingdom God hates.

The Ouija board may seem like an innocent toy. But it isn't. It is really an instrument used to contact spirits who are not of God. Your parents aren't trying to control your life. They are trying to guide you in the ways God wants you to go. This is one of the reasons why God gives us parents—to guide us and protect us from evil.

Jordan

you are to set aside three more cities. ¹⁰Do this so that innocent blood will not be shed in your land, which the LORD your God is giving you as your inheritance, and so that you will not be guilty of bloodshed.

¹¹But if out of hate someone lies in wait, assaults and kills a neighbor, and then flees to one of these cities, ¹²the killer shall be sent for by the town elders, be brought back from the city, and be handed over to the avenger of blood to die. ¹³Show no pity. You must purge from Israel the guilt of shedding innocent blood, so that it may go well with you.

¹⁴Do not move your neighbor's boundary stone set up by your predecessors in the inheritance you receive in the land the LORD your God is giving you to possess.

Witnesses

¹⁵One witness is not enough to convict anyone accused of any crime or offense they may have committed. A matter must be established by the testimony of two or three witnesses.

¹⁶If a malicious witness takes the stand to accuse someone of a crime, ¹⁷the two people involved in the dispute must stand in the presence of the LORD before the priests and the judges who are in office at the time. ¹⁸The judges must make a thorough investigation, and if the witness proves to be a liar, giving false testimony against a fellow Israelite, ¹⁹then do to the false witness as that witness intended to do to the other party. You must purge the evil from among you. ²⁰The rest of the people will hear of this and be afraid, and never again will such an evil thing be done among you. ²¹Show no pity: life for life, eye for eye, tooth for tooth, hand for hand, foot for foot.

Going to War

20 When you go to war against your enemies and see horses and chariots and an army greater than yours, do not be afraid of them, because the LORD your God, who brought you up out of Egypt, will be with you. ²When you are about to go into battle, the priest shall come forward and address the army. ³He shall say: "Hear, Israel: Today you are going into battle against your enemies. Do not be fainthearted or afraid; do not panic or be terrified by them. ⁴For the LORD your God is the one who goes with you to fight for you against your enemies to give you victory."

⁵The officers shall say to the army: "Has anyone built a new house and not yet begun to live in it? Let him go home, or he may die in battle and someone else may begin to live in it. ⁶Has anyone planted a vineyard and not begun to enjoy it? Let him go home, or he may die in battle and someone else enjoy it. ⁷Has anyone become pledged to a woman and not married her? Let him go home, or he may die in battle and someone else marry her." ⁸Then the officers shall add, "Is anyone afraid or fainthearted? Let him go home so that his fellow soldiers will not become disheartened too." ⁹When the officers have finished speaking to the army, they shall appoint commanders over it.

¹⁰When you march up to attack a city, make its people an offer of peace. ¹¹If they accept and open their gates, all the people in it shall be subject to forced labor and shall work for you. ¹²If they refuse to make peace and they engage you in battle, lay siege to that city. ¹³When the LORD your God delivers it into your hand, put to the sword all the men in it. ¹⁴As for the women, the children, the livestock and everything else in the city, you may take these as plunder for yourselves. And you may use the plunder the LORD your God gives you from your enemies. ¹⁵This is how you are to treat all the cities that are at a distance from you and do not belong to the nations nearby.

¹⁶However, in the cities of the nations the LORD your God is giving you as an inheritance, do not leave alive anything that breathes. ¹⁷Completely destroyᵃ them— the Hittites, Amorites, Canaanites, Perizzites, Hivites and Jebusites—as the LORD your God has commanded you. ¹⁸Otherwise, they will teach you to follow all the detestable things they do in worshiping

---

ᵃ 17 The Hebrew term refers to the irrevocable giving over of things or persons to the LORD, often by totally destroying them.

their gods, and you will sin against the LORD your God.

[19]When you lay siege to a city for a long time, fighting against it to capture it, do not destroy its trees by putting an ax to them, because you can eat their fruit. Do not cut them down. Are the trees people, that you should besiege them?[a] [20]However, you may cut down trees that you know are not fruit trees and use them to build siege works until the city at war with you falls.

Atonement for an Unsolved Murder

21 If someone is found slain, lying in a field in the land the LORD your God is giving you to possess, and it is not known who the killer was, [2]your elders and judges shall go out and measure the distance from the body to the neighboring towns. [3]Then the elders of the town nearest the body shall take a heifer that has never been worked and has never worn a yoke [4]and lead it down to a valley that has not been plowed or planted and where there is a flowing stream. There in the valley they are to break the heifer's neck. [5]The Levitical priests shall step forward, for the LORD your God has chosen them to minister and to pronounce blessings in the name of the LORD and to decide all cases of dispute and assault. [6]Then all the elders of the town nearest the body shall wash their hands over the heifer whose neck was broken in the valley, [7]and they shall declare: "Our hands did not shed this blood, nor did

[a] 19 Or down to use in the siege, for the fruit trees are for the benefit of people.

TO THE POINT

Destroy Them?

How could a loving God tell his people to "completely destroy" the Canaanites (Deuteronomy 20:16–17)? God gave this command to protect his people. Deuteronomy 20:18 explains clearly that if any Canaanites were left alive they would teach the Israelites to worship idols.

Archaeology has revealed much about Canaanite religion, which featured prostitution, immorality, even burning children alive to please their gods. And because the Israelites did not exterminate these people, exactly what God warned about did happen. The Canaanites turned the Israelites to idolatry.

So was God being brutal and bloodthirsty when he gave this command? Not at all. It was the Canaanites who were bloodthirsty, brutal and immoral. God was protecting his people and punishing the Canaanites, as they deserved.

our eyes see it done. [8]Accept this atonement for your people Israel, whom you have redeemed, LORD, and do not hold your people guilty of the blood of an innocent person." Then the bloodshed will be atoned for, [9]and you will have purged from yourselves the guilt of shedding innocent blood, since you have done what is right in the eyes of the LORD.

Marrying a Captive Woman

[10]When you go to war against your enemies and the LORD your God delivers them into your hands and you take captives, [11]if you notice among the captives a beautiful woman and are attracted to her, you may take her as your wife. [12]Bring her into your home and have her shave her head, trim her nails [13]and put aside the clothes she was wearing when captured. After she has lived in your house and mourned her father and mother for a full month, then you may go to her and be her husband and she shall be your wife. [14]If you are not pleased with her, let her go wherever she wishes. You must not sell her or treat her as a slave, since you have dishonored her.

The Right of the Firstborn

[15]If a man has two wives, and he loves one but not the other, and both bear him sons but the firstborn is the son of the wife he does not love, [16]when he wills his property to his sons, he must not give the rights of the firstborn to the son of the wife he loves in preference to his actual firstborn, the son of the wife he does not love. [17]He must acknowledge the son of his unloved wife as the firstborn by giving him a double share of all he has. That son is the first sign of his father's strength. The right of the firstborn belongs to him.

A Rebellious Son

[18]If someone has a stubborn and rebellious son who does not obey his father and mother and will not listen to them when they discipline him, [19]his father and mother shall take hold of him and bring

him to the elders at the gate of his town. [20]They shall say to the elders, "This son of ours is stubborn and rebellious. He will not obey us. He is a glutton and a drunkard." [21]Then all the men of his town are to stone him to death. You must purge the evil from among you. All Israel will hear of it and be afraid.

Various Laws

[22]If someone guilty of a capital offense is put to death and their body is exposed on a pole, [23]you must not leave the body hanging on the pole overnight. Be sure to bury it that same day, because anyone who is hung on a pole is under God's curse. You must not desecrate the land the LORD your God is giving you as an inheritance.

22 If you see your fellow Israelite's ox or sheep straying, do not ignore it but be sure to take it back to its owner. [2]If they do not live near you or if you do not know who owns it, take it home with you and keep it until they come looking for it. Then give it back. [3]Do the same if you find their donkey or cloak or anything else they have lost. Do not ignore it.

[4]If you see your fellow Israelite's donkey or ox fallen on the road, do not ignore it. Help the owner get it to its feet.

[5]A woman must not wear men's clothing, nor a man wear women's clothing, for the LORD your God detests anyone who does this.

[6]If you come across a bird's nest beside the road, either in a tree or on the ground, and the mother is sitting on the young or on the eggs, do not take the mother with the young. [7]You may take the young, but be sure to let the mother go, so that it may go well with you and you may have a long life.

[8]When you build a new house, make a parapet around your roof so that you may not bring the guilt of bloodshed on your house if someone falls from the roof.

[9]Do not plant two kinds of seed in your vineyard; if you do, not only the crops you plant but also the fruit of the vineyard will be defiled.[a]

---

[a] 9 Or *be forfeited to the sanctuary*

D ad says, "Be home at 10:00." And you get home at 10:45. Mom says, "No internet." You sneak over to your laptop and get online while she's in the kitchen. Even though your parents might not be too happy with you, chances are you won't get grounded—much less stoned to death. But what about open rebellion? Dad says be in by 10:00, and son is gone all night. Every day Mom says, "Get up and go to school," and every day daughter rolls over and ignores her. Now that's disobedience. Is it serious? Check out this passage—you may re-think rebellion at home is a minor sin.

{Deuteronomy 21:18–21}

» INSTANT ACCESS

approached her, I did not find proof of her virginity," ¹⁵then the young woman's father and mother shall bring to the town elders at the gate proof that she was a virgin. ¹⁶Her father will say to the elders, "I gave my daughter in marriage to this man, but he dislikes her. ¹⁷Now he has slandered her and said, 'I did not find your daughter to be a virgin.' But here is the proof of my daughter's virginity." Then her parents shall display the cloth before the elders of the town, ¹⁸and the elders shall take the man and punish him. ¹⁹They shall fine him a hundred shekels[a] of silver and give them to the young woman's father, because this man has given an Israelite virgin a bad name. She shall continue to be his wife; he must not divorce her as long as he lives.

²⁰If, however, the charge is true and no proof of the young woman's virginity can be found, ²¹she shall be brought to the door of her father's house and there the men of her town shall stone her to death. She has done an outrageous thing in Israel by being promiscuous while still in her father's house. You must purge the evil from among you.

²²If a man is found sleeping with another man's wife, both the man who slept with her and the woman must die. You must purge the evil from Israel.

²³If a man happens to meet in a town a virgin pledged to be married and he sleeps with her, ²⁴you shall take both of them to the gate of that town and stone them to death—the young woman because she was in a town and did not scream for help, and the man because he violated another man's wife. You must purge the evil from among you.

²⁵But if out in the country a man happens to meet a young woman pledged to be married and rapes her, only the man who has done this shall die. ²⁶Do nothing to the woman; she has committed no sin deserving death. This case is like that of someone who attacks and murders a neighbor, ²⁷for the man found the young woman out in the country, and though the betrothed woman screamed, there was no one to rescue her.

¹⁰Do not plow with an ox and a donkey yoked together.

¹¹Do not wear clothes of wool and linen woven together.

¹²Make tassels on the four corners of the cloak you wear.

Marriage Violations

¹³If a man takes a wife and, after sleeping with her, dislikes her ¹⁴and slanders her and gives her a bad name, saying, "I married this woman, but when I

---

^a 19 That is, about 2 1/2 pounds or about 1.2 kilograms

> I was at a party and drank some beer. We were playing truth or dare and before I knew it, I was alone in a room with a boy I didn't know. I tried to stop him, but I couldn't. I feel sick and used. What can I do?
>
> **>> Unsigned**

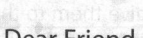

Dear Friend,

There are several steps that you need to take. But first you need to know that getting raped was not your fault. You were the victim. Deuteronomy 22:25–27 tells us God holds the violator accountable, not the victim.

I hope you will tell your mom what happened. You need to see a doctor as you could have been given a sexually transmitted disease. Most of these have no symptoms until damage has already been done. Be sure to tell the doctor what happened so the right tests will be run.

Rape is a serious crime. In addition to seeing a doctor, seeing a good counselor can help you with the emotional and psychological trauma.

Please remember to pray for your healing also. God is our maker and he can bring healing to us even in these terrible circumstances.

No one should have to try to cope with this alone. Please let your mom help you get the help you need. God bless you.

Jordan

²⁸ If a man happens to meet a virgin who is not pledged to be married and rapes her and they are discovered, ²⁹ he shall pay her father fifty shekels*ᵃ* of silver. He must marry the young woman, for he has violated her. He can never divorce her as long as he lives.

³⁰ A man is not to marry his father's wife; he must not dishonor his father's bed.*ᵇ*

Exclusion From the Assembly

23 *ᶜ* No one who has been emasculated by crushing or cutting may enter the assembly of the LORD.

² No one born of a forbidden marriage*ᵈ* nor any of their descendants may enter the assembly of the LORD, not even in the tenth generation.

³ No Ammonite or Moabite or any of their descendants may enter the assembly of the LORD, not even in the tenth generation. ⁴ For they did not come to meet you with bread and water on your way when you came out of Egypt, and they hired Balaam son of Beor from Pethor in Aram Naharaim*ᵉ* to pronounce a curse on you. ⁵ However, the LORD your God would not listen to Balaam but turned the curse into a blessing for you, because the LORD your God loves you. ⁶ Do not seek a treaty of friendship with them as long as you live.

⁷ Do not despise an Edomite, for the Edomites are related to you. Do not despise an Egyptian, because you resided as foreigners in their country. ⁸ The third generation of children born to them may enter the assembly of the LORD.

Uncleanness in the Camp

⁹ When you are encamped against your enemies, keep away from everything impure. ¹⁰ If one of your men is unclean because of a nocturnal emission, he is to go outside the camp and stay there. ¹¹ But as evening approaches he is to wash himself, and at sunset he may return to the camp.

¹² Designate a place outside the camp where you can go to relieve yourself. ¹³ As part of your equipment have something to dig with, and when you relieve yourself, dig a hole and cover up your excrement. ¹⁴ For the LORD your God moves about in your camp to protect you and to deliver your enemies to you. Your camp must be holy, so that he will not see among you anything indecent and turn away from you.

Miscellaneous Laws

¹⁵ If a slave has taken refuge with you, do not hand them over to their master. ¹⁶ Let them live among you wherever they like and in whatever town they choose. Do not oppress them.

¹⁷ No Israelite man or woman is to become a shrine prostitute. ¹⁸ You must not bring the earnings of a female prostitute or of a male prostitute*ᶠ* into the house of the LORD your God to pay any vow, because the LORD your God detests them both.

¹⁹ Do not charge a fellow Israelite interest, whether on money or food or anything else that may earn interest. ²⁰ You may charge a foreigner interest, but not a fellow Israelite, so that the LORD your God may bless you in everything you put your hand to in the land you are entering to possess.

²¹ If you make a vow to the LORD your God, do not be slow to pay it, for the LORD your God will certainly demand it of you and you will be guilty of sin. ²² But if you refrain from making a vow, you will not be guilty. ²³ Whatever your lips utter you must be sure to do, because you made your vow freely to the LORD your God with your own mouth.

²⁴ If you enter your neighbor's vineyard, you may eat all the grapes you want, but do not put any in your basket. ²⁵ If you enter your neighbor's grainfield, you may pick kernels with your hands, but you must not put a sickle to their standing grain.

24 If a man marries a woman who becomes displeasing to him because he finds something indecent about her, and he writes her a certificate of divorce, gives it to her and sends her from

---

ᵃ 29 That is, about 1 1/4 pounds or about 575 grams   *ᵇ 30* In Hebrew texts this verse (22:30) is numbered 23:1.
ᶜ In Hebrew texts 23:1-25 is numbered 23:2-26.   *ᵈ 2* Or *one of illegitimate birth*   *ᵉ 4* That is, Northwest Mesopotamia
ᶠ 18 Hebrew *of a dog*

his house, ²and if after she leaves his house she becomes the wife of another man, ³and her second husband dislikes her and writes her a certificate of divorce, gives it to her and sends her from his house, or if he dies, ⁴then her first husband, who divorced her, is not allowed to marry her again after she has been defiled. That would be detestable in the eyes of the LORD. Do not bring sin upon the land the LORD your God is giving you as an inheritance.

⁵If a man has recently married, he must not be sent to war or have any other duty laid on him. For one year he is to be free to stay at home and bring happiness to the wife he has married.

⁶Do not take a pair of millstones—not even the upper one—as security for a debt, because that would be taking a person's livelihood as security.

⁷If someone is caught kidnapping a fellow Israelite and treating or selling them as a slave, the kidnapper must die. You must purge the evil from among you.

⁸In cases of defiling skin diseases,ᵃ be very careful to do exactly as the Levitical priests instruct you. You must follow carefully what I have commanded them.

⁹Remember what the LORD your God did to Miriam along the way after you came out of Egypt.

¹⁰When you make a loan of any kind to your neighbor, do not go into their house to get what is offered to you as a pledge. ¹¹Stay outside and let the neighbor to whom you are making the loan bring the pledge out to you. ¹²If the neighbor is poor, do not go to sleep with their pledge in your possession. ¹³Return their cloak by sunset so that your neighbor may sleep in it. Then they will thank you, and it will be regarded as a righteous act in the sight of the LORD your God.

¹⁴Do not take advantage of a hired worker who is poor and needy, whether that worker is a fellow Israelite or a foreigner residing in one of your towns. ¹⁵Pay them their wages each day before sunset, because they are poor and are counting on it. Otherwise they may cry to the LORD against you, and you will be guilty of sin.

¹⁶Parents are not to be put to death for their children, nor children put to death for their parents; each will die for their own sin.

¹⁷Do not deprive the foreigner or the fatherless of justice, or take the cloak of the widow as a pledge. ¹⁸Remember that you were slaves in Egypt and the LORD your God redeemed you from there. That is why I command you to do this.

¹⁹When you are harvesting in your field and you overlook a sheaf, do not go back to get it. Leave it for the foreigner, the fatherless and the widow, so that the LORD your God may bless you in all the work of your hands. ²⁰When you beat the olives from your trees, do not go over the branches a second time. Leave what remains for the foreigner, the fatherless and the widow. ²¹When you harvest the grapes in your vineyard, do not go over the vines again. Leave what remains for the foreigner, the fatherless and the widow. ²²Remember that you were slaves in Egypt. That is why I command you to do this.

Deuteronomy 24

Q: How long a honeymoon did the Old Testament law permit?

BONUS: What was the purpose of the honeymoon?

Answers on next page

ᵃ 8 The Hebrew word for *defiling skin diseases*, traditionally translated "leprosy," was used for various diseases affecting the skin.

25 When people have a dispute, they are to take it to court and the judges will decide the case, acquitting the innocent and condemning the guilty. ²If the guilty person deserves to be beaten, the judge shall make them lie down and have them flogged in his presence with the number of lashes the crime deserves, ³but the judge must not impose more than forty lashes. If the guilty party is flogged more than that, your fellow Israelite will be degraded in your eyes.

⁴Do not muzzle an ox while it is treading out the grain.

⁵If brothers are living together and one of them dies without a son, his widow must not marry outside the family. Her husband's brother shall take her and marry her and fulfill the duty of a brother-in-law to her. ⁶The first son she bears shall carry on the name of the dead brother so that his name will not be blotted out from Israel.

⁷However, if a man does not want to marry his brother's wife, she shall go to the elders at the town gate and say, "My husband's brother refuses to carry on his brother's name in Israel. He will not fulfill the duty of a brother-in-law to me." ⁸Then the elders of his town shall summon him and talk to him. If he persists in saying, "I do not want to marry her," ⁹his brother's widow shall go up to him in the presence of the elders, take off one of his sandals, spit in his face and say, "This is what is done to the man who will not build up his brother's family line." ¹⁰That man's line shall be known in Israel as The Family of the Unsandaled.

¹¹If two men are fighting and the wife of one of them comes to rescue her husband from his assailant, and she reaches out and seizes him by his private parts, ¹²you shall cut off her hand. Show her no pity.

¹³Do not have two differing weights in your bag—one heavy, one light. ¹⁴Do not have two differing measures in your house—one large, one small. ¹⁵You must have accurate and honest weights and measures, so that you may live long in the land the LORD your God is giving you. ¹⁶For the LORD your God detests any-

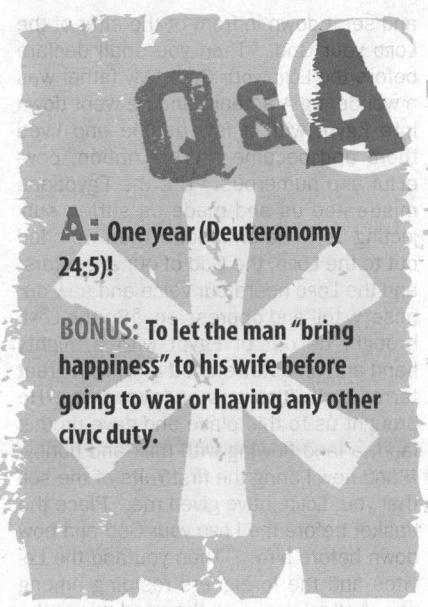

A: One year (Deuteronomy 24:5)!

BONUS: To let the man "bring happiness" to his wife before going to war or having any other civic duty.

one who does these things, anyone who deals dishonestly.

¹⁷Remember what the Amalekites did to you along the way when you came out of Egypt. ¹⁸When you were weary and worn out, they met you on your journey and attacked all who were lagging behind; they had no fear of God. ¹⁹When the LORD your God gives you rest from all the enemies around you in the land he is giving you to possess as an inheritance, you shall blot out the name of Amalek from under heaven. Do not forget!

Firstfruits and Tithes

26 When you have entered the land the LORD your God is giving you as an inheritance and have taken possession of it and settled in it, ²take some of the firstfruits of all that you produce from the soil of the land the LORD your God is giving you and put them in a basket. Then go to the place the LORD your God will choose as a dwelling for his Name ³and say to the priest in office at the time, "I declare today to the LORD your God that I have come to the land the LORD swore to our ancestors to give us." ⁴The priest shall take the basket from your hands and set it down in front of the altar of the LORD your God. ⁵Then you shall declare before the LORD your God: "My father was a wandering Aramean, and he went down into Egypt with a few people and lived there and became a great nation, powerful and numerous. ⁶But the Egyptians mistreated us and made us suffer, subjecting us to harsh labor. ⁷Then we cried out to the LORD, the God of our ancestors, and the LORD heard our voice and saw our misery, toil and oppression. ⁸So the LORD brought us out of Egypt with a mighty hand and an outstretched arm, with great terror and with signs and wonders. ⁹He brought us to this place and gave us this land, a land flowing with milk and honey; ¹⁰and now I bring the firstfruits of the soil that you, LORD, have given me." Place the basket before the LORD your God and bow down before him. ¹¹Then you and the Levites and the foreigners residing among you shall rejoice in all the good things the LORD your God has given to you and your household.

¹²When you have finished setting aside a tenth of all your produce in the third year, the year of the tithe, you shall give it to the Levite, the foreigner, the fatherless and the widow, so that they may eat in your towns and be satisfied. ¹³Then say to the LORD your God: "I have removed from my house the sacred portion and have given it to the Levite, the foreigner, the fatherless and the widow, according to all you commanded. I have not turned aside from your commands nor have I forgotten any of them. ¹⁴I have not eaten any of the sacred portion while I was in mourning, nor have I removed any of it while I was unclean, nor have I offered any of it to the dead. I have obeyed the LORD my God; I have done everything you commanded me. ¹⁵Look down from heaven, your holy dwelling place, and bless your people Israel and the land you have given us as you promised on oath to our ancestors, a land flowing with milk and honey."

Follow the LORD's Commands

¹⁶The LORD your God commands you this day to follow these decrees and laws; carefully observe them with all your heart and with all your soul. ¹⁷You have declared this day that the LORD is your God and that you will walk in obedience to him, that you will keep his decrees, commands and laws—that you will listen to him. ¹⁸And the LORD has declared this day that you are his people, his treasured possession as he promised, and that you are to keep all his commands. ¹⁹He has declared that he will set you in praise, fame and honor high above all the nations he has made and that you will be a people holy to the LORD your God, as he promised.

The Altar on Mount Ebal

27 Moses and the elders of Israel commanded the people: "Keep all these commands that I give you today. ²When you have crossed the Jordan into the land the LORD your God is giving you, set up some large stones and coat them with plaster. ³Write on them all the words of this law when you have crossed over to enter the land the LORD your God is giving you, a land flowing with milk and honey, just as the LORD, the God of your ancestors, promised you. ⁴And when you have crossed the Jordan, set up these stones on Mount Ebal, as I command you today, and coat them with plaster. ⁵Build there an altar to the LORD your God, an altar of stones. Do not use any iron tool on them. ⁶Build the altar of the LORD your God with fieldstones and offer burnt offerings on it to the LORD your God. ⁷Sacrifice fellowship offerings there, eating them and rejoicing in the presence of the LORD your God. ⁸And you shall write very clearly all the words of this law on these stones you have set up."

Curses From Mount Ebal

⁹Then Moses and the Levitical priests said to all Israel, "Be silent, Israel, and listen! You have now become the people of the LORD your God. ¹⁰Obey the LORD your God and follow his commands and decrees that I give you today."

¹¹On the same day Moses commanded the people:

Does it bother you when kids who go to church regularly swear or tell dirty jokes at school? When someone in your youth group cheats on tests? Or when a teen who is oh-so-pious at church mocks Christian kids at school? Maybe you wonder if they're real Christians at all. That question is one you and I can't answer. But for real Christians, their walk and their talk are supposed to be the same. Maybe you can't judge whether another person is a real Christian or not. But you *can* make sure that no one has any doubts about you! If you say you're a Christian, live a Christian life at school, at home, everywhere!

{Deuteronomy 26:16–19}

INSTANT ACCESS

¹²When you have crossed the Jordan, these tribes shall stand on Mount Gerizim to bless the people: Simeon, Levi, Judah, Issachar, Joseph and Benjamin. ¹³And these tribes shall stand on Mount Ebal to pronounce curses: Reuben, Gad, Asher, Zebulun, Dan and Naphtali.

¹⁴The Levites shall recite to all the people of Israel in a loud voice:

¹⁵"Cursed is anyone who makes an idol—a thing detestable to the LORD, the work of skilled hands—and sets it up in secret."

Then all the people shall say, "Amen!"

¹⁶"Cursed is anyone who dishonors their father or mother."

Then all the people shall say, "Amen!"

¹⁷"Cursed is anyone who moves their neighbor's boundary stone."

Then all the people shall say, "Amen!"

¹⁸"Cursed is anyone who leads the blind astray on the road."

Then all the people shall say, "Amen!"

¹⁹"Cursed is anyone who withholds justice from the foreigner, the fatherless or the widow."

Then all the people shall say, "Amen!"

²⁰"Cursed is anyone who sleeps with his father's wife, for he dishonors his father's bed."

Then all the people shall say, "Amen!"

²¹"Cursed is anyone who has sexual relations with any animal."

Then all the people shall say, "Amen!"

²²"Cursed is anyone who sleeps with his sister, the daughter of his father or the daughter of his mother."

Then all the people shall say, "Amen!"

²³"Cursed is anyone who sleeps with his mother-in-law."

Then all the people shall say, "Amen!"

²⁴"Cursed is anyone who kills their neighbor secretly."

Then all the people shall say, "Amen!"

²⁵"Cursed is anyone who accepts a bribe to kill an innocent person."

Then all the people shall say, "Amen!"

²⁶"Cursed is anyone who does not uphold the words of this law by carrying them out."

Then all the people shall say, "Amen!"

Blessings for Obedience

28 If you fully obey the Lord your God and carefully follow all his commands I give you today, the Lord your God will set you high above all the nations on earth. ²All these blessings will come on you and accompany you if you obey the Lord your God:

³You will be blessed in the city and blessed in the country.

⁴The fruit of your womb will be blessed, and the crops of your land and the young of your livestock—the calves of your herds and the lambs of your flocks.

⁵Your basket and your kneading trough will be blessed.

⁶You will be blessed when you come in and blessed when you go out.

⁷The Lord will grant that the enemies who rise up against you will be defeated before you. They will come at you from one direction but flee from you in seven.

⁸The Lord will send a blessing on your barns and on everything you put your hand to. The Lord your God will bless you in the land he is giving you.

⁹The Lord will establish you as his holy people, as he promised you on oath, if you keep the commands of the Lord your God and walk in obedience to him. ¹⁰Then all the peoples on earth will see that you are called by the name of the Lord, and they will fear you. ¹¹The Lord will grant you abundant prosperity—in the fruit of your womb, the young of your livestock and the crops of your ground—in the land he swore to your ancestors to give you.

¹²The Lord will open the heavens, the storehouse of his bounty, to send rain on your land in season and to bless all the work of your hands. You will lend to many nations but will borrow from none. ¹³The Lord will make you the head, not the tail. If you pay attention to the commands of the Lord your God that I give you this day and carefully follow them, you will always

be at the top, never at the bottom. ¹⁴Do not turn aside from any of the commands I give you today, to the right or to the left, following other gods and serving them.

Curses for Disobedience

¹⁵However, if you do not obey the Lord your God and do not carefully follow all his commands and decrees I am giving you today, all these curses will come on you and overtake you:

¹⁶You will be cursed in the city and cursed in the country.

¹⁷Your basket and your kneading trough will be cursed.

¹⁸The fruit of your womb will be cursed, and the crops of your land, and the calves of your herds and the lambs of your flocks.

¹⁹You will be cursed when you come in and cursed when you go out.

²⁰The Lord will send on you curses, confusion and rebuke in everything you put your hand to, until you are destroyed and come to sudden ruin because of the evil you have done in forsaking him.[a] ²¹The Lord will plague you with diseases until he has destroyed you from the land you are entering to possess. ²²The Lord will strike you with wasting disease, with fever and inflammation, with scorching heat and drought, with blight and mildew, which will plague you until you perish. ²³The sky over your head will be bronze, the ground beneath you iron. ²⁴The Lord will turn the rain of your country into dust and powder; it will come down from the skies until you are destroyed.

²⁵The Lord will cause you to be defeated before your enemies. You will come at them from one direction but flee from them in seven, and you will become a thing of horror to all the kingdoms on earth. ²⁶Your carcasses will be food for all the birds and the wild animals, and there will be no one to frighten them away. ²⁷The Lord will afflict you with the boils of Egypt and with tumors, festering sores and the itch, from which you can-

---

not be cured. ²⁸The Lord will afflict you with madness, blindness and confusion of mind. ²⁹At midday you will grope about like a blind person in the dark. You will be unsuccessful in everything you do; day after day you will be oppressed and robbed, with no one to rescue you.

³⁰You will be pledged to be married to a woman, but another will take her and rape her. You will build a house, but you will not live in it. You will plant a vineyard, but you will not even begin to enjoy its fruit. ³¹Your ox will be slaughtered before your eyes, but you will eat none of it. Your donkey will be forcibly taken from you and will not be returned. Your sheep will be given to your enemies, and no one will rescue them. ³²Your sons and daughters will be given to another nation, and you will wear out your eyes watching for them day after day, powerless to lift a hand. ³³A people that you do not know will eat what your land and labor produce, and you will have nothing but cruel oppression all your days. ³⁴The sights you see will drive you mad. ³⁵The Lord will afflict your knees and legs with painful boils that cannot be cured, spreading from the soles of your feet to the top of your head.

³⁶The Lord will drive you and the king you set over you to a nation unknown to you or your ancestors. There you will worship other gods, gods of wood and stone. ³⁷You will become a thing of horror, a byword and an object of ridicule among all the peoples where the Lord will drive you.

³⁸You will sow much seed in the field but you will harvest little, because locusts will devour it. ³⁹You will plant vineyards and cultivate them but you will not drink the wine or gather the grapes, because worms will eat them. ⁴⁰You will have olive trees throughout your country but you will not use the oil, because the olives will drop off. ⁴¹You will have sons and daughters but you will not keep them, because they will go into captivity. ⁴²Swarms of lo-

custs will take over all your trees and the crops of your land.

⁴³The foreigners who reside among you will rise above you higher and higher, but you will sink lower and lower. ⁴⁴They will lend to you, but you will not lend to them. They will be the head, but you will be the tail.

⁴⁵All these curses will come on you. They will pursue you and overtake you until you are destroyed, because you did not obey the Lord your God and observe the commands and decrees he gave you. ⁴⁶They will be a sign and a wonder to you and your descendants forever. ⁴⁷Because you did not serve the Lord your God joyfully and gladly in the time of prosperity, ⁴⁸therefore in hunger and thirst, in nakedness and dire poverty, you will serve the enemies the Lord sends against you. He will put an iron yoke on your neck until he has destroyed you.

⁴⁹The Lord will bring a nation against you from far away, from the ends of the earth, like an eagle swooping down, a nation whose language you will not understand, ⁵⁰a fierce-looking nation without respect for the old or pity for the young. ⁵¹They will devour the young of your livestock and the crops of your land until you are destroyed. They will leave you no grain, new wine or olive oil, nor any calves of your herds or lambs of your flocks until you are ruined. ⁵²They will lay siege to all the cities throughout your land until the high fortified walls in which you trust fall down. They will besiege all the cities throughout the land the Lord your God is giving you.

⁵³Because of the suffering that your enemy will inflict on you during the siege, you will eat the fruit of the womb, the flesh of the sons and daughters the Lord your God has given you. ⁵⁴Even the most gentle and sensitive man among you will have no compassion on his own brother or the wife he loves or his surviving children,

The Lord will establish you as his holy people.
Deuteronomy 28:9

I'm starting 9th grade in the fall and still my parents have rules for everything. Between God's laws and their rules, when can I do what I want to do? Why should I try to obey when I just want to live my own life?

>> Ethan

Dear Jordan

Dear Ethan,

It is understandable that as we grow up we want more independence. So it's easy to get impatient when it comes to wanting to make our own decisions. But since you rely on your parents to meet your needs, you still need to follow their rules. But you're in good company. If you look at Luke 2:51 you'll discover that even Jesus had to obey his parents. He wanted to be in the temple with God, but he knew for that time he still had to follow the wishes of his parents.

In the Bible we find obedience linked with blessing many times, so it's not surprising that we also find disobedience linked with painful consequences. Just look at Deuteronomy 28:1,15. When we do what is right, we are in a place where God chooses to bless people. When we do what is wrong, do you think God will bless you any more than your parents would?

In addition to blessings for our obedience, we will also be protected from many things that can harm us. I suspect many of your parents' rules are there just for that purpose, to protect you and not to make you miserable. So for a little while longer try to obey your parents. It may not always seem fun, but neither is being disobedient and suffering the consequences.

Jordan

⁵⁵and he will not give to one of them any of the flesh of his children that he is eating. It will be all he has left because of the suffering your enemy will inflict on you during the siege of all your cities. ⁵⁶The most gentle and sensitive woman among you— so sensitive and gentle that she would not venture to touch the ground with the sole of her foot—will begrudge the husband she loves and her own son or daughter ⁵⁷the afterbirth from her womb and the children she bears. For in her dire need she intends to eat them secretly because of the suffering your enemy will inflict on you during the siege of your cities.

⁵⁸If you do not carefully follow all the words of this law, which are written in this book, and do not revere this glorious and awesome name—the Lᴏʀᴅ your God— ⁵⁹the Lᴏʀᴅ will send fearful plagues on you and your descendants, harsh and prolonged disasters, and severe and lingering illnesses. ⁶⁰He will bring on you all the diseases of Egypt that you dreaded, and they will cling to you. ⁶¹The Lᴏʀᴅ will also bring on you every kind of sickness and disaster not recorded in this Book of the Law, until you are destroyed. ⁶²You who were as numerous as the stars in the sky will be left but few in number, because you did not obey the Lᴏʀᴅ your God. ⁶³Just as it pleased the Lᴏʀᴅ to make you prosper and increase in number, so it will please him to ruin and destroy you. You will be uprooted from the land you are entering to possess.

⁶⁴Then the Lᴏʀᴅ will scatter you among all nations, from one end of the earth to the other. There you will worship other gods—gods of wood and stone, which neither you nor your ancestors have known. ⁶⁵Among those nations you will find no repose, no resting place for the sole of your foot. There the Lᴏʀᴅ will give you an anxious mind, eyes weary with longing, and a despairing heart. ⁶⁶You will live in constant suspense, filled with dread both night and day, never sure of your life. ⁶⁷In the morning you will say, "If only it were evening!" and in the evening, "If only it were morning!"—because

of the terror that will fill your hearts and the sights that your eyes will see. ⁶⁸The Lᴏʀᴅ will send you back in ships to Egypt on a journey I said you should never make again. There you will offer yourselves for sale to your enemies as male and female slaves, but no one will buy you.

Renewal of the Covenant

29 ᵃ These are the terms of the covenant the Lᴏʀᴅ commanded Moses to make with the Israelites in Moab, in addition to the covenant he had made with them at Horeb.

²Moses summoned all the Israelites and said to them:

Your eyes have seen all that the Lᴏʀᴅ did in Egypt to Pharaoh, to all his officials and to all his land. ³With your own eyes you saw those great trials, those signs and great wonders. ⁴But to this day the Lᴏʀᴅ has not given you a mind that understands or eyes that see or ears that hear. ⁵Yet the Lᴏʀᴅ says, "During the forty years that I led you through the wilderness, your clothes did not wear out, nor did the sandals on your feet. ⁶You ate no bread and drank no wine or other fermented drink. I did this so that you might know that I am the Lᴏʀᴅ your God."

⁷When you reached this place, Sihon king of Heshbon and Og king of Bashan came out to fight against us, but we defeated them. ⁸We took their land and gave it as an inheritance to the Reubenites, the Gadites and the half-tribe of Manasseh.

⁹Carefully follow the terms of this covenant, so that you may prosper in everything you do. ¹⁰All of you are standing today in the presence of the Lᴏʀᴅ your God—your leaders and chief men, your elders and officials, and all the other men of Israel, ¹¹together with your children and your wives, and the foreigners living in your camps who chop your wood and carry your water. ¹²You are standing here in order to enter into a covenant with the Lᴏʀᴅ your God, a covenant the Lᴏʀᴅ is making with you this day and sealing

ᵃ In Hebrew texts 29:1 is numbered 28:69, and 29:2-29 is numbered 29:1-28.

with an oath, 13to confirm you this day as his people, that he may be your God as he promised you and as he swore to your fathers, Abraham, Isaac and Jacob. 14I am making this covenant, with its oath, not only with you 15who are standing here with us today in the presence of the LORD our God but also with those who are not here today.

16You yourselves know how we lived in Egypt and how we passed through the countries on the way here. 17You saw among them their detestable images and idols of wood and stone, of silver and gold. 18Make sure there is no man or woman, clan or tribe among you today whose heart turns away from the LORD our God to go and worship the gods of those nations; make sure there is no root among you that produces such bitter poison.

19When such a person hears the words of this oath and they invoke a blessing on themselves, thinking, "I will be safe, even though I persist in going my own way," they will bring disaster on the watered land as well as the dry. 20The LORD will never be willing to forgive them; his wrath and zeal will burn against them. All the curses written in this book will fall on them, and the LORD will blot out their names from under heaven. 21The LORD will single them out from all the tribes of Israel for disaster, according to all the curses of the covenant written in this Book of the Law.

22Your children who follow you in later generations and foreigners who come from distant lands will see the calamities that have fallen on the land and the diseases with which the LORD has afflicted it. 23The whole land will be a burning waste of salt and sulfur—nothing planted, nothing sprouting, no vegetation growing on it. It will be like the destruction of Sodom and Gomorrah, Admah and Zeboyim, which the LORD overthrew in fierce anger. 24All the nations will ask: "Why has the LORD done this to this land? Why this fierce, burning anger?"

25And the answer will be: "It is because this people abandoned the covenant of the LORD, the God of their ancestors, the covenant he made with them when he

>> INSTANT ACCESS

You check out one test answer in the book and get caught. Kyle cheats regularly, and nobody catches him! Life sure isn't fair. To Kyle. That's right. Actually, the worst thing that can happen to a person is to get away with doing wrong. Kyle smirks when you get hauled up in front of class. He thinks he'll never get caught. The longer people get away with doing wrong, the more they think they'll never get caught. Eventually they do something serious and come face to face with disaster. If you're caught and punished when you step out of line, don't complain. God is being more than fair to you. It's Kyle, not you, who's in trouble!

{Deuteronomy 29:19–21}

brought them out of Egypt. 26They went off and worshiped other gods and bowed down to them, gods they did not know, gods he had not given them. 27Therefore the LORD's anger burned against this land, so that he brought on it all the curses written in this book. 28In furious anger and in great wrath the LORD uprooted them from their land and thrust them into another land, as it is now."

29The secret things belong to the LORD our God, but the things revealed belong to us and to our children forever, that we may follow all the words of this law.

Prosperity After Turning to the LORD

30 When all these blessings and curses I have set before you come on you and you take them to heart wherever the LORD your God disperses you among the nations, ²and when you and your children return to the LORD your God and obey him with all your heart and with all your soul according to everything I command you today, ³then the LORD your God will restore your fortunes[a] and have compassion on you and gather you again from all the nations where he scattered you. ⁴Even if you have been banished to the most distant land under the heavens, from there the LORD your God will gather you and bring you back. ⁵He will bring you to the land that belonged to your ancestors, and you will take possession of it. He will make you more prosperous and numerous than your ancestors. ⁶The LORD your God will circumcise your hearts and the hearts of your descendants, so that you may love him with all your heart and with all your soul, and live. ⁷The LORD your God will put all these curses on your enemies who hate and persecute you. ⁸You will again obey the LORD and follow all his commands I am giving you today. ⁹Then

the LORD your God will make you most prosperous in all the work of your hands and in the fruit of your womb, the young of your livestock and the crops of your land. The LORD will again delight in you and make you prosperous, just as he delighted in your ancestors, ¹⁰if you obey the LORD your God and keep his commands and decrees that are written in this Book of the Law and turn to the LORD your God with all your heart and with all your soul.

The Offer of Life or Death

¹¹Now what I am commanding you today is not too difficult for you or beyond your reach. ¹²It is not up in heaven, so that you have to ask, "Who will ascend into heaven to get it and proclaim it to us so we may obey it?" ¹³Nor is it beyond the sea, so that you have to ask, "Who will cross the sea to get it and proclaim it to us so we may obey it?" ¹⁴No, the word is very near you; it is in your mouth and in your heart so you may obey it.

¹⁵See, I set before you today life and prosperity, death and destruction. ¹⁶For I command you today to love the LORD your God, to walk in obedience to him, and to keep his commands, decrees and laws; then you will live and increase, and the LORD your God will bless you in the land you are entering to possess.

---

a 3 Or will bring you back from captivity

¹⁷But if your heart turns away and you are not obedient, and if you are drawn away to bow down to other gods and worship them, ¹⁸I declare to you this day that you will certainly be destroyed. You will not live long in the land you are crossing the Jordan to enter and possess.

¹⁹This day I call the heavens and the earth as witnesses against you that I have set before you life and death, blessings and curses. Now choose life, so that you and your children may live ²⁰and that you may love the LORD your God, listen to his voice, and hold fast to him. For the LORD is your life, and he will give you many years in the land he swore to give to your fathers, Abraham, Isaac and Jacob.

Joshua to Succeed Moses

31 Then Moses went out and spoke these words to all Israel: ²"I am now a hundred and twenty years old and I am no longer able to lead you. The LORD has said to me, 'You shall not cross the Jordan.' ³The LORD your God himself will cross over ahead of you. He will destroy these nations before you, and you will take possession of their land. Joshua also will cross over ahead of you, as the LORD said. ⁴And the LORD will do to them what he did to Sihon and Og, the kings of the Amorites, whom he destroyed along with their land. ⁵The LORD will deliver them to you, and you must do to them all that I have commanded you. ⁶Be strong and courageous. Do not be afraid or terrified because of them, for the LORD your God goes with you; he will never leave you nor forsake you."

⁷Then Moses summoned Joshua and said to him in the presence of all Israel, "Be strong and courageous, for you must go with this people into the land that the LORD swore to their ancestors to give them, and you must divide it among them as their inheritance. ⁸The LORD himself goes before you and will be with you; he will never leave you nor forsake you. Do not be afraid; do not be discouraged."

Public Reading of the Law

⁹So Moses wrote down this law and gave it to the Levitical priests, who carried the ark of the covenant of the LORD, and to all the elders of Israel. ¹⁰Then Moses commanded them: "At the end of every seven years, in the year for canceling debts, during the Festival of Tabernacles, ¹¹when all Israel comes to appear before the LORD your God at the place he will choose, you shall read this law before them in their hearing. ¹²Assemble the people—men, women and children, and the foreigners residing in your towns—so they can listen and learn to fear the LORD your God and follow carefully all the words of this law. ¹³Their children, who do not know this law, must hear it and learn to fear the LORD your God as long as you live in the land you are crossing the Jordan to possess."

Israel's Rebellion Predicted

¹⁴The LORD said to Moses, "Now the day of your death is near. Call Joshua and present yourselves at the tent of meeting, where I will commission him." So Moses and Joshua came and presented themselves at the tent of meeting.

¹⁵Then the LORD appeared at the tent in a pillar of cloud, and the cloud stood over the entrance to the tent. ¹⁶And the LORD said to Moses: "You are going to rest with your ancestors, and these people will soon prostitute themselves to the foreign gods of the land they are entering. They will forsake me and break the covenant I made with them. ¹⁷And in that day I will become angry with them and forsake them; I will hide my face from them, and they will be destroyed. Many disasters and calamities will come on them, and in that day they will ask, 'Have not these disasters come on us because our God is not with us?' ¹⁸And I will certainly hide my face in that day because of all their wickedness in turning to other gods.

¹⁹"Now write down this song and teach it to the Israelites and have them sing it, so that it may be a witness for me against them. ²⁰When I have brought them into the land flowing with milk and honey, the land I promised on oath to their ancestors, and when they eat their fill and

thrive, they will turn to other gods and worship them, rejecting me and breaking my covenant. ²¹And when many disasters and calamities come on them, this song will testify against them, because it will not be forgotten by their descendants. I know what they are disposed to do, even before I bring them into the land I promised them on oath." ²²So Moses wrote down this song that day and taught it to the Israelites.

²³The LORD gave this command to Joshua son of Nun: "Be strong and courageous, for you will bring the Israelites into the land I promised them on oath, and I myself will be with you."

²⁴After Moses finished writing in a book the words of this law from beginning to end, ²⁵he gave this command to the Levites who carried the ark of the covenant of the LORD: ²⁶"Take this Book of the Law and place it beside the ark of the covenant of the LORD your God. There it will remain as a witness against you. ²⁷For I know how rebellious and stiff-necked you are. If you have been rebellious against the LORD while I am still alive and with you, how much more will you rebel after I die! ²⁸Assemble before me all the elders of your tribes and all your officials, so that I can speak these words in their hearing and call the heavens and the earth to testify against them. ²⁹For I know that after my death you are sure to become utterly corrupt and to turn from the way I have commanded you. In days to come, disaster will fall on you because you will do evil in the sight of the LORD and arouse his anger by what your hands have made."

TO THE POINT

Fear God

The Bible doesn't say, "Be scared of God." To "fear the LORD" (Deuteronomy 31:12) means something very different. And very important.

"Fear sharks" means that you don't go splashing around in the ocean when sharks are near. "Fear fire" means that you remember what fire can do and don't toss lighted matches around your bedroom. In each of these cases "fear" means "to have respect for"—to give sharks or fire serious consideration.

That's what the Bible means when it says to fear God. You give God serious consideration in your life. You have a growing respect for him. Some people don't fear God at all. They ignore him, as if he didn't exist. But you're wiser than that. You're not scared of God, because you know he loves you. But you do fear him, because you know he deserves all your respect.

The Song of Moses

30 And Moses recited the words of this song from beginning to end in the hearing of the whole assembly of Israel:

32 Listen, you heavens, and I will speak;
  hear, you earth, the words of my mouth.
2 Let my teaching fall like rain
  and my words descend like dew,
  like showers on new grass,
  like abundant rain on tender plants.

3 I will proclaim the name of the LORD.
  Oh, praise the greatness of our God!
4 He is the Rock, his works are perfect,
  and all his ways are just.
  A faithful God who does no wrong,
  upright and just is he.

5 They are corrupt and not his children;
  to their shame they are a warped
    and crooked generation.
6 Is this the way you repay the LORD,
  you foolish and unwise people?
  Is he not your Father, your Creator,[a]
  who made you and formed you?

7 Remember the days of old;
  consider the generations long past.
  Ask your father and he will tell you,
  your elders, and they will explain to you.
8 When the Most High gave the nations
    their inheritance,
  when he divided all mankind,
  he set up boundaries for the peoples
    according to the number of the
    sons of Israel.[b]
9 For the LORD's portion is his people,
  Jacob his allotted inheritance.

10 In a desert land he found him,
  in a barren and howling waste.
  He shielded him and cared for him;
  he guarded him as the apple of his eye,
11 like an eagle that stirs up its nest
  and hovers over its young,
  that spreads its wings to catch them
  and carries them aloft.

12 The LORD alone led him;
  no foreign god was with him.

13 He made him ride on the heights of
    the land
  and fed him with the fruit of the
    fields.
  He nourished him with honey from the
    rock,
  and with oil from the flinty crag,
14 with curds and milk from herd and
    flock
  and with fattened lambs and goats,
  with choice rams of Bashan
  and the finest kernels of wheat.
  You drank the foaming blood of the
    grape.

15 Jeshurun[c] grew fat and kicked;
  filled with food, they became heavy
    and sleek.
  They abandoned the God who made
    them
  and rejected the Rock their Savior.
16 They made him jealous with their
    foreign gods
  and angered him with their
    detestable idols.
17 They sacrificed to false gods, which
    are not God—
  gods they had not known,
  gods that recently appeared,
  gods your ancestors did not fear.
18 You deserted the Rock, who fathered
    you;
  you forgot the God who gave you
    birth.

19 The LORD saw this and rejected them
  because he was angered by his
    sons and daughters.
20 "I will hide my face from them," he
    said,
  "and see what their end will be;
  for they are a perverse generation,
  children who are unfaithful.
21 They made me jealous by what is no
    god
  and angered me with their
    worthless idols.
  I will make them envious by those who
    are not a people;

---

a 6 Or *Father, who bought you*   b 8 Masoretic Text; Dead Sea Scrolls (see also Septuagint) *sons of God*   c 15 *Jeshurun* means *the upright one,* that is, Israel.

I will make them angry by a nation
    that has no understanding.
22 For a fire will be kindled by my wrath,
    one that burns down to the realm of
    the dead below.
It will devour the earth and its
    harvests
    and set afire the foundations of the
    mountains.
23 "I will heap calamities on them
    and spend my arrows against them.
24 I will send wasting famine against
    them,
    consuming pestilence and deadly
    plague;
I will send against them the fangs of
    wild beasts,
    the venom of vipers that glide in the
    dust.
25 In the street the sword will make them
    childless;
    in their homes terror will reign.
The young men and young women will
    perish,
    the infants and those with gray hair.
26 I said I would scatter them
    and erase their name from human
    memory,
27 but I dreaded the taunt of the enemy,
    lest the adversary misunderstand
and say, 'Our hand has triumphed;
    the LORD has not done all this.' "

28 They are a nation without sense,
    there is no discernment in them.
29 If only they were wise and would
    understand this
    and discern what their end will be!
30 How could one man chase a
    thousand,
    or two put ten thousand to flight,
unless their Rock had sold them,
    unless the LORD had given them up?
31 For their rock is not like our Rock,
    as even our enemies concede.
32 Their vine comes from the vine of
    Sodom
and from the fields of Gomorrah.
Their grapes are filled with poison,
    and their clusters with bitterness.

33 Their wine is the venom of serpents,
    the deadly poison of cobras.

34 "Have I not kept this in reserve
    and sealed it in my vaults?
35 It is mine to avenge; I will repay.
    In due time their foot will slip;
their day of disaster is near
    and their doom rushes upon them."

36 The LORD will vindicate his people
    and relent concerning his servants
when he sees their strength is gone
    and no one is left, slave or free.[a]
37 He will say: "Now where are their
    gods,
    the rock they took refuge in,
38 the gods who ate the fat of their
    sacrifices
    and drank the wine of their drink
    offerings?
Let them rise up to help you!
    Let them give you shelter!

39 "See now that I myself am he!
    There is no god besides me.
I put to death and I bring to life,
    I have wounded and I will heal,
    and no one can deliver out of my
    hand.
40 I lift my hand to heaven and solemnly
    swear:
    As surely as I live forever,
41 when I sharpen my flashing sword
    and my hand grasps it in judgment,
I will take vengeance on my
    adversaries
    and repay those who hate me.
42 I will make my arrows drunk with
    blood,
    while my sword devours flesh:
the blood of the slain and the
    captives,
    the heads of the enemy leaders."

43 Rejoice, you nations, with his
    people,[b,c]
    for he will avenge the blood of his
    servants;
he will take vengeance on his enemies
    and make atonement for his land
    and people.

---

[a] 36 Or and they are without a ruler or leader   [b] 43 Or Make his people rejoice, you nations   [c] 43 Masoretic Text; Dead Sea Scrolls (see also Septuagint) people, / and let all the angels worship him, /

44 Moses came with Joshua[a] son of Nun and spoke all the words of this song in the hearing of the people. 45 When Moses finished reciting all these words to all Israel, 46 he said to them, "Take to heart all the words I have solemnly declared to you this day, so that you may command your children to obey carefully all the words of this law. 47 They are not just idle words for you—they are your life. By them you will live long in the land you are crossing the Jordan to possess."

Moses to Die on Mount Nebo

48 On that same day the LORD told Moses, 49 "Go up into the Abarim Range to Mount Nebo in Moab, across from Jericho, and view Canaan, the land I am giving the Israelites as their own possession. 50 There on the mountain that you have climbed you will die and be gathered to your people, just as your brother Aaron died on Mount Hor and was gathered to his people. 51 This is because both of you broke faith with me in the presence of the Israelites at the waters of Meribah Kadesh in the Desert of Zin and because you did not uphold my holiness among the Israelites. 52 Therefore, you will see the land only from a distance; you will not enter the land I am giving to the people of Israel."

Moses Blesses the Tribes

33 This is the blessing that Moses the man of God pronounced on the Israelites before his death. 2 He said:

"The LORD came from Sinai
    and dawned over them from Seir;
    he shone forth from Mount Paran.
He came with[b] myriads of holy ones
    from the south, from his mountain
        slopes.[c]
3 Surely it is you who love the people;
    all the holy ones are in your hand.
At your feet they all bow down,
    and from you receive instruction,
4 the law that Moses gave us,
    the possession of the assembly of
        Jacob.

5 He was king over Jeshurun[d]
    when the leaders of the people
        assembled,
    along with the tribes of Israel.

6 "Let Reuben live and not die,
    nor[e] his people be few."

7 And this he said about Judah:

"Hear, LORD, the cry of Judah;
    bring him to his people.
With his own hands he defends his
        cause.
    Oh, be his help against his foes!"

8 About Levi he said:

"Your Thummim and Urim belong
    to your faithful servant.
You tested him at Massah;
    you contended with him at the
        waters of Meribah.
9 He said of his father and mother,
    'I have no regard for them.'
He did not recognize his brothers
    or acknowledge his own children,
but he watched over your word
    and guarded your covenant.
10 He teaches your precepts to Jacob
    and your law to Israel.
He offers incense before you
    and whole burnt offerings on your
        altar.
11 Bless all his skills, LORD,
    and be pleased with the work of his
        hands.
Strike down those who rise against
        him,
    his foes till they rise no more."

12 About Benjamin he said:

"Let the beloved of the LORD rest
        secure in him,
    for he shields him all day long,
    and the one the LORD loves rests
        between his shoulders."

13 About Joseph he said:

"May the LORD bless his land
    with the precious dew from heaven
        above

---

and with the deep waters that lie
below;
14 with the best the sun brings forth
and the finest the moon can
yield;
15 with the choicest gifts of the ancient
mountains
and the fruitfulness of the
everlasting hills;
16 with the best gifts of the earth and its
fullness
and the favor of him who dwelt in
the burning bush.
Let all these rest on the head of
Joseph,
on the brow of the prince among*a*
his brothers.
17 In majesty he is like a firstborn bull;
his horns are the horns of a wild ox.
With them he will gore the nations,
even those at the ends of the
earth.
Such are the ten thousands of
Ephraim;
such are the thousands of
Manasseh."

18 About Zebulun he said:

"Rejoice, Zebulun, in your going out,
and you, Issachar, in your tents.
19 They will summon peoples to the
mountain
and there offer the sacrifices of the
righteous;
they will feast on the abundance of
the seas,
on the treasures hidden in the
sand."

20 About Gad he said:

"Blessed is he who enlarges Gad's
domain!
Gad lives there like a lion,
tearing at arm or head.
21 He chose the best land for himself;
the leader's portion was kept for
him.
When the heads of the people
assembled,
he carried out the LORD's righteous
will,

and his judgments concerning
Israel."

22 About Dan he said:

"Dan is a lion's cub,
springing out of Bashan."

23 About Naphtali he said:

"Naphtali is abounding with the favor
of the LORD
and is full of his blessing;
he will inherit southward to the
lake."

24 About Asher he said:

"Most blessed of sons is Asher;
let him be favored by his brothers,
and let him bathe his feet in oil.
25 The bolts of your gates will be iron
and bronze,
and your strength will equal your
days.

26 "There is no one like the God of
Jeshurun,
who rides across the heavens to
help you
and on the clouds in his
majesty.

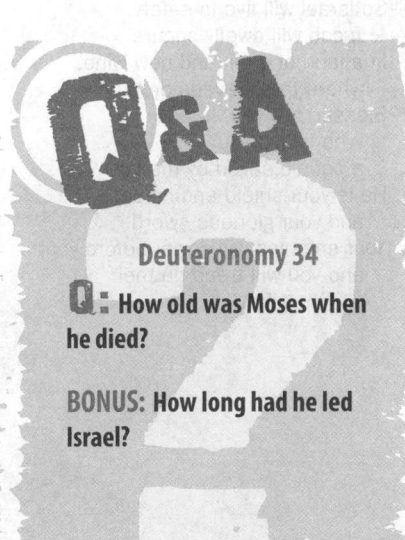

Deuteronomy 34

Q: How old was Moses when
he died?

BONUS: How long had he led
Israel?

Answers on next page

---

a 16 Or *of the one separated from*

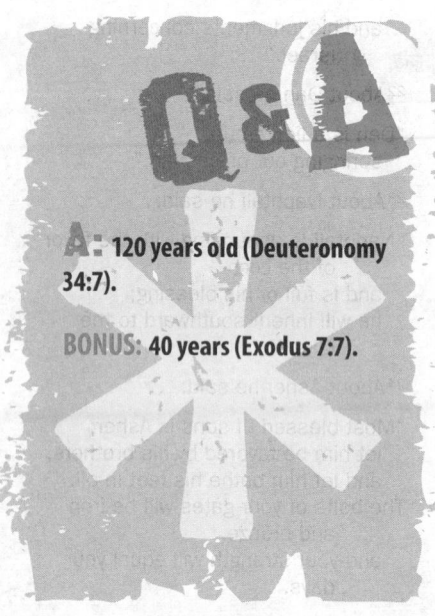

A: 120 years old (Deuteronomy 34:7).

BONUS: 40 years (Exodus 7:7).

27 The eternal God is your refuge,
    and underneath are the everlasting
      arms.
He will drive out your enemies before
      you,
    saying, 'Destroy them!'
28 So Israel will live in safety;
    Jacob will dwell[a] secure
in a land of grain and new wine,
    where the heavens drop dew.
29 Blessed are you, Israel!
    Who is like you,
    a people saved by the LORD?
He is your shield and helper
    and your glorious sword.
Your enemies will cower before you,
    and you will tread on their
      heights."

The Death of Moses

34 Then Moses climbed Mount Nebo from the plains of Moab to the top of Pisgah, across from Jericho. There the LORD showed him the whole land—from Gilead to Dan, 2 all of Naphtali, the territory of Ephraim and Manasseh, all the land of Judah as far as the Mediterranean Sea, 3 the Negev and the whole region from the Valley of Jericho, the City of Palms, as far as Zoar. 4 Then the LORD said to him, "This is the land I promised on oath to Abraham, Isaac and Jacob when I said, 'I will give it to your descendants.' I have let you see it with your eyes, but you will not cross over into it."

5 And Moses the servant of the LORD died there in Moab, as the LORD had said. 6 He buried him[b] in Moab, in the valley opposite Beth Peor, but to this day no one knows where his grave is. 7 Moses was a hundred and twenty years old when he died, yet his eyes were not weak nor his strength gone. 8 The Israelites grieved for Moses in the plains of Moab thirty days, until the time of weeping and mourning was over.

9 Now Joshua son of Nun was filled with the spirit[c] of wisdom because Moses had laid his hands on him. So the Israelites listened to him and did what the LORD had commanded Moses.

10 Since then, no prophet has risen in Israel like Moses, whom the LORD knew face to face, 11 who did all those signs and wonders the LORD sent him to do in Egypt—to Pharaoh and to all his officials and to his whole land. 12 For no one has ever shown the mighty power or performed the awesome deeds that Moses did in the sight of all Israel.

---

a 28 Septuagint; Hebrew *Jacob's spring is*   b 6 Or *He was buried*   c 9 Or *Spirit*

JOSHUA

The Winner!

What does it take to win? In sports it takes dedication, practice, and hard work. Spiritual victories take dedication too. And something else: obedience. You can enjoy spiritual victories if you keep looking to God for guidance and then live by his Word.

Joshua is a book about victory and defeat. Moses, who led the Israelites out of slavery, has died. Now under a new leader, God's people must invade a heavily populated land. At Jericho and Ai, Israel learns the importance of obedience. It takes 10 years, but finally Canaan is subdued and the promised land is divided among Israel's 12 tribes.

>> **ONE SIZE ADVICE FITS ALL**
Success principles summarized, Joshua 1:9

>> **SHOUTS STUN JERICHO CITIZENS**
Report from the front lines, see Joshua 6:12–21

>> **SINNER WELCOMED BY GOD'S PEOPLE**
Woman's past forgiven, report in Joshua 6:22–25

>> **CAPITAL PUNISHMENT DEBATE RESOLVED**
Legal principles defined, see Joshua 20

>> **JOSHUA SAYS, CHOOSE**
Retiring leader's challenge quoted in Joshua 24:15

preview

Joshua's name means "The LORD saves."

Only one man who was a slave in Egypt lives to enter Canaan: Caleb (Joshua 14:6–15)

Joshua casts lots to divide the land to let God choose which tribe settles where.

As the Israelites are at war in Canaan, the capital city of Crete is destroyed by fire. Several board games are carved on the flat roof of a temple in Kuma, Egypt.

Joshua Installed as Leader

1 After the death of Moses the servant of the LORD, the LORD said to Joshua son of Nun, Moses' aide: ² "Moses my servant is dead. Now then, you and all these people, get ready to cross the Jordan River into the land I am about to give to them—to the Israelites. ³ I will give you every place where you set your foot, as I promised Moses. ⁴ Your territory will extend from the desert to Lebanon, and from the great river, the Euphrates—all the Hittite country—to the Mediterranean Sea in the west. ⁵ No one will be able to stand against you all the days of your life. As I was with Moses, so I will be with you; I will never leave you nor forsake you. ⁶ Be strong and courageous, because you will lead these people to inherit the land I swore to their ancestors to give them.

⁷ "Be strong and very courageous. Be careful to obey all the law my servant Moses gave you; do not turn from it to the right or to the left, that you may be successful wherever you go. ⁸ Keep this Book of the Law always on your lips; meditate on it day and night, so that you may be careful to do everything written in it. Then you will be prosperous and successful. ⁹ Have I not commanded you? Be strong and courageous. Do not be afraid; do not be discouraged, for the LORD your God will be with you wherever you go."

¹⁰ So Joshua ordered the officers of the people: ¹¹ "Go through the camp and tell the people, 'Get your provisions ready. Three days from now you will cross the Jordan here to go in and take possession of the land the LORD your God is giving you for your own.' "

¹² But to the Reubenites, the Gadites and the half-tribe of Manasseh, Joshua said, ¹³ "Remember the command that Moses the servant of the LORD gave you after he said, 'The LORD your God will give you rest by giving you this land.' ¹⁴ Your wives, your children and your livestock may stay in the land that Moses gave you east of the Jordan, but all your fighting men, ready for battle, must cross over ahead of your fellow Israelites. You are to help them ¹⁵ until the LORD gives them rest, as he has done for you, and until they too have taken possession of the land the LORD your God is giving them. After that, you may go back and occupy your own land, which Moses the servant of the LORD gave you east of the Jordan toward the sunrise."

¹⁶ Then they answered Joshua, "Whatever you have commanded us we will do, and wherever you send us we will go. ¹⁷ Just as we fully obeyed Moses, so we will obey you. Only may the LORD your God be with you as he was with Moses. ¹⁸ Whoever rebels against your word and does not obey it, whatever you may command them, will be put to death. Only be strong and courageous!"

Rahab and the Spies

2 Then Joshua son of Nun secretly sent two spies from Shittim. "Go, look over the land," he said, "especially Jericho." So they went and entered the house of a prostitute named Rahab and stayed there.

² The king of Jericho was told, "Look, some of the Israelites have come here tonight to spy out the land." ³ So the king of Jericho sent this message to Rahab: "Bring out the men who came to you and entered your house, because they have come to spy out the whole land."

⁴ But the woman had taken the two men and hidden them. She said, "Yes, the men came to me, but I did not know where they had come from. ⁵ At dusk, when it was time to close the city gate, they left. I don't know which way they went. Go after them quickly. You may catch up with them." ⁶ (But she had taken them up to the roof and hidden them under the stalks of flax she had laid out on the roof.) ⁷ So the men set out in pursuit of the spies on the road

> *Be strong and very courageous ... that you may be successful.*
> Joshua 1:7

that leads to the fords of the Jordan, and as soon as the pursuers had gone out, the gate was shut.

⁸Before the spies lay down for the night, she went up on the roof ⁹and said to them, "I know that the LORD has given you this land and that a great fear of you has fallen on us, so that all who live in this country are melting in fear because of you. ¹⁰We have heard how the LORD dried up the water of the Red Sea[a] for you when you came out of Egypt, and what you did to Sihon and Og, the two kings of the Amorites east of the Jordan, whom you completely destroyed.[b] ¹¹When we heard of it, our hearts melted in fear and everyone's courage failed because of you, for the LORD your God is God in heaven above and on the earth below.

¹²"Now then, please swear to me by the LORD that you will show kindness to my family, because I have shown kindness to you. Give me a sure sign ¹³that you will spare the lives of my father and mother, my brothers and sisters, and all who belong to them—and that you will save us from death."

¹⁴"Our lives for your lives!" the men assured her. "If you don't tell what we are doing, we will treat you kindly and faithfully when the LORD gives us the land."

¹⁵So she let them down by a rope through the window, for the house she lived in was part of the city wall. ¹⁶She said to them, "Go to the hills so the pursuers will not find you. Hide yourselves there three days until they return, and then go on your way."

¹⁷Now the men had said to her, "This oath you made us swear will not be binding on us ¹⁸unless, when we enter the land, you have tied this scarlet cord in the window through which you let us down, and unless you have brought your father and mother, your brothers and all your family into your house. ¹⁹If any of them go outside your house into the street, their blood will be on their own heads; we will not be responsible. As for those who are in the house with you, their blood will be on our head if a hand is laid on them. ²⁰But if you tell what we are doing, we will be released from the oath you made us swear."

²¹"Agreed," she replied. "Let it be as you say."

So she sent them away, and they departed. And she tied the scarlet cord in the window.

²²When they left, they went into the hills and stayed there three days, until the pursuers had searched all along the road and returned without finding them. ²³Then the two men started back. They went down out of the hills, forded the river and came to Joshua son of Nun and told him everything that had happened to them. ²⁴They said to Joshua, "The LORD has surely given the whole land into our hands; all the people are melting in fear because of us."

Crossing the Jordan

3 Early in the morning Joshua and all the Israelites set out from Shittim and went to the Jordan, where they camped before crossing over. ²After three days the officers went throughout the camp, ³giving orders to the people: "When you see the ark of the covenant

Q&A

Joshua 2

Q: Where did Rahab hide the Israelite spies?

BONUS: Why did she hide them?

Answers on next page

---

[a] *10 Or the Sea of Reeds*   [b] *10 The Hebrew term refers to the irrevocable giving over of things or persons to the LORD, often by totally destroying them.*

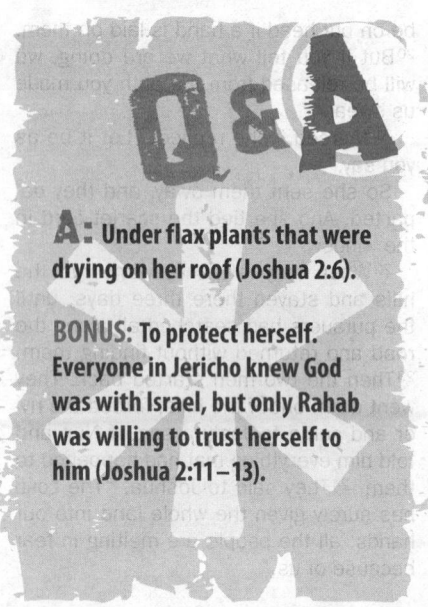

A: Under flax plants that were drying on her roof (Joshua 2:6).

BONUS: To protect herself. Everyone in Jericho knew God was with Israel, but only Rahab was willing to trust herself to him (Joshua 2:11–13).

gashites, Amorites and Jebusites. [11]See, the ark of the covenant of the Lord of all the earth will go into the Jordan ahead of you. [12]Now then, choose twelve men from the tribes of Israel, one from each tribe. [13]And as soon as the priests who carry the ark of the LORD—the Lord of all the earth—set foot in the Jordan, its waters flowing downstream will be cut off and stand up in a heap."

[14]So when the people broke camp to cross the Jordan, the priests carrying the ark of the covenant went ahead of them. [15]Now the Jordan is at flood stage all during harvest. Yet as soon as the priests who carried the ark reached the Jordan and their feet touched the water's edge, [16]the water from upstream stopped flowing. It piled up in a heap a great distance away, at a town called Adam in the vicinity of Zarethan, while the water flowing down to the Sea of the Arabah (that is, the Dead Sea) was completely cut off. So the people crossed over opposite Jericho. [17]The priests who carried the ark of the covenant of the LORD stopped in the middle of the Jordan and stood on dry ground, while all Israel passed by until the whole nation had completed the crossing on dry ground.

4 When the whole nation had finished crossing the Jordan, the LORD said to Joshua, [2]"Choose twelve men from among the people, one from each tribe, [3]and tell them to take up twelve stones from the middle of the Jordan, from right where the priests are standing, and carry them over with you and put them down at the place where you stay tonight."

[4]So Joshua called together the twelve men he had appointed from the Israelites, one from each tribe, [5]and said to them, "Go over before the ark of the LORD your God into the middle of the Jordan. Each of you is to take up a stone on his shoulder, according to the number of the tribes of the Israelites, [6]to serve as a sign among you. In the future, when your children ask you, 'What do these stones mean?' [7]tell them that the flow of the Jordan was cut off before the ark of the

of the LORD your God, and the Levitical priests carrying it, you are to move out from your positions and follow it. [4]Then you will know which way to go, since you have never been this way before. But keep a distance of about two thousand cubits[a] between you and the ark; do not go near it."

[5]Joshua told the people, "Consecrate yourselves, for tomorrow the LORD will do amazing things among you."

[6]Joshua said to the priests, "Take up the ark of the covenant and pass on ahead of the people." So they took it up and went ahead of them.

[7]And the LORD said to Joshua, "Today I will begin to exalt you in the eyes of all Israel, so they may know that I am with you as I was with Moses. [8]Tell the priests who carry the ark of the covenant: 'When you reach the edge of the Jordan's waters, go and stand in the river.'"

[9]Joshua said to the Israelites, "Come here and listen to the words of the LORD your God. [10]This is how you will know that the living God is among you and that he will certainly drive out before you the Canaanites, Hittites, Hivites, Perizzites, Girgashites,

---

[a] 4 That is, about 3,000 feet or about 900 meters

covenant of the Lord. When it crossed the Jordan, the waters of the Jordan were cut off. These stones are to be a memorial to the people of Israel forever."

⁸So the Israelites did as Joshua commanded them. They took twelve stones from the middle of the Jordan, according to the number of the tribes of the Israelites, as the Lord had told Joshua; and they carried them over with them to their camp, where they put them down. ⁹Joshua set up the twelve stones that had been*ᵃ* in the middle of the Jordan at the spot where the priests who carried the ark of the covenant had stood. And they are there to this day.

¹⁰Now the priests who carried the ark remained standing in the middle of the Jordan until everything the Lord had commanded Joshua was done by the people, just as Moses had directed Joshua. The people hurried over, ¹¹and as soon as all of them had crossed, the ark of the Lord and the priests came to the other side while the people watched. ¹²The men of Reuben, Gad and the half-tribe of Manasseh crossed over, ready for battle, in front of the Israelites, as Moses had directed them. ¹³About forty thousand armed for battle crossed over before the Lord to the plains of Jericho for war.

¹⁴That day the Lord exalted Joshua in the sight of all Israel; and they stood in awe of him all the days of his life, just as they had stood in awe of Moses.

¹⁵Then the Lord said to Joshua, ¹⁶"Command the priests carrying the ark of the covenant law to come up out of the Jordan."

¹⁷So Joshua commanded the priests, "Come up out of the Jordan."

¹⁸And the priests came up out of the river carrying the ark of the covenant of the Lord. No sooner had they set their feet on the dry ground than the waters of the Jordan returned to their place and ran at flood stage as before.

¹⁹On the tenth day of the first month the people went up from the Jordan and camped at Gilgal on the eastern border of Jericho. ²⁰And Joshua set up at Gilgal the twelve stones they had taken out of the Jordan. ²¹He said to the Israelites, "In the future when your descendants ask their parents, 'What do these stones mean?' ²²tell them, 'Israel crossed the Jordan on dry ground.' ²³For the Lord your God dried up the Jordan before you until you had crossed over. The Lord your God did to the Jordan what he had done to the Red Sea*ᵇ* when he dried it up before us until we had crossed over. ²⁴He did this so that all the peoples of the earth might know that the hand of the Lord is powerful and so that you might always fear the Lord your God."

5 Now when all the Amorite kings west of the Jordan and all the Canaanite kings along the coast heard how the Lord had dried up the Jordan before the Israelites until they*ᶜ* had crossed over, their hearts melted in fear and they no longer had the courage to face the Israelites.

Circumcision and Passover at Gilgal

²At that time the Lord said to Joshua, "Make flint knives and circumcise the Israelites again." ³So Joshua made flint knives and circumcised the Israelites at Gibeath Haaraloth.*ᵈ*

⁴Now this is why he did so: All those who came out of Egypt—all the men of military age—died in the wilderness on the way after leaving Egypt. ⁵All the people that came out had been circumcised, but all the people born in the wilderness during the journey from Egypt had not. ⁶The Israelites had moved about in the wilderness forty years until all the men who were of military age when they left Egypt had died, since they had not obeyed the Lord. For the Lord had sworn to them that they would not see the land he had solemnly promised their ancestors to give us, a land flowing with milk and honey. ⁷So he raised up their sons in their place, and these were the ones Joshua circumcised. They were still uncircumcised because they had not been circumcised on the way. ⁸And after the

---

ᵃ 9 Or *Joshua also set up twelve stones*   *ᵇ* 23 Or *the Sea of Reeds*   *ᶜ* 1 Another textual tradition *we*   *ᵈ* 3 *Gibeath Haaraloth* means *the hill of foreskins.*

whole nation had been circumcised, they remained where they were in camp until they were healed.

⁹Then the LORD said to Joshua, "Today I have rolled away the reproach of Egypt from you." So the place has been called Gilgal[a] to this day.

¹⁰On the evening of the fourteenth day of the month, while camped at Gilgal on the plains of Jericho, the Israelites celebrated the Passover. ¹¹The day after the Passover, that very day, they ate some of the produce of the land: unleavened bread and roasted grain. ¹²The manna stopped the day after[b] they ate this food from the land; there was no longer any manna for the Israelites, but that year they ate the produce of Canaan.

The Fall of Jericho

¹³Now when Joshua was near Jericho, he looked up and saw a man standing in front of him with a drawn sword in his hand. Joshua went up to him and asked, "Are you for us or for our enemies?"

¹⁴"Neither," he replied, "but as commander of the army of the LORD I have now come." Then Joshua fell facedown to the ground in reverence, and asked him, "What message does my Lord[c] have for his servant?"

¹⁵The commander of the LORD's army replied, "Take off your sandals, for the place where you are standing is holy." And Joshua did so.

6 Now the gates of Jericho were securely barred because of the Israelites. No one went out and no one came in.

²Then the LORD said to Joshua, "See, I have delivered Jericho into your hands, along with its king and its fighting men. ³March around the city once with all the armed men. Do this for six days. ⁴Have seven priests carry trumpets of rams' horns in front of the ark. On the seventh day, march around the city seven times, with the priests blowing the trumpets. ⁵When you hear them sound a long blast on the trumpets, have the whole army give a loud shout; then the wall of the city will collapse and the army will go up, everyone straight in."

⁶So Joshua son of Nun called the priests and said to them, "Take up the ark of the covenant of the LORD and have seven priests carry trumpets in front of it." ⁷And he ordered the army, "Advance! March around the city, with an armed guard going ahead of the ark of the LORD."

⁸When Joshua had spoken to the people, the seven priests carrying the seven trumpets before the LORD went forward, blowing their trumpets, and the ark of the LORD's covenant followed them. ⁹The armed guard marched ahead of the priests who blew the trumpets, and the rear guard followed the ark. All this time the trumpets were sounding. ¹⁰But Joshua had commanded the army, "Do not give a war cry, do not raise your voices, do not say a word until the day I tell you to shout. Then shout!" ¹¹So he had the ark of the LORD carried around the city, circling it once. Then the army returned to camp and spent the night there.

¹²Joshua got up early the next morning and the priests took up the ark of the LORD. ¹³The seven priests carrying the seven trumpets went forward, marching before the ark of the LORD and blowing the trumpets. The armed men went ahead of them and the rear guard followed the ark of the LORD, while the trumpets kept sounding. ¹⁴So on the second day they marched around the city once and returned to the camp. They did this for six days.

¹⁵On the seventh day, they got up at daybreak and marched around the city seven times in the same manner, except that on that day they circled the city seven times. ¹⁶The seventh time around, when the priests sounded the trumpet blast, Joshua commanded the army, "Shout! For the LORD has given you the city! ¹⁷The city and all that is in it are to be devoted[d] to the LORD. Only Rahab the prostitute and all who are with her in her house shall be spared, because she hid the spies we sent. ¹⁸But keep away from the devoted things, so that you will not

---

a 9 *Gilgal* sounds like the Hebrew for *roll.*   b 12 Or *the day*   c 14 Or *lord*   d 17 The Hebrew term refers to the irrevocable giving over of things or persons to the LORD, often by totally destroying them; also in verses 18 and 21.

bring about your own destruction by taking any of them. Otherwise you will make the camp of Israel liable to destruction and bring trouble on it. ¹⁹All the silver and gold and the articles of bronze and iron are sacred to the LORD and must go into his treasury."

²⁰When the trumpets sounded, the army shouted, and at the sound of the trumpet, when the men gave a loud shout, the wall collapsed; so everyone charged straight in, and they took the city. ²¹They devoted the city to the LORD and destroyed with the sword every living thing in it—men and women, young and old, cattle, sheep and donkeys.

²²Joshua said to the two men who had spied out the land, "Go into the prostitute's house and bring her out and all who belong to her, in accordance with your oath to her." ²³So the young men who had done the spying went in and brought out Rahab, her father and mother, her brothers and sisters and all who belonged to her. They brought out her entire family and put them in a place outside the camp of Israel.

²⁴Then they burned the whole city and everything in it, but they put the silver and gold and the articles of bronze and iron into the treasury of the LORD's house. ²⁵But Joshua spared Rahab the prostitute, with her family and all who belonged to her, because she hid the men Joshua had sent as spies to Jericho—and she lives among the Israelites to this day.

²⁶At that time Joshua pronounced this solemn oath: "Cursed before the LORD is the one who undertakes to rebuild this city, Jericho:

"At the cost of his firstborn son
  he will lay its foundations;
at the cost of his youngest
  he will set up its gates."

²⁷So the LORD was with Joshua, and his fame spread throughout the land.

Achan's Sin

7 But the Israelites were unfaithful in regard to the devoted things[a]; Achan son of Karmi, the son of Zimri,[b] the son of Zerah, of the tribe of Judah, took some of them. So the LORD's anger burned against Israel.

²Now Joshua sent men from Jericho to Ai, which is near Beth Aven to the east of Bethel, and told them, "Go up and spy out the region." So the men went up and spied out Ai.

³When they returned to Joshua, they said, "Not all the army will have to go up against Ai. Send two or three thousand men to take it and do not weary the whole army, for only a few people live there." ⁴So about three thousand went up; but they were routed by the men of Ai, ⁵who killed about thirty-six of them. They chased the Israelites from the city gate as far as the stone quarries and struck them down on the slopes. At this the hearts of the people melted in fear and became like water.

⁶Then Joshua tore his clothes and fell facedown to the ground before the ark of the LORD, remaining there till evening. The elders of Israel did the same, and

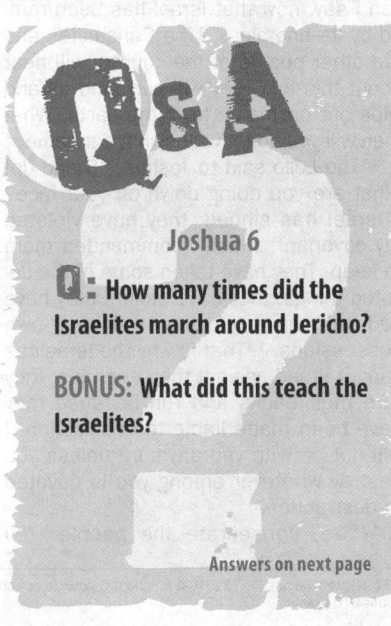

Joshua 6

Q: How many times did the Israelites march around Jericho?

BONUS: What did this teach the Israelites?

Answers on next page

ª 1 The Hebrew term refers to the irrevocable giving over of things or persons to the LORD, often by totally destroying them; also in verses 11, 12, 13 and 15.
ᵇ 1 See Septuagint and 1 Chron. 2:6; Hebrew *Zabdi*; also in verses 17 and 18.

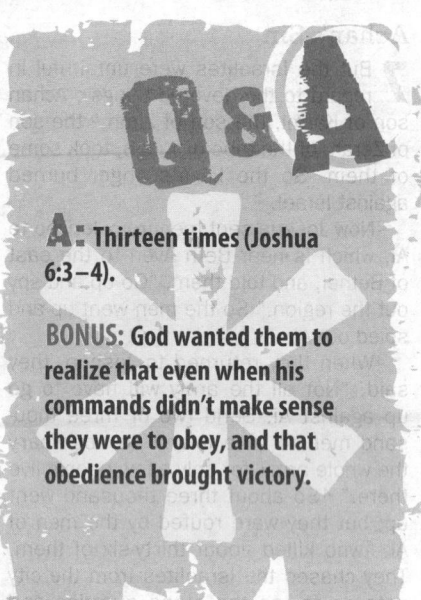

A: Thirteen times (Joshua 6:3–4).

BONUS: God wanted them to realize that even when his commands didn't make sense they were to obey, and that obedience brought victory.

sprinkled dust on their heads. ⁷And Joshua said, "Alas, Sovereign LORD, why did you ever bring this people across the Jordan to deliver us into the hands of the Amorites to destroy us? If only we had been content to stay on the other side of the Jordan! ⁸Pardon your servant, Lord. What can I say, now that Israel has been routed by its enemies? ⁹The Canaanites and the other people of the country will hear about this and they will surround us and wipe out our name from the earth. What then will you do for your own great name?"

¹⁰The LORD said to Joshua, "Stand up! What are you doing down on your face? ¹¹Israel has sinned; they have violated my covenant, which I commanded them to keep. They have taken some of the devoted things; they have stolen, they have lied, they have put them with their own possessions. ¹²That is why the Israelites cannot stand against their enemies; they turn their backs and run because they have been made liable to destruction. I will not be with you anymore unless you destroy whatever among you is devoted to destruction.

¹³"Go, consecrate the people. Tell them, 'Consecrate yourselves in preparation for tomorrow; for this is what the LORD, the God of Israel, says: There are devoted things among you, Israel. You cannot stand against your enemies until you remove them.

¹⁴"'In the morning, present yourselves tribe by tribe. The tribe the LORD chooses shall come forward clan by clan; the clan the LORD chooses shall come forward family by family; and the family the LORD chooses shall come forward man by man. ¹⁵Whoever is caught with the devoted things shall be destroyed by fire, along with all that belongs to him. He has violated the covenant of the LORD and has done an outrageous thing in Israel!' "

¹⁶Early the next morning Joshua had Israel come forward by tribes, and Judah was chosen. ¹⁷The clans of Judah came forward, and the Zerahites were chosen. He had the clan of the Zerahites come forward by families, and Zimri was chosen. ¹⁸Joshua had his family come forward man by man, and Achan son of Karmi, the son of Zimri, the son of Zerah, of the tribe of Judah, was chosen.

¹⁹Then Joshua said to Achan, "My son, give glory to the LORD, the God of Israel, and honor him. Tell me what you have done; do not hide it from me."

²⁰Achan replied, "It is true! I have sinned against the LORD, the God of Israel. This is what I have done: ²¹When I saw in the plunder a beautiful robe from Babylonia,ᵃ two hundred shekelsᵇ of silver and a bar of gold weighing fifty shekels,ᶜ I coveted them and took them. They are hidden in the ground inside my tent, with the silver underneath."

²²So Joshua sent messengers, and they ran to the tent, and there it was, hidden in his tent, with the silver underneath. ²³They took the things from the tent, brought them to Joshua and all the Israelites and spread them out before the LORD.

²⁴Then Joshua, together with all Israel, took Achan son of Zerah, the silver, the robe, the gold bar, his sons and daughters, his cattle, donkeys and sheep, his tent and all that he had, to the Valley

---

ᵃ 21 Hebrew *Shinar*   ᵇ 21 That is, about 5 pounds or about 2.3 kilograms   ᶜ 21 That is, about 1 1/4 pounds or about 575 grams

Consider a teen who's grounded for sneaking out the window at night—the third time this week. Two minutes later he goes to his dad and says, "Dad, will you take me to the mall for new basketball shoes?" He's sort of like Christians who knowingly do wrong and then can't understand why God doesn't answer their prayers. When an Israelite broke God's command, God's people suffered defeat in their next battle. God explained: "Israel has sinned . . . I will not be with you anymore" (Joshua 7:11–12). If you want God's blessing, don't make a habit of disobeying.

{Joshua 7:10–12}

≫ INSTANT ACCESS

Take the whole army with you, and go up and attack Ai. For I have delivered into your hands the king of Ai, his people, his city and his land. ²You shall do to Ai and its king as you did to Jericho and its king, except that you may carry off their plunder and livestock for yourselves. Set an ambush behind the city."

³So Joshua and the whole army moved out to attack Ai. He chose thirty thousand of his best fighting men and sent them out at night ⁴with these orders: "Listen carefully. You are to set an ambush behind the city. Don't go very far from it. All of you be on the alert. ⁵I and all those with me will advance on the city, and when the men come out against us, as they did before, we will flee from them. ⁶They will pursue us until we have lured them away from the city, for they will say, 'They are running away from us as they did before.' So when we flee from them, ⁷you are to rise up from ambush and take the city. The LORD your God will give it into your hand. ⁸When you have taken the city, set it on fire. Do what the LORD has commanded. See to it; you have my orders."

⁹Then Joshua sent them off, and they went to the place of ambush and lay in wait between Bethel and Ai, to the west of Ai—but Joshua spent that night with the people.

¹⁰Early the next morning Joshua mustered his army, and he and the leaders of Israel marched before them to Ai. ¹¹The entire force that was with him marched up and approached the city and arrived in front of it. They set up camp north of Ai, with the valley between them and the city. ¹²Joshua had taken about five thousand men and set them in ambush between Bethel and Ai, to the west of the city. ¹³So the soldiers took up their positions—with the main camp to the north of the city and the ambush to the west of it. That night Joshua went into the valley.

¹⁴When the king of Ai saw this, he and all the men of the city hurried out early in the morning to meet Israel in battle at a certain place overlooking the Arabah. But he did not know that an ambush had been

of Achor. ²⁵Joshua said, "Why have you brought this trouble on us? The LORD will bring trouble on you today."

Then all Israel stoned him, and after they had stoned the rest, they burned them. ²⁶Over Achan they heaped up a large pile of rocks, which remains to this day. Then the LORD turned from his fierce anger. Therefore that place has been called the Valley of Achor[a] ever since.

Ai Destroyed

8 Then the LORD said to Joshua, "Do not be afraid; do not be discouraged.

---

[a] 26 *Achor* means *trouble*.

set against him behind the city. ¹⁵Joshua and all Israel let themselves be driven back before them, and they fled toward the wilderness. ¹⁶All the men of Ai were called to pursue them, and they pursued Joshua and were lured away from the city. ¹⁷Not a man remained in Ai or Bethel who did not go after Israel. They left the city open and went in pursuit of Israel.

¹⁸Then the Lᴏʀᴅ said to Joshua, "Hold out toward Ai the javelin that is in your hand, for into your hand I will deliver the city." So Joshua held out toward the city the javelin that was in his hand. ¹⁹As soon as he did this, the men in the ambush rose quickly from their position and rushed forward. They entered the city and captured it and quickly set it on fire.

²⁰The men of Ai looked back and saw the smoke of the city rising up into the sky, but they had no chance to escape in any direction; the Israelites who had been fleeing toward the wilderness had turned back against their pursuers. ²¹For when Joshua and all Israel saw that the ambush had taken the city and that smoke was going up from it, they turned around and attacked the men of Ai. ²²Those in the ambush also came out of the city against them, so that they were caught in the middle, with Israelites on both sides. Israel cut them down, leaving them neither survivors nor fugitives. ²³But they took the king of Ai alive and brought him to Joshua.

²⁴When Israel had finished killing all the men of Ai in the fields and in the wilderness where they had chased them, and when every one of them had been put to the sword, all the Israelites returned to Ai and killed those who were in it. ²⁵Twelve thousand men and women fell that day—all the people of Ai. ²⁶For Joshua did not draw back the hand that held out his javelin until he had destroyedᵃ all who lived in Ai. ²⁷But Israel did carry off for themselves the livestock and plunder of this city, as the Lᴏʀᴅ had instructed Joshua.

²⁸So Joshua burned Aiᵇ and made it a permanent heap of ruins, a desolate place to this day. ²⁹He impaled the body of the king of Ai on a pole and left it there until evening. At sunset, Joshua ordered them to take the body from the pole and throw it down at the entrance of the city gate. And they raised a large pile of rocks over it, which remains to this day.

The Covenant Renewed at Mount Ebal

³⁰Then Joshua built on Mount Ebal an altar to the Lᴏʀᴅ, the God of Israel, ³¹as Moses the servant of the Lᴏʀᴅ had commanded the Israelites. He built it according to what is written in the Book of the Law of Moses—an altar of uncut stones, on which no iron tool had been used. On it they offered to the Lᴏʀᴅ burnt offerings and sacrificed fellowship offerings. ³²There, in the presence of the Israelites, Joshua wrote on stones a copy of the law of Moses. ³³All the Israelites, with their elders, officials and judges, were standing on both sides of the ark of the covenant of the Lᴏʀᴅ, facing the Levitical priests who carried it. Both the foreigners living among them and the native-born were there. Half of the people stood in front of Mount Gerizim and half of them in front of Mount Ebal, as Moses the servant of the Lᴏʀᴅ had formerly commanded when he gave instructions to bless the people of Israel.

³⁴Afterward, Joshua read all the words of the law—the blessings and the curses—just as it is written in the Book of the Law. ³⁵There was not a word of all that Moses had commanded that Joshua did not read to the whole assembly of Israel, including the women and children, and the foreigners who lived among them.

The Gibeonite Deception

9 Now when all the kings west of the Jordan heard about these things— the kings in the hill country, in the western foothills, and along the entire coast of the Mediterranean Sea as far as Lebanon (the kings of the Hittites, Amorites,

---

ᵃ *26* The Hebrew term refers to the irrevocable giving over of things or persons to the Lᴏʀᴅ, often by totally destroying them.   ᵇ *28* *Ai* means *the ruin.*

Sometimes keeping your word can be hard, and sometimes it's just not fun. For instance, you promise to help Amanda with her algebra. Then another friend invites you to the mall. What do you do when keeping your word hurts? The Gibeonites fooled the leaders of Israel into making a treaty with them by pretending to live a long way away. Then the Israelites learned that the Gibeonites were neighbors. The Israelites were upset, but they kept their word. God wants you to be people of your word too. Christians represent a God who always keeps his word. It is important to be trustworthy.

{Joshua 9:16-21}

≫ INSTANT ACCESS

Gilgal and said to him and the Israelites, "We have come from a distant country; make a treaty with us."

7 The Israelites said to the Hivites, "But perhaps you live near us, so how can we make a treaty with you?"

8 "We are your servants," they said to Joshua.

But Joshua asked, "Who are you and where do you come from?"

9 They answered: "Your servants have come from a very distant country because of the fame of the LORD your God. For we have heard reports of him: all that he did in Egypt, 10 and all that he did to the two kings of the Amorites east of the Jordan—Sihon king of Heshbon, and Og king of Bashan, who reigned in Ashtaroth. 11 And our elders and all those living in our country said to us, 'Take provisions for your journey; go and meet them and say to them, "We are your servants; make a treaty with us."' 12 This bread of ours was warm when we packed it at home on the day we left to come to you. But now see how dry and moldy it is. 13 And these wineskins that we filled were new, but see how cracked they are. And our clothes and sandals are worn out by the very long journey."

14 The Israelites sampled their provisions but did not inquire of the LORD. 15 Then Joshua made a treaty of peace with them to let them live, and the leaders of the assembly ratified it by oath.

16 Three days after they made the treaty with the Gibeonites, the Israelites heard that they were neighbors, living near them. 17 So the Israelites set out and on the third day came to their cities: Gibeon, Kephirah, Beeroth and Kiriath Jearim. 18 But the Israelites did not attack them, because the leaders of the assembly had sworn an oath to them by the LORD, the God of Israel.

The whole assembly grumbled against the leaders, 19 but all the leaders answered, "We have given them our oath by the LORD, the God of Israel, and we cannot touch them now. 20 This is what we will do to them: We will let them live,

Canaanites, Perizzites, Hivites and Jebusites)— 2 they came together to wage war against Joshua and Israel.

3 However, when the people of Gibeon heard what Joshua had done to Jericho and Ai, 4 they resorted to a ruse: They went as a delegation whose donkeys were loaded[a] with worn-out sacks and old wineskins, cracked and mended. 5 They put worn and patched sandals on their feet and wore old clothes. All the bread of their food supply was dry and moldy. 6 Then they went to Joshua in the camp at

---

[a] 4 Most Hebrew manuscripts; some Hebrew manuscripts, Vulgate and Syriac (see also Septuagint) *They prepared provisions and loaded their donkeys*

so that God's wrath will not fall on us for breaking the oath we swore to them." ²¹They continued, "Let them live, but let them be woodcutters and water carriers in the service of the whole assembly." So the leaders' promise to them was kept.

²²Then Joshua summoned the Gibeonites and said, "Why did you deceive us by saying, 'We live a long way from you,' while actually you live near us? ²³You are now under a curse: You will never be released from service as woodcutters and water carriers for the house of my God."

²⁴They answered Joshua, "Your servants were clearly told how the LORD your God had commanded his servant Moses to give you the whole land and to wipe out all its inhabitants from before you. So we feared for our lives because of you, and that is why we did this. ²⁵We are now in your hands. Do to us whatever seems good and right to you."

²⁶So Joshua saved them from the Israelites, and they did not kill them. ²⁷That day he made the Gibeonites woodcutters and water carriers for the assembly, to provide for the needs of the altar of the LORD at the place the LORD would choose. And that is what they are to this day.

The Sun Stands Still

10 Now Adoni-Zedek king of Jerusalem heard that Joshua had taken Ai and totally destroyedᵃ it, doing to Ai and its king as he had done to Jericho and its king, and that the people of Gibeon had made a treaty of peace with Israel and had become their allies. ²He and his people were very much alarmed at this, because Gibeon was an important city, like one of the royal cities; it was larger than Ai, and all its men were good fighters. ³So Adoni-Zedek king of Jerusalem appealed to Hoham king of Hebron, Piram king of Jarmuth, Japhia king of Lachish and Debir king of Eglon. ⁴"Come up and help me attack Gibeon," he said, "because it has made peace with Joshua and the Israelites."

⁵Then the five kings of the Amorites—the kings of Jerusalem, Hebron, Jarmuth, Lachish and Eglon—joined forces. They moved up with all their troops and took up positions against Gibeon and attacked it.

⁶The Gibeonites then sent word to Joshua in the camp at Gilgal: "Do not abandon your servants. Come up to us quickly and save us! Help us, because all the Amorite kings from the hill country have joined forces against us."

⁷So Joshua marched up from Gilgal with his entire army, including all the best fighting men. ⁸The LORD said to Joshua, "Do not be afraid of them; I have given them into your hand. Not one of them will be able to withstand you."

⁹After an all-night march from Gilgal, Joshua took them by surprise. ¹⁰The LORD threw them into confusion before Israel, so Joshua and the Israelites defeated them completely at Gibeon. Israel pursued them along the road going up to Beth Horon and cut them down all the way to Azekah and Makkedah. ¹¹As they fled before Israel on the road down from Beth Horon to Azekah, the LORD hurled large hailstones down on them, and more of them died from the hail than were killed by the swords of the Israelites.

¹²On the day the LORD gave the Amorites over to Israel, Joshua said to the LORD in the presence of Israel:

"Sun, stand still over Gibeon,
    and you, moon, over the Valley of Aijalon."
¹³So the sun stood still,
    and the moon stopped,
    till the nation avenged itself onᵇ its enemies,

as it is written in the Book of Jashar.

The sun stopped in the middle of the sky and delayed going down about a full day. ¹⁴There has never been a day like it before or since, a day when the LORD listened to a human being. Surely the LORD was fighting for Israel!

¹⁵Then Joshua returned with all Israel to the camp at Gilgal.

ᵃ 1 The Hebrew term refers to the irrevocable giving over of things or persons to the LORD, often by totally destroying them; also in verses 28, 35, 37, 39 and 40.   ᵇ 13 Or nation triumphed over

Five Amorite Kings Killed

16 Now the five kings had fled and hidden in the cave at Makkedah. 17 When Joshua was told that the five kings had been found hiding in the cave at Makkedah, 18 he said, "Roll large rocks up to the mouth of the cave, and post some men there to guard it. 19 But don't stop; pursue your enemies! Attack them from the rear and don't let them reach their cities, for the LORD your God has given them into your hand."

20 So Joshua and the Israelites defeated them completely, but a few survivors managed to reach their fortified cities. 21 The whole army then returned safely to Joshua in the camp at Makkedah, and no one uttered a word against the Israelites.

22 Joshua said, "Open the mouth of the cave and bring those five kings out to me." 23 So they brought the five kings out of the cave—the kings of Jerusalem, Hebron, Jarmuth, Lachish and Eglon. 24 When they had brought these kings to Joshua, he summoned all the men of Israel and said to the army commanders who had come with him, "Come here and put your feet on the necks of these kings." So they came forward and placed their feet on their necks.

25 Joshua said to them, "Do not be afraid; do not be discouraged. Be strong and courageous. This is what the LORD will do to all the enemies you are going to fight." 26 Then Joshua put the kings to death and exposed their bodies on five poles, and they were left hanging on the poles until evening.

27 At sunset Joshua gave the order and they took them down from the poles and threw them into the cave where they had been hiding. At the mouth of the cave they placed large rocks, which are there to this day.

Southern Cities Conquered

28 That day Joshua took Makkedah. He put the city and its king to the sword and totally destroyed everyone in it. He left no survivors. And he did to the king of Makkedah as he had done to the king of Jericho.

29 Then Joshua and all Israel with him moved on from Makkedah to Libnah and attacked it. 30 The LORD also gave that city and its king into Israel's hand. The city and everyone in it Joshua put to the sword. He left no survivors there. And he did to its king as he had done to the king of Jericho.

31 Then Joshua and all Israel with him moved on from Libnah to Lachish; he took up positions against it and attacked it. 32 The LORD gave Lachish into Israel's hands, and Joshua took it on the second day. The city and everyone in it he put to the sword, just as he had done to Libnah. 33 Meanwhile, Horam king of Gezer had come up to help Lachish, but Joshua defeated him and his army—until no survivors were left.

34 Then Joshua and all Israel with him moved on from Lachish to Eglon; they took up positions against it and attacked it. 35 They captured it that same day and put it to the sword and totally destroyed everyone in it, just as they had done to Lachish.

36 Then Joshua and all Israel with him went up from Eglon to Hebron and attacked it. 37 They took the city and put it to the sword, together with its king, its villages and everyone in it. They left no survivors. Just as at Eglon, they totally destroyed it and everyone in it.

38 Then Joshua and all Israel with him turned around and attacked Debir. 39 They took the city, its king and its villages, and put them to the sword. Everyone in it they totally destroyed. They left no survivors. They did to Debir and its king as they had done to Libnah and its king and to Hebron.

40 So Joshua subdued the whole region, including the hill country, the Negev, the western foothills and the mountain slopes, together with all their kings. He left no survivors. He totally destroyed all who breathed, just as the LORD, the God of Israel, had commanded. 41 Joshua subdued them from Kadesh Barnea to Gaza and from the whole region of Goshen to Gibeon. 42 All these kings and their lands Joshua conquered in one campaign, because the LORD, the God of Israel, fought for Israel.

43 Then Joshua returned with all Israel to the camp at Gilgal.

Northern Kings Defeated

11 When Jabin king of Hazor heard of this, he sent word to Jobab king of Madon, to the kings of Shimron and Akshaph, 2 and to the northern kings who were in the mountains, in the Arabah south of Kinnereth, in the western foothills and in Naphoth Dor on the west; 3 to the Canaanites in the east and west; to the Amorites, Hittites, Perizzites and Jebusites in the hill country; and to the Hivites below Hermon in the region of Mizpah. 4 They came out with all their troops and a large number of horses and chariots—a huge army, as numerous as the sand on the seashore. 5 All these kings joined forces and made camp together at the Waters of Merom to fight against Israel.

6 The LORD said to Joshua, "Do not be afraid of them, because by this time tomorrow I will hand all of them, slain, over to Israel. You are to hamstring their horses and burn their chariots."

7 So Joshua and his whole army came against them suddenly at the Waters of Merom and attacked them, 8 and the LORD gave them into the hand of Israel. They defeated them and pursued them all the way to Greater Sidon, to Misrephoth Maim, and to the Valley of Mizpah on the east, until no survivors were left. 9 Joshua did to them as the LORD had directed: He hamstrung their horses and burned their chariots.

10 At that time Joshua turned back and captured Hazor and put its king to the sword. (Hazor had been the head of all these kingdoms.) 11 Everyone in it they put to the sword. They totally destroyed[a] them, not sparing anyone that breathed, and he burned Hazor itself.

12 Joshua took all these royal cities and their kings and put them to the sword. He totally destroyed them, as Moses the servant of the LORD had commanded. 13 Yet Israel did not burn any of the cities built on their mounds—except Hazor, which Joshua burned. 14 The Israelites carried off for themselves all the plunder and livestock of these cities, but all the people they put to the sword until they completely destroyed them, not sparing anyone that breathed. 15 As the LORD commanded his servant Moses, so Moses commanded Joshua, and Joshua did it; he left nothing undone of all that the LORD commanded Moses.

16 So Joshua took this entire land: the hill country, all the Negev, the whole region of Goshen, the western foothills, the Arabah and the mountains of Israel with their foothills, 17 from Mount Halak, which rises toward Seir, to Baal Gad in the Valley of Lebanon below Mount Hermon. He captured all their kings and put them to death. 18 Joshua waged war against all these kings for a long time. 19 Except for the Hivites living in Gibeon, not one city made a treaty of peace with the Israelites, who took them all in battle. 20 For it was the LORD himself who hardened their hearts to wage war against Israel, so that he might destroy them totally, exterminating them without mercy, as the LORD had commanded Moses.

21 At that time Joshua went and destroyed the Anakites from the hill country: from Hebron, Debir and Anab, from all the hill country of Judah, and from all the hill country of Israel. Joshua totally destroyed them and their towns. 22 No Anakites were left in Israelite territory; only in Gaza, Gath and Ashdod did any survive.

23 So Joshua took the entire land, just as the LORD had directed Moses, and he gave it as an inheritance to Israel according to their tribal divisions. Then the land had rest from war.

List of Defeated Kings

12 These are the kings of the land whom the Israelites had defeated and whose territory they took over east of the Jordan, from the Arnon Gorge to Mount Hermon, including all the eastern side of the Arabah:

---

a 11 The Hebrew term refers to the irrevocable giving over of things or persons to the LORD, often by totally destroying them; also in verses 12, 20 and 21.

2 Sihon king of the Amorites, who reigned in Heshbon.

He ruled from Aroer on the rim of the Arnon Gorge—from the middle of the gorge—to the Jabbok River, which is the border of the Ammonites. This included half of Gilead. 3 He also ruled over the eastern Arabah from the Sea of Galilee[a] to the Sea of the Arabah (that is, the Dead Sea), to Beth Jeshimoth, and then southward below the slopes of Pisgah.

4 And the territory of Og king of Bashan, one of the last of the Rephaites, who reigned in Ashtaroth and Edrei.

5 He ruled over Mount Hermon, Salekah, all of Bashan to the border of the people of Geshur and Maakah, and half of Gilead to the border of Sihon king of Heshbon.

6 Moses, the servant of the LORD, and the Israelites conquered them. And Moses the servant of the LORD gave their land to the Reubenites, the Gadites and the half-tribe of Manasseh to be their possession.

7 Here is a list of the kings of the land that Joshua and the Israelites conquered on the west side of the Jordan, from Baal Gad in the Valley of Lebanon to Mount Halak, which rises toward Seir. Joshua gave their lands as an inheritance to the tribes of Israel according to their tribal divisions. 8 The lands included the hill country, the western foothills, the Arabah, the mountain slopes, the wilderness and the Negev. These were the lands of the Hittites, Amorites, Canaanites, Perizzites, Hivites and Jebusites. These were the kings:

9 the king of Jericho	one
the king of Ai (near Bethel)	one
10 the king of Jerusalem	one
the king of Hebron	one
11 the king of Jarmuth	one
the king of Lachish	one
12 the king of Eglon	one
the king of Gezer	one
13 the king of Debir	one
the king of Geder	one
14 the king of Hormah	one
the king of Arad	one
15 the king of Libnah	one
the king of Adullam	one
16 the king of Makkedah	one
the king of Bethel	one
17 the king of Tappuah	one
the king of Hepher	one
18 the king of Aphek	one
the king of Lasharon	one
19 the king of Madon	one
the king of Hazor	one
20 the king of Shimron Meron	one
the king of Akshaph	one
21 the king of Taanach	one
the king of Megiddo	one
22 the king of Kedesh	one
the king of Jokneam in Carmel	one
23 the king of Dor (in Naphoth Dor)	one
the king of Goyim in Gilgal	one
24 the king of Tirzah	one
thirty-one kings in all.	

Land Still to Be Taken

13 When Joshua had grown old, the LORD said to him, "You are now very old, and there are still very large areas of land to be taken over.

2 "This is the land that remains: all the regions of the Philistines and Geshurites, 3 from the Shihor River on the east of Egypt to the territory of Ekron on the north, all of it counted as Canaanite though held by the five Philistine rulers in Gaza, Ashdod, Ashkelon, Gath and Ekron; the territory of the Avvites 4 on the south; all the land of the Canaanites, from Arah of the Sidonians as far as Aphek and the border of the Amorites; 5 the area of Byblos; and all Lebanon to the east, from Baal Gad below Mount Hermon to Lebo Hamath.

6 "As for all the inhabitants of the mountain regions from Lebanon to Misrephoth

---

a 3 Hebrew Kinnereth

Maim, that is, all the Sidonians, I myself will drive them out before the Israelites. Be sure to allocate this land to Israel for an inheritance, as I have instructed you, [7] and divide it as an inheritance among the nine tribes and half of the tribe of Manasseh."

Division of the Land East of the Jordan

[8] The other half of Manasseh,[a] the Reubenites and the Gadites had received the inheritance that Moses had given them east of the Jordan, as he, the servant of the LORD, had assigned it to them.

[9] It extended from Aroer on the rim of the Arnon Gorge, and from the town in the middle of the gorge, and included the whole plateau of Medeba as far as Dibon, [10] and all the towns of Sihon king of the Amorites, who ruled in Heshbon, out to the border of the Ammonites. [11] It also included Gilead, the territory of the people of Geshur and Maakah, all of Mount Hermon and all Bashan as far as Salekah— [12] that is, the whole kingdom of Og in Bashan, who had reigned in Ashtaroth and Edrei. (He was the last of the Rephaites.) Moses had defeated them and taken over their land. [13] But the Israelites did not drive out the people of Geshur and Maakah, so they continue to live among the Israelites to this day.

[14] But to the tribe of Levi he gave no inheritance, since the food offerings presented to the LORD, the God of Israel, are their inheritance, as he promised them.

[15] This is what Moses had given to the tribe of Reuben, according to its clans:

[16] The territory from Aroer on the rim of the Arnon Gorge, and from the town in the middle of the gorge, and the whole plateau past Medeba [17] to Heshbon and all its towns on the plateau, including Dibon, Bamoth Baal, Beth Baal Meon, [18] Jahaz, Kedemoth, Mephaath, [19] Kiriathaim, Sibmah, Zereth Shahar on the hill in the valley, [20] Beth Peor, the slopes of Pisgah, and Beth Jeshimoth— [21] all the towns on the plateau and the entire realm of Sihon king of the Amorites, who ruled at Heshbon. Moses had defeated him and the Midianite chiefs, Evi, Rekem, Zur, Hur and Reba—princes allied with Sihon—who lived in that country. [22] In addition to those slain in battle, the Israelites had put to the sword Balaam son of Beor, who practiced divination. [23] The boundary of the Reubenites was the bank of the Jordan. These towns and their villages were the inheritance of the Reubenites, according to their clans.

[24] This is what Moses had given to the tribe of Gad, according to its clans:

[25] The territory of Jazer, all the towns of Gilead and half the Ammonite country as far as Aroer, near Rabbah; [26] and from Heshbon to Ramath Mizpah and Betonim, and from Mahanaim to the territory of Debir; [27] and in the valley, Beth Haram, Beth Nimrah, Sukkoth and Zaphon with the rest of the realm of Sihon king of Heshbon (the east side of the Jordan, the territory up to the end of the Sea of Galilee[b]). [28] These towns and their villages were the inheritance of the Gadites, according to their clans.

[29] This is what Moses had given to the half-tribe of Manasseh, that is, to half the family of the descendants of Manasseh, according to its clans:

[30] The territory extending from Mahanaim and including all of Bashan, the entire realm of Og king of Bashan— all the settlements of Jair in Bashan, sixty towns, [31] half of Gilead, and Ashtaroth and Edrei (the royal cities of Og in Bashan). This was for the descendants of Makir son of Manasseh—for half of the sons of Makir, according to their clans.

---

[a] 8 Hebrew With it (that is, with the other half of Manasseh)   [b] 27 Hebrew Kinnereth

³²This is the inheritance Moses had given when he was in the plains of Moab across the Jordan east of Jericho. ³³But to the tribe of Levi, Moses had given no inheritance; the Lᴏʀᴅ, the God of Israel, is their inheritance, as he promised them.

Division of the Land West of the Jordan

14 Now these are the areas the Israelites received as an inheritance in the land of Canaan, which Eleazar the priest, Joshua son of Nun and the heads of the tribal clans of Israel allotted to them. ²Their inheritances were assigned by lot to the nine and a half tribes, as the Lᴏʀᴅ had commanded through Moses. ³Moses had granted the two and a half tribes their inheritance east of the Jordan but had not granted the Levites an inheritance among the rest, ⁴for Joseph's descendants had become two tribes—Manasseh and Ephraim. The Levites received no share of the land but only towns to live in, with pasturelands for their flocks and herds. ⁵So the Israelites divided the land, just as the Lᴏʀᴅ had commanded Moses.

Allotment for Caleb

⁶Now the people of Judah approached Joshua at Gilgal, and Caleb son of Jephunneh the Kenizzite said to him, "You know what the Lᴏʀᴅ said to Moses the man of God at Kadesh Barnea about you and me. ⁷I was forty years old when Moses the servant of the Lᴏʀᴅ sent me from Kadesh Barnea to explore the land. And I brought him back a report according to my convictions, ⁸but my fellow Israelites who went up with me made the hearts of the people melt in fear. I, however, followed the Lᴏʀᴅ my God wholeheartedly. ⁹So on that day Moses swore to me, 'The land on which your feet have walked will be your inheritance and that of your children forever, because you have followed the Lᴏʀᴅ my God wholeheartedly.'ᵃ

¹⁰"Now then, just as the Lᴏʀᴅ promised, he has kept me alive for forty-five years since the time he said this to Moses, while Israel moved about in the wilderness. So here I am today, eighty-five years old! ¹¹I am still as strong today as the day Moses sent me out; I'm just as vigorous to go out to battle now as I was then. ¹²Now give me this hill country that the Lᴏʀᴅ promised me that day. You yourself heard then that the Anakites were there and their cities were large and fortified, but, the Lᴏʀᴅ helping me, I will drive them out just as he said."

¹³Then Joshua blessed Caleb son of Jephunneh and gave him Hebron as his inheritance. ¹⁴So Hebron has belonged to Caleb son of Jephunneh the Kenizzite ever since, because he followed the Lᴏʀᴅ, the God of Israel, wholeheartedly. ¹⁵(Hebron used to be called Kiriath Arba after Arba, who was the greatest man among the Anakites.)

Then the land had rest from war.

Allotment for Judah

15 The allotment for the tribe of Judah, according to its clans, extended down to the territory of Edom, to the Desert of Zin in the extreme south.

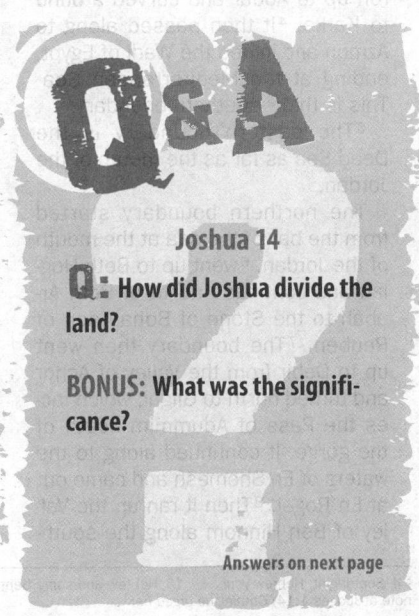

Joshua 14

Q: How did Joshua divide the land?

BONUS: What was the significance?

Answers on next page

ᵃ 9 Deut. 1:36

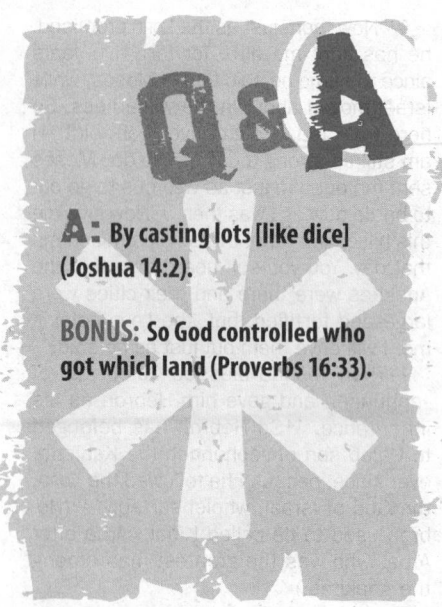

A: By casting lots [like dice] (Joshua 14:2).

BONUS: So God controlled who got which land (Proverbs 16:33).

ern slope of the Jebusite city (that is, Jerusalem). From there it climbed to the top of the hill west of the Hinnom Valley at the northern end of the Valley of Rephaim. ⁹From the hilltop the boundary headed toward the spring of the waters of Nephtoah, came out at the towns of Mount Ephron and went down toward Baalah (that is, Kiriath Jearim). ¹⁰Then it curved westward from Baalah to Mount Seir, ran along the northern slope of Mount Jearim (that is, Kesalon), continued down to Beth Shemesh and crossed to Timnah. ¹¹It went to the northern slope of Ekron, turned toward Shikkeron, passed along to Mount Baalah and reached Jabneel. The boundary ended at the sea.

¹²The western boundary is the coastline of the Mediterranean Sea.

These are the boundaries around the people of Judah by their clans.

²Their southern boundary started from the bay at the southern end of the Dead Sea, ³crossed south of Scorpion Pass, continued on to Zin and went over to the south of Kadesh Barnea. Then it ran past Hezron up to Addar and curved around to Karka. ⁴It then passed along to Azmon and joined the Wadi of Egypt, ending at the Mediterranean Sea. This is their[a] southern boundary.

⁵The eastern boundary is the Dead Sea as far as the mouth of the Jordan.

The northern boundary started from the bay of the sea at the mouth of the Jordan, ⁶went up to Beth Hoglah and continued north of Beth Arabah to the Stone of Bohan son of Reuben. ⁷The boundary then went up to Debir from the Valley of Achor and turned north to Gilgal, which faces the Pass of Adummim south of the gorge. It continued along to the waters of En Shemesh and came out at En Rogel. ⁸Then it ran up the Valley of Ben Hinnom along the south-

¹³In accordance with the Lord's command to him, Joshua gave to Caleb son of Jephunneh a portion in Judah—Kiriath Arba, that is, Hebron. (Arba was the forefather of Anak.) ¹⁴From Hebron Caleb drove out the three Anakites—Sheshai, Ahiman and Talmai, the sons of Anak. ¹⁵From there he marched against the people living in Debir (formerly called Kiriath Sepher). ¹⁶And Caleb said, "I will give my daughter Aksah in marriage to the man who attacks and captures Kiriath Sepher." ¹⁷Othniel son of Kenaz, Caleb's brother, took it; so Caleb gave his daughter Aksah to him in marriage.

¹⁸One day when she came to Othniel, she urged him[b] to ask her father for a field. When she got off her donkey, Caleb asked her, "What can I do for you?"

¹⁹She replied, "Do me a special favor. Since you have given me land in the Negev, give me also springs of water." So Caleb gave her the upper and lower springs.

²⁰This is the inheritance of the tribe of Judah, according to its clans:

[a] 4 Septuagint; Hebrew your   [b] 18 Hebrew and some Septuagint manuscripts; other Septuagint manuscripts (see also note at Judges 1:14) Othniel, he urged her

21 The southernmost towns of the tribe of Judah in the Negev toward the boundary of Edom were:

Kabzeel, Eder, Jagur, 22 Kinah, Dimonah, Adadah, 23 Kedesh, Hazor, Ithnan, 24 Ziph, Telem, Bealoth, 25 Hazor Hadattah, Kerioth Hezron (that is, Hazor), 26 Amam, Shema, Moladah, 27 Hazar Gaddah, Heshmon, Beth Pelet, 28 Hazar Shual, Beersheba, Biziothiah, 29 Baalah, Iyim, Ezem, 30 Eltolad, Kesil, Hormah, 31 Ziklag, Madmannah, Sansannah, 32 Lebaoth, Shilhim, Ain and Rimmon—a total of twenty-nine towns and their villages.

33 In the western foothills:

Eshtaol, Zorah, Ashnah, 34 Zanoah, En Gannim, Tappuah, Enam, 35 Jarmuth, Adullam, Sokoh, Azekah, 36 Shaaraim, Adithaim and Gederah (or Gederothaim)[a]—fourteen towns and their villages.

37 Zenan, Hadashah, Migdal Gad, 38 Dilean, Mizpah, Joktheel, 39 Lachish, Bozkath, Eglon, 40 Kabbon, Lahmas, Kitlish, 41 Gederoth, Beth Dagon, Naamah and Makkedah—sixteen towns and their villages.

42 Libnah, Ether, Ashan, 43 Iphtah, Ashnah, Nezib, 44 Keilah, Akzib and Mareshah—nine towns and their villages.

45 Ekron, with its surrounding settlements and villages; 46 west of Ekron, all that were in the vicinity of Ashdod, together with their villages; 47 Ashdod, its surrounding settlements and villages; and Gaza, its settlements and villages, as far as the Wadi of Egypt and the coastline of the Mediterranean Sea.

48 In the hill country:

Shamir, Jattir, Sokoh, 49 Dannah, Kiriath Sannah (that is, Debir), 50 Anab, Eshtemoh, Anim, 51 Goshen, Holon and Giloh—eleven towns and their villages.

52 Arab, Dumah, Eshan, 53 Janim, Beth Tappuah, Aphekah, 54 Humtah, Kiriath Arba (that is, Hebron) and Zior—nine towns and their villages.

55 Maon, Carmel, Ziph, Juttah, 56 Jezreel, Jokdeam, Zanoah, 57 Kain, Gibeah and Timnah—ten towns and their villages.

58 Halhul, Beth Zur, Gedor, 59 Maarath, Beth Anoth and Eltekon—six towns and their villages.[b]

60 Kiriath Baal (that is, Kiriath Jearim) and Rabbah—two towns and their villages.

61 In the wilderness:

Beth Arabah, Middin, Sekakah, 62 Nibshan, the City of Salt and En Gedi—six towns and their villages.

63 Judah could not dislodge the Jebusites, who were living in Jerusalem; to this day the Jebusites live there with the people of Judah.

Allotment for Ephraim and Manasseh

16 The allotment for Joseph began at the Jordan, east of the springs of Jericho, and went up from there through the desert into the hill country of Bethel. 2 It went on from Bethel (that is, Luz),[c] crossed over to the territory of the Arkites in Ataroth, 3 descended westward to the territory of the Japhletites as far as the region of Lower Beth Horon and on to Gezer, ending at the Mediterranean Sea.

4 So Manasseh and Ephraim, the descendants of Joseph, received their inheritance.

5 This was the territory of Ephraim, according to its clans:

The boundary of their inheritance went from Ataroth Addar in the east to Upper Beth Horon 6 and continued to the Mediterranean Sea. From Mikmethath on the north it curved eastward to Taanath Shiloh, passing by it to Janoah on the east. 7 Then it went down from Janoah to Ataroth and Naarah, touched Jericho and came

---

a 36 Or *Gederah and Gederothaim*   b 59 The Septuagint adds another district of eleven towns, including Tekoa and Ephrathah (Bethlehem).   c 2 Septuagint; Hebrew *Bethel to Luz*

out at the Jordan. 8From Tappuah the border went west to the Kanah Ravine and ended at the Mediterranean Sea. This was the inheritance of the tribe of the Ephraimites, according to its clans. 9It also included all the towns and their villages that were set aside for the Ephraimites within the inheritance of the Manassites.

10They did not dislodge the Canaanites living in Gezer; to this day the Canaanites live among the people of Ephraim but are required to do forced labor.

17 This was the allotment for the tribe of Manasseh as Joseph's firstborn, that is, for Makir, Manasseh's firstborn. Makir was the ancestor of the Gileadites, who had received Gilead and Bashan because the Makirites were great soldiers. 2So this allotment was for the rest of the people of Manasseh—the clans of Abiezer, Helek, Asriel, Shechem, Hepher and Shemida. These are the other male descendants of Manasseh son of Joseph by their clans.

3Now Zelophehad son of Hepher, the son of Gilead, the son of Makir, the son of Manasseh, had no sons but only daughters, whose names were Mahlah, Noah, Hoglah, Milkah and Tirzah. 4They went to Eleazar the priest, Joshua son of Nun, and the leaders and said, "The LORD commanded Moses to give us an inheritance among our relatives." So Joshua gave them an inheritance along with the brothers of their father, according to the LORD's command. 5Manasseh's share consisted of ten tracts of land besides Gilead and Bashan east of the Jordan, 6because the daughters of the tribe of Manasseh received an inheritance among the sons. The land of Gilead belonged to the rest of the descendants of Manasseh.

7The territory of Manasseh extended from Asher to Mikmethath east of Shechem. The boundary ran southward from there to include the people living at En Tappuah. 8(Manasseh had the land of Tappuah, but Tappuah itself, on the boundary of Manasseh, belonged to the Ephraimites.) 9Then the boundary continued south to the Kanah Ravine. There were towns belonging to Ephraim lying among the towns of Manasseh, but the boundary of Manasseh was the northern side of the ravine and ended at the Mediterranean Sea. 10On the south the land belonged to Ephraim, on the north to Manasseh. The territory of Manasseh reached the Mediterranean Sea and bordered Asher on the north and Issachar on the east.

11Within Issachar and Asher, Manasseh also had Beth Shan, Ibleam and the people of Dor, Endor, Taanach and Megiddo, together with their surrounding settlements (the third in the list is Naphoth[a]). 12Yet the Manassites were not able to occupy these towns, for the Canaanites were determined to live in that region. 13However, when the Israelites grew stronger, they subjected the Canaanites to forced labor but did not drive them out completely.

14The people of Joseph said to Joshua, "Why have you given us only one allotment and one portion for an inheritance? We are a numerous people, and the LORD has blessed us abundantly."

15"If you are so numerous," Joshua answered, "and if the hill country of Ephraim is too small for you, go up into the forest and clear land for yourselves there in the land of the Perizzites and Rephaites."

16The people of Joseph replied, "The hill country is not enough for us, and all the Canaanites who live in the plain have chariots fitted with iron, both those in Beth Shan and its settlements and those in the Valley of Jezreel."

17But Joshua said to the tribes of Joseph—to Ephraim and Manasseh—"You are numerous and very powerful. You will have not only one allotment 18but the forested hill country as well. Clear it, and its farthest limits will be yours; though the Canaanites have chariots fitted with iron

---

a 11 That is, Naphoth Dor

and though they are strong, you can drive them out."

Division of the Rest of the Land

18 The whole assembly of the Israelites gathered at Shiloh and set up the tent of meeting there. The country was brought under their control, ²but there were still seven Israelite tribes who had not yet received their inheritance.

³So Joshua said to the Israelites: "How long will you wait before you begin to take possession of the land that the LORD, the God of your ancestors, has given you? ⁴Appoint three men from each tribe. I will send them out to make a survey of the land and to write a description of it, according to the inheritance of each. Then they will return to me. ⁵You are to divide the land into seven parts. Judah is to remain in its territory on the south and the tribes of Joseph in their territory on the north. ⁶After you have written descriptions of the seven parts of the land, bring them here to me and I will cast lots for you in the presence of the LORD our God. ⁷The Levites, however, do not get a portion among you, because the priestly service of the LORD is their inheritance. And Gad, Reuben and the half-tribe of Manasseh have already received their inheritance on the east side of the Jordan. Moses the servant of the LORD gave it to them."

⁸As the men started on their way to map out the land, Joshua instructed them, "Go and make a survey of the land and write a description of it. Then return to me, and I will cast lots for you here at Shiloh in the presence of the LORD." ⁹So the men left and went through the land. They wrote its description on a scroll, town by town, in seven parts, and returned to Joshua in the camp at Shiloh. ¹⁰Joshua then cast lots for them in Shiloh in the presence of the LORD, and there he distributed the land to the Israelites according to their tribal divisions.

Allotment for Benjamin

¹¹The first lot came up for the tribe of Benjamin according to its clans. Their allotted territory lay between the tribes of Judah and Joseph:

¹²On the north side their boundary began at the Jordan, passed the northern slope of Jericho and headed west into the hill country, coming out at the wilderness of Beth Aven. ¹³From there it crossed to the south slope of Luz (that is, Bethel) and went down to Ataroth Addar on the hill south of Lower Beth Horon.

¹⁴From the hill facing Beth Horon on the south the boundary turned south along the western side and came out at Kiriath Baal (that is, Kiriath Jearim), a town of the people of Judah. This was the western side.

¹⁵The southern side began at the outskirts of Kiriath Jearim on the west, and the boundary came out at the spring of the waters of Nephtoah. ¹⁶The boundary went down to the foot of the hill facing the Valley of Ben Hinnom, north of the Valley of Rephaim. It continued down the Hinnom Valley along the southern slope of the Jebusite city and so to En Rogel. ¹⁷It then curved north, went to En Shemesh, continued to Geliloth, which faces the Pass of Adummim,

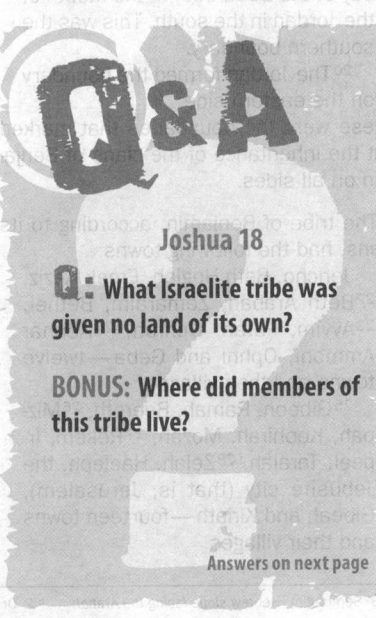

Joshua 18

Q: What Israelite tribe was given no land of its own?

BONUS: Where did members of this tribe live?

Answers on next page

A: Every tribe but the Levites was given a plot of land (Joshua 18:7).

BONUS: The Levites had towns in the lands of the other tribes (Joshua 21:2–3), so they could teach everyone God's law (2 Chronicles 35:3).

and ran down to the Stone of Bohan son of Reuben. [18] It continued to the northern slope of Beth Arabah[a] and on down into the Arabah. [19] It then went to the northern slope of Beth Hoglah and came out at the northern bay of the Dead Sea, at the mouth of the Jordan in the south. This was the southern boundary.

[20] The Jordan formed the boundary on the eastern side.

These were the boundaries that marked out the inheritance of the clans of Benjamin on all sides.

[21] The tribe of Benjamin, according to its clans, had the following towns:

Jericho, Beth Hoglah, Emek Keziz, [22] Beth Arabah, Zemaraim, Bethel, [23] Avvim, Parah, Ophrah, [24] Kephar Ammoni, Ophni and Geba—twelve towns and their villages.

[25] Gibeon, Ramah, Beeroth, [26] Mizpah, Kephirah, Mozah, [27] Rekem, Irpeel, Taralah, [28] Zelah, Haeleph, the Jebusite city (that is, Jerusalem), Gibeah and Kiriath—fourteen towns and their villages.

This was the inheritance of Benjamin for its clans.

Allotment for Simeon

19 The second lot came out for the tribe of Simeon according to its clans. Their inheritance lay within the territory of Judah. [2] It included:

Beersheba (or Sheba),[b] Moladah, [3] Hazar Shual, Balah, Ezem, [4] Eltolad, Bethul, Hormah, [5] Ziklag, Beth Markaboth, Hazar Susah, [6] Beth Lebaoth and Sharuhen—thirteen towns and their villages;

[7] Ain, Rimmon, Ether and Ashan—four towns and their villages— [8] and all the villages around these towns as far as Baalath Beer (Ramah in the Negev).

This was the inheritance of the tribe of the Simeonites, according to its clans. [9] The inheritance of the Simeonites was taken from the share of Judah, because Judah's portion was more than they needed. So the Simeonites received their inheritance within the territory of Judah.

Allotment for Zebulun

[10] The third lot came up for Zebulun according to its clans:

The boundary of their inheritance went as far as Sarid. [11] Going west it ran to Maralah, touched Dabbesheth, and extended to the ravine near Jokneam. [12] It turned east from Sarid toward the sunrise to the territory of Kisloth Tabor and went on to Daberath and up to Japhia. [13] Then it continued eastward to Gath Hepher and Eth Kazin; it came out at Rimmon and turned toward Neah. [14] There the boundary went around on the north to Hannathon and ended at the Valley of Iphtah El. [15] Included were Kattath, Nahalal, Shimron, Idalah and Bethlehem. There were twelve towns and their villages. [16] These towns and their villages were the inheritance of Zebulun, according to its clans.

Allotment for Issachar

¹⁷The fourth lot came out for Issachar according to its clans. ¹⁸Their territory included:

Jezreel, Kesulloth, Shunem, ¹⁹Hapharaim, Shion, Anaharath, ²⁰Rabbith, Kishion, Ebez, ²¹Remeth, En Gannim, En Haddah and Beth Pazzez. ²²The boundary touched Tabor, Shahazumah and Beth Shemesh, and ended at the Jordan. There were sixteen towns and their villages.

²³These towns and their villages were the inheritance of the tribe of Issachar, according to its clans.

Allotment for Asher

²⁴The fifth lot came out for the tribe of Asher according to its clans. ²⁵Their territory included:

Helkath, Hali, Beten, Akshaph, ²⁶Allammelek, Amad and Mishal. On the west the boundary touched Carmel and Shihor Libnath. ²⁷It then turned east toward Beth Dagon, touched Zebulun and the Valley of Iphtah El, and went north to Beth Emek and Neiel, passing Kabul on the left. ²⁸It went to Abdon,^a Rehob, Hammon and Kanah, as far as Greater Sidon. ²⁹The boundary then turned back toward Ramah and went to the fortified city of Tyre, turned toward Hosah and came out at the Mediterranean Sea in the region of Akzib, ³⁰Ummah, Aphek and Rehob. There were twenty-two towns and their villages.

³¹These towns and their villages were the inheritance of the tribe of Asher, according to its clans.

Allotment for Naphtali

³²The sixth lot came out for Naphtali according to its clans:

³³Their boundary went from Heleph and the large tree in Zaanannim, passing Adami Nekeb and Jabneel to Lakkum and ending at the Jordan. ³⁴The boundary ran west through Aznoth Tabor and came out at Hukkok. It touched Zebulun on the south, Asher on the west and the Jordan^b on the east. ³⁵The fortified towns were Ziddim, Zer, Hammath, Rakkath, Kinnereth, ³⁶Adamah, Ramah, Hazor, ³⁷Kedesh, Edrei, En Hazor, ³⁸Iron, Migdal El, Horem, Beth Anath and Beth Shemesh. There were nineteen towns and their villages.

³⁹These towns and their villages were the inheritance of the tribe of Naphtali, according to its clans.

Allotment for Dan

⁴⁰The seventh lot came out for the tribe of Dan according to its clans. ⁴¹The territory of their inheritance included:

---

^a 28 Some Hebrew manuscripts (see also 21:30); most Hebrew manuscripts *Ebron*   ^b 34 Septuagint; Hebrew *west, and Judah, the Jordan,*

PANORAMA

The Winner!

Joshua is a book about victory and defeat. God's people must invade a heavily populated land. After ten years, the promised land is theirs and is divided among Israel's twelve tribes.

{JOSHUA}

Zorah, Eshtaol, Ir Shemesh, 42Shaalabbin, Aijalon, Ithlah, 43Elon, Timnah, Ekron, 44Eltekeh, Gibbethon, Baalath, 45Jehud, Bene Berak, Gath Rimmon, 46Me Jarkon and Rakkon, with the area facing Joppa.

47(When the territory of the Danites was lost to them, they went up and attacked Leshem, took it, put it to the sword and occupied it. They settled in Leshem and named it Dan after their ancestor.)

48These towns and their villages were the inheritance of the tribe of Dan, according to its clans.

Allotment for Joshua

49When they had finished dividing the land into its allotted portions, the Israelites gave Joshua son of Nun an inheritance among them, 50as the LORD had commanded. They gave him the town he asked for—Timnath Serah[a] in the hill country of Ephraim. And he built up the town and settled there.

51These are the territories that Eleazar the priest, Joshua son of Nun and the heads of the tribal clans of Israel assigned by lot at Shiloh in the presence of the LORD at the entrance to the tent of meeting. And so they finished dividing the land.

Cities of Refuge

20 Then the LORD said to Joshua: 2"Tell the Israelites to designate the cities of refuge, as I instructed you through Moses, 3so that anyone who kills a person accidentally and unintentionally may flee there and find protection from the avenger of blood. 4When they flee to one of these cities, they are to stand in the entrance of the city gate and state their case before the elders of that city. Then the elders are to admit the fugitive into their city and provide a place to live among them. 5If the avenger of blood comes in pursuit, the elders must not surrender the fugitive, because the fugitive killed their neighbor unintentionally and without malice aforethought. 6They

are to stay in that city until they have stood trial before the assembly and until the death of the high priest who is serving at that time. Then they may go back to their own home in the town from which they fled."

7So they set apart Kedesh in Galilee in the hill country of Naphtali, Shechem in the hill country of Ephraim, and Kiriath Arba (that is, Hebron) in the hill country of Judah. 8East of the Jordan (on the other side from Jericho) they designated Bezer in the wilderness on the plateau in the tribe of Reuben, Ramoth in Gilead in the tribe of Gad, and Golan in Bashan in the tribe of Manasseh. 9Any of the Israelites or any foreigner residing among them who killed someone accidentally could flee to these designated cities and not be killed by the avenger of blood prior to standing trial before the assembly.

Towns for the Levites

21 Now the family heads of the Levites approached Eleazar the priest, Joshua son of Nun, and the heads of the other tribal families of Israel 2at Shiloh in Canaan and said to them, "The LORD commanded through Moses that you give us towns to live in, with pasturelands for our livestock." 3So, as the LORD had commanded, the Israelites gave the Levites the following towns and pasturelands out of their own inheritance:

4The first lot came out for the Kohathites, according to their clans. The Levites who were descendants of Aaron the priest were allotted thirteen towns from the tribes of Judah, Simeon and Benjamin. 5The rest of Kohath's descendants were allotted ten towns from the clans of the tribes of Ephraim, Dan and half of Manasseh.

6The descendants of Gershon were allotted thirteen towns from the clans of the tribes of Issachar, Asher, Naphtali and the half-tribe of Manasseh in Bashan.

7The descendants of Merari, according to their clans, received twelve towns from the tribes of Reuben, Gad and Zebulun.

8So the Israelites allotted to the Levites

---

a 50 Also known as Timnath Heres (see Judges 2:9)

these towns and their pasturelands, as the LORD had commanded through Moses.

9 From the tribes of Judah and Simeon they allotted the following towns by name 10 (these towns were assigned to the descendants of Aaron who were from the Kohathite clans of the Levites, because the first lot fell to them):

11 They gave them Kiriath Arba (that is, Hebron), with its surrounding pastureland, in the hill country of Judah. (Arba was the forefather of Anak.) 12 But the fields and villages around the city they had given to Caleb son of Jephunneh as his possession.

13 So to the descendants of Aaron the priest they gave Hebron (a city of refuge for one accused of murder), Libnah, 14 Jattir, Eshtemoa, 15 Holon, Debir, 16 Ain, Juttah and Beth Shemesh, together with their pasturelands—nine towns from these two tribes.

17 And from the tribe of Benjamin they gave them Gibeon, Geba, 18 Anathoth and Almon, together with their pasturelands—four towns.

19 The total number of towns for the priests, the descendants of Aaron, came to thirteen, together with their pasturelands.

20 The rest of the Kohathite clans of the Levites were allotted towns from the tribe of Ephraim:

21 In the hill country of Ephraim they were given Shechem (a city of refuge for one accused of murder) and Gezer, 22 Kibzaim and Beth Horon, together with their pasturelands—four towns.

23 Also from the tribe of Dan they received Eltekeh, Gibbethon, 24 Aijalon and Gath Rimmon, together with their pasturelands—four towns.

25 From half the tribe of Manasseh they received Taanach and Gath Rimmon, together with their pasturelands—two towns.

26 All these ten towns and their pasturelands were given to the rest of the Kohathite clans.

27 The Levite clans of the Gershonites were given:

from the half-tribe of Manasseh, Golan in Bashan (a city of refuge for one accused of murder) and Be Eshterah, together with their pasturelands—two towns;

28 from the tribe of Issachar, Kishion, Daberath, 29 Jarmuth and En Gannim, together with their pasturelands—four towns;

30 from the tribe of Asher, Mishal, Abdon, 31 Helkath and Rehob, together with their pasturelands—four towns;

32 from the tribe of Naphtali, Kedesh in Galilee (a city of refuge for one accused of murder), Hammoth Dor and Kartan, together with their pasturelands—three towns.

33 The total number of towns of the Gershonite clans came to thirteen, together with their pasturelands.

34 The Merarite clans (the rest of the Levites) were given:

from the tribe of Zebulun, Jokneam, Kartah, 35 Dimnah and Nahalal, together with their pasturelands—four towns;

36 from the tribe of Reuben, Bezer, Jahaz, 37 Kedemoth and Mephaath, together with their pasturelands—four towns;

38 from the tribe of Gad, Ramoth in Gilead (a city of refuge for one accused of murder), Mahanaim, 39 Heshbon and Jazer, together with their pasturelands—four towns in all.

40 The total number of towns allotted to the Merarite clans, who were the rest of the Levites, came to twelve.

41 The towns of the Levites in the territory held by the Israelites were forty-eight in all, together with their pasturelands. 42 Each of these towns had pasturelands surrounding it; this was true for all these towns.

43 So the LORD gave Israel all the land he had sworn to give their ancestors, and they took possession of it and settled there. 44 The LORD gave them rest on every

side, just as he had sworn to their ancestors. Not one of their enemies withstood them; the LORD gave all their enemies into their hands. ⁴⁵Not one of all the LORD's good promises to Israel failed; every one was fulfilled.

Eastern Tribes Return Home

22 Then Joshua summoned the Reubenites, the Gadites and the half-tribe of Manasseh ²and said to them, "You have done all that Moses the servant of the LORD commanded, and you have obeyed me in everything I commanded. ³For a long time now—to this very day—you have not deserted your fellow Israelites but have carried out the mission the LORD your God gave you. ⁴Now that the LORD your God has given them rest as he promised, return to your homes in the land that Moses the servant of the LORD gave you on the other side of the Jordan. ⁵But be very careful to keep the commandment and the law that Moses the servant of the LORD gave you: to love the LORD your God, to walk in obedience to him, to keep his commands, to hold fast to him and to serve him with all your heart and with all your soul."

⁶Then Joshua blessed them and sent them away, and they went to their homes. ⁷(To the half-tribe of Manasseh Moses had given land in Bashan, and to the other half of the tribe Joshua gave land on the west side of the Jordan along with their fellow Israelites.) When Joshua sent them home, he blessed them, ⁸saying, "Return to your homes with your great wealth—with large herds of livestock, with silver, gold, bronze and iron, and a great quantity of clothing—and divide the plunder from your enemies with your fellow Israelites."

⁹So the Reubenites, the Gadites and the half-tribe of Manasseh left the Israelites at Shiloh in Canaan to return to Gilead, their own land, which they had acquired in accordance with the command of the LORD through Moses.

¹⁰When they came to Geliloth near the Jordan in the land of Canaan, the Reubenites, the Gadites and the half-tribe of Manasseh built an imposing altar there by the Jordan. ¹¹And when the Israelites heard that they had built the altar on the border of Canaan at Geliloth near the Jordan on the Israelite side, ¹²the whole assembly of Israel gathered at Shiloh to go to war against them.

¹³So the Israelites sent Phinehas son of Eleazar, the priest, to the land of Gilead—to Reuben, Gad and the half-tribe of Manasseh. ¹⁴With him they sent ten of the chief men, one from each of the tribes of Israel, each the head of a family division among the Israelite clans.

¹⁵When they went to Gilead—to Reuben, Gad and the half-tribe of Manasseh—they said to them: ¹⁶"The whole assembly of the LORD says: 'How could you break faith with the God of Israel like this? How could you turn away from the LORD and build yourselves an altar in rebellion against him now? ¹⁷Was not the sin of Peor enough for us? Up to this very day we have not cleansed ourselves from that sin, even though a plague fell on the community of the LORD! ¹⁸And are you now turning away from the LORD?

"'If you rebel against the LORD today, tomorrow he will be angry with the whole community of Israel. ¹⁹If the land you possess is defiled, come over to the LORD's land, where the LORD's tabernacle stands, and share the land with us. But do not rebel against the LORD or against us by building an altar for yourselves, other than the altar of the LORD our God. ²⁰When Achan son of Zerah was unfaithful in regard to the devoted things,ᵃ did

Not one of all the LORD's good promises ... failed; every one was fulfilled.

Joshua 21:45

ᵃ 20 The Hebrew term refers to the irrevocable giving over of things or persons to the LORD, often by totally destroying them.

> I asked a boy in my math class about our homework assignment. It spread all over school and within a couple of days people were saying I was kissing him. Now his girlfriend and her friends want to fight me and my friends. I'm scared and upset. Now what am I supposed to do?
>
> >> Ashley

Dear Jordan

Dear Ashley,

Most people don't think gossip and rumors are that big of a deal. But they're wrong, as your letter points out. It's not a new problem either. Joshua 22 tells of a rumor which nearly caused a war. A story was getting around that some of Israel's tribes who lived across the Jordan River had built an altar for worship, which was forbidden. The other tribes were afraid they would be punished for what the tribes across the river had done.

Fortunately, a group of people were sent across the Jordan River to confront the tribes over there. They discovered that the altar was a remembrance and was not to be used in worship. If the main section of Israel had not gone and talked to the others, there would have been a war because a rumor had been spread around.

It doesn't sound all that much different from what you're describing. Try to get the word out that all you did was ask that guy about a homework assignment. And try to spread it around that gossip and rumors can be very harmful.

Jordan

not wrath come on the whole community of Israel? He was not the only one who died for his sin.'"

²¹Then Reuben, Gad and the half-tribe of Manasseh replied to the heads of the clans of Israel: ²²"The Mighty One, God, the LORD! The Mighty One, God, the LORD! He knows! And let Israel know! If this has been in rebellion or disobedience to the LORD, do not spare us this day. ²³If we have built our own altar to turn away from the LORD and to offer burnt offerings and grain offerings, or to sacrifice fellowship offerings on it, may the LORD himself call us to account.

²⁴"No! We did it for fear that some day your descendants might say to ours, 'What do you have to do with the LORD, the God of Israel? ²⁵The LORD has made the Jordan a boundary between us and you—you Reubenites and Gadites! You have no share in the LORD.' So your descendants might cause ours to stop fearing the LORD.

²⁶"That is why we said, 'Let us get ready and build an altar—but not for burnt offerings or sacrifices.' ²⁷On the contrary, it is to be a witness between us and you and the generations that follow, that we will worship the LORD at his sanctuary with our burnt offerings, sacrifices and fellowship offerings. Then in the future your descendants will not be able to say to ours, 'You have no share in the LORD.'

²⁸"And we said, 'If they ever say this to us, or to our descendants, we will answer: Look at the replica of the LORD's altar, which our ancestors built, not for burnt offerings and sacrifices, but as a witness between us and you.'

²⁹"Far be it from us to rebel against the LORD and turn away from him today by building an altar for burnt offerings, grain offerings and sacrifices, other than the altar of the LORD our God that stands before his tabernacle."

³⁰When Phinehas the priest and the leaders of the community—the heads of the clans of the Israelites—heard what Reuben, Gad and Manasseh had to say, they were pleased. ³¹And Phinehas son of Eleazar, the priest, said to Reuben, Gad and Manasseh, "Today we know that the LORD is with us, because you have not been unfaithful to the LORD in this matter. Now you have rescued the Israelites from the LORD's hand."

³²Then Phinehas son of Eleazar, the priest, and the leaders returned to Canaan from their meeting with the Reubenites and Gadites in Gilead and reported to the Israelites. ³³They were glad to hear the report and praised God. And they talked no more about going to war against them to devastate the country where the Reubenites and the Gadites lived.

³⁴And the Reubenites and the Gadites gave the altar this name: A Witness Between Us—that the LORD is God.

Joshua's Farewell to the Leaders

23 After a long time had passed and the LORD had given Israel rest from all their enemies around them, Joshua, by then a very old man, ²summoned all Israel—their elders, leaders, judges and officials—and said to them: "I am very old. ³You yourselves have seen everything the LORD your God has done to all these nations for your sake; it was the LORD your God who fought for you. ⁴Remember how I have allotted as an inheritance for your tribes all the land of the nations that remain—the nations I conquered—between the Jordan and the Mediterranean Sea in the west. ⁵The LORD your God himself will push them out for your sake. He will drive them out before you, and you will take possession of their land, as the LORD your God promised you.

⁶"Be very strong; be careful to obey all that is written in the Book of the Law of Moses, without turning aside to the right or to the left. ⁷Do not associate with these nations that remain among you; do not invoke the names of their gods or swear by them. You must not serve them or bow down to them. ⁸But you are to hold fast to the LORD your God, as you have until now.

⁹"The LORD has driven out before you great and powerful nations; to this day no one has been able to withstand you. ¹⁰One of you routs a thousand, because

Years ago a good-looking guy or girl was a "dreamboat." In the sixties he or she was "groovy." The words change year by year, but whatever you call an attractive person now, don't get carried away by mere looks. God warned his people not to intermarry with the neighboring Canaanites. They might have looked like "dreamboats," but they weren't committed to God and would draw God's people away from him. There's nothing wrong with good looks or with being attracted to good-looking guys or girls. Just make sure that the person you like loves the Lord and will help instead of hinder your Christian life.

{Joshua 23:6–13}

INSTANT ACCESS

the LORD your God fights for you, just as he promised. ¹¹So be very careful to love the LORD your God.

¹²"But if you turn away and ally yourselves with the survivors of these nations that remain among you and if you intermarry with them and associate with them, ¹³then you may be sure that the LORD your God will no longer drive out these nations before you. Instead, they will become snares and traps for you, whips on your backs and thorns in your

eyes, until you perish from this good land, which the LORD your God has given you.

¹⁴"Now I am about to go the way of all the earth. You know with all your heart and soul that not one of all the good promises the LORD your God gave you has failed. Every promise has been fulfilled; not one has failed. ¹⁵But just as all the good things the LORD your God has promised you have come to you, so he will bring on you all the evil things he has threatened, until the LORD your God has destroyed you from this good land he has given you. ¹⁶If you violate the covenant of the LORD your God, which he commanded you, and go and serve other gods and bow down to them, the LORD's anger will burn against you, and you will quickly perish from the good land he has given you."

The Covenant Renewed at Shechem

24 Then Joshua assembled all the tribes of Israel at Shechem. He summoned the elders, leaders, judges and officials of Israel, and they presented themselves before God.

²Joshua said to all the people, "This is what the LORD, the God of Israel, says: 'Long ago your ancestors, including Terah the father of Abraham and Nahor, lived beyond the Euphrates River and worshiped other gods. ³But I took your father Abraham from the land beyond the Euphrates and led him throughout Canaan and gave him many descendants. I gave him Isaac, ⁴and to Isaac I gave Jacob and Esau. I assigned the hill country of Seir to Esau, but Jacob and his family went down to Egypt.

⁵"'Then I sent Moses and Aaron, and I afflicted the Egyptians by what I did there, and I brought you out. ⁶When I brought your people out of Egypt, you came to the sea, and the Egyptians pursued them with chariots and horsemen*a* as far as the Red Sea.*b* ⁷But they cried to the LORD for help, and he put darkness between you and the Egyptians; he brought the sea over them and covered them. You saw with your own eyes what I did to the Egyptians. Then you lived in the wilderness for a long time.

---

a 6 Or charioteers   *b 6 Or the Sea of Reeds*

8 " 'I brought you to the land of the Amorites who lived east of the Jordan. They fought against you, but I gave them into your hands. I destroyed them from before you, and you took possession of their land. 9When Balak son of Zippor, the king of Moab, prepared to fight against Israel, he sent for Balaam son of Beor to put a curse on you. 10But I would not listen to Balaam, so he blessed you again and again, and I delivered you out of his hand.

11 " 'Then you crossed the Jordan and came to Jericho. The citizens of Jericho fought against you, as did also the Amorites, Perizzites, Canaanites, Hittites, Girgashites, Hivites and Jebusites, but I gave them into your hands. 12I sent the hornet ahead of you, which drove them out before you—also the two Amorite kings. You did not do it with your own sword and bow. 13So I gave you a land on which you did not toil and cities you did not build; and you live in them and eat from vineyards and olive groves that you did not plant.'

14 "Now fear the LORD and serve him with all faithfulness. Throw away the gods your ancestors worshiped beyond the Euphrates River and in Egypt, and serve the LORD. 15But if serving the LORD seems undesirable to you, then choose for yourselves this day whom you will serve, whether the gods your ancestors served beyond the Euphrates, or the gods of the Amorites, in whose land you are living. But as for me and my household, we will serve the LORD."

16Then the people answered, "Far be it from us to forsake the LORD to serve other gods! 17It was the LORD our God himself who brought us and our parents up out of Egypt, from that land of slavery, and performed those great signs before our eyes. He protected us on our entire journey and among all the nations through which we traveled. 18And the LORD drove out before us all the nations, including the Amorites, who lived in the land. We too will serve the LORD, because he is our God."

19Joshua said to the people, "You are not able to serve the LORD. He is a holy God; he is a jealous God. He will not forgive your rebellion and your sins. 20If you forsake the LORD and serve foreign gods, he will turn and bring disaster on you and

INSTANT ACCESS

Your parents make you go to church? Even if you don't want to? Well, that's their right as long as you live in their home. Not that they think dragging you to church makes you a Christian any more than sitting in a school classroom makes you an A student. Going to church just gives you the chance to learn about God. But you have to decide to make a personal commitment. Joshua knew this very well. When he was old and about to die, he challenged all the Israelites: "Choose for yourselves this day whom you will serve" (Joshua 24:15). That's a challenge every person faces. Including you.

{Joshua 24:14–21}

make an end of you, after he has been good to you."

21But the people said to Joshua, "No! We will serve the LORD."

22Then Joshua said, "You are witnesses against yourselves that you have chosen to serve the LORD."

"Yes, we are witnesses," they replied.

23 "Now then," said Joshua, "throw away the foreign gods that are among you and yield your hearts to the LORD, the God of Israel."

24And the people said to Joshua, "We will serve the LORD our God and obey him."

²⁵On that day Joshua made a covenant for the people, and there at Shechem he reaffirmed for them decrees and laws. ²⁶And Joshua recorded these things in the Book of the Law of God. Then he took a large stone and set it up there under the oak near the holy place of the LORD.

²⁷"See!" he said to all the people. "This stone will be a witness against us. It has heard all the words the LORD has said to us. It will be a witness against you if you are untrue to your God."

²⁸Then Joshua dismissed the people, each to their own inheritance.

Buried in the Promised Land

²⁹After these things, Joshua son of Nun, the servant of the LORD, died at the age of a hundred and ten. ³⁰And they buried him in the land of his inheritance, at Timnath Serah^a in the hill country of Ephraim, north of Mount Gaash.

³¹Israel served the LORD throughout the lifetime of Joshua and of the elders who outlived him and who had experienced everything the LORD had done for Israel.

³²And Joseph's bones, which the Israelites had brought up from Egypt, were buried at Shechem in the tract of land that Jacob bought for a hundred pieces of silver^b from the sons of Hamor, the father of Shechem. This became the inheritance of Joseph's descendants.

³³And Eleazar son of Aaron died and was buried at Gibeah, which had been allotted to his son Phinehas in the hill country of Ephraim.

---

^a 30 Also known as *Timnath Heres* (see Judges 2:9)   ^b 32 Hebrew *hundred kesitahs*; a kesitah was a unit of money of unknown weight and value.

JUDGES

preview

"Judges" led the Israelites from about 1375 to 1040 B.C.

The "judges" were military, political and spiritual leaders.

Events in this book follow a common pattern: Israel sins, suffers, turns to God, is saved by a judge, experiences a time of peace, but soon sins again.

Rules.

What if no one at school followed the rules? What if no one obeyed traffic lights when driving? There certainly would be one big mess. And probably a lot of people would get hurt.

Judges tells about a time when the Israelites didn't follow God's rules. Again and again they forgot him and worshiped idols. Each time they got in trouble. And each time, when they turned back to the Lord, he sent a leader to save them from their enemies. Judges is a reminder that God is faithful even when you don't follow his rules. But Judges also reminds you that you're in for trouble if you don't do things God's way!

>>**DISOBEDIENCE BRINGS DEFEAT**
   200 years of history explained, Judges 2:6–23

>>**WOMAN LEADS ISRAEL TO VICTORY**
   General relies on female judge, Judges 4

>>**GIDEON TO GOD: PLEASE SHOW ME**
   Hesitant leader begs for a sign, Judges 6:33–40

>>**SO STRONG, YET SO WEAK**
   Jock judge falls short, Judges 16

>>**FORGETTING GOD BRINGS MORAL MESS**
   Shocking events described in Judges 19

During the time of the judges, wheeled chariots spread to China from central Asia. Zoroaster establishes a religion in what is now Iran.

Israel Fights the Remaining Canaanites

1 After the death of Joshua, the Israelites asked the LORD, "Who of us is to go up first to fight against the Canaanites?"

[2] The LORD answered, "Judah shall go up; I have given the land into their hands."

[3] The men of Judah then said to the Simeonites their fellow Israelites, "Come up with us into the territory allotted to us, to fight against the Canaanites. We in turn will go with you into yours." So the Simeonites went with them.

[4] When Judah attacked, the LORD gave the Canaanites and Perizzites into their hands, and they struck down ten thousand men at Bezek. [5] It was there that they found Adoni-Bezek and fought against him, putting to rout the Canaanites and Perizzites. [6] Adoni-Bezek fled, but they chased him and caught him, and cut off his thumbs and big toes.

[7] Then Adoni-Bezek said, "Seventy kings with their thumbs and big toes cut off have picked up scraps under my table. Now God has paid me back for what I did to them." They brought him to Jerusalem, and he died there.

[8] The men of Judah attacked Jerusalem also and took it. They put the city to the sword and set it on fire.

[9] After that, Judah went down to fight against the Canaanites living in the hill country, the Negev and the western foothills. [10] They advanced against the Canaanites living in Hebron (formerly called Kiriath Arba) and defeated Sheshai, Ahiman and Talmai. [11] From there they advanced against the people living in Debir (formerly called Kiriath Sepher).

[12] And Caleb said, "I will give my daughter Aksah in marriage to the man who attacks and captures Kiriath Sepher." [13] Othniel son of Kenaz, Caleb's younger brother, took it; so Caleb gave his daughter Aksah to him in marriage.

[14] One day when she came to Othniel, she urged him[a] to ask her father for a field. When she got off her donkey, Caleb asked her, "What can I do for you?"

[15] She replied, "Do me a special favor. Since you have given me land in the Negev, give me also springs of water." So Caleb gave her the upper and lower springs.

[16] The descendants of Moses' father-in-law, the Kenite, went up from the City of Palms[b] with the people of Judah to live among the inhabitants of the Desert of Judah in the Negev near Arad.

[17] Then the men of Judah went with the Simeonites their fellow Israelites and attacked the Canaanites living in Zephath, and they totally destroyed[c] the city. Therefore it was called Hormah.[d] [18] Judah also took[e] Gaza, Ashkelon and Ekron — each city with its territory.

[19] The LORD was with the men of Judah. They took possession of the hill country, but they were unable to drive the people from the plains, because they had chariots fitted with iron. [20] As Moses had promised, Hebron was given to Caleb, who drove from it the three sons of Anak. [21] The Benjamites, however, did not drive out the Jebusites, who were living in Jerusalem; to this day the Jebusites live there with the Benjamites.

[22] Now the tribes of Joseph attacked Bethel, and the LORD was with them. [23] When they sent men to spy out Bethel (formerly called Luz), [24] the spies saw a man coming out of the city and they said to him, "Show us how to get into the city and we will see that you are treated well." [25] So he showed them, and they put the city to the sword but spared the man and his whole family. [26] He then went to the land of the Hittites, where he built a city and called it Luz, which is its name to this day.

[27] But Manasseh did not drive out the people of Beth Shan or Taanach or Dor or Ibleam or Megiddo and their surrounding settlements, for the Canaanites were determined to live in that land. [28] When Israel became strong, they pressed the Canaanites into forced labor but never drove them

---

a 14 Hebrew; Septuagint and Vulgate *Othniel, he urged her*   *b 16* That is, Jericho   *c 17* The Hebrew term refers to the irrevocable giving over of things or persons to the LORD, often by totally destroying them.   *d 17 Hormah* means *destruction.*   *e 18* Hebrew; Septuagint *Judah did not take*

out completely. [29] Nor did Ephraim drive out the Canaanites living in Gezer, but the Canaanites continued to live there among them. [30] Neither did Zebulun drive out the Canaanites living in Kitron or Nahalol, so these Canaanites lived among them, but Zebulun did subject them to forced labor. [31] Nor did Asher drive out those living in Akko or Sidon or Ahlab or Akzib or Helbah or Aphek or Rehob. [32] The Asherites lived among the Canaanite inhabitants of the land because they did not drive them out. [33] Neither did Naphtali drive out those living in Beth Shemesh or Beth Anath; but the Naphtalites too lived among the Canaanite inhabitants of the land, and those living in Beth Shemesh and Beth Anath became forced laborers for them. [34] The Amorites confined the Danites to the hill country, not allowing them to come down into the plain. [35] And the Amorites were determined also to hold out in Mount Heres, Aijalon and Shaalbim, but when the power of the tribes of Joseph increased, they too were pressed into forced labor. [36] The boundary of the Amorites was from Scorpion Pass to Sela and beyond.

The Angel of the LORD at Bokim

2 The angel of the LORD went up from Gilgal to Bokim and said, "I brought you up out of Egypt and led you into the land I swore to give to your ancestors. I said, 'I will never break my covenant with you, [2] and you shall not make a covenant with the people of this land, but you shall break down their altars.' Yet you have disobeyed me. Why have you done this? [3] And I have also said, 'I will not drive them out before you; they will become traps for you, and their gods will become snares to you.' "

[4] When the angel of the LORD had spoken these things to all the Israelites, the people wept aloud, [5] and they called that place Bokim.[a] There they offered sacrifices to the LORD.

Disobedience and Defeat

[6] After Joshua had dismissed the Israelites, they went to take possession of the land, each to their own inheritance. [7] The people served the LORD throughout the lifetime of Joshua and of the elders who outlived him and who had seen all the great things the LORD had done for Israel.

[8] Joshua son of Nun, the servant of the LORD, died at the age of a hundred and ten. [9] And they buried him in the land of his inheritance, at Timnath Heres[b] in the hill country of Ephraim, north of Mount Gaash.

[10] After that whole generation had been gathered to their ancestors, another generation grew up who knew neither the LORD nor what he had done for Israel. [11] Then the Israelites did evil in the eyes of the LORD and served the Baals. [12] They forsook the LORD, the God of their ancestors, who had brought them out of Egypt. They followed and worshiped various gods of the peoples around them. They aroused the LORD's anger [13] because they forsook him and served Baal and the Ashtoreths. [14] In his anger against Israel the LORD gave them into the hands of raiders who plundered them. He sold them into the hands of their enemies all around, whom they were no longer able to resist. [15] Whenever Israel went out to fight, the hand of the LORD was against them to defeat them, just as he had sworn to them. They were in great distress.

[16] Then the LORD raised up judges,[c] who saved them out of the hands of these raiders. [17] Yet they would not listen to their judges but prostituted themselves to other gods and worshiped them. They quickly turned from the ways of their ancestors, who had been obedient to the LORD's commands. [18] Whenever the LORD raised up a judge for them, he was with the judge and saved them out of the hands of their enemies as long as the judge lived; for the LORD relented because of their groaning under those who oppressed and afflicted them. [19] But when the judge died, the people returned to ways even more corrupt than those of their ancestors, following other gods and serving and worshiping them. They refused to give up their evil practices and stubborn ways.

---

[a] 5 *Bokim* means weepers.   [b] 9 Also known as *Timnath Serah* (see Joshua 19:50 and 24:30)   [c] 16 Or *leaders*; similarly in verses 17-19

20 Therefore the LORD was very angry with Israel and said, "Because this nation has violated the covenant I ordained for their ancestors and has not listened to me, 21 I will no longer drive out before them any of the nations Joshua left when he died. 22 I will use them to test Israel and see whether they will keep the way of the LORD and walk in it as their ancestors did." 23 The LORD had allowed those nations to remain; he did not drive them out at once by giving them into the hands of Joshua.

3 These are the nations the LORD left to test all those Israelites who had not experienced any of the wars in Canaan 2 (he did this only to teach warfare to the descendants of the Israelites who had not had previous battle experience): 3 the five rulers of the Philistines, all the Canaanites, the Sidonians, and the Hivites living in the Lebanon mountains from Mount Baal Hermon to Lebo Hamath. 4 They were left to test the Israelites to see whether they would obey the LORD's commands, which he had given their ancestors through Moses.

5 The Israelites lived among the Canaanites, Hittites, Amorites, Perizzites, Hivites and Jebusites. 6 They took their daughters in marriage and gave their own daughters to their sons, and served their gods.

Othniel

7 The Israelites did evil in the eyes of the LORD; they forgot the LORD their God and served the Baals and the Asherahs. 8 The anger of the LORD burned against Israel so that he sold them into the hands of Cushan-Rishathaim king of Aram Naharaim,[a] to whom the Israelites were subject for eight years. 9 But when they cried out to the LORD, he raised up for them a deliverer, Othniel son of Kenaz, Caleb's younger brother, who saved them. 10 The Spirit of the LORD came on him, so that he became Israel's judge[b] and went to war. The LORD gave Cushan-Rishathaim king of Aram into the hands of Othniel, who overpowered him. 11 So the land had peace for forty years, until Othniel son of Kenaz died.

Ehud

12 Again the Israelites did evil in the eyes of the LORD, and because they did this evil the LORD gave Eglon king of Moab power over Israel. 13 Getting the Ammonites and Amalekites to join him, Eglon came and attacked Israel, and they took possession of the City of Palms.[c] 14 The Israelites were subject to Eglon king of Moab for eighteen years.

15 Again the Israelites cried out to the LORD, and he gave them a deliverer—Ehud, a left-handed man, the son of Gera the Benjamite. The Israelites sent him with tribute to Eglon king of Moab. 16 Now Ehud had made a double-edged sword about a cubit[d] long, which he strapped to his right thigh under his clothing. 17 He presented the tribute to Eglon king of Moab, who was a very fat man. 18 After Ehud had presented the tribute, he sent on their way those who had carried it. 19 But on reaching the stone images near Gilgal he himself went back to Eglon and said, "Your Majesty, I have a secret message for you."

Judges 3

Q: What strange weapon did Shamgar use to fight the Philistines?

BONUS: What other strange weapon is mentioned in Judges?

Answers on next page

---

a 8 That is, Northwest Mesopotamia   b 10 Or leader
c 13 That is, Jericho   d 16 That is, about 18 inches or about 45 centimeters

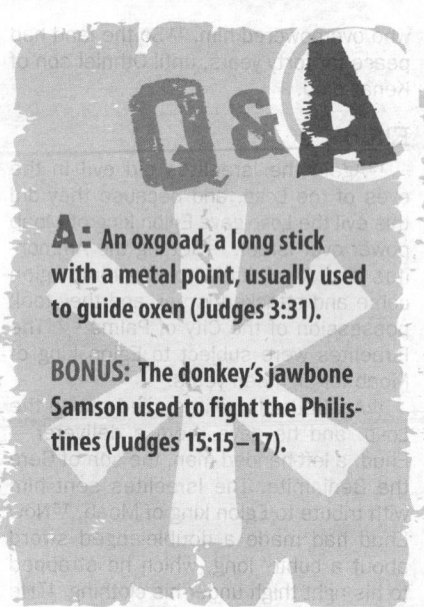

A: An oxgoad, a long stick with a metal point, usually used to guide oxen (Judges 3:31).

BONUS: The donkey's jawbone Samson used to fight the Philistines (Judges 15:15–17).

The king said to his attendants, "Leave us!" And they all left.

²⁰ Ehud then approached him while he was sitting alone in the upper room of his palace*a* and said, "I have a message from God for you." As the king rose from his seat, ²¹ Ehud reached with his left hand, drew the sword from his right thigh and plunged it into the king's belly. ²² Even the handle sank in after the blade, and his bowels discharged. Ehud did not pull the sword out, and the fat closed in over it. ²³ Then Ehud went out to the porch*b*; he shut the doors of the upper room behind him and locked them.

²⁴ After he had gone, the servants came and found the doors of the upper room locked. They said, "He must be relieving himself in the inner room of the palace." ²⁵ They waited to the point of embarrassment, but when he did not open the doors of the room, they took a key and unlocked them. There they saw their lord fallen to the floor, dead.

²⁶ While they waited, Ehud got away. He passed by the stone images and escaped to Seirah. ²⁷ When he arrived there,

he blew a trumpet in the hill country of Ephraim, and the Israelites went down with him from the hills, with him leading them.

²⁸ "Follow me," he ordered, "for the LORD has given Moab, your enemy, into your hands." So they followed him down and took possession of the fords of the Jordan that led to Moab; they allowed no one to cross over. ²⁹ At that time they struck down about ten thousand Moabites, all vigorous and strong; not one escaped. ³⁰ That day Moab was made subject to Israel, and the land had peace for eighty years.

Shamgar

³¹ After Ehud came Shamgar son of Anath, who struck down six hundred Philistines with an oxgoad. He too saved Israel.

Deborah

4 Again the Israelites did evil in the eyes of the LORD, now that Ehud was dead. ² So the LORD sold them into the hands of Jabin king of Canaan, who reigned in Hazor. Sisera, the commander of his army, was based in Harosheth Haggoyim. ³ Because he had nine hundred chariots fitted with iron and had cruelly oppressed the Israelites for twenty years, they cried to the LORD for help.

⁴ Now Deborah, a prophet, the wife of Lappidoth, was leading*c* Israel at that time. ⁵ She held court under the Palm of Deborah between Ramah and Bethel in the hill country of Ephraim, and the Israelites went up to her to have their disputes decided. ⁶ She sent for Barak son of Abinoam from Kedesh in Naphtali and said to him, "The LORD, the God of Israel, commands you: 'Go, take with you ten thousand men of Naphtali and Zebulun and lead them up to Mount Tabor. ⁷ I will lead Sisera, the commander of Jabin's army, with his chariots and his troops to the Kishon River and give him into your hands.'"

⁸ Barak said to her, "If you go with me,

---

a 20 The meaning of the Hebrew for this word is uncertain; also in verse 24.   *b 23* The meaning of the Hebrew for this word is uncertain.   *c 4* Traditionally *judging*

> I hear a lot of talk about whether women should be allowed to be leaders in the church. This isn't the Dark Ages. What are people thinking?
>
> >> Jonathan

Dear Jordan

Dear Jonathan,

Many denominations still have lots of conflict about this issue. Feelings run strong on both sides. If you read Judges 4–5, you will learn about a woman named Deborah. She was chosen by God to be a prophetess and the leader of Israel.

This story shows that God not only permits women to be leaders, but sometimes even appoints them. God gives the gift of leadership to both men and women. And he calls on each person to obey him and to use the gifts he has given.

Some denominations in the church interpret the Bible in a way that allows women to have many roles. Others limit how women are allowed to use their gifts. We must try to respect those who believe differently and study God's Word carefully. God desires love, respect, and the studying of his Word among his people.

Jordan

I will go; but if you don't go with me, I won't go."

⁹ "Certainly I will go with you," said Deborah. "But because of the course you are taking, the honor will not be yours, for the LORD will deliver Sisera into the hands of a woman." So Deborah went with Barak to Kedesh. ¹⁰ There Barak summoned Zebulun and Naphtali, and ten thousand men went up under his command. Deborah also went up with him.

¹¹ Now Heber the Kenite had left the other Kenites, the descendants of Hobab, Moses' brother-in-law,ᵃ and pitched his tent by the great tree in Zaanannim near Kedesh.

¹² When they told Sisera that Barak son of Abinoam had gone up to Mount Tabor, ¹³ Sisera summoned from Harosheth Haggoyim to the Kishon River all his men and his nine hundred chariots fitted with iron. ¹⁴ Then Deborah said to Barak, "Go! This is the day the LORD has given Sisera into your hands. Has not the LORD gone ahead of you?" So Barak went down Mount Tabor, with ten thousand men following him. ¹⁵ At Barak's advance, the LORD routed Sisera and all his chariots and army by the sword, and Sisera got down from his chariot and fled on foot.

¹⁶ Barak pursued the chariots and army as far as Harosheth Haggoyim, and all Sisera's troops fell by the sword; not a man was left. ¹⁷ Sisera, meanwhile, fled on foot to the tent of Jael, the wife of Heber the Kenite, because there was an alliance between Jabin king of Hazor and the family of Heber the Kenite.

¹⁸ Jael went out to meet Sisera and said to him, "Come, my lord, come right in. Don't be afraid." So he entered her tent, and she covered him with a blanket.

¹⁹ "I'm thirsty," he said. "Please give me some water." She opened a skin of milk, gave him a drink, and covered him up.

²⁰ "Stand in the doorway of the tent," he told her. "If someone comes by and asks you, 'Is anyone in there?' say 'No.'"

²¹ But Jael, Heber's wife, picked up a tent peg and a hammer and went quietly to him while he lay fast asleep, exhausted. She drove the peg through his temple into the ground, and he died.

²² Just then Barak came by in pursuit of Sisera, and Jael went out to meet him. "Come," she said, "I will show you the man you're looking for." So he went in with her, and there lay Sisera with the tent peg through his temple—dead.

²³ On that day God subdued Jabin king of Canaan before the Israelites. ²⁴ And the hand of the Israelites pressed harder and harder against Jabin king of Canaan until they destroyed him.

The Song of Deborah

5 On that day Deborah and Barak son of Abinoam sang this song:

² "When the princes in Israel take the lead,
 when the people willingly offer themselves—
 praise the LORD!

³ "Hear this, you kings! Listen, you rulers!
 I, even I, will sing toᵇ the LORD;
 I will praise the LORD, the God of Israel, in song.

⁴ "When you, LORD, went out from Seir,
 when you marched from the land of Edom,
 the earth shook, the heavens poured,
 the clouds poured down water.
⁵ The mountains quaked before the LORD, the One of Sinai,
 before the LORD, the God of Israel.

⁶ "In the days of Shamgar son of Anath,
 in the days of Jael, the highways were abandoned;
 travelers took to winding paths.
⁷ Villagers in Israel would not fight;
 they held back until I, Deborah, arose,
 until I arose, a mother in Israel.
⁸ God chose new leaders
 when war came to the city gates,
 but not a shield or spear was seen among forty thousand in Israel.

ᵃ 11 Or *father-in-law*   ᵇ 3 Or *of*

⁹My heart is with Israel's princes,
  with the willing volunteers among
    the people.
  Praise the LORD!

¹⁰"You who ride on white donkeys,
  sitting on your saddle blankets,
  and you who walk along the road,
  consider ¹¹the voice of the singers[a] at
    the watering places.
  They recite the victories of the LORD,
  the victories of his villagers in
    Israel.

"Then the people of the LORD
  went down to the city gates.
¹²'Wake up, wake up, Deborah!
  Wake up, wake up, break out in
    song!
  Arise, Barak!
  Take captive your captives, son of
    Abinoam.'

¹³"The remnant of the nobles came
    down;
  the people of the LORD came down
    to me against the mighty.
¹⁴Some came from Ephraim, whose
    roots were in Amalek;
  Benjamin was with the people who
    followed you.
  From Makir captains came down,
  from Zebulun those who bear a
    commander's[a] staff.
¹⁵The princes of Issachar were with
    Deborah;
  yes, Issachar was with Barak,
  sent under his command into the
    valley.
  In the districts of Reuben
  there was much searching of heart.
¹⁶Why did you stay among the sheep
    pens[b]
  to hear the whistling for the flocks?
  In the districts of Reuben
  there was much searching of heart.
¹⁷Gilead stayed beyond the Jordan.
  And Dan, why did he linger by the
    ships?
  Asher remained on the coast
  and stayed in his coves.
¹⁸The people of Zebulun risked their
    very lives;

so did Naphtali on the terraced
    fields.

¹⁹"Kings came, they fought,
  the kings of Canaan fought.
  At Taanach, by the waters of Megiddo,
  they took no plunder of silver.
²⁰From the heavens the stars fought,
  from their courses they fought
    against Sisera.
²¹The river Kishon swept them away,
  the age-old river, the river Kishon.
  March on, my soul; be strong!
²²Then thundered the horses' hooves—
  galloping, galloping go his mighty
    steeds.
²³'Curse Meroz,' said the angel of the
    LORD.
  'Curse its people bitterly,
  because they did not come to help the
    LORD,
  to help the LORD against the mighty.'

²⁴"Most blessed of women be Jael,
  the wife of Heber the Kenite,
  most blessed of tent-dwelling
    women.
²⁵He asked for water, and she gave him
    milk;
  in a bowl fit for nobles she brought
    him curdled milk.
²⁶Her hand reached for the tent peg,
  her right hand for the workman's
    hammer.
  She struck Sisera, she crushed his
    head,
  she shattered and pierced his
    temple.
²⁷At her feet he sank,
  he fell; there he lay.
  At her feet he sank, he fell;
  where he sank, there he fell—
    dead.

²⁸"Through the window peered Sisera's
    mother;
  behind the lattice she cried out,
  'Why is his chariot so long in coming?
  Why is the clatter of his chariots
    delayed?'
²⁹The wisest of her ladies answer her;
  indeed, she keeps saying to
    herself,

ᵃ 11,14 The meaning of the Hebrew for this word is uncertain. ᵇ 16 Or the campfires; or the saddlebags

30 'Are they not finding and dividing the
   spoils:
   a woman or two for each man,
colorful garments as plunder for
   Sisera,
   colorful garments embroidered,
highly embroidered garments for my
   neck—
   all this as plunder?'

31 "So may all your enemies perish,
   LORD!
   But may all who love you be like the
   sun
   when it rises in its strength."

Then the land had peace forty years.

Gideon

6 The Israelites did evil in the eyes of
the LORD, and for seven years he gave
them into the hands of the Midianites.
2 Because the power of Midian was so oppressive, the Israelites prepared shelters
for themselves in mountain clefts, caves
and strongholds. 3 Whenever the Israelites planted their crops, the Midianites,
Amalekites and other eastern peoples invaded the country. 4 They camped on the
land and ruined the crops all the way to
Gaza and did not spare a living thing for
Israel, neither sheep nor cattle nor donkeys. 5 They came up with their livestock
and their tents like swarms of locusts.
It was impossible to count them or their
camels; they invaded the land to ravage
it. 6 Midian so impoverished the Israelites
that they cried out to the LORD for help.

7 When the Israelites cried out to the
LORD because of Midian, 8 he sent them a
prophet, who said, "This is what the LORD,
the God of Israel, says: I brought you up
out of Egypt, out of the land of slavery. 9 I
rescued you from the hand of the Egyptians. And I delivered you from the hand
of all your oppressors; I drove them out
before you and gave you their land. 10 I
said to you, 'I am the LORD your God; do
not worship the gods of the Amorites, in
whose land you live.' But you have not
listened to me."

11 The angel of the LORD came and sat

down under the oak in Ophrah that belonged to Joash the Abiezrite, where his
son Gideon was threshing wheat in a
winepress to keep it from the Midianites.
12 When the angel of the LORD appeared
to Gideon, he said, "The LORD is with you,
mighty warrior."

13 "Pardon me, my lord," Gideon replied, "but if the LORD is with us, why has
all this happened to us? Where are all his
wonders that our ancestors told us about
when they said, 'Did not the LORD bring us
up out of Egypt?' But now the LORD has
abandoned us and given us into the hand
of Midian."

14 The LORD turned to him and said, "Go
in the strength you have and save Israel
out of Midian's hand. Am I not sending
you?"

15 "Pardon me, my lord," Gideon replied, "but how can I save Israel? My clan
is the weakest in Manasseh, and I am the
least in my family."

16 The LORD answered, "I will be with
you, and you will strike down all the Midianites, leaving none alive."

17 Gideon replied, "If now I have found
favor in your eyes, give me a sign that it is
really you talking to me. 18 Please do not
go away until I come back and bring my
offering and set it before you."

And the LORD said, "I will wait until you
return."

19 Gideon went inside, prepared a
young goat, and from an ephaha of flour
he made bread without yeast. Putting the
meat in a basket and its broth in a pot,
he brought them out and offered them to
him under the oak.

20 The angel of God said to him, "Take
the meat and the unleavened bread,
place them on this rock, and pour out the
broth." And Gideon did so. 21 Then the angel of the LORD touched the meat and the
unleavened bread with the tip of the staff
that was in his hand. Fire flared from the
rock, consuming the meat and the bread.
And the angel of the LORD disappeared.
22 When Gideon realized that it was the
angel of the LORD, he exclaimed, "Alas,
Sovereign LORD! I have seen the angel of
the LORD face to face!"

a 19 That is, probably about 36 pounds or about 16 kilograms

Gideon had a problem with his self-image. When God told him to save Israel from the Midianites, Gideon responded, "My clan is the weakest in Manasseh, and I am the least in my family" (Judges 6:15). But God said, "Go in the strength you have" (Judges 6:14). Gideon had strengths he hadn't yet discovered. And so do you! God has given you abilities that make you unique and strengths that make you able to triumph over your challenges. Sure, you feel as inadequate as Gideon did sometimes. But God has given you strengths that are greater than your weaknesses. And he has said to you as he did to Gideon, "I will be with you" (Judges 6:16).

{Judges 6:14–16}

INSTANT ACCESS

23 But the LORD said to him, "Peace! Do not be afraid. You are not going to die."

24 So Gideon built an altar to the LORD there and called it The LORD Is Peace. To this day it stands in Ophrah of the Abiezrites.

25 That same night the LORD said to him, "Take the second bull from your father's herd, the one seven years old.[a] Tear down your father's altar to Baal and cut down the Asherah pole[b] beside it. 26 Then build a proper kind of[c] altar to the LORD your God on the top of this height. Using the wood of the Asherah pole that you cut down, offer the second[d] bull as a burnt offering."

27 So Gideon took ten of his servants and did as the LORD told him. But because he was afraid of his family and the townspeople, he did it at night rather than in the daytime.

28 In the morning when the people of the town got up, there was Baal's altar, demolished, with the Asherah pole beside it cut down and the second bull sacrificed on the newly built altar!

29 They asked each other, "Who did this?"

When they carefully investigated, they were told, "Gideon son of Joash did it."

30 The people of the town demanded of Joash, "Bring out your son. He must die, because he has broken down Baal's altar and cut down the Asherah pole beside it."

31 But Joash replied to the hostile crowd around him, "Are you going to plead Baal's cause? Are you trying to save him? Whoever fights for him shall be put to death by morning! If Baal really is a god, he can defend himself when someone breaks down his altar." 32 So because Gideon broke down Baal's altar, they gave him the name Jerub-Baal[e] that day, saying, "Let Baal contend with him."

33 Now all the Midianites, Amalekites and other eastern peoples joined forces and crossed over the Jordan and camped in the Valley of Jezreel. 34 Then the Spirit of the LORD came on Gideon, and he blew a trumpet, summoning the Abiezrites to follow him. 35 He sent messengers throughout Manasseh, calling them to arms, and also into Asher, Zebulun and Naphtali, so that they too went up to meet them.

36 Gideon said to God, "If you will save Israel by my hand as you have promised— 37 look, I will place a wool fleece on the threshing floor. If there is dew only on the fleece and all the ground is dry, then I will know that you will save Israel by

---

[a] 25 Or Take a full-grown, mature bull from your father's herd, also in verses 26, 28 and 30   [c] 26 Or build with layers of stone an Baal probably means let Baal contend.   [b] 25 That is, a wooden symbol of the goddess Asherah;   [d] 26 Or full-grown; also in verse 28   [e] 32 Jerub-

my hand, as you said." 38And that is what happened. Gideon rose early the next day; he squeezed the fleece and wrung out the dew—a bowlful of water.

39Then Gideon said to God, "Do not be angry with me. Let me make just one more request. Allow me one more test with the fleece, but this time make the fleece dry and let the ground be covered with dew." 40That night God did so. Only the fleece was dry; all the ground was covered with dew.

Gideon Defeats the Midianites

7 Early in the morning, Jerub-Baal (that is, Gideon) and all his men camped at the spring of Harod. The camp of Midian was north of them in the valley near the hill of Moreh. 2The LORD said to Gideon, "You have too many men. I cannot deliver Midian into their hands, or Israel would boast against me, 'My own strength has saved me.' 3Now announce to the army, 'Anyone who trembles with fear may turn back and leave Mount Gilead.'" So twenty-two thousand men left, while ten thousand remained.

4But the LORD said to Gideon, "There are still too many men. Take them down to the water, and I will thin them out for you there. If I say, 'This one shall go with you,' he shall go; but if I say, 'This one shall not go with you,' he shall not go."

5So Gideon took the men down to the water. There the LORD told him, "Separate those who lap the water with their tongues as a dog laps from those who kneel down to drink." 6Three hundred of them drank from cupped hands, lapping like dogs. All the rest got down on their knees to drink.

7The LORD said to Gideon, "With the three hundred men that lapped I will save you and give the Midianites into your hands. Let all the others go home." 8So Gideon sent the rest of the Israelites home but kept the three hundred, who took over the provisions and trumpets of the others.

Now the camp of Midian lay below him in the valley. 9During that night the LORD said to Gideon, "Get up, go down against the camp, because I am going to give it into your hands. 10If you are afraid to attack, go down to the camp with your servant Purah 11and listen to what they are saying. Afterward, you will be encouraged to attack the camp." So he and Purah his servant went down to the outposts of the camp. 12The Midianites, the Amalekites and all the other eastern peoples had settled in the valley, thick as locusts. Their camels could no more be counted than the sand on the seashore.

13Gideon arrived just as a man was telling a friend his dream. "I had a dream," he was saying. "A round loaf of barley bread came tumbling into the Midianite camp. It struck the tent with such force that the tent overturned and collapsed."

14His friend responded, "This can be nothing other than the sword of Gideon son of Joash, the Israelite. God has given the Midianites and the whole camp into his hands."

15When Gideon heard the dream and its interpretation, he bowed down and worshiped. He returned to the camp of Israel and called out, "Get up! The LORD has given the Midianite camp into your hands." 16Dividing the three hundred men into three companies, he placed trumpets and empty jars in the hands of all of them, with torches inside.

17"Watch me," he told them. "Follow my lead. When I get to the edge of the camp, do exactly as I do. 18When I and all who are with me blow our trumpets, then from all around the camp blow yours and shout, 'For the LORD and for Gideon.'"

19Gideon and the hundred men with him reached the edge of the camp at the beginning of the middle watch, just after they had changed the guard. They blew their trumpets and broke the jars that were in their hands. 20The three companies blew the trumpets and smashed the jars. Grasping the torches in their left hands and holding in their right hands the trumpets they were to blow, they shouted, "A sword for the LORD and for Gideon!" 21While each man held his position around the camp, all the Midianites ran, crying out as they fled.

22When the three hundred trumpets sounded, the LORD caused the men throughout the camp to turn on each other with their swords. The army fled to Beth Shittah toward Zererah as far as the border of Abel Meholah near Tabbath. [23]Israelites from Naphtali, Asher and all Manasseh were called out, and they pursued the Midianites. [24]Gideon sent messengers throughout the hill country of Ephraim, saying, "Come down against the Midianites and seize the waters of the Jordan ahead of them as far as Beth Barah."

So all the men of Ephraim were called out and they seized the waters of the Jordan as far as Beth Barah. [25]They also captured two of the Midianite leaders, Oreb and Zeeb. They killed Oreb at the rock of Oreb, and Zeeb at the winepress of Zeeb. They pursued the Midianites and brought the heads of Oreb and Zeeb to Gideon, who was by the Jordan.

Zebah and Zalmunna

8 Now the Ephraimites asked Gideon, "Why have you treated us like this? Why didn't you call us when you went to fight Midian?" And they challenged him vigorously.

[2]But he answered them, "What have I accomplished compared to you? Aren't the gleanings of Ephraim's grapes better than the full grape harvest of Abiezer? [3]God gave Oreb and Zeeb, the Midianite leaders, into your hands. What was I able to do compared to you?" At this, their resentment against him subsided.

[4]Gideon and his three hundred men, exhausted yet keeping up the pursuit, came to the Jordan and crossed it. [5]He said to the men of Sukkoth, "Give my troops some bread; they are worn out, and I am still pursuing Zebah and Zalmunna, the kings of Midian."

[6]But the officials of Sukkoth said, "Do you already have the hands of Zebah and Zalmunna in your possession? Why should we give bread to your troops?"

[7]Then Gideon replied, "Just for that, when the LORD has given Zebah and Zalmunna into my hand, I will tear your flesh with desert thorns and briers."

[8]From there he went up to Peniel[a] and made the same request of them, but they answered as the men of Sukkoth had. [9]So he said to the men of Peniel, "When I return in triumph, I will tear down this tower."

[10]Now Zebah and Zalmunna were in Karkor with a force of about fifteen thousand men, all that were left of the armies of the eastern peoples; a hundred and twenty thousand swordsmen had fallen. [11]Gideon went up by the route of the nomads east of Nobah and Jogbehah and attacked the unsuspecting army. [12]Zebah and Zalmunna, the two kings of Midian, fled, but he pursued them and captured them, routing their entire army.

[13]Gideon son of Joash then returned from the battle by the Pass of Heres. [14]He caught a young man of Sukkoth and questioned him, and the young man wrote down for him the names of the seventy-seven officials of Sukkoth, the elders of the town. [15]Then Gideon came and said to the men of Sukkoth, "Here are Zebah and Zalmunna, about whom you taunted me by saying, 'Do you already have the hands of Zebah and Zalmunna in your possession? Why should we give bread to your exhausted men?'" [16]He took the elders of the town and taught the men of Sukkoth a lesson by punishing them with desert thorns and briers. [17]He also pulled down the tower of Peniel and killed the men of the town.

[18]Then he asked Zebah and Zalmunna, "What kind of men did you kill at Tabor?"

"Men like you," they answered, "each one with the bearing of a prince."

[19]Gideon replied, "Those were my brothers, the sons of my own mother. As surely as the LORD lives, if you had spared their lives, I would not kill you." [20]Turning to Jether, his oldest son, he said, "Kill them!" But Jether did not draw his sword, because he was only a boy and was afraid.

[21]Zebah and Zalmunna said, "Come, do it yourself. 'As is the man, so is his strength.'" So Gideon stepped forward and killed them, and took the ornaments off their camels' necks.

---

[a] 8 Hebrew *Penuel*, a variant of *Peniel*; also in verses 9 and 17

Gideon's Ephod

²²The Israelites said to Gideon, "Rule over us—you, your son and your grandson—because you have saved us from the hand of Midian."

²³But Gideon told them, "I will not rule over you, nor will my son rule over you. The LORD will rule over you." ²⁴And he said, "I do have one request, that each of you give me an earring from your share of the plunder." (It was the custom of the Ishmaelites to wear gold earrings.)

²⁵They answered, "We'll be glad to give them." So they spread out a garment, and each of them threw a ring from his plunder onto it. ²⁶The weight of the gold rings he asked for came to seventeen hundred shekels,ᵃ not counting the ornaments, the pendants and the purple garments worn by the kings of Midian or the chains that were on their camels' necks. ²⁷Gideon made the gold into an ephod, which he placed in Ophrah, his town. All Israel prostituted themselves by worshiping it there, and it became a snare to Gideon and his family.

Gideon's Death

²⁸Thus Midian was subdued before the Israelites and did not raise its head again. During Gideon's lifetime, the land had peace forty years.

²⁹Jerub-Baal son of Joash went back home to live. ³⁰He had seventy sons of his own, for he had many wives. ³¹His concubine, who lived in Shechem, also bore him a son, whom he named Abimelek. ³²Gideon son of Joash died at a good old age and was buried in the tomb of his father Joash in Ophrah of the Abiezrites.

³³No sooner had Gideon died than the Israelites again prostituted themselves to the Baals. They set up Baal-Berith as their god ³⁴and did not remember the LORD their God, who had rescued them from the hands of all their enemies on every side. ³⁵They also failed to show any loyalty to the family of Jerub-Baal (that is, Gideon) in spite of all the good things he had done for them.

Abimelek

9 Abimelek son of Jerub-Baal went to his mother's brothers in Shechem and said to them and to all his mother's clan, ²"Ask all the citizens of Shechem, 'Which is better for you: to have all seventy of Jerub-Baal's sons rule over you, or just one man?' Remember, I am your flesh and blood."

³When the brothers repeated all this to the citizens of Shechem, they were inclined to follow Abimelek, for they said, "He is related to us." ⁴They gave him seventy shekelsᵇ of silver from the temple of Baal-Berith, and Abimelek used it to hire reckless scoundrels, who became his followers. ⁵He went to his father's home in Ophrah and on one stone murdered his seventy brothers, the sons of Jerub-Baal. But Jotham, the youngest son of Jerub-Baal, escaped by hiding. ⁶Then all the citizens of Shechem and Beth Millo gathered beside the great tree at the pillar in Shechem to crown Abimelek king.

⁷When Jotham was told about this, he climbed up on the top of Mount Gerizim and shouted to them, "Listen to me, citizens of Shechem, so that God may listen to you. ⁸One day the trees went out to anoint a king for themselves. They said to the olive tree, 'Be our king.'

⁹"But the olive tree answered, 'Should I give up my oil, by which both gods and humans are honored, to hold sway over the trees?'

¹⁰"Next, the trees said to the fig tree, 'Come and be our king.'

¹¹"But the fig tree replied, 'Should I give up my fruit, so good and sweet, to hold sway over the trees?'

¹²"Then the trees said to the vine, 'Come and be our king.'

¹³"But the vine answered, 'Should I give up my wine, which cheers both gods and humans, to hold sway over the trees?'

¹⁴"Finally all the trees said to the thornbush, 'Come and be our king.'

¹⁵"The thornbush said to the trees, 'If you really want to anoint me king over

---

ᵃ 26 That is, about 43 pounds or about 20 kilograms   ᵇ 4 That is, about 1 3/4 pounds or about 800 grams

How important is it to trust people you call your friends? Judges 9 raises the question by describing the relationship between Abimelek and the citizens of Shechem, who plotted together to make Abimelek king. The story makes it very clear that people who get together to do wrong can't trust each other. True friendship is different. It's not based on doing wrong together; it's based on caring. As friendship deepens, friends share and learn that they can trust each other. What keeps you and your friends together? Can you trust them? Abimelek's "friends" weren't really friends. Are yours?

{Judges 9}

》》 INSTANT ACCESS

have murdered his seventy sons on a single stone and have made Abimelek, the son of his female slave, king over the citizens of Shechem because he is related to you. 19 So have you acted honorably and in good faith toward Jerub-Baal and his family today? If you have, may Abimelek be your joy, and may you be his, too! 20 But if you have not, let fire come out from Abimelek and consume you, the citizens of Shechem and Beth Millo, and let fire come out from you, the citizens of Shechem and Beth Millo, and consume Abimelek!"

21 Then Jotham fled, escaping to Beer, and he lived there because he was afraid of his brother Abimelek.

22 After Abimelek had governed Israel three years, 23 God stirred up animosity between Abimelek and the citizens of Shechem so that they acted treacherously against Abimelek. 24 God did this in order that the crime against Jerub-Baal's seventy sons, the shedding of their blood, might be avenged on their brother Abimelek and on the citizens of Shechem, who had helped him murder his brothers. 25 In opposition to him these citizens of Shechem set men on the hilltops to ambush and rob everyone who passed by, and this was reported to Abimelek.

26 Now Gaal son of Ebed moved with his clan into Shechem, and its citizens put their confidence in him. 27 After they had gone out into the fields and gathered the grapes and trodden them, they held a festival in the temple of their god. While they were eating and drinking, they cursed Abimelek. 28 Then Gaal son of Ebed said, "Who is Abimelek, and why should we Shechemites be subject to him? Isn't he Jerub-Baal's son, and isn't Zebul his deputy? Serve the family of Hamor, Shechem's father! Why should we serve Abimelek? 29 If only this people were under my command! Then I would get rid of him. I would say to Abimelek, 'Call out your whole army!' "[a]

30 When Zebul the governor of the city heard what Gaal son of Ebed said, he was very angry. 31 Under cover he sent messengers to Abimelek, saying, "Gaal son

you, come and take refuge in my shade; but if not, then let fire come out of the thornbush and consume the cedars of Lebanon!'

16 "Have you acted honorably and in good faith by making Abimelek king? Have you been fair to Jerub-Baal and his family? Have you treated him as he deserves? 17 Remember that my father fought for you and risked his life to rescue you from the hand of Midian. 18 But today you have revolted against my father's family. You

---

a 29 Septuagint; Hebrew *him.*" Then he said to Abimelek, "Call out your whole army!"

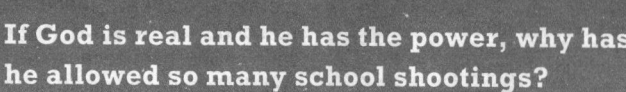

> If God is real and he has the power, why has he allowed so many school shootings?
>
> >> Blake

Dear Jordan

Dear Blake,

God is not a puppet master. Because we are made in his image and likeness, he gave us the opportunity to choose good or evil. He gave us free will. It would delight God if everyone chose to worship him and accepted Christ as Lord and Savior. But he won't force us.

Some people become very twisted and choose to do unimaginable violence to others. In the story of Abimelek found in Judges 9, a young man kills all of his brothers and sets himself up as king. We know God wants us to love one another. It grieves him just as it does us when we learn about school shootings and other needless violence.

Make no mistake about it. God is in control and God detests these murderous acts. One day, people will be called to account for their actions. Until then, people will suffer at the hands of evil ones. Not because God doesn't care, but because God is not running a puppet show.

Keep in mind Proverbs 24:1–2: "Do not envy the wicked, do not desire their company; for their hearts plot violence, and their lips talk about making trouble." We all make choices about who we hang out with and what we will do. We must be sure our focus remains on what is good in God's sight.

Jordan

of Ebed and his clan have come to Shechem and are stirring up the city against you. ³²Now then, during the night you and your men should come and lie in wait in the fields. ³³In the morning at sunrise, advance against the city. When Gaal and his men come out against you, seize the opportunity to attack them."

³⁴So Abimelek and all his troops set out by night and took up concealed positions near Shechem in four companies. ³⁵Now Gaal son of Ebed had gone out and was standing at the entrance of the city gate just as Abimelek and his troops came out from their hiding place.

³⁶When Gaal saw them, he said to Zebul, "Look, people are coming down from the tops of the mountains!"

Zebul replied, "You mistake the shadows of the mountains for men."

³⁷But Gaal spoke up again: "Look, people are coming down from the central hill,ª and a company is coming from the direction of the diviners' tree."

³⁸Then Zebul said to him, "Where is your big talk now, you who said, 'Who is Abimelek that we should be subject to him?' Aren't these the men you ridiculed? Go out and fight them!"

³⁹So Gaal led outᵇ the citizens of Shechem and fought Abimelek. ⁴⁰Abimelek chased him all the way to the entrance of the gate, and many were killed as they fled. ⁴¹Then Abimelek stayed in Arumah, and Zebul drove Gaal and his clan out of Shechem.

⁴²The next day the people of Shechem went out to the fields, and this was reported to Abimelek. ⁴³So he took his men, divided them into three companies and set an ambush in the fields. When he saw the people coming out of the city, he rose to attack them. ⁴⁴Abimelek and the companies with him rushed forward to a position at the entrance of the city gate. Then two companies attacked those in the fields and struck them down. ⁴⁵All that day Abimelek pressed his attack against the city until he had captured it and killed its people. Then he destroyed the city and scattered salt over it.

⁴⁶On hearing this, the citizens in the tower of Shechem went into the stronghold of the temple of El-Berith. ⁴⁷When Abimelek heard that they had assembled there, ⁴⁸he and all his men went up Mount Zalmon. He took an ax and cut off some branches, which he lifted to his shoulders. He ordered the men with him, "Quick! Do what you have seen me do!" ⁴⁹So all the men cut branches and followed Abimelek. They piled them against the stronghold and set it on fire with the people still inside. So all the people in the tower of Shechem, about a thousand men and women, also died.

⁵⁰Next Abimelek went to Thebez and besieged it and captured it. ⁵¹Inside the city, however, was a strong tower, to which all the men and women—all the people of the city—had fled. They had locked themselves in and climbed up on the tower roof. ⁵²Abimelek went to the tower and attacked it. But as he approached the entrance to the tower to set it on fire, ⁵³a woman dropped an upper millstone on his head and cracked his skull.

⁵⁴Hurriedly he called to his armor-bearer, "Draw your sword and kill me, so that they can't say, 'A woman killed him.'" So his servant ran him through, and he died. ⁵⁵When the Israelites saw that Abimelek was dead, they went home.

⁵⁶Thus God repaid the wickedness that Abimelek had done to his father by murdering his seventy brothers. ⁵⁷God also made the people of Shechem pay for all their wickedness. The curse of Jotham son of Jerub-Baal came on them.

Tola

10 After the time of Abimelek, a man of Issachar named Tola son of Puah, the son of Dodo, rose to save Israel. He lived in Shamir, in the hill country of Ephraim. ²He ledᶜ Israel twenty-three years; then he died, and was buried in Shamir.

Jair

³He was followed by Jair of Gilead, who led Israel twenty-two years. ⁴He had thirty sons, who rode thirty donkeys. They

---

ª 37 The Hebrew for this phrase means *the navel of the earth.*   ᵇ 39 Or *Gaal went out in the sight of*   ᶜ 2 Traditionally *judged*; also in verse 3

controlled thirty towns in Gilead, which to this day are called Havvoth Jair.ᵃ ⁵When Jair died, he was buried in Kamon.

Jephthah

⁶Again the Israelites did evil in the eyes of the LORD. They served the Baals and the Ashtoreths, and the gods of Aram, the gods of Sidon, the gods of Moab, the gods of the Ammonites and the gods of the Philistines. And because the Israelites forsook the LORD and no longer served him, ⁷he became angry with them. He sold them into the hands of the Philistines and the Ammonites, ⁸who that year shattered and crushed them. For eighteen years they oppressed all the Israelites on the east side of the Jordan in Gilead, the land of the Amorites. ⁹The Ammonites also crossed the Jordan to fight against Judah, Benjamin and Ephraim; Israel was in great distress. ¹⁰Then the Israelites cried out to the LORD, "We have sinned against you, forsaking our God and serving the Baals."

¹¹The LORD replied, "When the Egyptians, the Amorites, the Ammonites, the Philistines, ¹²the Sidonians, the Amalekites and the Maonitesᵇ oppressed you and you cried to me for help, did I not save you from their hands? ¹³But you have forsaken me and served other gods, so I will no longer save you. ¹⁴Go and cry out to the gods you have chosen. Let them save you when you are in trouble!"

¹⁵But the Israelites said to the LORD, "We have sinned. Do with us whatever you think best, but please rescue us now." ¹⁶Then they got rid of the foreign gods among them and served the LORD. And he could bear Israel's misery no longer.

¹⁷When the Ammonites were called to arms and camped in Gilead, the Israelites assembled and camped at Mizpah. ¹⁸The leaders of the people of Gilead said to each other, "Whoever will take the lead in attacking the Ammonites will be head over all who live in Gilead."

11 Jephthah the Gileadite was a mighty warrior. His father was Gilead; his mother was a prostitute. ²Gilead's wife also bore him sons, and when they were grown up, they drove Jephthah away. "You are not going to get any inheritance in our family," they said, "because you are the son of another woman." ³So Jephthah fled from his brothers and settled in the land of Tob, where a gang of scoundrels gathered around him and followed him.

⁴Some time later, when the Ammonites were fighting against Israel, ⁵the elders of Gilead went to get Jephthah from the land of Tob. ⁶"Come," they said, "be our commander, so we can fight the Ammonites."

⁷Jephthah said to them, "Didn't you hate me and drive me from my father's house? Why do you come to me now, when you're in trouble?"

⁸The elders of Gilead said to him, "Nevertheless, we are turning to you now; come with us to fight the Ammonites, and you will be head over all of us who live in Gilead."

⁹Jephthah answered, "Suppose you take me back to fight the Ammonites and the LORD gives them to me—will I really be your head?"

¹⁰The elders of Gilead replied, "The LORD is our witness; we will certainly do

Judges 10

Q: What were Baals and Ashtoreths?

BONUS: Why was it wrong to have anything to do with them?

Answers on next page

ᵃ 4 Or called the settlements of Jair   ᵇ 12 Hebrew; some Septuagint manuscripts Midianites

as you say." [11] So Jephthah went with the elders of Gilead, and the people made him head and commander over them. And he repeated all his words before the LORD in Mizpah.

[12] Then Jephthah sent messengers to the Ammonite king with the question: "What do you have against me that you have attacked my country?"

[13] The king of the Ammonites answered Jephthah's messengers, "When Israel came up out of Egypt, they took away my land from the Arnon to the Jabbok, all the way to the Jordan. Now give it back peaceably."

[14] Jephthah sent back messengers to the Ammonite king, [15] saying:

"This is what Jephthah says: Israel did not take the land of Moab or the land of the Ammonites. [16] But when they came up out of Egypt, Israel went through the wilderness to the Red Sea[a] and on to Kadesh. [17] Then Israel sent messengers to the king of Edom, saying, 'Give us permission to go through your country,' but the king of Edom would not listen. They sent also to the king of Moab, and he refused. So Israel stayed at Kadesh.

[18] "Next they traveled through the wilderness, skirted the lands of Edom and Moab, passed along the eastern side of the country of Moab, and camped on the other side of the Arnon. They did not enter the territory of Moab, for the Arnon was its border.

[19] "Then Israel sent messengers to Sihon king of the Amorites, who ruled in Heshbon, and said to him, 'Let us pass through your country to our own place.' [20] Sihon, however, did not trust Israel[b] to pass through his territory. He mustered all his troops and encamped at Jahaz and fought with Israel.

[21] "Then the LORD, the God of Israel, gave Sihon and his whole army into Israel's hands, and they defeated them. Israel took over all the land of the Amorites who lived in that country, [22] capturing all of it from the

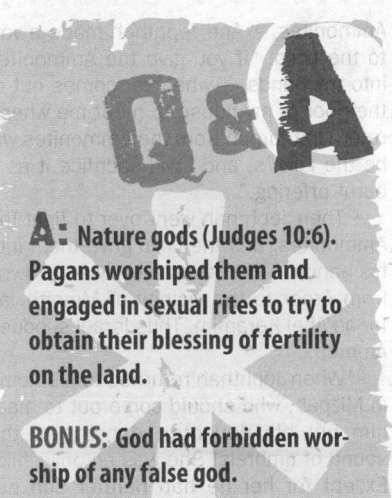

A: Nature gods (Judges 10:6). Pagans worshiped them and engaged in sexual rites to try to obtain their blessing of fertility on the land.

BONUS: God had forbidden worship of any false god.

Arnon to the Jabbok and from the desert to the Jordan.

[23] "Now since the LORD, the God of Israel, has driven the Amorites out before his people Israel, what right have you to take it over? [24] Will you not take what your god Chemosh gives you? Likewise, whatever the LORD our God has given us, we will possess. [25] Are you any better than Balak son of Zippor, king of Moab? Did he ever quarrel with Israel or fight with them? [26] For three hundred years Israel occupied Heshbon, Aroer, the surrounding settlements and all the towns along the Arnon. Why didn't you retake them during that time? [27] I have not wronged you, but you are doing me wrong by waging war against me. Let the LORD, the Judge, decide the dispute this day between the Israelites and the Ammonites."

[28] The king of Ammon, however, paid no attention to the message Jephthah sent him.

[29] Then the Spirit of the LORD came on Jephthah. He crossed Gilead and Manasseh, passed through Mizpah of Gilead, and from there he advanced against the

---

[a] 16 Or the Sea of Reeds   [b] 20 Or however, would not make an agreement for Israel

Ammonites. 30And Jephthah made a vow to the LORD: "If you give the Ammonites into my hands, 31whatever comes out of the door of my house to meet me when I return in triumph from the Ammonites will be the LORD's, and I will sacrifice it as a burnt offering."

32Then Jephthah went over to fight the Ammonites, and the LORD gave them into his hands. 33He devastated twenty towns from Aroer to the vicinity of Minnith, as far as Abel Keramim. Thus Israel subdued Ammon.

34When Jephthah returned to his home in Mizpah, who should come out to meet him but his daughter, dancing to the sound of timbrels! She was an only child. Except for her he had neither son nor daughter. 35When he saw her, he tore his clothes and cried, "Oh no, my daughter! You have brought me down and I am devastated. I have made a vow to the LORD that I cannot break."

36"My father," she replied, "you have given your word to the LORD. Do to me just as you promised, now that the LORD has avenged you of your enemies, the Ammonites. 37But grant me this one request," she said. "Give me two months to roam the hills and weep with my friends, because I will never marry."

38"You may go," he said. And he let her go for two months. She and her friends went into the hills and wept because she would never marry. 39After the two months, she returned to her father, and he did to her as he had vowed. And she was a virgin.

From this comes the Israelite tradition 40that each year the young women of Israel go out for four days to commemorate the daughter of Jephthah the Gileadite.

Jephthah and Ephraim

12 The Ephraimite forces were called out, and they crossed over to Zaphon. They said to Jephthah, "Why did you go to fight the Ammonites without calling us to go with you? We're going to burn down your house over your head."

2Jephthah answered, "I and my people

were engaged in a great struggle with the Ammonites, and although I called, you didn't save me out of their hands. 3When I saw that you wouldn't help, I took my life in my hands and crossed over to fight the Ammonites, and the LORD gave me the victory over them. Now why have you come up today to fight me?"

4Jephthah then called together the men of Gilead and fought against Ephraim. The Gileadites struck them down because the Ephraimites had said, "You Gileadites are renegades from Ephraim and Manasseh." 5The Gileadites captured the fords of the Jordan leading to Ephraim, and whenever a survivor of Ephraim said, "Let me cross over," the men of Gilead asked him, "Are you an Ephraimite?" If he replied, "No," 6they said, "All right, say 'Shibboleth.'" If he said, "Sibboleth," because he could not pronounce the word correctly, they seized him and killed him at the fords of the Jordan. Forty-two thousand Ephraimites were killed at that time.

7Jephthah led[a] Israel six years. Then Jephthah the Gileadite died and was buried in a town in Gilead.

Ibzan, Elon and Abdon

8After him, Ibzan of Bethlehem led Israel. 9He had thirty sons and thirty daughters. He gave his daughters away in marriage to those outside his clan, and for his sons he brought in thirty young women as wives from outside his clan. Ibzan led Israel seven years. 10Then Ibzan died and was buried in Bethlehem.

11After him, Elon the Zebulunite led Israel ten years. 12Then Elon died and was buried in Aijalon in the land of Zebulun.

13After him, Abdon son of Hillel, from Pirathon, led Israel. 14He had forty sons and thirty grandsons, who rode on seventy donkeys. He led Israel eight years. 15Then Abdon son of Hillel died and was buried at Pirathon in Ephraim, in the hill country of the Amalekites.

The Birth of Samson

13 Again the Israelites did evil in the eyes of the LORD, so the LORD de-

a 7 Traditionally judged; also in verses 8-14

INSTANT ACCESS

How often do you thank God for your parents? Are your mom and dad like Manoah and his wife? Do they look to God "to teach [them] how to bring up" you and your brothers or sisters? If so, you've got a lot to be thankful for. That doesn't mean your parents are perfect. Maybe you feel they're a little too strict. Or that they expect too much of you. Or that they don't give you the freedom you deserve. But if you sit down and make a list, chances are the positive things about your parents will outweigh the negatives.

{Judges 13:8}

livered them into the hands of the Philistines for forty years.

²A certain man of Zorah, named Manoah, from the clan of the Danites, had a wife who was childless, unable to give birth. ³The angel of the LORD appeared to her and said, "You are barren and childless, but you are going to become pregnant and give birth to a son. ⁴Now see to it that you drink no wine or other fermented drink and that you do not eat anything unclean. ⁵You will become pregnant and have a son whose head is never to be touched by a razor because the boy is to be a Nazirite, dedicated to God from the womb. He will take the lead in delivering Israel from the hands of the Philistines."

⁶Then the woman went to her husband and told him, "A man of God came to me. He looked like an angel of God, very awesome. I didn't ask him where he came from, and he didn't tell me his name. ⁷But he said to me, 'You will become pregnant and have a son. Now then, drink no wine or other fermented drink and do not eat anything unclean, because the boy will be a Nazirite of God from the womb until the day of his death.'"

⁸Then Manoah prayed to the LORD: "Pardon your servant, Lord. I beg you to let the man of God you sent to us come again to teach us how to bring up the boy who is to be born."

⁹God heard Manoah, and the angel of God came again to the woman while she was out in the field; but her husband Manoah was not with her. ¹⁰The woman hurried to tell her husband, "He's here! The man who appeared to me the other day!"

¹¹Manoah got up and followed his wife. When he came to the man, he said, "Are you the man who talked to my wife?"

"I am," he said.

¹²So Manoah asked him, "When your words are fulfilled, what is to be the rule that governs the boy's life and work?"

¹³The angel of the LORD answered, "Your wife must do all that I have told her. ¹⁴She must not eat anything that comes from the grapevine, nor drink any wine or other fermented drink nor eat anything unclean. She must do everything I have commanded her."

¹⁵Manoah said to the angel of the LORD, "We would like you to stay until we prepare a young goat for you."

¹⁶The angel of the LORD replied, "Even though you detain me, I will not eat any of your food. But if you prepare a burnt offering, offer it to the LORD." (Manoah did not realize that it was the angel of the LORD.)

¹⁷Then Manoah inquired of the angel of the LORD, "What is your name, so that we may honor you when your word comes true?"

¹⁸He replied, "Why do you ask my name? It is beyond understanding.ᵃ" ¹⁹Then Manoah took a young goat, together

---

ᵃ 18 Or is wonderful

with the grain offering, and sacrificed it on a rock to the LORD. And the LORD did an amazing thing while Manoah and his wife watched: 20As the flame blazed up from the altar toward heaven, the angel of the LORD ascended in the flame. Seeing this, Manoah and his wife fell with their faces to the ground. 21When the angel of the LORD did not show himself again to Manoah and his wife, Manoah realized that it was the angel of the LORD.

22"We are doomed to die!" he said to his wife. "We have seen God!"

23But his wife answered, "If the LORD had meant to kill us, he would not have accepted a burnt offering and grain offering from our hands, nor shown us all these things or now told us this."

24The woman gave birth to a boy and named him Samson. He grew and the LORD blessed him, 25and the Spirit of the LORD began to stir him while he was in Mahaneh Dan, between Zorah and Eshtaol.

Samson's Marriage

14 Samson went down to Timnah and saw there a young Philistine woman. 2When he returned, he said to his father and mother, "I have seen a Philistine woman in Timnah; now get her for me as my wife."

3His father and mother replied, "Isn't there an acceptable woman among your relatives or among all our people? Must you go to the uncircumcised Philistines to get a wife?"

But Samson said to his father, "Get her for me. She's the right one for me." 4(His parents did not know that this was from the LORD, who was seeking an occasion to confront the Philistines; for at that time they were ruling over Israel.)

5Samson went down to Timnah together with his father and mother. As they approached the vineyards of Timnah, suddenly a young lion came roaring toward him. 6The Spirit of the LORD came powerfully upon him so that he tore the lion apart with his bare hands as he might have torn a young goat. But he told neither his father nor his mother what

he had done. 7Then he went down and talked with the woman, and he liked her.

8Some time later, when he went back to marry her, he turned aside to look at the lion's carcass, and in it he saw a swarm of bees and some honey. 9He scooped out the honey with his hands and ate as he went along. When he rejoined his parents, he gave them some, and they too ate it. But he did not tell them that he had taken the honey from the lion's carcass.

10Now his father went down to see the woman. And there Samson held a feast, as was customary for young men. 11When the people saw him, they chose thirty men to be his companions.

12"Let me tell you a riddle," Samson said to them. "If you can give me the answer within the seven days of the feast, I will give you thirty linen garments and thirty sets of clothes. 13If you can't tell me the answer, you must give me thirty linen garments and thirty sets of clothes."

"Tell us your riddle," they said. "Let's hear it."

14He replied,

"Out of the eater, something to eat;
    out of the strong, something
        sweet."

For three days they could not give the answer.

15On the fourtha day, they said to Samson's wife, "Coax your husband into explaining the riddle for us, or we will burn you and your father's household to death. Did you invite us here to steal our property?"

16Then Samson's wife threw herself on him, sobbing, "You hate me! You don't really love me. You've given my people a riddle, but you haven't told me the answer."

"I haven't even explained it to my father or mother," he replied, "so why should I explain it to you?" 17She cried the whole seven days of the feast. So on the seventh day he finally told her, because she continued to press him. She in turn explained the riddle to her people.

---

a 15 Some Septuagint manuscripts and Syriac; Hebrew seventh

Samson had great parents (see Judges 13). He had a strong body. But history's super-jock was a spiritual flop. For all his exploits, Samson failed to free his people from Philistine rule. In fact, he never tried! All his battles were for personal revenge: "I merely did to them what they did to me" (Judges 15:11). You may be very talented. Athletic. Artistic. Smart. But how you use your talent is what counts. Use it selfishly, and in the long run your talent won't help you or anyone else. Commit your talent to God and use it to serve others, and you'll be a success.

{Judges 15}

18 Before sunset on the seventh day the men of the town said to him,

"What is sweeter than honey?
    What is stronger than a lion?"

Samson said to them,

"If you had not plowed with my heifer,
    you would not have solved my
        riddle."

19 Then the Spirit of the LORD came powerfully upon him. He went down to Ashkelon, struck down thirty of their men, stripped them of everything and gave their clothes to those who had explained the riddle. Burning with anger, he returned to his father's home. 20 And Samson's wife was given to one of his companions who had attended him at the feast.

Samson's Vengeance on the Philistines

15 Later on, at the time of wheat harvest, Samson took a young goat and went to visit his wife. He said, "I'm going to my wife's room." But her father would not let him go in.

2 "I was so sure you hated her," he said, "that I gave her to your companion. Isn't her younger sister more attractive? Take her instead."

3 Samson said to them, "This time I have a right to get even with the Philistines; I will really harm them." 4 So he went out and caught three hundred foxes and tied them tail to tail in pairs. He then fastened a torch to every pair of tails, 5 lit the torches and let the foxes loose in the standing grain of the Philistines. He burned up the shocks and standing grain, together with the vineyards and olive groves.

6 When the Philistines asked, "Who did this?" they were told, "Samson, the Timnite's son-in-law, because his wife was given to his companion."

So the Philistines went up and burned her and her father to death. 7 Samson said to them, "Since you've acted like this, I swear that I won't stop until I get my revenge on you." 8 He attacked them viciously and slaughtered many of them. Then he went down and stayed in a cave in the rock of Etam.

9 The Philistines went up and camped in Judah, spreading out near Lehi. 10 The people of Judah asked, "Why have you come to fight us?"

"We have come to take Samson prisoner," they answered, "to do to him as he did to us."

11 Then three thousand men from Judah went down to the cave in the rock of Etam and said to Samson, "Don't you realize that the Philistines are rulers over us? What have you done to us?"

He answered, "I merely did to them what they did to me."

12 They said to him, "We've come to tie you up and hand you over to the Philistines."

Samson said, "Swear to me that you won't kill me yourselves."

¹³"Agreed," they answered. "We will only tie you up and hand you over to them. We will not kill you." So they bound him with two new ropes and led him up from the rock. ¹⁴As he approached Lehi, the Philistines came toward him shouting. The Spirit of the LORD came powerfully upon him. The ropes on his arms became like charred flax, and the bindings dropped from his hands. ¹⁵Finding a fresh jawbone of a donkey, he grabbed it and struck down a thousand men.

¹⁶Then Samson said,

"With a donkey's jawbone
  I have made donkeys of them.ᵃ
With a donkey's jawbone
  I have killed a thousand men."

¹⁷When he finished speaking, he threw away the jawbone; and the place was called Ramath Lehi.ᵇ

¹⁸Because he was very thirsty, he cried out to the LORD, "You have given your servant this great victory. Must I now die of thirst and fall into the hands of the uncircumcised?" ¹⁹Then God opened up the hollow place in Lehi, and water came out of it. When Samson drank, his strength returned and he revived. So the spring was called En Hakkore,ᶜ and it is still there in Lehi.

²⁰Samson ledᵈ Israel for twenty years in the days of the Philistines.

Samson and Delilah

16 One day Samson went to Gaza, where he saw a prostitute. He went in to spend the night with her. ²The people of Gaza were told, "Samson is here!" So they surrounded the place and lay in wait for him all night at the city gate. They made no move during the night, saying, "At dawn we'll kill him."

³But Samson lay there only until the middle of the night. Then he got up and took hold of the doors of the city gate, together with the two posts, and tore them loose, bar and all. He lifted them to his

shoulders and carried them to the top of the hill that faces Hebron.

⁴Some time later, he fell in love with a woman in the Valley of Sorek whose name was Delilah. ⁵The rulers of the Philistines went to her and said, "See if you can lure him into showing you the secret of his great strength and how we can overpower him so we may tie him up and subdue him. Each one of us will give you eleven hundred shekelsᵉ of silver."

⁶So Delilah said to Samson, "Tell me the secret of your great strength and how you can be tied up and subdued."

⁷Samson answered her, "If anyone ties me with seven fresh bowstrings that have not been dried, I'll become as weak as any other man."

⁸Then the rulers of the Philistines brought her seven fresh bowstrings that had not been dried, and she tied him with them. ⁹With men hidden in the room, she called to him, "Samson, the Philistines are upon you!" But he snapped the bowstrings as easily as a piece of string snaps when it comes close to a flame. So the secret of his strength was not discovered.

¹⁰Then Delilah said to Samson, "You have made a fool of me; you lied to me. Come now, tell me how you can be tied."

¹¹He said, "If anyone ties me securely with new ropes that have never been used, I'll become as weak as any other man."

¹²So Delilah took new ropes and tied him with them. Then, with men hidden in the room, she called to him, "Samson, the Philistines are upon you!" But he snapped the ropes off his arms as if they were threads.

¹³Delilah then said to Samson, "All this time you have been making a fool of me and lying to me. Tell me how you can be tied."

He replied, "If you weave the seven braids of my head into the fabric on the loom and tighten it with the pin, I'll become as weak as any other man." So while he was sleeping, Delilah took the

---

ᵃ 16 Or *made a heap or two*; the Hebrew for *donkey* sounds like the Hebrew for *heap*.   ᵇ 17 *Ramath Lehi* means *jawbone hill.*   ᶜ 19 *En Hakkore* means *caller's spring.*   ᵈ 20 Traditionally *judged*   ᵉ 5 That is, about 28 pounds or about 13 kilograms

seven braids of his head, wove them into the fabric [14] and[a] tightened it with the pin.

Again she called to him, "Samson, the Philistines are upon you!" He awoke from his sleep and pulled up the pin and the loom, with the fabric.

[15] Then she said to him, "How can you say, 'I love you,' when you won't confide in me? This is the third time you have made a fool of me and haven't told me the secret of your great strength." [16] With such nagging she prodded him day after day until he was sick to death of it.

[17] So he told her everything. "No razor has ever been used on my head," he said, "because I have been a Nazirite dedicated to God from my mother's womb. If my head were shaved, my strength would leave me, and I would become as weak as any other man."

[18] When Delilah saw that he had told her everything, she sent word to the rulers of the Philistines, "Come back once more; he has told me everything." So the rulers of the Philistines returned with the silver in their hands. [19] After putting him to sleep on her lap, she called for someone to shave off the seven braids of his hair, and so began to subdue him.[b] And his strength left him.

[20] Then she called, "Samson, the Philistines are upon you!"

He awoke from his sleep and thought, "I'll go out as before and shake myself free." But he did not know that the LORD had left him.

[21] Then the Philistines seized him, gouged out his eyes and took him down to Gaza. Binding him with bronze shackles, they set him to grinding grain in the prison. [22] But the hair on his head began to grow again after it had been shaved.

The Death of Samson

[23] Now the rulers of the Philistines assembled to offer a great sacrifice to Dagon their god and to celebrate, saying, "Our god has delivered Samson, our enemy, into our hands."

[24] When the people saw him, they praised their god, saying,

"Our god has delivered our enemy
    into our hands,
the one who laid waste our land
    and multiplied our slain."

[25] While they were in high spirits, they shouted, "Bring out Samson to entertain us." So they called Samson out of the prison, and he performed for them.

When they stood him among the pillars, [26] Samson said to the servant who held his hand, "Put me where I can feel the pillars that support the temple, so that I may lean against them." [27] Now the temple was crowded with men and women; all the rulers of the Philistines were there, and on the roof were about three thousand men and women watching Samson perform. [28] Then Samson prayed to the LORD, "Sovereign LORD, remember me. Please, God, strengthen me just once more, and let me with one blow get revenge on the Philistines for my two eyes." [29] Then Samson reached toward the two central pillars on which the temple stood. Bracing himself against them, his right hand on the one and his left hand on the

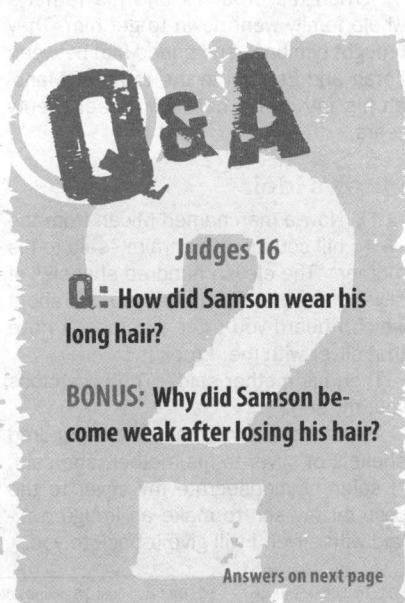

Judges 16

Q: How did Samson wear his long hair?

BONUS: Why did Samson become weak after losing his hair?

Answers on next page

---

[a] 13,14 Some Septuagint manuscripts; Hebrew *replied, "I can if you weave the seven braids of my head into the fabric on the loom."* [14] *So she*   [b] 19 Hebrew; some Septuagint manuscripts *and he began to weaken*

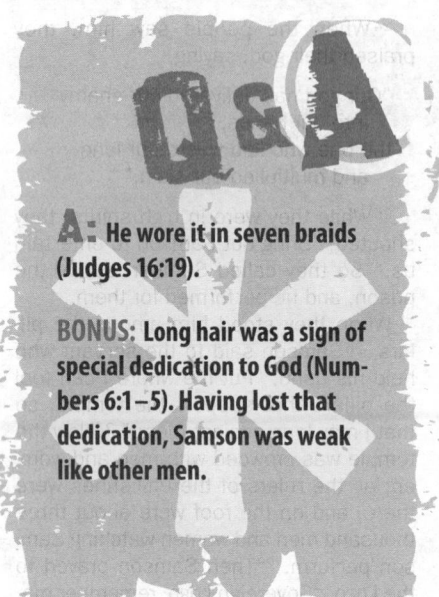

A: He wore it in seven braids (Judges 16:19).

BONUS: Long hair was a sign of special dedication to God (Numbers 6:1–5). Having lost that dedication, Samson was weak like other men.

other, ³⁰Samson said, "Let me die with the Philistines!" Then he pushed with all his might, and down came the temple on the rulers and all the people in it. Thus he killed many more when he died than while he lived.

³¹Then his brothers and his father's whole family went down to get him. They brought him back and buried him between Zorah and Eshtaol in the tomb of Manoah his father. He had led[a] Israel twenty years.

Micah's Idols

17 Now a man named Micah from the hill country of Ephraim ²said to his mother, "The eleven hundred shekels[b] of silver that were taken from you and about which I heard you utter a curse—I have that silver with me; I took it."

Then his mother said, "The LORD bless you, my son!"

³When he returned the eleven hundred shekels of silver to his mother, she said, "I solemnly consecrate my silver to the LORD for my son to make an image overlaid with silver. I will give it back to you."

⁴So after he returned the silver to his mother, she took two hundred shekels[c] of silver and gave them to a silversmith, who used them to make the idol. And it was put in Micah's house.

⁵Now this man Micah had a shrine, and he made an ephod and some household gods and installed one of his sons as his priest. ⁶In those days Israel had no king; everyone did as they saw fit.

⁷A young Levite from Bethlehem in Judah, who had been living within the clan of Judah, ⁸left that town in search of some other place to stay. On his way[d] he came to Micah's house in the hill country of Ephraim.

⁹Micah asked him, "Where are you from?"

"I'm a Levite from Bethlehem in Judah," he said, "and I'm looking for a place to stay."

¹⁰Then Micah said to him, "Live with me and be my father and priest, and I'll give you ten shekels[e] of silver a year, your clothes and your food." ¹¹So the Levite agreed to live with him, and the young man became like one of his sons to him. ¹²Then Micah installed the Levite, and the young man became his priest and lived in his house. ¹³And Micah said, "Now I know that the LORD will be good to me, since this Levite has become my priest."

The Danites Settle in Laish

18 In those days Israel had no king.

And in those days the tribe of the Danites was seeking a place of their own where they might settle, because they had not yet come into an inheritance among the tribes of Israel. ²So the Danites sent five of their leading men from Zorah and Eshtaol to spy out the land and explore it. These men represented all the Danites. They told them, "Go, explore the land."

So they entered the hill country of Ephraim and came to the house of Micah, where they spent the night. ³When they were near Micah's house, they recognized the voice of the young Levite; so they turned in there and asked him, "Who

a 31 Traditionally *judged*   b 2 That is, about 28 pounds or about 13 kilograms   c 4 That is, about 5 pounds or about 2.3 kilograms   d 8 Or *To carry on his profession*   e 10 That is, about 4 ounces or about 115 grams

brought you here? What are you doing in this place? Why are you here?"

[4] He told them what Micah had done for him, and said, "He has hired me and I am his priest."

[5] Then they said to him, "Please inquire of God to learn whether our journey will be successful."

[6] The priest answered them, "Go in peace. Your journey has the LORD's approval."

[7] So the five men left and came to Laish, where they saw that the people were living in safety, like the Sidonians, at peace and secure. And since their land lacked nothing, they were prosperous.[a] Also, they lived a long way from the Sidonians and had no relationship with anyone else.[b]

[8] When they returned to Zorah and Eshtaol, their fellow Danites asked them, "How did you find things?"

[9] They answered, "Come on, let's attack them! We have seen the land, and it is very good. Aren't you going to do something? Don't hesitate to go there and take it over. [10] When you get there, you will find an unsuspecting people and a spacious land that God has put into your hands, a land that lacks nothing whatever."

[11] Then six hundred men of the Danites, armed for battle, set out from Zorah and Eshtaol. [12] On their way they set up camp near Kiriath Jearim in Judah. This

is why the place west of Kiriath Jearim is called Mahaneh Dan[c] to this day. [13] From there they went on to the hill country of Ephraim and came to Micah's house.

[14] Then the five men who had spied out the land of Laish said to their fellow Danites, "Do you know that one of these houses has an ephod, some household gods and an image overlaid with silver? Now you know what to do." [15] So they turned in there and went to the house of the young Levite at Micah's place and greeted him. [16] The six hundred Danites, armed for battle, stood at the entrance of the gate. [17] The five men who had spied out the land went inside and took the idol, the ephod and the household gods while the priest and the six hundred armed men stood at the entrance of the gate.

[18] When the five men went into Micah's house and took the idol, the ephod and the household gods, the priest said to them, "What are you doing?"

[19] They answered him, "Be quiet! Don't say a word. Come with us, and be our father and priest. Isn't it better that you serve a tribe and clan in Israel as priest rather than just one man's household?" [20] The priest was very pleased. He took the ephod, the household gods and the idol and went along with the people. [21] Putting their little children, their livestock and their possessions in front of them, they turned away and left.

---

[a] 7 The meaning of the Hebrew for this clause is uncertain. Arameans   [c] 12 *Mahaneh Dan* means *Dan's camp.*   [b] 7 Hebrew; some Septuagint manuscripts *with the*

Rules.

This book tells what happened to the Israelites when they didn't follow them. Not a pretty picture.

PANORAMA

{JUDGES}

22When they had gone some distance from Micah's house, the men who lived near Micah were called together and overtook the Danites. 23As they shouted after them, the Danites turned and said to Micah, "What's the matter with you that you called out your men to fight?"

24He replied, "You took the gods I made, and my priest, and went away. What else do I have? How can you ask, 'What's the matter with you?'"

25The Danites answered, "Don't argue with us, or some of the men may get angry and attack you, and you and your family will lose your lives." 26So the Danites went their way, and Micah, seeing that they were too strong for him, turned around and went back home.

27Then they took what Micah had made, and his priest, and went on to Laish, against a people at peace and secure. They attacked them with the sword and burned down their city. 28There was no one to rescue them because they lived a long way from Sidon and had no relationship with anyone else. The city was in a valley near Beth Rehob.

The Danites rebuilt the city and settled there. 29They named it Dan after their ancestor Dan, who was born to Israel—though the city used to be called Laish. 30There the Danites set up for themselves the idol, and Jonathan son of Gershom, the son of Moses,a and his sons were priests for the tribe of Dan until the time of the captivity of the land. 31They continued to use the idol Micah had made, all the time the house of God was in Shiloh.

A Levite and His Concubine

19 In those days Israel had no king. Now a Levite who lived in a remote area in the hill country of Ephraim took a concubine from Bethlehem in Judah. 2But she was unfaithful to him. She left him and went back to her parents' home in Bethlehem, Judah. After she had been there four months, 3her husband went to her to persuade her to return. He had with him his servant and two donkeys.

She took him into her parents' home, and when her father saw him, he gladly welcomed him. 4His father-in-law, the woman's father, prevailed on him to stay; so he remained with him three days, eating and drinking, and sleeping there.

5On the fourth day they got up early and he prepared to leave, but the woman's father said to his son-in-law, "Refresh yourself with something to eat; then you can go." 6So the two of them sat down to eat and drink together. Afterward the woman's father said, "Please stay tonight and enjoy yourself." 7And when the man got up to go, his father-in-law persuaded him, so he stayed there that night. 8On the morning of the fifth day, when he rose to go, the woman's father said, "Refresh yourself. Wait till afternoon!" So the two of them ate together.

9Then when the man, with his concubine and his servant, got up to leave, his father-in-law, the woman's father, said, "Now look, it's almost evening. Spend the night here; the day is nearly over. Stay and enjoy yourself. Early tomorrow morning you can get up and be on your way home." 10But, unwilling to stay another night, the man left and went toward Jebus (that is, Jerusalem), with his two saddled donkeys and his concubine.

11When they were near Jebus and the day was almost gone, the servant said to his master, "Come, let's stop at this city of the Jebusites and spend the night."

12His master replied, "No. We won't go into any city whose people are not Israelites. We will go on to Gibeah." 13He added, "Come, let's try to reach Gibeah or Ramah and spend the night in one of those places." 14So they went on, and the sun set as they neared Gibeah in Benjamin. 15There they stopped to spend the night. They went and sat in the city square, but no one took them in for the night.

16That evening an old man from the hill country of Ephraim, who was living in Gibeah (the inhabitants of the place were Benjamites), came in from his work in the fields. 17When he looked and saw the

---

a 30 Many Hebrew manuscripts, some Septuagint manuscripts and Vulgate; many other Hebrew manuscripts and some other Septuagint manuscripts *Manasseh*

Have you ever heard someone defend X-rated books and movies by saying the Bible has the same kinds of stories? Like this one. It's got homosexuality, gang rape, even the cutting up of a dead body. Hey, it's just like today's movies! There is one difference though. X-rated books and movies cater to passion. They're intended to excite or thrill. The Bible's real-life stories, however, underline how terrible these sins are. So don't fall for the argument that sex and violence in movies is the same as sex and violence in the Bible. Today's books and movies try to make sin glamorous. The Bible shows sin for what it really is.

{Judges 19}

INSTANT ACCESS

traveler in the city square, the old man asked, "Where are you going? Where did you come from?"

¹⁸He answered, "We are on our way from Bethlehem in Judah to a remote area in the hill country of Ephraim where I live. I have been to Bethlehem in Judah and now I am going to the house of the LORD.ᵃ No one has taken me in for the night. ¹⁹We have both straw and fodder for our donkeys and bread and wine for ourselves your servants—me, the wom-

an and the young man with us. We don't need anything."

²⁰"You are welcome at my house," the old man said. "Let me supply whatever you need. Only don't spend the night in the square." ²¹So he took him into his house and fed his donkeys. After they had washed their feet, they had something to eat and drink.

²²While they were enjoying themselves, some of the wicked men of the city surrounded the house. Pounding on the door, they shouted to the old man who owned the house, "Bring out the man who came to your house so we can have sex with him."

²³The owner of the house went outside and said to them, "No, my friends, don't be so vile. Since this man is my guest, don't do this outrageous thing. ²⁴Look, here is my virgin daughter, and his concubine. I will bring them out to you now, and you can use them and do to them whatever you wish. But as for this man, don't do such an outrageous thing."

²⁵But the men would not listen to him. So the man took his concubine and sent her outside to them, and they raped her and abused her throughout the night, and at dawn they let her go. ²⁶At daybreak the woman went back to the house where her master was staying, fell down at the door and lay there until daylight.

²⁷When her master got up in the morning and opened the door of the house and stepped out to continue on his way, there lay his concubine, fallen in the doorway of the house, with her hands on the threshold. ²⁸He said to her, "Get up; let's go." But there was no answer. Then the man put her on his donkey and set out for home.

²⁹When he reached home, he took a knife and cut up his concubine, limb by limb, into twelve parts and sent them into all the areas of Israel. ³⁰Everyone who saw it was saying to one another, "Such a thing has never been seen or done, not since the day the Israelites came up out of Egypt. Just imagine! We must do something! So speak up!"

ᵃ *18* Hebrew, Vulgate, Syriac and Targum; Septuagint *going home*

The Israelites Punish the Benjamites

20 Then all Israel from Dan to Beersheba and from the land of Gilead came together as one and assembled before the LORD in Mizpah. ²The leaders of all the people of the tribes of Israel took their places in the assembly of God's people, four hundred thousand men armed with swords. ³(The Benjamites heard that the Israelites had gone up to Mizpah.) Then the Israelites said, "Tell us how this awful thing happened."

⁴So the Levite, the husband of the murdered woman, said, "I and my concubine came to Gibeah in Benjamin to spend the night. ⁵During the night the men of Gibeah came after me and surrounded the house, intending to kill me. They raped my concubine, and she died. ⁶I took my concubine, cut her into pieces and sent one piece to each region of Israel's inheritance, because they committed this lewd and outrageous act in Israel. ⁷Now, all you Israelites, speak up and tell me what you have decided to do."

⁸All the men rose up together as one, saying, "None of us will go home. No, not one of us will return to his house. ⁹But now this is what we'll do to Gibeah: We'll go up against it in the order decided by casting lots. ¹⁰We'll take ten men out of every hundred from all the tribes of Israel, and a hundred from a thousand, and a thousand from ten thousand, to get provisions for the army. Then, when the army arrives at Gibeahᵃ in Benjamin, it can give them what they deserve for this outrageous act done in Israel." ¹¹So all the Israelites got together and united as one against the city.

¹²The tribes of Israel sent messengers throughout the tribe of Benjamin, saying, "What about this awful crime that was committed among you? ¹³Now turn those wicked men of Gibeah over to us so that we may put them to death and purge the evil from Israel."

But the Benjamites would not listen to their fellow Israelites. ¹⁴From their towns they came together at Gibeah to fight against the Israelites. ¹⁵At once the Benjamites mobilized twenty-six thousand swordsmen from their towns, in addition to seven hundred able young men from those living in Gibeah. ¹⁶Among all these soldiers there were seven hundred select troops who were left-handed, each of whom could sling a stone at a hair and not miss.

¹⁷Israel, apart from Benjamin, mustered four hundred thousand swordsmen, all of them fit for battle.

¹⁸The Israelites went up to Bethelᵇ and inquired of God. They said, "Who of us is to go up first to fight against the Benjamites?"

The LORD replied, "Judah shall go first."

¹⁹The next morning the Israelites got up and pitched camp near Gibeah. ²⁰The Israelites went out to fight the Benjamites and took up battle positions against them at Gibeah. ²¹The Benjamites came out of Gibeah and cut down twenty-two thousand Israelites on the battlefield that day. ²²But the Israelites encouraged one another and again took up their positions where they had stationed themselves the first day. ²³The Israelites went up and wept before the LORD until evening, and they inquired of the LORD. They said, "Shall we go up again to fight against the Benjamites, our fellow Israelites?"

The LORD answered, "Go up against them."

²⁴Then the Israelites drew near to Benjamin the second day. ²⁵This time, when the Benjamites came out from Gibeah to oppose them, they cut down another eighteen thousand Israelites, all of them armed with swords.

²⁶Then all the Israelites, the whole army, went up to Bethel, and there they sat weeping before the LORD. They fasted that day until evening and presented burnt offerings and fellowship offerings to the LORD. ²⁷And the Israelites inquired of the LORD. (In those days the ark of the covenant of God was there, ²⁸with Phinehas son of Eleazar, the son of Aaron, ministering before it.) They asked, "Shall

---

ᵃ 10 One Hebrew manuscript; most Hebrew manuscripts *Geba*, a variant of *Gibeah*   ᵇ 18 Or *to the house of God*; also in verse 26

we go up again to fight against the Benjamites, our fellow Israelites, or not?"

The Lord responded, "Go, for tomorrow I will give them into your hands."

²⁹Then Israel set an ambush around Gibeah. ³⁰They went up against the Benjamites on the third day and took up positions against Gibeah as they had done before. ³¹The Benjamites came out to meet them and were drawn away from the city. They began to inflict casualties on the Israelites as before, so that about thirty men fell in the open field and on the roads—the one leading to Bethel and the other to Gibeah. ³²While the Benjamites were saying, "We are defeating them as before," the Israelites were saying, "Let's retreat and draw them away from the city to the roads."

³³All the men of Israel moved from their places and took up positions at Baal Tamar, and the Israelite ambush charged out of its place on the west*a* of Gibeah.*b* ³⁴Then ten thousand of Israel's able young men made a frontal attack on Gibeah. The fighting was so heavy that the Benjamites did not realize how near disaster was. ³⁵The Lord defeated Benjamin before Israel, and on that day the Israelites struck down 25,100 Benjamites, all armed with swords. ³⁶Then the Benjamites saw that they were beaten.

Now the men of Israel had given way before Benjamin, because they relied on the ambush they had set near Gibeah. ³⁷Those who had been in ambush made a sudden dash into Gibeah, spread out and put the whole city to the sword. ³⁸The Israelites had arranged with the ambush that they should send up a great cloud of smoke from the city, ³⁹and then the Israelites would counterattack.

The Benjamites had begun to inflict casualties on the Israelites (about thirty), and they said, "We are defeating them as in the first battle." ⁴⁰But when the column of smoke began to rise from the city, the Benjamites turned and saw the whole city going up in smoke. ⁴¹Then the Israelites counterattacked, and the Benjamites were terrified, because they realized that disaster had come on them. ⁴²So they fled before the Israelites in the direction of the wilderness, but they could not escape the battle. And the Israelites who came out of the towns cut them down there. ⁴³They surrounded the Benjamites, chased them and easily*c* overran them in the vicinity of Gibeah on the east. ⁴⁴Eighteen thousand Benjamites fell, all of them valiant fighters. ⁴⁵As they turned and fled toward the wilderness to the rock of Rimmon, the Israelites cut down five thousand men along the roads. They kept pressing after the Benjamites as far as Gidom and struck down two thousand more.

⁴⁶On that day twenty-five thousand Benjamite swordsmen fell, all of them valiant fighters. ⁴⁷But six hundred of them turned and fled into the wilderness to the rock of Rimmon, where they stayed four months. ⁴⁸The men of Israel went back to Benjamin and put all the towns to the sword, including the animals and everything else they found. All the towns they came across they set on fire.

Wives for the Benjamites

21 The men of Israel had taken an oath at Mizpah: "Not one of us will give his daughter in marriage to a Benjamite."

²The people went to Bethel,*d* where they sat before God until evening, raising their voices and weeping bitterly. ³"Lord, God of Israel," they cried, "why has this happened to Israel? Why should one tribe be missing from Israel today?"

⁴Early the next day the people built an altar and presented burnt offerings and fellowship offerings.

⁵Then the Israelites asked, "Who from all the tribes of Israel has failed to assemble before the Lord?" For they had taken a solemn oath that anyone who failed to assemble before the Lord at Mizpah was to be put to death.

⁶Now the Israelites grieved for the tribe of Benjamin, their fellow Israelites. "Today one tribe is cut off from Israel," they said. ⁷"How can we provide wives for

---

a 33 Some Septuagint manuscripts and Vulgate; the meaning of the Hebrew for this word is uncertain.   *b 33* Hebrew *Geba,* a variant of *Gibeah*   *c 43* The meaning of the Hebrew for this word is uncertain.   *d 2* Or *to the house of God*

those who are left, since we have taken an oath by the LORD not to give them any of our daughters in marriage?" ⁸Then they asked, "Which one of the tribes of Israel failed to assemble before the LORD at Mizpah?" They discovered that no one from Jabesh Gilead had come to the camp for the assembly. ⁹For when they counted the people, they found that none of the people of Jabesh Gilead were there.

¹⁰So the assembly sent twelve thousand fighting men with instructions to go to Jabesh Gilead and put to the sword those living there, including the women and children. ¹¹"This is what you are to do," they said. "Kill every male and every woman who is not a virgin." ¹²They found among the people living in Jabesh Gilead four hundred young women who had never slept with a man, and they took them to the camp at Shiloh in Canaan.

¹³Then the whole assembly sent an offer of peace to the Benjamites at the rock of Rimmon. ¹⁴So the Benjamites returned at that time and were given the women of Jabesh Gilead who had been spared. But there were not enough for all of them.

¹⁵The people grieved for Benjamin, because the LORD had made a gap in the tribes of Israel. ¹⁶And the elders of the assembly said, "With the women of Benjamin destroyed, how shall we provide wives for the men who are left? ¹⁷The Benjamite survivors must have heirs,"

they said, "so that a tribe of Israel will not be wiped out. ¹⁸We can't give them our daughters as wives, since we Israelites have taken this oath: 'Cursed be anyone who gives a wife to a Benjamite.' ¹⁹But look, there is the annual festival of the LORD in Shiloh, which lies north of Bethel, east of the road that goes from Bethel to Shechem, and south of Lebonah."

²⁰So they instructed the Benjamites, saying, "Go and hide in the vineyards ²¹and watch. When the young women of Shiloh come out to join in the dancing, rush from the vineyards and each of you seize one of them to be your wife. Then return to the land of Benjamin. ²²When their fathers or brothers complain to us, we will say to them, 'Do us the favor of helping them, because we did not get wives for them during the war. You will not be guilty of breaking your oath because you did not give your daughters to them.' "

²³So that is what the Benjamites did. While the young women were dancing, each man caught one and carried her off to be his wife. Then they returned to their inheritance and rebuilt the towns and settled in them.

²⁴At that time the Israelites left that place and went home to their tribes and clans, each to his own inheritance.

²⁵In those days Israel had no king; everyone did as they saw fit.

RUTH

Friends.

What makes someone a good friend?

A friend is someone you like being with and can talk to. Someone you can count on when you're feeling down, need help, or just want to have fun.

Ruth was a Moabite widow who was a true friend to her Israelite mother-in-law, Naomi. That friendship led Ruth to accept Naomi's God and to go and live with Naomi in Israel. People admired Ruth for her devotion to Naomi, and Ruth soon remarried. But Ruth is remembered for more than friendship: she was an ancestor of King David and of Jesus Christ.

>>**RUTH PROVES HER FRIENDSHIP**
 "I'll never leave," widow pledges. Report in Ruth 1

>>**RUTH'S GOOD REPUTATION PAYS**
 Immigrant welcomed, Ruth 2

>>**CHILD HEALS HEARTACHES**
 Infant heals aged widow's pain, Ruth 4

preview

The name "Ruth" means "friendship."

Ruth lived during the time of the judges.

In those days a close relative who helped a widow was called the "guardian-redeemer."

God's Son became a human being so he could be our redeemer.

During this period Phoenician ships trade all along the Mediterranean coast. Troy is attacked by the Greeks. And silk fabrics are woven in China.

Naomi Loses Her Husband and Sons

1 In the days when the judges ruled,[a] there was a famine in the land. So a man from Bethlehem in Judah, together with his wife and two sons, went to live for a while in the country of Moab. ²The man's name was Elimelek, his wife's name was Naomi, and the names of his two sons were Mahlon and Kilion. They were Ephrathites from Bethlehem, Judah. And they went to Moab and lived there.

³Now Elimelek, Naomi's husband, died, and she was left with her two sons. ⁴They married Moabite women, one named Orpah and the other Ruth. After they had lived there about ten years, ⁵both Mahlon and Kilion also died, and Naomi was left without her two sons and her husband.

Naomi and Ruth Return to Bethlehem

⁶When Naomi heard in Moab that the LORD had come to the aid of his people by providing food for them, she and her daughters-in-law prepared to return home from there. ⁷With her two daughters-in-law she left the place where she had been living and set out on the road that would take them back to the land of Judah.

⁸Then Naomi said to her two daughters-in-law, "Go back, each of you, to your mother's home. May the LORD show you kindness, as you have shown kindness to your dead husbands and to me. ⁹May the LORD grant that each of you will find rest in the home of another husband."

Then she kissed them goodbye and they wept aloud ¹⁰and said to her, "We will go back with you to your people."

¹¹But Naomi said, "Return home, my daughters. Why would you come with me? Am I going to have any more sons, who could become your husbands? ¹²Return home, my daughters; I am too old to have another husband. Even if I thought there was still hope for me—even if I had a husband tonight and then gave birth to sons— ¹³would you wait until they grew up? Would you remain unmarried for them? No, my daughters. It is more bitter for me than for you, because the LORD's hand has turned against me!"

¹⁴At this they wept aloud again. Then Orpah kissed her mother-in-law goodbye, but Ruth clung to her.

¹⁵"Look," said Naomi, "your sister-in-law is going back to her people and her gods. Go back with her."

¹⁶But Ruth replied, "Don't urge me to leave you or to turn back from you. Where you go I will go, and where you stay I will stay. Your people will be my people and your God my God. ¹⁷Where you die I will die, and there I will be buried. May the LORD deal with me, be it ever so severely, if even death separates you and me." ¹⁸When Naomi realized that Ruth was determined to go with her, she stopped urging her.

¹⁹So the two women went on until they came to Bethlehem. When they arrived in Bethlehem, the whole town was stirred because of them, and the women exclaimed, "Can this be Naomi?"

²⁰"Don't call me Naomi,[b]" she told them. "Call me Mara,[c] because the Almighty[d] has made my life very bitter. ²¹I went away full, but the LORD has brought me back empty. Why call me Naomi? The LORD has afflicted[e] me; the Almighty has brought misfortune upon me."

²²So Naomi returned from Moab accompanied by Ruth the Moabite, her daughter-in-law, arriving in Bethlehem as the barley harvest was beginning.

Ruth Meets Boaz in the Grain Field

2 Now Naomi had a relative on her husband's side, a man of standing from the clan of Elimelek, whose name was Boaz.

²And Ruth the Moabite said to Naomi, "Let me go to the fields and pick up the leftover grain behind anyone in whose eyes I find favor."

Naomi said to her, "Go ahead, my daugh-

---

a 1 Traditionally *judged*   *b* 20 *Naomi* means *pleasant.*   *c* 20 *Mara* means *bitter.*   *d* 20 Hebrew *Shaddai*; also in verse 21   *e* 21 Or *has testified against*

ter." ³So she went out, entered a field and began to glean behind the harvesters. As it turned out, she was working in a field belonging to Boaz, who was from the clan of Elimelek.

⁴Just then Boaz arrived from Bethlehem and greeted the harvesters, "The LORD be with you!"

"The LORD bless you!" they answered.

⁵Boaz asked the overseer of his harvesters, "Who does that young woman belong to?"

⁶The overseer replied, "She is the Moabite who came back from Moab with Naomi. ⁷She said, 'Please let me glean and gather among the sheaves behind the harvesters.' She came into the field and has remained here from morning till now, except for a short rest in the shelter."

⁸So Boaz said to Ruth, "My daughter, listen to me. Don't go and glean in another field and don't go away from here. Stay here with the women who work for me. ⁹Watch the field where the men are harvesting, and follow along after the women. I have told the men not to lay a hand on you. And whenever you are thirsty, go and get a drink from the water jars the men have filled."

¹⁰At this, she bowed down with her face to the ground. She asked him, "Why have I found such favor in your eyes that you notice me—a foreigner?"

¹¹Boaz replied, "I've been told all about what you have done for your mother-in-law since the death of your husband—how you left your father and mother and your homeland and came to live with a people you did not know before. ¹²May the LORD repay you for what you have done. May you be richly rewarded by the LORD, the God of Israel, under whose wings you have come to take refuge."

¹³"May I continue to find favor in your eyes, my lord," she said. "You have put me at ease by speaking kindly to your servant—though I do not have the standing of one of your servants."

¹⁴At mealtime Boaz said to her, "Come over here. Have some bread and dip it in the wine vinegar."

When she sat down with the harvesters, he offered her some roasted grain. She ate all she wanted and had some left over. ¹⁵As she got up to glean, Boaz gave orders to his men, "Let her gather among the sheaves and don't reprimand her. ¹⁶Even pull out some stalks for her from the bundles and leave them for her to pick up, and don't rebuke her."

¹⁷So Ruth gleaned in the field until evening. Then she threshed the barley she had gathered, and it amounted to about an ephah.ᵃ ¹⁸She carried it back to town, and her mother-in-law saw how much she had gathered. Ruth also brought out and gave her what she had left over after she had eaten enough.

¹⁹Her mother-in-law asked her, "Where did you glean today? Where did you work?

ᵃ 17 That is, probably about 30 pounds or about 13 kilograms

PANORAMA

Friends.

Ruth was a great example of true friendship and devotion. A friend is someone you like being with and can talk to. It's someone you can count on.

{RUTH}

Blessed be the man who took notice of you!"

Then Ruth told her mother-in-law about the one at whose place she had been working. "The name of the man I worked with today is Boaz," she said.

20 "The LORD bless him!" Naomi said to her daughter-in-law. "He has not stopped showing his kindness to the living and the dead." She added, "That man is our close relative; he is one of our guardian-redeemers.*a*"

21 Then Ruth the Moabite said, "He even said to me, 'Stay with my workers until they finish harvesting all my grain.'"

22 Naomi said to Ruth her daughter-in-law, "It will be good for you, my daughter, to go with the women who work for him, because in someone else's field you might be harmed."

23 So Ruth stayed close to the women of Boaz to glean until the barley and wheat harvests were finished. And she lived with her mother-in-law.

Ruth and Boaz at the Threshing Floor

3 One day Ruth's mother-in-law Naomi said to her, "My daughter, I must find a home*b* for you, where you will be well provided for. 2 Now Boaz, with whose women you have worked, is a relative of ours. Tonight he will be winnowing barley on the threshing floor. 3 Wash, put on perfume, and get dressed in your best clothes. Then go down to the threshing floor, but don't let him know you are there until he has finished eating and drinking. 4 When he lies down, note the place where he is lying. Then go and uncover his feet and lie down. He will tell you what to do."

5 "I will do whatever you say," Ruth answered. 6 So she went down to the threshing floor and did everything her mother-in-law told her to do.

7 When Boaz had finished eating and drinking and was in good spirits, he went over to lie down at the far end of the grain pile. Ruth approached quietly, uncovered

his feet and lay down. 8 In the middle of the night something startled the man; he turned—and there was a woman lying at his feet!

9 "Who are you?" he asked.

"I am your servant Ruth," she said. "Spread the corner of your garment over me, since you are a guardian-redeemer*c* of our family."

10 "The LORD bless you, my daughter," he replied. "This kindness is greater than that which you showed earlier: You have not run after the younger men, whether rich or poor. 11 And now, my daughter, don't be afraid. I will do for you all you ask. All the people of my town know that you are a woman of noble character.

» INSTANT ACCESS

Do you get upset if someone gossips about you or spreads lies on the web? No one can blame you for being upset. A good reputation is precious. But in the end your reputation doesn't depend on lies others spread. It depends on how you live. Ruth earned her reputation, and Boaz could say, "All the people of my town know that you are a woman of noble character" (Ruth 3:11). Concentrate on living a noble life. The reputation that will be ruined is the reputation of the person who gossips and lies about you.

{Ruth 3:11}

---

a 20 The Hebrew word for *guardian-redeemer* is a legal term for one who has the obligation to redeem a relative in serious difficulty (see Lev. 25:25-55).   *b* 1 Hebrew *find rest* (see 1:9)   *c* 9 The Hebrew word for *guardian-redeemer* is a legal term for one who has the obligation to redeem a relative in serious difficulty (see Lev. 25:25-55); also in verses 12 and 13.

My mom and I argue a lot about how I get ready to go out—clothes, hair, makeup—that type of thing. I want to look attractive. Is there anything wrong with that?

>> Yasmina

Dear Jordan

Dear Yasmina,

Ask your mom if she will discuss finding a middle ground policy which is good for both of you. Sometimes it helps to have a third party like an aunt or an older sister to help keep things moving along in a positive way.

It might be a good idea to read chapter 3 of Ruth. Ruth was a young widow whose mother-in-law gave her some advice on getting a new husband. Of course you're not looking for a husband yet, but I understand that you want to look nice.

Another thought I have comes from an email I received from a teenage guy. He told me he has feelings of lust toward girls which is not helped by the way girls at his school dress. I am reminded of some verses in 1 Peter 3:3–5: "Your beauty should not come from outward adornment, such as elaborate hairstyles and the wearing of gold jewelry or fine clothes. Rather, it should be that of your inner self … a gentle and quiet spirit, which is of great worth in God's sight."

Shiny hair, a warm smile, dressing modestly—these are great ways to be attractive.

Jordan

¹²Although it is true that I am a guardian-redeemer of our family, there is another who is more closely related than I. ¹³Stay here for the night, and in the morning if he wants to do his duty as your guardian-redeemer, good; let him redeem you. But if he is not willing, as surely as the LORD lives I will do it. Lie here until morning."

¹⁴So she lay at his feet until morning, but got up before anyone could be recognized; and he said, "No one must know that a woman came to the threshing floor."

¹⁵He also said, "Bring me the shawl you are wearing and hold it out." When she did so, he poured into it six measures of barley and placed the bundle on her. Then he*ᵃ* went back to town.

¹⁶When Ruth came to her mother-in-law, Naomi asked, "How did it go, my daughter?"

Then she told her everything Boaz had done for her ¹⁷and added, "He gave me these six measures of barley, saying, 'Don't go back to your mother-in-law empty-handed.'"

¹⁸Then Naomi said, "Wait, my daughter, until you find out what happens. For the man will not rest until the matter is settled today."

Boaz Marries Ruth

4 Meanwhile Boaz went up to the town gate and sat down there just as the guardian-redeemer*ᵇ* he had mentioned came along. Boaz said, "Come over here, my friend, and sit down." So he went over and sat down.

²Boaz took ten of the elders of the town and said, "Sit here," and they did so. ³Then he said to the guardian-redeemer, "Naomi, who has come back from Moab, is selling the piece of land that belonged to our relative Elimelek. ⁴I thought I should bring the matter to your attention and suggest that you buy it in the presence of these seated here and in the presence of the elders of my people. If you will redeem it, do so. But if you*ᶜ* will

not, tell me, so I will know. For no one has the right to do it except you, and I am next in line."

"I will redeem it," he said.

⁵Then Boaz said, "On the day you buy the land from Naomi, you also acquire Ruth the Moabite, the*ᵈ* dead man's widow, in order to maintain the name of the dead with his property."

⁶At this, the guardian-redeemer said, "Then I cannot redeem it because I might endanger my own estate. You redeem it yourself. I cannot do it."

⁷(Now in earlier times in Israel, for the redemption and transfer of property to become final, one party took off his sandal and gave it to the other. This was the method of legalizing transactions in Israel.)

⁸So the guardian-redeemer said to Boaz, "Buy it yourself." And he removed his sandal.

⁹Then Boaz announced to the elders and all the people, "Today you are witnesses that I have bought from Naomi all the property of Elimelek, Kilion and Mahlon. ¹⁰I have also acquired Ruth the Moabite, Mahlon's widow, as my wife, in order to maintain the name of the dead with his property, so that his name will not disappear from among his family or from his hometown. Today you are witnesses!"

¹¹Then the elders and all the people at the gate said, "We are witnesses. May the LORD make the woman who is coming into your home like Rachel and Leah, who together built up the family of Israel. May you have standing in Ephrathah and be famous in Bethlehem. ¹²Through the offspring the LORD gives you by this young woman, may your family be like that of Perez, whom Tamar bore to Judah."

Naomi Gains a Son

¹³So Boaz took Ruth and she became his wife. When he made love to her, the LORD enabled her to conceive, and she gave birth to a son. ¹⁴The women said to Naomi: "Praise be to the LORD, who

---

ᵃ 15 Most Hebrew manuscripts; many Hebrew manuscripts, Vulgate and Syriac *she*   *ᵇ* 1 The Hebrew word for *guardian-redeemer* is a legal term for one who has the obligation to redeem a relative in serious difficulty (see Lev. 25:25-55); also in verses 3, 6, 8 and 14.   *ᶜ* 4 Many Hebrew manuscripts, Septuagint, Vulgate and Syriac; most Hebrew manuscripts *he*   *ᵈ* 5 Vulgate and Syriac; Hebrew (see also Septuagint) *Naomi and from Ruth the Moabite, you acquire the*

this day has not left you without a guardian-redeemer. May he become famous throughout Israel! [15]He will renew your life and sustain you in your old age. For your daughter-in-law, who loves you and who is better to you than seven sons, has given him birth."

[16]Then Naomi took the child in her arms and cared for him. [17]The women living there said, "Naomi has a son!" And they named him Obed. He was the father of Jesse, the father of David.

The Genealogy of David

[18]This, then, is the family line of Perez:

Perez was the father of Hezron,
[19]Hezron the father of Ram,
Ram the father of Amminadab,
[20]Amminadab the father of Nahshon,
Nahshon the father of Salmon,[a]
[21]Salmon the father of Boaz,
Boaz the father of Obed,
[22]Obed the father of Jesse,
and Jesse the father of David.

---

a 20 A few Hebrew manuscripts, some Septuagint manuscripts and Vulgate (see also verse 21 and Septuagint of 1 Chron. 2:11); most Hebrew manuscripts *Salma*

1 SAMUEL

The cast in this book features a judge, Samuel; a king, Saul; and a shepherd boy, David.

Iron weapons give the Philistines military superiority. God gives Israel ... victory.

Events in this book take place between 1060 and 1010 B.C.

Change.

Change can be hard. Especially big changes such as moving or changing schools, living through your parents' divorce, or trying to adjust to a stepmother or stepfather.

Israel and David were experiencing some big changes. When Samuel, Israel's last judge, grew old, the people demanded a king. Saul, the first king, was disobedient. So God chose a young man named David to replace him. But many difficult years passed before David became king, because Saul was jealous of David and became hostile. The book of 1 Samuel tells the story of those difficult years.

>>**MOM DEDICATES BABY TO GOD**
Story in 1 Samuel 1

>>**WEAK KING LOSES CROWN**
No dynasty for disobedient ruler, 1 Samuel 15

>>**BOY ROCKS PHILISTINE HERO**
Giant loses his head, 1 Samuel 17

>>**DAVID LETS GO, LETS GOD**
Fugitive's restraint saves king's life, 1 Samuel 26

As Saul tries to murder David, Tiglath-pileser is establishing the Assyrian empire.
Athens abolishes the monarchy to become the world's first republic.
In China mathematicians measure the height of the sun.

The Birth of Samuel

1 There was a certain man from Rama-thaim, a Zuphite[a] from the hill country of Ephraim, whose name was Elkanah son of Jeroham, the son of Elihu, the son of Tohu, the son of Zuph, an Ephraimite. [2]He had two wives; one was called Hannah and the other Peninnah. Peninnah had children, but Hannah had none.

[3]Year after year this man went up from his town to worship and sacrifice to the LORD Almighty at Shiloh, where Hophni and Phinehas, the two sons of Eli, were priests of the LORD. [4]Whenever the day came for Elkanah to sacrifice, he would give portions of the meat to his wife Peninnah and to all her sons and daughters. [5]But to Hannah he gave a double portion because he loved her, and the LORD had closed her womb. [6]Because the LORD had closed Hannah's womb, her rival kept provoking her in order to irritate her. [7]This went on year after year. Whenever Hannah went up to the house of the LORD, her rival provoked her till she wept and would not eat. [8]Her husband Elkanah would say to her, "Hannah, why are you weeping? Why don't you eat? Why are you downhearted? Don't I mean more to you than ten sons?"

[9]Once when they had finished eating and drinking in Shiloh, Hannah stood up. Now Eli the priest was sitting on his chair by the doorpost of the LORD's house. [10]In her deep anguish Hannah prayed to the LORD, weeping bitterly. [11]And she made a vow, saying, "LORD Almighty, if you will only look on your servant's misery and remember me, and not forget your servant but give her a son, then I will give him to the LORD for all the days of his life, and no razor will ever be used on his head."

[12]As she kept on praying to the LORD, Eli observed her mouth. [13]Hannah was praying in her heart, and her lips were moving but her voice was not heard. Eli thought she was drunk [14]and said to her, "How long are you going to stay drunk? Put away your wine."

[15]"Not so, my lord," Hannah replied, "I am a woman who is deeply troubled. I have not been drinking wine or beer; I was pouring out my soul to the LORD. [16]Do not take your servant for a wicked woman; I have been praying here out of my great anguish and grief."

[17]Eli answered, "Go in peace, and may the God of Israel grant you what you have asked of him."

[18]She said, "May your servant find favor in your eyes." Then she went her way and ate something, and her face was no longer downcast.

[19]Early the next morning they arose and worshiped before the LORD and then went back to their home at Ramah. Elkanah made love to his wife Hannah, and the LORD remembered her. [20]So in the course of time Hannah became pregnant and gave birth to a son. She named him Samuel,[b] saying, "Because I asked the LORD for him."

Hannah Dedicates Samuel

[21]When her husband Elkanah went up with all his family to offer the annual sacrifice to the LORD and to fulfill his vow, [22]Hannah did not go. She said to her husband, "After the boy is weaned, I will take him and present him before the LORD, and he will live there always."[c]

[23]"Do what seems best to you," her husband Elkanah told her. "Stay here until you have weaned him; only may the LORD make good his[d] word." So the woman stayed at home and nursed her son until she had weaned him.

[24]After he was weaned, she took the boy with her, young as he was, along with a three-year-old bull,[e] an ephah[f] of flour and a skin of wine, and brought him to the house of the LORD at Shiloh. [25]When the bull had been sacrificed, they brought the boy to Eli, [26]and she said to him, "Pardon me, my lord. As surely as you live, I am the woman who stood here beside you praying to the LORD. [27]I prayed for this child, and the LORD has granted

me what I asked of him. ²⁸So now I give him to the LORD. For his whole life he will be given over to the LORD." And he worshiped the LORD there.

Hannah's Prayer

2 Then Hannah prayed and said:

"My heart rejoices in the LORD;
    in the LORD my horn*a* is lifted high.
My mouth boasts over my enemies,
    for I delight in your deliverance.

² "There is no one holy like the LORD;
    there is no one besides you;
    there is no Rock like our God.

³ "Do not keep talking so proudly
    or let your mouth speak such arrogance,
for the LORD is a God who knows,
    and by him deeds are weighed.

⁴ "The bows of the warriors are broken,
    but those who stumbled are armed with strength.
⁵ Those who were full hire themselves out for food,
    but those who were hungry are hungry no more.
She who was barren has borne seven children,
    but she who has had many sons pines away.

⁶ "The LORD brings death and makes alive;
    he brings down to the grave and raises up.
⁷ The LORD sends poverty and wealth;
    he humbles and he exalts.
⁸ He raises the poor from the dust
    and lifts the needy from the ash heap;
he seats them with princes
    and has them inherit a throne of honor.

"For the foundations of the earth are the LORD's;
    on them he has set the world.
⁹ He will guard the feet of his faithful servants,
    but the wicked will be silenced in the place of darkness.

"It is not by strength that one prevails;
¹⁰   those who oppose the LORD will be broken.
The Most High will thunder from heaven;
    the LORD will judge the ends of the earth.

"He will give strength to his king
    and exalt the horn of his anointed."

¹¹ Then Elkanah went home to Ramah, but the boy ministered before the LORD under Eli the priest.

Eli's Wicked Sons

¹²Eli's sons were scoundrels; they had no regard for the LORD. ¹³Now it was the practice of the priests that, whenever any of the people offered a sacrifice, the priest's servant would come with a three-pronged fork in his hand while the meat was being boiled ¹⁴and would plunge the fork into the pan or kettle or caldron or pot. Whatever the fork brought up the priest would take for himself. This is how they treated all the Israelites who came to Shiloh. ¹⁵But even before the fat was burned, the priest's servant would come and say to the person who was sacrificing, "Give the priest some meat to roast; he won't accept boiled meat from you, but only raw."

¹⁶If the person said to him, "Let the fat be burned first, and then take whatever you want," the servant would answer, "No, hand it over now; if you don't, I'll take it by force."

> *He will guard the feet of his faithful servants.*
> 1 Samuel 2:9

---

a 1 Horn here symbolizes strength; also in verse 10.

If you were to build a house and knew you had to live in it for the next 50 years, wouldn't you be very careful when laying the foundation? Of course. Why risk cracks and tumbledown walls? It's the same with your life. The choices you make each day are the foundation you lay for your future. The choices made by a priest named Eli and by his two sons are described in 1 Samuel 2. Their choices ruined their lives. But 1 Samuel 2:35 tells how you can guarantee a very different future. If you "do according to what is in [God's] heart and mind," then God will "firmly establish" you and make your life worthwhile.

{1 Samuel 2:35}

INSTANT ACCESS

¹⁷This sin of the young men was very great in the Lord's sight, for they[a] were treating the Lord's offering with contempt.

¹⁸But Samuel was ministering before the Lord—a boy wearing a linen ephod. ¹⁹Each year his mother made him a little robe and took it to him when she went up with her husband to offer the annual sacrifice. ²⁰Eli would bless Elkanah and his wife, saying, "May the Lord give you children by this woman to take the place of the one she prayed for and gave to[b] the

Lord." Then they would go home. ²¹And the Lord was gracious to Hannah; she gave birth to three sons and two daughters. Meanwhile, the boy Samuel grew up in the presence of the Lord.

²²Now Eli, who was very old, heard about everything his sons were doing to all Israel and how they slept with the women who served at the entrance to the tent of meeting. ²³So he said to them, "Why do you do such things? I hear from all the people about these wicked deeds of yours. ²⁴No, my sons; the report I hear spreading among the Lord's people is not good. ²⁵If one person sins against another, God[c] may mediate for the offender; but if anyone sins against the Lord, who will intercede for them?" His sons, however, did not listen to their father's rebuke, for it was the Lord's will to put them to death.

²⁶And the boy Samuel continued to grow in stature and in favor with the Lord and with people.

Prophecy Against the House of Eli

²⁷Now a man of God came to Eli and said to him, "This is what the Lord says: 'Did I not clearly reveal myself to your ancestor's family when they were in Egypt under Pharaoh? ²⁸I chose your ancestor out of all the tribes of Israel to be my priest, to go up to my altar, to burn incense, and to wear an ephod in my presence. I also gave your ancestor's family all the food offerings presented by the Israelites. ²⁹Why do you[d] scorn my sacrifice and offering that I prescribed for my dwelling? Why do you honor your sons more than me by fattening yourselves on the choice parts of every offering made by my people Israel?'

³⁰"Therefore the Lord, the God of Israel, declares: 'I promised that members of your family would minister before me forever.' But now the Lord declares: 'Far be it from me! Those who honor me I will honor, but those who despise me will be disdained. ³¹The time is coming when I will cut short your strength and the strength

---

[a] 17 Dead Sea Scrolls and Septuagint; Masoretic Text *people*   [b] 20 Dead Sea Scrolls; Masoretic Text *and asked from*
[c] 25 Or *the judges*   [d] 29 The Hebrew is plural.

of your priestly house, so that no one in it will reach old age, 32 and you will see distress in my dwelling. Although good will be done to Israel, no one in your family line will ever reach old age. 33 Every one of you that I do not cut off from serving at my altar I will spare only to destroy your sight and sap your strength, and all your descendants will die in the prime of life.

34 " 'And what happens to your two sons, Hophni and Phinehas, will be a sign to you—they will both die on the same day. 35 I will raise up for myself a faithful priest, who will do according to what is in my heart and mind. I will firmly establish his priestly house, and they will minister before my anointed one always. 36 Then everyone left in your family line will come and bow down before him for a piece of silver and a loaf of bread and plead, "Appoint me to some priestly office so I can have food to eat." ' "

The LORD Calls Samuel

3 The boy Samuel ministered before the LORD under Eli. In those days the word of the LORD was rare; there were not many visions.

2 One night Eli, whose eyes were becoming so weak that he could barely see, was lying down in his usual place. 3 The lamp of God had not yet gone out, and Samuel was lying down in the house of the LORD, where the ark of God was. 4 Then the LORD called Samuel.

Samuel answered, "Here I am." 5 And he ran to Eli and said, "Here I am; you called me."

But Eli said, "I did not call; go back and lie down." So he went and lay down.

6 Again the LORD called, "Samuel!" And Samuel got up and went to Eli and said, "Here I am; you called me."

"My son," Eli said, "I did not call; go back and lie down."

7 Now Samuel did not yet know the LORD: The word of the LORD had not yet been revealed to him.

8 A third time the LORD called, "Samuel!" And Samuel got up and went to Eli and said, "Here I am; you called me."

Then Eli realized that the LORD was calling the boy. 9 So Eli told Samuel, "Go and lie down, and if he calls you, say, 'Speak, LORD, for your servant is listening.' " So Samuel went and lay down in his place.

10 The LORD came and stood there, calling as at the other times, "Samuel! Samuel!"

Then Samuel said, "Speak, for your servant is listening."

11 And the LORD said to Samuel: "See, I am about to do something in Israel that will make the ears of everyone who hears about it tingle. 12 At that time I will carry out against Eli everything I spoke against his family—from beginning to end. 13 For I told him that I would judge his family forever because of the sin he knew about; his sons blasphemed God,[a] and he failed to restrain them. 14 Therefore I swore to the house of Eli, 'The guilt of Eli's house will never be atoned for by sacrifice or offering.' "

15 Samuel lay down until morning and then opened the doors of the house of the LORD. He was afraid to tell Eli the vision, 16 but Eli called him and said, "Samuel, my son."

Samuel answered, "Here I am."

17 "What was it he said to you?" Eli asked. "Do not hide it from me. May God deal with you, be it ever so severely, if you hide from me anything he told you." 18 So Samuel told him everything, hiding nothing from him. Then Eli said, "He is the LORD; let him do what is good in his eyes."

19 The LORD was with Samuel as he grew up, and he let none of Samuel's words fall to the ground. 20 And all Israel from Dan to Beersheba recognized that Samuel was attested as a prophet of the LORD. 21 The LORD continued to appear at Shiloh, and there he revealed himself to Samuel through his word.

4 And Samuel's word came to all Israel.

The Philistines Capture the Ark

Now the Israelites went out to fight against the Philistines. The Israelites camped at Ebenezer, and the Philistines

---

a 13 An ancient Hebrew scribal tradition (see also Septuagint); Masoretic Text *sons made themselves contemptible*

Do you think your dad is too strict? In 1 Samuel 3:13 God told Eli that he would judge Eli's family forever because his sons were sinful and because Eli had failed to restrain them. Maybe that strict dad of yours is just taking his responsibility seriously! Most parents don't enjoy "restraining" their children. Saying no isn't parents' idea of a good time. It's a lot easier to be laid back and let kids do whatever they want. It may be easier, but it's not right. Failing to "restrain" fails God, and as Eli realized when both his sons died, failing to restrain means failing one's children as well.

{1 Samuel 3:13}

INSTANT ACCESS

at Aphek. [2] The Philistines deployed their forces to meet Israel, and as the battle spread, Israel was defeated by the Philistines, who killed about four thousand of them on the battlefield. [3] When the soldiers returned to camp, the elders of Israel asked, "Why did the LORD bring defeat on us today before the Philistines? Let us bring the ark of the LORD's covenant from Shiloh, so that he may go with us and save us from the hand of our enemies."

[4] So the people sent men to Shiloh, and they brought back the ark of the covenant of the LORD Almighty, who is enthroned between the cherubim. And Eli's two sons, Hophni and Phinehas, were there with the ark of the covenant of God.

[5] When the ark of the LORD's covenant came into the camp, all Israel raised such a great shout that the ground shook. [6] Hearing the uproar, the Philistines asked, "What's all this shouting in the Hebrew camp?"

When they learned that the ark of the LORD had come into the camp, [7] the Philistines were afraid. "A god has[a] come into the camp," they said. "Oh no! Nothing like this has happened before. [8] We're doomed! Who will deliver us from the hand of these mighty gods? They are the gods who struck the Egyptians with all kinds of plagues in the wilderness. [9] Be strong, Philistines! Be men, or you will be subject to the Hebrews, as they have been to you. Be men, and fight!"

[10] So the Philistines fought, and the Israelites were defeated and every man fled to his tent. The slaughter was very great; Israel lost thirty thousand foot soldiers. [11] The ark of God was captured, and Eli's two sons, Hophni and Phinehas, died.

Death of Eli

[12] That same day a Benjamite ran from the battle line and went to Shiloh with his clothes torn and dust on his head. [13] When he arrived, there was Eli sitting on his chair by the side of the road, watching, because his heart feared for the ark of God. When the man entered the town and told what had happened, the whole town sent up a cry.

[14] Eli heard the outcry and asked, "What is the meaning of this uproar?"

The man hurried over to Eli, [15] who was ninety-eight years old and whose eyes had failed so that he could not see. [16] He told Eli, "I have just come from the battle line; I fled from it this very day."

Eli asked, "What happened, my son?"

[17] The man who brought the news replied, "Israel fled before the Philistines, and the army has suffered heavy losses. Also your two sons, Hophni and Phinehas, are dead, and the ark of God has been captured."

[a] 7 Or "Gods have (see Septuagint)

18When he mentioned the ark of God, Eli fell backward off his chair by the side of the gate. His neck was broken and he died, for he was an old man, and he was heavy. He had led[a] Israel forty years.

19His daughter-in-law, the wife of Phinehas, was pregnant and near the time of delivery. When she heard the news that the ark of God had been captured and that her father-in-law and her husband were dead, she went into labor and gave birth, but was overcome by her labor pains. 20As she was dying, the women attending her said, "Don't despair; you have given birth to a son." But she did not respond or pay any attention.

21She named the boy Ichabod,[b] saying, "The Glory has departed from Israel"—because of the capture of the ark of God and the deaths of her father-in-law and her husband. 22She said, "The Glory has departed from Israel, for the ark of God has been captured."

The Ark in Ashdod and Ekron

5 After the Philistines had captured the ark of God, they took it from Ebenezer to Ashdod. 2Then they carried the ark into Dagon's temple and set it beside Dagon. 3When the people of Ashdod rose early the next day, there was Dagon, fallen on his face on the ground before the ark of the LORD! They took Dagon and put him back in his place. 4But the following morning when they rose, there was Dagon, fallen on his face on the ground before the ark of the LORD! His head and hands had been broken off and were lying on the threshold; only his body remained. 5That is why to this day neither the priests of Dagon nor any others who enter Dagon's temple at Ashdod step on the threshold.

6The LORD's hand was heavy on the people of Ashdod and its vicinity; he brought devastation on them and afflicted them with tumors.[c] 7When the people of Ashdod saw what was happening, they said, "The ark of the god of Israel must not stay here with us, because his hand is heavy on us and on Dagon our god." 8So they called together all the rulers of the Philistines and asked them, "What shall we do with the ark of the god of Israel?"

They answered, "Have the ark of the god of Israel moved to Gath." So they moved the ark of the God of Israel.

9But after they had moved it, the LORD's hand was against that city, throwing it into a great panic. He afflicted the people of the city, both young and old, with an outbreak of tumors.[d] 10So they sent the ark of God to Ekron.

As the ark of God was entering Ekron, the people of Ekron cried out, "They have brought the ark of the god of Israel around to us to kill us and our people." 11So they called together all the rulers of the Philistines and said, "Send the ark of the god of Israel away; let it go back to its own place, or it[e] will kill us and our people." For death had filled the city with panic; God's hand was very heavy on it. 12Those who did not die were afflicted with tumors, and the outcry of the city went up to heaven.

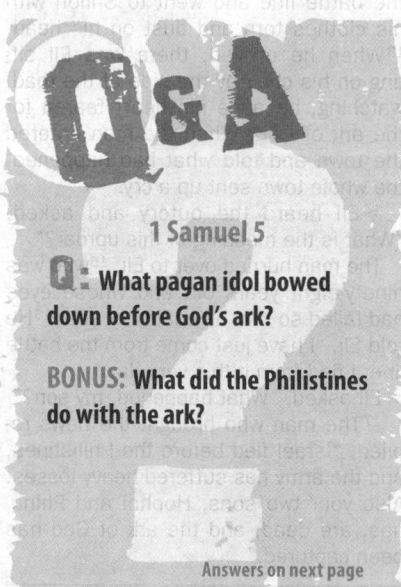

1 Samuel 5

Q: What pagan idol bowed down before God's ark?

BONUS: What did the Philistines do with the ark?

Answers on next page

a 18 Traditionally judged   b 21 Ichabod means no glory.
c 6 Hebrew; Septuagint and Vulgate tumors. And rats appeared in their land, and there was death and destruction throughout the city   d 9 Or with tumors in the groin (see Septuagint)   e 11 Or he

The Ark Returned to Israel

6 When the ark of the LORD had been in Philistine territory seven months, ²the Philistines called for the priests and the diviners and said, "What shall we do with the ark of the LORD? Tell us how we should send it back to its place."

³They answered, "If you return the ark of the god of Israel, do not send it back to him without a gift; by all means send a guilt offering to him. Then you will be healed, and you will know why his hand has not been lifted from you."

⁴The Philistines asked, "What guilt offering should we send to him?"

They replied, "Five gold tumors and five gold rats, according to the number of the Philistine rulers, because the same plague has struck both you and your rulers. ⁵Make models of the tumors and of the rats that are destroying the country, and give glory to Israel's god. Perhaps he will lift his hand from you and your gods and your land. ⁶Why do you harden your hearts as the Egyptians and Pharaoh did? When Israel's god dealt harshly with them, did they not send the Israelites out so they could go on their way?

⁷"Now then, get a new cart ready, with two cows that have calved and have never been yoked. Hitch the cows to the cart, but take their calves away and pen them up. ⁸Take the ark of the LORD and put it on the cart, and in a chest beside it put the gold objects you are sending back to him as a guilt offering. Send it on its way, ⁹but keep watching it. If it goes up to its own territory, toward Beth Shemesh, then the LORD has brought this great disaster on us. But if it does not, then we will know that it was not his hand that struck us but that it happened to us by chance."

¹⁰So they did this. They took two such cows and hitched them to the cart and penned up their calves. ¹¹They placed the ark of the LORD on the cart and along with it the chest containing the gold rats and the models of the tumors. ¹²Then the cows went straight up toward Beth Shemesh, keeping on the road and lowing all the way; they did not turn to the right or to the left. The rulers of the Philistines followed them as far as the border of Beth Shemesh.

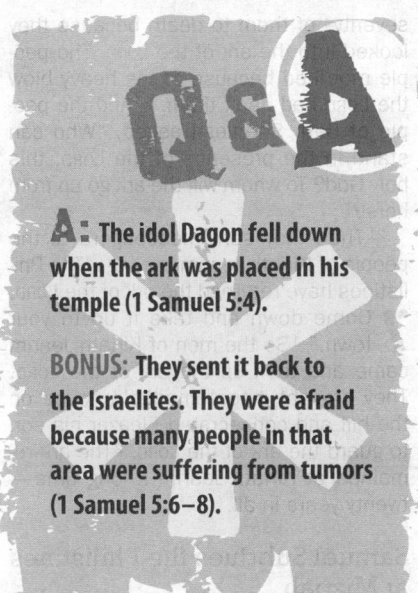

A: The idol Dagon fell down when the ark was placed in his temple (1 Samuel 5:4).

BONUS: They sent it back to the Israelites. They were afraid because many people in that area were suffering from tumors (1 Samuel 5:6–8).

¹³Now the people of Beth Shemesh were harvesting their wheat in the valley, and when they looked up and saw the ark, they rejoiced at the sight. ¹⁴The cart came to the field of Joshua of Beth Shemesh, and there it stopped beside a large rock. The people chopped up the wood of the cart and sacrificed the cows as a burnt offering to the LORD. ¹⁵The Levites took down the ark of the LORD, together with the chest containing the gold objects, and placed them on the large rock. On that day the people of Beth Shemesh offered burnt offerings and made sacrifices to the LORD. ¹⁶The five rulers of the Philistines saw all this and then returned that same day to Ekron.

¹⁷These are the gold tumors the Philistines sent as a guilt offering to the LORD—one each for Ashdod, Gaza, Ashkelon, Gath and Ekron. ¹⁸And the number of the gold rats was according to the number of Philistine towns belonging to the five rulers—the fortified towns with their country villages. The large rock on which the Levites set the ark of the LORD is a witness to this day in the field of Joshua of Beth Shemesh.

¹⁹But God struck down some of the inhabitants of Beth Shemesh, putting

seventy[a] of them to death because they looked into the ark of the LORD. The people mourned because of the heavy blow the LORD had dealt them. [20]And the people of Beth Shemesh asked, "Who can stand in the presence of the LORD, this holy God? To whom will the ark go up from here?"

[21]Then they sent messengers to the people of Kiriath Jearim, saying, "The Philistines have returned the ark of the LORD. Come down and take it up to your town." [1]So the men of Kiriath Jearim came and took up the ark of the LORD. They brought it to Abinadab's house on the hill and consecrated Eleazar his son to guard the ark of the LORD. [2]The ark remained at Kiriath Jearim a long time— twenty years in all.

Samuel Subdues the Philistines at Mizpah

Then all the people of Israel turned back to the LORD. [3]So Samuel said to all the Israelites, "If you are returning to the LORD with all your hearts, then rid yourselves of the foreign gods and the Ashtoreths and commit yourselves to the LORD and serve him only, and he will deliver you out of the hand of the Philistines." [4]So the Israelites put away their Baals and Ashtoreths, and served the LORD only.

[5]Then Samuel said, "Assemble all Israel at Mizpah, and I will intercede with the LORD for you." [6]When they had assembled at Mizpah, they drew water and poured it out before the LORD. On that day they fasted and there they confessed, "We have sinned against the LORD." Now Samuel was serving as leader[b] of Israel at Mizpah.

[7]When the Philistines heard that Israel had assembled at Mizpah, the rulers of the Philistines came up to attack them. When the Israelites heard of it, they were afraid because of the Philistines. [8]They said to Samuel, "Do not stop crying out to the LORD our God for us, that he may rescue us from the hand of the Philistines." [9]Then Samuel took a suckling lamb and sacrificed it as a whole burnt offering to the LORD. He cried out to the LORD on Israel's behalf, and the LORD answered him.

[10]While Samuel was sacrificing the burnt offering, the Philistines drew near to engage Israel in battle. But that day the LORD thundered with loud thunder against the Philistines and threw them into such a panic that they were routed before the Israelites. [11]The men of Israel rushed out of Mizpah and pursued the Philistines, slaughtering them along the way to a point below Beth Kar.

[12]Then Samuel took a stone and set it up between Mizpah and Shen. He named it Ebenezer,[c] saying, "Thus far the LORD has helped us."

[13]So the Philistines were subdued and they stopped invading Israel's territory. Throughout Samuel's lifetime, the hand of the LORD was against the Philistines. [14]The towns from Ekron to Gath that the Philistines had captured from Israel were restored to Israel, and Israel delivered the neighboring territory from the hands of the Philistines. And there was peace between Israel and the Amorites.

[15]Samuel continued as Israel's leader all the days of his life. [16]From year to year he went on a circuit from Bethel to Gilgal to Mizpah, judging Israel in all those places. [17]But he always went back to Ramah, where his home was, and there he also held court for Israel. And he built an altar there to the LORD.

Israel Asks for a King

When Samuel grew old, he appointed his sons as Israel's leaders.[d] [2]The name of his firstborn was Joel and the name of his second was Abijah, and they served at Beersheba. [3]But his sons did not follow his ways. They turned aside after dishonest gain and accepted bribes and perverted justice.

[4]So all the elders of Israel gathered together and came to Samuel at Ramah. [5]They said to him, "You are old, and your sons do not follow your ways; now ap-

---

[a] 19 A few Hebrew manuscripts; most Hebrew manuscripts and Septuagint 50,070   [b] 6 Traditionally *judge*; also in verse 15   [c] 12 *Ebenezer* means *stone of help*.   [d] 1 Traditionally *judges*

Want to be a cheerleader? Eager to be accepted by the popular kids in your class? Want to be elected class president? Great! There's nothing wrong with those ambitions—in themselves. Of course, you have to watch your motives. The people of Israel wanted a king. That wasn't wrong in itself, but they wanted a king to "be like all the other nations" (1 Samuel 8:20). They weren't satisfied to be different, even though God's people are supposed to be different in very special ways. Motives do count. It's OK to have ambitions. Just be sure your ambition isn't to "be like all the others," rather than to be different in a positive, godly way.

{1 Samuel 8}

>> INSTANT ACCESS

point a king to lead[a] us, such as all the other nations have."

6 But when they said, "Give us a king to lead us," this displeased Samuel; so he prayed to the LORD. 7 And the LORD told him: "Listen to all that the people are saying to you; it is not you they have rejected, but they have rejected me as their king. 8 As they have done from the day I brought them up out of Egypt until this day, forsaking me and serving other gods, so they are doing to you. 9 Now listen to them; but warn them solemnly and let them know what the king who will reign over them will claim as his rights."

10 Samuel told all the words of the LORD to the people who were asking him for a king. 11 He said, "This is what the king who will reign over you will claim as his rights: He will take your sons and make them serve with his chariots and horses, and they will run in front of his chariots. 12 Some he will assign to be commanders of thousands and commanders of fifties, and others to plow his ground and reap his harvest, and still others to make weapons of war and equipment for his chariots. 13 He will take your daughters to be perfumers and cooks and bakers. 14 He will take the best of your fields and vineyards and olive groves and give them to his attendants. 15 He will take a tenth of your grain and of your vintage and give it to his officials and attendants. 16 Your male and female servants and the best of your cattle[b] and donkeys he will take for his own use. 17 He will take a tenth of your flocks, and you yourselves will become his slaves. 18 When that day comes, you will cry out for relief from the king you have chosen, but the LORD will not answer you in that day."

19 But the people refused to listen to Samuel. "No!" they said. "We want a king over us. 20 Then we will be like all the other nations, with a king to lead us and to go out before us and fight our battles."

21 When Samuel heard all that the people said, he repeated it before the LORD. 22 The LORD answered, "Listen to them and give them a king."

Then Samuel said to the Israelites, "Everyone go back to your own town."

Samuel Anoints Saul

9 There was a Benjamite, a man of standing, whose name was Kish son of Abiel, the son of Zeror, the son of Bekorath, the son of Aphiah of Benjamin. 2 Kish had a son named Saul, as handsome a young man as could be found anywhere in Israel, and he was a head taller than anyone else.

[a] 5 Traditionally judge; also in verses 6 and 20   [b] 16 Septuagint; Hebrew young men

³Now the donkeys belonging to Saul's father Kish were lost, and Kish said to his son Saul, "Take one of the servants with you and go and look for the donkeys." ⁴So he passed through the hill country of Ephraim and through the area around Shalisha, but they did not find them. They went on into the district of Shaalim, but the donkeys were not there. Then he passed through the territory of Benjamin, but they did not find them.

⁵When they reached the district of Zuph, Saul said to the servant who was with him, "Come, let's go back, or my father will stop thinking about the donkeys and start worrying about us."

⁶But the servant replied, "Look, in this town there is a man of God; he is highly respected, and everything he says comes true. Let's go there now. Perhaps he will tell us what way to take."

⁷Saul said to his servant, "If we go, what can we give the man? The food in our sacks is gone. We have no gift to take to the man of God. What do we have?"

⁸The servant answered him again. "Look," he said, "I have a quarter of a shekelᵃ of silver. I will give it to the man of God so that he will tell us what way to take." ⁹(Formerly in Israel, if someone went to inquire of God, they would say, "Come, let us go to the seer," because the prophet of today used to be called a seer.)

¹⁰"Good," Saul said to his servant. "Come, let's go." So they set out for the town where the man of God was.

¹¹As they were going up the hill to the town, they met some young women coming out to draw water, and they asked them, "Is the seer here?"

¹²"He is," they answered. "He's ahead of you. Hurry now; he has just come to our town today, for the people have a sacrifice at the high place. ¹³As soon as you enter the town, you will find him before he goes up to the high place to eat. The people will not begin eating until he comes, because he must bless the sacrifice; afterward, those who are invited will eat. Go up now; you should find him about this time."

¹⁴They went up to the town, and as they were entering it, there was Samuel, coming toward them on his way up to the high place.

¹⁵Now the day before Saul came, the LORD had revealed this to Samuel: ¹⁶"About this time tomorrow I will send you a man from the land of Benjamin. Anoint him ruler over my people Israel; he will deliver them from the hand of the Philistines. I have looked on my people, for their cry has reached me."

¹⁷When Samuel caught sight of Saul, the LORD said to him, "This is the man I spoke to you about; he will govern my people."

¹⁸Saul approached Samuel in the gateway and asked, "Would you please tell me where the seer's house is?"

¹⁹"I am the seer," Samuel replied. "Go up ahead of me to the high place, for today you are to eat with me, and in the morning I will send you on your way and will tell you all that is in your heart. ²⁰As for the donkeys you lost three days ago, do not worry about them; they have been found. And to whom is all the desire of Israel turned, if not to you and your whole family line?"

²¹Saul answered, "But am I not a Benjamite, from the smallest tribe of Israel, and is not my clan the least of all the clans of the tribe of Benjamin? Why do you say such a thing to me?"

²²Then Samuel brought Saul and his servant into the hall and seated them at the head of those who were invited— about thirty in number. ²³Samuel said to the cook, "Bring the piece of meat I gave you, the one I told you to lay aside."

²⁴So the cook took up the thigh with what was on it and set it in front of Saul. Samuel said, "Here is what has been kept for you. Eat, because it was set aside for you for this occasion from the time I said, 'I have invited guests.'" And Saul dined with Samuel that day.

²⁵After they came down from the high place to the town, Samuel talked with Saul on the roof of his house. ²⁶They rose about daybreak, and Samuel called

---

ᵃ 8 That is, about 1/10 ounce or about 3 grams

to Saul on the roof, "Get ready, and I will send you on your way." When Saul got ready, he and Samuel went outside together. 27As they were going down to the edge of the town, Samuel said to Saul, "Tell the servant to go on ahead of us"—and the servant did so—"but you stay here for a while, so that I may give you a message from God."

10 Then Samuel took a flask of olive oil and poured it on Saul's head and kissed him, saying, "Has not the LORD anointed you ruler over his inheritance?a 2When you leave me today, you will meet two men near Rachel's tomb, at Zelzah on the border of Benjamin. They will say to you, 'The donkeys you set out to look for have been found. And now your father has stopped thinking about them and is worried about you. He is asking, "What shall I do about my son?"'

3"Then you will go on from there until you reach the great tree of Tabor. Three men going up to worship God at Bethel will meet you there. One will be carrying three young goats, another three loaves of bread, and another a skin of wine. 4They will greet you and offer you two loaves of bread, which you will accept from them.

5"After that you will go to Gibeah of God, where there is a Philistine outpost. As you approach the town, you will meet a procession of prophets coming down from the high place with lyres, timbrels, pipes and harps being played before them, and they will be prophesying. 6The Spirit of the LORD will come powerfully upon you, and you will prophesy with them; and you will be changed into a different person. 7Once these signs are fulfilled, do whatever your hand finds to do, for God is with you.

8"Go down ahead of me to Gilgal. I will surely come down to you to sacrifice

burnt offerings and fellowship offerings, but you must wait seven days until I come to you and tell you what you are to do."

Saul Made King

9As Saul turned to leave Samuel, God changed Saul's heart, and all these signs were fulfilled that day. 10When he and his servant arrived at Gibeah, a procession of prophets met him; the Spirit of God came powerfully upon him, and he joined in their prophesying. 11When all those who had formerly known him saw him prophesying with the prophets, they asked each other, "What is this that has happened to the son of Kish? Is Saul also among the prophets?"

12A man who lived there answered, "And who is their father?" So it became a saying: "Is Saul also among the prophets?" 13After Saul stopped prophesying, he went to the high place.

14Now Saul's uncle asked him and his servant, "Where have you been?"

"Looking for the donkeys," he said. "But when we saw they were not to be found, we went to Samuel."

15Saul's uncle said, "Tell me what Samuel said to you."

16Saul replied, "He assured us that the donkeys had been found." But he did not tell his uncle what Samuel had said about the kingship.

17Samuel summoned the people of Israel to the LORD at Mizpah 18and said to them, "This is what the LORD, the God of Israel, says: 'I brought Israel up out of Egypt, and I delivered you from the power of Egypt and all the kingdoms that oppressed you.' 19But you have now rejected your God, who saves you out of all your disasters and calamities. And you have said, 'No, appoint a king over us.' So now present yourselves before the LORD by your tribes and clans."

> The Spirit of the LORD will come powerfully upon you . . . and you will be changed.
>
> 1 Samuel 10:6

---

a 1 Hebrew; Septuagint and Vulgate *over his people Israel? You will reign over the LORD's people and save them from the power of their enemies round about. And this will be a sign to you that the LORD has anointed you ruler over his inheritance:*

20 When Samuel had all Israel come forward by tribes, the tribe of Benjamin was taken by lot. 21 Then he brought forward the tribe of Benjamin, clan by clan, and Matri's clan was taken. Finally Saul son of Kish was taken. But when they looked for him, he was not to be found. 22 So they inquired further of the LORD, "Has the man come here yet?"

And the LORD said, "Yes, he has hidden himself among the supplies."

23 They ran and brought him out, and as he stood among the people he was a head taller than any of the others. 24 Samuel said to all the people, "Do you see the man the LORD has chosen? There is no one like him among all the people."

Then the people shouted, "Long live the king!"

25 Samuel explained to the people the rights and duties of kingship. He wrote them down on a scroll and deposited it before the LORD. Then Samuel dismissed the people to go to their own homes.

26 Saul also went to his home in Gibeah, accompanied by valiant men whose hearts God had touched. 27 But some scoundrels said, "How can this fellow save us?" They despised him and brought him no gifts. But Saul kept silent.

Saul Rescues the City of Jabesh

11 Nahash[a] the Ammonite went up and besieged Jabesh Gilead. And all the men of Jabesh said to him, "Make a treaty with us, and we will be subject to you."

2 But Nahash the Ammonite replied, "I will make a treaty with you only on the condition that I gouge out the right eye of every one of you and so bring disgrace on all Israel."

3 The elders of Jabesh said to him, "Give us seven days so we can send messengers throughout Israel; if no one comes to rescue us, we will surrender to you."

4 When the messengers came to Gibeah of Saul and reported these terms to the people, they all wept aloud. 5 Just

then Saul was returning from the fields, behind his oxen, and he asked, "What is wrong with everyone? Why are they weeping?" Then they repeated to him what the men of Jabesh had said.

6 When Saul heard their words, the Spirit of God came powerfully upon him, and he burned with anger. 7 He took a pair of oxen, cut them into pieces, and sent the pieces by messengers throughout Israel, proclaiming, "This is what will be done to the oxen of anyone who does not follow Saul and Samuel." Then the terror of the LORD fell on the people, and they came out together as one. 8 When Saul mustered them at Bezek, the men of Israel numbered three hundred thousand and those of Judah thirty thousand.

9 They told the messengers who had come, "Say to the men of Jabesh Gilead, 'By the time the sun is hot tomorrow, you will be rescued.' " When the messengers went and reported this to the men of Jabesh, they were elated. 10 They said to the Ammonites, "Tomorrow we will surrender to you, and you can do to us whatever you like."

11 The next day Saul separated his men into three divisions; during the last watch of the night they broke into the camp of the Ammonites and slaughtered them until the heat of the day. Those who survived were scattered, so that no two of them were left together.

Saul Confirmed as King

12 The people then said to Samuel, "Who was it that asked, 'Shall Saul reign over us?' Turn these men over to us so that we may put them to death."

13 But Saul said, "No one will be put to death today, for this day the LORD has rescued Israel."

14 Then Samuel said to the people, "Come, let us go to Gilgal and there renew the kingship." 15 So all the people went to Gilgal and made Saul king in the presence of the LORD. There they sacrificed fellowship offerings before the LORD,

---

a 1 Masoretic Text; Dead Sea Scrolls gifts. Now Nahash king of the Ammonites oppressed the Gadites and Reubenites severely. He gouged out all their right eyes and struck terror and dread in Israel. Not a man remained among the Israelites beyond the Jordan whose right eye was not gouged out by Nahash king of the Ammonites, except that seven thousand men fled from the Ammonites and entered Jabesh Gilead. About a month later, 1Nahash

Surveys show that lots of teens are concerned about improving their self-image, but they wonder how to go about it. Probably the best way to begin to feel good about yourself is to keep making good choices. Take a look at what Samuel says in this farewell speech to Israel, and how the people responded. Then, like Samuel, live a caring, honest and godly life. You'll not only develop a good self-image, other people will respect you too.

{1 Samuel 12:1–4}

and Saul and all the Israelites held a great celebration.

Samuel's Farewell Speech

12 Samuel said to all Israel, "I have listened to everything you said to me and have set a king over you. 2 Now you have a king as your leader. As for me, I am old and gray, and my sons are here with you. I have been your leader from my youth until this day. 3 Here I stand. Testify against me in the presence of the LORD and his anointed. Whose ox have I taken? Whose donkey have I taken? Whom have I cheated? Whom have I oppressed? From whose hand have I accepted a bribe to make me shut my eyes? If I have done any of these things, I will make it right."

4 "You have not cheated or oppressed us," they replied. "You have not taken anything from anyone's hand."

5 Samuel said to them, "The LORD is witness against you, and also his anointed is witness this day, that you have not found anything in my hand."

"He is witness," they said.

6 Then Samuel said to the people, "It is the LORD who appointed Moses and Aaron and brought your ancestors up out of Egypt. 7 Now then, stand here, because I am going to confront you with evidence before the LORD as to all the righteous acts performed by the LORD for you and your ancestors.

8 "After Jacob entered Egypt, they cried to the LORD for help, and the LORD sent Moses and Aaron, who brought your ancestors out of Egypt and settled them in this place.

9 "But they forgot the LORD their God; so he sold them into the hand of Sisera, the commander of the army of Hazor, and into the hands of the Philistines and the king of Moab, who fought against them. 10 They cried out to the LORD and said, 'We have sinned; we have forsaken the LORD and served the Baals and the Ashtoreths. But now deliver us from the hands of our enemies, and we will serve you.' 11 Then the LORD sent Jerub-Baal,a Barak,b Jephthah and Samuel,c and he delivered you from the hands of your enemies all around you, so that you lived in safety.

12 "But when you saw that Nahash king of the Ammonites was moving against you, you said to me, 'No, we want a king to rule over us' — even though the LORD your God was your king. 13 Now here is the king you have chosen, the one you asked for; see, the LORD has set a king over you. 14 If you fear the LORD and serve and obey him and do not rebel against his commands, and if both you and the king who reigns over you follow the LORD your God — good! 15 But if you do not obey the LORD, and if you rebel against his commands, his hand will be against you, as it was against your ancestors.

16 "Now then, stand still and see this great thing the LORD is about to do before your eyes! 17 Is it not wheat harvest now? I will call on the LORD to send thunder and

---

a 11 Also called *Gideon*   b 11 Some Septuagint manuscripts and Syriac; Hebrew *Bedan*   c 11 Hebrew; some Septuagint manuscripts and Syriac *Samson*

rain. And you will realize what an evil thing you did in the eyes of the LORD when you asked for a king."

¹⁸Then Samuel called on the LORD, and that same day the LORD sent thunder and rain. So all the people stood in awe of the LORD and of Samuel.

¹⁹The people all said to Samuel, "Pray to the LORD your God for your servants so that we will not die, for we have added to all our other sins the evil of asking for a king."

²⁰"Do not be afraid," Samuel replied. "You have done all this evil; yet do not turn away from the LORD, but serve the LORD with all your heart. ²¹Do not turn away after useless idols. They can do you no good, nor can they rescue you, because they are useless. ²²For the sake of his great name the LORD will not reject his people, because the LORD was pleased to make you his own. ²³As for me, far be it from me that I should sin against the LORD by failing to pray for you. And I will teach you the way that is good and right. ²⁴But be sure to fear the LORD and serve him faithfully with all your heart; consider what great things he has done for you.

1 Samuel 13

Q: Why didn't Saul's army carry swords or spears?

BONUS: What two men did have a sword or spear?

Answers on next page

²⁵Yet if you persist in doing evil, both you and your king will perish."

Samuel Rebukes Saul

13 Saul was thirty*ᵃ* years old when he became king, and he reigned over Israel forty-*ᵇ* two years.

²Saul chose three thousand men from Israel; two thousand were with him at Mikmash and in the hill country of Bethel, and a thousand were with Jonathan at Gibeah in Benjamin. The rest of the men he sent back to their homes.

³Jonathan attacked the Philistine outpost at Geba, and the Philistines heard about it. Then Saul had the trumpet blown throughout the land and said, "Let the Hebrews hear!" ⁴So all Israel heard the news: "Saul has attacked the Philistine outpost, and now Israel has become obnoxious to the Philistines." And the people were summoned to join Saul at Gilgal.

⁵The Philistines assembled to fight Israel, with three thousand*ᶜ* chariots, six thousand charioteers, and soldiers as numerous as the sand on the seashore. They went up and camped at Mikmash, east of Beth Aven. ⁶When the Israelites saw that their situation was critical and that their army was hard pressed, they hid in caves and thickets, among the rocks, and in pits and cisterns. ⁷Some Hebrews even crossed the Jordan to the land of Gad and Gilead.

Saul remained at Gilgal, and all the troops with him were quaking with fear. ⁸He waited seven days, the time set by Samuel; but Samuel did not come to Gilgal, and Saul's men began to scatter. ⁹So he said, "Bring me the burnt offering and the fellowship offerings." And Saul offered up the burnt offering. ¹⁰Just as he finished making the offering, Samuel arrived, and Saul went out to greet him.

¹¹"What have you done?" asked Samuel.

Saul replied, "When I saw that the men were scattering, and that you did not come at the set time, and that the

---

ᵃ 1 A few late manuscripts of the Septuagint; Hebrew does not have *thirty.* *ᵇ 1* Probable reading of the original Hebrew text (see Acts 13:21); Masoretic Text does not have *forty-.* *ᶜ 5* Some Septuagint manuscripts and Syriac; Hebrew *thirty thousand*

Philistines were assembling at Mikmash, [12] I thought, 'Now the Philistines will come down against me at Gilgal, and I have not sought the LORD's favor.' So I felt compelled to offer the burnt offering."

[13] "You have done a foolish thing," Samuel said. "You have not kept the command the LORD your God gave you; if you had, he would have established your kingdom over Israel for all time. [14] But now your kingdom will not endure; the LORD has sought out a man after his own heart and appointed him ruler of his people, because you have not kept the LORD's command."

[15] Then Samuel left Gilgal[a] and went up to Gibeah in Benjamin, and Saul counted the men who were with him. They numbered about six hundred.

Israel Without Weapons

[16] Saul and his son Jonathan and the men with them were staying in Gibeah[b] in Benjamin, while the Philistines camped at Mikmash. [17] Raiding parties went out from the Philistine camp in three detachments. One turned toward Ophrah in the vicinity of Shual, [18] another toward Beth Horon, and the third toward the borderland overlooking the Valley of Zeboyim facing the wilderness.

[19] Not a blacksmith could be found in the whole land of Israel, because the Philistines had said, "Otherwise the Hebrews will make swords or spears!" [20] So all Israel went down to the Philistines to have their plow points, mattocks, axes and sickles[c] sharpened. [21] The price was two-thirds of a shekel[d] for sharpening plow points and mattocks, and a third of a shekel[e] for sharpening forks and axes and for repointing goads.

[22] So on the day of the battle not a soldier with Saul and Jonathan had a sword or spear in his hand; only Saul and his son Jonathan had them.

Jonathan Attacks the Philistines

14 [23] Now a detachment of Philistines had gone out to the pass at Mikmash. [1] One day Jonathan son of Saul

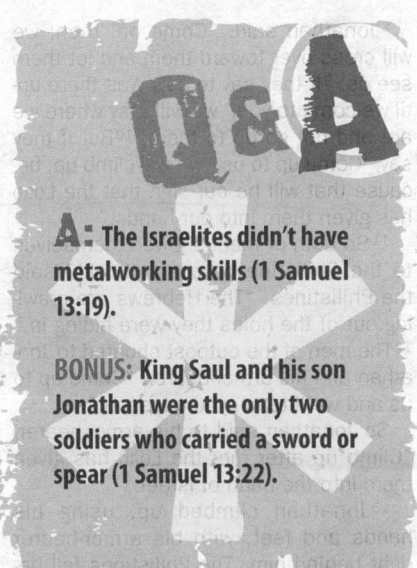

A: The Israelites didn't have metalworking skills (1 Samuel 13:19).

BONUS: King Saul and his son Jonathan were the only two soldiers who carried a sword or spear (1 Samuel 13:22).

said to his young armor-bearer, "Come, let's go over to the Philistine outpost on the other side." But he did not tell his father.

[2] Saul was staying on the outskirts of Gibeah under a pomegranate tree in Migron. With him were about six hundred men, [3] among whom was Ahijah, who was wearing an ephod. He was a son of Ichabod's brother Ahitub son of Phinehas, the son of Eli, the LORD's priest in Shiloh. No one was aware that Jonathan had left.

[4] On each side of the pass that Jonathan intended to cross to reach the Philistine outpost was a cliff; one was called Bozez and the other Seneh. [5] One cliff stood to the north toward Mikmash, the other to the south toward Geba.

[6] Jonathan said to his young armor-bearer, "Come, let's go over to the outpost of those uncircumcised men. Perhaps the LORD will act in our behalf. Nothing can hinder the LORD from saving, whether by many or by few."

[7] "Do all that you have in mind," his armor-bearer said. "Go ahead; I am with you heart and soul."

---

a 15 Hebrew; Septuagint *Gilgal and went his way; the rest of the people went after Saul to meet the army, and they went out of Gilgal*   *b* 16 Two Hebrew manuscripts; most Hebrew manuscripts *Geba,* a variant of *Gibeah*   *c* 20 Septuagint; Hebrew *plow points*   *d* 21 That is, about 1/4 ounce or about 8 grams   *e* 21 That is, about 1/8 ounce or about 4 grams

8 Jonathan said, "Come on, then; we will cross over toward them and let them see us. 9 If they say to us, 'Wait there until we come to you,' we will stay where we are and not go up to them. 10 But if they say, 'Come up to us,' we will climb up, because that will be our sign that the LORD has given them into our hands."

11 So both of them showed themselves to the Philistine outpost. "Look!" said the Philistines. "The Hebrews are crawling out of the holes they were hiding in." 12 The men of the outpost shouted to Jonathan and his armor-bearer, "Come up to us and we'll teach you a lesson."

So Jonathan said to his armor-bearer, "Climb up after me; the LORD has given them into the hand of Israel."

13 Jonathan climbed up, using his hands and feet, with his armor-bearer right behind him. The Philistines fell before Jonathan, and his armor-bearer followed and killed behind him. 14 In that first attack Jonathan and his armor-bearer killed some twenty men in an area of about half an acre.

Israel Routs the Philistines

15 Then panic struck the whole army— those in the camp and field, and those in the outposts and raiding parties—and the ground shook. It was a panic sent by God.[a]

16 Saul's lookouts at Gibeah in Benjamin saw the army melting away in all directions. 17 Then Saul said to the men who were with him, "Muster the forces and see who has left us." When they did, it was Jonathan and his armor-bearer who were not there.

18 Saul said to Ahijah, "Bring the ark of God." (At that time it was with the Israelites.)[b] 19 While Saul was talking to the priest, the tumult in the Philistine camp increased more and more. So Saul said to the priest, "Withdraw your hand."

20 Then Saul and all his men assembled and went to the battle. They found the Philistines in total confusion, striking each other with their swords. 21 Those He-

brews who had previously been with the Philistines and had gone up with them to their camp went over to the Israelites who were with Saul and Jonathan. 22 When all the Israelites who had hidden in the hill country of Ephraim heard that the Philistines were on the run, they joined the battle in hot pursuit. 23 So on that day the LORD saved Israel, and the battle moved on beyond Beth Aven.

Jonathan Eats Honey

24 Now the Israelites were in distress that day, because Saul had bound the people under an oath, saying, "Cursed be anyone who eats food before evening comes, before I have avenged myself on my enemies!" So none of the troops tasted food.

25 The entire army entered the woods, and there was honey on the ground. 26 When they went into the woods, they saw the honey oozing out; yet no one put his hand to his mouth, because they feared the oath. 27 But Jonathan had not heard that his father had bound the people with the oath, so he reached out the end of the staff that was in his hand and dipped it into the honeycomb. He raised his hand to his mouth, and his eyes brightened.[c] 28 Then one of the soldiers told him, "Your father bound the army under a strict oath, saying, 'Cursed be anyone who eats food today!' That is why the men are faint."

29 Jonathan said, "My father has made trouble for the country. See how my eyes brightened when I tasted a little of this honey. 30 How much better it would have been if the men had eaten today some of the plunder they took from their enemies. Would not the slaughter of the Philistines have been even greater?"

31 That day, after the Israelites had struck down the Philistines from Mikmash to Aijalon, they were exhausted. 32 They pounced on the plunder and, taking sheep, cattle and calves, they butchered them on the ground and ate them, together with the blood. 33 Then someone

---

[a] 15 Or a terrible panic   [b] 18 Hebrew; Septuagint "Bring the ephod." (At that time he wore the ephod before the Israelites.)
[c] 27 Or his strength was renewed; similarly in verse 29

said to Saul, "Look, the men are sinning against the LORD by eating meat that has blood in it."

"You have broken faith," he said. "Roll a large stone over here at once." ³⁴Then he said, "Go out among the men and tell them, 'Each of you bring me your cattle and sheep, and slaughter them here and eat them. Do not sin against the LORD by eating meat with blood still in it.'"

So everyone brought his ox that night and slaughtered it there. ³⁵Then Saul built an altar to the LORD; it was the first time he had done this.

³⁶Saul said, "Let us go down and pursue the Philistines by night and plunder them till dawn, and let us not leave one of them alive."

"Do whatever seems best to you," they replied.

But the priest said, "Let us inquire of God here."

³⁷So Saul asked God, "Shall I go down and pursue the Philistines? Will you give them into Israel's hand?" But God did not answer him that day.

³⁸Saul therefore said, "Come here, all you who are leaders of the army, and let us find out what sin has been committed today. ³⁹As surely as the LORD who rescues Israel lives, even if the guilt lies with my son Jonathan, he must die." But not one of them said a word.

⁴⁰Saul then said to all the Israelites, "You stand over there; I and Jonathan my son will stand over here."

"Do what seems best to you," they replied.

⁴¹Then Saul prayed to the LORD, the God of Israel, "Why have you not answered your servant today? If the fault is in me or my son Jonathan, respond with Urim, but if the men of Israel are at fault,ᵃ respond with Thummim." Jonathan and Saul were taken by lot, and the men were cleared. ⁴²Saul said, "Cast the lot between me and Jonathan my son." And Jonathan was taken.

⁴³Then Saul said to Jonathan, "Tell me what you have done."

So Jonathan told him, "I tasted a little honey with the end of my staff. And now I must die!"

⁴⁴Saul said, "May God deal with me, be it ever so severely, if you do not die, Jonathan."

⁴⁵But the men said to Saul, "Should Jonathan die—he who has brought about this great deliverance in Israel? Never! As surely as the LORD lives, not a hair of his head will fall to the ground, for he did this today with God's help." So the men rescued Jonathan, and he was not put to death.

⁴⁶Then Saul stopped pursuing the Philistines, and they withdrew to their own land.

⁴⁷After Saul had assumed rule over Israel, he fought against their enemies on every side: Moab, the Ammonites, Edom, the kingsᵇ of Zobah, and the Philistines. Wherever he turned, he inflicted punishment on them.ᶜ ⁴⁸He fought valiantly and defeated the Amalekites, delivering Israel from the hands of those who had plundered them.

Saul's Family

⁴⁹Saul's sons were Jonathan, Ishvi and Malki-Shua. The name of his older daughter was Merab, and that of the younger was Michal. ⁵⁰His wife's name was Ahinoam daughter of Ahimaaz. The name of the commander of Saul's army was Abner son of Ner, and Ner was Saul's uncle. ⁵¹Saul's father Kish and Abner's father Ner were sons of Abiel.

⁵²All the days of Saul there was bitter war with the Philistines, and whenever Saul saw a mighty or brave man, he took him into his service.

The LORD Rejects Saul as King

15 Samuel said to Saul, "I am the one the LORD sent to anoint you king over his people Israel; so listen now to the message from the LORD. ²This is what the LORD Almighty says: 'I will punish the Amalekites for what they did to Israel when they waylaid them as they came up from Egypt. ³Now go, attack the Amalekites

---

ᵃ 41 Septuagint; Hebrew does not have "Why . . . at fault." ᵇ 47 Masoretic Text; Dead Sea Scrolls and Septuagint king
ᶜ 47 Hebrew; Septuagint he was victorious

and totally destroy[a] all that belongs to them. Do not spare them; put to death men and women, children and infants, cattle and sheep, camels and donkeys.' "

4 So Saul summoned the men and mustered them at Telaim—two hundred thousand foot soldiers and ten thousand from Judah. 5 Saul went to the city of Amalek and set an ambush in the ravine. 6 Then he said to the Kenites, "Go away, leave the Amalekites so that I do not destroy you along with them; for you showed kindness to all the Israelites when they came up out of Egypt." So the Kenites moved away from the Amalekites.

7 Then Saul attacked the Amalekites all the way from Havilah to Shur, near the eastern border of Egypt. 8 He took Agag king of the Amalekites alive, and all his people he totally destroyed with the sword. 9 But Saul and the army spared Agag and the best of the sheep and cattle, the fat calves[b] and lambs—everything that was good. These they were unwilling to destroy completely, but everything that was despised and weak they totally destroyed.

10 Then the word of the LORD came to Samuel: 11 "I regret that I have made Saul king, because he has turned away from me and has not carried out my instructions." Samuel was angry, and he cried out to the LORD all that night.

12 Early in the morning Samuel got up and went to meet Saul, but he was told, "Saul has gone to Carmel. There he has set up a monument in his own honor and has turned and gone on down to Gilgal."

13 When Samuel reached him, Saul said, "The LORD bless you! I have carried out the LORD's instructions."

14 But Samuel said, "What then is this bleating of sheep in my ears? What is this lowing of cattle that I hear?"

15 Saul answered, "The soldiers brought them from the Amalekites; they spared the best of the sheep and cattle to sacrifice to the LORD your God, but we totally destroyed the rest."

16 "Enough!" Samuel said to Saul. "Let

me tell you what the LORD said to me last night."

"Tell me," Saul replied.

17 Samuel said, "Although you were once small in your own eyes, did you not become the head of the tribes of Israel? The LORD anointed you king over Israel. 18 And he sent you on a mission, saying, 'Go and completely destroy those wicked

INSTANT ACCESS

Your mom tells you to put your dirty dishes in the dishwasher, then goes off to watch TV and leaves her dishes on the table. That can be upsetting. It doesn't seem fair to hold others to a higher standard than you hold yourself. That's what Saul did. Saul knowingly disobeyed God (1 Samuel 13). But when Jonathan unknowingly violated Saul's command, Saul was ready to execute him! Before you get too upset with Saul, or with your mom, stop and think. Do you get upset with friends for gossiping about you—when you gossip just as much about them? Don't use the Bible as a hammer to beat up on others. Use it as a mirror to better see yourself!

{1 Samuel 14:44}

people, the Amalekites; wage war against them until you have wiped them out.' 19 Why did you not obey the LORD? Why did you pounce on the plunder and do evil in the eyes of the LORD?"

20 "But I did obey the LORD," Saul said. "I went on the mission the LORD assigned me. I completely destroyed the Amalekites and brought back Agag their king. 21 The soldiers took sheep and cattle from the plunder, the best of what was devoted to God, in order to sacrifice them to the LORD your God at Gilgal."

22 But Samuel replied:

"Does the LORD delight in burnt
        offerings and sacrifices
    as much as in obeying the LORD?
To obey is better than sacrifice,
    and to heed is better than the fat of
        rams.
23 For rebellion is like the sin of
        divination,
    and arrogance like the evil of
        idolatry.
Because you have rejected the word
        of the LORD,
    he has rejected you as king."

24 Then Saul said to Samuel, "I have sinned. I violated the LORD's command and your instructions. I was afraid of the men and so I gave in to them. 25 Now I beg you, forgive my sin and come back with me, so that I may worship the LORD."

26 But Samuel said to him, "I will not go back with you. You have rejected the word of the LORD, and the LORD has rejected you as king over Israel!"

27 As Samuel turned to leave, Saul caught hold of the hem of his robe, and it tore. 28 Samuel said to him, "The LORD has torn the kingdom of Israel from you today and has given it to one of your neighbors—to one better than you. 29 He who is the Glory of Israel does not lie or change his mind; for he is not a human being, that he should change his mind."

30 Saul replied, "I have sinned. But please honor me before the elders of my people and before Israel; come back with me, so that I may worship the LORD your God." 31 So Samuel went back with Saul, and Saul worshiped the LORD.

32 Then Samuel said, "Bring me Agag king of the Amalekites."

Agag came to him in chains.[a] And he thought, "Surely the bitterness of death is past."

33 But Samuel said,

"As your sword has made women
        childless,
    so will your mother be childless
        among women."

And Samuel put Agag to death before the LORD at Gilgal.

34 Then Samuel left for Ramah, but Saul went up to his home in Gibeah of Saul. 35 Until the day Samuel died, he did not go to see Saul again, though Samuel mourned for him. And the LORD regretted that he had made Saul king over Israel.

Samuel Anoints David

16 The LORD said to Samuel, "How long will you mourn for Saul, since I have rejected him as king over Israel? Fill your horn with oil and be on your way; I am sending you to Jesse of Bethlehem. I have chosen one of his sons to be king."

2 But Samuel said, "How can I go? If Saul hears about it, he will kill me."

The LORD said, "Take a heifer with you and say, 'I have come to sacrifice to the LORD.' 3 Invite Jesse to the sacrifice, and I will show you what to do. You are to anoint for me the one I indicate."

4 Samuel did what the LORD said. When he arrived at Bethlehem, the elders of the town trembled when they met him. They asked, "Do you come in peace?"

5 Samuel replied, "Yes, in peace; I have come to sacrifice to the LORD. Consecrate yourselves and come to the sacrifice with me." Then he consecrated Jesse and his sons and invited them to the sacrifice.

6 When they arrived, Samuel saw Eliab and thought, "Surely the LORD's anointed stands here before the LORD."

7 But the LORD said to Samuel, "Do not consider his appearance or his height, for I have rejected him. The LORD does not

---

[a] 32 The meaning of the Hebrew for this phrase is uncertain.

> I'm on the short side and have some problems with breaking out. I feel embarrassed about what girls think of the way I look most of the time. People don't understand how self-conscious I feel. >> Christopher

Dear Jordan

Dear Christopher,

I have heard similar stories so often. We see all those air-brushed pictures from Hollywood and then see our own imperfections too clearly. As far as your complexion goes, there are many products that are effective over the counter. If you've already tried those, see your doctor if you are able to.

Speaking of appearances, you might find it interesting to know how God looks at us. In 1 Samuel 16, God tells Samuel to anoint a king from Jesse's sons. Samuel saw one of the sons and thought he was the one. But God said, "Do not consider his appearance or his height ... The LORD does not look at the things people look at. People look at the outward appearance, but the LORD looks at the heart."

A nice smile, a good personality, confidence and kindness are very attractive to most girls.

Jordan

look at the things people look at. People look at the outward appearance, but the LORD looks at the heart."

8Then Jesse called Abinadab and had him pass in front of Samuel. But Samuel said, "The LORD has not chosen this one either." 9Jesse then had Shammah pass by, but Samuel said, "Nor has the LORD chosen this one." 10Jesse had seven of his sons pass before Samuel, but Samuel said to him, "The LORD has not chosen these." 11So he asked Jesse, "Are these all the sons you have?"

"There is still the youngest," Jesse answered. "He is tending the sheep."

Samuel said, "Send for him; we will not sit down until he arrives."

12So he sent for him and had him brought in. He was glowing with health and had a fine appearance and handsome features.

Then the LORD said, "Rise and anoint him; this is the one."

13So Samuel took the horn of oil and anointed him in the presence of his brothers, and from that day on the Spirit of the LORD came powerfully upon David. Samuel then went to Ramah.

David in Saul's Service

14Now the Spirit of the LORD had departed from Saul, and an evil[a] spirit from the LORD tormented him.

15Saul's attendants said to him, "See, an evil spirit from God is tormenting you. 16Let our lord command his servants here to search for someone who can play the lyre. He will play when the evil spirit from God comes on you, and you will feel better."

17So Saul said to his attendants, "Find someone who plays well and bring him to me."

18One of the servants answered, "I have seen a son of Jesse of Bethlehem who knows how to play the lyre. He is a brave man and a warrior. He speaks well and is a fine-looking man. And the LORD is with him."

19Then Saul sent messengers to Jesse and said, "Send me your son David, who is with the sheep." 20So Jesse took a donkey loaded with bread, a skin of wine and a young goat and sent them with his son David to Saul.

21David came to Saul and entered his service. Saul liked him very much, and David became one of his armor-bearers. 22Then Saul sent word to Jesse, saying, "Allow David to remain in my service, for I am pleased with him."

23Whenever the spirit from God came on Saul, David would take up his lyre and play. Then relief would come to Saul; he would feel better, and the evil spirit would leave him.

David and Goliath

17 Now the Philistines gathered their forces for war and assembled at Sokoh in Judah. They pitched camp at Ephes Dammim, between Sokoh and Azekah. 2Saul and the Israelites assembled and camped in the Valley of Elah and drew up their battle line to meet the Philistines. 3The Philistines occupied one hill and the Israelites another, with the valley between them.

4A champion named Goliath, who was from Gath, came out of the Philistine camp. His height was six cubits and a span.[b] 5He had a bronze helmet on his head and wore a coat of scale armor of bronze weighing five thousand shekels[c]; 6on his legs he wore bronze greaves, and a bronze javelin was slung on his back. 7His spear shaft was like a weaver's rod, and its iron point weighed six hundred shekels.[d] His shield bearer went ahead of him.

8Goliath stood and shouted to the ranks of Israel, "Why do you come out and line up for battle? Am I not a Philistine, and are you not the servants of Saul? Choose a man and have him come down to me. 9If he is able to fight and kill me, we will become your subjects; but if I overcome him and kill him, you will become our subjects and serve us." 10Then the Philistine said, "This day I defy the armies of Israel! Give me a man and let us fight each other." 11On hearing the Philistine's

---

a 14 Or *and a harmful*; similarly in verses 15, 16 and 23   b 4 That is, about 9 feet 9 inches or about 3 meters
c 5 That is, about 125 pounds or about 58 kilograms   d 7 That is, about 15 pounds or about 6.9 kilograms

words, Saul and all the Israelites were dismayed and terrified.

¹²Now David was the son of an Ephrathite named Jesse, who was from Bethlehem in Judah. Jesse had eight sons, and in Saul's time he was very old. ¹³Jesse's three oldest sons had followed Saul to the war: The firstborn was Eliab; the second, Abinadab; and the third, Shammah. ¹⁴David was the youngest. The three oldest followed Saul, ¹⁵but David went back and forth from Saul to tend his father's sheep at Bethlehem.

¹⁶For forty days the Philistine came forward every morning and evening and took his stand.

¹⁷Now Jesse said to his son David, "Take this ephah*a* of roasted grain and these ten loaves of bread for your brothers and hurry to their camp. ¹⁸Take along these ten cheeses to the commander of their unit. See how your brothers are and bring back some assurance*b* from them. ¹⁹They are with Saul and all the men of Israel in the Valley of Elah, fighting against the Philistines."

²⁰Early in the morning David left the flock in the care of a shepherd, loaded up and set out, as Jesse had directed. He reached the camp as the army was going out to its battle positions, shouting the war cry. ²¹Israel and the Philistines were drawing up their lines facing each other. ²²David left his things with the keeper of supplies, ran to the battle lines and asked his brothers how they were. ²³As he was talking with them, Goliath, the Philistine champion from Gath, stepped out from his lines and shouted his usual defiance, and David heard it. ²⁴Whenever the Israelites saw the man, they all fled from him in great fear.

²⁵Now the Israelites had been saying, "Do you see how this man keeps coming out? He comes out to defy Israel. The king will give great wealth to the man who kills him. He will also give him his daughter in marriage and will exempt his family from taxes in Israel."

²⁶David asked the men standing near him, "What will be done for the man who kills this Philistine and removes this disgrace from Israel? Who is this uncircumcised Philistine that he should defy the armies of the living God?"

²⁷They repeated to him what they had been saying and told him, "This is what will be done for the man who kills him."

²⁸When Eliab, David's oldest brother, heard him speaking with the men, he burned with anger at him and asked, "Why have you come down here? And with whom did you leave those few sheep in the wilderness? I know how conceited you are and how wicked your heart is; you came down only to watch the battle."

²⁹"Now what have I done?" said David. "Can't I even speak?" ³⁰He then turned away to someone else and brought up the same matter, and the men answered him as before. ³¹What David said was overheard and reported to Saul, and Saul sent for him.

³²David said to Saul, "Let no one lose heart on account of this Philistine; your servant will go and fight him."

³³Saul replied, "You are not able to go out against this Philistine and fight him; you are only a young man, and he has been a warrior from his youth."

Q&A

1 Samuel 17

Q: Was Goliath tall enough to play NBA basketball?

BONUS: Was the stone David used to kill Goliath closer to the size of a golf ball or a tennis ball?

Answers on next page

---

a 17 That is, probably about 36 pounds or about 16 kilograms   *b* 18 Or some token; or some pledge of spoils

³⁴But David said to Saul, "Your servant has been keeping his father's sheep. When a lion or a bear came and carried off a sheep from the flock, ³⁵I went after it, struck it and rescued the sheep from its mouth. When it turned on me, I seized it by its hair, struck it and killed it. ³⁶Your servant has killed both the lion and the bear; this uncircumcised Philistine will be like one of them, because he has defied the armies of the living God. ³⁷The LORD who rescued me from the paw of the lion and the paw of the bear will rescue me from the hand of this Philistine."

Saul said to David, "Go, and the LORD be with you."

³⁸Then Saul dressed David in his own tunic. He put a coat of armor on him and a bronze helmet on his head. ³⁹David fastened on his sword over the tunic and tried walking around, because he was not used to them.

"I cannot go in these," he said to Saul, "because I am not used to them." So he took them off. ⁴⁰Then he took his staff in his hand, chose five smooth stones from the stream, put them in the pouch of his shepherd's bag and, with his sling in his hand, approached the Philistine.

⁴¹Meanwhile, the Philistine, with his shield bearer in front of him, kept coming closer to David. ⁴²He looked David over and saw that he was little more than a boy, glowing with health and handsome, and he despised him. ⁴³He said to David, "Am I a dog, that you come at me with sticks?" And the Philistine cursed David by his gods. ⁴⁴"Come here," he said, "and I'll give your flesh to the birds and the wild animals!"

⁴⁵David said to the Philistine, "You come against me with sword and spear and javelin, but I come against you in the name of the LORD Almighty, the God of the armies of Israel, whom you have defied. ⁴⁶This day the LORD will deliver you into my hands, and I'll strike you down and cut off your head. This very day I will give the carcasses of the Philistine army to the birds and the wild animals, and the whole world will know that there is a God in Is-

rael. ⁴⁷All those gathered here will know that it is not by sword or spear that the LORD saves; for the battle is the LORD's, and he will give all of you into our hands."

⁴⁸As the Philistine moved closer to attack him, David ran quickly toward the battle line to meet him. ⁴⁹Reaching into his bag and taking out a stone, he slung it and struck the Philistine on the forehead. The stone sank into his forehead, and he fell facedown on the ground.

⁵⁰So David triumphed over the Philistine with a sling and a stone; without a sword in his hand he struck down the Philistine and killed him.

⁵¹David ran and stood over him. He took hold of the Philistine's sword and drew it from the sheath. After he killed him, he cut off his head with the sword.

When the Philistines saw that their hero was dead, they turned and ran. ⁵²Then the men of Israel and Judah surged forward with a shout and pursued the Philistines to the entrance of Gathᵃ and to the gates of Ekron. Their dead were strewn along the Shaaraim road to Gath and Ekron. ⁵³When the Israelites returned from

A: You bet! He was over nine feet tall (1 Samuel 17:4)!

BONUS: Many sling stones have been found on battlegrounds in Israel. These heavy stones were just a little smaller than a tennis ball.

chasing the Philistines, they plundered their camp.

54 David took the Philistine's head and brought it to Jerusalem; he put the Philistine's weapons in his own tent.

55 As Saul watched David going out to meet the Philistine, he said to Abner, commander of the army, "Abner, whose son is that young man?"

Abner replied, "As surely as you live, Your Majesty, I don't know."

56 The king said, "Find out whose son this young man is."

57 As soon as David returned from killing the Philistine, Abner took him and brought him before Saul, with David still holding the Philistine's head.

58 "Whose son are you, young man?" Saul asked him.

David said, "I am the son of your servant Jesse of Bethlehem."

Saul's Growing Fear of David

18 After David had finished talking with Saul, Jonathan became one in spirit with David, and he loved him as himself. 2 From that day Saul kept David with him and did not let him return home to his family. 3 And Jonathan made a covenant with David because he loved him as himself. 4 Jonathan took off the robe he was wearing and gave it to David, along with his tunic, and even his sword, his bow and his belt.

5 Whatever mission Saul sent him on, David was so successful that Saul gave him a high rank in the army. This pleased all the troops, and Saul's officers as well.

6 When the men were returning home after David had killed the Philistine, the women came out from all the towns of Israel to meet King Saul with singing and dancing, with joyful songs and with timbrels and lyres. 7 As they danced, they sang:

"Saul has slain his thousands,
    and David his tens of thousands."

8 Saul was very angry; this refrain displeased him greatly. "They have credited David with tens of thousands," he

---

INSTANT ACCESS

Ashley is going out with the guy you like. Matt is the quarterback and you're on the bench. These are just two reasons why teens get jealous of each other. You could probably name more. King Saul was jealous of David because David was successful. But what's important here is to see what jealousy leads to. Instead of being David's friend, Saul became David's enemy (1 Samuel 18:15). Jealousy drives people apart. It creates suspicion and fear. What can you do about jealousy? First, remember that God loves you and gives you what's best for you. Second, pray for the person you're jealous of. It's really hard to hate or fear someone you're praying for!

{1 Samuel 18:1–15}

---

thought, "but me with only thousands. What more can he get but the kingdom?" 9 And from that time on Saul kept a close eye on David.

10 The next day an evil[a] spirit from God came forcefully on Saul. He was prophesying in his house, while David was playing the lyre, as he usually did. Saul had a spear in his hand 11 and he hurled it, saying to himself, "I'll pin David to the wall." But David eluded him twice.

12 Saul was afraid of David, because

---

a 10 Or a harmful

the Lord was with David but had departed from Saul. ¹³So he sent David away from him and gave him command over a thousand men, and David led the troops in their campaigns. ¹⁴In everything he did he had great success, because the Lord was with him. ¹⁵When Saul saw how successful he was, he was afraid of him. ¹⁶But all Israel and Judah loved David, because he led them in their campaigns.

¹⁷Saul said to David, "Here is my older daughter Merab. I will give her to you in marriage; only serve me bravely and fight the battles of the Lord." For Saul said to himself, "I will not raise a hand against him. Let the Philistines do that!"

¹⁸But David said to Saul, "Who am I, and what is my family or my clan in Israel, that I should become the king's son-in-law?" ¹⁹Soᵃ when the time came for Merab, Saul's daughter, to be given to David, she was given in marriage to Adriel of Meholah.

²⁰Now Saul's daughter Michal was in love with David, and when they told Saul about it, he was pleased. ²¹"I will give her to him," he thought, "so that she may be a snare to him and so that the hand of the Philistines may be against him." So Saul said to David, "Now you have a second opportunity to become my son-in-law."

²²Then Saul ordered his attendants: "Speak to David privately and say, 'Look, the king likes you, and his attendants all love you; now become his son-in-law.'"

²³They repeated these words to David. But David said, "Do you think it is a small matter to become the king's son-in-law? I'm only a poor man and little known."

²⁴When Saul's servants told him what David had said, ²⁵Saul replied, "Say to David, 'The king wants no other price for the bride than a hundred Philistine foreskins, to take revenge on his enemies.'" Saul's plan was to have David fall by the hands of the Philistines.

²⁶When the attendants told David these things, he was pleased to become the king's son-in-law. So before the allotted time elapsed, ²⁷David took his men with him and went out and killed two hundred Philistines and brought back their foreskins. They counted out the full number to the king so that David might become the king's son-in-law. Then Saul gave him his daughter Michal in marriage.

²⁸When Saul realized that the Lord was with David and that his daughter Michal loved David, ²⁹Saul became still more afraid of him, and he remained his enemy the rest of his days.

³⁰The Philistine commanders continued to go out to battle, and as often as they did, David met with more success than the rest of Saul's officers, and his name became well known.

Saul Tries to Kill David

19 Saul told his son Jonathan and all the attendants to kill David. But Jonathan had taken a great liking to David ²and warned him, "My father Saul is looking for a chance to kill you. Be on your guard tomorrow morning; go into hiding and stay there. ³I will go out and stand with my father in the field where you are. I'll speak to him about you and will tell you what I find out."

⁴Jonathan spoke well of David to Saul his father and said to him, "Let not the king do wrong to his servant David; he has not wronged you, and what he has done has benefited you greatly. ⁵He took his life in his hands when he killed the Philistine. The Lord won a great victory for all Israel, and you saw it and were glad. Why then would you do wrong to an innocent man like David by killing him for no reason?"

⁶Saul listened to Jonathan and took this oath: "As surely as the Lord lives, David will not be put to death."

⁷So Jonathan called David and told him the whole conversation. He brought him to Saul, and David was with Saul as before.

⁸Once more war broke out, and David went out and fought the Philistines. He struck them with such force that they fled before him.

⁹But an evilᵇ spirit from the Lord came on Saul as he was sitting in his house with

ᵃ 19 Or However, ᵇ 9 Or But a harmful

his spear in his hand. While David was playing the lyre, [10]Saul tried to pin him to the wall with his spear, but David eluded him as Saul drove the spear into the wall. That night David made good his escape.

[11]Saul sent men to David's house to watch it and to kill him in the morning. But Michal, David's wife, warned him, "If you don't run for your life tonight, tomorrow you'll be killed." [12]So Michal let David down through a window, and he fled and escaped. [13]Then Michal took an idol and laid it on the bed, covering it with a garment and putting some goats' hair at the head.

[14]When Saul sent the men to capture David, Michal said, "He is ill."

[15]Then Saul sent the men back to see David and told them, "Bring him up to me in his bed so that I may kill him." [16]But when the men entered, there was the idol in the bed, and at the head was some goats' hair.

[17]Saul said to Michal, "Why did you deceive me like this and send my enemy away so that he escaped?"

Michal told him, "He said to me, 'Let me get away. Why should I kill you?'"

[18]When David had fled and made his escape, he went to Samuel at Ramah and told him all that Saul had done to him. Then he and Samuel went to Naioth and stayed there. [19]Word came to Saul: "David is in Naioth at Ramah"; [20]so he sent men to capture him. But when they saw a group of prophets prophesying, with Samuel standing there as their leader, the Spirit of God came on Saul's men, and they also prophesied. [21]Saul was told about it, and he sent more men, and they prophesied too. Saul sent men a third time, and they also prophesied. [22]Finally, he himself left for Ramah and went to the great cistern at Seku. And he asked, "Where are Samuel and David?"

"Over in Naioth at Ramah," they said.

[23]So Saul went to Naioth at Ramah. But the Spirit of God came even on him, and he walked along prophesying until he came to Naioth. [24]He stripped off his garments, and he too prophesied in Samuel's presence. He lay naked all that day and all that night. This is why people say, "Is Saul also among the prophets?"

David and Jonathan

20 Then David fled from Naioth at Ramah and went to Jonathan and asked, "What have I done? What is my crime? How have I wronged your father, that he is trying to kill me?"

[2]"Never!" Jonathan replied. "You are not going to die! Look, my father doesn't do anything, great or small, without letting me know. Why would he hide this from me? It isn't so!"

[3]But David took an oath and said, "Your father knows very well that I have found favor in your eyes, and he has said to himself, 'Jonathan must not know this or he will be grieved.' Yet as surely as the

PANORAMA

Change.

This book tells about the difficult years between the time when Israel had judges to lead them and then kings to lead them. It was a rocky start with King Saul.

{1 SAMUEL}

LORD lives and as you live, there is only a step between me and death."

⁴Jonathan said to David, "Whatever you want me to do, I'll do for you."

⁵So David said, "Look, tomorrow is the New Moon feast, and I am supposed to dine with the king; but let me go and hide in the field until the evening of the day after tomorrow. ⁶If your father misses me at all, tell him, 'David earnestly asked my permission to hurry to Bethlehem, his hometown, because an annual sacrifice is being made there for his whole clan.' ⁷If he says, 'Very well,' then your servant is safe. But if he loses his temper, you can be sure that he is determined to harm me. ⁸As for you, show kindness to your servant, for you have brought him into a covenant with you before the LORD. If I am guilty, then kill me yourself! Why hand me over to your father?"

⁹"Never!" Jonathan said. "If I had the least inkling that my father was determined to harm you, wouldn't I tell you?"

¹⁰David asked, "Who will tell me if your father answers you harshly?"

¹¹"Come," Jonathan said, "let's go out into the field." So they went there together.

¹²Then Jonathan said to David, "I swear by the LORD, the God of Israel, that I will surely sound out my father by this time the day after tomorrow! If he is favorably disposed toward you, will I not send you word and let you know? ¹³But if my father intends to harm you, may the LORD deal with Jonathan, be it ever so severely, if I do not let you know and send you away in peace. May the LORD be with you as he has been with my father. ¹⁴But show me unfailing kindness like the LORD's kindness as long as I live, so that I may not be killed, ¹⁵and do not ever cut off your kindness from my family—not even when the LORD has cut off every one of David's enemies from the face of the earth."

¹⁶So Jonathan made a covenant with the house of David, saying, "May the LORD call David's enemies to account." ¹⁷And Jonathan had David reaffirm his oath out of love for him, because he loved him as he loved himself.

¹⁸Then Jonathan said to David, "Tomorrow is the New Moon feast. You will be missed, because your seat will be empty. ¹⁹The day after tomorrow, toward evening, go to the place where you hid when this trouble began, and wait by the stone Ezel. ²⁰I will shoot three arrows to the side of it, as though I were shooting at a target. ²¹Then I will send a boy and say, 'Go, find the arrows.' If I say to him, 'Look, the arrows are on this side of you; bring them here,' then come, because, as surely as the LORD lives, you are safe; there is no danger. ²²But if I say to the boy, 'Look, the arrows are beyond you,' then you must go, because the LORD has sent you away. ²³And about the matter you and I discussed—remember, the LORD is witness between you and me forever."

²⁴So David hid in the field, and when the New Moon feast came, the king sat down to eat. ²⁵He sat in his customary place by the wall, opposite Jonathan,ᵃ and Abner sat next to Saul, but David's place was empty. ²⁶Saul said nothing that day, for he thought, "Something must have happened to David to make him ceremonially unclean—surely he is

1 Samuel 20

Q: What happened to Jonathan?

BONUS: How did David show his friendship?

Answers on next page

ᵃ 25 Septuagint; Hebrew *wall. Jonathan arose*

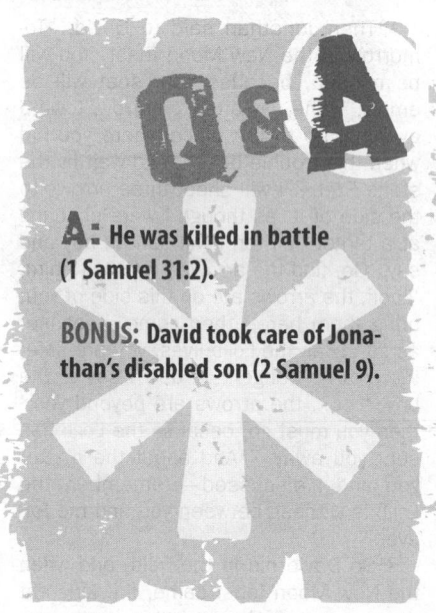

A: He was killed in battle
(1 Samuel 31:2).

BONUS: David took care of Jonathan's disabled son (2 Samuel 9).

to kill him. Then Jonathan knew that his father intended to kill David.

³⁴ Jonathan got up from the table in fierce anger; on that second day of the feast he did not eat, because he was grieved at his father's shameful treatment of David.

³⁵ In the morning Jonathan went out to the field for his meeting with David. He had a small boy with him, ³⁶ and he said to the boy, "Run and find the arrows I shoot." As the boy ran, he shot an arrow beyond him. ³⁷ When the boy came to the place where Jonathan's arrow had fallen, Jonathan called out after him, "Isn't the arrow beyond you?" ³⁸ Then he shouted, "Hurry! Go quickly! Don't stop!" The boy picked up the arrow and returned to his master. ³⁹ (The boy knew nothing about all this; only Jonathan and David knew.) ⁴⁰ Then Jonathan gave his weapons to the boy and said, "Go, carry them back to town."

⁴¹ After the boy had gone, David got up from the south side of the stone and bowed down before Jonathan three times, with his face to the ground. Then they kissed each other and wept together— but David wept the most.

⁴² Jonathan said to David, "Go in peace, for we have sworn friendship with each other in the name of the LORD, saying, 'The LORD is witness between you and me, and between your descendants and my descendants forever.' " Then David left, and Jonathan went back to the town.ᵃ

unclean." ²⁷ But the next day, the second day of the month, David's place was empty again. Then Saul said to his son Jonathan, "Why hasn't the son of Jesse come to the meal, either yesterday or today?"

²⁸ Jonathan answered, "David earnestly asked me for permission to go to Bethlehem. ²⁹ He said, 'Let me go, because our family is observing a sacrifice in the town and my brother has ordered me to be there. If I have found favor in your eyes, let me get away to see my brothers.' That is why he has not come to the king's table."

³⁰ Saul's anger flared up at Jonathan and he said to him, "You son of a perverse and rebellious woman! Don't I know that you have sided with the son of Jesse to your own shame and to the shame of the mother who bore you? ³¹ As long as the son of Jesse lives on this earth, neither you nor your kingdom will be established. Now send someone to bring him to me, for he must die!"

³² "Why should he be put to death? What has he done?" Jonathan asked his father. ³³ But Saul hurled his spear at him

David at Nob

21 ᵇ David went to Nob, to Ahimelek the priest. Ahimelek trembled when he met him, and asked, "Why are you alone? Why is no one with you?"

² David answered Ahimelek the priest, "The king sent me on a mission and said to me, 'No one is to know anything about the mission I am sending you on.' As for my men, I have told them to meet me at a certain place. ³ Now then, what do you have on hand? Give me five loaves of bread, or whatever you can find."

ᵃ 42 In Hebrew texts this sentence (20:42b) is numbered 21:1.   ᵇ In Hebrew texts 21:1-15 is numbered 21:2-16.

4 But the priest answered David, "I don't have any ordinary bread on hand; however, there is some consecrated bread here—provided the men have kept themselves from women."

5 David replied, "Indeed women have been kept from us, as usual whenever[a] I set out. The men's bodies are holy even on missions that are not holy. How much more so today!" 6 So the priest gave him the consecrated bread, since there was no bread there except the bread of the Presence that had been removed from before the LORD and replaced by hot bread on the day it was taken away.

7 Now one of Saul's servants was there that day, detained before the LORD; he was Doeg the Edomite, Saul's chief shepherd.

8 David asked Ahimelek, "Don't you have a spear or a sword here? I haven't brought my sword or any other weapon, because the king's mission was urgent."

9 The priest replied, "The sword of Goliath the Philistine, whom you killed in the Valley of Elah, is here; it is wrapped in a cloth behind the ephod. If you want it, take it; there is no sword here but that one."

David said, "There is none like it; give it to me."

David at Gath

10 That day David fled from Saul and went to Achish king of Gath. 11 But the servants of Achish said to him, "Isn't this David, the king of the land? Isn't he the one they sing about in their dances:

a 5 Or from us in the past few days since

Lies Don't Help

Have you ever been tempted to get out of trouble by telling a lie? Most everyone has. Even Bible heroes were tempted to lie.

+ Abram lied and said Sarai was his sister—and got into trouble in Egypt (Genesis 12:10–20).

+ Jacob lied to his father—and made his brother so angry that Jacob had to run to safety (Genesis 27:34–45).

+ David lied in order to get help from Ahimelek the priest—and later King Saul killed the innocent priest and his family for helping David escape (1 Samuel 21–22).

When tempted to lie, remember: "The LORD detests lying lips, but he delights in people who are trustworthy" (Proverbs 12:22).

" 'Saul has slain his thousands,
and David his tens of thousands'?"

¹²David took these words to heart and was very much afraid of Achish king of Gath. ¹³So he pretended to be insane in their presence; and while he was in their hands he acted like a madman, making marks on the doors of the gate and letting saliva run down his beard.

¹⁴Achish said to his servants, "Look at the man! He is insane! Why bring him to me? ¹⁵Am I so short of madmen that you have to bring this fellow here to carry on like this in front of me? Must this man come into my house?"

David at Adullam and Mizpah

22 David left Gath and escaped to the cave of Adullam. When his brothers and his father's household heard about it, they went down to him there. ²All those who were in distress or in debt or discontented gathered around him, and he became their commander. About four hundred men were with him.

³From there David went to Mizpah in Moab and said to the king of Moab, "Would you let my father and mother come and stay with you until I learn what God will do for me?" ⁴So he left them with the king of Moab, and they stayed with him as long as David was in the stronghold.

⁵But the prophet Gad said to David, "Do not stay in the stronghold. Go into the land of Judah." So David left and went to the forest of Hereth.

Saul Kills the Priests of Nob

⁶Now Saul heard that David and his men had been discovered. And Saul was seated, spear in hand, under the tamarisk tree on the hill at Gibeah, with all his officials standing at his side. ⁷He said to them, "Listen, men of Benjamin! Will the son of Jesse give all of you fields and vineyards? Will he make all of you commanders of thousands and commanders of hundreds? ⁸Is that why you have all conspired against me? No one tells me when my son makes a covenant with the son of Jesse. None of you is concerned

about me or tells me that my son has incited my servant to lie in wait for me, as he does today."

⁹But Doeg the Edomite, who was standing with Saul's officials, said, "I saw the son of Jesse come to Ahimelek son of Ahitub at Nob. ¹⁰Ahimelek inquired of the Lᴏʀᴅ for him; he also gave him provisions and the sword of Goliath the Philistine."

¹¹Then the king sent for the priest Ahimelek son of Ahitub and all the men of his family, who were the priests at Nob, and they all came to the king. ¹²Saul said, "Listen now, son of Ahitub."

"Yes, my lord," he answered.

¹³Saul said to him, "Why have you conspired against me, you and the son of Jesse, giving him bread and a sword and inquiring of God for him, so that he has rebelled against me and lies in wait for me, as he does today?"

¹⁴Ahimelek answered the king, "Who of all your servants is as loyal as David, the king's son-in-law, captain of your bodyguard and highly respected in your household? ¹⁵Was that day the first time I inquired of God for him? Of course not! Let not the king accuse your servant or any of his father's family, for your servant knows nothing at all about this whole affair."

¹⁶But the king said, "You will surely die, Ahimelek, you and your whole family."

¹⁷Then the king ordered the guards at his side: "Turn and kill the priests of the Lᴏʀᴅ, because they too have sided with David. They knew he was fleeing, yet they did not tell me."

But the king's officials were unwilling to raise a hand to strike the priests of the Lᴏʀᴅ.

¹⁸The king then ordered Doeg, "You turn and strike down the priests." So Doeg the Edomite turned and struck them down. That day he killed eighty-five men who wore the linen ephod. ¹⁹He also put to the sword Nob, the town of the priests, with its men and women, its children and infants, and its cattle, donkeys and sheep.

²⁰But one son of Ahimelek son of Ahitub, named Abiathar, escaped and fled to join David. ²¹He told David that Saul

Y ou helped the neighbor wash her car, and she didn't pay you? You rescued a cat stuck up in a tree, and it bit you? You worked all day cleaning up at church, and they left your name out of the bulletin? Look what happened to David: He and his men rescued the people of a little town, yet the people of that town were ready to turn him over to Saul. But so what? Did the ingratitude of those people make David's rescue foolish? Or even more noble? Sure, you want to be recognized for the good things you do. But even when you don't get credit or appreciation, you have the inner satisfaction of knowing you did right.

{1 Samuel 23:1–13}

INSTANT ACCESS

²he inquired of the LORD, saying, "Shall I go and attack these Philistines?"

The LORD answered him, "Go, attack the Philistines and save Keilah."

³But David's men said to him, "Here in Judah we are afraid. How much more, then, if we go to Keilah against the Philistine forces!"

⁴Once again David inquired of the LORD, and the LORD answered him, "Go down to Keilah, for I am going to give the Philistines into your hand." ⁵So David and his men went to Keilah, fought the Philistines and carried off their livestock. He inflicted heavy losses on the Philistines and saved the people of Keilah. ⁶(Now Abiathar son of Ahimelek had brought the ephod down with him when he fled to David at Keilah.)

Saul Pursues David

⁷Saul was told that David had gone to Keilah, and he said, "God has delivered him into my hands, for David has imprisoned himself by entering a town with gates and bars." ⁸And Saul called up all his forces for battle, to go down to Keilah to besiege David and his men.

⁹When David learned that Saul was plotting against him, he said to Abiathar the priest, "Bring the ephod." ¹⁰David said, "LORD, God of Israel, your servant has heard definitely that Saul plans to come to Keilah and destroy the town on account of me. ¹¹Will the citizens of Keilah surrender me to him? Will Saul come down, as your servant has heard? LORD, God of Israel, tell your servant."

And the LORD said, "He will."

¹²Again David asked, "Will the citizens of Keilah surrender me and my men to Saul?"

And the LORD said, "They will."

¹³So David and his men, about six hundred in number, left Keilah and kept moving from place to place. When Saul was told that David had escaped from Keilah, he did not go there.

¹⁴David stayed in the wilderness strongholds and in the hills of the Desert of Ziph. Day after day Saul searched for him, but God did not give David into his hands.

had killed the priests of the LORD. ²²Then David said to Abiathar, "That day, when Doeg the Edomite was there, I knew he would be sure to tell Saul. I am responsible for the death of your whole family. ²³Stay with me; don't be afraid. The man who wants to kill you is trying to kill me too. You will be safe with me."

David Saves Keilah

23 When David was told, "Look, the Philistines are fighting against Keilah and are looting the threshing floors,"

15 While David was at Horesh in the Desert of Ziph, he learned that[a] Saul had come out to take his life. 16 And Saul's son Jonathan went to David at Horesh and helped him find strength in God. 17 "Don't be afraid," he said. "My father Saul will not lay a hand on you. You will be king over Israel, and I will be second to you. Even my father Saul knows this." 18 The two of them made a covenant before the LORD. Then Jonathan went home, but David remained at Horesh.

19 The Ziphites went up to Saul at Gibeah and said, "Is not David hiding among us in the strongholds at Horesh, on the hill of Hakilah, south of Jeshimon? 20 Now, Your Majesty, come down whenever it pleases you to do so, and we will be responsible for giving him into your hands."

21 Saul replied, "The LORD bless you for your concern for me. 22 Go and get more information. Find out where David usually goes and who has seen him there. They tell me he is very crafty. 23 Find out about all the hiding places he uses and come back to me with definite information. Then I will go with you; if he is in the area, I will track him down among all the clans of Judah."

24 So they set out and went to Ziph ahead of Saul. Now David and his men were in the Desert of Maon, in the Arabah south of Jeshimon. 25 Saul and his men began the search, and when David was told about it, he went down to the rock and stayed in the Desert of Maon. When Saul heard this, he went into the Desert of Maon in pursuit of David.

26 Saul was going along one side of the mountain, and David and his men were on the other side, hurrying to get away from Saul. As Saul and his forces were closing in on David and his men to capture them, 27 a messenger came to Saul, saying, "Come quickly! The Philistines are raiding the land." 28 Then Saul broke off his pursuit of David and went to meet the Philistines. That is why they call this place Sela Hammahlekoth.[b] 29 And David went up from there and lived in the strongholds of En Gedi.[c]

David Spares Saul's Life

24[d] After Saul returned from pursuing the Philistines, he was told, "David is in the Desert of En Gedi." 2 So Saul took three thousand able young men from all Israel and set out to look for David and his men near the Crags of the Wild Goats.

3 He came to the sheep pens along the way; a cave was there, and Saul went in to relieve himself. David and his men were far back in the cave. 4 The men said, "This is the day the LORD spoke of when he said[e] to you, 'I will give your enemy into your hands for you to deal with as you wish.' " Then David crept up unnoticed and cut off a corner of Saul's robe.

5 Afterward, David was conscience-stricken for having cut off a corner of his robe. 6 He said to his men, "The LORD forbid that I should do such a thing to my master, the LORD's anointed, or lay my hand on him; for he is the anointed of the LORD." 7 With these words David sharply rebuked his men and did not allow them to attack Saul. And Saul left the cave and went his way.

8 Then David went out of the cave and called out to Saul, "My lord the king!" When Saul looked behind him, David bowed down and prostrated himself with his face to the ground. 9 He said to Saul, "Why do you listen when men say, 'David is bent on harming you'? 10 This day you have seen with your own eyes how the LORD delivered you into my hands in the cave. Some urged me to kill you, but I spared you; I said, 'I will not lay my hand on my lord, because he is the LORD's anointed.' 11 See, my father, look at this piece of your robe in my hand! I cut off the corner of your robe but did not kill you. See that there is nothing in my hand to indicate that I am guilty of wrongdoing or rebellion. I have not wronged you, but you are hunting me down to take my life. 12 May the LORD judge between you and me. And may the LORD avenge the wrongs you have done to me, but my hand will not touch you. 13 As the old saying goes,

---

[a] 15 Or he was afraid because   [b] 28 Sela Hammahlekoth means rock of parting.   [c] 29 In Hebrew texts this verse (23:29) is numbered 24:1.   [d] In Hebrew texts 24:1-22 is numbered 24:2-23.   [e] 4 Or "Today the LORD is saying

What's the first thing you want to do when someone tells a lie about you? You want to talk to the people who heard the lie and tell them it isn't true. And you may want to beat up the person who told the lie. David gives you another option. Saul labeled David a traitor and set out to kill him. But when David had the chance to kill Saul, he let him live. David's action did more to disprove the lies told about him than anything he could have said. Sure, it's upsetting to hear someone is saying bad things about you. But keep on living a good life and prove by your actions how wrong those accusations are.

{1 Samuel 24}

INSTANT ACCESS

'From evildoers come evil deeds,' so my hand will not touch you.

14 "Against whom has the king of Israel come out? Who are you pursuing? A dead dog? A flea? 15 May the LORD be our judge and decide between us. May he consider my cause and uphold it; may he vindicate me by delivering me from your hand."

16 When David finished saying this, Saul asked, "Is that your voice, David my son?" And he wept aloud. 17 "You are more righteous than I," he said. "You

have treated me well, but I have treated you badly. 18 You have just now told me about the good you did to me; the LORD delivered me into your hands, but you did not kill me. 19 When a man finds his enemy, does he let him get away unharmed? May the LORD reward you well for the way you treated me today. 20 I know that you will surely be king and that the kingdom of Israel will be established in your hands. 21 Now swear to me by the LORD that you will not kill off my descendants or wipe out my name from my father's family."

22 So David gave his oath to Saul. Then Saul returned home, but David and his men went up to the stronghold.

David, Nabal and Abigail

25 Now Samuel died, and all Israel assembled and mourned for him; and they buried him at his home in Ramah. Then David moved down into the Desert of Paran.[a]

2 A certain man in Maon, who had property there at Carmel, was very wealthy. He had a thousand goats and three thousand sheep, which he was shearing in Carmel. 3 His name was Nabal and his wife's name was Abigail. She was an intelligent and beautiful woman, but her husband was surly and mean in his dealings—he was a Calebite.

4 While David was in the wilderness, he heard that Nabal was shearing sheep. 5 So he sent ten young men and said to them, "Go up to Nabal at Carmel and greet him in my name. 6 Say to him: 'Long life to you! Good health to you and your household! And good health to all that is yours!

7 "'Now I hear that it is sheep-shearing time. When your shepherds were with us, we did not mistreat them, and the whole time they were at Carmel nothing of theirs was missing. 8 Ask your own servants and they will tell you. Therefore be favorable toward my men, since we come at a festive time. Please give your servants and your son David whatever you can find for them.'"

9 When David's men arrived, they gave

> Sometimes I get so mad I say or do something I'm sorry for later. I've gotten into trouble many times because I can't control my anger. Any suggestions?
>
> >> Wyatt

Dear Jordan

Dear Wyatt,

You're not alone in having trouble controlling your anger. But do you realize anger is a choice? Everyone has stressful situations pop up. It's how people choose to react that makes the difference.

David was very angry about the way he'd been treated by a wealthy man named Nabal (which means "fool"). David was so offended he decided he would kill Nabal (1 Samuel 25). Fortunately, this foolish man had a very wise wife, Abigail. She went to David and begged for forgiveness for her husband. She reminded David that just because her husband had done something foolish and insulting didn't mean that David had to take revenge.

David recognized the wisdom of her words. He saw that he had almost committed murder because he had been treated so badly. He chose not to seek revenge and blessed Abigail for keeping him from bloodshed.

Instead of lashing out at people when you're angry, try doing something physical like running or bike riding. Some people find it helpful to count to themselves until their angry feelings subside. Plan ahead, and next time you get angry, you'll have some options to try other than losing control.

Jordan

Nabal this message in David's name. Then they waited.

10 Nabal answered David's servants, "Who is this David? Who is this son of Jesse? Many servants are breaking away from their masters these days. 11 Why should I take my bread and water, and the meat I have slaughtered for my shearers, and give it to men coming from who knows where?"

12 David's men turned around and went back. When they arrived, they reported every word. 13 David said to his men, "Each of you strap on your sword!" So they did, and David strapped his on as well. About four hundred men went up with David, while two hundred stayed with the supplies.

14 One of the servants told Abigail, Nabal's wife, "David sent messengers from the wilderness to give our master his greetings, but he hurled insults at them. 15 Yet these men were very good to us. They did not mistreat us, and the whole time we were out in the fields near them nothing was missing. 16 Night and day they were a wall around us the whole time we were herding our sheep near them. 17 Now think it over and see what you can do, because disaster is hanging over our master and his whole household. He is such a wicked man that no one can talk to him."

18 Abigail acted quickly. She took two hundred loaves of bread, two skins of wine, five dressed sheep, five seahs[a] of roasted grain, a hundred cakes of raisins and two hundred cakes of pressed figs, and loaded them on donkeys. 19 Then she told her servants, "Go on ahead; I'll follow you." But she did not tell her husband Nabal.

20 As she came riding her donkey into a mountain ravine, there were David and his men descending toward her, and she met them. 21 David had just said, "It's been useless—all my watching over this fellow's property in the wilderness so that nothing of his was missing. He has paid me back evil for good. 22 May God deal with David,[b] be it ever so severely,

if by morning I leave alive one male of all who belong to him!"

23 When Abigail saw David, she quickly got off her donkey and bowed down before David with her face to the ground. 24 She fell at his feet and said: "Pardon your servant, my lord, and let me speak to you; hear what your servant has to say. 25 Please pay no attention, my lord, to that wicked man Nabal. He is just like his name—his name means Fool, and folly goes with him. And as for me, your servant, I did not see the men my lord sent. 26 And now, my lord, as surely as the LORD your God lives and as you live, since the LORD has kept you from bloodshed and from avenging yourself with your own hands, may your enemies and all who are intent on harming my lord be like Nabal. 27 And let this gift, which your servant has brought to my lord, be given to the men who follow you.

28 "Please forgive your servant's presumption. The LORD your God will certainly make a lasting dynasty for my lord, because you fight the LORD's battles, and no wrongdoing will be found in you as long as you live. 29 Even though someone is pursuing you to take your life, the life of my lord will be bound securely in the bundle of the living by the LORD your God, but the lives of your enemies he will hurl away as from the pocket of a sling. 30 When the LORD has fulfilled for my lord every good thing he promised concerning him and has appointed him ruler over Israel, 31 my lord will not have on his conscience the staggering burden of needless bloodshed or of having avenged himself. And when the LORD your God has brought my lord success, remember your servant."

32 David said to Abigail, "Praise be to the LORD, the God of Israel, who has sent you today to meet me. 33 May you be blessed for your good judgment and for keeping me from bloodshed this day and from avenging myself with my own hands. 34 Otherwise, as surely as the LORD, the God of Israel, lives, who has kept me from harming you, if you had not come quickly to meet me, not one male belonging to

---

[a] 18 That is, probably about 60 pounds or about 27 kilograms   [b] 22 Some Septuagint manuscripts; Hebrew with David's
enemies

Nabal would have been left alive by daybreak."

35 Then David accepted from her hand what she had brought him and said, "Go home in peace. I have heard your words and granted your request."

36 When Abigail went to Nabal, he was in the house holding a banquet like that of a king. He was in high spirits and very drunk. So she told him nothing at all until daybreak. 37 Then in the morning, when Nabal was sober, his wife told him all these things, and his heart failed him and he became like a stone. 38 About ten days later, the LORD struck Nabal and he died.

39 When David heard that Nabal was dead, he said, "Praise be to the LORD, who has upheld my cause against Nabal for treating me with contempt. He has kept his servant from doing wrong and has brought Nabal's wrongdoing down on his own head."

Then David sent word to Abigail, asking her to become his wife. 40 His servants went to Carmel and said to Abigail, "David has sent us to you to take you to become his wife."

41 She bowed down with her face to the ground and said, "I am your servant and am ready to serve you and wash the feet of my lord's servants." 42 Abigail quickly got on a donkey and, attended by her five female servants, went with David's messengers and became his wife. 43 David had also married Ahinoam of Jezreel, and they both were his wives. 44 But Saul had given his daughter Michal, David's wife, to Paltiel[a] son of Laish, who was from Gallim.

David Again Spares Saul's Life

26 The Ziphites went to Saul at Gibeah and said, "Is not David hiding on the hill of Hakilah, which faces Jeshimon?"

2 So Saul went down to the Desert of Ziph, with his three thousand select Israelite troops, to search there for David. 3 Saul made his camp beside the road on the hill of Hakilah facing Jeshimon, but David stayed in the wilderness. When he

saw that Saul had followed him there, 4 he sent out scouts and learned that Saul had definitely arrived.

5 Then David set out and went to the place where Saul had camped. He saw where Saul and Abner son of Ner, the commander of the army, had lain down. Saul was lying inside the camp, with the army encamped around him.

6 David then asked Ahimelek the Hittite and Abishai son of Zeruiah, Joab's brother, "Who will go down into the camp with me to Saul?"

"I'll go with you," said Abishai.

7 So David and Abishai went to the army by night, and there was Saul, lying asleep inside the camp with his spear stuck in the ground near his head. Abner and the soldiers were lying around him.

8 Abishai said to David, "Today God has delivered your enemy into your hands. Now let me pin him to the ground with one thrust of the spear; I won't strike him twice."

9 But David said to Abishai, "Don't destroy him! Who can lay a hand on the LORD's anointed and be guiltless? 10 As surely as the LORD lives," he said, "the LORD himself will strike him, or his time will come and he will die, or he will go into battle and perish. 11 But the LORD forbid that I should lay a hand on the LORD's anointed. Now get the spear and water jug that are near his head, and let's go."

12 So David took the spear and water jug near Saul's head, and they left. No one saw or knew about it, nor did anyone wake up. They were all sleeping, because the LORD had put them into a deep sleep.

13 Then David crossed over to the other side and stood on top of the hill some distance away; there was a wide space between them. 14 He called out to the army and to Abner son of Ner, "Aren't you going to answer me, Abner?"

Abner replied, "Who are you who calls to the king?"

15 David said, "You're a man, aren't you? And who is like you in Israel? Why didn't you guard your lord the king? Someone came to destroy your lord the

---

a 44 Hebrew *Palti*, a variant of *Paltiel*

Sometimes being nice doesn't work. Just look at David. Twice he had the chance to kill Saul. Twice David let Saul live. But Saul kept on trying to kill David anyway. Being nice to Saul didn't change Saul one bit. So what do you do when nice doesn't work? David states a basic principle: "I would not lay a hand on the LORD's anointed" (1 Samuel 26:11,23). Nice didn't work. But revenge or getting even doesn't work either! Instead what David says is "may the LORD avenge the wrongs you have done to me" (1 Samuel 24:12). Any payback for being wronged is to come from God. Not from David. And not from anyone else.

{1 Samuel 26:9–12}

INSTANT ACCESS

me, then may he accept an offering. If, however, people have done it, may they be cursed before the LORD! They have driven me today from my share in the LORD's inheritance and have said, 'Go, serve other gods.' 20Now do not let my blood fall to the ground far from the presence of the LORD. The king of Israel has come out to look for a flea—as one hunts a partridge in the mountains."

21Then Saul said, "I have sinned. Come back, David my son. Because you considered my life precious today, I will not try to harm you again. Surely I have acted like a fool and have been terribly wrong."

22"Here is the king's spear," David answered. "Let one of your young men come over and get it. 23The LORD rewards everyone for their righteousness and faithfulness. The LORD delivered you into my hands today, but I would not lay a hand on the LORD's anointed. 24As surely as I valued your life today, so may the LORD value my life and deliver me from all trouble."

25Then Saul said to David, "May you be blessed, David my son; you will do great things and surely triumph."

So David went on his way, and Saul returned home.

David Among the Philistines

27 But David thought to himself, "One of these days I will be destroyed by the hand of Saul. The best thing I can do is to escape to the land of the Philistines. Then Saul will give up searching for me anywhere in Israel, and I will slip out of his hand."

2So David and the six hundred men with him left and went over to Achish son of Maok king of Gath. 3David and his men settled in Gath with Achish. Each man had his family with him, and David had his two wives: Ahinoam of Jezreel and Abigail of Carmel, the widow of Nabal. 4When Saul was told that David had fled to Gath, he no longer searched for him.

5Then David said to Achish, "If I have found favor in your eyes, let a place be assigned to me in one of the country towns, that I may live there. Why should your servant live in the royal city with you?"

6So on that day Achish gave him Ziklag,

king. 16What you have done is not good. As surely as the LORD lives, you and your men must die, because you did not guard your master, the LORD's anointed. Look around you. Where are the king's spear and water jug that were near his head?"

17Saul recognized David's voice and said, "Is that your voice, David my son?"

David replied, "Yes it is, my lord the king." 18And he added, "Why is my lord pursuing his servant? What have I done, and what wrong am I guilty of? 19Now let my lord the king listen to his servant's words. If the LORD has incited you against

and it has belonged to the kings of Judah ever since. 7David lived in Philistine territory a year and four months.

8Now David and his men went up and raided the Geshurites, the Girzites and the Amalekites. (From ancient times these peoples had lived in the land extending to Shur and Egypt.) 9Whenever David attacked an area, he did not leave a man or woman alive, but took sheep and cattle, donkeys and camels, and clothes. Then he returned to Achish.

10When Achish asked, "Where did you go raiding today?" David would say, "Against the Negev of Judah" or "Against the Negev of Jerahmeel" or "Against the Negev of the Kenites." 11He did not leave a man or woman alive to be brought to Gath, for he thought, "They might inform on us and say, 'This is what David did.'" And such was his practice as long as he lived in Philistine territory. 12Achish trusted David and said to himself, "He has become so obnoxious to his people, the Israelites, that he will be my servant for life."

28 In those days the Philistines gathered their forces to fight against Israel. Achish said to David, "You must understand that you and your men will accompany me in the army."

2David said, "Then you will see for yourself what your servant can do."

Achish replied, "Very well, I will make you my bodyguard for life."

Saul and the Medium at Endor

3Now Samuel was dead, and all Israel had mourned for him and buried him in his own town of Ramah. Saul had expelled the mediums and spiritists from the land.

4The Philistines assembled and came and set up camp at Shunem, while Saul gathered all Israel and set up camp at Gilboa. 5When Saul saw the Philistine army, he was afraid; terror filled his heart. 6He inquired of the LORD, but the LORD did not answer him by dreams or Urim or prophets. 7Saul then said to his attendants, "Find me a woman who is a medium, so I may go and inquire of her."

"There is one in Endor," they said.

8So Saul disguised himself, putting on other clothes, and at night he and two men went to the woman. "Consult a spirit for me," he said, "and bring up for me the one I name."

9But the woman said to him, "Surely you know what Saul has done. He has cut off the mediums and spiritists from the land. Why have you set a trap for my life to bring about my death?"

10Saul swore to her by the LORD, "As surely as the LORD lives, you will not be punished for this."

11Then the woman asked, "Whom shall I bring up for you?"

"Bring up Samuel," he said.

12When the woman saw Samuel, she cried out at the top of her voice and said to Saul, "Why have you deceived me? You are Saul!"

13The king said to her, "Don't be afraid. What do you see?"

The woman said, "I see a ghostly figure[a] coming up out of the earth."

14"What does he look like?" he asked.

"An old man wearing a robe is coming up," she said.

Then Saul knew it was Samuel, and he bowed down and prostrated himself with his face to the ground.

15Samuel said to Saul, "Why have you disturbed me by bringing me up?"

"I am in great distress," Saul said. "The Philistines are fighting against me, and God has departed from me. He no longer answers me, either by prophets or by dreams. So I have called on you to tell me what to do."

16Samuel said, "Why do you consult me, now that the LORD has departed from you and become your enemy? 17The LORD has done what he predicted through me. The LORD has torn the kingdom out of your hands and given it to one of your neighbors—to David. 18Because you did not obey the LORD or carry out his fierce wrath against the Amalekites, the LORD has done this to you today. 19The LORD will deliver both Israel and you into the hands of the Philistines, and tomorrow you and

---

a 13 Or see spirits; or see gods

How much power do witches have? Didn't the witch of Endor call Samuel back from the dead? Doesn't that prove spiritists and mediums really can reach the dead, as they claim? Read the story closely, and you discover the most surprised person in the witch's house was the witch herself (1 Samuel 28:12–14)! She may have expected some evil spirit to manifest itself, but she surely didn't expect Samuel himself to appear. Don't be fooled. People who dabble in the occult may touch supernatural powers, but they're dabbling with danger.

{1 Samuel 28}

him, and he listened to them. He got up from the ground and sat on the couch.

24 The woman had a fattened calf at the house, which she butchered at once. She took some flour, kneaded it and baked bread without yeast. 25 Then she set it before Saul and his men, and they ate. That same night they got up and left.

Achish Sends David Back to Ziklag

29 The Philistines gathered all their forces at Aphek, and Israel camped by the spring in Jezreel. 2 As the Philistine rulers marched with their units of hundreds and thousands, David and his men were marching at the rear with Achish. 3 The commanders of the Philistines asked, "What about these Hebrews?"

Achish replied, "Is this not David, who was an officer of Saul king of Israel? He has already been with me for over a year, and from the day he left Saul until now, I have found no fault in him."

4 But the Philistine commanders were angry with Achish and said, "Send the man back, that he may return to the place you assigned him. He must not go with us into battle, or he will turn against us during the fighting. How better could he regain his master's favor than by taking the heads of our own men? 5 Isn't this the David they sang about in their dances:

" 'Saul has slain his thousands,
and David his tens of thousands'?"

6 So Achish called David and said to him, "As surely as the LORD lives, you have been reliable, and I would be pleased to have you serve with me in the army. From the day you came to me until today, I have found no fault in you, but the rulers don't approve of you. 7 Now turn back and go in peace; do nothing to displease the Philistine rulers."

8 "But what have I done?" asked David. "What have you found against your servant from the day I came to you until now? Why can't I go and fight against the enemies of my lord the king?"

your sons will be with me. The LORD will also give the army of Israel into the hands of the Philistines."

20 Immediately Saul fell full length on the ground, filled with fear because of Samuel's words. His strength was gone, for he had eaten nothing all that day and all that night.

21 When the woman came to Saul and saw that he was greatly shaken, she said, "Look, your servant has obeyed you. I took my life in my hands and did what you told me to do. 22 Now please listen to your servant and let me give you some food so you may eat and have the strength to go on your way."

23 He refused and said, "I will not eat." But his men joined the woman in urging

9Achish answered, "I know that you have been as pleasing in my eyes as an angel of God; nevertheless, the Philistine commanders have said, 'He must not go up with us into battle.' 10Now get up early, along with your master's servants who have come with you, and leave in the morning as soon as it is light."

11So David and his men got up early in the morning to go back to the land of the Philistines, and the Philistines went up to Jezreel.

David Destroys the Amalekites

30 David and his men reached Ziklag on the third day. Now the Amalekites had raided the Negev and Ziklag. They had attacked Ziklag and burned it, 2and had taken captive the women and everyone else in it, both young and old. They killed none of them, but carried them off as they went on their way.

3When David and his men reached Ziklag, they found it destroyed by fire and their wives and sons and daughters taken captive. 4So David and his men wept aloud until they had no strength left to weep. 5David's two wives had been captured—Ahinoam of Jezreel and Abigail, the widow of Nabal of Carmel. 6David was greatly distressed because the men were talking of stoning him; each one was bitter in spirit because of his sons and daughters. But David found strength in the LORD his God.

7Then David said to Abiathar the priest, the son of Ahimelek, "Bring me the ephod." Abiathar brought it to him, 8and David inquired of the LORD, "Shall I pursue this raiding party? Will I overtake them?"

TO THE POINT

God Is at Work

The story in 1 Samuel 29 illustrates God's providence, how he works to make sure things turn out according to his plan.

David had fled his homeland and settled with the Philistines. When the Philistines went to war against Israel, David was expected to fight against his own people. But God had chosen David to be the king of Israel (1 Samuel 16). He would never become king if he fought on the side of the Philistines. Then, because some Philistine rulers questioned David's loyalties, they refused to let him go to war with them. God was at work, making sure that David became king.

It's comforting to know that God is at work for you too, isn't it? You may not see miracles. You may not hear God speak. But in all that happens, God is at work for your good (Romans 8:28).

"Pursue them," he answered. "You will certainly overtake them and succeed in the rescue."

9 David and the six hundred men with him came to the Besor Valley, where some stayed behind. 10 Two hundred of them were too exhausted to cross the valley, but David and the other four hundred continued the pursuit.

11 They found an Egyptian in a field and brought him to David. They gave him water to drink and food to eat— 12 part of a cake of pressed figs and two cakes of raisins. He ate and was revived, for he had not eaten any food or drunk any water for three days and three nights.

13 David asked him, "Who do you belong to? Where do you come from?"

He said, "I am an Egyptian, the slave of an Amalekite. My master abandoned me when I became ill three days ago. 14 We raided the Negev of the Kerethites, some territory belonging to Judah and the Negev of Caleb. And we burned Ziklag."

15 David asked him, "Can you lead me down to this raiding party?"

He answered, "Swear to me before God that you will not kill me or hand me over to my master, and I will take you down to them."

16 He led David down, and there they were, scattered over the countryside, eating, drinking and reveling because of the great amount of plunder they had taken from the land of the Philistines and from Judah. 17 David fought them from dusk until the evening of the next day, and none of them got away, except four hundred young men who rode off on camels and fled. 18 David recovered everything the Amalekites had taken, including his two wives. 19 Nothing was missing: young or old, boy or girl, plunder or anything else they had taken. David brought everything back. 20 He took all the flocks and herds, and his men drove them ahead of the other livestock, saying, "This is David's plunder."

21 Then David came to the two hundred men who had been too exhausted to follow him and who were left behind at the Besor Valley. They came out to meet David and the men with him. As David and his men approached, he asked them how they were. 22 But all the evil men and troublemakers among David's followers said, "Because they did not go out with us, we will not share with them the plunder we recovered. However, each man may take his wife and children and go."

23 David replied, "No, my brothers, you must not do that with what the LORD has given us. He has protected us and delivered into our hands the raiding party that came against us. 24 Who will listen to what you say? The share of the man who stayed with the supplies is to be the same as that of him who went down to the battle. All will share alike." 25 David made this a statute and ordinance for Israel from that day to this.

26 When David reached Ziklag, he sent some of the plunder to the elders of Judah, who were his friends, saying, "Here is a gift for you from the plunder of the LORD's enemies."

27 David sent it to those who were in Bethel, Ramoth Negev and Jattir; 28 to those in Aroer, Siphmoth, Eshtemoa 29 and Rakal; to those in the towns of the Jerahmeelites and the Kenites; 30 to those in Hormah, Bor Ashan, Athak 31 and Hebron; and to those in all the other places where he and his men had roamed.

Saul Takes His Life

31 Now the Philistines fought against Israel; the Israelites fled before them, and many fell dead on Mount Gilboa. 2 The Philistines were in hot pursuit of Saul and his sons, and they killed his sons Jonathan, Abinadab and Malki-Shua. 3 The fighting grew fierce around Saul, and when the archers overtook him, they wounded him critically.

4 Saul said to his armor-bearer, "Draw your sword and run me through, or these uncircumcised fellows will come and run me through and abuse me."

But his armor-bearer was terrified and would not do it; so Saul took his own sword and fell on it. 5 When the armor-bearer saw that Saul was dead, he too fell on his sword and died with him. 6 So Saul and his three sons and his armor-bearer and all his men died together that same day.

⁷When the Israelites along the valley and those across the Jordan saw that the Israelite army had fled and that Saul and his sons had died, they abandoned their towns and fled. And the Philistines came and occupied them.

⁸The next day, when the Philistines came to strip the dead, they found Saul and his three sons fallen on Mount Gilboa. ⁹They cut off his head and stripped off his armor, and they sent messengers throughout the land of the Philistines to proclaim the news in the temple of their idols and among their people. ¹⁰They put his armor in the temple of the Ashtoreths and fastened his body to the wall of Beth Shan.

¹¹When the people of Jabesh Gilead heard what the Philistines had done to Saul, ¹²all their valiant men marched through the night to Beth Shan. They took down the bodies of Saul and his sons from the wall of Beth Shan and went to Jabesh, where they burned them. ¹³Then they took their bones and buried them under a tamarisk tree at Jabesh, and they fasted seven days.

2 SAMUEL

Dream On.

What if all your dreams were to come true? You make it in the movies or become president. You become the next missionary in a far-away country, or your process for turning sunlight into energy makes you a billionaire. Will your life be easier then?

David's dreams did come true. Saul died; David was crowned king over all Israel. His armies pushed back Israel's enemies until Israel had ten times as much land as before. And David led his people to worship God in Jerusalem. But despite his successes, David's life wasn't easy. He made some choices that hurt him and his people.

>>**DREAMS COME TRUE FOR 30-YEAR OLD**
Young ruler super-successful, see 2 Samuel 5

>>**GOD PROMISES A "FOREVER" KINGDOM**
King amazed by divine commitment, 2 Samuel 7

>>**DAVID REPENTS, CONFESSES SIN**
Flawed ruler sets example for flawed people, 2 Samuel 12, Psalm 51

>>**TROUBLES DOG DAVID'S FAMILY**
Good king, bad father. Commentary in 2 Samuel 13–15

preview

David rules Israel from 1010 to 970 B.C.

Samuel didn't write either of the books named for him. The author is unknown.

David is an ancestor of Jesus. Jesus is the promised King who will rule "forever."

As David rules in Israel, Greek colonists settle in Asia Minor. Aristocratic Egyptians and Assyrians begin to wear wigs. In China math textbooks include geometry and algebraic equations. And a prosperous American Indian culture develops in the Ohio River valley.

David Hears of Saul's Death

1 After the death of Saul, David returned from striking down the Amalekites and stayed in Ziklag two days. ²On the third day a man arrived from Saul's camp with his clothes torn and dust on his head. When he came to David, he fell to the ground to pay him honor.

³"Where have you come from?" David asked him.

He answered, "I have escaped from the Israelite camp."

⁴"What happened?" David asked. "Tell me."

"The men fled from the battle," he replied. "Many of them fell and died. And Saul and his son Jonathan are dead."

⁵Then David said to the young man who brought him the report, "How do you know that Saul and his son Jonathan are dead?"

⁶"I happened to be on Mount Gilboa," the young man said, "and there was Saul, leaning on his spear, with the chariots and their drivers in hot pursuit. ⁷When he turned around and saw me, he called out to me, and I said, 'What can I do?'

⁸"He asked me, 'Who are you?'

" 'An Amalekite,' I answered.

⁹"Then he said to me, 'Stand here by me and kill me! I'm in the throes of death, but I'm still alive.'

¹⁰"So I stood beside him and killed him, because I knew that after he had fallen he could not survive. And I took the crown that was on his head and the band on his arm and have brought them here to my lord."

¹¹Then David and all the men with him took hold of their clothes and tore them. ¹²They mourned and wept and fasted till evening for Saul and his son Jonathan, and for the army of the LORD and for the nation of Israel, because they had fallen by the sword.

¹³David said to the young man who brought him the report, "Where are you from?"

"I am the son of a foreigner, an Amalekite," he answered.

¹⁴David asked him, "Why weren't you afraid to lift your hand to destroy the LORD's anointed?"

¹⁵Then David called one of his men and said, "Go, strike him down!" So he struck him down, and he died. ¹⁶For David had said to him, "Your blood be on your own head. Your own mouth testified against you when you said, 'I killed the LORD's anointed.' "

David's Lament for Saul and Jonathan

¹⁷David took up this lament concerning Saul and his son Jonathan, ¹⁸and he ordered that the people of Judah be taught this lament of the bow (it is written in the Book of Jashar):

¹⁹"A gazelle*ᵃ* lies slain on your heights, Israel.
How the mighty have fallen!

²⁰"Tell it not in Gath,
proclaim it not in the streets of Ashkelon,
lest the daughters of the Philistines be glad,
lest the daughters of the uncircumcised rejoice.

²¹"Mountains of Gilboa,
may you have neither dew nor rain,
may no showers fall on your terraced fields.*ᵇ*
For there the shield of the mighty was despised,
the shield of Saul—no longer rubbed with oil.

²²"From the blood of the slain,
from the flesh of the mighty,
the bow of Jonathan did not turn back,
the sword of Saul did not return unsatisfied.

²³"Saul and Jonathan—
in life they were loved and admired,
and in death they were not parted.
They were swifter than eagles,
they were stronger than lions.

²⁴"Daughters of Israel,
weep for Saul,
who clothed you in scarlet and finery,

ᵃ 19 Gazelle here symbolizes a human dignitary. *ᵇ 21* Or / nor fields that yield grain for offerings

who adorned your garments with
  ornaments of gold.

25 "How the mighty have fallen in battle!
  Jonathan lies slain on your heights.
26 I grieve for you, Jonathan my brother;
  you were very dear to me.
  Your love for me was wonderful,
    more wonderful than that of
    women.

27 "How the mighty have fallen!
  The weapons of war have perished!"

David Anointed King Over Judah

2 In the course of time, David inquired of the LORD. "Shall I go up to one of the towns of Judah?" he asked.

The LORD said, "Go up."

David asked, "Where shall I go?"

"To Hebron," the LORD answered.

2 So David went up there with his two wives, Ahinoam of Jezreel and Abigail, the widow of Nabal of Carmel. 3 David also took the men who were with him, each with his family, and they settled in Hebron and its towns. 4 Then the men of Judah came to Hebron, and there they anointed David king over the tribe of Judah.

When David was told that it was the men from Jabesh Gilead who had buried Saul, 5 he sent messengers to them to say to them, "The LORD bless you for showing this kindness to Saul your master by burying him. 6 May the LORD now show you kindness and faithfulness, and I too will show you the same favor because you have done this. 7 Now then, be strong and brave, for Saul your master is dead, and the people of Judah have anointed me king over them."

War Between the Houses of David and Saul

8 Meanwhile, Abner son of Ner, the commander of Saul's army, had taken Ish-Bosheth son of Saul and brought him over to Mahanaim. 9 He made him king over Gilead, Ashuri and Jezreel, and also over Ephraim, Benjamin and all Israel.

10 Ish-Bosheth son of Saul was forty years old when he became king over Israel, and he reigned two years. The tribe of Judah, however, remained loyal to David. 11 The length of time David was king in Hebron over Judah was seven years and six months.

12 Abner son of Ner, together with the men of Ish-Bosheth son of Saul, left Mahanaim and went to Gibeon. 13 Joab son of Zeruiah and David's men went out and met them at the pool of Gibeon. One group sat down on one side of the pool and one group on the other side.

14 Then Abner said to Joab, "Let's have some of the young men get up and fight hand to hand in front of us."

"All right, let them do it," Joab said.

15 So they stood up and were counted off—twelve men for Benjamin and Ish-Bosheth son of Saul, and twelve for David. 16 Then each man grabbed his opponent by the head and thrust his dagger into his opponent's side, and they fell down together. So that place in Gibeon was called Helkath Hazzurim.[a]

17 The battle that day was very fierce, and Abner and the Israelites were defeated by David's men.

18 The three sons of Zeruiah were there: Joab, Abishai and Asahel. Now Asahel was as fleet-footed as a wild gazelle. 19 He chased Abner, turning neither to the right nor to the left as he pursued him. 20 Abner looked behind him and asked, "Is that you, Asahel?"

"It is," he answered.

21 Then Abner said to him, "Turn aside to the right or to the left; take on one of the young men and strip him of his weapons." But Asahel would not stop chasing him.

22 Again Abner warned Asahel, "Stop chasing me! Why should I strike you down? How could I look your brother Joab in the face?"

23 But Asahel refused to give up the pursuit; so Abner thrust the butt of his spear into Asahel's stomach, and the spear came out through his back. He fell there and died on the spot. And every

---

a 16 *Helkath Hazzurim* means *field of daggers* or *field of hostilities.*

man stopped when he came to the place where Asahel had fallen and died. 24But Joab and Abishai pursued Abner, and as the sun was setting, they came to the hill of Ammah, near Giah on the way to the wasteland of Gibeon. 25Then the men of Benjamin rallied behind Abner. They formed themselves into a group and took their stand on top of a hill.

26Abner called out to Joab, "Must the sword devour forever? Don't you realize that this will end in bitterness? How long before you order your men to stop pursuing their fellow Israelites?"

27Joab answered, "As surely as God lives, if you had not spoken, the men would have continued pursuing them until morning."

28So Joab blew the trumpet, and all the troops came to a halt; they no longer pursued Israel, nor did they fight anymore.

29All that night Abner and his men marched through the Arabah. They crossed the Jordan, continued through the morning hours[a] and came to Mahanaim.

30Then Joab stopped pursuing Abner and assembled the whole army. Besides Asahel, nineteen of David's men were found missing. 31But David's men had killed three hundred and sixty Benjamites who were with Abner. 32They took Asahel and buried him in his father's tomb at Bethlehem. Then Joab and his men marched all night and arrived at Hebron by daybreak.

3 The war between the house of Saul and the house of David lasted a long time. David grew stronger and stronger, while the house of Saul grew weaker and weaker.

2Sons were born to David in Hebron:

His firstborn was Amnon the son of Ahinoam of Jezreel;

3his second, Kileab the son of Abigail the widow of Nabal of Carmel; the third, Absalom the son of Maakah daughter of Talmai king of Geshur;

4the fourth, Adonijah the son of Haggith;

the fifth, Shephatiah the son of Abital;

5and the sixth, Ithream the son of David's wife Eglah.

These were born to David in Hebron.

Abner Goes Over to David

6During the war between the house of Saul and the house of David, Abner had been strengthening his own position in the house of Saul. 7Now Saul had had a concubine named Rizpah daughter of Aiah. And Ish-Bosheth said to Abner, "Why did you sleep with my father's concubine?"

8Abner was very angry because of what Ish-Bosheth said. So he answered, "Am I a dog's head—on Judah's side? This very day I am loyal to the house of your father Saul and to his family and friends. I haven't handed you over to David. Yet now you accuse me of an offense involving this woman! 9May God deal with Abner, be it ever so severely, if I do not do for David what the LORD promised him on oath 10and transfer the kingdom from the house of Saul and establish David's throne over Israel and Judah from Dan to Beersheba." 11Ish-Bosheth did not dare to say another word to Abner, because he was afraid of him.

12Then Abner sent messengers on his behalf to say to David, "Whose land is it? Make an agreement with me, and I will help you bring all Israel over to you."

13"Good," said David. "I will make an agreement with you. But I demand one thing of you: Do not come into my presence unless you bring Michal daughter of Saul when you come to see me." 14Then David sent messengers to Ish-Bosheth son of Saul, demanding, "Give me my wife Michal, whom I betrothed to myself for the price of a hundred Philistine foreskins."

15So Ish-Bosheth gave orders and had her taken away from her husband Paltiel son of Laish. 16Her husband, however, went with her, weeping behind her all the way to Bahurim. Then Abner said to him, "Go back home!" So he went back.

---

[a] 29 See Septuagint; the meaning of the Hebrew for this phrase is uncertain.

¹⁷Abner conferred with the elders of Israel and said, "For some time you have wanted to make David your king. ¹⁸Now do it! For the LORD promised David, 'By my servant David I will rescue my people Israel from the hand of the Philistines and from the hand of all their enemies.'"

¹⁹Abner also spoke to the Benjamites in person. Then he went to Hebron to tell David everything that Israel and the whole tribe of Benjamin wanted to do. ²⁰When Abner, who had twenty men with him, came to David at Hebron, David prepared a feast for him and his men. ²¹Then Abner said to David, "Let me go at once and assemble all Israel for my lord the king, so that they may make a covenant with you, and that you may rule over all that your heart desires." So David sent Abner away, and he went in peace.

Joab Murders Abner

²²Just then David's men and Joab returned from a raid and brought with them a great deal of plunder. But Abner was no longer with David in Hebron, because David had sent him away, and he had gone in peace. ²³When Joab and all the soldiers with him arrived, he was told that Abner son of Ner had come to the king and that the king had sent him away and that he had gone in peace.

²⁴So Joab went to the king and said, "What have you done? Look, Abner came to you. Why did you let him go? Now he is gone! ²⁵You know Abner son of Ner; he came to deceive you and observe your movements and find out everything you are doing."

²⁶Joab then left David and sent messengers after Abner, and they brought him back from the cistern at Sirah. But David did not know it. ²⁷Now when Abner returned to Hebron, Joab took him aside into an inner chamber, as if to speak with him privately. And there, to avenge the blood of his brother Asahel, Joab stabbed him in the stomach, and he died.

²⁸Later, when David heard about this,

he said, "I and my kingdom are forever innocent before the LORD concerning the blood of Abner son of Ner. ²⁹May his blood fall on the head of Joab and on his whole family! May Joab's family never be without someone who has a running sore or leprosyᵃ or who leans on a crutch or who falls by the sword or who lacks food."

³⁰(Joab and his brother Abishai murdered Abner because he had killed their brother Asahel in the battle at Gibeon.)

³¹Then David said to Joab and all the people with him, "Tear your clothes and put on sackcloth and walk in mourning in front of Abner." King David himself walked behind the bier. ³²They buried Abner in Hebron, and the king wept aloud at Abner's tomb. All the people wept also.

³³The king sang this lament for Abner:

"Should Abner have died as the
    lawless die?
³⁴   Your hands were not bound,
      your feet were not fettered.
You fell as one falls before the
    wicked."

And all the people wept over him again.

³⁵Then they all came and urged David to eat something while it was still day;

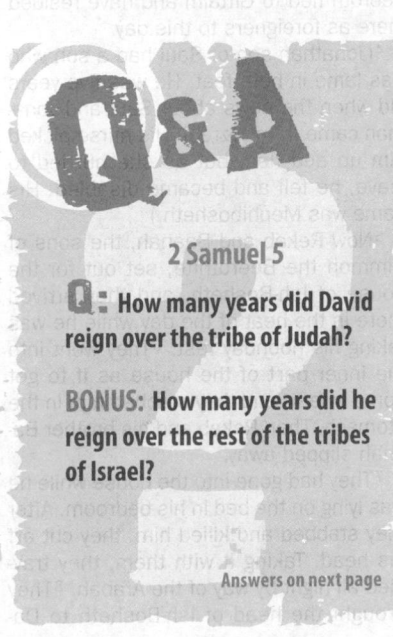

2 Samuel 5

Q: How many years did David reign over the tribe of Judah?

BONUS: How many years did he reign over the rest of the tribes of Israel?

Answers on next page

ᵃ 29 The Hebrew for *leprosy* was used for various diseases affecting the skin.

but David took an oath, saying, "May God deal with me, be it ever so severely, if I taste bread or anything else before the sun sets!"

36 All the people took note and were pleased; indeed, everything the king did pleased them. 37 So on that day all the people there and all Israel knew that the king had no part in the murder of Abner son of Ner.

38 Then the king said to his men, "Do you not realize that a commander and a great man has fallen in Israel this day? 39 And today, though I am the anointed king, I am weak, and these sons of Zeruiah are too strong for me. May the LORD repay the evildoer according to his evil deeds!"

Ish-Bosheth Murdered

4 When Ish-Bosheth son of Saul heard that Abner had died in Hebron, he lost courage, and all Israel became alarmed. 2 Now Saul's son had two men who were leaders of raiding bands. One was named Baanah and the other Rekab; they were sons of Rimmon the Beerothite from the tribe of Benjamin—Beeroth is considered part of Benjamin, 3 because the people of Beeroth fled to Gittaim and have resided there as foreigners to this day.

4 (Jonathan son of Saul had a son who was lame in both feet. He was five years old when the news about Saul and Jonathan came from Jezreel. His nurse picked him up and fled, but as she hurried to leave, he fell and became disabled. His name was Mephibosheth.)

5 Now Rekab and Baanah, the sons of Rimmon the Beerothite, set out for the house of Ish-Bosheth, and they arrived there in the heat of the day while he was taking his noonday rest. 6 They went into the inner part of the house as if to get some wheat, and they stabbed him in the stomach. Then Rekab and his brother Baanah slipped away.

7 They had gone into the house while he was lying on the bed in his bedroom. After they stabbed and killed him, they cut off his head. Taking it with them, they traveled all night by way of the Arabah. 8 They brought the head of Ish-Bosheth to David at Hebron and said to the king, "Here is the head of Ish-Bosheth son of Saul, your enemy, who tried to kill you. This day the LORD has avenged my lord the king against Saul and his offspring."

9 David answered Rekab and his brother Baanah, the sons of Rimmon the Beerothite, "As surely as the LORD lives, who has delivered me out of every trouble, 10 when someone told me, 'Saul is dead,' and thought he was bringing good news, I seized him and put him to death in Ziklag. That was the reward I gave him for his news! 11 How much more—when wicked men have killed an innocent man in his own house and on his own bed—should I not now demand his blood from your hand and rid the earth of you!"

12 So David gave an order to his men, and they killed them. They cut off their hands and feet and hung the bodies by the pool in Hebron. But they took the head of Ish-Bosheth and buried it in Abner's tomb at Hebron.

David Becomes King Over Israel

5 All the tribes of Israel came to David at Hebron and said, "We are your own flesh and blood. 2 In the past, while Saul was king over us, you were the one who led Israel on their military campaigns. And the LORD said to you, 'You will shepherd my people Israel, and you will become their ruler.' "

3 When all the elders of Israel had come to King David at Hebron, the king made a covenant with them at Hebron before the LORD, and they anointed David king over Israel.

4 David was thirty years old when he became king, and he reigned forty years. 5 In Hebron he reigned over Judah seven years and six months, and in Jerusalem he reigned over all Israel and Judah thirty-three years.

David Conquers Jerusalem

6 The king and his men marched to Jerusalem to attack the Jebusites, who lived there. The Jebusites said to David, "You will not get in here; even the blind and the lame can ward you off."

They thought, "David cannot get in here." [7] Nevertheless, David captured the fortress of Zion—which is the City of David.

[8] On that day David had said, "Anyone who conquers the Jebusites will have to use the water shaft to reach those 'lame and blind' who are David's enemies.[a]" That is why they say, "The 'blind and lame' will not enter the palace."

[9] David then took up residence in the fortress and called it the City of David. He built up the area around it, from the terraces[b] inward. [10] And he became more and more powerful, because the LORD God Almighty was with him.

[11] Now Hiram king of Tyre sent envoys to David, along with cedar logs and carpenters and stonemasons, and they built a palace for David. [12] Then David knew that the LORD had established him as king over Israel and had exalted his kingdom for the sake of his people Israel.

[13] After he left Hebron, David took more concubines and wives in Jerusalem, and more sons and daughters were born to him. [14] These are the names of the children born to him there: Shammua, Shobab, Nathan, Solomon, [15] Ibhar, Elishua, Nepheg, Japhia, [16] Elishama, Eliada and Eliphelet.

David Defeats the Philistines

[17] When the Philistines heard that David had been anointed king over Israel, they went up in full force to search for him, but David heard about it and went down to the stronghold. [18] Now the Philistines had come and spread out in the Valley of Rephaim; [19] so David inquired of the LORD, "Shall I go and attack the Philistines? Will you deliver them into my hands?"

The LORD answered him, "Go, for I will surely deliver the Philistines into your hands."

[20] So David went to Baal Perazim, and there he defeated them. He said, "As waters break out, the LORD has broken out against my enemies before me." So that place was called Baal Perazim.[c] [21] The Philistines abandoned their idols there, and David and his men carried them off.

[22] Once more the Philistines came up and spread out in the Valley of Rephaim; [23] so David inquired of the LORD, and he answered, "Do not go straight up, but circle around behind them and attack them in front of the poplar trees. [24] As soon as you hear the sound of marching in the tops of the poplar trees, move quickly, because that will mean the LORD has gone out in front of you to strike the Philistine army." [25] So David did as the LORD commanded him, and he struck down the Philistines all the way from Gibeon[d] to Gezer.

The Ark Brought to Jerusalem

6 David again brought together all the able young men of Israel—thirty thousand. [2] He and all his men went to Baalah[e] in Judah to bring up from there the ark of God, which is called by the Name,[f] the name of the LORD Almighty, who is enthroned between the cherubim on the ark. [3] They set the ark of God on a new cart and brought it from the house of Abinadab, which was on the hill. Uzzah

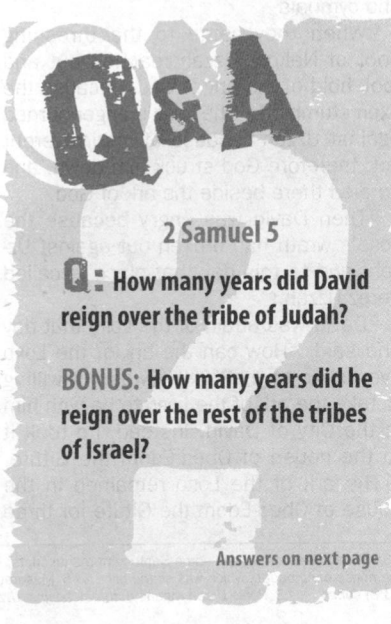

2 Samuel 5

Q: How many years did David reign over the tribe of Judah?

BONUS: How many years did he reign over the rest of the tribes of Israel?

Answers on next page

---

[a] 8 Or are hated by David   [b] 9 Or the Millo
[c] 20 Baal Perazim means the lord who breaks out.
[d] 25 Septuagint (see also 1 Chron. 14:16); Hebrew Geba   [e] 2 That is, Kiriath Jearim (see 1 Chron. 13:6)
[f] 2 Hebrew; Septuagint and Vulgate do not have the Name.

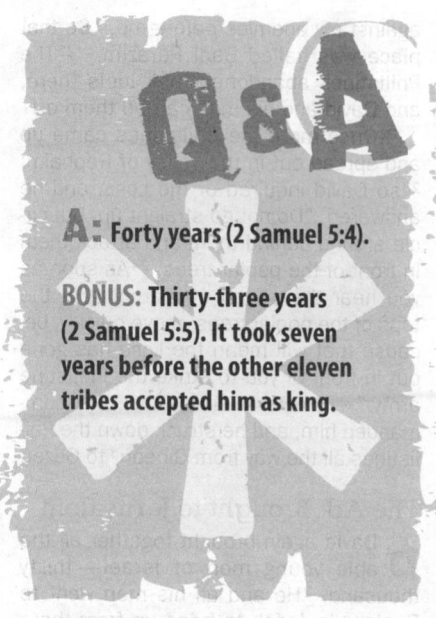

A: Forty years (2 Samuel 5:4).

BONUS: Thirty-three years (2 Samuel 5:5). It took seven years before the other eleven tribes accepted him as king.

and Ahio, sons of Abinadab, were guiding the new cart [4]with the ark of God on it,[a] and Ahio was walking in front of it. [5]David and all Israel were celebrating with all their might before the LORD, with castanets,[b] harps, lyres, timbrels, sistrums and cymbals.

[6]When they came to the threshing floor of Nakon, Uzzah reached out and took hold of the ark of God, because the oxen stumbled. [7]The LORD's anger burned against Uzzah because of his irreverent act; therefore God struck him down, and he died there beside the ark of God.

[8]Then David was angry because the LORD's wrath had broken out against Uzzah, and to this day that place is called Perez Uzzah.[c]

[9]David was afraid of the LORD that day and said, "How can the ark of the LORD ever come to me?" [10]He was not willing to take the ark of the LORD to be with him in the City of David. Instead, he took it to the house of Obed-Edom the Gittite. [11]The ark of the LORD remained in the house of Obed-Edom the Gittite for three months, and the LORD blessed him and his entire household.

[12]Now King David was told, "The LORD has blessed the household of Obed-Edom and everything he has, because of the ark of God." So David went to bring up the ark of God from the house of Obed-Edom to the City of David with rejoicing. [13]When those who were carrying the ark of the LORD had taken six steps, he sacrificed a bull and a fattened calf. [14]Wearing a linen ephod, David was dancing before the LORD with all his might, [15]while he and all Israel were bringing up the ark of the LORD with shouts and the sound of trumpets.

[16]As the ark of the LORD was entering the City of David, Michal daughter of Saul watched from a window. And when she saw King David leaping and dancing before the LORD, she despised him in her heart.

[17]They brought the ark of the LORD and set it in its place inside the tent that David had pitched for it, and David sacrificed burnt offerings and fellowship offerings before the LORD. [18]After he had finished sacrificing the burnt offerings and fellowship offerings, he blessed the people in the name of the LORD Almighty. [19]Then he gave a loaf of bread, a cake of dates and a cake of raisins to each person in the whole crowd of Israelites, both men and women. And all the people went to their homes.

[20]When David returned home to bless his household, Michal daughter of Saul came out to meet him and said, "How the king of Israel has distinguished himself today, going around half-naked in full view of the slave girls of his servants as any vulgar fellow would!"

[21]David said to Michal, "It was before the LORD, who chose me rather than your father or anyone from his house when he appointed me ruler over the LORD's people Israel—I will celebrate before the LORD. [22]I will become even more undignified than this, and I will be humiliated in my own eyes. But by these slave girls you spoke of, I will be held in honor."

---

[a] 3,4 Dead Sea Scrolls and some Septuagint manuscripts; Masoretic Text cart [4]and they brought it with the ark of God from the house of Abinadab, which was on the hill   [b] 5 Masoretic Text; Dead Sea Scrolls and Septuagint (see also 1 Chron. 13:8) songs   [c] 8 Perez Uzzah means outbreak against Uzzah.

23And Michal daughter of Saul had no children to the day of her death.

God's Promise to David

7 After the king was settled in his palace and the LORD had given him rest from all his enemies around him, 2he said to Nathan the prophet, "Here I am, living in a house of cedar, while the ark of God remains in a tent."

3Nathan replied to the king, "Whatever you have in mind, go ahead and do it, for the LORD is with you."

4But that night the word of the LORD came to Nathan, saying:

5"Go and tell my servant David, 'This is what the LORD says: Are you the one to build me a house to dwell in? 6I have not dwelt in a house from the day I brought the Israelites up out of Egypt to this day. I have been moving from place to place with a tent as my dwelling. 7Wherever I have moved with all the Israelites, did I ever say to any of their rulers whom I commanded to shepherd my people Israel, "Why have you not built me a house of cedar?"'

8"Now then, tell my servant David, 'This is what the LORD Almighty says: I took you from the pasture, from tending the flock, and appointed you ruler over my people Israel. 9I have been with you wherever you have gone, and I have cut off all your enemies from before you. Now I will make your name great, like the names of the greatest men on earth. 10And I will provide a place for my people Israel and will plant them so that they can have a home of their

TO THE P**O**INT

David's Son Will Rule!

Sometimes words in the Bible are hard to understand. Take God's promise to David: "Your *house* and your kingdom will endure forever before me; your *throne* will be established *forever*" (2 Samuel 7:16, italics added). David knew what God was saying, but do you?

+ In the Bible, *house* can mean "family" as well as a building.

+ In the Bible, *throne* often stands for a king's rule.

+ In the Bible, *forever* means forever.

This verse promises that someone born into David's family will be a king who will rule forever. Does anyone qualify? Yes! Jesus was a descendant of David (Matthew 1:1). Raised from the dead, he is "KING OF KINGS AND LORD OF LORDS" (Revelation 19:16). "And he will reign for ever and ever" (Revelation 11:15).

own and no longer be disturbed. Wicked people will not oppress them anymore, as they did at the beginning [11]and have done ever since the time I appointed leaders[a] over my people Israel. I will also give you rest from all your enemies.

" 'The LORD declares to you that the LORD himself will establish a house for you: [12]When your days are over and you rest with your ancestors, I will raise up your offspring to succeed you, your own flesh and blood, and I will establish his kingdom. [13]He is the one who will build a house for my Name, and I will establish the throne of his kingdom forever. [14]I will be his father, and he will be my son. When he does wrong, I will punish him with a rod wielded by men, with floggings inflicted by human hands. [15]But my love will never be taken away from him, as I took it away from Saul, whom I removed from before you. [16]Your house and your kingdom will endure forever before me[b]; your throne will be established forever.' "

[17]Nathan reported to David all the words of this entire revelation.

David's Prayer

[18]Then King David went in and sat before the LORD, and he said:

"Who am I, Sovereign LORD, and what is my family, that you have brought me this far? [19]And as if this were not enough in your sight, Sovereign LORD, you have also spoken about the future of the house of your servant—and this decree, Sovereign LORD, is for a mere human![c]

[20]"What more can David say to you? For you know your servant, Sovereign LORD. [21]For the sake of your word and according to your will, you have done this great thing and made it known to your servant.

[22]"How great you are, Sovereign LORD! There is no one like you, and there is no God but you, as we have heard with our own ears. [23]And who is like your people Israel—the one nation on earth that God went out to redeem as a people for himself, and to make a name for himself, and to perform great and awesome wonders by driving out nations and their gods from before your people, whom you redeemed from Egypt?[d] [24]You have established your people Israel as your very own forever, and you, LORD, have become their God.

[25]"And now, LORD God, keep forever the promise you have made concerning your servant and his house. Do as you promised, [26]so that your name will be great forever. Then people will say, 'The LORD Almighty is God over Israel!' And the house of your servant David will be established in your sight.

[27]"LORD Almighty, God of Israel, you have revealed this to your servant, saying, 'I will build a house for you.' So your servant has found courage to pray this prayer to you. [28]Sovereign LORD, you are God! Your covenant is trustworthy, and you have promised these good things to your servant. [29]Now be pleased to bless the house of your servant, that it may continue forever in your sight; for you, Sovereign LORD, have spoken, and with your blessing the house of your servant will be blessed forever."

David's Victories

8 In the course of time, David defeated the Philistines and subdued them, and he took Metheg Ammah from the control of the Philistines.

[2]David also defeated the Moabites. He made them lie down on the ground and measured them off with a length of cord. Every two lengths of them were put to death, and the third length was allowed to live. So the Moabites became subject to David and brought him tribute.

[3]Moreover, David defeated Hadade-

---

[a] 11 Traditionally judges   [b] 16 Some Hebrew manuscripts and Septuagint; most Hebrew manuscripts you   [c] 19 Or for the human race   [d] 23 See Septuagint and 1 Chron. 17:21; Hebrew wonders for your land and before your people, whom you redeemed from Egypt, from the nations and their gods.

Do you ever wonder if what you're asking for in prayer is OK with God? You can gain confidence in prayer by "claiming God's promises." This is what David did in 2 Samuel 7:25–26. God through the prophet Nathan gave David a wonderful promise. So David thanked God and then claimed the promise: he asked God to "keep forever the promise you have made." In keeping his promises God shows the universe that he is faithful to his word, that he can be trusted. As you read your Bible, underline the promises you find. Then when you pray, claim God's promises and become more and more confident about prayer.

{2 Samuel 7:25–26}

INSTANT ACCESS

⁵When the Arameans of Damascus came to help Hadadezer king of Zobah, David struck down twenty-two thousand of them. ⁶He put garrisons in the Aramean kingdom of Damascus, and the Arameans became subject to him and brought tribute. The Lord gave David victory wherever he went.

⁷David took the gold shields that belonged to the officers of Hadadezer and brought them to Jerusalem. ⁸From Tebah*c* and Berothai, towns that belonged to Hadadezer, King David took a great quantity of bronze.

⁹When Tou*d* king of Hamath heard that David had defeated the entire army of Hadadezer, ¹⁰he sent his son Joram*e* to King David to greet him and congratulate him on his victory in battle over Hadadezer, who had been at war with Tou. Joram brought with him articles of silver, of gold and of bronze.

¹¹King David dedicated these articles to the Lord, as he had done with the silver and gold from all the nations he had subdued: ¹²Edom*f* and Moab, the Ammonites and the Philistines, and Amalek. He also dedicated the plunder taken from Hadadezer son of Rehob, king of Zobah.

¹³And David became famous after he returned from striking down eighteen thousand Edomites*g* in the Valley of Salt.

¹⁴He put garrisons throughout Edom, and all the Edomites became subject to David. The Lord gave David victory wherever he went.

David's Officials

¹⁵David reigned over all Israel, doing what was just and right for all his people. ¹⁶Joab son of Zeruiah was over the army; Jehoshaphat son of Ahilud was recorder; ¹⁷Zadok son of Ahitub and Ahimelek son of Abiathar were priests; Seraiah was secretary; ¹⁸Benaiah son of Jehoiada was over the Kerethites and Pelethites; and David's sons were priests.*h*

zer son of Rehob, king of Zobah, when he went to restore his monument at*a* the Euphrates River. ⁴David captured a thousand of his chariots, seven thousand charioteers*b* and twenty thousand foot soldiers. He hamstrung all but a hundred of the chariot horses.

---

a 3 Or *his control along*   *b 4* Septuagint (see also Dead Sea Scrolls and 1 Chron. 18:4); Masoretic Text *captured seventeen hundred of his charioteers*   *c 8* See some Septuagint manuscripts (see also 1 Chron. 18:8); Hebrew *Betah*.   *d 9* Hebrew *Toi,* a variant of *Tou;* also in verse 10   *e 10* A variant of *Hadoram*   *f 12* Some Hebrew manuscripts, Septuagint and Syriac (see also 1 Chron. 18:11); most Hebrew manuscripts *Aram*   *g 13* A few Hebrew manuscripts, Septuagint and Syriac (see also 1 Chron. 18:12); most Hebrew manuscripts *Aram* (that is, Arameans)   *h 18* Or *were chief officials* (see Septuagint and Targum; see also 1 Chron. 18:17)

David and Mephibosheth

9 David asked, "Is there anyone still left of the house of Saul to whom I can show kindness for Jonathan's sake?"

2 Now there was a servant of Saul's household named Ziba. They summoned him to appear before David, and the king said to him, "Are you Ziba?"

"At your service," he replied.

3 The king asked, "Is there no one still alive from the house of Saul to whom I can show God's kindness?"

Ziba answered the king, "There is still a son of Jonathan; he is lame in both feet."

4 "Where is he?" the king asked.

Ziba answered, "He is at the house of Makir son of Ammiel in Lo Debar."

5 So King David had him brought from Lo Debar, from the house of Makir son of Ammiel.

6 When Mephibosheth son of Jonathan, the son of Saul, came to David, he bowed down to pay him honor.

David said, "Mephibosheth!"

"At your service," he replied.

7 "Don't be afraid," David said to him, "for I will surely show you kindness for the sake of your father Jonathan. I will restore to you all the land that belonged to your grandfather Saul, and you will always eat at my table."

8 Mephibosheth bowed down and said, "What is your servant, that you should notice a dead dog like me?"

9 Then the king summoned Ziba, Saul's steward, and said to him, "I have given your master's grandson everything that belonged to Saul and his family. 10 You and your sons and your servants are to farm the land for him and bring in the crops, so that your master's grandson may be provided for. And Mephibosheth, grandson of your master, will always eat at my table." (Now Ziba had fifteen sons and twenty servants.)

11 Then Ziba said to the king, "Your servant will do whatever my lord the king commands his servant to do." So Mephibosheth ate at David's[a] table like one of the king's sons.

12 Mephibosheth had a young son named Mika, and all the members of Ziba's household were servants of Mephibosheth. 13 And Mephibosheth lived in Jerusalem, because he always ate at the king's table; he was lame in both feet.

David Defeats the Ammonites

10 In the course of time, the king of the Ammonites died, and his son Hanun succeeded him as king. 2 David thought, "I will show kindness to Hanun

---

≫ INSTANT ACCESS

Sure, Christians should be "different." But how? By carrying a Bible with your books? By listening to Christian music? By writing Bible verses on your homework? When David became king over Israel, he searched for descendants of Saul in order to show kindness to them (2 Samuel 9:1). Rulers in that day usually searched for members of the previous king's family, not to show kindness but to kill them! David was different, in a godly way. How can you be different? You can be polite to classmates who don't like you. You can be nice to unpopular teachers. Keep on being "different," and you'll be surprised how many of your friends will be interested in you and in Christ.

{2 Samuel 9:1–11}

---

a 11 Septuagint; Hebrew *my*

son of Nahash, just as his father showed kindness to me." So David sent a delegation to express his sympathy to Hanun concerning his father.

When David's men came to the land of the Ammonites, [3]the Ammonite commanders said to Hanun their lord, "Do you think David is honoring your father by sending envoys to you to express sympathy? Hasn't David sent them to you only to explore the city and spy it out and overthrow it?" [4]So Hanun seized David's envoys, shaved off half of each man's beard, cut off their garments at the buttocks, and sent them away.

[5]When David was told about this, he sent messengers to meet the men, for they were greatly humiliated. The king said, "Stay at Jericho till your beards have grown, and then come back."

[6]When the Ammonites realized that they had become obnoxious to David, they hired twenty thousand Aramean foot soldiers from Beth Rehob and Zobah, as well as the king of Maakah with a thousand men, and also twelve thousand men from Tob.

[7]On hearing this, David sent Joab out with the entire army of fighting men. [8]The Ammonites came out and drew up in battle formation at the entrance of their city gate, while the Arameans of Zobah and Rehob and the men of Tob and Maakah were by themselves in the open country.

[9]Joab saw that there were battle lines in front of him and behind him; so he selected some of the best troops in Israel and deployed them against the Arameans. [10]He put the rest of the men under the command of Abishai his brother and deployed them against the Ammonites. [11]Joab said, "If the Arameans are too strong for me, then you are to come to my rescue; but if the Ammonites are too strong for you, then I will come to rescue you. [12]Be strong, and let us fight bravely for our people and the cities of our God. The LORD will do what is good in his sight."

[13]Then Joab and the troops with him advanced to fight the Arameans, and they fled before him. [14]When the Ammonites

realized that the Arameans were fleeing, they fled before Abishai and went inside the city. So Joab returned from fighting the Ammonites and came to Jerusalem.

[15]After the Arameans saw that they had been routed by Israel, they regrouped. [16]Hadadezer had Arameans brought from beyond the Euphrates River; they went to Helam, with Shobak the commander of Hadadezer's army leading them.

[17]When David was told of this, he gathered all Israel, crossed the Jordan and went to Helam. The Arameans formed their battle lines to meet David and fought against him. [18]But they fled before Israel, and David killed seven hundred of their charioteers and forty thousand of their foot soldiers.[a] He also struck down Shobak the commander of their army, and he died there. [19]When all the kings who were vassals of Hadadezer saw that they had been routed by Israel, they made peace with the Israelites and became subject to them.

So the Arameans were afraid to help the Ammonites anymore.

David and Bathsheba

11 In the spring, at the time when kings go off to war, David sent Joab out with the king's men and the whole Israelite army. They destroyed the Ammonites and besieged Rabbah. But David remained in Jerusalem.

[2]One evening David got up from his bed and walked around on the roof of the palace. From the roof he saw a woman bathing. The woman was very beautiful, [3]and David sent someone to find out about her. The man said, "She is Bathsheba, the daughter of Eliam and the wife of Uriah the Hittite." [4]Then David sent messengers to get her. She came to him, and he slept with her. (Now she was purifying herself from her monthly uncleanness.) Then she went back home. [5]The woman conceived and sent word to David, saying, "I am pregnant."

[6]So David sent this word to Joab: "Send me Uriah the Hittite." And Joab sent him to David. [7]When Uriah came to

---

[a] 18 Some Septuagint manuscripts (see also 1 Chron. 19:18); Hebrew *horsemen*

him, David asked him how Joab was, how the soldiers were and how the war was going. [8] Then David said to Uriah, "Go down to your house and wash your feet." So Uriah left the palace, and a gift from the king was sent after him. [9] But Uriah slept at the entrance to the palace with all his master's servants and did not go down to his house.

[10] David was told, "Uriah did not go home." So he asked Uriah, "Haven't you just come from a military campaign? Why didn't you go home?"

[11] Uriah said to David, "The ark and Israel and Judah are staying in tents,[a] and my commander Joab and my lord's men are camped in the open country. How could I go to my house to eat and drink and make love to my wife? As surely as you live, I will not do such a thing!"

[12] Then David said to him, "Stay here one more day, and tomorrow I will send you back." So Uriah remained in Jerusalem that day and the next. [13] At David's invitation, he ate and drank with him, and David made him drunk. But in the evening Uriah went out to sleep on his mat among his master's servants; he did not go home.

[14] In the morning David wrote a letter to Joab and sent it with Uriah. [15] In it he wrote, "Put Uriah out in front where the fighting is fiercest. Then withdraw from him so he will be struck down and die."

[16] So while Joab had the city under siege, he put Uriah at a place where he knew the strongest defenders were. [17] When the men of the city came out and fought against Joab, some of the men in David's army fell; moreover, Uriah the Hittite died.

[18] Joab sent David a full account of the battle. [19] He instructed the messenger: "When you have finished giving the king this account of the battle, [20] the king's anger may flare up, and he may ask you, 'Why did you get so close to the city to fight? Didn't you know they would shoot arrows from the wall? [21] Who killed Abimelek son of Jerub-Besheth[b]? Didn't a woman drop an upper millstone on him

from the wall, so that he died in Thebez? Why did you get so close to the wall?' If he asks you this, then say to him, 'Moreover, your servant Uriah the Hittite is dead.'"

[22] The messenger set out, and when he arrived he told David everything Joab had sent him to say. [23] The messenger said to David, "The men overpowered us and came out against us in the open, but we drove them back to the entrance of the city gate. [24] Then the archers shot arrows at your servants from the wall, and some of the king's men died. Moreover, your servant Uriah the Hittite is dead."

[25] David told the messenger, "Say this to Joab: 'Don't let this upset you; the sword devours one as well as another. Press the attack against the city and destroy it.' Say this to encourage Joab."

[26] When Uriah's wife heard that her husband was dead, she mourned for him. [27] After the time of mourning was over, David had her brought to his house, and she became his wife and bore him a son. But the thing David had done displeased the LORD.

Nathan Rebukes David

12 The LORD sent Nathan to David. When he came to him, he said, "There were two men in a certain town, one rich and the other poor. [2] The rich man had a very large number of sheep and cattle, [3] but the poor man had nothing except one little ewe lamb he had bought. He raised it, and it grew up with him and his children. It shared his food, drank from his cup and even slept in his arms. It was like a daughter to him.

[4] "Now a traveler came to the rich man, but the rich man refrained from taking one of his own sheep or cattle to prepare a meal for the traveler who had come to him. Instead, he took the ewe lamb that belonged to the poor man and prepared it for the one who had come to him."

[5] David burned with anger against the man and said to Nathan, "As surely as the LORD lives, the man who did this must die! [6] He must pay for that lamb four

---

[a] 11 Or *staying at Sukkoth*   [b] 21 Also known as *Jerub-Baal* (that is, Gideon)

The brownies your sister baked are half gone. You're the only one home, yet you look her in the eye and say, "But I didn't eat them." Even without that brown smear on your upper lip, she knows you did it. What's worse, God knows. And you know. When David tried to hide his sin with Bathsheba, God didn't let him rest. Finally, when confronted by the prophet Nathan, David confessed his sin. Then he wrote Psalm 51 to describe the sense of release that came when he admitted his sin and let God cleanse him. Check out this psalm, and you may find a better way to react than to claim, "But I didn't do it," when you really did.

{2 Samuel 12:13}

INSTANT ACCESS

word of the LORD by doing what is evil in his eyes? You struck down Uriah the Hittite with the sword and took his wife to be your own. You killed him with the sword of the Ammonites. 10Now, therefore, the sword will never depart from your house, because you despised me and took the wife of Uriah the Hittite to be your own.'

11"This is what the LORD says: 'Out of your own household I am going to bring calamity on you. Before your very eyes I will take your wives and give them to one who is close to you, and he will sleep with your wives in broad daylight. 12You did it in secret, but I will do this thing in broad daylight before all Israel.'"

13Then David said to Nathan, "I have sinned against the LORD."

Nathan replied, "The LORD has taken away your sin. You are not going to die. 14But because by doing this you have shown utter contempt for*a* the LORD, the son born to you will die."

15After Nathan had gone home, the LORD struck the child that Uriah's wife had borne to David, and he became ill. 16David pleaded with God for the child. He fasted and spent the nights lying in sackcloth*b* on the ground. 17The elders of his household stood beside him to get him up from the ground, but he refused, and he would not eat any food with them.

18On the seventh day the child died. David's attendants were afraid to tell him that the child was dead, for they thought, "While the child was still living, he wouldn't listen to us when we spoke to him. How can we now tell him the child is dead? He may do something desperate."

19David noticed that his attendants were whispering among themselves, and he realized the child was dead. "Is the child dead?" he asked.

"Yes," they replied, "he is dead."

20Then David got up from the ground. After he had washed, put on lotions and changed his clothes, he went into the house of the LORD and worshiped. Then he went to his own house, and at his request they served him food, and he ate.

times over, because he did such a thing and had no pity."

7Then Nathan said to David, "You are the man! This is what the LORD, the God of Israel, says: 'I anointed you king over Israel, and I delivered you from the hand of Saul. 8I gave your master's house to you, and your master's wives into your arms. I gave you all Israel and Judah. And if all this had been too little, I would have given you even more. 9Why did you despise the

---

a 14 An ancient Hebrew scribal tradition; Masoretic Text *for the enemies of* Masoretic Text does not have *in sackcloth*.   *b 16* Dead Sea Scrolls and Septuagint;

²¹His attendants asked him, "Why are you acting this way? While the child was alive, you fasted and wept, but now that the child is dead, you get up and eat!"

²²He answered, "While the child was still alive, I fasted and wept. I thought, 'Who knows? The LORD may be gracious to me and let the child live.' ²³But now that he is dead, why should I go on fasting? Can I bring him back again? I will go to him, but he will not return to me."

²⁴Then David comforted his wife Bathsheba, and he went to her and made love to her. She gave birth to a son, and they named him Solomon. The LORD loved him; ²⁵and because the LORD loved him, he sent word through Nathan the prophet to name him Jedidiah.ᵃ

²⁶Meanwhile Joab fought against Rabbah of the Ammonites and captured the royal citadel. ²⁷Joab then sent messengers to David, saying, "I have fought against Rabbah and taken its water supply. ²⁸Now muster the rest of the troops and besiege the city and capture it. Otherwise I will take the city, and it will be named after me."

²⁹So David mustered the entire army and went to Rabbah, and attacked and captured it. ³⁰David took the crown from their king'sᵇ head, and it was placed on his own head. It weighed a talentᶜ of gold, and it was set with precious stones. David took a great quantity of plunder from the city ³¹and brought out the people who were there, consigning them to labor with saws and with iron picks and axes, and he made them work at brickmaking.ᵈ David did this to all the Ammonite towns. Then he and his entire army returned to Jerusalem.

Amnon and Tamar

13 In the course of time, Amnon son of David fell in love with Tamar, the beautiful sister of Absalom son of David.

²Amnon became so obsessed with his sister Tamar that he made himself ill. She was a virgin, and it seemed impossible for him to do anything to her.

³Now Amnon had an adviser named Jonadab son of Shimeah, David's brother. Jonadab was a very shrewd man. ⁴He asked Amnon, "Why do you, the king's son, look so haggard morning after morning? Won't you tell me?"

Amnon said to him, "I'm in love with Tamar, my brother Absalom's sister."

⁵"Go to bed and pretend to be ill," Jonadab said. "When your father comes to see you, say to him, 'I would like my sister Tamar to come and give me something to eat. Let her prepare the food in my sight so I may watch her and then eat it from her hand.'"

⁶So Amnon lay down and pretended to be ill. When the king came to see him, Amnon said to him, "I would like my sister Tamar to come and make some special bread in my sight, so I may eat from her hand."

⁷David sent word to Tamar at the palace: "Go to the house of your brother Amnon and prepare some food for him." ⁸So Tamar went to the house of her brother Amnon, who was lying down. She took some dough, kneaded it, made the bread in his sight and baked it. ⁹Then she took the pan and served him the bread, but he refused to eat.

"Send everyone out of here," Amnon said. So everyone left him. ¹⁰Then Amnon said to Tamar, "Bring the food here into my bedroom so I may eat from your hand." And Tamar took the bread she had prepared and brought it to her brother Amnon in his bedroom. ¹¹But when she took it to him to eat, he grabbed her and said, "Come to bed with me, my sister."

¹²"No, my brother!" she said to him. "Don't force me! Such a thing should not be done in Israel! Don't do this wicked thing. ¹³What about me? Where could I get rid of my disgrace? And what about you? You would be like one of the wicked fools in Israel. Please speak to the king; he will not keep me from being married to you." ¹⁴But he refused to listen to her, and since he was stronger than she, he raped her.

¹⁵Then Amnon hated her with intense

ᵃ 25 *Jedidiah* means *loved by the LORD.*   ᵇ 30 Or *from Milkom's* (that is, Molek's)   ᶜ 30 That is, about 75 pounds or about 34 kilograms   ᵈ 31 The meaning of the Hebrew for this clause is uncertain.

> My best friend had the worst thing done to her by her uncle. He abused her in the worst way. I'm the only one she has told. She's hardly been eating and she's very depressed. I promised I wouldn't tell anyone. I'm scared. What can I do? >> Holland, MI

Dear Jordan

Dear Friend,

I am so saddened by your letter. A vile thing has been done to your friend. Try to get her to tell someone. She needs help. She is lucky to have a friend like you.

There is a story in 2 Samuel 13 about a girl named Tamar. She was raped by her half brother, Amnon. This led to a series of terrible events. One of her other brothers, Absalom, tried to help her, but he gave her poor advice. Tamar's father, King David, heard about what had been done and was furious, but he did nothing.

Eventually, Absalom killed Amnon and was later also killed. Now two of David's sons were dead and Tamar never was given the help she needed. The Bible said she "lived in her brother Absalom's house, a desolate woman" (verse 20).

Rape and incest are wicked and very damaging to the victim as well as the perpetrator. With the help of a good counselor and the love and support of those around her, your friend can experience amazing healing. She can grow up and have healthy relationships. Remember to pray for your friend. God is the greatest mender of brokenness.

Jordan

hatred. In fact, he hated her more than he had loved her. Amnon said to her, "Get up and get out!"

16 "No!" she said to him. "Sending me away would be a greater wrong than what you have already done to me."

But he refused to listen to her. 17 He called his personal servant and said, "Get this woman out of my sight and bolt the door after her." 18 So his servant put her out and bolted the door after her. She was wearing an ornate*a* robe, for this was the kind of garment the virgin daughters of the king wore. 19 Tamar put ashes on her head and tore the ornate robe she was wearing. She put her hands on her head and went away, weeping aloud as she went.

20 Her brother Absalom said to her, "Has that Amnon, your brother, been with you? Be quiet for now, my sister; he is your brother. Don't take this thing to heart." And Tamar lived in her brother Absalom's house, a desolate woman.

21 When King David heard all this, he was furious. 22 And Absalom never said a word to Amnon, either good or bad; he hated Amnon because he had disgraced his sister Tamar.

Absalom Kills Amnon

23 Two years later, when Absalom's sheepshearers were at Baal Hazor near the border of Ephraim, he invited all the king's sons to come there. 24 Absalom went to the king and said, "Your servant has had shearers come. Will the king and his attendants please join me?"

25 "No, my son," the king replied. "All of us should not go; we would only be a burden to you." Although Absalom urged him, he still refused to go but gave him his blessing.

26 Then Absalom said, "If not, please let my brother Amnon come with us."

The king asked him, "Why should he go with you?" 27 But Absalom urged him, so he sent with him Amnon and the rest of the king's sons.

28 Absalom ordered his men, "Listen! When Amnon is in high spirits from drink-

ing wine and I say to you, 'Strike Amnon down,' then kill him. Don't be afraid. Haven't I given you this order? Be strong and brave." 29 So Absalom's men did to Amnon what Absalom had ordered. Then all the king's sons got up, mounted their mules and fled.

30 While they were on their way, the report came to David: "Absalom has struck down all the king's sons; not one of them is left." 31 The king stood up, tore his clothes and lay down on the ground; and all his attendants stood by with their clothes torn.

32 But Jonadab son of Shimeah, David's brother, said, "My lord should not think that they killed all the princes; only Amnon is dead. This has been Absalom's express intention ever since the day Amnon raped his sister Tamar. 33 My lord the king should not be concerned about the report that all the king's sons are dead. Only Amnon is dead."

34 Meanwhile, Absalom had fled.

Now the man standing watch looked up and saw many people on the road west of him, coming down the side of the hill. The watchman went and told the king, "I see men in the direction of Horonaim, on the side of the hill."*b*

35 Jonadab said to the king, "See, the king's sons have come; it has happened just as your servant said."

36 As he finished speaking, the king's sons came in, wailing loudly. The king, too, and all his attendants wept very bitterly.

37 Absalom fled and went to Talmai son of Ammihud, the king of Geshur. But King David mourned many days for his son.

38 After Absalom fled and went to Geshur, he stayed there three years. 39 And King David longed to go to Absalom, for he was consoled concerning Amnon's death.

Absalom Returns to Jerusalem

14 Joab son of Zeruiah knew that the king's heart longed for Absalom. 2 So Joab sent someone to Tekoa and had a wise woman brought from there.

---

a 18 The meaning of the Hebrew for this word is uncertain; also in verse 19. *b* 34 Septuagint; Hebrew does not have this sentence.

He said to her, "Pretend you are in mourning. Dress in mourning clothes, and don't use any cosmetic lotions. Act like a woman who has spent many days grieving for the dead. ³Then go to the king and speak these words to him." And Joab put the words in her mouth.

⁴When the woman from Tekoa went[a] to the king, she fell with her face to the ground to pay him honor, and she said, "Help me, Your Majesty!"

⁵The king asked her, "What is troubling you?"

She said, "I am a widow; my husband is dead. ⁶I your servant had two sons. They got into a fight with each other in the field, and no one was there to separate them. One struck the other and killed him. ⁷Now the whole clan has risen up against your servant; they say, 'Hand over the one who struck his brother down, so that we may put him to death for the life of his brother whom he killed; then we will get rid of the heir as well.' They would put out the only burning coal I have left, leaving my husband neither name nor descendant on the face of the earth."

⁸The king said to the woman, "Go home, and I will issue an order in your behalf."

⁹But the woman from Tekoa said to him, "Let my lord the king pardon me and my family, and let the king and his throne be without guilt."

¹⁰The king replied, "If anyone says anything to you, bring them to me, and they will not bother you again."

¹¹She said, "Then let the king invoke the Lᴏʀᴅ his God to prevent the avenger of blood from adding to the destruction, so that my son will not be destroyed."

"As surely as the Lᴏʀᴅ lives," he said, "not one hair of your son's head will fall to the ground."

¹²Then the woman said, "Let your servant speak a word to my lord the king."

"Speak," he replied.

¹³The woman said, "Why then have you devised a thing like this against the people of God? When the king says this, does he not convict himself, for the king has not brought back his banished son? ¹⁴Like water spilled on the ground, which cannot be recovered, so we must die. But that is not what God desires; rather, he devises ways so that a banished person does not remain banished from him.

¹⁵"And now I have come to say this to my lord the king because the people have made me afraid. Your servant thought, 'I will speak to the king; perhaps he will grant his servant's request. ¹⁶Perhaps the king will agree to deliver his servant from the hand of the man who is trying to cut off both me and my son from God's inheritance.'

¹⁷"And now your servant says, 'May the word of my lord the king secure my inheritance, for my lord the king is like an angel of God in discerning good and evil. May the Lᴏʀᴅ your God be with you.' "

¹⁸Then the king said to the woman, "Don't keep from me the answer to what I am going to ask you."

"Let my lord the king speak," the woman said.

¹⁹The king asked, "Isn't the hand of Joab with you in all this?"

The woman answered, "As surely as you live, my lord the king, no one can turn to the right or to the left from anything my lord the king says. Yes, it was your servant Joab who instructed me to do this and who put all these words into the mouth of your servant. ²⁰Your servant Joab did this to change the present situation. My lord has wisdom like that of an angel of God—he knows everything that happens in the land."

²¹The king said to Joab, "Very well, I will do it. Go, bring back the young man Absalom."

²²Joab fell with his face to the ground to pay him honor, and he blessed the king. Joab said, "Today your servant knows that he has found favor in your eyes, my lord the king, because the king has granted his servant's request."

²³Then Joab went to Geshur and brought Absalom back to Jerusalem. ²⁴But the king said, "He must go to his own house; he must not see my face." So

---

ᵃ 4 Many Hebrew manuscripts, Septuagint, Vulgate and Syriac; most Hebrew manuscripts *spoke*

Absalom went to his own house and did not see the face of the king.

25 In all Israel there was not a man so highly praised for his handsome appearance as Absalom. From the top of his head to the sole of his foot there was no blemish in him. 26 Whenever he cut the hair of his head—he used to cut his hair once a year because it became too heavy for him—he would weigh it, and its weight was two hundred shekels[a] by the royal standard.

27 Three sons and a daughter were born to Absalom. His daughter's name was Tamar, and she became a beautiful woman.

28 Absalom lived two years in Jerusalem without seeing the king's face. 29 Then Absalom sent for Joab in order to send him to the king, but Joab refused to come to him. So he sent a second time, but he refused to come. 30 Then he said to his servants, "Look, Joab's field is next to mine, and he has barley there. Go and set it on fire." So Absalom's servants set the field on fire.

31 Then Joab did go to Absalom's house, and he said to him, "Why have your servants set my field on fire?"

32 Absalom said to Joab, "Look, I sent word to you and said, 'Come here so I can send you to the king to ask, "Why have I come from Geshur? It would be better for me if I were still there!"' Now then, I want to see the king's face, and if I am guilty of anything, let him put me to death."

33 So Joab went to the king and told him this. Then the king summoned Absalom, and he came in and bowed down with his face to the ground before the king. And the king kissed Absalom.

Absalom's Conspiracy

15 In the course of time, Absalom provided himself with a chariot and horses and with fifty men to run ahead of him. 2 He would get up early and stand by the side of the road leading to the city gate. Whenever anyone came with a complaint to be placed before the king for a decision, Absalom would call out to him, "What town are you from?" He would

---

INSTANT ACCESS

Parents do make mistakes. David made a big one with his son Absalom. When Absalom killed his brother Amnon, David neither punished Absalom nor forgave him. By failing to act, David left Absalom without moral direction and was at least partly responsible when his son later rebelled. Are your parents quick to ground you when you get out of line? Or are they more likely to talk it over and give you a hug? Believe it or not, both kinds of discipline work. What counts is that Mom and Dad have well-defined moral standards and let you know by their actions that they care whether the choices you make are right or wrong.

{2 Samuel 14:23–24}

---

answer, "Your servant is from one of the tribes of Israel." 3 Then Absalom would say to him, "Look, your claims are valid and proper, but there is no representative of the king to hear you." 4 And Absalom would add, "If only I were appointed judge in the land! Then everyone who has a complaint or case could come to me and I would see that they receive justice." 5 Also, whenever anyone approached him to bow down before him, Absalom would reach out his hand, take hold of

---

him and kiss him. ⁶Absalom behaved in this way toward all the Israelites who came to the king asking for justice, and so he stole the hearts of the people of Israel.

⁷At the end of four*ᵃ* years, Absalom said to the king, "Let me go to Hebron and fulfill a vow I made to the LORD. ⁸While your servant was living at Geshur in Aram, I made this vow: 'If the LORD takes me back to Jerusalem, I will worship the LORD in Hebron.*ᵇ*'"

⁹The king said to him, "Go in peace." So he went to Hebron.

¹⁰Then Absalom sent secret messengers throughout the tribes of Israel to say, "As soon as you hear the sound of the trumpets, then say, 'Absalom is king in Hebron.'" ¹¹Two hundred men from Jerusalem had accompanied Absalom. They had been invited as guests and went quite innocently, knowing nothing about the matter. ¹²While Absalom was offering sacrifices, he also sent for Ahithophel the Gilonite, David's counselor, to come from Giloh, his hometown. And so the conspiracy gained strength, and Absalom's following kept on increasing.

David Flees

¹³A messenger came and told David, "The hearts of the people of Israel are with Absalom."

¹⁴Then David said to all his officials who were with him in Jerusalem, "Come! We must flee, or none of us will escape from Absalom. We must leave immediately, or he will move quickly to overtake us and bring ruin on us and put the city to the sword."

¹⁵The king's officials answered him, "Your servants are ready to do whatever our lord the king chooses."

¹⁶The king set out, with his entire household following him; but he left ten concubines to take care of the palace. ¹⁷So the king set out, with all the people following him, and they halted at the edge of the city. ¹⁸All his men marched past him, along with all the Kerethites and Pelethites; and all the six hundred

Gittites who had accompanied him from Gath marched before the king.

¹⁹The king said to Ittai the Gittite, "Why should you come along with us? Go back and stay with King Absalom. You are a foreigner, an exile from your homeland. ²⁰You came only yesterday. And today shall I make you wander about with us, when I do not know where I am going? Go back, and take your people with you. May the LORD show you kindness and faithfulness."*ᶜ*

²¹But Ittai replied to the king, "As surely as the LORD lives, and as my lord the king lives, wherever my lord the king may be, whether it means life or death, there will your servant be."

²²David said to Ittai, "Go ahead, march on." So Ittai the Gittite marched on with all his men and the families that were with him.

²³The whole countryside wept aloud as all the people passed by. The king also crossed the Kidron Valley, and all the people moved on toward the wilderness.

²⁴Zadok was there, too, and all the Levites who were with him were carrying the ark of the covenant of God. They set down the ark of God, and Abiathar offered sacrifices until all the people had finished leaving the city.

²⁵Then the king said to Zadok, "Take the ark of God back into the city. If I find favor in the LORD's eyes, he will bring me back and let me see it and his dwelling place again. ²⁶But if he says, 'I am not pleased with you,' then I am ready; let him do to me whatever seems good to him."

²⁷The king also said to Zadok the priest, "Do you understand? Go back to the city with my blessing. Take your son Ahimaaz with you, and also Abiathar's son Jonathan. You and Abiathar return with your two sons. ²⁸I will wait at the fords in the wilderness until word comes from you to inform me." ²⁹So Zadok and Abiathar took the ark of God back to Jerusalem and stayed there.

³⁰But David continued up the Mount of Olives, weeping as he went; his head was

---

ᵃ 7 Some Septuagint manuscripts, Syriac and Josephus; Hebrew forty   *ᵇ 8 Some Septuagint manuscripts; Hebrew does not have* in Hebron.   *ᶜ 20 Septuagint; Hebrew* May kindness and faithfulness be with you

covered and he was barefoot. All the people with him covered their heads too and were weeping as they went up. ³¹Now David had been told, "Ahithophel is among the conspirators with Absalom." So David prayed, "LORD, turn Ahithophel's counsel into foolishness."

³²When David arrived at the summit, where people used to worship God, Hushai the Arkite was there to meet him, his robe torn and dust on his head. ³³David said to him, "If you go with me, you will be a burden to me. ³⁴But if you return to the city and say to Absalom, 'Your Majesty, I will be your servant; I was your father's servant in the past, but now I will be your servant,' then you can help me by frustrating Ahithophel's advice. ³⁵Won't the priests Zadok and Abiathar be there with you? Tell them anything you hear in the king's palace. ³⁶Their two sons, Ahimaaz son of Zadok and Jonathan son of Abiathar, are there with them. Send them to me with anything you hear."

³⁷So Hushai, David's confidant, arrived at Jerusalem as Absalom was entering the city.

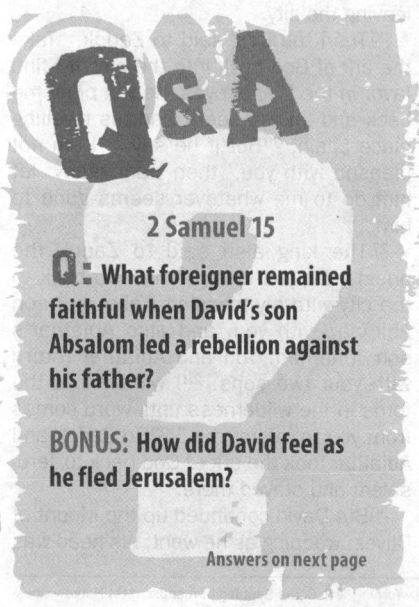

2 Samuel 15

Q: What foreigner remained faithful when David's son Absalom led a rebellion against his father?

BONUS: How did David feel as he fled Jerusalem?

Answers on next page

David and Ziba

16 When David had gone a short distance beyond the summit, there was Ziba, the steward of Mephibosheth, waiting to meet him. He had a string of donkeys saddled and loaded with two hundred loaves of bread, a hundred cakes of raisins, a hundred cakes of figs and a skin of wine.

²The king asked Ziba, "Why have you brought these?"

Ziba answered, "The donkeys are for the king's household to ride on, the bread and fruit are for the men to eat, and the wine is to refresh those who become exhausted in the wilderness."

³The king then asked, "Where is your master's grandson?"

Ziba said to him, "He is staying in Jerusalem, because he thinks, 'Today the Israelites will restore to me my grandfather's kingdom.'"

⁴Then the king said to Ziba, "All that belonged to Mephibosheth is now yours."

"I humbly bow," Ziba said. "May I find favor in your eyes, my lord the king."

Shimei Curses David

⁵As King David approached Bahurim, a man from the same clan as Saul's family came out from there. His name was Shimei son of Gera, and he cursed as he came out. ⁶He pelted David and all the king's officials with stones, though all the troops and the special guard were on David's right and left. ⁷As he cursed, Shimei said, "Get out, get out, you murderer, you scoundrel! ⁸The LORD has repaid you for all the blood you shed in the household of Saul, in whose place you have reigned. The LORD has given the kingdom into the hands of your son Absalom. You have come to ruin because you are a murderer!"

⁹Then Abishai son of Zeruiah said to the king, "Why should this dead dog curse my lord the king? Let me go over and cut off his head."

¹⁰But the king said, "What does this have to do with you, you sons of Zeruiah? If he is cursing because the LORD said to him, 'Curse David,' who can ask, 'Why do you do this?'"

¹¹David then said to Abishai and all his officials, "My son, my own flesh and blood, is trying to kill me. How much more, then, this Benjamite! Leave him alone; let him curse, for the LORD has told him to. ¹²It may be that the LORD will look upon my misery and restore to me his covenant blessing instead of his curse today."

¹³So David and his men continued along the road while Shimei was going along the hillside opposite him, cursing as he went and throwing stones at him and showering him with dirt. ¹⁴The king and all the people with him arrived at their destination exhausted. And there he refreshed himself.

The Advice of Ahithophel and Hushai

¹⁵Meanwhile, Absalom and all the men of Israel came to Jerusalem, and Ahithophel was with him. ¹⁶Then Hushai the Arkite, David's confidant, went to Absalom and said to him, "Long live the king! Long live the king!"

¹⁷Absalom said to Hushai, "So this is the love you show your friend? If he's your friend, why didn't you go with him?"

¹⁸Hushai said to Absalom, "No, the one chosen by the LORD, by these people, and by all the men of Israel—his I will be, and I will remain with him. ¹⁹Furthermore, whom should I serve? Should I not serve the son? Just as I served your father, so I will serve you."

²⁰Absalom said to Ahithophel, "Give us your advice. What should we do?"

²¹Ahithophel answered, "Sleep with your father's concubines whom he left to take care of the palace. Then all Israel will hear that you have made yourself obnoxious to your father, and the hands of everyone with you will be more resolute." ²²So they pitched a tent for Absalom on the roof, and he slept with his father's concubines in the sight of all Israel.

²³Now in those days the advice Ahithophel gave was like that of one who inquires of God. That was how both David and Absalom regarded all of Ahithophel's advice.

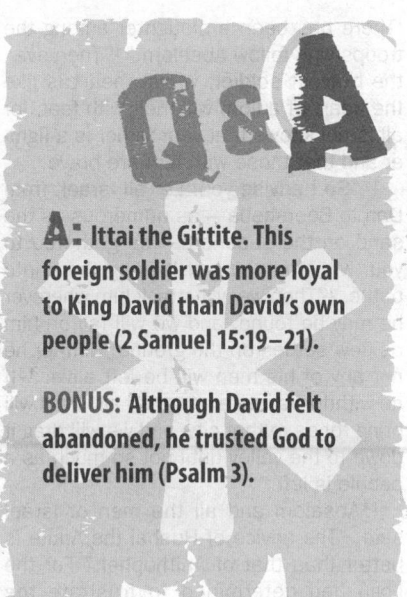

A: Ittai the Gittite. This foreign soldier was more loyal to King David than David's own people (2 Samuel 15:19–21).

BONUS: Although David felt abandoned, he trusted God to deliver him (Psalm 3).

17 Ahithophel said to Absalom, "I would[a] choose twelve thousand men and set out tonight in pursuit of David. ²I would attack him while he is weary and weak. I would strike him with terror, and then all the people with him will flee. I would strike down only the king ³and bring all the people back to you. The death of the man you seek will mean the return of all; all the people will be unharmed." ⁴This plan seemed good to Absalom and to all the elders of Israel.

⁵But Absalom said, "Summon also Hushai the Arkite, so we can hear what he has to say as well." ⁶When Hushai came to him, Absalom said, "Ahithophel has given this advice. Should we do what he says? If not, give us your opinion."

⁷Hushai replied to Absalom, "The advice Ahithophel has given is not good this time. ⁸You know your father and his men; they are fighters, and as fierce as a wild bear robbed of her cubs. Besides, your father is an experienced fighter; he will not spend the night with the troops. ⁹Even now, he is hidden in a cave or some other place. If he should attack your troops first,[b] whoever hears about it will say,

---

[a] 1 Or *Let me*   [b] 9 Or *When some of the men fall at the first attack*

'There has been a slaughter among the troops who follow Absalom.' [10] Then even the bravest soldier, whose heart is like the heart of a lion, will melt with fear, for all Israel knows that your father is a fighter and that those with him are brave.

[11] "So I advise you: Let all Israel, from Dan to Beersheba—as numerous as the sand on the seashore—be gathered to you, with you yourself leading them into battle. [12] Then we will attack him wherever he may be found, and we will fall on him as dew settles on the ground. Neither he nor any of his men will be left alive. [13] If he withdraws into a city, then all Israel will bring ropes to that city, and we will drag it down to the valley until not so much as a pebble is left."

[14] Absalom and all the men of Israel said, "The advice of Hushai the Arkite is better than that of Ahithophel." For the LORD had determined to frustrate the good advice of Ahithophel in order to bring disaster on Absalom.

[15] Hushai told Zadok and Abiathar, the priests, "Ahithophel has advised Absalom and the elders of Israel to do such and such, but I have advised them to do so and so. [16] Now send a message at once and tell David, 'Do not spend the night at the fords in the wilderness; cross over without fail, or the king and all the people with him will be swallowed up.'"

[17] Jonathan and Ahimaaz were staying at En Rogel. A female servant was to go and inform them, and they were to go and tell King David, for they could not risk being seen entering the city. [18] But a young man saw them and told Absalom. So the two of them left at once and went to the house of a man in Bahurim. He had a well in his courtyard, and they climbed down into it. [19] His wife took a covering and spread it out over the opening of the well and scattered grain over it. No one knew anything about it.

[20] When Absalom's men came to the woman at the house, they asked, "Where are Ahimaaz and Jonathan?"

The woman answered them, "They crossed over the brook."[a] The men

searched but found no one, so they returned to Jerusalem.

[21] After they had gone, the two climbed out of the well and went to inform King David. They said to him, "Set out and cross the river at once; Ahithophel has advised such and such against you." [22] So David and all the people with him set out and crossed the Jordan. By daybreak, no one was left who had not crossed the Jordan.

[23] When Ahithophel saw that his advice had not been followed, he saddled his donkey and set out for his house in his hometown. He put his house in order and

INSTANT ACCESS

You ask Jenny what she thinks, and she says you should tell. Kendra says don't tell. You ask Karen, and she says you should tell only if you're asked. Sarah says you should pick up the phone and tell right away. So you ask Chrissy, and she . . . Somehow, when you want advice, everyone seems to have a different opinion. It may be good to get different views, but in the end you're the one who has to make the decision. Even if all agree that one choice is better (2 Samuel 17:14), they may be wrong. In the end you have to decide. Ask God for help with your decisions. And do what you think is right.

{2 Samuel 17:1–14}

[a] 20 Or "They passed by the sheep pen toward the water."

then hanged himself. So he died and was buried in his father's tomb.

Absalom's Death

24 David went to Mahanaim, and Absalom crossed the Jordan with all the men of Israel. 25 Absalom had appointed Amasa over the army in place of Joab. Amasa was the son of Jether,[a] an Ishmaelite[b] who had married Abigal, the daughter of Nahash and sister of Zeruiah the mother of Joab. 26 The Israelites and Absalom camped in the land of Gilead.

27 When David came to Mahanaim, Shobi son of Nahash from Rabbah of the Ammonites, and Makir son of Ammiel from Lo Debar, and Barzillai the Gileadite from Rogelim 28 brought bedding and bowls and articles of pottery. They also brought wheat and barley, flour and roasted grain, beans and lentils,[c] 29 honey and curds, sheep, and cheese from cows' milk for David and his people to eat. For they said, "The people have become exhausted and hungry and thirsty in the wilderness."

18 David mustered the men who were with him and appointed over them commanders of thousands and commanders of hundreds. 2 David sent out his troops, a third under the command of Joab, a third under Joab's brother Abishai son of Zeruiah, and a third under Ittai the Gittite. The king told the troops, "I myself will surely march out with you."

3 But the men said, "You must not go out; if we are forced to flee, they won't care about us. Even if half of us die, they won't care; but you are worth ten thousand of us.[d] It would be better now for you to give us support from the city."

4 The king answered, "I will do whatever seems best to you."

So the king stood beside the gate while all his men marched out in units of hundreds and of thousands. 5 The king commanded Joab, Abishai and Ittai, "Be gentle with the young man Absalom for my sake." And all the troops heard the king giving orders concerning Absalom to each of the commanders.

6 David's army marched out of the city to fight Israel, and the battle took place in the forest of Ephraim. 7 There Israel's troops were routed by David's men, and the casualties that day were great — twenty thousand men. 8 The battle spread out over the whole countryside, and the forest swallowed up more men that day than the sword.

9 Now Absalom happened to meet David's men. He was riding his mule, and as the mule went under the thick branches of a large oak, Absalom's hair got caught in the tree. He was left hanging in mid-air, while the mule he was riding kept on going.

10 When one of the men saw what had happened, he told Joab, "I just saw Absalom hanging in an oak tree."

11 Joab said to the man who had told him this, "What! You saw him? Why didn't you strike him to the ground right there? Then I would have had to give you ten shekels[e] of silver and a warrior's belt."

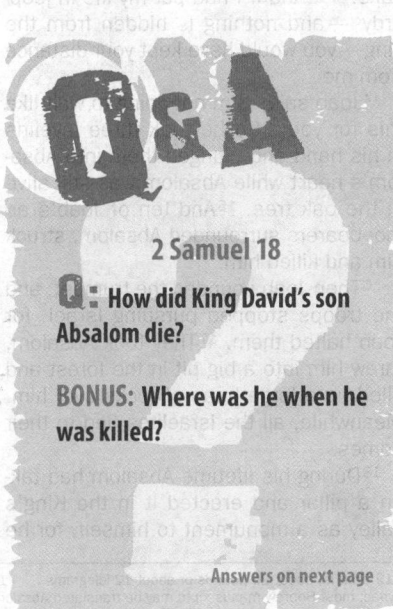

2 Samuel 18

Q: How did King David's son Absalom die?

BONUS: Where was he when he was killed?

Answers on next page

---

a 25 Hebrew *Ithra*, a variant of *Jether*   b 25 Some Septuagint manuscripts (see also 1 Chron. 2:17); Hebrew and other Septuagint manuscripts *Israelite*   c 28 Most Septuagint manuscripts and Syriac; Hebrew *lentils, and roasted grain*   d 3 Two Hebrew manuscripts, some Septuagint manuscripts and Vulgate; most Hebrew manuscripts *care; for now there are ten thousand like us*   e 11 That is, about 4 ounces or about 115 grams

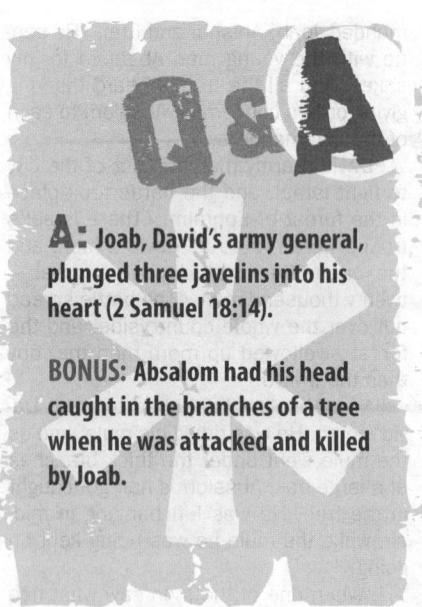

A: Joab, David's army general, plunged three javelins into his heart (2 Samuel 18:14).

BONUS: Absalom had his head caught in the branches of a tree when he was attacked and killed by Joab.

¹²But the man replied, "Even if a thousand shekels[a] were weighed out into my hands, I would not lay a hand on the king's son. In our hearing the king commanded you and Abishai and Ittai, 'Protect the young man Absalom for my sake.[b]' ¹³And if I had put my life in jeopardy[c] — and nothing is hidden from the king — you would have kept your distance from me."

¹⁴Joab said, "I'm not going to wait like this for you." So he took three javelins in his hand and plunged them into Absalom's heart while Absalom was still alive in the oak tree. ¹⁵And ten of Joab's armor-bearers surrounded Absalom, struck him and killed him.

¹⁶Then Joab sounded the trumpet, and the troops stopped pursuing Israel, for Joab halted them. ¹⁷They took Absalom, threw him into a big pit in the forest and piled up a large heap of rocks over him. Meanwhile, all the Israelites fled to their homes.

¹⁸During his lifetime Absalom had taken a pillar and erected it in the King's Valley as a monument to himself, for he thought, "I have no son to carry on the memory of my name." He named the pillar after himself, and it is called Absalom's Monument to this day.

David Mourns

¹⁹Now Ahimaaz son of Zadok said, "Let me run and take the news to the king that the Lᴏʀᴅ has vindicated him by delivering him from the hand of his enemies."

²⁰"You are not the one to take the news today," Joab told him. "You may take the news another time, but you must not do so today, because the king's son is dead."

²¹Then Joab said to a Cushite, "Go, tell the king what you have seen." The Cushite bowed down before Joab and ran off.

²²Ahimaaz son of Zadok again said to Joab, "Come what may, please let me run behind the Cushite."

But Joab replied, "My son, why do you want to go? You don't have any news that will bring you a reward."

²³He said, "Come what may, I want to run."

So Joab said, "Run!" Then Ahimaaz ran by way of the plain[d] and outran the Cushite.

²⁴While David was sitting between the inner and outer gates, the watchman went up to the roof of the gateway by the wall. As he looked out, he saw a man running alone. ²⁵The watchman called out to the king and reported it.

The king said, "If he is alone, he must have good news." And the runner came closer and closer.

²⁶Then the watchman saw another runner, and he called down to the gatekeeper, "Look, another man running alone!"

The king said, "He must be bringing good news, too."

²⁷The watchman said, "It seems to me that the first one runs like Ahimaaz son of Zadok."

"He's a good man," the king said. "He comes with good news."

²⁸Then Ahimaaz called out to the king, "All is well!" He bowed down before the

---

a 12 That is, about 25 pounds or about 12 kilograms   *b 12* A few Hebrew manuscripts, Septuagint, Vulgate and Syriac; most Hebrew manuscripts may be translated *Absalom, whoever you may be.*   *c 13* Or *Otherwise, if I had acted treacherously toward him*   *d 23* That is, the plain of the Jordan

king with his face to the ground and said, "Praise be to the Lord your God! He has delivered up those who lifted their hands against my lord the king."

29 The king asked, "Is the young man Absalom safe?"

Ahimaaz answered, "I saw great confusion just as Joab was about to send the king's servant and me, your servant, but I don't know what it was."

30 The king said, "Stand aside and wait here." So he stepped aside and stood there.

31 Then the Cushite arrived and said, "My lord the king, hear the good news! The Lord has vindicated you today by delivering you from the hand of all who rose up against you."

32 The king asked the Cushite, "Is the young man Absalom safe?"

The Cushite replied, "May the enemies of my lord the king and all who rise up to harm you be like that young man."

33 The king was shaken. He went up to the room over the gateway and wept. As he went, he said: "O my son Absalom! My son, my son Absalom! If only I had died instead of you—O Absalom, my son, my son!"*a*

19 *b* Joab was told, "The king is weeping and mourning for Absalom." 2 And for the whole army the victory that day was turned into mourning, because on that day the troops heard it said, "The king is grieving for his son." 3 The men stole into the city that day as men steal in who are ashamed when they flee from battle. 4 The king covered his face and cried aloud, "O my son Absalom! O Absalom, my son, my son!"

5 Then Joab went into the house to the king and said, "Today you have humiliated all your men, who have just saved your life and the lives of your sons and daughters and the lives of your wives and concubines. 6 You love those who hate you and hate those who love you. You have made it clear today that the commanders and their men mean nothing to you. I see that you would be pleased if Absalom were alive today and all of us were dead.

7 Now go out and encourage your men. I swear by the Lord that if you don't go out, not a man will be left with you by nightfall. This will be worse for you than all the calamities that have come on you from your youth till now."

8 So the king got up and took his seat in the gateway. When the men were told, "The king is sitting in the gateway," they all came before him.

Meanwhile, the Israelites had fled to their homes.

David Returns to Jerusalem

9 Throughout the tribes of Israel, all the people were arguing among themselves, saying, "The king delivered us from the hand of our enemies; he is the one who rescued us from the hand of the Philistines. But now he has fled the country to escape from Absalom; 10 and Absalom, whom we anointed to rule over us, has died in battle. So why do you say nothing about bringing the king back?"

11 King David sent this message to Zadok and Abiathar, the priests: "Ask the elders of Judah, 'Why should you be the last to bring the king back to his palace, since what is being said throughout Israel has reached the king at his quarters? 12 You are my relatives, my own flesh and blood. So why should you be the last to bring back the king?' 13 And say to Amasa, 'Are you not my own flesh and blood? May God deal with me, be it ever so severely, if you are not the commander of my army for life in place of Joab.'"

14 He won over the hearts of the men of Judah so that they were all of one mind. They sent word to the king, "Return, you and all your men." 15 Then the king returned and went as far as the Jordan.

Now the men of Judah had come to Gilgal to go out and meet the king and bring him across the Jordan. 16 Shimei son of Gera, the Benjamite from Bahurim, hurried down with the men of Judah to meet King David. 17 With him were a thousand Benjamites, along with Ziba, the steward of Saul's household, and his fifteen sons and twenty servants. They rushed

---

a 33 In Hebrew texts this verse (18:33) is numbered 19:1.   *b* In Hebrew texts 19:1-43 is numbered 19:2-44.

to the Jordan, where the king was. ¹⁸They crossed at the ford to take the king's household over and to do whatever he wished.

When Shimei son of Gera crossed the Jordan, he fell prostrate before the king ¹⁹and said to him, "May my lord not hold me guilty. Do not remember how your servant did wrong on the day my lord the king left Jerusalem. May the king put it out of his mind. ²⁰For I your servant know that I have sinned, but today I have come here as the first from the tribes of Joseph to come down and meet my lord the king."

²¹Then Abishai son of Zeruiah said, "Shouldn't Shimei be put to death for this? He cursed the LORD's anointed."

²²David replied, "What does this have to do with you, you sons of Zeruiah? What right do you have to interfere? Should anyone be put to death in Israel today? Don't I know that today I am king over Israel?" ²³So the king said to Shimei, "You shall not die." And the king promised him on oath.

²⁴Mephibosheth, Saul's grandson, also went down to meet the king. He had not taken care of his feet or trimmed his mustache or washed his clothes from the day the king left until the day he returned safely. ²⁵When he came from Jerusalem to meet the king, the king asked him, "Why didn't you go with me, Mephibosheth?"

²⁶He said, "My lord the king, since I your servant am lame, I said, 'I will have my donkey saddled and will ride on it, so I can go with the king.' But Ziba my servant betrayed me. ²⁷And he has slandered your servant to my lord the king. My lord the king is like an angel of God; so do whatever you wish. ²⁸All my grandfather's descendants deserved nothing but death from my lord the king, but you gave your servant a place among those who eat at your table. So what right do I have to make any more appeals to the king?"

²⁹The king said to him, "Why say more? I order you and Ziba to divide the land."

³⁰Mephibosheth said to the king, "Let him take everything, now that my lord the king has returned home safely."

³¹Barzillai the Gileadite also came down from Rogelim to cross the Jordan with the king and to send him on his way from there. ³²Now Barzillai was very old, eighty years of age. He had provided for the king during his stay in Mahanaim, for he was a very wealthy man. ³³The king said to Barzillai, "Cross over with me and stay with me in Jerusalem, and I will provide for you."

³⁴But Barzillai answered the king, "How many more years will I live, that I should go up to Jerusalem with the king? ³⁵I am now eighty years old. Can I tell the difference between what is enjoyable and what is not? Can your servant taste what he eats and drinks? Can I still hear the voices of male and female singers? Why should your servant be an added burden to my lord the king? ³⁶Your servant will

---

PANORAMA

{2 SAMUEL}

Dreams Come True.

David's dreams come true. He is crowned king over all Israel. His armies pushed back the enemies until Israel had ten times as much land as before. David also led his people to worship in Jerusalem. Despite his successes, David made some choices that hurt him and his people.

cross over the Jordan with the king for a short distance, but why should the king reward me in this way? ³⁷Let your servant return, that I may die in my own town near the tomb of my father and mother. But here is your servant Kimham. Let him cross over with my lord the king. Do for him whatever you wish."

³⁸The king said, "Kimham shall cross over with me, and I will do for him whatever you wish. And anything you desire from me I will do for you."

³⁹So all the people crossed the Jordan, and then the king crossed over. The king kissed Barzillai and bid him farewell, and Barzillai returned to his home.

⁴⁰When the king crossed over to Gilgal, Kimham crossed with him. All the troops of Judah and half the troops of Israel had taken the king over.

⁴¹Soon all the men of Israel were coming to the king and saying to him, "Why did our brothers, the men of Judah, steal the king away and bring him and his household across the Jordan, together with all his men?"

⁴²All the men of Judah answered the men of Israel, "We did this because the king is closely related to us. Why are you angry about it? Have we eaten any of the king's provisions? Have we taken anything for ourselves?"

⁴³Then the men of Israel answered the men of Judah, "We have ten shares in the king; so we have a greater claim on David than you have. Why then do you treat us with contempt? Weren't we the first to speak of bringing back our king?"

But the men of Judah pressed their claims even more forcefully than the men of Israel.

Sheba Rebels Against David

20 Now a troublemaker named Sheba son of Bikri, a Benjamite, happened to be there. He sounded the trumpet and shouted,

"We have no share in David,
  no part in Jesse's son!
Every man to his tent, Israel!"

²So all the men of Israel deserted David to follow Sheba son of Bikri. But the men of Judah stayed by their king all the way from the Jordan to Jerusalem.

³When David returned to his palace in Jerusalem, he took the ten concubines he had left to take care of the palace and put them in a house under guard. He provided for them but had no sexual relations with them. They were kept in confinement till the day of their death, living as widows.

⁴Then the king said to Amasa, "Summon the men of Judah to come to me within three days, and be here yourself." ⁵But when Amasa went to summon Judah, he took longer than the time the king had set for him.

⁶David said to Abishai, "Now Sheba son of Bikri will do us more harm than Absalom did. Take your master's men and pursue him, or he will find fortified cities and escape from us."ᵃ ⁷So Joab's men and the Kerethites and Pelethites and all the mighty warriors went out under the command of Abishai. They marched out from Jerusalem to pursue Sheba son of Bikri.

⁸While they were at the great rock in Gibeon, Amasa came to meet them. Joab was wearing his military tunic, and strapped over it at his waist was a belt with a dagger in its sheath. As he stepped forward, it dropped out of its sheath.

⁹Joab said to Amasa, "How are you, my brother?" Then Joab took Amasa by the beard with his right hand to kiss him. ¹⁰Amasa was not on his guard against the dagger in Joab's hand, and Joab plunged it into his belly, and his intestines spilled out on the ground. Without being stabbed again, Amasa died. Then Joab and his brother Abishai pursued Sheba son of Bikri.

¹¹One of Joab's men stood beside Amasa and said, "Whoever favors Joab, and whoever is for David, let him follow Joab!" ¹²Amasa lay wallowing in his blood in the middle of the road, and the man saw that all the troops came to a halt there. When he realized that everyone who came up to Amasa stopped, he dragged him from

ᵃ 6 Or and do us serious injury

the road into a field and threw a garment over him. ¹³After Amasa had been removed from the road, everyone went on with Joab to pursue Sheba son of Bikri.

¹⁴Sheba passed through all the tribes of Israel to Abel Beth Maakah and through the entire region of the Bikrites,ᵃ who gathered together and followed him. ¹⁵All the troops with Joab came and besieged Sheba in Abel Beth Maakah. They built a siege ramp up to the city, and it stood against the outer fortifications. While they were battering the wall to bring it down, ¹⁶a wise woman called from the city, "Listen! Listen! Tell Joab to come here so I can speak to him." ¹⁷He went toward her, and she asked, "Are you Joab?"

"I am," he answered.

She said, "Listen to what your servant has to say."

"I'm listening," he said.

¹⁸She continued, "Long ago they used to say, 'Get your answer at Abel,' and that settled it. ¹⁹We are the peaceful and faithful in Israel. You are trying to destroy a city that is a mother in Israel. Why do you want to swallow up the LORD's inheritance?"

²⁰"Far be it from me!" Joab replied, "Far be it from me to swallow up or destroy! ²¹That is not the case. A man named Sheba son of Bikri, from the hill country of Ephraim, has lifted up his hand against the king, against David. Hand over this one man, and I'll withdraw from the city."

The woman said to Joab, "His head will be thrown to you from the wall."

²²Then the woman went to all the people with her wise advice, and they cut off the head of Sheba son of Bikri and threw it to Joab. So he sounded the trumpet, and his men dispersed from the city, each returning to his home. And Joab went back to the king in Jerusalem.

David's Officials

²³Joab was over Israel's entire army; Benaiah son of Jehoiada was over the Kerethites and Pelethites; ²⁴Adoniramᵇ was in charge of forced labor; Jehoshaphat son of Ahilud was recorder; ²⁵Sheva was secretary; Zadok and Abiathar were priests; ²⁶and Ira the Jairiteᶜ was David's priest.

The Gibeonites Avenged

21 During the reign of David, there was a famine for three successive years; so David sought the face of the LORD. The LORD said, "It is on account of Saul and his blood-stained house; it is because he put the Gibeonites to death."

²The king summoned the Gibeonites and spoke to them. (Now the Gibeonites were not a part of Israel but were survivors of the Amorites; the Israelites had sworn to spare them, but Saul in his zeal for Israel and Judah had tried to annihilate them.) ³David asked the Gibeonites, "What shall I do for you? How shall I make atonement so that you will bless the LORD's inheritance?"

⁴The Gibeonites answered him, "We have no right to demand silver or gold from Saul or his family, nor do we have the right to put anyone in Israel to death."

"What do you want me to do for you?" David asked.

⁵They answered the king, "As for the man who destroyed us and plotted against us so that we have been decimated and have no place anywhere in Israel, ⁶let seven of his male descendants be given to us to be killed and their bodies exposed before the LORD at Gibeah of Saul—the LORD's chosen one."

So the king said, "I will give them to you."

⁷The king spared Mephibosheth son of Jonathan, the son of Saul, because of the oath before the LORD between David and Jonathan son of Saul. ⁸But the king took Armoni and Mephibosheth, the two sons of Aiah's daughter Rizpah, whom she had borne to Saul, together with the five sons of Saul's daughter Merab,ᵈ whom she had borne to Adriel son of Barzillai

---

ᵃ 14 See Septuagint and Vulgate; Hebrew *Berites*.   ᵇ 24 Some Septuagint manuscripts (see also 1 Kings 4:6 and 5:14); Hebrew *Adoram*   ᶜ 26 Hebrew; some Septuagint manuscripts and Syriac (see also 23:38) *Ithrite*   ᵈ 8 Two Hebrew manuscripts, some Septuagint manuscripts and Syriac (see also 1 Samuel 18:19); most Hebrew and Septuagint manuscripts *Michal*

the Meholathite. ⁹He handed them over to the Gibeonites, who killed them and exposed their bodies on a hill before the Lᴏʀᴅ. All seven of them fell together; they were put to death during the first days of the harvest, just as the barley harvest was beginning.

¹⁰Rizpah daughter of Aiah took sackcloth and spread it out for herself on a rock. From the beginning of the harvest till the rain poured down from the heavens on the bodies, she did not let the birds touch them by day or the wild animals by night. ¹¹When David was told what Aiah's daughter Rizpah, Saul's concubine, had done, ¹²he went and took the bones of Saul and his son Jonathan from the citizens of Jabesh Gilead. (They had stolen their bodies from the public square at Beth Shan, where the Philistines had hung them after they struck Saul down on Gilboa.) ¹³David brought the bones of Saul and his son Jonathan from there, and the bones of those who had been killed and exposed were gathered up.

¹⁴They buried the bones of Saul and his son Jonathan in the tomb of Saul's father Kish, at Zela in Benjamin, and did everything the king commanded. After that, God answered prayer in behalf of the land.

Wars Against the Philistines

¹⁵Once again there was a battle between the Philistines and Israel. David went down with his men to fight against the Philistines, and he became exhausted. ¹⁶And Ishbi-Benob, one of the descendants of Rapha, whose bronze spearhead weighed three hundred shekels[a] and who was armed with a new sword, said he would kill David. ¹⁷But Abishai son of Zeruiah came to David's rescue; he struck the Philistine down and killed him. Then David's men swore to him, saying, "Never again will you go out with us to battle, so that the lamp of Israel will not be extinguished."

¹⁸In the course of time, there was another battle with the Philistines, at Gob. At that time Sibbekai the Hushathite killed Saph, one of the descendants of Rapha.

¹⁹In another battle with the Philistines at Gob, Elhanan son of Jair[b] the Bethlehemite killed the brother of[c] Goliath the Gittite, who had a spear with a shaft like a weaver's rod.

²⁰In still another battle, which took place at Gath, there was a huge man with six fingers on each hand and six toes on each foot—twenty-four in all. He also was descended from Rapha. ²¹When he taunted Israel, Jonathan son of Shimeah, David's brother, killed him.

²²These four were descendants of Rapha in Gath, and they fell at the hands of David and his men.

David's Song of Praise

22 David sang to the Lᴏʀᴅ the words of this song when the Lᴏʀᴅ delivered him from the hand of all his enemies and from the hand of Saul. ²He said:

> "The Lᴏʀᴅ is my rock, my fortress and
>   my deliverer;
> 3   my God is my rock, in whom I take
>   refuge,
>   my shield[d] and the horn[e] of my
>   salvation.
> He is my stronghold, my refuge and
>   my savior—
>   from violent people you save me.
>
> 4 "I called to the Lᴏʀᴅ, who is worthy of
>   praise,
>   and have been saved from my
>   enemies.
> 5 The waves of death swirled about me;
>   the torrents of destruction
>   overwhelmed me.

My God is my rock, in whom I take refuge.
2 Samuel 22:3

---

a 16 That is, about 7 1/2 pounds or about 3.5 kilograms   b 19 See 1 Chron. 20:5; Hebrew Jaare-Oregim.   c 19 See 1 Chron. 20:5; Hebrew does not have the brother of.   d 3 Or sovereign   e 3 Horn here symbolizes strength.

6 The cords of the grave coiled around
me;
the snares of death confronted me.

7 "In my distress I called to the LORD;
I called out to my God.
From his temple he heard my voice;
my cry came to his ears.

8 The earth trembled and quaked,
the foundations of the heavens[a]
shook;
they trembled because he was
angry.

9 Smoke rose from his nostrils;
consuming fire came from his
mouth,
burning coals blazed out of it.

10 He parted the heavens and came
down;
dark clouds were under his feet.

11 He mounted the cherubim and flew;
he soared[b] on the wings of the
wind.

12 He made darkness his canopy around
him—
the dark[c] rain clouds of the sky.

13 Out of the brightness of his
presence
bolts of lightning blazed forth.

14 The LORD thundered from heaven;
the voice of the Most High
resounded.

15 He shot his arrows and scattered the
enemy,
with great bolts of lightning he
routed them.

16 The valleys of the sea were exposed
and the foundations of the earth
laid bare
at the rebuke of the LORD,
at the blast of breath from his
nostrils.

17 "He reached down from on high and
took hold of me;
he drew me out of deep waters.

18 He rescued me from my powerful
enemy,
from my foes, who were too strong
for me.

19 They confronted me in the day of my
disaster,
but the LORD was my support.

20 He brought me out into a spacious
place;
he rescued me because he
delighted in me.

21 "The LORD has dealt with me according
to my righteousness;
according to the cleanness of my
hands he has rewarded me.

22 For I have kept the ways of the LORD;
I am not guilty of turning from my
God.

23 All his laws are before me;
I have not turned away from his
decrees.

24 I have been blameless before him
and have kept myself from sin.

25 The LORD has rewarded me according
to my righteousness,
according to my cleanness[d] in his
sight.

26 "To the faithful you show yourself
faithful,
to the blameless you show yourself
blameless,

27 to the pure you show yourself pure,
but to the devious you show
yourself shrewd.

28 You save the humble,
but your eyes are on the haughty to
bring them low.

29 You, LORD, are my lamp;
the LORD turns my darkness into
light.

30 With your help I can advance against a
troop[e];
with my God I can scale a wall.

31 "As for God, his way is perfect:
The LORD's word is flawless;
he shields all who take refuge in
him.

32 For who is God besides the LORD?
And who is the Rock except our
God?

33 It is God who arms me with strength[f]
and keeps my way secure.

God . . . shields all who take refuge in him.

2 Samuel 22:31

34 He makes my feet like the feet of a
     deer;
  he causes me to stand on the
     heights.
35 He trains my hands for battle;
  my arms can bend a bow of bronze.
36 You make your saving help my shield;
  your help has made[a] me great.
37 You provide a broad path for my feet,
  so that my ankles do not give way.

38 "I pursued my enemies and crushed
     them;
  I did not turn back till they were
     destroyed.
39 I crushed them completely, and they
     could not rise;
  they fell beneath my feet.
40 You armed me with strength for battle;
  you humbled my adversaries before
     me.
41 You made my enemies turn their
     backs in flight,
  and I destroyed my foes.
42 They cried for help, but there was no
     one to save them—
  to the LORD, but he did not answer.
43 I beat them as fine as the dust of the
     earth;
  I pounded and trampled them like
     mud in the streets.

44 "You have delivered me from the
     attacks of the peoples;
  you have preserved me as the head
     of nations.
  People I did not know now serve
     me,

45   foreigners cower before me;
  as soon as they hear of me, they
     obey me.
46 They all lose heart;
  they come trembling[b] from their
     strongholds.

47 "The LORD lives! Praise be to my Rock!
  Exalted be my God, the Rock, my
     Savior!
48 He is the God who avenges me,
  who puts the nations under me,
49   who sets me free from my enemies.
  You exalted me above my foes;
  from a violent man you rescued me.
50 Therefore I will praise you, LORD,
     among the nations;
  I will sing the praises of your name.

51 "He gives his king great victories;
  he shows unfailing kindness to his
     anointed,
  to David and his descendants
     forever."

David's Last Words

23 These are the last words of David:

"The inspired utterance of David son of
     Jesse,
  the utterance of the man exalted by
     the Most High,
  the man anointed by the God of
     Jacob,
  the hero of Israel's songs:

2 "The Spirit of the LORD spoke through
     me;
  his word was on my tongue.
3 The God of Israel spoke,
  the Rock of Israel said to me:
'When one rules over people in
     righteousness,
  when he rules in the fear of God,
4 he is like the light of morning at
     sunrise
  on a cloudless morning,
  like the brightness after rain
  that brings grass from the earth.'
5 "If my house were not right with God,
  surely he would not have made with
     me an everlasting covenant,

---

a 36 Dead Sea Scrolls; Masoretic Text *shield; / you stoop down to make*   b 46 Some Septuagint manuscripts and
Vulgate (see also Psalm 18:45); Masoretic Text *they arm themselves*

arranged and secured in every
part;
surely he would not bring to fruition
my salvation
and grant me my every desire.
⁶But evil men are all to be cast aside
like thorns,
which are not gathered with the
hand.
⁷Whoever touches thorns
uses a tool of iron or the shaft of a
spear;
they are burned up where they lie."

David's Mighty Warriors

⁸These are the names of David's
mighty warriors:

Josheb-Basshebeth,ᵃ a Tahkemonite,ᵇ
was chief of the Three; he raised his
spear against eight hundred men, whom
he killedᶜ in one encounter.

⁹Next to him was Eleazar son of Dodai
the Ahohite. As one of the three mighty
warriors, he was with David when they
taunted the Philistines gathered at Pas
Dammimᵈ for battle. Then the Israelites
retreated, ¹⁰but Eleazar stood his ground
and struck down the Philistines till his
hand grew tired and froze to the sword.
The LORD brought about a great victory
that day. The troops returned to Eleazar,
but only to strip the dead.

¹¹Next to him was Shammah son of
Agee the Hararite. When the Philistines
banded together at a place where there
was a field full of lentils, Israel's troops
fled from them. ¹²But Shammah took his
stand in the middle of the field. He defended it and struck the Philistines down,
and the LORD brought about a great victory.

¹³During harvest time, three of the
thirty chief warriors came down to David
at the cave of Adullam, while a band of
Philistines was encamped in the Valley
of Rephaim. ¹⁴At that time David was in
the stronghold, and the Philistine garrison
was at Bethlehem. ¹⁵David longed for water and said, "Oh, that someone would

get me a drink of water from the well near
the gate of Bethlehem!" ¹⁶So the three
mighty warriors broke through the Philistine lines, drew water from the well near
the gate of Bethlehem and carried it back
to David. But he refused to drink it; instead, he poured it out before the LORD.
¹⁷"Far be it from me, LORD, to do this!"
he said. "Is it not the blood of men who
went at the risk of their lives?" And David
would not drink it.

Such were the exploits of the three
mighty warriors.

¹⁸Abishai the brother of Joab son
of Zeruiah was chief of the Three.ᵉ He
raised his spear against three hundred
men, whom he killed, and so he became
as famous as the Three. ¹⁹Was he not
held in greater honor than the Three? He
became their commander, even though
he was not included among them.

²⁰Benaiah son of Jehoiada, a valiant
fighter from Kabzeel, performed great exploits. He struck down Moab's two mightiest warriors. He also went down into a
pit on a snowy day and killed a lion. ²¹And
he struck down a huge Egyptian. Although
the Egyptian had a spear in his hand, Benaiah went against him with a club. He
snatched the spear from the Egyptian's
hand and killed him with his own spear.
²²Such were the exploits of Benaiah son
of Jehoiada; he too was as famous as
the three mighty warriors. ²³He was held
in greater honor than any of the Thirty,
but he was not included among the Three.
And David put him in charge of his bodyguard.

²⁴Among the Thirty were:
Asahel the brother of Joab,
Elhanan son of Dodo from Bethle-
hem,
²⁵Shammah the Harodite,
Elika the Harodite,
²⁶Helez the Paltite,
Ira son of Ikkesh from Tekoa,
²⁷Abiezer from Anathoth,
Sibbekaiᶠ the Hushathite,

ᵃ 8 Hebrew; some Septuagint manuscripts suggest *Ish-Bosheth*, that is, *Esh-Baal* (see also 1 Chron. 11:11 *Jashobeam*).
ᵇ 8 Probably a variant of *Hakmonite* (see 1 Chron. 11:11)   ᶜ 8 Some Septuagint manuscripts (see also 1 Chron. 11:11);
Hebrew and other Septuagint manuscripts *Three; it was Adino the Eznite who killed eight hundred men*   ᵈ 9 See 1 Chron.
11:13; Hebrew *gathered there.*   ᵉ 18 Most Hebrew manuscripts (see also 1 Chron. 11:20); two Hebrew manuscripts
and Syriac *Thirty*   ᶠ 27 Some Septuagint manuscripts (see also 21:18; 1 Chron. 11:29); Hebrew *Mebunnai*

28 Zalmon the Ahohite,
   Maharai the Netophathite,
29 Heled[a] son of Baanah the Netophathite,
   Ithai son of Ribai from Gibeah in Benjamin,
30 Benaiah the Pirathonite,
   Hiddai[b] from the ravines of Gaash,
31 Abi-Albon the Arbathite,
   Azmaveth the Barhumite,
32 Eliahba the Shaalbonite,
   the sons of Jashen,
   Jonathan 33 son of[c] Shammah the Hararite,
   Ahiam son of Sharar[d] the Hararite,
34 Eliphelet son of Ahasbai the Maakathite,
   Eliam son of Ahithophel the Gilonite,
35 Hezro the Carmelite,
   Paarai the Arbite,
36 Igal son of Nathan from Zobah,
   the son of Hagri,[e]
37 Zelek the Ammonite,
   Naharai the Beerothite, the armor-bearer of Joab son of Zeruiah,
38 Ira the Ithrite,
   Gareb the Ithrite
39 and Uriah the Hittite.
   There were thirty-seven in all.

David Enrolls the Fighting Men

24 Again the anger of the LORD burned against Israel, and he incited David against them, saying, "Go and take a census of Israel and Judah."

2 So the king said to Joab and the army commanders[f] with him, "Go throughout the tribes of Israel from Dan to Beersheba and enroll the fighting men, so that I may know how many there are."

3 But Joab replied to the king, "May the LORD your God multiply the troops a hundred times over, and may the eyes of my lord the king see it. But why does my lord the king want to do such a thing?"

4 The king's word, however, overruled Joab and the army commanders; so they left the presence of the king to enroll the fighting men of Israel.

5 After crossing the Jordan, they camped near Aroer, south of the town in the gorge, and then went through Gad and on to Jazer. 6 They went to Gilead and the region of Tahtim Hodshi, and on to Dan Jaan and around toward Sidon. 7 Then they went toward the fortress of Tyre and all the towns of the Hivites and Canaanites. Finally, they went on to Beersheba in the Negev of Judah.

8 After they had gone through the entire land, they came back to Jerusalem at the end of nine months and twenty days.

9 Joab reported the number of the fighting men to the king: In Israel there were eight hundred thousand able-bodied men who could handle a sword, and in Judah five hundred thousand.

10 David was conscience-stricken after he had counted the fighting men, and he said to the LORD, "I have sinned greatly in what I have done. Now, LORD, I beg you, take away the guilt of your servant. I have done a very foolish thing."

11 Before David got up the next morning, the word of the LORD had come to Gad the prophet, David's seer: 12 "Go and tell David, 'This is what the LORD says: I am giving you three options. Choose one of them for me to carry out against you.'"

13 So Gad went to David and said to him, "Shall there come on you three[g] years of famine in your land? Or three months of fleeing from your enemies while they pursue you? Or three days of plague in your land? Now then, think it over and decide how I should answer the one who sent me."

14 David said to Gad, "I am in deep distress. Let us fall into the hands of the LORD, for his mercy is great; but do not let me fall into human hands."

15 So the LORD sent a plague on Israel from that morning until the end of the time designated, and seventy thousand of the people from Dan to Beersheba died. 16 When the angel stretched out his

---

[a] 29 Some Hebrew manuscripts and Vulgate (see also 1 Chron. 11:30); most Hebrew manuscripts *Heleb*   [b] 30 Hebrew; some Septuagint manuscripts (see also 1 Chron. 11:32) *Hurai*   [c] 33 Some Septuagint manuscripts (see also 1 Chron. 11:34); Hebrew does not have *son of*.   [d] 33 Hebrew; some Septuagint manuscripts (see also 1 Chron. 11:35) *Sakar*   [e] 36 Some Septuagint manuscripts (see also 1 Chron. 11:38); Hebrew *Haggadi*   [f] 2 Septuagint (see also verse 4 and 1 Chron. 21:2); Hebrew *Joab the army commander*   [g] 13 Septuagint (see also 1 Chron. 21:12); Hebrew *seven*

hand to destroy Jerusalem, the LORD relented concerning the disaster and said to the angel who was afflicting the people, "Enough! Withdraw your hand." The angel of the LORD was then at the threshing floor of Araunah the Jebusite.

17 When David saw the angel who was striking down the people, he said to the LORD, "I have sinned; I, the shepherd,[a] have done wrong. These are but sheep. What have they done? Let your hand fall on me and my family."

David Builds an Altar

18 On that day Gad went to David and said to him, "Go up and build an altar to the LORD on the threshing floor of Araunah the Jebusite." 19 So David went up, as the LORD had commanded through Gad. 20 When Araunah looked and saw the king and his officials coming toward him, he went out and bowed down before the king with his face to the ground.

21 Araunah said, "Why has my lord the king come to his servant?"

"To buy your threshing floor," David answered, "so I can build an altar to the LORD, that the plague on the people may be stopped."

22 Araunah said to David, "Let my lord the king take whatever he wishes and offer it up. Here are oxen for the burnt offering, and here are threshing sledges and ox yokes for the wood. 23 Your Majesty, Araunah[b] gives all this to the king." Araunah also said to him, "May the LORD your God accept you."

24 But the king replied to Araunah, "No, I insist on paying you for it. I will not sacrifice to the LORD my God burnt offerings that cost me nothing."

So David bought the threshing floor and the oxen and paid fifty shekels[c] of silver for them. 25 David built an altar to the LORD there and sacrificed burnt offerings and fellowship offerings. Then the LORD answered his prayer in behalf of the land, and the plague on Israel was stopped.

>> INSTANT ACCESS

Have you ever wondered if something you wanted to do was right or wrong? How can you tell if there's no commandment about it in the Bible? There's no commandment in the Old Testament against taking a military census. But after David counted the fighting men in Israel, the Bible says he "was conscience-stricken" (2 Samuel 24:10). Somehow David knew he'd done wrong. Even though there was no command against a census, David's motive was wrong. He had begun to rely on numbers instead of on God. When you have a decision to make and there's no clear command in the Bible, check your motive. Even right things done for the wrong reasons are wrong.

{2 Samuel 24:1–10}

1 KINGS

Justice.

Sometimes you see other kids do wrong and get away with it, and you wonder, why doesn't the school do something? Why don't their parents? Why doesn't God? But just because someone doesn't get punished doesn't mean justice won't be done.

Solomon held on to the great kingdom of his father David. But after Solomon died the kingdom split in two, Israel and Judah. God sent prophets to warn both kingdoms to return to him. But they didn't listen. Would both kingdoms get away with abandoning God? The stories in this book are a reminder: no one gets away with anything! Justice will be done.

>>**GOOD TAKE OFF, CRASH LANDING**
   Wives corrupt David's son. Story in 1 Kings 11

>>**FEARFUL KING CORRUPTS ISRAEL**
   Counterfeit religion established, see 1 Kings 12:25–33

>>**NOT ONE GOOD KING IN ISRAEL!**
   North's kings all disobey God's Word, 1 Kings 16

>>**ONE WHIPS FOUR HUNDRED FIFTY!**
   Occult powers useless. See story, 1 Kings 18:16–45

preview

The authors use royal records, called "annals," to write this history.

The false gods the Israelites worship are called "baals," which means "lord" or "master."

Events recorded in this book took place between about 930 and 850 B.C.

During these years the later Vedas and the Upanishads are written in India. A village is erected on Rome's Palatine hill. In Peru part-human, part-animal deities are worshiped by the Chavin cult.

Adonijah Sets Himself Up as King

1 When King David was very old, he could not keep warm even when they put covers over him. ²So his attendants said to him, "Let us look for a young virgin to serve the king and take care of him. She can lie beside him so that our lord the king may keep warm."

³Then they searched throughout Israel for a beautiful young woman and found Abishag, a Shunammite, and brought her to the king. ⁴The woman was very beautiful; she took care of the king and waited on him, but the king had no sexual relations with her.

⁵Now Adonijah, whose mother was Haggith, put himself forward and said, "I will be king." So he got chariots and horses^a ready, with fifty men to run ahead of him. ⁶(His father had never rebuked him by asking, "Why do you behave as you do?" He was also very handsome and was born next after Absalom.)

⁷Adonijah conferred with Joab son of Zeruiah and with Abiathar the priest, and they gave him their support. ⁸But Zadok the priest, Benaiah son of Jehoiada, Nathan the prophet, Shimei and Rei and David's special guard did not join Adonijah.

⁹Adonijah then sacrificed sheep, cattle and fattened calves at the Stone of Zoheleth near En Rogel. He invited all his brothers, the king's sons, and all the royal officials of Judah, ¹⁰but he did not invite Nathan the prophet or Benaiah or the special guard or his brother Solomon.

¹¹Then Nathan asked Bathsheba, Solomon's mother, "Have you not heard that Adonijah, the son of Haggith, has become king, and our lord David knows nothing about it? ¹²Now then, let me advise you how you can save your own life and the life of your son Solomon. ¹³Go in to King David and say to him, 'My lord the king, did you not swear to me your servant: "Surely Solomon your son shall be king after me, and he will sit on my throne"? Why then has Adonijah become king?' ¹⁴While you are still there talking to the king, I will come in and add my word to what you have said."

¹⁵So Bathsheba went to see the aged king in his room, where Abishag the Shunammite was attending him. ¹⁶Bathsheba bowed down, prostrating herself before the king.

"What is it you want?" the king asked.

¹⁷She said to him, "My lord, you yourself swore to me your servant by the LORD your God: 'Solomon your son shall be king after me, and he will sit on my throne.' ¹⁸But now Adonijah has become king, and you, my lord the king, do not know about it. ¹⁹He has sacrificed great numbers of cattle, fattened calves, and sheep, and has invited all the king's sons, Abiathar the priest and Joab the commander of the army, but he has not invited Solomon your servant. ²⁰My lord the king, the eyes of all Israel are on you, to learn from you who will sit on the throne of my lord the king after him. ²¹Otherwise, as soon as my lord the king is laid to rest with his ancestors, I and my son Solomon will be treated as criminals."

²²While she was still speaking with the king, Nathan the prophet arrived. ²³And the king was told, "Nathan the prophet is here." So he went before the king and bowed with his face to the ground.

²⁴Nathan said, "Have you, my lord the king, declared that Adonijah shall be king after you, and that he will sit on your throne? ²⁵Today he has gone down and sacrificed great numbers of cattle, fattened calves, and sheep. He has invited all the king's sons, the commanders of the army and Abiathar the priest. Right now they are eating and drinking with him and saying, 'Long live King Adonijah!' ²⁶But me your servant, and Zadok the priest, and Benaiah son of Jehoiada, and your servant Solomon he did not invite. ²⁷Is this something my lord the king has done without letting his servants know who should sit on the throne of my lord the king after him?"

David Makes Solomon King

²⁸Then King David said, "Call in Bathsheba." So she came into the king's presence and stood before him.

---

^a 5 Or *charioteers*

You know you have to get your homework done. But maybe later, after you spend some time online. And you have to write a report for English. But soon the guys want you to play basketball. Guess you can write it later. David took the "maybe later" approach, and it almost cost the life of Bathsheba and Solomon. Because David put off announcing a successor, another son tried to steal the throne. Fortunately, Bathsheba and the prophet Nathan stepped in. (Sort of like Mom or Dad making you study!) Putting off homework or even missing a report probably won't ruin your life. But if putting things off becomes a habit, it might!

{1 Kings 1:1–27}

INSTANT ACCESS

29 The king then took an oath: "As surely as the LORD lives, who has delivered me out of every trouble, 30 I will surely carry out this very day what I swore to you by the LORD, the God of Israel: Solomon your son shall be king after me, and he will sit on my throne in my place."

31 Then Bathsheba bowed down with her face to the ground, prostrating herself before the king, and said, "May my lord King David live forever!"

32 King David said, "Call in Zadok the priest, Nathan the prophet and Benaiah son of Jehoiada." When they came be-fore the king, 33 he said to them: "Take your lord's servants with you and have Solomon my son mount my own mule and take him down to Gihon. 34 There have Zadok the priest and Nathan the proph-et anoint him king over Israel. Blow the trumpet and shout, 'Long live King Solo-mon!' 35 Then you are to go up with him, and he is to come and sit on my throne and reign in my place. I have appointed him ruler over Israel and Judah."

36 Benaiah son of Jehoiada answered the king, "Amen! May the LORD, the God of my lord the king, so declare it. 37 As the LORD was with my lord the king, so may he be with Solomon to make his throne even greater than the throne of my lord King David!"

38 So Zadok the priest, Nathan the prophet, Benaiah son of Jehoiada, the Kerethites and the Pelethites went down and had Solomon mount King David's mule, and they escorted him to Gihon. 39 Zadok the priest took the horn of oil from the sacred tent and anointed Solo-mon. Then they sounded the trumpet and all the people shouted, "Long live King Solomon!" 40 And all the people went up after him, playing pipes and rejoicing greatly, so that the ground shook with the sound.

41 Adonijah and all the guests who were with him heard it as they were finishing their feast. On hearing the sound of the trumpet, Joab asked, "What's the mean-ing of all the noise in the city?"

42 Even as he was speaking, Jonathan son of Abiathar the priest arrived. Adoni-jah said, "Come in. A worthy man like you must be bringing good news."

43 "Not at all!" Jonathan answered. "Our lord King David has made Solomon king. 44 The king has sent with him Zadok the priest, Nathan the prophet, Benaiah son of Jehoiada, the Kerethites and the Pelethites, and they have put him on the king's mule, 45 and Zadok the priest and Nathan the prophet have anointed him king at Gihon. From there they have gone up cheering, and the city resounds with it. That's the noise you hear. 46 Moreover, Solomon has taken his seat on the roy-al throne. 47 Also, the royal officials have

come to congratulate our lord King David, saying, 'May your God make Solomon's name more famous than yours and his throne greater than yours!' And the king bowed in worship on his bed ⁴⁸and said, 'Praise be to the LORD, the God of Israel, who has allowed my eyes to see a successor on my throne today.' "

⁴⁹At this, all Adonijah's guests rose in alarm and dispersed. ⁵⁰But Adonijah, in fear of Solomon, went and took hold of the horns of the altar. ⁵¹Then Solomon was told, "Adonijah is afraid of King Solomon and is clinging to the horns of the altar. He says, 'Let King Solomon swear to me today that he will not put his servant to death with the sword.' "

⁵²Solomon replied, "If he shows himself to be worthy, not a hair of his head will fall to the ground; but if evil is found in him, he will die." ⁵³Then King Solomon sent men, and they brought him down from the altar. And Adonijah came and bowed down to King Solomon, and Solomon said, "Go to your home."

David's Charge to Solomon

2 When the time drew near for David to die, he gave a charge to Solomon his son.

²"I am about to go the way of all the earth," he said. "So be strong, act like a man, ³and observe what the LORD your God requires: Walk in obedience to him, and keep his decrees and commands, his laws and regulations, as written in the Law of Moses. Do this so that you may prosper in all you do and wherever you go ⁴and that the LORD may keep his promise to me: 'If your descendants watch how they live, and if they walk faithfully before me with all their heart and soul, you will never fail to have a successor on the throne of Israel.'

⁵"Now you yourself know what Joab son of Zeruiah did to me—what he did to the two commanders of Israel's armies, Abner son of Ner and Amasa son of Jether. He killed them, shedding their blood in peacetime as if in battle, and with that blood he stained the belt around his waist and the sandals on his feet. ⁶Deal with him according to your wisdom, but

do not let his gray head go down to the grave in peace.

⁷"But show kindness to the sons of Barzillai of Gilead and let them be among those who eat at your table. They stood by me when I fled from your brother Absalom.

⁸"And remember, you have with you Shimei son of Gera, the Benjamite from Bahurim, who called down bitter curses on me the day I went to Mahanaim. When he came down to meet me at the Jordan, I swore to him by the LORD: 'I will not put you to death by the sword.' ⁹But now, do not consider him innocent. You are a man of wisdom; you will know what to do to him. Bring his gray head down to the grave in blood."

¹⁰Then David rested with his ancestors and was buried in the City of David. ¹¹He had reigned forty years over Israel—seven years in Hebron and thirty-three in Jerusalem. ¹²So Solomon sat on the throne of his father David, and his rule was firmly established.

Solomon's Throne Established

¹³Now Adonijah, the son of Haggith, went to Bathsheba, Solomon's mother. Bathsheba asked him, "Do you come peacefully?"

He answered, "Yes, peacefully." ¹⁴Then he added, "I have something to say to you."

"You may say it," she replied.

¹⁵"As you know," he said, "the kingdom was mine. All Israel looked to me as their king. But things changed, and the kingdom has gone to my brother; for it has come to him from the LORD. ¹⁶Now I have one request to make of you. Do not refuse me."

"You may make it," she said.

¹⁷So he continued, "Please ask King Solomon—he will not refuse you—to give me Abishag the Shunammite as my wife."

¹⁸"Very well," Bathsheba replied, "I will speak to the king for you."

¹⁹When Bathsheba went to King Solomon to speak to him for Adonijah, the king stood up to meet her, bowed down to her and sat down on his throne. He had a

throne brought for the king's mother, and she sat down at his right hand.

²⁰"I have one small request to make of you," she said. "Do not refuse me."

The king replied, "Make it, my mother; I will not refuse you."

²¹So she said, "Let Abishag the Shunammite be given in marriage to your brother Adonijah."

²²King Solomon answered his mother, "Why do you request Abishag the Shunammite for Adonijah? You might as well request the kingdom for him—after all, he is my older brother—yes, for him and for Abiathar the priest and Joab son of Zeruiah!"

²³Then King Solomon swore by the LORD: "May God deal with me, be it ever so severely, if Adonijah does not pay with his life for this request! ²⁴And now, as surely as the LORD lives—he who has established me securely on the throne of my father David and has founded a dynasty for me as he promised—Adonijah shall be put to death today!" ²⁵So King Solomon gave orders to Benaiah son of Jehoiada, and he struck down Adonijah and he died.

²⁶To Abiathar the priest the king said, "Go back to your fields in Anathoth. You deserve to die, but I will not put you to death now, because you carried the ark of the Sovereign LORD before my father David and shared all my father's hardships." ²⁷So Solomon removed Abiathar from the priesthood of the LORD, fulfilling the word the LORD had spoken at Shiloh about the house of Eli.

²⁸When the news reached Joab, who had conspired with Adonijah though not with Absalom, he fled to the tent of the LORD and took hold of the horns of the altar. ²⁹King Solomon was told that Joab had fled to the tent of the LORD and was beside the altar. Then Solomon ordered Benaiah son of Jehoiada, "Go, strike him down!"

³⁰So Benaiah entered the tent of the LORD and said to Joab, "The king says, 'Come out!'"

But he answered, "No, I will die here."

Benaiah reported to the king, "This is how Joab answered me."

³¹Then the king commanded Benaiah, "Do as he says. Strike him down and bury him, and so clear me and my whole family of the guilt of the innocent blood that Joab shed. ³²The LORD will repay him for the blood he shed, because without my father David knowing it he attacked two men and killed them with the sword. Both of them—Abner son of Ner, commander of Israel's army, and Amasa son of Jether, commander of Judah's army—were better men and more upright than he. ³³May the guilt of their blood rest on the head of Joab and his descendants forever. But on David and his descendants, his house and his throne, may there be the LORD's peace forever."

³⁴So Benaiah son of Jehoiada went up and struck down Joab and killed him, and he was buried at his home out in the country. ³⁵The king put Benaiah son of Jehoiada over the army in Joab's position and replaced Abiathar with Zadok the priest.

³⁶Then the king sent for Shimei and said to him, "Build yourself a house in Jerusalem and live there, but do not go anywhere else. ³⁷The day you leave and cross the Kidron Valley, you can be sure you will die; your blood will be on your own head."

³⁸Shimei answered the king, "What you say is good. Your servant will do as my lord the king has said." And Shimei stayed in Jerusalem for a long time.

³⁹But three years later, two of Shimei's slaves ran off to Achish son of Maakah, king of Gath, and Shimei was told, "Your slaves are in Gath." ⁴⁰At this, he saddled his donkey and went to Achish at Gath in search of his slaves. So Shimei went away and brought the slaves back from Gath.

Walk in obedience to him . . . so that you may prosper in all you do.
1 Kings 2:3

41 When Solomon was told that Shimei had gone from Jerusalem to Gath and had returned, 42 the king summoned Shimei and said to him, "Did I not make you swear by the LORD and warn you, 'On the day you leave to go anywhere else, you can be sure you will die'? At that time you said to me, 'What you say is good. I will obey.' 43 Why then did you not keep your oath to the LORD and obey the command I gave you?"

44 The king also said to Shimei, "You know in your heart all the wrong you did to my father David. Now the LORD will repay you for your wrongdoing. 45 But King Solomon will be blessed, and David's throne will remain secure before the LORD forever."

46 Then the king gave the order to Benaiah son of Jehoiada, and he went out and struck Shimei down and he died.

The kingdom was now established in Solomon's hands.

Solomon Asks for Wisdom

3 Solomon made an alliance with Pharaoh king of Egypt and married his daughter. He brought her to the City of David until he finished building his palace and the temple of the LORD, and the wall around Jerusalem. 2 The people, however, were still sacrificing at the high places, because a temple had not yet been built for the Name of the LORD. 3 Solomon showed his love for the LORD by walking according to the instructions given him by his father David, except that he offered sacrifices and burned incense on the high places.

4 The king went to Gibeon to offer sacrifices, for that was the most important high place, and Solomon offered a thousand burnt offerings on that altar. 5 At Gibeon the LORD appeared to Solomon during the night in a dream, and God said, "Ask for whatever you want me to give you."

6 Solomon answered, "You have shown great kindness to your servant, my father David, because he was faithful to you and righteous and upright in heart. You have continued this great kindness to him and have given him a son to sit on his throne this very day.

7 "Now, LORD my God, you have made your servant king in place of my father David. But I am only a little child and do not know how to carry out my duties. 8 Your servant is here among the people you have chosen, a great people, too numerous to count or number. 9 So give your servant a discerning heart to govern your people and to distinguish between right and wrong. For who is able to govern this great people of yours?"

10 The Lord was pleased that Solomon had asked for this. 11 So God said to him, "Since you have asked for this and not for long life or wealth for yourself, nor have asked for the death of your enemies but for discernment in administering justice, 12 I will do what you have asked. I will give you a wise and discerning heart, so that there will never have been anyone like you, nor will there ever be. 13 Moreover, I will give you what you have not asked for—both wealth and honor—so that in your lifetime you will have no equal among kings. 14 And if you walk in obedience to me and keep my decrees and commands as David your father did, I will give you a long life." 15 Then Solomon awoke—and he realized it had been a dream.

Q&A

1 Kings 3

Q: What did Solomon get that he hadn't asked for?

BONUS: What was Solomon's yearly income?

Answers on next page

He returned to Jerusalem, stood before the ark of the Lord's covenant and sacrificed burnt offerings and fellowship offerings. Then he gave a feast for all his court.

A Wise Ruling

16 Now two prostitutes came to the king and stood before him. 17 One of them said, "Pardon me, my lord. This woman and I live in the same house, and I had a baby while she was there with me. 18 The third day after my child was born, this woman also had a baby. We were alone; there was no one in the house but the two of us.

19 "During the night this woman's son died because she lay on him. 20 So she got up in the middle of the night and took my son from my side while I your servant was asleep. She put him by her breast and put her dead son by my breast. 21 The next morning, I got up to nurse my son — and he was dead! But when I looked at him closely in the morning light, I saw that it wasn't the son I had borne."

22 The other woman said, "No! The living one is my son; the dead one is yours."

But the first one insisted, "No! The dead one is yours; the living one is mine." And so they argued before the king.

23 The king said, "This one says, 'My son is alive and your son is dead,' while that one says, 'No! Your son is dead and mine is alive.'"

24 Then the king said, "Bring me a sword." So they brought a sword for the king. 25 He then gave an order: "Cut the living child in two and give half to one and half to the other."

26 The woman whose son was alive was deeply moved out of love for her son and said to the king, "Please, my lord, give her the living baby! Don't kill him!"

But the other said, "Neither I nor you shall have him. Cut him in two!"

27 Then the king gave his ruling: "Give the living baby to the first woman. Do not kill him; she is his mother."

28 When all Israel heard the verdict the king had given, they held the king in awe, because they saw that he had wisdom from God to administer justice.

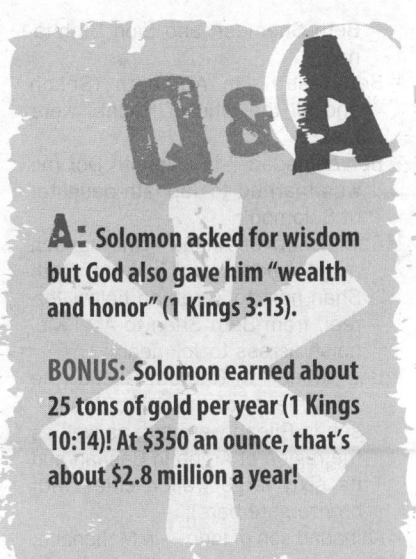

A: Solomon asked for wisdom but God also gave him "wealth and honor" (1 Kings 3:13).

BONUS: Solomon earned about 25 tons of gold per year (1 Kings 10:14)! At $350 an ounce, that's about $2.8 million a year!

Solomon's Officials and Governors

4 So King Solomon ruled over all Israel. 2 And these were his chief officials:

Azariah son of Zadok — the priest;
3 Elihoreph and Ahijah, sons of Shisha — secretaries;
Jehoshaphat son of Ahilud — recorder;
4 Benaiah son of Jehoiada — commander in chief;
Zadok and Abiathar — priests;
5 Azariah son of Nathan — in charge of the district governors;
Zabud son of Nathan — a priest and adviser to the king;
6 Ahishar — palace administrator;
Adoniram son of Abda — in charge of forced labor.

7 Solomon had twelve district governors over all Israel, who supplied provisions for the king and the royal household. Each one had to provide supplies for one month in the year. 8 These are their names:

Ben-Hur — in the hill country of Ephraim;
9 Ben-Deker — in Makaz, Shaalbim,

Beth Shemesh and Elon Bethha-
nan;

10 Ben-Hesed — in Arubboth (Sokoh
and all the land of Hepher were
his);

11 Ben-Abinadab — in Naphoth Dor (he
was married to Taphath daughter
of Solomon);

12 Baana son of Ahilud — in Taanach
and Megiddo, and in all of Beth
Shan next to Zarethan below Jezreel, from Beth Shan to Abel Meholah across to Jokmeam;

13 Ben-Geber — in Ramoth Gilead (the
settlements of Jair son of Manasseh in Gilead were his, as well as
the region of Argob in Bashan and
its sixty large walled cities with
bronze gate bars);

14 Ahinadab son of Iddo — in Mahanaim;

15 Ahimaaz — in Naphtali (he had married Basemath daughter of Solomon);

16 Baana son of Hushai — in Asher and
in Aloth;

17 Jehoshaphat son of Paruah — in Issachar;

18 Shimei son of Ela — in Benjamin;

19 Geber son of Uri — in Gilead (the
country of Sihon king of the Amorites and the country of Og king of
Bashan). He was the only governor
over the district.

Solomon's Daily Provisions

20 The people of Judah and Israel were
as numerous as the sand on the seashore; they ate, they drank and they were
happy. 21 And Solomon ruled over all the
kingdoms from the Euphrates River to
the land of the Philistines, as far as the
border of Egypt. These countries brought
tribute and were Solomon's subjects all
his life.

22 Solomon's daily provisions were thirty cors[a] of the finest flour and sixty cors[b]
of meal, 23 ten head of stall-fed cattle,
twenty of pasture-fed cattle and a hundred sheep and goats, as well as deer,
gazelles, roebucks and choice fowl. 24 For

he ruled over all the kingdoms west of the
Euphrates River, from Tiphsah to Gaza,
and had peace on all sides. 25 During Solomon's lifetime Judah and Israel, from
Dan to Beersheba, lived in safety, everyone under their own vine and under their
own fig tree.

26 Solomon had four[c] thousand stalls
for chariot horses, and twelve thousand
horses.[d]

27 The district governors, each in his
month, supplied provisions for King Solomon and all who came to the king's table.
They saw to it that nothing was lacking.
28 They also brought to the proper place
their quotas of barley and straw for the
chariot horses and the other horses.

Solomon's Wisdom

29 God gave Solomon wisdom and very
great insight, and a breadth of understanding as measureless as the sand on
the seashore. 30 Solomon's wisdom was
greater than the wisdom of all the people
of the East, and greater than all the wisdom of Egypt. 31 He was wiser than anyone else, including Ethan the Ezrahite —
wiser than Heman, Kalkol and Darda, the
sons of Mahol. And his fame spread to
all the surrounding nations. 32 He spoke
three thousand proverbs and his songs
numbered a thousand and five. 33 He
spoke about plant life, from the cedar of
Lebanon to the hyssop that grows out of
walls. He also spoke about animals and
birds, reptiles and fish. 34 From all nations
people came to listen to Solomon's wisdom, sent by all the kings of the world,
who had heard of his wisdom.[e]

Preparations for Building the Temple

5[f] When Hiram king of Tyre heard that
Solomon had been anointed king to
succeed his father David, he sent his envoys to Solomon, because he had always
been on friendly terms with David. 2 Solomon sent back this message to Hiram:

3 "You know that because of the
wars waged against my father David

---

a 22 That is, probably about 5 1/2 tons or about 5 metric tons   b 22 That is, probably about 11 tons or about 10 metric
tons   c 26 Some Septuagint manuscripts (see also 2 Chron. 9:25); Hebrew forty   d 26 Or charioteers   e 34 In
Hebrew texts 4:21-34 is numbered 5:1-14.   f In Hebrew texts 5:1-18 is numbered 5:15-32.

from all sides, he could not build a temple for the Name of the LORD his God until the LORD put his enemies under his feet. ⁴But now the LORD my God has given me rest on every side, and there is no adversary or disaster. ⁵I intend, therefore, to build a temple for the Name of the LORD my God, as the LORD told my father David, when he said, 'Your son whom I will put on the throne in your place will build the temple for my Name.'

⁶"So give orders that cedars of Lebanon be cut for me. My men will work with yours, and I will pay you for your men whatever wages you set. You know that we have no one so skilled in felling timber as the Sidonians."

⁷When Hiram heard Solomon's message, he was greatly pleased and said, "Praise be to the LORD today, for he has given David a wise son to rule over this great nation."

⁸So Hiram sent word to Solomon:

"I have received the message you sent me and will do all you want in providing the cedar and juniper logs. ⁹My men will haul them down from Lebanon to the Mediterranean Sea, and I will float them as rafts by sea to the place you specify. There I will separate them and you can take them away. And you are to grant my wish by providing food for my royal household."

¹⁰In this way Hiram kept Solomon supplied with all the cedar and juniper logs he wanted, ¹¹and Solomon gave Hiram twenty thousand cors[a] of wheat as food for his household, in addition to twenty thousand baths[b,c] of pressed olive oil. Solomon continued to do this for Hiram year after year. ¹²The LORD gave Solomon wisdom, just as he had promised him. There were peaceful relations between

Hiram and Solomon, and the two of them made a treaty.

¹³King Solomon conscripted laborers from all Israel—thirty thousand men. ¹⁴He sent them off to Lebanon in shifts of ten thousand a month, so that they spent one month in Lebanon and two months at home. Adoniram was in charge of the forced labor. ¹⁵Solomon had seventy thousand carriers and eighty thousand stonecutters in the hills, ¹⁶as well as thirty-three hundred[d] foremen who supervised the project and directed the workers. ¹⁷At the king's command they removed from the quarry large blocks of high-grade stone to provide a foundation of dressed stone for the temple. ¹⁸The craftsmen of Solomon and Hiram and workers from Byblos cut and prepared the timber and stone for the building of the temple.

Solomon Builds the Temple

6 In the four hundred and eightieth[e] year after the Israelites came out of Egypt, in the fourth year of Solomon's reign over Israel, in the month of Ziv, the second month, he began to build the temple of the LORD.

²The temple that King Solomon built for the LORD was sixty cubits long, twenty wide and thirty high.[f] ³The portico at the front of the main hall of the temple extended the width of the temple, that is twenty cubits,[g] and projected ten cubits[h] from the front of the temple. ⁴He made narrow windows high up in the temple walls. ⁵Against the walls of the main hall and inner sanctuary he built a structure around the building, in which there were side rooms. ⁶The lowest floor was five cubits[i] wide, the middle floor six cubits[j] and the third floor seven.[k] He made offset ledges around the outside of the temple so that nothing would be inserted into the temple walls.

⁷In building the temple, only blocks

a 11 That is, probably about 3,600 tons or about 3,250 metric tons   b 11 Septuagint (see also 2 Chron. 2:10); Hebrew twenty cors   c 11 That is, about 120,000 gallons or about 440,000 liters   d 16 Hebrew; some Septuagint manuscripts (see also 2 Chron. 2:2,18) thirty-six hundred   e 1 Hebrew; Septuagint four hundred and fortieth   f 2 That is, about 90 feet long, 30 feet wide and 45 feet high or about 27 meters long, 9 meters wide and 14 meters high   g 3 That is, about 30 feet or about 9 meters; also in verses 16 and 20   h 3 That is, about 15 feet or about 4.5 meters; also in verses 23-26   i 6 That is, about 7 1/2 feet or about 2.3 meters; also in verses 10 and 24   j 6 That is, about 9 feet or about 2.7 meters   k 6 That is, about 11 feet or about 3.2 meters

Dear Jordan

Dear Alejandro,

This is a question that many teens and adults ask. I like to look at the example that wise King Solomon gives. He had a friend named Hiram, King of Tyre, who did not worship God. Solomon explained in a message to Hiram that he was building a temple for the Lord and needed materials from Tyre (1 Kings 5:10–11). Hiram was happy to provide what his friend Solomon needed.

These men respected each other even though they didn't worship the same God. Each man dealt honestly with the other. Solomon paid Hiram back with grain and olive oil. The king of Tyre did nothing that would entice or encourage Solomon to disobey his God.

If you have friends who are not Christians, it's okay as long as they're not tempting you to sin (see 1 Corinthians 5:9–11). And who knows, maybe they will see you've made some changes and you can share with them about Jesus. Each friendship is unique. You'll have to decide if each friendship is built on mutual respect like that of these two kings. If it is, it's probably a keeper.

Jordan

dressed at the quarry were used, and no hammer, chisel or any other iron tool was heard at the temple site while it was being built.

[8] The entrance to the lowest[a] floor was on the south side of the temple; a stairway led up to the middle level and from there to the third. [9] So he built the temple and completed it, roofing it with beams and cedar planks. [10] And he built the side rooms all along the temple. The height of each was five cubits, and they were attached to the temple by beams of cedar.

[11] The word of the LORD came to Solomon: [12] "As for this temple you are building, if you follow my decrees, observe my laws and keep all my commands and obey them, I will fulfill through you the promise I gave to David your father. [13] And I will live among the Israelites and will not abandon my people Israel."

[14] So Solomon built the temple and completed it. [15] He lined its interior walls with cedar boards, paneling them from the floor of the temple to the ceiling, and covered the floor of the temple with planks of juniper. [16] He partitioned off twenty cubits at the rear of the temple with cedar boards from floor to ceiling to form within the temple an inner sanctuary, the Most Holy Place. [17] The main hall in front of this room was forty cubits[b] long. [18] The inside of the temple was cedar, carved with gourds and open flowers. Everything was cedar; no stone was to be seen.

[19] He prepared the inner sanctuary within the temple to set the ark of the covenant of the LORD there. [20] The inner sanctuary was twenty cubits long, twenty wide and twenty high. He overlaid the inside with pure gold, and he also overlaid the altar of cedar. [21] Solomon covered the inside of the temple with pure gold, and he extended gold chains across the front of the inner sanctuary, which was overlaid with gold. [22] So he overlaid the whole interior with gold. He also overlaid with gold the altar that belonged to the inner sanctuary.

[23] For the inner sanctuary he made a pair of cherubim out of olive wood, each ten cubits high. [24] One wing of the first cherub was five cubits long, and the other wing five cubits—ten cubits from wing tip to wing tip. [25] The second cherub also measured ten cubits, for the two cherubim were identical in size and shape. [26] The height of each cherub was ten cubits. [27] He placed the cherubim inside the innermost room of the temple, with their wings spread out. The wing of one cherub touched one wall, while the wing of the other touched the other wall, and their wings touched each other in the middle of the room. [28] He overlaid the cherubim with gold.

[29] On the walls all around the temple, in both the inner and outer rooms, he carved cherubim, palm trees and open flowers. [30] He also covered the floors of both the inner and outer rooms of the temple with gold.

[31] For the entrance to the inner sanctuary he made doors out of olive wood that were one fifth of the width of the sanctuary. [32] And on the two olive-wood doors he carved cherubim, palm trees and open flowers, and overlaid the cherubim and palm trees with hammered gold. [33] In the

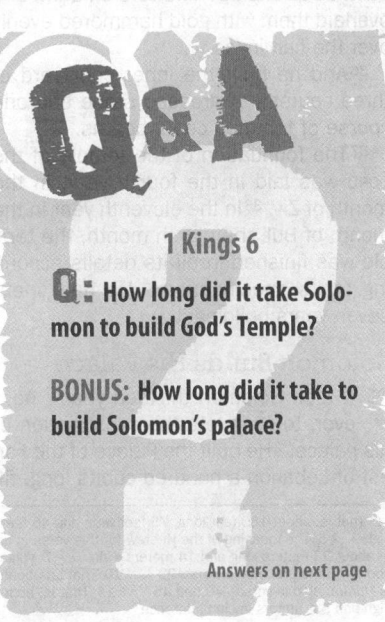

1 Kings 6

Q: How long did it take Solomon to build God's Temple?

BONUS: How long did it take to build Solomon's palace?

Answers on next page

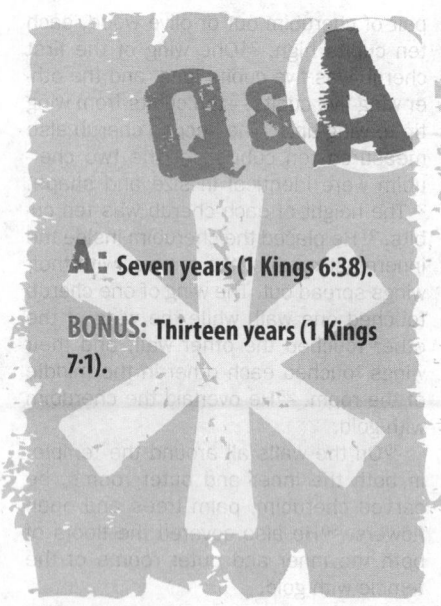

same way, for the entrance to the main hall he made doorframes out of olive wood that were one fourth of the width of the hall. ³⁴He also made two doors out of juniper wood, each having two leaves that turned in sockets. ³⁵He carved cherubim, palm trees and open flowers on them and overlaid them with gold hammered evenly over the carvings.

³⁶And he built the inner courtyard of three courses of dressed stone and one course of trimmed cedar beams.

³⁷The foundation of the temple of the Lord was laid in the fourth year, in the month of Ziv. ³⁸In the eleventh year in the month of Bul, the eighth month, the temple was finished in all its details according to its specifications. He had spent seven years building it.

Solomon Builds His Palace

7 It took Solomon thirteen years, however, to complete the construction of his palace. ²He built the Palace of the Forest of Lebanon a hundred cubits long, fif-ty wide and thirty high,[a] with four rows of cedar columns supporting trimmed cedar beams. ³It was roofed with cedar above the beams that rested on the columns—forty-five beams, fifteen to a row. ⁴Its windows were placed high in sets of three, facing each other. ⁵All the doorways had rectangular frames; they were in the front part in sets of three, facing each other.[b]

⁶He made a colonnade fifty cubits long and thirty wide.[c] In front of it was a portico, and in front of that were pillars and an overhanging roof.

⁷He built the throne hall, the Hall of Justice, where he was to judge, and he covered it with cedar from floor to ceiling.[d] ⁸And the palace in which he was to live, set farther back, was similar in design. Solomon also made a palace like this hall for Pharaoh's daughter, whom he had married.

⁹All these structures, from the outside to the great courtyard and from foundation to eaves, were made of blocks of high-grade stone cut to size and smoothed on their inner and outer faces. ¹⁰The foundations were laid with large stones of good quality, some measuring ten cubits[e] and some eight.[f] ¹¹Above were high-grade stones, cut to size, and cedar beams. ¹²The great courtyard was surrounded by a wall of three courses of dressed stone and one course of trimmed cedar beams, as was the inner courtyard of the temple of the Lord with its portico.

The Temple's Furnishings

¹³King Solomon sent to Tyre and brought Huram,[g] ¹⁴whose mother was a widow from the tribe of Naphtali and whose father was from Tyre and a skilled craftsman in bronze. Huram was filled with wisdom, with understanding and with knowledge to do all kinds of bronze work. He came to King Solomon and did all the work assigned to him.

¹⁵He cast two bronze pillars, each eighteen cubits high and twelve cubits in circumference.[h] ¹⁶He also made two capi-

ᵃ 2 That is, about 150 feet long, 75 feet wide and 45 feet high or about 45 meters long, 23 meters wide and 14 meters high   ᵇ 5 The meaning of the Hebrew for this verse is uncertain.   ᶜ 6 That is, about 75 feet long and 45 feet wide or about 23 meters long and 14 meters wide   ᵈ 7 Vulgate and Syriac; Hebrew *floor*   ᵉ 10 That is, about 15 feet or about 4.5 meters; also in verse 23   ᶠ 10 That is, about 12 feet or about 3.6 meters   ᵍ 13 Hebrew *Hiram*, a variant of *Huram*; also in verses 40 and 45   ʰ 15 That is, about 27 feet high and 18 feet in circumference or about 8.1 meters high and 5.4 meters in circumference

tals of cast bronze to set on the tops of the pillars; each capital was five cubits[a] high. [17]A network of interwoven chains adorned the capitals on top of the pillars, seven for each capital. [18]He made pomegranates in two rows[b] encircling each network to decorate the capitals on top of the pillars.[c] He did the same for each capital. [19]The capitals on top of the pillars in the portico were in the shape of lilies, four cubits[d] high. [20]On the capitals of both pillars, above the bowl-shaped part next to the network, were the two hundred pomegranates in rows all around. [21]He erected the pillars at the portico of the temple. The pillar to the south he named Jakin[e] and the one to the north Boaz.[f] [22]The capitals on top were in the shape of lilies. And so the work on the pillars was completed.

[23]He made the Sea of cast metal, circular in shape, measuring ten cubits from rim to rim and five cubits high. It took a line of thirty cubits[g] to measure around it. [24]Below the rim, gourds encircled it—ten to a cubit. The gourds were cast in two rows in one piece with the Sea.

[25]The Sea stood on twelve bulls, three facing north, three facing west, three facing south and three facing east. The Sea rested on top of them, and their hindquarters were toward the center. [26]It was a handbreadth[h] in thickness, and its rim was like the rim of a cup, like a lily blossom. It held two thousand baths.[i]

[27]He also made ten movable stands of bronze; each was four cubits long, four wide and three high.[j] [28]This is how the stands were made: They had side panels attached to uprights. [29]On the panels between the uprights were lions, bulls and cherubim—and on the uprights as well. Above and below the lions and bulls were wreaths of hammered work. [30]Each stand had four bronze wheels with bronze axles, and each had a basin resting on

four supports, cast with wreaths on each side. [31]On the inside of the stand there was an opening that had a circular frame one cubit[k] deep. This opening was round, and with its basework it measured a cubit and a half.[l] Around its opening there was engraving. The panels of the stands were square, not round. [32]The four wheels were under the panels, and the axles of the wheels were attached to the stand. The diameter of each wheel was a cubit and a half. [33]The wheels were made like chariot wheels; the axles, rims, spokes and hubs were all of cast metal.

[34]Each stand had four handles, one on each corner, projecting from the stand. [35]At the top of the stand there was a circular band half a cubit[m] deep. The supports and panels were attached to the top of the stand. [36]He engraved cherubim, lions and palm trees on the surfaces of the supports and on the panels, in every available space, with wreaths all around. [37]This is the way he made the ten stands. They were all cast in the same molds and were identical in size and shape.

[38]He then made ten bronze basins, each holding forty baths[n] and measuring four cubits across, one basin to go on each of the ten stands. [39]He placed five of the stands on the south side of the temple and five on the north. He placed the Sea on the south side, at the southeast corner of the temple. [40]He also made the pots[o] and shovels and sprinkling bowls.

So Huram finished all the work he had undertaken for King Solomon in the temple of the LORD:

[41]the two pillars;
the two bowl-shaped capitals on top of the pillars;
the two sets of network decorating the two bowl-shaped capitals on top of the pillars;

---

[a] 16 That is, about 7 1/2 feet or about 2.3 meters; also in verse 23   [b] 18 Two Hebrew manuscripts and Septuagint; most Hebrew manuscripts *made the pillars, and there were two rows*   [c] 18 Many Hebrew manuscripts and Syriac; most Hebrew manuscripts *pomegranates*   [d] 19 That is, about 6 feet or about 1.8 meters; also in verse 38   [e] 21 *Jakin* probably means *he establishes*.   [f] 21 *Boaz* probably means *in him is strength*.   [g] 23 That is, about 45 feet or about 14 meters   [h] 26 That is, about 3 inches or about 7.5 centimeters   [i] 26 That is, about 12,000 gallons or about 44,000 liters; the Septuagint does not have this sentence.   [j] 27 That is, about 6 feet long and wide and about 4 1/2 feet high or about 1.8 meters long and wide and 1.4 meters high   [k] 31 That is, about 18 inches or about 45 centimeters   [l] 31 That is, about 2 1/4 feet or about 68 centimeters; also in verse 32   [m] 35 That is, about 9 inches or about 23 centimeters   [n] 38 That is, about 240 gallons or about 880 liters   [o] 40 Many Hebrew manuscripts, Septuagint, Syriac and Vulgate (see also verse 45 and 2 Chron. 4:11); many other Hebrew manuscripts *basins*

⁴²the four hundred pomegranates for the two sets of network (two rows of pomegranates for each network decorating the bowl-shaped capitals on top of the pillars);
⁴³the ten stands with their ten basins;
⁴⁴the Sea and the twelve bulls under it;
⁴⁵the pots, shovels and sprinkling bowls.

All these objects that Huram made for King Solomon for the temple of the LORD were of burnished bronze. ⁴⁶The king had them cast in clay molds in the plain of the Jordan between Sukkoth and Zarethan. ⁴⁷Solomon left all these things unweighed, because there were so many; the weight of the bronze was not determined.

⁴⁸Solomon also made all the furnishings that were in the LORD's temple:

the golden altar;
the golden table on which was the bread of the Presence;
⁴⁹the lampstands of pure gold (five on the right and five on the left, in front of the inner sanctuary);
the gold floral work and lamps and tongs;
⁵⁰the pure gold basins, wick trimmers, sprinkling bowls, dishes and censers;
and the gold sockets for the doors of the innermost room, the Most Holy Place, and also for the doors of the main hall of the temple.

⁵¹When all the work King Solomon had done for the temple of the LORD was finished, he brought in the things his father David had dedicated—the silver and gold and the furnishings—and he placed them in the treasuries of the LORD's temple.

The Ark Brought to the Temple

8 Then King Solomon summoned into his presence at Jerusalem the elders of Israel, all the heads of the tribes and the chiefs of the Israelite families, to bring up the ark of the LORD's covenant from Zion, the City of David. ²All the Israelites came together to King Solomon at the time of the festival in the month of Ethanim, the seventh month.

³When all the elders of Israel had arrived, the priests took up the ark, ⁴and they brought up the ark of the LORD and the tent of meeting and all the sacred furnishings in it. The priests and Levites carried them up, ⁵and King Solomon and the entire assembly of Israel that had gathered about him were before the ark, sacrificing so many sheep and cattle that they could not be recorded or counted.

⁶The priests then brought the ark of the LORD's covenant to its place in the inner sanctuary of the temple, the Most Holy Place, and put it beneath the wings of the cherubim. ⁷The cherubim spread their wings over the place of the ark and overshadowed the ark and its carrying poles. ⁸These poles were so long that their ends could be seen from the Holy Place in front of the inner sanctuary, but not from outside the Holy Place; and they are still there today. ⁹There was nothing in the ark except the two stone tablets that Moses had placed in it at Horeb, where the LORD made a covenant with the Israelites after they came out of Egypt.

¹⁰When the priests withdrew from the Holy Place, the cloud filled the temple of the LORD. ¹¹And the priests could not perform their service because of the cloud, for the glory of the LORD filled his temple.

¹²Then Solomon said, "The LORD has said that he would dwell in a dark cloud; ¹³I have indeed built a magnificent temple for you, a place for you to dwell forever."

¹⁴While the whole assembly of Israel was standing there, the king turned around and blessed them. ¹⁵Then he said:

"Praise be to the LORD, the God of Israel, who with his own hand has fulfilled what he promised with his own mouth to my father David. For he said, ¹⁶'Since the day I brought my people Israel out of Egypt, I have not chosen a city in any tribe of Israel to have a temple built so that my Name might be there, but I have chosen David to rule my people Israel.'

17 "My father David had it in his heart to build a temple for the Name of the Lord, the God of Israel. 18 But the Lord said to my father David, 'You did well to have it in your heart to build a temple for my Name. 19 Nevertheless, you are not the one to build the temple, but your son, your own flesh and blood—he is the one who will build the temple for my Name.'

20 "The Lord has kept the promise he made: I have succeeded David my father and now I sit on the throne of Israel, just as the Lord promised, and I have built the temple for the Name of the Lord, the God of Israel. 21 I have provided a place there for the ark, in which is the covenant of the Lord that he made with our ancestors when he brought them out of Egypt."

Solomon's Prayer of Dedication

22 Then Solomon stood before the altar of the Lord in front of the whole assembly of Israel, spread out his hands toward heaven 23 and said:

"Lord, the God of Israel, there is no God like you in heaven above or on earth below—you who keep your covenant of love with your servants who continue wholeheartedly in your way. 24 You have kept your promise to your servant David my father; with your mouth you have promised and with your hand you have fulfilled it—as it is today. 25 "Now Lord, the God of Israel, keep for your servant David my father the promises you made to him when you said, 'You shall never fail to have a successor to sit before me on the throne of Israel, if only your descendants are careful in all they do to walk before me faithfully as you have done.' 26 And now, God of Israel, let your word that you promised your servant David my father come true.

27 "But will God really dwell on earth? The heavens, even the highest heaven, cannot contain you. How much less this temple I have built! 28 Yet give attention to your servant's prayer and his plea for mercy, Lord my God. Hear the cry and the prayer that your servant is praying in your presence this day. 29 May your eyes be open toward this temple night and day, this place of which you said, 'My Name shall be there,' so that you will hear the prayer your servant prays toward this place. 30 Hear the supplication of your servant and of your people Israel when they pray toward this place. Hear from heaven, your dwelling place, and when you hear, forgive.

31 "When anyone wrongs their neighbor and is required to take an oath and they come and swear the oath before your altar in this temple, 32 then hear from heaven and act. Judge between your servants, condemning the guilty by bringing down on their heads what they have done, and vindicating the innocent by treating them in accordance with their innocence.

33 "When your people Israel have been defeated by an enemy because they have sinned against you, and when they turn back to you and give praise to your name, praying and making supplication to you in this temple, 34 then hear from heaven and forgive the sin of your people Israel and bring them back to the land you gave to their ancestors.

35 "When the heavens are shut up and there is no rain because your people have sinned against you, and when they pray toward this place and give praise to your name and turn from their sin because you have afflicted them, 36 then hear from heaven and forgive the sin of your servants, your people Israel. Teach them the right way to live, and send rain on the land you gave your people for an inheritance.

37 "When famine or plague comes to the land, or blight or mildew, locusts or grasshoppers, or when an

enemy besieges them in any of their cities, whatever disaster or disease may come, ³⁸and when a prayer or plea is made by anyone among your people Israel—being aware of the afflictions of their own hearts, and spreading out their hands toward this temple— ³⁹then hear from heaven, your dwelling place. Forgive and act; deal with everyone according to all they do, since you know their hearts (for you alone know every human heart), ⁴⁰so that they will fear you all the time they live in the land you gave our ancestors.

⁴¹"As for the foreigner who does not belong to your people Israel but has come from a distant land because of your name— ⁴²for they will hear of your great name and your mighty hand and your outstretched arm—when they come and pray toward this temple, ⁴³then hear from heaven, your dwelling place. Do whatever the foreigner asks of you, so that all the peoples of the earth may know your name and fear you, as do your own people Israel, and may know that this house I have built bears your Name.

⁴⁴"When your people go to war against their enemies, wherever you send them, and when they pray to the LORD toward the city you have chosen and the temple I have built for your Name, ⁴⁵then hear from heaven their prayer and their plea, and uphold their cause.

⁴⁶"When they sin against you—for there is no one who does not sin— and you become angry with them and give them over to their enemies, who take them captive to their own lands, far away or near; ⁴⁷and if they have a change of heart in the land where they are held captive, and repent and plead with you in the land of their captors and say, 'We have sinned, we have done wrong, we have acted wickedly'; ⁴⁸and if they turn back to you with all their heart and soul in the land of their enemies who took them captive, and pray to you toward the land you gave their ancestors, toward the city you have chosen and the temple I have built for your Name; ⁴⁹then from heaven, your dwelling place, hear their prayer and their plea, and uphold their cause. ⁵⁰And forgive your people, who have sinned against you; forgive all the offenses they have committed against you, and cause their captors to show them mercy; ⁵¹for they are your people and your inheritance, whom you brought out of Egypt, out of that iron-smelting furnace.

⁵²"May your eyes be open to your servant's plea and to the plea of your people Israel, and may you listen to them whenever they cry out to you. ⁵³For you singled them out from all the nations of the world to be your own inheritance, just as you declared through your servant Moses when you, Sovereign LORD, brought our ancestors out of Egypt."

⁵⁴When Solomon had finished all these prayers and supplications to the LORD, he rose from before the altar of the LORD, where he had been kneeling with his hands spread out toward heaven. ⁵⁵He stood and blessed the whole assembly of Israel in a loud voice, saying:

⁵⁶"Praise be to the LORD, who has given rest to his people Israel just as he promised. Not one word has failed of all the good promises he gave through his servant Moses. ⁵⁷May the LORD our God be with us as he was with our ancestors; may he never leave us nor forsake us. ⁵⁸May he turn our hearts to him, to walk in obedience to him and keep the commands, decrees and laws he gave our ancestors. ⁵⁹And may these words of mine, which I have prayed before the LORD, be near to the LORD our God day and night, that he may uphold the cause of his servant and the cause of his people Israel according to each day's need, ⁶⁰so that all the peoples of the earth may know that the LORD is God and that there is no other. ⁶¹And may

your hearts be fully committed to the LORD our God, to live by his decrees and obey his commands, as at this time."

The Dedication of the Temple

62 Then the king and all Israel with him offered sacrifices before the LORD. 63 Solomon offered a sacrifice of fellowship offerings to the LORD: twenty-two thousand cattle and a hundred and twenty thousand sheep and goats. So the king and all the Israelites dedicated the temple of the LORD.

64 On that same day the king consecrated the middle part of the courtyard in front of the temple of the LORD, and there he offered burnt offerings, grain offerings and the fat of the fellowship offerings, because the bronze altar that stood before the LORD was too small to hold the burnt offerings, the grain offerings and the fat of the fellowship offerings.

65 So Solomon observed the festival at that time, and all Israel with him—a vast assembly, people from Lebo Hamath to the Wadi of Egypt. They celebrated it before the LORD our God for seven days and seven days more, fourteen days in all. 66 On the following day he sent the people away. They blessed the king and then went home, joyful and glad in heart for all the good things the LORD had done for his servant David and his people Israel.

The LORD Appears to Solomon

9 When Solomon had finished building the temple of the LORD and the royal palace, and had achieved all he had desired to do, 2 the LORD appeared to him a second time, as he had appeared to him at Gibeon. 3 The LORD said to him:

"I have heard the prayer and plea you have made before me; I have consecrated this temple, which you have built, by putting my Name there forever. My eyes and my heart will always be there.

4 "As for you, if you walk before me faithfully with integrity of heart and uprightness, as David your father did, and do all I command and observe my decrees and laws, 5 I will establish your royal throne over Israel forever, as I promised David your father when I said, 'You shall never fail to have a successor on the throne of Israel.'

6 "But if you[a] or your descendants turn away from me and do not observe the commands and decrees I have given you[a] and go off to serve other gods and worship them, 7 then I will cut off Israel from the land I have given them and will reject this temple I have consecrated for my Name. Israel will then become a byword and an object of ridicule among all peoples. 8 This temple will become a heap of rubble. All[b] who pass by will be appalled and will scoff and say, 'Why has the LORD done such a thing to this land and to this temple?' 9 People will answer, 'Because they have forsaken the LORD their God, who brought their ancestors out of Egypt, and have embraced other gods, worshiping and serving them—that is why the LORD brought all this disaster on them.'"

Solomon's Other Activities

10 At the end of twenty years, during which Solomon built these two buildings—the temple of the LORD and the royal palace— 11 King Solomon gave twenty towns in Galilee to Hiram king of Tyre, because Hiram had supplied him with all the cedar and juniper and gold he wanted. 12 But when Hiram went from

> *May the LORD our God ... never leave us nor forsake us.*
> 1 Kings 8:57

---

a 6 The Hebrew is plural.   b 8 See some Septuagint manuscripts, Old Latin, Syriac, Arabic and Targum; Hebrew *And though this temple is now imposing, all*

Tyre to see the towns that Solomon had given him, he was not pleased with them. [13] "What kind of towns are these you have given me, my brother?" he asked. And he called them the Land of Kabul,[a] a name they have to this day. [14] Now Hiram had sent to the king 120 talents[b] of gold.

[15] Here is the account of the forced labor King Solomon conscripted to build the LORD's temple, his own palace, the terraces,[c] the wall of Jerusalem, and Hazor, Megiddo and Gezer. [16] (Pharaoh king of Egypt had attacked and captured Gezer. He had set it on fire. He killed its Canaanite inhabitants and then gave it as a wedding gift to his daughter, Solomon's wife. [17] And Solomon rebuilt Gezer.) He built up Lower Beth Horon, [18] Baalath, and Tadmor[d] in the desert, within his land, [19] as well as all his store cities and the towns for his chariots and for his horses[e] — whatever he desired to build in Jerusalem, in Lebanon and throughout all the territory he ruled.

[20] There were still people left from the Amorites, Hittites, Perizzites, Hivites and Jebusites (these peoples were not Israelites). [21] Solomon conscripted the descendants of all these peoples remaining in the land — whom the Israelites could not exterminate[f] — to serve as slave labor, as it is to this day. [22] But Solomon did not make slaves of any of the Israelites; they were his fighting men, his government officials, his officers, his captains, and the commanders of his chariots and charioteers. [23] They were also the chief officials in charge of Solomon's projects — 550 officials supervising those who did the work.

[24] After Pharaoh's daughter had come up from the City of David to the palace Solomon had built for her, he constructed the terraces.

[25] Three times a year Solomon sacrificed burnt offerings and fellowship offerings on the altar he had built for the LORD, burning incense before the LORD along with them, and so fulfilled the temple obligations.

[26] King Solomon also built ships at Ezion Geber, which is near Elath in Edom, on the shore of the Red Sea.[g] [27] And Hiram sent his men — sailors who knew the sea — to serve in the fleet with Solomon's men. [28] They sailed to Ophir and brought back 420 talents[h] of gold, which they delivered to King Solomon.

The Queen of Sheba Visits Solomon

10 When the queen of Sheba heard about the fame of Solomon and his relationship to the LORD, she came to test Solomon with hard questions. [2] Arriving at Jerusalem with a very great caravan — with camels carrying spices, large quantities of gold, and precious stones — she came to Solomon and talked with him about all that she had on her mind. [3] Solomon answered all her questions; nothing was too hard for the king to explain to her. [4] When the queen of Sheba saw all the wisdom of Solomon and the palace he had built, [5] the food on his table, the seating of his officials, the attending servants in their robes, his cupbearers, and the burnt offerings he made at[i] the temple of the LORD, she was overwhelmed.

[6] She said to the king, "The report I heard in my own country about your achievements and your wisdom is true. [7] But I did not believe these things until I came and saw with my own eyes. Indeed, not even half was told me; in wisdom and wealth you have far exceeded the report I heard. [8] How happy your people must be! How happy your officials, who continually stand before you and hear your wisdom! [9] Praise be to the LORD your God, who has delighted in you and placed you on the throne of Israel. Because of the LORD's eternal love for Israel, he has made you king to maintain justice and righteousness."

[10] And she gave the king 120 talents[b] of gold, large quantities of spices, and precious stones. Never again were so

---

[a] *13 Kabul sounds like the Hebrew for good-for-nothing.*   [b] *14,10 That is, about 4 1/2 tons or about 4 metric tons*   [c] *15 Or the Millo; also in verse 24*   [d] *18 The Hebrew may also be read Tamar.*   [e] *19 Or charioteers*   [f] *21 The Hebrew term refers to the irrevocable giving over of things or persons to the LORD, often by totally destroying them.*   [g] *26 Or the Sea of Reeds*   [h] *28 That is, about 16 tons or about 14 metric tons*   [i] *5 Or the ascent by which he went up to*

So you hear one science teacher is really tough. Do you make sure you avoid her? Sometimes it pays to check things out for yourself. If you talk to some students who had her class, you might hear things like "Yeah, she's hard. But I learned more in her class than in all my other science classes put together." And, "She made things interesting." Sometimes it's a good thing to be a bit like the Queen of Sheba. She had heard reports about Solomon and his wisdom and riches, but she came to check him out herself. Her motto was a pretty good one to follow: "I came and saw with my own eyes" (1 Kings 10:7).

{1 Kings 10:1–7}

INSTANT ACCESS

ba all she desired and asked for, besides what he had given her out of his royal bounty. Then she left and returned with her retinue to her own country.

Solomon's Splendor

14 The weight of the gold that Solomon received yearly was 666 talents,[c] 15 not including the revenues from merchants and traders and from all the Arabian kings and the governors of the territories.

16 King Solomon made two hundred large shields of hammered gold; six hundred shekels[d] of gold went into each shield. 17 He also made three hundred small shields of hammered gold, with three minas[e] of gold in each shield. The king put them in the Palace of the Forest of Lebanon.

18 Then the king made a great throne covered with ivory and overlaid with fine gold. 19 The throne had six steps, and its back had a rounded top. On both sides of the seat were armrests, with a lion standing beside each of them. 20 Twelve lions stood on the six steps, one at either end of each step. Nothing like it had ever been made for any other kingdom. 21 All King Solomon's goblets were gold, and all the household articles in the Palace of the Forest of Lebanon were pure gold. Nothing was made of silver, because silver was considered of little value in Solomon's days. 22 The king had a fleet of trading ships[f] at sea along with the ships of Hiram. Once every three years it returned, carrying gold, silver and ivory, and apes and baboons.

23 King Solomon was greater in riches and wisdom than all the other kings of the earth. 24 The whole world sought audience with Solomon to hear the wisdom God had put in his heart. 25 Year after year, everyone who came brought a gift—articles of silver and gold, robes, weapons and spices, and horses and mules.

26 Solomon accumulated chariots and horses; he had fourteen hundred chariots and twelve thousand horses,[g] which

many spices brought in as those the queen of Sheba gave to King Solomon.

11 (Hiram's ships brought gold from Ophir; and from there they brought great cargoes of almugwood[a] and precious stones. 12 The king used the almugwood to make supports[b] for the temple of the LORD and for the royal palace, and to make harps and lyres for the musicians. So much almugwood has never been imported or seen since that day.)

13 King Solomon gave the queen of She-

---

a 11 Probably a variant of algumwood; also in verse 12   b 12 The meaning of the Hebrew for this word is uncertain.
c 14 That is, about 25 tons or about 23 metric tons   d 16 That is, about 15 pounds or about 6.9 kilograms; also in verse 29   e 17 That is, about 3 3/4 pounds or about 1.7 kilograms; or perhaps reference is to double minas, that is, about 7 1/2 pounds or about 3.5 kilograms.   f 22 Hebrew of ships of Tarshish   g 26 Or charioteers

he kept in the chariot cities and also with him in Jerusalem. ²⁷ The king made silver as common in Jerusalem as stones, and cedar as plentiful as sycamore-fig trees in the foothills. ²⁸ Solomon's horses were imported from Egypt and from Kue[a] — the royal merchants purchased them from Kue at the current price. ²⁹ They imported a chariot from Egypt for six hundred shekels of silver, and a horse for a hundred and fifty.[b] They also exported them to all the kings of the Hittites and of the Arameans.

Solomon's Wives

11 King Solomon, however, loved many foreign women besides Pharaoh's daughter — Moabites, Ammonites, Edomites, Sidonians and Hittites. ² They were from nations about which the LORD had told the Israelites, "You must not intermarry with them, because they will surely turn your hearts after their gods." Nevertheless, Solomon held fast to them in love. ³ He had seven hundred wives of royal birth and three hundred concubines, and his wives led him astray. ⁴ As Solomon grew old, his wives turned his heart after other gods, and his heart was not fully devoted to the LORD his God, as the heart of David his father had been. ⁵ He followed Ashtoreth the goddess of the Sidonians, and Molek the detestable god of the Ammonites. ⁶ So Solomon did evil in the eyes of the LORD; he did not follow the LORD completely, as David his father had done.

⁷ On a hill east of Jerusalem, Solomon built a high place for Chemosh the detestable god of Moab, and for Molek the detestable god of the Ammonites. ⁸ He did the same for all his foreign wives, who burned incense and offered sacrifices to their gods.

⁹ The LORD became angry with Solomon because his heart had turned away from the LORD, the God of Israel, who had appeared to him twice. ¹⁰ Although he had forbidden Solomon to follow other gods, Solomon did not keep the LORD's command. ¹¹ So the LORD said to Solomon,

---

Holding hands. Kissing. A hug or kiss is exciting, even if you don't really like the guy or girl that much. Your hormones are pumping. Add the stimulation from TV, music and movies, and it's no surprise they work overtime. Solomon's hormones pumped too, and he didn't control them. The king may have been wise, but he sure wasn't smart when it came to women. "His wives turned his heart after other gods" (1 Kings 11:4). You don't need to be ashamed of your hormones. It was God who designed you this way. But you do need to be careful that hormones don't turn your heart away from obedience to the Lord.

{1 Kings 11:1–10}

"Since this is your attitude and you have not kept my covenant and my decrees, which I commanded you, I will most certainly tear the kingdom away from you and give it to one of your subordinates. ¹² Nevertheless, for the sake of David your father, I will not do it during your lifetime. I will tear it out of the hand of your son. ¹³ Yet I will not tear the whole kingdom from him, but will give him one tribe for the sake of David my servant

---

[a] 28 Probably *Cilicia*   [b] 29 That is, about 3 3/4 pounds or about 1.7 kilograms

and for the sake of Jerusalem, which I have chosen."

Solomon's Adversaries

14 Then the LORD raised up against Solomon an adversary, Hadad the Edomite, from the royal line of Edom. 15 Earlier when David was fighting with Edom, Joab the commander of the army, who had gone up to bury the dead, had struck down all the men in Edom. 16 Joab and all the Israelites stayed there for six months, until they had destroyed all the men in Edom. 17 But Hadad, still only a boy, fled to Egypt with some Edomite officials who had served his father. 18 They set out from Midian and went to Paran. Then taking people from Paran with them, they went to Egypt, to Pharaoh king of Egypt, who gave Hadad a house and land and provided him with food.

19 Pharaoh was so pleased with Hadad that he gave him a sister of his own wife, Queen Tahpenes, in marriage. 20 The sister of Tahpenes bore him a son named Genubath, whom Tahpenes brought up in the royal palace. There Genubath lived with Pharaoh's own children.

21 While he was in Egypt, Hadad heard that David rested with his ancestors and that Joab the commander of the army was also dead. Then Hadad said to Pharaoh, "Let me go, that I may return to my own country."

22 "What have you lacked here that you want to go back to your own country?" Pharaoh asked.

"Nothing," Hadad replied, "but do let me go!"

23 And God raised up against Solomon another adversary, Rezon son of Eliada, who had fled from his master, Hadadezer king of Zobah. 24 When David destroyed Zobah's army, Rezon gathered a band of men around him and became their leader; they went to Damascus, where they settled and took control. 25 Rezon was Israel's adversary as long as Solomon lived, adding to the trouble caused by Hadad. So Rezon ruled in Aram and was hostile toward Israel.

Jeroboam Rebels Against Solomon

26 Also, Jeroboam son of Nebat rebelled against the king. He was one of Solomon's officials, an Ephraimite from Zeredah, and his mother was a widow named Zeruah.

27 Here is the account of how he rebelled against the king: Solomon had built the terraces[a] and had filled in the gap in the wall of the city of David his father. 28 Now Jeroboam was a man of standing, and when Solomon saw how well the young man did his work, he put him in charge of the whole labor force of the tribes of Joseph.

29 About that time Jeroboam was going out of Jerusalem, and Ahijah the prophet of Shiloh met him on the way, wearing a new cloak. The two of them were alone out in the country, 30 and Ahijah took hold of the new cloak he was wearing and tore it into twelve pieces. 31 Then he said to Jeroboam, "Take ten pieces for yourself, for this is what the LORD, the God of Israel, says: 'See, I am going to tear the kingdom out of Solomon's hand and give you ten tribes. 32 But for the sake of my servant David and the city of Jerusalem, which I have chosen out of all the tribes of Israel, he will have one tribe. 33 I will do this because they have[b] forsaken me and worshiped Ashtoreth the goddess of the Sidonians, Chemosh the god of the Moabites, and Molek the god of the Ammonites, and have not walked in obedience to me, nor done what is right in my eyes, nor kept my decrees and laws as David, Solomon's father, did.

34 " 'But I will not take the whole kingdom out of Solomon's hand; I have made him ruler all the days of his life for the sake of David my servant, whom I chose and who obeyed my commands and decrees. 35 I will take the kingdom from his son's hands and give you ten tribes. 36 I will give one tribe to his son so that David my servant may always have a lamp before me in Jerusalem, the city where I chose to put my Name. 37 However, as for you, I will take you, and you will rule

a 27 Or the Millo   b 33 Hebrew; Septuagint, Vulgate and Syriac because he has over all that your heart desires; you will be king over Israel. ³⁸If you do whatever I command you and walk in obedience to me and do what is right in my eyes by obeying my decrees and commands, as David my servant did, I will be with you. I will build you a dynasty as enduring as the one I built for David and will give Israel to you. ³⁹I will humble David's descendants because of this, but not forever.' "

⁴⁰Solomon tried to kill Jeroboam, but Jeroboam fled to Egypt, to Shishak the king, and stayed there until Solomon's death.

Solomon's Death

⁴¹As for the other events of Solomon's reign—all he did and the wisdom he displayed—are they not written in the book of the annals of Solomon? ⁴²Solomon reigned in Jerusalem over all Israel forty years. ⁴³Then he rested with his ancestors and was buried in the city of David his father. And Rehoboam his son succeeded him as king.

Israel Rebels Against Rehoboam

12 Rehoboam went to Shechem, for all Israel had gone there to make him king. ²When Jeroboam son of Nebat heard this (he was still in Egypt, where he had fled from King Solomon), he returned from*a* Egypt. ³So they sent for Jeroboam, and he and the whole assembly of Israel went to Rehoboam and said to him: ⁴"Your father put a heavy yoke on us, but now lighten the harsh labor and the heavy yoke he put on us, and we will serve you."

⁵Rehoboam answered, "Go away for three days and then come back to me." So the people went away.

⁶Then King Rehoboam consulted the elders who had served his father Solomon during his lifetime. "How would you advise me to answer these people?" he asked.

⁷They replied, "If today you will be a servant to these people and serve them and give them a favorable answer, they will always be your servants."

INSTANT ACCESS

Have you ever noticed how some of your friends look like their parents? Or have their mannerisms? Like Melissa, who has her mom's way of sputtering when she's upset. If you were to make a list of ways you want to be like your dad or your mom, what would the top three traits be? How might you go about developing those traits? Solomon's problems can be traced to the fact that he failed to imitate his father David in one thing. David was faithful to God all his life and walked in obedience to God (1 Kings 11:33). David wasn't perfect. But he honestly tried to put God first. That's a family tradition you'll want to follow. Or begin!

{1 Kings 11:29–33}

---

⁸But Rehoboam rejected the advice the elders gave him and consulted the young men who had grown up with him and were serving him. ⁹He asked them, "What is your advice? How should we answer these people who say to me, 'Lighten the yoke your father put on us'?"

¹⁰The young men who had grown up with him replied, "These people have said to you, 'Your father put a heavy yoke on us, but make our yoke lighter.' Now tell them, 'My little finger is thicker than my

---

a 2 Or he remained in

father's waist. ¹¹My father laid on you a heavy yoke; I will make it even heavier. My father scourged you with whips; I will scourge you with scorpions.'"

¹²Three days later Jeroboam and all the people returned to Rehoboam, as the king had said, "Come back to me in three days." ¹³The king answered the people harshly. Rejecting the advice given him by the elders, ¹⁴he followed the advice of the young men and said, "My father made your yoke heavy; I will make it even heavier. My father scourged you with whips; I will scourge you with scorpions." ¹⁵So the king did not listen to the people, for this turn of events was from the LORD, to fulfill the word the LORD had spoken to Jeroboam son of Nebat through Ahijah the Shilonite.

¹⁶When all Israel saw that the king refused to listen to them, they answered the king:

"What share do we have in David,
    what part in Jesse's son?
To your tents, Israel!
    Look after your own house, David!"

So the Israelites went home. ¹⁷But as for the Israelites who were living in the towns of Judah, Rehoboam still ruled over them.

¹⁸King Rehoboam sent out Adoniram,ᵃ who was in charge of forced labor, but all Israel stoned him to death. King Rehoboam, however, managed to get into his chariot and escape to Jerusalem. ¹⁹So Israel has been in rebellion against the house of David to this day.

²⁰When all the Israelites heard that Jeroboam had returned, they sent and called him to the assembly and made him king over all Israel. Only the tribe of Judah remained loyal to the house of David.

²¹When Rehoboam arrived in Jerusalem, he mustered all Judah and the tribe of Benjamin—a hundred and eighty thousand able young men—to go to war against Israel and to regain the kingdom for Rehoboam son of Solomon.

²²But this word of God came to Shemaiah the man of God: ²³"Say to Rehoboam son of Solomon king of Judah, to all Ju-

dah and Benjamin, and to the rest of the people, ²⁴'This is what the LORD says: Do not go up to fight against your brothers, the Israelites. Go home, every one of you, for this is my doing.'" So they obeyed the word of the LORD and went home again, as the LORD had ordered.

Golden Calves at Bethel and Dan

²⁵Then Jeroboam fortified Shechem in the hill country of Ephraim and lived there. From there he went out and built up Peniel.ᵇ

²⁶Jeroboam thought to himself, "The kingdom will now likely revert to the house of David. ²⁷If these people go up to offer sacrifices at the temple of the LORD in Jerusalem, they will again give their allegiance to their lord, Rehoboam king of Judah. They will kill me and return to King Rehoboam."

²⁸After seeking advice, the king made two golden calves. He said to the people, "It is too much for you to go up to Jerusalem. Here are your gods, Israel, who brought you up out of Egypt." ²⁹One he set up in Bethel, and the other in Dan. ³⁰And this thing became a sin; the people came to worship the one at Bethel and went as far as Dan to worship the other.ᶜ

³¹Jeroboam built shrines on high places and appointed priests from all sorts of people, even though they were not Levites. ³²He instituted a festival on the fifteenth day of the eighth month, like the festival held in Judah, and offered sacrifices on the altar. This he did in Bethel, sacrificing to the calves he had made. And at Bethel he also installed priests at the high places he had made. ³³On the fifteenth day of the eighth month, a month of his own choosing, he offered sacrifices on the altar he had built at Bethel. So he instituted the festival for the Israelites and went up to the altar to make offerings.

The Man of God From Judah

13 By the word of the LORD a man of God came from Judah to Bethel,

---

ᵃ 18 Some Septuagint manuscripts and Syriac (see also 4:6 and 5:14); Hebrew *Adoram*   ᵇ 25 Hebrew *Penuel*, a variant of *Peniel*   ᶜ 30 Probable reading of the original Hebrew text; Masoretic Text *people went to the one as far as Dan*

as Jeroboam was standing by the altar to make an offering. ²By the word of the LORD he cried out against the altar: "Altar, altar! This is what the LORD says: 'A son named Josiah will be born to the house of David. On you he will sacrifice the priests of the high places who make offerings here, and human bones will be burned on you.'" ³That same day the man of God gave a sign: "This is the sign the LORD has declared: The altar will be split apart and the ashes on it will be poured out."

⁴When King Jeroboam heard what the man of God cried out against the altar at Bethel, he stretched out his hand from the altar and said, "Seize him!" But the hand he stretched out toward the man shriveled up, so that he could not pull it back. ⁵Also, the altar was split apart and its ashes poured out according to the sign given by the man of God by the word of the LORD.

⁶Then the king said to the man of God, "Intercede with the LORD your God and pray for me that my hand may be restored." So the man of God interceded with the LORD, and the king's hand was restored and became as it was before.

⁷The king said to the man of God, "Come home with me for a meal, and I will give you a gift."

⁸But the man of God answered the king, "Even if you were to give me half your possessions, I would not go with you, nor would I eat bread or drink water here. ⁹For I was commanded by the word of the LORD: 'You must not eat bread or drink water or return by the way you came.'" ¹⁰So he took another road and did not return by the way he had come to Bethel.

¹¹Now there was a certain old prophet living in Bethel, whose sons came and told him all that the man of God had done there that day. They also told their father what he had said to the king. ¹²Their father asked them, "Which way did he go?" And his sons showed him which road the man of God from Judah had taken. ¹³So he said to his sons, "Saddle the donkey for me." And when they had saddled the donkey for him, he mounted it ¹⁴and rode after the man of God. He found him sit-ting under an oak tree and asked, "Are you the man of God who came from Judah?"

"I am," he replied.

¹⁵So the prophet said to him, "Come home with me and eat."

¹⁶The man of God said, "I cannot turn back and go with you, nor can I eat bread or drink water with you in this place. ¹⁷I have been told by the word of the LORD: 'You must not eat bread or drink water there or return by the way you came.'"

¹⁸The old prophet answered, "I too am a prophet, as you are. And an angel said to me by the word of the LORD: 'Bring him back with you to your house so that he may eat bread and drink water.'" (But he was lying to him.) ¹⁹So the man of God returned with him and ate and drank in his house.

²⁰While they were sitting at the table, the word of the LORD came to the old prophet who had brought him back. ²¹He cried out to the man of God who had come from Judah, "This is what the LORD says: 'You have defied the word of the LORD and have not kept the command the LORD your God gave you. ²²You came back and ate bread and drank water in the place where he told you not to eat or drink. Therefore your body will not be buried in the tomb of your ancestors.'"

²³When the man of God had finished eating and drinking, the prophet who had brought him back saddled his donkey for him. ²⁴As he went on his way, a lion met him on the road and killed him, and his body was left lying on the road, with both the donkey and the lion standing beside it. ²⁵Some people who passed by saw the body lying there, with the lion standing beside the body, and they went and reported it in the city where the old prophet lived.

²⁶When the prophet who had brought him back from his journey heard of it, he said, "It is the man of God who defied the word of the LORD. The LORD has given him over to the lion, which has mauled him and killed him, as the word of the LORD had warned him."

²⁷The prophet said to his sons, "Saddle the donkey for me," and they did so. ²⁸Then he went out and found the body

lying on the road, with the donkey and the lion standing beside it. The lion had neither eaten the body nor mauled the donkey. ²⁹So the prophet picked up the body of the man of God, laid it on the donkey, and brought it back to his own city to mourn for him and bury him. ³⁰Then he laid the body in his own tomb, and they mourned over him and said, "Alas, my brother!"

³¹After burying him, he said to his sons, "When I die, bury me in the grave where the man of God is buried; lay my bones beside his bones. ³²For the message he declared by the word of the LORD against the altar in Bethel and against all the shrines on the high places in the towns of Samaria will certainly come true."

³³Even after this, Jeroboam did not change his evil ways, but once more appointed priests for the high places from all sorts of people. Anyone who wanted to become a priest he consecrated for the high places. ³⁴This was the sin of the house of Jeroboam that led to its downfall and to its destruction from the face of the earth.

Ahijah's Prophecy Against Jeroboam

14 At that time Abijah son of Jeroboam became ill, ²and Jeroboam said to his wife, "Go, disguise yourself, so you won't be recognized as the wife of Jeroboam. Then go to Shiloh. Ahijah the prophet is there—the one who told me I would be king over this people. ³Take ten loaves of bread with you, some cakes and a jar of honey, and go to him. He will tell you what will happen to the boy." ⁴So Jeroboam's wife did what he said and went to Ahijah's house in Shiloh.

Now Ahijah could not see; his sight was gone because of his age. ⁵But the LORD had told Ahijah, "Jeroboam's wife is coming to ask you about her son, for he is ill, and you are to give her such and such an answer. When she arrives, she will pretend to be someone else."

⁶So when Ahijah heard the sound of her footsteps at the door, he said, "Come in, wife of Jeroboam. Why this pretense? I have been sent to you with bad news. ⁷Go, tell Jeroboam that this is what the LORD, the God of Israel, says: 'I raised you up from among the people and appointed you ruler over my people Israel. ⁸I tore the kingdom away from the house of David and gave it to you, but you have not been like my servant David, who kept my commands and followed me with all his heart, doing only what was right in my eyes. ⁹You have done more evil than all who lived before you. You have made for yourself other gods, idols made of metal; you have aroused my anger and turned your back on me.

¹⁰" 'Because of this, I am going to bring disaster on the house of Jeroboam. I will cut off from Jeroboam every last male in Israel—slave or free.ᵃ I will burn up the house of Jeroboam as one burns up dung, until it is all gone. ¹¹Dogs will eat those belonging to Jeroboam who die in the city, and the birds will feed on those who die in the country. The LORD has spoken!'

¹²"As for you, go back home. When you set foot in your city, the boy will die. ¹³All Israel will mourn for him and bury him. He is the only one belonging to Jeroboam who will be buried, because he is the only one in the house of Jeroboam in whom the LORD, the God of Israel, has found anything good.

¹⁴"The LORD will raise up for himself a king over Israel who will cut off the family of Jeroboam. Even now this is beginning to happen.ᵇ ¹⁵And the LORD will strike Israel, so that it will be like a reed swaying in the water. He will uproot Israel from this good land that he gave to their ancestors and scatter them beyond the Euphrates River, because they aroused the LORD's anger by making Asherah poles.ᶜ ¹⁶And he will give Israel up because of the sins Jeroboam has committed and has caused Israel to commit."

¹⁷Then Jeroboam's wife got up and left and went to Tirzah. As soon as she stepped over the threshold of the house,

---

ᵃ 10 Or Israel—every ruler or leader   ᵇ 14 The meaning of the Hebrew for this sentence is uncertain.   ᶜ 15 That is, wooden symbols of the goddess Asherah; here and elsewhere in 1 Kings

the boy died. [18]They buried him, and all Israel mourned for him, as the LORD had said through his servant the prophet Ahijah.

[19]The other events of Jeroboam's reign, his wars and how he ruled, are written in the book of the annals of the kings of Israel. [20]He reigned for twenty-two years and then rested with his ancestors. And Nadab his son succeeded him as king.

Rehoboam King of Judah

[21]Rehoboam son of Solomon was king in Judah. He was forty-one years old when he became king, and he reigned seventeen years in Jerusalem, the city the LORD had chosen out of all the tribes of Israel in which to put his Name. His mother's name was Naamah; she was an Ammonite.

[22]Judah did evil in the eyes of the LORD. By the sins they committed they stirred up his jealous anger more than those who were before them had done. [23]They also set up for themselves high places, sacred stones and Asherah poles on every high hill and under every spreading tree. [24]There were even male shrine prostitutes in the land; the people engaged in all the detestable practices of the nations the LORD had driven out before the Israelites.

[25]In the fifth year of King Rehoboam, Shishak king of Egypt attacked Jerusalem. [26]He carried off the treasures of the temple of the LORD and the treasures of the royal palace. He took everything, including all the gold shields Solomon had made. [27]So King Rehoboam made bronze shields to replace them and assigned these to the commanders of the guard on duty at the entrance to the royal palace. [28]Whenever the king went to the LORD's temple, the guards bore the shields, and afterward they returned them to the guardroom.

[29]As for the other events of Rehoboam's reign, and all he did, are they not written in the book of the annals of the kings of Judah? [30]There was continual warfare between Rehoboam and Jeroboam. [31]And Rehoboam rested with his ancestors and was buried with them in the City of David. His mother's name was Naamah; she was an Ammonite. And Abijah[a] his son succeeded him as king.

Abijah King of Judah

15 In the eighteenth year of the reign of Jeroboam son of Nebat, Abijah[b] became king of Judah, [2]and he reigned in Jerusalem three years. His mother's name was Maakah daughter of Abishalom.[c]

[3]He committed all the sins his father had done before him; his heart was not fully devoted to the LORD his God, as the heart of David his forefather had been. [4]Nevertheless, for David's sake the LORD his God gave him a lamp in Jerusalem by raising up a son to succeed him and by making Jerusalem strong. [5]For David had done what was right in the eyes of the LORD and had not failed to keep any of the LORD's commands all the days of his life—except in the case of Uriah the Hittite.

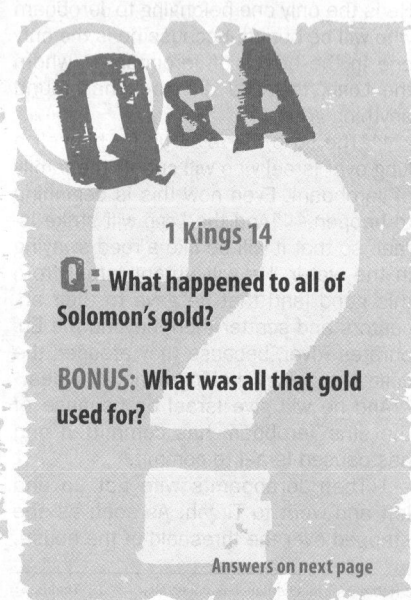

1 Kings 14

Q: What happened to all of Solomon's gold?

BONUS: What was all that gold used for?

Answers on next page

a 31 Some Hebrew manuscripts and Septuagint (see also 2 Chron. 12:16); most Hebrew manuscripts Abijam   b 1 Some Hebrew manuscripts and Septuagint (see also 2 Chron. 12:16); most Hebrew manuscripts Abijam; also in verses 7 and 8   c 2 A variant of Absalom; also in verse 10

⁶There was war between Abijahᵃ and Jeroboam throughout Abijah's lifetime. ⁷As for the other events of Abijah's reign, and all he did, are they not written in the book of the annals of the kings of Judah? There was war between Abijah and Jeroboam. ⁸And Abijah rested with his ancestors and was buried in the City of David. And Asa his son succeeded him as king.

Asa King of Judah

⁹In the twentieth year of Jeroboam king of Israel, Asa became king of Judah, ¹⁰and he reigned in Jerusalem forty-one years. His grandmother's name was Maakah daughter of Abishalom.

¹¹Asa did what was right in the eyes of the LORD, as his father David had done. ¹²He expelled the male shrine prostitutes from the land and got rid of all the idols his ancestors had made. ¹³He even deposed his grandmother Maakah from her position as queen mother, because she had made a repulsive image for the worship of Asherah. Asa cut it down and burned it in the Kidron Valley. ¹⁴Although he did not remove the high places, Asa's heart was fully committed to the LORD all his life. ¹⁵He brought into the temple of the LORD the silver and gold and the articles that he and his father had dedicated.

¹⁶There was war between Asa and Baasha king of Israel throughout their reigns. ¹⁷Baasha king of Israel went up against Judah and fortified Ramah to prevent anyone from leaving or entering the territory of Asa king of Judah.

¹⁸Asa then took all the silver and gold that was left in the treasuries of the LORD's temple and of his own palace. He entrusted it to his officials and sent them to Ben-Hadad son of Tabrimmon, the son of Hezion, the king of Aram, who was ruling in Damascus. ¹⁹"Let there be a treaty between me and you," he said, "as there was between my father and your father. See, I am sending you a gift of silver and gold. Now break your treaty with Baasha king of Israel so he will withdraw from me."

²⁰Ben-Hadad agreed with King Asa

A: After Judah abandoned the Lord, Shishak king of Egypt captured Jerusalem and took Solomon's gold (1 Kings 14:25–26).

BONUS: It was used to beautify the temples of Egypt's gods.

and sent the commanders of his forces against the towns of Israel. He conquered Ijon, Dan, Abel Beth Maakah and all Kinnereth in addition to Naphtali. ²¹When Baasha heard this, he stopped building Ramah and withdrew to Tirzah. ²²Then King Asa issued an order to all Judah— no one was exempt—and they carried away from Ramah the stones and timber Baasha had been using there. With them King Asa built up Geba in Benjamin, and also Mizpah.

²³As for all the other events of Asa's reign, all his achievements, all he did and the cities he built, are they not written in the book of the annals of the kings of Judah? In his old age, however, his feet became diseased. ²⁴Then Asa rested with his ancestors and was buried with them in the city of his father David. And Jehoshaphat his son succeeded him as king.

Nadab King of Israel

²⁵Nadab son of Jeroboam became king of Israel in the second year of Asa king of Judah, and he reigned over Israel two years. ²⁶He did evil in the eyes of the

ᵃ 6 Some Hebrew manuscripts and Syriac *Abijam* (that is, Abijah); most Hebrew manuscripts *Rehoboam*

LORD, following the ways of his father and committing the same sin his father had caused Israel to commit.

27 Baasha son of Ahijah from the tribe of Issachar plotted against him, and he struck him down at Gibbethon, a Philistine town, while Nadab and all Israel were besieging it. 28 Baasha killed Nadab in the third year of Asa king of Judah and succeeded him as king.

29 As soon as he began to reign, he killed Jeroboam's whole family. He did not leave Jeroboam anyone that breathed, but destroyed them all, according to the word of the LORD given through his servant Ahijah the Shilonite. 30 This happened because of the sins Jeroboam had committed and had caused Israel to commit, and because he aroused the anger of the LORD, the God of Israel.

31 As for the other events of Nadab's reign, and all he did, are they not written in the book of the annals of the kings of Israel? 32 There was war between Asa and Baasha king of Israel throughout their reigns.

Baasha King of Israel

33 In the third year of Asa king of Judah, Baasha son of Ahijah became king of all Israel in Tirzah, and he reigned twenty-four years. 34 He did evil in the eyes of the LORD, following the ways of Jeroboam and committing the same sin Jeroboam had caused Israel to commit.

16 Then the word of the LORD came to Jehu son of Hanani concerning Baasha: 2 "I lifted you up from the dust and appointed you ruler over my people Israel, but you followed the ways of Jeroboam and caused my people Israel to sin and to arouse my anger by their sins. 3 So I am about to wipe out Baasha and his house, and I will make your house like that of Jeroboam son of Nebat. 4 Dogs will eat those belonging to Baasha who die in the city, and birds will feed on those who die in the country."

5 As for the other events of Baasha's reign, what he did and his achievements, are they not written in the book of the annals of the kings of Israel? 6 Baasha rested with his ancestors and was bur-

ied in Tirzah. And Elah his son succeeded him as king.

7 Moreover, the word of the LORD came through the prophet Jehu son of Hanani to Baasha and his house, because of all the evil he had done in the eyes of the LORD, arousing his anger by the things he did, becoming like the house of Jeroboam—and also because he destroyed it.

Elah King of Israel

8 In the twenty-sixth year of Asa king of Judah, Elah son of Baasha became king of Israel, and he reigned in Tirzah two years.

9 Zimri, one of his officials, who had command of half his chariots, plotted against him. Elah was in Tirzah at the time, getting drunk in the home of Arza, the palace administrator at Tirzah. 10 Zimri came in, struck him down and killed him in the twenty-seventh year of Asa king of Judah. Then he succeeded him as king.

11 As soon as he began to reign and was seated on the throne, he killed off Baasha's whole family. He did not spare a single male, whether relative or friend. 12 So Zimri destroyed the whole family of Baasha, in accordance with the word of the LORD spoken against Baasha through the prophet Jehu— 13 because of all the sins Baasha and his son Elah had committed and had caused Israel to commit, so that they aroused the anger of the LORD, the God of Israel, by their worthless idols.

14 As for the other events of Elah's reign, and all he did, are they not written in the book of the annals of the kings of Israel?

Zimri King of Israel

15 In the twenty-seventh year of Asa king of Judah, Zimri reigned in Tirzah seven days. The army was encamped near Gibbethon, a Philistine town. 16 When the Israelites in the camp heard that Zimri had plotted against the king and murdered him, they proclaimed Omri, the commander of the army, king over Israel that very day there in the camp. 17 Then Omri and all the Israelites with him withdrew from Gibbethon and laid siege to

Tirzah. [18]When Zimri saw that the city was taken, he went into the citadel of the royal palace and set the palace on fire around him. So he died, [19]because of the sins he had committed, doing evil in the eyes of the LORD and following the ways of Jeroboam and committing the same sin Jeroboam had caused Israel to commit.

[20]As for the other events of Zimri's reign, and the rebellion he carried out, are they not written in the book of the annals of the kings of Israel?

Omri King of Israel

[21]Then the people of Israel were split into two factions; half supported Tibni son of Ginath for king, and the other half supported Omri. [22]But Omri's followers proved stronger than those of Tibni son of Ginath. So Tibni died and Omri became king.

[23]In the thirty-first year of Asa king of Judah, Omri became king of Israel, and he reigned twelve years, six of them in Tirzah. [24]He bought the hill of Samaria from Shemer for two talents[a] of silver and built a city on the hill, calling it Samaria, after Shemer, the name of the former owner of the hill.

[25]But Omri did evil in the eyes of the LORD and sinned more than all those before him. [26]He followed completely the ways of Jeroboam son of Nebat, committing the same sin Jeroboam had caused Israel to commit, so that they aroused the anger of the LORD, the God of Israel, by their worthless idols.

[27]As for the other events of Omri's reign, what he did and the things he achieved, are they not written in the book of the annals of the kings of Israel? [28]Omri rested with his ancestors and was buried in Samaria. And Ahab his son succeeded him as king.

Ahab Becomes King of Israel

[29]In the thirty-eighth year of Asa king of Judah, Ahab son of Omri became king of Israel, and he reigned in Samaria over Israel twenty-two years. [30]Ahab son of Omri did more evil in the eyes of the LORD than any of those before him. [31]He not only considered it trivial to commit the sins of Jeroboam son of Nebat, but he also married Jezebel daughter of Ethbaal king of the Sidonians, and began to serve Baal and worship him. [32]He set up an altar for Baal in the temple of Baal that he built in Samaria. [33]Ahab also made an Asherah pole and did more to arouse the anger of the LORD, the God of Israel, than did all the kings of Israel before him.

[34]In Ahab's time, Hiel of Bethel rebuilt Jericho. He laid its foundations at the cost of his firstborn son Abiram, and he set up its gates at the cost of his youngest son Segub, in accordance with the word of the LORD spoken by Joshua son of Nun.

[a] 24 That is, about 150 pounds or about 68 kilograms

PANORAMA

{1 KINGS}

Justice.

Solomon held on to the great kingdom of his father David. But after Solomon died, the kingdom split into two, Israel and Judah. Both kingdoms wandered away from, and abandoned, God. But not without consequences.

Elijah Announces a Great Drought

17 Now Elijah the Tishbite, from Tishbe*ª* in Gilead, said to Ahab, "As the LORD, the God of Israel, lives, whom I serve, there will be neither dew nor rain in the next few years except at my word."

Elijah Fed by Ravens

² Then the word of the LORD came to Elijah: ³ "Leave here, turn eastward and hide in the Kerith Ravine, east of the Jordan. ⁴ You will drink from the brook, and I have directed the ravens to supply you with food there."

⁵ So he did what the LORD had told him. He went to the Kerith Ravine, east of the Jordan, and stayed there. ⁶ The ravens brought him bread and meat in the morning and bread and meat in the evening, and he drank from the brook.

Elijah and the Widow at Zarephath

⁷ Some time later the brook dried up because there had been no rain in the land. ⁸ Then the word of the LORD came to him: ⁹ "Go at once to Zarephath in the region of Sidon and stay there. I have directed a widow there to supply you with food." ¹⁰ So he went to Zarephath. When he came to the town gate, a widow was there gathering sticks. He called to her and asked, "Would you bring me a little water in a jar so I may have a drink?" ¹¹ As she was going to get it, he called, "And bring me, please, a piece of bread."

¹² "As surely as the LORD your God lives," she replied, "I don't have any bread—only a handful of flour in a jar and a little olive oil in a jug. I am gathering a few sticks to take home and make a meal for myself and my son, that we may eat it—and die."

¹³ Elijah said to her, "Don't be afraid. Go home and do as you have said. But first make a small loaf of bread for me from what you have and bring it to me, and then make something for yourself and your son. ¹⁴ For this is what the LORD,

the God of Israel, says: 'The jar of flour will not be used up and the jug of oil will not run dry until the day the LORD sends rain on the land.'"

¹⁵ She went away and did as Elijah had told her. So there was food every day for Elijah and for the woman and her family. ¹⁶ For the jar of flour was not used up and the jug of oil did not run dry, in keeping with the word of the LORD spoken by Elijah.

¹⁷ Some time later the son of the woman who owned the house became ill. He grew worse and worse, and finally stopped breathing. ¹⁸ She said to Elijah, "What do you have against me, man of God? Did you come to remind me of my sin and kill my son?"

¹⁹ "Give me your son," Elijah replied. He took him from her arms, carried him to the upper room where he was staying, and laid him on his bed. ²⁰ Then he cried out to the LORD, "LORD my God, have you brought tragedy even on this widow I am staying with, by causing her son to die?" ²¹ Then he stretched himself out on the boy three times and cried out to the LORD, "LORD my God, let this boy's life return to him!"

²² The LORD heard Elijah's cry, and the boy's life returned to him, and he lived. ²³ Elijah picked up the child and carried him down from the room into the house. He gave him to his mother and said, "Look, your son is alive!"

²⁴ Then the woman said to Elijah, "Now I know that you are a man of God and that the word of the LORD from your mouth is the truth."

Elijah and Obadiah

18 After a long time, in the third year, the word of the LORD came to Elijah: "Go and present yourself to Ahab, and I will send rain on the land." ² So Elijah went to present himself to Ahab.

Now the famine was severe in Samaria, ³ and Ahab had summoned Obadiah, his palace administrator. (Obadiah was a devout believer in the LORD. ⁴ While Jezebel was killing off the LORD's prophets, Obadi-

---

ª 1 Or Tishbite, of the settlers

widow in a town called Zarephath had just enough food for one meal for herself and her son. The prophet Elijah told her not to be afraid, but to "first make a small loaf of bread for me" (1 Kings 17:13). Put God's prophet first? When there wasn't enough for the woman and her son? If you remember the story, you know that God made the woman's pot of oil and jar of flour last for years. She put God first, and God provided for her needs. Can you apply this story to your life? You bet! Don't act just because you feel you have to have something "right now." Put God first in all you do, and he'll meet your needs too.

{1 Kings 17:13–14}

INSTANT ACCESS

8 "Yes," he replied. "Go tell your master, 'Elijah is here.'"

9 "What have I done wrong," asked Obadiah, "that you are handing your servant over to Ahab to be put to death? 10 As surely as the LORD your God lives, there is not a nation or kingdom where my master has not sent someone to look for you. And whenever a nation or kingdom claimed you were not there, he made them swear they could not find you. 11 But now you tell me to go to my master and say, 'Elijah is here.' 12 I don't know where the Spirit of the LORD may carry you when I leave you. If I go and tell Ahab and he doesn't find you, he will kill me. Yet I your servant have worshiped the LORD since my youth. 13 Haven't you heard, my lord, what I did while Jezebel was killing the prophets of the LORD? I hid a hundred of the LORD's prophets in two caves, fifty in each, and supplied them with food and water. 14 And now you tell me to go to my master and say, 'Elijah is here.' He will kill me!"

15 Elijah said, "As the LORD Almighty lives, whom I serve, I will surely present myself to Ahab today."

Elijah on Mount Carmel

16 So Obadiah went to meet Ahab and told him, and Ahab went to meet Elijah. 17 When he saw Elijah, he said to him, "Is that you, you troubler of Israel?"

18 "I have not made trouble for Israel," Elijah replied. "But you and your father's family have. You have abandoned the LORD's commands and have followed the Baals. 19 Now summon the people from all over Israel to meet me on Mount Carmel. And bring the four hundred and fifty prophets of Baal and the four hundred prophets of Asherah, who eat at Jezebel's table."

20 So Ahab sent word throughout all Israel and assembled the prophets on Mount Carmel. 21 Elijah went before the people and said, "How long will you waver between two opinions? If the LORD is God, follow him; but if Baal is God, follow him."

But the people said nothing.

22 Then Elijah said to them, "I am the only one of the LORD's prophets left, but

ah had taken a hundred prophets and hidden them in two caves, fifty in each, and had supplied them with food and water.) 5 Ahab had said to Obadiah, "Go through the land to all the springs and valleys. Maybe we can find some grass to keep the horses and mules alive so we will not have to kill any of our animals." 6 So they divided the land they were to cover, Ahab going in one direction and Obadiah in another.

7 As Obadiah was walking along, Elijah met him. Obadiah recognized him, bowed down to the ground, and said, "Is it really you, my lord Elijah?"

Baal has four hundred and fifty prophets. 23 Get two bulls for us. Let Baal's prophets choose one for themselves, and let them cut it into pieces and put it on the wood but not set fire to it. I will prepare the other bull and put it on the wood but not set fire to it. 24 Then you call on the name of your god, and I will call on the name of the LORD. The god who answers by fire — he is God."

Then all the people said, "What you say is good."

25 Elijah said to the prophets of Baal, "Choose one of the bulls and prepare it first, since there are so many of you. Call on the name of your god, but do not light the fire." 26 So they took the bull given them and prepared it.

Then they called on the name of Baal from morning till noon. "Baal, answer us!" they shouted. But there was no response; no one answered. And they danced around the altar they had made.

27 At noon Elijah began to taunt them. "Shout louder!" he said. "Surely he is a god! Perhaps he is deep in thought, or busy, or traveling. Maybe he is sleeping and must be awakened." 28 So they shouted louder and slashed themselves with swords and spears, as was their custom, until their blood flowed. 29 Midday passed, and they continued their frantic prophesying until the time for the evening sacrifice. But there was no response, no one answered, no one paid attention.

30 Then Elijah said to all the people, "Come here to me." They came to him, and he repaired the altar of the LORD, which had been torn down. 31 Elijah took twelve stones, one for each of the tribes descended from Jacob, to whom the word of the LORD had come, saying, "Your name shall be Israel." 32 With the stones he built an altar in the name of the LORD, and he dug a trench around it large enough to hold two seahs[a] of seed. 33 He arranged the wood, cut the bull into pieces and laid it on the wood. Then he said to them, "Fill four large jars with water and pour it on the offering and on the wood."

34 "Do it again," he said, and they did it again.

"Do it a third time," he ordered, and they did it the third time. 35 The water ran down around the altar and even filled the trench.

36 At the time of sacrifice, the prophet Elijah stepped forward and prayed: "LORD, the God of Abraham, Isaac and Israel, let it be known today that you are God in Israel and that I am your servant and have done all these things at your command. 37 Answer me, LORD, answer me, so these people will know that you, LORD, are God, and that you are turning their hearts back again."

38 Then the fire of the LORD fell and burned up the sacrifice, the wood, the stones and the soil, and also licked up the water in the trench.

39 When all the people saw this, they fell prostrate and cried, "The LORD — he is God! The LORD — he is God!"

40 Then Elijah commanded them, "Seize the prophets of Baal. Don't let anyone get away!" They seized them, and Elijah had them brought down to the Kishon Valley and slaughtered there.

41 And Elijah said to Ahab, "Go, eat and drink, for there is the sound of a heavy rain." 42 So Ahab went off to eat and drink, but Elijah climbed to the top of Carmel, bent down to the ground and put his face between his knees.

43 "Go and look toward the sea," he told his servant. And he went up and looked.

"There is nothing there," he said.

Seven times Elijah said, "Go back."

44 The seventh time the servant reported, "A cloud as small as a man's hand is rising from the sea."

So Elijah said, "Go and tell Ahab, 'Hitch up your chariot and go down before the rain stops you.'"

45 Meanwhile, the sky grew black with clouds, the wind rose, a heavy rain started falling and Ahab rode off to Jezreel. 46 The power of the LORD came on Elijah and, tucking his cloak into his belt, he ran ahead of Ahab all the way to Jezreel.

---

a 32 That is, probably about 24 pounds or about 11 kilograms

Elijah Flees to Horeb

19 Now Ahab told Jezebel everything Elijah had done and how he had killed all the prophets with the sword. ²So Jezebel sent a messenger to Elijah to say, "May the gods deal with me, be it ever so severely, if by this time tomorrow I do not make your life like that of one of them."

³Elijah was afraid[a] and ran for his life. When he came to Beersheba in Judah, he left his servant there, ⁴while he himself went a day's journey into the wilderness. He came to a broom bush, sat down under it and prayed that he might die. "I have had enough, LORD," he said. "Take my life; I am no better than my ancestors." ⁵Then he lay down under the bush and fell asleep.

All at once an angel touched him and said, "Get up and eat." ⁶He looked around, and there by his head was some bread baked over hot coals, and a jar of water. He ate and drank and then lay down again.

⁷The angel of the LORD came back a second time and touched him and said, "Get up and eat, for the journey is too much for you." ⁸So he got up and ate and drank. Strengthened by that food, he traveled forty days and forty nights until he reached Horeb, the mountain of God. ⁹There he went into a cave and spent the night.

The LORD Appears to Elijah

And the word of the LORD came to him: "What are you doing here, Elijah?"

¹⁰He replied, "I have been very zealous for the LORD God Almighty. The Israelites have rejected your covenant, torn down your altars, and put your prophets to death with the sword. I am the only one left, and now they are trying to kill me too."

¹¹The LORD said, "Go out and stand on the mountain in the presence of the LORD, for the LORD is about to pass by."

Then a great and powerful wind tore the mountains apart and shattered the rocks before the LORD, but the LORD was not in the wind. After the wind there was an earthquake, but the LORD was not in the earthquake. ¹²After the earthquake came a fire, but the LORD was not in the fire. And after the fire came a gentle whisper. ¹³When Elijah heard it, he pulled his cloak over his face and went out and stood at the mouth of the cave.

Then a voice said to him, "What are you doing here, Elijah?"

¹⁴He replied, "I have been very zealous for the LORD God Almighty. The Israelites have rejected your covenant, torn down your altars, and put your prophets to death with the sword. I am the only one left, and now they are trying to kill me too."

¹⁵The LORD said to him, "Go back the way you came, and go to the Desert of Damascus. When you get there, anoint Hazael king over Aram. ¹⁶Also, anoint Jehu son of Nimshi king over Israel, and anoint Elisha son of Shaphat from Abel Meholah to succeed you as prophet. ¹⁷Jehu will put to death any who escape the sword of Hazael, and Elisha will put to death any who escape the sword of Jehu. ¹⁸Yet I reserve seven thousand in Israel—all whose knees have not bowed down to Baal and whose mouths have not kissed him."

The Call of Elisha

¹⁹So Elijah went from there and found Elisha son of Shaphat. He was plowing with twelve yoke of oxen, and he himself was driving the twelfth pair. Elijah went up to him and threw his cloak around him. ²⁰Elisha then left his oxen and ran after Elijah. "Let me kiss my father and mother goodbye," he said, "and then I will come with you."

"Go back," Elijah replied. "What have I done to you?"

²¹So Elisha left him and went back. He took his yoke of oxen and slaughtered them. He burned the plowing equipment to cook the meat and gave it to the people, and they ate. Then he set out to follow Elijah and became his servant.

Ben-Hadad Attacks Samaria

20 Now Ben-Hadad king of Aram mustered his entire army. Accompanied by thirty-two kings with their horses

---

ᵃ 3 Or *Elijah saw*

> I feel sad most of the time. I cry a lot and sometimes I think about doing something bad to myself. Are these normal feelings?
>
> **>> Mariah**

Dear Mariah,

Just about everyone feels a little sad from time to time. But deep sadness that doesn't go away for a couple weeks or more is depression. It can be very serious. More teenagers are depressed than ever before which explains the growing number of teens who take their own lives, or try to.

You must tell your parent or a responsible adult about your feelings. Depression is serious but treatable. Do not seek a permanent solution to a temporary problem.

Even during Bible times, many godly people suffered with depression. The prophet Elijah was so depressed he asked God to take his life (1 Kings 19:4). You can find the rest of his story in 1 Kings 19. Elijah was stressed out, exhausted and in danger. But great stress is only one reason people can have depression. Some people have a chemical imbalance. Some have experienced a sad event like a death or divorce. Sometimes people start making some bad choices and start feeling depressed. They don't know how to get their lives turned back around.

There are many things that can cause depression. But the best way to deal with it is to get help. God loves you and he wants you to be happy and live your life. He gave you parents to help you, so let them.

Jordan

and chariots, he went up and besieged Samaria and attacked it. ²He sent messengers into the city to Ahab king of Israel, saying, "This is what Ben-Hadad says: ³'Your silver and gold are mine, and the best of your wives and children are mine.'"

⁴The king of Israel answered, "Just as you say, my lord the king. I and all I have are yours."

⁵The messengers came again and said, "This is what Ben-Hadad says: 'I sent to demand your silver and gold, your wives and your children. ⁶But about this time tomorrow I am going to send my officials to search your palace and the houses of your officials. They will seize everything you value and carry it away.'"

⁷The king of Israel summoned all the elders of the land and said to them, "See how this man is looking for trouble! When he sent for my wives and my children, my silver and my gold, I did not refuse him."

⁸The elders and the people all answered, "Don't listen to him or agree to his demands."

⁹So he replied to Ben-Hadad's messengers, "Tell my lord the king, 'Your servant will do all you demanded the first time, but this demand I cannot meet.'" They left and took the answer back to Ben-Hadad.

¹⁰Then Ben-Hadad sent another message to Ahab: "May the gods deal with me, be it ever so severely, if enough dust remains in Samaria to give each of my men a handful."

¹¹The king of Israel answered, "Tell him: 'One who puts on his armor should not boast like one who takes it off.'"

¹²Ben-Hadad heard this message while he and the kings were drinking in their tents,ᵃ and he ordered his men: "Prepare to attack." So they prepared to attack the city.

Ahab Defeats Ben-Hadad

¹³Meanwhile a prophet came to Ahab king of Israel and announced, "This is what the LORD says: 'Do you see this vast army? I will give it into your hand today, and then you will know that I am the LORD.'"

¹⁴"But who will do this?" asked Ahab.

The prophet replied, "This is what the LORD says: 'The junior officers under the provincial commanders will do it.'"

"And who will start the battle?" he asked.

The prophet answered, "You will."

¹⁵So Ahab summoned the 232 junior officers under the provincial commanders. Then he assembled the rest of the Israelites, 7,000 in all. ¹⁶They set out at noon while Ben-Hadad and the 32 kings allied with him were in their tents getting drunk. ¹⁷The junior officers under the provincial commanders went out first.

Now Ben-Hadad had dispatched scouts, who reported, "Men are advancing from Samaria."

¹⁸He said, "If they have come out for peace, take them alive; if they have come out for war, take them alive."

¹⁹The junior officers under the provincial commanders marched out of the city with the army behind them ²⁰and each one struck down his opponent. At that, the Arameans fled, with the Israelites in pursuit. But Ben-Hadad king of Aram escaped on horseback with some of his horsemen. ²¹The king of Israel advanced and overpowered the horses and chariots and inflicted heavy losses on the Arameans.

²²Afterward, the prophet came to the king of Israel and said, "Strengthen your position and see what must be done, because next spring the king of Aram will attack you again."

²³Meanwhile, the officials of the king of Aram advised him, "Their gods are gods of the hills. That is why they were too strong for us. But if we fight them on the plains, surely we will be stronger than they. ²⁴Do this: Remove all the kings from their commands and replace them with other officers. ²⁵You must also raise an army like the one you lost—horse for horse and chariot for chariot—so we can fight Israel on the plains. Then surely we will be stronger than they." He agreed with them and acted accordingly.

²⁶The next spring Ben-Hadad mustered the Arameans and went up to Aphek to fight against Israel. ²⁷When the Israelites were also mustered and given provisions,

---

ᵃ 12 Or *in Sukkoth*; also in verse 16

they marched out to meet them. The Israelites camped opposite them like two small flocks of goats, while the Arameans covered the countryside.

28 The man of God came up and told the king of Israel, "This is what the LORD says: 'Because the Arameans think the LORD is a god of the hills and not a god of the valleys, I will deliver this vast army into your hands, and you will know that I am the LORD.' "

29 For seven days they camped opposite each other, and on the seventh day the battle was joined. The Israelites inflicted a hundred thousand casualties on the Aramean foot soldiers in one day. 30 The rest of them escaped to the city of Aphek, where the wall collapsed on twenty-seven thousand of them. And Ben-Hadad fled to the city and hid in an inner room.

31 His officials said to him, "Look, we have heard that the kings of Israel are merciful. Let us go to the king of Israel with sackcloth around our waists and ropes around our heads. Perhaps he will spare your life."

32 Wearing sackcloth around their waists and ropes around their heads, they went to the king of Israel and said, "Your servant Ben-Hadad says: 'Please let me live.' "

The king answered, "Is he still alive? He is my brother."

33 The men took this as a good sign and were quick to pick up his word. "Yes, your brother Ben-Hadad!" they said.

"Go and get him," the king said. When Ben-Hadad came out, Ahab had him come up into his chariot.

34 "I will return the cities my father took from your father," Ben-Hadad offered. "You may set up your own market areas in Damascus, as my father did in Samaria."

Ahab said, "On the basis of a treaty I will set you free." So he made a treaty with him, and let him go.

A Prophet Condemns Ahab

35 By the word of the LORD one of the company of the prophets said to his companion, "Strike me with your weapon," but he refused.

36 So the prophet said, "Because you have not obeyed the LORD, as soon as you leave me a lion will kill you." And after the man went away, a lion found him and killed him.

37 The prophet found another man and said, "Strike me, please." So the man struck him and wounded him. 38 Then the prophet went and stood by the road waiting for the king. He disguised himself with his headband down over his eyes. 39 As the king passed by, the prophet called out to him, "Your servant went into the thick of the battle, and someone came to me with a captive and said, 'Guard this man. If he is missing, it will be your life for his life, or you must pay a talent*a* of silver.' 40 While your servant was busy here and there, the man disappeared."

"That is your sentence," the king of Israel said. "You have pronounced it yourself."

41 Then the prophet quickly removed the headband from his eyes, and the king of Israel recognized him as one of the prophets. 42 He said to the king, "This is what the LORD says: 'You have set free a man I had determined should die.*b* Therefore it is your life for his life, your people for his people.' " 43 Sullen and angry, the king of Israel went to his palace in Samaria.

Naboth's Vineyard

21 Some time later there was an incident involving a vineyard belonging to Naboth the Jezreelite. The vineyard was in Jezreel, close to the palace of Ahab king of Samaria. 2 Ahab said to Naboth, "Let me have your vineyard to use for a vegetable garden, since it is close to my palace. In exchange I will give you a better vineyard or, if you prefer, I will pay you whatever it is worth."

3 But Naboth replied, "The LORD forbid that I should give you the inheritance of my ancestors."

4 So Ahab went home, sullen and angry because Naboth the Jezreelite had said, "I will not give you the inheritance of my

---

a 39 That is, about 75 pounds or about 34 kilograms   *b 42* The Hebrew term refers to the irrevocable giving over of things or persons to the LORD, often by totally destroying them.

ancestors." He lay on his bed sulking and refused to eat.

[5]His wife Jezebel came in and asked him, "Why are you so sullen? Why won't you eat?"

[6]He answered her, "Because I said to Naboth the Jezreelite, 'Sell me your vineyard; or if you prefer, I will give you another vineyard in its place.' But he said, 'I will not give you my vineyard.'"

[7]Jezebel his wife said, "Is this how you act as king over Israel? Get up and eat! Cheer up. I'll get you the vineyard of Naboth the Jezreelite."

[8]So she wrote letters in Ahab's name, placed his seal on them, and sent them to the elders and nobles who lived in Naboth's city with him. [9]In those letters she wrote:

"Proclaim a day of fasting and seat Naboth in a prominent place among the people. [10]But seat two scoundrels opposite him and have them bring charges that he has cursed both God and the king. Then take him out and stone him to death."

[11]So the elders and nobles who lived in Naboth's city did as Jezebel directed in the letters she had written to them. [12]They proclaimed a fast and seated Naboth in a prominent place among the people. [13]Then two scoundrels came and sat opposite him and brought charges against Naboth before the people, saying, "Naboth has cursed both God and the king." So they took him outside the city and stoned him to death. [14]Then they sent word to Jezebel: "Naboth has been stoned to death."

[15]As soon as Jezebel heard that Naboth had been stoned to death, she said to Ahab, "Get up and take possession of the vineyard of Naboth the Jezreelite that he refused to sell you. He is no longer alive, but dead." [16]When Ahab heard that Naboth was dead, he got up and went down to take possession of Naboth's vineyard.

[17]Then the word of the LORD came to Elijah the Tishbite: [18]"Go down to meet Ahab king of Israel, who rules in Samaria.

He is now in Naboth's vineyard, where he has gone to take possession of it. [19]Say to him, 'This is what the LORD says: Have you not murdered a man and seized his property?' Then say to him, 'This is what the LORD says: In the place where dogs licked up Naboth's blood, dogs will lick up your blood—yes, yours!'"

[20]Ahab said to Elijah, "So you have found me, my enemy!"

"I have found you," he answered, "because you have sold yourself to do evil in the eyes of the LORD. [21]He says, 'I am going to bring disaster on you. I will wipe out your descendants and cut off from Ahab every last male in Israel—slave or free.[a] [22]I will make your house like that of Jeroboam son of Nebat and that of Baasha son of Ahijah, because you have aroused my anger and have caused Israel to sin.'

[23]"And also concerning Jezebel the LORD says: 'Dogs will devour Jezebel by the wall of[b] Jezreel.'

[24]"Dogs will eat those belonging to Ahab who die in the city, and the birds will feed on those who die in the country."

[25](There was never anyone like Ahab, who sold himself to do evil in the eyes of the LORD, urged on by Jezebel his wife. [26]He behaved in the vilest manner by going after idols, like the Amorites the LORD drove out before Israel.)

[27]When Ahab heard these words, he tore his clothes, put on sackcloth and fasted. He lay in sackcloth and went around meekly.

[28]Then the word of the LORD came to Elijah the Tishbite: [29]"Have you noticed how Ahab has humbled himself before me? Because he has humbled himself, I will not bring this disaster in his day, but I will bring it on his house in the days of his son."

Micaiah Prophesies Against Ahab

22 For three years there was no war between Aram and Israel. [2]But in the third year Jehoshaphat king of Judah went down to see the king of Israel. [3]The

---

[a] 21 Or *Israel—every ruler or leader*   [b] 23 Most Hebrew manuscripts; a few Hebrew manuscripts, Vulgate and Syriac (see also 2 Kings 9:26) *the plot of ground at*

king of Israel had said to his officials, "Don't you know that Ramoth Gilead belongs to us and yet we are doing nothing to retake it from the king of Aram?"

[4] So he asked Jehoshaphat, "Will you go with me to fight against Ramoth Gilead?"

Jehoshaphat replied to the king of Israel, "I am as you are, my people as your people, my horses as your horses." [5] But Jehoshaphat also said to the king of Israel, "First seek the counsel of the Lord."

[6] So the king of Israel brought together the prophets—about four hundred men—and asked them, "Shall I go to war against Ramoth Gilead, or shall I refrain?"

"Go," they answered, "for the Lord will give it into the king's hand."

[7] But Jehoshaphat asked, "Is there no longer a prophet of the Lord here whom we can inquire of?"

[8] The king of Israel answered Jehoshaphat, "There is still one prophet through whom we can inquire of the Lord, but I hate him because he never prophesies anything good about me, but always bad. He is Micaiah son of Imlah."

"The king should not say such a thing," Jehoshaphat replied.

[9] So the king of Israel called one of his officials and said, "Bring Micaiah son of Imlah at once."

[10] Dressed in their royal robes, the king of Israel and Jehoshaphat king of Judah were sitting on their thrones at the threshing floor by the entrance of the gate of Samaria, with all the prophets prophesying before them. [11] Now Zedekiah son of Kenaanah had made iron horns and he declared, "This is what the Lord says: 'With these you will gore the Arameans until they are destroyed.'"

[12] All the other prophets were prophesying the same thing. "Attack Ramoth Gilead and be victorious," they said, "for the Lord will give it into the king's hand."

[13] The messenger who had gone to summon Micaiah said to him, "Look, the other prophets without exception are predicting success for the king. Let your word agree with theirs, and speak favorably."

[14] But Micaiah said, "As surely as the Lord lives, I can tell him only what the Lord tells me."

[15] When he arrived, the king asked him, "Micaiah, shall we go to war against Ramoth Gilead, or not?"

"Attack and be victorious," he answered, "for the Lord will give it into the king's hand."

[16] The king said to him, "How many times must I make you swear to tell me nothing but the truth in the name of the Lord?"

[17] Then Micaiah answered, "I saw all Israel scattered on the hills like sheep without a shepherd, and the Lord said, 'These people have no master. Let each one go home in peace.'"

[18] The king of Israel said to Jehoshaphat, "Didn't I tell you that he never prophesies anything good about me, but only bad?"

[19] Micaiah continued, "Therefore hear the word of the Lord: I saw the Lord sitting on his throne with all the multitudes of heaven standing around him on his right and on his left. [20] And the Lord said, 'Who will entice Ahab into attacking Ramoth Gilead and going to his death there?'

"One suggested this, and another that. [21] Finally, a spirit came forward, stood before the Lord and said, 'I will entice him.'

[22] "'By what means?' the Lord asked.

"'I will go out and be a deceiving spirit in the mouths of all his prophets,' he said.

"'You will succeed in enticing him,' said the Lord. 'Go and do it.'

[23] "So now the Lord has put a deceiving spirit in the mouths of all these prophets of yours. The Lord has decreed disaster for you."

[24] Then Zedekiah son of Kenaanah went up and slapped Micaiah in the face. "Which way did the spirit from[a] the Lord go when he went from me to speak to you?" he asked.

[25] Micaiah replied, "You will find out on the day you go to hide in an inner room."

[26] The king of Israel then ordered, "Take Micaiah and send him back to Amon the ruler of the city and to Joash the king's son [27] and say, 'This is what the king says: Put

---

[a] 24 Or Spirit of

INSTANT ACCESS

Who is a real friend? Someone who tells you what you want to hear? Or someone who tells you the truth? King Ahab didn't want to hear the truth, so he locked out a prophet of God and invited some prophets of Baal to speak. When he did finally hear what God's prophet had to say, Ahab learned he was going to die. If only Ahab had listened to God's prophet earlier, he might have had a very different end. God made sure that Ahab heard the truth. But even when Ahab heard, he refused to believe. Value friends who tell you the truth even when it isn't pleasant. Act on what they say, and you may avoid tragedy in your life.

{1 Kings 22}

but you wear your royal robes." So the king of Israel disguised himself and went into battle.

31 Now the king of Aram had ordered his thirty-two chariot commanders, "Do not fight with anyone, small or great, except the king of Israel." 32 When the chariot commanders saw Jehoshaphat, they thought, "Surely this is the king of Israel." So they turned to attack him, but when Jehoshaphat cried out, 33 the chariot commanders saw that he was not the king of Israel and stopped pursuing him.

34 But someone drew his bow at random and hit the king of Israel between the sections of his armor. The king told his chariot driver, "Wheel around and get me out of the fighting. I've been wounded." 35 All day long the battle raged, and the king was propped up in his chariot facing the Arameans. The blood from his wound ran onto the floor of the chariot, and that evening he died. 36 As the sun was setting, a cry spread through the army: "Every man to his town. Every man to his land!"

37 So the king died and was brought to Samaria, and they buried him there. 38 They washed the chariot at a pool in Samaria (where the prostitutes bathed),[a] and the dogs licked up his blood, as the word of the LORD had declared.

39 As for the other events of Ahab's reign, including all he did, the palace he built and adorned with ivory, and the cities he fortified, are they not written in the book of the annals of the kings of Israel? 40 Ahab rested with his ancestors. And Ahaziah his son succeeded him as king.

Jehoshaphat King of Judah

41 Jehoshaphat son of Asa became king of Judah in the fourth year of Ahab king of Israel. 42 Jehoshaphat was thirty-five years old when he became king, and he reigned in Jerusalem twenty-five years. His mother's name was Azubah daughter of Shilhi. 43 In everything he followed the ways of his father Asa and did not stray from them; he did what was right in the

this fellow in prison and give him nothing but bread and water until I return safely.' "

28 Micaiah declared, "If you ever return safely, the LORD has not spoken through me." Then he added, "Mark my words, all you people!"

Ahab Killed at Ramoth Gilead

29 So the king of Israel and Jehoshaphat king of Judah went up to Ramoth Gilead. 30 The king of Israel said to Jehoshaphat, "I will enter the battle in disguise,

---

[a] 38 Or Samaria and cleaned the weapons

eyes of the LORD. The high places, however, were not removed, and the people continued to offer sacrifices and burn incense there.[a] 44 Jehoshaphat was also at peace with the king of Israel.

45 As for the other events of Jehoshaphat's reign, the things he achieved and his military exploits, are they not written in the book of the annals of the kings of Judah? 46 He rid the land of the rest of the male shrine prostitutes who remained there even after the reign of his father Asa. 47 There was then no king in Edom; a provincial governor ruled.

48 Now Jehoshaphat built a fleet of trading ships[b] to go to Ophir for gold, but they never set sail—they were wrecked at Ezion Geber. 49 At that time Ahaziah son of Ahab said to Jehoshaphat, "Let my men sail with yours," but Jehoshaphat refused.

50 Then Jehoshaphat rested with his ancestors and was buried with them in the city of David his father. And Jehoram his son succeeded him as king.

Ahaziah King of Israel

51 Ahaziah son of Ahab became king of Israel in Samaria in the seventeenth year of Jehoshaphat king of Judah, and he reigned over Israel two years. 52 He did evil in the eyes of the LORD, because he followed the ways of his father and mother and of Jeroboam son of Nebat, who caused Israel to sin. 53 He served and worshiped Baal and aroused the anger of the LORD, the God of Israel, just as his father had done.

---

a 43 In Hebrew texts this sentence (22:43b) is numbered 22:44, and 22:44-53 is numbered 22:45-54.   b 48 Hebrew of ships of Tarshish

2 KINGS

Warnings?

You don't want to hear them? Nothing will happen to you? Actually, most people think this way when they're determined to do something they know is dangerous or wrong.

The book of 2 Kings is full of stories telling how God warned his people and how they refused to listen. Even when the northern Israelite kingdom was taken into captivity by the Assyrians in 722 B.C., the southern kingdom wouldn't change its ways. Some people think the stories about these kings are boring. But what you can learn from them might save your life.

>>**WOMAN'S ONLY SON SAVED!**
   Miracle report in 2 Kings 4:1–37

>>**RELIGIOUS LEADERS EXECUTED**
   Pagan priests killed. See 2 Kings 10:18–36

>>**GODLY KING'S PRAYER SAVES JUDAH**
   Prayer recorded in 2 Kings 18:17 — 19:20

>>**JOSIAH LEADS JUDAH CLEAN UP**
   For a full report, see 2 Kings 23

《preview

For all its 108 years the northern kingdom, Israel, has not one good king.

The southern kingdom, Judah, is led by godly kings for 234 of its 344 years.

In the end the people of Judah turn from God, and Jerusalem is destroyed in 586 B.C. The survivors are deported to Babylon.

During these years the city of Rome is founded. The Greek poet Hesiod writes his *Theogony*. The first recorded Olympic Games are celebrated. Spoked wheels and horseshoes are developed in Europe.

The LORD's Judgment on Ahaziah

1 After Ahab's death, Moab rebelled against Israel. ²Now Ahaziah had fallen through the lattice of his upper room in Samaria and injured himself. So he sent messengers, saying to them, "Go and consult Baal-Zebub, the god of Ekron, to see if I will recover from this injury."

³But the angel of the LORD said to Elijah the Tishbite, "Go up and meet the messengers of the king of Samaria and ask them, 'Is it because there is no God in Israel that you are going off to consult Baal-Zebub, the god of Ekron?' ⁴Therefore this is what the LORD says: 'You will not leave the bed you are lying on. You will certainly die!' " So Elijah went.

⁵When the messengers returned to the king, he asked them, "Why have you come back?"

⁶"A man came to meet us," they replied. "And he said to us, 'Go back to the king who sent you and tell him, "This is what the LORD says: Is it because there is no God in Israel that you are sending messengers to consult Baal-Zebub, the god of Ekron? Therefore you will not leave the bed you are lying on. You will certainly die!" ' "

⁷The king asked them, "What kind of man was it who came to meet you and told you this?"

⁸They replied, "He had a garment of hair[a] and had a leather belt around his waist."

The king said, "That was Elijah the Tishbite."

⁹Then he sent to Elijah a captain with his company of fifty men. The captain went up to Elijah, who was sitting on the top of a hill, and said to him, "Man of God, the king says, 'Come down!' "

¹⁰Elijah answered the captain, "If I am a man of God, may fire come down from heaven and consume you and your fifty men!" Then fire fell from heaven and consumed the captain and his men.

¹¹At this the king sent to Elijah another captain with his fifty men. The captain

> ## » INSTANT ACCESS
>
> Do you have a parent who gets upset over the clothes you wear or your hairstyle? Maybe both you and your parent can get some help from this passage. As soon as the king's messengers described the clothes Elijah wore, Ahaziah knew who he was. In the same way, teens tell each other who they are by their clothes and hairstyles. The trouble is, you might feel like your parent doesn't know the trends. So if they object to what you want to wear, don't get upset. Talk it over with them. Explain that the clothes you wear identify you as one of the good guys.
>
> {2 Kings 1:6–8}

said to him, "Man of God, this is what the king says, 'Come down at once!' "

¹²"If I am a man of God," Elijah replied, "may fire come down from heaven and consume you and your fifty men!" Then the fire of God fell from heaven and consumed him and his fifty men.

¹³So the king sent a third captain with his fifty men. This third captain went up and fell on his knees before Elijah. "Man of God," he begged, "please have respect for my life and the lives of these fifty men, your servants! ¹⁴See, fire has fallen from heaven and consumed the first two cap-

---

[a] 8 Or *He was a hairy man*

tains and all their men. But now have respect for my life!"

[15] The angel of the LORD said to Elijah, "Go down with him; do not be afraid of him." So Elijah got up and went down with him to the king.

[16] He told the king, "This is what the LORD says: Is it because there is no God in Israel for you to consult that you have sent messengers to consult Baal-Zebub, the god of Ekron? Because you have done this, you will never leave the bed you are lying on. You will certainly die!" [17] So he died, according to the word of the LORD that Elijah had spoken.

Because Ahaziah had no son, Joram[a] succeeded him as king in the second year of Jehoram son of Jehoshaphat king of Judah. [18] As for all the other events of Ahaziah's reign, and what he did, are they not written in the book of the annals of the kings of Israel?

Elijah Taken Up to Heaven

2 When the LORD was about to take Elijah up to heaven in a whirlwind, Elijah and Elisha were on their way from Gilgal. [2] Elijah said to Elisha, "Stay here; the LORD has sent me to Bethel."

But Elisha said, "As surely as the LORD lives and as you live, I will not leave you." So they went down to Bethel.

[3] The company of the prophets at Bethel came out to Elisha and asked, "Do you know that the LORD is going to take your master from you today?"

"Yes, I know," Elisha replied, "so be quiet."

[4] Then Elijah said to him, "Stay here, Elisha; the LORD has sent me to Jericho."

And he replied, "As surely as the LORD lives and as you live, I will not leave you." So they went to Jericho.

[5] The company of the prophets at Jericho went up to Elisha and asked him, "Do you know that the LORD is going to take your master from you today?"

"Yes, I know," he replied, "so be quiet."

[6] Then Elijah said to him, "Stay here; the LORD has sent me to the Jordan."

And he replied, "As surely as the LORD

lives and as you live, I will not leave you." So the two of them walked on.

[7] Fifty men from the company of the prophets went and stood at a distance, facing the place where Elijah and Elisha had stopped at the Jordan. [8] Elijah took his cloak, rolled it up and struck the water with it. The water divided to the right and to the left, and the two of them crossed over on dry ground.

[9] When they had crossed, Elijah said to Elisha, "Tell me, what can I do for you before I am taken from you?"

"Let me inherit a double portion of your spirit," Elisha replied.

[10] "You have asked a difficult thing," Elijah said, "yet if you see me when I am taken from you, it will be yours—otherwise, it will not."

[11] As they were walking along and talking together, suddenly a chariot of fire and horses of fire appeared and separated the two of them, and Elijah went up to heaven in a whirlwind. [12] Elisha saw this and cried out, "My father! My father! The chariots and horsemen of Israel!" And Elisha saw him no more. Then he took hold of his garment and tore it in two.

[13] Elisha then picked up Elijah's cloak

2 Kings 2

Q: Who asked for a double portion of Elijah's spirit?

BONUS: What did that request mean?

Answers on next page

---

[a] 17 Hebrew *Jehoram*, a variant of *Joram*

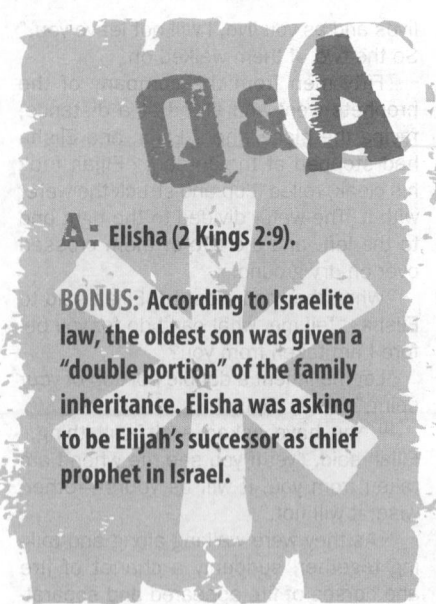

A: Elisha (2 Kings 2:9).

BONUS: According to Israelite law, the oldest son was given a "double portion" of the family inheritance. Elisha was asking to be Elijah's successor as chief prophet in Israel.

that had fallen from him and went back and stood on the bank of the Jordan. ¹⁴He took the cloak that had fallen from Elijah and struck the water with it. "Where now is the LORD, the God of Elijah?" he asked. When he struck the water, it divided to the right and to the left, and he crossed over.

¹⁵The company of the prophets from Jericho, who were watching, said, "The spirit of Elijah is resting on Elisha." And they went to meet him and bowed to the ground before him. ¹⁶"Look," they said, "we your servants have fifty able men. Let them go and look for your master. Perhaps the Spirit of the LORD has picked him up and set him down on some mountain or in some valley."

"No," Elisha replied, "do not send them."

¹⁷But they persisted until he was too embarrassed to refuse. So he said, "Send them." And they sent fifty men, who searched for three days but did not find him. ¹⁸When they returned to Elisha, who was staying in Jericho, he said to them, "Didn't I tell you not to go?"

Healing of the Water

¹⁹The people of the city said to Elisha, "Look, our lord, this town is well situated, as you can see, but the water is bad and the land is unproductive."

²⁰"Bring me a new bowl," he said, "and put salt in it." So they brought it to him.

²¹Then he went out to the spring and threw the salt into it, saying, "This is what the LORD says: 'I have healed this water. Never again will it cause death or make the land unproductive.'" ²²And the water has remained pure to this day, according to the word Elisha had spoken.

Elisha Is Jeered

²³From there Elisha went up to Bethel. As he was walking along the road, some boys came out of the town and jeered at him. "Get out of here, baldy!" they said. "Get out of here, baldy!" ²⁴He turned around, looked at them and called down a curse on them in the name of the LORD. Then two bears came out of the woods and mauled forty-two of the boys. ²⁵And he went on to Mount Carmel and from there returned to Samaria.

Moab Revolts

3 Joram*ᵃ* son of Ahab became king of Israel in Samaria in the eighteenth year of Jehoshaphat king of Judah, and he reigned twelve years. ²He did evil in the eyes of the LORD, but not as his father and mother had done. He got rid of the sacred stone of Baal that his father had made. ³Nevertheless he clung to the sins of Jeroboam son of Nebat, which he had caused Israel to commit; he did not turn away from them.

⁴Now Mesha king of Moab raised sheep, and he had to pay the king of Israel a tribute of a hundred thousand lambs and the wool of a hundred thousand rams. ⁵But after Ahab died, the king of Moab rebelled against the king of Israel. ⁶So at that time King Joram set out from Samaria and mobilized all Israel. ⁷He also sent this message to Jehoshaphat king of Judah: "The king of Moab has re-

---

ᵃ 1 Hebrew Jehoram, a variant of Joram; also in verse 6

belled against me. Will you go with me to fight against Moab?"

"I will go with you," he replied. "I am as you are, my people as your people, my horses as your horses."

8 "By what route shall we attack?" he asked.

"Through the Desert of Edom," he answered.

9 So the king of Israel set out with the king of Judah and the king of Edom. After a roundabout march of seven days, the army had no more water for themselves or for the animals with them.

10 "What!" exclaimed the king of Israel. "Has the LORD called us three kings together only to deliver us into the hands of Moab?"

11 But Jehoshaphat asked, "Is there no prophet of the LORD here, through whom we may inquire of the LORD?"

An officer of the king of Israel answered, "Elisha son of Shaphat is here. He used to pour water on the hands of Elijah.ᵃ"

12 Jehoshaphat said, "The word of the LORD is with him." So the king of Israel and Jehoshaphat and the king of Edom went down to him.

13 Elisha said to the king of Israel, "Why do you want to involve me? Go to the prophets of your father and the prophets of your mother."

"No," the king of Israel answered, "because it was the LORD who called us three kings together to deliver us into the hands of Moab."

14 Elisha said, "As surely as the LORD Almighty lives, whom I serve, if I did not have respect for the presence of Jehoshaphat king of Judah, I would not pay any attention to you. 15 But now bring me a harpist."

While the harpist was playing, the hand of the LORD came on Elisha 16 and he said, "This is what the LORD says: I will fill this valley with pools of water. 17 For this is what the LORD says: You will see neither wind nor rain, yet this valley will be filled with water, and you, your cattle and your other animals will drink. 18 This is an easy

thing in the eyes of the LORD; he will also deliver Moab into your hands. 19 You will overthrow every fortified city and every major town. You will cut down every good tree, stop up all the springs, and ruin every good field with stones."

20 The next morning, about the time for offering the sacrifice, there it was—water flowing from the direction of Edom! And the land was filled with water.

21 Now all the Moabites had heard that the kings had come to fight against them; so every man, young and old, who could bear arms was called up and stationed on the border. 22 When they got up early in the morning, the sun was shining on the water. To the Moabites across the way, the water looked red—like blood. 23 "That's blood!" they said. "Those kings must have fought and slaughtered each other. Now to the plunder, Moab!"

24 But when the Moabites came to the camp of Israel, the Israelites rose up and fought them until they fled. And the Israelites invaded the land and slaughtered the Moabites. 25 They destroyed the towns, and each man threw a stone on every good field until it was covered. They stopped up all the springs and cut down every good tree. Only Kir Hareseth was left with its stones in place, but men armed with slings surrounded it and attacked it.

26 When the king of Moab saw that the battle had gone against him, he took with him seven hundred swordsmen to break through to the king of Edom, but they failed. 27 Then he took his firstborn son, who was to succeed him as king, and offered him as a sacrifice on the city wall. The fury against Israel was great; they withdrew and returned to their own land.

The Widow's Olive Oil

4 The wife of a man from the company of the prophets cried out to Elisha, "Your servant my husband is dead, and you know that he revered the LORD. But now his creditor is coming to take my two boys as his slaves."

2 Elisha replied to her, "How can I help

ᵃ 11 That is, he was Elijah's personal servant.

you? Tell me, what do you have in your house?"

"Your servant has nothing there at all," she said, "except a small jar of olive oil."

³Elisha said, "Go around and ask all your neighbors for empty jars. Don't ask for just a few. ⁴Then go inside and shut the door behind you and your sons. Pour oil into all the jars, and as each is filled, put it to one side."

⁵She left him and shut the door behind her and her sons. They brought the jars to her and she kept pouring. ⁶When all the jars were full, she said to her son, "Bring me another one."

But he replied, "There is not a jar left." Then the oil stopped flowing.

⁷She went and told the man of God, and he said, "Go, sell the oil and pay your debts. You and your sons can live on what is left."

The Shunammite's Son Restored to Life

⁸One day Elisha went to Shunem. And a well-to-do woman was there, who urged him to stay for a meal. So whenever he came by, he stopped there to eat. ⁹She said to her husband, "I know that this man who often comes our way is a holy man of God. ¹⁰Let's make a small room on the roof and put in it a bed and a table, a chair and a lamp for him. Then he can stay there whenever he comes to us."

¹¹One day when Elisha came, he went up to his room and lay down there. ¹²He said to his servant Gehazi, "Call the Shunammite." So he called her, and she stood before him. ¹³Elisha said to him, "Tell her, 'You have gone to all this trouble for us. Now what can be done for you? Can we speak on your behalf to the king or the commander of the army?'"

She replied, "I have a home among my own people."

¹⁴"What can be done for her?" Elisha asked.

Gehazi said, "She has no son, and her husband is old."

¹⁵Then Elisha said, "Call her." So he called her, and she stood in the doorway. ¹⁶"About this time next year," Elisha said, "you will hold a son in your arms."

"No, my lord!" she objected. "Please, man of God, don't mislead your servant!"

¹⁷But the woman became pregnant, and the next year about that same time she gave birth to a son, just as Elisha had told her.

¹⁸The child grew, and one day he went out to his father, who was with the reapers. ¹⁹He said to his father, "My head! My head!"

His father told a servant, "Carry him to his mother." ²⁰After the servant had lifted him up and carried him to his mother, the boy sat on her lap until noon, and then he died. ²¹She went up and laid him on the bed of the man of God, then shut the door and went out.

²²She called her husband and said, "Please send me one of the servants and a donkey so I can go to the man of God quickly and return."

²³"Why go to him today?" he asked. "It's not the New Moon or the Sabbath."

"That's all right," she said.

²⁴She saddled the donkey and said to her servant, "Lead on; don't slow down for me unless I tell you." ²⁵So she set out and came to the man of God at Mount Carmel.

When he saw her in the distance, the man of God said to his servant Gehazi, "Look! There's the Shunammite! ²⁶Run to meet her and ask her, 'Are you all right? Is your husband all right? Is your child all right?'"

"Everything is all right," she said.

²⁷When she reached the man of God at the mountain, she took hold of his feet. Gehazi came over to push her away, but the man of God said, "Leave her alone! She is in bitter distress, but the Lᴏʀᴅ has hidden it from me and has not told me why."

²⁸"Did I ask you for a son, my lord?" she said. "Didn't I tell you, 'Don't raise my hopes'?"

²⁹Elisha said to Gehazi, "Tuck your cloak into your belt, take my staff in your hand and run. Don't greet anyone you meet, and if anyone greets you, do not answer. Lay my staff on the boy's face."

³⁰But the child's mother said, "As surely as the Lᴏʀᴅ lives and as you live, I will

> A girl I know told a huge secret to someone she thought was her friend. Spreading this girl's story became her "friend's" mission. After all this, I'm worried about telling my friends things. How can I know if I can trust my friends?   >> Gabriella

Dear Jordan

Dear Gabriella,

Ben Franklin said, "Three can keep a secret if two of them are dead." It sounds funny, but there's lots of truth in it. I mention that because if something is that damaging, perhaps telling a friend isn't the best idea. It's fun to share some things with friends, however.

The prophet Elisha was friends with a woman in Shunem. When her son died, she went to see Elisha. His servant asked her what was wrong. "Everything is all right," she replied (2 Kings 4:26). But when she got to Elisha, she told him that her son had died. She believed that her friend could help her and spoke only to him about her situation. She showed wisdom confiding in the person she thought could help her with her great trouble.

Like this woman, choose who you share with carefully when you have something important to share. Galatians 6:2 says, "Carry each other's burdens." Sometimes it's nice to have someone to talk to. If you keep your friends' trust, perhaps they will see you are someone to be trusted and will try to do the same for you.

Jordan

not leave you." So he got up and followed her.

³¹Gehazi went on ahead and laid the staff on the boy's face, but there was no sound or response. So Gehazi went back to meet Elisha and told him, "The boy has not awakened."

³²When Elisha reached the house, there was the boy lying dead on his couch. ³³He went in, shut the door on the two of them and prayed to the LORD. ³⁴Then he got on the bed and lay on the boy, mouth to mouth, eyes to eyes, hands to hands. As he stretched himself out on him, the boy's body grew warm. ³⁵Elisha turned away and walked back and forth in the room and then got on the bed and stretched out on him once more. The boy sneezed seven times and opened his eyes.

³⁶Elisha summoned Gehazi and said, "Call the Shunammite." And he did. When she came, he said, "Take your son." ³⁷She came in, fell at his feet and bowed to the ground. Then she took her son and went out.

Death in the Pot

³⁸Elisha returned to Gilgal and there was a famine in that region. While the company of the prophets was meeting with him, he said to his servant, "Put on the large pot and cook some stew for these prophets."

³⁹One of them went out into the fields to gather herbs and found a wild vine and picked as many of its gourds as his garment could hold. When he returned, he cut them up into the pot of stew, though no one knew what they were. ⁴⁰The stew was poured out for the men, but as they began to eat it, they cried out, "Man of God, there is death in the pot!" And they could not eat it.

⁴¹Elisha said, "Get some flour." He put it into the pot and said, "Serve it to the people to eat." And there was nothing harmful in the pot.

Feeding of a Hundred

⁴²A man came from Baal Shalishah, bringing the man of God twenty loaves of barley bread baked from the first ripe grain, along with some heads of new grain. "Give it to the people to eat," Elisha said.

⁴³"How can I set this before a hundred men?" his servant asked.

But Elisha answered, "Give it to the people to eat. For this is what the LORD says: 'They will eat and have some left over.'" ⁴⁴Then he set it before them, and they ate and had some left over, according to the word of the LORD.

Naaman Healed of Leprosy

5 Now Naaman was commander of the army of the king of Aram. He was a great man in the sight of his master and highly regarded, because through him the LORD had given victory to Aram. He was a valiant soldier, but he had leprosy.ᵃ

²Now bands of raiders from Aram had gone out and had taken captive a young girl from Israel, and she served Naaman's wife. ³She said to her mistress, "If only my master would see the prophet who is in Samaria! He would cure him of his leprosy."

⁴Naaman went to his master and told him what the girl from Israel had said. ⁵"By all means, go," the king of Aram replied. "I will send a letter to the king of Israel." So Naaman left, taking with him ten talentsᵇ of silver, six thousand shekelsᶜ of gold and ten sets of clothing. ⁶The letter that he took to the king of Israel read: "With this letter I am sending my servant Naaman to you so that you may cure him of his leprosy."

⁷As soon as the king of Israel read the letter, he tore his robes and said, "Am I God? Can I kill and bring back to life? Why does this fellow send someone to me to be cured of his leprosy? See how he is trying to pick a quarrel with me!"

⁸When Elisha the man of God heard that the king of Israel had torn his robes, he sent him this message: "Why have you torn your robes? Have the man come to me and he will know that there is a prophet in Israel." ⁹So Naaman went with his horses and chariots and stopped at the door of

---

ᵃ 1 The Hebrew for *leprosy* was used for various diseases affecting the skin; also in verses 3, 6, 7, 11 and 27.
ᵇ 5 That is, about 750 pounds or about 340 kilograms   ᶜ 5 That is, about 150 pounds or about 69 kilograms

>> INSTANT ACCESS

Take a look at Gehazi in this Bible story. He was upset when his boss, Elisha, wouldn't take the wealth offered him for healing Naaman. So Gehazi ran after Naaman and begged for 150 pounds of silver and two suits of clothing. When Gehazi returned to Elisha, he was punished with leprosy for his lie. Suddenly Gehazi learned there are more important things in life than possessions. Things like health. Things like self-respect and the respect of others. Don't be a Gehazi. Don't buy into the notion that possessions are the most important things in life.

{2 Kings 5}

Elisha's house. ¹⁰ Elisha sent a messenger to say to him, "Go, wash yourself seven times in the Jordan, and your flesh will be restored and you will be cleansed."

¹¹ But Naaman went away angry and said, "I thought that he would surely come out to me and stand and call on the name of the LORD his God, wave his hand over the spot and cure me of my leprosy. ¹² Are not Abana and Pharpar, the rivers of Damascus, better than all the waters of Israel? Couldn't I wash in them and be cleansed?" So he turned and went off in a rage.

¹³ Naaman's servants went to him and said, "My father, if the prophet had told you to do some great thing, would

you not have done it? How much more, then, when he tells you, 'Wash and be cleansed'!" ¹⁴ So he went down and dipped himself in the Jordan seven times, as the man of God had told him, and his flesh was restored and became clean like that of a young boy.

¹⁵ Then Naaman and all his attendants went back to the man of God. He stood before him and said, "Now I know that there is no God in all the world except in Israel. So please accept a gift from your servant."

¹⁶ The prophet answered, "As surely as the LORD lives, whom I serve, I will not accept a thing." And even though Naaman urged him, he refused.

¹⁷ "If you will not," said Naaman, "please let me, your servant, be given as much earth as a pair of mules can carry, for your servant will never again make burnt offerings and sacrifices to any other god but the LORD. ¹⁸ But may the LORD forgive your servant for this one thing: When my master enters the temple of Rimmon to bow down and he is leaning on my arm and I have to bow there also — when I bow down in the temple of Rimmon, may the LORD forgive your servant for this."

¹⁹ "Go in peace," Elisha said.

After Naaman had traveled some distance, ²⁰ Gehazi, the servant of Elisha the man of God, said to himself, "My master was too easy on Naaman, this Aramean, by not accepting from him what he brought. As surely as the LORD lives, I will run after him and get something from him."

²¹ So Gehazi hurried after Naaman. When Naaman saw him running toward him, he got down from the chariot to meet him. "Is everything all right?" he asked.

²² "Everything is all right," Gehazi answered. "My master sent me to say, 'Two young men from the company of the prophets have just come to me from the hill country of Ephraim. Please give them a talent[a] of silver and two sets of clothing.'"

²³ "By all means, take two talents," said Naaman. He urged Gehazi to accept them, and then tied up the two talents of silver in two bags, with two sets

---

[a] 22 That is, about 75 pounds or about 34 kilograms

of clothing. He gave them to two of his servants, and they carried them ahead of Gehazi. 24 When Gehazi came to the hill, he took the things from the servants and put them away in the house. He sent the men away and they left.

25 When he went in and stood before his master, Elisha asked him, "Where have you been, Gehazi?"

"Your servant didn't go anywhere," Gehazi answered.

26 But Elisha said to him, "Was not my spirit with you when the man got down from his chariot to meet you? Is this the time to take money or to accept clothes—or olive groves and vineyards, or flocks and herds, or male and female slaves? 27 Naaman's leprosy will cling to you and to your descendants forever." Then Gehazi went from Elisha's presence and his skin was leprous—it had become as white as snow.

An Axhead Floats

6 The company of the prophets said to Elisha, "Look, the place where we meet with you is too small for us. 2 Let us go to the Jordan, where each of us can get a pole; and let us build a place there for us to meet."

And he said, "Go."

3 Then one of them said, "Won't you please come with your servants?"

"I will," Elisha replied. 4 And he went with them.

They went to the Jordan and began to cut down trees. 5 As one of them was cutting down a tree, the iron axhead fell into the water. "Oh no, my lord!" he cried out. "It was borrowed!"

6 The man of God asked, "Where did it fall?" When he showed him the place, Elisha cut a stick and threw it there, and made the iron float. 7 "Lift it out," he said. Then the man reached out his hand and took it.

Elisha Traps Blinded Arameans

8 Now the king of Aram was at war with Israel. After conferring with his officers, he said, "I will set up my camp in such and such a place."

9 The man of God sent word to the king of Israel: "Beware of passing that place, because the Arameans are going down there." 10 So the king of Israel checked on the place indicated by the man of God. Time and again Elisha warned the king, so that he was on his guard in such places.

11 This enraged the king of Aram. He summoned his officers and demanded of them, "Tell me! Which of us is on the side of the king of Israel?"

12 "None of us, my lord the king," said one of his officers, "but Elisha, the prophet who is in Israel, tells the king of Israel the very words you speak in your bedroom."

13 "Go, find out where he is," the king ordered, "so I can send men and capture him." The report came back: "He is in Dothan." 14 Then he sent horses and chariots and a strong force there. They went by night and surrounded the city.

15 When the servant of the man of God got up and went out early the next morning, an army with horses and chariots had surrounded the city. "Oh no, my lord! What shall we do?" the servant asked.

16 "Don't be afraid," the prophet answered. "Those who are with us are more than those who are with them."

17 And Elisha prayed, "Open his eyes, LORD, so that he may see." Then the LORD opened the servant's eyes, and he looked and saw the hills full of horses and chariots of fire all around Elisha.

18 As the enemy came down toward him, Elisha prayed to the LORD, "Strike this army with blindness." So he struck them with blindness, as Elisha had asked.

19 Elisha told them, "This is not the road and this is not the city. Follow me, and I will lead you to the man you are looking for." And he led them to Samaria.

20 After they entered the city, Elisha said, "LORD, open the eyes of these men so they can see." Then the LORD opened their eyes and they looked, and there they were, inside Samaria.

21 When the king of Israel saw them, he asked Elisha, "Shall I kill them, my father? Shall I kill them?"

22 "Do not kill them," he answered.

"Would you kill those you have captured with your own sword or bow? Set food and water before them so that they may eat and drink and then go back to their master." 23 So he prepared a great feast for them, and after they had finished eating and drinking, he sent them away, and they returned to their master. So the bands from Aram stopped raiding Israel's territory.

Famine in Besieged Samaria

24 Some time later, Ben-Hadad king of Aram mobilized his entire army and marched up and laid siege to Samaria. 25 There was a great famine in the city; the siege lasted so long that a donkey's head sold for eighty shekels[a] of silver, and a quarter of a cab[b] of seed pods[c] for five shekels.[d]

26 As the king of Israel was passing by on the wall, a woman cried to him, "Help me, my lord the king!"

27 The king replied, "If the LORD does not help you, where can I get help for you? From the threshing floor? From the winepress?" 28 Then he asked her, "What's the matter?"

She answered, "This woman said to me, 'Give up your son so we may eat him today, and tomorrow we'll eat my son.' 29 So we cooked my son and ate him. The next day I said to her, 'Give up your son so we may eat him,' but she had hidden him."

---

[a] 25 That is, about 2 pounds or about 920 grams   [b] 25 That is, probably about 1/4 pound or about 100 grams
[c] 25 Or of doves' dung   [d] 25 That is, about 2 ounces or about 58 grams

---

TO THE POINT

Angels Are Around

Elisha's servant couldn't see God's protecting army until God opened his eyes. Then he saw "horses and chariots of fire all around" (2 Kings 6:15–17), protecting Elisha from the enemy army. Do God's angels protect ordinary people like you and me, or just prophets? Here are some things the Bible says about angels:

+ Angels minister to Christians (Hebrews 1:14).

+ Angels protect people from their enemies (Psalm 91:11–14).

+ Angels guard children (Matthew 18:10) and churches (Revelation 2–3).

Pretty exciting, isn't it? Look around you. You may not see them with your eyes, but you can be sure they are there.

30When the king heard the woman's words, he tore his robes. As he went along the wall, the people looked, and they saw that, under his robes, he had sackcloth on his body. 31He said, "May God deal with me, be it ever so severely, if the head of Elisha son of Shaphat remains on his shoulders today!"

32Now Elisha was sitting in his house, and the elders were sitting with him. The king sent a messenger ahead, but before he arrived, Elisha said to the elders, "Don't you see how this murderer is sending someone to cut off my head? Look, when the messenger comes, shut the door and hold it shut against him. Is not the sound of his master's footsteps behind him?" 33While he was still talking to them, the messenger came down to him.

The king said, "This disaster is from the LORD. Why should I wait for the LORD any longer?"

7 Elisha replied, "Hear the word of the LORD. This is what the LORD says: About this time tomorrow, a seah*a* of the finest flour will sell for a shekel*b* and two seahs*c* of barley for a shekel at the gate of Samaria."

2The officer on whose arm the king was leaning said to the man of God, "Look, even if the LORD should open the floodgates of the heavens, could this happen?"

"You will see it with your own eyes," answered Elisha, "but you will not eat any of it!"

The Siege Lifted

3Now there were four men with leprosy*d* at the entrance of the city gate. They said to each other, "Why stay here until we die? 4If we say, 'We'll go into the city'—the famine is there, and we will die. And if we stay here, we will die. So let's go over to the camp of the Arameans and surrender. If they spare us, we live; if they kill us, then we die."

5At dusk they got up and went to the camp of the Arameans. When they reached the edge of the camp, no one was there, 6for the Lord had caused the Arameans to hear the sound of chariots and horses and a great army, so that they said to one another, "Look, the king of Israel has hired the Hittite and Egyptian kings to attack us!" 7So they got up and fled in the dusk and abandoned their tents and their horses and donkeys. They left the camp as it was and ran for their lives.

8The men who had leprosy reached the edge of the camp, entered one of the tents and ate and drank. Then they took silver, gold and clothes, and went off and hid them. They returned and entered another tent and took some things from it and hid them also.

9Then they said to each other, "What we're doing is not right. This is a day of good news and we are keeping it to ourselves. If we wait until daylight, punishment will overtake us. Let's go at once and report this to the royal palace."

10So they went and called out to the city gatekeepers and told them, "We went into the Aramean camp and no one was there—not a sound of anyone—only tethered horses and donkeys, and the tents left just as they were." 11The gatekeepers shouted the news, and it was reported within the palace.

12The king got up in the night and said to his officers, "I will tell you what the Arameans have done to us. They know we are starving; so they have left the camp to hide in the countryside, thinking, 'They will surely come out, and then we will take them alive and get into the city.'"

13One of his officers answered, "Have some men take five of the horses that are left in the city. Their plight will be like that of all the Israelites left here—yes, they will only be like all these Israelites who are doomed. So let us send them to find out what happened."

14So they selected two chariots with their horses, and the king sent them after the Aramean army. He commanded the drivers, "Go and find out what has happened." 15They followed them as far

---

a 1 That is, probably about 12 pounds or about 5.5 kilograms of flour; also in verses 16 and 18   *b* 1 That is, about 2/5 ounce or about 12 grams; also in verses 16 and 18   *c* 1 That is, probably about 20 pounds or about 9 kilograms of barley; also in verses 16 and 18   *d* 3 The Hebrew for *leprosy* was used for various diseases affecting the skin; also in verse 8.

as the Jordan, and they found the whole road strewn with the clothing and equipment the Arameans had thrown away in their headlong flight. So the messengers returned and reported to the king. [16]Then the people went out and plundered the camp of the Arameans. So a seah of the finest flour sold for a shekel, and two seahs of barley sold for a shekel, as the LORD had said.

[17]Now the king had put the officer on whose arm he leaned in charge of the gate, and the people trampled him in the gateway, and he died, just as the man of God had foretold when the king came down to his house. [18]It happened as the man of God had said to the king: "About this time tomorrow, a seah of the finest flour will sell for a shekel and two seahs of barley for a shekel at the gate of Samaria."

[19]The officer had said to the man of God, "Look, even if the LORD should open the floodgates of the heavens, could this happen?" The man of God had replied, "You will see it with your own eyes, but you will not eat any of it!" [20]And that is exactly what happened to him, for the people trampled him in the gateway, and he died.

The Shunammite's Land Restored

8 Now Elisha had said to the woman whose son he had restored to life, "Go away with your family and stay for a while wherever you can, because the LORD has decreed a famine in the land that will last seven years." [2]The woman proceeded to do as the man of God said. She and her family went away and stayed in the land of the Philistines seven years.

[3]At the end of the seven years she came back from the land of the Philistines and went to appeal to the king for her house and land. [4]The king was talking to Gehazi, the servant of the man of God, and had said, "Tell me about all the great things Elisha has done." [5]Just as Gehazi was telling the king how Elisha had restored the dead to life, the woman whose son Elisha had brought back to life came to appeal to the king for her house and land.

Gehazi said, "This is the woman, my lord the king, and this is her son whom Elisha restored to life." [6]The king asked the woman about it, and she told him.

Then he assigned an official to her case and said to him, "Give back everything that belonged to her, including all the income from her land from the day she left the country until now."

Hazael Murders Ben-Hadad

[7]Elisha went to Damascus, and Ben-Hadad king of Aram was ill. When the king was told, "The man of God has come all the way up here," [8]he said to Hazael,

"Take a gift with you and go to meet the man of God. Consult the LORD through him; ask him, 'Will I recover from this illness?'"

⁹Hazael went to meet Elisha, taking with him as a gift forty camel-loads of all the finest wares of Damascus. He went in and stood before him, and said, "Your son Ben-Hadad king of Aram has sent me to ask, 'Will I recover from this illness?'" ¹⁰Elisha answered, "Go and say to him, 'You will certainly recover.' Nevertheless,ᵃ the LORD has revealed to me that he will in fact die." ¹¹He stared at him with a fixed gaze until Hazael was embarrassed. Then the man of God began to weep.

¹²"Why is my lord weeping?" asked Hazael.

"Because I know the harm you will do to the Israelites," he answered. "You will set fire to their fortified places, kill their young men with the sword, dash their little children to the ground, and rip open their pregnant women." ¹³Hazael said, "How could your servant, a mere dog, accomplish such a feat?"

"The LORD has shown me that you will become king of Aram," answered Elisha.

¹⁴Then Hazael left Elisha and returned to his master. When Ben-Hadad asked, "What did Elisha say to you?" Hazael replied, "He told me that you would certainly recover." ¹⁵But the next day he took a thick cloth, soaked it in water and spread it over the king's face, so that he died. Then Hazael succeeded him as king.

Jehoram King of Judah

¹⁶In the fifth year of Joram son of Ahab king of Israel, when Jehoshaphat was king of Judah, Jehoram son of Jehoshaphat began his reign as king of Judah. ¹⁷He was thirty-two years old when he became king, and he reigned in Jerusalem eight years. ¹⁸He followed the ways of the kings of Israel, as the house of Ahab had done, for he married a daughter of Ahab. He did evil in the eyes of the LORD. ¹⁹Nevertheless, for the sake of his servant David, the LORD was not willing to destroy Ju-

dah. He had promised to maintain a lamp for David and his descendants forever.

²⁰In the time of Jehoram, Edom rebelled against Judah and set up its own king. ²¹So Jehoramᵇ went to Zair with all his chariots. The Edomites surrounded him and his chariot commanders, but he rose up and broke through by night; his army, however, fled back home. ²²To this day Edom has been in rebellion against Judah. Libnah revolted at the same time.

²³As for the other events of Jehoram's reign, and all he did, are they not written in the book of the annals of the kings of Judah? ²⁴Jehoram rested with his ancestors and was buried with them in the City of David. And Ahaziah his son succeeded him as king.

Ahaziah King of Judah

²⁵In the twelfth year of Joram son of Ahab king of Israel, Ahaziah son of Jehoram king of Judah began to reign. ²⁶Ahaziah was twenty-two years old when he became king, and he reigned in Jerusalem one year. His mother's name was Athaliah, a granddaughter of Omri king of Israel. ²⁷He followed the ways of the house of Ahab and did evil in the eyes of the LORD, as the house of Ahab had done, for he was related by marriage to Ahab's family.

²⁸Ahaziah went with Joram son of Ahab to war against Hazael king of Aram at Ramoth Gilead. The Arameans wounded Joram; ²⁹so King Joram returned to Jezreel to recover from the wounds the Arameans had inflicted on him at Ramothᶜ in his battle with Hazael king of Aram.

Then Ahaziah son of Jehoram king of Judah went down to Jezreel to see Joram son of Ahab, because he had been wounded.

Jehu Anointed King of Israel

9 The prophet Elisha summoned a man from the company of the prophets and said to him, "Tuck your cloak into your belt, take this flask of olive oil with you and go to Ramoth Gilead. ²When you get there, look for Jehu son of Jehosha-

---

ᵃ 10 The Hebrew may also be read Go and say, 'You will certainly not recover,' for.   ᵇ 21 Hebrew Joram, a variant of Jehoram; also in verses 23 and 24   ᶜ 29 Hebrew Ramah, a variant of Ramoth

phat, the son of Nimshi. Go to him, get him away from his companions and take him into an inner room. ³Then take the flask and pour the oil on his head and declare, 'This is what the LORD says: I anoint you king over Israel.' Then open the door and run; don't delay!"

⁴So the young prophet went to Ramoth Gilead. ⁵When he arrived, he found the army officers sitting together. "I have a message for you, commander," he said.

"For which of us?" asked Jehu.

"For you, commander," he replied.

⁶Jehu got up and went into the house. Then the prophet poured the oil on Jehu's head and declared, "This is what the LORD, the God of Israel, says: 'I anoint you king over the LORD's people Israel. ⁷You are to destroy the house of Ahab your master, and I will avenge the blood of my servants the prophets and the blood of all the LORD's servants shed by Jezebel. ⁸The whole house of Ahab will perish. I will cut off from Ahab every last male in Israel—slave or free.ᵃ ⁹I will make the house of Ahab like the house of Jeroboam son of Nebat and like the house of Baasha son of Ahijah. ¹⁰As for Jezebel, dogs will devour her on the plot of ground at Jezreel, and no one will bury her.'" Then he opened the door and ran.

¹¹When Jehu went out to his fellow officers, one of them asked him, "Is everything all right? Why did this maniac come to you?"

"You know the man and the sort of things he says," Jehu replied.

¹²"That's not true!" they said. "Tell us."

Jehu said, "Here is what he told me: 'This is what the LORD says: I anoint you king over Israel.'"

¹³They quickly took their cloaks and spread them under him on the bare steps. Then they blew the trumpet and shouted, "Jehu is king!"

Jehu Kills Joram and Ahaziah

¹⁴So Jehu son of Jehoshaphat, the son of Nimshi, conspired against Joram. (Now Joram and all Israel had been defending Ramoth Gilead against Hazael king of Aram, ¹⁵but King Joramᵇ had returned to Jezreel to recover from the wounds the Arameans had inflicted on him in the battle with Hazael king of Aram.) Jehu said, "If you desire to make me king, don't let anyone slip out of the city to go and tell the news in Jezreel." ¹⁶Then he got into his chariot and rode to Jezreel, because Joram was resting there and Ahaziah king of Judah had gone down to see him.

¹⁷When the lookout standing on the tower in Jezreel saw Jehu's troops approaching, he called out, "I see some troops coming."

"Get a horseman," Joram ordered. "Send him to meet them and ask, 'Do you come in peace?'"

¹⁸The horseman rode off to meet Jehu and said, "This is what the king says: 'Do you come in peace?'"

"What do you have to do with peace?" Jehu replied. "Fall in behind me."

The lookout reported, "The messenger has reached them, but he isn't coming back."

¹⁹So the king sent out a second horseman. When he came to them he said,

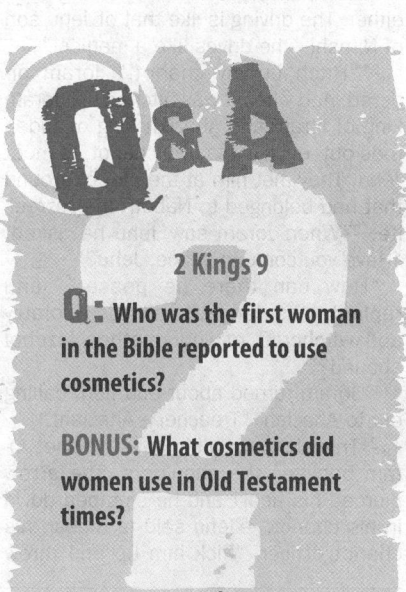

2 Kings 9

Q: Who was the first woman in the Bible reported to use cosmetics?

BONUS: What cosmetics did women use in Old Testament times?

Answers on next page

ᵃ 8 Or Israel—every ruler or leader   ᵇ 15 Hebrew Jehoram, a variant of Joram; also in verses 17 and 21-24

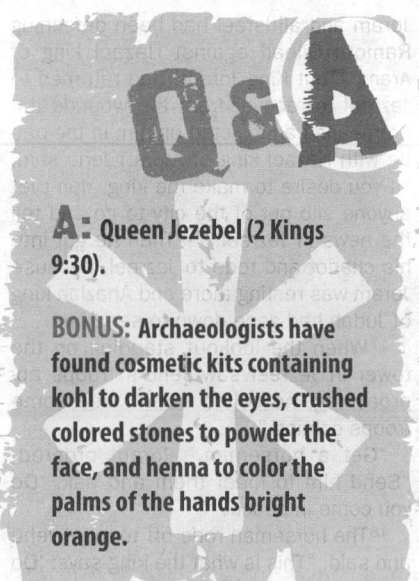

A: Queen Jezebel (2 Kings 9:30).

BONUS: Archaeologists have found cosmetic kits containing kohl to darken the eyes, crushed colored stones to powder the face, and henna to color the palms of the hands bright orange.

"This is what the king says: 'Do you come in peace?'"

Jehu replied, "What do you have to do with peace? Fall in behind me."

²⁰The lookout reported, "He has reached them, but he isn't coming back either. The driving is like that of Jehu son of Nimshi—he drives like a maniac."

²¹"Hitch up my chariot," Joram ordered. And when it was hitched up, Joram king of Israel and Ahaziah king of Judah rode out, each in his own chariot, to meet Jehu. They met him at the plot of ground that had belonged to Naboth the Jezreelite. ²²When Joram saw Jehu he asked, "Have you come in peace, Jehu?"

"How can there be peace," Jehu replied, "as long as all the idolatry and witchcraft of your mother Jezebel abound?"

²³Joram turned about and fled, calling out to Ahaziah, "Treachery, Ahaziah!"

²⁴Then Jehu drew his bow and shot Joram between the shoulders. The arrow pierced his heart and he slumped down in his chariot. ²⁵Jehu said to Bidkar, his chariot officer, "Pick him up and throw him on the field that belonged to Naboth the Jezreelite. Remember how you and I were riding together in chariots behind Ahab his father when the LORD spoke this prophecy against him: ²⁶'Yesterday I saw the blood of Naboth and the blood of his sons, declares the LORD, and I will surely make you pay for it on this plot of ground, declares the LORD.'ª Now then, pick him up and throw him on that plot, in accordance with the word of the LORD."

²⁷When Ahaziah king of Judah saw what had happened, he fled up the road to Beth Haggan.ᵇ Jehu chased him, shouting, "Kill him too!" They wounded him in his chariot on the way up to Gur near Ibleam, but he escaped to Megiddo and died there. ²⁸His servants took him by chariot to Jerusalem and buried him with his ancestors in his tomb in the City of David. ²⁹(In the eleventh year of Joram son of Ahab, Ahaziah had become king of Judah.)

Jezebel Killed

³⁰Then Jehu went to Jezreel. When Jezebel heard about it, she put on eye makeup, arranged her hair and looked out of a window. ³¹As Jehu entered the gate, she asked, "Have you come in peace, you Zimri, you murderer of your master?"ᶜ

³²He looked up at the window and called out, "Who is on my side? Who?" Two or three eunuchs looked down at him. ³³"Throw her down!" Jehu said. So they threw her down, and some of her blood spattered the wall and the horses as they trampled her underfoot.

³⁴Jehu went in and ate and drank. "Take care of that cursed woman," he said, "and bury her, for she was a king's daughter." ³⁵But when they went out to bury her, they found nothing except her skull, her feet and her hands. ³⁶They went back and told Jehu, who said, "This is the word of the LORD that he spoke through his servant Elijah the Tishbite: On the plot of ground at Jezreel dogs will devour Jezebel's flesh.ᵈ ³⁷Jezebel's body will be like dung on the ground in the plot at Jezreel, so that no one will be able to say, 'This is Jezebel.'"

ª 26 See 1 Kings 21:19.   ᵇ 27 Or fled by way of the garden house   ᶜ 31 Or "Was there peace for Zimri, who murdered his master?"   ᵈ 36 See 1 Kings 21:23.

Ahab's Family Killed

10 Now there were in Samaria seventy sons of the house of Ahab. So Jehu wrote letters and sent them to Samaria: to the officials of Jezreel,[a] to the elders and to the guardians of Ahab's children. He said, 2 "You have your master's sons with you and you have chariots and horses, a fortified city and weapons. Now as soon as this letter reaches you, 3 choose the best and most worthy of your master's sons and set him on his father's throne. Then fight for your master's house."

4 But they were terrified and said, "If two kings could not resist him, how can we?"

5 So the palace administrator, the city governor, the elders and the guardians sent this message to Jehu: "We are your servants and we will do anything you say. We will not appoint anyone as king; you do whatever you think best."

6 Then Jehu wrote them a second letter, saying, "If you are on my side and will obey me, take the heads of your master's sons and come to me in Jezreel by this time tomorrow."

Now the royal princes, seventy of them, were with the leading men of the city, who were rearing them. 7 When the letter arrived, these men took the princes and slaughtered all seventy of them. They put their heads in baskets and sent them to Jehu in Jezreel. 8 When the messenger arrived, he told Jehu, "They have brought the heads of the princes."

Then Jehu ordered, "Put them in two piles at the entrance of the city gate until morning."

9 The next morning Jehu went out. He stood before all the people and said, "You are innocent. It was I who conspired against my master and killed him, but who killed all these? 10 Know, then, that not a word the LORD has spoken against the house of Ahab will fail. The LORD has done what he announced through his servant Elijah." 11 So Jehu killed everyone in Jezreel who remained of the house of Ahab, as well as all his chief men, his close friends and his priests, leaving him no survivor.

12 Jehu then set out and went toward Samaria. At Beth Eked of the Shepherds, 13 he met some relatives of Ahaziah king of Judah and asked, "Who are you?"

They said, "We are relatives of Ahaziah, and we have come down to greet the families of the king and of the queen mother."

14 "Take them alive!" he ordered. So they took them alive and slaughtered them by the well of Beth Eked—forty-two of them. He left no survivor.

15 After he left there, he came upon Jehonadab son of Rekab, who was on his way to meet him. Jehu greeted him and

a 1 Hebrew; some Septuagint manuscripts and Vulgate *of the city*

PANORAMA

Warnings?

God warned his people, but they refused to listen. Even when Israel was taken captive by Assyria, Judah still wouldn't change its ways and return to God.

{2 KINGS}

said, "Are you in accord with me, as I am with you?"

"I am," Jehonadab answered.

"If so," said Jehu, "give me your hand." So he did, and Jehu helped him up into the chariot. ¹⁶Jehu said, "Come with me and see my zeal for the LORD." Then he had him ride along in his chariot.

¹⁷When Jehu came to Samaria, he killed all who were left there of Ahab's family; he destroyed them, according to the word of the LORD spoken to Elijah.

Servants of Baal Killed

¹⁸Then Jehu brought all the people together and said to them, "Ahab served Baal a little; Jehu will serve him much. ¹⁹Now summon all the prophets of Baal, all his servants and all his priests. See that no one is missing, because I am going to hold a great sacrifice for Baal. Anyone who fails to come will no longer live." But Jehu was acting deceptively in order to destroy the servants of Baal.

²⁰Jehu said, "Call an assembly in honor of Baal." So they proclaimed it. ²¹Then he sent word throughout Israel, and all the servants of Baal came; not one stayed away. They crowded into the temple of Baal until it was full from one end to the other. ²²And Jehu said to the keeper of the wardrobe, "Bring robes for all the servants of Baal." So he brought out robes for them.

²³Then Jehu and Jehonadab son of Rekab went into the temple of Baal. Jehu said to the servants of Baal, "Look around and see that no one who serves the LORD is here with you—only servants of Baal." ²⁴So they went in to make sacrifices and burnt offerings. Now Jehu had posted eighty men outside with this warning: "If one of you lets any of the men I am placing in your hands escape, it will be your life for his life."

²⁵As soon as Jehu had finished making the burnt offering, he ordered the guards and officers: "Go in and kill them; let no one escape." So they cut them down with the sword. The guards and officers threw the bodies out and then entered the inner shrine of the temple of Baal. ²⁶They brought the sacred stone out of the temple of Baal and burned it. ²⁷They demolished the sacred stone of Baal and tore down the temple of Baal, and people have used it for a latrine to this day.

²⁸So Jehu destroyed Baal worship in Israel. ²⁹However, he did not turn away from the sins of Jeroboam son of Nebat, which he had caused Israel to commit—the worship of the golden calves at Bethel and Dan.

³⁰The LORD said to Jehu, "Because you have done well in accomplishing what is right in my eyes and have done to the house of Ahab all I had in mind to do, your descendants will sit on the throne of Israel to the fourth generation." ³¹Yet Jehu was not careful to keep the law of the LORD, the God of Israel, with all his heart. He did not turn away from the sins of Jeroboam, which he had caused Israel to commit.

³²In those days the LORD began to reduce the size of Israel. Hazael overpowered the Israelites throughout their territory ³³east of the Jordan in all the land of Gilead (the region of Gad, Reuben and Manasseh), from Aroer by the Arnon Gorge through Gilead to Bashan.

³⁴As for the other events of Jehu's reign, all he did, and all his achievements, are they not written in the book of the annals of the kings of Israel?

³⁵Jehu rested with his ancestors and was buried in Samaria. And Jehoahaz his son succeeded him as king. ³⁶The time that Jehu reigned over Israel in Samaria was twenty-eight years.

Athaliah and Joash

11 When Athaliah the mother of Ahaziah saw that her son was dead, she proceeded to destroy the whole royal family. ²But Jehosheba, the daughter of King Jehoram[a] and sister of Ahaziah, took Joash son of Ahaziah and stole him away from among the royal princes, who were about to be murdered. She put him and his nurse in a bedroom to hide him from Athaliah; so he was not killed. ³He

---

ᵃ 2 Hebrew Joram, a variant of Jehoram

There are some things you just have to wait for. Like a license to drive. Like graduating from school and getting a good job. Marriage is another "wait" kind of thing. After all, it would be hard to have a home or raise kids on wages you'd earn flipping burgers at the local fast-food place. It was hard for the priest Jehoiada to wait for six long years during the rule of evil Queen Athaliah until he was able to reveal the hidden boy king, Joash. But Jehoiada had to wait. Waiting is always hard. But the outcome of this Bible story reminds you that waiting on God's timing in life really is best.

{2 Kings 11:1–12}

≫ INSTANT ACCESS

Gate, and a third at the gate behind the guard, who take turns guarding the temple— [7] and you who are in the other two companies that normally go off Sabbath duty are all to guard the temple for the king. [8] Station yourselves around the king, each of you with weapon in hand. Anyone who approaches your ranks[a] is to be put to death. Stay close to the king wherever he goes."

[9] The commanders of units of a hundred did just as Jehoiada the priest ordered. Each one took his men—those who were going on duty on the Sabbath and those who were going off duty—and came to Jehoiada the priest. [10] Then he gave the commanders the spears and shields that had belonged to King David and that were in the temple of the LORD. [11] The guards, each with weapon in hand, stationed themselves around the king—near the altar and the temple, from the south side to the north side of the temple.

[12] Jehoiada brought out the king's son and put the crown on him; he presented him with a copy of the covenant and proclaimed him king. They anointed him, and the people clapped their hands and shouted, "Long live the king!"

[13] When Athaliah heard the noise made by the guards and the people, she went to the people at the temple of the LORD. [14] She looked and there was the king, standing by the pillar, as the custom was. The officers and the trumpeters were beside the king, and all the people of the land were rejoicing and blowing trumpets. Then Athaliah tore her robes and called out, "Treason! Treason!"

[15] Jehoiada the priest ordered the commanders of units of a hundred, who were in charge of the troops: "Bring her out between the ranks[b] and put to the sword anyone who follows her." For the priest had said, "She must not be put to death in the temple of the LORD." [16] So they seized her as she reached the place where the horses enter the palace grounds, and there she was put to death.

[17] Jehoiada then made a covenant between the LORD and the king and people

remained hidden with his nurse at the temple of the LORD for six years while Athaliah ruled the land.

[4] In the seventh year Jehoiada sent for the commanders of units of a hundred, the Carites and the guards and had them brought to him at the temple of the LORD. He made a covenant with them and put them under oath at the temple of the LORD. Then he showed them the king's son. [5] He commanded them, saying, "This is what you are to do: You who are in the three companies that are going on duty on the Sabbath—a third of you guarding the royal palace, [6] a third at the Sur

---

[a] 8 Or approaches the precincts   [b] 15 Or out from the precincts

that they would be the LORD's people. He also made a covenant between the king and the people. [18] All the people of the land went to the temple of Baal and tore it down. They smashed the altars and idols to pieces and killed Mattan the priest of Baal in front of the altars.

Then Jehoiada the priest posted guards at the temple of the LORD. [19] He took with him the commanders of hundreds, the Carites, the guards and all the people of the land, and together they brought the king down from the temple of the LORD and went into the palace, entering by way of the gate of the guards. The king then took his place on the royal throne. [20] All the people of the land rejoiced, and the city was calm, because Athaliah had been slain with the sword at the palace.

[21] Joash[a] was seven years old when he began to reign.[b]

Joash Repairs the Temple

12[c] In the seventh year of Jehu, Joash[d] became king, and he reigned in Jerusalem forty years. His mother's name was Zibiah; she was from Beersheba. [2] Joash did what was right in the eyes of the LORD all the years Jehoiada the priest instructed him. [3] The high places, however, were not removed; the people continued to offer sacrifices and burn incense there.

[4] Joash said to the priests, "Collect all the money that is brought as sacred offerings to the temple of the LORD — the money collected in the census, the money received from personal vows and the money brought voluntarily to the temple. [5] Let every priest receive the money from one of the treasurers, then use it to repair whatever damage is found in the temple."

[6] But by the twenty-third year of King Joash the priests still had not repaired the temple. [7] Therefore King Joash summoned Jehoiada the priest and the other priests and asked them, "Why aren't you repairing the damage done to the temple? Take no more money from your trea-

surers, but hand it over for repairing the temple." [8] The priests agreed that they would not collect any more money from the people and that they would not repair the temple themselves.

[9] Jehoiada the priest took a chest and bored a hole in its lid. He placed it beside the altar, on the right side as one enters the temple of the LORD. The priests who guarded the entrance put into the chest all the money that was brought to the temple of the LORD. [10] Whenever they saw that there was a large amount of money in the chest, the royal secretary and the high priest came, counted the money that had been brought into the temple of the LORD and put it into bags. [11] When the amount had been determined, they gave the money to the men appointed to supervise the work on the temple. With it they paid those who worked on the temple of the LORD — the carpenters and builders, [12] the masons and stonecutters. They purchased timber and blocks of dressed stone for the repair of the temple of the LORD, and met all the other expenses of restoring the temple.

[13] The money brought into the temple was not spent for making silver basins, wick trimmers, sprinkling bowls, trumpets or any other articles of gold or silver for the temple of the LORD; [14] it was paid to the workers, who used it to repair the temple. [15] They did not require an accounting from those to whom they gave the money to pay the workers, because they acted with complete honesty. [16] The money from the guilt offerings and sin offerings[e] was not brought into the temple of the LORD; it belonged to the priests.

[17] About this time Hazael king of Aram went up and attacked Gath and captured it. Then he turned to attack Jerusalem. [18] But Joash king of Judah took all the sacred objects dedicated by his predecessors — Jehoshaphat, Jehoram and Ahaziah, the kings of Judah — and the gifts he himself had dedicated and all the gold found in the treasuries of the temple of the LORD and of the royal palace, and he

---

[a] 21 Hebrew *Jehoash*, a variant of *Joash*   [b] 21 In Hebrew texts this verse (11:21) is numbered 12:1.   [c] In Hebrew texts 12:1-21 is numbered 12:2-22.   [d] 1 Hebrew *Jehoash*, a variant of *Joash*; also in verses 2, 4, 6, 7 and 18
[e] 16 Or *purification offerings*

sent them to Hazael king of Aram, who then withdrew from Jerusalem.

¹⁹As for the other events of the reign of Joash, and all he did, are they not written in the book of the annals of the kings of Judah? ²⁰His officials conspired against him and assassinated him at Beth Millo, on the road down to Silla. ²¹The officials who murdered him were Jozabad son of Shimeath and Jehozabad son of Shomer. He died and was buried with his ancestors in the City of David. And Amaziah his son succeeded him as king.

Jehoahaz King of Israel

13 In the twenty-third year of Joash son of Ahaziah king of Judah, Jehoahaz son of Jehu became king of Israel in Samaria, and he reigned seventeen years. ²He did evil in the eyes of the Lord by following the sins of Jeroboam son of Nebat, which he had caused Israel to commit, and he did not turn away from them. ³So the Lord's anger burned against Israel, and for a long time he kept them under the power of Hazael king of Aram and Ben-Hadad his son.

⁴Then Jehoahaz sought the Lord's favor, and the Lord listened to him, for he saw how severely the king of Aram was oppressing Israel. ⁵The Lord provided a deliverer for Israel, and they escaped from the power of Aram. So the Israelites lived in their own homes as they had before. ⁶But they did not turn away from the sins of the house of Jeroboam, which he had caused Israel to commit; they continued in them. Also, the Asherah pole[a] remained standing in Samaria.

⁷Nothing had been left of the army of Jehoahaz except fifty horsemen, ten chariots and ten thousand foot soldiers, for the king of Aram had destroyed the rest and made them like the dust at threshing time. ⁸As for the other events of the reign of Jehoahaz, all he did and his achievements, are they not written in the book of the annals of the kings of Israel? ⁹Jehoahaz rested with his ancestors and was buried in Samaria. And Jehoash[b] his son succeeded him as king.

Jehoash King of Israel

¹⁰In the thirty-seventh year of Joash king of Judah, Jehoash son of Jehoahaz became king of Israel in Samaria, and he reigned sixteen years. ¹¹He did evil in the eyes of the Lord and did not turn away from any of the sins of Jeroboam son of Nebat, which he had caused Israel to commit; he continued in them.

¹²As for the other events of the reign of Jehoash, all he did and his achievements, including his war against Amaziah king of Judah, are they not written in the book of the annals of the kings of Israel? ¹³Jehoash rested with his ancestors, and Jeroboam succeeded him on the throne. Jehoash was buried in Samaria with the kings of Israel.

¹⁴Now Elisha had been suffering from the illness from which he died. Jehoash king of Israel went down to see him and wept over him. "My father! My father!" he cried. "The chariots and horsemen of Israel!"

¹⁵Elisha said, "Get a bow and some arrows," and he did so. ¹⁶"Take the bow in your hands," he said to the king of Israel. When he had taken it, Elisha put his hands on the king's hands.

¹⁷"Open the east window," he said, and he opened it. "Shoot!" Elisha said, and he shot. "The Lord's arrow of victory, the arrow of victory over Aram!" Elisha declared. "You will completely destroy the Arameans at Aphek."

¹⁸Then he said, "Take the arrows," and the king took them. Elisha told him, "Strike the ground." He struck it three times and stopped. ¹⁹The man of God was angry with him and said, "You should have struck the ground five or six times; then you would have defeated Aram and completely destroyed it. But now you will defeat it only three times."

²⁰Elisha died and was buried.

Now Moabite raiders used to enter the country every spring. ²¹Once while some Israelites were burying a man, suddenly they saw a band of raiders; so they threw the man's body into Elisha's tomb.

---

[a] 6 That is, a wooden symbol of the goddess Asherah; here and elsewhere in 2 Kings   [b] 9 Hebrew *Joash*, a variant of *Jehoash*; also in verses 12-14 and 25

When the body touched Elisha's bones, the man came to life and stood up on his feet.

²² Hazael king of Aram oppressed Israel throughout the reign of Jehoahaz. ²³ But the LORD was gracious to them and had compassion and showed concern for them because of his covenant with Abraham, Isaac and Jacob. To this day he has been unwilling to destroy them or banish them from his presence.

²⁴ Hazael king of Aram died, and Ben-Hadad his son succeeded him as king. ²⁵ Then Jehoash son of Jehoahaz recaptured from Ben-Hadad son of Hazael the towns he had taken in battle from his father Jehoahaz. Three times Jehoash defeated him, and so he recovered the Israelite towns.

Amaziah King of Judah

14 In the second year of Jehoash[a] son of Jehoahaz king of Israel, Amaziah son of Joash king of Judah began to reign. ² He was twenty-five years old when he became king, and he reigned in Jerusalem twenty-nine years. His mother's name was Jehoaddan; she was from Jerusalem. ³ He did what was right in the eyes of the LORD, but not as his father David had done. In everything he followed the example of his father Joash. ⁴ The high places, however, were not removed; the people continued to offer sacrifices and burn incense there.

⁵ After the kingdom was firmly in his grasp, he executed the officials who had murdered his father the king. ⁶ Yet he did not put the children of the assassins to death, in accordance with what is written in the Book of the Law of Moses where the LORD commanded: "Parents are not to be put to death for their children, nor children put to death for their parents; each will die for their own sin."[b]

⁷ He was the one who defeated ten thousand Edomites in the Valley of Salt and captured Sela in battle, calling it Joktheel, the name it has to this day.

⁸ Then Amaziah sent messengers to Jehoash son of Jehoahaz, the son of Jehu, king of Israel, with the challenge: "Come, let us face each other in battle."

⁹ But Jehoash king of Israel replied to Amaziah king of Judah: "A thistle in Lebanon sent a message to a cedar in Lebanon, 'Give your daughter to my son in marriage.' Then a wild beast in Lebanon came along and trampled the thistle underfoot. ¹⁰ You have indeed defeated Edom and now you are arrogant. Glory in your victory, but stay at home! Why ask for trouble and cause your own downfall and that of Judah also?"

¹¹ Amaziah, however, would not listen, so Jehoash king of Israel attacked. He and Amaziah king of Judah faced each other at Beth Shemesh in Judah. ¹² Judah was routed by Israel, and every man fled to his home. ¹³ Jehoash king of Israel captured Amaziah king of Judah, the son of Joash, the son of Ahaziah, at Beth Shemesh. Then Jehoash went to Jerusalem and broke down the wall of Jerusalem from the Ephraim Gate to the Corner Gate—a section about four hundred cubits long.[c] ¹⁴ He took all the gold and silver and all the articles found in the temple of the LORD and in the treasuries of the royal palace. He also took hostages and returned to Samaria.

¹⁵ As for the other events of the reign of Jehoash, what he did and his achievements, including his war against Amaziah king of Judah, are they not written in the book of the annals of the kings of Israel? ¹⁶ Jehoash rested with his ancestors and was buried in Samaria with the kings of Israel. And Jeroboam his son succeeded him as king.

¹⁷ Amaziah son of Joash king of Judah lived for fifteen years after the death of Jehoash son of Jehoahaz king of Israel. ¹⁸ As for the other events of Amaziah's reign, are they not written in the book of the annals of the kings of Judah?

¹⁹ They conspired against him in Jerusalem, and he fled to Lachish, but they sent men after him to Lachish and killed him there. ²⁰ He was brought back by horse and was buried in Jerusalem with his ancestors, in the City of David.

---

a 1 Hebrew *Joash,* a variant of *Jehoash;* also in verses 13, 23 and 27   *b 6* Deut. 24:16   *c 13* That is, about 600 feet or about 180 meters

21 Then all the people of Judah took Azariah,[a] who was sixteen years old, and made him king in place of his father Amaziah. 22 He was the one who rebuilt Elath and restored it to Judah after Amaziah rested with his ancestors.

Jeroboam II King of Israel

23 In the fifteenth year of Amaziah son of Joash king of Judah, Jeroboam son of Jehoash king of Israel became king in Samaria, and he reigned forty-one years. 24 He did evil in the eyes of the LORD and did not turn away from any of the sins of Jeroboam son of Nebat, which he had caused Israel to commit. 25 He was the one who restored the boundaries of Israel from Lebo Hamath to the Dead Sea,[b] in accordance with the word of the LORD, the God of Israel, spoken through his servant Jonah son of Amittai, the prophet from Gath Hepher.

26 The LORD had seen how bitterly everyone in Israel, whether slave or free, was suffering;[c] there was no one to help them. 27 And since the LORD had not said he would blot out the name of Israel from under heaven, he saved them by the hand of Jeroboam son of Jehoash.

28 As for the other events of Jeroboam's reign, all he did, and his military achievements, including how he recovered for Israel both Damascus and Hamath, which had belonged to Judah, are they not written in the book of the annals of the kings of Israel? 29 Jeroboam rested with his ancestors, the kings of Israel. And Zechariah his son succeeded him as king.

Azariah King of Judah

15 In the twenty-seventh year of Jeroboam king of Israel, Azariah[d] son of Amaziah king of Judah began to reign. 2 He was sixteen years old when he became king, and he reigned in Jerusalem fifty-two years. His mother's name was Jekoliah; she was from Jerusalem. 3 He did what was right in the eyes of the LORD, just as his father Amaziah had done. 4 The high places, however, were not removed; the people continued to offer sacrifices and burn incense there.

5 The LORD afflicted the king with leprosy[e] until the day he died, and he lived in a separate house.[f] Jotham the king's son had charge of the palace and governed the people of the land.

6 As for the other events of Azariah's reign, and all he did, are they not written in the book of the annals of the kings of Judah? 7 Azariah rested with his ancestors and was buried near them in the City of David. And Jotham his son succeeded him as king.

Zechariah King of Israel

8 In the thirty-eighth year of Azariah king of Judah, Zechariah son of Jeroboam became king of Israel in Samaria, and he reigned six months. 9 He did evil in the eyes of the LORD, as his predecessors had done. He did not turn away from the sins of Jeroboam son of Nebat, which he had caused Israel to commit.

10 Shallum son of Jabesh conspired against Zechariah. He attacked him in front of the people,[g] assassinated him and succeeded him as king. 11 The other events of Zechariah's reign are written in the book of the annals of the kings of Israel. 12 So the word of the LORD spoken to Jehu was fulfilled: "Your descendants will sit on the throne of Israel to the fourth generation."[h]

Shallum King of Israel

13 Shallum son of Jabesh became king in the thirty-ninth year of Uzziah king of Judah, and he reigned in Samaria one month. 14 Then Menahem son of Gadi went from Tirzah up to Samaria. He attacked Shallum son of Jabesh in Samaria, assassinated him and succeeded him as king.

15 The other events of Shallum's reign, and the conspiracy he led, are written in the book of the annals of the kings of Israel.

---

a 21 Also called *Uzziah*   b 25 Hebrew *the Sea of the Arabah*   c 26 Or *Israel was suffering. They were without a ruler or leader, and*   d 1 Also called *Uzziah*; also in verses 6, 7, 8, 17, 23 and 27   e 5 The Hebrew for *leprosy* was used for various diseases affecting the skin.   f 5 Or *in a house where he was relieved of responsibilities*   g 10 Hebrew; some Septuagint manuscripts *in Ibleam*   h 12 2 Kings 10:30

16At that time Menahem, starting out from Tirzah, attacked Tiphsah and everyone in the city and its vicinity, because they refused to open their gates. He sacked Tiphsah and ripped open all the pregnant women.

Menahem King of Israel

17In the thirty-ninth year of Azariah king of Judah, Menahem son of Gadi became king of Israel, and he reigned in Samaria ten years. 18He did evil in the eyes of the LORD. During his entire reign he did not turn away from the sins of Jeroboam son of Nebat, which he had caused Israel to commit.

19Then Pula king of Assyria invaded the land, and Menahem gave him a thousand talentsb of silver to gain his support and strengthen his own hold on the kingdom.

---

a 19 Also called *Tiglath-Pileser*   b 19 That is, about 38 tons or about 34 metric tons

---

TO THE POINT

Good Parents, Bad Parents

Are you destined to become just like your parents? Abusive? Alcoholic? Generous? Loving? Bitter? For some teens, turning out like their parents would be terrible; for others, terrific. You can have terrific parents and go wrong, or you can have terrible parents and become a good person. Follow this family's story (2 Kings 8–21):

+ Ahaz was a wicked king; his son Joash was godly.

+ Joash's son Amaziah was godly, and so was Amaziah's son Uzziah.

+ Uzziah's son Jotham was godly, but Jotham's son Ahaz was wicked.

+ Ahaz's son Hezekiah was godly, but Hezekiah's son Manasseh was the most wicked of all Judah's kings.

What does this pattern tell you? Having good parents won't make you good. And bad parents won't make you bad. The kind of person you become is up to you.

20 Menahem exacted this money from Israel. Every wealthy person had to contribute fifty shekels[a] of silver to be given to the king of Assyria. So the king of Assyria withdrew and stayed in the land no longer.

21 As for the other events of Menahem's reign, and all he did, are they not written in the book of the annals of the kings of Israel? 22 Menahem rested with his ancestors. And Pekahiah his son succeeded him as king.

Pekahiah King of Israel

23 In the fiftieth year of Azariah king of Judah, Pekahiah son of Menahem became king of Israel in Samaria, and he reigned two years. 24 Pekahiah did evil in the eyes of the LORD. He did not turn away from the sins of Jeroboam son of Nebat, which he had caused Israel to commit. 25 One of his chief officers, Pekah son of Remaliah, conspired against him. Taking fifty men of Gilead with him, he assassinated Pekahiah, along with Argob and Arieh, in the citadel of the royal palace at Samaria. So Pekah killed Pekahiah and succeeded him as king.

26 The other events of Pekahiah's reign, and all he did, are written in the book of the annals of the kings of Israel.

Pekah King of Israel

27 In the fifty-second year of Azariah king of Judah, Pekah son of Remaliah became king of Israel in Samaria, and he reigned twenty years. 28 He did evil in the eyes of the LORD. He did not turn away from the sins of Jeroboam son of Nebat, which he had caused Israel to commit.

29 In the time of Pekah king of Israel, Tiglath-Pileser king of Assyria came and took Ijon, Abel Beth Maakah, Janoah, Kedesh and Hazor. He took Gilead and Galilee, including all the land of Naphtali, and deported the people to Assyria. 30 Then Hoshea son of Elah conspired against Pekah son of Remaliah. He attacked and assassinated him, and then succeeded him as king in the twentieth year of Jotham son of Uzziah.

31 As for the other events of Pekah's reign, and all he did, are they not written in the book of the annals of the kings of Israel?

Jotham King of Judah

32 In the second year of Pekah son of Remaliah king of Israel, Jotham son of Uzziah king of Judah began to reign. 33 He was twenty-five years old when he became king, and he reigned in Jerusalem sixteen years. His mother's name was Jerusha daughter of Zadok. 34 He did what was right in the eyes of the LORD, just as his father Uzziah had done. 35 The high places, however, were not removed; the people continued to offer sacrifices and burn incense there. Jotham rebuilt the Upper Gate of the temple of the LORD.

36 As for the other events of Jotham's reign, and what he did, are they not written in the book of the annals of the kings of Judah? 37 (In those days the LORD began to send Rezin king of Aram and Pekah son of Remaliah against Judah.) 38 Jotham rested with his ancestors and was buried with them in the City of David, the city of his father. And Ahaz his son succeeded him as king.

Ahaz King of Judah

16 In the seventeenth year of Pekah son of Remaliah, Ahaz son of Jotham king of Judah began to reign. 2 Ahaz was twenty years old when he became king, and he reigned in Jerusalem sixteen years. Unlike David his father, he did not do what was right in the eyes of the LORD his God. 3 He followed the ways of the kings of Israel and even sacrificed his son in the fire, engaging in the detestable practices of the nations the LORD had driven out before the Israelites. 4 He offered sacrifices and burned incense at the high places, on the hilltops and under every spreading tree.

5 Then Rezin king of Aram and Pekah son of Remaliah king of Israel marched up to fight against Jerusalem and besieged Ahaz, but they could not overpower him. 6 At that time, Rezin king of

---

a 20 That is, about 1 1/4 pounds or about 575 grams

Aram recovered Elath for Aram by driving out the people of Judah. Edomites then moved into Elath and have lived there to this day.

⁷Ahaz sent messengers to say to Tiglath-Pileser king of Assyria, "I am your servant and vassal. Come up and save me out of the hand of the king of Aram and of the king of Israel, who are attacking me." ⁸And Ahaz took the silver and gold found in the temple of the LORD and in the treasuries of the royal palace and sent it as a gift to the king of Assyria. ⁹The king of Assyria complied by attacking Damascus and capturing it. He deported its inhabitants to Kir and put Rezin to death.

¹⁰Then King Ahaz went to Damascus to meet Tiglath-Pileser king of Assyria. He saw an altar in Damascus and sent to Uriah the priest a sketch of the altar, with detailed plans for its construction. ¹¹So Uriah the priest built an altar in accordance with all the plans that King Ahaz had sent from Damascus and finished it before King Ahaz returned. ¹²When the king came back from Damascus and saw the altar, he approached it and presented offerings[a] on it. ¹³He offered up his burnt offering and grain offering, poured out his drink offering, and splashed the blood of his fellowship offerings against the altar. ¹⁴As for the bronze altar that stood before the LORD, he brought it from the front of the temple—from between the new altar and the temple of the LORD—and put it on the north side of the new altar.

¹⁵King Ahaz then gave these orders to Uriah the priest: "On the large new altar, offer the morning burnt offering and the evening grain offering, the king's burnt offering and his grain offering, and the burnt offering of all the people of the land, and their grain offering and their drink offering. Splash against this altar the blood of all the burnt offerings and sacrifices. But I will use the bronze altar for seeking guidance." ¹⁶And Uriah the priest did just as King Ahaz had ordered.

¹⁷King Ahaz cut off the side panels and removed the basins from the movable stands. He removed the Sea from the bronze bulls that supported it and set it on a stone base. ¹⁸He took away the Sabbath canopy[b] that had been built at the temple and removed the royal entryway outside the temple of the LORD, in deference to the king of Assyria.

¹⁹As for the other events of the reign of Ahaz, and what he did, are they not written in the book of the annals of the kings of Judah? ²⁰Ahaz rested with his ancestors and was buried with them in the City of David. And Hezekiah his son succeeded him as king.

Hoshea Last King of Israel

17 In the twelfth year of Ahaz king of Judah, Hoshea son of Elah became king of Israel in Samaria, and he reigned nine years. ²He did evil in the eyes of the LORD, but not like the kings of Israel who preceded him.

³Shalmaneser king of Assyria came up to attack Hoshea, who had been Shalmaneser's vassal and had paid him tribute. ⁴But the king of Assyria discovered that Hoshea was a traitor, for he had sent envoys to So[c] king of Egypt, and he no longer paid tribute to the king of Assyria, as he had done year by year. Therefore Shalmaneser seized him and put him in prison. ⁵The king of Assyria invaded the entire land, marched against Samaria and laid siege to it for three years. ⁶In the ninth year of Hoshea, the king of Assyria captured Samaria and deported the Israelites to Assyria. He settled them in Halah, in Gozan on the Habor River and in the towns of the Medes.

Israel Exiled Because of Sin

⁷All this took place because the Israelites had sinned against the LORD their God, who had brought them up out of Egypt from under the power of Pharaoh king of Egypt. They worshiped other gods ⁸and followed the practices of the nations the LORD had driven out before them, as well as the practices that the kings of Israel had introduced. ⁹The Israelites secretly

---

a 12 Or *and went up*   *b* 18 Or *the dais of his throne* (see Septuagint)   *c* 4 *So* is probably an abbreviation for *Osorkon.*

did things against the LORD their God that were not right. From watchtower to fortified city they built themselves high places in all their towns. ¹⁰They set up sacred stones and Asherah poles on every high hill and under every spreading tree. ¹¹At every high place they burned incense, as the nations whom the LORD had driven out before them had done. They did wicked things that aroused the LORD's anger. ¹²They worshiped idols, though the LORD had said, "You shall not do this."ᵃ ¹³The LORD warned Israel and Judah through all his prophets and seers: "Turn from your evil ways. Observe my commands and decrees, in accordance with the entire Law that I commanded your ancestors to obey and that I delivered to you through my servants the prophets."

¹⁴But they would not listen and were as stiff-necked as their ancestors, who did not trust in the LORD their God. ¹⁵They rejected his decrees and the covenant he had made with their ancestors and the statutes he had warned them to keep. They followed worthless idols and themselves became worthless. They imitated the nations around them although the LORD had ordered them, "Do not do as they do."

¹⁶They forsook all the commands of the LORD their God and made for themselves two idols cast in the shape of calves, and an Asherah pole. They bowed down to all the starry hosts, and they worshiped Baal. ¹⁷They sacrificed their sons and daughters in the fire. They practiced divination and sought omens and sold themselves to do evil in the eyes of the LORD, arousing his anger.

¹⁸So the LORD was very angry with Israel and removed them from his presence. Only the tribe of Judah was left, ¹⁹and even Judah did not keep the commands of the LORD their God. They followed the practices Israel had introduced. ²⁰Therefore the LORD rejected all the people of Israel; he afflicted them and gave them into the hands of plunderers, until he thrust them from his presence.

²¹When he tore Israel away from the house of David, they made Jeroboam son of Nebat their king. Jeroboam enticed Israel away from following the LORD and caused them to commit a great sin. ²²The Israelites persisted in all the sins of Jeroboam and did not turn away from them ²³until the LORD removed them from his presence, as he had warned through all his servants the prophets. So the people of Israel were taken from their homeland into exile in Assyria, and they are still there.

Samaria Resettled

²⁴The king of Assyria brought people from Babylon, Kuthah, Avva, Hamath and Sepharvaim and settled them in the towns of Samaria to replace the Israelites. They took over Samaria and lived in its towns. ²⁵When they first lived there, they did not worship the LORD; so he sent lions among them and they killed some of the people. ²⁶It was reported to the king of Assyria: "The people you deported and resettled in the towns of Samaria do not know what the god of that country requires. He has sent lions among them, which are killing them off, because the people do not know what he requires."

²⁷Then the king of Assyria gave this order: "Have one of the priests you took captive from Samaria go back to live there and teach the people what the god of the land requires." ²⁸So one of the priests who had been exiled from Samaria came to live in Bethel and taught them how to worship the LORD.

²⁹Nevertheless, each national group made its own gods in the several towns where they settled, and set them up in the shrines the people of Samaria had made at the high places. ³⁰The people from Babylon made Sukkoth Benoth, those from Kuthah made Nergal, and those from Hamath made Ashima; ³¹the Avvites made Nibhaz and Tartak, and the Sepharvites burned their children in the fire as sacrifices to Adrammelek and Anammelek, the gods of Sepharvaim. ³²They worshiped the LORD, but they also appointed all sorts of their own people

---

ᵃ 12 Exodus 20:4,5

to officiate for them as priests in the shrines at the high places. ³³They worshiped the LORD, but they also served their own gods in accordance with the customs of the nations from which they had been brought.

³⁴To this day they persist in their former practices. They neither worship the LORD nor adhere to the decrees and regulations, the laws and commands that the LORD gave the descendants of Jacob, whom he named Israel. ³⁵When the LORD made a covenant with the Israelites, he commanded them: "Do not worship any other gods or bow down to them, serve them or sacrifice to them. ³⁶But the LORD, who brought you up out of Egypt with mighty power and outstretched arm, is the one you must worship. To him you shall bow down and to him offer sacrifices. ³⁷You must always be careful to keep the decrees and regulations, the laws and commands he wrote for you. Do not worship other gods. ³⁸Do not forget the covenant I have made with you, and do not worship other gods. ³⁹Rather, worship the LORD your God; it is he who will deliver you from the hand of all your enemies."

⁴⁰They would not listen, however, but persisted in their former practices. ⁴¹Even while these people were worshiping the LORD, they were serving their idols. To this day their children and grandchildren continue to do as their ancestors did.

Hezekiah King of Judah

18 In the third year of Hoshea son of Elah king of Israel, Hezekiah son of Ahaz king of Judah began to reign. ²He was twenty-five years old when he became king, and he reigned in Jerusalem twenty-nine years. His mother's name was Abijah[a] daughter of Zechariah. ³He did what was right in the eyes of the LORD, just as his father David had done. ⁴He removed the high places, smashed the sacred stones and cut down the Asherah poles. He broke into pieces the bronze snake Moses had made, for up to that

time the Israelites had been burning incense to it. (It was called Nehushtan.[b])

⁵Hezekiah trusted in the LORD, the God of Israel. There was no one like him among all the kings of Judah, either before him or after him. ⁶He held fast to the LORD and did not stop following him; he kept the commands the LORD had given Moses. ⁷And the LORD was with him; he was successful in whatever he undertook. He rebelled against the king of Assyria and did not serve him. ⁸From watchtower to fortified city, he defeated the Philistines, as far as Gaza and its territory.

⁹In King Hezekiah's fourth year, which was the seventh year of Hoshea son of Elah king of Israel, Shalmaneser king of Assyria marched against Samaria and laid siege to it. ¹⁰At the end of three years the Assyrians took it. So Samaria was captured in Hezekiah's sixth year, which was the ninth year of Hoshea king of Israel. ¹¹The king of Assyria deported Israel to Assyria and settled them in Halah, in Gozan on the Habor River and in towns of the Medes. ¹²This happened because they had not obeyed the LORD their God, but had violated his covenant—all that Moses the servant of the LORD commanded. They neither listened to the commands nor carried them out.

¹³In the fourteenth year of King Hezekiah's reign, Sennacherib king of Assyria attacked all the fortified cities of Judah and captured them. ¹⁴So Hezekiah king of Judah sent this message to the king of Assyria at Lachish: "I have done wrong. Withdraw from me, and I will pay whatever you demand of me." The king of Assyria exacted from Hezekiah king of Judah three hundred talents[c] of silver and thirty talents[d] of gold. ¹⁵So Hezekiah gave him all the silver that was found in the temple of the LORD and in the treasuries of the royal palace.

¹⁶At this time Hezekiah king of Judah stripped off the gold with which he had covered the doors and doorposts of the temple of the LORD, and gave it to the king of Assyria.

---

[a] 2 Hebrew *Abi*, a variant of *Abijah*   [b] 4 *Nehushtan* sounds like the Hebrew for both *bronze* and *snake*.   [c] 14 That is, about 11 tons or about 10 metric tons   [d] 14 That is, about 1 ton or about 1 metric ton

Sennacherib Threatens Jerusalem

17 The king of Assyria sent his supreme commander, his chief officer and his field commander with a large army, from Lachish to King Hezekiah at Jerusalem. They came up to Jerusalem and stopped at the aqueduct of the Upper Pool, on the road to the Washerman's Field. 18 They called for the king; and Eliakim son of Hilkiah the palace administrator, Shebna the secretary, and Joah son of Asaph the recorder went out to them.

19 The field commander said to them, "Tell Hezekiah:

" 'This is what the great king, the king of Assyria, says: On what are you basing this confidence of yours? 20 You say you have the counsel and the might for war—but you speak only empty words. On whom are you depending, that you rebel against me? 21 Look, I know you are depending on Egypt, that splintered reed of a staff, which pierces the hand of anyone who leans on it! Such is Pharaoh king of Egypt to all who depend on him. 22 But if you say to me, "We are depending on the Lord our God"—isn't he the one whose high places and altars Hezekiah removed, saying to Judah and Jerusalem, "You must worship before this altar in Jerusalem"?

23 " 'Come now, make a bargain with my master, the king of Assyria: I will give you two thousand horses—if you can put riders on them! 24 How can you repulse one officer of the least of my master's officials, even though you are depending on Egypt for chariots and horsemen[a]? 25 Furthermore, have I come to attack and destroy this place without word from the Lord? The Lord himself told me to march against this country and destroy it.' "

26 Then Eliakim son of Hilkiah, and Shebna and Joah said to the field com-mander, "Please speak to your servants in Aramaic, since we understand it. Don't speak to us in Hebrew in the hearing of the people on the wall."

27 But the commander replied, "Was it only to your master and you that my master sent me to say these things, and not to the people sitting on the wall—who, like you, will have to eat their own excrement and drink their own urine?"

28 Then the commander stood and called out in Hebrew, "Hear the word of the great king, the king of Assyria! 29 This is what the king says: Do not let Hezekiah deceive you. He cannot deliver you from my hand. 30 Do not let Hezekiah persuade you to trust in the Lord when he says, 'The Lord will surely deliver us; this city will not be given into the hand of the king of Assyria.'

31 "Do not listen to Hezekiah. This is what the king of Assyria says: Make peace with me and come out to me. Then each of you will eat fruit from your own vine and fig tree and drink water from your own cistern, 32 until I come and take you to a land like your own—a land of grain and new wine, a land of bread and vineyards, a land of olive trees and honey. Choose life and not death!

"Do not listen to Hezekiah, for he is misleading you when he says, 'The Lord will deliver us.' 33 Has the god of any nation ever delivered his land from the hand of the king of Assyria? 34 Where are the gods of Hamath and Arpad? Where are the gods of Sepharvaim, Hena and Ivvah? Have they rescued Samaria from my hand? 35 Who of all the gods of these countries has been able to save his land from me? How then can the Lord deliver Jerusalem from my hand?"

36 But the people remained silent and said nothing in reply, because the king had commanded, "Do not answer him."

37 Then Eliakim son of Hilkiah the palace administrator, Shebna the secretary, and Joah son of Asaph the recorder went to Hezekiah, with their clothes torn, and told him what the field commander had said.

---

a 24 Or charioteers

Jerusalem's Deliverance Foretold

19 When King Hezekiah heard this, he tore his clothes and put on sackcloth and went into the temple of the LORD. ²He sent Eliakim the palace administrator, Shebna the secretary and the leading priests, all wearing sackcloth, to the prophet Isaiah son of Amoz. ³They told him, "This is what Hezekiah says: This day is a day of distress and rebuke and disgrace, as when children come to the moment of birth and there is no strength to deliver them. ⁴It may be that the LORD your God will hear all the words of the field commander, whom his master, the king of Assyria, has sent to ridicule the living God, and that he will rebuke him for the words the LORD your God has heard. Therefore pray for the remnant that still survives."

⁵When King Hezekiah's officials came to Isaiah, ⁶Isaiah said to them, "Tell your master, 'This is what the LORD says: Do not be afraid of what you have heard—those words with which the underlings of the king of Assyria have blasphemed me. ⁷Listen! When he hears a certain report, I will make him want to return to his own country, and there I will have him cut down with the sword.'"

⁸When the field commander heard that the king of Assyria had left Lachish, he withdrew and found the king fighting against Libnah.

⁹Now Sennacherib received a report that Tirhakah, the king of Cush,ᵃ was marching out to fight against him. So he again sent messengers to Hezekiah with this word: ¹⁰"Say to Hezekiah king of Judah: Do not let the god you depend on deceive you when he says, 'Jerusalem will not be given into the hands of the king of Assyria.' ¹¹Surely you have heard what the kings of Assyria have done to all the countries, destroying them completely. And will you be delivered? ¹²Did the gods of the nations that were destroyed by my predecessors deliver them—the gods of Gozan, Harran, Rezeph and the people of Eden who were in Tel Assar? ¹³Where is the king of Hamath or the king of Arpad? Where are the kings of Lair, Sepharvaim, Hena and Ivvah?"

Hezekiah's Prayer

¹⁴Hezekiah received the letter from the messengers and read it. Then he went up to the temple of the LORD and spread it out before the LORD. ¹⁵And Hezekiah prayed to the LORD: "LORD, the God of Israel, enthroned between the cherubim, you alone are God over all the kingdoms of the earth. You have made heaven and earth. ¹⁶Give ear, LORD, and hear; open your eyes, LORD, and see; listen to the words Sennacherib has sent to ridicule the living God.

¹⁷"It is true, LORD, that the Assyrian kings have laid waste these nations and their lands. ¹⁸They have thrown their gods into the fire and destroyed them, for they were not gods but only wood and stone, fashioned by human hands. ¹⁹Now, LORD our God, deliver us from his hand, so that all the kingdoms of the earth may know that you alone, LORD, are God."

Isaiah Prophesies Sennacherib's Fall

²⁰Then Isaiah son of Amoz sent a message to Hezekiah: "This is what the LORD, the God of Israel, says: I have heard your prayer concerning Sennacherib king of Assyria. ²¹This is the word that the LORD has spoken against him:

" 'Virgin Daughter Zion
  despises you and mocks you.
Daughter Jerusalem
  tosses her head as you flee.
²²Who is it you have ridiculed and
    blasphemed?
  Against whom have you raised your
    voice
and lifted your eyes in pride?
  Against the Holy One of Israel!
²³By your messengers
  you have ridiculed the Lord.
And you have said,
  "With my many chariots
I have ascended the heights of the
    mountains,

ᵃ 9 That is, the upper Nile region

Have you ever wondered why God answers prayers? Because he loves you? Because you've been good and deserve a reward? Because you keep on asking? Because you ask in faith? It's not really possible to say why God chooses to answer a particular prayer. But King Hezekiah's experience is educational. An Assyrian army threatened Jerusalem, yet Hezekiah didn't plead for the lives of his people. He asked God to deliver the city "so that all the kingdoms on earth may know that you alone, LORD, are God" (2 Kings 19:19). When you can honestly ask God to answer your prayers for his glory, there's a good chance he will say yes.

{2 Kings 19:14–19}

≫ INSTANT ACCESS

the utmost heights of Lebanon.
I have cut down its tallest cedars,
    the choicest of its junipers.
I have reached its remotest parts,
    the finest of its forests.
24 I have dug wells in foreign lands
    and drunk the water there.
With the soles of my feet
    I have dried up all the streams
        of Egypt."

25 " 'Have you not heard?
    Long ago I ordained it.
In days of old I planned it;
    now I have brought it to pass,
that you have turned fortified cities
    into piles of stone.
26 Their people, drained of power,
    are dismayed and put to shame.
They are like plants in the field,
    like tender green shoots,
like grass sprouting on the roof,
    scorched before it grows up.

27 " 'But I know where you are
    and when you come and go
    and how you rage against me.
28 Because you rage against me
    and because your insolence has
        reached my ears,
I will put my hook in your nose
    and my bit in your mouth,
and I will make you return
    by the way you came.'

29 "This will be the sign for you, Hezekiah:

"This year you will eat what grows by
        itself,
    and the second year what springs
        from that.
But in the third year sow and reap,
    plant vineyards and eat their fruit.
30 Once more a remnant of the kingdom
        of Judah
    will take root below and bear fruit
        above.
31 For out of Jerusalem will come a
        remnant,
    and out of Mount Zion a band of
        survivors.

"The zeal of the LORD Almighty will accomplish this.

32 "Therefore this is what the LORD says concerning the king of Assyria:

" 'He will not enter this city
    or shoot an arrow here.
He will not come before it with shield
    or build a siege ramp against it.
33 By the way that he came he will
        return;
    he will not enter this city,
            declares the LORD.
34 I will defend this city and save it,
    for my sake and for the sake of
        David my servant.' "

35 That night the angel of the LORD went out and put to death a hundred and eighty-five thousand in the Assyrian camp. When the people got up the next morning—there were all the dead bodies! 36 So Sennacherib king of Assyria broke camp and withdrew. He returned to Nineveh and stayed there.

37 One day, while he was worshiping in the temple of his god Nisrok, his sons Adrammelek and Sharezer killed him with the sword, and they escaped to the land of Ararat. And Esarhaddon his son succeeded him as king.

Hezekiah's Illness

20 In those days Hezekiah became ill and was at the point of death. The prophet Isaiah son of Amoz went to him and said, "This is what the LORD says: Put your house in order, because you are going to die; you will not recover."

2 Hezekiah turned his face to the wall and prayed to the LORD, 3 "Remember, LORD, how I have walked before you faithfully and with wholehearted devotion and have done what is good in your eyes." And Hezekiah wept bitterly.

4 Before Isaiah had left the middle court, the word of the LORD came to him: 5 "Go back and tell Hezekiah, the ruler of my people, 'This is what the LORD, the God of your father David, says: I have heard your prayer and seen your tears; I will heal you. On the third day from now you will go up to the temple of the LORD. 6 I will add fifteen years to your life. And I will deliver you and this city from the hand of the king of Assyria. I will defend this city for my sake and for the sake of my servant David.'"

7 Then Isaiah said, "Prepare a poultice of figs." They did so and applied it to the boil, and he recovered.

8 Hezekiah had asked Isaiah, "What will be the sign that the LORD will heal me and that I will go up to the temple of the LORD on the third day from now?"

9 Isaiah answered, "This is the LORD's sign to you that the LORD will do what he has promised: Shall the shadow go forward ten steps, or shall it go back ten steps?"

10 "It is a simple matter for the shadow to go forward ten steps," said Hezekiah. "Rather, have it go back ten steps."

11 Then the prophet Isaiah called on the LORD, and the LORD made the shadow go back the ten steps it had gone down on the stairway of Ahaz.

Envoys From Babylon

12 At that time Marduk-Baladan son of Baladan king of Babylon sent Hezekiah letters and a gift, because he had heard of Hezekiah's illness. 13 Hezekiah received the envoys and showed them all that was in his storehouses—the silver, the gold, the spices and the fine olive oil—his armory and everything found among his treasures. There was nothing in his palace or in all his kingdom that Hezekiah did not show them.

14 Then Isaiah the prophet went to King Hezekiah and asked, "What did those men say, and where did they come from?"

"From a distant land," Hezekiah replied. "They came from Babylon."

15 The prophet asked, "What did they see in your palace?"

"They saw everything in my palace," Hezekiah said. "There is nothing among my treasures that I did not show them."

16 Then Isaiah said to Hezekiah, "Hear the word of the LORD: 17 The time will surely come when everything in your palace, and all that your predecessors have stored up until this day, will be carried off to Babylon. Nothing will be left, says the LORD. 18 And some of your descendants, your own flesh and blood who will be born to you, will be taken away, and they will become eunuchs in the palace of the king of Babylon."

19 "The word of the LORD you have spoken is good," Hezekiah replied. For he thought, "Will there not be peace and security in my lifetime?"

20 As for the other events of Hezekiah's reign, all his achievements and how he made the pool and the tunnel by which he brought water into the city, are they not written in the book of the annals of the kings of Judah? 21 Hezekiah rested with his ancestors. And Manasseh his son succeeded him as king.

Manasseh King of Judah

21 Manasseh was twelve years old when he became king, and he reigned in Jerusalem fifty-five years. His mother's name was Hephzibah. ²He did evil in the eyes of the LORD, following the detestable practices of the nations the LORD had driven out before the Israelites. ³He rebuilt the high places his father Hezekiah had destroyed; he also erected altars to Baal and made an Asherah pole, as Ahab king of Israel had done. He bowed down to all the starry hosts and worshiped them. ⁴He built altars in the temple of the LORD, of which the LORD had said, "In Jerusalem I will put my Name." ⁵In the two courts of the temple of the LORD, he built altars to all the starry hosts. ⁶He sacrificed his own son in the fire, practiced divination, sought omens, and consulted mediums and spiritists. He did much evil in the eyes of the LORD, arousing his anger.

⁷He took the carved Asherah pole he had made and put it in the temple, of which the LORD had said to David and to his son Solomon, "In this temple and in Jerusalem, which I have chosen out of all the tribes of Israel, I will put my Name forever. ⁸I will not again make the feet of the Israelites wander from the land I gave their ancestors, if only they will be careful to do everything I commanded them and will keep the whole Law that my servant Moses gave them." ⁹But the people did not listen. Manasseh led them astray, so that they did more evil than the nations the LORD had destroyed before the Israelites.

¹⁰The LORD said through his servants the prophets: ¹¹"Manasseh king of Judah has committed these detestable sins. He has done more evil than the Amorites who preceded him and has led Judah into sin with his idols. ¹²Therefore this is what the LORD, the God of Israel, says: I am going to bring such disaster on Jerusalem and Judah that the ears of everyone who hears of it will tingle. ¹³I will stretch out over Jerusalem the measuring line used against Samaria and the plumb line used against the house of Ahab. I will wipe out Jerusalem as one wipes a dish, wiping it and turning it upside down. ¹⁴I will forsake the remnant of my inheritance and give them into the hands of enemies. They will be looted and plundered by all their enemies; ¹⁵they have done evil in my eyes and have aroused my anger from the day their ancestors came out of Egypt until this day."

¹⁶Moreover, Manasseh also shed so much innocent blood that he filled Jerusalem from end to end—besides the sin that he had caused Judah to commit, so that they did evil in the eyes of the LORD.

¹⁷As for the other events of Manasseh's reign, and all he did, including the sin he committed, are they not written in the book of the annals of the kings of Judah? ¹⁸Manasseh rested with his ancestors and was buried in his palace garden, the garden of Uzza. And Amon his son succeeded him as king.

Amon King of Judah

¹⁹Amon was twenty-two years old when he became king, and he reigned in Jerusalem two years. His mother's name was Meshullemeth daughter of Haruz; she was from Jotbah. ²⁰He did evil in the eyes of the LORD, as his father Manasseh had

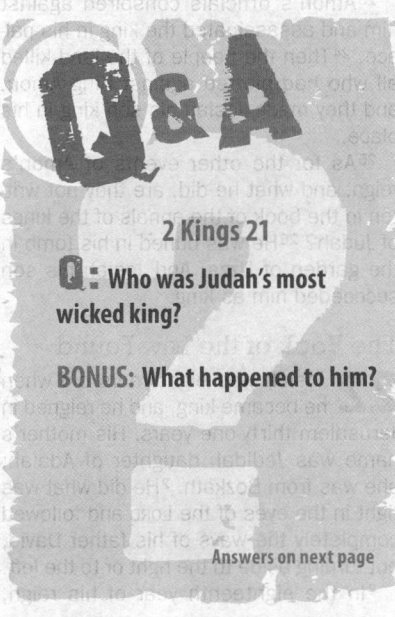

Q&A

2 Kings 21

Q: Who was Judah's most wicked king?

BONUS: What happened to him?

Answers on next page

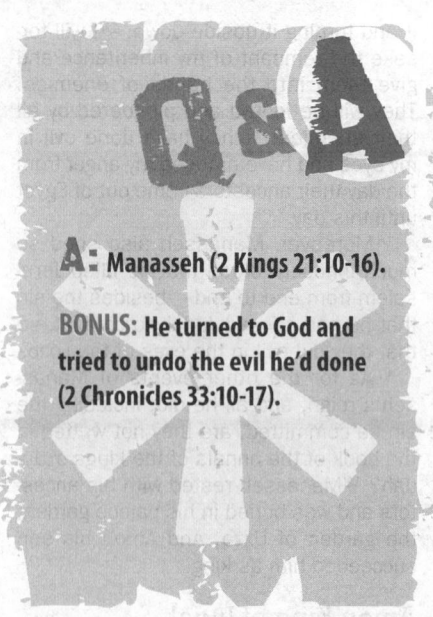

A: Manasseh (2 Kings 21:10-16).

BONUS: He turned to God and tried to undo the evil he'd done (2 Chronicles 33:10-17).

King Josiah sent the secretary, Shaphan son of Azaliah, the son of Meshullam, to the temple of the LORD. He said: 4 "Go up to Hilkiah the high priest and have him get ready the money that has been brought into the temple of the LORD, which the doorkeepers have collected from the people. 5 Have them entrust it to the men appointed to supervise the work on the temple. And have these men pay the workers who repair the temple of the LORD— 6 the carpenters, the builders and the masons. Also have them purchase timber and dressed stone to repair the temple. 7 But they need not account for the money entrusted to them, because they are honest in their dealings."

8 Hilkiah the high priest said to Shaphan the secretary, "I have found the Book of the Law in the temple of the LORD." He gave it to Shaphan, who read it. 9 Then Shaphan the secretary went to the king and reported to him: "Your officials have paid out the money that was in the temple of the LORD and have entrusted it to the workers and supervisors at the temple." 10 Then Shaphan the secretary informed the king, "Hilkiah the priest has given me a book." And Shaphan read from it in the presence of the king.

11 When the king heard the words of the Book of the Law, he tore his robes. 12 He gave these orders to Hilkiah the priest, Ahikam son of Shaphan, Akbor son of Micaiah, Shaphan the secretary and Asaiah the king's attendant: 13 "Go and inquire of the LORD for me and for the people and for all Judah about what is written in this book that has been found. Great is the LORD's anger that burns against us because those who have gone before us have not obeyed the words of this book; they have not acted in accordance with all that is written there concerning us."

14 Hilkiah the priest, Ahikam, Akbor, Shaphan and Asaiah went to speak to the prophet Huldah, who was the wife of Shallum son of Tikvah, the son of Harhas, keeper of the wardrobe. She lived in Jerusalem, in the New Quarter.

15 She said to them, "This is what the LORD, the God of Israel, says: Tell the man who sent you to me, 16 'This is what the

done. 21 He followed completely the ways of his father, worshiping the idols his father had worshiped, and bowing down to them. 22 He forsook the LORD, the God of his ancestors, and did not walk in obedience to him.

23 Amon's officials conspired against him and assassinated the king in his palace. 24 Then the people of the land killed all who had plotted against King Amon, and they made Josiah his son king in his place.

25 As for the other events of Amon's reign, and what he did, are they not written in the book of the annals of the kings of Judah? 26 He was buried in his tomb in the garden of Uzza. And Josiah his son succeeded him as king.

The Book of the Law Found

22 Josiah was eight years old when he became king, and he reigned in Jerusalem thirty-one years. His mother's name was Jedidah daughter of Adaiah; she was from Bozkath. 2 He did what was right in the eyes of the LORD and followed completely the ways of his father David, not turning aside to the right or to the left.

3 In the eighteenth year of his reign,

LORD says: I am going to bring disaster on this place and its people, according to everything written in the book the king of Judah has read. ¹⁷Because they have forsaken me and burned incense to other gods and aroused my anger by all the idols their hands have made,ᵃ my anger will burn against this place and will not be quenched.' ¹⁸Tell the king of Judah, who sent you to inquire of the LORD, 'This is what the LORD, the God of Israel, says concerning the words you heard: ¹⁹Because your heart was responsive and you humbled yourself before the LORD when you heard what I have spoken against this place and its people—that they would become a curseᵇ and be laid waste—and because you tore your robes and wept in my presence, I also have heard you, declares the LORD. ²⁰Therefore I will gather you to your ancestors, and you will be buried in peace. Your eyes will not see all the disaster I am going to bring on this place.' "

So they took her answer back to the king.

Josiah Renews the Covenant

23 Then the king called together all the elders of Judah and Jerusalem. ²He went up to the temple of the LORD with the people of Judah, the inhabitants of Jerusalem, the priests and the prophets—all the people from the least to the greatest. He read in their hearing all the words of the Book of the Covenant, which had been found in the temple of the LORD. ³The king stood by the pillar and renewed the covenant in the presence of the LORD—to follow the LORD and keep his commands, statutes and decrees with all his heart and all his soul, thus confirming the words of the covenant written in this book. Then all the people pledged themselves to the covenant.

⁴The king ordered Hilkiah the high priest, the priests next in rank and the doorkeepers to remove from the temple of the LORD all the articles made for Baal and Asherah and all the starry hosts. He burned them outside Jerusalem in the fields of the Kidron Valley and took the ashes to Bethel. ⁵He did away with the idolatrous priests appointed by the kings of Judah to burn incense on the high places of the towns of Judah and on those around Jerusalem—those who burned incense to Baal, to the sun and moon, to the constellations and to all the starry hosts. ⁶He took the Asherah pole from the temple of the LORD to the Kidron Valley outside Jerusalem and burned it there. He ground it to powder and scattered the dust over the graves of the common people. ⁷He also tore down the quarters of the male shrine prostitutes that were in the temple of the LORD, the quarters where women did weaving for Asherah.

⁸Josiah brought all the priests from the towns of Judah and desecrated the high places, from Geba to Beersheba, where the priests had burned incense. He broke down the gateway at the entrance of the Gate of Joshua, the city governor, which was on the left of the city gate. ⁹Although the priests of the high places did not serve at the altar of the LORD in Jerusalem, they ate unleavened bread with their fellow priests.

¹⁰He desecrated Topheth, which was in the Valley of Ben Hinnom, so no one could use it to sacrifice their son or daughter in the fire to Molek. ¹¹He removed from the entrance to the temple of the LORD the horses that the kings of Judah had dedicated to the sun. They were in the courtᶜ near the room of an official named Nathan-Melek. Josiah then burned the chariots dedicated to the sun.

¹²He pulled down the altars the kings of Judah had erected on the roof near the upper room of Ahaz, and the altars Manasseh had built in the two courts of the temple of the LORD. He removed them from there, smashed them to pieces and threw the rubble into the Kidron Valley. ¹³The king also desecrated the high places that were east of Jerusalem on the south of the Hill of Corruption—the ones Solomon king of Israel had built for Ashtoreth the vile goddess of the Sidonians, for Chemosh the vile god of Moab, and for

---

ᵃ 17 Or by everything they have done   ᵇ 19 That is, their names would be used in cursing (see Jer. 29:22); or, others would see that they are cursed.   ᶜ 11 The meaning of the Hebrew for this word is uncertain.

Molek the detestable god of the people of Ammon. ¹⁴Josiah smashed the sacred stones and cut down the Asherah poles and covered the sites with human bones.

¹⁵Even the altar at Bethel, the high place made by Jeroboam son of Nebat, who had caused Israel to sin—even that altar and high place he demolished. He burned the high place and ground it to powder, and burned the Asherah pole also. ¹⁶Then Josiah looked around, and when he saw the tombs that were there on the hillside, he had the bones removed from them and burned on the altar to defile it, in accordance with the word of the LORD proclaimed by the man of God who foretold these things.

¹⁷The king asked, "What is that tombstone I see?"

The people of the city said, "It marks the tomb of the man of God who came from Judah and pronounced against the altar of Bethel the very things you have done to it."

¹⁸"Leave it alone," he said. "Don't let anyone disturb his bones." So they spared his bones and those of the prophet who had come from Samaria.

¹⁹Just as he had done at Bethel, Josiah removed all the shrines at the high places that the kings of Israel had built in the towns of Samaria and that had aroused the LORD's anger. ²⁰Josiah slaughtered all the priests of those high places on the altars and burned human bones on them. Then he went back to Jerusalem.

²¹The king gave this order to all the people: "Celebrate the Passover to the LORD your God, as it is written in this Book of the Covenant." ²²Neither in the days of the judges who led Israel nor in the days of the kings of Israel and the kings of Judah had any such Passover been observed. ²³But in the eighteenth year of King Josiah, this Passover was celebrated to the LORD in Jerusalem.

²⁴Furthermore, Josiah got rid of the mediums and spiritists, the household gods, the idols and all the other detestable things seen in Judah and Jerusalem. This he did to fulfill the requirements of the law written in the book that Hilkiah the priest had discovered in the temple of the LORD. ²⁵Neither before nor after Josiah was there a king like him who turned to the LORD as he did—with all his heart and with all his soul and with all his strength, in accordance with all the Law of Moses.

²⁶Nevertheless, the LORD did not turn away from the heat of his fierce anger, which burned against Judah because of all that Manasseh had done to arouse his anger. ²⁷So the LORD said, "I will remove Judah also from my presehce as I removed Israel, and I will reject Jerusalem, the city I chose, and this temple, about which I said, 'My Name shall be there.'ᵃ"

²⁸As for the other events of Josiah's reign, and all he did, are they not written in the book of the annals of the kings of Judah?

²⁹While Josiah was king, Pharaoh Necho king of Egypt went up to the Euphrates River to help the king of Assyria. King Josiah marched out to meet him in battle, but Necho faced him and killed him at Megiddo. ³⁰Josiah's servants brought his body in a chariot from Megiddo to Jerusalem and buried him in his own tomb. And the people of the land took Jehoahaz son of Josiah and anointed him and made him king in place of his father.

Jehoahaz King of Judah

³¹Jehoahaz was twenty-three years old when he became king, and he reigned in Jerusalem three months. His mother's name was Hamutal daughter of Jeremiah; she was from Libnah. ³²He did evil in the eyes of the LORD, just as his predecessors had done. ³³Pharaoh Necho put him in chains at Riblah in the land of Hamath so that he might not reign in Jerusalem, and he imposed on Judah a levy of a hundred talentsᵇ of silver and a talentᶜ of gold. ³⁴Pharaoh Necho made Eliakim son of Josiah king in place of his father Josiah and changed Eliakim's name to Jehoiakim. But he took Jehoahaz and carried him off to Egypt, and there he died. ³⁵Jehoiakim paid Pharaoh Necho the sil-

---

ᵃ 27 1 Kings 8:29   ᵇ 33 That is, about 3 3/4 tons or about 3.4 metric tons   ᶜ 33 That is, about 75 pounds or about 34 kilograms

Chris was a popular guy in high school. He was on the varsity football and baseball teams. He was elected to the student council and was president of a few school clubs. Chris is now studying for the ministry. Maybe Chris doesn't fit the stereotype some people have of a "godly" teenager, but he fits this description of young King Josiah. Josiah was committed to getting rid of everything in Judah that was corrupting and sinful. Chris is just as committed to being personally pure. Josiah was committed to worship. Chris is committed to worship too. Commitment to the Lord does bring challenges. But it also brings a satisfying lifestyle.

{2 Kings 23:25}

ver and gold he demanded. In order to do so, he taxed the land and exacted the silver and gold from the people of the land according to their assessments.

Jehoiakim King of Judah

³⁶ Jehoiakim was twenty-five years old when he became king, and he reigned in Jerusalem eleven years. His mother's name was Zebidah daughter of Pedaiah; she was from Rumah. ³⁷ And he did evil in the eyes of the LORD, just as his predecessors had done.

24 During Jehoiakim's reign, Nebuchadnezzar king of Babylon invaded the land, and Jehoiakim became his vassal for three years. But then he turned against Nebuchadnezzar and rebelled. ² The LORD sent Babylonian,ᵃ Aramean, Moabite and Ammonite raiders against him to destroy Judah, in accordance with the word of the LORD proclaimed by his servants the prophets. ³ Surely these things happened to Judah according to the LORD's command, in order to remove them from his presence because of the sins of Manasseh and all he had done, ⁴ including the shedding of innocent blood. For he had filled Jerusalem with innocent blood, and the LORD was not willing to forgive.

⁵ As for the other events of Jehoiakim's reign, and all he did, are they not written in the book of the annals of the kings of Judah? ⁶ Jehoiakim rested with his ancestors. And Jehoiachin his son succeeded him as king.

⁷ The king of Egypt did not march out from his own country again, because the king of Babylon had taken all his territory, from the Wadi of Egypt to the Euphrates River.

Jehoiachin King of Judah

⁸ Jehoiachin was eighteen years old when he became king, and he reigned in Jerusalem three months. His mother's name was Nehushta daughter of Elnathan; she was from Jerusalem. ⁹ He did evil in the eyes of the LORD, just as his father had done.

¹⁰ At that time the officers of Nebuchadnezzar king of Babylon advanced on Jerusalem and laid siege to it, ¹¹ and Nebuchadnezzar himself came up to the city while his officers were besieging it. ¹² Jehoiachin king of Judah, his mother, his attendants, his nobles and his officials all surrendered to him.

In the eighth year of the reign of the king of Babylon, he took Jehoiachin prisoner. ¹³ As the LORD had declared, Nebuchadnezzar removed the treasures from

ᵃ 2 Or Chaldean

the temple of the LORD and from the royal palace, and cut up the gold articles that Solomon king of Israel had made for the temple of the LORD. [14]He carried all Jerusalem into exile: all the officers and fighting men, and all the skilled workers and artisans—a total of ten thousand. Only the poorest people of the land were left.

[15]Nebuchadnezzar took Jehoiachin captive to Babylon. He also took from Jerusalem to Babylon the king's mother, his wives, his officials and the prominent people of the land. [16]The king of Babylon also deported to Babylon the entire force of seven thousand fighting men, strong and fit for war, and a thousand skilled workers and artisans. [17]He made Mattaniah, Jehoiachin's uncle, king in his place and changed his name to Zedekiah.

Zedekiah King of Judah

[18]Zedekiah was twenty-one years old when he became king, and he reigned in Jerusalem eleven years. His mother's name was Hamutal daughter of Jeremiah; she was from Libnah. [19]He did evil in the eyes of the LORD, just as Jehoiakim had done. [20]It was because of the LORD's anger that all this happened to Jerusalem and Judah, and in the end he thrust them from his presence.

The Fall of Jerusalem

Now Zedekiah rebelled against the king of Babylon.

25 So in the ninth year of Zedekiah's reign, on the tenth day of the tenth month, Nebuchadnezzar king of Babylon marched against Jerusalem with his whole army. He encamped outside the city and built siege works all around it. [2]The city was kept under siege until the eleventh year of King Zedekiah. [3]By the ninth day of the fourth[a] month the famine in the city had become so severe that there was no food for the people to eat. [4]Then the city wall was broken through, and the whole army fled at night through the gate between the two walls near the king's garden, though the

Babylonians[b] were surrounding the city. They fled toward the Arabah,[c] [5]but the Babylonian[d] army pursued the king and overtook him in the plains of Jericho. All his soldiers were separated from him and scattered, [6]and he was captured.

He was taken to the king of Babylon at Riblah, where sentence was pronounced on him. [7]They killed the sons of Zedekiah before his eyes. Then they put out his eyes, bound him with bronze shackles and took him to Babylon.

[8]On the seventh day of the fifth month, in the nineteenth year of Nebuchadnezzar king of Babylon, Nebuzaradan commander of the imperial guard, an official of the king of Babylon, came to Jerusalem. [9]He set fire to the temple of the LORD, the royal palace and all the houses of Jerusalem. Every important building he burned down. [10]The whole Babylonian army under the commander of the imperial guard broke down the walls around Jerusalem. [11]Nebuzaradan the commander of the guard carried into exile the people who remained in the city, along with the rest of the populace and those who had deserted to the king of Babylon. [12]But the commander left behind some of the poorest people of the land to work the vineyards and fields.

[13]The Babylonians broke up the bronze pillars, the movable stands and the bronze Sea that were at the temple of the LORD and they carried the bronze to Babylon. [14]They also took away the pots, shovels, wick trimmers, dishes and all the bronze articles used in the temple service. [15]The commander of the imperial guard took away the censers and sprinkling bowls—all that were made of pure gold or silver.

[16]The bronze from the two pillars, the Sea and the movable stands, which Solomon had made for the temple of the LORD, was more than could be weighed. [17]Each pillar was eighteen cubits[e] high. The bronze capital on top of one pillar was three cubits[f] high and was decorated with a network and pomegranates of bronze all

---

[a] 3 Probable reading of the original Hebrew text (see Jer. 52:6); Masoretic Text does not have *fourth*.   [b] 4 Or *Chaldeans*; also in verses 13, 25 and 26   [c] 4 Or *the Jordan Valley*   [d] 5 Or *Chaldean*; also in verses 10 and 24   [e] 17 That is, about 27 feet or about 8.1 meters   [f] 17 That is, about 4 1/2 feet or about 1.4 meters

around. The other pillar, with its network, was similar.

¹⁸ The commander of the guard took as prisoners Seraiah the chief priest, Zephaniah the priest next in rank and the three doorkeepers. ¹⁹ Of those still in the city, he took the officer in charge of the fighting men, and five royal advisers. He also took the secretary who was chief officer in charge of conscripting the people of the land and sixty of the conscripts who were found in the city. ²⁰ Nebuzaradan the commander took them all and brought them to the king of Babylon at Riblah. ²¹ There at Riblah, in the land of Hamath, the king had them executed.

So Judah went into captivity, away from her land.

²² Nebuchadnezzar king of Babylon appointed Gedaliah son of Ahikam, the son of Shaphan, to be over the people he had left behind in Judah. ²³ When all the army officers and their men heard that the king of Babylon had appointed Gedaliah as governor, they came to Gedaliah at Mizpah — Ishmael son of Nethaniah, Johanan son of Kareah, Seraiah son of Tanhumeth the Netophathite, Jaazaniah the son of the Maakathite, and their men. ²⁴ Gedaliah took an oath to reassure them and their men. "Do not be afraid of the Babylonian officials," he said. "Settle down in the land and serve the king of Babylon, and it will go well with you."

²⁵ In the seventh month, however, Ishmael son of Nethaniah, the son of Elishama, who was of royal blood, came with ten men and assassinated Gedaliah and also the men of Judah and the Babylonians who were with him at Mizpah. ²⁶ At this, all the people from the least to the greatest, together with the army officers, fled to Egypt for fear of the Babylonians.

Jehoiachin Released

²⁷ In the thirty-seventh year of the exile of Jehoiachin king of Judah, in the year Awel-Marduk became king of Babylon, he released Jehoiachin king of Judah from prison. He did this on the twenty-seventh day of the twelfth month. ²⁸ He spoke kindly to him and gave him a seat of honor higher than those of the other kings who were with him in Babylon. ²⁹ So Jehoiachin put aside his prison clothes and for the rest of his life ate regularly at the king's table. ³⁰ Day by day the king gave Jehoiachin a regular allowance as long as he lived.

1 CHRONICLES

preview

The Chronicles are written after the Babylonian captivity, about 440 B.C.

Events in 1 Chronicles take place between 1010 and 970 B.C.

The book focuses on worship and construction of the Jerusalem Temple.

Journals.

Some teens like to keep a journal. They record not only what happens to them but also what they think about it and how they feel. Wouldn't it be interesting if God kept a journal about you? What do you suppose he'd think was important enough to record?

The book of 1 Chronicles contains, in genealogies, a religious history of the Israelite nation from creation to the return of the captives in 538 B.C. In a way it's God's journal, his record of what was important in his people's lives. This book emphasizes good kings and good things rather than sins. Isn't it good to know that God is more interested in your successes than your failures?

>>**GOD REMEMBERS EVERYONE'S NAME**
Long list a reminder, see 1 Chronicles 1–9

>>**DON'T ASK, DON'T SUCCEED**
See editorial, 1 Chronicles 15

>>**DAVID TOO STUNNED TO STAND**
King has to sit down, according to 1 Chronicles 17

>>**SON TO FINISH WHAT FATHER BEGAN**
See report in 1 Chronicles 22

As David prepares for the Temple, a distinct Polynesian culture develops on Figi and Samoa. Wet rice cultivation is introduced in Korea. The Etruscans arrive in Italy. In California the Pinto Indians live in huts made of wood and reeds covered with mud.

Historical Records From Adam to Abraham

To Noah's Sons

1 Adam, Seth, Enosh, ²Kenan, Mahalalel, Jared, ³Enoch, Methuselah, Lamech, Noah.

⁴ The sons of Noah:ᵃ
  Shem, Ham and Japheth.

The Japhethites

⁵ The sonsᵇ of Japheth:
  Gomer, Magog, Madai, Javan, Tubal, Meshek and Tiras.
⁶ The sons of Gomer:
  Ashkenaz, Riphathᶜ and Togarmah.
⁷ The sons of Javan:
  Elishah, Tarshish, the Kittites and the Rodanites.

The Hamites

⁸ The sons of Ham:
  Cush, Egypt, Put and Canaan.
⁹ The sons of Cush:
  Seba, Havilah, Sabta, Raamah and Sabteka.
  The sons of Raamah:
  Sheba and Dedan.
¹⁰ Cush was the fatherᵈ of
  Nimrod, who became a mighty warrior on earth.
¹¹ Egypt was the father of
  the Ludites, Anamites, Lehabites, Naphtuhites, ¹²Pathrusites, Kasluhites (from whom the Philistines came) and Caphtorites.
¹³ Canaan was the father of
  Sidon his firstborn,ᵉ and of the Hittites, ¹⁴Jebusites, Amorites, Girgashites, ¹⁵Hivites, Arkites, Sinites, ¹⁶Arvadites, Zemarites and Hamathites.

The Semites

¹⁷ The sons of Shem:
  Elam, Ashur, Arphaxad, Lud and Aram.

The sons of Aram:ᶠ
  Uz, Hul, Gether and Meshek.
¹⁸ Arphaxad was the father of Shelah,
  and Shelah the father of Eber.
¹⁹ Two sons were born to Eber:
  One was named Peleg,ᵍ because in his time the earth was divided; his brother was named Joktan.
²⁰ Joktan was the father of
  Almodad, Sheleph, Hazarmaveth, Jerah, ²¹Hadoram, Uzal, Diklah, ²²Obal,ʰ Abimael, Sheba, ²³Ophir, Havilah and Jobab. All these were sons of Joktan.

²⁴ Shem, Arphaxad,ⁱ Shelah,
²⁵ Eber, Peleg, Reu,
²⁶ Serug, Nahor, Terah
²⁷ and Abram (that is, Abraham).

The Family of Abraham

²⁸ The sons of Abraham:
  Isaac and Ishmael.

Descendants of Hagar

²⁹ These were their descendants:
  Nebaioth the firstborn of Ishmael, Kedar, Adbeel, Mibsam, ³⁰Mishma, Dumah, Massa, Hadad, Tema, ³¹Jetur, Naphish and Kedemah. These were the sons of Ishmael.

Descendants of Keturah

³² The sons born to Keturah, Abraham's concubine:
  Zimran, Jokshan, Medan, Midian, Ishbak and Shuah.
  The sons of Jokshan:
  Sheba and Dedan.
³³ The sons of Midian:
  Ephah, Epher, Hanok, Abida and Eldaah.
  All these were descendants of Keturah.

Descendants of Sarah

³⁴ Abraham was the father of Isaac.
  The sons of Isaac:
  Esau and Israel.

ᵃ 4 Septuagint; Hebrew does not have this line. ᵇ 5 Sons may mean descendants or successors or nations; also in verses 6-9, 17 and 23. ᶜ 6 Many Hebrew manuscripts and Vulgate (see also Septuagint and Gen. 10:3); most Hebrew manuscripts Diphath ᵈ 10 Father may mean ancestor or predecessor or founder; also in verses 11, 13, 18 and 20. ᵉ 13 Or of the Sidonians, the foremost ᶠ 17 One Hebrew manuscript and some Septuagint manuscripts (see also Gen. 10:23); most Hebrew manuscripts do not have this line. ᵍ 19 Peleg means division. ʰ 22 Some Hebrew manuscripts and Syriac (see also Gen. 10:28); most Hebrew manuscripts Ebal ⁱ 24 Hebrew; some Septuagint manuscripts Arphaxad, Cainan (see also note at Gen. 11:10)

Esau's Sons

35 The sons of Esau:

Eliphaz, Reuel, Jeush, Jalam and Korah.

36 The sons of Eliphaz:

Teman, Omar, Zepho,*a* Gatam and Kenaz;

by Timna: Amalek.*b*

37 The sons of Reuel:

Nahath, Zerah, Shammah and Mizzah.

The People of Seir in Edom

38 The sons of Seir:

Lotan, Shobal, Zibeon, Anah, Dishon, Ezer and Dishan.

39 The sons of Lotan:

Hori and Homam. Timna was Lotan's sister.

40 The sons of Shobal:

Alvan,*c* Manahath, Ebal, Shepho and Onam.

The sons of Zibeon:

Aiah and Anah.

41 The son of Anah:

Dishon.

The sons of Dishon:

Hemdan,*d* Eshban, Ithran and Keran.

42 The sons of Ezer:

Bilhan, Zaavan and Akan.*e*

The sons of Dishan*f*:

Uz and Aran.

The Rulers of Edom

43 These were the kings who reigned in Edom before any Israelite king reigned:

Bela son of Beor, whose city was named Dinhabah.

44 When Bela died, Jobab son of Zerah from Bozrah succeeded him as king.

45 When Jobab died, Husham from the land of the Temanites succeeded him as king.

46 When Husham died, Hadad son of Bedad, who defeated Midian in the country of Moab, succeeded him as king. His city was named Avith.

47 When Hadad died, Samlah from Masrekah succeeded him as king.

48 When Samlah died, Shaul from Rehoboth on the river*g* succeeded him as king.

49 When Shaul died, Baal-Hanan son of Akbor succeeded him as king.

50 When Baal-Hanan died, Hadad succeeded him as king. His city was named Pau,*h* and his wife's name was Mehetabel daughter of Matred, the daughter of Me-Zahab.

51 Hadad also died.

The chiefs of Edom were:

Timna, Alvah, Jetheth, 52 Oholibamah, Elah, Pinon, 53 Kenaz, Teman, Mibzar, 54 Magdiel and Iram. These were the chiefs of Edom.

Israel's Sons

2 These were the sons of Israel:

Reuben, Simeon, Levi, Judah, Issachar, Zebulun, 2 Dan, Joseph, Benjamin, Naphtali, Gad and Asher.

Judah

To Hezron's Sons

3 The sons of Judah:

Er, Onan and Shelah. These three were born to him by a Canaanite woman, the daughter of Shua. Er, Judah's firstborn, was wicked in the Lord's sight; so the Lord put him to death. 4 Judah's daughter-in-law Tamar bore Perez and Zerah to Judah. He had five sons in all.

5 The sons of Perez:

Hezron and Hamul.

6 The sons of Zerah:

---

a 36 Many Hebrew manuscripts, some Septuagint manuscripts and Syriac (see also Gen. 36:11); most Hebrew manuscripts *Zephi*   *b 36* Some Septuagint manuscripts (see also Gen. 36:12); Hebrew *Gatam, Kenaz, Timna and Amalek*   *c 40* Many Hebrew manuscripts and some Septuagint manuscripts (see also Gen. 36:23); most Hebrew manuscripts *Alian*   *d 41* Many Hebrew manuscripts and some Septuagint manuscripts (see also Gen. 36:26); most Hebrew manuscripts *Hamran*   *e 42* Many Hebrew and Septuagint manuscripts (see also Gen. 36:27); most Hebrew manuscripts *Zaavan, Jaakan*   *f 42* See Gen. 36:28; Hebrew *Dishon*, a variant of *Dishan*   *g 48* Possibly the Euphrates   *h 50* Many Hebrew manuscripts, some Septuagint manuscripts, Vulgate and Syriac (see also Gen. 36:39); most Hebrew manuscripts *Pai*

Zimri, Ethan, Heman, Kalkol and Darda[a]—five in all.

[7] The son of Karmi:

Achar,[b] who brought trouble on Israel by violating the ban on taking devoted things.[c]

[8] The son of Ethan:

Azariah.

[9] The sons born to Hezron were:

Jerahmeel, Ram and Caleb.[d]

From Ram Son of Hezron

[10] Ram was the father of Amminadab, and Amminadab the father of Nahshon, the leader of the people of Judah. [11] Nahshon was the father of Salmon,[e] Salmon the father of Boaz, [12] Boaz the father of Obed and Obed the father of Jesse.

[13] Jesse was the father of Eliab his firstborn; the second son was Abinadab, the third Shimea, [14] the fourth Nethanel, the fifth Raddai, [15] the sixth Ozem and the seventh David. [16] Their sisters were Zeruiah and Abigail. Zeruiah's three sons were Abishai, Joab and Asahel. [17] Abigail was the mother of Amasa, whose father was Jether the Ishmaelite.

Caleb Son of Hezron

[18] Caleb son of Hezron had children by his wife Azubah (and by Jerioth). These were her sons: Jesher, Shobab and Ardon. [19] When Azubah died, Caleb married Ephrath, who bore him Hur. [20] Hur was the father of Uri, and Uri the father of Bezalel.

[21] Later, Hezron, when he was sixty years old, married the daughter of Makir the father of Gilead. He made love to her, and she bore him Segub. [22] Segub was the father of Jair, who controlled twenty-three towns in Gilead. [23] (But Geshur and Aram captured Havvoth Jair,[f] as well as Kenath with its surrounding settlements—sixty towns.) All these were descendants of Makir the father of Gilead.

[24] After Hezron died in Caleb Ephrathah, Abijah the wife of Hezron bore him Ashhur the father[g] of Tekoa.

Jerahmeel Son of Hezron

[25] The sons of Jerahmeel the firstborn of Hezron:

Ram his firstborn, Bunah, Oren, Ozem and[h] Ahijah. [26] Jerahmeel had another wife, whose name was Atarah; she was the mother of Onam.

[27] The sons of Ram the firstborn of Jerahmeel:

Maaz, Jamin and Eker.

[28] The sons of Onam:

Shammai and Jada.

The sons of Shammai:

Nadab and Abishur.

[29] Abishur's wife was named Abihail, who bore him Ahban and Molid.

[30] The sons of Nadab:

Seled and Appaim. Seled died without children.

[31] The son of Appaim:

Ishi, who was the father of Sheshan.

Sheshan was the father of Ahlai.

[32] The sons of Jada, Shammai's brother:

Jether and Jonathan. Jether died without children.

[33] The sons of Jonathan:

Peleth and Zaza.

These were the descendants of Jerahmeel.

[34] Sheshan had no sons—only daughters.

He had an Egyptian servant named Jarha. [35] Sheshan gave his daughter in marriage to his servant Jarha, and she bore him Attai.

[36] Attai was the father of Nathan, Nathan the father of Zabad,

---

[a] 6 Many Hebrew manuscripts, some Septuagint manuscripts and Syriac (see also 1 Kings 4:31); most Hebrew manuscripts *Dara*   [b] 7 *Achar* means *trouble*; *Achar* is called *Achan* in Joshua.   [c] 7 The Hebrew term refers to the irrevocable giving over of things or persons to the LORD, often by totally destroying them.   [d] 9 Hebrew *Kelubai*, a variant of *Caleb*   [e] 11 Septuagint (see also Ruth 4:21); Hebrew *Salma*   [f] 23 Or *captured the settlements of Jair*   [g] 24 *Father* may mean *civic leader* or *military leader*; also in verses 42, 45, 49-52 and possibly elsewhere.   [h] 25 Or *Oren and Ozem, by*

37 Zabad the father of Ephlal,
Ephlal the father of Obed,
38 Obed the father of Jehu,
Jehu the father of Azariah,
39 Azariah the father of Helez,
Helez the father of Eleasah,
40 Eleasah the father of Sismai,
Sismai the father of Shallum,
41 Shallum the father of Jekamiah,
and Jekamiah the father of Elishama.

The Clans of Caleb

42 The sons of Caleb the brother of Jerahmeel:
Mesha his firstborn, who was the father of Ziph, and his son Mareshah,*a* who was the father of Hebron.
43 The sons of Hebron:
Korah, Tappuah, Rekem and Shema. 44 Shema was the father of Raham, and Raham the father of Jorkeam. Rekem was the father of Shammai. 45 The son of Shammai was Maon, and Maon was the father of Beth Zur.
46 Caleb's concubine Ephah was the mother of Haran, Moza and Gazez. Haran was the father of Gazez.
47 The sons of Jahdai:
Regem, Jotham, Geshan, Pelet, Ephah and Shaaph.
48 Caleb's concubine Maakah was the mother of Sheber and Tirhanah. 49 She also gave birth to Shaaph the father of Madmannah and to Sheva the father of Makbenah and Gibea. Caleb's daughter was Aksah. 50 These were the descendants of Caleb.

The sons of Hur the firstborn of Ephrathah:
Shobal the father of Kiriath Jearim, 51 Salma the father of Bethlehem, and Hareph the father of Beth Gader.
52 The descendants of Shobal the father of Kiriath Jearim were:
Haroeh, half the Manahathites, 53 and the clans of Kiriath Jearim: the Ithrites, Puthites, Shumathites and Mishraites. From these descended the Zorathites and Eshtaolites.
54 The descendants of Salma:
Bethlehem, the Netophathites, Atroth Beth Joab, half the Manahathites, the Zorites, 55 and the clans of scribes*b* who lived at Jabez: the Tirathites, Shimeathites and Sucathites. These are the Kenites who came from Hammath, the father of the Rekabites.*c*

The Sons of David

3 These were the sons of David born to him in Hebron:
The firstborn was Amnon the son of Ahinoam of Jezreel;
the second, Daniel the son of Abigail of Carmel;
2 the third, Absalom the son of Maakah daughter of Talmai king of Geshur;
the fourth, Adonijah the son of Haggith;
3 the fifth, Shephatiah the son of Abital;
and the sixth, Ithream, by his wife Eglah.
4 These six were born to David in Hebron, where he reigned seven years and six months.
David reigned in Jerusalem thirty-three years, 5 and these were the children born to him there:
Shammua,*d* Shobab, Nathan and Solomon. These four were by Bathsheba*e* daughter of Ammiel. 6 There were also Ibhar, Elishua,*f* Eliphelet, 7 Nogah, Nepheg, Japhia, 8 Elishama, Eliada and Eliphelet—nine in all. 9 All these were the sons of David, besides his sons by his concubines. And Tamar was their sister.

a 42 The meaning of the Hebrew for this phrase is uncertain.   *b* 55 Or of the Sopherites   *c* 55 Or father of Beth Rekab
d 5 Hebrew Shimea, a variant of Shammua   *e* 5 One Hebrew manuscript and Vulgate (see also Septuagint and 2 Samuel 11:3); most Hebrew manuscripts Bathshua   *f* 6 Two Hebrew manuscripts (see also 2 Samuel 5:15 and 1 Chron. 14:5); most Hebrew manuscripts Elishama

The Kings of Judah

10 Solomon's son was Rehoboam,
    Abijah his son,
    Asa his son,
    Jehoshaphat his son,
11 Jehoram[a] his son,
    Ahaziah his son,
    Joash his son,
12 Amaziah his son,
    Azariah his son,
    Jotham his son,
13 Ahaz his son,
    Hezekiah his son,
    Manasseh his son,
14 Amon his son,
    Josiah his son.
15 The sons of Josiah:
    Johanan the firstborn,
    Jehoiakim the second son,
    Zedekiah the third,
    Shallum the fourth.
16 The successors of Jehoiakim:
    Jehoiachin[b] his son,
    and Zedekiah.

The Royal Line After the Exile

17 The descendants of Jehoiachin the
    captive:
    Shealtiel his son, 18 Malkiram,
    Pedaiah, Shenazzar, Jekamiah,
    Hoshama and Nedabiah.
19 The sons of Pedaiah:
    Zerubbabel and Shimei.
    The sons of Zerubbabel:
    Meshullam and Hananiah.
    Shelomith was their sister.
20 There were also five others:
    Hashubah, Ohel, Berekiah, Hasa-
    diah and Jushab-Hesed.
21 The descendants of Hananiah:
    Pelatiah and Jeshaiah, and the
    sons of Rephaiah, of Arnan, of
    Obadiah and of Shekaniah.
22 The descendants of Shekaniah:
    Shemaiah and his sons:
    Hattush, Igal, Bariah, Neariah and
    Shaphat—six in all.
23 The sons of Neariah:
    Elioenai, Hizkiah and Azrikam—
    three in all.

24 The sons of Elioenai:
    Hodaviah, Eliashib, Pelaiah, Ak-
    kub, Johanan, Delaiah and Ana-
    ni—seven in all.

Other Clans of Judah

4 The descendants of Judah:
    Perez, Hezron, Karmi, Hur and
    Shobal.
2 Reaiah son of Shobal was the father
    of Jahath, and Jahath the father
    of Ahumai and Lahad. These were
    the clans of the Zorathites.
3 These were the sons[c] of Etam:
    Jezreel, Ishma and Idbash. Their
    sister was named Hazzelelponi.
4 Penuel was the father of Gedor,
    and Ezer the father of Hushah.
    These were the descendants of Hur,
    the firstborn of Ephrathah and fa-
    ther[d] of Bethlehem.
5 Ashhur the father of Tekoa had two
    wives, Helah and Naarah.
6 Naarah bore him Ahuzzam, Hepher,
    Temeni and Haahashtari. These
    were the descendants of Naarah.
7 The sons of Helah:
    Zereth, Zohar, Ethnan, 8 and Koz,
    who was the father of Anub and
    Hazzobebah and of the clans of
    Aharhel son of Harum.

9 Jabez was more honorable than his
brothers. His mother had named him Jabez,[e] saying, "I gave birth to him in pain."
10 Jabez cried out to the God of Israel, "Oh,
that you would bless me and enlarge my
territory! Let your hand be with me, and
keep me from harm so that I will be free
from pain." And God granted his request.

11 Kelub, Shuhah's brother, was the
    father of Mehir, who was the fa-
    ther of Eshton. 12 Eshton was the
    father of Beth Rapha, Paseah and
    Tehinnah the father of Ir Nahash.[f]
    These were the men of Rekah.

13 The sons of Kenaz:
    Othniel and Seraiah.

---

a 11 Hebrew *Joram*, a variant of *Jehoram*   b 16 Hebrew *Jeconiah*, a variant of *Jehoiachin*; also in verse 17   c 3 Some
Septuagint manuscripts (see also Vulgate); Hebrew *father*   d 4 *Father* may mean *civic leader* or *military leader*; also in
verses 12, 14, 17, 18 and possibly elsewhere.   e 9 *Jabez* sounds like the Hebrew for *pain.*   f 12 Or *of the city of
Nahash*

The sons of Othniel:
Hathath and Meonothai.[a] 14Meonothai was the father of Ophrah.
Seraiah was the father of Joab,
the father of Ge Harashim.[b] It was called this because its people were skilled workers.
15The sons of Caleb son of Jephunneh:
Iru, Elah and Naam.
The son of Elah:
Kenaz.
16The sons of Jehallelel:
Ziph, Ziphah, Tiria and Asarel.
17The sons of Ezrah:
Jether, Mered, Epher and Jalon. One of Mered's wives gave birth to Miriam, Shammai and Ishbah the father of Eshtemoa. 18(His wife from the tribe of Judah gave birth to Jered the father of Gedor, Heber the father of Soko, and Jekuthiel the father of Zanoah.) These were the children of Pharaoh's daughter Bithiah, whom Mered had married.
19The sons of Hodiah's wife, the sister of Naham:
the father of Keilah the Garmite, and Eshtemoa the Maakathite.
20The sons of Shimon:
Amnon, Rinnah, Ben-Hanan and Tilon.
The descendants of Ishi:
Zoheth and Ben-Zoheth.
21The sons of Shelah son of Judah:
Er the father of Lekah, Laadah the father of Mareshah and the clans of the linen workers at Beth Ashbea, 22Jokim, the men of Kozeba, and Joash and Saraph, who ruled in Moab and Jashubi Lehem. (These records are from ancient times.) 23They were the potters who lived at Netaim and Gederah; they stayed there and worked for the king.

Simeon

24The descendants of Simeon:
Nemuel, Jamin, Jarib, Zerah and Shaul;

25Shallum was Shaul's son, Mibsam his son and Mishma his son.
26The descendants of Mishma:
Hammuel his son, Zakkur his son and Shimei his son.
27Shimei had sixteen sons and six daughters, but his brothers did not have many children; so their entire clan did not become as numerous as the people of Judah. 28They lived in Beersheba, Moladah, Hazar Shual, 29Bilhah, Ezem, Tolad, 30Bethuel, Hormah, Ziklag, 31Beth Markaboth, Hazar Susim, Beth Biri and Shaaraim. These were their towns until the reign of David. 32Their surrounding villages were Etam, Ain, Rimmon, Token and Ashan—five towns— 33and all the villages around these towns as far as Baalath.[c] These were their settlements. And they kept a genealogical record.

34Meshobab, Jamlech, Joshah son of Amaziah, 35Joel, Jehu son of Joshibiah, the son of Seraiah, the son of Asiel, 36also Elioenai, Jaakobah, Jeshohaiah, Asaiah, Adiel, Jesimiel, Benaiah, 37and Ziza son of Shiphi, the son of Allon, the son of Jedaiah, the son of Shimri, the son of Shemaiah.

38The men listed above by name were leaders of their clans. Their families increased greatly, 39and they went to the outskirts of Gedor to the east of the valley in search of pasture for their flocks. 40They found rich, good pasture, and the land was spacious, peaceful and quiet. Some Hamites had lived there formerly.

41The men whose names were listed came in the days of Hezekiah king of Judah. They attacked the Hamites in their dwellings and also the Meunites who were there and completely destroyed[d] them, as is evident to this day. Then they settled in their place, because there was pasture for their flocks. 42And five hundred of these Simeonites, led by Pelatiah, Neariah, Rephaiah and Uzziel, the sons of Ishi, invaded the hill country of Seir. 43They killed the remaining Amalekites

---

[a] 13 Some Septuagint manuscripts and Vulgate; Hebrew does not have and Meonothai.   [b] 14 Ge Harashim means valley of skilled workers.   [c] 33 Some Septuagint manuscripts (see also Joshua 19:8); Hebrew Baal   [d] 41 The Hebrew term refers to the irrevocable giving over of things or persons to the Lord, often by totally destroying them.

who had escaped, and they have lived there to this day.

Reuben

5 The sons of Reuben the firstborn of Israel (he was the firstborn, but when he defiled his father's marriage bed, his rights as firstborn were given to the sons of Joseph son of Israel; so he could not be listed in the genealogical record in accordance with his birthright, ²and though Judah was the strongest of his brothers and a ruler came from him, the rights of the firstborn belonged to Joseph)— ³the sons of Reuben the firstborn of Israel:

Hanok, Pallu, Hezron and Karmi.

⁴The descendants of Joel:
Shemaiah his son, Gog his son, Shimei his son, ⁵Micah his son, Reaiah his son, Baal his son, ⁶and Beerah his son, whom Tiglath-Pileser[a] king of Assyria took into exile. Beerah was a leader of the Reubenites.

⁷Their relatives by clans, listed according to their genealogical records:
Jeiel the chief, Zechariah, ⁸and Bela son of Azaz, the son of Shema, the son of Joel. They settled in the area from Aroer to Nebo and Baal Meon. ⁹To the east they occupied the land up to the edge of the desert that extends to the Euphrates River, because their livestock had increased in Gilead.

¹⁰During Saul's reign they waged war against the Hagrites, who were defeated at their hands; they occupied the dwellings of the Hagrites throughout the entire region east of Gilead.

Gad

¹¹The Gadites lived next to them in Bashan, as far as Salekah:

¹²Joel was the chief, Shapham the second, then Janai and Shaphat, in Bashan.

¹³Their relatives, by families, were:
Michael, Meshullam, Sheba, Jorai, Jakan, Zia and Eber—seven in all.

¹⁴These were the sons of Abihail son of Huri, the son of Jaroah, the son of Gilead, the son of Michael, the son of Jeshishai, the son of Jahdo, the son of Buz.

¹⁵Ahi son of Abdiel, the son of Guni, was head of their family.

¹⁶The Gadites lived in Gilead, in Bashan and its outlying villages, and on all the pasturelands of Sharon as far as they extended.

¹⁷All these were entered in the genealogical records during the reigns of Jotham king of Judah and Jeroboam king of Israel.

¹⁸The Reubenites, the Gadites and the half-tribe of Manasseh had 44,760 men ready for military service—able-bodied men who could handle shield and sword, who could use a bow, and who were trained for battle. ¹⁹They waged war against the Hagrites, Jetur, Naphish and Nodab. ²⁰They were helped in fighting them, and God delivered the Hagrites and all their allies into their hands, because they cried out to him during the battle. He answered their prayers, because they trusted in him. ²¹They seized the livestock of the Hagrites—fifty thousand camels, two hundred fifty thousand sheep and two thousand donkeys. They also took one hundred thousand people captive, ²²and many others fell slain, because the battle was God's. And they occupied the land until the exile.

The Half-Tribe of Manasseh

²³The people of the half-tribe of Manasseh were numerous; they settled in the land from Bashan to Baal Hermon, that is, to Senir (Mount Hermon).

²⁴These were the heads of their families: Epher, Ishi, Eliel, Azriel, Jeremiah, Hodaviah and Jahdiel. They were brave warriors, famous men, and heads of their families. ²⁵But they were unfaithful to the God of their ancestors and prostituted themselves to the gods of the peoples of the land, whom God had destroyed before them. ²⁶So the God of Israel stirred up the spirit of Pul king of Assyria (that

---

a 6 Hebrew *Tilgath-Pilneser*, a variant of *Tiglath-Pileser*; also in verse 26

is, Tiglath-Pileser king of Assyria), who took the Reubenites, the Gadites and the half-tribe of Manasseh into exile. He took them to Halah, Habor, Hara and the river of Gozan, where they are to this day.

Levi

6 ^a The sons of Levi:
Gershon, Kohath and Merari.

² The sons of Kohath:
Amram, Izhar, Hebron and Uzziel.
³ The children of Amram:
Aaron, Moses and Miriam.
The sons of Aaron:
Nadab, Abihu, Eleazar and Itha-
mar.
⁴ Eleazar was the father of Phine-
has,
Phinehas the father of Abishua,
⁵ Abishua the father of Bukki,
Bukki the father of Uzzi,
⁶ Uzzi the father of Zerahiah,
Zerahiah the father of Meraioth,
⁷ Meraioth the father of Amariah,
Amariah the father of Ahitub,
⁸ Ahitub the father of Zadok,
Zadok the father of Ahimaaz,
⁹ Ahimaaz the father of Azariah,
Azariah the father of Johanan,
¹⁰ Johanan the father of Azariah (it
was he who served as priest in
the temple Solomon built in Jeru-
salem),
¹¹ Azariah the father of Amariah,
Amariah the father of Ahitub,
¹² Ahitub the father of Zadok,
Zadok the father of Shallum,
¹³ Shallum the father of Hilkiah,
Hilkiah the father of Azariah,
¹⁴ Azariah the father of Seraiah,
and Seraiah the father of Joza-
dak.^b
¹⁵ Jozadak was deported when the
LORD sent Judah and Jerusalem into
exile by the hand of Nebuchadnezzar.

¹⁶ The sons of Levi:
Gershon,^c Kohath and Merari.

¹⁷ These are the names of the sons of
Gershon:
Libni and Shimei.
¹⁸ The sons of Kohath:
Amram, Izhar, Hebron and Uzziel.
¹⁹ The sons of Merari:
Mahli and Mushi.
These are the clans of the Levites
listed according to their fathers:
²⁰ Of Gershon:
Libni his son, Jahath his son,
Zimmah his son, ²¹ Joah his son,
Iddo his son, Zerah his son
and Jeatherai his son.
²² The descendants of Kohath:
Amminadab his son, Korah his
son,
Assir his son, ²³ Elkanah his son,
Ebiasaph his son, Assir his son,
²⁴ Tahath his son, Uriel his son,
Uzziah his son and Shaul his son.
²⁵ The descendants of Elkanah:
Amasai, Ahimoth,
²⁶ Elkanah his son,^d Zophai his son,
Nahath his son, ²⁷ Eliab his son,
Jeroham his son, Elkanah his son
and Samuel his son.^e
²⁸ The sons of Samuel:
Joel^f the firstborn
and Abijah the second son.
²⁹ The descendants of Merari:
Mahli, Libni his son,
Shimei his son, Uzzah his son,
³⁰ Shimea his son, Haggiah his son
and Asaiah his son.

The Temple Musicians

³¹ These are the men David put in charge of the music in the house of the LORD after the ark came to rest there. ³² They ministered with music before the tabernacle, the tent of meeting, until Solomon built the temple of the LORD in Jerusalem. They performed their duties according to the regulations laid down for them. ³³ Here are the men who served, to-gether with their sons:

---

^a In Hebrew texts 6:1-15 is numbered 5:27-41, and 6:16-81 is numbered 6:1-66.   ^b 14 Hebrew *Jehozadak*, a variant of *Jozadak*; also in verse 15   ^c 16 Hebrew *Gershom*, a variant of *Gershon*; also in verses 17, 20, 43, 62 and 71   ^d 26 Some Hebrew manuscripts, Septuagint and Syriac; most Hebrew manuscripts *Ahimoth* ²⁶*and Elkanah. The sons of Elkanah:*   ^e 27 Some Septuagint manuscripts (see also 1 Samuel 1:19,20 and 1 Chron. 6:33,34); Hebrew does not have *and Samuel his son.*   ^f 28 Some Septuagint manuscripts and Syriac (see also 1 Samuel 8:2 and 1 Chron. 6:33); Hebrew does not have *Joel.*

From the Kohathites:
Heman, the musician,
the son of Joel, the son of Samuel,
³⁴the son of Elkanah, the son of Jeroham,
the son of Eliel, the son of Toah,
³⁵the son of Zuph, the son of Elkanah,
the son of Mahath, the son of Amasai,
³⁶the son of Elkanah, the son of Joel,
the son of Azariah, the son of Zephaniah,
³⁷the son of Tahath, the son of Assir,
the son of Ebiasaph, the son of Korah,
³⁸the son of Izhar, the son of Kohath,
the son of Levi, the son of Israel;
³⁹and Heman's associate Asaph, who served at his right hand:
Asaph son of Berekiah, the son of Shimea,
⁴⁰the son of Michael, the son of Baaseiah,ᵃ
the son of Malkijah, ⁴¹the son of Ethni,
the son of Zerah, the son of Adaiah,
⁴²the son of Ethan, the son of Zimmah,
the son of Shimei, ⁴³the son of Jahath,
the son of Gershon, the son of Levi;
⁴⁴and from their associates, the Merarites, at his left hand:
Ethan son of Kishi, the son of Abdi,
the son of Malluk, ⁴⁵the son of Hashabiah,
the son of Amaziah, the son of Hilkiah,
⁴⁶the son of Amzi, the son of Bani,
the son of Shemer, ⁴⁷the son of Mahli,
the son of Mushi, the son of Merari,
the son of Levi.
⁴⁸Their fellow Levites were assigned to all the other duties of the tabernacle, the house of God. ⁴⁹But Aaron and his descendants were the ones who presented offerings on the altar of burnt offering and on the altar of incense in connection with all that was done in the Most Holy Place, making atonement for Israel, in accordance with all that Moses the servant of God had commanded.

⁵⁰These were the descendants of Aaron:
Eleazar his son, Phinehas his son,
Abishua his son, ⁵¹Bukki his son,
Uzzi his son, Zerahiah his son,
⁵²Meraioth his son, Amariah his son,
Ahitub his son, ⁵³Zadok his son
and Ahimaaz his son.

⁵⁴These were the locations of their settlements allotted as their territory (they were assigned to the descendants of Aaron who were from the Kohathite clan, because the first lot was for them): ⁵⁵They were given Hebron in Judah with its surrounding pasturelands. ⁵⁶But the fields and villages around the city were given to Caleb son of Jephunneh. ⁵⁷So the descendants of Aaron were given Hebron (a city of refuge), and Libnah,ᵇ Jattir, Eshtemoa, ⁵⁸Hilen, Debir, ⁵⁹Ashan, Juttahᶜ and Beth Shemesh, together with their pasturelands. ⁶⁰And from the tribe of Benjamin they were given Gibeon,ᵈ Geba, Alemeth and Anathoth, together with their pasturelands.

The total number of towns distributed among the Kohathite clans came to thirteen.

⁶¹The rest of Kohath's descendants were allotted ten towns from the clans of half the tribe of Manasseh.

⁶²The descendants of Gershon, clan by clan, were allotted thirteen towns from the tribes of Issachar, Asher and Naphtali, and from the part of the tribe of Manasseh that is in Bashan.

ᵃ 40 Most Hebrew manuscripts; some Hebrew manuscripts, one Septuagint manuscript and Syriac *Maaseiah*
ᵇ 57 See Joshua 21:13; Hebrew *given the cities of refuge: Hebron, Libnah.*   ᶜ 59 Syriac (see also Septuagint and Joshua 21:16); Hebrew does not have *Juttah.*   ᵈ 60 See Joshua 21:17; Hebrew does not have *Gibeon.*

63 The descendants of Merari, clan by clan, were allotted twelve towns from the tribes of Reuben, Gad and Zebulun.

64 So the Israelites gave the Levites these towns and their pasturelands. 65 From the tribes of Judah, Simeon and Benjamin they allotted the previously named towns.

66 Some of the Kohathite clans were given as their territory towns from the tribe of Ephraim.

67 In the hill country of Ephraim they were given Shechem (a city of refuge), and Gezer,ᵃ 68 Jokmeam, Beth Horon, 69 Aijalon and Gath Rimmon, together with their pasturelands.

70 And from half the tribe of Manasseh the Israelites gave Aner and Bileam, together with their pasturelands, to the rest of the Kohathite clans.

71 The Gershonites received the following:

From the clan of the half-tribe of Manasseh
they received Golan in Bashan and also Ashtaroth, together with their pasturelands;
72 from the tribe of Issachar
they received Kedesh, Daberath, 73 Ramoth and Anem, together with their pasturelands;
74 from the tribe of Asher
they received Mashal, Abdon, 75 Hukok and Rehob, together with their pasturelands;
76 and from the tribe of Naphtali
they received Kedesh in Galilee, Hammon and Kiriathaim, together with their pasturelands.

77 The Merarites (the rest of the Levites) received the following:

From the tribe of Zebulun
they received Jokneam, Kartah,ᵇ Rimmono and Tabor, together with their pasturelands;
78 from the tribe of Reuben across the Jordan east of Jericho
they received Bezer in the wilderness, Jahzah, 79 Kedemoth and Mephaath, together with their pasturelands;
80 and from the tribe of Gad
they received Ramoth in Gilead, Mahanaim, 81 Heshbon and Jazer, together with their pasturelands.

Issachar

7 The sons of Issachar:
Tola, Puah, Jashub and Shimron— four in all.
2 The sons of Tola:
Uzzi, Rephaiah, Jeriel, Jahmai, Ibsam and Samuel—heads of their families. During the reign of David, the descendants of Tola listed as fighting men in their genealogy numbered 22,600.
3 The son of Uzzi:
Izrahiah.
The sons of Izrahiah:
Michael, Obadiah, Joel and Ishiah. All five of them were chiefs. 4 According to their family genealogy, they had 36,000 men ready for battle, for they had many wives and children.
5 The relatives who were fighting men belonging to all the clans of Issachar, as listed in their genealogy, were 87,000 in all.

Benjamin

6 Three sons of Benjamin:
Bela, Beker and Jediael.
7 The sons of Bela:
Ezbon, Uzzi, Uzziel, Jerimoth and Iri, heads of families—five in all. Their genealogical record listed 22,034 fighting men.
8 The sons of Beker:
Zemirah, Joash, Eliezer, Elioenai, Omri, Jeremoth, Abijah, Anathoth and Alemeth. All these were the sons of Beker. 9 Their genealogical record listed the heads of families and 20,200 fighting men.
10 The son of Jediael:
Bilhan.

ᵃ 67 See Joshua 21:21; Hebrew *given the cities of refuge: Shechem, Gezer.*   ᵇ 77 See Septuagint and Joshua 21:34; Hebrew does not have *Jokneam, Kartah.*

The sons of Bilhan:

Jeush, Benjamin, Ehud, Kenaanah, Zethan, Tarshish and Ahishahar. [11]All these sons of Jediael were heads of families. There were 17,200 fighting men ready to go out to war.

[12]The Shuppites and Huppites were the descendants of Ir, and the Hushites[a] the descendants of Aher.

Naphtali

[13]The sons of Naphtali:

Jahziel, Guni, Jezer and Shillem[b]—the descendants of Bilhah.

Manasseh

[14]The descendants of Manasseh:

Asriel was his descendant through his Aramean concubine. She gave birth to Makir the father of Gilead. [15]Makir took a wife from among the Huppites and Shuppites. His sister's name was Maakah.

Another descendant was named Zelophehad, who had only daughters.

[16]Makir's wife Maakah gave birth to a son and named him Peresh. His brother was named Sheresh, and his sons were Ulam and Rakem.

[17]The son of Ulam:

Bedan.

These were the sons of Gilead son of Makir, the son of Manasseh. [18]His sister Hammoleketh gave birth to Ishhod, Abiezer and Mahlah.

[19]The sons of Shemida were:

Ahian, Shechem, Likhi and Aniam.

Ephraim

[20]The descendants of Ephraim:

Shuthelah, Bered his son,
Tahath his son, Eleadah his son,
Tahath his son, [21]Zabad his son
and Shuthelah his son.

Ezer and Elead were killed by the native-born men of Gath, when they went down to seize their livestock.

[22]Their father Ephraim mourned for them many days, and his relatives came to comfort him. [23]Then he made love to his wife again, and she became pregnant and gave birth to a son. He named him Beriah,[c] because there had been misfortune in his family. [24]His daughter was Sheerah, who built Lower and Upper Beth Horon as well as Uzzen Sheerah.

[25]Rephah was his son, Resheph his son,[d]
Telah his son, Tahan his son,
[26]Ladan his son, Ammihud his son,
Elishama his son, [27]Nun his son
and Joshua his son.

[28]Their lands and settlements included Bethel and its surrounding villages, Naaran to the east, Gezer and its villages to the west, and Shechem and its villages all the way to Ayyah and its villages. [29]Along the borders of Manasseh were Beth Shan, Taanach, Megiddo and Dor, together with their villages. The descendants of Joseph son of Israel lived in these towns.

Asher

[30]The sons of Asher:

Imnah, Ishvah, Ishvi and Beriah. Their sister was Serah.

[31]The sons of Beriah:

Heber and Malkiel, who was the father of Birzaith.

[32]Heber was the father of Japhlet, Shomer and Hotham and of their sister Shua.

[33]The sons of Japhlet:

Pasak, Bimhal and Ashvath.

These were Japhlet's sons.

[34]The sons of Shomer:

Ahi, Rohgah,[e] Hubbah and Aram.

[35]The sons of his brother Helem:

Zophah, Imna, Shelesh and Amal.

[36]The sons of Zophah:

Suah, Harnepher, Shual, Beri, Imrah, [37]Bezer, Hod, Shamma, Shilshah, Ithran[f] and Beera.

[38]The sons of Jether:

Jephunneh, Pispah and Ara.

---

[a] 12 Or Ir. The sons of Dan: Hushim, (see Gen. 46:23); Hebrew does not have The sons of Dan.   [b] 13 Some Hebrew and Septuagint manuscripts (see also Gen. 46:24 and Num. 26:49); most Hebrew manuscripts Shallum   [c] 23 Beriah sounds like the Hebrew for misfortune.   [d] 25 Some Septuagint manuscripts; Hebrew does not have his son.   [e] 34 Or of his brother Shomer: Rohgah   [f] 37 Possibly a variant of Jether

39 The sons of Ulla:

Arah, Hanniel and Rizia.

40 All these were descendants of Asher—heads of families, choice men, brave warriors and outstanding leaders. The number of men ready for battle, as listed in their genealogy, was 26,000.

The Genealogy of Saul the Benjamite

8 Benjamin was the father of Bela his firstborn,

Ashbel the second son, Aharah the third,

2 Nohah the fourth and Rapha the fifth.

3 The sons of Bela were:

Addar, Gera, Abihud,[a] 4 Abishua, Naaman, Ahoah, 5 Gera, Shephuphan and Huram.

6 These were the descendants of Ehud, who were heads of families of those living in Geba and were deported to Manahath:

7 Naaman, Ahijah, and Gera, who deported them and who was the father of Uzza and Ahihud.

8 Sons were born to Shaharaim in Moab after he had divorced his wives Hushim and Baara. 9 By his wife Hodesh he had Jobab, Zibia, Mesha, Malkam, 10 Jeuz, Sakia and Mirmah. These were his sons, heads of families. 11 By Hushim he had Abitub and Elpaal.

12 The sons of Elpaal:

Eber, Misham, Shemed (who built Ono and Lod with its surrounding villages), 13 and Beriah and Shema, who were heads of families of those living in Aijalon and who drove out the inhabitants of Gath.

14 Ahio, Shashak, Jeremoth, 15 Zebadiah, Arad, Eder, 16 Michael, Ishpah and Joha were the sons of Beriah.

17 Zebadiah, Meshullam, Hizki, Heber, 18 Ishmerai, Izliah and Jobab were the sons of Elpaal.

19 Jakim, Zikri, Zabdi, 20 Elienai, Zillethai, Eliel, 21 Adaiah, Beraiah and Shimrath were the sons of Shimei.

22 Ishpan, Eber, Eliel, 23 Abdon, Zikri, Hanan, 24 Hananiah, Elam, Anthothijah, 25 Iphdeiah and Penuel were the sons of Shashak.

26 Shamsherai, Shehariah, Athaliah, 27 Jaareshiah, Elijah and Zikri were the sons of Jeroham.

28 All these were heads of families, chiefs as listed in their genealogy, and they lived in Jerusalem.

29 Jeiel[b] the father[c] of Gibeon lived in Gibeon.

His wife's name was Maakah, 30 and his firstborn son was Abdon, followed by Zur, Kish, Baal, Ner,[d] Nadab, 31 Gedor, Ahio, Zeker 32 and Mikloth, who was the father of Shimeah. They too lived near their relatives in Jerusalem.

33 Ner was the father of Kish, Kish the father of Saul, and Saul the father of Jonathan, Malki-Shua, Abinadab and Esh-Baal.[e]

34 The son of Jonathan:

Merib-Baal,[f] who was the father of Micah.

35 The sons of Micah:

Pithon, Melek, Tarea and Ahaz.

36 Ahaz was the father of Jehoaddah, Jehoaddah was the father of Alemeth, Azmaveth and Zimri, and Zimri was the father of Moza.

37 Moza was the father of Binea; Raphah was his son, Eleasah his son and Azel his son.

38 Azel had six sons, and these were their names:

Azrikam, Bokeru, Ishmael, Sheariah, Obadiah and Hanan. All these were the sons of Azel.

39 The sons of his brother Eshek:

Ulam his firstborn, Jeush the second son and Eliphelet the third.

40 The sons of Ulam were brave warriors who could handle the bow. They had many sons and grandsons—150 in all.

---

a 3 Or Gera the father of Ehud   b 29 Some Septuagint manuscripts (see also 9:35); Hebrew does not have Jeiel.
c 29 Father may mean civic leader or military leader.   d 30 Some Septuagint manuscripts (see also 9:36); Hebrew does not have Ner.   e 33 Also known as Ish-Bosheth   f 34 Also known as Mephibosheth

All these were the descendants of Benjamin.

9 All Israel was listed in the genealogies recorded in the book of the kings of Israel and Judah. They were taken captive to Babylon because of their unfaithfulness.

The People in Jerusalem

2 Now the first to resettle on their own property in their own towns were some Israelites, priests, Levites and temple servants.

3 Those from Judah, from Benjamin, and from Ephraim and Manasseh who lived in Jerusalem were:

4 Uthai son of Ammihud, the son of Omri, the son of Imri, the son of Bani, a descendant of Perez son of Judah.

5 Of the Shelanites[a]:

Asaiah the firstborn and his sons.

6 Of the Zerahites:

Jeuel.

The people from Judah numbered 690.

7 Of the Benjamites:

Sallu son of Meshullam, the son of Hodaviah, the son of Hassenuah;

8 Ibneiah son of Jeroham; Elah son of Uzzi, the son of Mikri; and Meshullam son of Shephatiah, the son of Reuel, the son of Ibnijah.

9 The people from Benjamin, as listed in their genealogy, numbered 956. All these men were heads of their families.

10 Of the priests:

Jedaiah; Jehoiarib; Jakin;

11 Azariah son of Hilkiah, the son of Meshullam, the son of Zadok, the son of Meraioth, the son of Ahitub, the official in charge of the house of God;

12 Adaiah son of Jeroham, the son of Pashhur, the son of Malkijah; and Maasai son of Adiel, the son of Jahzerah, the son of Meshullam, the son of Meshillemith, the son of Immer.

13 The priests, who were heads of families, numbered 1,760. They were able men, responsible for ministering in the house of God.

14 Of the Levites:

Shemaiah son of Hasshub, the son of Azrikam, the son of Hashabiah, a Merarite; 15 Bakbakkar, Heresh, Galal and Mattaniah son of Mika, the son of Zikri, the son of Asaph; 16 Obadiah son of Shemaiah, the son of Galal, the son of Jeduthun; and Berekiah son of Asa, the son of Elkanah, who lived in the villages of the Netophathites.

17 The gatekeepers:

Shallum, Akkub, Talmon, Ahiman and their fellow Levites, Shallum their chief 18 being stationed at the King's Gate on the east, up to the present time. These were the gatekeepers belonging to the camp of the Levites. 19 Shallum son of Kore, the son of Ebiasaph, the son of Korah, and his fellow gatekeepers from his family (the Korahites) were responsible for guarding the thresholds of the tent just as their ancestors had been responsible for guarding the entrance to the dwelling of the LORD. 20 In earlier times Phinehas son of Eleazar was the official in charge of the gatekeepers, and the LORD was with him. 21 Zechariah son of Meshelemiah was the gatekeeper at the entrance to the tent of meeting.

22 Altogether, those chosen to be gatekeepers at the thresholds numbered 212. They were registered by genealogy in their villages. The gatekeepers had been assigned to their positions of trust by David and Samuel the seer. 23 They and their descendants were in charge of guarding the gates of the house of the LORD—the house called the tent of meeting. 24 The gatekeepers were on the four sides: east, west, north and south. 25 Their fellow Levites in their villages had to come from

---

a 5 See Num. 26:20; Hebrew *Shilonites*.

time to time and share their duties for seven-day periods. 26 But the four principal gatekeepers, who were Levites, were entrusted with the responsibility for the rooms and treasuries in the house of God. 27 They would spend the night stationed around the house of God, because they had to guard it; and they had charge of the key for opening it each morning.

28 Some of them were in charge of the articles used in the temple service; they counted them when they were brought in and when they were taken out. 29 Others were assigned to take care of the furnishings and all the other articles of the sanctuary, as well as the special flour and wine, and the olive oil, incense and spices. 30 But some of the priests took care of mixing the spices. 31 A Levite named Mattithiah, the firstborn son of Shallum the Korahite, was entrusted with the responsibility for baking the offering bread. 32 Some of the Kohathites, their fellow Levites, were in charge of preparing for every Sabbath the bread set out on the table.

33 Those who were musicians, heads of Levite families, stayed in the rooms of the temple and were exempt from other duties because they were responsible for the work day and night.

34 All these were heads of Levite families, chiefs as listed in their genealogy, and they lived in Jerusalem.

The Genealogy of Saul

35 Jeiel the father[a] of Gibeon lived in Gibeon.

His wife's name was Maakah, 36 and his firstborn son was Abdon, followed by Zur, Kish, Baal, Ner, Nadab, 37 Gedor, Ahio, Zechariah and Mikloth. 38 Mikloth was the father of Shimeam. They too lived near their relatives in Jerusalem.

39 Ner was the father of Kish, Kish the father of Saul, and Saul the father of Jonathan, Malki-Shua, Abinadab and Esh-Baal.[b]

40 The son of Jonathan:

Merib-Baal,[c] who was the father of Micah.

41 The sons of Micah:

Pithon, Melek, Tahrea and Ahaz.[d]

42 Ahaz was the father of Jadah, Jadah[e] was the father of Alemeth, Azmaveth and Zimri, and Zimri was the father of Moza. 43 Moza was the father of Binea; Rephaiah was his son, Eleasah his son and Azel his son.

44 Azel had six sons, and these were their names:

Azrikam, Bokeru, Ishmael, Sheariah, Obadiah and Hanan. These were the sons of Azel.

Saul Takes His Life

10 Now the Philistines fought against Israel; the Israelites fled before them, and many fell dead on Mount Gilboa. 2 The Philistines were in hot pursuit of Saul and his sons, and they killed his sons Jonathan, Abinadab and Malki-Shua. 3 The fighting grew fierce around Saul, and when the archers overtook him, they wounded him.

4 Saul said to his armor-bearer, "Draw your sword and run me through, or these uncircumcised fellows will come and abuse me."

But his armor-bearer was terrified and would not do it; so Saul took his own sword and fell on it. 5 When the armor-bearer saw that Saul was dead, he too fell on his sword and died. 6 So Saul and his three sons died, and all his house died together.

7 When all the Israelites in the valley saw that the army had fled and that Saul and his sons had died, they abandoned their towns and fled. And the Philistines came and occupied them.

8 The next day, when the Philistines came to strip the dead, they found Saul and his sons fallen on Mount Gilboa. 9 They stripped him and took his head and his armor, and sent messengers throughout the land of the Philistines to proclaim

---

a 35 Father may mean civic leader or military leader.   b 39 Also known as Ish-Bosheth   c 40 Also known as Mephibosheth   d 41 Vulgate and Syriac (see also Septuagint and 8:35); Hebrew does not have and Ahaz.   e 42 Some Hebrew manuscripts and Septuagint (see also 8:36); most Hebrew manuscripts Jarah, Jarah

the news among their idols and their people. [10]They put his armor in the temple of their gods and hung up his head in the temple of Dagon.

[11]When all the inhabitants of Jabesh Gilead heard what the Philistines had done to Saul, [12]all their valiant men went and took the bodies of Saul and his sons and brought them to Jabesh. Then they buried their bones under the great tree in Jabesh, and they fasted seven days.

[13]Saul died because he was unfaithful to the LORD; he did not keep the word of the LORD and even consulted a medium for guidance, [14]and did not inquire of the LORD. So the LORD put him to death and turned the kingdom over to David son of Jesse.

David Becomes King Over Israel

11 All Israel came together to David at Hebron and said, "We are your own flesh and blood. [2]In the past, even while Saul was king, you were the one who led Israel on their military campaigns. And the LORD your God said to you, 'You will shepherd my people Israel, and you will become their ruler.'"

[3]When all the elders of Israel had come to King David at Hebron, he made a covenant with them at Hebron before the LORD, and they anointed David king over Israel, as the LORD had promised through Samuel.

David Conquers Jerusalem

[4]David and all the Israelites marched to Jerusalem (that is, Jebus). The Jebusites who lived there [5]said to David, "You will not get in here." Nevertheless, David captured the fortress of Zion—which is the City of David.

[6]David had said, "Whoever leads the attack on the Jebusites will become commander-in-chief." Joab son of Zeruiah went up first, and so he received the command.

[7]David then took up residence in the fortress, and so it was called the City of David. [8]He built up the city around it, from the terraces[a] to the surrounding wall, while Joab restored the rest of the city. [9]And David became more and more powerful, because the LORD Almighty was with him.

David's Mighty Warriors

[10]These were the chiefs of David's mighty warriors—they, together with all Israel, gave his kingship strong support to extend it over the whole land, as the LORD had promised— [11]this is the list of David's mighty warriors:

Jashobeam,[b] a Hakmonite, was chief of the officers[c]; he raised his spear against three hundred men, whom he killed in one encounter.

[12]Next to him was Eleazar son of Dodai the Ahohite, one of the three mighty warriors. [13]He was with David at Pas Dammim when the Philistines gathered there for battle. At a place where there was a field full of barley, the troops fled from the Philistines. [14]But they took their stand in the middle of the field. They defended it and struck the Philistines down, and the LORD brought about a great victory.

[15]Three of the thirty chiefs came down to David to the rock at the cave of Adullam, while a band of Philistines was encamped in the Valley of Rephaim. [16]At that time David was in the stronghold, and the Philistine garrison was at Bethlehem. [17]David longed for water and said, "Oh, that someone would get me a drink of water from the well near the gate of Bethlehem!" [18]So the Three broke through the Philistine lines, drew water from the well near the gate of Bethlehem and carried it back to David. But he refused to drink it; instead, he poured it out to the LORD. [19]"God forbid that I should do this!" he said. "Should I drink the blood of these men who went at the risk of their lives?" Because they risked their lives to bring it back, David would not drink it.

Such were the exploits of the three mighty warriors.

[20]Abishai the brother of Joab was chief

---

a 8 Or *the Millo*   *b 11* Possibly a variant of *Jashob-Baal*   *c 11* Or *Thirty*; some Septuagint manuscripts *Three* (see also 2 Samuel 23:8)

of the Three. He raised his spear against three hundred men, whom he killed, and so he became as famous as the Three. 21He was doubly honored above the Three and became their commander, even though he was not included among them.

22Benaiah son of Jehoiada, a valiant fighter from Kabzeel, performed great exploits. He struck down Moab's two mightiest warriors. He also went down into a pit on a snowy day and killed a lion. 23And he struck down an Egyptian who was five cubits[a] tall. Although the Egyptian had a spear like a weaver's rod in his hand, Benaiah went against him with a club. He snatched the spear from the Egyptian's hand and killed him with his own spear. 24Such were the exploits of Benaiah son of Jehoiada; he too was as famous as the three mighty warriors. 25He was held in greater honor than any of the Thirty, but he was not included among the Three. And David put him in charge of his bodyguard.

26The mighty warriors were:
Asahel the brother of Joab,
Elhanan son of Dodo from Bethlehem,
27Shammoth the Harorite,
Helez the Pelonite,
28Ira son of Ikkesh from Tekoa,
Abiezer from Anathoth,
29Sibbekai the Hushathite,
Ilai the Ahohite,
30Maharai the Netophathite,
Heled son of Baanah the Netophathite,
31Ithai son of Ribai from Gibeah in Benjamin,
Benaiah the Pirathonite,
32Hurai from the ravines of Gaash,
Abiel the Arbathite,
33Azmaveth the Baharumite,
Eliahba the Shaalbonite,
34the sons of Hashem the Gizonite,
Jonathan son of Shagee the Hararite,
35Ahiam son of Sakar the Hararite,
Eliphal son of Ur,
36Hepher the Mekerathite,
Ahijah the Pelonite,
37Hezro the Carmelite,
Naarai son of Ezbai,
38Joel the brother of Nathan,
Mibhar son of Hagri,
39Zelek the Ammonite,
Naharai the Berothite, the armorbearer of Joab son of Zeruiah,
40Ira the Ithrite,
Gareb the Ithrite,
41Uriah the Hittite,
Zabad son of Ahlai,
42Adina son of Shiza the Reubenite, who was chief of the Reubenites, and the thirty with him,
43Hanan son of Maakah,
Joshaphat the Mithnite,
44Uzzia the Ashterathite,
Shama and Jeiel the sons of Hotham the Aroerite,
45Jediael the son of Shimri,
his brother Joha the Tizite,
46Eliel the Mahavite,
Jeribai and Joshaviah the sons of Elnaam,
Ithmah the Moabite,
47Eliel, Obed and Jaasiel the Mezobaite.

Warriors Join David

12 These were the men who came to David at Ziklag, while he was banished from the presence of Saul son of Kish (they were among the warriors who helped him in battle; 2they were armed with bows and were able to shoot arrows or to sling stones right-handed or left-handed; they were relatives of Saul from the tribe of Benjamin):

3Ahiezer their chief and Joash the sons of Shemaah the Gibeathite; Jeziel and Pelet the sons of Azmaveth; Berakah, Jehu the Anathothite, 4and Ishmaiah the Gibeonite, a mighty warrior among the Thirty, who was a leader of the Thirty; Jeremiah, Jahaziel, Johanan, Jozabad the Gederathite,[b] 5Eluzai, Jerimoth, Bealiah, Shemariah and Shephatiah the Ha-

---

[a] 23 That is, about 7 feet 6 inches or about 2.3 meters   [b] 4 In Hebrew texts the second half of this verse (Jeremiah ... Gederathite) is numbered 12:5, and 12:5-40 is numbered 12:6-41.

ruphite; [6] Elkanah, Ishiah, Azarel, Joezer and Jashobeam the Korahites; [7] and Joelah and Zebadiah the sons of Jeroham from Gedor.

[8] Some Gadites defected to David at his stronghold in the wilderness. They were brave warriors, ready for battle and able to handle the shield and spear. Their faces were the faces of lions, and they were as swift as gazelles in the mountains.

[9] Ezer was the chief,
Obadiah the second in command, Eliab the third,
[10] Mishmannah the fourth, Jeremiah the fifth,
[11] Attai the sixth, Eliel the seventh,
[12] Johanan the eighth, Elzabad the ninth,
[13] Jeremiah the tenth and Makbannai the eleventh.

[14] These Gadites were army commanders; the least was a match for a hundred, and the greatest for a thousand. [15] It was they who crossed the Jordan in the first month when it was overflowing all its banks, and they put to flight everyone living in the valleys, to the east and to the west.

[16] Other Benjamites and some men from Judah also came to David in his stronghold. [17] David went out to meet them and said to them, "If you have come to me in peace to help me, I am ready for you to join me. But if you have come to betray me to my enemies when my hands are free from violence, may the God of our ancestors see it and judge you."

[18] Then the Spirit came on Amasai, chief of the Thirty, and he said:

"We are yours, David!
We are with you, son of Jesse!
Success, success to you,
and success to those who help you,
for your God will help you."

So David received them and made them leaders of his raiding bands.

Success, success to you . . . for your God will help you.
1 Chronicles 12:18

[19] Some of the tribe of Manasseh defected to David when he went with the Philistines to fight against Saul. (He and his men did not help the Philistines because, after consultation, their rulers sent him away. They said, "It will cost us our heads if he deserts to his master Saul.") [20] When David went to Ziklag, these were the men of Manasseh who defected to him: Adnah, Jozabad, Jediael, Michael, Jozabad, Elihu and Zillethai, leaders of units of a thousand in Manasseh. [21] They helped David against raiding bands, for all of them were brave warriors, and they were commanders in his army. [22] Day after day men came to help David, until he had a great army, like the army of God.[a]

Others Join David at Hebron

[23] These are the numbers of the men armed for battle who came to David at Hebron to turn Saul's kingdom over to him, as the LORD had said:
[24] from Judah, carrying shield and spear—6,800 armed for battle;
[25] from Simeon, warriors ready for battle—7,100;
[26] from Levi—4,600, [27] including Jehoiada, leader of the family of Aaron, with 3,700 men, [28] and Zadok, a brave young warrior, with 22 officers from his family;
[29] from Benjamin, Saul's tribe—3,000, most of whom had remained loyal to Saul's house until then;
[30] from Ephraim, brave warriors, famous in their own clans—20,800;
[31] from half the tribe of Manasseh, designated by name to come and make David king—18,000;
[32] from Issachar, men who understood the times and knew what Israel should do—200 chiefs, with all their relatives under their command;

---

[a] 22 Or *a great and mighty army*

33 from Zebulun, experienced soldiers prepared for battle with every type of weapon, to help David with undivided loyalty—50,000;

34 from Naphtali—1,000 officers, together with 37,000 men carrying shields and spears;

35 from Dan, ready for battle—28,600;

36 from Asher, experienced soldiers prepared for battle—40,000;

37 and from east of the Jordan, from Reuben, Gad and the half-tribe of Manasseh, armed with every type of weapon—120,000.

38 All these were fighting men who volunteered to serve in the ranks. They came to Hebron fully determined to make David king over all Israel. All the rest of the Israelites were also of one mind to make David king. 39 The men spent three days there with David, eating and drinking, for their families had supplied provisions for them. 40 Also, their neighbors from as far away as Issachar, Zebulun and Naphtali came bringing food on donkeys, camels, mules and oxen. There were plentiful supplies of flour, fig cakes, raisin cakes, wine, olive oil, cattle and sheep, for there was joy in Israel.

Bringing Back the Ark

13 David conferred with each of his officers, the commanders of thousands and commanders of hundreds. 2 He then said to the whole assembly of Israel, "If it seems good to you and if it is the will of the LORD our God, let us send word far and wide to the rest of our people throughout the territories of Israel, and also to the priests and Levites who are with them in their towns and pasturelands, to come and join us. 3 Let us bring the ark of our God back to us, for we did not inquire of[a] it[b] during the reign of Saul." 4 The whole assembly agreed to do this, because it seemed right to all the people.

5 So David assembled all Israel, from the Shihor River in Egypt to Lebo Hamath, to bring the ark of God from Kiriath Jearim. 6 David and all Israel went to Baalah

» INSTANT ACCESS

If you've been a leader in your youth group, you've probably found out how frustrating leadership can be. You've pushed and prodded and poked, and you've probably found out that it just doesn't work. David's way of leading is better. David set out to accomplish a task. When others saw what he was doing, they joined him. His volunteer team grew "until he had a great army." That's how spiritual leadership works. Set out to accomplish something important, and rely on those who are willing to volunteer. Leading by example is always more effective than getting behind others and trying to push.

{1 Chronicles 12:22}

of Judah (Kiriath Jearim) to bring up from there the ark of God the LORD, who is enthroned between the cherubim—the ark that is called by the Name.

7 They moved the ark of God from Abinadab's house on a new cart, with Uzzah and Ahio guiding it. 8 David and all the Israelites were celebrating with all their might before God, with songs and with harps, lyres, timbrels, cymbals and trumpets.

9 When they came to the threshing floor of Kidon, Uzzah reached out his hand to steady the ark, because the oxen stum-

---

a 3 Or we neglected   b 3 Or him

bled. [10]The LORD's anger burned against Uzzah, and he struck him down because he had put his hand on the ark. So he died there before God.

[11]Then David was angry because the LORD's wrath had broken out against Uzzah, and to this day that place is called Perez Uzzah.[a]

[12]David was afraid of God that day and asked, "How can I ever bring the ark of God to me?" [13]He did not take the ark to be with him in the City of David. Instead, he took it to the house of Obed-Edom the Gittite. [14]The ark of God remained with the family of Obed-Edom in his house for three months, and the LORD blessed his household and everything he had.

David's House and Family

14 Now Hiram king of Tyre sent messengers to David, along with cedar logs, stonemasons and carpenters to build a palace for him. [2]And David knew that the LORD had established him as king over Israel and that his kingdom had been highly exalted for the sake of his people Israel.

[3]In Jerusalem David took more wives and became the father of more sons and daughters. [4]These are the names of the children born to him there: Shammua, Shobab, Nathan, Solomon, [5]Ibhar, Elishua, Elpelet, [6]Nogah, Nepheg, Japhia, [7]Elishama, Beeliada[b] and Eliphelet.

David Defeats the Philistines

[8]When the Philistines heard that David had been anointed king over all Israel, they went up in full force to search for him, but David heard about it and went out to meet them. [9]Now the Philistines had come and raided the Valley of Rephaim; [10]so David inquired of God: "Shall I go and attack the Philistines? Will you deliver them into my hands?"

The LORD answered him, "Go, I will deliver them into your hands."

[11]So David and his men went up to Baal Perazim, and there he defeated

them. He said, "As waters break out, God has broken out against my enemies by my hand." So that place was called Baal Perazim.[c] [12]The Philistines had abandoned their gods there, and David gave orders to burn them in the fire.

[13]Once more the Philistines raided the valley; [14]so David inquired of God again, and God answered him, "Do not go directly after them, but circle around them and attack them in front of the poplar trees. [15]As soon as you hear the sound of marching in the tops of the poplar trees, move out to battle, because that will mean God has gone out in front of you to strike the Philistine army." [16]So David did as God commanded him, and they struck down the Philistine army, all the way from Gibeon to Gezer.

[17]So David's fame spread throughout every land, and the LORD made all the nations fear him.

The Ark Brought to Jerusalem

15 After David had constructed buildings for himself in the City of David, he prepared a place for the ark of God and pitched a tent for it. [2]Then David said, "No one but the Levites may carry

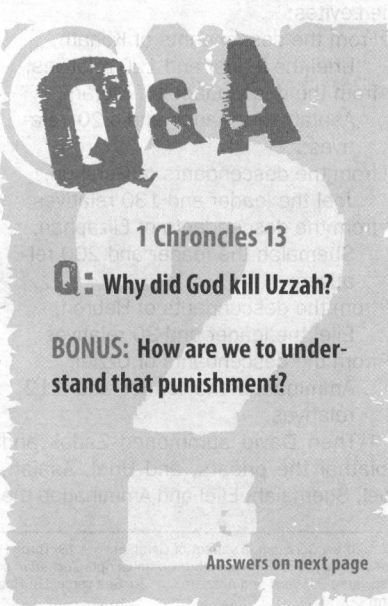

1 Chronicles 13

Q: Why did God kill Uzzah?

BONUS: How are we to understand that punishment?

Answers on next page

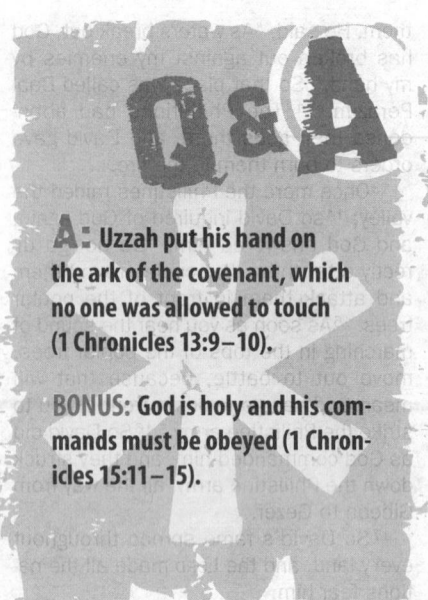

A: Uzzah put his hand on the ark of the covenant, which no one was allowed to touch (1 Chronicles 13:9–10).

BONUS: God is holy and his commands must be obeyed (1 Chronicles 15:11–15).

the ark of God, because the LORD chose them to carry the ark of the LORD and to minister before him forever."

³ David assembled all Israel in Jerusalem to bring up the ark of the LORD to the place he had prepared for it. ⁴ He called together the descendants of Aaron and the Levites:

⁵ From the descendants of Kohath,
Uriel the leader and 120 relatives;
⁶ from the descendants of Merari,
Asaiah the leader and 220 relatives;
⁷ from the descendants of Gershon,ᵃ
Joel the leader and 130 relatives;
⁸ from the descendants of Elizaphan,
Shemaiah the leader and 200 relatives;
⁹ from the descendants of Hebron,
Eliel the leader and 80 relatives;
¹⁰ from the descendants of Uzziel,
Amminadab the leader and 112 relatives.

¹¹ Then David summoned Zadok and Abiathar the priests, and Uriel, Asaiah, Joel, Shemaiah, Eliel and Amminadab the Levites. ¹² He said to them, "You are the heads of the Levitical families; you and your fellow Levites are to consecrate yourselves and bring up the ark of the LORD, the God of Israel, to the place I have prepared for it. ¹³ It was because you, the Levites, did not bring it up the first time that the LORD our God broke out in anger against us. We did not inquire of him about how to do it in the prescribed way." ¹⁴ So the priests and Levites consecrated themselves in order to bring up the ark of the LORD, the God of Israel. ¹⁵ And the Levites carried the ark of God with the poles on their shoulders, as Moses had commanded in accordance with the word of the LORD.

¹⁶ David told the leaders of the Levites to appoint their fellow Levites as musicians to make a joyful sound with musical instruments: lyres, harps and cymbals.

¹⁷ So the Levites appointed Heman son of Joel; from his relatives, Asaph son of Berekiah; and from their relatives the Merarites, Ethan son of Kushaiah; ¹⁸ and with them their relatives next in rank: Zechariah,ᵇ Jaaziel, Shemiramoth, Jehiel, Unni, Eliab, Benaiah, Maaseiah, Mattithiah, Eliphelehu, Mikneiah, Obed-Edom and Jeiel,ᶜ the gatekeepers.

¹⁹ The musicians Heman, Asaph and Ethan were to sound the bronze cymbals; ²⁰ Zechariah, Jaaziel,ᵈ Shemiramoth, Jehiel, Unni, Eliab, Maaseiah and Benaiah were to play the lyres according to alamoth,ᵉ ²¹ and Mattithiah, Eliphelehu, Mikneiah, Obed-Edom, Jeiel and Azaziah were to play the harps, directing according to sheminith.ᵉ ²² Kenaniah the head Levite was in charge of the singing; that was his responsibility because he was skillful at it.

²³ Berekiah and Elkanah were to be doorkeepers for the ark. ²⁴ Shebaniah, Joshaphat, Nethanel, Amasai, Zechariah, Benaiah and Eliezer the priests were to blow trumpets before the ark of God. Obed-Edom and Jehiah were also to be doorkeepers for the ark.

ᵃ 7 Hebrew Gershom, a variant of Gershon   ᵇ 18 Three Hebrew manuscripts and most Septuagint manuscripts (see also verse 20 and 16:5); most Hebrew manuscripts Zechariah son and or Zechariah, Ben and   ᶜ 18 Hebrew; Septuagint (see also verse 21) Jeiel and Azaziah   ᵈ 20 See verse 18; Hebrew Aziel, a variant of Jaaziel.   ᵉ 20,21 Probably a musical term

25 So David and the elders of Israel and the commanders of units of a thousand went to bring up the ark of the covenant of the LORD from the house of Obed-Edom, with rejoicing. 26 Because God had helped the Levites who were carrying the ark of the covenant of the LORD, seven bulls and seven rams were sacrificed. 27 Now David was clothed in a robe of fine linen, as were all the Levites who were carrying the ark, and as were the musicians, and Kenaniah, who was in charge of the singing of the choirs. David also wore a linen ephod. 28 So all Israel brought up the ark of the covenant of the LORD with shouts, with the sounding of rams' horns and trumpets, and of cymbals, and the playing of lyres and harps.

29 As the ark of the covenant of the LORD was entering the City of David, Michal daughter of Saul watched from a window. And when she saw King David dancing and celebrating, she despised him in her heart.

Ministering Before the Ark

16 They brought the ark of God and set it inside the tent that David had pitched for it, and they presented burnt offerings and fellowship offerings before God. 2 After David had finished sacrificing the burnt offerings and fellowship offerings, he blessed the people in the name of the LORD. 3 Then he gave a loaf

of bread, a cake of dates and a cake of raisins to each Israelite man and woman.

4 He appointed some of the Levites to minister before the ark of the LORD, to extol,[a] thank, and praise the LORD, the God of Israel: 5 Asaph was the chief, and next to him in rank were Zechariah, then Jaaziel,[b] Shemiramoth, Jehiel, Mattithiah, Eliab, Benaiah, Obed-Edom and Jeiel. They were to play the lyres and harps, Asaph was to sound the cymbals, 6 and Benaiah and Jahaziel the priests were to blow the trumpets regularly before the ark of the covenant of God.

7 That day David first appointed Asaph and his associates to give praise to the LORD in this manner:

8 Give praise to the LORD, proclaim his name;
   make known among the nations
      what he has done.
9 Sing to him, sing praise to him;
   tell of all his wonderful acts.
10 Glory in his holy name;
   let the hearts of those who seek
      the LORD rejoice.
11 Look to the LORD and his strength;
   seek his face always.

12 Remember the wonders he has done,
   his miracles, and the judgments he
      pronounced,
13 you his servants, the descendants of
      Israel,

---

[a] 4 Or *petition*; or *invoke*   [b] 5 See 15:18,20; Hebrew *Jeiel*, possibly another name for *Jaaziel*.

his chosen ones, the children of
Jacob.
¹⁴ He is the Lord our God;
his judgments are in all the earth.

¹⁵ He remembersᵃ his covenant forever,
the promise he made, for a
thousand generations,
¹⁶ the covenant he made with Abraham,
the oath he swore to Isaac.
¹⁷ He confirmed it to Jacob as a decree,
to Israel as an everlasting covenant:
¹⁸ "To you I will give the land of Canaan
as the portion you will inherit."

¹⁹ When they were but few in number,
few indeed, and strangers in it,
²⁰ theyᵇ wandered from nation to nation,
from one kingdom to another.
²¹ He allowed no one to oppress them;
for their sake he rebuked kings:
²² "Do not touch my anointed ones;
do my prophets no harm."

²³ Sing to the Lord, all the earth;
proclaim his salvation day after day.
²⁴ Declare his glory among the nations,
his marvelous deeds among all
peoples.

²⁵ For great is the Lord and most worthy
of praise;
he is to be feared above all gods.
²⁶ For all the gods of the nations are
idols,
but the Lord made the heavens.
²⁷ Splendor and majesty are before him;
strength and joy are in his dwelling
place.

²⁸ Ascribe to the Lord, all you families of
nations,
ascribe to the Lord glory and
strength.
²⁹ Ascribe to the Lord the glory due his
name;
bring an offering and come before
him.
Worship the Lord in the splendor of
hisᶜ holiness.
³⁰ Tremble before him, all the earth!
The world is firmly established; it
cannot be moved.

³¹ Let the heavens rejoice, let the earth
be glad;
let them say among the nations,
"The Lord reigns!"
³² Let the sea resound, and all that is in
it;
let the fields be jubilant, and
everything in them!
³³ Let the trees of the forest sing,
let them sing for joy before the
Lord,
for he comes to judge the earth.

³⁴ Give thanks to the Lord, for he is
good;
his love endures forever.
³⁵ Cry out, "Save us, God our Savior;
gather us and deliver us from the
nations,
that we may give thanks to your holy
name,
and glory in your praise."
³⁶ Praise be to the Lord, the God of
Israel,
from everlasting to everlasting.

Then all the people said "Amen" and
"Praise the Lord."

³⁷ David left Asaph and his associates
before the ark of the covenant of the Lord
to minister there regularly, according to
each day's requirements. ³⁸ He also left
Obed-Edom and his sixty-eight associates to minister with them. Obed-Edom
son of Jeduthun, and also Hosah, were
gatekeepers.

³⁹ David left Zadok the priest and his
fellow priests before the tabernacle of
the Lord at the high place in Gibeon ⁴⁰ to
present burnt offerings to the Lord on
the altar of burnt offering regularly, morning and evening, in accordance with everything written in the Law of the Lord,
which he had given Israel. ⁴¹ With them
were Heman and Jeduthun and the rest
of those chosen and designated by name
to give thanks to the Lord, "for his love
endures forever." ⁴² Heman and Jeduthun
were responsible for the sounding of the
trumpets and cymbals and for the playing
of the other instruments for sacred song.

ᵃ 15 Some Septuagint manuscripts (see also Psalm 105:8); Hebrew *Remember*   ᵇ 18-20 One Hebrew manuscript,
Septuagint and Vulgate (see also Psalm 105:12); most Hebrew manuscripts *inherit, / ¹⁹though you are but few in number, /
few indeed, and strangers in it." / ²⁰They*   ᶜ 29 Or *Lord with the splendor of*

The sons of Jeduthun were stationed at the gate.

⁴³Then all the people left, each for their own home, and David returned home to bless his family.

God's Promise to David

17 After David was settled in his palace, he said to Nathan the prophet, "Here I am, living in a house of cedar, while the ark of the covenant of the Lord is under a tent."

²Nathan replied to David, "Whatever you have in mind, do it, for God is with you."

³But that night the word of God came to Nathan, saying:

⁴"Go and tell my servant David, 'This is what the Lord says: You are not the one to build me a house to dwell in. ⁵I have not dwelt in a house from the day I brought Israel up out of Egypt to this day. I have moved from one tent site to another, from one dwelling place to another. ⁶Wherever I have moved with all the Israelites, did I ever say to any of their leaders[a] whom I commanded to shepherd my people, "Why have you not built me a house of cedar?" '

⁷"Now then, tell my servant David, 'This is what the Lord Almighty says: I took you from the pasture, from tending the flock, and appointed you ruler over my people Israel. ⁸I have been with you wherever you have gone, and I have cut off all your enemies from before you. Now I will make your name like the names of the greatest men on earth. ⁹And I will provide a place for my people Israel and will plant them so that they can have a home of their own and no longer be disturbed. Wicked people will not oppress them anymore, as they did at the beginning ¹⁰and have

done ever since the time I appointed leaders over my people Israel. I will also subdue all your enemies.

" 'I declare to you that the Lord will build a house for you: ¹¹When your days are over and you go to be with your ancestors, I will raise up your offspring to succeed you, one of your own sons, and I will establish his kingdom. ¹²He is the one who will build a house for me, and I will establish his throne forever. ¹³I will be his father, and he will be my son. I will never take my love away from him, as I took it away from your predecessor. ¹⁴I will set him over my house and my kingdom forever; his throne will be established forever.' "

¹⁵Nathan reported to David all the words of this entire revelation.

David's Prayer

¹⁶Then King David went in and sat before the Lord, and he said:

"Who am I, Lord God, and what is my family, that you have brought me this far? ¹⁷And as if this were not enough in your sight, my God, you have spoken about the future of the house of your servant. You, Lord God, have looked on me as though I were the most exalted of men.

¹⁸"What more can David say to you for honoring your servant? For you know your servant, ¹⁹Lord. For the sake of your servant and according to your will, you have done this great thing and made known all these great promises.

²⁰"There is no one like you, Lord, and there is no God but you, as we have heard with our own ears. ²¹And who is like your people Israel—the one nation on earth whose God went out to redeem a people for himself,

> **Let the hearts of those who seek the Lord rejoice.**
> 1 Chronicles 16:10

ᵃ 6 Traditionally *judges*; also in verse 10

and to make a name for yourself, and to perform great and awesome wonders by driving out nations from before your people, whom you redeemed from Egypt? ²²You made your people Israel your very own forever, and you, LORD, have become their God.

²³"And now, LORD, let the promise you have made concerning your servant and his house be established forever. Do as you promised, ²⁴so that it will be established and that your name will be great forever. Then people will say, 'The LORD Almighty, the God over Israel, is Israel's God!' And the house of your servant David will be established before you.

²⁵"You, my God, have revealed to your servant that you will build a house for him. So your servant has found courage to pray to you. ²⁶You, LORD, are God! You have promised these good things to your servant. ²⁷Now you have been pleased to bless the house of your servant, that it may continue forever in your sight; for you, LORD, have blessed it, and it will be blessed forever."

David's Victories

18 In the course of time, David defeated the Philistines and subdued them, and he took Gath and its surrounding villages from the control of the Philistines.

²David also defeated the Moabites, and they became subject to him and brought him tribute.

³Moreover, David defeated Hadadezer king of Zobah, in the vicinity of Hamath, when he went to set up his monument at^a the Euphrates River. ⁴David captured a thousand of his chariots, seven thousand charioteers and twenty thousand foot soldiers. He hamstrung all but a hundred of the chariot horses.

⁵When the Arameans of Damascus came to help Hadadezer king of Zobah, David struck down twenty-two thousand of them. ⁶He put garrisons in the Aramean kingdom of Damascus, and the Arameans became subject to him and brought him tribute. The LORD gave David victory wherever he went.

⁷David took the gold shields carried by the officers of Hadadezer and brought them to Jerusalem. ⁸From Tebah^b and Kun, towns that belonged to Hadadezer, David took a great quantity of bronze, which Solomon used to make the bronze Sea, the pillars and various bronze articles.

⁹When Tou king of Hamath heard that David had defeated the entire army of Hadadezer king of Zobah, ¹⁰he sent his son Hadoram to King David to greet him and congratulate him on his victory in battle over Hadadezer, who had been at war with Tou. Hadoram brought all kinds of articles of gold, of silver and of bronze.

¹¹King David dedicated these articles to the LORD, as he had done with the silver and gold he had taken from all these nations: Edom and Moab, the Ammonites and the Philistines, and Amalek.

¹²Abishai son of Zeruiah struck down eighteen thousand Edomites in the Valley of Salt. ¹³He put garrisons in Edom, and all the Edomites became subject to David. The LORD gave David victory wherever he went.

David's Officials

¹⁴David reigned over all Israel, doing what was just and right for all his people. ¹⁵Joab son of Zeruiah was over the army; Jehoshaphat son of Ahilud was recorder; ¹⁶Zadok son of Ahitub and Ahimelek^c son of Abiathar were priests; Shavsha was secretary; ¹⁷Benaiah son of Jehoiada

Give thanks to the LORD, for he is good; his love endures forever.
1 Chronicles 16:34

---

was over the Kerethites and Pelethites; and David's sons were chief officials at the king's side.

David Defeats the Ammonites

19 In the course of time, Nahash king of the Ammonites died, and his son succeeded him as king. ²David thought, "I will show kindness to Hanun son of Nahash, because his father showed kindness to me." So David sent a delegation to express his sympathy to Hanun concerning his father.

When David's envoys came to Hanun in the land of the Ammonites to express sympathy to him, ³the Ammonite commanders said to Hanun, "Do you think David is honoring your father by sending envoys to you to express sympathy? Haven't his envoys come to you only to explore and spy out the country and overthrow it?" ⁴So Hanun seized David's envoys, shaved them, cut off their garments at the buttocks, and sent them away.

⁵When someone came and told David about the men, he sent messengers to meet them, for they were greatly humiliated. The king said, "Stay at Jericho till your beards have grown, and then come back."

⁶When the Ammonites realized that they had become obnoxious to David, Hanun and the Ammonites sent a thousand talentsᵃ of silver to hire chariots and charioteers from Aram Naharaim,ᵇ Aram Maakah and Zobah. ⁷They hired thirty-two thousand chariots and charioteers, as well as the king of Maakah with his troops, who came and camped near Medeba, while the Ammonites were mustered from their towns and moved out for battle.

⁸On hearing this, David sent Joab out with the entire army of fighting men. ⁹The Ammonites came out and drew up in battle formation at the entrance to their city, while the kings who had come were by themselves in the open country.

¹⁰Joab saw that there were battle lines in front of him and behind him; so he selected some of the best troops in Israel and deployed them against the Arameans. ¹¹He put the rest of the men under the command of Abishai his brother, and they were deployed against the Ammonites. ¹²Joab said, "If the Arameans are too strong for me, then you are to rescue me; but if the Ammonites are too strong for you, then I will rescue you. ¹³Be strong, and let us fight bravely for our people and the cities of our God. The Lord will do what is good in his sight."

¹⁴Then Joab and the troops with him advanced to fight the Arameans, and they fled before him. ¹⁵When the Ammonites realized that the Arameans were fleeing, they too fled before his brother Abishai and went inside the city. So Joab went back to Jerusalem.

¹⁶After the Arameans saw that they had been routed by Israel, they sent messengers and had Arameans brought from beyond the Euphrates River, with Shophak the commander of Hadadezer's army leading them.

¹⁷When David was told of this, he gathered all Israel and crossed the Jordan; he advanced against them and formed his battle lines opposite them. David formed his lines to meet the Arameans in battle, and they fought against him. ¹⁸But they fled before Israel, and David killed seven thousand of their charioteers and forty thousand of their foot soldiers. He also killed Shophak the commander of their army.

¹⁹When the vassals of Hadadezer saw that they had been routed by Israel, they made peace with David and became subject to him.

So the Arameans were not willing to help the Ammonites anymore.

The Capture of Rabbah

20 In the spring, at the time when kings go off to war, Joab led out the armed forces. He laid waste the land of the Ammonites and went to Rabbah and besieged it, but David remained in Jerusalem. Joab attacked Rabbah and left it in ruins. ²David took the crown from the

---

ᵃ 6 That is, about 38 tons or about 34 metric tons   ᵇ 6 That is, Northwest Mesopotamia

head of their king[a]—its weight was found to be a talent[b] of gold, and it was set with precious stones—and it was placed on David's head. He took a great quantity of plunder from the city ³and brought out the people who were there, consigning them to labor with saws and with iron picks and axes. David did this to all the Ammonite towns. Then David and his entire army returned to Jerusalem.

War With the Philistines

⁴In the course of time, war broke out with the Philistines, at Gezer. At that time Sibbekai the Hushathite killed Sippai, one of the descendants of the Rephaites, and the Philistines were subjugated.

⁵In another battle with the Philistines, Elhanan son of Jair killed Lahmi the brother of Goliath the Gittite, who had a spear with a shaft like a weaver's rod.

⁶In still another battle, which took place at Gath, there was a huge man with six fingers on each hand and six toes on each foot—twenty-four in all. He also was descended from Rapha. ⁷When he taunted Israel, Jonathan son of Shimea, David's brother, killed him.

⁸These were descendants of Rapha in Gath, and they fell at the hands of David and his men.

David Counts the Fighting Men

21 Satan rose up against Israel and incited David to take a census of Israel. ²So David said to Joab and the commanders of the troops, "Go and count the Israelites from Beersheba to Dan. Then report back to me so that I may know how many there are."

³But Joab replied, "May the LORD multiply his troops a hundred times over. My lord the king, are they not all my lord's subjects? Why does my lord want to do this? Why should he bring guilt on Israel?"

⁴The king's word, however, overruled Joab; so Joab left and went throughout Israel and then came back to Jerusalem. ⁵Joab reported the number of the fighting men to David: In all Israel there were one million one hundred thousand men

INSTANT ACCESS

Do your parents have trouble understanding why you just can't wear the clothes they think you should wear? Try this Bible story. A foreign king humiliated David's messengers by shaving off their beards and cutting up their clothes. David let his messengers stay in Jericho until their beards had grown back and they could return to Jerusalem without embarrassment. Ask your mom and dad to be as sensitive as David. It can be humiliating if your clothing is too different from that of other teens. If your parents understand just how you feel, they just might give you more freedom to dress the way you want.

{1 Chronicles 19:4–5}

who could handle a sword, including four hundred and seventy thousand in Judah.

⁶But Joab did not include Levi and Benjamin in the numbering, because the king's command was repulsive to him. ⁷This command was also evil in the sight of God; so he punished Israel.

⁸Then David said to God, "I have sinned greatly by doing this. Now, I beg you, take away the guilt of your servant. I have done a very foolish thing."

⁹The LORD said to Gad, David's seer,

ᵃ 2 Or of *Milkom*, that is, Molek   ᵇ 2 That is, about 75 pounds or about 34 kilograms

10 "Go and tell David, 'This is what the LORD says: I am giving you three options. Choose one of them for me to carry out against you.'"

11 So Gad went to David and said to him, "This is what the LORD says: 'Take your choice: 12 three years of famine, three months of being swept away*a* before your enemies, with their swords overtaking you, or three days of the sword of the LORD—days of plague in the land, with the angel of the LORD ravaging every part of Israel.' Now then, decide how I should answer the one who sent me."

13 David said to Gad, "I am in deep distress. Let me fall into the hands of the LORD, for his mercy is very great; but do not let me fall into human hands."

14 So the LORD sent a plague on Israel, and seventy thousand men of Israel fell dead. 15 And God sent an angel to destroy Jerusalem. But as the angel was doing so, the LORD saw it and relented concerning the disaster and said to the angel who was destroying the people, "Enough! Withdraw your hand." The angel of the LORD was then standing at the threshing floor of Araunah*b* the Jebusite.

16 David looked up and saw the angel of the LORD standing between heaven and earth, with a drawn sword in his hand extended over Jerusalem. Then David and the elders, clothed in sackcloth, fell facedown.

17 David said to God, "Was it not I who ordered the fighting men to be counted?

a 12 Hebrew; Septuagint and Vulgate (see also 2 Samuel 24:13) *of fleeing*   *b 15* Hebrew *Ornan,* a variant of *Araunah;* also in verses 18-28

TO THE POINT

The Devil Didn't Make You

"The devil made me do it!" Some people actually believe that Satan is responsible when they do something that's wrong. But is he?

First Chronicles 21:1 tells you that Satan "incited" David to do something wrong. When David was later confronted by God, he didn't say, "The devil made me do it." He said, "I, the shepherd, have sinned and done wrong" (1 Chronicles 21:17). Satan may tempt you, but he can't make you sin. It's your choice, and you don't have to choose to do wrong. You're free to choose what is right.

So what should you do when Satan tempts you?

+ Remember what the Bible teaches and act on it (Matthew 4:1–11).
+ "Resist the devil, and he will flee" (James 4:7).
+ Remember: Christ is far more powerful than Satan (1 John 4:4).

I, the shepherd,[a] have sinned and done wrong. These are but sheep. What have they done? Lord my God, let your hand fall on me and my family, but do not let this plague remain on your people."

David Builds an Altar

[18]Then the angel of the Lord ordered Gad to tell David to go up and build an altar to the Lord on the threshing floor of Araunah the Jebusite. [19]So David went up in obedience to the word that Gad had spoken in the name of the Lord.

[20]While Araunah was threshing wheat, he turned and saw the angel; his four sons who were with him hid themselves. [21]Then David approached, and when Araunah looked and saw him, he left the threshing floor and bowed down before David with his face to the ground.

[22]David said to him, "Let me have the site of your threshing floor so I can build an altar to the Lord, that the plague on the people may be stopped. Sell it to me at the full price."

[23]Araunah said to David, "Take it! Let my lord the king do whatever pleases him. Look, I will give the oxen for the burnt offerings, the threshing sledges for the wood, and the wheat for the grain offering. I will give all this."

[24]But King David replied to Araunah, "No, I insist on paying the full price. I will not take for the Lord what is yours, or sacrifice a burnt offering that costs me nothing."

[25]So David paid Araunah six hundred shekels[b] of gold for the site. [26]David built an altar to the Lord there and sacrificed burnt offerings and fellowship offerings. He called on the Lord, and the Lord answered him with fire from heaven on the altar of burnt offering.

[27]Then the Lord spoke to the angel, and he put his sword back into its sheath. [28]At that time, when David saw that the Lord had answered him on the threshing floor of Araunah the Jebusite, he offered sacrifices there. [29]The tabernacle of the Lord, which Moses had made in the wilderness, and the altar of burnt offering were at that time on the high place at Gibeon. [30]But David could not go before it to inquire of God, because he was afraid of the sword of the angel of the Lord.

22 Then David said, "The house of the Lord God is to be here, and also the altar of burnt offering for Israel."

Preparations for the Temple

[2]So David gave orders to assemble the foreigners residing in Israel, and from among them he appointed stonecutters to prepare dressed stone for building the house of God. [3]He provided a large amount of iron to make nails for the doors of the gateways and for the fittings, and more bronze than could be weighed. [4]He also provided more cedar logs than could be counted, for the Sidonians and Tyrians had brought large numbers of them to David.

[5]David said, "My son Solomon is young and inexperienced, and the house to be built for the Lord should be of great magnificence and fame and splendor in the sight of all the nations. Therefore I will make preparations for it." So David made extensive preparations before his death.

[6]Then he called for his son Solomon and charged him to build a house for the Lord, the God of Israel. [7]David said to Solomon: "My son, I had it in my heart to build a house for the Name of the Lord my God. [8]But this word of the Lord came to me: 'You have shed much blood and have fought many wars. You are not to build a house for my Name, because you have shed much blood on the earth in my sight. [9]But you will have a son who will be a man of peace and rest, and I will give him rest from all his enemies on every side. His name will be Solomon,[c] and I will grant Israel peace and quiet during his reign. [10]He is the one who will build a house for my Name. He will be my son, and I will be his father. And I will establish the throne of his kingdom over Israel forever.'

[11]"Now, my son, the Lord be with you, and may you have success and build the

a 17 Probable reading of the original Hebrew text (see 2 Samuel 24:17 and note); Masoretic Text does not have the shepherd.   b 25 That is, about 15 pounds or about 6.9 kilograms   c 9 Solomon sounds like and may be derived from the Hebrew for peace.

INSTANT ACCESS

Can you sense David's concern in this verse: "My son Solomon is young and inexperienced"? We know Solomon as history's wisest man, but to David, Solomon was still his little boy. Most parents worry about their children. "He's gone for the evening with all his friends. Will he be OK?" "This is her first real date. I won't sleep until she gets home safely." It's not that they don't trust you. It's just love. Yes, it can be irritating at times, but part of loving is being concerned about the person you love. Maybe if you sense the love, the feeling that Mom or Dad is hanging over your shoulder watching will be a little easier to deal with.

{1 Chronicles 22:5}

house of the LORD your God, as he said you would. ¹²May the LORD give you discretion and understanding when he puts you in command over Israel, so that you may keep the law of the LORD your God. ¹³Then you will have success if you are careful to observe the decrees and laws that the LORD gave Moses for Israel. Be strong and courageous. Do not be afraid or discouraged.

¹⁴"I have taken great pains to provide for the temple of the LORD a hundred thousand talents[a] of gold, a million talents[b] of silver, quantities of bronze and iron too great to be weighed, and wood and stone. And you may add to them. ¹⁵You have many workers: stonecutters, masons and carpenters, as well as those skilled in every kind of work ¹⁶in gold and silver, bronze and iron—craftsmen beyond number. Now begin the work, and the LORD be with you."

¹⁷Then David ordered all the leaders of Israel to help his son Solomon. ¹⁸He said to them, "Is not the LORD your God with you? And has he not granted you rest on every side? For he has given the inhabitants of the land into my hands, and the land is subject to the LORD and to his people. ¹⁹Now devote your heart and soul to seeking the LORD your God. Begin to build the sanctuary of the LORD God, so that you may bring the ark of the covenant of the LORD and the sacred articles belonging to God into the temple that will be built for the Name of the LORD."

The Levites

23 When David was old and full of years, he made his son Solomon king over Israel.

²He also gathered together all the leaders of Israel, as well as the priests and Levites. ³The Levites thirty years old or more were counted, and the total number of men was thirty-eight thousand. ⁴David said, "Of these, twenty-four thousand are to be in charge of the work of the temple of the LORD and six thousand are to be officials and judges. ⁵Four thousand are to be gatekeepers and four thousand are to praise the LORD with the musical instruments I have provided for that purpose."

⁶David separated the Levites into divisions corresponding to the sons of Levi: Gershon, Kohath and Merari.

Gershonites

⁷Belonging to the Gershonites:
Ladan and Shimei.
⁸The sons of Ladan:

---

[a] 14 That is, about 3,750 tons or about 3,400 metric tons   [b] 14 That is, about 37,500 tons or about 34,000 metric tons

Jehiel the first, Zetham and Joel—
three in all.
⁹The sons of Shimei:
Shelomoth, Haziel and Haran—
three in all.
These were the heads of the families of Ladan.
¹⁰And the sons of Shimei:
Jahath, Ziza,ᵃ Jeush and Beriah.
These were the sons of Shimei—
four in all.
¹¹Jahath was the first and Ziza the
second, but Jeush and Beriah did
not have many sons; so they were
counted as one family with one assignment.

Kohathites

¹²The sons of Kohath:
Amram, Izhar, Hebron and Uzziel—four in all.
¹³The sons of Amram:
Aaron and Moses.
Aaron was set apart, he and his
descendants forever, to consecrate the most holy things, to offer
sacrifices before the LORD, to minister before him and to pronounce
blessings in his name forever.
¹⁴The sons of Moses the man of
God were counted as part of the
tribe of Levi.
¹⁵The sons of Moses:
Gershom and Eliezer.
¹⁶The descendants of Gershom:
Shubael was the first.
¹⁷The descendants of Eliezer:
Rehabiah was the first.
Eliezer had no other sons, but the
sons of Rehabiah were very numerous.
¹⁸The sons of Izhar:
Shelomith was the first.
¹⁹The sons of Hebron:
Jeriah the first, Amariah the second, Jahaziel the third and Jekameam the fourth.
²⁰The sons of Uzziel:
Micah the first and Ishiah the second.

Merarites

²¹The sons of Merari:
Mahli and Mushi.
The sons of Mahli:
Eleazar and Kish.
²²Eleazar died without having sons:
he had only daughters. Their cousins, the sons of Kish, married
them.
²³The sons of Mushi:
Mahli, Eder and Jerimoth—three
in all.

²⁴These were the descendants of Levi
by their families—the heads of families as they were registered under their
names and counted individually, that is,
the workers twenty years old or more who
served in the temple of the LORD. ²⁵For
David had said, "Since the LORD, the God
of Israel, has granted rest to his people
and has come to dwell in Jerusalem forever, ²⁶the Levites no longer need to carry
the tabernacle or any of the articles used
in its service." ²⁷According to the last
instructions of David, the Levites were
counted from those twenty years old or
more.
²⁸The duty of the Levites was to help
Aaron's descendants in the service of
the temple of the LORD: to be in charge of
the courtyards, the side rooms, the purification of all sacred things and the performance of other duties at the house of
God. ²⁹They were in charge of the bread
set out on the table, the special flour for
the grain offerings, the thin loaves made
without yeast, the baking and the mixing,
and all measurements of quantity and
size. ³⁰They were also to stand every
morning to thank and praise the LORD.
They were to do the same in the evening
³¹and whenever burnt offerings were presented to the LORD on the Sabbaths, at
the New Moon feasts and at the appointed festivals. They were to serve before
the LORD regularly in the proper number
and in the way prescribed for them.
³²And so the Levites carried out their
responsibilities for the tent of meeting,
for the Holy Place and, under their rela-

tives the descendants of Aaron, for the service of the temple of the LORD.

The Divisions of Priests

24 These were the divisions of the descendants of Aaron:

The sons of Aaron were Nadab, Abihu, Eleazar and Ithamar. [2]But Nadab and Abihu died before their father did, and they had no sons; so Eleazar and Ithamar served as the priests. [3]With the help of Zadok a descendant of Eleazar and Ahimelek a descendant of Ithamar, David separated them into divisions for their appointed order of ministering. [4]A larger number of leaders were found among Eleazar's descendants than among Ithamar's, and they were divided accordingly: sixteen heads of families from Eleazar's descendants and eight heads of families from Ithamar's descendants. [5]They divided them impartially by casting lots, for there were officials of the sanctuary and officials of God among the descendants of both Eleazar and Ithamar.

[6]The scribe Shemaiah son of Nethanel, a Levite, recorded their names in the presence of the king and of the officials: Zadok the priest, Ahimelek son of Abiathar and the heads of families of the priests and of the Levites — one family being taken from Eleazar and then one from Ithamar.

[7]The first lot fell to Jehoiarib,
the second to Jedaiah,
[8]the third to Harim,
the fourth to Seorim,
[9]the fifth to Malkijah,
the sixth to Mijamin,
[10]the seventh to Hakkoz,
the eighth to Abijah,
[11]the ninth to Jeshua,
the tenth to Shekaniah,
[12]the eleventh to Eliashib,
the twelfth to Jakim,
[13]the thirteenth to Huppah,
the fourteenth to Jeshebeab,
[14]the fifteenth to Bilgah,
the sixteenth to Immer,
[15]the seventeenth to Hezir,
the eighteenth to Happizzez,
[16]the nineteenth to Pethahiah,
the twentieth to Jehezkel,
[17]the twenty-first to Jakin,
the twenty-second to Gamul,
[18]the twenty-third to Delaiah
and the twenty-fourth to Maaziah.

[19]This was their appointed order of ministering when they entered the temple of the LORD, according to the regulations prescribed for them by their ancestor Aaron, as the LORD, the God of Israel, had commanded him.

The Rest of the Levites

[20]As for the rest of the descendants of Levi:

from the sons of Amram: Shubael;
from the sons of Shubael: Jehdeiah.
[21]As for Rehabiah, from his sons:
Ishiah was the first.
[22]From the Izharites: Shelomoth;
from the sons of Shelomoth: Jahath.
[23]The sons of Hebron: Jeriah the first,[a]
Amariah the second, Jahaziel the third and Jekameam the fourth.
[24]The son of Uzziel: Micah;
from the sons of Micah: Shamir.
[25]The brother of Micah: Ishiah;
from the sons of Ishiah: Zechariah.
[26]The sons of Merari: Mahli and Mushi.
The son of Jaaziah: Beno.
[27]The sons of Merari:
from Jaaziah: Beno, Shoham, Zakkur and Ibri.
[28]From Mahli: Eleazar, who had no sons.
[29]From Kish: the son of Kish:
Jerahmeel.
[30]And the sons of Mushi: Mahli, Eder and Jerimoth.

These were the Levites, according to their families. [31]They also cast lots, just as their relatives the descendants of Aaron did, in the presence of King David and of Zadok, Ahimelek, and the heads of families of the priests and of the Levites. The families of the oldest brother

---

[a] 23 Two Hebrew manuscripts and some Septuagint manuscripts (see also 23:19); most Hebrew manuscripts *The sons of Jeriah:*

were treated the same as those of the youngest.

The Musicians

25 David, together with the commanders of the army, set apart some of the sons of Asaph, Heman and Jeduthun for the ministry of prophesying, accompanied by harps, lyres and cymbals. Here is the list of the men who performed this service:

2 From the sons of Asaph:
Zakkur, Joseph, Nethaniah and Asarelah. The sons of Asaph were under the supervision of Asaph, who prophesied under the king's supervision.
3 As for Jeduthun, from his sons:
Gedaliah, Zeri, Jeshaiah, Shimei,[a] Hashabiah and Mattithiah, six in all, under the supervision of their father Jeduthun, who prophesied, using the harp in thanking and praising the Lord.
4 As for Heman, from his sons:
Bukkiah, Mattaniah, Uzziel, Shubael and Jerimoth; Hananiah, Hanani, Eliathah, Giddalti and Romamti-Ezer; Joshbekashah, Mallothi, Hothir and Mahazioth. 5 (All these were sons of Heman the king's seer. They were given him through the promises of God to exalt him. God gave Heman fourteen sons and three daughters.)

6 All these men were under the supervision of their father for the music of the temple of the Lord, with cymbals, lyres and harps, for the ministry at the house of God.

Asaph, Jeduthun and Heman were under the supervision of the king. 7 Along with their relatives — all of them trained and skilled in music for the Lord — they numbered 288. 8 Young and old alike, teacher as well as student, cast lots for their duties.

9 The first lot, which was for Asaph, fell to Joseph,
his sons and relatives[b] 12[c]

I t's easy to feel lost in church. You sit there in the pew. You stand up to sing or say the responsive reading. And nobody cares if you're there or not. Or so it may seem. Read some of the weird names in this passage: Zeri, Shimei, Hashabiah, Uzziel, Jerimoth, Mallothi, Hothir, and so on. Who in the world are these people, and why are they in the Bible? They're people who served God by leading in worship. And, although no one today knows who they are, God knows them and gave them a place in his Word. Don't ever feel lost in church. God knows you're there. And he lists you among his worshipers.

INSTANT ACCESS

{1 Chronicles 25:1–7}

the second to Gedaliah,
him and his relatives and
sons 12
10 the third to Zakkur,
his sons and relatives 12
11 the fourth to Izri,[d]
his sons and relatives 12
12 the fifth to Nethaniah,
his sons and relatives 12
13 the sixth to Bukkiah,
his sons and relatives 12

---

a 3 One Hebrew manuscript and some Septuagint manuscripts (see also verse 17); most Hebrew manuscripts do not have Shimei.   b 9 See Septuagint; Hebrew does not have his sons and relatives.   c 9 See the total in verse 7; Hebrew does not have twelve.   d 11 A variant of Zeri

¹⁴the seventh to Jesarelah,ᵃ
  his sons and relatives   12
¹⁵the eighth to Jeshaiah,
  his sons and relatives   12
¹⁶the ninth to Mattaniah,
  his sons and relatives   12
¹⁷the tenth to Shimei,
  his sons and relatives   12
¹⁸the eleventh to Azarel,ᵇ
  his sons and relatives   12
¹⁹the twelfth to Hashabiah,
  his sons and relatives   12
²⁰the thirteenth to Shubael,
  his sons and relatives   12
²¹the fourteenth to Mattithiah,
  his sons and relatives   12
²²the fifteenth to Jerimoth,
  his sons and relatives   12
²³the sixteenth to Hananiah,
  his sons and relatives   12
²⁴the seventeenth to
  Joshbekashah,
  his sons and relatives   12
²⁵the eighteenth to Hanani,
  his sons and relatives   12
²⁶the nineteenth to Mallothi,
  his sons and relatives   12
²⁷the twentieth to Eliathah,
  his sons and relatives   12
²⁸the twenty-first to Hothir,
  his sons and relatives   12
²⁹the twenty-second to Giddalti,
  his sons and relatives   12
³⁰the twenty-third to Mahazioth,
  his sons and relatives   12
³¹the twenty-fourth to Romamti-
  Ezer,
  his sons and relatives   12.

The Gatekeepers

26 The divisions of the gatekeepers:

From the Korahites: Meshelemiah son of Kore, one of the sons of Asaph.

²Meshelemiah had sons:
  Zechariah the firstborn,
  Jediael the second,
  Zebadiah the third,
  Jathniel the fourth,
³Elam the fifth,

Jehohanan the sixth
and Eliehoenai the seventh.
⁴Obed-Edom also had sons:
  Shemaiah the firstborn,
  Jehozabad the second,
  Joah the third,
  Sakar the fourth,
  Nethanel the fifth,
⁵Ammiel the sixth,
  Issachar the seventh
  and Peullethai the eighth.
  (For God had blessed Obed-
  Edom.)

⁶Obed-Edom's son Shemaiah also had sons, who were leaders in their father's family because they were very capable men. ⁷The sons of Shemaiah: Othni, Rephael, Obed and Elzabad; his relatives Elihu and Semakiah were also able men. ⁸All these were descendants of Obed-Edom; they and their sons and their relatives were capable men with the strength to do the work—descendants of Obed-Edom, 62 in all.

⁹Meshelemiah had sons and relatives, who were able men—18 in all.

¹⁰Hosah the Merarite had sons: Shimri the first (although he was not the firstborn, his father had appointed him the first), ¹¹Hilkiah the second, Tabaliah the third and Zechariah the fourth. The sons and relatives of Hosah were 13 in all.

¹²These divisions of the gatekeepers, through their leaders, had duties for ministering in the temple of the LORD, just as their relatives had. ¹³Lots were cast for each gate, according to their families, young and old alike.

¹⁴The lot for the East Gate fell to Shelemiah.ᶜ Then lots were cast for his son Zechariah, a wise counselor, and the lot for the North Gate fell to him. ¹⁵The lot for the South Gate fell to Obed-Edom, and the lot for the storehouse fell to his sons. ¹⁶The lots for the West Gate and

---

ᵃ 14 A variant of Asarelah   ᵇ 18 A variant of Uzziel   ᶜ 14 A variant of Meshelemiah

the Shalleketh Gate on the upper road fell to Shuppim and Hosah.

Guard was alongside of guard: [17]There were six Levites a day on the east, four a day on the north, four a day on the south and two at a time at the storehouse. [18]As for the court[a] to the west, there were four at the road and two at the court[a] itself.

[19]These were the divisions of the gatekeepers who were descendants of Korah and Merari.

The Treasurers and Other Officials

[20]Their fellow Levites were[b] in charge of the treasuries of the house of God and the treasuries for the dedicated things.

[21]The descendants of Ladan, who were Gershonites through Ladan and who were heads of families belonging to Ladan the Gershonite, were Jehieli, [22]the sons of Jehieli, Zetham and his brother Joel. They were in charge of the treasuries of the temple of the LORD.

[23]From the Amramites, the Izharites, the Hebronites and the Uzzielites:

[24]Shubael, a descendant of Gershom son of Moses, was the official in charge of the treasuries. [25]His relatives through Eliezer: Rehabiah his son, Jeshaiah his son, Joram his son, Zikri his son and Shelomith his son. [26]Shelomith and his relatives were in charge of all the treasuries for the things dedicated by King David, by the heads of families who were the commanders of thousands and commanders of hundreds, and by the other army commanders. [27]Some of the plunder taken in battle they dedicated for the repair of the temple of the LORD. [28]And everything dedicated by Samuel the seer and by Saul son of Kish, Abner son of Ner and Joab son of Zeruiah, and all the other dedicated things were in the care of Shelomith and his relatives.

[29]From the Izharites: Kenaniah and his sons were assigned duties away from the temple, as officials and judges over Israel.

[30]From the Hebronites: Hashabiah and his relatives—seventeen hundred able men—were responsible in Israel west of the Jordan for all the work of the LORD and for the king's service. [31]As for the Hebronites, Jeriah was their chief according to the genealogical records of their families. In the fortieth year of David's reign a search was made in the records, and capable men among the Hebronites were found at Jazer in Gilead. [32]Jeriah had twenty-seven hundred relatives, who were able men and heads of families, and King David put them in charge of the Reubenites, the Gadites and the half-tribe of Manasseh for every matter pertaining to God and for the affairs of the king.

Army Divisions

27 This is the list of the Israelites—heads of families, commanders of thousands and commanders of hundreds, and their officers, who served the king in all that concerned the army divisions that were on duty month by month throughout the year. Each division consisted of 24,000 men.

[2]In charge of the first division, for the first month, was Jashobeam son of Zabdiel. There were 24,000 men in his division. [3]He was a descendant of Perez and chief of all the army officers for the first month. [4]In charge of the division for the second month was Dodai the Ahohite; Mikloth was the leader of his division. There were 24,000 men in his division. [5]The third army commander, for the third month, was Benaiah son of Jehoiada the priest. He was chief and there were 24,000 men in his

---

[a] 18 The meaning of the Hebrew for this word is uncertain.   [b] 20 Septuagint; Hebrew *As for the Levites, Ahijah was*

division. 6 This was the Benaiah who was a mighty warrior among the Thirty and was over the Thirty. His son Ammizabad was in charge of his division.

7 The fourth, for the fourth month, was Asahel the brother of Joab; his son Zebadiah was his successor. There were 24,000 men in his division.

8 The fifth, for the fifth month, was the commander Shamhuth the Izrahite. There were 24,000 men in his division.

9 The sixth, for the sixth month, was Ira the son of Ikkesh the Tekoite. There were 24,000 men in his division.

10 The seventh, for the seventh month, was Helez the Pelonite, an Ephraimite. There were 24,000 men in his division.

11 The eighth, for the eighth month, was Sibbekai the Hushathite, a Zerahite. There were 24,000 men in his division.

12 The ninth, for the ninth month, was Abiezer the Anathothite, a Benjamite. There were 24,000 men in his division.

13 The tenth, for the tenth month, was Maharai the Netophathite, a Zerahite. There were 24,000 men in his division.

14 The eleventh, for the eleventh month, was Benaiah the Pirathonite, an Ephraimite. There were 24,000 men in his division.

15 The twelfth, for the twelfth month, was Heldai the Netophathite, from the family of Othniel. There were 24,000 men in his division.

Leaders of the Tribes

16 The leaders of the tribes of Israel:

over the Reubenites: Eliezer son of Zikri;

over the Simeonites: Shephatiah son of Maakah;

17 over Levi: Hashabiah son of Kemuel;

over Aaron: Zadok;

18 over Judah: Elihu, a brother of David;

over Issachar: Omri son of Michael;

19 over Zebulun: Ishmaiah son of Obadiah;

over Naphtali: Jerimoth son of Azriel;

20 over the Ephraimites: Hoshea son of Azaziah;

over half the tribe of Manasseh: Joel son of Pedaiah;

21 over the half-tribe of Manasseh in Gilead: Iddo son of Zechariah;

over Benjamin: Jaasiel son of Abner;

22 over Dan: Azarel son of Jeroham.

These were the leaders of the tribes of Israel.

23 David did not take the number of the men twenty years old or less, because the LORD had promised to make Israel as numerous as the stars in the sky. 24 Joab son of Zeruiah began to count the men but did not finish. God's wrath came on Israel on account of this numbering, and the number was not entered in the book[a] of the annals of King David.

The King's Overseers

25 Azmaveth son of Adiel was in charge of the royal storehouses.

Jonathan son of Uzziah was in charge of the storehouses in the outlying districts, in the towns, the villages and the watchtowers.

26 Ezri son of Kelub was in charge of the workers who farmed the land.

27 Shimei the Ramathite was in charge of the vineyards.

Zabdi the Shiphmite was in charge of the produce of the vineyards for the wine vats.

28 Baal-Hanan the Gederite was in charge of the olive and sycamore-fig trees in the western foothills.

Joash was in charge of the supplies of olive oil.

29 Shitrai the Sharonite was in charge of the herds grazing in Sharon.

Shaphat son of Adlai was in charge of the herds in the valleys.

30 Obil the Ishmaelite was in charge of the camels.

Jehdeiah the Meronothite was in charge of the donkeys.

---

a 24 Septuagint; Hebrew number

31 Jaziz the Hagrite was in charge of the flocks.

All these were the officials in charge of King David's property.

32 Jonathan, David's uncle, was a counselor, a man of insight and a scribe. Jehiel son of Hakmoni took care of the king's sons.

33 Ahithophel was the king's counselor. Hushai the Arkite was the king's confidant. 34 Ahithophel was succeeded by Jehoiada son of Benaiah and by Abiathar.

Joab was the commander of the royal army.

David's Plans for the Temple

28 David summoned all the officials of Israel to assemble at Jerusalem: the officers over the tribes, the commanders of the divisions in the service of the king, the commanders of thousands and commanders of hundreds, and the officials in charge of all the property and livestock belonging to the king and his sons, together with the palace officials, the warriors and all the brave fighting men.

2 King David rose to his feet and said: "Listen to me, my fellow Israelites, my people. I had it in my heart to build a house as a place of rest for the ark of the covenant of the LORD, for the footstool of our God, and I made plans to build it. 3 But God said to me, 'You are not to build a house for my Name, because you are a warrior and have shed blood.'

4 "Yet the LORD, the God of Israel, chose me from my whole family to be king over Israel forever. He chose Judah as leader, and from the tribe of Judah he chose my family, and from my father's sons he was pleased to make me king over all Israel. 5 Of all my sons—and the LORD has given me many—he has chosen my son Solomon to sit on the throne of the kingdom of the LORD over Israel. 6 He said to me: 'Solomon your son is the one who will build my house and my courts, for I have chosen him to be my son, and I will be his father. 7 I will establish his kingdom forever if he is unswerving in carrying out

my commands and laws, as is being done at this time.'

8 "So now I charge you in the sight of all Israel and of the assembly of the LORD, and in the hearing of our God: Be careful to follow all the commands of the LORD your God, that you may possess this good land and pass it on as an inheritance to your descendants forever.

9 "And you, my son Solomon, acknowledge the God of your father, and serve him with wholehearted devotion and with a willing mind, for the LORD searches every heart and understands every desire and every thought. If you seek him, he will be found by you; but if you forsake him, he will reject you forever. 10 Consider now, for the LORD has chosen you to build a house as the sanctuary. Be strong and do the work."

11 Then David gave his son Solomon the plans for the portico of the temple, its buildings, its storerooms, its upper parts, its inner rooms and the place of atonement. 12 He gave him the plans of all that the Spirit had put in his mind for the courts of the temple of the LORD and all the surrounding rooms, for the treasuries of the temple of God and for the treasuries for the dedicated things. 13 He gave him instructions for the divisions of the priests and Levites, and for all the work of serving in the temple of the LORD, as well as for all the articles to be used in its service. 14 He designated the weight of gold for all the gold articles to be used in various kinds of service, and the weight of silver for all the silver articles to be used in various kinds of service: 15 the weight of gold for the gold lampstands and their lamps, with the weight for each lampstand and its lamps; and the weight of silver for each silver lampstand and its lamps, according to the use of each lampstand; 16 the weight of gold for each table for consecrated bread; the weight of silver for the silver tables; 17 the weight of pure gold for the forks, sprinkling bowls and pitchers; the weight of gold for each gold dish; the weight of silver for each silver dish; 18 and the weight of the refined gold for the altar of incense. He also gave him

INSTANT ACCESS

Can God truly be real to you? Lots of kids believe in God but aren't sure how to experience him. Read David's advice to Solomon: Acknowledge God and "serve him with whole-hearted devotion and with a willing mind." Then David promises: "If you seek him, he will be found by you." And he gives this assurance: God "searches every heart and understands every desire and every thought." You won't always obey the Lord. You'll fall short at times. But God won't evaluate you only by what you do. He'll look deeper. And if you are committed to serving God with wholehearted devotion, he'll know you. And you'll know him.

{1 Chronicles 28:9}

the plan for the chariot, that is, the cherubim of gold that spread their wings and overshadow the ark of the covenant of the LORD.

19 "All this," David said, "I have in writing as a result of the LORD's hand on me, and he enabled me to understand all the details of the plan."

20 David also said to Solomon his son, "Be strong and courageous, and do the work. Do not be afraid or discouraged, for the LORD God, my God, is with you. He will not fail you or forsake you until all the work for the service of the temple of the LORD is finished. 21 The divisions of the priests and Levites are ready for all the work on the temple of God, and every willing person skilled in any craft will help you in all the work. The officials and all the people will obey your every command."

Gifts for Building the Temple

29 Then King David said to the whole assembly: "My son Solomon, the one whom God has chosen, is young and inexperienced. The task is great, because this palatial structure is not for man but for the LORD God. 2 With all my resources I have provided for the temple of my God—gold for the gold work, silver for the silver, bronze for the bronze, iron for the iron and wood for the wood, as well as onyx for the settings, turquoise,[a] stones of various colors, and all kinds of fine stone and marble—all of these in large quantities. 3 Besides, in my devotion to the temple of my God I now give my personal treasures of gold and silver for the temple of my God, over and above everything I have provided for this holy temple: 4 three thousand talents[b] of gold (gold of Ophir) and seven thousand talents[c] of refined silver, for the overlaying of the walls of the buildings, 5 for the gold work and the silver work, and for all the work to be done by the craftsmen. Now, who is willing to consecrate themselves to the LORD today?"

6 Then the leaders of families, the officers of the tribes of Israel, the commanders of thousands and commanders of hundreds, and the officials in charge of the king's work gave willingly. 7 They gave toward the work on the temple of God five thousand talents[d] and ten thousand darics[e] of gold, ten thousand talents[f] of silver, eighteen thousand talents[g] of bronze and a hundred thousand talents[h] of iron.

---

[a] 2 The meaning of the Hebrew for this word is uncertain.   [b] 4 That is, about 110 tons or about 100 metric tons
[c] 4 That is, about 260 tons or about 235 metric tons   [d] 7 That is, about 190 tons or about 170 metric tons   [e] 7 That is, about 185 pounds or about 84 kilograms   [f] 7 That is, about 380 tons or about 340 metric tons   [g] 7 That is, about 675 tons or about 610 metric tons   [h] 7 That is, about 3,800 tons or about 3,400 metric tons

⁸Anyone who had precious stones gave them to the treasury of the temple of the LORD in the custody of Jehiel the Gershonite. ⁹The people rejoiced at the willing response of their leaders, for they had given freely and wholeheartedly to the LORD. David the king also rejoiced greatly.

David's Prayer

¹⁰David praised the LORD in the presence of the whole assembly, saying,

"Praise be to you, LORD,
  the God of our father
    Israel,
  from everlasting to everlasting.
¹¹Yours, LORD, is the greatness and the
    power
  and the glory and the majesty and
    the splendor,
  for everything in heaven and earth
    is yours.
Yours, LORD, is the kingdom;
  you are exalted as head over all.
¹²Wealth and honor come from you;
  you are the ruler of all things.
In your hands are strength and power
  to exalt and give strength to all.
¹³Now, our God, we give you thanks,
  and praise your glorious name.

¹⁴"But who am I, and who are my people, that we should be able to give as generously as this? Everything comes from you, and we have given you only what comes from your hand. ¹⁵We are foreigners and strangers in your sight, as were all our ancestors. Our days on earth are like a shadow, without hope. ¹⁶LORD our God, all this abundance that we have provided for building you a temple for your Holy Name comes from your hand, and all of it belongs to you. ¹⁷I know, my God, that you test the heart and are pleased with integrity. All these things I have given willingly and with honest intent. And now I have seen with joy how willingly your people who are here have given to you. ¹⁸LORD, the God of our fathers Abraham, Isaac and Israel, keep these desires and thoughts in the hearts of your people forever, and keep their hearts loyal to you. ¹⁹And give my son Solomon the wholehearted devotion to keep your commands, statutes and decrees and to do everything to build the palatial structure for which I have provided."

²⁰Then David said to the whole assembly, "Praise the LORD your God." So they all praised the LORD, the God of their fathers; they bowed down, prostrating themselves before the LORD and the king.

Now, our God, we give you thanks, and praise your glorious name.
1 Chronicles 29:13

Solomon Acknowledged as King

²¹The next day they made sacrifices to the LORD and presented burnt offerings to him: a thousand bulls, a thousand rams and a thousand male lambs, together with their drink offerings, and other sacrifices in abundance for all Israel. ²²They ate and drank with great joy in the presence of the LORD that day.

Then they acknowledged Solomon son of David as king a second time, anointing him before the LORD to be ruler and Zadok to be priest. ²³So Solomon sat on the throne of the LORD as king in place of his father David. He prospered and all Israel obeyed him. ²⁴All the officers and warriors, as well as all of King David's sons, pledged their submission to King Solomon.

²⁵The LORD highly exalted Solomon in the sight of all Israel and bestowed on him royal splendor such as no king over Israel ever had before.

The Death of David

²⁶David son of Jesse was king over all Israel. ²⁷He ruled over Israel forty years—seven in Hebron and thirty-three in Jerusalem. ²⁸He died at a good old age, having enjoyed long life, wealth and honor. His son Solomon succeeded him as king.

29 As for the events of King David's reign, from beginning to end, they are written in the records of Samuel the seer, the records of Nathan the prophet and the records of Gad the seer, 30 together with the details of his reign and power, and the circumstances that surrounded him and Israel and the kingdoms of all the other lands.

2 CHRONICLES

preview

The stories in this book emphasize staying close to God to experience his blessing.

The first step in returning to God is to revive worship.

Five kings begin to reign while in their teens or younger: Joash (7), Uzziah (16), Manasseh (12), Josiah (8), and Jehoiachin (18).

Friends.

You probably have some friends who are good examples and others who are not so good. Even bad. If you could study one of these groups of kids to see what made them like they are, which would you study: the kids who are good examples or the kids who are bad?

The book of 2 Chronicles tells the story of the southern kingdom of Judah from Solomon to the Babylonian captivity. The writer quickly passes over Judah's bad kings. But he looks in depth at the godly rulers, all to make an important point. When the nation's rulers and people were faithful to God, he blessed them. Get the picture?

>> **SOLOMON TOLD THE REASON**
God reveals secret of success, see 2 Chronicles 7:11–22

>> **PROPHET JAILED FOR TELLING TRUTH**
King believes lying spirits, 2 Chronicles 18

>> **JOASH TAKES UP WITH ASHERAH**
Report in 2 Chronicles 24:1–22

>> **JUDAH'S LAST HOPE KILLED IN BATTLE**
Last good king dies, see 2 Chronicles 35

>> **JERUSALEM BURNS!**
Eyewitness report in 2 Chronicles 36:15–21

As these kings reign, the first coins are minted in Asia Minor. Hilltop fortresses are built in Germany and France. The Olmecs in Central America play ritual ball games. In India elephants are used in warfare.

Solomon Asks for Wisdom

1 Solomon son of David established himself firmly over his kingdom, for the LORD his God was with him and made him exceedingly great.

2 Then Solomon spoke to all Israel—to the commanders of thousands and commanders of hundreds, to the judges and to all the leaders in Israel, the heads of families— 3 and Solomon and the whole assembly went to the high place at Gibeon, for God's tent of meeting was there, which Moses the LORD's servant had made in the wilderness. 4 Now David had brought up the ark of God from Kiriath Jearim to the place he had prepared for it, because he had pitched a tent for it in Jerusalem. 5 But the bronze altar that Bezalel son of Uri, the son of Hur, had made was in Gibeon in front of the tabernacle of the LORD; so Solomon and the assembly inquired of him there. 6 Solomon went up to the bronze altar before the LORD in the tent of meeting and offered a thousand burnt offerings on it.

7 That night God appeared to Solomon and said to him, "Ask for whatever you want me to give you."

8 Solomon answered God, "You have shown great kindness to David my father and have made me king in his place. 9 Now, LORD God, let your promise to my father David be confirmed, for you have made me king over a people who are as numerous as the dust of the earth. 10 Give me wisdom and knowledge, that I may lead this people, for who is able to govern this great people of yours?"

11 God said to Solomon, "Since this is your heart's desire and you have not asked for wealth, possessions or honor, nor for the death of your enemies, and since you have not asked for a long life but for wisdom and knowledge to govern my people over whom I have made you king, 12 therefore wisdom and knowledge will be given you. And I will also give you wealth, possessions and honor, such as no king who was before you ever had and none after you will have."

13 Then Solomon went to Jerusalem from the high place at Gibeon, from before the tent of meeting. And he reigned over Israel.

14 Solomon accumulated chariots and horses; he had fourteen hundred chariots and twelve thousand horses,[a] which he kept in the chariot cities and also with him in Jerusalem. 15 The king made silver and gold as common in Jerusalem as stones, and cedar as plentiful as sycamore-fig trees in the foothills. 16 Solomon's horses were imported from Egypt and from Kue[b]—the royal merchants purchased them from Kue at the current price. 17 They imported a chariot from Egypt for six hundred shekels[c] of silver, and a horse for a hundred and fifty.[d] They also exported them to all the kings of the Hittites and of the Arameans.

Preparations for Building the Temple

2[e] Solomon gave orders to build a temple for the Name of the LORD and a royal palace for himself. 2 He conscripted 70,000 men as carriers and 80,000 as stonecutters in the hills and 3,600 as foremen over them.

3 Solomon sent this message to Hiram[f] king of Tyre:

"Send me cedar logs as you did for my father David when you sent him cedar to build a palace to live in. 4 Now I am about to build a temple for the Name of the LORD my God and to dedicate it to him for burning fragrant incense before him, for setting out the consecrated bread regularly, and for making burnt offerings every morning and evening and on the Sabbaths, at the New Moons and at the appointed festivals of the LORD our God. This is a lasting ordinance for Israel.

5 "The temple I am going to build will be great, because our God is greater than all other gods. 6 But who is able to build a temple for him,

---

[a] 14 Or charioteers   [b] 16 Probably Cilicia   [c] 17 That is, about 15 pounds or about 6.9 kilograms   [d] 17 That is, about 3 3/4 pounds or about 1.7 kilograms   [e] In Hebrew texts 2:1 is numbered 1:18, and 2:2-18 is numbered 2:1-17.
[f] 3 Hebrew Huram, a variant of Hiram; also in verses 11 and 12

since the heavens, even the highest
heavens, cannot contain him? Who
then am I to build a temple for him,
except as a place to burn sacrifices
before him?
7 "Send me, therefore, a man
skilled to work in gold and silver,
bronze and iron, and in purple, crimson and blue yarn, and experienced in the art of engraving, to work in Judah
and Jerusalem with
my skilled workers,
whom my father Da-
vid provided.
8 "Send me also
cedar, juniper and
algum[a] logs from
Lebanon, for I know
that your servants are
skilled in cutting timber
there. My servants will
work with yours 9 to provide
me with plenty of lumber, because
the temple I build must be large and
magnificent. 10 I will give your servants, the woodsmen who cut the
timber, twenty thousand cors[b] of
ground wheat, twenty thousand cors[c]
of barley, twenty thousand baths[d] of
wine and twenty thousand baths of
olive oil."

11 Hiram king of Tyre replied by letter
to Solomon:

"Because the LORD loves his people, he has made you their king."

12 And Hiram added:

"Praise be to the LORD, the God of
Israel, who made heaven and earth!
He has given King David a wise son,
endowed with intelligence and discernment, who will build a temple
for the LORD and a palace for himself.
13 "I am sending you Huram-Abi,
a man of great skill, 14 whose mother was from Dan and whose father
was from Tyre. He is trained to work
in gold and silver, bronze and iron,
stone and wood, and with purple and
blue and crimson yarn and fine linen.
He is experienced in all kinds of engraving and can execute any design
given to him. He will work with your
skilled workers and with those of my
lord, David your father.
15 "Now let my lord send his
servants the wheat and
barley and the olive oil
and wine he promised,
16 and we will cut all
the logs from Leba-
non that you need
and will float them as
rafts by sea down to
Joppa. You can then
take them up to Jeru-
salem."

Our God is greater than all other gods.

2 Chronicles 2:5

17 Solomon took a census
of all the foreigners residing in
Israel, after the census his father David had taken; and they were found to be
153,600. 18 He assigned 70,000 of them
to be carriers and 80,000 to be stonecutters in the hills, with 3,600 foremen over
them to keep the people working.

Solomon Builds the Temple

3 Then Solomon began to build the
temple of the LORD in Jerusalem on
Mount Moriah, where the LORD had appeared to his father David. It was on the
threshing floor of Araunah[e] the Jebusite,
the place provided by David. 2 He began
building on the second day of the second
month in the fourth year of his reign.
3 The foundation Solomon laid for building the temple of God was sixty cubits
long and twenty cubits wide[f] (using the
cubit of the old standard). 4 The portico at
the front of the temple was twenty cubits[g]
long across the width of the building and
twenty[h] cubits high.
He overlaid the inside with pure gold.
5 He paneled the main hall with juniper
and covered it with fine gold and decorat-

[a] 8 Probably a variant of *almug* [b] 10 That is, probably about 3,600 tons or about 3,200 metric tons of wheat
[c] 10 That is, probably about 3,000 tons or about 2,700 metric tons of barley [d] 10 That is, about 120,000 gallons or about 440,000 liters [e] 1 Hebrew *Ornan,* a variant of *Araunah* [f] 3 That is, about 90 feet long and 30 feet wide or about 27 meters long and 9 meters wide [g] 4 That is, about 30 feet or about 9 meters; also in verses 8, 11 and 13
[h] 4 Some Septuagint and Syriac manuscripts; Hebrew *and a hundred and twenty*

ed it with palm tree and chain designs. [6]He adorned the temple with precious stones. And the gold he used was gold of Parvaim. [7]He overlaid the ceiling beams, doorframes, walls and doors of the temple with gold, and he carved cherubim on the walls.

[8]He built the Most Holy Place, its length corresponding to the width of the temple—twenty cubits long and twenty cubits wide. He overlaid the inside with six hundred talents[a] of fine gold. [9]The gold nails weighed fifty shekels.[b] He also overlaid the upper parts with gold.

[10]For the Most Holy Place he made a pair of sculptured cherubim and overlaid them with gold. [11]The total wingspan of the cherubim was twenty cubits. One wing of the first cherub was five cubits[c] long and touched the temple wall, while its other wing, also five cubits long, touched the wing of the other cherub. [12]Similarly one wing of the second cherub was five cubits long and touched the other temple wall, and its other wing, also five cubits long, touched the wing of the first cherub. [13]The wings of these cherubim extended twenty cubits. They stood on their feet, facing the main hall.[d]

[14]He made the curtain of blue, purple and crimson yarn and fine linen, with cherubim worked into it.

[15]For the front of the temple he made two pillars, which together were thirty-five cubits[e] long, each with a capital five cubits high. [16]He made interwoven chains[f] and put them on top of the pillars. He also made a hundred pomegranates and attached them to the chains. [17]He erected the pillars in the front of the temple, one to the south and one to the north. The one to the south he named Jakin[g] and the one to the north Boaz.[h]

The Temple's Furnishings

4 He made a bronze altar twenty cubits long, twenty cubits wide and ten cu-

bits high.[i] [2]He made the Sea of cast metal, circular in shape, measuring ten cubits from rim to rim and five cubits[j] high. It took a line of thirty cubits[k] to measure around it. [3]Below the rim, figures of bulls encircled it—ten to a cubit.[l] The bulls were cast in two rows in one piece with the Sea.

[4]The Sea stood on twelve bulls, three facing north, three facing west, three facing south and three facing east. The Sea rested on top of them, and their hindquarters were toward the center. [5]It was a handbreadth[m] in thickness, and its rim was like the rim of a cup, like a lily blossom. It held three thousand baths.[n]

[6]He then made ten basins for washing and placed five on the south side and five on the north. In them the things to be used for the burnt offerings were rinsed, but the Sea was to be used by the priests for washing.

[7]He made ten gold lampstands according to the specifications for them and placed them in the temple, five on the south side and five on the north.

[8]He made ten tables and placed them in the temple, five on the south side and five on the north. He also made a hundred gold sprinkling bowls.

[9]He made the courtyard of the priests, and the large court and the doors for the court, and overlaid the doors with bronze. [10]He placed the Sea on the south side, at the southeast corner.

[11]And Huram also made the pots and shovels and sprinkling bowls.

So Huram finished the work he had undertaken for King Solomon in the temple of God:

[12]the two pillars;
  the two bowl-shaped capitals on top
    of the pillars;
  the two sets of network decorating
    the two bowl-shaped capitals on
    top of the pillars;

---

[a] 8 That is, about 23 tons or about 21 metric tons   [b] 9 That is, about 1 1/4 pounds or about 575 grams   [c] 11 That is, about 7 1/2 feet or about 2.3 meters; also in verse 15   [d] 13 Or facing inward   [e] 15 That is, about 53 feet or about 16 meters   [f] 16 Or possibly made chains in the inner sanctuary; the meaning of the Hebrew for this phrase is uncertain.   [g] 17 Jakin probably means he establishes.   [h] 17 Boaz probably means in him is strength.   [i] 1 That is, about 30 feet long and wide and 15 feet high or about 9 meters long and wide and 4.5 meters high   [j] 2 That is, about 7 1/2 feet or about 2.3 meters   [k] 2 That is, about 45 feet or about 14 meters   [l] 3 That is, about 18 inches or about 45 centimeters   [m] 5 That is, about 3 inches or about 7.5 centimeters   [n] 5 That is, about 18,000 gallons or about 66,000 liters

13 the four hundred pomegranates for the two sets of network (two rows of pomegranates for each network, decorating the bowl-shaped capitals on top of the pillars);
14 the stands with their basins;
15 the Sea and the twelve bulls under it;
16 the pots, shovels, meat forks and all related articles.

All the objects that Huram-Abi made for King Solomon for the temple of the LORD were of polished bronze. 17 The king had them cast in clay molds in the plain of the Jordan between Sukkoth and Zarethan.[a] 18 All these things that Solomon made amounted to so much that the weight of the bronze could not be calculated.

19 Solomon also made all the furnishings that were in God's temple:

the golden altar;
the tables on which was the bread of the Presence;
20 the lampstands of pure gold with their lamps, to burn in front of the inner sanctuary as prescribed;
21 the gold floral work and lamps and tongs (they were solid gold);
22 the pure gold wick trimmers, sprinkling bowls, dishes and censers; and the gold doors of the temple: the inner doors to the Most Holy Place and the doors of the main hall.

5 When all the work Solomon had done for the temple of the LORD was finished, he brought in the things his father David had dedicated—the silver and gold and all the furnishings—and he placed them in the treasuries of God's temple.

The Ark Brought to the Temple

2 Then Solomon summoned to Jerusalem the elders of Israel, all the heads of the tribes and the chiefs of the Israelite families, to bring up the ark of the LORD's covenant from Zion, the City of David. 3 And all the Israelites came together to the king at the time of the festival in the seventh month.

4 When all the elders of Israel had arrived, the Levites took up the ark, 5 and they brought up the ark and the tent of meeting and all the sacred furnishings in it. The Levitical priests carried them up; 6 and King Solomon and the entire assembly of Israel that had gathered about him were before the ark, sacrificing so many sheep and cattle that they could not be recorded or counted.

7 The priests then brought the ark of the LORD's covenant to its place in the inner sanctuary of the temple, the Most Holy Place, and put it beneath the wings of the cherubim. 8 The cherubim spread their wings over the place of the ark and covered the ark and its carrying poles. 9 These poles were so long that their ends, extending from the ark, could be seen from in front of the inner sanctuary, but not from outside the Holy Place; and they are still there today. 10 There was nothing in the ark except the two tablets that Moses had placed in it at Horeb, where the LORD made a covenant with the Israelites after they came out of Egypt.

11 The priests then withdrew from the Holy Place. All the priests who were there had consecrated themselves, regardless of their divisions. 12 All the Levites who were musicians—Asaph, Heman, Jeduthun and their sons and relatives—stood on the east side of the altar, dressed in fine linen and playing cymbals, harps and lyres. They were accompanied by 120 priests sounding trumpets. 13 The trumpeters and musicians joined in unison to give praise and thanks to the LORD. Accompanied by trumpets, cymbals and other instruments, the singers raised their voices in praise to the LORD and sang:

"He is good;
his love endures forever."

Then the temple of the LORD was filled with the cloud, 14 and the priests could not perform their service because of the cloud, for the glory of the LORD filled the temple of God.

---

[a] 17 Hebrew *Zeredatha*, a variant of *Zarethan*

6 Then Solomon said, "The LORD has said that he would dwell in a dark cloud; ²I have built a magnificent temple for you, a place for you to dwell forever."

³While the whole assembly of Israel was standing there, the king turned around and blessed them. ⁴Then he said:

"Praise be to the LORD, the God of Israel, who with his hands has fulfilled what he promised with his mouth to my father David. For he said, ⁵'Since the day I brought my people out of Egypt, I have not chosen a city in any tribe of Israel to have a temple built so that my Name might be there, nor have I chosen anyone to be ruler over my people Israel. ⁶But now I have chosen Jerusalem for my Name to be there, and I have chosen David to rule my people Israel.'

⁷"My father David had it in his heart to build a temple for the Name of the LORD, the God of Israel. ⁸But the LORD said to my father David, 'You did well to have it in your heart to build a temple for my Name. ⁹Nevertheless, you are not the one to build the temple, but your son, your own flesh and blood—he is the one who will build the temple for my Name.'

¹⁰"The LORD has kept the promise he made. I have succeeded David my father and now I sit on the throne of Israel, just as the LORD promised, and I have built the temple for the Name of the LORD, the God of Israel. ¹¹There I have placed the ark, in which is the covenant of the LORD that he made with the people of Israel."

Solomon's Prayer of Dedication

¹²Then Solomon stood before the altar of the LORD in front of the whole assembly of Israel and spread out his hands. ¹³Now he had made a bronze platform, five cubits long, five cubits wide and three cubits high,ᵃ and had placed it in the center of the outer court. He stood on the platform and then knelt down before the whole assembly of Israel and spread out his hands toward heaven. ¹⁴He said:

"LORD, the God of Israel, there is no God like you in heaven or on earth—you who keep your covenant of love with your servants who continue wholeheartedly in your way. ¹⁵You have kept your promise to your servant David my father; with your mouth you have promised and with your hand you have fulfilled it—as it is today.

¹⁶"Now, LORD, the God of Israel, keep for your servant David my father the promises you made to him when you said, 'You shall never fail to have a successor to sit before me on the throne of Israel, if only your descendants are careful in all they do to walk before me according to my law, as you have done.' ¹⁷And now, LORD, the God of Israel, let your word that you promised your servant David come true.

¹⁸"But will God really dwell on earth with humans? The heavens, even the highest heavens, cannot contain you. How much less this temple I have built! ¹⁹Yet, LORD my God, give attention to your servant's prayer and his plea for mercy. Hear the cry and the prayer that your servant is praying in your presence. ²⁰May your eyes be open toward this temple day and night, this place of which you said you would put your Name there. May you hear the prayer your servant prays toward this place. ²¹Hear the supplications of your servant and of your people Israel when they pray toward this place. Hear from heaven, your dwelling place; and when you hear, forgive.

²²"When anyone wrongs their neighbor and is required to take an oath and they come and swear the oath before your altar in this temple, ²³then hear from heaven and act. Judge between your servants, condemning the guilty and bringing

---

ᵃ 13 That is, about 7 1/2 feet long and wide and 4 1/2 feet high or about 2.3 meters long and wide and 1.4 meters high

down on their heads what they have done, and vindicating the innocent by treating them in accordance with their innocence.

24 "When your people Israel have been defeated by an enemy because they have sinned against you and when they turn back and give praise to your name, praying and making supplication before you in this temple, 25 then hear from heaven and forgive the sin of your people Israel and bring them back to the land you gave to them and their ancestors.

26 "When the heavens are shut up and there is no rain because your people have sinned against you, and when they pray toward this place and give praise to your name and turn from their sin because you have afflicted them, 27 then hear from heaven and forgive the sin of your servants, your people Israel. Teach them the right way to live, and send rain on the land you gave your people for an inheritance.

28 "When famine or plague comes to the land, or blight or mildew, locusts or grasshoppers, or when enemies besiege them in any of their cities, whatever disaster or disease may come, 29 and when a prayer or plea is made by anyone among your people Israel—being aware of their afflictions and pains, and spreading out their hands toward this temple— 30 then hear from heaven, your dwelling place. Forgive, and deal with everyone according to all they do, since you know their hearts (for you alone know the human heart), 31 so that they will fear you and walk in obedience to you all the time they live in the land you gave our ancestors.

32 "As for the foreigner who does not belong to your people Israel but has come from a distant land because of your great name and your mighty hand and your outstretched arm—when they come and pray toward this temple, 33 then hear from heaven, your dwelling place. Do whatever the foreigner asks of you, so that all the peoples of the earth may know your name and fear you, as do your own people Israel, and may know that this house I have built bears your Name.

34 "When your people go to war against their enemies, wherever you send them, and when they pray to you toward this city you have chosen and the temple I have built for your Name, 35 then hear from heaven their prayer and their plea, and uphold their cause.

36 "When they sin against you—for there is no one who does not sin— and you become angry with them and give them over to the enemy, who takes them captive to a land far away or near; 37 and if they have a change of heart in the land where they are held captive, and repent and plead with you in the land of their captivity and say, 'We have sinned, we have done wrong and acted wickedly'; 38 and if they turn back to you with all their heart and soul in the land of their captivity where they were taken, and pray toward the land you gave their ancestors, toward the city you have chosen and toward the temple I have built for your Name; 39 then from heaven, your dwelling place, hear their prayer and their pleas, and uphold their cause. And forgive your people, who have sinned against you.

40 "Now, my God, may your eyes be open and your ears attentive to the prayers offered in this place.

41 "Now arise, Lord God, and
come to your resting
place,
you and the ark of your
might.
May your priests, Lord God, be
clothed with salvation,
may your faithful people
rejoice in your
goodness.
42 Lord God, do not reject your
anointed one.
Remember the great love
promised to David your
servant."

> My parents told me I couldn't hang around
> with certain kids. I think I should be able to
> choose my own friends, so I've been lying and
> sneaking out. Now I feel guilty every time I
> try to pray. Why is everything so confusing?
> What should I do?   >> Alex

Dear Jordan

Dear Alex,

You have two separate problems here. Your first problem is you felt your parents were too controlling of your choice of friends. Your second problem is you chose to solve this problem by lying to your parents and being disobedient. This is sinning against your parents who God told you to honor.

You mentioned feeling guilty when you pray. God expects you to obey your parents, even when you don't want to in the worst way. That's one reason you're feeling guilty. Lying and disobedience are sins in God's eyes. Sin takes us out of fellowship with God. King Solomon understood it was necessary for people to stop disobeying God in order to receive God's blessings (2 Chronicles 6:26–27).

Seek forgiveness and do what's right. Perhaps if your parents can get to know your friends, they'll even lift their restrictions. Feeling better will be a bonus.

Jordan

The Dedication of the Temple

7 When Solomon finished praying, fire came down from heaven and consumed the burnt offering and the sacrifices, and the glory of the LORD filled the temple. ² The priests could not enter the temple of the LORD because the glory of the LORD filled it. ³ When all the Israelites saw the fire coming down and the glory of the LORD above the temple, they knelt on the pavement with their faces to the ground, and they worshiped and gave thanks to the LORD, saying,

"He is good;
his love endures forever."

⁴ Then the king and all the people offered sacrifices before the LORD. ⁵ And King Solomon offered a sacrifice of twenty-two thousand head of cattle and a hundred and twenty thousand sheep and goats. So the king and all the people dedicated the temple of God. ⁶ The priests took their positions, as did the Levites with the LORD's musical instruments, which King David had made for praising the LORD and which were used when he gave thanks, saying, "His love endures forever." Opposite the Levites, the priests blew their trumpets, and all the Israelites were standing.

⁷ Solomon consecrated the middle part of the courtyard in front of the temple of the LORD, and there he offered burnt offerings and the fat of the fellowship offerings, because the bronze altar he had made could not hold the burnt offerings, the grain offerings and the fat portions.

⁸ So Solomon observed the festival at that time for seven days, and all Israel with him—a vast assembly, people from Lebo Hamath to the Wadi of Egypt. ⁹ On the eighth day they held an assembly, for they had celebrated the dedication of the altar for seven days and the festival for seven days more. ¹⁰ On the twenty-third day of the seventh month he sent the people to their homes, joyful and glad in heart for the good things the LORD had done for David and Solomon and for his people Israel.

The LORD Appears to Solomon

¹¹ When Solomon had finished the temple of the LORD and the royal palace, and had succeeded in carrying out all he had in mind to do in the temple of the LORD and in his own palace, ¹² the LORD appeared to him at night and said:

"I have heard your prayer and have chosen this place for myself as a temple for sacrifices.

¹³ "When I shut up the heavens so that there is no rain, or command locusts to devour the land or send a plague among my people, ¹⁴ if my people, who are called by my name, will humble themselves and pray and seek my face and turn from their wicked ways, then I will hear from heaven, and I will forgive their sin and will heal their land. ¹⁵ Now my eyes will be open and my ears attentive to the prayers offered in this place. ¹⁶ I have chosen and consecrated this temple so that my Name may be there forever. My eyes and my heart will always be there.

¹⁷ "As for you, if you walk before me faithfully as David your father did, and do all I command, and ob-

serve my decrees and laws, 18I will establish your royal throne, as I covenanted with David your father when I said, 'You shall never fail to have a successor to rule over Israel.'

19 "But if you*a* turn away and forsake the decrees and commands I have given you*a* and go off to serve other gods and worship them, 20then I will uproot Israel from my land, which I have given them, and will reject this temple I have consecrated for my Name. I will make it a byword and an object of ridicule among all peoples. 21This temple will become a heap of rubble. All*b* who pass by will be appalled and say, 'Why has the LORD done such a thing to this land and to this temple?' 22People will answer, 'Because they have forsaken the LORD, the God of their ancestors, who brought them out of Egypt, and have embraced other gods, worshiping and serving them—that is why he brought all this disaster on them.' "

Solomon's Other Activities

8 At the end of twenty years, during which Solomon built the temple of the LORD and his own palace, 2Solomon rebuilt the villages that Hiram*c* had given him, and settled Israelites in them. 3Solomon then went to Hamath Zobah and captured it. 4He also built up Tadmor in the desert and all the store cities he had built in Hamath. 5He rebuilt Upper Beth Horon and Lower Beth Horon as fortified cities, with walls and with gates and bars, 6as well as Baalath and all his store cities, and all the cities for his chariots and for his horses*d*—whatever he desired to build in Jerusalem, in Lebanon and throughout all the territory he ruled.

7There were still people left from the Hittites, Amorites, Perizzites, Hivites and Jebusites (these people were not Israelites). 8Solomon conscripted the descendants of all these people remaining in the land—whom the Israelites had not

A: He sacrificed 22,000 head of cattle and 120,000 sheep and goats (2 Chronicles 7:5).

BONUS: The "glory of the LORD," a bright, glowing cloud, filled the temple (2 Chronicles 7:1–3).

destroyed—to serve as slave labor, as it is to this day. 9But Solomon did not make slaves of the Israelites for his work; they were his fighting men, commanders of his captains, and commanders of his chariots and charioteers. 10They were also King Solomon's chief officials—two hundred and fifty officials supervising the men.

11Solomon brought Pharaoh's daughter up from the City of David to the palace he had built for her, for he said, "My wife must not live in the palace of David king of Israel, because the places the ark of the LORD has entered are holy."

12On the altar of the LORD that he had built in front of the portico, Solomon sacrificed burnt offerings to the LORD, 13according to the daily requirement for offerings commanded by Moses for the Sabbaths, the New Moons and the three annual festivals—the Festival of Unleavened Bread, the Festival of Weeks and the Festival of Tabernacles. 14In keeping with the ordinance of his father David, he appointed the divisions of the priests for their duties, and the Levites to lead the

---

a 19 The Hebrew is plural.   *b 21* See some Septuagint manuscripts, Old Latin, Syriac, Arabic and Targum; Hebrew *And though this temple is now so imposing, all*   *c 2* Hebrew *Huram,* a variant of *Hiram;* also in verse 18   *d 6* Or *charioteers*

praise and to assist the priests according to each day's requirement. He also appointed the gatekeepers by divisions for the various gates, because this was what David the man of God had ordered. ¹⁵They did not deviate from the king's commands to the priests or to the Levites in any matter, including that of the treasuries.

¹⁶All Solomon's work was carried out, from the day the foundation of the temple of the LORD was laid until its completion. So the temple of the LORD was finished.

¹⁷Then Solomon went to Ezion Geber and Elath on the coast of Edom. ¹⁸And Hiram sent him ships commanded by his own men, sailors who knew the sea. These, with Solomon's men, sailed to Ophir and brought back four hundred and fifty talents[a] of gold, which they delivered to King Solomon.

The Queen of Sheba Visits Solomon

9 When the queen of Sheba heard of Solomon's fame, she came to Jerusalem to test him with hard questions. Arriving with a very great caravan—with camels carrying spices, large quantities of gold, and precious stones—she came to Solomon and talked with him about all she had on her mind. ²Solomon answered all her questions; nothing was too hard for him to explain to her. ³When the queen of Sheba saw the wisdom of Solomon, as well as the palace he had built, ⁴the food on his table, the seating of his officials, the attending servants in their robes, the cupbearers in their robes and the burnt offerings he made at[b] the temple of the LORD, she was overwhelmed.

⁵She said to the king, "The report I heard in my own country about your achievements and your wisdom is true. ⁶But I did not believe what they said until I came and saw with my own eyes. Indeed, not even half the greatness of your wisdom was told me; you have far exceeded the report I heard. ⁷How happy your people must be! How happy your of-

INSTANT ACCESS

Some prayers are always answered with an enthusiastic "Yes!" God promises: "If my people, who are called by my name, will humble themselves and pray and seek my face and turn from their wicked ways, then will I hear from heaven, and I will forgive their sin." What a great promise for those times when guilt gets you down. You feel ashamed. Even dirty. You wonder how you'll ever be able to face yourself or God. And then you hear the promise: "Pray. Seek my face. Turn from your wicked ways." And you remember God always answers "Yes!" to prayers for forgiveness. He has promised, "I will hear and will forgive."

{2 Chronicles 7:14}

ficials, who continually stand before you and hear your wisdom! ⁸Praise be to the LORD your God, who has delighted in you and placed you on his throne as king to rule for the LORD your God. Because of the love of your God for Israel and his desire to uphold them forever, he has made you king over them, to maintain justice and righteousness."

⁹Then she gave the king 120 talents[c] of gold, large quantities of spices, and

---

[a] 18 That is, about 17 tons or about 15 metric tons   [b] 4 Or and the ascent by which he went up to   [c] 9 That is, about 4 1/2 tons or about 4 metric tons

precious stones. There had never been such spices as those the queen of Sheba gave to King Solomon.

¹⁰(The servants of Hiram and the servants of Solomon brought gold from Ophir; they also brought algumwood[a] and precious stones. ¹¹The king used the algumwood to make steps for the temple of the LORD and for the royal palace, and to make harps and lyres for the musicians. Nothing like them had ever been seen in Judah.)

¹²King Solomon gave the queen of Sheba all she desired and asked for; he gave her more than she had brought to him. Then she left and returned with her retinue to her own country.

Solomon's Splendor

¹³The weight of the gold that Solomon received yearly was 666 talents,[b] ¹⁴not including the revenues brought in by merchants and traders. Also all the kings of Arabia and the governors of the territories brought gold and silver to Solomon.

¹⁵King Solomon made two hundred large shields of hammered gold; six hundred shekels[c] of hammered gold went into each shield. ¹⁶He also made three hundred small shields of hammered gold, with three hundred shekels[d] of gold in each shield. The king put them in the Palace of the Forest of Lebanon.

¹⁷Then the king made a great throne covered with ivory and overlaid with pure gold. ¹⁸The throne had six steps, and a footstool of gold was attached to it. On both sides of the seat were armrests, with a lion standing beside each of them. ¹⁹Twelve lions stood on the six steps, one at either end of each step. Nothing like it had ever been made for any other kingdom. ²⁰All King Solomon's goblets were gold, and all the household articles in the Palace of the Forest of Lebanon were pure gold. Nothing was made of silver, because silver was considered of little value in Solomon's day. ²¹The king had a fleet

of trading ships[e] manned by Hiram's[f] servants. Once every three years it returned, carrying gold, silver and ivory, and apes and baboons.

²²King Solomon was greater in riches and wisdom than all the other kings of the earth. ²³All the kings of the earth sought audience with Solomon to hear the wisdom God had put in his heart. ²⁴Year after year, everyone who came brought a gift—articles of silver and gold, and robes, weapons and spices, and horses and mules.

²⁵Solomon had four thousand stalls for horses and chariots, and twelve thousand horses,[g] which he kept in the chariot cities and also with him in Jerusalem. ²⁶He ruled over all the kings from the Euphrates River to the land of the Philistines, as far as the border of Egypt. ²⁷The king made silver as common in Jerusalem as stones, and cedar as plentiful as sycamore-fig trees in the foothills. ²⁸Solomon's horses were imported from Egypt and from all other countries.

Solomon's Death

²⁹As for the other events of Solomon's reign, from beginning to end, are they

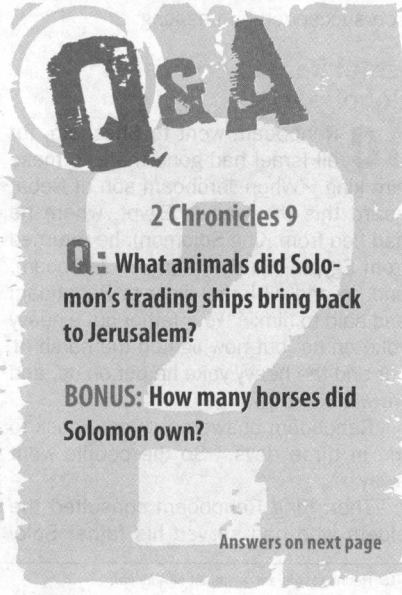

2 Chronicles 9

Q: What animals did Solomon's trading ships bring back to Jerusalem?

BONUS: How many horses did Solomon own?

Answers on next page

ᵃ 10 Probably a variant of *almugwood*   ᵇ 13 That is, about 25 tons or about 23 metric tons   ᶜ 15 That is, about 15 pounds or about 6.9 kilograms   ᵈ 16 That is, about 7 1/2 pounds or about 3.5 kilograms   ᵉ 21 Hebrew of *ships that could go to Tarshish*   ᶠ 21 Hebrew *Huram*, a variant of *Hiram*   ᵍ 25 Or *charioteers*

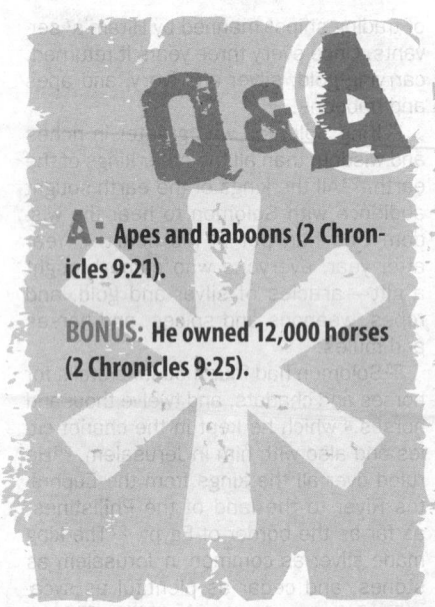

A: Apes and baboons (2 Chronicles 9:21).

BONUS: He owned 12,000 horses (2 Chronicles 9:25).

not written in the records of Nathan the prophet, in the prophecy of Ahijah the Shilonite and in the visions of Iddo the seer concerning Jeroboam son of Nebat? 30 Solomon reigned in Jerusalem over all Israel forty years. 31 Then he rested with his ancestors and was buried in the city of David his father. And Rehoboam his son succeeded him as king.

Israel Rebels Against Rehoboam

10 Rehoboam went to Shechem, for all Israel had gone there to make him king. 2 When Jeroboam son of Nebat heard this (he was in Egypt, where he had fled from King Solomon), he returned from Egypt. 3 So they sent for Jeroboam, and he and all Israel went to Rehoboam and said to him: 4 "Your father put a heavy yoke on us, but now lighten the harsh labor and the heavy yoke he put on us, and we will serve you."

5 Rehoboam answered, "Come back to me in three days." So the people went away.

6 Then King Rehoboam consulted the elders who had served his father Solomon during his lifetime. "How would you advise me to answer these people?" he asked.

7 They replied, "If you will be kind to these people and please them and give them a favorable answer, they will always be your servants."

8 But Rehoboam rejected the advice the elders gave him and consulted the young men who had grown up with him and were serving him. 9 He asked them, "What is your advice? How should we answer these people who say to me, 'Lighten the yoke your father put on us'?"

10 The young men who had grown up with him replied, "The people have said to you, 'Your father put a heavy yoke on us, but make our yoke lighter.' Now tell them, 'My little finger is thicker than my father's waist. 11 My father laid on you a heavy yoke; I will make it even heavier. My father scourged you with whips; I will scourge you with scorpions.' "

12 Three days later Jeroboam and all the people returned to Rehoboam, as the king had said, "Come back to me in three days." 13 The king answered them harshly. Rejecting the advice of the elders, 14 he followed the advice of the young men and said, "My father made your yoke heavy; I will make it even heavier. My father scourged you with whips; I will scourge you with scorpions." 15 So the king did not listen to the people, for this turn of events was from God, to fulfill the word the LORD had spoken to Jeroboam son of Nebat through Ahijah the Shilonite.

16 When all Israel saw that the king refused to listen to them, they answered the king:

"What share do we have in David,
     what part in Jesse's son?
To your tents, Israel!
     Look after your own house, David!"

So all the Israelites went home. 17 But as for the Israelites who were living in the towns of Judah, Rehoboam still ruled over them.

18 King Rehoboam sent out Adoniram,[a] who was in charge of forced labor, but

> " "
>
> Why are my parents always saying, "Don't do this. Don't do that?" Why can't I just live my life and find out things for myself?
>
> ## >> Elizabeth

Dear Elizabeth,

Let's pretend two of your friends invited you to go on a family vacation with them. You wanted to go to both places but didn't know which place was better. Your mom said go to place B, and somebody you know at school said she would go to place A. So you go to place A. You find out this island has no air conditioning and lots of bugs. When you get home you see photos of location B where your other friend stayed. You go and tell your mom what you learned and she says, "I know, I've been to both places."

You could have had the time of your life. Instead you're covered with bug bites and came home sick. But you listened to your friend and not your parents who really knew something.

A young king in Israel named Rehoboam felt the same as you. He sought the advice of those who had served his father and had much experience and wisdom. But then he talked to his friends and decided to take their advice instead. Disaster followed (2 Chronicles 10:16–19).

Your parents can help you make better choices that will help make life easier and happier. I know the world has changed since they were your age, but many things are still the same. Your parents know a lot more than you think. They really are on your side. Of course you can choose to learn every lesson the hard way. But why would you want to?

Jordan

the Israelites stoned him to death. King Rehoboam, however, managed to get into his chariot and escape to Jerusalem. [19]So Israel has been in rebellion against the house of David to this day.

11 When Rehoboam arrived in Jerusalem, he mustered Judah and Benjamin—a hundred and eighty thousand able young men—to go to war against Israel and to regain the kingdom for Rehoboam.

[2]But this word of the LORD came to Shemaiah the man of God: [3]"Say to Rehoboam son of Solomon king of Judah and to all Israel in Judah and Benjamin, [4]'This is what the LORD says: Do not go up to fight against your fellow Israelites. Go home, every one of you, for this is my doing.'" So they obeyed the words of the LORD and turned back from marching against Jeroboam.

Rehoboam Fortifies Judah

[5]Rehoboam lived in Jerusalem and built up towns for defense in Judah: [6]Bethlehem, Etam, Tekoa, [7]Beth Zur, Soko, Adullam, [8]Gath, Mareshah, Ziph, [9]Adoraim, Lachish, Azekah, [10]Zorah, Aijalon and Hebron. These were fortified cities in Judah and Benjamin. [11]He strengthened their defenses and put commanders in them, with supplies of food, olive oil and wine. [12]He put shields and spears in all the cities, and made them very strong. So Judah and Benjamin were his.

[13]The priests and Levites from all their districts throughout Israel sided with him. [14]The Levites even abandoned their pasturelands and property and came to Judah and Jerusalem, because Jeroboam and his sons had rejected them as priests of the LORD [15]when he appointed his own priests for the high places and for the goat and calf idols he had made. [16]Those from every tribe of Israel who set their hearts on seeking the LORD, the God of Israel, followed the Levites to Jerusalem to offer sacrifices to the LORD, the God of their ancestors. [17]They strengthened the kingdom of Judah and supported Rehoboam son of Solomon three years, following the ways of David and Solomon during this time.

Rehoboam's Family

[18]Rehoboam married Mahalath, who was the daughter of David's son Jerimoth and of Abihail, the daughter of Jesse's son Eliab. [19]She bore him sons: Jeush, Shemariah and Zaham. [20]Then he married Maakah daughter of Absalom, who bore him Abijah, Attai, Ziza and Shelomith. [21]Rehoboam loved Maakah daughter of Absalom more than any of his other wives and concubines. In all, he had eighteen wives and sixty concubines, twenty-eight sons and sixty daughters.

[22]Rehoboam appointed Abijah son of Maakah as crown prince among his brothers, in order to make him king. [23]He acted wisely, dispersing some of his sons throughout the districts of Judah and Benjamin, and to all the fortified cities. He gave them abundant provisions and took many wives for them.

Shishak Attacks Jerusalem

12 After Rehoboam's position as king was established and he had become strong, he and all Israel[a] with him abandoned the law of the LORD. [2]Because they had been unfaithful to the LORD, Shishak king of Egypt attacked Jerusalem in the fifth year of King Rehoboam. [3]With twelve hundred chariots and sixty thousand horsemen and the innumerable troops of Libyans, Sukkites and Cushites[b] that came with him from Egypt, [4]he captured the fortified cities of Judah and came as far as Jerusalem.

[5]Then the prophet Shemaiah came to Rehoboam and to the leaders of Judah who had assembled in Jerusalem for fear of Shishak, and he said to them, "This is what the LORD says, 'You have abandoned me; therefore, I now abandon you to Shishak.'"

[6]The leaders of Israel and the king humbled themselves and said, "The LORD is just."

[7]When the LORD saw that they humbled themselves, this word of the LORD came

---

[a] 1 That is, Judah, as frequently in 2 Chronicles   [b] 3 That is, people from the upper Nile region

to Shemaiah: "Since they have humbled themselves, I will not destroy them but will soon give them deliverance. My wrath will not be poured out on Jerusalem through Shishak. 8 They will, however, become subject to him, so that they may learn the difference between serving me and serving the kings of other lands."

9 When Shishak king of Egypt attacked Jerusalem, he carried off the treasures of the temple of the LORD and the treasures of the royal palace. He took everything, including the gold shields Solomon had made. 10 So King Rehoboam made bronze shields to replace them and assigned these to the commanders of the guard on duty at the entrance to the royal palace. 11 Whenever the king went to the LORD's temple, the guards went with him, bearing the shields, and afterward they returned them to the guardroom.

12 Because Rehoboam humbled himself, the LORD's anger turned from him, and he was not totally destroyed. Indeed, there was some good in Judah.

13 King Rehoboam established himself firmly in Jerusalem and continued as king. He was forty-one years old when he became king, and he reigned seventeen years in Jerusalem, the city the LORD had chosen out of all the tribes of Israel in which to put his Name. His mother's name was Naamah; she was an Ammonite. 14 He did evil because he had not set his heart on seeking the LORD.

15 As for the events of Rehoboam's reign, from beginning to end, are they not written in the records of Shemaiah the prophet and of Iddo the seer that deal with genealogies? There was continual warfare between Rehoboam and Jeroboam. 16 Rehoboam rested with his ancestors and was buried in the City of David. And Abijah his son succeeded him as king.

Abijah King of Judah

13 In the eighteenth year of the reign of Jeroboam, Abijah became king of Judah, 2 and he reigned in Jerusalem three years. His mother's name was Maakah,a a daughterb of Uriel of Gibeah.

There was war between Abijah and Jeroboam. 3 Abijah went into battle with an army of four hundred thousand able fighting men, and Jeroboam drew up a battle line against him with eight hundred thousand able troops.

4 Abijah stood on Mount Zemaraim, in the hill country of Ephraim, and said, "Jeroboam and all Israel, listen to me! 5 Don't you know that the LORD, the God of Israel, has given the kingship of Israel to David and his descendants forever by a covenant of salt? 6 Yet Jeroboam son of Nebat, an official of Solomon son of David, rebelled against his master. 7 Some worthless scoundrels gathered around him and opposed Rehoboam son of Solomon when he was young and indecisive and not strong enough to resist them.

8 "And now you plan to resist the kingdom of the LORD, which is in the hands of David's descendants. You are indeed a vast army and have with you the golden calves that Jeroboam made to be your gods. 9 But didn't you drive out the priests of the LORD, the sons of Aaron, and the Levites, and make priests of your own as the peoples of other lands do? Whoever comes to consecrate himself with a young bull and seven rams may become a priest of what are not gods.

10 "As for us, the LORD is our God, and we have not forsaken him. The priests who serve the LORD are sons of Aaron, and the Levites assist them. 11 Every morning and evening they present burnt offerings and fragrant incense to the LORD. They set out the bread on the ceremonially clean table and light the lamps on the gold lampstand every evening. We are observing the requirements of the LORD our God. But you have forsaken him. 12 God is with us; he is our leader. His priests with their trumpets will sound the battle cry against you. People of Israel, do not fight against the LORD, the God of your ancestors, for you will not succeed."

13 Now Jeroboam had sent troops around to the rear, so that while he was in front of Judah the ambush was behind them. 14 Judah turned and saw that they

---

a 2 Most Septuagint manuscripts and Syriac (see also 11:20 and 1 Kings 15:2); Hebrew *Micaiah*   b 2 Or *granddaughter*

were being attacked at both front and rear. Then they cried out to the LORD. The priests blew their trumpets ¹⁵and the men of Judah raised the battle cry. At the sound of their battle cry, God routed Jeroboam and all Israel before Abijah and Judah. ¹⁶The Israelites fled before Judah, and God delivered them into their hands. ¹⁷Abijah and his troops inflicted heavy losses on them, so that there were five hundred thousand casualties among Israel's able men. ¹⁸The Israelites were subdued on that occasion, and the people of Judah were victorious because they relied on the LORD, the God of their ancestors.

¹⁹Abijah pursued Jeroboam and took from him the towns of Bethel, Jeshanah and Ephron, with their surrounding villages. ²⁰Jeroboam did not regain power during the time of Abijah. And the LORD struck him down and he died.

²¹But Abijah grew in strength. He married fourteen wives and had twenty-two sons and sixteen daughters.

²²The other events of Abijah's reign, what he did and what he said, are written in the annotations of the prophet Iddo.

14 *ᵃ* And Abijah rested with his ancestors and was buried in the City of David. Asa his son succeeded him as king, and in his days the country was at peace for ten years.

Asa King of Judah

²Asa did what was good and right in the eyes of the LORD his God. ³He removed the foreign altars and the high places, smashed the sacred stones and cut down the Asherah poles.*ᵇ* ⁴He commanded Judah to seek the LORD, the God of their ancestors, and to obey his laws and commands. ⁵He removed the high places and incense altars in every town in Judah, and the kingdom was at peace under him. ⁶He built up the fortified cities of Judah, since the land was at peace. No one was at war with him during those years, for the LORD gave him rest.

⁷"Let us build up these towns," he said to Judah, "and put walls around them, with towers, gates and bars. The land is

>> INSTANT ACCESS

Do you ever feel the odds are stacked against you? The guys in the locker room mock you because you don't join in the sex talk? Everyone in your science class laughs at you when you say you believe in creation? You face kids in a gang when you get on the bus? How do you keep your courage up? When one king of Judah was forced to face an army twice as big as his (2 Chronicles 13:3), he was absolutely confident. He cried out, "The LORD is our God ... God is with us" (1 Chronicles 13:10–12). Keep on being faithful to the Lord and have courage. The odds may seem to be against you, but one person plus God is a majority!

{2 Chronicles 13:10–18}

still ours, because we have sought the LORD our God; we sought him and he has given us rest on every side." So they built and prospered.

⁸Asa had an army of three hundred thousand men from Judah, equipped with large shields and with spears, and two hundred and eighty thousand from Benjamin, armed with small shields and with bows. All these were brave fighting men.

⁹Zerah the Cushite marched out against them with an army of thousands

---

ᵃ In Hebrew texts 14:1 is numbered 13:23, and 14:2-15 is numbered 14:1-14.   *ᵇ* 3 That is, wooden symbols of the goddess Asherah; here and elsewhere in 2 Chronicles

upon thousands and three hundred chariots, and came as far as Mareshah. [10]Asa went out to meet him, and they took up battle positions in the Valley of Zephathah near Mareshah.

[11]Then Asa called to the LORD his God and said, "LORD, there is no one like you to help the powerless against the mighty. Help us, LORD our God, for we rely on you, and in your name we have come against this vast army. LORD, you are our God; do not let mere mortals prevail against you."

[12]The LORD struck down the Cushites before Asa and Judah. The Cushites fled, [13]and Asa and his army pursued them as far as Gerar. Such a great number of Cushites fell that they could not recover; they were crushed before the LORD and his forces. The men of Judah carried off a large amount of plunder. [14]They destroyed all the villages around Gerar, for the terror of the LORD had fallen on them. They looted all these villages, since there was much plunder there. [15]They also attacked the camps of the herders and carried off droves of sheep and goats and camels. Then they returned to Jerusalem.

Asa's Reform

15 The Spirit of God came on Azariah son of Oded. [2]He went out to meet Asa and said to him, "Listen to me, Asa and all Judah and Benjamin. The LORD is with you when you are with him. If you seek him, he will be found by you, but if you forsake him, he will forsake you. [3]For a long time Israel was without the true God, without a priest to teach and without the law. [4]But in their distress they turned to the LORD, the God of Israel, and sought him, and he was found by them. [5]In those days it was not safe to travel about, for all the inhabitants of the lands were in great turmoil. [6]One nation was being crushed by another and one city by another, because God was troubling them with every kind of distress. [7]But as for you, be strong and do not give up, for your work will be rewarded."

[8]When Asa heard these words and the prophecy of Azariah son of[a] Oded the prophet, he took courage. He removed the detestable idols from the whole land of Judah and Benjamin and from the towns he had captured in the hills of Ephraim. He repaired the altar of the LORD that was in front of the portico of the LORD's temple.

[9]Then he assembled all Judah and Benjamin and the people from Ephraim, Manasseh and Simeon who had settled among them, for large numbers had come over to him from Israel when they saw that the LORD his God was with him.

[10]They assembled at Jerusalem in the third month of the fifteenth year of Asa's reign. [11]At that time they sacrificed to the LORD seven hundred head of cattle and seven thousand sheep and goats from the plunder they had brought back. [12]They entered into a covenant to seek the LORD, the God of their ancestors, with all their heart and soul. [13]All who would not seek the LORD, the God of Israel, were to be put to death, whether small or great, man or woman. [14]They took an oath to the LORD with loud acclamation, with shouting and with trumpets and horns. [15]All Judah rejoiced about the oath because they had sworn it wholeheartedly. They sought God eagerly, and he was found by them. So the LORD gave them rest on every side.

[16]King Asa also deposed his grandmother Maakah from her position as queen mother, because she had made a repulsive image for the worship of Asherah. Asa cut it down, broke it up and burned it in the Kidron Valley. [17]Although he did not remove the high places from Israel, Asa's heart was fully committed to the LORD all

> *The LORD is with you when you are with him. If you seek him, he will be found by you.*
>
> **2 Chronicles 15:2**

---

[a] 8 Vulgate and Syriac (see also Septuagint and verse 1); Hebrew does not have *Azariah son of*.

It seems like I have to work so much harder at things than other people I know. I get good grades (not all A's) but spend twice as long on my homework as other kids. I tried out for cheerleading and didn't make the final cut. What's the point in trying this hard when I can't get ahead?

>> Jenny

Dear Jenny,

Don't give up! Think of all the practice that goes into becoming an Olympic athlete. In the long run, you'll be prepared for life. For some people many things come easily. They never learn to work through the hard things. When they get into the real world, they don't know how to keep working at something when things don't go as planned.

"But as for you, be strong and do not give up, for your work will be rewarded" (2 Chronicles 15:7). This passage gives you a great promise. You can depend on it every day as life's discouragements come your way. The world's values are so different from yours. Do you ever feel like you're swimming against the current? Like you're going the wrong way on a one-way street? (Or perhaps you're the one going the *right* way!) It's good to remember that your work will be rewarded by God if you stay strong and don't give up.

How great of God to include these encouraging words for us in the Bible.

Jordan

his life. ¹⁸He brought into the temple of God the silver and gold and the articles that he and his father had dedicated.

¹⁹There was no more war until the thirty-fifth year of Asa's reign.

Asa's Last Years

16 In the thirty-sixth year of Asa's reign Baasha king of Israel went up against Judah and fortified Ramah to prevent anyone from leaving or entering the territory of Asa king of Judah.

²Asa then took the silver and gold out of the treasuries of the LORD's temple and of his own palace and sent it to Ben-Hadad king of Aram, who was ruling in Damascus. ³"Let there be a treaty between me and you," he said, "as there was between my father and your father. See, I am sending you silver and gold. Now break your treaty with Baasha king of Israel so he will withdraw from me."

⁴Ben-Hadad agreed with King Asa and sent the commanders of his forces against the towns of Israel. They conquered Ijon, Dan, Abel Maimᵃ and all the store cities of Naphtali. ⁵When Baasha heard this, he stopped building Ramah and abandoned his work. ⁶Then King Asa brought all the men of Judah, and they carried away from Ramah the stones and timber Baasha had been using. With them he built up Geba and Mizpah.

⁷At that time Hanani the seer came to Asa king of Judah and said to him: "Because you relied on the king of Aram and not on the LORD your God, the army of the king of Aram has escaped from your hand. ⁸Were not the Cushitesᵇ and Libyans a mighty army with great numbers of chariots and horsemenᶜ? Yet when you relied on the LORD, he delivered them into your hand. ⁹For the eyes of the LORD range throughout the earth to strengthen those whose hearts are fully committed to him. You have done a foolish thing, and from now on you will be at war."

¹⁰Asa was angry with the seer because of this; he was so enraged that he put him in prison. At the same time Asa brutally oppressed some of the people.

¹¹The events of Asa's reign, from beginning to end, are written in the book of the kings of Judah and Israel. ¹²In the thirty-ninth year of his reign Asa was afflicted with a disease in his feet. Though his disease was severe, even in his illness he did not seek help from the LORD, but only from the physicians. ¹³Then in the forty-first year of his reign Asa died and rested with his ancestors. ¹⁴They buried him in the tomb that he had cut out for himself in the City of David. They laid him on a bier covered with spices and various blended perfumes, and they made a huge fire in his honor.

Jehoshaphat King of Judah

17 Jehoshaphat his son succeeded him as king and strengthened himself against Israel. ²He stationed troops in all the fortified cities of Judah and put garrisons in Judah and in the towns of Ephraim that his father Asa had captured.

³The LORD was with Jehoshaphat because he followed the ways of his father David before him. He did not consult the Baals ⁴but sought the God of his father and followed his commands rather than the practices of Israel. ⁵The LORD established the kingdom under his control; and all Judah brought gifts to Jehoshaphat, so that he had great wealth and honor. ⁶His heart was devoted to the ways of the LORD; furthermore, he removed the high places and the Asherah poles from Judah.

⁷In the third year of his reign he sent his officials Ben-Hail, Obadiah, Zechariah, Nethanel and Micaiah to teach in the towns of Judah. ⁸With them were certain Levites—Shemaiah, Nethaniah, Zebadiah, Asahel, Shemiramoth, Jehonathan, Adonijah, Tobijah and Tob-Adonijah—and the priests Elishama and Jehoram. ⁹They taught throughout Judah, taking with them the Book of the Law of the LORD; they went around to all the towns of Judah and taught the people.

¹⁰The fear of the LORD fell on all the kingdoms of the lands surrounding Judah, so that they did not go to war against

---

ᵃ 4 Also known as *Abel Beth Maakah*   ᵇ 8 That is, people from the upper Nile region   ᶜ 8 Or *charioteers*

Jehoshaphat. ¹¹Some Philistines brought Jehoshaphat gifts and silver as tribute, and the Arabs brought him flocks: seven thousand seven hundred rams and seven thousand seven hundred goats.

¹²Jehoshaphat became more and more powerful; he built forts and store cities in Judah ¹³and had large supplies in the towns of Judah. He also kept experienced fighting men in Jerusalem. ¹⁴Their enrollment by families was as follows:

> From Judah, commanders of units of 1,000:
> Adnah the commander, with 300,000 fighting men;
> ¹⁵next, Jehohanan the commander, with 280,000;
> ¹⁶next, Amasiah son of Zikri, who volunteered himself for the service of the LORD, with 200,000.

¹⁷From Benjamin:
> Eliada, a valiant soldier, with 200,000 men armed with bows and shields;
> ¹⁸next, Jehozabad, with 180,000 men armed for battle.

¹⁹These were the men who served the king, besides those he stationed in the fortified cities throughout Judah.

Micaiah Prophesies Against Ahab

18 Now Jehoshaphat had great wealth and honor, and he allied himself with Ahab by marriage. ²Some years later he went down to see Ahab in Samaria. Ahab slaughtered many sheep and cattle for him and the people with him and urged him to attack Ramoth Gil-

TO THE POINT

Doctors and God

Some people think going to a doctor shows a lack of faith. They think someone who's sick should just pray. They point to 2 Chronicles 16:12 and say that if Asa had relied only on God he would have been healed for sure. Of course, the Bible actually says that Asa was wrong to rely *only* on doctors and not to ask for God's help.

Jesus' miracles show that God can heal even the most terrible sicknesses. Many Christians will tell you that God answered their prayers for healing. But most of them will also tell you that they followed the doctors' orders and expected God to use the knowledge of the doctors to make them well. (Who do you suppose gave them that knowledge in the first place?)

It's always important to rely on the Lord. But that doesn't mean you can't seek and find help from doctors.

ead. ³Ahab king of Israel asked Jehoshaphat king of Judah, "Will you go with me against Ramoth Gilead?"

Jehoshaphat replied, "I am as you are, and my people as your people; we will join you in the war." ⁴But Jehoshaphat also said to the king of Israel, "First seek the counsel of the LORD."

⁵So the king of Israel brought together the prophets—four hundred men—and asked them, "Shall we go to war against Ramoth Gilead, or shall I not?"

"Go," they answered, "for God will give it into the king's hand."

⁶But Jehoshaphat asked, "Is there no longer a prophet of the LORD here whom we can inquire of?"

⁷The king of Israel answered Jehoshaphat, "There is still one prophet through whom we can inquire of the LORD, but I hate him because he never prophesies anything good about me, but always bad. He is Micaiah son of Imlah."

"The king should not say such a thing," Jehoshaphat replied.

⁸So the king of Israel called one of his officials and said, "Bring Micaiah son of Imlah at once."

⁹Dressed in their royal robes, the king of Israel and Jehoshaphat king of Judah were sitting on their thrones at the threshing floor by the entrance of the gate of Samaria, with all the prophets prophesying before them. ¹⁰Now Zedekiah son of Kenaanah had made iron horns, and he declared, "This is what the LORD says: 'With these you will gore the Arameans until they are destroyed.' "

¹¹All the other prophets were prophesying the same thing. "Attack Ramoth Gilead and be victorious," they said, "for the LORD will give it into the king's hand."

¹²The messenger who had gone to summon Micaiah said to him, "Look, the other prophets without exception are predicting success for the king. Let your word agree with theirs, and speak favorably."

¹³But Micaiah said, "As surely as the LORD lives, I can tell him only what my God says."

¹⁴When he arrived, the king asked him,

"Micaiah, shall we go to war against Ramoth Gilead, or shall I not?"

"Attack and be victorious," he answered, "for they will be given into your hand."

¹⁵The king said to him, "How many times must I make you swear to tell me nothing but the truth in the name of the LORD?"

¹⁶Then Micaiah answered, "I saw all Israel scattered on the hills like sheep without a shepherd, and the LORD said, 'These people have no master. Let each one go home in peace.' "

¹⁷The king of Israel said to Jehoshaphat, "Didn't I tell you that he never prophesies anything good about me, but only bad?"

¹⁸Micaiah continued, "Therefore hear the word of the LORD: I saw the LORD sitting on his throne with all the multitudes of heaven standing on his right and on his left. ¹⁹And the LORD said, 'Who will entice Ahab king of Israel into attacking Ramoth Gilead and going to his death there?'

"One suggested this, and another that. ²⁰Finally, a spirit came forward, stood before the LORD and said, 'I will entice him.'

" 'By what means?' the LORD asked.

²¹" 'I will go and be a deceiving spirit in the mouths of all his prophets,' he said.

" 'You will succeed in enticing him,' said the LORD. 'Go and do it.'

²²"So now the LORD has put a deceiving spirit in the mouths of these prophets of yours. The LORD has decreed disaster for you."

²³Then Zedekiah son of Kenaanah went up and slapped Micaiah in the face. "Which way did the spirit from[a] the LORD go when he went from me to speak to you?" he asked.

²⁴Micaiah replied, "You will find out on the day you go to hide in an inner room."

²⁵The king of Israel then ordered, "Take Micaiah and send him back to Amon the ruler of the city and to Joash the king's son, ²⁶and say, 'This is what the king says: Put this fellow in prison and give him nothing but bread and water until I return safely.' "

ᵃ 23 Or *Spirit of*

27 Micaiah declared, "If you ever return safely, the LORD has not spoken through me." Then he added, "Mark my words, all you people!"

Ahab Killed at Ramoth Gilead

28 So the king of Israel and Jehoshaphat king of Judah went up to Ramoth Gilead. 29 The king of Israel said to Jehoshaphat, "I will enter the battle in disguise, but you wear your royal robes." So the king of Israel disguised himself and went into battle.

30 Now the king of Aram had ordered his chariot commanders, "Do not fight with anyone, small or great, except the king of Israel." 31 When the chariot commanders saw Jehoshaphat, they thought, "This is the king of Israel." So they turned to attack him, but Jehoshaphat cried out, and the LORD helped him. God drew them away from him, 32 for when the chariot commanders saw that he was not the king of Israel, they stopped pursuing him.

33 But someone drew his bow at random and hit the king of Israel between the breastplate and the scale armor. The king told the chariot driver, "Wheel around and get me out of the fighting. I've been wounded." 34 All day long the battle raged, and the king of Israel propped himself up in his chariot facing the Arameans until evening. Then at sunset he died.

19 When Jehoshaphat king of Judah returned safely to his palace in Je-rusalem, 2 Jehu the seer, the son of Hanani, went out to meet him and said to the king, "Should you help the wicked and love[a] those who hate the LORD? Because of this, the wrath of the LORD is on you. 3 There is, however, some good in you, for you have rid the land of the Asherah poles and have set your heart on seeking God."

Jehoshaphat Appoints Judges

4 Jehoshaphat lived in Jerusalem, and he went out again among the people from Beersheba to the hill country of Ephraim and turned them back to the LORD, the God of their ancestors. 5 He appointed judges in the land, in each of the fortified cities of Judah. 6 He told them, "Consider carefully what you do, because you are not judging for mere mortals but for the LORD, who is with you whenever you give a verdict. 7 Now let the fear of the LORD be on you. Judge carefully, for with the LORD our God there is no injustice or partiality or bribery."

8 In Jerusalem also, Jehoshaphat appointed some of the Levites, priests and heads of Israelite families to administer the law of the LORD and to settle disputes. And they lived in Jerusalem. 9 He gave them these orders: "You must serve faithfully and wholeheartedly in the fear of the LORD. 10 In every case that comes before you from your people who live in the cities—whether bloodshed or other concerns of the law, commands, decrees

a 2 Or and make alliances with

PANORAMA

{2 CHRONICLES}

Friends.

This book tells the story of the southern kingdom of Judah, from Solomon to the Babylonian captivity. It tells about bad kings and good kings. When the nation's rulers and God's people were faithful to God, he blessed them.

or regulations—you are to warn them not to sin against the LORD; otherwise his wrath will come on you and your people. Do this, and you will not sin.

¹¹"Amariah the chief priest will be over you in any matter concerning the LORD, and Zebadiah son of Ishmael, the leader of the tribe of Judah, will be over you in any matter concerning the king, and the Levites will serve as officials before you. Act with courage, and may the LORD be with those who do well."

Jehoshaphat Defeats Moab and Ammon

20 After this, the Moabites and Ammonites with some of the Meunitesª came to wage war against Jehoshaphat.

²Some people came and told Jehoshaphat, "A vast army is coming against you from Edom,ᵇ from the other side of the Dead Sea. It is already in Hazezon Tamar" (that is, En Gedi). ³Alarmed, Jehoshaphat resolved to inquire of the LORD, and he proclaimed a fast for all Judah. ⁴The people of Judah came together to seek help from the LORD; indeed, they came from every town in Judah to seek him.

⁵Then Jehoshaphat stood up in the assembly of Judah and Jerusalem at the temple of the LORD in the front of the new courtyard ⁶and said:

"LORD, the God of our ancestors, are you not the God who is in heaven? You rule over all the kingdoms of the nations. Power and might are in your hand, and no one can withstand you. ⁷Our God, did you not drive out the inhabitants of this land before your people Israel and give it forever to the descendants of Abraham your friend? ⁸They have lived in it and have built in it a sanctuary for your Name, saying, ⁹'If calamity comes upon us, whether the sword of judgment, or plague or famine, we will stand in your presence before this temple that bears your Name and will cry out to you in our distress, and you will hear us and save us.'

¹⁰"But now here are men from Ammon, Moab and Mount Seir, whose territory you would not allow Israel to invade when they came from Egypt; so they turned away from them and did not destroy them. ¹¹See how they are repaying us by coming to drive us out of the possession you gave us as an inheritance. ¹²Our God, will you not judge them? For we have no power to face this vast army that is attacking us. We do not know what to do, but our eyes are on you."

¹³All the men of Judah, with their wives and children and little ones, stood there before the LORD.

¹⁴Then the Spirit of the LORD came on Jahaziel son of Zechariah, the son of Benaiah, the son of Jeiel, the son of Mattaniah, a Levite and descendant of Asaph, as he stood in the assembly.

¹⁵He said: "Listen, King Jehoshaphat and all who live in Judah and Jerusalem! This is what the LORD says to you: 'Do not be afraid or discouraged because of this vast army. For the battle is not yours, but God's. ¹⁶Tomorrow march down against them. They will be climbing up by the Pass of Ziz, and you will find them at the end of the gorge in the Desert of Jeruel. ¹⁷You will not have to fight this battle. Take up your positions; stand firm and see the deliverance the LORD will give you, Judah and Jerusalem. Do not be afraid; do not be discouraged. Go out to face them tomorrow, and the LORD will be with you.'"

¹⁸Jehoshaphat bowed down with his face to the ground, and all the people of Judah and Jerusalem fell down in worship before the LORD. ¹⁹Then some Levites from the Kohathites and Korahites stood up and praised the LORD, the God of Israel, with a very loud voice.

²⁰Early in the morning they left for the Desert of Tekoa. As they set out, Jehoshaphat stood and said, "Listen to me, Judah and people of Jerusalem! Have faith in the LORD your God and you will be upheld;

ª 1 Some Septuagint manuscripts; Hebrew *Ammonites*   ᵇ 2 One Hebrew manuscript; most Hebrew manuscripts, Septuagint and Vulgate *Aram* have faith in his prophets and you will be successful." [21]After consulting the people, Jehoshaphat appointed men to sing to the LORD and to praise him for the splendor of his[a] holiness as they went out at the head of the army, saying:

"Give thanks to the LORD,
    for his love endures forever."

[22]As they began to sing and praise, the LORD set ambushes against the men of Ammon and Moab and Mount Seir who were invading Judah, and they were defeated. [23]The Ammonites and Moabites rose up against the men from Mount Seir to destroy and annihilate them. After they finished slaughtering the men from Seir, they helped to destroy one another.

[24]When the men of Judah came to the place that overlooks the desert and looked toward the vast army, they saw only dead bodies lying on the ground; no one had escaped. [25]So Jehoshaphat and his men went to carry off their plunder, and they found among them a great amount of equipment and clothing[b] and also articles of value—more than they could take away. There was so much plunder that it took three days to collect it. [26]On the fourth day they assembled in the Valley of Berakah, where they praised the LORD. This is why it is called the Valley of Berakah[c] to this day.

[27]Then, led by Jehoshaphat, all the men of Judah and Jerusalem returned joyfully to Jerusalem, for the LORD had given them cause to rejoice over their enemies. [28]They entered Jerusalem and went to the temple of the LORD with harps and lyres and trumpets.

[29]The fear of God came on all the surrounding kingdoms when they heard how the LORD had fought against the enemies of Israel. [30]And the kingdom of Jehoshaphat was at peace, for his God had given him rest on every side.

The End of Jehoshaphat's Reign

[31]So Jehoshaphat reigned over Judah. He was thirty-five years old when he became king of Judah, and he reigned in Jerusalem twenty-five years. His mother's name was Azubah daughter of Shilhi. [32]He followed the ways of his father Asa and did not stray from them; he did what was right in the eyes of the LORD. [33]The high places, however, were not removed, and the people still had not set their hearts on the God of their ancestors.

[34]The other events of Jehoshaphat's reign, from beginning to end, are written in the annals of Jehu son of Hanani, which are recorded in the book of the kings of Israel.

[35]Later, Jehoshaphat king of Judah made an alliance with Ahaziah king of Israel, whose ways were wicked. [36]He agreed with him to construct a fleet of trading ships.[d] After these were built at Ezion Geber, [37]Eliezer son of Dodavahu of Mareshah prophesied against Jehoshaphat, saying, "Because you have made an alliance with Ahaziah, the LORD will destroy what you have made." The ships were wrecked and were not able to set sail to trade.[e]

21 Then Jehoshaphat rested with his ancestors and was buried with them in the City of David. And Jehoram his son succeeded him as king. [2]Jehoram's brothers, the sons of Jehoshaphat, were Azariah, Jehiel, Zechariah, Azariahu, Michael and Shephatiah. All these were sons of Jehoshaphat king of Israel.[f] [3]Their father had given them many gifts of silver and gold and articles of value, as well as fortified cities in Judah, but he had given the kingdom to Jehoram because he was his firstborn son.

Have faith in the LORD your God and you will be upheld.
2 Chronicles 20:20

---

[a] 21 Or him with the splendor of   [b] 25 Some Hebrew manuscripts and Vulgate; most Hebrew manuscripts corpses
[c] 26 Berakah means praise.   [d] 36 Hebrew of ships that could go to Tarshish   [e] 37 Hebrew sail for Tarshish   [f] 2 That is, Judah, as frequently in 2 Chronicles

Jehoram King of Judah

⁴When Jehoram established himself firmly over his father's kingdom, he put all his brothers to the sword along with some of the officials of Israel. ⁵Jehoram was thirty-two years old when he became king, and he reigned in Jerusalem eight years. ⁶He followed the ways of the kings of Israel, as the house of Ahab had done, for he married a daughter of Ahab. He did evil in the eyes of the LORD. ⁷Nevertheless, because of the covenant the LORD had made with David, the LORD was not willing to destroy the house of David. He had promised to maintain a lamp for him and his descendants forever.

⁸In the time of Jehoram, Edom rebelled against Judah and set up its own king. ⁹So Jehoram went there with his officers and all his chariots. The Edomites surrounded him and his chariot commanders, but he rose up and broke through by night. ¹⁰To this day Edom has been in rebellion against Judah.

Libnah revolted at the same time, because Jehoram had forsaken the LORD, the God of his ancestors. ¹¹He had also built high places on the hills of Judah and had caused the people of Jerusalem to prostitute themselves and had led Judah astray.

¹²Jehoram received a letter from Elijah the prophet, which said:

"This is what the LORD, the God of your father David, says: 'You have not followed the ways of your father Jehoshaphat or of Asa king of Judah. ¹³But you have followed the ways of the kings of Israel, and you have led Judah and the people of Jerusalem to prostitute themselves, just as the house of Ahab did. You have also murdered your own brothers, members of your own family, men who were better than you. ¹⁴So now the LORD is about to strike your people, your sons, your wives and everything that is yours, with a heavy blow. ¹⁵You yourself will be very ill with a lingering disease of the bowels, until the disease causes your bowels to come out.' "

¹⁶The LORD aroused against Jehoram the hostility of the Philistines and of the Arabs who lived near the Cushites. ¹⁷They attacked Judah, invaded it and carried off all the goods found in the king's palace, together with his sons and wives. Not a son was left to him except Ahaziah,ᵃ the youngest.

¹⁸After all this, the LORD afflicted Jehoram with an incurable disease of the bowels. ¹⁹In the course of time, at the end of the second year, his bowels came out because of the disease, and he died in great pain. His people made no funeral fire in his honor, as they had for his predecessors.

²⁰Jehoram was thirty-two years old when he became king, and he reigned in Jerusalem eight years. He passed away, to no one's regret, and was buried in the City of David, but not in the tombs of the kings.

Ahaziah King of Judah

22 The people of Jerusalem made Ahaziah, Jehoram's youngest son, king in his place, since the raiders, who came with the Arabs into the camp, had killed all the older sons. So Ahaziah son of Jehoram king of Judah began to reign.

²Ahaziah was twenty-twoᵇ years old when he became king, and he reigned in Jerusalem one year. His mother's name was Athaliah, a granddaughter of Omri.

³He too followed the ways of the house of Ahab, for his mother encouraged him to act wickedly. ⁴He did evil in the eyes of the LORD, as the house of Ahab had done, for after his father's death they became his advisers, to his undoing. ⁵He also followed their counsel when he went with Joramᶜ son of Ahab king of Israel to wage war against Hazael king of Aram at Ramoth Gilead. The Arameans wounded Joram; ⁶so he returned to Jezreel to recover from the wounds they had inflicted on him at Ramothᵈ in his battle with Hazael king of Aram.

ᵃ 17 Hebrew *Jehoahaz*, a variant of *Ahaziah*   ᵇ 2 Some Septuagint manuscripts and Syriac (see also 2 Kings 8:26); Hebrew *forty-two*   ᶜ 5 Hebrew *Jehoram*, a variant of *Joram*; also in verses 6 and 7   ᵈ 6 Hebrew *Ramah*, a variant of *Ramoth*

Dear Jordan

Dear Meghan,

Would you believe that keeping children safe has been a
difficult thing for thousands of years? There was a young
boy named Joash in the Bible who found himself in a very
dangerous home. His father, the king, had died and Joash's
grandmother decided that she would like to be queen. All
that stood in her way was her grandchildren. So she decided to kill them. Fortunately, Joash had an aunt named
Jehosheba who rescued Joash and hid him in the temple
for six years (2 Chronicles 22).

Just as Joash was protected, there must be some
places of safety for you. If the person you told didn't believe
you, think of another trustworthy and responsible adult
who will. Do you have an aunt or grandmother who might
be able to help? Do you have a good friend whose parents
would be willing to offer you a safe place when you need it?
If you can go to your room and play some Christian music
with your headphones on, while not a perfect solution, it
would at least get you away from something bad and give
you something good to replace it.

Don't give up trying to find a safe place. You deserve
it. And pray for yourself and your parents.

Jordan

Then Ahaziah[a] son of Jehoram king of Judah went down to Jezreel to see Joram son of Ahab because he had been wounded.

[7] Through Ahaziah's visit to Joram, God brought about Ahaziah's downfall. When Ahaziah arrived, he went out with Joram to meet Jehu son of Nimshi, whom the LORD had anointed to destroy the house of Ahab. [8] While Jehu was executing judgment on the house of Ahab, he found the officials of Judah and the sons of Ahaziah's relatives, who had been attending Ahaziah, and he killed them. [9] He then went in search of Ahaziah, and his men captured him while he was hiding in Samaria. He was brought to Jehu and put to death. They buried him, for they said, "He was a son of Jehoshaphat, who sought the LORD with all his heart." So there was no one in the house of Ahaziah powerful enough to retain the kingdom.

Athaliah and Joash

[10] When Athaliah the mother of Ahaziah saw that her son was dead, she proceeded to destroy the whole royal family of the house of Judah. [11] But Jehosheba,[b] the daughter of King Jehoram, took Joash son of Ahaziah and stole him away from among the royal princes who were about to be murdered and put him and his nurse in a bedroom. Because Jehosheba,[b] the daughter of King Jehoram and wife of the priest Jehoiada, was Ahaziah's sister, she hid the child from Athaliah so she could not kill him. [12] He remained hidden with them at the temple of God for six years while Athaliah ruled the land.

23 In the seventh year Jehoiada showed his strength. He made a covenant with the commanders of units of a hundred: Azariah son of Jeroham, Ishmael son of Jehohanan, Azariah son of Obed, Maaseiah son of Adaiah, and Elishaphat son of Zikri. [2] They went throughout Judah and gathered the Levites and the heads of Israelite families from all the

towns. When they came to Jerusalem, [3] the whole assembly made a covenant with the king at the temple of God.

Jehoiada said to them, "The king's son shall reign, as the LORD promised concerning the descendants of David. [4] Now this is what you are to do: A third of you priests and Levites who are going on duty on the Sabbath are to keep watch at the doors, [5] a third of you at the royal palace and a third at the Foundation Gate, and all the others are to be in the courtyards of the temple of the LORD. [6] No one is to enter the temple of the LORD except the priests and Levites on duty; they may enter because they are consecrated, but all the others are to observe the LORD's command not to enter.[c] [7] The Levites are to station themselves around the king, each with weapon in hand. Anyone who enters the temple is to be put to death. Stay close to the king wherever he goes."

[8] The Levites and all the men of Judah did just as Jehoiada the priest ordered. Each one took his men—those who were going on duty on the Sabbath and those who were going off duty—for Jehoiada the priest had not released any of the divisions. [9] Then he gave the commanders

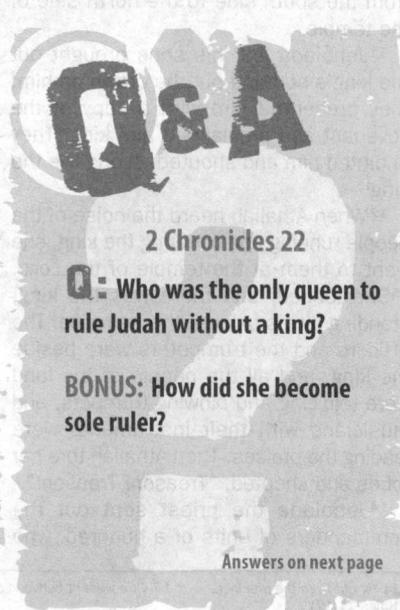

Q&A

2 Chronicles 22

Q: Who was the only queen to rule Judah without a king?

BONUS: How did she become sole ruler?

Answers on next page

---

[a] 6 Some Hebrew manuscripts, Septuagint, Vulgate and Syriac (see also 2 Kings 8:29); most Hebrew manuscripts *Azariah*   [b] 11 Hebrew *Jehoshabeath*, a variant of *Jehosheba*   [c] 6 Or *are to stand guard where the LORD has assigned them*

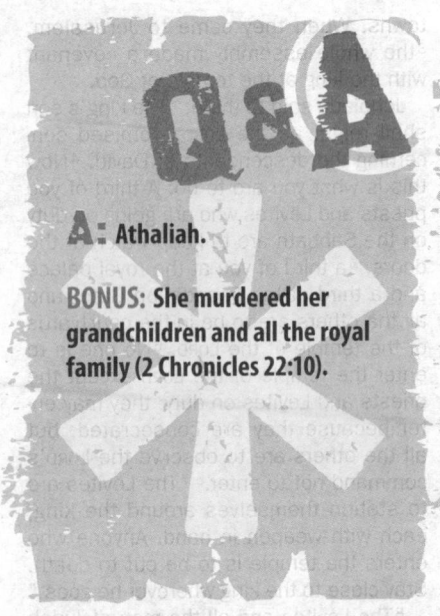

A: Athaliah.

BONUS: She murdered her grandchildren and all the royal family (2 Chronicles 22:10).

of units of a hundred the spears and the large and small shields that had belonged to King David and that were in the temple of God. ¹⁰He stationed all the men, each with his weapon in his hand, around the king—near the altar and the temple, from the south side to the north side of the temple.

¹¹Jehoiada and his sons brought out the king's son and put the crown on him; they presented him with a copy of the covenant and proclaimed him king. They anointed him and shouted, "Long live the king!"

¹²When Athaliah heard the noise of the people running and cheering the king, she went to them at the temple of the Lord. ¹³She looked, and there was the king, standing by his pillar at the entrance. The officers and the trumpeters were beside the king, and all the people of the land were rejoicing and blowing trumpets, and musicians with their instruments were leading the praises. Then Athaliah tore her robes and shouted, "Treason! Treason!"

¹⁴Jehoiada the priest sent out the commanders of units of a hundred, who were in charge of the troops, and said to them: "Bring her out between the ranksª and put to the sword anyone who follows her." For the priest had said, "Do not put her to death at the temple of the Lord." ¹⁵So they seized her as she reached the entrance of the Horse Gate on the palace grounds, and there they put her to death.

¹⁶Jehoiada then made a covenant that he, the people and the kingᵇ would be the Lord's people. ¹⁷All the people went to the temple of Baal and tore it down. They smashed the altars and idols and killed Mattan the priest of Baal in front of the altars.

¹⁸Then Jehoiada placed the oversight of the temple of the Lord in the hands of the Levitical priests, to whom David had made assignments in the temple, to present the burnt offerings of the Lord as written in the Law of Moses, with rejoicing and singing, as David had ordered. ¹⁹He also stationed gatekeepers at the gates of the Lord's temple so that no one who was in any way unclean might enter.

²⁰He took with him the commanders of hundreds, the nobles, the rulers of the people and all the people of the land and brought the king down from the temple of the Lord. They went into the palace through the Upper Gate and seated the king on the royal throne. ²¹All the people of the land rejoiced, and the city was calm, because Athaliah had been slain with the sword.

Joash Repairs the Temple

24 Joash was seven years old when he became king, and he reigned in Jerusalem forty years. His mother's name was Zibiah; she was from Beersheba. ²Joash did what was right in the eyes of the Lord all the years of Jehoiada the priest. ³Jehoiada chose two wives for him, and he had sons and daughters.

⁴Some time later Joash decided to restore the temple of the Lord. ⁵He called together the priests and Levites and said to them, "Go to the towns of Judah and collect the money due annually from all

---

ª 14 Or *out from the precincts*   ᵇ 16 Or *covenant between the Lord and the people and the king that they* (see 2 Kings 11:17)

Israel, to repair the temple of your God. Do it now." But the Levites did not act at once.

⁶Therefore the king summoned Jehoiada the chief priest and said to him, "Why haven't you required the Levites to bring in from Judah and Jerusalem the tax imposed by Moses the servant of the Lord and by the assembly of Israel for the tent of the covenant law?"

⁷Now the sons of that wicked woman Athaliah had broken into the temple of God and had used even its sacred objects for the Baals.

⁸At the king's command, a chest was made and placed outside, at the gate of the temple of the Lord. ⁹A proclamation was then issued in Judah and Jerusalem that they should bring to the Lord the tax that Moses the servant of God had required of Israel in the wilderness. ¹⁰All the officials and all the people brought their contributions gladly, dropping them into the chest until it was full. ¹¹Whenever the chest was brought in by the Levites to the king's officials and they saw that there was a large amount of money, the royal secretary and the officer of the chief priest would come and empty the chest and carry it back to its place. They did this regularly and collected a great amount of money. ¹²The king and Jehoiada gave it to those who carried out the work required for the temple of the Lord. They hired masons and carpenters to restore the Lord's temple, and also workers in iron and bronze to repair the temple.

¹³The men in charge of the work were diligent, and the repairs progressed under them. They rebuilt the temple of God according to its original design and reinforced it. ¹⁴When they had finished, they brought the rest of the money to the king and Jehoiada, and with it were made articles for the Lord's temple: articles for the service and for the burnt offerings, and also dishes and other objects of gold and silver. As long as Jehoiada lived, burnt offerings were presented continually in the temple of the Lord.

¹⁵Now Jehoiada was old and full of years, and he died at the age of a hundred and thirty. ¹⁶He was buried with the kings in the City of David, because of the good he had done in Israel for God and his temple.

The Wickedness of Joash

¹⁷After the death of Jehoiada, the officials of Judah came and paid homage to the king, and he listened to them. ¹⁸They abandoned the temple of the Lord, the God of their ancestors, and worshiped Asherah poles and idols. Because of their guilt, God's anger came on Judah and Jerusalem. ¹⁹Although the Lord sent prophets to the people to bring them back to him, and though they testified against them, they would not listen.

²⁰Then the Spirit of God came on Zechariah son of Jehoiada the priest. He stood before the people and said, "This is what God says: 'Why do you disobey the Lord's commands? You will not prosper. Because you have forsaken the Lord, he has forsaken you.'"

²¹But they plotted against him, and by order of the king they stoned him to death in the courtyard of the Lord's temple. ²²King Joash did not remember the kindness Zechariah's father Jehoiada had shown him but killed his son, who said as he lay dying, "May the Lord see this and call you to account."

²³At the turn of the year,ᵃ the army of Aram marched against Joash; it invaded Judah and Jerusalem and killed all the leaders of the people. They sent all the plunder to their king in Damascus. ²⁴Although the Aramean army had come with only a few men, the Lord delivered into their hands a much larger army. Because Judah had forsaken the Lord, the God of their ancestors, judgment was executed on Joash. ²⁵When the Arameans withdrew, they left Joash severely wounded. His officials conspired against him for murdering the son of Jehoiada the priest, and they killed him in his bed. So he died and was buried in the City of David, but not in the tombs of the kings. ²⁶Those who conspired against him

---

ᵃ 23 Probably in the spring

were Zabad,[a] son of Shimeath an Ammonite woman, and Jehozabad, son of Shimrith[b] a Moabite woman. 27 The account of his sons, the many prophecies about him, and the record of the restoration of the temple of God are written in the annotations on the book of the kings. And Amaziah his son succeeded him as king.

Amaziah King of Judah

25 Amaziah was twenty-five years old when he became king, and he reigned in Jerusalem twenty-nine years. His mother's name was Jehoaddan; she was from Jerusalem. 2 He did what was right in the eyes of the LORD, but not wholeheartedly. 3 After the kingdom was firmly in his control, he executed the officials who had murdered his father the king. 4 Yet he did not put their children to death, but acted in accordance with what is written in the Law, in the Book of Moses, where the LORD commanded: "Parents shall not be put to death for their children, nor children be put to death for their parents; each will die for their own sin."[c]

5 Amaziah called the people of Judah together and assigned them according to their families to commanders of thousands and commanders of hundreds for all Judah and Benjamin. He then mustered those twenty years old or more and found that there were three hundred thousand men fit for military service, able to handle the spear and shield. 6 He also hired a hundred thousand fighting men from Israel for a hundred talents[d] of silver.

7 But a man of God came to him and said, "Your Majesty, these troops from Israel must not march with you, for the LORD is not with Israel — not with any of the people of Ephraim. 8 Even if you go and fight courageously in battle, God will overthrow you before the enemy, for God has the power to help or to overthrow."

9 Amaziah asked the man of God, "But what about the hundred talents I paid for these Israelite troops?"

INSTANT ACCESS

"You look so great today!" Words like that can make you feel good — that is, until the person who said them adds, "Can you loan me $20?" Then you realize the compliment was only flattery. Your friend was buttering you up. Some people are easily swayed by flattery. King Joash was. After the death of his adviser, Judah's officials came and "paid homage to" (meaning "flattered") the king. And Joash let his people persuade him to serve pagan gods. Watch out when insincere people rush up to compliment you. That's flattery. You don't have to pay flatterers back by doing what they want.

{2 Chronicles 24:17}

The man of God replied, "The LORD can give you much more than that."

10 So Amaziah dismissed the troops who had come to him from Ephraim and sent them home. They were furious with Judah and left for home in a great rage.

11 Amaziah then marshaled his strength and led his army to the Valley of Salt, where he killed ten thousand men of Seir. 12 The army of Judah also captured ten thousand men alive, took them to the top of a cliff and threw them down so that all were dashed to pieces.

---

[a] 26 A variant of *Jozabad*   [b] 26 A variant of *Shomer*   [c] 4 Deut. 24:16   [d] 6 That is, about 3 3/4 tons or about 3.4 metric tons; also in verse 9

¹³Meanwhile the troops that Amaziah had sent back and had not allowed to take part in the war raided towns belonging to Judah from Samaria to Beth Horon. They killed three thousand people and carried off great quantities of plunder.

¹⁴When Amaziah returned from slaughtering the Edomites, he brought back the gods of the people of Seir. He set them up as his own gods, bowed down to them and burned sacrifices to them. ¹⁵The anger of the LORD burned against Amaziah, and he sent a prophet to him, who said, "Why do you consult this people's gods, which could not save their own people from your hand?"

¹⁶While he was still speaking, the king said to him, "Have we appointed you an adviser to the king? Stop! Why be struck down?"

So the prophet stopped but said, "I know that God has determined to destroy you, because you have done this and have not listened to my counsel."

¹⁷After Amaziah king of Judah consulted his advisers, he sent this challenge to Jehoash[a] son of Jehoahaz, the son of Jehu, king of Israel: "Come, let us face each other in battle."

¹⁸But Jehoash king of Israel replied to Amaziah king of Judah: "A thistle in Lebanon sent a message to a cedar in Lebanon, 'Give your daughter to my son in marriage.' Then a wild beast in Lebanon came along and trampled the thistle underfoot. ¹⁹You say to yourself that you have defeated Edom, and now you are arrogant and proud. But stay at home! Why ask for trouble and cause your own downfall and that of Judah also?"

²⁰Amaziah, however, would not listen, for God so worked that he might deliver them into the hands of Jehoash, because they sought the gods of Edom. ²¹So Jehoash king of Israel attacked. He and Amaziah king of Judah faced each other at Beth Shemesh in Judah. ²²Judah was routed by Israel, and every man fled to his home. ²³Jehoash king of Israel captured Amazi-ah king of Judah, the son of Joash, the son of Ahaziah,[b] at Beth Shemesh. Then Jehoash brought him to Jerusalem and broke down the wall of Jerusalem from the Ephraim Gate to the Corner Gate—a section about four hundred cubits[c] long. ²⁴He took all the gold and silver and all the articles found in the temple of God that had been in the care of Obed-Edom, together with the palace treasures and the hostages, and returned to Samaria.

²⁵Amaziah son of Joash king of Judah lived for fifteen years after the death of Jehoash son of Jehoahaz king of Israel. ²⁶As for the other events of Amaziah's reign, from beginning to end, are they not written in the book of the kings of Judah and Israel? ²⁷From the time that Amaziah turned away from following the LORD, they conspired against him in Jerusalem and he fled to Lachish, but they sent men after him to Lachish and killed him there. ²⁸He was brought back by horse and was buried with his ancestors in the City of Judah.[d]

Uzziah King of Judah

26 Then all the people of Judah took Uzziah,[e] who was sixteen years old, and made him king in place of his father Amaziah. ²He was the one who rebuilt Elath and restored it to Judah after Amaziah rested with his ancestors.

³Uzziah was sixteen years old when he became king, and he reigned in Jerusalem fifty-two years. His mother's name was Jekoliah; she was from Jerusalem. ⁴He did what was right in the eyes of the LORD, just as his father Amaziah had done. ⁵He sought God during the days of Zechariah, who instructed him in the fear[f] of God. As long as he sought the LORD, God gave him success.

⁶He went to war against the Philistines and broke down the walls of Gath, Jabneh and Ashdod. He then rebuilt towns near Ashdod and elsewhere among the Philistines. ⁷God helped him against the Philistines and against the Arabs who lived in

---

a 17 Hebrew *Joash,* a variant of *Jehoash;* also in verses 18, 21, 23 and 25   *b 23* Hebrew *Jehoahaz,* a variant of *Ahaziah*
c 23 That is, about 600 feet or about 180 meters   *d 28* Most Hebrew manuscripts; some Hebrew manuscripts,
Septuagint, Vulgate and Syriac (see also 2 Kings 14:20) *David*   *e 1* Also called *Azariah*   *f 5* Many Hebrew
manuscripts, Septuagint and Syriac; other Hebrew manuscripts *vision*

Gur Baal and against the Meunites. [8]The Ammonites brought tribute to Uzziah, and his fame spread as far as the border of Egypt, because he had become very powerful.

[9]Uzziah built towers in Jerusalem at the Corner Gate, at the Valley Gate and at the angle of the wall, and he fortified them. [10]He also built towers in the wilderness and dug many cisterns, because he had much livestock in the foothills and in the plain. He had people working his fields and vineyards in the hills and in the fertile lands, for he loved the soil.

[11]Uzziah had a well-trained army, ready to go out by divisions according to their numbers as mustered by Jeiel the secretary and Maaseiah the officer under the direction of Hananiah, one of the royal officials. [12]The total number of family leaders over the fighting men was 2,600. [13]Under their command was an army of 307,500 men trained for war, a powerful force to support the king against his enemies. [14]Uzziah provided shields, spears, helmets, coats of armor, bows and slingstones for the entire army. [15]In Jerusalem he made devices invented for use on the towers and on the corner defenses so that soldiers could shoot arrows and hurl large stones from the walls. His fame spread far and wide, for he was greatly helped until he became powerful.

[16]But after Uzziah became powerful, his pride led to his downfall. He was unfaithful to the LORD his God, and entered the temple of the LORD to burn incense on the altar of incense. [17]Azariah the priest with eighty other courageous priests of the LORD followed him in. [18]They confronted King Uzziah and said, "It is not right for you, Uzziah, to burn incense to the LORD. That is for the priests, the descendants of Aaron, who have been consecrated to burn incense. Leave the sanctuary, for

> As long as he sought the LORD, God gave him success.
>
> 2 Chronicles 26:5

you have been unfaithful; and you will not be honored by the LORD God."

[19]Uzziah, who had a censer in his hand ready to burn incense, became angry. While he was raging at the priests in their presence before the incense altar in the LORD's temple, leprosy[a] broke out on his forehead. [20]When Azariah the chief priest and all the other priests looked at him, they saw that he had leprosy on his forehead, so they hurried him out. Indeed, he himself was eager to leave, because the LORD had afflicted him.

[21]King Uzziah had leprosy until the day he died. He lived in a separate house[b]—leprous, and banned from the temple of the LORD. Jotham his son had charge of the palace and governed the people of the land.

[22]The other events of Uzziah's reign, from beginning to end, are recorded by the prophet Isaiah son of Amoz. [23]Uzziah rested with his ancestors and was buried near them in a cemetery that belonged to the kings, for people said, "He had leprosy." And Jotham his son succeeded him as king.

Jotham King of Judah

27 Jotham was twenty-five years old when he became king, and he reigned in Jerusalem sixteen years. His mother's name was Jerusha daughter of Zadok. [2]He did what was right in the eyes of the LORD, just as his father Uzziah had done, but unlike him he did not enter the temple of the LORD. The people, however, continued their corrupt practices. [3]Jotham rebuilt the Upper Gate of the temple of the LORD and did extensive work on the wall at the hill of Ophel. [4]He built towns in the hill country of Judah and forts and towers in the wooded areas.

[5]Jotham waged war against the king of the Ammonites and conquered them. That year the Ammonites paid him a

---

[a] 19 The Hebrew for leprosy was used for various diseases affecting the skin; also in verses 20, 21 and 23.   [b] 21 Or in a house where he was relieved of responsibilities

Sometimes even Christians can become proud. Of good grades. Of popularity. Of athletic ability. Want to know if you are proud? You can recognize pride by the feeling that you don't have to live by normal rules. You're so beautiful you don't have to be nice to "ugly" people. You're so popular you don't talk to kids who are "out" socially. King Uzziah became so rich and powerful that he didn't think he had to live by the rules either. He found out the hard way that pride does go before a painful fall (Proverbs 16:18). Watch out for pride. It hurts others first. Then it really hurts—you.

{2 Chronicles 26:16–21}

≫INSTANT ACCESS

hundred talents^a of silver, ten thousand cors^b of wheat and ten thousand cors^c of barley. The Ammonites brought him the same amount also in the second and third years.

⁶Jotham grew powerful because he walked steadfastly before the LORD his God.

⁷The other events in Jotham's reign, including all his wars and the other things he did, are written in the book of the kings of Israel and Judah. ⁸He was twenty-five years old when he became king, and he reigned in Jerusalem sixteen years. ⁹Jotham rested with his ancestors and was

buried in the City of David. And Ahaz his son succeeded him as king.

Ahaz King of Judah

28 Ahaz was twenty years old when he became king, and he reigned in Jerusalem sixteen years. Unlike David his father, he did not do what was right in the eyes of the LORD. ²He followed the ways of the kings of Israel and also made idols for worshiping the Baals. ³He burned sacrifices in the Valley of Ben Hinnom and sacrificed his children in the fire, engaging in the detestable practices of the nations the LORD had driven out before the Israelites. ⁴He offered sacrifices and burned incense at the high places, on the hilltops and under every spreading tree.

⁵Therefore the LORD his God delivered him into the hands of the king of Aram. The Arameans defeated him and took many of his people as prisoners and brought them to Damascus.

He was also given into the hands of the king of Israel, who inflicted heavy casualties on him. ⁶In one day Pekah son of Remaliah killed a hundred and twenty thousand soldiers in Judah—because Judah had forsaken the LORD, the God of their ancestors. ⁷Zikri, an Ephraimite warrior, killed Maaseiah the king's son, Azrikam the officer in charge of the palace, and Elkanah, second to the king. ⁸The men of Israel took captive from their fellow Israelites who were from Judah two hundred thousand wives, sons and daughters. They also took a great deal of plunder, which they carried back to Samaria.

⁹But a prophet of the LORD named Oded was there, and he went out to meet the army when it returned to Samaria. He said to them, "Because the LORD, the God of your ancestors, was angry with Judah, he gave them into your hand. But you have slaughtered them in a rage that reaches to heaven. ¹⁰And now you intend to make the men and women of Judah and Jerusalem your slaves. But aren't you also guilty of sins against the LORD your

^a 5 That is, about 3 3/4 tons or about 3.4 metric tons ^b 5 That is, probably about 1,800 tons or about 1,600 metric tons of wheat ^c 5 That is, probably about 1,500 tons or about 1,350 metric tons of barley

God? ¹¹Now listen to me! Send back your fellow Israelites you have taken as prisoners, for the LORD's fierce anger rests on you."

¹²Then some of the leaders in Ephraim—Azariah son of Jehohanan, Berekiah son of Meshillemoth, Jehizkiah son of Shallum, and Amasa son of Hadlai—confronted those who were arriving from the war. ¹³"You must not bring those prisoners here," they said, "or we will be guilty before the LORD. Do you intend to add to our sin and guilt? For our guilt is already great, and his fierce anger rests on Israel."

¹⁴So the soldiers gave up the prisoners and plunder in the presence of the officials and all the assembly. ¹⁵The men designated by name took the prisoners, and from the plunder they clothed all who were naked. They provided them with clothes and sandals, food and drink, and healing balm. All those who were weak they put on donkeys. So they took them back to their fellow Israelites at Jericho, the City of Palms, and returned to Samaria.

¹⁶At that time King Ahaz sent to the kingsᵃ of Assyria for help. ¹⁷The Edomites had again come and attacked Judah and carried away prisoners, ¹⁸while the Philistines had raided towns in the foothills and in the Negev of Judah. They captured and occupied Beth Shemesh, Aijalon and Gederoth, as well as Soko, Timnah and Gimzo, with their surrounding villages. ¹⁹The LORD had humbled Judah because of Ahaz king of Israel,ᵇ for he had promoted wickedness in Judah and had been most unfaithful to the LORD. ²⁰Tiglath-Pileserᶜ king of Assyria came to him, but he gave him trouble instead of help. ²¹Ahaz took some of the things from the temple of the LORD and from the royal palace and from the officials and presented them to the king of Assyria, but that did not help him.

²²In his time of trouble King Ahaz became even more unfaithful to the LORD. ²³He offered sacrifices to the gods of Damascus, who had defeated him; for he thought, "Since the gods of the kings of Aram have helped them, I will sacrifice to

them so they will help me." But they were his downfall and the downfall of all Israel. ²⁴Ahaz gathered together the furnishings from the temple of God and cut them in pieces. He shut the doors of the LORD's temple and set up altars at every street corner in Jerusalem. ²⁵In every town in Judah he built high places to burn sacrifices to other gods and aroused the anger of the LORD, the God of his ancestors.

²⁶The other events of his reign and all his ways, from beginning to end, are written in the book of the kings of Judah and Israel. ²⁷Ahaz rested with his ancestors and was buried in the city of Jerusalem, but he was not placed in the tombs of the kings of Israel. And Hezekiah his son succeeded him as king.

Hezekiah Purifies the Temple

29 Hezekiah was twenty-five years old when he became king, and he reigned in Jerusalem twenty-nine years. His mother's name was Abijah daughter of Zechariah. ²He did what was right in the eyes of the LORD, just as his father David had done.

³In the first month of the first year of his reign, he opened the doors of the temple of the LORD and repaired them. ⁴He brought in the priests and the Levites, assembled them in the square on the east side ⁵and said: "Listen to me, Levites! Consecrate yourselves now and consecrate the temple of the LORD, the God of your ancestors. Remove all defilement from the sanctuary. ⁶Our parents were unfaithful; they did evil in the eyes of the LORD our God and forsook him. They turned their faces away from the LORD's dwelling place and turned their backs on him. ⁷They also shut the doors of the portico and put out the lamps. They did not burn incense or present any burnt offerings at the sanctuary to the God of Israel. ⁸Therefore, the anger of the LORD has fallen on Judah and Jerusalem; he has made them an object of dread and horror and scorn, as you can see with your own eyes. ⁹This is why our fathers have fallen by the sword and why our sons and

---

ᵃ 16 Most Hebrew manuscripts; one Hebrew manuscript, Septuagint and Vulgate (see also 2 Kings 16:7) king
ᵇ 19 That is, Judah, as frequently in 2 Chronicles   ᶜ 20 Hebrew Tilgath-Pilneser, a variant of Tiglath-Pileser

daughters and our wives are in captivity. [10] Now I intend to make a covenant with the LORD, the God of Israel, so that his fierce anger will turn away from us. [11] My sons, do not be negligent now, for the LORD has chosen you to stand before him and serve him, to minister before him and to burn incense."

[12] Then these Levites set to work:

from the Kohathites,

Mahath son of Amasai and Joel son of Azariah;

from the Merarites,

Kish son of Abdi and Azariah son of Jehallelel;

from the Gershonites,

Joah son of Zimmah and Eden son of Joah;

[13] from the descendants of Elizaphan, Shimri and Jeiel;

from the descendants of Asaph, Zechariah and Mattaniah;

[14] from the descendants of Heman, Jehiel and Shimei;

from the descendants of Jeduthun, Shemaiah and Uzziel.

[15] When they had assembled their fellow Levites and consecrated themselves, they went in to purify the temple of the LORD, as the king had ordered, following the word of the LORD. [16] The priests went into the sanctuary of the LORD to purify it. They brought out to the courtyard of the LORD's temple everything unclean that they found in the temple of the LORD. The Levites took it and carried it out to the Kidron Valley. [17] They began the consecration on the first day of the first month, and by the eighth day of the month they reached the portico of the LORD. For eight more days they consecrated the temple of the LORD itself, finishing on the sixteenth day of the first month.

[18] Then they went in to King Hezekiah and reported: "We have purified the entire temple of the LORD, the altar of burnt offering with all its utensils, and the table for setting out the consecrated bread, with all its articles. [19] We have prepared and consecrated all the articles that King Ahaz removed in his unfaithfulness while

he was king. They are now in front of the LORD's altar."

[20] Early the next morning King Hezekiah gathered the city officials together and went up to the temple of the LORD. [21] They brought seven bulls, seven rams, seven male lambs and seven male goats as a sin offering[a] for the kingdom, for the sanctuary and for Judah. The king commanded the priests, the descendants of Aaron, to offer these on the altar of the LORD. [22] So they slaughtered the bulls, and the priests took the blood and splashed it against the altar; next they slaughtered the rams and splashed their blood against the altar; then they slaughtered the lambs and splashed their blood against the altar. [23] The goats for the sin offering were brought before the king and the assembly, and they laid their hands on them. [24] The priests then slaughtered the goats and presented their blood on the altar for a sin offering to atone for all Israel, because the king had ordered the burnt offering and the sin offering for all Israel.

[25] He stationed the Levites in the temple of the LORD with cymbals, harps and lyres in the way prescribed by David and Gad the king's seer and Nathan the prophet; this was commanded by the LORD through his prophets. [26] So the Levites stood ready with David's instruments, and the priests with their trumpets.

[27] Hezekiah gave the order to sacrifice the burnt offering on the altar. As the offering began, singing to the LORD began also, accompanied by trumpets and the instruments of David king of Israel. [28] The whole assembly bowed in worship, while the musicians played and the trumpets sounded. All this continued until the sacrifice of the burnt offering was completed.

[29] When the offerings were finished, the king and everyone present with him knelt down and worshiped. [30] King Hezekiah and his officials ordered the Levites to praise the LORD with the words of David and of Asaph the seer. So they sang praises with gladness and bowed down and worshiped.

---

[a] 21 Or purification offering; also in verses 23 and 24

³¹Then Hezekiah said, "You have now dedicated yourselves to the LORD. Come and bring sacrifices and thank offerings to the temple of the LORD." So the assembly brought sacrifices and thank offerings, and all whose hearts were willing brought burnt offerings.

³²The number of burnt offerings the assembly brought was seventy bulls, a hundred rams and two hundred male lambs—all of them for burnt offerings to the LORD. ³³The animals consecrated as sacrifices amounted to six hundred bulls and three thousand sheep and goats. ³⁴The priests, however, were too few to skin all the burnt offerings; so their relatives the Levites helped them until the task was finished and until other priests had been consecrated, for the Levites had been more conscientious in consecrating themselves than the priests had been. ³⁵There were burnt offerings in abundance, together with the fat of the fellowship offerings and the drink offerings that accompanied the burnt offerings.

So the service of the temple of the LORD was reestablished. ³⁶Hezekiah and all the people rejoiced at what God had brought about for his people, because it was done so quickly.

Hezekiah Celebrates the Passover

30 Hezekiah sent word to all Israel and Judah and also wrote letters to Ephraim and Manasseh, inviting them to come to the temple of the LORD in Jerusalem and celebrate the Passover to the LORD, the God of Israel. ²The king and his officials and the whole assembly in Jerusalem decided to celebrate the Passover in the second month. ³They had not been able to celebrate it at the regular time because not enough priests had consecrated themselves and the people had not assembled in Jerusalem. ⁴The plan seemed right both to the king and to the whole assembly. ⁵They decided to send a proclamation throughout Israel, from Beersheba to Dan, calling the people to come to Jerusalem and celebrate the Passover to the LORD, the God of Israel. It

had not been celebrated in large numbers according to what was written.

⁶At the king's command, couriers went throughout Israel and Judah with letters from the king and from his officials, which read:

"People of Israel, return to the LORD, the God of Abraham, Isaac and Israel, that he may return to you who are left, who have escaped from the hand of the kings of Assyria. ⁷Do not be like your parents and your fellow Israelites, who were unfaithful to the LORD, the God of their ancestors, so that he made them an object of horror, as you see. ⁸Do not be stiff-necked, as your ancestors were; submit to the LORD. Come to his sanctuary, which he has consecrated forever. Serve the LORD your God, so that his fierce anger will turn away from you. ⁹If you return to the LORD, then your fellow Israelites and your children will be shown compassion by their captors and will return to this land, for the LORD your God is gracious and compassionate. He will not turn his face from you if you return to him."

¹⁰The couriers went from town to town in Ephraim and Manasseh, as far as Zebulun, but people scorned and ridiculed them. ¹¹Nevertheless, some from Asher, Manasseh and Zebulun humbled themselves and went to Jerusalem. ¹²Also in Judah the hand of God was on the people to give them unity of mind to carry out what the king and his officials had ordered, following the word of the LORD.

¹³A very large crowd of people assembled in Jerusalem to celebrate the Festival of Unleavened Bread in the second month. ¹⁴They removed the altars in Jerusalem and cleared away the incense altars and threw them into the Kidron Valley.

¹⁵They slaughtered the Passover lamb on the fourteenth day of the second month. The priests and the Levites were ashamed and consecrated themselves and brought burnt offerings to the temple of the LORD. ¹⁶Then they took up

their regular positions as prescribed in the Law of Moses the man of God. The priests splashed against the altar the blood handed to them by the Levites. [17] Since many in the crowd had not consecrated themselves, the Levites had to kill the Passover lambs for all those who were not ceremonially clean and could not consecrate their lambs[a] to the LORD. [18] Although most of the many people who came from Ephraim, Manasseh, Issachar and Zebulun had not purified themselves, yet they ate the Passover, contrary to what was written. But Hezekiah prayed for them, saying, "May the LORD, who is good, pardon everyone [19] who sets their heart on seeking God — the LORD, the God of their ancestors — even if they are not clean according to the rules of the sanctuary." [20] And the LORD heard Hezekiah and healed the people.

[21] The Israelites who were present in Jerusalem celebrated the Festival of Unleavened Bread for seven days with great rejoicing, while the Levites and priests praised the LORD every day with resounding instruments dedicated to the LORD.[b]

[22] Hezekiah spoke encouragingly to all the Levites, who showed good understanding of the service of the LORD. For the seven days they ate their assigned portion and offered fellowship offerings and praised[c] the LORD, the God of their ancestors.

[23] The whole assembly then agreed to celebrate the festival seven more days; so for another seven days they celebrated joyfully. [24] Hezekiah king of Judah provided a thousand bulls and seven thousand sheep and goats for the assembly, and the officials provided them with a thousand bulls and ten thousand sheep and goats. A great number of priests consecrated themselves. [25] The entire assembly of Judah rejoiced, along with the priests and Levites and all who had assembled from Israel, including the foreigners who had come from Israel and also those who resided in Judah. [26] There was great joy in Jerusalem, for since the days of Sol-

omon son of David king of Israel there had been nothing like this in Jerusalem. [27] The priests and the Levites stood to bless the people, and God heard them, for their prayer reached heaven, his holy dwelling place.

31 When all this had ended, the Israelites who were there went out to the towns of Judah, smashed the sacred stones and cut down the Asherah poles. They destroyed the high places and the altars throughout Judah and Benjamin and in Ephraim and Manasseh. After they had destroyed all of them, the Israelites returned to their own towns and to their own property.

Contributions for Worship

[2] Hezekiah assigned the priests and Levites to divisions — each of them according to their duties as priests or Levites — to offer burnt offerings and fellowship offerings, to minister, to give thanks and to sing praises at the gates of the LORD's dwelling. [3] The king contributed from his own possessions for the morning and evening burnt offerings and for the burnt offerings on the Sabbaths, at the New Moons and at the appointed festivals as

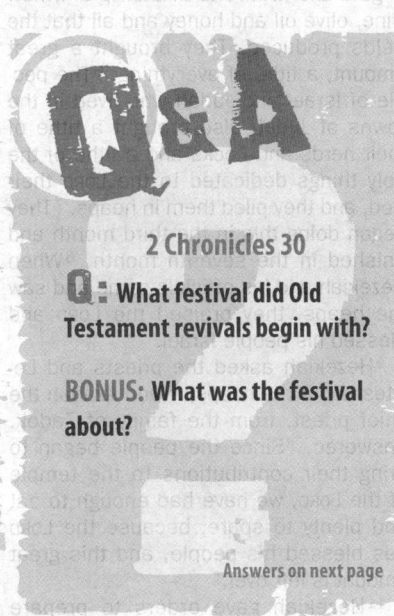

2 Chronicles 30

Q: What festival did Old Testament revivals begin with?

BONUS: What was the festival about?

Answers on next page

---

a 17 Or *consecrate themselves*   b 21 Or *priests sang to the LORD every day, accompanied by the LORD's instruments of praise*   c 22 Or *and confessed their sins to*

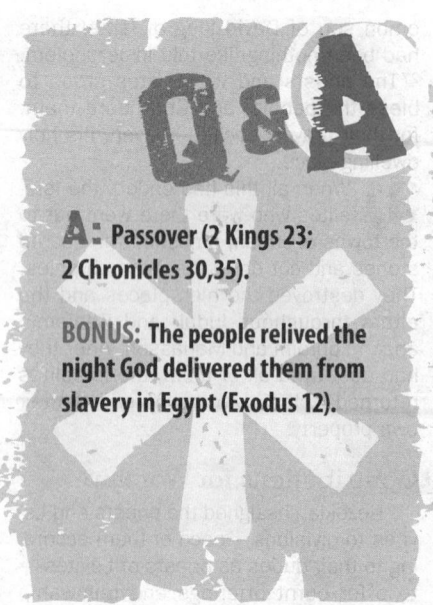

A: Passover (2 Kings 23; 2 Chronicles 30,35).

BONUS: The people relived the night God delivered them from slavery in Egypt (Exodus 12).

written in the Law of the LORD. ⁴He ordered the people living in Jerusalem to give the portion due the priests and Levites so they could devote themselves to the Law of the LORD. ⁵As soon as the order went out, the Israelites generously gave the firstfruits of their grain, new wine, olive oil and honey and all that the fields produced. They brought a great amount, a tithe of everything. ⁶The people of Israel and Judah who lived in the towns of Judah also brought a tithe of their herds and flocks and a tithe of the holy things dedicated to the LORD their God, and they piled them in heaps. ⁷They began doing this in the third month and finished in the seventh month. ⁸When Hezekiah and his officials came and saw the heaps, they praised the LORD and blessed his people Israel.

⁹Hezekiah asked the priests and Levites about the heaps; ¹⁰and Azariah the chief priest, from the family of Zadok, answered, "Since the people began to bring their contributions to the temple of the LORD, we have had enough to eat and plenty to spare, because the LORD has blessed his people, and this great amount is left over."

¹¹Hezekiah gave orders to prepare storerooms in the temple of the LORD, and this was done. ¹²Then they faithfully brought in the contributions, tithes and dedicated gifts. Konaniah, a Levite, was the overseer in charge of these things, and his brother Shimei was next in rank. ¹³Jehiel, Azaziah, Nahath, Asahel, Jerimoth, Jozabad, Eliel, Ismakiah, Mahath and Benaiah were assistants of Konaniah and Shimei his brother. All these served by appointment of King Hezekiah and Azariah the official in charge of the temple of God.

¹⁴Kore son of Imnah the Levite, keeper of the East Gate, was in charge of the freewill offerings given to God, distributing the contributions made to the LORD and also the consecrated gifts. ¹⁵Eden, Miniamin, Jeshua, Shemaiah, Amariah and Shekaniah assisted him faithfully in the towns of the priests, distributing to their fellow priests according to their divisions, old and young alike.

¹⁶In addition, they distributed to the males three years old or more whose names were in the genealogical records—all who would enter the temple of the LORD to perform the daily duties of their various tasks, according to their responsibilities and their divisions. ¹⁷And they distributed to the priests enrolled by their families in the genealogical records and likewise to the Levites twenty years old or more, according to their responsibilities and their divisions. ¹⁸They included all the little ones, the wives, and the sons and daughters of the whole community listed in these genealogical records. For they were faithful in consecrating themselves.

¹⁹As for the priests, the descendants of Aaron, who lived on the farmlands around their towns or in any other towns, men were designated by name to distribute portions to every male among them and to all who were recorded in the genealogies of the Levites.

²⁰This is what Hezekiah did throughout Judah, doing what was good and right and faithful before the LORD his God. ²¹In everything that he undertook in the service of God's temple and in obedience to the law and the commands, he sought his

God and worked wholeheartedly. And so he prospered.

Sennacherib Threatens Jerusalem

32 After all that Hezekiah had so faithfully done, Sennacherib king of Assyria came and invaded Judah. He laid siege to the fortified cities, thinking to conquer them for himself. ²When Hezekiah saw that Sennacherib had come and that he intended to wage war against Jerusalem, ³he consulted with his officials and military staff about blocking off the water from the springs outside the city, and they helped him. ⁴They gathered a large group of people who blocked all the springs and the stream that flowed through the land. "Why should the kings^a of Assyria come and find plenty of water?" they said. ⁵Then he worked hard repairing all the broken sections of the wall and building towers on it. He built another wall outside that one and reinforced the terraces^b of the City of David. He also made large numbers of weapons and shields.

⁶He appointed military officers over the people and assembled them before him in the square at the city gate and encouraged them with these words: ⁷"Be strong and courageous. Do not be afraid or discouraged because of the king of Assyria and the vast army with him, for there is a greater power with us than with him. ⁸With him is only the arm of flesh, but with us is the LORD our God to help us and to fight our battles." And the people gained confidence from what Hezekiah the king of Judah said.

⁹Later, when Sennacherib king of Assyria and all his forces were laying siege to Lachish, he sent his officers to Jerusalem with this message for Hezekiah king of Judah and for all the people of Judah who were there:

¹⁰"This is what Sennacherib king of Assyria says: On what are you basing your confidence, that you remain in Jerusalem under siege? ¹¹When Hezekiah says, 'The LORD our God will save us from the hand of the king of Assyria,' he is misleading you, to let you die of hunger and thirst. ¹²Did not Hezekiah himself remove this god's high places and altars, saying to Judah and Jerusalem, 'You must worship before one altar and burn sacrifices on it'?

¹³"Do you not know what I and my predecessors have done to all the peoples of the other lands? Were the gods of those nations ever able to deliver their land from my hand? ¹⁴Who of all the gods of these nations that my predecessors destroyed has been able to save his people from me? How then can your god deliver you from my hand? ¹⁵Now do not let Hezekiah deceive you and mislead you like this. Do not believe him, for no god of any nation or kingdom has been able to deliver his people from my hand or the hand of my predecessors. How much less will your god deliver you from my hand!"

¹⁶Sennacherib's officers spoke further against the LORD God and against his servant Hezekiah. ¹⁷The king also wrote letters ridiculing the LORD, the God of Israel, and saying this against him: "Just as the gods of the peoples of the other lands did not rescue their people from my hand, so the god of Hezekiah will not rescue his people from my hand." ¹⁸Then they called out in Hebrew to the people of Jerusalem who were on the wall, to terrify them and make them afraid in order to capture the city. ¹⁹They spoke about the God of Jerusalem as they did about the gods of the other peoples of the world—the work of human hands.

²⁰King Hezekiah and the prophet Isaiah son of Amoz cried out in prayer to heaven about this. ²¹And the LORD sent an angel, who annihilated all the fighting men and the commanders and officers in the camp of the Assyrian king. So he withdrew to his own land in disgrace. And when he went into the temple of his god, some of his sons, his own flesh and blood, cut him down with the sword.

---

^a 4 Hebrew; Septuagint and Syriac *king*   ^b 5 Or *the Millo*

²²So the LORD saved Hezekiah and the people of Jerusalem from the hand of Sennacherib king of Assyria and from the hand of all others. He took care of them[a] on every side. ²³Many brought offerings to Jerusalem for the LORD and valuable gifts for Hezekiah king of Judah. From then on he was highly regarded by all the nations.

Hezekiah's Pride, Success and Death

²⁴In those days Hezekiah became ill and was at the point of death. He prayed to the LORD, who answered him and gave him a miraculous sign. ²⁵But Hezekiah's heart was proud and he did not respond to the kindness shown him; therefore the LORD's wrath was on him and on Judah and Jerusalem. ²⁶Then Hezekiah repented of the pride of his heart, as did the people of Jerusalem; therefore the LORD's wrath did not come on them during the days of Hezekiah.

²⁷Hezekiah had very great wealth and honor, and he made treasuries for his silver and gold and for his precious stones, spices, shields and all kinds of valuables. ²⁸He also made buildings to store the harvest of grain, new wine and olive oil; and he made stalls for various kinds of cattle, and pens for the flocks. ²⁹He built villages and acquired great numbers of flocks and herds, for God had given him very great riches.

³⁰It was Hezekiah who blocked the upper outlet of the Gihon spring and channeled the water down to the west side of the City of David. He succeeded in everything he undertook. ³¹But when envoys were sent by the rulers of Babylon to ask him about the miraculous sign that had occurred in the land, God left him to test him and to know everything that was in his heart.

³²The other events of Hezekiah's reign and his acts of devotion are written in the vision of the prophet Isaiah son of Amoz in the book of the kings of Judah and Israel. ³³Hezekiah rested with his ancestors and was buried on the hill where the tombs of David's descendants are. All Judah and the people of Jerusalem honored him when he died. And Manasseh his son succeeded him as king.

Manasseh King of Judah

33 Manasseh was twelve years old when he became king, and he reigned in Jerusalem fifty-five years. ²He did evil in the eyes of the LORD, following the detestable practices of the nations the LORD had driven out before the Israelites. ³He rebuilt the high places his father Hezekiah had demolished; he also erected altars to the Baals and made Asherah poles. He bowed down to all the starry hosts and worshiped them. ⁴He built altars in the temple of the LORD, of which the LORD had said, "My Name will remain in Jerusalem forever." ⁵In both courts of the temple of the LORD, he built altars to all the starry hosts. ⁶He sacrificed his children in the fire in the Valley of Ben Hinnom, practiced divination and witchcraft, sought omens, and consulted mediums and spiritists. He did much evil in the eyes of the LORD, arousing his anger.

⁷He took the image he had made and put it in God's temple, of which God had said to David and to his son Solomon, "In this temple and in Jerusalem, which I have chosen out of all the tribes of Israel, I will put my Name forever. ⁸I will not again make the feet of the Israelites leave the land I assigned to your ancestors, if only they will be careful to do everything I commanded them concerning all the laws, decrees and regulations given through Moses." ⁹But Manasseh led Judah and the people of Jerusalem astray, so that they did more evil than the nations the LORD had destroyed before the Israelites.

¹⁰The LORD spoke to Manasseh and his people, but they paid no attention. ¹¹So the LORD brought against them the army commanders of the king of Assyria, who took Manasseh prisoner, put a hook in his nose, bound him with bronze shackles and took him to Babylon. ¹²In his distress he sought the favor of the LORD his

a 22 Hebrew; Septuagint and Vulgate He gave them rest

God and humbled himself greatly before the God of his ancestors. ¹³And when he prayed to him, the LORD was moved by his entreaty and listened to his plea; so he brought him back to Jerusalem and to his kingdom. Then Manasseh knew that the LORD is God.

¹⁴Afterward he rebuilt the outer wall of the City of David, west of the Gihon spring in the valley, as far as the entrance of the Fish Gate and encircling the hill of Ophel; he also made it much higher. He stationed military commanders in all the fortified cities in Judah.

¹⁵He got rid of the foreign gods and removed the image from the temple of the LORD, as well as all the altars he had built on the temple hill and in Jerusalem; and he threw them out of the city. ¹⁶Then he restored the altar of the LORD and sacrificed fellowship offerings and thank offerings on it, and told Judah to serve the LORD, the God of Israel. ¹⁷The people, however, continued to sacrifice at the high places, but only to the LORD their God.

¹⁸The other events of Manasseh's reign, including his prayer to his God and the words the seers spoke to him in the name of the LORD, the God of Israel, are written in the annals of the kings of Israel.ᵃ ¹⁹His prayer and how God was moved by his entreaty, as well as all his sins and unfaithfulness, and the sites where he built high places and set up Asherah poles and idols before he humbled himself—all these are written in the records of the seers.ᵇ ²⁰Manasseh rested with his ancestors and was buried in his palace. And Amon his son succeeded him as king.

Amon King of Judah

²¹Amon was twenty-two years old when he became king, and he reigned in Jerusalem two years. ²²He did evil in the eyes of the LORD, as his father Manasseh had done. Amon worshiped and offered sacrifices to all the idols Manasseh had made. ²³But unlike his father Manasseh, he did not humble himself before the LORD; Amon increased his guilt.

²⁴Amon's officials conspired against him and assassinated him in his palace. ²⁵Then the people of the land killed all who had plotted against King Amon, and they made Josiah his son king in his place.

Josiah's Reforms

34 Josiah was eight years old when he became king, and he reigned in Jerusalem thirty-one years. ²He did what was right in the eyes of the LORD and followed the ways of his father David, not turning aside to the right or to the left.

³In the eighth year of his reign, while he was still young, he began to seek the God of his father David. In his twelfth year he began to purge Judah and Jerusalem of high places, Asherah poles and idols. ⁴Under his direction the altars of the Baals were torn down; he cut to pieces the incense altars that were above them, and smashed the Asherah poles and the idols. These he broke to pieces and scattered over the graves of those who had sacrificed to them. ⁵He burned the bones of the priests on their altars, and so he purged Judah and Jerusalem. ⁶In the towns of Manasseh, Ephraim and Simeon, as far as Naphtali, and in the ruins around them, ⁷he tore down the altars and the Asherah poles and crushed the idols to powder and cut to pieces all the incense altars throughout Israel. Then he went back to Jerusalem.

⁸In the eighteenth year of Josiah's reign, to purify the land and the temple, he sent Shaphan son of Azaliah and Maaseiah the ruler of the city, with Joah son of Joahaz, the recorder, to repair the temple of the LORD his God.

⁹They went to Hilkiah the high priest and gave him the money that had been brought into the temple of God, which the Levites who were the gatekeepers had collected from the people of Manasseh, Ephraim and the entire remnant of Israel and from all the people of Judah and Benjamin and the inhabitants of Jerusalem. ¹⁰Then they entrusted it to the men appointed to supervise the work on the

---

ᵃ 18 That is, Judah, as frequently in 2 Chronicles   ᵇ 19 One Hebrew manuscript and Septuagint; most Hebrew manuscripts *of Hozai*

LORD's temple. These men paid the workers who repaired and restored the temple. [11] They also gave money to the carpenters and builders to purchase dressed stone, and timber for joists and beams for the buildings that the kings of Judah had allowed to fall into ruin.

[12] The workers labored faithfully. Over them to direct them were Jahath and Obadiah, Levites descended from Merari, and Zechariah and Meshullam, descended from Kohath. The Levites—all who were skilled in playing musical instruments— [13] had charge of the laborers and supervised all the workers from job to job. Some of the Levites were secretaries, scribes and gatekeepers.

The Book of the Law Found

[14] While they were bringing out the money that had been taken into the temple of the LORD, Hilkiah the priest found the Book of the Law of the LORD that had been given through Moses. [15] Hilkiah said to Shaphan the secretary, "I have found the Book of the Law in the temple of the LORD." He gave it to Shaphan.

[16] Then Shaphan took the book to the king and reported to him: "Your officials are doing everything that has been committed to them. [17] They have paid out the money that was in the temple of the LORD and have entrusted it to the supervisors and workers." [18] Then Shaphan the secretary informed the king, "Hilkiah the priest has given me a book." And Shaphan read from it in the presence of the king.

[19] When the king heard the words of the Law, he tore his robes. [20] He gave these orders to Hilkiah, Ahikam son of Shaphan, Abdon son of Micah,[a] Shaphan the secretary and Asaiah the king's attendant: [21] "Go and inquire of the LORD for me and for the remnant in Israel and Judah about what is written in this book that has been found. Great is the LORD's anger that is poured out on us because those who have gone before us have not kept the word of the LORD; they have not acted in accordance with all that is written in this book."

> Y ou don't have to be an adult for God to use you. Six-year-old Sarah explained to her cousin that "Jesus loves you." And it was a 12-year-old who was so moved by the plight of the homeless that he launched a winter crusade to supply street people with blankets. At age 16 young King Josiah "began to seek the God of his father," and before he was 21 he led his nation in a great religious revival. Seek God now, and look for ways to serve him. God uses faithful followers of any age.
>
> {2 Chronicles 34:1–3}

[22] Hilkiah and those the king had sent with him[b] went to speak to the prophet Huldah, who was the wife of Shallum son of Tokhath,[c] the son of Hasrah,[d] keeper of the wardrobe. She lived in Jerusalem, in the New Quarter.

[23] She said to them, "This is what the LORD, the God of Israel, says: Tell the man who sent you to me, [24] 'This is what the LORD says: I am going to bring disaster on this place and its people—all the curses written in the book that has been read in the presence of the king of Judah. [25] Because they have forsaken me and burned incense to other gods and aroused my anger by all that their hands have made,[e] my anger will be poured out on this place and will not be quenched.' [26] Tell the king of Judah, who sent you to inquire of the LORD, 'This is what the LORD, the God of

a 20 Also called Akbor son of Micaiah   b 22 One Hebrew manuscript, Vulgate and Syriac; most Hebrew manuscripts do not have had sent with him.   c 22 Also called Tikvah   d 22 Also called Harhas   e 25 Or by everything they have done

Israel, says concerning the words you heard: 27 Because your heart was responsive and you humbled yourself before God when you heard what he spoke against this place and its people, and because you humbled yourself before me and tore your robes and wept in my presence, I have heard you, declares the LORD. 28 Now I will gather you to your ancestors, and you will be buried in peace. Your eyes will not see all the disaster I am going to bring on this place and on those who live here.' "

So they took her answer back to the king.

29 Then the king called together all the elders of Judah and Jerusalem. 30 He went up to the temple of the LORD with the people of Judah, the inhabitants of Jerusalem, the priests and the Levites—all the people from the least to the greatest. He read in their hearing all the words of the Book of the Covenant, which had been found in the temple of the LORD. 31 The king stood by his pillar and renewed the covenant in the presence of the LORD—to follow the LORD and keep his commands, statutes and decrees with all his heart and all his soul, and to obey the words of the covenant written in this book.

32 Then he had everyone in Jerusalem and Benjamin pledge themselves to it; the people of Jerusalem did this in accordance with the covenant of God, the God of their ancestors.

33 Josiah removed all the detestable idols from all the territory belonging to the Israelites, and he had all who were present in Israel serve the LORD their God. As long as he lived, they did not fail to follow the LORD, the God of their ancestors.

Josiah Celebrates the Passover

35 Josiah celebrated the Passover to the LORD in Jerusalem, and the Passover lamb was slaughtered on the fourteenth day of the first month. 2 He appointed the priests to their duties and encouraged them in the service of the LORD's temple. 3 He said to the Levites, who instructed all Israel and who had been consecrated to the LORD: "Put the sacred ark in the temple that Solomon son of David king of Israel built. It is not to be carried about on your shoulders. Now serve the LORD your God and his people Israel. 4 Prepare yourselves by families in your divisions, according to the instructions written by David king of Israel and by his son Solomon.

5 "Stand in the holy place with a group of Levites for each subdivision of the families of your fellow Israelites, the lay people. 6 Slaughter the Passover lambs, consecrate yourselves and prepare the lambs for your fellow Israelites, doing what the LORD commanded through Moses."

7 Josiah provided for all the lay people who were there a total of thirty thousand lambs and goats for the Passover offerings, and also three thousand cattle—all from the king's own possessions.

8 His officials also contributed voluntarily to the people and the priests and Levites. Hilkiah, Zechariah and Jehiel, the officials in charge of God's temple, gave the priests twenty-six hundred Passover offerings and three hundred cattle. 9 Also Konaniah along with Shemaiah and Nethanel, his brothers, and Hashabiah, Jeiel and Jozabad, the leaders of the Levites, provided five thousand Passover offerings and five hundred head of cattle for the Levites.

10 The service was arranged and the priests stood in their places with the Levites in their divisions as the king had ordered. 11 The Passover lambs were slaughtered, and the priests splashed against the altar the blood handed to them, while the Levites skinned the animals. 12 They set aside the burnt offerings to give them to the subdivisions of the families of the people to offer to the LORD, as it is written in the Book of Moses. They did the same with the cattle. 13 They roasted the Passover animals over the fire as prescribed, and boiled the holy offerings in pots, caldrons and pans and served them quickly to all the people. 14 After this, they made preparations for themselves and for the priests, because the priests, the descendants of Aaron, were sacrificing the burnt offerings and the fat portions until nightfall.

So the Levites made preparations for themselves and for the Aaronic priests.

[15] The musicians, the descendants of Asaph, were in the places prescribed by David, Asaph, Heman and Jeduthun the king's seer. The gatekeepers at each gate did not need to leave their posts, because their fellow Levites made the preparations for them.

[16] So at that time the entire service of the LORD was carried out for the celebration of the Passover and the offering of burnt offerings on the altar of the LORD, as King Josiah had ordered. [17] The Israelites who were present celebrated the Passover at that time and observed the Festival of Unleavened Bread for seven days. [18] The Passover had not been observed like this in Israel since the days of the prophet Samuel; and none of the kings of Israel had ever celebrated such a Passover as did Josiah, with the priests, the Levites and all Judah and Israel who were there with the people of Jerusalem. [19] This Passover was celebrated in the eighteenth year of Josiah's reign.

The Death of Josiah

[20] After all this, when Josiah had set the temple in order, Necho king of Egypt went up to fight at Carchemish on the Euphrates, and Josiah marched out to meet him in battle. [21] But Necho sent messengers to him, saying, "What quarrel is there, king of Judah, between you and me? It is not you I am attacking at this time, but the house with which I am at war. God has told me to hurry; so stop opposing God, who is with me, or he will destroy you."

TO THE POINT

Passover

Second Chronicles 35 tells a story of a very special Passover in Israel. What was Passover anyway, and why was it important? When God's angel killed the firstborn sons of the Egyptians, the angel "passed over" the homes of God's people (Exodus 12:13). Passover was a celebration of that event.

On the first Passover the blood of a lamb was used to tell the angel that the people who lived there were God's own. The New Testament calls Jesus your "Passover lamb" (1 Corinthians 5:7). Because Jesus shed his blood, you are now God's own.

Did you know that it was the very week of Passover that Jesus was crucified? So every Easter Christians have their own special Passover. Easter can remind you of Jesus, your Passover lamb, and of God's promise that through Jesus you have everlasting life.

²²Josiah, however, would not turn away from him, but disguised himself to engage him in battle. He would not listen to what Necho had said at God's command but went to fight him on the plain of Megiddo. ²³Archers shot King Josiah, and he told his officers, "Take me away; I am badly wounded." ²⁴So they took him out of his chariot, put him in his other chariot and brought him to Jerusalem, where he died. He was buried in the tombs of his ancestors, and all Judah and Jerusalem mourned for him.

²⁵Jeremiah composed laments for Josiah, and to this day all the male and female singers commemorate Josiah in the laments. These became a tradition in Israel and are written in the Laments.

²⁶The other events of Josiah's reign and his acts of devotion in accordance with what is written in the Law of the LORD— ²⁷all the events, from beginning to end, are written in the book of the kings **36** of Israel and Judah. ¹And the people of the land took Jehoahaz son of Josiah and made him king in Jerusalem in place of his father.

Jehoahaz King of Judah

²Jehoahaz*ᵃ* was twenty-three years old when he became king, and he reigned in Jerusalem three months. ³The king of Egypt dethroned him in Jerusalem and imposed on Judah a levy of a hundred talents*ᵇ* of silver and a talent*ᶜ* of gold. ⁴The king of Egypt made Eliakim, a brother of Jehoahaz, king over Judah and Jerusalem and changed Eliakim's name to Jehoiakim. But Necho took Eliakim's brother Jehoahaz and carried him off to Egypt.

Jehoiakim King of Judah

⁵Jehoiakim was twenty-five years old when he became king, and he reigned in Jerusalem eleven years. He did evil in the eyes of the LORD his God. ⁶Nebuchadnezzar king of Babylon attacked him and bound him with bronze shackles to take

him to Babylon. ⁷Nebuchadnezzar also took to Babylon articles from the temple of the LORD and put them in his temple*ᵈ* there.

⁸The other events of Jehoiakim's reign, the detestable things he did and all that was found against him, are written in the book of the kings of Israel and Judah. And Jehoiachin his son succeeded him as king.

Jehoiachin King of Judah

⁹Jehoiachin was eighteen*ᵉ* years old when he became king, and he reigned in Jerusalem three months and ten days. He did evil in the eyes of the LORD. ¹⁰In the spring, King Nebuchadnezzar sent for him and brought him to Babylon, together with articles of value from the temple of the LORD, and he made Jehoiachin's uncle,*ᶠ* Zedekiah, king over Judah and Jerusalem.

Zedekiah King of Judah

¹¹Zedekiah was twenty-one years old when he became king, and he reigned in Jerusalem eleven years. ¹²He did evil in the eyes of the LORD his God and did not humble himself before Jeremiah the prophet, who spoke the word of the LORD. ¹³He also rebelled against King Nebuchadnezzar, who had made him take an oath in God's name. He became stiff-necked and hardened his heart and would not turn to the LORD, the God of Israel. ¹⁴Furthermore, all the leaders of the priests and the people became more and more unfaithful, following all the detestable practices of the nations and defiling the temple of the LORD, which he had consecrated in Jerusalem.

The Fall of Jerusalem

¹⁵The LORD, the God of their ancestors, sent word to them through his messengers again and again, because he had pity on his people and on his dwelling place. ¹⁶But they mocked God's messengers, despised his words and scoffed at

---

ᵃ 2 Hebrew *Joahaz*, a variant of *Jehoahaz*; also in verse 4   *ᵇ 3* That is, about 3 3/4 tons or about 3.4 metric tons
ᶜ 3 That is, about 75 pounds or about 34 kilograms   *ᵈ 7* Or *palace*   *ᵉ 9* One Hebrew manuscript, some Septuagint
manuscripts and Syriac (see also 2 Kings 24:8); most Hebrew manuscripts *eight*   *ᶠ 10* Hebrew *brother*, that is, relative
(see 2 Kings 24:17)

his prophets until the wrath of the LORD was aroused against his people and there was no remedy. [17]He brought up against them the king of the Babylonians,[a] who killed their young men with the sword in the sanctuary, and did not spare young men or young women, the elderly or the infirm. God gave them all into the hands of Nebuchadnezzar. [18]He carried to Babylon all the articles from the temple of God, both large and small, and the treasures of the LORD's temple and the treasures of the king and his officials. [19]They set fire to God's temple and broke down the wall of Jerusalem; they burned all the palaces and destroyed everything of value there.

[20]He carried into exile to Babylon the remnant, who escaped from the sword, and they became servants to him and his successors until the kingdom of Persia

came to power. [21]The land enjoyed its sabbath rests; all the time of its desolation it rested, until the seventy years were completed in fulfillment of the word of the LORD spoken by Jeremiah.

[22]In the first year of Cyrus king of Persia, in order to fulfill the word of the LORD spoken by Jeremiah, the LORD moved the heart of Cyrus king of Persia to make a proclamation throughout his realm and also to put it in writing:

[23]"This is what Cyrus king of Persia says:

"'The LORD, the God of heaven, has given me all the kingdoms of the earth and he has appointed me to build a temple for him at Jerusalem in Judah. Any of his people among you may go up, and may the LORD their God be with them.'"

EZRA

Coming Home.

After a rough day at school or a long trip, it feels pretty good to come home, doesn't it? But what if you were gone for years, and when you got back your house had burned down and your hometown was deserted? You might be glad to get back, but you'd be disappointed too.

Ezra tells the story of the Israelites' return to their empty and ruined homeland after 70 years of captivity in Babylon. It was especially tough because the Jews' neighbors were hostile. If their attempt to rebuild their homeland was going to succeed in the face of harsh opposition, they had to remain faithful to God!

>>**CYRUS SENDS JEWS PACKING**.
New ruler changes policy, see Ezra 1:1–8

>>**EZRA SETS LIFE-GOAL**
Example reported, Ezra 7:10

>>**DISGRACEFUL MARRIAGES STUN EZRA**
See report in Ezra 9

>>**EZRA: SHOW UP, OR ELSE!**
Edict recorded in Ezra 10:7–17

preview

Isaiah predicts Cyrus' conquest of Babylon a hundred years before it happens: Isaiah 45:1–6

Only 50,000 Jews return. Hundreds of thousands stay in Babylon.

Events recorded in this book take place between 538 B.C. and 438 B.C.

During these years the Greeks defeat invading Persian armies. Roman laws are recorded on Twelve Tablets. Celts settle in the British Isles. In India Buddha dies. He is not resurrected.

Cyrus Helps the Exiles to Return

1 In the first year of Cyrus king of Persia, in order to fulfill the word of the LORD spoken by Jeremiah, the LORD moved the heart of Cyrus king of Persia to make a proclamation throughout his realm and also to put it in writing:

2 "This is what Cyrus king of Persia says:

" 'The LORD, the God of heaven, has given me all the kingdoms of the earth and he has appointed me to build a temple for him at Jerusalem in Judah. 3 Any of his people among you may go up to Jerusalem in Judah and build the temple of the LORD, the God of Israel, the God who is in Jerusalem, and may their God be with them. 4 And in any locality where survivors may now be living, the people are to provide them with silver and gold, with goods and livestock, and with freewill offerings for the temple of God in Jerusalem.' "

5 Then the family heads of Judah and Benjamin, and the priests and Levites—everyone whose heart God had moved—prepared to go up and build the house of the LORD in Jerusalem. 6 All their neighbors assisted them with articles of silver and gold, with goods and livestock, and with valuable gifts, in addition to all the freewill offerings.

7 Moreover, King Cyrus brought out the articles belonging to the temple of the LORD, which Nebuchadnezzar had carried away from Jerusalem and had placed in the temple of his god.[a] 8 Cyrus king of Persia had them brought by Mithredath the treasurer, who counted them out to Sheshbazzar the prince of Judah.

9 This was the inventory:

gold dishes	30
silver dishes	1,000
silver pans[b]	29
10 gold bowls	30
matching silver bowls	410
other articles	1,000

11 In all, there were 5,400 articles of gold and of silver. Sheshbazzar brought all these along with the exiles when they came up from Babylon to Jerusalem.

The List of the Exiles Who Returned

2 Now these are the people of the province who came up from the captivity of the exiles, whom Nebuchadnezzar king of Babylon had taken captive to Babylon (they returned to Jerusalem and Judah, each to their own town, 2 in company with Zerubbabel, Joshua, Nehemiah, Seraiah, Reelaiah, Mordecai, Bilshan, Mispar, Bigvai, Rehum and Baanah):

The list of the men of the people of Israel:

3 the descendants of Parosh	2,172
4 of Shephatiah	372
5 of Arah	775
6 of Pahath-Moab (through the line of Jeshua and Joab)	2,812
7 of Elam	1,254
8 of Zattu	945
9 of Zakkai	760
10 of Bani	642
11 of Bebai	623
12 of Azgad	1,222
13 of Adonikam	666
14 of Bigvai	2,056
15 of Adin	454
16 of Ater (through Hezekiah)	98
17 of Bezai	323
18 of Jorah	112
19 of Hashum	223
20 of Gibbar	95
21 the men of Bethlehem	123
22 of Netophah	56
23 of Anathoth	128
24 of Azmaveth	42
25 of Kiriath Jearim,[c] Kephirah and Beeroth	743
26 of Ramah and Geba	621
27 of Mikmash	122
28 of Bethel and Ai	223
29 of Nebo	52
30 of Magbish	156

[31] of the other Elam	1,254
[32] of Harim	320
[33] of Lod, Hadid and Ono	725
[34] of Jericho	345
[35] of Senaah	3,630

[36] The priests:

the descendants of Jedaiah
(through the family of
Jeshua) 973
[37] of Immer 1,052
[38] of Pashhur 1,247
[39] of Harim 1,017

[40] The Levites:

the descendants of Jeshua
and Kadmiel (of the line of
Hodaviah) 74

[41] The musicians:

the descendants of Asaph 128

[42] The gatekeepers of the temple:

the descendants of
Shallum, Ater, Talmon,
Akkub, Hatita and Shobai 139

[43] The temple servants:

the descendants of
Ziha, Hasupha, Tabbaoth,
[44] Keros, Siaha, Padon,
[45] Lebanah, Hagabah, Akkub,
[46] Hagab, Shalmai, Hanan,
[47] Giddel, Gahar, Reaiah,
[48] Rezin, Nekoda, Gazzam,
[49] Uzza, Paseah, Besai,
[50] Asnah, Meunim, Nephusim,
[51] Bakbuk, Hakupha, Harhur,
[52] Bazluth, Mehida, Harsha,
[53] Barkos, Sisera, Temah,
[54] Neziah and Hatipha

[55] The descendants of the servants
of Solomon:

the descendants of
Sotai, Hassophereth, Peruda,
[56] Jaala, Darkon, Giddel,
[57] Shephatiah, Hattil,
Pokereth-Hazzebaim and Ami

[58] The temple servants and the
descendants of the servants of
Solomon 392

[59] The following came up from
the towns of Tel Melah, Tel Harsha,
Kerub, Addon and Immer, but they
could not show that their families
were descended from Israel:

[60] The descendants of
Delaiah, Tobiah and Nekoda
652

[61] And from among the priests:

The descendants of
Hobaiah, Hakkoz and Barzillai
(a man who had married
a daughter of Barzillai the
Gileadite and was called by
that name).

[62] These searched for their family records, but they could not find them and so were excluded from the priesthood as unclean. [63] The governor ordered them not to eat any of the most sacred food until there was a priest ministering with the Urim and Thummim.

[64] The whole company numbered 42,360, [65] besides their 7,337 male and female slaves; and they also had 200 male and female singers. [66] They had 736 horses, 245 mules, [67] 435 camels and 6,720 donkeys.

[68] When they arrived at the house of the LORD in Jerusalem, some of the heads of the families gave freewill offerings toward the rebuilding of the house of God on its site. [69] According to their ability they gave to the treasury for this work 61,000 darics[a] of gold, 5,000 minas[b] of silver and 100 priestly garments.

[70] The priests, the Levites, the musicians, the gatekeepers and the temple servants settled in their own towns, along with some of the other people, and the rest of the Israelites settled in their towns.

Rebuilding the Altar

3 When the seventh month came and the Israelites had settled in their towns, the people assembled together as one in Jerusalem. [2] Then Joshua son of

---

[a] 69 That is, about 1,100 pounds or about 500 kilograms   [b] 69 That is, about 3 tons or about 2.8 metric tons

Jozadak and his fellow priests and Zerubbabel son of Shealtiel and his associates began to build the altar of the God of Israel to sacrifice burnt offerings on it, in accordance with what is written in the Law of Moses the man of God. ³Despite their fear of the peoples around them, they built the altar on its foundation and sacrificed burnt offerings on it to the LORD, both the morning and evening sacrifices. ⁴Then in accordance with what is written, they celebrated the Festival of Tabernacles with the required number of burnt offerings prescribed for each day. ⁵After that, they presented the regular burnt offerings, the New Moon sacrifices and the sacrifices for all the appointed sacred festivals of the LORD, as well as those brought as freewill offerings to the LORD. ⁶On the first day of the seventh month they began to offer burnt offerings to the LORD, though the foundation of the LORD's temple had not yet been laid.

Rebuilding the Temple

⁷Then they gave money to the masons and carpenters, and gave food and drink and olive oil to the people of Sidon and Tyre, so that they would bring cedar logs by sea from Lebanon to Joppa, as authorized by Cyrus king of Persia.

⁸In the second month of the second year after their arrival at the house of God in Jerusalem, Zerubbabel son of Shealtiel, Joshua son of Jozadak and the rest of the people (the priests and the Levites and all who had returned from the captivity to Jerusalem) began the work. They appointed Levites twenty years old and older to supervise the building of the house of the LORD. ⁹Joshua and his sons and brothers and Kadmiel and his sons (descendants of Hodaviahª) and the sons of Henadad and their sons and brothers — all Levites — joined together in supervising those working on the house of God.

¹⁰When the builders laid the foundation of the temple of the LORD, the priests in their vestments and with trumpets, and the Levites (the sons of Asaph) with cymbals, took their places to praise the LORD,

INSTANT ACCESS

You woke up grumpy. Called your sister a name. Talked back to your mom. Got in a fight at the bus stop. Tripped a kid in gym. You feel awful. If only you could start the day over! No one can go back and live a day over again. But you can make a fresh start, even in the middle of a bad day. The people of Judah had a bad century. They sinned willfully. Their homeland was destroyed, and they were carried as captives to Babylon. Now they were back. And the first thing they did was worship the Lord. Fresh starts begin by turning to the Lord. Admit your failures. Thank God for his forgiveness. And the rest of the day really will be new.

{Ezra 3:1–6}

as prescribed by David king of Israel. ¹¹With praise and thanksgiving they sang to the LORD:

"He is good;
   his love toward Israel endures
      forever."

And all the people gave a great shout of praise to the LORD, because the foundation of the house of the LORD was laid. ¹²But many of the older priests and Levites and family heads, who had seen the

---

ª 9 Hebrew *Yehudah*, a variant of *Hodaviah*

former temple, wept aloud when they saw the foundation of this temple being laid, while many others shouted for joy. ¹³No one could distinguish the sound of the shouts of joy from the sound of weeping, because the people made so much noise. And the sound was heard far away.

Opposition to the Rebuilding

4 When the enemies of Judah and Benjamin heard that the exiles were building a temple for the Lord, the God of Israel, ²they came to Zerubbabel and to the heads of the families and said, "Let us help you build because, like you, we seek your God and have been sacrificing to him since the time of Esarhaddon king of Assyria, who brought us here."

³But Zerubbabel, Joshua and the rest of the heads of the families of Israel answered, "You have no part with us in building a temple to our God. We alone will build it for the Lord, the God of Israel, as King Cyrus, the king of Persia, commanded us."

⁴Then the peoples around them set out to discourage the people of Judah and make them afraid to go on building.ᵃ ⁵They bribed officials to work against them and frustrate their plans during the entire reign of Cyrus king of Persia and down to the reign of Darius king of Persia.

Later Opposition Under Xerxes and Artaxerxes

⁶At the beginning of the reign of Xerxes,ᵇ they lodged an accusation against the people of Judah and Jerusalem.

⁷And in the days of Artaxerxes king of Persia, Bishlam, Mithredath, Tabeel and the rest of his associates wrote a letter to Artaxerxes. The letter was written in Aramaic script and in the Aramaic language.ᶜ,ᵈ

⁸Rehum the commanding officer and Shimshai the secretary wrote a letter against Jerusalem to Artaxerxes the king as follows:

⁹Rehum the commanding officer and Shimshai the secretary, together with

the rest of their associates—the judges, officials and administrators over the people from Persia, Uruk and Babylon, the Elamites of Susa, ¹⁰and the other people whom the great and honorable Ashurbanipal deported and settled in the city of Samaria and elsewhere in Trans-Euphrates.

¹¹(This is a copy of the letter they sent him.)

To King Artaxerxes,

From your servants in Trans-Euphrates:

¹²The king should know that the people who came up to us from you have gone to Jerusalem and are rebuilding that rebellious and wicked city. They are restoring the walls and repairing the foundations.

¹³Furthermore, the king should know that if this city is built and its walls are restored, no more taxes, tribute or duty will be paid, and eventually the royal revenues will suffer.ᵉ ¹⁴Now since we are under obligation to the palace and it is not proper for us to see the king dishonored, we are sending this message to inform the king, ¹⁵so that a search may be made in the archives of your predecessors. In these records you will find that this city is a rebellious city, troublesome to kings and provinces, a place with a long history of sedition. That is why this city was destroyed. ¹⁶We inform the king that if this city is built and its walls are restored, you will be left with nothing in Trans-Euphrates.

¹⁷The king sent this reply:

To Rehum the commanding officer, Shimshai the secretary and the rest of their associates living in Samaria and elsewhere in Trans-Euphrates:

Greetings.

¹⁸The letter you sent us has been read and translated in my presence.

ᵃ 4 Or and troubled them as they built   ᵇ 6 Hebrew Ahasuerus   ᶜ 7 Or written in Aramaic and translated
ᵈ 7 The text of 4:8–6:18 is in Aramaic.   ᵉ 13 The meaning of the Aramaic for this clause is uncertain.

19 I issued an order and a search was made, and it was found that this city has a long history of revolt against kings and has been a place of rebellion and sedition. 20 Jerusalem has had powerful kings ruling over the whole of Trans-Euphrates, and taxes, tribute and duty were paid to them. 21 Now issue an order to these men to stop work, so that this city will not be rebuilt until I so order. 22 Be careful not to neglect this matter. Why let this threat grow, to the detriment of the royal interests?

23 As soon as the copy of the letter of King Artaxerxes was read to Rehum and Shimshai the secretary and their associates, they went immediately to the Jews in Jerusalem and compelled them by force to stop.

24 Thus the work on the house of God in Jerusalem came to a standstill until the second year of the reign of Darius king of Persia.

Tattenai's Letter to Darius

5 Now Haggai the prophet and Zechariah the prophet, a descendant of Iddo, prophesied to the Jews in Judah and Jerusalem in the name of the God of Israel, who was over them. 2 Then Zerubbabel son of Shealtiel and Joshua son of Jozadak set to work to rebuild the house of God in Jerusalem. And the prophets of God were with them, supporting them.

3 At that time Tattenai, governor of Trans-Euphrates, and Shethar-Bozenai and their associates went to them and asked, "Who authorized you to rebuild this temple and to finish it?" 4 They[a] also asked, "What are the names of those who are constructing this building?" 5 But the eye of their God was watching over the elders of the Jews, and they were not stopped until a report could go to Darius and his written reply be received.

6 This is a copy of the letter that Tattenai, governor of Trans-Euphrates, and Shethar-Bozenai and their associates, the officials of Trans-Euphrates, sent to King Darius. 7 The report they sent him read as follows:

To King Darius:

Cordial greetings.

8 The king should know that we went to the district of Judah, to the temple of the great God. The people are building it with large stones and placing the timbers in the walls. The work is being carried on with diligence and is making rapid progress under their direction.

9 We questioned the elders and asked them, "Who authorized you to rebuild this temple and to finish it?" 10 We also asked them their names, so that we could write down the names of their leaders for your information.

11 This is the answer they gave us:

"We are the servants of the God of heaven and earth, and we are rebuilding the temple that was built many years ago, one that a great king of Israel built and finished. 12 But because our ancestors angered the God of heaven, he gave them into the hands of Nebuchadnezzar the Chaldean, king of Babylon, who destroyed this temple and deported the people to Babylon.

13 "However, in the first year of Cyrus king of Babylon, King Cyrus issued a decree to rebuild this house of God. 14 He even removed from the temple[b] of Babylon the gold and silver articles of the house of God, which Nebuchadnezzar had taken from the temple in Jerusalem and brought to the temple[b] in Babylon. Then King Cyrus gave them to a man named Sheshbazzar, whom he had appointed governor, 15 and he told him, 'Take these articles and go and deposit them in the temple in Jerusalem. And rebuild the house of God on its site.'

16 "So this Sheshbazzar came and laid the foundations of the house of

a 4 See Septuagint; Aramaic We.   b 14 Or palace

God in Jerusalem. From that day to the present it has been under construction but is not yet finished."

17 Now if it pleases the king, let a search be made in the royal archives of Babylon to see if King Cyrus did in fact issue a decree to rebuild this house of God in Jerusalem. Then let the king send us his decision in this matter.

The Decree of Darius

6 King Darius then issued an order, and they searched in the archives stored in the treasury at Babylon. 2 A scroll was found in the citadel of Ecbatana in the province of Media, and this was written on it:

Memorandum:

3 In the first year of King Cyrus, the king issued a decree concerning the temple of God in Jerusalem:

Let the temple be rebuilt as a place to present sacrifices, and let its foundations be laid. It is to be sixty cubits[a] high and sixty cubits wide, 4 with three courses of large stones and one of timbers. The costs are to be paid by the royal treasury. 5 Also, the gold and silver articles of the house of God, which Nebuchadnezzar took from the temple in Jerusalem and brought to Babylon, are to be returned to their places in the temple in Jerusalem; they are to be deposited in the house of God.

6 Now then, Tattenai, governor of Trans-Euphrates, and Shethar-Bozenai and you other officials of that province, stay away from there. 7 Do not interfere with the work on this temple of God. Let the governor of the Jews and the Jewish elders rebuild this house of God on its site.

8 Moreover, I hereby decree what you are to do for these elders of the Jews in the construction of this house of God:

Their expenses are to be fully paid out of the royal treasury, from the revenues of Trans-Euphrates, so that the work will not stop. 9 Whatever is needed—young bulls, rams, male lambs for burnt offerings to the God of heaven, and wheat, salt, wine and olive oil, as requested by the priests in Jerusalem—must be given them daily without fail, 10 so that they may offer sacrifices pleasing to the God of heaven and pray for the well-being of the king and his sons.

11 Furthermore, I decree that if anyone defies this edict, a beam is to be pulled from their house and they are to be impaled on it. And for this crime their house is to be made a pile of rubble. 12 May God, who has caused his Name to dwell there, overthrow any king or people who lifts a hand to change this decree or to destroy this temple in Jerusalem.

I Darius have decreed it. Let it be carried out with diligence.

Completion and Dedication of the Temple

13 Then, because of the decree King Darius had sent, Tattenai, governor of Trans-Euphrates, and Shethar-Bozenai and their associates carried it out with diligence. 14 So the elders of the Jews continued to build and prosper under the preaching of Haggai the prophet and Zechariah, a descendant of Iddo. They finished building the temple according to the command of the God of Israel and the decrees of Cyrus, Darius and Artaxerxes, kings of Persia. 15 The temple was completed on the third day of the month Adar, in the sixth year of the reign of King Darius.

16 Then the people of Israel—the priests, the Levites and the rest of the exiles—celebrated the dedication of the house of God with joy. 17 For the dedication of this house of God they offered a hundred bulls, two hundred rams, four hundred male lambs and, as a sin offering[b] for all Israel, twelve male goats, one

---

[a] 3 That is, about 90 feet or about 27 meters   [b] 17 Or purification offering

> I spent a month at my uncle's farm during the summer, and when I came home I found out my brother had told people I had gone into drug rehab. Now it's all over school. Some people at school are actually avoiding me. Will I ever get my reputation back?   >> Justin

Dear Jordan

Dear Justin,

Rumors can be vicious. That's one reason God warns people not to gossip. This is clearly an embarrassing situation for you. But you will get your reputation back.

Did you know the people of Israel had to stop a bad rumor? The Israelites were rebuilding the temple. Their enemies wrote letters to their ruler and started a rumor saying the Israelites were rebellious and wicked (Ezra 4:11–16). The leader ordered the rebuilding to stop until the rumor was checked out. Eventually, the truth was found out and the rebuilding of the temple continued (Ezra 6:3–10). It caused trouble and stress, but the truth came out and the Israelites were found innocent of the charges.

When the truth is known about where you were, your reputation will be restored. It may take some time but things will get back to normal. Did your aunt or uncle take pictures of you on the farm? If so, ask for some to be sent to you. Take them in to show your friends the nice visit you had with your family. The truth can fly around as fast as a lie.

Jordan

for each of the tribes of Israel. ¹⁸And they installed the priests in their divisions and the Levites in their groups for the service of God at Jerusalem, according to what is written in the Book of Moses.

The Passover

¹⁹On the fourteenth day of the first month, the exiles celebrated the Passover. ²⁰The priests and Levites had purified themselves and were all ceremonially clean. The Levites slaughtered the Passover lamb for all the exiles, for their relatives the priests and for themselves. ²¹So the Israelites who had returned from the exile ate it, together with all who had separated themselves from the unclean practices of their Gentile neighbors in order to seek the LORD, the God of Israel. ²²For seven days they celebrated with joy the Festival of Unleavened Bread, because the LORD had filled them with joy by changing the attitude of the king of Assyria so that he assisted them in the work on the house of God, the God of Israel.

Ezra Comes to Jerusalem

7 After these things, during the reign of Artaxerxes king of Persia, Ezra son of Seraiah, the son of Azariah, the son of Hilkiah, ²the son of Shallum, the son of Zadok, the son of Ahitub, ³the son of Amariah, the son of Azariah, the son of Meraioth, ⁴the son of Zerahiah, the son of Uzzi, the son of Bukki, ⁵the son of Abishua, the son of Phinehas, the son of Eleazar, the son of Aaron the chief priest— ⁶this Ezra came up from Babylon. He was a teacher well versed in the Law of Moses, which the LORD, the God of Israel, had given. The king had granted him everything he asked, for the hand of the LORD his God was on him. ⁷Some of the Israelites, including priests, Levites, musicians, gatekeepers and temple servants, also came up to Jerusalem in the seventh year of King Artaxerxes.

⁸Ezra arrived in Jerusalem in the fifth month of the seventh year of the king. ⁹He had begun his journey from Babylon on the first day of the first month, and he arrived in Jerusalem on the first day of the fifth month, for the gracious hand of

his God was on him. ¹⁰For Ezra had devoted himself to the study and observance of the Law of the LORD, and to teaching its decrees and laws in Israel.

King Artaxerxes' Letter to Ezra

¹¹This is a copy of the letter King Artaxerxes had given to Ezra the priest, a teacher of the Law, a man learned in matters concerning the commands and decrees of the LORD for Israel:

¹²Artaxerxes, king of kings,

To Ezra the priest, teacher of the Law of the God of heaven:

Greetings.

¹³Now I decree that any of the Israelites in my kingdom, including priests and Levites, who volunteer to go to Jerusalem with you, may go. ¹⁴You are sent by the king and his seven advisers to inquire about Judah and Jerusalem with regard to the Law of your God, which is in your hand. ¹⁵Moreover, you are to take with you the silver and gold that the king and his advisers have freely given to the God of Israel, whose dwelling is in Jerusalem, ¹⁶together with all the silver and gold you may obtain from the province of Babylon, as well as the freewill offerings of the people and priests for the temple of their God in Jerusalem. ¹⁷With this money be sure to buy bulls, rams and male lambs, together with their grain offerings and drink offerings, and sacrifice them on the altar of the temple of your God in Jerusalem.

¹⁸You and your fellow Israelites may then do whatever seems best with the rest of the silver and gold, in accordance with the will of your God. ¹⁹Deliver to the God of Jerusalem all the articles entrusted to you for worship in the temple of your God. ²⁰And anything else needed for the temple of your God that you are responsible to supply, you may provide from the royal treasury.

²¹Now I, King Artaxerxes, decree that all the treasurers of

Trans-Euphrates are to provide with diligence whatever Ezra the priest, the teacher of the Law of the God of heaven, may ask of you— 22 up to a hundred talents[a] of silver, a hundred cors[b] of wheat, a hundred baths[c] of wine, a hundred baths[c] of olive oil, and salt without limit. 23 Whatever the God of heaven has prescribed, let it be done with diligence for the temple of the God of heaven. Why should his wrath fall on the realm of the king and of his sons? 24 You are also to know that you have no authority to impose taxes, tribute or duty on any of the priests, Levites, musicians, gatekeepers, temple servants or other workers at this house of God.

25 And you, Ezra, in accordance with the wisdom of your God, which you possess, appoint magistrates and judges to administer justice to all the people of Trans-Euphrates— all who know the laws of your God. And you are to teach any who do not know them. 26 Whoever does not obey the law of your God and the law of the king must surely be punished by death, banishment, confiscation of property, or imprisonment.[d]

27 Praise be to the LORD, the God of our ancestors, who has put it into the king's heart to bring honor to the house of the LORD in Jerusalem in this way 28 and who has extended his good favor to me before the king and his advisers and all the king's powerful officials. Because the hand of the LORD my God was on me, I took courage and gathered leaders from Israel to go up with me.

List of the Family Heads Returning With Ezra

8 These are the family heads and those registered with them who came up with me from Babylon during the reign of King Artaxerxes:

2 of the descendants of Phinehas, Gershom;

You want to be a leader? It doesn't just happen. You have to prepare yourself to be a leader. To be a leading scientist, you'd better start now to master math. To be a top athlete, you'd better practice daily. It's the same way with the spiritual. If you want to be a leader in God's kingdom, you need to follow Ezra's path. He devoted himself to studying and practicing God's Word and to teaching it to others. Leaders aren't born. People become leaders because they're dedicated to excellence in their field. Wouldn't it be great to follow Ezra's path to leadership?

{Ezra 7:10}

INSTANT ACCESS

---

of the descendants of Ithamar, Daniel;

of the descendants of David, Hattush 3 of the descendants of Shekaniah;

of the descendants of Parosh, Zechariah, and with him were registered 150 men;

4 of the descendants of Pahath-Moab, Eliehoenai son of Zerahiah, and with him 200 men;

5 of the descendants of Zattu,[e] Shekaniah son of Jahaziel, and with him 300 men;

6 of the descendants of Adin, Ebed

---

[a] 22 That is, about 3 3/4 tons or about 3.4 metric tons   [b] 22 That is, probably about 18 tons or about 16 metric tons   [c] 22 That is, about 600 gallons or about 2,200 liters   [d] 26 The text of 7:12-26 is in Aramaic.   [e] 5 Some Septuagint manuscripts (also 1 Esdras 8:32); Hebrew does not have Zattu.

son of Jonathan, and with him 50 men;

⁷of the descendants of Elam, Jeshaiah son of Athaliah, and with him 70 men;

⁸of the descendants of Shephatiah, Zebadiah son of Michael, and with him 80 men;

⁹of the descendants of Joab, Obadiah son of Jehiel, and with him 218 men;

¹⁰of the descendants of Bani,ᵃ Shelomith son of Josiphiah, and with him 160 men;

¹¹of the descendants of Bebai, Zechariah son of Bebai, and with him 28 men;

¹²of the descendants of Azgad, Johanan son of Hakkatan, and with him 110 men;

¹³of the descendants of Adonikam, the last ones, whose names were Eliphelet, Jeuel and Shemaiah, and with them 60 men;

¹⁴of the descendants of Bigvai, Uthai and Zakkur, and with them 70 men.

The Return to Jerusalem

¹⁵I assembled them at the canal that flows toward Ahava, and we camped there three days. When I checked among the people and the priests, I found no Levites there. ¹⁶So I summoned Eliezer, Ariel, Shemaiah, Elnathan, Jarib, Elnathan, Nathan, Zechariah and Meshullam, who were leaders, and Joiarib and Elnathan, who were men of learning, ¹⁷and I ordered them to go to Iddo, the leader in Kasiphia. I told them what to say to Iddo and his fellow Levites, the temple servants in Kasiphia, so that they might bring attendants to us for the house of our God. ¹⁸Because the gracious hand of our God was on us, they brought us Sherebiah, a capable man, from the descendants of Mahli son of Levi, the son of Israel, and Sherebiah's sons and brothers, 18 in all; ¹⁹and Hashabiah, together with Jeshaiah from the descendants of Merari, and his brothers and nephews, 20 in all. ²⁰They also brought 220 of the temple servants—a body that David and the officials had established to assist the Levites. All were registered by name.

²¹There, by the Ahava Canal, I proclaimed a fast, so that we might humble ourselves before our God and ask him for a safe journey for us and our children, with all our possessions. ²²I was ashamed to ask the king for soldiers and horsemen to protect us from enemies on the road, because we had told the king, "The gracious hand of our God is on everyone who looks to him, but his great anger is against all who forsake him." ²³So we fasted and petitioned our God about this, and he answered our prayer.

ᵃ 10 Some Septuagint manuscripts (also 1 Esdras 8:36); Hebrew does not have Bani.

24 Then I set apart twelve of the leading priests, namely, Sherebiah, Hashabiah and ten of their brothers, 25 and I weighed out to them the offering of silver and gold and the articles that the king, his advisers, his officials and all Israel present there had donated for the house of our God. 26 I weighed out to them 650 talents[a] of silver, silver articles weighing 100 talents,[b] 100 talents[b] of gold, 27 20 bowls of gold valued at 1,000 darics,[c] and two fine articles of polished bronze, as precious as gold.

28 I said to them, "You as well as these articles are consecrated to the LORD. The silver and gold are a freewill offering to the LORD, the God of your ancestors. 29 Guard them carefully until you weigh them out in the chambers of the house of the LORD in Jerusalem before the leading priests and the Levites and the family heads of Israel." 30 Then the priests and Levites received the silver and gold and sacred articles that had been weighed out to be taken to the house of our God in Jerusalem.

31 On the twelfth day of the first month we set out from the Ahava Canal to go to Jerusalem. The hand of our God was on us, and he protected us from enemies and bandits along the way. 32 So we arrived in Jerusalem, where we rested three days.

33 On the fourth day, in the house of our God, we weighed out the silver and gold and the sacred articles into the hands of Meremoth son of Uriah, the priest. Eleazar son of Phinehas was with him, and so were the Levites Jozabad son of Jeshua and Noadiah son of Binnui. 34 Everything was accounted for by number and weight, and the entire weight was recorded at that time.

35 Then the exiles who had returned from captivity sacrificed burnt offerings to the God of Israel: twelve bulls for all Israel, ninety-six rams, seventy-seven male lambs and, as a sin offering,[d] twelve male goats. All this was a burnt offering to the LORD. 36 They also delivered the king's orders to the royal satraps and to the governors of Trans-Euphrates, who then gave assistance to the people and to the house of God.

Ezra's Prayer About Intermarriage

9 After these things had been done, the leaders came to me and said, "The people of Israel, including the priests and the Levites, have not kept themselves separate from the neighboring peoples with their detestable practices, like those of the Canaanites, Hittites, Perizzites, Jebusites, Ammonites, Moabites, Egyptians and Amorites. 2 They have taken some of their daughters as wives for themselves and their sons, and have mingled the holy race with the peoples around them. And the leaders and officials have led the way in this unfaithfulness."

3 When I heard this, I tore my tunic and cloak, pulled hair from my head and beard and sat down appalled. 4 Then everyone who trembled at the words of the God of Israel gathered around me because of this unfaithfulness of the exiles. And I sat there appalled until the evening sacrifice.

5 Then, at the evening sacrifice, I rose from my self-abasement, with my tunic and cloak torn, and fell on my knees with my hands spread out to the LORD my God 6 and prayed:

"I am too ashamed and disgraced, my God, to lift up my face to you, because our sins are higher than our heads and our guilt has reached to the heavens. 7 From the days of our ancestors until now, our guilt has been great. Because of our sins, we and our kings and our priests have been subjected to the sword and captivity, to pillage and humiliation at the hand of foreign kings, as it is today.

8 "But now, for a brief moment, the LORD our God has been gracious in leaving us a remnant and giving us

> How important is it to have friends who are Christians? Regular friends and boyfriends? And what about more serious relationships?

>> Chloe

Dear Jordan

Dear Chloe,

Many people say they are Christians, but their walk is off the path. As you make friends, it's important to see if a person is living a life honoring God. If your friends' lives show respect for God, it makes it easier for you to do the same. There isn't anything wrong with having friends who are not Christians. The problems begin when your friends—whether they are or are not Christians—act or speak in ways that are offensive to God.

Those are the people to stay away from. If you spend all your time with people who say and do things that are offensive to God, you are on slippery ground. Try to find some people who share your interests so you can have fun together doing something worthwhile. Your life will be less stressful and you can succeed in the things that are important to you and your family.

Then as you get older, you'll have a pattern of good habits with friends. This will also help you when you want to find a husband or wife. The values of this world are not the values of God. The Bible is clear that Christians should not marry non-Christians (Ezra 9; 2 Corinthians 6:14). But marriage is for a time in the future and so should be "more serious" relationships. Being young doesn't last long. So honor God in all your relationships. He will bless you for it.

Jordan

a firm place[a] in his sanctuary, and so our God gives light to our eyes and a little relief in our bondage. [9]Though we are slaves, our God has not forsaken us in our bondage. He has shown us kindness in the sight of the kings of Persia: He has granted us new life to rebuild the house of our God and repair its ruins, and he has given us a wall of protection in Judah and Jerusalem.

[10]"But now, our God, what can we say after this? For we have forsaken the commands [11]you gave through your servants the prophets when you said: 'The land you are entering to possess is a land polluted by the corruption of its peoples. By their detestable practices they have filled it with their impurity from one end to the other. [12]Therefore, do not give your daughters in marriage to their sons or take their daughters for your sons. Do not seek a treaty of friendship with them at any time, that you may be strong and eat the good things of the land and leave it to your children as an everlasting inheritance.'

[13]"What has happened to us is a result of our evil deeds and our great guilt, and yet, our God, you have punished us less than our sins deserved and have given us a remnant like this. [14]Shall we then break your commands again and intermarry with the peoples who commit such detestable practices? Would you not be angry enough with us to destroy us, leaving us no remnant or survivor? [15]LORD, the God of Israel, you are righteous! We are left this day as a remnant. Here we are before you in our guilt, though because of it not one of us can stand in your presence."

The People's Confession of Sin

10 While Ezra was praying and confessing, weeping and throwing himself down before the house of God, a large crowd of Israelites—men, women and children—gathered around him. They too wept bitterly. [2]Then Shekaniah son of Jehiel, one of the descendants of Elam, said to Ezra, "We have been unfaithful to our God by marrying foreign women from the peoples around us. But in spite of this, there is still hope for Israel. [3]Now let us make a covenant before our God to send away all these women and their children, in accordance with the counsel of my lord and of those who fear the commands of our God. Let it be done according to the Law. [4]Rise up; this matter is in your hands. We will support you, so take courage and do it."

[5]So Ezra rose up and put the leading priests and Levites and all Israel under oath to do what had been suggested. And they took the oath. [6]Then Ezra withdrew from before the house of God and went to the room of Jehohanan son of Eliashib. While he was there, he ate no food and drank no water, because he continued to mourn over the unfaithfulness of the exiles.

[7]A proclamation was then issued throughout Judah and Jerusalem for all the exiles to assemble in Jerusalem. [8]Anyone who failed to appear within three days would forfeit all his property, in accordance with the decision of the officials and elders, and would himself be expelled from the assembly of the exiles.

[9]Within the three days, all the men of Judah and Benjamin had gathered in Jerusalem. And on the twentieth day of the ninth month, all the people were sitting in the square before the house of God, greatly distressed by the occasion and because of the rain. [10]Then Ezra the priest stood up and said to them, "You have been unfaithful; you have married foreign women, adding to Israel's guilt. [11]Now honor[a] the LORD, the God of your ancestors, and do his will. Separate yourselves from the peoples around you and from your foreign wives."

[12]The whole assembly responded with a loud voice: "You are right! We must do as you say. [13]But there are many people

<hr/>

[a] 8 Or a foothold   *[b] 11 Or Now make confession to*

R ob comes home, and his dad says, "Looks like you've got a lot of homework." "You're right," Rob says (and heads out to play soccer). "Megan, it's your turn to empty the dishwasher." "OK," Megan says (and picks up her cell phone to call Allison). Knowing you should do something, and doing it, are two different things. The people of Ezra's time set a good example. Ezra pointed out an area in which many had disobeyed God. The people not only said, "You are right," but added, "We must do as you say." Be a Christian who not only says, "You're right," but also says, "We should do that." Then do it!

{Ezra 10:12}

≫ INSTANT ACCESS

here and it is the rainy season; so we cannot stand outside. Besides, this matter cannot be taken care of in a day or two, because we have sinned greatly in this thing. 14 Let our officials act for the whole assembly. Then let everyone in our towns who has married a foreign woman come at a set time, along with the elders and judges of each town, until the fierce anger of our God in this matter is turned away from us." 15 Only Jonathan son of Asahel and Jahzeiah son of Tikvah, supported by Meshullam and Shabbethai the Levite, opposed this.

16 So the exiles did as was proposed. Ezra the priest selected men who were family heads, one from each family division, and all of them designated by name. On the first day of the tenth month they sat down to investigate the cases, 17 and by the first day of the first month they finished dealing with all the men who had married foreign women.

Those Guilty of Intermarriage

18 Among the descendants of the priests, the following had married foreign women:

From the descendants of Joshua son of Jozadak, and his brothers: Maaseiah, Eliezer, Jarib and Gedaliah. 19 (They all gave their hands in pledge to put away their wives, and for their guilt they each presented a ram from the flock as a guilt offering.)

20 From the descendants of Immer: Hanani and Zebadiah.

21 From the descendants of Harim: Maaseiah, Elijah, Shemaiah, Jehiel and Uzziah.

22 From the descendants of Pashhur: Elioenai, Maaseiah, Ishmael, Nethanel, Jozabad and Elasah.

23 Among the Levites:

Jozabad, Shimei, Kelaiah (that is, Kelita), Pethahiah, Judah and Eliezer.

24 From the musicians:
Eliashib.
From the gatekeepers:
Shallum, Telem and Uri.

25 And among the other Israelites:

From the descendants of Parosh: Ramiah, Izziah, Malkijah, Mijamin, Eleazar, Malkijah and Benaiah.

26 From the descendants of Elam: Mattaniah, Zechariah, Jehiel, Abdi, Jeremoth and Elijah.

27 From the descendants of Zattu: Elioenai, Eliashib, Mattaniah, Jeremoth, Zabad and Aziza.

28 From the descendants of Bebai:

Jehohanan, Hananiah, Zabbai and Athlai.

29 From the descendants of Bani:
Meshullam, Malluk, Adaiah, Jashub, Sheal and Jeremoth.

30 From the descendants of Pahath-Moab:
Adna, Kelal, Benaiah, Maaseiah, Mattaniah, Bezalel, Binnui and Manasseh.

31 From the descendants of Harim:
Eliezer, Ishijah, Malkijah, Shemaiah, Shimeon, 32 Benjamin, Malluk and Shemariah.

33 From the descendants of Hashum:
Mattenai, Mattattah, Zabad, Eliphelet, Jeremai, Manasseh and Shimei.

34 From the descendants of Bani:
Maadai, Amram, Uel, 35 Benaiah, Bedeiah, Keluhi, 36 Vaniah, Meremoth, Eliashib, 37 Mattaniah, Mattenai and Jaasu.

38 From the descendants of Binnui:[a]
Shimei, 39 Shelemiah, Nathan, Adaiah, 40 Maknadebai, Shashai, Sharai, 41 Azarel, Shelemiah, Shemariah, 42 Shallum, Amariah and Joseph.

43 From the descendants of Nebo:
Jeiel, Mattithiah, Zabad, Zebina, Jaddai, Joel and Benaiah.

44 All these had married foreign women, and some of them had children by these wives.[b]

---

[a] 37,38 See Septuagint (also 1 Esdras 9:34); Hebrew *Jaasu* 38 *and Bani and Binnui,*   [b] 44 Or *and they sent them away with their children*

NEHEMIAH

Courage.

So many things call for courage. Speaking up in class. Saying no when friends pressure you to do something wrong. Making a decision and sticking with it when things don't turn out as you expect.

This book is about one man's courage. Nehemiah was a high official in the Persian empire. He was so upset when he heard of poverty and weakness in his homeland that he asked to be made governor of that tiny province. There Nehemiah battled hostile neighbors, threats, and the indifference of his own people. Nehemiah's success reminds you that faith plus courage wins.

>>**FEARFUL NEHEMIAH SPEAKS UP**
Prays, then speaks. See Nehemiah 2:1–8
>>**LOCALS PLOT TO STOP REBUILDING**
Story in Nehemiah 6
>>**ALL STAND FOR READING OF GOD'S LAW**
Day-long Bible study report, Nehemiah 8
>>**NEHEMIAH INSTITUTES REFORMS**
Changes explained in Nehemiah 13

preview

Nehemiah governs Judah from 444 to 433 B.C.

In Bible times, no walls mean a city gets no respect.

This is one of the few Old Testament books written in the first person, "I."

As Nehemiah governs Judah, the Parthenon is built in Athens.
Athens and Sparta agree to a 30-year truce.

Nehemiah's Prayer

1 The words of Nehemiah son of Hakaliah:

In the month of Kislev in the twentieth year, while I was in the citadel of Susa, [2]Hanani, one of my brothers, came from Judah with some other men, and I questioned them about the Jewish remnant that had survived the exile, and also about Jerusalem.

[3]They said to me, "Those who survived the exile and are back in the province are in great trouble and disgrace. The wall of Jerusalem is broken down, and its gates have been burned with fire."

[4]When I heard these things, I sat down and wept. For some days I mourned and fasted and prayed before the God of heaven. [5]Then I said:

"LORD, the God of heaven, the great and awesome God, who keeps his covenant of love with those who love him and keep his commandments, [6]let your ear be attentive and your eyes open to hear the prayer your servant is praying before you day and night for your servants, the people of Israel. I confess the sins we Israelites, including myself and my father's family, have committed against you. [7]We have acted very wickedly toward you. We have not obeyed the commands, decrees and laws you gave your servant Moses.

[8]"Remember the instruction you gave your servant Moses, saying, 'If you are unfaithful, I will scatter you among the nations, [9]but if you return to me and obey my commands, then even if your exiled people are at the farthest horizon, I will gather them from there and bring them to the place I have chosen as a dwelling for my Name.'

[10]"They are your servants and your people, whom you redeemed by your great strength and your mighty hand. [11]Lord, let your ear be attentive to the prayer of this your servant and to the prayer of your servants who delight in revering your name.

>> INSTANT ACCESS

Martin Luther once said, "I've got so much work to do today, I'd better spend two hours in prayer instead of one." Got tons of homework? Feel overwhelmed and rushed? Maybe the best way to get everything done is to stop and pray. Nehemiah was a man of action. He became governor of Judah and quickly got everyone to work building the walls of Jerusalem. But the first thing Nehemiah did "for some days" was to mourn and fast and pray (Nehemiah 1:4). If you're going to get any job done well, you need God's help. The time you take to pray before you act isn't wasted. It's the most important time of all.

{Nehemiah 1:1-11}

Give your servant success today by granting him favor in the presence of this man."

I was cupbearer to the king.

Artaxerxes Sends Nehemiah to Jerusalem

2 In the month of Nisan in the twentieth year of King Artaxerxes, when wine was brought for him, I took the wine and gave it to the king. I had not been sad in his presence before, [2]so the king asked me, "Why does your face look so sad when you are not ill? This can be nothing but sadness of heart."

I was very much afraid, [3] but I said to the king, "May the king live forever! Why should my face not look sad when the city where my ancestors are buried lies in ruins, and its gates have been destroyed by fire?"

[4] The king said to me, "What is it you want?"

Then I prayed to the God of heaven, [5] and I answered the king, "If it pleases the king and if your servant has found favor in his sight, let him send me to the city in Judah where my ancestors are buried so that I can rebuild it."

[6] Then the king, with the queen sitting beside him, asked me, "How long will your journey take, and when will you get back?" It pleased the king to send me; so I set a time.

[7] I also said to him, "If it pleases the king, may I have letters to the governors of Trans-Euphrates, so that they will provide me safe-conduct until I arrive in Judah? [8] And may I have a letter to Asaph, keeper of the royal park, so he will give me timber to make beams for the gates of the citadel by the temple and for the city wall and for the residence I will occupy?" And because the gracious hand of my God was on me, the king granted my requests. [9] So I went to the governors of Trans-Euphrates and gave them the king's letters. The king had also sent army officers and cavalry with me.

[10] When Sanballat the Horonite and Tobiah the Ammonite official heard about this, they were very much disturbed that someone had come to promote the welfare of the Israelites.

Nehemiah Inspects Jerusalem's Walls

[11] I went to Jerusalem, and after staying there three days [12] I set out during the night with a few others. I had not told anyone what my God had put in my heart to do for Jerusalem. There were no mounts with me except the one I was riding on.

[13] By night I went out through the Valley Gate toward the Jackal[a] Well and the Dung Gate, examining the walls of Jerusalem, which had been broken down, and its gates, which had been destroyed by fire. [14] Then I moved on toward the Fountain Gate and the King's Pool, but there was not enough room for my mount to get through; [15] so I went up the valley by night, examining the wall. Finally, I turned back and reentered through the Valley Gate. [16] The officials did not know where I had gone or what I was doing, because as yet I had said nothing to the Jews or the priests or nobles or officials or any others who would be doing the work.

The God of heaven will give us success.
Nehemiah 2:20

[17] Then I said to them, "You see the trouble we are in: Jerusalem lies in ruins, and its gates have been burned with fire. Come, let us rebuild the wall of Jerusalem, and we will no longer be in disgrace." [18] I also told them about the gracious hand of my God on me and what the king had said to me.

They replied, "Let us start rebuilding." So they began this good work.

[19] But when Sanballat the Horonite, Tobiah the Ammonite official and Geshem the Arab heard about it, they mocked and ridiculed us. "What is this you are doing?" they asked. "Are you rebelling against the king?"

[20] I answered them by saying, "The God of heaven will give us success. We his servants will start rebuilding, but as for you, you have no share in Jerusalem or any claim or historic right to it."

Builders of the Wall

3 Eliashib the high priest and his fellow priests went to work and rebuilt the

---

Sheep Gate. They dedicated it and set its doors in place, building as far as the Tower of the Hundred, which they dedicated, and as far as the Tower of Hananel. [2] The men of Jericho built the adjoining section, and Zakkur son of Imri built next to them.

[3] The Fish Gate was rebuilt by the sons of Hassenaah. They laid its beams and put its doors and bolts and bars in place. [4] Meremoth son of Uriah, the son of Hakkoz, repaired the next section. Next to him Meshullam son of Berekiah, the son of Meshezabel, made repairs, and next to him Zadok son of Baana also made repairs. [5] The next section was repaired by the men of Tekoa, but their nobles would not put their shoulders to the work under their supervisors.[a]

[6] The Jeshanah[b] Gate was repaired by Joiada son of Paseah and Meshullam son of Besodeiah. They laid its beams and put its doors with their bolts and bars in place. [7] Next to them, repairs were made by men from Gibeon and Mizpah—Melatiah of Gibeon and Jadon of Meronoth—places under the authority of the governor of Trans-Euphrates. [8] Uzziel son of Harhaiah, one of the goldsmiths, repaired the next section; and Hananiah, one of the perfume-makers, made repairs next to that. They restored Jerusalem as far as the Broad Wall. [9] Rephaiah son of Hur, ruler of a half-district of Jerusalem, repaired the next section. [10] Adjoining this, Jedaiah son of Harumaph made repairs opposite his house, and Hattush son of Hashabneiah made repairs next to him. [11] Malkijah son of Harim and Hasshub son of Pahath-Moab repaired another section and the Tower of the Ovens. [12] Shallum son of Hallohesh, ruler of a half-district of Jerusalem, repaired the next section with the help of his daughters.

[13] The Valley Gate was repaired by Hanun and the residents of Zanoah. They rebuilt it and put its doors with their bolts and bars in place. They also repaired a thousand cubits[c] of the wall as far as the Dung Gate.

[14] The Dung Gate was repaired by Malkijah son of Rekab, ruler of the district of Beth Hakkerem. He rebuilt it and put its doors with their bolts and bars in place.

[15] The Fountain Gate was repaired by Shallun son of Kol-Hozeh, ruler of the district of Mizpah. He rebuilt it, roofing it over and putting its doors and bolts and bars in place. He also repaired the wall of the Pool of Siloam,[d] by the King's Garden, as far as the steps going down from the City of David. [16] Beyond him, Nehemiah son of Azbuk, ruler of a half-district of Beth Zur, made repairs up to a point opposite the tombs[e] of David, as far as the artificial pool and the House of the Heroes.

[17] Next to him, the repairs were made by the Levites under Rehum son of Bani. Beside him, Hashabiah, ruler of half the district of Keilah, carried out repairs for his district. [18] Next to him, the repairs were made by their fellow Levites under Binnui[f] son of Henadad, ruler of the other half-district of Keilah. [19] Next to him, Ezer

Nehemiah 3

Q: How long did it take to rebuild the walls of Jerusalem?

BONUS: Why could only half the men work at one time?

Answers on next page

---

[a] 5 Or *their Lord* or *the governor*   [b] 6 Or *Old*
[c] 13 That is, about 1,500 feet or about 450 meters
[d] 15 Hebrew *Shelah*, a variant of *Shiloah*, that is, Siloam
[e] 16 Hebrew; Septuagint, some Vulgate manuscripts and Syriac *tomb*   [f] 18 Two Hebrew manuscripts and Syriac (see also Septuagint and verse 24); most Hebrew manuscripts *Bavvai*

son of Jeshua, ruler of Mizpah, repaired another section, from a point facing the ascent to the armory as far as the angle of the wall. 20 Next to him, Baruch son of Zabbai zealously repaired another section, from the angle to the entrance of the house of Eliashib the high priest. 21 Next to him, Meremoth son of Uriah, the son of Hakkoz, repaired another section, from the entrance of Eliashib's house to the end of it.

22 The repairs next to him were made by the priests from the surrounding region. 23 Beyond them, Benjamin and Hasshub made repairs in front of their house; and next to them, Azariah son of Maaseiah, the son of Ananiah, made repairs beside his house. 24 Next to him, Binnui son of Henadad repaired another section, from Azariah's house to the angle and the corner, 25 and Palal son of Uzai worked opposite the angle and the tower projecting from the upper palace near the court of the guard. Next to him, Pedaiah son of Parosh 26 and the temple servants living on the hill of Ophel made repairs up to a point opposite the Water Gate toward the east and the projecting tower. 27 Next to them, the men of Tekoa repaired another section, from the great projecting tower to the wall of Ophel.

28 Above the Horse Gate, the priests made repairs, each in front of his own house. 29 Next to them, Zadok son of Immer made repairs opposite his house. Next to him, Shemaiah son of Shekaniah, the guard at the East Gate, made repairs. 30 Next to him, Hananiah son of Shelemiah, and Hanun, the sixth son of Zalaph, repaired another section. Next to them, Meshullam son of Berekiah made repairs opposite his living quarters. 31 Next to him, Malkijah, one of the goldsmiths, made repairs as far as the house of the temple servants and the merchants, opposite the Inspection Gate, and as far as the room above the corner; 32 and between the room above the corner and the Sheep Gate the goldsmiths and merchants made repairs.

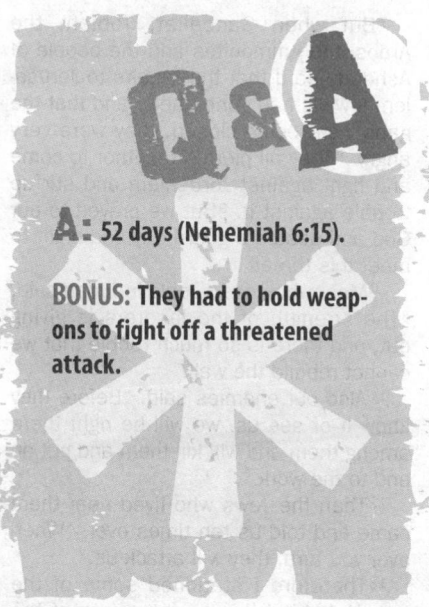

A: 52 days (Nehemiah 6:15).

BONUS: They had to hold weapons to fight off a threatened attack.

Opposition to the Rebuilding

4 [a] When Sanballat heard that we were rebuilding the wall, he became angry and was greatly incensed. He ridiculed the Jews, 2 and in the presence of his associates and the army of Samaria, he said, "What are those feeble Jews doing? Will they restore their wall? Will they offer sacrifices? Will they finish in a day? Can they bring the stones back to life from those heaps of rubble—burned as they are?"

3 Tobiah the Ammonite, who was at his side, said, "What they are building—even a fox climbing up on it would break down their wall of stones!"

4 Hear us, our God, for we are despised. Turn their insults back on their own heads. Give them over as plunder in a land of captivity. 5 Do not cover up their guilt or blot out their sins from your sight, for they have thrown insults in the face of [b] the builders.

6 So we rebuilt the wall till all of it reached half its height, for the people worked with all their heart.

---

[a] In Hebrew texts 4:1-6 is numbered 3:33-38, and 4:7-23 is numbered 4:1-17.   [b] 5 Or *have aroused your anger before*

7 But when Sanballat, Tobiah, the Arabs, the Ammonites and the people of Ashdod heard that the repairs to Jerusalem's walls had gone ahead and that the gaps were being closed, they were very angry. 8 They all plotted together to come and fight against Jerusalem and stir up trouble against it. 9 But we prayed to our God and posted a guard day and night to meet this threat.

10 Meanwhile, the people in Judah said, "The strength of the laborers is giving out, and there is so much rubble that we cannot rebuild the wall."

11 Also our enemies said, "Before they know it or see us, we will be right there among them and will kill them and put an end to the work."

12 Then the Jews who lived near them came and told us ten times over, "Wherever you turn, they will attack us."

13 Therefore I stationed some of the people behind the lowest points of the wall at the exposed places, posting them by families, with their swords, spears and bows. 14 After I looked things over, I stood up and said to the nobles, the officials and the rest of the people, "Don't be afraid of them. Remember the Lord, who is great and awesome, and fight for your families, your sons and your daughters, your wives and your homes."

15 When our enemies heard that we were aware of their plot and that God had frustrated it, we all returned to the wall, each to our own work.

16 From that day on, half of my men did the work, while the other half were equipped with spears, shields, bows and armor. The officers posted themselves behind all the people of Judah 17 who were building the wall. Those who carried materials did their work with one hand and held a weapon in the other, 18 and each of the builders wore his sword at his side as he worked. But the man who sounded the trumpet stayed with me.

19 Then I said to the nobles, the officials and the rest of the people, "The work is extensive and spread out, and we are widely separated from each other

along the wall. 20 Wherever you hear the sound of the trumpet, join us there. Our God will fight for us!"

21 So we continued the work with half the men holding spears, from the first light of dawn till the stars came out. 22 At that time I also said to the people, "Have every man and his helper stay inside Jerusalem at night, so they can serve us as guards by night and as workers by day." 23 Neither I nor my brothers nor my men nor the guards with me took off our clothes; each had his weapon, even when he went for water.[a]

Nehemiah Helps the Poor

5 Now the men and their wives raised a great outcry against their fellow Jews. 2 Some were saying, "We and our sons and daughters are numerous; in order for us to eat and stay alive, we must get grain."

3 Others were saying, "We are mortgaging our fields, our vineyards and our homes to get grain during the famine."

4 Still others were saying, "We have had to borrow money to pay the king's tax on our fields and vineyards. 5 Although we are of the same flesh and blood as our fellow Jews and though our children are as good as theirs, yet we have to subject our sons and daughters to slavery. Some of our daughters have already been enslaved, but we are powerless, because our fields and our vineyards belong to others."

6 When I heard their outcry and these charges, I was very angry. 7 I pondered them in my mind and then accused the nobles and officials. I told them, "You are charging your own people interest!" So I called together a large meeting to deal with them 8 and said: "As far as possible, we have bought back our fellow Jews who were sold to the Gentiles. Now you are selling your own people, only for them to be sold back to us!" They kept quiet, because they could find nothing to say.

9 So I continued, "What you are doing is not right. Shouldn't you walk in the fear of our God to avoid the reproach of our

---

a 23 The meaning of the Hebrew for this clause is uncertain.

Gentile enemies? ¹⁰I and my brothers and my men are also lending the people money and grain. But let us stop charging interest! ¹¹Give back to them immediately their fields, vineyards, olive groves and houses, and also the interest you are charging them—one percent of the money, grain, new wine and olive oil."

¹²"We will give it back," they said. "And we will not demand anything more from them. We will do as you say."

Then I summoned the priests and made the nobles and officials take an oath to do what they had promised. ¹³I also shook out the folds of my robe and said, "In this way may God shake out of their house and possessions anyone who does not keep this promise. So may such a person be shaken out and emptied!"

At this the whole assembly said, "Amen," and praised the LORD. And the people did as they had promised.

¹⁴Moreover, from the twentieth year of King Artaxerxes, when I was appointed to be their governor in the land of Judah, until his thirty-second year—twelve years—neither I nor my brothers ate the food allotted to the governor. ¹⁵But the earlier governors—those preceding me—placed a heavy burden on the people and took forty shekels*ᵃ* of silver from them in addition to food and wine. Their assistants also lorded it over the people. But out of reverence for God I did not act like that. ¹⁶Instead, I devoted myself to the work on this wall. All my men were assembled there for the work; we*ᵇ* did not acquire any land.

¹⁷Furthermore, a hundred and fifty Jews and officials ate at my table, as well as those who came to us from the surrounding nations. ¹⁸Each day one ox, six choice sheep and some poultry were prepared for me, and every ten days an abundant supply of wine of all kinds. In spite of all this, I never demanded the food allotted to the governor, because the demands were heavy on these people.

¹⁹Remember me with favor, my God, for all I have done for these people.

Further Opposition to the Rebuilding

6 When word came to Sanballat, Tobiah, Geshem the Arab and the rest of our enemies that I had rebuilt the wall and not a gap was left in it—though up to that time I had not set the doors in the gates— ²Sanballat and Geshem sent me this message: "Come, let us meet together in one of the villages*ᶜ* on the plain of Ono."

But they were scheming to harm me; ³so I sent messengers to them with this reply: "I am carrying on a great project and cannot go down. Why should the work stop while I leave it and go down to you?" ⁴Four times they sent me the same message, and each time I gave them the same answer.

⁵Then, the fifth time, Sanballat sent his aide to me with the same message, and in his hand was an unsealed letter ⁶in which was written:

"It is reported among the nations—and Geshem*ᵈ* says it is true—that you and the Jews are plotting to revolt, and therefore you are building the wall. Moreover, according to these reports you are about to become their king ⁷and have even appointed prophets to make this proclamation about you in Jerusalem: 'There is a king in Judah!' Now this report will get back to the king; so come, let us meet together."

⁸I sent him this reply: "Nothing like what you are saying is happening; you are just making it up out of your head."

⁹They were all trying to frighten us, thinking, "Their hands will get too weak for the work, and it will not be completed."

But I prayed, "Now strengthen my hands."

¹⁰One day I went to the house of Shemaiah son of Delaiah, the son of Mehetabel, who was shut in at his home. He said, "Let us meet in the house of God, inside the temple, and let us close the temple

doors, because men are coming to kill you—by night they are coming to kill you."

¹¹But I said, "Should a man like me run away? Or should someone like me go into the temple to save his life? I will not go!" ¹²I realized that God had not sent him, but that he had prophesied against me because Tobiah and Sanballat had hired him. ¹³He had been hired to intimidate me so that I would commit a sin by doing this, and then they would give me a bad name to discredit me.

¹⁴Remember Tobiah and Sanballat, my God, because of what they have done; remember also the prophet Noadiah and how she and the rest of the prophets have been trying to intimidate me. ¹⁵So the wall was completed on the twenty-fifth of Elul, in fifty-two days.

Opposition to the Completed Wall

¹⁶When all our enemies heard about this, all the surrounding nations were afraid and lost their self-confidence, because they realized that this work had been done with the help of our God.

¹⁷Also, in those days the nobles of Judah were sending many letters to Tobiah, and replies from Tobiah kept coming to them. ¹⁸For many in Judah were under oath to him, since he was son-in-law to Shekaniah son of Arah, and his son Jehohanan had married the daughter of Meshullam son of Berekiah. ¹⁹Moreover, they kept reporting to me his good deeds and then telling him what I said. And Tobiah sent letters to intimidate me.

7 After the wall had been rebuilt and I had set the doors in place, the gatekeepers, the musicians and the Levites were appointed. ²I put in charge of Jerusalem my brother Hanani, along with Hananiah the commander of the citadel, because he was a man of integrity and feared God more than most people do. ³I said to them, "The gates of Jerusalem are not to be opened until the sun is hot. While the gatekeepers are still on duty, have them shut the doors and bar them. Also appoint residents of Jerusalem as guards, some at their posts and some near their own houses."

INSTANT ACCESS

Have you ever looked in the mirror and thought to yourself, "I am so ugly"? Or have you done something at school and later in the day thought, "I'm so useless"? Most people, both adults and teens, at times have trouble dealing with their self-image. Nehemiah had a strong, positive self-image. He wasn't about to be frightened into doing something he knew was wrong. Wouldn't it be great to have such a strong self-image that you would do what's right no matter what? Nehemiah wasn't born with a strong self-image. He developed it by making right choices. If you want a strong, positive self-image, you can build one the same way.

{Nehemiah 6:11}

The List of the Exiles Who Returned

⁴Now the city was large and spacious, but there were few people in it, and the houses had not yet been rebuilt. ⁵So my God put it into my heart to assemble the nobles, the officials and the common people for registration by families. I found the genealogical record of those who had been the first to return. This is what I found written there:

6These are the people of the province who came up from the captivity of the exiles whom Nebuchadnezzar king of Babylon had taken captive (they returned to Jerusalem and Judah, each to his own town, 7in company with Zerubbabel, Joshua, Nehemiah, Azariah, Raamiah, Nahamani, Mordecai, Bilshan, Mispereth, Bigvai, Nehum and Baanah):

The list of the men of Israel:

8the descendants of Parosh	2,172
9of Shephatiah	372
10of Arah	652
11of Pahath-Moab (through the line of Jeshua and Joab)	2,818
12of Elam	1,254
13of Zattu	845
14of Zakkai	760
15of Binnui	648
16of Bebai	628
17of Azgad	2,322
18of Adonikam	667
19of Bigvai	2,067
20of Adin	655
21of Ater (through Hezekiah)	98
22of Hashum	328
23of Bezai	324
24of Hariph	112
25of Gibeon	95
26the men of Bethlehem and Netophah	188
27of Anathoth	128
28of Beth Azmaveth	42
29of Kiriath Jearim, Kephirah and Beeroth	743
30of Ramah and Geba	621
31of Mikmash	122
32of Bethel and Ai	123
33of the other Nebo	52
34of the other Elam	1,254
35of Harim	320
36of Jericho	345
37of Lod, Hadid and Ono	721
38of Senaah	3,930

39The priests:

the descendants of Jedaiah (through the family of Jeshua)	973
40of Immer	1,052
41of Pashhur	1,247
42of Harim	1,017

43The Levites:

the descendants of Jeshua (through Kadmiel through the line of Hodaviah)	74

44The musicians:

the descendants of Asaph	148

45The gatekeepers:

the descendants of Shallum, Ater, Talmon, Akkub, Hatita and Shobai	138

46The temple servants:

the descendants of
Ziha, Hasupha, Tabbaoth,
47Keros, Sia, Padon,
48Lebana, Hagaba, Shalmai,
49Hanan, Giddel, Gahar,
50Reaiah, Rezin, Nekoda,
51Gazzam, Uzza, Paseah,
52Besai, Meunim, Nephusim,
53Bakbuk, Hakupha, Harhur,
54Bazluth, Mehida, Harsha,
55Barkos, Sisera, Temah,
56Neziah and Hatipha

57The descendants of the servants of Solomon:

the descendants of
Sotai, Sophereth, Perida,
58Jaala, Darkon, Giddel,
59Shephatiah, Hattil,
Pokereth-Hazzebaim and Amon

60The temple servants and the descendants of the servants of Solomon	392

61The following came up from the towns of Tel Melah, Tel Harsha, Kerub, Addon and Immer, but they could not show that their families were descended from Israel:

62the descendants of Delaiah, Tobiah and Nekoda	642

63And from among the priests:

the descendants of
Hobaiah, Hakkoz and Barzillai
(a man who had married

a daughter of Barzillai the Gileadite and was called by that name).

⁶⁴These searched for their family records, but they could not find them and so were excluded from the priesthood as unclean. ⁶⁵The governor, therefore, ordered them not to eat any of the most sacred food until there should be a priest ministering with the Urim and Thummim.

⁶⁶The whole company numbered 42,360, ⁶⁷besides their 7,337 male and female slaves; and they also had 245 male and female singers. ⁶⁸There were 736 horses, 245 mules,ᵃ ⁶⁹435 camels and 6,720 donkeys.

⁷⁰Some of the heads of the families contributed to the work. The governor gave to the treasury 1,000 daricsᵇ of gold, 50 bowls and 530 garments for priests. ⁷¹Some of the heads of the families gave to the treasury for the work 20,000 daricsᶜ of gold and 2,200 minasᵈ of silver. ⁷²The total given by the rest of the people was 20,000 darics of gold, 2,000 minasᵉ of silver and 67 garments for priests.

⁷³The priests, the Levites, the gatekeepers, the musicians and the temple servants, along with certain of the people and the rest of the Israelites, settled in their own towns.

Ezra Reads the Law

When the seventh month came and the Israelites had settled in their towns, **8** ¹all the people came together as one in the square before the Water Gate. They told Ezra the teacher of the Law to bring out the Book of the Law of Moses, which the LORD had commanded for Israel.

²So on the first day of the seventh month Ezra the priest brought the Law before the assembly, which was made up of men and women and all who were able to understand. ³He read it aloud from daybreak till noon as he faced the square before the Water Gate in the presence of the men, women and others who could understand. And all the people listened attentively to the Book of the Law.

⁴Ezra the teacher of the Law stood on a high wooden platform built for the occasion. Beside him on his right stood Mattithiah, Shema, Anaiah, Uriah, Hilkiah and Maaseiah; and on his left were Pedaiah, Mishael, Malkijah, Hashum, Hashbaddanah, Zechariah and Meshullam.

⁵Ezra opened the book. All the people could see him because he was standing above them; and as he opened it, the people all stood up. ⁶Ezra praised the

---

ᵃ 68 Some Hebrew manuscripts (see also Ezra 2:66); most Hebrew manuscripts do not have this verse.   ᵇ 70 That is, about 19 pounds or about 8.4 kilograms   ᶜ 71 That is, about 375 pounds or about 170 kilograms; also in verse 72   ᵈ 71 That is, about 1 1/3 tons or about 1.2 metric tons   ᵉ 72 That is, about 1 1/4 tons or about 1.1 metric tons

PANORAMA

Courage.

This book is about one man's courage. Nehemiah was a high official in the Persian Empire. He was so upset when he heard of poverty and weakness in his homeland that he asked to be made governor of that tiny province. Nehemiah's success reminds you that faith plus courage wins.

{NEHEMIAH}

LORD, the great God; and all the people lifted their hands and responded, "Amen! Amen!" Then they bowed down and worshiped the LORD with their faces to the ground.

7 The Levites—Jeshua, Bani, Sherebiah, Jamin, Akkub, Shabbethai, Hodiah, Maaseiah, Kelita, Azariah, Jozabad, Hanan and Pelaiah—instructed the people in the Law while the people were standing there. 8 They read from the Book of the Law of God, making it clear[a] and giving the meaning so that the people understood what was being read.

9 Then Nehemiah the governor, Ezra the priest and teacher of the Law, and the Levites who were instructing the people said to them all, "This day is holy to the LORD your God. Do not mourn or weep." For all the people had been weeping as they listened to the words of the Law.

10 Nehemiah said, "Go and enjoy choice food and sweet drinks, and send some to those who have nothing prepared. This day is holy to our Lord. Do not grieve, for the joy of the LORD is your strength."

11 The Levites calmed all the people, saying, "Be still, for this is a holy day. Do not grieve."

12 Then all the people went away to eat and drink, to send portions of food and to celebrate with great joy, because they now understood the words that had been made known to them.

13 On the second day of the month, the heads of all the families, along with the priests and the Levites, gathered around Ezra the teacher to give attention to the words of the Law. 14 They found written in the Law, which the LORD had commanded through Moses, that the Israelites were to live in temporary shelters during the festival of the seventh month 15 and that they should proclaim this word and spread it throughout their towns and in Jerusalem: "Go out into the hill country and bring back branches from olive and wild olive trees, and from myrtles, palms and shade trees, to make temporary shelters"—as it is written.[b]

16 So the people went out and brought back branches and built themselves temporary shelters on their own roofs, in their courtyards, in the courts of the house of God and in the square by the Water Gate and the one by the Gate of Ephraim. 17 The whole company that had returned from exile built temporary shelters and lived in them. From the days of Joshua son of Nun until that day, the Israelites had not celebrated it like this. And their joy was very great.

18 Day after day, from the first day to the last, Ezra read from the Book of the Law of God. They celebrated the festival for seven days, and on the eighth day, in accordance with the regulation, there was an assembly.

The Israelites Confess Their Sins

9 On the twenty-fourth day of the same month, the Israelites gathered together, fasting and wearing sackcloth and putting dust on their heads. 2 Those of Israelite descent had separated themselves from all foreigners. They stood in their places and confessed their sins and the sins of their ancestors. 3 They stood where they were and read from the Book of the Law of the LORD their God for a quarter of the day, and spent another quarter in confession and in worshiping the LORD their God. 4 Standing on the stairs of the Levites were Jeshua, Bani, Kadmiel, Shebaniah, Bunni, Sherebiah, Bani and Kenani. They cried out with loud voices to the LORD their God. 5 And the Levites—Jeshua, Kadmiel, Bani, Hashabneiah, Sherebiah, Hodiah, Shebaniah and Pethahiah—said: "Stand up and praise the LORD your God, who is from everlasting to everlasting.[c]"

"Blessed be your glorious name, and may it be exalted above all blessing and praise. 6 You alone are the LORD. You made the heavens, even the highest heavens, and all their starry host, the earth and all that is on it, the seas and all that is in them. You give life to everything,

---

a 8 Or God, translating it   b 15 See Lev. 23:37-40.   c 5 Or God for ever and ever

and the multitudes of heaven worship you.

7 "You are the LORD God, who chose Abram and brought him out of Ur of the Chaldeans and named him Abraham. 8 You found his heart faithful to you, and you made a covenant with him to give to his descendants the land of the Canaanites, Hittites, Amorites, Perizzites, Jebusites and Girgashites. You have kept your promise because you are righteous.

9 "You saw the suffering of our ancestors in Egypt; you heard their cry at the Red Sea.[a] 10 You sent signs and wonders against Pharaoh, against all his officials and all the people of his land, for you knew how arrogantly the Egyptians treated them. You made a name for yourself, which remains to this day. 11 You divided the sea before them, so that they passed through it on dry ground, but you hurled their pursuers into the depths, like a stone into mighty waters. 12 By day you led them with a pillar of cloud, and by night with a pillar of fire to give them light on the way they were to take.

13 "You came down on Mount Sinai; you spoke to them from heaven. You gave them regulations and laws that are just and right, and decrees and commands that are good. 14 You made known to them your holy Sabbath and gave them commands, decrees and laws through your servant Moses. 15 In their hunger you gave them bread from heaven and in their thirst you brought them water from the rock; you told them to go in and take possession of the land you had sworn with uplifted hand to give them.

16 "But they, our ancestors, became arrogant and stiff-necked, and they did not obey your commands. 17 They refused to listen and failed to remember the miracles you performed among them. They became stiff-necked and in their rebellion ap-

›› INSTANT ACCESS

How would you describe a good time? What would you do? Think about it for a minute—what's the most fun thing you can think of to do? Fun! Just because you're a Christian doesn't mean you aren't supposed to have fun. Sure there are some activities you shouldn't participate in, but there are plenty of things you *can* do. Nehemiah told his people, "Go and enjoy choice food and sweet drinks." Time to party! Have a good time and enjoy yourselves, for "this day is sacred to our LORD." Don't ever apologize for having a good time. God has given you life. Celebrate it, and enjoy God's good gifts.

{Nehemiah 8:10}

pointed a leader in order to return to their slavery. But you are a forgiving God, gracious and compassionate, slow to anger and abounding in love. Therefore you did not desert them, 18 even when they cast for themselves an image of a calf and said, 'This is your god, who brought you up out of Egypt,' or when they committed awful blasphemies.

19 "Because of your great compassion you did not abandon them in the

---

a 9 Or the Sea of Reeds

wilderness. By day the pillar of cloud did not fail to guide them on their path, nor the pillar of fire by night to shine on the way they were to take. 20 You gave your good Spirit to instruct them. You did not withhold your manna from their mouths, and you gave them water for their thirst. 21 For forty years you sustained them in the wilderness; they lacked nothing, their clothes did not wear out nor did their feet become swollen.

22 "You gave them kingdoms and nations, allotting to them even the remotest frontiers. They took over the country of Sihon[a] king of Heshbon and the country of Og king of Bashan. 23 You made their children as numerous as the stars in the sky, and you brought them into the land that you told their parents to enter and possess. 24 Their children went in and took possession of the land. You subdued before them the Canaanites, who lived in the land; you gave the Canaanites into their hands, along with their kings and the peoples of the land, to deal with them as they pleased. 25 They captured fortified cities and fertile land; they took possession of houses filled with all kinds of good things, wells already dug, vineyards, olive groves and fruit trees in abundance. They ate to the full and were well-nourished; they reveled in your great goodness.

26 "But they were disobedient and rebelled against you; they turned their backs on your law. They killed your prophets, who had warned them in order to turn them back to you; they committed awful blasphemies. 27 So you delivered them into the hands of their enemies, who oppressed them. But when they were oppressed they cried out to you. From heaven you heard them, and in your great compassion you gave them deliverers, who rescued them from the hand of their enemies.

28 "But as soon as they were at rest, they again did what was evil in your sight. Then you abandoned them to the hand of their enemies so that they ruled over them. And when they cried out to you again, you heard from heaven, and in your compassion you delivered them time after time.

29 "You warned them in order to turn them back to your law, but they became arrogant and disobeyed your commands. They sinned against your ordinances, of which you said, 'The person who obeys them will live by them.' Stubbornly they turned their backs on you, became stiff-necked and refused to listen. 30 For many years you were patient with them. By your Spirit you warned them through your prophets. Yet they paid no attention, so you gave them into the hands of the neighboring peoples. 31 But in your great mercy you did not put an end to them or abandon them, for you are a gracious and merciful God.

32 "Now therefore, our God, the great God, mighty and awesome, who keeps his covenant of love, do not let all this hardship seem trifling in your eyes—the hardship that has come on us, on our kings and leaders, on our priests and prophets, on our ancestors and all your people, from the days of the kings of Assyria until today. 33 In all that has happened to us, you have remained righteous; you have acted faithfully, while we acted wickedly. 34 Our kings, our leaders, our priests and our ancestors did not follow your law; they did not pay attention to your commands or the statutes you warned them to keep. 35 Even while they were in their kingdom, enjoying your great goodness to them in the spacious and fertile land you gave them, they did not serve you or turn from their evil ways.

36 "But see, we are slaves today,

---

a 22 One Hebrew manuscript and Septuagint; most Hebrew manuscripts Sihon, that is, the country of the

slaves in the land you gave our ancestors so they could eat its fruit and the other good things it produces. ³⁷Because of our sins, its abundant harvest goes to the kings you have placed over us. They rule over our bodies and our cattle as they please. We are in great distress.

The Agreement of the People

³⁸"In view of all this, we are making a binding agreement, putting it in writing, and our leaders, our Levites and our priests are affixing their seals to it."ª

10 ^b Those who sealed it were:

Nehemiah the governor, the son of Hakaliah.

Zedekiah, ²Seraiah, Azariah, Jeremiah,
³Pashhur, Amariah, Malkijah,
⁴Hattush, Shebaniah, Malluk,
⁵Harim, Meremoth, Obadiah,
⁶Daniel, Ginnethon, Baruch,
⁷Meshullam, Abijah, Mijamin,
⁸Maaziah, Bilgai and Shemaiah.
These were the priests.

⁹The Levites:

Jeshua son of Azaniah, Binnui of the sons of Henadad, Kadmiel,
¹⁰and their associates: Shebaniah, Hodiah, Kelita, Pelaiah, Hanan,
¹¹Mika, Rehob, Hashabiah,
¹²Zakkur, Sherebiah, Shebaniah,
¹³Hodiah, Bani and Beninu.

¹⁴The leaders of the people:

Parosh, Pahath-Moab, Elam, Zattu, Bani,
¹⁵Bunni, Azgad, Bebai,
¹⁶Adonijah, Bigvai, Adin,
¹⁷Ater, Hezekiah, Azzur,
¹⁸Hodiah, Hashum, Bezai,
¹⁹Hariph, Anathoth, Nebai,
²⁰Magpiash, Meshullam, Hezir,
²¹Meshezabel, Zadok, Jaddua,
²²Pelatiah, Hanan, Anaiah,
²³Hoshea, Hananiah, Hasshub,
²⁴Hallohesh, Pilha, Shobek,
²⁵Rehum, Hashabnah, Maaseiah,
²⁶Ahiah, Hanan, Anan,
²⁷Malluk, Harim and Baanah.

²⁸"The rest of the people—priests, Levites, gatekeepers, musicians, temple servants and all who separated themselves from the neighboring peoples for the sake of the Law of God, together with their wives and all their sons and daughters who are able to understand—²⁹all these now join their fellow Israelites the nobles, and bind themselves with a curse and an oath to follow the Law of God given through Moses the servant of God and to obey carefully all the commands, regulations and decrees of the LORD our Lord.

³⁰"We promise not to give our daughters in marriage to the peoples around us or take their daughters for our sons.

³¹"When the neighboring peoples bring merchandise or grain to sell on the Sabbath, we will not buy from them on the Sabbath or on any holy day. Every seventh year we will forgo working the land and will cancel all debts.

³²"We assume the responsibility for carrying out the commands to give a third of a shekel^c each year for the service of the house of our God: ³³for the bread set out on the table; for the regular grain offerings and burnt offerings; for the offerings on the Sabbaths, at the New Moon feasts and at the appointed festivals; for the holy offerings; for sin offerings^d to make atonement for Israel; and for all the duties of the house of our God.

³⁴"We—the priests, the Levites and the people—have cast lots to determine when each of our families is to bring to the house of our God at set times each year a contribution of wood to burn on the altar of the LORD our God, as it is written in the Law.

---

^a 38 In Hebrew texts this verse (9:38) is numbered 10:1. ^b In Hebrew texts 10:1-39 is numbered 10:2-40.
^c 32 That is, about 1/8 ounce or about 4 grams ^d 33 Or purification offerings

New Year's resolutions are kind of a joke. Give up candy? Sure. Do your homework right away—all of it? You bet. Those resolutions may be broken by January 2! There's another kind of resolution you're more likely to keep. You make a bad mistake, and you say, "Boy, I won't do that again." You hurt a friend, and you say, "I'm sorry, I'll never do it again." The mistakes made you feel bad, and you decided not to make them again. Nehemiah 10:28–39 lists seven resolutions the people of Judah made because of past mistakes. Now think of mistakes you've made. What personal resolutions will you make to avoid them in the future?

{Nehemiah 10:28–39}

35 "We also assume responsibility for bringing to the house of the LORD each year the firstfruits of our crops and of every fruit tree.

36 "As it is also written in the Law, we will bring the firstborn of our sons and of our cattle, of our herds and of our flocks to the house of our God, to the priests ministering there.

37 "Moreover, we will bring to the storerooms of the house of our God, to the priests, the first of our ground meal, of our grain offerings, of the fruit of all our trees and of our new wine and olive oil. And we will bring a tithe of our crops to the Levites, for it is the Levites who collect the tithes in all the towns where we work. 38 A priest descended from Aaron is to accompany the Levites when they receive the tithes, and the Levites are to bring a tenth of the tithes up to the house of our God, to the storerooms of the treasury. 39 The people of Israel, including the Levites, are to bring their contributions of grain, new wine and olive oil to the storerooms, where the articles for the sanctuary and for the ministering priests, the gatekeepers and the musicians are also kept.

"We will not neglect the house of our God."

The New Residents of Jerusalem

11 Now the leaders of the people settled in Jerusalem. The rest of the people cast lots to bring one out of every ten of them to live in Jerusalem, the holy city, while the remaining nine were to stay in their own towns. 2 The people commended all who volunteered to live in Jerusalem.

3 These are the provincial leaders who settled in Jerusalem (now some Israelites, priests, Levites, temple servants and descendants of Solomon's servants lived in the towns of Judah, each on their own property in the various towns, 4 while other people from both Judah and Benjamin lived in Jerusalem):

From the descendants of Judah:

Athaiah son of Uzziah, the son of Zechariah, the son of Amariah, the son of Shephatiah, the son of Mahalalel, a descendant of Perez; 5 and Maaseiah son of Baruch, the son of Kol-Hozeh, the son of Hazaiah, the son of Adaiah, the son of Joiarib, the son of Zechariah, a descendant of Shelah. 6 The descendants of Perez who lived in Jerusalem totaled 468 men of standing.

7 From the descendants of Benjamin:

Sallu son of Meshullam, the son of Joed, the son of Pedaiah, the son of Kolaiah, the son of Maaseiah, the son of Ithiel, the son of Jeshaiah, 8 and his followers, Gabbai and Sallai—928 men. 9 Joel son of Zikri was their chief officer, and Judah son of Hassenuah was over the New Quarter of the city.

10 From the priests:

Jedaiah; the son of Joiarib; Jakin; 11 Seraiah son of Hilkiah, the son of Meshullam, the son of Zadok, the son of Meraioth, the son of Ahitub, the official in charge of the house of God, 12 and their associates, who carried on work for the temple—822 men; Adaiah son of Jeroham, the son of Pelaliah, the son of Amzi, the son of Zechariah, the son of Pashhur, the son of Malkijah, 13 and his associates, who were heads of families—242 men; Amashsai son of Azarel, the son of Ahzai, the son of Meshillemoth, the son of Immer, 14 and hisª associates, who were men of standing—128. Their chief officer was Zabdiel son of Haggedolim.

15 From the Levites:

Shemaiah son of Hasshub, the son of Azrikam, the son of Hashabiah, the son of Bunni; 16 Shabbethai and Jozabad, two of the heads of the Levites, who had charge of the outside work of the house of God; 17 Mattaniah son of Mika, the son of Zabdi, the son of Asaph, the director who led in thanksgiving and prayer; Bakbukiah, second among his associates; and Abda son of Shammua, the son of Galal, the son of Jeduthun. 18 The Levites in the holy city totaled 284.

19 The gatekeepers:

Akkub, Talmon and their associates, who kept watch at the gates—172 men.

20 The rest of the Israelites, with the priests and Levites, were in all the towns of Judah, each on their ancestral property.
21 The temple servants lived on the hill of Ophel, and Ziha and Gishpa were in charge of them.
22 The chief officer of the Levites in Jerusalem was Uzzi son of Bani, the son of Hashabiah, the son of Mattaniah, the son of Mika. Uzzi was one of Asaph's descendants, who were the musicians responsible for the service of the house of God. 23 The musicians were under the king's orders, which regulated their daily activity.
24 Pethahiah son of Meshezabel, one of the descendants of Zerah son of Judah, was the king's agent in all affairs relating to the people.
25 As for the villages with their fields, some of the people of Judah lived in Kiriath Arba and its surrounding settlements, in Dibon and its settlements, in Jekabzeel and its villages, 26 in Jeshua, in Moladah, in Beth Pelet, 27 in Hazar Shual, in Beersheba and its settlements, 28 in Ziklag, in Mekonah and its settlements, 29 in En Rimmon, in Zorah, in Jarmuth, 30 Zanoah, Adullam and their villages, in Lachish and

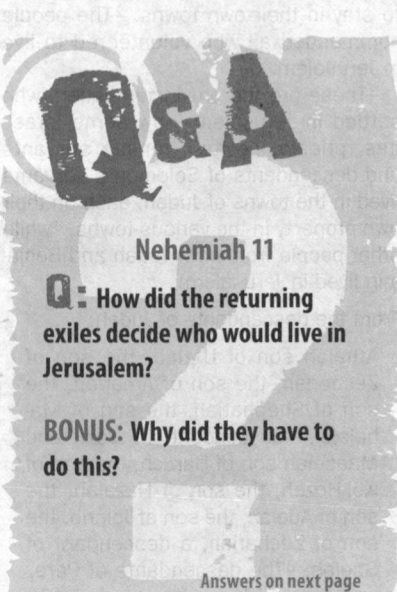

Nehemiah 11

Q: How did the returning exiles decide who would live in Jerusalem?

BONUS: Why did they have to do this?

Answers on next page

ª 14 Most Septuagint manuscripts; Hebrew *their*

its fields, and in Azekah and its settlements. So they were living all the way from Beersheba to the Valley of Hinnom.

31 The descendants of the Benjamites from Geba lived in Mikmash, Aija, Bethel and its settlements, 32 in Anathoth, Nob and Ananiah, 33 in Hazor, Ramah and Gittaim, 34 in Hadid, Zeboim and Neballat, 35 in Lod and Ono, and in Ge Harashim.

36 Some of the divisions of the Levites of Judah settled in Benjamin.

Priests and Levites

12 These were the priests and Levites who returned with Zerubbabel son of Shealtiel and with Joshua:
Seraiah, Jeremiah, Ezra,
2 Amariah, Malluk, Hattush,
3 Shekaniah, Rehum, Meremoth,
4 Iddo, Ginnethon,^a Abijah,
5 Mijamin,^b Moadiah, Bilgah,
6 Shemaiah, Joiarib, Jedaiah,
7 Sallu, Amok, Hilkiah and Jedaiah.
These were the leaders of the priests and their associates in the days of Joshua.

8 The Levites were Jeshua, Binnui, Kadmiel, Sherebiah, Judah, and also Mattaniah, who, together with his associates, was in charge of the songs of thanksgiving. 9 Bakbukiah and Unni, their associates, stood opposite them in the services.

10 Joshua was the father of Joiakim, Joiakim the father of Eliashib, Eliashib the father of Joiada, 11 Joiada the father of Jonathan, and Jonathan the father of Jaddua.

12 In the days of Joiakim, these were the heads of the priestly families:
of Seraiah's family, Meraiah;
of Jeremiah's, Hananiah;
13 of Ezra's, Meshullam;
of Amariah's, Jehohanan;
14 of Malluk's, Jonathan;
of Shekaniah's,^c Joseph;
15 of Harim's, Adna;
of Meremoth's,^d Helkai;
16 of Iddo's, Zechariah;
of Ginnethon's, Meshullam;
17 of Abijah's, Zikri;

of Miniamin's and of Moadiah's, Piltai;
18 of Bilgah's, Shammua;
of Shemaiah's, Jehonathan;
19 of Joiarib's, Mattenai;
of Jedaiah's, Uzzi;
20 of Sallu's, Kallai;
of Amok's, Eber;
21 of Hilkiah's, Hashabiah;
of Jedaiah's, Nethanel.

22 The family heads of the Levites in the days of Eliashib, Joiada, Johanan and Jaddua, as well as those of the priests, were recorded in the reign of Darius the Persian. 23 The family heads among the descendants of Levi up to the time of Johanan son of Eliashib were recorded in the book of the annals. 24 And the leaders of the Levites were Hashabiah, Sherebiah, Jeshua son of Kadmiel, and their associates, who stood opposite them to give praise and thanksgiving, one section responding to the other, as prescribed by David the man of God.

25 Mattaniah, Bakbukiah, Obadiah, Meshullam, Talmon and Akkub were gate-

---

^a 4 Many Hebrew manuscripts and Vulgate (see also verse 16); most Hebrew manuscripts *Ginnethoi*   ^b 5 A variant of *Miniamin*   ^c 14 Very many Hebrew manuscripts, some Septuagint manuscripts and Syriac (see also verse 3); most Hebrew manuscripts *Shebaniah's*   ^d 15 Some Septuagint manuscripts (see also verse 3); Hebrew *Meraioth's*

keepers who guarded the storerooms at the gates. 26They served in the days of Joiakim son of Joshua, the son of Jozadak, and in the days of Nehemiah the governor and of Ezra the priest, the teacher of the Law.

Dedication of the Wall of Jerusalem

27At the dedication of the wall of Jerusalem, the Levites were sought out from where they lived and were brought to Jerusalem to celebrate joyfully the dedication with songs of thanksgiving and with the music of cymbals, harps and lyres. 28The musicians also were brought together from the region around Jerusalem—from the villages of the Netophathites, 29from Beth Gilgal, and from the area of Geba and Azmaveth, for the musicians had built villages for themselves around Jerusalem. 30When the priests and Levites had purified themselves ceremonially, they purified the people, the gates and the wall.

31I had the leaders of Judah go up on top ofª the wall. I also assigned two large choirs to give thanks. One was to proceed on top ofᵇ the wall to the right, toward the Dung Gate. 32Hoshaiah and half the leaders of Judah followed them, 33along with Azariah, Ezra, Meshullam, 34Judah, Benjamin, Shemaiah, Jeremiah, 35as well as some priests with trumpets, and also Zechariah son of Jonathan, the son of Shemaiah, the son of Mattaniah, the son of Micaiah, the son of Zakkur, the son of Asaph, 36and his associates—Shemaiah, Azarel, Milalai, Gilalai, Maai, Nethanel, Judah and Hanani—with musical instruments prescribed by David the man of God. Ezra the teacher of the Law led the procession. 37At the Fountain Gate they continued directly up the steps of the City of David on the ascent to the wall and passed above the site of David's palace to the Water Gate on the east.

38The second choir proceeded in the opposite direction. I followed them on top ofᶜ the wall, together with half the people—past the Tower of the Ovens to the Broad Wall, 39over the Gate of Ephraim, the Jeshanahᵈ Gate, the Fish Gate, the Tower of Hananel and the Tower of the Hundred, as far as the Sheep Gate. At the Gate of the Guard they stopped.

40The two choirs that gave thanks then took their places in the house of God; so did I, together with half the officials, 41as well as the priests—Eliakim, Maaseiah, Miniamin, Micaiah, Elioenai, Zechariah and Hananiah with their trumpets— 42and also Maaseiah, Shemaiah, Eleazar, Uzzi, Jehohanan, Malkijah, Elam and Ezer. The choirs sang under the direction of Jezrahiah. 43And on that day they offered great sacrifices, rejoicing because God had given them great joy. The women and children also rejoiced. The sound of rejoicing in Jerusalem could be heard far away.

44At that time men were appointed to be in charge of the storerooms for the contributions, firstfruits and tithes. From the fields around the towns they were to bring into the storerooms the portions required by the Law for the priests and the Levites, for Judah was pleased with the ministering priests and Levites. 45They performed the service of their God and the service of purification, as did also the musicians and gatekeepers, according to the commands of David and his son Solomon. 46For long ago, in the days of David and Asaph, there had been directors for the musicians and for the songs of praise and thanksgiving to God. 47So in the days of Zerubbabel and of Nehemiah, all Israel contributed the daily portions for the musicians and the gatekeepers. They also set aside the portion for the other Levites, and the Levites set aside the portion for the descendants of Aaron.

Nehemiah's Final Reforms

13 On that day the Book of Moses was read aloud in the hearing of the people and there it was found written that no Ammonite or Moabite should ever be admitted into the assembly of God, 2because they had not met the Israelites with food and water but had hired Balaam to call a curse down on them. (Our God,

---

ª 31 Or go alongside   ᵇ 31 Or proceed alongside   ᶜ 38 Or them alongside   ᵈ 39 Or Old

however, turned the curse into a blessing.) ³When the people heard this law, they excluded from Israel all who were of foreign descent.

⁴Before this, Eliashib the priest had been put in charge of the storerooms of the house of our God. He was closely associated with Tobiah, ⁵and he had provided him with a large room formerly used to store the grain offerings and incense and temple articles, and also the tithes of grain, new wine and olive oil prescribed for the Levites, musicians and gatekeepers, as well as the contributions for the priests.

⁶But while all this was going on, I was not in Jerusalem, for in the thirty-second year of Artaxerxes king of Babylon I had returned to the king. Some time later I asked his permission ⁷and came back to Jerusalem. Here I learned about the evil thing Eliashib had done in providing Tobiah a room in the courts of the house of God. ⁸I was greatly displeased and threw all Tobiah's household goods out of the room. ⁹I gave orders to purify the rooms, and then I put back into them the equipment of the house of God, with the grain offerings and the incense.

¹⁰I also learned that the portions assigned to the Levites had not been given to them, and that all the Levites and musicians responsible for the service had gone back to their own fields. ¹¹So I rebuked the officials and asked them, "Why is the house of God neglected?" Then I called them together and stationed them at their posts.

¹²All Judah brought the tithes of grain, new wine and olive oil into the storerooms. ¹³I put Shelemiah the priest, Zadok the scribe, and a Levite named Pedaiah in charge of the storerooms and made Hanan son of Zakkur, the son of Mattaniah, their assistant, because they were considered trustworthy. They were made responsible for distributing the supplies to their fellow Levites.

¹⁴Remember me for this, my God, and do not blot out what I have so faithfully done for the house of my God and its services.

¹⁵In those days I saw people in Judah treading winepresses on the Sabbath and bringing in grain and loading it on donkeys, together with wine, grapes, figs and all other kinds of loads. And they were bringing all this into Jerusalem on the Sabbath. Therefore I warned them against selling food on that day. ¹⁶People from Tyre who lived in Jerusalem were bringing in fish and all kinds of merchandise and selling them in Jerusalem on the Sabbath to the people of Judah. ¹⁷I rebuked the nobles of Judah and said to them, "What is this wicked thing you are doing—desecrating the Sabbath day? ¹⁸Didn't your ancestors do the same things, so that our God brought all this calamity on us and on this city? Now you are stirring up more wrath against Israel by desecrating the Sabbath."

¹⁹When evening shadows fell on the gates of Jerusalem before the Sabbath, I ordered the doors to be shut and not opened until the Sabbath was over. I stationed some of my own men at the gates so that no load could be brought in on the Sabbath day. ²⁰Once or twice the merchants and sellers of all kinds of goods spent the night outside Jerusalem. ²¹But

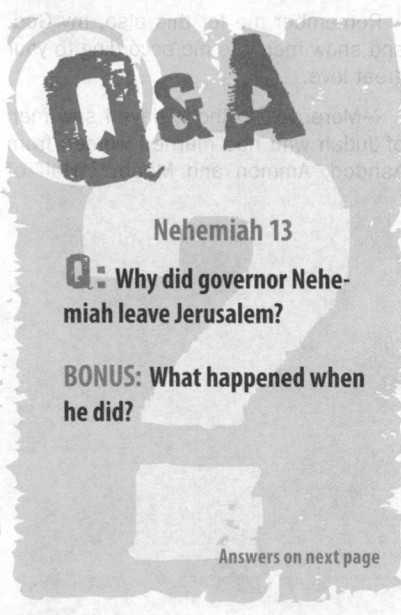

Nehemiah 13

Q: Why did governor Nehemiah leave Jerusalem?

BONUS: What happened when he did?

Answers on next page

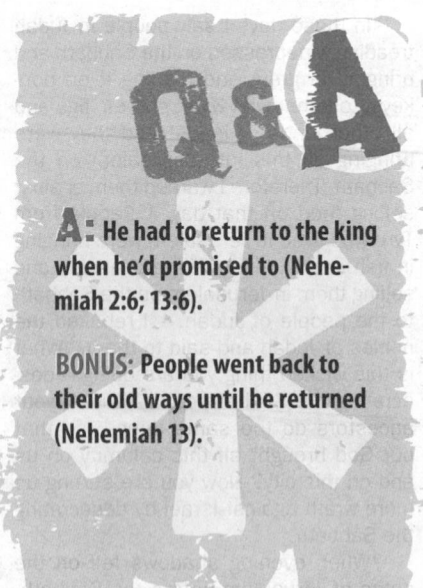

A: He had to return to the king when he'd promised to (Nehemiah 2:6; 13:6).

BONUS: People went back to their old ways until he returned (Nehemiah 13).

I warned them and said, "Why do you spend the night by the wall? If you do this again, I will arrest you." From that time on they no longer came on the Sabbath. 22 Then I commanded the Levites to purify themselves and go and guard the gates in order to keep the Sabbath day holy.

Remember me for this also, my God, and show mercy to me according to your great love.

23 Moreover, in those days I saw men of Judah who had married women from Ashdod, Ammon and Moab. 24 Half of their children spoke the language of Ashdod or the language of one of the other peoples, and did not know how to speak the language of Judah. 25 I rebuked them and called curses down on them. I beat some of the men and pulled out their hair. I made them take an oath in God's name and said: "You are not to give your daughters in marriage to their sons, nor are you to take their daughters in marriage for your sons or for yourselves. 26 Was it not because of marriages like these that Solomon king of Israel sinned? Among the many nations there was no king like him. He was loved by his God, and God made him king over all Israel, but even he was led into sin by foreign women. 27 Must we hear now that you too are doing all this terrible wickedness and are being unfaithful to our God by marrying foreign women?"

28 One of the sons of Joiada son of Eliashib the high priest was son-in-law to Sanballat the Horonite. And I drove him away from me.

29 Remember them, my God, because they defiled the priestly office and the covenant of the priesthood and of the Levites.

30 So I purified the priests and the Levites of everything foreign, and assigned them duties, each to his own task. 31 I also made provision for contributions of wood at designated times, and for the firstfruits.

Remember me with favor, my God.

ESTHER

Making Plans.

Is God putting your life together according to some plan? Or do you "just happen" to have your looks, your brain, your talents, and abilities? You can't look ahead and know what God is preparing you for. But God definitely has something special in mind.

Esther was an orphan, raised by her cousin. Yet she became Queen of Persia and saved an entire nation. God isn't mentioned once in this book named for the orphan queen. But it's clear that God was at work, arranging things behind the scenes, just as he's at work behind the scenes in your life.

>>**KING XERXES DIVORCES DEFIANT QUEEN**
Husbands fear wives will rebel, see Esther 1

>>**ESTHER HIDES JEWISH IDENTITY**
Cousin advises secrecy, story in Esther 2

>>**PLOT TO EXTERMINATE JEWS FAILS**
Queen plays central role, report in Esther 7

>>**CELEBRATE DELIVERANCE! ENJOY PURIM**
New Jewish holiday established, see Esther 9:18–32

«preview

Esther's husband, Xerxes, rules Persia 486–459 B.C.

Xerxes tries to invade Europe, is defeated by the Greeks.

The Book of Esther reminds us: God doesn't need to do miracles to protect his own.

While Xerxes rules Persia, the caste system is introduced in India. The Indian surgeon Susrata performs cataract surgery. Hypocrites, the "father of medicine," practices in Greece.

Queen Vashti Deposed

1 This is what happened during the time of Xerxes,[a] the Xerxes who ruled over 127 provinces stretching from India to Cush[b]: ²At that time King Xerxes reigned from his royal throne in the citadel of Susa, ³and in the third year of his reign he gave a banquet for all his nobles and officials. The military leaders of Persia and Media, the princes, and the nobles of the provinces were present.

⁴For a full 180 days he displayed the vast wealth of his kingdom and the splendor and glory of his majesty. ⁵When these days were over, the king gave a banquet, lasting seven days, in the enclosed garden of the king's palace, for all the people from the least to the greatest who were in the citadel of Susa. ⁶The garden had hangings of white and blue linen, fastened with cords of white linen and purple material to silver rings on marble pillars. There were couches of gold and silver on a mosaic pavement of porphyry, marble, mother-of-pearl and other costly stones. ⁷Wine was served in goblets of gold, each one different from the other, and the royal wine was abundant, in keeping with the king's liberality. ⁸By the king's command each guest was allowed to drink with no restrictions, for the king instructed all the wine stewards to serve each man what he wished.

⁹Queen Vashti also gave a banquet for the women in the royal palace of King Xerxes.

¹⁰On the seventh day, when King Xerxes was in high spirits from wine, he commanded the seven eunuchs who served him—Mehuman, Biztha, Harbona, Bigtha, Abagtha, Zethar and Karkas— ¹¹to bring before him Queen Vashti, wearing her royal crown, in order to display her beauty to the people and nobles, for she was lovely to look at. ¹²But when the attendants delivered the king's command, Queen Vashti refused to come. Then the king became furious and burned with anger.

¹³Since it was customary for the king to consult experts in matters of law and justice, he spoke with the wise men who understood the times ¹⁴and were closest to the king—Karshena, Shethar, Admatha, Tarshish, Meres, Marsena and Memukan, the seven nobles of Persia and Media who had special access to the king and were highest in the kingdom.

¹⁵"According to law, what must be done to Queen Vashti?" he asked. "She has not obeyed the command of King Xerxes that the eunuchs have taken to her."

¹⁶Then Memukan replied in the presence of the king and the nobles, "Queen Vashti has done wrong, not only against the king but also against all the nobles and the peoples of all the provinces of King Xerxes. ¹⁷For the queen's conduct will become known to all the women, and so they will despise their husbands and say, 'King Xerxes commanded Queen Vashti to be brought before him, but she would not come.' ¹⁸This very day the Persian and Median women of the nobility who have heard about the queen's conduct will respond to all the king's nobles in the same way. There will be no end of disrespect and discord.

¹⁹"Therefore, if it pleases the king, let him issue a royal decree and let it be

Esther 1

Q: Who was one of the first women's rights advocates?

BONUS: What happened to her?

Answers on next page

---

[a] 1 Hebrew *Ahasuerus*; here and throughout Esther
[b] 1 That is, the upper Nile region

written in the laws of Persia and Media, which cannot be repealed, that Vashti is never again to enter the presence of King Xerxes. Also let the king give her royal position to someone else who is better than she. ²⁰Then when the king's edict is proclaimed throughout all his vast realm, all the women will respect their husbands, from the least to the greatest."

²¹The king and his nobles were pleased with this advice, so the king did as Memukan proposed. ²²He sent dispatches to all parts of the kingdom, to each province in its own script and to each people in their own language, proclaiming that every man should be ruler over his own household, using his native tongue.

Esther Made Queen

2 Later when King Xerxes' fury had subsided, he remembered Vashti and what she had done and what he had decreed about her. ²Then the king's personal attendants proposed, "Let a search be made for beautiful young virgins for the king. ³Let the king appoint commissioners in every province of his realm to bring all these beautiful young women into the harem at the citadel of Susa. Let them be placed under the care of Hegai, the king's eunuch, who is in charge of the women; and let beauty treatments be given to them. ⁴Then let the young woman who pleases the king be queen instead of Vashti." This advice appealed to the king, and he followed it.

⁵Now there was in the citadel of Susa a Jew of the tribe of Benjamin, named Mordecai son of Jair, the son of Shimei, the son of Kish, ⁶who had been carried into exile from Jerusalem by Nebuchadnezzar king of Babylon, among those taken captive with Jehoiachin[a] king of Judah. ⁷Mordecai had a cousin named Hadassah, whom he had brought up because she had neither father nor mother. This young woman, who was also known as Esther, had a lovely figure and was beautiful. Mordecai had taken her as his own daughter when her father and mother died.

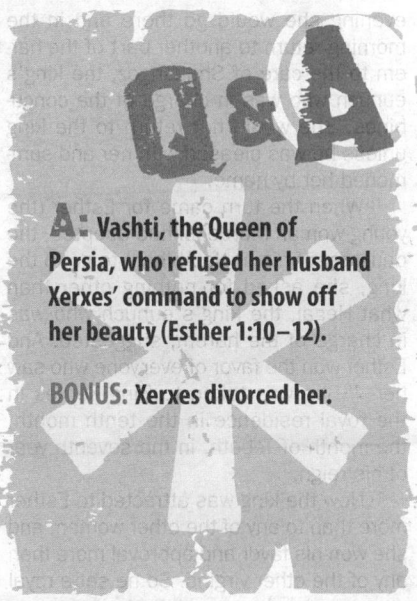

A: Vashti, the Queen of Persia, who refused her husband Xerxes' command to show off her beauty (Esther 1:10–12).

BONUS: Xerxes divorced her.

⁸When the king's order and edict had been proclaimed, many young women were brought to the citadel of Susa and put under the care of Hegai. Esther also was taken to the king's palace and entrusted to Hegai, who had charge of the harem. ⁹She pleased him and won his favor. Immediately he provided her with her beauty treatments and special food. He assigned to her seven female attendants selected from the king's palace and moved her and her attendants into the best place in the harem.

¹⁰Esther had not revealed her nationality and family background, because Mordecai had forbidden her to do so. ¹¹Every day he walked back and forth near the courtyard of the harem to find out how Esther was and what was happening to her.

¹²Before a young woman's turn came to go in to King Xerxes, she had to complete twelve months of beauty treatments prescribed for the women, six months with oil of myrrh and six with perfumes and cosmetics. ¹³And this is how she would go to the king: Anything she wanted was given her to take with her from the harem to the king's palace. ¹⁴In the

---

[a] 6 Hebrew *Jeconiah*, a variant of *Jehoiachin*

evening she would go there and in the morning return to another part of the harem to the care of Shaashgaz, the king's eunuch who was in charge of the concubines. She would not return to the king unless he was pleased with her and summoned her by name.

¹⁵When the turn came for Esther (the young woman Mordecai had adopted, the daughter of his uncle Abihail) to go to the king, she asked for nothing other than what Hegai, the king's eunuch who was in charge of the harem, suggested. And Esther won the favor of everyone who saw her. ¹⁶She was taken to King Xerxes in the royal residence in the tenth month, the month of Tebeth, in the seventh year of his reign.

¹⁷Now the king was attracted to Esther more than to any of the other women, and she won his favor and approval more than any of the other virgins. So he set a royal crown on her head and made her queen instead of Vashti. ¹⁸And the king gave a great banquet, Esther's banquet, for all his nobles and officials. He proclaimed a holiday throughout the provinces and distributed gifts with royal liberality.

Mordecai Uncovers a Conspiracy

¹⁹When the virgins were assembled a second time, Mordecai was sitting at the king's gate. ²⁰But Esther had kept secret her family background and nationality just as Mordecai had told her to do, for she continued to follow Mordecai's instructions as she had done when he was bringing her up.

²¹During the time Mordecai was sitting at the king's gate, Bigthana[a] and Teresh, two of the king's officers who guarded the doorway, became angry and conspired to assassinate King Xerxes. ²²But Mordecai found out about the plot and told Queen Esther, who in turn reported it to the king, giving credit to Mordecai. ²³And when the report was investigated and found to be true, the two officials were impaled on poles. All this was re-

corded in the book of the annals in the presence of the king.

Haman's Plot to Destroy the Jews

3 After these events, King Xerxes honored Haman son of Hammedatha, the Agagite, elevating him and giving him a seat of honor higher than that of all the other nobles. ²All the royal officials at the king's gate knelt down and paid honor to Haman, for the king had commanded this concerning him. But Mordecai would not kneel down or pay him honor.

³Then the royal officials at the king's gate asked Mordecai, "Why do you disobey the king's command?" ⁴Day after day they spoke to him but he refused to comply. Therefore they told Haman about it to see whether Mordecai's behavior would be tolerated, for he had told them he was a Jew.

⁵When Haman saw that Mordecai would not kneel down or pay him honor, he was enraged. ⁶Yet having learned who Mordecai's people were, he scorned the idea of killing only Mordecai. Instead Haman looked for a way to destroy all Mordecai's people, the Jews, throughout the whole kingdom of Xerxes.

⁷In the twelfth year of King Xerxes, in the first month, the month of Nisan, the *pur* (that is, the lot) was cast in the presence of Haman to select a day and month. And the lot fell on[b] the twelfth month, the month of Adar.

⁸Then Haman said to King Xerxes, "There is a certain people dispersed among the peoples in all the provinces of your kingdom who keep themselves separate. Their customs are different from those of all other people, and they do not obey the king's laws; it is not in the king's best interest to tolerate them. ⁹If it pleases the king, let a decree be issued to destroy them, and I will give ten thousand talents[c] of silver to the king's administrators for the royal treasury."

¹⁰So the king took his signet ring from his finger and gave it to Haman son of

---

a 21 Hebrew *Bigthan*, a variant of *Bigthana*   *b* 7 Septuagint; Hebrew does not have *And the lot fell on*.   *c* 9 That is, about 375 tons or about 340 metric tons

Have you ever noticed that some friends forgive you quickly? Then there are others who get mad and hold a grudge for days or weeks. Their pride is hurt, and they're not about to forgive you. The pagan official Haman was like that. He thought the Jew Mordecai had insulted him, and he held such a grudge that he plotted to wipe out the whole Jewish race. He didn't succeed, but holding that grudge was the sign of a hateful and wicked man. Aren't you glad God doesn't hold grudges when you do something wrong? God is eager to forgive. And God is eager for his people to follow his example of forgiveness and to not hold grudges.

{Esther 3:1–6}

≫INSTANT ACCESS

Hammedatha, the Agagite, the enemy of the Jews. ¹¹"Keep the money," the king said to Haman, "and do with the people as you please."

¹²Then on the thirteenth day of the first month the royal secretaries were summoned. They wrote out in the script of each province and in the language of each people all Haman's orders to the king's satraps, the governors of the various provinces and the nobles of the various peoples. These were written in the name of King Xerxes himself and sealed with his own ring. ¹³Dispatches were sent by couriers to all the king's provinces with the order to destroy, kill and annihilate all the Jews—young and old, women and children—on a single day, the thirteenth day of the twelfth month, the month of Adar, and to plunder their goods. ¹⁴A copy of the text of the edict was to be issued as law in every province and made known to the people of every nationality so they would be ready for that day.

¹⁵The couriers went out, spurred on by the king's command, and the edict was issued in the citadel of Susa. The king and Haman sat down to drink, but the city of Susa was bewildered.

Mordecai Persuades Esther to Help

4 When Mordecai learned of all that had been done, he tore his clothes, put on sackcloth and ashes, and went out into the city, wailing loudly and bitterly. ²But he went only as far as the king's gate, because no one clothed in sackcloth was allowed to enter it. ³In every province to which the edict and order of the king came, there was great mourning among the Jews, with fasting, weeping and wailing. Many lay in sackcloth and ashes.

⁴When Esther's eunuchs and female attendants came and told her about Mordecai, she was in great distress. She sent clothes for him to put on instead of his sackcloth, but he would not accept them. ⁵Then Esther summoned Hathak, one of the king's eunuchs assigned to attend her, and ordered him to find out what was troubling Mordecai and why.

⁶So Hathak went out to Mordecai in the open square of the city in front of the king's gate. ⁷Mordecai told him everything that had happened to him, including the exact amount of money Haman had promised to pay into the royal treasury for the destruction of the Jews. ⁸He also gave him a copy of the text of the edict for their annihilation, which had been published in Susa, to show to Esther and explain it to her, and he told him to instruct her to go into the king's presence to beg for mercy and plead with him for her people.

⁹Hathak went back and reported to Esther what Mordecai had said. ¹⁰Then she instructed him to say to Mordecai, ¹¹"All the king's officials and the people of the royal provinces know that for any man or woman who approaches the king in the inner court without being summoned the king has but one law: that they be put to death unless the king extends the gold scepter to them and spares their lives. But thirty days have passed since I was called to go to the king."

¹²When Esther's words were reported to Mordecai, ¹³he sent back this answer: "Do not think that because you are in the king's house you alone of all the Jews will escape. ¹⁴For if you remain silent at this time, relief and deliverance for the Jews will arise from another place, but you and your father's family will perish. And who knows but that you have come to your royal position for such a time as this?"

¹⁵Then Esther sent this reply to Mordecai: ¹⁶"Go, gather together all the Jews who are in Susa, and fast for me. Do not eat or drink for three days, night or day. I and my attendants will fast as you do. When this is done, I will go to the king, even though it is against the law. And if I perish, I perish."

¹⁷So Mordecai went away and carried out all of Esther's instructions.

Esther's Request to the King

5 On the third day Esther put on her royal robes and stood in the inner court of the palace, in front of the king's hall. The king was sitting on his royal throne in the hall, facing the entrance. ²When he saw Queen Esther standing in the court, he was pleased with her and held out to her the gold scepter that was in his hand. So Esther approached and touched the tip of the scepter.

³Then the king asked, "What is it, Queen Esther? What is your request? Even up to half the kingdom, it will be given you."

⁴"If it pleases the king," replied Esther, "let the king, together with Haman, come today to a banquet I have prepared for him."

INSTANT ACCESS

Three girls you know are kicking a younger girl. You feel like you ought to step in. But it's scary. So you . . . Queen Esther was frightened when her cousin Mordecai asked her to see the king about Haman's plot. King Xerxes was unpredictable. If Esther went to see him uninvited, she might be killed! Mordecai had an answer for her: "Who knows but that you have come to your royal position for such a time as this?" (Esther 4:14). Did God make Esther queen so she could step in and help? Ask yourself the same thing the next time you feel you should speak up but are afraid. Maybe God put you in that situation just so you could help.

{Esther 4}

---

⁵"Bring Haman at once," the king said, "so that we may do what Esther asks."

So the king and Haman went to the banquet Esther had prepared. ⁶As they were drinking wine, the king again asked Esther, "Now what is your petition? It will be given you. And what is your request? Even up to half the kingdom, it will be granted."

⁷Esther replied, "My petition and my request is this: ⁸If the king regards me with favor and if it pleases the king to grant my petition and fulfill my request, let the king and Haman come tomorrow to the

> My family is moving at the end of the school year. I have to leave all my friends, and who knows what I'll find at my new school. I get lonely thinking about it. How will I ever make new friends? **>> Emma**

Dear Jordan

Dear Emma,

Moving is a very stressful experience, and your feelings are certainly valid. When you get to your new neighborhood, try taking some walks or bike rides. Keep your eyes open for someone your age. Put on your confidence. A big smile will help you look like a good prospect as a friend.

When school starts, look into joining a club or team. Finding some others with similar interests is a good place to start. Also, when your family finds a church, get involved with a Sunday school class or youth group.

There's always the chance that you're at this new school because God wants you there for a special purpose. Esther found that God had prepared her for a very special job (Esther 4:14). It wasn't easy, and she wasn't sure that she wanted it. But she followed God and served him, and she saved a whole nation of people.

Perhaps you won't be used to save a whole nation, but you could be in your new school to impact someone's life for God. That's a wonderful thing. Keep your heart open and your eyes on him. I'm excited for all you will do for him!

Jordan

banquet I will prepare for them. Then I will answer the king's question."

Haman's Rage Against Mordecai

⁹Haman went out that day happy and in high spirits. But when he saw Mordecai at the king's gate and observed that he neither rose nor showed fear in his presence, he was filled with rage against Mordecai. ¹⁰Nevertheless, Haman restrained himself and went home.

Calling together his friends and Zeresh, his wife, ¹¹Haman boasted to them about his vast wealth, his many sons, and all the ways the king had honored him and how he had elevated him above the other nobles and officials. ¹²"And that's not all," Haman added. "I'm the only person Queen Esther invited to accompany the king to the banquet she gave. And she has invited me along with the king tomorrow. ¹³But all this gives me no satisfaction as long as I see that Jew Mordecai sitting at the king's gate."

¹⁴His wife Zeresh and all his friends said to him, "Have a pole set up, reaching to a height of fifty cubits,ᵃ and ask the king in the morning to have Mordecai impaled on it. Then go with the king to the banquet and enjoy yourself." This suggestion delighted Haman, and he had the pole set up.

Mordecai Honored

6 That night the king could not sleep; so he ordered the book of the chronicles, the record of his reign, to be brought in and read to him. ²It was found recorded there that Mordecai had exposed Bigthana and Teresh, two of the king's officers who guarded the doorway, who had conspired to assassinate King Xerxes.

³"What honor and recognition has Mordecai received for this?" the king asked.

"Nothing has been done for him," his attendants answered.

⁴The king said, "Who is in the court?" Now Haman had just entered the outer court of the palace to speak to the king about impaling Mordecai on the pole he had set up for him.

⁵His attendants answered, "Haman is standing in the court."

"Bring him in," the king ordered.

⁶When Haman entered, the king asked him, "What should be done for the man the king delights to honor?"

Now Haman thought to himself, "Who is there that the king would rather honor than me?" ⁷So he answered the king, "For the man the king delights to honor, ⁸have them bring a royal robe the king has worn and a horse the king has ridden, one with a royal crest placed on its head. ⁹Then let the robe and horse be entrusted to one of the king's most noble princes. Let them robe the man the king delights to honor, and lead him on the horse through the city streets, proclaiming before him, 'This is what is done for the man the king delights to honor!'"

¹⁰"Go at once," the king commanded Haman. "Get the robe and the horse and do just as you have suggested for Mordecai the Jew, who sits at the king's gate. Do not neglect anything you have recommended."

¹¹So Haman got the robe and the horse. He robed Mordecai, and led him on horseback through the city streets, proclaiming before him, "This is what is done for the man the king delights to honor!"

¹²Afterward Mordecai returned to the king's gate. But Haman rushed home, with his head covered in grief, ¹³and told Zeresh his wife and all his friends everything that had happened to him.

His advisers and his wife Zeresh said to him, "Since Mordecai, before whom your downfall has started, is of Jewish origin, you cannot stand against him—you will surely come to ruin!" ¹⁴While they were still talking with him, the king's eunuchs arrived and hurried Haman away to the banquet Esther had prepared.

Haman Impaled

7 So the king and Haman went to Queen Esther's banquet, ²and as they were drinking wine on the second day, the king

---

ᵃ 14 That is, about 75 feet or about 23 meters

A voice swears in the back of the bus and someone says, "Tyler did it!" Everybody snickers. Tyler didn't do it, but the bus driver still writes him up. Someone may even try to get you in trouble because they don't like you. They don't want a laugh. They want to hurt you. And sometimes they succeed. If you've ever been the victim of a prank or a plot, you know how unfair it is. But take comfort in this Bible story. The more someone tries to harm you, the more likely it is the plot will backfire. Like Haman, hanged on the same gallows he built for Mordecai, your tormentor is more likely to hurt him or herself!

{Esther 7}

» INSTANT ACCESS

kept quiet, because no such distress would justify disturbing the king.[a]"

5 King Xerxes asked Queen Esther, "Who is he? Where is he—the man who has dared to do such a thing?"

6 Esther said, "An adversary and enemy! This vile Haman!"

Then Haman was terrified before the king and queen. 7 The king got up in a rage, left his wine and went out into the palace garden. But Haman, realizing that the king had already decided his fate, stayed behind to beg Queen Esther for his life.

8 Just as the king returned from the palace garden to the banquet hall, Haman was falling on the couch where Esther was reclining.

The king exclaimed, "Will he even molest the queen while she is with me in the house?"

As soon as the word left the king's mouth, they covered Haman's face. 9 Then Harbona, one of the eunuchs attending the king, said, "A pole reaching to a height of fifty cubits[b] stands by Haman's house. He had it set up for Mordecai, who spoke up to help the king."

The king said, "Impale him on it!" 10 So they impaled Haman on the pole he had set up for Mordecai. Then the king's fury subsided.

The King's Edict in Behalf of the Jews

8 That same day King Xerxes gave Queen Esther the estate of Haman, the enemy of the Jews. And Mordecai came into the presence of the king, for Esther had told how he was related to her. 2 The king took off his signet ring, which he had reclaimed from Haman, and presented it to Mordecai. And Esther appointed him over Haman's estate.

3 Esther again pleaded with the king, falling at his feet and weeping. She begged him to put an end to the evil plan of Haman the Agagite, which he had devised against the Jews. 4 Then the king

again asked, "Queen Esther, what is your petition? It will be given you. What is your request? Even up to half the kingdom, it will be granted."

3 Then Queen Esther answered, "If I have found favor with you, Your Majesty, and if it pleases you, grant me my life— this is my petition. And spare my people— this is my request. 4 For I and my people have been sold to be destroyed, killed and annihilated. If we had merely been sold as male and female slaves, I would have

---

[a] 4 Or quiet, but the compensation our adversary offers cannot be compared with the loss the king would suffer   [b] 9 That is, about 75 feet or about 23 meters

extended the gold scepter to Esther and she arose and stood before him.

⁵ "If it pleases the king," she said, "and if he regards me with favor and thinks it the right thing to do, and if he is pleased with me, let an order be written overruling the dispatches that Haman son of Hammedatha, the Agagite, devised and wrote to destroy the Jews in all the king's provinces. ⁶ For how can I bear to see disaster fall on my people? How can I bear to see the destruction of my family?"

⁷ King Xerxes replied to Queen Esther and to Mordecai the Jew, "Because Haman attacked the Jews, I have given his estate to Esther, and they have impaled him on the pole he set up. ⁸ Now write another decree in the king's name in behalf of the Jews as seems best to you, and seal it with the king's signet ring—for no document written in the king's name and sealed with his ring can be revoked."

⁹ At once the royal secretaries were summoned—on the twenty-third day of the third month, the month of Sivan. They wrote out all Mordecai's orders to the Jews, and to the satraps, governors and nobles of the 127 provinces stretching from India to Cush.ᵃ These orders were written in the script of each province and the language of each people and also to the Jews in their own script and language. ¹⁰ Mordecai wrote in the name of King Xerxes, sealed the dispatches with the king's signet ring, and sent them by mounted couriers, who rode fast horses especially bred for the king.

¹¹ The king's edict granted the Jews in every city the right to assemble and protect themselves; to destroy, kill and annihilate the armed men of any nationality or province who might attack them and their women and children,ᵇ and to plunder the property of their enemies. ¹² The day appointed for the Jews to do this in all the provinces of King Xerxes was the thirteenth day of the twelfth month, the month of Adar. ¹³ A copy of the text of the edict was to be issued as law in every province and made known to the people of every nationality so that the Jews would be ready on that day to avenge themselves on their enemies.

¹⁴ The couriers, riding the royal horses, went out, spurred on by the king's command, and the edict was issued in the citadel of Susa.

The Triumph of the Jews

¹⁵ When Mordecai left the king's presence, he was wearing royal garments of blue and white, a large crown of gold and a purple robe of fine linen. And the city of Susa held a joyous celebration. ¹⁶ For the Jews it was a time of happiness and joy, gladness and honor. ¹⁷ In every province and in every city to which the edict of the king came, there was joy and gladness

---

ᵃ 9 That is, the upper Nile region   ᵇ 11 Or province, together with their women and children, who might attack them;

PANORAMA

Making Plans.

We aren't able to look ahead and know what God is preparing us for. But God definitely has something special in mind. God put Esther's life together according to a plan. She was an orphan, raised by her cousin. Yet she became the Queen of Persia and saved an entire nation.

{ESTHER}

among the Jews, with feasting and celebrating. And many people of other nationalities became Jews because fear of the Jews had seized them.

9 On the thirteenth day of the twelfth month, the month of Adar, the edict commanded by the king was to be carried out. On this day the enemies of the Jews had hoped to overpower them, but now the tables were turned and the Jews got the upper hand over those who hated them. ²The Jews assembled in their cities in all the provinces of King Xerxes to attack those determined to destroy them. No one could stand against them, because the people of all the other nationalities were afraid of them. ³And all the nobles of the provinces, the satraps, the governors and the king's administrators helped the Jews, because fear of Mordecai had seized them. ⁴Mordecai was prominent in the palace; his reputation spread throughout the provinces, and he became more and more powerful.

⁵The Jews struck down all their enemies with the sword, killing and destroying them, and they did what they pleased to those who hated them. ⁶In the citadel of Susa, the Jews killed and destroyed five hundred men. ⁷They also killed Parshandatha, Dalphon, Aspatha, ⁸Poratha, Adalia, Aridatha, ⁹Parmashta, Arisai, Aridai and Vaizatha, ¹⁰the ten sons of Haman son of Hammedatha, the enemy of the Jews. But they did not lay their hands on the plunder.

¹¹The number of those killed in the citadel of Susa was reported to the king that same day. ¹²The king said to Queen Esther, "The Jews have killed and destroyed five hundred men and the ten sons of Haman in the citadel of Susa. What have they done in the rest of the king's provinces? Now what is your petition? It will be given you. What is your request? It will also be granted."

¹³"If it pleases the king," Esther answered, "give the Jews in Susa permission to carry out this day's edict tomorrow also, and let Haman's ten sons be impaled on poles."

¹⁴So the king commanded that this be done. An edict was issued in Susa, and they impaled the ten sons of Haman. ¹⁵The Jews in Susa came together on the fourteenth day of the month of Adar, and they put to death in Susa three hundred men, but they did not lay their hands on the plunder.

¹⁶Meanwhile, the remainder of the Jews who were in the king's provinces also assembled to protect themselves and get relief from their enemies. They killed seventy-five thousand of them but did not lay their hands on the plunder. ¹⁷This happened on the thirteenth day of the month of Adar, and on the fourteenth they rested and made it a day of feasting and joy.

¹⁸The Jews in Susa, however, had assembled on the thirteenth and fourteenth, and then on the fifteenth they rested and made it a day of feasting and joy.

¹⁹That is why rural Jews—those living in villages—observe the fourteenth of the month of Adar as a day of joy and feasting, a day for giving presents to each other.

Purim Established

²⁰Mordecai recorded these events, and he sent letters to all the Jews through-

Esther 9

Q: What Jewish holiday is mentioned in this book?

BONUS: What did it celebrate?

Answers on next page

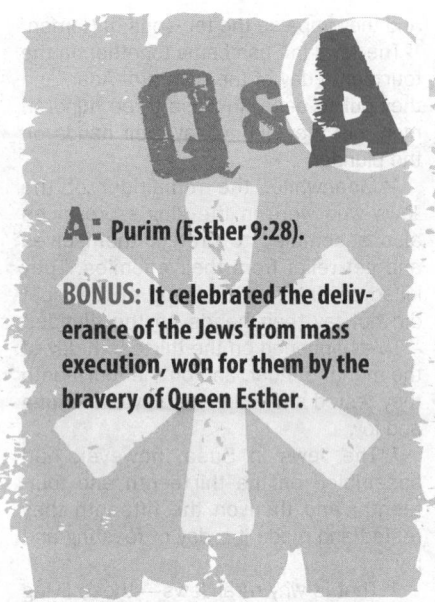

A: Purim (Esther 9:28).

BONUS: It celebrated the deliverance of the Jews from mass execution, won for them by the bravery of Queen Esther.

out the provinces of King Xerxes, near and far, [21] to have them celebrate annually the fourteenth and fifteenth days of the month of Adar [22] as the time when the Jews got relief from their enemies, and as the month when their sorrow was turned into joy and their mourning into a day of celebration. He wrote them to observe the days as days of feasting and joy and giving presents of food to one another and gifts to the poor.

[23] So the Jews agreed to continue the celebration they had begun, doing what Mordecai had written to them. [24] For Haman son of Hammedatha, the Agagite, the enemy of all the Jews, had plotted against the Jews to destroy them and had cast the *pur* (that is, the lot) for their ruin and destruction. [25] But when the plot came to the king's attention,[a] he issued written orders that the evil scheme Haman had devised against the Jews should come back onto his own head, and that he and his sons should be impaled on

poles. [26] (Therefore these days were called Purim, from the word *pur*.) Because of everything written in this letter and because of what they had seen and what had happened to them, [27] the Jews took it on themselves to establish the custom that they and their descendants and all who join them should without fail observe these two days every year, in the way prescribed and at the time appointed. [28] These days should be remembered and observed in every generation by every family, and in every province and in every city. And these days of Purim should never fail to be celebrated by the Jews—nor should the memory of these days die out among their descendants.

[29] So Queen Esther, daughter of Abihail, along with Mordecai the Jew, wrote with full authority to confirm this second letter concerning Purim. [30] And Mordecai sent letters to all the Jews in the 127 provinces of Xerxes' kingdom—words of goodwill and assurance— [31] to establish these days of Purim at their designated times, as Mordecai the Jew and Queen Esther had decreed for them, and as they had established for themselves and their descendants in regard to their times of fasting and lamentation. [32] Esther's decree confirmed these regulations about Purim, and it was written down in the records.

The Greatness of Mordecai

10 King Xerxes imposed tribute throughout the empire, to its distant shores. [2] And all his acts of power and might, together with a full account of the greatness of Mordecai, whom the king had promoted, are they not written in the book of the annals of the kings of Media and Persia? [3] Mordecai the Jew was second in rank to King Xerxes, preeminent among the Jews, and held in high esteem by his many fellow Jews, because he worked for the good of his people and spoke up for the welfare of all the Jews.

---

[a] 25 Or *when Esther came before the king*

JOB

Tough Times.

You plan a vacation and get sick the day before you're supposed to leave. Your grandma gets cancer, and even though you pray hard, she dies. Your dad, a good person, loses his job and can't find work. Do you ever wonder why God lets bad things happen to good people?

Job wondered too. He was a good person, but one day he lost all his wealth, all his children and his health. Job's friends said God must be punishing him for secret sins. Job knew he'd been faithful to God, but he couldn't explain why God was letting him suffer.

>>**SATAN ALLOWED TO TORMENT JOB**
God removes protection, story in Job 1:8–12

>>**FRIENDS AGREE, JOB HAS SINNED**
Accusation hurts the sufferer, see Job 8:1–7

>>**JOB CLAIMS HE'S INNOCENT**
Job's testimony recorded in Job 31

>>**ELIHU: GOD'S TOO BIG TO UNDERSTAND**
Younger man breaks impasse, report in Job 33

>>**GOD VISITS JOB, RESTORES HIM**
Blessings follow test of faith, see Job 42

preview

God calls Job "blameless and upright" (Job 1:8).

Job's suffering isn't punishment for sin—but the reason isn't fully explained. Like Job, we sometimes have to simply trust God in our hard times.

Job probably lived around the time of Abraham.

As Job struggles with suffering, Canaanite tribes settle in the Holy Land. Egyptians discover how to make paper from papyrus and develop an alphabet of 24 signs. The earliest pottery is fired in South America.

Prologue

1 In the land of Uz there lived a man whose name was Job. This man was blameless and upright; he feared God and shunned evil. ²He had seven sons and three daughters, ³and he owned seven thousand sheep, three thousand camels, five hundred yoke of oxen and five hundred donkeys, and had a large number of servants. He was the greatest man among all the people of the East.

⁴His sons used to hold feasts in their homes on their birthdays, and they would invite their three sisters to eat and drink with them. ⁵When a period of feasting had run its course, Job would make arrangements for them to be purified. Early in the morning he would sacrifice a burnt offering for each of them, thinking, "Perhaps my children have sinned and cursed God in their hearts." This was Job's regular custom.

⁶One day the angels[a] came to present themselves before the Lord, and Satan[b] also came with them. ⁷The Lord said to Satan, "Where have you come from?"

Satan answered the Lord, "From roaming throughout the earth, going back and forth on it."

⁸Then the Lord said to Satan, "Have you considered my servant Job? There is no one on earth like him; he is blameless and upright, a man who fears God and shuns evil."

⁹"Does Job fear God for nothing?" Satan replied. ¹⁰"Have you not put a hedge around him and his household and everything he has? You have blessed the work of his hands, so that his flocks and herds are spread throughout the land. ¹¹But now stretch out your hand and strike everything he has, and he will surely curse you to your face."

¹²The Lord said to Satan, "Very well, then, everything he has is in your power, but on the man himself do not lay a finger."

Then Satan went out from the presence of the Lord.

¹³One day when Job's sons and daughters were feasting and drinking wine at the oldest brother's house, ¹⁴a messenger came to Job and said, "The oxen were plowing and the donkeys were grazing nearby, ¹⁵and the Sabeans attacked and made off with them. They put the servants to the sword, and I am the only one who has escaped to tell you!"

¹⁶While he was still speaking, another messenger came and said, "The fire of God fell from the heavens and burned up the sheep and the servants, and I am the only one who has escaped to tell you!"

¹⁷While he was still speaking, another messenger came and said, "The Chaldeans formed three raiding parties and swept down on your camels and made off with them. They put the servants to the sword, and I am the only one who has escaped to tell you!"

¹⁸While he was still speaking, yet another messenger came and said, "Your sons and daughters were feasting and drinking wine at the oldest brother's house, ¹⁹when suddenly a mighty wind swept in from the desert and struck the four corners of the house. It collapsed on them and they are dead, and I am the only one who has escaped to tell you!"

²⁰At this, Job got up and tore his robe and shaved his head. Then he fell to the ground in worship ²¹and said:

"Naked I came from my mother's
    womb,
    and naked I will depart.[c]
The Lord gave and the Lord has taken
    away;
    may the name of the Lord be
    praised."

²²In all this, Job did not sin by charging God with wrongdoing.

2 On another day the angels[a] came to present themselves before the Lord, and Satan also came with them to present himself before him. ²And the Lord said to Satan, "Where have you come from?"

Satan answered the Lord, "From roaming throughout the earth, going back and forth on it."

ᵃ 6,1 Hebrew *the sons of God*   ᵇ 6 Hebrew *satan means adversary.*   ᶜ 21 Or *will return there*

Your friend's mother died yesterday. You know you should go over and talk to her, comfort her. But you just can't. You have no idea what to say. Well, this passage suggests that maybe you don't need to say anything! Job was so sad that when his friends came to comfort him, "they could hardly recognize him" (Job 2:12). What did they do? They sat "with him for seven days and seven nights. No one said a word to him" (Job 2:13)! Many times, when someone is sad or upset, words aren't necessary. Just your presence speaks of your love and caring. Don't be afraid. Go visit your friend. You don't have to say a word.

{Job 2:11–13}

≫ INSTANT ACCESS

³Then the LORD said to Satan, "Have you considered my servant Job? There is no one on earth like him; he is blameless and upright, a man who fears God and shuns evil. And he still maintains his integrity, though you incited me against him to ruin him without any reason."

⁴"Skin for skin!" Satan replied. "A man will give all he has for his own life. ⁵But now stretch out your hand and strike his flesh and bones, and he will surely curse you to your face."

⁶The LORD said to Satan, "Very well, then, he is in your hands; but you must spare his life."

⁷So Satan went out from the presence of the LORD and afflicted Job with painful sores from the soles of his feet to the crown of his head. ⁸Then Job took a piece of broken pottery and scraped himself with it as he sat among the ashes.

⁹His wife said to him, "Are you still maintaining your integrity? Curse God and die!"

¹⁰He replied, "You are talking like a foolish[a] woman. Shall we accept good from God, and not trouble?"

In all this, Job did not sin in what he said.

¹¹When Job's three friends, Eliphaz the Temanite, Bildad the Shuhite and Zophar the Naamathite, heard about all the troubles that had come upon him, they set out from their homes and met together by agreement to go and sympathize with him and comfort him. ¹²When they saw him from a distance, they could hardly recognize him; they began to weep aloud, and they tore their robes and sprinkled dust on their heads. ¹³Then they sat on the ground with him for seven days and seven nights. No one said a word to him, because they saw how great his suffering was.

Job Speaks

3 After this, Job opened his mouth and cursed the day of his birth. ²He said:

³ "May the day of my birth perish,
  and the night that said, 'A boy is
    conceived!'
⁴ That day—may it turn to darkness;
  may God above not care
    about it;
  may no light shine on it.
⁵ May gloom and utter darkness claim it
    once more;
  may a cloud settle over it;
  may blackness overwhelm it.
⁶ That night—may thick darkness
    seize it;

─────────────
a 10 The Hebrew word rendered *foolish* denotes moral deficiency.

Dear Jordan

Dear Zack,

I am sorry that you have lost a classmate. It is very shocking when someone so young dies, not only for his friends but also for his family. I don't know why some people we pray for are healed and others aren't. God does hear all of our prayers. We don't always get our prayers answered the way we desire them to be, even when they are wonderful, godly prayers.

In the book of Job, we read the story of a very godly and wealthy man. God is pleased because Job is so faithful. But Satan tells God it's easy to be faithful when one is so blessed. So God allowed Satan to attack all that Job had. All of Job's livestock died, his servants were killed, and so were his ten children (Job 1). But Job remained faithful to God.

Eventually, Satan was allowed to make Job sick (Job 2:7). Then his friends came and told him he must have done something wrong or God never would have let all these terrible things happen to him. But God speaks and explains that Job had done right, not wrong.

Job finally realized people cannot fully understand the purposes of God (42:1–3). In the end God gave him back twice the number of camels, sheep, and oxen that he had owned before. But he gave him only ten more children, not twenty. That's because God knew that Job's other 10 children were not lost. They were waiting in heaven for Job.

God didn't heal your friend the way you hoped he would. But even now he is healed and waiting for his family and friends who today miss him so.

Jordan

may it not be included among the
days of the year
nor be entered in any of the
months.
⁷ May that night be barren;
may no shout of joy be heard in it.
⁸ May those who curse days^a curse that
day,
those who are ready to rouse
Leviathan.
⁹ May its morning stars become dark;
may it wait for daylight in vain
and not see the first rays of
dawn,
¹⁰ for it did not shut the doors of the
womb on me
to hide trouble from my eyes.

¹¹ "Why did I not perish at birth,
and die as I came from the
womb?
¹² Why were there knees to receive me
and breasts that I might be
nursed?
¹³ For now I would be lying down in
peace;
I would be asleep and at rest
¹⁴ with kings and rulers of the earth,
who built for themselves places
now lying in ruins,
¹⁵ with princes who had gold,
who filled their houses with silver.
¹⁶ Or why was I not hidden away in the
ground like a stillborn child,
like an infant who never saw the
light of day?
¹⁷ There the wicked cease from turmoil,
and there the weary are at rest.
¹⁸ Captives also enjoy their ease;
they no longer hear the slave
driver's shout.
¹⁹ The small and the great are there,
and the slaves are freed from their
owners.

²⁰ "Why is light given to those in
misery,
and life to the bitter of soul,
²¹ to those who long for death that does
not come,
who search for it more than for
hidden treasure,

²² who are filled with gladness
and rejoice when they reach the
grave?
²³ Why is life given to a man
whose way is hidden,
whom God has hedged in?
²⁴ For sighing has become my daily
food;
my groans pour out like water.
²⁵ What I feared has come upon me;
what I dreaded has happened
to me.
²⁶ I have no peace, no quietness;
I have no rest, but only turmoil."

Eliphaz

4 Then Eliphaz the Temanite replied:

² "If someone ventures a word with you,
will you be impatient?
But who can keep from speaking?
³ Think how you have instructed
many,
how you have strengthened feeble
hands.
⁴ Your words have supported those who
stumbled;
you have strengthened faltering
knees.
⁵ But now trouble comes to you, and
you are discouraged;
it strikes you, and you are
dismayed.
⁶ Should not your piety be your
confidence
and your blameless ways your
hope?

⁷ "Consider now: Who, being innocent,
has ever perished?
Where were the upright ever
destroyed?
⁸ As I have observed, those who plow
evil
and those who sow trouble
reap it.
⁹ At the breath of God they perish;
at the blast of his anger they are no
more.
¹⁰ The lions may roar and growl,
yet the teeth of the great lions are
broken.

¹¹ The lion perishes for lack of prey,
  and the cubs of the lioness are
   scattered.

¹² "A word was secretly brought to me,
  my ears caught a whisper of it.
¹³ Amid disquieting dreams in the night,
  when deep sleep falls on people,
¹⁴ fear and trembling seized me
  and made all my bones shake.
¹⁵ A spirit glided past my face,
  and the hair on my body stood
   on end.
¹⁶ It stopped,
  but I could not tell what it was.
 A form stood before my eyes,
  and I heard a hushed voice:
¹⁷ 'Can a mortal be more righteous than
   God?
  Can even a strong man be more
   pure than his Maker?
¹⁸ If God places no trust in his
   servants,
  if he charges his angels with error,
¹⁹ how much more those who live in
   houses of clay,
  whose foundations are in the
   dust,
  who are crushed more readily than
   a moth!
²⁰ Between dawn and dusk they are
   broken to pieces;
  unnoticed, they perish forever.
²¹ Are not the cords of their tent pulled
   up,
  so that they die without wisdom?'

5 "Call if you will, but who will answer
  you?
  To which of the holy ones will you
   turn?
² Resentment kills a fool,
  and envy slays the simple.
³ I myself have seen a fool taking root,
  but suddenly his house was cursed.
⁴ His children are far from safety,
  crushed in court without a
   defender.
⁵ The hungry consume his harvest,
  taking it even from among thorns,
  and the thirsty pant after his
   wealth.

⁶ For hardship does not spring from the
   soil,
  nor does trouble sprout from the
   ground.
⁷ Yet man is born to trouble
  as surely as sparks fly upward.

⁸ "But if I were you, I would appeal to
   God;
  I would lay my cause before him.
⁹ He performs wonders that cannot be
   fathomed,
  miracles that cannot be counted.
¹⁰ He provides rain for the earth;
  he sends water on the countryside.
¹¹ The lowly he sets on high,
  and those who mourn are lifted to
   safety.
¹² He thwarts the plans of the crafty,
  so that their hands achieve no
   success.
¹³ He catches the wise in their
   craftiness,
  and the schemes of the wily are
   swept away.
¹⁴ Darkness comes upon them in the
   daytime;
  at noon they grope as in the night.
¹⁵ He saves the needy from the sword in
   their mouth;
  he saves them from the clutches of
   the powerful.
¹⁶ So the poor have hope,
  and injustice shuts its mouth.

¹⁷ "Blessed is the one whom God
   corrects;
  so do not despise the discipline of
   the Almighty.ᵃ
¹⁸ For he wounds, but he also binds up;
  he injures, but his hands also heal.
¹⁹ From six calamities he will rescue
   you;
  in seven no harm will touch you.
²⁰ In famine he will deliver you from
   death,
  and in battle from the stroke of the
   sword.
²¹ You will be protected from the lash of
   the tongue,
  and need not fear when destruction
   comes.

ᵃ *17* Hebrew *Shaddai*; here and throughout Job

22 You will laugh at destruction and famine,
and need not fear the wild animals.
23 For you will have a covenant with the stones of the field,
and the wild animals will be at peace with you.
24 You will know that your tent is secure;
you will take stock of your property and find nothing missing.
25 You will know that your children will be many,
and your descendants like the grass of the earth.
26 You will come to the grave in full vigor,
like sheaves gathered in season.

27 "We have examined this, and it is true.
So hear it and apply it to yourself."

Job

6

Then Job replied:

2 "If only my anguish could be weighed
and all my misery be placed on the scales!
3 It would surely outweigh the sand of the seas—
no wonder my words have been impetuous.
4 The arrows of the Almighty are in me,
my spirit drinks in their poison;
God's terrors are marshaled against me.
5 Does a wild donkey bray when it has grass,
or an ox bellow when it has fodder?
6 Is tasteless food eaten without salt,
or is there flavor in the sap of the mallow[a]?
7 I refuse to touch it;
such food makes me ill.

8 "Oh, that I might have my request,
that God would grant what I hope for,
9 that God would be willing to crush me,
to let loose his hand and cut off my life!

10 Then I would still have this consolation—
my joy in unrelenting pain—
that I had not denied the words of the Holy One.

11 "What strength do I have, that I should still hope?
What prospects, that I should be patient?
12 Do I have the strength of stone?
Is my flesh bronze?
13 Do I have any power to help myself,
now that success has been driven from me?

14 "Anyone who withholds kindness from a friend
forsakes the fear of the Almighty.
15 But my brothers are as undependable as intermittent streams,
as the streams that overflow
16 when darkened by thawing ice
and swollen with melting snow,
17 but that stop flowing in the dry season,
and in the heat vanish from their channels.
18 Caravans turn aside from their routes;
they go off into the wasteland and perish.
19 The caravans of Tema look for water,
the traveling merchants of Sheba look in hope.
20 They are distressed, because they had been confident;
they arrive there, only to be disappointed.
21 Now you too have proved to be of no help;
you see something dreadful and are afraid.
22 Have I ever said, 'Give something on my behalf,
pay a ransom for me from your wealth,
23 deliver me from the hand of the enemy,
rescue me from the clutches of the ruthless'?

---

a 6 The meaning of the Hebrew for this phrase is uncertain.

24 "Teach me, and I will be quiet;
    show me where I have been wrong.
25 How painful are honest words!
    But what do your arguments prove?
26 Do you mean to correct what I say,
    and treat my desperate words as
        wind?
27 You would even cast lots for the
        fatherless
    and barter away your friend.

28 "But now be so kind as to look at me.
    Would I lie to your face?
29 Relent, do not be unjust;
    reconsider, for my integrity is at
        stake.[a]
30 Is there any wickedness on my lips?
    Can my mouth not discern
        malice?

7 "Do not mortals have hard service
        on earth?
    Are not their days like those of
        hired laborers?
2 Like a slave longing for the evening
        shadows,
    or a hired laborer waiting to be
        paid,
3 so I have been allotted months of
        futility,
    and nights of misery have been
        assigned to me.
4 When I lie down I think, 'How long
        before I get up?'
    The night drags on, and I toss and
        turn until dawn.
5 My body is clothed with worms and
        scabs,
    my skin is broken and festering.

6 "My days are swifter than a weaver's
        shuttle,
    and they come to an end without
        hope.
7 Remember, O God, that my life is but
        a breath;
    my eyes will never see happiness
        again.
8 The eye that now sees me will see me
        no longer;
    you will look for me, but I will be no
        more.

9 As a cloud vanishes and is gone,
    so one who goes down to the grave
        does not return.
10 He will never come to his house
        again;
    his place will know him no more.

11 "Therefore I will not keep silent;
    I will speak out in the anguish of my
        spirit,
    I will complain in the bitterness of
        my soul.
12 Am I the sea, or the monster of the
        deep,
    that you put me under guard?
13 When I think my bed will comfort me
    and my couch will ease my
        complaint,
14 even then you frighten me with
        dreams
    and terrify me with visions,
15 so that I prefer strangling and death,
    rather than this body of mine.
16 I despise my life; I would not live
        forever.
    Let me alone; my days have no
        meaning.

17 "What is mankind that you make so
        much of them,
    that you give them so much
        attention,
18 that you examine them every morning
    and test them every moment?
19 Will you never look away from me,
    or let me alone even for an instant?
20 If I have sinned, what have I done to
        you,
    you who sees everything we do?
    Why have you made me your target?
    Have I become a burden to you?[b]
21 Why do you not pardon my offenses
    and forgive my sins?
    For I will soon lie down in the dust;
    you will search for me, but I will be
        no more."

Bildad

8 Then Bildad the Shuhite replied:

2 "How long will you say such things?
    Your words are a blustering wind.

---

a 29 Or *my righteousness still stands*   b 20 A few manuscripts of the Masoretic Text, an ancient Hebrew scribal tradition and Septuagint; most manuscripts of the Masoretic Text *I have become a burden to myself.*

3 Does God pervert justice?
  Does the Almighty pervert what is
    right?
4 When your children sinned against
    him,
  he gave them over to the penalty of
    their sin.
5 But if you will seek God earnestly
  and plead with the Almighty,
6 if you are pure and upright,
  even now he will rouse himself on
    your behalf
  and restore you to your prosperous
    state.
7 Your beginnings will seem humble,
  so prosperous will your future be.

8 "Ask the former generation
  and find out what their ancestors
    learned,
9 for we were born only yesterday and
    know nothing,
  and our days on earth are but a
    shadow.
10 Will they not instruct you and tell you?
  Will they not bring forth words from
    their understanding?
11 Can papyrus grow tall where there is
    no marsh?
  Can reeds thrive without water?
12 While still growing and uncut,
  they wither more quickly than grass.
13 Such is the destiny of all who forget
    God;
  so perishes the hope of the
    godless.
14 What they trust in is fragile*;
  what they rely on is a spider's web.
15 They lean on the web, but it gives
    way;
  they cling to it, but it does not hold.
16 They are like a well-watered plant in
    the sunshine,
  spreading its shoots over the
    garden;
17 it entwines its roots around a pile of
    rocks
  and looks for a place among the
    stones.
18 But when it is torn from its spot,
  that place disowns it and says, 'I
    never saw you.'

19 Surely its life withers away,
  and* from the soil other plants
    grow.
20 "Surely God does not reject one who
    is blameless
  or strengthen the hands of
    evildoers.
21 He will yet fill your mouth with
    laughter
  and your lips with shouts of joy.
22 Your enemies will be clothed in
    shame,
  and the tents of the wicked will be
    no more."

Job

9

Then Job replied:

2 "Indeed, I know that this is true.
  But how can mere mortals prove
    their innocence before God?
3 Though they wished to dispute with
    him,
  they could not answer him one time
    out of a thousand.
4 His wisdom is profound, his power is
    vast.
  Who has resisted him and come out
    unscathed?
5 He moves mountains without their
    knowing it
  and overturns them in his anger.
6 He shakes the earth from its place
  and makes its pillars tremble.
7 He speaks to the sun and it does not
    shine;
  he seals off the light of the stars.
8 He alone stretches out the heavens
  and treads on the waves of the
    sea.
9 He is the Maker of the Bear* and
    Orion,
  the Pleiades and the constellations
    of the south.
10 He performs wonders that cannot be
    fathomed,
  miracles that cannot be counted.
11 When he passes me, I cannot see
    him;
  when he goes by, I cannot perceive
    him.

---

a 14 The meaning of the Hebrew for this word is uncertain.   b 19 Or Surely all the joy it has / is that   c 9 Or of Leo

12 If he snatches away, who can stop him?
    Who can say to him, 'What are you doing?'

13 God does not restrain his anger;
    even the cohorts of Rahab cowered at his feet.

14 "How then can I dispute with him?
    How can I find words to argue with him?

15 Though I were innocent, I could not answer him;
    I could only plead with my Judge for mercy.

16 Even if I summoned him and he responded,
    I do not believe he would give me a hearing.

17 He would crush me with a storm
    and multiply my wounds for no reason.

18 He would not let me catch my breath
    but would overwhelm me with misery.

19 If it is a matter of strength, he is mighty!
    And if it is a matter of justice, who can challenge him?[a]

20 Even if I were innocent, my mouth would condemn me;
    if I were blameless, it would pronounce me guilty.

21 "Although I am blameless,
    I have no concern for myself;
    I despise my own life.

22 It is all the same; that is why I say,
    'He destroys both the blameless and the wicked.'

23 When a scourge brings sudden death,
    he mocks the despair of the innocent.

24 When a land falls into the hands of the wicked,
    he blindfolds its judges.
    If it is not he, then who is it?

25 "My days are swifter than a runner;
    they fly away without a glimpse of joy.

26 They skim past like boats of papyrus,
    like eagles swooping down on their prey.

27 If I say, 'I will forget my complaint,
    I will change my expression, and smile,'

28 I still dread all my sufferings,
    for I know you will not hold me innocent.

29 Since I am already found guilty,
    why should I struggle in vain?

30 Even if I washed myself with soap
    and my hands with cleansing powder,

31 you would plunge me into a slime pit
    so that even my clothes would detest me.

32 "He is not a mere mortal like me that I might answer him,
    that we might confront each other in court.

33 If only there were someone to mediate between us,
    someone to bring us together,

34 someone to remove God's rod from me,
    so that his terror would frighten me no more.

35 Then I would speak up without fear of him,
    but as it now stands with me, I cannot.

10 "I loathe my very life;
    therefore I will give free rein to my complaint
    and speak out in the bitterness of my soul.

2 I say to God: Do not declare me guilty,
    but tell me what charges you have against me.

3 Does it please you to oppress me,
    to spurn the work of your hands,
    while you smile on the plans of the wicked?

4 Do you have eyes of flesh?
    Do you see as a mortal sees?

5 Are your days like those of a mortal
    or your years like those of a strong man,

6 that you must search out my faults
    and probe after my sin—

---

⁷though you know that I am not guilty
and that no one can rescue me
from your hand?

⁸ "Your hands shaped me and made me.
Will you now turn and destroy me?
⁹Remember that you molded me like
clay.
Will you now turn me to dust again?
¹⁰Did you not pour me out like milk
and curdle me like cheese,
¹¹clothe me with skin and flesh
and knit me together with bones
and sinews?
¹²You gave me life and showed me
kindness,
and in your providence watched
over my spirit.

¹³ "But this is what you concealed in
your heart,
and I know that this was in your
mind:
¹⁴If I sinned, you would be watching me
and would not let my offense go
unpunished.
¹⁵If I am guilty—woe to me!
Even if I am innocent, I cannot lift
my head,
for I am full of shame
and drowned in ᵃ my affliction.
¹⁶If I hold my head high, you stalk me
like a lion
and again display your awesome
power against me.
¹⁷You bring new witnesses against me
and increase your anger toward me;
your forces come against me wave
upon wave.

¹⁸ "Why then did you bring me out of
the womb?
I wish I had died before any eye
saw me.
¹⁹If only I had never come into being,
or had been carried straight from
the womb to the grave!
²⁰Are not my few days almost over?
Turn away from me so I can have a
moment's joy
²¹before I go to the place of no return,
to the land of gloom and utter
darkness,

> *You gave me life and
> showed me kindness,
> and in your providence
> watched over my spirit.*
>
> Job 10:12

²²to the land of deepest night,
of utter darkness and disorder,
where even the light is like
darkness."

Zophar

11 Then Zophar the Naamathite replied:

² "Are all these words to go
unanswered?
Is this talker to be vindicated?
³Will your idle talk reduce others to
silence?
Will no one rebuke you when you
mock?
⁴You say to God, 'My beliefs are
flawless
and I am pure in your sight.'
⁵Oh, how I wish that God would speak,
that he would open his lips against
you
⁶and disclose to you the secrets of
wisdom,
for true wisdom has two sides.
Know this: God has even forgotten
some of your sin.

⁷ "Can you fathom the mysteries of
God?
Can you probe the limits of the
Almighty?
⁸They are higher than the heavens
above—what can you do?
They are deeper than the depths
below—what can you know?

ᵃ 15 Or and aware of

9 Their measure is longer than the earth
  and wider than the sea.

10 "If he comes along and confines you
     in prison
   and convenes a court, who can
     oppose him?
11 Surely he recognizes deceivers;
   and when he sees evil, does he not
     take note?
12 But the witless can no more become
     wise
   than a wild donkey's colt can be
     born human.*a*

13 "Yet if you devote your heart to him
   and stretch out your hands to him,
14 if you put away the sin that is in your
     hand
   and allow no evil to dwell in your
     tent,
15 then, free of fault, you will lift up your
     face;
   you will stand firm and without fear.
16 You will surely forget your trouble,
   recalling it only as waters gone by.
17 Life will be brighter than noonday,
   and darkness will become like
     morning.
18 You will be secure, because there is
     hope;
   you will look about you and take
     your rest in safety.
19 You will lie down, with no one to make
     you afraid,
   and many will court your favor.
20 But the eyes of the wicked will fail,
   and escape will elude them;
   their hope will become a dying
     gasp."

Job

12 Then Job replied:

2 "Doubtless you are the only people
     who matter,
   and wisdom will die with you!
3 But I have a mind as well as you;
   I am not inferior to you.
   Who does not know all these
     things?

4 "I have become a laughingstock to my
     friends,
   though I called on God and he
     answered—
   a mere laughingstock, though
     righteous and blameless!
5 Those who are at ease have contempt
     for misfortune
   as the fate of those whose feet are
     slipping.
6 The tents of marauders are
     undisturbed,
   and those who provoke God are
     secure—
   those God has in his hand.*b*

7 "But ask the animals, and they will
     teach you,
   or the birds in the sky, and they will
     tell you;
8 or speak to the earth, and it will teach
     you,
   or let the fish in the sea inform you.
9 Which of all these does not know
   that the hand of the LORD has done
     this?
10 In his hand is the life of every
     creature
   and the breath of all mankind.
11 Does not the ear test words
   as the tongue tastes food?
12 Is not wisdom found among the aged?
   Does not long life bring
     understanding?

13 "To God belong wisdom and power;
   counsel and understanding are his.
14 What he tears down cannot be rebuilt;
   those he imprisons cannot be
     released.
15 If he holds back the waters, there is
     drought;
   if he lets them loose, they
     devastate the land.
16 To him belong strength and insight;
   both deceived and deceiver are his.
17 He leads rulers away stripped
   and makes fools of judges.
18 He takes off the shackles put on by
     kings
   and ties a loincloth*c* around their
     waist.

---

a 12 Or *wild donkey can be born tame*   *b* 6 Or *those whose god is in their own hand*   *c* 18 Or *shackles of kings / and ties a belt*

¹⁹He leads priests away stripped
and overthrows officials long
established.
²⁰He silences the lips of trusted
advisers
and takes away the discernment of
elders.
²¹He pours contempt on nobles
and disarms the mighty.
²²He reveals the deep things of
darkness
and brings utter darkness into the
light.
²³He makes nations great, and destroys
them;
he enlarges nations, and disperses
them.
²⁴He deprives the leaders of the earth
of their reason;
he makes them wander in a
trackless waste.
²⁵They grope in darkness with no
light;
he makes them stagger like
drunkards.

13 "My eyes have seen all this,
my ears have heard and
understood it.
²What you know, I also know;
I am not inferior to you.
³But I desire to speak to the Almighty
and to argue my case with God.
⁴You, however, smear me with lies;
you are worthless physicians, all of
you!
⁵If only you would be altogether
silent!
For you, that would be wisdom.
⁶Hear now my argument;
listen to the pleas of my lips.
⁷Will you speak wickedly on God's
behalf?
Will you speak deceitfully for him?
⁸Will you show him partiality?
Will you argue the case for God?
⁹Would it turn out well if he examined
you?
Could you deceive him as you might
deceive a mortal?
¹⁰He would surely call you to account
if you secretly showed partiality.

¹¹Would not his splendor terrify you?
Would not the dread of him fall on
you?
¹²Your maxims are proverbs of ashes;
your defenses are defenses of clay.

¹³"Keep silent and let me speak;
then let come to me what may.
¹⁴Why do I put myself in jeopardy
and take my life in my hands?
¹⁵Though he slay me, yet will I hope in
him;
I will surely*a* defend my ways to his
face.
¹⁶Indeed, this will turn out for my
deliverance,
for no godless person would dare
come before him!
¹⁷Listen carefully to what I say;
let my words ring in your ears.
¹⁸Now that I have prepared my case,
I know I will be vindicated.
¹⁹Can anyone bring charges
against me?
If so, I will be silent and die.

²⁰"Only grant me these two things, God,
and then I will not hide from you:
²¹Withdraw your hand far from me,
and stop frightening me with your
terrors.
²²Then summon me and I will answer,
or let me speak, and you reply to me.
²³How many wrongs and sins have I
committed?
Show me my offense and my sin.
²⁴Why do you hide your face
and consider me your enemy?
²⁵Will you torment a windblown leaf?
Will you chase after dry chaff?
²⁶For you write down bitter things
against me
and make me reap the sins of my
youth.
²⁷You fasten my feet in shackles;
you keep close watch on all my
paths
by putting marks on the soles of my
feet.
²⁸"So man wastes away like something
rotten,
like a garment eaten by moths.

---

a 15 Or *He will surely slay me; I have no hope* — / *yet I will*

14 "Mortals, born of woman,
    are of few days and full of
    trouble.
2 They spring up like flowers and wither
        away;
    like fleeting shadows, they do not
        endure.
3 Do you fix your eye on them?
    Will you bring them[a] before you for
        judgment?
4 Who can bring what is pure from the
        impure?
    No one!
5 A person's days are determined;
    you have decreed the number of his
        months
    and have set limits he cannot
        exceed.
6 So look away from him and let him
        alone,
    till he has put in his time like a
        hired laborer.

7 "At least there is hope for a tree:
    If it is cut down, it will sprout again,
    and its new shoots will not fail.
8 Its roots may grow old in the ground
    and its stump die in the soil,
9 yet at the scent of water it will bud
    and put forth shoots like a plant.
10 But a man dies and is laid low;
    he breathes his last and is no
        more.
11 As the water of a lake dries up
    or a riverbed becomes parched and
        dry,
12 so he lies down and does not rise;
    till the heavens are no more, people
        will not awake
    or be roused from their sleep.

13 "If only you would hide me in the grave
    and conceal me till your anger has
        passed!
    If only you would set me a time
    and then remember me!
14 If someone dies, will they live again?
    All the days of my hard service
    I will wait for my renewal[b] to come.
15 You will call and I will answer you;
    you will long for the creature your
        hands have made.

16 Surely then you will count my steps
    but not keep track of my sin.
17 My offenses will be sealed up in a
        bag;
    you will cover over my sin.

18 "But as a mountain erodes and
        crumbles
    and as a rock is moved from its
        place,
19 as water wears away stones
    and torrents wash away the soil,
    so you destroy a person's hope.
20 You overpower them once for all, and
        they are gone;
    you change their countenance and
        send them away.
21 If their children are honored, they do
        not know it;
    if their offspring are brought low,
        they do not see it.
22 They feel but the pain of their own
        bodies
    and mourn only for themselves."

Eliphaz

15 Then Eliphaz the Temanite replied:

2 "Would a wise person answer with
        empty notions
    or fill their belly with the hot east
        wind?
3 Would they argue with useless words,
    with speeches that have no value?
4 But you even undermine piety
    and hinder devotion to God.
5 Your sin prompts your mouth;
    you adopt the tongue of the crafty.
6 Your own mouth condemns you, not
        mine;
    your own lips testify against you.

7 "Are you the first man ever born?
    Were you brought forth before the
        hills?
8 Do you listen in on God's council?
    Do you have a monopoly on
        wisdom?
9 What do you know that we do not
        know?
    What insights do you have that we
        do not have?

---

[a] 3 Septuagint, Vulgate and Syriac; Hebrew *me*   [b] 14 Or *release*

10 The gray-haired and the aged are on
     our side,
     men even older than your father.
11 Are God's consolations not enough for
     you,
     words spoken gently to you?
12 Why has your heart carried you away,
     and why do your eyes flash,
13 so that you vent your rage against God
     and pour out such words from your
     mouth?
14 "What are mortals, that they could be
     pure,
     or those born of woman, that they
     could be righteous?
15 If God places no trust in his holy
     ones,
     if even the heavens are not pure in
     his eyes,
16 how much less mortals, who are vile
     and corrupt,
     who drink up evil like water!

17 "Listen to me and I will explain
     to you;
     let me tell you what I have seen,
18 what the wise have declared,
     hiding nothing received from their
     ancestors
19 (to whom alone the land was given
     when no foreigners moved among
     them):
20 All his days the wicked man suffers
     torment,
     the ruthless man through all the
     years stored up for him.

21 Terrifying sounds fill his ears;
     when all seems well, marauders
     attack him.
22 He despairs of escaping the realm of
     darkness;
     he is marked for the sword.
23 He wanders about for food like a
     vulture;
     he knows the day of darkness is at
     hand.
24 Distress and anguish fill him with
     terror;
     troubles overwhelm him, like a king
     poised to attack,
25 because he shakes his fist at God
     and vaunts himself against the
     Almighty,
26 defiantly charging against him
     with a thick, strong shield.

27 "Though his face is covered with
     fat
     and his waist bulges with flesh,
28 he will inhabit ruined towns
     and houses where no one lives,
     houses crumbling to rubble.
29 He will no longer be rich and his
     wealth will not endure,
     nor will his possessions spread
     over the land.
30 He will not escape the darkness;
     a flame will wither his shoots,
     and the breath of God's mouth will
     carry him away.
31 Let him not deceive himself by
     trusting what is worthless,
     for he will get nothing in return.

PANORAMA

{JOB}

Tough Times.

Bad things happen to good people. Job was
a good person, but one day he lost all his
money, all his children and his health. Job
was faithful to God, and he couldn't explain
why God was letting him suffer.

32 Before his time he will wither,
and his branches will not flourish.
33 He will be like a vine stripped of its
unripe grapes,
like an olive tree shedding its
blossoms.
34 For the company of the godless will be
barren,
and fire will consume the tents of
those who love bribes.
35 They conceive trouble and give birth to
evil;
their womb fashions deceit."

Job
16
Then Job replied:

2 "I have heard many things like these;
you are miserable comforters, all of
you!
3 Will your long-winded speeches never
end?
What ails you that you keep on
arguing?
4 I also could speak like you,
if you were in my place;
I could make fine speeches against
you
and shake my head at you.
5 But my mouth would encourage you;
comfort from my lips would bring
you relief.

6 "Yet if I speak, my pain is not relieved;
and if I refrain, it does not go away.
7 Surely, God, you have worn me out;
you have devastated my entire
household.
8 You have shriveled me up—and it has
become a witness;
my gauntness rises up and testifies
against me.
9 God assails me and tears me in his
anger
and gnashes his teeth at me;
my opponent fastens on me his
piercing eyes.
10 People open their mouths to jeer
at me;
they strike my cheek in scorn
and unite together against me.

11 God has turned me over to the
ungodly
and thrown me into the clutches of
the wicked.
12 All was well with me, but he
shattered me;
he seized me by the neck and
crushed me.
He has made me his target;
13 his archers surround me.
Without pity, he pierces my kidneys
and spills my gall on the ground.
14 Again and again he bursts upon me;
he rushes at me like a warrior.

15 "I have sewed sackcloth over my skin
and buried my brow in the dust.
16 My face is red with weeping,
dark shadows ring my eyes;
17 yet my hands have been free of
violence
and my prayer is pure.

18 "Earth, do not cover my blood;
may my cry never be laid to rest!
19 Even now my witness is in heaven;
my advocate is on high.
20 My intercessor is my friend[a]
as my eyes pour out tears to God;
21 on behalf of a man he pleads with
God
as one pleads for a friend.

22 "Only a few years will pass
before I take the path of no return.
17
1 My spirit is broken,
my days are cut short,
the grave awaits me.
2 Surely mockers surround me;
my eyes must dwell on their
hostility.

3 "Give me, O God, the pledge you
demand.
Who else will put up security for
me?
4 You have closed their minds to
understanding;
therefore you will not let them
triumph.
5 If anyone denounces their friends for
reward,
the eyes of their children will fail.

---

[a] 20 Or *My friends treat me with scorn*

6 "God has made me a byword to everyone,
a man in whose face people spit.
7 My eyes have grown dim with grief;
my whole frame is but a shadow.
8 The upright are appalled at this;
the innocent are aroused against the ungodly.
9 Nevertheless, the righteous will hold to their ways,
and those with clean hands will grow stronger.

10 "But come on, all of you, try again!
I will not find a wise man among you.
11 My days have passed, my plans are shattered.
Yet the desires of my heart
12 turn night into day;
in the face of the darkness light is near.
13 If the only home I hope for is the grave,
if I spread out my bed in the realm of darkness,
14 if I say to corruption, 'You are my father,'
and to the worm, 'My mother' or 'My sister,'
15 where then is my hope—
who can see any hope for me?
16 Will it go down to the gates of death?
Will we descend together into the dust?"

Bildad

18 Then Bildad the Shuhite replied:

2 "When will you end these speeches?
Be sensible, and then we can talk.
3 Why are we regarded as cattle
and considered stupid in your sight?
4 You who tear yourself to pieces in your anger,
is the earth to be abandoned for your sake?
Or must the rocks be moved from their place?

5 "The lamp of a wicked man is snuffed out;
the flame of his fire stops burning.

6 The light in his tent becomes dark;
the lamp beside him goes out.
7 The vigor of his step is weakened;
his own schemes throw him down.
8 His feet thrust him into a net;
he wanders into its mesh.
9 A trap seizes him by the heel;
a snare holds him fast.
10 A noose is hidden for him on the ground;
a trap lies in his path.
11 Terrors startle him on every side
and dog his every step.
12 Calamity is hungry for him;
disaster is ready for him when he falls.
13 It eats away parts of his skin;
death's firstborn devours his limbs.
14 He is torn from the security of his tent
and marched off to the king of terrors.
15 Fire resides[a] in his tent;
burning sulfur is scattered over his dwelling.
16 His roots dry up below
and his branches wither above.
17 The memory of him perishes from the earth;
he has no name in the land.
18 He is driven from light into the realm of darkness
and is banished from the world.
19 He has no offspring or descendants among his people,
no survivor where once he lived.
20 People of the west are appalled at his fate;
those of the east are seized with horror.
21 Surely such is the dwelling of an evil man;
such is the place of one who does not know God."

Job

19 Then Job replied:

2 "How long will you torment me
and crush me with words?
3 Ten times now you have reproached me;

---

a 15 Or *Nothing he had remains*

shamelessly you attack me.
⁴ If it is true that I have gone astray,
my error remains my concern alone.
⁵ If indeed you would exalt yourselves
above me
and use my humiliation against me,
⁶ then know that God has wronged me
and drawn his net around me.

⁷ "Though I cry, 'Violence!' I get no
response;
though I call for help, there is no
justice.
⁸ He has blocked my way so I cannot
pass;
he has shrouded my paths in
darkness.
⁹ He has stripped me of my honor
and removed the crown from my
head.
¹⁰ He tears me down on every side till I
am gone;
he uproots my hope like a tree.
¹¹ His anger burns against me;
he counts me among his enemies.
¹² His troops advance in force;
they build a siege ramp against me
and encamp around my tent.

¹³ "He has alienated my family from me;
my acquaintances are completely
estranged from me.
¹⁴ My relatives have gone away;
my closest friends have
forgotten me.
¹⁵ My guests and my female servants
count me a foreigner;
they look on me as on a stranger.
¹⁶ I summon my servant, but he does
not answer,
though I beg him with my own
mouth.
¹⁷ My breath is offensive to my wife;
I am loathsome to my own family.
¹⁸ Even the little boys scorn me;
when I appear, they ridicule me.
¹⁹ All my intimate friends detest me;
those I love have turned
against me.
²⁰ I am nothing but skin and bones;
I have escaped only by the skin of
my teeth.ᵃ

²¹ "Have pity on me, my friends, have
pity,
for the hand of God has struck me.
²² Why do you pursue me as God does?
Will you never get enough of my
flesh?

²³ "Oh, that my words were recorded,
that they were written on a scroll,
²⁴ that they were inscribed with an iron
tool onᵇ lead,
or engraved in rock forever!
²⁵ I know that my redeemerᶜ lives,
and that in the end he will stand on
the earth.ᵈ
²⁶ And after my skin has been
destroyed,
yetᵉ inᶠ my flesh I will see God;
²⁷ I myself will see him
with my own eyes—I, and not
another.
How my heart yearns within me!

²⁸ "If you say, 'How we will hound him,
since the root of the trouble lies in
him,ᵍ'
²⁹ you should fear the sword
yourselves;
for wrath will bring punishment by
the sword,
and then you will know that there is
judgment.ʰ"

Zophar

20 Then Zophar the Naamathite replied:

² "My troubled thoughts prompt me to
answer
because I am greatly disturbed.
³ I hear a rebuke that dishonors me,
and my understanding inspires me
to reply.

⁴ "Surely you know how it has been
from of old,
ever since mankindⁱ was placed on
the earth,
⁵ that the mirth of the wicked is brief,
the joy of the godless lasts but a
moment.

ᵃ 20 Or only by my gums   ᵇ 24 Or and   ᶜ 25 Or vindicator   ᵈ 25 Or on my grave   ᵉ 26 Or And after I awake,
/ though this body has been destroyed, / then   ᶠ 26 Or destroyed, / apart from   ᵍ 28 Many Hebrew manuscripts,
Septuagint and Vulgate; most Hebrew manuscripts me   ʰ 29 Or sword, / that you may come to know the Almighty
ⁱ 4 Or Adam

6 Though the pride of the godless
person reaches to the heavens
and his head touches the clouds,
7 he will perish forever, like his own
dung;
those who have seen him will say,
'Where is he?'
8 Like a dream he flies away, no more
to be found,
banished like a vision of the night.
9 The eye that saw him will not see him
again;
his place will look on him no more.
10 His children must make amends to
the poor;
his own hands must give back his
wealth.
11 The youthful vigor that fills his bones
will lie with him in the dust.

12 "Though evil is sweet in his mouth
and he hides it under his tongue,
13 though he cannot bear to let it go
and lets it linger in his mouth,
14 yet his food will turn sour in his
stomach;
it will become the venom of
serpents within him.
15 He will spit out the riches he
swallowed;
God will make his stomach vomit
them up.
16 He will suck the poison of serpents;
the fangs of an adder will kill him.
17 He will not enjoy the streams,
the rivers flowing with honey and
cream.
18 What he toiled for he must give back
uneaten;
he will not enjoy the profit from his
trading.
19 For he has oppressed the poor and
left them destitute;
he has seized houses he did not
build.

20 "Surely he will have no respite from
his craving;
he cannot save himself by his
treasure.
21 Nothing is left for him to devour;
his prosperity will not endure.

22 In the midst of his plenty, distress will
overtake him;
the full force of misery will come
upon him.
23 When he has filled his belly,
God will vent his burning anger
against him
and rain down his blows on him.
24 Though he flees from an iron weapon,
a bronze-tipped arrow pierces him.
25 He pulls it out of his back,
the gleaming point out of his liver.
Terrors will come over him;
26 total darkness lies in wait for his
treasures.
A fire unfanned will consume him
and devour what is left in his tent.
27 The heavens will expose his guilt;
the earth will rise up against him.
28 A flood will carry off his house,
rushing waters[a] on the day of God's
wrath.
29 Such is the fate God allots the wicked,
the heritage appointed for them by
God."

Job

21 Then Job replied:

2 "Listen carefully to my words;
let this be the consolation you
give me.
3 Bear with me while I speak,
and after I have spoken, mock on.

4 "Is my complaint directed to a human
being?
Why should I not be impatient?
5 Look at me and be appalled;
clap your hand over your mouth.
6 When I think about this, I am terrified;
trembling seizes my body.
7 Why do the wicked live on,
growing old and increasing in
power?
8 They see their children established
around them,
their offspring before their eyes.
9 Their homes are safe and free from
fear;
the rod of God is not on them.

---

a 28 Or *The possessions in his house will be carried off, / washed away*

10 Their bulls never fail to breed;
   their cows calve and do not
      miscarry.
11 They send forth their children as a
      flock;
   their little ones dance about.
12 They sing to the music of timbrel and
      lyre;
   they make merry to the sound of
      the pipe.
13 They spend their years in prosperity
   and go down to the grave in
      peace.*a*
14 Yet they say to God, 'Leave us alone!
   We have no desire to know your
      ways.
15 Who is the Almighty, that we should
      serve him?
   What would we gain by praying to
      him?'
16 But their prosperity is not in their own
      hands,
   so I stand aloof from the plans of
      the wicked.

17 "Yet how often is the lamp of the
      wicked snuffed out?
   How often does calamity come upon
      them,
   the fate God allots in his anger?
18 How often are they like straw before
      the wind,
   like chaff swept away by a gale?
19 It is said, 'God stores up the
      punishment of the wicked for
      their children.'
   Let him repay the wicked, so
      that they themselves will
      experience it!
20 Let their own eyes see their
      destruction;
   let them drink the cup of the wrath
      of the Almighty.
21 For what do they care about the
      families they leave behind
   when their allotted months come to
      an end?
22 "Can anyone teach knowledge to God,
   since he judges even the highest?
23 One person dies in full vigor,
   completely secure and at ease,

INSTANT ACCESS

Do doubts and questions show a lack of faith? Shouldn't we just say, "The Bible says ..." and stop asking hard questions? When Job's friends insisted that God punishes the wicked, Job asked a hard question: "Why then do we know wicked people who seem happier and better off than we are?" God wasn't upset with Job. In fact, God said that Job was right to ask the hard questions (Job 42:7). We can be honest about our doubts and questions. Like Job, we can know God has the answer. We just don't know the answer ... yet.

{Job 21}

24 well nourished in body,*b*
   bones rich with marrow.
25 Another dies in bitterness of soul,
   never having enjoyed anything good.
26 Side by side they lie in the dust,
   and worms cover them both.

27 "I know full well what you are thinking,
   the schemes by which you would
      wrong me.
28 You say, 'Where now is the house of
      the great,
   the tents where the wicked lived?'
29 Have you never questioned those who
      travel?
   Have you paid no regard to their
      accounts—

a 13 Or in an instant   b 24 The meaning of the Hebrew for this word is uncertain.

30 that the wicked are spared from the
day of calamity,
that they are delivered from[a] the
day of wrath?
31 Who denounces their conduct to their
face?
Who repays them for what they
have done?
32 They are carried to the grave,
and watch is kept over their tombs.
33 The soil in the valley is sweet to them;
everyone follows after them,
and a countless throng goes[b]
before them.
34 "So how can you console me with your
nonsense?
Nothing is left of your answers but
falsehood!"

Eliphaz

22 Then Eliphaz the Temanite replied:

2 "Can a man be of benefit to God?
Can even a wise person benefit
him?
3 What pleasure would it give the
Almighty if you were righteous?
What would he gain if your ways
were blameless?

4 "Is it for your piety that he rebukes
you
and brings charges against you?
5 Is not your wickedness great?
Are not your sins endless?
6 You demanded security from your
relatives for no reason;
you stripped people of their
clothing, leaving them naked.
7 You gave no water to the weary
and you withheld food from the
hungry,
8 though you were a powerful man,
owning land—
an honored man, living on it.
9 And you sent widows away empty-
handed
and broke the strength of the
fatherless.
10 That is why snares are all around you,
why sudden peril terrifies you,

11 why it is so dark you cannot see,
and why a flood of water covers you.

12 "Is not God in the heights of heaven?
And see how lofty are the highest
stars!
13 Yet you say, 'What does God know?
Does he judge through such
darkness?
14 Thick clouds veil him, so he does not
see us
as he goes about in the vaulted
heavens.'
15 Will you keep to the old path
that the wicked have trod?
16 They were carried off before their
time,
their foundations washed away by a
flood.
17 They said to God, 'Leave us alone!
What can the Almighty do to us?'
18 Yet it was he who filled their houses
with good things,
so I stand aloof from the plans of
the wicked.
19 The righteous see their ruin and
rejoice;
the innocent mock them, saying,
20 'Surely our foes are destroyed,
and fire devours their wealth.'

21 "Submit to God and be at peace with
him;
in this way prosperity will come to
you.
22 Accept instruction from his mouth
and lay up his words in your heart.
23 If you return to the Almighty, you will
be restored:
If you remove wickedness far from
your tent
24 and assign your nuggets to the dust,
your gold of Ophir to the rocks in
the ravines,
25 then the Almighty will be your gold,
the choicest silver for you.
26 Surely then you will find delight in the
Almighty
and will lift up your face to God.
27 You will pray to him, and he will hear
you,
and you will fulfill your vows.

---

a 30 Or wicked are reserved for the day of calamity, / that they are brought forth to   b 33 Or them, / as a countless throng
went

28 What you decide on will be done,
  and light will shine on your ways.
29 When people are brought low and you
    say, 'Lift them up!'
  then he will save the downcast.
30 He will deliver even one who is not
    innocent,
  who will be delivered through the
    cleanness of your hands."

Job

23 Then Job replied:

2 "Even today my complaint is bitter;[a]
  his hand[a] is heavy in spite of[b] my
    groaning.
3 If only I knew where to find him;
  if only I could go to his dwelling!
4 I would state my case before him
  and fill my mouth with arguments.
5 I would find out what he would
    answer me,
  and consider what he would say
    to me.
6 Would he vigorously oppose me?
  No, he would not press charges
    against me.
7 There the upright can establish their
    innocence before him,
  and there I would be delivered
    forever from my judge.

8 "But if I go to the east, he is not there;
  if I go to the west, I do not find him.
9 When he is at work in the north, I do
    not see him;
  when he turns to the south, I catch
    no glimpse of him.
10 But he knows the way that I take;
  when he has tested me, I will come
    forth as gold.
11 My feet have closely followed his steps;
  I have kept to his way without
    turning aside.
12 I have not departed from the
    commands of his lips;
  I have treasured the words of his
    mouth more than my daily
    bread.

13 "But he stands alone, and who can
    oppose him?
  He does whatever he pleases.

14 He carries out his decree against me,
  and many such plans he still has in
    store.
15 That is why I am terrified before him;
  when I think of all this, I fear him.
16 God has made my heart faint;
  the Almighty has terrified me.
17 Yet I am not silenced by the
    darkness,
  by the thick darkness that covers
    my face.

24 "Why does the Almighty not set
    times for judgment?
  Why must those who know him look
    in vain for such days?
2 There are those who move boundary
    stones;
  they pasture flocks they have
    stolen.
3 They drive away the orphan's donkey
  and take the widow's ox in pledge.
4 They thrust the needy from the path
  and force all the poor of the land
    into hiding.
5 Like wild donkeys in the desert,
  the poor go about their labor of
    foraging food;
  the wasteland provides food for
    their children.
6 They gather fodder in the fields
  and glean in the vineyards of the
    wicked.
7 Lacking clothes, they spend the night
    naked;
  they have nothing to cover
    themselves in the cold.
8 They are drenched by mountain rains
  and hug the rocks for lack of
    shelter.
9 The fatherless child is snatched from
    the breast;
  the infant of the poor is seized for a
    debt.
10 Lacking clothes, they go about naked;
  they carry the sheaves, but still go
    hungry.
11 They crush olives among the
    terraces[c];
  they tread the winepresses, yet
    suffer thirst.

---

a 2 Septuagint and Syriac; Hebrew / *the hand on me*   *b 2* Or *heavy on me in*   *c 11* The meaning of the Hebrew for this word is uncertain.

12 The groans of the dying rise from the
city,
and the souls of the wounded cry
out for help.
But God charges no one with
wrongdoing.

13 "There are those who rebel against
the light,
who do not know its ways
or stay in its paths.

14 When daylight is gone, the murderer
rises up,
kills the poor and needy,
and in the night steals forth like a
thief.

15 The eye of the adulterer watches for
dusk;
he thinks, 'No eye will see me,'
and he keeps his face concealed.

16 In the dark, thieves break into houses,
but by day they shut themselves in;
they want nothing to do with the
light.

17 For all of them, midnight is their
morning;
they make friends with the terrors
of darkness.

18 "Yet they are foam on the surface of
the water;
their portion of the land is cursed,
so that no one goes to the
vineyards.

19 As heat and drought snatch away the
melted snow,
so the grave snatches away those
who have sinned.

20 The womb forgets them,
the worm feasts on them;
the wicked are no longer remembered
but are broken like a tree.

21 They prey on the barren and childless
woman,
and to the widow they show no
kindness.

22 But God drags away the mighty by his
power;
though they become established,
they have no assurance of life.

23 He may let them rest in a feeling of
security,
but his eyes are on their ways.

24 For a little while they are exalted, and
then they are gone;
they are brought low and gathered
up like all others;
they are cut off like heads of grain.

25 "If this is not so, who can prove me
false
and reduce my words to nothing?"

Bildad

25 Then Bildad the Shuhite replied:

2 "Dominion and awe belong to God;
he establishes order in the heights
of heaven.

3 Can his forces be numbered?
On whom does his light not rise?

4 How then can a mortal be righteous
before God?
How can one born of woman be
pure?

5 If even the moon is not bright
and the stars are not pure in his
eyes,

6 how much less a mortal, who is but a
maggot—
a human being, who is only a
worm!"

Job

26 Then Job replied:

2 "How you have helped the
powerless!
How you have saved the arm that is
feeble!

3 What advice you have offered to one
without wisdom!
And what great insight you have
displayed!

4 Who has helped you utter these
words?
And whose spirit spoke from your
mouth?

5 "The dead are in deep anguish,
those beneath the waters and all
that live in them.

6 The realm of the dead is naked before
God;
Destruction[a] lies uncovered.

---

a 6 Hebrew *Abaddon*

7 He spreads out the northern skies
over empty space;
he suspends the earth over
nothing.
8 He wraps up the waters in his clouds,
yet the clouds do not burst under
their weight.
9 He covers the face of the full moon,
spreading his clouds over it.
10 He marks out the horizon on the face
of the waters
for a boundary between light and
darkness.
11 The pillars of the heavens quake,
aghast at his rebuke.
12 By his power he churned up the sea;
by his wisdom he cut Rahab to
pieces.
13 By his breath the skies became fair;
his hand pierced the gliding
serpent.
14 And these are but the outer fringe of
his works;
how faint the whisper we hear of
him!
Who then can understand the
thunder of his power?"

Job's Final Word to His Friends

27 And Job continued his discourse:

2 "As surely as God lives, who has
denied me justice,
the Almighty, who has made my life
bitter,
3 as long as I have life within me,
the breath of God in my nostrils,
4 my lips will not say anything wicked,
and my tongue will not utter lies.
5 I will never admit you are in the right;
till I die, I will not deny my integrity.
6 I will maintain my innocence and never
let go of it;
my conscience will not reproach me
as long as I live.

7 "May my enemy be like the wicked,
my adversary like the unjust!
8 For what hope have the godless when
they are cut off,
when God takes away their life?
9 Does God listen to their cry
when distress comes upon them?

10 Will they find delight in the Almighty?
Will they call on God at all times?

11 "I will teach you about the power of
God;
the ways of the Almighty I will not
conceal.
12 You have all seen this yourselves.
Why then this meaningless talk?

13 "Here is the fate God allots to the
wicked,
the heritage a ruthless man
receives from the Almighty:
14 However many his children, their fate
is the sword;
his offspring will never have enough
to eat.
15 The plague will bury those who survive
him,
and their widows will not weep for
them.
16 Though he heaps up silver like dust
and clothes like piles of clay,
17 what he lays up the righteous will wear,
and the innocent will divide his
silver.
18 The house he builds is like a moth's
cocoon,
like a hut made by a watchman.
19 He lies down wealthy, but will do so
no more;
when he opens his eyes, all is
gone.
20 Terrors overtake him like a flood;
a tempest snatches him away in
the night.
21 The east wind carries him off, and he
is gone;
it sweeps him out of his place.
22 It hurls itself against him without
mercy
as he flees headlong from its
power.
23 It claps its hands in derision
and hisses him out of his place."

Interlude: Where Wisdom Is Found

28 There is a mine for silver
and a place where gold is
refined.
2 Iron is taken from the earth,
and copper is smelted from ore.

3 Mortals put an end to the darkness;
  they search out the farthest
    recesses
  for ore in the blackest darkness.
4 Far from human dwellings they cut a
    shaft,
  in places untouched by human feet;
  far from other people they dangle
    and sway.
5 The earth, from which food comes,
  is transformed below as by fire;
6 lapis lazuli comes from its rocks,
  and its dust contains nuggets of
    gold.
7 No bird of prey knows that hidden path,
  no falcon's eye has seen it.
8 Proud beasts do not set foot on it,
  and no lion prowls there.
9 People assault the flinty rock with
    their hands
  and lay bare the roots of the
    mountains.
10 They tunnel through the rock;
  their eyes see all its treasures.
11 They search*a* the sources of the rivers
  and bring hidden things to light.

12 But where can wisdom be found?
  Where does understanding dwell?
13 No mortal comprehends its worth;
  it cannot be found in the land of the
    living.
14 The deep says, "It is not in me";
  the sea says, "It is not with me."
15 It cannot be bought with the finest gold,
  nor can its price be weighed out in
    silver.
16 It cannot be bought with the gold of
    Ophir,
  with precious onyx or lapis lazuli.
17 Neither gold nor crystal can compare
    with it,
  nor can it be had for jewels of gold.
18 Coral and jasper are not worthy of
    mention;
  the price of wisdom is beyond rubies.
19 The topaz of Cush cannot compare
    with it;
  it cannot be bought with pure gold.

20 Where then does wisdom come from?
  Where does understanding dwell?

21 It is hidden from the eyes of every
    living thing,
  concealed even from the birds in
    the sky.
22 Destruction*b* and Death say,
  "Only a rumor of it has reached our
    ears."
23 God understands the way to it
  and he alone knows where it dwells,
24 for he views the ends of the earth
  and sees everything under the
    heavens.
25 When he established the force of the
    wind
  and measured out the waters,
26 when he made a decree for the rain
  and a path for the thunderstorm,
27 then he looked at wisdom and
    appraised it;
  he confirmed it and tested it.
28 And he said to the human race,
  "The fear of the Lord—that is
    wisdom,
  and to shun evil is understanding."

Job's Final Defense

29 Job continued his discourse:

2 "How I long for the months gone by,
  for the days when God watched
    over me,
3 when his lamp shone on my head
  and by his light I walked through
    darkness!
4 Oh, for the days when I was in my
    prime,
  when God's intimate friendship
    blessed my house,
5 when the Almighty was still with me
  and my children were around me,
6 when my path was drenched with
    cream
  and the rock poured out for me
    streams of olive oil.

7 "When I went to the gate of the city
  and took my seat in the public
    square,
8 the young men saw me and stepped
    aside
  and the old men rose to their feet;

---

a 11 Septuagint, Aquila and Vulgate; Hebrew *They dam up*   *b* 22 Hebrew *Abaddon*

9 the chief men refrained from speaking
  and covered their mouths with their
    hands;
10 the voices of the nobles were hushed,
  and their tongues stuck to the roof
    of their mouths.
11 Whoever heard me spoke well of me,
  and those who saw me
    commended me,
12 because I rescued the poor who cried
    for help,
  and the fatherless who had none to
    assist them.
13 The one who was dying blessed me;
  I made the widow's heart sing.
14 I put on righteousness as my clothing;
  justice was my robe and my turban.
15 I was eyes to the blind
  and feet to the lame.
16 I was a father to the needy;
  I took up the case of the stranger.
17 I broke the fangs of the wicked
  and snatched the victims from their
    teeth.

18 "I thought, 'I will die in my own house,
  my days as numerous as the grains
    of sand.
19 My roots will reach to the water,
  and the dew will lie all night on my
    branches.
20 My glory will not fade;
  the bow will be ever new in my hand.'

21 "People listened to me expectantly,
  waiting in silence for my counsel.
22 After I had spoken, they spoke no
    more;
  my words fell gently on their ears.
23 They waited for me as for showers
  and drank in my words as the
    spring rain.
24 When I smiled at them, they scarcely
    believed it;
  the light of my face was precious to
    them.[a]
25 I chose the way for them and sat as
    their chief;
  I dwelt as a king among his troops;
  I was like one who comforts
    mourners.

30 "But now they mock me,
    men younger than I,
  whose fathers I would have disdained
    to put with my sheep dogs.
2 Of what use was the strength of their
    hands to me,
  since their vigor had gone from
    them?
3 Haggard from want and hunger,
  they roamed[b] the parched land
  in desolate wastelands at night.
4 In the brush they gathered salt herbs,
  and their food[c] was the root of the
    broom bush.
5 They were banished from human
    society,
  shouted at as if they were thieves.
6 They were forced to live in the dry
    stream beds,
  among the rocks and in holes in the
    ground.
7 They brayed among the bushes
  and huddled in the undergrowth.
8 A base and nameless brood,
  they were driven out of the land.

9 "And now those young men mock me
    in song;
  I have become a byword among
    them.
10 They detest me and keep their
    distance;
  they do not hesitate to spit in my
    face.
11 Now that God has unstrung my bow
    and afflicted me,
  they throw off restraint in my
    presence.
12 On my right the tribe[d] attacks;
  they lay snares for my feet,
  they build their siege ramps
    against me.
13 They break up my road;
  they succeed in destroying me.
  'No one can help him,' they say.
14 They advance as through a gaping
    breach;
  amid the ruins they come rolling in.
15 Terrors overwhelm me;
  my dignity is driven away as by the
    wind,
  my safety vanishes like a cloud.

---

[a] 24 The meaning of the Hebrew for this clause is uncertain. Hebrew for this word is uncertain. [b] 3 Or gnawed [c] 4 Or fuel [d] 12 The meaning of the Hebrew for this word is uncertain.

16 "And now my life ebbs away;
  days of suffering grip me.
17 Night pierces my bones;
  my gnawing pains never rest.
18 In his great power God becomes like
    clothing to me^a;
  he binds me like the neck of my
    garment.
19 He throws me into the mud,
  and I am reduced to dust and ashes.

20 "I cry out to you, God, but you do not
    answer;
  I stand up, but you merely look
    at me.
21 You turn on me ruthlessly;
  with the might of your hand you
    attack me.
22 You snatch me up and drive me before
    the wind;
  you toss me about in the storm.
23 I know you will bring me down to
    death,
  to the place appointed for all the
    living.

24 "Surely no one lays a hand on a
    broken man
  when he cries for help in his
    distress.
25 Have I not wept for those in trouble?
  Has not my soul grieved for the
    poor?
26 Yet when I hoped for good, evil came;
  when I looked for light, then came
    darkness.
27 The churning inside me never stops;
  days of suffering confront me.
28 I go about blackened, but not by the
    sun;
  I stand up in the assembly and cry
    for help.
29 I have become a brother of jackals,
  a companion of owls.
30 My skin grows black and peels;
  my body burns with fever.
31 My lyre is tuned to mourning,
  and my pipe to the sound of
    wailing.

31 "I made a covenant with my eyes
  not to look lustfully at a young
    woman.

2 For what is our lot from God above,
  our heritage from the Almighty on
    high?
3 Is it not ruin for the wicked,
  disaster for those who do wrong?
4 Does he not see my ways
  and count my every step?

5 "If I have walked with falsehood
  or my foot has hurried after
    deceit—
6 let God weigh me in honest scales
  and he will know that I am
    blameless—
7 if my steps have turned from the path,
  if my heart has been led by my
    eyes,
  or if my hands have been defiled,
8 then may others eat what I have
    sown,
  and may my crops be uprooted.

9 "If my heart has been enticed by a
    woman,
  or if I have lurked at my neighbor's
    door,
10 then may my wife grind another man's
    grain,
  and may other men sleep with her.
11 For that would have been wicked,
  a sin to be judged.
12 It is a fire that burns to Destruction^b;
  it would have uprooted my harvest.

13 "If I have denied justice to any of my
    servants,
  whether male or female,
  when they had a grievance
    against me,
14 what will I do when God confronts me?
  What will I answer when called to
    account?
15 Did not he who made me in the womb
    make them?
  Did not the same one form us both
    within our mothers?

16 "If I have denied the desires of the
    poor
  or let the eyes of the widow grow
    weary,
17 if I have kept my bread to myself,
  not sharing it with the fatherless—

---

^a 18 Hebrew; Septuagint *power he grasps my clothing*   ^b 12 Hebrew *Abaddon*

¹⁸ but from my youth I reared them as a
father would,
and from my birth I guided the
widow—
¹⁹ if I have seen anyone perishing for
lack of clothing,
or the needy without garments,
²⁰ and their hearts did not bless me
for warming them with the fleece
from my sheep,
²¹ if I have raised my hand against the
fatherless,
knowing that I had influence in court,
²² then let my arm fall from the shoulder,
let it be broken off at the joint.
²³ For I dreaded destruction from God,
and for fear of his splendor I could
not do such things.

²⁴ "If I have put my trust in gold
or said to pure gold, 'You are my
security,'
²⁵ if I have rejoiced over my great wealth,
the fortune my hands had gained,
²⁶ if I have regarded the sun in its
radiance
or the moon moving in splendor,
²⁷ so that my heart was secretly enticed
and my hand offered them a kiss of
homage,
²⁸ then these also would be sins to be
judged,
for I would have been unfaithful to
God on high.

²⁹ "If I have rejoiced at my enemy's
misfortune
or gloated over the trouble that
came to him—
³⁰ I have not allowed my mouth to sin
by invoking a curse against their
life—
³¹ if those of my household have never
said,
'Who has not been filled with Job's
meat?'—
³² but no stranger had to spend the night
in the street,
for my door was always open to the
traveler—
³³ if I have concealed my sin as
people do,ᵃ
by hiding my guilt in my heart

³⁴ because I so feared the crowd
and so dreaded the contempt of the
clans
that I kept silent and would not go
outside—

³⁵ ("Oh, that I had someone to hear me!
I sign now my defense—let the
Almighty answer me;
let my accuser put his indictment in
writing.
³⁶ Surely I would wear it on my shoulder,
I would put it on like a crown.
³⁷ I would give him an account of my
every step;
I would present it to him as to a
ruler.)—

³⁸ "if my land cries out against me
and all its furrows are wet with
tears,
³⁹ if I have devoured its yield without
payment
or broken the spirit of its tenants,
⁴⁰ then let briers come up instead of
wheat
and stinkweed instead of barley."

The words of Job are ended.

Elihu

32 So these three men stopped answering Job, because he was righteous in his own eyes. ² But Elihu son of Barakel the Buzite, of the family of Ram, became very angry with Job for justifying himself rather than God. ³ He was also angry with the three friends, because they had found no way to refute Job, and yet had condemned him.ᵇ ⁴ Now Elihu had waited before speaking to Job because they were older than he. ⁵ But when he saw that the three men had nothing more to say, his anger was aroused.

⁶ So Elihu son of Barakel the Buzite said:

"I am young in years,
and you are old;
that is why I was fearful,
not daring to tell you what I know.
⁷ I thought, 'Age should speak;
advanced years should teach
wisdom.'

ᵃ 33 Or as Adam did   ᵇ 3 Masoretic Text; an ancient Hebrew scribal tradition *Job, and so had condemned God*

8 But it is the spirit*a* in a person,
  the breath of the Almighty, that
    gives them understanding.
9 It is not only the old*b* who are wise,
  not only the aged who understand
    what is right.

10 "Therefore I say: Listen to me;
   I too will tell you what I know.
11 I waited while you spoke,
   I listened to your reasoning;
  while you were searching for words,
12   I gave you my full attention.
   But not one of you has proved Job
     wrong;
     none of you has answered his
       arguments.
13 Do not say, 'We have found wisdom;
   let God, not a man, refute him.'
14 But Job has not marshaled his words
     against me,
   and I will not answer him with your
     arguments.

15 "They are dismayed and have no more
     to say;
   words have failed them.
16 Must I wait, now that they are silent,
   now that they stand there with no
     reply?
17 I too will have my say;
   I too will tell what I know.
18 For I am full of words,
   and the spirit within me compels me;
19 inside I am like bottled-up wine,
   like new wineskins ready to burst.
20 I must speak and find relief;
   I must open my lips and reply.
21 I will show no partiality,
   nor will I flatter anyone;
22 for if I were skilled in flattery,
   my Maker would soon take me
     away.

33
"But now, Job, listen to my
     words;
   pay attention to everything I say.
2 I am about to open my mouth;
   my words are on the tip of my
     tongue.
3 My words come from an upright heart;
   my lips sincerely speak what I know.

4 The Spirit of God has made me;
   the breath of the Almighty gives me
     life.
5 Answer me then, if you can;
   stand up and argue your case
     before me.
6 I am the same as you in God's sight;
   I too am a piece of clay.
7 No fear of me should alarm you,
   nor should my hand be heavy on
     you.

8 "But you have said in my hearing—
   I heard the very words—
9 'I am pure, I have done no wrong;
   I am clean and free from sin.
10 Yet God has found fault with me;
   he considers me his enemy.
11 He fastens my feet in shackles;
   he keeps close watch on all my
     paths.'

12 "But I tell you, in this you are not
     right,
   for God is greater than any mortal.
13 Why do you complain to him
   that he responds to no one's
     words*c*?
14 For God does speak—now one way,
     now another—
   though no one perceives it.
15 In a dream, in a vision of the night,
   when deep sleep falls on people
   as they slumber in their beds,
16 he may speak in their ears
   and terrify them with warnings,
17 to turn them from wrongdoing
   and keep them from pride,
18 to preserve them from the pit,
   their lives from perishing by the
     sword.*d*

19 "Or someone may be chastened on a
     bed of pain
   with constant distress in their
     bones,
20 so that their body finds food repulsive
   and their soul loathes the choicest
     meal.
21 Their flesh wastes away to nothing,
   and their bones, once hidden, now
     stick out.

---

a 8 Or *Spirit*; also in verse 18   *b* 9 Or *many*; *or great*   *c* 13 Or *that he does not answer for any of his actions*
d 18 Or *from crossing the river*

22 They draw near to the pit,
  and their life to the messengers of
    death.ᵃ
23 Yet if there is an angel at their side,
  a messenger, one out of a
    thousand,
  sent to tell them how to be upright,
24 and he is gracious to that person and
    says to God,
  'Spare them from going down to the
    pit;
  I have found a ransom for them—
25 let their flesh be renewed like a
    child's;
  let them be restored as in the days
    of their youth'—
26 then that person can pray to God and
    find favor with him,
  they will see God's face and shout
    for joy;
  he will restore them to full well-
    being.
27 And they will go to others and say,
  'I have sinned, I have perverted
    what is right,
  but I did not get what I deserved.
28 God has delivered me from going
    down to the pit,
  and I shall live to enjoy the light of
    life.'

29 "God does all these things to a
    person—
  twice, even three times—
30 to turn them back from the pit,
  that the light of life may shine on
    them.

31 "Pay attention, Job, and listen to me;
  be silent, and I will speak.
32 If you have anything to say, answer me;
  speak up, for I want to vindicate
    you.
33 But if not, then listen to me;
  be silent, and I will teach you
    wisdom."

34 Then Elihu said:

2 "Hear my words, you wise men;
  listen to me, you men of learning.
3 For the ear tests words
  as the tongue tastes food.

4 Let us discern for ourselves what is
    right;
  let us learn together what is good.

5 "Job says, 'I am innocent,
  but God denies me justice.
6 Although I am right,
  I am considered a liar;
  although I am guiltless,
  his arrow inflicts an incurable
    wound.'
7 Is there anyone like Job,
  who drinks scorn like water?
8 He keeps company with evildoers;
  he associates with the wicked.
9 For he says, 'There is no profit
  in trying to please God.'

10 "So listen to me, you men of
    understanding.
  Far be it from God to do evil,
  from the Almighty to do wrong.
11 He repays everyone for what they
    have done;
  he brings on them what their
    conduct deserves.
12 It is unthinkable that God would do
    wrong,
  that the Almighty would pervert
    justice.
13 Who appointed him over the earth?
  Who put him in charge of the whole
    world?
14 If it were his intention
  and he withdrew his spiritᵇ and
    breath,
15 all humanity would perish together
  and mankind would return to the
    dust.

16 "If you have understanding, hear this;
  listen to what I say.
17 Can someone who hates justice
    govern?
  Will you condemn the just and
    mighty One?
18 Is he not the One who says to kings,
  'You are worthless,'
  and to nobles, 'You are wicked,'
19 who shows no partiality to princes
  and does not favor the rich over the
    poor,
  for they are all the work of his
    hands?

ᵃ 22 Or *to the place of the dead*   ᵇ 14 Or *Spirit*

20 They die in an instant, in the middle of
the night;
   the people are shaken and they
      pass away;
   the mighty are removed without
      human hand.
21 "His eyes are on the ways of mortals;
   he sees their every step.
22 There is no deep shadow, no utter
      darkness,
   where evildoers can hide.
23 God has no need to examine people
      further,
   that they should come before him
      for judgment.
24 Without inquiry he shatters the mighty
   and sets up others in their place.
25 Because he takes note of their deeds,
   he overthrows them in the night
      and they are crushed.
26 He punishes them for their
      wickedness
   where everyone can see them,
27 because they turned from following
      him
   and had no regard for any of his
      ways.
28 They caused the cry of the poor to
      come before him,
   so that he heard the cry of the
      needy.
29 But if he remains silent, who can
      condemn him?
   If he hides his face, who can see
      him?
   Yet he is over individual and nation
      alike,
30   to keep the godless from ruling,
   from laying snares for the people.
31 "Suppose someone says to God,
   'I am guilty but will offend no more.
32 Teach me what I cannot see;
   if I have done wrong, I will not do so
      again.'
33 Should God then reward you on your
      terms,
   when you refuse to repent?
   You must decide, not I;
   so tell me what you know.
34 "Men of understanding declare,
   wise men who hear me say to me,

35 'Job speaks without knowledge;
   his words lack insight.'
36 Oh, that Job might be tested to the
      utmost
   for answering like a wicked man!
37 To his sin he adds rebellion;
   scornfully he claps his hands
      among us
   and multiplies his words against
      God."

35

Then Elihu said:

2 "Do you think this is just?
   You say, 'I am in the right, not God.'
3 Yet you ask him, 'What profit is it
      to me,ᵃ
   and what do I gain by not sinning?'

4 "I would like to reply to you
   and to your friends with you.
5 Look up at the heavens and see;
   gaze at the clouds so high above
      you.
6 If you sin, how does that affect him?
   If your sins are many, what does
      that do to him?
7 If you are righteous, what do you give
      to him,
   or what does he receive from your
      hand?
8 Your wickedness only affects humans
      like yourself,
   and your righteousness only other
      people.

9 "People cry out under a load of
      oppression;
   they plead for relief from the arm of
      the powerful.
10 But no one says, 'Where is God my
      Maker,
   who gives songs in the night,
11 who teaches us more than he
      teachesᵇ the beasts of the
      earth
   and makes us wiser thanᶜ the birds
      in the sky?'
12 He does not answer when people cry
      out
   because of the arrogance of the
      wicked.

ᵃ 3 Or you   ᵇ 10,11 Or night, / ¹¹who teaches us by   ᶜ 11 Or us wise by

13 Indeed, God does not listen to their
empty plea;
the Almighty pays no attention to it.
14 How much less, then, will he listen
when you say that you do not see
him,
that your case is before him
and you must wait for him,
15 and further, that his anger never
punishes
and he does not take the least
notice of wickedness.*ᵃ*
16 So Job opens his mouth with empty
talk;
without knowledge he multiplies
words."

36
Elihu continued:

2 "Bear with me a little longer and I will
show you
that there is more to be said in
God's behalf.
3 I get my knowledge from afar;
I will ascribe justice to my Maker.
4 Be assured that my words are not
false;
one who has perfect knowledge is
with you.

5 "God is mighty, but despises no one;
he is mighty, and firm in his
purpose.
6 He does not keep the wicked alive
but gives the afflicted their rights.
7 He does not take his eyes off the
righteous;
he enthrones them with kings
and exalts them forever.
8 But if people are bound in chains,
held fast by cords of affliction,
9 he tells them what they have done—
that they have sinned arrogantly.
10 He makes them listen to correction
and commands them to repent of
their evil.
11 If they obey and serve him,
they will spend the rest of their
days in prosperity
and their years in contentment.
12 But if they do not listen,

they will perish by the sword*ᵇ*
and die without knowledge.

13 "The godless in heart harbor
resentment;
even when he fetters them, they do
not cry for help.
14 They die in their youth,
among male prostitutes of the
shrines.
15 But those who suffer he delivers in
their suffering;
he speaks to them in their
affliction.

16 "He is wooing you from the jaws of
distress
to a spacious place free from
restriction,
to the comfort of your table laden
with choice food.
17 But now you are laden with the
judgment due the wicked;
judgment and justice have taken
hold of you.
18 Be careful that no one entices you by
riches;
do not let a large bribe turn you
aside.
19 Would your wealth or even all your
mighty efforts
sustain you so you would not be in
distress?
20 Do not long for the night,
to drag people away from their
homes.*ᶜ*
21 Beware of turning to evil,
which you seem to prefer to
affliction.

22 "God is exalted in his power.
Who is a teacher like him?
23 Who has prescribed his ways for him,
or said to him, 'You have done
wrong'?
24 Remember to extol his work,
which people have praised in song.
25 All humanity has seen it;
mortals gaze on it from afar.
26 How great is God—beyond our
understanding!
The number of his years is past
finding out.

ᵃ 15 Symmachus, Theodotion and Vulgate; the meaning of the Hebrew for this word is uncertain.   *ᵇ 12* Or *will cross the river*   *ᶜ 20* The meaning of the Hebrew for verses 18-20 is uncertain.

27 "He draws up the drops of water,
　which distill as rain to the streams*a*;
28 the clouds pour down their moisture
　and abundant showers fall on
　mankind.
29 Who can understand how he spreads
　out the clouds,
　how he thunders from his pavilion?
30 See how he scatters his lightning
　about him,
　bathing the depths of the sea.
31 This is the way he governs*b* the
　nations
　and provides food in abundance.
32 He fills his hands with lightning
　and commands it to strike its mark.
33 His thunder announces the coming
　storm;
　even the cattle make known its
　approach.*c*

37

"At this my heart pounds
　and leaps from its place.
2 Listen! Listen to the roar of his voice,
　to the rumbling that comes from his
　mouth.
3 He unleashes his lightning beneath
　the whole heaven
　and sends it to the ends of the
　earth.
4 After that comes the sound of his
　roar;
　he thunders with his majestic voice.
When his voice resounds,
　he holds nothing back.
5 God's voice thunders in marvelous
　ways;
　he does great things beyond our
　understanding.
6 He says to the snow, 'Fall on the
　earth,'
　and to the rain shower, 'Be a mighty
　downpour.'
7 So that everyone he has made may
　know his work,
　he stops all people from their
　labor.*d*
8 The animals take cover;
　they remain in their dens.
9 The tempest comes out from its
　chamber,
　the cold from the driving winds.

10 The breath of God produces ice,
　and the broad waters become
　frozen.
11 He loads the clouds with moisture;
　he scatters his lightning through
　them.
12 At his direction they swirl around
　over the face of the whole earth
　to do whatever he commands them.
13 He brings the clouds to punish
　people,
　or to water his earth and show his
　love.

14 "Listen to this, Job;
　stop and consider God's wonders.
15 Do you know how God controls the
　clouds
　and makes his lightning flash?
16 Do you know how the clouds hang
　poised,
　those wonders of him who has
　perfect knowledge?
17 You who swelter in your clothes
　when the land lies hushed under
　the south wind,
18 can you join him in spreading out the
　skies,
　hard as a mirror of cast bronze?

19 "Tell us what we should say to him;
　we cannot draw up our case
　because of our darkness.
20 Should he be told that I want to
　speak?
　Would anyone ask to be
　swallowed up?
21 Now no one can look at the sun,
　bright as it is in the skies
　after the wind has swept them
　clean.
22 Out of the north he comes in golden
　splendor;
　God comes in awesome majesty.
23 The Almighty is beyond our reach and
　exalted in power;
　in his justice and great
　righteousness, he does not
　oppress.
24 Therefore, people revere him,
　for does he not have regard for all
　the wise in heart?*e*".

---

a 27 Or *distill from the mist as rain*　　*b* 31 Or *nourishes*　　*c* 33 Or *announces his coming— / the One zealous against evil*
d 7 Or *work, / he fills all people with fear by his power*　　*e* 24 Or *for he does not have regard for any who think they are wise.*

The LORD Speaks

38 Then the LORD spoke to Job out of the storm. He said:

2 "Who is this that obscures my plans
    with words without knowledge?
3 Brace yourself like a man;
    I will question you,
    and you shall answer me.

4 "Where were you when I laid the
        earth's foundation?
    Tell me, if you understand.
5 Who marked off its dimensions?
        Surely you know!
    Who stretched a measuring line
        across it?
6 On what were its footings set,
    or who laid its cornerstone—

7 while the morning stars sang together
    and all the angels*a* shouted for joy?

8 "Who shut up the sea behind doors
        when it burst forth from the womb,
9 when I made the clouds its garment
        and wrapped it in thick darkness,
10 when I fixed limits for it
        and set its doors and bars in place,
11 when I said, 'This far you may come
            and no farther;
        here is where your proud waves
            halt'?

12 "Have you ever given orders to the
            morning,
        or shown the dawn its place,
13 that it might take the earth by the
            edges
        and shake the wicked out of it?

---

a 7 Hebrew *the sons of God*

TO THE POINT

Where Were You?

Many of today's science books discuss evolution as if scientists know what happened at creation years ago. But God once asked Job, "Where were you when I laid the earth's foundation?" (Job 38:4).

Scientists have only one way of learning things. They observe things and develop hypotheses. Then they run and rerun experiments to test the hypotheses. Does water boil at 212°F? Test it and see. Of course, there's no way to experiment with creation or evolution. So this "best way" can't be used by scientists to find out what happened long ago.

"Where were you?" is still a good question to ask when scientists talk as if they know for sure how the earth came to be. It's good for everyone to remember that while scientists weren't there, *God* was.

14 The earth takes shape like clay under
a seal;
   its features stand out like those of
   a garment.
15 The wicked are denied their light,
   and their upraised arm is broken.

16 "Have you journeyed to the springs of
the sea
   or walked in the recesses of the
   deep?
17 Have the gates of death been shown
to you?
   Have you seen the gates of the
   deepest darkness?
18 Have you comprehended the vast
expanses of the earth?
   Tell me, if you know all this.

19 "What is the way to the abode of
light?
   And where does darkness
   reside?
20 Can you take them to their places?
   Do you know the paths to their
   dwellings?
21 Surely you know, for you were already
born!
   You have lived so many years!

22 "Have you entered the storehouses of
the snow
   or seen the storehouses of the
   hail,
23 which I reserve for times of trouble,
   for days of war and battle?
24 What is the way to the place where
the lightning is dispersed,
   or the place where the east winds
   are scattered over the earth?
25 Who cuts a channel for the torrents of
rain,
   and a path for the thunderstorm,
26 to water a land where no one lives,
   an uninhabited desert,
27 to satisfy a desolate wasteland
   and make it sprout with grass?
28 Does the rain have a father?
   Who fathers the drops of dew?
29 From whose womb comes the ice?
   Who gives birth to the frost from
   the heavens

30 when the waters become hard as
stone,
   when the surface of the deep is
   frozen?
31 "Can you bind the chains[a] of the
Pleiades?
   Can you loosen Orion's belt?
32 Can you bring forth the constellations
in their seasons[b]
   or lead out the Bear[c] with its cubs?
33 Do you know the laws of the heavens?
   Can you set up God's[d] dominion
   over the earth?

34 "Can you raise your voice to the
clouds
   and cover yourself with a flood of
   water?
35 Do you send the lightning bolts on
their way?
   Do they report to you, 'Here we
   are'?
36 Who gives the ibis wisdom[e]
   or gives the rooster
   understanding?[f]
37 Who has the wisdom to count the
clouds?
   Who can tip over the water jars of
   the heavens
38 when the dust becomes hard
   and the clods of earth stick
   together?

39 "Do you hunt the prey for the lioness
   and satisfy the hunger of the lions
40 when they crouch in their dens
   or lie in wait in a thicket?
41 Who provides food for the raven
   when its young cry out to God
   and wander about for lack of food?

39 "Do you know when the
mountain goats give birth?
   Do you watch when the doe bears
   her fawn?
2 Do you count the months till they
bear?
   Do you know the time they give
   birth?
3 They crouch down and bring forth their
young;
   their labor pains are ended.

---

a 31 Septuagint; Hebrew beauty   b 32 Or the morning star in its season   c 32 Or out Leo   d 33 Or their
e 36 That is, wisdom about the flooding of the Nile   f 36 That is, understanding of when to crow; the meaning of the
Hebrew for this verse is uncertain.

4 Their young thrive and grow strong in
the wilds;
they leave and do not return.

5 "Who let the wild donkey go free?
Who untied its ropes?
6 I gave it the wasteland as its home,
the salt flats as its habitat.
7 It laughs at the commotion in the
town;
it does not hear a driver's shout.
8 It ranges the hills for its pasture
and searches for any green thing.

9 "Will the wild ox consent to serve
you?
Will it stay by your manger at night?
10 Can you hold it to the furrow with a
harness?
Will it till the valleys behind you?
11 Will you rely on it for its great
strength?
Will you leave your heavy work to it?
12 Can you trust it to haul in your grain
and bring it to your threshing floor?

13 "The wings of the ostrich flap joyfully,
though they cannot compare
with the wings and feathers of the
stork.
14 She lays her eggs on the ground
and lets them warm in the sand,
15 unmindful that a foot may crush them,
that some wild animal may trample
them.
16 She treats her young harshly, as if
they were not hers;
she cares not that her labor was in
vain,
17 for God did not endow her with
wisdom
or give her a share of good sense.
18 Yet when she spreads her feathers to
run,
she laughs at horse and rider.

19 "Do you give the horse its strength
or clothe its neck with a flowing
mane?
20 Do you make it leap like a locust,
striking terror with its proud
snorting?
21 It paws fiercely, rejoicing in its
strength,
and charges into the fray.

22 It laughs at fear, afraid of nothing;
it does not shy away from the
sword.
23 The quiver rattles against its side,
along with the flashing spear and
lance.
24 In frenzied excitement it eats up the
ground;
it cannot stand still when the
trumpet sounds.
25 At the blast of the trumpet it snorts,
'Aha!'
It catches the scent of battle from
afar,
the shout of commanders and the
battle cry.

26 "Does the hawk take flight by your
wisdom
and spread its wings toward the
south?
27 Does the eagle soar at your command
and build its nest on high?
28 It dwells on a cliff and stays there at
night;
a rocky crag is its stronghold.
29 From there it looks for food;
its eyes detect it from afar.
30 Its young ones feast on blood,
and where the slain are, there it is."

40 The LORD said to Job:

2 "Will the one who contends with the
Almighty correct him?
Let him who accuses God answer
him!"

3 Then Job answered the LORD:

4 "I am unworthy—how can I reply to
you?
I put my hand over my mouth.
5 I spoke once, but I have no answer—
twice, but I will say no more."

6 Then the LORD spoke to Job out of the
storm:

7 "Brace yourself like a man;
I will question you,
and you shall answer me.

8 "Would you discredit my justice?
Would you condemn me to justify
yourself?

⁹ Do you have an arm like God's,
  and can your voice thunder like his?
¹⁰ Then adorn yourself with glory and
  splendor,
  and clothe yourself in honor and
  majesty.
¹¹ Unleash the fury of your wrath,
  look at all who are proud and bring
  them low,
¹² look at all who are proud and humble
  them,
  crush the wicked where they stand.
¹³ Bury them all in the dust together;
  shroud their faces in the grave.
¹⁴ Then I myself will admit to you
  that your own right hand can save
  you.

¹⁵ "Look at Behemoth,
  which I made along with you
  and which feeds on grass like an
  ox.
¹⁶ What strength it has in its loins,
  what power in the muscles of its
  belly!
¹⁷ Its tail sways like a cedar;
  the sinews of its thighs are close-
  knit.
¹⁸ Its bones are tubes of bronze,
  its limbs like rods of iron.
¹⁹ It ranks first among the works of God,
  yet its Maker can approach it with
  his sword.
²⁰ The hills bring it their produce,
  and all the wild animals play nearby.
²¹ Under the lotus plants it lies,
  hidden among the reeds in the
  marsh.
²² The lotuses conceal it in their shadow;
  the poplars by the stream
  surround it.
²³ A raging river does not alarm it;
  it is secure, though the Jordan
  should surge against its
  mouth.
²⁴ Can anyone capture it by the eyes,
  or trap it and pierce its nose?

41 ᵃ "Can you pull in Leviathan with a
  fishhook
  or tie down its tongue with a rope?

² Can you put a cord through its nose
  or pierce its jaw with a hook?
³ Will it keep begging you for mercy?
  Will it speak to you with gentle
  words?
⁴ Will it make an agreement with you
  for you to take it as your slave
  for life?
⁵ Can you make a pet of it like a bird
  or put it on a leash for the young
  women in your house?
⁶ Will traders barter for it?
  Will they divide it up among the
  merchants?
⁷ Can you fill its hide with harpoons
  or its head with fishing spears?
⁸ If you lay a hand on it,
  you will remember the struggle and
  never do it again!
⁹ Any hope of subduing it is false;
  the mere sight of it is overpowering.
¹⁰ No one is fierce enough to rouse it.
  Who then is able to stand
  against me?
¹¹ Who has a claim against me that I
  must pay?
  Everything under heaven belongs
  to me.

¹² "I will not fail to speak of Leviathan's
  limbs,
  its strength and its graceful form.
¹³ Who can strip off its outer coat?
  Who can penetrate its double coat
  of armorᵇ?
¹⁴ Who dares open the doors of its
  mouth,
  ringed about with fearsome
  teeth?
¹⁵ Its back hasᶜ rows of shields
  tightly sealed together;
¹⁶ each is so close to the next
  that no air can pass between.
¹⁷ They are joined fast to one another;
  they cling together and cannot be
  parted.
¹⁸ Its snorting throws out flashes of
  light;
  its eyes are like the rays of dawn.
¹⁹ Flames stream from its mouth;
  sparks of fire shoot out.

ᵃ In Hebrew texts 41:1-8 is numbered 40:25-32, and 41:9-34 is numbered 41:1-26.   ᵇ 13 Septuagint; Hebrew *double
bridle*   ᶜ 15 Or *Its pride is its*

20 Smoke pours from its nostrils
    as from a boiling pot over burning
        reeds.
21 Its breath sets coals ablaze,
    and flames dart from its
        mouth.
22 Strength resides in its neck;
    dismay goes before it.
23 The folds of its flesh are tightly
        joined;
    they are firm and immovable.
24 Its chest is hard as rock,
    hard as a lower millstone.
25 When it rises up, the mighty are
        terrified;
    they retreat before its thrashing.
26 The sword that reaches it has no
        effect,
    nor does the spear or the dart or
        the javelin.
27 Iron it treats like straw
    and bronze like rotten wood.
28 Arrows do not make it flee;
    slingstones are like chaff to it.
29 A club seems to it but a piece of
        straw;
    it laughs at the rattling of the
        lance.
30 Its undersides are jagged
        potsherds,
    leaving a trail in the mud like a
        threshing sledge.
31 It makes the depths churn like a
        boiling caldron
    and stirs up the sea like a pot of
        ointment.
32 It leaves a glistening wake behind it;
    one would think the deep had white
        hair.
33 Nothing on earth is its equal —
    a creature without fear.
34 It looks down on all that are
        haughty;
    it is king over all that are proud."

Job

42
Then Job replied to the Lord:

2 "I know that you can do all things;
    no purpose of yours can be
        thwarted.

3 You asked, 'Who is this that obscures
    my plans without knowledge?'
    Surely I spoke of things I did not
        understand,
    things too wonderful for me to
        know.

4 "You said, 'Listen now, and I will
        speak;
    I will question you,
    and you shall answer me.'
5 My ears had heard of you
    but now my eyes have seen you.
6 Therefore I despise myself
    and repent in dust and
        ashes."

Epilogue

7 After the Lord had said these things
to Job, he said to Eliphaz the Temanite, "I
am angry with you and your two friends,
because you have not spoken the truth
about me, as my servant Job has. 8 So
now take seven bulls and seven rams
and go to my servant Job and sacrifice a
burnt offering for yourselves. My servant
Job will pray for you, and I will accept his
prayer and not deal with you according to
your folly. You have not spoken the truth
about me, as my servant Job has." 9 So
Eliphaz the Temanite, Bildad the Shuhite
and Zophar the Naamathite did what the
Lord told them; and the Lord accepted
Job's prayer.

10 After Job had prayed for his friends,
the Lord restored his fortunes and gave
him twice as much as he had before.
11 All his brothers and sisters and everyone who had known him before came and
ate with him in his house. They comforted
and consoled him over all the trouble the
Lord had brought on him, and each one
gave him a piece of silver[a] and a gold ring.

12 The Lord blessed the latter part of
Job's life more than the former part. He
had fourteen thousand sheep, six thousand camels, a thousand yoke of oxen
and a thousand donkeys. 13 And he also
had seven sons and three daughters.
14 The first daughter he named Jemimah,
the second Keziah and the third Keren-

---

a 11 Hebrew *him a kesitah;* a kesitah was a unit of money of unknown weight and value.

Happuch. 15 Nowhere in all the land were there found women as beautiful as Job's daughters, and their father granted them an inheritance along with their brothers.

16 After this, Job lived a hundred and forty years; he saw his children and their children to the fourth generation. 17 And so Job died, an old man and full of years.

PSALMS

Friends.

Friends are people to whom you can really talk. You can tell a friend when you feel upset or afraid. You know a friend won't criticize you for being angry and will be patient when you mess up. A friend is someone with whom you can laugh—or cry.

Maybe that's why believers have loved the book of Psalms for thousands of years. The psalmists talk to God as a friend. They tell him just how they feel. And they praise God, not only for listening but also for his help. One of the best ways to grow close to God is to read a psalm every day and then use that psalm as a model for your own prayers.

>>**PSALM PREDICTS SUFFERING OF CHRIST**
See thousand-year prophecy, Psalm 22

>>**RICH AND FAMOUS ON SLIPPERY SLOPE**
"Don't envy the wicked," says psalmist. See Psalm 73

>>**GOD'S WORD: THEME OF LONGEST PSALM**
Values of Bible reading listed, Psalm 119

>>**GOD'S LOVE PRAISED IN SHORTEST PSALM**
Psalmist reminds of God's kindness and truth, Psalm 117

As the Hebrews praise God with psalms, Plato writes his dialogs. Homer describes skilled battlefield surgery. Aramaic develops as a Middle Eastern language. The Phoenicians circumnavigate Africa in a three-year voyage.

BOOK I

Psalms 1 – 41

Psalm 1

1 Blessed is the one
　who does not walk in step with the
　　wicked
or stand in the way that sinners take
　or sit in the company of mockers,
2 but whose delight is in the law of the
　LORD,
　and who meditates on his law day
　　and night.
3 That person is like a tree planted by
　streams of water,
　which yields its fruit in season
and whose leaf does not wither—
　whatever they do prospers.

4 Not so the wicked!
　They are like chaff
　that the wind blows away.
5 Therefore the wicked will not stand in
　the judgment,
　nor sinners in the assembly of the
　　righteous.

6 For the LORD watches over the way of
　the righteous,
　but the way of the wicked leads to
　　destruction.

Psalm 2

1 Why do the nations conspire[a]
　and the peoples plot in vain?
2 The kings of the earth rise up
　and the rulers band together
　against the LORD and against his
　　anointed, saying,
3 "Let us break their chains
　and throw off their shackles."

4 The One enthroned in heaven laughs;
　the Lord scoffs at them.
5 He rebukes them in his anger
　and terrifies them in his wrath,
　　saying,
6 "I have installed my king
　on Zion, my holy mountain."

7 I will proclaim the LORD's decree:

He said to me, "You are my son;
　today I have become your father.
8 Ask me,
　and I will make the nations your
　　inheritance,
　the ends of the earth your
　　possession.
9 You will break them with a rod of iron[b];
　you will dash them to pieces like
　　pottery."

10 Therefore, you kings, be wise;
　be warned, you rulers of the earth.
11 Serve the LORD with fear
　and celebrate his rule with
　　trembling.
12 Kiss his son, or he will be angry
　and your way will lead to your
　　destruction,
for his wrath can flare up in a
　　moment.
　Blessed are all who take refuge in
　　him.

Psalm 3[c]

A psalm of David. When he fled from his
son Absalom.

1 LORD, how many are my foes!
　How many rise up against me!
2 Many are saying of me,
　"God will not deliver him."[d]

3 But you, LORD, are a shield around me,
　my glory, the One who lifts my head
　　high.
4 I call out to the LORD,
　and he answers me from his holy
　　mountain.

5 I lie down and sleep;
　I wake again, because the LORD
　　sustains me.
6 I will not fear though tens of
　thousands
　assail me on every side.

7 Arise, LORD!
　Deliver me, my God!
Strike all my enemies on the jaw;
　break the teeth of the wicked.

---

a 1 Hebrew; Septuagint rage　　b 9 Or will rule them with an iron scepter (see Septuagint and Syriac)　　c In Hebrew texts
3:1-8 is numbered 3:2-9.　　d 2 The Hebrew has Selah (a word of uncertain meaning) here and at the end of verses 4
and 8.

8 From the LORD comes deliverance.
  May your blessing be on your
      people.

Psalm 4 [a]

For the director of music. With stringed
instruments. A psalm of David.

1 Answer me when I call to you,
    my righteous God.
  Give me relief from my distress;
    have mercy on me and hear my
        prayer.

2 How long will you people turn my glory
      into shame?
  How long will you love delusions
    and seek false gods [b]? [c]
3 Know that the LORD has set apart his
    faithful servant for himself;
  the LORD hears when I call to him.

4 Tremble and [d] do not sin;
    when you are on your beds,
  search your hearts and be silent.

> *The LORD has set
> apart his faithful servant
> for himself; the LORD hears
> when I call to him.*
>
> **Psalm 4:3**

5 Offer the sacrifices of the righteous
    and trust in the LORD.

6 Many, LORD, are asking, "Who will
      bring us prosperity?"
  Let the light of your face shine
      on us.
7 Fill my heart with joy
    when their grain and new wine
        abound.

8 In peace I will lie down and sleep,
    for you alone, LORD,
  make me dwell in safety.

Psalm 5 [e]

For the director of music. For pipes. A psalm
of David.

1 Listen to my words, LORD,
    consider my lament.
2 Hear my cry for help,
    my King and my God,
  for to you I pray.

3 In the morning, LORD, you hear my
      voice;
  in the morning I lay my requests
      before you
  and wait expectantly.
4 For you are not a God who is pleased
      with wickedness;
  with you, evil people are not
      welcome.
5 The arrogant cannot stand
    in your presence.
  You hate all who do wrong;
6   you destroy those who tell lies.
  The bloodthirsty and deceitful
    you, LORD, detest.
7 But I, by your great love,
    can come into your house;
  in reverence I bow down
    toward your holy temple.

8 Lead me, LORD, in your righteousness
    because of my enemies—
  make your way straight before me.
9 Not a word from their mouth can be
      trusted;
  their heart is filled with malice.
  Their throat is an open grave;
    with their tongues they tell lies.
10 Declare them guilty, O God!
    Let their intrigues be their
        downfall.
  Banish them for their many sins,
    for they have rebelled against
        you.
11 But let all who take refuge in you be
      glad;
  let them ever sing for joy.

---

[a] In Hebrew texts 4:1-8 is numbered 4:2-9.   [b] 2 Or seek lies   [c] 2 The Hebrew has Selah (a word of uncertain meaning)
here and at the end of verse 4.   [d] 4 Or In your anger (see Septuagint)   [e] In Hebrew texts 5:1-12 is numbered 5:2-13.

Spread your protection over them,
that those who love your name may
rejoice in you.
¹²Surely, LORD, you bless the righteous;
you surround them with your favor
as with a shield.

Psalm 6ᵃ

For the director of music. With stringed
instruments. According to *sheminith*.ᵇ
A psalm of David.

¹LORD, do not rebuke me in your anger
or discipline me in your wrath.
²Have mercy on me, LORD, for I am faint;
heal me, LORD, for my bones are in
agony.
³My soul is in deep anguish.
How long, LORD, how long?

⁴Turn, LORD, and deliver me;
save me because of your unfailing
love.
⁵Among the dead no one proclaims
your name.
Who praises you from the grave?

⁶I am worn out from my groaning.

All night long I flood my bed with
weeping
and drench my couch with tears.
⁷My eyes grow weak with sorrow;
they fail because of all my foes.

⁸Away from me, all you who do evil,
for the LORD has heard my weeping.
⁹The LORD has heard my cry for mercy;
the LORD accepts my prayer.
¹⁰All my enemies will be overwhelmed
with shame and anguish;
they will turn back and suddenly be
put to shame.

Psalm 7ᶜ

A *shiggaion*ᵈ of David, which he sang to the
LORD concerning Cush, a Benjamite.

¹LORD my God, I take refuge in you;
save and deliver me from all who
pursue me,

²or they will tear me apart like a lion
and rip me to pieces with no one to
rescue me.

³LORD my God, if I have done this
and there is guilt on my hands—
⁴if I have repaid my ally with evil
or without cause have robbed my
foe—
⁵then let my enemy pursue and
overtake me;
let him trample my life to the
ground
and make me sleep in the dust.ᵉ

⁶Arise, LORD, in your anger;
rise up against the rage of my
enemies.
Awake, my God; decree justice.
⁷Let the assembled peoples gather
around you,
while you sit enthroned over them
on high.
⁸ Let the LORD judge the peoples.
Vindicate me, LORD, according to my
righteousness,
according to my integrity, O Most
High.
⁹Bring to an end the violence of the
wicked
and make the righteous secure—
you, the righteous God
who probes minds and hearts.

¹⁰My shieldᶠ is God Most High,
who saves the upright in heart.
¹¹God is a righteous judge,
a God who displays his wrath every
day.
¹²If he does not relent,
heᵍ will sharpen his sword;
he will bend and string his bow.
¹³He has prepared his deadly
weapons;
he makes ready his flaming
arrows.

¹⁴Whoever is pregnant with evil
conceives trouble and gives birth to
disillusionment.
¹⁵Whoever digs a hole and scoops it out
falls into the pit they have made.

ᵃ In Hebrew texts 6:1-10 is numbered 6:2-11.   ᵇ Title: Probably a musical term   ᶜ In Hebrew texts 7:1-17 is numbered
7:2-18.   ᵈ Title: Probably a literary or musical term   ᵉ 5 The Hebrew has *Selah* (a word of uncertain meaning) here.
ᶠ 10 Or *sovereign*   ᵍ 12 Or *If anyone does not repent, / God*

16 The trouble they cause recoils on them;
 their violence comes down on their
 own heads.

17 I will give thanks to the LORD because
 of his righteousness;
 I will sing the praises of the name
 of the LORD Most High.

Psalm 8[a]

For the director of music. According to
 gittith.[b] A psalm of David.

1 LORD, our Lord,
 how majestic is your name in all the
 earth!

You have set your glory
 in the heavens.

2 Through the praise of children and
 infants
 you have established a stronghold
 against your enemies,
 to silence the foe and the
 avenger.

3 When I consider your heavens,
 the work of your fingers,
 the moon and the stars,
 which you have set in place,

4 what is mankind that you are mindful
 of them,
 human beings that you care for
 them?[c]

5 You have made them[d] a little lower
 than the angels[e]
 and crowned them[d] with glory and
 honor.

---

[a] In Hebrew texts 8:1-9 is numbered 8:2-10. [b] Title: Probably a musical term [c] 4 Or what is a human being that you are mindful of him, / a son of man that you care for him? [d] 5 Or him [e] 5 Or than God

TO THE POINT

Guard the Earth

Environment is a familiar word these days. More and more people have begun to realize that we are seriously polluting and damaging the earth.

When God first created human beings in his image, he said, "Rule over the fish in the sea and the birds in the sky and over every living creature" (Genesis 1:28). That word *rule* doesn't mean "use." It means "take care of." That's what Psalm 8 is saying. God gave you a special honor (Psalm 8:5). God made you the ruler over all he made, to take care of it for him for the benefit of future generations and for the benefit of the other living creatures he created (Psalm 8:6–9).

6 You made them rulers over the works
of your hands;
you put everything under their*a* feet:
7 all flocks and herds,
and the animals of the wild,
8 the birds in the sky,
and the fish in the sea,
all that swim the paths of the seas.

9 LORD, our Lord,
how majestic is your name in all the
earth!

Psalm 9 *b,c*

For the director of music. To the tune of
"The Death of the Son." A psalm of David.

1 I will give thanks to you, LORD, with all
my heart;
I will tell of all your wonderful
deeds.
2 I will be glad and rejoice in you;
I will sing the praises of your name,
O Most High.

3 My enemies turn back;
they stumble and perish before you.
4 For you have upheld my right and my
cause,
sitting enthroned as the righteous
judge.
5 You have rebuked the nations and
destroyed the wicked;
you have blotted out their name for
ever and ever.
6 Endless ruin has overtaken my
enemies,
you have uprooted their cities;
even the memory of them has
perished.

7 The LORD reigns forever;
he has established his throne for
judgment.
8 He rules the world in righteousness
and judges the peoples with equity.
9 The LORD is a refuge for the
oppressed,
a stronghold in times of trouble.
10 Those who know your name trust in
you,

for you, LORD, have never forsaken
those who seek you.

11 Sing the praises of the LORD,
enthroned in Zion;
proclaim among the nations what
he has done.
12 For he who avenges blood
remembers;
he does not ignore the cries of the
afflicted.

13 LORD, see how my enemies
persecute me!
Have mercy and lift me up from the
gates of death,
14 that I may declare your praises
in the gates of Daughter Zion,
and there rejoice in your salvation.

15 The nations have fallen into the pit
they have dug;
their feet are caught in the net they
have hidden.
16 The LORD is known by his acts of
justice;
the wicked are ensnared by the
work of their hands.*d*
17 The wicked go down to the realm of
the dead,
all the nations that forget God.
18 But God will never forget the needy;
the hope of the afflicted will never
perish.

19 Arise, LORD, do not let mortals triumph;
let the nations be judged in your
presence.
20 Strike them with terror, LORD;
let the nations know they are only
mortal.

Psalm 10 *b*

1 Why, LORD, do you stand far off?
Why do you hide yourself in times of
trouble?

2 In his arrogance the wicked man
hunts down the weak,
who are caught in the schemes he
devises.

---

a 6 Or *made him ruler . . . ; / . . . his*   *b* Psalms 9 and 10 may originally have been a single acrostic poem in which
alternating lines began with the successive letters of the Hebrew alphabet. In the Septuagint they constitute one psalm.
c In Hebrew texts 9:1-20 is numbered 9:2-21.   *d* 16 The Hebrew has *Higgaion* and *Selah* (words of uncertain meaning)
here; *Selah* occurs also at the end of verse 20.

³He boasts about the cravings of his
    heart;
  he blesses the greedy and reviles
    the Lord.
⁴In his pride the wicked man does not
    seek him;
  in all his thoughts there is no room
    for God.
⁵His ways are always prosperous;
  your laws are rejected byᵃ him;
  he sneers at all his enemies.
⁶He says to himself, "Nothing will ever
    shake me."
  He swears, "No one will ever do me
    harm."

⁷His mouth is full of lies and threats;
  trouble and evil are under his
    tongue.
⁸He lies in wait near the villages;
  from ambush he murders the
    innocent.
  His eyes watch in secret for his victims;
9   like a lion in cover he lies in wait.
  He lies in wait to catch the helpless;
  he catches the helpless and drags
    them off in his net.
¹⁰His victims are crushed, they
    collapse;
  they fall under his strength.
¹¹He says to himself, "God will never
    notice;
  he covers his face and never sees."

¹²Arise, Lord! Lift up your hand, O God.
  Do not forget the helpless.
¹³Why does the wicked man revile God?
  Why does he say to himself,
  "He won't call me to account"?

¹⁴But you, God, see the trouble of the
    afflicted;
  you consider their grief and take it
    in hand.
  The victims commit themselves to
    you;
  you are the helper of the fatherless.
¹⁵Break the arm of the wicked man;
  call the evildoer to account for his
    wickedness
  that would not otherwise be found
    out.

¹⁶The Lord is King for ever and ever;
  the nations will perish from his
    land.
¹⁷You, Lord, hear the desire of the
    afflicted;
  you encourage them, and you listen
    to their cry,
¹⁸defending the fatherless and the
    oppressed,
  so that mere earthly mortals
  will never again strike terror.

Psalm 11

For the director of music. Of David.

¹In the Lord I take refuge.
  How then can you say to me:
  "Flee like a bird to your mountain.
²For look, the wicked bend their bows;
  they set their arrows against the
    strings
  to shoot from the shadows
  at the upright in heart.
³When the foundations are being
    destroyed,
  what can the righteous do?"

⁴The Lord is in his holy temple;
  the Lord is on his heavenly
    throne.
  He observes everyone on earth;
  his eyes examine them.
⁵The Lord examines the righteous,
  but the wicked, those who love
    violence,
  he hates with a passion.
⁶On the wicked he will rain
  fiery coals and burning sulfur;
  a scorching wind will be their lot.

> *You, Lord, hear the desire of the afflicted; you encourage them, and you listen to their cry.*
> **Psalm 10:17**

ᵃ 5 See Septuagint; Hebrew / they are haughty, and your laws are far from

INSTANT ACCESS

Brittany is upset because her friends talk about her behind her back and call her names. That happens to most of us. It even happened in Bible times. Check out verse 3 of this psalm. When people talked down to King David, he remembered God's attitude toward such people. And David remembered God's promise: "I will protect them from those who malign them" (Psalm 12:5). When others talk behind our backs, we can follow David's example and trust God to protect us from such people forever (verse 7).

{Psalm 12}

7 For the LORD is righteous,
  he loves justice;
  the upright will see his face.

Psalm 12ᵃ

For the director of music. According to
*sheminith.*ᵇ A psalm of David.

1 Help, LORD, for no one is faithful
    anymore;
  those who are loyal have vanished
    from the human race.
2 Everyone lies to their neighbor;
  they flatter with their lips
  but harbor deception in their hearts.

3 May the LORD silence all flattering lips
    and every boastful tongue—
4 those who say,
    "By our tongues we will prevail;
    our own lips will defend us—who is
      lord over us?"

5 "Because the poor are plundered and
      the needy groan,
  I will now arise," says the LORD.
  "I will protect them from those who
      malign them."
6 And the words of the LORD are
      flawless,
  like silver purified in a crucible,
  like goldᶜ refined seven times.

7 You, LORD, will keep the needy safe
  and will protect us forever from the
      wicked,
8 who freely strut about
  when what is vile is honored by the
      human race.

Psalm 13ᵈ

For the director of music.
A psalm of David.

1 How long, LORD? Will you forget me
    forever?
  How long will you hide your face
    from me?
2 How long must I wrestle with my
      thoughts
  and day after day have sorrow in my
      heart?
  How long will my enemy triumph
    over me?

3 Look on me and answer, LORD my
      God.
  Give light to my eyes, or I will sleep
    in death,
4 and my enemy will say, "I have
      overcome him,"
  and my foes will rejoice when I
    fall.

5 But I trust in your unfailing love;
  my heart rejoices in your
      salvation.
6 I will sing the LORD's praise,
  for he has been good to me.

ᵃ In Hebrew texts 12:1-8 is numbered 12:2-9.   ᵇ Title: Probably a musical term   ᶜ 6 Probable reading of the original
Hebrew text; Masoretic Text *earth*   ᵈ In Hebrew texts 13:1-6 is numbered 13:2-6.

Psalm 14

For the director of music. Of David.

1 The fool[a] says in his heart,
    "There is no God."
They are corrupt, their deeds are vile;
    there is no one who does good.

2 The LORD looks down from heaven
    on all mankind
to see if there are any who
    understand,
    any who seek God.
3 All have turned away, all have become
    corrupt;
    there is no one who does good,
    not even one.

4 Do all these evildoers know nothing?

They devour my people as though
    eating bread;
    they never call on the LORD.
5 But there they are, overwhelmed with
    dread,
    for God is present in the company
    of the righteous.
6 You evildoers frustrate the plans of
    the poor,
    but the LORD is their refuge.

7 Oh, that salvation for Israel would
    come out of Zion!
When the LORD restores his people,
    let Jacob rejoice and Israel be
    glad!

a 1 The Hebrew words rendered *fool* in Psalms denote one who is morally deficient.

TO THE POINT

Don't Be Foolish

Very intelligent people can also be very foolish. In fact, the Old Testament uses several different words for *fool*, and none of them has anything to do with intelligence.

The word *fool* used in Psalm 14:1 describes the person who commits gross sins. The actions of such persons show that they don't believe God exists. If they believed in God and knew that one day God would declare judgment, they would change.

Believing in God makes a moral difference. It won't make you more intelligent, but it will make a difference in the way you live your life. And that's what's really important.

INSTANT ACCESS

Why am I here? What's my purpose in life? Many teens ask that question. "What's my purpose in life?" is a question that probably can't be answered yet. Looking back on his life, King David wrote, "You are my portion and my cup." He realized God's plan for him was a "delightful inheritance." But as a teen taking care of sheep, David didn't know his future. None of us knows ahead of time what our future holds. But as long as you look to God for advice and guidance each day (verse 7), he'll lead you to the "delightful inheritance" he's planned for you.

{Psalm 16:5-7}

Psalm 15

A psalm of David.

¹ LORD, who may dwell in your sacred tent?
  Who may live on your holy mountain?

² The one whose walk is blameless,
  who does what is righteous,
  who speaks the truth from their heart;
³ whose tongue utters no slander,
  who does no wrong to a neighbor,
  and casts no slur on others;

⁴ who despises a vile person
  but honors those who fear the LORD;
 who keeps an oath even when it hurts,
  and does not change their mind;
⁵ who lends money to the poor without interest;
  who does not accept a bribe
  against the innocent.

 Whoever does these things
  will never be shaken.

Psalm 16

A miktam[a] of David.

¹ Keep me safe, my God,
  for in you I take refuge.

² I say to the LORD, "You are my Lord;
  apart from you I have no good thing."
³ I say of the holy people who are in the land,
  "They are the noble ones in whom is all my delight."
⁴ Those who run after other gods will suffer more and more.
  I will not pour out libations of blood to such gods
  or take up their names on my lips.

⁵ LORD, you alone are my portion and my cup;
  you make my lot secure.
⁶ The boundary lines have fallen for me in pleasant places;
  surely I have a delightful inheritance.
⁷ I will praise the LORD, who counsels me;
  even at night my heart instructs me.
⁸ I keep my eyes always on the LORD.
  With him at my right hand, I will not be shaken.

⁹ Therefore my heart is glad and my tongue rejoices;
  my body also will rest secure,
¹⁰ because you will not abandon me to the realm of the dead,
  nor will you let your faithful[b] one see decay.

---

a Title: Probably a literary or musical term   b 10 Or holy

11 You make known to me the path of life;
  you will fill me with joy in your
    presence,
  with eternal pleasures at your right
    hand.

Psalm 17

A prayer of David.

1 Hear me, LORD, my plea is just;
  listen to my cry.
Hear my prayer—
  it does not rise from deceitful lips.
2 Let my vindication come from you;
  may your eyes see what is right.

3 Though you probe my heart,
  though you examine me at night
    and test me,
you will find that I have planned no evil;
  my mouth has not transgressed.
4 Though people tried to bribe me,
  I have kept myself from the ways of
    the violent
  through what your lips have
    commanded.
5 My steps have held to your paths;
  my feet have not stumbled.

6 I call on you, my God, for you will
    answer me;
  turn your ear to me and hear my
    prayer.
7 Show me the wonders of your great
    love,
  you who save by your right hand
  those who take refuge in you from
    their foes.

> I call on you, my God,
> for you will answer me;
> turn your ear to me
> and hear my prayer.
>
> Psalm 17:6

8 Keep me as the apple of your eye;
  hide me in the shadow of your
    wings
9 from the wicked who are out to
    destroy me,
  from my mortal enemies who
    surround me.

10 They close up their callous hearts,
  and their mouths speak with
    arrogance.
11 They have tracked me down, they now
    surround me,
  with eyes alert, to throw me to the
    ground.
12 They are like a lion hungry for prey,
  like a fierce lion crouching in cover.

13 Rise up, LORD, confront them, bring
    them down;
  with your sword rescue me from the
    wicked.
14 By your hand save me from such
    people, LORD,
  from those of this world whose
    reward is in this life.
May what you have stored up for the
    wicked fill their bellies;
  may their children gorge themselves
    on it,
  and may there be leftovers for their
    little ones.

15 As for me, I will be vindicated and will
    see your face;
  when I awake, I will be satisfied
    with seeing your likeness.

Psalm 18[a]

For the director of music. Of David the
servant of the LORD. He sang to the LORD the
words of this song when the LORD delivered
him from the hand of all his enemies and
from the hand of Saul. He said:

1 I love you, LORD, my strength.

2 The LORD is my rock, my fortress and
    my deliverer;
  my God is my rock, in whom I take
    refuge,
  my shield[b] and the horn[c] of my
    salvation, my stronghold.

---

[a] In Hebrew texts 18:1-50 is numbered 18:2-51.   [b] 2 Or sovereign   [c] 2 Horn here symbolizes strength.

Morgan is fearful. She says her biggest problem is not having confidence that God will protect her. We do live in a dangerous world. Terrible things happen to teens every day. And sometimes the terrible things happen to Christians. So what are believers to do? Just what David did when he was being pursued by enemies out to kill him—he remembered how great God is (verses 30–31). He counted on God to give him strength and help him meet the dangers ahead (verses 32–34). David trusted God to bring him through every danger (verses 35–36). Let's not forget that God can strengthen us to meet any dangers the future may hold.

{Psalm 18}

>> INSTANT ACCESS

³ I called to the LORD, who is worthy of praise,
    and I have been saved from my enemies.
⁴ The cords of death entangled me;
    the torrents of destruction overwhelmed me.
⁵ The cords of the grave coiled around me;
    the snares of death confronted me.

⁶ In my distress I called to the LORD;
    I cried to my God for help.
From his temple he heard my voice;
    my cry came before him, into his ears.
⁷ The earth trembled and quaked,
    and the foundations of the mountains shook;
    they trembled because he was angry.
⁸ Smoke rose from his nostrils;
    consuming fire came from his mouth,
    burning coals blazed out of it.
⁹ He parted the heavens and came down;
    dark clouds were under his feet.
¹⁰ He mounted the cherubim and flew;
    he soared on the wings of the wind.
¹¹ He made darkness his covering, his canopy around him—
    the dark rain clouds of the sky.
¹² Out of the brightness of his presence clouds advanced,
    with hailstones and bolts of lightning.
¹³ The LORD thundered from heaven;
    the voice of the Most High resounded.ᵃ
¹⁴ He shot his arrows and scattered the enemy,
    with great bolts of lightning he routed them.
¹⁵ The valleys of the sea were exposed
    and the foundations of the earth laid bare
at your rebuke, LORD,
    at the blast of breath from your nostrils.

¹⁶ He reached down from on high and took hold of me;
    he drew me out of deep waters.
¹⁷ He rescued me from my powerful enemy,
    from my foes, who were too strong for me.
¹⁸ They confronted me in the day of my disaster,
    but the LORD was my support.
¹⁹ He brought me out into a spacious place;
    he rescued me because he delighted in me.

ᵃ 13 Some Hebrew manuscripts and Septuagint (see also 2 Samuel 22:14); most Hebrew manuscripts *resounded, / amid hailstones and bolts of lightning*

²⁰ The L<small>ORD</small> has dealt with me according
 to my righteousness;
 according to the cleanness of my
 hands he has rewarded me.
²¹ For I have kept the ways of the L<small>ORD</small>;
 I am not guilty of turning from my
 God.
²² All his laws are before me;
 I have not turned away from his
 decrees.
²³ I have been blameless before him
 and have kept myself from sin.
²⁴ The L<small>ORD</small> has rewarded me according
 to my righteousness,
 according to the cleanness of my
 hands in his sight.

²⁵ To the faithful you show yourself
 faithful,
 to the blameless you show yourself
 blameless,
²⁶ to the pure you show yourself pure,
 but to the devious you show
 yourself shrewd.
²⁷ You save the humble
 but bring low those whose eyes are
 haughty.
²⁸ You, L<small>ORD</small>, keep my lamp burning;
 my God turns my darkness into
 light.
²⁹ With your help I can advance against a
 troop^a;
 with my God I can scale a wall.

³⁰ As for God, his way is perfect:
 The L<small>ORD</small>'s word is flawless;
 he shields all who take refuge
 in him.
³¹ For who is God besides the L<small>ORD</small>?
 And who is the Rock except our
 God?
³² It is God who arms me with strength
 and keeps my way secure.
³³ He makes my feet like the feet of a
 deer;
 he causes me to stand on the
 heights.
³⁴ He trains my hands for battle;
 my arms can bend a bow of bronze.
³⁵ You make your saving help my shield,
 and your right hand sustains me;
 your help has made me great.

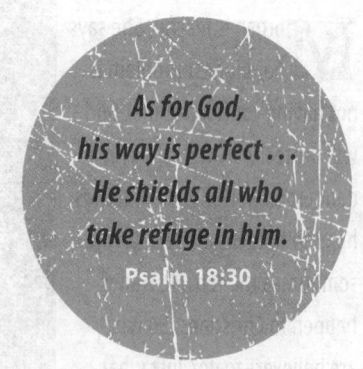

*As for God,
his way is perfect . . .
He shields all who
take refuge in him.*

Psalm 18:30

³⁶ You provide a broad path for my feet,
 so that my ankles do not give way.

³⁷ I pursued my enemies and overtook
 them;
 I did not turn back till they were
 destroyed.
³⁸ I crushed them so that they could not
 rise;
 they fell beneath my feet.
³⁹ You armed me with strength for battle;
 you humbled my adversaries
 before me.
⁴⁰ You made my enemies turn their
 backs in flight,
 and I destroyed my foes.
⁴¹ They cried for help, but there was no
 one to save them—
 to the L<small>ORD</small>, but he did not answer.
⁴² I beat them as fine as windblown
 dust;
 I trampled them^b like mud in the
 streets.
⁴³ You have delivered me from the
 attacks of the people;
 you have made me the head of
 nations.
People I did not know now serve me,
⁴⁴ foreigners cower before me;
 as soon as they hear of me, they
 obey me.
⁴⁵ They all lose heart;
 they come trembling from their
 strongholds.

⁴⁶ The L<small>ORD</small> lives! Praise be to my Rock!
 Exalted be God my Savior!

---

^a 29 Or *can run through a barricade* ^b 42 Many Hebrew manuscripts, Septuagint, Syriac and Targum (see also
2 Samuel 22:43); Masoretic Text *I poured them out*

47 He is the God who avenges me,
who subdues nations under me,
48 who saves me from my enemies.
You exalted me above my foes;
from a violent man you rescued me.
49 Therefore I will praise you, Lord,
among the nations;
I will sing the praises of your name.

50 He gives his king great victories;
he shows unfailing love to his
anointed,
to David and to his descendants
forever.

Psalm 19 [a]

For the director of music. A psalm of David.

1 The heavens declare the glory of God;
the skies proclaim the work of his
hands.
2 Day after day they pour forth speech;
night after night they reveal
knowledge.
3 They have no speech, they use no
words;
no sound is heard from them.
4 Yet their voice [b] goes out into all the
earth,
their words to the ends of the world.
In the heavens God has pitched a
tent for the sun.
5 It is like a bridegroom coming out
of his chamber,
like a champion rejoicing to run his
course.
6 It rises at one end of the heavens
and makes its circuit to the other;
nothing is deprived of its warmth.

7 The law of the Lord is perfect,
refreshing the soul.
The statutes of the Lord are
trustworthy,
making wise the simple.
8 The precepts of the Lord are right,
giving joy to the heart.
The commands of the Lord are
radiant,
giving light to the eyes.
9 The fear of the Lord is pure,
enduring forever.

The decrees of the Lord are firm,
and all of them are righteous.
10 They are more precious than gold,
than much pure gold;
they are sweeter than honey,
than honey from the honeycomb.
11 By them your servant is warned;
in keeping them there is great
reward.
12 But who can discern their own errors?
Forgive my hidden faults.
13 Keep your servant also from willful sins;
may they not rule over me.
Then I will be blameless,
innocent of great transgression.

14 May these words of my mouth and
this meditation of my heart
be pleasing in your sight,
Lord, my Rock and my Redeemer.

Psalm 20 [c]

For the director of music. A psalm of David.

1 May the Lord answer you when you
are in distress;
may the name of the God of Jacob
protect you.

Psalm 20

Q: What is a psalm super-scription?

BONUS: What does it do?

---

[a] In Hebrew texts 19:1-14 is numbered 19:2-15.
[b] 4 Septuagint, Jerome and Syriac; Hebrew *measuring line*   [c] In Hebrew texts 20:1-9 is numbered 20:2-10.

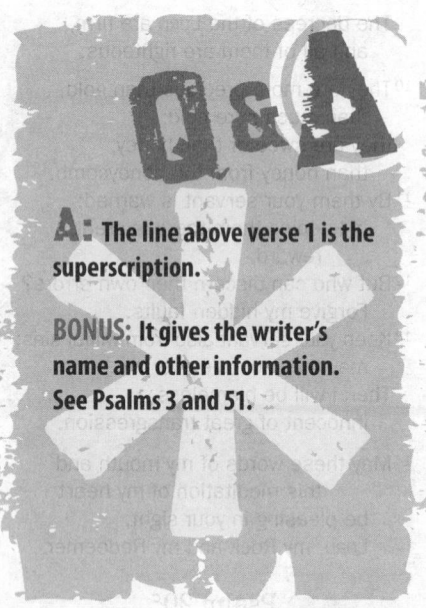

A: The line above verse 1 is the superscription.

BONUS: It gives the writer's name and other information. See Psalms 3 and 51.

2 May he send you help from the sanctuary
and grant you support from Zion.
3 May he remember all your sacrifices
and accept your burnt offerings.[a]
4 May he give you the desire of your heart
and make all your plans succeed.
5 May we shout for joy over your victory
and lift up our banners in the name of our God.

May the LORD grant all your requests.

6 Now this I know:
The LORD gives victory to his anointed.
He answers him from his heavenly sanctuary
with the victorious power of his right hand.
7 Some trust in chariots and some in horses,
but we trust in the name of the LORD our God.
8 They are brought to their knees and fall,
but we rise up and stand firm.
9 LORD, give victory to the king!
Answer us when we call!

Psalm 21[b]

For the director of music. A psalm of David.

1 The king rejoices in your strength, LORD.
How great is his joy in the victories you give!
2 You have granted him his heart's desire
and have not withheld the request of his lips.[a]
3 You came to greet him with rich blessings
and placed a crown of pure gold on his head.
4 He asked you for life, and you gave it to him—
length of days, for ever and ever.
5 Through the victories you gave, his glory is great;
you have bestowed on him splendor and majesty.
6 Surely you have granted him unending blessings
and made him glad with the joy of your presence.
7 For the king trusts in the LORD;
through the unfailing love of the Most High
he will not be shaken.
8 Your hand will lay hold on all your enemies;
your right hand will seize your foes.
9 When you appear for battle,
you will burn them up as in a blazing furnace.
The LORD will swallow them up in his wrath,
and his fire will consume them.
10 You will destroy their descendants from the earth,
their posterity from mankind.
11 Though they plot evil against you
and devise wicked schemes, they cannot succeed.
12 You will make them turn their backs
when you aim at them with drawn bow.

---

[a] 3,2 The Hebrew has Selah (a word of uncertain meaning) here.   [b] In Hebrew texts 21:1-13 is numbered 21:2-14.

Josh wonders, "Why is life so hard?" It is hard, for everyone. In this messianic Psalm (a prophecy about Jesus), we even hear Christ say, "Do not be far from me, for trouble is near and there is no one to help" (verse 11). Reading this psalm reminds us that life was hard for Jesus. No wonder it's hard for us. Jesus' troubles made him look to God the Father. That may be one reason God lets hard things into our lives. If everything were easy, we probably wouldn't think we need to rely on God or stay near to him. The great thing is that when our life is hard and we look to the Lord, he gives us the strength we need to live life his way.

{Psalm 22}

INSTANT ACCESS

13 Be exalted in your strength, LORD;
  we will sing and praise your might.

Psalm 22 [a]

For the director of music. To the tune of "The Doe of the Morning." A psalm of David.

1 My God, my God, why have you
    forsaken me?
  Why are you so far from saving me,
  so far from my cries of anguish?

2 My God, I cry out by day, but you do
    not answer,
  by night, but I find no rest. [b]

3 Yet you are enthroned as the Holy
    One;
  you are the one Israel praises. [c]

4 In you our ancestors put their trust;
  they trusted and you delivered
    them.

5 To you they cried out and were
    saved;
  in you they trusted and were not put
    to shame.

6 But I am a worm and not a man,
  scorned by everyone, despised by
    the people.

7 All who see me mock me;
  they hurl insults, shaking their
    heads.

8 "He trusts in the LORD," they say,
  "let the LORD rescue him.
  Let him deliver him,
    since he delights in him."

9 Yet you brought me out of the womb;
  you made me trust in you, even at
    my mother's breast.

10 From birth I was cast on you;
  from my mother's womb you have
    been my God.

11 Do not be far from me,
  for trouble is near
  and there is no one to help.

12 Many bulls surround me;
  strong bulls of Bashan encircle me.

13 Roaring lions that tear their prey
  open their mouths wide against me.

14 I am poured out like water,
  and all my bones are out of joint.
  My heart has turned to wax;
  it has melted within me.

15 My mouth [d] is dried up like a potsherd,
  and my tongue sticks to the roof of
    my mouth;
  you lay me in the dust of death.

16 Dogs surround me,
  a pack of villains encircles me;
  they pierce [e] my hands and my feet.

---

a In Hebrew texts 22:1-31 is numbered 22:2-32.   b 2 Or night, and am not silent   c 3 Or Yet you are holy, / enthroned on the praises of Israel   d 15 Probable reading of the original Hebrew text; Masoretic Text strength   e 16 Dead Sea Scrolls and some manuscripts of the Masoretic Text, Septuagint and Syriac; most manuscripts of the Masoretic Text me, / like a lion

Why does God allow people to suffer so much from hurricanes and tsunamis?

>> Tyler

Dear Jordan

Dear Tyler,

I don't understand why there is so much suffering in this world. But I do know that God knows when his people suffer. Psalm 22 tells us, "For he has not despised or scorned the suffering of the afflicted one; he has not hidden his face from him but has listened to his cry for help" (verse 24).

God created an amazing universe with a set of natural laws such as gravity. He set the planets into motion and the whole solar system has been operating for thousands of years. He gave us the sun and rain and all of the natural consequences that come with such a complex system.

As we have seen, sometimes there are massive and destructive storms, earthquakes and volcanic eruptions. It seems as a general rule, God does not intervene in these natural phenomena. But we hear stories of miraculous rescues and people surviving things that no one should have been able to. Are some people saved by guardian angels? I wish I knew the answers to all these questions. Some things are mysteries to us.

Sometimes disasters come along and damage or destroy even the best people. Not because God doesn't care and not because God doesn't see the suffering people endure. We can't stop natural disasters, but we can share the love and compassion God has given us.

Jordan

17 All my bones are on display;
    people stare and gloat over me.
18 They divide my clothes among them
    and cast lots for my garment.

19 But you, LORD, do not be far from me.
    You are my strength; come quickly
        to help me.
20 Deliver me from the sword,
    my precious life from the power of
        the dogs.
21 Rescue me from the mouth of the
        lions;
    save me from the horns of the wild
        oxen.

22 I will declare your name to my
        people;
    in the assembly I will praise you.
23 You who fear the LORD, praise him!
    All you descendants of Jacob, honor
        him!
    Revere him, all you descendants of
        Israel!
24 For he has not despised or scorned
        the suffering of the afflicted one;
    he has not hidden his face from him
        but has listened to his cry for
        help.

25 From you comes the theme of my
        praise in the great assembly;
    before those who fear you[a] I will
        fulfill my vows.
26 The poor will eat and be satisfied;
    those who seek the LORD will praise
        him—
    may your hearts live forever!

27 All the ends of the earth
    will remember and turn to the
        LORD,
    and all the families of the nations
    will bow down before him,
28 for dominion belongs to the LORD
    and he rules over the nations.

29 All the rich of the earth will feast and
        worship;
    all who go down to the dust will
        kneel before him—
    those who cannot keep themselves
        alive.

30 Posterity will serve him;
    future generations will be told about
        the Lord.
31 They will proclaim his righteousness,
    declaring to a people yet
        unborn:
    He has done it!

Psalm 23

A psalm of David.

1 The LORD is my shepherd, I lack
    nothing.
2   He makes me lie down in green
        pastures,
    he leads me beside quiet waters,
3   he refreshes my soul.
    He guides me along the right
        paths
    for his name's sake.
4 Even though I walk
    through the darkest valley,[b]
I will fear no evil,
    for you are with me;
your rod and your staff,
    they comfort me.

5 You prepare a table before me
    in the presence of my enemies.
You anoint my head with oil;
    my cup overflows.
6 Surely your goodness and love will
        follow me
    all the days of my life,
and I will dwell in the house
        of the LORD
    forever.

Psalm 24

Of David. A psalm.

1 The earth is the LORD's, and
        everything in it,
    the world, and all who live in it;
2 for he founded it on the seas
    and established it on the waters.

3 Who may ascend the mountain of the
        LORD?
    Who may stand in his holy
        place?

---

a 25 Hebrew him   b 4 Or the valley of the shadow of death

4 The one who has clean hands and a
    pure heart,
  who does not trust in an idol
  or swear by a false god.*a*

5 They will receive blessing from the Lord
    and vindication from God their
    Savior.
6 Such is the generation of those who
    seek him,
  who seek your face, God of Jacob.*b,c*

7 Lift up your heads, you gates;
    be lifted up, you ancient doors,
  that the King of glory may come in.
8 Who is this King of glory?
    The Lord strong and mighty,
    the Lord mighty in battle.
9 Lift up your heads, you gates;
    lift them up, you ancient doors,
  that the King of glory may come in.
10 Who is he, this King of glory?
    The Lord Almighty—
    he is the King of glory.

Psalm 25*d*

Of David.

1 In you, Lord my God,
    I put my trust.

2 I trust in you;
    do not let me be put to shame,
    nor let my enemies triumph over me.
3 No one who hopes in you
    will ever be put to shame,
  but shame will come on those
    who are treacherous without cause.

4 Show me your ways, Lord,
    teach me your paths.
5 Guide me in your truth and teach me,
    for you are God my Savior,
    and my hope is in you all day long.
6 Remember, Lord, your great mercy
    and love,
  for they are from of old.
7 Do not remember the sins of my youth
    and my rebellious ways;
  according to your love remember me,
    for you, Lord, are good.

One teen writes, "The hardest thing is walking with God every day." What would you tell her if she'd written to you? I suspect King David might say something like he wrote in Psalm 25: "Ask God to show you his ways and guide you all day long" (verses 4–5). And if you go wrong, look to God for "mercy and forgiveness" (verses 6–7). Will God really do this for you? Sure he will. Because God loves you, and because he is good (verse 7).

{Psalm 25:4–7}

INSTANT ACCESS

8 Good and upright is the Lord;
    therefore he instructs sinners in his
    ways.
9 He guides the humble in what is right
    and teaches them his way.
10 All the ways of the Lord are loving and
    faithful
    toward those who keep the
    demands of his covenant.
11 For the sake of your name, Lord,
    forgive my iniquity, though it is
    great.
12 Who, then, are those who fear the
    Lord?
    He will instruct them in the ways
    they should choose.*e*

---

a 4 Or *swear falsely*   *b* 6 Two Hebrew manuscripts and Syriac (see also Septuagint); most Hebrew manuscripts *face, Jacob*   *c* 6 The Hebrew has *Selah* (a word of uncertain meaning) here and at the end of verse 10.   *d* This psalm is an acrostic poem, the verses of which begin with the successive letters of the Hebrew alphabet.   *e* 12 Or *ways he chooses*

13 They will spend their days in prosperity,
and their descendants will inherit
the land.
14 The LORD confides in those who fear
him;
he makes his covenant known to
them.
15 My eyes are ever on the LORD,
for only he will release my feet from
the snare.

16 Turn to me and be gracious to me,
for I am lonely and afflicted.
17 Relieve the troubles of my heart
and free me from my anguish.
18 Look on my affliction and my distress
and take away all my sins.
19 See how numerous are my enemies
and how fiercely they hate me!

20 Guard my life and rescue me;
do not let me be put to shame,
for I take refuge in you.
21 May integrity and uprightness
protect me,
because my hope, LORD,ᵃ is in you.

22 Deliver Israel, O God,
from all their troubles!

Psalm 26

Of David.

1 Vindicate me, LORD,
for I have led a blameless life;
I have trusted in the LORD
and have not faltered.
2 Test me, LORD, and try me,
examine my heart and my mind;
3 for I have always been mindful of your
unfailing love
and have lived in reliance on your
faithfulness.

4 I do not sit with the deceitful,
nor do I associate with hypocrites.
5 I abhor the assembly of evildoers
and refuse to sit with the wicked.
6 I wash my hands in innocence,
and go about your altar, LORD,
7 proclaiming aloud your praise
and telling of all your wonderful
deeds.

8 LORD, I love the house where you live,
the place where your glory dwells.
9 Do not take away my soul along with
sinners,
my life with those who are
bloodthirsty,
10 in whose hands are wicked schemes,
whose right hands are full of bribes.
11 I lead a blameless life;
deliver me and be merciful to me.
12 My feet stand on level ground;
in the great congregation I will
praise the LORD.

Psalm 27

Of David.

1 The LORD is my light and my salvation—
whom shall I fear?
The LORD is the stronghold of my
life—
of whom shall I be afraid?
2 When the wicked advance against me
to devourᵇ me,
it is my enemies and my foes
who will stumble and fall.
3 Though an army besiege me,
my heart will not fear;
though war break out against me,
even then I will be confident.

4 One thing I ask from the LORD,
this only do I seek:
that I may dwell in the house of the
LORD
all the days of my life,
to gaze on the beauty of the LORD
and to seek him in his temple.
5 For in the day of trouble
he will keep me safe in his dwelling;
he will hide me in the shelter of his
sacred tent
and set me high upon a rock.
6 Then my head will be exalted
above the enemies who
surround me;
at his sacred tent I will sacrifice with
shouts of joy;
I will sing and make music to the
LORD.

ᵃ 21 Septuagint; Hebrew does not have LORD.   ᵇ 2 Or *slander*

[7] Hear my voice when I call, LORD;
  be merciful to me and answer me.
[8] My heart says of you, "Seek his face!"
  Your face, LORD, I will seek.
[9] Do not hide your face from me,
  do not turn your servant away in
    anger;
  you have been my helper.
  Do not reject me or forsake me,
  God my Savior.
[10] Though my father and mother
    forsake me,
  the LORD will receive me.
[11] Teach me your way, LORD;
  lead me in a straight path
  because of my oppressors.
[12] Do not turn me over to the desire of
    my foes,
  for false witnesses rise up
    against me,
  spouting malicious accusations.

[13] I remain confident of this:
  I will see the goodness of the LORD
  in the land of the living.
[14] Wait for the LORD;
  be strong and take heart
  and wait for the LORD.

Psalm 28

Of David.

[1] To you, LORD, I call;
  you are my Rock,
  do not turn a deaf ear to me.
  For if you remain silent,
  I will be like those who go down to
    the pit.
[2] Hear my cry for mercy
  as I call to you for help,
  as I lift up my hands
  toward your Most Holy Place.

[3] Do not drag me away with the wicked,
  with those who do evil,
  who speak cordially with their
    neighbors
  but harbor malice in their hearts.
[4] Repay them for their deeds
  and for their evil work;
  repay them for what their hands have
    done

and bring back on them what they
    deserve.
[5] Because they have no regard for the
    deeds of the LORD
  and what his hands have done,
  he will tear them down
  and never build them up again.
[6] Praise be to the LORD,
  for he has heard my cry for
    mercy.
[7] The LORD is my strength and my
    shield;
  my heart trusts in him, and he
    helps me.
  My heart leaps for joy,
  and with my song I praise him.

[8] The LORD is the strength of his
    people,
  a fortress of salvation for his
    anointed one.
[9] Save your people and bless your
    inheritance;
  be their shepherd and carry them
    forever.

Psalm 29

A psalm of David.

[1] Ascribe to the LORD, you heavenly
    beings,
  ascribe to the LORD glory and
    strength.
[2] Ascribe to the LORD the glory due his
    name;
  worship the LORD in the splendor of
    his[a] holiness.
[3] The voice of the LORD is over the
    waters;
  the God of glory thunders,
  the LORD thunders over the mighty
    waters.
[4] The voice of the LORD is powerful;
  the voice of the LORD is majestic.
[5] The voice of the LORD breaks the
    cedars;
  the LORD breaks in pieces the
    cedars of Lebanon.
[6] He makes Lebanon leap like a calf,
  Sirion[b] like a young wild ox.

---

[a] 2 Or LORD with the splendor of   [b] 6 That is, Mount Hermon

7 The voice of the LORD strikes
with flashes of lightning.
8 The voice of the LORD shakes the
desert;
the LORD shakes the Desert of
Kadesh.
9 The voice of the LORD twists the oaks^a
and strips the forests bare.
And in his temple all cry, "Glory!"

10 The LORD sits enthroned over the
flood;
the LORD is enthroned as King
forever.
11 The LORD gives strength to his people;
the LORD blesses his people with
peace.

Psalm 30 ^b

A psalm. A song. For the dedication of the
temple.^c Of David.

1 I will exalt you, LORD,
for you lifted me out of the depths
and did not let my enemies gloat
over me.
2 LORD my God, I called to you for help,
and you healed me.
3 You, LORD, brought me up from the
realm of the dead;
you spared me from going down to
the pit.

4 Sing the praises of the LORD, you his
faithful people;
praise his holy name.
5 For his anger lasts only a moment,
but his favor lasts a lifetime;
weeping may stay for the night,
but rejoicing comes in the morning.

6 When I felt secure, I said,
"I will never be shaken."
7 LORD, when you favored me,
you made my royal mountain^d stand
firm;
but when you hid your face,
I was dismayed.

8 To you, LORD, I called;
to the Lord I cried for mercy:
9 "What is gained if I am silenced,

if I go down to the pit?
Will the dust praise you?
Will it proclaim your faithfulness?
10 Hear, LORD, and be merciful to me;
LORD, be my help."

11 You turned my wailing into dancing;
you removed my sackcloth and
clothed me with joy,
12 that my heart may sing your praises
and not be silent.
LORD my God, I will praise you
forever.

Psalm 31 ^e

For the director of music. A psalm of David.

1 In you, LORD, I have taken refuge;
let me never be put to shame;
deliver me in your righteousness.
2 Turn your ear to me,
come quickly to my rescue;
be my rock of refuge,
a strong fortress to save me.
3 Since you are my rock and my
fortress,
for the sake of your name lead and
guide me.
4 Keep me free from the trap that is set
for me,
for you are my refuge.
5 Into your hands I commit my spirit;
deliver me, LORD, my faithful God.

6 I hate those who cling to worthless
idols;
as for me, I trust in the LORD.
7 I will be glad and rejoice in your love,
for you saw my affliction
and knew the anguish of my soul.
8 You have not given me into the hands
of the enemy
but have set my feet in a spacious
place.

9 Be merciful to me, LORD, for I am in
distress;
my eyes grow weak with sorrow,
my soul and body with grief.
10 My life is consumed by anguish
and my years by groaning;

---

^a 9 Or LORD *makes the deer give birth*   ^b In Hebrew texts 30:1-12 is numbered 30:2-13.   ^c Title: Or *palace*   ^d 7 That
is, Mount Zion   ^e In Hebrew texts 31:1-24 is numbered 31:2-25.

my strength fails because of my
affliction,[a]
and my bones grow weak.
11 Because of all my enemies,
I am the utter contempt of my
neighbors
and an object of dread to my closest
friends—
those who see me on the street
flee from me.
12 I am forgotten as though I were dead;
I have become like broken pottery.
13 For I hear many whispering,
"Terror on every side!"
They conspire against me
and plot to take my life.

14 But I trust in you, Lord;
I say, "You are my God."
15 My times are in your hands;
deliver me from the hands of my
enemies,
from those who pursue me.
16 Let your face shine on your servant;
save me in your unfailing love.
17 Let me not be put to shame, Lord,
for I have cried out to you;
but let the wicked be put to shame
and be silent in the realm of the
dead.
18 Let their lying lips be silenced,
for with pride and contempt
they speak arrogantly against the
righteous.

19 How abundant are the good things
that you have stored up for those
who fear you,
that you bestow in the sight of all,
on those who take refuge in you.
20 In the shelter of your presence you
hide them
from all human intrigues;
you keep them safe in your
dwelling
from accusing tongues.
21 Praise be to the Lord,
for he showed me the wonders of
his love
when I was in a city under siege.
22 In my alarm I said,
"I am cut off from your sight!"

INSTANT ACCESS

They're constantly talking about me, and it hurts." Maybe you feel this way too. Most teens are gossiped about at some time or other … or even most of the time. When that happens, you may feel a lot like David, who writes, "My life is consumed by anguish … I am the utter contempt of my neighbors" (verses 10–11). The trouble with slander is you really can't fight it or strike back. What can you do?

(1) Remember, your "times" are in God's hands. It won't last.

(2) Rely on God to deliver you from your enemies and to silence them.

It may not happen right away. But keep asking God and he will show you his wonderful love (verse 21).

{Psalm 31:9–18}

Yet you heard my cry for mercy
when I called to you for help.

23 Love the Lord, all his faithful people!
The Lord preserves those who are
true to him,
but the proud he pays back in full.
24 Be strong and take heart,
all you who hope in the Lord.

---

[a] 10 Or guilt

Psalm 32

Of David. A *maskil*.[a]

[1] Blessed is the one
    whose transgressions are forgiven,
    whose sins are covered.
[2] Blessed is the one
    whose sin the LORD does not count
        against them
    and in whose spirit is no deceit.

[3] When I kept silent,
    my bones wasted away
    through my groaning all day long.
[4] For day and night
    your hand was heavy on me;
my strength was sapped
    as in the heat of summer.[b]

[5] Then I acknowledged my sin to you
    and did not cover up my iniquity.
I said, "I will confess
    my transgressions to the LORD."
And you forgave
    the guilt of my sin.

[6] Therefore let all the faithful pray to you
    while you may be found;
surely the rising of the mighty waters
    will not reach them.
[7] You are my hiding place;
    you will protect me from trouble
    and surround me with songs of
        deliverance.

[8] I will instruct you and teach you in the
        way you should go;
    I will counsel you with my loving eye
        on you.
[9] Do not be like the horse or the mule,
    which have no understanding
but must be controlled by bit and
        bridle
    or they will not come to you.
[10] Many are the woes of the wicked,
    but the LORD's unfailing love
    surrounds the one who trusts in
        him.

[11] Rejoice in the LORD and be glad, you
        righteous;
    sing, all you who are upright in
        heart!

Psalm 33

[1] Sing joyfully to the LORD, you
        righteous;
    it is fitting for the upright to praise
        him.
[2] Praise the LORD with the harp;
    make music to him on the ten-
        stringed lyre.
[3] Sing to him a new song;
    play skillfully, and shout for joy.

[4] For the word of the LORD is right and
        true;
    he is faithful in all he does.
[5] The LORD loves righteousness and
        justice;
    the earth is full of his unfailing
        love.

[6] By the word of the LORD the heavens
        were made,
    their starry host by the breath of his
        mouth.
[7] He gathers the waters of the sea into
        jars[c];
    he puts the deep into storehouses.
[8] Let all the earth fear the LORD;
    let all the people of the world revere
        him.
[9] For he spoke, and it came to be;
    he commanded, and it stood
        firm.

[10] The LORD foils the plans of the
        nations;
    he thwarts the purposes of the
        peoples.
[11] But the plans of the LORD stand firm
        forever,
    the purposes of his heart through
        all generations.

[12] Blessed is the nation whose God is
        the LORD,
    the people he chose for his
        inheritance.
[13] From heaven the LORD looks down
    and sees all mankind;
[14] from his dwelling place he watches
    all who live on earth—
[15] he who forms the hearts of all,
    who considers everything they do.

---

[a] Title: Probably a literary or musical term   [b] 4 The Hebrew has *Selah* (a word of uncertain meaning) here and at the end of verses 5 and 7.   [c] 7 Or *sea as into a heap*

> I feel guilty about so many things. Is this normal? How can I make these feelings go away?
>
> >> Sarah

Dear Jordan

Dear Sarah,

That's a good question. Many times people feel guilty when they shouldn't. Sometimes you may feel guilty over an argument your parents had, even though you had nothing to do with the situation. It's important not to spend emotional energy feeling guilty and asking for forgiveness when you're not at fault.

But what about those times when you really are guilty? Believe it or not, feeling guilt for doing wrong shows that the Holy Spirit is at work, guiding you to repent. Repentance means apologizing and asking for forgiveness, but it also means making a commitment to stop sinning.

David said that when he tried to keep quiet about the wrong things he had done, he became ill (Psalm 32:3–4). If this is how you feel, you need to do what David did: admit your sin to God, ask for forgiveness and stop that sin. Do you know what happens then? God forgives you. Have you ever watched a teacher erasing a whiteboard? That's how God removes your sin. Completely! Remember that and you will no longer experience guilt but the peace of God's forgiveness.

Jordan

16 No king is saved by the size of his
army;
 no warrior escapes by his great
strength.
17 A horse is a vain hope for deliverance;
 despite all its great strength it
cannot save.
18 But the eyes of the LORD are on those
who fear him,
 on those whose hope is in his
unfailing love,
19 to deliver them from death
 and keep them alive in famine.

20 We wait in hope for the LORD;
 he is our help and our shield.
21 In him our hearts rejoice,
 for we trust in his holy name.
22 May your unfailing love be with us,
LORD,
 even as we put our hope in you.

Psalm 34*a,b*

Of David. When he pretended to be
insane before Abimelek, who drove him
away, and he left.

1 I will extol the LORD at all times;
 his praise will always be on my lips.
2 I will glory in the LORD;
 let the afflicted hear and rejoice.
3 Glorify the LORD with me;
 let us exalt his name together.

4 I sought the LORD, and he
answered me;
 he delivered me from all my fears.
5 Those who look to him are radiant;
 their faces are never covered with
shame.
6 This poor man called, and the LORD
heard him;
 he saved him out of all his troubles.
7 The angel of the LORD encamps
around those who fear him,
 and he delivers them.

8 Taste and see that the LORD is good;
 blessed is the one who takes
refuge in him.
9 Fear the LORD, you his holy people,
 for those who fear him lack nothing.

10 The lions may grow weak and hungry,
 but those who seek the LORD lack
no good thing.
11 Come, my children, listen to me;
 I will teach you the fear of the LORD.
12 Whoever of you loves life
 and desires to see many good days,
13 keep your tongue from evil
 and your lips from telling lies.
14 Turn from evil and do good;
 seek peace and pursue it.

15 The eyes of the LORD are on the
righteous,
 and his ears are attentive to their
cry;
16 but the face of the LORD is against
those who do evil,
 to blot out their name from the
earth.

17 The righteous cry out, and the LORD
hears them;
 he delivers them from all their
troubles.
18 The LORD is close to the
brokenhearted
 and saves those who are crushed
in spirit.

19 The righteous person may have many
troubles,
 but the LORD delivers him from them
all;
20 he protects all his bones,
 not one of them will be broken.

21 Evil will slay the wicked;
 the foes of the righteous will be
condemned.
22 The LORD will rescue his servants;
 no one who takes refuge in him will
be condemned.

Psalm 35

Of David.

1 Contend, LORD, with those who
contend with me;
 fight against those who fight
against me.
2 Take up shield and armor;
 arise and come to my aid.

---

a This psalm is an acrostic poem, the verses of which begin with the successive letters of the Hebrew alphabet. *b* In Hebrew texts 34:1-22 is numbered 34:2-23.

3 Brandish spear and javelin[a]
   against those who pursue me.
Say to me,
   "I am your salvation."

4 May those who seek my life
   be disgraced and put to shame;
may those who plot my ruin
   be turned back in dismay.
5 May they be like chaff before the
   wind,
   with the angel of the LORD driving
      them away;
6 may their path be dark and slippery,
   with the angel of the LORD pursuing
      them.
7 Since they hid their net for me without
   cause
   and without cause dug a pit
      for me,
8 may ruin overtake them by surprise—
   may the net they hid entangle them,
   may they fall into the pit, to their
      ruin.
9 Then my soul will rejoice in the LORD
   and delight in his salvation.
10 My whole being will exclaim,
   "Who is like you, LORD?
You rescue the poor from those too
   strong for them,
   the poor and needy from those who
      rob them."

11 Ruthless witnesses come forward;
   they question me on things I know
      nothing about.
12 They repay me evil for good
   and leave me like one bereaved.
13 Yet when they were ill, I put on
   sackcloth
   and humbled myself with fasting.
When my prayers returned to me
   unanswered,
14   I went about mourning
   as though for my friend or brother.
I bowed my head in grief
   as though weeping for my mother.
15 But when I stumbled, they gathered in
   glee;
   assailants gathered against me
      without my knowledge.
They slandered me without ceasing.

INSTANT ACCESS

Brandon asks, "Why should I keep away from sin?" From the outside, many things labeled "sin" look like fun. But in this psalm, David has a good answer to Brandon's question. David reminds us that if we want to "see many good days," we need to "turn from evil and do good" (verses 12 and 14). God is watching, and he's on the side of the righteous. That doesn't mean we won't have troubles. But God will hear our prayers and will deliver us from the troubles we have. At first, sin can look appealing. Eventually the evil things get in the way and cause huge problems in people's lives. Like a lot of teachings in the Bible, this is one you can take on faith: Keep away from sin. Or you can try out sin for yourself, and learn the hard way.

{Psalm 34:11–22}

16 Like the ungodly they maliciously
   mocked;[b]
   they gnashed their teeth at me.

17 How long, Lord, will you look on?
   Rescue me from their ravages,
   my precious life from these
      lions.

---

[a] 3 Or and block the way   [b] 16 Septuagint; Hebrew may mean Like an ungodly circle of mockers,

18 I will give you thanks in the great
assembly;
among the throngs I will praise you.
19 Do not let those gloat over me
who are my enemies without cause;
do not let those who hate me without
reason
maliciously wink the eye.
20 They do not speak peaceably,
but devise false accusations
against those who live quietly in the
land.
21 They sneer at me and say, "Aha! Aha!
With our own eyes we have seen it."

22 LORD, you have seen this; do not be
silent.
Do not be far from me, Lord.
23 Awake, and rise to my defense!
Contend for me, my God and Lord.
24 Vindicate me in your righteousness,
LORD my God;
do not let them gloat over me.
25 Do not let them think, "Aha, just what
we wanted!"
or say, "We have swallowed him up."

26 May all who gloat over my distress
be put to shame and confusion;
may all who exalt themselves over me
be clothed with shame and disgrace.
27 May those who delight in my
vindication
shout for joy and gladness;
may they always say, "The LORD be
exalted,
who delights in the well-being of his
servant."
28 My tongue will proclaim your
righteousness,
your praises all day long.

Psalm 36^a

For the director of music. Of David the
servant of the LORD.

1 I have a message from God in my heart
concerning the sinfulness of the
wicked:^b
There is no fear of God
before their eyes.

2 In their own eyes they flatter
themselves
too much to detect or hate their sin.
3 The words of their mouths are wicked
and deceitful;
they fail to act wisely or do good.
4 Even on their beds they plot evil;
they commit themselves to a sinful
course
and do not reject what is wrong.

5 Your love, LORD, reaches to the
heavens,
your faithfulness to the skies.
6 Your righteousness is like the highest
mountains,
your justice like the great deep.
You, LORD, preserve both people
and animals.
7 How priceless is your unfailing love,
O God!
People take refuge in the shadow of
your wings.
8 They feast on the abundance of your
house;
you give them drink from your river
of delights.
9 For with you is the fountain of life;
in your light we see light.

10 Continue your love to those who know
you,
your righteousness to the upright in
heart.
11 May the foot of the proud not come
against me,
nor the hand of the wicked drive me
away.
12 See how the evildoers lie fallen—
thrown down, not able to rise!

Psalm 37^c

Of David.

1 Do not fret because of those who are
evil
or be envious of those who do
wrong;
2 for like the grass they will soon wither,
like green plants they will soon die
away.

---

^a In Hebrew texts 36:1-12 is numbered 36:2-13.   ^b 1 Or A message from God: The transgression of the wicked / resides in their
hearts.   ^c This psalm is an acrostic poem, the stanzas of which begin with the successive letters of the Hebrew alphabet.

3 Trust in the Lord and do good;
   dwell in the land and enjoy safe
      pasture.
4 Take delight in the Lord,
   and he will give you the desires of
      your heart.

5 Commit your way to the Lord;
   trust in him and he will do this:
6 He will make your righteous reward
      shine like the dawn,
   your vindication like the noonday
      sun.

7 Be still before the Lord
   and wait patiently for him;
  do not fret when people succeed in
      their ways,
   when they carry out their wicked
      schemes.

8 Refrain from anger and turn from
      wrath;
   do not fret—it leads only to evil.
9 For those who are evil will be
      destroyed,
   but those who hope in the Lord will
      inherit the land.

10 A little while, and the wicked will be no
      more;
   though you look for them, they will
      not be found.
11 But the meek will inherit the land
   and enjoy peace and prosperity.

12 The wicked plot against the righteous
   and gnash their teeth at them;
13 but the Lord laughs at the wicked,
   for he knows their day is coming.

14 The wicked draw the sword
   and bend the bow
  to bring down the poor and needy,
   to slay those whose ways are
      upright.
15 But their swords will pierce their own
      hearts,
   and their bows will be broken.

16 Better the little that the righteous have
   than the wealth of many wicked;
17 for the power of the wicked will be
      broken,
   but the Lord upholds the righteous.

18 The blameless spend their days under
   the Lord's care,

INSTANT ACCESS

Talk about pressure! Sometimes life is just too overwhelming. We have a ton of stuff to do, and not enough time to do it. People expect too much . . . teachers, parents, coaches, friends, youth group leaders, brothers and sisters. What can you do when so much stuff piles up you feel like you can't stand it any more? In Psalm 37 Dr. David prescribes six remedies. Check out verses 3 though 9. Find the six and write them down. Chances are, whatever situation you find yourself in, one of the six will apply and help you deal with the pressure.

{Psalm 37:3–9}

and their inheritance will endure
      forever.
19 In times of disaster they will not
      wither;
   in days of famine they will enjoy
      plenty.

20 But the wicked will perish:
   Though the Lord's enemies are like
      the flowers of the field,
   they will be consumed, they will go
      up in smoke.

21 The wicked borrow and do not repay,
   but the righteous give generously;
22 those the Lord blesses will inherit the
      land,
   but those he curses will be
      destroyed.

23 The Lord makes firm the steps
   of the one who delights in him;
24 though he may stumble, he will not
      fall,
   for the Lord upholds him with his
      hand.

25 I was young and now I am old,
   yet I have never seen the righteous
      forsaken
   or their children begging bread.
26 They are always generous and lend
      freely;
   their children will be a blessing.a

27 Turn from evil and do good;
   then you will dwell in the land
      forever.
28 For the Lord loves the just
   and will not forsake his faithful ones.

   Wrongdoers will be completely
      destroyedb;
   the offspring of the wicked will
      perish.
29 The righteous will inherit the land
   and dwell in it forever.

30 The mouths of the righteous utter
      wisdom,
   and their tongues speak what is just.
31 The law of their God is in their hearts;
   their feet do not slip.

32 The wicked lie in wait for the
      righteous,
   intent on putting them to death;
33 but the Lord will not leave them in the
      power of the wicked
   or let them be condemned when
      brought to trial.

34 Hope in the Lord
   and keep his way.
   He will exalt you to inherit the land;
   when the wicked are destroyed, you
      will see it.

35 I have seen a wicked and ruthless man
   flourishing like a luxuriant native tree,
36 but he soon passed away and was no
      more;
   though I looked for him, he could
      not be found.

37 Consider the blameless, observe the
      upright;
   a future awaits those who seek
      peace.c
38 But all sinners will be destroyed;
   there will be no futured for the
      wicked.

39 The salvation of the righteous comes
      from the Lord;
   he is their stronghold in time of
      trouble.
40 The Lord helps them and delivers them;
   he delivers them from the wicked
      and saves them,
   because they take refuge in him.

Psalm 38e

A psalm of David. A petition.

1 Lord, do not rebuke me in your anger
   or discipline me in your wrath.
2 Your arrows have pierced me,
   and your hand has come down
      on me.
3 Because of your wrath there is no
      health in my body;
   there is no soundness in my bones
      because of my sin.
4 My guilt has overwhelmed me
   like a burden too heavy to bear.

5 My wounds fester and are loathsome
   because of my sinful folly.
6 I am bowed down and brought very
      low;
   all day long I go about mourning.
7 My back is filled with searing pain;
   there is no health in my body.
8 I am feeble and utterly crushed;
   I groan in anguish of heart.

9 All my longings lie open before you,
      Lord;
   my sighing is not hidden from you.
10 My heart pounds, my strength fails me;
   even the light has gone from my
      eyes.
11 My friends and companions avoid me
      because of my wounds;
   my neighbors stay far away.

---

a 26 Or freely; / the names of their children will be used in blessings (see Gen. 48:20); or freely; / others will see that their children are blessed   b 28 See Septuagint; Hebrew They will be protected forever   c 37 Or upright; / those who seek peace will have posterity   d 38 Or posterity   e In Hebrew texts 38:1-22 is numbered 38:2-23.

12 Those who want to kill me set their
    traps,
  those who would harm me talk of
    my ruin;
  all day long they scheme and lie.

13 I am like the deaf, who cannot hear,
  like the mute, who cannot speak;
14 I have become like one who does not
    hear,
  whose mouth can offer no reply.
15 Lord, I wait for you;
  you will answer, Lord my God.
16 For I said, "Do not let them gloat
  or exalt themselves over me when
    my feet slip."

17 For I am about to fall,
  and my pain is ever with me.
18 I confess my iniquity;
  I am troubled by my sin.
19 Many have become my enemies
    without cause[a];
  those who hate me without reason
    are numerous.
20 Those who repay my good with evil
  lodge accusations against me,
  though I seek only to do what is
    good.

21 Lord, do not forsake me;
  do not be far from me, my God.
22 Come quickly to help me,
  my Lord and my Savior.

Psalm 39[b]

For the director of music. For Jeduthun.
A psalm of David.

1 I said, "I will watch my ways
  and keep my tongue from sin;
  I will put a muzzle on my mouth
  while in the presence of the wicked."
2 So I remained utterly silent,
  not even saying anything good.
  But my anguish increased;
3   my heart grew hot within me.
  While I meditated, the fire burned;
  then I spoke with my tongue:

4 "Show me, Lord, my life's end
  and the number of my days;
  let me know how fleeting my life is.

5 You have made my days a mere
    handbreadth;
  the span of my years is as nothing
    before you.
  Everyone is but a breath,
  even those who seem secure.[c]

6 "Surely everyone goes around like a
    mere phantom;
  in vain they rush about, heaping up
    wealth
  without knowing whose it will
    finally be.

7 "But now, Lord, what do I look for?
  My hope is in you.
8 Save me from all my transgressions;
  do not make me the scorn of fools.
9 I was silent; I would not open my
    mouth,
  for you are the one who has done
    this.
10 Remove your scourge from me;
  I am overcome by the blow of your
    hand.
11 When you rebuke and discipline
    anyone for their sin,
  you consume their wealth like a
    moth—
  surely everyone is but a breath.

12 "Hear my prayer, Lord,
  listen to my cry for help;
  do not be deaf to my weeping.
  I dwell with you as a foreigner,
  a stranger, as all my ancestors were.
13 Look away from me, that I may enjoy
    life again
  before I depart and am no more."

Psalm 40[d]

For the director of music. Of David. A psalm.

1 I waited patiently for the Lord;
  he turned to me and heard my cry.
2 He lifted me out of the slimy pit,
  out of the mud and mire;
  he set my feet on a rock
  and gave me a firm place to stand.
3 He put a new song in my mouth,
  a hymn of praise to our God.

---

a 19 One Dead Sea Scrolls manuscript; Masoretic Text my vigorous enemies   b In Hebrew texts 39:1-13 is numbered
39:2-14.   c 5 The Hebrew has Selah (a word of uncertain meaning) here and at the end of verse 11.   d In Hebrew
texts 40:1-17 is numbered 40:2-18.

Many will see and fear the Lord
and put their trust in him.

4 Blessed is the one
who trusts in the Lord,
who does not look to the proud,
to those who turn aside to false
gods.[a]
5 Many, Lord my God,
are the wonders you have done,
the things you planned for us.
None can compare with you;
were I to speak and tell of your
deeds,
they would be too many to declare.

6 Sacrifice and offering you did not
desire—
but my ears you have opened[b]—
burnt offerings and sin offerings[c]
you did not require.
7 Then I said, "Here I am, I have come—
it is written about me in the scroll.[d]
8 I desire to do your will, my God;
your law is within my heart."

9 I proclaim your saving acts in the
great assembly;
I do not seal my lips, Lord,
as you know.
10 I do not hide your righteousness in my
heart;
I speak of your faithfulness and
your saving help.
I do not conceal your love and your
faithfulness
from the great assembly.

11 Do not withhold your mercy from me,
Lord;
may your love and faithfulness
always protect me.
12 For troubles without number
surround me;
my sins have overtaken me, and I
cannot see.
They are more than the hairs of my
head,
and my heart fails within me.
13 Be pleased to save me, Lord;
come quickly, Lord, to help me.

14 May all who want to take my life
be put to shame and confusion;

may all who desire my ruin
be turned back in disgrace.
15 May those who say to me, "Aha! Aha!"
be appalled at their own shame.
16 But may all who seek you
rejoice and be glad in you;
may those who long for your saving
help always say,
"The Lord is great!"

17 But as for me, I am poor and needy;
may the Lord think of me.
You are my help and my deliverer;
you are my God, do not delay.

Psalm 41[e]

For the director of music. A psalm of David.

1 Blessed are those who have regard
for the weak;
the Lord delivers them in times of
trouble.
2 The Lord protects and preserves
them—
they are counted among the
blessed in the land—
he does not give them over to the
desire of their foes.
3 The Lord sustains them on their
sickbed
and restores them from their bed of
illness.

4 I said, "Have mercy on me, Lord;
heal me, for I have sinned against
you."
5 My enemies say of me in malice,
"When will he die and his name
perish?"
6 When one of them comes to see me,
he speaks falsely, while his heart
gathers slander;
then he goes out and spreads it
around.

7 All my enemies whisper together
against me;
they imagine the worst for me,
saying,
8 "A vile disease has afflicted him;
he will never get up from the place
where he lies."

---

a 4 Or to lies   b 6 Hebrew; some Septuagint manuscripts *but a body you have prepared for me*   c 6 Or *purification
offerings*   d 7 Or *come / with the scroll written for me*   e In Hebrew texts 41:1-13 is numbered 41:2-14.

⁹Even my close friend,
   someone I trusted,
one who shared my bread,
   has turned[a] against me.

¹⁰But may you have mercy on me, LORD;
   raise me up, that I may repay them.
¹¹I know that you are pleased with me,
   for my enemy does not triumph
      over me.
¹²Because of my integrity you uphold me
   and set me in your presence
      forever.

¹³Praise be to the LORD, the God of Israel,
   from everlasting to everlasting.
      Amen and Amen.

BOOK II

Psalms 42 – 72

Psalm 42[b,c]

For the director of music. A maskil[d] of the
Sons of Korah.

¹As the deer pants for streams of
      water,
   so my soul pants for you, my God.
²My soul thirsts for God, for the living
      God.
   When can I go and meet with God?
³My tears have been my food
      day and night,
while people say to me all day long,
   "Where is your God?"
⁴These things I remember
   as I pour out my soul:
how I used to go to the house of God
   under the protection of the Mighty
      One[e]
with shouts of joy and praise
   among the festive throng.

⁵Why, my soul, are you downcast?
   Why so disturbed within me?
Put your hope in God,
   for I will yet praise him,
      my Savior and my God.

⁶My soul is downcast within me;
   therefore I will remember you

from the land of the Jordan,
   the heights of Hermon—from
      Mount Mizar.
⁷Deep calls to deep
   in the roar of your waterfalls;
all your waves and breakers
   have swept over me.

⁸By day the LORD directs his love,
   at night his song is with me—
a prayer to the God of my life.

⁹I say to God my Rock,
   "Why have you forgotten me?
Why must I go about mourning,
   oppressed by the enemy?"
¹⁰My bones suffer mortal agony
   as my foes taunt me,
saying to me all day long,
   "Where is your God?"

¹¹Why, my soul, are you downcast?
   Why so disturbed within me?
Put your hope in God,
   for I will yet praise him,
      my Savior and my God.

Psalm 43[b]

¹Vindicate me, my God,
   and plead my cause
      against an unfaithful nation.
Rescue me from those who are
   deceitful and wicked.
²You are God my stronghold.
   Why have you rejected me?
Why must I go about mourning,
   oppressed by the enemy?
³Send me your light and your faithful
      care,
   let them lead me;
let them bring me to your holy
      mountain,
   to the place where you dwell.
⁴Then I will go to the altar of God,
   to God, my joy and my delight.
I will praise you with the lyre,
   O God, my God.

⁵Why, my soul, are you downcast?
   Why so disturbed within me?
Put your hope in God,
   for I will yet praise him,
      my Savior and my God.

---

[a] 9 Hebrew has lifted up his heel   [b] In many Hebrew manuscripts Psalms 42 and 43 constitute one psalm.   [c] In Hebrew texts 42:1-11 is numbered 42:2-12.   [d] Title: Probably a literary or musical term   [e] 4 See Septuagint and Syriac; the meaning of the Hebrew for this line is uncertain.

Sometimes it feels like there's no hope—that even God has written you off. As one teen put it, "I feel like the whole world is against me." David put it this way: "my soul is downcast" and "disturbed." It can help to read a psalm like this one and realize others have felt the same way you do. All 11 of the verses of this psalm express those "down" feelings you experience. But in two of the verses, David remembers that when things are darkest, there's still one ray of sunshine. What is it? Check out verses 5 and 11.

{Psalm 42}

INSTANT ACCESS

Psalm 44 [a]

For the director of music. Of the Sons of Korah. A *maskil*.[b]

1 We have heard it with our ears, O God;
     our ancestors have told us
what you did in their days,
     in days long ago.
2 With your hand you drove out the
          nations
     and planted our ancestors;
you crushed the peoples
     and made our ancestors flourish.
3 It was not by their sword that they won
          the land,
     nor did their arm bring them victory;

it was your right hand, your arm,
     and the light of your face, for you
          loved them.

4 You are my King and my God,
     who decrees[c] victories for Jacob.
5 Through you we push back our
          enemies;
     through your name we trample our
          foes.
6 I put no trust in my bow,
     my sword does not bring me victory;
7 but you give us victory over our
          enemies,
     you put our adversaries to shame.
8 In God we make our boast all day
          long,
     and we will praise your name
          forever.[d]

9 But now you have rejected and
          humbled us;
     you no longer go out with our
          armies.
10 You made us retreat before the
          enemy,
     and our adversaries have
          plundered us.
11 You gave us up to be devoured like
          sheep
     and have scattered us among the
          nations.
12 You sold your people for a pittance,
     gaining nothing from their sale.

13 You have made us a reproach to our
          neighbors,
     the scorn and derision of those
          around us.
14 You have made us a byword among
          the nations;
     the peoples shake their heads
          at us.
15 I live in disgrace all day long,
     and my face is covered with shame
16 at the taunts of those who reproach
          and revile me,
     because of the enemy, who is bent
          on revenge.

17 All this came upon us,
     though we had not forgotten you;
     we had not been false to your
          covenant.

---

a In Hebrew texts 44:1-26 is numbered 44:2-27.   b Title: Probably a literary or musical term   c 4 Septuagint, Aquila
and Syriac; Hebrew King, O God; / command   d 8 The Hebrew has Selah (a word of uncertain meaning) here.

18 Our hearts had not turned back;
   our feet had not strayed from your
      path.
19 But you crushed us and made us a
      haunt for jackals;
   you covered us over with deep
      darkness.

20 If we had forgotten the name of our
      God
   or spread out our hands to a foreign
      god,
21 would not God have discovered it,
   since he knows the secrets of the
      heart?
22 Yet for your sake we face death all day
      long;
   we are considered as sheep to be
      slaughtered.

23 Awake, Lord! Why do you sleep?
   Rouse yourself! Do not reject us
      forever.
24 Why do you hide your face
   and forget our misery and
      oppression?

25 We are brought down to the dust;
   our bodies cling to the ground.
26 Rise up and help us;
   rescue us because of your unfailing
      love.

Psalm 45 [a]

For the director of music. To the tune of
"Lilies." Of the Sons of Korah. A maskil.[b]
A wedding song.

1 My heart is stirred by a noble theme
   as I recite my verses for the king;
   my tongue is the pen of a skillful
      writer.

2 You are the most excellent of men
   and your lips have been anointed
      with grace,
   since God has blessed you
      forever.

3 Gird your sword on your side, you
      mighty one;
   clothe yourself with splendor and
      majesty.

4 In your majesty ride forth victoriously
   in the cause of truth, humility and
      justice;
   let your right hand achieve
      awesome deeds.
5 Let your sharp arrows pierce the
      hearts of the king's enemies;
   let the nations fall beneath your
      feet.
6 Your throne, O God,[c] will last for ever
      and ever;
   a scepter of justice will be the
      scepter of your kingdom.
7 You love righteousness and hate
      wickedness;
   therefore God, your God, has set
      you above your companions
   by anointing you with the oil of joy.
8 All your robes are fragrant with myrrh
      and aloes and cassia;
   from palaces adorned with ivory
      the music of the strings makes you
      glad.
9 Daughters of kings are among your
      honored women;
   at your right hand is the royal bride
      in gold of Ophir.

10 Listen, daughter, and pay careful
      attention:
   Forget your people and your father's
      house.
11 Let the king be enthralled by your
      beauty;
   honor him, for he is your lord.
12 The city of Tyre will come with a gift,[d]
   people of wealth will seek your
      favor.
13 All glorious is the princess within her
      chamber;
   her gown is interwoven with gold.
14 In embroidered garments she is led to
      the king;
   her virgin companions follow her—
   those brought to be with her.
15 Led in with joy and gladness,
   they enter the palace of the king.

16 Your sons will take the place of your
      fathers;
   you will make them princes
      throughout the land.

---

a In Hebrew texts 45:1-17 is numbered 45:2-18.   b Title: Probably a literary or musical term   c 6 Here the king is
addressed as God's representative.   d 12 Or A Tyrian robe is among the gifts

17 I will perpetuate your memory through
all generations;
therefore the nations will praise you
for ever and ever.

Psalm 46[a]

For the director of music. Of the Sons of
Korah. According to *alamoth*.[b] A song.

1 God is our refuge and strength,
an ever-present help in trouble.
2 Therefore we will not fear, though the
earth give way
and the mountains fall into the
heart of the sea,
3 though its waters roar and foam
and the mountains quake with their
surging.[c]

4 There is a river whose streams make
glad the city of God,
the holy place where the Most High
dwells.
5 God is within her, she will not fall;
God will help her at break of day.
6 Nations are in uproar, kingdoms fall;
he lifts his voice, the earth melts.

7 The Lord Almighty is with us;
the God of Jacob is our fortress.

8 Come and see what the Lord has done,
the desolations he has brought on
the earth.
9 He makes wars cease
to the ends of the earth.
He breaks the bow and shatters the
spear;
he burns the shields[d] with fire.

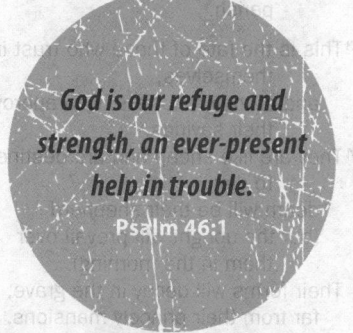

*God is our refuge and
strength, an ever-present
help in trouble.*

Psalm 46:1

10 He says, "Be still, and know that I am
God;
I will be exalted among the nations,
I will be exalted in the earth."

11 The Lord Almighty is with us;
the God of Jacob is our fortress.

Psalm 47[e]

For the director of music. Of the Sons of
Korah. A psalm.

1 Clap your hands, all you nations;
shout to God with cries of joy.

2 For the Lord Most High is awesome,
the great King over all the earth.
3 He subdued nations under us,
peoples under our feet.
4 He chose our inheritance for us,
the pride of Jacob, whom he
loved.[f]

5 God has ascended amid shouts of joy,
the Lord amid the sounding of
trumpets.
6 Sing praises to God, sing praises;
sing praises to our King, sing
praises.
7 For God is the King of all the earth;
sing to him a psalm of praise.

8 God reigns over the nations;
God is seated on his holy throne.
9 The nobles of the nations assemble
as the people of the God of
Abraham,
for the kings[g] of the earth belong to
God;
he is greatly exalted.

Psalm 48[h]

A song. A psalm of the Sons of Korah.

1 Great is the Lord, and most worthy of
praise,
in the city of our God, his holy
mountain.

2 Beautiful in its loftiness,
the joy of the whole earth,

---

a In Hebrew texts 46:1-11 is numbered 46:2-12.   b Title: Probably a musical term   c 3 The Hebrew has *Selah* (a word
of uncertain meaning) here and at the end of verses 7 and 11.   d 9 Or *chariots*   e In Hebrew texts 47:1-9 is numbered
47:2-10.   f 4 The Hebrew has *Selah* (a word of uncertain meaning) here.   g 9 Or *shields*   h In Hebrew texts 48:1-14
is numbered 48:2-15.

like the heights of Zaphon[a] is Mount
  Zion,
  the city of the Great King.
3 God is in her citadels;
  he has shown himself to be her
    fortress.

4 When the kings joined forces,
  when they advanced together,
5 they saw her and were astounded;
  they fled in terror.
6 Trembling seized them there,
  pain like that of a woman in labor.
7 You destroyed them like ships of
    Tarshish
  shattered by an east wind.

8 As we have heard,
  so we have seen
  in the city of the LORD Almighty,
  in the city of our God:
  God makes her secure
    forever.[b]

9 Within your temple, O God,
  we meditate on your unfailing love.
10 Like your name, O God,
  your praise reaches to the ends of
    the earth;
  your right hand is filled with
    righteousness.
11 Mount Zion rejoices,
  the villages of Judah are glad
  because of your judgments.

12 Walk about Zion, go around her,
  count her towers,
13 consider well her ramparts,
  view her citadels,
  that you may tell of them
  to the next generation.

14 For this God is our God for ever and
    ever;
  he will be our guide even to the end.

Psalm 49[c]

For the director of music. Of the Sons of
  Korah. A psalm.

1 Hear this, all you peoples;
  listen, all who live in this world,

2 both low and high,
  rich and poor alike:
3 My mouth will speak words of
    wisdom;
  the meditation of my heart will give
    you understanding.
4 I will turn my ear to a proverb;
  with the harp I will expound my
    riddle:

5 Why should I fear when evil days
    come,
  when wicked deceivers
    surround me—
6 those who trust in their wealth
  and boast of their great riches?
7 No one can redeem the life of
    another
  or give to God a ransom for
    them—
8 the ransom for a life is costly,
  no payment is ever enough—
9 so that they should live on forever
  and not see decay.
10 For all can see that the wise die,
  that the foolish and the senseless
    also perish,
  leaving their wealth to others.
11 Their tombs will remain their houses[d]
    forever,
  their dwellings for endless
    generations,
  though they had[e] named lands after
    themselves.

12 People, despite their wealth, do not
    endure;
  they are like the beasts that
    perish.

13 This is the fate of those who trust in
    themselves,
  and of their followers, who approve
    their sayings.[f]
14 They are like sheep and are destined
    to die;
  death will be their shepherd
  (but the upright will prevail over
    them in the morning).
  Their forms will decay in the grave,
  far from their princely mansions.

---

a 2 Zaphon was the most sacred mountain of the Canaanites.
here.   c In Hebrew texts 49:1-20 is numbered 49:2-21.
houses will remain   e 11 Or generations, / for they have
here and at the end of verse 15.

b 8 The Hebrew has Selah (a word of uncertain meaning)
d 11 Septuagint and Syriac; Hebrew In their thoughts their
f 13 The Hebrew has Selah (a word of uncertain meaning)

INSTANT ACCESS

Bad things do happen to good people. One girl who helped with this Bible was upset because her dad lost his business because of an untrustworthy contractor. Her question is, "Why do things like this happen?" It's too easy to say it's because people are sinners. Or even that God has something better for her family. The question is, Why does God let such people get away with it? In this Bible passage, God has a word of warning to the wicked. What this psalm says won't make the pain of being cheated go away. But it is helpful to remember that God himself is judge, and no wicked act goes unpunished.

{Psalm 50:6–22}

their splendor will not descend with
   them.
18 Though while they live they count
      themselves blessed—
   and people praise you when you
      prosper—
19 they will join those who have gone
      before them,
   who will never again see the light of
      life.
20 People who have wealth but lack
      understanding
   are like the beasts that perish.

Psalm 50

A psalm of Asaph.

1 The Mighty One, God, the LORD,
   speaks and summons the earth
   from the rising of the sun to where
      it sets.
2 From Zion, perfect in beauty,
   God shines forth.
3 Our God comes
   and will not be silent;
 a fire devours before him,
   and around him a tempest rages.
4 He summons the heavens above,
   and the earth, that he may judge
      his people:
5 "Gather to me this consecrated
      people,
   who made a covenant with me by
      sacrifice."
6 And the heavens proclaim his
      righteousness,
   for he is a God of justice.[a,b]

7 "Listen, my people, and I will speak;
   I will testify against you, Israel:
   I am God, your God.
8 I bring no charges against you
      concerning your sacrifices
   or concerning your burnt offerings,
      which are ever before me.
9 I have no need of a bull from your
      stall
   or of goats from your pens,
10 for every animal of the forest is mine,
   and the cattle on a thousand hills.

15 But God will redeem me from the
      realm of the dead;
   he will surely take me to himself.
16 Do not be overawed when others grow
      rich,
   when the splendor of their houses
      increases;
17 for they will take nothing with them
   when they die,

---

[a] 6 With a different word division of the Hebrew; Masoretic Text *for God himself is judge*   [b] 6 The Hebrew has *Selah* (a word of uncertain meaning) here.

¹¹I know every bird in the mountains,
    and the insects in the fields are
        mine.
¹²If I were hungry I would not tell you,
    for the world is mine, and all that is
        in it.
¹³Do I eat the flesh of bulls
    or drink the blood of goats?

¹⁴"Sacrifice thank offerings to God,
    fulfill your vows to the Most High,
¹⁵and call on me in the day of trouble;
    I will deliver you, and you will
        honor me."

¹⁶But to the wicked person, God says:

"What right have you to recite my laws
    or take my covenant on your lips?
¹⁷You hate my instruction
    and cast my words behind you.
¹⁸When you see a thief, you join with
        him;
    you throw in your lot with adulterers.
¹⁹You use your mouth for evil
    and harness your tongue to deceit.
²⁰You sit and testify against your brother
    and slander your own mother's son.
²¹When you did these things and I kept
        silent,
    you thought I was exactlyᵃ like you.
    But I now arraign you
        and set my accusations before you.

²²"Consider this, you who forget God,
    or I will tear you to pieces, with no
        one to rescue you:
²³Those who sacrifice thank offerings
        honor me,
    and to the blamelessᵇ I will show
        my salvation."

Psalm 51ᶜ

For the director of music. A psalm of David.
When the prophet Nathan came to him
after David had committed adultery with
Bathsheba.

¹Have mercy on me, O God,
    according to your unfailing love;
    according to your great compassion
        blot out my transgressions.

²Wash away all my iniquity
    and cleanse me from my sin.

³For I know my transgressions,
    and my sin is always before me.
⁴Against you, you only, have I sinned
    and done what is evil in your
        sight;
so you are right in your verdict
    and justified when you judge.
⁵Surely I was sinful at birth,
    sinful from the time my mother
        conceived me.
⁶Yet you desired faithfulness even in
        the womb;
    you taught me wisdom in that
        secret place.

⁷Cleanse me with hyssop, and I will be
        clean;
    wash me, and I will be whiter than
        snow.
⁸Let me hear joy and gladness;
    let the bones you have crushed
        rejoice.
⁹Hide your face from my sins
    and blot out all my iniquity.

¹⁰Create in me a pure heart, O God,
    and renew a steadfast spirit
        within me.
¹¹Do not cast me from your
        presence
    or take your Holy Spirit
        from me.
¹²Restore to me the joy of your
        salvation
    and grant me a willing spirit, to
        sustain me.

¹³Then I will teach transgressors your
        ways,
    so that sinners will turn back to
        you.
¹⁴Deliver me from the guilt of
        bloodshed, O God,
    you who are God my Savior,
    and my tongue will sing of your
        righteousness.
¹⁵Open my lips, Lord,
    and my mouth will declare your
        praise.

ᵃ 21 Or thought the 'I AM' was   ᵇ 23 Probable reading of the original Hebrew text; the meaning of the Masoretic Text for
this phrase is uncertain.   ᶜ In Hebrew texts 51:1-19 is numbered 51:3-21.

16 You do not delight in sacrifice, or I
would bring it;
you do not take pleasure in burnt
offerings.
17 My sacrifice, O God, is*a* a broken
spirit;
a broken and contrite heart
you, God, will not despise.

18 May it please you to prosper Zion,
to build up the walls of
Jerusalem.
19 Then you will delight in the sacrifices
of the righteous,
in burnt offerings offered
whole;
then bulls will be offered on your
altar.

Psalm 52*b*

For the director of music. A *maskil*c of David.
When Doeg the Edomite had gone to Saul
and told him: "David has gone to the house
of Ahimelek."

1 Why do you boast of evil, you mighty
hero?
Why do you boast all day long,
you who are a disgrace in the eyes
of God?
2 You who practice deceit,
your tongue plots destruction;
it is like a sharpened razor.
3 You love evil rather than good,
falsehood rather than speaking the
truth.*d*

---

a 17 Or *The sacrifices of God are*   *b* In Hebrew texts 52:1-9 is numbered 52:3-11.   *c* Title: Probably a literary or
musical term   *d* 3 The Hebrew has *Selah* (a word of uncertain meaning) here and at the end of verse 5.

TO THE POINT

Confess Sins

When David confessed his sin with Bathsheba to the Lord, he
asked God to cleanse him, to purify his heart and to restore the
joy of salvation (Psalm 51:7–12). And God did forgive him.

But King David didn't only confess to God. Other people knew
what he had done, and his sin set a terrible example for his
people. That's why the introduction to this psalm is important.
David sent it to "the director of music." David's confession
wasn't made just to God. It was made publicly as well.

If you sin in a way that doesn't involve others, confess it to God
and accept his forgiveness. But if others know what you've
done, you need to make sure they also know you've confessed
to God and received forgiveness—and you need to ask them to
forgive you too.

4 You love every harmful word,
 you deceitful tongue!

5 Surely God will bring you down to
 everlasting ruin:
He will snatch you up and pluck you
 from your tent;
he will uproot you from the land of
 the living.
6 The righteous will see and fear;
 they will laugh at you, saying,
7 "Here now is the man
 who did not make God his
 stronghold
but trusted in his great wealth
 and grew strong by destroying
 others!"

8 But I am like an olive tree
 flourishing in the house of God;
I trust in God's unfailing love
 for ever and ever.
9 For what you have done I will always
 praise you
 in the presence of your faithful
 people.
And I will hope in your name,
 for your name is good.

Psalm 53[a]

For the director of music. According to
mahalath.[b] A *maskil*[c] of David.

1 The fool says in his heart,
 "There is no God."
They are corrupt, and their ways are
 vile;
 there is no one who does good.

2 God looks down from heaven
 on all mankind
to see if there are any who
 understand,
 any who seek God.
3 Everyone has turned away, all have
 become corrupt;
 there is no one who does good,
 not even one.

4 Do all these evildoers know nothing?

They devour my people as though
 eating bread;
 they never call on God.

5 But there they are, overwhelmed with
 dread,
 where there was nothing to dread.
God scattered the bones of those who
 attacked you;
 you put them to shame, for God
 despised them.

6 Oh, that salvation for Israel would
 come out of Zion!
When God restores his people,
 let Jacob rejoice and Israel be glad!

Psalm 54[d]

For the director of music. With stringed
instruments. A *maskil*[c] of David. When the
Ziphites had gone to Saul and said, "Is not
David hiding among us?"

1 Save me, O God, by your name;
 vindicate me by your might.
2 Hear my prayer, O God;
 listen to the words of my mouth.

3 Arrogant foes are attacking me;
 ruthless people are trying to
 kill me—
people without regard for God.[e]

4 Surely God is my help;
 the Lord is the one who sustains me.

5 Let evil recoil on those who slander me;
 in your faithfulness destroy them.

6 I will sacrifice a freewill offering to
 you;
 I will praise your name, LORD, for it
 is good.
7 You have delivered me from all my
 troubles,
 and my eyes have looked in triumph
 on my foes.

Psalm 55[f]

For the director of music. With stringed
instruments. A *maskil*[c] of David.

1 Listen to my prayer, O God,
 do not ignore my plea;
2   hear me and answer me.
My thoughts trouble me and I am
 distraught

---

[a] In Hebrew texts 53:1-6 is numbered 53:2-7.   [b] Title: Probably a musical term   [c] Title: Probably a literary or musical
term   [d] In Hebrew texts 54:1-7 is numbered 54:3-9.   [e] 3 The Hebrew has *Selah* (a word of uncertain meaning) here.
[f] In Hebrew texts 55:1-23 is numbered 55:2-24.

How do you handle feelings? Strong feelings, like anger. Or fear. Or loneliness. Or shame. Feelings that are hard to share with parents or even close friends. The book of Psalms can show you what to do with strong feelings. David knew that however he felt, he could express his emotions to God. God wouldn't be angry with him or say, "You shouldn't feel that way!" God cares how you feel, and just expressing your emotions to him can often make you feel better. You could look for words about feelings in different psalms and make a list. Then when you have one of those feelings, read that psalm as your prayer.

{Psalm 55:1–8}

INSTANT ACCESS

7 I would flee far away
 and stay in the desert;[a]
8 I would hurry to my place of shelter,
 far from the tempest and storm."

9 Lord, confuse the wicked, confound their words,
 for I see violence and strife in the city.
10 Day and night they prowl about on its walls;
 malice and abuse are within it.
11 Destructive forces are at work in the city;
 threats and lies never leave its streets.

12 If an enemy were insulting me,
 I could endure it;
 if a foe were rising against me,
 I could hide.
13 But it is you, a man like myself,
 my companion, my close friend,
14 with whom I once enjoyed sweet fellowship
 at the house of God,
 as we walked about
 among the worshipers.

15 Let death take my enemies by surprise;
 let them go down alive to the realm of the dead,
 for evil finds lodging among them.

16 As for me, I call to God,
 and the Lord saves me.
17 Evening, morning and noon
 I cry out in distress,
 and he hears my voice.
18 He rescues me unharmed
 from the battle waged against me,
 even though many oppose me.
19 God, who is enthroned from of old,
 who does not change—
 he will hear them and humble them,
 because they have no fear of God.

20 My companion attacks his friends;
 he violates his covenant.
21 His talk is smooth as butter,
 yet war is in his heart;
 his words are more soothing than oil,
 yet they are drawn swords.

3 because of what my enemy is saying,
 because of the threats of the wicked;
 for they bring down suffering on me
 and assail me in their anger.

4 My heart is in anguish within me;
 the terrors of death have fallen on me.
5 Fear and trembling have beset me;
 horror has overwhelmed me.
6 I said, "Oh, that I had the wings of a dove!
 I would fly away and be at rest.

---

[a] 7 The Hebrew has *Selah* (a word of uncertain meaning) here and in the middle of verse 19.

22 Cast your cares on the LORD
    and he will sustain you;
  he will never let
    the righteous be shaken.
23 But you, God, will bring down the
      wicked
    into the pit of decay;
  the bloodthirsty and deceitful
    will not live out half their days.

  But as for me, I trust in you.

Psalm 56^a

For the director of music. To the tune
of "A Dove on Distant Oaks." Of David.
A *miktam.*^b When the Philistines had
    seized him in Gath.

1 Be merciful to me, my God,
    for my enemies are in hot pursuit;
  all day long they press their attack.
2 My adversaries pursue me all day
      long;
  in their pride many are attacking me.

3 When I am afraid, I put my trust in you.
4   In God, whose word I praise—
  in God I trust and am not afraid.
    What can mere mortals do to me?

5 All day long they twist my words;
    all their schemes are for my ruin.
6 They conspire, they lurk,
    they watch my steps,
    hoping to take my life.
7 Because of their wickedness do not^c
      let them escape;
  in your anger, God, bring the
      nations down.

8 Record my misery;
    list my tears on your scroll^d—
  are they not in your record?
9 Then my enemies will turn back
    when I call for help.
  By this I will know that God is for me.

10 In God, whose word I praise,
  in the LORD, whose word I praise—
11 in God I trust and am not afraid.
    What can man do to me?

12 I am under vows to you, my God;
  I will present my thank offerings to
      you.
13 For you have delivered me from death
    and my feet from stumbling,
  that I may walk before God
    in the light of life.

Psalm 57^e

For the director of music. To the tune of
"Do Not Destroy." Of David. A *miktam.*^b
When he had fled from Saul into the cave.

1 Have mercy on me, my God, have
      mercy on me,
    for in you I take refuge.
  I will take refuge in the shadow of your
      wings
    until the disaster has passed.

2 I cry out to God Most High,
    to God, who vindicates me.
3 He sends from heaven and saves me,
  rebuking those who hotly
      pursue me—^f
  God sends forth his love and his
      faithfulness.

4 I am in the midst of lions;
    I am forced to dwell among
      ravenous beasts—
  men whose teeth are spears and
      arrows,
    whose tongues are sharp swords.

5 Be exalted, O God, above the
      heavens;
    let your glory be over all the earth.

6 They spread a net for my feet—
    I was bowed down in distress.
  They dug a pit in my path—
    but they have fallen into it
      themselves.

7 My heart, O God, is steadfast,
    my heart is steadfast;
  I will sing and make music.
8 Awake, my soul!
  Awake, harp and lyre!
    I will awaken the dawn.

---

^a In Hebrew texts 56:1-13 is numbered 56:2-14.   ^b Title: Probably a literary or musical term   ^c 7 Probable reading
of the original Hebrew text; Masoretic Text does not have *do not*.   ^d 8 Or *misery; / put my tears in your wineskin*   ^e In
Hebrew texts 57:1-11 is numbered 57:2-12.   ^f 3 The Hebrew has *Selah* (a word of uncertain meaning) here and at the
end of verse 6.

⁹ I will praise you, Lord, among the
  nations;
 I will sing of you among the
  peoples.
¹⁰ For great is your love, reaching to the
  heavens;
 your faithfulness reaches to the
  skies.
¹¹ Be exalted, O God, above the heavens;
 let your glory be over all the earth.

Psalm 58[a]

For the director of music. To the tune of
"Do Not Destroy." Of David. A *miktam.*[b]

¹ Do you rulers indeed speak justly?
 Do you judge people with equity?
² No, in your heart you devise injustice,
 and your hands mete out violence
  on the earth.

³ Even from birth the wicked go astray;
 from the womb they are wayward,
  spreading lies.
⁴ Their venom is like the venom of a
  snake,
 like that of a cobra that has
  stopped its ears,
⁵ that will not heed the tune of the
  charmer,
 however skillful the enchanter
  may be.

⁶ Break the teeth in their mouths,
  O God;
 LORD, tear out the fangs of those
  lions!
⁷ Let them vanish like water that flows
  away;
 when they draw the bow, let their
  arrows fall short.
⁸ May they be like a slug that melts
  away as it moves along,
 like a stillborn child that never sees
  the sun.

⁹ Before your pots can feel the heat of
  the thorns—
 whether they be green or dry—the
  wicked will be swept away.[c]
¹⁰ The righteous will be glad when they
  are avenged,
 when they dip their feet in the blood
  of the wicked.
¹¹ Then people will say,
 "Surely the righteous still are
  rewarded;
 surely there is a God who judges
  the earth."

Psalm 59[d]

For the director of music. To the tune of
"Do Not Destroy." Of David. A *miktam.*[b]
When Saul had sent men to watch David's
house in order to kill him.

¹ Deliver me from my enemies, O God;
 be my fortress against those who
  are attacking me.
² Deliver me from evildoers
 and save me from those who are
  after my blood.

³ See how they lie in wait for me!
 Fierce men conspire against me
 for no offense or sin of mine, LORD.
⁴ I have done no wrong, yet they are
  ready to attack me.
 Arise to help me; look on my plight!
⁵ You, LORD God Almighty,
 you who are the God of Israel,
rouse yourself to punish all the
  nations;
 show no mercy to wicked traitors.[e]

⁶ They return at evening,
 snarling like dogs,
 and prowl about the city.
⁷ See what they spew from their
  mouths—
 the words from their lips are sharp
  as swords,
 and they think, "Who can hear us?"
⁸ But you laugh at them, LORD;
 you scoff at all those nations.

⁹ You are my strength, I watch for you;
 you, God, are my fortress,
¹⁰ my God on whom I can rely.

God will go before me
 and will let me gloat over those who
  slander me.
¹¹ But do not kill them, Lord our shield,[f]
 or my people will forget.

---

[a] In Hebrew texts 58:1-11 is numbered 58:2-12. [b] Title: Probably a literary or musical term [c] 9 The meaning of the Hebrew for this verse is uncertain. [d] In Hebrew texts 59:1-17 is numbered 59:2-18. [e] 5 The Hebrew has *Selah* (a word of uncertain meaning) here and at the end of verse 13. [f] 11 Or *sovereign*

In your might uproot them
and bring them down.
12 For the sins of their mouths,
for the words of their lips,
let them be caught in their pride.
For the curses and lies they utter,
13 consume them in your wrath,
consume them till they are no
more.
Then it will be known to the ends of
the earth
that God rules over Jacob.

14 They return at evening,
snarling like dogs,
and prowl about the city.
15 They wander about for food
and howl if not satisfied.
16 But I will sing of your strength,
in the morning I will sing of your
love;
for you are my fortress,
my refuge in times of trouble.

17 You are my strength, I sing praise to
you;
you, God, are my fortress,
my God on whom I can rely.

Psalm 60 ^a

For the director of music. To the tune of
"The Lily of the Covenant." A *miktam*^b
of David. For teaching. When he fought
Aram Naharaim^c and Aram Zobah,^d and
when Joab returned and struck down twelve
thousand Edomites in the Valley of Salt.

1 You have rejected us, God, and burst
upon us;
you have been angry—now restore
us!
2 You have shaken the land and torn it
open;
mend its fractures, for it is quaking.
3 You have shown your people
desperate times;
you have given us wine that makes
us stagger.
4 But for those who fear you, you have
raised a banner
to be unfurled against the bow.^e

5 Save us and help us with your right
hand,
that those you love may be
delivered.
6 God has spoken from his sanctuary:
"In triumph I will parcel out
Shechem
and measure off the Valley of
Sukkoth.
7 Gilead is mine, and Manasseh is
mine;
Ephraim is my helmet,
Judah is my scepter.
8 Moab is my washbasin,
on Edom I toss my sandal;
over Philistia I shout in triumph."

9 Who will bring me to the fortified
city?
Who will lead me to Edom?
10 Is it not you, God, you who have now
rejected us
and no longer go out with our
armies?
11 Give us aid against the enemy,
for human help is worthless.
12 With God we will gain the victory,
and he will trample down our
enemies.

Psalm 61 ^f

For the director of music. With stringed
instruments. Of David.

1 Hear my cry, O God;
listen to my prayer.

2 From the ends of the earth I call to
you,
I call as my heart grows faint;
lead me to the rock that is higher
than I.
3 For you have been my refuge,
a strong tower against the foe.

4 I long to dwell in your tent forever
and take refuge in the shelter of
your wings.^e
5 For you, God, have heard my vows;
you have given me the heritage of
those who fear your name.

---

^a In Hebrew texts 60:1-12 is numbered 60:3-14.   ^b Title: Probably a literary or musical term   ^c Title: That is, Arameans
of Northwest Mesopotamia   ^d Title: That is, Arameans of central Syria   ^e 4 The Hebrew has *Selah* (a word of uncertain
meaning) here.   ^f In Hebrew texts 61:1-8 is numbered 61:2-9.

INSTANT ACCESS

They're talking behind your back again? Teens we surveyed while writing the notes in this Bible raised this issue again and again. They feel a lot like David. Sometimes friends are determined to bring each other down. Sometimes we can't understand others' motives. We just know that it's wrong, and that it hurts. When King David hurt, he remembered two important things. He spells them out in verses 11 and 12. Why do you suppose these comforted David? Can they comfort you too?

{Psalm 62}

⁶ Increase the days of the king's life,
    his years for many generations.
⁷ May he be enthroned in God's
        presence forever;
    appoint your love and faithfulness
        to protect him.

⁸ Then I will ever sing in praise of your
        name
    and fulfill my vows day after day.

Psalm 62ᵃ

For the director of music. For Jeduthun.
A psalm of David.

¹ Truly my soul finds rest in God;

my salvation comes from him.
² Truly he is my rock and my salvation;
    he is my fortress, I will never be
        shaken.

³ How long will you assault me?
    Would all of you throw me down—
    this leaning wall, this tottering
        fence?
⁴ Surely they intend to topple me
    from my lofty place;
    they take delight in lies.
With their mouths they bless,
    but in their hearts they curse.ᵇ

⁵ Yes, my soul, find rest in God;
    my hope comes from him.
⁶ Truly he is my rock and my salvation;
    he is my fortress, I will not be
        shaken.
⁷ My salvation and my honor depend on
        Godᶜ;
    he is my mighty rock, my refuge.
⁸ Trust in him at all times, you people;
    pour out your hearts to him,
    for God is our refuge.

⁹ Surely the lowborn are but a breath,
    the highborn are but a lie.
If weighed on a balance, they are
        nothing;
    together they are only a breath.
¹⁰ Do not trust in extortion
    or put vain hope in stolen goods;
though your riches increase,
    do not set your heart on them.

¹¹ One thing God has spoken,
    two things I have heard:
"Power belongs to you, God,
¹²   and with you, Lord, is unfailing love";
and, "You reward everyone
    according to what they have done."

Psalm 63ᵈ

A psalm of David. When he was in the
Desert of Judah.

¹ You, God, are my God,
    earnestly I seek you;
I thirst for you,
    my whole being longs for you,

ᵃ In Hebrew texts 62:1-12 is numbered 62:2-13.   ᵇ 4 The Hebrew has Selah (a word of uncertain meaning) here and at the end of verse 8.   ᶜ 7 Or / God Most High is my salvation and my honor   ᵈ In Hebrew texts 63:1-11 is numbered 63:2-12.

in a dry and parched land
where there is no water.

2 I have seen you in the sanctuary
and beheld your power and your
glory.
3 Because your love is better than life,
my lips will glorify you.
4 I will praise you as long as I live,
and in your name I will lift up my
hands.
5 I will be fully satisfied as with the
richest of foods;
with singing lips my mouth will
praise you.

6 On my bed I remember you;
I think of you through the watches
of the night.
7 Because you are my help,
I sing in the shadow of your wings.
8 I cling to you;
your right hand upholds me.

9 Those who want to kill me will be
destroyed;
they will go down to the depths of
the earth.
10 They will be given over to the sword
and become food for jackals.

11 But the king will rejoice in God;
all who swear by God will glory in
him,
while the mouths of liars will be
silenced.

Psalm 64 [a]

For the director of music.
A psalm of David.

1 Hear me, my God, as I voice my
complaint;
protect my life from the threat of
the enemy.

2 Hide me from the conspiracy of the
wicked,
from the plots of evildoers.
3 They sharpen their tongues like swords
and aim cruel words like deadly
arrows.
4 They shoot from ambush at the
innocent;

they shoot suddenly, without fear.

5 They encourage each other in evil
plans,
they talk about hiding their snares;
they say, "Who will see it [b]?"
6 They plot injustice and say,
"We have devised a perfect plan!"
Surely the human mind and heart
are cunning.

7 But God will shoot them with his
arrows;
they will suddenly be struck down.
8 He will turn their own tongues against
them
and bring them to ruin;
all who see them will shake their
heads in scorn.
9 All people will fear;
they will proclaim the works of God
and ponder what he has done.

10 The righteous will rejoice in the LORD
and take refuge in him;
all the upright in heart will glory in
him!

Psalm 65 [c]

For the director of music.
A psalm of David. A song.

1 Praise awaits [d] you, our God, in Zion;
to you our vows will be fulfilled.
2 You who answer prayer,
to you all people will come.
3 When we were overwhelmed by sins,
you forgave [e] our transgressions.
4 Blessed are those you choose
and bring near to live in your courts!
We are filled with the good things of
your house,
of your holy temple.

5 You answer us with awesome and
righteous deeds,
God our Savior,
the hope of all the ends of the earth
and of the farthest seas,
6 who formed the mountains by your
power,
having armed yourself with strength,

---

a In Hebrew texts 64:1-10 is numbered 64:2-11.   *b 5* Or *us*   *c* In Hebrew texts 65:1-13 is numbered 65:2-14.
d 1 Or *befits*; the meaning of the Hebrew for this word is uncertain.   *e 3* Or *made atonement for*

When we were overwhelmed by sins, you forgave our transgressions.

Psalm 65:3

⁷who stilled the roaring of the seas,
  the roaring of their waves,
  and the turmoil of the nations.
⁸The whole earth is filled with awe at
    your wonders;
  where morning dawns, where
    evening fades,
  you call forth songs of joy.

⁹You care for the land and water it;
  you enrich it abundantly.
  The streams of God are filled with
    water
  to provide the people with grain,
  for so you have ordained it.ᵃ
¹⁰You drench its furrows and level its
    ridges;
  you soften it with showers and
    bless its crops.
¹¹You crown the year with your bounty,
  and your carts overflow with
    abundance.
¹²The grasslands of the wilderness
    overflow;
  the hills are clothed with gladness.
¹³The meadows are covered with flocks
  and the valleys are mantled with
    grain;
  they shout for joy and sing.

Psalm 66

For the director of music.
A song. A psalm.

¹Shout for joy to God, all the earth!
² Sing the glory of his name;
  make his praise glorious.

³Say to God, "How awesome are your
    deeds!
  So great is your power
  that your enemies cringe before
    you.
⁴All the earth bows down to you;
  they sing praise to you,
  they sing the praises of your
    name."ᵇ
⁵Come and see what God has done,
  his awesome deeds for mankind!
⁶He turned the sea into dry land,
  they passed through the waters on
    foot—
  come, let us rejoice in him.
⁷He rules forever by his power,
  his eyes watch the nations—
  let not the rebellious rise up against
    him.

⁸Praise our God, all peoples,
  let the sound of his praise be
    heard;
⁹he has preserved our lives
  and kept our feet from slipping.
¹⁰For you, God, tested us;
  you refined us like silver.
¹¹You brought us into prison
  and laid burdens on our backs.
¹²You let people ride over our heads;
  we went through fire and water,
  but you brought us to a place of
    abundance.

¹³I will come to your temple with burnt
    offerings
  and fulfill my vows to you—
¹⁴vows my lips promised and my mouth
    spoke
  when I was in trouble.
¹⁵I will sacrifice fat animals to you
  and an offering of rams;
  I will offer bulls and goats.

¹⁶Come and hear, all you who fear God;
  let me tell you what he has done
    for me.
¹⁷I cried out to him with my mouth;
  his praise was on my tongue.
¹⁸If I had cherished sin in my heart,
  the Lord would not have listened;

ᵃ 9 Or *for that is how you prepare the land* ᵇ 4 The Hebrew has *Selah* (a word of uncertain meaning) here and at the end of verses 7 and 15.

19 but God has surely listened
　　and has heard my prayer.
20 Praise be to God,
　　who has not rejected my prayer
　　or withheld his love from me!

Psalm 67 [a]

For the director of music. With stringed
　　instruments. A psalm. A song.

1 May God be gracious to us and
　　bless us
　　and make his face shine on us— [b]
2 so that your ways may be known on
　　earth,
　　your salvation among all nations.

3 May the peoples praise you, God;
　　may all the peoples praise you.
4 May the nations be glad and sing for
　　joy,
　　for you rule the peoples with equity
　　and guide the nations of the earth.
5 May the peoples praise you, God;
　　may all the peoples praise you.

6 The land yields its harvest;
　　God, our God, blesses us.
7 May God bless us still,
　　so that all the ends of the earth will
　　fear him.

Psalm 68 [c]

For the director of music. Of David. A psalm.
　　A song.

1 May God arise, may his enemies be
　　scattered;
　　may his foes flee before him.
2 May you blow them away like
　　smoke—
　　as wax melts before the fire,
　　may the wicked perish before
　　God.
3 But may the righteous be glad
　　and rejoice before God;
　　may they be happy and joyful.

4 Sing to God, sing in praise of his
　　name,

extol him who rides on the clouds [d];
　　rejoice before him—his name is
　　the LORD.
5 A father to the fatherless, a defender
　　of widows,
　　is God in his holy dwelling.
6 God sets the lonely in families, [e]
　　he leads out the prisoners with
　　singing;
　　but the rebellious live in a sun-
　　scorched land.

7 When you, God, went out before your
　　people,
　　when you marched through the
　　wilderness, [f]
8 the earth shook, the heavens poured
　　down rain,
　　before God, the One of Sinai,
　　before God, the God of Israel.
9 You gave abundant showers, O God;
　　you refreshed your weary
　　inheritance.
10 Your people settled in it,
　　and from your bounty, God, you
　　provided for the poor.

11 The Lord announces the word,
　　and the women who proclaim it are
　　a mighty throng:
12 "Kings and armies flee in haste;
　　the women at home divide the
　　plunder.
13 Even while you sleep among the
　　sheep pens, [g]
　　the wings of my dove are sheathed
　　with silver,
　　its feathers with shining gold."
14 When the Almighty [h] scattered the
　　kings in the land,
　　it was like snow fallen on Mount
　　Zalmon.

15 Mount Bashan, majestic mountain,
　　Mount Bashan, rugged mountain,
16 why gaze in envy, you rugged
　　mountain,
　　at the mountain where God chooses
　　to reign,
　　where the LORD himself will dwell
　　forever?

---

a In Hebrew texts 67:1-7 is numbered 67:2-8.　　b 1 The Hebrew has Selah (a word of uncertain meaning) here and at the
end of verse 4.　　c In Hebrew texts 68:1-35 is numbered 68:2-36.　　d 4 Or name, / prepare the way for him who rides
through the deserts　　e 6 Or the desolate in a homeland　　f 7 The Hebrew has Selah (a word of uncertain meaning) here
and at the end of verses 19 and 32.　　g 13 Or the campfires; or the saddlebags　　h 14 Hebrew Shaddai

17 The chariots of God are tens of
thousands
and thousands of thousands;
the Lord has come from Sinai into
his sanctuary.*a*
18 When you ascended on high,
you took many captives;
you received gifts from people,
even from*b* the rebellious—
that you,*c* Lord God, might dwell
there.

19 Praise be to the Lord, to God our
Savior,
who daily bears our burdens.
20 Our God is a God who saves;
from the Sovereign Lord comes
escape from death.
21 Surely God will crush the heads of his
enemies,
the hairy crowns of those who go
on in their sins.
22 The Lord says, "I will bring them from
Bashan;
I will bring them from the depths of
the sea,
23 that your feet may wade in the blood
of your foes,
while the tongues of your dogs have
their share."

24 Your procession, God, has come into
view,
the procession of my God and King
into the sanctuary.
25 In front are the singers, after them the
musicians;
with them are the young women
playing the timbrels.
26 Praise God in the great congregation;
praise the Lord in the assembly of
Israel.
27 There is the little tribe of Benjamin,
leading them,
there the great throng of Judah's
princes,
and there the princes of Zebulun
and of Naphtali.

28 Summon your power, God*d*;
show us your strength, our God, as
you have done before.

29 Because of your temple at Jerusalem
kings will bring you gifts.
30 Rebuke the beast among the reeds,
the herd of bulls among the calves
of the nations.
Humbled, may the beast bring bars of
silver.
Scatter the nations who delight in
war.
31 Envoys will come from Egypt;
Cush*e* will submit herself to God.

32 Sing to God, you kingdoms of the earth,
sing praise to the Lord,
33 to him who rides across the highest
heavens, the ancient heavens,
who thunders with mighty voice.
34 Proclaim the power of God,
whose majesty is over Israel,
whose power is in the heavens.
35 You, God, are awesome in your
sanctuary;
the God of Israel gives power and
strength to his people.

Praise be to God!

Psalm 69*f*

For the director of music. To the tune of
"Lilies." Of David.

1 Save me, O God,
for the waters have come up to my
neck.
2 I sink in the miry depths,
where there is no foothold.
I have come into the deep waters;
the floods engulf me.
3 I am worn out calling for help;
my throat is parched.
My eyes fail,
looking for my God.
4 Those who hate me without reason
outnumber the hairs of my head;
many are my enemies without cause,
those who seek to destroy me.
I am forced to restore
what I did not steal.

5 You, God, know my folly;
my guilt is not hidden from you.

---

a 17 Probable reading of the original Hebrew text; Masoretic Text *Lord is among them at Sinai in holiness*   *b* 18 Or *gifts for
people, / even*   *c* 18 Or *they*   *d* 28 Many Hebrew manuscripts, Septuagint and Syriac; most Hebrew manuscripts *Your
God has summoned power for you*   *e* 31 That is, the upper Nile region   *f* In Hebrew texts 69:1-36 is numbered 69:2-37.

⁶Lord, the LORD Almighty,
   may those who hope in you
      not be disgraced because of me;
   God of Israel,
   may those who seek you
      not be put to shame because
         of me.
⁷For I endure scorn for your sake,
   and shame covers my face.
⁸I am a foreigner to my own family,
   a stranger to my own mother's
      children;
⁹for zeal for your house consumes me,
   and the insults of those who insult
      you fall on me.
¹⁰When I weep and fast,
   I must endure scorn;
¹¹when I put on sackcloth,
   people make sport of me.
¹²Those who sit at the gate mock me,
   and I am the song of the drunkards.

¹³But I pray to you, LORD,
   in the time of your favor;
   in your great love, O God,
      answer me with your sure salvation.
¹⁴Rescue me from the mire,
   do not let me sink;
   deliver me from those who hate me,
      from the deep waters.
¹⁵Do not let the floodwaters engulf me
   or the depths swallow me up
   or the pit close its mouth over me.
¹⁶Answer me, LORD, out of the goodness
      of your love;
   in your great mercy turn to me.
¹⁷Do not hide your face from your
      servant;
   answer me quickly, for I am in
      trouble.
¹⁸Come near and rescue me;
   deliver me because of my foes.

¹⁹You know how I am scorned,
   disgraced and shamed;
   all my enemies are before you.
²⁰Scorn has broken my heart
   and has left me helpless;
   I looked for sympathy, but there was
      none,
   for comforters, but I found none.
²¹They put gall in my food
   and gave me vinegar for my thirst.

INSTANT ACCESS

Did anyone ever tell you, "I just don't like you"? They didn't have any particular reason to be your enemy. They just were. That's what David is talking about in Psalm 69. That and being worn out by trying to stand up to those who are his enemies without a cause. What can we do when we're in pain and distress because everyone seems to be against us? Find out David's surprising answer in verse 30. Even better, try it out. Let David's solution shift your focus away from your enemies and discover for yourself what happens.

{Psalm 69}

²²May the table set before them
      become a snare;
   may it become retribution andᵃ a
      trap.
²³May their eyes be darkened so they
      cannot see,
   and their backs be bent forever.
²⁴Pour out your wrath on them;
   let your fierce anger overtake
      them.
²⁵May their place be deserted;
   let there be no one to dwell in their
      tents.
²⁶For they persecute those you wound

ᵃ 22 Or snare / and their fellowship become

and talk about the pain of those you
hurt.
27 Charge them with crime upon crime;
do not let them share in your
salvation.
28 May they be blotted out of the book of
life
and not be listed with the righteous.

29 But as for me, afflicted and in pain—
may your salvation, God, protect me.

30 I will praise God's name in song
and glorify him with thanksgiving.
31 This will please the LORD more than
an ox,
more than a bull with its horns and
hooves.
32 The poor will see and be glad—
you who seek God, may your hearts
live!
33 The LORD hears the needy
and does not despise his captive
people.
34 Let heaven and earth praise him,
the seas and all that move in them,
35 for God will save Zion
and rebuild the cities of Judah.
Then people will settle there and
possess it;
36 the children of his servants will
inherit it,
and those who love his name will
dwell there.

Psalm 70[a]

For the director of music. Of David.
A petition.

1 Hasten, O God, to save me;
come quickly, LORD, to help me.

2 May those who want to take my life
be put to shame and confusion;
may all who desire my ruin
be turned back in disgrace.
3 May those who say to me, "Aha! Aha!"
turn back because of their shame.
4 But may all who seek you
rejoice and be glad in you;
may those who long for your saving
help always say,
"The LORD is great!"

5 But as for me, I am poor and needy;
come quickly to me, O God.
You are my help and my deliverer;
LORD, do not delay.

Psalm 71

1 In you, LORD, I have taken refuge;
let me never be put to shame.
2 In your righteousness, rescue me and
deliver me;
turn your ear to me and save me.
3 Be my rock of refuge,
to which I can always go;
give the command to save me,
for you are my rock and my
fortress.
4 Deliver me, my God, from the hand of
the wicked,
from the grasp of those who are evil
and cruel.

5 For you have been my hope, Sovereign
LORD,
my confidence since my youth.
6 From birth I have relied on you;
you brought me forth from my
mother's womb.
I will ever praise you.
7 I have become a sign to many;
you are my strong refuge.
8 My mouth is filled with your praise,
declaring your splendor all day
long.

9 Do not cast me away when I am old;
do not forsake me when my
strength is gone.
10 For my enemies speak against me;
those who wait to kill me conspire
together.
11 They say, "God has forsaken him;
pursue him and seize him,
for no one will rescue him."
12 Do not be far from me, my God;
come quickly, God, to help me.
13 May my accusers perish in shame;
may those who want to harm me
be covered with scorn and
disgrace.

14 As for me, I will always have hope;
I will praise you more and more.

15 My mouth will tell of your righteous
   deeds,
   of your saving acts all day long—
   though I know not how to relate
   them all.
16 I will come and proclaim your mighty
   acts, Sovereign LORD;
   I will proclaim your righteous deeds,
   yours alone.
17 Since my youth, God, you have
   taught me,
   and to this day I declare your
   marvelous deeds.
18 Even when I am old and gray,
   do not forsake me, my God,
   till I declare your power to the next
   generation,
   your mighty acts to all who are to
   come.

19 Your righteousness, God, reaches to
   the heavens,
   you who have done great things.
   Who is like you, God?
20 Though you have made me see
   troubles,
   many and bitter,
   you will restore my life again;
   from the depths of the earth
   you will again bring me up.
21 You will increase my honor
   and comfort me once more.

22 I will praise you with the harp
   for your faithfulness, my God;
   I will sing praise to you with the lyre,
   Holy One of Israel.
23 My lips will shout for joy
   when I sing praise to you—
   I whom you have delivered.
24 My tongue will tell of your righteous
   acts
   all day long,
   for those who wanted to harm me
   have been put to shame and
   confusion.

Psalm 72

Of Solomon.

1 Endow the king with your justice,
   O God,
   the royal son with your
   righteousness.

You will increase my honor and comfort me once more.

Psalm 71:21

2 May he judge your people in
   righteousness,
   your afflicted ones with justice.
3 May the mountains bring prosperity to
   the people,
   the hills the fruit of righteousness.
4 May he defend the afflicted among
   the people
   and save the children of the needy;
   may he crush the oppressor.
5 May he endure[a] as long as the sun,
   as long as the moon, through all
   generations.
6 May he be like rain falling on a mown
   field,
   like showers watering the earth.
7 In his days may the righteous
   flourish
   and prosperity abound till the moon
   is no more.

8 May he rule from sea to sea
   and from the River[b] to the ends of
   the earth.
9 May the desert tribes bow before him
   and his enemies lick the dust.
10 May the kings of Tarshish and of
   distant shores
   bring tribute to him.
   May the kings of Sheba and Seba
   present him gifts.
11 May all kings bow down to him
   and all nations serve him.

12 For he will deliver the needy who cry
   out,
   the afflicted who have no one to
   help.

---

[a] 5 Septuagint; Hebrew *You will be feared*   [b] 8 That is, the Euphrates

13 He will take pity on the weak and the
   needy
     and save the needy from death.
14 He will rescue them from oppression
   and violence,
     for precious is their blood in his
       sight.

15 Long may he live!
     May gold from Sheba be given him.
   May people ever pray for him
     and bless him all day long.
16 May grain abound throughout the
   land;
     on the tops of the hills may it sway.
   May the crops flourish like Lebanon
     and thrive*a* like the grass of the
       field.
17 May his name endure forever;
     may it continue as long as the sun.

   Then all nations will be blessed
     through him,*b*
   and they will call him blessed.

18 Praise be to the LORD God, the God of
   Israel,
     who alone does marvelous deeds.
19 Praise be to his glorious name
   forever;
     may the whole earth be filled with
       his glory.
         Amen and Amen.

20 This concludes the prayers of David
   son of Jesse.

BOOK III

Psalms 73–89

Psalm 73

A psalm of Asaph.

1 Surely God is good to Israel,
     to those who are pure in heart.

2 But as for me, my feet had almost
   slipped;
     I had nearly lost my foothold.

3 For I envied the arrogant
     when I saw the prosperity of the
       wicked.

4 They have no struggles;
     their bodies are healthy and
       strong.*c*
5 They are free from common human
   burdens;
     they are not plagued by human ills.
6 Therefore pride is their necklace;
     they clothe themselves with
       violence.
7 From their callous hearts comes
   iniquity*d*;
     their evil imaginations have no
       limits.
8 They scoff, and speak with malice;
     with arrogance they threaten
       oppression.
9 Their mouths lay claim to heaven,
     and their tongues take possession
       of the earth.
10 Therefore their people turn to them
     and drink up waters in abundance.*e*
11 They say, "How would God know?
     Does the Most High know
       anything?"

12 This is what the wicked are like—
     always free of care, they go on
       amassing wealth.

13 Surely in vain I have kept my heart
   pure
     and have washed my hands in
       innocence.
14 All day long I have been afflicted,
     and every morning brings new
       punishments.

15 If I had spoken out like that,
     I would have betrayed your children.
16 When I tried to understand all this,
     it troubled me deeply
17 till I entered the sanctuary of God;
     then I understood their final
       destiny.

18 Surely you place them on slippery
   ground;
     you cast them down to ruin.

---

a 16 Probable reading of the original Hebrew text; Masoretic Text Lebanon, / from the city   b 17 Or will use his name in blessings (see Gen. 48:20)   c 4 With a different word division of the Hebrew; Masoretic Text struggles at their death; / their bodies are healthy   d 7 Syriac (see also Septuagint); Hebrew Their eyes bulge with fat   e 10 The meaning of the Hebrew for this verse is uncertain.

Dear Jordan

Dear Gavin,

It seems to be more and more difficult to live with Christian values. Young people see and hear so many sinful things they become desensitized—that means they are so used to hearing and seeing sinful things that those things don't even seem wrong anymore. Music, movies, the internet, drugs, alcohol, promiscuous sex, abortion—all these chip away at our understanding of what's right and what's wrong. And those who are most sinful are often most popular (or at least it seems that way).

This is nothing new, however. Many centuries ago the psalmist said he was jealous of wicked people because they seemed to have everything (Psalm 73:3–12). He felt he had gotten nowhere by trying to do the right thing (verse 13).

It wasn't until he entered "the sanctuary of God" that God gave the psalmist understanding. Eventually the wicked get into trouble so deep they are destroyed (Psalm 73:16–19). They don't rely on God because they are enjoying doing what's wrong. But God is always there for us. He gives strength to those who rely on him. It may be hard to live as God wants, but who will be there for you when you need him? People change from one day to the next. But God never changes.

Jordan

19 How suddenly are they destroyed,
   completely swept away by terrors!
20 They are like a dream when one
   awakes;
   when you arise, Lord,
   you will despise them as
   fantasies.

21 When my heart was grieved
   and my spirit embittered,
22 I was senseless and ignorant;
   I was a brute beast before you.

23 Yet I am always with you;
   you hold me by my right hand.
24 You guide me with your counsel,
   and afterward you will take me into
   glory.
25 Whom have I in heaven but you?
   And earth has nothing I desire
   besides you.
26 My flesh and my heart may fail,
   but God is the strength of my
   heart
   and my portion forever.

27 Those who are far from you will
   perish;
   you destroy all who are unfaithful to
   you.
28 But as for me, it is good to be near
   God.
   I have made the Sovereign LORD my
   refuge;
   I will tell of all your deeds.

Psalm 74

A *maskil*[a] of Asaph.

1 O God, why have you rejected us
   forever?
   Why does your anger smolder
   against the sheep of your
   pasture?
2 Remember the nation you purchased
   long ago,
   the people of your inheritance,
   whom you redeemed—
   Mount Zion, where you dwelt.
3 Turn your steps toward these
   everlasting ruins,
   all this destruction the enemy has
   brought on the sanctuary.

4 Your foes roared in the place where
   you met with us;
   they set up their standards as
   signs.
5 They behaved like men wielding
   axes
   to cut through a thicket of trees.
6 They smashed all the carved
   paneling
   with their axes and hatchets.
7 They burned your sanctuary to the
   ground;
   they defiled the dwelling place of
   your Name.
8 They said in their hearts, "We will
   crush them completely!"
   They burned every place where God
   was worshiped in the land.

9 We are given no signs from God;
   no prophets are left,
   and none of us knows how long this
   will be.
10 How long will the enemy mock you,
   God?
   Will the foe revile your name
   forever?
11 Why do you hold back your hand, your
   right hand?
   Take it from the folds of your
   garment and destroy them!

12 But God is my King from long ago;
   he brings salvation on the earth.

13 It was you who split open the sea by
   your power;
   you broke the heads of the monster
   in the waters.
14 It was you who crushed the heads of
   Leviathan
   and gave it as food to the creatures
   of the desert.
15 It was you who opened up springs and
   streams;
   you dried up the ever-flowing
   rivers.
16 The day is yours, and yours also the
   night;
   you established the sun and moon.
17 It was you who set all the boundaries
   of the earth;
   you made both summer and winter.

---

a Title: Probably a literary or musical term

18 Remember how the enemy has
mocked you, LORD,
how foolish people have reviled your
name.
19 Do not hand over the life of your dove
to wild beasts;
do not forget the lives of your
afflicted people forever.
20 Have regard for your covenant,
because haunts of violence fill the
dark places of the land.
21 Do not let the oppressed retreat in
disgrace;
may the poor and needy praise your
name.
22 Rise up, O God, and defend your
cause;
remember how fools mock you all
day long.
23 Do not ignore the clamor of your
adversaries,
the uproar of your enemies, which
rises continually.

Psalm 75[a]

For the director of music. To the tune of "Do
Not Destroy." A psalm of Asaph. A song.

1 We praise you, God,
we praise you, for your Name is
near;
people tell of your wonderful deeds.

2 You say, "I choose the appointed time;
it is I who judge with equity.
3 When the earth and all its people
quake,
it is I who hold its pillars firm.[b]
4 To the arrogant I say, 'Boast no more,'
and to the wicked, 'Do not lift up
your horns.[c]
5 Do not lift your horns against heaven;
do not speak so defiantly.'"

6 No one from the east or the west
or from the desert can exalt
themselves.
7 It is God who judges:
He brings one down, he exalts
another.

8 In the hand of the LORD is a cup
full of foaming wine mixed with
spices;
he pours it out, and all the wicked of
the earth
drink it down to its very dregs.

9 As for me, I will declare this forever;
I will sing praise to the God of
Jacob,
10 who says, "I will cut off the horns of
all the wicked,
but the horns of the righteous will
be lifted up."

Psalm 76[d]

For the director of music. With stringed
instruments. A psalm of Asaph. A song.

1 God is renowned in Judah;
in Israel his name is great.
2 His tent is in Salem,
his dwelling place in Zion.
3 There he broke the flashing arrows,
the shields and the swords, the
weapons of war.[e]

4 You are radiant with light,
more majestic than mountains rich
with game.
5 The valiant lie plundered,
they sleep their last sleep;
not one of the warriors
can lift his hands.
6 At your rebuke, God of Jacob,
both horse and chariot lie still.

7 It is you alone who are to be feared.
Who can stand before you when you
are angry?
8 From heaven you pronounced
judgment,
and the land feared and was
quiet—
9 when you, God, rose up to judge,
to save all the afflicted of the land.
10 Surely your wrath against mankind
brings you praise,
and the survivors of your wrath are
restrained.[f]

---

[a] In Hebrew texts 75:1-10 is numbered 75:2-11.   [b] 3 The Hebrew has Selah (a word of uncertain meaning) here.
[c] 4 Horns here symbolize strength; also in verses 5 and 10.   [d] In Hebrew texts 76:1-12 is numbered 76:2-13.
[e] 3 The Hebrew has Selah (a word of uncertain meaning) here and at the end of verse 9.   [f] 10 Or Surely the wrath of
mankind brings you praise, / and with the remainder of wrath you arm yourself

Sometimes it seems like God just isn't listening. Or if he is, he's decided to ignore us. And sometimes we ask, "Will God ever answer my prayer?" The person who wrote Psalm 77 understands. He prayed too, but God didn't seem to hear. Finally the psalmist figured out how to deal with prayers that go unanswered. He focused on the fact that God *can* perform miracles (Psalm 77:10–20). God can do anything ... but God chooses what he *will* do. If the Lord chooses not to answer your prayer (yet), then he has a good reason— even if you don't know what that reason is.

{Psalm 77}

≫ INSTANT ACCESS

² When I was in distress, I sought the
Lord;
at night I stretched out untiring
hands,
and I would not be comforted.

³ I remembered you, God, and I
groaned;
I meditated, and my spirit grew faint.*b*
⁴ You kept my eyes from closing;
I was too troubled to speak.
⁵ I thought about the former days,
the years of long ago;
⁶ I remembered my songs in the night.
My heart meditated and my spirit
asked:

⁷ "Will the Lord reject forever?
Will he never show his favor again?
⁸ Has his unfailing love vanished
forever?
Has his promise failed for all time?
⁹ Has God forgotten to be merciful?
Has he in anger withheld his
compassion?"

¹⁰ Then I thought, "To this I will appeal:
the years when the Most High
stretched out his right hand.
¹¹ I will remember the deeds of the Lord;
yes, I will remember your miracles
of long ago.
¹² I will consider all your works
and meditate on all your mighty
deeds."

¹³ Your ways, God, are holy.
What god is as great as our God?
¹⁴ You are the God who performs
miracles;
you display your power among the
peoples.
¹⁵ With your mighty arm you redeemed
your people,
the descendants of Jacob and
Joseph.

¹⁶ The waters saw you, God,
the waters saw you and writhed;
the very depths were convulsed.
¹⁷ The clouds poured down water,
the heavens resounded with
thunder;
your arrows flashed back and forth.

¹¹ Make vows to the Lord your God and
fulfill them;
let all the neighboring lands
bring gifts to the One to be feared.
¹² He breaks the spirit of rulers;
he is feared by the kings of the earth.

Psalm 77*a*

For the director of music. For Jeduthun.
Of Asaph. A psalm.

¹ I cried out to God for help;
I cried out to God to hear me.

---

a In Hebrew texts 77:1-20 is numbered 77:2-21.   *b* 3 The Hebrew has *Selah* (a word of uncertain meaning) here and at the end of verses 9 and 15.

18 Your thunder was heard in the
whirlwind,
your lightning lit up the world;
the earth trembled and quaked.
19 Your path led through the sea,
your way through the mighty waters,
though your footprints were not
seen.

20 You led your people like a flock
by the hand of Moses and Aaron.

Psalm 78

A *maskil*[a] of Asaph.

1 My people, hear my teaching;
listen to the words of my mouth.
2 I will open my mouth with a parable;
I will utter hidden things, things
from of old—
3 things we have heard and known,
things our ancestors have told us.
4 We will not hide them from their
descendants;
we will tell the next generation
the praiseworthy deeds of the LORD,
his power, and the wonders he has
done.
5 He decreed statutes for Jacob
and established the law in Israel,
which he commanded our ancestors
to teach their children,
6 so the next generation would know
them,
even the children yet to be born,
and they in turn would tell their
children.
7 Then they would put their trust in God
and would not forget his deeds
but would keep his commands.
8 They would not be like their
ancestors—
a stubborn and rebellious
generation,
whose hearts were not loyal to God,
whose spirits were not faithful to
him.
9 The men of Ephraim, though armed
with bows,
turned back on the day of battle;
10 they did not keep God's covenant

and refused to live by his law.
11 They forgot what he had done,
the wonders he had shown them.
12 He did miracles in the sight of their
ancestors
in the land of Egypt, in the region of
Zoan.
13 He divided the sea and led them
through;
he made the water stand up like a
wall.
14 He guided them with the cloud by day
and with light from the fire all night.
15 He split the rocks in the wilderness
and gave them water as abundant
as the seas;
16 he brought streams out of a rocky
crag
and made water flow down like
rivers.

17 But they continued to sin against him,
rebelling in the wilderness against
the Most High.
18 They willfully put God to the test
by demanding the food they craved.
19 They spoke against God;
they said, "Can God really
spread a table in the wilderness?
20 True, he struck the rock,
and water gushed out,
streams flowed abundantly,
but can he also give us bread?
Can he supply meat for his
people?"
21 When the LORD heard them, he was
furious;
his fire broke out against Jacob,
and his wrath rose against Israel,
22 for they did not believe in God
or trust in his deliverance.
23 Yet he gave a command to the skies
above
and opened the doors of the
heavens;
24 he rained down manna for the people
to eat,
he gave them the grain of heaven.
25 Human beings ate the bread of
angels;
he sent them all the food they could
eat.

---

a Title: Probably a literary or musical term

26 He let loose the east wind from the
heavens
and by his power made the south
wind blow.
27 He rained meat down on them like
dust,
birds like sand on the seashore.
28 He made them come down inside their
camp,
all around their tents.
29 They ate till they were gorged—
he had given them what they
craved.
30 But before they turned from what they
craved,
even while the food was still in their
mouths,
31 God's anger rose against them;
he put to death the sturdiest among
them,
cutting down the young men of
Israel.

32 In spite of all this, they kept on
sinning;
in spite of his wonders, they did not
believe.
33 So he ended their days in futility
and their years in terror.
34 Whenever God slew them, they would
seek him;
they eagerly turned to him again.
35 They remembered that God was their
Rock,
that God Most High was their
Redeemer.
36 But then they would flatter him with
their mouths,
lying to him with their tongues;
37 their hearts were not loyal to him,
they were not faithful to his
covenant.
38 Yet he was merciful;
he forgave their iniquities
and did not destroy them.
Time after time he restrained his
anger
and did not stir up his full
wrath.
39 He remembered that they were but
flesh,
a passing breeze that does not
return.

40 How often they rebelled against him in
the wilderness
and grieved him in the wasteland!
41 Again and again they put God to the
test;
they vexed the Holy One of Israel.
42 They did not remember his power—
the day he redeemed them from the
oppressor,
43 the day he displayed his signs in
Egypt,
his wonders in the region of Zoan.
44 He turned their river into blood;
they could not drink from their
streams.
45 He sent swarms of flies that devoured
them,
and frogs that devastated them.
46 He gave their crops to the
grasshopper,
their produce to the locust.
47 He destroyed their vines with hail
and their sycamore-figs with sleet.
48 He gave over their cattle to the hail,
their livestock to bolts of lightning.
49 He unleashed against them his hot
anger,
his wrath, indignation and
hostility—
a band of destroying angels.
50 He prepared a path for his anger;
he did not spare them from death
but gave them over to the plague.
51 He struck down all the firstborn of
Egypt,
the firstfruits of manhood in the
tents of Ham.
52 But he brought his people out like a
flock;
he led them like sheep through the
wilderness.
53 He guided them safely, so they were
unafraid;
but the sea engulfed their enemies.
54 And so he brought them to the border
of his holy land,
to the hill country his right hand had
taken.
55 He drove out nations before them
and allotted their lands to them as
an inheritance;
he settled the tribes of Israel in
their homes.

56 But they put God to the test
    and rebelled against the Most High;
    they did not keep his statutes.
57 Like their ancestors they were disloyal
    and faithless,
    as unreliable as a faulty bow.
58 They angered him with their high
    places;
    they aroused his jealousy with their
    idols.
59 When God heard them, he was
    furious;
    he rejected Israel completely.
60 He abandoned the tabernacle of
    Shiloh,
    the tent he had set up among
    humans.
61 He sent the ark of his might into
    captivity,
    his splendor into the hands of the
    enemy.
62 He gave his people over to the
    sword;
    he was furious with his inheritance.
63 Fire consumed their young men,
    and their young women had no
    wedding songs;
64 their priests were put to the sword,
    and their widows could not weep.

65 Then the Lord awoke as from sleep,
    as a warrior wakes from the stupor
    of wine.
66 He beat back his enemies;
    he put them to everlasting shame.
67 Then he rejected the tents of Joseph,
    he did not choose the tribe of
    Ephraim;
68 but he chose the tribe of Judah,
    Mount Zion, which he loved.
69 He built his sanctuary like the heights,
    like the earth that he established
    forever.
70 He chose David his servant
    and took him from the sheep pens;
71 from tending the sheep he brought
    him
    to be the shepherd of his people
    Jacob,
    of Israel his inheritance.
72 And David shepherded them with
    integrity of heart;
    with skillful hands he led them.

Psalm 79

A psalm of Asaph.

1 O God, the nations have invaded your
    inheritance;
    they have defiled your holy temple,
    they have reduced Jerusalem to
    rubble.
2 They have left the dead bodies of your
    servants
    as food for the birds of the sky,
    the flesh of your own people for the
    animals of the wild.
3 They have poured out blood like
    water
    all around Jerusalem,
    and there is no one to bury the
    dead.
4 We are objects of contempt to our
    neighbors,
    of scorn and derision to those
    around us.

5 How long, LORD? Will you be angry
    forever?
    How long will your jealousy burn like
    fire?
6 Pour out your wrath on the nations
    that do not acknowledge you,
  on the kingdoms
    that do not call on your name;
7 for they have devoured Jacob
    and devastated his homeland.

8 Do not hold against us the sins of
    past generations;
    may your mercy come quickly to
    meet us,
    for we are in desperate need.
9 Help us, God our Savior,
    for the glory of your name;
  deliver us and forgive our sins
    for your name's sake.
10 Why should the nations say,
    "Where is their God?"

Before our eyes, make known among
    the nations
    that you avenge the outpoured
    blood of your servants.
11 May the groans of the prisoners come
    before you;
    with your strong arm preserve those
    condemned to die.

¹²Pay back into the laps of our
neighbors seven times
the contempt they have hurled at
you, Lord.
¹³Then we your people, the sheep of
your pasture,
will praise you forever;
from generation to generation
we will proclaim your praise.

Psalm 80ᵃ

For the director of music. To the tune of
"The Lilies of the Covenant." Of Asaph.
A psalm.

¹Hear us, Shepherd of Israel,
you who lead Joseph like a flock.
You who sit enthroned between the
cherubim,
shine forth ²before Ephraim,
Benjamin and Manasseh.
Awaken your might;
come and save us.

³Restore us, O God;
make your face shine on us,
that we may be saved.

⁴How long, LORD God Almighty,
will your anger smolder
against the prayers of your
people?
⁵You have fed them with the bread of
tears;

you have made them drink tears by
the bowlful.
⁶You have made us an object of
derisionᵇ to our neighbors,
and our enemies mock us.

⁷Restore us, God Almighty;
make your face shine on us,
that we may be saved.

⁸You transplanted a vine from Egypt;
you drove out the nations and
planted it.
⁹You cleared the ground for it,
and it took root and filled the land.
¹⁰The mountains were covered with its
shade,
the mighty cedars with its branches.
¹¹Its branches reached as far as the
Sea,ᶜ
its shoots as far as the River.ᵈ

¹²Why have you broken down its walls
so that all who pass by pick its
grapes?
¹³Boars from the forest ravage it,
and insects from the fields feed
on it.
¹⁴Return to us, God Almighty!
Look down from heaven and see!
Watch over this vine,
15   the root your right hand has
planted,
the sonᵉ you have raised up for
yourself.

ᵃ In Hebrew texts 80:1-19 is numbered 80:2-20.   ᵇ 6 Probable reading of the original Hebrew text; Masoretic Text
contention   ᶜ 11 Probably the Mediterranean   ᵈ 11 That is, the Euphrates   ᵉ 15 Or branch

---

PANORAMA

Friends.

In this book, the psalmists talk to God as a
friend. They tell him just how they feel. And
they praise God, not only for listening but
also for his help.

{PSALMS}

16 Your vine is cut down, it is burned with
fire;
  at your rebuke your people perish.
17 Let your hand rest on the man at your
right hand,
  the son of man you have raised up
for yourself.
18 Then we will not turn away from you;
  revive us, and we will call on your
name.

19 Restore us, LORD God Almighty;
  make your face shine on us,
  that we may be saved.

Psalm 81 [a]

For the director of music. According to
gittith. [b] Of Asaph.

1 Sing for joy to God our strength;
  shout aloud to the God of Jacob!
2 Begin the music, strike the timbrel,
  play the melodious harp and
lyre.

3 Sound the ram's horn at the New
Moon,
  and when the moon is full, on the
day of our festival;
4 this is a decree for Israel,
  an ordinance of the God of
Jacob.
5 When God went out against Egypt,
  he established it as a statute for
Joseph.

I heard an unknown voice say:

6 "I removed the burden from their
shoulders;
  their hands were set free from the
basket.
7 In your distress you called and I
rescued you,
  I answered you out of a
thundercloud;
  I tested you at the waters of
Meribah. [c]
8 Hear me, my people, and I will warn
you—
  if you would only listen to me,
Israel!

9 You shall have no foreign god among
you;
  you shall not worship any god other
than me.
10 I am the LORD your God,
  who brought you up out of Egypt.
Open wide your mouth and I will fill it.

11 "But my people would not listen
to me;
  Israel would not submit to me.
12 So I gave them over to their stubborn
hearts
  to follow their own devices.

13 "If my people would only listen to me,
  if Israel would only follow my ways,
14 how quickly I would subdue their
enemies
  and turn my hand against their
foes!
15 Those who hate the LORD would cringe
before him,
  and their punishment would last
forever.
16 But you would be fed with the finest of
wheat;
  with honey from the rock I would
satisfy you."

Psalm 82

A psalm of Asaph.

1 God presides in the great assembly;
  he renders judgment among the
"gods":

2 "How long will you [d] defend the
unjust
  and show partiality to the wicked? [c]
3 Defend the weak and the fatherless;
  uphold the cause of the poor and
the oppressed.
4 Rescue the weak and the needy;
  deliver them from the hand of the
wicked.

5 "The 'gods' know nothing, they
understand nothing.
  They walk about in darkness;
  all the foundations of the earth are
shaken.

---

[a] In Hebrew texts 81:1-16 is numbered 81:2-17.   [b] Title: Probably a musical term   [c] 7,2 The Hebrew has *Selah* (a word
of uncertain meaning) here.   [d] 2 The Hebrew is plural.

6 "I said, 'You are "gods";
   you are all sons of the Most High.'
7 But you will die like mere mortals;
   you will fall like every other ruler.'"

8 Rise up, O God, judge the earth,
   for all the nations are your
      inheritance.

Psalm 83[a]

A song. A psalm of Asaph.

1 O God, do not remain silent;
   do not turn a deaf ear,
   do not stand aloof, O God.
2 See how your enemies growl,
   how your foes rear their heads.
3 With cunning they conspire against
      your people;
   they plot against those you cherish.

4 "Come," they say, "let us destroy
      them as a nation,
   so that Israel's name is
      remembered no more."

5 With one mind they plot together;
   they form an alliance against you—
6 the tents of Edom and the
      Ishmaelites,
   of Moab and the Hagrites,
7 Byblos, Ammon and Amalek,
   Philistia, with the people of Tyre.
8 Even Assyria has joined them
   to reinforce Lot's descendants.[b]

9 Do to them as you did to Midian,
   as you did to Sisera and Jabin at
      the river Kishon,
10 who perished at Endor
   and became like dung on the
      ground.

---

a In Hebrew texts 83:1-18 is numbered 83:2-19.   b 8 The Hebrew has *Selah* (a word of uncertain meaning) here.

TO THE POINT

Adoption's an Option

Sometimes Christians are criticized for being "pro-life." Abortion advocates talk about how terrible it is to be an "unwanted" child. They think if a child is unwanted, he or she is sure to be neglected or abused.

We need to remember that adoption is an option. Believers are called to "defend the weak and the fatherless" and to "rescue the weak and needy" (Psalm 82:3–4). If you should ever face the choice, please consider options other than an abortion. Many Christian couples want a baby to love—couples who would be glad to do God's will by caring for a fatherless child and rescuing you and your baby from this very difficult situation.

11 Make their nobles like Oreb and Zeeb,
   all their princes like Zebah and
   Zalmunna,
12 who said, "Let us take possession
   of the pasturelands of God."

13 Make them like tumbleweed, my
   God,
   like chaff before the wind.
14 As fire consumes the forest
   or a flame sets the mountains
   ablaze,
15 so pursue them with your tempest
   and terrify them with your storm.
16 Cover their faces with shame, LORD,
   so that they will seek your name.

17 May they ever be ashamed and
   dismayed;
   may they perish in disgrace.
18 Let them know that you, whose name
   is the LORD—
   that you alone are the Most High
   over all the earth.

Psalm 84[a]

For the director of music. According to
gittith.[b] Of the Sons of Korah. A psalm.

1 How lovely is your dwelling place,
   LORD Almighty!
2 My soul yearns, even faints,
   for the courts of the LORD;
   my heart and my flesh cry out
   for the living God.
3 Even the sparrow has found a
   home,
   and the swallow a nest for herself,
   where she may have her young—
   a place near your altar,
   LORD Almighty, my King and my
   God.
4 Blessed are those who dwell in your
   house;
   they are ever praising you.[c]

5 Blessed are those whose strength is
   in you,
   whose hearts are set on
   pilgrimage.
6 As they pass through the Valley of
   Baka,

they make it a place of springs;
   the autumn rains also cover it with
   pools.[d]
7 They go from strength to strength,
   till each appears before God in
   Zion.

8 Hear my prayer, LORD God Almighty;
   listen to me, God of Jacob.
9 Look on our shield,[e] O God;
   look with favor on your anointed
   one.

INSTANT ACCESS

It's never wrong to pray for people who are sick. It's also not even wrong to pray for things you need, or even things you don't really need but want. But don't miss out on the most important thing about prayer. What's that? Prayer is a time to relax and just be near God. That's what this psalm is talking about. Psalms use different word pictures. But they are all about how good it feels to just enjoy being with the Lord. So when you pray, it's not wrong to request this or that from God. But take an extra couple of minutes just to tell the Lord how wonderful you think he is. You'll feel a lot closer to God all day.

{Psalm 84}

---

a In Hebrew texts 84:1-12 is numbered 84:2-13.   b Title: Probably a musical term   c 4 The Hebrew has Selah (a word of uncertain meaning) here and at the end of verse 8.   d 6 Or blessings   e 9 Or sovereign

10 Better is one day in your courts
  than a thousand elsewhere;
 I would rather be a doorkeeper in the
  house of my God
  than dwell in the tents of the
  wicked.
11 For the Lord God is a sun and
  shield;
  the Lord bestows favor and
  honor;
 no good thing does he withhold
  from those whose walk is
  blameless.

12 Lord Almighty,
  blessed is the one who trusts in
  you.

Psalm 85 [a]

For the director of music. Of the Sons of
Korah. A psalm.

1 You, Lord, showed favor to your land;
  you restored the fortunes of Jacob.
2 You forgave the iniquity of your
  people
  and covered all their sins. [b]
3 You set aside all your wrath
  and turned from your fierce anger.

4 Restore us again, God our Savior,
  and put away your displeasure
  toward us.
5 Will you be angry with us forever?
  Will you prolong your anger through
  all generations?
6 Will you not revive us again,
  that your people may rejoice in you?
7 Show us your unfailing love, Lord,
  and grant us your salvation.

8 I will listen to what God the Lord
  says;
  he promises peace to his people,
  his faithful servants—
  but let them not turn to folly.
9 Surely his salvation is near those who
  fear him,
  that his glory may dwell in our land.

10 Love and faithfulness meet together;
  righteousness and peace kiss each
  other.

11 Faithfulness springs forth from the
  earth,
  and righteousness looks down from
  heaven.
12 The Lord will indeed give what is good,
  and our land will yield its harvest.
13 Righteousness goes before him
  and prepares the way for his steps.

Psalm 86

A prayer of David.

1 Hear me, Lord, and answer me,
  for I am poor and needy.
2 Guard my life, for I am faithful to you;
  save your servant who trusts in you.
 You are my God; 3 have mercy on me,
  Lord,
  for I call to you all day long.
4 Bring joy to your servant, Lord,
  for I put my trust in you.

5 You, Lord, are forgiving and good,
  abounding in love to all who call to
  you.
6 Hear my prayer, Lord;
  listen to my cry for mercy.
7 When I am in distress, I call to you,
  because you answer me.

8 Among the gods there is none like
  you, Lord;
  no deeds can compare with yours.
9 All the nations you have made
  will come and worship before you,
  Lord;
  they will bring glory to your name.
10 For you are great and do marvelous
  deeds;
  you alone are God.

11 Teach me your way, Lord,
  that I may rely on your faithfulness;
 give me an undivided heart,
  that I may fear your name.
12 I will praise you, Lord my God, with all
  my heart;
  I will glorify your name forever.
13 For great is your love toward me;
  you have delivered me from the
  depths,
  from the realm of the dead.

---

a In Hebrew texts 85:1-13 is numbered 85:2-14.   b 2 The Hebrew has Selah (a word of uncertain meaning) here.

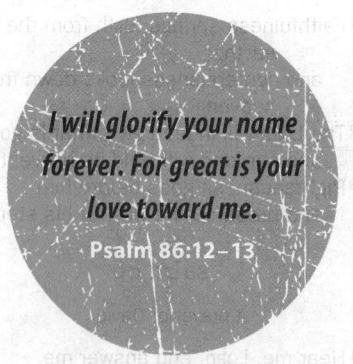

I will glorify your name forever. For great is your love toward me.

Psalm 86:12–13

¹⁴ Arrogant foes are attacking me, O God;
ruthless people are trying to
kill me—
they have no regard for you.
¹⁵ But you, Lord, are a compassionate
and gracious God,
slow to anger, abounding in love
and faithfulness.
¹⁶ Turn to me and have mercy on me;
show your strength in behalf of your
servant;
save me, because I serve you
just as my mother did.
¹⁷ Give me a sign of your goodness,
that my enemies may see it and be
put to shame,
for you, Lord, have helped me and
comforted me.

Psalm 87

Of the Sons of Korah. A psalm. A song.

¹ He has founded his city on the holy
mountain.
² The Lord loves the gates of Zion
more than all the other dwellings of
Jacob.

³ Glorious things are said of you,
city of God:^a
⁴ "I will record Rahab^b and Babylon
among those who acknowledge me—
Philistia too, and Tyre, along with
Cush^c—
and will say, 'This one was born in
Zion.'"^d

⁵ Indeed, of Zion it will be said,
"This one and that one were born in
her,
and the Most High himself will
establish her."
⁶ The Lord will write in the register of
the peoples:
"This one was born in Zion."

⁷ As they make music they will sing,
"All my fountains are in you."

Psalm 88^e

A song. A psalm of the Sons of Korah.
For the director of music. According
to *mahalath leannoth.*^f A *maskil*^g of
Heman the Ezrahite.

¹ Lord, you are the God who saves me;
day and night I cry out to you.
² May my prayer come before you;
turn your ear to my cry.

³ I am overwhelmed with troubles
and my life draws near to death.
⁴ I am counted among those who go
down to the pit;
I am like one without strength.
⁵ I am set apart with the dead,
like the slain who lie in the grave,
whom you remember no more,
who are cut off from your care.

⁶ You have put me in the lowest pit,
in the darkest depths.
⁷ Your wrath lies heavily on me;
you have overwhelmed me with all
your waves.^h
⁸ You have taken from me my closest
friends
and have made me repulsive to
them.
I am confined and cannot escape;
⁹ my eyes are dim with grief.

I call to you, Lord, every day;
I spread out my hands to you.
¹⁰ Do you show your wonders to the
dead?
Do their spirits rise up and praise
you?

---

^a 3 The Hebrew has *Selah* (a word of uncertain meaning) here and at the end of verse 6.   ^b 4 A poetic name for Egypt
^c 4 That is, the upper Nile region   ^d 4 Or *"I will record concerning those who acknowledge me: / 'This one was born in
Zion.' / Hear this, Rahab and Babylon, / and you too, Philistia, Tyre and Cush."*   ^e In Hebrew texts 88:1-18 is numbered
88:2-19.   ^f Title: Possibly a tune, "The Suffering of Affliction"   ^g Title: Probably a literary or musical term   ^h 7 The
Hebrew has *Selah* (a word of uncertain meaning) here and at the end of verse 10.

11 Is your love declared in the grave,
   your faithfulness in Destruction*a*?
12 Are your wonders known in the place
      of darkness,
   or your righteous deeds in the land
      of oblivion?
13 But I cry to you for help, LORD;
   in the morning my prayer comes
      before you.
14 Why, LORD, do you reject me
   and hide your face from me?

15 From my youth I have suffered and
      been close to death;
   I have borne your terrors and am in
      despair.
16 Your wrath has swept over me;
   your terrors have destroyed me.
17 All day long they surround me like a
      flood;
   they have completely engulfed me.
18 You have taken from me friend and
      neighbor—
   darkness is my closest friend.

Psalm 89*b*

A *maskil*c of Ethan the Ezrahite.

1 I will sing of the LORD's great love
      forever;
   with my mouth I will make your
      faithfulness known
   through all generations.
2 I will declare that your love stands
      firm forever,
   that you have established your
      faithfulness in heaven itself.
3 You said, "I have made a covenant
      with my chosen one,
   I have sworn to David my servant,
4 'I will establish your line forever
   and make your throne firm through
      all generations.' "*d*

5 The heavens praise your wonders,
      LORD,
   your faithfulness too, in the
      assembly of the holy ones.
6 For who in the skies above can
      compare with the LORD?

Who is like the LORD among the
      heavenly beings?
7 In the council of the holy ones God is
      greatly feared;
   he is more awesome than all who
      surround him.
8 Who is like you, LORD God Almighty?
   You, LORD, are mighty, and your
      faithfulness surrounds you.
9 You rule over the surging sea;
   when its waves mount up, you still
      them.
10 You crushed Rahab like one of the
      slain;
   with your strong arm you scattered
      your enemies.
11 The heavens are yours, and yours also
      the earth;
   you founded the world and all that
      is in it.
12 You created the north and the south;
   Tabor and Hermon sing for joy at
      your name.
13 Your arm is endowed with power;
   your hand is strong, your right hand
      exalted.

14 Righteousness and justice are the
      foundation of your throne;
   love and faithfulness go before you.
15 Blessed are those who have learned
      to acclaim you,
   who walk in the light of your
      presence, LORD.
16 They rejoice in your name all day
      long;
   they celebrate your righteousness.
17 For you are their glory and strength,
   and by your favor you exalt our
      horn.*e*
18 Indeed, our shield*f* belongs to the
      LORD,
   our king to the Holy One of Israel.

19 Once you spoke in a vision,
   to your faithful people you said:
"I have bestowed strength on a
      warrior;
   I have raised up a young man from
      among the people.

---

a 11 Hebrew *Abaddon*   *b* In Hebrew texts 89:1-52 is numbered 89:2-53.   *c* Title: Probably a literary or musical term
d 4 The Hebrew has *Selah* (a word of uncertain meaning) here and at the end of verses 37, 45 and 48.   *e* 17 *Horn* here
symbolizes strong one.   *f* 18 Or *sovereign*

20 I have found David my servant;
    with my sacred oil I have anointed
        him.
21 My hand will sustain him;
    surely my arm will strengthen him.
22 The enemy will not get the better of
        him;
    the wicked will not oppress him.
23 I will crush his foes before him
    and strike down his adversaries.
24 My faithful love will be with him,
    and through my name his horn^a will
        be exalted.
25 I will set his hand over the sea,
    his right hand over the rivers.
26 He will call out to me, 'You are my
        Father,
    my God, the Rock my Savior.'
27 And I will appoint him to be my
        firstborn,
    the most exalted of the kings of the
        earth.
28 I will maintain my love to him forever,
    and my covenant with him will never
        fail.
29 I will establish his line forever,
    his throne as long as the heavens
        endure.

30 "If his sons forsake my law
    and do not follow my statutes,
31 if they violate my decrees
    and fail to keep my commands,
32 I will punish their sin with the rod,
    their iniquity with flogging;
33 but I will not take my love from him,
    nor will I ever betray my
        faithfulness.
34 I will not violate my covenant
    or alter what my lips have uttered.
35 Once for all, I have sworn by my
        holiness—
    and I will not lie to David—
36 that his line will continue forever
    and his throne endure before me
        like the sun;
37 it will be established forever like the
        moon,
    the faithful witness in the sky."

38 But you have rejected, you have
        spurned,
    you have been very angry with your
        anointed one.

39 You have renounced the covenant with
        your servant
    and have defiled his crown in the
        dust.
40 You have broken through all his
        walls
    and reduced his strongholds to
        ruins.
41 All who pass by have plundered
        him;
    he has become the scorn of his
        neighbors.
42 You have exalted the right hand of his
        foes;
    you have made all his enemies
        rejoice.
43 Indeed, you have turned back the
        edge of his sword
    and have not supported him in
        battle.
44 You have put an end to his splendor
    and cast his throne to the ground.
45 You have cut short the days of his
        youth;
    you have covered him with a mantle
        of shame.

46 How long, LORD? Will you hide yourself
        forever?
    How long will your wrath burn like
        fire?
47 Remember how fleeting is my life.
    For what futility you have created all
        humanity!
48 Who can live and not see death,
    or who can escape the power of the
        grave?
49 Lord, where is your former great
        love,
    which in your faithfulness you swore
        to David?
50 Remember, Lord, how your servant
        has^b been mocked,
    how I bear in my heart the taunts of
        all the nations,
51 the taunts with which your enemies,
    LORD, have mocked,
    with which they have mocked every
        step of your anointed one.

52 Praise be to the LORD forever!
    Amen and Amen.

---

^a 24 Horn here symbolizes strength.   ^b 50 Or your servants have

We Believe...

"in God Almighty"

✝ Did you learn Bible stories as a child? Stories about the miracles that forced Pharaoh to free the Israelite slaves. About God parting the Red Sea so his people could pass through it on dry ground. And the stories about Jesus' miracles: telling a raging storm to stop, casting out demons and healing the sick.

That's part of what being "All-mighty" means: God is able do whatever he chooses any time, any place.

A number of Bible passages show how powerful our God is. Like Psalm 89:5–13. Or Job 38 and 39, where God challenges Job to consider his greatness.

One truly special passage in Isaiah 40 quotes God asking, "To whom will you compare me?" and points out that God not only created the universe but he sustains it. It is only "because of his great power and mighty strength" that not a star is missing from the heavens (see verses 25–26).

But what makes this Isaiah passage special isn't just that it helps us see our God as Almighty. What's special is that God uses his power to give "strength to the weary." Whenever things seem to be too much for us, or we feel we just can't go on, we can look to the Lord God Almighty who will use his power to "increase our strength."

Go to page 3 for the next We Believe

BOOK IV

Psalms 90–106

Psalm 90

A prayer of Moses the man of God.

1 Lord, you have been our dwelling
    place
  throughout all generations.
2 Before the mountains were born
  or you brought forth the whole
    world,
  from everlasting to everlasting you
    are God.

3 You turn people back to dust,
  saying, "Return to dust, you
    mortals."
4 A thousand years in your sight
  are like a day that has just gone by,
  or like a watch in the night.
5 Yet you sweep people away in the
    sleep of death—
  they are like the new grass of the
    morning:
6 In the morning it springs up new,
  but by evening it is dry and
    withered.

7 We are consumed by your anger
  and terrified by your indignation.
8 You have set our iniquities before
    you,
  our secret sins in the light of your
    presence.
9 All our days pass away under your
    wrath;
  we finish our years with a moan.
10 Our days may come to seventy years,
  or eighty, if our strength endures;
  yet the best of them are but trouble
    and sorrow,
  for they quickly pass, and we fly
    away.
11 If only we knew the power of your
    anger!
  Your wrath is as great as the fear
    that is your due.
12 Teach us to number our days,
  that we may gain a heart of
    wisdom.

13 Relent, LORD! How long will it be?
  Have compassion on your
    servants.
14 Satisfy us in the morning with your
    unfailing love,
  that we may sing for joy and be glad
    all our days.
15 Make us glad for as many days as you
    have afflicted us,
  for as many years as we have seen
    trouble.
16 May your deeds be shown to your
    servants,
  your splendor to their children.

17 May the favor[a] of the Lord our God
    rest on us;
  establish the work of our hands for
    us—
  yes, establish the work of our
    hands.

Psalm 91

1 Whoever dwells in the shelter of the
    Most High
  will rest in the shadow of the
    Almighty.[b]
2 I will say of the LORD, "He is my refuge
    and my fortress,
  my God, in whom I trust."

3 Surely he will save you
  from the fowler's snare
  and from the deadly pestilence.
4 He will cover you with his feathers,
  and under his wings you will find
    refuge;
  his faithfulness will be your shield
    and rampart.
5 You will not fear the terror of night,
  nor the arrow that flies by day,
6 nor the pestilence that stalks in the
    darkness,
  nor the plague that destroys at
    midday.
7 A thousand may fall at your side,
  ten thousand at your right hand,
  but it will not come near you.
8 You will only observe with your
    eyes
  and see the punishment of the
    wicked.

---

a 17 Or *beauty*   b 1 Hebrew *Shaddai*

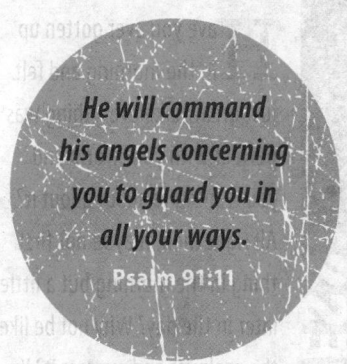

He will command his angels concerning you to guard you in all your ways.

Psalm 91:11

⁹ If you say, "The LORD is my refuge,"
and you make the Most High your
dwelling,
¹⁰ no harm will overtake you,
no disaster will come near your
tent.
¹¹ For he will command his angels
concerning you
to guard you in all your ways;
¹² they will lift you up in their hands,
so that you will not strike your foot
against a stone.
¹³ You will tread on the lion and the
cobra;
you will trample the great lion and
the serpent.
¹⁴ "Because heᵃ loves me," says the
LORD, "I will rescue him;
I will protect him, for he
acknowledges my name.
¹⁵ He will call on me, and I will answer
him;
I will be with him in trouble,
I will deliver him and honor him.
¹⁶ With long life I will satisfy him
and show him my salvation."

Psalm 92ᵇ

A psalm. A song. For the Sabbath day.

¹ It is good to praise the LORD
and make music to your name,
O Most High,
² proclaiming your love in the
morning
and your faithfulness at night,

³ to the music of the ten-stringed lyre
and the melody of the harp.
⁴ For you make me glad by your deeds,
LORD;
I sing for joy at what your hands
have done.
⁵ How great are your works, LORD,
how profound your thoughts!
⁶ Senseless people do not know,
fools do not understand,
⁷ that though the wicked spring up like
grass
and all evildoers flourish,
they will be destroyed forever.

⁸ But you, LORD, are forever exalted.

⁹ For surely your enemies, LORD,
surely your enemies will perish;
all evildoers will be scattered.
¹⁰ You have exalted my hornᶜ like that of
a wild ox;
fine oils have been poured
on me.
¹¹ My eyes have seen the defeat of my
adversaries;
my ears have heard the rout of my
wicked foes.

¹² The righteous will flourish like a palm
tree,
they will grow like a cedar of
Lebanon;
¹³ planted in the house of the LORD,
they will flourish in the courts of our
God.
¹⁴ They will still bear fruit in old age,
they will stay fresh and green,
¹⁵ proclaiming, "The LORD is upright;
he is my Rock, and there is no
wickedness in him."

Psalm 93

¹ The LORD reigns, he is robed in
majesty;
the LORD is robed in majesty and
armed with strength;
indeed, the world is established,
firm and secure.
² Your throne was established long ago;
you are from all eternity.

ᵃ 14 That is, probably the king   ᵇ In Hebrew texts 92:1-15 is numbered 92:2-16.   ᶜ 10 Horn here symbolizes
strength.

3 The seas have lifted up, Lord,
the seas have lifted up their voice;
the seas have lifted up their
pounding waves.
4 Mightier than the thunder of the great
waters,
mightier than the breakers of the
sea—
the Lord on high is mighty.

5 Your statutes, Lord, stand firm;
holiness adorns your house
for endless days.

Psalm 94

1 The Lord is a God who avenges.
O God who avenges, shine forth.
2 Rise up, Judge of the earth;
pay back to the proud what they
deserve.
3 How long, Lord, will the wicked,
how long will the wicked be jubilant?

4 They pour out arrogant words;
all the evildoers are full of boasting.
5 They crush your people, Lord;
they oppress your inheritance.
6 They slay the widow and the
foreigner;
they murder the fatherless.
7 They say, "The Lord does not see;
the God of Jacob takes no notice."

8 Take notice, you senseless ones
among the people;
you fools, when will you become
wise?
9 Does he who fashioned the ear not
hear?
Does he who formed the eye not
see?
10 Does he who disciplines nations not
punish?
Does he who teaches mankind lack
knowledge?
11 The Lord knows all human plans;
he knows that they are futile.

12 Blessed is the one you discipline,
Lord,
the one you teach from your law;
13 you grant them relief from days of
trouble,
till a pit is dug for the wicked.

INSTANT ACCESS

Have you ever gotten up in the morning and felt just great? Like everything was perfect with your world and you wanted to shout about it? All right then, maybe not first thing in the morning but a little later in the day? Why not be like the psalmist and express it? You don't have to write a poem, but you could give your mom a big smile and a hug. You could pat a friend on the back. You could sing. Or dance. However you feel comfortable expressing your joy. The psalmist praised God for his happiness. Maybe you could do that too!

{Psalm 92}

14 For the Lord will not reject his people;
he will never forsake his inheritance.
15 Judgment will again be founded on
righteousness,
and all the upright in heart will
follow it.

16 Who will rise up for me against the
wicked?
Who will take a stand for me
against evildoers?
17 Unless the Lord had given me help,
I would soon have dwelt in the
silence of death.
18 When I said, "My foot is slipping,"
your unfailing love, Lord,
supported me.
19 When anxiety was great within me,
your consolation brought me joy.

20 Can a corrupt throne be allied with
   you—
   a throne that brings on misery by
   its decrees?
21 The wicked band together against the
   righteous
   and condemn the innocent to
   death.
22 But the LORD has become my fortress,
   and my God the rock in whom I take
   refuge.
23 He will repay them for their sins
   and destroy them for their
   wickedness;
   the LORD our God will destroy them.

Psalm 95

1 Come, let us sing for joy to the LORD;
   let us shout aloud to the Rock of
   our salvation.
2 Let us come before him with
   thanksgiving
   and extol him with music and song.
3 For the LORD is the great God,
   the great King above all gods.
4 In his hand are the depths of the
   earth,
   and the mountain peaks belong to
   him.
5 The sea is his, for he made it,
   and his hands formed the dry land.

6 Come, let us bow down in worship,
   let us kneel before the LORD our
   Maker;
7 for he is our God
   and we are the people of his
   pasture,
   the flock under his care.

Today, if only you would hear his
   voice,
8 "Do not harden your hearts as you did
   at Meribah,[a]
   as you did that day at Massah[b] in
   the wilderness,
9 where your ancestors tested me;
   they tried me, though they had seen
   what I did.
10 For forty years I was angry with that
   generation;

I said, 'They are a people whose
   hearts go astray,
   and they have not known my ways.'
11 So I declared on oath in my anger,
   'They shall never enter my rest.' "

Psalm 96

1 Sing to the LORD a new song;
   sing to the LORD, all the earth.
2 Sing to the LORD, praise his name;
   proclaim his salvation day after
   day.
3 Declare his glory among the nations,
   his marvelous deeds among all
   peoples.

4 For great is the LORD and most worthy
   of praise;
   he is to be feared above all gods.
5 For all the gods of the nations are
   idols,
   but the LORD made the heavens.
6 Splendor and majesty are before him;
   strength and glory are in his
   sanctuary.

7 Ascribe to the LORD, all you families of
   nations,
   ascribe to the LORD glory and
   strength.
8 Ascribe to the LORD the glory due his
   name;
   bring an offering and come into his
   courts.
9 Worship the LORD in the splendor of
   his[c] holiness;
   tremble before him, all the earth.
10 Say among the nations, "The LORD
   reigns."
   The world is firmly established, it
   cannot be moved;
   he will judge the peoples with
   equity.

11 Let the heavens rejoice, let the earth
   be glad;
   let the sea resound, and all that is
   in it.
12 Let the fields be jubilant, and
   everything in them;
   let all the trees of the forest sing
   for joy.

---

a 8 Meribah means quarreling.   b 8 Massah means testing.   c 9 Or LORD with the splendor of

¹³ Let all creation rejoice before the
    LORD, for he comes,
he comes to judge the earth.
He will judge the world in
    righteousness
and the peoples in his faithfulness.

Psalm 97

¹ The LORD reigns, let the earth be glad;
    let the distant shores rejoice.
² Clouds and thick darkness surround
    him;
    righteousness and justice are the
    foundation of his throne.
³ Fire goes before him
    and consumes his foes on every
    side.
⁴ His lightning lights up the world;
    the earth sees and trembles.
⁵ The mountains melt like wax before
    the LORD,
    before the Lord of all the earth.
⁶ The heavens proclaim his
    righteousness,
    and all peoples see his glory.

⁷ All who worship images are put to
    shame,
    those who boast in idols—
    worship him, all you gods!

⁸ Zion hears and rejoices
    and the villages of Judah are glad
    because of your judgments, LORD.
⁹ For you, LORD, are the Most High over
    all the earth;
    you are exalted far above all gods.

> *Let those who love
> the LORD hate evil,
> for he guards the lives
> of his faithful ones.*
> **Psalm 97:10**

¹⁰ Let those who love the LORD hate evil,
    for he guards the lives of his faithful
    ones
    and delivers them from the hand of
    the wicked.
¹¹ Light shines^a on the righteous
    and joy on the upright in heart.
¹² Rejoice in the LORD, you who are
    righteous,
    and praise his holy name.

Psalm 98

A psalm.

¹ Sing to the LORD a new song,
    for he has done marvelous things;
his right hand and his holy arm
    have worked salvation for him.
² The LORD has made his salvation
    known
    and revealed his righteousness to
    the nations.
³ He has remembered his love
    and his faithfulness to Israel;
all the ends of the earth have seen
    the salvation of our God.

⁴ Shout for joy to the LORD, all the
    earth,
    burst into jubilant song with
    music;
⁵ make music to the LORD with the
    harp,
    with the harp and the sound of
    singing,
⁶ with trumpets and the blast of the
    ram's horn—
    shout for joy before the LORD, the
    King.

⁷ Let the sea resound, and everything
    in it,
    the world, and all who live in it.
⁸ Let the rivers clap their hands,
    let the mountains sing together for
    joy;
⁹ let them sing before the LORD,
    for he comes to judge the earth.
He will judge the world in
    righteousness
    and the peoples with equity.

---

^a *11* One Hebrew manuscript and ancient versions (see also
112:4); most Hebrew manuscripts *Light is sown*

Psalm 99

1 The LORD reigns,
  let the nations tremble;
he sits enthroned between the
    cherubim,
  let the earth shake.
2 Great is the LORD in Zion;
  he is exalted over all the nations.
3 Let them praise your great and
    awesome name—
  he is holy.

4 The King is mighty, he loves justice—
  you have established equity;
in Jacob you have done
  what is just and right.
5 Exalt the LORD our God
  and worship at his footstool;
  he is holy.

6 Moses and Aaron were among his
    priests,
  Samuel was among those who
    called on his name;
they called on the LORD
  and he answered them.
7 He spoke to them from the pillar of
    cloud;
  they kept his statutes and the
    decrees he gave them.

8 LORD our God,
  you answered them;
you were to Israel a forgiving God,
  though you punished their
    misdeeds.a
9 Exalt the LORD our God
  and worship at his holy mountain,
  for the LORD our God is holy.

Psalm 100

A psalm. For giving grateful praise.

1 Shout for joy to the LORD, all the
    earth.
2   Worship the LORD with gladness;
  come before him with joyful songs.
3 Know that the LORD is God.
  It is he who made us, and we are
    hisb;
  we are his people, the sheep of his
    pasture.

4 Enter his gates with thanksgiving
  and his courts with praise;
  give thanks to him and praise his
    name.
5 For the LORD is good and his love
    endures forever;
  his faithfulness continues through
    all generations.

Psalm 101

Of David. A psalm.

1 I will sing of your love and justice;
  to you, LORD, I will sing praise.
2 I will be careful to lead a blameless
    life—
  when will you come to me?

I will conduct the affairs of my
    house
  with a blameless heart.
3 I will not look with approval
  on anything that is vile.

I hate what faithless people do;
  I will have no part in it.
4 The perverse of heart shall be far
    from me;
  I will have nothing to do with what is
    evil.

5 Whoever slanders their neighbor in
    secret,
  I will put to silence;
whoever has haughty eyes and a
    proud heart,
  I will not tolerate.

6 My eyes will be on the faithful in the
    land,
  that they may dwell with me;
the one whose walk is blameless
  will minister to me.

7 No one who practices deceit
  will dwell in my house;
no one who speaks falsely
  will stand in my presence.

8 Every morning I will put to
    silence
  all the wicked in the land;
I will cut off every evildoer
  from the city of the LORD.

---

a 8 Or God, / an avenger of the wrongs done to them   b 3 Or and not we ourselves

Psalm 102[a]

A prayer of an afflicted person who
has grown weak and pours out a
lament before the LORD.

1 Hear my prayer, LORD;
    let my cry for help come to you.
2 Do not hide your face from me
    when I am in distress.
  Turn your ear to me;
    when I call, answer me quickly.

3 For my days vanish like smoke;
    my bones burn like glowing embers.
4 My heart is blighted and withered like
        grass;
    I forget to eat my food.
5 In my distress I groan aloud
    and am reduced to skin and
        bones.
6 I am like a desert owl,
    like an owl among the ruins.
7 I lie awake; I have become
    like a bird alone on a roof.
8 All day long my enemies taunt me;
    those who rail against me use my
        name as a curse.
9 For I eat ashes as my food
    and mingle my drink with tears
10 because of your great wrath,
    for you have taken me up and
        thrown me aside.
11 My days are like the evening
        shadow;
    I wither away like grass.

12 But you, LORD, sit enthroned forever;
    your renown endures through all
        generations.
13 You will arise and have compassion
        on Zion,
    for it is time to show favor to her;
    the appointed time has come.
14 For her stones are dear to your
        servants;
    her very dust moves them to pity.
15 The nations will fear the name of the
        LORD,
    all the kings of the earth will revere
        your glory.
16 For the LORD will rebuild Zion
    and appear in his glory.

17 He will respond to the prayer of the
        destitute;
    he will not despise their plea.

18 Let this be written for a future
        generation,
    that a people not yet created may
        praise the LORD:
19 "The LORD looked down from his
        sanctuary on high,
    from heaven he viewed the earth,
20 to hear the groans of the prisoners
    and release those condemned to
        death."
21 So the name of the LORD will be
        declared in Zion
    and his praise in Jerusalem
22 when the peoples and the kingdoms
    assemble to worship the LORD.

23 In the course of my life[b] he broke my
        strength;
    he cut short my days.
24 So I said:
  "Do not take me away, my God, in the
        midst of my days;
    your years go on through all
        generations.
25 In the beginning you laid the
        foundations of the earth,
    and the heavens are the work of
        your hands.
26 They will perish, but you remain;
    they will all wear out like a
        garment.
  Like clothing you will change them
    and they will be discarded.
27 But you remain the same,
    and your years will never end.
28 The children of your servants will live
        in your presence;
    their descendants will be
        established before you."

Psalm 103

Of David.

1 Praise the LORD, my soul;
    all my inmost being, praise his holy
        name.
2 Praise the LORD, my soul,
    and forget not all his benefits—

---

a In Hebrew texts 102:1-28 is numbered 102:2-29.   b 23 Or By his power

What is "praise"? It's telling a person all the good things you've noticed and appreciate about him or her. Praise is also something we appreciate. You know how you feel when Mom or Dad or a teacher praises you? It makes you feel good. You may never have thought of it this way, but when you praise God it makes him feel good too. And really, there's so much about God that's worthy of praise. Just for fun, make a list of everything you can think of that's good and wonderful about God. Then read Psalm 103, and add things to your list. Finally, not just for fun but because he deserves it, praise God for everything on your list.

{Psalm 103}

INSTANT ACCESS

3 who forgives all your sins
    and heals all your diseases,
4 who redeems your life from the
        pit
    and crowns you with love and
        compassion,
5 who satisfies your desires with
        good things
    so that your youth is renewed like
        the eagle's.

6 The LORD works righteousness
    and justice for all the oppressed.

7 He made known his ways to Moses,
    his deeds to the people of Israel:
8 The LORD is compassionate and
        gracious,
    slow to anger, abounding in love.
9 He will not always accuse,
    nor will he harbor his anger
        forever;
10 he does not treat us as our sins
        deserve
    or repay us according to our
        iniquities.
11 For as high as the heavens are above
        the earth,
    so great is his love for those who
        fear him;
12 as far as the east is from the west,
    so far has he removed our
        transgressions from us.

13 As a father has compassion on his
        children,
    so the LORD has compassion on
        those who fear him;
14 for he knows how we are formed,
    he remembers that we are dust.
15 The life of mortals is like grass,
    they flourish like a flower of the
        field;
16 the wind blows over it and it is gone,
    and its place remembers it no
        more.
17 But from everlasting to everlasting
    the LORD's love is with those who
        fear him,
    and his righteousness with their
        children's children—
18 with those who keep his covenant
    and remember to obey his
        precepts.

19 The LORD has established his throne
        in heaven,
    and his kingdom rules over all.

20 Praise the LORD, you his angels,
    you mighty ones who do his
        bidding,
    who obey his word.
21 Praise the LORD, all his heavenly
        hosts,
    you his servants who do his will.

"in God the Father"

✝ That word, "Father," may trouble you if your dad doesn't love you. Or if he loves you but just isn't there for you. Some dads may get drunk and beat their kids. A few even abuse daughters sexually. For anyone who has a dad who's failed him or her, it can be uncomfortable to think of God as "the Father."

But the Bible assures us that God is a *loving* Father. Psalm 103:8 says, "The LORD is compassionate and gracious, slow to anger, abounding in love." And Jesus encourages us to see God as a Father who never fails us; a Father who takes care of us and gives us good gifts.

Here are some Bible passages that picture God as Father. Take a look at them. You'll see what a father is supposed to be like. And you'll discover that you can count on God the Father to love you and be there for you—even if your dad has fallen short.

* Psalm 103:8–18
* Matthew 6:25–34
* Matthew 7:7–11
* Hebrews 12:5–11

If you still feel a little uncertain about God, remember something Jesus said. When one of his followers asked Jesus to show him the Father, Jesus told him, "Anyone who has seen me has seen the Father" (John 14:9). God the Father is just like Jesus . . . just as loving, just as kind, and just as powerful and caring as God the Son.

Go to page 727 for the next We Believe

22 Praise the LORD, all his works
everywhere in his dominion.

Praise the LORD, my soul.

Psalm 104

1 Praise the LORD, my soul.

LORD my God, you are very great;
you are clothed with splendor and
majesty.

2 The LORD wraps himself in light as with
a garment;
he stretches out the heavens like a
tent

3 and lays the beams of his upper
chambers on their waters.
He makes the clouds his chariot
and rides on the wings of the wind.

4 He makes winds his messengers,[a]
flames of fire his servants.

5 He set the earth on its foundations;
it can never be moved.

6 You covered it with the watery depths
as with a garment;
the waters stood above the
mountains.

7 But at your rebuke the waters fled,
at the sound of your thunder they
took to flight;

8 they flowed over the mountains,
they went down into the valleys,
to the place you assigned for them.

9 You set a boundary they cannot
cross;
never again will they cover the
earth.

10 He makes springs pour water into the
ravines;
it flows between the mountains.

11 They give water to all the beasts of
the field;
the wild donkeys quench their thirst.

12 The birds of the sky nest by the
waters;
they sing among the branches.

13 He waters the mountains from his
upper chambers;
the land is satisfied by the fruit of
his work.

14 He makes grass grow for the cattle,
and plants for people to cultivate—
bringing forth food from the earth:

15 wine that gladdens human hearts,
oil to make their faces shine,
and bread that sustains their
hearts.

16 The trees of the LORD are well
watered,
the cedars of Lebanon that he
planted.

17 There the birds make their nests;
the stork has its home in the
junipers.

18 The high mountains belong to the wild
goats;
the crags are a refuge for the hyrax.

19 He made the moon to mark the
seasons,
and the sun knows when to go
down.

20 You bring darkness, it becomes night,
and all the beasts of the forest
prowl.

21 The lions roar for their prey
and seek their food from God.

22 The sun rises, and they steal away;
they return and lie down in their
dens.

23 Then people go out to their work,
to their labor until evening.

24 How many are your works, LORD!
In wisdom you made them all;
the earth is full of your creatures.

25 There is the sea, vast and spacious,
teeming with creatures beyond
number—
living things both large and small.

26 There the ships go to and fro,
and Leviathan, which you formed to
frolic there.

27 All creatures look to you
to give them their food at the proper
time.

28 When you give it to them,
they gather it up;
when you open your hand,
they are satisfied with good things.

29 When you hide your face,
they are terrified;

---

a 4 Or angels

when you take away their breath,
    they die and return to the dust.
30 When you send your Spirit,
    they are created,
    and you renew the face of the
       ground.

31 May the glory of the Lord endure
      forever;
    may the Lord rejoice in his works—
32 he who looks at the earth, and it
      trembles,
    who touches the mountains, and
      they smoke.

33 I will sing to the Lord all my life;
    I will sing praise to my God as long
      as I live.
34 May my meditation be pleasing to
      him,
    as I rejoice in the Lord.
35 But may sinners vanish from the earth
    and the wicked be no more.

    Praise the Lord, my soul.

    Praise the Lord.[a]

Psalm 105

1 Give praise to the Lord, proclaim his
      name;
    make known among the nations
      what he has done.
2 Sing to him, sing praise to him;
    tell of all his wonderful acts.
3 Glory in his holy name;
    let the hearts of those who seek
      the Lord rejoice.
4 Look to the Lord and his strength;
    seek his face always.

5 Remember the wonders he has done,
    his miracles, and the judgments he
      pronounced,
6 you his servants, the descendants of
      Abraham,
    his chosen ones, the children of
      Jacob.
7 He is the Lord our God;
    his judgments are in all the earth.

8 He remembers his covenant forever,
    the promise he made, for a
      thousand generations,
9 the covenant he made with Abraham,
    the oath he swore to Isaac.
10 He confirmed it to Jacob as a decree,
    to Israel as an everlasting
      covenant:
11 "To you I will give the land of
      Canaan
    as the portion you will inherit."

12 When they were but few in number,
    few indeed, and strangers in it,
13 they wandered from nation to nation,
    from one kingdom to another.
14 He allowed no one to oppress
      them;
    for their sake he rebuked kings:
15 "Do not touch my anointed ones;
    do my prophets no harm."

16 He called down famine on the land
    and destroyed all their supplies of
      food;
17 and he sent a man before them—
    Joseph, sold as a slave.
18 They bruised his feet with shackles,
    his neck was put in irons,
19 till what he foretold came to pass,
    till the word of the Lord proved him
      true.
20 The king sent and released him,
    the ruler of peoples set him free.
21 He made him master of his
      household,
    ruler over all he possessed,
22 to instruct his princes as he
      pleased
    and teach his elders wisdom.

23 Then Israel entered Egypt;
    Jacob resided as a foreigner in the
      land of Ham.
24 The Lord made his people very
      fruitful;
    he made them too numerous for
      their foes,
25 whose hearts he turned to hate his
      people,
    to conspire against his servants.
26 He sent Moses his servant,
    and Aaron, whom he had chosen.
27 They performed his signs among
      them,
    his wonders in the land of Ham.

---

a 35 Hebrew Hallelu Yah; in the Septuagint this line stands at the beginning of Psalm 105.

28 He sent darkness and made the land
dark—
for had they not rebelled against his
words?
29 He turned their waters into blood,
causing their fish to die.
30 Their land teemed with frogs,
which went up into the bedrooms of
their rulers.
31 He spoke, and there came swarms of
flies,
and gnats throughout their country.
32 He turned their rain into hail,
with lightning throughout their
land;
33 he struck down their vines and fig
trees
and shattered the trees of their
country.
34 He spoke, and the locusts came,
grasshoppers without number;
35 they ate up every green thing in their
land,
ate up the produce of their soil.
36 Then he struck down all the firstborn
in their land,
the firstfruits of all their manhood.
37 He brought out Israel, laden with silver
and gold,
and from among their tribes no one
faltered.
38 Egypt was glad when they left,
because dread of Israel had fallen
on them.

39 He spread out a cloud as a covering,
and a fire to give light at night.
40 They asked, and he brought them
quail;
he fed them well with the bread of
heaven.
41 He opened the rock, and water
gushed out;
it flowed like a river in the desert.

42 For he remembered his holy promise
given to his servant Abraham.
43 He brought out his people with
rejoicing,
his chosen ones with shouts of
joy;
44 he gave them the lands of the
nations,

and they fell heir to what others had
toiled for—
45 that they might keep his precepts
and observe his laws.

Praise the LORD.ᵃ

Psalm 106

1 Praise the LORD.ᵇ

Give thanks to the LORD, for he is
good;
his love endures forever.

2 Who can proclaim the mighty acts of
the LORD
or fully declare his praise?
3 Blessed are those who act justly,
who always do what is right.

4 Remember me, LORD, when you show
favor to your people,
come to my aid when you save
them,
5 that I may enjoy the prosperity of your
chosen ones,
that I may share in the joy of your
nation
and join your inheritance in giving
praise.

6 We have sinned, even as our
ancestors did;
we have done wrong and acted
wickedly.
7 When our ancestors were in Egypt,
they gave no thought to your
miracles;
they did not remember your many
kindnesses,
and they rebelled by the sea, the
Red Sea.ᶜ
8 Yet he saved them for his name's
sake,
to make his mighty power known.
9 He rebuked the Red Sea, and it dried
up;
he led them through the depths as
through a desert.
10 He saved them from the hand of the
foe;
from the hand of the enemy he
redeemed them.

ᵃ 45 Hebrew *Hallelu Yah*   ᵇ 1 Hebrew *Hallelu Yah*; also in verse 48   ᶜ 7 Or *the Sea of Reeds*; also in verses 9 and 22

11 The waters covered their adversaries;
  not one of them survived.
12 Then they believed his promises
  and sang his praise.

13 But they soon forgot what he had
    done
  and did not wait for his plan to
    unfold.
14 In the desert they gave in to their
    craving;
  in the wilderness they put God to
    the test.
15 So he gave them what they asked for,
  but sent a wasting disease among
    them.

16 In the camp they grew envious of
    Moses
  and of Aaron, who was consecrated
    to the LORD.
17 The earth opened up and swallowed
    Dathan;
  it buried the company of Abiram.
18 Fire blazed among their followers;
  a flame consumed the wicked.
19 At Horeb they made a calf
  and worshiped an idol cast from
    metal.
20 They exchanged their glorious God
  for an image of a bull, which eats
    grass.
21 They forgot the God who saved them,
  who had done great things in Egypt,
22 miracles in the land of Ham
  and awesome deeds by the Red
    Sea.
23 So he said he would destroy them—
  had not Moses, his chosen one,
  stood in the breach before him
  to keep his wrath from destroying
    them.

24 Then they despised the pleasant land;
  they did not believe his promise.
25 They grumbled in their tents
  and did not obey the LORD.
26 So he swore to them with uplifted
    hand
  that he would make them fall in the
    wilderness,
27 make their descendants fall among
    the nations

and scatter them throughout the
    lands.

28 They yoked themselves to the Baal of
    Peor
  and ate sacrifices offered to lifeless
    gods;
29 they aroused the LORD's anger by their
    wicked deeds,
  and a plague broke out among
    them.
30 But Phinehas stood up and
    intervened,
  and the plague was checked.
31 This was credited to him as
    righteousness
  for endless generations to come.
32 By the waters of Meribah they angered
    the LORD,
  and trouble came to Moses
    because of them;
33 for they rebelled against the Spirit of
    God,
  and rash words came from Moses'
    lips.[a]

34 They did not destroy the peoples
  as the LORD had commanded
    them,
35 but they mingled with the nations
  and adopted their customs.
36 They worshiped their idols,
  which became a snare to them.
37 They sacrificed their sons
  and their daughters to false gods.
38 They shed innocent blood,
  the blood of their sons and
    daughters,
  whom they sacrificed to the idols of
    Canaan,
  and the land was desecrated by
    their blood.
39 They defiled themselves by what they
    did;
  by their deeds they prostituted
    themselves.
40 Therefore the LORD was angry with his
    people
  and abhorred his inheritance.
41 He gave them into the hands of the
    nations,
  and their foes ruled over them.

---

a 33 Or against his spirit, / and rash words came from his lips

⁴²Their enemies oppressed them
and subjected them to their power.
⁴³Many times he delivered them,
but they were bent on rebellion
and they wasted away in their sin.
⁴⁴Yet he took note of their distress
when he heard their cry;
⁴⁵for their sake he remembered his
covenant
and out of his great love he
relented.
⁴⁶He caused all who held them captive
to show them mercy.

⁴⁷Save us, Lord our God,
and gather us from the nations,
that we may give thanks to your holy
name
and glory in your praise.

⁴⁸Praise be to the Lord, the God of
Israel,
from everlasting to everlasting.

Let all the people say, "Amen!"

Praise the Lord.

BOOK V

Psalms 107–150

Psalm 107

¹Give thanks to the Lord, for he is
good;
his love endures forever.

²Let the redeemed of the Lord tell their
story—
those he redeemed from the hand
of the foe,
³those he gathered from the lands,
from east and west, from north and
south.ᵃ

⁴Some wandered in desert wastelands,
finding no way to a city where they
could settle.
⁵They were hungry and thirsty,
and their lives ebbed away.
⁶Then they cried out to the Lord in their
trouble,
and he delivered them from their
distress.

⁷He led them by a straight way
to a city where they could settle.
⁸Let them give thanks to the Lord for
his unfailing love
and his wonderful deeds for
mankind,
⁹for he satisfies the thirsty
and fills the hungry with good things.

¹⁰Some sat in darkness, in utter
darkness,
prisoners suffering in iron chains,
¹¹because they rebelled against God's
commands
and despised the plans of the Most
High.
¹²So he subjected them to bitter labor;
they stumbled, and there was no
one to help.
¹³Then they cried to the Lord in their
trouble,
and he saved them from their
distress.
¹⁴He brought them out of darkness, the
utter darkness,
and broke away their chains.
¹⁵Let them give thanks to the Lord for
his unfailing love
and his wonderful deeds for
mankind,
¹⁶for he breaks down gates of bronze
and cuts through bars of iron.

¹⁷Some became fools through their
rebellious ways
and suffered affliction because of
their iniquities.
¹⁸They loathed all food
and drew near the gates of death.

*Let them
give thanks to the Lord …
for he satisfies the thirsty
and fills the hungry with
good things.*
Psalm 107:8-9

ᵃ 3 Hebrew *north and the sea*

19 Then they cried to the Lord in their trouble,
and he saved them from their distress.
20 He sent out his word and healed them;
he rescued them from the grave.
21 Let them give thanks to the Lord for his unfailing love
and his wonderful deeds for mankind.
22 Let them sacrifice thank offerings
and tell of his works with songs of joy.

23 Some went out on the sea in ships;
they were merchants on the mighty waters.
24 They saw the works of the Lord,
his wonderful deeds in the deep.
25 For he spoke and stirred up a tempest
that lifted high the waves.
26 They mounted up to the heavens and went down to the depths;
in their peril their courage melted away.
27 They reeled and staggered like drunkards;
they were at their wits' end.
28 Then they cried out to the Lord in their trouble,
and he brought them out of their distress.
29 He stilled the storm to a whisper;
the waves of the sea[a] were hushed.
30 They were glad when it grew calm,
and he guided them to their desired haven.
31 Let them give thanks to the Lord for his unfailing love
and his wonderful deeds for mankind.
32 Let them exalt him in the assembly of the people
and praise him in the council of the elders.

33 He turned rivers into a desert,
flowing springs into thirsty ground,
34 and fruitful land into a salt waste,
because of the wickedness of those who lived there.
35 He turned the desert into pools of water
and the parched ground into flowing springs;
36 there he brought the hungry to live,
and they founded a city where they could settle.
37 They sowed fields and planted vineyards
that yielded a fruitful harvest;
38 he blessed them, and their numbers greatly increased,
and he did not let their herds diminish.

39 Then their numbers decreased, and they were humbled
by oppression, calamity and sorrow;
40 he who pours contempt on nobles
made them wander in a trackless waste.
41 But he lifted the needy out of their affliction
and increased their families like flocks.
42 The upright see and rejoice,
but all the wicked shut their mouths.

43 Let the one who is wise heed these things
and ponder the loving deeds of the Lord.

Psalm 108[b]

A song. A psalm of David.

1 My heart, O God, is steadfast;
I will sing and make music with all my soul.
2 Awake, harp and lyre!
I will awaken the dawn.
3 I will praise you, Lord, among the nations;
I will sing of you among the peoples.
4 For great is your love, higher than the heavens;
your faithfulness reaches to the skies.
5 Be exalted, O God, above the heavens;
let your glory be over all the earth.

6 Save us and help us with your right hand,

---

a 29 Dead Sea Scrolls; Masoretic Text / their waves   b In Hebrew texts 108:1-13 is numbered 108:2-14.

that those you love may be
   delivered.
7 God has spoken from his sanctuary:
   "In triumph I will parcel out
     Shechem
   and measure off the Valley of
     Sukkoth.
8 Gilead is mine, Manasseh is mine;
   Ephraim is my helmet,
   Judah is my scepter.
9 Moab is my washbasin,
   on Edom I toss my sandal;
   over Philistia I shout in triumph."

10 Who will bring me to the fortified city?
   Who will lead me to Edom?
11 Is it not you, God, you who have
     rejected us
   and no longer go out with our
     armies?
12 Give us aid against the enemy,
   for human help is worthless.
13 With God we will gain the victory,
   and he will trample down our
     enemies.

Psalm 109

For the director of music.
Of David. A psalm.

1 My God, whom I praise,
   do not remain silent,
2 for people who are wicked and
     deceitful
   have opened their mouths
     against me;
   they have spoken against me with
     lying tongues.
3 With words of hatred they surround me;
   they attack me without cause.
4 In return for my friendship they
     accuse me,
   but I am a man of prayer.
5 They repay me evil for good,
   and hatred for my friendship.

6 Appoint someone evil to oppose my
     enemy;
   let an accuser stand at his right
     hand.
7 When he is tried, let him be found
     guilty,
   and may his prayers condemn him.

8 May his days be few;
   may another take his place of
     leadership.
9 May his children be fatherless
   and his wife a widow.
10 May his children be wandering
     beggars;
   may they be driven[a] from their
     ruined homes.
11 May a creditor seize all he has;
   may strangers plunder the fruits of
     his labor.
12 May no one extend kindness to him
   or take pity on his fatherless
     children.
13 May his descendants be cut off,
   their names blotted out from the
     next generation.
14 May the iniquity of his fathers be
     remembered before the
     LORD;
   may the sin of his mother never be
     blotted out.
15 May their sins always remain before
     the LORD,
   that he may blot out their name
     from the earth.

16 For he never thought of doing a
     kindness,
   but hounded to death the poor
   and the needy and the
     brokenhearted.
17 He loved to pronounce a curse—
   may it come back on him.
   He found no pleasure in blessing—
   may it be far from him.
18 He wore cursing as his garment;
   it entered into his body like water,
   into his bones like oil.
19 May it be like a cloak wrapped about
     him,
   like a belt tied forever around
     him.
20 May this be the LORD's payment to my
     accusers,
   to those who speak evil of me.

21 But you, Sovereign LORD,
   help me for your name's sake;
   out of the goodness of your love,
     deliver me.

---

a 10 Septuagint; Hebrew *sought*

22 For I am poor and needy,
   and my heart is wounded within me.
23 I fade away like an evening shadow;
   I am shaken off like a locust.
24 My knees give way from fasting;
   my body is thin and gaunt.
25 I am an object of scorn to my accusers;
   when they see me, they shake their
      heads.
26 Help me, LORD my God;
   save me according to your unfailing
      love.
27 Let them know that it is your hand,
   that you, LORD, have done it.
28 While they curse, may you bless;
   may those who attack me be put to
      shame,
   but may your servant rejoice.
29 May my accusers be clothed with
      disgrace
   and wrapped in shame as in a
      cloak.

30 With my mouth I will greatly extol the
      LORD;
   in the great throng of worshipers I
      will praise him.
31 For he stands at the right hand of the
      needy,
   to save their lives from those who
      would condemn them.

Psalm 110

Of David. A psalm.

1 The LORD says to my lord:[a]

"Sit at my right hand
   until I make your enemies
   a footstool for your feet."

2 The LORD will extend your mighty
      scepter from Zion, saying,
   "Rule in the midst of your
      enemies!"
3 Your troops will be willing
   on your day of battle.
Arrayed in holy splendor,
   your young men will come to you
   like dew from the morning's womb.[b]

>> INSTANT ACCESS

It comes up again and again in Psalms, just like it comes up again and again in life. People gossip and ridicule you. And it hurts. You can feel the hurt when you read this psalm. But there's comfort here too. God is on the side of the one who is hurt, not of the gossips'. As the psalmist says, "While they curse, may you bless; may those who attack me be put to shame" (verse 28).

{Psalm 109}

4 The LORD has sworn
   and will not change his mind:
"You are a priest forever,
   in the order of Melchizedek."
5 The Lord is at your right hand[c];
   he will crush kings on the day of his
      wrath.
6 He will judge the nations, heaping up
      the dead
   and crushing the rulers of the whole
      earth.
7 He will drink from a brook along the
      way,[d]
   and so he will lift his head high.

Psalm 111[e]

1 Praise the LORD.[f]

I will extol the LORD with all my heart
   in the council of the upright and in
      the assembly.

---

[a] 1 Or Lord   [b] 3 The meaning of the Hebrew for this sentence is uncertain.   [c] 5 Or My lord is at your right hand, LORD
[d] 7 The meaning of the Hebrew for this clause is uncertain.   [e] This psalm is an acrostic poem, the lines of which begin
with the successive letters of the Hebrew alphabet.   [f] 1 Hebrew Hallelu Yah

2 Great are the works of the LORD;
   they are pondered by all who delight
      in them.
3 Glorious and majestic are his deeds,
   and his righteousness endures
      forever.
4 He has caused his wonders to be
      remembered;
   the LORD is gracious and
      compassionate.
5 He provides food for those who fear
      him;
   he remembers his covenant forever.
6 He has shown his people the power of
      his works,
   giving them the lands of other
      nations.
7 The works of his hands are faithful
      and just;
   all his precepts are trustworthy.
8 They are established for ever and
      ever,
   enacted in faithfulness and
      uprightness.
9 He provided redemption for his
      people;
   he ordained his covenant forever—
      holy and awesome is his name.
10 The fear of the LORD is the beginning
      of wisdom;
   all who follow his precepts have
      good understanding.
   To him belongs eternal praise.

Psalm 112[a]

1 Praise the LORD.[b]

Blessed are those who fear the LORD,
   who find great delight in his
      commands.
2 Their children will be mighty in the
      land;
   the generation of the upright will be
      blessed.
3 Wealth and riches are in their houses,
   and their righteousness endures
      forever.
4 Even in darkness light dawns for the
      upright,

for those who are gracious and
   compassionate and righteous.
5 Good will come to those who are
      generous and lend freely,
   who conduct their affairs with
      justice.
6 Surely the righteous will never be
      shaken;
   they will be remembered forever.
7 They will have no fear of bad news;
   their hearts are steadfast, trusting
      in the LORD.
8 Their hearts are secure, they will have
      no fear;
   in the end they will look in triumph
      on their foes.
9 They have freely scattered their gifts
      to the poor,
   their righteousness endures forever;
   their horn[c] will be lifted high in honor.
10 The wicked will see and be vexed,
   they will gnash their teeth and
      waste away;
   the longings of the wicked will come
      to nothing.

Psalm 113

1 Praise the LORD.[d]

Praise the LORD, you his servants;
   praise the name of the LORD.
2 Let the name of the LORD be praised,
   both now and forevermore.
3 From the rising of the sun to the place
      where it sets,
   the name of the LORD is to be
      praised.
4 The LORD is exalted over all the
      nations,
   his glory above the heavens.
5 Who is like the LORD our God,
   the One who sits enthroned on
      high,
6 who stoops down to look
   on the heavens and the earth?

7 He raises the poor from the dust
   and lifts the needy from the ash
      heap;

---

a This psalm is an acrostic poem, the lines of which begin with the successive letters of the Hebrew alphabet.
b 1 Hebrew Hallelu Yah   c 9 Horn here symbolizes dignity.   d 1 Hebrew Hallelu Yah; also in verse 9

⁸he seats them with princes,
with the princes of his people.
⁹He settles the childless woman in her
home
as a happy mother of children.

Praise the LORD.

Psalm 114

¹When Israel came out of Egypt,
Jacob from a people of foreign
tongue,
²Judah became God's sanctuary,
Israel his dominion.

³The sea looked and fled,
the Jordan turned back;
⁴the mountains leaped like rams,
the hills like lambs.

⁵Why was it, sea, that you fled?
Why, Jordan, did you turn back?
⁶Why, mountains, did you leap like rams,
you hills, like lambs?

⁷Tremble, earth, at the presence of the
Lord,
at the presence of the God of
Jacob,
⁸who turned the rock into a pool,
the hard rock into springs of water.

Psalm 115

¹Not to us, LORD, not to us
but to your name be the glory,
because of your love and
faithfulness.

²Why do the nations say,
"Where is their God?"
³Our God is in heaven;
he does whatever pleases him.
⁴But their idols are silver and gold,
made by human hands.
⁵They have mouths, but cannot speak,
eyes, but cannot see.
⁶They have ears, but cannot hear,
noses, but cannot smell.
⁷They have hands, but cannot feel,
feet, but cannot walk,
nor can they utter a sound with their
throats.

⁸Those who make them will be like
them,
and so will all who trust in them.

⁹All you Israelites, trust in the LORD—
he is their help and shield.
¹⁰House of Aaron, trust in the LORD—
he is their help and shield.
¹¹You who fear him, trust in the LORD—
he is their help and shield.

¹²The LORD remembers us and will
bless us:
He will bless his people Israel,
he will bless the house of Aaron,
¹³he will bless those who fear the
LORD—
small and great alike.

¹⁴May the LORD cause you to flourish,
both you and your children.
¹⁵May you be blessed by the LORD,
the Maker of heaven and earth.

¹⁶The highest heavens belong to the
LORD,
but the earth he has given to
mankind.
¹⁷It is not the dead who praise the LORD,
those who go down to the place of
silence;
¹⁸it is we who extol the LORD,
both now and forevermore.

Praise the LORD.ª

Psalm 116

¹I love the LORD, for he heard my voice;
he heard my cry for mercy.
²Because he turned his ear to me,
I will call on him as long as I live.

³The cords of death entangled me,
the anguish of the grave came
over me;
I was overcome by distress and
sorrow.
⁴Then I called on the name of the LORD:
"LORD, save me!"

⁵The LORD is gracious and righteous;
our God is full of compassion.
⁶The LORD protects the unwary;
when I was brought low, he
saved me.

ª 18 Hebrew *Hallelu Yah*

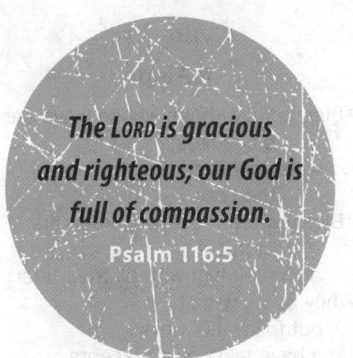

*The LORD is gracious
and righteous; our God is
full of compassion.*

Psalm 116:5

⁷Return to your rest, my soul,
for the LORD has been good to you.

⁸For you, LORD, have delivered me from
death,
my eyes from tears,
my feet from stumbling,
⁹that I may walk before the LORD
in the land of the living.

¹⁰I trusted in the LORD when I said,
"I am greatly afflicted";
¹¹in my alarm I said,
"Everyone is a liar."

¹²What shall I return to the LORD
for all his goodness to me?

¹³I will lift up the cup of salvation
and call on the name of the LORD.
¹⁴I will fulfill my vows to the LORD
in the presence of all his people.

¹⁵Precious in the sight of the LORD
is the death of his faithful
servants.
¹⁶Truly I am your servant, LORD;
I serve you just as my mother
did;
you have freed me from my
chains.

¹⁷I will sacrifice a thank offering to you
and call on the name of the LORD.
¹⁸I will fulfill my vows to the LORD
in the presence of all his people,
¹⁹in the courts of the house of the
LORD—
in your midst, Jerusalem.

Praise the LORD.ᵃ

Psalm 117

¹Praise the LORD, all you nations;
extol him, all you peoples.
²For great is his love toward us,
and the faithfulness of the LORD
endures forever.

Praise the LORD.ᵃ

Psalm 118

¹Give thanks to the LORD, for he is
good;
his love endures forever.

²Let Israel say:
"His love endures forever."
³Let the house of Aaron say:
"His love endures forever."
⁴Let those who fear the LORD say:
"His love endures forever."

⁵When hard pressed, I cried to the
LORD;
he brought me into a spacious
place.
⁶The LORD is with me; I will not be
afraid.
What can mere mortals do to me?
⁷The LORD is with me; he is my
helper.
I look in triumph on my enemies.

⁸It is better to take refuge in the LORD
than to trust in humans.
⁹It is better to take refuge in the LORD
than to trust in princes.
¹⁰All the nations surrounded me,
but in the name of the LORD I cut
them down.
¹¹They surrounded me on every side,
but in the name of the LORD I cut
them down.
¹²They swarmed around me like bees,
but they were consumed as quickly
as burning thorns;
in the name of the LORD I cut them
down.
¹³I was pushed back and about to fall,
but the LORD helped me.
¹⁴The LORD is my strength and my
defenseᵇ;
he has become my salvation.

ᵃ 19,2 Hebrew *Hallelu Yah*   ᵇ 14 Or *song*

15 Shouts of joy and victory
　　resound in the tents of the
　　righteous:
　　"The LORD's right hand has done
　　　mighty things!
16　The LORD's right hand is lifted high;
　　the LORD's right hand has done
　　　mighty things!"
17 I will not die but live,
　　and will proclaim what the LORD has
　　　done.
18 The LORD has chastened me
　　severely,
　　but he has not given me over to
　　　death.
19 Open for me the gates of the
　　righteous;
　　I will enter and give thanks to the
　　　LORD.
20 This is the gate of the LORD
　　through which the righteous may
　　　enter.
21 I will give you thanks, for you
　　answered me;
　　you have become my salvation.

22 The stone the builders rejected
　　has become the cornerstone;
23 the LORD has done this,
　　and it is marvelous in our eyes.
24 The LORD has done it this very day;
　　let us rejoice today and be glad.

25 LORD, save us!
　　LORD, grant us success!
26 Blessed is he who comes in the name
　　of the LORD.
　　From the house of the LORD we
　　　bless you.a
27 The LORD is God,
　　and he has made his light shine
　　　on us.
　　With boughs in hand, join in the festal
　　procession
　　upb to the horns of the altar.

28 You are my God, and I will praise you;
　　you are my God, and I will exalt you.
29 Give thanks to the LORD, for he is
　　good;
　　his love endures forever.

Psalm 119c

א Aleph

1 Blessed are those whose ways are
　　blameless,
　　who walk according to the law of
　　　the LORD.
2 Blessed are those who keep his
　　statutes
　　and seek him with all their heart—
3 they do no wrong
　　but follow his ways.
4 You have laid down precepts
　　that are to be fully obeyed.
5 Oh, that my ways were steadfast
　　in obeying your decrees!
6 Then I would not be put to shame
　　when I consider all your commands.
7 I will praise you with an upright heart
　　as I learn your righteous laws.
8 I will obey your decrees;
　　do not utterly forsake me.

ב Beth

9 How can a young person stay on the
　　path of purity?
　　By living according to your word.
10 I seek you with all my heart;
　　do not let me stray from your
　　　commands.
11 I have hidden your word in my
　　heart
　　that I might not sin against you.
12 Praise be to you, LORD;
　　teach me your decrees.
13 With my lips I recount
　　all the laws that come from your
　　　mouth.
14 I rejoice in following your statutes
　　as one rejoices in great riches.
15 I meditate on your precepts
　　and consider your ways.
16 I delight in your decrees;
　　I will not neglect your word.

ג Gimel

17 Be good to your servant while I
　　live,
　　that I may obey your word.

---

a 26 The Hebrew is plural.　　b 27 Or *Bind the festal sacrifice with ropes / and take it*　　c This psalm is an acrostic poem,
the stanzas of which begin with successive letters of the Hebrew alphabet; moreover, the verses of each stanza begin with
the same letter of the Hebrew alphabet.

18 Open my eyes that I may see
  wonderful things in your law.
19 I am a stranger on earth;
  do not hide your commands
    from me.
20 My soul is consumed with longing
  for your laws at all times.
21 You rebuke the arrogant, who are
    accursed,
  those who stray from your
    commands.
22 Remove from me their scorn and
    contempt,
  for I keep your statutes.
23 Though rulers sit together and slander
    me,
  your servant will meditate on your
    decrees.
24 Your statutes are my delight;
  they are my counselors.

ד **Daleth**

25 I am laid low in the dust;
  preserve my life according to your
    word.
26 I gave an account of my ways and you
    answered me;
  teach me your decrees.
27 Cause me to understand the way of
    your precepts,
  that I may meditate on your
    wonderful deeds.
28 My soul is weary with sorrow;
  strengthen me according to your
    word.
29 Keep me from deceitful ways;
  be gracious to me and teach me
    your law.
30 I have chosen the way of faithfulness;
  I set my heart on your laws.

TO THE POINT

Use God's Word

It's great to know that God's Word is trustworthy, but how do you use it? Psalm 119:105 says, "Your word is a lamp for my feet, a light on my path." For a lamp to do you any good, you have to light it and hold it so its light can show you the way. The same goes for God's Word. To do any good, you have to read it and let it show the way to live. Here is what the longest chapter in the Bible tells you about how to use God's Word:

+ Live according to its laws (Psalm 119:1).

+ Hide its words in your heart (Psalm 119:11).

+ Obey its words (Psalm 119:57).

+ Meditate on its teachings (Psalm 119:78).

+ Rejoice in its promises (Psalm 119:162).

³¹ I hold fast to your statutes, Lord;
  do not let me be put to shame.
³² I run in the path of your commands,
  for you have broadened my
    understanding.

ה He

³³ Teach me, Lord, the way of your
    decrees,
  that I may follow it to the end.^a
³⁴ Give me understanding, so that I may
    keep your law
  and obey it with all my heart.
³⁵ Direct me in the path of your
    commands,
  for there I find delight.
³⁶ Turn my heart toward your statutes
  and not toward selfish gain.
³⁷ Turn my eyes away from worthless
    things;
  preserve my life according to your
    word.^b
³⁸ Fulfill your promise to your servant,
  so that you may be feared.
³⁹ Take away the disgrace I dread,
  for your laws are good.
⁴⁰ How I long for your precepts!
  In your righteousness preserve my
    life.

ו Waw

⁴¹ May your unfailing love come to me,
    Lord,
  your salvation, according to your
    promise;
⁴² then I can answer anyone who
    taunts me,
  for I trust in your word.
⁴³ Never take your word of truth from my
    mouth,
  for I have put my hope in your
    laws.
⁴⁴ I will always obey your law,
  for ever and ever.
⁴⁵ I will walk about in freedom,
  for I have sought out your
    precepts.
⁴⁶ I will speak of your statutes before
    kings
  and will not be put to shame,

⁴⁷ for I delight in your commands
  because I love them.
⁴⁸ I reach out for your commands, which
    I love,
  that I may meditate on your
    decrees.

ז Zayin

⁴⁹ Remember your word to your
    servant,
  for you have given me hope.
⁵⁰ My comfort in my suffering is this:
  Your promise preserves my life.
⁵¹ The arrogant mock me unmercifully,
  but I do not turn from your law.
⁵² I remember, Lord, your ancient
    laws,
  and I find comfort in them.
⁵³ Indignation grips me because of the
    wicked,
  who have forsaken your law.
⁵⁴ Your decrees are the theme of my
    song
  wherever I lodge.
⁵⁵ In the night, Lord, I remember your
    name,
  that I may keep your law.
⁵⁶ This has been my practice:
  I obey your precepts.

ח Heth

⁵⁷ You are my portion, Lord;
  I have promised to obey your
    words.
⁵⁸ I have sought your face with all my
    heart;
  be gracious to me according to your
    promise.
⁵⁹ I have considered my ways
  and have turned my steps to your
    statutes.
⁶⁰ I will hasten and not delay
  to obey your commands.
⁶¹ Though the wicked bind me with
    ropes,
  I will not forget your law.
⁶² At midnight I rise to give you thanks
  for your righteous laws.
⁶³ I am a friend to all who fear you,
  to all who follow your precepts.

---

^a 33 Or *follow it for its reward* ^b 37 Two manuscripts of the Masoretic Text and Dead Sea Scrolls; most manuscripts of the Masoretic Text *life in your way*

64 The earth is filled with your love, LORD;
  teach me your decrees.

ט Teth

65 Do good to your servant
  according to your word, LORD.
66 Teach me knowledge and good
    judgment,
  for I trust your commands.
67 Before I was afflicted I went astray,
  but now I obey your word.
68 You are good, and what you do is
    good;
  teach me your decrees.
69 Though the arrogant have smeared
    me with lies,
  I keep your precepts with all my
    heart.
70 Their hearts are callous and
    unfeeling,
  but I delight in your law.
71 It was good for me to be afflicted
  so that I might learn your
    decrees.
72 The law from your mouth is more
    precious to me
  than thousands of pieces of silver
    and gold.

י Yodh

73 Your hands made me and formed me;
  give me understanding to learn your
    commands.
74 May those who fear you rejoice when
    they see me,
  for I have put my hope in your
    word.
75 I know, LORD, that your laws are
    righteous,
  and that in faithfulness you have
    afflicted me.
76 May your unfailing love be my
    comfort,
  according to your promise to your
    servant.
77 Let your compassion come to me that
    I may live,
  for your law is my delight.
78 May the arrogant be put to shame for
    wronging me without cause;
  but I will meditate on your
    precepts.

79 May those who fear you turn to me,
  those who understand your
    statutes.
80 May I wholeheartedly follow your
    decrees,
  that I may not be put to shame.

כ Kaph

81 My soul faints with longing for your
    salvation,
  but I have put my hope in your
    word.
82 My eyes fail, looking for your
    promise;
  I say, "When will you comfort me?"
83 Though I am like a wineskin in the
    smoke,
  I do not forget your decrees.
84 How long must your servant wait?
  When will you punish my
    persecutors?
85 The arrogant dig pits to trap me,
  contrary to your law.
86 All your commands are trustworthy;
  help me, for I am being persecuted
    without cause.
87 They almost wiped me from the
    earth,
  but I have not forsaken your
    precepts.
88 In your unfailing love preserve my
    life,
  that I may obey the statutes of your
    mouth.

ל Lamedh

89 Your word, LORD, is eternal;
  it stands firm in the heavens.
90 Your faithfulness continues through all
    generations;
  you established the earth, and it
    endures.
91 Your laws endure to this day,
  for all things serve you.
92 If your law had not been my delight,
  I would have perished in my
    affliction.
93 I will never forget your precepts,
  for by them you have preserved my
    life.
94 Save me, for I am yours;
  I have sought out your precepts.

95 The wicked are waiting to destroy me,
   but I will ponder your statutes.
96 To all perfection I see a limit,
   but your commands are boundless.

‌מ Mem

97 Oh, how I love your law!
   I meditate on it all day long.
98 Your commands are always with me
   and make me wiser than my
      enemies.
99 I have more insight than all my
      teachers,
   for I meditate on your statutes.
100 I have more understanding than the
      elders,
   for I obey your precepts.
101 I have kept my feet from every evil
      path
   so that I might obey your word.
102 I have not departed from your laws,
   for you yourself have taught me.
103 How sweet are your words to my taste,
   sweeter than honey to my mouth!
104 I gain understanding from your
      precepts;
   therefore I hate every wrong path.

‌נ Nun

105 Your word is a lamp for my feet,
   a light on my path.
106 I have taken an oath and
      confirmed it,
   that I will follow your righteous laws.
107 I have suffered much;
   preserve my life, LORD, according to
      your word.
108 Accept, LORD, the willing praise of my
      mouth,
   and teach me your laws.
109 Though I constantly take my life in my
      hands,
   I will not forget your law.
110 The wicked have set a snare for me,
   but I have not strayed from your
      precepts.
111 Your statutes are my heritage forever;
   they are the joy of my heart.
112 My heart is set on keeping your
      decrees
   to the very end.ᵃ

INSTANT ACCESS

Many teens today wonder what's ahead. One 15-year old writes, "What's God's plan for my life and am I on the right path?" The Bible doesn't reveal God's plans for individuals. But it does talk about being on the right path. This psalm says God's Word is "a lamp for my feet" and a "light on my path." The light in Bible-time lamps came from candles. In the span of their dim light, a person could only see enough to take the next step. Lamps weren't like flashlights that allow a person today to see a long way down the path ahead. So this verse is a reminder. Let God's Word guide your next step. Do that every day, and you'll be on the path that leads to God's plan for your life.

{Psalm 119:105}

‌ס Samekh

113 I hate double-minded people,
   but I love your law.
114 You are my refuge and my shield;
   I have put my hope in your word.
115 Away from me, you evildoers,
   that I may keep the commands of
      my God!

ᵃ 112 Or decrees / for their enduring reward

116 Sustain me, my God, according to
  your promise, and I will live;
  do not let my hopes be dashed.
117 Uphold me, and I will be delivered;
  I will always have regard for your
  decrees.
118 You reject all who stray from your
  decrees,
  for their delusions come to nothing.
119 All the wicked of the earth you
  discard like dross;
  therefore I love your statutes.
120 My flesh trembles in fear of you;
  I stand in awe of your laws.

ע Ayin

121 I have done what is righteous and
  just;
  do not leave me to my oppressors.
122 Ensure your servant's well-being;
  do not let the arrogant oppress me.
123 My eyes fail, looking for your
  salvation,
  looking for your righteous promise.
124 Deal with your servant according to
  your love
  and teach me your decrees.
125 I am your servant; give me
  discernment
  that I may understand your
  statutes.
126 It is time for you to act, LORD;
  your law is being broken.
127 Because I love your commands
  more than gold, more than pure
  gold,
128 and because I consider all your
  precepts right,
  I hate every wrong path.

פ Pe

129 Your statutes are wonderful;
  therefore I obey them.
130 The unfolding of your words gives
  light;
  it gives understanding to the
  simple.
131 I open my mouth and pant,
  longing for your commands.
132 Turn to me and have mercy on me,
  as you always do to those who love
  your name.

133 Direct my footsteps according to your
  word;
  let no sin rule over me.
134 Redeem me from human oppression,
  that I may obey your precepts.
135 Make your face shine on your
  servant
  and teach me your decrees.
136 Streams of tears flow from my
  eyes,
  for your law is not obeyed.

צ Tsadhe

137 You are righteous, LORD,
  and your laws are right.
138 The statutes you have laid down are
  righteous;
  they are fully trustworthy.
139 My zeal wears me out,
  for my enemies ignore your words.
140 Your promises have been thoroughly
  tested,
  and your servant loves them.
141 Though I am lowly and despised,
  I do not forget your precepts.
142 Your righteousness is everlasting
  and your law is true.
143 Trouble and distress have come
  upon me,
  but your commands give me
  delight.
144 Your statutes are always righteous;
  give me understanding that I may
  live.

ק Qoph

145 I call with all my heart; answer me,
  LORD,
  and I will obey your decrees.
146 I call out to you; save me
  and I will keep your statutes.
147 I rise before dawn and cry for
  help;
  I have put my hope in your word.
148 My eyes stay open through the
  watches of the night,
  that I may meditate on your
  promises.
149 Hear my voice in accordance with
  your love;
  preserve my life, LORD, according to
  your laws.

150 Those who devise wicked schemes
are near,
but they are far from your law.
151 Yet you are near, LORD,
and all your commands are true.
152 Long ago I learned from your statutes
that you established them to last
forever.

ר Resh

153 Look on my suffering and deliver me,
for I have not forgotten your law.
154 Defend my cause and redeem me;
preserve my life according to your
promise.
155 Salvation is far from the wicked,
for they do not seek out your
decrees.
156 Your compassion, LORD, is great;
preserve my life according to your
laws.
157 Many are the foes who persecute me,
but I have not turned from your
statutes.
158 I look on the faithless with loathing,
for they do not obey your word.
159 See how I love your precepts;
preserve my life, LORD, in
accordance with your love.
160 All your words are true;
all your righteous laws are
eternal.

ש Sin and Shin

161 Rulers persecute me without
cause,
but my heart trembles at your
word.
162 I rejoice in your promise
like one who finds great spoil.
163 I hate and detest falsehood
but I love your law.
164 Seven times a day I praise you
for your righteous laws.
165 Great peace have those who love
your law,
and nothing can make them
stumble.
166 I wait for your salvation, LORD,
and I follow your commands.
167 I obey your statutes,
for I love them greatly.

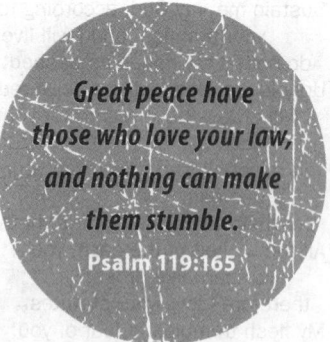

*Great peace have
those who love your law,
and nothing can make
them stumble.*

Psalm 119:165

168 I obey your precepts and your
statutes,
for all my ways are known to you.

ת Taw

169 May my cry come before you, LORD;
give me understanding according to
your word.
170 May my supplication come before you;
deliver me according to your
promise.
171 May my lips overflow with praise,
for you teach me your decrees.
172 May my tongue sing of your word,
for all your commands are
righteous.
173 May your hand be ready to help me,
for I have chosen your precepts.
174 I long for your salvation, LORD,
and your law gives me delight.
175 Let me live that I may praise you,
and may your laws sustain me.
176 I have strayed like a lost sheep.
Seek your servant,
for I have not forgotten your
commands.

Psalm 120

A song of ascents.

1 I call on the LORD in my distress,
and he answers me.
2 Save me, LORD,
from lying lips
and from deceitful tongues.

3 What will he do to you,
and what more besides,
you deceitful tongue?

4 He will punish you with a warrior's
  sharp arrows,
    with burning coals of the broom
    bush.

5 Woe to me that I dwell in Meshek,
    that I live among the tents of
    Kedar!
6 Too long have I lived
    among those who hate peace.
7 I am for peace;
    but when I speak, they are for war.

Psalm 121

A song of ascents.

1 I lift up my eyes to the mountains—
    where does my help come from?
2 My help comes from the LORD,
    the Maker of heaven and earth.

3 He will not let your foot slip—
    he who watches over you will not
    slumber;
4 indeed, he who watches over Israel
    will neither slumber nor sleep.

5 The LORD watches over you—
    the LORD is your shade at your right
    hand;
6 the sun will not harm you by day,
    nor the moon by night.

7 The LORD will keep you from all
    harm—
    he will watch over your life;
8 the LORD will watch over your coming
    and going
    both now and forevermore.

Psalm 122

A song of ascents. Of David.

1 I rejoiced with those who said to me,
    "Let us go to the house of the
    LORD."
2 Our feet are standing
    in your gates, Jerusalem.

3 Jerusalem is built like a city
    that is closely compacted
    together.
4 That is where the tribes go up—
    the tribes of the LORD—
  to praise the name of the LORD

according to the statute given to
    Israel.
5 There stand the thrones for judgment,
    the thrones of the house of David.

6 Pray for the peace of Jerusalem:
    "May those who love you be secure.
7 May there be peace within your walls
    and security within your citadels."
8 For the sake of my family and friends,
    I will say, "Peace be within you."
9 For the sake of the house of the LORD
    our God,
    I will seek your prosperity.

Psalm 123

A song of ascents.

1 I lift up my eyes to you,
    to you who sit enthroned in heaven.
2 As the eyes of slaves look to the hand
        of their master,
    as the eyes of a female slave look
        to the hand of her mistress,
  so our eyes look to the LORD our God,
    till he shows us his mercy.

3 Have mercy on us, LORD, have mercy
        on us,
    for we have endured no end of
        contempt.
4 We have endured no end
    of ridicule from the arrogant,
    of contempt from the proud.

Psalm 124

A song of ascents. Of David.

1 If the LORD had not been on our
        side—
    let Israel say—
2 if the LORD had not been on our side
    when people attacked us,
3 they would have swallowed us alive
    when their anger flared against us;
4 the flood would have engulfed us,
    the torrent would have swept
        over us,
5 the raging waters
    would have swept us away.

6 Praise be to the LORD,
    who has not let us be torn by their
    teeth.

7 We have escaped like a bird
    from the fowler's snare;
the snare has been broken,
    and we have escaped.
8 Our help is in the name of the LORD,
    the Maker of heaven and earth.

Psalm 125

A song of ascents.

1 Those who trust in the LORD are like
    Mount Zion,
which cannot be shaken but
    endures forever.
2 As the mountains surround
    Jerusalem,
so the LORD surrounds his people
    both now and forevermore.

3 The scepter of the wicked will not
    remain
    over the land allotted to the
    righteous,
for then the righteous might use
    their hands to do evil.

4 LORD, do good to those who are good,
    to those who are upright in heart.
5 But those who turn to crooked ways
    the LORD will banish with the
    evildoers.

Peace be on Israel.

Psalm 126

A song of ascents.

1 When the LORD restored the fortunes
    ofª Zion,
    we were like those who dreamed.ᵇ
2 Our mouths were filled with laughter,
    our tongues with songs of joy.
Then it was said among the nations,
    "The LORD has done great things for
    them."
3 The LORD has done great things for us,
    and we are filled with joy.

4 Restore our fortunes,ᶜ LORD,
    like streams in the Negev.
5 Those who sow with tears
    will reap with songs of joy.

6 Those who go out weeping,
    carrying seed to sow,
will return with songs of joy,
    carrying sheaves with them.

Psalm 127

A song of ascents. Of Solomon.

1 Unless the LORD builds the house,
    the builders labor in vain.
Unless the LORD watches over the
    city,
    the guards stand watch in vain.
2 In vain you rise early
    and stay up late,
toiling for food to eat—
    for he grants sleep toᵈ those he
    loves.

3 Children are a heritage from the LORD,
    offspring a reward from him.
4 Like arrows in the hands of a warrior
    are children born in one's youth.
5 Blessed is the man
    whose quiver is full of them.
They will not be put to shame
    when they contend with their
    opponents in court.

Psalm 128

A song of ascents.

1 Blessed are all who fear the LORD,
    who walk in obedience to him.
2 You will eat the fruit of your labor;
    blessings and prosperity will be
    yours.
3 Your wife will be like a fruitful vine
    within your house;
your children will be like olive shoots
    around your table.
4 Yes, this will be the blessing
    for the man who fears the LORD.

5 May the LORD bless you from Zion;
    may you see the prosperity of
    Jerusalem
all the days of your life.
6 May you live to see your children's
    children—
    peace be on Israel.

ª 1 Or LORD brought back the captives to   ᵇ 1 Or those restored to health   ᶜ 4 Or Bring back our captives
ᵈ 2 Or eat — / for while they sleep he provides for

Most teens who ask about God's plan for their lives mean, "Will I be or do something really special?" Could be. But God's plan for most believers is summed up in Psalm 128. God plans for us to do and be good, to work hard, to live with our spouse and see our families grow up. That kind of life probably won't make you a celebrity. But it sure will make you "blessed."

{Psalm 128}

Psalm 129

A song of ascents.

1 "They have greatly oppressed me from my youth,"
   let Israel say;
2 "they have greatly oppressed me from my youth,
   but they have not gained the victory over me.
3 Plowmen have plowed my back
   and made their furrows long.
4 But the LORD is righteous;
   he has cut me free from the cords of the wicked."

5 May all who hate Zion
   be turned back in shame.
6 May they be like grass on the roof,
   which withers before it can grow;
7 a reaper cannot fill his hands with it,
   nor one who gathers fill his arms.

8 May those who pass by not say to them,
   "The blessing of the LORD be on you;
   we bless you in the name of the LORD."

Psalm 130

A song of ascents.

1 Out of the depths I cry to you, LORD;
2   Lord, hear my voice.
   Let your ears be attentive
   to my cry for mercy.

3 If you, LORD, kept a record of sins,
   Lord, who could stand?
4 But with you there is forgiveness,
   so that we can, with reverence, serve you.

5 I wait for the LORD, my whole being waits,
   and in his word I put my hope.
6 I wait for the Lord
   more than watchmen wait for the morning,
   more than watchmen wait for the morning.

7 Israel, put your hope in the LORD,
   for with the LORD is unfailing love
   and with him is full redemption.
8 He himself will redeem Israel
   from all their sins.

Psalm 131

A song of ascents. Of David.

1 My heart is not proud, LORD,
   my eyes are not haughty;
   I do not concern myself with great matters
   or things too wonderful for me.
2 But I have calmed and quieted myself,
   I am like a weaned child with its mother;
   like a weaned child I am content.

3 Israel, put your hope in the LORD
   both now and forevermore.

Psalm 132

A song of ascents.

1 LORD, remember David
   and all his self-denial.

2 He swore an oath to the LORD,
he made a vow to the Mighty One of
Jacob:
3 "I will not enter my house
or go to my bed,
4 I will allow no sleep to my eyes
or slumber to my eyelids,
5 till I find a place for the LORD,
a dwelling for the Mighty One of
Jacob."

6 We heard it in Ephrathah,
we came upon it in the fields of
Jaar:[a]
7 "Let us go to his dwelling place,
let us worship at his footstool,
saying,
8 'Arise, LORD, and come to your resting
place,
you and the ark of your might.
9 May your priests be clothed with your
righteousness;
may your faithful people sing for
joy.' "

10 For the sake of your servant David,
do not reject your anointed one.

11 The LORD swore an oath to David,
a sure oath he will not revoke:
"One of your own descendants
I will place on your throne.
12 If your sons keep my covenant
and the statutes I teach them,
then their sons will sit
on your throne for ever and ever."

13 For the LORD has chosen Zion,
he has desired it for his dwelling,
saying,
14 "This is my resting place for ever and
ever;
here I will sit enthroned, for I have
desired it.
15 I will bless her with abundant
provisions;
her poor I will satisfy with food.
16 I will clothe her priests with salvation,
and her faithful people will ever sing
for joy.

17 "Here I will make a horn[b] grow for
David
and set up a lamp for my anointed
one.

18 I will clothe his enemies with shame,
but his head will be adorned with a
radiant crown."

Psalm 133

A song of ascents. Of David.

1 How good and pleasant it is
when God's people live together in
unity!

2 It is like precious oil poured on the
head,
running down on the beard,
running down on Aaron's beard,
down on the collar of his robe.
3 It is as if the dew of Hermon
were falling on Mount Zion.
For there the LORD bestows his
blessing,
even life forevermore.

Psalm 134

A song of ascents.

1 Praise the LORD, all you servants of
the LORD
who minister by night in the house
of the LORD.
2 Lift up your hands in the sanctuary
and praise the LORD.

3 May the LORD bless you from Zion,
he who is the Maker of heaven and
earth.

Psalm 135

1 Praise the LORD.[c]

Praise the name of the LORD;
praise him, you servants of the
LORD,
2 you who minister in the house of the
LORD,
in the courts of the house of our
God.

3 Praise the LORD, for the LORD is good;
sing praise to his name, for that is
pleasant.
4 For the LORD has chosen Jacob to be
his own,

---

[a] 6 Or heard of it in Ephrathah, / we found it in the fields of Jearim. (See 1 Chron. 13:5,6) (And no quotation marks around verses 7-9)   [b] 17 Horn here symbolizes strong one, that is, king.   [c] 1 Hebrew Hallelu Yah; also in verses 3 and 21

Israel to be his treasured
possession.

⁵I know that the Lord is great,
that our Lord is greater than all gods.
⁶The Lord does whatever pleases him,
in the heavens and on the earth,
in the seas and all their depths.
⁷He makes clouds rise from the ends
of the earth;
he sends lightning with the rain
and brings out the wind from his
storehouses.

⁸He struck down the firstborn of Egypt,
the firstborn of people and animals.
⁹He sent his signs and wonders into
your midst, Egypt,
against Pharaoh and all his servants.
¹⁰He struck down many nations
and killed mighty kings—
¹¹Sihon king of the Amorites,
Og king of Bashan,
and all the kings of Canaan—
¹²and he gave their land as an
inheritance,
an inheritance to his people Israel.

¹³Your name, Lord, endures forever,
your renown, Lord, through all
generations.
¹⁴For the Lord will vindicate his people
and have compassion on his
servants.

¹⁵The idols of the nations are silver and
gold,
made by human hands.
¹⁶They have mouths, but cannot speak,
eyes, but cannot see.
¹⁷They have ears, but cannot hear,
nor is there breath in their mouths.
¹⁸Those who make them will be like
them,
and so will all who trust in them.

¹⁹All you Israelites, praise the Lord;
house of Aaron, praise the Lord;
²⁰house of Levi, praise the Lord;
you who fear him, praise the Lord.
²¹Praise be to the Lord from Zion,
to him who dwells in Jerusalem.

Praise the Lord.

Psalm 136

¹Give thanks to the Lord, for he is
good.
His love endures forever.
²Give thanks to the God of gods.
His love endures forever.
³Give thanks to the Lord of lords:
His love endures forever.

⁴to him who alone does great wonders,
His love endures forever.
⁵who by his understanding made the
heavens,
His love endures forever.
⁶who spread out the earth upon the
waters,
His love endures forever.
⁷who made the great lights—
His love endures forever.
⁸the sun to govern the day,
His love endures forever.
⁹the moon and stars to govern the
night;
His love endures forever.

¹⁰to him who struck down the firstborn
of Egypt
His love endures forever.
¹¹and brought Israel out from among
them
His love endures forever.
¹²with a mighty hand and outstretched
arm;
His love endures forever.
¹³to him who divided the Red Sea[a]
asunder
His love endures forever.

> **Give thanks to the
> Lord, for he is good. His
> love endures forever.**
>
> Psalm 136:1

---

a 13 Or *the Sea of Reeds*; also in verse 15

14 and brought Israel through the midst of it,
His love endures forever.
15 but swept Pharaoh and his army into the Red Sea;
His love endures forever.
16 to him who led his people through the wilderness;
His love endures forever.
17 to him who struck down great kings,
His love endures forever.
18 and killed mighty kings—
His love endures forever.
19 Sihon king of the Amorites
His love endures forever.
20 and Og king of Bashan—
His love endures forever.
21 and gave their land as an inheritance,
His love endures forever.
22 an inheritance to his servant Israel.
His love endures forever.
23 He remembered us in our low estate
His love endures forever.
24 and freed us from our enemies.
His love endures forever.
25 He gives food to every creature.
His love endures forever.
26 Give thanks to the God of heaven.
His love endures forever.

Psalm 137

1 By the rivers of Babylon we sat and wept
when we remembered Zion.
2 There on the poplars
we hung our harps,
3 for there our captors asked us for songs,
our tormentors demanded songs of joy;
they said, "Sing us one of the songs of Zion!"
4 How can we sing the songs of the LORD
while in a foreign land?
5 If I forget you, Jerusalem,
may my right hand forget its skill.
6 May my tongue cling to the roof of my mouth
if I do not remember you,

Repeat it: *"His love endures forever."* Say again: *"His love endures forever."* Once more: *"His love endures forever."* A lot of repeats? Yes. But an important reminder. Think about what God has done for you. Then change that "His" to "Your"… and praise God for the fact that "Your love endures forever." That's the essence of praise. Talk directly to God. Focus on something special about him. And let him know how much you appreciate him.

>> INSTANT ACCESS

{Psalm 136}

if I do not consider Jerusalem
my highest joy.

7 Remember, LORD, what the Edomites did
on the day Jerusalem fell.
"Tear it down," they cried,
"tear it down to its foundations!"
8 Daughter Babylon, doomed to destruction,
happy is the one who repays you
according to what you have done to us.
9 Happy is the one who seizes your infants
and dashes them against the rocks.

Psalm 138

Of David.

1 I will praise you, LORD, with all my heart;

before the "gods" I will sing your
    praise.
2 I will bow down toward your holy temple
    and will praise your name
for your unfailing love and your
    faithfulness,
for you have so exalted your solemn
    decree
that it surpasses your fame.
3 When I called, you answered me;
    you greatly emboldened me.

4 May all the kings of the earth praise
    you, LORD,
when they hear what you have
    decreed.
5 May they sing of the ways of the LORD,
    for the glory of the LORD is great.

6 Though the LORD is exalted, he looks
    kindly on the lowly;

though lofty, he sees them from
    afar.
7 Though I walk in the midst of trouble,
    you preserve my life.
You stretch out your hand against the
    anger of my foes;
with your right hand you save me.
8 The LORD will vindicate me;
    your love, LORD, endures forever—
do not abandon the works of your
    hands.

Psalm 139

For the director of music. Of David. A psalm.

1 You have searched me, LORD,
    and you know me.
2 You know when I sit and when I rise;
    you perceive my thoughts from afar.

TO THE POINT

God Is Pro-life

The whole abortion debate hinges on one issue. Is a fetus really part of the woman's body, so she can do what she chooses with it? Or is the fetus a separate, distinct human being?

Every human being throughout history has had a unique, individual genetic code stamped on every cell in his or her body. Both the mother and the fetus she carries have a genetic code stamped on their genes and chromosomes. Are they the same? No! The fetus's genetic code is different from the mother's. To say a woman can do whatever she wants with her own body may be true. But it is not true that a fetus is merely part of the mother's body.

As Psalm 139 teaches, even in his mother's womb, David was David, a unique person being shaped by God for a special role in God's plan.

3 You discern my going out and my lying
     down;
   you are familiar with all my
     ways.
4 Before a word is on my tongue
   you, LORD, know it completely.
5 You hem me in behind and before,
   and you lay your hand upon me.
6 Such knowledge is too wonderful
     for me,
   too lofty for me to attain.

7 Where can I go from your Spirit?
   Where can I flee from your
     presence?
8 If I go up to the heavens, you are
     there;
   if I make my bed in the depths, you
     are there.
9 If I rise on the wings of the dawn,
   if I settle on the far side of the
     sea,
10 even there your hand will guide me,
   your right hand will hold me fast.
11 If I say, "Surely the darkness will
     hide me
   and the light become night
     around me,"
12 even the darkness will not be dark to
     you;
   the night will shine like the day,
   for darkness is as light to you.

13 For you created my inmost being;
   you knit me together in my mother's
     womb.
14 I praise you because I am fearfully
     and wonderfully made;
   your works are wonderful,
   I know that full well.
15 My frame was not hidden from you
   when I was made in the secret
     place,
   when I was woven together in the
     depths of the earth.
16 Your eyes saw my unformed body;
   all the days ordained for me were
     written in your book
   before one of them came to be.
17 How precious to me are your
     thoughts,a God!
   How vast is the sum of them!

INSTANT ACCESS

Ever get really down and feel like no one understands you? Whenever you do, it's a good time to read Psalm 139:13–16. These verses remind you that God understands you better than you understand yourself. Best of all, God loves you and watches over you. God is all around you. He has laid his hand on you (verse 5). You are his, and he is yours.

{Psalm 139:13–16}

18 Were I to count them,
   they would outnumber the grains of
     sand—
   when I awake, I am still with you.

19 If only you, God, would slay the
     wicked!
   Away from me, you who are
     bloodthirsty!
20 They speak of you with evil intent;
   your adversaries misuse your
     name.
21 Do I not hate those who hate you,
     LORD,
   and abhor those who are in
     rebellion against you?
22 I have nothing but hatred for them;
   I count them my enemies.
23 Search me, God, and know my
     heart;
   test me and know my anxious
     thoughts.
24 See if there is any offensive way
     in me,
   and lead me in the way
     everlasting.

---

a 17 Or How amazing are your thoughts concerning me

Psalm 140[a]

For the director of music. A psalm of David.

¹Rescue me, LORD, from evildoers;
  protect me from the violent,
²who devise evil plans in their hearts
  and stir up war every day.
³They make their tongues as sharp as
    a serpent's;
  the poison of vipers is on their
    lips.[b]

⁴Keep me safe, LORD, from the hands
    of the wicked;
  protect me from the violent,
  who devise ways to trip my feet.
⁵The arrogant have hidden a snare for
    me;
  they have spread out the cords of
    their net
  and have set traps for me along my
    path.

⁶I say to the LORD, "You are my God."
  Hear, LORD, my cry for mercy.
⁷Sovereign LORD, my strong deliverer,
  you shield my head in the day of
    battle.
⁸Do not grant the wicked their desires,
    LORD;
  do not let their plans succeed.

⁹Those who surround me proudly rear
    their heads;
  may the mischief of their lips engulf
    them.
¹⁰May burning coals fall on them;
  may they be thrown into the fire,
  into miry pits, never to rise.
¹¹May slanderers not be established in
    the land;
  may disaster hunt down the
    violent.

¹²I know that the LORD secures justice
    for the poor
  and upholds the cause of the
    needy.
¹³Surely the righteous will praise your
    name,
  and the upright will live in your
    presence.

Psalm 141

A psalm of David.

¹I call to you, LORD, come quickly to me;
  hear me when I call to you.
²May my prayer be set before you like
    incense;
  may the lifting up of my hands be
    like the evening sacrifice.

³Set a guard over my mouth, LORD;
  keep watch over the door of my lips.
⁴Do not let my heart be drawn to what
    is evil
  so that I take part in wicked deeds
along with those who are evildoers;
  do not let me eat their delicacies.

⁵Let a righteous man strike me—that
    is a kindness;
  let him rebuke me—that is oil on
    my head.
My head will not refuse it,
  for my prayer will still be against the
    deeds of evildoers.

⁶Their rulers will be thrown down from
    the cliffs,
  and the wicked will learn that my
    words were well spoken.
⁷They will say, "As one plows and
    breaks up the earth,
  so our bones have been scattered
    at the mouth of the grave."

⁸But my eyes are fixed on you,
    Sovereign LORD;
  in you I take refuge—do not give
    me over to death.
⁹Keep me safe from the traps set by
    evildoers,
  from the snares they have laid
    for me.
¹⁰Let the wicked fall into their own nets,
  while I pass by in safety.

Psalm 142[c]

A *maskil*[d] of David. When he was in the
cave. A prayer.

¹I cry aloud to the LORD;
  I lift up my voice to the LORD for
    mercy.

---

a In Hebrew texts 140:1-13 is numbered 140:2-14.   b 3 The Hebrew has *Selah* (a word of uncertain meaning) here and at
the end of verses 5 and 8.   c In Hebrew texts 142:1-7 is numbered 142:2-8.   d Title: Probably a literary or musical term

2I pour out before him my complaint;
   before him I tell my trouble.

3When my spirit grows faint within me,
   it is you who watch over my way.
In the path where I walk
   people have hidden a snare for me.
4Look and see, there is no one at my
      right hand;
   no one is concerned for me.
I have no refuge;
   no one cares for my life.

5I cry to you, LORD;
   I say, "You are my refuge,
   my portion in the land of the
      living."

6Listen to my cry,
   for I am in desperate need;
rescue me from those who
      pursue me,
   for they are too strong for me.
7Set me free from my prison,
   that I may praise your name.
Then the righteous will gather
      about me
   because of your goodness to me.

Psalm 143

A psalm of David.

1LORD, hear my prayer,
   listen to my cry for mercy;
in your faithfulness and righteousness
   come to my relief.
2Do not bring your servant into
      judgment,
   for no one living is righteous before
      you.
3The enemy pursues me,
   he crushes me to the ground;
he makes me dwell in the darkness
   like those long dead.
4So my spirit grows faint within me;
   my heart within me is dismayed.
5I remember the days of long ago;
   I meditate on all your works
   and consider what your hands have
      done.
6I spread out my hands to you;
   I thirst for you like a parched land.*a*

7Answer me quickly, LORD;
   my spirit fails.
Do not hide your face from me
   or I will be like those who go down
      to the pit.
8Let the morning bring me word of your
      unfailing love,
   for I have put my trust in you.
Show me the way I should go,
   for to you I entrust my life.
9Rescue me from my enemies, LORD,
   for I hide myself in you.
10Teach me to do your will,
   for you are my God;
may your good Spirit
   lead me on level ground.

11For your name's sake, LORD, preserve
      my life;
   in your righteousness, bring me out
      of trouble.
12In your unfailing love, silence my
      enemies;
   destroy all my foes,
   for I am your servant.

Psalm 144

Of David.

1Praise be to the LORD my Rock,
   who trains my hands for war,
   my fingers for battle.
2He is my loving God and my fortress,
   my stronghold and my deliverer,
my shield, in whom I take refuge,
   who subdues peoples*b* under me.

3LORD, what are human beings that you
      care for them,
   mere mortals that you think of
      them?
4They are like a breath;
   their days are like a fleeting
      shadow.

5Part your heavens, LORD, and come
      down;
   touch the mountains, so that they
      smoke.
6Send forth lightning and scatter the
      enemy;
   shoot your arrows and rout them.

---

a 6 The Hebrew has *Selah* (a word of uncertain meaning) here.   *b* 2 Many manuscripts of the Masoretic Text, Dead Sea Scrolls, Aquila, Jerome and Syriac; most manuscripts of the Masoretic Text *subdues my people*

7 Reach down your hand from on high;
    deliver me and rescue me
from the mighty waters,
    from the hands of foreigners
8 whose mouths are full of lies,
    whose right hands are deceitful.

9 I will sing a new song to you, my
        God;
    on the ten-stringed lyre I will make
        music to you,
10 to the One who gives victory to kings,
    who delivers his servant David.

From the deadly sword 11 deliver me;
    rescue me from the hands of
        foreigners
whose mouths are full of lies,
    whose right hands are deceitful.

12 Then our sons in their youth
    will be like well-nurtured plants,
and our daughters will be like pillars
    carved to adorn a palace.
13 Our barns will be filled
    with every kind of provision.
Our sheep will increase by
        thousands,
    by tens of thousands in our fields;
14   our oxen will draw heavy loads. *a*
There will be no breaching of walls,
    no going into captivity,
    no cry of distress in our streets.
15 Blessed is the people of whom this is
        true;
    blessed is the people whose God is
        the LORD.

Psalm 145 *b*

A psalm of praise. Of David.

1 I will exalt you, my God the King;
    I will praise your name for ever and
        ever.
2 Every day I will praise you
    and extol your name for ever and
        ever.
3 Great is the LORD and most worthy of
        praise;
    his greatness no one can fathom.

4 One generation commends your works
        to another;
    they tell of your mighty acts.
5 They speak of the glorious splendor of
        your majesty—
    and I will meditate on your
        wonderful works. *c*
6 They tell of the power of your
        awesome works—
    and I will proclaim your great
        deeds.
7 They celebrate your abundant
        goodness
    and joyfully sing of your
        righteousness.

8 The LORD is gracious and
        compassionate,
    slow to anger and rich in love.

9 The LORD is good to all;
    he has compassion on all he has
        made.
10 All your works praise you, LORD;
    your faithful people extol you.
11 They tell of the glory of your kingdom
    and speak of your might,
12 so that all people may know of your
        mighty acts
    and the glorious splendor of your
        kingdom.
13 Your kingdom is an everlasting
        kingdom,
    and your dominion endures through
        all generations.

The LORD is trustworthy in all he
        promises
    and faithful in all he does. *d*
14 The LORD upholds all who fall
    and lifts up all who are bowed
        down.
15 The eyes of all look to you,
    and you give them their food at the
        proper time.
16 You open your hand
    and satisfy the desires of every
        living thing.

17 The LORD is righteous in all his ways
    and faithful in all he does.

---

a 14 Or *our chieftains will be firmly established*   *b* This psalm is an acrostic poem, the verses of which (including
verse 13b) begin with the successive letters of the Hebrew alphabet.   *c 5* Dead Sea Scrolls and Syriac (see also
Septuagint); Masoretic Text *On the glorious splendor of your majesty / and on your wonderful works I will meditate*
d 13 One manuscript of the Masoretic Text, Dead Sea Scrolls and Syriac (see also Septuagint); most manuscripts of the
Masoretic Text do not have the last two lines of verse 13.

The Lord is trustworthy in all he promises and faithful in all he does.

Psalm 145:13

18 The Lord is near to all who call on
   him,
   to all who call on him in truth.
19 He fulfills the desires of those who
   fear him;
   he hears their cry and saves
   them.
20 The Lord watches over all who love
   him,
   but all the wicked he will destroy.

21 My mouth will speak in praise of the
   Lord.
   Let every creature praise his holy
   name
   for ever and ever.

Psalm 146

1 Praise the Lord.[a]

Praise the Lord, my soul.

2 I will praise the Lord all my life;
   I will sing praise to my God as long
   as I live.
3 Do not put your trust in princes,
   in human beings, who cannot save.
4 When their spirit departs, they return
   to the ground;
   on that very day their plans come to
   nothing.
5 Blessed are those whose help is the
   God of Jacob,
   whose hope is in the Lord their
   God.

6 He is the Maker of heaven and earth,
   the sea, and everything in them—
   he remains faithful forever.

7 He upholds the cause of the
   oppressed
   and gives food to the hungry.
   The Lord sets prisoners free,
8   the Lord gives sight to the blind,
   the Lord lifts up those who are bowed
   down,
   the Lord loves the righteous.
9 The Lord watches over the foreigner
   and sustains the fatherless and the
   widow,
   but he frustrates the ways of the
   wicked.

10 The Lord reigns forever,
   your God, O Zion, for all
   generations.

Praise the Lord.

Psalm 147

1 Praise the Lord.[b]

How good it is to sing praises to our
   God,
   how pleasant and fitting to praise
   him!

2 The Lord builds up Jerusalem;
   he gathers the exiles of Israel.
3 He heals the brokenhearted
   and binds up their wounds.
4 He determines the number of the
   stars
   and calls them each by name.
5 Great is our Lord and mighty in power;
   his understanding has no limit.
6 The Lord sustains the humble
   but casts the wicked to the ground.

7 Sing to the Lord with grateful praise;
   make music to our God on the harp.

8 He covers the sky with clouds;
   he supplies the earth with rain
   and makes grass grow on the hills.
9 He provides food for the cattle
   and for the young ravens when they
   call.

10 His pleasure is not in the strength of
   the horse,
   nor his delight in the legs of the
   warrior;

---

a 1 Hebrew *Hallelu Yah*; also in verse 10   b 1 Hebrew *Hallelu Yah*; also in verse 20

> I have been sexually abused. Sometimes I feel so angry I want to die. I feel used and worthless. Is there anything I can do?
>
> **>> Alone**

Dear Jordan

Dear Friend,

There are some things you must do. First, you need to try to make sure this doesn't happen again. You probably have feelings of great shame. But the shame is not yours. It belongs to the person who did this. You must tell someone that you trust. If that person won't believe you, tell someone else. No one deserves to be sexually abused. Most victims are abused by someone they know. The person who abused you might have threatened you or told you it was your fault. It was NOT your fault. That is a lie to keep you quiet. Tell a parent, your doctor, your guidance counselor … tell someone.

Second, pray often. Pour out your heart to God. He made you, and he will heal you. Psalm 147:3 has a wonderful promise for you: "He heals the brokenhearted and binds up their wounds."

Third, get some help. A good counselor or therapist can help you work through the terrible feelings you have. You deserve to be angry. And you deserve to get help to work through those feelings as well.

I am saddened when I read letters such as yours. I know God is very saddened also. Be brave and ask for help. Do not believe the lies this person tells you. Do not let fear or embarrassment stop you from protecting yourself.

God bless you.

Jordan

11 the Lord delights in those who fear
      him,
    who put their hope in his unfailing
      love.

12 Extol the Lord, Jerusalem;
    praise your God, Zion.

13 He strengthens the bars of your gates
    and blesses your people within you.
14 He grants peace to your borders
    and satisfies you with the finest of
      wheat.

15 He sends his command to the earth;
    his word runs swiftly.
16 He spreads the snow like wool
    and scatters the frost like ashes.
17 He hurls down his hail like pebbles.
    Who can withstand his icy blast?
18 He sends his word and melts them;
    he stirs up his breezes, and the
      waters flow.

19 He has revealed his word to Jacob,
    his laws and decrees to Israel.
20 He has done this for no other nation;
    they do not know his laws.ᵃ

    Praise the Lord.

Psalm 148

1 Praise the Lord.ᵇ

  Praise the Lord from the heavens;
    praise him in the heights above.
2 Praise him, all his angels;
    praise him, all his heavenly hosts.
3 Praise him, sun and moon;
    praise him, all you shining stars.
4 Praise him, you highest heavens
    and you waters above the skies.

5 Let them praise the name of the Lord,
    for at his command they were
      created,
6 and he established them for ever and
      ever—
    he issued a decree that will never
      pass away.

7 Praise the Lord from the earth,
    you great sea creatures and all
      ocean depths,

8 lightning and hail, snow and clouds,
    stormy winds that do his bidding,
9 you mountains and all hills,
    fruit trees and all cedars,
10 wild animals and all cattle,
    small creatures and flying birds,
11 kings of the earth and all nations,
    you princes and all rulers on earth,
12 young men and women,
    old men and children.

13 Let them praise the name of the Lord,
    for his name alone is exalted;
    his splendor is above the earth and
      the heavens.
14 And he has raised up for his people a
      horn,ᶜ
    the praise of all his faithful
      servants,
    of Israel, the people close to his
      heart.

    Praise the Lord.

Psalm 149

1 Praise the Lord.ᵈ

  Sing to the Lord a new song,
    his praise in the assembly of his
      faithful people.

2 Let Israel rejoice in their Maker;
    let the people of Zion be glad in
      their King.
3 Let them praise his name with
      dancing
    and make music to him with timbrel
      and harp.
4 For the Lord takes delight in his
      people;
    he crowns the humble with victory.
5 Let his faithful people rejoice in this
      honor
    and sing for joy on their beds.

6 May the praise of God be in their
      mouths
    and a double-edged sword in their
      hands,
7 to inflict vengeance on the nations
    and punishment on the peoples,
8 to bind their kings with fetters,
    their nobles with shackles of iron,

ᵃ 20 Masoretic Text; Dead Sea Scrolls and Septuagint *nation; / he has not made his laws known to them*   ᵇ 1 Hebrew
Hallelu Yah; also in verse 14   ᶜ 14 *Horn* here symbolizes strength.   ᵈ 1 Hebrew *Hallelu Yah*; also in verse 9

9 to carry out the sentence written
against them—
this is the glory of all his faithful
people.

Praise the LORD.

Psalm 150

1 Praise the LORD.[a]

Praise God in his sanctuary;
praise him in his mighty heavens.
2 Praise him for his acts of power;
praise him for his surpassing
greatness.

3 Praise him with the sounding of the
trumpet,
praise him with the harp and lyre,
4 praise him with timbrel and dancing,
praise him with the strings and
pipe,
5 praise him with the clash of
cymbals,
praise him with resounding
cymbals.

6 Let everything that has breath praise
the LORD.

Praise the LORD.

---

[a] 1 Hebrew *Hallelu Yah*; also in verse 6

PROVERBS

preview

Solomon contributes many of the proverbs. The collection is finished about 250 years after Solomon dies.

To "fear the LORD" means to show him respect by living a moral life.

Good Advice.

How can you get along with someone who doesn't like you? What is the best way to make friends? Lots of good advice is what you'll find in the book of Proverbs.

Proverbs are short sayings that help people make wise choices. The advice found in Proverbs makes good sense for both Christians and non-Christians. Take, for example, "a gentle answer turns away wrath" (Proverbs 15:1). It's better to be polite than to yell back insults when someone is angry at you. Usually this will stop a fight. But not always. Proverbs describe what usually happens, not necessarily what God promises to do.

》》WISDOM BEATS KNOWLEDGE
Its importance described, Proverbs 2

》》DON'T BE A DUMB OX
Don't go for the wrong woman, says Proverbs 7:6–27

》》TELL THE TRUTH? WHY?
See Proverbs 6:16–17; 12:17–19; 17:4,20

》》WANT TO GET RICH QUICK?
Don't try this at home. Proverbs 10:4; 11:4,28; 15:16

During the years the proverbs are being collected, the *Iliad* and *Odyssey* are written down. Carthage is founded as a Phoenician trade colony. Tradition says Rome is founded by Romulus. Mayans spread into the Yucatan peninsula.

Purpose and Theme

1 The proverbs of Solomon son of David, king of Israel:

2 for gaining wisdom and instruction;
  for understanding words of insight;
3 for receiving instruction in prudent
    behavior,
  doing what is right and just and fair;
4 for giving prudence to those who are
    simple,*a*
  knowledge and discretion to the
    young—
5 let the wise listen and add to their
    learning,
  and let the discerning get
    guidance—
6 for understanding proverbs and
    parables,
  the sayings and riddles of the
    wise.*b*

7 The fear of the Lord is the beginning
    of knowledge,
  but fools*c* despise wisdom and
    instruction.

Prologue: Exhortations to Embrace Wisdom

Warning Against the Invitation of Sinful Men

8 Listen, my son, to your father's
    instruction
  and do not forsake your mother's
    teaching.
9 They are a garland to grace your
    head
  and a chain to adorn your neck.

10 My son, if sinful men entice you,
  do not give in to them.
11 If they say, "Come along with us;
  let's lie in wait for innocent blood,
  let's ambush some harmless
    soul;
12 let's swallow them alive, like the
    grave,
  and whole, like those who go down
    to the pit;

13 we will get all sorts of valuable things
    and fill our houses with plunder;
14 cast lots with us;
  we will all share the loot"—
15 my son, do not go along with them,
  do not set foot on their paths;
16 for their feet rush into evil,
  they are swift to shed blood.
17 How useless to spread a net
  where every bird can see it!
18 These men lie in wait for their own
    blood;
  they ambush only themselves!
19 Such are the paths of all who go after
    ill-gotten gain;
  it takes away the life of those who
    get it.

Wisdom's Rebuke

20 Out in the open wisdom calls aloud,
  she raises her voice in the public
    square;
21 on top of the wall*d* she cries out,
  at the city gate she makes her
    speech:

22 "How long will you who are simple
    love your simple ways?
  How long will mockers delight in
    mockery
  and fools hate knowledge?
23 Repent at my rebuke!
  Then I will pour out my thoughts to
    you,
  I will make known to you my
    teachings.
24 But since you refuse to listen when I
    call
  and no one pays attention when I
    stretch out my hand,
25 since you disregard all my advice
  and do not accept my rebuke,
26 I in turn will laugh when disaster
    strikes you;
  I will mock when calamity overtakes
    you—
27 when calamity overtakes you like a
    storm,
  when disaster sweeps over you like
    a whirlwind,

---

a 4 The Hebrew word rendered *simple* in Proverbs denotes a person who is gullible, without moral direction and inclined to evil.   *b* 6 Or *understanding a proverb, namely, a parable, / and the sayings of the wise, their riddles*   *c* 7 The Hebrew words rendered *fool* in Proverbs, and often elsewhere in the Old Testament, denote a person who is morally deficient.
d 21 Septuagint; Hebrew / *at noisy street corners*

when distress and trouble
overwhelm you.

28 "Then they will call to me but I will not
answer;
they will look for me but will not
find me,
29 since they hated knowledge
and did not choose to fear the
LORD.
30 Since they would not accept my
advice
and spurned my rebuke,
31 they will eat the fruit of their ways
and be filled with the fruit of their
schemes.
32 For the waywardness of the simple will
kill them,
and the complacency of fools will
destroy them;

33 but whoever listens to me will live in
safety
and be at ease, without fear of
harm."

Moral Benefits of Wisdom

2 My son, if you accept my words
and store up my commands within
you,
2 turning your ear to wisdom
and applying your heart to
understanding—
3 indeed, if you call out for insight
and cry aloud for understanding,
4 and if you look for it as for silver
and search for it as for hidden
treasure,
5 then you will understand the fear of
the LORD
and find the knowledge of God.

TO THE POINT

God Gives Advice

Most teens don't want advice from adults. Especially from
parents! Sure they've lived longer, you say, but do they really
understand the world I live in?

Of course, you can't say that about God. When you read God's
Word, you listen to God and learn how to live right every day.
What will you gain if you read the Bible for advice?

• You will understand what is right and just
(Proverbs 2:9).

• You will gain wisdom and be protected by it
(Proverbs 2:10–11).

• You will be saved from the ways of the wicked
(Proverbs 2:12).

The Bible is filled with treasures that can be yours if only you
look (Proverbs 2:4).

⁶ For the LORD gives wisdom;
from his mouth come knowledge
and understanding.
⁷ He holds success in store for the
upright,
he is a shield to those whose walk
is blameless,
⁸ for he guards the course of the just
and protects the way of his faithful
ones.

⁹ Then you will understand what is right
and just
and fair—every good path.
¹⁰ For wisdom will enter your heart,
and knowledge will be pleasant to
your soul.
¹¹ Discretion will protect you,
and understanding will guard you.

¹² Wisdom will save you from the ways of
wicked men,
from men whose words are
perverse,
¹³ who have left the straight paths
to walk in dark ways,
¹⁴ who delight in doing wrong
and rejoice in the perverseness of
evil,
¹⁵ whose paths are crooked
and who are devious in their ways.

¹⁶ Wisdom will save you also from the
adulterous woman,
from the wayward woman with her
seductive words,
¹⁷ who has left the partner of her youth
and ignored the covenant she made
before God.ᵃ
¹⁸ Surely her house leads down to
death
and her paths to the spirits of the
dead.
¹⁹ None who go to her return
or attain the paths of life.
²⁰ Thus you will walk in the ways of the
good
and keep to the paths of the
righteous.
²¹ For the upright will live in the land,
and the blameless will remain in it;

²² but the wicked will be cut off from the
land,
and the unfaithful will be torn
from it.

Wisdom Bestows Well-Being

3 My son, do not forget my teaching,
but keep my commands in your
heart,
² for they will prolong your life many
years
and bring you peace and prosperity.

³ Let love and faithfulness never leave
you;
bind them around your neck,
write them on the tablet of your
heart.
⁴ Then you will win favor and a good
name
in the sight of God and man.

⁵ Trust in the LORD with all your heart
and lean not on your own
understanding;
⁶ in all your ways submit to him,
and he will make your paths
straight.ᵇ

⁷ Do not be wise in your own eyes;
fear the LORD and shun evil.
⁸ This will bring health to your body
and nourishment to your bones.

⁹ Honor the LORD with your wealth,
with the firstfruits of all your
crops;
¹⁰ then your barns will be filled to
overflowing,
and your vats will brim over with
new wine.

¹¹ My son, do not despise the LORD's
discipline,
and do not resent his rebuke,
¹² because the LORD disciplines those he
loves,
as a father the son he delights in.ᶜ
¹³ Blessed are those who find wisdom,
those who gain understanding,
¹⁴ for she is more profitable than silver
and yields better returns than gold.

ᵃ 17 Or covenant of her God ᵇ 6 Or will direct your paths ᶜ 12 Hebrew; Septuagint loves, / and he chastens everyone
he accepts as his child

15 She is more precious than rubies;
　　nothing you desire can compare
　　　with her.
16 Long life is in her right hand;
　　in her left hand are riches and
　　　honor.
17 Her ways are pleasant ways,
　　and all her paths are peace.
18 She is a tree of life to those who take
　　hold of her;
　　those who hold her fast will be
　　　blessed.

19 By wisdom the LORD laid the earth's
　　foundations,
　　by understanding he set the
　　　heavens in place;
20 by his knowledge the watery depths
　　were divided,
　　and the clouds let drop the dew.

21 My son, do not let wisdom and
　　understanding out of your
　　　sight,
　　preserve sound judgment and
　　　discretion;
22 they will be life for you,
　　an ornament to grace your neck.
23 Then you will go on your way in safety,
　　and your foot will not stumble.
24 When you lie down, you will not be
　　afraid;
　　when you lie down, your sleep will
　　　be sweet.
25 Have no fear of sudden disaster
　　or of the ruin that overtakes the
　　　wicked,
26 for the LORD will be at your side
　　and will keep your foot from being
　　　snared.

27 Do not withhold good from those to
　　whom it is due,
　　when it is in your power to act.
28 Do not say to your neighbor,
　　"Come back tomorrow and I'll give
　　it to you" —
　　when you already have it with you.
29 Do not plot harm against your
　　neighbor,
　　who lives trustfully near you.
30 Do not accuse anyone for no
　　reason —
　　when they have done you no harm.

31 Do not envy the violent
　　or choose any of their ways.
32 For the LORD detests the perverse
　　but takes the upright into his
　　　confidence.
33 The LORD's curse is on the house of
　　the wicked,
　　but he blesses the home of the
　　　righteous.
34 He mocks proud mockers
　　but shows favor to the humble and
　　　oppressed.
35 The wise inherit honor,
　　but fools get only shame.

Get Wisdom at Any Cost

4 Listen, my sons, to a father's
　　instruction;
　　pay attention and gain
　　　understanding.
2 I give you sound learning,
　　so do not forsake my teaching.
3 For I too was a son to my father,
　　still tender, and cherished by my
　　　mother.
4 Then he taught me, and he said to me,
　　"Take hold of my words with all your
　　　heart;
　　keep my commands, and you will
　　　live.
5 Get wisdom, get understanding;
　　do not forget my words or turn away
　　　from them.
6 Do not forsake wisdom, and she will
　　protect you;
　　love her, and she will watch over you.
7 The beginning of wisdom is this: Get[a]
　　wisdom.
　　Though it cost all you have,[b] get
　　　understanding.
8 Cherish her, and she will exalt you;
　　embrace her, and she will honor
　　　you.
9 She will give you a garland to grace
　　your head
　　and present you with a glorious
　　　crown."

10 Listen, my son, accept what I say,
　　and the years of your life will be
　　　many.

---

[a] 7 Or *Wisdom is supreme; therefore get*　　[b] 7 Or *wisdom. / Whatever else you get*

INSTANT ACCESS

Ever imagine that this Bible would have a word about pornographic websites? It does. Not that it mentions them by name. What it says is "guard your heart" (verse 23). Don't let the essential "you" become corrupted. Look straight ahead, not out of the corner of your eyes at stuff you wouldn't want others to know you're watching. Also, you know the expression "Garbage in, garbage out"? Your mind works that way too. If you want to keep garbage out of your life, don't let it in.

{Proverbs 4:23–27}

11 I instruct you in the way of wisdom
    and lead you along straight paths.
12 When you walk, your steps will not be
        hampered;
    when you run, you will not
        stumble.
13 Hold on to instruction, do not let
        it go;
    guard it well, for it is your life.
14 Do not set foot on the path of the
        wicked
    or walk in the way of evildoers.
15 Avoid it, do not travel on it;
    turn from it and go on your way.
16 For they cannot rest until they do
        evil;
    they are robbed of sleep till they
        make someone stumble.
17 They eat the bread of wickedness
    and drink the wine of violence.

18 The path of the righteous is like the
        morning sun,
    shining ever brighter till the full light
        of day.
19 But the way of the wicked is like deep
        darkness;
    they do not know what makes them
        stumble.

20 My son, pay attention to what I say;
    turn your ear to my words.
21 Do not let them out of your sight,
    keep them within your heart;
22 for they are life to those who find
        them
    and health to one's whole body.
23 Above all else, guard your heart,
    for everything you do flows
        from it.
24 Keep your mouth free of perversity;
    keep corrupt talk far from your
        lips.
25 Let your eyes look straight ahead;
    fix your gaze directly before you.
26 Give careful thought to the[a] paths for
        your feet
    and be steadfast in all your ways.
27 Do not turn to the right or the left;
    keep your foot from evil.

Warning Against Adultery

5 My son, pay attention to my wisdom,
    turn your ear to my words of insight,
2 that you may maintain discretion
    and your lips may preserve
        knowledge.
3 For the lips of the adulterous woman
        drip honey,
    and her speech is smoother than
        oil;
4 but in the end she is bitter as gall,
    sharp as a double-edged sword.
5 Her feet go down to death;
    her steps lead straight to the
        grave.
6 She gives no thought to the way of
        life;
    her paths wander aimlessly, but she
        does not know it.

7 Now then, my sons, listen to me;
    do not turn aside from what I say.

a 26 Or *Make level*

8 Keep to a path far from her,
do not go near the door of her
house,
9 lest you lose your honor to others
and your dignity[a] to one who is
cruel,
10 lest strangers feast on your wealth
and your toil enrich the house of
another.
11 At the end of your life you will groan,
when your flesh and body are spent.
12 You will say, "How I hated discipline!
How my heart spurned correction!
13 I would not obey my teachers
or turn my ear to my instructors.
14 And I was soon in serious trouble
in the assembly of God's people."

15 Drink water from your own cistern,
running water from your own well.
16 Should your springs overflow in the
streets,
your streams of water in the public
squares?
17 Let them be yours alone,
never to be shared with strangers.
18 May your fountain be blessed,
and may you rejoice in the wife of
your youth.
19 A loving doe, a graceful deer—
may her breasts satisfy you always,
may you ever be intoxicated with
her love.
20 Why, my son, be intoxicated with
another man's wife?
Why embrace the bosom of a
wayward woman?

21 For your ways are in full view of the
LORD,
and he examines all your paths.
22 The evil deeds of the wicked ensnare
them;
the cords of their sins hold them
fast.
23 For lack of discipline they will die,
led astray by their own great folly.

Warnings Against Folly

6 My son, if you have put up security
for your neighbor,
if you have shaken hands in pledge
for a stranger,

2 you have been trapped by what you
said,
ensnared by the words of your
mouth.
3 So do this, my son, to free yourself,
since you have fallen into your
neighbor's hands:
Go—to the point of exhaustion—[b]
and give your neighbor no rest!
4 Allow no sleep to your eyes,
no slumber to your eyelids.
5 Free yourself, like a gazelle from the
hand of the hunter,
like a bird from the snare of the
fowler.

6 Go to the ant, you sluggard;
consider its ways and be wise!
7 It has no commander,
no overseer or ruler,
8 yet it stores its provisions in summer
and gathers its food at harvest.

9 How long will you lie there, you
sluggard?
When will you get up from your
sleep?
10 A little sleep, a little slumber,
a little folding of the hands to
rest—
11 and poverty will come on you like a
thief
and scarcity like an armed man.

12 A troublemaker and a villain,
who goes about with a corrupt
mouth,
13 who winks maliciously with his eye,
signals with his feet
and motions with his fingers,
14 who plots evil with deceit in his
heart—
he always stirs up conflict.
15 Therefore disaster will overtake him in
an instant;
he will suddenly be destroyed—
without remedy.

16 There are six things the LORD hates,
seven that are detestable to him:
17 haughty eyes,
a lying tongue,
hands that shed innocent blood,

¹⁸   a heart that devises wicked
          schemes,
        feet that are quick to rush into
          evil,
¹⁹   a false witness who pours out
          lies
        and a person who stirs up conflict
          in the community.

Warning Against Adultery

²⁰ My son, keep your father's command
        and do not forsake your mother's
          teaching.
²¹ Bind them always on your heart;
        fasten them around your neck.
²² When you walk, they will guide you;
        when you sleep, they will watch over
          you;
        when you awake, they will speak to
          you.
²³ For this command is a lamp,
        this teaching is a light,
      and correction and instruction
        are the way to life,
²⁴ keeping you from your neighbor's wife,
        from the smooth talk of a wayward
          woman.

²⁵ Do not lust in your heart after her
          beauty
        or let her captivate you with her
          eyes.
²⁶ For a prostitute can be had for a loaf
          of bread,
        but another man's wife preys on
          your very life.
²⁷ Can a man scoop fire into his lap
        without his clothes being burned?
²⁸ Can a man walk on hot coals
        without his feet being scorched?
²⁹ So is he who sleeps with another
          man's wife;
        no one who touches her will go
          unpunished.

³⁰ People do not despise a thief if he
          steals
        to satisfy his hunger when he is
          starving.
³¹ Yet if he is caught, he must pay
          sevenfold,
        though it costs him all the wealth of
          his house.

³² But a man who commits adultery has
          no sense;
        whoever does so destroys himself.
³³ Blows and disgrace are his lot,
        and his shame will never be wiped
          away.
³⁴ For jealousy arouses a husband's fury,
        and he will show no mercy when he
          takes revenge.
³⁵ He will not accept any compensation;
        he will refuse a bribe, however great
          it is.

Warning Against the Adulterous Woman

7 My son, keep my words
        and store up my commands within
          you.
² Keep my commands and you will live;
        guard my teachings as the apple of
          your eye.
³ Bind them on your fingers;
        write them on the tablet of your
          heart.
⁴ Say to wisdom, "You are my sister,"
        and to insight, "You are my
          relative."
⁵ They will keep you from the adulterous
          woman,
        from the wayward woman with her
          seductive words.

⁶ At the window of my house
        I looked down through the lattice.
⁷ I saw among the simple,
        I noticed among the young men,
        a youth who had no sense.
⁸ He was going down the street near
          her corner,
        walking along in the direction of her
          house
⁹ at twilight, as the day was fading,
        as the dark of night set in.

¹⁰ Then out came a woman to meet him,
        dressed like a prostitute and with
          crafty intent.
¹¹ (She is unruly and defiant,
        her feet never stay at home;
¹² now in the street, now in the squares,
        at every corner she lurks.)
¹³ She took hold of him and kissed him
        and with a brazen face she said:

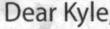

If God made sex for people to enjoy, why do some people get AIDS and other STDs?

>> Kyle

Dear Jordan

Dear Kyle,

Did you ever get a present and have to read the instructions before you used it? When microwave ovens were first available, a woman used one to warm her cat. It did warm the pet, but it cooked its organs and killed the cat. The oven was wonderful, but its owner didn't read the instructions on how to use it and how not to use it. Does that mean microwave ovens are too dangerous or that you shouldn't use them? No, but you need to follow the instructions in order to enjoy them without getting hurt.

The urge to have sex can be very powerful as well as very dangerous. You need to know and follow God's instructions for this wonderful gift. God knew marriage would be a difficult, lifelong commitment. So he gave husbands and wives a special gift, a way to bond together. Sex in marriage helps a man and a woman stay close in body and soul.

When people who aren't married to each other have sex, it's sort of like putting a pet in the microwave. Someone could be burned, damaged or killed (Proverbs 6:26–28). Having sex before marriage can bring an unwanted pregnancy or STDs (sexually transmitted diseases), many of which have no cure, some of which are fatal. And did you know promiscuous sex is also linked with serious depression? Why take the chance? It is much better to follow God's instructions and enjoy this precious gift only after you are married, just as God intended.

Jordan

14 "Today I fulfilled my vows,
  and I have food from my fellowship
    offering at home.
15 So I came out to meet you;
  I looked for you and have found you!
16 I have covered my bed
  with colored linens from Egypt.
17 I have perfumed my bed
  with myrrh, aloes and cinnamon.
18 Come, let's drink deeply of love till
    morning;
  let's enjoy ourselves with love!
19 My husband is not at home;
  he has gone on a long journey.
20 He took his purse filled with money
  and will not be home till full moon."

21 With persuasive words she led him
    astray;
  she seduced him with her smooth
    talk.
22 All at once he followed her
  like an ox going to the slaughter,
  like a deer[a] stepping into a noose[b]
23   till an arrow pierces his liver,
  like a bird darting into a snare,
    little knowing it will cost him his life.

24 Now then, my sons, listen to me;
  pay attention to what I say.
25 Do not let your heart turn to her ways
  or stray into her paths.
26 Many are the victims she has brought
    down;
  her slain are a mighty throng.
27 Her house is a highway to the grave,
  leading down to the chambers of
    death.

Wisdom's Call

8 Does not wisdom call out?
  Does not understanding raise her
    voice?
2 At the highest point along the way,
  where the paths meet, she takes
    her stand;
3 beside the gate leading into the city,
  at the entrance, she cries aloud:
4 "To you, O people, I call out;
  I raise my voice to all mankind.

5 You who are simple, gain prudence;
  you who are foolish, set your hearts
    on it.[c]
6 Listen, for I have trustworthy things to
    say;
  I open my lips to speak what is
    right.
7 My mouth speaks what is true,
  for my lips detest wickedness.
8 All the words of my mouth are just;
  none of them is crooked or perverse.
9 To the discerning all of them are right;
  they are upright to those who have
    found knowledge.
10 Choose my instruction instead of
    silver,
  knowledge rather than choice gold,
11 for wisdom is more precious than
    rubies,
  and nothing you desire can
    compare with her.

12 "I, wisdom, dwell together with
    prudence;
  I possess knowledge and
    discretion.
13 To fear the LORD is to hate evil;
  I hate pride and arrogance,
    evil behavior and perverse speech.

Proverbs 8

Q: What is more valuable than
gold, silver or rubies?

**BONUS: What's the difference
between being smart and being
wise?**

---

a 22 Syriac (see also Septuagint); Hebrew *fool*
b 22 The meaning of the Hebrew for this line is uncertain.
c 5 Septuagint; Hebrew *foolish, instruct your minds*

A: Knowledge and wisdom (Proverbs 8:10–11).

BONUS: Smarts might earn you good grades in school, but wisdom will guide you to good choices all your life.

¹⁴ Counsel and sound judgment are
    mine;
    I have insight, I have power.
¹⁵ By me kings reign
    and rulers issue decrees that are
    just;
¹⁶ by me princes govern,
    and nobles—all who rule on
    earth.ᵃ
¹⁷ I love those who love me,
    and those who seek me find me.
¹⁸ With me are riches and honor,
    enduring wealth and prosperity.
¹⁹ My fruit is better than fine gold;
    what I yield surpasses choice silver.
²⁰ I walk in the way of righteousness,
    along the paths of justice,
²¹ bestowing a rich inheritance on those
    who love me
    and making their treasuries full.

²² "The Lᴏʀᴅ brought me forth as the
    first of his works,ᵇ,ᶜ
    before his deeds of old;
²³ I was formed long ages ago,
    at the very beginning, when the
    world came to be.

²⁴ When there were no watery depths, I
    was given birth,
    when there were no springs
    overflowing with water;
²⁵ before the mountains were settled in
    place,
    before the hills, I was given birth,
²⁶ before he made the world or its
    fields
    or any of the dust of the earth.
²⁷ I was there when he set the heavens
    in place,
    when he marked out the horizon on
    the face of the deep,
²⁸ when he established the clouds
    above
    and fixed securely the fountains of
    the deep,
²⁹ when he gave the sea its boundary
    so the waters would not overstep
    his command,
    and when he marked out the
    foundations of the earth.
³⁰   Then I was constantlyᵈ at his side.
    I was filled with delight day after day,
    rejoicing always in his presence,
³¹ rejoicing in his whole world
    and delighting in mankind.
³² "Now then, my children, listen to me;
    blessed are those who keep my
    ways.
³³ Listen to my instruction and be
    wise;
    do not disregard it.
³⁴ Blessed are those who listen to me,
    watching daily at my doors,
    waiting at my doorway.
³⁵ For those who find me find life
    and receive favor from the Lᴏʀᴅ.
³⁶ But those who fail to find me harm
    themselves;
    all who hate me love death."

Invitations of Wisdom and Folly

9 Wisdom has built her house;
    she has set upᵉ its seven pillars.
² She has prepared her meat and mixed
    her wine;
    she has also set her table.

ᵃ 16 Some Hebrew manuscripts and Septuagint; other Hebrew manuscripts *all righteous rulers*   ᵇ 22 Or *way*; or
dominion   ᶜ 22 Or *The Lᴏʀᴅ possessed me at the beginning of his work*; or *The Lᴏʀᴅ brought me forth at the beginning of
his work*   ᵈ 30 Or *was the artisan*; or *was a little child*   ᵉ 1 Septuagint, Syriac and Targum; Hebrew *has hewn out*

³She has sent out her servants, and she calls
from the highest point of the city,

⁴ "Let all who are simple come to my house!"
To those who have no sense she says,

⁵ "Come, eat my food
and drink the wine I have mixed.

⁶Leave your simple ways and you will live;
walk in the way of insight."

⁷Whoever corrects a mocker invites insults;
whoever rebukes the wicked incurs abuse.

⁸Do not rebuke mockers or they will hate you;
rebuke the wise and they will love you.

⁹Instruct the wise and they will be wiser still;
teach the righteous and they will add to their learning.

¹⁰The fear of the LORD is the beginning of wisdom,
and knowledge of the Holy One is understanding.

¹¹For through wisdomᵃ your days will be many,
and years will be added to your life.

¹²If you are wise, your wisdom will reward you;
if you are a mocker, you alone will suffer.

> **The fear of the LORD is the beginning of wisdom.**
> Proverbs 9:10

¹³Folly is an unruly woman;
she is simple and knows nothing.

¹⁴She sits at the door of her house,
on a seat at the highest point of the city,

¹⁵calling out to those who pass by,
who go straight on their way,

¹⁶ "Let all who are simple come to my house!"
To those who have no sense she says,

¹⁷ "Stolen water is sweet;
food eaten in secret is delicious!"

¹⁸But little do they know that the dead are there,
that her guests are deep in the realm of the dead.

Proverbs of Solomon

10 The proverbs of Solomon:

A wise son brings joy to his father,
but a foolish son brings grief to his mother.

²Ill-gotten treasures have no lasting value,
but righteousness delivers from death.

³The LORD does not let the righteous go hungry,
but he thwarts the craving of the wicked.

⁴Lazy hands make for poverty,
but diligent hands bring wealth.

⁵He who gathers crops in summer is a prudent son,
but he who sleeps during harvest is a disgraceful son.

⁶Blessings crown the head of the righteous,
but violence overwhelms the mouth of the wicked.ᵇ

⁷The name of the righteous is used in blessings,ᶜ
but the name of the wicked will rot.

ᵃ 11 Septuagint, Syriac and Targum; Hebrew *me* ᵇ 6 Or *righteous, / but the mouth of the wicked conceals violence*
ᶜ 7 See Gen. 48:20.

8 The wise in heart accept commands,
  but a chattering fool comes to ruin.

9 Whoever walks in integrity walks
  securely,
  but whoever takes crooked paths
  will be found out.

10 Whoever winks maliciously causes
  grief,
  and a chattering fool comes to
  ruin.

11 The mouth of the righteous is a
  fountain of life,
  but the mouth of the wicked
  conceals violence.

12 Hatred stirs up conflict,
  but love covers over all wrongs.

13 Wisdom is found on the lips of the
  discerning,
  but a rod is for the back of one who
  has no sense.

14 The wise store up knowledge,
  but the mouth of a fool invites ruin.

15 The wealth of the rich is their fortified
  city,
  but poverty is the ruin of the poor.

16 The wages of the righteous is life,
  but the earnings of the wicked are
  sin and death.

17 Whoever heeds discipline shows the
  way to life,
  but whoever ignores correction
  leads others astray.

18 Whoever conceals hatred with lying
  lips
  and spreads slander is a fool.

19 Sin is not ended by multiplying
  words,
  but the prudent hold their
  tongues.

20 The tongue of the righteous is choice
  silver,
  but the heart of the wicked is of
  little value.

21 The lips of the righteous nourish
  many,
  but fools die for lack of sense.

22 The blessing of the Lord brings
  wealth,
  without painful toil for it.

23 A fool finds pleasure in wicked
  schemes,
  but a person of understanding
  delights in wisdom.

24 What the wicked dread will overtake
  them;
  what the righteous desire will be
  granted.

25 When the storm has swept by, the
  wicked are gone,
  but the righteous stand firm forever.

26 As vinegar to the teeth and smoke to
  the eyes,
  so are sluggards to those who send
  them.

27 The fear of the Lord adds length to
  life,
  but the years of the wicked are cut
  short.

28 The prospect of the righteous is joy,
  but the hopes of the wicked come
  to nothing.

29 The way of the Lord is a refuge for the
  blameless,
  but it is the ruin of those who do
  evil.

30 The righteous will never be uprooted,
  but the wicked will not remain in the
  land.

31 From the mouth of the righteous
  comes the fruit of wisdom,
  but a perverse tongue will be
  silenced.

32 The lips of the righteous know what
  finds favor,
  but the mouth of the wicked only
  what is perverse.

11 The Lord detests dishonest
  scales,
  but accurate weights find favor with
  him.

2 When pride comes, then comes
  disgrace,
  but with humility comes wisdom.

³The integrity of the upright guides
   them,
   but the unfaithful are destroyed by
     their duplicity.

⁴Wealth is worthless in the day of
   wrath,
   but righteousness delivers from
     death.

⁵The righteousness of the blameless
   makes their paths straight,
   but the wicked are brought down by
     their own wickedness.

⁶The righteousness of the upright
   delivers them,
   but the unfaithful are trapped by evil
     desires.

⁷Hopes placed in mortals die with
   them;
   all the promise ofᵃ their power
     comes to nothing.

⁸The righteous person is rescued from
   trouble,
   and it falls on the wicked instead.

⁹With their mouths the godless destroy
   their neighbors,
   but through knowledge the
     righteous escape.

¹⁰When the righteous prosper, the city
   rejoices;
   when the wicked perish, there are
     shouts of joy.

¹¹Through the blessing of the upright a
   city is exalted,
   but by the mouth of the wicked it is
     destroyed.

¹²Whoever derides their neighbor has no
   sense,
   but the one who has understanding
     holds their tongue.

¹³A gossip betrays a confidence,
   but a trustworthy person keeps a
     secret.

¹⁴For lack of guidance a nation falls,
   but victory is won through many
     advisers.

¹⁵Whoever puts up security for a
   stranger will surely suffer,
   but whoever refuses to shake
     hands in pledge is safe.

¹⁶A kindhearted woman gains honor,
   but ruthless men gain only wealth.

¹⁷Those who are kind benefit themselves,
   but the cruel bring ruin on
     themselves.

¹⁸A wicked person earns deceptive
   wages,
   but the one who sows
     righteousness reaps a sure
     reward.

¹⁹Truly the righteous attain life,
   but whoever pursues evil finds death.

²⁰The LORD detests those whose hearts
   are perverse,
   but he delights in those whose
     ways are blameless.

²¹Be sure of this: The wicked will not go
   unpunished,
   but those who are righteous will go
     free.

²²Like a gold ring in a pig's snout
   is a beautiful woman who shows no
     discretion.

²³The desire of the righteous ends only
   in good,
   but the hope of the wicked only in
     wrath.

²⁴One person gives freely, yet gains
   even more;
   another withholds unduly, but
     comes to poverty.

²⁵A generous person will prosper;
   whoever refreshes others will be
     refreshed.

²⁶People curse the one who hoards
   grain,
   but they pray God's blessing on the
     one who is willing to sell.

²⁷Whoever seeks good finds favor,
   but evil comes to one who searches
     for it.

ᵃ 7 Two Hebrew manuscripts; most Hebrew manuscripts, Vulgate, Syriac and Targum *When the wicked die, their hope perishes; / all they expected from*

²⁸ Those who trust in their riches will fall,
but the righteous will thrive like a
green leaf.

²⁹ Whoever brings ruin on their family will
inherit only wind,
and the fool will be servant to the
wise.

³⁰ The fruit of the righteous is a tree of
life,
and the one who is wise saves lives.

³¹ If the righteous receive their due on
earth,
how much more the ungodly and
the sinner!

12 Whoever loves discipline loves
knowledge,
but whoever hates correction is
stupid.

² Good people obtain favor from the
LORD,
but he condemns those who devise
wicked schemes.

³ No one can be established through
wickedness,
but the righteous cannot be
uprooted.

Proverbs 12

Q: What effect does a noble
wife have on her husband?

BONUS: What effect does a
disgraceful wife have on her
husband?

⁴ A wife of noble character is her
husband's crown,
but a disgraceful wife is like decay
in his bones.

⁵ The plans of the righteous are just,
but the advice of the wicked is
deceitful.

⁶ The words of the wicked lie in wait for
blood,
but the speech of the upright
rescues them.

⁷ The wicked are overthrown and are no
more,
but the house of the righteous
stands firm.

⁸ A person is praised according to their
prudence,
and one with a warped mind is
despised.

⁹ Better to be a nobody and yet have a
servant
than pretend to be somebody and
have no food.

¹⁰ The righteous care for the needs of
their animals,
but the kindest acts of the wicked
are cruel.

¹¹ Those who work their land will have
abundant food,
but those who chase fantasies have
no sense.

¹² The wicked desire the stronghold of
evildoers,
but the root of the righteous
endures.

¹³ Evildoers are trapped by their sinful
talk,
and so the innocent escape trouble.

¹⁴ From the fruit of their lips people are
filled with good things,
and the work of their hands brings
them reward.

¹⁵ The way of fools seems right to them,
but the wise listen to advice.

¹⁶ Fools show their annoyance at once,
but the prudent overlook an
insult.

¹⁷ An honest witness tells the truth,
  but a false witness tells lies.
¹⁸ The words of the reckless pierce like
    swords,
  but the tongue of the wise brings
    healing.
¹⁹ Truthful lips endure forever,
  but a lying tongue lasts only a
    moment.
²⁰ Deceit is in the hearts of those who
    plot evil,
  but those who promote peace have
    joy.
²¹ No harm overtakes the righteous,
  but the wicked have their fill of
    trouble.
²² The LORD detests lying lips,
  but he delights in people who are
    trustworthy.

²³ The prudent keep their knowledge to
    themselves,
  but a fool's heart blurts out folly.
²⁴ Diligent hands will rule,
  but laziness ends in forced
    labor.
²⁵ Anxiety weighs down the heart,
  but a kind word cheers it up.
²⁶ The righteous choose their friends
    carefully,
  but the way of the wicked leads
    them astray.
²⁷ The lazy do not roast[a] any game,
  but the diligent feed on the riches
    of the hunt.
²⁸ In the way of righteousness there is
    life;
  along that path is immortality.

13 A wise son heeds his father's
    instruction,
  but a mocker does not respond to
    rebukes.
² From the fruit of their lips people
    enjoy good things,
  but the unfaithful have an appetite
    for violence.

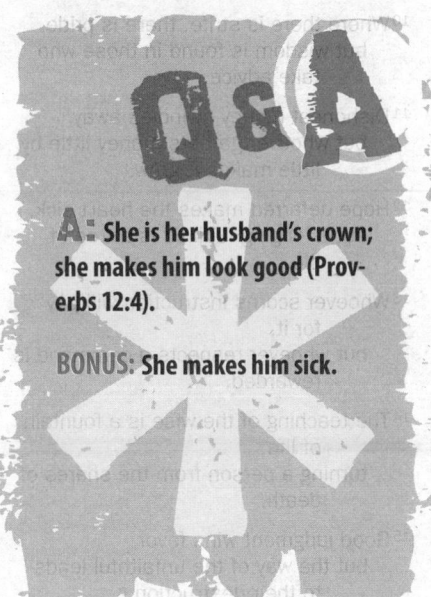

A: She is her husband's crown;
she makes him look good (Proverbs 12:4).

BONUS: She makes him sick.

³ Those who guard their lips preserve
    their lives,
  but those who speak rashly will
    come to ruin.
⁴ A sluggard's appetite is never filled,
  but the desires of the diligent are
    fully satisfied.
⁵ The righteous hate what is false,
  but the wicked make themselves a
    stench
  and bring shame on themselves.
⁶ Righteousness guards the person of
    integrity,
  but wickedness overthrows the
    sinner.
⁷ One person pretends to be rich, yet
    has nothing;
  another pretends to be poor, yet
    has great wealth.
⁸ A person's riches may ransom their life,
  but the poor cannot respond to
    threatening rebukes.
⁹ The light of the righteous shines
    brightly,
  but the lamp of the wicked is
    snuffed out.

ᵃ 27 The meaning of the Hebrew for this word is uncertain.

10 Where there is strife, there is pride,
   but wisdom is found in those who
      take advice.

11 Dishonest money dwindles away,
   but whoever gathers money little by
      little makes it grow.

12 Hope deferred makes the heart sick,
   but a longing fulfilled is a tree of
      life.

13 Whoever scorns instruction will pay
      for it,
   but whoever respects a command is
      rewarded.

14 The teaching of the wise is a fountain
      of life,
   turning a person from the snares of
      death.

15 Good judgment wins favor,
   but the way of the unfaithful leads
      to their destruction.*a*

16 All who are prudent act with*b*
      knowledge,
   but fools expose their folly.

17 A wicked messenger falls into
      trouble,
   but a trustworthy envoy brings
      healing.

18 Whoever disregards discipline comes
      to poverty and shame,
   but whoever heeds correction is
      honored.

19 A longing fulfilled is sweet to the
      soul,
   but fools detest turning from evil.

20 Walk with the wise and become
      wise,
   for a companion of fools suffers
      harm.

21 Trouble pursues the sinner,
   but the righteous are rewarded with
      good things.

22 A good person leaves an inheritance
      for their children's children,
   but a sinner's wealth is stored up
      for the righteous.

INSTANT ACCESS

There are some things in the Bible we just don't like to hear, like, "Whoever loves discipline loves knowledge" and "Whoever hates correction is stupid." Hey, aren't you old enough to make your own decisions about your own life? Maybe you are. But "discipline"—a word that means "training" as well as "correction" (and sometimes "punishment")—is something everyone needs. The point of this proverb is that it's stupid to rebel. Instead, make the best of your limits and learn all you can from them. Then when you're on your own, chances are you'll make more wise choices than stupid ones.

{Proverbs 12:1}

23 An unplowed field produces food for
      the poor,
   but injustice sweeps it away.

24 Whoever spares the rod hates their
      children,
   but the one who loves their children
      is careful to discipline them.

25 The righteous eat to their hearts'
      content,
   but the stomach of the wicked goes
      hungry.

---

a 15 Septuagint and Syriac; the meaning of the Hebrew for this phrase is uncertain.   *b* 16 Or *prudent protect themselves through*

14

The wise woman builds her house,
but with her own hands the foolish one tears hers down.

2 Whoever fears the LORD walks uprightly,
but those who despise him are devious in their ways.

3 A fool's mouth lashes out with pride,
but the lips of the wise protect them.

4 Where there are no oxen, the manger is empty,
but from the strength of an ox come abundant harvests.

5 An honest witness does not deceive,
but a false witness pours out lies.

6 The mocker seeks wisdom and finds none,
but knowledge comes easily to the discerning.

7 Stay away from a fool,
for you will not find knowledge on their lips.

8 The wisdom of the prudent is to give thought to their ways,
but the folly of fools is deception.

9 Fools mock at making amends for sin,
but goodwill is found among the upright.

10 Each heart knows its own bitterness,
and no one else can share its joy.

11 The house of the wicked will be destroyed,
but the tent of the upright will flourish.

12 There is a way that appears to be right,
but in the end it leads to death.

13 Even in laughter the heart may ache,
and rejoicing may end in grief.

14 The faithless will be fully repaid for their ways,
and the good rewarded for theirs.

15 The simple believe anything,
but the prudent give thought to their steps.

16 The wise fear the LORD and shun evil,
but a fool is hotheaded and yet feels secure.

17 A quick-tempered person does foolish things,
and the one who devises evil schemes is hated.

18 The simple inherit folly,
but the prudent are crowned with knowledge.

19 Evildoers will bow down in the presence of the good,
and the wicked at the gates of the righteous.

20 The poor are shunned even by their neighbors,
but the rich have many friends.

21 It is a sin to despise one's neighbor,
but blessed is the one who is kind to the needy.

22 Do not those who plot evil go astray?
But those who plan what is good find[a] love and faithfulness.

23 All hard work brings a profit,
but mere talk leads only to poverty.

24 The wealth of the wise is their crown,
but the folly of fools yields folly.

25 A truthful witness saves lives,
but a false witness is deceitful.

26 Whoever fears the LORD has a secure fortress,
and for their children it will be a refuge.

27 The fear of the LORD is a fountain of life,
turning a person from the snares of death.

28 A large population is a king's glory,
but without subjects a prince is ruined.

---

a 22 Or show

29 Whoever is patient has great
   understanding,
   but one who is quick-tempered
   displays folly.

30 A heart at peace gives life to the body,
   but envy rots the bones.

31 Whoever oppresses the poor shows
   contempt for their Maker,
   but whoever is kind to the needy
   honors God.

32 When calamity comes, the wicked are
   brought down,
   but even in death the righteous
   seek refuge in God.

33 Wisdom reposes in the heart of the
   discerning
   and even among fools she lets
   herself be known.*a*

34 Righteousness exalts a nation,
   but sin condemns any people.

35 A king delights in a wise servant,
   but a shameful servant arouses his
   fury.

15 A gentle answer turns away
   wrath,
   but a harsh word stirs up anger.

2 The tongue of the wise adorns
   knowledge,
   but the mouth of the fool gushes
   folly.

3 The eyes of the LORD are everywhere,
   keeping watch on the wicked and
   the good.

4 The soothing tongue is a tree of life,
   but a perverse tongue crushes the
   spirit.

5 A fool spurns a parent's discipline,
   but whoever heeds correction
   shows prudence.

6 The house of the righteous contains
   great treasure,
   but the income of the wicked brings
   ruin.

7 The lips of the wise spread knowledge,
   but the hearts of fools are not
   upright.

8 The LORD detests the sacrifice of the
   wicked,
   but the prayer of the upright
   pleases him.

9 The LORD detests the way of the
   wicked,
   but he loves those who pursue
   righteousness.

10 Stern discipline awaits anyone who
   leaves the path;
   the one who hates correction will
   die.

11 Death and Destruction*b* lie open
   before the LORD—
   how much more do human hearts!

---

a 33 Hebrew; Septuagint and Syriac *discerning / but in the heart of fools she is not known*   *b* 11 Hebrew *Abaddon*

PANORAMA

Good Advice.

**Proverbs are short sayings that help people
make wise choices.**

{PROVERBS}

12 Mockers resent correction,
   so they avoid the wise.

13 A happy heart makes the face
      cheerful,
   but heartache crushes the spirit.

14 The discerning heart seeks
      knowledge,
   but the mouth of a fool feeds on
      folly.

15 All the days of the oppressed are
      wretched,
   but the cheerful heart has a
      continual feast.

16 Better a little with the fear of the Lord
   than great wealth with turmoil.

17 Better a small serving of vegetables
      with love
   than a fattened calf with hatred.

18 A hot-tempered person stirs up
      conflict,
   but the one who is patient calms a
      quarrel.

19 The way of the sluggard is blocked
      with thorns,
   but the path of the upright is a
      highway.

20 A wise son brings joy to his father,
   but a foolish man despises his
      mother.

21 Folly brings joy to one who has no
      sense,
   but whoever has understanding
      keeps a straight course.

22 Plans fail for lack of counsel,
   but with many advisers they
      succeed.

23 A person finds joy in giving an apt
      reply—
   and how good is a timely word!

24 The path of life leads upward for the
      prudent
   to keep them from going down to
      the realm of the dead.

25 The Lord tears down the house of the
      proud,
   but he sets the widow's boundary
      stones in place.

26 The Lord detests the thoughts of the
      wicked,
   but gracious words are pure in his
      sight.

27 The greedy bring ruin to their
      households,
   but the one who hates bribes will
      live.

28 The heart of the righteous weighs its
      answers,
   but the mouth of the wicked gushes
      evil.

29 The Lord is far from the wicked,
   but he hears the prayer of the
      righteous.

30 Light in a messenger's eyes brings joy
      to the heart,
   and good news gives health to the
      bones.

31 Whoever heeds life-giving correction
   will be at home among the wise.

32 Those who disregard discipline
      despise themselves,
   but the one who heeds correction
      gains understanding.

33 Wisdom's instruction is to fear the
      Lord,
   and humility comes before honor.

16 To humans belong the plans of
      the heart,
   but from the Lord comes the proper
      answer of the tongue.

2 All a person's ways seem pure to
      them,
   but motives are weighed by the
      Lord.

3 Commit to the Lord whatever
      you do,
   and he will establish your plans.

4 The Lord works out everything to its
      proper end—
   even the wicked for a day of
      disaster.

5 The Lord detests all the proud of
      heart.
   Be sure of this: They will not go
      unpunished.

⁶Through love and faithfulness sin is
  atoned for;
    through the fear of the LORD evil is
    avoided.

⁷When the LORD takes pleasure in
  anyone's way,
    he causes their enemies to make
    peace with them.

⁸Better a little with righteousness
  than much gain with injustice.

⁹In their hearts humans plan their
  course,
    but the LORD establishes their steps.

¹⁰The lips of a king speak as an oracle,
  and his mouth does not betray
  justice.

¹¹Honest scales and balances belong to
  the LORD;
    all the weights in the bag are of his
    making.

¹²Kings detest wrongdoing,
  for a throne is established through
  righteousness.

¹³Kings take pleasure in honest lips;
  they value the one who speaks
  what is right.

¹⁴A king's wrath is a messenger of death,
  but the wise will appease it.

¹⁵When a king's face brightens, it
  means life;
    his favor is like a rain cloud in
    spring.

> **Commit to the LORD
> whatever you do, and he
> will establish your plans.**
> Proverbs 16:3

¹⁶How much better to get wisdom than
  gold,
    to get insight rather than silver!

¹⁷The highway of the upright avoids evil;
  those who guard their ways
  preserve their lives.

¹⁸Pride goes before destruction,
  a haughty spirit before a fall.

¹⁹Better to be lowly in spirit along with
  the oppressed
    than to share plunder with the
    proud.

²⁰Whoever gives heed to instruction
  prospers,ᵃ
    and blessed is the one who trusts
    in the LORD.

²¹The wise in heart are called
  discerning,
    and gracious words promote
    instruction.ᵇ

²²Prudence is a fountain of life to the
  prudent,
    but folly brings punishment to fools.

²³The hearts of the wise make their
  mouths prudent,
    and their lips promote instruction.ᶜ

²⁴Gracious words are a honeycomb,
  sweet to the soul and healing to the
  bones.

²⁵There is a way that appears to be
  right,
    but in the end it leads to death.

²⁶The appetite of laborers works for
  them;
    their hunger drives them on.

²⁷A scoundrel plots evil,
  and on their lips it is like a
  scorching fire.

²⁸A perverse person stirs up conflict,
  and a gossip separates close
  friends.

²⁹A violent person entices their neighbor
  and leads them down a path that is
  not good.

ᵃ 20 Or whoever speaks prudently finds what is good   ᵇ 21 Or words make a person persuasive   ᶜ 23 Or prudent / and
make their lips persuasive

Ever been the guest of honor at a surprise party? Well, you will be. And God is going to be the host. It's a good idea to look ahead and plan for your future. Maybe you want to be a crime scene investigator, or have a career in science or sales. Maybe you have plans to be a physical therapist or a cosmetologist. It's smart to take classes now that will get you where you want to go. But the one guarantee you have as you plan your "life path," is that the Lord determines your steps. God is planning that surprise for you, and you can count on your future holding something great!

{Proverbs 16:9}

INSTANT ACCESS

30 Whoever winks with their eye is
plotting perversity;
whoever purses their lips is bent on
evil.

31 Gray hair is a crown of splendor;
it is attained in the way of
righteousness.

32 Better a patient person than a
warrior,
one with self-control than one who
takes a city.

33 The lot is cast into the lap,
but its every decision is from the
LORD.

17 Better a dry crust with peace and
quiet
than a house full of feasting, with
strife.

2 A prudent servant will rule over a
disgraceful son
and will share the inheritance as
one of the family.

3 The crucible for silver and the furnace
for gold,
but the LORD tests the heart.

4 A wicked person listens to deceitful
lips;
a liar pays attention to a destructive
tongue.

5 Whoever mocks the poor shows
contempt for their Maker;
whoever gloats over disaster will
not go unpunished.

6 Children's children are a crown to the
aged,
and parents are the pride of their
children.

7 Eloquent lips are unsuited to a
godless fool—
how much worse lying lips to a
ruler!

8 A bribe is seen as a charm by the one
who gives it;
they think success will come at
every turn.

9 Whoever would foster love covers over
an offense,
but whoever repeats the matter
separates close friends.

10 A rebuke impresses a discerning
person
more than a hundred lashes a fool.

11 Evildoers foster rebellion against
God;
the messenger of death will be sent
against them.

12 Better to meet a bear robbed of her
cubs
than a fool bent on folly.

13 Evil will never leave the house
of one who pays back evil for good.

14 Starting a quarrel is like breaching a
dam;
so drop the matter before a dispute
breaks out.

15 Acquitting the guilty and condemning
the innocent—
the LORD detests them both.

16 Why should fools have money in hand
to buy wisdom,
when they are not able to
understand it?

17 A friend loves at all times,
and a brother is born for a time of
adversity.

18 One who has no sense shakes hands
in pledge
and puts up security for a neighbor.

19 Whoever loves a quarrel loves sin;
whoever builds a high gate invites
destruction.

20 One whose heart is corrupt does not
prosper;
one whose tongue is perverse falls
into trouble.

21 To have a fool for a child brings grief;
there is no joy for the parent of a
godless fool.

22 A cheerful heart is good medicine,
but a crushed spirit dries up the
bones.

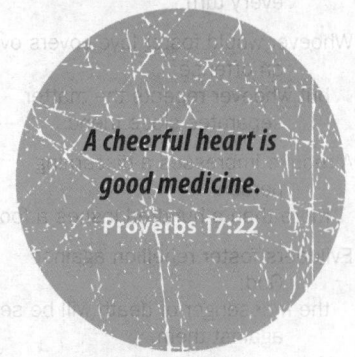

*A cheerful heart is
good medicine.*
Proverbs 17:22

23 The wicked accept bribes in secret
to pervert the course of justice.

24 A discerning person keeps wisdom in
view,

but a fool's eyes wander to the
ends of the earth.

25 A foolish son brings grief to his father
and bitterness to the mother who
bore him.

26 If imposing a fine on the innocent is
not good,
surely to flog honest officials is not
right.

27 The one who has knowledge uses
words with restraint,
and whoever has understanding is
even-tempered.

28 Even fools are thought wise if they
keep silent,
and discerning if they hold their
tongues.

18 An unfriendly person pursues
selfish ends
and against all sound judgment
starts quarrels.

2 Fools find no pleasure in
understanding
but delight in airing their own
opinions.

3 When wickedness comes, so does
contempt,
and with shame comes reproach.

4 The words of the mouth are deep
waters,
but the fountain of wisdom is a
rushing stream.

5 It is not good to be partial to the
wicked
and so deprive the innocent of
justice.

6 The lips of fools bring them strife,
and their mouths invite a beating.

7 The mouths of fools are their undoing,
and their lips are a snare to their
very lives.

8 The words of a gossip are like choice
morsels;
they go down to the inmost parts.

9 One who is slack in his work
is brother to one who destroys.

One of the hardest things in life is to say nothing. Suppose you find out that Jenny said something mean about you. Your first instinct is to get on the phone and tell Nikki what she did. And Nikki will tell someone else, and pretty soon it will get back to Jenny and then the whole thing will escalate. You know. You've seen it happen. So what do you do? The advice in this proverb is, do nothing. Say nothing. Chances are Jenny didn't mean it . . . or that Jenny didn't even say what someone told you she said. It's hard to say nothing. But saying nothing ends the cruel circle. And gossiping may separate even the closest of friends.

{Proverbs 17:9}

»INSTANT ACCESS

10 The name of the LORD is a fortified
tower;
the righteous run to it and are safe.

11 The wealth of the rich is their fortified
city;
they imagine it a wall too high to
scale.

12 Before a downfall the heart is
haughty,
but humility comes before honor.

13 To answer before listening—
that is folly and shame.

14 The human spirit can endure in
sickness,
but a crushed spirit who can bear?

15 The heart of the discerning acquires
knowledge,
for the ears of the wise seek it out.

16 A gift opens the way
and ushers the giver into the
presence of the great.

17 In a lawsuit the first to speak seems
right,
until someone comes forward and
cross-examines.

18 Casting the lot settles disputes
and keeps strong opponents apart.

19 A brother wronged is more unyielding
than a fortified city;
disputes are like the barred gates
of a citadel.

20 From the fruit of their mouth a
person's stomach is filled;
with the harvest of their lips they
are satisfied.

21 The tongue has the power of life and
death,
and those who love it will eat its
fruit.

22 He who finds a wife finds what is good
and receives favor from the LORD.

23 The poor plead for mercy,
but the rich answer harshly.

24 One who has unreliable friends soon
comes to ruin,
but there is a friend who sticks
closer than a brother.

19 Better the poor whose walk is
blameless
than a fool whose lips are perverse.

2 Desire without knowledge is not
good—
how much more will hasty feet miss
the way!

3 A person's own folly leads to their
ruin,
yet their heart rages against the
LORD.

4 Wealth attracts many friends,
    but even the closest friend of the
    poor person deserts them.

5 A false witness will not go
    unpunished,
    and whoever pours out lies will not
    go free.

6 Many curry favor with a ruler,
    and everyone is the friend of one
    who gives gifts.

7 The poor are shunned by all their
    relatives—
    how much more do their friends
    avoid them!
  Though the poor pursue them with
    pleading,
    they are nowhere to be found.[a]

8 The one who gets wisdom loves life;
    the one who cherishes
    understanding will soon
    prosper.

9 A false witness will not go
    unpunished,
    and whoever pours out lies will
    perish.

10 It is not fitting for a fool to live in
    luxury—
    how much worse for a slave to rule
    over princes!

11 A person's wisdom yields patience;
    it is to one's glory to overlook an
    offense.

12 A king's rage is like the roar of a lion,
    but his favor is like dew on the
    grass.

13 A foolish child is a father's ruin,
    and a quarrelsome wife is like
    the constant dripping of a leaky roof.

14 Houses and wealth are inherited from
    parents,
    but a prudent wife is from the
    LORD.

15 Laziness brings on deep sleep,
    and the shiftless go hungry.

16 Whoever keeps commandments
    keeps their life,
    but whoever shows contempt for
    their ways will die.

17 Whoever is kind to the poor lends to
    the LORD,
    and he will reward them for what
    they have done.

18 Discipline your children, for in that
    there is hope;
    do not be a willing party to their
    death.

19 A hot-tempered person must pay the
    penalty;
    rescue them, and you will have to
    do it again.

20 Listen to advice and accept discipline,
    and at the end you will be counted
    among the wise.

21 Many are the plans in a person's
    heart,
    but it is the LORD's purpose that
    prevails.

22 What a person desires is unfailing
    love[b];
    better to be poor than a liar.

23 The fear of the LORD leads to life;
    then one rests content, untouched
    by trouble.

24 A sluggard buries his hand in the
    dish;
    he will not even bring it back to his
    mouth!

25 Flog a mocker, and the simple will
    learn prudence;
    rebuke the discerning, and they will
    gain knowledge.

26 Whoever robs their father and drives
    out their mother
  is a child who brings shame and
    disgrace.

27 Stop listening to instruction, my son,
    and you will stray from the words of
    knowledge.

28 A corrupt witness mocks at justice,
    and the mouth of the wicked gulps
    down evil.

29 Penalties are prepared for mockers,
    and beatings for the backs of fools.

---

a 7 The meaning of the Hebrew for this sentence is uncertain.   b 22 Or *Greed is a person's shame*

20 Wine is a mocker and beer a
brawler;
 whoever is led astray by them is not
wise.

2 A king's wrath strikes terror like the
roar of a lion;
 those who anger him forfeit their
lives.

3 It is to one's honor to avoid strife,
 but every fool is quick to quarrel.

4 Sluggards do not plow in season;
 so at harvest time they look but
find nothing.

5 The purposes of a person's heart are
deep waters,
 but one who has insight draws them
out.

6 Many claim to have unfailing love,
 but a faithful person who can find?

7 The righteous lead blameless lives;
 blessed are their children after
them.

8 When a king sits on his throne to
judge,
 he winnows out all evil with his
eyes.

9 Who can say, "I have kept my heart
pure;
 I am clean and without sin"?

10 Differing weights and differing
measures—
 the Lord detests them both.

11 Even small children are known by
their actions,
 so is their conduct really pure and
upright?

12 Ears that hear and eyes that see—
 the Lord has made them both.

13 Do not love sleep or you will grow
poor;
 stay awake and you will have food
to spare.

14 "It's no good, it's no good!" says the
buyer—
 then goes off and boasts about the
purchase.

15 Gold there is, and rubies in
abundance,
 but lips that speak knowledge are a
rare jewel.

16 Take the garment of one who puts up
security for a stranger;
 hold it in pledge if it is done for an
outsider.

17 Food gained by fraud tastes sweet,
 but one ends up with a mouth full of
gravel.

18 Plans are established by seeking
advice;
 so if you wage war, obtain guidance.

19 A gossip betrays a confidence;
 so avoid anyone who talks too much.

20 If someone curses their father or
mother,
 their lamp will be snuffed out in
pitch darkness.

21 An inheritance claimed too soon
 will not be blessed at the end.

22 Do not say, "I'll pay you back for this
wrong!"
 Wait for the Lord, and he will
avenge you.

Proverbs 20

Q: What kind of person is it
good to avoid?

**BONUS: What does a gossip do
with the secret you told him or
her?**

A: A person who talks too much (Proverbs 20:19).

BONUS: He or she "betrays a confidence" and shares your secret with someone else.

23 The LORD detests differing weights,
and dishonest scales do not please
him.

24 A person's steps are directed by the
LORD.
How then can anyone understand
their own way?

25 It is a trap to dedicate something
rashly
and only later to consider one's
vows.

26 A wise king winnows out the wicked;
he drives the threshing wheel over
them.

27 The human spirit is[a] the lamp of the
LORD
that sheds light on one's inmost
being.

28 Love and faithfulness keep a king
safe;
through love his throne is made
secure.

29 The glory of young men is their
strength,
gray hair the splendor of the old.

30 Blows and wounds scrub away evil,
and beatings purge the inmost
being.

21 In the LORD's hand the king's
heart is a stream of water
that he channels toward all who
please him.

2 A person may think their own ways are
right,
but the LORD weighs the heart.

3 To do what is right and just
is more acceptable to the LORD than
sacrifice.

4 Haughty eyes and a proud heart—
the unplowed field of the wicked—
produce sin.

5 The plans of the diligent lead to profit
as surely as haste leads to poverty.

6 A fortune made by a lying tongue
is a fleeting vapor and a deadly
snare.[b]

7 The violence of the wicked will drag
them away,
for they refuse to do what is right.

8 The way of the guilty is devious,
but the conduct of the innocent is
upright.

9 Better to live on a corner of the roof
than share a house with a
quarrelsome wife.

10 The wicked crave evil;
their neighbors get no mercy from
them.

11 When a mocker is punished, the
simple gain wisdom;
by paying attention to the wise they
get knowledge.

12 The Righteous One[c] takes note of the
house of the wicked
and brings the wicked to ruin.

13 Whoever shuts their ears to the cry of
the poor
will also cry out and not be
answered.

---

a 27 Or *A person's words are
for those who seek death   b 6* Some Hebrew manuscripts, Septuagint and Vulgate; most Hebrew manuscripts *vapor*
c 12 Or *The righteous person*

> My boyfriend usually offers me a beer when we are hanging out. He says it will relax me and that it's okay because we're not getting drunk. My parents would ground me for life if they knew I was drinking, but is it really that bad to relax a little? >> Zoe

Dear Jordan

Dear Zoe,

Sometimes young people feel very grown up when they act like adults. But drinking alcohol is against the law until you become an adult for many good reasons. It can do a lot of damage quickly to bodies that aren't yet mature. And it has other dangers too. Alcohol affects the part of your brain that inhibits or stops you from doing things you know you shouldn't. And you don't have to be drunk; sometimes a little alcohol is all it takes. When inhibitions are numbed away, many people become sexually active, only to regret it the next day. Perhaps this is why Proverbs 20:1 says, "Wine is a mocker and beer a brawler; whoever is led astray by them is not wise."

   Tell your boyfriend you prefer not to drink alcohol and you don't want him to keep asking you to. If he really cares about you, he won't try to get you to do something you don't want to. And if he doesn't care about you enough to stop offering, maybe it's time for you to move on without him.

Jordan

¹⁴A gift given in secret soothes anger,
  and a bribe concealed in the cloak
    pacifies great wrath.

¹⁵When justice is done, it brings joy to
    the righteous
  but terror to evildoers.

¹⁶Whoever strays from the path of
    prudence
  comes to rest in the company of the
    dead.

¹⁷Whoever loves pleasure will become
    poor;
  whoever loves wine and olive oil will
    never be rich.

¹⁸The wicked become a ransom for the
    righteous,
  and the unfaithful for the upright.

¹⁹Better to live in a desert
  than with a quarrelsome and
    nagging wife.

²⁰The wise store up choice food and
    olive oil,
  but fools gulp theirs down.

²¹Whoever pursues righteousness and
    love
  finds life, prosperity^a and honor.

²²One who is wise can go up against the
    city of the mighty
  and pull down the stronghold in
    which they trust.

²³Those who guard their mouths and
    their tongues
  keep themselves from calamity.

²⁴The proud and arrogant person—
    "Mocker" is his name—
  behaves with insolent fury.

²⁵The craving of a sluggard will be the
    death of him,
  because his hands refuse to work.
²⁶All day long he craves for more,
  but the righteous give without
    sparing.

²⁷The sacrifice of the wicked is
    detestable—
  how much more so when brought
    with evil intent!

²⁸A false witness will perish,

  but a careful listener will testify
    successfully.
²⁹The wicked put up a bold front,
  but the upright give thought to their
    ways.

³⁰There is no wisdom, no insight, no
    plan
  that can succeed against the
    LORD.

³¹The horse is made ready for the day
    of battle,
  but victory rests with the LORD.

22 A good name is more desirable
    than great riches;
  to be esteemed is better than silver
    or gold.

²Rich and poor have this in common:
  The LORD is the Maker of them all.

³The prudent see danger and take
    refuge,
  but the simple keep going and pay
    the penalty.

⁴Humility is the fear of the LORD;
  its wages are riches and honor and
    life.

⁵In the paths of the wicked are snares
    and pitfalls,
  but those who would preserve their
    life stay far from them.

⁶Start children off on the way they
    should go,
  and even when they are old they will
    not turn from it.

⁷The rich rule over the poor,
  and the borrower is slave to the
    lender.

⁸Whoever sows injustice reaps
    calamity,
  and the rod they wield in fury will be
    broken.

⁹The generous will themselves be
    blessed,
  for they share their food with the
    poor.

¹⁰Drive out the mocker, and out goes
    strife;
  quarrels and insults are ended.

---

^a 21 Or *righteousness*

11 One who loves a pure heart and who
  speaks with grace
  will have the king for a friend.

12 The eyes of the LORD keep watch over
  knowledge,
  but he frustrates the words of the
  unfaithful.

13 The sluggard says, "There's a lion
  outside!
  I'll be killed in the public square!"

14 The mouth of an adulterous woman is
  a deep pit;
  a man who is under the LORD's
  wrath falls into it.

15 Folly is bound up in the heart of a
  child,
  but the rod of discipline will drive it
  far away.

16 One who oppresses the poor to
  increase his wealth
  and one who gives gifts to the
  rich—both come to poverty.

Thirty Sayings of the Wise
Saying 1
17 Pay attention and turn your ear to the
  sayings of the wise;
  apply your heart to what I teach,
18 for it is pleasing when you keep them
  in your heart
  and have all of them ready on your
  lips.
19 So that your trust may be in the LORD,
  I teach you today, even you.
20 Have I not written thirty sayings for you,
  sayings of counsel and knowledge,
21 teaching you to be honest and to
  speak the truth,
  so that you bring back truthful
  reports
  to those you serve?

Saying 2
22 Do not exploit the poor because they
  are poor
  and do not crush the needy in
  court,
23 for the LORD will take up their case
  and will exact life for life.

Saying 3
24 Do not make friends with a hot-
  tempered person,
  do not associate with one easily
  angered,
25 or you may learn their ways
  and get yourself ensnared.

Saying 4
26 Do not be one who shakes hands in
  pledge
  or puts up security for debts;
27 if you lack the means to pay,
  your very bed will be snatched from
  under you.

Saying 5
28 Do not move an ancient boundary
  stone
  set up by your ancestors.

Saying 6
29 Do you see someone skilled in their
  work?
  They will serve before kings;
  they will not serve before officials
  of low rank.

Saying 7
23 When you sit to dine with a ruler,
  note well what[a] is before you,
2 and put a knife to your throat
  if you are given to gluttony.
3 Do not crave his delicacies,
  for that food is deceptive.

Saying 8
4 Do not wear yourself out to get rich;
  do not trust your own cleverness.
5 Cast but a glance at riches, and they
  are gone,
  for they will surely sprout wings
  and fly off to the sky like an
  eagle.

Saying 9
6 Do not eat the food of a begrudging
  host,
  do not crave his delicacies;
7 for he is the kind of person
  who is always thinking about the
  cost.[b]

---

a 1 Or who   b 7 Or for as he thinks within himself, / so he is; or for as he puts on a feast, / so he is

"Eat and drink," he says to you,
but his heart is not with you.
8 You will vomit up the little you have
eaten
and will have wasted your
compliments.

Saying 10

9 Do not speak to fools,
for they will scorn your prudent
words.

Saying 11

10 Do not move an ancient boundary
stone
or encroach on the fields of the
fatherless,
11 for their Defender is strong;
he will take up their case against
you.

Saying 12

12 Apply your heart to instruction
and your ears to words of knowledge.

Saying 13

13 Do not withhold discipline from a child;
if you punish them with the rod,
they will not die.
14 Punish them with the rod
and save them from death.

Saying 14

15 My son, if your heart is wise,
then my heart will be glad indeed;
16 my inmost being will rejoice
when your lips speak what is right.

Saying 15

17 Do not let your heart envy sinners,
but always be zealous for the fear
of the LORD.
18 There is surely a future hope for you,
and your hope will not be cut off.

Saying 16

19 Listen, my son, and be wise,
and set your heart on the right path:
20 Do not join those who drink too much
wine
or gorge themselves on meat,
21 for drunkards and gluttons become
poor,
and drowsiness clothes them in
rags.

Saying 17

22 Listen to your father, who gave you life,
and do not despise your mother
when she is old.
23 Buy the truth and do not sell it—
wisdom, instruction and insight as
well.
24 The father of a righteous child has
great joy;
a man who fathers a wise son
rejoices in him.
25 May your father and mother rejoice;
may she who gave you birth be joyful!

Saying 18

26 My son, give me your heart
and let your eyes delight in my ways,
27 for an adulterous woman is a deep pit,
and a wayward wife is a narrow well.
28 Like a bandit she lies in wait
and multiplies the unfaithful among
men.

Saying 19

29 Who has woe? Who has sorrow?
Who has strife? Who has complaints?
Who has needless bruises? Who
has bloodshot eyes?
30 Those who linger over wine,
who go to sample bowls of mixed
wine.
31 Do not gaze at wine when it is red,
when it sparkles in the cup,
when it goes down smoothly!
32 In the end it bites like a snake
and poisons like a viper.
33 Your eyes will see strange sights,
and your mind will imagine
confusing things.
34 You will be like one sleeping on the
high seas,
lying on top of the rigging.
35 "They hit me," you will say, "but I'm
not hurt!
They beat me, but I don't feel it!
When will I wake up
so I can find another drink?"

Saying 20

24 Do not envy the wicked,
do not desire their company;
2 for their hearts plot violence,
and their lips talk about making
trouble.

Five high schoolers were killed in alcohol-related accidents in one month. All went to the same school. Two weeks later eleven students from the same school were arrested at a party for underage drinking. People may drink because they think it makes them look cool, or to fit in with friends, or even as self-medication. But as these proverbs remind us, "in the end it bites like a snake and poisons like a viper" (verse 32). Each of the five teens killed probably thought, "It can't happen to me." But don't kid yourself. It can happen to anyone. Even you.

{Proverbs 23:29–33}

>> INSTANT ACCESS

Saying 21

3 By wisdom a house is built,
  and through understanding it is
    established;
4 through knowledge its rooms are
    filled
  with rare and beautiful treasures.

Saying 22

5 The wise prevail through great power,
  and those who have knowledge
    muster their strength.
6 Surely you need guidance to wage war,
  and victory is won through many
    advisers.

Saying 23

7 Wisdom is too high for fools;
  in the assembly at the gate they
    must not open their mouths.

Saying 24

8 Whoever plots evil
  will be known as a schemer.
9 The schemes of folly are sin,
  and people detest a mocker.

Saying 25

10 If you falter in a time of trouble,
  how small is your strength!
11 Rescue those being led away to
    death;
  hold back those staggering toward
    slaughter.
12 If you say, "But we knew nothing
    about this,"
  does not he who weighs the heart
    perceive it?
  Does not he who guards your life
    know it?
  Will he not repay everyone
    according to what they have
    done?

Saying 26

13 Eat honey, my son, for it is good;
  honey from the comb is sweet to
    your taste.
14 Know also that wisdom is like honey
    for you:
  If you find it, there is a future hope
    for you,
  and your hope will not be cut off.

Saying 27

15 Do not lurk like a thief near the house
    of the righteous,
  do not plunder their dwelling place;
16 for though the righteous fall seven
    times, they rise again,
  but the wicked stumble when
    calamity strikes.

Saying 28

17 Do not gloat when your enemy falls;
  when they stumble, do not let your
    heart rejoice,
18 or the LORD will see and disapprove
  and turn his wrath away from them.

Saying 29

19 Do not fret because of evildoers
   or be envious of the wicked,
20 for the evildoer has no future hope,
   and the lamp of the wicked will be
      snuffed out.

Saying 30

21 Fear the LORD and the king, my son,
   and do not join with rebellious
      officials,
22 for those two will send sudden
      destruction on them,
   and who knows what calamities
      they can bring?

Further Sayings of the Wise

23 These also are sayings of the wise:

To show partiality in judging is not
   good:
24 Whoever says to the guilty, "You are
      innocent,"
   will be cursed by peoples and
      denounced by nations.
25 But it will go well with those who
      convict the guilty,
   and rich blessing will come on them.

26 An honest answer
   is like a kiss on the lips.

27 Put your outdoor work in order
   and get your fields ready;
   after that, build your house.

28 Do not testify against your neighbor
      without cause—
   would you use your lips to mislead?
29 Do not say, "I'll do to them as they
      have done to me;
   I'll pay them back for what they
      did."

30 I went past the field of a sluggard,
   past the vineyard of someone who
      has no sense;
31 thorns had come up everywhere,
   the ground was covered with weeds,
   and the stone wall was in ruins.
32 I applied my heart to what I observed
   and learned a lesson from what I
      saw:

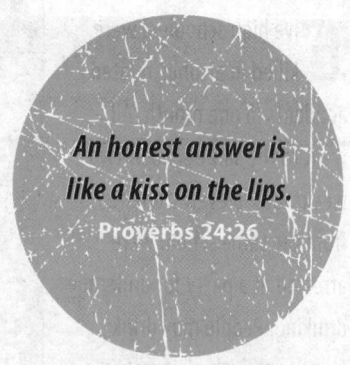

An honest answer is like a kiss on the lips.
Proverbs 24:26

33 A little sleep, a little slumber,
   a little folding of the hands to
      rest—
34 and poverty will come on you like a
      thief
   and scarcity like an armed
      man.

More Proverbs of Solomon

25 These are more proverbs of Solomon, compiled by the men of Hezekiah king of Judah:

2 It is the glory of God to conceal a
      matter;
   to search out a matter is the glory
      of kings.
3 As the heavens are high and the earth
      is deep,
   so the hearts of kings are
      unsearchable.

4 Remove the dross from the silver,
   and a silversmith can produce a
      vessel;
5 remove wicked officials from the
      king's presence,
   and his throne will be established
      through righteousness.

6 Do not exalt yourself in the king's
      presence,
   and do not claim a place among his
      great men;
7 it is better for him to say to you,
      "Come up here,"
   than for him to humiliate you before
      his nobles.

What you have seen with your eyes
8 do not bring[a] hastily to court,
for what will you do in the end
if your neighbor puts you to shame?

9 If you take your neighbor to court,
do not betray another's confidence,
10 or the one who hears it may shame you
and the charge against you will
stand.

11 Like apples[b] of gold in settings of silver
is a ruling rightly given.
12 Like an earring of gold or an ornament
of fine gold
is the rebuke of a wise judge to a
listening ear.

13 Like a snow-cooled drink at harvest
time
is a trustworthy messenger to the
one who sends him;
he refreshes the spirit of his
master.
14 Like clouds and wind without rain
is one who boasts of gifts never
given.

15 Through patience a ruler can be
persuaded,
and a gentle tongue can break a
bone.

16 If you find honey, eat just enough—
too much of it, and you will vomit.
17 Seldom set foot in your neighbor's
house—
too much of you, and they will hate
you.

18 Like a club or a sword or a sharp arrow
is one who gives false testimony
against a neighbor.
19 Like a broken tooth or a lame foot
is reliance on the unfaithful in a
time of trouble.

20 Like one who takes away a garment
on a cold day,
or like vinegar poured on a wound,
is one who sings songs to a heavy
heart.

21 If your enemy is hungry, give him food
to eat;
if he is thirsty, give him water to
drink.

22 In doing this, you will heap burning
coals on his head,
and the LORD will reward you.

23 Like a north wind that brings
unexpected rain
is a sly tongue—which provokes a
horrified look.

24 Better to live on a corner of the roof
than share a house with a
quarrelsome wife.

25 Like cold water to a weary soul
is good news from a distant land.
26 Like a muddied spring or a polluted
well
are the righteous who give way to
the wicked.

27 It is not good to eat too much honey,
nor is it honorable to search out
matters that are too deep.

28 Like a city whose walls are broken
through
is a person who lacks self-control.

26 Like snow in summer or rain in
harvest,
honor is not fitting for a fool.
2 Like a fluttering sparrow or a darting
swallow,
an undeserved curse does not
come to rest.
3 A whip for the horse, a bridle for the
donkey,
and a rod for the backs of fools!
4 Do not answer a fool according to his
folly,
or you yourself will be just like him.
5 Answer a fool according to his folly,
or he will be wise in his own eyes.
6 Sending a message by the hands of a
fool
is like cutting off one's feet or
drinking poison.
7 Like the useless legs of one who is
lame
is a proverb in the mouth of a fool.
8 Like tying a stone in a sling
is the giving of honor to a fool.
9 Like a thornbush in a drunkard's
hand
is a proverb in the mouth of a fool.

---

[a] 7,8 Or nobles / on whom you had set your eyes. / [8]Do not go   [b] 11 Or possibly apricots

10 Like an archer who wounds at random
   is one who hires a fool or any
      passer-by.
11 As a dog returns to its vomit,
   so fools repeat their folly.
12 Do you see a person wise in their own
      eyes?
   There is more hope for a fool than
      for them.
13 A sluggard says, "There's a lion in the
      road,
   a fierce lion roaming the streets!"
14 As a door turns on its hinges,
   so a sluggard turns on his bed.
15 A sluggard buries his hand in the dish;
   he is too lazy to bring it back to his
      mouth.
16 A sluggard is wiser in his own eyes
   than seven people who answer
      discreetly.
17 Like one who grabs a stray dog by the
      ears
   is someone who rushes into a
      quarrel not their own.
18 Like a maniac shooting
   flaming arrows of death
19 is one who deceives their neighbor
   and says, "I was only joking!"
20 Without wood a fire goes out;
   without a gossip a quarrel dies down.
21 As charcoal to embers and as wood to
      fire,
   so is a quarrelsome person for
      kindling strife.
22 The words of a gossip are like choice
      morsels;
   they go down to the inmost parts.
23 Like a coating of silver dross on
      earthenware
   are ferventa lips with an evil heart.
24 Enemies disguise themselves with
      their lips,
   but in their hearts they harbor deceit.
25 Though their speech is charming, do
      not believe them,
   for seven abominations fill their
      hearts.
26 Their malice may be concealed by
      deception,
   but their wickedness will be
      exposed in the assembly.

INSTANT ACCESS

Want some "friendly" advice? There's a lot of it in proverbs. Like, "wounds from a friend can be trusted, but an enemy multiplies kisses." "Do not forsake your friend" (27:10). "Gossip separates close friends" (16:28). "Do not make friends with a hot-tempered person" (22:24). "The righteous choose their friends carefully" (12:26). A true "friend loves at all times" (17:17). Be wise choosing your friends. Life will be richer . . . and easier.

{Proverbs 27:6}

27 Whoever digs a pit will fall into it;
   if someone rolls a stone, it will roll
      back on them.
28 A lying tongue hates those it hurts,
   and a flattering mouth works ruin.

27 Do not boast about tomorrow,
   for you do not know what a day
      may bring.

2 Let someone else praise you, and not
      your own mouth;
   an outsider, and not your own lips.

3 Stone is heavy and sand a burden,
   but a fool's provocation is heavier
      than both.

4 Anger is cruel and fury overwhelming,
   but who can stand before jealousy?

5 Better is open rebuke
   than hidden love.

---

a 23 Hebrew; Septuagint smooth

⁶Wounds from a friend can be trusted,
  but an enemy multiplies kisses.

⁷One who is full loathes honey from the comb,
  but to the hungry even what is bitter tastes sweet.

⁸Like a bird that flees its nest
  is anyone who flees from home.

⁹Perfume and incense bring joy to the heart,
  and the pleasantness of a friend springs from their heartfelt advice.

¹⁰Do not forsake your friend or a friend of your family,
  and do not go to your relative's house when disaster strikes you—
  better a neighbor nearby than a relative far away.

¹¹Be wise, my son, and bring joy to my heart;
  then I can answer anyone who treats me with contempt.

¹²The prudent see danger and take refuge,
  but the simple keep going and pay the penalty.

¹³Take the garment of one who puts up security for a stranger;
  hold it in pledge if it is done for an outsider.

¹⁴If anyone loudly blesses their neighbor early in the morning,
  it will be taken as a curse.

¹⁵A quarrelsome wife is like the dripping of a leaky roof in a rainstorm;
¹⁶restraining her is like restraining the wind
  or grasping oil with the hand.

¹⁷As iron sharpens iron,
  so one person sharpens another.

¹⁸The one who guards a fig tree will eat its fruit,
  and whoever protects their master will be honored.

¹⁹As water reflects the face,
  so one's life reflects the heart.ᵃ

²⁰Death and Destructionᵇ are never satisfied,
  and neither are human eyes.

²¹The crucible for silver and the furnace for gold,
  but people are tested by their praise.

²²Though you grind a fool in a mortar,
  grinding them like grain with a pestle,
  you will not remove their folly from them.

²³Be sure you know the condition of your flocks,
  give careful attention to your herds;
²⁴for riches do not endure forever,
  and a crown is not secure for all generations.
²⁵When the hay is removed and new growth appears
  and the grass from the hills is gathered in,
²⁶the lambs will provide you with clothing,
  and the goats with the price of a field.
²⁷You will have plenty of goats' milk to feed your family
  and to nourish your female servants.

Proverbs 28

Q: When is it better to be poor than rich?

BONUS: What don't those who want to be rich understand?

ᵃ 19 Or *so others reflect your heart back to you*
ᵇ 20 Hebrew *Abaddon*

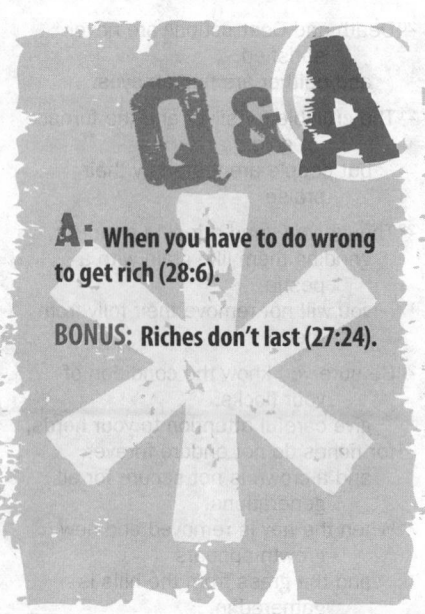

A: When you have to do wrong to get rich (28:6).

BONUS: Riches don't last (27:24).

28 The wicked flee though no one pursues,
but the righteous are as bold as a lion.

[2] When a country is rebellious, it has many rulers,
but a ruler with discernment and knowledge maintains order.

[3] A ruler[a] who oppresses the poor
is like a driving rain that leaves no crops.

[4] Those who forsake instruction praise the wicked,
but those who heed it resist them.

[5] Evildoers do not understand what is right,
but those who seek the LORD understand it fully.

[6] Better the poor whose walk is blameless
than the rich whose ways are perverse.

[7] A discerning son heeds instruction,
but a companion of gluttons disgraces his father.

[8] Whoever increases wealth by taking interest or profit from the poor
amasses it for another, who will be kind to the poor.

[9] If anyone turns a deaf ear to my instruction,
even their prayers are detestable.

[10] Whoever leads the upright along an evil path
will fall into their own trap,
but the blameless will receive a good inheritance.

[11] The rich are wise in their own eyes;
one who is poor and discerning sees how deluded they are.

[12] When the righteous triumph, there is great elation;
but when the wicked rise to power, people go into hiding.

[13] Whoever conceals their sins does not prosper,
but the one who confesses and renounces them finds mercy.

[14] Blessed is the one who always trembles before God,
but whoever hardens their heart falls into trouble.

[15] Like a roaring lion or a charging bear
is a wicked ruler over a helpless people.

[16] A tyrannical ruler practices extortion,
but one who hates ill-gotten gain will enjoy a long reign.

[17] Anyone tormented by the guilt of murder
will seek refuge in the grave;
let no one hold them back.

[18] The one whose walk is blameless is kept safe,
but the one whose ways are perverse will fall into the pit.[b]

[19] Those who work their land will have abundant food,
but those who chase fantasies will have their fill of poverty.

---

[a] 3 Or A poor person   [b] 18 Syriac (see Septuagint); Hebrew into one

Why care about justice for the poor? Because having concern for others is a mark of righteousness. "Justice for the poor" means making sure that everyone has a chance for an education and access to a job. It means making sure the rich aren't taking advantage of the poor. And it also means making sure that the children of the poor have food to eat and clothes to wear. Many churches actively minister to the poor in their communities. What do Christians in your community do? And what can you do to help?

{Proverbs 28:7}

20 A faithful person will be richly blessed,
but one eager to get rich will not go
unpunished.

21 To show partiality is not good—
yet a person will do wrong for a
piece of bread.

22 The stingy are eager to get rich
and are unaware that poverty
awaits them.

23 Whoever rebukes a person will in the
end gain favor
rather than one who has a flattering
tongue.

24 Whoever robs their father or mother
and says, "It's not wrong,"
is partner to one who destroys.

25 The greedy stir up conflict,
but those who trust in the LORD will
prosper.

26 Those who trust in themselves are
fools,
but those who walk in wisdom are
kept safe.

27 Those who give to the poor will lack
nothing,
but those who close their eyes to
them receive many curses.

28 When the wicked rise to power, people
go into hiding;
but when the wicked perish, the
righteous thrive.

29 Whoever remains stiff-necked
after many rebukes
will suddenly be destroyed—
without remedy.

2 When the righteous thrive, the people
rejoice;
when the wicked rule, the people
groan.

3 A man who loves wisdom brings joy to
his father,
but a companion of prostitutes
squanders his wealth.

4 By justice a king gives a country
stability,
but those who are greedy for[a]
bribes tear it down.

5 Those who flatter their neighbors
are spreading nets for their feet.

6 Evildoers are snared by their own sin,
but the righteous shout for joy and
are glad.

7 The righteous care about justice for
the poor,
but the wicked have no such
concern.

8 Mockers stir up a city,
but the wise turn away anger.

9 If a wise person goes to court with a
fool,
the fool rages and scoffs, and there
is no peace.

---

a 4 Or who give

A faithful person will be richly blessed.

Proverbs 28:20

¹⁰ The bloodthirsty hate a person of integrity
and seek to kill the upright.

¹¹ Fools give full vent to their rage,
but the wise bring calm in the end.

¹² If a ruler listens to lies,
all his officials become wicked.

¹³ The poor and the oppressor have this in common:
The LORD gives sight to the eyes of both.

¹⁴ If a king judges the poor with fairness,
his throne will be established forever.

¹⁵ A rod and a reprimand impart wisdom,
but a child left undisciplined disgraces its mother.

¹⁶ When the wicked thrive, so does sin,
but the righteous will see their downfall.

¹⁷ Discipline your children, and they will give you peace;
they will bring you the delights you desire.

¹⁸ Where there is no revelation, people cast off restraint;
but blessed is the one who heeds wisdom's instruction.

¹⁹ Servants cannot be corrected by mere words;
though they understand, they will not respond.

²⁰ Do you see someone who speaks in haste?
There is more hope for a fool than for them.

²¹ A servant pampered from youth
will turn out to be insolent.

²² An angry person stirs up conflict,
and a hot-tempered person commits many sins.

²³ Pride brings a person low,
but the lowly in spirit gain honor.

²⁴ The accomplices of thieves are their own enemies;
they are put under oath and dare not testify.

²⁵ Fear of man will prove to be a snare,
but whoever trusts in the LORD is kept safe.

²⁶ Many seek an audience with a ruler,
but it is from the LORD that one gets justice.

²⁷ The righteous detest the dishonest;
the wicked detest the upright.

Sayings of Agur

30 The sayings of Agur son of Jakeh—an inspired utterance.

This man's utterance to Ithiel:

"I am weary, God,
but I can prevail.ᵃ
² Surely I am only a brute, not a man;
I do not have human understanding.
³ I have not learned wisdom,
nor have I attained to the knowledge of the Holy One.
⁴ Who has gone up to heaven and come down?
Whose hands have gathered up the wind?
Who has wrapped up the waters in a cloak?
Who has established all the ends of the earth?
What is his name, and what is the name of his son?
Surely you know!

ᵃ 1 With a different word division of the Hebrew; Masoretic Text *utterance to Ithiel, / to Ithiel and Ukal:*

5 "Every word of God is flawless;
  he is a shield to those who take
    refuge in him.
6 Do not add to his words,
  or he will rebuke you and prove you
    a liar.

7 "Two things I ask of you, LORD;
  do not refuse me before I die:
8 Keep falsehood and lies far from me;
  give me neither poverty nor riches,
  but give me only my daily bread.
9 Otherwise, I may have too much and
    disown you
  and say, 'Who is the LORD?'
  Or I may become poor and steal,
  and so dishonor the name of my
    God.

10 "Do not slander a servant to their
    master,
  or they will curse you, and you will
    pay for it.

11 "There are those who curse their
    fathers
  and do not bless their mothers;
12 those who are pure in their own eyes
  and yet are not cleansed of their filth;
13 those whose eyes are ever so
    haughty,
  whose glances are so disdainful;
14 those whose teeth are swords
  and whose jaws are set with knives
  to devour the poor from the earth
  and the needy from among
    mankind.

15 "The leech has two daughters.
  'Give! Give!' they cry.

  "There are three things that are never
    satisfied,
  four that never say, 'Enough!':
16 the grave, the barren womb,
  land, which is never satisfied with
    water,
  and fire, which never says,
    'Enough!'

17 "The eye that mocks a father,
  that scorns an aged mother,
  will be pecked out by the ravens of the
    valley,
  will be eaten by the vultures.

18 "There are three things that are too
    amazing for me,
  four that I do not understand:
19 the way of an eagle in the sky,
  the way of a snake on a rock,
  the way of a ship on the high seas,
  and the way of a man with a young
    woman.

20 "This is the way of an adulterous
    woman:
  She eats and wipes her mouth
  and says, 'I've done nothing wrong.'

21 "Under three things the earth
    trembles,
  under four it cannot bear up:
22 a servant who becomes king,
  a godless fool who gets plenty to
    eat,
23 a contemptible woman who gets
    married,
  and a servant who displaces her
    mistress.

24 "Four things on earth are small,
  yet they are extremely wise:
25 Ants are creatures of little strength,
  yet they store up their food in the
    summer;
26 hyraxes are creatures of little power,
  yet they make their home in the
    crags;
27 locusts have no king,
  yet they advance together in ranks;
28 a lizard can be caught with the hand,
  yet it is found in kings' palaces.

29 "There are three things that are
    stately in their stride,
  four that move with stately bearing:
30 a lion, mighty among beasts,
  who retreats before nothing;
31 a strutting rooster, a he-goat,
  and a king secure against revolt.[a]

32 "If you play the fool and exalt yourself,
  or if you plan evil,
  clap your hand over your mouth!
33 For as churning cream produces
    butter,
  and as twisting the nose produces
    blood,
  so stirring up anger produces
    strife."

---

[a] 31 The meaning of the Hebrew for this phrase is uncertain.

Sayings of King Lemuel

31 The sayings of King Lemuel—an inspired utterance his mother taught him.

² Listen, my son! Listen, son of my womb!
Listen, my son, the answer to my prayers!

³ Do not spend your strength[a] on women,
your vigor on those who ruin kings.

⁴ It is not for kings, Lemuel—
it is not for kings to drink wine,
not for rulers to crave beer,

⁵ lest they drink and forget what has been decreed,

---

a 3 Or wealth

TO THE POINT

No "Men's Work"

Have you ever heard that women aren't supposed to do "men's work"? That they are supposed to stay home, clean house and cook?

In Old Testament times most men worked the land. They hired workers, they bought and sold produce, they gave to the poor, they took care of their families. That's what is fascinating about Proverbs 31. The noble wife does much the same work as her husband:

+ She supervises employees (Proverbs 31:15).

+ She buys and sells land (Proverbs 31:16).

+ She invests her earnings (Proverbs 31:16).

+ She makes a profit trading her produce (Proverbs 31:18).

+ She gives to the poor (Proverbs 31:20).

+ And she cares for the needs of her family (Proverbs 31:21).

God has given abilities to both men and women. There is nothing wrong with being a stay-at-home mom, or with having a career.

and deprive all the oppressed of
their rights.
⁶ Let beer be for those who are
perishing,
wine for those who are in anguish!
⁷ Let them drink and forget their
poverty
and remember their misery no
more.

⁸ Speak up for those who cannot speak
for themselves,
for the rights of all who are
destitute.
⁹ Speak up and judge fairly;
defend the rights of the poor and
needy.

Epilogue: The Wife of Noble Character

¹⁰ᵃ A wife of noble character who can
find?
She is worth far more than rubies.
¹¹ Her husband has full confidence in
her
and lacks nothing of value.
¹² She brings him good, not harm,
all the days of her life.
¹³ She selects wool and flax
and works with eager hands.
¹⁴ She is like the merchant ships,
bringing her food from afar.
¹⁵ She gets up while it is still night;
she provides food for her family
and portions for her female
servants.
¹⁶ She considers a field and buys it;
out of her earnings she plants a
vineyard.
¹⁷ She sets about her work vigorously;
her arms are strong for her tasks.
¹⁸ She sees that her trading is
profitable,
and her lamp does not go out at
night.

¹⁹ In her hand she holds the distaff
and grasps the spindle with her
fingers.
²⁰ She opens her arms to the poor
and extends her hands to the
needy.
²¹ When it snows, she has no fear for
her household;
for all of them are clothed in
scarlet.
²² She makes coverings for her bed;
she is clothed in fine linen and
purple.
²³ Her husband is respected at the city
gate,
where he takes his seat among the
elders of the land.
²⁴ She makes linen garments and sells
them,
and supplies the merchants with
sashes.
²⁵ She is clothed with strength and
dignity;
she can laugh at the days to come.
²⁶ She speaks with wisdom,
and faithful instruction is on her
tongue.
²⁷ She watches over the affairs of her
household
and does not eat the bread of
idleness.
²⁸ Her children arise and call her
blessed;
her husband also, and he praises
her:
²⁹ "Many women do noble things,
but you surpass them all."
³⁰ Charm is deceptive, and beauty is
fleeting;
but a woman who fears the Lᴏʀᴅ is
to be praised.
³¹ Honor her for all that her hands have
done,
and let her works bring her praise at
the city gate.

ᵃ 10 Verses 10-31 are an acrostic poem, the verses of which begin with the successive letters of the Hebrew alphabet.

ECCLESIASTES

preview

Solomon writes this near the end of his life. He relies on reasoning since he has abandoned God.

Solomon's personal income is 50,000 pounds of gold a year. (That's $320 million!) And he's miserably unhappy.

What's the Use?

Have you ever asked yourself that question? What's the use of studying? What's the use of trying to get along with others? What's the use of trying to do the right thing when all your friends just laugh at you? Do you ever feel that life is meaningless?

One book in the Bible agrees: life is empty. Everything is meaningless. At least that's what King Solomon thought after he'd turned away from God. But Solomon was wrong! If you listen to what God's Word tells about the Lord and his plan for you, you'll find life isn't meaningless at all.

>>**HOW TO BE UNHAPPY**
Solomon tries everything, see Ecclesiastes 2:1–11

>>**WORKING WITH MILLIONS**
Report given in Ecclesiastes 5:8–20

>>**DECISIONS, DECISIONS**
You do have choices, King reminds, Ecclesiastes 7:1–14

>>**TAKE IT FROM ME**
Wise advice recorded in Ecclesiastes 12:1

While Solomon experiments with pleasure and accomplishments, Athens empire-builds. Greeks worship a pagan pantheon. Pantheism develops in India. In China rationalist philosophy replaces earlier mysticism.

Everything Is Meaningless

1 The words of the Teacher,[a] son of David, king in Jerusalem:

2 "Meaningless! Meaningless!"
    says the Teacher.
"Utterly meaningless!
    Everything is meaningless."

3 What do people gain from all their
        labors
    at which they toil under the sun?
4 Generations come and generations go,
    but the earth remains forever.
5 The sun rises and the sun sets,
    and hurries back to where it rises.
6 The wind blows to the south
    and turns to the north;
round and round it goes,
    ever returning on its course.
7 All streams flow into the sea,
    yet the sea is never full.
To the place the streams come from,
    there they return again.
8 All things are wearisome,
    more than one can say.
The eye never has enough of seeing,
    nor the ear its fill of hearing.
9 What has been will be again,
    what has been done will be done
        again;
    there is nothing new under the sun.
10 Is there anything of which one can
        say,
    "Look! This is something new"?
It was here already, long ago;
    it was here before our time.
11 No one remembers the former
        generations,
    and even those yet to come
will not be remembered
    by those who follow them.

Wisdom Is Meaningless

12 I, the Teacher, was king over Israel in Jerusalem. 13 I applied my mind to study and to explore by wisdom all that is done under the heavens. What a heavy burden God has laid on mankind! 14 I have seen all the things that are done under the sun; all of them are meaningless, a chasing after the wind.

15 What is crooked cannot be
        straightened;
    what is lacking cannot be counted.

16 I said to myself, "Look, I have increased in wisdom more than anyone who has ruled over Jerusalem before me; I have experienced much of wisdom and knowledge." 17 Then I applied myself to the understanding of wisdom, and also of madness and folly, but I learned that this, too, is a chasing after the wind.

18 For with much wisdom comes much
        sorrow;
    the more knowledge, the more grief.

Pleasures Are Meaningless

2 I said to myself, "Come now, I will test you with pleasure to find out what is good." But that also proved to be meaningless. 2 "Laughter," I said, "is madness. And what does pleasure accomplish?" 3 I tried cheering myself with wine, and embracing folly—my mind still guiding me with wisdom. I wanted to see what was good for people to do under the heavens during the few days of their lives.

4 I undertook great projects: I built houses for myself and planted vineyards. 5 I made gardens and parks and planted all kinds of fruit trees in them. 6 I made reservoirs to water groves of flourishing trees. 7 I bought male and female slaves and had other slaves who were born in my house. I also owned more herds and flocks than anyone in Jerusalem before me. 8 I amassed silver and gold for myself, and the treasure of kings and provinces. I acquired male and female singers, and a harem[b] as well—the delights of a man's heart. 9 I became greater by far than anyone in Jerusalem before me. In all this my wisdom stayed with me.

10 I denied myself nothing my eyes
        desired;
    I refused my heart no pleasure.
My heart took delight in all my labor,
    and this was the reward for all my
        toil.

---

a 1 Or the leader of the assembly; also in verses 2 and 12   b 8 The meaning of the Hebrew for this phrase is uncertain.

11 Yet when I surveyed all that my hands
had done
and what I had toiled to achieve,
everything was meaningless, a
chasing after the wind;
nothing was gained under the sun.

Wisdom and Folly Are Meaningless

12 Then I turned my thoughts to consider
wisdom,
and also madness and folly.
What more can the king's
successor do
than what has already been done?
13 I saw that wisdom is better than folly,
just as light is better than darkness.
14 The wise have eyes in their heads,
while the fool walks in the
darkness;
but I came to realize
that the same fate overtakes them
both.

15 Then I said to myself,

"The fate of the fool will overtake me
also.
What then do I gain by being wise?"
I said to myself,
"This too is meaningless."
16 For the wise, like the fool, will not be
long remembered;
the days have already come when
both have been forgotten.
Like the fool, the wise too must die!

Toil Is Meaningless

17 So I hated life, because the work that
is done under the sun was grievous to
me. All of it is meaningless, a chasing after the wind. 18 I hated all the things I had
toiled for under the sun, because I must
leave them to the one who comes after
me. 19 And who knows whether that person will be wise or foolish? Yet they will
have control over all the fruit of my toil
into which I have poured my effort and
skill under the sun. This too is meaningless. 20 So my heart began to despair over
all my toilsome labor under the sun. 21 For
a person may labor with wisdom, knowledge and skill, and then they must leave

INSTANT ACCESS

Toys. That tractor you loved when you were three. That game you played all the time when you were five. Your baby doll with all the clothes. A popular bumper sticker says, "The one who has the most toys when he dies, wins." Some adults never grow up. Their toys just change. Solomon had so much money and power that he got anything he wanted. Later in life he looked back and decided everything he had was meaningless. Possessions hadn't made him happy at all. Those who feel like they just have to have "things" haven't grown up spiritually. It's not the things you have, but the kind of person you are that makes life worthwhile.

{Ecclesiastes 2:1–11}

all they own to another who has not toiled
for it. This too is meaningless and a great
misfortune. 22 What do people get for all
the toil and anxious striving with which
they labor under the sun? 23 All their days
their work is grief and pain; even at night
their minds do not rest. This too is meaningless.

24 A person can do nothing better than
to eat and drink and find satisfaction in
their own toil. This too, I see, is from the
hand of God, 25 for without him, who can

eat or find enjoyment? ²⁶To the person who pleases him, God gives wisdom, knowledge and happiness, but to the sinner he gives the task of gathering and storing up wealth to hand it over to the one who pleases God. This too is meaningless, a chasing after the wind.

A Time for Everything

3 There is a time for everything,
and a season for every activity
under the heavens:

2 a time to be born and a time to
die,
a time to plant and a time to
uproot,
3 a time to kill and a time to heal,
a time to tear down and a time to
build,

4 a time to weep and a time to
laugh,
a time to mourn and a time to
dance,
5 a time to scatter stones and a time
to gather them,
a time to embrace and a time to
refrain from embracing,
6 a time to search and a time to
give up,
a time to keep and a time to throw
away,
7 a time to tear and a time to
mend,
a time to be silent and a time to
speak,
8 a time to love and a time to hate,
a time for war and a time for
peace.

TO THE POINT

Can't Buy Happiness

Solomon's income was probably over $200 million a year. He says, "I denied myself nothing my eyes desired; I refused my heart no pleasure" (Ecclesiastes 2:10). But in despair he also wrote, "Meaningless! Everything is meaningless." What good is money anyway? A lot, if you follow a few simple rules:

+ Work so you won't be dependent on anyone
(1 Thessalonians 4:11–12).

+ Rely on God, not on your money (1 Timothy 6:17).

+ Be generous and willing to share (1 Timothy 6:18).

+ Store up treasures in heaven, not on earth
(Matthew 6:19–21).

If money is the most important thing in your life, you'll be miserable. But if God's values are most important, and if his values shape the way you use your money, you'll be happy indeed.

I'm always waiting to be old enough to do things—date, get a job, drive, get my braces off. Will I ever be the right age to do the stuff I want to do?

>> Joshua

Dear Jordan

Dear Joshua,

Don't wish your youth away! Did you notice that sixth grade went by faster than kindergarten? And eighth grade went by faster than sixth? Of course they didn't really go any faster, it just seemed that way. When you were 5, a year was 1/5 of your life. When you were 10, a year was 1/10 of your life. So the more years you live, the shorter a year seems. The older you get, the faster time seems to pass.

Be happy for each day. Do the things this year that you can do, and when next year comes, enjoy new opportunities. But don't be so impatient that one day you regret you didn't take the time to enjoy each step. Remember: "There is a time for everything, and a season for every activity under the heavens" (Ecclesiastes 3:1).

Jordan

⁹What do workers gain from their toil? ¹⁰I have seen the burden God has laid on the human race. ¹¹He has made everything beautiful in its time. He has also set eternity in the human heart; yetᵃ no one can fathom what God has done from beginning to end. ¹²I know that there is nothing better for people than to be happy and to do good while they live. ¹³That each of them may eat and drink, and find satisfaction in all their toil—this is the gift of God. ¹⁴I know that everything God does will endure forever; nothing can be added to it and nothing taken from it. God does it so that people will fear him.

¹⁵Whatever is has already been,
    and what will be has been before;
    and God will call the past to
        account.ᵇ

¹⁶And I saw something else under the sun:

In the place of judgment—wickedness
        was there,
    in the place of justice—wickedness
        was there.

¹⁷I said to myself,

"God will bring into judgment
    both the righteous and the wicked,
for there will be a time for every
        activity,
    a time to judge every deed."

¹⁸I also said to myself, "As for humans, God tests them so that they may see that they are like the animals. ¹⁹Surely the fate of human beings is like that of the animals; the same fate awaits them both: As one dies, so dies the other. All have the same breathᶜ; humans have no advantage over animals. Everything is meaningless. ²⁰All go to the same place; all come from dust, and to dust all return. ²¹Who knows if the human spirit rises upward and if the spirit of the animal goes down into the earth?"

²²So I saw that there is nothing better for a person than to enjoy their work, because that is their lot. For who can bring them to see what will happen after them?

Oppression, Toil, Friendlessness

4 Again I looked and saw all the oppression that was taking place under the sun:

I saw the tears of the oppressed—
    and they have no comforter;
power was on the side of their
        oppressors—
    and they have no comforter.
²And I declared that the dead,
    who had already died,
are happier than the living,
    who are still alive.
³But better than both
    is the one who has never been
        born,
who has not seen the evil
    that is done under the sun.

⁴And I saw that all toil and all achievement spring from one person's envy of another. This too is meaningless, a chasing after the wind.

⁵Fools fold their hands
    and ruin themselves.
⁶Better one handful with tranquillity
    than two handfuls with toil
    and chasing after the wind.

⁷Again I saw something meaningless under the sun:

⁸There was a man all alone;
    he had neither son nor brother.
There was no end to his toil,
    yet his eyes were not content with
        his wealth.
"For whom am I toiling," he asked,
    "and why am I depriving myself of
        enjoyment?"
This too is meaningless—
    a miserable business!

⁹Two are better than one,
    because they have a good return for
        their labor:
¹⁰If either of them falls down,
    one can help the other up.
But pity anyone who falls
    and has no one to help them up.

ᵃ 11 Or *also placed ignorance in the human heart, so that*   ᵇ 15 Or *God calls back the past*   ᶜ 19 Or *spirit*

11 Also, if two lie down together, they will keep warm.
But how can one keep warm alone?
12 Though one may be overpowered,
two can defend themselves.
A cord of three strands is not quickly broken.

Advancement Is Meaningless

13 Better a poor but wise youth than an old but foolish king who no longer knows how to heed a warning. 14 The youth may have come from prison to the kingship, or he may have been born in poverty within his kingdom. 15 I saw that all who lived and walked under the sun followed the youth, the king's successor. 16 There was no end to all the people who were before them. But those who came later were not pleased with the successor. This too is meaningless, a chasing after the wind.

Fulfill Your Vow to God

5 *a* Guard your steps when you go to the house of God. Go near to listen rather than to offer the sacrifice of fools, who do not know that they do wrong.

2 Do not be quick with your mouth,
do not be hasty in your heart
to utter anything before God.
God is in heaven
and you are on earth,
so let your words be few.
3 A dream comes when there are many cares,
and many words mark the speech of a fool.

4 When you make a vow to God, do not delay to fulfill it. He has no pleasure in fools; fulfill your vow. 5 It is better not to make a vow than to make one and not fulfill it. 6 Do not let your mouth lead you into sin. And do not protest to the temple messenger, "My vow was a mistake." Why should God be angry at what you say and destroy the work of your hands? 7 Much dreaming and many words are meaningless. Therefore fear God.

Riches Are Meaningless

8 If you see the poor oppressed in a

INSTANT ACCESS

Many teens these days promise not to have sex before marriage. But studies show these same abstainers come down with as many sexually transmitted diseases (STD's) as teens who admit to having sex. Why? Because people lie to themselves about what is and isn't "sex." There's more to sex than going "all the way." Deep down you can read through what your friends think is OK. Girls and guys can be "technical virgins"—but no one who plays with sex can escape the emotional turmoil and emotional scars. And many won't escape a sexually transmitted disease. So if you're going to promise God to be sexually pure, keep your promise. Don't pretend oral sex isn't sex. God knows, and you know, that's just a technicality.

{Ecclesiastes 5:4}

district, and justice and rights denied, do not be surprised at such things; for one official is eyed by a higher one, and over them both are others higher still. 9 The increase from the land is taken by all; the king himself profits from the fields.

---

a In Hebrew texts 5:1 is numbered 4:17, and 5:2-20 is numbered 5:1-19.

¹⁰Whoever loves money never has
enough;
whoever loves wealth is never
satisfied with their income.
This too is meaningless.

¹¹As goods increase,
so do those who consume them.
And what benefit are they to the
owners
except to feast their eyes on them?

¹²The sleep of a laborer is sweet,
whether they eat little or much,
but as for the rich, their abundance
permits them no sleep.

¹³I have seen a grievous evil under the
sun:

wealth hoarded to the harm of its
owners,
¹⁴ or wealth lost through some
misfortune,
so that when they have children
there is nothing left for them to
inherit.
¹⁵Everyone comes naked from their
mother's womb,
and as everyone comes, so they
depart.
They take nothing from their toil
that they can carry in their hands.

¹⁶This too is a grievous evil:

As everyone comes, so they depart,
and what do they gain,
since they toil for the wind?

¹⁷All their days they eat in darkness,
with great frustration, affliction and
anger.

¹⁸This is what I have observed to be
good: that it is appropriate for a person
to eat, to drink and to find satisfaction in
their toilsome labor under the sun during
the few days of life God has given them—
for this is their lot. ¹⁹Moreover, when God
gives someone wealth and possessions,
and the ability to enjoy them, to accept
their lot and be happy in their toil—this
is a gift of God. ²⁰They seldom reflect on
the days of their life, because God keeps
them occupied with gladness of heart.

6 I have seen another evil under the
sun, and it weighs heavily on mankind: ²God gives some people wealth,
possessions and honor, so that they lack
nothing their hearts desire, but God does
not grant them the ability to enjoy them,
and strangers enjoy them instead. This is
meaningless, a grievous evil.

³A man may have a hundred children
and live many years; yet no matter how
long he lives, if he cannot enjoy his prosperity and does not receive proper burial,
I say that a stillborn child is better off
than he. ⁴It comes without meaning, it
departs in darkness, and in darkness its
name is shrouded. ⁵Though it never saw
the sun or knew anything, it has more
rest than does that man— ⁶even if he
lives a thousand years twice over but fails
to enjoy his prosperity. Do not all go to
the same place?

7 Everyone's toil is for their mouth,
  yet their appetite is never satisfied.
8 What advantage have the wise over
    fools?
  What do the poor gain
    by knowing how to conduct
      themselves before others?
9 Better what the eye sees
  than the roving of the appetite.
  This too is meaningless,
    a chasing after the wind.

10 Whatever exists has already been
    named,
  and what humanity is has been
    known;
  no one can contend
    with someone who is stronger.
11 The more the words,
  the less the meaning,
  and how does that profit anyone?

12 For who knows what is good for a person in life, during the few and meaningless days they pass through like a shadow? Who can tell them what will happen under the sun after they are gone?

Wisdom

7 A good name is better than fine
    perfume,
  and the day of death better than the
    day of birth.
2 It is better to go to a house of
    mourning
  than to go to a house of feasting,
  for death is the destiny of everyone;
    the living should take this to heart.
3 Frustration is better than laughter,
  because a sad face is good for the
    heart.
4 The heart of the wise is in the house
    of mourning,
  but the heart of fools is in the
    house of pleasure.
5 It is better to heed the rebuke of a
    wise person
  than to listen to the song of fools.
6 Like the crackling of thorns under the
    pot,
  so is the laughter of fools.
  This too is meaningless.

7 Extortion turns a wise person into a
    fool,
  and a bribe corrupts the heart.
8 The end of a matter is better than its
    beginning,
  and patience is better than pride.
9 Do not be quickly provoked in your
    spirit,
  for anger resides in the lap of fools.

10 Do not say, "Why were the old days
    better than these?"
  For it is not wise to ask such
    questions.
11 Wisdom, like an inheritance, is a good
    thing
  and benefits those who see the
    sun.
12 Wisdom is a shelter
  as money is a shelter,
  but the advantage of knowledge is
    this:
    Wisdom preserves those who
      have it.
13 Consider what God has done:

  Who can straighten
    what he has made crooked?
14 When times are good, be happy;
  but when times are bad, consider
    this:
  God has made the one
    as well as the other.
  Therefore, no one can discover
    anything about their future.

15 In this meaningless life of mine I have seen both of these:

  the righteous perishing in their
    righteousness,
  and the wicked living long in their
    wickedness.
16 Do not be overrighteous,
  neither be overwise—
  why destroy yourself?
17 Do not be overwicked,
  and do not be a fool—
  why die before your time?
18 It is good to grasp the one
  and not let go of the other.
  Whoever fears God will avoid all
    extremes.[a]

---

[a] 18 Or will follow them both

Have you ever heard someone say something bad about you? Or have you ever overheard someone you like say something about you and then laugh? It's hard not to be sensitive to what others say about you. Maybe sometimes you're too sensitive. Solomon says, "Do not pay attention to every word people say." He's wise, because lots of times people say things they don't really mean. If you think about it, you can probably remember times when you have said things about others that you didn't mean. If you remember that human beings are weak and often say things they don't really mean, it will help you follow Solomon's good advice.

{Ecclesiastes 7:21–22}

19 Wisdom makes one wise person more powerful
than ten rulers in a city.

20 Indeed, there is no one on earth who is righteous,
no one who does what is right and never sins.

21 Do not pay attention to every word people say,
or you may hear your servant cursing you—

22 for you know in your heart
that many times you yourself have cursed others.

23 All this I tested by wisdom and I said,

"I am determined to be wise"—
but this was beyond me.
24 Whatever exists is far off and most profound—
who can discover it?
25 So I turned my mind to understand,
to investigate and to search out wisdom and the scheme of things
and to understand the stupidity of wickedness
and the madness of folly.
26 I find more bitter than death
the woman who is a snare,
whose heart is a trap
and whose hands are chains.
The man who pleases God will escape her,
but the sinner she will ensnare.

27 "Look," says the Teacher,[a] "this is what I have discovered:

"Adding one thing to another to discover the scheme of things—
28 while I was still searching but not finding—
I found one upright man among a thousand,
but not one upright woman among them all.
29 This only have I found:
God created mankind upright,
but they have gone in search of many schemes."

8 Who is like the wise?
Who knows the explanation of things?
A person's wisdom brightens their face
and changes its hard appearance.

Obey the King

2 Obey the king's command, I say, because you took an oath before God. 3 Do

---

a 27 Or the leader of the assembly

not be in a hurry to leave the king's presence. Do not stand up for a bad cause, for he will do whatever he pleases. [4]Since a king's word is supreme, who can say to him, "What are you doing?"

[5]Whoever obeys his command will
come to no harm,
and the wise heart will know the
proper time and procedure.
[6]For there is a proper time and
procedure for every matter,
though a person may be weighed
down by misery.

[7]Since no one knows the future,
who can tell someone else what is
to come?
[8]As no one has power over the wind to
contain it,
so[a] no one has power over the time
of their death.
As no one is discharged in time of
war,
so wickedness will not release
those who practice it.

[9]All this I saw, as I applied my mind to everything done under the sun. There is a time when a man lords it over others to his own[b] hurt. [10]Then too, I saw the wicked buried—those who used to come and go from the holy place and receive praise[c] in the city where they did this. This too is meaningless.

[11]When the sentence for a crime is not quickly carried out, people's hearts are filled with schemes to do wrong. [12]Although a wicked person who commits a hundred crimes may live a long time, I know that it will go better with those who fear God, who are reverent before him. [13]Yet because the wicked do not fear God, it will not go well with them, and their days will not lengthen like a shadow.

[14]There is something else meaningless that occurs on earth: the righteous who get what the wicked deserve, and the wicked who get what the righteous deserve. This too, I say, is meaningless. [15]So I commend the enjoyment of life, because there is nothing better for a person under the sun than to eat and drink and be glad. Then joy will accompany them in their toil all the days of the life God has given them under the sun.

[16]When I applied my mind to know wisdom and to observe the labor that is done on earth—people getting no sleep day or night— [17]then I saw all that God has done. No one can comprehend what goes on under the sun. Despite all their efforts to search it out, no one can discover its meaning. Even if the wise claim they know, they cannot really comprehend it.

A Common Destiny for All

9 So I reflected on all this and concluded that the righteous and the wise and what they do are in God's hands, but no one knows whether love or hate awaits them. [2]All share a common destiny—the righteous and the wicked, the good and the bad,[d] the clean and the unclean, those who offer sacrifices and those who do not.

As it is with the good,
so with the sinful;
as it is with those who take oaths,
so with those who are afraid to take
them.

[3]This is the evil in everything that happens under the sun: The same destiny overtakes all. The hearts of people, moreover, are full of evil and there is madness in their hearts while they live, and afterward they join the dead. [4]Anyone who is among the living has hope[e]—even a live dog is better off than a dead lion!

[5]For the living know that they will
die,
but the dead know nothing;
they have no further reward,
and even their name is forgotten.
[6]Their love, their hate
and their jealousy have long since
vanished;
never again will they have a part
in anything that happens under the
sun.

---

[a] *8 Or over the human spirit to retain it, / and so*   [b] *9 Or to their*   [c] *10 Some Hebrew manuscripts and Septuagint (Aquila); most Hebrew manuscripts and are forgotten*   [d] *2 Septuagint (Aquila), Vulgate and Syriac; Hebrew does not have and the bad.*   [e] *4 Or What then is to be chosen? With all who live, there is hope*

7Go, eat your food with gladness, and drink your wine with a joyful heart, for God has already approved what you do. 8Always be clothed in white, and always anoint your head with oil. 9Enjoy life with your wife, whom you love, all the days of this meaningless life that God has given you under the sun—all your meaningless days. For this is your lot in life and in your toilsome labor under the sun. 10Whatever your hand finds to do, do it with all your might, for in the realm of the dead, where you are going, there is neither working nor planning nor knowledge nor wisdom.

11I have seen something else under the sun:

The race is not to the swift
    or the battle to the strong,
nor does food come to the wise
    or wealth to the brilliant
    or favor to the learned;
but time and chance happen to them
    all.

12Moreover, no one knows when their hour will come:

As fish are caught in a cruel net,
    or birds are taken in a snare,
so people are trapped by evil times
    that fall unexpectedly upon them.

Wisdom Better Than Folly

13I also saw under the sun this example of wisdom that greatly impressed me: 14There was once a small city with only a few people in it. And a powerful king came against it, surrounded it and built huge siege works against it. 15Now there lived in that city a man poor but wise, and

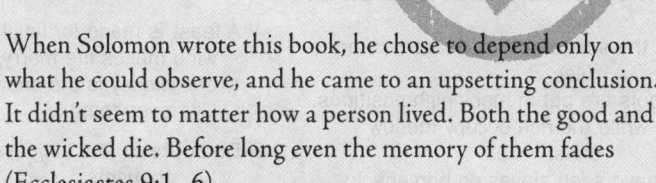

Look Again

When Solomon wrote this book, he chose to depend only on what he could observe, and he came to an upsetting conclusion. It didn't seem to matter how a person lived. Both the good and the wicked die. Before long even the memory of them fades (Ecclesiastes 9:1–6).

That's what's special about the Bible. In it God pulls back the curtain and lets you look beyond the physical. You learn that there is a very real invisible world. You learn that every person who has died still exists. The body dies. But the person—the real person, who thinks and feels and remembers—continues to exist.

You don't have to be a Solomon to know that things aren't always fair here on earth. But don't be discouraged. This life isn't the end, and God promises you "an inheritance" (1 Peter 1:4).

he saved the city by his wisdom. But nobody remembered that poor man. ¹⁶So I said, "Wisdom is better than strength." But the poor man's wisdom is despised, and his words are no longer heeded.

¹⁷ The quiet words of the wise are more
    to be heeded
  than the shouts of a ruler of fools.
¹⁸ Wisdom is better than weapons of
    war,
  but one sinner destroys much
    good.

10 As dead flies give perfume a bad
    smell,
  so a little folly outweighs wisdom
    and honor.
² The heart of the wise inclines to the
    right,
  but the heart of the fool to the
    left.
³ Even as fools walk along the road,
    they lack sense
  and show everyone how stupid they
    are.
⁴ If a ruler's anger rises against you,
    do not leave your post;
  calmness can lay great offenses to
    rest.

⁵ There is an evil I have seen under the
    sun,
  the sort of error that arises from a
    ruler:
⁶ Fools are put in many high positions,
  while the rich occupy the low
    ones.
⁷ I have seen slaves on horseback,
  while princes go on foot like
    slaves.

⁸ Whoever digs a pit may fall into it;
  whoever breaks through a wall may
    be bitten by a snake.
⁹ Whoever quarries stones may be
    injured by them;
  whoever splits logs may be
    endangered by them.
¹⁰ If the ax is dull
    and its edge unsharpened,
  more strength is needed,
  but skill will bring success.

¹¹ If a snake bites before it is charmed,
  the charmer receives no fee.

¹² Words from the mouth of the wise are
    gracious,
  but fools are consumed by their
    own lips.
¹³ At the beginning their words are folly;
  at the end they are wicked
    madness—
¹⁴   and fools multiply words.

No one knows what is coming—
  who can tell someone else what will
    happen after them?

¹⁵ The toil of fools wearies them;
  they do not know the way to town.

¹⁶ Woe to the land whose king was a
    servantᵃ
  and whose princes feast in the
    morning.
¹⁷ Blessed is the land whose king is of
    noble birth
  and whose princes eat at a proper
    time—
  for strength and not for
    drunkenness.

¹⁸ Through laziness, the rafters sag;
  because of idle hands, the house
    leaks.

¹⁹ A feast is made for laughter,
  wine makes life merry,
  and money is the answer for
    everything.

²⁰ Do not revile the king even in your
    thoughts,
  or curse the rich in your bedroom,
  because a bird in the sky may carry
    your words,
  and a bird on the wing may report
    what you say.

Invest in Many Ventures

11 Ship your grain across the sea;
  after many days you may receive
    a return.
² Invest in seven ventures, yes, in
    eight;
  you do not know what disaster may
    come upon the land.

ᵃ 16 Or *king is a child*

or how the body is formed[a] in a mother's womb,
so you cannot understand the work of God,
the Maker of all things.

6 Sow your seed in the morning,
and at evening let your hands not be idle,
for you do not know which will succeed,
whether this or that,
or whether both will do equally well.

Remember Your Creator While Young

7 Light is sweet,
and it pleases the eyes to see the sun.
8 However many years anyone may live,
let them enjoy them all.
But let them remember the days of darkness,
for there will be many.
Everything to come is meaningless.

9 You who are young, be happy while you are young,
and let your heart give you joy in the days of your youth.
Follow the ways of your heart
and whatever your eyes see,
but know that for all these things
God will bring you into judgment.
10 So then, banish anxiety from your heart
and cast off the troubles of your body,
for youth and vigor are meaningless.

12 Remember your Creator
in the days of your youth,
before the days of trouble come
and the years approach when you will say,
"I find no pleasure in them"—
2 before the sun and the light
and the moon and the stars grow dark,
and the clouds return after the rain;

I f God is "the Maker of all things," why did he make you like you are? Oh, there are some things about yourself you don't like? That nose just a bit off center? You have to study hard while your older sister breezes through school without cracking a book? OK, you're not perfect. But that's not the point. The point is that God, "the Maker of all things," shaped you from the beginning. Instead of worrying about flaws, why not make a list of good things about yourself? You may not get a lot of things down the first time you try. But keep the list around and add things when you think of them. Then enjoy—and celebrate—yourself!

{Ecclesiastes 11:5}

INSTANT ACCESS

---

3 If clouds are full of water,
they pour rain on the earth.
Whether a tree falls to the south or to the north,
in the place where it falls, there it will lie.
4 Whoever watches the wind will not plant;
whoever looks at the clouds will not reap.

5 As you do not know the path of the wind,

---

a 5 Or know how life (or the spirit) / enters the body being formed

³when the keepers of the house
    tremble,
  and the strong men stoop,
when the grinders cease because they
    are few,
  and those looking through the
    windows grow dim;
⁴when the doors to the street are
    closed
  and the sound of grinding fades;
when people rise up at the sound of
    birds,
  but all their songs grow faint;
⁵when people are afraid of heights
  and of dangers in the streets;
when the almond tree blossoms
  and the grasshopper drags itself
    along
  and desire no longer is stirred.
Then people go to their eternal
    home
  and mourners go about the
    streets.

⁶Remember him—before the silver
    cord is severed,
  and the golden bowl is broken;
before the pitcher is shattered at the
    spring,
  and the wheel broken at the well,
⁷and the dust returns to the ground it
    came from,

and the spirit returns to God who
    gave it.
⁸"Meaningless! Meaningless!" says the
    Teacher.ᵃ
  "Everything is meaningless!"

The Conclusion of the Matter

⁹Not only was the Teacher wise, but he
also imparted knowledge to the people.
He pondered and searched out and set
in order many proverbs. ¹⁰The Teacher
searched to find just the right words, and
what he wrote was upright and true.

¹¹The words of the wise are like goads,
their collected sayings like firmly embedded nails—given by one shepherd.ᵇ ¹²Be
warned, my son, of anything in addition
to them.

Of making many books there is no end,
and much study wearies the body.

¹³Now all has been heard;
  here is the conclusion of the
    matter:
Fear God and keep his
    commandments,
  for this is the duty of all mankind.
¹⁴For God will bring every deed into
    judgment,
  including every hidden thing,
  whether it is good or evil.

ᵃ 8 Or the leader of the assembly; also in verses 9 and 10   ᵇ 11 Or Shepherd

SONG OF SONGS

Love Letters.

Have you ever written one? Have you ever received one? Love is great! No wonder there are so many popular songs about love between a man and woman.

You don't need to be surprised to find love poems in the Bible. God made human beings male and female. He intended love between men and women to be a wonderful, beautiful thing. Song of Songs is a collection of love poems, telling how a man and his bride feel about each other.

>>**A HUSBAND'S LOVE LETTERS**
(See "He" sections)

>>**A WIFE'S LOVE LETTERS**
(See "She" sections)

>>**ROMANCE AHEAD**
(See Song of Songs 5:8; 6:4)

Solomon wrote Song of Songs.

Gardens were prized in Bible times. These love poems feature garden trees, plants and flowers.

Some Christians see Song of Songs as a picture of Christ's love for the church.

When Solomon wrote this love poem, European men were giving their beloveds embossed gold jewelry, and a distinct Polynesian culture was developing in Figi and Samoa.

1 Solomon's Song of Songs.

She[a]

2 Let him kiss me with the kisses of his
mouth—
for your love is more delightful than
wine.
3 Pleasing is the fragrance of your
perfumes;
your name is like perfume poured
out.
No wonder the young women love
you!
4 Take me away with you—let us hurry!
Let the king bring me into his
chambers.

Friends

We rejoice and delight in you[b];
we will praise your love more than
wine.

She

How right they are to adore you!

5 Dark am I, yet lovely,
daughters of Jerusalem,
dark like the tents of Kedar,
like the tent curtains of Solomon.[c]
6 Do not stare at me because I am
dark,
because I am darkened by the sun.
My mother's sons were angry with me
and made me take care of the
vineyards;
my own vineyard I had to neglect.
7 Tell me, you whom I love,
where you graze your flock
and where you rest your sheep at
midday.
Why should I be like a veiled woman
beside the flocks of your friends?

Friends

8 If you do not know, most beautiful of
women,
follow the tracks of the sheep
and graze your young goats
by the tents of the shepherds.

He

9 I liken you, my darling, to a mare
among Pharaoh's chariot horses.
10 Your cheeks are beautiful with
earrings,
your neck with strings of jewels.
11 We will make you earrings of gold,
studded with silver.

She

12 While the king was at his table,
my perfume spread its fragrance.
13 My beloved is to me a sachet of
myrrh
resting between my breasts.
14 My beloved is to me a cluster of
henna blossoms
from the vineyards of En Gedi.

He

15 How beautiful you are, my darling!
Oh, how beautiful!
Your eyes are doves.

She

16 How handsome you are, my beloved!
Oh, how charming!
And our bed is verdant.

He

17 The beams of our house are cedars;
our rafters are firs.

She[d]

2 I am a rose[e] of Sharon,
a lily of the valleys.

He

2 Like a lily among thorns
is my darling among the young
women.

She

3 Like an apple[f] tree among the trees of
the forest
is my beloved among the young
men.
I delight to sit in his shade,
and his fruit is sweet to my taste.

---

[a] The main male and female speakers (identified primarily on the basis of the gender of the relevant Hebrew forms)
are indicated by the captions *He* and *She* respectively. The words of others are marked *Friends*. In some instances
the divisions and their captions are debatable.   [b] 4 The Hebrew is masculine singular.   [c] 5 Or *Salma*   [d] Or *He*
[e] 1 Probably a member of the crocus family   [f] 3 Or possibly *apricot*; here and elsewhere in Song of Songs

How can each time you fall in love seem like the first time? That's part of the magic. Each time it's exciting, fresh and new. The song that Solomon wrote to celebrate love can help you realize that God isn't a prude, frowning at you when your heart beats faster. It can also help you realize that when Hollywood tries to tell you it's all just sex, Hollywood is dead wrong. Solomon is right: that "Look, here he [or she] comes" that sets your heart beating faster is something special you can enjoy no matter what your age.

{Song of Songs 2:8–13}

≫ INSTANT ACCESS

⁴ Let him lead me to the banquet hall,
    and let his banner over me be love.
⁵ Strengthen me with raisins,
    refresh me with apples,
    for I am faint with love.
⁶ His left arm is under my head,
    and his right arm embraces me.
⁷ Daughters of Jerusalem, I charge you
    by the gazelles and by the does of
        the field:
Do not arouse or awaken love
    until it so desires.

⁸ Listen! My beloved!
    Look! Here he comes,
leaping across the mountains,
    bounding over the hills.

⁹ My beloved is like a gazelle or a young
        stag.
    Look! There he stands behind our
        wall,
gazing through the windows,
    peering through the lattice.
¹⁰ My beloved spoke and said to me,
    "Arise, my darling,
    my beautiful one, come with me.
¹¹ See! The winter is past;
    the rains are over and gone.
¹² Flowers appear on the earth;
    the season of singing has come,
    the cooing of doves
    is heard in our land.
¹³ The fig tree forms its early fruit;
    the blossoming vines spread their
        fragrance.
    Arise, come, my darling;
    my beautiful one, come with me."

He

¹⁴ My dove in the clefts of the rock,
    in the hiding places on the
        mountainside,
show me your face,
    let me hear your voice;
for your voice is sweet,
    and your face is lovely.
¹⁵ Catch for us the foxes,
    the little foxes
that ruin the vineyards,
    our vineyards that are in bloom.

She

¹⁶ My beloved is mine and I am his;
    he browses among the lilies.
¹⁷ Until the day breaks
    and the shadows flee,
turn, my beloved,
    and be like a gazelle
or like a young stag
    on the rugged hills.ᵃ

3 All night long on my bed
    I looked for the one my heart loves;
    I looked for him but did not find
        him.
² I will get up now and go about the city,
    through its streets and squares;
    I will search for the one my heart
        loves.

ᵃ 17 Or the hills of Bether

So I looked for him but did not find
    him.
³ The watchmen found me
    as they made their rounds in the
        city.
    "Have you seen the one my heart
        loves?"
⁴ Scarcely had I passed them
    when I found the one my heart
        loves.
    I held him and would not let him go
        till I had brought him to my
            mother's house,
    to the room of the one who
        conceived me.
⁵ Daughters of Jerusalem, I charge
        you
    by the gazelles and by the does of
        the field:
    Do not arouse or awaken love
        until it so desires.

⁶ Who is this coming up from the
        wilderness
    like a column of smoke,
    perfumed with myrrh and incense
        made from all the spices of the
            merchant?
⁷ Look! It is Solomon's carriage,
    escorted by sixty warriors,
        the noblest of Israel,
⁸ all of them wearing the sword,
    all experienced in battle,
    each with his sword at his side,
        prepared for the terrors of the
            night.
⁹ King Solomon made for himself the
        carriage;
    he made it of wood from Lebanon.
¹⁰ Its posts he made of silver,
    its base of gold.
    Its seat was upholstered with purple,
        its interior inlaid with love.
    Daughters of Jerusalem, ¹¹come out,
        and look, you daughters of Zion.
    Lookᵃ on King Solomon wearing a
        crown,
        the crown with which his mother
            crowned him
    on the day of his wedding,
        the day his heart rejoiced.

He

4 How beautiful you are, my darling!
    Oh, how beautiful!
    Your eyes behind your veil are
        doves.
    Your hair is like a flock of goats
        descending from the hills of
            Gilead.
² Your teeth are like a flock of sheep
        just shorn,
    coming up from the washing.
    Each has its twin;
        not one of them is alone.
³ Your lips are like a scarlet ribbon;
    your mouth is lovely.
    Your temples behind your veil
        are like the halves of a
            pomegranate.
⁴ Your neck is like the tower of David,
    built with courses of stoneᵇ;
    on it hang a thousand shields,
        all of them shields of warriors.
⁵ Your breasts are like two fawns,
    like twin fawns of a gazelle
        that browse among the lilies.
⁶ Until the day breaks
    and the shadows flee,
    I will go to the mountain of myrrh
        and to the hill of incense.
⁷ You are altogether beautiful, my
        darling;
    there is no flaw in you.

⁸ Come with me from Lebanon, my
        bride,
    come with me from Lebanon.
    Descend from the crest of Amana,
        from the top of Senir, the summit of
            Hermon,
    from the lions' dens
        and the mountain haunts of
            leopards.
⁹ You have stolen my heart, my sister,
        my bride;
    you have stolen my heart
    with one glance of your eyes,
        with one jewel of your necklace.
¹⁰ How delightful is your love, my sister,
        my bride!
    How much more pleasing is your
        love than wine,

ᵃ 10,11 Or interior lovingly inlaid / by the daughters of Jerusalem. / ¹¹Come out, you daughters of Zion, / and look
ᵇ 4 The meaning of the Hebrew for this phrase is uncertain.

and the fragrance of your perfume
  more than any spice!
¹¹ Your lips drop sweetness as the
    honeycomb, my bride;
  milk and honey are under your
    tongue.
The fragrance of your garments
  is like the fragrance of Lebanon.
¹² You are a garden locked up, my sister,
    my bride;
  you are a spring enclosed, a sealed
    fountain.
¹³ Your plants are an orchard of
    pomegranates
  with choice fruits,
  with henna and nard,
¹⁴   nard and saffron,
  calamus and cinnamon,
  with every kind of incense tree,
  with myrrh and aloes
  and all the finest spices.
¹⁵ You are^a a garden fountain,
  a well of flowing water
  streaming down from Lebanon.

She

¹⁶ Awake, north wind,
  and come, south wind!
Blow on my garden,
  that its fragrance may spread
    everywhere.
Let my beloved come into his
    garden
  and taste its choice fruits.

He

5 I have come into my garden, my
    sister, my bride;
  I have gathered my myrrh with my
    spice.
I have eaten my honeycomb and my
    honey;
  I have drunk my wine and my
    milk.

Friends

  Eat, friends, and drink;
    drink your fill of love.

She

² I slept but my heart was awake.
  Listen! My beloved is knocking:
"Open to me, my sister, my darling,
  my dove, my flawless one.
My head is drenched with dew,
  my hair with the dampness of the
    night."
³ I have taken off my robe—
  must I put it on again?
I have washed my feet—
  must I soil them again?
⁴ My beloved thrust his hand through
    the latch-opening;
  my heart began to pound for him.
⁵ I arose to open for my beloved,
  and my hands dripped with
    myrrh,
  my fingers with flowing myrrh,
  on the handles of the bolt.

---

^a 15 Or *I am* (spoken by *She*)

⁶I opened for my beloved,
   but my beloved had left; he was
      gone.
My heart sank at his departure.ª
I looked for him but did not find him.
I called him but he did not answer.
⁷The watchmen found me
   as they made their rounds in the
      city.
They beat me, they bruised me;
   they took away my cloak,
      those watchmen of the walls!
⁸Daughters of Jerusalem, I charge
      you—
   if you find my beloved,
what will you tell him?
   Tell him I am faint with love.

ª 6 Or *heart had gone out to him when he spoke*

Friends

⁹How is your beloved better than
      others,
   most beautiful of women?
How is your beloved better than
      others,
   that you so charge us?

She

¹⁰My beloved is radiant and ruddy,
   outstanding among ten thousand.
¹¹His head is purest gold;
   his hair is wavy
      and black as a raven.
¹²His eyes are like doves
   by the water streams,

TO THE POINT

Romance Ahead

Romance is a pretty special thing. You know, those feelings that grow as you get to know a special person.

Song of Songs gives you a preview of what romance is all about. The woman talks about being "faint with love," and the man talks about how beautiful and wonderful she is (Song of Songs 5:8; 6:4).

Some teens miss out on romantic love altogether. They confuse romantic love with sex and think that having sex is love. They never realize that sex can spoil their chances to find lasting romantic love.

Don't make that mistake. Read Song of Songs to discover how special romantic love can be. If you want that kind of love, you'll be wise enough to wait for it.

washed in milk,
  mounted like jewels.
13 His cheeks are like beds of spice
  yielding perfume.
His lips are like lilies
  dripping with myrrh.
14 His arms are rods of gold
  set with topaz.
His body is like polished ivory
  decorated with lapis lazuli.
15 His legs are pillars of marble
  set on bases of pure gold.
His appearance is like Lebanon,
  choice as its cedars.
16 His mouth is sweetness itself;
  he is altogether lovely.
This is my beloved, this is my friend,
  daughters of Jerusalem.

Friends

6 Where has your beloved gone,
  most beautiful of women?
Which way did your beloved turn,
  that we may look for him with you?

She

2 My beloved has gone down to his
  garden,
  to the beds of spices,
to browse in the gardens
  and to gather lilies.
3 I am my beloved's and my beloved is
  mine;
  he browses among the lilies.

He

4 You are as beautiful as Tirzah, my
  darling,
  as lovely as Jerusalem,
  as majestic as troops with banners.
5 Turn your eyes from me;
  they overwhelm me.
Your hair is like a flock of goats
  descending from Gilead.
6 Your teeth are like a flock of sheep
  coming up from the washing.
Each has its twin,
  not one of them is missing.
7 Your temples behind your veil
  are like the halves of a
  pomegranate.

8 Sixty queens there may be,
  and eighty concubines,
  and virgins beyond number;
9 but my dove, my perfect one, is
  unique,
  the only daughter of her mother,
  the favorite of the one who bore
  her.
The young women saw her and called
  her blessed;
  the queens and concubines praised
  her.

Friends

10 Who is this that appears like the
  dawn,
  fair as the moon, bright as the sun,
  majestic as the stars in
  procession?

He

11 I went down to the grove of nut trees
  to look at the new growth in the
  valley,
  to see if the vines had budded
  or the pomegranates were in bloom.
12 Before I realized it,
  my desire set me among the royal
  chariots of my people. *a*

Friends

13 Come back, come back,
  O Shulammite;
  come back, come back, that we
  may gaze on you!

He

Why would you gaze on the
  Shulammite
  as on the dance of Mahanaim? *b*

7 *c* How beautiful your sandaled feet,
  O prince's daughter!
Your graceful legs are like jewels,
  the work of an artist's hands.
2 Your navel is a rounded goblet
  that never lacks blended wine.
Your waist is a mound of wheat
  encircled by lilies.
3 Your breasts are like two fawns,
  like twin fawns of a gazelle.

---

a 12 Or *among the chariots of Amminadab; or among the chariots of the people of the prince*   *b 13* In Hebrew texts this
verse (6:13) is numbered 7:1.   *c* In Hebrew texts 7:1-13 is numbered 7:2-14.

⁴ Your neck is like an ivory tower.
  Your eyes are the pools of Heshbon
    by the gate of Bath Rabbim.
  Your nose is like the tower of Lebanon
    looking toward Damascus.
⁵ Your head crowns you like Mount
    Carmel.
  Your hair is like royal tapestry;
    the king is held captive by its
      tresses.
⁶ How beautiful you are and how
    pleasing,
  my love, with your delights!
⁷ Your stature is like that of the palm,
    and your breasts like clusters of
      fruit.
⁸ I said, "I will climb the palm tree;
    I will take hold of its fruit."
  May your breasts be like clusters of
    grapes on the vine,
  the fragrance of your breath like
    apples,
⁹ and your mouth like the best wine.

She

May the wine go straight to my
    beloved,
  flowing gently over lips and teeth.ᵃ
¹⁰ I belong to my beloved,
  and his desire is for me.
¹¹ Come, my beloved, let us go to the
    countryside,
  let us spend the night in the
    villages.ᵇ
¹² Let us go early to the vineyards
    to see if the vines have budded,
  if their blossoms have opened,
    and if the pomegranates are in
      bloom—
  there I will give you my love.
¹³ The mandrakes send out their
    fragrance,
  and at our door is every delicacy,
    both new and old,
  that I have stored up for you, my
    beloved.

8 If only you were to me like a brother,
  who was nursed at my mother's
    breasts!
  Then, if I found you outside,
    I would kiss you,
  and no one would despise me.

Someday you'll stop falling in love with someone new every month. Someday love will last for weeks and months and stretch on into years. When that lasting love comes—a love "as strong as death," a love "many waters cannot quench"—then you'll know you've found the right one. Then love will lead you to the commitment of marriage. You'll want to be with that one person for the rest of your life. Don't get "being in love" mixed up with "lasting love." It's so tempting to think the guy you met last week is "the one." But you can't tell until being "in love" has stood the test of time and become "lasting love."

{Song of Songs 8:6–7}

INSTANT ACCESS

² I would lead you
    and bring you to my mother's
      house—
  she who has taught me.
  I would give you spiced wine to drink,
    the nectar of my pomegranates.
³ His left arm is under my head
    and his right arm embraces me.
⁴ Daughters of Jerusalem, I charge
    you:
  Do not arouse or awaken love
    until it so desires.

ᵃ 9 Septuagint, Aquila, Vulgate and Syriac; Hebrew *lips of sleepers*   ᵇ 11 Or *the henna bushes*

Friends

⁵Who is this coming up from the
wilderness
leaning on her beloved?

She

Under the apple tree I roused you;
there your mother conceived you,
there she who was in labor gave
you birth.
⁶Place me like a seal over your heart,
like a seal on your arm;
for love is as strong as death,
its jealousy*a* unyielding as the
grave.
It burns like blazing fire,
like a mighty flame.*b*
⁷Many waters cannot quench love;
rivers cannot sweep it away.
If one were to give
all the wealth of one's house for
love,
it*c* would be utterly scorned.

Friends

⁸We have a little sister,
and her breasts are not yet grown.
What shall we do for our sister
on the day she is spoken for?
⁹If she is a wall,
we will build towers of silver on her.
If she is a door,
we will enclose her with panels of
cedar.

She

¹⁰I am a wall,
and my breasts are like towers.
Thus I have become in his eyes
like one bringing contentment.
¹¹Solomon had a vineyard in Baal
Hamon;
he let out his vineyard to tenants.
Each was to bring for its fruit
a thousand shekels*d* of silver.
¹²But my own vineyard is mine to
give;
the thousand shekels are for you,
Solomon,
and two hundred*e* are for those who
tend its fruit.

He

¹³You who dwell in the gardens
with friends in attendance,
let me hear your voice!

She

¹⁴Come away, my beloved,
and be like a gazelle
or like a young stag
on the spice-laden mountains.

---

a 6 Or ardor   *b* 6 Or fire, / like the very flame of the Lord   *c* 7 Or he   *d* 11 That is, about 25 pounds or about 12 kilograms; also in verse 12   *e* 12 That is, about 5 pounds or about 2.3 kilograms

ISAIAH

Bullies.

Sooner or later you'll probably meet one—
someone who's mean and just doesn't like you.
Wouldn't it be great to know ahead of time that
everything will turn out OK next time you're
confronted by a bully?

In Isaiah's time, Assyria was a bully, a powerful nation determined to invade Israel. In 722
B.C. Assyria crushed the northern kingdom of
Israel. Isaiah made it clear that the southern
kingdom of Judah would be invaded too. But
the nation would survive. Isaiah also promised
that one day God would send a Savior to deliver his people from sin and to set up God's
kingdom on earth.

>>**CHECK WITH GOD, NOT A SPIRITIST**
   Only God has answers, says Isaiah 8:19–22

>>**ISAIAH TELLS THE FUTURE**
   Secret revealed, see Isaiah 46:8–10

>>**SEE JESUS, 700 YEARS BEFORE HE COMES**
   Prophecy explains the cross, Isaiah 53

>>**NEW WORLD COMING!**
   Look into the future found in Isaiah 65:17–25

While Isaiah urges the people of Judah to be faithful to God, American Indians establish
permanent farming villages in the southeastern U.S. In India the notion of transmigration
of souls develops. Kallinos, the earliest known songwriter, pens his "Battle Hymn."

1 The vision concerning Judah and Jerusalem that Isaiah son of Amoz saw during the reigns of Uzziah, Jotham, Ahaz and Hezekiah, kings of Judah.

A Rebellious Nation

² Hear me, you heavens! Listen, earth!
    For the LORD has spoken:
"I reared children and brought
        them up,
    but they have rebelled against me.
³ The ox knows its master,
    the donkey its owner's manger,
but Israel does not know,
    my people do not understand."

⁴ Woe to the sinful nation,
    a people whose guilt is great,
a brood of evildoers,
    children given to corruption!
They have forsaken the LORD;
    they have spurned the Holy One of
        Israel
    and turned their backs on him.

⁵ Why should you be beaten anymore?
    Why do you persist in rebellion?
Your whole head is injured,
    your whole heart afflicted.
⁶ From the sole of your foot to the top
        of your head
    there is no soundness—
only wounds and welts
    and open sores,
not cleansed or bandaged
    or soothed with olive oil.

⁷ Your country is desolate,
    your cities burned with fire;
your fields are being stripped by
        foreigners
    right before you,
    laid waste as when overthrown by
        strangers.
⁸ Daughter Zion is left
    like a shelter in a vineyard,
like a hut in a cucumber field,
    like a city under siege.
⁹ Unless the LORD Almighty
    had left us some survivors,
we would have become like Sodom,
    we would have been like
        Gomorrah.

¹⁰ Hear the word of the LORD,
    you rulers of Sodom;
listen to the instruction of our God,
    you people of Gomorrah!
¹¹ "The multitude of your sacrifices—
    what are they to me?" says the
        LORD.
"I have more than enough of burnt
        offerings,
    of rams and the fat of fattened
        animals;
I have no pleasure
    in the blood of bulls and lambs and
        goats.
¹² When you come to appear before me,
    who has asked this of you,
    this trampling of my courts?
¹³ Stop bringing meaningless offerings!
    Your incense is detestable to me.
New Moons, Sabbaths and
        convocations—
    I cannot bear your worthless
        assemblies.
¹⁴ Your New Moon feasts and your
        appointed festivals
    I hate with all my being.
They have become a burden to me;
    I am weary of bearing them.
¹⁵ When you spread out your hands in
        prayer,
    I hide my eyes from you;
even when you offer many prayers,
    I am not listening.

Your hands are full of blood!

¹⁶ Wash and make yourselves clean.
    Take your evil deeds out of my sight;
    stop doing wrong.
¹⁷ Learn to do right; seek justice.
    Defend the oppressed.ᵃ
Take up the cause of the fatherless;
    plead the case of the widow.

¹⁸ "Come now, let us settle the matter,"
    says the LORD.
"Though your sins are like scarlet,
    they shall be as white as snow;
though they are red as crimson,
    they shall be like wool.
¹⁹ If you are willing and obedient,
    you will eat the good things of the
        land;

ᵃ 17 Or justice. / Correct the oppressor

20 but if you resist and rebel,
    you will be devoured by the sword."
        For the mouth of the LORD
            has spoken.

21 See how the faithful city
    has become a prostitute!
  She once was full of justice;
    righteousness used to dwell in her—
        but now murderers!
22 Your silver has become dross,
    your choice wine is diluted with
        water.
23 Your rulers are rebels,
    partners with thieves;
  they all love bribes
    and chase after gifts.
  They do not defend the cause of the
        fatherless;
    the widow's case does not come
        before them.

24 Therefore the Lord, the LORD Almighty,
    the Mighty One of Israel, declares:
  "Ah! I will vent my wrath on my foes
    and avenge myself on my enemies.
25 I will turn my hand against you;[a]
    I will thoroughly purge away your
        dross
    and remove all your impurities.
26 I will restore your leaders as in days
        of old,
    your rulers as at the beginning.
  Afterward you will be called
    the City of Righteousness,
    the Faithful City."

27 Zion will be delivered with justice,
    her penitent ones with
        righteousness.
28 But rebels and sinners will both be
        broken,
    and those who forsake the LORD will
        perish.

29 "You will be ashamed because of the
        sacred oaks
    in which you have delighted;
  you will be disgraced because of the
        gardens
    that you have chosen.
30 You will be like an oak with fading
        leaves,
    like a garden without water.

INSTANT ACCESS

How bad is too bad? When do you step over the line, so there's no chance of turning back? When you take the family car and wreck it? When you try that new drug and find you're hooked? When you flunk out of school? Hey, it's best not to take any of those steps. But even if you have, it's never too late. God cried out to a sinful Judah, whose hands were "full of blood" (Isaiah 1:15), and urged them to change. "Though your sins are like scarlet," God promised, "they shall be as white as snow" (Isaiah 1:18). Don't give up. It's not too late to experience God's forgiveness, and to change.

{Isaiah 1:15–20}

31 The mighty man will become
        tinder
    and his work a spark;
  both will burn together,
    with no one to quench the fire."

The Mountain of the LORD

2 This is what Isaiah son of Amoz saw
  concerning Judah and Jerusalem:

2 In the last days

  the mountain of the LORD's temple will
        be established
    as the highest of the mountains;

---

[a] 25 That is, against Jerusalem

it will be exalted above the hills,
and all nations will stream to it.

³Many peoples will come and say,

"Come, let us go up to the mountain
of the LORD,
to the temple of the God of Jacob.
He will teach us his ways,
so that we may walk in his paths."
The law will go out from Zion,
the word of the LORD from
Jerusalem.
⁴He will judge between the nations
and will settle disputes for many
peoples.
They will beat their swords into
plowshares
and their spears into pruning hooks.
Nation will not take up sword against
nation,
nor will they train for war anymore.

⁵Come, descendants of Jacob,
let us walk in the light of the LORD.

The Day of the LORD

⁶You, LORD, have abandoned your
people,
the descendants of Jacob.
They are full of superstitions from the
East;
they practice divination like the
Philistines
and embrace pagan customs.
⁷Their land is full of silver and gold;
there is no end to their treasures.
Their land is full of horses;
there is no end to their chariots.
⁸Their land is full of idols;
they bow down to the work of their
hands,
to what their fingers have made.
⁹So people will be brought low
and everyone humbled—
do not forgive them.^a

¹⁰Go into the rocks, hide in the ground
from the fearful presence of the LORD
and the splendor of his majesty!
¹¹The eyes of the arrogant will be
humbled
and human pride brought low;
the LORD alone will be exalted in that
day.

¹²The LORD Almighty has a day in store
for all the proud and lofty,
for all that is exalted
(and they will be humbled),
¹³for all the cedars of Lebanon, tall and
lofty,
and all the oaks of Bashan,
¹⁴for all the towering mountains
and all the high hills,
¹⁵for every lofty tower
and every fortified wall,
¹⁶for every trading ship^b
and every stately vessel.
¹⁷The arrogance of man will be brought
low
and human pride humbled;
the LORD alone will be exalted in that
day,
¹⁸   and the idols will totally disappear.

¹⁹People will flee to caves in the rocks
and to holes in the ground
from the fearful presence of the LORD
and the splendor of his majesty,
when he rises to shake the earth.
²⁰In that day people will throw away
to the moles and bats
their idols of silver and idols of gold,
which they made to worship.
²¹They will flee to caverns in the rocks
and to the overhanging crags
from the fearful presence of the LORD
and the splendor of his majesty,
when he rises to shake the earth.

²²Stop trusting in mere humans,
who have but a breath in their
nostrils.
Why hold them in esteem?

Judgment on Jerusalem and Judah

3 See now, the Lord,
the LORD Almighty,
is about to take from Jerusalem and
Judah
both supply and support:
all supplies of food and all supplies of
water,
²   the hero and the warrior,
the judge and the prophet,
the diviner and the elder,

---

^a 9 Or *not raise them up*   ^b 16 Hebrew *every ship of Tarshish*

³the captain of fifty and the man of rank,
  the counselor, skilled craftsman
    and clever enchanter.

⁴ "I will make mere youths their
    officials;
  children will rule over them."

⁵People will oppress each other—
    man against man, neighbor against
    neighbor.
The young will rise up against the old,
  the nobody against the honored.

⁶A man will seize one of his brothers
  in his father's house, and say,
"You have a cloak, you be our leader;
  take charge of this heap of ruins!"
⁷But in that day he will cry out,
  "I have no remedy.
I have no food or clothing in my house;
  do not make me the leader of the
    people."

⁸Jerusalem staggers,
  Judah is falling;
their words and deeds are against the
    LORD,
  defying his glorious presence.
⁹The look on their faces testifies
    against them;
  they parade their sin like Sodom;
    they do not hide it.
Woe to them!
  They have brought disaster upon
    themselves.

¹⁰Tell the righteous it will be well with
    them,
  for they will enjoy the fruit of their
    deeds.
¹¹Woe to the wicked!
  Disaster is upon them!
They will be paid back
  for what their hands have done.

¹²Youths oppress my people,
  women rule over them.
My people, your guides lead you
    astray;
  they turn you from the path.

¹³The LORD takes his place in court;
  he rises to judge the people.
¹⁴The LORD enters into judgment
  against the elders and leaders of
    his people:

Your school is rough.
  Drugs. Fights. Even guns
and knives. Your neighborhood is rough too. You may
be pressured to join a gang
just for safety. It's not easy to
live like a Christian in a hostile
world. Isaiah knew what it
meant to live in a society where
the "words and deeds" of the
people are against everything
God stands for. But the Lord had
a word of encouragement for
the Jews of Isaiah's day and for
you: "Tell the righteous it will
be well with them, for they will
enjoy the fruit of their deeds"
(Isaiah 3:10).

{Isaiah 3:8–10}

INSTANT ACCESS

"It is you who have ruined my
    vineyard;
  the plunder from the poor is in your
    houses.
¹⁵What do you mean by crushing my
    people
  and grinding the faces of the poor?"
    declares the Lord,
      the LORD Almighty.

¹⁶The LORD says,
  "The women of Zion are haughty,
walking along with outstretched
    necks,
  flirting with their eyes,
strutting along with swaying hips,
  with ornaments jingling on their
    ankles.

17 Therefore the Lord will bring sores
on the heads of the women of
Zion;
the LORD will make their scalps
bald."

18 In that day the Lord will snatch away
their finery: the bangles and headbands
and crescent necklaces, 19 the earrings
and bracelets and veils, 20 the headdress-
es and anklets and sashes, the perfume
bottles and charms, 21 the signet rings
and nose rings, 22 the fine robes and the
capes and cloaks, the purses 23 and mirrors, and the linen garments and tiaras
and shawls.

24 Instead of fragrance there will be a
stench;
instead of a sash, a rope;
instead of well-dressed hair, baldness;
instead of fine clothing, sackcloth;
instead of beauty, branding.
25 Your men will fall by the sword,
your warriors in battle.
26 The gates of Zion will lament and
mourn;
destitute, she will sit on the
ground.

4 1 In that day seven women
will take hold of one man
and say, "We will eat our own food
and provide our own clothes;
only let us be called by your name.
Take away our disgrace!"

The Branch of the LORD

2 In that day the Branch of the LORD will
be beautiful and glorious, and the fruit of
the land will be the pride and glory of the
survivors in Israel. 3 Those who are left
in Zion, who remain in Jerusalem, will be
called holy, all who are recorded among
the living in Jerusalem. 4 The Lord will
wash away the filth of the women of Zion;
he will cleanse the bloodstains from Jerusalem by a spirit[a] of judgment and a
spirit[a] of fire. 5 Then the LORD will create
over all of Mount Zion and over those who
assemble there a cloud of smoke by day
and a glow of flaming fire by night; over
everything the glory[b] will be a canopy. 6 It

will be a shelter and shade from the heat
of the day, and a refuge and hiding place
from the storm and rain.

The Song of the Vineyard

5 I will sing for the one I love
a song about his vineyard:
My loved one had a vineyard
on a fertile hillside.
2 He dug it up and cleared it of stones
and planted it with the choicest
vines.
He built a watchtower in it
and cut out a winepress as well.
Then he looked for a crop of good
grapes,
but it yielded only bad fruit.

3 "Now you dwellers in Jerusalem and
people of Judah,
judge between me and my vineyard.
4 What more could have been done for
my vineyard
than I have done for it?
When I looked for good grapes,
why did it yield only bad?
5 Now I will tell you
what I am going to do to my
vineyard:
I will take away its hedge,
and it will be destroyed;
I will break down its wall,
and it will be trampled.
6 I will make it a wasteland,
neither pruned nor cultivated,
and briers and thorns will grow
there.
I will command the clouds
not to rain on it."

7 The vineyard of the LORD Almighty
is the nation of Israel,
and the people of Judah
are the vines he delighted in.
And he looked for justice, but saw
bloodshed;
for righteousness, but heard cries
of distress.

Woes and Judgments

8 Woe to you who add house to house
and join field to field

till no space is left
and you live alone in the land.

⁹The LORD Almighty has declared in my hearing:

"Surely the great houses will become
desolate,
the fine mansions left without
occupants.
¹⁰A ten-acre vineyard will produce only a
bathᵃ of wine;
a homerᵇ of seed will yield only an
ephahᶜ of grain."

¹¹Woe to those who rise early in the
morning
to run after their drinks,
who stay up late at night
till they are inflamed with wine.
¹²They have harps and lyres at their
banquets,
pipes and timbrels and wine,
but they have no regard for the deeds
of the LORD,
no respect for the work of his
hands.
¹³Therefore my people will go into
exile
for lack of understanding;
those of high rank will die of hunger
and the common people will be
parched with thirst.
¹⁴Therefore Death expands its jaws,
opening wide its mouth;
into it will descend their nobles and
masses
with all their brawlers and revelers.
¹⁵So people will be brought low
and everyone humbled,
the eyes of the arrogant humbled.
¹⁶But the LORD Almighty will be exalted
by his justice,
and the holy God will be proved holy
by his righteous acts.
¹⁷Then sheep will graze as in their own
pasture;
lambs will feedᵈ among the ruins of
the rich.

¹⁸Woe to those who draw sin along with
cords of deceit,
and wickedness as with cart ropes,

¹⁹to those who say, "Let God hurry;
let him hasten his work
so we may see it.
The plan of the Holy One of Israel—
let it approach, let it come into
view,
so we may know it."

²⁰Woe to those who call evil good
and good evil,
who put darkness for light
and light for darkness,
who put bitter for sweet
and sweet for bitter.

²¹Woe to those who are wise in their
own eyes
and clever in their own sight.

²²Woe to those who are heroes at
drinking wine
and champions at mixing drinks,
²³who acquit the guilty for a bribe,
but deny justice to the innocent.
²⁴Therefore, as tongues of fire lick up
straw
and as dry grass sinks down in the
flames,
so their roots will decay
and their flowers blow away like
dust;
for they have rejected the law of the
LORD Almighty
and spurned the word of the Holy
One of Israel.
²⁵Therefore the LORD's anger burns
against his people;
his hand is raised and he strikes
them down.
The mountains shake,
and the dead bodies are like refuse
in the streets.

Yet for all this, his anger is not turned
away,
his hand is still upraised.

²⁶He lifts up a banner for the distant
nations,
he whistles for those at the ends of
the earth.
Here they come,
swiftly and speedily!

ᵃ 10 That is, about 6 gallons or about 22 liters   ᵇ 10 That is, probably about 360 pounds or about 160 kilograms
ᶜ 10 That is, probably about 36 pounds or about 16 kilograms   ᵈ 17 Septuagint; Hebrew / strangers will eat

27 Not one of them grows tired or
    stumbles,
  not one slumbers or sleeps;
  not a belt is loosened at the waist,
    not a sandal strap is broken.
28 Their arrows are sharp,
  all their bows are strung;
  their horses' hooves seem like flint,
    their chariot wheels like a whirlwind.
29 Their roar is like that of the lion,
  they roar like young lions;
  they growl as they seize their prey
    and carry it off with no one to
    rescue.
30 In that day they will roar over it
  like the roaring of the sea.
And if one looks at the land,
  there is only darkness and distress;
  even the sun will be darkened by
    clouds.

Isaiah's Commission

6 In the year that King Uzziah died, I saw the Lord, high and exalted, seated on a throne; and the train of his robe filled the temple. 2 Above him were seraphim, each with six wings: With two wings they covered their faces, with two they covered their feet, and with two they were flying. 3 And they were calling to one another:

"Holy, holy, holy is the Lord Almighty;
  the whole earth is full of his glory."

4 At the sound of their voices the doorposts and thresholds shook and the temple was filled with smoke.

5 "Woe to me!" I cried. "I am ruined! For I am a man of unclean lips, and I live among a people of unclean lips, and my eyes have seen the King, the Lord Almighty."

TO THE POINT

God Is Holy

Lots of people think being holy means never having any fun. They think God is disgusted whenever they enjoy themselves.

Actually, God enjoys a good time. The Bible says that God "provides us with everything for our enjoyment" (1 Timothy 6:17). When Jesus was on earth, he was criticized for going to dinner parties (Matthew 9:9–11). But holiness doesn't mean being miserable.

To say that God is holy means that he is committed to doing what is right and loving—and that he wants his people to do what is right and loving too. Isaiah describes rich people who care nothing for the poor, then goes on to warn that "the holy God will be proved holy by his righteous acts" (Isaiah 5:16). Because God is holy, he will punish the wicked and will see justice done.

Jesus was "born of the virgin Mary"

✚ Can you predict what will happen next week? How about predicting something that will happen in 730 years? And just to make it harder, try to predict something impossible.

That's what the prophet Isaiah did. Of course, he had help. He was saying what God told him to say: "The virgin will conceive and give birth to a son, and will call him Immanuel" (Isaiah 7:14).

Actually, there are two "impossible" predictions here. The first is that a virgin will have a child. And the second is that the child will be *Immanuel*, a Hebrew word that means "God with us." For hundreds of years those who studied the Old Testament must have puzzled over this prediction. How could a virgin have a child? How could a human child be "God with us?"

And then 730 years after Isaiah's prophecy it happened! An angel came to a teenage Jewish girl named Mary. The angel told her she would have a child who would be the Son of God. She did, and today we celebrate Christmas to honor Jesus, God's one and only Son, born of the virgin Mary.

We're so familiar with Christmas that sometimes we forget the miracle. A virgin bore a child. That child was God, come in the flesh to be with us and to die for us. And it was all foretold 730 years before it happened!

Go to page 902 for the next We Believe

⁶Then one of the seraphim flew to me with a live coal in his hand, which he had taken with tongs from the altar. ⁷With it he touched my mouth and said, "See, this has touched your lips; your guilt is taken away and your sin atoned for."

⁸Then I heard the voice of the Lord saying, "Whom shall I send? And who will go for us?"

And I said, "Here am I. Send me!"

⁹He said, "Go and tell this people:

" 'Be ever hearing, but never
       understanding;
   be ever seeing, but never
       perceiving.'
¹⁰Make the heart of this people
       calloused;
   make their ears dull
   and close their eyes.ᵃ
Otherwise they might see with their
       eyes,
   hear with their ears,
   understand with their hearts,
   and turn and be healed."

¹¹Then I said, "For how long, Lord?"

And he answered:

"Until the cities lie ruined
   and without inhabitant,
until the houses are left deserted
   and the fields ruined and
       ravaged,
¹²until the LORD has sent everyone far
       away
   and the land is utterly forsaken.
¹³And though a tenth remains in the
       land,
   it will again be laid waste.
But as the terebinth and oak
   leave stumps when they are cut
       down,
   so the holy seed will be the stump
       in the land."

The Sign of Immanuel

7 When Ahaz son of Jotham, the son of Uzziah, was king of Judah, King Rezin of Aram and Pekah son of Remaliah king of Israel marched up to fight against Jerusalem, but they could not overpower it.

²Now the house of David was told, "Aram has allied itself withᵇ Ephraim"; so the hearts of Ahaz and his people were shaken, as the trees of the forest are shaken by the wind.

³Then the LORD said to Isaiah, "Go out, you and your son Shear-Jashub,ᶜ to meet Ahaz at the end of the aqueduct of the Upper Pool, on the road to the Launderer's Field. ⁴Say to him, 'Be careful, keep calm and don't be afraid. Do not lose heart because of these two smoldering stubs of firewood — because of the fierce anger of Rezin and Aram and of the son of Remaliah. ⁵Aram, Ephraim and Remaliah's son have plotted your ruin, saying, ⁶"Let us invade Judah; let us tear it apart and divide it among ourselves, and make the son of Tabeel king over it." ⁷Yet this is what the Sovereign LORD says:

" 'It will not take place,
       it will not happen,
⁸for the head of Aram is Damascus,
   and the head of Damascus is only
       Rezin.
Within sixty-five years
   Ephraim will be too shattered to be
       a people.

Isaiah 7

Q: What does the name Immanuel mean?

BONUS: When was the prophecy of Isaiah 7:14 fulfilled?

Answers on next page

ᵃ 9,10 Hebrew; Septuagint 'You will be ever hearing, but never understanding; / you will be ever seeing, but never perceiving.' / ¹⁰This people's heart has become calloused; / they hardly hear with their ears, / and they have closed their eyes   ᵇ 2 Or has set up camp in   ᶜ 3 Shear-Jashub means a remnant will return.

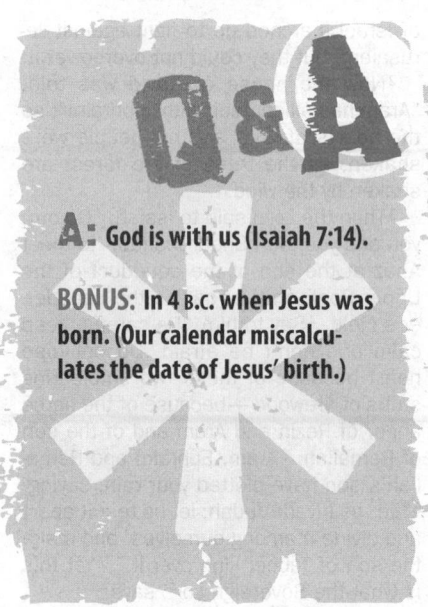

A: God is with us (Isaiah 7:14).

BONUS: In 4 B.C. when Jesus was born. (Our calendar miscalculates the date of Jesus' birth.)

9 The head of Ephraim is Samaria,
and the head of Samaria is only
Remaliah's son.
If you do not stand firm in your faith,
you will not stand at all.' "

10 Again the LORD spoke to Ahaz, 11 "Ask the LORD your God for a sign, whether in the deepest depths or in the highest heights."

12 But Ahaz said, "I will not ask; I will not put the LORD to the test."

13 Then Isaiah said, "Hear now, you house of David! Is it not enough to try the patience of humans? Will you try the patience of my God also? 14 Therefore the Lord himself will give you*a* a sign: The virgin*b* will conceive and give birth to a son, and*c* will call him Immanuel.*d* 15 He will be eating curds and honey when he knows enough to reject the wrong and choose the right, 16 for before the boy knows enough to reject the wrong and choose the right, the land of the two kings you dread will be laid waste. 17 The LORD will bring on you and on your people and on the house of your father a time unlike any since Ephraim broke away from Judah— he will bring the king of Assyria."

Assyria, the LORD's Instrument

18 In that day the LORD will whistle for flies from the Nile delta in Egypt and for bees from the land of Assyria. 19 They will all come and settle in the steep ravines and in the crevices in the rocks, on all the thornbushes and at all the water holes. 20 In that day the Lord will use a razor hired from beyond the Euphrates River—the king of Assyria—to shave your head and private parts, and to cut off your beard also. 21 In that day, a person will keep alive a young cow and two goats. 22 And because of the abundance of the milk they give, there will be curds to eat. All who remain in the land will eat curds and honey. 23 In that day, in every place where there were a thousand vines worth a thousand silver shekels,*e* there will be only briers and thorns. 24 Hunters will go there with bow and arrow, for the land will be covered with briers and thorns. 25 As for all the hills once cultivated by the hoe, you will no longer go there for fear of the briers and thorns; they will become places where cattle are turned loose and where sheep run.

Isaiah and His Children as Signs

8 The LORD said to me, "Take a large scroll and write on it with an ordinary pen: Maher-Shalal-Hash-Baz."*f* 2 So I called in Uriah the priest and Zechariah son of Jeberekiah as reliable witnesses for me. 3 Then I made love to the prophetess, and she conceived and gave birth to a son. And the LORD said to me, "Name him Maher-Shalal-Hash-Baz. 4 For before the boy knows how to say 'My father' or 'My mother,' the wealth of Damascus and the plunder of Samaria will be carried off by the king of Assyria."

5 The LORD spoke to me again:

6 "Because this people has rejected
the gently flowing waters of Shiloah
and rejoices over Rezin
and the son of Remaliah,

---

a 14 The Hebrew is plural.   *b 14* Or *young woman*   *c 14* Masoretic Text; Dead Sea Scrolls *son, and he* or *son, and they*
d 14 Immanuel means *God with us.*   *e 23* That is, about 25 pounds or about 12 kilograms   *f 1* *Maher-Shalal-Hash-Baz*
means *quick to the plunder, swift to the spoil*; also in verse 3.

7 therefore the Lord is about to bring
against them
the mighty floodwaters of the
Euphrates—
the king of Assyria with all his pomp.
It will overflow all its channels,
run over all its banks
8 and sweep on into Judah, swirling
over it,
passing through it and reaching up
to the neck.
Its outspread wings will cover the
breadth of your land,
Immanuel[a]!"

9 Raise the war cry,[b] you nations, and
be shattered!
Listen, all you distant lands.
Prepare for battle, and be shattered!
Prepare for battle, and be shattered!
10 Devise your strategy, but it will be
thwarted;
propose your plan, but it will not
stand,
for God is with us.[c]

11 This is what the Lord says to me with
his strong hand upon me, warning me not
to follow the way of this people:

12 "Do not call conspiracy
everything this people calls a
conspiracy;
do not fear what they fear,
and do not dread it.
13 The Lord Almighty is the one you are
to regard as holy,
he is the one you are to fear,
he is the one you are to dread.
14 He will be a holy place;
for both Israel and Judah he will be
a stone that causes people to
stumble
and a rock that makes them fall.
And for the people of Jerusalem he
will be
a trap and a snare.
15 Many of them will stumble;
they will fall and be broken,
they will be snared and captured."

16 Bind up this testimony of warning
and seal up God's instruction
among my disciples.

17 I will wait for the Lord,
who is hiding his face from the
descendants of Jacob.
I will put my trust in him.

18 Here am I, and the children the Lord
has given me. We are signs and symbols in Israel from the Lord Almighty, who
dwells on Mount Zion.

The Darkness Turns to Light

19 When someone tells you to consult
mediums and spiritists, who whisper
and mutter, should not a people inquire
of their God? Why consult the dead on
behalf of the living? 20 Consult God's instruction and the testimony of warning.
If anyone does not speak according to
this word, they have no light of dawn.
21 Distressed and hungry, they will roam
through the land; when they are famished, they will become enraged and,
looking upward, will curse their king and
their God. 22 Then they will look toward
the earth and see only distress and darkness and fearful gloom, and they will be
thrust into utter darkness.

9[d] Nevertheless, there will be no more
gloom for those who were in distress. In the past he humbled the land
of Zebulun and the land of Naphtali, but
in the future he will honor Galilee of the
nations, by the Way of the Sea, beyond
the Jordan—

2 The people walking in darkness
have seen a great light;
on those living in the land of deep
darkness
a light has dawned.
3 You have enlarged the nation
and increased their joy;
they rejoice before you
as people rejoice at the harvest,
as warriors rejoice
when dividing the plunder.
4 For as in the day of Midian's defeat,
you have shattered
the yoke that burdens them,
the bar across their shoulders,
the rod of their oppressor.

---

[a] 8 Immanuel means God with us.   [b] 9 Or Do your worst   [c] 10 Hebrew Immanuel   [d] In Hebrew texts 9:1 is
numbered 8:23, and 9:2-21 is numbered 9:1-20.

5 Every warrior's boot used in battle
   and every garment rolled in blood
 will be destined for burning,
   will be fuel for the fire.
6 For to us a child is born,
   to us a son is given,
   and the government will be on his
      shoulders.
 And he will be called
   Wonderful Counselor, Mighty God,
   Everlasting Father, Prince of Peace.
7 Of the greatness of his government
      and peace
   there will be no end.
 He will reign on David's throne
   and over his kingdom,
 establishing and upholding it
   with justice and righteousness
   from that time on and forever.
 The zeal of the LORD Almighty
   will accomplish this.

The LORD's Anger Against Israel

8 The Lord has sent a message against
      Jacob;
   it will fall on Israel.
9 All the people will know it—
   Ephraim and the inhabitants of
      Samaria—
 who say with pride
   and arrogance of heart,
10 "The bricks have fallen down,
   but we will rebuild with dressed
      stone;
 the fig trees have been felled,
   but we will replace them with
      cedars."
11 But the LORD has strengthened Rezin's
      foes against them
   and has spurred their enemies on.
12 Arameans from the east and
      Philistines from the west
 have devoured Israel with open
      mouth.

 Yet for all this, his anger is not turned
      away,
   his hand is still upraised.

13 But the people have not returned to
      him who struck them,
   nor have they sought the LORD
      Almighty.

14 So the LORD will cut off from Israel
      both head and tail,
   both palm branch and reed in a
      single day;
15 the elders and dignitaries are the head,
   the prophets who teach lies are the
      tail.
16 Those who guide this people mislead
      them,
   and those who are guided are led
      astray.
17 Therefore the Lord will take no
      pleasure in the young men,
   nor will he pity the fatherless and
      widows,
 for everyone is ungodly and wicked,
   every mouth speaks folly.

 Yet for all this, his anger is not turned
      away,
   his hand is still upraised.

18 Surely wickedness burns like a fire;
   it consumes briers and thorns,
 it sets the forest thickets ablaze,
   so that it rolls upward in a column
      of smoke.
19 By the wrath of the LORD Almighty
   the land will be scorched
 and the people will be fuel for the fire;
   they will not spare one another.
20 On the right they will devour,
   but still be hungry;
 on the left they will eat,
   but not be satisfied.
 Each will feed on the flesh of their
      own offspringª:
21   Manasseh will feed on Ephraim,
      and Ephraim on Manasseh;
   together they will turn against
      Judah.

 Yet for all this, his anger is not turned
      away,
   his hand is still upraised.

10 Woe to those who make unjust
      laws,
   to those who issue oppressive
      decrees,
2 to deprive the poor of their rights
   and withhold justice from the
      oppressed of my people,

ª 20 Or arm

making widows their prey
    and robbing the fatherless.
³What will you do on the day of
        reckoning,
    when disaster comes from afar?
To whom will you run for help?
    Where will you leave your
        riches?
⁴Nothing will remain but to cringe
        among the captives
    or fall among the slain.

Yet for all this, his anger is not turned
        away,
    his hand is still upraised.

God's Judgment on Assyria

⁵"Woe to the Assyrian, the rod of my
        anger,
    in whose hand is the club of my
        wrath!
⁶I send him against a godless nation,
    I dispatch him against a people who
        anger me,
to seize loot and snatch plunder,
    and to trample them down like mud
        in the streets.
⁷But this is not what he intends,
    this is not what he has in mind;
his purpose is to destroy,
    to put an end to many nations.
⁸'Are not my commanders all kings?'
    he says.
⁹   'Has not Kalno fared like
        Carchemish?
Is not Hamath like Arpad,
    and Samaria like Damascus?
¹⁰As my hand seized the kingdoms of
        the idols,
    kingdoms whose images excelled
        those of Jerusalem and
        Samaria—
¹¹shall I not deal with Jerusalem and
        her images
    as I dealt with Samaria and her
        idols?'"

¹²When the Lord has finished all his
work against Mount Zion and Jerusalem,
he will say, "I will punish the king of Assyria for the willful pride of his heart and the
haughty look in his eyes. ¹³For he says:

"'By the strength of my hand I have
        done this,
    and by my wisdom, because I have
        understanding.
I removed the boundaries of nations,
    I plundered their treasures;
    like a mighty one I subdued[a] their
        kings.
¹⁴As one reaches into a nest,
    so my hand reached for the wealth
        of the nations;
as people gather abandoned eggs,
    so I gathered all the countries;
not one flapped a wing,
    or opened its mouth to chirp.'"

¹⁵Does the ax raise itself above the
        person who swings it,
    or the saw boast against the one
        who uses it?
As if a rod were to wield the person
        who lifts it up,
    or a club brandish the one who is
        not wood!
¹⁶Therefore, the Lord, the LORD Almighty,
    will send a wasting disease upon
        his sturdy warriors;
under his pomp a fire will be kindled
    like a blazing flame.
¹⁷The Light of Israel will become a fire,
    their Holy One a flame;
in a single day it will burn and consume
    his thorns and his briers.
¹⁸The splendor of his forests and fertile
        fields
    it will completely destroy,
    as when a sick person wastes away.
¹⁹And the remaining trees of his forests
        will be so few
    that a child could write them down.

The Remnant of Israel

²⁰In that day the remnant of Israel,
    the survivors of Jacob,
will no longer rely on him
    who struck them down
but will truly rely on the LORD,
    the Holy One of Israel.
²¹A remnant will return,[b] a remnant of
        Jacob
    will return to the Mighty God.

ª 13 Or treasures; / I subdued the mighty,   ᵇ 21 Hebrew shear-jashub (see 7:3 and note); also in verse 22

²²Though your people be like the sand
    by the sea, Israel,
  only a remnant will return.
  Destruction has been decreed,
    overwhelming and righteous.
²³The Lord, the LORD Almighty, will carry
    out
    the destruction decreed upon the
      whole land.

²⁴Therefore this is what the Lord, the
LORD Almighty, says:

  "My people who live in Zion,
    do not be afraid of the Assyrians,
  who beat you with a rod
    and lift up a club against you, as
      Egypt did.
²⁵Very soon my anger against you will
    end
    and my wrath will be directed to
      their destruction."

²⁶The LORD Almighty will lash them with
    a whip,
    as when he struck down Midian at
      the rock of Oreb;
  and he will raise his staff over the
    waters,
    as he did in Egypt.
²⁷In that day their burden will be lifted
    from your shoulders,
    their yoke from your neck;
  the yoke will be broken
    because you have grown so fat.ᵃ

²⁸They enter Aiath;
    they pass through Migron;
    they store supplies at Mikmash.
²⁹They go over the pass, and say,
    "We will camp overnight at
      Geba."
  Ramah trembles;
    Gibeah of Saul flees.
³⁰Cry out, Daughter Gallim!
    Listen, Laishah!
    Poor Anathoth!
³¹Madmenah is in flight;
    the people of Gebim take cover.
³²This day they will halt at Nob;
    they will shake their fist
  at the mount of Daughter Zion,
    at the hill of Jerusalem.

³³See, the Lord, the LORD Almighty,
    will lop off the boughs with great
      power.
  The lofty trees will be felled,
    the tall ones will be brought
      low.
³⁴He will cut down the forest thickets
    with an ax;
    Lebanon will fall before the Mighty
      One.

The Branch From Jesse

11 A shoot will come up from the
      stump of Jesse;
    from his roots a Branch will bear
      fruit.
²The Spirit of the LORD will rest on
    him—
    the Spirit of wisdom and of
      understanding,
    the Spirit of counsel and of
      might,
    the Spirit of the knowledge and fear
      of the LORD—
³and he will delight in the fear of the
    LORD.

  He will not judge by what he sees with
    his eyes,
    or decide by what he hears with his
      ears;
⁴but with righteousness he will judge
    the needy,
    with justice he will give decisions
      for the poor of the earth.
  He will strike the earth with the rod of
    his mouth;
    with the breath of his lips he will
      slay the wicked.
⁵Righteousness will be his belt
    and faithfulness the sash around
      his waist.

⁶The wolf will live with the lamb,
    the leopard will lie down with the
      goat,
  the calf and the lion and the yearlingᵇ
    together;
    and a little child will lead them.
⁷The cow will feed with the bear,
    their young will lie down together,
    and the lion will eat straw like
      the ox.

ᵃ 27 Hebrew; Septuagint *broken / from your shoulders*   ᵇ 6 Hebrew; Septuagint *lion will feed*

8 The infant will play near the cobra's den,
 the young child will put its hand into the viper's nest.
9 They will neither harm nor destroy on all my holy mountain,
 for the earth will be filled with the knowledge of the LORD
 as the waters cover the sea.

10 In that day the Root of Jesse will stand as a banner for the peoples; the nations will rally to him, and his resting place will be glorious. 11 In that day the Lord will reach out his hand a second time to reclaim the surviving remnant of his people from Assyria, from Lower Egypt, from Upper Egypt, from Cush,ᵃ from Elam, from Babylonia,ᵇ from Hamath and from the islands of the Mediterranean.

12 He will raise a banner for the nations and gather the exiles of Israel;
 he will assemble the scattered people of Judah
 from the four quarters of the earth.
13 Ephraim's jealousy will vanish, and Judah's enemiesᶜ will be destroyed;
 Ephraim will not be jealous of Judah, nor Judah hostile toward Ephraim.
14 They will swoop down on the slopes of Philistia to the west;
 together they will plunder the people to the east.

ᵃ 11 That is, the upper Nile region   ᵇ 11 Hebrew Shinar   ᶜ 13 Or hostility

TO THE POINT

Animals Fell Too

Why is nature so cruel? Predators kill weaker animals. Why did God create animals that hurt and kill other animals? The Bible tells you that the sin of Adam and Eve spoiled nature as well as the human race. The ground itself was cursed, and even vegetation changed (Genesis 3:17). When Adam and Eve sinned, plants and animals felt the effects of the fall too.

Take a look at Isaiah 11:6–9. In the future God will actually change the nature of wild animals. "The wolf will live with the lamb," and "the cow will feed with the bear."

This world is beautiful now. Imagine how beautiful it was before Adam and Eve sinned. One day this world will be perfect again. No wonder Romans 8:19–21 says that creation itself can hardly wait.

They will subdue Edom and Moab,
and the Ammonites will be subject
to them.
15 The LORD will dry up
the gulf of the Egyptian sea;
with a scorching wind he will sweep
his hand
over the Euphrates River.
He will break it up into seven
streams
so that anyone can cross over in
sandals.
16 There will be a highway for the
remnant of his people
that is left from Assyria,
as there was for Israel
when they came up from Egypt.

Songs of Praise

12 In that day you will say:

"I will praise you, LORD.
Although you were angry with me,
your anger has turned away
and you have comforted me.
2 Surely God is my salvation;
I will trust and not be afraid.
The LORD, the LORD himself, is my
strength and my defense[a];
he has become my salvation."
3 With joy you will draw water
from the wells of salvation.

4 In that day you will say:

"Give praise to the LORD, proclaim his
name;
make known among the nations
what he has done,
and proclaim that his name is
exalted.
5 Sing to the LORD, for he has done
glorious things;
let this be known to all the world.
6 Shout aloud and sing for joy, people of
Zion,
for great is the Holy One of Israel
among you."

A Prophecy Against Babylon

13 A prophecy against Babylon that
Isaiah son of Amoz saw:

2 Raise a banner on a bare hilltop,
shout to them;
beckon to them
to enter the gates of the nobles.
3 I have commanded those I prepared
for battle;
I have summoned my warriors to
carry out my wrath—
those who rejoice in my triumph.

4 Listen, a noise on the mountains,
like that of a great multitude!
Listen, an uproar among the
kingdoms,
like nations massing together!
The LORD Almighty is mustering
an army for war.
5 They come from faraway lands,
from the ends of the heavens—
the LORD and the weapons of his
wrath—
to destroy the whole country.

6 Wail, for the day of the LORD is
near;
it will come like destruction from
the Almighty.[b]
7 Because of this, all hands will go
limp,
every heart will melt with fear.
8 Terror will seize them,
pain and anguish will grip them;
they will writhe like a woman in
labor.
They will look aghast at each other,
their faces aflame.

9 See, the day of the LORD is coming
—a cruel day, with wrath and fierce
anger—
to make the land desolate
and destroy the sinners within it.
10 The stars of heaven and their
constellations
will not show their light.
The rising sun will be darkened
and the moon will not give its light.
11 I will punish the world for its evil,
the wicked for their sins.
I will put an end to the arrogance of
the haughty
and will humble the pride of the
ruthless.

---

a 2 Or song   b 6 Hebrew Shaddai

¹²I will make people scarcer than pure
 gold,
 more rare than the gold of Ophir.
¹³Therefore I will make the heavens
 tremble;
 and the earth will shake from its
 place
 at the wrath of the LORD Almighty,
 in the day of his burning anger.

¹⁴Like a hunted gazelle,
 like sheep without a shepherd,
 they will all return to their own people,
 they will flee to their native land.
¹⁵Whoever is captured will be thrust
 through;
 all who are caught will fall by the
 sword.
¹⁶Their infants will be dashed to pieces
 before their eyes;
 their houses will be looted and their
 wives violated.

¹⁷See, I will stir up against them the
 Medes,
 who do not care for silver
 and have no delight in gold.
¹⁸Their bows will strike down the young
 men;
 they will have no mercy on infants,
 nor will they look with compassion
 on children.
¹⁹Babylon, the jewel of kingdoms,
 the pride and glory of the
 Babylonians,ᵃ
 will be overthrown by God
 like Sodom and Gomorrah.
²⁰She will never be inhabited
 or lived in through all generations;
 there no nomads will pitch their tents,
 there no shepherds will rest their
 flocks.
²¹But desert creatures will lie there,
 jackals will fill her houses;
 there the owls will dwell,
 and there the wild goats will leap
 about.
²²Hyenas will inhabit her strongholds,
 jackals her luxurious palaces.
 Her time is at hand,
 and her days will not be prolonged.

14 The LORD will have compassion
 on Jacob;
 once again he will choose Israel
 and will settle them in their own
 land.
Foreigners will join them
 and unite with the descendants of
 Jacob.
²Nations will take them
 and bring them to their own place.
And Israel will take possession of the
 nations
 and make them male and female
 servants in the LORD's land.
They will make captives of their
 captors
 and rule over their oppressors.

³On the day the LORD gives you relief
from your suffering and turmoil and from
the harsh labor forced on you, ⁴you will
take up this taunt against the king of
Babylon:

How the oppressor has come to an end!
 How his furyᵇ has ended!
⁵The LORD has broken the rod of the
 wicked,
 the scepter of the rulers,
⁶which in anger struck down peoples
 with unceasing blows,
 and in fury subdued nations
 with relentless aggression.
⁷All the lands are at rest and at peace;
 they break into singing.
⁸Even the junipers and the cedars of
 Lebanon
 gloat over you and say,
"Now that you have been laid low,
 no one comes to cut us down."

⁹The realm of the dead below is all
 astir
 to meet you at your coming;
it rouses the spirits of the departed to
 greet you—
 all those who were leaders in the
 world;
it makes them rise from their
 thrones—
 all those who were kings over the
 nations.

ᵃ 19 Or *Chaldeans*   ᵇ 4 Dead Sea Scrolls, Septuagint and Syriac; the meaning of the word in the Masoretic Text is
uncertain.

10 They will all respond,
    they will say to you,
"You also have become weak, as we
    are;
you have become like us."
11 All your pomp has been brought down
    to the grave,
    along with the noise of your harps;
maggots are spread out beneath you
    and worms cover you.

12 How you have fallen from heaven,
    morning star, son of the dawn!
You have been cast down to the earth,
    you who once laid low the nations!
13 You said in your heart,
    "I will ascend to the heavens;
I will raise my throne
    above the stars of God;
I will sit enthroned on the mount of
    assembly,
    on the utmost heights of Mount
    Zaphon.ᵃ
14 I will ascend above the tops of the
    clouds;
    I will make myself like the Most
    High."
15 But you are brought down to the realm
    of the dead,
    to the depths of the pit.

Isaiah 14

Q: Why do people think
14:13–17 is about Satan?

BONUS: What was Satan's sin?

16 Those who see you stare at you,
    they ponder your fate:
"Is this the man who shook the earth
    and made kingdoms tremble,
17 the man who made the world a
    wilderness,
    who overthrew its cities
    and would not let his captives go
    home?"

18 All the kings of the nations lie in
    state,
    each in his own tomb.
19 But you are cast out of your tomb
    like a rejected branch;
you are covered with the slain,
    with those pierced by the sword,
    those who descend to the stones of
    the pit.
Like a corpse trampled underfoot,
20   you will not join them in burial,
for you have destroyed your land
    and killed your people.

Let the offspring of the wicked
    never be mentioned again.
21 Prepare a place to slaughter his
    children
    for the sins of their ancestors;
they are not to rise to inherit the land
    and cover the earth with their cities.

22 "I will rise up against them,"
    declares the Lᴏʀᴅ Almighty.
"I will wipe out Babylon's name and
    survivors,
    her offspring and descendants,"
             declares the Lᴏʀᴅ.
23 "I will turn her into a place for owls
    and into swampland;
I will sweep her with the broom of
    destruction,"
    declares the Lᴏʀᴅ Almighty.

24 The Lᴏʀᴅ Almighty has sworn,

"Surely, as I have planned, so it will be,
    and as I have purposed, so it will
    happen.
25 I will crush the Assyrian in my land;
    on my mountains I will trample him
    down.

ᵃ 13 Or of the north; Zaphon was the most sacred
mountain of the Canaanites.

His yoke will be taken from my people,
and his burden removed from their
shoulders."

26 This is the plan determined for the
whole world;
this is the hand stretched out over
all nations.
27 For the LORD Almighty has purposed,
and who can thwart him?
His hand is stretched out, and who
can turn it back?

A Prophecy Against the Philistines

28 This prophecy came in the year King
Ahaz died:

29 Do not rejoice, all you Philistines,
that the rod that struck you is
broken;
from the root of that snake will spring
up a viper,
its fruit will be a darting, venomous
serpent.
30 The poorest of the poor will find
pasture,
and the needy will lie down in
safety.
But your root I will destroy by famine;
it will slay your survivors.

31 Wail, you gate! Howl, you city!
Melt away, all you Philistines!
A cloud of smoke comes from the
north,
and there is not a straggler in its
ranks.
32 What answer shall be given
to the envoys of that nation?
"The LORD has established Zion,
and in her his afflicted people will
find refuge."

A Prophecy Against Moab

15 A prophecy against Moab:

Ar in Moab is ruined,
destroyed in a night!
Kir in Moab is ruined,
destroyed in a night!
2 Dibon goes up to its temple,
to its high places to weep;
Moab wails over Nebo and Medeba.

A: He's called Lucifer ["morning star"] and he fell from heaven (14:13).

BONUS: He wanted to be greater than God (14:13–14).

Every head is shaved
and every beard cut off.
3 In the streets they wear sackcloth;
on the roofs and in the public
squares
they all wail,
prostrate with weeping.
4 Heshbon and Elealeh cry out,
their voices are heard all the way to
Jahaz.
Therefore the armed men of Moab cry
out,
and their hearts are faint.
5 My heart cries out over Moab;
her fugitives flee as far as
Zoar,
as far as Eglath Shelishiyah.
They go up the hill to Luhith,
weeping as they go;
on the road to Horonaim
they lament their destruction.
6 The waters of Nimrim are dried up
and the grass is withered;
the vegetation is gone
and nothing green is left.
7 So the wealth they have acquired and
stored up
they carry away over the Ravine of
the Poplars.

8 Their outcry echoes along the border
of Moab;
their wailing reaches as far as
Eglaim,
their lamentation as far as Beer
Elim.
9 The waters of Dimon*a* are full of blood,
but I will bring still more upon
Dimon*a*—
a lion upon the fugitives of Moab
and upon those who remain in the
land.

16 Send lambs as tribute
to the ruler of the land,
from Sela, across the desert,
to the mount of Daughter Zion.
2 Like fluttering birds
pushed from the nest,
so are the women of Moab
at the fords of the Arnon.

3 "Make up your mind," Moab says.
"Render a decision.
Make your shadow like night—
at high noon.
Hide the fugitives,
do not betray the refugees.
4 Let the Moabite fugitives stay with
you;
be their shelter from the destroyer."

The oppressor will come to an end,
and destruction will cease;
the aggressor will vanish from the
land.
5 In love a throne will be established;
in faithfulness a man will sit on it—
one from the house*b* of David—
one who in judging seeks justice
and speeds the cause of
righteousness.

6 We have heard of Moab's pride—
how great is her arrogance!—
of her conceit, her pride and her
insolence;
but her boasts are empty.
7 Therefore the Moabites wail,
they wail together for Moab.
Lament and grieve
for the raisin cakes of Kir Hareseth.

8 The fields of Heshbon wither,
the vines of Sibmah also.
The rulers of the nations
have trampled down the choicest
vines,
which once reached Jazer
and spread toward the desert.
Their shoots spread out
and went as far as the sea.*c*
9 So I weep, as Jazer weeps,
for the vines of Sibmah.
Heshbon and Elealeh,
I drench you with tears!
The shouts of joy over your ripened
fruit
and over your harvests have been
stilled.
10 Joy and gladness are taken away from
the orchards;
no one sings or shouts in the
vineyards;
no one treads out wine at the
presses,
for I have put an end to the
shouting.
11 My heart laments for Moab like a
harp,
my inmost being for Kir Hareseth.
12 When Moab appears at her high
place,
she only wears herself out;
when she goes to her shrine to pray,
it is to no avail.

13 This is the word the LORD has already
spoken concerning Moab. 14 But now the
LORD says: "Within three years, as a servant bound by contract would count them,
Moab's splendor and all her many people
will be despised, and her survivors will be
very few and feeble."

A Prophecy Against Damascus

17 A prophecy against Damascus:

"See, Damascus will no longer be a
city
but will become a heap of ruins.
2 The cities of Aroer will be deserted
and left to flocks, which will lie
down,
with no one to make them afraid.

---

a 9 Dimon, a wordplay on *Dibon* (see verse 2), sounds like the Hebrew for *blood*. *b 5* Hebrew *tent* *c 8* Probably the
Dead Sea

3 The fortified city will disappear from
    Ephraim,
  and royal power from Damascus;
the remnant of Aram will be
  like the glory of the Israelites,"
         declares the LORD Almighty.

4 "In that day the glory of Jacob will
    fade;
  the fat of his body will waste away.
5 It will be as when reapers harvest the
    standing grain,
  gathering the grain in their arms—
as when someone gleans heads of
    grain
  in the Valley of Rephaim.
6 Yet some gleanings will remain,
  as when an olive tree is beaten,
leaving two or three olives on the
    topmost branches,
  four or five on the fruitful boughs,"
       declares the LORD, the God
                of Israel.

7 In that day people will look to their
    Maker
  and turn their eyes to the Holy One
    of Israel.
8 They will not look to the altars,
  the work of their hands,
and they will have no regard for the
    Asherah poles[a]
  and the incense altars their fingers
    have made.

9 In that day their strong cities, which
they left because of the Israelites, will be
like places abandoned to thickets and undergrowth. And all will be desolation.

10 You have forgotten God your Savior;
  you have not remembered the Rock,
    your fortress.
Therefore, though you set out the
    finest plants
  and plant imported vines,
11 though on the day you set them out,
  you make them grow,
  and on the morning when you plant
    them, you bring them to bud,
yet the harvest will be as nothing
  in the day of disease and incurable
    pain.

12 Woe to the many nations that rage—
  they rage like the raging sea!
Woe to the peoples who roar—
  they roar like the roaring of great
    waters!
13 Although the peoples roar like the roar
  of surging waters,
  when he rebukes them they flee far
    away,
driven before the wind like chaff on
    the hills,
  like tumbleweed before a gale.
14 In the evening, sudden terror!
  Before the morning, they are gone!
This is the portion of those who
    loot us,
  the lot of those who plunder us.

A Prophecy Against Cush

18   Woe to the land of whirring
         wings[b]
along the rivers of Cush,[c]
2 which sends envoys by sea
  in papyrus boats over the water.

Go, swift messengers,
to a people tall and smooth-skinned,
  to a people feared far and wide,
an aggressive nation of strange
    speech,
  whose land is divided by rivers.

3 All you people of the world,
  you who live on the earth,
when a banner is raised on the
    mountains,
  you will see it,
and when a trumpet sounds,
  you will hear it.
4 This is what the LORD says to me:
  "I will remain quiet and will look on
    from my dwelling place,
like shimmering heat in the
    sunshine,
  like a cloud of dew in the heat of
    harvest."
5 For, before the harvest, when the
    blossom is gone
  and the flower becomes a ripening
    grape,
he will cut off the shoots with pruning
    knives,

---

a 8 That is, wooden symbols of the goddess Asherah   *b* 1 Or *of locusts*   *c* 1 That is, the upper Nile region

and cut down and take away the
spreading branches.
6 They will all be left to the mountain
birds of prey
and to the wild animals;
the birds will feed on them all
summer,
the wild animals all winter.

7 At that time gifts will be brought to the
LORD Almighty

from a people tall and smooth-
skinned,
from a people feared far and
wide,
an aggressive nation of strange
speech,
whose land is divided by rivers—

the gifts will be brought to Mount Zion,
the place of the Name of the LORD Almighty.

A Prophecy Against Egypt

19 A prophecy against Egypt:

See, the LORD rides on a swift cloud
and is coming to Egypt.
The idols of Egypt tremble before
him,
and the hearts of the Egyptians
melt with fear.

2 "I will stir up Egyptian against
Egyptian—
brother will fight against brother,
neighbor against neighbor,
city against city,
kingdom against kingdom.
3 The Egyptians will lose heart,
and I will bring their plans to
nothing;
they will consult the idols and the
spirits of the dead,
the mediums and the spiritists.
4 I will hand the Egyptians over
to the power of a cruel master,
and a fierce king will rule over them,"
declares the Lord, the LORD
Almighty.
5 The waters of the river will dry up,
and the riverbed will be parched
and dry.

6 The canals will stink;
the streams of Egypt will dwindle
and dry up.
The reeds and rushes will wither,
7   also the plants along the Nile,
at the mouth of the river.
Every sown field along the Nile
will become parched, will blow away
and be no more.
8 The fishermen will groan and lament,
all who cast hooks into the Nile;
those who throw nets on the water
will pine away.
9 Those who work with combed flax will
despair,
the weavers of fine linen will lose
hope.
10 The workers in cloth will be dejected,
and all the wage earners will be
sick at heart.

11 The officials of Zoan are nothing but
fools;
the wise counselors of Pharaoh give
senseless advice.
How can you say to Pharaoh,
"I am one of the wise men,
a disciple of the ancient kings"?

12 Where are your wise men now?
Let them show you and make
known
what the LORD Almighty
has planned against Egypt.
13 The officials of Zoan have become
fools,
the leaders of Memphis are
deceived;
the cornerstones of her peoples
have led Egypt astray.
14 The LORD has poured into them
a spirit of dizziness;
they make Egypt stagger in all that
she does,
as a drunkard staggers around in
his vomit.
15 There is nothing Egypt can do—
head or tail, palm branch or reed.

16 In that day the Egyptians will become
weaklings. They will shudder with fear at
the uplifted hand that the LORD Almighty
raises against them. 17 And the land of
Judah will bring terror to the Egyptians;

everyone to whom Judah is mentioned will be terrified, because of what the LORD Almighty is planning against them.

¹⁸In that day five cities in Egypt will speak the language of Canaan and swear allegiance to the LORD Almighty. One of them will be called the City of the Sun.ᵃ

¹⁹In that day there will be an altar to the LORD in the heart of Egypt, and a monument to the LORD at its border. ²⁰It will be a sign and witness to the LORD Almighty in the land of Egypt. When they cry out to the LORD because of their oppressors, he will send them a savior and defender, and he will rescue them. ²¹So the LORD will make himself known to the Egyptians, and in that day they will acknowledge the LORD. They will worship with sacrifices and grain offerings; they will make vows to the LORD and keep them. ²²The LORD will strike Egypt with a plague; he will strike them and heal them. They will turn to the LORD, and he will respond to their pleas and heal them.

²³In that day there will be a highway from Egypt to Assyria. The Assyrians will go to Egypt and the Egyptians to Assyria. The Egyptians and Assyrians will worship together. ²⁴In that day Israel will be the third, along with Egypt and Assyria, a blessingᵇ on the earth. ²⁵The LORD Almighty will bless them, saying, "Blessed be Egypt my people, Assyria my handiwork, and Israel my inheritance."

A Prophecy Against Egypt and Cush

20 In the year that the supreme commander, sent by Sargon king of Assyria, came to Ashdod and attacked and captured it— ²at that time the LORD spoke through Isaiah son of Amoz. He said to him, "Take off the sackcloth from your body and the sandals from your feet." And he did so, going around stripped and barefoot.

³Then the LORD said, "Just as my servant Isaiah has gone stripped and barefoot for three years, as a sign and portent against Egypt and Cush,ᶜ ⁴so the king of Assyria will lead away stripped and barefoot the Egyptian captives and Cushite exiles, young and old, with buttocks bared—to Egypt's shame. ⁵Those who trusted in Cush and boasted in Egypt will be dismayed and put to shame. ⁶In that day the people who live on this coast will say, 'See what has happened to those we relied on, those we fled to for help and deliverance from the king of Assyria! How then can we escape?'"

A Prophecy Against Babylon

21 A prophecy against the Desert by the Sea:

Like whirlwinds sweeping through the
        southland,
    an invader comes from the desert,
    from a land of terror.

²A dire vision has been shown to me:
    The traitor betrays, the looter takes
        loot.
    Elam, attack! Media, lay siege!
    I will bring to an end all the groaning
        she caused.

³At this my body is racked with pain,
    pangs seize me, like those of a
        woman in labor;
    I am staggered by what I hear,
    I am bewildered by what I see.
⁴My heart falters,
    fear makes me tremble;
    the twilight I longed for
    has become a horror to me.

⁵They set the tables,
    they spread the rugs,
    they eat, they drink!
    Get up, you officers,
    oil the shields!

⁶This is what the Lord says to me:

"Go, post a lookout
    and have him report what he
        sees.
⁷When he sees chariots
    with teams of horses,
    riders on donkeys
    or riders on camels,

let him be alert,
    fully alert."

[8] And the lookout[a] shouted,

"Day after day, my lord, I stand on the
        watchtower;
    every night I stay at my post.
[9] Look, here comes a man in a
        chariot
    with a team of horses.
And he gives back the answer:
    'Babylon has fallen, has fallen!
All the images of its gods
    lie shattered on the ground!'"

[10] My people who are crushed on the
        threshing floor,
    I tell you what I have heard
from the LORD Almighty,
    from the God of Israel.

A Prophecy Against Edom

[11] A prophecy against Dumah[b]:

Someone calls to me from
        Seir,
    "Watchman, what is left of the
        night?
    Watchman, what is left of the
        night?"
[12] The watchman replies,
    "Morning is coming, but also the
        night.
If you would ask, then ask;
    and come back yet again."

A Prophecy Against Arabia

[13] A prophecy against Arabia:

You caravans of Dedanites,
    who camp in the thickets of Arabia,
[14] bring water for the thirsty;
you who live in Tema,
    bring food for the fugitives.
[15] They flee from the sword,
    from the drawn sword,
from the bent bow
    and from the heat of battle.

[16] This is what the Lord says to me:
"Within one year, as a servant bound by
contract would count it, all the splendor
of Kedar will come to an end. [17] The survivors of the archers, the warriors of Kedar,
will be few." The LORD, the God of Israel,
has spoken.

A Prophecy About Jerusalem

22 A prophecy against the Valley of
    Vision:

What troubles you now,
    that you have all gone up on the
        roofs,
[2] you town so full of commotion,
    you city of tumult and revelry?
Your slain were not killed by the sword,
    nor did they die in battle.
[3] All your leaders have fled together;
    they have been captured without
        using the bow.

---

[a] 8 Dead Sea Scrolls and Syriac; Masoretic Text *A lion*   [b] 11 *Dumah*, a wordplay on *Edom*, means *silence* or *stillness*.

All you who were caught were taken
prisoner together,
having fled while the enemy was
still far away.
4 Therefore I said, "Turn away from me;
let me weep bitterly.
Do not try to console me
over the destruction of my people."

5 The Lord, the LORD Almighty, has a day
of tumult and trampling and terror
in the Valley of Vision,
a day of battering down walls
and of crying out to the mountains.
6 Elam takes up the quiver,
with her charioteers and horses;
Kir uncovers the shield.
7 Your choicest valleys are full of
chariots,
and horsemen are posted at the
city gates.

8 The Lord stripped away the defenses
of Judah,
and you looked in that day
to the weapons in the Palace of the
Forest.
9 You saw that the walls of the City of
David
were broken through in many
places;
you stored up water
in the Lower Pool.
10 You counted the buildings in
Jerusalem
and tore down houses to strengthen
the wall.
11 You built a reservoir between the two
walls
for the water of the Old Pool,
but you did not look to the One who
made it,
or have regard for the One who
planned it long ago.

12 The Lord, the LORD Almighty,
called you on that day
to weep and to wail,
to tear out your hair and put on
sackcloth.
13 But see, there is joy and revelry,
slaughtering of cattle and killing of
sheep,
eating of meat and drinking of wine!

"Let us eat and drink," you say,
"for tomorrow we die!"

14 The LORD Almighty has revealed this
in my hearing: "Till your dying day this sin
will not be atoned for," says the Lord, the
LORD Almighty.

15 This is what the Lord, the LORD Almighty, says:

"Go, say to this steward,
to Shebna the palace administrator:
16 What are you doing here and who
gave you permission
to cut out a grave for yourself here,
hewing your grave on the height
and chiseling your resting place in
the rock?

17 "Beware, the LORD is about to take
firm hold of you
and hurl you away, you mighty man.
18 He will roll you up tightly like a ball
and throw you into a large country.
There you will die
and there the chariots you were so
proud of
will become a disgrace to your
master's house.
19 I will depose you from your office,
and you will be ousted from your
position.

20 "In that day I will summon my servant, Eliakim son of Hilkiah. 21 I will clothe
him with your robe and fasten your sash
around him and hand your authority over
to him. He will be a father to those who
live in Jerusalem and to the people of Judah. 22 I will place on his shoulder the key
to the house of David; what he opens no
one can shut, and what he shuts no one
can open. 23 I will drive him like a peg into
a firm place; he will become a seat[a] of
honor for the house of his father. 24 All
the glory of his family will hang on him:
its offspring and offshoots—all its lesser vessels, from the bowls to all the jars.

25 "In that day," declares the LORD Almighty, "the peg driven into the firm place
will give way; it will be sheared off and will
fall, and the load hanging on it will be cut
down." The LORD has spoken.

a 23 Or throne

A Prophecy Against Tyre

23 A prophecy against Tyre:

Wail, you ships of Tarshish!
  For Tyre is destroyed
  and left without house or harbor.
From the land of Cyprus
  word has come to them.

² Be silent, you people of the island
  and you merchants of Sidon,
    whom the seafarers have
      enriched.
³ On the great waters
  came the grain of the Shihor;
the harvest of the Nile[a] was the
      revenue of Tyre,
  and she became the marketplace of
      the nations.

⁴ Be ashamed, Sidon, and you fortress
      of the sea,
  for the sea has spoken:
"I have neither been in labor nor given
      birth;
  I have neither reared sons nor
      brought up daughters."
⁵ When word comes to Egypt,
  they will be in anguish at the report
      from Tyre.

⁶ Cross over to Tarshish;
  wail, you people of the island.
⁷ Is this your city of revelry,
  the old, old city,
whose feet have taken her
  to settle in far-off lands?
⁸ Who planned this against Tyre,
  the bestower of crowns,
whose merchants are princes,
  whose traders are renowned in the
      earth?
⁹ The LORD Almighty planned it,
  to bring down her pride in all her
      splendor
  and to humble all who are
      renowned on the earth.

¹⁰ Till[b] your land as they do along the
      Nile,
  Daughter Tarshish,
  for you no longer have a harbor.

¹¹ The LORD has stretched out his hand
      over the sea
  and made its kingdoms tremble.
He has given an order concerning
      Phoenicia
  that her fortresses be destroyed.
¹² He said, "No more of your reveling,
  Virgin Daughter Sidon, now
      crushed!

"Up, cross over to Cyprus;
  even there you will find no rest."
¹³ Look at the land of the Babylonians,[c]
  this people that is now of no
      account!
The Assyrians have made it
  a place for desert creatures;
they raised up their siege towers,
  they stripped its fortresses bare
  and turned it into a ruin.

¹⁴ Wail, you ships of Tarshish;
  your fortress is destroyed!

¹⁵ At that time Tyre will be forgotten for seventy years, the span of a king's life. But at the end of these seventy years, it will happen to Tyre as in the song of the prostitute:

¹⁶ "Take up a harp, walk through the city,
  you forgotten prostitute;
play the harp well, sing many a song,
  so that you will be remembered."

¹⁷ At the end of seventy years, the LORD will deal with Tyre. She will return to her lucrative prostitution and will ply her trade with all the kingdoms on the face of the earth. ¹⁸ Yet her profit and her earnings will be set apart for the LORD; they will not be stored up or hoarded. Her profits will go to those who live before the LORD, for abundant food and fine clothes.

The LORD's Devastation of the Earth

24 See, the LORD is going to lay
      waste the earth
  and devastate it;
he will ruin its face
  and scatter its inhabitants—

---

[a] 2,3 Masoretic Text; Dead Sea Scrolls *Sidon, / who cross over the sea; / your envoys* ³*are on the great waters. / The grain of the Shihor, / the harvest of the Nile,*   [b] 10 Dead Sea Scrolls and some Septuagint manuscripts; Masoretic Text *Go through*   [c] 13 Or *Chaldeans*

2 it will be the same
 for priest as for people,
 for the master as for his servant,
 for the mistress as for her servant,
 for seller as for buyer,
 for borrower as for lender,
 for debtor as for creditor.
3 The earth will be completely laid
  waste
 and totally plundered.
  The Lord has spoken this word.

4 The earth dries up and withers,
 the world languishes and withers,
 the heavens languish with the
  earth.
5 The earth is defiled by its people;
 they have disobeyed the laws,
violated the statutes
 and broken the everlasting
  covenant.
6 Therefore a curse consumes the
  earth;
 its people must bear their guilt.
Therefore earth's inhabitants are
  burned up,
 and very few are left.
7 The new wine dries up and the vine
  withers;
 all the merrymakers groan.
8 The joyful timbrels are stilled,
 the noise of the revelers has
  stopped,
 the joyful harp is silent.
9 No longer do they drink wine with a
  song;
 the beer is bitter to its drinkers.
10 The ruined city lies desolate;
 the entrance to every house is
  barred.
11 In the streets they cry out for
  wine;
 all joy turns to gloom,
 all joyful sounds are banished from
  the earth.
12 The city is left in ruins,
 its gate is battered to pieces.
13 So will it be on the earth
 and among the nations,
as when an olive tree is beaten,
 or as when gleanings are left after
  the grape harvest.

14 They raise their voices, they shout for
  joy;
 from the west they acclaim the
  Lord's majesty.
15 Therefore in the east give glory to the
  Lord;
 exalt the name of the Lord, the God
  of Israel,
 in the islands of the sea.
16 From the ends of the earth we hear
  singing:
 "Glory to the Righteous One."

But I said, "I waste away, I waste
  away!
 Woe to me!
The treacherous betray!
 With treachery the treacherous
  betray!"
17 Terror and pit and snare await you,
 people of the earth.
18 Whoever flees at the sound of terror
 will fall into a pit;
 whoever climbs out of the pit
 will be caught in a snare.

The floodgates of the heavens are
  opened,
 the foundations of the earth
  shake.
19 The earth is broken up,
 the earth is split asunder,
 the earth is violently shaken.
20 The earth reels like a drunkard,
 it sways like a hut in the wind;
so heavy upon it is the guilt of its
  rebellion
 that it falls—never to rise again.

21 In that day the Lord will punish
 the powers in the heavens above
 and the kings on the earth below.
22 They will be herded together
 like prisoners bound in a dungeon;
they will be shut up in prison
 and be punished[a] after many
  days.
23 The moon will be dismayed,
 the sun ashamed;
for the Lord Almighty will reign
 on Mount Zion and in Jerusalem,
 and before its elders—with great
  glory.

---

a 22 Or *released*

Praise to the LORD

25 LORD, you are my God;
I will exalt you and praise your
name,
for in perfect faithfulness
you have done wonderful things,
things planned long ago.
2 You have made the city a heap of
rubble,
the fortified town a ruin,
the foreigners' stronghold a city no
more;
it will never be rebuilt.
3 Therefore strong peoples will honor
you;
cities of ruthless nations will revere
you.
4 You have been a refuge for the poor,
a refuge for the needy in their
distress,
a shelter from the storm
and a shade from the heat.
For the breath of the ruthless
is like a storm driving against a wall
5 and like the heat of the desert.
You silence the uproar of foreigners;
as heat is reduced by the shadow
of a cloud,
so the song of the ruthless is
stilled.

6 On this mountain the LORD Almighty
will prepare
a feast of rich food for all peoples,
a banquet of aged wine—
the best of meats and the finest of
wines.
7 On this mountain he will destroy
the shroud that enfolds all peoples,
the sheet that covers all nations;
8 he will swallow up death forever.
The Sovereign LORD will wipe away the
tears
from all faces;
he will remove his people's disgrace
from all the earth.
The LORD has spoken.

9 In that day they will say,

"Surely this is our God;
we trusted in him, and he saved us.

> **LORD, you are my God . . . in perfect faithfulness you have done wonderful things.**
>
> Isaiah 25:1

This is the LORD, we trusted in him;
let us rejoice and be glad in his
salvation."
10 The hand of the LORD will rest on this
mountain;
but Moab will be trampled in their
land
as straw is trampled down in the
manure.
11 They will stretch out their hands in it,
as swimmers stretch out their
hands to swim.
God will bring down their pride
despite the cleverness[a] of their
hands.
12 He will bring down your high fortified
walls
and lay them low;
he will bring them down to the ground,
to the very dust.

A Song of Praise

26 In that day this song will be sung
in the land of Judah:

We have a strong city;
God makes salvation
its walls and ramparts.
2 Open the gates
that the righteous nation may enter,
the nation that keeps faith.
3 You will keep in perfect peace
those whose minds are steadfast,
because they trust in you.
4 Trust in the LORD forever,
for the LORD, the LORD himself, is
the Rock eternal.

---

a 11 The meaning of the Hebrew for this word is uncertain.

⁵He humbles those who dwell on high,
　he lays the lofty city low;
　he levels it to the ground
　and casts it down to the dust.
⁶Feet trample it down—
　the feet of the oppressed,
　the footsteps of the poor.

⁷The path of the righteous is level;
　you, the Upright One, make the way
　　of the righteous smooth.
⁸Yes, Lord, walking in the way of your
　laws,ᵃ
　we wait for you;
　your name and renown
　are the desire of our hearts.
⁹My soul yearns for you in the night;
　in the morning my spirit longs for
　　you.
When your judgments come upon the
　earth,
　the people of the world learn
　　righteousness.
¹⁰But when grace is shown to the
　wicked,
　they do not learn righteousness;
　even in a land of uprightness they go
　　on doing evil
　and do not regard the majesty of
　　the Lord.
¹¹Lord, your hand is lifted high,
　but they do not see it.
Let them see your zeal for your people
　and be put to shame;
　let the fire reserved for your
　enemies consume them.

¹²Lord, you establish peace for us;
　all that we have accomplished you
　have done for us.
¹³Lord our God, other lords besides you
　have ruled over us,
　but your name alone do we honor.
¹⁴They are now dead, they live no
　more;
　their spirits do not rise.
You punished them and brought them
　to ruin;
　you wiped out all memory of
　them.
¹⁵You have enlarged the nation, Lord;
　you have enlarged the nation.

You have gained glory for yourself;
　you have extended all the borders
　　of the land.
¹⁶Lord, they came to you in their
　distress;
　when you disciplined them,
　they could barely whisper a prayer.ᵇ
¹⁷As a pregnant woman about to give
　birth
　writhes and cries out in her pain,
　so were we in your presence, Lord.
¹⁸We were with child, we writhed in
　labor,
　but we gave birth to wind.
We have not brought salvation to the
　earth,
　and the people of the world have
　not come to life.

¹⁹But your dead will live, Lord;
　their bodies will rise—
let those who dwell in the dust
　wake up and shout for joy—
your dew is like the dew of the
　morning;
　the earth will give birth to her dead.

²⁰Go, my people, enter your rooms
　and shut the doors behind you;
hide yourselves for a little while
　until his wrath has passed by.
²¹See, the Lord is coming out of his
　dwelling
　to punish the people of the earth
　for their sins.
The earth will disclose the blood shed
　on it;
　the earth will conceal its slain no
　longer.

Deliverance of Israel

27 In that day,

　the Lord will punish with his sword—
　his fierce, great and powerful
　　sword—
Leviathan the gliding serpent,
　Leviathan the coiling serpent;
　he will slay the monster of the sea.

²In that day—

　"Sing about a fruitful vineyard:

ᵃ 8 Or *judgments*　　ᵇ 16 The meaning of the Hebrew for this clause is uncertain.

³ I, the LORD, watch over it;
    I water it continually.
I guard it day and night
    so that no one may harm it.
⁴   I am not angry.
If only there were briers and thorns
    confronting me!
    I would march against them in battle;
    I would set them all on fire.
⁵ Or else let them come to me for
    refuge;
    let them make peace with me,
    yes, let them make peace with me."

⁶ In days to come Jacob will take root,
    Israel will bud and blossom
    and fill all the world with fruit.

⁷ Has the LORD struck her
    as he struck down those who struck
    her?
Has she been killed
    as those were killed who killed her?
⁸ By warfare[a] and exile you contend
    with her—
    with his fierce blast he drives her
    out,
    as on a day the east wind blows.
⁹ By this, then, will Jacob's guilt be
    atoned for,
    and this will be the full fruit of the
    removal of his sin:
When he makes all the altar stones
    to be like limestone crushed to
    pieces,
    no Asherah poles[b] or incense altars
    will be left standing.
¹⁰ The fortified city stands desolate,
    an abandoned settlement, forsaken
    like the wilderness;
there the calves graze,
    there they lie down;
    they strip its branches bare.
¹¹ When its twigs are dry, they are
    broken off
    and women come and make fires
    with them.
For this is a people without
    understanding;
    so their Maker has no compassion
    on them,
    and their Creator shows them no
    favor.

¹² In that day the LORD will thresh from the flowing Euphrates to the Wadi of Egypt, and you, Israel, will be gathered up one by one. ¹³ And in that day a great trumpet will sound. Those who were perishing in Assyria and those who were exiled in Egypt will come and worship the LORD on the holy mountain in Jerusalem.

Woe to the Leaders of Ephraim and Judah

28 Woe to that wreath, the pride of
    Ephraim's drunkards,
    to the fading flower, his glorious
    beauty,
set on the head of a fertile valley—
    to that city, the pride of those laid
    low by wine!
² See, the Lord has one who is powerful
    and strong.
    Like a hailstorm and a destructive
    wind,
like a driving rain and a flooding
    downpour,
    he will throw it forcefully to the
    ground.
³ That wreath, the pride of Ephraim's
    drunkards,
    will be trampled underfoot.
⁴ That fading flower, his glorious beauty,
    set on the head of a fertile valley,
will be like figs ripe before harvest—
    as soon as people see them and
    take them in hand,
    they swallow them.

⁵ In that day the LORD Almighty
    will be a glorious crown,
a beautiful wreath
    for the remnant of his people.
⁶ He will be a spirit of justice
    to the one who sits in judgment,
a source of strength
    to those who turn back the battle at
    the gate.

⁷ And these also stagger from wine
    and reel from beer:
Priests and prophets stagger from
    beer
    and are befuddled with wine;

---

[a] 8 See Septuagint; the meaning of the Hebrew for this word is uncertain.   [b] 9 That is, wooden symbols of the goddess Asherah

they reel from beer,
  they stagger when seeing visions,
  they stumble when rendering
    decisions.
8 All the tables are covered with vomit
  and there is not a spot without
    filth.

9 "Who is it he is trying to teach?
  To whom is he explaining his
    message?
To children weaned from their milk,
  to those just taken from the
    breast?
10 For it is:
  Do this, do that,
  a rule for this, a rule for that[a];
  a little here, a little there."

11 Very well then, with foreign lips and
    strange tongues
  God will speak to this people,
12 to whom he said,
  "This is the resting place, let the
    weary rest";
and, "This is the place of repose" —
  but they would not listen.
13 So then, the word of the LORD to them
    will become:
  Do this, do that,
  a rule for this, a rule for that;
  a little here, a little there —
so that as they go they will fall
    backward;
  they will be injured and snared and
    captured.

14 Therefore hear the word of the LORD,
    you scoffers
  who rule this people in Jerusalem.
15 You boast, "We have entered into a
    covenant with death,
  with the realm of the dead we have
    made an agreement.
When an overwhelming scourge
    sweeps by,
  it cannot touch us,
for we have made a lie our refuge
  and falsehood[b] our hiding place."

16 So this is what the Sovereign LORD
says:

"See, I lay a stone in Zion, a tested
    stone,
  a precious cornerstone for a sure
    foundation;
the one who relies on it
  will never be stricken with panic.
17 I will make justice the measuring line
  and righteousness the plumb line;
hail will sweep away your refuge, the
    lie,
  and water will overflow your hiding
    place.
18 Your covenant with death will be
    annulled;
  your agreement with the realm of
    the dead will not stand.
When the overwhelming scourge
    sweeps by,
  you will be beaten down by it.
19 As often as it comes it will carry you
    away;
  morning after morning, by day and
    by night,
  it will sweep through."

The understanding of this message
  will bring sheer terror.
20 The bed is too short to stretch
    out on,
  the blanket too narrow to wrap
    around you.
21 The LORD will rise up as he did at
    Mount Perazim,
  he will rouse himself as in the
    Valley of Gibeon —
to do his work, his strange work,
  and perform his task, his alien
    task.
22 Now stop your mocking,
  or your chains will become heavier;
the Lord, the LORD Almighty, has
    told me
  of the destruction decreed against
    the whole land.

23 Listen and hear my voice;
  pay attention and hear what I say.
24 When a farmer plows for planting,
  does he plow continually?
  Does he keep on breaking up and
    working the soil?

---

a 10 Hebrew / sav lasav sav lasav / kav lakav kav lakav (probably meaningless sounds mimicking the prophet's words);
also in verse 13   b 15 Or false gods

²⁵When he has leveled the surface,
  does he not sow caraway and
    scatter cumin?
Does he not plant wheat in its place,ᵃ
  barley in its plot,ᵃ
  and spelt in its field?
²⁶His God instructs him
  and teaches him the right way.

²⁷Caraway is not threshed with a
    sledge,
  nor is the wheel of a cart rolled
    over cumin;
caraway is beaten out with a rod,
  and cumin with a stick.
²⁸Grain must be ground to make bread;
  so one does not go on threshing it
    forever.
The wheels of a threshing cart may be
    rolled over it,
  but one does not use horses to
    grind grain.
²⁹All this also comes from the LORD
    Almighty,
  whose plan is wonderful,
  whose wisdom is magnificent.

Woe to David's City

29 Woe to you, Ariel, Ariel,
  the city where David settled!
Add year to year
  and let your cycle of festivals go on.
²Yet I will besiege Ariel;
  she will mourn and lament,
  she will be to me like an altar
    hearth.ᵇ
³I will encamp against you on all sides;
  I will encircle you with towers
  and set up my siege works against
    you.
⁴Brought low, you will speak from the
    ground;
  your speech will mumble out of the
    dust.
Your voice will come ghostlike from
    the earth;
  out of the dust your speech will
    whisper.

⁵But your many enemies will become
  like fine dust,
  the ruthless hordes like blown
    chaff.
Suddenly, in an instant,
⁶ the LORD Almighty will come
with thunder and earthquake and
    great noise,
  with windstorm and tempest and
    flames of a devouring fire.
⁷Then the hordes of all the nations that
  fight against Ariel,
  that attack her and her fortress and
    besiege her,
will be as it is with a dream,
  with a vision in the night—
⁸as when a hungry person dreams of
    eating,
  but awakens hungry still;
as when a thirsty person dreams of
    drinking,
  but awakens faint and thirsty
    still.
So will it be with the hordes of all the
    nations
  that fight against Mount Zion.

⁹Be stunned and amazed,
  blind yourselves and be sightless;
be drunk, but not from wine,
  stagger, but not from beer.
¹⁰The LORD has brought over you a deep
    sleep:
  He has sealed your eyes (the
    prophets);
  he has covered your heads (the
    seers).

¹¹For you this whole vision is nothing but words sealed in a scroll. And if you give the scroll to someone who can read, and say, "Read this, please," they will answer, "I can't; it is sealed." ¹²Or if you give the scroll to someone who cannot read, and say, "Read this, please," they will answer, "I don't know how to read."

¹³The Lord says:

"These people come near to me with
  their mouth
  and honor me with their lips,
  but their hearts are far from me.
Their worship of me
  is based on merely human rules
    they have been taught.ᶜ

ᵃ 25 The meaning of the Hebrew for this word is uncertain.　ᵇ 2 The Hebrew for *altar hearth* sounds like the Hebrew for *Ariel*.　ᶜ 13 Hebrew; Septuagint *They worship me in vain; / their teachings are merely human rules*

14 Therefore once more I will astound
these people
with wonder upon wonder;
the wisdom of the wise will perish,
the intelligence of the intelligent will
vanish."
15 Woe to those who go to great depths
to hide their plans from the LORD,
who do their work in darkness and
think,
"Who sees us? Who will know?"
16 You turn things upside down,
as if the potter were thought to be
like the clay!
Shall what is formed say to the one
who formed it,
"You did not make me"?
Can the pot say to the potter,
"You know nothing"?
17 In a very short time, will not Lebanon
be turned into a fertile field
and the fertile field seem like a
forest?
18 In that day the deaf will hear the
words of the scroll,
and out of gloom and darkness
the eyes of the blind will see.
19 Once more the humble will rejoice in
the LORD;
the needy will rejoice in the Holy
One of Israel.
20 The ruthless will vanish,
the mockers will disappear,
and all who have an eye for evil will
be cut down—
21 those who with a word make someone
out to be guilty,
who ensnare the defender in court
and with false testimony deprive the
innocent of justice.

22 Therefore this is what the LORD, who
redeemed Abraham, says to the descendants of Jacob:

"No longer will Jacob be ashamed;
no longer will their faces grow pale.
23 When they see among them their
children,
the work of my hands,
they will keep my name holy;
they will acknowledge the holiness
of the Holy One of Jacob,

and will stand in awe of the God of
Israel.
24 Those who are wayward in spirit will
gain understanding;
those who complain will accept
instruction."

Woe to the Obstinate Nation

30 "Woe to the obstinate children,"
declares the LORD,
"to those who carry out plans that are
not mine,
forming an alliance, but not by my
Spirit,
heaping sin upon sin;
2 who go down to Egypt
without consulting me;
who look for help to Pharaoh's
protection,
to Egypt's shade for refuge.
3 But Pharaoh's protection will be to
your shame,
Egypt's shade will bring you
disgrace.
4 Though they have officials in
Zoan
and their envoys have arrived in
Hanes,

Isaiah 30

**Q: What do rebellious people
want to hear?**

**BONUS: What don't they want
to hear?**

Answers on next page

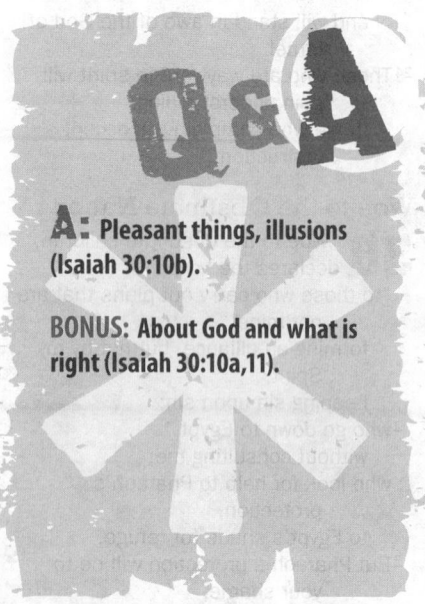

A: Pleasant things, illusions (Isaiah 30:10b).

BONUS: About God and what is right (Isaiah 30:10a,11).

5 everyone will be put to shame
because of a people useless to
them,
who bring neither help nor advantage,
but only shame and disgrace."

6 A prophecy concerning the animals of
the Negev:

Through a land of hardship and
distress,
of lions and lionesses,
of adders and darting snakes,
the envoys carry their riches on
donkeys' backs,
their treasures on the humps of
camels,
to that unprofitable nation,
7   to Egypt, whose help is utterly
useless.
Therefore I call her
Rahab the Do-Nothing.

8 Go now, write it on a tablet for them,
inscribe it on a scroll,
that for the days to come
it may be an everlasting witness.
9 For these are rebellious people,
deceitful children,
children unwilling to listen to the
LORD's instruction.

10 They say to the seers,
"See no more visions!"
and to the prophets,
"Give us no more visions of what is
right!
Tell us pleasant things,
prophesy illusions.
11 Leave this way,
get off this path,
and stop confronting us
with the Holy One of Israel!"

12 Therefore this is what the Holy One
of Israel says:

"Because you have rejected this
message,
relied on oppression
and depended on deceit,
13 this sin will become for you
like a high wall, cracked and
bulging,
that collapses suddenly, in an
instant.
14 It will break in pieces like pottery,
shattered so mercilessly
that among its pieces not a fragment
will be found
for taking coals from a hearth
or scooping water out of a cistern."

15 This is what the Sovereign LORD, the
Holy One of Israel, says:

"In repentance and rest is your
salvation,
in quietness and trust is your
strength,
but you would have none of it.
16 You said, 'No, we will flee on horses.'
Therefore you will flee!
You said, 'We will ride off on swift
horses.'
Therefore your pursuers will be swift!
17 A thousand will flee
at the threat of one;
at the threat of five
you will all flee away,
till you are left
like a flagstaff on a mountaintop,
like a banner on a hill."

18 Yet the LORD longs to be gracious to
you;
therefore he will rise up to show you
compassion.

For the Lᴏʀᴅ is a God of justice.
Blessed are all who wait for him!

¹⁹People of Zion, who live in Jerusalem, you will weep no more. How gracious he will be when you cry for help! As soon as he hears, he will answer you. ²⁰Although the Lord gives you the bread of adversity and the water of affliction, your teachers will be hidden no more; with your own eyes you will see them. ²¹Whether you turn to the right or to the left, your ears will hear a voice behind you, saying, "This is the way; walk in it." ²²Then you will desecrate your idols overlaid with silver and your images covered with gold; you will throw them away like a menstrual cloth and say to them, "Away with you!"

²³He will also send you rain for the seed you sow in the ground, and the food that comes from the land will be rich and plentiful. In that day your cattle will graze in broad meadows. ²⁴The oxen and donkeys that work the soil will eat fodder and mash, spread out with fork and shovel. ²⁵In the day of great slaughter, when the towers fall, streams of water will flow on every high mountain and every lofty hill. ²⁶The moon will shine like the sun, and the sunlight will be seven times brighter, like the light of seven full days, when the Lᴏʀᴅ binds up the bruises of his people and heals the wounds he inflicted.

²⁷See, the Name of the Lᴏʀᴅ comes
from afar,
with burning anger and dense
clouds of smoke;
his lips are full of wrath,
and his tongue is a consuming fire.
²⁸His breath is like a rushing torrent,
rising up to the neck.
He shakes the nations in the sieve of
destruction;
he places in the jaws of the peoples
a bit that leads them astray.
²⁹And you will sing
as on the night you celebrate a holy
festival;
your hearts will rejoice
as when people playing pipes go up
to the mountain of the Lᴏʀᴅ,
to the Rock of Israel.

³⁰The Lᴏʀᴅ will cause people to hear his
majestic voice
and will make them see his arm
coming down
with raging anger and consuming fire,
with cloudburst, thunderstorm and
hail.
³¹The voice of the Lᴏʀᴅ will shatter
Assyria;
with his rod he will strike them
down.
³²Every stroke the Lᴏʀᴅ lays on them
with his punishing club
will be to the music of timbrels and
harps,
as he fights them in battle with the
blows of his arm.
³³Topheth has long been prepared;
it has been made ready for the king.
Its fire pit has been made deep and
wide,
with an abundance of fire and
wood;
the breath of the Lᴏʀᴅ,
like a stream of burning sulfur,
sets it ablaze.

Woe to Those Who Rely on Egypt

31 Woe to those who go down to
Egypt for help,
who rely on horses,
who trust in the multitude of their
chariots
and in the great strength of their
horsemen,
but do not look to the Holy One of
Israel,
or seek help from the Lᴏʀᴅ.
²Yet he too is wise and can bring
disaster;
he does not take back his words.
He will rise up against that wicked
nation,
against those who help evildoers.
³But the Egyptians are mere mortals
and not God;
their horses are flesh and not spirit.
When the Lᴏʀᴅ stretches out his hand,
those who help will stumble,
those who are helped will fall;
all will perish together.

⁴This is what the LORD says to me:

"As a lion growls,
  a great lion over its prey—
and though a whole band of
    shepherds
  is called together against it,
it is not frightened by their shouts
  or disturbed by their clamor—
so the LORD Almighty will come down
  to do battle on Mount Zion and on
    its heights.
⁵Like birds hovering overhead,
  the LORD Almighty will shield
    Jerusalem;
he will shield it and deliver it,
  he will 'pass over' it and will
    rescue it."

⁶Return, you Israelites, to the One you
have so greatly revolted against. ⁷For in
that day every one of you will reject the
idols of silver and gold your sinful hands
have made.

⁸ "Assyria will fall by no human sword;
  a sword, not of mortals, will devour
    them.
They will flee before the sword
  and their young men will be put to
    forced labor.
⁹Their stronghold will fall because of
    terror;
  at the sight of the battle standard
    their commanders will
      panic,"
declares the LORD,
  whose fire is in Zion,
  whose furnace is in Jerusalem.

The Kingdom of Righteousness

32 See, a king will reign in
  righteousness
  and rulers will rule with justice.
²Each one will be like a shelter from
    the wind
  and a refuge from the storm,
like streams of water in the desert
  and the shadow of a great rock in a
    thirsty land.
³Then the eyes of those who see will
    no longer be closed,
  and the ears of those who hear will
    listen.

⁴The fearful heart will know and
    understand,
  and the stammering tongue will be
    fluent and clear.
⁵No longer will the fool be called noble
  nor the scoundrel be highly
    respected.
⁶For fools speak folly,
  their hearts are bent on evil:
They practice ungodliness
  and spread error concerning the
    LORD;
the hungry they leave empty
  and from the thirsty they withhold
    water.
⁷Scoundrels use wicked methods,
  they make up evil schemes
to destroy the poor with lies,
  even when the plea of the needy is
    just.
⁸But the noble make noble plans,
  and by noble deeds they stand.

The Women of Jerusalem

⁹You women who are so complacent,
  rise up and listen to me;
you daughters who feel secure,
  hear what I have to say!
¹⁰In little more than a year
  you who feel secure will tremble;
the grape harvest will fail,
  and the harvest of fruit will not
    come.
¹¹Tremble, you complacent women;
  shudder, you daughters who feel
    secure!
Strip off your fine clothes
  and wrap yourselves in rags.
¹²Beat your breasts for the pleasant
    fields,
  for the fruitful vines
¹³and for the land of my people,
  a land overgrown with thorns and
    briers—
yes, mourn for all houses of
    merriment
  and for this city of revelry.
¹⁴The fortress will be abandoned,
  the noisy city deserted;
citadel and watchtower will become a
    wasteland forever,
  the delight of donkeys, a pasture
    for flocks,

¹⁵ till the Spirit is poured on us from on
high,
and the desert becomes a fertile
field,
and the fertile field seems like a
forest.
¹⁶ The LORD's justice will dwell in the
desert,
his righteousness live in the fertile
field.
¹⁷ The fruit of that righteousness will be
peace;
its effect will be quietness and
confidence forever.
¹⁸ My people will live in peaceful dwelling
places,
in secure homes,
in undisturbed places of rest.
¹⁹ Though hail flattens the forest
and the city is leveled completely,

²⁰ how blessed you will be,
sowing your seed by every stream,
and letting your cattle and donkeys
range free.

Distress and Help

33 Woe to you, destroyer,
you who have not been
destroyed!
Woe to you, betrayer,
you who have not been betrayed!
When you stop destroying,
you will be destroyed;
when you stop betraying,
you will be betrayed.

² LORD, be gracious to us;
we long for you.
Be our strength every morning,
our salvation in time of distress.

TO THE POINT

Yes to World Peace

Today world peace seems closer than it did when the United
States and the Soviet Union had missiles aimed at each other.
However, every day thousands of people live in terror. You
might feel safer, but someone on the other side of the world
might not. *World* peace is peace everywhere, for all people.

When the United Nations tries to stop terrorism or sends help
to the victims of war, you can be glad. But however hard they
try, they'll never be able to bring world peace. As long as people
are moved by anger and hatred and a lust for power, peace is
impossible.

When Jesus returns to rule, he'll bring world peace by changing the hearts of those who live in this world. "The fruit of
that righteousness will be peace; its effect will be quietness and
confidence forever" (Isaiah 32:17).

3 At the uproar of your army, the
     peoples flee;
  when you rise up, the nations
     scatter.
4 Your plunder, O nations, is harvested
     as by young locusts;
  like a swarm of locusts people
     pounce on it.

5 The LORD is exalted, for he dwells on
     high;
  he will fill Zion with his justice and
     righteousness.
6 He will be the sure foundation for your
     times,
  a rich store of salvation and wisdom
     and knowledge;
  the fear of the LORD is the key to
     this treasure.ᵃ

7 Look, their brave men cry aloud in the
     streets;
  the envoys of peace weep bitterly.
8 The highways are deserted,
  no travelers are on the roads.
  The treaty is broken,
  its witnessesᵇ are despised,
  no one is respected.
9 The land dries up and wastes away,
  Lebanon is ashamed and withers;
  Sharon is like the Arabah,
  and Bashan and Carmel drop their
     leaves.

10 "Now will I arise," says the LORD.
  "Now will I be exalted;
  now will I be lifted up.
11 You conceive chaff,
  you give birth to straw;
  your breath is a fire that consumes
     you.
12 The peoples will be burned to ashes;
  like cut thornbushes they will be set
     ablaze."

13 You who are far away, hear what I
     have done;
  you who are near, acknowledge my
     power!
14 The sinners in Zion are terrified;
  trembling grips the godless:
  "Who of us can dwell with the
     consuming fire?

Who of us can dwell with everlasting
     burning?"
15 Those who walk righteously
  and speak what is right,
  who reject gain from extortion
  and keep their hands from
     accepting bribes,
  who stop their ears against plots of
     murder
  and shut their eyes against
     contemplating evil—
16 they are the ones who will dwell on
     the heights,
  whose refuge will be the mountain
     fortress.
  Their bread will be supplied,
  and water will not fail them.

17 Your eyes will see the king in his
     beauty
  and view a land that stretches afar.
18 In your thoughts you will ponder the
     former terror:
  "Where is that chief officer?
  Where is the one who took the
     revenue?
  Where is the officer in charge of the
     towers?"
19 You will see those arrogant people no
     more,
  people whose speech is obscure,
  whose language is strange and
     incomprehensible.

20 Look on Zion, the city of our festivals;
  your eyes will see Jerusalem,
  a peaceful abode, a tent that will
     not be moved;
  its stakes will never be pulled up,
  nor any of its ropes broken.
21 There the LORD will be our Mighty One.
  It will be like a place of broad rivers
     and streams.
  No galley with oars will ride them,
  no mighty ship will sail them.
22 For the LORD is our judge,
  the LORD is our lawgiver,
  the LORD is our king;
  it is he who will save us.

23 Your rigging hangs loose:
  The mast is not held secure,
  the sail is not spread.

ᵃ 6 Or is a treasure from him   ᵇ 8 Dead Sea Scrolls; Masoretic Text / the cities

Then an abundance of spoils will be
divided
and even the lame will carry off
plunder.
24 No one living in Zion will say, "I am
ill";
and the sins of those who dwell
there will be forgiven.

Judgment Against the Nations

34 Come near, you nations, and
listen;
pay attention, you peoples!
Let the earth hear, and all that is
in it,
the world, and all that comes out
of it!
2 The LORD is angry with all nations;
his wrath is on all their armies.
He will totally destroy[a] them,
he will give them over to
slaughter.
3 Their slain will be thrown out,
their dead bodies will stink;
the mountains will be soaked with
their blood.
4 All the stars in the sky will be
dissolved
and the heavens rolled up like a
scroll;
all the starry host will fall
like withered leaves from the
vine,
like shriveled figs from the fig
tree.

5 My sword has drunk its fill in the
heavens;
see, it descends in judgment on
Edom,
the people I have totally
destroyed.
6 The sword of the LORD is bathed in
blood,
it is covered with fat—
the blood of lambs and goats,
fat from the kidneys of rams.
For the LORD has a sacrifice in
Bozrah
and a great slaughter in the land of
Edom.

7 And the wild oxen will fall with them,
the bull calves and the great bulls.
Their land will be drenched with
blood,
and the dust will be soaked with
fat.

8 For the LORD has a day of vengeance,
a year of retribution, to uphold
Zion's cause.
9 Edom's streams will be turned into
pitch,
her dust into burning sulfur;
her land will become blazing
pitch!
10 It will not be quenched night or day;
its smoke will rise forever.
From generation to generation it will
lie desolate;
no one will ever pass through it
again.
11 The desert owl[b] and screech owl[b] will
possess it;
the great owl[b] and the raven will
nest there.
God will stretch out over Edom
the measuring line of chaos
and the plumb line of desolation.
12 Her nobles will have nothing there to
be called a kingdom,
all her princes will vanish away.
13 Thorns will overrun her citadels,
nettles and brambles her
strongholds.
She will become a haunt for jackals,
a home for owls.
14 Desert creatures will meet with
hyenas,
and wild goats will bleat to each
other;
there the night creatures will also lie
down
and find for themselves places of
rest.
15 The owl will nest there and lay
eggs,
she will hatch them, and care for
her young
under the shadow of her wings;
there also the falcons will gather,
each with its mate.

---

a 2 The Hebrew term refers to the irrevocable giving over of things or persons to the LORD, often by totally destroying them;
also in verse 5. b 11 The precise identification of these birds is uncertain.

¹⁶Look in the scroll of the LORD and read:

None of these will be missing,
  not one will lack her mate.
For it is his mouth that has given the
    order,
  and his Spirit will gather them
    together.
¹⁷He allots their portions;
  his hand distributes them by
    measure.
They will possess it forever
  and dwell there from generation to
    generation.

Joy of the Redeemed

35 The desert and the parched land
    will be glad;
  the wilderness will rejoice and
    blossom.
Like the crocus, ²it will burst into
    bloom;
  it will rejoice greatly and shout for
    joy.
The glory of Lebanon will be given to it,
  the splendor of Carmel and
    Sharon;
they will see the glory of the LORD,
  the splendor of our God.

³Strengthen the feeble hands,
  steady the knees that give way;
⁴say to those with fearful hearts,
  "Be strong, do not fear;
your God will come,
  he will come with vengeance;
with divine retribution
  he will come to save you."

⁵Then will the eyes of the blind be
    opened
  and the ears of the deaf unstopped.
⁶Then will the lame leap like a deer,
  and the mute tongue shout for joy.
Water will gush forth in the
    wilderness
  and streams in the desert.
⁷The burning sand will become a pool,
  the thirsty ground bubbling springs.
In the haunts where jackals once lay,
  grass and reeds and papyrus will
    grow.

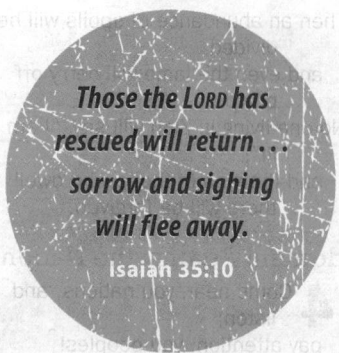

Those the LORD has rescued will return . . . sorrow and sighing will flee away.

Isaiah 35:10

⁸And a highway will be there;
  it will be called the Way of Holiness;
  it will be for those who walk on that
    Way.
The unclean will not journey on it;
  wicked fools will not go about on it.
⁹No lion will be there,
  nor any ravenous beast;
  they will not be found there.
But only the redeemed will walk there,
¹⁰ and those the LORD has rescued will
    return.
They will enter Zion with singing;
  everlasting joy will crown their
    heads.
Gladness and joy will overtake them,
  and sorrow and sighing will flee
    away.

Sennacherib Threatens Jerusalem

36 In the fourteenth year of King Hez-
    ekiah's reign, Sennacherib king
of Assyria attacked all the fortified cities
of Judah and captured them. ²Then the
king of Assyria sent his field commander
with a large army from Lachish to King
Hezekiah at Jerusalem. When the commander stopped at the aqueduct of the
Upper Pool, on the road to the Launderer's Field, ³Eliakim son of Hilkiah the palace administrator, Shebna the secretary,
and Joah son of Asaph the recorder went
out to him.

⁴The field commander said to them,
"Tell Hezekiah:

" 'This is what the great king, the
king of Assyria, says: On what are

you basing this confidence of yours? ⁵You say you have counsel and might for war—but you speak only empty words. On whom are you depending, that you rebel against me? ⁶Look, I know you are depending on Egypt, that splintered reed of a staff, which pierces the hand of anyone who leans on it! Such is Pharaoh king of Egypt to all who depend on him. ⁷But if you say to me, "We are depending on the LORD our God"—isn't he the one whose high places and altars Hezekiah removed, saying to Judah and Jerusalem, "You must worship before this altar"?

⁸"'Come now, make a bargain with my master, the king of Assyria: I will give you two thousand horses—if you can put riders on them! ⁹How then can you repulse one officer of the least of my master's officials, even though you are depending on Egypt for chariots and horsemen[a]? ¹⁰Furthermore, have I come to attack and destroy this land without the LORD? The LORD himself told me to march against this country and destroy it.' "

¹¹Then Eliakim, Shebna and Joah said to the field commander, "Please speak to your servants in Aramaic, since we understand it. Don't speak to us in Hebrew in the hearing of the people on the wall."

¹²But the commander replied, "Was it only to your master and you that my master sent me to say these things, and not to the people sitting on the wall—who, like you, will have to eat their own excrement and drink their own urine?"

¹³Then the commander stood and called out in Hebrew, "Hear the words of the great king, the king of Assyria! ¹⁴This is what the king says: Do not let Hezekiah deceive you. He cannot deliver you! ¹⁵Do not let Hezekiah persuade you to trust in the LORD when he says, 'The LORD will surely deliver us; this city will not be given into the hand of the king of Assyria.'

¹⁶"Do not listen to Hezekiah. This is what the king of Assyria says: Make peace with me and come out to me. Then each of you will eat fruit from your own vine and fig tree and drink water from your own cistern, ¹⁷until I come and take you to a land like your own—a land of grain and new wine, a land of bread and vineyards.

¹⁸"Do not let Hezekiah mislead you when he says, 'The LORD will deliver us.' Have the gods of any nations ever delivered their lands from the hand of the king of Assyria? ¹⁹Where are the gods of Hamath and Arpad? Where are the gods of Sepharvaim? Have they rescued Samaria from my hand? ²⁰Who of all the gods of these countries have been able to save their lands from me? How then can the LORD deliver Jerusalem from my hand?"

²¹But the people remained silent and said nothing in reply, because the king had commanded, "Do not answer him."

²²Then Eliakim son of Hilkiah the palace administrator, Shebna the secretary and Joah son of Asaph the recorder went to Hezekiah, with their clothes torn, and told him what the field commander had said.

Jerusalem's Deliverance Foretold

37 When King Hezekiah heard this, he tore his clothes and put on sackcloth and went into the temple of the LORD. ²He sent Eliakim the palace administrator, Shebna the secretary, and the leading priests, all wearing sackcloth, to the prophet Isaiah son of Amoz. ³They told him, "This is what Hezekiah says: This day is a day of distress and rebuke and disgrace, as when children come to the moment of birth and there is no strength to deliver them. ⁴It may be that the LORD your God will hear the words of the field commander, whom his master, the king of Assyria, has sent to ridicule the living God, and that he will rebuke him for the words the LORD your God has heard. Therefore pray for the remnant that still survives."

⁵When King Hezekiah's officials came to Isaiah, ⁶Isaiah said to them, "Tell your

---

[a] 9 Or charioteers

master, 'This is what the LORD says: Do not be afraid of what you have heard—those words with which the underlings of the king of Assyria have blasphemed me. [7]Listen! When he hears a certain report, I will make him want to return to his own country, and there I will have him cut down with the sword.' "

[8]When the field commander heard that the king of Assyria had left Lachish, he withdrew and found the king fighting against Libnah.

[9]Now Sennacherib received a report that Tirhakah, the king of Cush,[a] was marching out to fight against him. When he heard it, he sent messengers to Hezekiah with this word: [10]"Say to Hezekiah king of Judah: Do not let the god you depend on deceive you when he says, 'Jerusalem will not be given into the hands of the king of Assyria.' [11]Surely you have heard what the kings of Assyria have done to all the countries, destroying them completely. And will you be delivered? [12]Did the gods of the nations that were destroyed by my predecessors deliver them—the gods of Gozan, Harran, Rezeph and the people of Eden who were in

Tel Assar? [13]Where is the king of Hamath or the king of Arpad? Where are the kings of Lair, Sepharvaim, Hena and Ivvah?"

Hezekiah's Prayer

[14]Hezekiah received the letter from the messengers and read it. Then he went up to the temple of the LORD and spread it out before the LORD. [15]And Hezekiah prayed to the LORD: [16]"LORD Almighty, the God of Israel, enthroned between the cherubim, you alone are God over all the kingdoms of the earth. You have made heaven and earth. [17]Give ear, LORD, and hear; open your eyes, LORD, and see; listen to all the words Sennacherib has sent to ridicule the living God.

[18]"It is true, LORD, that the Assyrian kings have laid waste all these peoples and their lands. [19]They have thrown their gods into the fire and destroyed them, for they were not gods but only wood and stone, fashioned by human hands. [20]Now, LORD our God, deliver us from his hand, so that all the kingdoms of the earth may know that you, LORD, are the only God.[b]"

Sennacherib's Fall

[21]Then Isaiah son of Amoz sent a message to Hezekiah: "This is what the LORD, the God of Israel, says: Because you have prayed to me concerning Sennacherib king of Assyria, [22]this is the word the LORD has spoken against him:

"Virgin Daughter Zion
        despises and mocks you.
Daughter Jerusalem
        tosses her head as you flee.
[23]Who is it you have ridiculed and
                blasphemed?
        Against whom have you raised your
                voice
        and lifted your eyes in pride?
        Against the Holy One of Israel!
[24]By your messengers
        you have ridiculed the Lord.
And you have said,
        'With my many chariots

Q&A

Isaiah 37

Q: How many Assyrian soldiers did the angel of the LORD kill?

BONUS: Do any other historical sources report this incident?

Answers on next page

---

[a] 9 That is, the upper Nile region   [b] 20 Dead Sea Scrolls (see also 2 Kings 19:19); Masoretic Text *you alone are the LORD*

I have ascended the heights of the
     mountains,
  the utmost heights of Lebanon.
I have cut down its tallest cedars,
  the choicest of its junipers.
I have reached its remotest heights,
  the finest of its forests.
²⁵ I have dug wells in foreign lands^a
  and drunk the water there.
With the soles of my feet
  I have dried up all the streams of
     Egypt.'

²⁶ "Have you not heard?
  Long ago I ordained it.
In days of old I planned it;
  now I have brought it to pass,
that you have turned fortified
     cities
  into piles of stone.
²⁷ Their people, drained of power,
  are dismayed and put to shame.
They are like plants in the field,
  like tender green shoots,
like grass sprouting on the roof,
  scorched^b before it grows up.

²⁸ "But I know where you are
  and when you come and go
  and how you rage against me.
²⁹ Because you rage against me
  and because your insolence has
     reached my ears,
I will put my hook in your nose
  and my bit in your mouth,
and I will make you return
  by the way you came.

³⁰ "This will be the sign for you, Hez-
ekiah:

"This year you will eat what grows by
     itself,
  and the second year what springs
     from that.
But in the third year sow and reap,
  plant vineyards and eat their
     fruit.
³¹ Once more a remnant of the kingdom
     of Judah
  will take root below and bear fruit
     above.

A: He killed 185,000 (Isaiah 37:36)!

BONUS: According to the Greek historian Herodotus, field mice attacked Sennacherib's army and ate their weapons. Perhaps God used plague-infested mice to deliver his people.

³² For out of Jerusalem will come a
     remnant,
  and out of Mount Zion a band of
     survivors.
The zeal of the LORD Almighty
  will accomplish this.

³³ "Therefore this is what the LORD says
concerning the king of Assyria:

"He will not enter this city
  or shoot an arrow here.
He will not come before it with shield
  or build a siege ramp against it.
³⁴ By the way that he came he will
     return;
  he will not enter this city,"
                    declares the LORD.
³⁵ "I will defend this city and save it,
  for my sake and for the sake of
     David my servant!"

³⁶ Then the angel of the LORD went out
and put to death a hundred and eighty-five
thousand in the Assyrian camp. When the
people got up the next morning—there
were all the dead bodies! ³⁷ So Sennacherib king of Assyria broke camp and

^a 25 Dead Sea Scrolls (see also 2 Kings 19:24); Masoretic Text does not have *in foreign lands.*   ^b 27 Some
manuscripts of the Masoretic Text, Dead Sea Scrolls and some Septuagint manuscripts (see also 2 Kings 19:26); most
manuscripts of the Masoretic Text *roof / and terraced fields*

withdrew. He returned to Nineveh and stayed there.

38 One day, while he was worshiping in the temple of his god Nisrok, his sons Adrammelek and Sharezer killed him with the sword, and they escaped to the land of Ararat. And Esarhaddon his son succeeded him as king.

Hezekiah's Illness

38 In those days Hezekiah became ill and was at the point of death. The prophet Isaiah son of Amoz went to him and said, "This is what the LORD says: Put your house in order, because you are going to die; you will not recover."

2 Hezekiah turned his face to the wall and prayed to the LORD, 3 "Remember, LORD, how I have walked before you faithfully and with wholehearted devotion and have done what is good in your eyes." And Hezekiah wept bitterly.

4 Then the word of the LORD came to Isaiah: 5 "Go and tell Hezekiah, 'This is what the LORD, the God of your father David, says: I have heard your prayer and seen your tears; I will add fifteen years to your life. 6 And I will deliver you and this city from the hand of the king of Assyria. I will defend this city.

7 "'This is the LORD's sign to you that the LORD will do what he has promised: 8 I will make the shadow cast by the sun go back the ten steps it has gone down on the stairway of Ahaz.'" So the sunlight went back the ten steps it had gone down.

9 A writing of Hezekiah king of Judah after his illness and recovery:

10 I said, "In the prime of my life
must I go through the gates of death
and be robbed of the rest of my years?"
11 I said, "I will not again see the LORD himself
in the land of the living;
no longer will I look on my fellow man,
or be with those who now dwell in this world.
12 Like a shepherd's tent my house
has been pulled down and taken from me.

Like a weaver I have rolled up my life,
and he has cut me off from the loom;
day and night you made an end of me.
13 I waited patiently till dawn,
but like a lion he broke all my bones;
day and night you made an end of me.
14 I cried like a swift or thrush,
I moaned like a mourning dove.
My eyes grew weak as I looked to the heavens.
I am being threatened; Lord, come to my aid!"

15 But what can I say?
He has spoken to me, and he himself has done this.
I will walk humbly all my years
because of this anguish of my soul.
16 Lord, by such things people live;
and my spirit finds life in them too.
You restored me to health
and let me live.
17 Surely it was for my benefit
that I suffered such anguish.
In your love you kept me
from the pit of destruction;
you have put all my sins
behind your back.
18 For the grave cannot praise you,
death cannot sing your praise;
those who go down to the pit
cannot hope for your faithfulness.
19 The living, the living—they praise you,
as I am doing today;
parents tell their children
about your faithfulness.

20 The LORD will save me,
and we will sing with stringed instruments
all the days of our lives
in the temple of the LORD.

21 Isaiah had said, "Prepare a poultice of figs and apply it to the boil, and he will recover."

²²Hezekiah had asked, "What will be the sign that I will go up to the temple of the LORD?"

Envoys From Babylon

39 At that time Marduk-Baladan son of Baladan king of Babylon sent Hezekiah letters and a gift, because he had heard of his illness and recovery. ²Hezekiah received the envoys gladly and showed them what was in his storehouses—the silver, the gold, the spices, the fine olive oil—his entire armory and everything found among his treasures. There was nothing in his palace or in all his kingdom that Hezekiah did not show them.

³Then Isaiah the prophet went to King Hezekiah and asked, "What did those men say, and where did they come from?"

"From a distant land," Hezekiah replied. "They came to me from Babylon."

⁴The prophet asked, "What did they see in your palace?"

"They saw everything in my palace," Hezekiah said. "There is nothing among my treasures that I did not show them."

⁵Then Isaiah said to Hezekiah, "Hear the word of the LORD Almighty: ⁶The time will surely come when everything in your palace, and all that your predecessors have stored up until this day, will be carried off to Babylon. Nothing will be left, says the LORD. ⁷And some of your descendants, your own flesh and blood who will be born to you, will be taken away, and they will become eunuchs in the palace of the king of Babylon."

⁸"The word of the LORD you have spoken is good," Hezekiah replied. For he thought, "There will be peace and security in my lifetime."

Comfort for God's People

40 Comfort, comfort my people, says your God.
²Speak tenderly to Jerusalem,
    and proclaim to her
that her hard service has been
        completed,
    that her sin has been paid for,

that she has received from the LORD's
        hand
    double for all her sins.

³A voice of one calling:
"In the wilderness prepare
    the way for the LORDᵃ;
make straight in the desert
    a highway for our God.ᵇ
⁴Every valley shall be raised up,
    every mountain and hill made low;
the rough ground shall become level,
    the rugged places a plain.
⁵And the glory of the LORD will be
        revealed,
    and all people will see it together.
            For the mouth of the LORD
                    has spoken."

⁶A voice says, "Cry out."
    And I said, "What shall I cry?"

"All people are like grass,
    and all their faithfulness is like the
        flowers of the field.
⁷The grass withers and the flowers fall,
    because the breath of the LORD
        blows on them.
    Surely the people are grass.
⁸The grass withers and the flowers fall,
    but the word of our God endures
        forever."

⁹You who bring good news to Zion,
    go up on a high mountain.
You who bring good news to
        Jerusalem,ᶜ
    lift up your voice with a shout,
lift it up, do not be afraid;
    say to the towns of Judah,
    "Here is your God!"
¹⁰See, the Sovereign LORD comes with
        power,
    and he rules with a mighty arm.
See, his reward is with him,
    and his recompense accompanies
        him.
¹¹He tends his flock like a shepherd:
    He gathers the lambs in his arms
and carries them close to his heart;
    he gently leads those that have
        young.

ᵃ 3 Or *A voice of one calling in the wilderness: / "Prepare the way for the LORD*   ᵇ 3 Hebrew; Septuagint *make straight the paths of our God*   ᶜ 9 Or *Zion, bringer of good news, / go up on a high mountain. / Jerusalem, bringer of good news*

¹²Who has measured the waters in the
hollow of his hand,
or with the breadth of his hand
marked off the heavens?
Who has held the dust of the earth in
a basket,
or weighed the mountains on the
scales
and the hills in a balance?
¹³Who can fathom the Spirit[a] of the
Lᴏʀᴅ,
or instruct the Lᴏʀᴅ as his
counselor?
¹⁴Whom did the Lᴏʀᴅ consult to
enlighten him,
and who taught him the right way?
Who was it that taught him
knowledge,
or showed him the path of
understanding?

¹⁵Surely the nations are like a drop in a
bucket;
they are regarded as dust on the
scales;
he weighs the islands as though
they were fine dust.
¹⁶Lebanon is not sufficient for altar
fires,
nor its animals enough for burnt
offerings.
¹⁷Before him all the nations are as
nothing;
they are regarded by him as
worthless
and less than nothing.

¹⁸With whom, then, will you compare
God?
To what image will you liken him?
¹⁹As for an idol, a metalworker casts it,
and a goldsmith overlays it with
gold
and fashions silver chains for it.
²⁰A person too poor to present such an
offering
selects wood that will not rot;
they look for a skilled worker
to set up an idol that will not
topple.

²¹Do you not know?
Have you not heard?
Has it not been told you from the
beginning?
Have you not understood since the
earth was founded?
²²He sits enthroned above the circle of
the earth,
and its people are like
grasshoppers.
He stretches out the heavens like a
canopy,
and spreads them out like a tent to
live in.
²³He brings princes to naught
and reduces the rulers of this world
to nothing.
²⁴No sooner are they planted,
no sooner are they sown,
no sooner do they take root in the
ground,
than he blows on them and they wither,
and a whirlwind sweeps them away
like chaff.

²⁵"To whom will you compare me?
Or who is my equal?" says the Holy
One.
²⁶Lift up your eyes and look to the
heavens:
Who created all these?
He who brings out the starry host one
by one
and calls forth each of them by
name.
Because of his great power and
mighty strength,
not one of them is missing.

²⁷Why do you complain, Jacob?
Why do you say, Israel,
"My way is hidden from the Lᴏʀᴅ;
my cause is disregarded by my
God"?
²⁸Do you not know?
Have you not heard?
The Lᴏʀᴅ is the everlasting God,
the Creator of the ends of the
earth.
He will not grow tired or weary,
and his understanding no one can
fathom.
²⁹He gives strength to the weary
and increases the power of the
weak.

ᵃ 13 Or *mind*

> The guys in the locker room are all over me about being a virgin. They're now asking if I'm gay. I also take a lot of heat because I don't go out and get drunk with them. I'm beginning to feel like I really am a loser. My willpower is getting weak.   >> Hunter

Dear Jordan

Dear Hunter,

Lots of kids say they're Christians, but the way they live doesn't show it. You have the courage to live your faith. You have a clear conscience because you're not living in sin.

I'm concerned that you're feeling worn down saying no. Next time the guys are getting on your case you could say something like, "Hey, I don't get on you because of the choices you make. How about returning the favor?" People need to feel comfortable with their choices, and you deserve the right to choose. I'm guessing after a while of getting the same answer, they'll decide to leave you alone.

Maybe you could also find some other guys and girls who honor God in their lives. Does your church have a youth group? Does your school have a Fellowship of Christian Athletes group? If so, you might find some others whose choices are more like yours.

One great thing to remember is that God will give you strength to help you continue to honor him. Take a look at Isaiah 40:28–31: "Even youths grow tired and weary, and young men stumble and fall; but those who hope in the LORD will renew their strength. They will soar on wings like eagles; they will run and not grow weary ..." (verses 30–31). Stay strong. You not only honor God with your life, but you may also be helping someone else who needs someone to look up to.

Jordan

> *Those who hope in the Lord will renew their strength. They will soar on wings like eagles.*
>
> Isaiah 40:31

30 Even youths grow tired and weary,
   and young men stumble and fall;
31 but those who hope in the Lord
   will renew their strength.
   They will soar on wings like eagles;
   they will run and not grow weary,
   they will walk and not be faint.

The Helper of Israel

41 "Be silent before me, you
   islands!
   Let the nations renew their
      strength!
   Let them come forward and speak;
   let us meet together at the place of
      judgment.

2 "Who has stirred up one from the
   east,
   calling him in righteousness to his
      service[a]?
   He hands nations over to him
   and subdues kings before him.
   He turns them to dust with his sword,
   to windblown chaff with his bow.
3 He pursues them and moves on
   unscathed,
   by a path his feet have not traveled
      before.
4 Who has done this and carried it
   through,
   calling forth the generations from
      the beginning?
   I, the Lord—with the first of them
   and with the last—I am he."

5 The islands have seen it and fear;
   the ends of the earth tremble.

   They approach and come forward;
6   they help each other
     and say to their companions, "Be
        strong!"
7 The metalworker encourages the
     goldsmith,
   and the one who smooths with the
     hammer
   spurs on the one who strikes the
     anvil.
   One says of the welding, "It is good."
   The other nails down the idol so it
     will not topple.

8 "But you, Israel, my servant,
   Jacob, whom I have chosen,
   you descendants of Abraham my
     friend,
9 I took you from the ends of the earth,
   from its farthest corners I called
     you.
   I said, 'You are my servant';
   I have chosen you and have not
     rejected you.
10 So do not fear, for I am with you;
   do not be dismayed, for I am your
     God.
   I will strengthen you and help you;
   I will uphold you with my righteous
     right hand.

11 "All who rage against you
   will surely be ashamed and
     disgraced;
   those who oppose you
   will be as nothing and perish.
12 Though you search for your enemies,
   you will not find them.
   Those who wage war against you
   will be as nothing at all.
13 For I am the Lord your God
   who takes hold of your right hand
   and says to you, Do not fear;
   I will help you.
14 Do not be afraid, you worm Jacob,
   little Israel, do not fear,
   for I myself will help you," declares
     the Lord,
   your Redeemer, the Holy One of
     Israel.
15 "See, I will make you into a threshing
     sledge,
   new and sharp, with many teeth.

---

a 2 Or east, / whom victory meets at every step

You will thresh the mountains and
crush them,
and reduce the hills to chaff.
16 You will winnow them, the wind will
pick them up,
and a gale will blow them away.
But you will rejoice in the LORD
and glory in the Holy One of Israel.

17 "The poor and needy search for
water,
but there is none;
their tongues are parched with
thirst.
But I the LORD will answer them;
I, the God of Israel, will not forsake
them.
18 I will make rivers flow on barren
heights,
and springs within the valleys.
I will turn the desert into pools of
water,
and the parched ground into
springs.
19 I will put in the desert
the cedar and the acacia, the
myrtle and the olive.
I will set junipers in the wasteland,
the fir and the cypress together,
20 so that people may see and know,
may consider and understand,
that the hand of the LORD has done
this,
that the Holy One of Israel has
created it.

21 "Present your case," says the LORD.
"Set forth your arguments," says
Jacob's King.
22 "Tell us, you idols,
what is going to happen.
Tell us what the former things were,
so that we may consider them
and know their final outcome.
Or declare to us the things to come,
23 tell us what the future holds,
so we may know that you are gods.
Do something, whether good or bad,
so that we will be dismayed and
filled with fear.
24 But you are less than nothing
and your works are utterly
worthless;
whoever chooses you is detestable.

25 "I have stirred up one from the north,
and he comes—
one from the rising sun who calls
on my name.
He treads on rulers as if they were
mortar,
as if he were a potter treading the
clay.
26 Who told of this from the beginning,
so we could know,
or beforehand, so we could say, 'He
was right'?
No one told of this,
no one foretold it,
no one heard any words from you.
27 I was the first to tell Zion, 'Look, here
they are!'
I gave to Jerusalem a messenger of
good news.
28 I look but there is no one—
no one among the gods to give
counsel,
no one to give answer when I ask
them.
29 See, they are all false!
Their deeds amount to nothing;
their images are but wind and
confusion.

The Servant of the LORD

42 "Here is my servant, whom I
uphold,
my chosen one in whom I delight;
I will put my Spirit on him,
and he will bring justice to the
nations.
2 He will not shout or cry out,
or raise his voice in the streets.
3 A bruised reed he will not break,
and a smoldering wick he will not
snuff out.
In faithfulness he will bring forth
justice;
4 he will not falter or be discouraged
till he establishes justice on earth.
In his teaching the islands will put
their hope."

5 This is what God the LORD says—
the Creator of the heavens, who
stretches them out,
who spreads out the earth with all
that springs from it,

who gives breath to its people,
and life to those who walk on it:
6 "I, the LORD, have called you in
righteousness;
I will take hold of your hand.
I will keep you and will make you
to be a covenant for the people
and a light for the Gentiles,
7 to open eyes that are blind,
to free captives from prison
and to release from the dungeon
those who sit in darkness.

8 "I am the LORD; that is my name!
I will not yield my glory to another
or my praise to idols.
9 See, the former things have taken
place,
and new things I declare;
before they spring into being
I announce them to you."

Song of Praise to the LORD

10 Sing to the LORD a new song,
his praise from the ends of the
earth,
you who go down to the sea, and all
that is in it,
you islands, and all who live in
them.
11 Let the wilderness and its towns raise
their voices;
let the settlements where Kedar
lives rejoice.
Let the people of Sela sing for joy;
let them shout from the
mountaintops.
12 Let them give glory to the LORD
and proclaim his praise in the
islands.
13 The LORD will march out like a
champion,
like a warrior he will stir up his zeal;
with a shout he will raise the battle cry
and will triumph over his enemies.

14 "For a long time I have kept silent,
I have been quiet and held myself
back.
But now, like a woman in childbirth,
I cry out, I gasp and pant.
15 I will lay waste the mountains and
hills
and dry up all their vegetation;

I will turn rivers into islands
and dry up the pools.
16 I will lead the blind by ways they have
not known,
along unfamiliar paths I will guide
them;
I will turn the darkness into light
before them
and make the rough places
smooth.
These are the things I will do;
I will not forsake them.
17 But those who trust in idols,
who say to images, 'You are our
gods,'
will be turned back in utter shame.

>> INSTANT ACCESS

When you go to school tomorrow or the next day, take a look around you. What about that girl with the bad complexion? Or the guy with the bad reputation? Or the group that dresses in black and walks around looking angry? They're outsiders who make you feel uncomfortable. Do you just write them off? This passage in Isaiah describes the outsider as a "bruised reed" and as a "smoldering wick." Neither is of much use. Isaiah says that people whom society sees as worthless are important to the Lord. Try to look at the "outsiders" at school with Christ's eyes, and reach out to them.

{Isaiah 42:3}

Israel Blind and Deaf

18 "Hear, you deaf;
    look, you blind, and see!
19 Who is blind but my servant,
    and deaf like the messenger I send?
Who is blind like the one in covenant
    with me,
    blind like the servant of the LORD?
20 You have seen many things, but you
    pay no attention;
    your ears are open, but you do not
    listen."
21 It pleased the LORD
    for the sake of his righteousness
    to make his law great and glorious.
22 But this is a people plundered and
    looted,
    all of them trapped in pits
    or hidden away in prisons.
They have become plunder,
    with no one to rescue them;
they have been made loot,
    with no one to say, "Send them
    back."

23 Which of you will listen to this
    or pay close attention in time to
    come?
24 Who handed Jacob over to become
    loot,
    and Israel to the plunderers?
Was it not the LORD,
    against whom we have sinned?
For they would not follow his ways;
    they did not obey his law.
25 So he poured out on them his burning
    anger,
    the violence of war.
It enveloped them in flames, yet they
    did not understand;
    it consumed them, but they did not
    take it to heart.

Israel's Only Savior

43 But now, this is what the LORD
    says—
    he who created you, Jacob,
    he who formed you, Israel:
"Do not fear, for I have redeemed you;
    I have summoned you by name; you
    are mine.

2 When you pass through the waters,
    I will be with you;
and when you pass through the
    rivers,
    they will not sweep over you.
When you walk through the fire,
    you will not be burned;
    the flames will not set you ablaze.
3 For I am the LORD your God,
    the Holy One of Israel, your
    Savior;
I give Egypt for your ransom,
    Cush[a] and Seba in your stead.
4 Since you are precious and honored in
    my sight,
    and because I love you,
I will give people in exchange for you,
    nations in exchange for your life.
5 Do not be afraid, for I am with you;
    I will bring your children from the
    east
    and gather you from the west.
6 I will say to the north, 'Give them up!'
    and to the south, 'Do not hold them
    back.'
Bring my sons from afar
    and my daughters from the ends of
    the earth—
7 everyone who is called by my name,
    whom I created for my glory,
    whom I formed and made."

8 Lead out those who have eyes but are
    blind,
    who have ears but are deaf.
9 All the nations gather together
    and the peoples assemble.
Which of their gods foretold this
    and proclaimed to us the former
    things?
Let them bring in their witnesses to
    prove they were right,
    so that others may hear and say, "It
    is true."
10 "You are my witnesses," declares the
    LORD,
    "and my servant whom I have
    chosen,
so that you may know and believe me
    and understand that I am he.
Before me no god was formed,
    nor will there be one after me.

---

a 3 That is, the upper Nile region

11 I, even I, am the LORD,
and apart from me there is no
savior.
12 I have revealed and saved and
proclaimed—
I, and not some foreign god among
you.
You are my witnesses," declares the
LORD, "that I am God.
13 Yes, and from ancient days I am he.
No one can deliver out of my hand.
When I act, who can reverse it?"

God's Mercy and Israel's Unfaithfulness

14 This is what the LORD says—
your Redeemer, the Holy One of
Israel:
"For your sake I will send to Babylon
and bring down as fugitives all the
Babylonians,[a]
in the ships in which they took
pride.
15 I am the LORD, your Holy One,
Israel's Creator, your King."

16 This is what the LORD says—
he who made a way through the
sea,
a path through the mighty waters,
17 who drew out the chariots and horses,
the army and reinforcements
together,
and they lay there, never to rise
again,
extinguished, snuffed out like a
wick:
18 "Forget the former things;
do not dwell on the past.
19 See, I am doing a new thing!
Now it springs up; do you not
perceive it?
I am making a way in the wilderness
and streams in the wasteland.
20 The wild animals honor me,
the jackals and the owls,
because I provide water in the
wilderness
and streams in the wasteland,
to give drink to my people, my chosen,

21 the people I formed for myself
that they may proclaim my praise.

22 "Yet you have not called on me,
Jacob,
you have not wearied yourselves
for[b] me, Israel.
23 You have not brought me sheep for
burnt offerings,
nor honored me with your sacrifices.
I have not burdened you with grain
offerings
nor wearied you with demands for
incense.
24 You have not bought any fragrant
calamus for me,
or lavished on me the fat of your
sacrifices.
But you have burdened me with your
sins
and wearied me with your offenses.

25 "I, even I, am he who blots out
your transgressions, for my own
sake,
and remembers your sins no more.
26 Review the past for me,
let us argue the matter together;
state the case for your innocence.
27 Your first father sinned;
those I sent to teach you rebelled
against me.
28 So I disgraced the dignitaries of your
temple;
I consigned Jacob to destruction[c]
and Israel to scorn.

Israel the Chosen

44 "But now listen, Jacob, my
servant,
Israel, whom I have chosen.
2 This is what the LORD says—
he who made you, who formed you
in the womb,
and who will help you:
Do not be afraid, Jacob, my servant,
Jeshurun,[d] whom I have chosen.
3 For I will pour water on the thirsty
land,
and streams on the dry ground;

---

[a] 14 Or Chaldeans   [b] 22 Or Jacob; / surely you have grown weary of   [c] 28 The Hebrew term refers to the irrevocable
giving over of things or persons to the LORD, often by totally destroying them.   [d] 2 Jeshurun means the upright one, that
is, Israel.

I will pour out my Spirit on your
offspring,
and my blessing on your
descendants.
⁴ They will spring up like grass in a
meadow,
like poplar trees by flowing streams.
⁵ Some will say, 'I belong to the LORD';
others will call themselves by the
name of Jacob;
still others will write on their hand,
'The LORD's,'
and will take the name Israel.

The LORD, Not Idols

⁶ "This is what the LORD says—
Israel's King and Redeemer, the
LORD Almighty:
I am the first and I am the last;
apart from me there is no God.

⁷ Who then is like me? Let him
proclaim it.
Let him declare and lay out
before me
what has happened since I
established my ancient people,
and what is yet to come—
yes, let them foretell what will
come.
⁸ Do not tremble, do not be afraid.
Did I not proclaim this and foretell it
long ago?
You are my witnesses. Is there any
God besides me?
No, there is no other Rock; I know
not one."

⁹ All who make idols are nothing,
and the things they treasure are
worthless.

TO THE POINT

Idols Can't Help

In chapter 44:6–20, Isaiah pokes fun at people who cut down a
tree, use part of it for firewood and carve an idol from the rest.
Then they bow down and pray to that hunk of wood!

People today are often just as foolish, counting on the wrong
things to help them. Some count on wealth, others on popularity. Some count on stylish clothes, others on athletic talent. But
in the end, you can't count on any of these things.

What you can count on is God. Don't misunderstand. It's not
wrong to have money or nice clothes. What's wrong is to count
on these things as if they are what life is all about. That's idolatry. And that's foolish. Living God's way and making what's
important to him important to you will lead you to a happy
tomorrow and a happy forever.

Those who would speak up for them
are blind;
they are ignorant, to their own
shame.
10 Who shapes a god and casts an idol,
which can profit nothing?
11 People who do that will be put to
shame;
such craftsmen are only human
beings.
Let them all come together and take
their stand;
they will be brought down to terror
and shame.

12 The blacksmith takes a tool
and works with it in the coals;
he shapes an idol with hammers,
he forges it with the might of his
arm.
He gets hungry and loses his strength;
he drinks no water and grows faint.
13 The carpenter measures with a line
and makes an outline with a
marker;
he roughs it out with chisels
and marks it with compasses.
He shapes it in human form,
human form in all its glory,
that it may dwell in a shrine.
14 He cut down cedars,
or perhaps took a cypress or oak.
He let it grow among the trees of the
forest,
or planted a pine, and the rain
made it grow.
15 It is used as fuel for burning;
some of it he takes and warms
himself,
he kindles a fire and bakes bread.
But he also fashions a god and
worships it;
he makes an idol and bows down
to it.
16 Half of the wood he burns in the fire;
over it he prepares his meal,
he roasts his meat and eats his fill.
He also warms himself and says,
"Ah! I am warm; I see the fire."
17 From the rest he makes a god, his
idol;
he bows down to it and worships.
He prays to it and says,
"Save me! You are my god!"

18 They know nothing, they understand
nothing;
their eyes are plastered over so
they cannot see,
and their minds closed so they
cannot understand.
19 No one stops to think,
no one has the knowledge or
understanding to say,
"Half of it I used for fuel;
I even baked bread over its coals,
I roasted meat and I ate.
Shall I make a detestable thing from
what is left?
Shall I bow down to a block of
wood?"
20 Such a person feeds on ashes; a
deluded heart misleads him;
he cannot save himself, or say,
"Is not this thing in my right hand a
lie?"

21 "Remember these things, Jacob,
for you, Israel, are my servant.
I have made you, you are my servant;
Israel, I will not forget you.
22 I have swept away your offenses like
a cloud,
your sins like the morning mist.
Return to me,
for I have redeemed you."

23 Sing for joy, you heavens, for the LORD
has done this;
shout aloud, you earth beneath.
Burst into song, you mountains,
you forests and all your trees,
for the LORD has redeemed Jacob,
he displays his glory in Israel.

Jerusalem to Be Inhabited

24 "This is what the LORD says—
your Redeemer, who formed you in
the womb:

I am the LORD,
the Maker of all things,
who stretches out the heavens,
who spreads out the earth by
myself,
25 who foils the signs of false prophets
and makes fools of diviners,
who overthrows the learning of the
wise
and turns it into nonsense,

²⁶who carries out the words of his
　　servants
　　and fulfills the predictions of his
　　　messengers,

who says of Jerusalem, 'It shall be
　　inhabited,'
　　of the towns of Judah, 'They shall
　　　be rebuilt,'
　　and of their ruins, 'I will restore
　　　them,'
²⁷who says to the watery deep, 'Be dry,
　　and I will dry up your streams,'
²⁸who says of Cyrus, 'He is my
　　shepherd
　　and will accomplish all that I
　　　please;
　　he will say of Jerusalem, "Let it be
　　　rebuilt,"
　　and of the temple, "Let its
　　　foundations be laid." '

45 "This is what the LORD says to
　　his anointed,
　　to Cyrus, whose right hand I take
　　　hold of
　to subdue nations before him
　　and to strip kings of their armor,
　to open doors before him
　　so that gates will not be shut:
²I will go before you
　　and will level the mountains^a;
　I will break down gates of bronze
　　and cut through bars of iron.
³I will give you hidden treasures,
　　riches stored in secret places,
　so that you may know that I am the
　　　LORD,
　　the God of Israel, who summons
　　　you by name.
⁴For the sake of Jacob my servant,
　　of Israel my chosen,
　I summon you by name
　　and bestow on you a title of honor,
　　though you do not acknowledge me.
⁵I am the LORD, and there is no other;
　　apart from me there is no God.
　I will strengthen you,
　　though you have not
　　　acknowledged me,
⁶so that from the rising of the sun
　　to the place of its setting

people may know there is none
　　besides me.
　I am the LORD, and there is no
　　　other.
⁷I form the light and create darkness,
　　I bring prosperity and create
　　　disaster;
　I, the LORD, do all these things.

⁸"You heavens above, rain down my
　　righteousness;
　　let the clouds shower it down.
Let the earth open wide,
　　let salvation spring up,
let righteousness flourish with it;
　　I, the LORD, have created it.

⁹"Woe to those who quarrel with their
　　Maker,
　　those who are nothing but
　　　potsherds
　　among the potsherds on the
　　　ground.
Does the clay say to the potter,
　　'What are you making?'
Does your work say,
　　'The potter has no hands'?
¹⁰Woe to the one who says to a
　　father,
　　'What have you begotten?'
　or to a mother,
　　'What have you brought to birth?'

¹¹"This is what the LORD says—
　　the Holy One of Israel, and its
　　　Maker:
Concerning things to come,
　　do you question me about my
　　　children,
　　or give me orders about the work of
　　　my hands?
¹²It is I who made the earth
　　and created mankind on it.
My own hands stretched out the
　　heavens;
　　I marshaled their starry hosts.
¹³I will raise up Cyrus^b in my
　　righteousness:
　　I will make all his ways straight.
He will rebuild my city
　　and set my exiles free,
but not for a price or reward,
　　says the LORD Almighty."

---

^a 2 Dead Sea Scrolls and Septuagint; the meaning of the word in the Masoretic Text is uncertain.　^b 13 Hebrew *him*

¹⁴This is what the LORD says:

"The products of Egypt and the
     merchandise of Cush,ᵃ
and those tall Sabeans—
they will come over to you
     and will be yours;
they will trudge behind you,
     coming over to you in chains.
They will bow down before you
     and plead with you, saying,
'Surely God is with you, and there is
     no other;
there is no other god.'"

¹⁵Truly you are a God who has been
     hiding himself,
the God and Savior of Israel.
¹⁶All the makers of idols will be put to
     shame and disgraced;
they will go off into disgrace
     together.
¹⁷But Israel will be saved by the LORD
     with an everlasting salvation;
you will never be put to shame or
     disgraced,
     to ages everlasting.

¹⁸For this is what the LORD says—
he who created the heavens,
     he is God;
he who fashioned and made the
     earth,
     he founded it;
he did not create it to be empty,
     but formed it to be inhabited—
he says:
"I am the LORD,
     and there is no other.
¹⁹I have not spoken in secret,
     from somewhere in a land of
          darkness;
I have not said to Jacob's
     descendants,
'Seek me in vain.'
I, the LORD, speak the truth;
     I declare what is right.

²⁰"Gather together and come;
     assemble, you fugitives from the
          nations.
Ignorant are those who carry about
     idols of wood,
who pray to gods that cannot save.

²¹Declare what is to be, present it—
     let them take counsel together.
Who foretold this long ago,
     who declared it from the distant
          past?
Was it not I, the LORD?
     And there is no God apart from me,
a righteous God and a Savior;
     there is none but me.

²²"Turn to me and be saved,
     all you ends of the earth;
for I am God, and there is no other.
²³By myself I have sworn,
     my mouth has uttered in all integrity
          a word that will not be revoked:
Before me every knee will bow;
     by me every tongue will swear.
²⁴They will say of me, 'In the LORD alone
     are deliverance and strength.'"
All who have raged against him
     will come to him and be put to
          shame.
²⁵But all the descendants of Israel
     will find deliverance in the LORD
     and will make their boast in him.

Gods of Babylon

46 Bel bows down, Nebo stoops
          low;
     their idols are borne by beasts of
          burden.ᵇ
The images that are carried about are
     burdensome,
     a burden for the weary.
²They stoop and bow down together;
     unable to rescue the burden,
they themselves go off into captivity.

³"Listen to me, you descendants of
     Jacob,
all the remnant of the people of
     Israel,
you whom I have upheld since your
     birth,
     and have carried since you were
          born.
⁴Even to your old age and gray hairs
     I am he, I am he who will sustain
          you.
I have made you and I will carry you;
     I will sustain you and I will rescue
          you.

ᵃ 14 That is, the upper Nile region   ᵇ 1 Or are but beasts and cattle

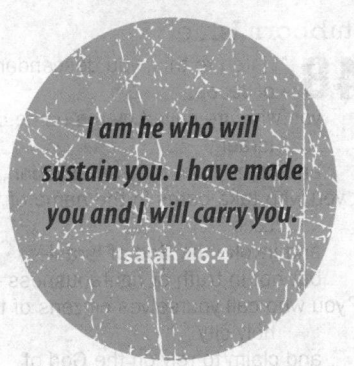

I am he who will sustain you. I have made you and I will carry you.

Isaiah 46:4

5 "With whom will you compare me or
    count me equal?
  To whom will you liken me that we
    may be compared?
6 Some pour out gold from their bags
    and weigh out silver on the scales;
  they hire a goldsmith to make it into a
    god,
    and they bow down and worship it.
7 They lift it to their shoulders and
    carry it;
    they set it up in its place, and there
      it stands.
  From that spot it cannot move.
  Even though someone cries out to it,
    it cannot answer;
    it cannot save them from their
      troubles.

8 "Remember this, keep it in mind,
    take it to heart, you rebels.
9 Remember the former things, those of
    long ago;
  I am God, and there is no other;
    I am God, and there is none like me.
10 I make known the end from the
    beginning,
    from ancient times, what is still to
      come.
  I say, 'My purpose will stand,
    and I will do all that I please.'
11 From the east I summon a bird of
    prey;
    from a far-off land, a man to fulfill
      my purpose.
  What I have said, that I will bring
    about;
    what I have planned, that I will do.

12 Listen to me, you stubborn-hearted,
    you who are now far from my
      righteousness.
13 I am bringing my righteousness
    near,
    it is not far away;
  and my salvation will not be
    delayed.
  I will grant salvation to Zion,
    my splendor to Israel.

The Fall of Babylon

47 "Go down, sit in the dust,
    Virgin Daughter Babylon;
  sit on the ground without a throne,
    queen city of the Babylonians.[a]
  No more will you be called
    tender or delicate.
2 Take millstones and grind flour;
    take off your veil.
  Lift up your skirts, bare your legs,
    and wade through the streams.
3 Your nakedness will be exposed
    and your shame uncovered.
  I will take vengeance;
    I will spare no one."

4 Our Redeemer—the Lord Almighty is
    his name—
  is the Holy One of Israel.

5 "Sit in silence, go into darkness,
    queen city of the Babylonians;
  no more will you be called
    queen of kingdoms.
6 I was angry with my people
    and desecrated my inheritance;
  I gave them into your hand,
    and you showed them no mercy.
  Even on the aged
    you laid a very heavy yoke.
7 You said, 'I am forever—
    the eternal queen!'
  But you did not consider these
    things
    or reflect on what might happen.

8 "Now then, listen, you lover of
    pleasure,
    lounging in your security
  and saying to yourself,
    'I am, and there is none
      besides me.

ᵃ 1 Or *Chaldeans*; also in verse 5

I will never be a widow
   or suffer the loss of children.'
⁹ Both of these will overtake you
   in a moment, on a single day:
    loss of children and widowhood.
They will come upon you in full
    measure,
   in spite of your many sorceries
    and all your potent spells.
¹⁰ You have trusted in your wickedness
   and have said, 'No one sees me.'
Your wisdom and knowledge mislead
    you
   when you say to yourself,
   'I am, and there is none besides
    me.'
¹¹ Disaster will come upon you,
   and you will not know how to
    conjure it away.
A calamity will fall upon you
   that you cannot ward off with a
    ransom;
a catastrophe you cannot foresee
   will suddenly come upon you.

¹² "Keep on, then, with your magic
    spells
   and with your many sorceries,
   which you have labored at since
    childhood.
Perhaps you will succeed,
   perhaps you will cause terror.
¹³ All the counsel you have received has
    only worn you out!
Let your astrologers come
    forward,
those stargazers who make
    predictions month by
    month,
let them save you from what is
    coming upon you.
¹⁴ Surely they are like stubble;
   the fire will burn them up.
They cannot even save themselves
   from the power of the flame.
These are not coals for warmth;
   this is not a fire to sit by.
¹⁵ That is all they are to you—
   these you have dealt with
   and labored with since childhood.
All of them go on in their error;
   there is not one that can save
    you.

Stubborn Israel

48 "Listen to this, you descendants
    of Jacob,
   you who are called by the name of
    Israel
   and come from the line of Judah,
you who take oaths in the name of the
    LORD
   and invoke the God of Israel—
   but not in truth or righteousness—
² you who call yourselves citizens of the
    holy city
   and claim to rely on the God of
    Israel—
   the LORD Almighty is his name:
³ I foretold the former things long
    ago,
   my mouth announced them and I
    made them known;
   then suddenly I acted, and they
    came to pass.
⁴ For I knew how stubborn you were;
   your neck muscles were iron,
   your forehead was bronze.
⁵ Therefore I told you these things long
    ago;
   before they happened I announced
    them to you
so that you could not say,
   'My images brought them about;
   my wooden image and metal god
    ordained them.'
⁶ You have heard these things; look at
    them all.
   Will you not admit them?

"From now on I will tell you of new
    things,
   of hidden things unknown to
    you.
⁷ They are created now, and not long
    ago;
   you have not heard of them before
    today.
So you cannot say,
   'Yes, I knew of them.'
⁸ You have neither heard nor
    understood;
   from of old your ears have not been
    open.
Well do I know how treacherous you
    are;
   you were called a rebel from birth.

Do you wish you had more independence? That's good. You're not a child anymore. You make many decisions on your own. But probably not all of them. So it's easy to see why some kids resent authority. It's your life, and you want to make your own decisions. But remember one thing: even adults need guidance. Not someone to say, "You have to do this!" But someone to suggest, "This way is best." Don't resent God's authority. He isn't standing over you with a whip. He's standing beside you saying, "Let me help you. I just want what's best for you."

{Isaiah 48:17}

INSTANT ACCESS

9 For my own name's sake I delay my
    wrath;
  for the sake of my praise I hold it
    back from you,
  so as not to destroy you
    completely.
10 See, I have refined you, though not as
    silver;
  I have tested you in the furnace of
    affliction.
11 For my own sake, for my own sake, I
    do this.
  How can I let myself be
    defamed?
  I will not yield my glory to
    another.

Israel Freed

12 "Listen to me, Jacob,
    Israel, whom I have called:
  I am he;
    I am the first and I am the last.
13 My own hand laid the foundations of
    the earth,
  and my right hand spread out the
    heavens;
  when I summon them,
    they all stand up together.

14 "Come together, all of you, and listen:
    Which of the idols has foretold
      these things?
  The LORD's chosen ally
    will carry out his purpose against
      Babylon;
  his arm will be against the
    Babylonians.[a]
15 I, even I, have spoken;
    yes, I have called him.
  I will bring him,
    and he will succeed in his mission.

16 "Come near me and listen to this:

"From the first announcement I have
    not spoken in secret;
  at the time it happens, I am there."

And now the Sovereign LORD has
    sent me,
  endowed with his Spirit.

17 This is what the LORD says—
    your Redeemer, the Holy One of
      Israel:
  "I am the LORD your God,
    who teaches you what is best for
      you,
  who directs you in the way you
    should go.
18 If only you had paid attention to my
    commands,
  your peace would have been like a
    river,
  your well-being like the waves of the
    sea.
19 Your descendants would have been
    like the sand,
  your children like its numberless
    grains;

---

a 14 Or Chaldeans; also in verse 20

their name would never be blotted out
nor destroyed from before me."

20 Leave Babylon,
   flee from the Babylonians!
Announce this with shouts of joy
   and proclaim it.
Send it out to the ends of the earth;
   say, "The LORD has redeemed his
      servant Jacob."
21 They did not thirst when he led them
      through the deserts;
   he made water flow for them from
      the rock;
   he split the rock
      and water gushed out.

22 "There is no peace," says the LORD,
   "for the wicked."

The Servant of the LORD

49 Listen to me, you islands;
   hear this, you distant nations:
Before I was born the LORD called me;
   from my mother's womb he has
      spoken my name.
2 He made my mouth like a sharpened
      sword,
   in the shadow of his hand he hid me;
he made me into a polished arrow
   and concealed me in his quiver.
3 He said to me, "You are my servant,
   Israel, in whom I will display my
      splendor."
4 But I said, "I have labored in vain;
   I have spent my strength for nothing
      at all.
Yet what is due me is in the LORD's
      hand,
   and my reward is with my God."

5 And now the LORD says—
   he who formed me in the womb to
      be his servant
to bring Jacob back to him
   and gather Israel to himself,
for I am[a] honored in the eyes of the
      LORD
   and my God has been my
      strength—
6 he says:
"It is too small a thing for you to be
   my servant

to restore the tribes of Jacob
   and bring back those of Israel I
      have kept.
I will also make you a light for the
      Gentiles,
   that my salvation may reach to the
      ends of the earth."

7 This is what the LORD says—
   the Redeemer and Holy One of
      Israel—
to him who was despised and
      abhorred by the nation,
   to the servant of rulers:
"Kings will see you and stand up,
   princes will see and bow down,
because of the LORD, who is faithful,
   the Holy One of Israel, who has
      chosen you."

Restoration of Israel

8 This is what the LORD says:

"In the time of my favor I will answer
   you,
   and in the day of salvation I will
      help you;
I will keep you and will make you
   to be a covenant for the people,
to restore the land
   and to reassign its desolate
      inheritances,
9 to say to the captives, 'Come out,'
   and to those in darkness, 'Be free!'

"They will feed beside the roads
   and find pasture on every barren
      hill.
10 They will neither hunger nor thirst,
   nor will the desert heat or the sun
      beat down on them.
He who has compassion on them will
      guide them
   and lead them beside springs of
      water.
11 I will turn all my mountains into
      roads,
   and my highways will be raised up.
12 See, they will come from afar—
   some from the north, some from
      the west,
   some from the region of Aswan.[b]"

---

a 5 Or *him, / but Israel would not be gathered; / yet I will be*   b 12 Dead Sea Scrolls; Masoretic Text *Sinim*

13 Shout for joy, you heavens;
   rejoice, you earth;
   burst into song, you mountains!
For the LORD comforts his people
   and will have compassion on his
   afflicted ones.

14 But Zion said, "The LORD has
   forsaken me,
   the Lord has forgotten me."

15 "Can a mother forget the baby at her
   breast
   and have no compassion on the
   child she has borne?
Though she may forget,
   I will not forget you!

16 See, I have engraved you on the
   palms of my hands;
   your walls are ever before me.

17 Your children hasten back,
   and those who laid you waste
   depart from you.

18 Lift up your eyes and look around;
   all your children gather and come to
   you.
As surely as I live," declares the LORD,
   "you will wear them all as
   ornaments;
   you will put them on, like a bride.

19 "Though you were ruined and made
   desolate
   and your land laid waste,
now you will be too small for your
   people,
   and those who devoured you will be
   far away.

20 The children born during your
   bereavement
will yet say in your hearing,
   'This place is too small for us;
   give us more space to live in.'

21 Then you will say in your heart,
   'Who bore me these?
I was bereaved and barren;
   I was exiled and rejected.
Who brought these up?
I was left all alone,
   but these—where have they come
   from?'"

22 This is what the Sovereign LORD says:

"See, I will beckon to the nations,
   I will lift up my banner to the
   peoples;
they will bring your sons in their arms
   and carry your daughters on their
   hips.

23 Kings will be your foster fathers,
   and their queens your nursing
   mothers.
They will bow down before you with
   their faces to the ground;
   they will lick the dust at your feet.
Then you will know that I am the LORD;
   those who hope in me will not be
   disappointed."

24 Can plunder be taken from warriors,
   or captives be rescued from the
   fierce[a]?

25 But this is what the LORD says:

"Yes, captives will be taken from
   warriors,
   and plunder retrieved from the
   fierce;
I will contend with those who contend
   with you,
   and your children I will save.

26 I will make your oppressors eat their
   own flesh;
   they will be drunk on their own
   blood, as with wine.
Then all mankind will know
   that I, the LORD, am your Savior,
   your Redeemer, the Mighty One of
   Jacob."

Israel's Sin and the Servant's Obedience

50 This is what the LORD says:

"Where is your mother's certificate of
   divorce
   with which I sent her away?
Or to which of my creditors
   did I sell you?
Because of your sins you were sold;
   because of your transgressions your
   mother was sent away.

2 When I came, why was there no one?
   When I called, why was there no
   one to answer?

---

[a] 24 Dead Sea Scrolls, Vulgate and Syriac (see also Septuagint and verse 25); Masoretic Text *righteous*

Was my arm too short to deliver you?
  Do I lack the strength to rescue
    you?
By a mere rebuke I dry up the sea,
  I turn rivers into a desert;
their fish rot for lack of water
  and die of thirst.
3 I clothe the heavens with darkness
  and make sackcloth its covering."

4 The Sovereign Lord has given me a
    well-instructed tongue,
  to know the word that sustains the
    weary.
He wakens me morning by morning,
  wakens my ear to listen like one
    being instructed.
5 The Sovereign Lord has opened my
    ears;
  I have not been rebellious,
  I have not turned away.
6 I offered my back to those who
    beat me,
  my cheeks to those who pulled out
    my beard;
I did not hide my face
  from mocking and spitting.
7 Because the Sovereign Lord helps me,
  I will not be disgraced.
Therefore have I set my face like
    flint,
  and I know I will not be put to
    shame.
8 He who vindicates me is near.
  Who then will bring charges
    against me?
  Let us face each other!
Who is my accuser?
  Let him confront me!
9 It is the Sovereign Lord who helps me.
  Who is he that will condemn me?
They will all wear out like a garment;
  the moths will eat them up.

10 Who among you fears the Lord
  and obeys the word of his servant?
Let the one who walks in the dark,
  who has no light,
trust in the name of the Lord
  and rely on their God.
11 But now, all you who light fires
  and provide yourselves with flaming
    torches,

go, walk in the light of your fires
  and of the torches you have set
    ablaze.
This is what you shall receive from my
    hand:
  You will lie down in torment.

Everlasting Salvation for Zion

51 "Listen to me, you who pursue
    righteousness
  and who seek the Lord:
Look to the rock from which you were
    cut
  and to the quarry from which you
    were hewn;
2 look to Abraham, your father,
  and to Sarah, who gave you birth.
When I called him he was only one
    man,
  and I blessed him and made him
    many.
3 The Lord will surely comfort Zion
  and will look with compassion on all
    her ruins;
he will make her deserts like Eden,
  her wastelands like the garden of
    the Lord.
Joy and gladness will be found in her,
  thanksgiving and the sound of
    singing.

4 "Listen to me, my people;
  hear me, my nation:
Instruction will go out from me;
  my justice will become a light to the
    nations.
5 My righteousness draws near speedily,
  my salvation is on the way,
  and my arm will bring justice to the
    nations.
The islands will look to me
  and wait in hope for my arm.
6 Lift up your eyes to the heavens,
  look at the earth beneath;
the heavens will vanish like smoke,
  the earth will wear out like a
    garment
  and its inhabitants die like flies.
But my salvation will last forever,
  my righteousness will never fail.

7 "Hear me, you who know what is right,
  you people who have taken my
    instruction to heart:

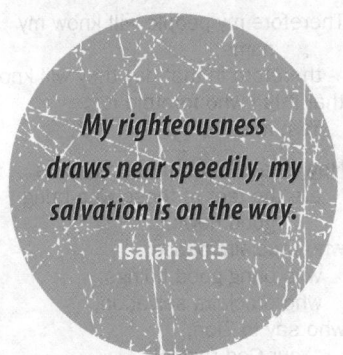

My righteousness draws near speedily, my salvation is on the way.

Isaiah 51:5

Do not fear the reproach of mere
    mortals
    or be terrified by their insults.
8 For the moth will eat them up like a
    garment;
    the worm will devour them like
    wool.
But my righteousness will last
    forever,
    my salvation through all
    generations."

9 Awake, awake, arm of the LORD,
    clothe yourself with strength!
Awake, as in days gone by,
    as in generations of old.
Was it not you who cut Rahab to
    pieces,
    who pierced that monster through?
10 Was it not you who dried up the sea,
    the waters of the great deep,
who made a road in the depths of the
    sea
    so that the redeemed might cross
    over?
11 Those the LORD has rescued will
    return.
    They will enter Zion with singing;
    everlasting joy will crown their
    heads.
Gladness and joy will overtake them,
    and sorrow and sighing will flee
    away.

12 "I, even I, am he who comforts you.
    Who are you that you fear mere
    mortals,
    human beings who are but grass,

13 that you forget the LORD your Maker,
    who stretches out the heavens
    and who lays the foundations of the
    earth,
that you live in constant terror every
    day
    because of the wrath of the
    oppressor,
    who is bent on destruction?
For where is the wrath of the
    oppressor?
14   The cowering prisoners will soon be
    set free;
they will not die in their dungeon,
    nor will they lack bread.
15 For I am the LORD your God,
    who stirs up the sea so that its
    waves roar—
    the LORD Almighty is his name.
16 I have put my words in your mouth
    and covered you with the shadow of
    my hand—
I who set the heavens in place,
    who laid the foundations of the
    earth,
    and who say to Zion, 'You are my
    people.'"

The Cup of the LORD's Wrath

17 Awake, awake!
    Rise up, Jerusalem,
you who have drunk from the hand of
    the LORD
    the cup of his wrath,
you who have drained to its dregs
    the goblet that makes people
    stagger.
18 Among all the children she bore
    there was none to guide her;
among all the children she reared
    there was none to take her by the
    hand.
19 These double calamities have come
    upon you—
    who can comfort you?—
ruin and destruction, famine and
    sword—
    who can[a] console you?
20 Your children have fainted;
    they lie at every street corner,
    like antelope caught in a net.

---

[a] 19 Dead Sea Scrolls, Septuagint, Vulgate and Syriac; Masoretic Text / how can I

They are filled with the wrath of the
Lord,
with the rebuke of your God.

21 Therefore hear this, you afflicted one,
made drunk, but not with wine.
22 This is what your Sovereign Lord says,
your God, who defends his people:
"See, I have taken out of your hand
the cup that made you stagger;
from that cup, the goblet of my
wrath,
you will never drink again.
23 I will put it into the hands of your
tormentors,
who said to you,
'Fall prostrate that we may walk on
you.'
And you made your back like the
ground,
like a street to be walked on."

52

Awake, awake, Zion,
clothe yourself with strength!
Put on your garments of splendor,
Jerusalem, the holy city.
The uncircumcised and defiled
will not enter you again.
2 Shake off your dust;
rise up, sit enthroned, Jerusalem.
Free yourself from the chains on your
neck,
Daughter Zion, now a captive.

3 For this is what the Lord says:

"You were sold for nothing,
and without money you will be
redeemed."

4 For this is what the Sovereign Lord
says:

"At first my people went down to Egypt
to live;
lately, Assyria has oppressed them.

5 "And now what do I have here?" declares the Lord.

"For my people have been taken away
for nothing,
and those who rule them mock,*a*"
declares the Lord.
"And all day long
my name is constantly blasphemed.

6 Therefore my people will know my
name;
therefore in that day they will know
that it is I who foretold it.
Yes, it is I."

7 How beautiful on the mountains
are the feet of those who bring
good news,
who proclaim peace,
who bring good tidings,
who proclaim salvation,
who say to Zion,
"Your God reigns!"
8 Listen! Your watchmen lift up their
voices;
together they shout for joy.
When the Lord returns to Zion,
they will see it with their own eyes.
9 Burst into songs of joy together,
you ruins of Jerusalem,
for the Lord has comforted his
people,
he has redeemed Jerusalem.
10 The Lord will lay bare his holy arm
in the sight of all the nations,
and all the ends of the earth will see
the salvation of our God.

11 Depart, depart, go out from there!
Touch no unclean thing!
Come out from it and be pure,
you who carry the articles of the
Lord's house.
12 But you will not leave in haste
or go in flight;
for the Lord will go before you,
the God of Israel will be your rear
guard.

The Suffering and Glory of the Servant

13 See, my servant will act wisely*b*;
he will be raised and lifted up and
highly exalted.
14 Just as there were many who were
appalled at him*c*—
his appearance was so disfigured
beyond that of any human
being
and his form marred beyond human
likeness—

---

a 5 Dead Sea Scrolls and Vulgate; Masoretic Text *wail*   *b* 13 Or *will prosper*   *c* 14 Hebrew *you*

15 so he will sprinkle many nations,[a]
  and kings will shut their mouths
    because of him.
  For what they were not told, they will
      see,
  and what they have not heard, they
      will understand.

53 Who has believed our message
  and to whom has the arm of the
    LORD been revealed?
2 He grew up before him like a tender
      shoot,
  and like a root out of dry ground.
  He had no beauty or majesty to attract
      us to him,
  nothing in his appearance that we
      should desire him.
3 He was despised and rejected by
      mankind,
  a man of suffering, and familiar with
      pain.
  Like one from whom people hide their
      faces
  he was despised, and we held him
      in low esteem.

4 Surely he took up our pain
  and bore our suffering,
yet we considered him punished by
      God,
  stricken by him, and afflicted.
5 But he was pierced for our
      transgressions,
  he was crushed for our iniquities;
the punishment that brought us peace
      was on him,
  and by his wounds we are healed.
6 We all, like sheep, have gone astray,
  each of us has turned to our own
      way;
  and the LORD has laid on him
    the iniquity of us all.

7 He was oppressed and afflicted,
  yet he did not open his mouth;
he was led like a lamb to the
      slaughter,
  and as a sheep before its shearers
      is silent,
  so he did not open his mouth.

8 By oppression[b] and judgment he was
      taken away.
  Yet who of his generation
      protested?
  For he was cut off from the land of the
      living;
  for the transgression of my people
      he was punished.[c]
9 He was assigned a grave with the
      wicked,
  and with the rich in his death,
though he had done no violence,
  nor was any deceit in his mouth.

10 Yet it was the LORD's will to crush him
  and cause him to suffer,
  and though the LORD makes[d] his life
    an offering for sin,
he will see his offspring and prolong
      his days,
  and the will of the LORD will prosper
      in his hand.
11 After he has suffered,
  he will see the light of life[e] and be
      satisfied[f];
by his knowledge[g] my righteous
      servant will justify many,
  and he will bear their iniquities.
12 Therefore I will give him a portion
      among the great,[h]
  and he will divide the spoils with
      the strong,[i]
because he poured out his life unto
      death,
  and was numbered with the
      transgressors.
For he bore the sin of many,
  and made intercession for the
      transgressors.

The Future Glory of Zion

54 "Sing, barren woman,
  you who never bore a child;
burst into song, shout for joy,
  you who were never in labor;
because more are the children of the
      desolate woman
  than of her who has a husband,"
                    says the LORD.

---

a 15 Or so will many nations be amazed at him (see also Septuagint)   b 8 Or From arrest   c 8 Or generation
considered / that he was cut off from the land of the living, / that he was punished for the transgression of my people?
d 10 Hebrew though you make   e 11 Dead Sea Scrolls (see also Septuagint); Masoretic Text does not have the light of
life.   f 11 Or (with Masoretic Text) 11He will see the fruit of his suffering / and will be satisfied   g 11 Or by knowledge of
him   h 12 Or many   i 12 Or numerous

We Believe...

"Jesus suffered under Pontius Pilate, was crucified"

✝ Historical records tell us that Pontius Pilate was the Roman governor of Judea for ten years. There's no doubt he was there; no doubt that he reluctantly ordered the death of Jesus of Nazareth. No doubt that Pilate lost his position when his patron, a man named Sejanus who was captain of the Emperor's personal guard, was executed. The historical fact is that Jesus did "suffer under Pontius Pilate" (see John 18:28—19:19).

Yet 700 years before Pilate became governor, the prophet Isaiah described Jesus' suffering:

* Jesus' hands and feet were pierced (Isaiah 53:5).

* Jesus was hung on a cross between two criminals (Isaiah 53:9).

* Jesus was buried in a rich man's tomb (Isaiah 53:9).

Isaiah also tells us why Jesus died. He took the punishment that you deserve so you could have peace with God (Isaiah 53:4–6). And Isaiah saw beyond the cross. After Jesus' pain he rose from the grave, knew that your salvation had been won, and he said, "It was worth it!" (Isaiah 53:11).

Go to page 1221 for the next We Believe

2 "Enlarge the place of your tent,
   stretch your tent curtains wide,
   do not hold back;
 lengthen your cords,
   strengthen your stakes.
3 For you will spread out to the right and
      to the left;
   your descendants will dispossess
      nations
   and settle in their desolate cities.

4 "Do not be afraid; you will not be put
      to shame.
   Do not fear disgrace; you will not be
      humiliated.
 You will forget the shame of your youth
   and remember no more the
      reproach of your widowhood.
5 For your Maker is your husband—
   the LORD Almighty is his name—
 the Holy One of Israel is your
      Redeemer;
   he is called the God of all the earth.
6 The LORD will call you back
   as if you were a wife deserted and
      distressed in spirit—
 a wife who married young,
   only to be rejected," says your God.
7 "For a brief moment I abandoned you,
   but with deep compassion I will
      bring you back.
8 In a surge of anger
   I hid my face from you for a
      moment,
 but with everlasting kindness
   I will have compassion on you,"
   says the LORD your Redeemer.

9 "To me this is like the days of Noah,
   when I swore that the waters of
      Noah would never again cover
      the earth.
 So now I have sworn not to be angry
      with you,
   never to rebuke you again.
10 Though the mountains be shaken
   and the hills be removed,
 yet my unfailing love for you will not be
      shaken
   nor my covenant of peace be
      removed,"
   says the LORD, who has compassion
      on you.

11 "Afflicted city, lashed by storms and
      not comforted,
   I will rebuild you with stones of
      turquoise,[a]
   your foundations with lapis lazuli.
12 I will make your battlements of
      rubies,
   your gates of sparkling jewels,
   and all your walls of precious
      stones.
13 All your children will be taught by the
      LORD,
   and great will be their peace.
14 In righteousness you will be
      established:
 Tyranny will be far from you;
   you will have nothing to fear.
 Terror will be far removed;
   it will not come near you.
15 If anyone does attack you, it will not
      be my doing;
   whoever attacks you will surrender
      to you.

16 "See, it is I who created the
      blacksmith
   who fans the coals into flame
   and forges a weapon fit for its
      work.
 And it is I who have created the
      destroyer to wreak havoc;
17   no weapon forged against you will
      prevail,
   and you will refute every tongue
      that accuses you.
 This is the heritage of the servants of
      the LORD,
   and this is their vindication
      from me,"
                    declares the LORD.

Invitation to the Thirsty

55 "Come, all you who are thirsty,
      come to the waters;
 and you who have no money,
   come, buy and eat!
 Come, buy wine and milk
   without money and without cost.
2 Why spend money on what is not
      bread,
   and your labor on what does not
      satisfy?

---

a 11 The meaning of the Hebrew for this word is uncertain.

Listen, listen to me, and eat what is
good,
and you will delight in the richest of
fare.
[3] Give ear and come to me;
listen, that you may live.
I will make an everlasting covenant
with you,
my faithful love promised to
David.
[4] See, I have made him a witness to the
peoples,
a ruler and commander of the
peoples.
[5] Surely you will summon nations you
know not,
and nations you do not know will
come running to you,
because of the LORD your God,
the Holy One of Israel,
for he has endowed you with
splendor."

[6] Seek the LORD while he may be
found;
call on him while he is near.
[7] Let the wicked forsake their ways
and the unrighteous their
thoughts.
Let them turn to the LORD, and he will
have mercy on them,
and to our God, for he will freely
pardon.

[8] "For my thoughts are not your
thoughts,
neither are your ways my ways,"
declares the LORD.
[9] "As the heavens are higher than the
earth,
so are my ways higher than your
ways
and my thoughts than your
thoughts.
[10] As the rain and the snow
come down from heaven,
and do not return to it
without watering the earth
and making it bud and flourish,
so that it yields seed for the sower
and bread for the eater,
[11] so is my word that goes out from my
mouth:
It will not return to me empty,

*Let the wicked
forsake their ways ... Let
them turn to the LORD, and
he will ... freely pardon.*

Isaiah 55:7

but will accomplish what I desire
and achieve the purpose for which I
sent it.
[12] You will go out in joy
and be led forth in peace;
the mountains and hills
will burst into song before you,
and all the trees of the field
will clap their hands.
[13] Instead of the thornbush will grow the
juniper,
and instead of briers the myrtle will
grow.
This will be for the LORD's renown,
for an everlasting sign,
that will endure forever."

Salvation for Others

56 This is what the LORD says:

"Maintain justice
and do what is right,
for my salvation is close at hand
and my righteousness will soon be
revealed.
[2] Blessed is the one who does
this—
the person who holds it fast,
who keeps the Sabbath without
desecrating it,
and keeps their hands from doing
any evil."

[3] Let no foreigner who is bound to the
LORD say,
"The LORD will surely exclude me
from his people."
And let no eunuch complain,
"I am only a dry tree."

⁴For this is what the LORD says:

"To the eunuchs who keep my
    Sabbaths,
  who choose what pleases me
    and hold fast to my covenant—
⁵to them I will give within my temple
    and its walls
  a memorial and a name
    better than sons and daughters;
  I will give them an everlasting name
    that will endure forever.
⁶And foreigners who bind themselves
    to the LORD
  to minister to him,
to love the name of the LORD,
    and to be his servants,
  all who keep the Sabbath without
    desecrating it
  and who hold fast to my covenant—
⁷these I will bring to my holy mountain
    and give them joy in my house of
    prayer.
  Their burnt offerings and sacrifices
    will be accepted on my altar;
  for my house will be called
    a house of prayer for all nations."
⁸The Sovereign LORD declares—
    he who gathers the exiles of
    Israel:
  "I will gather still others to them
    besides those already gathered."

God's Accusation Against the Wicked

⁹Come, all you beasts of the field,
    come and devour, all you beasts of
    the forest!
¹⁰Israel's watchmen are blind,
    they all lack knowledge;
  they are all mute dogs,
    they cannot bark;
  they lie around and dream,
    they love to sleep.
¹¹They are dogs with mighty appetites;
    they never have enough.
  They are shepherds who lack
    understanding;
  they all turn to their own way,
    they seek their own gain.
¹²"Come," each one cries, "let me get
    wine!
  Let us drink our fill of beer!

And tomorrow will be like today,
    or even far better."

57 The righteous perish,
    and no one takes it to heart;
  the devout are taken away,
    and no one understands
  that the righteous are taken away
    to be spared from evil.
²Those who walk uprightly
    enter into peace;
  they find rest as they lie in
    death.

³"But you—come here, you children of
    a sorceress,
  you offspring of adulterers and
    prostitutes!
⁴Who are you mocking?
    At whom do you sneer
    and stick out your tongue?
  Are you not a brood of rebels,
    the offspring of liars?
⁵You burn with lust among the oaks
    and under every spreading tree;
  you sacrifice your children in the
    ravines
    and under the overhanging
    crags.

Isaiah 57

Q: What are the wicked like?

BONUS: What don't the wicked have?

Answers on next page

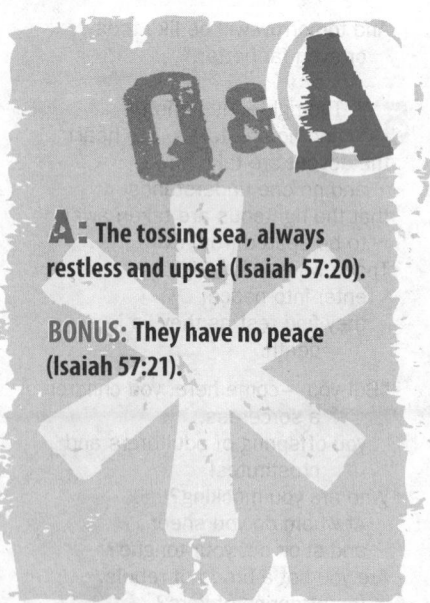

A: The tossing sea, always restless and upset (Isaiah 57:20).

BONUS: They have no peace (Isaiah 57:21).

6 The idols among the smooth stones of
    the ravines are your portion;
  indeed, they are your lot.
Yes, to them you have poured out
    drink offerings
  and offered grain offerings.
  In view of all this, should I relent?
7 You have made your bed on a high
    and lofty hill;
  there you went up to offer your
    sacrifices.
8 Behind your doors and your doorposts
    you have put your pagan symbols.
  Forsaking me, you uncovered your
    bed,
  you climbed into it and opened it
    wide;
  you made a pact with those whose
    beds you love,
  and you looked with lust on their
    naked bodies.
9 You went to Molek[a] with olive oil
  and increased your perfumes.
  You sent your ambassadors[b] far away;
  you descended to the very realm of
    the dead!
10 You wearied yourself by such going
    about,

but you would not say, 'It is
    hopeless.'
  You found renewal of your strength,
  and so you did not faint.

11 "Whom have you so dreaded and
    feared
  that you have not been true to me,
  and have neither remembered me
  nor taken this to heart?
  Is it not because I have long been
    silent
  that you do not fear me?
12 I will expose your righteousness and
    your works,
  and they will not benefit you.
13 When you cry out for help,
  let your collection of idols save you!
  The wind will carry all of them off,
  a mere breath will blow them
    away.
  But whoever takes refuge in me
  will inherit the land
  and possess my holy mountain."

Comfort for the Contrite

14 And it will be said:

"Build up, build up, prepare the road!
  Remove the obstacles out of the
    way of my people."
15 For this is what the high and exalted
    One says—
  he who lives forever, whose name is
    holy:
"I live in a high and holy place,
  but also with the one who is
    contrite and lowly in spirit,
  to revive the spirit of the lowly
  and to revive the heart of the
    contrite.
16 I will not accuse them forever,
  nor will I always be angry,
  for then they would faint away
    because of me—
  the very people I have created.
17 I was enraged by their sinful greed;
  I punished them, and hid my face in
    anger,
  yet they kept on in their willful ways.
18 I have seen their ways, but I will heal
    them;

---

a 9 Or to the king   b 9 Or idols

INSTANT ACCESS

ack writes, "My biggest temptation is living the way others want me to instead of how God wants me to live." Everybody—adults and teens—has that temptation. It may help to remember Isaiah's warning to the people of Israel, who were tempted to live the way the pagan people around them lived. God said through the prophet, do it and you'll be all churned up inside. For "there is no peace for the wicked." Living the way that non-Christians do just isn't worth it.

{Isaiah 57:21}

I will guide them and restore
    comfort to Israel's mourners,
19 creating praise on their lips.
Peace, peace, to those far and
        near,"
    says the LORD. "And I will heal
        them."
20 But the wicked are like the tossing
        sea,
    which cannot rest,
    whose waves cast up mire and
        mud.
21 "There is no peace," says my God,
    "for the wicked."

True Fasting

58 "Shout it aloud, do not hold
        back.
    Raise your voice like a trumpet.
Declare to my people their rebellion

    and to the descendants of Jacob
        their sins.
2 For day after day they seek me out;
    they seem eager to know my
        ways,
as if they were a nation that does
        what is right
    and has not forsaken the
        commands of its God.
They ask me for just decisions
    and seem eager for God to come
        near them.
3 'Why have we fasted,' they say,
    'and you have not seen it?
Why have we humbled ourselves,
    and you have not noticed?'

"Yet on the day of your fasting, you do
        as you please
    and exploit all your workers.
4 Your fasting ends in quarreling and
        strife,
    and in striking each other with
        wicked fists.
You cannot fast as you do today
    and expect your voice to be heard
        on high.
5 Is this the kind of fast I have chosen,
    only a day for people to humble
        themselves?
Is it only for bowing one's head like a
        reed
    and for lying in sackcloth and
        ashes?
Is that what you call a fast,
    a day acceptable to the LORD?

6 "Is not this the kind of fasting I have
        chosen:
to loose the chains of injustice
    and untie the cords of the yoke,
to set the oppressed free
    and break every yoke?
7 Is it not to share your food with the
        hungry
    and to provide the poor wanderer
        with shelter—
when you see the naked, to clothe
        them,
    and not to turn away from your own
        flesh and blood?
8 Then your light will break forth like the
        dawn,
    and your healing will quickly appear;

then your righteousness[a] will go
before you,
and the glory of the LORD will be
your rear guard.
⁹Then you will call, and the LORD will
answer;
you will cry for help, and he will say:
Here am I.

"If you do away with the yoke of
oppression,
with the pointing finger and
malicious talk,
¹⁰and if you spend yourselves in behalf
of the hungry
and satisfy the needs of the
oppressed,

> *You will call, and the
> LORD will answer; you
> will cry for help, and he
> will say: Here am I.*
>
> **Isaiah 58:9**

then your light will rise in the
darkness,
and your night will become like the
noonday.
¹¹The LORD will guide you always;
he will satisfy your needs in a sun-
scorched land
and will strengthen your frame.
You will be like a well-watered
garden,
like a spring whose waters never
fail.
¹²Your people will rebuild the ancient
ruins
and will raise up the age-old
foundations;
you will be called Repairer of Broken
Walls,
Restorer of Streets with Dwellings.

¹³"If you keep your feet from breaking
the Sabbath
and from doing as you please on my
holy day,
if you call the Sabbath a delight
and the LORD's holy day honorable,
and if you honor it by not going your
own way
and not doing as you please or
speaking idle words,
¹⁴then you will find your joy in the LORD,
and I will cause you to ride in
triumph on the heights of the
land
and to feast on the inheritance of
your father Jacob."
For the mouth of the LORD
has spoken.

Sin, Confession and Redemption

59 Surely the arm of the LORD is not
too short to save,
nor his ear too dull to hear.
²But your iniquities have separated
you from your God;
your sins have hidden his face from
you,
so that he will not hear.
³For your hands are stained with blood,
your fingers with guilt.
Your lips have spoken falsely,
and your tongue mutters wicked
things.
⁴No one calls for justice;
no one pleads a case with integrity.
They rely on empty arguments, they
utter lies;
they conceive trouble and give birth
to evil.
⁵They hatch the eggs of vipers
and spin a spider's web.
Whoever eats their eggs will die,
and when one is broken, an adder
is hatched.
⁶Their cobwebs are useless for clothing;
they cannot cover themselves with
what they make.
Their deeds are evil deeds,
and acts of violence are in their
hands.

---

a 8 Or your righteous One

7 Their feet rush into sin;
  they are swift to shed innocent
    blood.
They pursue evil schemes;
  acts of violence mark their ways.
8 The way of peace they do not know;
  there is no justice in their paths.
They have turned them into crooked
    roads;
  no one who walks along them will
    know peace.

9 So justice is far from us,
  and righteousness does not
    reach us.
We look for light, but all is darkness;
  for brightness, but we walk in deep
    shadows.
10 Like the blind we grope along the
    wall,
  feeling our way like people without
    eyes.
At midday we stumble as if it were
    twilight;
  among the strong, we are like the
    dead.
11 We all growl like bears;
  we moan mournfully like doves.
We look for justice, but find none;
  for deliverance, but it is far away.

12 For our offenses are many in your
    sight,
  and our sins testify against us.
Our offenses are ever with us,
  and we acknowledge our iniquities:
13 rebellion and treachery against the
    LORD,
  turning our backs on our God,
inciting revolt and oppression,
  uttering lies our hearts have
    conceived.
14 So justice is driven back,
  and righteousness stands at a
    distance;
  truth has stumbled in the streets,
    honesty cannot enter.
15 Truth is nowhere to be found,
  and whoever shuns evil becomes a
    prey.

The LORD looked and was displeased
  that there was no justice.

16 He saw that there was no one,
  he was appalled that there was no
    one to intervene;
so his own arm achieved salvation for
    him,
  and his own righteousness
    sustained him.
17 He put on righteousness as his
    breastplate,
  and the helmet of salvation on his
    head;
he put on the garments of vengeance
  and wrapped himself in zeal as in a
    cloak.
18 According to what they have done,
  so will he repay
wrath to his enemies
  and retribution to his foes;
  he will repay the islands their
    due.
19 From the west, people will fear the
    name of the LORD,
  and from the rising of the sun, they
    will revere his glory.
For he will come like a pent-up flood
  that the breath of the LORD drives
    along.[a]

20 "The Redeemer will come to Zion,
  to those in Jacob who repent of
    their sins,"
                    declares the LORD.

21 "As for me, this is my covenant with
them," says the LORD. "My Spirit, who is
on you, will not depart from you, and my
words that I have put in your mouth will
always be on your lips, on the lips of your
children and on the lips of their descendants—from this time on and forever,"
says the LORD.

The Glory of Zion

60 "Arise, shine, for your light has
    come,
  and the glory of the LORD rises upon
    you.
2 See, darkness covers the earth
  and thick darkness is over the
    peoples,
but the LORD rises upon you
  and his glory appears over you.

---

a 19 Or When enemies come in like a flood, / the Spirit of the LORD will put them to flight

3 Nations will come to your light,
    and kings to the brightness of your
        dawn.

4 "Lift up your eyes and look about you:
    All assemble and come to you;
your sons come from afar,
    and your daughters are carried on
        the hip.
5 Then you will look and be radiant,
    your heart will throb and swell with
        joy;
the wealth on the seas will be brought
        to you,
    to you the riches of the nations will
        come.
6 Herds of camels will cover your land,
    young camels of Midian and
        Ephah.
And all from Sheba will come,
    bearing gold and incense
    and proclaiming the praise of the
        Lord.
7 All Kedar's flocks will be gathered to
        you,
    the rams of Nebaioth will serve you;
they will be accepted as offerings on
        my altar,
    and I will adorn my glorious temple.

8 "Who are these that fly along like
        clouds,
    like doves to their nests?
9 Surely the islands look to me;
    in the lead are the ships of
        Tarshish,[a]
bringing your children from afar,
    with their silver and gold,
to the honor of the Lord your God,
    the Holy One of Israel,
    for he has endowed you with
        splendor.

10 "Foreigners will rebuild your walls,
    and their kings will serve you.
Though in anger I struck you,
    in favor I will show you compassion.
11 Your gates will always stand open,
    they will never be shut, day or night,
so that people may bring you the
        wealth of the nations—
    their kings led in triumphal
        procession.

12 For the nation or kingdom that will not
        serve you will perish;
    it will be utterly ruined.

13 "The glory of Lebanon will come to
        you,
    the juniper, the fir and the cypress
        together,
to adorn my sanctuary;
    and I will glorify the place for my
        feet.
14 The children of your oppressors will
        come bowing before you;
    all who despise you will bow down
        at your feet
and will call you the City of the Lord,
    Zion of the Holy One of Israel.

15 "Although you have been forsaken and
        hated,
    with no one traveling through,
I will make you the everlasting pride
    and the joy of all generations.
16 You will drink the milk of nations
    and be nursed at royal breasts.
Then you will know that I, the Lord,
        am your Savior,
    your Redeemer, the Mighty One of
        Jacob.
17 Instead of bronze I will bring you gold,
    and silver in place of iron.
Instead of wood I will bring you
        bronze,
    and iron in place of stones.
I will make peace your governor
    and well-being your ruler.
18 No longer will violence be heard in
        your land,
    nor ruin or destruction within your
        borders,
but you will call your walls Salvation
    and your gates Praise.
19 The sun will no more be your light by
        day,
    nor will the brightness of the moon
        shine on you,
for the Lord will be your everlasting
        light,
    and your God will be your glory.
20 Your sun will never set again,
    and your moon will wane no more;
the Lord will be your everlasting light,
    and your days of sorrow will end.

---

a 9 Or the trading ships

21 Then all your people will be righteous
    and they will possess the land
      forever.
  They are the shoot I have planted,
    the work of my hands,
    for the display of my splendor.
22 The least of you will become a
      thousand,
    the smallest a mighty nation.
  I am the Lord;
    in its time I will do this swiftly."

The Year of the Lord's Favor

61 The Spirit of the Sovereign Lord
       is on me,
    because the Lord has anointed me
    to proclaim good news to the poor.
  He has sent me to bind up the
      brokenhearted,
    to proclaim freedom for the captives
    and release from darkness for the
      prisoners,[a]
2 to proclaim the year of the Lord's
      favor
    and the day of vengeance of our
      God,
  to comfort all who mourn,
3   and provide for those who grieve in
      Zion—
  to bestow on them a crown of beauty
    instead of ashes,
  the oil of joy
    instead of mourning,
  and a garment of praise
    instead of a spirit of despair.
  They will be called oaks of
    righteousness,
    a planting of the Lord
    for the display of his splendor.

4 They will rebuild the ancient ruins
    and restore the places long
      devastated;
  they will renew the ruined cities
    that have been devastated for
      generations.
5 Strangers will shepherd your flocks;
    foreigners will work your fields and
      vineyards.
6 And you will be called priests of the
      Lord,
    you will be named ministers of our
      God.

You will feed on the wealth of nations,
    and in their riches you will boast.

7 Instead of your shame
    you will receive a double portion,
  and instead of disgrace
    you will rejoice in your inheritance.
  And so you will inherit a double
      portion in your land,
    and everlasting joy will be yours.

8 "For I, the Lord, love justice;
    I hate robbery and wrongdoing.
  In my faithfulness I will reward my
      people
    and make an everlasting covenant
      with them.
9 Their descendants will be known
      among the nations
    and their offspring among the
      peoples.
  All who see them will acknowledge
    that they are a people the Lord has
      blessed."

10 I delight greatly in the Lord;
    my soul rejoices in my God.
  For he has clothed me with garments
      of salvation
    and arrayed me in a robe of his
      righteousness,
  as a bridegroom adorns his head like
      a priest,
    and as a bride adorns herself with
      her jewels.
11 For as the soil makes the sprout
      come up
    and a garden causes seeds to grow,
  so the Sovereign Lord will make
      righteousness
    and praise spring up before all
      nations.

Zion's New Name

62 For Zion's sake I will not keep
       silent,
    for Jerusalem's sake I will not
      remain quiet,
  till her vindication shines out like the
      dawn,
    her salvation like a blazing torch.
2 The nations will see your vindication,
    and all kings your glory;

---

a 1 Hebrew; Septuagint *the blind*

you will be called by a new name
that the mouth of the LORD will
bestow.
³ You will be a crown of splendor in the
LORD's hand,
a royal diadem in the hand of your
God.
⁴ No longer will they call you Deserted,
or name your land Desolate.
But you will be called Hephzibah,ᵃ
and your land Beulahᵇ;
for the LORD will take delight in you,
and your land will be married.
⁵ As a young man marries a young
woman,
so will your Builder marry you;
as a bridegroom rejoices over his
bride,
so will your God rejoice over you.

⁶ I have posted watchmen on your
walls, Jerusalem;
they will never be silent day or
night.
You who call on the LORD,
give yourselves no rest,
⁷ and give him no rest till he
establishes Jerusalem
and makes her the praise of the
earth.

⁸ The LORD has sworn by his right hand
and by his mighty arm:
"Never again will I give your grain
as food for your enemies,
and never again will foreigners drink
the new wine
for which you have toiled;
⁹ but those who harvest it will eat it
and praise the LORD,
and those who gather the grapes will
drink it
in the courts of my sanctuary."

¹⁰ Pass through, pass through the gates!
Prepare the way for the people.
Build up, build up the highway!
Remove the stones.
Raise a banner for the nations.

¹¹ The LORD has made proclamation
to the ends of the earth:
"Say to Daughter Zion,
'See, your Savior comes!

See, his reward is with him,
and his recompense accompanies
him.'"
¹² They will be called the Holy People,
the Redeemed of the LORD;
and you will be called Sought After,
the City No Longer Deserted.

God's Day of Vengeance and Redemption

63 Who is this coming from Edom,
from Bozrah, with his garments
stained crimson?
Who is this, robed in splendor,
striding forward in the greatness of
his strength?

"It is I, proclaiming victory,
mighty to save."

² Why are your garments red,
like those of one treading the
winepress?

³ "I have trodden the winepress alone;
from the nations no one was
with me.
I trampled them in my anger
and trod them down in my wrath;
their blood spattered my garments,
and I stained all my clothing.
⁴ It was for me the day of vengeance;
the year for me to redeem had
come.
⁵ I looked, but there was no one to
help,
I was appalled that no one gave
support;
so my own arm achieved salvation
for me,
and my own wrath sustained me.
⁶ I trampled the nations in my anger;
in my wrath I made them drunk
and poured their blood on the
ground."

Praise and Prayer

⁷ I will tell of the kindnesses of the
LORD,
the deeds for which he is to be
praised,
according to all the LORD has done
for us—

ᵃ 4 *Hephzibah* means *my delight is in her.*   ᵇ 4 *Beulah* means *married.*

yes, the many good things
he has done for Israel,
according to his compassion and
many kindnesses.
[8] He said, "Surely they are my people,
children who will be true to me";
and so he became their Savior.
[9] In all their distress he too was
distressed,
and the angel of his presence
saved them.[a]
In his love and mercy he redeemed
them;
he lifted them up and carried them
all the days of old.
[10] Yet they rebelled
and grieved his Holy Spirit.
So he turned and became their enemy
and he himself fought against
them.

[11] Then his people recalled[b] the days of
old,
the days of Moses and his
people—
where is he who brought them through
the sea,
with the shepherd of his flock?
Where is he who set
his Holy Spirit among them,
[12] who sent his glorious arm of power
to be at Moses' right hand,
who divided the waters before them,
to gain for himself everlasting
renown,
[13] who led them through the depths?
Like a horse in open country,
they did not stumble;
[14] like cattle that go down to the plain,
they were given rest by the Spirit of
the LORD.
This is how you guided your people
to make for yourself a glorious
name.

[15] Look down from heaven and see,
from your lofty throne, holy and
glorious.
Where are your zeal and your might?
Your tenderness and compassion
are withheld from us.

[16] But you are our Father,
though Abraham does not know us
or Israel acknowledge us;
you, LORD, are our Father,
our Redeemer from of old is your
name.
[17] Why, LORD, do you make us wander
from your ways
and harden our hearts so we do not
revere you?
Return for the sake of your servants,
the tribes that are your inheritance.
[18] For a little while your people
possessed your holy place,
but now our enemies have trampled
down your sanctuary.
[19] We are yours from of old;
but you have not ruled over them,
they have not been called[c] by your
name.

64 [d] Oh, that you would rend the
heavens and come down,
that the mountains would tremble
before you!
[2] As when fire sets twigs ablaze
and causes water to boil,
come down to make your name known
to your enemies
and cause the nations to quake
before you!
[3] For when you did awesome things that
we did not expect,
you came down, and the mountains
trembled before you.
[4] Since ancient times no one has heard,
no ear has perceived,
no eye has seen any God besides you,
who acts on behalf of those who
wait for him.
[5] You come to the help of those who
gladly do right,
who remember your ways.
But when we continued to sin against
them,
you were angry.
How then can we be saved?
[6] All of us have become like one who is
unclean,
and all our righteous acts are like
filthy rags;

---

[a] 9 Or Savior [9] in their distress. / It was no envoy or angel / but his own presence that saved them   [b] 11 Or But may he recall   [c] 19 Or We are like those you have never ruled, / like those never called   [d] In Hebrew texts 64:1 is numbered 63:19b, and 64:2-12 is numbered 64:1-11.

we all shrivel up like a leaf,
    and like the wind our sins sweep us
        away.
7 No one calls on your name
    or strives to lay hold of you;
for you have hidden your face from us
    and have given us over to*a* our sins.

8 Yet you, LORD, are our Father.
    We are the clay, you are the potter;
    we are all the work of your hand.
9 Do not be angry beyond measure,
    LORD;
    do not remember our sins forever.
Oh, look on us, we pray,
    for we are all your people.
10 Your sacred cities have become a
        wasteland;
    even Zion is a wasteland,
    Jerusalem a desolation.
11 Our holy and glorious temple, where
        our ancestors praised you,
    has been burned with fire,
    and all that we treasured lies in
        ruins.
12 After all this, LORD, will you hold
        yourself back?
    Will you keep silent and punish us
        beyond measure?

Isaiah 65

Q: Where will some Jewish
people be living at history's end?

BONUS: Between 1840 and 1980
the world's population doubled.
During this time how much did
the Jewish population of Israel
grow?

Answers on next page

Judgment and Salvation

65 "I revealed myself to those who
    did not ask for me;
    I was found by those who did not
        seek me.
To a nation that did not call on my
        name,
    I said, 'Here am I, here am I.'
2 All day long I have held out my hands
    to an obstinate people,
who walk in ways not good,
    pursuing their own imaginations—
3 a people who continually provoke me
    to my very face,
offering sacrifices in gardens
    and burning incense on altars of
        brick;
4 who sit among the graves
    and spend their nights keeping
        secret vigil;
who eat the flesh of pigs,
    and whose pots hold broth of
        impure meat;
5 who say, 'Keep away; don't come
        near me,
    for I am too sacred for you!'
Such people are smoke in my
        nostrils,
    a fire that keeps burning all day.

6 "See, it stands written before me:
    I will not keep silent but will pay
        back in full;
    I will pay it back into their laps—
7 both your sins and the sins of your
        ancestors,"
    says the LORD.
"Because they burned sacrifices on
        the mountains
    and defied me on the hills,
I will measure into their laps
    the full payment for their former
        deeds."

8 This is what the LORD says:

"As when juice is still found in a
        cluster of grapes
    and people say, 'Don't destroy it,
        there is still a blessing in it,'
so will I do in behalf of my servants;
    I will not destroy them all.

---

a 7 Septuagint, Syriac and Targum; Hebrew *have made us
melt because of*

9 I will bring forth descendants from
Jacob,
and from Judah those who will
possess my mountains;
my chosen people will inherit them,
and there will my servants live.
10 Sharon will become a pasture for
flocks,
and the Valley of Achor a resting
place for herds,
for my people who seek me.

11 "But as for you who forsake the LORD
and forget my holy mountain,
who spread a table for Fortune
and fill bowls of mixed wine for
Destiny,
12 I will destine you for the sword,
and all of you will fall in the
slaughter;
for I called but you did not answer,
I spoke but you did not listen.
You did evil in my sight
and chose what displeases me."

13 Therefore this is what the Sovereign
LORD says:

"My servants will eat,
but you will go hungry;
my servants will drink,
but you will go thirsty;
my servants will rejoice,
but you will be put to shame.
14 My servants will sing
out of the joy of their hearts,
but you will cry out
from anguish of heart
and wail in brokenness of spirit.
15 You will leave your name
for my chosen ones to use in their
curses;
the Sovereign LORD will put you to
death,
but to his servants he will give
another name.
16 Whoever invokes a blessing in the
land
will do so by the one true God;
whoever takes an oath in the land
will swear by the one true God.
For the past troubles will be forgotten
and hidden from my eyes.

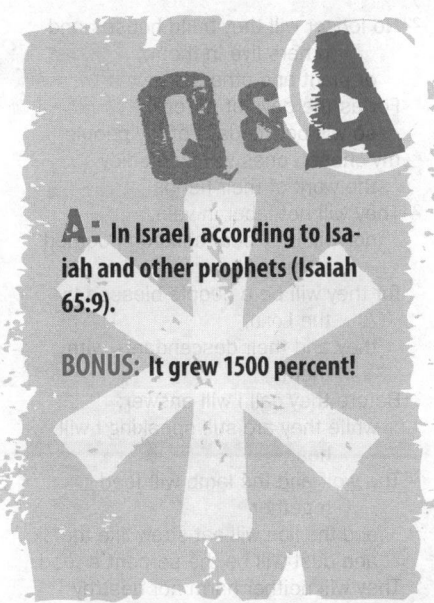

A: In Israel, according to Isaiah and other prophets (Isaiah
65:9).

BONUS: It grew 1500 percent!

New Heavens and a New Earth

17 "See, I will create
new heavens and a new earth.
The former things will not be
remembered,
nor will they come to mind.
18 But be glad and rejoice forever
in what I will create,
for I will create Jerusalem to be a
delight
and its people a joy.
19 I will rejoice over Jerusalem
and take delight in my people;
the sound of weeping and of crying
will be heard in it no more.

20 "Never again will there be in it
an infant who lives but a few days,
or an old man who does not live out
his years;
the one who dies at a hundred
will be thought a mere child;
the one who fails to reach[a] a hundred
will be considered accursed.
21 They will build houses and dwell in
them;
they will plant vineyards and eat
their fruit.

---

[a] 20 Or the sinner who reaches

²²No longer will they build houses and
others live in them,
or plant and others eat.
For as the days of a tree,
so will be the days of my people;
my chosen ones will long enjoy
the work of their hands.
²³They will not labor in vain,
nor will they bear children doomed
to misfortune;
for they will be a people blessed by
the LORD,
they and their descendants with
them.
²⁴Before they call I will answer;
while they are still speaking I will
hear.
²⁵The wolf and the lamb will feed
together,
and the lion will eat straw like the ox,
and dust will be the serpent's food.
They will neither harm nor destroy
on all my holy mountain,"
says the LORD.

Judgment and Hope

66 This is what the LORD says:

"Heaven is my throne,
and the earth is my footstool.
Where is the house you will build
for me?
Where will my resting place be?
²Has not my hand made all these
things,
and so they came into being?"
declares the LORD.

"These are the ones I look on with
favor:
those who are humble and contrite
in spirit,
and who tremble at my word.
³But whoever sacrifices a bull
is like one who kills a person,
and whoever offers a lamb
is like one who breaks a dog's
neck;
whoever makes a grain offering
is like one who presents pig's
blood,
and whoever burns memorial incense
is like one who worships an idol.

They have chosen their own ways,
and they delight in their
abominations;
⁴so I also will choose harsh treatment
for them
and will bring on them what they
dread.
For when I called, no one answered,
when I spoke, no one listened.
They did evil in my sight
and chose what displeases me."

⁵Hear the word of the LORD,
you who tremble at his word:
"Your own people who hate you,
and exclude you because of my
name, have said,
'Let the LORD be glorified,
that we may see your joy!'
Yet they will be put to shame.
⁶Hear that uproar from the city,
hear that noise from the temple!
It is the sound of the LORD
repaying his enemies all they
deserve.

⁷"Before she goes into labor,
she gives birth;
before the pains come upon her,
she delivers a son.
⁸Who has ever heard of such things?
Who has ever seen things like
this?
Can a country be born in a day
or a nation be brought forth in a
moment?
Yet no sooner is Zion in labor
than she gives birth to her children.
⁹Do I bring to the moment of birth
and not give delivery?" says the
LORD.
"Do I close up the womb
when I bring to delivery?" says your
God.
¹⁰"Rejoice with Jerusalem and be glad
for her,
all you who love her;
rejoice greatly with her,
all you who mourn over her.
¹¹For you will nurse and be satisfied
at her comforting breasts;
you will drink deeply
and delight in her overflowing
abundance."

Have you heard the latest on the "end of the world"? Global warming? A new ice age? Giant asteroids that knock the earth out of its orbit? All these theories make the future sound pretty grim. And then you turn to the Bible and get a different view. Yes, this earth will be destroyed (Isaiah 51:6; 2 Peter 3:10–13). But God will then create a new heaven and earth to be the home of a purified humanity. What will life on earth be like after God acts? Check it out in Isaiah 65:17–25. Sure, scientists predict scary pictures of the end of the world. But what God has in store for you is nothing but good!

{Isaiah 66:22}

INSTANT ACCESS

14 When you see this, your heart will rejoice
and you will flourish like grass;
the hand of the LORD will be made known to his servants,
but his fury will be shown to his foes.
15 See, the LORD is coming with fire,
and his chariots are like a whirlwind;
he will bring down his anger with fury,
and his rebuke with flames of fire.
16 For with fire and with his sword
the LORD will execute judgment on all people,
and many will be those slain by the LORD.

17 "Those who consecrate and purify themselves to go into the gardens, following one who is among those who eat the flesh of pigs, rats and other unclean things—they will meet their end together with the one they follow," declares the LORD.

18 "And I, because of what they have planned and done, am about to come[a] and gather the people of all nations and languages, and they will come and see my glory.

19 "I will set a sign among them, and I will send some of those who survive to the nations—to Tarshish, to the Libyans[b] and Lydians (famous as archers), to Tubal and Greece, and to the distant islands that have not heard of my fame or seen my glory. They will proclaim my glory among the nations. 20 And they will bring all your people, from all the nations, to my holy mountain in Jerusalem as an offering to the LORD—on horses, in chariots and wagons, and on mules and camels," says the LORD. "They will bring them, as the Israelites bring their grain offerings, to the temple of the LORD in ceremonially clean vessels. 21 And I will select some of them also to be priests and Levites," says the LORD.

22 "As the new heavens and the new earth that I make will endure before me," declares the LORD, "so will your name and

12 For this is what the LORD says:

"I will extend peace to her like a river,
and the wealth of nations like a flooding stream;
you will nurse and be carried on her arm
and dandled on her knees.
13 As a mother comforts her child,
so will I comfort you;
and you will be comforted over Jerusalem."

---

a 18 The meaning of the Hebrew for this clause is uncertain.   b 19 Some Septuagint manuscripts *Put* (Libyans); Hebrew *Pul*

descendants endure. [23] From one New Moon to another and from one Sabbath to another, all mankind will come and bow down before me," says the LORD. [24] "And they will go out and look on the dead bodies of those who rebelled against me; the worms that eat them will not die, the fire that burns them will not be quenched, and they will be loathsome to all mankind."

JEREMIAH

Change.

Is it ever too late to change? No, but sometimes it's too late to avoid punishment. You can say you're sorry and you'll never do it again, but you'll probably still be punished. And if you refuse to change, well, then you can be sure there's more trouble ahead!

Jeremiah's contemporaries refused to change. For 40 years God's prophet urged the people of Judah to turn back to God. If they didn't change, God was going to destroy the nation. Instead of changing, the people of Judah got mad at Jeremiah. Finally what Jeremiah predicted happened. Judah and Jerusalem were destroyed by Babylon, and the people were taken captive.

≫GOD PROMISES TO ACT, "IF"
Conditions explained, see Jeremiah 4:1–4

≫FALSE PROPHET PAYS THE PRICE
Liar condemned, report in Jeremiah 28

≫NEW DAY COMING
For good news, check Jeremiah 31:27–34

≫SOME PEOPLE NEVER LEARN
Story in Jeremiah 44

preview

Jeremiah warns Judah for 40 years. His words are ignored and he's called a traitor to Judah.

When Jerusalem falls to Babylon in 586 B.C., as Jeremiah predicted, the survivors still won't listen to God's prophet.

As Jeremiah faithfully warns Judah, Babylon defeats Assyria. Hinduism emerges in India. Aesop spins fables in Greece. The Romans build their first stone bridge.

1 The words of Jeremiah son of Hilkiah, one of the priests at Anathoth in the territory of Benjamin. ²The word of the LORD came to him in the thirteenth year of the reign of Josiah son of Amon king of Judah, ³and through the reign of Jehoiakim son of Josiah king of Judah, down to the fifth month of the eleventh year of Zedekiah son of Josiah king of Judah, when the people of Jerusalem went into exile.

The Call of Jeremiah

⁴The word of the LORD came to me, saying,

⁵"Before I formed you in the womb I
        knew*a* you,
     before you were born I set you
        apart;
     I appointed you as a prophet to the
        nations."

⁶"Alas, Sovereign LORD," I said, "I do not know how to speak; I am too young."

⁷But the LORD said to me, "Do not say, 'I am too young.' You must go to everyone I send you to and say whatever I command you. ⁸Do not be afraid of them, for I am with you and will rescue you," declares the LORD.

⁹Then the LORD reached out his hand and touched my mouth and said to me, "I have put my words in your mouth. ¹⁰See, today I appoint you over nations and kingdoms to uproot and tear down, to destroy and overthrow, to build and to plant."

¹¹The word of the LORD came to me: "What do you see, Jeremiah?"

"I see the branch of an almond tree," I replied.

¹²The LORD said to me, "You have seen correctly, for I am watching*b* to see that my word is fulfilled."

¹³The word of the LORD came to me again: "What do you see?"

"I see a pot that is boiling," I answered. "It is tilting toward us from the north."

¹⁴The LORD said to me, "From the north disaster will be poured out on all who live in the land. ¹⁵I am about to summon all the peoples of the northern kingdoms," declares the LORD.

"Their kings will come and set up their
        thrones
     in the entrance of the gates of
        Jerusalem;
they will come against all her
        surrounding walls
     and against all the towns of Judah.
¹⁶I will pronounce my judgments on my
        people
     because of their wickedness in
        forsaking me,
in burning incense to other gods
     and in worshiping what their hands
        have made.

¹⁷"Get yourself ready! Stand up and say to them whatever I command you. Do not be terrified by them, or I will terrify you before them. ¹⁸Today I have made you a fortified city, an iron pillar and a bronze wall to stand against the whole land—against the kings of Judah, its officials, its priests and the people of the land. ¹⁹They will fight against you but will not overcome you, for I am with you and will rescue you," declares the LORD.

Israel Forsakes God

2 The word of the LORD came to me: ²"Go and proclaim in the hearing of Jerusalem:

"This is what the LORD says:

" 'I remember the devotion of your
        youth,
     how as a bride you loved me
and followed me through the
        wilderness,
     through a land not sown.
³Israel was holy to the LORD,
     the firstfruits of his harvest;
all who devoured her were held guilty,
     and disaster overtook them,' "
                    declares the LORD.

⁴Hear the word of the LORD, you
        descendants of Jacob,
     all you clans of Israel.

⁵This is what the LORD says:

"What fault did your ancestors find in
        me,
     that they strayed so far from me?

---

a 5 Or *chose*   *b* 12 The Hebrew for *watching* sounds like the Hebrew for *almond tree.*

> The U.S. Supreme Court says abortion is legal. Why shouldn't Christians get them if they need to? Does the Bible even talk about abortion?
>
> >> Ashley

Dear Ashley,

As Christians, we are called on to live by the laws of man. But more importantly, we are called on to live by God's law. He is our highest authority.

People who defend abortion say that a woman has the right to control her own body. But consider this. Each cell in your body has your unique genetic stamp. Whether a living cell is taken from your tongue or your toe, it contains the stamp of your identity. From the moment a sperm meets an egg, the cells which start multiplying carry their own genetic code, different from the mother's. An unborn child is therefore not a part of the woman's body. It is a separate individual with its own genetic code. If it were a part of the woman's body, it would have the woman's genetic code.

Old Testament laws said if someone caused a woman's unborn child to die, compensation should be paid. The unborn child was seen as more than just an extension of the woman's body (Exodus 21:22–23).

For Christians, the issue is even clearer. The Bible says God formed you in the womb and prepared you for your life before you were born (Jeremiah 1:5). You were carefully made by God from the moment of conception (Psalm 139:13–16). The unborn are individuals known by God. No one has the right to destroy them.

Jordan

They followed worthless idols
and became worthless themselves.
⁶They did not ask, 'Where is the LORD,
who brought us up out of Egypt
and led us through the barren
wilderness,
through a land of deserts and
ravines,
a land of drought and utter darkness,
a land where no one travels and no
one lives?'
⁷I brought you into a fertile land
to eat its fruit and rich produce.
But you came and defiled my land
and made my inheritance
detestable.
⁸The priests did not ask,
'Where is the LORD?'
Those who deal with the law did not
know me;
the leaders rebelled against me.
The prophets prophesied by Baal,
following worthless idols.

⁹"Therefore I bring charges against you
again,"
            declares the LORD.
"And I will bring charges against
your children's children.
¹⁰Cross over to the coasts of Cyprus
and look,
send to Kedarᵃ and observe closely;
see if there has ever been anything
like this:
¹¹Has a nation ever changed its gods?
(Yet they are not gods at all.)
But my people have exchanged their
glorious God
for worthless idols.
¹²Be appalled at this, you heavens,
and shudder with great horror,"
            declares the LORD.
¹³"My people have committed two sins:
They have forsaken me,
the spring of living water,
and have dug their own cisterns,
broken cisterns that cannot hold
water.
¹⁴Is Israel a servant, a slave by birth?
Why then has he become plunder?
¹⁵Lions have roared;
they have growled at him.

They have laid waste his land;
his towns are burned and deserted.
¹⁶Also, the men of Memphis and
Tahpanhes
have cracked your skull.
¹⁷Have you not brought this on
yourselves
by forsaking the LORD your God
when he led you in the way?
¹⁸Now why go to Egypt
to drink water from the Nileᵇ?
And why go to Assyria
to drink water from the Euphrates?
¹⁹Your wickedness will punish you;
your backsliding will rebuke you.
Consider then and realize
how evil and bitter it is for you
when you forsake the LORD your God
and have no awe of me,"
            declares the Lord,
            the LORD Almighty.

²⁰"Long ago you broke off your yoke
and tore off your bonds;
you said, 'I will not serve you!'
Indeed, on every high hill
and under every spreading tree
you lay down as a prostitute.
²¹I had planted you like a choice vine
of sound and reliable stock.
How then did you turn against me
into a corrupt, wild vine?
²²Although you wash yourself with
soap
and use an abundance of cleansing
powder,
the stain of your guilt is still
before me,"
            declares the Sovereign LORD.
²³"How can you say, 'I am not defiled;
I have not run after the Baals'?
See how you behaved in the valley;
consider what you have done.
You are a swift she-camel
running here and there,
²⁴a wild donkey accustomed to the
desert,
sniffing the wind in her craving—
in her heat who can restrain her?
Any males that pursue her need not
tire themselves;
at mating time they will find her.

ᵃ 10 In the Syro-Arabian desert   ᵇ 18 Hebrew Shihor; that is, a branch of the Nile

25 Do not run until your feet are bare
   and your throat is dry.
   But you said, 'It's no use!
   I love foreign gods,
   and I must go after them.'

26 "As a thief is disgraced when he is
   caught,
   so the people of Israel are
   disgraced—
   they, their kings and their officials,
   their priests and their prophets.
27 They say to wood, 'You are my
   father,'
   and to stone, 'You gave me birth.'
   They have turned their backs to me
   and not their faces;
   yet when they are in trouble, they
   say,
   'Come and save us!'
28 Where then are the gods you made for
   yourselves?
   Let them come if they can save
   you
   when you are in trouble!
   For you, Judah, have as many gods
   as you have towns.

29 "Why do you bring charges
   against me?
   You have all rebelled against me,"
                    declares the LORD.
30 "In vain I punished your people;
   they did not respond to correction.
   Your sword has devoured your
   prophets
   like a ravenous lion.

31 "You of this generation, consider the
   word of the LORD:

   "Have I been a desert to Israel
   or a land of great darkness?
   Why do my people say, 'We are free to
   roam;
   we will come to you no more'?
32 Does a young woman forget her
   jewelry,
   a bride her wedding ornaments?
   Yet my people have forgotten me,
   days without number.
33 How skilled you are at pursuing
   love!
   Even the worst of women can learn
   from your ways.

34 On your clothes is found
   the lifeblood of the innocent poor,
   though you did not catch them
   breaking in.
   Yet in spite of all this
35   you say, 'I am innocent;
   he is not angry with me.'
   But I will pass judgment on you
   because you say, 'I have not
   sinned.'
36 Why do you go about so much,
   changing your ways?
   You will be disappointed by Egypt
   as you were by Assyria.
37 You will also leave that place
   with your hands on your head,
   for the LORD has rejected those you
   trust;
   you will not be helped by them.

3 "If a man divorces his wife
   and she leaves him and marries
   another man,
   should he return to her again?
   Would not the land be completely
   defiled?
   But you have lived as a prostitute with
   many lovers—
   would you now return to me?"
                    declares the LORD.
2 "Look up to the barren heights and
   see.
   Is there any place where you have
   not been ravished?
   By the roadside you sat waiting for
   lovers,
   sat like a nomad in the desert.
   You have defiled the land
   with your prostitution and
   wickedness.
3 Therefore the showers have been
   withheld,
   and no spring rains have fallen.
   Yet you have the brazen look of a
   prostitute;
   you refuse to blush with shame.
4 Have you not just called to me:
   'My Father, my friend from my
   youth,
5 will you always be angry?
   Will your wrath continue forever?'
   This is how you talk,
   but you do all the evil you can."

Unfaithful Israel

⁶During the reign of King Josiah, the LORD said to me, "Have you seen what faithless Israel has done? She has gone up on every high hill and under every spreading tree and has committed adultery there. ⁷I thought that after she had done all this she would return to me but she did not, and her unfaithful sister Judah saw it. ⁸I gave faithless Israel her certificate of divorce and sent her away because of all her adulteries. Yet I saw that her unfaithful sister Judah had no fear; she also went out and committed adultery. ⁹Because Israel's immorality mattered so little to her, she defiled the land and committed adultery with stone and wood. ¹⁰In spite of all this, her unfaithful sister Judah did not return to me with all her heart, but only in pretense," declares the LORD.

¹¹The LORD said to me, "Faithless Israel is more righteous than unfaithful Judah. ¹²Go, proclaim this message toward the north:

" 'Return, faithless Israel,' declares the LORD,
'I will frown on you no longer,
for I am faithful,' declares the LORD,
'I will not be angry forever.
¹³Only acknowledge your guilt—
you have rebelled against the LORD your God,
you have scattered your favors to foreign gods
under every spreading tree,
and have not obeyed me,' "
declares the LORD.

¹⁴"Return, faithless people," declares the LORD, "for I am your husband. I will choose you—one from a town and two from a clan—and bring you to Zion. ¹⁵Then I will give you shepherds after my own heart, who will lead you with knowledge and understanding. ¹⁶In those days, when your numbers have increased greatly in the land," declares the LORD, "people will no longer say, 'The ark of the covenant of the LORD.' It will never enter their minds or be remembered; it will not be missed, nor will another one

be made. ¹⁷At that time they will call Jerusalem The Throne of the LORD, and all nations will gather in Jerusalem to honor the name of the LORD. No longer will they follow the stubbornness of their evil hearts. ¹⁸In those days the people of Judah will join the people of Israel, and together they will come from a northern land to the land I gave your ancestors as an inheritance.

¹⁹"I myself said,

" 'How gladly would I treat you like my children
and give you a pleasant land,
the most beautiful inheritance of any nation.'

INSTANT ACCESS

Six kids from the same high school died in car wrecks in one year. They all thought, "I can drink and drive. Nothing will happen to me." Most sexually active teens think, "I won't get an STD." Assyria had destroyed the Israelites. It was God's judgment on them for their idolatry. But the idolaters in Judah thought, "Hey, that can't happen to us," and went right on sinning. It's wise to learn from your own mistakes. But it's better to learn from others' mistakes. The next time you catch yourself thinking, "That can't happen to me," think again.

{Jeremiah 3:6–13}

I thought you would call me 'Father'
and not turn away from following me.
20 But like a woman unfaithful to her
husband,
so you, Israel, have been unfaithful
to me,"
declares the LORD.

21 A cry is heard on the barren heights,
the weeping and pleading of the
people of Israel,
because they have perverted their
ways
and have forgotten the LORD their
God.

22 "Return, faithless people;
I will cure you of backsliding."

"Yes, we will come to you,
for you are the LORD our God.
23 Surely the idolatrous commotion on
the hills
and mountains is a deception;
surely in the LORD our God
is the salvation of Israel.
24 From our youth shameful gods have
consumed
the fruits of our ancestors'
labor—
their flocks and herds,
their sons and daughters.
25 Let us lie down in our shame,
and let our disgrace cover us.
We have sinned against the LORD our
God,
both we and our ancestors;
from our youth till this day
we have not obeyed the LORD our
God."

4 "If you, Israel, will return,
then return to me,"
declares the LORD.
"If you put your detestable idols out of
my sight
and no longer go astray,
2 and if in a truthful, just and righteous
way
you swear, 'As surely as the LORD
lives,'
then the nations will invoke blessings
by him
and in him they will boast."

3 This is what the LORD says to the people of Judah and to Jerusalem:

"Break up your unplowed ground
and do not sow among thorns.
4 Circumcise yourselves to the LORD,
circumcise your hearts,
you people of Judah and inhabitants
of Jerusalem,
or my wrath will flare up and burn like
fire
because of the evil you have
done—
burn with no one to quench it.

Disaster From the North

5 "Announce in Judah and proclaim in
Jerusalem and say:
'Sound the trumpet throughout the
land!'
Cry aloud and say:
'Gather together!
Let us flee to the fortified cities!'
6 Raise the signal to go to Zion!
Flee for safety without delay!
For I am bringing disaster from the
north,
even terrible destruction."

7 A lion has come out of his lair;
a destroyer of nations has set out.
He has left his place
to lay waste your land.
Your towns will lie in ruins
without inhabitant.
8 So put on sackcloth,
lament and wail,
for the fierce anger of the LORD
has not turned away from us.

9 "In that day," declares the LORD,
"the king and the officials will lose
heart,
the priests will be horrified,
and the prophets will be appalled."

10 Then I said, "Alas, Sovereign LORD!
How completely you have deceived this
people and Jerusalem by saying, 'You will
have peace,' when the sword is at our
throats!"

11 At that time this people and Jerusalem will be told, "A scorching wind from
the barren heights in the desert blows
toward my people, but not to winnow

or cleanse; ¹²a wind too strong for that comes from me. Now I pronounce my judgments against them."

¹³ Look! He advances like the clouds,
  his chariots come like a whirlwind,
his horses are swifter than eagles.
  Woe to us! We are ruined!
¹⁴ Jerusalem, wash the evil from your heart and be saved.
  How long will you harbor wicked thoughts?
¹⁵ A voice is announcing from Dan,
  proclaiming disaster from the hills of Ephraim.
¹⁶ "Tell this to the nations,
  proclaim concerning Jerusalem:
'A besieging army is coming from a distant land,
  raising a war cry against the cities of Judah.
¹⁷ They surround her like men guarding a field,
  because she has rebelled against me,'"
                    declares the LORD.
¹⁸ "Your own conduct and actions
  have brought this on you.
This is your punishment.
  How bitter it is!
  How it pierces to the heart!"

¹⁹ Oh, my anguish, my anguish!
  I writhe in pain.
Oh, the agony of my heart!
  My heart pounds within me,
  I cannot keep silent.
For I have heard the sound of the trumpet;
  I have heard the battle cry.
²⁰ Disaster follows disaster;
  the whole land lies in ruins.
In an instant my tents are destroyed,
  my shelter in a moment.
²¹ How long must I see the battle standard
  and hear the sound of the trumpet?

²² "My people are fools;
  they do not know me.
They are senseless children;
  they have no understanding.
They are skilled in doing evil;
  they know not how to do good."

²³ I looked at the earth,
  and it was formless and empty;
and at the heavens,
  and their light was gone.
²⁴ I looked at the mountains,
  and they were quaking;
  all the hills were swaying.
²⁵ I looked, and there were no people;
  every bird in the sky had flown away.
²⁶ I looked, and the fruitful land was a desert;
  all its towns lay in ruins
  before the LORD, before his fierce anger.

²⁷ This is what the LORD says:

"The whole land will be ruined,
  though I will not destroy it completely.
²⁸ Therefore the earth will mourn
  and the heavens above grow dark,
because I have spoken and will not relent,
  I have decided and will not turn back."

²⁹ At the sound of horsemen and archers
  every town takes to flight.
Some go into the thickets;
  some climb up among the rocks.
All the towns are deserted;
  no one lives in them.

³⁰ What are you doing, you devastated one?
  Why dress yourself in scarlet
  and put on jewels of gold?
Why highlight your eyes with makeup?
  You adorn yourself in vain.
Your lovers despise you;
  they want to kill you.

³¹ I hear a cry as of a woman in labor,
  a groan as of one bearing her first child—
the cry of Daughter Zion gasping for breath,
  stretching out her hands and saying,
"Alas! I am fainting;
  my life is given over to murderers."

Not One Is Upright

5 "Go up and down the streets of
Jerusalem,
look around and consider,
search through her squares.
If you can find but one person
who deals honestly and seeks the
truth,
I will forgive this city.
2 Although they say, 'As surely as the
LORD lives,'
still they are swearing falsely."

3 LORD, do not your eyes look for
truth?
You struck them, but they felt no
pain;
you crushed them, but they refused
correction.
They made their faces harder than
stone
and refused to repent.
4 I thought, "These are only the poor;
they are foolish,
for they do not know the way of the
LORD,
the requirements of their God.
5 So I will go to the leaders
and speak to them;
surely they know the way of the
LORD,
the requirements of their God."
But with one accord they too had
broken off the yoke
and torn off the bonds.
6 Therefore a lion from the forest will
attack them,
a wolf from the desert will ravage
them,
a leopard will lie in wait near their
towns
to tear to pieces any who venture
out,
for their rebellion is great
and their backslidings many.

7 "Why should I forgive you?
Your children have forsaken me
and sworn by gods that are not
gods.
I supplied all their needs,
yet they committed adultery
and thronged to the houses of
prostitutes.

8 They are well-fed, lusty stallions,
each neighing for another man's
wife.
9 Should I not punish them for this?"
declares the LORD.
"Should I not avenge myself
on such a nation as this?

10 "Go through her vineyards and ravage
them,
but do not destroy them completely.
Strip off her branches,
for these people do not belong to
the LORD.
11 The people of Israel and the people of
Judah
have been utterly unfaithful to me,"
declares the LORD.

12 They have lied about the LORD;
they said, "He will do nothing!
No harm will come to us;
we will never see sword or famine.
13 The prophets are but wind
and the word is not in them;
so let what they say be done to
them."

14 Therefore this is what the LORD God
Almighty says:

"Because the people have spoken
these words,
I will make my words in your mouth
a fire
and these people the wood it
consumes.
15 People of Israel," declares the LORD,
"I am bringing a distant nation
against you—
an ancient and enduring nation,
a people whose language you do
not know,
whose speech you do not
understand.
16 Their quivers are like an open grave;
all of them are mighty warriors.
17 They will devour your harvests and
food,
devour your sons and daughters;
they will devour your flocks and herds,
devour your vines and fig trees.
With the sword they will destroy
the fortified cities in which you
trust.

18 "Yet even in those days," declares the LORD, "I will not destroy you completely. 19 And when the people ask, 'Why has the LORD our God done all this to us?' you will tell them, 'As you have forsaken me and served foreign gods in your own land, so now you will serve foreigners in a land not your own.'

20 "Announce this to the descendants of Jacob
and proclaim it in Judah:
21 Hear this, you foolish and senseless people,
who have eyes but do not see,
who have ears but do not hear:
22 Should you not fear me?" declares the LORD.
"Should you not tremble in my presence?
I made the sand a boundary for the sea,
an everlasting barrier it cannot cross.
The waves may roll, but they cannot prevail;
they may roar, but they cannot cross it.
23 But these people have stubborn and rebellious hearts;
they have turned aside and gone away.
24 They do not say to themselves,
'Let us fear the LORD our God,
who gives autumn and spring rains in season,
who assures us of the regular weeks of harvest.'
25 Your wrongdoings have kept these away;
your sins have deprived you of good.
26 "Among my people are the wicked
who lie in wait like men who snare birds
and like those who set traps to catch people.
27 Like cages full of birds,
their houses are full of deceit;
they have become rich and powerful
28 and have grown fat and sleek.
Their evil deeds have no limit;
they do not seek justice.

They do not promote the case of the fatherless;
they do not defend the just cause of the poor.
29 Should I not punish them for this?"
declares the LORD.
"Should I not avenge myself
on such a nation as this?
30 "A horrible and shocking thing
has happened in the land:
31 The prophets prophesy lies,

INSTANT ACCESS

What does God do all day? Sit back and watch you? Make lists of the good and bad things you do? Or does he ignore you and think his own thoughts? Whatever God does, many people pretty much ignore him. They may not consciously think it, but their actions show that they assume, "He will do nothing. No harm will come to us." It's not safe to think of the Lord as a do-nothing God. God may be patient and delay punishment while he gives people a chance to repent. But people who persist in doing wrong aren't safe at all. God really is the judge of his universe, and there are painful consequences for people who keep on doing wrong.

{Jeremiah 5:11-17}

the priests rule by their own
authority,
and my people love it this way.
But what will you do in the end?

Jerusalem Under Siege

6 "Flee for safety, people of Benjamin!
Flee from Jerusalem!
Sound the trumpet in Tekoa!
Raise the signal over Beth
Hakkerem!
For disaster looms out of the north,
even terrible destruction.
2 I will destroy Daughter Zion,
so beautiful and delicate.
3 Shepherds with their flocks will come
against her;
they will pitch their tents around
her,
each tending his own portion."

4 "Prepare for battle against her!
Arise, let us attack at noon!
But, alas, the daylight is fading,
and the shadows of evening grow
long.
5 So arise, let us attack at night
and destroy her fortresses!"

6 This is what the LORD Almighty says:

"Cut down the trees
and build siege ramps against
Jerusalem.
This city must be punished;
it is filled with oppression.
7 As a well pours out its water,
so she pours out her wickedness.
Violence and destruction resound in
her;
her sickness and wounds are ever
before me.
8 Take warning, Jerusalem,
or I will turn away from you
and make your land desolate
so no one can live in it."

9 This is what the LORD Almighty says:

"Let them glean the remnant of Israel
as thoroughly as a vine;
pass your hand over the branches
again,
like one gathering grapes."

10 To whom can I speak and give
warning?
Who will listen to me?
Their ears are closed[a]
so they cannot hear.
The word of the LORD is offensive to
them;
they find no pleasure in it.
11 But I am full of the wrath of the LORD,
and I cannot hold it in.

"Pour it out on the children in the
street
and on the young men gathered
together;
both husband and wife will be caught
in it,
and the old, those weighed down
with years.
12 Their houses will be turned over to
others,
together with their fields and their
wives,
when I stretch out my hand
against those who live in the land,"
declares the LORD.
13 "From the least to the greatest,
all are greedy for gain;
prophets and priests alike,
all practice deceit.
14 They dress the wound of my people
as though it were not serious.
'Peace, peace,' they say,
when there is no peace.
15 Are they ashamed of their detestable
conduct?
No, they have no shame at all;
they do not even know how to blush.
So they will fall among the fallen;
they will be brought down when I
punish them,"
says the LORD.

16 This is what the LORD says:

"Stand at the crossroads and look;
ask for the ancient paths,
ask where the good way is, and walk
in it,
and you will find rest for your souls.
But you said, 'We will not walk in it.'
17 I appointed watchmen over you and
said,

---

a 10 Hebrew uncircumcised

'Listen to the sound of the
trumpet!'
But you said, 'We will not listen.'
18 Therefore hear, you nations;
you who are witnesses,
observe what will happen to them.
19 Hear, you earth:
I am bringing disaster on this
people,
the fruit of their schemes,
because they have not listened to my
words
and have rejected my law.
20 What do I care about incense from
Sheba
or sweet calamus from a distant
land?
Your burnt offerings are not
acceptable;
your sacrifices do not please me."

21 Therefore this is what the Lord says:

"I will put obstacles before this
people.
Parents and children alike will
stumble over them;
neighbors and friends will perish."

22 This is what the Lord says:

"Look, an army is coming
from the land of the north;
a great nation is being stirred up
from the ends of the earth.
23 They are armed with bow and spear;
they are cruel and show no mercy.
They sound like the roaring sea
as they ride on their horses;
they come like men in battle formation
to attack you, Daughter Zion."

24 We have heard reports about them,
and our hands hang limp.
Anguish has gripped us,
pain like that of a woman in labor.
25 Do not go out to the fields
or walk on the roads,
for the enemy has a sword,
and there is terror on every side.
26 Put on sackcloth, my people,
and roll in ashes;
mourn with bitter wailing

as for an only son,
for suddenly the destroyer
will come upon us.

27 "I have made you a tester of metals
and my people the ore,
that you may observe
and test their ways.
28 They are all hardened rebels,
going about to slander.
They are bronze and iron;
they all act corruptly.
29 The bellows blow fiercely
to burn away the lead with fire,
but the refining goes on in vain;
the wicked are not purged out.
30 They are called rejected silver,
because the Lord has rejected
them."

False Religion Worthless

7 This is the word that came to Jeremiah from the Lord: 2 "Stand at the gate of the Lord's house and there proclaim this message:

"'Hear the word of the Lord, all you people of Judah who come through these gates to worship the Lord. 3 This is what the Lord Almighty, the God of Israel, says: Reform your ways and your actions, and I will let you live in this place. 4 Do not trust in deceptive words and say, "This is the temple of the Lord, the temple of the Lord, the temple of the Lord!" 5 If you really change your ways and your actions and deal with each other justly, 6 if you do not oppress the foreigner, the fatherless or the widow and do not shed innocent blood in this place, and if you do not follow other gods to your own harm, 7 then I will let you live in this place, in the land I gave your ancestors for ever and ever. 8 But look, you are trusting in deceptive words that are worthless.

9 "'Will you steal and murder, commit adultery and perjury,[a] burn incense to Baal and follow other gods you have not known, 10 and then come and stand before me in this house, which bears my Name, and say, "We are safe"—safe to do all these detestable things? 11 Has

---

a 9 Or *and swear by false gods*

this house, which bears my Name, become a den of robbers to you? But I have been watching! declares the LORD.

12 " 'Go now to the place in Shiloh where I first made a dwelling for my Name, and see what I did to it because of the wickedness of my people Israel. 13While you were doing all these things, declares the LORD, I spoke to you again and again, but you did not listen; I called you, but you did not answer. 14Therefore, what I did to Shiloh I will now do to the house that bears my Name, the temple you trust in, the place I gave to you and your ancestors. 15I will thrust you from my presence, just as I did all your fellow Israelites, the people of Ephraim.'

16 "So do not pray for this people nor offer any plea or petition for them; do not plead with me, for I will not listen to you. 17Do you not see what they are doing in the towns of Judah and in the streets of Jerusalem? 18The children gather wood, the fathers light the fire, and the women knead the dough and make cakes to offer to the Queen of Heaven. They pour out drink offerings to other gods to arouse my anger. 19But am I the one they are provoking? declares the LORD. Are they not rather harming themselves, to their own shame?

20 " 'Therefore this is what the Sovereign LORD says: My anger and my wrath will be poured out on this place—on man and beast, on the trees of the field and on the crops of your land—and it will burn and not be quenched.

21 " 'This is what the LORD Almighty, the God of Israel, says: Go ahead, add your burnt offerings to your other sacrifices and eat the meat yourselves! 22For when I brought your ancestors out of Egypt and spoke to them, I did not just give them commands about burnt offerings and sacrifices, 23but I gave them this command: Obey me, and I will be your God and you will be my people. Walk in obedience to all I command you, that it may go well with you. 24But they did not listen or pay attention; instead, they followed the stubborn inclinations of their evil hearts. They went backward and not forward. 25From the time your ancestors left Egypt until now, day after day, again and again I sent

you my servants the prophets. 26But they did not listen to me or pay attention. They were stiff-necked and did more evil than their ancestors.'

27 "When you tell them all this, they will not listen to you; when you call to them, they will not answer. 28Therefore say to them, 'This is the nation that has not obeyed the LORD its God or responded to correction. Truth has perished; it has vanished from their lips.

29 " 'Cut off your hair and throw it away; take up a lament on the barren heights, for the LORD has rejected and abandoned this generation that is under his wrath.

The Valley of Slaughter

30 " 'The people of Judah have done evil in my eyes, declares the LORD. They have set up their detestable idols in the house that bears my Name and have defiled it. 31They have built the high places of Topheth in the Valley of Ben Hinnom to burn their sons and daughters in the fire—something I did not command, nor did it enter my mind. 32So beware, the days are coming, declares the LORD, when people will no longer call it Topheth or the Valley of Ben Hinnom, but the Valley of Slaughter, for they will bury the dead in Topheth until there is no more room. 33Then the carcasses of this people will become food for the birds and the wild animals, and there will be no one to frighten them away. 34I will bring an end to the sounds of joy and gladness and to the voices of bride and bridegroom in the towns of Judah and the streets of Jerusalem, for the land will become desolate.

8 " 'At that time, declares the LORD, the bones of the kings and officials of Judah, the bones of the priests and prophets, and the bones of the people of Jerusalem will be removed from their graves. 2They will be exposed to the sun and the moon and all the stars of the heavens, which they have loved and served and which they have followed and consulted and worshiped. They will not be gathered up or buried, but will be like dung lying on the ground. 3Wherever I banish them, all the survivors of this evil nation will prefer death to life, declares the LORD Almighty.'

Sin and Punishment

⁴"Say to them, 'This is what the LORD says:

" 'When people fall down, do they not
get up?
When someone turns away, do they
not return?
⁵Why then have these people turned
away?
Why does Jerusalem always turn
away?
They cling to deceit;
they refuse to return.
⁶I have listened attentively,
but they do not say what is right.
None of them repent of their
wickedness,
saying, "What have I done?"
Each pursues their own course
like a horse charging into battle.
⁷Even the stork in the sky
knows her appointed seasons,
and the dove, the swift and the
thrush
observe the time of their
migration.
But my people do not know
the requirements of the LORD.

⁸" 'How can you say, "We are wise,
for we have the law of the LORD,"
when actually the lying pen of the
scribes
has handled it falsely?
⁹The wise will be put to shame;
they will be dismayed and trapped.
Since they have rejected the word of
the LORD,
what kind of wisdom do they have?
¹⁰Therefore I will give their wives to
other men
and their fields to new owners.
From the least to the greatest,
all are greedy for gain;
prophets and priests alike,
all practice deceit.
¹¹They dress the wound of my people
as though it were not serious.
"Peace, peace," they say,
when there is no peace.

¹²Are they ashamed of their detestable
conduct?
No, they have no shame at all;
they do not even know how to
blush.
So they will fall among the fallen;
they will be brought down when they
are punished,
says the LORD.

¹³" 'I will take away their harvest,
declares the LORD.
There will be no grapes on the vine.
There will be no figs on the tree,
and their leaves will wither.
What I have given them
will be taken from them.ᵃ' "

¹⁴Why are we sitting here?
Gather together!
Let us flee to the fortified cities
and perish there!
For the LORD our God has doomed us
to perish
and given us poisoned water to
drink,
because we have sinned against
him.
¹⁵We hoped for peace
but no good has come,
for a time of healing
but there is only terror.
¹⁶The snorting of the enemy's horses
is heard from Dan;
at the neighing of their stallions
the whole land trembles.
They have come to devour
the land and everything in it,
the city and all who live there.

¹⁷"See, I will send venomous snakes
among you,
vipers that cannot be charmed,
and they will bite you,"
declares the LORD.

¹⁸You who are my Comforterᵇ in sorrow,
my heart is faint within me.
¹⁹Listen to the cry of my people
from a land far away:
"Is the LORD not in Zion?
Is her King no longer there?"

ᵃ 13 The meaning of the Hebrew for this sentence is uncertain.   ᵇ 18 The meaning of the Hebrew for this word is uncertain.

"Why have they aroused my anger with
their images,
with their worthless foreign idols?"

20 "The harvest is past,
the summer has ended,
and we are not saved."

21 Since my people are crushed, I am
crushed;
I mourn, and horror grips me.
22 Is there no balm in Gilead?
Is there no physician there?
Why then is there no healing
for the wound of my people?

9 [a] 1 Oh, that my head were a spring of
water
and my eyes a fountain of tears!
I would weep day and night
for the slain of my people.
2 Oh, that I had in the desert
a lodging place for travelers,
so that I might leave my people
and go away from them;
for they are all adulterers,
a crowd of unfaithful people.

3 "They make ready their tongue
like a bow, to shoot lies;
it is not by truth
that they triumph[b] in the land.
They go from one sin to another;
they do not acknowledge me,"
declares the LORD.
4 "Beware of your friends;
do not trust anyone in your clan.
For every one of them is a deceiver,[c]
and every friend a slanderer.
5 Friend deceives friend,
and no one speaks the truth.
They have taught their tongues to lie;
they weary themselves with sinning.
6 You[d] live in the midst of deception;
in their deceit they refuse to
acknowledge me,"
declares the LORD.

7 Therefore this is what the LORD Almighty says:

"See, I will refine and test them,
for what else can I do
because of the sin of my people?

8 Their tongue is a deadly arrow;
it speaks deceitfully.
With their mouths they all speak
cordially to their neighbors,
but in their hearts they set traps for
them.
9 Should I not punish them for this?"
declares the LORD.
"Should I not avenge myself
on such a nation as this?"

10 I will weep and wail for the mountains
and take up a lament concerning
the wilderness grasslands.
They are desolate and untraveled,
and the lowing of cattle is not
heard.
The birds have all fled
and the animals are gone.

11 "I will make Jerusalem a heap of
ruins,
a haunt of jackals;
and I will lay waste the towns of Judah
so no one can live there."

12 Who is wise enough to understand
this? Who has been instructed by the
LORD and can explain it? Why has the land
been ruined and laid waste like a desert
that no one can cross?

13 The LORD said, "It is because they
have forsaken my law, which I set before them; they have not obeyed me or
followed my law. 14 Instead, they have followed the stubbornness of their hearts;
they have followed the Baals, as their ancestors taught them." 15 Therefore this is
what the LORD Almighty, the God of Israel,
says: "See, I will make this people eat bitter food and drink poisoned water. 16 I will
scatter them among nations that neither
they nor their ancestors have known, and
I will pursue them with the sword until I
have made an end of them."

17 This is what the LORD Almighty says:

"Consider now! Call for the wailing
women to come;
send for the most skillful of them.
18 Let them come quickly
and wail over us

---

[a] In Hebrew texts 9:1 is numbered 8:23, and 9:2-26 is numbered 9:1-25.   [b] 3 Or lies; / they are not valiant for truth
[c] 4 Or a deceiving Jacob   [d] 6 That is, Jeremiah (the Hebrew is singular)

till our eyes overflow with tears
and water streams from our eyelids.
19 The sound of wailing is heard from
Zion:
'How ruined we are!
How great is our shame!
We must leave our land
because our houses are in ruins.' "

20 Now, you women, hear the word of the
LORD;
open your ears to the words of his
mouth.
Teach your daughters how to wail;
teach one another a lament.
21 Death has climbed in through our
windows
and has entered our fortresses;
it has removed the children from the
streets
and the young men from the public
squares.

22 Say, "This is what the LORD declares:

" 'Dead bodies will lie
like dung on the open field,
like cut grain behind the reaper,
with no one to gather them.' "

23 This is what the LORD says:

"Let not the wise boast of their
wisdom
or the strong boast of their strength
or the rich boast of their riches,
24 but let the one who boasts boast
about this:
that they have the understanding to
know me,
that I am the LORD, who exercises
kindness,
justice and righteousness on earth,
for in these I delight,"
declares the LORD.

25 "The days are coming," declares the
LORD, "when I will punish all who are circumcised only in the flesh— 26 Egypt, Judah, Edom, Ammon, Moab and all who
live in the wilderness in distant places.ᵃ
For all these nations are really uncircumcised, and even the whole house of Israel
is uncircumcised in heart."

>> INSTANT ACCESS

Only about 1 person out of 100 comes anywhere near being a genius. That means that 99 aren't as smart. Comparing yourself to others can make you feel inferior. Even dumb. And that's not a comfortable feeling at all. There are more important things than being smart. Or being strong or rich or athletic. Jeremiah says there is only one thing you should boast about: that you understand and know God (Jeremiah 9:24). Knowing God makes you special in a way that being smarter or stronger than others never could. Knowing God makes you a child of the King, and you're important to him.

{Jeremiah 9:23-24}

God and Idols

10 Hear what the LORD says to you, people of Israel. 2 This is what the LORD says:

"Do not learn the ways of the nations
or be terrified by signs in the
heavens,
though the nations are terrified by
them.
3 For the practices of the peoples are
worthless;

ᵃ 26 Or wilderness and who clip the hair by their foreheads

they cut a tree out of the forest,
and a craftsman shapes it with his
chisel.
4 They adorn it with silver and gold;
they fasten it with hammer and
nails
so it will not totter.
5 Like a scarecrow in a cucumber field,
their idols cannot speak;
they must be carried
because they cannot walk.
Do not fear them;
they can do no harm
nor can they do any good."

6 No one is like you, Lord;
you are great,
and your name is mighty in power.
7 Who should not fear you,
King of the nations?
This is your due.
Among all the wise leaders of the
nations
and in all their kingdoms,
there is no one like you.

8 They are all senseless and foolish;
they are taught by worthless
wooden idols.
9 Hammered silver is brought from
Tarshish
and gold from Uphaz.
What the craftsman and goldsmith
have made
is then dressed in blue and
purple—
all made by skilled workers.
10 But the Lord is the true God;
he is the living God, the eternal
King.
When he is angry, the earth trembles;
the nations cannot endure his
wrath.

11 "Tell them this: 'These gods, who did
not make the heavens and the earth, will
perish from the earth and from under the
heavens.' "*a*

12 But God made the earth by his power;
he founded the world by his wisdom
and stretched out the heavens by
his understanding.

13 When he thunders, the waters in the
heavens roar;
he makes clouds rise from the ends
of the earth.
He sends lightning with the rain
and brings out the wind from his
storehouses.

14 Everyone is senseless and without
knowledge;
every goldsmith is shamed by his
idols.
The images he makes are a fraud;
they have no breath in them.
15 They are worthless, the objects of
mockery;
when their judgment comes, they
will perish.
16 He who is the Portion of Jacob is not
like these,
for he is the Maker of all things,
including Israel, the people of his
inheritance—
the Lord Almighty is his name.

Coming Destruction

17 Gather up your belongings to leave the
land,
you who live under siege.
18 For this is what the Lord says:
"At this time I will hurl out
those who live in this land;
I will bring distress on them
so that they may be captured."

19 Woe to me because of my injury!
My wound is incurable!
Yet I said to myself,
"This is my sickness, and I must
endure it."
20 My tent is destroyed;
all its ropes are snapped.
My children are gone from me and are
no more;
no one is left now to pitch my tent
or to set up my shelter.
21 The shepherds are senseless
and do not inquire of the Lord;
so they do not prosper
and all their flock is scattered.
22 Listen! The report is coming—
a great commotion from the land of
the north!

---

a 11 The text of this verse is in Aramaic.

It will make the towns of Judah
desolate,
a haunt of jackals.

Jeremiah's Prayer

23 LORD, I know that people's lives are
not their own;
it is not for them to direct their
steps.
24 Discipline me, LORD, but only in due
measure—
not in your anger,
or you will reduce me to nothing.
25 Pour out your wrath on the nations
that do not acknowledge you,
on the peoples who do not call on
your name.
For they have devoured Jacob;
they have devoured him completely
and destroyed his homeland.

The Covenant Is Broken

11 This is the word that came to Jeremiah from the LORD: 2 "Listen to the terms of this covenant and tell them to the people of Judah and to those who live in Jerusalem. 3 Tell them that this is what the LORD, the God of Israel, says: 'Cursed is the one who does not obey the terms of this covenant— 4 the terms I commanded your ancestors when I brought them out of Egypt, out of the iron-smelting furnace.' I said, 'Obey me and do everything I command you, and you will be my people, and I will be your God. 5 Then I will fulfill the oath I swore to your ancestors, to give them a land flowing with milk and honey'—the land you possess today."

I answered, "Amen, LORD."

6 The LORD said to me, "Proclaim all these words in the towns of Judah and in the streets of Jerusalem: 'Listen to the terms of this covenant and follow them. 7 From the time I brought your ancestors up from Egypt until today, I warned them again and again, saying, "Obey me." 8 But they did not listen or pay attention; instead, they followed the stubbornness of their evil hearts. So I brought on them all the curses of the covenant I had commanded them to follow but that they did not keep.' "

9 Then the LORD said to me, "There is a conspiracy among the people of Judah and those who live in Jerusalem. 10 They have returned to the sins of their ancestors, who refused to listen to my words. They have followed other gods to serve them. Both Israel and Judah have broken the covenant I made with their ancestors. 11 Therefore this is what the LORD says: 'I will bring on them a disaster they cannot escape. Although they cry out to me, I will not listen to them. 12 The towns of Judah and the people of Jerusalem will go and cry out to the gods to whom they burn incense, but they will not help them at all when disaster strikes. 13 You, Judah, have as many gods as you have towns; and the altars you have set up to burn incense to that shameful god Baal are as many as the streets of Jerusalem.'

14 "Do not pray for this people or offer any plea or petition for them, because I will not listen when they call to me in the time of their distress.

15 "What is my beloved doing in my
temple
as she, with many others, works out
her evil schemes?
Can consecrated meat avert your
punishment?
When you engage in your wickedness,
then you rejoice. [a]"

16 The LORD called you a thriving olive
tree
with fruit beautiful in form.
But with the roar of a mighty storm
he will set it on fire,
and its branches will be broken.

17 The LORD Almighty, who planted you, has decreed disaster for you, because the people of both Israel and Judah have done evil and aroused my anger by burning incense to Baal.

Plot Against Jeremiah

18 Because the LORD revealed their plot to me, I knew it, for at that time he showed me what they were doing. 19 I had been like a gentle lamb led to the slaugh-

---

a 15 Or Could consecrated meat avert your punishment? / Then you would rejoice

ter; I did not realize that they had plotted against me, saying,

"Let us destroy the tree and its fruit;
let us cut him off from the land of the living,
that his name be remembered no more."

20 But you, LORD Almighty, who judge righteously
and test the heart and mind,
let me see your vengeance on them,
for to you I have committed my cause.

21 Therefore this is what the LORD says about the people of Anathoth who are threatening to kill you, saying, "Do not prophesy in the name of the LORD or you will die by our hands"— 22 therefore this is what the LORD Almighty says: "I will punish them. Their young men will die by the sword, their sons and daughters by famine. 23 Not even a remnant will be left to them, because I will bring disaster on the people of Anathoth in the year of their punishment."

Jeremiah's Complaint

12 You are always righteous, LORD,
when I bring a case before you.
Yet I would speak with you about your justice:
Why does the way of the wicked prosper?
Why do all the faithless live at ease?
2 You have planted them, and they have taken root;
they grow and bear fruit.
You are always on their lips
but far from their hearts.
3 Yet you know me, LORD;
you see me and test my thoughts about you.
Drag them off like sheep to be butchered!
Set them apart for the day of slaughter!
4 How long will the land lie parched
and the grass in every field be withered?

Because those who live in it are wicked,
the animals and birds have perished.
Moreover, the people are saying,
"He will not see what happens to us."

God's Answer

5 "If you have raced with men on foot
and they have worn you out,
how can you compete with horses?
If you stumble^a in safe country,
how will you manage in the thickets by^b the Jordan?
6 Your relatives, members of your own family—
even they have betrayed you;
they have raised a loud cry against you.
Do not trust them,
though they speak well of you.

7 "I will forsake my house,
abandon my inheritance;
I will give the one I love
into the hands of her enemies.
8 My inheritance has become to me
like a lion in the forest.
She roars at me;
therefore I hate her.
9 Has not my inheritance become to me
like a speckled bird of prey
that other birds of prey surround and attack?
Go and gather all the wild beasts;
bring them to devour.
10 Many shepherds will ruin my vineyard
and trample down my field;
they will turn my pleasant field
into a desolate wasteland.
11 It will be made a wasteland,
parched and desolate before me;
the whole land will be laid waste
because there is no one who cares.
12 Over all the barren heights in the desert
destroyers will swarm,
for the sword of the LORD will devour
from one end of the land to the other;
no one will be safe.

---

^a 5 Or *you feel secure only*   ^b 5 Or *the flooding of*

13 They will sow wheat but reap thorns;
　　they will wear themselves out but
　　　gain nothing.
　They will bear the shame of their
　　　harvest
　　because of the LORD's fierce anger."

14 This is what the LORD says: "As for all my wicked neighbors who seize the inheritance I gave my people Israel, I will uproot them from their lands and I will uproot the people of Judah from among them. 15 But after I uproot them, I will again have compassion and will bring each of them back to their own inheritance and their own country. 16 And if they learn well the ways of my people and swear by my name, saying, 'As surely as the LORD lives'—even as they once taught my people to swear by Baal—then they will be established among my people. 17 But if any nation does not listen, I will completely uproot and destroy it," declares the LORD.

A Linen Belt

13 This is what the LORD said to me: "Go and buy a linen belt and put it around your waist, but do not let it touch water." 2 So I bought a belt, as the LORD directed, and put it around my waist.

3 Then the word of the LORD came to me a second time: 4 "Take the belt you bought and are wearing around your waist, and go now to Perath[a] and hide it there in a crevice in the rocks." 5 So I went and hid it at Perath, as the LORD told me.

6 Many days later the LORD said to me, "Go now to Perath and get the belt I told you to hide there." 7 So I went to Perath and dug up the belt and took it from the place where I had hidden it, but now it was ruined and completely useless.

8 Then the word of the LORD came to me: 9 "This is what the LORD says: 'In the same way I will ruin the pride of Judah and the great pride of Jerusalem. 10 These wicked people, who refuse to listen to my words, who follow the stubbornness of their hearts and go after other gods to serve and worship them, will be like this belt—completely useless! 11 For as a belt is bound around the waist, so I bound all

the people of Israel and all the people of Judah to me,' declares the LORD, 'to be my people for my renown and praise and honor. But they have not listened.'

Wineskins

12 "Say to them: 'This is what the LORD, the God of Israel, says: Every wineskin should be filled with wine.' And if they say to you, 'Don't we know that every wineskin should be filled with wine?' 13 then tell them, 'This is what the LORD says: I

INSTANT ACCESS

Over and over in the Bible believers get upset and say things like, "Why does the way of the wicked prosper?" (Jeremiah 12:1). You probably know how they feel. It's the guy who lies and gossips about girls who gets the date with the one you like. And how about the girl whose mom types and corrects (and rewrites) her book report? She gets an A while you get a C. Sometimes it's easy to wonder, "Where is God, anyway?" But be sure to remember: Nobody gets away with doing wrong in the end. It's just frustrating now. But try not to get discouraged in doing good. God does know. And in the end you'll be the one who wins.

{Jeremiah 12:1–4}

---

am going to fill with drunkenness all who live in this land, including the kings who sit on David's throne, the priests, the prophets and all those living in Jerusalem. ¹⁴I will smash them one against the other, parents and children alike, declares the LORD. I will allow no pity or mercy or compassion to keep me from destroying them.'"

Threat of Captivity

¹⁵Hear and pay attention,
    do not be arrogant,
    for the LORD has spoken.
¹⁶Give glory to the LORD your God
    before he brings the darkness,
    before your feet stumble
    on the darkening hills.
You hope for light,
    but he will turn it to utter
        darkness
    and change it to deep gloom.
¹⁷If you do not listen,
    I will weep in secret
    because of your pride;
my eyes will weep bitterly,
    overflowing with tears,
    because the LORD's flock will be
        taken captive.

¹⁸Say to the king and to the queen
        mother,
    "Come down from your thrones,
    for your glorious crowns
    will fall from your heads."
¹⁹The cities in the Negev will be
        shut up,
    and there will be no one to open
        them.
All Judah will be carried into exile,
    carried completely away.

²⁰Look up and see
    those who are coming from the
        north.
Where is the flock that was entrusted
    to you,
    the sheep of which you boasted?
²¹What will you say when the LORD sets
        over you
    those you cultivated as your special
        allies?

Will not pain grip you
    like that of a woman in labor?
²²And if you ask yourself,
    "Why has this happened to me?" —
it is because of your many sins
    that your skirts have been torn off
    and your body mistreated.
²³Can an Ethiopianᵃ change his skin
    or a leopard its spots?
Neither can you do good
    who are accustomed to doing evil.

²⁴"I will scatter you like chaff
    driven by the desert wind.
²⁵This is your lot,
    the portion I have decreed for you,"
        declares the LORD,
    "because you have forgotten me
    and trusted in false gods.
²⁶I will pull up your skirts over your face
    that your shame may be seen—
²⁷your adulteries and lustful neighings,
    your shameless prostitution!
I have seen your detestable acts
    on the hills and in the fields.
Woe to you, Jerusalem!
    How long will you be unclean?"

Drought, Famine, Sword

14 This is the word of the LORD that came to Jeremiah concerning the drought:

²"Judah mourns,
    her cities languish;
they wail for the land,
    and a cry goes up from Jerusalem.
³The nobles send their servants for
        water;
    they go to the cisterns
    but find no water.
They return with their jars unfilled;
    dismayed and despairing,
    they cover their heads.
⁴The ground is cracked
    because there is no rain in the
        land;
the farmers are dismayed
    and cover their heads.
⁵Even the doe in the field
    deserts her newborn fawn
    because there is no grass.

ᵃ 23 Hebrew *Cushite* (probably a person from the upper Nile region)

⁶Wild donkeys stand on the barren
heights
and pant like jackals;
their eyes fail
for lack of food."

⁷Although our sins testify against us,
do something, LORD, for the sake of
your name.
For we have often rebelled;
we have sinned against you.
⁸You who are the hope of Israel,
its Savior in times of distress,
why are you like a stranger in the
land,
like a traveler who stays only a
night?
⁹Why are you like a man taken by
surprise,
like a warrior powerless to
save?
You are among us, LORD,
and we bear your name;
do not forsake us!

¹⁰This is what the LORD says about this
people:

"They greatly love to wander;
they do not restrain their feet.
So the LORD does not accept them;
he will now remember their
wickedness
and punish them for their sins."

¹¹Then the LORD said to me, "Do not
pray for the well-being of this people. ¹²Although they fast, I will not listen to their
cry; though they offer burnt offerings and
grain offerings, I will not accept them. Instead, I will destroy them with the sword,
famine and plague."

¹³But I said, "Alas, Sovereign LORD! The
prophets keep telling them, 'You will not
see the sword or suffer famine. Indeed, I
will give you lasting peace in this place.'"

¹⁴Then the LORD said to me, "The
prophets are prophesying lies in my
name. I have not sent them or appointed
them or spoken to them. They are prophesying to you false visions, divinations,
idolatries*a* and the delusions of their own
minds. ¹⁵Therefore this is what the LORD

says about the prophets who are prophesying in my name: I did not send them, yet
they are saying, 'No sword or famine will
touch this land.' Those same prophets
will perish by sword and famine. ¹⁶And
the people they are prophesying to will be
thrown out into the streets of Jerusalem
because of the famine and sword. There
will be no one to bury them, their wives,
their sons and their daughters. I will pour
out on them the calamity they deserve.

¹⁷"Speak this word to them:

"'Let my eyes overflow with tears
night and day without ceasing;
for the Virgin Daughter, my people,
has suffered a grievous wound,
a crushing blow.
¹⁸If I go into the country,
I see those slain by the sword;
if I go into the city,
I see the ravages of famine.
Both prophet and priest
have gone to a land they know not.'"

¹⁹Have you rejected Judah completely?
Do you despise Zion?
Why have you afflicted us
so that we cannot be healed?
We hoped for peace
but no good has come,
for a time of healing
but there is only terror.
²⁰We acknowledge our wickedness,
LORD,
and the guilt of our ancestors;
we have indeed sinned against
you.
²¹For the sake of your name do not
despise us;
do not dishonor your glorious
throne.
Remember your covenant with us
and do not break it.
²²Do any of the worthless idols of the
nations bring rain?
Do the skies themselves send down
showers?
No, it is you, LORD our God.
Therefore our hope is in you,
for you are the one who does all
this.

---

a 14 Or *visions, worthless divinations*

15 Then the LORD said to me: "Even if Moses and Samuel were to stand before me, my heart would not go out to this people. Send them away from my presence! Let them go! ²And if they ask you, 'Where shall we go?' tell them, 'This is what the LORD says:

" 'Those destined for death, to death;
    those for the sword, to the sword;
those for starvation, to starvation;
    those for captivity, to captivity.'

³ "I will send four kinds of destroyers against them," declares the LORD, "the sword to kill and the dogs to drag away and the birds and the wild animals to devour and destroy. ⁴I will make them abhorrent to all the kingdoms of the earth because of what Manasseh son of Hezekiah king of Judah did in Jerusalem.

⁵ "Who will have pity on you,
        Jerusalem?
    Who will mourn for you?
    Who will stop to ask how you are?
⁶ You have rejected me," declares the
        LORD.
    "You keep on backsliding.
So I will reach out and destroy you;
    I am tired of holding back.
⁷ I will winnow them with a winnowing
        fork
    at the city gates of the land.
I will bring bereavement and
        destruction on my people,
    for they have not changed their
        ways.
⁸ I will make their widows more
        numerous
    than the sand of the sea.
At midday I will bring a destroyer
    against the mothers of their young
        men;
suddenly I will bring down on them
    anguish and terror.
⁹ The mother of seven will grow
        faint
    and breathe her last.
Her sun will set while it is still day;
    she will be disgraced and
        humiliated.

I will put the survivors to the sword
    before their enemies,"
                    declares the LORD.

¹⁰ Alas, my mother, that you gave me
        birth,
    a man with whom the whole land
        strives and contends!
I have neither lent nor borrowed,
    yet everyone curses me.

¹¹ The LORD said,

"Surely I will deliver you for a good
        purpose;
    surely I will make your enemies
        plead with you
in times of disaster and times of
    distress.

¹² "Can a man break iron—
    iron from the north—or
        bronze?

¹³ "Your wealth and your treasures
    I will give as plunder, without
        charge,
because of all your sins
    throughout your country.
¹⁴ I will enslave you to your enemies
    in[a] a land you do not know,
for my anger will kindle a fire
    that will burn against you."

¹⁵ LORD, you understand;
    remember me and care for me.
    Avenge me on my persecutors.
You are long-suffering—do not take
        me away;
    think of how I suffer reproach for
        your sake.
¹⁶ When your words came, I ate them;
    they were my joy and my heart's
        delight,
for I bear your name,
    LORD God Almighty.
¹⁷ I never sat in the company of
        revelers,
    never made merry with them;
I sat alone because your hand was
        on me
    and you had filled me with
        indignation.

---

[a] 14 Some Hebrew manuscripts, Septuagint and Syriac (see also 17:4); most Hebrew manuscripts *I will cause your enemies to bring you / into*

LORD, you understand;
remember me
and care for me.

Jeremiah 15:15

¹⁸Why is my pain unending
    and my wound grievous and
        incurable?
You are to me like a deceptive brook,
    like a spring that fails.

¹⁹Therefore this is what the LORD says:

"If you repent, I will restore you
    that you may serve me;
if you utter worthy, not worthless,
        words,
    you will be my spokesman.
Let this people turn to you,
    but you must not turn to them.
²⁰I will make you a wall to this people,
    a fortified wall of bronze;
they will fight against you
    but will not overcome you,
for I am with you
    to rescue and save you,"
                    declares the LORD.
²¹"I will save you from the hands of the
        wicked
    and deliver you from the grasp of
        the cruel."

Day of Disaster

16 Then the word of the LORD came to me: ²"You must not marry and have sons or daughters in this place." ³For this is what the LORD says about the sons and daughters born in this land and about the women who are their mothers and the men who are their fathers: ⁴"They will die of deadly diseases. They will not be mourned or buried but will be like dung lying on the ground. They will perish by sword and famine, and their dead bod-

ies will become food for the birds and the wild animals."

⁵For this is what the LORD says: "Do not enter a house where there is a funeral meal; do not go to mourn or show sympathy, because I have withdrawn my blessing, my love and my pity from this people," declares the LORD. ⁶"Both high and low will die in this land. They will not be buried or mourned, and no one will cut themselves or shave their head for the dead. ⁷No one will offer food to comfort those who mourn for the dead—not even for a father or a mother—nor will anyone give them a drink to console them.

⁸"And do not enter a house where there is feasting and sit down to eat and drink. ⁹For this is what the LORD Almighty, the God of Israel, says: Before your eyes and in your days I will bring an end to the sounds of joy and gladness and to the voices of bride and bridegroom in this place.

¹⁰"When you tell these people all this and they ask you, 'Why has the LORD decreed such a great disaster against us? What wrong have we done? What sin have we committed against the LORD our God?' ¹¹then say to them, 'It is because your ancestors forsook me,' declares the LORD, 'and followed other gods and served and worshiped them. They forsook me and did not keep my law. ¹²But you have behaved more wickedly than your ancestors. See how all of you are following the stubbornness of your evil hearts instead of obeying me. ¹³So I will throw you out of this land into a land neither you nor your ancestors have known, and there you will serve other gods day and night, for I will show you no favor.'

¹⁴"However, the days are coming," declares the LORD, "when it will no longer be said, 'As surely as the LORD lives, who brought the Israelites up out of Egypt,' ¹⁵but it will be said, 'As surely as the LORD lives, who brought the Israelites up out of the land of the north and out of all the countries where he had banished them.' For I will restore them to the land I gave their ancestors.

¹⁶"But now I will send for many fishermen," declares the LORD, "and they will

catch them. After that I will send for many hunters, and they will hunt them down on every mountain and hill and from the crevices of the rocks. ¹⁷My eyes are on all their ways; they are not hidden from me, nor is their sin concealed from my eyes. ¹⁸I will repay them double for their wickedness and their sin, because they have defiled my land with the lifeless forms of their vile images and have filled my inheritance with their detestable idols."

¹⁹Lord, my strength and my fortress,
  my refuge in time of distress,
to you the nations will come
  from the ends of the earth and
    say,
"Our ancestors possessed nothing but
    false gods,
  worthless idols that did them no
    good.
²⁰Do people make their own gods?
  Yes, but they are not gods!"

²¹"Therefore I will teach them—
  this time I will teach them
  my power and might.
Then they will know
  that my name is the Lord.

17

"Judah's sin is engraved with an
    iron tool,
  inscribed with a flint point,
on the tablets of their hearts
  and on the horns of their altars.
²Even their children remember
  their altars and Asherah poles[a]
beside the spreading trees
  and on the high hills.
³My mountain in the land
  and your[b] wealth and all your
    treasures
I will give away as plunder,
  together with your high places,
  because of sin throughout your
    country.
⁴Through your own fault you will
    lose
  the inheritance I gave you.
I will enslave you to your enemies
  in a land you do not know,
for you have kindled my anger,
  and it will burn forever."

⁵This is what the Lord says:

"Cursed is the one who trusts in
    man,
  who draws strength from mere
    flesh
  and whose heart turns away from
    the Lord.
⁶That person will be like a bush in the
    wastelands;
  they will not see prosperity when it
    comes.
They will dwell in the parched places
    of the desert,
  in a salt land where no one lives.

⁷"But blessed is the one who trusts in
    the Lord,
  whose confidence is in him.
⁸They will be like a tree planted by the
    water
  that sends out its roots by the
    stream.
It does not fear when heat comes;
  its leaves are always green.
It has no worries in a year of
    drought
  and never fails to bear fruit."

⁹The heart is deceitful above all
    things
  and beyond cure.
  Who can understand it?

¹⁰"I the Lord search the heart
  and examine the mind,
to reward each person according to
    their conduct,
  according to what their deeds
    deserve."

¹¹Like a partridge that hatches eggs it
    did not lay
  are those who gain riches by unjust
    means.
When their lives are half gone, their
    riches will desert them,
  and in the end they will prove to be
    fools.

¹²A glorious throne, exalted from the
    beginning,
  is the place of our sanctuary.

---

a 2 That is, wooden symbols of the goddess Asherah   b 2,3 Or hills / ³and the mountains of the land. / Your

13 LORD, you are the hope of Israel;
　　all who forsake you will be put to
　　　shame.
　　Those who turn away from you will be
　　　written in the dust
　　　because they have forsaken the
　　　　LORD,
　　　the spring of living water.

14 Heal me, LORD, and I will be healed;
　　save me and I will be saved,
　　for you are the one I praise.

15 They keep saying to me,
　　"Where is the word of the LORD?
　　Let it now be fulfilled!"

16 I have not run away from being your
　　　shepherd;
　　you know I have not desired the day
　　　of despair.
　　What passes my lips is open before
　　　you.

17 Do not be a terror to me;
　　you are my refuge in the day of
　　　disaster.

18 Let my persecutors be put to shame,
　　but keep me from shame;
　　let them be terrified,
　　but keep me from terror.
　　Bring on them the day of disaster;
　　destroy them with double
　　　destruction.

Keeping the Sabbath Day Holy

19 This is what the LORD said to me:
"Go and stand at the Gate of the People,[a] through which the kings of Judah
go in and out; stand also at all the other
gates of Jerusalem. 20 Say to them, 'Hear
the word of the LORD, you kings of Judah
and all people of Judah and everyone living in Jerusalem who come through these
gates. 21 This is what the LORD says: Be
careful not to carry a load on the Sabbath day or bring it through the gates of
Jerusalem. 22 Do not bring a load out of
your houses or do any work on the Sabbath, but keep the Sabbath day holy, as
I commanded your ancestors. 23 Yet they
did not listen or pay attention; they were
stiff-necked and would not listen or respond to discipline. 24 But if you are careful to obey me, declares the LORD, and

---

INSTANT ACCESS

Even teens brought up in Christian homes will challenge their parents' standards of right and wrong. And they'll question the Bible too. That's OK, because questioning is a first step toward developing personal convictions. The problems begin when you decide to accept the standards of society and ignore God's standards. Jeremiah warns that "the heart is deceitful" (Jeremiah 17:9). People don't decide against God's ways because they've thought things through. People decide against God's ways because they're attracted to sin. Read this passage and begin to think for yourself and depend on God.

{Jeremiah 17:5–9}

---

bring no load through the gates of this
city on the Sabbath, but keep the Sabbath day holy by not doing any work on
it, 25 then kings who sit on David's throne
will come through the gates of this city
with their officials. They and their officials
will come riding in chariots and on horses, accompanied by the men of Judah
and those living in Jerusalem, and this
city will be inhabited forever. 26 People will
come from the towns of Judah and the
villages around Jerusalem, from the ter-

---

a 19 Or *Army*

ritory of Benjamin and the western foot-hills, from the hill country and the Negev, bringing burnt offerings and sacrifices, grain offerings and incense, and bringing thank offerings to the house of the LORD. 27 But if you do not obey me to keep the Sabbath day holy by not carrying any load as you come through the gates of Jerusalem on the Sabbath day, then I will kindle an unquenchable fire in the gates of Jerusalem that will consume her fortresses.' "

At the Potter's House

18 This is the word that came to Jeremiah from the LORD: 2 "Go down to the potter's house, and there I will give you my message." 3 So I went down to the potter's house, and I saw him working at the wheel. 4 But the pot he was shaping from the clay was marred in his hands; so the potter formed it into another pot, shaping it as seemed best to him.

5 Then the word of the LORD came to me. 6 He said, "Can I not do with you, Israel, as this potter does?" declares the LORD. "Like clay in the hand of the potter, so are you in my hand, Israel. 7 If at any time I announce that a nation or kingdom is to be uprooted, torn down and destroyed, 8 and if that nation I warned repents of its evil, then I will relent and not inflict on it the disaster I had planned. 9 And if at another time I announce that a nation or kingdom is to be built up and planted, 10 and if it does evil in my sight and does not obey me, then I will reconsider the good I had intended to do for it.

11 "Now therefore say to the people of Judah and those living in Jerusalem, 'This is what the LORD says: Look! I am preparing a disaster for you and devising a plan against you. So turn from your evil ways, each one of you, and reform your ways and your actions.' 12 But they will reply, 'It's no use. We will continue with our own plans; we will all follow the stubbornness of our evil hearts.' "

13 Therefore this is what the LORD says:

"Inquire among the nations:
    Who has ever heard anything like
        this?

A most horrible thing has been done
    by Virgin Israel.
14 Does the snow of Lebanon
    ever vanish from its rocky slopes?
Do its cool waters from distant
        sources
    ever stop flowing?[a]
15 Yet my people have forgotten me;
    they burn incense to worthless
        idols,
which made them stumble in their
        ways,
    in the ancient paths.
They made them walk in byways,
    on roads not built up.
16 Their land will be an object of horror
    and of lasting scorn;
all who pass by will be appalled
    and will shake their heads.
17 Like a wind from the east,
    I will scatter them before their
        enemies;
I will show them my back and not my
        face
    in the day of their disaster."

18 They said, "Come, let's make plans against Jeremiah; for the teaching of the law by the priest will not cease, nor will counsel from the wise, nor the word from the prophets. So come, let's attack him with our tongues and pay no attention to anything he says."

19 Listen to me, LORD;
    hear what my accusers are saying!
20 Should good be repaid with evil?
    Yet they have dug a pit for me.
Remember that I stood before you
    and spoke in their behalf
    to turn your wrath away from them.
21 So give their children over to famine;
    hand them over to the power of the
        sword.
Let their wives be made childless and
        widows;
    let their men be put to death,
    their young men slain by the sword
        in battle.
22 Let a cry be heard from their houses
    when you suddenly bring invaders
        against them,

---

a 14 The meaning of the Hebrew for this sentence is uncertain.

for they have dug a pit to capture me
 and have hidden snares for my feet.
²³ But you, Lord, know
 all their plots to kill me.
Do not forgive their crimes
 or blot out their sins from your
 sight.
Let them be overthrown before you;
 deal with them in the time of your
 anger.

19 This is what the Lord says: "Go and buy a clay jar from a potter. Take along some of the elders of the people and of the priests ² and go out to the Valley of Ben Hinnom, near the entrance of the Potsherd Gate. There proclaim the words I tell you, ³ and say, 'Hear the word of the Lord, you kings of Judah and people of Jerusalem. This is what the Lord Almighty, the God of Israel, says: Listen! I am going to bring a disaster on this place that will make the ears of everyone who hears of it tingle. ⁴ For they have forsaken me and made this a place of foreign gods; they have burned incense in it to gods that neither they nor their ancestors nor the kings of Judah ever knew, and they have filled this place with the blood of the innocent. ⁵ They have built the high places of Baal to burn their children in the fire as offerings to Baal—something I did not command or mention, nor did it enter my mind. ⁶ So beware, the days are coming, declares the Lord, when people will no longer call this place Topheth or the Valley of Ben Hinnom, but the Valley of Slaughter.

⁷ " 'In this place I will ruinᵃ the plans of Judah and Jerusalem. I will make them fall by the sword before their enemies, at the hands of those who want to kill them, and I will give their carcasses as food to the birds and the wild animals. ⁸ I will devastate this city and make it an object of horror and scorn; all who pass by will be appalled and will scoff because of all its wounds. ⁹ I will make them eat the flesh of their sons and daughters, and they will eat one another's flesh because their enemies will press the siege so hard against them to destroy them.'

¹⁰ "Then break the jar while those who go with you are watching, ¹¹ and say to them, 'This is what the Lord Almighty says: I will smash this nation and this city just as this potter's jar is smashed and cannot be repaired. They will bury the dead in Topheth until there is no more room. ¹² This is what I will do to this place and to those who live here, declares the Lord. I will make this city like Topheth. ¹³ The houses in Jerusalem and those of the kings of Judah will be defiled like this place, Topheth—all the houses where they burned incense on the roofs to all the starry hosts and poured out drink offerings to other gods.' "

¹⁴ Jeremiah then returned from Topheth, where the Lord had sent him to prophesy, and stood in the court of the Lord's temple and said to all the people, ¹⁵ "This is what the Lord Almighty, the God of Israel, says: 'Listen! I am going to bring on this city and all the villages around it every disaster I pronounced against them, because they were stiff-necked and would not listen to my words.' "

Jeremiah and Pashhur

20 When the priest Pashhur son of Immer, the official in charge of the temple of the Lord, heard Jeremiah prophesying these things, ² he had Jeremiah the prophet beaten and put in the stocks at the Upper Gate of Benjamin at the Lord's temple. ³ The next day, when Pashhur released him from the stocks, Jeremiah said to him, "The Lord's name for you is not Pashhur, but Terror on Every Side. ⁴ For this is what the Lord says: 'I will make you a terror to yourself and to all your friends; with your own eyes you will see them fall by the sword of their enemies. I will give all Judah into the hands of the king of Babylon, who will carry them away to Babylon or put them to the sword. ⁵ I will deliver all the wealth of this city into the hands of their enemies—all its products, all its valuables and all the treasures of the kings of Judah. They will take it away as plunder and carry it off to Babylon. ⁶ And you, Pashhur, and all

---

ᵃ 7 The Hebrew for *ruin* sounds like the Hebrew for *jar* (see verses 1 and 10).

who live in your house will go into exile to Babylon. There you will die and be buried, you and all your friends to whom you have prophesied lies.'"

Jeremiah's Complaint

[7] You deceived[a] me, LORD, and I was deceived[a];
　you overpowered me and prevailed.
I am ridiculed all day long;
　everyone mocks me.
[8] Whenever I speak, I cry out
　proclaiming violence and
　　destruction.
So the word of the LORD has
　brought me
　insult and reproach all day long.
[9] But if I say, "I will not mention his
　word
　or speak anymore in his name,"
his word is in my heart like a fire,
　a fire shut up in my bones.
I am weary of holding it in;
　indeed, I cannot.
[10] I hear many whispering,
　"Terror on every side!
　Denounce him! Let's denounce
　　him!"
All my friends
　are waiting for me to slip, saying,
"Perhaps he will be deceived;
　then we will prevail over him
　and take our revenge on him."

[11] But the LORD is with me like a mighty
　warrior;
　so my persecutors will stumble and
　　not prevail.
They will fail and be thoroughly
　disgraced;
　their dishonor will never be
　　forgotten.
[12] LORD Almighty, you who examine the
　righteous
　and probe the heart and mind,
let me see your vengeance on them,
　for to you I have committed my
　　cause.

[13] Sing to the LORD!
　Give praise to the LORD!

He rescues the life of the needy
　from the hands of the wicked.

[14] Cursed be the day I was born!
　May the day my mother bore me not
　　be blessed!
[15] Cursed be the man who brought my
　father the news,
　who made him very glad, saying,
　"A child is born to you—a son!"
[16] May that man be like the towns
　the LORD overthrew without pity.
May he hear wailing in the morning,
　a battle cry at noon.
[17] For he did not kill me in the womb,
　with my mother as my grave,
　her womb enlarged forever.
[18] Why did I ever come out of the womb
　to see trouble and sorrow
　and to end my days in shame?

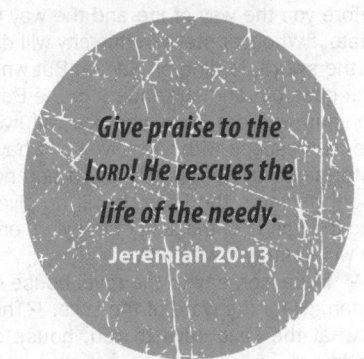

Give praise to the LORD! He rescues the life of the needy.
Jeremiah 20:13

God Rejects Zedekiah's Request

21 The word came to Jeremiah from the LORD when King Zedekiah sent to him Pashhur son of Malkijah and the priest Zephaniah son of Maaseiah. They said: [2] "Inquire now of the LORD for us because Nebuchadnezzar[b] king of Babylon is attacking us. Perhaps the LORD will perform wonders for us as in times past so that he will withdraw from us."

[3] But Jeremiah answered them, "Tell Zedekiah, [4] 'This is what the LORD, the God of Israel, says: I am about to turn against you the weapons of war that are

[a] 7 Or persuaded　[b] 2 Hebrew Nebuchadrezzar, of which Nebuchadnezzar is a variant; here and often in Jeremiah and Ezekiel

in your hands, which you are using to fight the king of Babylon and the Babylonians[a] who are outside the wall besieging you. And I will gather them inside this city. [5]I myself will fight against you with an outstretched hand and a mighty arm in furious anger and in great wrath. [6]I will strike down those who live in this city—both man and beast—and they will die of a terrible plague. [7]After that, declares the Lord, I will give Zedekiah king of Judah, his officials and the people in this city who survive the plague, sword and famine, into the hands of Nebuchadnezzar king of Babylon and to their enemies who want to kill them. He will put them to the sword; he will show them no mercy or pity or compassion.'

[8]"Furthermore, tell the people, 'This is what the Lord says: See, I am setting before you the way of life and the way of death. [9]Whoever stays in this city will die by the sword, famine or plague. But whoever goes out and surrenders to the Babylonians who are besieging you will live; they will escape with their lives. [10]I have determined to do this city harm and not good, declares the Lord. It will be given into the hands of the king of Babylon, and he will destroy it with fire.'

[11]"Moreover, say to the royal house of Judah, 'Hear the word of the Lord. [12]This is what the Lord says to you, house of David:

" 'Administer justice every
        morning;
    rescue from the hand of the
        oppressor
    the one who has been robbed,
    or my wrath will break out and burn
        like fire
    because of the evil you have
        done—
    burn with no one to quench it.
[13]I am against you, Jerusalem,
    you who live above this valley
    on the rocky plateau, declares the
        Lord—
you who say, "Who can come
        against us?
    Who can enter our refuge?"

[14]I will punish you as your deeds
        deserve,
    declares the Lord.
I will kindle a fire in your forests
    that will consume everything around
        you.' "

Judgment Against Wicked Kings

22 This is what the Lord says: "Go down to the palace of the king of Judah and proclaim this message there: [2]'Hear the word of the Lord to you, king of Judah, you who sit on David's throne— you, your officials and your people who come through these gates. [3]This is what the Lord says: Do what is just and right. Rescue from the hand of the oppressor the one who has been robbed. Do no wrong or violence to the foreigner, the fatherless or the widow, and do not shed innocent blood in this place. [4]For if you are careful to carry out these commands, then kings who sit on David's throne will come through the gates of this palace, riding in chariots and on horses, accompanied by their officials and their people. [5]But if you do not obey these commands, declares the Lord, I swear by myself that this palace will become a ruin.' "

[6]For this is what the Lord says about the palace of the king of Judah:

"Though you are like Gilead to me,
    like the summit of Lebanon,
I will surely make you like a
        wasteland,
    like towns not inhabited.
[7]I will send destroyers against
        you,
    each man with his weapons,
and they will cut up your fine cedar
        beams
    and throw them into the fire.

[8]"People from many nations will pass by this city and will ask one another, 'Why has the Lord done such a thing to this great city?' [9]And the answer will be: 'Because they have forsaken the covenant of the Lord their God and have worshiped and served other gods.' "

---

[a] 4 Or Chaldeans; also in verse 9

10 Do not weep for the dead king or
  mourn his loss;
rather, weep bitterly for him who is
  exiled,
because he will never return
  nor see his native land again.

11 For this is what the LORD says about Shallum[a] son of Josiah, who succeeded his father as king of Judah but has gone from
this place: "He will never return. 12 He will
die in the place where they have led him
captive; he will not see this land again."

13 "Woe to him who builds his palace by
  unrighteousness,
his upper rooms by injustice,
making his own people work for
  nothing,
  not paying them for their labor.

14 He says, 'I will build myself a great
  palace
with spacious upper rooms.'
So he makes large windows in it,
  panels it with cedar
  and decorates it in red.

15 "Does it make you a king
  to have more and more cedar?
Did not your father have food and
  drink?
He did what was right and just,
  so all went well with him.
16 He defended the cause of the poor
  and needy,
  and so all went well.
Is that not what it means to
  know me?"
  declares the LORD.

a 11 Also called *Jehoahaz*

TO THE POINT

Care About People

Ever dream about having a sports car? Or a designer wardrobe? Some people feel they have to have such things. They'll do anything to get them.

One king in Jeremiah's day felt that way. Jeremiah warned him that since his eyes and his heart were set only on dishonest gain (Jeremiah 22:13), he would soon die and have the "burial of a donkey" (Jeremiah 22:19). To that king possessions were more important than people. He didn't care if he hurt others as long as he got what he wanted.

It's important to remember that people are more important than possessions. If you set your heart on what is right and just, if you defend the cause of the poor and needy, then you'll know God better, and all will go well with you (Jeremiah 22:15–16).

17 "But your eyes and your heart
  are set only on dishonest gain,
on shedding innocent blood
  and on oppression and extortion."

18 Therefore this is what the LORD says about Jehoiakim son of Josiah king of Judah:

"They will not mourn for him:
  'Alas, my brother! Alas, my
    sister!'
They will not mourn for him:
  'Alas, my master! Alas, his
    splendor!'
19 He will have the burial of a donkey—
  dragged away and thrown
  outside the gates of Jerusalem."

20 "Go up to Lebanon and cry out,
  let your voice be heard in Bashan,
cry out from Abarim,
  for all your allies are crushed.
21 I warned you when you felt secure,
  but you said, 'I will not listen!'
This has been your way from your
    youth;
  you have not obeyed me.
22 The wind will drive all your shepherds
    away,
  and your allies will go into exile.
Then you will be ashamed and
    disgraced
  because of all your wickedness.
23 You who live in 'Lebanon,ᵃ'
  who are nestled in cedar buildings,
how you will groan when pangs come
    upon you,
  pain like that of a woman in labor!

24 "As surely as I live," declares the LORD, "even if you, Jehoiachinᵇ son of Jehoiakim king of Judah, were a signet ring on my right hand, I would still pull you off. 25 I will deliver you into the hands of those who want to kill you, those you fear—Nebuchadnezzar king of Babylon and the Babylonians.ᶜ 26 I will hurl you and the mother who gave you birth into another country, where neither of you was born, and there you both will die. 27 You will never come back to the land you long to return to."

28 Is this man Jehoiachin a despised,
    broken pot,
  an object no one wants?
Why will he and his children be hurled
    out,
  cast into a land they do not know?
29 O land, land, land,
  hear the word of the LORD!
30 This is what the LORD says:
"Record this man as if childless,
  a man who will not prosper in his
    lifetime,
for none of his offspring will prosper,
  none will sit on the throne of David
  or rule anymore in Judah."

The Righteous Branch

23 "Woe to the shepherds who are destroying and scattering the sheep of my pasture!" declares the LORD. 2 Therefore this is what the LORD, the God of Israel, says to the shepherds who tend my people: "Because you have scattered my flock and driven them away and have not bestowed care on them, I will bestow punishment on you for the evil you have done," declares the LORD. 3 "I myself will gather the remnant of my flock out of all the countries where I have driven them and will bring them back to their pasture, where they will be fruitful and increase in number. 4 I will place shepherds over them who will tend them, and they will no longer be afraid or terrified, nor will any be missing," declares the LORD.

5 "The days are coming," declares the
    LORD,
  "when I will raise up for Davidᵈ a
    righteous Branch,
a King who will reign wisely
  and do what is just and right in the
    land.
6 In his days Judah will be saved
  and Israel will live in safety.
This is the name by which he will be
    called:
  The LORD Our Righteous Savior.

7 "So then, the days are coming," declares the LORD, "when people will no lon-

---

ᵃ 23 That is, the palace in Jerusalem (see 1 Kings 7:2)   ᵇ 24 Hebrew Koniah, a variant of Jehoiachin; also in verse 28
ᶜ 25 Or Chaldeans   ᵈ 5 Or up from David's line

ger say, 'As surely as the LORD lives, who brought the Israelites up out of Egypt,' [8]but they will say, 'As surely as the LORD lives, who brought the descendants of Israel up out of the land of the north and out of all the countries where he had banished them.' Then they will live in their own land."

Lying Prophets

[9]Concerning the prophets:

My heart is broken within me;
 all my bones tremble.
I am like a drunken man,
 like a strong man overcome by
  wine,
because of the LORD
 and his holy words.
[10]The land is full of adulterers;
 because of the curse[a] the land lies
  parched
 and the pastures in the wilderness
  are withered.
The prophets follow an evil course
 and use their power unjustly.

[11]"Both prophet and priest are godless;
 even in my temple I find their
  wickedness,"
   declares the LORD.
[12]"Therefore their path will become
  slippery;
 they will be banished to darkness
  and there they will fall.
I will bring disaster on them
 in the year they are punished,"
   declares the LORD.

[13]"Among the prophets of Samaria
 I saw this repulsive thing:
They prophesied by Baal
 and led my people Israel astray.
[14]And among the prophets of Jerusalem
 I have seen something horrible:
 They commit adultery and live a lie.
They strengthen the hands of
  evildoers,
 so that not one of them turns from
  their wickedness.
They are all like Sodom to me;
 the people of Jerusalem are like
  Gomorrah."

[15]Therefore this is what the LORD Almighty says concerning the prophets:

"I will make them eat bitter food
 and drink poisoned water,
because from the prophets of
  Jerusalem
 ungodliness has spread throughout
  the land."

[16]This is what the LORD Almighty says:

"Do not listen to what the prophets
 are prophesying to you;
 they fill you with false hopes.
They speak visions from their own
  minds,
 not from the mouth of the LORD.
[17]They keep saying to those who
  despise me,
 'The LORD says: You will have
  peace.'
And to all who follow the
  stubbornness of their hearts
 they say, 'No harm will come to
  you.'
[18]But which of them has stood in the
  council of the LORD
 to see or to hear his word?
Who has listened and heard his
  word?
[19]See, the storm of the LORD
 will burst out in wrath,
a whirlwind swirling down
 on the heads of the wicked.
[20]The anger of the LORD will not turn
  back
 until he fully accomplishes
 the purposes of his heart.
In days to come
 you will understand it clearly.
[21]I did not send these prophets,
 yet they have run with their
  message;
I did not speak to them,
 yet they have prophesied.
[22]But if they had stood in my council,
 they would have proclaimed my
  words to my people
and would have turned them from
  their evil ways
 and from their evil deeds.

---

[a] 10 Or because of these things

23 "Am I only a God nearby,"
　　　　declares the LORD,
　　"and not a God far away?
24 Who can hide in secret places
　　so that I cannot see them?"
　　　　declares the LORD.
　　"Do not I fill heaven and earth?"
　　　　declares the LORD.

25 "I have heard what the prophets say who prophesy lies in my name. They say, 'I had a dream! I had a dream!' 26 How long will this continue in the hearts of these lying prophets, who prophesy the delusions of their own minds? 27 They think the dreams they tell one another will make my people forget my name, just as their ancestors forgot my name through Baal worship. 28 Let the prophet who has a dream recount the dream, but let the one who has my word speak it faithfully. For what has straw to do with grain?" declares the LORD. 29 "Is not my word like fire," declares the LORD, "and like a hammer that breaks a rock in pieces?

30 "Therefore," declares the LORD, "I am against the prophets who steal from one another words supposedly from me. 31 Yes," declares the LORD, "I am against the prophets who wag their own tongues and yet declare, 'The LORD declares.' 32 Indeed, I am against those who prophesy false dreams," declares the LORD. "They tell them and lead my people astray with their reckless lies, yet I did not send or appoint them. They do not benefit these people in the least," declares the LORD.

False Prophecy

33 "When these people, or a prophet or a priest, ask you, 'What is the message from the LORD?' say to them, 'What message? I will forsake you, declares the LORD.' 34 If a prophet or a priest or anyone else claims, 'This is a message from the LORD,' I will punish them and their household. 35 This is what each of you keeps saying to your friends and other Israelites: 'What is the LORD's answer?' or 'What has the LORD spoken?' 36 But you must not mention 'a message from the LORD' again, because each one's word becomes their own message. So you distort the words of the living God, the LORD Almighty, our God. 37 This is what you keep saying to a prophet: 'What is the LORD's answer to you?' or 'What has the LORD spoken?' 38 Although you claim, 'This is a message from the LORD,' this is what the LORD says: You used the words, 'This is a message from the LORD,' even though I told you that you must not claim, 'This is a message from the LORD.' 39 Therefore, I will surely forget you and cast you out of my presence along with the city I gave to you and your ancestors. 40 I will bring on you everlasting disgrace—everlasting shame that will not be forgotten."

Two Baskets of Figs

24 After Jehoiachin[a] son of Jehoiakim king of Judah and the officials, the skilled workers and the artisans of Judah were carried into exile from Jerusalem to Babylon by Nebuchadnezzar king of Babylon, the LORD showed me two baskets of figs placed in front of the temple of the LORD. 2 One basket had very good figs, like those that ripen early; the other basket had very bad figs, so bad they could not be eaten.

3 Then the LORD asked me, "What do you see, Jeremiah?"

"Figs," I answered. "The good ones are very good, but the bad ones are so bad they cannot be eaten."

4 Then the word of the LORD came to me: 5 "This is what the LORD, the God of Israel, says: 'Like these good figs, I regard as good the exiles from Judah, whom I sent away from this place to the land of the Babylonians.[b] 6 My eyes will watch over them for their good, and I will bring them

> *I will give them a heart to know me . . . They will be my people, and I will be their God.*
>
> **Jeremiah 24:7**

---

a 1 Hebrew *Jeconiah*, a variant of *Jehoiachin*　　b 5 Or *Chaldeans*

back to this land. I will build them up and not tear them down; I will plant them and not uproot them. ⁷I will give them a heart to know me, that I am the LORD. They will be my people, and I will be their God, for they will return to me with all their heart.

⁸"'But like the bad figs, which are so bad they cannot be eaten,' says the LORD, 'so will I deal with Zedekiah king of Judah, his officials and the survivors from Jerusalem, whether they remain in this land or live in Egypt. ⁹I will make them abhorrent and an offense to all the kingdoms of the earth, a reproach and a byword, a curse[a] and an object of ridicule, wherever I banish them. ¹⁰I will send the sword, famine and plague against them until they are destroyed from the land I gave to them and their ancestors.'"

Seventy Years of Captivity

25 The word came to Jeremiah concerning all the people of Judah in the fourth year of Jehoiakim son of Josiah king of Judah, which was the first year of Nebuchadnezzar king of Babylon. ²So Jeremiah the prophet said to all the people of Judah and to all those living in Jerusalem: ³For twenty-three years—from the thirteenth year of Josiah son of Amon king of Judah until this very day—the word of the LORD has come to me and I have spoken to you again and again, but you have not listened.

⁴And though the LORD has sent all his servants the prophets to you again and again, you have not listened or paid any attention. ⁵They said, "Turn now, each of you, from your evil ways and your evil practices, and you can stay in the land the LORD gave to you and your ancestors for ever and ever. ⁶Do not follow other gods to serve and worship them; do not arouse my anger with what your hands have made. Then I will not harm you."

⁷"But you did not listen to me," declares the LORD, "and you have aroused my anger with what your hands have made, and you have brought harm to yourselves."

⁸Therefore the LORD Almighty says this: "Because you have not listened to my words, ⁹I will summon all the peoples of the north and my servant Nebuchadnezzar king of Babylon," declares the LORD, "and I will bring them against this land and its inhabitants and against all the surrounding nations. I will completely destroy[b] them and make them an object of horror and scorn, and an everlasting ruin. ¹⁰I will banish from them the sounds of joy and gladness, the voices of bride and bridegroom, the sound of millstones and the light of the lamp. ¹¹This whole country will become a desolate wasteland, and these nations will serve the king of Babylon seventy years.

¹²"But when the seventy years are fulfilled, I will punish the king of Babylon and his nation, the land of the Babylonians,[c] for their guilt," declares the LORD, "and will make it desolate forever. ¹³I will bring on that land all the things I have spoken against it, all that are written in this book and prophesied by Jeremiah against all the nations. ¹⁴They themselves will be enslaved by many nations and great kings; I will repay them according to their deeds and the work of their hands."

The Cup of God's Wrath

¹⁵This is what the LORD, the God of Israel, said to me: "Take from my hand this cup filled with the wine of my wrath and make all the nations to whom I send you drink it. ¹⁶When they drink it, they will stagger and go mad because of the sword I will send among them."

¹⁷So I took the cup from the LORD's hand and made all the nations to whom he sent me drink it: ¹⁸Jerusalem and the towns of Judah, its kings and officials, to make them a ruin and an object of horror and scorn, a curse[d]—as they are today; ¹⁹Pharaoh king of Egypt, his attendants, his officials and all his people, ²⁰and all the foreign people there; all the kings of Uz; all the kings of the Philistines (those of Ashkelon, Gaza, Ekron, and the people left at Ashdod); ²¹Edom, Moab and Am-

---

[a] 9 That is, their names will be used in cursing (see 29:22); or, others will see that they are cursed.   [b] 9 The Hebrew term refers to the irrevocable giving over of things or persons to the LORD, often by totally destroying them.   [c] 12 Or Chaldeans   [d] 18 That is, their names to be used in cursing (see 29:22); or, to be seen by others as cursed

mon; 22 all the kings of Tyre and Sidon; the kings of the coastlands across the sea; 23 Dedan, Tema, Buz and all who are in distant places*a*; 24 all the kings of Arabia and all the kings of the foreign people who live in the wilderness; 25 all the kings of Zimri, Elam and Media; 26 and all the kings of the north, near and far, one after the other—all the kingdoms on the face of the earth. And after all of them, the king of Sheshak*b* will drink it too.

27 "Then tell them, 'This is what the LORD Almighty, the God of Israel, says: Drink, get drunk and vomit, and fall to rise no more because of the sword I will send among you.' 28 But if they refuse to take the cup from your hand and drink, tell them, 'This is what the LORD Almighty says: You must drink it! 29 See, I am beginning to bring disaster on the city that bears my Name, and will you indeed go unpunished? You will not go unpunished, for I am calling down a sword on all who live on the earth, declares the LORD Almighty.'

30 "Now prophesy all these words against them and say to them:

" 'The LORD will roar from on high;
    he will thunder from his holy dwelling
    and roar mightily against his land.
He will shout like those who tread the grapes,
    shout against all who live on the earth.
31 The tumult will resound to the ends of the earth,
    for the LORD will bring charges against the nations;
he will bring judgment on all mankind
    and put the wicked to the sword,' "
                    declares the LORD.

32 This is what the LORD Almighty says:

"Look! Disaster is spreading
    from nation to nation;
a mighty storm is rising
    from the ends of the earth."

33 At that time those slain by the LORD will be everywhere—from one end of the earth to the other. They will not be

mourned or gathered up or buried, but will be like dung lying on the ground.

34 Weep and wail, you shepherds;
    roll in the dust, you leaders of the flock.
For your time to be slaughtered has come;
    you will fall like the best of the rams.*c*
35 The shepherds will have nowhere to flee,
    the leaders of the flock no place to escape.
36 Hear the cry of the shepherds,
    the wailing of the leaders of the flock,
    for the LORD is destroying their pasture.
37 The peaceful meadows will be laid waste
    because of the fierce anger of the LORD.
38 Like a lion he will leave his lair,
    and their land will become desolate
because of the sword*d* of the oppressor
    and because of the LORD's fierce anger.

Jeremiah Threatened With Death

26 Early in the reign of Jehoiakim son of Josiah king of Judah, this word came from the LORD: 2 "This is what the LORD says: Stand in the courtyard of the LORD's house and speak to all the people of the towns of Judah who come to worship in the house of the LORD. Tell them everything I command you; do not omit a word. 3 Perhaps they will listen and each will turn from their evil ways. Then I will relent and not inflict on them the disaster I was planning because of the evil they have done. 4 Say to them, 'This is what the LORD says: If you do not listen to me and follow my law, which I have set before you, 5 and if you do not listen to the words of my servants the prophets, whom I have sent to you again and again (though you have not listened), 6 then I will make this

---

a 23 Or *who clip the hair by their foreheads*   *b* 26 *Sheshak* is a cryptogram for Babylon.   *c* 34 Septuagint; Hebrew *fall and be shattered like fine pottery*   *d* 38 Some Hebrew manuscripts and Septuagint (see also 46:16 and 50:16); most Hebrew manuscripts *anger*

Do you know how many people have been killed because they spoke up for God? Acts 7 records the story of the first Christian martyr. Tradition says Peter and Paul were executed for spreading the Christian message. A book called *Foxe's Book of Martyrs* tells about hundreds more. When Jeremiah delivered God's message, he was threatened with death too. Witnessing has never been easy. At times believers have faced death and still shared God's Word. Compared to that, maybe it's worth taking a look at your reasons not to.

{Jeremiah 26:8}

>> INSTANT ACCESS

house like Shiloh and this city a curse[a] among all the nations of the earth.'"

7 The priests, the prophets and all the people heard Jeremiah speak these words in the house of the LORD. 8 But as soon as Jeremiah finished telling all the people everything the LORD had commanded him to say, the priests, the prophets and all the people seized him and said, "You must die! 9 Why do you prophesy in the LORD's name that this house will be like Shiloh and this city will be desolate and deserted?" And all the people crowded around Jeremiah in the house of the LORD.

10 When the officials of Judah heard about these things, they went up from the royal palace to the house of the LORD

and took their places at the entrance of the New Gate of the LORD's house. 11 Then the priests and the prophets said to the officials and all the people, "This man should be sentenced to death because he has prophesied against this city. You have heard it with your own ears!"

12 Then Jeremiah said to all the officials and all the people: "The LORD sent me to prophesy against this house and this city all the things you have heard. 13 Now reform your ways and your actions and obey the LORD your God. Then the LORD will relent and not bring the disaster he has pronounced against you. 14 As for me, I am in your hands; do with me whatever you think is good and right. 15 Be assured, however, that if you put me to death, you will bring the guilt of innocent blood on yourselves and on this city and on those who live in it, for in truth the LORD has sent me to you to speak all these words in your hearing."

16 Then the officials and all the people said to the priests and the prophets, "This man should not be sentenced to death! He has spoken to us in the name of the LORD our God."

17 Some of the elders of the land stepped forward and said to the entire assembly of people, 18 "Micah of Moresheth prophesied in the days of Hezekiah king of Judah. He told all the people of Judah, 'This is what the LORD Almighty says:

" 'Zion will be plowed like a field,
    Jerusalem will become a heap of
        rubble,
    the temple hill a mound overgrown
        with thickets.'[b]

19 "Did Hezekiah king of Judah or anyone else in Judah put him to death? Did not Hezekiah fear the LORD and seek his favor? And did not the LORD relent, so that he did not bring the disaster he pronounced against them? We are about to bring a terrible disaster on ourselves!"

20 (Now Uriah son of Shemaiah from Kiriath Jearim was another man who prophesied in the name of the LORD; he prophesied the same things against this city

---

[a] 6 That is, its name will be used in cursing (see 29:22); or, others will see that it is cursed.   [b] 18 Micah 3:12

and this land as Jeremiah did. ²¹When King Jehoiakim and all his officers and officials heard his words, the king was determined to put him to death. But Uriah heard of it and fled in fear to Egypt. ²²King Jehoiakim, however, sent Elnathan son of Akbor to Egypt, along with some other men. ²³They brought Uriah out of Egypt and took him to King Jehoiakim, who had him struck down with a sword and his body thrown into the burial place of the common people.)

²⁴Furthermore, Ahikam son of Shaphan supported Jeremiah, and so he was not handed over to the people to be put to death.

Judah to Serve Nebuchadnezzar

27 Early in the reign of Zedekiah^a son of Josiah king of Judah, this word came to Jeremiah from the LORD: ²This is what the LORD said to me: "Make a yoke out of straps and crossbars and put it on your neck. ³Then send word to the kings of Edom, Moab, Ammon, Tyre and Sidon through the envoys who have come to Jerusalem to Zedekiah king of Judah. ⁴Give them a message for their masters and say, 'This is what the LORD Almighty, the God of Israel, says: "Tell this to your masters: ⁵With my great power and outstretched arm I made the earth and its people and the animals that are on it, and I give it to anyone I please. ⁶Now I will give all your countries into the hands of my servant Nebuchadnezzar king of Babylon; I will make even the wild animals subject to him. ⁷All nations will serve him and his son and his grandson until the time for his land comes; then many nations and great kings will subjugate him.

⁸"'"If, however, any nation or kingdom will not serve Nebuchadnezzar king of Babylon or bow its neck under his yoke, I will punish that nation with the sword, famine and plague, declares the LORD, until I destroy it by his hand. ⁹So do not listen to your prophets, your diviners, your interpreters of dreams, your mediums or your sorcerers who tell you, 'You will not serve the king of Babylon.' ¹⁰They prophesy lies to you that will only serve to remove you far from your lands; I will banish you and you will perish. ¹¹But if any nation will bow its neck under the yoke of the king of Babylon and serve him, I will let that nation remain in its own land to till it and to live there, declares the LORD."'"

¹²I gave the same message to Zedekiah king of Judah. I said, "Bow your neck under the yoke of the king of Babylon; serve him and his people, and you will live. ¹³Why will you and your people die by the sword, famine and plague with which the LORD has threatened any nation that will not serve the king of Babylon? ¹⁴Do not listen to the words of the prophets who say to you, 'You will not serve the king of Babylon,' for they are prophesying lies to you. ¹⁵'I have not sent them,' declares the LORD. 'They are prophesying lies in my name. Therefore, I will banish you and you will perish, both you and the prophets who prophesy to you.'"

¹⁶Then I said to the priests and all these people, "This is what the LORD says: Do not listen to the prophets who say, 'Very soon now the articles from the LORD's house will be brought back from Babylon.' They are prophesying lies to you. ¹⁷Do not listen to them. Serve the king of Babylon, and you will live. Why should this city become a ruin? ¹⁸If they are prophets and have the word of the LORD, let them plead with the LORD Almighty that the articles remaining in the house of the LORD and in the palace of the king of Judah and in Jerusalem not be taken to Babylon. ¹⁹For this is what the LORD Almighty says about the pillars, the bronze Sea, the movable stands and the other articles that are left in this city, ²⁰which Nebuchadnezzar king of Babylon did not take away when he carried Jehoiachin^b son of Jehoiakim king of Judah into exile from Jerusalem to Babylon, along with all the nobles of Judah and Jerusalem— ²¹yes, this is what the LORD Al-

^a 1 A few Hebrew manuscripts and Syriac (see also 27:3,12 and 28:1); most Hebrew manuscripts Jehoiakim (Most Septuagint manuscripts do not have this verse.)   ^b 20 Hebrew Jeconiah, a variant of Jehoiachin

mighty, the God of Israel, says about the things that are left in the house of the LORD and in the palace of the king of Judah and in Jerusalem: 22'They will be taken to Babylon and there they will remain until the day I come for them,' declares the LORD. 'Then I will bring them back and restore them to this place.'"

The False Prophet Hananiah

28 In the fifth month of that same year, the fourth year, early in the reign of Zedekiah king of Judah, the prophet Hananiah son of Azzur, who was from Gibeon, said to me in the house of the LORD in the presence of the priests and all the people: 2"This is what the LORD Almighty, the God of Israel, says: 'I will break the yoke of the king of Babylon. 3Within two years I will bring back to this place all the articles of the LORD's house that Nebuchadnezzar king of Babylon removed from here and took to Babylon. 4I will also bring back to this place Jehoiachin[a] son of Jehoiakim king of Judah and all the other exiles from Judah who went to Babylon,' declares the LORD, 'for I will break the yoke of the king of Babylon.'"

5Then the prophet Jeremiah replied to the prophet Hananiah before the priests and all the people who were standing in the house of the LORD. 6He said, "Amen! May the LORD do so! May the LORD fulfill the words you have prophesied by bringing the articles of the LORD's house and all the exiles back to this place from Babylon. 7Nevertheless, listen to what I have to say in your hearing and in the hearing of all the people: 8From early times the prophets who preceded you and me have prophesied war, disaster and plague against many countries and great kingdoms. 9But the prophet who prophesies peace will be recognized as one truly sent by the LORD only if his prediction comes true."

10Then the prophet Hananiah took the yoke off the neck of the prophet Jeremiah and broke it, 11and he said before all the people, "This is what the LORD says: 'In the same way I will break the yoke of

Nebuchadnezzar king of Babylon off the neck of all the nations within two years.' " At this, the prophet Jeremiah went on his way.

12After the prophet Hananiah had broken the yoke off the neck of the prophet Jeremiah, the word of the LORD came to Jeremiah: 13"Go and tell Hananiah, 'This is what the LORD says: You have broken a wooden yoke, but in its place you will get a yoke of iron. 14This is what the LORD Almighty, the God of Israel, says: I will put an iron yoke on the necks of all these nations to make them serve Nebuchadnezzar king of Babylon, and they will serve him. I will even give him control over the wild animals.' "

15Then the prophet Jeremiah said to Hananiah the prophet, "Listen, Hananiah! The LORD has not sent you, yet you have persuaded this nation to trust in lies. 16Therefore this is what the LORD says: 'I am about to remove you from the face of the earth. This very year you are going to die, because you have preached rebellion against the LORD.' "

17In the seventh month of that same year, Hananiah the prophet died.

Jeremiah 28

Q: Hananiah predicted the Jews would return from Babylon in two years (Jeremiah 28:3). Was he right?

BONUS: What did Jeremiah predict would happen to Hananiah?

Answers on next page

---

a 4 Hebrew *Jeconiah*, a variant of *Jehoiachin*

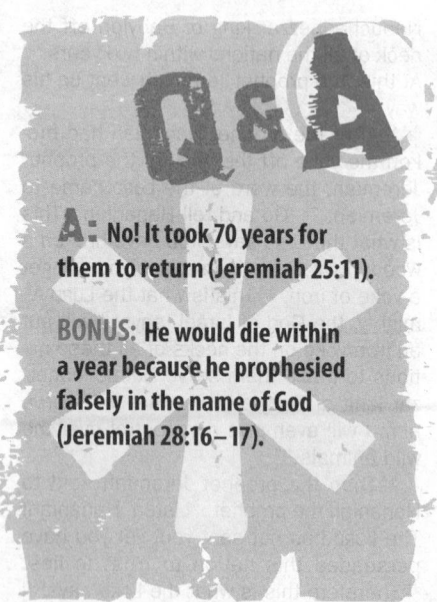

A: No! It took 70 years for them to return (Jeremiah 25:11).

BONUS: He would die within a year because he prophesied falsely in the name of God (Jeremiah 28:16–17).

A Letter to the Exiles

29 This is the text of the letter that the prophet Jeremiah sent from Jerusalem to the surviving elders among the exiles and to the priests, the prophets and all the other people Nebuchadnezzar had carried into exile from Jerusalem to Babylon. ²(This was after King Jehoiachin[a] and the queen mother, the court officials and the leaders of Judah and Jerusalem, the skilled workers and the artisans had gone into exile from Jerusalem.) ³He entrusted the letter to Elasah son of Shaphan and to Gemariah son of Hilkiah, whom Zedekiah king of Judah sent to King Nebuchadnezzar in Babylon. It said:

⁴This is what the LORD Almighty, the God of Israel, says to all those I carried into exile from Jerusalem to Babylon: ⁵"Build houses and settle down; plant gardens and eat what they produce. ⁶Marry and have sons and daughters; find wives for your sons and give your daughters in marriage, so that they too may have sons and daughters. Increase in number there; do not decrease.

⁷Also, seek the peace and prosperity of the city to which I have carried you into exile. Pray to the LORD for it, because if it prospers, you too will prosper." ⁸Yes, this is what the LORD Almighty, the God of Israel, says: "Do not let the prophets and diviners among you deceive you. Do not listen to the dreams you encourage them to have. ⁹They are prophesying lies to you in my name. I have not sent them," declares the LORD.

¹⁰This is what the LORD says: "When seventy years are completed for Babylon, I will come to you and fulfill my good promise to bring you back to this place. ¹¹For I know the plans I have for you," declares the LORD, "plans to prosper you and not to harm you, plans to give you hope and a future. ¹²Then you will call on me and come and pray to me, and I will listen to you. ¹³You will seek me and find me when you seek me with all your heart. ¹⁴I will be found by you," declares the LORD, "and will bring you back from captivity.[b] I will gather you from all the nations and places where I have banished you," declares the LORD, "and will bring you back to the place from which I carried you into exile."

¹⁵You may say, "The LORD has raised up prophets for us in Babylon," ¹⁶but this is what the LORD says about the king who sits on David's throne and all the people who remain in this city, your fellow citizens who did not go with you into exile— ¹⁷yes, this is what the LORD Almighty says: "I will send the sword, famine and plague against them and I will make them like figs that are so bad they cannot be eaten. ¹⁸I will pursue them with the sword, famine and plague and will make them abhorrent to all the kingdoms of the earth, a curse[c] and an object of horror, of scorn and reproach, among all the nations where I drive them. ¹⁹For they have not listened to my words,"

> No one really notices or cares about me. Nobody loves me or listens to a thing I say. I don't seem to do anything right. Lots of times I wish I was dead and wonder if I can make that come true. I don't want to hurt anyone, but I'm tired of feeling this way. What can I do?
>
> >> Morgan

Dear Jordan

Dear Morgan,

You are not alone. Many young people have feelings of great sadness and feelings of worthlessness. But feelings can and do change. Please tell your parents, your doctor, a teacher or guidance counselor. Find an adult you can trust, and tell them you need help. You said you don't want to hurt anyone else, but how do you think your parents, brothers, sisters and friends would feel if you weren't there anymore? They would be devastated. You are thinking of a permanent solution to a temporary problem.

God has good plans for you, plans that include hope and a future (Jeremiah 29:11–13). Seek God. Give your family the chance to get you some help from your doctor or a counselor. There is help for people who are depressed. God can bless you in more ways than you can even imagine. Give him a chance. And give those around you a chance to help you. Give yourself the chance to live your life.

Jordan

declares the LORD, "words that I sent to them again and again by my servants the prophets. And you exiles have not listened either," declares the LORD.

20 Therefore, hear the word of the LORD, all you exiles whom I have sent away from Jerusalem to Babylon. 21 This is what the LORD Almighty, the God of Israel, says about Ahab son of Kolaiah and Zedekiah son of Maaseiah, who are prophesying lies to you in my name: "I will deliver them into the hands of Nebuchadnezzar king of Babylon, and he will put them to death before your very eyes. 22 Because of them, all the exiles from Judah who are in Babylon will use this curse: 'May the LORD treat you like Zedekiah and Ahab, whom the king of Babylon burned in the fire.' 23 For they have done outrageous things in Israel; they have committed adultery with their neighbors' wives, and in my name they have uttered lies—which I did not authorize. I know it and am a witness to it," declares the LORD.

Message to Shemaiah

24 Tell Shemaiah the Nehelamite, 25 "This is what the LORD Almighty, the God of Israel, says: You sent letters in your own name to all the people in Jerusalem, to the priest Zephaniah son of Maaseiah, and to all the other priests. You said to Zephaniah, 26 'The LORD has appointed you priest in place of Jehoiada to be in charge of the house of the LORD; you should put any maniac who acts like a prophet into the stocks and neck-irons. 27 So why have you not reprimanded Jeremiah from Anathoth, who poses as a prophet among you? 28 He has sent this message to us in Babylon: It will be a long time. Therefore build houses and settle down; plant gardens and eat what they produce.'"

29 Zephaniah the priest, however, read the letter to Jeremiah the prophet. 30 Then the word of the LORD came to Jeremiah: 31 "Send this message to all the exiles: 'This is what the LORD says about Shema-

iah the Nehelamite: Because Shemaiah has prophesied to you, even though I did not send him, and has persuaded you to trust in lies, 32 this is what the LORD says: I will surely punish Shemaiah the Nehelamite and his descendants. He will have no one left among this people, nor will he see the good things I will do for my people, declares the LORD, because he has preached rebellion against me.'"

Restoration of Israel

30 This is the word that came to Jeremiah from the LORD: 2 "This is what the LORD, the God of Israel, says: 'Write in a book all the words I have spoken to you. 3 The days are coming,' declares the LORD, 'when I will bring my people Israel and Judah back from captivity[a] and restore them to the land I gave their ancestors to possess,' says the LORD."

4 These are the words the LORD spoke concerning Israel and Judah: 5 "This is what the LORD says:

" 'Cries of fear are heard—
    terror, not peace.
6 Ask and see:
    Can a man bear children?
Then why do I see every strong man
    with his hands on his stomach like
        a woman in labor,
    every face turned deathly pale?
7 How awful that day will be!
    No other will be like it.
It will be a time of trouble for Jacob,
    but he will be saved out of it.

8 " 'In that day,' declares the LORD
        Almighty,
    'I will break the yoke off their necks
and will tear off their bonds;
    no longer will foreigners enslave
        them.
9 Instead, they will serve the LORD their
        God
    and David their king,
    whom I will raise up for them.

10 " 'So do not be afraid, Jacob my
        servant;
    do not be dismayed, Israel,'
                declares the LORD.

---

a 3 Or will restore the fortunes of my people Israel and Judah

'I will surely save you out of a distant
place,
your descendants from the land of
their exile.
Jacob will again have peace and
security,
and no one will make him afraid.
¹¹ I am with you and will save you,'
declares the LORD.
'Though I completely destroy all the
nations
among which I scatter you,
I will not completely destroy you.
I will discipline you but only in due
measure;
I will not let you go entirely
unpunished.'

¹² "This is what the LORD says:

" 'Your wound is incurable,
your injury beyond healing.
¹³ There is no one to plead your cause,
no remedy for your sore,
no healing for you.
¹⁴ All your allies have forgotten you;
they care nothing for you.
I have struck you as an enemy
would
and punished you as would the
cruel,
because your guilt is so great
and your sins so many.
¹⁵ Why do you cry out over your wound,
your pain that has no cure?
Because of your great guilt and many
sins
I have done these things to you.

¹⁶ " 'But all who devour you will be
devoured;
all your enemies will go into exile.
Those who plunder you will be
plundered;
all who make spoil of you I will
despoil.
¹⁷ But I will restore you to health
and heal your wounds,'
declares the LORD,
'because you are called an outcast,
Zion for whom no one cares.'

¹⁸ "This is what the LORD says:

" 'I will restore the fortunes of Jacob's
tents
and have compassion on his
dwellings;
the city will be rebuilt on her ruins,
and the palace will stand in its
proper place.
¹⁹ From them will come songs of
thanksgiving
and the sound of rejoicing.
I will add to their numbers,
and they will not be decreased;
I will bring them honor,
and they will not be disdained.
²⁰ Their children will be as in days of old,
and their community will be
established before me;
I will punish all who oppress them.
²¹ Their leader will be one of their own;
their ruler will arise from among
them.
I will bring him near and he will come
close to me—
for who is he who will devote
himself
to be close to me?'
declares the LORD.
²² " 'So you will be my people,
and I will be your God.' "

²³ See, the storm of the LORD
will burst out in wrath,
a driving wind swirling down
on the heads of the wicked.
²⁴ The fierce anger of the LORD will not
turn back
until he fully accomplishes
the purposes of his heart.
In days to come
you will understand this.

31 "At that time," declares the LORD,
"I will be the God of all the families of Israel, and they will be my people."
² This is what the LORD says:

"The people who survive the sword
will find favor in the wilderness;
I will come to give rest to Israel."

³ The LORD appeared to us in the past,ᵃ
saying:

ᵃ 3 Or LORD has appeared to us from afar

"I have loved you with an everlasting
love;
I have drawn you with unfailing
kindness.
⁴I will build you up again,
and you, Virgin Israel, will be rebuilt.
Again you will take up your timbrels
and go out to dance with the
joyful.
⁵Again you will plant vineyards
on the hills of Samaria;
the farmers will plant them
and enjoy their fruit.
⁶There will be a day when watchmen
cry out
on the hills of Ephraim,
'Come, let us go up to Zion,
to the LORD our God.'"

⁷This is what the LORD says:

"Sing with joy for Jacob;
shout for the foremost of the
nations.
Make your praises heard, and say,
'LORD, save your people,
the remnant of Israel.'
⁸See, I will bring them from the land of
the north
and gather them from the ends of
the earth.
Among them will be the blind and the
lame,
expectant mothers and women in
labor;
a great throng will return.
⁹They will come with weeping;
they will pray as I bring them back.
I will lead them beside streams of
water
on a level path where they will not
stumble,
because I am Israel's father,
and Ephraim is my firstborn son.

¹⁰"Hear the word of the LORD, you
nations;
proclaim it in distant coastlands:
'He who scattered Israel will gather
them
and will watch over his flock like a
shepherd.'
¹¹For the LORD will deliver Jacob
and redeem them from the hand of
those stronger than they.

¹²They will come and shout for joy on
the heights of Zion;
they will rejoice in the bounty of the
LORD—
the grain, the new wine and the olive
oil,
the young of the flocks and herds.
They will be like a well-watered
garden,
and they will sorrow no more.
¹³Then young women will dance and be
glad,
young men and old as well.
I will turn their mourning into
gladness;
I will give them comfort and joy
instead of sorrow.
¹⁴I will satisfy the priests with
abundance,
and my people will be filled with my
bounty,"
declares the LORD.

¹⁵This is what the LORD says:

"A voice is heard in Ramah,
mourning and great weeping,
Rachel weeping for her children
and refusing to be comforted,
because they are no more."

¹⁶This is what the LORD says:

"Restrain your voice from weeping
and your eyes from tears,
for your work will be rewarded,"
declares the LORD.
"They will return from the land of
the enemy.
¹⁷So there is hope for your
descendants,"
declares the LORD.
"Your children will return to their
own land.

¹⁸"I have surely heard Ephraim's
moaning:
'You disciplined me like an unruly
calf,
and I have been disciplined.
Restore me, and I will return,
because you are the LORD my God.
¹⁹After I strayed,
I repented;
after I came to understand,
I beat my breast.

We Believe...

"in the forgiveness of sins"

✝ Jeremiah kept warning God's people. They had sinned, and unless they changed their ways the little nation of Judah would be destroyed. No one listened and, sure enough, the Babylonian war machine trampled Jerusalem, destroyed the temple and carried the people off as captives.

But Jeremiah, the bad news prophet, also delivered some good news. One day God would make a new covenant with his people. And in that covenant God would guarantee to change people's hearts (Jeremiah 31:33), and forgive their wickedness and sins (Jeremiah 31:34).

When Jesus died on the cross God kept his promise of a new covenant. The book of Hebrews assures us that Jesus' death was a sacrifice for sins offered "for all time," and that by "one sacrifice" Jesus did everything necessary to provide the forgiveness we need and perfect us for heaven (Hebrews 10:12,14). Because Jesus died for us, the sins of those who believe in him "have been forgiven" (Hebrews 10:18). Ephesians 1:7 says, in Jesus "we have redemption through his blood, the forgiveness of sins, in accordance with the riches of God's grace."

What a wonderful thing forgiveness is. You know what it means to feel guilty and ashamed after you've done something you know you shouldn't. Because of Jesus you can experience God's forgiveness now. That guilt and shame can be taken away, and you can feel whole and good about yourself again. Claim the forgiveness God offers you in Jesus. Give yourself a fresh start. And next time, don't choose to do what you know is wrong.

Go to page 1084 for the next We Believe

I was ashamed and humiliated
  because I bore the disgrace of my
    youth.'
20 Is not Ephraim my dear son,
  the child in whom I delight?
Though I often speak against him,
  I still remember him.
Therefore my heart yearns for him;
  I have great compassion for him,"
                declares the LORD.

21 "Set up road signs;
  put up guideposts.
Take note of the highway,
  the road that you take.
Return, Virgin Israel,
  return to your towns.
22 How long will you wander,
  unfaithful Daughter Israel?
The LORD will create a new thing on
    earth—
  the woman will return to*a* the man."

23 This is what the LORD Almighty, the God of Israel, says: "When I bring them back from captivity,*b* the people in the land of Judah and in its towns will once again use these words: 'The LORD bless you, you prosperous city, you sacred mountain.' 24 People will live together in Judah and all its towns—farmers and those who move about with their flocks. 25 I will refresh the weary and satisfy the faint."

26 At this I awoke and looked around. My sleep had been pleasant to me.

27 "The days are coming," declares the LORD, "when I will plant the kingdoms of Israel and Judah with the offspring of people and of animals. 28 Just as I watched over them to uproot and tear down, and to overthrow, destroy and bring disaster, so I will watch over them to build and to plant," declares the LORD. 29 "In those days people will no longer say,

'The parents have eaten sour grapes,
  and the children's teeth are set on
    edge.'

30 Instead, everyone will die for their own sin; whoever eats sour grapes—their own teeth will be set on edge.

31 "The days are coming," declares the
      LORD,
  "when I will make a new covenant
with the people of Israel
  and with the people of Judah.
32 It will not be like the covenant
  I made with their ancestors
when I took them by the hand
  to lead them out of Egypt,
because they broke my covenant,
  though I was a husband to*c* them,*d*"
                declares the LORD.
33 "This is the covenant I will make with
      the people of Israel
  after that time," declares the LORD.
"I will put my law in their minds
  and write it on their hearts.
I will be their God,
  and they will be my people.
34 No longer will they teach their
      neighbor,
  or say to one another, 'Know the
      LORD,'
because they will all know me,
  from the least of them to the
      greatest,"
                declares the LORD.

Q&A

Jeremiah 31

Q: What promise does God make in Jeremiah 31?

BONUS: Why is it so special?

Answers on next page

---

a 22 Or *will protect*   *b* 23 Or *I restore their fortunes*
c 32 Hebrew; Septuagint and Syriac / *and I turned away from*   *d* 32 Or *was their master*

"For I will forgive their wickedness
and will remember their sins no
more."

35 This is what the LORD says,

he who appoints the sun
to shine by day,
who decrees the moon and stars
to shine by night,
who stirs up the sea
so that its waves roar—
the LORD Almighty is his name:
36 "Only if these decrees vanish from my
sight,"
declares the LORD,
"will Israel ever cease
being a nation before me."

37 This is what the LORD says:

"Only if the heavens above can be
measured
and the foundations of the earth
below be searched out
will I reject all the descendants of
Israel
because of all they have done,"
declares the LORD.

38 "The days are coming," declares
the LORD, "when this city will be rebuilt
for me from the Tower of Hananel to the
Corner Gate. 39 The measuring line will
stretch from there straight to the hill of
Gareb and then turn to Goah. 40 The whole
valley where dead bodies and ashes are
thrown, and all the terraces out to the
Kidron Valley on the east as far as the
corner of the Horse Gate, will be holy to
the LORD. The city will never again be uprooted or demolished."

Jeremiah Buys a Field

32 This is the word that came to Jeremiah from the LORD in the tenth
year of Zedekiah king of Judah, which was
the eighteenth year of Nebuchadnezzar.
2 The army of the king of Babylon was
then besieging Jerusalem, and Jeremiah
the prophet was confined in the courtyard
of the guard in the royal palace of Judah.
3 Now Zedekiah king of Judah had imprisoned him there, saying, "Why do you

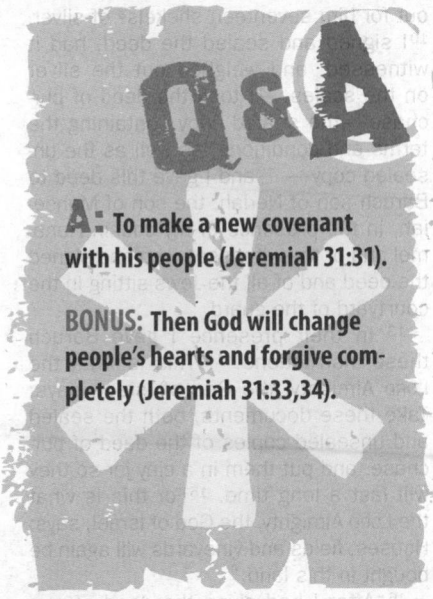

A: To make a new covenant
with his people (Jeremiah 31:31).

BONUS: Then God will change
people's hearts and forgive completely (Jeremiah 31:33,34).

prophesy as you do? You say, 'This is
what the LORD says: I am about to give
this city into the hands of the king of
Babylon, and he will capture it. 4 Zedekiah king of Judah will not escape the Babylonians*a* but will certainly be given into
the hands of the king of Babylon, and will
speak with him face to face and see him
with his own eyes. 5 He will take Zedekiah
to Babylon, where he will remain until I
deal with him, declares the LORD. If you
fight against the Babylonians, you will not
succeed.'"

6 Jeremiah said, "The word of the LORD
came to me: 7 Hanamel son of Shallum
your uncle is going to come to you and
say, 'Buy my field at Anathoth, because
as nearest relative it is your right and duty
to buy it.'

8 "Then, just as the LORD had said, my
cousin Hanamel came to me in the courtyard of the guard and said, 'Buy my field
at Anathoth in the territory of Benjamin.
Since it is your right to redeem it and possess it, buy it for yourself.'

"I knew that this was the word of the
LORD; 9 so I bought the field at Anathoth
from my cousin Hanamel and weighed

---

a 4 Or Chaldeans; also in verses 5, 24, 25, 28, 29 and 43

out for him seventeen shekels[a] of silver. ¹⁰I signed and sealed the deed, had it witnessed, and weighed out the silver on the scales. ¹¹I took the deed of purchase—the sealed copy containing the terms and conditions, as well as the unsealed copy— ¹²and I gave this deed to Baruch son of Neriah, the son of Mahseiah, in the presence of my cousin Hanamel and of the witnesses who had signed the deed and of all the Jews sitting in the courtyard of the guard.

¹³"In their presence I gave Baruch these instructions: ¹⁴'This is what the LORD Almighty, the God of Israel, says: Take these documents, both the sealed and unsealed copies of the deed of purchase, and put them in a clay jar so they will last a long time. ¹⁵For this is what the LORD Almighty, the God of Israel, says: Houses, fields and vineyards will again be bought in this land.'

¹⁶"After I had given the deed of purchase to Baruch son of Neriah, I prayed to the LORD:

¹⁷"Ah, Sovereign LORD, you have made the heavens and the earth by your great power and outstretched arm. Nothing is too hard for you. ¹⁸You show love to thousands but bring the punishment for the parents' sins into the laps of their children after them. Great and mighty God, whose name is the LORD Almighty, ¹⁹great are your purposes and mighty are your deeds. Your eyes are open to the ways of all mankind; you reward each person according to their conduct and as their deeds deserve. ²⁰You performed signs and wonders in Egypt and have continued them to this day, in Israel and among all mankind, and have gained the renown that is still yours. ²¹You brought your people Israel out of Egypt with signs and wonders, by a mighty hand and an outstretched arm and with great terror. ²²You gave them this land you had sworn to give their ancestors, a land flowing with milk and honey. ²³They came in and took possession of it, but they did not obey you or follow your law; they did not do what you commanded them to do. So you brought all this disaster on them.

²⁴"See how the siege ramps are built up to take the city. Because of the sword, famine and plague, the city will be given into the hands of the Babylonians who are attacking it. What you said has happened, as you now see. ²⁵And though the city will be given into the hands of the Babylonians, you, Sovereign LORD, say to me, 'Buy the field with silver and have the transaction witnessed.'"

²⁶Then the word of the LORD came to Jeremiah: ²⁷"I am the LORD, the God of all mankind. Is anything too hard for me? ²⁸Therefore this is what the LORD says: I am about to give this city into the hands of the Babylonians and to Nebuchadnezzar king of Babylon, who will capture it. ²⁹The Babylonians who are attacking this city will come in and set it on fire; they will burn it down, along with the houses where the people aroused my anger by burning incense on the roofs to Baal and by pouring out drink offerings to other gods.

³⁰"The people of Israel and Judah have done nothing but evil in my sight from their youth; indeed, the people of Israel have done nothing but arouse my anger with what their hands have made, declares the LORD. ³¹From the day it was built until now, this city has so aroused my anger and wrath that I must remove it from my sight. ³²The people of Israel and Judah have provoked me by all the evil they have done—they, their kings and officials, their priests and prophets, the people of Judah and those living in Jerusalem. ³³They turned their backs to me and not their faces; though I taught them again and again, they would not listen or respond to discipline. ³⁴They set up their vile images in the house that bears my Name and defiled it. ³⁵They built high places for Baal in the Valley of Ben Hinnom to sacrifice their sons and

---

[a] 9 That is, about 7 ounces or about 200 grams

daughters to Molek, though I never commanded—nor did it enter my mind—that they should do such a detestable thing and so make Judah sin.

36 "You are saying about this city, 'By the sword, famine and plague it will be given into the hands of the king of Babylon'; but this is what the LORD, the God of Israel, says: 37 I will surely gather them from all the lands where I banish them in my furious anger and great wrath; I will bring them back to this place and let them live in safety. 38 They will be my people, and I will be their God. 39 I will give them singleness of heart and action, so that they will always fear me and that all will then go well for them and for their children after them. 40 I will make an everlasting covenant with them: I will never stop doing good to them, and I will inspire them to fear me, so that they will never turn away from me. 41 I will rejoice in doing them good and will assuredly plant them in this land with all my heart and soul.

42 "This is what the LORD says: As I have brought all this great calamity on this people, so I will give them all the prosperity I have promised them. 43 Once more fields will be bought in this land of which you say, 'It is a desolate waste, without people or animals, for it has been given into the hands of the Babylonians.' 44 Fields will be bought for silver, and deeds will be signed, sealed and witnessed in the territory of Benjamin, in the villages around Jerusalem, in the towns of Judah and in the towns of the hill country, of the western foothills and of the Negev, because I will restore their fortunes,[a] declares the LORD."

Promise of Restoration

33 While Jeremiah was still confined in the courtyard of the guard, the word of the LORD came to him a second time: 2 "This is what the LORD says, he who made the earth, the LORD who formed it and established it—the LORD is his name: 3 'Call to me and I will answer you and tell you great and unsearchable things you do not know.' 4 For this is what the LORD, the God of Israel, says about the houses in this city and the royal palaces of Judah that have been torn down to be used against the siege ramps and the sword 5 in the fight with the Babylonians[b]: 'They will be filled with the dead bodies of the people I will slay in my anger and wrath. I will hide my face from this city because of all its wickedness.

6 " 'Nevertheless, I will bring health and healing to it; I will heal my people and will let them enjoy abundant peace and security. 7 I will bring Judah and Israel back from captivity[c] and will rebuild them as they were before. 8 I will cleanse them from all the sin they have committed against me and will forgive all their sins of rebellion against me. 9 Then this city will bring me renown, joy, praise and honor before all nations on earth that hear of all the good things I do for it; and they will be in awe and will tremble at the abundant prosperity and peace I provide for it.'

10 "This is what the LORD says: 'You say about this place, "It is a desolate waste, without people or animals." Yet in the towns of Judah and the streets of Jerusalem that are deserted, inhabited by neither people nor animals, there will be heard once more 11 the sounds of joy and gladness, the voices of bride and bridegroom, and the voices of those who bring thank offerings to the house of the LORD, saying,

"Give thanks to the LORD Almighty,
    for the LORD is good;
    his love endures forever."

For I will restore the fortunes of the land as they were before,' says the LORD. 12 "This is what the LORD Almighty says:

I will never stop doing good to them.
Jeremiah 32:40

---

a 44 Or will bring them back from captivity   b 5 Or Chaldeans   c 7 Or will restore the fortunes of Judah and Israel

'In this place, desolate and without people or animals—in all its towns there will again be pastures for shepherds to rest their flocks. ¹³In the towns of the hill country, of the western foothills and of the Negev, in the territory of Benjamin, in the villages around Jerusalem and in the towns of Judah, flocks will again pass under the hand of the one who counts them,' says the Lord.

¹⁴ " 'The days are coming,' declares the Lord, 'when I will fulfill the good promise I made to the people of Israel and Judah.

¹⁵ " 'In those days and at that time
    I will make a righteous Branch
        sprout from David's line;
    he will do what is just and right in
        the land.
¹⁶ In those days Judah will be saved
    and Jerusalem will live in safety.
    This is the name by which it*a* will be
        called:
    The Lord Our Righteous Savior.'

¹⁷ For this is what the Lord says: 'David will never fail to have a man to sit on the throne of Israel, ¹⁸nor will the Levitical priests ever fail to have a man to stand before me continually to offer burnt offerings, to burn grain offerings and to present sacrifices.' "

¹⁹ The word of the Lord came to Jeremiah: ²⁰ "This is what the Lord says: 'If you can break my covenant with the day and my covenant with the night, so that day and night no longer come at their appointed time, ²¹then my covenant with David my servant—and my covenant with the Levites who are priests ministering before me—can be broken and David will no longer have a descendant to reign on his throne. ²²I will make the descendants of David my servant and the Levites who minister before me as countless as the stars in the sky and as measureless as the sand on the seashore.' "

²³ The word of the Lord came to Jeremiah: ²⁴ "Have you not noticed that these people are saying, 'The Lord has rejected the two kingdoms*b* he chose'? So they despise my people and no longer regard them as a nation. ²⁵This is what the Lord says: 'If I have not made my covenant with day and night and established the laws of heaven and earth, ²⁶then I will reject the descendants of Jacob and David my servant and will not choose one of his sons to rule over the descendants of Abraham, Isaac and Jacob. For I will restore their fortunes*c* and have compassion on them.' "

Warning to Zedekiah

34 While Nebuchadnezzar king of Babylon and all his army and all the kingdoms and peoples in the empire he ruled were fighting against Jerusalem and all its surrounding towns, this word came to Jeremiah from the Lord: ²"This is what the Lord, the God of Israel, says: Go to Zedekiah king of Judah and tell him, 'This is what the Lord says: I am about to give this city into the hands of the king of Babylon, and he will burn it down. ³You will not escape from his grasp but will surely be captured and given into his hands. You will see the king of Babylon with your own eyes, and he will speak with you face to face. And you will go to Babylon.

⁴ " 'Yet hear the Lord's promise to you, Zedekiah king of Judah. This is what the Lord says concerning you: You will not die by the sword; ⁵you will die peacefully. As people made a funeral fire in honor of your predecessors, the kings who ruled before you, so they will make a fire in your honor and lament, "Alas, master!" I myself make this promise, declares the Lord.' "

⁶ Then Jeremiah the prophet told all this to Zedekiah king of Judah, in Jerusalem, ⁷while the army of the king of Babylon was fighting against Jerusalem and the other cities of Judah that were still holding out—Lachish and Azekah. These were the only fortified cities left in Judah.

Freedom for Slaves

⁸ The word came to Jeremiah from the Lord after King Zedekiah had made a covenant with all the people in Jerusalem to proclaim freedom for the slaves. ⁹Every-

---

a 16 Or *he*   *b* 24 Or *families*   *c* 26 Or *will bring them back from captivity* one was to free their Hebrew slaves, both male and female; no one was to hold a fellow Hebrew in bondage. ¹⁰So all the officials and people who entered into this covenant agreed that they would free their male and female slaves and no longer hold them in bondage. They agreed, and set them free. ¹¹But afterward they changed their minds and took back the slaves they had freed and enslaved them again.

¹²Then the word of the LORD came to Jeremiah: ¹³"This is what the LORD, the God of Israel, says: I made a covenant with your ancestors when I brought them out of Egypt, out of the land of slavery. I said, ¹⁴'Every seventh year each of you must free any fellow Hebrews who have sold themselves to you. After they have served you six years, you must let them go free.'ᵃ Your ancestors, however, did not listen to me or pay attention to me. ¹⁵Recently you repented and did what is right in my sight: Each of you proclaimed freedom to your own people. You even made a covenant before me in the house that bears my Name. ¹⁶But now you have turned around and profaned my name; each of you has taken back the male and female slaves you had set free to go where they wished. You have forced them to become your slaves again.

¹⁷"Therefore this is what the LORD says: You have not obeyed me; you have not proclaimed freedom to your own people. So I now proclaim 'freedom' for you, declares the LORD— 'freedom' to fall by the sword, plague and famine. I will make you abhorrent to all the kingdoms of the earth. ¹⁸Those who have violated my covenant and have not fulfilled the terms of the covenant they made before me, I will treat like the calf they cut in two and then walked between its pieces. ¹⁹The leaders of Judah and Jerusalem, the court officials, the priests and all the people of the land who walked between the pieces of the calf, ²⁰I will deliver into the hands of their enemies who want to kill them. Their dead bodies will become food for the birds and the wild animals.

²¹"I will deliver Zedekiah king of Judah and his officials into the hands of their enemies who want to kill them, to the army of the king of Babylon, which has withdrawn from you. ²²I am going to give the order, declares the LORD, and I will bring them back to this city. They will fight against it, take it and burn it down. And I will lay waste the towns of Judah so no one can live there."

The Rekabites

35 This is the word that came to Jeremiah from the LORD during the reign of Jehoiakim son of Josiah king of Judah: ²"Go to the Rekabite family and invite them to come to one of the side rooms of the house of the LORD and give them wine to drink."

³So I went to get Jaazaniah son of Jeremiah, the son of Habazziniah, and his brothers and all his sons—the whole family of the Rekabites. ⁴I brought them into the house of the LORD, into the room of the sons of Hanan son of Igdaliah the man of God. It was next to the room of the officials, which was over that of Maaseiah son of Shallum the doorkeeper. ⁵Then I set bowls full of wine and some cups before the Rekabites and said to them, "Drink some wine."

⁶But they replied, "We do not drink wine, because our forefather Jehonadabᵇ son of Rekab gave us this command: 'Neither you nor your descendants must ever drink wine. ⁷Also you must never build houses, sow seed or plant vineyards; you must never have any of these things, but must always live in tents. Then you will live a long time in the land where you are nomads.' ⁸We have obeyed everything our forefather Jehonadab son of Rekab commanded us. Neither we nor our wives nor our sons and daughters have ever drunk wine ⁹or built houses to live in or had vineyards, fields or crops. ¹⁰We have lived in tents and have fully obeyed everything our forefather Jehonadab commanded us. ¹¹But when Nebuchadnezzar king of Babylon invaded this land, we said, 'Come, we must go to Jerusalem to escape the Babylonianᶜ and Aramean armies.' So we have remained in Jerusalem."

ᵃ 14 Deut. 15:12   ᵇ 6 Hebrew *Jonadab*, a variant of *Jehonadab*; here and often in this chapter   ᶜ 11 Or *Chaldean*

12 Then the word of the LORD came to Jeremiah, saying: 13 "This is what the LORD Almighty, the God of Israel, says: Go and tell the people of Judah and those living in Jerusalem, 'Will you not learn a lesson and obey my words?' declares the LORD. 14 'Jehonadab son of Rekab ordered his descendants not to drink wine and this command has been kept. To this day they do not drink wine, because they obey their forefather's command. But I have spoken to you again and again, yet you have not obeyed me. 15 Again and again I sent all my servants the prophets to you. They said, "Each of you must turn from your wicked ways and reform your actions; do not follow other gods to serve them. Then you will live in the land I have given to you and your ancestors." But you have not paid attention or listened to me. 16 The descendants of Jehonadab son of Rekab have carried out the command their forefather gave them, but these people have not obeyed me.'

17 "Therefore this is what the LORD God Almighty, the God of Israel, says: 'Listen! I am going to bring on Judah and on everyone living in Jerusalem every disaster I pronounced against them. I spoke to them, but they did not listen; I called to them, but they did not answer.'"

18 Then Jeremiah said to the family of the Rekabites, "This is what the LORD Almighty, the God of Israel, says: 'You have obeyed the command of your forefather Jehonadab and have followed all his instructions and have done everything he ordered.' 19 Therefore this is what the LORD Almighty, the God of Israel, says: 'Jehonadab son of Rekab will never fail to have a descendant to serve me.'"

Jehoiakim Burns Jeremiah's Scroll

36 In the fourth year of Jehoiakim son of Josiah king of Judah, this word came to Jeremiah from the LORD: 2 "Take a scroll and write on it all the words I have spoken to you concerning Israel, Judah and all the other nations from the time I began speaking to you in the reign of Josiah till now. 3 Perhaps when the people of Judah hear about every di-

INSTANT ACCESS

Read the end of the story first. The LORD tells the family, "You have obeyed the command of your forefather" (Jeremiah 35:18). As a result, God promised to bless them. When the Bible says honor your parents, it doesn't just mean you should be polite. Part of honoring parents is respecting their beliefs and values and seriously considering making their beliefs and values your own. So don't talk about your parents "forcing" you to go to church. Go, listen actively and seriously consider the claims of Christ. Mom and Dad can't believe for you, but you can honor them by taking an honest, open look at their faith.

{Jeremiah 35}

saster I plan to inflict on them, they will each turn from their wicked ways; then I will forgive their wickedness and their sin."

4 So Jeremiah called Baruch son of Neriah, and while Jeremiah dictated all the words the LORD had spoken to him, Baruch wrote them on the scroll. 5 Then Jeremiah told Baruch, "I am restricted; I am not allowed to go to the LORD's temple. 6 So you go to the house of the LORD on a day of fasting and read to the people from the scroll the words of the LORD that you wrote as I dictated. Read them to all the

people of Judah who come in from their towns. ⁷Perhaps they will bring their petition before the LORD and will each turn from their wicked ways, for the anger and wrath pronounced against this people by the LORD are great."

⁸Baruch son of Neriah did everything Jeremiah the prophet told him to do; at the LORD's temple he read the words of the LORD from the scroll. ⁹In the ninth month of the fifth year of Jehoiakim son of Josiah king of Judah, a time of fasting before the LORD was proclaimed for all the people in Jerusalem and those who had come from the towns of Judah. ¹⁰From the room of Gemariah son of Shaphan the secretary, which was in the upper courtyard at the entrance of the New Gate of the temple, Baruch read to all the people at the LORD's temple the words of Jeremiah from the scroll.

¹¹When Micaiah son of Gemariah, the son of Shaphan, heard all the words of the LORD from the scroll, ¹²he went down to the secretary's room in the royal palace, where all the officials were sitting: Elishama the secretary, Delaiah son of Shemaiah, Elnathan son of Akbor, Gemariah son of Shaphan, Zedekiah son of Hananiah, and all the other officials. ¹³After Micaiah told them everything he had heard Baruch read to the people from the scroll, ¹⁴all the officials sent Jehudi son of Nethaniah, the son of Shelemiah, the son of Cushi, to say to Baruch, "Bring the scroll from which you have read to the people and come." So Baruch son of Neriah went to them with the scroll in his hand. ¹⁵They said to him, "Sit down, please, and read it to us."

So Baruch read it to them. ¹⁶When they heard all these words, they looked at each other in fear and said to Baruch, "We must report all these words to the king." ¹⁷Then they asked Baruch, "Tell us, how did you come to write all this? Did Jeremiah dictate it?"

¹⁸"Yes," Baruch replied, "he dictated all these words to me, and I wrote them in ink on the scroll."

¹⁹Then the officials said to Baruch, "You and Jeremiah, go and hide. Don't let anyone know where you are."

²⁰After they put the scroll in the room of Elishama the secretary, they went to the king in the courtyard and reported everything to him. ²¹The king sent Jehudi to get the scroll, and Jehudi brought it from the room of Elishama the secretary and read it to the king and all the officials standing beside him. ²²It was the ninth month and the king was sitting in the winter apartment, with a fire burning in the firepot in front of him. ²³Whenever Jehudi had read three or four columns of the scroll, the king cut them off with a scribe's knife and threw them into the firepot, until the entire scroll was burned in the fire. ²⁴The king and all his attendants who heard all these words showed no fear, nor did they tear their clothes. ²⁵Even though Elnathan, Delaiah and Gemariah urged the king not to burn the scroll, he would not listen to them. ²⁶Instead, the king commanded Jerahmeel, a son of the king, Seraiah son of Azriel and Shelemiah son of Abdeel to arrest Baruch the scribe and Jeremiah the prophet. But the LORD had hidden them.

²⁷After the king burned the scroll containing the words that Baruch had written at Jeremiah's dictation, the word of the

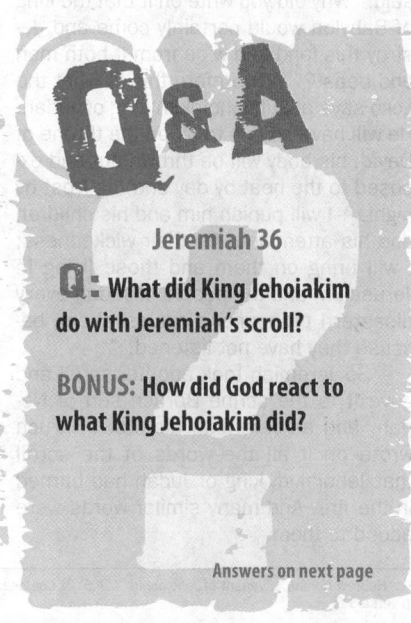

Jeremiah 36

Q: What did King Jehoiakim do with Jeremiah's scroll?

BONUS: How did God react to what King Jehoiakim did?

Answers on next page

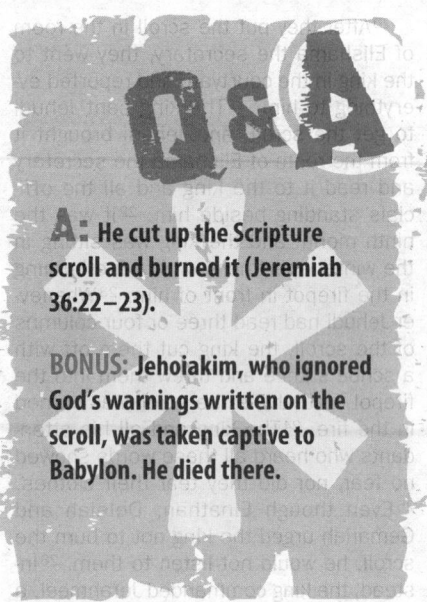

A: He cut up the Scripture scroll and burned it (Jeremiah 36:22–23).

BONUS: Jehoiakim, who ignored God's warnings written on the scroll, was taken captive to Babylon. He died there.

LORD came to Jeremiah: ²⁸"Take another scroll and write on it all the words that were on the first scroll, which Jehoiakim king of Judah burned up. ²⁹Also tell Jehoiakim king of Judah, 'This is what the LORD says: You burned that scroll and said, "Why did you write on it that the king of Babylon would certainly come and destroy this land and wipe from it both man and beast?" ³⁰Therefore this is what the LORD says about Jehoiakim king of Judah: He will have no one to sit on the throne of David; his body will be thrown out and exposed to the heat by day and the frost by night. ³¹I will punish him and his children and his attendants for their wickedness; I will bring on them and those living in Jerusalem and the people of Judah every disaster I pronounced against them, because they have not listened.'"

³²So Jeremiah took another scroll and gave it to the scribe Baruch son of Neriah, and as Jeremiah dictated, Baruch wrote on it all the words of the scroll that Jehoiakim king of Judah had burned in the fire. And many similar words were added to them.

Jeremiah in Prison

37 Zedekiah son of Josiah was made king of Judah by Nebuchadnezzar king of Babylon; he reigned in place of Jehoiachin[a] son of Jehoiakim. ²Neither he nor his attendants nor the people of the land paid any attention to the words the LORD had spoken through Jeremiah the prophet.

³King Zedekiah, however, sent Jehukal son of Shelemiah with the priest Zephaniah son of Maaseiah to Jeremiah the prophet with this message: "Please pray to the LORD our God for us."

⁴Now Jeremiah was free to come and go among the people, for he had not yet been put in prison. ⁵Pharaoh's army had marched out of Egypt, and when the Babylonians[b] who were besieging Jerusalem heard the report about them, they withdrew from Jerusalem.

⁶Then the word of the LORD came to Jeremiah the prophet: ⁷"This is what the LORD, the God of Israel, says: Tell the king of Judah, who sent you to inquire of me, 'Pharaoh's army, which has marched out to support you, will go back to its own land, to Egypt. ⁸Then the Babylonians will return and attack this city; they will capture it and burn it down.'

⁹"This is what the LORD says: Do not deceive yourselves, thinking, 'The Babylonians will surely leave us.' They will not! ¹⁰Even if you were to defeat the entire Babylonian[c] army that is attacking you and only wounded men were left in their tents, they would come out and burn this city down."

¹¹After the Babylonian army had withdrawn from Jerusalem because of Pharaoh's army, ¹²Jeremiah started to leave the city to go to the territory of Benjamin to get his share of the property among the people there. ¹³But when he reached the Benjamin Gate, the captain of the guard, whose name was Irijah son of Shelemiah, the son of Hananiah, arrested him and said, "You are deserting to the Babylonians!"

¹⁴"That's not true!" Jeremiah said. "I

ᵃ 1 Hebrew Koniah, a variant of Jehoiachin   ᵇ 5 Or Chaldeans; also in verses 8, 9, 13 and 14   ᶜ 10 Or Chaldean; also in verse 11

am not deserting to the Babylonians."
But Irijah would not listen to him; instead,
he arrested Jeremiah and brought him to
the officials. 15 They were angry with Jeremiah and had him beaten and imprisoned
in the house of Jonathan the secretary,
which they had made into a prison.

16 Jeremiah was put into a vaulted cell
in a dungeon, where he remained a long
time. 17 Then King Zedekiah sent for him
and had him brought to the palace, where
he asked him privately, "Is there any word
from the LORD?"

"Yes," Jeremiah replied, "you will be
delivered into the hands of the king of
Babylon."

18 Then Jeremiah said to King Zedekiah, "What crime have I committed against
you or your attendants or this people, that
you have put me in prison? 19 Where are
your prophets who prophesied to you,
'The king of Babylon will not attack you or
this land'? 20 But now, my lord the king,
please listen. Let me bring my petition
before you: Do not send me back to the
house of Jonathan the secretary, or I will
die there."

21 King Zedekiah then gave orders for
Jeremiah to be placed in the courtyard of
the guard and given a loaf of bread from
the street of the bakers each day until all
the bread in the city was gone. So Jeremiah remained in the courtyard of the guard.

Jeremiah Thrown Into a Cistern

38 Shephatiah son of Mattan, Gedaliah son of Pashhur, Jehukal[a] son
of Shelemiah, and Pashhur son of Malkijah heard what Jeremiah was telling all
the people when he said, 2 "This is what
the LORD says: 'Whoever stays in this city
will die by the sword, famine or plague,
but whoever goes over to the Babylonians[b] will live. They will escape with their
lives; they will live.' 3 And this is what the
LORD says: 'This city will certainly be given
into the hands of the army of the king of
Babylon, who will capture it.' "

4 Then the officials said to the king,
"This man should be put to death. He is

discouraging the soldiers who are left in
this city, as well as all the people, by the
things he is saying to them. This man is
not seeking the good of these people but
their ruin."

5 "He is in your hands," King Zedekiah
answered. "The king can do nothing to
oppose you."

6 So they took Jeremiah and put him
into the cistern of Malkijah, the king's
son, which was in the courtyard of the
guard. They lowered Jeremiah by ropes
into the cistern; it had no water in it, only
mud, and Jeremiah sank down into the
mud.

7 But Ebed-Melek, a Cushite,[c] an official[d] in the royal palace, heard that they
had put Jeremiah into the cistern. While
the king was sitting in the Benjamin Gate,
8 Ebed-Melek went out of the palace and
said to him, 9 "My lord the king, these
men have acted wickedly in all they have
done to Jeremiah the prophet. They have
thrown him into a cistern, where he will
starve to death when there is no longer
any bread in the city."

10 Then the king commanded Ebed-Melek the Cushite, "Take thirty men from
here with you and lift Jeremiah the prophet out of the cistern before he dies."

11 So Ebed-Melek took the men with
him and went to a room under the treasury in the palace. He took some old rags
and worn-out clothes from there and let
them down with ropes to Jeremiah in the
cistern. 12 Ebed-Melek the Cushite said
to Jeremiah, "Put these old rags and
worn-out clothes under your arms to pad
the ropes." Jeremiah did so, 13 and they
pulled him up with the ropes and lifted
him out of the cistern. And Jeremiah remained in the courtyard of the guard.

Zedekiah Questions Jeremiah Again

14 Then King Zedekiah sent for Jeremiah the prophet and had him brought to
the third entrance to the temple of the
LORD. "I am going to ask you something,"
the king said to Jeremiah. "Do not hide
anything from me."

---

a 1 Hebrew *Jukal*, a variant of *Jehukal*   b 2 Or *Chaldeans*; also in verses 18, 19 and 23   c 7 Probably from the upper
Nile region   d 7 Or a *eunuch*

15 Jeremiah said to Zedekiah, "If I give you an answer, will you not kill me? Even if I did give you counsel, you would not listen to me."

16 But King Zedekiah swore this oath secretly to Jeremiah: "As surely as the LORD lives, who has given us breath, I will neither kill you nor hand you over to those who want to kill you."

17 Then Jeremiah said to Zedekiah, "This is what the LORD God Almighty, the God of Israel, says: 'If you surrender to the officers of the king of Babylon, your life will be spared and this city will not be burned down; you and your family will live. 18 But if you will not surrender to the officers of the king of Babylon, this city will be given into the hands of the Babylonians and they will burn it down; you yourself will not escape from them.'"

19 King Zedekiah said to Jeremiah, "I am afraid of the Jews who have gone over to the Babylonians, for the Babylonians may hand me over to them and they will mistreat me."

20 "They will not hand you over," Jeremiah replied. "Obey the LORD by doing what I tell you. Then it will go well with you, and your life will be spared. 21 But if you refuse to surrender, this is what the LORD has revealed to me: 22 All the women left in the palace of the king of Judah will be brought out to the officials of the king of Babylon. Those women will say to you:

" 'They misled you and overcame you—
    those trusted friends of yours.
Your feet are sunk in the mud;
    your friends have deserted you.'

23 "All your wives and children will be brought out to the Babylonians. You yourself will not escape from their hands but will be captured by the king of Babylon; and this city will*a* be burned down."

24 Then Zedekiah said to Jeremiah, "Do not let anyone know about this conversation, or you may die. 25 If the officials hear that I talked with you, and they come to you and say, 'Tell us what you said to the king and what the king said to you; do not hide it from us or we will kill you,' 26 then tell them, 'I was pleading with the king not to send me back to Jonathan's house to die there.'"

27 All the officials did come to Jeremiah and question him, and he told them everything the king had ordered him to say. So they said no more to him, for no one had heard his conversation with the king.

28 And Jeremiah remained in the courtyard of the guard until the day Jerusalem was captured.

The Fall of Jerusalem

39 This is how Jerusalem was taken: 1 In the ninth year of Zedekiah king of Judah, in the tenth month, Nebuchad-

---

a 23 Or *and you will cause this city to*

PANORAMA

Change.

It's never too late to change, but sometimes it's too late to avoid punishment. That's what happened to Judah and Jerusalem. They were given 40 years to repent, but they didn't, so they were destroyed and the people were taken captive to Babylon.

{JEREMIAH}

nezzar king of Babylon marched against Jerusalem with his whole army and laid siege to it. ²And on the ninth day of the fourth month of Zedekiah's eleventh year, the city wall was broken through. ³Then all the officials of the king of Babylon came and took seats in the Middle Gate: Nergal-Sharezer of Samgar, Nebo-Sarsekim a chief officer, Nergal-Sharezer a high official and all the other officials of the king of Babylon. ⁴When Zedekiah king of Judah and all the soldiers saw them, they fled; they left the city at night by way of the king's garden, through the gate between the two walls, and headed toward the Arabah.ᵃ

⁵But the Babylonianᵇ army pursued them and overtook Zedekiah in the plains of Jericho. They captured him and took him to Nebuchadnezzar king of Babylon at Riblah in the land of Hamath, where he pronounced sentence on him. ⁶There at Riblah the king of Babylon slaughtered the sons of Zedekiah before his eyes and also killed all the nobles of Judah. ⁷Then he put out Zedekiah's eyes and bound him with bronze shackles to take him to Babylon.

⁸The Babyloniansᵇ set fire to the royal palace and the houses of the people and broke down the walls of Jerusalem. ⁹Nebuzaradan commander of the imperial guard carried into exile to Babylon the people who remained in the city, along with those who had gone over to him, and the rest of the people. ¹⁰But Nebuzaradan the commander of the guard left behind in the land of Judah some of the poor people, who owned nothing; and at that time he gave them vineyards and fields.

¹¹Now Nebuchadnezzar king of Babylon had given these orders about Jeremiah through Nebuzaradan commander of the imperial guard: ¹²"Take him and look after him; don't harm him but do for him whatever he asks." ¹³So Nebuzaradan the commander of the guard, Nebushazban a chief officer, Nergal-Sharezer a high official and all the other officers of the king of Babylon ¹⁴sent and had Jeremiah

taken out of the courtyard of the guard. They turned him over to Gedaliah son of Ahikam, the son of Shaphan, to take him back to his home. So he remained among his own people.

¹⁵While Jeremiah had been confined in the courtyard of the guard, the word of the LORD came to him: ¹⁶"Go and tell Ebed-Melek the Cushite, 'This is what the LORD Almighty, the God of Israel, says: I am about to fulfill my words against this city—words concerning disaster, not prosperity. At that time they will be fulfilled before your eyes. ¹⁷But I will rescue you on that day, declares the LORD; you will not be given into the hands of those you fear. ¹⁸I will save you; you will not fall by the sword but will escape with your life, because you trust in me, declares the LORD.'"

Jeremiah Freed

40 The word came to Jeremiah from the LORD after Nebuzaradan commander of the imperial guard had released him at Ramah. He had found Jeremiah bound in chains among all the captives from Jerusalem and Judah who were being carried into exile to Babylon. ²When the commander of the guard found Jeremiah, he said to him, "The LORD your God decreed this disaster for this place. ³And now the LORD has brought it about; he has done just as he said he would. All this happened because you people sinned against the LORD and did not obey him. ⁴But today I am freeing you from the chains on your wrists. Come with me to Babylon, if you like, and I will look after you; but if you do not want to, then don't come. Look, the whole country lies before you; go wherever you please." ⁵However, before Jeremiah turned to go,ᶜ Nebuzaradan added, "Go back to Gedaliah son of Ahikam, the son of Shaphan, whom the king of Babylon has appointed over the towns of Judah, and live with him among the people, or go anywhere else you please."

Then the commander gave him provisions and a present and let him go. ⁶So

ᵃ 4 Or the Jordan Valley   ᵇ 5,8 Or Chaldean   ᶜ 5 Or Jeremiah answered

Jeremiah went to Gedaliah son of Ahikam at Mizpah and stayed with him among the people who were left behind in the land.

Gedaliah Assassinated

[7] When all the army officers and their men who were still in the open country heard that the king of Babylon had appointed Gedaliah son of Ahikam as governor over the land and had put him in charge of the men, women and children who were the poorest in the land and who had not been carried into exile to Babylon, [8] they came to Gedaliah at Mizpah — Ishmael son of Nethaniah, Johanan and Jonathan the sons of Kareah, Seraiah son of Tanhumeth, the sons of Ephai the Netophathite, and Jaazaniah[a] the son of the Maakathite, and their men. [9] Gedaliah son of Ahikam, the son of Shaphan, took an oath to reassure them and their men. "Do not be afraid to serve the Babylonians,[b]" he said. "Settle down in the land and serve the king of Babylon, and it will go well with you. [10] I myself will stay at Mizpah to represent you before the Babylonians who come to us, but you are to harvest the wine, summer fruit and olive oil, and put them in your storage jars, and live in the towns you have taken over."

[11] When all the Jews in Moab, Ammon, Edom and all the other countries heard that the king of Babylon had left a remnant in Judah and had appointed Gedaliah son of Ahikam, the son of Shaphan, as governor over them, [12] they all came back to the land of Judah, to Gedaliah at Mizpah, from all the countries where they had been scattered. And they harvested an abundance of wine and summer fruit.

[13] Johanan son of Kareah and all the army officers still in the open country came to Gedaliah at Mizpah [14] and said to him, "Don't you know that Baalis king of the Ammonites has sent Ishmael son of Nethaniah to take your life?" But Gedaliah son of Ahikam did not believe them.

[15] Then Johanan son of Kareah said privately to Gedaliah in Mizpah, "Let me go and kill Ishmael son of Nethaniah, and no one will know it. Why should he take your life and cause all the Jews who are gathered around you to be scattered and the remnant of Judah to perish?"

[16] But Gedaliah son of Ahikam said to Johanan son of Kareah, "Don't do such a thing! What you are saying about Ishmael is not true."

41 In the seventh month Ishmael son of Nethaniah, the son of Elishama, who was of royal blood and had been one of the king's officers, came with ten men to Gedaliah son of Ahikam at Mizpah. While they were eating together there, [2] Ishmael son of Nethaniah and the ten men who were with him got up and struck down Gedaliah son of Ahikam, the son of Shaphan, with the sword, killing the one whom the king of Babylon had appointed as governor over the land. [3] Ishmael also killed all the men of Judah who were with Gedaliah at Mizpah, as well as the Babylonian[c] soldiers who were there.

[4] The day after Gedaliah's assassination, before anyone knew about it, [5] eighty men who had shaved off their beards, torn their clothes and cut themselves came from Shechem, Shiloh and Samaria, bringing grain offerings and incense with them to the house of the LORD. [6] Ishmael son of Nethaniah went out from Mizpah to meet them, weeping as he went. When he met them, he said, "Come to Gedaliah son of Ahikam." [7] When they went into the city, Ishmael son of Nethaniah and the men who were with him slaughtered them and threw them into a cistern. [8] But ten of them said to Ishmael, "Don't kill us! We have wheat and barley, olive oil and honey, hidden in a field." So he let them alone and did not kill them with the others. [9] Now the cistern where he threw all the bodies of the men he had killed along with Gedaliah was the one King Asa had made as part of his defense against Baasha king of Israel. Ishmael son of Nethaniah filled it with the dead.

[10] Ishmael made captives of all the rest of the people who were in Mizpah — the king's daughters along with all the others who were left there, over whom Nebuzaradan commander of the imperial guard had

---

[a] 8 Hebrew *Jezaniah*, a variant of *Jaazaniah*   [b] 9 Or *Chaldeans*; also in verse 10   [c] 3 Or *Chaldean*

appointed Gedaliah son of Ahikam. Ishmael son of Nethaniah took them captive and set out to cross over to the Ammonites.

[11] When Johanan son of Kareah and all the army officers who were with him heard about all the crimes Ishmael son of Nethaniah had committed, [12] they took all their men and went to fight Ishmael son of Nethaniah. They caught up with him near the great pool in Gibeon. [13] When all the people Ishmael had with him saw Johanan son of Kareah and the army officers who were with him, they were glad. [14] All the people Ishmael had taken captive at Mizpah turned and went over to Johanan son of Kareah. [15] But Ishmael son of Nethaniah and eight of his men escaped from Johanan and fled to the Ammonites.

Flight to Egypt

[16] Then Johanan son of Kareah and all the army officers who were with him led away all the people of Mizpah who had survived, whom Johanan had recovered from Ishmael son of Nethaniah after Ishmael had assassinated Gedaliah son of Ahikam—the soldiers, women, children and court officials he had recovered from Gibeon. [17] And they went on, stopping at Geruth Kimham near Bethlehem on their way to Egypt [18] to escape the Babylonians.[a] They were afraid of them because Ishmael son of Nethaniah had killed Gedaliah son of Ahikam, whom the king of Babylon had appointed as governor over the land.

42 Then all the army officers, including Johanan son of Kareah and Jezaniah[b] son of Hoshaiah, and all the people from the least to the greatest approached [2] Jeremiah the prophet and said to him, "Please hear our petition and pray to the LORD your God for this entire remnant. For as you now see, though we were once many, now only a few are left. [3] Pray that the LORD your God will tell us where we should go and what we should do."

[4] "I have heard you," replied Jeremiah the prophet. "I will certainly pray to the LORD your God as you have requested; I will tell you everything the LORD says and will keep nothing back from you."

[5] Then they said to Jeremiah, "May the LORD be a true and faithful witness against us if we do not act in accordance with everything the LORD your God sends you to tell us. [6] Whether it is favorable or unfavorable, we will obey the LORD our God, to whom we are sending you, so that it will go well with us, for we will obey the LORD our God."

[7] Ten days later the word of the LORD came to Jeremiah. [8] So he called together Johanan son of Kareah and all the army officers who were with him and all the people from the least to the greatest. [9] He said to them, "This is what the LORD, the God of Israel, to whom you sent me to present your petition, says: [10] 'If you stay in this land, I will build you up and not tear you down; I will plant you and not uproot you, for I have relented concerning the disaster I have inflicted on you. [11] Do not be afraid of the king of Babylon, whom you now fear. Do not be afraid of him, declares the LORD, for I am with you and will save you and deliver you from his hands. [12] I will show you compassion so that he will have compassion on you and restore you to your land.'

[13] "However, if you say, 'We will not stay in this land,' and so disobey the LORD your God, [14] and if you say, 'No, we will go and live in Egypt, where we will not see war or hear the trumpet or be hungry for bread,' [15] then hear the word of the LORD, you remnant of Judah. This is what the LORD Almighty, the God of Israel, says: 'If you are determined to go to Egypt and you do go to settle there, [16] then the sword you fear will overtake you there, and the famine you dread will follow you into Egypt, and there you will die. [17] Indeed, all who are determined to go to Egypt to settle there will die by the sword, famine and plague; not one of them will survive or escape the disaster I will bring on them.' [18] This is what the LORD Almighty, the God of Israel, says: 'As my anger and wrath have been poured out on those who lived in Jerusalem, so will my wrath be poured out on you when you go to Egypt. You will be a curse[c] and an object of horror, a curse[c] and an object of reproach; you will never see this place again.'

---

[a] 18 Or Chaldeans   [b] 1 Hebrew; Septuagint (see also 43:2) Azariah   [c] 18 That is, your name will be used in cursing (see 29:22); or, others will see that you are cursed.

¹⁹"Remnant of Judah, the LORD has told you, 'Do not go to Egypt.' Be sure of this: I warn you today ²⁰that you made a fatal mistake when you sent me to the LORD your God and said, 'Pray to the LORD our God for us; tell us everything he says and we will do it.' ²¹I have told you today, but you still have not obeyed the LORD your God in all he sent me to tell you. ²²So now, be sure of this: You will die by the sword, famine and plague in the place where you want to go to settle."

43 When Jeremiah had finished telling the people all the words of the LORD their God—everything the LORD had sent him to tell them— ²Azariah son of Hoshaiah and Johanan son of Kareah and all the arrogant men said to Jeremiah, "You are lying! The LORD our God has not sent you to say, 'You must not go to Egypt to settle there.' ³But Baruch son of Neriah is inciting you against us to hand us over to the Babylonians,ᵃ so they may kill us or carry us into exile to Babylon."

⁴So Johanan son of Kareah and all the army officers and all the people disobeyed the LORD's command to stay in the land of Judah. ⁵Instead, Johanan son of Kareah and all the army officers led away all the remnant of Judah who had come back to live in the land of Judah from all the nations where they had been scattered. ⁶They also led away all those whom Nebuzaradan commander of the imperial guard had left with Gedaliah son of Ahikam, the son of Shaphan—the men, the women, the children and the king's daughters. And they took Jeremiah the prophet and Baruch son of Neriah along with them. ⁷So they entered Egypt in disobedience to the LORD and went as far as Tahpanhes.

⁸In Tahpanhes the word of the LORD came to Jeremiah: ⁹"While the Jews are watching, take some large stones with you and bury them in clay in the brick pavement at the entrance to Pharaoh's palace in Tahpanhes. ¹⁰Then say to them, 'This is what the LORD Almighty, the God of Israel, says: I will send for my servant Nebuchadnezzar king of Babylon, and I will set his throne over these stones I have buried here; he will spread his royal canopy above them. ¹¹He will come and attack Egypt, bringing death to those destined for death, captivity to those destined for captivity, and the sword to those destined for the sword. ¹²He will set fire to the temples of the gods of Egypt; he will burn their temples and take their gods captive. As a shepherd picks his garment clean of lice, so he will pick Egypt clean and depart. ¹³There in the temple of the sunᵇ in Egypt he will demolish the sacred pillars and will burn down the temples of the gods of Egypt.'"

Disaster Because of Idolatry

44 This word came to Jeremiah concerning all the Jews living in Lower Egypt—in Migdol, Tahpanhes and Memphis—and in Upper Egypt: ²"This is what the LORD Almighty, the God of Israel, says: You saw the great disaster I brought on Jerusalem and on all the towns of Judah. Today they lie deserted and in ruins ³because of the evil they have done. They aroused my anger by burning incense to and worshiping other gods that neither they nor you nor your ancestors ever knew. ⁴Again and again I sent my servants the prophets, who said, 'Do not do this detestable thing that I hate!' ⁵But they did not listen or pay attention; they did not turn from their wickedness or stop burning incense to other gods. ⁶Therefore, my fierce anger was poured out; it raged against the towns of Judah and the streets of Jerusalem and made them the desolate ruins they are today.

⁷"Now this is what the LORD God Almighty, the God of Israel, says: Why bring such great disaster on yourselves by cutting off from Judah the men and women, the children and infants, and so leave yourselves without a remnant? ⁸Why arouse my anger with what your hands have made, burning incense to other gods in Egypt, where you have come to live? You will destroy yourselves and make yourselves a curseᶜ and an object

---

ᵃ 3 Or Chaldeans   ᵇ 13 Or in Heliopolis   ᶜ 8 That is, your name will be used in cursing (see 29:22); or, others will see that you are cursed; also in verse 12; similarly in verse 22.

of reproach among all the nations on earth. ⁹Have you forgotten the wickedness committed by your ancestors and by the kings and queens of Judah and the wickedness committed by you and your wives in the land of Judah and the streets of Jerusalem? ¹⁰To this day they have not humbled themselves or shown reverence, nor have they followed my law and the decrees I set before you and your ancestors.

¹¹"Therefore this is what the Lᴏʀᴅ Almighty, the God of Israel, says: I am determined to bring disaster on you and to destroy all Judah. ¹²I will take away the remnant of Judah who were determined to go to Egypt to settle there. They will all perish in Egypt; they will fall by the sword or die from famine. From the least to the greatest, they will die by sword or famine. They will become a curse and an object of horror, a curse and an object of reproach. ¹³I will punish those who live in Egypt with the sword, famine and plague, as I punished Jerusalem. ¹⁴None of the remnant of Judah who have gone to live in Egypt will escape or survive to return to the land of Judah, to which they long to return and live; none will return except a few fugitives."

¹⁵Then all the men who knew that their wives were burning incense to other gods, along with all the women who were present—a large assembly—and all the people living in Lower and Upper Egypt, said to Jeremiah, ¹⁶"We will not listen to the message you have spoken to us in the name of the Lᴏʀᴅ! ¹⁷We will certainly do everything we said we would: We will burn incense to the Queen of Heaven and will pour out drink offerings to her just as we and our ancestors, our kings and our officials did in the towns of Judah and in the streets of Jerusalem. At that time we had plenty of food and were well off and suffered no harm. ¹⁸But ever since we stopped burning incense to the Queen of Heaven and pouring out drink offerings to her, we have had nothing and have been perishing by sword and famine."

¹⁹The women added, "When we burned incense to the Queen of Heaven and poured out drink offerings to her, did not our husbands know that we were making cakes impressed with her image and pouring out drink offerings to her?"

²⁰Then Jeremiah said to all the people, both men and women, who were answering him, ²¹"Did not the Lᴏʀᴅ remember and call to mind the incense burned in the towns of Judah and the streets of Jerusalem by you and your ancestors, your kings and your officials and the people of the land? ²²When the Lᴏʀᴅ could no longer endure your wicked actions and the detestable things you did, your land became a curse and a desolate waste without inhabitants, as it is today. ²³Because you have burned incense and have sinned against the Lᴏʀᴅ and have not obeyed him or followed his law or his decrees or his stipulations, this disaster has come upon you, as you now see."

²⁴Then Jeremiah said to all the people, including the women, "Hear the word of the Lᴏʀᴅ, all you people of Judah in Egypt. ²⁵This is what the Lᴏʀᴅ Almighty, the God of Israel, says: You and your wives have done what you said you would do when you promised, 'We will certainly carry out the vows we made to burn incense and pour out drink offerings to the Queen of Heaven.'

"Go ahead then, do what you promised! Keep your vows! ²⁶But hear the word of the Lᴏʀᴅ, all you Jews living in Egypt: 'I swear by my great name,' says the Lᴏʀᴅ, 'that no one from Judah living anywhere in Egypt will ever again invoke my name or swear, "As surely as the Sovereign Lᴏʀᴅ lives." ²⁷For I am watching over them for harm, not for good; the Jews in Egypt will perish by sword and famine until they are all destroyed. ²⁸Those who escape the sword and return to the land of Judah from Egypt will be very few. Then the whole remnant of Judah who came to live in Egypt will know whose word will stand—mine or theirs.

²⁹"'This will be the sign to you that I will punish you in this place,' declares the Lᴏʀᴅ, 'so that you will know that my threats of harm against you will surely stand.' ³⁰This is what the Lᴏʀᴅ says: 'I am going to deliver Pharaoh Hophra king of Egypt into the hands of his enemies

who want to kill him, just as I gave Zedekiah king of Judah into the hands of Nebuchadnezzar king of Babylon, the enemy who wanted to kill him.' "

A Message to Baruch

45 When Baruch son of Neriah wrote on a scroll the words Jeremiah the prophet dictated in the fourth year of Jehoiakim son of Josiah king of Judah, Jeremiah said this to Baruch: ² "This is what the Lord, the God of Israel, says to you, Baruch: ³ You said, 'Woe to me! The Lord has added sorrow to my pain; I am worn out with groaning and find no rest.' ⁴ But the Lord has told me to say to you, 'This is what the Lord says: I will overthrow what I have built and uproot what I have planted, throughout the earth. ⁵ Should you then seek great things for yourself? Do not seek them. For I will bring disaster on all people, declares the Lord, but wherever you go I will let you escape with your life.' "

A Message About Egypt

46 This is the word of the Lord that came to Jeremiah the prophet concerning the nations:

² Concerning Egypt:

This is the message against the army of Pharaoh Necho king of Egypt, which was defeated at Carchemish on the Euphrates River by Nebuchadnezzar king of Babylon in the fourth year of Jehoiakim son of Josiah king of Judah:

³ "Prepare your shields, both large and
　　small,
　　and march out for battle!
⁴ Harness the horses,
　　mount the steeds!
Take your positions
　　with helmets on!
Polish your spears,
　　put on your armor!
⁵ What do I see?
　　They are terrified,
they are retreating,
　　their warriors are defeated.

They flee in haste
　　without looking back,
　　and there is terror on every side,"
　　　　　declares the Lord.
⁶ "The swift cannot flee
　　nor the strong escape.
In the north by the River Euphrates
　　they stumble and fall.

⁷ "Who is this that rises like the
　　Nile,
　　like rivers of surging waters?
⁸ Egypt rises like the Nile,
　　like rivers of surging waters.
She says, 'I will rise and cover the
　　earth;
　　I will destroy cities and their
　　people.'
⁹ Charge, you horses!
　　Drive furiously, you charioteers!
March on, you warriors—men of
　　Cush[a] and Put who carry
　　shields,
　　men of Lydia who draw the bow.
¹⁰ But that day belongs to the Lord, the
　　Lord Almighty—
　　a day of vengeance, for vengeance
　　on his foes.
The sword will devour till it is
　　satisfied,
　　till it has quenched its thirst with
　　blood.
For the Lord, the Lord Almighty, will
　　offer sacrifice
　　in the land of the north by the River
　　Euphrates.

¹¹ "Go up to Gilead and get balm,
　　Virgin Daughter Egypt.
But you try many medicines in
　　vain;
　　there is no healing for you.
¹² The nations will hear of your
　　shame;
　　your cries will fill the earth.
One warrior will stumble over
　　another;
　　both will fall down together."

¹³ This is the message the Lord spoke to Jeremiah the prophet about the coming of Nebuchadnezzar king of Babylon to attack Egypt:

ª 9 That is, the upper Nile region

14 "Announce this in Egypt, and proclaim
it in Migdol;
   proclaim it also in Memphis and
Tahpanhes:
'Take your positions and get ready,
   for the sword devours those around
you.'
15 Why will your warriors be laid low?
They cannot stand, for the LORD will
push them down.
16 They will stumble repeatedly;
   they will fall over each other.
They will say, 'Get up, let us go
back
   to our own people and our native
lands,
   away from the sword of the
oppressor.'
17 There they will exclaim,
   'Pharaoh king of Egypt is only a loud
noise;
   he has missed his opportunity.'

18 "As surely as I live," declares the
King,
   whose name is the LORD Almighty,
"one will come who is like Tabor
   among the mountains,
   like Carmel by the sea.
19 Pack your belongings for exile,
   you who live in Egypt,
for Memphis will be laid waste
   and lie in ruins without
inhabitant.

20 "Egypt is a beautiful heifer,
   but a gadfly is coming
   against her from the north.
21 The mercenaries in her ranks
   are like fattened calves.
They too will turn and flee together,
   they will not stand their ground,
for the day of disaster is coming upon
them,
   the time for them to be punished.
22 Egypt will hiss like a fleeing
serpent
   as the enemy advances in force;
they will come against her with
axes,
   like men who cut down trees.
23 They will chop down her forest,"
               declares the LORD,
"dense though it be.

They are more numerous than
locusts,
   they cannot be counted.
24 Daughter Egypt will be put to
shame,
   given into the hands of the people
of the north."

25 The LORD Almighty, the God of Israel, says: "I am about to bring punishment on Amon god of Thebes, on Pharaoh, on Egypt and her gods and her kings, and on those who rely on Pharaoh. 26 I will give them into the hands of those who want to kill them—Nebuchadnezzar king of Babylon and his officers. Later, however, Egypt will be inhabited as in times past," declares the LORD.

27 "Do not be afraid, Jacob my
servant;
   do not be dismayed, Israel.
I will surely save you out of a distant
place,
   your descendants from the land of
their exile.
Jacob will again have peace and
security,
   and no one will make him afraid.
28 Do not be afraid, Jacob my
servant,
   for I am with you," declares the
LORD.
"Though I completely destroy all the
nations
   among which I scatter you,
I will not completely destroy you.
I will discipline you but only in due
measure;
   I will not let you go entirely
unpunished."

A Message About the Philistines

47 This is the word of the LORD that came to Jeremiah the prophet concerning the Philistines before Pharaoh attacked Gaza:

2 This is what the LORD says:

"See how the waters are rising in the
north;
   they will become an overflowing
torrent.

They will overflow the land and
everything in it,
the towns and those who live in
them.
The people will cry out;
all who dwell in the land will wail
³at the sound of the hooves of
galloping steeds,
at the noise of enemy chariots
and the rumble of their wheels.
Parents will not turn to help their
children;
their hands will hang limp.
⁴For the day has come
to destroy all the Philistines
and to remove all survivors
who could help Tyre and Sidon.
The LORD is about to destroy the
Philistines,
the remnant from the coasts of
Caphtor.ᵃ
⁵Gaza will shave her head in mourning;
Ashkelon will be silenced.
You remnant on the plain,
how long will you cut yourselves?

⁶" 'Alas, sword of the LORD,
how long till you rest?
Return to your sheath;
cease and be still.'
⁷But how can it rest
when the LORD has commanded it,
when he has ordered it
to attack Ashkelon and the coast?"

A Message About Moab

48

Concerning Moab:

This is what the LORD Almighty, the God
of Israel, says:

"Woe to Nebo, for it will be ruined.
Kiriathaim will be disgraced and
captured;
the strongholdᵇ will be disgraced
and shattered.
²Moab will be praised no more;
in Heshbonᶜ people will plot her
downfall:
'Come, let us put an end to that
nation.'

You, the people of Madmen,ᵈ will also
be silenced;
the sword will pursue you.
³Cries of anguish arise from
Horonaim,
cries of great havoc and
destruction.
⁴Moab will be broken;
her little ones will cry out.ᵉ
⁵They go up the hill to Luhith,
weeping bitterly as they go;
on the road down to Horonaim
anguished cries over the
destruction are heard.
⁶Flee! Run for your lives;
become like a bushᶠ in the
desert.
⁷Since you trust in your deeds and
riches,
you too will be taken captive,
and Chemosh will go into exile,
together with his priests and
officials.
⁸The destroyer will come against every
town,
and not a town will escape.
The valley will be ruined
and the plateau destroyed,
because the LORD has spoken.
⁹Put salt on Moab,
for she will be laid wasteᵍ;
her towns will become desolate,
with no one to live in them.

¹⁰"A curse on anyone who is lax in doing
the LORD's work!
A curse on anyone who keeps their
sword from bloodshed!

¹¹"Moab has been at rest from youth,
like wine left on its dregs,
not poured from one jar to
another—
she has not gone into exile.
So she tastes as she did,
and her aroma is unchanged.
¹²But days are coming,"
declares the LORD,
"when I will send men who pour from
pitchers,
and they will pour her out;

ᵃ 4 That is, Crete   ᵇ 1 Or captured; / Misgab   ᶜ 2 The Hebrew for Heshbon sounds like the Hebrew for plot.
ᵈ 2 The name of the Moabite town Madmen sounds like the Hebrew for be silenced.   ᵉ 4 Hebrew; Septuagint / proclaim
it to Zoar   ᶠ 6 Or like Aroer   ᵍ 9 Or Give wings to Moab, / for she will fly away

they will empty her pitchers
and smash her jars.
¹³ Then Moab will be ashamed of
Chemosh,
as Israel was ashamed
when they trusted in Bethel.

¹⁴ "How can you say, 'We are warriors,
men valiant in battle'?
¹⁵ Moab will be destroyed and her towns
invaded;
her finest young men will go down
in the slaughter,"
declares the King, whose name is
the Lord Almighty.
¹⁶ "The fall of Moab is at hand;
her calamity will come quickly.
¹⁷ Mourn for her, all who live around
her,
all who know her fame;
say, 'How broken is the mighty
scepter,
how broken the glorious staff!'

¹⁸ "Come down from your glory
and sit on the parched ground,
you inhabitants of Daughter Dibon,
for the one who destroys Moab
will come up against you
and ruin your fortified cities.
¹⁹ Stand by the road and watch,
you who live in Aroer.
Ask the man fleeing and the woman
escaping,
ask them, 'What has happened?'
²⁰ Moab is disgraced, for she is
shattered.
Wail and cry out!
Announce by the Arnon
that Moab is destroyed.
²¹ Judgment has come to the plateau—
to Holon, Jahzah and Mephaath,
²² to Dibon, Nebo and Beth
Diblathaim,
²³ to Kiriathaim, Beth Gamul and Beth
Meon,
²⁴ to Kerioth and Bozrah—
to all the towns of Moab, far and
near.
²⁵ Moab's horn[a] is cut off;
her arm is broken,"
declares the Lord.

²⁶ "Make her drunk,
for she has defied the Lord.
Let Moab wallow in her vomit;
let her be an object of ridicule.
²⁷ Was not Israel the object of your
ridicule?
Was she caught among thieves,
that you shake your head in scorn
whenever you speak of her?
²⁸ Abandon your towns and dwell among
the rocks,
you who live in Moab.
Be like a dove that makes its nest
at the mouth of a cave.

²⁹ "We have heard of Moab's pride—
how great is her arrogance!—
of her insolence, her pride, her
conceit
and the haughtiness of her
heart.
³⁰ I know her insolence but it is
futile,"
declares the Lord,
"and her boasts accomplish
nothing.
³¹ Therefore I wail over Moab,
for all Moab I cry out,
I moan for the people of Kir
Hareseth.

Jeremiah 48

Q: What are Jeremiah 46–51
about?

**BONUS: Name three of Judah's
enemies.**

Answers on next page

ᵃ 25 *Horn* here symbolizes strength.

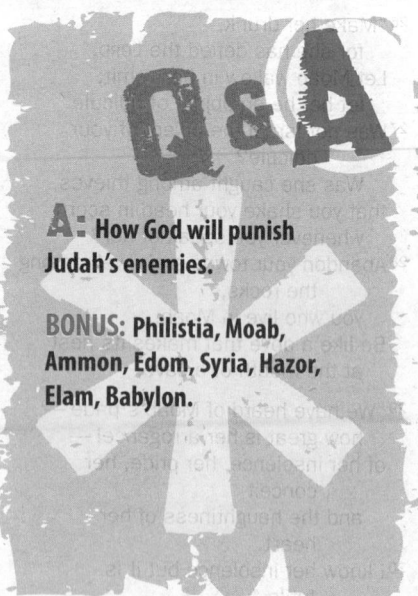

A: How God will punish Judah's enemies.

BONUS: Philistia, Moab, Ammon, Edom, Syria, Hazor, Elam, Babylon.

32 I weep for you, as Jazer weeps,
   you vines of Sibmah.
Your branches spread as far as the sea[a];
   they reached as far as[b] Jazer.
The destroyer has fallen
   on your ripened fruit and grapes.
33 Joy and gladness are gone
   from the orchards and fields of Moab.
I have stopped the flow of wine from the presses;
   no one treads them with shouts of joy.
Although there are shouts,
   they are not shouts of joy.

34 "The sound of their cry rises
   from Heshbon to Elealeh and Jahaz,
from Zoar as far as Horonaim and Eglath Shelishiyah,
   for even the waters of Nimrim are dried up.
35 In Moab I will put an end
   to those who make offerings on the high places
and burn incense to their gods,"
            declares the Lord.

36 "So my heart laments for Moab like
      the music of a pipe;
   it laments like a pipe for the people
      of Kir Hareseth.
   The wealth they acquired is gone.
37 Every head is shaved
   and every beard cut off;
every hand is slashed
   and every waist is covered with sackcloth.
38 On all the roofs in Moab
   and in the public squares
there is nothing but mourning,
   for I have broken Moab
   like a jar that no one wants,"
            declares the Lord.
39 "How shattered she is! How they wail!
   How Moab turns her back in shame!
Moab has become an object of ridicule,
   an object of horror to all those around her."

40 This is what the Lord says:

"Look! An eagle is swooping down,
   spreading its wings over Moab.
41 Kerioth[c] will be captured
   and the strongholds taken.
In that day the hearts of Moab's warriors
   will be like the heart of a woman in labor.
42 Moab will be destroyed as a nation
   because she defied the Lord.
43 Terror and pit and snare await you,
   you people of Moab,"
            declares the Lord.
44 "Whoever flees from the terror
   will fall into a pit,
whoever climbs out of the pit
   will be caught in a snare;
for I will bring on Moab
   the year of her punishment,"
            declares the Lord.

45 "In the shadow of Heshbon
   the fugitives stand helpless,
for a fire has gone out from Heshbon,
   a blaze from the midst of Sihon;
it burns the foreheads of Moab,
   the skulls of the noisy boasters.

---

a 32 Probably the Dead Sea   b 32 Two Hebrew manuscripts and Septuagint; most Hebrew manuscripts as far as the Sea of   c 41 Or The cities

46 Woe to you, Moab!
The people of Chemosh are
destroyed;
your sons are taken into exile
and your daughters into captivity.
47 "Yet I will restore the fortunes of
Moab
in days to come,"
declares the LORD.

Here ends the judgment on Moab.

A Message About Ammon

49 Concerning the Ammonites:

This is what the LORD says:

"Has Israel no sons?
Has Israel no heir?
Why then has Molek[a] taken
possession of Gad?
Why do his people live in its towns?
2 But the days are coming,"
declares the LORD,
"when I will sound the battle cry
against Rabbah of the Ammonites;
it will become a mound of ruins,
and its surrounding villages will be
set on fire.
Then Israel will drive out
those who drove her out,"
says the LORD.
3 "Wail, Heshbon, for Ai is destroyed!
Cry out, you inhabitants of Rabbah!
Put on sackcloth and mourn;
rush here and there inside the
walls,
for Molek will go into exile,
together with his priests and
officials.
4 Why do you boast of your valleys,
boast of your valleys so fruitful?
Unfaithful Daughter Ammon,
you trust in your riches and say,
'Who will attack me?'
5 I will bring terror on you
from all those around you,"
declares the Lord,
the LORD Almighty.
"Every one of you will be driven away,
and no one will gather the fugitives.

6 "Yet afterward, I will restore the
fortunes of the Ammonites,"
declares the LORD.

A Message About Edom

7 Concerning Edom:

This is what the LORD Almighty says:

"Is there no longer wisdom in Teman?
Has counsel perished from the
prudent?
Has their wisdom decayed?
8 Turn and flee, hide in deep caves,
you who live in Dedan,
for I will bring disaster on Esau
at the time when I punish him.
9 If grape pickers came to you,
would they not leave a few grapes?
If thieves came during the night,
would they not steal only as much
as they wanted?
10 But I will strip Esau bare;
I will uncover his hiding places,
so that he cannot conceal himself.
His armed men are destroyed,
also his allies and neighbors,
so there is no one to say,
11 'Leave your fatherless children; I will
keep them alive.
Your widows too can depend
on me.'"

12 This is what the LORD says: "If those
who do not deserve to drink the cup must
drink it, why should you go unpunished?
You will not go unpunished, but must
drink it. 13 I swear by myself," declares the
LORD, "that Bozrah will become a ruin and
a curse,[b] an object of horror and reproach;
and all its towns will be in ruins forever."

14 I have heard a message from the LORD;
an envoy was sent to the nations to
say,
"Assemble yourselves to attack it!
Rise up for battle!"
15 "Now I will make you small among the
nations,
despised by mankind.
16 The terror you inspire
and the pride of your heart have
deceived you,

---

a 1 Or *their king*; also in verse 3   b 13 That is, its name will be used in cursing (see 29:22); or, others will see that it is cursed.

you who live in the clefts of the rocks,
who occupy the heights of the hill.
Though you build your nest as high as
the eagle's,
from there I will bring you down,"
declares the LORD.
17 "Edom will become an object of horror;
all who pass by will be appalled and
will scoff
because of all its wounds.
18 As Sodom and Gomorrah were
overthrown,
along with their neighboring towns,"
says the LORD,
"so no one will live there;
no people will dwell in it.

19 "Like a lion coming up from Jordan's
thickets
to a rich pastureland,
I will chase Edom from its land in an
instant.
Who is the chosen one I will appoint
for this?
Who is like me and who can
challenge me?
And what shepherd can stand
against me?"

20 Therefore, hear what the LORD has
planned against Edom,
what he has purposed against
those who live in Teman:
The young of the flock will be dragged
away;
their pasture will be appalled at
their fate.
21 At the sound of their fall the earth will
tremble;
their cry will resound to the Red
Sea.*a*
22 Look! An eagle will soar and swoop
down,
spreading its wings over Bozrah.
In that day the hearts of Edom's
warriors
will be like the heart of a woman in
labor.

A Message About Damascus

23 Concerning Damascus:

"Hamath and Arpad are dismayed,
for they have heard bad news.

They are disheartened,
troubled like*b* the restless sea.
24 Damascus has become feeble,
she has turned to flee
and panic has gripped her;
anguish and pain have seized her,
pain like that of a woman in labor.
25 Why has the city of renown not been
abandoned,
the town in which I delight?
26 Surely, her young men will fall in the
streets;
all her soldiers will be silenced in
that day,"
declares the LORD Almighty.
27 "I will set fire to the walls of
Damascus;
it will consume the fortresses of
Ben-Hadad."

A Message About Kedar
and Hazor

28 Concerning Kedar and the kingdoms
of Hazor, which Nebuchadnezzar king of
Babylon attacked:

This is what the LORD says:

"Arise, and attack Kedar
and destroy the people of the East.
29 Their tents and their flocks will be
taken;
their shelters will be carried off
with all their goods and camels.
People will shout to them,
'Terror on every side!'

30 "Flee quickly away!
Stay in deep caves, you who live in
Hazor,"
declares the LORD.
"Nebuchadnezzar king of Babylon has
plotted against you;
he has devised a plan against you.

31 "Arise and attack a nation at ease,
which lives in confidence,"
declares the LORD,
"a nation that has neither gates nor
bars;
its people live far from danger.
32 Their camels will become plunder,
and their large herds will be spoils
of war.

---

a 21 Or *the Sea of Reeds*   *b* 23 Hebrew *on* or *by*

I will scatter to the winds those who
are in distant places[a]
and will bring disaster on them from
every side,"
declares the LORD.
33 "Hazor will become a haunt of jackals,
a desolate place forever.
No one will live there;
no people will dwell in it."

A Message About Elam

34 This is the word of the LORD that came to Jeremiah the prophet concerning Elam, early in the reign of Zedekiah king of Judah:

35 This is what the LORD Almighty says:

"See, I will break the bow of Elam,
the mainstay of their might.
36 I will bring against Elam the four winds
from the four quarters of heaven;
I will scatter them to the four winds,
and there will not be a nation
where Elam's exiles do not go.
37 I will shatter Elam before their foes,
before those who want to kill them;
I will bring disaster on them,
even my fierce anger,"
declares the LORD.
"I will pursue them with the sword
until I have made an end of them.
38 I will set my throne in Elam
and destroy her king and officials,"
declares the LORD.

39 "Yet I will restore the fortunes of Elam
in days to come,"
declares the LORD.

A Message About Babylon

50 This is the word the LORD spoke through Jeremiah the prophet concerning Babylon and the land of the Babylonians[b]:

2 "Announce and proclaim among the
nations,
lift up a banner and proclaim it;
keep nothing back, but say,
'Babylon will be captured;
Bel will be put to shame,
Marduk filled with terror.

Her images will be put to shame
and her idols filled with terror.'
3 A nation from the north will attack her
and lay waste her land.
No one will live in it;
both people and animals will flee
away.

4 "In those days, at that time,"
declares the LORD,
"the people of Israel and the people
of Judah together
will go in tears to seek the LORD
their God.
5 They will ask the way to Zion
and turn their faces toward it.
They will come and bind themselves
to the LORD
in an everlasting covenant
that will not be forgotten.

6 "My people have been lost sheep;
their shepherds have led them
astray
and caused them to roam on the
mountains.
They wandered over mountain and
hill
and forgot their own resting place.
7 Whoever found them devoured
them;
their enemies said, 'We are not
guilty,
for they sinned against the LORD, their
verdant pasture,
the LORD, the hope of their
ancestors.'

8 "Flee out of Babylon;
leave the land of the Babylonians,
and be like the goats that lead the
flock.
9 For I will stir up and bring against
Babylon
an alliance of great nations from
the land of the north.
They will take up their positions
against her,
and from the north she will be
captured.
Their arrows will be like skilled
warriors
who do not return empty-handed.

---

[a] 32 Or who clip the hair by their foreheads   [b] 1 Or Chaldeans; also in verses 8, 25, 35 and 45

¹⁰So Babylonia^a will be plundered;
  all who plunder her will have their
    fill,"
                    declares the Lord.

¹¹"Because you rejoice and are glad,
  you who pillage my inheritance,
  because you frolic like a heifer
    threshing grain
  and neigh like stallions,
¹²your mother will be greatly ashamed;
  she who gave you birth will be
    disgraced.
  She will be the least of the nations—
    a wilderness, a dry land, a desert.
¹³Because of the Lord's anger she will
    not be inhabited
  but will be completely desolate.
  All who pass Babylon will be appalled;
    they will scoff because of all her
      wounds.

¹⁴"Take up your positions around
    Babylon,
  all you who draw the bow.
  Shoot at her! Spare no arrows,
    for she has sinned against the
      Lord.
¹⁵Shout against her on every side!
  She surrenders, her towers fall,
    her walls are torn down.
  Since this is the vengeance of the
    Lord,
    take vengeance on her;
    do to her as she has done to
      others.
¹⁶Cut off from Babylon the sower,
  and the reaper with his sickle at
    harvest.
  Because of the sword of the
    oppressor
  let everyone return to their own
    people,
  let everyone flee to their own land.

¹⁷"Israel is a scattered flock
  that lions have chased away.
  The first to devour them
    was the king of Assyria;
  the last to crush their bones
    was Nebuchadnezzar king of
      Babylon."

¹⁸Therefore this is what the Lord Almighty, the God of Israel, says:

"I will punish the king of Babylon and
    his land
  as I punished the king of Assyria.
¹⁹But I will bring Israel back to their own
    pasture,
  and they will graze on Carmel and
    Bashan;
  their appetite will be satisfied
    on the hills of Ephraim and Gilead.
²⁰In those days, at that time,"
                    declares the Lord,
  "search will be made for Israel's guilt,
    but there will be none,
  and for the sins of Judah,
    but none will be found,
  for I will forgive the remnant I spare.

²¹"Attack the land of Merathaim
  and those who live in Pekod.
  Pursue, kill and completely destroy^b
    them,"
                    declares the Lord.
  "Do everything I have commanded
    you.
²²The noise of battle is in the land,
    the noise of great destruction!
²³How broken and shattered
    is the hammer of the whole earth!
  How desolate is Babylon
    among the nations!
²⁴I set a trap for you, Babylon,
    and you were caught before you
      knew it;
  you were found and captured
    because you opposed the Lord.
²⁵The Lord has opened his arsenal
    and brought out the weapons of his
      wrath,
  for the Sovereign Lord Almighty has
    work to do
    in the land of the Babylonians.
²⁶Come against her from afar.
  Break open her granaries;
    pile her up like heaps of grain.
  Completely destroy her
    and leave her no remnant.
²⁷Kill all her young bulls;
    let them go down to the slaughter!

---

^a 10 Or *Chaldea*   ^b 21 The Hebrew term refers to the irrevocable giving over of things or persons to the Lord, often by totally destroying them; also in verse 26.

Woe to them! For their day has come,
the time for them to be punished.
28 Listen to the fugitives and refugees
from Babylon
declaring in Zion
how the LORD our God has taken
vengeance,
vengeance for his temple.

29 "Summon archers against Babylon,
all those who draw the bow.
Encamp all around her;
let no one escape.
Repay her for her deeds;
do to her as she has done.
For she has defied the LORD,
the Holy One of Israel.
30 Therefore, her young men will fall in
the streets;
all her soldiers will be silenced in
that day,"
declares the LORD.
31 "See, I am against you, you arrogant
one,"
declares the Lord, the LORD
Almighty,
"for your day has come,
the time for you to be punished.
32 The arrogant one will stumble and fall
and no one will help her up;
I will kindle a fire in her towns
that will consume all who are
around her."

33 This is what the LORD Almighty says:

"The people of Israel are oppressed,
and the people of Judah as well.
All their captors hold them fast,
refusing to let them go.
34 Yet their Redeemer is strong;
the LORD Almighty is his name.
He will vigorously defend their cause
so that he may bring rest to their
land,
but unrest to those who live in
Babylon.

35 "A sword against the Babylonians!"
declares the LORD—
"against those who live in Babylon
and against her officials and wise
men!
36 A sword against her false prophets!
They will become fools.
A sword against her warriors!
They will be filled with terror.
37 A sword against her horses and
chariots
and all the foreigners in her ranks!
They will become weaklings.
A sword against her treasures!
They will be plundered.
38 A drought on[a] her waters!
They will dry up.
For it is a land of idols,
idols that will go mad with terror.

39 "So desert creatures and hyenas will
live there,
and there the owl will dwell.
It will never again be inhabited
or lived in from generation to
generation.
40 As I overthrew Sodom and Gomorrah
along with their neighboring towns,"
declares the LORD,
"so no one will live there;
no people will dwell in it.

41 "Look! An army is coming from the
north;
a great nation and many kings
are being stirred up from the ends
of the earth.
42 They are armed with bows and spears;
they are cruel and without mercy.
They sound like the roaring sea
as they ride on their horses;
they come like men in battle formation
to attack you, Daughter Babylon.
43 The king of Babylon has heard reports
about them,
and his hands hang limp.
Anguish has gripped him,
pain like that of a woman in labor.
44 Like a lion coming up from Jordan's
thickets
to a rich pastureland,
I will chase Babylon from its land in an
instant.
Who is the chosen one I will appoint
for this?
Who is like me and who can
challenge me?

---

a 38 Or A sword against

And what shepherd can stand
    against me?"

45 Therefore, hear what the LORD has
    planned against Babylon,
  what he has purposed against the
    land of the Babylonians:
The young of the flock will be dragged
    away;
  their pasture will be appalled at
    their fate.
46 At the sound of Babylon's capture the
    earth will tremble;
  its cry will resound among the
    nations.

51 This is what the LORD says:

"See, I will stir up the spirit of a
    destroyer
  against Babylon and the people of
    Leb Kamai.[a]
2 I will send foreigners to Babylon
    to winnow her and to devastate her
      land;
  they will oppose her on every side
    in the day of her disaster.
3 Let not the archer string his
    bow,
  nor let him put on his armor.
Do not spare her young men;
  completely destroy[b] her army.
4 They will fall down slain in
    Babylon,[c]
  fatally wounded in her streets.
5 For Israel and Judah have not been
    forsaken
  by their God, the LORD Almighty,
though their land[d] is full of guilt
  before the Holy One of Israel.

6 "Flee from Babylon!
    Run for your lives!
  Do not be destroyed because of her
      sins.
It is time for the LORD's vengeance;
  he will repay her what she
    deserves.
7 Babylon was a gold cup in the LORD's
    hand;
  she made the whole earth
    drunk.

The nations drank her wine;
  therefore they have now gone
    mad.
8 Babylon will suddenly fall and be
    broken.
  Wail over her!
Get balm for her pain;
  perhaps she can be healed.

9 " 'We would have healed Babylon,
    but she cannot be healed;
let us leave her and each go to our
    own land,
  for her judgment reaches to the
    skies,
  it rises as high as the heavens.'

10 " 'The LORD has vindicated us;
    come, let us tell in Zion
  what the LORD our God has done.'

11 "Sharpen the arrows,
    take up the shields!
The LORD has stirred up the kings of
    the Medes,
  because his purpose is to destroy
    Babylon.
The LORD will take vengeance,
  vengeance for his temple.
12 Lift up a banner against the walls of
    Babylon!
  Reinforce the guard,
station the watchmen,
  prepare an ambush!
The LORD will carry out his purpose,
  his decree against the people of
    Babylon.
13 You who live by many waters
    and are rich in treasures,
  your end has come,
    the time for you to be destroyed.
14 The LORD Almighty has sworn by
    himself:
  I will surely fill you with troops, as
    with a swarm of locusts,
  and they will shout in triumph over
    you.

15 "He made the earth by his power;
  he founded the world by his wisdom
  and stretched out the heavens by
    his understanding.

---

a 1 Leb Kamai is a cryptogram for Chaldea, that is, Babylonia.   *b 3* The Hebrew term refers to the irrevocable giving over
of things or persons to the LORD, often by totally destroying them.   *c 4* Or Chaldea   *d 5* Or Almighty, / and the land of
the Babylonians

16 When he thunders, the waters in the
   heavens roar;
     he makes clouds rise from the ends
       of the earth.
   He sends lightning with the rain
     and brings out the wind from his
       storehouses.
17 "Everyone is senseless and without
   knowledge;
     every goldsmith is shamed by his
       idols.
   The images he makes are a fraud;
     they have no breath in them.
18 They are worthless, the objects of
   mockery;
     when their judgment comes, they
       will perish.
19 He who is the Portion of Jacob is not
   like these,
     for he is the Maker of all things,
   including the people of his
       inheritance—
     the Lord Almighty is his name.

20 "You are my war club,
     my weapon for battle—
   with you I shatter nations,
     with you I destroy kingdoms,
21 with you I shatter horse and rider,
     with you I shatter chariot and driver,
22 with you I shatter man and woman,
     with you I shatter old man and
       youth,
     with you I shatter young man and
       young woman,
23 with you I shatter shepherd and flock,
     with you I shatter farmer and oxen,
     with you I shatter governors and
       officials.

24 "Before your eyes I will repay Babylon
and all who live in Babylonia*a* for all the
wrong they have done in Zion," declares
the Lord.

25 "I am against you, you destroying
   mountain,
     you who destroy the whole earth,"
       declares the Lord.
   "I will stretch out my hand against you,
     roll you off the cliffs,
     and make you a burned-out
       mountain.

26 No rock will be taken from you for a
   cornerstone,
     nor any stone for a foundation,
   for you will be desolate forever,"
       declares the Lord.

27 "Lift up a banner in the land!
     Blow the trumpet among the
       nations!
   Prepare the nations for battle against
       her;
     summon against her these
       kingdoms:
     Ararat, Minni and Ashkenaz.
   Appoint a commander against her;
     send up horses like a swarm of
       locusts.
28 Prepare the nations for battle against
   her—
     the kings of the Medes,
   their governors and all their officials,
     and all the countries they rule.
29 The land trembles and writhes,
     for the Lord's purposes against
       Babylon stand—
   to lay waste the land of Babylon
     so that no one will live there.
30 Babylon's warriors have stopped
   fighting;
     they remain in their strongholds.

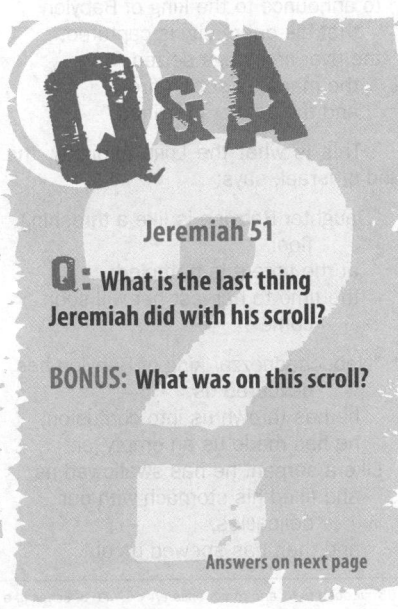

Jeremiah 51

Q: What is the last thing
Jeremiah did with his scroll?

BONUS: What was on this scroll?

Answers on next page

---

a 24 Or *Chaldea*; also in verse 35

A: He gave Seraiah the scroll and told him to read it, to tie a rock to it and to throw it in the Euphrates River when he arrived in Babylon (Jeremiah 51:59–64).

BONUS: All the disasters that would come to Babylon.

Their strength is exhausted;
  they have become weaklings.
Her dwellings are set on fire;
  the bars of her gates are broken.
³¹ One courier follows another
  and messenger follows
    messenger
to announce to the king of Babylon
  that his entire city is captured,
³² the river crossings seized,
  the marshes set on fire,
  and the soldiers terrified."

³³ This is what the LORD Almighty, the God of Israel, says:

"Daughter Babylon is like a threshing
    floor
  at the time it is trampled;
  the time to harvest her will soon
    come."

³⁴ "Nebuchadnezzar king of Babylon has
    devoured us,
  he has thrown us into confusion,
  he has made us an empty jar.
Like a serpent he has swallowed us
  and filled his stomach with our
    delicacies,
  and then has spewed us out.

³⁵ May the violence done to our flesh^a be
    on Babylon,"
  say the inhabitants of Zion.
"May our blood be on those who live
    in Babylonia,"
  says Jerusalem.

³⁶ Therefore this is what the LORD says:

"See, I will defend your cause
  and avenge you;
I will dry up her sea
  and make her springs dry.
³⁷ Babylon will be a heap of ruins,
  a haunt of jackals,
an object of horror and scorn,
  a place where no one lives.
³⁸ Her people all roar like young lions,
  they growl like lion cubs.
³⁹ But while they are aroused,
  I will set out a feast for them
  and make them drunk,
so that they shout with laughter—
  then sleep forever and not awake,"
    declares the LORD.
⁴⁰ "I will bring them down
  like lambs to the slaughter,
  like rams and goats.

⁴¹ "How Sheshak^b will be captured,
  the boast of the whole earth
    seized!
How desolate Babylon will be
  among the nations!
⁴² The sea will rise over Babylon;
  its roaring waves will cover her.
⁴³ Her towns will be desolate,
  a dry and desert land,
a land where no one lives,
  through which no one travels.
⁴⁴ I will punish Bel in Babylon
  and make him spew out what he
    has swallowed.
The nations will no longer stream to
    him.
  And the wall of Babylon will fall.

⁴⁵ "Come out of her, my people!
  Run for your lives!
  Run from the fierce anger of the
    LORD.
⁴⁶ Do not lose heart or be afraid
  when rumors are heard in the land;

---

^{a} 35 Or *done to us and to our children* ^{b} 41 *Sheshak* is a cryptogram for Babylon.

one rumor comes this year, another
the next,
rumors of violence in the land
and of ruler against ruler.
⁴⁷For the time will surely come
when I will punish the idols of
Babylon;
her whole land will be disgraced
and her slain will all lie fallen within
her.
⁴⁸Then heaven and earth and all that is
in them
will shout for joy over Babylon,
for out of the north
destroyers will attack her,"
declares the LORD.

⁴⁹"Babylon must fall because of Israel's
slain,
just as the slain in all the earth
have fallen because of Babylon.
⁵⁰You who have escaped the sword,
leave and do not linger!
Remember the LORD in a distant land,
and call to mind Jerusalem."

⁵¹"We are disgraced,
for we have been insulted
and shame covers our faces,
because foreigners have entered
the holy places of the LORD's
house."

⁵²"But days are coming," declares the
LORD,
"when I will punish her idols,
and throughout her land
the wounded will groan.
⁵³Even if Babylon ascends to the
heavens
and fortifies her lofty stronghold,
I will send destroyers against her,"
declares the LORD.

⁵⁴"The sound of a cry comes from
Babylon,
the sound of great destruction
from the land of the Babylonians.ᵃ
⁵⁵The LORD will destroy Babylon;
he will silence her noisy din.
Waves of enemies will rage like great
waters;
the roar of their voices will resound.

⁵⁶A destroyer will come against
Babylon;
her warriors will be captured,
and their bows will be broken.
For the LORD is a God of retribution;
he will repay in full.
⁵⁷I will make her officials and wise men
drunk,
her governors, officers and warriors
as well;
they will sleep forever and not
awake,"
declares the King, whose name is
the LORD Almighty.

⁵⁸This is what the LORD Almighty says:

"Babylon's thick wall will be leveled
and her high gates set on fire;
the peoples exhaust themselves for
nothing,
the nations' labor is only fuel for
the flames."

⁵⁹This is the message Jeremiah the
prophet gave to the staff officer Seraiah
son of Neriah, the son of Mahseiah, when
he went to Babylon with Zedekiah king
of Judah in the fourth year of his reign.
⁶⁰Jeremiah had written on a scroll about
all the disasters that would come upon
Babylon—all that had been recorded concerning Babylon. ⁶¹He said to Seraiah,
"When you get to Babylon, see that you
read all these words aloud. ⁶²Then say,
'LORD, you have said you will destroy this
place, so that neither people nor animals
will live in it; it will be desolate forever.'
⁶³When you finish reading this scroll, tie
a stone to it and throw it into the Euphrates. ⁶⁴Then say, 'So will Babylon sink to
rise no more because of the disaster I will
bring on her. And her people will fall.'"

The words of Jeremiah end here.

The Fall of Jerusalem

52 Zedekiah was twenty-one years
old when he became king, and he
reigned in Jerusalem eleven years. His
mother's name was Hamutal daughter
of Jeremiah; she was from Libnah. ²He
did evil in the eyes of the LORD, just as

ᵃ 54 Or Chaldeans

Jehoiakim had done. ³It was because of the LORD's anger that all this happened to Jerusalem and Judah, and in the end he thrust them from his presence.

Now Zedekiah rebelled against the king of Babylon.

⁴So in the ninth year of Zedekiah's reign, on the tenth day of the tenth month, Nebuchadnezzar king of Babylon marched against Jerusalem with his whole army. They encamped outside the city and built siege works all around it. ⁵The city was kept under siege until the eleventh year of King Zedekiah.

⁶By the ninth day of the fourth month the famine in the city had become so severe that there was no food for the people to eat. ⁷Then the city wall was broken through, and the whole army fled. They left the city at night through the gate between the two walls near the king's garden, though the Babylonians*a* were surrounding the city. They fled toward the Arabah,*b* ⁸but the Babylonian*c* army pursued King Zedekiah and overtook him in the plains of Jericho. All his soldiers were separated from him and scattered, ⁹and he was captured.

He was taken to the king of Babylon at Riblah in the land of Hamath, where he pronounced sentence on him. ¹⁰There at Riblah the king of Babylon killed the sons of Zedekiah before his eyes; he also killed all the officials of Judah. ¹¹Then he put out Zedekiah's eyes, bound him with bronze shackles and took him to Babylon, where he put him in prison till the day of his death.

¹²On the tenth day of the fifth month, in the nineteenth year of Nebuchadnezzar king of Babylon, Nebuzaradan commander of the imperial guard, who served the king of Babylon, came to Jerusalem. ¹³He set fire to the temple of the LORD, the royal palace and all the houses of Jerusalem. Every important building he burned down. ¹⁴The whole Babylonian army, under the commander of the imperial guard, broke down all the walls around Jerusa-

lem. ¹⁵Nebuzaradan the commander of the guard carried into exile some of the poorest people and those who remained in the city, along with the rest of the craftsmen*d* and those who had deserted to the king of Babylon. ¹⁶But Nebuzaradan left behind the rest of the poorest people of the land to work the vineyards and fields.

¹⁷The Babylonians broke up the bronze pillars, the movable stands and the bronze Sea that were at the temple of the LORD and they carried all the bronze to Babylon. ¹⁸They also took away the pots, shovels, wick trimmers, sprinkling bowls, dishes and all the bronze articles used in the temple service. ¹⁹The commander of the imperial guard took away the basins, censers, sprinkling bowls, pots, lampstands, dishes and bowls used for drink offerings—all that were made of pure gold or silver.

²⁰The bronze from the two pillars, the Sea and the twelve bronze bulls under it, and the movable stands, which King Solomon had made for the temple of the LORD, was more than could be weighed. ²¹Each pillar was eighteen cubits high and twelve cubits in circumference*e*; each was four fingers thick, and hollow. ²²The bronze capital on top of one pillar was five cubits*f* high and was decorated with a network and pomegranates of bronze all around. The other pillar, with its pomegranates, was similar. ²³There were ninety-six pomegranates on the sides; the total number of pomegranates above the surrounding network was a hundred.

²⁴The commander of the guard took as prisoners Seraiah the chief priest, Zephaniah the priest next in rank and the three doorkeepers. ²⁵Of those still in the city, he took the officer in charge of the fighting men, and seven royal advisers. He also took the secretary who was chief officer in charge of conscripting the people of the land, sixty of whom were found in the city. ²⁶Nebuzaradan the commander took them all and brought them to the

---

a 7 Or *Chaldeans; also in verse 17*   *b 7* Or *the Jordan Valley*   *c 8* Or *Chaldean; also in verse 14*   *d 15* Or *the populace*   *e 21* That is, about 27 feet high and 18 feet in circumference or about 8.1 meters high and 5.4 meters in circumference   *f 22* That is, about 7 1/2 feet or about 2.3 meters

king of Babylon at Riblah. ²⁷There at Riblah, in the land of Hamath, the king had them executed.

So Judah went into captivity, away from her land. ²⁸This is the number of the people Nebuchadnezzar carried into exile:

in the seventh year, 3,023 Jews;
²⁹in Nebuchadnezzar's eighteenth year,
832 people from Jerusalem;
³⁰in his twenty-third year,
745 Jews taken into exile by Nebuzaradan the commander of the imperial guard.
There were 4,600 people in all.

Jehoiachin Released

³¹In the thirty-seventh year of the exile of Jehoiachin king of Judah, in the year Awel-Marduk became king of Babylon, on the twenty-fifth day of the twelfth month, he released Jehoiachin king of Judah and freed him from prison. ³²He spoke kindly to him and gave him a seat of honor higher than those of the other kings who were with him in Babylon. ³³So Jehoiachin put aside his prison clothes and for the rest of his life ate regularly at the king's table. ³⁴Day by day the king of Babylon gave Jehoiachin a regular allowance as long as he lived, till the day of his death.

LAMENTATIONS

Lamentations means "funeral songs."

These poems are probably written in Babylon by Jeremiah.

Each poem is an acrostic: the first word in each verse begins with one of the 22 consonants of the Hebrew alphabet.

You Feel Terrible!

You lost the big game. You dropped your tray of spaghetti in the cafeteria. You got permanent black marker all over your new jeans. If this kind of thing happened to you every day, you'd feel terrible and you'd be in the right mood for this book.

Lamentations is a book of five poems. They are called "dirges" because they express how awful the Jews felt after the Babylonians destroyed Jerusalem and God's temple. It was terrible for the Jews to look back and realize what happened was their own fault.

>>SORRY DOESN'T MAKE IT GO AWAY
Lesson learned too late. Report in Lamentations 1:18–22

>>SUFFERING CAN'T QUENCH HOPE
See Lamentations 3:19–24

>>"HOW LONG" IS UP TO GOD
Hard lesson learned, report in Lamentations 5:1–22

While the Jews are captives in Babylon, Buddha is born in Asia. Confucius is born in China. In Peru natives weave brightly colored textiles. Frankincense and myrrh are exported from southern Arabia.

1 *a* How deserted lies the city,
  once so full of people!
How like a widow is she,
  who once was great among the
    nations!
She who was queen among the
    provinces
  has now become a slave.

2 Bitterly she weeps at night,
  tears are on her cheeks.
Among all her lovers
  there is no one to comfort her.
All her friends have betrayed her;
  they have become her enemies.

3 After affliction and harsh labor,
  Judah has gone into exile.
She dwells among the nations;
  she finds no resting place.
All who pursue her have overtaken her
  in the midst of her distress.

4 The roads to Zion mourn,
  for no one comes to her appointed
    festivals.
All her gateways are desolate,
  her priests groan,
her young women grieve,
  and she is in bitter anguish.

5 Her foes have become her masters;
  her enemies are at ease.
The Lord has brought her grief
  because of her many sins.
Her children have gone into exile,
  captive before the foe.

6 All the splendor has departed
  from Daughter Zion.
Her princes are like deer
  that find no pasture;
in weakness they have fled
  before the pursuer.

7 In the days of her affliction and
    wandering
  Jerusalem remembers all the
    treasures
  that were hers in days of old.
When her people fell into enemy
    hands,
  there was no one to help her.

Her enemies looked at her
  and laughed at her destruction.

8 Jerusalem has sinned greatly
  and so has become unclean.
All who honored her despise her,
  for they have all seen her
    naked;
she herself groans
  and turns away.

9 Her filthiness clung to her skirts;
  she did not consider her future.
Her fall was astounding;
  there was none to comfort her.
"Look, Lord, on my affliction,
  for the enemy has triumphed."

10 The enemy laid hands
  on all her treasures;
she saw pagan nations
  enter her sanctuary—
those you had forbidden
  to enter your assembly.

11 All her people groan
  as they search for bread;
they barter their treasures for food
  to keep themselves alive.
"Look, Lord, and consider,
  for I am despised."

12 "Is it nothing to you, all you who
    pass by?
  Look around and see.
Is any suffering like my suffering
  that was inflicted on me,
that the Lord brought on me
  in the day of his fierce anger?

13 "From on high he sent fire,
  sent it down into my bones.
He spread a net for my feet
  and turned me back.
He made me desolate,
  faint all the day long.

14 "My sins have been bound into a
    yoke*b*;
  by his hands they were woven
    together.
They have been hung on my neck,
  and the Lord has sapped my
    strength.

---

a This chapter is an acrostic poem, the verses of which begin with the successive letters of the Hebrew alphabet.
b 14 Most Hebrew manuscripts; many Hebrew manuscripts and Septuagint *He kept watch over my sins*

He has given me into the hands
　of those I cannot withstand.

15 "The Lord has rejected
　all the warriors in my midst;
he has summoned an army against me
　to*a* crush my young men.
In his winepress the Lord has
　　trampled
　Virgin Daughter Judah.

16 "This is why I weep
　and my eyes overflow with tears.
No one is near to comfort me,
　no one to restore my spirit.
My children are destitute
　because the enemy has prevailed."

17 Zion stretches out her hands,
　but there is no one to comfort her.
The LORD has decreed for Jacob
　that his neighbors become his foes;
Jerusalem has become
　an unclean thing among them.

18 "The LORD is righteous,
　yet I rebelled against his command.
Listen, all you peoples;
　look on my suffering.
My young men and young women
　have gone into exile.

19 "I called to my allies
　but they betrayed me.
My priests and my elders
　perished in the city
while they searched for food
　to keep themselves alive.

20 "See, LORD, how distressed I am!
　I am in torment within,
and in my heart I am disturbed,
　for I have been most rebellious.
Outside, the sword bereaves;
　inside, there is only death.

21 "People have heard my groaning,
　but there is no one to comfort me.
All my enemies have heard of my
　　distress;
　they rejoice at what you have done.
May you bring the day you have
　　announced
so they may become like me.

INSTANT ACCESS

Have you ever experienced the consequences of a poor choice? Like being grounded because you skipped a few math assignments? Or finding out the hard way that you can be arrested for vandalizing a teacher's car? Lamentations is a collection of mournful poems expressing how distressed, disturbed and tormented the people of Judah felt in their captivity. They looked back and realized how foolish they had been to go against God's ways. There's a powerful lesson in Lamentations for everyone: Think first. After you've made a wrong choice, there's often nothing you can do to avoid agonizing consequences.

{Lamentations 1:20–22}

22 "Let all their wickedness come before
　　you;
　deal with them
as you have dealt with me
　because of all my sins.
My groans are many
　and my heart is faint."

2*b* How the Lord has covered Daughter
　　Zion
　with the cloud of his anger*c*!

---

a 15 Or *has set a time for me / when he will*   *b* This chapter is an acrostic poem, the verses of which begin with the successive letters of the Hebrew alphabet.   *c* 1 Or *How the Lord in his anger / has treated Daughter Zion with contempt*

He has hurled down the splendor of
Israel
from heaven to earth;
he has not remembered his footstool
in the day of his anger.

2 Without pity the Lord has swallowed
up
all the dwellings of Jacob;
in his wrath he has torn down
the strongholds of Daughter Judah.
He has brought her kingdom and its
princes
down to the ground in dishonor.

3 In fierce anger he has cut off
every horn[a,b] of Israel.
He has withdrawn his right hand
at the approach of the enemy.
He has burned in Jacob like a flaming
fire
that consumes everything
around it.

4 Like an enemy he has strung his
bow;
his right hand is ready.
Like a foe he has slain
all who were pleasing to the eye;
he has poured out his wrath like fire
on the tent of Daughter Zion.

5 The Lord is like an enemy;
he has swallowed up Israel.
He has swallowed up all her palaces
and destroyed her strongholds.
He has multiplied mourning and
lamentation
for Daughter Judah.

6 He has laid waste his dwelling like a
garden;
he has destroyed his place of
meeting.
The LORD has made Zion forget
her appointed festivals and her
Sabbaths;
in his fierce anger he has spurned
both king and priest.

7 The Lord has rejected his altar
and abandoned his sanctuary.
He has given the walls of her palaces
into the hands of the enemy;

they have raised a shout in the house
of the LORD
as on the day of an appointed
festival.

8 The LORD determined to tear down
the wall around Daughter Zion.
He stretched out a measuring line
and did not withhold his hand from
destroying.
He made ramparts and walls lament;
together they wasted away.

9 Her gates have sunk into the ground;
their bars he has broken and
destroyed.
Her king and her princes are exiled
among the nations,
the law is no more,
and her prophets no longer find
visions from the LORD.

10 The elders of Daughter Zion
sit on the ground in silence;
they have sprinkled dust on their
heads
and put on sackcloth.
The young women of Jerusalem
have bowed their heads to the
ground.

11 My eyes fail from weeping,
I am in torment within;
my heart is poured out on the
ground
because my people are destroyed,
because children and infants faint
in the streets of the city.

12 They say to their mothers,
"Where is bread and wine?"
as they faint like the wounded
in the streets of the city,
as their lives ebb away
in their mothers' arms.

13 What can I say for you?
With what can I compare you,
Daughter Jerusalem?
To what can I liken you,
that I may comfort you,
Virgin Daughter Zion?
Your wound is as deep as the sea.
Who can heal you?

---

a 3 Or *off / all the strength*; or *every king*   *b* 3 *Horn* here symbolizes strength.

14 The visions of your prophets
    were false and worthless;
they did not expose your sin
    to ward off your captivity.
The prophecies they gave you
    were false and misleading.

15 All who pass your way
    clap their hands at you;
they scoff and shake their heads
    at Daughter Jerusalem:
"Is this the city that was called
    the perfection of beauty,
    the joy of the whole earth?"

16 All your enemies open their mouths
    wide against you;
they scoff and gnash their teeth
    and say, "We have swallowed
        her up.
This is the day we have waited for;
    we have lived to see it."

17 The LORD has done what he planned;
    he has fulfilled his word,
    which he decreed long ago.
He has overthrown you without pity,
    he has let the enemy gloat over
        you,
    he has exalted the horn[a] of your
        foes.

18 The hearts of the people
    cry out to the Lord.
You walls of Daughter Zion,
    let your tears flow like a river
    day and night;
give yourself no relief,
    your eyes no rest.

19 Arise, cry out in the night,
    as the watches of the night begin;
pour out your heart like water
    in the presence of the Lord.
Lift up your hands to him
    for the lives of your children,
who faint from hunger
    at every street corner.

20 "Look, LORD, and consider:
    Whom have you ever treated like
        this?
Should women eat their offspring,
    the children they have cared for?

Should priest and prophet be killed
    in the sanctuary of the Lord?

21 "Young and old lie together
    in the dust of the streets;
my young men and young women
    have fallen by the sword.
You have slain them in the day of your
        anger;
    you have slaughtered them without
        pity.

22 "As you summon to a feast day,
    so you summoned against me
        terrors on every side.
In the day of the LORD's anger
    no one escaped or survived;
those I cared for and reared
    my enemy has destroyed."

3 [b] I am the man who has seen
        affliction
    by the rod of the LORD's wrath.
2 He has driven me away and made me
        walk
    in darkness rather than light;
3 indeed, he has turned his hand
        against me
    again and again, all day long.

4 He has made my skin and my flesh
        grow old
    and has broken my bones.
5 He has besieged me and
        surrounded me
    with bitterness and hardship.
6 He has made me dwell in darkness
    like those long dead.

7 He has walled me in so I cannot
        escape;
    he has weighed me down with
        chains.
8 Even when I call out or cry for help,
    he shuts out my prayer.
9 He has barred my way with blocks of
        stone;
    he has made my paths crooked.

10 Like a bear lying in wait,
    like a lion in hiding,
11 he dragged me from the path and
        mangled me
    and left me without help.

---

[a] 17 Horn here symbolizes strength.   [b] This chapter is an acrostic poem; the verses of each stanza begin with the successive letters of the Hebrew alphabet, and the verses within each stanza begin with the same letter.

12 He drew his bow
   and made me the target for his
       arrows.

13 He pierced my heart
   with arrows from his quiver.
14 I became the laughingstock of all my
       people;
   they mock me in song all day long.
15 He has filled me with bitter herbs
   and given me gall to drink.

16 He has broken my teeth with gravel;
   he has trampled me in the dust.
17 I have been deprived of peace;
   I have forgotten what prosperity is.
18 So I say, "My splendor is gone
   and all that I had hoped from the
       LORD."

19 I remember my affliction and my
       wandering,
   the bitterness and the gall.
20 I well remember them,
   and my soul is downcast
       within me.
21 Yet this I call to mind
   and therefore I have hope:

22 Because of the LORD's great love we
       are not consumed,
   for his compassions never fail.
23 They are new every morning;
   great is your faithfulness.
24 I say to myself, "The LORD is my
       portion;
   therefore I will wait for him."

25 The LORD is good to those whose hope
       is in him,
   to the one who seeks him;
26 it is good to wait quietly
   for the salvation of the LORD.
27 It is good for a man to bear the yoke
   while he is young.

28 Let him sit alone in silence,
   for the LORD has laid it on him.
29 Let him bury his face in the dust—
   there may yet be hope.
30 Let him offer his cheek to one who
       would strike him,
   and let him be filled with disgrace.

31 For no one is cast off
   by the Lord forever.

> **Because of
> the LORD's great love we
> are not consumed, for his
> compassions never fail. They
> are new every morning.**
>
> **Lamentations
> 3:22-23**

32 Though he brings grief, he will show
       compassion,
   so great is his unfailing love.
33 For he does not willingly bring
       affliction
   or grief to anyone.

34 To crush underfoot
   all prisoners in the land,
35 to deny people their rights
   before the Most High,
36 to deprive them of justice—
   would not the Lord see such
       things?

37 Who can speak and have it happen
   if the Lord has not decreed it?
38 Is it not from the mouth of the Most
       High
   that both calamities and good
       things come?
39 Why should the living complain
   when punished for their sins?

40 Let us examine our ways and test
       them,
   and let us return to the LORD.
41 Let us lift up our hearts and our
       hands
   to God in heaven, and say:
42 "We have sinned and rebelled
   and you have not forgiven.

43 "You have covered yourself with anger
       and pursued us;
   you have slain without pity.
44 You have covered yourself with a
       cloud
   so that no prayer can get through.
45 You have made us scum and refuse
       among the nations.

46 "All our enemies have opened their
     mouths
     wide against us.
47 We have suffered terror and
     pitfalls,
     ruin and destruction."
48 Streams of tears flow from my eyes
     because my people are destroyed.

49 My eyes will flow unceasingly,
     without relief,
50 until the LORD looks down
     from heaven and sees.
51 What I see brings grief to my soul
     because of all the women of my
     city.

52 Those who were my enemies without
     cause
     hunted me like a bird.
53 They tried to end my life in a pit
     and threw stones at me;
54 the waters closed over my head,
     and I thought I was about to
     perish.

55 I called on your name, LORD,
     from the depths of the pit.
56 You heard my plea: "Do not close your
     ears
     to my cry for relief."
57 You came near when I called you,
     and you said, "Do not fear."

58 You, Lord, took up my case;
     you redeemed my life.
59 LORD, you have seen the wrong done
     to me.
     Uphold my cause!
60 You have seen the depth of their
     vengeance,
     all their plots against me.

61 LORD, you have heard their insults,
     all their plots against me—
62 what my enemies whisper and
     mutter
     against me all day long.
63 Look at them! Sitting or standing,
     they mock me in their songs.

64 Pay them back what they deserve,
     LORD,
     for what their hands have done.

INSTANT ACCESS

The writer of this poem knows that God is punishing him for his sins (Lamentations 3:1). And he wonders: Is there any hope for a person who has done wrong? Will God punish me forever? The answer comes in Lamentations 3:25–27. Even if you've done wrong and are suffering for it, you can still have hope. God "is good to those whose hope is in him" (Lamentations 3:25), and he will forgive you and give you another chance as well. The writer warns that you may have to live through some hard times while you wait for that next chance to come (Lamentations 3:26). But don't give up. Keep on hoping in God, and he will be good to you.

{Lamentations 3:25–27}

65 Put a veil over their hearts,
     and may your curse be on them!
66 Pursue them in anger and destroy
     them
     from under the heavens of the LORD.

4 *a* How the gold has lost its luster,
     the fine gold become dull!
The sacred gems are scattered
     at every street corner.

---

a This chapter is an acrostic poem, the verses of which begin with the successive letters of the Hebrew alphabet.

2 How the precious children of Zion,
  once worth their weight in gold,
are now considered as pots of clay,
  the work of a potter's hands!

3 Even jackals offer their breasts
  to nurse their young,
but my people have become
  heartless
  like ostriches in the desert.

4 Because of thirst the infant's
  tongue
  sticks to the roof of its mouth;
the children beg for bread,
  but no one gives it to them.

5 Those who once ate delicacies
  are destitute in the streets.
Those brought up in royal purple
  now lie on ash heaps.

6 The punishment of my people
  is greater than that of Sodom,
which was overthrown in a moment
  without a hand turned to help her.

7 Their princes were brighter than
  snow
  and whiter than milk,
their bodies more ruddy than rubies,
  their appearance like lapis lazuli.

8 But now they are blacker than soot;
  they are not recognized in the
  streets.
Their skin has shriveled on their
  bones;
  it has become as dry as a stick.

9 Those killed by the sword are better
  off
  than those who die of famine;
racked with hunger, they waste
  away
  for lack of food from the field.

10 With their own hands compassionate
  women
  have cooked their own children,
who became their food
  when my people were destroyed.

11 The LORD has given full vent to his
  wrath;
  he has poured out his fierce
  anger.
He kindled a fire in Zion
  that consumed her foundations.

12 The kings of the earth did not
  believe,
  nor did any of the peoples of the
  world,
that enemies and foes could enter
  the gates of Jerusalem.

13 But it happened because of the sins
  of her prophets
  and the iniquities of her priests,
who shed within her
  the blood of the righteous.

14 Now they grope through the streets
  as if they were blind.
They are so defiled with blood
  that no one dares to touch their
  garments.

PANORAMA

You Feel Terrible!

The Jews felt awful after the Babylonians destroyed Jerusalem and God's temple. They realized it was their fault.

{LAMENTATIONS}

15 "Go away! You are unclean!" people
  cry to them.
    "Away! Away! Don't touch us!"
When they flee and wander about,
  people among the nations say,
    "They can stay here no longer."

16 The LORD himself has scattered them;
  he no longer watches over them.
The priests are shown no honor,
  the elders no favor.

17 Moreover, our eyes failed,
  looking in vain for help;
from our towers we watched
  for a nation that could not save us.

18 People stalked us at every step,
  so we could not walk in our streets.
Our end was near, our days were
  numbered,
    for our end had come.

19 Our pursuers were swifter
  than eagles in the sky;
they chased us over the mountains
  and lay in wait for us in the desert.

20 The LORD's anointed, our very life
  breath,
    was caught in their traps.
We thought that under his shadow
  we would live among the nations.

21 Rejoice and be glad, Daughter Edom,
  you who live in the land of Uz.
But to you also the cup will be
  passed;
    you will be drunk and stripped
      naked.

22 Your punishment will end, Daughter
  Zion;
    he will not prolong your exile.
But he will punish your sin, Daughter
  Edom,
    and expose your wickedness.

5 Remember, LORD, what has
  happened to us;
    look, and see our disgrace.
2 Our inheritance has been turned over
  to strangers,
    our homes to foreigners.
3 We have become fatherless,
  our mothers are widows.

4 We must buy the water we drink;
  our wood can be had only at a
    price.
5 Those who pursue us are at our
  heels;
    we are weary and find no rest.
6 We submitted to Egypt and Assyria
  to get enough bread.
7 Our ancestors sinned and are no
  more,
    and we bear their punishment.
8 Slaves rule over us,
  and there is no one to free us from
    their hands.
9 We get our bread at the risk of our
  lives
    because of the sword in the
      desert.
10 Our skin is hot as an oven,
  feverish from hunger.
11 Women have been violated in Zion,
  and virgins in the towns of Judah.
12 Princes have been hung up by their
  hands;
    elders are shown no respect.
13 Young men toil at the millstones;
  boys stagger under loads of wood.
14 The elders are gone from the city
  gate;
    the young men have stopped their
      music.
15 Joy is gone from our hearts;
  our dancing has turned to
    mourning.
16 The crown has fallen from our head.
  Woe to us, for we have sinned!
17 Because of this our hearts are faint,
  because of these things our eyes
    grow dim
18 for Mount Zion, which lies desolate,
  with jackals prowling over it.

19 You, LORD, reign forever;
  your throne endures from
    generation to generation.
20 Why do you always forget us?
  Why do you forsake us so long?
21 Restore us to yourself, LORD, that we
  may return;
    renew our days as of old
22 unless you have utterly rejected us
  and are angry with us beyond
    measure.

EZEKIEL

Picture It.

Do you ever wonder what God looks like? Like a dark, angry cloud hurling bolts of lightning? Like an old man with a long white beard? No matter how you use your imagination, it's hard to picture God.

Ezekiel was in Babylon with Jewish captives just before the final invasion of their homeland. He saw God as a fire, about to destroy Jerusalem. God would show his holiness in this terrible judgment. Years after the city was destroyed, Ezekiel preached again. God would now show his love and bring the Jews home to build a new temple.

>>**EZEKIEL'S ACTIONS LOUDER THAN WORDS**
Act it out, prophet told. Report in Ezekiel 4

>>**GOD COULDN'T TAKE IT ANY LONGER**
Stunning vision recorded in Ezekiel 9–11

>>**DON'T BLAME DAD FOR YOUR CHOICES**
"Individuals responsible," God says. See Ezekiel 18

>>**IT'S ALL ABOUT SATAN**
Report in Ezekiel 28:11–19

As Ezekiel preaches in Babylon, Jerusalem and the temple are razed by Nebuchadnezzar. A solar eclipse is correctly predicted by Thales. The Greek mathematician Pythagoras is born.

Ezekiel's Inaugural Vision

1 In my thirtieth year, in the fourth month on the fifth day, while I was among the exiles by the Kebar River, the heavens were opened and I saw visions of God.

[2] On the fifth of the month—it was the fifth year of the exile of King Jehoiachin— [3] the word of the LORD came to Ezekiel the priest, the son of Buzi, by the Kebar River in the land of the Babylonians.[a] There the hand of the LORD was on him.

[4] I looked, and I saw a windstorm coming out of the north—an immense cloud with flashing lightning and surrounded by brilliant light. The center of the fire looked like glowing metal, [5] and in the fire was what looked like four living creatures. In appearance their form was human, [6] but each of them had four faces and four wings. [7] Their legs were straight; their feet were like those of a calf and gleamed like burnished bronze. [8] Under their wings on their four sides they had human hands. All four of them had faces and wings, [9] and the wings of one touched the wings of another. Each one went straight ahead; they did not turn as they moved.

[10] Their faces looked like this: Each of the four had the face of a human being, and on the right side each had the face of a lion, and on the left the face of an ox; each also had the face of an eagle. [11] Such were their faces. They each had two wings spreading out upward, each wing touching that of the creature on either side; and each had two other wings covering its body. [12] Each one went straight ahead. Wherever the spirit would go, they would go, without turning as they went. [13] The appearance of the living creatures was like burning coals of fire or like torches. Fire moved back and forth among the creatures; it was bright, and lightning flashed out of it. [14] The creatures sped back and forth like flashes of lightning.

[15] As I looked at the living creatures, I saw a wheel on the ground beside each creature with its four faces. [16] This was the appearance and structure of the wheels: They sparkled like topaz, and all four looked alike. Each appeared to be made like a wheel intersecting a wheel. [17] As they moved, they would go in any one of the four directions the creatures faced; the wheels did not change direction as the creatures went. [18] Their rims were high and awesome, and all four rims were full of eyes all around.

[19] When the living creatures moved, the wheels beside them moved; and when the living creatures rose from the ground, the wheels also rose. [20] Wherever the spirit would go, they would go, and the wheels would rise along with them, because the spirit of the living creatures was in the wheels. [21] When the creatures moved, they also moved; when the creatures stood still, they also stood still; and when the creatures rose from the ground, the wheels rose along with them, because the spirit of the living creatures was in the wheels.

[22] Spread out above the heads of the living creatures was what looked something like a vault, sparkling like crystal, and awesome. [23] Under the vault their wings were stretched out one toward the other, and each had two wings covering its body. [24] When the creatures moved, I heard the sound of their wings, like the roar of rushing waters, like the voice of the Almighty,[b] like the tumult of an army. When they stood still, they lowered their wings.

[25] Then there came a voice from above the vault over their heads as they stood with lowered wings. [26] Above the vault over their heads was what looked like a throne of lapis lazuli, and high above on the throne was a figure like that of a man. [27] I saw that from what appeared to be his waist up he looked like glowing metal, as if full of fire, and that from there down he looked like fire; and brilliant light surrounded him. [28] Like the appearance of a rainbow in the clouds on a rainy day, so was the radiance around him.

This was the appearance of the likeness of the glory of the LORD. When I saw it, I fell facedown, and I heard the voice of one speaking.

---

[a] 3 Or *Chaldeans*   [b] 24 Hebrew *Shaddai*

Sticks and stones can break my bones, but names will never hurt me." Have you ever heard that old saying? It's not true, you know. If you've ever heard anyone laugh and make a rude comment about your looks, you know words can hurt. If anyone has ever started a rumor about you, you know words can hurt. But words can also heal. A word of encouragement, a simple compliment or an expression of appreciation can make you feel liked and confident. God reminded Ezekiel not to fear the words of his enemies but to "speak my words" to all. Be aware of the words you speak. Be sure they are words that heal rather than hurt.

{Ezekiel 2:6–7}

>> INSTANT ACCESS

Ezekiel's Call to Be a Prophet

2 He said to me, "Son of man,[a] stand up on your feet and I will speak to you." [2] As he spoke, the Spirit came into me and raised me to my feet, and I heard him speaking to me.

[3] He said: "Son of man, I am sending you to the Israelites, to a rebellious nation that has rebelled against me; they and their ancestors have been in revolt against me to this very day. [4] The people to whom I am sending you are obstinate and stubborn. Say to them, 'This is what the Sovereign LORD says.' [5] And whether they listen or fail to listen—for they are a rebellious people—they will know that a prophet has been among them. [6] And you, son of man, do not be afraid of them or their words. Do not be afraid, though briers and thorns are all around you and you live among scorpions. Do not be afraid of what they say or be terrified by them, though they are a rebellious people. [7] You must speak my words to them, whether they listen or fail to listen, for they are rebellious. [8] But you, son of man, listen to what I say to you. Do not rebel like that rebellious people; open your mouth and eat what I give you."

[9] Then I looked, and I saw a hand stretched out to me. In it was a scroll, [10] which he unrolled before me. On both sides of it were written words of lament and mourning and woe.

3 And he said to me, "Son of man, eat what is before you, eat this scroll; then go and speak to the people of Israel." [2] So I opened my mouth, and he gave me the scroll to eat.

[3] Then he said to me, "Son of man, eat this scroll I am giving you and fill your stomach with it." So I ate it, and it tasted as sweet as honey in my mouth.

[4] He then said to me: "Son of man, go now to the people of Israel and speak my words to them. [5] You are not being sent to a people of obscure speech and strange language, but to the people of Israel— [6] not to many peoples of obscure speech and strange language, whose words you cannot understand. Surely if I had sent you to them, they would have listened to you. [7] But the people of Israel are not willing to listen to you because they are not willing to listen to me, for all the Israelites are hardened and obstinate. [8] But I will make you as unyielding and hardened as they are. [9] I will make your forehead like the hardest stone, harder than flint. Do not be afraid of them or terrified by them, though they are a rebellious people."

[10] And he said to me, "Son of man, listen carefully and take to heart all the words I speak to you. [11] Go now to your

---

a 1 The Hebrew phrase *ben adam* means *human being*. The phrase *son of man* is retained as a form of address here and throughout Ezekiel because of its possible association with "Son of Man" in the New Testament.

people in exile and speak to them. Say to them, 'This is what the Sovereign LORD says,' whether they listen or fail to listen."

[12] Then the Spirit lifted me up, and I heard behind me a loud rumbling sound as the glory of the LORD rose from the place where it was standing.[a] [13] It was the sound of the wings of the living creatures brushing against each other and the sound of the wheels beside them, a loud rumbling sound. [14] The Spirit then lifted me up and took me away, and I went in bitterness and in the anger of my spirit, with the strong hand of the LORD on me. [15] I came to the exiles who lived at Tel Aviv near the Kebar River. And there, where they were living, I sat among them for seven days—deeply distressed.

Ezekiel's Task as Watchman

[16] At the end of seven days the word of the LORD came to me: [17] "Son of man, I have made you a watchman for the people of Israel; so hear the word I speak and give them warning from me. [18] When I say to a wicked person, 'You will surely die,' and you do not warn them or speak out to dissuade them from their evil ways in order to save their life, that wicked person will die for[b] their sin, and I will hold you accountable for their blood. [19] But if you do warn the wicked person and they do not turn from their wickedness or from their evil ways, they will die for their sin; but you will have saved yourself.

[20] "Again, when a righteous person turns from their righteousness and does evil, and I put a stumbling block before them, they will die. Since you did not warn them, they will die for their sin. The righteous things that person did will not be remembered, and I will hold you accountable for their blood. [21] But if you do warn the righteous person not to sin and they do not sin, they will surely live because they took warning, and you will have saved yourself."

[22] The hand of the LORD was on me there, and he said to me, "Get up and go out to the plain, and there I will speak to you." [23] So I got up and went out to the plain. And the glory of the LORD was standing there, like the glory I had seen by the Kebar River, and I fell facedown.

[24] Then the Spirit came into me and raised me to my feet. He spoke to me and said: "Go, shut yourself inside your house. [25] And you, son of man, they will tie with ropes; you will be bound so that you cannot go out among the people. [26] I will make your tongue stick to the roof of your mouth so that you will be silent and unable to rebuke them, for they are a rebellious people. [27] But when I speak to you, I will open your mouth and you shall say to them, 'This is what the Sovereign LORD says.' Whoever will listen let them listen, and whoever will refuse let them refuse; for they are a rebellious people.

Siege of Jerusalem Symbolized

4 "Now, son of man, take a block of clay, put it in front of you and draw the city of Jerusalem on it. [2] Then lay siege to it: Erect siege works against it, build a ramp up to it, set up camps against it and put battering rams around it. [3] Then take an iron pan, place it as an iron wall between you and the city and turn your face toward it. It will be under siege, and you shall besiege it. This will be a sign to the people of Israel.

Ezekiel 3

Q: What strange meal did Ezekiel eat?

BONUS: What would have been the ingredients of the main dish?

Answers on next page

---

[a] 12 Probable reading of the original Hebrew text; Masoretic Text *sound—may the glory of the LORD be praised from his place* [b] 18 Or *in*; also in verses 19 and 20

4 "Then lie on your left side and put the sin of the people of Israel upon yourself.[a] You are to bear their sin for the number of days you lie on your side. 5 I have assigned you the same number of days as the years of their sin. So for 390 days you will bear the sin of the people of Israel.

6 "After you have finished this, lie down again, this time on your right side, and bear the sin of the people of Judah. I have assigned you 40 days, a day for each year. 7 Turn your face toward the siege of Jerusalem and with bared arm prophesy against her. 8 I will tie you up with ropes so that you cannot turn from one side to the other until you have finished the days of your siege.

9 "Take wheat and barley, beans and lentils, millet and spelt; put them in a storage jar and use them to make bread for yourself. You are to eat it during the 390 days you lie on your side. 10 Weigh out twenty shekels[b] of food to eat each day and eat it at set times. 11 Also measure out a sixth of a hin[c] of water and drink it at set times. 12 Eat the food as you would a loaf of barley bread; bake it in the sight of the people, using human excrement for fuel." 13 The Lord said, "In this way the people of Israel will eat defiled food among the nations where I will drive them."

14 Then I said, "Not so, Sovereign Lord! I have never defiled myself. From my youth until now I have never eaten anything found dead or torn by wild animals. No impure meat has ever entered my mouth."

15 "Very well," he said, "I will let you bake your bread over cow dung instead of human excrement."

16 He then said to me: "Son of man, I am about to cut off the food supply in Jerusalem. The people will eat rationed food in anxiety and drink rationed water in despair, 17 for food and water will be scarce. They will be appalled at the sight of each other and will waste away because of[d] their sin.

God's Razor of Judgment

5 "Now, son of man, take a sharp sword and use it as a barber's razor to shave your head and your beard. Then

A: A scroll (Ezekiel 3:2).

BONUS: Rolled sheets of leather or paper. The books of Old Testament times were made of rolled sheets of leather or heavy paper.

take a set of scales and divide up the hair. 2 When the days of your siege come to an end, burn a third of the hair inside the city. Take a third and strike it with the sword all around the city. And scatter a third to the wind. For I will pursue them with drawn sword. 3 But take a few hairs and tuck them away in the folds of your garment. 4 Again, take a few of these and throw them into the fire and burn them up. A fire will spread from there to all Israel.

5 "This is what the Sovereign Lord says: This is Jerusalem, which I have set in the center of the nations, with countries all around her. 6 Yet in her wickedness she has rebelled against my laws and decrees more than the nations and countries around her. She has rejected my laws and has not followed my decrees.

7 "Therefore this is what the Sovereign Lord says: You have been more unruly than the nations around you and have not followed my decrees or kept my laws. You have not even[e] conformed to the standards of the nations around you.

8 "Therefore this is what the Sovereign Lord says: I myself am against you, Jerusalem, and I will inflict punishment on

---

you in the sight of the nations. ⁹Because of all your detestable idols, I will do to you what I have never done before and will never do again. ¹⁰Therefore in your midst parents will eat their children, and children will eat their parents. I will inflict punishment on you and will scatter all your survivors to the winds. ¹¹Therefore as surely as I live, declares the Sovereign Lᴏʀᴅ, because you have defiled my sanctuary with all your vile images and detestable practices, I myself will shave you; I will not look on you with pity or spare you. ¹²A third of your people will die of the plague or perish by famine inside you; a third will fall by the sword outside your walls; and a third I will scatter to the winds and pursue with drawn sword.

¹³"Then my anger will cease and my wrath against them will subside, and I will be avenged. And when I have spent my wrath on them, they will know that I the Lᴏʀᴅ have spoken in my zeal.

¹⁴"I will make you a ruin and a reproach among the nations around you, in the sight of all who pass by. ¹⁵You will be a reproach and a taunt, a warning and an object of horror to the nations around you when I inflict punishment on you in anger and in wrath and with stinging rebuke. I the Lᴏʀᴅ have spoken. ¹⁶When I shoot at you with my deadly and destructive arrows of famine, I will shoot to destroy you. I will bring more and more famine upon you and cut off your supply of food. ¹⁷I will send famine and wild beasts against you, and they will leave you childless. Plague and bloodshed will sweep through you, and I will bring the sword against you. I the Lᴏʀᴅ have spoken."

Doom for the Mountains of Israel

6 The word of the Lᴏʀᴅ came to me: ²"Son of man, set your face against the mountains of Israel; prophesy against them ³and say: 'You mountains of Israel, hear the word of the Sovereign Lᴏʀᴅ. This is what the Sovereign Lᴏʀᴅ says to the mountains and hills, to the ravines and valleys: I am about to bring a sword against you, and I will destroy your high places. ⁴Your altars will be demolished and your incense altars will be smashed; and I will slay your people in front of your idols. ⁵I will lay the dead bodies of the Israelites in front of their idols, and I will scatter your bones around your altars. ⁶Wherever you live, the towns will be laid waste and the high places demolished, so that your altars will be laid waste and devastated, your idols smashed and ruined, your incense altars broken down, and what you have made wiped out. ⁷Your people will fall slain among you, and you will know that I am the Lᴏʀᴅ.

⁸"'But I will spare some, for some of you will escape the sword when you are scattered among the lands and nations. ⁹Then in the nations where they have been carried captive, those who escape will remember me—how I have been grieved by their adulterous hearts, which have turned away from me, and by their eyes, which have lusted after their idols. They will loathe themselves for the evil they have done and for all their detestable practices. ¹⁰And they will know that I am the Lᴏʀᴅ; I did not threaten in vain to bring this calamity on them.

¹¹"'This is what the Sovereign Lᴏʀᴅ says: Strike your hands together and stamp your feet and cry out "Alas!" because of all the wicked and detestable practices of the people of Israel, for they will fall by the sword, famine and plague. ¹²One who is far away will die of the plague, and one who is near will fall by the sword, and anyone who survives and is spared will die of famine. So will I pour out my wrath on them. ¹³And they will know that I am the Lᴏʀᴅ, when their people lie slain among their idols around their altars, on every high hill and on all the mountaintops, under every spreading tree and every leafy oak—places where they offered fragrant incense to all their idols. ¹⁴And I will stretch out my hand against them and make the land a desolate waste from the desert to Diblah[a]—wherever they live. Then they will know that I am the Lᴏʀᴅ.'"

ᵃ 14 Most Hebrew manuscripts; a few Hebrew manuscripts *Riblah*

The End Has Come

7 The word of the LORD came to me: 2 "Son of man, this is what the Sovereign LORD says to the land of Israel:

" 'The end! The end has come
upon the four corners of the land!
3 The end is now upon you,
and I will unleash my anger against
you.
I will judge you according to your
conduct
and repay you for all your
detestable practices.
4 I will not look on you with pity;
I will not spare you.
I will surely repay you for your conduct
and for the detestable practices
among you.

" 'Then you will know that I am the LORD.'

5 "This is what the Sovereign LORD says:

" 'Disaster! Unheard-of[a] disaster!
See, it comes!
6 The end has come!
The end has come!
It has roused itself against you.
See, it comes!
7 Doom has come upon you,
upon you who dwell in the land.
The time has come! The day is near!
There is panic, not joy, on the
mountains.
8 I am about to pour out my wrath on you
and spend my anger against you.
I will judge you according to your
conduct
and repay you for all your
detestable practices.
9 I will not look on you with pity;
I will not spare you.

---

a 5 Most Hebrew manuscripts; some Hebrew manuscripts and Syriac *Disaster after*

TO THE POINT

Talk to the Hills?

In Ezekiel 6:2–3 God tells Ezekiel to speak to the mountains. Mountains can't hear. Why talk to them?

Like other literature, the Bible uses literary devices. A writer uses literary devices to create a powerful image for the reader. Speaking as if mountains were people is a literary device called "personification." God used this powerful way to tell the people that he knew about the altars they had built on top of the mountains. And he would soon smash those places of pagan worship and destroy the people who worshiped there (Ezekiel 6:3–7).

When the Bible writers used these literary devices, they hoped to create a picture in your mind that would help you better understand God's message to you today.

I will repay you for your conduct
and for the detestable practices
among you.

" 'Then you will know that it is I the LORD
who strikes you.

¹⁰ " 'See, the day!
See, it comes!
Doom has burst forth,
the rod has budded,
arrogance has blossomed!
¹¹ Violence has arisen,ᵃ
a rod to punish the wicked.
None of the people will be left,
none of that crowd—
none of their wealth,
nothing of value.
¹² The time has come!
The day has arrived!
Let not the buyer rejoice
nor the seller grieve,
for my wrath is on the whole crowd.
¹³ The seller will not recover
the property that was sold—
as long as both buyer and seller
live.
For the vision concerning the whole
crowd
will not be reversed.
Because of their sins, not one of them
will preserve their life.

¹⁴ " 'They have blown the trumpet,
they have made all things ready,
but no one will go into battle,
for my wrath is on the whole crowd.
¹⁵ Outside is the sword;
inside are plague and famine.
Those in the country
will die by the sword;
those in the city
will be devoured by famine and
plague.
¹⁶ The fugitives who escape
will flee to the mountains.
Like doves of the valleys,
they will all moan,
each for their own sins.
¹⁷ Every hand will go limp;
every leg will be wet with urine.
¹⁸ They will put on sackcloth
and be clothed with terror.

Every face will be covered with
shame,
and every head will be shaved.

¹⁹ " 'They will throw their silver into the
streets,
and their gold will be treated as a
thing unclean.
Their silver and gold
will not be able to deliver them
in the day of the LORD's wrath.
It will not satisfy their hunger
or fill their stomachs,
for it has caused them to stumble
into sin.
²⁰ They took pride in their beautiful jewelry
and used it to make their
detestable idols.
They made it into vile images;
therefore I will make it a thing
unclean for them.
²¹ I will give their wealth as plunder to
foreigners
and as loot to the wicked of the
earth,
who will defile it.
²² I will turn my face away from the
people,
and robbers will desecrate the
place I treasure.
They will enter it
and will defile it.

²³ " 'Prepare chains!
For the land is full of bloodshed,
and the city is full of violence.
²⁴ I will bring the most wicked of nations
to take possession of their houses.
I will put an end to the pride of the
mighty,
and their sanctuaries will be
desecrated.
²⁵ When terror comes,
they will seek peace in vain.
²⁶ Calamity upon calamity will come,
and rumor upon rumor.
They will go searching for a vision
from the prophet,
priestly instruction in the law will
cease,
the counsel of the elders will come
to an end.

ᵃ 11 Or *The violent one has become*

The people in Judah thought they were safe from the Babylonians because God's temple stood in Jerusalem. But in a vision from God Ezekiel saw the "glory of the LORD" (Ezekiel 10:18), God's visible expression, actually leave the temple. Without God the temple was a beautiful but empty heap of stones, and no protection at all. The Babylonian army did sweep down on the little Jewish state. It crushed their defenses, captured the city and destroyed the temple. That terrible defeat is a reminder of an important truth: Just because you belong to the Lord does not mean that he will protect you from the consequences of doing wrong.

{Ezekiel 8–11}

>> INSTANT ACCESS

27 The king will mourn,
    the prince will be clothed with
        despair,
    and the hands of the people of the
        land will tremble.
I will deal with them according to their
        conduct,
    and by their own standards I will
        judge them.
" 'Then they will know that I am the
LORD.' "

---

a 2 Or saw a fiery figure

Idolatry in the Temple

8 In the sixth year, in the sixth month on the fifth day, while I was sitting in my house and the elders of Judah were sitting before me, the hand of the Sovereign LORD came on me there. ² I looked, and I saw a figure like that of a man.ᵃ From what appeared to be his waist down he was like fire, and from there up his appearance was as bright as glowing metal. ³ He stretched out what looked like a hand and took me by the hair of my head. The Spirit lifted me up between earth and heaven and in visions of God he took me to Jerusalem, to the entrance of the north gate of the inner court, where the idol that provokes to jealousy stood. ⁴ And there before me was the glory of the God of Israel, as in the vision I had seen in the plain.

⁵ Then he said to me, "Son of man, look toward the north." So I looked, and in the entrance north of the gate of the altar I saw this idol of jealousy.

⁶ And he said to me, "Son of man, do you see what they are doing—the utterly detestable things the Israelites are doing here, things that will drive me far from my sanctuary? But you will see things that are even more detestable."

⁷ Then he brought me to the entrance to the court. I looked, and I saw a hole in the wall. ⁸ He said to me, "Son of man, now dig into the wall." So I dug into the wall and saw a doorway there.

⁹ And he said to me, "Go in and see the wicked and detestable things they are doing here." ¹⁰ So I went in and looked, and I saw portrayed all over the walls all kinds of crawling things and unclean animals and all the idols of Israel. ¹¹ In front of them stood seventy elders of Israel, and Jaazaniah son of Shaphan was standing among them. Each had a censer in his hand, and a fragrant cloud of incense was rising.

¹² He said to me, "Son of man, have you seen what the elders of Israel are doing in the darkness, each at the shrine of his own idol? They say, 'The LORD does not see us; the LORD has forsaken the land.' "
¹³ Again, he said, "You will see them doing things that are even more detestable."
¹⁴ Then he brought me to the entrance

of the north gate of the house of the LORD, and I saw women sitting there, mourning the god Tammuz. ¹⁵He said to me, "Do you see this, son of man? You will see things that are even more detestable than this."

¹⁶He then brought me into the inner court of the house of the LORD, and there at the entrance to the temple, between the portico and the altar, were about twenty-five men. With their backs toward the temple of the LORD and their faces toward the east, they were bowing down to the sun in the east.

¹⁷He said to me, "Have you seen this, son of man? Is it a trivial matter for the people of Judah to do the detestable things they are doing here? Must they also fill the land with violence and continually arouse my anger? Look at them putting the branch to their nose! ¹⁸Therefore I will deal with them in anger; I will not look on them with pity or spare them. Although they shout in my ears, I will not listen to them."

Judgment on the Idolaters

9 Then I heard him call out in a loud voice, "Bring near those who are appointed to execute judgment on the city, each with a weapon in his hand." ²And I saw six men coming from the direction of the upper gate, which faces north, each

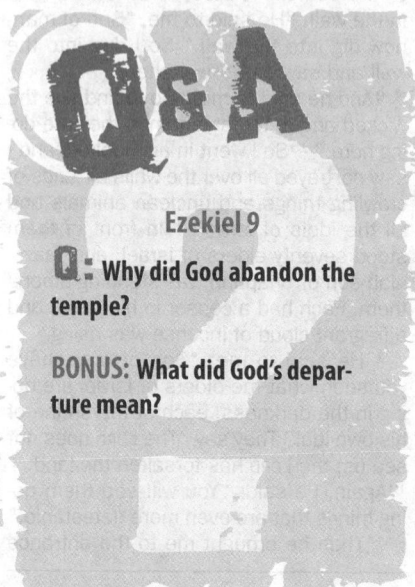

Ezekiel 9

Q: Why did God abandon the temple?

BONUS: What did God's departure mean?

with a deadly weapon in his hand. With them was a man clothed in linen who had a writing kit at his side. They came in and stood beside the bronze altar.

³Now the glory of the God of Israel went up from above the cherubim, where it had been, and moved to the threshold of the temple. Then the LORD called to the man clothed in linen who had the writing kit at his side ⁴and said to him, "Go throughout the city of Jerusalem and put a mark on the foreheads of those who grieve and lament over all the detestable things that are done in it."

⁵As I listened, he said to the others, "Follow him through the city and kill, without showing pity or compassion. ⁶Slaughter the old men, the young men and women, the mothers and children, but do not touch anyone who has the mark. Begin at my sanctuary." So they began with the old men who were in front of the temple.

⁷Then he said to them, "Defile the temple and fill the courts with the slain. Go!" So they went out and began killing throughout the city. ⁸While they were killing and I was left alone, I fell facedown, crying out, "Alas, Sovereign LORD! Are you going to destroy the entire remnant of Israel in this outpouring of your wrath on Jerusalem?"

⁹He answered me, "The sin of the people of Israel and Judah is exceedingly great; the land is full of bloodshed and the city is full of injustice. They say, 'The LORD has forsaken the land; the LORD does not see.' ¹⁰So I will not look on them with pity or spare them, but I will bring down on their own heads what they have done."

¹¹Then the man in linen with the writing kit at his side brought back word, saying, "I have done as you commanded."

God's Glory Departs From the Temple

10 I looked, and I saw the likeness of a throne of lapis lazuli above the vault that was over the heads of the cherubim. ²The LORD said to the man clothed in linen, "Go in among the wheels beneath the cherubim. Fill your hands with burning coals from among the cherubim and scatter them over the city." And as I watched, he went in.

³Now the cherubim were standing on

the south side of the temple when the man went in, and a cloud filled the inner court. [4]Then the glory of the LORD rose from above the cherubim and moved to the threshold of the temple. The cloud filled the temple, and the court was full of the radiance of the glory of the LORD. [5]The sound of the wings of the cherubim could be heard as far away as the outer court, like the voice of God Almighty[a] when he speaks.

[6]When the LORD commanded the man in linen, "Take fire from among the wheels, from among the cherubim," the man went in and stood beside a wheel. [7]Then one of the cherubim reached out his hand to the fire that was among them. He took up some of it and put it into the hands of the man in linen, who took it and went out. [8](Under the wings of the cherubim could be seen what looked like human hands.)

[9]I looked, and I saw beside the cherubim four wheels, one beside each of the cherubim; the wheels sparkled like topaz. [10]As for their appearance, the four of them looked alike; each was like a wheel intersecting a wheel. [11]As they moved, they would go in any one of the four directions the cherubim faced; the wheels did not turn about[b] as the cherubim went. The cherubim went in whatever direction the head faced, without turning as they went. [12]Their entire bodies, including their backs, their hands and their wings, were completely full of eyes, as were their four wheels. [13]I heard the wheels being called "the whirling wheels." [14]Each of the cherubim had four faces: One face was that of a cherub, the second the face of a human being, the third the face of a lion, and the fourth the face of an eagle.

[15]Then the cherubim rose upward. These were the living creatures I had seen by the Kebar River. [16]When the cherubim moved, the wheels beside them moved; and when the cherubim spread their wings to rise from the ground, the wheels did not leave their side. [17]When the cherubim stood still, they also stood still; and when the cherubim rose, they rose with them, because the spirit of the living creatures was in them.

[18]Then the glory of the LORD departed from over the threshold of the temple and

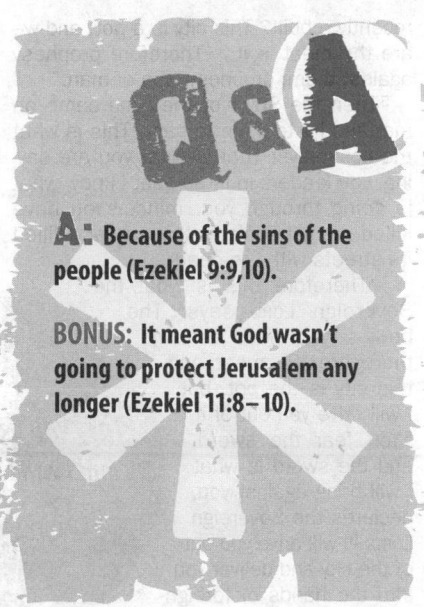

A: Because of the sins of the people (Ezekiel 9:9,10).

BONUS: It meant God wasn't going to protect Jerusalem any longer (Ezekiel 11:8–10).

stopped above the cherubim. [19]While I watched, the cherubim spread their wings and rose from the ground, and as they went, the wheels went with them. They stopped at the entrance of the east gate of the LORD's house, and the glory of the God of Israel was above them.

[20]These were the living creatures I had seen beneath the God of Israel by the Kebar River, and I realized that they were cherubim. [21]Each had four faces and four wings, and under their wings was what looked like human hands. [22]Their faces had the same appearance as those I had seen by the Kebar River. Each one went straight ahead.

God's Sure Judgment on Jerusalem

11 Then the Spirit lifted me up and brought me to the gate of the house of the LORD that faces east. There at the entrance of the gate were twenty-five men, and I saw among them Jaazaniah son of Azzur and Pelatiah son of Benaiah, leaders of the people. [2]The LORD said to me, "Son of man, these are the men who are plotting evil and giving wicked advice in this city. [3]They say, 'Haven't our houses been recently rebuilt? This city is a pot, and we are the meat in it.' [4] Therefore prophesy against them; prophesy, son of man."

[5] Then the Spirit of the LORD came on me, and he told me to say: "This is what the LORD says: That is what you are saying, you leaders in Israel, but I know what is going through your mind. [6] You have killed many people in this city and filled its streets with the dead.

[7] "Therefore this is what the Sovereign LORD says: The bodies you have thrown there are the meat and this city is the pot, but I will drive you out of it. [8] You fear the sword, and the sword is what I will bring against you, declares the Sovereign LORD. [9] I will drive you out of the city and deliver you into the hands of foreigners and inflict punishment on you. [10] You will fall by the sword, and I will execute judgment on you at the borders of Israel. Then you will know that I am the LORD. [11] This city will not be a pot for you, nor will you be the meat in it; I will execute judgment on you at the borders of Israel. [12] And you will know that I am the LORD, for you have not followed my decrees or kept my laws but have conformed to the standards of the nations around you."

[13] Now as I was prophesying, Pelatiah son of Benaiah died. Then I fell facedown and cried out in a loud voice, "Alas, Sovereign LORD! Will you completely destroy the remnant of Israel?"

The Promise of Israel's Return

[14] The word of the LORD came to me: [15] "Son of man, the people of Jerusalem have said of your fellow exiles and all the other Israelites, 'They are far away from the LORD; this land was given to us as our possession.'

[16] "Therefore say: 'This is what the Sovereign LORD says: Although I sent them far away among the nations and scattered them among the countries, yet for a little while I have been a sanctuary for them in the countries where they have gone.'

[17] "Therefore say: 'This is what the Sovereign LORD says: I will gather you from the nations and bring you back from the countries where you have been scattered, and I will give you back the land of Israel again.'

[18] "They will return to it and remove all its vile images and detestable idols. [19] I will give them an undivided heart and put a new spirit in them; I will remove from them their heart of stone and give them a heart of flesh. [20] Then they will follow my decrees and be careful to keep my laws. They will be my people, and I will be their God. [21] But as for those whose hearts are devoted to their vile images and detestable idols, I will bring down on their own heads what they have done, declares the Sovereign LORD."

[22] Then the cherubim, with the wheels beside them, spread their wings, and the glory of the God of Israel was above them. [23] The glory of the LORD went up from within the city and stopped above the mountain east of it. [24] The Spirit lifted me up and brought me to the exiles in Babylonia[a] in the vision given by the Spirit of God.

Then the vision I had seen went up from me, [25] and I told the exiles everything the LORD had shown me.

The Exile Symbolized

12 The word of the LORD came to me: [2] "Son of man, you are living among a rebellious people. They have eyes to see but do not see and ears to hear but do not hear, for they are a rebellious people.

[3] "Therefore, son of man, pack your belongings for exile and in the daytime, as they watch, set out and go from where you are to another place. Perhaps they will understand, though they are a rebellious people. [4] During the daytime, while they watch, bring out your belongings packed for exile. Then in the evening, while they are watching, go out like those who go into exile. [5] While they watch, dig

They will be my people, and I will be their God.
Ezekiel 11:20

---

[a] 24 Or Chaldea

through the wall and take your belongings out through it. ⁶Put them on your shoulder as they are watching and carry them out at dusk. Cover your face so that you cannot see the land, for I have made you a sign to the Israelites."

⁷So I did as I was commanded. During the day I brought out my things packed for exile. Then in the evening I dug through the wall with my hands. I took my belongings out at dusk, carrying them on my shoulders while they watched.

⁸In the morning the word of the LORD came to me: ⁹"Son of man, did not the Israelites, that rebellious people, ask you, 'What are you doing?'

¹⁰"Say to them, 'This is what the Sovereign LORD says: This prophecy concerns the prince in Jerusalem and all the Israelites who are there.' ¹¹Say to them, 'I am a sign to you.'

"As I have done, so it will be done to them. They will go into exile as captives.

¹²"The prince among them will put his things on his shoulder at dusk and leave, and a hole will be dug in the wall for him to go through. He will cover his face so that he cannot see the land. ¹³I will spread my net for him, and he will be caught in my snare; I will bring him to Babylonia, the land of the Chaldeans, but he will not see it, and there he will die. ¹⁴I will scatter to the winds all those around him—his staff and all his troops—and I will pursue them with drawn sword.

¹⁵"They will know that I am the LORD, when I disperse them among the nations and scatter them through the countries. ¹⁶But I will spare a few of them from the sword, famine and plague, so that in the nations where they go they may acknowledge all their detestable practices. Then they will know that I am the LORD."

¹⁷The word of the LORD came to me: ¹⁸"Son of man, tremble as you eat your food, and shudder in fear as you drink your water. ¹⁹Say to the people of the land: 'This is what the Sovereign LORD says about those living in Jerusalem and in the land of Israel: They will eat their food in anxiety and drink their water in despair, for their land will be stripped of everything in it because of the violence of all who live

there. ²⁰The inhabited towns will be laid waste and the land will be desolate. Then you will know that I am the LORD.'"

There Will Be No Delay

²¹The word of the LORD came to me: ²²"Son of man, what is this proverb you have in the land of Israel: 'The days go by and every vision comes to nothing'? ²³Say to them, 'This is what the Sovereign LORD says: I am going to put an end to this proverb, and they will no longer quote it in Israel.' Say to them, 'The days are near when every vision will be fulfilled. ²⁴For there will be no more false visions or flattering divinations among the people of Israel. ²⁵But I the LORD will speak what I will, and it shall be fulfilled without delay. For in your days, you rebellious people, I will fulfill whatever I say, declares the Sovereign LORD.'"

²⁶The word of the LORD came to me: ²⁷"Son of man, the Israelites are saying, 'The vision he sees is for many years from now, and he prophesies about the distant future.'

²⁸"Therefore say to them, 'This is what the Sovereign LORD says: None of my words will be delayed any longer; whatever I say will be fulfilled, declares the Sovereign LORD.'"

False Prophets Condemned

13 The word of the LORD came to me: ²"Son of man, prophesy against the prophets of Israel who are now prophesying. Say to those who prophesy out of their own imagination: 'Hear the word of the LORD! ³This is what the Sovereign LORD says: Woe to the foolishᵃ prophets who follow their own spirit and have seen nothing! ⁴Your prophets, Israel, are like jackals among ruins. ⁵You have not gone up to the breaches in the wall to repair it for the people of Israel so that it will stand firm in the battle on the day of the LORD. ⁶Their visions are false and their divinations a lie. Even though the LORD has not sent them, they say, "The LORD declares," and expect him to fulfill their words. ⁷Have you not seen false visions and uttered lying divinations when you say, "The LORD declares," though I have not spoken?

ᵃ 3 Or wicked

8 " 'Therefore this is what the Sovereign LORD says: Because of your false words and lying visions, I am against you, declares the Sovereign LORD. 9My hand will be against the prophets who see false visions and utter lying divinations. They will not belong to the council of my people or be listed in the records of Israel, nor will they enter the land of Israel. Then you will know that I am the Sovereign LORD.

10 " 'Because they lead my people astray, saying, "Peace," when there is no peace, and because, when a flimsy wall is built, they cover it with whitewash, 11therefore tell those who cover it with whitewash that it is going to fall. Rain will come in torrents, and I will send hailstones hurtling down, and violent winds will burst forth. 12When the wall collapses, will people not ask you, "Where is the whitewash you covered it with?"

13 " 'Therefore this is what the Sovereign LORD says: In my wrath I will unleash a violent wind, and in my anger hailstones and torrents of rain will fall with destructive fury. 14I will tear down the wall you have covered with whitewash and will level it to the ground so that its foundation will be laid bare. When it[a] falls, you will be destroyed in it; and you will know that I am the LORD. 15So I will pour out my wrath against the wall and against those who covered it with whitewash. I will say to you, "The wall is gone and so are those who whitewashed it, 16those prophets of Israel who prophesied to Jerusalem and saw visions of peace for her when there was no peace, declares the Sovereign LORD." '

17 "Now, son of man, set your face against the daughters of your people who prophesy out of their own imagination. Prophesy against them 18and say, 'This is what the Sovereign LORD says: Woe to the women who sew magic charms on all their wrists and make veils of various lengths for their heads in order to ensnare people. Will you ensnare the lives of my people but preserve your own? 19You have profaned me among my people for a few handfuls of barley and scraps of bread. By lying to my people, who listen to lies, you have killed those who should not have died and have spared those who should not live.

20 " 'Therefore this is what the Sovereign LORD says: I am against your magic charms with which you ensnare people like birds and I will tear them from your arms; I will set free the people that you ensnare like birds. 21I will tear off your veils and save my people from your hands, and they will no longer fall prey to your power. Then you will know that I am the LORD. 22Because you disheartened the righteous with your lies, when I had brought them no grief, and because you encouraged the wicked not to turn from their evil ways and so save their lives, 23therefore you will no longer see false visions or practice divination. I will save my people from your hands. And then you will know that I am the LORD.' "

Idolaters Condemned

14 Some of the elders of Israel came to me and sat down in front of me. 2Then the word of the LORD came to me: 3 "Son of man, these men have set up idols in their hearts and put wicked stumbling blocks before their faces. Should I let them inquire of me at all? 4Therefore speak to them and tell them, 'This is what the Sovereign LORD says: When any of the Israelites set up idols in their hearts and put a wicked stumbling block before their faces and then go to a prophet, I the LORD will answer them myself in keeping with their great idolatry. 5I will do this to recapture the hearts of the people of Israel, who have all deserted me for their idols.'

6 "Therefore say to the people of Israel, 'This is what the Sovereign LORD says: Repent! Turn from your idols and renounce all your detestable practices!

7 " 'When any of the Israelites or any foreigner residing in Israel separate themselves from me and set up idols in their hearts and put a wicked stumbling block before their faces and then go to a prophet to inquire of me, I the LORD will answer them myself. 8I will set my face against them and make them an example and a byword. I will remove them from my people. Then you will know that I am the LORD.

9 " 'And if the prophet is enticed to utter a prophecy, I the LORD have enticed that prophet, and I will stretch out my hand against him and destroy him from among

---

a 14 Or the city

my people Israel. ¹⁰They will bear their guilt—the prophet will be as guilty as the one who consults him. ¹¹Then the people of Israel will no longer stray from me, nor will they defile themselves anymore with all their sins. They will be my people, and I will be their God, declares the Sovereign Lord.'"

Jerusalem's Judgment Inescapable

¹²The word of the Lord came to me: ¹³"Son of man, if a country sins against me by being unfaithful and I stretch out my hand against it to cut off its food supply and send famine upon it and kill its people and their animals, ¹⁴even if these three men—Noah, Daniel[a] and Job—were in it, they could save only themselves by their righteousness, declares the Sovereign Lord.

¹⁵"Or if I send wild beasts through that country and they leave it childless and it becomes desolate so that no one can pass through it because of the beasts, ¹⁶as surely as I live, declares the Sovereign Lord, even if these three men were in it, they could not save their own sons or daughters. They alone would be saved, but the land would be desolate.

¹⁷"Or if I bring a sword against that country and say, 'Let the sword pass throughout the land,' and I kill its people and their animals, ¹⁸as surely as I live, declares the Sovereign Lord, even if these three men were in it, they could not save their own sons or daughters. They alone would be saved.

¹⁹"Or if I send a plague into that land and pour out my wrath on it through bloodshed, killing its people and their animals, ²⁰as surely as I live, declares the Sovereign Lord, even if Noah, Daniel and Job were in it, they could save neither son nor daughter. They would save only themselves by their righteousness.

²¹"For this is what the Sovereign Lord says: How much worse will it be when I send against Jerusalem my four dreadful judgments—sword and famine and wild beasts and plague—to kill its men and their animals! ²²Yet there will be some

survivors—sons and daughters who will be brought out of it. They will come to you, and when you see their conduct and their actions, you will be consoled regarding the disaster I have brought on Jerusalem—every disaster I have brought on it. ²³You will be consoled when you see their conduct and their actions, for you will know that I have done nothing in it without cause, declares the Sovereign Lord."

Jerusalem as a Useless Vine

15 The word of the Lord came to me: ²"Son of man, how is the wood of a vine different from that of a branch from any of the trees in the forest? ³Is wood ever taken from it to make anything useful? Do they make pegs from it to hang things on? ⁴And after it is thrown on the fire as fuel and the fire burns both ends and chars the middle, is it then useful for anything? ⁵If it was not useful for anything when it was whole, how much less can it be made into something useful when the fire has burned it and it is charred?

⁶"Therefore this is what the Sovereign Lord says: As I have given the wood of the vine among the trees of the forest as fuel for the fire, so will I treat the people living in Jerusalem. ⁷I will set my face against them. Although they have come out of the fire, the fire will yet consume them. And when I set my face against them, you will know that I am the Lord. ⁸I will make the land desolate because they have been unfaithful, declares the Sovereign Lord."

Jerusalem as an Adulterous Wife

16 The word of the Lord came to me: ²"Son of man, confront Jerusalem with her detestable practices ³and say, 'This is what the Sovereign Lord says to Jerusalem: Your ancestry and birth were in the land of the Canaanites; your father was an Amorite and your mother a Hittite. ⁴On the day you were born your cord was not cut, nor were you washed with water to make you clean, nor were you rubbed with salt or wrapped in cloths. ⁵No one looked on you with pity or had compassion enough to do any of these things for

---

[a] 14 Or *Danel*, a man of renown in ancient literature; also in verse 20

you. Rather, you were thrown out into the open field, for on the day you were born you were despised.

6 " 'Then I passed by and saw you kicking about in your blood, and as you lay there in your blood I said to you, "Live!"[a] 7 I made you grow like a plant of the field. You grew and developed and entered puberty. Your breasts had formed and your hair had grown, yet you were stark naked.

8 " 'Later I passed by, and when I looked at you and saw that you were old enough for love, I spread the corner of my garment over you and covered your naked body. I gave you my solemn oath and entered into a covenant with you, declares the Sovereign LORD, and you became mine.

9 " 'I bathed you with water and washed the blood from you and put ointments on you. 10 I clothed you with an embroidered dress and put sandals of fine leather on you. I dressed you in fine linen and covered you with costly garments. 11 I adorned you with jewelry: I put bracelets on your arms and a necklace around your neck, 12 and I put a ring on your nose, earrings on your ears and a beautiful crown on your head. 13 So you were adorned with gold and silver; your clothes were of fine linen and costly fabric and embroidered cloth. Your food was honey, olive oil and the finest flour. You became very beautiful and rose to be a queen. 14 And your fame spread among the nations on account of your beauty, because the splendor I had given you made your beauty perfect, declares the Sovereign LORD.

15 " 'But you trusted in your beauty and used your fame to become a prostitute. You lavished your favors on anyone who passed by and your beauty became his. 16 You took some of your garments to make gaudy high places, where you carried on your prostitution. You went to him, and he possessed your beauty.[b] 17 You also took the fine jewelry I gave you, the jewelry made of my gold and silver, and you made for yourself male idols and engaged in prostitution with them. 18 And you took your embroidered clothes to put on them, and you offered my oil and incense

before them. 19 Also the food I provided for you — the flour, olive oil and honey I gave you to eat — you offered as fragrant incense before them. That is what happened, declares the Sovereign LORD.

20 " 'And you took your sons and daughters whom you bore to me and sacrificed them as food to the idols. Was your prostitution not enough? 21 You slaughtered my children and sacrificed them to the idols. 22 In all your detestable practices and your prostitution you did not remember the days of your youth, when you were naked and bare, kicking about in your blood.

23 " 'Woe! Woe to you, declares the Sovereign LORD. In addition to all your other wickedness, 24 you built a mound for yourself and made a lofty shrine in every public square. 25 At every street corner you built your lofty shrines and degraded your beauty, spreading your legs with increasing promiscuity to anyone who passed by. 26 You engaged in prostitution with the Egyptians, your neighbors with large genitals, and aroused my anger with your increasing promiscuity. 27 So I stretched out my hand against you and reduced your territory; I gave you over to the greed of your enemies, the daughters of the Philistines, who were shocked by your lewd conduct. 28 You engaged in prostitution with the Assyrians too, because you were insatiable; and even after that, you still were not satisfied. 29 Then you increased your promiscuity to include Babylonia,[c] a land of merchants, but even with this you were not satisfied.

30 " 'I am filled with fury against you,[d] declares the Sovereign LORD, when you do all these things, acting like a brazen prostitute! 31 When you built your mounds at every street corner and made your lofty shrines in every public square, you were unlike a prostitute, because you scorned payment.

32 " 'You adulterous wife! You prefer strangers to your own husband! 33 All prostitutes receive gifts, but you give gifts to all your lovers, bribing them to come to you from everywhere for your illicit favors. 34 So in your prostitution you are the opposite of others; no one runs after you for

---

[a] 6 A few Hebrew manuscripts, Septuagint and Syriac; most Hebrew manuscripts repeat *and as you lay there in your blood I said to you, "Live!"*   [b] 16 The meaning of the Hebrew for this sentence is uncertain.   [c] 29 Or *Chaldea*   [d] 30 Or *How feverish is your heart,*

your favors. You are the very opposite, for you give payment and none is given to you.

35 " 'Therefore, you prostitute, hear the word of the LORD! 36 This is what the Sovereign LORD says: Because you poured out your lust and exposed your naked body in your promiscuity with your lovers, and because of all your detestable idols, and because you gave them your children's blood, 37 therefore I am going to gather all your lovers, with whom you found pleasure, those you loved as well as those you hated. I will gather them against you from all around and will strip you in front of them, and they will see you stark naked. 38 I will sentence you to the punishment of women who commit adultery and who shed blood; I will bring on you the blood vengeance of my wrath and jealous anger. 39 Then I will deliver you into the hands of your lovers, and they will tear down your mounds and destroy your lofty shrines. They will strip you of your clothes and take your fine jewelry and leave you stark naked. 40 They will bring a mob against you, who will stone you and hack you to pieces with their swords. 41 They will burn down your houses and inflict punishment on you in the sight of many women. I will put a stop to your prostitution, and you will no longer pay your lovers. 42 Then my wrath against you will subside and my jealous anger will turn away from you; I will be calm and no longer angry.

43 " 'Because you did not remember the days of your youth but enraged me with all these things, I will surely bring down on your head what you have done, declares the Sovereign LORD. Did you not add lewdness to all your other detestable practices?

44 " 'Everyone who quotes proverbs will quote this proverb about you: "Like mother, like daughter." 45 You are a true daughter of your mother, who despised her husband and her children; and you are a true sister of your sisters, who despised their husbands and their children. Your mother was a Hittite and your father an Amorite. 46 Your older sister was Samaria, who

lived to the north of you with her daughters; and your younger sister, who lived to the south of you with her daughters, was Sodom. 47 You not only followed their ways and copied their detestable practices, but in all your ways you soon became more depraved than they. 48 As surely as I live, declares the Sovereign LORD, your sister Sodom and her daughters never did what you and your daughters have done.

49 " 'Now this was the sin of your sister Sodom: She and her daughters were arrogant, overfed and unconcerned; they did not help the poor and needy. 50 They were haughty and did detestable things before me. Therefore I did away with them as you have seen. 51 Samaria did not commit half the sins you did. You have done more detestable things than they, and have made your sisters seem righteous by all these things you have done. 52 Bear your disgrace, for you have furnished some justification for your sisters. Because your sins were more vile than theirs, they appear more righteous than you. So then, be ashamed and bear your disgrace, for you have made your sisters appear righteous.

53 " 'However, I will restore the fortunes of Sodom and her daughters and of Samaria and her daughters, and your fortunes along with them, 54 so that you may bear your disgrace and be ashamed of all you have done in giving them comfort. 55 And your sisters, Sodom with her daughters and Samaria with her daughters, will return to what they were before; and you and your daughters will return to what you were before. 56 You would not even mention your sister Sodom in the day of your pride, 57 before your wickedness was uncovered. Even so, you are now scorned by the daughters of Edom[a] and all her neighbors and the daughters of the Philistines—all those around you who despise you. 58 You will bear the consequences of your lewdness and your detestable practices, declares the LORD.

59 " 'This is what the Sovereign LORD says: I will deal with you as you deserve, because you have despised my oath by breaking the covenant. 60 Yet I will

---

[a] 57 Many Hebrew manuscripts and Syriac; most Hebrew manuscripts, Septuagint and Vulgate Aram

remember the covenant I made with you in the days of your youth, and I will establish an everlasting covenant with you. 61 Then you will remember your ways and be ashamed when you receive your sisters, both those who are older than you and those who are younger. I will give them to you as daughters, but not on the basis of my covenant with you. 62 So I will establish my covenant with you, and you will know that I am the LORD. 63 Then, when I make atonement for you for all you have done, you will remember and be ashamed and never again open your mouth because of your humiliation, declares the Sovereign LORD.' "

Two Eagles and a Vine

17 The word of the LORD came to me: 2 "Son of man, set forth an allegory and tell it to the Israelites as a parable. 3 Say to them, 'This is what the Sovereign LORD says: A great eagle with powerful wings, long feathers and full plumage of varied colors came to Lebanon. Taking hold of the top of a cedar, 4 he broke off its topmost shoot and carried it away to a land of merchants, where he planted it in a city of traders.

5 " 'He took one of the seedlings of the land and put it in fertile soil. He planted it like a willow by abundant water, 6 and it sprouted and became a low, spreading vine. Its branches turned toward him, but its roots remained under it. So it became a vine and produced branches and put out leafy boughs.

7 " 'But there was another great eagle with powerful wings and full plumage. The vine now sent out its roots toward him from the plot where it was planted and stretched out its branches to him for water. 8 It had been planted in good soil by abundant water so that it would produce branches, bear fruit and become a splendid vine.'

9 "Say to them, 'This is what the Sovereign LORD says: Will it thrive? Will it not be uprooted and stripped of its fruit so that it withers? All its new growth will wither. It will not take a strong arm or many people to pull it up by the roots. 10 It has been planted, but will it thrive? Will it not wither completely when the east wind strikes it—wither away in the plot where it grew?' "

11 Then the word of the LORD came to me: 12 "Say to this rebellious people, 'Do you not know what these things mean?' Say to them: 'The king of Babylon went to Jerusalem and carried off her king and her nobles, bringing them back with him to Babylon. 13 Then he took a member of the royal family and made a treaty with him, putting him under oath. He also carried away the leading men of the land, 14 so that the kingdom would be brought low, unable to rise again, surviving only by keeping his treaty. 15 But the king rebelled against him by sending his envoys to Egypt to get horses and a large army. Will he succeed? Will he who does such things escape? Will he break the treaty and yet escape?

16 " 'As surely as I live, declares the Sovereign LORD, he shall die in Babylon, in the land of the king who put him on the throne, whose oath he despised and whose treaty he broke. 17 Pharaoh with his mighty army and great horde will be of no help to him in war, when ramps are built and siege works erected to destroy many lives. 18 He despised the oath by breaking the covenant. Because he had given his hand in pledge and yet did all these things, he shall not escape.

19 " 'Therefore this is what the Sovereign LORD says: As surely as I live, I will repay him for despising my oath and breaking my covenant. 20 I will spread my net for him, and he will be caught in my snare. I will bring him to Babylon and execute judgment on him there because he was unfaithful to me. 21 All his choice troops will fall by the sword, and the survivors will be scattered to the winds. Then you will know that I the LORD have spoken.

22 " 'This is what the Sovereign LORD says: I myself will take a shoot from the very top of a cedar and plant it; I will break off a tender sprig from its topmost shoots and plant it on a high and lofty mountain. 23 On the mountain heights of Israel I will plant it; it will produce branches and bear fruit and become a splendid cedar. Birds of every kind will nest in it;

they will find shelter in the shade of its branches. ²⁴All the trees of the forest will know that I the LORD bring down the tall tree and make the low tree grow tall. I dry up the green tree and make the dry tree flourish.

" 'I the LORD have spoken, and I will do it.' "

The One Who Sins Will Die

18 The word of the LORD came to me: ²"What do you people mean by quoting this proverb about the land of Israel:

" 'The parents eat sour grapes,
      and the children's teeth are set on
         edge'?

³"As surely as I live, declares the Sovereign LORD, you will no longer quote this proverb in Israel. ⁴For everyone belongs to me, the parent as well as the child— both alike belong to me. The one who sins is the one who will die.

⁵"Suppose there is a righteous man
      who does what is just and right.
⁶He does not eat at the mountain
         shrines
      or look to the idols of Israel.
   He does not defile his neighbor's wife
      or have sexual relations with a
         woman during her period.
⁷He does not oppress anyone,
      but returns what he took in pledge
         for a loan.
   He does not commit robbery
      but gives his food to the hungry
      and provides clothing for the
         naked.
⁸He does not lend to them at interest
      or take a profit from them.
   He withholds his hand from doing
         wrong
      and judges fairly between two
         parties.
⁹He follows my decrees
      and faithfully keeps my laws.
   That man is righteous;
      he will surely live,
         declares the Sovereign LORD.

¹⁰"Suppose he has a violent son, who sheds blood or does any of these other things[a] ¹¹(though the father has done none of them):

"He eats at the mountain shrines.
   He defiles his neighbor's wife.
¹²He oppresses the poor and needy.
   He commits robbery.
   He does not return what he took in
         pledge.
   He looks to the idols.
   He does detestable things.
¹³He lends at interest and takes a
         profit.

Will such a man live? He will not! Because he has done all these detestable things, he is to be put to death; his blood will be on his own head.

¹⁴"But suppose this son has a son who sees all the sins his father commits, and though he sees them, he does not do such things:

¹⁵"He does not eat at the mountain
         shrines
      or look to the idols of Israel.
   He does not defile his neighbor's wife.
¹⁶He does not oppress anyone
      or require a pledge for a loan.
   He does not commit robbery
      but gives his food to the hungry
      and provides clothing for the naked.
¹⁷He withholds his hand from
         mistreating the poor
      and takes no interest or profit from
         them.
   He keeps my laws and follows my
         decrees.

He will not die for his father's sin; he will surely live. ¹⁸But his father will die for his own sin, because he practiced extortion, robbed his brother and did what was wrong among his people.

¹⁹"Yet you ask, 'Why does the son not share the guilt of his father?' Since the son has done what is just and right and has been careful to keep all my decrees, he will surely live. ²⁰The one who sins is the one who will die. The child will not share the guilt of the parent, nor will the

---

a 10 Or *things to a brother*

> A year ago my mom and dad got divorced. I really miss being together as a family. Sometimes my parents would argue when I did something stupid. I feel like it was my fault or something that they got divorced. Can I do anything to get them back together?
> >> Makayla

Dear Jordan

Dear Makayla,

Sadly, about half of all marriages end in divorce. When a divorce takes place, sometimes the children feel somehow responsible. But really, it was your parents' decision to get married, and it was their decision to get divorced. It was not your fault at all. God tells us in Ezekiel 18:20, "The child will not share the guilt of the parent, nor will the parent share the guilt of the child." You are responsible to God when you sin, but it is not your fault if someone else falls short of God's standard.

There is a lot of sadness and anger when two people get divorced. And it's hard for the whole family. It kind of feels like somebody died, but there's no body to bury. It's normal to feel a sense of loss when parents get divorced. Sometimes it helps to talk about your feelings with somebody who can understand what you're going through. But one thing you can feel good about: It wasn't your fault. God doesn't blame you and he doesn't want you to blame yourself either.

Jordan

parent share the guilt of the child. The righteousness of the righteous will be credited to them, and the wickedness of the wicked will be charged against them.

21 "But if a wicked person turns away from all the sins they have committed and keeps all my decrees and does what is just and right, that person will surely live; they will not die. 22 None of the offenses they have committed will be remembered against them. Because of the righteous things they have done, they will live. 23 Do I take any pleasure in the death of the wicked? declares the Sovereign Lord. Rather, am I not pleased when they turn from their ways and live?

24 "But if a righteous person turns from their righteousness and commits sin and does the same detestable things the wicked person does, will they live? None of the righteous things that person has done will be remembered. Because of the unfaithfulness they are guilty of and because of the sins they have committed, they will die.

25 "Yet you say, 'The way of the Lord is not just.' Hear, you Israelites: Is my way unjust? Is it not your ways that are unjust? 26 If a righteous person turns from their righteousness and commits sin, they will die for it; because of the sin they have committed they will die. 27 But if a wicked person turns away from the wickedness they have committed and does what is just and right, they will save their life. 28 Because they consider all the offenses they have committed and turn away from them, that person will surely live; they will not die. 29 Yet the Israelites say, 'The way of the Lord is not just.' Are my ways unjust, people of Israel? Is it not your ways that are unjust?

30 "Therefore, you Israelites, I will judge each of you according to your own ways, declares the Sovereign Lord. Repent! Turn away from all your offenses; then sin will not be your downfall. 31 Rid yourselves of all the offenses you have committed, and get a new heart and a new spirit. Why will you die, people of Israel? 32 For I take no pleasure in the death of anyone, declares the Sovereign Lord. Repent and live!

A Lament Over Israel's Princes

19 "Take up a lament concerning the princes of Israel 2 and say:

" 'What a lioness was your mother
    among the lions!
She lay down among them
    and reared her cubs.
3 She brought up one of her cubs,
    and he became a strong lion.
He learned to tear the prey
    and he became a man-eater.
4 The nations heard about him,
    and he was trapped in their pit.
They led him with hooks
    to the land of Egypt.

5 " 'When she saw her hope unfulfilled,
    her expectation gone,
she took another of her cubs
    and made him a strong lion.
6 He prowled among the lions,
    for he was now a strong lion.
He learned to tear the prey
    and he became a man-eater.
7 He broke down[a] their strongholds
    and devastated their towns.
The land and all who were in it
    were terrified by his roaring.
8 Then the nations came against him,
    those from regions round about.
They spread their net for him,
    and he was trapped in their pit.
9 With hooks they pulled him into a
        cage
    and brought him to the king of
        Babylon.
They put him in prison,
    so his roar was heard no longer
    on the mountains of Israel.

10 " 'Your mother was like a vine in your
        vineyard[b]
    planted by the water;
it was fruitful and full of branches
    because of abundant water.
11 Its branches were strong,
    fit for a ruler's scepter.
It towered high
    above the thick foliage,
conspicuous for its height
    and for its many branches.

---

a 7 Targum (see Septuagint); Hebrew *He knew*   b 10 Two Hebrew manuscripts; most Hebrew manuscripts *your blood*

¹²But it was uprooted in fury
and thrown to the ground.
The east wind made it shrivel,
it was stripped of its fruit;
its strong branches withered
and fire consumed them.
¹³Now it is planted in the desert,
in a dry and thirsty land.
¹⁴Fire spread from one of its main^a
branches
and consumed its fruit.
No strong branch is left on it
fit for a ruler's scepter.'

"This is a lament and is to be used as a lament."

Rebellious Israel Purged

20 In the seventh year, in the fifth month on the tenth day, some of the elders of Israel came to inquire of the LORD, and they sat down in front of me.

²Then the word of the LORD came to me: ³"Son of man, speak to the elders of Israel and say to them, 'This is what the Sovereign LORD says: Have you come to inquire of me? As surely as I live, I will not let you inquire of me, declares the Sovereign LORD.'

⁴"Will you judge them? Will you judge them, son of man? Then confront them with the detestable practices of their ancestors ⁵and say to them: 'This is what the Sovereign LORD says: On the day I chose Israel, I swore with uplifted hand to the descendants of Jacob and revealed myself to them in Egypt. With uplifted hand I said to them, "I am the LORD your God." ⁶On that day I swore to them that I would bring them out of Egypt into a land I had searched out for them, a land flowing with milk and honey, the most beautiful of all lands. ⁷And I said to them, "Each of you, get rid of the vile images you have set your eyes on, and do not defile yourselves with the idols of Egypt. I am the LORD your God."

⁸"'But they rebelled against me and would not listen to me; they did not get rid of the vile images they had set their eyes on, nor did they forsake the idols of Egypt. So I said I would pour out my wrath on them and spend my anger against them in Egypt. ⁹But for the sake of my name, I brought them out of Egypt. I did it to keep my name from being profaned in the eyes of the nations among whom they lived and in whose sight I had revealed myself to the Israelites. ¹⁰Therefore I led them out of Egypt and brought them into the wilderness. ¹¹I gave them my decrees and made known to them my laws, by which the person who obeys them will live. ¹²Also I gave them my Sabbaths as a sign between us, so they would know that I the LORD made them holy.

¹³"'Yet the people of Israel rebelled against me in the wilderness. They did not follow my decrees but rejected my laws—by which the person who obeys them will live—and they utterly desecrated my Sabbaths. So I said I would pour out my wrath on them and destroy them in the wilderness. ¹⁴But for the sake of my name I did what would keep it from being profaned in the eyes of the nations in whose sight I had brought them out. ¹⁵Also with uplifted hand I swore to them in the wilderness that I would not bring them into the land I had given them— a land flowing with milk and honey, the most beautiful of all lands— ¹⁶because they rejected my laws and did not follow my decrees and desecrated my Sabbaths. For their hearts were devoted to their idols. ¹⁷Yet I looked on them with pity and did not destroy them or put an end to them in the wilderness. ¹⁸I said to their children in the wilderness, "Do not follow the statutes of your parents or keep their laws or defile yourselves with their idols. ¹⁹I am the LORD your God; follow my decrees and be careful to keep my laws. ²⁰Keep my Sabbaths holy, that they may be a sign between us. Then you will know that I am the LORD your God."

²¹"'But the children rebelled against me: They did not follow my decrees, they were not careful to keep my laws, of which I said, "The person who obeys them will live by them," and they desecrated my Sabbaths. So I said I would pour out my wrath on them and spend my anger against them in the wilderness.

---

^a 14 Or from under its

22 But I withheld my hand, and for the sake of my name I did what would keep it from being profaned in the eyes of the nations in whose sight I had brought them out. 23 Also with uplifted hand I swore to them in the wilderness that I would disperse them among the nations and scatter them through the countries, 24 because they had not obeyed my laws but had rejected my decrees and desecrated my Sabbaths, and their eyes lusted after their parents' idols. 25 So I gave them other statutes that were not good and laws through which they could not live; 26 I defiled them through their gifts—the sacrifice of every firstborn—that I might fill them with horror so they would know that I am the LORD.'

27 "Therefore, son of man, speak to the people of Israel and say to them, 'This is what the Sovereign LORD says: In this also your ancestors blasphemed me by being unfaithful to me: 28 When I brought them into the land I had sworn to give them and they saw any high hill or any leafy tree, there they offered their sacrifices, made offerings that aroused my anger, presented their fragrant incense and poured out their drink offerings. 29 Then I said to them: What is this high place you go to?' " (It is called Bamah[a] to this day.)

Rebellious Israel Renewed

30 "Therefore say to the Israelites: 'This is what the Sovereign LORD says: Will you defile yourselves the way your ancestors did and lust after their vile images? 31 When you offer your gifts—the sacrifice of your children in the fire—you continue to defile yourselves with all your idols to this day. Am I to let you inquire of me, you Israelites? As surely as I live, declares the Sovereign LORD, I will not let you inquire of me.

32 " 'You say, "We want to be like the nations, like the peoples of the world, who serve wood and stone." But what you have in mind will never happen. 33 As surely as I live, declares the Sovereign LORD, I will reign over you with a mighty hand and an outstretched arm and with outpoured wrath. 34 I will bring you from the nations and gather you from the countries where you have been scattered—with a mighty hand and an outstretched arm and with outpoured wrath. 35 I will bring you into the wilderness of the nations and there, face to face, I will execute judgment upon you. 36 As I judged your ancestors in the wilderness of the land of Egypt, so I will judge you, declares the Sovereign LORD. 37 I will take note of you as you pass under my rod, and I will bring you into the bond of the covenant. 38 I will purge you of those who revolt and rebel against me. Although I will bring them out of the land where they are living, yet they will not enter the land of Israel. Then you will know that I am the LORD.

39 " 'As for you, people of Israel, this is what the Sovereign LORD says: Go and serve your idols, every one of you! But afterward you will surely listen to me and no longer profane my holy name with your gifts and idols. 40 For on my holy mountain, the high mountain of Israel, declares the Sovereign LORD, there in the land all the people of Israel will serve me, and there I will accept them. There I will require your offerings and your choice gifts,[b] along with all your holy sacrifices. 41 I will accept you as fragrant incense when I bring you out from the nations and gather you from the countries where you have been scattered, and I will be proved holy through you in the sight of the nations. 42 Then you will know that I am the LORD, when I bring you into the land of Israel, the land I had sworn with uplifted hand to give to your ancestors. 43 There you will remember your conduct and all the actions by which you have defiled yourselves, and you will loathe yourselves for all the evil you have done. 44 You will know that I am the LORD, when I deal with you for my name's sake and not according to your evil ways and your corrupt practices, you people of Israel, declares the Sovereign LORD.' "

Prophecy Against the South

45 The word of the LORD came to me: 46 "Son of man, set your face toward

---

a 29 Bamah means high place.   b 40 Or and the gifts of your firstfruits the south; preach against the south and prophesy against the forest of the southland. ⁴⁷Say to the southern forest: 'Hear the word of the LORD. This is what the Sovereign LORD says: I am about to set fire to you, and it will consume all your trees, both green and dry. The blazing flame will not be quenched, and every face from south to north will be scorched by it. ⁴⁸Everyone will see that I the LORD have kindled it; it will not be quenched.' "

⁴⁹Then I said, "Sovereign LORD, they are saying of me, 'Isn't he just telling parables?' "ᵃ

Babylon as God's Sword of Judgment

21 ᵇThe word of the LORD came to me: ²"Son of man, set your face against Jerusalem and preach against the sanctuary. Prophesy against the land of Israel ³and say to her: 'This is what the LORD says: I am against you. I will draw my sword from its sheath and cut off from you both the righteous and the wicked. ⁴Because I am going to cut off the righteous and the wicked, my sword will be unsheathed against everyone from south to north. ⁵Then all people will know that I the LORD have drawn my sword from its sheath; it will not return again.'

⁶"Therefore groan, son of man! Groan before them with broken heart and bitter grief. ⁷And when they ask you, 'Why are you groaning?' you shall say, 'Because of the news that is coming. Every heart will melt with fear and every hand go limp; every spirit will become faint and every leg will be wet with urine.' It is coming! It will surely take place, declares the Sovereign LORD."

⁸The word of the LORD came to me: ⁹"Son of man, prophesy and say, 'This is what the Lord says:

" 'A sword, a sword,
      sharpened and polished—
¹⁰sharpened for the slaughter,
      polished to flash like lightning!

" 'Shall we rejoice in the scepter of my royal son? The sword despises every such stick.

Many of you have family members or friends who don't know the Lord. It hurts when you witness to people you love and they just won't listen. The people of Ezekiel's day didn't listen to God's prophet either. But God gave them a special promise through Ezekiel. "Afterward you will surely listen . . ." A person you love may not listen to you until after he or she suffers the consequences of wrong choices. Sure you'd like your loved ones to avoid being hurt. But some are only willing to listen "afterward." Don't stop praying for your loved ones. And don't give up hope.

{Ezekiel 20:39}

¹¹" 'The sword is appointed to be polished,
      to be grasped with the hand;
it is sharpened and polished,
      made ready for the hand of the slayer.
¹²Cry out and wail, son of man,
      for it is against my people;
      it is against all the princes of Israel.
They are thrown to the sword
      along with my people.
Therefore beat your breast.

ᵃ 49 In Hebrew texts 20:45-49 is numbered 21:1-5.   ᵇ In Hebrew texts 21:1-32 is numbered 21:6-37.

13 " 'Testing will surely come. And what if even the scepter, which the sword despises, does not continue? declares the Sovereign LORD.'

14 "So then, son of man, prophesy
and strike your hands together.
Let the sword strike twice,
even three times.
It is a sword for slaughter—
a sword for great slaughter,
closing in on them from every side.
15 So that hearts may melt with fear
and the fallen be many,
I have stationed the sword for
slaughter[a]
at all their gates.
Look! It is forged to strike like
lightning,
it is grasped for slaughter.
16 Slash to the right, you sword,
then to the left,
wherever your blade is turned.
17 I too will strike my hands together,
and my wrath will subside.
I the LORD have spoken."

18 The word of the LORD came to me: 19 "Son of man, mark out two roads for the sword of the king of Babylon to take, both starting from the same country. Make a signpost where the road branches off to the city. 20 Mark out one road for the sword to come against Rabbah of the Ammonites and another against Judah and fortified Jerusalem. 21 For the king of Babylon will stop at the fork in the road, at the junction of the two roads, to seek an omen: He will cast lots with arrows, he will consult his idols, he will examine the liver. 22 Into his right hand will come the lot for Jerusalem, where he is to set up battering rams, to give the command to slaughter, to sound the battle cry, to set battering rams against the gates, to build a ramp and to erect siege works. 23 It will seem like a false omen to those who have sworn allegiance to him, but he will remind them of their guilt and take them captive.

24 "Therefore this is what the Sovereign LORD says: 'Because you people have brought to mind your guilt by your open re-

bellion, revealing your sins in all that you do—because you have done this, you will be taken captive.

25 " 'You profane and wicked prince of Israel, whose day has come, whose time of punishment has reached its climax, 26 this is what the Sovereign LORD says: Take off the turban, remove the crown. It will not be as it was: The lowly will be exalted and the exalted will be brought low. 27 A ruin! A ruin! I will make it a ruin! The crown will not be restored until he to whom it rightfully belongs shall come; to him I will give it.'

28 "And you, son of man, prophesy and say, 'This is what the Sovereign LORD says about the Ammonites and their insults:

" 'A sword, a sword,
drawn for the slaughter,
polished to consume
and to flash like lightning!
29 Despite false visions concerning you
and lying divinations about you,
it will be laid on the necks
of the wicked who are to be slain,
whose day has come,
whose time of punishment has
reached its climax.
30 " 'Let the sword return to its sheath.
In the place where you were created,
in the land of your ancestry,
I will judge you.
31 I will pour out my wrath on you
and breathe out my fiery anger
against you;
I will deliver you into the hands of
brutal men,
men skilled in destruction.
32 You will be fuel for the fire,
your blood will be shed in your land,
you will be remembered no more;
for I the LORD have spoken.' "

Judgment on Jerusalem's Sins

22 The word of the LORD came to me:

2 "Son of man, will you judge her? Will you judge this city of bloodshed? Then confront her with all her detestable practices 3 and say: 'This is what the

---

a 15 Septuagint; the meaning of the Hebrew for this word is uncertain.

Sovereign LORD says: You city that brings on herself doom by shedding blood in her midst and defiles herself by making idols, 4you have become guilty because of the blood you have shed and have become defiled by the idols you have made. You have brought your days to a close, and the end of your years has come. Therefore I will make you an object of scorn to the nations and a laughingstock to all the countries. 5Those who are near and those who are far away will mock you, you infamous city, full of turmoil.

6 " 'See how each of the princes of Israel who are in you uses his power to shed blood. 7In you they have treated father and mother with contempt; in you they have oppressed the foreigner and mistreated the fatherless and the widow. 8You have despised my holy things and desecrated my Sabbaths. 9In you are slanderers who are bent on shedding blood; in you are those who eat at the mountain shrines and commit lewd acts. 10In you are those who dishonor their father's bed; in you are those who violate women during their period, when they are ceremonially unclean. 11In you one man commits a detestable offense with his neighbor's wife, another shamefully defiles his daughter-in-law, and another violates his sister, his own father's daughter. 12In you are people who accept bribes to shed blood; you take interest and make a profit from the poor. You extort unjust gain from your neighbors. And you have forgotten me, declares the Sovereign LORD.

13 " 'I will surely strike my hands together at the unjust gain you have made and at the blood you have shed in your midst. 14Will your courage endure or your hands be strong in the day I deal with you? I the LORD have spoken, and I will do it. 15I will disperse you among the nations and scatter you through the countries; and I will put an end to your uncleanness. 16When you have been defileda in the eyes of the nations, you will know that I am the LORD.' "

17Then the word of the LORD came to me: 18"Son of man, the people of Israel have become dross to me; all of them are the copper, tin, iron and lead left inside a furnace. They are but the dross of silver. 19Therefore this is what the Sovereign LORD says: 'Because you have all become dross, I will gather you into Jerusalem. 20As silver, copper, iron, lead and tin are gathered into a furnace to be melted with a fiery blast, so will I gather you in my anger and my wrath and put you inside the city and melt you. 21I will gather you and I will blow on you with my fiery wrath, and you will be melted inside her. 22As silver is melted in a furnace, so you will be melted inside her, and you will know that I the LORD have poured out my wrath on you.' "

23Again the word of the LORD came to me: 24"Son of man, say to the land, 'You are a land that has not been cleansed or rained on in the day of wrath.' 25There is a conspiracy of her princesb within her like a roaring lion tearing its prey; they devour people, take treasures and precious things and make many widows within her. 26Her priests do violence to my law and profane my holy things; they do not distinguish between the holy and the common; they teach that there is no difference between the unclean and the clean; and they shut their eyes to the keeping of my Sabbaths, so that I am profaned among them. 27Her officials within her are like wolves tearing their prey; they shed blood and kill people to make unjust gain. 28Her prophets whitewash these deeds for them by false visions and lying divinations. They say, 'This is what the Sovereign LORD says'—when the LORD has not spoken. 29The people of the land practice extortion and commit robbery; they oppress the poor and needy and mistreat the foreigner, denying them justice.

30"I looked for someone among them who would build up the wall and stand before me in the gap on behalf of the land so I would not have to destroy it, but I found no one. 31So I will pour out my wrath on them and consume them with my fiery anger, bringing down on their own heads all they have done, declares the Sovereign LORD."

---

a 16 Or When I have allotted you your inheritance   b 25 Septuagint; Hebrew prophets

Two Adulterous Sisters

23 The word of the LORD came to me: 2 "Son of man, there were two women, daughters of the same mother. 3 They became prostitutes in Egypt, engaging in prostitution from their youth. In that land their breasts were fondled and their virgin bosoms caressed. 4 The older was named Oholah, and her sister was Oholibah. They were mine and gave birth to sons and daughters. Oholah is Samaria, and Oholibah is Jerusalem.

5 "Oholah engaged in prostitution while she was still mine; and she lusted after her lovers, the Assyrians—warriors 6 clothed in blue, governors and commanders, all of them handsome young men, and mounted horsemen. 7 She gave herself as a prostitute to all the elite of the Assyrians and defiled herself with all the idols of everyone she lusted after. 8 She did not give up the prostitution she began in Egypt, when during her youth men slept with her, caressed her virgin bosom and poured out their lust on her.

9 "Therefore I delivered her into the hands of her lovers, the Assyrians, for whom she lusted. 10 They stripped her naked, took away her sons and daughters and killed her with the sword. She became a byword among women, and punishment was inflicted on her.

11 "Her sister Oholibah saw this, yet in her lust and prostitution she was more depraved than her sister. 12 She too lusted after the Assyrians—governors and commanders, warriors in full dress, mounted horsemen, all handsome young men. 13 I saw that she too defiled herself; both of them went the same way.

14 "But she carried her prostitution still further. She saw men portrayed on a wall, figures of Chaldeans[a] portrayed in red, 15 with belts around their waists and flowing turbans on their heads; all of them looked like Babylonian chariot officers, natives of Chaldea.[b] 16 As soon as she saw them, she lusted after them and sent messengers to them in Chaldea. 17 Then the Babylonians came to her, to the bed of love, and in their lust they defiled her. After she had been defiled by them, she turned away from them in disgust. 18 When she carried on her prostitution openly and exposed her naked body, I turned away from her in disgust, just as I had turned away from her sister. 19 Yet she became more and more promiscuous as she recalled the days of her youth, when she was a prostitute in Egypt. 20 There she lusted after her lovers, whose genitals were like those of donkeys and whose emission was like that of horses. 21 So you longed for the lewdness of your youth, when in Egypt your bosom was caressed and your young breasts fondled.[c]

22 "Therefore, Oholibah, this is what the Sovereign LORD says: I will stir up your lovers against you, those you turned away from in disgust, and I will bring them against you from every side— 23 the Babylonians and all the Chaldeans, the men of Pekod and Shoa and Koa, and all the Assyrians with them, handsome young men, all of them governors and commanders, chariot officers and men of high rank, all mounted on horses. 24 They will come against you with weapons,[d] chariots and wagons and with a throng of people; they will take up positions against you on every side with large and small shields and with helmets. I will turn you over to them for punishment, and they will punish you according to their standards. 25 I will direct my jealous anger against you, and they will deal with you in fury. They will cut off your noses and your ears, and those of you who are left will fall by the sword. They will take away your sons and daughters, and those of you who are left will be consumed by fire. 26 They will also strip you of your clothes and take your fine jewelry. 27 So I will put a stop to the lewdness and prostitution you began in Egypt. You will not look on these things with longing or remember Egypt anymore.

28 "For this is what the Sovereign LORD says: I am about to deliver you into the hands of those you hate, to those you turned away from in disgust. 29 They will

---

a 14 Or *Babylonians your young breasts*   *b* 15 Or *Babylonia*; also in verse 16   *c* 21 Syriac (see also verse 3); Hebrew *caressed because of*   *d* 24 The meaning of the Hebrew for this word is uncertain.

deal with you in hatred and take away everything you have worked for. They will leave you stark naked, and the shame of your prostitution will be exposed. Your lewdness and promiscuity ³⁰have brought this on you, because you lusted after the nations and defiled yourself with their idols. ³¹You have gone the way of your sister; so I will put her cup into your hand.

³²"This is what the Sovereign LORD says:

> "You will drink your sister's cup,
> a cup large and deep;
> it will bring scorn and derision,
> for it holds so much.
> ³³You will be filled with drunkenness
> and sorrow,
> the cup of ruin and desolation,
> the cup of your sister Samaria.
> ³⁴You will drink it and drain it dry
> and chew on its pieces—
> and you will tear your breasts.

I have spoken, declares the Sovereign LORD.

³⁵"Therefore this is what the Sovereign LORD says: Since you have forgotten me and turned your back on me, you must bear the consequences of your lewdness and prostitution."

³⁶The LORD said to me: "Son of man, will you judge Oholah and Oholibah? Then confront them with their detestable practices, ³⁷for they have committed adultery and blood is on their hands. They committed adultery with their idols; they even sacrificed their children, whom they bore to me, as food for them. ³⁸They have also done this to me: At that same time they defiled my sanctuary and desecrated my Sabbaths. ³⁹On the very day they sacrificed their children to their idols, they entered my sanctuary and desecrated it. That is what they did in my house.

⁴⁰"They even sent messengers for men who came from far away, and when they arrived you bathed yourself for them, applied eye makeup and put on your jewelry. ⁴¹You sat on an elegant couch, with a table spread before it on which you had placed the incense and olive oil that belonged to me.

⁴²"The noise of a carefree crowd was around her; drunkards were brought from the desert along with men from the rabble, and they put bracelets on the wrists of the woman and her sister and beautiful crowns on their heads. ⁴³Then I said about the one worn out by adultery, 'Now let them use her as a prostitute, for that is all she is.' ⁴⁴And they slept with her. As men sleep with a prostitute, so they slept with those lewd women, Oholah and Oholibah. ⁴⁵But righteous judges will sentence them to the punishment of women who commit adultery and shed blood, because they are adulterous and blood is on their hands.

⁴⁶"This is what the Sovereign LORD says: Bring a mob against them and give them over to terror and plunder. ⁴⁷The mob will stone them and cut them down with their swords; they will kill their sons and daughters and burn down their houses.

⁴⁸"So I will put an end to lewdness in the land, that all women may take warning and not imitate you. ⁴⁹You will suffer the penalty for your lewdness and bear the consequences of your sins of idolatry. Then you will know that I am the Sovereign LORD."

Jerusalem as a Cooking Pot

24 In the ninth year, in the tenth month on the tenth day, the word of the LORD came to me: ²"Son of man, record this date, this very date, because the king of Babylon has laid siege to Jerusalem this very day. ³Tell this rebellious people a parable and say to them: 'This is what the Sovereign LORD says:

> "'Put on the cooking pot; put it on
> and pour water into it.
> ⁴Put into it the pieces of meat,
> all the choice pieces—the leg and
> the shoulder.
> Fill it with the best of these bones;
> ⁵ take the pick of the flock.
> Pile wood beneath it for the bones;
> bring it to a boil
> and cook the bones in it.

⁶"'For this is what the Sovereign LORD says:

> "'Woe to the city of bloodshed,
> to the pot now encrusted,
> whose deposit will not go away!

Take the meat out piece by piece
in whatever order it comes.

7 " 'For the blood she shed is in her
midst:
She poured it on the bare rock;
she did not pour it on the ground,
where the dust would cover it.
8 To stir up wrath and take revenge
I put her blood on the bare rock,
so that it would not be covered.

9 " 'Therefore this is what the Sovereign
Lord says:

" 'Woe to the city of bloodshed!
I, too, will pile the wood high.
10 So heap on the wood
and kindle the fire.
Cook the meat well,
mixing in the spices;
and let the bones be charred.
11 Then set the empty pot on the
coals
till it becomes hot and its copper
glows,
so that its impurities may be melted
and its deposit burned away.
12 It has frustrated all efforts;
its heavy deposit has not been
removed,
not even by fire.

13 " 'Now your impurity is lewdness.
Because I tried to cleanse you but you
would not be cleansed from your impurity,
you will not be clean again until my wrath
against you has subsided.

14 " 'I the Lord have spoken. The time
has come for me to act. I will not hold
back; I will not have pity, nor will I relent.
You will be judged according to your conduct and your actions, declares the Sovereign Lord.' "

Ezekiel's Wife Dies

15 The word of the Lord came to me:
16 "Son of man, with one blow I am about
to take away from you the delight of your
eyes. Yet do not lament or weep or shed
any tears. 17 Groan quietly; do not mourn
for the dead. Keep your turban fastened
and your sandals on your feet; do not cov-

er your mustache and beard or eat the
customary food of mourners."

18 So I spoke to the people in the morning, and in the evening my wife died. The
next morning I did as I had been commanded.

19 Then the people asked me, "Won't
you tell us what these things have to do
with us? Why are you acting like this?"

20 So I said to them, "The word of the
Lord came to me: 21 Say to the people of
Israel, 'This is what the Sovereign Lord
says: I am about to desecrate my sanctuary—the stronghold in which you take
pride, the delight of your eyes, the object
of your affection. The sons and daughters you left behind will fall by the sword.
22 And you will do as I have done. You will
not cover your mustache and beard or eat
the customary food of mourners. 23 You
will keep your turbans on your heads
and your sandals on your feet. You will
not mourn or weep but will waste away
because of[a] your sins and groan among
yourselves. 24 Ezekiel will be a sign to you;
you will do just as he has done. When
this happens, you will know that I am the
Sovereign Lord.'

25 "And you, son of man, on the day
I take away their stronghold, their joy
and glory, the delight of their eyes, their
heart's desire, and their sons and daughters as well— 26 on that day a fugitive will
come to tell you the news. 27 At that time
your mouth will be opened; you will speak
with him and will no longer be silent. So
you will be a sign to them, and they will
know that I am the Lord."

A Prophecy Against Ammon

25 The word of the Lord came to
me: 2 "Son of man, set your face
against the Ammonites and prophesy
against them. 3 Say to them, 'Hear the
word of the Sovereign Lord. This is what
the Sovereign Lord says: Because you
said "Aha!" over my sanctuary when it
was desecrated and over the land of Israel when it was laid waste and over the
people of Judah when they went into exile, 4 therefore I am going to give you to
the people of the East as a possession.

---

a 23 Or away in

They will set up their camps and pitch their tents among you; they will eat your fruit and drink your milk. ⁵I will turn Rabbah into a pasture for camels and Ammon into a resting place for sheep. Then you will know that I am the Lord. ⁶For this is what the Sovereign Lord says: Because you have clapped your hands and stamped your feet, rejoicing with all the malice of your heart against the land of Israel, ⁷therefore I will stretch out my hand against you and give you as plunder to the nations. I will wipe you out from among the nations and exterminate you from the countries. I will destroy you, and you will know that I am the Lord.' "

A Prophecy Against Moab

⁸"This is what the Sovereign Lord says: 'Because Moab and Seir said, "Look, Judah has become like all the other nations," ⁹therefore I will expose the flank of Moab, beginning at its frontier towns— Beth Jeshimoth, Baal Meon and Kiriathaim—the glory of that land. ¹⁰I will give Moab along with the Ammonites to the people of the East as a possession, so that the Ammonites will not be remembered among the nations; ¹¹and I will inflict punishment on Moab. Then they will know that I am the Lord.' "

A Prophecy Against Edom

¹²"This is what the Sovereign Lord says: 'Because Edom took revenge on Judah and became very guilty by doing so, ¹³therefore this is what the Sovereign Lord says: I will stretch out my hand against Edom and kill both man and beast. I will lay it waste, and from Teman to Dedan they will fall by the sword. ¹⁴I will take vengeance on Edom by the hand of my people Israel, and they will deal with Edom in accordance with my anger and my wrath; they will know my vengeance, declares the Sovereign Lord.' "

A Prophecy Against Philistia

¹⁵"This is what the Sovereign Lord says: 'Because the Philistines acted in vengeance and took revenge with malice in their hearts, and with ancient hostility sought to destroy Judah, ¹⁶therefore this is what the Sovereign Lord says: I am about to stretch out my hand against the Philistines, and I will wipe out the Kerethites and destroy those remaining along the coast. ¹⁷I will carry out great vengeance on them and punish them in my wrath. Then they will know that I am the Lord, when I take vengeance on them.' "

A Prophecy Against Tyre

26 In the eleventh month of the twelfth[a] year, on the first day of the month, the word of the Lord came to me: ²"Son of man, because Tyre has said of Jerusalem, 'Aha! The gate to the nations is broken, and its doors have swung open to me; now that she lies in ruins I will prosper,' ³therefore this is what the Sovereign Lord says: I am against you, Tyre, and I will bring many nations against you, like the sea casting up its waves. ⁴They will destroy the walls of Tyre and pull down her towers; I will scrape away her rubble and make her a bare rock. ⁵Out in the sea she will become a place to spread fishnets, for I have spoken, declares the Sovereign Lord. She will become plunder for the nations, ⁶and her settlements on the mainland will be ravaged by the sword. Then they will know that I am the Lord.

⁷"For this is what the Sovereign Lord says: From the north I am going to bring against Tyre Nebuchadnezzar[b] king of Babylon, king of kings, with horses and chariots, with horsemen and a great army. ⁸He will ravage your settlements on the mainland with the sword; he will set up siege works against you, build a ramp up to your walls and raise his shields against you. ⁹He will direct the blows of his battering rams against your walls and demolish your towers with his weapons. ¹⁰His horses will be so many that they will cover you with dust. Your walls will tremble at the noise of the warhorses, wagons and chariots when he enters your gates

---

[a] 1 Probable reading of the original Hebrew text; Masoretic Text does not have *month of the twelfth*.   [b] 7 Hebrew *Nebuchadrezzar*, of which *Nebuchadnezzar* is a variant; here and often in Ezekiel and Jeremiah

as men enter a city whose walls have been broken through. 11 The hooves of his horses will trample all your streets; he will kill your people with the sword, and your strong pillars will fall to the ground. 12 They will plunder your wealth and loot your merchandise; they will break down your walls and demolish your fine houses and throw your stones, timber and rubble into the sea. 13 I will put an end to your noisy songs, and the music of your harps will be heard no more. 14 I will make you a bare rock, and you will become a place to spread fishnets. You will never be rebuilt, for I the LORD have spoken, declares the Sovereign LORD.

15 "This is what the Sovereign LORD says to Tyre: Will not the coastlands tremble at the sound of your fall, when the wounded groan and the slaughter takes place in you? 16 Then all the princes of the coast will step down from their thrones and lay aside their robes and take off their embroidered garments. Clothed with terror, they will sit on the ground, trembling every moment, appalled at you. 17 Then they will take up a lament concerning you and say to you:

" 'How you are destroyed, city of renown,
    peopled by men of the sea!
You were a power on the seas,
    you and your citizens;
you put your terror
    on all who lived there.
18 Now the coastlands tremble
    on the day of your fall;
the islands in the sea
    are terrified at your collapse.'

19 "This is what the Sovereign LORD says: When I make you a desolate city, like cities no longer inhabited, and when I bring the ocean depths over you and its vast waters cover you, 20 then I will bring you down with those who go down to the pit, to the people of long ago. I will make you dwell in the earth below, as in ancient ruins, with those who go down to the pit, and you will not return or take your place[a] in the land of the living. 21 I

will bring you to a horrible end and you will be no more. You will be sought, but you will never again be found, declares the Sovereign LORD."

A Lament Over Tyre

27 The word of the LORD came to me: 2 "Son of man, take up a lament concerning Tyre. 3 Say to Tyre, situated at the gateway to the sea, merchant of peoples on many coasts, 'This is what the Sovereign LORD says:

" 'You say, Tyre,
    "I am perfect in beauty."
4 Your domain was on the high seas;
    your builders brought your beauty to
        perfection.
5 They made all your timbers
    of juniper from Senir[b];
they took a cedar from Lebanon
    to make a mast for you.
6 Of oaks from Bashan
    they made your oars;
of cypress wood[c] from the coasts of
        Cyprus
    they made your deck, adorned with
        ivory.
7 Fine embroidered linen from Egypt
    was your sail
    and served as your banner;
your awnings were of blue and
        purple
    from the coasts of Elishah.
8 Men of Sidon and Arvad were your
        oarsmen;
    your skilled men, Tyre, were aboard
        as your sailors.
9 Veteran craftsmen of Byblos were on
        board
    as shipwrights to caulk your
        seams.
All the ships of the sea and their
        sailors
    came alongside to trade for your
        wares.
10 " 'Men of Persia, Lydia and Put
    served as soldiers in your army.
They hung their shields and helmets
        on your walls,
    bringing you splendor.

---

a 20 Septuagint; Hebrew *return, and I will give glory*   b 5 That is, Mount Hermon   c 6 Targum; the Masoretic Text has a different division of the consonants.

11 Men of Arvad and Helek
    guarded your walls on every side;
    men of Gammad
    were in your towers.
They hung their shields around your
        walls;
    they brought your beauty to
        perfection.

12 " 'Tarshish did business with you because of your great wealth of goods; they exchanged silver, iron, tin and lead for your merchandise.

13 " 'Greece, Tubal and Meshek did business with you; they traded human beings and articles of bronze for your wares.

14 " 'Men of Beth Togarmah exchanged chariot horses, cavalry horses and mules for your merchandise.

15 " 'The men of Rhodes[a] traded with you, and many coastlands were your customers; they paid you with ivory tusks and ebony.

16 " 'Aram[b] did business with you because of your many products; they exchanged turquoise, purple fabric, embroidered work, fine linen, coral and rubies for your merchandise.

17 " 'Judah and Israel traded with you; they exchanged wheat from Minnith and confections,[c] honey, olive oil and balm for your wares.

18 " 'Damascus did business with you because of your many products and great wealth of goods. They offered wine from Helbon, wool from Zahar 19 and casks of wine from Izal in exchange for your wares: wrought iron, cassia and calamus.

---

a 15 Septuagint; Hebrew *Dedan*   *b 16* Most Hebrew manuscripts; some Hebrew manuscripts and Syriac *Edom*
c 17 The meaning of the Hebrew for this word is uncertain.

TO THE POINT

Accurate? You Bet!

Every now and then you'll hear someone say that the Bible can't be trusted, that it's not historically accurate, that things just didn't happen the way the Old Testament says they did.

Then you come to a passage like Ezekiel 27. Tyre was one of the great trade cities of the ancient world. Its ships traveled all over the Mediterranean. And where do you suppose historians look to learn about trade in those ancient days? They look in Ezekiel 27! They've learned that everything in this chapter is accurate. Archaeological finds have shown that the prophet was right about the trade routes the ships traveled and the goods they carried.

Oh, some people will tell you that you can't trust the Bible. Don't believe them. The Bible is accurate. It's God's Word, and it's not full of mistakes.

20 " 'Dedan traded in saddle blankets with you.

21 " 'Arabia and all the princes of Kedar were your customers; they did business with you in lambs, rams and goats.

22 " 'The merchants of Sheba and Ra-amah traded with you; for your merchandise they exchanged the finest of all kinds of spices and precious stones, and gold.

23 " 'Harran, Kanneh and Eden and merchants of Sheba, Ashur and Kilmad traded with you. 24 In your marketplace they traded with you beautiful garments, blue fabric, embroidered work and multicolored rugs with cords twisted and tightly knotted.

25 " 'The ships of Tarshish serve
   as carriers for your wares.
You are filled with heavy cargo
   as you sail the sea.
26 Your oarsmen take you
   out to the high seas.
But the east wind will break you to
      pieces
   far out at sea.
27 Your wealth, merchandise and wares,
   your mariners, sailors and
      shipwrights,
your merchants and all your soldiers,
   and everyone else on board
will sink into the heart of the sea
   on the day of your shipwreck.
28 The shorelands will quake
   when your sailors cry out.
29 All who handle the oars
   will abandon their ships;
the mariners and all the sailors
   will stand on the shore.
30 They will raise their voice
   and cry bitterly over you;
they will sprinkle dust on their heads
   and roll in ashes.
31 They will shave their heads because
      of you
   and will put on sackcloth.
They will weep over you with anguish
      of soul
   and with bitter mourning.
32 As they wail and mourn over you,
   they will take up a lament
      concerning you:

"Who was ever silenced like Tyre,
   surrounded by the sea?"
33 When your merchandise went out on
      the seas,
   you satisfied many nations;
with your great wealth and your wares
   you enriched the kings of the earth.
34 Now you are shattered by the sea
   in the depths of the waters;
your wares and all your company
   have gone down with you.
35 All who live in the coastlands
   are appalled at you;
their kings shudder with horror
   and their faces are distorted with
      fear.
36 The merchants among the nations
      scoff at you;
   you have come to a horrible end
   and will be no more.' "

A Prophecy Against the King of Tyre

28 The word of the LORD came to me: 2 "Son of man, say to the ruler of Tyre, 'This is what the Sovereign LORD says:

" 'In the pride of your heart
   you say, "I am a god;
I sit on the throne of a god
   in the heart of the seas."
But you are a mere mortal and not a
      god,
   though you think you are as wise as
      a god.
3 Are you wiser than Daniel[a]?
   Is no secret hidden from you?
4 By your wisdom and understanding
   you have gained wealth for yourself
and amassed gold and silver
   in your treasuries.
5 By your great skill in trading
   you have increased your wealth,
and because of your wealth
   your heart has grown proud.

6 " 'Therefore this is what the Sovereign LORD says:

" 'Because you think you are wise,
   as wise as a god,

---

a 3 Or *Danel*, a man of renown in ancient literature

7 I am going to bring foreigners against
    you,
  the most ruthless of nations;
they will draw their swords against
    your beauty and wisdom
  and pierce your shining splendor.
8 They will bring you down to the pit,
  and you will die a violent death
  in the heart of the seas.
9 Will you then say, "I am a god,"
  in the presence of those who kill
    you?
  You will be but a mortal, not a god,
  in the hands of those who slay
    you.
10 You will die the death of the
    uncircumcised
  at the hands of foreigners.

I have spoken, declares the Sovereign
Lord.'"

11 The word of the Lord came to me:
12 "Son of man, take up a lament concerning the king of Tyre and say to him: 'This is what the Sovereign Lord says:

  "'You were the seal of perfection,
    full of wisdom and perfect in
    beauty.
13 You were in Eden,
  the garden of God;
every precious stone adorned you:
  carnelian, chrysolite and emerald,
  topaz, onyx and jasper,
  lapis lazuli, turquoise and beryl.[a]
Your settings and mountings[b] were
    made of gold;
  on the day you were created they
    were prepared.
14 You were anointed as a guardian
    cherub,
  for so I ordained you.
You were on the holy mount of God;
  you walked among the fiery
    stones.
15 You were blameless in your ways
  from the day you were created
  till wickedness was found in you.
16 Through your widespread trade
  you were filled with violence,
  and you sinned.

So I drove you in disgrace from the
    mount of God,
  and I expelled you, guardian cherub,
  from among the fiery stones.
17 Your heart became proud
  on account of your beauty,
and you corrupted your wisdom
  because of your splendor.
So I threw you to the earth;
  I made a spectacle of you before
    kings.
18 By your many sins and dishonest
    trade
  you have desecrated your
    sanctuaries.
So I made a fire come out from you,
  and it consumed you,
and I reduced you to ashes on the
    ground
  in the sight of all who were
    watching.
19 All the nations who knew you
  are appalled at you;
you have come to a horrible end
  and will be no more.'"

A Prophecy Against Sidon

20 The word of the Lord came to me:
21 "Son of man, set your face against Sidon; prophesy against her 22 and say: 'This is what the Sovereign Lord says:

  "'I am against you, Sidon,
    and among you I will display my
    glory.
You will know that I am the Lord,
  when I inflict punishment on you
  and within you am proved to be
    holy.
23 I will send a plague upon you
  and make blood flow in your
    streets.
The slain will fall within you,
  with the sword against you on every
    side.
Then you will know that I am the Lord.

24 "'No longer will the people of Israel have malicious neighbors who are painful briers and sharp thorns. Then they will know that I am the Sovereign Lord.

---

[a] 13 The precise identification of some of these precious stones is uncertain.   [b] 13 The meaning of the Hebrew for this phrase is uncertain.

25 " 'This is what the Sovereign LORD says: When I gather the people of Israel from the nations where they have been scattered, I will be proved holy through them in the sight of the nations. Then they will live in their own land, which I gave to my servant Jacob. 26 They will live there in safety and will build houses and plant vineyards; they will live in safety when I inflict punishment on all their neighbors who maligned them. Then they will know that I am the LORD their God.' "

A Prophecy Against Egypt
Judgment on Pharaoh

29 In the tenth year, in the tenth month on the twelfth day, the word of the LORD came to me: 2 "Son of man, set your face against Pharaoh king of Egypt and prophesy against him and against all Egypt. 3 Speak to him and say: 'This is what the Sovereign LORD says:

" 'I am against you, Pharaoh king of
    Egypt,
  you great monster lying among your
    streams.
You say, "The Nile belongs to me;
  I made it for myself."
4 But I will put hooks in your jaws
  and make the fish of your streams
    stick to your scales.
I will pull you out from among your
    streams,
  with all the fish sticking to your
    scales.
5 I will leave you in the desert,
  you and all the fish of your streams.
You will fall on the open field
  and not be gathered or picked up.
I will give you as food
  to the beasts of the earth and the
    birds of the sky.

6 Then all who live in Egypt will know that I am the LORD.

" 'You have been a staff of reed for the people of Israel. 7 When they grasped you with their hands, you splintered and you tore open their shoulders; when they leaned on you, you broke and their backs were wrenched.[a]

8 " 'Therefore this is what the Sovereign LORD says: I will bring a sword against you and kill both man and beast. 9 Egypt will become a desolate wasteland. Then they will know that I am the LORD.

" 'Because you said, "The Nile is mine; I made it," 10 therefore I am against you and against your streams, and I will make the land of Egypt a ruin and a desolate waste from Migdol to Aswan, as far as the border of Cush.[b] 11 The foot of neither man nor beast will pass through it; no one will live there for forty years. 12 I will make the land of Egypt desolate among devastated lands, and her cities will lie desolate forty years among ruined cities. And I will disperse the Egyptians among the nations and scatter them through the countries.

13 " 'Yet this is what the Sovereign LORD says: At the end of forty years I will gather the Egyptians from the nations where they were scattered. 14 I will bring them back from captivity and return them to Upper Egypt, the land of their ancestry. There they will be a lowly kingdom. 15 It will be the lowliest of kingdoms and will never again exalt itself above the other nations. I will make it so weak that it will never again rule over the nations. 16 Egypt will no longer be a source of confidence for the people of Israel but will be a reminder of their sin in turning to her for help. Then they will know that I am the Sovereign LORD.' "

Nebuchadnezzar's Reward

17 In the twenty-seventh year, in the first month on the first day, the word of the LORD came to me: 18 "Son of man, Nebuchadnezzar king of Babylon drove his army in a hard campaign against Tyre; every head was rubbed bare and every shoulder made raw. Yet he and his army got no reward from the campaign he led against Tyre. 19 Therefore this is what the Sovereign LORD says: I am going to give Egypt to Nebuchadnezzar king of Babylon, and he will carry off its wealth. He will loot and plunder the land as pay for his army. 20 I have given him Egypt as a reward for his efforts because he and his army did it for me, declares the Sovereign LORD.

---

a 7 Syriac (see also Septuagint and Vulgate); Hebrew *and you caused their backs to stand*   b 10 That is, the upper Nile region

21 "On that day I will make a horn[a] grow for the Israelites, and I will open your mouth among them. Then they will know that I am the Lord."

A Lament Over Egypt

30 The word of the Lord came to me: 2 "Son of man, prophesy and say: 'This is what the Sovereign Lord says:

" 'Wail and say,
    "Alas for that day!"
3 For the day is near,
    the day of the Lord is near—
a day of clouds,
    a time of doom for the nations.
4 A sword will come against Egypt,
    and anguish will come upon Cush.[b]
When the slain fall in Egypt,
    her wealth will be carried away
    and her foundations torn down.

5 Cush and Libya, Lydia and all Arabia, Kub and the people of the covenant land will fall by the sword along with Egypt.

6 " 'This is what the Lord says:

" 'The allies of Egypt will fall
    and her proud strength will fail.
From Migdol to Aswan
    they will fall by the sword within
        her,
            declares the Sovereign Lord.
7 " 'They will be desolate
    among desolate lands,
and their cities will lie
    among ruined cities.
8 Then they will know that I am the
        Lord,
    when I set fire to Egypt
    and all her helpers are crushed.

9 " 'On that day messengers will go out from me in ships to frighten Cush out of her complacency. Anguish will take hold of them on the day of Egypt's doom, for it is sure to come.

10 " 'This is what the Sovereign Lord says:

" 'I will put an end to the hordes of
        Egypt
    by the hand of Nebuchadnezzar king
        of Babylon.

11 He and his army—the most ruthless
        of nations—
    will be brought in to destroy the
        land.
They will draw their swords against
        Egypt
    and fill the land with the slain.
12 I will dry up the waters of the Nile
    and sell the land to an evil nation;
by the hand of foreigners
    I will lay waste the land and
        everything in it.

I the Lord have spoken.

13 " 'This is what the Sovereign Lord says:

" 'I will destroy the idols
    and put an end to the images in
        Memphis.
No longer will there be a prince in
        Egypt,
    and I will spread fear throughout
        the land.
14 I will lay waste Upper Egypt,
    set fire to Zoan
    and inflict punishment on Thebes.
15 I will pour out my wrath on Pelusium,
    the stronghold of Egypt,
    and wipe out the hordes of
        Thebes.
16 I will set fire to Egypt;
    Pelusium will writhe in agony.
Thebes will be taken by storm;
    Memphis will be in constant
        distress.
17 The young men of Heliopolis and
        Bubastis
    will fall by the sword,
    and the cities themselves will go
        into captivity.
18 Dark will be the day at Tahpanhes
    when I break the yoke of Egypt;
    there her proud strength will come
        to an end.
She will be covered with clouds,
    and her villages will go into
        captivity.
19 So I will inflict punishment on
        Egypt,
    and they will know that I am the
        Lord.' "

---

[a] 21 *Horn* here symbolizes strength.   [b] 4 That is, the upper Nile region; also in verses 5 and 9

Pharaoh's Arms Are Broken

20 In the eleventh year, in the first month on the seventh day, the word of the LORD came to me: 21 "Son of man, I have broken the arm of Pharaoh king of Egypt. It has not been bound up to be healed or put in a splint so that it may become strong enough to hold a sword. 22 Therefore this is what the Sovereign LORD says: I am against Pharaoh king of Egypt. I will break both his arms, the good arm as well as the broken one, and make the sword fall from his hand. 23 I will disperse the Egyptians among the nations and scatter them through the countries. 24 I will strengthen the arms of the king of Babylon and put my sword in his hand, but I will break the arms of Pharaoh, and he will groan before him like a mortally wounded man. 25 I will strengthen the arms of the king of Babylon, but the arms of Pharaoh will fall limp. Then they will know that I am the LORD, when I put my sword into the hand of the king of Babylon and he brandishes it against Egypt. 26 I will disperse the Egyptians among the nations and scatter them through the countries. Then they will know that I am the LORD."

Pharaoh as a Felled Cedar of Lebanon

31 In the eleventh year, in the third month on the first day, the word of the LORD came to me: 2 "Son of man, say to Pharaoh king of Egypt and to his hordes:

" 'Who can be compared with you in
  majesty?
3 Consider Assyria, once a cedar in
    Lebanon,
  with beautiful branches
    overshadowing the forest;
  it towered on high,
    its top above the thick foliage.
4 The waters nourished it,
    deep springs made it grow tall;
  their streams flowed
    all around its base
  and sent their channels
    to all the trees of the field.
5 So it towered higher
    than all the trees of the field;
  its boughs increased
    and its branches grew long,
    spreading because of abundant
      waters.
6 All the birds of the sky
    nested in its boughs,
  all the animals of the wild
    gave birth under its branches;
  all the great nations
    lived in its shade.
7 It was majestic in beauty,
    with its spreading boughs,
  for its roots went down
    to abundant waters.
8 The cedars in the garden of God
    could not rival it,
  nor could the junipers
    equal its boughs,
  nor could the plane trees
    compare with its branches—

Picture It.

What does God look like in this book? Angry like a thunderstorm but then showing love after the storm and bringing the Jews home to build a new temple.

no tree in the garden of God
could match its beauty.
⁹I made it beautiful
with abundant branches,
the envy of all the trees of Eden
in the garden of God.

¹⁰ " 'Therefore this is what the Sovereign LORD says: Because the great cedar towered over the thick foliage, and because it was proud of its height, ¹¹I gave it into the hands of the ruler of the nations, for him to deal with according to its wickedness. I cast it aside, ¹²and the most ruthless of foreign nations cut it down and left it. Its boughs fell on the mountains and in all the valleys; its branches lay broken in all the ravines of the land. All the nations of the earth came out from under its shade and left it. ¹³All the birds settled on the fallen tree, and all the wild animals lived among its branches. ¹⁴Therefore no other trees by the waters are ever to tower proudly on high, lifting their tops above the thick foliage. No other trees so well-watered are ever to reach such a height; they are all destined for death, for the earth below, among mortals who go down to the realm of the dead.

¹⁵ "This is what the Sovereign LORD says: On the day it was brought down to the realm of the dead I covered the deep springs with mourning for it; I held back its streams, and its abundant waters were restrained. Because of it I clothed Lebanon with gloom, and all the trees of the field withered away. ¹⁶I made the nations tremble at the sound of its fall when I brought it down to the realm of the dead to be with those who go down to the pit. Then all the trees of Eden, the choicest and best of Lebanon, the well-watered trees, were consoled in the earth below. ¹⁷They too, like the great cedar, had gone down to the realm of the dead, to those killed by the sword, along with the armed men who lived in its shade among the nations.

¹⁸ " 'Which of the trees of Eden can be compared with you in splendor and majesty? Yet you, too, will be brought down with the trees of Eden to the earth below;

you will lie among the uncircumcised, with those killed by the sword.

" 'This is Pharaoh and all his hordes, declares the Sovereign LORD.' "

A Lament Over Pharaoh

32 In the twelfth year, in the twelfth month on the first day, the word of the LORD came to me: ²"Son of man, take up a lament concerning Pharaoh king of Egypt and say to him:

" 'You are like a lion among the
nations;
you are like a monster in the seas
thrashing about in your streams,
churning the water with your feet
and muddying the streams.

³ " 'This is what the Sovereign LORD says:

" 'With a great throng of people
I will cast my net over you,
and they will haul you up in my net.
⁴I will throw you on the land
and hurl you on the open field.
I will let all the birds of the sky settle
on you
and all the animals of the wild
gorge themselves on you.
⁵I will spread your flesh on the
mountains
and fill the valleys with your remains.
⁶I will drench the land with your flowing
blood
all the way to the mountains,
and the ravines will be filled with
your flesh.
⁷When I snuff you out, I will cover the
heavens
and darken their stars;
I will cover the sun with a cloud,
and the moon will not give its light.
⁸All the shining lights in the heavens
I will darken over you;
I will bring darkness over your land,
declares the Sovereign LORD.
⁹I will trouble the hearts of many
peoples
when I bring about your destruction
among the nations,
amongᵃ lands you have not known.

ᵃ 9 Hebrew; Septuagint *bring you into captivity among the nations, / to*

10 I will cause many peoples to be
appalled at you,
and their kings will shudder with
horror because of you
when I brandish my sword before
them.
On the day of your downfall
each of them will tremble
every moment for his life.

11 " 'For this is what the Sovereign LORD
says:

" 'The sword of the king of Babylon
will come against you.
12 I will cause your hordes to fall
by the swords of mighty men —
the most ruthless of all nations.
They will shatter the pride of Egypt,
and all her hordes will be
overthrown.
13 I will destroy all her cattle
from beside abundant waters
no longer to be stirred by the foot of
man
or muddied by the hooves of cattle.
14 Then I will let her waters settle
and make her streams flow like oil,
declares the Sovereign LORD.
15 When I make Egypt desolate
and strip the land of everything in it,
when I strike down all who live there,
then they will know that I am the
LORD.'

16 "This is the lament they will chant
for her. The daughters of the nations
will chant it; for Egypt and all her hordes
they will chant it, declares the Sovereign
LORD."

Egypt's Descent Into the Realm of the Dead

17 In the twelfth year, on the fifteenth
day of the month, the word of the LORD
came to me: 18 "Son of man, wail for the
hordes of Egypt and consign to the earth
below both her and the daughters of
mighty nations, along with those who go
down to the pit. 19 Say to them, 'Are you
more favored than others? Go down and
be laid among the uncircumcised.' 20 They
will fall among those killed by the sword.

The sword is drawn; let her be dragged
off with all her hordes. 21 From within the
realm of the dead the mighty leaders will
say of Egypt and her allies, 'They have
come down and they lie with the uncircumcised, with those killed by the sword.'

22 "Assyria is there with her whole army;
she is surrounded by the graves of all her
slain, all who have fallen by the sword.
23 Their graves are in the depths of the pit
and her army lies around her grave. All
who had spread terror in the land of the
living are slain, fallen by the sword.

24 "Elam is there, with all her hordes
around her grave. All of them are slain,
fallen by the sword. All who had spread
terror in the land of the living went down
uncircumcised to the earth below. They
bear their shame with those who go down
to the pit. 25 A bed is made for her among
the slain, with all her hordes around her
grave. All of them are uncircumcised,
killed by the sword. Because their terror
had spread in the land of the living, they
bear their shame with those who go down
to the pit; they are laid among the slain.

26 "Meshek and Tubal are there, with
all their hordes around their graves. All
of them are uncircumcised, killed by the
sword because they spread their terror in
the land of the living. 27 But they do not lie
with the fallen warriors of old,[a] who went
down to the realm of the dead with their
weapons of war — their swords placed under their heads and their shields[b] resting
on their bones — though these warriors
also had terrorized the land of the living.

28 "You too, Pharaoh, will be broken and
will lie among the uncircumcised, with
those killed by the sword.

29 "Edom is there, her kings and all her
princes; despite their power, they are laid
with those killed by the sword. They lie
with the uncircumcised, with those who
go down to the pit.

30 "All the princes of the north and
all the Sidonians are there; they went
down with the slain in disgrace despite
the terror caused by their power. They lie
uncircumcised with those killed by the
sword and bear their shame with those
who go down to the pit.

---

[a] 27 Septuagint; Hebrew *warriors who were uncircumcised*   [b] 27 Probable reading of the original Hebrew text; Masoretic
Text *punishment*

31 "Pharaoh—he and all his army—will see them and he will be consoled for all his hordes that were killed by the sword, declares the Sovereign LORD. 32 Although I had him spread terror in the land of the living, Pharaoh and all his hordes will be laid among the uncircumcised, with those killed by the sword, declares the Sovereign LORD."

Renewal of Ezekiel's Call as Watchman

33 The word of the LORD came to me: 2 "Son of man, speak to your people and say to them: 'When I bring the sword against a land, and the people of the land choose one of their men and make him their watchman, 3 and he sees the sword coming against the land and blows the trumpet to warn the people, 4 then if anyone hears the trumpet but does not heed the warning and the sword comes and takes their life, their blood will be on their own head. 5 Since they heard the sound of the trumpet but did not heed the warning, their blood will be on their own head. If they had heeded the warning, they would have saved themselves. 6 But if the watchman sees the sword coming and does not blow the trumpet to warn the people and the sword comes and takes someone's life, that person's life will be taken because of their sin, but I will hold the watchman accountable for their blood.'

7 "Son of man, I have made you a watchman for the people of Israel; so hear the word I speak and give them warning from me. 8 When I say to the wicked, 'You wicked person, you will surely die,' and you do not speak out to dissuade them from their ways, that wicked person will die for[a] their sin, and I will hold you accountable for their blood. 9 But if you do warn the wicked person to turn from their ways and they do not do so, they will die for their sin, though you yourself will be saved.

10 "Son of man, say to the Israelites, 'This is what you are saying: "Our offenses and sins weigh us down, and we are wasting away because of[b] them. How then can we live?"' 11 Say to them, 'As surely as I live, declares the Sovereign LORD, I take no pleasure in the death of the wicked, but rather that they turn from their ways and live. Turn! Turn from your evil ways! Why will you die, people of Israel?'

12 "Therefore, son of man, say to your people, 'If someone who is righteous disobeys, that person's former righteousness will count for nothing. And if someone who is wicked repents, that person's former wickedness will not bring condemnation. The righteous person who sins will not be allowed to live even though they were formerly righteous.' 13 If I tell a righteous person that they will surely live, but then they trust in their righteousness and do evil, none of the righteous things that person has done will be remembered; they will die for the evil they have done. 14 And if I say to a wicked person, 'You will surely die,' but they then turn away from their sin and do what is just and right— 15 if they give back what they took in pledge for a loan, return what they have stolen, follow the decrees that give life, and do no evil—that person will surely live; they will not die. 16 None of the sins that person has committed will be remembered against them. They have done what is just and right; they will surely live.

17 "Yet your people say, 'The way of the Lord is not just.' But it is their way that is not just. 18 If a righteous person turns from their righteousness and does evil, they will die for it. 19 And if a wicked person turns away from their wickedness and does what is just and right, they will live by doing so. 20 Yet you Israelites say, 'The way of the Lord is not just.' But I will judge each of you according to your own ways."

Jerusalem's Fall Explained

21 In the twelfth year of our exile, in the tenth month on the fifth day, a man who had escaped from Jerusalem came to me and said, "The city has fallen!" 22 Now the evening before the man arrived, the hand of the LORD was on me, and he opened my mouth before the man came to me in the morning. So my mouth was opened and I was no longer silent.

---

[a] 8 Or in; also in verse 9   [b] 10 Or away in

> Last week in youth group our leader asked if some of us would share a time we witnessed to somebody. I didn't say anything; I have never done that. Is everybody supposed to witness to people? >> Elijah

Dear Jordan

Dear Elijah,

Sharing about what God is doing in your life seems very easy to some people. For others, it's scary or it seems weird. If it doesn't come easily to you, you should at least make a decision to be prepared to speak up if the Lord calls out to you. If you feel that urging inside of you to speak up, then you should.

Ezekiel was told by God to be a watchman. He was supposed to warn people who were living sinful lives. If he did not give the warning, he was guilty. If he gave the warning but people didn't pay attention, they were responsible (Ezekiel 33:7–9).

Whether God asks you to warn someone, tell how God has answered a prayer, explain about salvation or share your faith in another way, be willing to obey his call. Ask God to give you the words. That's a job the Holy Spirit does for us. The rest is up to God and the person you share with.

Jordan

23Then the word of the LORD came to me: 24"Son of man, the people living in those ruins in the land of Israel are saying, 'Abraham was only one man, yet he possessed the land. But we are many; surely the land has been given to us as our possession.' 25Therefore say to them, 'This is what the Sovereign LORD says: Since you eat meat with the blood still in it and look to your idols and shed blood, should you then possess the land? 26You rely on your sword, you do detestable things, and each of you defiles his neighbor's wife. Should you then possess the land?'

27"Say this to them: 'This is what the Sovereign LORD says: As surely as I live, those who are left in the ruins will fall by the sword, those out in the country I will give to the wild animals to be devoured, and those in strongholds and caves will die of a plague. 28I will make the land a desolate waste, and her proud strength will come to an end, and the mountains of Israel will become desolate so that no one will cross them. 29Then they will know that I am the LORD, when I have made the land a desolate waste because of all the detestable things they have done.'

30"As for you, son of man, your people are talking together about you by the walls and at the doors of the houses, saying to each other, 'Come and hear the message that has come from the LORD.' 31My people come to you, as they usually do, and sit before you to hear your words, but they do not put them into practice. Their mouths speak of love, but their hearts are greedy for unjust gain. 32Indeed, to them you are nothing more than one who sings love songs with a beautiful voice and plays an instrument well, for they hear your words but do not put them into practice.

33"When all this comes true—and it surely will—then they will know that a prophet has been among them."

The LORD Will Be Israel's Shepherd

34 The word of the LORD came to me: 2"Son of man, prophesy against the shepherds of Israel; prophesy and say to them: 'This is what the Sovereign LORD says: Woe to you shepherds of Israel who only take care of yourselves! Should not shepherds take care of the flock? 3You eat the curds, clothe yourselves with the wool and slaughter the choice animals, but you do not take care of the flock. 4You have not strengthened the weak or healed the sick or bound up the injured. You have not brought back the strays or searched for the lost. You have ruled them harshly and brutally. 5So they were scattered because there was no shepherd, and when they were scattered they became food for all the wild animals. 6My sheep wandered over all the mountains and on every high hill. They were scattered over the whole earth, and no one searched or looked for them.

7" 'Therefore, you shepherds, hear the word of the LORD: 8As surely as I live, declares the Sovereign LORD, because my flock lacks a shepherd and so has been plundered and has become food for all the wild animals, and because my shepherds did not search for my flock but cared for themselves rather than for my flock, 9therefore, you shepherds, hear the word of the LORD: 10This is what the Sovereign LORD says: I am against the shepherds and will hold them accountable for my flock. I will remove them from tending the flock so that the shepherds can no longer feed themselves. I will rescue my flock from their mouths, and it will no longer be food for them.

11" 'For this is what the Sovereign LORD says: I myself will search for my sheep and look after them. 12As a shepherd looks after his scattered flock when he is with them, so will I look after my sheep. I will rescue them from all the places where they were scattered on a day of clouds and darkness. 13I will bring them out from the nations and gather them from the countries, and I will bring them into their own land. I will pasture them on the mountains of Israel, in the ravines and in all the settlements in the land. 14I will tend them in a good pasture, and the mountain heights of Israel will be their grazing land. There they will lie down in good grazing land, and there they will feed in a rich pasture on the mountains of Israel. 15I myself will tend my sheep and have them lie down, declares the Sovereign LORD. ¹⁶I will search for the lost and bring back the strays. I will bind up the injured and strengthen the weak, but the sleek and the strong I will destroy. I will shepherd the flock with justice.

¹⁷ " 'As for you, my flock, this is what the Sovereign LORD says: I will judge between one sheep and another, and between rams and goats. ¹⁸Is it not enough for you to feed on the good pasture? Must you also trample the rest of your pasture with your feet? Is it not enough for you to drink clear water? Must you also muddy the rest with your feet? ¹⁹Must my flock feed on what you have trampled and drink what you have muddied with your feet?

²⁰ " 'Therefore this is what the Sovereign LORD says to them: See, I myself will judge between the fat sheep and the lean sheep. ²¹Because you shove with flank and shoulder, butting all the weak sheep with your horns until you have driven them away, ²²I will save my flock, and they will no longer be plundered. I will judge between one sheep and another. ²³I will place over them one shepherd, my servant David, and he will tend them; he will tend them and be their shepherd. ²⁴I the LORD will be their God, and my servant David will be prince among them. I the LORD have spoken.

²⁵ " 'I will make a covenant of peace with them and rid the land of savage beasts so that they may live in the wilderness and sleep in the forests in safety. ²⁶I will make them and the places surrounding my hill a blessing.ᵃ I will send down showers in season; there will be showers of blessing. ²⁷The trees will yield their fruit and the ground will yield its crops; the people will be secure in their land. They will know that I am the LORD, when I break the bars of their yoke

As a shepherd looks after his scattered flock ... so will I look after my sheep.

Ezekiel 34:12

and rescue them from the hands of those who enslaved them. ²⁸They will no longer be plundered by the nations, nor will wild animals devour them. They will live in safety, and no one will make them afraid. ²⁹I will provide for them a land renowned for its crops, and they will no longer be victims of famine in the land or bear the scorn of the nations. ³⁰Then they will know that I, the LORD their God, am with them and that they, the Israelites, are my people, declares the Sovereign LORD. ³¹You are my sheep, the sheep of my pasture, and I am your God, declares the Sovereign LORD.' "

A Prophecy Against Edom

35 The word of the LORD came to me: ²"Son of man, set your face against Mount Seir; prophesy against it ³and say: 'This is what the Sovereign LORD says: I am against you, Mount Seir, and I will stretch out my hand against you and make you a desolate waste. ⁴I will turn your towns into ruins and you will be desolate. Then you will know that I am the LORD.

⁵ " 'Because you harbored an ancient hostility and delivered the Israelites over to the sword at the time of their calamity, the time their punishment reached its climax, ⁶therefore as surely as I live, declares the Sovereign LORD, I will give you over to bloodshed and it will pursue you. Since you did not hate bloodshed, bloodshed will pursue you. ⁷I will make Mount Seir a desolate waste and cut off from it all who come and go. ⁸I will fill your mountains with the slain; those killed by the sword will fall on your hills and in your valleys and in all your ravines. ⁹I will make you desolate forever; your towns will not be inhabited. Then you will know that I am the LORD.

¹⁰ " 'Because you have said, "These two nations and countries will be ours

---

ᵃ 26 Or I will cause them and the places surrounding my hill to be named in blessings (see Gen. 48:20); or I will cause them and the places surrounding my hill to be seen as blessed

and we will take possession of them," even though I the LORD was there, 11 therefore as surely as I live, declares the Sovereign LORD, I will treat you in accordance with the anger and jealousy you showed in your hatred of them and I will make myself known among them when I judge you. 12 Then you will know that I the LORD have heard all the contemptible things you have said against the mountains of Israel. You said, "They have been laid waste and have been given over to us to devour." 13 You boasted against me and spoke against me without restraint, and I heard it. 14 This is what the Sovereign LORD says: While the whole earth rejoices, I will make you desolate. 15 Because you rejoiced when the inheritance of Israel became desolate, that is how I will treat you. You will be desolate, Mount Seir, you and all of Edom. Then they will know that I am the LORD.' "

Hope for the Mountains of Israel

36 "Son of man, prophesy to the mountains of Israel and say, 'Mountains of Israel, hear the word of the LORD. 2 This is what the Sovereign LORD says: The enemy said of you, "Aha! The ancient heights have become our possession." ' 3 Therefore prophesy and say, 'This is what the Sovereign LORD says: Because they ravaged and crushed you from every side so that you became the possession of the rest of the nations and the object of people's malicious talk and slander, 4 therefore, mountains of Israel, hear the word of the Sovereign LORD: This is what the Sovereign LORD says to the mountains and hills, to the ravines and valleys, to the desolate ruins and the deserted towns that have been plundered and ridiculed by the rest of the nations around you— 5 this is what the Sovereign LORD says: In my burning zeal I have spoken against the rest of the nations, and against all Edom, for with glee and with malice in their hearts they made my land their own possession so that they might plunder its pastureland.' 6 Therefore prophesy concerning the land of Israel and say to the mountains and hills, to the ravines and valleys: 'This is what the Sovereign LORD says: I speak in my jealous wrath because you have suffered the scorn of the nations. 7 Therefore this is what the Sovereign LORD says: I swear with uplifted hand that the nations around you will also suffer scorn.

8 " 'But you, mountains of Israel, will produce branches and fruit for my people Israel, for they will soon come home. 9 I am concerned for you and will look on you with favor; you will be plowed and sown, 10 and I will cause many people to live on you—yes, all of Israel. The towns will be inhabited and the ruins rebuilt. 11 I will increase the number of people and animals living on you, and they will be fruitful and become numerous. I will settle people on you as in the past and will make you prosper more than before. Then you will know that I am the LORD. 12 I will cause people, my people Israel, to live on you. They will possess you, and you will be their inheritance; you will never again deprive them of their children.

13 " 'This is what the Sovereign LORD says: Because some say to you, "You devour people and deprive your nation of its children," 14 therefore you will no longer devour people or make your nation childless, declares the Sovereign LORD. 15 No longer will I make you hear the taunts of the nations, and no longer will you suffer the scorn of the peoples or cause your nation to fall, declares the Sovereign LORD.' "

Israel's Restoration Assured

16 Again the word of the LORD came to me: 17 "Son of man, when the people of Israel were living in their own land, they defiled it by their conduct and their actions. Their conduct was like a woman's monthly uncleanness in my sight. 18 So I poured out my wrath on them because they had shed blood in the land and because they had defiled it with their idols. 19 I dispersed them among the nations, and they were scattered through the countries; I judged them according to their conduct and their actions. 20 And wherever they went among the nations they profaned my holy name, for it was

said of them, 'These are the LORD's people, and yet they had to leave his land.' ²¹I had concern for my holy name, which the people of Israel profaned among the nations where they had gone.

²²"Therefore say to the Israelites, 'This is what the Sovereign LORD says: It is not for your sake, people of Israel, that I am going to do these things, but for the sake of my holy name, which you have profaned among the nations where you have gone. ²³I will show the holiness of my great name, which has been profaned among the nations, the name you have profaned among them. Then the nations will know that I am the LORD, declares the Sovereign LORD, when I am proved holy through you before their eyes.

²⁴"'For I will take you out of the nations; I will gather you from all the countries and bring you back into your own land. ²⁵I will sprinkle clean water on you, and you will be clean; I will cleanse you from all your impurities and from all your idols. ²⁶I will give you a new heart and put a new spirit in you; I will remove from you your heart of stone and give you a heart of flesh. ²⁷And I will put my Spirit in you and move you to follow my decrees and be careful to keep my laws. ²⁸Then you will live in the land I gave your ancestors; you will be my people, and I will be your God. ²⁹I will save you from all your uncleanness. I will call for the grain and make it plentiful and will not bring famine upon you. ³⁰I will increase the fruit of the trees and the crops of the field, so that you will no longer suffer disgrace among the nations because of famine. ³¹Then you will remember your evil ways and wicked deeds, and you will loathe yourselves for your sins and detestable practices. ³²I want you to know that I am not doing this for your sake, declares the Sovereign LORD. Be ashamed and disgraced for your conduct, people of Israel!

³³"'This is what the Sovereign LORD says: On the day I cleanse you from all your sins, I will resettle your towns, and the ruins will be rebuilt. ³⁴The desolate land will be cultivated instead of lying desolate in the sight of all who pass through it. ³⁵They will say, "This land that was laid waste has become like the garden of Eden; the cities that were lying in ruins, desolate and destroyed, are now fortified and inhabited." ³⁶Then the nations around you that remain will know that I the LORD have rebuilt what was destroyed and have replanted what was desolate. I the LORD have spoken, and I will do it.'

³⁷"This is what the Sovereign LORD says: Once again I will yield to Israel's plea and do this for them: I will make their people as numerous as sheep, ³⁸as numerous as the flocks for offerings at Jerusalem during her appointed festivals. So will the ruined cities be filled with flocks of people. Then they will know that I am the LORD."

The Valley of Dry Bones

37 The hand of the LORD was on me, and he brought me out by the Spirit of the LORD and set me in the middle of a valley; it was full of bones. ²He led me back and forth among them, and I saw a great many bones on the floor of the valley, bones that were very dry. ³He asked me, "Son of man, can these bones live?"

I said, "Sovereign LORD, you alone know."

⁴Then he said to me, "Prophesy to these bones and say to them, 'Dry bones, hear the word of the LORD! ⁵This is what the Sovereign LORD says to these bones: I will make breathᵃ enter you, and you will come to life. ⁶I will attach tendons to you and make flesh come upon you and cover you with skin; I will put breath in you, and you will come to life. Then you will know that I am the LORD.'"

⁷So I prophesied as I was commanded. And as I was prophesying, there was a noise, a rattling sound, and the bones came together, bone to bone. ⁸I looked, and tendons and flesh appeared on them and skin covered them, but there was no breath in them.

⁹Then he said to me, "Prophesy to the breath; prophesy, son of man, and say to it, 'This is what the Sovereign LORD says:

ᵃ 5 The Hebrew for this word can also mean *wind* or *spirit* (see verses 6-14).

Come, breath, from the four winds and breathe into these slain, that they may live.'" [10] So I prophesied as he commanded me, and breath entered them; they came to life and stood up on their feet— a vast army.

[11] Then he said to me: "Son of man, these bones are the people of Israel. They say, 'Our bones are dried up and our hope is gone; we are cut off.' [12] Therefore prophesy and say to them: 'This is what the Sovereign Lord says: My people, I am going to open your graves and bring you up from them; I will bring you back to the land of Israel. [13] Then you, my people, will know that I am the Lord, when I open your graves and bring you up from them. [14] I will put my Spirit in you and you will live, and I will settle you in your own land. Then you will know that I the Lord have spoken, and I have done it, declares the Lord.'"

One Nation Under One King

[15] The word of the Lord came to me: [16] "Son of man, take a stick of wood and write on it, 'Belonging to Judah and the Israelites associated with him.' Then take another stick of wood, and write on it, 'Belonging to Joseph (that is, to Ephraim) and all the Israelites associated with him.' [17] Join them together into one stick so that they will become one in your hand.

[18] "When your people ask you, 'Won't you tell us what you mean by this?' [19] say to them, 'This is what the Sovereign Lord says: I am going to take the stick of Joseph—which is in Ephraim's hand—and of the Israelite tribes associated with him, and join it to Judah's stick. I will make them into a single stick of wood, and they will become one in my hand.' [20] Hold before their eyes the sticks you have written on [21] and say to them, 'This is what the Sovereign Lord says: I will take the Israelites out of the nations where they have gone. I will gather them from all around and bring them back into their own land. [22] I will make them one nation in the land, on the mountains of Israel. There will be one king over all of them and they will

never again be two nations or be divided into two kingdoms. [23] They will no longer defile themselves with their idols and vile images or with any of their offenses, for I will save them from all their sinful backsliding,[a] and I will cleanse them. They will be my people, and I will be their God.

[24] "'My servant David will be king over them, and they will all have one shepherd. They will follow my laws and be careful to keep my decrees. [25] They will live in the land I gave to my servant Jacob, the land where your ancestors lived. They and their children and their children's children will live there forever, and David my servant will be their prince forever. [26] I will make a covenant of peace with them; it will be an everlasting covenant. I will establish them and increase their numbers, and I will put my sanctuary among them forever. [27] My dwelling place will be with them; I will be their God, and they will be my people. [28] Then the nations will know that I the Lord make Israel holy, when my sanctuary is among them forever.'"

The Lord's Great Victory Over the Nations

38 The word of the Lord came to me: [2] "Son of man, set your face against Gog, of the land of Magog, the chief prince of[b] Meshek and Tubal; prophesy against him [3] and say: 'This is what the Sovereign Lord says: I am against you, Gog, chief prince of[c] Meshek and Tubal. [4] I will turn you around, put hooks in your jaws and bring you out with your whole army—your horses, your horsemen fully armed, and a great horde with large and small shields, all of them brandishing their swords. [5] Persia, Cush[d] and Put will be with them, all with shields and helmets, [6] also Gomer with all its troops, and Beth Togarmah from the far north with all its troops—the many nations with you.

[7] "'Get ready; be prepared, you and all the hordes gathered about you, and take command of them. [8] After many days you will be called to arms. In future years you will invade a land that has recovered from

---

[a] 23 Many Hebrew manuscripts (see also Septuagint); most Hebrew manuscripts *all their dwelling places where they sinned*
[b] 2 Or *the prince of Rosh,*   [c] 3 Or *Gog, prince of Rosh,*   [d] 5 That is, the upper Nile region

war, whose people were gathered from many nations to the mountains of Israel, which had long been desolate. They had been brought out from the nations, and now all of them live in safety. [9]You and all your troops and the many nations with you will go up, advancing like a storm; you will be like a cloud covering the land.

[10]" 'This is what the Sovereign LORD says: On that day thoughts will come into your mind and you will devise an evil scheme. [11]You will say, "I will invade a land of unwalled villages; I will attack a peaceful and unsuspecting people—all of them living without walls and without gates and bars. [12]I will plunder and loot and turn my hand against the resettled ruins and the people gathered from the nations, rich in livestock and goods, living at the center of the land.[a]" [13]Sheba and Dedan and the merchants of Tarshish and all her villages[b] will say to you, "Have you come to plunder? Have you gathered your hordes to loot, to carry off silver and gold, to take away livestock and goods and to seize much plunder?" '

[14]"Therefore, son of man, prophesy and say to Gog: 'This is what the Sovereign LORD says: In that day, when my people Israel are living in safety, will you not take notice of it? [15]You will come from your place in the far north, you and many nations with you, all of them riding on horses, a great horde, a mighty army. [16]You will advance against my people Israel like a cloud that covers the land. In days to come, Gog, I will bring you against my land, so that the nations may know me when I am proved holy through you before their eyes.

[17]" 'This is what the Sovereign LORD says: You are the one I spoke of in former days by my servants the prophets of Israel. At that time they prophesied for years that I would bring you against them. [18]This is what will happen in that day: When Gog attacks the land of Israel, my hot anger will be aroused, declares the Sovereign LORD. [19]In my zeal and fiery wrath I declare that at that time there

shall be a great earthquake in the land of Israel. [20]The fish in the sea, the birds in the sky, the beasts of the field, every creature that moves along the ground, and all the people on the face of the earth will tremble at my presence. The mountains will be overturned, the cliffs will crumble and every wall will fall to the ground. [21]I will summon a sword against Gog on all my mountains, declares the Sovereign LORD. Every man's sword will be against his brother. [22]I will execute judgment on him with plague and bloodshed; I will pour down torrents of rain, hailstones and burning sulfur on him and on his troops and on the many nations with him. [23]And so I will show my greatness and my holiness, and I will make myself known in the sight of many nations. Then they will know that I am the LORD.'

39 "Son of man, prophesy against Gog and say: 'This is what the Sovereign LORD says: I am against you, Gog, chief prince of[c] Meshek and Tubal. [2]I will turn you around and drag you along. I will bring you from the far north and send you against the mountains of Israel. [3]Then I will strike your bow from your left hand and make your arrows drop from your right hand. [4]On the mountains of

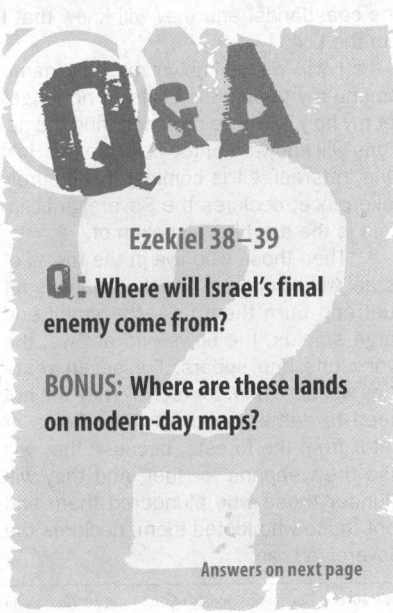

Ezekiel 38–39

Q: Where will Israel's final enemy come from?

BONUS: Where are these lands on modern-day maps?

Answers on next page

---

[a] 12 The Hebrew for this phrase means *the navel of the earth.*   [b] 13 Or *her strong lions*   [c] 1 Or Gog, *prince of Rosh,*

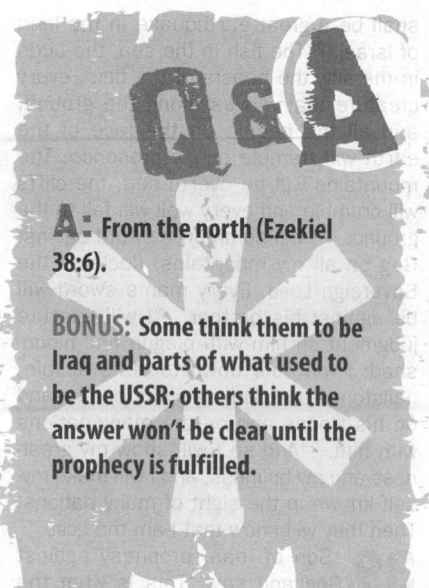

Israel you will fall, you and all your troops and the nations with you. I will give you as food to all kinds of carrion birds and to the wild animals. [5]You will fall in the open field, for I have spoken, declares the Sovereign LORD. [6]I will send fire on Magog and on those who live in safety in the coastlands, and they will know that I am the LORD.

[7]" 'I will make known my holy name among my people Israel. I will no longer let my holy name be profaned, and the nations will know that I the LORD am the Holy One in Israel. [8]It is coming! It will surely take place, declares the Sovereign LORD. This is the day I have spoken of.

[9]" 'Then those who live in the towns of Israel will go out and use the weapons for fuel and burn them up—the small and large shields, the bows and arrows, the war clubs and spears. For seven years they will use them for fuel. [10]They will not need to gather wood from the fields or cut it from the forests, because they will use the weapons for fuel. And they will plunder those who plundered them and loot those who looted them, declares the Sovereign LORD.

[11]" 'On that day I will give Gog a burial place in Israel, in the valley of those who travel east of the Sea. It will block the way of travelers, because Gog and all his hordes will be buried there. So it will be called the Valley of Hamon Gog.[a]

[12]" 'For seven months the Israelites will be burying them in order to cleanse the land. [13]All the people of the land will bury them, and the day I display my glory will be a memorable day for them, declares the Sovereign LORD. [14]People will be continually employed in cleansing the land. They will spread out across the land and, along with others, they will bury any bodies that are lying on the ground.

" 'After the seven months they will carry out a more detailed search. [15]As they go through the land, anyone who sees a human bone will leave a marker beside it until the gravediggers bury it in the Valley of Hamon Gog, [16]near a town called Hamonah.[b] And so they will cleanse the land.'

[17]"Son of man, this is what the Sovereign LORD says: Call out to every kind of bird and all the wild animals: 'Assemble and come together from all around to the sacrifice I am preparing for you, the great sacrifice on the mountains of Israel. There you will eat flesh and drink blood. [18]You will eat the flesh of mighty men and drink the blood of the princes of the earth as if they were rams and lambs, goats and bulls—all of them fattened animals from Bashan. [19]At the sacrifice I am preparing for you, you will eat fat till you are glutted and drink blood till you are drunk. [20]At my table you will eat your fill of horses and riders, mighty men and soldiers of every kind,' declares the Sovereign LORD.

[21]"I will display my glory among the nations, and all the nations will see the punishment I inflict and the hand I lay on them. [22]From that day forward the people of Israel will know that I am the LORD their God. [23]And the nations will know that the people of Israel went into exile for their sin, because they were unfaithful to me. So I hid my face from them and

---

[a] 11 Hamon Gog means hordes of Gog.   [b] 16 Hamonah means horde.

handed them over to their enemies, and they all fell by the sword. ²⁴I dealt with them according to their uncleanness and their offenses, and I hid my face from them.

²⁵ "Therefore this is what the Sovereign Lord says: I will now restore the fortunes of Jacob^a and will have compassion on all the people of Israel, and I will be zealous for my holy name. ²⁶They will forget their shame and all the unfaithfulness they showed toward me when they lived in safety in their land with no one to make them afraid. ²⁷When I have brought them back from the nations and have gathered them from the countries of their enemies, I will be proved holy through them in the sight of many nations. ²⁸Then they will know that I am the Lord their God, for though I sent them into exile among the nations, I will gather them to their own land, not leaving any behind. ²⁹I will no longer hide my face from them, for I will pour out my Spirit on the people of Israel, declares the Sovereign Lord."

The Temple Area Restored

40 In the twenty-fifth year of our exile, at the beginning of the year, on the tenth of the month, in the fourteenth year after the fall of the city—on that very day the hand of the Lord was on me and he took me there. ²In visions of God he took me to the land of Israel and set me on a very high mountain, on whose south side were some buildings that looked like a city. ³He took me there, and I saw a man whose appearance was like bronze; he was standing in the gateway with a linen cord and a measuring rod in his hand. ⁴The man said to me, "Son of man, look carefully and listen closely and pay attention to everything I am going to show you, for that is why you have been brought here. Tell the people of Israel everything you see."

The East Gate to the Outer Court

⁵I saw a wall completely surrounding the temple area. The length of the measuring rod in the man's hand was six long cubits,^b each of which was a cubit and a handbreadth. He measured the wall; it was one measuring rod thick and one rod high.

⁶Then he went to the east gate. He climbed its steps and measured the threshold of the gate; it was one rod deep. ⁷The alcoves for the guards were one rod long and one rod wide, and the projecting walls between the alcoves were five cubits^c thick. And the threshold of the gate next to the portico facing the temple was one rod deep.

⁸Then he measured the portico of the gateway; ⁹it^d was eight cubits^e deep and its jambs were two cubits^f thick. The portico of the gateway faced the temple.

¹⁰Inside the east gate were three alcoves on each side; the three had the same measurements, and the faces of the projecting walls on each side had the same measurements. ¹¹Then he measured the width of the entrance of the gateway; it was ten cubits and its length was thirteen cubits.^g ¹²In front of each alcove was a wall one cubit high, and the alcoves were six cubits square. ¹³Then he measured the gateway from the top of the rear wall of one alcove to the top of the opposite one; the distance was twenty-five cubits^h from one parapet opening to the opposite one. ¹⁴He measured along the faces of the projecting walls all around the inside of the gateway—sixty cubits.ⁱ The measurement was up to the portico^j facing the courtyard.^k ¹⁵The distance from the entrance of the gateway to the far end of its portico was fifty cubits.^l ¹⁶The alcoves and the projecting walls inside the gateway were surmounted by narrow parapet openings all around, as was the portico; the openings all around

---

^a 25 Or now bring Jacob back from captivity   ^b 5 That is, about 11 feet or about 3.2 meters; also in verse 12. The long cubit of about 21 inches or about 53 centimeters is the basic unit of measurement of length throughout chapters 40–48.   ^c 7 That is, about 8 3/4 feet or about 2.7 meters; also in verse 48   ^d 8,9 Many Hebrew manuscripts, Septuagint, Vulgate and Syriac; most Hebrew manuscripts gateway facing the temple; it was one rod deep. ⁹Then he measured the portico of the gateway; it   ^e 9 That is, about 14 feet or about 4.2 meters   ^f 9 That is, about 3 1/2 feet or about 1 meter   ^g 11 That is, about 18 feet wide and 23 feet long or about 5.3 meters wide and 6.9 meters long   ^h 13 That is, about 44 feet or about 13 meters; also in verses 21, 25, 29, 30, 33 and 36   ⁱ 14 That is, about 105 feet or about 32 meters   ^j 14 Septuagint; Hebrew projecting wall   ^k 14 The meaning of the Hebrew for this verse is uncertain.   ^l 15 That is, about 88 feet or about 27 meters; also in verses 21, 25, 29, 33 and 36

faced inward. The faces of the projecting walls were decorated with palm trees.

The Outer Court

17 Then he brought me into the outer court. There I saw some rooms and a pavement that had been constructed all around the court; there were thirty rooms along the pavement. 18 It abutted the sides of the gateways and was as wide as they were long; this was the lower pavement. 19 Then he measured the distance from the inside of the lower gateway to the outside of the inner court; it was a hundred cubits*a* on the east side as well as on the north.

The North Gate

20 Then he measured the length and width of the north gate, leading into the outer court. 21 Its alcoves—three on each side—its projecting walls and its portico had the same measurements as those of the first gateway. It was fifty cubits long and twenty-five cubits wide. 22 Its openings, its portico and its palm tree decorations had the same measurements as those of the gate facing east. Seven steps led up to it, with its portico opposite them. 23 There was a gate to the inner court facing the north gate, just as there was on the east. He measured from one gate to the opposite one; it was a hundred cubits.

The South Gate

24 Then he led me to the south side and I saw the south gate. He measured its jambs and its portico, and they had the same measurements as the others. 25 The gateway and its portico had narrow openings all around, like the openings of the others. It was fifty cubits long and twenty-five cubits wide. 26 Seven steps led up to it, with its portico opposite them; it had palm tree decorations on the faces of the projecting walls on each side. 27 The inner court also had a gate facing south, and he measured from this gate to the outer gate on the south side; it was a hundred cubits.

The Gates to the Inner Court

28 Then he brought me into the inner court through the south gate, and he measured the south gate; it had the same measurements as the others. 29 Its alcoves, its projecting walls and its portico had the same measurements as the others. The gateway and its portico had openings all around. It was fifty cubits long and twenty-five cubits wide. 30 (The porticoes of the gateways around the inner court were twenty-five cubits wide and five cubits deep.) 31 Its portico faced the outer court; palm trees decorated its jambs, and eight steps led up to it.

32 Then he brought me to the inner court on the east side, and he measured the gateway; it had the same measurements as the others. 33 Its alcoves, its projecting walls and its portico had the same measurements as the others. The gateway and its portico had openings all around. It was fifty cubits long and twenty-five cubits wide. 34 Its portico faced the outer court; palm trees decorated the jambs on either side, and eight steps led up to it.

35 Then he brought me to the north gate and measured it. It had the same measurements as the others, 36 as did its alcoves, its projecting walls and its portico, and it had openings all around. It was fifty cubits long and twenty-five cubits wide. 37 Its portico*b* faced the outer court; palm trees decorated the jambs on either side, and eight steps led up to it.

The Rooms for Preparing Sacrifices

38 A room with a doorway was by the portico in each of the inner gateways, where the burnt offerings were washed. 39 In the portico of the gateway were two tables on each side, on which the burnt offerings, sin offerings*c* and guilt offerings were slaughtered. 40 By the outside wall of the portico of the gateway, near the steps at the entrance of the north gateway were two tables, and on the other side of the steps were two tables. 41 So there were four tables on one side of the

---

a 19 That is, about 175 feet or about 53 meters; also in verses 23, 27 and 47   *b 37* Septuagint (see also verses 31 and 34); Hebrew *jambs*   *c 39* Or *purification offerings*

gateway and four on the other—eight tables in all—on which the sacrifices were slaughtered. [42]There were also four tables of dressed stone for the burnt offerings, each a cubit and a half long, a cubit and a half wide and a cubit high.[a] On them were placed the utensils for slaughtering the burnt offerings and the other sacrifices. [43]And double-pronged hooks, each a handbreadth[b] long, were attached to the wall all around. The tables were for the flesh of the offerings.

The Rooms for the Priests

[44]Outside the inner gate, within the inner court, were two rooms, one[c] at the side of the north gate and facing south, and another at the side of the south[d] gate and facing north. [45]He said to me, "The room facing south is for the priests who guard the temple, [46]and the room facing north is for the priests who guard the altar. These are the sons of Zadok, who are the only Levites who may draw near to the LORD to minister before him."

[47]Then he measured the court: It was square—a hundred cubits long and a hundred cubits wide. And the altar was in front of the temple.

The New Temple

[48]He brought me to the portico of the temple and measured the jambs of the portico; they were five cubits wide on either side. The width of the entrance was fourteen cubits[e] and its projecting walls were[f] three cubits[g] wide on either side. [49]The portico was twenty cubits[h] wide, and twelve[i] cubits[j] from front to back. It was reached by a flight of stairs,[k] and there were pillars on each side of the jambs.

41 Then the man brought me to the main hall and measured the jambs; the width of the jambs was six cubits[l] on each side.[m] [2]The entrance was ten cubits[n] wide, and the projecting walls on each side of it were five cubits[o] wide. He also measured the main hall; it was forty cubits long and twenty cubits wide.[p]

[3]Then he went into the inner sanctuary and measured the jambs of the entrance; each was two cubits[q] wide. The entrance was six cubits wide, and the projecting walls on each side of it were seven cubits[r] wide. [4]And he measured the length of the inner sanctuary; it was twenty cubits, and its width was twenty cubits across the end of the main hall. He said to me, "This is the Most Holy Place."

[5]Then he measured the wall of the temple; it was six cubits thick, and each side room around the temple was four cubits[s] wide. [6]The side rooms were on three levels, one above another, thirty on each level. There were ledges all around the wall of the temple to serve as supports for the side rooms, so that the supports were not inserted into the wall of the temple. [7]The side rooms all around the temple were wider at each successive level. The structure surrounding the temple was built in ascending stages, so that the rooms widened as one went upward. A stairway went up from the lowest floor to the top floor through the middle floor.

[8]I saw that the temple had a raised base all around it, forming the foundation of the side rooms. It was the length of the rod, six long cubits. [9]The outer wall of the side rooms was five cubits thick. The open area between the side rooms of the temple [10]and the priests' rooms was twenty cubits wide all around the temple. [11]There were entrances to the side rooms from the open area, one on the north and another on the south; and the base adjoining the open area was five cubits wide all around.

[12]The building facing the temple court-

a 42 That is, about 2 2/3 feet long and wide and 21 inches high or about 80 centimeters long and wide and 53 centimeters high   b 43 That is, about 3 1/2 inches or about 9 centimeters   c 44 Septuagint; Hebrew were rooms for singers, which were   d 44 Septuagint; Hebrew east   e 48 That is, about 25 feet or about 7.4 meters   f 48 Septuagint; Hebrew entrance was   g 48 That is, about 5 1/4 feet or about 1.6 meters   h 49 That is, about 35 feet or about 11 meters   i 49 Septuagint; Hebrew eleven   j 49 That is, about 21 feet or about 6.4 meters   k 49 Hebrew; Septuagint Ten steps led up to it   l 1 That is, about 11 feet or about 3.2 meters; also in verses 3, 5 and 8   m 1 One Hebrew manuscript and Septuagint; most Hebrew manuscripts side, the width of the tent   n 2 That is, about 18 feet or about 5.3 meters   o 2 That is, about 8 3/4 feet or about 2.7 meters; also in verses 9, 11 and 12   p 2 That is, about 70 feet long and 35 feet wide or about 21 meters long and 11 meters wide   q 3 That is, about 3 1/2 feet or about 1.1 meters; also in verse 22   r 3 That is, about 12 feet or about 3.7 meters   s 5 That is, about 7 feet or about 2.1 meters

yard on the west side was seventy cubits[a] wide. The wall of the building was five cubits thick all around, and its length was ninety cubits.[b]

13 Then he measured the temple; it was a hundred cubits[c] long, and the temple courtyard and the building with its walls were also a hundred cubits long. 14 The width of the temple courtyard on the east, including the front of the temple, was a hundred cubits.

15 Then he measured the length of the building facing the courtyard at the rear of the temple, including its galleries on each side; it was a hundred cubits.

The main hall, the inner sanctuary and the portico facing the court, 16 as well as the thresholds and the narrow windows and galleries around the three of them—everything beyond and including the threshold was covered with wood. The floor, the wall up to the windows, and the windows were covered. 17 In the space above the outside of the entrance to the inner sanctuary and on the walls at regular intervals all around the inner and outer sanctuary 18 were carved cherubim and palm trees. Palm trees alternated with cherubim. Each cherub had two faces: 19 the face of a human being toward the palm tree on one side and the face of a lion toward the palm tree on the other. They were carved all around the whole temple. 20 From the floor to the area above the entrance, cherubim and palm trees were carved on the wall of the main hall.

21 The main hall had a rectangular doorframe, and the one at the front of the Most Holy Place was similar. 22 There was a wooden altar three cubits[d] high and two cubits square[e]; its corners, its base[f] and its sides were of wood. The man said to me, "This is the table that is before the LORD." 23 Both the main hall and the Most Holy Place had double doors. 24 Each door had two leaves—two hinged leaves for each door. 25 And on the doors of the main hall were carved cherubim and palm trees like those carved on the walls, and there was a wooden overhang on the front of the portico. 26 On the sidewalls of the portico were narrow windows with palm trees carved on each side. The side rooms of the temple also had overhangs.

The Rooms for the Priests

42 Then the man led me northward into the outer court and brought me to the rooms opposite the temple courtyard and opposite the outer wall on the north side. 2 The building whose door faced north was a hundred cubits long and fifty cubits wide.[g] 3 Both in the section twenty cubits[h] from the inner court and in the section opposite the pavement of the outer court, gallery faced gallery at the three levels. 4 In front of the rooms was an inner passageway ten cubits wide and a hundred cubits[i] long.[j] Their doors were on the north. 5 Now the upper rooms were narrower, for the galleries took more space from them than from the rooms on the lower and middle floors of the building. 6 The rooms on the top floor had no pillars, as the courts had; so they were smaller in floor space than those on the lower and middle floors. 7 There was an outer wall parallel to the rooms and the outer court; it extended in front of the rooms for fifty cubits. 8 While the row of rooms on the side next to the outer court was fifty cubits long, the row on the side nearest the sanctuary was a hundred cubits long. 9 The lower rooms had an entrance on the east side as one enters them from the outer court.

10 On the south side[k] along the length of the wall of the outer court, adjoining the temple courtyard and opposite the outer wall, were rooms 11 with a passageway in front of them. These were like the rooms on the north; they had the same length and width, with similar exits and dimensions. Similar to the doorways on the north 12 were the doorways of the rooms

---

[a] 12 That is, about 123 feet or about 37 meters   [b] 12 That is, about 158 feet or about 48 meters   [c] 13 That is, about 175 feet or about 53 meters; also in verses 14 and 15   [d] 22 That is, about 5 1/4 feet or about 1.5 meters   [e] 22 Septuagint; Hebrew long   [f] 22 Septuagint; Hebrew length   [g] 2 That is, about 175 feet long and 88 feet wide or about 53 meters long and 27 meters wide   [h] 3 That is, about 35 feet or about 11 meters   [i] 4 Septuagint and Syriac; Hebrew and one cubit   [j] 4 That is, about 18 feet wide and 175 feet long or about 5.3 meters wide and 53 meters long   [k] 10 Septuagint; Hebrew Eastward

on the south. There was a doorway at the beginning of the passageway that was parallel to the corresponding wall extending eastward, by which one enters the rooms.

[13] Then he said to me, "The north and south rooms facing the temple courtyard are the priests' rooms, where the priests who approach the LORD will eat the most holy offerings. There they will put the most holy offerings — the grain offerings, the sin offerings[a] and the guilt offerings — for the place is holy. [14] Once the priests enter the holy precincts, they are not to go into the outer court until they leave behind the garments in which they minister, for these are holy. They are to put on other clothes before they go near the places that are for the people."

[15] When he had finished measuring what was inside the temple area, he led me out by the east gate and measured the area all around: [16] He measured the east side with the measuring rod; it was five hundred cubits.[b,c] [17] He measured the north side; it was five hundred cubits[d] by the measuring rod. [18] He measured the south side; it was five hundred cubits by the measuring rod. [19] Then he turned to the west side and measured; it was five hundred cubits by the measuring rod. [20] So he measured the area on all four sides. It had a wall around it, five hundred cubits long and five hundred cubits wide, to separate the holy from the common.

God's Glory Returns to the Temple

43 Then the man brought me to the gate facing east, [2] and I saw the glory of the God of Israel coming from the east. His voice was like the roar of rushing waters, and the land was radiant with his glory. [3] The vision I saw was like the vision I had seen when he[e] came to destroy the city and like the visions I had seen by the Kebar River, and I fell facedown. [4] The glory of the LORD entered the temple through the

gate facing east. [5] Then the Spirit lifted me up and brought me into the inner court, and the glory of the LORD filled the temple.

[6] While the man was standing beside me, I heard someone speaking to me from inside the temple. [7] He said: "Son of man, this is the place of my throne and the place for the soles of my feet. This is where I will live among the Israelites forever. The people of Israel will never again defile my holy name — neither they nor their kings — by their prostitution and the funeral offerings[f] for their kings at their death.[g] [8] When they placed their threshold next to my threshold and their doorposts beside my doorposts, with only a wall between me and them, they defiled my holy name by their detestable practices. So I destroyed them in my anger. [9] Now let them put away from me their prostitution and the funeral offerings for their kings, and I will live among them forever.

[10] "Son of man, describe the temple to the people of Israel, that they may be ashamed of their sins. Let them consider its perfection, [11] and if they are ashamed of all they have done, make known to them the design of the temple — its arrangement, its exits and entrances — its

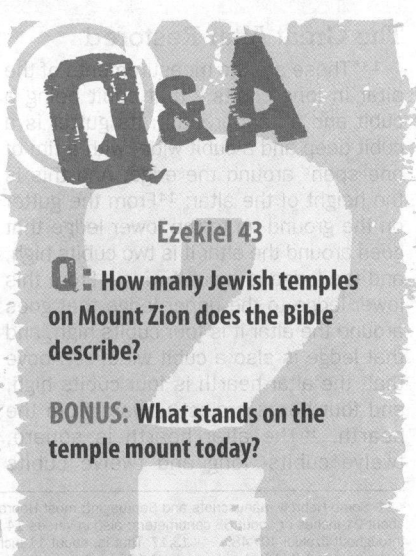

Ezekiel 43

Q: How many Jewish temples on Mount Zion does the Bible describe?

BONUS: What stands on the temple mount today?

---

a 13 Or *purification offerings* b 16 See Septuagint of verse 17; Hebrew *rods*; also in verses 18 and 19.
c 16 Five hundred cubits equal about 875 feet or about 265 meters; also in verses 17, 18 and 19. d 17 Septuagint; Hebrew *rods* e 3 Some Hebrew manuscripts and Vulgate; most Hebrew manuscripts *I* f 7 Or *the memorial monuments*; also in verse 9 g 7 Or *their high places*

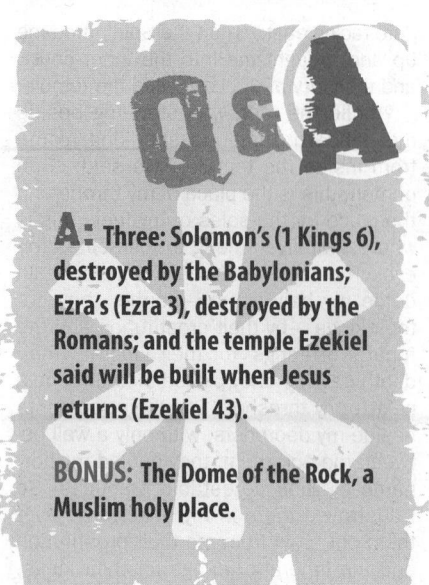

A: Three: Solomon's (1 Kings 6), destroyed by the Babylonians; Ezra's (Ezra 3), destroyed by the Romans; and the temple Ezekiel said will be built when Jesus returns (Ezekiel 43).

BONUS: The Dome of the Rock, a Muslim holy place.

whole design and all its regulations*a* and laws. Write these down before them so that they may be faithful to its design and follow all its regulations.

12 "This is the law of the temple: All the surrounding area on top of the mountain will be most holy. Such is the law of the temple.

The Great Altar Restored

13 "These are the measurements of the altar in long cubits,*b* that cubit being a cubit and a handbreadth: Its gutter is a cubit deep and a cubit wide, with a rim of one span*c* around the edge. And this is the height of the altar: 14 From the gutter on the ground up to the lower ledge that goes around the altar it is two cubits high, and the ledge is a cubit wide.*d* From this lower ledge to the upper ledge that goes around the altar it is four cubits high, and that ledge is also a cubit wide.*e* 15 Above that, the altar hearth is four cubits high, and four horns project upward from the hearth. 16 The altar hearth is square, twelve cubits*f* long and twelve cubits

wide. 17 The upper ledge also is square, fourteen cubits*g* long and fourteen cubits wide. All around the altar is a gutter of one cubit with a rim of half a cubit.*c* The steps of the altar face east."

18 Then he said to me, "Son of man, this is what the Sovereign LORD says: These will be the regulations for sacrificing burnt offerings and splashing blood against the altar when it is built: 19 You are to give a young bull as a sin offering*h* to the Levitical priests of the family of Zadok, who come near to minister before me, declares the Sovereign LORD. 20 You are to take some of its blood and put it on the four horns of the altar and on the four corners of the upper ledge and all around the rim, and so purify the altar and make atonement for it. 21 You are to take the bull for the sin offering and burn it in the designated part of the temple area outside the sanctuary.

22 "On the second day you are to offer a male goat without defect for a sin offering, and the altar is to be purified as it was purified with the bull. 23 When you have finished purifying it, you are to offer a young bull and a ram from the flock, both without defect. 24 You are to offer them before the LORD, and the priests are to sprinkle salt on them and sacrifice them as a burnt offering to the LORD.

25 "For seven days you are to provide a male goat daily for a sin offering; you are also to provide a young bull and a ram from the flock, both without defect. 26 For seven days they are to make atonement for the altar and cleanse it; thus they will dedicate it. 27 At the end of these days, from the eighth day on, the priests are to present your burnt offerings and fellowship offerings on the altar. Then I will accept you, declares the Sovereign LORD."

The Priesthood Restored

44 Then the man brought me back to the outer gate of the sanctuary, the one facing east, and it was shut. 2 The LORD said to me, "This gate is to remain shut. It must not be opened; no one

---

a 11 Some Hebrew manuscripts and Septuagint; most Hebrew manuscripts *regulations and its whole design*   *b 13* That is, about 21 inches or about 53 centimeters; also in verses 14 and 17. The long cubit is the basic unit for linear measurement throughout Ezekiel 40–48.   *c 13,17* That is, about 11 inches or about 27 centimeters   *d 14* That is, about 3 1/2 feet high and 1 3/4 feet wide or about 105 centimeters high and 53 centimeters wide   *e 14* That is, about 7 feet high and 1 3/4 feet wide or about 2.1 meters high and 53 centimeters wide   *f 16* That is, about 21 feet or about 6.4 meters   *g 17* That is, about 25 feet or about 7.4 meters   *h 19* Or *purification offering*; also in verses 21, 22 and 25

may enter through it. It is to remain shut because the LORD, the God of Israel, has entered through it. ³The prince himself is the only one who may sit inside the gateway to eat in the presence of the LORD. He is to enter by way of the portico of the gateway and go out the same way."

⁴Then the man brought me by way of the north gate to the front of the temple. I looked and saw the glory of the LORD filling the temple of the LORD, and I fell facedown.

⁵The LORD said to me, "Son of man, look carefully, listen closely and give attention to everything I tell you concerning all the regulations and instructions regarding the temple of the LORD. Give attention to the entrance to the temple and all the exits of the sanctuary. ⁶Say to rebellious Israel, 'This is what the Sovereign LORD says: Enough of your detestable practices, people of Israel! ⁷In addition to all your other detestable practices, you brought foreigners uncircumcised in heart and flesh into my sanctuary, desecrating my temple while you offered me food, fat and blood, and you broke my covenant. ⁸Instead of carrying out your duty in regard to my holy things, you put others in charge of my sanctuary. ⁹This is what the Sovereign LORD says: No foreigner uncircumcised in heart and flesh is to enter my sanctuary, not even the foreigners who live among the Israelites.

¹⁰"'The Levites who went far from me when Israel went astray and who wandered from me after their idols must bear the consequences of their sin. ¹¹They may serve in my sanctuary, having charge of the gates of the temple and serving in it; they may slaughter the burnt offerings and sacrifices for the people and stand before the people and serve them. ¹²But because they served them in the presence of their idols and made the people of Israel fall into sin, therefore I have sworn with uplifted hand that they must bear the consequences of their sin, declares the Sovereign LORD. ¹³They are not to come near to serve me as priests or come near any of my holy things or my most holy offerings; they must bear the shame of their detestable practices. ¹⁴And I will ap-

point them to guard the temple for all the work that is to be done in it.

¹⁵"'But the Levitical priests, who are descendants of Zadok and who guarded my sanctuary when the Israelites went astray from me, are to come near to minister before me; they are to stand before me to offer sacrifices of fat and blood, declares the Sovereign LORD. ¹⁶They alone are to enter my sanctuary; they alone are to come near my table to minister before me and serve me as guards.

¹⁷"'When they enter the gates of the inner court, they are to wear linen clothes; they must not wear any woolen garment while ministering at the gates of the inner court or inside the temple. ¹⁸They are to wear linen turbans on their heads and linen undergarments around their waists. They must not wear anything that makes them perspire. ¹⁹When they go out into the outer court where the people are, they are to take off the clothes they have been ministering in and are to leave them in the sacred rooms, and put on other clothes, so that the people are not consecrated through contact with their garments.

²⁰"'They must not shave their heads or let their hair grow long, but they are to keep the hair of their heads trimmed. ²¹No priest is to drink wine when he enters the inner court. ²²They must not marry widows or divorced women; they may marry only virgins of Israelite descent or widows of priests. ²³They are to teach my people the difference between the holy and the common and show them how to distinguish between the unclean and the clean.

²⁴"'In any dispute, the priests are to serve as judges and decide it according to my ordinances. They are to keep my laws and my decrees for all my appointed festivals, and they are to keep my Sabbaths holy.

²⁵"'A priest must not defile himself by going near a dead person; however, if the dead person was his father or mother, son or daughter, brother or unmarried sister, then he may defile himself. ²⁶After he is cleansed, he must wait seven days. ²⁷On the day he goes into the inner court of the sanctuary to minister in the

sanctuary, he is to offer a sin offering[a] for himself, declares the Sovereign LORD. [28] " 'I am to be the only inheritance the priests have. You are to give them no possession in Israel; I will be their possession. [29] They will eat the grain offerings, the sin offerings and the guilt offerings; and everything in Israel devoted[b] to the LORD will belong to them. [30] The best of all the firstfruits and of all your special gifts will belong to the priests. You are to give them the first portion of your ground meal so that a blessing may rest on your household. [31] The priests must not eat anything, whether bird or animal, found dead or torn by wild animals.

Israel Fully Restored

45 " 'When you allot the land as an inheritance, you are to present to the LORD a portion of the land as a sacred district, 25,000 cubits[c] long and 20,000[d] cubits[e] wide; the entire area will be holy. [2] Of this, a section 500 cubits[f] square is to be for the sanctuary, with 50 cubits[g] around it for open land. [3] In the sacred district, measure off a section 25,000 cubits long and 10,000 cubits[h] wide. In it will be the sanctuary, the Most Holy Place. [4] It will be the sacred portion of the land for the priests, who minister in the sanctuary and who draw near to minister before the LORD. It will be a place for their houses as well as a holy place for the sanctuary. [5] An area 25,000 cubits long and 10,000 cubits wide will belong to the Levites, who serve in the temple, as their possession for towns to live in.[i]

[6] " 'You are to give the city as its property an area 5,000 cubits[j] wide and 25,000 cubits long, adjoining the sacred portion; it will belong to all Israel.

[7] " 'The prince will have the land bordering each side of the area formed by the sacred district and the property of the city. It will extend westward from the west side and eastward from the east side, running lengthwise from the western to the eastern border parallel to one of the tribal portions. [8] This land will be his possession in Israel. And my princes will no longer oppress my people but will allow the people of Israel to possess the land according to their tribes.

[9] " 'This is what the Sovereign LORD says: You have gone far enough, princes of Israel! Give up your violence and oppression and do what is just and right. Stop dispossessing my people, declares the Sovereign LORD. [10] You are to use accurate scales, an accurate ephah[k] and an accurate bath.[l] [11] The ephah and the bath are to be the same size, the bath containing a tenth of a homer and the ephah a tenth of a homer; the homer is to be the standard measure for both. [12] The shekel[m] is to consist of twenty gerahs. Twenty shekels plus twenty-five shekels plus fifteen shekels equal one mina.[n]

[13] " 'This is the special gift you are to offer: a sixth of an ephah[o] from each homer of wheat and a sixth of an ephah[p] from each homer of barley. [14] The prescribed portion of olive oil, measured by the bath, is a tenth of a bath[q] from each cor (which consists of ten baths or one homer, for ten baths are equivalent to a homer). [15] Also one sheep is to be taken from every flock of two hundred from the well-watered pastures of Israel. These will be used for the grain offerings, burnt offerings and fellowship offerings to make atonement for the people, declares the Sovereign LORD. [16] All the people of the land will be required to give this special offering to the prince in Israel. [17] It will be the duty of the prince to provide the burnt offerings, grain offerings and drink offerings at the festivals, the New Moons and the Sabbaths—at all the appointed festivals of Israel. He will provide the sin

---

[a] 27 Or purification offering; also in verse 29   [b] 29 The Hebrew term refers to the irrevocable giving over of things or persons to the LORD.   [c] 1 That is, about 8 miles or about 13 kilometers; also in verses 3, 5 and 6   [d] 1 Septuagint (see also verses 3 and 5 and 48:9); Hebrew 10,000   [e] 1 That is, about 6 1/2 miles or about 11 kilometers   [f] 2 That is, about 875 feet or about 265 meters   [g] 2 That is, about 88 feet or about 27 meters   [h] 3 That is, about 3 1/3 miles or about 5.3 kilometers; also in verse 5   [i] 5 Septuagint; Hebrew temple; they will have as their possession 20 rooms   [j] 6 That is, about 1 2/3 miles or about 2.7 kilometers   [k] 10 An ephah was a dry measure having the capacity of about 3/5 bushel or about 22 liters.   [l] 10 A bath was a liquid measure equaling about 6 gallons or about 22 liters.   [m] 12 A shekel weighed about 2/5 ounce or about 12 grams.   [n] 12 That is, 60 shekels; the common mina was 50 shekels. Sixty shekels were about 1 1/2 pounds or about 690 grams.   [o] 13 That is, probably about 6 pounds or about 2.7 kilograms   [p] 13 That is, probably about 5 pounds or about 2.3 kilograms   [q] 14 That is, about 2 1/2 quarts or about 2.2 liters

offerings,[a] grain offerings, burnt offerings and fellowship offerings to make atonement for the Israelites.

18 "'This is what the Sovereign LORD says: In the first month on the first day you are to take a young bull without defect and purify the sanctuary. 19 The priest is to take some of the blood of the sin offering and put it on the doorposts of the temple, on the four corners of the upper ledge of the altar and on the gateposts of the inner court. 20 You are to do the same on the seventh day of the month for anyone who sins unintentionally or through ignorance; so you are to make atonement for the temple.

21 "'In the first month on the fourteenth day you are to observe the Passover, a festival lasting seven days, during which you shall eat bread made without yeast. 22 On that day the prince is to provide a bull as a sin offering for himself and for all the people of the land. 23 Every day during the seven days of the festival he is to provide seven bulls and seven rams without defect as a burnt offering to the LORD, and a male goat for a sin offering. 24 He is to provide as a grain offering an ephah for each bull and an ephah for each ram, along with a hin[b] of olive oil for each ephah.

25 "'During the seven days of the festival, which begins in the seventh month on the fifteenth day, he is to make the same provision for sin offerings, burnt offerings, grain offerings and oil.

46 "'This is what the Sovereign LORD says: The gate of the inner court facing east is to be shut on the six working days, but on the Sabbath day and on the day of the New Moon it is to be opened. 2 The prince is to enter from the outside through the portico of the gateway and stand by the gatepost. The priests are to sacrifice his burnt offering and his fellowship offerings. He is to bow down in worship at the threshold of the gateway and then go out, but the gate will not be shut until evening. 3 On the Sabbaths and New Moons the people of the land are to worship in the presence of the LORD at the entrance of that gateway. 4 The burnt offering the prince brings to the LORD on the Sabbath day is to be six male lambs and a ram, all without defect. 5 The grain offering given with the ram is to be an ephah,[c] and the grain offering with the lambs is to be as much as he pleases, along with a hin[d] of olive oil for each ephah. 6 On the day of the New Moon he is to offer a young bull, six lambs and a ram, all without defect. 7 He is to provide as a grain offering one ephah with the bull, one ephah with the ram, and with the lambs as much as he wants to give, along with a hin of oil for each ephah. 8 When the prince enters, he is to go in through the portico of the gateway, and he is to come out the same way.

9 "'When the people of the land come before the LORD at the appointed festivals, whoever enters by the north gate to worship is to go out the south gate; and whoever enters by the south gate is to go out the north gate. No one is to return through the gate by which they entered, but each is to go out the opposite gate. 10 The prince is to be among them, going in when they go in and going out when they go out. 11 At the feasts and the appointed festivals, the grain offering is to be an ephah with a bull, an ephah with a ram, and with the lambs as much as he pleases, along with a hin of oil for each ephah.

12 "'When the prince provides a freewill offering to the LORD—whether a burnt offering or fellowship offerings—the gate facing east is to be opened for him. He shall offer his burnt offering or his fellowship offerings as he does on the Sabbath day. Then he shall go out, and after he has gone out, the gate will be shut.

13 "'Every day you are to provide a year-old lamb without defect for a burnt offering to the LORD; morning by morning you shall provide it. 14 You are also to provide with it morning by morning a grain offering, consisting of a sixth of an ephah[e] with a third of a hin[f] of oil to moisten the flour. The presenting of this grain offering to the LORD is a lasting ordinance. 15 So the lamb and the grain offering and the

---

a 17 Or *purification offerings*; also in verses 19, 22, 23 and 25   b 24 That is, about 1 gallon or about 3.8 liters
c 5 That is, probably about 35 pounds or about 16 kilograms; also in verses 7 and 11   d 5 That is, about 1 gallon or about 3.8 liters; also in verses 7 and 11   e 14 That is, probably about 6 pounds or about 2.7 kilograms   f 14 That is, about 1 1/2 quarts or about 1.3 liters

oil shall be provided morning by morning for a regular burnt offering.

16 " 'This is what the Sovereign LORD says: If the prince makes a gift from his inheritance to one of his sons, it will also belong to his descendants; it is to be their property by inheritance. 17 If, however, he makes a gift from his inheritance to one of his servants, the servant may keep it until the year of freedom; then it will revert to the prince. His inheritance belongs to his sons only; it is theirs. 18 The prince must not take any of the inheritance of the people, driving them off their property. He is to give his sons their inheritance out of his own property, so that not one of my people will be separated from their property.' "

19 Then the man brought me through the entrance at the side of the gate to the sacred rooms facing north, which belonged to the priests, and showed me a place at the western end. 20 He said to me, "This is the place where the priests are to cook the guilt offering and the sin offering[a] and bake the grain offering, to avoid bringing them into the outer court and consecrating the people."

21 He then brought me to the outer court and led me around to its four corners, and I saw in each corner another court. 22 In the four corners of the outer court were enclosed[b] courts, forty cubits long and thirty cubits wide;[c] each of the courts in the four corners was the same size. 23 Around the inside of each of the four courts was a ledge of stone, with places for fire built all around under the ledge. 24 He said to me, "These are the kitchens where those who minister at the temple are to cook the sacrifices of the people."

The River From the Temple

47 The man brought me back to the entrance to the temple, and I saw water coming out from under the threshold of the temple toward the east (for the temple faced east). The water was coming down from under the south side of the temple, south of the altar. 2 He then brought me out through the north gate and led me around the outside to the outer gate facing east, and the water was trickling from the south side.

3 As the man went eastward with a measuring line in his hand, he measured off a thousand cubits[d] and then led me through water that was ankle-deep. 4 He measured off another thousand cubits and led me through water that was knee-deep. He measured off another thousand and led me through water that was up to the waist. 5 He measured off another thousand, but now it was a river that I could not cross, because the water had risen and was deep enough to swim in—a river that no one could cross. 6 He asked me, "Son of man, do you see this?"

Then he led me back to the bank of the river. 7 When I arrived there, I saw a great number of trees on each side of the river. 8 He said to me, "This water flows toward the eastern region and goes down into the Arabah,[e] where it enters the Dead Sea. When it empties into the sea, the salty water there becomes fresh. 9 Swarms of living creatures will live wherever the river flows. There will be large numbers of fish, because this water flows there and makes the salt water fresh; so where the river flows everything will live. 10 Fishermen will stand along the shore; from En Gedi to En Eglaim there will be places for spreading nets. The fish will be of many kinds—like the fish of the Mediterranean Sea. 11 But the swamps and marshes will not become fresh; they will be left for salt. 12 Fruit trees of all kinds will grow on both banks of the river. Their leaves will not wither, nor will their fruit fail. Every month they will bear fruit, because the water from the sanctuary flows to them. Their fruit will serve for food and their leaves for healing."

The Boundaries of the Land

13 This is what the Sovereign LORD says: "These are the boundaries of the land that you will divide among the twelve tribes of Israel as their inheritance, with two portions for Joseph. 14 You are to divide it equally among them. Because I swore with uplifted hand to give it to your ancestors, this land will become your inheritance.

---

[a] 20 Or *purification offering*   [b] 22 The meaning of the Hebrew for this word is uncertain.   [c] 22 That is, about 70 feet long and 53 feet wide or about 21 meters long and 16 meters wide   [d] 3 That is, about 1,700 feet or about 530 meters   [e] 8 Or *the Jordan Valley*

15 "This is to be the boundary of the land:

"On the north side it will run from the Mediterranean Sea by the Hethlon road past Lebo Hamath to Zedad, 16 Berothah[a] and Sibraim (which lies on the border between Damascus and Hamath), as far as Hazer Hattikon, which is on the border of Hauran. 17 The boundary will extend from the sea to Hazar Enan,[b] along the northern border of Damascus, with the border of Hamath to the north. This will be the northern boundary.

18 "On the east side the boundary will run between Hauran and Damascus, along the Jordan between Gilead and the land of Israel, to the Dead Sea and as far as Tamar.[c] This will be the eastern boundary.

19 "On the south side it will run from Tamar as far as the waters of Meribah Kadesh, then along the Wadi of Egypt to the Mediterranean Sea. This will be the southern boundary.

20 "On the west side, the Mediterranean Sea will be the boundary to a point opposite Lebo Hamath. This will be the western boundary.

21 "You are to distribute this land among yourselves according to the tribes of Israel. 22 You are to allot it as an inheritance for yourselves and for the foreigners residing among you and who have children. You are to consider them as native-born Israelites; along with you they are to be allotted an inheritance among the tribes of Israel. 23 In whatever tribe a foreigner resides, there you are to give them their inheritance," declares the Sovereign LORD.

The Division of the Land

48 "These are the tribes, listed by name: At the northern frontier, Dan will have one portion; it will follow the Hethlon road to Lebo Hamath; Hazar Enan and the northern border of Damascus next to Hamath will be part of its border from the east side to the west side.

2 "Asher will have one portion; it will border the territory of Dan from east to west.

3 "Naphtali will have one portion; it will border the territory of Asher from east to west.

4 "Manasseh will have one portion; it will border the territory of Naphtali from east to west.

5 "Ephraim will have one portion; it will border the territory of Manasseh from east to west.

6 "Reuben will have one portion; it will border the territory of Ephraim from east to west.

7 "Judah will have one portion; it will border the territory of Reuben from east to west.

8 "Bordering the territory of Judah from east to west will be the portion you are to present as a special gift. It will be 25,000 cubits[d] wide, and its length from east to west will equal one of the tribal portions; the sanctuary will be in the center of it.

9 "The special portion you are to offer to the LORD will be 25,000 cubits long and 10,000 cubits[e] wide. 10 This will be the sacred portion for the priests. It will be 25,000 cubits long on the north side, 10,000 cubits wide on the west side, 10,000 cubits wide on the east side and 25,000 cubits long on the south side. In the center of it will be the sanctuary of the LORD. 11 This will be for the consecrated priests, the Zadokites, who were faithful in serving me and did not go astray as the Levites did when the Israelites went astray. 12 It will be a special gift to them from the sacred portion of the land, a most holy portion, bordering the territory of the Levites.

13 "Alongside the territory of the priests, the Levites will have an allotment 25,000 cubits long and 10,000 cubits wide. Its total length will be 25,000 cubits and its width 10,000 cubits. 14 They must not sell or exchange any of it. This is the best of

---

a 15,16 See Septuagint and 48:1; Hebrew road to go into Zedad, 16Hamath, Berothah.   b 17 Hebrew Enon, a variant of Enan   c 18 See Syriac; Hebrew Israel. You will measure to the Dead Sea.   d 8 That is, about 8 miles or about 13 kilometers; also in verses 9, 10, 13, 15, 20 and 21   e 9 That is, about 3 1/3 miles or about 5.3 kilometers; also in verses 10, 13 and 18

the land and must not pass into other hands, because it is holy to the LORD.

15 "The remaining area, 5,000 cubits*a* wide and 25,000 cubits long, will be for the common use of the city, for houses and for pastureland. The city will be in the center of it 16 and will have these measurements: the north side 4,500 cubits,*b* the south side 4,500 cubits, the east side 4,500 cubits, and the west side 4,500 cubits. 17 The pastureland for the city will be 250 cubits*c* on the north, 250 cubits on the south, 250 cubits on the east, and 250 cubits on the west. 18 What remains of the area, bordering on the sacred portion and running the length of it, will be 10,000 cubits on the east side and 10,000 cubits on the west side. Its produce will supply food for the workers of the city. 19 The workers from the city who farm it will come from all the tribes of Israel. 20 The entire portion will be a square, 25,000 cubits on each side. As a special gift you will set aside the sacred portion, along with the property of the city.

21 "What remains on both sides of the area formed by the sacred portion and the property of the city will belong to the prince. It will extend eastward from the 25,000 cubits of the sacred portion to the eastern border, and westward from the 25,000 cubits to the western border. Both these areas running the length of the tribal portions will belong to the prince, and the sacred portion with the temple sanctuary will be in the center of them. 22 So the property of the Levites and the property of the city will lie in the center of the area that belongs to the prince. The area belonging to the prince will lie between the border of Judah and the border of Benjamin.

23 "As for the rest of the tribes: Benjamin will have one portion; it will extend from the east side to the west side.

24 "Simeon will have one portion; it will border the territory of Benjamin from east to west.

25 "Issachar will have one portion; it will border the territory of Simeon from east to west.

26 "Zebulun will have one portion; it will border the territory of Issachar from east to west.

27 "Gad will have one portion; it will border the territory of Zebulun from east to west.

28 "The southern boundary of Gad will run south from Tamar to the waters of Meribah Kadesh, then along the Wadi of Egypt to the Mediterranean Sea.

29 "This is the land you are to allot as an inheritance to the tribes of Israel, and these will be their portions," declares the Sovereign LORD.

The Gates of the New City

30 "These will be the exits of the city: Beginning on the north side, which is 4,500 cubits long, 31 the gates of the city will be named after the tribes of Israel. The three gates on the north side will be the gate of Reuben, the gate of Judah and the gate of Levi.

32 "On the east side, which is 4,500 cubits long, will be three gates: the gate of Joseph, the gate of Benjamin and the gate of Dan.

33 "On the south side, which measures 4,500 cubits, will be three gates: the gate of Simeon, the gate of Issachar and the gate of Zebulun.

34 "On the west side, which is 4,500 cubits long, will be three gates: the gate of Gad, the gate of Asher and the gate of Naphtali.

35 "The distance all around will be 18,000 cubits.*d*

"And the name of the city from that time on will be:

THE LORD IS THERE."

---

a 15 That is, about 1 2/3 miles or about 2.7 kilometers   *b 16* That is, about 1 1/2 miles or about 2.4 kilometers; also in verses 30, 32, 33 and 34   *c 17* That is, about 440 feet or about 135 meters   *d 35* That is, about 6 miles or about 9.5 kilometers

Convictions.

What makes it so hard to stand up for them? Do you find it hard to say, "I don't do that because I'm a Christian"? Or "I'm going to wait until marriage, because I know that's right." What others think about you is important, but it isn't *that* important.

Daniel was a teenager, a hostage in Babylon, when he had to decide: Would he stand up for what he believed or go along with pagan ways? Because Daniel decided to be loyal to God, God helped him become a powerful government official. Even the emperor came to admire Daniel for his faith.

>>**PRESSURED TEEN WON'T CONFORM**
Story in Daniel 1

>>**HE'S DREAMING OF A WHITE KINGDOM**
Dream reveals the future. Report in Daniel 2:24–49

>>**THESE BEASTS ARE REALLY SCARY!**
For a vision report, see Daniel 7

>>**ANGELS WAR OVER ANSWER TO PRAYER**
Glimpse of invisible war revealed. Report in Daniel 10:4–19

preview

Teenage Daniel is taken to Babylon. He becomes a high government official and lives into his 90's.

God gives Daniel visions of future world empires ... including a final kingdom to be set up by God.

As Daniel serves in Babylon from 605 to 535 B.C., Solon the law-giver revises Athens' constitution. In India, Buddha is born. In the Mediterranean, Carthage conquers Sicily and Sardinia.

Daniel's Training in Babylon

1 In the third year of the reign of Jehoiakim king of Judah, Nebuchadnezzar king of Babylon came to Jerusalem and besieged it. [2]And the Lord delivered Jehoiakim king of Judah into his hand, along with some of the articles from the temple of God. These he carried off to the temple of his god in Babylonia[a] and put in the treasure house of his god.

[3]Then the king ordered Ashpenaz, chief of his court officials, to bring into the king's service some of the Israelites from the royal family and the nobility— [4]young men without any physical defect, handsome, showing aptitude for every kind of learning, well informed, quick to understand, and qualified to serve in the king's palace. He was to teach them the language and literature of the Babylonians.[b] [5]The king assigned them a daily amount of food and wine from the king's table. They were to be trained for three years, and after that they were to enter the king's service.

[6]Among those who were chosen were some from Judah: Daniel, Hananiah, Mishael and Azariah. [7]The chief official gave them new names: to Daniel, the name Belteshazzar; to Hananiah, Shadrach; to Mishael, Meshach; and to Azariah, Abednego.

[8]But Daniel resolved not to defile himself with the royal food and wine, and he asked the chief official for permission not to defile himself this way. [9]Now God had caused the official to show favor and compassion to Daniel, [10]but the official told Daniel, "I am afraid of my lord the king, who has assigned your[c] food and drink. Why should he see you looking worse than the other young men your age? The king would then have my head because of you."

[11]Daniel then said to the guard whom the chief official had appointed over Daniel, Hananiah, Mishael and Azariah, [12]"Please test your servants for ten days: Give us nothing but vegetables to eat and water to drink. [13]Then compare our appearance with that of the young men who eat the royal food, and treat your servants in accordance with what you see." [14]So he agreed to this and tested them for ten days.

[15]At the end of the ten days they looked healthier and better nourished than any of the young men who ate the royal food. [16]So the guard took away their choice food and the wine they were to drink and gave them vegetables instead.

[17]To these four young men God gave knowledge and understanding of all kinds of literature and learning. And Daniel could understand visions and dreams of all kinds.

[18]At the end of the time set by the king to bring them into his service, the chief official presented them to Nebuchadnezzar. [19]The king talked with them, and he found none equal to Daniel, Hananiah, Mishael and Azariah; so they entered the king's service. [20]In every matter of wisdom and understanding about which the king questioned them, he found them ten times better than all the magicians and enchanters in his whole kingdom.

[21]And Daniel remained there until the first year of King Cyrus.

Nebuchadnezzar's Dream

2 In the second year of his reign, Nebuchadnezzar had dreams; his mind was troubled and he could not sleep. [2]So the king summoned the magicians, enchanters, sorcerers and astrologers[d] to tell him what he had dreamed. When they came in and stood before the king, [3]he said to them, "I have had a dream that troubles me and I want to know what it means.[e]"

[4]Then the astrologers answered the king,[f] "May the king live forever! Tell your servants the dream, and we will interpret it."

[5]The king replied to the astrologers, "This is what I have firmly decided: If you do not tell me what my dream was and interpret it, I will have you cut into pieces and your houses turned into piles of

---

[a] 2 Hebrew *Shinar*   [b] 4 Or *Chaldeans*   [c] 10 The Hebrew for *your* and *you* in this verse is plural; also in verses 4, 5 and 10   [d] 2 Or *Chaldeans*; also in verses 4, 5 and 10   [e] 3 Or *was*   [f] 4 At this point the Hebrew text has *in Aramaic*, indicating that the text from here through the end of chapter 7 is in Aramaic.

> Most of my friends aren't Christians. They swear and curse and do other stuff that I don't do. They don't make fun of me or anything, but sometimes I feel strange ... you know, just different. They're not troublemakers or anything. Is it so bad to try to fit in?
>
> >> Christopher

Dear Christopher,

You may feel different, but it sounds like you're well liked. Your friends include you when they do things and they don't make fun of you for your beliefs.

Take a look at Daniel. He was probably a teenager when he and some other guys were taken away from Judah. The young captives were given food and drink from the king's table. But Daniel did not want to eat foods that God had told his people were unclean. He went to an official and asked for vegetables and water for himself and his three friends.

To some perhaps that sounded like a strange request. Daniel asked for a ten-day trial period. If after ten days they didn't look as healthy as the other young men, they would eat as the others did. After the ten days, "They looked healthier and better nourished than any of the young men who ate the royal food ... To these four young men God gave knowledge and understanding ... And Daniel could understand visions and dreams of all kinds" (Daniel 1:15,17).

You may feel a little weird, but when you honor God with your obedience, he honors you with blessing.

Jordan

rubble. ⁶But if you tell me the dream and explain it, you will receive from me gifts and rewards and great honor. So tell me the dream and interpret it for me."

⁷Once more they replied, "Let the king tell his servants the dream, and we will interpret it."

⁸Then the king answered, "I am certain that you are trying to gain time, because you realize that this is what I have firmly decided: ⁹If you do not tell me the dream, there is only one penalty for you. You have conspired to tell me misleading and wicked things, hoping the situation will change. So then, tell me the dream, and I will know that you can interpret it for me."

¹⁰The astrologers answered the king, "There is no one on earth who can do what the king asks! No king, however great and mighty, has ever asked such a thing of any magician or enchanter or astrologer. ¹¹What the king asks is too difficult. No one can reveal it to the king except the gods, and they do not live among humans."

¹²This made the king so angry and furious that he ordered the execution of all the wise men of Babylon. ¹³So the decree was issued to put the wise men to death, and men were sent to look for Daniel and his friends to put them to death.

¹⁴When Arioch, the commander of the king's guard, had gone out to put to death the wise men of Babylon, Daniel spoke to him with wisdom and tact. ¹⁵He asked the king's officer, "Why did the king issue such a harsh decree?" Arioch then explained the matter to Daniel. ¹⁶At this, Daniel went in to the king and asked for time, so that he might interpret the dream for him.

¹⁷Then Daniel returned to his house and explained the matter to his friends Hananiah, Mishael and Azariah. ¹⁸He urged them to plead for mercy from the God of heaven concerning this mystery, so that he and his friends might not be executed with the rest of the wise men of Babylon. ¹⁹During the night the mystery was revealed to Daniel in a vision. Then Daniel praised the God of heaven ²⁰and said:

"Praise be to the name of God for
    ever and ever;
    wisdom and power are his.
²¹He changes times and seasons;
    he deposes kings and raises up
      others.
He gives wisdom to the wise
    and knowledge to the discerning.
²²He reveals deep and hidden things;
    he knows what lies in darkness,
    and light dwells with him.
²³I thank and praise you, God of my
      ancestors:
    You have given me wisdom and
      power,
you have made known to me what we
      asked of you,
    you have made known to us the
      dream of the king."

Daniel Interprets the Dream

²⁴Then Daniel went to Arioch, whom the king had appointed to execute the wise men of Babylon, and said to him, "Do not execute the wise men of Babylon. Take me to the king, and I will interpret his dream for him."

²⁵Arioch took Daniel to the king at once and said, "I have found a man among the exiles from Judah who can tell the king what his dream means."

²⁶The king asked Daniel (also called Belteshazzar), "Are you able to tell me what I saw in my dream and interpret it?"

²⁷Daniel replied, "No wise man, enchanter, magician or diviner can explain to the king the mystery he has asked about, ²⁸but there is a God in heaven who reveals mysteries. He has shown King Nebuchadnezzar what will happen in days to come. Your dream and the visions that passed through your mind as you were lying in bed are these:

²⁹"As Your Majesty was lying there, your mind turned to things to come, and the revealer of mysteries showed you what is going to happen. ³⁰As for me, this mystery has been revealed to me, not because I have greater wisdom than anyone else alive, but so that Your Majesty may know the interpretation and that you may understand what went through your mind.

³¹"Your Majesty looked, and there be-

fore you stood a large statue—an enormous, dazzling statue, awesome in appearance. [32] The head of the statue was made of pure gold, its chest and arms of silver, its belly and thighs of bronze, [33] its legs of iron, its feet partly of iron and partly of baked clay. [34] While you were watching, a rock was cut out, but not by human hands. It struck the statue on its feet of iron and clay and smashed them. [35] Then the iron, the clay, the bronze, the silver and the gold were all broken to pieces and became like chaff on a threshing floor in the summer. The wind swept them away without leaving a trace. But the rock that struck the statue became a huge mountain and filled the whole earth.

[36] "This was the dream, and now we will interpret it to the king. [37] Your Majesty, you are the king of kings. The God of heaven has given you dominion and power and might and glory; [38] in your hands he has placed all mankind and the beasts of the field and the birds in the sky. Wherever they live, he has made you ruler over them all. You are that head of gold.

[39] "After you, another kingdom will arise, inferior to yours. Next, a third kingdom, one of bronze, will rule over the whole earth. [40] Finally, there will be a fourth kingdom, strong as iron—for iron breaks and smashes everything—and as iron breaks things to pieces, so it will crush and break all the others. [41] Just as you saw that the feet and toes were partly of baked clay and partly of iron, so this will be a divided kingdom; yet it will have some of the strength of iron in it, even as you saw iron mixed with clay. [42] As the toes were partly iron and partly clay, so this kingdom will be partly strong and partly brittle. [43] And just as you saw the iron mixed with baked clay, so the people will be a mixture and will not remain united, any more than iron mixes with clay.

[44] "In the time of those kings, the God of heaven will set up a kingdom that will never be destroyed, nor will it be left to another people. It will crush all those kingdoms and bring them to an end, but it will itself endure forever. [45] This is the meaning of the vision of the rock cut out of a mountain, but not by human hands—a rock that broke the iron, the bronze, the clay, the silver and the gold to pieces.

"The great God has shown the king what will take place in the future. The dream is true and its interpretation is trustworthy."

[46] Then King Nebuchadnezzar fell prostrate before Daniel and paid him honor and ordered that an offering and incense be presented to him. [47] The king said to Daniel, "Surely your God is the God of gods and the Lord of kings and a revealer of mysteries, for you were able to reveal this mystery."

[48] Then the king placed Daniel in a high position and lavished many gifts on him. He made him ruler over the entire province of Babylon and placed him in charge of all its wise men. [49] Moreover, at Daniel's request the king appointed Shadrach, Meshach and Abednego administrators over the province of Babylon, while Daniel himself remained at the royal court.

The Image of Gold and the Blazing Furnace

3 King Nebuchadnezzar made an image of gold, sixty cubits high and six cubits wide,[a] and set it up on the plain of Dura in the province of Babylon. [2] He then summoned the satraps, prefects, governors, advisers, treasurers, judges, magistrates and all the other provincial officials to come to the dedication of the image he had set up. [3] So the satraps, prefects, governors, advisers, treasurers, judges, magistrates and all the other provincial officials assembled for the dedication of the image that King Nebuchadnezzar had set up, and they stood before it.

[4] Then the herald loudly proclaimed, "Nations and peoples of every language, this is what you are commanded to do: [5] As soon as you hear the sound of the horn, flute, zither, lyre, harp, pipe and all kinds of music, you must fall down and worship the image of gold that King Nebuchadnezzar has set up. [6] Whoever does not fall down and worship will immediately be thrown into a blazing furnace."

---

[a] 1 That is, about 90 feet high and 9 feet wide or about 27 meters high and 2.7 meters wide

⁷Therefore, as soon as they heard the sound of the horn, flute, zither, lyre, harp and all kinds of music, all the nations and peoples of every language fell down and worshiped the image of gold that King Nebuchadnezzar had set up.

⁸At this time some astrologers[a] came forward and denounced the Jews. ⁹They said to King Nebuchadnezzar, "May the king live forever! ¹⁰Your Majesty has issued a decree that everyone who hears the sound of the horn, flute, zither, lyre, harp, pipe and all kinds of music must fall down and worship the image of gold, ¹¹and that whoever does not fall down and worship will be thrown into a blazing furnace. ¹²But there are some Jews whom you have set over the affairs of the province of Babylon—Shadrach, Meshach and Abednego—who pay no attention to you, Your Majesty. They neither serve your gods nor worship the image of gold you have set up."

¹³Furious with rage, Nebuchadnezzar summoned Shadrach, Meshach and Abednego. So these men were brought before the king, ¹⁴and Nebuchadnezzar said to them, "Is it true, Shadrach, Meshach and Abednego, that you do not serve my gods or worship the image of gold I have set up? ¹⁵Now when you hear the sound of the horn, flute, zither, lyre, harp, pipe and all kinds of music, if you are ready to fall down and worship the image I made, very good. But if you do not worship it, you will be thrown immediately into a blazing furnace. Then what god will be able to rescue you from my hand?"

¹⁶Shadrach, Meshach and Abednego replied to him, "King Nebuchadnezzar, we do not need to defend ourselves before you in this matter. ¹⁷If we are thrown into the blazing furnace, the God we serve is able to deliver us from it, and he will deliver us[b] from Your Majesty's hand. ¹⁸But even if he does not, we want you to know, Your Majesty, that we will not serve your gods or worship the image of gold you have set up."

¹⁹Then Nebuchadnezzar was furious with Shadrach, Meshach and Abednego,

and his attitude toward them changed. He ordered the furnace heated seven times hotter than usual ²⁰and commanded some of the strongest soldiers in his army to tie up Shadrach, Meshach and Abednego and throw them into the blazing furnace. ²¹So these men, wearing their robes, trousers, turbans and other clothes, were bound and thrown into the blazing furnace. ²²The king's command was so urgent and the furnace so hot that

INSTANT ACCESS

Your convictions can be a hard thing to stick to at times. You can witness, but you can't tell whether the person you speak to will listen or laugh. You can say no when friends urge you to do something wrong, but you don't know whether they'll respect you or make fun of you. When threatened with death Daniel's three friends said, "The God we serve is able to save us ... But even if he does not ... we will not serve your gods." When you face a tough decision, you know that God is able to make things turn out right, but you never know for sure that he will. That's what faith is all about: being determined to do what is right, no matter what.

{Daniel 3:17–18}

the flames of the fire killed the soldiers who took up Shadrach, Meshach and Abednego, ²³ and these three men, firmly tied, fell into the blazing furnace.

²⁴ Then King Nebuchadnezzar leaped to his feet in amazement and asked his advisers, "Weren't there three men that we tied up and threw into the fire?"

They replied, "Certainly, Your Majesty."

²⁵ He said, "Look! I see four men walking around in the fire, unbound and unharmed, and the fourth looks like a son of the gods."

²⁶ Nebuchadnezzar then approached the opening of the blazing furnace and shouted, "Shadrach, Meshach and Abednego, servants of the Most High God, come out! Come here!"

So Shadrach, Meshach and Abednego came out of the fire, ²⁷ and the satraps, prefects, governors and royal advisers crowded around them. They saw that the fire had not harmed their bodies, nor was a hair of their heads singed; their robes were not scorched, and there was no smell of fire on them.

²⁸ Then Nebuchadnezzar said, "Praise be to the God of Shadrach, Meshach and Abednego, who has sent his angel and rescued his servants! They trusted in him and defied the king's command and were willing to give up their lives rather than serve or worship any god except their own God. ²⁹ Therefore I decree that the people of any nation or language who say anything against the God of Shadrach, Meshach and Abednego be cut into pieces and their houses be turned into piles of rubble, for no other god can save in this way."

³⁰ Then the king promoted Shadrach, Meshach and Abednego in the province of Babylon.

Nebuchadnezzar's Dream of a Tree

4 ^a King Nebuchadnezzar,

To the nations and peoples of every language, who live in all the earth:

May you prosper greatly!

² It is my pleasure to tell you about the miraculous signs and wonders that the Most High God has performed for me.

³ How great are his signs,
how mighty his wonders!
His kingdom is an eternal
kingdom;
his dominion endures
from generation to
generation.

⁴ I, Nebuchadnezzar, was at home in my palace, contented and prosperous. ⁵ I had a dream that made me afraid. As I was lying in bed, the images and visions that passed through my mind terrified me. ⁶ So I commanded that all the wise men of Babylon be brought before me to interpret the dream for me. ⁷ When the magicians, enchanters, astrologers^b and diviners came, I told them the dream, but they could not interpret it for me. ⁸ Finally, Daniel came into my presence and I told him the dream. (He is called Belteshazzar, after the name of my god, and the spirit of the holy gods is in him.)

⁹ I said, "Belteshazzar, chief of the magicians, I know that the spirit of the holy gods is in you, and no mystery is too difficult for you. Here is my dream; interpret it for me. ¹⁰ These are the visions I saw while lying in bed: I looked, and there before me stood a tree in the middle of the land. Its height was enormous. ¹¹ The tree grew large and strong and its top touched the sky; it was visible to the ends of the earth. ¹² Its leaves were beautiful, its fruit abundant, and on it was food for all. Under it the wild animals found shelter, and the birds lived in its branches; from it every creature was fed.

¹³ "In the visions I saw while lying in bed, I looked, and there before me was a holy one, a messenger,^c

---

^a In Aramaic texts 4:1-3 is numbered 3:31-33, and 4:4-37 is numbered 4:1-34.   ^b 7 Or *Chaldeans*   ^c 13 Or *watchman*; also in verses 17 and 23

coming down from heaven. ¹⁴He called in a loud voice: 'Cut down the tree and trim off its branches; strip off its leaves and scatter its fruit. Let the animals flee from under it and the birds from its branches. ¹⁵But let the stump and its roots, bound with iron and bronze, remain in the ground, in the grass of the field.

" 'Let him be drenched with the dew of heaven, and let him live with the animals among the plants of the earth. ¹⁶Let his mind be changed from that of a man and let him be given the mind of an animal, till seven times* pass by for him.

¹⁷" 'The decision is announced by messengers, the holy ones declare the verdict, so that the living may know that the Most High is sovereign over all kingdoms on earth and gives them to anyone he wishes and sets over them the lowliest of people.'

¹⁸"This is the dream that I, King Nebuchadnezzar, had. Now, Belteshazzar, tell me what it means, for none of the wise men in my kingdom can interpret it for me. But you can, because the spirit of the holy gods is in you."

Daniel Interprets the Dream

¹⁹Then Daniel (also called Belteshazzar) was greatly perplexed for a time, and his thoughts terrified him. So the king said, "Belteshazzar, do not let the dream or its meaning alarm you."

Belteshazzar answered, "My lord, if only the dream applied to your enemies and its meaning to your adversaries! ²⁰The tree you saw, which grew large and strong, with its top touching the sky, visible to the whole earth, ²¹with beautiful leaves and abundant fruit, providing food for all, giving shelter to the wild animals, and having nesting places in its branches for the birds— ²²Your Majesty, you are that tree! You have become great and strong; your great-

ness has grown until it reaches the sky, and your dominion extends to distant parts of the earth.

²³"Your Majesty saw a holy one, a messenger, coming down from heaven and saying, 'Cut down the tree and destroy it, but leave the stump, bound with iron and bronze, in the grass of the field, while its roots remain in the ground. Let him be drenched with the dew of heaven; let him live with the wild animals, until seven times pass by for him.'

²⁴"This is the interpretation, Your Majesty, and this is the decree the Most High has issued against my lord the king: ²⁵You will be driven away from people and will live with the wild animals; you will eat grass like the ox and be drenched with the dew of heaven. Seven times will pass by for you until you acknowledge that the Most High is sovereign over all kingdoms on earth and gives them to anyone he wishes. ²⁶The command to leave the stump of the tree with its roots means that your kingdom will be restored to you when you acknowledge that Heaven rules. ²⁷Therefore, Your Majesty, be pleased to accept my advice: Renounce your sins by doing what is right, and your wickedness by being kind to the oppressed. It may be that then your prosperity will continue."

The Dream Is Fulfilled

²⁸All this happened to King Nebuchadnezzar. ²⁹Twelve months later, as the king was walking on the roof of the royal palace of Babylon, ³⁰he said, "Is not this the great Babylon I have built as the royal residence, by my mighty power and for the glory of my majesty?"

³¹Even as the words were on his lips, a voice came from heaven, "This is what is decreed for you, King Nebuchadnezzar: Your royal authority has been taken from you. ³²You will be driven away from people and will

---

ᵃ 16 Or years; also in verses 23, 25 and 32

Pick a candidate for the person you know who's "least likely to become a Christian." Got him or her in mind? Then compare that person with Nebuchadnezzar of Babylon. That ruler was master of his world, an emperor whose word was law throughout the Middle East. He didn't believe in God. And he didn't feel any need for God. But read these verses, and you discover that Nebuchadnezzar did come to know and worship the Lord through Daniel's faithful witness and a personal tragedy. Don't give up, even on that person "least likely to become a Christian." You and God together may reach him or her after all!

{Daniel 4:33–37}

» INSTANT ACCESS

live with the wild animals; you will eat grass like the ox. Seven times will pass by for you until you acknowledge that the Most High is sovereign over all kingdoms on earth and gives them to anyone he wishes."

³³Immediately what had been said about Nebuchadnezzar was fulfilled. He was driven away from people and ate grass like the ox. His body was drenched with the dew of heaven until his hair grew like the feathers of

an eagle and his nails like the claws of a bird.

³⁴At the end of that time, I, Nebuchadnezzar, raised my eyes toward heaven, and my sanity was restored. Then I praised the Most High; I honored and glorified him who lives forever.

His dominion is an eternal dominion;
  his kingdom endures from
    generation to generation.
³⁵All the peoples of the earth
  are regarded as nothing.
He does as he pleases
  with the powers of heaven
  and the peoples of the earth.
No one can hold back his hand
  or say to him: "What have you
    done?"

³⁶At the same time that my sanity was restored, my honor and splendor were returned to me for the glory of my kingdom. My advisers and nobles sought me out, and I was restored to my throne and became even greater than before. ³⁷Now I, Nebuchadnezzar, praise and exalt and glorify the King of heaven, because everything he does is right and all his ways are just. And those who walk in pride he is able to humble.

The Writing on the Wall

5 King Belshazzar gave a great banquet for a thousand of his nobles and drank wine with them. ²While Belshazzar was drinking his wine, he gave orders to bring in the gold and silver goblets that Nebuchadnezzar his father[a] had taken from the temple in Jerusalem, so that the king and his nobles, his wives and his concubines might drink from them. ³So they brought in the gold goblets that had been taken from the temple of God in Jerusalem, and the king and his nobles, his wives and his concubines drank from them. ⁴As they drank the wine, they praised the gods of gold and silver, of bronze, iron, wood and stone.

ª 2 Or *ancestor*; or *predecessor*; also in verses 11, 13 and 18

5 Suddenly the fingers of a human hand appeared and wrote on the plaster of the wall, near the lampstand in the royal palace. The king watched the hand as it wrote. 6 His face turned pale and he was so frightened that his legs became weak and his knees were knocking.

7 The king summoned the enchanters, astrologers[a] and diviners. Then he said to these wise men of Babylon, "Whoever reads this writing and tells me what it means will be clothed in purple and have a gold chain placed around his neck, and he will be made the third highest ruler in the kingdom."

8 Then all the king's wise men came in, but they could not read the writing or tell the king what it meant. 9 So King Belshazzar became even more terrified and his face grew more pale. His nobles were baffled.

10 The queen,[b] hearing the voices of the king and his nobles, came into the banquet hall. "May the king live forever!" she said. "Don't be alarmed! Don't look so pale! 11 There is a man in your kingdom who has the spirit of the holy gods in him. In the time of your father he was found to have insight and intelligence and wisdom

Daniel 5

Q: How did God send a message to King Belshazzar?

BONUS: How did he react?

like that of the gods. Your father, King Nebuchadnezzar, appointed him chief of the magicians, enchanters, astrologers and diviners. 12 He did this because Daniel, whom the king called Belteshazzar, was found to have a keen mind and knowledge and understanding, and also the ability to interpret dreams, explain riddles and solve difficult problems. Call for Daniel, and he will tell you what the writing means."

13 So Daniel was brought before the king, and the king said to him, "Are you Daniel, one of the exiles my father the king brought from Judah? 14 I have heard that the spirit of the gods is in you and that you have insight, intelligence and outstanding wisdom. 15 The wise men and enchanters were brought before me to read this writing and tell me what it means, but they could not explain it. 16 Now I have heard that you are able to give interpretations and to solve difficult problems. If you can read this writing and tell me what it means, you will be clothed in purple and have a gold chain placed around your neck, and you will be made the third highest ruler in the kingdom."

17 Then Daniel answered the king, "You may keep your gifts for yourself and give your rewards to someone else. Nevertheless, I will read the writing for the king and tell him what it means.

18 "Your Majesty, the Most High God gave your father Nebuchadnezzar sovereignty and greatness and glory and splendor. 19 Because of the high position he gave him, all the nations and peoples of every language dreaded and feared him. Those the king wanted to put to death, he put to death; those he wanted to spare, he spared; those he wanted to promote, he promoted; and those he wanted to humble, he humbled. 20 But when his heart became arrogant and hardened with pride, he was deposed from his royal throne and stripped of his glory. 21 He was driven away from people and given the mind of an animal; he lived with the wild donkeys and ate grass like the ox; and his body was drenched with the dew of heaven, until he acknowledged that the Most High God is sovereign over all king-

---

[a] 7 Or *Chaldeans*; also in verse 11   [b] 10 Or *queen mother*

doms on earth and sets over them anyone he wishes.

22 "But you, Belshazzar, his son,[a] have not humbled yourself, though you knew all this. 23 Instead, you have set yourself up against the Lord of heaven. You had the goblets from his temple brought to you, and you and your nobles, your wives and your concubines drank wine from them. You praised the gods of silver and gold, of bronze, iron, wood and stone, which cannot see or hear or understand. But you did not honor the God who holds in his hand your life and all your ways. 24 Therefore he sent the hand that wrote the inscription.

25 "This is the inscription that was written:

MENE, MENE, TEKEL, PARSIN

26 "Here is what these words mean:

Mene[b]: God has numbered the days of your reign and brought it to an end.
27 *Tekel*[c]: You have been weighed on the scales and found wanting.
28 *Peres*[d]: Your kingdom is divided and given to the Medes and Persians."

29 Then at Belshazzar's command, Daniel was clothed in purple, a gold chain was placed around his neck, and he was proclaimed the third highest ruler in the kingdom.

30 That very night Belshazzar, king of the Babylonians,[e] was slain, 31 and Darius the Mede took over the kingdom, at the age of sixty-two.[f]

Daniel in the Den of Lions

6[g] It pleased Darius to appoint 120 satraps to rule throughout the kingdom, 2 with three administrators over them, one of whom was Daniel. The satraps were made accountable to them so that the king might not suffer loss. 3 Now Daniel so distinguished himself among

A: He wrote on the wall with "the fingers of a human hand" (Daniel 5:5).

BONUS: The Bible says, "His face turned pale and he was so frightened that his legs became weak and his knees were knocking" (Daniel 5:6).

the administrators and the satraps by his exceptional qualities that the king planned to set him over the whole kingdom. 4 At this, the administrators and the satraps tried to find grounds for charges against Daniel in his conduct of government affairs, but they were unable to do so. They could find no corruption in him, because he was trustworthy and neither corrupt nor negligent. 5 Finally these men said, "We will never find any basis for charges against this man Daniel unless it has something to do with the law of his God."

6 So these administrators and satraps went as a group to the king and said: "May King Darius live forever! 7 The royal administrators, prefects, satraps, advisers and governors have all agreed that the king should issue an edict and enforce the decree that anyone who prays to any god or human being during the next thirty days, except to you, Your Majesty, shall be thrown into the lions' den. 8 Now, Your Majesty, issue the decree and put it in writing so that it cannot be altered—

---

[a] 22 Or *descendant*; or *successor*   [b] 26 *Mene* can mean *numbered* or *mina* (a unit of money).   [c] 27 *Tekel* can mean *weighed* or *shekel*.   [d] 28 *Peres* (the singular of *Parsin*) can mean *divided* or *Persia* or *a half mina* or *a half shekel*.   [e] 30 Or *Chaldeans*   [f] 31 In Aramaic texts this verse (5:31) is numbered 6:1.   [g] In Aramaic texts 6:1-28 is numbered 6:2-29.

in accordance with the law of the Medes and Persians, which cannot be repealed." [9] So King Darius put the decree in writing.

[10] Now when Daniel learned that the decree had been published, he went home to his upstairs room where the windows opened toward Jerusalem. Three times a day he got down on his knees and prayed, giving thanks to his God, just as he had done before. [11] Then these men went as a group and found Daniel praying and asking God for help. [12] So they went to the king and spoke to him about his royal decree: "Did you not publish a decree that during the next thirty days anyone who prays to any god or human being except to you, Your Majesty, would be thrown into the lions' den?"

The king answered, "The decree stands — in accordance with the law of the Medes and Persians, which cannot be repealed."

[13] Then they said to the king, "Daniel, who is one of the exiles from Judah, pays no attention to you, Your Majesty, or to the decree you put in writing. He still prays three times a day." [14] When the king heard this, he was greatly distressed; he was determined to rescue Daniel and made every effort until sundown to save him.

[15] Then the men went as a group to King Darius and said to him, "Remember, Your Majesty, that according to the law of the Medes and Persians no decree or edict that the king issues can be changed."

[16] So the king gave the order, and they brought Daniel and threw him into the lions' den. The king said to Daniel, "May your God, whom you serve continually, rescue you!"

[17] A stone was brought and placed over the mouth of the den, and the king sealed it with his own signet ring and with the rings of his nobles, so that Daniel's situation might not be changed. [18] Then the king returned to his palace and spent the night without eating and without any entertainment being brought to him. And he could not sleep.

[19] At the first light of dawn, the king got up and hurried to the lions' den. [20] When he came near the den, he called to Daniel in an anguished voice, "Daniel, servant of the living God, has your God, whom you serve continually, been able to rescue you from the lions?"

[21] Daniel answered, "May the king live forever! [22] My God sent his angel, and he shut the mouths of the lions. They have not hurt me, because I was found innocent in his sight. Nor have I ever done any wrong before you, Your Majesty."

[23] The king was overjoyed and gave orders to lift Daniel out of the den. And when Daniel was lifted from the den, no wound was found on him, because he had trusted in his God.

[24] At the king's command, the men who had falsely accused Daniel were brought in and thrown into the lions' den, along with their wives and children. And before they reached the floor of the den, the lions overpowered them and crushed all their bones.

[25] Then King Darius wrote to all the nations and peoples of every language in all the earth:

"May you prosper greatly!

[26] "I issue a decree that in every part of my kingdom people must fear and reverence the God of Daniel.

"For he is the living God
    and he endures forever;
his kingdom will not be destroyed,
    his dominion will never end.
[27] He rescues and he saves;
    he performs signs and wonders
    in the heavens and on the earth.
He has rescued Daniel
    from the power of the lions."

[28] So Daniel prospered during the reign of Darius and the reign of Cyrus[a] the Persian.

Daniel's Dream of Four Beasts

7 In the first year of Belshazzar king of Babylon, Daniel had a dream, and visions passed through his mind as he was lying in bed. He wrote down the substance of his dream.

---

[a] 28 Or Darius, that is, the reign of Cyrus

[2] Daniel said: "In my vision at night I looked, and there before me were the four winds of heaven churning up the great sea. [3] Four great beasts, each different from the others, came up out of the sea.

[4] "The first was like a lion, and it had the wings of an eagle. I watched until its wings were torn off and it was lifted from the ground so that it stood on two feet like a human being, and the mind of a human was given to it.

[5] "And there before me was a second beast, which looked like a bear. It was raised up on one of its sides, and it had three ribs in its mouth between its teeth. It was told, 'Get up and eat your fill of flesh!'

[6] "After that, I looked, and there before me was another beast, one that looked like a leopard. And on its back it had four wings like those of a bird. This beast had four heads, and it was given authority to rule.

[7] "After that, in my vision at night I looked, and there before me was a fourth beast—terrifying and frightening and very powerful. It had large iron teeth; it crushed and devoured its victims and trampled underfoot whatever was left. It was different from all the former beasts, and it had ten horns.

[8] "While I was thinking about the horns, there before me was another horn, a little one, which came up among them; and three of the first horns were uprooted before it. This horn had eyes like the eyes of a human being and a mouth that spoke boastfully.

[9] "As I looked,

"thrones were set in place,
    and the Ancient of Days took his
        seat.
His clothing was as white as snow;
    the hair of his head was white like
        wool.
His throne was flaming with fire,
    and its wheels were all ablaze.
[10] A river of fire was flowing,
    coming out from before him.
Thousands upon thousands attended
        him;
    ten thousand times ten thousand
        stood before him.
The court was seated,
    and the books were opened.

[11] "Then I continued to watch because of the boastful words the horn was speaking. I kept looking until the beast was slain and its body destroyed and thrown into the blazing fire. [12] (The other beasts had been stripped of their authority, but were allowed to live for a period of time.)

[13] "In my vision at night I looked, and there before me was one like a son of man,[a] coming with the clouds of heaven. He approached the Ancient of Days and was led into his presence. [14] He was

---

[a] 13 The Aramaic phrase *bar enash* means *human being*. The phrase *son of man* is retained here because of its use in the New Testament as a title of Jesus, probably based largely on this verse.

PANORAMA

Convictions.

Daniel was a teenager, a hostage in Babylon, when he had to decide: Would he stand up for what he believed in? Daniel was loyal to God and God saved him.

given authority, glory and sovereign power; all nations and peoples of every language worshiped him. His dominion is an everlasting dominion that will not pass away, and his kingdom is one that will never be destroyed.

The Interpretation of the Dream

¹⁵ "I, Daniel, was troubled in spirit, and the visions that passed through my mind disturbed me. ¹⁶ I approached one of those standing there and asked him the meaning of all this.

"So he told me and gave me the interpretation of these things: ¹⁷ 'The four great beasts are four kings that will rise from the earth. ¹⁸ But the holy people of the Most High will receive the kingdom and will possess it forever—yes, for ever and ever.'

¹⁹ "Then I wanted to know the meaning of the fourth beast, which was different from all the others and most terrifying, with its iron teeth and bronze claws—the beast that crushed and devoured its victims and trampled underfoot whatever was left. ²⁰ I also wanted to know about the ten horns on its head and about the other horn that came up, before which three of them fell—the horn that looked more imposing than the others and that had eyes and a mouth that spoke boastfully. ²¹ As I watched, this horn was waging war against the holy people and defeating them, ²² until the Ancient of Days came and pronounced judgment in favor of the holy people of the Most High, and the time came when they possessed the kingdom.

²³ "He gave me this explanation: 'The fourth beast is a fourth kingdom that will appear on earth. It will be different from all the other kingdoms and will devour the whole earth, trampling it down and crushing it. ²⁴ The ten horns are ten kings who will come from this kingdom. After them another king will arise, different from the earlier ones; he will subdue three kings. ²⁵ He will speak against the Most High and oppress his holy people and try to

change the set times and the laws. The holy people will be delivered into his hands for a time, times and half a time.ᵃ

²⁶ " 'But the court will sit, and his power will be taken away and completely destroyed forever. ²⁷ Then the sovereignty, power and greatness of all the kingdoms under heaven will be handed over to the holy people of the Most High. His kingdom will be an everlasting kingdom, and all rulers will worship and obey him.'

²⁸ "This is the end of the matter. I, Daniel, was deeply troubled by my thoughts, and my face turned pale, but I kept the matter to myself."

Daniel's Vision of a Ram and a Goat

8 In the third year of King Belshazzar's reign, I, Daniel, had a vision, after the one that had already appeared to me. ² In my vision I saw myself in the citadel of Susa in the province of Elam; in the vision I was beside the Ulai Canal. ³ I looked up, and there before me was a ram with two horns, standing beside the canal, and the horns were long. One of the horns was longer than the other but grew up later. ⁴ I watched the ram as it charged toward the west and the north and the south. No animal could stand against it, and none could rescue from its power. It did as it pleased and became great.

⁵ As I was thinking about this, suddenly a goat with a prominent horn between its eyes came from the west, crossing the whole earth without touching the ground. ⁶ It came toward the two-horned ram I had seen standing beside the canal and charged at it in great rage. ⁷ I saw it attack the ram furiously, striking the ram and shattering its two horns. The ram was powerless to stand against it; the goat knocked it to the ground and trampled on it, and none could rescue the ram from its power. ⁸ The goat became very great, but at the height of its power the large horn was broken off, and in its place four prominent horns grew up toward the four winds of heaven.

⁹ Out of one of them came another horn, which started small but grew in

---

ᵃ 25 Or *for a year, two years and half a year*

power to the south and to the east and toward the Beautiful Land. ¹⁰It grew until it reached the host of the heavens, and it threw some of the starry host down to the earth and trampled on them. ¹¹It set itself up to be as great as the commander of the army of the LORD; it took away the daily sacrifice from the LORD, and his sanctuary was thrown down. ¹²Because of rebellion, the LORD's people*ᵃ* and the daily sacrifice were given over to it. It prospered in everything it did, and truth was thrown to the ground.

¹³Then I heard a holy one speaking, and another holy one said to him, "How long will it take for the vision to be fulfilled—the vision concerning the daily sacrifice, the rebellion that causes desolation, the surrender of the sanctuary and the trampling underfoot of the LORD's people?"

¹⁴He said to me, "It will take 2,300 evenings and mornings; then the sanctuary will be reconsecrated."

The Interpretation of the Vision

¹⁵While I, Daniel, was watching the vision and trying to understand it, there before me stood one who looked like a man. ¹⁶And I heard a man's voice from the Ulai calling, "Gabriel, tell this man the meaning of the vision."

¹⁷As he came near the place where I was standing, I was terrified and fell prostrate. "Son of man,"*ᵇ* he said to me, "understand that the vision concerns the time of the end."

¹⁸While he was speaking to me, I was in a deep sleep, with my face to the ground. Then he touched me and raised me to my feet.

¹⁹He said: "I am going to tell you what will happen later in the time of wrath, because the vision concerns the appointed time of the end.*ᶜ* ²⁰The two-horned ram that you saw represents the kings of Media and Persia. ²¹The shaggy goat is the king of Greece, and the large horn between its eyes is the first king. ²²The four horns that replaced the one that was

broken off represent four kingdoms that will emerge from his nation but will not have the same power.

²³"In the latter part of their reign, when rebels have become completely wicked, a fierce-looking king, a master of intrigue, will arise. ²⁴He will become very strong, but not by his own power. He will cause astounding devastation and will succeed in whatever he does. He will destroy those who are mighty, the holy people. ²⁵He will cause deceit to prosper, and he will consider himself superior. When they feel secure, he will destroy many and take his stand against the Prince of princes. Yet he will be destroyed, but not by human power.

²⁶"The vision of the evenings and mornings that has been given you is true, but seal up the vision, for it concerns the distant future."

²⁷I, Daniel, was worn out. I lay exhausted for several days. Then I got up and went about the king's business. I was appalled by the vision; it was beyond understanding.

Daniel's Prayer

9 In the first year of Darius son of Xerxes*ᵈ* (a Mede by descent), who was made ruler over the Babylonian*ᵉ* kingdom— ²in the first year of his reign, I, Daniel, understood from the Scriptures, according to the word of the LORD given to Jeremiah the prophet, that the desolation of Jerusalem would last seventy years. ³So I turned to the Lord God and pleaded with him in prayer and petition, in fasting, and in sackcloth and ashes.

⁴I prayed to the LORD my God and confessed:

"Lord, the great and awesome God, who keeps his covenant of love with those who love him and keep his commandments, ⁵we have sinned and done wrong. We have been wicked and have rebelled; we have turned away from your commands and laws. ⁶We have not listened to your servants the prophets,

---

ᵃ 12 Or *rebellion, the armies*   *ᵇ 17* The Hebrew phrase *ben adam* means *human being.* The phrase *son of man* is retained as a form of address here because of its possible association with "Son of Man" in the New Testament.
ᶜ 19 Or *because the end will be at the appointed time*   *ᵈ 1* Hebrew *Ahasuerus*   *ᵉ 1* Or *Chaldean*

who spoke in your name to our kings, our princes and our ancestors, and to all the people of the land.

7 "Lord, you are righteous, but this day we are covered with shame—the people of Judah and the inhabitants of Jerusalem and all Israel, both near and far, in all the countries where you have scattered us because of our unfaithfulness to you. 8We and our kings, our princes and our ancestors are covered with shame, LORD, because we have sinned against you. 9The Lord our God is merciful and forgiving, even though we have rebelled against him; 10we have not obeyed the LORD our God or kept the laws he gave us through his servants the prophets. 11All Israel has transgressed your law and turned away, refusing to obey you.

"Therefore the curses and sworn judgments written in the Law of Moses, the servant of God, have been poured out on us, because we have sinned against you. 12You have fulfilled the words spoken against us and against our rulers by bringing on us great disaster. Under the whole heaven nothing has ever been done like what has been done to Jerusalem. 13Just as it is written in the Law of Moses, all this disaster has come on us, yet we have not sought the favor of the LORD our God by turning from our sins and giving attention to your truth. 14The LORD did not hesitate to bring the disaster on us, for the LORD our God is righteous in everything he does; yet we have not obeyed him.

15 "Now, Lord our God, who brought your people out of Egypt with a mighty hand and who made for yourself a name that endures to this day, we have sinned, we have done wrong. 16Lord, in keeping with all your righteous acts, turn away your anger and your wrath from Jerusalem, your city, your holy hill. Our sins and the iniquities of our ancestors have made Jerusalem and your people an object of scorn to all those around us.

17 "Now, our God, hear the prayers and petitions of your servant. For your sake, Lord, look with favor on your desolate sanctuary. 18Give ear, our God, and hear; open your eyes and see the desolation of the city that bears your Name. We do not make requests of you because we are righteous, but because of your great mercy. 19Lord, listen! Lord, forgive! Lord, hear and act! For your sake, my God, do not delay, because your city and your people bear your Name."

The Seventy "Sevens"

20While I was speaking and praying, confessing my sin and the sin of my people Israel and making my request to the LORD my God for his holy hill— 21while I was still in prayer, Gabriel, the man I had seen in the earlier vision, came to me in swift flight about the time of the evening sacrifice. 22He instructed me and said to me, "Daniel, I have now come to give you insight and understanding. 23As soon as you began to pray, a word went out, which I have come to tell you, for you are highly esteemed. Therefore, consider the word and understand the vision:

24 "Seventy 'sevens'a are decreed for your people and your holy city to finishb transgression, to put an end to sin, to atone for wickedness, to bring in everlasting righteousness, to seal up vision and prophecy and to anoint the Most Holy Place.c

25 "Know and understand this: From the time the word goes out to restore and rebuild Jerusalem until the Anointed One,d the ruler, comes, there will be seven 'sevens,' and sixty-two 'sevens.' It will be rebuilt with streets and a trench, but in times of trouble. 26After the sixty-two 'sevens,' the Anointed One will be put to death and will have nothing.e The people of the ruler who will come will destroy the city and the sanctuary. The end will come like a flood: War will continue until the end, and desolations have been decreed.

---

a 24 Or 'weeks'; also in verses 25 and 26   b 24 Or restrain   c 24 Or the most holy One   d 25 Or an anointed one; also in verse 26   e 26 Or death and will have no one; or death, but not for himself

²⁷He will confirm a covenant with many for one 'seven.'ᵃ In the middle of the 'seven'ᵃ he will put an end to sacrifice and offering. And at the templeᵇ he will set up an abomination that causes desolation, until the end that is decreed is poured out on him.ᶜ"ᵈ

Daniel's Vision of a Man

10 In the third year of Cyrus king of Persia, a revelation was given to Daniel (who was called Belteshazzar). Its message was true and it concerned a great war.ᵉ The understanding of the message came to him in a vision.

²At that time I, Daniel, mourned for three weeks. ³I ate no choice food; no meat or wine touched my lips; and I used no lotions at all until the three weeks were over.

⁴On the twenty-fourth day of the first month, as I was standing on the bank of the great river, the Tigris, ⁵I looked up and there before me was a man dressed in linen, with a belt of fine gold from Uphaz around his waist. ⁶His body was like topaz, his face like lightning, his eyes like flaming torches, his arms and legs like the gleam of burnished bronze, and his voice like the sound of a multitude.

⁷I, Daniel, was the only one who saw the vision; those who were with me did not see it, but such terror overwhelmed them that they fled and hid themselves. ⁸So I was left alone, gazing at this great vision; I had no strength left, my face

ᵃ 27 Or 'week'   ᵇ 27 Septuagint and Theodotion; Hebrew *wing*   ᶜ 27 Or *it*   ᵈ 27 Or *And one who causes desolation will come upon the wing of the abominable temple, until the end that is decreed is poured out on the desolated city*   ᵉ 1 Or *true and burdensome*

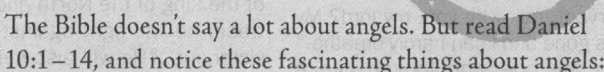

Angels

The Bible doesn't say a lot about angels. But read Daniel 10:1–14, and notice these fascinating things about angels:

+ The angels of God and the angels of Satan battle each other in an invisible war.

+ Angels seem to have rank. Daniel's "major" angel was stopped by an enemy "colonel" angel, until "general" Michael appeared.

+ Satan assigns angels to nations. The angel assigned to Persia is called "the prince of the Persian kingdom."

Most people are curious about angels and would like to know more. But the Bible focuses on things that are more important for human beings, like how to trust God and live in ways that please him. You'll learn all you need to know about angels when you get to heaven.

turned deathly pale and I was helpless. ⁹Then I heard him speaking, and as I listened to him, I fell into a deep sleep, my face to the ground.

¹⁰A hand touched me and set me trembling on my hands and knees. ¹¹He said, "Daniel, you who are highly esteemed, consider carefully the words I am about to speak to you, and stand up, for I have now been sent to you." And when he said this to me, I stood up trembling.

¹²Then he continued, "Do not be afraid, Daniel. Since the first day that you set your mind to gain understanding and to humble yourself before your God, your words were heard, and I have come in response to them. ¹³But the prince of the Persian kingdom resisted me twenty-one days. Then Michael, one of the chief princes, came to help me, because I was detained there with the king of Persia. ¹⁴Now I have come to explain to you what will happen to your people in the future, for the vision concerns a time yet to come."

¹⁵While he was saying this to me, I bowed with my face toward the ground and was speechless. ¹⁶Then one who looked like a man[a] touched my lips, and I opened my mouth and began to speak. I said to the one standing before me, "I am overcome with anguish because of the vision, my lord, and I feel very weak. ¹⁷How can I, your servant, talk with you, my lord? My strength is gone and I can hardly breathe."

¹⁸Again the one who looked like a man touched me and gave me strength. ¹⁹"Do not be afraid, you who are highly esteemed," he said. "Peace! Be strong now; be strong."

When he spoke to me, I was strengthened and said, "Speak, my lord, since you have given me strength."

²⁰So he said, "Do you know why I have come to you? Soon I will return to fight against the prince of Persia, and when I go, the prince of Greece will come; ²¹but first I will tell you what is written in the Book of Truth. (No one supports me against them except Michael, your prince.

11 ¹And in the first year of Darius the Mede, I took my stand to support and protect him.)

The Kings of the South and the North

²"Now then, I tell you the truth: Three more kings will arise in Persia, and then a fourth, who will be far richer than all the others. When he has gained power by his wealth, he will stir up everyone against the kingdom of Greece. ³Then a mighty king will arise, who will rule with great power and do as he pleases. ⁴After he has arisen, his empire will be broken up and parceled out toward the four winds of heaven. It will not go to his descendants, nor will it have the power he exercised, because his empire will be uprooted and given to others.

⁵"The king of the South will become strong, but one of his commanders will become even stronger than he and will rule his own kingdom with great power. ⁶After some years, they will become allies. The daughter of the king of the South will go to the king of the North to make an alliance, but she will not retain her power, and he and his power[b] will not last. In those days she will be betrayed, together with her royal escort and her father[c] and the one who supported her.

⁷"One from her family line will arise to take her place. He will attack the forces of the king of the North and enter his fortress; he will fight against them and be victorious. ⁸He will also seize their gods, their metal images and their valuable articles of silver and gold and carry them off to Egypt. For some years he will leave the king of the North alone. ⁹Then the king of the North will invade the realm of the king of the South but will retreat to his own country. ¹⁰His sons will prepare for war and assemble a great army, which will sweep on like an irresistible flood and carry the battle as far as his fortress.

¹¹"Then the king of the South will march out in a rage and fight against the king of the North, who will raise a large army, but it will be defeated. ¹²When the army is carried off, the king of the South will be filled with pride and will slaughter many thousands, yet he will not remain

---

a 16 Most manuscripts of the Masoretic Text; one manuscript of the Masoretic Text, Dead Sea Scrolls and Septuagint
Then something that looked like a human hand   b 6 Or offspring   c 6 Or child (see Vulgate and Syriac)

triumphant. [13]For the king of the North will muster another army, larger than the first; and after several years, he will advance with a huge army fully equipped.

[14]"In those times many will rise against the king of the South. Those who are violent among your own people will rebel in fulfillment of the vision, but without success. [15]Then the king of the North will come and build up siege ramps and will capture a fortified city. The forces of the South will be powerless to resist; even their best troops will not have the strength to stand. [16]The invader will do as he pleases; no one will be able to stand against him. He will establish himself in the Beautiful Land and will have the power to destroy it. [17]He will determine to come with the might of his entire kingdom and will make an alliance with the king of the South. And he will give him a daughter in marriage in order to overthrow the kingdom, but his plans[a] will not succeed or help him. [18]Then he will turn his attention to the coastlands and will take many of them, but a commander will put an end to his insolence and will turn his insolence back on him. [19]After this, he will turn back toward the fortresses of his own country but will stumble and fall, to be seen no more.

[20]"His successor will send out a tax collector to maintain the royal splendor. In a few years, however, he will be destroyed, yet not in anger or in battle.

[21]"He will be succeeded by a contemptible person who has not been given the honor of royalty. He will invade the kingdom when its people feel secure, and he will seize it through intrigue. [22]Then an overwhelming army will be swept away before him; both it and a prince of the covenant will be destroyed. [23]After coming to an agreement with him, he will act deceitfully, and with only a few people he will rise to power. [24]When the richest provinces feel secure, he will invade them and will achieve what neither his fathers nor his forefathers did. He will distribute plunder, loot and wealth among his followers. He will plot the overthrow of fortresses—but only for a time.

[25]"With a large army he will stir up his strength and courage against the king of the South. The king of the South will wage war with a large and very powerful army, but he will not be able to stand because of the plots devised against him. [26]Those who eat from the king's provisions will try to destroy him; his army will be swept away, and many will fall in battle. [27]The two kings, with their hearts bent on evil, will sit at the same table and lie to each other, but to no avail, because an end will still come at the appointed time. [28]The king of the North will return to his own country with great wealth, but his heart will be set against the holy covenant. He will take action against it and then return to his own country.

[29]"At the appointed time he will invade the South again, but this time the outcome will be different from what it was before. [30]Ships of the western coastlands will oppose him, and he will lose heart. Then he will turn back and vent his fury against the holy covenant. He will return and show favor to those who forsake the holy covenant.

[31]"His armed forces will rise up to desecrate the temple fortress and will abolish the daily sacrifice. Then they will set up the abomination that causes desolation. [32]With flattery he will corrupt those who have violated the covenant, but the people who know their God will firmly resist him.

[33]"Those who are wise will instruct many, though for a time they will fall by the sword or be burned or captured or plundered. [34]When they fall, they will receive a little help, and many who are not sincere will join them. [35]Some of the wise will stumble, so that they may be refined, purified and made spotless until the time of the end, for it will still come at the appointed time.

The King Who Exalts Himself

[36]"The king will do as he pleases. He will exalt and magnify himself above every god and will say unheard-of things against the God of gods. He will be successful until the time of wrath is complet-

a 17 Or but she

We Believe...

"in the resurrection of the body"

✝ The first specific teaching on the resurrection of the body is found in Daniel 12:2. There the Bible says that those who "sleep in the dust of the earth will awake: some to everlasting life, others to shame and everlasting contempt."

It's much clearer in the New Testament, where we're promised that when Jesus returns believers will be raised from the dead to meet Jesus in the air and will "be with the Lord forever" (1 Thessalonians 4:13 – 18).

Of course, the thing we want to know is what our resurrection bodies will look like. Will people still have zits? Will hair be curly or straight? Will people have all different heights and weights?

Even though those questions aren't answered directly, the Bible tells us a lot about our resurrection bodies in 1 Corinthians 15. Our bodies will be "raised in glory" and our weaknesses will be replaced with "power" (verse 43). And the best news of all is that our resurrection bodies will "bear the image of the heavenly man."

You can be sure the resurrection body of Jesus was the best that God could possibly invent. And your resurrection body will be like his—the best God can possibly provide!

Go to page 1585 for the next We Believe

ed, for what has been determined must take place. ³⁷He will show no regard for the gods of his ancestors or for the one desired by women, nor will he regard any god, but will exalt himself above them all. ³⁸Instead of them, he will honor a god of fortresses; a god unknown to his ancestors he will honor with gold and silver, with precious stones and costly gifts. ³⁹He will attack the mightiest fortresses with the help of a foreign god and will greatly honor those who acknowledge him. He will make them rulers over many people and will distribute the land at a price.ᵃ

⁴⁰"At the time of the end the king of the South will engage him in battle, and the king of the North will storm out against him with chariots and cavalry and a great fleet of ships. He will invade many countries and sweep through them like a flood. ⁴¹He will also invade the Beautiful Land. Many countries will fall, but Edom, Moab and the leaders of Ammon will be delivered from his hand. ⁴²He will extend his power over many countries; Egypt will not escape. ⁴³He will gain control of the treasures of gold and silver and all the riches of Egypt, with the Libyans and Cushitesᵇ in submission. ⁴⁴But reports from the east and the north will alarm him, and he will set out in a great rage to destroy and annihilate many. ⁴⁵He will pitch his royal tents between the seas atᶜ the beautiful holy mountain. Yet he will come to his end, and no one will help him.

ᵃ 39 Or land for a reward   ᵇ 43 That is, people from the upper Nile region   ᶜ 45 Or the sea and

Will We Live Again?

The New Testament teaches a resurrection, but what about the Old Testament? Did people then know that they would live again? They did if they believed the Scriptures:

+ God will "swallow up death forever" (Isaiah 25:8).

+ "Your dead will live; their bodies will rise" (Isaiah 26:19).

+ "Multitudes who sleep in the dust of the earth will awake: some to everlasting life, others to shame and everlasting contempt" (Daniel 12:2).

Old Testament passages don't speak about a resurrection as much as the New Testament—but the entire Bible tells about one God, who has always loved human beings and who has always planned that people who live by faith will live forever with him.

The End Times

12 "At that time Michael, the great prince who protects your people, will arise. There will be a time of distress such as has not happened from the beginning of nations until then. But at that time your people — everyone whose name is found written in the book — will be delivered. ²Multitudes who sleep in the dust of the earth will awake: some to everlasting life, others to shame and everlasting contempt. ³Those who are wise*a* will shine like the brightness of the heavens, and those who lead many to righteousness, like the stars for ever and ever. ⁴But you, Daniel, roll up and seal the words of the scroll until the time of the end. Many will go here and there to increase knowledge."

⁵Then I, Daniel, looked, and there before me stood two others, one on this bank of the river and one on the opposite bank. ⁶One of them said to the man clothed in linen, who was above the waters of the river, "How long will it be before these astonishing things are fulfilled?"

⁷The man clothed in linen, who was above the waters of the river, lifted his right hand and his left hand toward heaven, and I heard him swear by him who lives forever, saying, "It will be for a time, times and half a time.*b* When the power of the holy people has been finally broken, all these things will be completed."

⁸I heard, but I did not understand. So I asked, "My lord, what will the outcome of all this be?"

⁹He replied, "Go your way, Daniel, because the words are rolled up and sealed until the time of the end. ¹⁰Many will be purified, made spotless and refined, but the wicked will continue to be wicked. None of the wicked will understand, but those who are wise will understand.

¹¹"From the time that the daily sacrifice is abolished and the abomination that causes desolation is set up, there will be 1,290 days. ¹²Blessed is the one who waits for and reaches the end of the 1,335 days.

¹³"As for you, go your way till the end. You will rest, and then at the end of the days you will rise to receive your allotted inheritance."

---

a 3 Or *who impart wisdom*   *b* 7 Or *a year, two years and half a year*

HOSEA

Betrayal.

Have you ever written a very personal email to a friend and then had that friend turn around and forward the email to everyone? Or told your mom something confidential and later found out she told your grandma and two aunts? You probably felt betrayed.

The prophet Hosea must have felt the same way about his unfaithful wife. But God told Hosea to keep on loving her even though she hurt him. Why? Because Hosea was to be like God, who keeps on loving his people even when they're unfaithful to him. What you do can hurt the Lord. But even then he keeps on loving you.

>>**WHAT'S IN A NAME?**
  Decoded messages found in Hosea 1

>>**GOD WITHDRAWS FROM HIS PEOPLE**
  There are limits to love, suggests Hosea 5:1–6

>>**LOVE HURTS**
  God's heartbreak exposed. Report in Hosea 11:1–11

>>**LOVE HEALS**
  Reassuring words found in Hosea 14

preview

Hosea prophesies in the northern kingdom, Israel, about 850 B.C.

Hosea's wife is unfaithful but he keeps on loving her, just as God keeps on loving his people when they are unfaithful to him.

As Hosea prophesies in Israel, winged bulls are worshiped in most eastern Mediterranean countries. The ram is added to warships. The first known arched bridge is built in Smyrna (modern Turkey). The Chinese begin recording events by consecutive years.

1 The word of the LORD that came to Hosea son of Beeri during the reigns of Uzziah, Jotham, Ahaz and Hezekiah, kings of Judah, and during the reign of Jeroboam son of Jehoash[a] king of Israel:

Hosea's Wife and Children

² When the LORD began to speak through Hosea, the LORD said to him, "Go, marry a promiscuous woman and have children with her, for like an adulterous wife this land is guilty of unfaithfulness to the LORD." ³ So he married Gomer daughter of Diblaim, and she conceived and bore him a son.

⁴ Then the LORD said to Hosea, "Call him Jezreel, because I will soon punish the house of Jehu for the massacre at Jezreel, and I will put an end to the kingdom of Israel. ⁵ In that day I will break Israel's bow in the Valley of Jezreel."

⁶ Gomer conceived again and gave birth to a daughter. Then the LORD said to Hosea, "Call her Lo-Ruhamah (which means "not loved"), for I will no longer show love to Israel, that I should at all forgive them. ⁷ Yet I will show love to Judah; and I will save them—not by bow, sword or battle, or by horses and horsemen, but I, the LORD their God, will save them."

⁸ After she had weaned Lo-Ruhamah, Gomer had another son. ⁹ Then the LORD said, "Call him Lo-Ammi (which means "not my people"), for you are not my people, and I am not your God.[b]

¹⁰ "Yet the Israelites will be like the sand on the seashore, which cannot be measured or counted. In the place where it was said to them, 'You are not my people,' they will be called 'children of the living God.' ¹¹ The people of Judah and the people of Israel will come together; they will appoint one leader and will come up out of the land, for great will be the day of Jezreel.[c]

2[d] "Say of your brothers, 'My people,' and of your sisters, 'My loved one.'

Israel Punished and Restored

² "Rebuke your mother, rebuke her,
for she is not my wife,
and I am not her husband.
Let her remove the adulterous look
from her face
and the unfaithfulness from
between her breasts.
³ Otherwise I will strip her naked
and make her as bare as on the day
she was born;
I will make her like a desert,
turn her into a parched land,
and slay her with thirst.
⁴ I will not show my love to her children,
because they are the children of
adultery.
⁵ Their mother has been unfaithful
and has conceived them in disgrace.
She said, 'I will go after my lovers,
who give me my food and my water,
my wool and my linen, my olive oil
and my drink.'
⁶ Therefore I will block her path with
thornbushes;
I will wall her in so that she cannot
find her way.
⁷ She will chase after her lovers but not
catch them;
she will look for them but not find
them.
Then she will say,
'I will go back to my husband as at
first,
for then I was better off than now.'
⁸ She has not acknowledged that I was
the one
who gave her the grain, the new
wine and oil,
who lavished on her the silver and
gold—
which they used for Baal.

⁹ "Therefore I will take away my grain
when it ripens,
and my new wine when it is ready.
I will take back my wool and my linen,
intended to cover her naked body.
¹⁰ So now I will expose her lewdness
before the eyes of her lovers;
no one will take her out of my
hands.
¹¹ I will stop all her celebrations:
her yearly festivals, her New Moons,
her Sabbath days—all her
appointed festivals.

---

[a] 1 Hebrew *Joash*, a variant of *Jehoash*   [b] 9 Or *your I AM*   [c] 11 In Hebrew texts 1:10,11 is numbered 2:1,2.   [d] In Hebrew texts 2:1-23 is numbered 2:3-25.

¹²I will ruin her vines and her fig trees,
which she said were her pay from
her lovers;
I will make them a thicket,
and wild animals will devour them.
¹³I will punish her for the days
she burned incense to the Baals;
she decked herself with rings and
jewelry,
and went after her lovers,
but me she forgot,"
declares the LORD.
¹⁴"Therefore I am now going to allure
her;
I will lead her into the wilderness
and speak tenderly to her.
¹⁵There I will give her back her
vineyards,

and will make the Valley of Achor[a] a
door of hope.
There she will respond[b] as in the days
of her youth,
as in the day she came up out of
Egypt.
¹⁶"In that day," declares the LORD,
"you will call me 'my husband';
you will no longer call me 'my
master.[c]'
¹⁷I will remove the names of the Baals
from her lips;
no longer will their names be
invoked.
¹⁸In that day I will make a covenant for
them
with the beasts of the field, the
birds in the sky

---

[a] 15 Achor means trouble.   [b] 15 Or sing   [c] 16 Hebrew baal

---

TO THE POINT

God Is Jealous

Jealousy is a powerful emotion. When you feel jealous, you usually feel hateful and angry. So when the Bible says God is jealous (Exodus 20:5), does that mean he feels hateful and angry too?

Actually, the Bible doesn't say that God is jealous *against* anyone. Instead God is jealous *for* someone—his people. God cares so much that he becomes upset when the way you live keeps you from experiencing his very best.

Hosea 2 shows how God's jealousy works. God's people were unfaithful. No matter how good God was to them, they still worshiped idols. But God continued to love his people, knowing that without him they were lost. So he took away their good things—not to destroy them, but to bring them to their senses—so that once again they would turn to him and receive his blessing.

and the creatures that move along
    the ground.
Bow and sword and battle
    I will abolish from the land,
    so that all may lie down in safety.
¹⁹ I will betroth you to me forever;
    I will betroth you in^a righteousness
      and justice,
    in^a love and compassion.
²⁰ I will betroth you in^a faithfulness,
    and you will acknowledge the Lord.

²¹ "In that day I will respond,"
    declares the Lord—
 "I will respond to the skies,
    and they will respond to the earth;
²² and the earth will respond to the
    grain,
    the new wine and the olive oil,
    and they will respond to Jezreel.^b
²³ I will plant her for myself in the land;
    I will show my love to the one I
      called 'Not my loved one.^c'
 I will say to those called 'Not my
      people,^d' 'You are my people';
    and they will say, 'You are my
      God.'"

Hosea's Reconciliation With His Wife

3 The Lord said to me, "Go, show your love to your wife again, though she is loved by another man and is an adulteress. Love her as the Lord loves the Israelites, though they turn to other gods and love the sacred raisin cakes."

² So I bought her for fifteen shekels^e of silver and about a homer and a lethek^f of barley. ³ Then I told her, "You are to live with me many days; you must not be a prostitute or be intimate with any man, and I will behave the same way toward you."

⁴ For the Israelites will live many days without king or prince, without sacrifice or sacred stones, without ephod or household gods. ⁵ Afterward the Israelites will return and seek the Lord their God and David their king. They will come trembling to the Lord and to his blessings in the last days.

The Charge Against Israel

4 Hear the word of the Lord, you
    Israelites,
because the Lord has a charge to
    bring
    against you who live in the land:
"There is no faithfulness, no love,
    no acknowledgment of God in the
      land.
² There is only cursing,^g lying and
    murder,
    stealing and adultery;
 they break all bounds,
    and bloodshed follows bloodshed.
³ Because of this the land dries up,
    and all who live in it waste away;
 the beasts of the field, the birds in
      the sky
    and the fish in the sea are swept
      away.

⁴ "But let no one bring a charge,
    let no one accuse another,
 for your people are like those
    who bring charges against a priest.
⁵ You stumble day and night,
    and the prophets stumble with you.
 So I will destroy your mother—
⁶ my people are destroyed from lack
    of knowledge.

"Because you have rejected
    knowledge,
 I also reject you as my priests;
 because you have ignored the law of
    your God,
 I also will ignore your children.
⁷ The more priests there were,
    the more they sinned against me;
    they exchanged their glorious God^h
    for something disgraceful.
⁸ They feed on the sins of my people
    and relish their wickedness.
⁹ And it will be: Like people, like priests.
    I will punish both of them for their
      ways
    and repay them for their deeds.

---

^a *19,20* Or *with*   ^b *22 Jezreel* means *God plants.*   ^c *23* Hebrew *Lo-Ruhamah* (see 1:6)   ^d *23* Hebrew *Lo-Ammi* (see 1:9)   ^e *2* That is, about 6 ounces or about 170 grams   ^f *2* A homer and a lethek possibly weighed about 430 pounds or about 195 kilograms.   ^g *2* That is, to pronounce a curse on   ^h *7* Syriac (see also an ancient Hebrew scribal tradition); Masoretic Text *me; / I will exchange their glory*

10 "They will eat but not have enough;
    they will engage in prostitution but
        not flourish,
because they have deserted the LORD
    to give themselves 11to prostitution;
old wine and new wine
    take away their understanding.
12 My people consult a wooden idol,
    and a diviner's rod speaks to
        them.
A spirit of prostitution leads them
        astray;
    they are unfaithful to their God.
13 They sacrifice on the mountaintops
    and burn offerings on the hills,
under oak, poplar and terebinth,
    where the shade is pleasant.
Therefore your daughters turn to
        prostitution
    and your daughters-in-law to
        adultery.

14 "I will not punish your daughters
    when they turn to prostitution,
nor your daughters-in-law
    when they commit adultery,
because the men themselves consort
        with harlots
    and sacrifice with shrine
        prostitutes—
a people without understanding will
    come to ruin!

15 "Though you, Israel, commit
        adultery,
    do not let Judah become guilty.

"Do not go to Gilgal;
    do not go up to Beth Aven.a
    And do not swear, 'As surely as the
        LORD lives!'
16 The Israelites are stubborn,
    like a stubborn heifer.
How then can the LORD pasture them
    like lambs in a meadow?
17 Ephraim is joined to idols;
    leave him alone!
18 Even when their drinks are gone,
    they continue their prostitution;
    their rulers dearly love shameful
        ways.
19 A whirlwind will sweep them away,
    and their sacrifices will bring them
        shame.

Judgment Against Israel

5 "Hear this, you priests!
    Pay attention, you Israelites!
Listen, royal house!
    This judgment is against you:
You have been a snare at Mizpah,
    a net spread out on Tabor.
2 The rebels are knee-deep in
        slaughter.
    I will discipline all of them.
3 I know all about Ephraim;
    Israel is not hidden from me.
Ephraim, you have now turned to
        prostitution;
    Israel is corrupt.

4 "Their deeds do not permit them
    to return to their God.
A spirit of prostitution is in their heart;
    they do not acknowledge the LORD.

---

a 15 Beth Aven means house of wickedness (a derogatory name for Bethel, which means house of God).

5 Israel's arrogance testifies against
   them;
   the Israelites, even Ephraim,
      stumble in their sin;
   Judah also stumbles with them.
6 When they go with their flocks and
      herds
   to seek the LORD,
   they will not find him;
   he has withdrawn himself from
      them.
7 They are unfaithful to the LORD;
   they give birth to illegitimate
      children.
   When they celebrate their New Moon
      feasts,
   he will devour[a] their fields.

8 "Sound the trumpet in Gibeah,
   the horn in Ramah.
   Raise the battle cry in Beth Aven[b];
   lead on, Benjamin.
9 Ephraim will be laid waste
   on the day of reckoning.
   Among the tribes of Israel
   I proclaim what is certain.
10 Judah's leaders are like those
   who move boundary stones.
   I will pour out my wrath on them
   like a flood of water.
11 Ephraim is oppressed,
   trampled in judgment,
   intent on pursuing idols.[c]
12 I am like a moth to Ephraim,
   like rot to the people of Judah.

13 "When Ephraim saw his sickness,
   and Judah his sores,
   then Ephraim turned to Assyria,
   and sent to the great king for help.
   But he is not able to cure you,
   not able to heal your sores.
14 For I will be like a lion to Ephraim,
   like a great lion to Judah.
   I will tear them to pieces and go away;
   I will carry them off, with no one to
      rescue them.
15 Then I will return to my lair
   until they have borne their guilt
   and seek my face—
   in their misery
   they will earnestly seek me."

Israel Unrepentant

6 "Come, let us return to the LORD.
   He has torn us to pieces
   but he will heal us;
   he has injured us
   but he will bind up our wounds.
2 After two days he will revive us;
   on the third day he will restore us,
   that we may live in his presence.
3 Let us acknowledge the LORD;
   let us press on to acknowledge him.
   As surely as the sun rises,
   he will appear;
   he will come to us like the winter
      rains,
   like the spring rains that water the
      earth."

4 "What can I do with you, Ephraim?
   What can I do with you, Judah?
   Your love is like the morning mist,
   like the early dew that disappears.
5 Therefore I cut you in pieces with my
      prophets,
   I killed you with the words of my
      mouth—
   then my judgments go forth like the
      sun.[d]
6 For I desire mercy, not sacrifice,
   and acknowledgment of God rather
      than burnt offerings.
7 As at Adam,[e] they have broken the
      covenant;
   they were unfaithful to me there.
8 Gilead is a city of evildoers,
   stained with footprints of blood.
9 As marauders lie in ambush for a
      victim,
   so do bands of priests;
   they murder on the road to Shechem,
   carrying out their wicked schemes.
10 I have seen a horrible thing in Israel:
   There Ephraim is given to
      prostitution,
   Israel is defiled.

11 "Also for you, Judah,
   a harvest is appointed.

   "Whenever I would restore the
      fortunes of my people,

---

a 7 Or Now their New Moon feasts / will devour them and
for Bethel, which means house of God).   c 11 The meaning
of the Hebrew for this line is uncertain.   e 7 Or Like Adam; or Like human beings
b 8 Beth Aven means house of wickedness (a derogatory name
of the Hebrew for this word is uncertain.   d 5 The meaning

7 ¹whenever I would heal Israel,
the sins of Ephraim are exposed
and the crimes of Samaria
revealed.
They practice deceit,
thieves break into houses,
bandits rob in the streets;
²but they do not realize
that I remember all their evil
deeds.
Their sins engulf them;
they are always before me.

³"They delight the king with their
wickedness,
the princes with their lies.
⁴They are all adulterers,
burning like an oven
whose fire the baker need not stir
from the kneading of the dough till
it rises.
⁵On the day of the festival of our king
the princes become inflamed with
wine,
and he joins hands with the
mockers.
⁶Their hearts are like an oven;
they approach him with intrigue.
Their passion smolders all night;
in the morning it blazes like a
flaming fire.
⁷All of them are hot as an oven;
they devour their rulers.
All their kings fall,
and none of them calls on me.

⁸"Ephraim mixes with the nations;
Ephraim is a flat loaf not turned over.
⁹Foreigners sap his strength,
but he does not realize it.
His hair is sprinkled with gray,
but he does not notice.
¹⁰Israel's arrogance testifies against him,
but despite all this
he does not return to the Lord his God
or search for him.

¹¹"Ephraim is like a dove,
easily deceived and senseless—
now calling to Egypt,
now turning to Assyria.
¹²When they go, I will throw my net over
them;
I will pull them down like the birds
in the sky.
When I hear them flocking together,
I will catch them.
¹³Woe to them,
because they have strayed from me!
Destruction to them,
because they have rebelled
against me!
I long to redeem them
but they speak about me falsely.
¹⁴They do not cry out to me from their
hearts
but wail on their beds.
They slash themselves,ᵃ appealing to
their gods
for grain and new wine,
but they turn away from me.

ᵃ 14 Some Hebrew manuscripts and Septuagint; most Hebrew manuscripts *They gather together*

PANORAMA

Betrayal.

Hosea was betrayed by his unfaithful wife.
But he was told to act like God, and love her
anyway, even when she was unfaithful. It
hurts, but love prevails.

{HOSEA}

15 I trained them and strengthened their arms,
but they plot evil against me.
16 They do not turn to the Most High;
they are like a faulty bow.
Their leaders will fall by the sword
because of their insolent words.
For this they will be ridiculed
in the land of Egypt.

Israel to Reap the Whirlwind

8 "Put the trumpet to your lips!
An eagle is over the house of the LORD
because the people have broken my covenant
and rebelled against my law.
2 Israel cries out to me,
'Our God, we acknowledge you!'
3 But Israel has rejected what is good;
an enemy will pursue him.
4 They set up kings without my consent;
they choose princes without my approval.
With their silver and gold
they make idols for themselves
to their own destruction.
5 Samaria, throw out your calf-idol!
My anger burns against them.
How long will they be incapable of purity?
6   They are from Israel!
This calf—a metalworker has made it;
it is not God.
It will be broken in pieces,
that calf of Samaria.

7 "They sow the wind
and reap the whirlwind.
The stalk has no head;
it will produce no flour.
Were it to yield grain,
foreigners would swallow it up.
8 Israel is swallowed up;
now she is among the nations
like something no one wants.
9 For they have gone up to Assyria
like a wild donkey wandering alone.
Ephraim has sold herself to lovers.
10 Although they have sold themselves
among the nations,
I will now gather them together.
They will begin to waste away
under the oppression of the mighty king.

11 "Though Ephraim built many altars for sin offerings,
these have become altars for sinning.
12 I wrote for them the many things of my law,
but they regarded them as something foreign.
13 Though they offer sacrifices as gifts to me,
and though they eat the meat,
the LORD is not pleased with them.
Now he will remember their wickedness
and punish their sins:
They will return to Egypt.
14 Israel has forgotten their Maker
and built palaces;
Judah has fortified many towns.
But I will send fire on their cities
that will consume their fortresses."

Punishment for Israel

9 Do not rejoice, Israel;
do not be jubilant like the other nations.
For you have been unfaithful to your God;
you love the wages of a prostitute
at every threshing floor.
2 Threshing floors and winepresses will not feed the people;
the new wine will fail them.
3 They will not remain in the LORD's land;
Ephraim will return to Egypt
and eat unclean food in Assyria.
4 They will not pour out wine offerings to the LORD,
nor will their sacrifices please him.
Such sacrifices will be to them like the bread of mourners;
all who eat them will be unclean.
This food will be for themselves;
it will not come into the temple of the LORD.

5 What will you do on the day of your appointed festivals,
on the feast days of the LORD?

⁶Even if they escape from destruction,
  Egypt will gather them,
  and Memphis will bury them.
Their treasures of silver will be taken
    over by briers,
  and thorns will overrun their tents.
⁷The days of punishment are coming,
  the days of reckoning are at hand.
  Let Israel know this.
Because your sins are so many
  and your hostility so great,
the prophet is considered a fool,
  the inspired person a maniac.
⁸The prophet, along with my God,
  is the watchman over Ephraim,ᵃ
yet snares await him on all his
    paths,
  and hostility in the house of his
    God.
⁹They have sunk deep into corruption,
  as in the days of Gibeah.
God will remember their wickedness
  and punish them for their sins.

¹⁰"When I found Israel,
  it was like finding grapes in the
    desert;
when I saw your ancestors,
  it was like seeing the early fruit on
    the fig tree.
But when they came to Baal Peor,
  they consecrated themselves to
    that shameful idol
  and became as vile as the thing
    they loved.
¹¹Ephraim's glory will fly away like a
    bird—
  no birth, no pregnancy, no
    conception.
¹²Even if they rear children,
  I will bereave them of every one.
Woe to them
  when I turn away from them!
¹³I have seen Ephraim, like Tyre,
  planted in a pleasant place.
But Ephraim will bring out
  their children to the slayer."
¹⁴Give them, LORD—
  what will you give them?
Give them wombs that miscarry
  and breasts that are dry.

¹⁵"Because of all their wickedness in
    Gilgal,
  I hated them there.
Because of their sinful deeds,
  I will drive them out of my house.
I will no longer love them;
  all their leaders are rebellious.
¹⁶Ephraim is blighted,
  their root is withered,
  they yield no fruit.
Even if they bear children,
  I will slay their cherished offspring."

¹⁷My God will reject them
  because they have not obeyed him;
  they will be wanderers among the
    nations.

10 Israel was a spreading vine;
  he brought forth fruit for himself.
As his fruit increased,
  he built more altars;
as his land prospered,
  he adorned his sacred stones.
²Their heart is deceitful,
  and now they must bear their guilt.
The LORD will demolish their altars
  and destroy their sacred stones.

³Then they will say, "We have no king
  because we did not revere the LORD.
But even if we had a king,
  what could he do for us?"
⁴They make many promises,
  take false oaths
  and make agreements;
therefore lawsuits spring up
  like poisonous weeds in a plowed
    field.
⁵The people who live in Samaria fear
  for the calf-idol of Beth Aven.ᵇ
Its people will mourn over it,
  and so will its idolatrous priests,
those who had rejoiced over its
    splendor,
  because it is taken from them into
    exile.
⁶It will be carried to Assyria
  as tribute for the great king.
Ephraim will be disgraced;
  Israel will be ashamed of its foreign
    alliances.

ᵃ 8 Or *The prophet is the watchman over Ephraim, / the people of my God*   ᵇ 5 *Beth Aven* means *house of wickedness* (a
derogatory name for Bethel, which means *house of God*).

⁷Samaria's king will be destroyed,
  swept away like a twig on the
    surface of the waters.
⁸The high places of wickednessᵃ will be
      destroyed—
  it is the sin of Israel.
Thorns and thistles will grow up
  and cover their altars.
Then they will say to the mountains,
    "Cover us!"
  and to the hills, "Fall on us!"

⁹"Since the days of Gibeah, you have
    sinned, Israel,
  and there you have remained.ᵇ
Will not war again overtake
  the evildoers in Gibeah?
¹⁰When I please, I will punish them;
  nations will be gathered against
      them
  to put them in bonds for their
      double sin.
¹¹Ephraim is a trained heifer
    that loves to thresh;
  so I will put a yoke
    on her fair neck.
I will drive Ephraim,
    Judah must plow,
  and Jacob must break up the
      ground.

Hosea 11

Q: How did Israel repay God's
fatherly love?

BONUS: How did God feel about
them then?

Answers on next page

¹²Sow righteousness for yourselves,
  reap the fruit of unfailing love,
and break up your unplowed
      ground;
  for it is time to seek the Lᴏʀᴅ,
until he comes
  and showers his righteousness on
      you.
¹³But you have planted wickedness,
  you have reaped evil,
  you have eaten the fruit of
      deception.
Because you have depended on your
      own strength
  and on your many warriors,
¹⁴the roar of battle will rise against your
      people,
  so that all your fortresses will be
      devastated—
as Shalman devastated Beth Arbel on
      the day of battle,
  when mothers were dashed to the
      ground with their children.
¹⁵So will it happen to you, Bethel,
  because your wickedness is
      great.
When that day dawns,
  the king of Israel will be completely
      destroyed.

God's Love for Israel

11 "When Israel was a child, I loved
    him,
  and out of Egypt I called my son.
²But the more they were called,
  the more they went away from me.ᶜ
They sacrificed to the Baals
  and they burned incense to
      images.
³It was I who taught Ephraim to
      walk,
  taking them by the arms;
but they did not realize
  it was I who healed them.
⁴I led them with cords of human
      kindness,
  with ties of love.
To them I was like one who lifts
  a little child to the cheek,
  and I bent down to feed them.

ᵃ 8 Hebrew *aven*, a reference to Beth Aven (a derogatory
name for Bethel); see verse 5.   ᵇ 9 *Or there a stand was
taken*   ᶜ 2 Septuagint; Hebrew *them*

5 "Will they not return to Egypt
and will not Assyria rule over them
because they refuse to repent?
6 A sword will flash in their cities;
it will devour their false prophets
and put an end to their plans.
7 My people are determined to turn
from me.
Even though they call me God Most
High,
I will by no means exalt them.

8 "How can I give you up, Ephraim?
How can I hand you over, Israel?
How can I treat you like Admah?
How can I make you like Zeboyim?
My heart is changed within me;
all my compassion is aroused.
9 I will not carry out my fierce anger,
nor will I devastate Ephraim again.
For I am God, and not a man—
the Holy One among you.
I will not come against their
cities.
10 They will follow the LORD;
he will roar like a lion.
When he roars,
his children will come trembling
from the west.
11 They will come from Egypt,
trembling like sparrows,
from Assyria, fluttering like
doves.
I will settle them in their homes,"
declares the LORD.

Israel's Sin

12 Ephraim has surrounded me with lies,
Israel with deceit.
And Judah is unruly against God,
even against the faithful Holy One.[a]

12 [b] 1 Ephraim feeds on the wind;
he pursues the east wind all day
and multiplies lies and violence.
He makes a treaty with Assyria
and sends olive oil to Egypt.
2 The LORD has a charge to bring against
Judah;
he will punish Jacob[c] according to
his ways
and repay him according to his
deeds.

A: By deserting him for idols
(Hosea 11:2).

BONUS: He kept on loving them
(11:8).

3 In the womb he grasped his brother's
heel;
as a man he struggled with God.
4 He struggled with the angel and
overcame him;
he wept and begged for his favor.
He found him at Bethel
and talked with him there—
5 the LORD God Almighty,
the LORD is his name!
6 But you must return to your God;
maintain love and justice,
and wait for your God always.

7 The merchant uses dishonest scales
and loves to defraud.
8 Ephraim boasts,
"I am very rich; I have become
wealthy.
With all my wealth they will not find in
me
any iniquity or sin."

9 "I have been the LORD your God
ever since you came out of Egypt;
I will make you live in tents again,
as in the days of your appointed
festivals.

---

a 12 In Hebrew texts this verse (11:12) is numbered 12:1.   b In Hebrew texts 12:1-14 is numbered 12:2-15.
c 2 Jacob means he grasps the heel, a Hebrew idiom for he takes advantage of or he deceives.

¹⁰ I spoke to the prophets,
  gave them many visions
  and told parables through them."

¹¹ Is Gilead wicked?
  Its people are worthless!
  Do they sacrifice bulls in Gilgal?
  Their altars will be like piles of
    stones
  on a plowed field.
¹² Jacob fled to the country of Aram*ª*;
  Israel served to get a wife,
  and to pay for her he tended sheep.
¹³ The Lᴏʀᴅ used a prophet to bring
    Israel up from Egypt,
  by a prophet he cared for him.
¹⁴ But Ephraim has aroused his bitter
    anger;
  his Lord will leave on him the guilt
    of his bloodshed
  and will repay him for his contempt.

The Lᴏʀᴅ's Anger Against Israel

13 When Ephraim spoke, people
    trembled;
  he was exalted in Israel.
  But he became guilty of Baal
    worship and died.
² Now they sin more and more;
  they make idols for themselves
    from their silver,
  cleverly fashioned images,
  all of them the work of craftsmen.
  It is said of these people,
  "They offer human sacrifices!
  They kiss*ᵇ* calf-idols!"
³ Therefore they will be like the morning
    mist,
  like the early dew that disappears,
  like chaff swirling from a threshing
    floor,
  like smoke escaping through a
    window.

⁴ "But I have been the Lᴏʀᴅ your God
    ever since you came out of Egypt.
  You shall acknowledge no God
    but me,
  no Savior except me.
⁵ I cared for you in the wilderness,
  in the land of burning heat.

⁶ When I fed them, they were satisfied;
  when they were satisfied, they
    became proud;
  then they forgot me.
⁷ So I will be like a lion to them,
  like a leopard I will lurk by the path.
⁸ Like a bear robbed of her cubs,
  I will attack them and rip them
    open;
  like a lion I will devour them—
  a wild animal will tear them apart.

⁹ "You are destroyed, Israel,
  because you are against me,
    against your helper.
¹⁰ Where is your king, that he may save
    you?
  Where are your rulers in all your
    towns,
  of whom you said,
  'Give me a king and princes'?
¹¹ So in my anger I gave you a king,
  and in my wrath I took him away.
¹² The guilt of Ephraim is stored up,
  his sins are kept on record.
¹³ Pains as of a woman in childbirth
    come to him,
  but he is a child without wisdom;
  when the time arrives,
  he doesn't have the sense to come
    out of the womb.

¹⁴ "I will deliver this people from the
    power of the grave;
  I will redeem them from death.
  Where, O death, are your plagues?
  Where, O grave, is your
    destruction?

  "I will have no compassion,
¹⁵   even though he thrives among his
    brothers.
  An east wind from the Lᴏʀᴅ will come,
  blowing in from the desert;
  his spring will fail
  and his well dry up.
  His storehouse will be plundered
  of all its treasures.
¹⁶ The people of Samaria must bear their
    guilt,
  because they have rebelled against
    their God.
  They will fall by the sword;

ª 12 That is, Northwest Mesopotamia   *ᵇ* 2 Or *"Men who sacrifice / kiss*

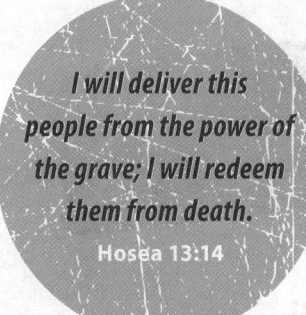

I will deliver this people from the power of the grave; I will redeem them from death.

Hosea 13:14

their little ones will be dashed to
the ground,
their pregnant women ripped
open."[a]

Repentance to Bring Blessing

14[b] Return, Israel, to the Lord your
God.
Your sins have been your downfall!
[2] Take words with you
and return to the Lord.
Say to him:
"Forgive all our sins
and receive us graciously,
that we may offer the fruit of our
lips.[c]
[3] Assyria cannot save us;
we will not mount warhorses.
We will never again say 'Our gods'
to what our own hands have made,
for in you the fatherless find
compassion."

[4] "I will heal their waywardness
and love them freely,
for my anger has turned away from
them.
[5] I will be like the dew to Israel;
he will blossom like a lily.
Like a cedar of Lebanon
he will send down his roots;
[6]   his young shoots will grow.
His splendor will be like an olive tree,
his fragrance like a cedar of
Lebanon.
[7] People will dwell again in his shade;
they will flourish like the grain,
they will blossom like the vine—
Israel's fame will be like the wine of
Lebanon.
[8] Ephraim, what more have I[d] to do with
idols?
I will answer him and care for him.
I am like a flourishing juniper;
your fruitfulness comes from me."

[9] Who is wise? Let them realize these
things.
Who is discerning? Let them
understand.
The ways of the Lord are right;
the righteous walk in them,
but the rebellious stumble in them.

---

[a] 16 In Hebrew texts this verse (13:16) is numbered 14:1.   [b] In Hebrew texts 14:1-9 is numbered 14:2-10.
[c] 2 Or offer our lips as sacrifices of bulls   [d] 8 Or Hebrew; Septuagint What more has Ephraim

JOEL

‹‹preview

Joel preaches in Judah. His prophecies are undated.

Locusts travel in great swarms, some covering 2,000 square miles. They eat every green plant, leaving empty, munched-down land when they move on.

Deuteronomy 28:42 identifies locusts as a divine judgment.

"The day of the LORD" in Old Testament prophecies usually refers to terrible judgments to come at history's end (Joel 1:15; 2:1,11,31; 3:14).

Divine Judgment.

Is a California earthquake a judgment from God? Is AIDS a divine warning? When something bad happens to you, is God shouting in your ear?

A terrible cloud of locusts destroyed all the vegetation in Israel. Animals and people were threatened with starvation. Joel saw this as a divine judgment. In the second half of his little book, Joel predicts that at history's end God will send a human army just as great to swarm into Israel and punish his sinning people. God does punish sin. But in the end God saves.

››THE BUZZ ON GOD'S WARNING SYSTEM
Disaster message, according to Joel 1

››"DAY OF THE LORD" MEANS DISASTER!
See descriptions in Joel 2:1–11

››GOOD NEWS "AFTERWARD"
Promises reported in Joel 2:28–32

When Joel described a locust swarm as a warning from God, leather scrolls were replacing clay tablets, Hesiod was penning wild stories about the creation of the world, and Etruscan city-states were emerging in Italy.

1 The word of the LORD that came to Joel son of Pethuel.

An Invasion of Locusts

2 Hear this, you elders;
   listen, all who live in the land.
   Has anything like this ever happened
      in your days
   or in the days of your ancestors?
3 Tell it to your children,
   and let your children tell it to their
      children,
   and their children to the next
      generation.
4 What the locust swarm has left
   the great locusts have eaten;
what the great locusts have left
   the young locusts have eaten;
what the young locusts have left
   other locusts^a have eaten.

5 Wake up, you drunkards, and weep!
   Wail, all you drinkers of wine;
wail because of the new wine,
   for it has been snatched from your
      lips.
6 A nation has invaded my land,
   a mighty army without number;
it has the teeth of a lion,
   the fangs of a lioness.
7 It has laid waste my vines
   and ruined my fig trees.
It has stripped off their bark
   and thrown it away,
   leaving their branches white.

8 Mourn like a virgin in sackcloth
   grieving for the betrothed of her
      youth.
9 Grain offerings and drink offerings
   are cut off from the house of the
      LORD.
The priests are in mourning,
   those who minister before the LORD.
10 The fields are ruined,
   the ground is dried up;
the grain is destroyed,
   the new wine is dried up,
   the olive oil fails.

11 Despair, you farmers,
   wail, you vine growers;

grieve for the wheat and the barley,
   because the harvest of the field is
      destroyed.
12 The vine is dried up
   and the fig tree is withered;
the pomegranate, the palm and the
   apple^b tree—
all the trees of the field—are
   dried up.
Surely the people's joy
   is withered away.

A Call to Lamentation

13 Put on sackcloth, you priests, and
      mourn;
   wail, you who minister before the
      altar.
Come, spend the night in
      sackcloth,
   you who minister before my
      God;
for the grain offerings and drink
      offerings
   are withheld from the house of your
      God.
14 Declare a holy fast;
   call a sacred assembly.
Summon the elders
   and all who live in the land
to the house of the LORD your God,
   and cry out to the LORD.

15 Alas for that day!
   For the day of the LORD is near;
   it will come like destruction from
      the Almighty.^c

16 Has not the food been cut off
   before our very eyes—
joy and gladness
   from the house of our God?
17 The seeds are shriveled
   beneath the clods.^d
The storehouses are in ruins,
   the granaries have been broken
      down,
   for the grain has dried up.
18 How the cattle moan!
   The herds mill about
because they have no pasture;
   even the flocks of sheep are
      suffering.

---

^a 4 The precise meaning of the four Hebrew words used here for locusts is uncertain.   ^b 12 Or possibly apricot
^c 15 Hebrew Shaddai   ^d 17 The meaning of the Hebrew for this word is uncertain.

¹⁹ To you, LORD, I call,
    for fire has devoured the pastures
        in the wilderness
    and flames have burned up all the
        trees of the field.
²⁰ Even the wild animals pant for you;
    the streams of water have dried up
    and fire has devoured the pastures
        in the wilderness.

An Army of Locusts

2 Blow the trumpet in Zion;
    sound the alarm on my holy hill.

Let all who live in the land tremble,
    for the day of the LORD is coming.
It is close at hand—
²   a day of darkness and gloom,
        a day of clouds and blackness.
Like dawn spreading across the
            mountains
    a large and mighty army comes,
such as never was in ancient times
    nor ever will be in ages to come.

³ Before them fire devours,
    behind them a flame blazes.
Before them the land is like the
            garden of Eden,
    behind them, a desert waste—
        nothing escapes them.
⁴ They have the appearance of
            horses;
    they gallop along like cavalry.
⁵ With a noise like that of chariots
    they leap over the mountaintops,
like a crackling fire consuming
            stubble,
    like a mighty army drawn up for
        battle.

⁶ At the sight of them, nations are in
            anguish;
    every face turns pale.
⁷ They charge like warriors;
    they scale walls like soldiers.
They all march in line,
    not swerving from their course.
⁸ They do not jostle each other;
    each marches straight ahead.
They plunge through defenses
    without breaking ranks.
⁹ They rush upon the city;
    they run along the wall.

They climb into the houses;
    like thieves they enter through the
        windows.

¹⁰ Before them the earth shakes,
    the heavens tremble,
the sun and moon are darkened,
    and the stars no longer shine.
¹¹ The LORD thunders
    at the head of his army;
his forces are beyond number,
    and mighty is the army that obeys
        his command.
The day of the LORD is great;
    it is dreadful.
Who can endure it?

Rend Your Heart

12 "Even now," declares the Lord,
    "return to me with all your heart,
    with fasting and weeping and
        mourning."

13 Rend your heart
    and not your garments.
Return to the Lord your God,
    for he is gracious and
        compassionate,
    slow to anger and abounding in love,
    and he relents from sending
        calamity.
14 Who knows? He may turn and relent
    and leave behind a blessing—
grain offerings and drink offerings
    for the Lord your God.

15 Blow the trumpet in Zion,
    declare a holy fast,
    call a sacred assembly.
16 Gather the people,
    consecrate the assembly;
    bring together the elders,
    gather the children,
    those nursing at the breast.
Let the bridegroom leave his room
    and the bride her chamber.
17 Let the priests, who minister before
        the Lord,
    weep between the portico and the
        altar.
Let them say, "Spare your people,
    Lord.
    Do not make your inheritance an
        object of scorn,
    a byword among the nations.
Why should they say among the
        peoples,
    'Where is their God?' "

The Lord's Answer

18 Then the Lord was jealous for his land
    and took pity on his people.

19 The Lord replied[a] to them:

"I am sending you grain, new wine and
        olive oil,
    enough to satisfy you fully;
never again will I make you
    an object of scorn to the nations.

20 "I will drive the northern horde far
        from you,
    pushing it into a parched and
        barren land;
its eastern ranks will drown in the
        Dead Sea
    and its western ranks in the
        Mediterranean Sea.
And its stench will go up;
    its smell will rise."

Surely he has done great things!
21   Do not be afraid, land of Judah;
    be glad and rejoice.
Surely the Lord has done great things!
22   Do not be afraid, you wild animals,
    for the pastures in the wilderness
        are becoming green.
The trees are bearing their fruit;
    the fig tree and the vine yield their
        riches.
23 Be glad, people of Zion,
    rejoice in the Lord your God,
for he has given you the autumn rains
        because he is faithful.
He sends you abundant showers,
    both autumn and spring rains, as
        before.
24 The threshing floors will be filled with
        grain;
    the vats will overflow with new wine
        and oil.

25 "I will repay you for the years the
        locusts have eaten—
    the great locust and the young
        locust,
    the other locusts and the locust
        swarm[b]—

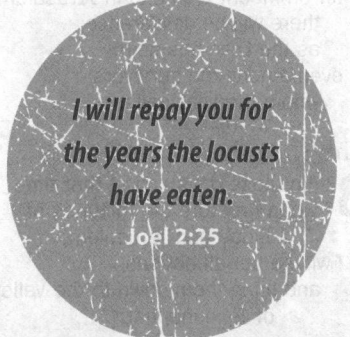

I will repay you for
the years the locusts
have eaten.
Joel 2:25

---

a 18,19 Or Lord will be jealous . . . / and take pity . . . / 19The Lord will reply   b 25 The precise meaning of the four
Hebrew words used here for locusts is uncertain.

my great army that I sent among you.
²⁶ You will have plenty to eat, until you
    are full,
    and you will praise the name of the
        LORD your God,
    who has worked wonders for you;
    never again will my people be
        shamed.
²⁷ Then you will know that I am in
    Israel,
    that I am the LORD your God,
    and that there is no other;
    never again will my people be
        shamed.

The Day of the LORD

²⁸ "And afterward,
    I will pour out my Spirit on all
        people.
    Your sons and daughters will
        prophesy,
    your old men will dream dreams,
    your young men will see visions.
²⁹ Even on my servants, both men and
    women,
    I will pour out my Spirit in those
        days.
³⁰ I will show wonders in the heavens
    and on the earth,
    blood and fire and billows of
        smoke.
³¹ The sun will be turned to darkness
    and the moon to blood
    before the coming of the great and
        dreadful day of the LORD.
³² And everyone who calls
    on the name of the LORD will be
        saved;
    for on Mount Zion and in Jerusalem
    there will be deliverance,
    as the LORD has said,
    even among the survivors
    whom the LORD calls.ᵃ

The Nations Judged

3 ᵇ "In those days and at that time,
    when I restore the fortunes of
        Judah and Jerusalem,
² I will gather all nations
    and bring them down to the Valley
        of Jehoshaphat.ᶜ

INSTANT ACCESS

Sometimes life just doesn't seem like it's worth living. One national survey indicated that about 24 percent of teenage girls consider suicide in any given year. Many attempt suicide. And some succeed. Joel describes some terrors that will drive many in Judah to despair. But he also gives them God's wonderful promise: "Return to me with all your heart . . . I will repay you for the years the locusts have eaten" (Joel 2:12,25). One day you too are likely to be so hurt or disappointed you feel life isn't worth living. But really, it is. Turn to God, and know that he will more than repay your pain with good things in your future.

{Joel 2:12–27}

There I will put them on trial
    for what they did to my inheritance,
        my people Israel,
    because they scattered my people
        among the nations
    and divided up my land.
³ They cast lots for my people
    and traded boys for prostitutes;
    they sold girls for wine to drink.

⁴ "Now what have you against me, Tyre
and Sidon and all you regions of Philistia?

ᵃ 32 In Hebrew texts 2:28-32 is numbered 3:1-5.   ᵇ In Hebrew texts 3:1-21 is numbered 4:1-21.   ᶜ 2 Jehoshaphat
means the LORD judges; also in verse 12.

Are you repaying me for something I have done? If you are paying me back, I will swiftly and speedily return on your own heads what you have done. ⁵For you took my silver and my gold and carried off my finest treasures to your temples.ᵃ ⁶You sold the people of Judah and Jerusalem to the Greeks, that you might send them far from their homeland.

⁷"See, I am going to rouse them out of the places to which you sold them, and I will return on your own heads what you have done. ⁸I will sell your sons and daughters to the people of Judah, and they will sell them to the Sabeans, a nation far away." The LORD has spoken.

⁹Proclaim this among the nations:
    Prepare for war!
Rouse the warriors!
    Let all the fighting men draw near
        and attack.
¹⁰Beat your plowshares into swords
    and your pruning hooks into spears.
Let the weakling say,
    "I am strong!"
¹¹Come quickly, all you nations from
        every side,
    and assemble there.

Bring down your warriors, LORD!

¹²"Let the nations be roused;
    let them advance into the Valley of
        Jehoshaphat,
for there I will sit
    to judge all the nations on every
        side.

¹³Swing the sickle,
    for the harvest is ripe.
Come, trample the grapes,
    for the winepress is full
    and the vats overflow—
so great is their wickedness!"

¹⁴Multitudes, multitudes
    in the valley of decision!
For the day of the LORD is near
    in the valley of decision.
¹⁵The sun and moon will be
        darkened,
    and the stars no longer shine.
¹⁶The LORD will roar from Zion
    and thunder from Jerusalem;
    the earth and the heavens will
        tremble.
But the LORD will be a refuge for his
        people,
    a stronghold for the people of
        Israel.

Blessings for God's People

¹⁷"Then you will know that I, the LORD
        your God,
    dwell in Zion, my holy hill.
Jerusalem will be holy;
    never again will foreigners invade
        her.

¹⁸"In that day the mountains will drip
        new wine,
    and the hills will flow with milk;
    all the ravines of Judah will run with
        water.

ᵃ 5 Or palaces

PANORAMA

Divine Judgment.

Joel predicts that at history's end God will send a human army to swarm into the Holy Land and punish his sinning people. God punishes sin. But in the end God saves.

{JOEL}

A fountain will flow out of the Lord's
    house
and will water the valley of acacias.[a]
19 But Egypt will be desolate,
    Edom a desert waste,
because of violence done to the
        people of Judah,
    in whose land they shed innocent
        blood.

20 Judah will be inhabited
        forever
    and Jerusalem through all
        generations.
21 Shall I leave their innocent blood
        unavenged?
    No, I will not."

The Lord dwells in Zion!

---

a 18 Or Valley of Shittim

AMOS

Tired of It?

Do you sometimes wish people would stop complaining about being poor? Why don't they go out and get a job? But isn't that kind of a selfish attitude? If you've got it so good, why shouldn't you share with those who don't?

The prophet Amos lived in Israel in a time of prosperity. Yet the rich cared more about their luxuries than about people. Amos warned that any society that isn't fair to poor people will be judged. Christians should be generous and should fight for justice for the poor.

>>**JUST LIKE TODAY'S TV NEWS**
Check it out in Amos 2:6–8

>>**HE SPOKE, THEY DIDN'T LISTEN**
Details in Amos 4:6–13

>>**IT'S NOT WISE TO DO WRONG**
Reasons explained, see Amos 5:10–17

>>**AMOS WON'T SHUT HIS MOUTH**
Story in Amos 7:10–17

preview

Amos is a rancher in Judah when God tells him to go preach in Israel.

Israel is rich and powerful in Amos' day, but the wealthy exploit the poor.

In the 760's B.C. as Amos preaches in Israel, barbarian tribes sack Hao in China, ending the Zhou dynasty. Duach I Fionn is High King of Ireland. Aischines wins the Stadion race in the Olympics.

1 The words of Amos, one of the shepherds of Tekoa—the vision he saw concerning Israel two years before the earthquake, when Uzziah was king of Judah and Jeroboam son of Jehoash[a] was king of Israel. ²He said:

"The LORD roars from Zion
    and thunders from Jerusalem;
the pastures of the shepherds
    dry up,
    and the top of Carmel withers."

Judgment on Israel's Neighbors

³This is what the LORD says:

"For three sins of Damascus,
    even for four, I will not relent.
Because she threshed Gilead
    with sledges having iron teeth,
⁴I will send fire on the house of
        Hazael
    that will consume the fortresses of
        Ben-Hadad.
⁵I will break down the gate of
        Damascus;
    I will destroy the king who is in[b] the
        Valley of Aven[c]
and the one who holds the scepter in
        Beth Eden.
The people of Aram will go into exile
        to Kir,"
                        says the LORD.

⁶This is what the LORD says:

"For three sins of Gaza,
    even for four, I will not relent.
Because she took captive whole
        communities
    and sold them to Edom,
⁷I will send fire on the walls of Gaza
    that will consume her fortresses.
⁸I will destroy the king[d] of Ashdod
    and the one who holds the scepter
        in Ashkelon.
I will turn my hand against Ekron,
    till the last of the Philistines are
        dead,"
            says the Sovereign LORD.

⁹This is what the LORD says:

"For three sins of Tyre,
    even for four, I will not relent.
Because she sold whole communities
        of captives to Edom,
    disregarding a treaty of
        brotherhood,
¹⁰I will send fire on the walls of Tyre
    that will consume her fortresses."

¹¹This is what the LORD says:

"For three sins of Edom,
    even for four, I will not relent.
Because he pursued his brother with
        a sword
    and slaughtered the women of the
        land,
because his anger raged continually
    and his fury flamed unchecked,
¹²I will send fire on Teman
    that will consume the fortresses of
        Bozrah."

¹³This is what the LORD says:

"For three sins of Ammon,
    even for four, I will not relent.
Because he ripped open the pregnant
        women of Gilead
    in order to extend his borders,
¹⁴I will set fire to the walls of Rabbah
    that will consume her fortresses
amid war cries on the day of battle,
    amid violent winds on a stormy
        day.
¹⁵Her king[e] will go into exile,
    he and his officials together,"
                        says the LORD.

2 This is what the LORD says:

"For three sins of Moab,
    even for four, I will not relent.
Because he burned to ashes
    the bones of Edom's king,
²I will send fire on Moab
    that will consume the fortresses of
        Kerioth.[f]
Moab will go down in great
        tumult
    amid war cries and the blast of the
        trumpet.

ᵃ 1 Hebrew *Joash,* a variant of *Jehoash*   ᵇ 5 Or *the inhabitants of*   ᶜ 5 *Aven* means *wickedness.*   ᵈ 8 Or *inhabitants*
ᵉ 15 Or / *Molek*   ᶠ 2 Or *of her cities*

³I will destroy her ruler
and kill all her officials with him,"
says the LORD.

⁴This is what the LORD says:

"For three sins of Judah,
even for four, I will not relent.
Because they have rejected the law of
the LORD
and have not kept his decrees,
because they have been led astray by
false gods,ᵃ
the godsᵇ their ancestors
followed,
⁵I will send fire on Judah
that will consume the fortresses of
Jerusalem."

Judgment on Israel

⁶This is what the LORD says:

"For three sins of Israel,
even for four, I will not relent.
They sell the innocent for silver,
and the needy for a pair of
sandals.
⁷They trample on the heads of the
poor
as on the dust of the ground
and deny justice to the
oppressed.
Father and son use the same girl
and so profane my holy name.
⁸They lie down beside every altar
on garments taken in pledge.

ᵃ 4 Or by lies   ᵇ 4 Or lies

TO THE POINT

Change

Were Bible times so different from today? Here's one way to check. Read today's newspaper, then read Amos 2:6–8. Were the events of Amos' day anything like the events recorded in today's news?

Every generation thinks things are different for them. It's true that your world is different from the world in which your parents grew up. But one thing never changes—the fact that you have a choice to make. You can choose to live God's way, even though it may be hard sometimes. Or you can choose to be greedy and sinful, to hurt rather than help others. Remember, God loves you—and that will never change.

In the house of their god
    they drink wine taken as fines.

9 "Yet I destroyed the Amorites before
    them,
    though they were tall as the
        cedars
    and strong as the oaks.
    I destroyed their fruit above
    and their roots below.
10 I brought you up out of Egypt
    and led you forty years in the
        wilderness
    to give you the land of the Amorites.

11 "I also raised up prophets from
        among your children
    and Nazirites from among your
        youths.
    Is this not true, people of Israel?"
                declares the LORD.
12 "But you made the Nazirites drink
        wine
    and commanded the prophets not
        to prophesy.

13 "Now then, I will crush you
    as a cart crushes when loaded with
        grain.
14 The swift will not escape,
    the strong will not muster their
        strength,
    and the warrior will not save his life.
15 The archer will not stand his
        ground,
    the fleet-footed soldier will not get
        away,
    and the horseman will not save his
        life.
16 Even the bravest warriors
    will flee naked on that day,"
                declares the LORD.

Witnesses Summoned Against Israel

3 Hear this word, people of Israel, the word the LORD has spoken against you—against the whole family I brought up out of Egypt:

2 "You only have I chosen
    of all the families of the earth;
    therefore I will punish you
    for all your sins."

3 Do two walk together
    unless they have agreed to do so?
4 Does a lion roar in the thicket
    when it has no prey?
    Does it growl in its den
    when it has caught nothing?
5 Does a bird swoop down to a trap on
        the ground
    when no bait is there?
    Does a trap spring up from the
        ground
    if it has not caught anything?
6 When a trumpet sounds in a city,
    do not the people tremble?
    When disaster comes to a city,
    has not the LORD caused it?

7 Surely the Sovereign LORD does
        nothing
    without revealing his plan
    to his servants the prophets.

8 The lion has roared—
    who will not fear?
    The Sovereign LORD has spoken—
    who can but prophesy?

9 Proclaim to the fortresses of
        Ashdod
    and to the fortresses of Egypt:
    "Assemble yourselves on the
        mountains of Samaria;
    see the great unrest within her
    and the oppression among her
        people."

10 "They do not know how to do right,"
        declares the LORD,
    "who store up in their fortresses
    what they have plundered and
        looted."

11 Therefore this is what the Sovereign
LORD says:

"An enemy will overrun your land,
    pull down your strongholds
    and plunder your fortresses."

12 This is what the LORD says:

"As a shepherd rescues from the
        lion's mouth
    only two leg bones or a piece of an
        ear,
    so will the Israelites living in Samaria
        be rescued,

with only the head of a bed
and a piece of fabric*ᵃ* from a
couch.*ᵇ*"

¹³ "Hear this and testify against the descendants of Jacob," declares the Lord,
the Lᴏʀᴅ God Almighty.

¹⁴ "On the day I punish Israel for her
sins,
I will destroy the altars of Bethel;
the horns of the altar will be cut off
and fall to the ground.
¹⁵ I will tear down the winter house
along with the summer house;
the houses adorned with ivory will be
destroyed
and the mansions will be
demolished,"
declares the Lᴏʀᴅ.

Israel Has Not Returned to God

4 Hear this word, you cows of Bashan
on Mount Samaria,
you women who oppress the poor
and crush the needy
and say to your husbands, "Bring
us some drinks!"
² The Sovereign Lᴏʀᴅ has sworn by his
holiness:
"The time will surely come
when you will be taken away with
hooks,
the last of you with fishhooks.*ᶜ*
³ You will each go straight out
through breaches in the wall,
and you will be cast out toward
Harmon,*ᵈ*"
declares the Lᴏʀᴅ.

⁴ "Go to Bethel and sin;
go to Gilgal and sin yet more.
Bring your sacrifices every morning,
your tithes every three years.*ᵉ*
⁵ Burn leavened bread as a thank
offering
and brag about your freewill
offerings—

boast about them, you Israelites,
for this is what you love to do,"
declares the Sovereign Lᴏʀᴅ.

⁶ "I gave you empty stomachs in every
city
and lack of bread in every town,
yet you have not returned to me,"
declares the Lᴏʀᴅ.

⁷ "I also withheld rain from you
when the harvest was still three
months away.
I sent rain on one town,
but withheld it from another.
One field had rain;
another had none and dried up.
⁸ People staggered from town to town
for water
but did not get enough to drink,
yet you have not returned to me,"
declares the Lᴏʀᴅ.

⁹ "Many times I struck your gardens
and vineyards,
destroying them with blight and
mildew.
Locusts devoured your fig and olive
trees,
yet you have not returned to me,"
declares the Lᴏʀᴅ.

Amos 4

Q: What did Amos call some of
the women of Israel?

BONUS: Why did he call them
this?

Answers on next page

ᵃ 12 The meaning of the Hebrew for this phrase is
uncertain.   *ᵇ 12* Or *Israelites be rescued, / those who sit
in Samaria / on the edge of their beds / and in Damascus
on their couches.*   *ᶜ 2* Or *away in baskets, / the last of
you in fish baskets*   *ᵈ 3* Masoretic Text; with a different
word division of the Hebrew (see Septuagint) *out, you
mountain of oppression*   *ᵉ 4* Or *days*

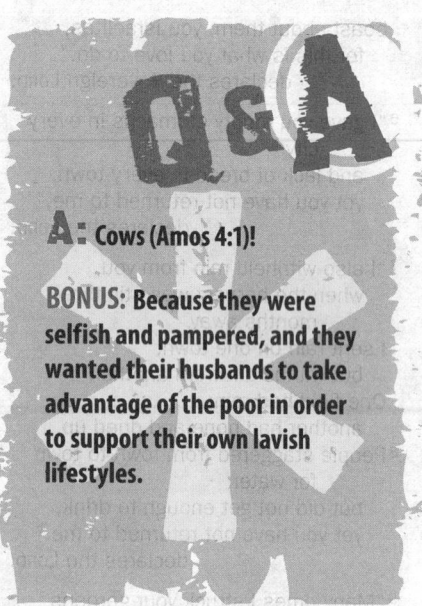

A: Cows (Amos 4:1)!

BONUS: Because they were selfish and pampered, and they wanted their husbands to take advantage of the poor in order to support their own lavish lifestyles.

10 "I sent plagues among you
as I did to Egypt.
I killed your young men with the
sword,
along with your captured horses.
I filled your nostrils with the stench of
your camps,
yet you have not returned to me,"
declares the LORD.

11 "I overthrew some of you
as I overthrew Sodom and
Gomorrah.
You were like a burning stick snatched
from the fire,
yet you have not returned to me,"
declares the LORD.

12 "Therefore this is what I will do to you,
Israel,
and because I will do this to you,
Israel,
prepare to meet your God."

13 He who forms the mountains,
who creates the wind,
and who reveals his thoughts to
mankind,

who turns dawn to darkness,
and treads on the heights of the
earth—
the LORD God Almighty is his name.

A Lament and Call to Repentance

5 Hear this word, Israel, this lament I
take up concerning you:

2 "Fallen is Virgin Israel,
never to rise again,
deserted in her own land,
with no one to lift her up."

3 This is what the Sovereign LORD says
to Israel:

"Your city that marches out a
thousand strong
will have only a hundred left;
your town that marches out a hundred
strong
will have only ten left."

4 This is what the LORD says to Israel:

"Seek me and live;
5   do not seek Bethel,
do not go to Gilgal,
do not journey to Beersheba.
For Gilgal will surely go into exile,
and Bethel will be reduced to
nothing.[a]"
6 Seek the LORD and live,
or he will sweep through the tribes
of Joseph like a fire;
it will devour them,
and Bethel will have no one to
quench it.

7 There are those who turn justice into
bitterness
and cast righteousness to the
ground.

8 He who made the Pleiades and Orion,
who turns midnight into dawn
and darkens day into night,
who calls for the waters of the sea
and pours them out over the face of
the land—
the LORD is his name.
9 With a blinding flash he destroys the
stronghold
and brings the fortified city to ruin.

---

a 5 Hebrew *aven*, a reference to Beth Aven (a derogatory name for Bethel); see Hosea 4:15.

10 There are those who hate the one who
   upholds justice in court
   and detest the one who tells the
   truth.

11 You levy a straw tax on the poor
   and impose a tax on their grain.
   Therefore, though you have built stone
   mansions,
   you will not live in them;
   though you have planted lush
   vineyards,
   you will not drink their wine.
12 For I know how many are your
   offenses
   and how great your sins.

There are those who oppress the
   innocent and take bribes
   and deprive the poor of justice in
   the courts.
13 Therefore the prudent keep quiet in
   such times,
   for the times are evil.

14 Seek good, not evil,
   that you may live.
   Then the LORD God Almighty will be
   with you,
   just as you say he is.
15 Hate evil, love good;
   maintain justice in the courts.
   Perhaps the LORD God Almighty will
   have mercy
   on the remnant of Joseph.

16 Therefore this is what the Lord, the
LORD God Almighty, says:

"There will be wailing in all the streets
   and cries of anguish in every public
   square.
The farmers will be summoned to
   weep
   and the mourners to wail.
17 There will be wailing in all the
   vineyards,
   for I will pass through your midst,"
                    says the LORD.

The Day of the LORD
18 Woe to you who long
   for the day of the LORD!
   Why do you long for the day of the
   LORD?
   That day will be darkness, not
   light.
19 It will be as though a man fled from a
   lion
   only to meet a bear,
   as though he entered his house
   and rested his hand on the wall
   only to have a snake bite him.
20 Will not the day of the LORD be
   darkness, not light—
   pitch-dark, without a ray of
   brightness?

21 "I hate, I despise your religious
   festivals;
   your assemblies are a stench to
   me.
22 Even though you bring me burnt
   offerings and grain offerings,
   I will not accept them.

PANORAMA

Tired of It?

**Amos warned that any society that isn't fair
to poor people will be judged. We should be
generous and fight for justice for the poor.**

{AMOS}

Though you bring choice fellowship
offerings,
I will have no regard for them.
23 Away with the noise of your songs!
I will not listen to the music of your
harps.
24 But let justice roll on like a river,
righteousness like a never-failing
stream!

25 "Did you bring me sacrifices and
offerings
forty years in the wilderness,
people of Israel?
26 You have lifted up the shrine of your
king,
the pedestal of your idols,
the star of your god*a* —
which you made for yourselves.
27 Therefore I will send you into exile
beyond Damascus,"
says the LORD, whose name is God
Almighty.

Woe to the Complacent

6 Woe to you who are complacent in
Zion,
and to you who feel secure on
Mount Samaria,
you notable men of the foremost
nation,
to whom the people of Israel
come!
2 Go to Kalneh and look at it;
go from there to great Hamath,
and then go down to Gath in
Philistia.
Are they better off than your two
kingdoms?
Is their land larger than yours?
3 You put off the day of disaster
and bring near a reign of terror.
4 You lie on beds adorned with ivory
and lounge on your couches.
You dine on choice lambs
and fattened calves.
5 You strum away on your harps like
David
and improvise on musical
instruments.

6 You drink wine by the bowlful
and use the finest lotions,
but you do not grieve over the ruin
of Joseph.
7 Therefore you will be among the first
to go into exile;
your feasting and lounging will end.

The LORD Abhors the Pride of Israel

8 The Sovereign LORD has sworn by himself—the LORD God Almighty declares:

"I abhor the pride of Jacob
and detest his fortresses;
I will deliver up the city
and everything in it."

9 If ten people are left in one house,
they too will die. 10 And if the relative who
comes to carry the bodies out of the
house to burn them*b* asks anyone who
might be hiding there, "Is anyone else
with you?" and he says, "No," then he will
go on to say, "Hush! We must not mention the name of the LORD."

11 For the LORD has given the
command,
and he will smash the great house
into pieces
and the small house into bits.

12 Do horses run on the rocky crags?
Does one plow the sea*c* with
oxen?
But you have turned justice into
poison
and the fruit of righteousness into
bitterness—
13 you who rejoice in the conquest of Lo
Debar*d*
and say, "Did we not take Karnaim*e*
by our own strength?"

14 For the LORD God Almighty declares,
"I will stir up a nation against you,
Israel,
that will oppress you all the way
from Lebo Hamath to the valley of
the Arabah."

Locusts, Fire and a Plumb Line

7 This is what the Sovereign LORD showed me: He was preparing swarms of locusts after the king's share had been harvested and just as the late crops were coming up. ²When they had stripped the land clean, I cried out, "Sovereign LORD, forgive! How can Jacob survive? He is so small!"

³So the LORD relented.

"This will not happen," the LORD said.

⁴This is what the Sovereign LORD showed me: The Sovereign LORD was calling for judgment by fire; it dried up the great deep and devoured the land. ⁵Then I cried out, "Sovereign LORD, I beg you, stop! How can Jacob survive? He is so small!"

⁶So the LORD relented.

"This will not happen either," the Sovereign LORD said.

⁷This is what he showed me: The Lord was standing by a wall that had been built true to plumb,ᵃ with a plumb lineᵇ in his hand. ⁸And the LORD asked me, "What do you see, Amos?"

"A plumb line," I replied.

Then the Lord said, "Look, I am setting a plumb line among my people Israel; I will spare them no longer.

⁹ "The high places of Isaac will be
        destroyed
    and the sanctuaries of Israel will be
        ruined;
    with my sword I will rise against the
        house of Jeroboam."

Amos and Amaziah

¹⁰Then Amaziah the priest of Bethel sent a message to Jeroboam king of Israel: "Amos is raising a conspiracy against you in the very heart of Israel. The land cannot bear all his words. ¹¹For this is what Amos is saying:

" 'Jeroboam will die by the sword,
    and Israel will surely go into exile,
        away from their native land.' "

¹²Then Amaziah said to Amos, "Get out, you seer! Go back to the land of Judah. Earn your bread there and do your prophesying there. ¹³Don't prophesy anymore at Bethel, because this is the king's sanctuary and the temple of the kingdom."

¹⁴Amos answered Amaziah, "I was neither a prophet nor the son of a prophet, but I was a shepherd, and I also took care of sycamore-fig trees. ¹⁵But the LORD took me from tending the flock and said to me, 'Go, prophesy to my people Israel.' ¹⁶Now then, hear the word of the LORD. You say,

" 'Do not prophesy against Israel,
    and stop preaching against the
        descendants of Isaac.'

¹⁷"Therefore this is what the LORD says:

" 'Your wife will become a prostitute in
        the city,
    and your sons and daughters will
        fall by the sword.
Your land will be measured and
        divided up,
    and you yourself will die in a paganᶜ
        country.
And Israel will surely go into exile,
    away from their native land.' "

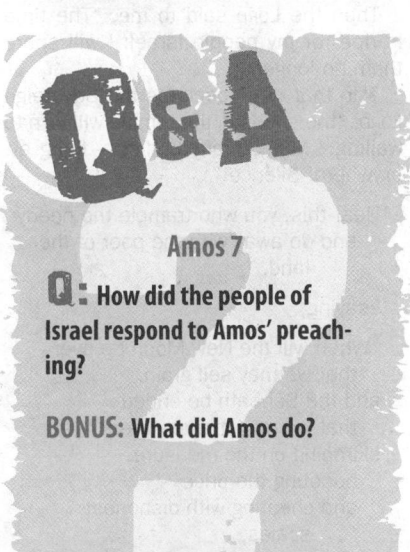

Amos 7

Q: How did the people of Israel respond to Amos' preaching?

BONUS: What did Amos do?

Answers on next page

ᵃ 7 The meaning of the Hebrew for this phrase is uncertain.   ᵇ 7 The meaning of the Hebrew for this phrase is uncertain; also in verse 8.   ᶜ 17 Hebrew *an unclean*

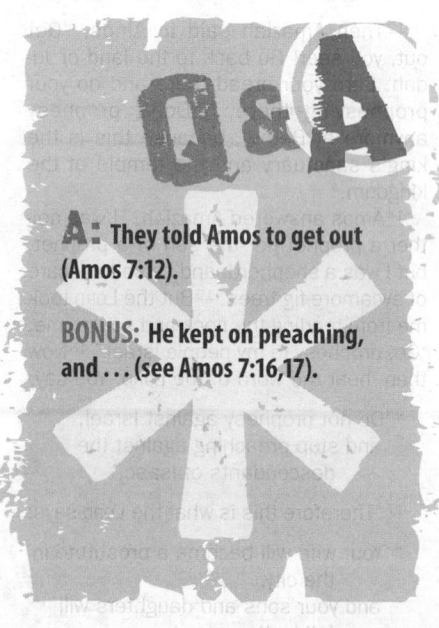

A: They told Amos to get out (Amos 7:12).

BONUS: He kept on preaching, and . . . (see Amos 7:16,17).

A Basket of Ripe Fruit

8 This is what the Sovereign LORD showed me: a basket of ripe fruit. 2 "What do you see, Amos?" he asked.

"A basket of ripe fruit," I answered.

Then the LORD said to me, "The time is ripe for my people Israel; I will spare them no longer.

3 "In that day," declares the Sovereign LORD, "the songs in the temple will turn to wailing.[a] Many, many bodies—flung everywhere! Silence!"

4 Hear this, you who trample the needy
　　and do away with the poor of the
　　land,

5 saying,

"When will the New Moon be over
　　that we may sell grain,
and the Sabbath be ended
　　that we may market wheat?"—
skimping on the measure,
　　boosting the price
　　and cheating with dishonest
　　scales,
6 buying the poor with silver
　　and the needy for a pair of
　　sandals,
selling even the sweepings with the
　　wheat.

7 The LORD has sworn by himself, the Pride of Jacob: "I will never forget anything they have done.

8 "Will not the land tremble for this,
　　and all who live in it mourn?
The whole land will rise like the Nile;
　　it will be stirred up and then sink
　　like the river of Egypt.

9 "In that day," declares the Sovereign LORD,

"I will make the sun go down at noon
　　and darken the earth in broad
　　daylight.
10 I will turn your religious festivals into
　　mourning
　　and all your singing into weeping.
I will make all of you wear sackcloth
　　and shave your heads.
I will make that time like mourning for
　　an only son
　　and the end of it like a bitter day.

11 "The days are coming," declares the
　　Sovereign LORD,
　　"when I will send a famine through
　　the land—
not a famine of food or a thirst for
　　water,
　　but a famine of hearing the words
　　of the LORD.
12 People will stagger from sea to sea
　　and wander from north to east,
searching for the word of the LORD,
　　but they will not find it.

13 "In that day

"the lovely young women and strong
　　young men
　　will faint because of thirst.
14 Those who swear by the sin of
　　Samaria—
who say, 'As surely as your god
　　lives, Dan,'
or, 'As surely as the god[b] of
　　Beersheba lives'—
　　they will fall, never to rise again."

---

a 3 Or "the temple singers will wail   b 14 Hebrew the way

Israel to Be Destroyed

9 I saw the Lord standing by the altar, and he said:

"Strike the tops of the pillars
  so that the thresholds shake.
Bring them down on the heads of all
    the people;
  those who are left I will kill with the
    sword.
Not one will get away,
  none will escape.
2 Though they dig down to the depths
    below,
  from there my hand will take
    them.
Though they climb up to the heavens
    above,
  from there I will bring them
    down.
3 Though they hide themselves on the
    top of Carmel,
  there I will hunt them down and
    seize them.
Though they hide from my eyes at the
    bottom of the sea,
  there I will command the serpent to
    bite them.
4 Though they are driven into exile by
    their enemies,
  there I will command the sword to
    slay them.

"I will keep my eye on them
  for harm and not for good."

5 The Lord, the LORD Almighty—
he touches the earth and it melts,
  and all who live in it mourn;
the whole land rises like the Nile,
  then sinks like the river of
    Egypt;
6 he builds his lofty palace*a* in the
    heavens
  and sets its foundation*b* on the
    earth;
he calls for the waters of the
    sea
  and pours them out over the face of
    the land—
  the LORD is his name.

7 "Are not you Israelites
  the same to me as the Cushites*c*?"
    declares the LORD.
"Did I not bring Israel up from Egypt,
  the Philistines from Caphtor*d*
  and the Arameans from Kir?

8 "Surely the eyes of the Sovereign LORD
  are on the sinful kingdom.
I will destroy it
  from the face of the earth.
Yet I will not totally destroy
  the descendants of Jacob,"
    declares the LORD.
9 "For I will give the command,
  and I will shake the people of
    Israel
  among all the nations
as grain is shaken in a sieve,
  and not a pebble will reach the
    ground.
10 All the sinners among my people
  will die by the sword,
all those who say,
  'Disaster will not overtake or
    meet us.'

Israel's Restoration

11 "In that day

"I will restore David's fallen
    shelter—
  I will repair its broken walls
  and restore its ruins—
  and will rebuild it as it used to be,
12 so that they may possess the remnant
    of Edom
  and all the nations that bear my
    name,*e*"
    declares the LORD,
    who will do these things.

13 "The days are coming," declares the
LORD,

"when the reaper will be overtaken by
    the plowman
  and the planter by the one treading
    grapes.
New wine will drip from the
    mountains
  and flow from all the hills,

---

a 6 The meaning of the Hebrew for this phrase is uncertain.   *b* 6 The meaning of the Hebrew for this word is uncertain.
c 7 That is, people from the upper Nile region   *d* 7 That is, Crete   *e* 12 Hebrew; Septuagint so that the remnant of
people / and all the nations that bear my name may seek me

14 and I will bring my people Israel
back from exile.[a]

"They will rebuild the ruined cities and
live in them.
They will plant vineyards and drink
their wine;

they will make gardens and eat
their fruit.
15 I will plant Israel in their own land,
never again to be uprooted
from the land I have given them,"

says the LORD your God.

OBADIAH

Getting Even.

Have you ever wanted to get even with someone who has hurt you? Is it kind of fun to plot revenge—like trashing his locker or stealing her sweater? You have to do something or that person will get away with what he or she did, right?

Obadiah's one-chapter prophecy expresses God's anger with Edom, an enemy of his people. Obadiah promises that the Edomites will be punished by God. You don't have to worry about revenge. God is the judge of his universe, and he'll handle those who hurt his people.

>>**NO BYSTANDERS ALLOWED**
    Sin described, see Obadiah 10–11

>>**PAYBACK TIME'S COMING**
    Punishment decreed, in Obadiah 15

No one knows when Obadiah preached.

The Edomites took part in at least three attacks on Jerusalem.

The Edomites disappeared as a people after 70 A.D.

King Herod the Great, who tried to kill Jesus, was an Idumean (Edomite).

preview

It is difficult to know what was happening in the surrounding countries and cultures when this book was written, since it is unknown.

Obadiah's Vision

¹The vision of Obadiah.

This is what the Sovereign LORD says about Edom—

We have heard a message from the LORD:
  An envoy was sent to the nations to say,
"Rise, let us go against her for battle"—

² "See, I will make you small among the nations;
  you will be utterly despised.
³ The pride of your heart has deceived you,
  you who live in the clefts of the rocks*a*
  and make your home on the heights,
you who say to yourself,
  'Who can bring me down to the ground?'
⁴ Though you soar like the eagle
  and make your nest among the stars,
  from there I will bring you down,"
    declares the LORD.
⁵ "If thieves came to you,
  if robbers in the night—
oh, what a disaster awaits you!—
  would they not steal only as much as they wanted?

If grape pickers came to you,
  would they not leave a few grapes?
⁶ But how Esau will be ransacked,
  his hidden treasures pillaged!
⁷ All your allies will force you to the border;
  your friends will deceive and overpower you;
  those who eat your bread will set a trap for you,*b*
  but you will not detect it.

⁸ "In that day," declares the LORD,
  "will I not destroy the wise men of Edom,
  those of understanding in the mountains of Esau?
⁹ Your warriors, Teman, will be terrified,
  and everyone in Esau's mountains
  will be cut down in the slaughter.
¹⁰ Because of the violence against your brother Jacob,
  you will be covered with shame;
  you will be destroyed forever.
¹¹ On the day you stood aloof
  while strangers carried off his wealth
and foreigners entered his gates
  and cast lots for Jerusalem,
  you were like one of them.
¹² You should not gloat over your brother
  in the day of his misfortune,

---

a 3 Or *of Sela*   *b 7* The meaning of the Hebrew for this clause is uncertain.

PANORAMA

Getting Even.

Obadiah expresses God's anger with Edom, an enemy of God's people, who will be punished.

{OBADIAH}

Fight! What do you do when you see some kids beating up another? Most will hurry over to watch. Some may cheer on the fighters. A few join in and help pound the victim. Maybe someone will run to get help, or even try to break it up. But it's really tough to decide in the moment. The short book of Obadiah helps us think about situations like this ahead of time. When God's people were attacked, the Edomites stood by and watched (verse 11) and then piled on the losers (verse 14)! God said, "because of the violence against your brother Jacob, you will be covered with shame" (verse 10). So what will you do when it happens in your school? Decide now, and you'll be ready to do the right thing then.

INSTANT ACCESS

nor rejoice over the people of Judah
  in the day of their destruction,
nor boast so much
  in the day of their trouble.
13 You should not march through the
    gates of my people
  in the day of their disaster,
nor gloat over them in their calamity
  in the day of their disaster,

nor seize their wealth
  in the day of their disaster.
14 You should not wait at the crossroads
    to cut down their fugitives,
nor hand over their survivors
  in the day of their trouble.

15 "The day of the LORD is near
    for all nations.
As you have done, it will be done to
    you;
  your deeds will return upon your
    own head.
16 Just as you drank on my holy hill,
  so all the nations will drink
    continually;
they will drink and drink
  and be as if they had never been.
17 But on Mount Zion will be
    deliverance;
  it will be holy,
and Jacob will possess his
    inheritance.
18 Jacob will be a fire
  and Joseph a flame;
Esau will be stubble,
  and they will set him on fire and
    destroy him.
There will be no survivors
  from Esau."
            The LORD has spoken.

19 People from the Negev will occupy
    the mountains of Esau,
and people from the foothills will
    possess
  the land of the Philistines.
They will occupy the fields of Ephraim
    and Samaria,
and Benjamin will possess Gilead.
20 This company of Israelite exiles who
    are in Canaan
  will possess the land as far as
    Zarephath;
the exiles from Jerusalem who are in
    Sepharad
  will possess the towns of the
    Negev.
21 Deliverers will go up on[a] Mount Zion
    to govern the mountains of Esau.
  And the kingdom will be the LORD's.

a 21 Or from

JONAH

preview

Nineveh is the capital of Assyria, Israel's enemy.

Jonah is sent there about 785 B.C. In 722 Assyria will attack and crush Jonah's country!

Mistakes.

We all make them. But does one mistake mean your life is ruined? Or does God give you another chance? Some bad decisions have lifelong consequences. Someone who drinks, drives and has an accident may well end up disabled. But God forgives and often gives another chance.

Jonah made a bad decision. When God told him to go north to Nineveh, Jonah took a ship going south and ended up in the stomach of a great fish! But did you notice that instead of punishing his prophet, God gave Jonah another chance to obey? This time Jonah did obey, and the people of Nineveh listened to God's warning.

>>**JONAH CONFESSES, SAVES SAILORS**
   Story in Jonah 1
>>**IT'S NOT TO LATE TO REMEMBER GOD**
   Desperate prayer answered. See Jonah 2
>>**SUCCESS PAINS ANGRY PROPHET**
   God comments on prophet's anger, in Jonah 4

As Jonah journeys to Nineveh, Egyptians worship Nut, the sky goddess who has the form of a pig. Near the headwaters of the Nile Alora, the king who unifies Nubia, dies. In Greece the "age of heroes" begins as *Iliad* and *Odyssey* are written down.

Jonah Flees From the LORD

1 The word of the LORD came to Jonah son of Amittai: 2 "Go to the great city of Nineveh and preach against it, because its wickedness has come up before me."

3 But Jonah ran away from the LORD and headed for Tarshish. He went down to Joppa, where he found a ship bound for that port. After paying the fare, he went aboard and sailed for Tarshish to flee from the LORD.

4 Then the LORD sent a great wind on the sea, and such a violent storm arose that the ship threatened to break up. 5 All the sailors were afraid and each cried out to his own god. And they threw the cargo into the sea to lighten the ship.

But Jonah had gone below deck, where he lay down and fell into a deep sleep. 6 The captain went to him and said, "How can you sleep? Get up and call on your god! Maybe he will take notice of us so that we will not perish."

7 Then the sailors said to each other, "Come, let us cast lots to find out who is responsible for this calamity." They cast lots and the lot fell on Jonah. 8 So they asked him, "Tell us, who is responsible for making all this trouble for us? What kind of work do you do? Where do you come from? What is your country? From what people are you?"

9 He answered, "I am a Hebrew and I worship the LORD, the God of heaven, who made the sea and the dry land."

10 This terrified them and they asked, "What have you done?" (They knew he was running away from the LORD, because he had already told them so.)

11 The sea was getting rougher and rougher. So they asked him, "What should we do to you to make the sea calm down for us?"

12 "Pick me up and throw me into the sea," he replied, "and it will become calm. I know that it is my fault that this great storm has come upon you."

13 Instead, the men did their best to row back to land. But they could not, for the sea grew even wilder than before. 14 Then they cried out to the LORD, "Please, LORD,

do not let us die for taking this man's life. Do not hold us accountable for killing an innocent man, for you, LORD, have done as you pleased." 15 Then they took Jonah and threw him overboard, and the raging sea grew calm. 16 At this the men greatly feared the LORD, and they offered a sacrifice to the LORD and made vows to him.

Jonah's Prayer

17 Now the LORD provided a huge fish to swallow Jonah, and Jonah was in the belly **2** *a* of the fish three days and three nights. 1 From inside the fish Jonah prayed to the LORD his God. 2 He said:

"In my distress I called to the LORD,
    and he answered me.
From deep in the realm of the dead I
        called for help,
    and you listened to my cry.
3 You hurled me into the depths,
    into the very heart of the
        seas,
    and the currents swirled
        about me;
all your waves and breakers
        swept over me.
4 I said, 'I have been banished
    from your sight;
yet I will look again
    toward your holy temple.'
5 The engulfing waters
        threatened me,*b*
    the deep surrounded me;
    seaweed was wrapped around my
        head.
6 To the roots of the mountains I sank
        down;
    the earth beneath barred me in
        forever.
But you, LORD my God,
    brought my life up from the pit.

7 "When my life was ebbing away,
    I remembered you, LORD,
and my prayer rose to you,
    to your holy temple.

8 "Those who cling to worthless idols
    turn away from God's love for
        them.

---

a In Hebrew texts 2:1 is numbered 1:17, and 2:1-10 is numbered 2:2-11.   *b* 5 Or *waters were at my throat*

9 But I, with shouts of grateful praise,
  will sacrifice to you.
What I have vowed I will make good.
  I will say, 'Salvation comes from the
  LORD.'"

10 And the LORD commanded the fish, and it vomited Jonah onto dry land.

Jonah Goes to Nineveh

3 Then the word of the LORD came to Jonah a second time: 2 "Go to the great city of Nineveh and proclaim to it the message I give you."

3 Jonah obeyed the word of the LORD and went to Nineveh. Now Nineveh was a very large city; it took three days to go through it. 4 Jonah began by going a day's journey into the city, proclaiming, "Forty more days and Nineveh will be overthrown." 5 The Ninevites believed God. A fast was proclaimed, and all of them, from the greatest to the least, put on sackcloth.

6 When Jonah's warning reached the king of Nineveh, he rose from his throne, took off his royal robes, covered himself with sackcloth and sat down in the dust. 7 This is the proclamation he issued in Nineveh:

"By the decree of the king and his nobles:

Do not let people or animals, herds or flocks, taste anything; do not let them eat or drink. 8 But let people and animals be covered with sackcloth. Let everyone call urgently on God. Let them give up their evil ways and their violence. 9 Who knows? God may yet relent and with compassion turn from his fierce anger so that we will not perish."

10 When God saw what they did and how they turned from their evil ways, he relented and did not bring on them the destruction he had threatened.

Jonah's Anger at the LORD's Compassion

4 But to Jonah this seemed very wrong, and he became angry. 2 He prayed to the LORD, "Isn't this what I said, LORD, when I was still at home? That is what I

INSTANT ACCESS

Have you ever felt like you have so many faults you just can't talk to anyone else about God? Take a look at Jonah. He ran away, deliberately disobeying God's command to go preach in Nineveh. When God sent a great storm, Jonah said it was his fault, because he was running away. As a result of Jonah's words and the great storm, all the sailors believed in the Lord and began to worship him. You don't have to be perfect to reach others for the Lord. God can even use people like Jonah, who are running away from him.

{Jonah 1:16}

---

tried to forestall by fleeing to Tarshish. I knew that you are a gracious and compassionate God, slow to anger and abounding in love, a God who relents from sending calamity. 3 Now, LORD, take away my life, for it is better for me to die than to live."

4 But the LORD replied, "Is it right for you to be angry?"

5 Jonah had gone out and sat down at a place east of the city. There he made himself a shelter, sat in its shade and waited to see what would happen to the city. 6 Then the LORD God provided a leafy plant[a] and made it grow up over Jonah to give shade for his head to ease his discomfort, and Jonah was very happy about the plant. 7 But at dawn the next day God

---

a 6 The precise identification of this plant is uncertain; also in verses 7, 9 and 10.

provided a worm, which chewed the plant so that it withered. ⁸When the sun rose, God provided a scorching east wind, and the sun blazed on Jonah's head so that he grew faint. He wanted to die, and said, "It would be better for me to die than to live."

⁹But God said to Jonah, "Is it right for you to be angry about the plant?"

"It is," he said. "And I'm so angry I wish I were dead."

¹⁰But the LORD said, "You have been concerned about this plant, though you did not tend it or make it grow. It sprang up overnight and died overnight. ¹¹And should I not have concern for the great city of Nineveh, in which there are more than a hundred and twenty thousand people who cannot tell their right hand from their left—and also many animals?"

PANORAMA

{JONAH}

Mistakes.

God gives us a second chance, like Jonah. At first, Jonah ran away from what God told him to do. But then he got a second chance. Jonah went to the people of Nineveh and warned them to change their ways from bad to good.

MICAH

Surprise!

Is God ever surprised? You make plans and then you have to change them. You get a summer job, and the store you were going to work in burns down. You get a ticket to the World Series, and, boom, there's an earthquake. You can plan, but you can't be sure what will happen.

God is never surprised. The prophet Micah warned Israel and Judah that because of their sins they would be conquered by enemy nations. Micah also saw ahead 700 years and predicted the town where the Savior would be born! Nothing in your future can surprise God. And nothing can shake his love for you.

>>**THE BEST LAID PLANS ... ARE GOD'S**
Helpful reminder reported in Micah 2:1–5

>>**IT'S NOT THAT HARD TO PLEASE GOD**
God explains. See Micah 6:6–8

>>**ONLY 700 YEARS BEFORE HE'S BORN!**
Amazing prophecy recorded, see Micah 5:1–4

>>**WHAT MAKES GOD SO SPECIAL?**
For details, see Micah 7:14–20

As Micah prophesies, water clocks are in use in Assyria. False teeth are invented in Italy. The Celts introduce the plow in Britain. Tradition says Rome is founded by Romulus.

1 The word of the LORD that came to Micah of Moresheth during the reigns of Jotham, Ahaz and Hezekiah, kings of Judah—the vision he saw concerning Samaria and Jerusalem.

2 Hear, you peoples, all of you,
   listen, earth and all who live in it,
that the Sovereign LORD may bear
      witness against you,
   the Lord from his holy temple.

Judgment Against Samaria and Jerusalem

3 Look! The LORD is coming from his
         dwelling place;
   he comes down and treads on the
         heights of the earth.
4 The mountains melt beneath him
   and the valleys split apart,
like wax before the fire,
   like water rushing down a slope.
5 All this is because of Jacob's
         transgression,
   because of the sins of the people
         of Israel.
What is Jacob's transgression?
   Is it not Samaria?
What is Judah's high place?
   Is it not Jerusalem?

6 "Therefore I will make Samaria a heap
         of rubble,
   a place for planting vineyards.
I will pour her stones into the valley
   and lay bare her foundations.
7 All her idols will be broken to pieces;
   all her temple gifts will be burned
         with fire;
   I will destroy all her images.
Since she gathered her gifts from the
         wages of prostitutes,
   as the wages of prostitutes they will
         again be used."

Weeping and Mourning

8 Because of this I will weep and wail;
   I will go about barefoot and naked.
I will howl like a jackal
   and moan like an owl.

9 For Samaria's plague is incurable;
   it has spread to Judah.
It has reached the very gate of my
         people,
   even to Jerusalem itself.
10 Tell it not in Gath*a*;
   weep not at all.
In Beth Ophrah*b*
   roll in the dust.
11 Pass by naked and in shame,
   you who live in Shaphir.*c*
Those who live in Zaanan*d*
   will not come out.
Beth Ezel is in mourning;
   it no longer protects you.
12 Those who live in Maroth*e* writhe in
         pain,
   waiting for relief,
because disaster has come from the
         LORD,
   even to the gate of Jerusalem.
13 You who live in Lachish,
   harness fast horses to the
         chariot.
You are where the sin of Daughter
         Zion began,
   for the transgressions of Israel
         were found in you.
14 Therefore you will give parting gifts
   to Moresheth Gath.
The town of Akzib*f* will prove
         deceptive
   to the kings of Israel.
15 I will bring a conqueror against you
   who live in Mareshah.*g*
The nobles of Israel
   will flee to Adullam.
16 Shave your head in mourning
   for the children in whom you
         delight;
make yourself as bald as the vulture,
   for they will go from you into exile.

Human Plans and God's Plans

2 Woe to those who plan iniquity,
   to those who plot evil on their beds!
At morning's light they carry it out
   because it is in their power to do it.
2 They covet fields and seize them,
   and houses, and take them.

---

a 10 Gath *sounds like the Hebrew for* tell.   *b 10* Beth Ophrah *means* house of dust.   *c 11* Shaphir *means* pleasant.
d 11 Zaanan *sounds like the Hebrew for* come out.   *e 12* Maroth *sounds like the Hebrew for* bitter.   *f 14* Akzib *means*
deception.   *g 15* Mareshah *sounds like the Hebrew for* conqueror.

They defraud people of their homes,
they rob them of their inheritance.

3 Therefore, the LORD says:

"I am planning disaster against this
people,
from which you cannot save
yourselves.
You will no longer walk proudly,
for it will be a time of calamity.
4 In that day people will ridicule you;
they will taunt you with this
mournful song:
'We are utterly ruined;
my people's possession is
divided up.
He takes it from me!
He assigns our fields to traitors.' "

5 Therefore you will have no one in the
assembly of the LORD
to divide the land by lot.

False Prophets

6 "Do not prophesy," their prophets say.
"Do not prophesy about these
things;
disgrace will not overtake us."
7 You descendants of Jacob, should it
be said,
"Does the LORD becomeª impatient?
Does he do such things?"

"Do not my words do good
to the one whose ways are upright?

ª 7 Or Is the Spirit of the LORD

8 Lately my people have risen up
like an enemy.
You strip off the rich robe
from those who pass by without a
care,
like men returning from battle.
9 You drive the women of my people
from their pleasant homes.
You take away my blessing
from their children forever.
10 Get up, go away!
For this is not your resting place,
because it is defiled,
it is ruined, beyond all remedy.
11 If a liar and deceiver comes and says,
'I will prophesy for you plenty of
wine and beer,'
that would be just the prophet for
this people!

Deliverance Promised

12 "I will surely gather all of you, Jacob;
I will surely bring together the
remnant of Israel.
I will bring them together like sheep in
a pen,
like a flock in its pasture;
the place will throng with people.
13 The One who breaks open the way will
go up before them;
they will break through the gate and
go out.
Their King will pass through before
them,
the LORD at their head."

PANORAMA

Surprise!

**God is never surprised. Nothing in the future
can surprise God. And nothing can shake his
love for you.**

{MICAH}

Leaders and Prophets Rebuked

3 Then I said,

"Listen, you leaders of Jacob,
 you rulers of Israel.
Should you not embrace justice,
2 you who hate good and love evil;
who tear the skin from my people
 and the flesh from their bones;
3 who eat my people's flesh,
 strip off their skin
 and break their bones in pieces;
who chop them up like meat for the
 pan,
 like flesh for the pot?"

4 Then they will cry out to the LORD,
 but he will not answer them.
At that time he will hide his face from
 them
 because of the evil they have done.

5 This is what the LORD says:

"As for the prophets
 who lead my people astray,
they proclaim 'peace'
 if they have something to eat,
but prepare to wage war against
 anyone
 who refuses to feed them.
6 Therefore night will come over you,
 without visions,
 and darkness, without divination.
The sun will set for the prophets,
 and the day will go dark for them.
7 The seers will be ashamed
 and the diviners disgraced.
They will all cover their faces
 because there is no answer from
 God."

8 But as for me, I am filled with power,
 with the Spirit of the LORD,
 and with justice and might,
to declare to Jacob his transgression,
 to Israel his sin.

9 Hear this, you leaders of Jacob,
 you rulers of Israel,
who despise justice
 and distort all that is right;
10 who build Zion with bloodshed,
 and Jerusalem with wickedness.

11 Her leaders judge for a bribe,
 her priests teach for a price,
 and her prophets tell fortunes for
 money.
Yet they look for the LORD's support
 and say,
 "Is not the LORD among us?
 No disaster will come upon us."
12 Therefore because of you,
 Zion will be plowed like a field,
Jerusalem will become a heap of
 rubble,
 the temple hill a mound overgrown
 with thickets.

The Mountain of the LORD

4 In the last days

the mountain of the LORD's temple will
 be established
 as the highest of the mountains;
it will be exalted above the hills,
 and peoples will stream to it.

2 Many nations will come and say,

"Come, let us go up to the mountain
 of the LORD,
 to the temple of the God of
 Jacob.
He will teach us his ways,
 so that we may walk in his paths."
The law will go out from Zion,
 the word of the LORD from
 Jerusalem.
3 He will judge between many
 peoples
 and will settle disputes for strong
 nations far and wide.

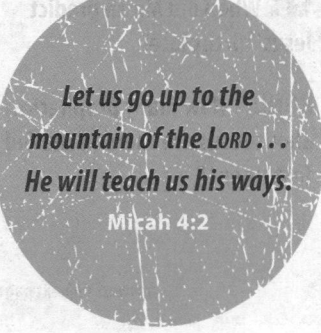

*Let us go up to the
mountain of the LORD . . .
He will teach us his ways.*

Micah 4:2

They will beat their swords into
plowshares
and their spears into pruning
hooks.
Nation will not take up sword against
nation,
nor will they train for war anymore.
⁴ Everyone will sit under their own vine
and under their own fig tree,
and no one will make them afraid,
for the LORD Almighty has spoken.
⁵ All the nations may walk
in the name of their gods,
but we will walk in the name of the
LORD
our God for ever and ever.

The LORD's Plan

⁶ "In that day," declares the LORD,

"I will gather the lame;
I will assemble the exiles
and those I have brought to grief.
⁷ I will make the lame my remnant,
those driven away a strong nation.
The LORD will rule over them in Mount
Zion
from that day and forever.
⁸ As for you, watchtower of the flock,
stronghold*a* of Daughter Zion,

the former dominion will be restored
to you;
kingship will come to Daughter
Jerusalem."

⁹ Why do you now cry aloud—
have you no king*b*?
Has your ruler*c* perished,
that pain seizes you like that of a
woman in labor?
¹⁰ Writhe in agony, Daughter Zion,
like a woman in labor,
for now you must leave the city
to camp in the open field.
You will go to Babylon;
there you will be rescued.
There the LORD will redeem you
out of the hand of your enemies.

¹¹ But now many nations
are gathered against you.
They say, "Let her be defiled,
let our eyes gloat over Zion!"
¹² But they do not know
the thoughts of the LORD;
they do not understand his plan,
that he has gathered them like
sheaves to the threshing floor.
¹³ "Rise and thresh, Daughter Zion,
for I will give you horns of iron;
I will give you hooves of bronze,
and you will break to pieces many
nations."
You will devote their ill-gotten gains to
the LORD,
their wealth to the Lord of all the
earth.

A Promised Ruler From Bethlehem

5 *d* Marshal your troops now, city of
troops,
for a siege is laid against us.
They will strike Israel's ruler
on the cheek with a rod.

² "But you, Bethlehem Ephrathah,
though you are small among the
clans*e* of Judah,
out of you will come for me
one who will be ruler over Israel,

Micah 5

Q: When did Micah predict Jesus' birthplace?

BONUS: How many prophecies about Jesus are there in the Old Testament?

Answers on next page

---

a 8 Or *hill*   *b* 9 Or *King*   *c* 9 Or *Ruler*   *d* In Hebrew
texts 5:1 is numbered 4:14, and 5:2-15 is numbered
5:1-14.   *e* 2 Or *rulers*

whose origins are from of old,
    from ancient times."

³ Therefore Israel will be abandoned
    until the time when she who is in
        labor bears a son,
and the rest of his brothers return
    to join the Israelites.

⁴ He will stand and shepherd his flock
    in the strength of the LORD,
    in the majesty of the name of the
        LORD his God.
And they will live securely, for then his
    greatness
will reach to the ends of the
    earth.

⁵ And he will be our peace
    when the Assyrians invade our
        land
    and march through our fortresses.
We will raise against them seven
    shepherds,
    even eight commanders,
⁶ who will rule*a* the land of Assyria with
    the sword,
    the land of Nimrod with drawn
        sword.*b*
He will deliver us from the Assyrians
    when they invade our land
    and march across our borders.

⁷ The remnant of Jacob will be
    in the midst of many peoples
like dew from the LORD,
    like showers on the grass,
which do not wait for anyone
    or depend on man.
⁸ The remnant of Jacob will be among
    the nations,
    in the midst of many peoples,
like a lion among the beasts of the
    forest,
    like a young lion among flocks of
        sheep,
which mauls and mangles as it
    goes,
    and no one can rescue.
⁹ Your hand will be lifted up in triumph
    over your enemies,
    and all your foes will be destroyed.

¹⁰ "In that day," declares the LORD,

A: About 720 years before
Christ was born (Micah 5:2)!

BONUS: There are 332 that have
already been fulfilled, and many
more that will be fulfilled when
Jesus returns.

"I will destroy your horses from among
    you
    and demolish your chariots.
¹¹ I will destroy the cities of your
    land
    and tear down all your strongholds.
¹² I will destroy your witchcraft
    and you will no longer cast spells.
¹³ I will destroy your idols
    and your sacred stones from among
        you;
you will no longer bow down
    to the work of your hands.
¹⁴ I will uproot from among you your
    Asherah poles*c*
    when I demolish your cities.
¹⁵ I will take vengeance in anger and
    wrath
    on the nations that have not
        obeyed me."

The LORD's Case Against Israel

6 Listen to what the LORD says:

"Stand up, plead my case before the
    mountains;
    let the hills hear what you have to
        say.

---

a 6 Or *crush*   *b* 6 Or *Nimrod in its gates*   *c* 14 That is, wooden symbols of the goddess Asherah

2 "Hear, you mountains, the LORD's
  accusation;
  listen, you everlasting foundations
    of the earth.
For the LORD has a case against his
    people;
  he is lodging a charge against Israel.

3 "My people, what have I done to you?
  How have I burdened you?
    Answer me.
4 I brought you up out of Egypt
  and redeemed you from the land of
    slavery.
I sent Moses to lead you,
  also Aaron and Miriam.
5 My people, remember
  what Balak king of Moab plotted
  and what Balaam son of Beor
    answered.
Remember your journey from Shittim
    to Gilgal,
  that you may know the righteous
    acts of the LORD."

6 With what shall I come before the LORD
  and bow down before the exalted
    God?
Shall I come before him with burnt
    offerings,
  with calves a year old?
7 Will the LORD be pleased with
    thousands of rams,
  with ten thousand rivers of olive oil?
Shall I offer my firstborn for my
    transgression,
  the fruit of my body for the sin of
    my soul?
8 He has shown you, O mortal, what is
    good.
  And what does the LORD require of
    you?
To act justly and to love mercy
  and to walk humbly[a] with your God.

Israel's Guilt and Punishment

9 Listen! The LORD is calling to the
    city—
  and to fear your name is wisdom—
  "Heed the rod and the One who
    appointed it.[b]

You probably feel at least some pressure to live up to others' expectations. You want to please your coach. You want Mom and Dad to be proud of you. You want to fit in with the other kids. It can be kind of confusing at times, trying to be the way all those different people expect you to be. The most important thing, of course, is to be the person God wants you to be. Micah 6:8 is a special verse because it describes what God expects of his followers. And there's a bonus involved: If you set your heart on being God's kind of person, just about everyone you care about will like and respect you too.

>> INSTANT ACCESS

{Micah 6:8}

10 Am I still to forget your ill-gotten
    treasures, you wicked house,
  and the short ephah,[c] which is
    accursed?
11 Shall I acquit someone with dishonest
    scales,
  with a bag of false weights?
12 Your rich people are violent;
  your inhabitants are liars
  and their tongues speak deceitfully.
13 Therefore, I have begun to destroy
    you,
  to ruin[d] you because of your sins.

---

a 8 Or prudently   b 9 The meaning of the Hebrew for this line is uncertain.   c 10 An ephah was a dry measure.
d 13 Or Therefore, I will make you ill and destroy you; / I will ruin

14 You will eat but not be satisfied;
  your stomach will still be empty.[a]
You will store up but save nothing,
  because what you save[b] I will give
    to the sword.
15 You will plant but not harvest;
  you will press olives but not use the
    oil,
  you will crush grapes but not drink
    the wine.
16 You have observed the statutes of
    Omri
  and all the practices of Ahab's
    house;
  you have followed their traditions.
Therefore I will give you over to ruin
  and your people to derision;
  you will bear the scorn of the
    nations.[c]"

Israel's Misery

7 What misery is mine!
  I am like one who gathers summer
    fruit
  at the gleaning of the vineyard;
there is no cluster of grapes to eat,
  none of the early figs that I crave.
2 The faithful have been swept from the
    land;
  not one upright person remains.
Everyone lies in wait to shed blood;
  they hunt each other with nets.
3 Both hands are skilled in doing evil;
  the ruler demands gifts,
  the judge accepts bribes,
    the powerful dictate what they
      desire—
  they all conspire together.
4 The best of them is like a brier,
  the most upright worse than a thorn
    hedge.
The day God visits you has come,
  the day your watchmen sound the
    alarm.
  Now is the time of your confusion.
5 Do not trust a neighbor;
  put no confidence in a friend.
Even with the woman who lies in your
    embrace
  guard the words of your lips.

6 For a son dishonors his father,
  a daughter rises up against her
    mother,
  a daughter-in-law against her
    mother-in-law—
  a man's enemies are the members
    of his own household.

7 But as for me, I watch in hope for the
    Lord,
  I wait for God my Savior;
  my God will hear me.

Israel Will Rise

8 Do not gloat over me, my enemy!
  Though I have fallen, I will rise.
Though I sit in darkness,
  the Lord will be my light.
9 Because I have sinned against him,
  I will bear the Lord's wrath,
until he pleads my case
  and upholds my cause.
He will bring me out into the light;
  I will see his righteousness.
10 Then my enemy will see it
  and will be covered with shame,
she who said to me,
  "Where is the Lord your God?"
My eyes will see her downfall;
  even now she will be trampled
    underfoot
  like mire in the streets.

11 The day for building your walls will
    come,
  the day for extending your
    boundaries.
12 In that day people will come to you
  from Assyria and the cities of Egypt,
  even from Egypt to the Euphrates
  and from sea to sea
  and from mountain to mountain.
13 The earth will become desolate
  because of its inhabitants,
  as the result of their deeds.

Prayer and Praise

14 Shepherd your people with your staff,
  the flock of your inheritance,
  which lives by itself in a forest,
  in fertile pasturelands.[d]

---

a 14 The meaning of the Hebrew for this word is uncertain.   *b 14* Or *You will press toward birth but not give birth, / and
what you bring to birth*   *c 16* Septuagint; Hebrew *scorn due my people*   *d 14* Or *in the middle of Carmel*

Let them feed in Bashan and Gilead
as in days long ago.

15 "As in the days when you came out of
Egypt,
I will show them my wonders."

16 Nations will see and be ashamed,
deprived of all their power.
They will put their hands over their
mouths
and their ears will become
deaf.
17 They will lick dust like a snake,
like creatures that crawl on the
ground.
They will come trembling out of their
dens;
they will turn in fear to the LORD our
God
and will be afraid of you.
18 Who is a God like you,
who pardons sin and forgives the
transgression
of the remnant of his
inheritance?

*You do not stay
angry forever but delight
to show mercy.*
Micah 7:18

You do not stay angry forever
but delight to show mercy.
19 You will again have compassion on us;
you will tread our sins underfoot
and hurl all our iniquities into the
depths of the sea.
20 You will be faithful to Jacob,
and show love to Abraham,
as you pledged on oath to our
ancestors
in days long ago.

NAHUM

Judgment.

When something bad happens to another person, it's not right to feel good about it. But what if that person has abused you for years or hurt you seriously? You just might cheer when he or she is judged and must pay for the harm done.

Nahum sees God as a judge, pronouncing sentence on Nineveh. Nineveh was the capital of Assyria, a nation that invaded Israel and carried 200,000 of her people into captivity. The prophet describes how the Assyrians will suffer when their own capital is attacked. After decades of terror, it was right for Judah to rejoice. It was Assyria's time to be judged.

>> **GOD CLAIMS RIGHT TO TAKE VENGEANCE**
See Nahum 1:1–8

>> **GOD TAKES A STAND AGAINST EVIL**
Report in Nahum 3:1–6

>> **ASSYRIA'S WOUNDS PROVE FATAL**
Fall of Nineveh described, see Nahum 3:18–19

preview

Nahum announces divine judgment on Nineveh.

Nineveh is enclosed by an 8-mile, 50-foot-high wall. But the city falls to the Babylonians, who use a strategy Nahum describes (2:5–9).

As Nahum preaches, Manasseh, the most evil of Judah's kings, rules in Jerusalem. The playwright Aeschylus dies. Greek philosophers speculate that earth is a flat disc covered by a dome of sky.

1 A prophecy concerning Nineveh. The book of the vision of Nahum the Elkoshite.

The LORD's Anger Against Nineveh

2 The LORD is a jealous and avenging
God;
the LORD takes vengeance and is
filled with wrath.
The LORD takes vengeance on his foes
and vents his wrath against his
enemies.
3 The LORD is slow to anger but great in
power;
the LORD will not leave the guilty
unpunished.
His way is in the whirlwind and the
storm,
and clouds are the dust of his feet.
4 He rebukes the sea and dries it up;
he makes all the rivers run dry.
Bashan and Carmel wither
and the blossoms of Lebanon fade.
5 The mountains quake before him
and the hills melt away.
The earth trembles at his presence,
the world and all who live in it.
6 Who can withstand his indignation?
Who can endure his fierce anger?
His wrath is poured out like fire;
the rocks are shattered before him.

7 The LORD is good,
a refuge in times of trouble.
He cares for those who trust in him,
8 but with an overwhelming flood
he will make an end of Nineveh;
he will pursue his foes into the
realm of darkness.

9 Whatever they plot against the LORD
he will bring[a] to an end;
trouble will not come a second time.
10 They will be entangled among thorns
and drunk from their wine;
they will be consumed like dry
stubble.[b]
11 From you, Nineveh, has one come
forth
who plots evil against the LORD
and devises wicked plans.

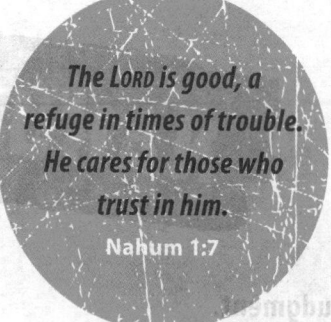

The LORD is good, a refuge in times of trouble. He cares for those who trust in him.

Nahum 1:7

12 This is what the LORD says:

"Although they have allies and are
numerous,
they will be destroyed and pass
away.
Although I have afflicted you, Judah,
I will afflict you no more.
13 Now I will break their yoke from your
neck
and tear your shackles away."

14 The LORD has given a command
concerning you, Nineveh:
"You will have no descendants to
bear your name.
I will destroy the images and idols
that are in the temple of your gods.
I will prepare your grave,
for you are vile."

15 Look, there on the mountains,
the feet of one who brings good
news,
who proclaims peace!
Celebrate your festivals, Judah,
and fulfill your vows.
No more will the wicked invade you;
they will be completely destroyed.[c]

Nineveh to Fall

2[d] An attacker advances against you,
Nineveh.
Guard the fortress,
watch the road,
brace yourselves,
marshal all your strength!

---

[a] 9 Or *What do you foes plot against the LORD? / He will bring it*
uncertain. [c] 15 In Hebrew texts this verse (1:15) is numbered 2:1. [d] In Hebrew texts 2:1-13 is numbered 2:2-14.
[b] 10 The meaning of the Hebrew for this verse is

2 The LORD will restore the splendor of
  Jacob
  like the splendor of Israel,
though destroyers have laid them waste
  and have ruined their vines.

3 The shields of the soldiers are red;
  the warriors are clad in scarlet.
The metal on the chariots flashes
  on the day they are made ready;
  the spears of juniper are
  brandished.ᵃ
4 The chariots storm through the
  streets,
  rushing back and forth through the
  squares.
They look like flaming torches;
  they dart about like lightning.

5 Nineveh summons her picked troops,
  yet they stumble on their way.
They dash to the city wall;
  the protective shield is put in place.
6 The river gates are thrown open
  and the palace collapses.
7 It is decreedᵇ that Nineveh
  be exiled and carried away.
Her female slaves moan like doves
  and beat on their breasts.
8 Nineveh is like a pool
  whose water is draining away.
"Stop! Stop!" they cry,
  but no one turns back.
9 Plunder the silver!
  Plunder the gold!

The supply is endless,
  the wealth from all its treasures!
10 She is pillaged, plundered, stripped!
  Hearts melt, knees give way,
  bodies tremble, every face grows
  pale.

11 Where now is the lions' den,
  the place where they fed their
  young,
where the lion and lioness went,
  and the cubs, with nothing to fear?
12 The lion killed enough for his cubs
  and strangled the prey for his mate,
filling his lairs with the kill
  and his dens with the prey.

13 "I am against you,"
  declares the LORD Almighty.
"I will burn up your chariots in smoke,
  and the sword will devour your
  young lions.
I will leave you no prey on the earth.
The voices of your messengers
  will no longer be heard."

Woe to Nineveh

3 Woe to the city of blood,
  full of lies,
full of plunder,
  never without victims!
2 The crack of whips,
  the clatter of wheels,
galloping horses
  and jolting chariots!

ᵃ 3 Hebrew; Septuagint and Syriac ready; / the horsemen rush to and fro.   ᵇ 7 The meaning of the Hebrew for this word is uncertain.

PANORAMA

Judgment.

Nahum sees God as a judge, pronouncing
the sentence of Nineveh. Nineveh was the
capital of Assyria, a nation that invaded
Israel and carried 200,000 of its people into
captivity.

³Charging cavalry,
  flashing swords
  and glittering spears!
Many casualties,
  piles of dead,
bodies without number,
  people stumbling over the
    corpses—
⁴all because of the wanton lust of a
    prostitute,
  alluring, the mistress of sorceries,
who enslaved nations by her
    prostitution
  and peoples by her witchcraft.

⁵"I am against you," declares the LORD
    Almighty.
  "I will lift your skirts over your face.
I will show the nations your nakedness
  and the kingdoms your shame.
⁶I will pelt you with filth,
  I will treat you with contempt
  and make you a spectacle.
⁷All who see you will flee from you and
    say,
  'Nineveh is in ruins—who will
    mourn for her?'
  Where can I find anyone to comfort
    you?"

⁸Are you better than Thebes,
  situated on the Nile,
  with water around her?
The river was her defense,
  the waters her wall.
⁹Cushᵃ and Egypt were her boundless
    strength;
  Put and Libya were among her
    allies.
¹⁰Yet she was taken captive
  and went into exile.
Her infants were dashed to pieces
  at every street corner.
Lots were cast for her nobles,
  and all her great men were put in
    chains.
¹¹You too will become drunk;
  you will go into hiding
  and seek refuge from the enemy.

¹²All your fortresses are like fig trees
  with their first ripe fruit;
when they are shaken,
  the figs fall into the mouth of the
    eater.
¹³Look at your troops—
  they are all weaklings.
The gates of your land
  are wide open to your enemies;
  fire has consumed the bars of your
    gates.

¹⁴Draw water for the siege,
  strengthen your defenses!
Work the clay,
  tread the mortar,
  repair the brickwork!
¹⁵There the fire will consume you;
  the sword will cut you down—
  they will devour you like a swarm of
    locusts.
Multiply like grasshoppers,
  multiply like locusts!
¹⁶You have increased the number of
    your merchants
  till they are more numerous than
    the stars in the sky,
but like locusts they strip the land
  and then fly away.
¹⁷Your guards are like locusts,
  your officials like swarms of locusts
  that settle in the walls on a cold
    day—
but when the sun appears they fly
    away,
  and no one knows where.

¹⁸King of Assyria, your shepherdsᵇ
    slumber;
  your nobles lie down to rest.
Your people are scattered on the
    mountains
  with no one to gather them.
¹⁹Nothing can heal you;
  your wound is fatal.
All who hear the news about you
  clap their hands at your fall,
for who has not felt
  your endless cruelty?

ᵃ 9 That is, the upper Nile region   ᵇ 18 That is, rulers

HABAKKUK

Life Isn't Fair.

Someone writes you a note, and you're the one who gets in trouble. Someone starts a fight with you, and you're the one who gets sent to the principal's office.

Habakkuk didn't think life was fair either. He was upset because it looked to him like the bad guys were winning. Why wasn't God doing something about it? God had an answer. Sinners would be punished. In the meantime success wouldn't make them happy. Think about it. Wouldn't you rather have little and be happy and right with God than have millions and always feel unsatisfied?

>> **SUCCESS BLINDS SINNERS TO REALITY**
   Insight revealed in Habakkuk 1:11

>> **PROPHET QUESTIONS GOD'S MOTIVES**
   Details in Habakkuk 1:12–13

>> **SINNERS GET AWAY WITH NOTHING**
   Stunning revelations recorded in Habakkuk 2

>> **CAUGHT IN THE CROSSFIRE, WE TRUST**
   Lessons summarized, see Habakkuk 3:16–19

preview

Habakkuk lives in Judah during Josiah's revival.

The return to religion fails to make Judah a just, moral community.

Habakkuk asks God to explain. God shows the prophet that he's punishing the wicked even as they seem most successful.

As Habakkuk dialogs with God, 16 Arian kingdoms spread across northern India. The Olmecs in Central America offer jade items to their deities. The temple of Artemis, one of the ancient world's seven wonders, is built in Ephesus.

1

The prophecy that Habakkuk the prophet received.

Habakkuk's Complaint

2 How long, LORD, must I call for help,
    but you do not listen?
Or cry out to you, "Violence!"
    but you do not save?
3 Why do you make me look at injustice?
    Why do you tolerate wrongdoing?
Destruction and violence are before me;
    there is strife, and conflict abounds.
4 Therefore the law is paralyzed,
    and justice never prevails.
The wicked hem in the righteous,
    so that justice is perverted.

The LORD's Answer

5 "Look at the nations and watch—
    and be utterly amazed.
For I am going to do something in your days
    that you would not believe,
    even if you were told.

6 I am raising up the Babylonians,[a]
    that ruthless and impetuous people,
who sweep across the whole earth
    to seize dwellings not their own.
7 They are a feared and dreaded people;
    they are a law to themselves
    and promote their own honor.
8 Their horses are swifter than leopards,
    fiercer than wolves at dusk.
Their cavalry gallops headlong;
    their horsemen come from afar.
They fly like an eagle swooping to devour;
9   they all come intent on violence.
Their hordes[b] advance like a desert wind
    and gather prisoners like sand.
10 They mock kings
    and scoff at rulers.
They laugh at all fortified cities;
    by building earthen ramps they capture them.
11 Then they sweep past like the wind and go on—
    guilty people, whose own strength is their god."

Habakkuk's Second Complaint

12 LORD, are you not from everlasting?
    My God, my Holy One, you[c] will never die.
You, LORD, have appointed them to execute judgment;
    you, my Rock, have ordained them to punish.
13 Your eyes are too pure to look on evil;
    you cannot tolerate wrongdoing.
Why then do you tolerate the treacherous?
    Why are you silent while the wicked swallow up those more righteous than themselves?
14 You have made people like the fish in the sea,
    like the sea creatures that have no ruler.

Q&A

Habakkuk 1

Q: What doesn't God look at?

BONUS: What doesn't God listen to?

Answers on next page

---

[a] 6 Or *Chaldeans*   [b] 9 The meaning of the Hebrew for this word is uncertain.   [c] 12 An ancient Hebrew scribal tradition; Masoretic Text *we*

¹⁵The wicked foe pulls all of them up
    with hooks,
  he catches them in his net,
he gathers them up in his dragnet;
    and so he rejoices and is glad.
¹⁶Therefore he sacrifices to his net
    and burns incense to his dragnet,
for by his net he lives in luxury
    and enjoys the choicest food.
¹⁷Is he to keep on emptying his net,
    destroying nations without mercy?

2 I will stand at my watch
    and station myself on the ramparts;
I will look to see what he will say
    to me,
    and what answer I am to give to this
      complaint.^a

The LORD's Answer

²Then the LORD replied:

"Write down the revelation
  and make it plain on tablets
    so that a herald^b may run with it.
³For the revelation awaits an appointed
    time;
  it speaks of the end
    and will not prove false.
Though it linger, wait for it;
  it^c will certainly come
    and will not delay.

⁴"See, the enemy is puffed up;
  his desires are not upright—
    but the righteous person will live by
      his faithfulness^d—
⁵indeed, wine betrays him;
  he is arrogant and never at rest.
Because he is as greedy as the grave
  and like death is never satisfied,
he gathers to himself all the nations
  and takes captive all the peoples.

⁶"Will not all of them taunt him with
ridicule and scorn, saying,

  " 'Woe to him who piles up stolen
    goods
  and makes himself wealthy by
    extortion!
  How long must this go on?'

A: Evil. Because his "eyes are
too pure to look on" it (Habakkuk 1:13).

BONUS: God can hear everything, but he does not listen to
those who won't listen to him
(Jeremiah 11:10–11).

⁷Will not your creditors suddenly arise?
  Will they not wake up and make you
    tremble?
  Then you will become their prey.
⁸Because you have plundered many
    nations,
  the peoples who are left will plunder
    you.
For you have shed human blood;
  you have destroyed lands and cities
    and everyone in them.

⁹"Woe to him who builds his house by
    unjust gain,
  setting his nest on high
    to escape the clutches of ruin!
¹⁰You have plotted the ruin of many
    peoples,
  shaming your own house and
    forfeiting your life.
¹¹The stones of the wall will cry out,
  and the beams of the woodwork will
    echo it.

¹²"Woe to him who builds a city with
    bloodshed
  and establishes a town by
    injustice!

---

^a 1 Or *and what to answer when I am rebuked*   ^b 2 Or *so that whoever reads it*   ^c 3 Or *Though he linger, wait for him; / he*
^d 4 Or *faith*

> I spend a lot of time getting all my homework done. I let one guy copy one day and now it's every day. I'm sick of it but I don't know how to get out of this. What can I do?
> >> Evan

Dear Evan,

It's just like in the book Habakkuk. When people do something they shouldn't, instead of being satisfied, they want more (Habakkuk 2:5). You tried to help out a friend in need, although, not in a wise way. Instead of being grateful and doing a better job of preparing for class, he began to use you. You probably know by now he wasn't much of a friend.

Perhaps you could tell him you are willing to tutor him if he needs some help but that you don't feel comfortable letting him copy anymore. Since you don't want to bring on more trouble for yourself, don't call him a cheater. Instead you could say, "I feel like I'm cheating, and it really bothers me."

You may find it helpful to avoid being in the usual place where he gets the work from you if it's possible.

Jordan

¹³Has not the LORD Almighty determined
  that the people's labor is only fuel
    for the fire,
  that the nations exhaust
    themselves for nothing?
¹⁴For the earth will be filled with the
    knowledge of the glory of the
    LORD
  as the waters cover the sea.

¹⁵"Woe to him who gives drink to his
    neighbors,
  pouring it from the wineskin till they
    are drunk,
  so that he can gaze on their naked
    bodies!
¹⁶You will be filled with shame instead
    of glory.
  Now it is your turn! Drink and let
    your nakedness be exposed[a]!
  The cup from the LORD's right hand is
    coming around to you,
  and disgrace will cover your glory.
¹⁷The violence you have done to
    Lebanon will overwhelm you,
  and your destruction of animals will
    terrify you.
  For you have shed human blood;
    you have destroyed lands and cities
    and everyone in them.

¹⁸"Of what value is an idol carved by a
    craftsman?
  Or an image that teaches lies?
For the one who makes it trusts in his
    own creation;
  he makes idols that cannot
    speak.
¹⁹Woe to him who says to wood, 'Come
    to life!'
  Or to lifeless stone, 'Wake up!'
Can it give guidance?
  It is covered with gold and silver;
    there is no breath in it."

²⁰The LORD is in his holy temple;
  let all the earth be silent before
    him.

Habakkuk's Prayer

3 A prayer of Habakkuk the prophet. On
  shigionoth.[b]

²LORD, I have heard of your fame;
  I stand in awe of your deeds, LORD.
Repeat them in our day,
  in our time make them known;
  in wrath remember mercy.

³God came from Teman,
  the Holy One from Mount Paran.[c]
His glory covered the heavens
  and his praise filled the earth.
⁴His splendor was like the sunrise;
  rays flashed from his hand,
  where his power was hidden.
⁵Plague went before him;
  pestilence followed his steps.

---

a 16 Masoretic Text; Dead Sea Scrolls, Aquila, Vulgate and Syriac (see also Septuagint) *and stagger*   *b 1* Probably a literary or musical term   *c 3* The Hebrew has *Selah* (a word of uncertain meaning) here and at the middle of verse 9 and at the end of verse 13.

{HABAKKUK}

PANORAMA

Life Isn't Fair.

It looked to Habakkuk like the bad guys were winning. But success wouldn't make them happy. Only God could and they didn't have that.

⁶He stood, and shook the earth;
  he looked, and made the nations
    tremble.
The ancient mountains crumbled
  and the age-old hills collapsed—
  but he marches on forever.
⁷I saw the tents of Cushan in distress,
  the dwellings of Midian in anguish.

⁸Were you angry with the rivers, Lᴏʀᴅ?
  Was your wrath against the
    streams?
Did you rage against the sea
  when you rode your horses
  and your chariots to victory?
⁹You uncovered your bow,
  you called for many arrows.
You split the earth with rivers;
¹⁰ the mountains saw you and writhed.
Torrents of water swept by;
  the deep roared
  and lifted its waves on high.

¹¹Sun and moon stood still in the
    heavens
  at the glint of your flying arrows,
  at the lightning of your flashing
    spear.
¹²In wrath you strode through the earth
  and in anger you threshed the
    nations.
¹³You came out to deliver your people,
  to save your anointed one.
You crushed the leader of the land of
    wickedness,
  you stripped him from head to foot.
¹⁴With his own spear you pierced his
    head
  when his warriors stormed out to
    scatter us,
  gloating as though about to devour
  the wretched who were in hiding.
¹⁵You trampled the sea with your
    horses,
  churning the great waters.

¹⁶I heard and my heart pounded,
  my lips quivered at the sound;
decay crept into my bones,
  and my legs trembled.
Yet I will wait patiently for the day of
    calamity
  to come on the nation invading us.
¹⁷Though the fig tree does not bud

and there are no grapes on the
    vines,
though the olive crop fails
  and the fields produce no food,
though there are no sheep in the pen
  and no cattle in the stalls,
¹⁸yet I will rejoice in the Lᴏʀᴅ,
  I will be joyful in God my Savior.

¹⁹The Sovereign Lᴏʀᴅ is my strength;
  he makes my feet like the feet of a
    deer,
  he enables me to tread on the
    heights.

For the director of music. On my
    stringed instruments.

≫ INSTANT ACCESS

For most people, family means security. Parents supply food and clothing and housing as well as love and support. But what happens if Dad loses his job? Or if Mom and Dad divorce? Or if a parent dies? Suddenly your whole future is in doubt. Look what happened to Habakkuk. God warned him that a terrible judgment was about to strike his homeland. Habakkuk was frightened (Habakkuk 3:16). But he came to realize that it isn't peace or prosperity that provides security: it's the Lord (Habakkuk 3:18–19). No matter how uncertain your future is, God can be your strength, today and tomorrow.

{Habakkuk 3:16–19}

of the Lord that came to   who fill the temple of their gods
with violence and deceit.

ZEPHANIAH

Do Something!

Does it ever bother you when there's a problem and no one does anything about it? The authorities complain about drunk driving but don't take action. Tough kids bug you on the school bus, but no one makes them stop. Why doesn't someone do something?

In Zephaniah's day the wicked grinned and thought, "The LORD will do nothing, either good or bad" (Zephaniah 1:12). But the prophet had a surprise for them. God was about to act and punish not only Judah, but also nearby nations. Zephaniah reminds you that God really does judge. God says that in his own time, "[He] will deal with all who oppressed you" (Zephaniah 3:19).

>>**A DO-NOTHING GOD? NO WAY**
God answers accusation, see Zephaniah 1:10–13

>>**PLEASE, DON'T LET ME BE LIKE THAT**
Check out plea in Zephaniah 3:1–5

>>**LOVE THOSE HAPPY ENDINGS**
How will it turn out? See Zephaniah 3:14–20

> **preview**
>
> Zephaniah means "the Lord protects."
>
> He preaches just before Josiah's religious revival. Within ten years of Josiah's death, Zephaniah's predictions come true.

As Zephaniah preaches, Lao-tzu, the founder of Taoism, is born in China.
Glaucus of Chios invents the soldering iron.

1 The word of the Lord that came to Zephaniah son of Cushi, the son of Gedaliah, the son of Amariah, the son of Hezekiah, during the reign of Josiah son of Amon king of Judah:

Judgment on the Whole Earth in the Day of the Lord

2 "I will sweep away everything
    from the face of the earth,"
                        declares the Lord.
3 "I will sweep away both man and
        beast;
    I will sweep away the birds in the sky
    and the fish in the sea—
    and the idols that cause the wicked
        to stumble."[a]

"When I destroy all mankind
    on the face of the earth,"
                        declares the Lord,
4 "I will stretch out my hand against
        Judah
    and against all who live in
        Jerusalem.
I will destroy every remnant of Baal
        worship in this place,
    the very names of the idolatrous
        priests—
5 those who bow down on the roofs
    to worship the starry host,
    those who bow down and swear by the
        Lord
    and who also swear by Molek,[b]
6 those who turn back from following
        the Lord
    and neither seek the Lord nor
        inquire of him."

7 Be silent before the Sovereign Lord,
    for the day of the Lord is near.
The Lord has prepared a sacrifice;
    he has consecrated those he has
        invited.

8 "On the day of the Lord's sacrifice
    I will punish the officials
    and the king's sons
and all those clad
    in foreign clothes.
9 On that day I will punish
    all who avoid stepping on the
        threshold,[c]

who fill the temple of their gods
    with violence and deceit.

10 "On that day,"
    declares the Lord,
"a cry will go up from the Fish Gate,
    wailing from the New Quarter,
    and a loud crash from the hills.
11 Wail, you who live in the market
        district[d];
    all your merchants will be wiped
        out,
    all who trade with[e] silver will be
        destroyed.
12 At that time I will search Jerusalem
        with lamps
    and punish those who are
        complacent,
    who are like wine left on its dregs,
who think, 'The Lord will do nothing,
    either good or bad.'
13 Their wealth will be plundered,
    their houses demolished.
Though they build houses,
    they will not live in them;
though they plant vineyards,
    they will not drink the wine."

14 The great day of the Lord is near—
    near and coming quickly.
The cry on the day of the Lord is
        bitter;
    the Mighty Warrior shouts his battle
        cry.
15 That day will be a day of wrath—
    a day of distress and anguish,
    a day of trouble and ruin,
    a day of darkness and gloom,
    a day of clouds and blackness—
16   a day of trumpet and battle cry
against the fortified cities
    and against the corner towers.

17 "I will bring such distress on all
        people
    that they will grope about like those
        who are blind,
    because they have sinned against
        the Lord.
Their blood will be poured out like
        dust
    and their entrails like dung.

---

[a] 3 The meaning of the Hebrew for this line is uncertain.   [b] 5 Hebrew *Malkam*   [c] 9 See 1 Samuel 5:5.   [d] 11 Or *the Mortar*   [e] 11 Or *in*

18 Neither their silver nor their
    gold
  will be able to save them
  on the day of the LORD's wrath."

In the fire of his jealousy
  the whole earth will be
    consumed,
for he will make a sudden end
  of all who live on the earth.

Judah and Jerusalem Judged Along With the Nations
Judah Summoned to Repent

2 Gather together, gather yourselves
    together,
  you shameful nation,
2 before the decree takes effect
  and that day passes like windblown
    chaff,

TO THE POINT

No "Do Nothing" God

In Zephaniah's day most of the people of Judah supposed they had a "do nothing" God. They thought they could do anything they wanted, and God would just sit there, frustrated, doing nothing at all.

Were they wrong! God brought enemy armies against his people, crushing their defenses. The people of Judah went off to captivity in Babylon. Do nothing? Hah!

It's good to remember that you don't have a "do nothing" God. Read Zephaniah to learn some of the things God says he will do:

+ God will punish those who abandon him (Zephaniah 1:4–6).

+ God will shelter those who do what he commands (Zephaniah 2:3).

+ God will bless those who trust in his name (Zephaniah 3:12–13).

+ God will deal with those who oppress his own (Zephaniah 3:19).

before the Lord's fierce anger
  comes upon you,
before the day of the Lord's wrath
  comes upon you.
3 Seek the Lord, all you humble of the
  land,
  you who do what he commands.
Seek righteousness, seek humility;
  perhaps you will be sheltered
  on the day of the Lord's anger.

Philistia

4 Gaza will be abandoned
  and Ashkelon left in ruins.
At midday Ashdod will be emptied
  and Ekron uprooted.
5 Woe to you who live by the sea,
  you Kerethite people;
the word of the Lord is against you,
  Canaan, land of the Philistines.
He says, "I will destroy you,
  and none will be left."
6 The land by the sea will become
  pastures
  having wells for shepherds
  and pens for flocks.
7 That land will belong
  to the remnant of the people of
  Judah;
  there they will find pasture.
In the evening they will lie down
  in the houses of Ashkelon.
The Lord their God will care for them;
  he will restore their fortunes.[a]

Moab and Ammon

8 "I have heard the insults of Moab
  and the taunts of the Ammonites,
who insulted my people
  and made threats against their land.
9 Therefore, as surely as I live,"
  declares the Lord Almighty,
  the God of Israel,
"surely Moab will become like Sodom,
  the Ammonites like Gomorrah—
a place of weeds and salt pits,
  a wasteland forever.
The remnant of my people will plunder
  them;
  the survivors of my nation will
  inherit their land."

10 This is what they will get in return for
  their pride,
  for insulting and mocking
  the people of the Lord Almighty.
11 The Lord will be awesome to them
  when he destroys all the gods of
  the earth.
Distant nations will bow down to him,
  all of them in their own lands.

Cush

12 "You Cushites,[b] too,
  will be slain by my sword."

Assyria

13 He will stretch out his hand against
  the north
  and destroy Assyria,

---

a 7 Or will bring back their captives   b 12 That is, people from the upper Nile region

PANORAMA

Do Something!

It bugs us when there's a problem and no one does anything about it. Zephaniah reminded the wicked people that God was about to act and punish them.

{ZEPHANIAH}

leaving Nineveh utterly desolate
and dry as the desert.
14 Flocks and herds will lie down there,
creatures of every kind.
The desert owl and the screech owl
will roost on her columns.
Their hooting will echo through the
windows,
rubble will fill the doorways,
the beams of cedar will be exposed.
15 This is the city of revelry
that lived in safety.
She said to herself,
"I am the one! And there is none
besides me."
What a ruin she has become,
a lair for wild beasts!
All who pass by her scoff
and shake their fists.

Jerusalem

3 Woe to the city of oppressors,
rebellious and defiled!
2 She obeys no one,
she accepts no correction.
She does not trust in the LORD,
she does not draw near to her God.
3 Her officials within her
are roaring lions;
her rulers are evening wolves,
who leave nothing for the morning.
4 Her prophets are unprincipled;
they are treacherous people.
Her priests profane the sanctuary
and do violence to the law.
5 The LORD within her is righteous;
he does no wrong.
Morning by morning he dispenses his
justice,
and every new day he does not fail,
yet the unrighteous know no
shame.

Jerusalem Remains Unrepentant

6 "I have destroyed nations;
their strongholds are demolished.
I have left their streets deserted,
with no one passing through.
Their cities are laid waste;
they are deserted and empty.

7 Of Jerusalem I thought,
'Surely you will fear me
and accept correction!'
Then her place of refuge[a] would not
be destroyed,
nor all my punishments come upon[b]
her.
But they were still eager
to act corruptly in all they did.
8 Therefore wait for me,"
declares the LORD,
"for the day I will stand up to
testify.[c]
I have decided to assemble the
nations,
to gather the kingdoms
and to pour out my wrath on them—
all my fierce anger.
The whole world will be consumed
by the fire of my jealous anger.

Restoration of Israel's Remnant

9 "Then I will purify the lips of the
peoples,
that all of them may call on the
name of the LORD
and serve him shoulder to
shoulder.
10 From beyond the rivers of Cush[d]
my worshipers, my scattered
people,
will bring me offerings.
11 On that day you, Jerusalem, will not
be put to shame
for all the wrongs you have done
to me,
because I will remove from you
your arrogant boasters.
Never again will you be haughty
on my holy hill.
12 But I will leave within you
the meek and humble.
The remnant of Israel
will trust in the name of the LORD.
13 They will do no wrong;
they will tell no lies.
A deceitful tongue
will not be found in their mouths.
They will eat and lie down
and no one will make them afraid."

---

a 7 Or her sanctuary   b 7 Or all those I appointed over   c 8 Septuagint and Syriac; Hebrew will rise up to plunder
d 10 That is, the upper Nile region

14 Sing, Daughter Zion;
  shout aloud, Israel!
Be glad and rejoice with all your heart,
  Daughter Jerusalem!
15 The LORD has taken away your
    punishment,
  he has turned back your enemy.
The LORD, the King of Israel, is with
    you;
  never again will you fear any harm.
16 On that day
  they will say to Jerusalem,
  "Do not fear, Zion;
  do not let your hands hang limp.
17 The LORD your God is with you,
  the Mighty Warrior who saves.
He will take great delight in you;
  in his love he will no longer rebuke
    you,
  but will rejoice over you with
    singing."
18 "I will remove from you
  all who mourn over the loss of your
    appointed festivals,
  which is a burden and reproach for
    you.
19 At that time I will deal
  with all who oppressed you.
I will rescue the lame;
  I will gather the exiles.
I will give them praise and honor
  in every land where they have
    suffered shame.
20 At that time I will gather you;
  at that time I will bring you home.

You're just one person. How can you make the world a better place? Should you get behind a political candidate? Start a Save the Bees foundation? Pass out "Bikes Don't Pollute" bumper stickers? Zephaniah 3:12–13 has a better idea. If you want to make the world better, the place to start is with you personally. Be meek and humble. Trust in the Lord. Don't do wrong. Don't tell lies. Live like this every day, and that part of the world where you live will be better because of you.

INSTANT ACCESS

{Zephaniah 3:9–13}

I will give you honor and praise
  among all the peoples of the earth
when I restore your fortunes[a]
  before your very eyes,"
        says the LORD.

---

a 20 Or I bring back your captives

HAGGAI

Write It Down.

When you listen to a sermon at church, do you take notes? Do you plan how you can put God's Word into practice right away? One problem most Old Testament prophets had was that people would listen, but they wouldn't respond to God's Word. They kept on living the same old way.

Haggai's preaching was different. He encouraged the people who had returned from captivity in Babylon to finish the temple they'd begun 18 years earlier. He preached one brief sermon, and the people immediately went to work! Because the people obeyed, God said, "From this day on I will bless you" (Haggai 2:19).

Haggai's sermons are preached on August 28, October 17, and December 16, in 520 B.C.

This temple has greater glory than Solomon's, for Jesus preached in it.

preview

>>**SO MUCH WORK, SO LITTLE MONEY**
Reasons explained, see Haggai 1:1–11

>>**A WORD ABOUT JESUS**
Prophecy provided in Haggai 2:8–9

>>**IT PAYS TO LISTEN TO THE PREACHER**
What will God do? See Haggai 2:15–19

The year Haggai preaches, Darius I of Persia completes a canal linking the Nile with the Red Sea. Cratinus, the author of Greek comedies, is born. A year earlier Buddha preaches his first sermon in India's holy city of Benares.

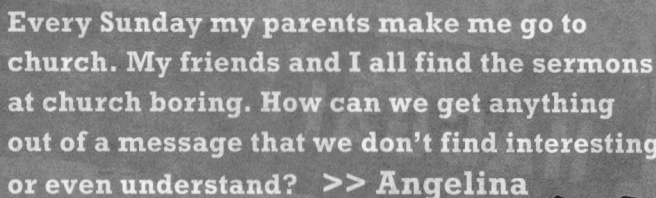

Every Sunday my parents make me go to church. My friends and I all find the sermons at church boring. How can we get anything out of a message that we don't find interesting or even understand? >> Angelina

Dear Jordan

Dear Angelina,

Young people are not the only ones who sometimes get lost or bored during sermons. Many adults have the same problem. But there's a lot more going on in church than just the sermon. God's people come together to praise and thank God. We come together to acknowledge and affirm our faith. We confess our sins and are reminded of God's faithfulness to forgive them.

It is also important to hear the reading of God's Word. Next Sunday try taking a pen and notebook to church. Write down one thing from the reading that you want to remember or that is especially meaningful to you.

The prophet Haggai had to warn his people because they were not tuned in to God's message. God had told them to rebuild the temple, but they were too busy doing their own thing to listen to God (Haggai 1:6–11).

Try each week to focus on the message. Jot down one or more things that hit you as meaningful or important. Good listening skills will help you in many ways in your life. And focusing on God's message (whether the pastor's sermon is interesting or not) is crucial in your life. How can you be obedient to God if you're not listening?

Jordan

A Call to Build the House of the LORD

1 In the second year of King Darius, on the first day of the sixth month, the word of the LORD came through the prophet Haggai to Zerubbabel son of Shealtiel, governor of Judah, and to Joshua[a] son of Jozadak,[b] the high priest:

2 This is what the LORD Almighty says: "These people say, 'The time has not yet come to rebuild the LORD's house.'"

3 Then the word of the LORD came through the prophet Haggai: 4 "Is it a time for you yourselves to be living in your paneled houses, while this house remains a ruin?"

5 Now this is what the LORD Almighty says: "Give careful thought to your ways. 6 You have planted much, but harvested little. You eat, but never have enough. You drink, but never have your fill. You put on clothes, but are not warm. You earn wages, only to put them in a purse with holes in it."

7 This is what the LORD Almighty says: "Give careful thought to your ways. 8 Go up into the mountains and bring down timber and build my house, so that I may take pleasure in it and be honored," says the LORD. 9 "You expected much, but see, it turned out to be little. What you brought home, I blew away. Why?" declares the LORD Almighty. "Because of my house, which remains a ruin, while each of you is busy with your own house. 10 Therefore, because of you the heavens have withheld their dew and the earth its crops. 11 I called for a drought on the fields and the mountains, on the grain, the new wine, the olive oil and everything else the ground produces, on people and livestock, and on all the labor of your hands."

12 Then Zerubbabel son of Shealtiel, Joshua son of Jozadak, the high priest, and the whole remnant of the people obeyed the voice of the LORD their God and the message of the prophet Haggai, because the LORD their God had sent him. And the people feared the LORD.

13 Then Haggai, the LORD's messenger, gave this message of the LORD to the people: "I am with you," declares the LORD. 14 So the LORD stirred up the spirit of Zerubbabel son of Shealtiel, governor of Judah, and the spirit of Joshua son of Jozadak, the high priest, and the spirit of the whole remnant of the people. They came and began to work on the house of the LORD Almighty, their God, 15 on the twenty-fourth day of the sixth month.

The Promised Glory of the New House

2 In the second year of King Darius, 1 on the twenty-first day of the seventh month, the word of the LORD came through the prophet Haggai: 2 "Speak to

---

a 1 A variant of *Jeshua*; here and elsewhere in Haggai and 14   *b* 1 Hebrew *Jehozadak*, a variant of *Jozadak*; also in verses 12 and 14

PANORAMA

Write It Down.

Haggai preached one sermon and the people got to work, finishing the temple they'd begun 18 years earlier.

Zerubbabel son of Shealtiel, governor of Judah, to Joshua son of Jozadak,[a] the high priest, and to the remnant of the people. Ask them, ³'Who of you is left who saw this house in its former glory? How does it look to you now? Does it not seem to you like nothing? ⁴But now be strong, Zerubbabel,' declares the LORD. 'Be strong, Joshua son of Jozadak, the high priest. Be strong, all you people of the land,' declares the LORD, 'and work. For I am with you,' declares the LORD Almighty. ⁵'This is what I covenanted with you when you came out of Egypt. And my Spirit remains among you. Do not fear.'

⁶"This is what the LORD Almighty says: 'In a little while I will once more shake the heavens and the earth, the sea and the dry land. ⁷I will shake all nations, and what is desired by all nations will come, and I will fill this house with glory,' says the LORD Almighty. ⁸'The silver is mine and the gold is mine,' declares the LORD Almighty. ⁹'The glory of this present house will be greater than the glory of the former house,' says the LORD Almighty. 'And in this place I will grant peace,' declares the LORD Almighty."

Blessings for a Defiled People

¹⁰On the twenty-fourth day of the ninth month, in the second year of Darius, the word of the LORD came to the prophet Haggai: ¹¹"This is what the LORD Almighty says: 'Ask the priests what the law says: ¹²If someone carries consecrated meat in the fold of their garment, and that fold touches some bread or stew, some wine, olive oil or other food, does it become consecrated?'"

The priests answered, "No."

¹³Then Haggai said, "If a person defiled by contact with a dead body touches one of these things, does it become defiled?"

"Yes," the priests replied, "it becomes defiled."

¹⁴Then Haggai said, "'So it is with this people and this nation in my sight,' declares the LORD. 'Whatever they do and whatever they offer there is defiled.

>> INSTANT ACCESS

Wouldn't it be great to hear God say to you, "From this day on I will bless you"? That's what God said to the people of Haggai's day. These people responded to Haggai's message and immediately set about finishing God's temple. Now, there's no guarantee that if you make a habit of responding to what God says all your problems will go away. Or that your family will suddenly be very rich. Or that you'll start getting all A's without studying. But there is one thing you can count on. If you put God's Word into practice, you put yourself in the place where God can bless you. And he will!

{Haggai 2:18–19}

---

¹⁵" 'Now give careful thought to this from this day on[b]—consider how things were before one stone was laid on another in the LORD's temple. ¹⁶When anyone came to a heap of twenty measures, there were only ten. When anyone went to a wine vat to draw fifty measures, there were only twenty. ¹⁷I struck all the work of your hands with blight, mildew and hail, yet you did not return to me,' declares the LORD. ¹⁸'From this day on, from this twenty-fourth day of the ninth month, give careful thought to the day when the foundation of the LORD's temple was laid. Give

---

careful thought: [19]Is there yet any seed left in the barn? Until now, the vine and the fig tree, the pomegranate and the olive tree have not borne fruit.

" 'From this day on I will bless you.' "

Zerubbabel the LORD's Signet Ring

[20]The word of the LORD came to Haggai a second time on the twenty-fourth day of the month: [21]"Tell Zerubbabel governor of Judah that I am going to shake the heavens and the earth. [22]I will overturn royal thrones and shatter the power of the foreign kingdoms. I will overthrow chariots and their drivers; horses and their riders will fall, each by the sword of his brother.

[23]" 'On that day,' declares the LORD Almighty, 'I will take you, my servant Zerubbabel son of Shealtiel,' declares the LORD, 'and I will make you like my signet ring, for I have chosen you,' declares the LORD Almighty."

ZECHARIAH

What's Ahead for the World?

Will there be a nuclear war? Will there be another Great Depression? Will pollution destroy our environment? No one can answer these questions, because the Bible doesn't mention the particular place where you live. But you can understand why people would like to know.

Haggai, who preached at the same time as Zechariah, said the Savior would enter the temple the returned exiles were rebuilding. Zechariah answers the questions "When?" and "What will happen when he comes?" Centuries would pass before God acted, but the time of God's intervention surely would come.

>> FLYING SCROLL HAS A MESSAGE
Vision explained, see Zechariah 5:1–4

>> DOES GIVING UP DINNER PLEASE GOD?
The scoop on fasting given in Zechariah 7

>> PALM SUNDAY PREDICTION
Read it in Zechariah 9:9

>> WORLD PEACE, OR ELSE
Path to peace explained. See Zechariah 14:16–21

As Zechariah brings God's message to the Jews, the Greek music composer Pindar is born. Pythagoras proposes that Earth is suspended in space, and that sun, moon, planets and stars all move around it. Public libraries open in Athens, Greece.

A Call to Return to the LORD

1 In the eighth month of the second year of Darius, the word of the LORD came to the prophet Zechariah son of Berekiah, the son of Iddo:

2 "The LORD was very angry with your ancestors. 3 Therefore tell the people: This is what the LORD Almighty says: 'Return to me,' declares the LORD Almighty, 'and I will return to you,' says the LORD Almighty. 4 Do not be like your ancestors, to whom the earlier prophets proclaimed: This is what the LORD Almighty says: 'Turn from your evil ways and your evil practices.' But they would not listen or pay attention to me, declares the LORD. 5 Where are your ancestors now? And the prophets, do they live forever? 6 But did not my words and my decrees, which I commanded my servants the prophets, overtake your ancestors?

"Then they repented and said, 'The LORD Almighty has done to us what our ways and practices deserve, just as he determined to do.' "

The Man Among the Myrtle Trees

7 On the twenty-fourth day of the eleventh month, the month of Shebat, in the second year of Darius, the word of the LORD came to the prophet Zechariah son of Berekiah, the son of Iddo.

8 During the night I had a vision, and there before me was a man mounted on a red horse. He was standing among the myrtle trees in a ravine. Behind him were red, brown and white horses.

9 I asked, "What are these, my lord?"

The angel who was talking with me answered, "I will show you what they are."

10 Then the man standing among the myrtle trees explained, "They are the ones the LORD has sent to go throughout the earth."

11 And they reported to the angel of the LORD who was standing among the myrtle trees, "We have gone throughout the earth and found the whole world at rest and in peace."

12 Then the angel of the LORD said, "LORD Almighty, how long will you with-

hold mercy from Jerusalem and from the towns of Judah, which you have been angry with these seventy years?" 13 So the LORD spoke kind and comforting words to the angel who talked with me.

14 Then the angel who was speaking to me said, "Proclaim this word: This is what the LORD Almighty says: 'I am very jealous for Jerusalem and Zion, 15 and I am very angry with the nations that feel secure. I was only a little angry, but they went too far with the punishment.'

16 "Therefore this is what the LORD says: 'I will return to Jerusalem with mercy, and there my house will be rebuilt. And the measuring line will be stretched out over Jerusalem,' declares the LORD Almighty.

17 "Proclaim further: This is what the LORD Almighty says: 'My towns will again overflow with prosperity, and the LORD will again comfort Zion and choose Jerusalem.' "

Four Horns and Four Craftsmen

18 Then I looked up, and there before me were four horns. 19 I asked the angel who was speaking to me, "What are these?"

He answered me, "These are the horns that scattered Judah, Israel and Jerusalem."

20 Then the LORD showed me four craftsmen. 21 I asked, "What are these coming to do?"

He answered, "These are the horns that scattered Judah so that no one could raise their head, but the craftsmen have come to terrify them and throw down these horns of the nations who lifted up their horns against the land of Judah to scatter its people."[a]

A Man With a Measuring Line

2[b] Then I looked up, and there before me was a man with a measuring line in his hand. 2 I asked, "Where are you going?"

He answered me, "To measure Jerusalem, to find out how wide and how long it is."

---

[a] 21 In Hebrew texts 1:18-21 is numbered 2:1-4. [b] In Hebrew texts 2:1-13 is numbered 2:5-17.

³While the angel who was speaking to me was leaving, another angel came to meet him ⁴and said to him: "Run, tell that young man, 'Jerusalem will be a city without walls because of the great number of people and animals in it. ⁵And I myself will be a wall of fire around it,' declares the LORD, 'and I will be its glory within.'

⁶"Come! Come! Flee from the land of the north," declares the LORD, "for I have scattered you to the four winds of heaven," declares the LORD.

⁷"Come, Zion! Escape, you who live in Daughter Babylon!" ⁸For this is what the LORD Almighty says: "After the Glorious One has sent me against the nations that have plundered you — for whoever touches you touches the apple of his eye— ⁹I will surely raise my hand against them so that their slaves will plunder them.ᵃ Then you will know that the LORD Almighty has sent me.

"I am coming, and I will live among you," declares the LORD.

Zechariah 2:10

¹⁰"Shout and be glad, Daughter Zion. For I am coming, and I will live among you," declares the LORD. ¹¹"Many nations will be joined with the LORD in that day and will become my people. I will live among you and you will know that the LORD Almighty has sent me to you. ¹²The LORD will inherit Judah as his portion in the holy land and will again choose Jerusalem. ¹³Be still before the LORD, all mankind, because he has roused himself from his holy dwelling."

Clean Garments for the High Priest

3 Then he showed me Joshuaᵇ the high priest standing before the angel of the LORD, and Satanᶜ standing at his right side to accuse him. ²The LORD said to Satan, "The LORD rebuke you, Satan! The LORD, who has chosen Jerusalem, rebuke you! Is not this man a burning stick snatched from the fire?"

³Now Joshua was dressed in filthy clothes as he stood before the angel. ⁴The angel said to those who were standing before him, "Take off his filthy clothes."

Then he said to Joshua, "See, I have taken away your sin, and I will put fine garments on you."

⁵Then I said, "Put a clean turban on his head." So they put a clean turban on his head and clothed him, while the angel of the LORD stood by.

⁶The angel of the LORD gave this charge to Joshua: ⁷"This is what the LORD Almighty says: 'If you will walk in obedience to me and keep my requirements, then you will govern my house and have charge of my courts, and I will give you a place among these standing here.

⁸"'Listen, High Priest Joshua, you and your associates seated before you, who are men symbolic of things to come: I am going to bring my servant, the Branch. ⁹See, the stone I have set in front of Joshua! There are seven eyesᵈ on that one stone, and I will engrave an inscription on it,' says the LORD Almighty, 'and I will remove the sin of this land in a single day.

¹⁰"'In that day each of you will invite your neighbor to sit under your vine and fig tree,' declares the LORD Almighty."

The Gold Lampstand and the Two Olive Trees

4 Then the angel who talked with me returned and woke me up, like someone awakened from sleep. ²He asked me, "What do you see?"

I answered, "I see a solid gold lampstand with a bowl at the top and seven lamps on it, with seven channels to the lamps. ³Also there are two olive trees by it, one on the right of the bowl and the other on its left."

⁴I asked the angel who talked with me, "What are these, my lord?"

ᵃ 8,9 Or *says after . . . eye:* ⁹"*I . . . plunder them.*"   ᵇ 1 A variant of *Jeshua*; here and elsewhere in Zechariah
ᶜ 1 Hebrew *satan* means *adversary.*   ᵈ 9 Or *facets*

⁵He answered, "Do you not know what these are?"

"No, my lord," I replied.

⁶So he said to me, "This is the word of the LORD to Zerubbabel: 'Not by might nor by power, but by my Spirit,' says the LORD Almighty.

⁷"What are you, mighty mountain? Before Zerubbabel you will become level ground. Then he will bring out the capstone to shouts of 'God bless it! God bless it!'"

⁸Then the word of the LORD came to me: ⁹"The hands of Zerubbabel have laid the foundation of this temple; his hands will also complete it. Then you will know that the LORD Almighty has sent me to you.

¹⁰"Who dares despise the day of small things, since the seven eyes of the LORD that range throughout the earth will rejoice when they see the chosen capstone*a* in the hand of Zerubbabel?"

¹¹Then I asked the angel, "What are these two olive trees on the right and the left of the lampstand?"

¹²Again I asked him, "What are these two olive branches beside the two gold pipes that pour out golden oil?"

¹³He replied, "Do you not know what these are?"

"No, my lord," I said.

¹⁴So he said, "These are the two who are anointed to*b* serve the Lord of all the earth."

The Flying Scroll

5 I looked again, and there before me was a flying scroll.

²He asked me, "What do you see?"

I answered, "I see a flying scroll, twenty cubits long and ten cubits wide.*c*"

³And he said to me, "This is the curse that is going out over the whole land; for according to what it says on one side, every thief will be banished, and according to what it says on the other, everyone who swears falsely will be banished. ⁴The LORD Almighty declares, 'I will send it out,

and it will enter the house of the thief and the house of anyone who swears falsely by my name. It will remain in that house and destroy it completely, both its timbers and its stones.'"

The Woman in a Basket

⁵Then the angel who was speaking to me came forward and said to me, "Look up and see what is appearing."

⁶I asked, "What is it?"

He replied, "It is a basket." And he added, "This is the iniquity*d* of the people throughout the land."

⁷Then the cover of lead was raised, and there in the basket sat a woman! ⁸He said, "This is wickedness," and he pushed her back into the basket and pushed its lead cover down on it.

⁹Then I looked up—and there before me were two women, with the wind in their wings! They had wings like those of a stork, and they lifted up the basket between heaven and earth.

¹⁰"Where are they taking the basket?" I asked the angel who was speaking to me.

¹¹He replied, "To the country of Babylonia*e* to build a house for it. When the

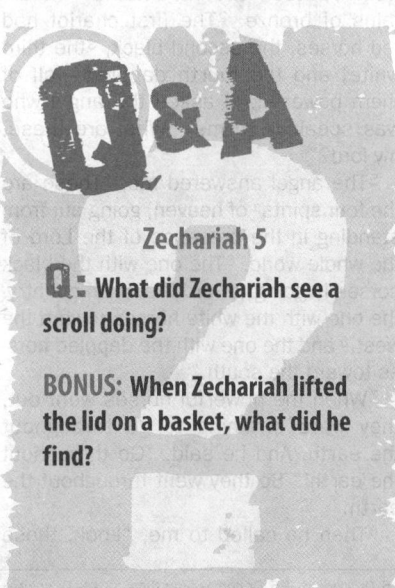

Zechariah 5

Q: What did Zechariah see a scroll doing?

BONUS: When Zechariah lifted the lid on a basket, what did he find?

---

a 10 Or *the plumb line*   *b* 14 Or *two who bring oil and*
c 2 That is, about 30 feet long and 15 feet wide or about
9 meters long and 4.5 meters wide   *d* 6 Or *appearance*
e 11 Hebrew *Shinar*

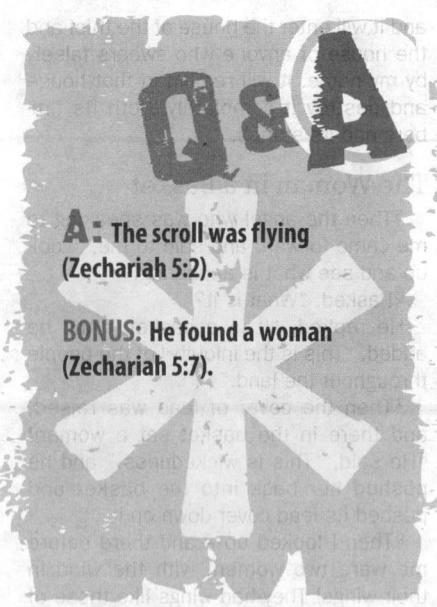

A: The scroll was flying (Zechariah 5:2).

BONUS: He found a woman (Zechariah 5:7).

house is ready, the basket will be set there in its place."

Four Chariots

6 I looked up again, and there before me were four chariots coming out from between two mountains—mountains of bronze. ²The first chariot had red horses, the second black, ³the third white, and the fourth dappled—all of them powerful. ⁴I asked the angel who was speaking to me, "What are these, my lord?"

⁵The angel answered me, "These are the four spirits[a] of heaven, going out from standing in the presence of the Lord of the whole world. ⁶The one with the black horses is going toward the north country, the one with the white horses toward the west,[b] and the one with the dappled horses toward the south."

⁷When the powerful horses went out, they were straining to go throughout the earth. And he said, "Go throughout the earth!" So they went throughout the earth.

⁸Then he called to me, "Look, those going toward the north country have given my Spirit[c] rest in the land of the north."

A Crown for Joshua

⁹The word of the Lord came to me: ¹⁰"Take silver and gold from the exiles Heldai, Tobijah and Jedaiah, who have arrived from Babylon. Go the same day to the house of Josiah son of Zephaniah. ¹¹Take the silver and gold and make a crown, and set it on the head of the high priest, Joshua son of Jozadak.[d] ¹²Tell him this is what the Lord Almighty says: 'Here is the man whose name is the Branch, and he will branch out from his place and build the temple of the Lord. ¹³It is he who will build the temple of the Lord, and he will be clothed with majesty and will sit and rule on his throne. And he[e] will be a priest on his throne. And there will be harmony between the two.' ¹⁴The crown will be given to Heldai,[f] Tobijah, Jedaiah and Hen[g] son of Zephaniah as a memorial in the temple of the Lord. ¹⁵Those who are far away will come and help to build the temple of the Lord, and you will know that the Lord Almighty has sent me to you. This will happen if you diligently obey the Lord your God."

Justice and Mercy, Not Fasting

7 In the fourth year of King Darius, the word of the Lord came to Zechariah on the fourth day of the ninth month, the month of Kislev. ²The people of Bethel had sent Sharezer and Regem-Melek, together with their men, to entreat the Lord ³by asking the priests of the house of the Lord Almighty and the prophets, "Should I mourn and fast in the fifth month, as I have done for so many years?"

⁴Then the word of the Lord Almighty came to me: ⁵"Ask all the people of the land and the priests, 'When you fasted and mourned in the fifth and seventh months for the past seventy years, was it really for me that you fasted? ⁶And when you were eating and drinking, were you not just feasting for yourselves? ⁷Are these not the words the Lord proclaimed

---

ᵃ 5 Or winds   ᵇ 6 Or horses after them   ᶜ 8 Or spirit   ᵈ 11 Hebrew Jehozadak, a variant of Jozadak   ᵉ 13 Or there
ᶠ 14 Syriac; Hebrew Helem   ᵍ 14 Or and the gracious one, the

through the earlier prophets when Jerusalem and its surrounding towns were at rest and prosperous, and the Negev and the western foothills were settled?' "

⁸And the word of the LORD came again to Zechariah: ⁹"This is what the LORD Almighty said: 'Administer true justice; show mercy and compassion to one another. ¹⁰Do not oppress the widow or the fatherless, the foreigner or the poor. Do not plot evil against each other.'

¹¹"But they refused to pay attention; stubbornly they turned their backs and covered their ears. ¹²They made their hearts as hard as flint and would not listen to the law or to the words that the LORD Almighty had sent by his Spirit through the earlier prophets. So the LORD Almighty was very angry.

¹³" 'When I called, they did not listen; so when they called, I would not listen,' says the LORD Almighty. ¹⁴'I scattered them with a whirlwind among all the nations, where they were strangers. The land they left behind them was so desolate that no one traveled through it. This is how they made the pleasant land desolate.' "

The LORD Promises to Bless Jerusalem

8 The word of the LORD Almighty came to me.

²This is what the LORD Almighty says: "I am very jealous for Zion; I am burning with jealousy for her."

³This is what the LORD says: "I will return to Zion and dwell in Jerusalem. Then Jerusalem will be called the Faithful City, and the mountain of the LORD Almighty will be called the Holy Mountain."

⁴This is what the LORD Almighty says: "Once again men and women of ripe old age will sit in the streets of Jerusalem, each of them with cane in hand because of their age. ⁵The city streets will be filled with boys and girls playing there."

⁶This is what the LORD Almighty says: "It may seem marvelous to the remnant of this people at that time, but will it seem marvelous to me?" declares the LORD Almighty.

⁷This is what the LORD Almighty says: "I will save my people from the countries of the east and the west. ⁸I will bring them back to live in Jerusalem; they will be my people, and I will be faithful and righteous to them as their God."

⁹This is what the LORD Almighty says: "Now hear these words, 'Let your hands be strong so that the temple may be built.' This is also what the prophets said who were present when the foundation was laid for the house of the LORD Almighty. ¹⁰Before that time there were no wages for people or hire for animals. No one could go about their business safely because of their enemies, since I had turned everyone against their neighbor. ¹¹But now I will not deal with the remnant of this people as I did in the past," declares the LORD Almighty.

¹²"The seed will grow well, the vine will yield its fruit, the ground will produce its crops, and the heavens will drop their dew. I will give all these things as an inheritance to the remnant of this people. ¹³Just as you, Judah and Israel, have been a curse[a] among the nations, so I will save you, and you will be a blessing.[b] Do not be afraid, but let your hands be strong."

¹⁴This is what the LORD Almighty says: "Just as I had determined to bring disaster on you and showed no pity when your ancestors angered me," says the LORD Almighty, ¹⁵"so now I have determined to do good again to Jerusalem and Judah. Do not be afraid. ¹⁶These are the things you are to do: Speak the truth to each other, and render true and sound judgment in your courts; ¹⁷do not plot evil against each other, and do not love to swear falsely. I hate all this," declares the LORD.

¹⁸The word of the LORD Almighty came to me.

¹⁹This is what the LORD Almighty says: "The fasts of the fourth, fifth, seventh and tenth months will become joyful and glad occasions and happy festivals for Judah. Therefore love truth and peace."

²⁰This is what the LORD Almighty says: "Many peoples and the inhabitants of many cities will yet come, ²¹and the inhabitants of one city will go to another and say, 'Let us go at once to entreat the LORD and seek the LORD Almighty. I myself am going.' ²²And many peoples and powerful nations will come to Jerusalem to seek the LORD Almighty and to entreat him."

²³This is what the LORD Almighty says: "In those days ten people from all languages and nations will take firm hold of one Jew by the hem of his robe and say, 'Let us go with you, because we have heard that God is with you.' "

Judgment on Israel's Enemies

9 A prophecy:

The word of the LORD is against the
  land of Hadrak
and will come to rest on
  Damascus—

for the eyes of all people and all the
    tribes of Israel
  are on the LORD—[c]
²and on Hamath too, which borders
    on it,
  and on Tyre and Sidon, though they
    are very skillful.
³Tyre has built herself a stronghold;
  she has heaped up silver like dust,
  and gold like the dirt of the streets.
⁴But the Lord will take away her
    possessions
  and destroy her power on the sea,
  and she will be consumed by fire.
⁵Ashkelon will see it and fear;
  Gaza will writhe in agony,
  and Ekron too, for her hope will
    wither.
Gaza will lose her king
  and Ashkelon will be deserted.
⁶A mongrel people will occupy Ashdod,
  and I will put an end to the pride of
    the Philistines.
⁷I will take the blood from their
    mouths,
  the forbidden food from between
    their teeth.
Those who are left will belong to our
    God
  and become a clan in Judah,
  and Ekron will be like the
    Jebusites.
⁸But I will encamp at my temple
  to guard it against marauding
    forces.
Never again will an oppressor overrun
    my people,
  for now I am keeping watch.

The Coming of Zion's King

⁹Rejoice greatly, Daughter Zion!
  Shout, Daughter Jerusalem!
See, your king comes to you,
  righteous and victorious,
lowly and riding on a donkey,
  on a colt, the foal of a donkey.
¹⁰I will take away the chariots from
    Ephraim
  and the warhorses from Jerusalem,
  and the battle bow will be broken.

---

[a] 13 That is, your name has been used in cursing (see Jer. 29:22); or, you have been regarded as under a curse.
[b] 13 Or and your name will be used in blessings (see Gen. 48:20); or and you will be seen as blessed   [c] 1 Or Damascus.
/ For the eye of the LORD is on all people, / as well as on the tribes of Israel,

This verse is a prophecy Jesus fulfilled on Palm Sunday (see Matthew 21:1–11). Do you know why riding a donkey was significant? When kings in the ancient world went to war, they rode horses. When they visited a city in peace, they rode donkeys. King Jesus rode a donkey into Jerusalem to show he threatened no one, even though religious leaders in that city treated him as an enemy. Why not follow Jesus' example? Be sure others realize you're no threat to them. You're not out to put them down or to win theological arguments. You're there to be like Jesus: loving, caring and eager to help others whether or not they know the Lord.

{Zechariah 9:9}

INSTANT ACCESS

He will proclaim peace to the nations.
His rule will extend from sea to sea
and from the River[a] to the ends of
the earth.
11 As for you, because of the blood of my
covenant with you,
I will free your prisoners from the
waterless pit.
12 Return to your fortress, you prisoners
of hope;
even now I announce that I will
restore twice as much to you.

13 I will bend Judah as I bend my bow
and fill it with Ephraim.
I will rouse your sons, Zion,
against your sons, Greece,
and make you like a warrior's
sword.

The LORD Will Appear

14 Then the LORD will appear over them;
his arrow will flash like lightning.
The Sovereign LORD will sound the
trumpet;
he will march in the storms of the
south,
15 and the LORD Almighty will shield
them.
They will destroy
and overcome with slingstones.
They will drink and roar as with wine;
they will be full like a bowl
used for sprinkling[b] the corners of
the altar.
16 The LORD their God will save his
people on that day
as a shepherd saves his flock.
They will sparkle in his land
like jewels in a crown.
17 How attractive and beautiful they
will be!
Grain will make the young men
thrive,
and new wine the young women.

The LORD Will Care for Judah

10 Ask the LORD for rain in the
springtime;
it is the LORD who sends the
thunderstorms.
He gives showers of rain to all people,
and plants of the field to everyone.
2 The idols speak deceitfully,
diviners see visions that lie;
they tell dreams that are false,
they give comfort in vain.
Therefore the people wander like
sheep
oppressed for lack of a shepherd.

3 "My anger burns against the
shepherds,
and I will punish the leaders;

---

a 10 That is, the Euphrates   b 15 Or bowl, / like

for the LORD Almighty will care
  for his flock, the people of Judah,
  and make them like a proud horse
    in battle.
⁴From Judah will come the
    cornerstone,
  from him the tent peg,
from him the battle bow,
  from him every ruler.
⁵Together theyᵃ will be like warriors in
    battle
  trampling their enemy into the mud
    of the streets.
They will fight because the LORD is
    with them,
  and they will put the enemy
    horsemen to shame.

⁶"I will strengthen Judah
  and save the tribes of Joseph.
I will restore them
  because I have compassion on
    them.
They will be as though
  I had not rejected them,
for I am the LORD their God
  and I will answer them.
⁷The Ephraimites will become like
    warriors,
  and their hearts will be glad as with
    wine.
Their children will see it and be joyful;
  their hearts will rejoice in the LORD.
⁸I will signal for them
  and gather them in.
Surely I will redeem them;
  they will be as numerous as before.
⁹Though I scatter them among the
    peoples,
  yet in distant lands they will
    remember me.
They and their children will survive,
  and they will return.
¹⁰I will bring them back from Egypt
  and gather them from Assyria.
I will bring them to Gilead and
    Lebanon,
  and there will not be room enough
    for them.
¹¹They will pass through the sea of
    trouble;
  the surging sea will be subdued

and all the depths of the Nile will
    dry up.
Assyria's pride will be brought down
  and Egypt's scepter will pass away.
¹²I will strengthen them in the LORD
  and in his name they will live
    securely,"
                    declares the LORD.

11 Open your doors, Lebanon,
     so that fire may devour your
       cedars!
²Wail, you juniper, for the cedar has
    fallen;
  the stately trees are ruined!
Wail, oaks of Bashan;
  the dense forest has been cut down!
³Listen to the wail of the shepherds;
  their rich pastures are destroyed!
Listen to the roar of the lions;
  the lush thicket of the Jordan is
    ruined!

Two Shepherds

⁴This is what the LORD my God says:
"Shepherd the flock marked for slaughter. ⁵Their buyers slaughter them and go
unpunished. Those who sell them say,
'Praise the LORD, I am rich!' Their own
shepherds do not spare them. ⁶For I will
no longer have pity on the people of the
land," declares the LORD. "I will give everyone into the hands of their neighbors
and their king. They will devastate the
land, and I will not rescue anyone from
their hands."

⁷So I shepherded the flock marked
for slaughter, particularly the oppressed
of the flock. Then I took two staffs and
called one Favor and the other Union, and
I shepherded the flock. ⁸In one month I
got rid of the three shepherds.

The flock detested me, and I grew weary of them ⁹and said, "I will not be your
shepherd. Let the dying die, and the perishing perish. Let those who are left eat
one another's flesh."

¹⁰Then I took my staff called Favor
and broke it, revoking the covenant I had
made with all the nations. ¹¹It was revoked on that day, and so the oppressed
of the flock who were watching me knew
it was the word of the LORD.

ᵃ 4,5 Or ruler, all of them together. / ⁵They

¹²I told them, "If you think it best, give me my pay; but if not, keep it." So they paid me thirty pieces of silver.

¹³And the LORD said to me, "Throw it to the potter"—the handsome price at which they valued me! So I took the thirty pieces of silver and threw them to the potter at the house of the LORD.

¹⁴Then I broke my second staff called Union, breaking the family bond between Judah and Israel.

¹⁵Then the LORD said to me, "Take again the equipment of a foolish shepherd. ¹⁶For I am going to raise up a shepherd over the land who will not care for the lost, or seek the young, or heal the injured, or feed the healthy, but will eat the meat of the choice sheep, tearing off their hooves.

¹⁷"Woe to the worthless shepherd,
   who deserts the flock!
May the sword strike his arm and his
      right eye!
May his arm be completely
      withered,
   his right eye totally blinded!"

Jerusalem's Enemies to Be Destroyed

12 A prophecy: The word of the LORD concerning Israel.

The LORD, who stretches out the heavens, who lays the foundation of the earth, and who forms the human spirit within a person, declares: ²"I am going to make Jerusalem a cup that sends all the surrounding peoples reeling. Judah will be besieged as well as Jerusalem. ³On that day, when all the nations of the earth are gathered against her, I will make Jerusalem an immovable rock for all the nations. All who try to move it will injure themselves. ⁴On that day I will strike every horse with panic and its rider with madness," declares the LORD. "I will keep a watchful eye over Judah, but I will blind all the horses of the nations. ⁵Then the clans of Judah will say in their hearts, 'The people of Jerusalem are strong, because the LORD Almighty is their God.'

⁶"On that day I will make the clans of Judah like a firepot in a woodpile, like a flaming torch among sheaves. They will consume all the surrounding peoples right and left, but Jerusalem will remain intact in her place.

⁷"The LORD will save the dwellings of Judah first, so that the honor of the house of David and of Jerusalem's inhabitants may not be greater than that of Judah. ⁸On that day the LORD will shield those who live in Jerusalem, so that the feeblest among them will be like David, and the house of David will be like God, like the angel of the LORD going before them. ⁹On that day I will set out to destroy all the nations that attack Jerusalem.

Mourning for the One They Pierced

¹⁰"And I will pour out on the house of David and the inhabitants of Jerusalem a spirit[a] of grace and supplication. They will look on[b] me, the one they have pierced, and they will mourn for him as one mourns for an only child, and grieve bitterly for him as one grieves for a first-born son. ¹¹On that day the weeping in Jerusalem will be as great as the weeping

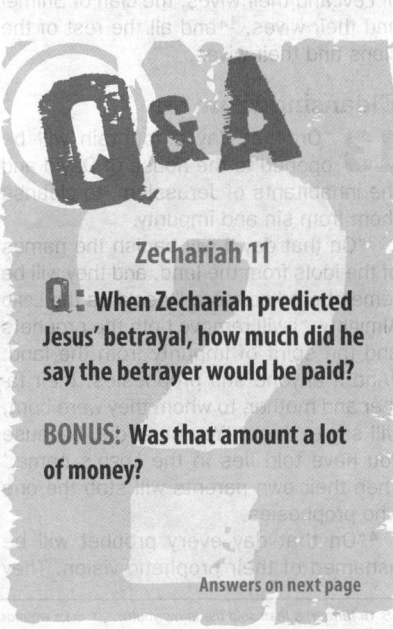

Zechariah 11

Q: When Zechariah predicted Jesus' betrayal, how much did he say the betrayer would be paid?

BONUS: Was that amount a lot of money?

Answers on next page

ᵃ 10 Or *the Spirit*   ᵇ 10 Or *to*

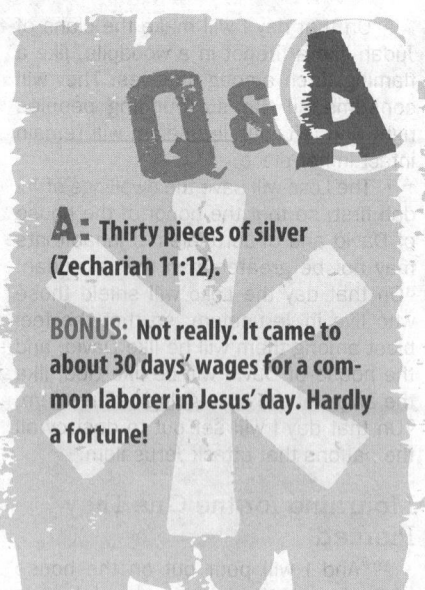

A: Thirty pieces of silver (Zechariah 11:12).

BONUS: Not really. It came to about 30 days' wages for a common laborer in Jesus' day. Hardly a fortune!

will not put on a prophet's garment of hair in order to deceive. ⁵Each will say, 'I am not a prophet. I am a farmer; the land has been my livelihood since my youth.ᵃ' ⁶If someone asks, 'What are these wounds on your bodyᵇ?' they will answer, 'The wounds I was given at the house of my friends.'

The Shepherd Struck, the Sheep Scattered

⁷ "Awake, sword, against my shepherd,
    against the man who is close to
        me!"
    declares the LORD Almighty.
"Strike the shepherd,
    and the sheep will be scattered,
    and I will turn my hand against the
        little ones.
⁸ In the whole land," declares the LORD,
    "two-thirds will be struck down and
        perish;
    yet one-third will be left in it.
⁹ This third I will put into the fire;
    I will refine them like silver
    and test them like gold.
They will call on my name
    and I will answer them;
I will say, 'They are my people,'
    and they will say, 'The LORD is our
        God.' "

of Hadad Rimmon in the plain of Megiddo. ¹²The land will mourn, each clan by itself, with their wives by themselves: the clan of the house of David and their wives, the clan of the house of Nathan and their wives, ¹³the clan of the house of Levi and their wives, the clan of Shimei and their wives, ¹⁴and all the rest of the clans and their wives.

Cleansing From Sin

13 "On that day a fountain will be opened to the house of David and the inhabitants of Jerusalem, to cleanse them from sin and impurity.

²"On that day, I will banish the names of the idols from the land, and they will be remembered no more," declares the LORD Almighty. "I will remove both the prophets and the spirit of impurity from the land. ³And if anyone still prophesies, their father and mother, to whom they were born, will say to them, 'You must die, because you have told lies in the LORD's name.' Then their own parents will stab the one who prophesies.

⁴"On that day every prophet will be ashamed of their prophetic vision. They

The LORD Comes and Reigns

14 A day of the LORD is coming, Jerusalem, when your possessions will be plundered and divided up within your very walls.

²I will gather all the nations to Jerusalem to fight against it; the city will be captured, the houses ransacked, and the women raped. Half of the city will go into exile, but the rest of the people will not be taken from the city. ³Then the LORD will go out and fight against those nations, as he fights on a day of battle. ⁴On that day his feet will stand on the Mount of Olives, east of Jerusalem, and the Mount of Olives will be split in two from east to west, forming a great valley, with half of the mountain moving north and half moving south. ⁵You will flee by my mountain

---

ᵃ 5 Or farmer; a man sold me in my youth   ᵇ 6 Or wounds between your hands valley, for it will extend to Azel. You will flee as you fled from the earthquake[a] in the days of Uzziah king of Judah. Then the LORD my God will come, and all the holy ones with him.

⁶On that day there will be neither sunlight nor cold, frosty darkness. ⁷It will be a unique day—a day known only to the LORD—with no distinction between day and night. When evening comes, there will be light.

⁸On that day living water will flow out from Jerusalem, half of it east to the Dead Sea and half of it west to the Mediterranean Sea, in summer and in winter. ⁹The LORD will be king over the whole earth. On that day there will be one LORD, and his name the only name.

¹⁰The whole land, from Geba to Rimmon, south of Jerusalem, will become like the Arabah. But Jerusalem will be raised up high from the Benjamin Gate to the site of the First Gate, to the Corner Gate, and from the Tower of Hananel to the royal winepresses, and will remain in its place. ¹¹It will be inhabited; never again will it be destroyed. Jerusalem will be secure.

¹²This is the plague with which the LORD will strike all the nations that fought against Jerusalem: Their flesh will rot while they are still standing on their feet, their eyes will rot in their sockets, and their tongues will rot in their mouths. ¹³On that day people will be stricken by the LORD with great panic. They will seize each other by the hand and attack one another. ¹⁴Judah too will fight at Jerusalem. The wealth of all the surrounding nations will be collected—great quantities of gold and silver and clothing. ¹⁵A similar plague will strike the horses and mules, the camels and donkeys, and all the animals in those camps.

¹⁶Then the survivors from all the nations that have attacked Jerusalem will go up year after year to worship the King, the LORD Almighty, and to celebrate the Festival of Tabernacles. ¹⁷If any of the peoples of the earth do not go up to Jerusalem to worship the King, the LORD Almighty, they will have no rain. ¹⁸If the Egyptian people do not go up and take part, they will have no rain. The LORD[b] will bring on them the plague he inflicts on the nations that do not go up to celebrate the Festival of Tabernacles. ¹⁹This will be the punishment of Egypt and the punishment of all the nations that do not go up to celebrate the Festival of Tabernacles.

²⁰On that day HOLY TO THE LORD will be inscribed on the bells of the horses, and the cooking pots in the LORD's house will be like the sacred bowls in front of the altar. ²¹Every pot in Jerusalem and Judah will be holy to the LORD Almighty, and all who come to sacrifice will take some of the pots and cook in them. And on that day there will no longer be a Canaanite[c] in the house of the LORD Almighty.

ᵃ 5 Or ⁵My mountain valley will be blocked and will extend to Azel. It will be blocked as it was blocked because of the earthquake   ᵇ 18 Or part, then the LORD   ᶜ 21 Or merchant

MALACHI

valley, for it will extend to Azel. You will flee as you fled from the earthquake in the days of Uzziah

preview

Malachi means "my messenger." God uses him to send a message to people who ignore the Lord.

Who, Me?

Have you ever seen someone play innocent? They do wrong, but they aren't going to admit it! It's almost funny. But it's frustrating too. What can you do with someone who won't admit anything, even when caught in the act?

In Malachi's day the "Who, me?" people were descendants of the captives who returned to Judah from Babylon. They'd become indifferent to God, and their lives showed it. No matter how they pretended, though, they couldn't fool the Lord. You might fool other people, but no one can fool God.

>>**DON'T HONOR GOD WITH CRUMBS**
People charged, see Malachi 1:6–11

>>**DO RESPECT AND TALK ABOUT HIM**
Something to do today, in Malachi 3:16–18

>>**STOMP THE WICKED? WHEN?**
Warning reported in Malachi 4:1–3

As Malachi preaches, about 430 B.C., war breaks out between Athens and Sparta. A plague kills 30,000 in Athens. Sophocles completes his play, "Oedipus the King." No more prophets will speak to God's people for over 400 years.

1 A prophecy: The word of the LORD to Israel through Malachi.[a]

Israel Doubts God's Love

2 "I have loved you," says the LORD.

"But you ask, 'How have you loved us?'

"Was not Esau Jacob's brother?" declares the LORD. "Yet I have loved Jacob, 3 but Esau I have hated, and I have turned his hill country into a wasteland and left his inheritance to the desert jackals."

4 Edom may say, "Though we have been crushed, we will rebuild the ruins."

But this is what the LORD Almighty says: "They may build, but I will demolish. They will be called the Wicked Land, a people always under the wrath of the LORD. 5 You will see it with your own eyes and say, 'Great is the LORD—even beyond the borders of Israel!'

Breaking Covenant Through Blemished Sacrifices

6 "A son honors his father, and a slave his master. If I am a father, where is the honor due me? If I am a master, where is the respect due me?" says the LORD Almighty.

"It is you priests who show contempt for my name.

"But you ask, 'How have we shown contempt for your name?'

7 "By offering defiled food on my altar.

"But you ask, 'How have we defiled you?'

"By saying that the LORD's table is contemptible. 8 When you offer blind animals for sacrifice, is that not wrong? When you sacrifice lame or diseased animals, is that not wrong? Try offering them to your governor! Would he be pleased with you? Would he accept you?" says the LORD Almighty.

9 "Now plead with God to be gracious to us. With such offerings from your hands, will he accept you?"—says the LORD Almighty.

10 "Oh, that one of you would shut the temple doors, so that you would not light useless fires on my altar! I am not pleased with you," says the LORD Almighty,

---

INSTANT ACCESS

Take a quick look at the first two verses in Malachi. Notice anything significant? The very first thing that God wanted to be sure his people knew was that *he loved them.* God had a lot of negative things to say to these people. He had a lot of scolding to do. But first he said, "I love you." In your relationships, especially with your family, is it easier to concentrate on what bugs you about them? What drives you nuts? Or just the fact that deep down you really love them? Keeping love at the front of your mind will make a big difference with how you treat others. Try to remember that when you're at home today.

{Malachi 1:1-2}

"and I will accept no offering from your hands. 11 My name will be great among the nations, from where the sun rises to where it sets. In every place incense and pure offerings will be brought to me, because my name will be great among the nations," says the LORD Almighty.

12 "But you profane it by saying, 'The Lord's table is defiled,' and, 'Its food is contemptible.' 13 And you say, 'What a burden!' and you sniff at it contemptuously," says the LORD Almighty.

---

[a] 1 Malachi means my messenger.

"When you bring injured, lame or diseased animals and offer them as sacrifices, should I accept them from your hands?" says the Lord. ¹⁴"Cursed is the cheat who has an acceptable male in his flock and vows to give it, but then sacrifices a blemished animal to the Lord. For I am a great king," says the Lord Almighty, "and my name is to be feared among the nations.

Additional Warning to the Priests

2 "And now, you priests, this warning is for you. ²If you do not listen, and if you do not resolve to honor my name," says the Lord Almighty, "I will send a curse on you, and I will curse your blessings. Yes, I have already cursed them, because you have not resolved to honor me.

³"Because of you I will rebuke your descendants[a]; I will smear on your faces the dung from your festival sacrifices, and you will be carried off with it. ⁴And you will know that I have sent you this warning so that my covenant with Levi may continue," says the Lord Almighty. ⁵"My covenant was with him, a covenant of life and peace, and I gave them to him; this called for reverence and he revered me and stood in awe of my name. ⁶True instruction was in his mouth and nothing false was found on his lips. He walked with me in peace and uprightness, and turned many from sin.

⁷"For the lips of a priest ought to preserve knowledge, because he is the messenger of the Lord Almighty and people seek instruction from his mouth. ⁸But you have turned from the way and by your teaching have caused many to stumble; you have violated the covenant with Levi," says the Lord Almighty. ⁹"So I have caused you to be despised and humiliated before all the people, because you have not followed my ways but have shown partiality in matters of the law."

Breaking Covenant Through Divorce

¹⁰Do we not all have one Father[b]? Did not one God create us? Why do we profane the covenant of our ancestors by being unfaithful to one another?

¹¹Judah has been unfaithful. A detestable thing has been committed in Israel and in Jerusalem: Judah has desecrated the sanctuary the Lord loves by marrying women who worship a foreign god. ¹²As for the man who does this, whoever he may be, may the Lord remove him from the tents of Jacob[c]—even though he brings an offering to the Lord Almighty.

¹³Another thing you do: You flood the Lord's altar with tears. You weep and wail because he no longer looks with favor on

---

a 3 Or will blight your grain   *b 10 Or father*   *c 12 Or ¹²May the Lord remove from the tents of Jacob anyone who gives testimony in behalf of the man who does this*

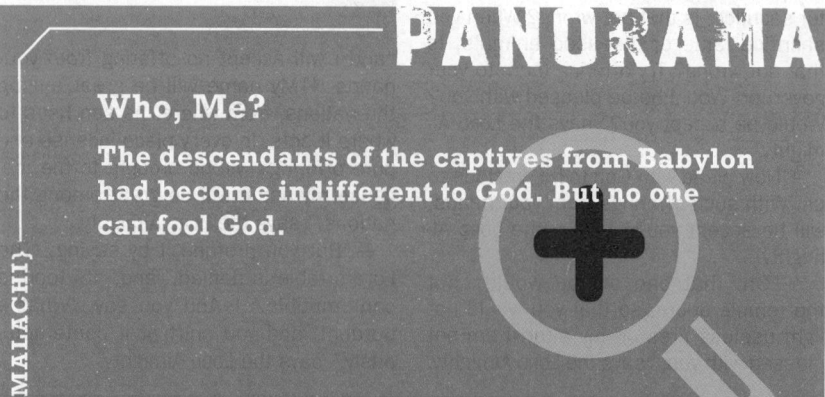

PANORAMA

Who, Me?
The descendants of the captives from Babylon had become indifferent to God. But no one can fool God.

{MALACHI}

your offerings or accepts them with pleasure from your hands. ¹⁴You ask, "Why?" It is because the LORD is the witness between you and the wife of your youth. You have been unfaithful to her, though she is your partner, the wife of your marriage covenant.

¹⁵Has not the one God made you? You belong to him in body and spirit. And what does the one God seek? Godly offspring.ᵃ So be on your guard, and do not be unfaithful to the wife of your youth.

¹⁶"The man who hates and divorces his wife," says the LORD, the God of Israel, "does violence to the one he should protect,"ᵇ says the LORD Almighty.

So be on your guard, and do not be unfaithful.

Breaking Covenant Through Injustice

¹⁷You have wearied the LORD with your words.

"How have we wearied him?" you ask.

By saying, "All who do evil are good in the eyes of the LORD, and he is pleased with them" or "Where is the God of justice?"

3 "I will send my messenger, who will prepare the way before me. Then suddenly the Lord you are seeking will come to his temple; the messenger of the covenant, whom you desire, will come," says the LORD Almighty.

²But who can endure the day of his coming? Who can stand when he appears? For he will be like a refiner's fire or a launderer's soap. ³He will sit as a refiner and purifier of silver; he will purify the Levites and refine them like gold and silver. Then the LORD will have men who will bring offerings in righteousness, ⁴and the offerings of Judah and Jerusalem will be acceptable to the LORD, as in days gone by, as in former years.

⁵"So I will come to put you on trial. I will be quick to testify against sorcerers, adulterers and perjurers, against those who defraud laborers of their wages, who oppress the widows and the fatherless, and deprive the foreigners among you of justice, but do not fear me," says the LORD Almighty.

Breaking Covenant by Withholding Tithes

⁶"I the LORD do not change. So you, the descendants of Jacob, are not destroyed. ⁷Ever since the time of your ancestors you have turned away from my decrees and have not kept them. Return to me, and I will return to you," says the LORD Almighty.

"But you ask, 'How are we to return?'

⁸"Will a mere mortal rob God? Yet you rob me.

"But you ask, 'How are we robbing you?'

"In tithes and offerings. ⁹You are under a curse—your whole nation—because you are robbing me. ¹⁰Bring the whole tithe into the storehouse, that there may be food in my house. Test me in this," says the LORD Almighty, "and see if I will not throw open the floodgates of heaven and pour out so much blessing that there will not be room enough to store it. ¹¹I will prevent pests from devouring your crops, and the vines in your fields will not drop their fruit before it is ripe," says the LORD Almighty. ¹²"Then all the nations will call you blessed, for yours will be a delightful land," says the LORD Almighty.

Israel Speaks Arrogantly Against God

¹³"You have spoken arrogantly against me," says the LORD.

"Yet you ask, 'What have we said against you?'

"On the day when I act," says the LORD Almighty, "they will be my treasured possession." Malachi 3:17

ᵃ 15 The meaning of the Hebrew for the first part of this verse is uncertain. ᵇ 16 Or "I hate divorce," says the LORD, the God of Israel, "because the man who divorces his wife covers his garment with violence,"

> The most popular girls at school go to parties and do things that I don't. I'm beginning to think the only way a boy is ever going to like me is if I go to those parties too. I get teased and called a prude. How bad can it be to join the crowd? >> Rachael

Dear Jordan

Dear Rachael,

Don't give in! Those girls may look happy, but girls (and guys) who are involved in what you have suggested often suffer depression and are vulnerable to many diseases as well as other bad things. Allowing yourself to be used by someone who will just be moving on to someone else in a few weeks or months is NOT a good trade off.

You may get some encouragement from Malachi 3:14–18. Those who were doing wrong seemed to be having such great lives while those who were obedient to God were walking around like mourners. But God does make a distinction between the righteous and the wicked. He knows and remembers those who are faithful to him.

Do you want to be remembered in ten years as a party girl or as a young woman who honored God and respected herself?

Jordan

14 "You have said, 'It is futile to serve God. What do we gain by carrying out his requirements and going about like mourners before the LORD Almighty? 15 But now we call the arrogant blessed. Certainly evildoers prosper, and even when they put God to the test, they get away with it.'"

The Faithful Remnant

16 Then those who feared the LORD talked with each other, and the LORD listened and heard. A scroll of remembrance was written in his presence concerning those who feared the LORD and honored his name.

17 "On the day when I act," says the LORD Almighty, "they will be my treasured possession. I will spare them, just as a father has compassion and spares his son who serves him. 18 And you will again see the distinction between the righteous and the wicked, between those who serve God and those who do not.

Judgment and Covenant Renewal

4 a "Surely the day is coming; it will burn like a furnace. All the arrogant and every evildoer will be stubble, and the day that is coming will set them on fire," says the LORD Almighty. "Not a root or a branch will be left to them. 2 But for you who revere my name, the sun of righteousness will rise with healing in its rays. And you will go out and frolic like well-fed calves. 3 Then you will trample on the wicked; they will be ashes under the soles of your feet on the day when I act," says the LORD Almighty.

4 "Remember the law of my servant Moses, the decrees and laws I gave him at Horeb for all Israel.

5 "See, I will send the prophet Elijah to you before that great and dreadful day of the LORD comes. 6 He will turn the hearts of the parents to their children, and the hearts of the children to their parents; or else I will come and strike the land with total destruction."

a In Hebrew texts 4:1-6 is numbered 3:19-24.

»NEW TESTAMENT

MATTHEW

preview

Looks.

Have you ever had someone describe a person to you? You get a mental picture of how that person looks. Then you meet him or her. Can that be the person? He or she sure doesn't look anything like you expected.

First-century Jews expected the promised Savior to be a conqueror. Jesus was a teacher. Instead of raising an army to defeat the Romans, he urged the people to trust him as God's Son. Matthew wrote to prove that Jesus really did fulfill the prophecies from the Old Testament and is the promised Savior. What Jesus conquered was sin. And the kingdom he rules today is in your heart.

Matthew is one of Jesus' twelve disciples.

Matthew quotes the Old Testament 53 times, to show that Jesus is the Messiah.

>> **FINAL SCORE: JESUS 3, SATAN 0**
Contest report found in Matthew 4:1–11

>> **RADICAL TEACHING SHOCKS PHARISEES**
"Not good enough," Jesus claims. See Matthew 5:17–30

>> **MIRACLE MAN RESTORES DEAD GIRL**
Story in Matthew 9:18–25

>> **JESUS' FOLLOWERS TO CARRY CROSSES?**
Private teaching puzzles followers. See Matthew 16:21–28

>> **ROMAN GOVERNOR CAVES IN TO PRESSURE**
Governor goes against conscience. See Matthew 27:11–26

When Jesus is born in 4 B.C., the Roman Empire is at peace. Augustus is in his 25th year as ruler. Herod the Great's expansion and beautification of the Jerusalem Temple is complete. Herod is about to die, and his kingdom will be divided among three of his children.

The Genealogy of Jesus the Messiah

1 This is the genealogy[a] of Jesus the Messiah[b] the son of David, the son of Abraham:

2 Abraham was the father of Isaac,
Isaac the father of Jacob,
Jacob the father of Judah and his brothers,
3 Judah the father of Perez and Zerah, whose mother was Tamar,
Perez the father of Hezron,
Hezron the father of Ram,
4 Ram the father of Amminadab,
Amminadab the father of Nahshon,
Nahshon the father of Salmon,
5 Salmon the father of Boaz, whose mother was Rahab,
Boaz the father of Obed, whose mother was Ruth,
Obed the father of Jesse,
6 and Jesse the father of King David.

David was the father of Solomon, whose mother had been Uriah's wife,
7 Solomon the father of Rehoboam,
Rehoboam the father of Abijah,
Abijah the father of Asa,
8 Asa the father of Jehoshaphat,
Jehoshaphat the father of Jehoram,
Jehoram the father of Uzziah,
9 Uzziah the father of Jotham,
Jotham the father of Ahaz,
Ahaz the father of Hezekiah,
10 Hezekiah the father of Manasseh,
Manasseh the father of Amon,
Amon the father of Josiah,
11 and Josiah the father of Jeconiah[c] and his brothers at the time of the exile to Babylon.

12 After the exile to Babylon:
Jeconiah was the father of Shealtiel,
Shealtiel the father of Zerubbabel,
13 Zerubbabel the father of Abihud,
Abihud the father of Eliakim,
Eliakim the father of Azor,
14 Azor the father of Zadok,
Zadok the father of Akim,
Akim the father of Elihud,
15 Elihud the father of Eleazar,
Eleazar the father of Matthan,
Matthan the father of Jacob,
16 and Jacob the father of Joseph, the husband of Mary, and Mary was the mother of Jesus who is called the Messiah.

17 Thus there were fourteen generations in all from Abraham to David, fourteen from David to the exile to Babylon, and fourteen from the exile to the Messiah.

Joseph Accepts Jesus as His Son

18 This is how the birth of Jesus the Messiah came about[d]: His mother Mary was pledged to be married to Joseph, but before they came together, she was found to be pregnant through the Holy Spirit. 19 Because Joseph her husband was faithful to the law, and yet[e] did not want to expose her to public disgrace, he had in mind to divorce her quietly.

20 But after he had considered this, an angel of the Lord appeared to him in a dream and said, "Joseph son of David, do not be afraid to take Mary home as your wife, because what is conceived in her is from the Holy Spirit. 21 She will give birth to a son, and you are to give him the name Jesus,[f] because he will save his people from their sins."

22 All this took place to fulfill what the Lord had said through the prophet: 23 "The virgin will conceive and give birth to a son, and they will call him Immanuel"[g] (which means "God with us").

24 When Joseph woke up, he did what the angel of the Lord had commanded him and took Mary home as his wife. 25 But he did not consummate their marriage until she gave birth to a son. And he gave him the name Jesus.

---

a 1 Or is an account of the origin   b 1 Or Jesus Christ. Messiah (Hebrew) and Christ (Greek) both mean Anointed One; also in verse 18.   c 11 That is, Jehoiachin; also in verse 12   d 18 Or The origin of Jesus the Messiah was like this   e 19 Or was a righteous man and   f 21 Jesus is the Greek form of Joshua, which means the LORD saves.
g 23 Isaiah 7:14

The Magi Visit the Messiah

2 After Jesus was born in Bethlehem in Judea, during the time of King Herod, Magi[a] from the east came to Jerusalem [2]and asked, "Where is the one who has been born king of the Jews? We saw his star when it rose and have come to worship him."

[3]When King Herod heard this he was disturbed, and all Jerusalem with him. [4]When he had called together all the people's chief priests and teachers of the law, he asked them where the Messiah was to be born. [5]"In Bethlehem in Judea," they replied, "for this is what the prophet has written:

[6]" 'But you, Bethlehem, in the land of
        Judah,
    are by no means least among the
        rulers of Judah;
    for out of you will come a ruler
    who will shepherd my people
        Israel.'[b]"

[7]Then Herod called the Magi secretly and found out from them the exact time the star had appeared. [8]He sent them to Bethlehem and said, "Go and search carefully for the child. As soon as you find him, report to me, so that I too may go and worship him."

[9]After they had heard the king, they went on their way, and the star they had seen when it rose went ahead of them until it stopped over the place where the child was. [10]When they saw the star, they were overjoyed. [11]On coming to the house, they saw the child with his mother Mary, and they bowed down and worshiped him. Then they opened their treasures and presented him with gifts of gold, frankincense and myrrh. [12]And having been warned in a dream not to go back to Herod, they returned to their country by another route.

The Escape to Egypt

[13]When they had gone, an angel of the Lord appeared to Joseph in a dream. "Get up," he said, "take the child and his mother and escape to Egypt. Stay there until I tell you, for Herod is going to search for the child to kill him."

[14]So he got up, took the child and his mother during the night and left for Egypt, [15]where he stayed until the death of Herod. And so was fulfilled what the Lord had said through the prophet: "Out of Egypt I called my son."[c]

[16]When Herod realized that he had been outwitted by the Magi, he was furious, and he gave orders to kill all the boys in Bethlehem and its vicinity who were two years old and under, in accordance with the time he had learned from the Magi. [17]Then what was said through the prophet Jeremiah was fulfilled:

[18]"A voice is heard in Ramah,
    weeping and great mourning,
Rachel weeping for her children
    and refusing to be comforted,
    because they are no more."[d]

The Return to Nazareth

[19]After Herod died, an angel of the Lord appeared in a dream to Joseph in Egypt [20]and said, "Get up, take the child and his mother and go to the land of Israel, for those who were trying to take the child's life are dead."

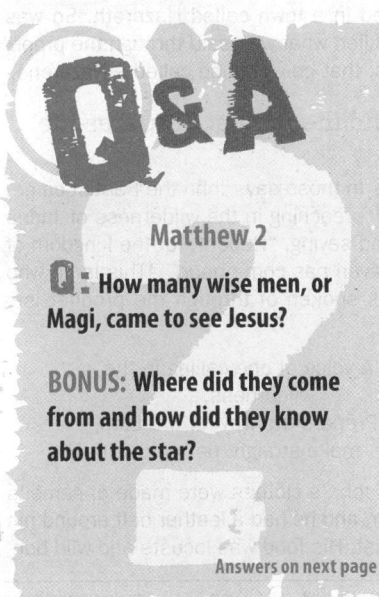

Matthew 2

Q: How many wise men, or Magi, came to see Jesus?

BONUS: Where did they come from and how did they know about the star?

Answers on next page

---

a 1 Traditionally *wise men*   b 6 Micah 5:2,4
c 15 Hosea 11:1   d 18 Jer. 31:15

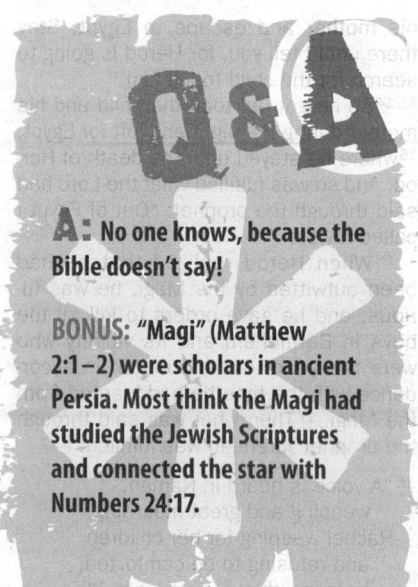

A: No one knows, because the Bible doesn't say!

BONUS: "Magi" (Matthew 2:1–2) were scholars in ancient Persia. Most think the Magi had studied the Jewish Scriptures and connected the star with Numbers 24:17.

21 So he got up, took the child and his mother and went to the land of Israel. 22 But when he heard that Archelaus was reigning in Judea in place of his father Herod, he was afraid to go there. Having been warned in a dream, he withdrew to the district of Galilee, 23 and he went and lived in a town called Nazareth. So was fulfilled what was said through the prophets, that he would be called a Nazarene.

John the Baptist Prepares the Way

3 In those days John the Baptist came, preaching in the wilderness of Judea 2 and saying, "Repent, for the kingdom of heaven has come near." 3 This is he who was spoken of through the prophet Isaiah:

"A voice of one calling in the
 wilderness,
'Prepare the way for the Lord,
 make straight paths for him.'"[a]

4 John's clothes were made of camel's hair, and he had a leather belt around his waist. His food was locusts and wild hon-

ey. 5 People went out to him from Jerusalem and all Judea and the whole region of the Jordan. 6 Confessing their sins, they were baptized by him in the Jordan River.

7 But when he saw many of the Pharisees and Sadducees coming to where he was baptizing, he said to them: "You brood of vipers! Who warned you to flee from the coming wrath? 8 Produce fruit in keeping with repentance. 9 And do not think you can say to yourselves, 'We have Abraham as our father.' I tell you that out of these stones God can raise up children for Abraham. 10 The ax is already at the root of the trees, and every tree that does not produce good fruit will be cut down and thrown into the fire.

11 "I baptize you with[b] water for repentance. But after me comes one who is more powerful than I, whose sandals I am not worthy to carry. He will baptize you with[b] the Holy Spirit and fire. 12 His winnowing fork is in his hand, and he will clear his threshing floor, gathering his wheat into the barn and burning up the chaff with unquenchable fire."

The Baptism of Jesus

13 Then Jesus came from Galilee to the Jordan to be baptized by John. 14 But John tried to deter him, saying, "I need to be baptized by you, and do you come to me?"

15 Jesus replied, "Let it be so now; it is proper for us to do this to fulfill all righteousness." Then John consented.

16 As soon as Jesus was baptized, he went up out of the water. At that moment heaven was opened, and he saw the Spirit of God descending like a dove and alighting on him. 17 And a voice from heaven said, "This is my Son, whom I love; with him I am well pleased."

Jesus Is Tested in the Wilderness

4 Then Jesus was led by the Spirit into the wilderness to be tempted[c] by the devil. 2 After fasting forty days and forty nights, he was hungry. 3 The tempter came

Did you hear about the preacher who asked his congregation, "Do you ever have trouble with giving in to temptation?" A voice from the choir answered, "Never. I can give in to temptation any time!" No doubt. But can you be tempted without giving in? Yes, if you follow Jesus' example. When Satan tempted him, Jesus looked to Scripture for guidance. Jesus knew that God's Word would show him what was right in each situation, and he put it into practice right then and there. If you trust God's Word as your guide to right and wrong, and if you choose to act on God's Word when you're tempted, you'll overcome your temptations too.

{Matthew 4:1–11}

to him and said, "If you are the Son of God, tell these stones to become bread."

⁴Jesus answered, "It is written: 'Man shall not live on bread alone, but on every word that comes from the mouth of God.'ᵃ"

⁵Then the devil took him to the holy city and had him stand on the highest point of the temple. ⁶"If you are the Son of God," he said, "throw yourself down. For it is written:

" 'He will command his angels
        concerning you,
    and they will lift you up in their
        hands,
      so that you will not strike your foot
        against a stone.'ᵇ"

⁷Jesus answered him, "It is also written: 'Do not put the Lord your God to the test.'ᶜ"

⁸Again, the devil took him to a very high mountain and showed him all the kingdoms of the world and their splendor. ⁹"All this I will give you," he said, "if you will bow down and worship me."

¹⁰Jesus said to him, "Away from me, Satan! For it is written: 'Worship the Lord your God, and serve him only.'ᵈ"

¹¹Then the devil left him, and angels came and attended him.

Jesus Begins to Preach

¹²When Jesus heard that John had been put in prison, he withdrew to Galilee. ¹³Leaving Nazareth, he went and lived in Capernaum, which was by the lake in the area of Zebulun and Naphtali— ¹⁴to fulfill what was said through the prophet Isaiah:

¹⁵"Land of Zebulun and land of
        Naphtali,
    the Way of the Sea, beyond the
        Jordan,
    Galilee of the Gentiles—
¹⁶the people living in darkness
    have seen a great light;
  on those living in the land of the
        shadow of death
    a light has dawned."ᵉ

¹⁷From that time on Jesus began to preach, "Repent, for the kingdom of heaven has come near."

Jesus Calls His First Disciples

¹⁸As Jesus was walking beside the Sea of Galilee, he saw two brothers, Simon called Peter and his brother Andrew. They were casting a net into the lake, for they were fishermen. ¹⁹"Come, follow me," Jesus said, "and I will send you out to

---

ᵃ 4 Deut. 8:3   ᵇ 6 Psalm 91:11,12   ᶜ 7 Deut. 6:16   ᵈ 10 Deut. 6:13   ᵉ 16 Isaiah 9:1,2

fish for people." [20] At once they left their nets and followed him.

[21] Going on from there, he saw two other brothers, James son of Zebedee and his brother John. They were in a boat with their father Zebedee, preparing their nets. Jesus called them, [22] and immediately they left the boat and their father and followed him.

Jesus Heals the Sick

[23] Jesus went throughout Galilee, teaching in their synagogues, proclaiming the good news of the kingdom, and healing every disease and sickness among the people. [24] News about him spread all over Syria, and people brought to him all who were ill with various diseases, those suffering severe pain, the demon-possessed, those having seizures, and the paralyzed; and he healed them. [25] Large crowds from Galilee, the Decapolis,[a] Jerusalem, Judea and the region across the Jordan followed him.

Introduction to the Sermon on the Mount

5 Now when Jesus saw the crowds, he went up on a mountainside and sat down. His disciples came to him, [2] and he began to teach them.

The Beatitudes

He said:

[3] "Blessed are the poor in spirit,
   for theirs is the kingdom of heaven.
[4] Blessed are those who mourn,
   for they will be comforted.
[5] Blessed are the meek,
   for they will inherit the earth.
[6] Blessed are those who hunger and
      thirst for righteousness,
   for they will be filled.
[7] Blessed are the merciful,
   for they will be shown mercy.
[8] Blessed are the pure in heart,
   for they will see God.
[9] Blessed are the peacemakers,
   for they will be called children of
      God.

[10] Blessed are those who are persecuted
      because of righteousness,
   for theirs is the kingdom of heaven.

[11] "Blessed are you when people insult you, persecute you and falsely say all kinds of evil against you because of me. [12] Rejoice and be glad, because great is your reward in heaven, for in the same way they persecuted the prophets who were before you.

Salt and Light

[13] "You are the salt of the earth. But if the salt loses its saltiness, how can it be made salty again? It is no longer good for anything, except to be thrown out and trampled underfoot.

[14] "You are the light of the world. A town built on a hill cannot be hidden. [15] Neither do people light a lamp and put it under a bowl. Instead they put it on its stand, and it gives light to everyone in the house. [16] In the same way, let your light shine before others, that they may see your good deeds and glorify your Father in heaven.

The Fulfillment of the Law

[17] "Do not think that I have come to abolish the Law or the Prophets; I have not come to abolish them but to fulfill them. [18] For truly I tell you, until heaven and earth disappear, not the smallest letter, not the least stroke of a pen, will by any means disappear from the Law until everything is accomplished. [19] Therefore anyone who sets aside one of the least of these commands and teaches others accordingly will be called least in the kingdom of heaven, but whoever practices and teaches these commands will be called great in the kingdom of heaven. [20] For I tell you that unless your righteousness surpasses that of the Pharisees and the teachers of the law, you will certainly not enter the kingdom of heaven.

Murder

[21] "You have heard that it was said to the people long ago, 'You shall not murder,[b] and anyone who murders will be

---

subject to judgment.' 22But I tell you that anyone who is angry with a brother or sister[a,b] will be subject to judgment. Again, anyone who says to a brother or sister, 'Raca,'[c] is answerable to the court. And anyone who says, 'You fool!' will be in danger of the fire of hell.

23"Therefore, if you are offering your gift at the altar and there remember that your brother or sister has something against you, 24leave your gift there in front of the altar. First go and be reconciled to them; then come and offer your gift.

25"Settle matters quickly with your adversary who is taking you to court. Do it while you are still together on the way, or your adversary may hand you over to the judge, and the judge may hand you over to the officer, and you may be thrown into prison. 26Truly I tell you, you will not get out until you have paid the last penny.

Adultery

27"You have heard that it was said, 'You shall not commit adultery.'[d] 28But I tell you that anyone who looks at a woman lustfully has already committed adultery with her in his heart. 29If your right eye causes you to stumble, gouge it out and throw it away. It is better for you to lose one part of your body than for your whole body to be thrown into hell. 30And if your right hand causes you to stumble, cut it off and throw it away. It is better for you to lose one part of your body than for your whole body to go into hell.

Divorce

31"It has been said, 'Anyone who divorces his wife must give her a certificate of divorce.'[e] 32But I tell you that anyone who divorces his wife, except for sexual immorality, makes her the victim of adul-

tery, and anyone who marries a divorced woman commits adultery.

Oaths

33"Again, you have heard that it was said to the people long ago, 'Do not break your oath, but fulfill to the Lord the vows you have made.' 34But I tell you, do not swear an oath at all: either by heaven, for it is God's throne; 35or by the earth, for it is his footstool; or by Jerusalem, for it is the city of the Great King. 36And do not swear by your head, for you cannot make even one hair white or black. 37All you need to say is simply 'Yes' or 'No'; anything beyond this comes from the evil one.[f]

Blessed are the pure in heart, for they will see God.
Matthew 5:8

Eye for Eye

38"You have heard that it was said, 'Eye for eye, and tooth for tooth.'[g] 39But I tell you, do not resist an evil person. If anyone slaps you on the right cheek, turn to them the other cheek also. 40And if anyone wants to sue you and take your shirt, hand over your coat as well. 41If anyone forces you to go one mile, go with them two miles. 42Give to the one who asks you, and do not turn away from the one who wants to borrow from you.

Love for Enemies

43"You have heard that it was said, 'Love your neighbor[h] and hate your enemy.' 44But I tell you, love your enemies and pray for those who persecute you, 45that you may be children of your Father in heaven. He causes his sun to rise on the evil and the good, and sends rain on the righteous and the unrighteous. 46If you love those who love you, what reward will you get? Are not even the tax collectors doing that? 47And if you greet only your own people, what are you doing

---

[a] 22 The Greek word for *brother or sister* (*adelphos*) refers here to a fellow disciple, whether man or woman; also in verse 23.   [b] 22 Some manuscripts *brother or sister without cause*   [c] 22 An Aramaic term of contempt
[d] 27 Exodus 20:14   [e] 31 Deut. 24:1   [f] 37 Or *from evil*   [g] 38 Exodus 21:24; Lev. 24:20; Deut. 19:21
[h] 43 Lev. 19:18

> A good friend betrayed me in the worst way. I don't want anything to do with her now. I don't want to be mean to her, but she has got to understand this. What's the best thing to do here?

>> Faith

Dear Jordan

Dear Faith,

It's hard to trust someone who has betrayed you. But since you asked what's the best thing to do, pray for her. Jesus said that even the pagans are kind to the people they love. So "love your enemies, and pray for those who persecute you" (Matthew 5:43–48).

This is not an easy thing, but it is a godly thing. It's amazing what happens when you pray for someone and even more amazing what happens to you. I hope you'll try it. Your friendship may or may not come back partially or all the way. But one great thing about praying for yourself and the person you're having a problem with is you won't be eaten up by negative feelings and thoughts. You may find you can even forgive your friend one day.

Love and forgiveness help us feel positive. Hatred and holding onto grudges can fill us with negative and bitter thoughts. Do something nice for yourself. Pray for your enemy and see what God does.

Jordan

No one likes the word *hypocrite*. Do you wonder sometimes if it applies to you? Does wanting to fit in with the other kids at school or wanting to be popular make you a hypocrite? No. It's natural to want to be accepted. Besides, how could you share your faith with others if everyone looked at you as an outsider? In the Bible a hypocrite is someone who is pretending, who is playing a role to impress others rather than being real. As long as you live by your convictions and don't pretend in order to fit in, you're no hypocrite. Not at all.

{Matthew 6:1–8}

>> INSTANT ACCESS

more than others? Do not even pagans do that? 48 Be perfect, therefore, as your heavenly Father is perfect.

Giving to the Needy

6 "Be careful not to practice your righteousness in front of others to be seen by them. If you do, you will have no reward from your Father in heaven.

2 "So when you give to the needy, do not announce it with trumpets, as the hypocrites do in the synagogues and on the streets, to be honored by others. Truly I tell you, they have received their reward in full. 3 But when you give to the needy, do not let your left hand know what your right hand is doing, 4 so that your giving may be in secret. Then your Father, who sees what is done in secret, will reward you.

Prayer

5 "And when you pray, do not be like the hypocrites, for they love to pray standing in the synagogues and on the street corners to be seen by others. Truly I tell you, they have received their reward in full. 6 But when you pray, go into your room, close the door and pray to your Father, who is unseen. Then your Father, who sees what is done in secret, will reward you. 7 And when you pray, do not keep on babbling like pagans, for they think they will be heard because of their many words. 8 Do not be like them, for your Father knows what you need before you ask him.

9 "This, then, is how you should pray:

" 'Our Father in heaven,
  hallowed be your name,
10 your kingdom come,
  your will be done,
    on earth as it is in heaven.
11 Give us today our daily bread.
12 And forgive us our debts,
    as we also have forgiven our
      debtors.
13 And lead us not into temptation,[a]
    but deliver us from the evil one.[b]'

14 For if you forgive other people when they sin against you, your heavenly Father will also forgive you. 15 But if you do not forgive others their sins, your Father will not forgive your sins.

Fasting

16 "When you fast, do not look somber as the hypocrites do, for they disfigure their faces to show others they are fasting. Truly I tell you, they have received their reward in full. 17 But when you fast, put oil on your head and wash your face, 18 so that it will not be obvious to others that you are fasting, but only to your Father, who is unseen; and your Father, who sees what is done in secret, will reward you.

---

a 13 The Greek for *temptation* can also mean *testing*.   b 13 Or *from evil*; some late manuscripts *one, / for yours is the kingdom and the power and the glory forever. Amen.*

Treasures in Heaven

19 "Do not store up for yourselves treasures on earth, where moths and vermin destroy, and where thieves break in and steal. 20 But store up for yourselves treasures in heaven, where moths and vermin do not destroy, and where thieves do not break in and steal. 21 For where your treasure is, there your heart will be also.

22 "The eye is the lamp of the body. If your eyes are healthy,*a* your whole body will be full of light. 23 But if your eyes are unhealthy,*b* your whole body will be full of darkness. If then the light within you is darkness, how great is that darkness!

24 "No one can serve two masters. Either you will hate the one and love the other, or you will be devoted to the one and despise the other. You cannot serve both God and money.

Do Not Worry

25 "Therefore I tell you, do not worry about your life, what you will eat or drink; or about your body, what you will wear. Is not life more than food, and the body more than clothes? 26 Look at the birds of the air; they do not sow or reap or store away in barns, and yet your heavenly Father feeds them. Are you not much more valuable than they? 27 Can any one of you by worrying add a single hour to your life*c*?

28 "And why do you worry about clothes? See how the flowers of the field grow. They do not labor or spin. 29 Yet I tell you that not even Solomon in all his splendor was dressed like one of these. 30 If that is how God clothes the grass of the field, which is here today and tomorrow is thrown into the fire, will he not much more clothe you—you of little faith? 31 So do not worry, saying, 'What shall we eat?' or 'What shall we drink?' or 'What shall we wear?' 32 For the pagans run after all these things, and

your heavenly Father knows that you need them. 33 But seek first his kingdom and his righteousness, and all these things will be given to you as well. 34 Therefore do not worry about tomorrow, for tomorrow will worry about itself. Each day has enough trouble of its own.

Judging Others

7 "Do not judge, or you too will be judged. 2 For in the same way you judge others, you will be judged, and with the measure you use, it will be measured to you.

3 "Why do you look at the speck of sawdust in your brother's eye and pay no attention to the plank in your own eye? 4 How can you say to your brother, 'Let me take the speck out of your eye,' when all the time there is a plank in your own eye? 5 You hypocrite, first take the plank out of your own eye, and then you will see clearly to remove the speck from your brother's eye.

6 "Do not give dogs what is sacred; do not throw your pearls to pigs. If you do, they may trample them under their feet, and turn and tear you to pieces.

Ask, Seek, Knock

7 "Ask and it will be given to you; seek and you will find; knock and the door will be opened to you. 8 For everyone who asks receives; the one who seeks finds; and to the one who knocks, the door will be opened.

9 "Which of you, if your son asks for bread, will give him a stone? 10 Or if he asks for a fish, will give him a snake? 11 If you, then, though you are evil, know how to give good gifts to your children, how much more will your Father in heaven give good gifts to those who ask him! 12 So in everything, do to others what you would have them do to you, for this sums up the Law and the Prophets.

Ask and it will be given to you; seek and you will find; knock and the door will be opened to you.

Matthew 7:7

---

a 22 The Greek for *healthy* here implies *generous*.   *b 23* The Greek for *unhealthy* here implies *stingy*.   *c 27* Or *single cubit to your height*

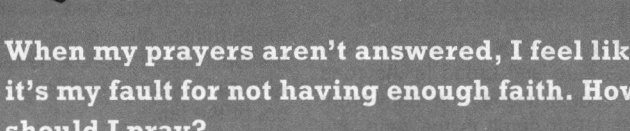

When my prayers aren't answered, I feel like it's my fault for not having enough faith. How should I pray?

>> Gabe

Dear Jordan

Dear Gabe,

Sometimes when Jesus addressed God he called him *Abba*, which is like us calling our fathers "daddy." Instead of the formal word, Jesus used an affectionate and familiar word used by little kids who rely on their parents for everything. Using this term might help you feel closer to God emotionally.

When Christ's disciples asked him how they should pray, he told them not to babble on and on as if the more words they used would help God hear their prayers better (Matthew 6:6–7). Verse 8 tells us that God knows what we need before we even ask. Jesus taught his disciples a short prayer which we now call the Lord's Prayer (Matthew 6:9–13). You can use it as a model for your own prayers.

When you pray, remember to thank God for what he has already done for you. Remember to praise his greatness each time you look at the beauty of the universe he's created. Take your needs and your pain to him. Ask for what you want but don't forget, we are to pray as Jesus did when he said, "Your will be done."

You said, "When my prayers aren't answered." Did you mean in the way you hoped? God answers our prayers. But like earthly parents, he sometimes answers with no or not yet. Sometimes his answer takes a long time. There are even times we can't see how God answered our prayers. But how God answers our prayers is up to him, so you don't have to feel like it's your fault when you don't see how the answer he's given will work out.

Jordan

The Narrow and Wide Gates

13 "Enter through the narrow gate. For wide is the gate and broad is the road that leads to destruction, and many enter through it. 14 But small is the gate and narrow the road that leads to life, and only a few find it.

True and False Prophets

15 "Watch out for false prophets. They come to you in sheep's clothing, but inwardly they are ferocious wolves. 16 By their fruit you will recognize them. Do people pick grapes from thornbushes, or figs from thistles? 17 Likewise, every good tree bears good fruit, but a bad tree bears bad fruit. 18 A good tree cannot bear bad fruit, and a bad tree cannot bear good fruit. 19 Every tree that does not bear good fruit is cut down and thrown into the fire. 20 Thus, by their fruit you will recognize them.

True and False Disciples

21 "Not everyone who says to me, 'Lord, Lord,' will enter the kingdom of heaven, but only the one who does the will of my Father who is in heaven. 22 Many will say to me on that day, 'Lord, Lord, did we not prophesy in your name and in your name drive out demons and in your name perform many miracles?' 23 Then I will tell them plainly, 'I never knew you. Away from me, you evildoers!'

The Wise and Foolish Builders

24 "Therefore everyone who hears these words of mine and puts them into practice is like a wise man who built his house on the rock. 25 The rain came down, the streams rose, and the winds blew and beat against that house; yet it did not fall, because it had its foundation on the rock. 26 But everyone who hears these words of mine and does not put them into practice is like a foolish man who built his house on sand. 27 The rain came down, the streams rose, and the winds blew and beat against that house, and it fell with a great crash."

28 When Jesus had finished saying these things, the crowds were amazed at his teaching, 29 because he taught as one who had authority, and not as their teachers of the law.

Jesus Heals a Man With Leprosy

8 When Jesus came down from the mountainside, large crowds followed him. 2 A man with leprosy[a] came and knelt before him and said, "Lord, if you are willing, you can make me clean."

3 Jesus reached out his hand and touched the man. "I am willing," he said. "Be clean!" Immediately he was cleansed of his leprosy. 4 Then Jesus said to him, "See that you don't tell anyone. But go, show yourself to the priest and offer the gift Moses commanded, as a testimony to them."

The Faith of the Centurion

5 When Jesus had entered Capernaum, a centurion came to him, asking for help. 6 "Lord," he said, "my servant lies at home paralyzed, suffering terribly."

7 Jesus said to him, "Shall I come and heal him?"

8 The centurion replied, "Lord, I do not deserve to have you come under my roof. But just say the word, and my servant will be healed. 9 For I myself am a man under authority, with soldiers under me. I tell this one, 'Go,' and he goes; and that one, 'Come,' and he comes. I say to my servant, 'Do this,' and he does it."

10 When Jesus heard this, he was amazed and said to those following him, "Truly I tell you, I have not found anyone in Israel with such great faith. 11 I say to you that many will come from the east and the west, and will take their places at the feast with Abraham, Isaac and Jacob in the kingdom of heaven. 12 But the subjects of the kingdom will be thrown outside, into the darkness, where there will be weeping and gnashing of teeth."

13 Then Jesus said to the centurion, "Go! Let it be done just as you believed it would." And his servant was healed at that moment.

---

a 2 The Greek word traditionally translated *leprosy* was used for various diseases affecting the skin.

Jesus Heals Many

¹⁴When Jesus came into Peter's house, he saw Peter's mother-in-law lying in bed with a fever. ¹⁵He touched her hand and the fever left her, and she got up and began to wait on him.

¹⁶When evening came, many who were demon-possessed were brought to him, and he drove out the spirits with a word and healed all the sick. ¹⁷This was to fulfill what was spoken through the prophet Isaiah:

"He took up our infirmities
and bore our diseases."ᵃ

The Cost of Following Jesus

¹⁸When Jesus saw the crowd around him, he gave orders to cross to the other side of the lake. ¹⁹Then a teacher of the law came to him and said, "Teacher, I will follow you wherever you go."

²⁰Jesus replied, "Foxes have dens and birds have nests, but the Son of Man has no place to lay his head."

²¹Another disciple said to him, "Lord, first let me go and bury my father."

²²But Jesus told him, "Follow me, and let the dead bury their own dead."

Jesus Calms the Storm

²³Then he got into the boat and his disciples followed him. ²⁴Suddenly a furious storm came up on the lake, so that the waves swept over the boat. But Jesus was sleeping. ²⁵The disciples went and woke him, saying, "Lord, save us! We're going to drown!"

ᵃ 17 Isaiah 53:4 (see Septuagint)

TO THE POINT

Demons Are Real

In the New Testament evil beings are called demons, or evil spirits (Matthew 8:28–34). Most believe that demons are angels who followed Satan in his rebellion against God. Those who practice witchcraft worship demons, not God or his angels (1 Corinthians 10:20).

It is important to remember that demons are the enemies of God and of human beings.

+ Demons are violent and malicious (Matthew 8:28).

+ Demons cause sickness (Matthew 4:24; 12:22; 17:15–18).

+ Demons corrupt morals (1 Timothy 4:1–3).

+ Demons aim their arsenal at believers (Ephesians 6:12).

Don't be tempted to toy with the occult. Remember to rely on Jesus. After all, Jesus easily overpowered every demon he met.

26 He replied, "You of little faith, why are you so afraid?" Then he got up and rebuked the winds and the waves, and it was completely calm.

27 The men were amazed and asked, "What kind of man is this? Even the winds and the waves obey him!"

Jesus Restores Two Demon-Possessed Men

28 When he arrived at the other side in the region of the Gadarenes,ᵃ two demon-possessed men coming from the tombs met him. They were so violent that no one could pass that way. 29 "What do you want with us, Son of God?" they shouted. "Have you come here to torture us before the appointed time?"

30 Some distance from them a large herd of pigs was feeding. 31 The demons begged Jesus, "If you drive us out, send us into the herd of pigs."

32 He said to them, "Go!" So they came out and went into the pigs, and the whole herd rushed down the steep bank into the lake and died in the water. 33 Those tending the pigs ran off, went into the town and reported all this, including what had happened to the demon-possessed men. 34 Then the whole town went out to meet Jesus. And when they saw him, they pleaded with him to leave their region.

Jesus Forgives and Heals a Paralyzed Man

9 Jesus stepped into a boat, crossed over and came to his own town. 2 Some men brought to him a paralyzed man, lying on a mat. When Jesus saw their faith, he said to the man, "Take heart, son; your sins are forgiven."

3 At this, some of the teachers of the law said to themselves, "This fellow is blaspheming!"

4 Knowing their thoughts, Jesus said, "Why do you entertain evil thoughts in your hearts? 5 Which is easier: to say, 'Your sins are forgiven,' or to say, 'Get up and walk'? 6 But I want you to know that the Son of Man has authority on earth to forgive sins." So he said to the para-lyzed man, "Get up, take your mat and go home." 7 Then the man got up and went home. 8 When the crowd saw this, they were filled with awe; and they praised God, who had given such authority to man.

The Calling of Matthew

9 As Jesus went on from there, he saw a man named Matthew sitting at the tax collector's booth. "Follow me," he told him, and Matthew got up and followed him.

10 While Jesus was having dinner at Matthew's house, many tax collectors and sinners came and ate with him and his disciples. 11 When the Pharisees saw this, they asked his disciples, "Why does your teacher eat with tax collectors and sinners?"

12 On hearing this, Jesus said, "It is not the healthy who need a doctor, but the sick. 13 But go and learn what this means: 'I desire mercy, not sacrifice.'ᵇ For I have not come to call the righteous, but sinners."

Jesus Questioned About Fasting

14 Then John's disciples came and asked him, "How is it that we and the Pharisees fast often, but your disciples do not fast?"

15 Jesus answered, "How can the guests of the bridegroom mourn while he is with them? The time will come when the bridegroom will be taken from them; then they will fast.

16 "No one sews a patch of unshrunk cloth on an old garment, for the patch will pull away from the garment, making the tear worse. 17 Neither do people pour new wine into old wineskins. If they do, the skins will burst; the wine will run out and the wineskins will be ruined. No, they pour new wine into new wineskins, and both are preserved."

Jesus Raises a Dead Girl and Heals a Sick Woman

18 While he was saying this, a synagogue leader came and knelt before him and said, "My daughter has just died. But come and put your hand on her, and she will live." 19 Jesus got up and went with him, and so did his disciples.

ᵃ 28 Some manuscripts *Gergesenes*; other manuscripts *Gerasenes*   ᵇ 13 Hosea 6:6

20 Just then a woman who had been subject to bleeding for twelve years came up behind him and touched the edge of his cloak. 21 She said to herself, "If I only touch his cloak, I will be healed."

22 Jesus turned and saw her. "Take heart, daughter," he said, "your faith has healed you." And the woman was healed at that moment.

23 When Jesus entered the synagogue leader's house and saw the noisy crowd and people playing pipes, 24 he said, "Go away. The girl is not dead but asleep." But they laughed at him. 25 After the crowd had been put outside, he went in and took the girl by the hand, and she got up. 26 News of this spread through all that region.

Jesus Heals the Blind and the Mute

27 As Jesus went on from there, two blind men followed him, calling out, "Have mercy on us, Son of David!"

28 When he had gone indoors, the blind men came to him, and he asked them, "Do you believe that I am able to do this?"

"Yes, Lord," they replied.

29 Then he touched their eyes and said, "According to your faith let it be done to you"; 30 and their sight was restored. Jesus warned them sternly, "See that no one knows about this." 31 But they went out and spread the news about him all over that region.

32 While they were going out, a man who was demon-possessed and could not talk was brought to Jesus. 33 And when the demon was driven out, the man who had been mute spoke. The crowd was amazed and said, "Nothing like this has ever been seen in Israel."

34 But the Pharisees said, "It is by the prince of demons that he drives out demons."

The Workers Are Few

35 Jesus went through all the towns and villages, teaching in their synagogues, proclaiming the good news of the kingdom and healing every disease and sickness.

36 When he saw the crowds, he had compassion on them, because they were harassed and helpless, like sheep without a shepherd. 37 Then he said to his disciples, "The harvest is plentiful but the workers are few. 38 Ask the Lord of the harvest, therefore, to send out workers into his harvest field."

Jesus Sends Out the Twelve

10 Jesus called his twelve disciples to him and gave them authority to drive out impure spirits and to heal every disease and sickness.

2 These are the names of the twelve apostles: first, Simon (who is called Peter) and his brother Andrew; James son of Zebedee, and his brother John; 3 Philip and Bartholomew; Thomas and Matthew the tax collector; James son of Alphaeus, and Thaddaeus; 4 Simon the Zealot and Judas Iscariot, who betrayed him.

5 These twelve Jesus sent out with the following instructions: "Do not go among the Gentiles or enter any town of the Samaritans. 6 Go rather to the lost sheep of Israel. 7 As you go, proclaim this message: 'The kingdom of heaven has come near.' 8 Heal the sick, raise the dead, cleanse those who have leprosy,ª drive out demons. Freely you have received; freely give.

9 "Do not get any gold or silver or copper to take with you in your belts— 10 no bag for the journey or extra shirt or sandals or a staff, for the worker is worth his keep. 11 Whatever town or village you enter, search there for some worthy person and stay at their house until you leave. 12 As you enter the home, give it your greeting. 13 If the home is deserving, let your peace rest on it; if it is not, let your peace return to you. 14 If anyone will not welcome you or listen to your words, leave that home or town and shake the dust off your feet. 15 Truly I tell you, it will be more bearable for Sodom and Gomorrah on the day of judgment than for that town.

16 "I am sending you out like sheep among wolves. Therefore be as shrewd as snakes and as innocent as doves.

ª 8 The Greek word traditionally translated *leprosy* was used for various diseases affecting the skin.

17 Be on your guard; you will be handed over to the local councils and be flogged in the synagogues. 18 On my account you will be brought before governors and kings as witnesses to them and to the Gentiles. 19 But when they arrest you, do not worry about what to say or how to say it. At that time you will be given what to say, 20 for it will not be you speaking, but the Spirit of your Father speaking through you.

21 "Brother will betray brother to death, and a father his child; children will rebel against their parents and have them put to death. 22 You will be hated by everyone because of me, but the one who stands firm to the end will be saved. 23 When you are persecuted in one place, flee to another. Truly I tell you, you will not finish going through the towns of Israel before the Son of Man comes.

24 "The student is not above the teacher, nor a servant above his master. 25 It is enough for students to be like their teachers, and servants like their masters. If the head of the house has been called Beelzebul, how much more the members of his household!

26 "So do not be afraid of them, for there is nothing concealed that will not be disclosed, or hidden that will not be made known. 27 What I tell you in the dark, speak in the daylight; what is whispered in your ear, proclaim from the roofs. 28 Do not be afraid of those who kill the body but cannot kill the soul. Rather, be afraid of the One who can destroy both soul and body in hell. 29 Are not two sparrows sold for a penny? Yet not one of them will fall to the ground outside your Father's care.[a] 30 And even the very hairs of your head are all numbered. 31 So don't be afraid; you are worth more than many sparrows.

32 "Whoever acknowledges me before others, I will also acknowledge before my Father in heaven. 33 But whoever disowns me before others, I will disown before my Father in heaven.

34 "Do not suppose that I have come to bring peace to the earth. I did not come to bring peace, but a sword. 35 For I have come to turn

INSTANT ACCESS

This is one of the hardest sayings in the New Testament. And it describes a hard experience. For some teens becoming a Christian creates real conflict in the family. Some parents will forbid a teen to go to a youth group or church of his or her choice. So what do you do? You're supposed to obey your parents. But you want to be with your Christian friends too. Usually it's best to honor your parents' wishes, read your Bible and try to meet with one or two friends to talk and pray. That way you can be faithful to the Lord and to your parents too. Only in the most unusual case will loving Christ mean a serious break with those at home.

{Matthew 10:34–38}

" 'a man against his father,
    a daughter against her mother,
a daughter-in-law against her mother-
    in-law—
36   a man's enemies will be the
    members of his own
    household.'[b]

37 "Anyone who loves their father or mother more than me is not worthy of me; anyone who loves their son or daughter more than me is not worthy of me.

---

[a] 29 Or will; or knowledge   [b] 36 Micah 7:6

[38]Whoever does not take up their cross and follow me is not worthy of me. [39]Whoever finds their life will lose it, and whoever loses their life for my sake will find it.

[40]"Anyone who welcomes you welcomes me, and anyone who welcomes me welcomes the one who sent me. [41]Whoever welcomes a prophet as a prophet will receive a prophet's reward, and whoever welcomes a righteous person as a righteous person will receive a righteous person's reward. [42]And if anyone gives even a cup of cold water to one of these little ones who is my disciple, truly I tell you, that person will certainly not lose their reward."

Jesus and John the Baptist

11 After Jesus had finished instructing his twelve disciples, he went on from there to teach and preach in the towns of Galilee.[a]

[2]When John, who was in prison, heard about the deeds of the Messiah, he sent his disciples [3]to ask him, "Are you the one who is to come, or should we expect someone else?"

[4]Jesus replied, "Go back and report to John what you hear and see: [5]The blind receive sight, the lame walk, those who have leprosy[b] are cleansed, the deaf hear, the dead are raised, and the good news is proclaimed to the poor. [6]Blessed is anyone who does not stumble on account of me."

[7]As John's disciples were leaving, Jesus began to speak to the crowd about John: "What did you go out into the wilderness to see? A reed swayed by the wind? [8]If not, what did you go out to see? A man dressed in fine clothes? No, those who wear fine clothes are in kings' palaces. [9]Then what did you go out to see? A prophet? Yes, I tell you, and more than a prophet. [10]This is the one about whom it is written:

" 'I will send my messenger ahead of
you,
who will prepare your way before
you.'[c]

[11]Truly I tell you, among those born of women there has not risen anyone greater than John the Baptist; yet whoever is least in the kingdom of heaven is greater than he. [12]From the days of John the Baptist until now, the kingdom of heaven has been subjected to violence,[d] and violent people have been raiding it. [13]For all the Prophets and the Law prophesied until John. [14]And if you are willing to accept it, he is the Elijah who was to come. [15]Whoever has ears, let them hear.

[16]"To what can I compare this generation? They are like children sitting in the marketplaces and calling out to others:

[17]" 'We played the pipe for you,
and you did not dance;
we sang a dirge,
and you did not mourn.'

[18]For John came neither eating nor drinking, and they say, 'He has a demon.' [19]The Son of Man came eating and drinking, and they say, 'Here is a glutton and a drunkard, a friend of tax collectors and sinners.' But wisdom is proved right by her deeds."

Woe on Unrepentant Towns

[20]Then Jesus began to denounce the towns in which most of his miracles had been performed, because they did not repent. [21]"Woe to you, Chorazin! Woe to you, Bethsaida! For if the miracles that were performed in you had been performed in Tyre and Sidon, they would have repented long ago in sackcloth and ashes. [22]But I tell you, it will be more bearable for Tyre and Sidon on the day of judgment than for you. [23]And you, Capernaum, will you be lifted to the heavens? No, you will go down to Hades.[e] For if the miracles that were performed in you had been performed in Sodom, it would have remained to this day. [24]But I tell you that it will be more bearable for Sodom on the day of judgment than for you."

The Father Revealed in the Son

[25]At that time Jesus said, "I praise you, Father, Lord of heaven and earth,

---

[a] 1 Greek *in their towns*   [b] 5 The Greek word traditionally translated *leprosy* was used for various diseases affecting the skin.   [c] 10 Mal. 3:1   [d] 12 Or *been forcefully advancing*   [e] 23 That is, the realm of the dead

because you have hidden these things from the wise and learned, and revealed them to little children. 26 Yes, Father, for this is what you were pleased to do.

27 "All things have been committed to me by my Father. No one knows the Son except the Father, and no one knows the Father except the Son and those to whom the Son chooses to reveal him.

28 "Come to me, all you who are weary and burdened, and I will give you rest. 29 Take my yoke upon you and learn from me, for I am gentle and humble in heart, and you will find rest for your souls. 30 For my yoke is easy and my burden is light."

Jesus Is Lord of the Sabbath

12 At that time Jesus went through the grainfields on the Sabbath. His disciples were hungry and began to pick some heads of grain and eat them. 2 When the Pharisees saw this, they said to him, "Look! Your disciples are doing what is unlawful on the Sabbath."

3 He answered, "Haven't you read what David did when he and his companions were hungry? 4 He entered the house of God, and he and his companions ate the consecrated bread—which was not lawful for them to do, but only for the priests. 5 Or haven't you read in the Law that the priests on Sabbath duty in the temple desecrate the Sabbath and yet are innocent? 6 I tell you that something greater than the temple is here. 7 If you had known what these words mean, 'I desire mercy, not sacrifice,'*a* you would not have condemned the innocent. 8 For the Son of Man is Lord of the Sabbath."

9 Going on from that place, he went into their synagogue, 10 and a man with a shriveled hand was there. Looking for a reason to bring charges against Jesus, they asked him, "Is it lawful to heal on the Sabbath?"

11 He said to them, "If any of you has a sheep and it falls into a pit on the Sabbath, will you not take hold of it and lift it out? 12 How much more valuable is a person than a sheep! Therefore it is lawful to do good on the Sabbath."

13 Then he said to the man, "Stretch out your hand." So he stretched it out and it was completely restored, just as sound as the other. 14 But the Pharisees went out and plotted how they might kill Jesus.

Come to me, all you who are weary and burdened, and I will give you rest.
Matthew 11:28

God's Chosen Servant

15 Aware of this, Jesus withdrew from that place. A large crowd followed him, and he healed all who were ill. 16 He warned them not to tell others about him. 17 This was to fulfill what was spoken through the prophet Isaiah:

18 "Here is my servant whom I have
    chosen,
    the one I love, in whom I delight;
I will put my Spirit on him,
    and he will proclaim justice to the
        nations.
19 He will not quarrel or cry out;
    no one will hear his voice in the
        streets.
20 A bruised reed he will not break,
    and a smoldering wick he will not
        snuff out,
    till he has brought justice through to
        victory.
21   In his name the nations will put
        their hope."*b*

Jesus and Beelzebul

22 Then they brought him a demon-possessed man who was blind and mute, and Jesus healed him, so that he could both talk and see. 23 All the people were astonished and said, "Could this be the Son of David?"

24 But when the Pharisees heard this, they said, "It is only by Beelzebul, the

---

a 7 Hosea 6:6   *b* 21 Isaiah 42:1-4

prince of demons, that this fellow drives out demons."

25 Jesus knew their thoughts and said to them, "Every kingdom divided against itself will be ruined, and every city or household divided against itself will not stand. 26 If Satan drives out Satan, he is divided against himself. How then can his kingdom stand? 27 And if I drive out demons by Beelzebul, by whom do your people drive them out? So then, they will be your judges. 28 But if it is by the Spirit of God that I drive out demons, then the kingdom of God has come upon you.

29 "Or again, how can anyone enter a strong man's house and carry off his possessions unless he first ties up the strong man? Then he can plunder his house.

30 "Whoever is not with me is against me, and whoever does not gather with me scatters. 31 And so I tell you, every kind of sin and slander can be forgiven, but blasphemy against the Spirit will not be forgiven. 32 Anyone who speaks a word against the Son of Man will be forgiven, but anyone who speaks against the Holy Spirit will not be forgiven, either in this age or in the age to come.

33 "Make a tree good and its fruit will be good, or make a tree bad and its fruit will be bad, for a tree is recognized by its fruit. 34 You brood of vipers, how can you who are evil say anything good? For the mouth speaks what the heart is full of. 35 A good man brings good things out of the good stored up in him, and an evil man brings evil things out of the evil stored up in him. 36 But I tell you that everyone will have to give account on the day of judgment for every empty word they have spoken. 37 For by your words you will be acquitted, and by your words you will be condemned."

The Sign of Jonah

38 Then some of the Pharisees and teachers of the law said to him, "Teacher, we want to see a sign from you."

39 He answered, "A wicked and adulterous generation asks for a sign! But none will be given it except the sign of the prophet Jonah. 40 For as Jonah was three days and three nights in the belly of a huge fish, so the Son of Man will be three days and three nights in the heart of the earth. 41 The men of Nineveh will stand up at the judgment with this generation and condemn it; for they repented at the preaching of Jonah, and now something greater than Jonah is here. 42 The Queen of the South will rise at the judgment with this generation and condemn it; for she came from the ends of the earth to listen to Solomon's wisdom, and now something greater than Solomon is here.

43 "When an impure spirit comes out of a person, it goes through arid places seeking rest and does not find it. 44 Then it says, 'I will return to the house I left.' When it arrives, it finds the house unoccupied, swept clean and put in order. 45 Then it goes and takes with it seven other spirits more wicked than itself, and they go in and live there. And the final condition of that person is worse than the first. That is how it will be with this wicked generation."

Jesus' Mother and Brothers

46 While Jesus was still talking to the crowd, his mother and brothers stood outside, wanting to speak to him. 47 Someone told him, "Your mother and brothers are standing outside, wanting to speak to you."

48 He replied to him, "Who is my mother, and who are my brothers?" 49 Pointing to his disciples, he said, "Here are my mother and my brothers. 50 For whoever does the will of my Father in heaven is my brother and sister and mother."

The Parable of the Sower

13 That same day Jesus went out of the house and sat by the lake. 2 Such large crowds gathered around him that he got into a boat and sat in it, while all the people stood on the shore. 3 Then he told them many things in parables, saying: "A farmer went out to sow his seed. 4 As he was scattering the seed, some fell along the path, and the birds came and ate it up. 5 Some fell on rocky places, where it did not have much soil.

It sprang up quickly, because the soil was shallow. [6]But when the sun came up, the plants were scorched, and they withered because they had no root. [7]Other seed fell among thorns, which grew up and choked the plants. [8]Still other seed fell on good soil, where it produced a crop— a hundred, sixty or thirty times what was sown. [9]Whoever has ears, let them hear."

[10]The disciples came to him and asked, "Why do you speak to the people in parables?"

[11]He replied, "Because the knowledge of the secrets of the kingdom of heaven has been given to you, but not to them. [12]Whoever has will be given more, and they will have an abundance. Whoever does not have, even what they have will be taken from them. [13]This is why I speak to them in parables:

"Though seeing, they do not see;
  though hearing, they do not hear or
    understand.

[14]In them is fulfilled the prophecy of Isaiah:

" 'You will be ever hearing but never
    understanding;
  you will be ever seeing but never
    perceiving.
[15]For this people's heart has become
    calloused;
  they hardly hear with their ears,
  and they have closed their eyes.
Otherwise they might see with their
    eyes,
  hear with their ears,
  understand with their hearts
and turn, and I would heal them.'[a]

[16]But blessed are your eyes because they see, and your ears because they hear. [17]For truly I tell you, many prophets and righteous people longed to see what you see but did not see it, and to hear what you hear but did not hear it.

[18]"Listen then to what the parable of the sower means: [19]When anyone hears the message about the kingdom and does not understand it, the evil one comes and snatches away what was sown in their

heart. This is the seed sown along the path. [20]The seed falling on rocky ground refers to someone who hears the word and at once receives it with joy. [21]But since they have no root, they last only a short time. When trouble or persecution comes because of the word, they quickly fall away. [22]The seed falling among the thorns refers to someone who hears the word, but the worries of this life and the deceitfulness of wealth choke the word, making it unfruitful. [23]But the seed falling on good soil refers to someone who hears the word and understands it. This is the one who produces a crop, yielding a hundred, sixty or thirty times what was sown."

The Parable of the Weeds

[24]Jesus told them another parable: "The kingdom of heaven is like a man who sowed good seed in his field. [25]But while everyone was sleeping, his enemy came and sowed weeds among the wheat, and went away. [26]When the wheat sprouted and formed heads, then the weeds also appeared.

[27]"The owner's servants came to him and said, 'Sir, didn't you sow good seed in your field? Where then did the weeds come from?'

[28]" 'An enemy did this,' he replied.

"The servants asked him, 'Do you want us to go and pull them up?'

[29]" 'No,' he answered, 'because while you are pulling the weeds, you may uproot the wheat with them. [30]Let both grow together until the harvest. At that time I will tell the harvesters: First collect the weeds and tie them in bundles to be burned; then gather the wheat and bring it into my barn.' "

The Parables of the Mustard Seed and the Yeast

[31]He told them another parable: "The kingdom of heaven is like a mustard seed, which a man took and planted in his field. [32]Though it is the smallest of all seeds, yet when it grows, it is the

---

[a] 15 Isaiah 6:9,10 (see Septuagint)

largest of garden plants and becomes a tree, so that the birds come and perch in its branches."

33 He told them still another parable: "The kingdom of heaven is like yeast that a woman took and mixed into about sixty pounds[a] of flour until it worked all through the dough."

34 Jesus spoke all these things to the crowd in parables; he did not say anything to them without using a parable. 35 So was fulfilled what was spoken through the prophet:

"I will open my mouth in parables,
     I will utter things hidden since the
          creation of the world."[b]

The Parable of the Weeds Explained

36 Then he left the crowd and went into the house. His disciples came to him and said, "Explain to us the parable of the weeds in the field."

37 He answered, "The one who sowed the good seed is the Son of Man. 38 The field is the world, and the good seed stands for the people of the kingdom. The weeds are the people of the evil one, 39 and the enemy who sows them is the devil. The harvest is the end of the age, and the harvesters are angels.

40 "As the weeds are pulled up and burned in the fire, so it will be at the end of the age. 41 The Son of Man will send out his angels, and they will weed out of his kingdom everything that causes sin and all who do evil. 42 They will throw them into the blazing furnace, where there will be weeping and gnashing of teeth. 43 Then the righteous will shine like the sun in the kingdom of their Father. Whoever has ears, let them hear.

The Parables of the Hidden Treasure and the Pearl

44 "The kingdom of heaven is like treasure hidden in a field. When a man found it, he hid it again, and then in his joy went and sold all he had and bought that field.

45 "Again, the kingdom of heaven is like a merchant looking for fine pearls. 46 When he found one of great value, he went away and sold everything he had and bought it.

The Parable of the Net

47 "Once again, the kingdom of heaven is like a net that was let down into the lake and caught all kinds of fish. 48 When it was full, the fishermen pulled it up on the shore. Then they sat down and collected the good fish in baskets, but threw the bad away. 49 This is how it will be at the end of the age. The angels will come and separate the wicked from the righteous 50 and throw them into the blazing furnace, where there will be weeping and gnashing of teeth.

51 "Have you understood all these things?" Jesus asked.

"Yes," they replied.

52 He said to them, "Therefore every teacher of the law who has become a disciple in the kingdom of heaven is like the owner of a house who brings out of his storeroom new treasures as well as old."

A Prophet Without Honor

53 When Jesus had finished these parables, he moved on from there. 54 Coming to his hometown, he began teaching the people in their synagogue, and they were amazed. "Where did this man get this wisdom and these miraculous powers?" they asked. 55 "Isn't this the carpenter's son? Isn't his mother's name Mary, and aren't his brothers James, Joseph, Simon and Judas? 56 Aren't all his sisters with us? Where then did this man get all these things?" 57 And they took offense at him.

But Jesus said to them, "A prophet is not without honor except in his own town and in his own home."

58 And he did not do many miracles there because of their lack of faith.

John the Baptist Beheaded

14 At that time Herod the tetrarch heard the reports about Jesus, 2 and he said to his attendants, "This is

John the Baptist; he has risen from the dead! That is why miraculous powers are at work in him."

3 Now Herod had arrested John and bound him and put him in prison because of Herodias, his brother Philip's wife, 4 for John had been saying to him: "It is not lawful for you to have her." 5 Herod wanted to kill John, but he was afraid of the people, because they considered John a prophet.

6 On Herod's birthday the daughter of Herodias danced for the guests and pleased Herod so much 7 that he promised with an oath to give her whatever she asked. 8 Prompted by her mother, she said, "Give me here on a platter the head of John the Baptist." 9 The king was distressed, but because of his oaths and his dinner guests, he ordered that her request be granted 10 and had John beheaded in the prison. 11 His head was brought in on a platter and given to the girl, who carried it to her mother. 12 John's disciples came and took his body and buried it. Then they went and told Jesus.

Jesus Feeds the Five Thousand

13 When Jesus heard what had happened, he withdrew by boat privately to a solitary place. Hearing of this, the crowds followed him on foot from the towns. 14 When Jesus landed and saw a large crowd, he had compassion on them and healed their sick.

15 As evening approached, the disciples came to him and said, "This is a remote place, and it's already getting late. Send the crowds away, so they can go to the villages and buy themselves some food."

16 Jesus replied, "They do not need to go away. You give them something to eat."

17 "We have here only five loaves of bread and two fish," they answered.

18 "Bring them here to me," he said. 19 And he directed the people to sit down on the grass. Taking the five loaves and the two fish and looking up to heaven, he gave thanks and broke the loaves. Then he gave them to the disciples, and the disciples gave them to the people.

20 They all ate and were satisfied, and the disciples picked up twelve basketfuls of broken pieces that were left over. 21 The number of those who ate was about five thousand men, besides women and children.

Jesus Walks on the Water

22 Immediately Jesus made the disciples get into the boat and go on ahead of him to the other side, while he dismissed the crowd. 23 After he had dismissed them, he went up on a mountainside by himself to pray. Later that night, he was there alone, 24 and the boat was already a considerable distance from land, buffeted by the waves because the wind was against it.

25 Shortly before dawn Jesus went out to them, walking on the lake. 26 When the disciples saw him walking on the lake, they were terrified. "It's a ghost," they said, and cried out in fear.

27 But Jesus immediately said to them: "Take courage! It is I. Don't be afraid."

28 "Lord, if it's you," Peter replied, "tell me to come to you on the water."

29 "Come," he said.

Then Peter got down out of the boat, walked on the water and came toward Jesus. 30 But when he saw the wind, he was afraid and, beginning to sink, cried out, "Lord, save me!"

31 Immediately Jesus reached out his hand and caught him. "You of little faith," he said, "why did you doubt?"

32 And when they climbed into the boat, the wind died down. 33 Then those who were in the boat worshiped him, saying, "Truly you are the Son of God."

34 When they had crossed over, they landed at Gennesaret. 35 And when the men of that place recognized Jesus, they sent word to all the surrounding country. People brought all their sick to him 36 and begged him to let the sick just touch the edge of his cloak, and all who touched it were healed.

That Which Defiles

15 Then some Pharisees and teachers of the law came to Jesus from

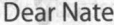

Why is it that it's okay for girls to cry in public, but not boys or men?

>> Nate

Dear Jordan

Dear Nate,

The "boys don't cry" mentality is a strange twist in American culture. The truth is boys (and men) do cry. It is also true that guys get the message it's *not* okay to cry. The Bible has stories about many emotional men. King David was one. He danced for joy and mourned deeply in grief, yet he was never known as a wimp. In fact he was a brave warrior and courageous leader.

Christ was another man who was in touch with his feelings. When he heard of his cousin John's death, he wanted to be by himself (Matthew 14:1–13). However, when the crowds followed him, he saw they were suffering and began to heal those who were sick (Matthew 14:14). When the temple was used as a marketplace, Jesus reacted with righteous anger (John 2:14–16). And after the death of his good friend Lazarus, Jesus wept (John 11:33–35).

There is a time for laughter and a time for tears (Ecclesiastes 3:4). It is normal to have feelings and it's okay to express them. If you feel uncomfortable in front of others, get some privacy and let it out. God made us so that when we cry, our brain chemicals change which helps us feel better. How awesome is that?

Jordan

Jerusalem and asked, 2 "Why do your disciples break the tradition of the elders? They don't wash their hands before they eat!"

3 Jesus replied, "And why do you break the command of God for the sake of your tradition? 4 For God said, 'Honor your father and mother'*a* and 'Anyone who curses their father or mother is to be put to death.'*b* 5 But you say that if anyone declares that what might have been used to help their father or mother is 'devoted to God,' 6 they are not to 'honor their father or mother' with it. Thus you nullify the word of God for the sake of your tradition. 7 You hypocrites! Isaiah was right when he prophesied about you:

8 " 'These people honor me with their lips,
    but their hearts are far from me.
9 They worship me in vain;
    their teachings are merely human rules.'*c*"

10 Jesus called the crowd to him and said, "Listen and understand. 11 What goes into someone's mouth does not defile them, but what comes out of their mouth, that is what defiles them."

12 Then the disciples came to him and asked, "Do you know that the Pharisees were offended when they heard this?"

13 He replied, "Every plant that my heavenly Father has not planted will be pulled up by the roots. 14 Leave them; they are blind guides.*d* If the blind lead the blind, both will fall into a pit."

15 Peter said, "Explain the parable to us."

16 "Are you still so dull?" Jesus asked them. 17 "Don't you see that whatever enters the mouth goes into the stomach and then out of the body? 18 But the things that come out of a person's mouth come from the heart, and these defile them. 19 For out of the heart come evil thoughts — murder, adultery, sexual immorality, theft, false testimony, slander. 20 These are what defile a person; but eating with unwashed hands does not defile them."

> It's scary to feel uncertain about your faith. But everybody wonders at times. Can I really believe the Bible? Am I truly saved? Is salvation for real? Am I fooling myself when I say I believe? Doubt is scary. But this Bible story helps. Peter believed in Jesus enough to get out of the boat and walk on water. But once out there, even Peter began to doubt. And to sink! What's important is that Jesus immediately caught him. Peter doubted, but Jesus was there anyway. Doubts don't drive Jesus away. He's there even when the doubts come. And you are much too important for Jesus to let you sink.
>
> **INSTANT ACCESS**
>
> {Matthew 14:22–36}

The Faith of a Canaanite Woman

21 Leaving that place, Jesus withdrew to the region of Tyre and Sidon. 22 A Canaanite woman from that vicinity came to him, crying out, "Lord, Son of David, have mercy on me! My daughter is demon-possessed and suffering terribly."

23 Jesus did not answer a word. So his disciples came to him and urged him, "Send her away, for she keeps crying out after us."

---

a 4 Exodus 20:12; Deut. 5:16   *b* 4 Exodus 21:17; Lev. 20:9   *c* 9 Isaiah 29:13   *d* 14 Some manuscripts *blind guides of the blind*

24 He answered, "I was sent only to the lost sheep of Israel."

25 The woman came and knelt before him. "Lord, help me!" she said.

26 He replied, "It is not right to take the children's bread and toss it to the dogs."

27 "Yes it is, Lord," she said. "Even the dogs eat the crumbs that fall from their master's table."

28 Then Jesus said to her, "Woman, you have great faith! Your request is granted." And her daughter was healed at that moment.

Jesus Feeds the Four Thousand

29 Jesus left there and went along the Sea of Galilee. Then he went up on a mountainside and sat down. 30 Great crowds came to him, bringing the lame, the blind, the crippled, the mute and many others, and laid them at his feet; and he healed them. 31 The people were amazed when they saw the mute speaking, the crippled made well, the lame walking and the blind seeing. And they praised the God of Israel.

32 Jesus called his disciples to him and said, "I have compassion for these people; they have already been with me three days and have nothing to eat. I do not want to send them away hungry, or they may collapse on the way."

33 His disciples answered, "Where could we get enough bread in this remote place to feed such a crowd?"

34 "How many loaves do you have?" Jesus asked.

"Seven," they replied, "and a few small fish."

35 He told the crowd to sit down on the ground. 36 Then he took the seven loaves and the fish, and when he had given thanks, he broke them and gave them to the disciples, and they in turn to the people. 37 They all ate and were satisfied. Afterward the disciples picked up seven basketfuls of broken pieces that were left over. 38 The number of those who ate was four thousand men, besides women and children. 39 After Jesus had sent the crowd away, he got into the boat and went to the vicinity of Magadan.

The Demand for a Sign

16 The Pharisees and Sadducees came to Jesus and tested him by asking him to show them a sign from heaven.

2 He replied, "When evening comes, you say, 'It will be fair weather, for the sky is red,' 3 and in the morning, 'Today it will be stormy, for the sky is red and overcast.' You know how to interpret the appearance of the sky, but you cannot interpret the signs of the times.ᵃ 4 A wicked and adulterous generation looks for a sign, but none will be given it except the sign of Jonah." Jesus then left them and went away.

The Yeast of the Pharisees and Sadducees

5 When they went across the lake, the disciples forgot to take bread. 6 "Be careful," Jesus said to them. "Be on your guard against the yeast of the Pharisees and Sadducees."

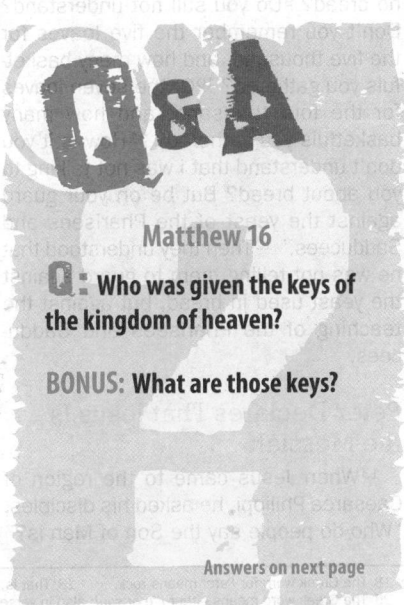

Matthew 16

Q: Who was given the keys of the kingdom of heaven?

BONUS: What are those keys?

Answers on next page

---

a 2,3 Some early manuscripts do not have *When evening comes . . . of the times.*

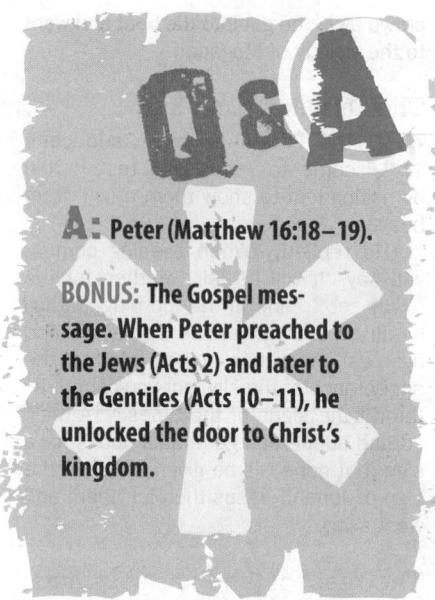

7 They discussed this among themselves and said, "It is because we didn't bring any bread."

8 Aware of their discussion, Jesus asked, "You of little faith, why are you talking among yourselves about having no bread? 9 Do you still not understand? Don't you remember the five loaves for the five thousand, and how many basketfuls you gathered? 10 Or the seven loaves for the four thousand, and how many basketfuls you gathered? 11 How is it you don't understand that I was not talking to you about bread? But be on your guard against the yeast of the Pharisees and Sadducees." 12 Then they understood that he was not telling them to guard against the yeast used in bread, but against the teaching of the Pharisees and Sadducees.

Peter Declares That Jesus Is the Messiah

13 When Jesus came to the region of Caesarea Philippi, he asked his disciples, "Who do people say the Son of Man is?"

14 They replied, "Some say John the Baptist; others say Elijah; and still others, Jeremiah or one of the prophets."

15 "But what about you?" he asked. "Who do you say I am?"

16 Simon Peter answered, "You are the Messiah, the Son of the living God."

17 Jesus replied, "Blessed are you, Simon son of Jonah, for this was not revealed to you by flesh and blood, but by my Father in heaven. 18 And I tell you that you are Peter,[a] and on this rock I will build my church, and the gates of Hades[b] will not overcome it. 19 I will give you the keys of the kingdom of heaven; whatever you bind on earth will be[c] bound in heaven, and whatever you loose on earth will be[c] loosed in heaven." 20 Then he ordered his disciples not to tell anyone that he was the Messiah.

Jesus Predicts His Death

21 From that time on Jesus began to explain to his disciples that he must go to Jerusalem and suffer many things at the hands of the elders, the chief priests and the teachers of the law, and that he must be killed and on the third day be raised to life.

22 Peter took him aside and began to rebuke him. "Never, Lord!" he said. "This shall never happen to you!"

23 Jesus turned and said to Peter, "Get behind me, Satan! You are a stumbling block to me; you do not have in mind the concerns of God, but merely human concerns."

24 Then Jesus said to his disciples, "Whoever wants to be my disciple must deny themselves and take up their cross and follow me. 25 For whoever wants to save their life[d] will lose it, but whoever loses their life for me will find it. 26 What good will it be for someone to gain the whole world, yet forfeit their soul? Or what can anyone give in exchange for their soul? 27 For the Son of Man is going to come in his Father's glory with his angels, and then he will reward each person according to what they have done.

---

a 18 The Greek word for *Peter* means *rock.*   *b 18* That is, the realm of the dead   *c 19* Or *will have been*
d 25 The Greek word means either *life* or *soul*; also in verse 26.

28 "Truly I tell you, some who are standing here will not taste death before they see the Son of Man coming in his kingdom."

The Transfiguration

17 After six days Jesus took with him Peter, James and John the brother of James, and led them up a high mountain by themselves. 2 There he was transfigured before them. His face shone like the sun, and his clothes became as white as the light. 3 Just then there appeared before them Moses and Elijah, talking with Jesus.

4 Peter said to Jesus, "Lord, it is good for us to be here. If you wish, I will put up three shelters—one for you, one for Moses and one for Elijah."

5 While he was still speaking, a bright cloud covered them, and a voice from the cloud said, "This is my Son, whom I love; with him I am well pleased. Listen to him!"

6 When the disciples heard this, they fell facedown to the ground, terrified. 7 But Jesus came and touched them. "Get up," he said. "Don't be afraid." 8 When they looked up, they saw no one except Jesus.

9 As they were coming down the mountain, Jesus instructed them, "Don't tell anyone what you have seen, until the Son of Man has been raised from the dead."

10 The disciples asked him, "Why then do the teachers of the law say that Elijah must come first?"

11 Jesus replied, "To be sure, Elijah comes and will restore all things. 12 But I tell you, Elijah has already come, and they did not recognize him, but have done to him everything they wished. In the same way the Son of Man is going to suffer at their hands." 13 Then the disciples understood that he was talking to them about John the Baptist.

Jesus Heals a Demon-Possessed Boy

14 When they came to the crowd, a man approached Jesus and knelt before him. 15 "Lord, have mercy on my son," he said. "He has seizures and is suffering greatly. He often falls into the fire or into the water. 16 I brought him to your disciples, but they could not heal him."

17 "You unbelieving and perverse generation," Jesus replied, "how long shall I stay with you? How long shall I put up with you? Bring the boy here to me." 18 Jesus rebuked the demon, and it came out of the boy, and he was healed at that moment.

19 Then the disciples came to Jesus in private and asked, "Why couldn't we drive it out?"

20 He replied, "Because you have so little faith. Truly I tell you, if you have faith

as small as a mustard seed, you can say to this mountain, 'Move from here to there,' and it will move. Nothing will be impossible for you." [21]a

Jesus Predicts His Death a Second Time

22 When they came together in Galilee, he said to them, "The Son of Man is going to be delivered into the hands of men. 23 They will kill him, and on the third day he will be raised to life." And the disciples were filled with grief.

The Temple Tax

24 After Jesus and his disciples arrived in Capernaum, the collectors of the two-drachma temple tax came to Peter and asked, "Doesn't your teacher pay the temple tax?"

25 "Yes, he does," he replied.

When Peter came into the house, Jesus was the first to speak. "What do you think, Simon?" he asked. "From whom do the kings of the earth collect duty and taxes—from their own children or from others?"

26 "From others," Peter answered.

"Then the children are exempt," Jesus said to him. 27 "But so that we may not cause offense, go to the lake and throw out your line. Take the first fish you catch; open its mouth and you will find a four-drachma coin. Take it and give it to them for my tax and yours."

The Greatest in the Kingdom of Heaven

18 At that time the disciples came to Jesus and asked, "Who, then, is the greatest in the kingdom of heaven?"

2 He called a little child to him, and placed the child among them. 3 And he said: "Truly I tell you, unless you change and become like little children, you will never enter the kingdom of heaven. 4 Therefore, whoever takes the lowly position of this child is the greatest in the kingdom of heaven. 5 And whoever welcomes one such child in my name welcomes me.

Causing to Stumble

6 "If anyone causes one of these little ones—those who believe in me—to stumble, it would be better for them to have a large millstone hung around their neck and to be drowned in the depths of the sea. 7 Woe to the world because of the things that cause people to stumble! Such things must come, but woe to the person through whom they come! 8 If your hand or your foot causes you to stumble, cut it off and throw it away. It is better for you to enter life maimed or crippled than to have two hands or two feet and be thrown into eternal fire. 9 And if your eye causes you to stumble, gouge it out and throw it away. It is better for you to enter life with one eye than to have two eyes and be thrown into the fire of hell.

The Parable of the Wandering Sheep

10 "See that you do not despise one of these little ones. For I tell you that their angels in heaven always see the face of my Father in heaven. [11]b

12 "What do you think? If a man owns a hundred sheep, and one of them wanders away, will he not leave the ninety-nine on the hills and go to look for the one that wandered off? 13 And if he finds it, truly I tell you, he is happier about that one sheep than about the ninety-nine that did not wander off. 14 In the same way your Father in heaven is not willing that any of these little ones should perish.

Dealing With Sin in the Church

15 "If your brother or sisterc sins,d go and point out their fault, just between the two of you. If they listen to you, you have won them over. 16 But if they will not listen, take one or two others along, so that 'every matter may be established by the testimony of two or three witnesses.'e 17 If they still refuse to listen, tell it to the church; and if they refuse to listen even to the church, treat them as you would a pagan or a tax collector.

---

a 21 Some manuscripts include here words similar to Mark 9:29.   b 11 Some manuscripts include here the words of Luke 19:10.   c 15 The Greek word for brother or sister (adelphos) refers here to a fellow disciple, whether man or woman; also in verses 21 and 35.   d 15 Some manuscripts sins against you   e 16 Deut. 19:15

18 "Truly I tell you, whatever you bind on earth will be*a* bound in heaven, and whatever you loose on earth will be*a* loosed in heaven.

19 "Again, truly I tell you that if two of you on earth agree about anything they ask for, it will be done for them by my Father in heaven. 20 For where two or three gather in my name, there am I with them."

The Parable of the Unmerciful Servant

21 Then Peter came to Jesus and asked, "Lord, how many times shall I forgive my brother or sister who sins against me? Up to seven times?"

22 Jesus answered, "I tell you, not seven times, but seventy-seven times.*b*

23 "Therefore, the kingdom of heaven is like a king who wanted to settle accounts with his servants. 24 As he began the settlement, a man who owed him ten thousand bags of gold*c* was brought to him. 25 Since he was not able to pay, the master ordered that he and his wife and his children and all that he had be sold to repay the debt.

26 "At this the servant fell on his knees before him. 'Be patient with me,' he begged, 'and I will pay back everything.' 27 The servant's master took pity on him, canceled the debt and let him go.

28 "But when that servant went out, he found one of his fellow servants who owed him a hundred silver coins.*d* He grabbed him and began to choke him. 'Pay back what you owe me!' he demanded.

29 "His fellow servant fell to his knees and begged him, 'Be patient with me, and I will pay it back.'

30 "But he refused. Instead, he went off and had the man thrown into prison until he could pay the debt. 31 When the other servants saw what had happened, they were outraged and went and told their master everything that had happened.

32 "Then the master called the servant in. 'You wicked servant,' he said, 'I canceled all that debt of yours because you begged me to. 33 Shouldn't you have had mercy on your fellow servant just as I had on you?' 34 In anger his master handed him over to the jailers to be tortured, until he should pay back all he owed.

35 "This is how my heavenly Father will treat each of you unless you forgive your brother or sister from your heart."

Divorce

19 When Jesus had finished saying these things, he left Galilee and went into the region of Judea to the other side of the Jordan. 2 Large crowds followed him, and he healed them there.

3 Some Pharisees came to him to test him. They asked, "Is it lawful for a man to divorce his wife for any and every reason?"

4 "Haven't you read," he replied, "that at the beginning the Creator 'made them male and female,'*e* 5 and said, 'For this reason a man will leave his father and mother and be united to his wife, and the two will become one flesh'*f*? 6 So they are no longer two, but one flesh. Therefore what God has joined together, let no one separate."

7 "Why then," they asked, "did Moses command that a man give his wife a certificate of divorce and send her away?"

8 Jesus replied, "Moses permitted you to divorce your wives because your hearts were hard. But it was not this way from the beginning. 9 I tell you that anyone who divorces his wife, except for sexual immorality, and marries another woman commits adultery."

10 The disciples said to him, "If this is the situation between a husband and wife, it is better not to marry."

11 Jesus replied, "Not everyone can accept this word, but only those to whom it has been given. 12 For there are eunuchs who were born that way, and there are eunuchs who have been made eunuchs by others—and there are those who choose to live like eunuchs for the sake of the kingdom of heaven. The one who can accept this should accept it."

a 18 Or *will have been*   *b 22* Or *seventy times seven*   *c 24* Greek *ten thousand talents*; a talent was worth about 20 years of a day laborer's wages.   *d 28* Greek *a hundred denarii*; a denarius was the usual daily wage of a day laborer (see 20:2).   *e 4* Gen. 1:27   *f 5* Gen. 2:24

The Little Children and Jesus

13 Then people brought little children to Jesus for him to place his hands on them and pray for them. But the disciples rebuked them.

14 Jesus said, "Let the little children come to me, and do not hinder them, for the kingdom of heaven belongs to such as these." 15 When he had placed his hands on them, he went on from there.

The Rich and the Kingdom of God

16 Just then a man came up to Jesus and asked, "Teacher, what good thing must I do to get eternal life?"

17 "Why do you ask me about what is good?" Jesus replied. "There is only One who is good. If you want to enter life, keep the commandments."

18 "Which ones?" he inquired.

Jesus replied, " 'You shall not murder, you shall not commit adultery, you shall not steal, you shall not give false testimony, 19 honor your father and mother,'[a] and 'love your neighbor as yourself.'[b]"

20 "All these I have kept," the young man said. "What do I still lack?"

21 Jesus answered, "If you want to be perfect, go, sell your possessions and give to the poor, and you will have treasure in heaven. Then come, follow me."

22 When the young man heard this, he went away sad, because he had great wealth.

---

a 19 Exodus 20:12-16; Deut. 5:16-20   b 19 Lev. 19:18

TO THE POINT

Divorce, Yes or No?

Some Christians feel believers can never get a divorce. Others feel it's OK for certain reasons. One thing is for sure. You want to take your time and pray about the person you choose as a life partner! Divorce hurts. It's painful for everyone involved.

In Matthew 19:1–12 Jesus said a few things about divorce:

+ God's ideal is a lifetime union (Matthew 19:4–6).

+ God never permits divorce just because a person wants to marry someone else. That's definitely wrong (Matthew 19:9).

If your parents are divorced, you know how much it can hurt. Do your best not to get involved in who's to blame. And don't think the divorce is your fault. Instead read the story that follows Jesus' teaching on divorce (Matthew 19:13–15), and remember Jesus places his hands on you and prays for you right now.

23 Then Jesus said to his disciples, "Truly I tell you, it is hard for someone who is rich to enter the kingdom of heaven. 24 Again I tell you, it is easier for a camel to go through the eye of a needle than for someone who is rich to enter the kingdom of God."

25 When the disciples heard this, they were greatly astonished and asked, "Who then can be saved?"

26 Jesus looked at them and said, "With man this is impossible, but with God all things are possible."

27 Peter answered him, "We have left everything to follow you! What then will there be for us?"

28 Jesus said to them, "Truly I tell you, at the renewal of all things, when the Son of Man sits on his glorious throne, you who have followed me will also sit on twelve thrones, judging the twelve tribes of Israel. 29 And everyone who has left houses or brothers or sisters or father or mother or wife[a] or children or fields for my sake will receive a hundred times as much and will inherit eternal life. 30 But many who are first will be last, and many who are last will be first.

The Parable of the Workers in the Vineyard

20 "For the kingdom of heaven is like a landowner who went out early in the morning to hire workers for his vineyard. 2 He agreed to pay them a denarius[b] for the day and sent them into his vineyard.

3 "About nine in the morning he went out and saw others standing in the marketplace doing nothing. 4 He told them, 'You also go and work in my vineyard, and I will pay you whatever is right.' 5 So they went.

"He went out again about noon and about three in the afternoon and did the same thing. 6 About five in the afternoon he went out and found still others standing around. He asked them, 'Why have you been standing here all day long doing nothing?'

7 " 'Because no one has hired us,' they answered.

"He said to them, 'You also go and work in my vineyard.'

8 "When evening came, the owner of the vineyard said to his foreman, 'Call the workers and pay them their wages, beginning with the last ones hired and going on to the first.'

9 "The workers who were hired about five in the afternoon came and each received a denarius. 10 So when those came who were hired first, they expected to receive more. But each one of them also received a denarius. 11 When they received it, they began to grumble against the landowner. 12 'These who were hired last worked only one hour,' they said, 'and you have made them equal to us who have borne the burden of the work and the heat of the day.'

13 "But he answered one of them, 'I am not being unfair to you, friend. Didn't you agree to work for a denarius? 14 Take your pay and go. I want to give the one who was hired last the same as I gave you. 15 Don't I have the right to do what I want with my own money? Or are you envious because I am generous?'

16 "So the last will be first, and the first will be last."

Jesus Predicts His Death a Third Time

17 Now Jesus was going up to Jerusalem. On the way, he took the Twelve aside and said to them, 18 "We are going up to Jerusalem, and the Son of Man will be delivered over to the chief priests and the teachers of the law. They will condemn him to death 19 and will hand him over to the Gentiles to be mocked and flogged and crucified. On the third day he will be raised to life!"

A Mother's Request

20 Then the mother of Zebedee's sons came to Jesus with her sons and, kneeling down, asked a favor of him.

21 "What is it you want?" he asked.

She said, "Grant that one of these two sons of mine may sit at your right and the other at your left in your kingdom."

---

a 29 Some manuscripts do not have *or wife*.   b 2 A denarius was the usual daily wage of a day laborer.

22 "You don't know what you are asking," Jesus said to them. "Can you drink the cup I am going to drink?"

"We can," they answered.

23 Jesus said to them, "You will indeed drink from my cup, but to sit at my right or left is not for me to grant. These places belong to those for whom they have been prepared by my Father."

24 When the ten heard about this, they were indignant with the two brothers. 25 Jesus called them together and said, "You know that the rulers of the Gentiles lord it over them, and their high officials exercise authority over them. 26 Not so with you. Instead, whoever wants to become great among you must be your servant, 27 and whoever wants to be first must be your slave— 28 just as the Son of Man did not come to be served, but to serve, and to give his life as a ransom for many."

Two Blind Men Receive Sight

29 As Jesus and his disciples were leaving Jericho, a large crowd followed him. 30 Two blind men were sitting by the roadside, and when they heard that Jesus was going by, they shouted, "Lord, Son of David, have mercy on us!"

31 The crowd rebuked them and told them to be quiet, but they shouted all the louder, "Lord, Son of David, have mercy on us!"

32 Jesus stopped and called them. "What do you want me to do for you?" he asked.

33 "Lord," they answered, "we want our sight."

34 Jesus had compassion on them and touched their eyes. Immediately they received their sight and followed him.

Jesus Comes to Jerusalem as King

21 As they approached Jerusalem and came to Bethphage on the Mount of Olives, Jesus sent two disciples, 2 saying to them, "Go to the village ahead of you, and at once you will find a donkey tied there, with her colt by her. Untie them

and bring them to me. 3 If anyone says anything to you, say that the Lord needs them, and he will send them right away."

4 This took place to fulfill what was spoken through the prophet:

5 "Say to Daughter Zion,
  'See, your king comes to you,
    gentle and riding on a donkey,
    and on a colt, the foal of a
      donkey.' "a

6 The disciples went and did as Jesus had instructed them. 7 They brought the donkey and the colt and placed their cloaks on them for Jesus to sit on. 8 A very large crowd spread their cloaks on the road, while others cut branches from the trees and spread them on the road. 9 The crowds that went ahead of him and those that followed shouted,

"Hosannab to the Son of David!"

"Blessed is he who comes in the
  name of the Lord!"c

"Hosannab in the highest heaven!"

10 When Jesus entered Jerusalem, the whole city was stirred and asked, "Who is this?"

11 The crowds answered, "This is Jesus, the prophet from Nazareth in Galilee."

Jesus at the Temple

12 Jesus entered the temple courts and drove out all who were buying and selling there. He overturned the tables of the money changers and the benches of those selling doves. 13 "It is written," he said to them, " 'My house will be called a house of prayer,'d but you are making it 'a den of robbers.'e"

14 The blind and the lame came to him at the temple, and he healed them. 15 But when the chief priests and the teachers of the law saw the wonderful things he did and the children shouting in the temple courts, "Hosanna to the Son of David," they were indignant.

16 "Do you hear what these children are saying?" they asked him.

---

a 5 Zech. 9:9   b 9 A Hebrew expression meaning "Save!" which became an exclamation of praise; also in verse 15
c 9 Psalm 118:25,26   d 13 Isaiah 56:7   e 13 Jer. 7:11

"Yes," replied Jesus, "have you never read,

" 'From the lips of children and infants you, Lord, have called forth your praise'*a*?"

17 And he left them and went out of the city to Bethany, where he spent the night.

Jesus Curses a Fig Tree

18 Early in the morning, as Jesus was on his way back to the city, he was hungry. 19 Seeing a fig tree by the road, he went up to it but found nothing on it except leaves. Then he said to it, "May you never bear fruit again!" Immediately the tree withered.

20 When the disciples saw this, they were amazed. "How did the fig tree wither so quickly?" they asked.

21 Jesus replied, "Truly I tell you, if you have faith and do not doubt, not only can you do what was done to the fig tree, but also you can say to this mountain, 'Go, throw yourself into the sea,' and it will be done. 22 If you believe, you will receive whatever you ask for in prayer."

The Authority of Jesus Questioned

23 Jesus entered the temple courts, and, while he was teaching, the chief priests and the elders of the people came to him. "By what authority are you doing these things?" they asked. "And who gave you this authority?"

24 Jesus replied, "I will also ask you one question. If you answer me, I will tell you by what authority I am doing these things. 25 John's baptism—where did it come from? Was it from heaven, or of human origin?"

They discussed it among themselves and said, "If we say, 'From heaven,' he will ask, 'Then why didn't you believe him?' 26 But if we say, 'Of human origin'—we are afraid of the people, for they all hold that John was a prophet."

27 So they answered Jesus, "We don't know."

Then he said, "Neither will I tell you by what authority I am doing these things.

The Parable of the Two Sons

28 "What do you think? There was a man who had two sons. He went to the first and said, 'Son, go and work today in the vineyard.'

29 " 'I will not,' he answered, but later he changed his mind and went.

30 "Then the father went to the other son and said the same thing. He answered, 'I will, sir,' but he did not go.

31 "Which of the two did what his father wanted?"

"The first," they answered.

Jesus said to them, "Truly I tell you, the tax collectors and the prostitutes are entering the kingdom of God ahead of you. 32 For John came to you to show you the way of righteousness, and you did not believe him, but the tax collectors and the prostitutes did. And even after you saw this, you did not repent and believe him.

The Parable of the Tenants

33 "Listen to another parable: There was a landowner who planted a vineyard. He put a wall around it, dug a winepress in it and built a watchtower. Then he rented the vineyard to some farmers and moved to another place. 34 When the harvest time approached, he sent his servants to the tenants to collect his fruit.

35 "The tenants seized his servants; they beat one, killed another, and stoned a third. 36 Then he sent other servants to them, more than the first time, and the tenants treated them the same way. 37 Last of all, he sent his son to them. 'They will respect my son,' he said.

38 "But when the tenants saw the son, they said to each other, 'This is the heir. Come, let's kill him and take his inheritance.' 39 So they took him and threw him out of the vineyard and killed him.

40 "Therefore, when the owner of the vineyard comes, what will he do to those tenants?"

41 "He will bring those wretches to a wretched end," they replied, "and he will rent the vineyard to other tenants, who will give him his share of the crop at harvest time."

---

a 16 Psalm 8:2 (see Septuagint)

42 Jesus said to them, "Have you never read in the Scriptures:

" 'The stone the builders rejected
    has become the cornerstone;
the Lord has done this,
    and it is marvelous in our eyes'ᵃ?

43 "Therefore I tell you that the kingdom of God will be taken away from you and given to a people who will produce its fruit. 44 Anyone who falls on this stone will be broken to pieces; anyone on whom it falls will be crushed."ᵇ

45 When the chief priests and the Pharisees heard Jesus' parables, they knew he was talking about them. 46 They looked for a way to arrest him, but they were afraid of the crowd because the people held that he was a prophet.

The Parable of the Wedding Banquet

22 Jesus spoke to them again in parables, saying: 2 "The kingdom of heaven is like a king who prepared a wedding banquet for his son. 3 He sent his servants to those who had been invited to the banquet to tell them to come, but they refused to come.

4 "Then he sent some more servants and said, 'Tell those who have been invited that I have prepared my dinner: My oxen and fattened cattle have been butchered, and everything is ready. Come to the wedding banquet.'

5 "But they paid no attention and went off—one to his field, another to his business. 6 The rest seized his servants, mistreated them and killed them. 7 The king was enraged. He sent his army and destroyed those murderers and burned their city.

8 "Then he said to his servants, 'The wedding banquet is ready, but those I invited did not deserve to come. 9 So go to the street corners and invite to the banquet anyone you find.' 10 So the servants went out into the streets and gathered all the people they could find, the bad as well as the good, and the wedding hall was filled with guests.

11 "But when the king came in to see the guests, he noticed a man there who was not wearing wedding clothes. 12 He asked, 'How did you get in here without wedding clothes, friend?' The man was speechless.

13 "Then the king told the attendants, 'Tie him hand and foot, and throw him outside, into the darkness, where there will be weeping and gnashing of teeth.'

14 "For many are invited, but few are chosen."

ᵃ 42 Psalm 118:22,23   ᵇ 44 Some manuscripts do not have verse 44.

Paying the Imperial Tax to Caesar

¹⁵Then the Pharisees went out and laid plans to trap him in his words. ¹⁶They sent their disciples to him along with the Herodians. "Teacher," they said, "we know that you are a man of integrity and that you teach the way of God in accordance with the truth. You aren't swayed by others, because you pay no attention to who they are. ¹⁷Tell us then, what is your opinion? Is it right to pay the imperial tax*ᵃ* to Caesar or not?"

¹⁸But Jesus, knowing their evil intent, said, "You hypocrites, why are you trying to trap me? ¹⁹Show me the coin used for paying the tax." They brought him a denarius, ²⁰and he asked them, "Whose image is this? And whose inscription?"

²¹"Caesar's," they replied.

Then he said to them, "So give back to Caesar what is Caesar's, and to God what is God's."

²²When they heard this, they were amazed. So they left him and went away.

Marriage at the Resurrection

²³That same day the Sadducees, who say there is no resurrection, came to him with a question. ²⁴"Teacher," they said, "Moses told us that if a man dies without having children, his brother must marry the widow and raise up offspring for him. ²⁵Now there were seven brothers among us. The first one married and died, and since he had no children, he left his wife to his brother. ²⁶The same thing happened to the second and third brother, right on down to the seventh. ²⁷Finally, the woman died. ²⁸Now then, at the resurrection, whose wife will she be of the seven, since all of them were married to her?"

²⁹Jesus replied, "You are in error because you do not know the Scriptures or the power of God. ³⁰At the resurrection people will neither marry nor be given in marriage; they will be like the angels in heaven. ³¹But about the resurrection of the dead—have you not read what God said to you, ³²'I am the God of Abraham, the God of Isaac, and the God of Jacob'*ᵇ*? He is not the God of the dead but of the living."

³³When the crowds heard this, they were astonished at his teaching.

The Greatest Commandment

³⁴Hearing that Jesus had silenced the Sadducees, the Pharisees got together. ³⁵One of them, an expert in the law, tested him with this question: ³⁶"Teacher, which is the greatest commandment in the Law?"

³⁷Jesus replied: " 'Love the Lord your God with all your heart and with all your soul and with all your mind.'*ᶜ* ³⁸This is the first and greatest commandment. ³⁹And the second is like it: 'Love your neighbor as yourself.'*ᵈ* ⁴⁰All the Law and the Prophets hang on these two commandments."

Whose Son Is the Messiah?

⁴¹While the Pharisees were gathered together, Jesus asked them, ⁴²"What do you think about the Messiah? Whose son is he?"

"The son of David," they replied.

⁴³He said to them, "How is it then that David, speaking by the Spirit, calls him 'Lord'? For he says,

⁴⁴ " 'The Lord said to my Lord:
  "Sit at my right hand
until I put your enemies
  under your feet." '*ᵉ*

⁴⁵If then David calls him 'Lord,' how can he be his son?" ⁴⁶No one could say a word in reply, and from that day on no one dared to ask him any more questions.

A Warning Against Hypocrisy

23 Then Jesus said to the crowds and to his disciples: ²"The teachers of the law and the Pharisees sit in Moses' seat. ³So you must be careful to do everything they tell you. But do not do what they do, for they do not practice what they preach. ⁴They tie up heavy, cumbersome loads and put them on other people's shoulders, but they themselves are not willing to lift a finger to move them.

ᵃ 17 A special tax levied on subject peoples, not on Roman citizens   *ᵇ* 32 Exodus 3:6   *ᶜ* 37 Deut. 6:5
ᵈ 39 Lev. 19:18   *ᵉ* 44 Psalm 110:1

5 "Everything they do is done for people to see: They make their phylacteries[a] wide and the tassels on their garments long; 6 they love the place of honor at banquets and the most important seats in the synagogues; 7 they love to be greeted with respect in the marketplaces and to be called 'Rabbi' by others.

8 "But you are not to be called 'Rabbi,' for you have one Teacher, and you are all brothers. 9 And do not call anyone on earth 'father,' for you have one Father, and he is in heaven. 10 Nor are you to be called instructors, for you have one Instructor, the Messiah. 11 The greatest among you will be your servant. 12 For those who exalt themselves will be humbled, and those who humble themselves will be exalted.

Seven Woes on the Teachers of the Law and the Pharisees

13 "Woe to you, teachers of the law and Pharisees, you hypocrites! You shut the door of the kingdom of heaven in people's faces. You yourselves do not enter, nor will you let those enter who are trying to. [14]b

15 "Woe to you, teachers of the law and Pharisees, you hypocrites! You travel over land and sea to win a single convert, and when you have succeeded, you make them twice as much a child of hell as you are.

16 "Woe to you, blind guides! You say, 'If anyone swears by the temple, it means nothing; but anyone who swears by the gold of the temple is bound by that oath.' 17 You blind fools! Which is greater: the gold, or the temple that makes the gold sacred? 18 You also say, 'If anyone swears by the altar, it means nothing; but anyone who swears by the gift on the altar is bound by that oath.' 19 You blind men! Which is greater: the gift, or the altar that makes the gift sacred? 20 Therefore, anyone who swears by the altar swears by it and by everything on it. 21 And anyone who swears by the temple swears by it and by the one who dwells in it. 22 And anyone who swears by heaven swears by God's throne and by the one who sits on it.

23 "Woe to you, teachers of the law and Pharisees, you hypocrites! You give a tenth of your spices — mint, dill and cumin. But you have neglected the more important matters of the law — justice, mercy and faithfulness. You should have practiced the latter, without neglecting the former. 24 You blind guides! You strain out a gnat but swallow a camel.

25 "Woe to you, teachers of the law and Pharisees, you hypocrites! You clean the outside of the cup and dish, but inside they are full of greed and self-indulgence. 26 Blind Pharisee! First clean the inside of the cup and dish, and then the outside also will be clean.

27 "Woe to you, teachers of the law and Pharisees, you hypocrites! You are like whitewashed tombs, which look beautiful on the outside but on the inside are full of the bones of the dead and everything unclean. 28 In the same way, on the outside you appear to people as righteous but on the inside you are full of hypocrisy and wickedness.

29 "Woe to you, teachers of the law and Pharisees, you hypocrites! You build tombs for the prophets and decorate the graves of the righteous. 30 And you say, 'If we had lived in the days of our ancestors, we would not have taken part with them in shedding the blood of the prophets.' 31 So you testify against yourselves that you are the descendants of those who murdered the prophets. 32 Go ahead, then, and complete what your ancestors started!

33 "You snakes! You brood of vipers! How will you escape being condemned to hell? 34 Therefore I am sending you prophets and sages and teachers. Some of them you will kill and crucify; others you will flog in your synagogues and pursue from town to town. 35 And so upon you will come all the righteous blood that has been shed on earth, from the blood of righteous Abel to the blood of Zechariah son of Berekiah, whom you murdered between the temple and the altar. 36 Truly I tell you, all this will come on this generation.

37 "Jerusalem, Jerusalem, you who kill the prophets and stone those sent to

---

a 5 That is, boxes containing Scripture verses, worn on forehead and arm   b 14 Some manuscripts include here words similar to Mark 12:40 and Luke 20:47.

you, how often I have longed to gather your children together, as a hen gathers her chicks under her wings, and you were not willing. ³⁸Look, your house is left to you desolate. ³⁹For I tell you, you will not see me again until you say, 'Blessed is he who comes in the name of the Lord.'ᵃ"

The Destruction of the Temple and Signs of the End Times

24 Jesus left the temple and was walking away when his disciples came up to him to call his attention to its buildings. ²"Do you see all these things?" he asked. "Truly I tell you, not one stone here will be left on another; every one will be thrown down."

³As Jesus was sitting on the Mount of Olives, the disciples came to him privately. "Tell us," they said, "when will this happen, and what will be the sign of your coming and of the end of the age?"

⁴Jesus answered: "Watch out that no one deceives you. ⁵For many will come in my name, claiming, 'I am the Messiah,' and will deceive many. ⁶You will hear of wars and rumors of wars, but see to it that you are not alarmed. Such things must happen, but the end is still to come. ⁷Nation will rise against nation, and kingdom against kingdom. There will be famines and earthquakes in various places. ⁸All these are the beginning of birth pains.

⁹"Then you will be handed over to be persecuted and put to death, and you will be hated by all nations because of me. ¹⁰At that time many will turn away from the faith and will betray and hate each other, ¹¹and many false prophets will appear and deceive many people. ¹²Because of the increase of wickedness, the love of most will grow cold, ¹³but the one who stands firm to the end will be saved. ¹⁴And this gospel of the kingdom will be preached in the whole world as a testimony to all nations, and then the end will come.

¹⁵"So when you see standing in the holy place 'the abomination that causes desolation,'ᵇ spoken of through the prophet Daniel—let the reader under-

stand— ¹⁶then let those who are in Judea flee to the mountains. ¹⁷Let no one on the housetop go down to take anything out of the house. ¹⁸Let no one in the field go back to get their cloak. ¹⁹How dreadful it will be in those days for pregnant women and nursing mothers! ²⁰Pray that your flight will not take place in winter or on the Sabbath. ²¹For then there will be great distress, unequaled from the beginning of the world until now—and never to be equaled again.

²²"If those days had not been cut short, no one would survive, but for the sake of the elect those days will be shortened. ²³At that time if anyone says to you, 'Look, here is the Messiah!' or, 'There he is!' do not believe it. ²⁴For false messiahs and false prophets will appear and perform great signs and wonders to deceive, if possible, even the elect. ²⁵See, I have told you ahead of time.

²⁶"So if anyone tells you, 'There he is, out in the wilderness,' do not go out; or, 'Here he is, in the inner rooms,' do not believe it. ²⁷For as lightning that comes from the east is visible even in the west, so will be the coming of the Son of Man. ²⁸Wherever there is a carcass, there the vultures will gather.

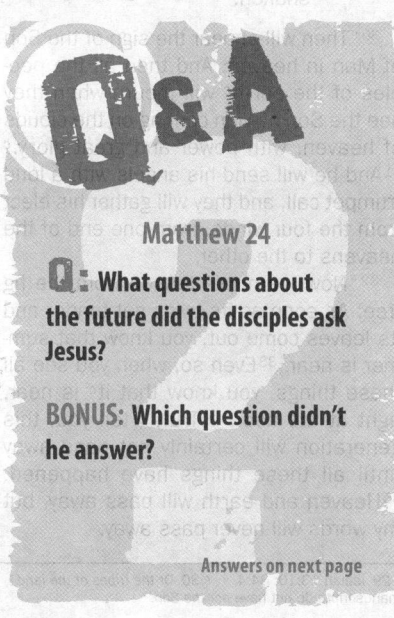

Matthew 24

Q: What questions about the future did the disciples ask Jesus?

BONUS: Which question didn't he answer?

Answers on next page

ᵃ 39 Psalm 118:26   ᵇ 15 Daniel 9:27; 11:31; 12:11

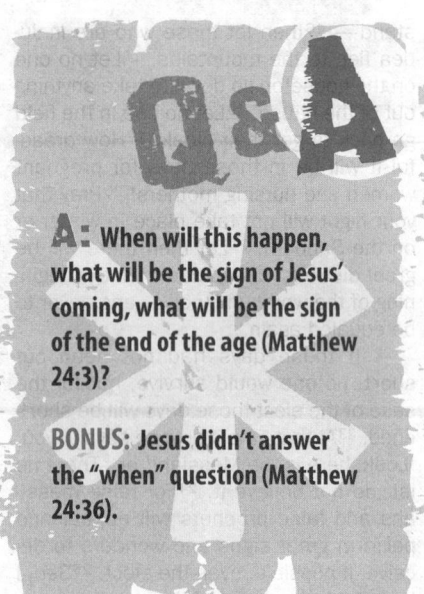

A: When will this happen, what will be the sign of Jesus' coming, what will be the sign of the end of the age (Matthew 24:3)?

BONUS: Jesus didn't answer the "when" question (Matthew 24:36).

The Day and Hour Unknown

36 "But about that day or hour no one knows, not even the angels in heaven, nor the Son,[e] but only the Father. 37 As it was in the days of Noah, so it will be at the coming of the Son of Man. 38 For in the days before the flood, people were eating and drinking, marrying and giving in marriage, up to the day Noah entered the ark; 39 and they knew nothing about what would happen until the flood came and took them all away. That is how it will be at the coming of the Son of Man. 40 Two men will be in the field; one will be taken and the other left. 41 Two women will be grinding with a hand mill; one will be taken and the other left.

42 "Therefore keep watch, because you do not know on what day your Lord will come. 43 But understand this: If the owner of the house had known at what time of night the thief was coming, he would have kept watch and would not have let his house be broken into. 44 So you also must be ready, because the Son of Man will come at an hour when you do not expect him.

45 "Who then is the faithful and wise servant, whom the master has put in charge of the servants in his household to give them their food at the proper time? 46 It will be good for that servant whose master finds him doing so when he returns. 47 Truly I tell you, he will put him in charge of all his possessions. 48 But suppose that servant is wicked and says to himself, 'My master is staying away a long time,' 49 and he then begins to beat his fellow servants and to eat and drink with drunkards. 50 The master of that servant will come on a day when he does not expect him and at an hour he is not aware of. 51 He will cut him to pieces and assign him a place with the hypocrites, where there will be weeping and gnashing of teeth.

29 "Immediately after the distress of those days

" 'the sun will be darkened,
    and the moon will not give its light;
the stars will fall from the sky,
    and the heavenly bodies will be
        shaken.'[a]

30 "Then will appear the sign of the Son of Man in heaven. And then all the peoples of the earth[b] will mourn when they see the Son of Man coming on the clouds of heaven, with power and great glory.[c] 31 And he will send his angels with a loud trumpet call, and they will gather his elect from the four winds, from one end of the heavens to the other.

32 "Now learn this lesson from the fig tree: As soon as its twigs get tender and its leaves come out, you know that summer is near. 33 Even so, when you see all these things, you know that it[d] is near, right at the door. 34 Truly I tell you, this generation will certainly not pass away until all these things have happened. 35 Heaven and earth will pass away, but my words will never pass away.

The Parable of the Ten Virgins

25 "At that time the kingdom of heaven will be like ten virgins who took their lamps and went out to meet the

---

bridegroom. ² Five of them were foolish and five were wise. ³ The foolish ones took their lamps but did not take any oil with them. ⁴ The wise ones, however, took oil in jars along with their lamps. ⁵ The bridegroom was a long time in coming, and they all became drowsy and fell asleep.

⁶ "At midnight the cry rang out: 'Here's the bridegroom! Come out to meet him!'

⁷ "Then all the virgins woke up and trimmed their lamps. ⁸ The foolish ones said to the wise, 'Give us some of your oil; our lamps are going out.'

⁹ " 'No,' they replied, 'there may not be enough for both us and you. Instead, go to those who sell oil and buy some for yourselves.'

¹⁰ "But while they were on their way to buy the oil, the bridegroom arrived. The virgins who were ready went in with him to the wedding banquet. And the door was shut.

¹¹ "Later the others also came. 'Lord, Lord,' they said, 'open the door for us!'

¹² "But he replied, 'Truly I tell you, I don't know you.'

¹³ "Therefore keep watch, because you do not know the day or the hour.

The Parable of the Bags of Gold

¹⁴ "Again, it will be like a man going on a journey, who called his servants and entrusted his wealth to them. ¹⁵ To one he gave five bags of gold, to another two bags, and to another one bag,ᵃ each according to his ability. Then he went on his journey. ¹⁶ The man who had received five bags of gold went at once and put his money to work and gained five bags more. ¹⁷ So also, the one with two bags of gold gained two more. ¹⁸ But the man who had received one bag went off, dug a hole in the ground and hid his master's money.

¹⁹ "After a long time the master of those servants returned and settled accounts with them. ²⁰ The man who had received five bags of gold brought the other five. 'Master,' he said, 'you entrusted me with five bags of gold. See, I have gained five more.'

²¹ "His master replied, 'Well done, good and faithful servant! You have been faithful with a few things; I will put you in charge of many things. Come and share your master's happiness!'

²² "The man with two bags of gold also came. 'Master,' he said, 'you entrusted me with two bags of gold; see, I have gained two more.'

²³ "His master replied, 'Well done, good and faithful servant! You have been faithful with a few things; I will put you in charge of many things. Come and share your master's happiness!'

²⁴ "Then the man who had received one bag of gold came. 'Master,' he said, 'I knew that you are a hard man, harvesting where you have not sown and gathering where you have not scattered seed. ²⁵ So I was afraid and went out and hid your gold in the ground. See, here is what belongs to you.'

²⁶ "His master replied, 'You wicked, lazy servant! So you knew that I harvest where I have not sown and gather where I have not scattered seed? ²⁷ Well then, you should have put my money on deposit with the bankers, so that when I returned I would have received it back with interest.

²⁸ " 'So take the bag of gold from him and give it to the one who has ten bags. ²⁹ For whoever has will be given more, and they will have an abundance. Whoever does not have, even what they have will be taken from them. ³⁰ And throw that worthless servant outside, into the darkness, where there will be weeping and gnashing of teeth.'

The Sheep and the Goats

³¹ "When the Son of Man comes in his glory, and all the angels with him, he will sit on his glorious throne. ³² All the nations will be gathered before him, and he will separate the people one from another as a shepherd separates the sheep from the goats. ³³ He will put the sheep on his right and the goats on his left.

³⁴ "Then the King will say to those on his right, 'Come, you who are blessed by

---

ᵃ 15 Greek *five talents . . . two talents . . . one talent*; also throughout this parable; a talent was worth about 20 years of a day laborer's wage.

my Father; take your inheritance, the kingdom prepared for you since the creation of the world. ³⁵For I was hungry and you gave me something to eat, I was thirsty and you gave me something to drink, I was a stranger and you invited me in, ³⁶I needed clothes and you clothed me, I was sick and you looked after me, I was in prison and you came to visit me.'

³⁷"Then the righteous will answer him, 'Lord, when did we see you hungry and feed you, or thirsty and give you something to drink? ³⁸When did we see you a stranger and invite you in, or needing clothes and clothe you? ³⁹When did we see you sick or in prison and go to visit you?'

⁴⁰"The King will reply, 'Truly I tell you, whatever you did for one of the least of these brothers and sisters of mine, you did for me.'

⁴¹"Then he will say to those on his left, 'Depart from me, you who are cursed, into the eternal fire prepared for the devil and his angels. ⁴²For I was hungry and you gave me nothing to eat, I was thirsty and you gave me nothing to drink, ⁴³I was a stranger and you did not invite me in, I needed clothes and you did not clothe me, I was sick and in prison and you did not look after me.'

⁴⁴"They also will answer, 'Lord, when did we see you hungry or thirsty or a stranger or needing clothes or sick or in prison, and did not help you?'

⁴⁵"He will reply, 'Truly I tell you, whatever you did not do for one of the least of these, you did not do for me.'

⁴⁶"Then they will go away to eternal punishment, but the righteous to eternal life."

Hell Is for Real!

Jesus told his listeners in no uncertain terms that hell is for real. He talked about "the fire of hell" (Matthew 5:22), and he described someone's "whole body [going] into hell" (Matthew 5:30). He also told a story about a man who was "in agony in this fire" (Luke 16:19–31).

The Bible mentions three things about hell:

+ It is permanent (Matthew 25:46).

+ It is a punishment for sin and disbelief (2 Thessalonians 1:8).

+ It is separation from God (2 Thessalonians 1:9).

The Bible also says that God doesn't want anyone to perish in hell (2 Peter 3:9). God was willing to send his Son to die in order to save everyone who believes from punishment in hell.

The Plot Against Jesus

26 When Jesus had finished saying all these things, he said to his disciples, 2 "As you know, the Passover is two days away—and the Son of Man will be handed over to be crucified."

3 Then the chief priests and the elders of the people assembled in the palace of the high priest, whose name was Caiaphas, 4 and they schemed to arrest Jesus secretly and kill him. 5 "But not during the festival," they said, "or there may be a riot among the people."

Jesus Anointed at Bethany

6 While Jesus was in Bethany in the home of Simon the Leper, 7 a woman came to him with an alabaster jar of very expensive perfume, which she poured on his head as he was reclining at the table. 8 When the disciples saw this, they were indignant. "Why this waste?" they asked. 9 "This perfume could have been sold at a high price and the money given to the poor."

10 Aware of this, Jesus said to them, "Why are you bothering this woman? She has done a beautiful thing to me. 11 The poor you will always have with you,[a] but you will not always have me. 12 When she poured this perfume on my body, she did it to prepare me for burial. 13 Truly I tell you, wherever this gospel is preached throughout the world, what she has done will also be told, in memory of her."

Judas Agrees to Betray Jesus

14 Then one of the Twelve—the one called Judas Iscariot—went to the chief priests 15 and asked, "What are you willing to give me if I deliver him over to you?" So they counted out for him thirty pieces of silver. 16 From then on Judas watched for an opportunity to hand him over.

The Last Supper

17 On the first day of the Festival of Unleavened Bread, the disciples came to Jesus and asked, "Where do you want us to make preparations for you to eat the Passover?"

18 He replied, "Go into the city to a certain man and tell him, 'The Teacher says: My appointed time is near. I am going to celebrate the Passover with my disciples at your house.'" 19 So the disciples did as Jesus had directed them and prepared the Passover.

20 When evening came, Jesus was reclining at the table with the Twelve. 21 And while they were eating, he said, "Truly I tell you, one of you will betray me."

22 They were very sad and began to say to him one after the other, "Surely you don't mean me, Lord?"

23 Jesus replied, "The one who has dipped his hand into the bowl with me will betray me. 24 The Son of Man will go just as it is written about him. But woe to that man who betrays the Son of Man! It would be better for him if he had not been born."

25 Then Judas, the one who would betray him, said, "Surely you don't mean me, Rabbi?"

Jesus answered, "You have said so."

26 While they were eating, Jesus took bread, and when he had given thanks, he broke it and gave it to his disciples, saying, "Take and eat; this is my body."

27 Then he took a cup, and when he had given thanks, he gave it to them, saying, "Drink from it, all of you. 28 This is my blood of the[b] covenant, which is poured out for many for the forgiveness of sins. 29 I tell you, I will not drink from this fruit of the vine from now on until that day when I drink it new with you in my Father's kingdom."

30 When they had sung a hymn, they went out to the Mount of Olives.

Jesus Predicts Peter's Denial

31 Then Jesus told them, "This very night you will all fall away on account of me, for it is written:

" 'I will strike the shepherd,
    and the sheep of the flock will be scattered.'[c]

32 But after I have risen, I will go ahead of you into Galilee."

---

a 11 See Deut. 15:11.   b 28 Some manuscripts *the new*   c 31 Zech. 13:7

33 Peter replied, "Even if all fall away on account of you, I never will."

34 "Truly I tell you," Jesus answered, "this very night, before the rooster crows, you will disown me three times."

35 But Peter declared, "Even if I have to die with you, I will never disown you." And all the other disciples said the same.

Gethsemane

36 Then Jesus went with his disciples to a place called Gethsemane, and he said to them, "Sit here while I go over there and pray." 37 He took Peter and the two sons of Zebedee along with him, and he began to be sorrowful and troubled. 38 Then he said to them, "My soul is overwhelmed with sorrow to the point of death. Stay here and keep watch with me."

39 Going a little farther, he fell with his face to the ground and prayed, "My Father, if it is possible, may this cup be taken from me. Yet not as I will, but as you will."

40 Then he returned to his disciples and found them sleeping. "Couldn't you men keep watch with me for one hour?" he asked Peter. 41 "Watch and pray so that you will not fall into temptation. The spirit is willing, but the flesh is weak."

42 He went away a second time and prayed, "My Father, if it is not possible for this cup to be taken away unless I drink it, may your will be done."

43 When he came back, he again found them sleeping, because their eyes were heavy. 44 So he left them and went away once more and prayed the third time, saying the same thing.

45 Then he returned to the disciples and said to them, "Are you still sleeping and resting? Look, the hour has come, and the Son of Man is delivered into the hands of sinners. 46 Rise! Let us go! Here comes my betrayer!"

Jesus Arrested

47 While he was still speaking, Judas, one of the Twelve, arrived. With him was a large crowd armed with swords and clubs, sent from the chief priests and the elders of the people. 48 Now the betray- er had arranged a signal with them: "The one I kiss is the man; arrest him." 49 Going at once to Jesus, Judas said, "Greetings, Rabbi!" and kissed him.

50 Jesus replied, "Do what you came for, friend."[a]

Then the men stepped forward, seized Jesus and arrested him. 51 With that, one of Jesus' companions reached for his sword, drew it out and struck the servant of the high priest, cutting off his ear.

52 "Put your sword back in its place," Jesus said to him, "for all who draw the sword will die by the sword. 53 Do you think I cannot call on my Father, and he will at once put at my disposal more than twelve legions of angels? 54 But how then would the Scriptures be fulfilled that say it must happen in this way?"

55 In that hour Jesus said to the crowd, "Am I leading a rebellion, that you have come out with swords and clubs to capture me? Every day I sat in the temple courts teaching, and you did not arrest me. 56 But this has all taken place that the writings of the prophets might be fulfilled." Then all the disciples deserted him and fled.

Jesus Before the Sanhedrin

57 Those who had arrested Jesus took him to Caiaphas the high priest, where the teachers of the law and the elders had assembled. 58 But Peter followed him at a distance, right up to the courtyard of the high priest. He entered and sat down with the guards to see the outcome.

59 The chief priests and the whole Sanhedrin were looking for false evidence against Jesus so that they could put him to death. 60 But they did not find any, though many false witnesses came forward.

Finally two came forward 61 and declared, "This fellow said, 'I am able to destroy the temple of God and rebuild it in three days.'"

62 Then the high priest stood up and said to Jesus, "Are you not going to answer? What is this testimony that these men are bringing against you?" 63 But Jesus remained silent.

[a] 50 Or "Why have you come, friend?"

I try so hard to do things right, but it seems like I never do. My mom told me to pray for strength to keep trying. But it's hard to keep trying when I always feel like such a loser. Are there people in the Bible who failed? If so, what did they do?   >> Thomas

Dear Jordan

Dear Thomas,

It's painful to try so hard and then feel like you've failed. You might be surprised, however, to discover that you're in great company.

Look at Peter's track record. He walked on water with Jesus but began to sink because of his lack of faith (Matthew 14:28–31). Yet later, Jesus praised Peter for his faith (Matthew 16:13–20). When Jesus predicted that Peter would disown him, Peter denied it fiercely. Peter loved Jesus so much he firmly believed he could never deny knowing him. But later that very night, his determination left him. Three times he swore he didn't know Jesus. When he heard the rooster crow, he remembered Jesus' words and "wept bitterly" (Matthew 26:69–75).

Quite a roller coaster, wouldn't you say? Up one moment, down the next. Did Christ ever tell Peter he was a failure? No. He knew what was in Peter's heart. Christ knows your heart too. He doesn't expect you to be perfect. He just wants your love and obedience and for you to do your best. Don't give up!

Jordan

The high priest said to him, "I charge you under oath by the living God: Tell us if you are the Messiah, the Son of God."

64 "You have said so," Jesus replied. "But I say to all of you: From now on you will see the Son of Man sitting at the right hand of the Mighty One and coming on the clouds of heaven."[a]

65 Then the high priest tore his clothes and said, "He has spoken blasphemy! Why do we need any more witnesses? Look, now you have heard the blasphemy. 66 What do you think?"

"He is worthy of death," they answered.

67 Then they spit in his face and struck him with their fists. Others slapped him 68 and said, "Prophesy to us, Messiah. Who hit you?"

Peter Disowns Jesus

69 Now Peter was sitting out in the courtyard, and a servant girl came to him. "You also were with Jesus of Galilee," she said.

70 But he denied it before them all. "I don't know what you're talking about," he said.

71 Then he went out to the gateway, where another servant girl saw him and said to the people there, "This fellow was with Jesus of Nazareth."

72 He denied it again, with an oath: "I don't know the man!"

73 After a little while, those standing there went up to Peter and said, "Surely you are one of them; your accent gives you away."

74 Then he began to call down curses, and he swore to them, "I don't know the man!"

Immediately a rooster crowed. 75 Then Peter remembered the word Jesus had spoken: "Before the rooster crows, you will disown me three times." And he went outside and wept bitterly.

Judas Hangs Himself

27 Early in the morning, all the chief priests and the elders of the people made their plans how to have Jesus executed. 2 So they bound him, led him away and handed him over to Pilate the governor.

3 When Judas, who had betrayed him, saw that Jesus was condemned, he was seized with remorse and returned the thirty pieces of silver to the chief priests and the elders. 4 "I have sinned," he said, "for I have betrayed innocent blood."

"What is that to us?" they replied. "That's your responsibility."

5 So Judas threw the money into the temple and left. Then he went away and hanged himself.

6 The chief priests picked up the coins and said, "It is against the law to put this into the treasury, since it is blood money." 7 So they decided to use the money to buy the potter's field as a burial place for foreigners. 8 That is why it has been called the Field of Blood to this day. 9 Then what was spoken by Jeremiah the prophet was fulfilled: "They took the thirty pieces of silver, the price set on him by the people of Israel, 10 and they used them to buy the potter's field, as the Lord commanded me."[b]

Jesus Before Pilate

11 Meanwhile Jesus stood before the governor, and the governor asked him, "Are you the king of the Jews?"

"You have said so," Jesus replied.

12 When he was accused by the chief priests and the elders, he gave no answer. 13 Then Pilate asked him, "Don't you hear the testimony they are bringing against you?" 14 But Jesus made no reply, not even to a single charge—to the great amazement of the governor.

15 Now it was the governor's custom at the festival to release a prisoner chosen by the crowd. 16 At that time they had a well-known prisoner whose name was Jesus[c] Barabbas. 17 So when the crowd had gathered, Pilate asked them, "Which one do you want me to release to you: Jesus Barabbas, or Jesus who is called the Messiah?" 18 For he knew it was out of self-interest that they had handed Jesus over to him.

---

[a] 64 See Psalm 110:1; Daniel 7:13.   [b] 10 See Zech. 11:12,13; Jer. 19:1-13; 32:6-9.   [c] 16 Many manuscripts do not have *Jesus*; also in verse 17.

We Believe...

Jesus was "dead and buried"

No one said Jesus didn't die. The chief priests paid the men who guarded Jesus' tomb to say the disciples stole his body (Matthew 28:11–15). But they never suggested Jesus hadn't been dead. There were too many people who knew better.

The Roman soldier who thrust a spear into Jesus' side knew he was dead (John 19:34).

The Roman officer who reported to Pilate knew that Jesus was dead (Mark 15:44–45).

Joseph and Nicodemus, who were members of the ruling council, wrapped Jesus' dead body in strips of linen (John 19:38–42; Luke 23:50–53). They knew he was dead.

There were just too many witnesses who knew that Jesus was dead and buried for enemies to suggest that maybe he hadn't died.

He was dead. He was buried in a tomb guarded by hired soldiers. And at first all Jesus' followers were heartbroken. Only later did they realize what Jesus' death meant—something the Apostle Paul tells us. Paul wrote, "You see, just at the right time, when we were still powerless, Christ died for the ungodly. Very rarely will anyone die for a righteous person, though for a good person someone might possibly dare to die. But God demonstrates his own love for us in this: While we were still sinners, Christ died for us" (Romans 5:6–8).

Jesus died . . . because he had to die to save us from the consequences of our sin. And now he lives to give us power to overcome the temptations we face every day (Romans 6:1–14). The phrase "descended into hell" found in some creeds does not mean that Jesus went to what we call hell today (the place of eternal punishment). In New Testament time *hades* simply meant the realm of the dead, the grave. Jesus truly died; his burial confirmed his death. And then he rose again.

Go to page 1303 for the next We Believe

19 While Pilate was sitting on the judge's seat, his wife sent him this message: "Don't have anything to do with that innocent man, for I have suffered a great deal today in a dream because of him."

20 But the chief priests and the elders persuaded the crowd to ask for Barabbas and to have Jesus executed.

21 "Which of the two do you want me to release to you?" asked the governor.

"Barabbas," they answered.

22 "What shall I do, then, with Jesus who is called the Messiah?" Pilate asked.

They all answered, "Crucify him!"

23 "Why? What crime has he committed?" asked Pilate.

But they shouted all the louder, "Crucify him!"

24 When Pilate saw that he was getting nowhere, but that instead an uproar was starting, he took water and washed his hands in front of the crowd. "I am innocent of this man's blood," he said. "It is your responsibility!"

25 All the people answered, "His blood is on us and on our children!"

26 Then he released Barabbas to them. But he had Jesus flogged, and handed him over to be crucified.

The Soldiers Mock Jesus

27 Then the governor's soldiers took Jesus into the Praetorium and gathered the whole company of soldiers around him. 28 They stripped him and put a scarlet robe on him, 29 and then twisted together a crown of thorns and set it on his head. They put a staff in his right hand. Then they knelt in front of him and mocked him. "Hail, king of the Jews!" they said. 30 They spit on him, and took the staff and struck him on the head again and again. 31 After they had mocked him, they took off the robe and put his own clothes on him. Then they led him away to crucify him.

The Crucifixion of Jesus

32 As they were going out, they met a man from Cyrene, named Simon, and they forced him to carry the cross. 33 They came to a place called Golgotha (which means "the place of the skull"). 34 There they offered Jesus wine to drink, mixed with gall; but after tasting it, he refused to drink it. 35 When they had crucified him, they divided up his clothes by casting lots. 36 And sitting down, they kept watch over him there. 37 Above his head they placed the written charge against him: THIS IS JESUS, THE KING OF THE JEWS.

38 Two rebels were crucified with him, one on his right and one on his left. 39 Those who passed by hurled insults at him, shaking their heads 40 and saying, "You who are going to destroy the temple and build it in three days, save yourself! Come down from the cross, if you are the Son of God!" 41 In the same way the chief priests, the teachers of the law and the elders mocked him. 42 "He saved others," they said, "but he can't save himself! He's the king of Israel! Let him come down now from the cross, and we will believe in him. 43 He trusts in God. Let God rescue him now if he wants him, for he said, 'I am the Son of God.' " 44 In the same way the rebels who were crucified with him also heaped insults on him.

The Death of Jesus

45 From noon until three in the afternoon darkness came over all the land. 46 About three in the afternoon Jesus cried out in a loud voice, *"Eli, Eli,*[a] *lema sabachthani?"* (which means "My God, my God, why have you forsaken me?").[b]

47 When some of those standing there heard this, they said, "He's calling Elijah."

48 Immediately one of them ran and got a sponge. He filled it with wine vinegar, put it on a staff, and offered it to Jesus to drink. 49 The rest said, "Now leave him alone. Let's see if Elijah comes to save him."

50 And when Jesus had cried out again in a loud voice, he gave up his spirit.

51 At that moment the curtain of the temple was torn in two from top to bottom. The earth shook, the rocks split 52 and the tombs broke open. The bodies of many holy people who had died

---

[a] 46 Some manuscripts *Eloi, Eloi*   [b] 46 Psalm 22:1

I t's an awful, empty feeling. Suddenly you feel totally alone. Your mom says she and your dad are going to divorce. Or your grandma dies. Or your closest friend ignores you. It's surprising how many things can make you feel completely alone. When Jesus hung on the cross, carrying our sins, God the Father himself looked away. Jesus knows what it feels like to be forsaken. To be left alone. But Jesus *volunteered* to be forsaken. He went to the cross knowing what it would mean. Why? So that even when you feel most alone, you won't be. No matter what happens, Christ will never forsake you or let you down.

{Matthew 27:45–50}

≫ INSTANT ACCESS

56 Among them were Mary Magdalene, Mary the mother of James and Joseph,[b] and the mother of Zebedee's sons.

The Burial of Jesus

57 As evening approached, there came a rich man from Arimathea, named Joseph, who had himself become a disciple of Jesus. 58 Going to Pilate, he asked for Jesus' body, and Pilate ordered that it be given to him. 59 Joseph took the body, wrapped it in a clean linen cloth, 60 and placed it in his own new tomb that he had cut out of the rock. He rolled a big stone in front of the entrance to the tomb and went away. 61 Mary Magdalene and the other Mary were sitting there opposite the tomb.

The Guard at the Tomb

62 The next day, the one after Preparation Day, the chief priests and the Pharisees went to Pilate. 63 "Sir," they said, "we remember that while he was still alive that deceiver said, 'After three days I will rise again.' 64 So give the order for the tomb to be made secure until the third day. Otherwise, his disciples may come and steal the body and tell the people that he has been raised from the dead. This last deception will be worse than the first."

65 "Take a guard," Pilate answered. "Go, make the tomb as secure as you know how." 66 So they went and made the tomb secure by putting a seal on the stone and posting the guard.

Jesus Has Risen

28 After the Sabbath, at dawn on the first day of the week, Mary Magdalene and the other Mary went to look at the tomb.

2 There was a violent earthquake, for an angel of the Lord came down from heaven and, going to the tomb, rolled back the stone and sat on it. 3 His appearance was like lightning, and his clothes were white as snow. 4 The guards were so afraid of him that they shook and became like dead men.

were raised to life. 53 They came out of the tombs after Jesus' resurrection and[a] went into the holy city and appeared to many people.

54 When the centurion and those with him who were guarding Jesus saw the earthquake and all that had happened, they were terrified, and exclaimed, "Surely he was the Son of God!"

55 Many women were there, watching from a distance. They had followed Jesus from Galilee to care for his needs.

---

a 53 Or *tombs, and after Jesus' resurrection they*   *b* 56 Greek *Joses*, a variant of *Joseph*

⁵The angel said to the women, "Do not be afraid, for I know that you are looking for Jesus, who was crucified. ⁶He is not here; he has risen, just as he said. Come and see the place where he lay. ⁷Then go quickly and tell his disciples: 'He has risen from the dead and is going ahead of you into Galilee. There you will see him.' Now I have told you."

⁸So the women hurried away from the tomb, afraid yet filled with joy, and ran to tell his disciples. ⁹Suddenly Jesus met them. "Greetings," he said. They came to him, clasped his feet and worshiped him. ¹⁰Then Jesus said to them, "Do not be afraid. Go and tell my brothers to go to Galilee; there they will see me."

The Guards' Report

¹¹While the women were on their way, some of the guards went into the city and reported to the chief priests everything that had happened. ¹²When the chief priests had met with the elders and de-vised a plan, they gave the soldiers a large sum of money, ¹³telling them, "You are to say, 'His disciples came during the night and stole him away while we were asleep.' ¹⁴If this report gets to the gover-nor, we will satisfy him and keep you out of trouble." ¹⁵So the soldiers took the money and did as they were in-structed. And this story has been widely circu-lated among the Jews to this very day.

The Great Commission

¹⁶Then the eleven disci-ples went to Galilee, to the mountain where Jesus had told them to go. ¹⁷When they saw him, they worshiped him; but some doubt-ed. ¹⁸Then Jesus came to them and said, "All authority in heaven and on earth has been given to me. ¹⁹Therefore go and make disciples of all nations, baptizing them in the name of the Father and of the Son and of the Holy Spirit, ²⁰and teaching them to obey everything I have command-ed you. And surely I am with you always, to the very end of the age."

Surely I am with you always, to the very end of the age.

Matthew 28:20

MARK

Who?

What kind of people do you like? The guys who play sports? The girls who are popular? Kids who study? Who are good-looking? Who dress in style? Or do you look for someone kind and friendly?

Mark wrote his Gospel to show that Jesus was the kind of person that the Romans in the empire would appreciate. Mark shows Jesus as a man of action, a man with authority. Jesus came to earth with a mission, and he didn't rest until he finished what he came here to do.

>>**DEMONS GIVE UP, PURSUE FUTURE IN PIGS**
Story in Mark 5:1–20

>>**DIRTY DINERS, NOT DIRTY DINNERS**
Teaching confounds Pharisees. See Mark 7:14–23

>>**"SERVANT" TOP JOB IN COMING KINGDOM**
Question gets unexpected answer. Report in Mark 10:35–45

>>**TEMPLE BUSINESSMEN BUSTED BY JESUS**
Exciting event reported in Mark 11:12–19

preview

Mark is not one of Jesus' twelve disciples. He records Peter's stories about Jesus.

A key word in this book is "immediately."

As Jesus grows to adulthood, Judea becomes a Roman province. Augustus dies, and Tiberius becomes Roman emperor.

The first Chinese census is taken. The Maya develop the "Long Count" calendar. The Roman poet Ovid dies in exile.

John the Baptist Prepares the Way

1 The beginning of the good news about Jesus the Messiah,[a] the Son of God,[b] ² as it is written in Isaiah the prophet:

"I will send my messenger ahead of you,
who will prepare your way"[c]—
³ "a voice of one calling in the wilderness,
'Prepare the way for the Lord,
make straight paths for him.' "[d]

⁴ And so John the Baptist appeared in the wilderness, preaching a baptism of repentance for the forgiveness of sins. ⁵ The whole Judean countryside and all the people of Jerusalem went out to him. Confessing their sins, they were baptized by him in the Jordan River. ⁶ John wore clothing made of camel's hair, with a leather belt around his waist, and he ate locusts and wild honey. ⁷ And this was his message: "After me comes the one more powerful than I, the straps of whose sandals I am not worthy to stoop down and untie. ⁸ I baptize you with[e] water, but he will baptize you with[e] the Holy Spirit."

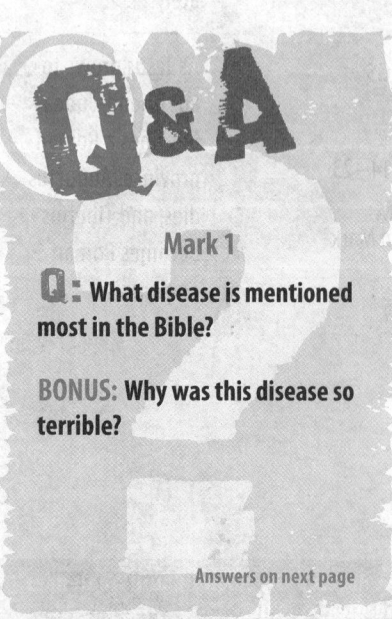

Mark 1

Q: What disease is mentioned most in the Bible?

BONUS: Why was this disease so terrible?

Answers on next page

The Baptism and Testing of Jesus

⁹ At that time Jesus came from Nazareth in Galilee and was baptized by John in the Jordan. ¹⁰ Just as Jesus was coming up out of the water, he saw heaven being torn open and the Spirit descending on him like a dove. ¹¹ And a voice came from heaven: "You are my Son, whom I love; with you I am well pleased."

¹² At once the Spirit sent him out into the wilderness, ¹³ and he was in the wilderness forty days, being tempted[f] by Satan. He was with the wild animals, and angels attended him.

Jesus Announces the Good News

¹⁴ After John was put in prison, Jesus went into Galilee, proclaiming the good news of God. ¹⁵ "The time has come," he said. "The kingdom of God has come near. Repent and believe the good news!"

Jesus Calls His First Disciples

¹⁶ As Jesus walked beside the Sea of Galilee, he saw Simon and his brother Andrew casting a net into the lake, for they were fishermen. ¹⁷ "Come, follow me," Jesus said, "and I will send you out to fish for people." ¹⁸ At once they left their nets and followed him.

¹⁹ When he had gone a little farther, he saw James son of Zebedee and his brother John in a boat, preparing their nets. ²⁰ Without delay he called them, and they left their father Zebedee in the boat with the hired men and followed him.

Jesus Drives Out an Impure Spirit

²¹ They went to Capernaum, and when the Sabbath came, Jesus went into the synagogue and began to teach. ²² The people were amazed at his teaching, because he taught them as one who had authority, not as the teachers of the law.

---

[a] 1 Or *Jesus Christ. Messiah* (Hebrew) and *Christ* (Greek) both mean *Anointed One.*   [b] 1 Some manuscripts do not have *the Son of God.*   [c] 2 Mal. 3:1   [d] 3 Isaiah 40:3   [e] 8 Or *in*   [f] 13 The Greek for *tempted* can also mean *tested.*

²³Just then a man in their synagogue who was possessed by an impure spirit cried out, ²⁴"What do you want with us, Jesus of Nazareth? Have you come to destroy us? I know who you are—the Holy One of God!"

²⁵"Be quiet!" said Jesus sternly. "Come out of him!" ²⁶The impure spirit shook the man violently and came out of him with a shriek.

²⁷The people were all so amazed that they asked each other, "What is this? A new teaching—and with authority! He even gives orders to impure spirits and they obey him." ²⁸News about him spread quickly over the whole region of Galilee.

Jesus Heals Many

²⁹As soon as they left the synagogue, they went with James and John to the home of Simon and Andrew. ³⁰Simon's mother-in-law was in bed with a fever, and they immediately told Jesus about her. ³¹So he went to her, took her hand and helped her up. The fever left her and she began to wait on them.

³²That evening after sunset the people brought to Jesus all the sick and demon-possessed. ³³The whole town gathered at the door, ³⁴and Jesus healed many who had various diseases. He also drove out many demons, but he would not let the demons speak because they knew who he was.

Jesus Prays in a Solitary Place

³⁵Very early in the morning, while it was still dark, Jesus got up, left the house and went off to a solitary place, where he prayed. ³⁶Simon and his companions went to look for him, ³⁷and when they found him, they exclaimed: "Everyone is looking for you!"

³⁸Jesus replied, "Let us go somewhere else—to the nearby villages—so I can preach there also. That is why I have come." ³⁹So he traveled throughout Galilee, preaching in their synagogues and driving out demons.

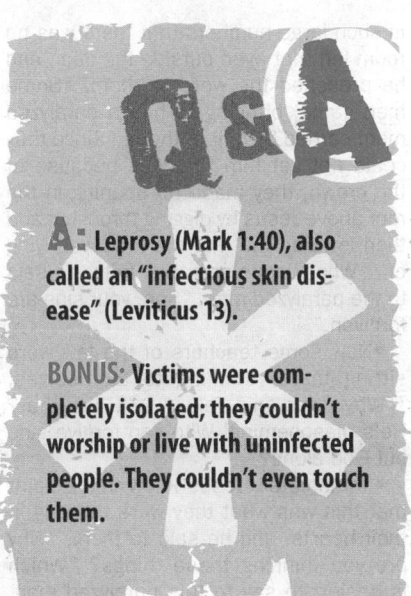

A: Leprosy (Mark 1:40), also called an "infectious skin disease" (Leviticus 13).

BONUS: Victims were completely isolated; they couldn't worship or live with uninfected people. They couldn't even touch them.

Jesus Heals a Man With Leprosy

⁴⁰A man with leprosy[a] came to him and begged him on his knees, "If you are willing, you can make me clean."

⁴¹Jesus was indignant.[b] He reached out his hand and touched the man. "I am willing," he said. "Be clean!" ⁴²Immediately the leprosy left him and he was cleansed.

⁴³Jesus sent him away at once with a strong warning: ⁴⁴"See that you don't tell this to anyone. But go, show yourself to the priest and offer the sacrifices that Moses commanded for your cleansing, as a testimony to them." ⁴⁵Instead he went out and began to talk freely, spreading the news. As a result, Jesus could no longer enter a town openly but stayed outside in lonely places. Yet the people still came to him from everywhere.

Jesus Forgives and Heals a Paralyzed Man

2 A few days later, when Jesus again entered Capernaum, the people heard that he had come home. ²They gathered

---

a 40 The Greek word traditionally translated *leprosy* was used for various diseases affecting the skin.   b 41 Many manuscripts *Jesus was filled with compassion*

in such large numbers that there was no room left, not even outside the door, and he preached the word to them. ³Some men came, bringing to him a paralyzed man, carried by four of them. ⁴Since they could not get him to Jesus because of the crowd, they made an opening in the roof above Jesus by digging through it and then lowered the mat the man was lying on. ⁵When Jesus saw their faith, he said to the paralyzed man, "Son, your sins are forgiven."

⁶Now some teachers of the law were sitting there, thinking to themselves, ⁷"Why does this fellow talk like that? He's blaspheming! Who can forgive sins but God alone?"

⁸Immediately Jesus knew in his spirit that this was what they were thinking in their hearts, and he said to them, "Why are you thinking these things? ⁹Which is easier: to say to this paralyzed man, 'Your sins are forgiven,' or to say, 'Get up, take your mat and walk'? ¹⁰But I want you to know that the Son of Man has authority on earth to forgive sins." So he said to the man, ¹¹"I tell you, get up, take your mat and go home." ¹²He got up, took his mat and walked out in full view of them all. This amazed everyone and they praised God, saying, "We have never seen anything like this!"

Jesus Calls Levi and Eats With Sinners

¹³Once again Jesus went out beside the lake. A large crowd came to him, and he began to teach them. ¹⁴As he walked along, he saw Levi son of Alphaeus sitting at the tax collector's booth. "Follow me," Jesus told him, and Levi got up and followed him.

¹⁵While Jesus was having dinner at Levi's house, many tax collectors and sinners were eating with him and his disciples, for there were many who followed him. ¹⁶When the teachers of the law who were Pharisees saw him eating with the sinners and tax collectors, they asked his disciples: "Why does he eat with tax collectors and sinners?"

¹⁷On hearing this, Jesus said to them, "It is not the healthy who need a doctor,

but the sick. I have not come to call the righteous, but sinners."

Jesus Questioned About Fasting

¹⁸Now John's disciples and the Pharisees were fasting. Some people came and asked Jesus, "How is it that John's disciples and the disciples of the Pharisees are fasting, but yours are not?"

¹⁹Jesus answered, "How can the guests of the bridegroom fast while he is with them? They cannot, so long as they

>> INSTANT ACCESS

You know that prayer is important. Everyone knows that. But it's not easy to find the time. Jesus was so busy it was hard for him to find time too. Mark says that Jesus' solution was to get up "very early in the morning, while it was still dark" and slip away to a "solitary place" where he could pray in private (Mark 1:35). Maybe you're not a "morning person." But setting your alarm just five or ten minutes early would give you time to start the day off right. And if you can't find a private place to pray, try the bathroom. You might find that getting up early for prayer can be important for you too.

{Mark 1:35–37}

have him with them. ²⁰But the time will come when the bridegroom will be taken from them, and on that day they will fast.

²¹"No one sews a patch of unshrunk cloth on an old garment. Otherwise, the new piece will pull away from the old, making the tear worse. ²²And no one pours new wine into old wineskins. Otherwise, the wine will burst the skins, and both the wine and the wineskins will be ruined. No, they pour new wine into new wineskins."

Jesus Is Lord of the Sabbath

²³One Sabbath Jesus was going through the grainfields, and as his disciples walked along, they began to pick some heads of grain. ²⁴The Pharisees said to him, "Look, why are they doing what is unlawful on the Sabbath?"

²⁵He answered, "Have you never read what David did when he and his companions were hungry and in need? ²⁶In the days of Abiathar the high priest, he entered the house of God and ate the consecrated bread, which is lawful only for priests to eat. And he also gave some to his companions."

²⁷Then he said to them, "The Sabbath was made for man, not man for the Sabbath. ²⁸So the Son of Man is Lord even of the Sabbath."

Jesus Heals on the Sabbath

3 Another time Jesus went into the synagogue, and a man with a shriveled hand was there. ²Some of them were looking for a reason to accuse Jesus, so they watched him closely to see if he would heal him on the Sabbath. ³Jesus said to the man with the shriveled hand, "Stand up in front of everyone."

⁴Then Jesus asked them, "Which is lawful on the Sabbath: to do good or to do evil, to save life or to kill?" But they remained silent.

⁵He looked around at them in anger and, deeply distressed at their stubborn hearts, said to the man, "Stretch out your hand." He stretched it out, and his hand was completely restored. ⁶Then the Pharisees went out and began to plot with the Herodians how they might kill Jesus.

Crowds Follow Jesus

⁷Jesus withdrew with his disciples to the lake, and a large crowd from Galilee followed. ⁸When they heard about all he was doing, many people came to him from Judea, Jerusalem, Idumea, and the regions across the Jordan and around Tyre and Sidon. ⁹Because of the crowd he told his disciples to have a small boat ready for him, to keep the people from crowding him. ¹⁰For he had healed many, so that those with diseases were pushing forward to touch him. ¹¹Whenever the impure spirits saw him, they fell down before him and cried out, "You are the Son of God." ¹²But he gave them strict orders not to tell others about him.

Jesus Appoints the Twelve

¹³Jesus went up on a mountainside and called to him those he wanted, and they came to him. ¹⁴He appointed twelveᵃ that they might be with him and that he might send them out to preach ¹⁵and to have authority to drive out demons. ¹⁶These are the twelve he appointed: Simon (to whom he gave the name Peter), ¹⁷James son of Zebedee and his brother John (to them he gave the name Boanerges, which means "sons of thunder"), ¹⁸Andrew, Philip, Bartholomew, Matthew, Thomas, James son of Alphaeus, Thaddaeus, Simon the Zealot ¹⁹and Judas Iscariot, who betrayed him.

Jesus Accused by His Family and by Teachers of the Law

²⁰Then Jesus entered a house, and again a crowd gathered, so that he and his disciples were not even able to eat. ²¹When his familyᵇ heard about this, they went to take charge of him, for they said, "He is out of his mind."

²²And the teachers of the law who came down from Jerusalem said, "He is possessed by Beelzebul! By the prince of demons he is driving out demons."

²³So Jesus called them over to him and began to speak to them in parables: "How can Satan drive out Satan?

ᵃ 14 Some manuscripts *twelve — designating them apostles —*   ᵇ 21 Or *his associates*

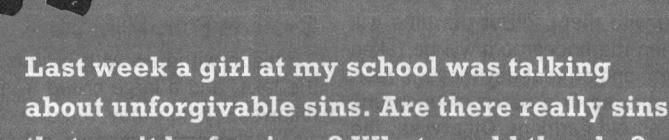

Last week a girl at my school was talking about unforgivable sins. Are there really sins that can't be forgiven? What would they be?

>> Kayla

Dear Jordan

Dear Kayla,

The Bible speaks of one sin that is unforgivable and that is blasphemy against the Holy Spirit (Mark 3:29). The word blasphemy means having contempt or hostility toward God.

In Mark 3, Jesus had been performing miracles of healing, giving clear evidence that he is God. But the teachers of the law began accusing him of doing these things by the power of Satan. Then they accused him of being possessed by the prince of demons. Instead of recognizing Jesus as the Son of God, they said his power was from Satan and he was possessed.

The men couldn't deny the great healing miracles Jesus performed, so instead they gave credit to Satan. This was the one unforgivable sin: saying Jesus had been given power by Satan.

Jesus paid the penalty for all our sins. We may ask for forgiveness and we are assured we have been washed clean.

Jordan

24 If a kingdom is divided against itself, that kingdom cannot stand. 25 If a house is divided against itself, that house cannot stand. 26 And if Satan opposes himself and is divided, he cannot stand; his end has come. 27 In fact, no one can enter a strong man's house without first tying him up. Then he can plunder the strong man's house. 28 Truly I tell you, people can be forgiven all their sins and every slander they utter, 29 but whoever blasphemes against the Holy Spirit will never be forgiven; they are guilty of an eternal sin."

30 He said this because they were saying, "He has an impure spirit."

31 Then Jesus' mother and brothers arrived. Standing outside, they sent someone in to call him. 32 A crowd was sitting around him, and they told him, "Your mother and brothers are outside looking for you."

33 "Who are my mother and my brothers?" he asked.

34 Then he looked at those seated in a circle around him and said, "Here are my mother and my brothers! 35 Whoever does God's will is my brother and sister and mother."

The Parable of the Sower

4 Again Jesus began to teach by the lake. The crowd that gathered around him was so large that he got into a boat and sat in it out on the lake, while all the people were along the shore at the water's edge. 2 He taught them many things by parables, and in his teaching said: 3 "Listen! A farmer went out to sow his seed. 4 As he was scattering the seed, some fell along the path, and the birds came and ate it up. 5 Some fell on rocky places, where it did not have much soil. It sprang up quickly, because the soil was shallow. 6 But when the sun came up, the plants were scorched, and they withered because they had no root. 7 Other seed fell among thorns, which grew up and choked the plants, so that they did not bear grain. 8 Still other seed fell on good soil. It came up, grew and produced a crop, some multiplying thirty, some sixty, some a hundred times."

9 Then Jesus said, "Whoever has ears to hear, let them hear."

10 When he was alone, the Twelve and the others around him asked him about the parables. 11 He told them, "The secret of the kingdom of God has been given to you. But to those on the outside everything is said in parables 12 so that,

" 'they may be ever seeing but never
   perceiving,
and ever hearing but never
   understanding;
otherwise they might turn and be
   forgiven!'^a"

13 Then Jesus said to them, "Don't you understand this parable? How then will you understand any parable? 14 The farmer sows the word. 15 Some people are like seed along the path, where the word is sown. As soon as they hear it, Satan comes and takes away the word that was sown in them. 16 Others, like seed sown on rocky places, hear the word and at once receive it with joy. 17 But since they have no root, they last only a short time. When trouble or persecution comes because of the word, they quickly fall away. 18 Still others, like seed sown among thorns, hear the word; 19 but the worries of this life, the deceitfulness of wealth and the desires for other things come in and choke the word, making it unfruitful. 20 Others, like seed sown on good soil, hear the word, accept it, and produce a crop—some thirty, some sixty, some a hundred times what was sown."

A Lamp on a Stand

21 He said to them, "Do you bring in a lamp to put it under a bowl or a bed? Instead, don't you put it on its stand? 22 For whatever is hidden is meant to be disclosed, and whatever is concealed is meant to be brought out into the open. 23 If anyone has ears to hear, let them hear."

24 "Consider carefully what you hear," he continued. "With the measure you use, it will be measured to you—and

---

^a 12 Isaiah 6:9,10

even more. 25Whoever has will be given more; whoever does not have, even what they have will be taken from them."

The Parable of the Growing Seed

26He also said, "This is what the kingdom of God is like. A man scatters seed on the ground. 27Night and day, whether he sleeps or gets up, the seed sprouts and grows, though he does not know how. 28All by itself the soil produces grain— first the stalk, then the head, then the full kernel in the head. 29As soon as the grain is ripe, he puts the sickle to it, because the harvest has come."

The Parable of the Mustard Seed

30Again he said, "What shall we say the kingdom of God is like, or what parable shall we use to describe it? 31It is like a mustard seed, which is the smallest of all seeds on earth. 32Yet when planted, it grows and becomes the largest of all garden plants, with such big branches that the birds can perch in its shade."

33With many similar parables Jesus spoke the word to them, as much as they could understand. 34He did not say anything to them without using a parable. But when he was alone with his own disciples, he explained everything.

Jesus Calms the Storm

35That day when evening came, he said to his disciples, "Let us go over to the other side." 36Leaving the crowd behind, they took him along, just as he was, in the boat. There were also other boats with him. 37A furious squall came up, and the waves broke over the boat, so that it was nearly swamped. 38Jesus was in the stern, sleeping on a cushion. The disciples woke him and said to him, "Teacher, don't you care if we drown?"

39He got up, rebuked the wind and said to the waves, "Quiet! Be still!" Then the wind died down and it was completely calm.

≫ INSTANT ACCESS

Do your friends know you're a Christian? Or hasn't the subject ever come up? Some teens (and adults too) hesitate to stand up for their faith. But as a Christian you really *are* different. When you try to hide who you are, it just isn't right. When people in Bible times lit a lamp, they didn't hide it. They put it on a stand so everyone could see. Jesus didn't come into your life to be hidden. He came into your life so you could be his light, so you could hold him up for others to see the way to eternal life.

{Mark 4:21–23}

40He said to his disciples, "Why are you so afraid? Do you still have no faith?"

41They were terrified and asked each other, "Who is this? Even the wind and the waves obey him!"

Jesus Restores a Demon-Possessed Man

5 They went across the lake to the region of the Gerasenes.[a] 2When Jesus got out of the boat, a man with an impure spirit came from the tombs to meet him. 3This man lived in the tombs, and no one could bind him anymore, not even with a chain. 4For he had often been chained hand and foot, but he tore the chains apart and broke the irons on his feet. No one was strong enough to subdue him.

---

[a] 1 Some manuscripts *Gadarenes*; other manuscripts *Gergesenes*

⁵Night and day among the tombs and in the hills he would cry out and cut himself with stones.

⁶When he saw Jesus from a distance, he ran and fell on his knees in front of him. ⁷He shouted at the top of his voice, "What do you want with me, Jesus, Son of the Most High God? In God's name don't torture me!" ⁸For Jesus had said to him, "Come out of this man, you impure spirit!"

⁹Then Jesus asked him, "What is your name?"

"My name is Legion," he replied, "for we are many." ¹⁰And he begged Jesus again and again not to send them out of the area.

¹¹A large herd of pigs was feeding on the nearby hillside. ¹²The demons begged Jesus, "Send us among the pigs; allow us to go into them." ¹³He gave them permission, and the impure spirits came out and went into the pigs. The herd, about two thousand in number, rushed down the steep bank into the lake and were drowned.

¹⁴Those tending the pigs ran off and reported this in the town and countryside, and the people went out to see what had happened. ¹⁵When they came to Jesus, they saw the man who had been possessed by the legion of demons, sitting there, dressed and in his right mind; and they were afraid. ¹⁶Those who had seen it told the people what had happened to the demon-possessed man—and told about the pigs as well. ¹⁷Then the people began to plead with Jesus to leave their region.

¹⁸As Jesus was getting into the boat, the man who had been demon-possessed begged to go with him. ¹⁹Jesus did not let him, but said, "Go home to your own people and tell them how much the Lord has done for you, and how he has had mercy on you." ²⁰So the man went away and began to tell in the Decapolis[a] how much Jesus had done for him. And all the people were amazed.

Jesus Raises a Dead Girl and Heals a Sick Woman

²¹When Jesus had again crossed over by boat to the other side of the lake, a large crowd gathered around him while he was by the lake. ²²Then one of the synagogue leaders, named Jairus, came, and when he saw Jesus, he fell at his feet. ²³He pleaded earnestly with him, "My little daughter is dying. Please come and put your hands on her so that she will be healed and live." ²⁴So Jesus went with him.

A large crowd followed and pressed around him. ²⁵And a woman was there who had been subject to bleeding for twelve years. ²⁶She had suffered a great deal under the care of many doctors and had spent all she had, yet instead of getting better she grew worse. ²⁷When she heard about Jesus, she came up behind him in the crowd and touched his cloak, ²⁸because she thought, "If I just touch his clothes, I will be healed." ²⁹Immediately her bleeding stopped and she felt in her body that she was freed from her suffering.

³⁰At once Jesus realized that power had gone out from him. He turned around in the crowd and asked, "Who touched my clothes?"

³¹"You see the people crowding against you," his disciples answered, "and yet you can ask, 'Who touched me?'"

³²But Jesus kept looking around to see who had done it. ³³Then the woman, knowing what had happened to her, came and fell at his feet and, trembling with fear, told him the whole truth. ³⁴He said to her, "Daughter, your faith has healed you. Go in peace and be freed from your suffering."

³⁵While Jesus was still speaking, some people came from the house of Jairus, the synagogue leader. "Your daughter is dead," they said. "Why bother the teacher anymore?"

³⁶Overhearing[b] what they said, Jesus told him, "Don't be afraid; just believe."

³⁷He did not let anyone follow him except Peter, James and John the brother of James. ³⁸When they came to the home of the synagogue leader, Jesus saw a commotion, with people crying and wailing

---

[a] 20 That is, the Ten Cities   [b] 36 Or *Ignoring*

loudly. ³⁹He went in and said to them, "Why all this commotion and wailing? The child is not dead but asleep." ⁴⁰But they laughed at him.

After he put them all out, he took the child's father and mother and the disciples who were with him, and went in where the child was. ⁴¹He took her by the hand and said to her, *"Talitha koum!"* (which means "Little girl, I say to you, get up!"). ⁴²Immediately the girl stood up and began to walk around (she was twelve years old). At this they were completely astonished. ⁴³He gave strict orders not to let anyone know about this, and told them to give her something to eat.

A Prophet Without Honor

6 Jesus left there and went to his hometown, accompanied by his disciples. ²When the Sabbath came, he began to teach in the synagogue, and many who heard him were amazed.

"Where did this man get these things?" they asked. "What's this wisdom that has been given him? What are these remarkable miracles he is performing? ³Isn't this the carpenter? Isn't this Mary's son and the brother of James, Joseph,ᵃ Judas and Simon? Aren't his sisters here with us?" And they took offense at him.

⁴Jesus said to them, "A prophet is not without honor except in his own town, among his relatives and in his own home." ⁵He could not do any miracles there, except lay his hands on a few sick people and heal them. ⁶He was amazed at their lack of faith.

Jesus Sends Out the Twelve

Then Jesus went around teaching from village to village. ⁷Calling the Twelve to him, he began to send them out two by two and gave them authority over impure spirits.

⁸These were his instructions: "Take nothing for the journey except a staff— no bread, no bag, no money in your belts. ⁹Wear sandals but not an extra shirt. ¹⁰Whenever you enter a house, stay

there until you leave that town. ¹¹And if any place will not welcome you or listen to you, leave that place and shake the dust off your feet as a testimony against them."

¹²They went out and preached that people should repent. ¹³They drove out many demons and anointed many sick people with oil and healed them.

John the Baptist Beheaded

¹⁴King Herod heard about this, for Jesus' name had become well known. Some were saying,ᵇ "John the Baptist has been raised from the dead, and that is why miraculous powers are at work in him."

¹⁵Others said, "He is Elijah."

And still others claimed, "He is a prophet, like one of the prophets of long ago."

¹⁶But when Herod heard this, he said, "John, whom I beheaded, has been raised from the dead!"

¹⁷For Herod himself had given orders to have John arrested, and he had him bound and put in prison. He did this because of Herodias, his brother Philip's wife, whom he had married. ¹⁸For John had been saying to Herod, "It is not lawful for you to have your brother's wife." ¹⁹So Herodias nursed a grudge against John and wanted to kill him. But she was not able to, ²⁰because Herod feared John and protected him, knowing him to be a righteous and holy man. When Herod heard John, he was greatly puzzledᶜ; yet he liked to listen to him.

²¹Finally the opportune time came. On his birthday Herod gave a banquet for his high officials and military commanders and the leading men of Galilee. ²²When the daughter ofᵈ Herodias came in and danced, she pleased Herod and his dinner guests.

The king said to the girl, "Ask me for anything you want, and I'll give it to you." ²³And he promised her with an oath, "Whatever you ask I will give you, up to half my kingdom."

²⁴She went out and said to her mother, "What shall I ask for?"

ᵃ 3 Greek *Joses*, a variant of *Joseph*   ᵇ 14 Some early manuscripts *He was saying*   ᶜ 20 Some early manuscripts *he did many things*   ᵈ 22 Some early manuscripts *When his daughter*

Have you ever tried to rewrite the end of a Bible story? Try this one. Herodias's daughter wanted John the Baptist beheaded. If the king hadn't been so worried about what his guests would think, what could he have said? Perhaps, "I said half my kingdom. I didn't say I'd kill someone for you." Or, "That's against God's law, my dear." Or, "What a terrible thing to ask. Guards, get her out of my sight!" There's always something you can do besides give in to peer pressure. Remember the last time you gave in? Try rewriting the end of that story. Now the next time you're under pressure, try out one of those different endings.

{Mark 6:14–29}

"The head of John the Baptist," she answered.

25 At once the girl hurried in to the king with the request: "I want you to give me right now the head of John the Baptist on a platter."

26 The king was greatly distressed, but because of his oaths and his dinner guests, he did not want to refuse her. 27 So he immediately sent an executioner with orders to bring John's head. The man went, beheaded John in the prison, 28 and brought back his head on a platter. He presented it to the girl, and she gave it to her mother. 29 On hearing of this, John's disciples came and took his body and laid it in a tomb.

Jesus Feeds the Five Thousand

30 The apostles gathered around Jesus and reported to him all they had done and taught. 31 Then, because so many people were coming and going that they did not even have a chance to eat, he said to them, "Come with me by yourselves to a quiet place and get some rest."

32 So they went away by themselves in a boat to a solitary place. 33 But many who saw them leaving recognized them and ran on foot from all the towns and got there ahead of them. 34 When Jesus landed and saw a large crowd, he had compassion on them, because they were like sheep without a shepherd. So he began teaching them many things.

35 By this time it was late in the day, so his disciples came to him. "This is a remote place," they said, "and it's already very late. 36 Send the people away so that they can go to the surrounding countryside and villages and buy themselves something to eat."

37 But he answered, "You give them something to eat."

They said to him, "That would take more than half a year's wages[a]! Are we to go and spend that much on bread and give it to them to eat?"

38 "How many loaves do you have?" he asked. "Go and see."

When they found out, they said, "Five—and two fish."

39 Then Jesus directed them to have all the people sit down in groups on the green grass. 40 So they sat down in groups of hundreds and fifties. 41 Taking the five loaves and the two fish and looking up to heaven, he gave thanks and broke the loaves. Then he gave them to his disciples to distribute to the people. He also divided the two fish among them all. 42 They all ate and were satisfied, 43 and the disciples picked up twelve basketfuls

---

[a] 37 Greek take two hundred denarii

of broken pieces of bread and fish. [44] The number of the men who had eaten was five thousand.

Jesus Walks on the Water

[45] Immediately Jesus made his disciples get into the boat and go on ahead of him to Bethsaida, while he dismissed the crowd. [46] After leaving them, he went up on a mountainside to pray.

[47] Later that night, the boat was in the middle of the lake, and he was alone on land. [48] He saw the disciples straining at the oars, because the wind was against them. Shortly before dawn he went out to them, walking on the lake. He was about to pass by them, [49] but when they saw him walking on the lake, they thought he was a ghost. They cried out, [50] because they all saw him and were terrified.

Immediately he spoke to them and said, "Take courage! It is I. Don't be afraid." [51] Then he climbed into the boat with them, and the wind died down. They were completely amazed, [52] for they had not understood about the loaves; their hearts were hardened.

[53] When they had crossed over, they landed at Gennesaret and anchored there. [54] As soon as they got out of the boat, people recognized Jesus. [55] They ran throughout that whole region and carried the sick on mats to wherever they heard he was. [56] And wherever he went—into villages, towns or countryside—they placed the sick in the marketplaces. They begged him to let them touch even the edge of his cloak, and all who touched it were healed.

That Which Defiles

7 The Pharisees and some of the teachers of the law who had come from Jerusalem gathered around Jesus [2] and saw some of his disciples eating food with hands that were defiled, that is, unwashed. [3] (The Pharisees and all the Jews do not eat unless they give their hands a ceremonial washing, holding to the tradition of the elders. [4] When they come from the marketplace they do not eat unless

they wash. And they observe many other traditions, such as the washing of cups, pitchers and kettles.[a])

[5] So the Pharisees and teachers of the law asked Jesus, "Why don't your disciples live according to the tradition of the elders instead of eating their food with defiled hands?"

[6] He replied, "Isaiah was right when he prophesied about you hypocrites; as it is written:

" 'These people honor me with their
    lips,
  but their hearts are far from me.
[7] They worship me in vain;
  their teachings are merely human
    rules.'[b]

[8] You have let go of the commands of God and are holding on to human traditions."

[9] And he continued, "You have a fine way of setting aside the commands of God in order to observe[c] your own traditions! [10] For Moses said, 'Honor your father and mother,'[d] and, 'Anyone who curses their father or mother is to be put to death.'[e] [11] But you say that if anyone declares that what might have been used to help their father or mother is Corban (that is, devoted to God)— [12] then you no longer let them do anything for their father or mother. [13] Thus you nullify the word of God by your tradition that you have handed down. And you do many things like that."

[14] Again Jesus called the crowd to him and said, "Listen to me, everyone, and understand this. [15] Nothing outside a person can defile them by going into them. Rather, it is what comes out of a person that defiles them." [16][f]

[17] After he had left the crowd and entered the house, his disciples asked him about this parable. [18] "Are you so dull?" he asked. "Don't you see that nothing that enters a person from the outside can defile them? [19] For it doesn't go into their heart but into their stomach, and then out of the body." (In saying this, Jesus declared all foods clean.)

---

[a] 4 Some early manuscripts *pitchers, kettles and dining couches*   [b] 6,7 Isaiah 29:13   [c] 9 Some manuscripts *set up*
[d] 10 Exodus 20:12; Deut. 5:16   [e] 10 Exodus 21:17; Lev. 20:9   [f] 16 Some manuscripts include here the words of 4:23.

20He went on: "What comes out of a person is what defiles them. 21For it is from within, out of a person's heart, that evil thoughts come—sexual immorality, theft, murder, 22adultery, greed, malice, deceit, lewdness, envy, slander, arrogance and folly. 23All these evils come from inside and defile a person."

Jesus Honors a Syrophoenician Woman's Faith

24Jesus left that place and went to the vicinity of Tyre.*a* He entered a house and did not want anyone to know it; yet he could not keep his presence secret. 25In fact, as soon as she heard about him, a woman whose little daughter was possessed by an impure spirit came and fell at his feet. 26The woman was a Greek, born in Syrian Phoenicia. She begged Jesus to drive the demon out of her daughter.

27"First let the children eat all they want," he told her, "for it is not right to take the children's bread and toss it to the dogs."

28"Lord," she replied, "even the dogs under the table eat the children's crumbs."

29Then he told her, "For such a reply, you may go; the demon has left your daughter."

30She went home and found her child lying on the bed, and the demon gone.

Jesus Heals a Deaf and Mute Man

31Then Jesus left the vicinity of Tyre and went through Sidon, down to the Sea of Galilee and into the region of the Decapolis.*b* 32There some people brought to him a man who was deaf and could hardly talk, and they begged Jesus to place his hand on him.

33After he took him aside, away from the crowd, Jesus put his fingers into the man's ears. Then he spit and touched the man's tongue. 34He looked up to heaven and with a deep sigh said to him, *"Ephphatha!"* (which means "Be opened!").

35At this, the man's ears were opened, his tongue was loosened and he began to speak plainly.

36Jesus commanded them not to tell anyone. But the more he did so, the more they kept talking about it. 37People were overwhelmed with amazement. "He has done everything well," they said. "He even makes the deaf hear and the mute speak."

Jesus Feeds the Four Thousand

8 During those days another large crowd gathered. Since they had nothing to eat, Jesus called his disciples to him and said, 2"I have compassion for these people; they have already been with me three days and have nothing to eat. 3If I send them home hungry, they will collapse on the way, because some of them have come a long distance."

4His disciples answered, "But where in this remote place can anyone get enough bread to feed them?"

5"How many loaves do you have?" Jesus asked.

"Seven," they replied.

6He told the crowd to sit down on the ground. When he had taken the seven loaves and given thanks, he broke them and gave them to his disciples to distribute to the people, and they did so. 7They had a few small fish as well; he gave thanks for them also and told the disciples to distribute them. 8The people ate and were satisfied. Afterward the disciples picked up seven basketfuls of broken pieces that were left over. 9About four thousand were present. After he had sent them away, 10he got into the boat with his disciples and went to the region of Dalmanutha.

11The Pharisees came and began to question Jesus. To test him, they asked him for a sign from heaven. 12He sighed deeply and said, "Why does this generation ask for a sign? Truly I tell you, no sign will be given to it." 13Then he left them, got back into the boat and crossed to the other side.

a 24 Many early manuscripts *Tyre and Sidon*   *b 31* That is, the Ten Cities

The Yeast of the Pharisees and Herod

14 The disciples had forgotten to bring bread, except for one loaf they had with them in the boat. 15 "Be careful," Jesus warned them. "Watch out for the yeast of the Pharisees and that of Herod."

16 They discussed this with one another and said, "It is because we have no bread."

17 Aware of their discussion, Jesus asked them: "Why are you talking about having no bread? Do you still not see or understand? Are your hearts hardened? 18 Do you have eyes but fail to see, and ears but fail to hear? And don't you remember? 19 When I broke the five loaves for the five thousand, how many basketfuls of pieces did you pick up?"

"Twelve," they replied.

20 "And when I broke the seven loaves for the four thousand, how many basketfuls of pieces did you pick up?"

They answered, "Seven."

21 He said to them, "Do you still not understand?"

Jesus Heals a Blind Man at Bethsaida

22 They came to Bethsaida, and some people brought a blind man and begged Jesus to touch him. 23 He took the blind man by the hand and led him outside the village. When he had spit on the man's eyes and put his hands on him, Jesus asked, "Do you see anything?"

24 He looked up and said, "I see people; they look like trees walking around."

25 Once more Jesus put his hands on the man's eyes. Then his eyes were opened,

TO THE POINT

Our Cross Is Different

Jesus said anyone who wants to follow him must "deny themselves and take up their cross" (Mark 8:34). The cross meant suffering and death for Jesus. Does that mean you'll have to suffer too?

The cross is more than a place where Jesus died. It is a symbol of our salvation and a symbol of God's will. The cross was God's will for Jesus. But your cross, God's will for your life, is different. What is Jesus telling you?

* Deny yourself. Choose what God wants, not what you want.

* Take up your cross. Do God's will each day.

* Keep on following Jesus.

Following Jesus will make a difference. The old you will be left behind, and you will become a new and beautiful person in Jesus.

his sight was restored, and he saw everything clearly. [26]Jesus sent him home, saying, "Don't even go into[a] the village."

Peter Declares That Jesus Is the Messiah

[27]Jesus and his disciples went on to the villages around Caesarea Philippi. On the way he asked them, "Who do people say I am?"

[28]They replied, "Some say John the Baptist; others say Elijah; and still others, one of the prophets."

[29]"But what about you?" he asked. "Who do you say I am?"

Peter answered, "You are the Messiah."

[30]Jesus warned them not to tell anyone about him.

Jesus Predicts His Death

[31]He then began to teach them that the Son of Man must suffer many things and be rejected by the elders, the chief priests and the teachers of the law, and that he must be killed and after three days rise again. [32]He spoke plainly about this, and Peter took him aside and began to rebuke him.

[33]But when Jesus turned and looked at his disciples, he rebuked Peter. "Get behind me, Satan!" he said. "You do not have in mind the concerns of God, but merely human concerns."

The Way of the Cross

[34]Then he called the crowd to him along with his disciples and said: "Whoever wants to be my disciple must deny themselves and take up their cross and follow me. [35]For whoever wants to save their life[b] will lose it, but whoever loses their life for me and for the gospel will save it. [36]What good is it for someone to gain the whole world, yet forfeit their soul? [37]Or what can anyone give in exchange for their soul? [38]If anyone is ashamed of me and my words in this adulterous and sinful generation, the Son of Man will be ashamed of them when he comes in his Father's glory with the holy angels."

9 And he said to them, "Truly I tell you, some who are standing here will not taste death before they see that the kingdom of God has come with power."

The Transfiguration

[2]After six days Jesus took Peter, James and John with him and led them up a high mountain, where they were all alone. There he was transfigured before them. [3]His clothes became dazzling white, whiter than anyone in the world could bleach them. [4]And there appeared before them Elijah and Moses, who were talking with Jesus.

[5]Peter said to Jesus, "Rabbi, it is good for us to be here. Let us put up three shelters—one for you, one for Moses and one for Elijah." [6](He did not know what to say, they were so frightened.)

[7]Then a cloud appeared and covered them, and a voice came from the cloud: "This is my Son, whom I love. Listen to him!"

[8]Suddenly, when they looked around, they no longer saw anyone with them except Jesus.

[9]As they were coming down the mountain, Jesus gave them orders not to tell anyone what they had seen until the Son of Man had risen from the dead. [10]They kept the matter to themselves, discussing what "rising from the dead" meant.

[11]And they asked him, "Why do the teachers of the law say that Elijah must come first?"

[12]Jesus replied, "To be sure, Elijah does come first, and restores all things. Why then is it written that the Son of Man must suffer much and be rejected? [13]But I tell you, Elijah has come, and they have done to him everything they wished, just as it is written about him."

Jesus Heals a Boy Possessed by an Impure Spirit

[14]When they came to the other disciples, they saw a large crowd around them and the teachers of the law arguing with them. [15]As soon as all the people saw Jesus, they were overwhelmed with wonder and ran to greet him.

---

[a] 26 Some manuscripts go and tell anyone in   [b] 35 The Greek word means either life or soul; also in verses 36 and 37.

¹⁶"What are you arguing with them about?" he asked.

¹⁷A man in the crowd answered, "Teacher, I brought you my son, who is possessed by a spirit that has robbed him of speech. ¹⁸Whenever it seizes him, it throws him to the ground. He foams at the mouth, gnashes his teeth and becomes rigid. I asked your disciples to drive out the spirit, but they could not."

¹⁹"You unbelieving generation," Jesus replied, "how long shall I stay with you? How long shall I put up with you? Bring the boy to me."

²⁰So they brought him. When the spirit saw Jesus, it immediately threw the boy into a convulsion. He fell to the ground and rolled around, foaming at the mouth.

²¹Jesus asked the boy's father, "How long has he been like this?"

"From childhood," he answered. ²²"It has often thrown him into fire or water to kill him. But if you can do anything, take pity on us and help us."

²³"'If you can'?" said Jesus. "Everything is possible for one who believes."

²⁴Immediately the boy's father exclaimed, "I do believe; help me overcome my unbelief!"

²⁵When Jesus saw that a crowd was running to the scene, he rebuked the impure spirit. "You deaf and mute spirit," he said, "I command you, come out of him and never enter him again."

²⁶The spirit shrieked, convulsed him violently and came out. The boy looked so much like a corpse that many said, "He's dead." ²⁷But Jesus took him by the hand and lifted him to his feet, and he stood up.

²⁸After Jesus had gone indoors, his disciples asked him privately, "Why couldn't we drive it out?"

²⁹He replied, "This kind can come out only by prayer.ᵃ"

Jesus Predicts His Death a Second Time

³⁰They left that place and passed through Galilee. Jesus did not want anyone to know where they were, ³¹because

he was teaching his disciples. He said to them, "The Son of Man is going to be delivered into the hands of men. They will kill him, and after three days he will rise." ³²But they did not understand what he meant and were afraid to ask him about it.

³³They came to Capernaum. When he was in the house, he asked them, "What were you arguing about on the road?" ³⁴But they kept quiet because on the way they had argued about who was the greatest.

³⁵Sitting down, Jesus called the Twelve and said, "Anyone who wants to be first

>> INSTANT ACCESS

Some teens feel uncomfortable with kids from other churches or denominations. They're uncertain about how big a difference their differences make. Even Christ's disciples were uncomfortable when they saw a man driving out demons in Jesus' name. He wasn't one of them. Jesus corrected them and said, "Whoever is not against us is for us." Christians don't agree on every belief. But all who trust Jesus as Savior become members of God's family. If you refuse to emphasize differences and instead emphasize commitment to Christ, you'll feel a lot more comfortable with Christian teens from other groups.

{Mark 9:38–41}

ᵃ 29 Some manuscripts *prayer and fasting*

must be the very last, and the servant of all."

36 He took a little child whom he placed among them. Taking the child in his arms, he said to them, 37 "Whoever welcomes one of these little children in my name welcomes me; and whoever welcomes me does not welcome me but the one who sent me."

Whoever Is Not Against Us Is for Us

38 "Teacher," said John, "we saw someone driving out demons in your name and we told him to stop, because he was not one of us."

39 "Do not stop him," Jesus said. "For no one who does a miracle in my name can in the next moment say anything bad about me, 40 for whoever is not against us is for us. 41 Truly I tell you, anyone who gives you a cup of water in my name because you belong to the Messiah will certainly not lose their reward.

Causing to Stumble

42 "If anyone causes one of these little ones — those who believe in me — to stumble, it would be better for them if a large millstone were hung around their neck and they were thrown into the sea. 43 If your hand causes you to stumble, cut it off. It is better for you to enter life maimed than with two hands to go into hell, where the fire never goes out. [44]a 45 And if your foot causes you to stumble, cut it off. It is better for you to enter life crippled than to have two feet and be thrown into hell. [46]a 47 And if your eye causes you to stumble, pluck it out. It is better for you to enter the kingdom of God with one eye than to have two eyes and be thrown into hell, 48 where

" 'the worms that eat them do not die, and the fire is not quenched.'b

49 Everyone will be salted with fire.

50 "Salt is good, but if it loses its saltiness, how can you make it salty again? Have salt among yourselves, and be at peace with each other."

Divorce

10 Jesus then left that place and went into the region of Judea and across the Jordan. Again crowds of people came to him, and as was his custom, he taught them.

2 Some Pharisees came and tested him by asking, "Is it lawful for a man to divorce his wife?"

3 "What did Moses command you?" he replied.

4 They said, "Moses permitted a man to write a certificate of divorce and send her away."

5 "It was because your hearts were hard that Moses wrote you this law," Jesus replied. 6 "But at the beginning of creation God 'made them male and female.'c 7 'For this reason a man will leave his father and mother and be united to his wife,d 8 and the two will become one flesh.'e So they are no longer two, but one flesh. 9 Therefore what God has joined together, let no one separate."

10 When they were in the house again, the disciples asked Jesus about this. 11 He answered, "Anyone who divorces his wife and marries another woman commits adultery against her. 12 And if she divorces her husband and marries another man, she commits adultery."

The Little Children and Jesus

13 People were bringing little children to Jesus for him to place his hands on them, but the disciples rebuked them. 14 When Jesus saw this, he was indignant. He said to them, "Let the little children come to me, and do not hinder them, for the kingdom of God belongs to such as these. 15 Truly I tell you, anyone who will not receive the kingdom of God like a little child will never enter it." 16 And he took the children in his arms, placed his hands on them and blessed them.

The Rich and the Kingdom of God

17 As Jesus started on his way, a man ran up to him and fell on his knees before

---

a 44,46 Some manuscripts include here the words of verse 48.   b 48 Isaiah 66:24   c 6 Gen. 1:27   d 7 Some early manuscripts do not have and be united to his wife.   e 8 Gen. 2:24

him. "Good teacher," he asked, "what must I do to inherit eternal life?"

18 "Why do you call me good?" Jesus answered. "No one is good—except God alone. 19 You know the commandments: 'You shall not murder, you shall not commit adultery, you shall not steal, you shall not give false testimony, you shall not defraud, honor your father and mother.'[a]"

20 "Teacher," he declared, "all these I have kept since I was a boy."

21 Jesus looked at him and loved him. "One thing you lack," he said. "Go, sell everything you have and give to the poor, and you will have treasure in heaven. Then come, follow me."

22 At this the man's face fell. He went away sad, because he had great wealth.

23 Jesus looked around and said to his disciples, "How hard it is for the rich to enter the kingdom of God!"

24 The disciples were amazed at his words. But Jesus said again, "Children, how hard it is[b] to enter the kingdom of God! 25 It is easier for a camel to go through the eye of a needle than for someone who is rich to enter the kingdom of God."

26 The disciples were even more amazed, and said to each other, "Who then can be saved?"

27 Jesus looked at them and said, "With man this is impossible, but not with God; all things are possible with God."

28 Then Peter spoke up, "We have left everything to follow you!"

29 "Truly I tell you," Jesus replied, "no one who has left home or brothers or sisters or mother or father or children or fields for me and the gospel 30 will fail to receive a hundred times as much in this present age: homes, brothers, sisters, mothers, children and fields—along with persecutions—and in the age to come eternal life. 31 But many who are first will be last, and the last first."

Jesus Predicts His Death a Third Time

32 They were on their way up to Jerusalem, with Jesus leading the way, and the disciples were astonished, while those who followed were afraid. Again he took

>> INSTANT ACCESS

Do you ever envy that rich girl at your school? The one whose dad hired a live band and Hummer limo for her birthday party? Do you feel cheated? In Bible times most people thought wealth was a sign of God's favor. So Jesus shocked his disciples when he said that it's hard for a rich person to "enter the kingdom of God" (Mark 10:23). What Jesus meant is that a rich person is likely to depend on possessions instead of on God. And a rich person is likely to value possessions more than pleasing God. It's not wrong to be rich. But this would be an appropriate label on all your possessions: "May be hazardous to your [spiritual] health."

{Mark 10:17-31}

the Twelve aside and told them what was going to happen to him. 33 "We are going up to Jerusalem," he said, "and the Son of Man will be delivered over to the chief priests and the teachers of the law. They will condemn him to death and will hand him over to the Gentiles, 34 who will mock him and spit on him, flog him and kill him. Three days later he will rise."

The Request of James and John

35 Then James and John, the sons of Zebedee, came to him. "Teacher," they

---

[a] 19 Exodus 20:12-16; Deut. 5:16-20   [b] 24 Some manuscripts *is for those who trust in riches*

said, "we want you to do for us whatever we ask."

36 "What do you want me to do for you?" he asked.

37 They replied, "Let one of us sit at your right and the other at your left in your glory."

38 "You don't know what you are asking," Jesus said. "Can you drink the cup I drink or be baptized with the baptism I am baptized with?"

39 "We can," they answered.

Jesus said to them, "You will drink the cup I drink and be baptized with the baptism I am baptized with, 40 but to sit at my right or left is not for me to grant. These places belong to those for whom they have been prepared."

41 When the ten heard about this, they became indignant with James and John. 42 Jesus called them together and said, "You know that those who are regarded as rulers of the Gentiles lord it over them, and their high officials exercise authority over them. 43 Not so with you. Instead, whoever wants to become great among you must be your servant, 44 and whoever wants to be first must be slave of all. 45 For even the Son of Man did not come to be served, but to serve, and to give his life as a ransom for many."

Blind Bartimaeus Receives His Sight

46 Then they came to Jericho. As Jesus and his disciples, together with a large crowd, were leaving the city, a blind man, Bartimaeus (which means "son of Timaeus"), was sitting by the roadside begging. 47 When he heard that it was Jesus of Nazareth, he began to shout, "Jesus, Son of David, have mercy on me!"

48 Many rebuked him and told him to be quiet, but he shouted all the more, "Son of David, have mercy on me!"

49 Jesus stopped and said, "Call him."

So they called to the blind man, "Cheer up! On your feet! He's calling you." 50 Throwing his cloak aside, he jumped to his feet and came to Jesus.

51 "What do you want me to do for you?" Jesus asked him.

The blind man said, "Rabbi, I want to see."

52 "Go," said Jesus, "your faith has healed you." Immediately he received his sight and followed Jesus along the road.

Jesus Comes to Jerusalem as King

11 As they approached Jerusalem and came to Bethphage and Bethany at the Mount of Olives, Jesus sent two of his disciples, 2 saying to them, "Go to the village ahead of you, and just as you enter it, you will find a colt tied there, which no one has ever ridden. Untie it and bring it here. 3 If anyone asks you, 'Why are you doing this?' say, 'The Lord needs it and will send it back here shortly.'"

4 They went and found a colt outside

PANORAMA

Who?

This book shows what Jesus was like—a man of action, a man with authority. He wouldn't rest until he finished what he came here to do.

{MARK}

> At a young people's retreat one of my friends went forward to accept Jesus as her Savior. Now she says it's all a bunch of nonsense, that it's what people who want to feel good do to feel good. How can she be saved when she acts like this?   >> Mackenzie

Dear Mackenzie,

On the first ever Palm Sunday, the crowds were praising Christ as he entered Jerusalem (Mark 11). Yet just a few days later, some of those same people shouted angrily to crucify him. Obviously, their excitement for Jesus showed no real commitment to him.

Faith isn't just going forward at a revival meeting. It's committing yourself to Jesus and trusting him enough to follow him. In Matthew 13 Christ told a story about a farmer sowing seeds. The birds ate the seed that fell on the path. Seed that fell on rocky places sprang up quickly but soon withered. Other seed fell among thorns that choked the young plants out. But some seed fell on good soil where it flourished and grew.

Your friend sounds like the rocky soil. The seed (the news of Christ) did not take root in her. It withered and died. It had no staying power. Perhaps the seed will lie dormant and one day take real root and grow. Perhaps not, but the choice is hers. Keep praying for her.

Jordan

in the street, tied at a doorway. As they untied it, ⁵some people standing there asked, "What are you doing, untying that colt?" ⁶They answered as Jesus had told them to, and the people let them go. ⁷When they brought the colt to Jesus and threw their cloaks over it, he sat on it. ⁸Many people spread their cloaks on the road, while others spread branches they had cut in the fields. ⁹Those who went ahead and those who followed shouted,

"Hosanna!ᵃ"

"Blessed is he who comes in the
    name of the Lord!"ᵇ

¹⁰"Blessed is the coming kingdom of
    our father David!"

"Hosanna in the highest heaven!"

¹¹Jesus entered Jerusalem and went into the temple courts. He looked around at everything, but since it was already late, he went out to Bethany with the Twelve.

Jesus Curses a Fig Tree and Clears the Temple Courts

¹²The next day as they were leaving Bethany, Jesus was hungry. ¹³Seeing in the distance a fig tree in leaf, he went to find out if it had any fruit. When he reached it, he found nothing but leaves, because it was not the season for figs. ¹⁴Then he said to the tree, "May no one ever eat fruit from you again." And his disciples heard him say it.

¹⁵On reaching Jerusalem, Jesus entered the temple courts and began driving out those who were buying and selling there. He overturned the tables of the money changers and the benches of those selling doves, ¹⁶and would not allow anyone to carry merchandise through the temple courts. ¹⁷And as he taught them, he said, "Is it not written: 'My house will be called a house of prayer for all nations'ᶜ? But you have made it 'a den of robbers.'ᵈ"

¹⁸The chief priests and the teachers of the law heard this and began looking for a way to kill him, for they feared him, because the whole crowd was amazed at his teaching.

¹⁹When evening came, Jesus and his disciplesᵉ went out of the city.

²⁰In the morning, as they went along, they saw the fig tree withered from the roots. ²¹Peter remembered and said to Jesus, "Rabbi, look! The fig tree you cursed has withered!"

²²"Have faith in God," Jesus answered. ²³"Trulyᶠ I tell you, if anyone says to this mountain, 'Go, throw yourself into the sea,' and does not doubt in their heart but believes that what they say will happen, it will be done for them. ²⁴Therefore I tell you, whatever you ask for in prayer, believe that you have received it, and it will be yours. ²⁵And when you stand praying, if you hold anything against anyone, forgive them, so that your Father in heaven may forgive you your sins." [26]ᵍ

The Authority of Jesus Questioned

²⁷They arrived again in Jerusalem, and while Jesus was walking in the temple courts, the chief priests, the teachers of the law and the elders came to him. ²⁸"By what authority are you doing these things?" they asked. "And who gave you authority to do this?"

²⁹Jesus replied, "I will ask you one question. Answer me, and I will tell you by what authority I am doing these things. ³⁰John's baptism—was it from heaven, or of human origin? Tell me!"

³¹They discussed it among themselves and said, "If we say, 'From heaven,' he will ask, 'Then why didn't you believe him?' ³²But if we say, 'Of human origin' . . ." (They feared the people, for everyone held that John really was a prophet.)

³³So they answered Jesus, "We don't know."

Jesus said, "Neither will I tell you by what authority I am doing these things."

ᵃ 9 A Hebrew expression meaning "Save!" which became an exclamation of praise; also in verse 10   ᵇ 9 Psalm 118:25,26   ᶜ 17 Isaiah 56:7   ᵈ 17 Jer. 7:11   ᵉ 19 Some early manuscripts came, Jesus   ᶠ 22,23 Some early manuscripts "If you have faith in God," Jesus answered, ²³"truly   ᵍ 26 Some manuscripts include here words similar to Matt. 6:15.

The Parable of the Tenants

12 Jesus then began to speak to them in parables: "A man planted a vineyard. He put a wall around it, dug a pit for the winepress and built a watchtower. Then he rented the vineyard to some farmers and moved to another place. ²At harvest time he sent a servant to the tenants to collect from them some of the fruit of the vineyard. ³But they seized him, beat him and sent him away empty-handed. ⁴Then he sent another servant to them; they struck this man on the head and treated him shamefully. ⁵He sent still another, and that one they killed. He sent many others; some of them they beat, others they killed.

⁶"He had one left to send, a son, whom he loved. He sent him last of all, saying, 'They will respect my son.'

⁷"But the tenants said to one another, 'This is the heir. Come, let's kill him, and the inheritance will be ours.' ⁸So they took him and killed him, and threw him out of the vineyard.

⁹"What then will the owner of the vineyard do? He will come and kill those tenants and give the vineyard to others. ¹⁰Haven't you read this passage of Scripture:

" 'The stone the builders rejected
has become the cornerstone;
¹¹the Lord has done this,
and it is marvelous in our eyes'ᵃ?"

¹²Then the chief priests, the teachers of the law and the elders looked for a way to arrest him because they knew he had spoken the parable against them. But they were afraid of the crowd; so they left him and went away.

Paying the Imperial Tax to Caesar

¹³Later they sent some of the Pharisees and Herodians to Jesus to catch him in his words. ¹⁴They came to him and said, "Teacher, we know that you are a man of integrity. You aren't swayed by others, because you pay no attention to who they are; but you teach the way of God in accordance with the truth. Is it right to pay the imperial taxᵇ to Caesar or not? ¹⁵Should we pay or shouldn't we?"

But Jesus knew their hypocrisy. "Why are you trying to trap me?" he asked. "Bring me a denarius and let me look at it." ¹⁶They brought the coin, and he asked them, "Whose image is this? And whose inscription?"

"Caesar's," they replied.

¹⁷Then Jesus said to them, "Give back to Caesar what is Caesar's and to God what is God's."

And they were amazed at him.

Marriage at the Resurrection

¹⁸Then the Sadducees, who say there is no resurrection, came to him with a question. ¹⁹"Teacher," they said, "Moses wrote for us that if a man's brother dies and leaves a wife but no children, the man must marry the widow and raise up offspring for his brother. ²⁰Now there were seven brothers. The first one married and died without leaving any children. ²¹The second one married the widow, but he also died, leaving no child. It was the same with the third. ²²In fact, none of the seven left any children. Last of all, the woman died too. ²³At the resurrectionᶜ whose wife will she be, since the seven were married to her?"

²⁴Jesus replied, "Are you not in error because you do not know the Scriptures or the power of God? ²⁵When the dead rise, they will neither marry nor be given in marriage; they will be like the angels in heaven. ²⁶Now about the dead rising—have you not read in the Book of Moses, in the account of the burning bush, how God said to him, 'I am the God of Abraham, the God of Isaac, and the God of Jacob'ᵈ? ²⁷He is not the God of the dead, but of the living. You are badly mistaken!"

The Greatest Commandment

²⁸One of the teachers of the law came and heard them debating. Noticing that Jesus had given them a good answer, he

---

ᵃ 11 Psalm 118:22,23   ᵇ 14 A special tax levied on subject peoples, not on Roman citizens   ᶜ 23 Some manuscripts resurrection, when people rise from the dead,   ᵈ 26 Exodus 3:6

INSTANT ACCESS

Did you ever try to list the things you do, or don't do, because you're a Christian? How many things would be on the "do" side, and how many on the "don't"? The rabbis in Jesus' time listed 622 "do" and "don't" commandments. Then one teacher of the law asked Jesus about "the most important" commandment. Jesus boiled all the rules down to just two: Love God completely, and love your neighbor as yourself. Make it your goal to love God and others. Your life will be one that pleases God.

{Mark 12:28–34}

asked him, "Of all the commandments, which is the most important?"

29 "The most important one," answered Jesus, "is this: 'Hear, O Israel: The Lord our God, the Lord is one.[a] 30 Love the Lord your God with all your heart and with all your soul and with all your mind and with all your strength.'[b] 31 The second is this: 'Love your neighbor as yourself.'[c] There is no commandment greater than these."

32 "Well said, teacher," the man replied. "You are right in saying that God is one and there is no other but him. 33 To love him with all your heart, with all your understanding and with all your strength, and to love your neighbor as yourself is more important than all burnt offerings and sacrifices."

34 When Jesus saw that he had answered wisely, he said to him, "You are not far from the kingdom of God." And from then on no one dared ask him any more questions.

Whose Son Is the Messiah?

35 While Jesus was teaching in the temple courts, he asked, "Why do the teachers of the law say that the Messiah is the son of David? 36 David himself, speaking by the Holy Spirit, declared:

" 'The Lord said to my Lord:
  "Sit at my right hand
until I put your enemies
  under your feet." '[d]

37 David himself calls him 'Lord.' How then can he be his son?"

The large crowd listened to him with delight.

Warning Against the Teachers of the Law

38 As he taught, Jesus said, "Watch out for the teachers of the law. They like to walk around in flowing robes and be greeted with respect in the marketplaces, 39 and have the most important seats in the synagogues and the places of honor at banquets. 40 They devour widows' houses and for a show make lengthy prayers. These men will be punished most severely."

The Widow's Offering

41 Jesus sat down opposite the place where the offerings were put and watched the crowd putting their money into the temple treasury. Many rich people threw in large amounts. 42 But a poor widow came and put in two very small copper coins, worth only a few cents.

43 Calling his disciples to him, Jesus said, "Truly I tell you, this poor widow has put more into the treasury than all the others. 44 They all gave out of their wealth; but she, out of her poverty, put in everything—all she had to live on."

---

[a] 29 Or *The Lord our God is one Lord* [b] 30 Deut. 6:4,5 [c] 31 Lev. 19:18 [d] 36 Psalm 110:1

The Destruction of the Temple and Signs of the End Times

13 As Jesus was leaving the temple, one of his disciples said to him, "Look, Teacher! What massive stones! What magnificent buildings!"

2 "Do you see all these great buildings?" replied Jesus. "Not one stone here will be left on another; every one will be thrown down."

3 As Jesus was sitting on the Mount of Olives opposite the temple, Peter, James, John and Andrew asked him privately, 4 "Tell us, when will these things happen? And what will be the sign that they are all about to be fulfilled?"

5 Jesus said to them: "Watch out that no one deceives you. 6 Many will come in my name, claiming, 'I am he,' and will deceive many. 7 When you hear of wars and rumors of wars, do not be alarmed. Such things must happen, but the end is still to come. 8 Nation will rise against nation, and kingdom against kingdom. There will be earthquakes in various places, and famines. These are the beginning of birth pains.

9 "You must be on your guard. You will be handed over to the local councils and flogged in the synagogues. On account of me you will stand before governors and kings as witnesses to them. 10 And the gospel must first be preached to all nations. 11 Whenever you are arrested and brought to trial, do not worry beforehand about what to say. Just say whatever is given you at the time, for it is not you speaking, but the Holy Spirit.

12 "Brother will betray brother to death, and a father his child. Children will rebel against their parents and have them put to death. 13 Everyone will hate you because of me, but the one who stands firm to the end will be saved.

14 "When you see 'the abomination that causes desolation'[a] standing where it[b] does not belong—let the reader understand—then let those who are in Judea flee to the mountains. 15 Let no one on the housetop go down or enter the house to take anything out. 16 Let no one in the field go back to get their cloak. 17 How dreadful it will be in those days for pregnant women and nursing mothers! 18 Pray that this will not take place in winter, 19 because those will be days of distress unequaled from the beginning, when God created the world, until now—and never to be equaled again.

20 "If the Lord had not cut short those days, no one would survive. But for the sake of the elect, whom he has chosen, he has shortened them. 21 At that time if anyone says to you, 'Look, here is the Messiah!' or, 'Look, there he is!' do not believe it. 22 For false messiahs and false prophets will appear and perform signs and wonders to deceive, if possible, even the elect. 23 So be on your guard; I have told you everything ahead of time.

24 "But in those days, following that distress,

" 'the sun will be darkened,
   and the moon will not give its light;
25 the stars will fall from the sky,
   and the heavenly bodies will be
      shaken.'[c]

26 "At that time people will see the Son of Man coming in clouds with great power and glory. 27 And he will send his angels and gather his elect from the four winds, from the ends of the earth to the ends of the heavens.

28 "Now learn this lesson from the fig tree: As soon as its twigs get tender and its leaves come out, you know that summer is near. 29 Even so, when you see these things happening, you know that it[b] is near, right at the door. 30 Truly I tell you, this generation will certainly not pass away until all these things have happened. 31 Heaven and earth will pass away, but my words will never pass away.

The Day and Hour Unknown

32 "But about that day or hour no one knows, not even the angels in heaven, nor the Son, but only the Father. 33 Be on guard! Be alert[d]! You do not know when that time will come. 34 It's like a man going away: He leaves his house and puts

---

a 14 Daniel 9:27; 11:31; 12:11   b 14,29 Or he   c 25 Isaiah 13:10; 34:4   d 33 Some manuscripts alert and pray

We Believe...

"he shall come"

✝ The Bible says that Jesus will return to earth. What do you know about his coming? Here are some things you can be sure about:

* Jesus will come in power and glory (Mark 13:26).

* Jesus will come back in person (Acts 1:11).

* Christians will rise from the dead (1 Thessalonians 4:13–18).

* Jesus will punish those who do not know God (2 Thessalonians 1:8–9).

No one knows just when Jesus will return. Some people think they'll change the way they live next week or next year. But Jesus warned that he might return at any time! Jesus urges you to "Be alert!" (Mark 13:33). If you expect Jesus to return at any moment, you'll be careful at all times to do the things that please him.

Go to page 1583 for the next We Believe

his servants in charge, each with their assigned task, and tells the one at the door to keep watch.

35 "Therefore keep watch because you do not know when the owner of the house will come back—whether in the evening, or at midnight, or when the rooster crows, or at dawn. 36 If he comes suddenly, do not let him find you sleeping. 37 What I say to you, I say to everyone: 'Watch!'"

Jesus Anointed at Bethany

14 Now the Passover and the Festival of Unleavened Bread were only two days away, and the chief priests and the teachers of the law were scheming to arrest Jesus secretly and kill him. 2 "But not during the festival," they said, "or the people may riot."

3 While he was in Bethany, reclining at the table in the home of Simon the Leper, a woman came with an alabaster jar of very expensive perfume, made of pure nard. She broke the jar and poured the perfume on his head.

4 Some of those present were saying indignantly to one another, "Why this waste of perfume? 5 It could have been sold for more than a year's wages[a] and the money given to the poor." And they rebuked her harshly.

6 "Leave her alone," said Jesus. "Why are you bothering her? She has done a beautiful thing to me. 7 The poor you will always have with you,[b] and you can help them any time you want. But you will not always have me. 8 She did what she could. She poured perfume on my body beforehand to prepare for my burial. 9 Truly I tell you, wherever the gospel is preached throughout the world, what she has done will also be told, in memory of her."

10 Then Judas Iscariot, one of the Twelve, went to the chief priests to betray Jesus to them. 11 They were delighted to hear this and promised to give him money. So he watched for an opportunity to hand him over.

The Last Supper

12 On the first day of the Festival of Unleavened Bread, when it was customary to sacrifice the Passover lamb, Jesus' disciples asked him, "Where do you want us to go and make preparations for you to eat the Passover?"

13 So he sent two of his disciples, telling them, "Go into the city, and a man carrying a jar of water will meet you. Follow him. 14 Say to the owner of the house he enters, 'The Teacher asks: Where is my guest room, where I may eat the Passover with my disciples?' 15 He will show you a large room upstairs, furnished and ready. Make preparations for us there."

16 The disciples left, went into the city and found things just as Jesus had told them. So they prepared the Passover.

17 When evening came, Jesus arrived with the Twelve. 18 While they were reclining at the table eating, he said, "Truly I tell you, one of you will betray me—one who is eating with me."

19 They were saddened, and one by one they said to him, "Surely you don't mean me?"

20 "It is one of the Twelve," he replied, "one who dips bread into the bowl with me. 21 The Son of Man will go just as it is written about him. But woe to that man who betrays the Son of Man! It would be better for him if he had not been born."

22 While they were eating, Jesus took bread, and when he had given thanks, he broke it and gave it to his disciples, saying, "Take it; this is my body."

23 Then he took a cup, and when he had given thanks, he gave it to them, and they all drank from it.

24 "This is my blood of the[c] covenant, which is poured out for many," he said to them. 25 "Truly I tell you, I will not drink again from the fruit of the vine until that day when I drink it new in the kingdom of God."

26 When they had sung a hymn, they went out to the Mount of Olives.

Jesus Predicts Peter's Denial

27 "You will all fall away," Jesus told them, "for it is written:

" 'I will strike the shepherd,
    and the sheep will be scattered.'[d]

---

28 But after I have risen, I will go ahead of you into Galilee."

29 Peter declared, "Even if all fall away, I will not."

30 "Truly I tell you," Jesus answered, "today—yes, tonight—before the rooster crows twice[a] you yourself will disown me three times."

31 But Peter insisted emphatically, "Even if I have to die with you, I will never disown you." And all the others said the same.

Gethsemane

32 They went to a place called Gethsemane, and Jesus said to his disciples, "Sit here while I pray." 33 He took Peter, James and John along with him, and he began to be deeply distressed and troubled. 34 "My soul is overwhelmed with sorrow to the point of death," he said to them. "Stay here and keep watch."

35 Going a little farther, he fell to the ground and prayed that if possible the hour might pass from him. 36 "Abba,[b] Father," he said, "everything is possible for you. Take this cup from me. Yet not what I will, but what you will."

37 Then he returned to his disciples and found them sleeping. "Simon," he said to Peter, "are you asleep? Couldn't you keep watch for one hour? 38 Watch and pray so that you will not fall into temptation. The spirit is willing, but the flesh is weak."

39 Once more he went away and prayed the same thing. 40 When he came back, he again found them sleeping, because their eyes were heavy. They did not know what to say to him.

41 Returning the third time, he said to them, "Are you still sleeping and resting? Enough! The hour has come. Look, the Son of Man is delivered into the hands of sinners. 42 Rise! Let us go! Here comes my betrayer!"

Jesus Arrested

43 Just as he was speaking, Judas, one of the Twelve, appeared. With him was a crowd armed with swords and clubs, sent from the chief priests, the teachers of the law, and the elders.

44 Now the betrayer had arranged a signal with them: "The one I kiss is the man; arrest him and lead him away under guard." 45 Going at once to Jesus, Judas said, "Rabbi!" and kissed him. 46 The men seized Jesus and arrested him. 47 Then one of those standing near drew his sword and struck the servant of the high priest, cutting off his ear.

48 "Am I leading a rebellion," said Jesus, "that you have come out with swords and clubs to capture me? 49 Every day I was with you, teaching in the temple courts, and you did not arrest me. But the Scriptures must be fulfilled." 50 Then everyone deserted him and fled.

51 A young man, wearing nothing but a linen garment, was following Jesus. When they seized him, 52 he fled naked, leaving his garment behind.

Jesus Before the Sanhedrin

53 They took Jesus to the high priest, and all the chief priests, the elders and the teachers of the law came together. 54 Peter followed him at a distance, right into the courtyard of the high priest. There he sat with the guards and warmed himself at the fire.

55 The chief priests and the whole Sanhedrin were looking for evidence against Jesus so that they could put him to death, but they did not find any. 56 Many testified falsely against him, but their statements did not agree.

57 Then some stood up and gave this false testimony against him: 58 "We heard him say, 'I will destroy this temple made with human hands and in three days will build another, not made with hands.'" 59 Yet even then their testimony did not agree.

60 Then the high priest stood up before them and asked Jesus, "Are you not going to answer? What is this testimony that these men are bringing against you?" 61 But Jesus remained silent and gave no answer.

Again the high priest asked him, "Are you the Messiah, the Son of the Blessed One?"

---

[a] 30 Some early manuscripts do not have *twice*. [b] 36 Aramaic for *father*

62 "I am," said Jesus. "And you will see the Son of Man sitting at the right hand of the Mighty One and coming on the clouds of heaven."

63 The high priest tore his clothes. "Why do we need any more witnesses?" he asked. 64 "You have heard the blasphemy. What do you think?"

They all condemned him as worthy of death. 65 Then some began to spit at him; they blindfolded him, struck him with their fists, and said, "Prophesy!" And the guards took him and beat him.

Peter Disowns Jesus

66 While Peter was below in the courtyard, one of the servant girls of the high priest came by. 67 When she saw Peter warming himself, she looked closely at him.

"You also were with that Nazarene, Jesus," she said.

68 But he denied it. "I don't know or understand what you're talking about," he said, and went out into the entryway.[a]

69 When the servant girl saw him there, she said again to those standing around, "This fellow is one of them." 70 Again he denied it.

After a little while, those standing near said to Peter, "Surely you are one of them, for you are a Galilean."

71 He began to call down curses, and he swore to them, "I don't know this man you're talking about."

72 Immediately the rooster crowed the second time.[b] Then Peter remembered the word Jesus had spoken to him: "Before the rooster crows twice[c] you will disown me three times." And he broke down and wept.

Jesus Before Pilate

15 Very early in the morning, the chief priests, with the elders, the teachers of the law and the whole Sanhedrin, made their plans. So they bound Jesus, led him away and handed him over to Pilate.

2 "Are you the king of the Jews?" asked Pilate.

"You have said so," Jesus replied.

3 The chief priests accused him of many things. 4 So again Pilate asked him, "Aren't you going to answer? See how many things they are accusing you of."

5 But Jesus still made no reply, and Pilate was amazed.

6 Now it was the custom at the festival to release a prisoner whom the people requested. 7 A man called Barabbas was in prison with the insurrectionists who had committed murder in the uprising. 8 The crowd came up and asked Pilate to do for them what he usually did.

9 "Do you want me to release to you the king of the Jews?" asked Pilate, 10 knowing it was out of self-interest that the chief priests had handed Jesus over to him. 11 But the chief priests stirred up the crowd to have Pilate release Barabbas instead.

12 "What shall I do, then, with the one you call the king of the Jews?" Pilate asked them.

13 "Crucify him!" they shouted.

14 "Why? What crime has he committed?" asked Pilate.

But they shouted all the louder, "Crucify him!"

15 Wanting to satisfy the crowd, Pilate released Barabbas to them. He had Jesus flogged, and handed him over to be crucified.

The Soldiers Mock Jesus

16 The soldiers led Jesus away into the palace (that is, the Praetorium) and called together the whole company of soldiers. 17 They put a purple robe on him, then twisted together a crown of thorns and set it on him. 18 And they began to call out to him, "Hail, king of the Jews!" 19 Again and again they struck him on the head with a staff and spit on him. Falling on their knees, they paid homage to him. 20 And when they had mocked him, they took off the purple robe and put his own clothes on him. Then they led him out to crucify him.

---

a 68 Some early manuscripts *entryway and the rooster crowed time.*   c 72 Some early manuscripts do not have *twice.*

b 72 Some early manuscripts do not have *the second*

Many who watched Jesus on the cross ridiculed and insulted him. Probably none of them understood that Christ's death was self-sacrifice. He was giving his life for them, and for you. Self-sacrifice is usually misunderstood. You give up good times to help take care of your little brothers and sisters. And the kids your age say you're a loner and think you don't like them. You get a job to help out because your dad can't work. And some teachers get on you because you fall asleep in class. Don't get discouraged. Yes, the sacrifices you make for others may be misunderstood. But you're following a perfect example: Jesus.

{Mark 15:29–32}

>> INSTANT ACCESS

The Crucifixion of Jesus

21 A certain man from Cyrene, Simon, the father of Alexander and Rufus, was passing by on his way in from the country, and they forced him to carry the cross. 22 They brought Jesus to the place called Golgotha (which means "the place of the skull"). 23 Then they offered him wine mixed with myrrh, but he did not take it. 24 And they crucified him. Dividing up his clothes, they cast lots to see what each would get.

25 It was nine in the morning when they crucified him. 26 The written notice of the charge against him read: THE KING OF THE JEWS.

27 They crucified two rebels with him, one on his right and one on his left. [28]*a* 29 Those who passed by hurled insults at him, shaking their heads and saying, "So! You who are going to destroy the temple and build it in three days, 30 come down from the cross and save yourself!" 31 In the same way the chief priests and the teachers of the law mocked him among themselves. "He saved others," they said, "but he can't save himself! 32 Let this Messiah, this king of Israel, come down now from the cross, that we may see and believe." Those crucified with him also heaped insults on him.

The Death of Jesus

33 At noon, darkness came over the whole land until three in the afternoon. 34 And at three in the afternoon Jesus cried out in a loud voice, *"Eloi, Eloi, lema sabachthani?"* (which means "My God, my God, why have you forsaken me?").*b*

35 When some of those standing near heard this, they said, "Listen, he's calling Elijah."

36 Someone ran, filled a sponge with wine vinegar, put it on a staff, and offered it to Jesus to drink. "Now leave him alone. Let's see if Elijah comes to take him down," he said.

37 With a loud cry, Jesus breathed his last.

38 The curtain of the temple was torn in two from top to bottom. 39 And when the centurion, who stood there in front of Jesus, saw how he died,*c* he said, "Surely this man was the Son of God!"

40 Some women were watching from a distance. Among them were Mary Magdalene, Mary the mother of James the younger and of Joseph,*d* and Salome. 41 In Galilee these women had followed him and cared for his needs. Many other women who had come up with him to Jerusalem were also there.

---

a 28 Some manuscripts include here words similar to Luke 22:37.   *b 34* Psalm 22:1   *c 39* Some manuscripts saw that he died with such a cry   *d 40* Greek Joses, a variant of Joseph; also in verse 47

The Burial of Jesus

42 It was Preparation Day (that is, the day before the Sabbath). So as evening approached, 43 Joseph of Arimathea, a prominent member of the Council, who was himself waiting for the kingdom of God, went boldly to Pilate and asked for Jesus' body. 44 Pilate was surprised to hear that he was already dead. Summoning the centurion, he asked him if Jesus had already died. 45 When he learned from the centurion that it was so, he gave the body to Joseph. 46 So Joseph bought some linen cloth, took down the body, wrapped it in the linen, and placed it in a tomb cut out of rock. Then he rolled a stone against the entrance of the tomb. 47 Mary Magdalene and Mary the mother of Joseph saw where he was laid.

Jesus Has Risen

16 When the Sabbath was over, Mary Magdalene, Mary the mother of James, and Salome bought spices so that they might go to anoint Jesus' body. 2 Very early on the first day of the week, just after sunrise, they were on their way to the tomb 3 and they asked each other, "Who will roll the stone away from the entrance of the tomb?"

4 But when they looked up, they saw that the stone, which was very large, had been rolled away. 5 As they entered the tomb, they saw a young man dressed in a white robe sitting on the right side, and they were alarmed.

6 "Don't be alarmed," he said. "You are looking for Jesus the Nazarene, who was crucified. He has risen! He is not here. See the place where they laid him. 7 But go, tell his disciples and Peter, 'He is going ahead of you into Galilee. There you will see him, just as he told you.'"

8 Trembling and bewildered, the women went out and fled from the tomb. They said nothing to anyone, because they were afraid.[a]

[The earliest manuscripts and some other ancient witnesses do not have verses 9–20.]

9 When Jesus rose early on the first day of the week, he appeared first to Mary Magdalene, out of whom he had driven seven demons. 10 She went and told those who had been with him and who were mourning and weeping. 11 When they heard that Jesus was alive and that she had seen him, they did not believe it.

12 Afterward Jesus appeared in a different form to two of them while they were walking in the country. 13 These returned and reported it to the rest; but they did not believe them either.

14 Later Jesus appeared to the Eleven as they were eating; he rebuked them for their lack of faith and their stubborn refusal to believe those who had seen him after he had risen.

15 He said to them, "Go into all the world and preach the gospel to all creation. 16 Whoever believes and is baptized will be saved, but whoever does not believe will be condemned. 17 And these signs will accompany those who believe: In my name they will drive out demons; they will speak in new tongues; 18 they will pick up snakes with their hands; and when they drink deadly poison, it will not hurt them at all; they will place their hands on sick people, and they will get well."

19 After the Lord Jesus had spoken to them, he was taken up into heaven and he sat at the right hand of God. 20 Then the disciples went out and preached everywhere, and the Lord worked with them and confirmed his word by the signs that accompanied it.

---

a 8 Some manuscripts have the following ending between verses 8 and 9, and one manuscript has it after verse 8 (omitting verses 9-20): *Then they quickly reported all these instructions to those around Peter. After this, Jesus himself also sent out through them from east to west the sacred and imperishable proclamation of eternal salvation. Amen.*

LUKE

Ignored.

It's no fun to be ignored. A teacher ignores your raised hand and doesn't answer your question. A parent butts in and ignores what you were trying to say. A friend walks away when you're talking.

Luke wants you to know Jesus wasn't like that. Jesus showed a loving interest in all kinds of people. He had time for children. He often spoke about caring for the poor and oppressed. And Luke was careful to mention by name the women Jesus met and spoke to. Luke will help you realize that, whoever you are, Jesus has time for you.

>>**YOUNG GIRL RISKS ALL ON GOD'S WORD**
   Mary sets example for all. See Luke 1:26–38

>>**WOMAN FORGIVEN MUCH, WASHES FEET**
   Report in Luke 7:36–50

>>**HEY "NEIGHBOR"**
   Jesus gives new definition. See Luke 10:25–37

>>**JESUS WARNS, USE IT OR LOSE IT**
   Exhortation recorded in Luke 19:11–26

preview

Luke interviews people who knew Jesus to get first-hand accounts.

Luke's stories show Jesus' love for all kinds of people.

As Jesus teaches and heals in Galilee and Judea, Romans learn the use of soap from the Gauls.

Pontius Pilate is appointed Prefect of Judea. Apricots are brought to Rome from Asia.

Introduction

1 Many have undertaken to draw up an account of the things that have been fulfilled[a] among us, [2]just as they were handed down to us by those who from the first were eyewitnesses and servants of the word. [3]With this in mind, since I myself have carefully investigated everything from the beginning, I too decided to write an orderly account for you, most excellent Theophilus, [4]so that you may know the certainty of the things you have been taught.

The Birth of John the Baptist Foretold

[5]In the time of Herod king of Judea there was a priest named Zechariah, who belonged to the priestly division of Abijah; his wife Elizabeth was also a descendant of Aaron. [6]Both of them were righteous in the sight of God, observing all the Lord's commands and decrees blamelessly. [7]But they were childless because Elizabeth was not able to conceive, and they were both very old.

[8]Once when Zechariah's division was on duty and he was serving as priest before God, [9]he was chosen by lot, according to the custom of the priesthood, to go into the temple of the Lord and burn incense. [10]And when the time for the burning of incense came, all the assembled worshipers were praying outside.

[11]Then an angel of the Lord appeared to him, standing at the right side of the altar of incense. [12]When Zechariah saw him, he was startled and was gripped with fear. [13]But the angel said to him: "Do not be afraid, Zechariah; your prayer has been heard. Your wife Elizabeth will bear you a son, and you are to call him John. [14]He will be a joy and delight to you, and many will rejoice because of his birth, [15]for he will be great in the sight of the Lord. He is never to take wine or other fermented drink, and he will be filled with the Holy Spirit even before he is born. [16]He will bring back many of the people of Israel to the Lord their God. [17]And he will go on before the Lord, in the spirit and power of Elijah, to turn the hearts of the parents to their children and the disobedient to the wisdom of the righteous—to make ready a people prepared for the Lord."

[18]Zechariah asked the angel, "How can I be sure of this? I am an old man and my wife is well along in years."

[19]The angel said to him, "I am Gabriel. I stand in the presence of God, and I have been sent to speak to you and to tell you this good news. [20]And now you will be silent and not able to speak until the day this happens, because you did not believe my words, which will come true at their appointed time."

[21]Meanwhile, the people were waiting for Zechariah and wondering why he stayed so long in the temple. [22]When he came out, he could not speak to them. They realized he had seen a vision in the temple, for he kept making signs to them but remained unable to speak.

[23]When his time of service was completed, he returned home. [24]After this his wife Elizabeth became pregnant and for five months remained in seclusion. [25]"The Lord has done this for me," she said. "In these days he has shown his favor and taken away my disgrace among the people."

The Birth of Jesus Foretold

[26]In the sixth month of Elizabeth's pregnancy, God sent the angel Gabriel to Nazareth, a town in Galilee, [27]to a virgin pledged to be married to a man named Joseph, a descendant of David. The virgin's name was Mary. [28]The angel went to her and said, "Greetings, you who are highly favored! The Lord is with you."

[29]Mary was greatly troubled at his words and wondered what kind of greeting this might be. [30]But the angel said to her, "Do not be afraid, Mary; you have found favor with God. [31]You will conceive and give birth to a son, and you are to call him Jesus. [32]He will be great and will be called the Son of the Most High. The Lord God will give him the throne of his father David, [33]and he will reign over

---

[a] 1 Or *been surely believed*

When you think of real heroes and heroines, you have to put a teenager named Mary at the top of the list. When this young virgin said she was willing to bear Jesus, she knew what it meant. She was engaged; her husband-to-be would think she was unfaithful. Everyone, even her parents, would think she'd had sex before marriage. It took a tremendous amount of courage to say, "I am the Lord's servant." There are still teenage heroes around. They're the ones who say no even when they're laughed at and called prudes. They're the ones who resist all the pressures to do wrong and instead echo Mary's words: "I am the Lord's servant" and choose to do God's will.

{Luke 1:26–38}

INSTANT ACCESS

going to have a child in her old age, and she who was said to be unable to conceive is in her sixth month. 37For no word from God will ever fail."

38"I am the Lord's servant," Mary answered. "May your word to me be fulfilled." Then the angel left her.

Mary Visits Elizabeth

39At that time Mary got ready and hurried to a town in the hill country of Judea, 40where she entered Zechariah's home and greeted Elizabeth. 41When Elizabeth heard Mary's greeting, the baby leaped in her womb, and Elizabeth was filled with the Holy Spirit. 42In a loud voice she exclaimed: "Blessed are you among women, and blessed is the child you will bear! 43But why am I so favored, that the mother of my Lord should come to me? 44As soon as the sound of your greeting reached my ears, the baby in my womb leaped for joy. 45Blessed is she who has believed that the Lord would fulfill his promises to her!"

Mary's Song

46And Mary said:

"My soul glorifies the Lord
47   and my spirit rejoices in God my
        Savior,
48for he has been mindful
        of the humble state of his servant.
    From now on all generations will call
        me blessed,
49   for the Mighty One has done great
        things for me—
    holy is his name.
50His mercy extends to those who fear
        him,
    from generation to generation.
51He has performed mighty deeds with
        his arm;
    he has scattered those who are
        proud in their inmost thoughts.
52He has brought down rulers from their
        thrones
    but has lifted up the humble.
53He has filled the hungry with good
        things
    but has sent the rich away empty.

Jacob's descendants forever; his kingdom will never end."

34"How will this be," Mary asked the angel, "since I am a virgin?"

35The angel answered, "The Holy Spirit will come on you, and the power of the Most High will overshadow you. So the holy one to be born will be called[a] the Son of God. 36Even Elizabeth your relative is

---

[a] 35 Or So the child to be born will be called holy,

Jesus was "conceived by the Holy Spirit"

✝ The angel who appeared to Mary shocked her. He told the teenager that she was going to have a son. Mary said, "How will this be, since I am a virgin?" (Luke 1:31–34).

Then the angel said something even more shocking. He told Mary that her child would be the "Son of God" (see the "We Believe" at John 1). God himself was going to take on human nature and be born as a human infant.

Mary might well have asked, "How can that be?" again. But the angel beat her to it. He explained that God the Holy Spirit, rather than a man, would energize the egg in her womb, so the child she produced would be the Son of God.

This had never happened before. And it would never happen again. But don't think it was impossible. After all, God did create Adam and Eve. He knows everything about how our bodies work. There's no reason to suppose that God the Holy Spirit couldn't blend deity and humanity so that the child Jesus was both God and Man, united in a single person. In fact that's what "conceived by the Holy Spirit" means. The Holy Spirit worked in Mary's body to blend deity and humanity so that Jesus, the one and only Son of God, was conceived.

To find out more about the Holy Spirit, see the "We Believe" at Acts 2.

Go to page 844 for the next We Believe

[54] He has helped his servant
Israel,
remembering to be merciful
[55] to Abraham and his descendants
forever,
just as he promised our
ancestors."

[56] Mary stayed with Elizabeth for about three months and then returned home.

The Birth of John the Baptist

[57] When it was time for Elizabeth to have her baby, she gave birth to a son. [58] Her neighbors and relatives heard that the Lord had shown her great mercy, and they shared her joy.

[59] On the eighth day they came to circumcise the child, and they were going to name him after his father Zechariah, [60] but his mother spoke up and said, "No! He is to be called John."

[61] They said to her, "There is no one among your relatives who has that name."

[62] Then they made signs to his father, to find out what he would like to name the child. [63] He asked for a writing tablet, and to everyone's astonishment he wrote, "His name is John." [64] Immediately his mouth was opened and his tongue set free, and he began to speak, praising God. [65] All the neighbors were filled with awe, and throughout the hill country of Judea people were talking about all these things. [66] Everyone who heard this wondered about it, asking, "What then is this child going to be?" For the Lord's hand was with him.

Zechariah's Song

[67] His father Zechariah was filled with the Holy Spirit and prophesied:

[68] "Praise be to the Lord, the God of
Israel,
because he has come to his people
and redeemed them.
[69] He has raised up a horn[a] of salvation
for us
in the house of his servant David
[70] (as he said through his holy prophets
of long ago),

[71] salvation from our enemies
and from the hand of all who hate
us—
[72] to show mercy to our ancestors
and to remember his holy covenant,
[73] the oath he swore to our father
Abraham:
[74] to rescue us from the hand of our
enemies,
and to enable us to serve him
without fear
[75] in holiness and righteousness
before him all our days.

[76] And you, my child, will be called a
prophet of the Most High;
for you will go on before the Lord to
prepare the way for him,
[77] to give his people the knowledge of
salvation
through the forgiveness of their sins,
[78] because of the tender mercy of our
God,
by which the rising sun will come to
us from heaven
[79] to shine on those living in darkness
and in the shadow of death,
to guide our feet into the path of
peace."

[80] And the child grew and became strong in spirit[b]; and he lived in the wilderness until he appeared publicly to Israel.

The Birth of Jesus

2 In those days Caesar Augustus issued a decree that a census should be taken of the entire Roman world. [2] (This was the first census that took place while[c] Quirinius was governor of Syria.) [3] And everyone went to their own town to register.

[4] So Joseph also went up from the town of Nazareth in Galilee to Judea, to Bethlehem the town of David, because he belonged to the house and line of David. [5] He went there to register with Mary, who was pledged to be married to him and was expecting a child. [6] While they were there, the time came for the baby to be born, [7] and she gave birth to her firstborn, a son. She wrapped him in cloths and

---

[a] 69 *Horn* here symbolizes a strong king.   [b] 80 Or *in the Spirit*   [c] 2 Or *This census took place before*

placed him in a manger, because there was no guest room available for them.

⁸And there were shepherds living out in the fields nearby, keeping watch over their flocks at night. ⁹An angel of the Lord appeared to them, and the glory of the Lord shone around them, and they were terrified. ¹⁰But the angel said to them, "Do not be afraid. I bring you good news that will cause great joy for all the people. ¹¹Today in the town of David a Savior has been born to you; he is the Messiah, the Lord. ¹²This will be a sign to you: You will find a baby wrapped in cloths and lying in a manger."

¹³Suddenly a great company of the heavenly host appeared with the angel, praising God and saying,

¹⁴ "Glory to God in the highest heaven,
    and on earth peace to those on
        whom his favor rests."

¹⁵When the angels had left them and gone into heaven, the shepherds said to one another, "Let's go to Bethlehem and see this thing that has happened, which the Lord has told us about."

¹⁶So they hurried off and found Mary and Joseph, and the baby, who was lying in the manger. ¹⁷When they had seen him, they spread the word concerning what had been told them about this child, ¹⁸and all who heard it were amazed at what the shepherds said to them. ¹⁹But Mary treasured up all these things and pondered them in her heart. ²⁰The shepherds returned, glorifying and praising God for all the things they had heard and seen, which were just as they had been told.

²¹On the eighth day, when it was time to circumcise the child, he was named Jesus, the name the angel had given him before he was conceived.

Jesus Presented in the Temple

²²When the time came for the purification rites required by the Law of Moses, Joseph and Mary took him to Jerusalem to present him to the Lord ²³(as it is written in the Law of the Lord, "Every firstborn male is to be consecrated to the Lord"ᵃ), ²⁴and to offer a sacrifice in keeping with what is said in the Law of the Lord: "a pair of doves or two young pigeons."ᵇ

²⁵Now there was a man in Jerusalem called Simeon, who was righteous and devout. He was waiting for the consolation of Israel, and the Holy Spirit was on him. ²⁶It had been revealed to him by the Holy Spirit that he would not die before he had seen the Lord's Messiah. ²⁷Moved by the Spirit, he went into the temple courts. When the parents brought in the child Jesus to do for him what the custom of the Law required, ²⁸Simeon took him in his arms and praised God, saying:

²⁹ "Sovereign Lord, as you have
        promised,
    you may now dismissᶜ your servant
        in peace.
³⁰For my eyes have seen your salvation,
³¹   which you have prepared in the
            sight of all nations:
³²a light for revelation to the Gentiles,
    and the glory of your people Israel."

³³The child's father and mother marveled at what was said about him. ³⁴Then

Luke 2

Q: Was Jesus born to a poor family or a rich one?

BONUS: How do we know?

Answers on next page

ᵃ 23 Exodus 13:2,12   ᵇ 24 Lev. 12:8
ᶜ 29 Or promised, / now dismiss

Simeon blessed them and said to Mary, his mother: "This child is destined to cause the falling and rising of many in Israel, and to be a sign that will be spoken against, [35]so that the thoughts of many hearts will be revealed. And a sword will pierce your own soul too."

[36]There was also a prophet, Anna, the daughter of Penuel, of the tribe of Asher. She was very old; she had lived with her husband seven years after her marriage, [37]and then was a widow until she was eighty-four.[a] She never left the temple but worshiped night and day, fasting and praying. [38]Coming up to them at that very moment, she gave thanks to God and spoke about the child to all who were looking forward to the redemption of Jerusalem.

[39]When Joseph and Mary had done everything required by the Law of the Lord, they returned to Galilee to their own town of Nazareth. [40]And the child grew and became strong; he was filled with wisdom, and the grace of God was on him.

The Boy Jesus at the Temple

[41]Every year Jesus' parents went to Jerusalem for the Festival of the Passover. [42]When he was twelve years old, they went up to the festival, according to the custom. [43]After the festival was over, while his parents were returning home, the boy Jesus stayed behind in Jerusalem, but they were unaware of it. [44]Thinking he was in their company, they traveled on for a day. Then they began looking for him among their relatives and friends. [45]When they did not find him, they went back to Jerusalem to look for him. [46]After three days they found him in the temple courts, sitting among the teachers, listening to them and asking them questions. [47]Everyone who heard him was amazed at his understanding and his answers. [48]When his parents saw him, they were astonished. His mother said to him, "Son, why have you treated us like this? Your father and I have been anxiously searching for you."

[49]"Why were you searching for me?" he

A: A poor family.

BONUS: Only the poor were allowed to offer two pigeons instead of a lamb (Luke 2:24; Leviticus 12:8).

asked. "Didn't you know I had to be in my Father's house?"[b] [50]But they did not understand what he was saying to them.

[51]Then he went down to Nazareth with them and was obedient to them. But his mother treasured all these things in her heart. [52]And Jesus grew in wisdom and stature, and in favor with God and man.

John the Baptist Prepares the Way

3 In the fifteenth year of the reign of Tiberius Caesar—when Pontius Pilate was governor of Judea, Herod tetrarch of Galilee, his brother Philip tetrarch of Iturea and Traconitis, and Lysanias tetrarch of Abilene— [2]during the high-priesthood of Annas and Caiaphas, the word of God came to John son of Zechariah in the wilderness. [3]He went into all the country around the Jordan, preaching a baptism of repentance for the forgiveness of sins. [4]As it is written in the book of the words of Isaiah the prophet:

"A voice of one calling in the wilderness,

---

[a] 37 Or then had been a widow for eighty-four years.   [b] 49 Or be about my Father's business

'Prepare the way for the Lord,
    make straight paths for him.
⁵Every valley shall be filled in,
    every mountain and hill made low.
The crooked roads shall become
        straight,
    the rough ways smooth.
⁶And all people will see God's
        salvation.' "ᵃ

⁷John said to the crowds coming out to be baptized by him, "You brood of vipers! Who warned you to flee from the coming wrath? ⁸Produce fruit in keeping with repentance. And do not begin to say to yourselves, 'We have Abraham as our father.' For I tell you that out of these stones God can raise up children for Abraham. ⁹The ax is already at the root of the trees, and every tree that does not produce good fruit will be cut down and thrown into the fire."

¹⁰"What should we do then?" the crowd asked.

¹¹John answered, "Anyone who has two shirts should share with the one who has none, and anyone who has food should do the same."

¹²Even tax collectors came to be baptized. "Teacher," they asked, "what should we do?"

¹³"Don't collect any more than you are required to," he told them.

¹⁴Then some soldiers asked him, "And what should we do?"

He replied, "Don't extort money and don't accuse people falsely—be content with your pay."

¹⁵The people were waiting expectantly and were all wondering in their hearts if John might possibly be the Messiah. ¹⁶John answered them all, "I baptize you withᵇ water. But one who is more powerful than I will come, the straps of whose sandals I am not worthy to untie. He will baptize you withᵇ the Holy Spirit and fire. ¹⁷His winnowing fork is in his hand to clear his threshing floor and to gather the wheat into his barn, but he will burn up the chaff with unquenchable fire." ¹⁸And with many other words John exhorted the

INSTANT ACCESS

Maybe you've been brought up in a Christian home. Mom and Dad take you to church every week. You pray at every meal, and Mom and Dad even talk about God around the house. That makes you a Christian. Right? Wrong. Going to church doesn't make you a Christian any more than going into a barn once a week would make you a cow. You have to be born a calf to be a cow. And you have to be born again to be a Christian. That's what John told the religious people who came to hear him. Only your own personal faith in Christ counts. Why not trust him now?

{Luke 3:7–9}

people and proclaimed the good news to them.

¹⁹But when John rebuked Herod the tetrarch because of his marriage to Herodias, his brother's wife, and all the other evil things he had done, ²⁰Herod added this to them all: He locked John up in prison.

The Baptism and Genealogy of Jesus

²¹When all the people were being baptized, Jesus was baptized too. And as he was praying, heaven was opened ²²and

---

ᵃ 6 Isaiah 40:3-5   ᵇ 16 Or in

the Holy Spirit descended on him in bodily form like a dove. And a voice came from heaven: "You are my Son, whom I love; with you I am well pleased."

23 Now Jesus himself was about thirty years old when he began his ministry. He was the son, so it was thought, of Joseph,

the son of Heli, 24 the son of Matthat,
the son of Levi, the son of Melki,
the son of Jannai, the son of Joseph,
25 the son of Mattathias, the son of Amos,
the son of Nahum, the son of Esli,
the son of Naggai, 26 the son of Maath,
the son of Mattathias, the son of Semein,
the son of Josek, the son of Joda,
27 the son of Joanan, the son of Rhesa,
the son of Zerubbabel, the son of Shealtiel,
the son of Neri, 28 the son of Melki,
the son of Addi, the son of Cosam,
the son of Elmadam, the son of Er,
29 the son of Joshua, the son of Eliezer,
the son of Jorim, the son of Matthat,
the son of Levi, 30 the son of Simeon,
the son of Judah, the son of Joseph,
the son of Jonam, the son of Eliakim,
31 the son of Melea, the son of Menna,
the son of Mattatha, the son of Nathan,
the son of David, 32 the son of Jesse,
the son of Obed, the son of Boaz,
the son of Salmon,^{a} the son of Nahshon,
33 the son of Amminadab, the son of Ram,^{b}
the son of Hezron, the son of Perez,
the son of Judah, 34 the son of Jacob,
the son of Isaac, the son of Abraham,
the son of Terah, the son of Nahor,
35 the son of Serug, the son of Reu,
the son of Peleg, the son of Eber,
the son of Shelah, 36 the son of Cainan,

the son of Arphaxad, the son of Shem,
the son of Noah, the son of Lamech,
37 the son of Methuselah, the son of Enoch,
the son of Jared, the son of Mahalalel,
the son of Kenan, 38 the son of Enosh,
the son of Seth, the son of Adam,
the son of God.

Jesus Is Tested in the Wilderness

4 Jesus, full of the Holy Spirit, left the Jordan and was led by the Spirit into the wilderness, 2 where for forty days he was tempted^c by the devil. He ate nothing during those days, and at the end of them he was hungry.

3 The devil said to him, "If you are the Son of God, tell this stone to become bread."

4 Jesus answered, "It is written: 'Man shall not live on bread alone.'^{d}"

5 The devil led him up to a high place and showed him in an instant all the kingdoms of the world. 6 And he said to him, "I

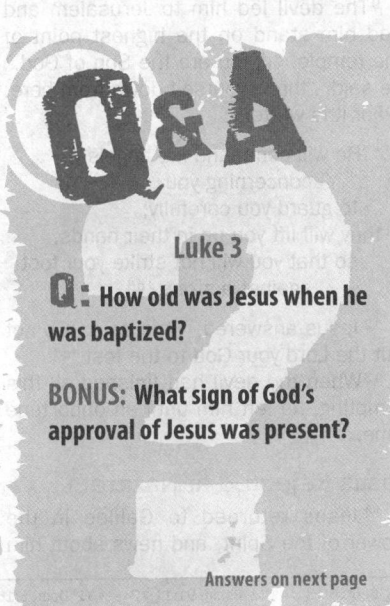

Luke 3

Q: How old was Jesus when he was baptized?

BONUS: What sign of God's approval of Jesus was present?

Answers on next page

---

^{a} 32 Some early manuscripts Sala ^{b} 33 Some manuscripts Amminadab, the son of Admin, the son of Arni; other manuscripts vary widely. ^{c} 2 The Greek for tempted can also mean tested. ^{d} 4 Deut. 8:3

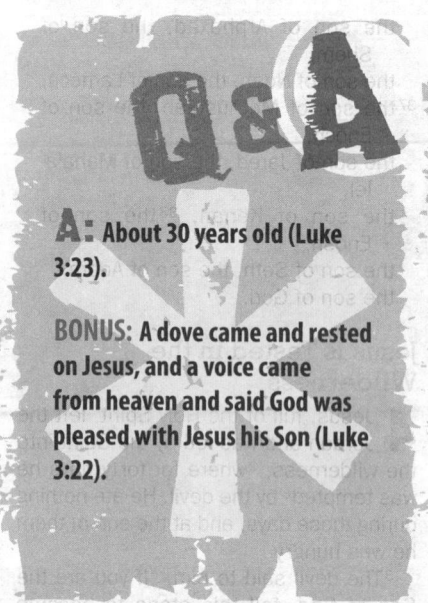

A: About 30 years old (Luke 3:23).

BONUS: A dove came and rested on Jesus, and a voice came from heaven and said God was pleased with Jesus his Son (Luke 3:22).

will give you all their authority and splendor; it has been given to me, and I can give it to anyone I want to. [7] If you worship me, it will all be yours."

[8] Jesus answered, "It is written: 'Worship the Lord your God and serve him only.'[a]"

[9] The devil led him to Jerusalem and had him stand on the highest point of the temple. "If you are the Son of God," he said, "throw yourself down from here. [10] For it is written:

" 'He will command his angels
        concerning you
    to guard you carefully;
[11] they will lift you up in their hands,
    so that you will not strike your foot
        against a stone.'[b]"

[12] Jesus answered, "It is said: 'Do not put the Lord your God to the test.'[c]"

[13] When the devil had finished all this tempting, he left him until an opportune time.

Jesus Rejected at Nazareth

[14] Jesus returned to Galilee in the power of the Spirit, and news about him spread through the whole countryside. [15] He was teaching in their synagogues, and everyone praised him.

[16] He went to Nazareth, where he had been brought up, and on the Sabbath day he went into the synagogue, as was his custom. He stood up to read, [17] and the scroll of the prophet Isaiah was handed to him. Unrolling it, he found the place where it is written:

[18] "The Spirit of the Lord is on me,
    because he has anointed me
    to proclaim good news to the poor.
He has sent me to proclaim freedom
        for the prisoners
    and recovery of sight for the blind,
to set the oppressed free,
[19]   to proclaim the year of the Lord's
        favor."[d]

[20] Then he rolled up the scroll, gave it back to the attendant and sat down. The eyes of everyone in the synagogue were fastened on him. [21] He began by saying to them, "Today this scripture is fulfilled in your hearing."

[22] All spoke well of him and were amazed at the gracious words that came from his lips. "Isn't this Joseph's son?" they asked.

[23] Jesus said to them, "Surely you will quote this proverb to me: 'Physician, heal yourself!' And you will tell me, 'Do here in your hometown what we have heard that you did in Capernaum.' "

[24] "Truly I tell you," he continued, "no prophet is accepted in his hometown. [25] I assure you that there were many widows in Israel in Elijah's time, when the sky was shut for three and a half years and there was a severe famine throughout the land. [26] Yet Elijah was not sent to any of them, but to a widow in Zarephath in the region of Sidon. [27] And there were many in Israel with leprosy[e] in the time of Elisha the prophet, yet not one of them was cleansed—only Naaman the Syrian."

[28] All the people in the synagogue were furious when they heard this. [29] They got up, drove him out of the town, and took

---

[a] 8 Deut. 6:13   [b] 11 Psalm 91:11,12   [c] 12 Deut. 6:16   [d] 19 Isaiah 61:1,2 (see Septuagint); Isaiah 58:6
[e] 27 The Greek word traditionally translated leprosy was used for various diseases affecting the skin.

him to the brow of the hill on which the town was built, in order to throw him off the cliff. 30 But he walked right through the crowd and went on his way.

Jesus Drives Out an Impure Spirit

31 Then he went down to Capernaum, a town in Galilee, and on the Sabbath he taught the people. 32 They were amazed at his teaching, because his words had authority.

33 In the synagogue there was a man possessed by a demon, an impure spirit. He cried out at the top of his voice, 34 "Go away! What do you want with us, Jesus of Nazareth? Have you come to destroy us? I know who you are—the Holy One of God!"

35 "Be quiet!" Jesus said sternly. "Come out of him!" Then the demon threw the man down before them all and came out without injuring him.

36 All the people were amazed and said to each other, "What words these are! With authority and power he gives orders to impure spirits and they come out!" 37 And the news about him spread throughout the surrounding area.

Jesus Heals Many

38 Jesus left the synagogue and went to the home of Simon. Now Simon's mother-in-law was suffering from a high fever, and they asked Jesus to help her. 39 So he bent over her and rebuked the fever, and it left her. She got up at once and began to wait on them.

40 At sunset, the people brought to Jesus all who had various kinds of sickness, and laying his hands on each one, he healed them. 41 Moreover, demons came out of many people, shouting, "You are the Son of God!" But he rebuked them and would not allow them to speak, because they knew he was the Messiah.

42 At daybreak, Jesus went out to a solitary place. The people were looking for him and when they came to where he was, they tried to keep him from leaving

them. 43 But he said, "I must proclaim the good news of the kingdom of God to the other towns also, because that is why I was sent." 44 And he kept on preaching in the synagogues of Judea.

Jesus Calls His First Disciples

5 One day as Jesus was standing by the Lake of Gennesaret,[a] the people were crowding around him and listening to the word of God. 2 He saw at the water's edge two boats, left there by the fishermen, who were washing their nets. 3 He got into one of the boats, the one belonging to Simon, and asked him to put out a little from shore. Then he sat down and taught the people from the boat.

4 When he had finished speaking, he said to Simon, "Put out into deep water, and let down the nets for a catch."

5 Simon answered, "Master, we've worked hard all night and haven't caught anything. But because you say so, I will let down the nets."

6 When they had done so, they caught such a large number of fish that their nets began to break. 7 So they signaled their partners in the other boat to come and help them, and they came and filled both boats so full that they began to sink.

8 When Simon Peter saw this, he fell at Jesus' knees and said, "Go away from me, Lord; I am a sinful man!" 9 For he and all his companions were astonished at the catch of fish they had taken, 10 and so were James and John, the sons of Zebedee, Simon's partners.

Then Jesus said to Simon, "Don't be afraid; from now on you will fish for people." 11 So they pulled their boats up on shore, left everything and followed him.

Jesus Heals a Man With Leprosy

12 While Jesus was in one of the towns, a man came along who was covered with leprosy.[b] When he saw Jesus, he fell with his face to the ground and begged him, "Lord, if you are willing, you can make me clean."

---

a 1 That is, the Sea of Galilee   *b* 12 The Greek word traditionally translated *leprosy* was used for various diseases affecting the skin.

13 Jesus reached out his hand and touched the man. "I am willing," he said. "Be clean!" And immediately the leprosy left him.

14 Then Jesus ordered him, "Don't tell anyone, but go, show yourself to the priest and offer the sacrifices that Moses commanded for your cleansing, as a testimony to them."

15 Yet the news about him spread all the more, so that crowds of people came to hear him and to be healed of their sicknesses. 16 But Jesus often withdrew to lonely places and prayed.

Jesus Forgives and Heals a Paralyzed Man

17 One day Jesus was teaching, and Pharisees and teachers of the law were sitting there. They had come from every village of Galilee and from Judea and Jerusalem. And the power of the Lord was with Jesus to heal the sick. 18 Some men came carrying a paralyzed man on a mat and tried to take him into the house to lay him before Jesus. 19 When they could not find a way to do this because of the crowd, they went up on the roof and lowered him on his mat through the tiles into the middle of the crowd, right in front of Jesus.

20 When Jesus saw their faith, he said, "Friend, your sins are forgiven."

21 The Pharisees and the teachers of the law began thinking to themselves, "Who is this fellow who speaks blasphemy? Who can forgive sins but God alone?"

22 Jesus knew what they were thinking and asked, "Why are you thinking these things in your hearts? 23 Which is easier: to say, 'Your sins are forgiven,' or to say, 'Get up and walk'? 24 But I want you to know that the Son of Man has authority on earth to forgive sins." So he said to the paralyzed man, "I tell you, get up, take your mat and go home." 25 Immediately he stood up in front of them, took what he had been lying on and went home praising God. 26 Everyone was amazed and gave praise to God. They were filled with awe and said, "We have seen remarkable things today."

INSTANT ACCESS

You've probably heard all the stories about Jesus' miracles and his kindness to hurting people. That's good, but that isn't all, nor is it enough. The first time they met, Peter not only realized Jesus was special but that he was powerful. After not catching any fish all night, at Jesus' command Peter and his friends filled their boats with a huge catch. The Bible says Peter was so "astonished" (Luke 5:9) that he fell on his knees and called Jesus "Lord!" Now that's something to experience. You go from knowing that Jesus is someone special, to calling him "Lord," confessing Jesus to be God—all in one day.

{Luke 5:1–11}

Jesus Calls Levi and Eats With Sinners

27 After this, Jesus went out and saw a tax collector by the name of Levi sitting at his tax booth. "Follow me," Jesus said to him, 28 and Levi got up, left everything and followed him.

29 Then Levi held a great banquet for Jesus at his house, and a large crowd of tax collectors and others were eating with them. 30 But the Pharisees and the teachers of the law who belonged to their sect complained to his disciples, "Why do you eat and drink with tax collectors and sinners?"

31 Jesus answered them, "It is not the healthy who need a doctor, but the sick. 32 I have not come to call the righteous, but sinners to repentance."

Jesus Questioned About Fasting

33 They said to him, "John's disciples often fast and pray, and so do the disciples of the Pharisees, but yours go on eating and drinking."

34 Jesus answered, "Can you make the friends of the bridegroom fast while he is with them? 35 But the time will come when the bridegroom will be taken from them; in those days they will fast."

36 He told them this parable: "No one tears a piece out of a new garment to patch an old one. Otherwise, they will have torn the new garment, and the patch from the new will not match the old. 37 And no one pours new wine into old wineskins. Otherwise, the new wine will burst the skins; the wine will run out and the wineskins will be ruined. 38 No, new wine must be poured into new wineskins. 39 And no one after drinking old wine wants the new, for they say, 'The old is better.' "

Jesus Is Lord of the Sabbath

6 One Sabbath Jesus was going through the grainfields, and his disciples began to pick some heads of grain, rub them in their hands and eat the kernels. 2 Some of the Pharisees asked, "Why are you doing what is unlawful on the Sabbath?"

3 Jesus answered them, "Have you never read what David did when he and his companions were hungry? 4 He entered the house of God, and taking the consecrated bread, he ate what is lawful only for priests to eat. And he also gave some to his companions." 5 Then Jesus said to them, "The Son of Man is Lord of the Sabbath."

6 On another Sabbath he went into the synagogue and was teaching, and a man was there whose right hand was shriveled. 7 The Pharisees and the teachers of the law were looking for a reason to accuse Jesus, so they watched him closely to see if he would heal on the Sabbath. 8 But Jesus knew what they were thinking and said to the man with the shriveled hand, "Get up and stand in front of everyone." So he got up and stood there.

9 Then Jesus said to them, "I ask you, which is lawful on the Sabbath: to do good or to do evil, to save life or to destroy it?"

10 He looked around at them all, and then said to the man, "Stretch out your hand." He did so, and his hand was completely restored. 11 But the Pharisees and the teachers of the law were furious and began to discuss with one another what they might do to Jesus.

The Twelve Apostles

12 One of those days Jesus went out to a mountainside to pray, and spent the night praying to God. 13 When morning came, he called his disciples to him and chose twelve of them, whom he also designated apostles: 14 Simon (whom he named Peter), his brother Andrew, James, John, Philip, Bartholomew, 15 Matthew, Thomas, James son of Alphaeus, Simon who was called the Zealot, 16 Judas son of James, and Judas Iscariot, who became a traitor.

Blessings and Woes

17 He went down with them and stood on a level place. A large crowd of his disciples was there and a great number of people from all over Judea, from Jerusalem, and from the coastal region around Tyre and Sidon, 18 who had come to hear him and to be healed of their diseases. Those troubled by impure spirits were cured, 19 and the people all tried to touch him, because power was coming from him and healing them all.

20 Looking at his disciples, he said:

"Blessed are you who are poor,
　for yours is the kingdom of God.
21 Blessed are you who hunger now,
　for you will be satisfied.
Blessed are you who weep now,
　for you will laugh.
22 Blessed are you when people hate you,
　when they exclude you and insult
　you

and reject your name as evil,
because of the Son of Man.

23 "Rejoice in that day and leap for joy, because great is your reward in heaven. For that is how their ancestors treated the prophets.

24 "But woe to you who are rich,
for you have already received your
comfort.
25 Woe to you who are well fed now,
for you will go hungry.
Woe to you who laugh now,
for you will mourn and weep.
26 Woe to you when everyone speaks
well of you,
for that is how their ancestors
treated the false prophets.

Love for Enemies

27 "But to you who are listening I say: Love your enemies, do good to those who hate you, 28 bless those who curse you, pray for those who mistreat you. 29 If someone slaps you on one cheek, turn to them the other also. If someone takes your coat, do not withhold your shirt from them. 30 Give to everyone who asks you, and if anyone takes what belongs to you, do not demand it back. 31 Do to others as you would have them do to you.

32 "If you love those who love you, what credit is that to you? Even sinners love those who love them. 33 And if you do good to those who are good to you, what credit is that to you? Even sinners do that. 34 And if you lend to those from whom you expect repayment, what credit is that to you? Even sinners lend to sinners, expecting to be repaid in full. 35 But love your enemies, do good to them, and lend to them without expecting to get anything back. Then your reward will be great, and you will be children of the Most High, because he is kind to the ungrateful and wicked. 36 Be merciful, just as your Father is merciful.

Judging Others

37 "Do not judge, and you will not be judged. Do not condemn, and you will not be condemned. Forgive, and you will be forgiven. 38 Give, and it will be given to you. A good measure, pressed down,

shaken together and running over, will be poured into your lap. For with the measure you use, it will be measured to you."

39 He also told them this parable: "Can the blind lead the blind? Will they not both fall into a pit? 40 The student is not above the teacher, but everyone who is fully trained will be like their teacher.

41 "Why do you look at the speck of sawdust in your brother's eye and pay no attention to the plank in your own eye? 42 How can you say to your brother, 'Brother, let me take the speck out of your eye,' when you yourself fail to see the plank in your own eye? You hypocrite, first take the plank out of your eye, and then you will see clearly to remove the speck from your brother's eye.

A Tree and Its Fruit

43 "No good tree bears bad fruit, nor does a bad tree bear good fruit. 44 Each tree is recognized by its own fruit. People do not pick figs from thornbushes, or grapes from briers. 45 A good man brings good things out of the good stored up in his heart, and an evil man brings evil things out of the evil stored up in his heart. For the mouth speaks what the heart is full of.

The Wise and Foolish Builders

46 "Why do you call me, 'Lord, Lord,' and do not do what I say? 47 As for everyone who comes to me and hears my words and puts them into practice, I will show you what they are like. 48 They are like a man building a house, who dug down deep and laid the foundation on rock. When a flood came, the torrent struck that house but could not shake it, because it was well built. 49 But the one who hears my words and does not put them into practice is like a man who built a house on the ground without a foundation. The moment the torrent struck that house, it collapsed and its destruction was complete."

The Faith of the Centurion

7 When Jesus had finished saying all this to the people who were listening, he entered Capernaum. 2 There a centurion's servant, whom his master valued

highly, was sick and about to die. ³The centurion heard of Jesus and sent some elders of the Jews to him, asking him to come and heal his servant. ⁴When they came to Jesus, they pleaded earnestly with him, "This man deserves to have you do this, ⁵because he loves our nation and has built our synagogue." ⁶So Jesus went with them.

He was not far from the house when the centurion sent friends to say to him: "Lord, don't trouble yourself, for I do not deserve to have you come under my roof. ⁷That is why I did not even consider myself worthy to come to you. But say the word, and my servant will be healed. ⁸For I myself am a man under authority, with soldiers under me. I tell this one, 'Go,' and he goes; and that one, 'Come,' and

he comes. I say to my servant, 'Do this,' and he does it."

⁹When Jesus heard this, he was amazed at him, and turning to the crowd following him, he said, "I tell you, I have not found such great faith even in Israel." ¹⁰Then the men who had been sent returned to the house and found the servant well.

Jesus Raises a Widow's Son

¹¹Soon afterward, Jesus went to a town called Nain, and his disciples and a large crowd went along with him. ¹²As he approached the town gate, a dead person was being carried out—the only son of his mother, and she was a widow. And a large crowd from the town was with her. ¹³When the Lord saw her, his heart went out to her and he said, "Don't cry."

TO THE POINT

God Sees You!

Some people are uncomfortable at the thought that God is everywhere. It means he sees everything they do! Certainly that's what the Bible says:

+ God "observes everyone on earth" (Psalm 11:4).

+ "The eyes of the Lord are on the righteous" (Psalm 34:15).

+ You can never run from God. He is everywhere (Psalm 139:7–8).

Of course, knowing God is everywhere doesn't make you uncomfortable unless you're making bad choices. In Luke 7:1–10 a Roman soldier asked Jesus to heal his servant. The soldier didn't insist Jesus go where the servant was. He just said, "Say the word, and my servant will be healed."

God can see you! He's right here with you—and he'll help you any time you ask.

¹⁴Then he went up and touched the bier they were carrying him on, and the bearers stood still. He said, "Young man, I say to you, get up!" ¹⁵The dead man sat up and began to talk, and Jesus gave him back to his mother.

¹⁶They were all filled with awe and praised God. "A great prophet has appeared among us," they said. "God has come to help his people." ¹⁷This news about Jesus spread throughout Judea and the surrounding country.

Jesus and John the Baptist

¹⁸John's disciples told him about all these things. Calling two of them, ¹⁹he sent them to the Lord to ask, "Are you the one who is to come, or should we expect someone else?"

²⁰When the men came to Jesus, they said, "John the Baptist sent us to you to ask, 'Are you the one who is to come, or should we expect someone else?' "

²¹At that very time Jesus cured many who had diseases, sicknesses and evil spirits, and gave sight to many who were blind. ²²So he replied to the messengers, "Go back and report to John what you have seen and heard: The blind receive sight, the lame walk, those who have leprosy*a* are cleansed, the deaf hear, the dead are raised, and the good news is proclaimed to the poor. ²³Blessed is anyone who does not stumble on account of me."

²⁴After John's messengers left, Jesus began to speak to the crowd about John: "What did you go out into the wilderness to see? A reed swayed by the wind? ²⁵If not, what did you go out to see? A man dressed in fine clothes? No, those who wear expensive clothes and indulge in luxury are in palaces. ²⁶But what did you go out to see? A prophet? Yes, I tell you, and more than a prophet. ²⁷This is the one about whom it is written:

" 'I will send my messenger ahead of
        you,
    who will prepare your way before
        you.'*b*

²⁸I tell you, among those born of women there is no one greater than John; yet the one who is least in the kingdom of God is greater than he."

²⁹(All the people, even the tax collectors, when they heard Jesus' words, acknowledged that God's way was right, because they had been baptized by John. ³⁰But the Pharisees and the experts in the law rejected God's purpose for themselves, because they had not been baptized by John.)

³¹Jesus went on to say, "To what, then, can I compare the people of this generation? What are they like? ³²They are like children sitting in the marketplace and calling out to each other:

" 'We played the pipe for you,
        and you did not dance;
    we sang a dirge,
        and you did not cry.'

³³For John the Baptist came neither eating bread nor drinking wine, and you say, 'He has a demon.' ³⁴The Son of Man came eating and drinking, and you say, 'Here is a glutton and a drunkard, a friend of tax collectors and sinners.' ³⁵But wisdom is proved right by all her children."

Jesus Anointed by a Sinful Woman

³⁶When one of the Pharisees invited Jesus to have dinner with him, he went to the Pharisee's house and reclined at the table. ³⁷A woman in that town who lived a sinful life learned that Jesus was eating at the Pharisee's house, so she came there with an alabaster jar of perfume. ³⁸As she stood behind him at his feet weeping, she began to wet his feet with her tears. Then she wiped them with her hair, kissed them and poured perfume on them.

³⁹When the Pharisee who had invited him saw this, he said to himself, "If this man were a prophet, he would know who is touching him and what kind of woman she is—that she is a sinner."

⁴⁰Jesus answered him, "Simon, I have something to tell you."

"Tell me, teacher," he said.

---

a 22 The Greek word traditionally translated *leprosy* was used for various diseases affecting the skin.   *b* 27 Mal. 3:1

C an you think of anyone—some "bad" person—you'd be shocked to see with someone from your church youth group? Someone who would make you say, "I never thought I'd see Dylan with her." Then you understand why the Pharisee was so shocked when a known prostitute slipped into his house and wept at Jesus' feet. It's hard. You're told to keep away from the wrong kind of people. But you're also told to love everyone and witness for Jesus. How can you do both? Begin by praying every day for at least one of those "bad" teenagers. Then if God opens up the door to be a friend to him or her, give it a try.

{Luke 7:36–50}

INSTANT ACCESS

41 "Two people owed money to a certain moneylender. One owed him five hundred denarii,[a] and the other fifty. 42 Neither of them had the money to pay him back, so he forgave the debts of both. Now which of them will love him more?"

43 Simon replied, "I suppose the one who had the bigger debt forgiven."

"You have judged correctly," Jesus said.

44 Then he turned toward the woman and said to Simon, "Do you see this woman? I came into your house. You did not give me any water for my feet, but she wet my feet with her tears and wiped them with her hair. 45 You did not give me a kiss, but this woman, from the time I entered, has not stopped kissing my feet. 46 You did not put oil on my head, but she has poured perfume on my feet. 47 Therefore, I tell you, her many sins have been forgiven—as her great love has shown. But whoever has been forgiven little loves little."

48 Then Jesus said to her, "Your sins are forgiven."

49 The other guests began to say among themselves, "Who is this who even forgives sins?"

50 Jesus said to the woman, "Your faith has saved you; go in peace."

The Parable of the Sower

8 After this, Jesus traveled about from one town and village to another, proclaiming the good news of the kingdom of God. The Twelve were with him, 2 and also some women who had been cured of evil spirits and diseases: Mary (called Magdalene) from whom seven demons had come out; 3 Joanna the wife of Chuza, the manager of Herod's household; Susanna; and many others. These women were helping to support them out of their own means.

4 While a large crowd was gathering and people were coming to Jesus from town after town, he told this parable: 5 "A farmer went out to sow his seed. As he was scattering the seed, some fell along the path; it was trampled on, and the birds ate it up. 6 Some fell on rocky ground, and when it came up, the plants withered because they had no moisture. 7 Other seed fell among thorns, which grew up with it and choked the plants. 8 Still other seed fell on good soil. It came up and yielded a crop, a hundred times more than was sown."

When he said this, he called out, "Whoever has ears to hear, let them hear."

9 His disciples asked him what this parable meant. 10 He said, "The knowledge of the secrets of the kingdom of God has been given to you, but to others I speak in parables, so that,

---

[a] 41 A denarius was the usual daily wage of a day laborer (see Matt. 20:2).

" 'though seeing, they may
    not see;
  though hearing, they may not
    understand.'[a]

11 "This is the meaning of the parable: The seed is the word of God. 12 Those along the path are the ones who hear, and then the devil comes and takes away the word from their hearts, so that they may not believe and be saved. 13 Those on the rocky ground are the ones who receive the word with joy when they hear it, but they have no root. They believe for a while, but in the time of testing they fall away. 14 The seed that fell among thorns stands for those who hear, but as they go on their way they are choked by life's worries, riches and pleasures, and they do not mature. 15 But the seed on good soil stands for those with a noble and good heart, who hear the word, retain it, and by persevering produce a crop.

A Lamp on a Stand

16 "No one lights a lamp and hides it in a clay jar or puts it under a bed. Instead, they put it on a stand, so that those who come in can see the light. 17 For there is nothing hidden that will not be disclosed, and nothing concealed that will not be known or brought out into the open. 18 Therefore consider carefully how you listen. Whoever has will be given more; whoever does not have, even what they think they have will be taken from them."

Jesus' Mother and Brothers

19 Now Jesus' mother and brothers came to see him, but they were not able to get near him because of the crowd. 20 Someone told him, "Your mother and brothers are standing outside, wanting to see you."

21 He replied, "My mother and brothers are those who hear God's word and put it into practice."

Jesus Calms the Storm

22 One day Jesus said to his disciples, "Let us go over to the other side of the lake." So they got into a boat and set out. 23 As they sailed, he fell asleep. A squall came down on the lake, so that the boat was being swamped, and they were in great danger.

24 The disciples went and woke him, saying, "Master, Master, we're going to drown!"

He got up and rebuked the wind and the raging waters; the storm subsided, and all was calm. 25 "Where is your faith?" he asked his disciples.

In fear and amazement they asked one another, "Who is this? He commands even the winds and the water, and they obey him."

Jesus Restores a Demon-Possessed Man

26 They sailed to the region of the Gerasenes,[b] which is across the lake from Galilee. 27 When Jesus stepped ashore, he was met by a demon-possessed man from the town. For a long time this man had not worn clothes or lived in a house, but had lived in the tombs. 28 When he saw Jesus, he cried out and fell at his feet, shouting at the top of his voice, "What do you want with me, Jesus, Son of the Most High God? I beg you, don't torture me!" 29 For Jesus had commanded the impure spirit to come out of the man. Many times it had seized him, and though he was chained hand and foot and kept under guard, he had broken his chains and had been driven by the demon into solitary places.

30 Jesus asked him, "What is your name?"

"Legion," he replied, because many demons had gone into him. 31 And they begged Jesus repeatedly not to order them to go into the Abyss.

32 A large herd of pigs was feeding there on the hillside. The demons begged Jesus to let them go into the pigs, and he gave them permission. 33 When the demons came out of the man, they went into the pigs, and the herd rushed down the steep bank into the lake and was drowned.

---

[a] 10 Isaiah 6:9   [b] 26 Some manuscripts *Gadarenes*; other manuscripts *Gergesenes*; also in verse 37

34 When those tending the pigs saw what had happened, they ran off and reported this in the town and countryside, 35 and the people went out to see what had happened. When they came to Jesus, they found the man from whom the demons had gone out, sitting at Jesus' feet, dressed and in his right mind; and they were afraid. 36 Those who had seen it told the people how the demon-possessed man had been cured. 37 Then all the people of the region of the Gerasenes asked Jesus to leave them, because they were overcome with fear. So he got into the boat and left.

38 The man from whom the demons had gone out begged to go with him, but Jesus sent him away, saying, 39 "Return home and tell how much God has done for you." So the man went away and told all over town how much Jesus had done for him.

Jesus Raises a Dead Girl and Heals a Sick Woman

40 Now when Jesus returned, a crowd welcomed him, for they were all expecting him. 41 Then a man named Jairus, a synagogue leader, came and fell at Jesus' feet, pleading with him to come to his house 42 because his only daughter, a girl of about twelve, was dying.

As Jesus was on his way, the crowds almost crushed him. 43 And a woman was there who had been subject to bleeding for twelve years,[a] but no one could heal her. 44 She came up behind him and touched the edge of his cloak, and immediately her bleeding stopped.

45 "Who touched me?" Jesus asked.

When they all denied it, Peter said, "Master, the people are crowding and pressing against you."

46 But Jesus said, "Someone touched me; I know that power has gone out from me."

47 Then the woman, seeing that she could not go unnoticed, came trembling and fell at his feet. In the presence of all the people, she told why she had touched him and how she had been instantly

healed. 48 Then he said to her, "Daughter, your faith has healed you. Go in peace."

49 While Jesus was still speaking, someone came from the house of Jairus, the synagogue leader. "Your daughter is dead," he said. "Don't bother the teacher anymore."

50 Hearing this, Jesus said to Jairus, "Don't be afraid; just believe, and she will be healed."

51 When he arrived at the house of Jairus, he did not let anyone go in with him except Peter, John and James, and the child's father and mother. 52 Meanwhile, all the people were wailing and mourning for her. "Stop wailing," Jesus said. "She is not dead but asleep."

53 They laughed at him, knowing that she was dead. 54 But he took her by the hand and said, "My child, get up!" 55 Her spirit returned, and at once she stood up. Then Jesus told them to give her something to eat. 56 Her parents were astonished, but he ordered them not to tell anyone what had happened.

Jesus Sends Out the Twelve

9 When Jesus had called the Twelve together, he gave them power and authority to drive out all demons and to cure diseases, 2 and he sent them out to proclaim the kingdom of God and to heal the sick. 3 He told them: "Take nothing for the journey—no staff, no bag, no bread, no money, no extra shirt. 4 Whatever house you enter, stay there until you leave that town. 5 If people do not welcome you, leave their town and shake the dust off your feet as a testimony against them." 6 So they set out and went from village to village, proclaiming the good news and healing people everywhere.

7 Now Herod the tetrarch heard about all that was going on. And he was perplexed because some were saying that John had been raised from the dead, 8 others that Elijah had appeared, and still others that one of the prophets of long ago had come back to life. 9 But Herod said, "I beheaded John. Who, then, is this I hear such things about?" And he tried to see him.

---

[a] 43 Many manuscripts years, and she had spent all she had on doctors

Jesus Feeds the Five Thousand

¹⁰When the apostles returned, they reported to Jesus what they had done. Then he took them with him and they withdrew by themselves to a town called Bethsaida, ¹¹but the crowds learned about it and followed him. He welcomed them and spoke to them about the kingdom of God, and healed those who needed healing.

¹²Late in the afternoon the Twelve came to him and said, "Send the crowd away so they can go to the surrounding villages and countryside and find food and lodging, because we are in a remote place here."

¹³He replied, "You give them something to eat."

They answered, "We have only five loaves of bread and two fish—unless we go and buy food for all this crowd." ¹⁴(About five thousand men were there.)

But he said to his disciples, "Have them sit down in groups of about fifty each." ¹⁵The disciples did so, and everyone sat down. ¹⁶Taking the five loaves and the two fish and looking up to heaven, he gave thanks and broke them. Then he gave them to the disciples to distribute to the people. ¹⁷They all ate and were satisfied, and the disciples picked up twelve basketfuls of broken pieces that were left over.

Peter Declares That Jesus Is the Messiah

¹⁸Once when Jesus was praying in private and his disciples were with him, he asked them, "Who do the crowds say I am?"

¹⁹They replied, "Some say John the Baptist; others say Elijah; and still others, that one of the prophets of long ago has come back to life."

²⁰"But what about you?" he asked. "Who do you say I am?"

Peter answered, "God's Messiah."

Jesus Predicts His Death

²¹Jesus strictly warned them not to tell this to anyone. ²²And he said, "The Son of Man must suffer many things and be rejected by the elders, the chief priests and the teachers of the law, and he must be killed and on the third day be raised to life."

²³Then he said to them all: "Whoever wants to be my disciple must deny themselves and take up their cross daily and follow me. ²⁴For whoever wants to save their life will lose it, but whoever loses their life for me will save it. ²⁵What good is it for someone to gain the whole world, and yet lose or forfeit their very self? ²⁶Whoever is ashamed of me and my words, the Son of Man will be ashamed of them when he comes in his glory and in the glory of the Father and of the holy angels.

²⁷"Truly I tell you, some who are standing here will not taste death before they see the kingdom of God."

The Transfiguration

²⁸About eight days after Jesus said this, he took Peter, John and James with him and went up onto a mountain to pray. ²⁹As he was praying, the appearance of his face changed, and his clothes became as bright as a flash of lightning. ³⁰Two men, Moses and Elijah, appeared in glorious splendor, talking with Jesus. ³¹They spoke about his departure,[a] which he was about to bring to fulfillment at Jerusalem. ³²Peter and his companions were very sleepy, but when they became fully awake, they saw his glory and the two men standing with him. ³³As the men were leaving Jesus, Peter said to him, "Master, it is good for us to be here. Let us put up three shelters—one for you, one for Moses and one for Elijah." (He did not know what he was saying.)

³⁴While he was speaking, a cloud appeared and covered them, and they were afraid as they entered the cloud. ³⁵A voice came from the cloud, saying, "This is my Son, whom I have chosen; listen to him." ³⁶When the voice had spoken, they found that Jesus was alone. The disciples kept this to themselves and did not tell anyone at that time what they had seen.

[a] 31 Greek *exodus*

Jesus Heals a Demon-Possessed Boy

37 The next day, when they came down from the mountain, a large crowd met him. 38 A man in the crowd called out, "Teacher, I beg you to look at my son, for he is my only child. 39 A spirit seizes him and he suddenly screams; it throws him into convulsions so that he foams at the mouth. It scarcely ever leaves him and is destroying him. 40 I begged your disciples to drive it out, but they could not."

41 "You unbelieving and perverse generation," Jesus replied, "how long shall I stay with you and put up with you? Bring your son here."

42 Even while the boy was coming, the demon threw him to the ground in a convulsion. But Jesus rebuked the impure spirit, healed the boy and gave him back to his father. 43 And they were all amazed at the greatness of God.

Jesus Predicts His Death a Second Time

While everyone was marveling at all that Jesus did, he said to his disciples, 44 "Listen carefully to what I am about to tell you: The Son of Man is going to be delivered into the hands of men." 45 But they did not understand what this meant. It was hidden from them, so that they did not grasp it, and they were afraid to ask him about it.

46 An argument started among the disciples as to which of them would be the greatest. 47 Jesus, knowing their thoughts, took a little child and had him stand beside him. 48 Then he said to them, "Whoever welcomes this little child in my name welcomes me; and whoever welcomes me welcomes the one who sent me. For it is the one who is least among you all who is the greatest."

49 "Master," said John, "we saw someone driving out demons in your name and we tried to stop him, because he is not one of us."

50 "Do not stop him," Jesus said, "for whoever is not against you is for you."

Samaritan Opposition

51 As the time approached for him to be taken up to heaven, Jesus resolutely set out for Jerusalem. 52 And he sent messengers on ahead, who went into a Samaritan village to get things ready for him; 53 but the people there did not welcome him, because he was heading for Jerusalem. 54 When the disciples James and John saw this, they asked, "Lord, do you want us to call fire down from heaven to destroy them*a*?" 55 But Jesus turned and rebuked them. 56 Then he and his disciples went to another village.

The Cost of Following Jesus

57 As they were walking along the road, a man said to him, "I will follow you wherever you go."

58 Jesus replied, "Foxes have dens and birds have nests, but the Son of Man has no place to lay his head."

59 He said to another man, "Follow me." But he replied, "Lord, first let me go and bury my father."

60 Jesus said to him, "Let the dead bury their own dead, but you go and proclaim the kingdom of God."

61 Still another said, "I will follow you, Lord; but first let me go back and say goodbye to my family."

62 Jesus replied, "No one who puts a hand to the plow and looks back is fit for service in the kingdom of God."

Jesus Sends Out the Seventy-Two

10 After this the Lord appointed seventy-two*b* others and sent them two by two ahead of him to every town and place where he was about to go. 2 He told them, "The harvest is plentiful, but the workers are few. Ask the Lord of the harvest, therefore, to send out workers into his harvest field. 3 Go! I am sending you out like lambs among wolves. 4 Do not take a purse or bag or sandals; and do not greet anyone on the road.

5 "When you enter a house, first say, 'Peace to this house.' 6 If someone who

---

a 54 Some manuscripts *them, just as Elijah did*   *b* 1 Some manuscripts *seventy*; also in verse 17

promotes peace is there, your peace will rest on them; if not, it will return to you. 7 Stay there, eating and drinking whatever they give you, for the worker deserves his wages. Do not move around from house to house.

8 "When you enter a town and are welcomed, eat what is offered to you. 9 Heal the sick who are there and tell them, 'The kingdom of God has come near to you.' 10 But when you enter a town and are not welcomed, go into its streets and say, 11 'Even the dust of your town we wipe from our feet as a warning to you. Yet be sure of this: The kingdom of God has come near.' 12 I tell you, it will be more bearable on that day for Sodom than for that town.

13 "Woe to you, Chorazin! Woe to you, Bethsaida! For if the miracles that were performed in you had been performed in Tyre and Sidon, they would have repented long ago, sitting in sackcloth and ashes. 14 But it will be more bearable for Tyre and Sidon at the judgment than for you. 15 And you, Capernaum, will you be lifted to the heavens? No, you will go down to Hades.*a*

16 "Whoever listens to you listens to me; whoever rejects you rejects me; but whoever rejects me rejects him who sent me."

17 The seventy-two returned with joy and said, "Lord, even the demons submit to us in your name."

18 He replied, "I saw Satan fall like lightning from heaven. 19 I have given you authority to trample on snakes and scorpions and to overcome all the power of the enemy; nothing will harm you. 20 However, do not rejoice that the spirits submit to you, but rejoice that your names are written in heaven."

21 At that time Jesus, full of joy through the Holy Spirit, said, "I praise you, Father, Lord of heaven and earth, because you have hidden these things from the wise and learned, and revealed them to little children. Yes, Father, for this is what you were pleased to do.

22 "All things have been committed to me by my Father. No one knows who the Son is except the Father, and no one knows who the Father is except the Son

and those to whom the Son chooses to reveal him."

23 Then he turned to his disciples and said privately, "Blessed are the eyes that see what you see. 24 For I tell you that many prophets and kings wanted to see what you see but did not see it, and to hear what you hear but did not hear it."

The Parable of the Good Samaritan

25 On one occasion an expert in the law stood up to test Jesus. "Teacher," he asked, "what must I do to inherit eternal life?"

26 "What is written in the Law?" he replied. "How do you read it?"

27 He answered, " 'Love the Lord your God with all your heart and with all your soul and with all your strength and with all your mind'*b*; and, 'Love your neighbor as yourself.'*c*"

28 "You have answered correctly," Jesus replied. "Do this and you will live."

29 But he wanted to justify himself, so he asked Jesus, "And who is my neighbor?"

30 In reply Jesus said: "A man was going down from Jerusalem to Jericho, when he was attacked by robbers. They stripped him of his clothes, beat him and went away, leaving him half dead. 31 A priest happened to be going down the same road, and when he saw the man, he passed by on the other side. 32 So too, a Levite, when he came to the place and saw him, passed by on the other side. 33 But a Samaritan, as he traveled, came where the man was; and when he saw him, he took pity on him. 34 He went to him and bandaged his wounds, pouring on oil and wine. Then he put the man on his own donkey, brought him to an inn and took care of him. 35 The next day he took out two denarii*d* and gave them to the innkeeper. 'Look after him,' he said, 'and when I return, I will reimburse you for any extra expense you may have.'

36 "Which of these three do you think was a neighbor to the man who fell into the hands of robbers?"

---

a 15 That is, the realm of the dead   *b* 27 Deut. 6:5   *c* 27 Lev. 19:18   *d* 35 A denarius was the usual daily wage of a day laborer (see Matt. 20:2).

³⁷ The expert in the law replied, "The one who had mercy on him."

Jesus told him, "Go and do likewise."

At the Home of Martha and Mary

³⁸ As Jesus and his disciples were on their way, he came to a village where a woman named Martha opened her home to him. ³⁹ She had a sister called Mary, who sat at the Lord's feet listening to what he said. ⁴⁰ But Martha was distracted by all the preparations that had to be made. She came to him and asked, "Lord, don't you care that my sister has left me to do the work by myself? Tell her to help me!"

⁴¹ "Martha, Martha," the Lord answered, "you are worried and upset about many things, ⁴² but few things are needed—or indeed only one.ª Mary has chosen what is better, and it will not be taken away from her."

Jesus' Teaching on Prayer

11 One day Jesus was praying in a certain place. When he finished, one of his disciples said to him, "Lord, teach us to pray, just as John taught his disciples."

² He said to them, "When you pray, say:

" 'Father,ᵇ
hallowed be your name,
your kingdom come.ᶜ
³ Give us each day our daily bread.
⁴ Forgive us our sins,

ª 42 Some manuscripts *but only one thing is needed*   ᵇ 2 Some manuscripts *Our Father in heaven*   ᶜ 2 Some manuscripts *come. May your will be done on earth as it is in heaven.*

TO THE POINT

Love Your Neighbor

The story of the Good Samaritan (Luke 10:25–37) teaches that being a neighbor is more than being friendly or being nice. Being a neighbor means being sensitive to others' problems and willing to help. Anyone who passes by a person in need is not being a neighbor. You may not feel safe stopping on a lonely highway to help change a tire. But you can call the police to let them know someone needs help.

It's even more personal with friends. Do you know anyone who is hurting or has problems? Then right now that person is your neighbor. You can be a Good Samaritan to him or her, as you "love your neighbor as yourself" (Leviticus 19:18).

for we also forgive everyone who
sins against us.ᵃ
And lead us not into temptation.ᵇ'"

5 Then Jesus said to them, "Suppose you have a friend, and you go to him at midnight and say, 'Friend, lend me three loaves of bread; 6 a friend of mine on a journey has come to me, and I have no food to offer him.' 7 And suppose the one inside answers, 'Don't bother me. The door is already locked, and my children and I are in bed. I can't get up and give you anything.' 8 I tell you, even though he will not get up and give you the bread because of friendship, yet because of your shameless audacityᶜ he will surely get up and give you as much as you need.

9 "So I say to you: Ask and it will be given to you; seek and you will find; knock and the door will be opened to you. 10 For everyone who asks receives; the one who seeks finds; and to the one who knocks, the door will be opened.

11 "Which of you fathers, if your son asks forᵈ a fish, will give him a snake instead? 12 Or if he asks for an egg, will give him a scorpion? 13 If you then, though you are evil, know how to give good gifts to your children, how much more will your Father in heaven give the Holy Spirit to those who ask him!"

Jesus and Beelzebul

14 Jesus was driving out a demon that was mute. When the demon left, the man who had been mute spoke, and the crowd was amazed. 15 But some of them said, "By Beelzebul, the prince of demons, he is driving out demons." 16 Others tested him by asking for a sign from heaven.

17 Jesus knew their thoughts and said to them: "Any kingdom divided against itself will be ruined, and a house divided against itself will fall. 18 If Satan is divided against himself, how can his kingdom stand? I say this because you claim that I drive out demons by Beelzebul. 19 Now if I drive out demons by Beelzebul, by whom do your followers drive them out? So then, they will be your judges. 20 But if I drive

---

INSTANT ACCESS

Does God hear your prayers? How can you know? Even if you get what you asked for, how can you know if it's an answer to prayer or if it would have happened anyway? This passage gives Jesus' answer. He asks you to think about what God is like. Is God a neighbor, who only gives you what you want so you will go away (Luke 11:5–8)? No, God is a good Father, who gives good gifts to his children. He has already given those who pray to him the best gift—his Holy Spirit (Luke 11:9–13). He will also answer all your prayers. Don't expect a yes to every request. Like every good father, there are times the Lord says no.

{Luke 11:5–13}

---

out demons by the finger of God, then the kingdom of God has come upon you.

21 "When a strong man, fully armed, guards his own house, his possessions are safe. 22 But when someone stronger attacks and overpowers him, he takes away the armor in which the man trusted and divides up his plunder.

23 "Whoever is not with me is against me, and whoever does not gather with me scatters.

ᵃ 4 Greek everyone who is indebted to us   ᵇ 4 Some manuscripts temptation, but deliver us from the evil one
ᶜ 8 Or yet to preserve his good name   ᵈ 11 Some manuscripts for bread, will give him a stone? Or if he asks for

24"When an impure spirit comes out of a person, it goes through arid places seeking rest and does not find it. Then it says, 'I will return to the house I left.' 25When it arrives, it finds the house swept clean and put in order. 26Then it goes and takes seven other spirits more wicked than itself, and they go in and live there. And the final condition of that person is worse than the first."

27As Jesus was saying these things, a woman in the crowd called out, "Blessed is the mother who gave you birth and nursed you."

28He replied, "Blessed rather are those who hear the word of God and obey it."

The Sign of Jonah

29As the crowds increased, Jesus said, "This is a wicked generation. It asks for a sign, but none will be given it except the sign of Jonah. 30For as Jonah was a sign to the Ninevites, so also will the Son of Man be to this generation. 31The Queen of the South will rise at the judgment with the people of this generation and condemn them, for she came from the ends of the earth to listen to Solomon's wisdom; and now something greater than Solomon is here. 32The men of Nineveh will stand up at the judgment with this generation and condemn it, for they repented at the preaching of Jonah; and now something greater than Jonah is here.

The Lamp of the Body

33"No one lights a lamp and puts it in a place where it will be hidden, or under a bowl. Instead they put it on its stand, so that those who come in may see the light. 34Your eye is the lamp of your body. When your eyes are healthy,*a* your whole body also is full of light. But when they are unhealthy,*b* your body also is full of darkness. 35See to it, then, that the light within you is not darkness. 36Therefore, if your whole body is full of light, and no part of it dark, it will be just as full of light as when a lamp shines its light on you."

Woes on the Pharisees and the Experts in the Law

37When Jesus had finished speaking, a Pharisee invited him to eat with him; so he went in and reclined at the table. 38But the Pharisee was surprised when he noticed that Jesus did not first wash before the meal.

39Then the Lord said to him, "Now then, you Pharisees clean the outside of the cup and dish, but inside you are full of greed and wickedness. 40You foolish people! Did not the one who made the outside make the inside also? 41But now as for what is inside you—be generous to the poor, and everything will be clean for you.

42"Woe to you Pharisees, because you give God a tenth of your mint, rue and all other kinds of garden herbs, but you neglect justice and the love of God. You should have practiced the latter without leaving the former undone.

43"Woe to you Pharisees, because you love the most important seats in the synagogues and respectful greetings in the marketplaces.

44"Woe to you, because you are like unmarked graves, which people walk over without knowing it."

45One of the experts in the law answered him, "Teacher, when you say these things, you insult us also."

46Jesus replied, "And you experts in the law, woe to you, because you load people down with burdens they can hardly carry, and you yourselves will not lift one finger to help them.

47"Woe to you, because you build tombs for the prophets, and it was your ancestors who killed them. 48So you testify that you approve of what your ancestors did; they killed the prophets, and you build their tombs. 49Because of this, God in his wisdom said, 'I will send them prophets and apostles, some of whom they will kill and others they will persecute.' 50Therefore this generation will be held responsible for the blood of all the prophets that has been shed since the beginning of the world, 51from the

---

a 34 The Greek for *healthy* here implies *generous*.   *b 34* The Greek for *unhealthy* here implies *stingy*.

blood of Abel to the blood of Zechariah, who was killed between the altar and the sanctuary. Yes, I tell you, this generation will be held responsible for it all.

52 "Woe to you experts in the law, because you have taken away the key to knowledge. You yourselves have not entered, and you have hindered those who were entering."

53 When Jesus went outside, the Pharisees and the teachers of the law began to oppose him fiercely and to besiege him with questions, 54 waiting to catch him in something he might say.

Warnings and Encouragements

12 Meanwhile, when a crowd of many thousands had gathered, so that they were trampling on one another, Jesus began to speak first to his disciples, saying: "Be[a] on your guard against the yeast of the Pharisees, which is hypocrisy. 2 There is nothing concealed that will not be disclosed, or hidden that will not be made known. 3 What you have said in the dark will be heard in the daylight, and what you have whispered in the ear in the inner rooms will be proclaimed from the roofs.

4 "I tell you, my friends, do not be afraid of those who kill the body and after that can do no more. 5 But I will show you whom you should fear: Fear him who, after your body has been killed, has authority to throw you into hell. Yes, I tell you, fear him. 6 Are not five sparrows sold for two pennies? Yet not one of them is forgotten by God. 7 Indeed, the very hairs of your head are all numbered. Don't be afraid; you are worth more than many sparrows.

8 "I tell you, whoever publicly acknowledges me before others, the Son of Man will also acknowledge before the angels of God. 9 But whoever disowns me before others will be disowned before the angels of God. 10 And everyone who speaks a word against the Son of Man will be forgiven, but anyone who blasphemes against the Holy Spirit will not be forgiven.

11 "When you are brought before synagogues, rulers and authorities, do not worry about how you will defend yourselves or what you will say, 12 for the Holy Spirit will teach you at that time what you should say."

The Parable of the Rich Fool

13 Someone in the crowd said to him, "Teacher, tell my brother to divide the inheritance with me."

14 Jesus replied, "Man, who appointed me a judge or an arbiter between you?" 15 Then he said to them, "Watch out! Be on your guard against all kinds of greed; life does not consist in an abundance of possessions."

16 And he told them this parable: "The ground of a certain rich man yielded an abundant harvest. 17 He thought to himself, 'What shall I do? I have no place to store my crops.'

18 "Then he said, 'This is what I'll do. I will tear down my barns and build bigger ones, and there I will store my surplus grain. 19 And I'll say to myself, "You have plenty of grain laid up for many years. Take life easy; eat, drink and be merry."'

20 "But God said to him, 'You fool! This very night your life will be demanded from you. Then who will get what you have prepared for yourself?'

21 "This is how it will be with whoever stores up things for themselves but is not rich toward God."

Do Not Worry

22 Then Jesus said to his disciples: "Therefore I tell you, do not worry about your life, what you will eat; or about your body, what you will wear. 23 For life is more than food, and the body more than clothes. 24 Consider the ravens: They do not sow or reap, they have no storeroom or barn; yet God feeds them. And how much more valuable you are than birds! 25 Who of you by worrying can add a single hour to your life[b]? 26 Since you cannot do this very little thing, why do you worry about the rest?

a 1 Or speak to his disciples, saying: "First of all, be   b 25 Or single cubit to your height

> I am a worrier. I worry about how I look. I worry about my clothes—you know, labels and style. I'm worried I won't measure up to the other kids at school. I'm worried people won't like me. I'm worried I'll say something stupid. Is there a way to stop worrying? **>> Lauren**

Dear Jordan

Dear Lauren,

This kind of anxiety is stressful and exhausting. Worry can be like a snowball rolling downhill. It just keeps getting bigger faster. Before long, there's nothing that doesn't get worried about.

Make a list of what is truly important in your life. Start with the most important person or thing and write down four more. Chances are your top 5 will include some of these: God, Mom, Dad, your dog and your best friend. Further down the list you'll come to hobbies, nice clothes, lots of friends. If your list is something like this, it shows you know what's truly important.

Do you know what Jesus taught about worrying? "Do not worry about your life, what you will eat; or about your body, what you will wear. For life is more than food, and the body more than clothes … Who of you by worrying can add a single hour to your life? Since you cannot do this very little thing, why do you worry about the rest?" (Luke 12:22–26).

Jesus encouraged people to keep focused on God. That keeps your perspective where it should be. The Apostle Paul understood this. He said at times he had much in his life, and at other times he had been hungry. But he had learned to be content in either situation (Philippians 4:11–13).

Jordan

27 "Consider how the wild flowers grow. They do not labor or spin. Yet I tell you, not even Solomon in all his splendor was dressed like one of these. 28 If that is how God clothes the grass of the field, which is here today, and tomorrow is thrown into the fire, how much more will he clothe you—you of little faith! 29 And do not set your heart on what you will eat or drink; do not worry about it. 30 For the pagan world runs after all such things, and your Father knows that you need them. 31 But seek his kingdom, and these things will be given to you as well.

32 "Do not be afraid, little flock, for your Father has been pleased to give you the kingdom. 33 Sell your possessions and give to the poor. Provide purses for yourselves that will not wear out, a treasure in heaven that will never fail, where no thief comes near and no moth destroys. 34 For where your treasure is, there your heart will be also.

Watchfulness

35 "Be dressed ready for service and keep your lamps burning, 36 like servants waiting for their master to return from a wedding banquet, so that when he comes and knocks they can immediately open the door for him. 37 It will be good for those servants whose master finds them watching when he comes. Truly I tell you, he will dress himself to serve, will have them recline at the table and will come and wait on them. 38 It will be good for those servants whose master finds them ready, even if he comes in the middle of the night or toward daybreak. 39 But understand this: If the owner of the house had known at what hour the thief was coming, he would not have let his house be broken into. 40 You also must be ready, because the Son of Man will come at an hour when you do not expect him."

41 Peter asked, "Lord, are you telling this parable to us, or to everyone?"

42 The Lord answered, "Who then is the faithful and wise manager, whom the master puts in charge of his servants to give them their food allowance at the proper time? 43 It will be good for that servant whom the master finds doing so

when he returns. 44 Truly I tell you, he will put him in charge of all his possessions. 45 But suppose the servant says to himself, 'My master is taking a long time in coming,' and he then begins to beat the other servants, both men and women, and to eat and drink and get drunk. 46 The master of that servant will come on a day when he does not expect him and at an hour he is not aware of. He will cut him to pieces and assign him a place with the unbelievers.

47 "The servant who knows the master's will and does not get ready or does not do what the master wants will be beaten with many blows. 48 But the one who does not know and does things deserving punishment will be beaten with few blows. From everyone who has been given much, much will be demanded; and from the one who has been entrusted with much, much more will be asked.

Not Peace but Division

49 "I have come to bring fire on the earth, and how I wish it were already kindled! 50 But I have a baptism to undergo, and what constraint I am under until it is completed! 51 Do you think I came to bring peace on earth? No, I tell you, but division. 52 From now on there will be five in one family divided against each other, three against two and two against three. 53 They will be divided, father against son and son against father, mother against daughter and daughter against mother, mother-in-law against daughter-in-law and daughter-in-law against mother-in-law."

Interpreting the Times

54 He said to the crowd: "When you see a cloud rising in the west, immediately you say, 'It's going to rain,' and it does. 55 And when the south wind blows, you say, 'It's going to be hot,' and it is. 56 Hypocrites! You know how to interpret the appearance of the earth and the sky. How is it that you don't know how to interpret this present time?

57 "Why don't you judge for yourselves what is right? 58 As you are going with your adversary to the magistrate, try hard to be reconciled on the way, or your adver-

sary may drag you off to the judge, and the judge turn you over to the officer, and the officer throw you into prison. 59 I tell you, you will not get out until you have paid the last penny."

Repent or Perish

13 Now there were some present at that time who told Jesus about the Galileans whose blood Pilate had mixed with their sacrifices. 2 Jesus answered, "Do you think that these Galileans were worse sinners than all the other Galileans because they suffered this way? 3 I tell you, no! But unless you repent, you too will all perish. 4 Or those eighteen who died when the tower in Siloam fell on them—do you think they were more guilty than all the others living in Jerusalem? 5 I tell you, no! But unless you repent, you too will all perish."

6 Then he told this parable: "A man had a fig tree growing in his vineyard, and he went to look for fruit on it but did not find any. 7 So he said to the man who took care of the vineyard, 'For three years now I've been coming to look for fruit on this fig tree and haven't found any. Cut it down! Why should it use up the soil?'

8 " 'Sir,' the man replied, 'leave it alone for one more year, and I'll dig around it and fertilize it. 9 If it bears fruit next year, fine! If not, then cut it down.' "

Jesus Heals a Crippled Woman on the Sabbath

10 On a Sabbath Jesus was teaching in one of the synagogues, 11 and a woman was there who had been crippled by a spirit for eighteen years. She was bent over and could not straighten up at all. 12 When Jesus saw her, he called her forward and said to her, "Woman, you are set free from your infirmity." 13 Then he put his hands on her, and immediately she straightened up and praised God.

14 Indignant because Jesus had healed on the Sabbath, the synagogue leader said to the people, "There are six days for work. So come and be healed on those days, not on the Sabbath."

15 The Lord answered him, "You hypocrites! Doesn't each of you on the Sabbath untie your ox or donkey from the stall and lead it out to give it water? 16 Then should not this woman, a daughter of Abraham, whom Satan has kept bound for eighteen long years, be set free on the Sabbath day from what bound her?"

17 When he said this, all his opponents were humiliated, but the people were delighted with all the wonderful things he was doing.

The Parables of the Mustard Seed and the Yeast

18 Then Jesus asked, "What is the kingdom of God like? What shall I compare it to? 19 It is like a mustard seed, which a man took and planted in his garden. It grew and became a tree, and the birds perched in its branches."

20 Again he asked, "What shall I compare the kingdom of God to? 21 It is like yeast that a woman took and mixed into about sixty pounds[a] of flour until it worked all through the dough."

The Narrow Door

22 Then Jesus went through the towns and villages, teaching as he made his way to Jerusalem. 23 Someone asked him, "Lord, are only a few people going to be saved?"

He said to them, 24 "Make every effort to enter through the narrow door, because many, I tell you, will try to enter and will not be able to. 25 Once the owner of the house gets up and closes the door, you will stand outside knocking and pleading, 'Sir, open the door for us.'

"But he will answer, 'I don't know you or where you come from.'

26 "Then you will say, 'We ate and drank with you, and you taught in our streets.'

27 "But he will reply, 'I don't know you or where you come from. Away from me, all you evildoers!'

28 "There will be weeping there, and gnashing of teeth, when you see Abraham, Isaac and Jacob and all the prophets in the kingdom of God, but you yourselves

---

a 21 Or about 27 kilograms

thrown out. [29] People will come from east and west and north and south, and will take their places at the feast in the kingdom of God. [30] Indeed there are those who are last who will be first, and first who will be last."

Jesus' Sorrow for Jerusalem

[31] At that time some Pharisees came to Jesus and said to him, "Leave this place and go somewhere else. Herod wants to kill you."

[32] He replied, "Go tell that fox, 'I will keep on driving out demons and healing people today and tomorrow, and on the third day I will reach my goal.' [33] In any case, I must press on today and tomorrow and the next day—for surely no prophet can die outside Jerusalem!

[34] "Jerusalem, Jerusalem, you who kill the prophets and stone those sent to you, how often I have longed to gather your children together, as a hen gathers her chicks under her wings, and you were not willing. [35] Look, your house is left to you desolate. I tell you, you will not see me again until you say, 'Blessed is he who comes in the name of the Lord.'[a]"

Jesus at a Pharisee's House

14 One Sabbath, when Jesus went to eat in the house of a prominent Pharisee, he was being carefully watched. [2] There in front of him was a man suffering from abnormal swelling of his body. [3] Jesus asked the Pharisees and experts in the law, "Is it lawful to heal on the Sabbath or not?" [4] But they remained silent. So taking hold of the man, he healed him and sent him on his way.

[5] Then he asked them, "If one of you has a child[b] or an ox that falls into a well on the Sabbath day, will you not immediately pull it out?" [6] And they had nothing to say.

[7] When he noticed how the guests picked the places of honor at the table, he told them this parable: [8] "When someone invites you to a wedding feast, do not take the place of honor, for a person more distinguished than you may have

been invited. [9] If so, the host who invited both of you will come and say to you, 'Give this person your seat.' Then, humiliated, you will have to take the least important place. [10] But when you are invited, take the lowest place, so that when your host comes, he will say to you, 'Friend, move up to a better place.' Then you will be honored in the presence of all the other guests. [11] For all those who exalt themselves will be humbled, and those who humble themselves will be exalted."

[12] Then Jesus said to his host, "When you give a luncheon or dinner, do not invite your friends, your brothers or sisters, your relatives, or your rich neighbors; if you do, they may invite you back and so you will be repaid. [13] But when you give a banquet, invite the poor, the crippled, the lame, the blind, [14] and you will be blessed. Although they cannot repay you, you will be repaid at the resurrection of the righteous."

The Parable of the Great Banquet

[15] When one of those at the table with him heard this, he said to Jesus, "Blessed is the one who will eat at the feast in the kingdom of God."

[16] Jesus replied: "A certain man was preparing a great banquet and invited many guests. [17] At the time of the banquet he sent his servant to tell those who had been invited, 'Come, for everything is now ready.'

[18] "But they all alike began to make excuses. The first said, 'I have just bought a field, and I must go and see it. Please excuse me.'

[19] "Another said, 'I have just bought five yoke of oxen, and I'm on my way to try them out. Please excuse me.'

[20] "Still another said, 'I just got married, so I can't come.'

[21] "The servant came back and reported this to his master. Then the owner of the house became angry and ordered his servant, 'Go out quickly into the streets and alleys of the town and bring in the poor, the crippled, the blind and the lame.'

---

[a] 35 Psalm 118:26   [b] 5 Some manuscripts *donkey*

Have you ever helped someone in math who later "didn't have time" when you needed help in history? Situations like that can upset you; they aren't fair. Most friendships are based, at least in part, on payback. You help each other out. You pick each other for teams. You email each other to check on school assignments. Adults do the same thing. They invite a couple over for dinner and expect to be invited back. But should all your relationships be based on payback? Jesus says no. You should try to do good things for people who can't pay you back. When you do, the payback you get will come from God!

{Luke 14:12–14}

²² " 'Sir,' the servant said, 'what you ordered has been done, but there is still room.'

²³ "Then the master told his servant, 'Go out to the roads and country lanes and compel them to come in, so that my house will be full. ²⁴ I tell you, not one of those who were invited will get a taste of my banquet.' "

The Cost of Being a Disciple

²⁵ Large crowds were traveling with Jesus, and turning to them he said: ²⁶ "If anyone comes to me and does not hate father and mother, wife and children, brothers and sisters—yes, even their own life—such a person cannot be my disciple. ²⁷ And whoever does not carry their cross and follow me cannot be my disciple.

²⁸ "Suppose one of you wants to build a tower. Won't you first sit down and estimate the cost to see if you have enough money to complete it? ²⁹ For if you lay the foundation and are not able to finish it, everyone who sees it will ridicule you, ³⁰ saying, 'This person began to build and wasn't able to finish.'

³¹ "Or suppose a king is about to go to war against another king. Won't he first sit down and consider whether he is able with ten thousand men to oppose the one coming against him with twenty thousand? ³² If he is not able, he will send a delegation while the other is still a long way off and will ask for terms of peace. ³³ In the same way, those of you who do not give up everything you have cannot be my disciples.

³⁴ "Salt is good, but if it loses its saltiness, how can it be made salty again? ³⁵ It is fit neither for the soil nor for the manure pile; it is thrown out.

"Whoever has ears to hear, let them hear."

The Parable of the Lost Sheep

15 Now the tax collectors and sinners were all gathering around to hear Jesus. ² But the Pharisees and the teachers of the law muttered, "This man welcomes sinners and eats with them."

³ Then Jesus told them this parable: ⁴ "Suppose one of you has a hundred sheep and loses one of them. Doesn't he leave the ninety-nine in the open country and go after the lost sheep until he finds it? ⁵ And when he finds it, he joyfully puts it on his shoulders ⁶ and goes home. Then he calls his friends and neighbors together and says, 'Rejoice with me; I have found my lost sheep.' ⁷ I tell you that in the same way there will be more rejoicing in heaven over one sinner who repents than over ninety-nine righteous persons who do not need to repent.

The Parable of the Lost Coin

⁸"Or suppose a woman has ten silver coinsᵃ and loses one. Doesn't she light a lamp, sweep the house and search carefully until she finds it? ⁹And when she finds it, she calls her friends and neighbors together and says, 'Rejoice with me; I have found my lost coin.' ¹⁰In the same way, I tell you, there is rejoicing in the presence of the angels of God over one sinner who repents."

The Parable of the Lost Son

¹¹Jesus continued: "There was a man who had two sons. ¹²The younger one said to his father, 'Father, give me my share of the estate.' So he divided his property between them.

¹³"Not long after that, the younger son got together all he had, set off for a distant country and there squandered his wealth in wild living. ¹⁴After he had spent everything, there was a severe famine in that whole country, and he began to be in need. ¹⁵So he went and hired himself out to a citizen of that country, who sent him to his fields to feed pigs. ¹⁶He longed to fill his stomach with the pods that the pigs were eating, but no one gave him anything.

¹⁷"When he came to his senses, he said, 'How many of my father's hired servants have food to spare, and here I am starving to death! ¹⁸I will set out and go back to my father and say to him: Father, I have sinned against heaven and against you. ¹⁹I am no longer worthy to be called your son; make me like one of your hired servants.' ²⁰So he got up and went to his father.

"But while he was still a long way off, his father saw him and was filled with compassion for him; he ran to his son, threw his arms around him and kissed him.

²¹"The son said to him, 'Father, I have sinned against heaven and against you. I am no longer worthy to be called your son.'

²²"But the father said to his servants, 'Quick! Bring the best robe and put it on

≫ INSTANT ACCESS

Some people think women didn't count in Bible times. They say the husband paid a "bride price" to the father to "buy" his wife. She was just property! But brides weren't bought and sold. The bride price compensated the father for the loss of his precious daughter. And then the father gave his daughter a dowry, so she wouldn't enter the marriage as a pauper, but as a partner. In Jesus' day the dowry was often made up of coins, with a hole drilled in the center so they could be strung like beads. The woman in this story was probably upset because she had lost a dowry coin. As today, women from Bible times were important.

{Luke 15:8–10}

him. Put a ring on his finger and sandals on his feet. ²³Bring the fattened calf and kill it. Let's have a feast and celebrate. ²⁴For this son of mine was dead and is alive again; he was lost and is found.' So they began to celebrate.

²⁵"Meanwhile, the older son was in the field. When he came near the house, he heard music and dancing. ²⁶So he called one of the servants and asked him what was going on. ²⁷'Your brother has come,'

ᵃ 8 Greek ten drachmas, each worth about a day's wages

he replied, 'and your father has killed the fattened calf because he has him back safe and sound.'

28 "The older brother became angry and refused to go in. So his father went out and pleaded with him. 29 But he answered his father, 'Look! All these years I've been slaving for you and never disobeyed your orders. Yet you never gave me even a young goat so I could celebrate with my friends. 30 But when this son of yours who has squandered your property with prostitutes comes home, you kill the fattened calf for him!'

31 " 'My son,' the father said, 'you are always with me, and everything I have is yours. 32 But we had to celebrate and be glad, because this brother of yours was dead and is alive again; he was lost and is found.' "

The Parable of the Shrewd Manager

16 Jesus told his disciples: "There was a rich man whose manager was accused of wasting his possessions. 2 So he called him in and asked him, 'What is this I hear about you? Give an account of your management, because you cannot be manager any longer.'

3 "The manager said to himself, 'What shall I do now? My master is taking away my job. I'm not strong enough to dig, and I'm ashamed to beg— 4 I know what I'll do so that, when I lose my job here, people will welcome me into their houses.'

5 "So he called in each one of his master's debtors. He asked the first, 'How much do you owe my master?'

6 " 'Nine hundred gallons[a] of olive oil,' he replied.

"The manager told him, 'Take your bill, sit down quickly, and make it four hundred and fifty.'

7 "Then he asked the second, 'And how much do you owe?'

" 'A thousand bushels[b] of wheat,' he replied.

"He told him, 'Take your bill and make it eight hundred.'

8 "The master commended the dishonest manager because he had acted shrewdly. For the people of this world are more shrewd in dealing with their own kind than are the people of the light. 9 I tell you, use worldly wealth to gain friends for yourselves, so that when it is gone, you will be welcomed into eternal dwellings.

10 "Whoever can be trusted with very little can also be trusted with much, and whoever is dishonest with very little will also be dishonest with much. 11 So if you have not been trustworthy in handling worldly wealth, who will trust you with true riches? 12 And if you have not been trustworthy with someone else's property, who will give you property of your own?

13 "No one can serve two masters. Either you will hate the one and love the other, or you will be devoted to the one and despise the other. You cannot serve both God and money."

14 The Pharisees, who loved money, heard all this and were sneering at Jesus. 15 He said to them, "You are the ones who justify yourselves in the eyes of others, but God knows your hearts. What people value highly is detestable in God's sight.

Additional Teachings

16 "The Law and the Prophets were proclaimed until John. Since that time, the good news of the kingdom of God is being preached, and everyone is forcing their way into it. 17 It is easier for heaven and earth to disappear than for the least stroke of a pen to drop out of the Law.

18 "Anyone who divorces his wife and marries another woman commits adultery, and the man who marries a divorced woman commits adultery.

The Rich Man and Lazarus

19 "There was a rich man who was dressed in purple and fine linen and lived in luxury every day. 20 At his gate was laid a beggar named Lazarus, covered with sores 21 and longing to eat what fell from the rich man's table. Even the dogs came and licked his sores.

---

a 6 Or about 3,000 liters   b 7 Or about 30 tons

22 "The time came when the beggar died and the angels carried him to Abraham's side. The rich man also died and was buried. 23 In Hades, where he was in torment, he looked up and saw Abraham far away, with Lazarus by his side. 24 So he called to him, 'Father Abraham, have pity on me and send Lazarus to dip the tip of his finger in water and cool my tongue, because I am in agony in this fire.'

25 "But Abraham replied, 'Son, remember that in your lifetime you received your good things, while Lazarus received bad things, but now he is comforted here and you are in agony. 26 And besides all this, between us and you a great chasm has been set in place, so that those who want to go from here to you cannot, nor can anyone cross over from there to us.'

27 "He answered, 'Then I beg you, father, send Lazarus to my family, 28 for I have five brothers. Let him warn them, so that they will not also come to this place of torment.'

29 "Abraham replied, 'They have Moses and the Prophets; let them listen to them.'

30 " 'No, father Abraham,' he said, 'but if someone from the dead goes to them, they will repent.'

31 "He said to him, 'If they do not listen to Moses and the Prophets, they will not be convinced even if someone rises from the dead.' "

Sin, Faith, Duty

17 Jesus said to his disciples: "Things that cause people to stumble

TO THE POINT

Death Isn't the End

Some people think that when a person dies, that's the end. The dead are just gone. Forever. But they're wrong.

Jesus made it very clear that death is not the end. He told a story about what happened after a rich man and a beggar died (Luke 16:19–31).

+ People remain conscious after their bodies die (Luke 16:25).

+ People have some kind of body after they die (Luke 16:24).

+ People can feel pleasure or pain after they die (Luke 16:25).

There really is no end for any human being. You will either live forever with God or live forever separated from him.

are bound to come, but woe to anyone through whom they come. ²It would be better for them to be thrown into the sea with a millstone tied around their neck than to cause one of these little ones to stumble. ³So watch yourselves.

"If your brother or sister[a] sins against you, rebuke them; and if they repent, forgive them. ⁴Even if they sin against you seven times in a day and seven times come back to you saying 'I repent,' you must forgive them."

⁵The apostles said to the Lord, "Increase our faith!"

⁶He replied, "If you have faith as small as a mustard seed, you can say to this mulberry tree, 'Be uprooted and planted in the sea,' and it will obey you.

⁷"Suppose one of you has a servant plowing or looking after the sheep. Will he say to the servant when he comes in from the field, 'Come along now and sit down to eat'? ⁸Won't he rather say, 'Prepare my supper, get yourself ready and wait on me while I eat and drink; after that you may eat and drink'? ⁹Will he thank the servant because he did what he was told to do? ¹⁰So you also, when you have done everything you were told to do, should say, 'We are unworthy servants; we have only done our duty.'"

Jesus Heals Ten Men With Leprosy

¹¹Now on his way to Jerusalem, Jesus traveled along the border between Samaria and Galilee. ¹²As he was going into a village, ten men who had leprosy[b] met him. They stood at a distance ¹³and called out in a loud voice, "Jesus, Master, have pity on us!"

¹⁴When he saw them, he said, "Go, show yourselves to the priests." And as they went, they were cleansed.

¹⁵One of them, when he saw he was healed, came back, praising God in a loud voice. ¹⁶He threw himself at Jesus' feet and thanked him—and he was a Samaritan.

¹⁷Jesus asked, "Were not all ten cleansed? Where are the other nine? ¹⁸Has no one returned to give praise to God except this foreigner?" ¹⁹Then he said to him, "Rise and go; your faith has made you well."

The Coming of the Kingdom of God

²⁰Once, on being asked by the Pharisees when the kingdom of God would come, Jesus replied, "The coming of the kingdom of God is not something that can be observed, ²¹nor will people say, 'Here it is,' or 'There it is,' because the kingdom of God is in your midst."[c]

²²Then he said to his disciples, "The time is coming when you will long to see one of the days of the Son of Man, but you will not see it. ²³People will tell you, 'There he is!' or 'Here he is!' Do not go running off after them. ²⁴For the Son of Man in his day[d] will be like the lightning, which flashes and lights up the sky from one end to the other. ²⁵But first he must suffer many things and be rejected by this generation.

²⁶"Just as it was in the days of Noah, so also will it be in the days of the Son of Man. ²⁷People were eating, drinking, marrying and being given in marriage up to the day Noah entered the ark. Then the flood came and destroyed them all.

²⁸"It was the same in the days of Lot. People were eating and drinking, buying and selling, planting and building. ²⁹But the day Lot left Sodom, fire and sulfur rained down from heaven and destroyed them all.

³⁰"It will be just like this on the day the Son of Man is revealed. ³¹On that day no one who is on the housetop, with possessions inside, should go down to get them. Likewise, no one in the field should go back for anything. ³²Remember Lot's wife! ³³Whoever tries to keep their life will lose it, and whoever loses their life will preserve it. ³⁴I tell you, on that night two people will be in one bed; one will be taken and the other left. ³⁵Two women

---

[a] 3 The Greek word for *brother or sister* (*adelphos*) refers here to a fellow disciple, whether man or woman.   [b] 12 The Greek word traditionally translated *leprosy* was used for various diseases affecting the skin.   [c] 21 Or *is within you*   [d] 24 Some manuscripts do not have *in his day*.

will be grinding grain together; one will be taken and the other left." [36]a

37 "Where, Lord?" they asked.

He replied, "Where there is a dead body, there the vultures will gather."

The Parable of the Persistent Widow

18 Then Jesus told his disciples a parable to show them that they should always pray and not give up. 2He said: "In a certain town there was a judge who neither feared God nor cared what people thought. 3And there was a widow in that town who kept coming to him with the plea, 'Grant me justice against my adversary.'

4 "For some time he refused. But finally he said to himself, 'Even though I don't fear God or care what people think, 5yet because this widow keeps bothering me, I will see that she gets justice, so that she won't eventually come and attack me!' "

6And the Lord said, "Listen to what the unjust judge says. 7And will not God bring about justice for his chosen ones, who cry out to him day and night? Will he keep putting them off? 8I tell you, he will see that they get justice, and quickly. However, when the Son of Man comes, will he find faith on the earth?"

The Parable of the Pharisee and the Tax Collector

9To some who were confident of their own righteousness and looked down on everyone else, Jesus told this parable: 10"Two men went up to the temple to pray, one a Pharisee and the other a tax collector. 11The Pharisee stood by himself and prayed: 'God, I thank you that I am not like other people—robbers, evildoers, adulterers—or even like this tax collector. 12I fast twice a week and give a tenth of all I get.'

13"But the tax collector stood at a distance. He would not even look up to heaven, but beat his breast and said, 'God, have mercy on me, a sinner.'

14"I tell you that this man, rather than the other, went home justified before

>> INSTANT ACCESS

Most of your days are pretty routine. School, homework, food, friends, family. And you expect the next day to be pretty much the same—unless you take Jesus' promised return seriously. Then you might wake up and wonder if today is the day Jesus will come back. Or you might go to bed and wonder if Jesus will give you your wake-up call instead of Mom. Most people are so busy with their own affairs they ignore the fact that Jesus is coming again. People who expect Jesus are a lot more careful about the choices they make. They know he's coming back soon and that everything they do matters.

{Luke 17:24–30}

God. For all those who exalt themselves will be humbled, and those who humble themselves will be exalted."

The Little Children and Jesus

15People were also bringing babies to Jesus for him to place his hands on them. When the disciples saw this, they rebuked them. 16But Jesus called the children to him and said, "Let the little children come to me, and do not hinder them, for the kingdom of God belongs to

---

a 36 Some manuscripts include here words similar to Matt. 24:40.

such as these. 17 Truly I tell you, anyone who will not receive the kingdom of God like a little child will never enter it."

The Rich and the Kingdom of God

18 A certain ruler asked him, "Good teacher, what must I do to inherit eternal life?"

19 "Why do you call me good?" Jesus answered. "No one is good—except God alone. 20 You know the commandments: 'You shall not commit adultery, you shall not murder, you shall not steal, you shall not give false testimony, honor your father and mother.'[a]"

21 "All these I have kept since I was a boy," he said.

22 When Jesus heard this, he said to him, "You still lack one thing. Sell everything you have and give to the poor, and you will have treasure in heaven. Then come, follow me."

23 When he heard this, he became very sad, because he was very wealthy. 24 Jesus looked at him and said, "How hard it is for the rich to enter the kingdom of God! 25 Indeed, it is easier for a camel to go through the eye of a needle than for someone who is rich to enter the kingdom of God."

26 Those who heard this asked, "Who then can be saved?"

27 Jesus replied, "What is impossible with man is possible with God."

28 Peter said to him, "We have left all we had to follow you!"

29 "Truly I tell you," Jesus said to them, "no one who has left home or wife or brothers or sisters or parents or children for the sake of the kingdom of God 30 will fail to receive many times as much in this age, and in the age to come eternal life."

Jesus Predicts His Death a Third Time

31 Jesus took the Twelve aside and told them, "We are going up to Jerusalem, and everything that is written by the prophets about the Son of Man will be fulfilled. 32 He will be delivered over to the Gentiles. They will mock him, insult him and spit on him; 33 they will flog him and kill him. On the third day he will rise again."

34 The disciples did not understand any of this. Its meaning was hidden from them, and they did not know what he was talking about.

A Blind Beggar Receives His Sight

35 As Jesus approached Jericho, a blind man was sitting by the roadside begging. 36 When he heard the crowd going by, he asked what was happening. 37 They told him, "Jesus of Nazareth is passing by."

---

[a] 20 Exodus 20:12-16; Deut. 5:16-20

PANORAMA

Ignored.

Jesus showed loving interest in all kinds of people—the poor, the oppressed, women, children. Jesus has time for you.

{LUKE}

38He called out, "Jesus, Son of David, have mercy on me!"

39Those who led the way rebuked him and told him to be quiet, but he shouted all the more, "Son of David, have mercy on me!"

40Jesus stopped and ordered the man to be brought to him. When he came near, Jesus asked him, **41**"What do you want me to do for you?"

"Lord, I want to see," he replied.

42Jesus said to him, "Receive your sight; your faith has healed you." **43**Immediately he received his sight and followed Jesus, praising God. When all the people saw it, they also praised God.

Zacchaeus the Tax Collector

19 Jesus entered Jericho and was passing through. **2**A man was there by the name of Zacchaeus; he was a chief tax collector and was wealthy. **3**He wanted to see who Jesus was, but because he was short he could not see over the crowd. **4**So he ran ahead and climbed a sycamore-fig tree to see him, since Jesus was coming that way.

5When Jesus reached the spot, he looked up and said to him, "Zacchaeus, come down immediately. I must stay at your house today." **6**So he came down at once and welcomed him gladly.

7All the people saw this and began to mutter, "He has gone to be the guest of a sinner."

8But Zacchaeus stood up and said to the Lord, "Look, Lord! Here and now I give half of my possessions to the poor, and if I have cheated anybody out of anything, I will pay back four times the amount."

9Jesus said to him, "Today salvation has come to this house, because this man, too, is a son of Abraham. **10**For the Son of Man came to seek and to save the lost."

The Parable of the Ten Minas

11While they were listening to this, he went on to tell them a parable, because he was near Jerusalem and the people thought that the kingdom of God was going to appear at once. **12**He said: "A man

Are you ready to haul out your TV, bike, laptop and various collections for a garage sale? No? Then how do you get around Luke 18:22? To understand a verse you need to see *who* the verse is directed to, *what* the context is and *how* the verse applies. Who: Jesus was speaking to a rich man. What: The rich man thought he could get to heaven by doing good things. How: Deep down the rich man put money first, not God. You don't have to get rid of all your stuff. This verse is important. Don't let anything you own or anything you want become more important to you than pleasing the Lord.

INSTANT ACCESS

{Luke 18:22}

of noble birth went to a distant country to have himself appointed king and then to return. **13**So he called ten of his servants and gave them ten minas.*a* 'Put this money to work,' he said, 'until I come back.'

14"But his subjects hated him and sent a delegation after him to say, 'We don't want this man to be our king.'

15"He was made king, however, and returned home. Then he sent for the servants to whom he had given the money, in order to find out what they had gained with it.

---

a 13 A mina was about three months' wages.

16 "The first one came and said, 'Sir, your mina has earned ten more.'

17 " 'Well done, my good servant!' his master replied. 'Because you have been trustworthy in a very small matter, take charge of ten cities.'

18 "The second came and said, 'Sir, your mina has earned five more.'

19 "His master answered, 'You take charge of five cities.'

20 "Then another servant came and said, 'Sir, here is your mina; I have kept it laid away in a piece of cloth. 21 I was afraid of you, because you are a hard man. You take out what you did not put in and reap what you did not sow.'

22 "His master replied, 'I will judge you by your own words, you wicked servant! You knew, did you, that I am a hard man, taking out what I did not put in, and reaping what I did not sow? 23 Why then didn't you put my money on deposit, so that when I came back, I could have collected it with interest?'

24 "Then he said to those standing by, 'Take his mina away from him and give it to the one who has ten minas.'

25 " 'Sir,' they said, 'he already has ten!'

26 "He replied, 'I tell you that to everyone who has, more will be given, but as for the one who has nothing, even what they have will be taken away. 27 But those enemies of mine who did not want me to be king over them—bring them here and kill them in front of me.' "

Jesus Comes to Jerusalem as King

28 After Jesus had said this, he went on ahead, going up to Jerusalem. 29 As he approached Bethphage and Bethany at the hill called the Mount of Olives, he sent two of his disciples, saying to them, 30 "Go to the village ahead of you, and as you enter it, you will find a colt tied there, which no one has ever ridden. Untie it and bring it here. 31 If anyone asks you, 'Why are you untying it?' say, 'The Lord needs it.' "

32 Those who were sent ahead went and found it just as he had told them.

33 As they were untying the colt, its owners asked them, "Why are you untying the colt?"

34 They replied, "The Lord needs it."

35 They brought it to Jesus, threw their cloaks on the colt and put Jesus on it. 36 As he went along, people spread their cloaks on the road.

37 When he came near the place where the road goes down the Mount of Olives, the whole crowd of disciples began joyfully to praise God in loud voices for all the miracles they had seen:

38 "Blessed is the king who comes in the name of the Lord!"[a]

"Peace in heaven and glory in the highest!"

39 Some of the Pharisees in the crowd said to Jesus, "Teacher, rebuke your disciples!"

40 "I tell you," he replied, "if they keep quiet, the stones will cry out."

41 As he approached Jerusalem and saw the city, he wept over it 42 and said, "If you, even you, had only known on this day what would bring you peace—but now it is hidden from your eyes. 43 The days will come upon you when your enemies will build an embankment against you and encircle you and hem you in on every side. 44 They will dash you to the ground, you and the children within your walls. They will not leave one stone on another, because you did not recognize the time of God's coming to you."

Jesus at the Temple

45 When Jesus entered the temple courts, he began to drive out those who were selling. 46 "It is written," he said to them, " 'My house will be a house of prayer'[b]; but you have made it 'a den of robbers.'[c]"

47 Every day he was teaching at the temple. But the chief priests, the teachers of the law and the leaders among the people were trying to kill him. 48 Yet they could not find any way to do it, because all the people hung on his words.

---

[a] 38 Psalm 118:26   [b] 46 Isaiah 56:7   [c] 46 Jer. 7:11

The Authority of Jesus Questioned

20 One day as Jesus was teaching the people in the temple courts and proclaiming the good news, the chief priests and the teachers of the law, together with the elders, came up to him. ² "Tell us by what authority you are doing these things," they said. "Who gave you this authority?"

³ He replied, "I will also ask you a question. Tell me: ⁴ John's baptism — was it from heaven, or of human origin?"

⁵ They discussed it among themselves and said, "If we say, 'From heaven,' he will ask, 'Why didn't you believe him?' ⁶ But if we say, 'Of human origin,' all the people will stone us, because they are persuaded that John was a prophet."

⁷ So they answered, "We don't know where it was from."

⁸ Jesus said, "Neither will I tell you by what authority I am doing these things."

The Parable of the Tenants

⁹ He went on to tell the people this parable: "A man planted a vineyard, rented it to some farmers and went away for a long time. ¹⁰ At harvest time he sent a servant to the tenants so they would give him some of the fruit of the vineyard. But the tenants beat him and sent him away empty-handed. ¹¹ He sent another servant, but that one also they beat and treated shamefully and sent away empty-handed. ¹² He sent still a third, and they wounded him and threw him out.

¹³ "Then the owner of the vineyard said, 'What shall I do? I will send my son, whom I love; perhaps they will respect him.'

¹⁴ "But when the tenants saw him, they talked the matter over. 'This is the heir,' they said. 'Let's kill him, and the inheritance will be ours.' ¹⁵ So they threw him out of the vineyard and killed him.

"What then will the owner of the vineyard do to them? ¹⁶ He will come and kill those tenants and give the vineyard to others."

When the people heard this, they said, "God forbid!"

≫ INSTANT ACCESS

Do you ever wonder why everyone doesn't believe in Jesus? Where else can you get eternal life as a free gift? One answer is found in this parable. When the owner of the vineyard sends his son, the tenants kill him. They just aren't willing to submit. They want to be their own god. Deep down people know that if they accept Christ as Savior, they no longer belong to themselves. They belong to the Lord. And they don't like the thought of not being their own boss. They want control. They want final say. But one thing they don't understand: giving control to Jesus frees people to be much more than they could ever be on their own.

{Luke 20:9–19}

---

¹⁷ Jesus looked directly at them and asked, "Then what is the meaning of that which is written:

" 'The stone the builders rejected
has become the cornerstone'[a]?

¹⁸ Everyone who falls on that stone will be broken to pieces; anyone on whom it falls will be crushed."

---

[a] 17 Psalm 118:22

[19] The teachers of the law and the chief priests looked for a way to arrest him immediately, because they knew he had spoken this parable against them. But they were afraid of the people.

Paying Taxes to Caesar

[20] Keeping a close watch on him, they sent spies, who pretended to be sincere. They hoped to catch Jesus in something he said, so that they might hand him over to the power and authority of the governor. [21] So the spies questioned him: "Teacher, we know that you speak and teach what is right, and that you do not show partiality but teach the way of God in accordance with the truth. [22] Is it right for us to pay taxes to Caesar or not?"

[23] He saw through their duplicity and said to them, [24] "Show me a denarius. Whose image and inscription are on it?"

"Caesar's," they replied.

[25] He said to them, "Then give back to Caesar what is Caesar's, and to God what is God's."

[26] They were unable to trap him in what he had said there in public. And astonished by his answer, they became silent.

The Resurrection and Marriage

[27] Some of the Sadducees, who say there is no resurrection, came to Jesus with a question. [28] "Teacher," they said, "Moses wrote for us that if a man's brother dies and leaves a wife but no children, the man must marry the widow and raise up offspring for his brother. [29] Now there were seven brothers. The first one married a woman and died childless. [30] The second [31] and then the third married her, and in the same way the seven died, leaving no children. [32] Finally, the woman died too. [33] Now then, at the resurrection whose wife will she be, since the seven were married to her?"

[34] Jesus replied, "The people of this age marry and are given in marriage. [35] But those who are considered worthy of taking part in the age to come and in the resurrection from the dead will neither marry nor be given in marriage, [36] and they can no longer die; for they are like the angels. They are God's children, since they are children of the resurrection. [37] But in the account of the burning bush, even Moses showed that the dead rise, for he calls the Lord 'the God of Abraham, and the God of Isaac, and the God of Jacob.'[a] [38] He is not the God of the dead, but of the living, for to him all are alive."

[39] Some of the teachers of the law responded, "Well said, teacher!" [40] And no one dared to ask him any more questions.

Whose Son Is the Messiah?

[41] Then Jesus said to them, "Why is it said that the Messiah is the son of David? [42] David himself declares in the Book of Psalms:

" 'The Lord said to my Lord:
"Sit at my right hand
[43] until I make your enemies
a footstool for your feet." '[b]

[44] David calls him 'Lord.' How then can he be his son?"

Warning Against the Teachers of the Law

[45] While all the people were listening, Jesus said to his disciples, [46] "Beware of the teachers of the law. They like to walk around in flowing robes and love to be greeted with respect in the marketplaces and have the most important seats in the synagogues and the places of honor at banquets. [47] They devour widows' houses and for a show make lengthy prayers. These men will be punished most severely."

The Widow's Offering

21 As Jesus looked up, he saw the rich putting their gifts into the temple treasury. [2] He also saw a poor widow put in two very small copper coins. [3] "Truly I tell you," he said, "this poor widow has put in more than all the others. [4] All these people gave their gifts out of their wealth; but she out of her poverty put in all she had to live on."

---

a 37 Exodus 3:6   *b* 43 Psalm 110:1

The Destruction of the Temple and Signs of the End Times

5 Some of his disciples were remarking about how the temple was adorned with beautiful stones and with gifts dedicated to God. But Jesus said, 6 "As for what you see here, the time will come when not one stone will be left on another; every one of them will be thrown down."

7 "Teacher," they asked, "when will these things happen? And what will be the sign that they are about to take place?"

8 He replied: "Watch out that you are not deceived. For many will come in my name, claiming, 'I am he,' and, 'The time is near.' Do not follow them. 9 When you hear of wars and uprisings, do not be frightened. These things must happen first, but the end will not come right away."

10 Then he said to them: "Nation will rise against nation, and kingdom against kingdom. 11 There will be great earthquakes, famines and pestilences in various places, and fearful events and great signs from heaven.

12 "But before all this, they will seize you and persecute you. They will hand you over to synagogues and put you in prison, and you will be brought before kings and governors, and all on account of my name. 13 And so you will bear testimony to me. 14 But make up your mind not to worry beforehand how you will defend yourselves. 15 For I will give you words and wisdom that none of your adversaries will be able to resist or contradict. 16 You will be betrayed even by parents, brothers and sisters, relatives and friends, and they

TO THE POINT

Dark before Dawn

Three Gospels report Jesus' teachings about the future (Matthew 24–25; Mark 13; Luke 21)—that it holds wars, revolutions, famines, and earthquakes. The Gospel writers also warn that at times Christians will be persecuted for their faith. But in the end Jesus will return with "power and great glory" (Luke 21:27).

How are you to live through the dark times before Jesus comes and brings the dawn?

+ Don't be frightened of terrible events (Luke 21:9).
+ Don't worry about how to defend yourself when persecuted (Luke 21:14).
+ Be careful to stay faithful to the Lord (Luke 21:34–36).

God doesn't promise you an easy life here, but he does promise to watch over you.

will put some of you to death. ¹⁷Everyone will hate you because of me. ¹⁸But not a hair of your head will perish. ¹⁹Stand firm, and you will win life.

²⁰"When you see Jerusalem being surrounded by armies, you will know that its desolation is near. ²¹Then let those who are in Judea flee to the mountains, let those in the city get out, and let those in the country not enter the city. ²²For this is the time of punishment in fulfillment of all that has been written. ²³How dreadful it will be in those days for pregnant women and nursing mothers! There will be great distress in the land and wrath against this people. ²⁴They will fall by the sword and will be taken as prisoners to all the nations. Jerusalem will be trampled on by the Gentiles until the times of the Gentiles are fulfilled.

²⁵"There will be signs in the sun, moon and stars. On the earth, nations will be in anguish and perplexity at the roaring and tossing of the sea. ²⁶People will faint from terror, apprehensive of what is coming on the world, for the heavenly bodies will be shaken. ²⁷At that time they will see the Son of Man coming in a cloud with power and great glory. ²⁸When these things begin to take place, stand up and lift up your heads, because your redemption is drawing near."

²⁹He told them this parable: "Look at the fig tree and all the trees. ³⁰When they sprout leaves, you can see for yourselves and know that summer is near. ³¹Even so, when you see these things happening, you know that the kingdom of God is near.

³²"Truly I tell you, this generation will certainly not pass away until all these things have happened. ³³Heaven and earth will pass away, but my words will never pass away.

³⁴"Be careful, or your hearts will be weighed down with carousing, drunkenness and the anxieties of life, and that day will close on you suddenly like a trap.

³⁵For it will come on all those who live on the face of the whole earth. ³⁶Be always on the watch, and pray that you may be able to escape all that is about to happen, and that you may be able to stand before the Son of Man."

³⁷Each day Jesus was teaching at the temple, and each evening he went out to spend the night on the hill called the Mount of Olives, ³⁸and all the people came early in the morning to hear him at the temple.

Judas Agrees to Betray Jesus

22 Now the Festival of Unleavened Bread, called the Passover, was approaching, ²and the chief priests and the teachers of the law were looking for some way to get rid of Jesus, for they were afraid of the people. ³Then Satan entered Judas, called Iscariot, one of the Twelve. ⁴And Judas went to the chief priests and the officers of the temple guard and discussed with them how he might betray Jesus. ⁵They were delighted and agreed to give him money. ⁶He consented, and watched for an opportunity to hand Jesus over to them when no crowd was present.

> *I will give you words and wisdom that none of your adversaries will be able to resist or contradict.*
>
> **Luke 21:15**

The Last Supper

⁷Then came the day of Unleavened Bread on which the Passover lamb had to be sacrificed. ⁸Jesus sent Peter and John, saying, "Go and make preparations for us to eat the Passover."

⁹"Where do you want us to prepare for it?" they asked.

¹⁰He replied, "As you enter the city, a man carrying a jar of water will meet you. Follow him to the house that he enters, ¹¹and say to the owner of the house, 'The Teacher asks: Where is the guest room, where I may eat the Passover with my disciples?' ¹²He will show you a large room upstairs, all furnished. Make preparations there."

My parents say I have to put part of my allowance in the offering every week. I feel stupid putting it in because it can't possibly make a difference anyway. Do you agree?

>> Logan

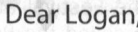

Dear Jordan

Dear Logan,

Giving is an interesting subject. Did you ever read about the poor widow in Luke 21 who put two tiny copper coins in the offering while all the rich people were putting in their large gifts? Jesus said, "Truly I tell you … this poor widow has put in more than all the others" (verse 3). The reason, he explained, was because she gave everything she had. The others gave a small portion of their great wealth.

Your offering may not be large, but it is a lot compared to what you have. Jesus sees your gift as generous. But remember, "God loves a cheerful giver" (2 Corinthians 9:7).

Jordan

¹³They left and found things just as Jesus had told them. So they prepared the Passover.

¹⁴When the hour came, Jesus and his apostles reclined at the table. ¹⁵And he said to them, "I have eagerly desired to eat this Passover with you before I suffer. ¹⁶For I tell you, I will not eat it again until it finds fulfillment in the kingdom of God."

¹⁷After taking the cup, he gave thanks and said, "Take this and divide it among you. ¹⁸For I tell you I will not drink again from the fruit of the vine until the kingdom of God comes."

¹⁹And he took bread, gave thanks and broke it, and gave it to them, saying, "This is my body given for you; do this in remembrance of me."

²⁰In the same way, after the supper he took the cup, saying, "This cup is the new covenant in my blood, which is poured out for you.ᵃ ²¹But the hand of him who is going to betray me is with mine on the table. ²²The Son of Man will go as it has been decreed. But woe to that man who betrays him!" ²³They began to question among themselves which of them it might be who would do this.

²⁴A dispute also arose among them as to which of them was considered to be greatest. ²⁵Jesus said to them, "The kings of the Gentiles lord it over them; and those who exercise authority over them call themselves Benefactors. ²⁶But you are not to be like that. Instead, the greatest among you should be like the youngest, and the one who rules like the one who serves. ²⁷For who is greater, the one who is at the table or the one who serves? Is it not the one who is at the table? But I am among you as one who serves. ²⁸You are those who have stood by me in my trials. ²⁹And I confer on you a kingdom, just as my Father conferred one on me, ³⁰so that you may eat and drink at my table in my kingdom and sit on thrones, judging the twelve tribes of Israel.

³¹"Simon, Simon, Satan has asked to sift all of you as wheat. ³²But I have prayed for you, Simon, that your faith may not fail. And when you have turned back, strengthen your brothers."

³³But he replied, "Lord, I am ready to go with you to prison and to death."

³⁴Jesus answered, "I tell you, Peter, before the rooster crows today, you will deny three times that you know me."

³⁵Then Jesus asked them, "When I sent you without purse, bag or sandals, did you lack anything?"

"Nothing," they answered.

³⁶He said to them, "But now if you have a purse, take it, and also a bag; and if you don't have a sword, sell your cloak and buy one. ³⁷It is written: 'And he was numbered with the transgressors'ᵇ; and I tell you that this must be fulfilled in me. Yes, what is written about me is reaching its fulfillment."

³⁸The disciples said, "See, Lord, here are two swords."

"That's enough!" he replied.

Jesus Prays on the Mount of Olives

³⁹Jesus went out as usual to the Mount of Olives, and his disciples followed him. ⁴⁰On reaching the place, he said to them, "Pray that you will not fall into temptation." ⁴¹He withdrew about a stone's throw beyond them, knelt down and prayed, ⁴²"Father, if you are willing, take this cup from me; yet not my will, but yours be done." ⁴³An angel from heaven appeared to him and strengthened him. ⁴⁴And being in anguish, he prayed more earnestly, and his sweat was like drops of blood falling to the ground.ᶜ

⁴⁵When he rose from prayer and went back to the disciples, he found them asleep, exhausted from sorrow. ⁴⁶"Why are you sleeping?" he asked them. "Get up and pray so that you will not fall into temptation."

Jesus Arrested

⁴⁷While he was still speaking a crowd came up, and the man who was called Judas, one of the Twelve, was leading them. He approached Jesus to kiss him, ⁴⁸but

---

ᵃ 19,20 Some manuscripts do not have *given for you . . . poured out for you.*   ᵇ 37 Isaiah 53:12   ᶜ 43,44 Many early manuscripts do not have verses 43 and 44.

Jesus asked him, "Judas, are you betraying the Son of Man with a kiss?"

⁴⁹When Jesus' followers saw what was going to happen, they said, "Lord, should we strike with our swords?" ⁵⁰And one of them struck the servant of the high priest, cutting off his right ear.

⁵¹But Jesus answered, "No more of this!" And he touched the man's ear and healed him.

⁵²Then Jesus said to the chief priests, the officers of the temple guard, and the elders, who had come for him, "Am I leading a rebellion, that you have come with swords and clubs? ⁵³Every day I was with you in the temple courts, and you did not lay a hand on me. But this is your hour— when darkness reigns."

Peter Disowns Jesus

⁵⁴Then seizing him, they led him away and took him into the house of the high priest. Peter followed at a distance. ⁵⁵And when some there had kindled a fire in the middle of the courtyard and had sat down together, Peter sat down with them. ⁵⁶A servant girl saw him seated there in the firelight. She looked closely at him and said, "This man was with him."

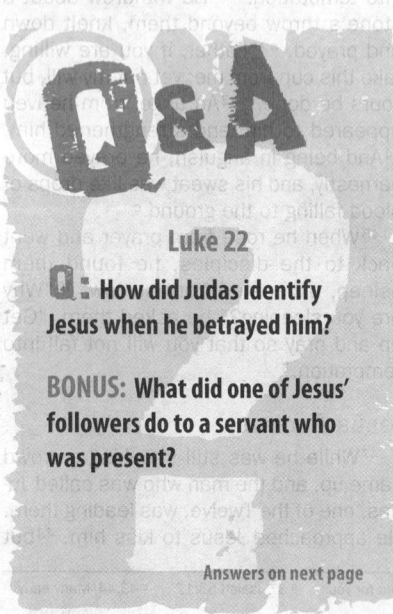

Luke 22

Q: How did Judas identify Jesus when he betrayed him?

BONUS: What did one of Jesus' followers do to a servant who was present?

Answers on next page

⁵⁷But he denied it. "Woman, I don't know him," he said.

⁵⁸A little later someone else saw him and said, "You also are one of them."

"Man, I am not!" Peter replied.

⁵⁹About an hour later another asserted, "Certainly this fellow was with him, for he is a Galilean."

⁶⁰Peter replied, "Man, I don't know what you're talking about!" Just as he was speaking, the rooster crowed. ⁶¹The Lord turned and looked straight at Peter. Then Peter remembered the word the Lord had spoken to him: "Before the rooster crows today, you will disown me three times." ⁶²And he went outside and wept bitterly.

The Guards Mock Jesus

⁶³The men who were guarding Jesus began mocking and beating him. ⁶⁴They blindfolded him and demanded, "Prophesy! Who hit you?" ⁶⁵And they said many other insulting things to him.

Jesus Before Pilate and Herod

⁶⁶At daybreak the council of the elders of the people, both the chief priests and the teachers of the law, met together, and Jesus was led before them. ⁶⁷"If you are the Messiah," they said, "tell us."

Jesus answered, "If I tell you, you will not believe me, ⁶⁸and if I asked you, you would not answer. ⁶⁹But from now on, the Son of Man will be seated at the right hand of the mighty God."

⁷⁰They all asked, "Are you then the Son of God?"

He replied, "You say that I am."

⁷¹Then they said, "Why do we need any more testimony? We have heard it from his own lips."

23 Then the whole assembly rose and led him off to Pilate. ²And they began to accuse him, saying, "We have found this man subverting our nation. He opposes payment of taxes to Caesar and claims to be Messiah, a king."

³So Pilate asked Jesus, "Are you the king of the Jews?"

"You have said so," Jesus replied.

⁴Then Pilate announced to the chief

priests and the crowd, "I find no basis for a charge against this man."

⁵But they insisted, "He stirs up the people all over Judea by his teaching. He started in Galilee and has come all the way here."

⁶On hearing this, Pilate asked if the man was a Galilean. ⁷When he learned that Jesus was under Herod's jurisdiction, he sent him to Herod, who was also in Jerusalem at that time.

⁸When Herod saw Jesus, he was greatly pleased, because for a long time he had been wanting to see him. From what he had heard about him, he hoped to see him perform a sign of some sort. ⁹He plied him with many questions, but Jesus gave him no answer. ¹⁰The chief priests and the teachers of the law were standing there, vehemently accusing him. ¹¹Then Herod and his soldiers ridiculed and mocked him. Dressing him in an elegant robe, they sent him back to Pilate. ¹²That day Herod and Pilate became friends—before this they had been enemies.

¹³Pilate called together the chief priests, the rulers and the people, ¹⁴and said to them, "You brought me this man as one who was inciting the people to rebellion. I have examined him in your presence and have found no basis for your charges against him. ¹⁵Neither has Herod, for he sent him back to us; as you can see, he has done nothing to deserve death. ¹⁶Therefore, I will punish him and then release him." [17]a

¹⁸But the whole crowd shouted, "Away with this man! Release Barabbas to us!" ¹⁹(Barabbas had been thrown into prison for an insurrection in the city, and for murder.)

²⁰Wanting to release Jesus, Pilate appealed to them again. ²¹But they kept shouting, "Crucify him! Crucify him!"

²²For the third time he spoke to them: "Why? What crime has this man committed? I have found in him no grounds for the death penalty. Therefore I will have him punished and then release him."

²³But with loud shouts they insistently

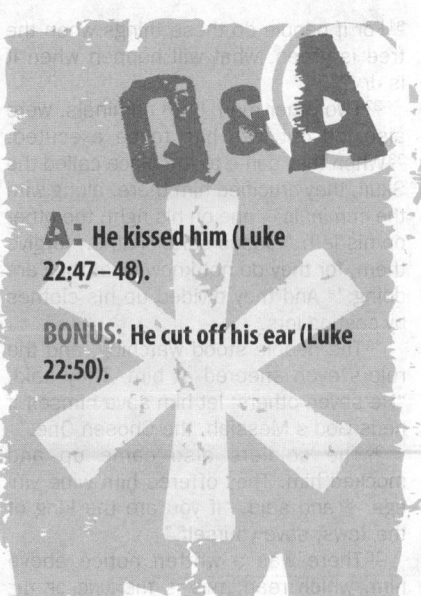

A: He kissed him (Luke 22:47–48).

BONUS: He cut off his ear (Luke 22:50).

demanded that he be crucified, and their shouts prevailed. ²⁴So Pilate decided to grant their demand. ²⁵He released the man who had been thrown into prison for insurrection and murder, the one they asked for, and surrendered Jesus to their will.

The Crucifixion of Jesus

²⁶As the soldiers led him away, they seized Simon from Cyrene, who was on his way in from the country, and put the cross on him and made him carry it behind Jesus. ²⁷A large number of people followed him, including women who mourned and wailed for him. ²⁸Jesus turned and said to them, "Daughters of Jerusalem, do not weep for me; weep for yourselves and for your children. ²⁹For the time will come when you will say, 'Blessed are the childless women, the wombs that never bore and the breasts that never nursed!' ³⁰Then

" 'they will say to the mountains, "Fall on us!"
and to the hills, "Cover us!" 'b

---

a 17 Some manuscripts include here words similar to Matt. 27:15 and Mark 15:6.   b 30 Hosea 10:8

31 For if people do these things when the tree is green, what will happen when it is dry?"

32 Two other men, both criminals, were also led out with him to be executed. 33 When they came to the place called the Skull, they crucified him there, along with the criminals—one on his right, the other on his left. 34 Jesus said, "Father, forgive them, for they do not know what they are doing."ᵃ And they divided up his clothes by casting lots.

35 The people stood watching, and the rulers even sneered at him. They said, "He saved others; let him save himself if he is God's Messiah, the Chosen One."

36 The soldiers also came up and mocked him. They offered him wine vinegar 37 and said, "If you are the king of the Jews, save yourself."

38 There was a written notice above him, which read: THIS IS THE KING OF THE JEWS.

39 One of the criminals who hung there hurled insults at him: "Aren't you the Messiah? Save yourself and us!"

40 But the other criminal rebuked him. "Don't you fear God," he said, "since you are under the same sentence? 41 We are punished justly, for we are getting what our deeds deserve. But this man has done nothing wrong."

42 Then he said, "Jesus, remember me when you come into your kingdom.ᵇ"

43 Jesus answered him, "Truly I tell you, today you will be with me in paradise."

The Death of Jesus

44 It was now about noon, and darkness came over the whole land until three in the afternoon, 45 for the sun stopped shining. And the curtain of the temple was torn in two. 46 Jesus called out with a loud voice, "Father, into your hands I commit my spirit."ᶜ When he had said this, he breathed his last.

47 The centurion, seeing what had happened, praised God and said, "Surely this was a righteous man." 48 When all the people who had gathered to witness this sight saw what took place, they beat their breasts and went away. 49 But all those who knew him, including the women who had followed him from Galilee, stood at a distance, watching these things.

The Burial of Jesus

50 Now there was a man named Joseph, a member of the Council, a good and upright man, 51 who had not consented to their decision and action. He came from the Judean town of Arimathea, and he himself was waiting for the kingdom of God. 52 Going to Pilate, he asked for Jesus' body. 53 Then he took it down, wrapped it in linen cloth and placed it in a tomb cut in the rock, one in which no one had yet been laid. 54 It was Preparation Day, and the Sabbath was about to begin.

55 The women who had come with Jesus from Galilee followed Joseph and saw the tomb and how his body was laid in it. 56 Then they went home and prepared spices and perfumes. But they rested on the Sabbath in obedience to the commandment.

Jesus Has Risen

24 On the first day of the week, very early in the morning, the women took the spices they had prepared and went to the tomb. 2 They found the stone rolled away from the tomb, 3 but when they entered, they did not find the body of the Lord Jesus. 4 While they were wondering about this, suddenly two men in clothes that gleamed like lightning stood beside them. 5 In their fright the women bowed down with their faces to the ground, but the men said to them, "Why do you look for the living among the dead? 6 He is not here; he has risen! Remember how he told you, while he was still with you in Galilee: 7 'The Son of Man must be delivered over to the hands of sinners, be crucified and on the third day be raised again.'" 8 Then they remembered his words.

9 When they came back from the tomb, they told all these things to the Eleven and to all the others. 10 It was Mary

We Believe...

"the third day he rose again"

✝ How do you know that Jesus rose from the dead? The resurrection of Jesus is one of the clearest teachings of the Bible. Many people witnessed it:

* Two disciples (Luke 24:13–31)
* The apostles (Luke 24:36–45; John 20–21)
* Several women (Matthew 28:8–10)
* Mary Magdalene (John 20:11–18)
* Paul (Acts 9:3–6)
* Stephen (Acts 7:55)
* Some 500 in Galilee (1 Corinthians 15:6)
* James (1 Corinthians 15:7)
* John (Revelation 1:10–18)

Jesus was seen alive again by many people. Because he rose from the dead, you can be sure that you will be resurrected too.

Go to page 1519 for the next We Believe

Magdalene, Joanna, Mary the mother of James, and the others with them who told this to the apostles. ¹¹But they did not believe the women, because their words seemed to them like nonsense. ¹²Peter, however, got up and ran to the tomb. Bending over, he saw the strips of linen lying by themselves, and he went away, wondering to himself what had happened.

On the Road to Emmaus

¹³Now that same day two of them were going to a village called Emmaus, about seven milesᵃ from Jerusalem. ¹⁴They were talking with each other about everything that had happened. ¹⁵As they talked and discussed these things with each other, Jesus himself came up and walked along with them; ¹⁶but they were kept from recognizing him.

¹⁷He asked them, "What are you discussing together as you walk along?"

They stood still, their faces downcast. ¹⁸One of them, named Cleopas, asked him, "Are you the only one visiting Jerusalem who does not know the things that have happened there in these days?"

¹⁹"What things?" he asked.

"About Jesus of Nazareth," they replied. "He was a prophet, powerful in word and deed before God and all the people. ²⁰The chief priests and our rulers handed him over to be sentenced to death, and they crucified him; ²¹but we had hoped that he was the one who was going to redeem Israel. And what is more, it is the third day since all this took place. ²²In addition, some of our women amazed us. They went to the tomb early this morning ²³but didn't find his body. They came and told us that they had seen a vision of angels, who said he was alive. ²⁴Then some of our companions went to the tomb and found it just as the women had said, but they did not see Jesus."

²⁵He said to them, "How foolish you are, and how slow to believe all that the prophets have spoken! ²⁶Did not the Messiah have to suffer these things and then enter his glory?" ²⁷And beginning with Moses and all the Prophets, he explained to them what was said in all the Scriptures concerning himself.

²⁸As they approached the village to which they were going, Jesus continued on as if he were going farther. ²⁹But they urged him strongly, "Stay with us, for it is nearly evening; the day is almost over." So he went in to stay with them.

³⁰When he was at the table with them, he took bread, gave thanks, broke it and began to give it to them. ³¹Then their eyes were opened and they recognized him, and he disappeared from their sight. ³²They asked each other, "Were not our hearts burning within us while he talked with us on the road and opened the Scriptures to us?"

³³They got up and returned at once to Jerusalem. There they found the Eleven and those with them, assembled together ³⁴and saying, "It is true! The Lord has risen and has appeared to Simon." ³⁵Then the two told what had happened on the way, and how Jesus was recognized by them when he broke the bread.

Jesus Appears to the Disciples

³⁶While they were still talking about this, Jesus himself stood among them and said to them, "Peace be with you."

³⁷They were startled and frightened, thinking they saw a ghost. ³⁸He said to them, "Why are you troubled, and why do doubts rise in your minds? ³⁹Look at my hands and my feet. It is I myself! Touch me and see; a ghost does not have flesh and bones, as you see I have."

⁴⁰When he had said this, he showed them his hands and feet. ⁴¹And while they still did not believe it because of joy and amazement, he asked them, "Do you have anything here to eat?" ⁴²They gave him a piece of broiled fish, ⁴³and he took it and ate it in their presence.

⁴⁴He said to them, "This is what I told you while I was still with you: Everything must be fulfilled that is written about me in the Law of Moses, the Prophets and the Psalms."

⁴⁵Then he opened their minds so they could understand the Scriptures. ⁴⁶He

---

ᵃ 13 Or about 11 kilometers

told them, "This is what is written: The Messiah will suffer and rise from the dead on the third day, [47] and repentance for the forgiveness of sins will be preached in his name to all nations, beginning at Jerusalem. [48] You are witnesses of these things. [49] I am going to send you what my Father has promised; but stay in the city until you have been clothed with power from on high."

The Ascension of Jesus

[50] When he had led them out to the vicinity of Bethany, he lifted up his hands and blessed them. [51] While he was blessing them, he left them and was taken up into heaven. [52] Then they worshiped him and returned to Jerusalem with great joy. [53] And they stayed continually at the temple, praising God.

JOHN

John the disciple wrote this book, not John the Baptist.

The key word in this Gospel is "love."

God?

Is Jesus really God? Some religions teach that Jesus is special but not that he is God the Son, who existed from all eternity and who created the universe and died to save you.

John makes sure you won't be confused. All the Gospels tell you that Jesus is the Son of God. But John emphasizes that Jesus is the God of the Old Testament, the God who loved you enough to come to earth to be with you and to save you from your sins.

>> **SALVATION PROMISE MADE TO "WHOEVER"**
Good news announcement, see John 3:16

>> **MIRACLE GIVES WITNESSES FOOD FOR THOUGHT**
Story in John 6:1–15

>> **NOT EVERYONE HAS GOD AS FATHER**
Stunning revelation reported in John 8:31–47

>> **MARY FIRST TO REPORT RESURRECTION**
Woman first evangelist? See John 20:10–18

As Jesus' life and death reveal the depths of God's love, two leading rabbis, Hillel and Shammai, die. Lavillia, the emperor Trajan's niece, is starved to death. A Roman physician advocates dissection of corpses. In China a water wheel drives bellows in an iron foundry.

The Word Became Flesh

1 In the beginning was the Word, and the Word was with God, and the Word was God. [2] He was with God in the beginning. [3] Through him all things were made; without him nothing was made that has been made. [4] In him was life, and that life was the light of all mankind. [5] The light shines in the darkness, and the darkness has not overcome[a] it.

[6] There was a man sent from God whose name was John. [7] He came as a witness to testify concerning that light, so that through him all might believe. [8] He himself was not the light; he came only as a witness to the light.

[9] The true light that gives light to everyone was coming into the world. [10] He was in the world, and though the world was made through him, the world did not recognize him. [11] He came to that which was his own, but his own did not receive him. [12] Yet to all who did receive him, to those who believed in his name, he gave the right to become children of God— [13] children born not of natural descent, nor of human decision or a husband's will, but born of God.

[14] The Word became flesh and made his dwelling among us. We have seen his glory, the glory of the one and only Son, who came from the Father, full of grace and truth.

[15] (John testified concerning him. He cried out, saying, "This is the one I spoke about when I said, 'He who comes after me has surpassed me because he was before me.'") [16] Out of his fullness we have all received grace in place of grace already given. [17] For the law was given through Moses; grace and truth came through Jesus Christ. [18] No one has ever seen God, but the one and only Son, who is himself God and[b] is in closest relationship with the Father, has made him known.

John the Baptist Denies Being the Messiah

[19] Now this was John's testimony when the Jewish leaders[c] in Jerusalem sent priests and Levites to ask him who he was. [20] He did not fail to confess, but confessed freely, "I am not the Messiah."

[21] They asked him, "Then who are you? Are you Elijah?"

He said, "I am not."

"Are you the Prophet?"

He answered, "No."

[22] Finally they said, "Who are you? Give us an answer to take back to those who sent us. What do you say about yourself?"

[23] John replied in the words of Isaiah the prophet, "I am the voice of one calling in the wilderness, 'Make straight the way for the Lord.'"[d]

[24] Now the Pharisees who had been sent [25] questioned him, "Why then do you baptize if you are not the Messiah, nor Elijah, nor the Prophet?"

[26] "I baptize with[e] water," John replied, "but among you stands one you do not know. [27] He is the one who comes after me, the straps of whose sandals I am not worthy to untie."

[28] This all happened at Bethany on the other side of the Jordan, where John was baptizing.

John Testifies About Jesus

[29] The next day John saw Jesus coming toward him and said, "Look, the Lamb of God, who takes away the sin of the world! [30] This is the one I meant when I said, 'A man who comes after me has surpassed me because he was before me.' [31] I myself did not know him, but the reason I came baptizing with water was that he might be revealed to Israel."

[32] Then John gave this testimony: "I saw the Spirit come down from heaven as a dove and remain on him. [33] And I myself did not know him, but the one who sent me to baptize with water told me, 'The man on whom you see the Spirit come down and remain is the one who will baptize with the Holy Spirit.' [34] I have seen and I testify that this is God's Chosen One."[f]

---

[a] 5 Or *understood*   [b] 18 Some manuscripts *but the only Son, who*   [c] 19 The Greek term traditionally translated *the Jews* (*hoi Ioudaioi*) refers here and elsewhere in John's Gospel to those Jewish leaders who opposed Jesus; also in 5:10, 15, 16; 7:1, 11, 13; 9:22; 18:14, 28, 36; 19:7, 12, 31, 38; 20:19.   [d] 23 Isaiah 40:3   [e] 26 Or *in*; also in verses 31 and 33 (twice)   [f] 34 See Isaiah 42:1; many manuscripts *is the Son of God*.

We Believe...

Jesus is "God's only Son"

✚ It's confusing. What does the Bible mean when it says Jesus is God's "one and only Son" (John 3:16)? The confusion is because in Bible days "son" could mean more than "descendant." For instance, "son of King Josiah" meant "successor"—even if the new king was from a different family. To call someone a "son of Israel" was a way of saying "Israelite." And "sons of the prophets" was a way of saying "prophets."

So to say Jesus is the "Son of God" is a way of saying "Jesus *is* God." To say that Jesus is the "one and only Son" means no other person is God. Christians are adopted into God's family as sons of God (Ephesians 1:5). But adoption doesn't make us God. Only *Jesus* is God.

What's fascinating is that Jesus often spoke of himself as the "Son of Man." When he did, Jesus was usually emphasizing the fact that he was a true human being as well as God.

John 1:1–14 sums up what the Bible teaches and what Christians believe. Jesus existed as God with God the Father before the universe was created. And then "the Word [an expression identifying the Son of God before Jesus was born] became flesh and made his dwelling among us."

Jesus, the Son of God—God himself!—was born into our world and became a Son of Man—a true human being. As God and Man, Jesus lived here on our planet. He died on a cross to pay for our sins. Today whoever believes in the one and only Son of God becomes a child of God and is welcomed into God's family forever.

Go to page 1408 for the next We Believe

Maybe the hardest thing a teen can do is witness to family. Especially if it's to unsaved parents. What can make family witness easier? Look how Andrew witnessed. He met Jesus personally. Then he said to his brother, "We have found the Messiah" (John 1:41). He didn't argue about the Bible or try to get his brother to go to church. He simply shared his own experience of having met Jesus. You don't have to convince your family and friends of anything. Just follow Jesus yourself and talk naturally about what he means to you. God the Holy Spirit will do the rest.

{John 1:40–42}

INSTANT ACCESS

John's Disciples Follow Jesus

35 The next day John was there again with two of his disciples. 36 When he saw Jesus passing by, he said, "Look, the Lamb of God!"

37 When the two disciples heard him say this, they followed Jesus. 38 Turning around, Jesus saw them following and asked, "What do you want?"

They said, "Rabbi" (which means "Teacher"), "where are you staying?"

39 "Come," he replied, "and you will see."

So they went and saw where he was staying, and they spent that day with him. It was about four in the afternoon.

40 Andrew, Simon Peter's brother, was one of the two who heard what John had said and who had followed Jesus. 41 The first thing Andrew did was to find his brother Simon and tell him, "We have found the Messiah" (that is, the Christ). 42 And he brought him to Jesus.

Jesus looked at him and said, "You are Simon son of John. You will be called Cephas" (which, when translated, is Peter[a]).

Jesus Calls Philip and Nathanael

43 The next day Jesus decided to leave for Galilee. Finding Philip, he said to him, "Follow me."

44 Philip, like Andrew and Peter, was from the town of Bethsaida. 45 Philip found Nathanael and told him, "We have found the one Moses wrote about in the Law, and about whom the prophets also wrote—Jesus of Nazareth, the son of Joseph."

46 "Nazareth! Can anything good come from there?" Nathanael asked.

"Come and see," said Philip.

47 When Jesus saw Nathanael approaching, he said of him, "Here truly is an Israelite in whom there is no deceit."

48 "How do you know me?" Nathanael asked.

Jesus answered, "I saw you while you were still under the fig tree before Philip called you."

49 Then Nathanael declared, "Rabbi, you are the Son of God; you are the king of Israel."

50 Jesus said, "You believe[b] because I told you I saw you under the fig tree. You will see greater things than that." 51 He then added, "Very truly I tell you,[c] you[c] will see 'heaven open, and the angels of God ascending and descending on'[d] the Son of Man."

Jesus Changes Water Into Wine

2 On the third day a wedding took place at Cana in Galilee. Jesus' mother was

---

[a] 42 Cephas (Aramaic) and Peter (Greek) both mean rock.   [b] 50 Or Do you believe . . . ?   [c] 51 The Greek is plural.
[d] 51 Gen. 28:12

there, ²and Jesus and his disciples had also been invited to the wedding. ³When the wine was gone, Jesus' mother said to him, "They have no more wine."

⁴"Woman,ᵃ why do you involve me?" Jesus replied. "My hour has not yet come."

⁵His mother said to the servants, "Do whatever he tells you."

⁶Nearby stood six stone water jars, the kind used by the Jews for ceremonial washing, each holding from twenty to thirty gallons.ᵇ

⁷Jesus said to the servants, "Fill the jars with water"; so they filled them to the brim.

⁸Then he told them, "Now draw some out and take it to the master of the banquet."

They did so, ⁹and the master of the banquet tasted the water that had been turned into wine. He did not realize where it had come from, though the servants who had drawn the water knew. Then he called the bridegroom aside ¹⁰and said, "Everyone brings out the choice wine first and then the cheaper wine after the guests have had too much to drink; but you have saved the best till now."

¹¹What Jesus did here in Cana of Galilee was the first of the signs through which he revealed his glory; and his disciples believed in him.

¹²After this he went down to Capernaum with his mother and brothers and his disciples. There they stayed for a few days.

Jesus Clears the Temple Courts

¹³When it was almost time for the Jewish Passover, Jesus went up to Jerusalem. ¹⁴In the temple courts he found people selling cattle, sheep and doves, and others sitting at tables exchanging money. ¹⁵So he made a whip out of cords, and drove all from the temple courts, both sheep and cattle; he scattered the coins of the money changers and overturned their tables. ¹⁶To those who sold doves he said, "Get these out of here! Stop turning my Father's house into a market!" ¹⁷His disciples remembered that it is written: "Zeal for your house will consume me."ᶜ

¹⁸The Jews then responded to him, "What sign can you show us to prove your authority to do all this?"

¹⁹Jesus answered them, "Destroy this temple, and I will raise it again in three days."

²⁰They replied, "It has taken forty-six years to build this temple, and you are going to raise it in three days?" ²¹But the temple he had spoken of was his body. ²²After he was raised from the dead, his disciples recalled what he had said. Then they believed the scripture and the words that Jesus had spoken.

²³Now while he was in Jerusalem at the Passover Festival, many people saw the signs he was performing and believed in his name.ᵈ ²⁴But Jesus would not entrust himself to them, for he knew all people. ²⁵He did not need any testimony about mankind, for he knew what was in each person.

Jesus Teaches Nicodemus

3 Now there was a Pharisee, a man named Nicodemus who was a member of the Jewish ruling council. ²He came to Jesus at night and said, "Rabbi, we know that you are a teacher who has come from God. For no one could perform the signs you are doing if God were not with him."

³Jesus replied, "Very truly I tell you, no one can see the kingdom of God unless they are born again.ᵉ"

⁴"How can someone be born when they are old?" Nicodemus asked. "Surely they cannot enter a second time into their mother's womb to be born!"

⁵Jesus answered, "Very truly I tell you, no one can enter the kingdom of God unless they are born of water and the Spirit. ⁶Flesh gives birth to flesh, but the Spiritᶠ gives birth to spirit. ⁷You should not be surprised at my saying, 'Youᵍ must be born again.' ⁸The wind blows wherever it

---

ᵃ 4 The Greek for *Woman* does not denote any disrespect.   ᵇ 6 Or from about 75 to about 115 liters   ᶜ 17 Psalm 69:9   ᵈ 23 Or *in him*   ᵉ 3 The Greek for *again* also means *from above*; also in verse 7.   ᶠ 6 Or *but spirit*   ᵍ 7 The Greek is plural.

pleases. You hear its sound, but you cannot tell where it comes from or where it is going. So it is with everyone born of the Spirit."[a]

9 "How can this be?" Nicodemus asked.

10 "You are Israel's teacher," said Jesus, "and do you not understand these things? 11 Very truly I tell you, we speak of what we know, and we testify to what we have seen, but still you people do not accept our testimony. 12 I have spoken to you of earthly things and you do not believe; how then will you believe if I speak of heavenly things? 13 No one has ever gone into heaven except the one who came from heaven — the Son of Man.[b] 14 Just as Moses lifted up the snake in the wilderness, so the Son of Man must be lifted up,[c] 15 that everyone who believes may have eternal life in him."[d]

16 For God so loved the world that he gave his one and only Son, that whoever believes in him shall not perish but have eternal life. 17 For God did not send his Son into the world to condemn the world, but to save the world through him. 18 Whoever believes in him is not condemned, but whoever does not believe stands condemned already because they have not believed in the name of God's one and only Son. 19 This is the verdict: Light has come into the world, but people loved darkness instead of light because their deeds were evil. 20 Everyone who does

---

[a] 8 The Greek for *Spirit* is the same as that for *wind*.   [b] 13 Some manuscripts *Man, who is in heaven*   [c] 14 The Greek for *lifted up* also means *exalted*.   [d] 15 Some interpreters end the quotation with verse 21.

TO THE POINT

You Can Know

If someone asked you if you're saved, what would you say? Some people say, "I hope I'll be saved." Some people say, "I think I'm saved." And then other people say, "I know I'm saved!"

A verse that is probably the most famous one in the Bible tells you that you can *know*. Take a minute to read John 3:16. Now read verse 17 also. It's pretty clear. God sent his Son to give everlasting life to whoever believes in him. And whoever believes in him is not condemned.

Try something. Take out that "whoever," and put your own name there. Read the verse again with your name in it, and think about it. Do you believe in Jesus? Then you have God's own word that you are saved.

We Believe...

"We believe"

✝ John 3:16 says, "For God so loved the world that he gave his one and only Son, that whoever believes in him shall not perish but have eternal life."

What does "believe" mean? First, it doesn't mean "know the facts about." We know a lot of facts about Napoleon and George Washington, for instance. But believing those facts—accepting them as true—doesn't make an eternal difference.

What makes believing in Jesus or any Bible truth different is that little word, "in." To "believe in" is different from believing information "about." To "believe in" means *we put our trust in* Jesus. We *rely on* Jesus; we *count on him* and count on truths found in the Bible.

A circus performer was about to walk a tightrope stretched over Niagara Falls. He asked the crowd, "Who believes I can carry a man across on my back?" One man shouted out, "I do! I do!"

The circus performer said, "All right, you're first." The man ran away as fast as he could. He believed something about the performer, but he didn't believe *in* the performer.

To "believe in" Jesus means trusting ourselves to him completely. To "believe in" what the Bible says means we rely on God's Word so completely that we build our lives on its teachings.

Check out what Jesus said one day. It's recorded in Matthew 7:24–27. And then decide to believe *in* Jesus.

Go to page 736 for the next We Believe

evil hates the light, and will not come into the light for fear that their deeds will be exposed. [21] But whoever lives by the truth comes into the light, so that it may be seen plainly that what they have done has been done in the sight of God.

John Testifies Again About Jesus

[22] After this, Jesus and his disciples went out into the Judean countryside, where he spent some time with them, and baptized. [23] Now John also was baptizing at Aenon near Salim, because there was plenty of water, and people were coming and being baptized. [24] (This was before John was put in prison.) [25] An argument developed between some of John's disciples and a certain Jew over the matter of ceremonial washing. [26] They came to John and said to him, "Rabbi, that man who was with you on the other side of the Jordan—the one you testified about—look, he is baptizing, and everyone is going to him."

[27] To this John replied, "A person can receive only what is given them from heaven. [28] You yourselves can testify that I said, 'I am not the Messiah but am sent ahead of him.' [29] The bride belongs to the bridegroom. The friend who attends the bridegroom waits and listens for him, and is full of joy when he hears the bridegroom's voice. That joy is mine, and it is now complete. [30] He must become greater; I must become less."[a]

[31] The one who comes from above is above all; the one who is from the earth belongs to the earth, and speaks as one from the earth. The one who comes from heaven is above all. [32] He testifies to what he has seen and heard, but no one accepts his testimony. [33] Whoever has accepted it has certified that God is truthful. [34] For the one whom God has sent speaks the words of God, for God[b] gives the Spirit without limit. [35] The Father loves the Son and has placed everything in his hands. [36] Whoever believes in the Son has eternal life, but whoever rejects the Son will not see life, for God's wrath remains on them.

Jesus Talks With a Samaritan Woman

4 Now Jesus learned that the Pharisees had heard that he was gaining and baptizing more disciples than John— [2] although in fact it was not Jesus who baptized, but his disciples. [3] So he left Judea and went back once more to Galilee.

[4] Now he had to go through Samaria. [5] So he came to a town in Samaria called Sychar, near the plot of ground Jacob had given to his son Joseph. [6] Jacob's well was there, and Jesus, tired as he was from the journey, sat down by the well. It was about noon.

[7] When a Samaritan woman came to draw water, Jesus said to her, "Will you give me a drink?" [8] (His disciples had gone into the town to buy food.)

[9] The Samaritan woman said to him, "You are a Jew and I am a Samaritan woman. How can you ask me for a drink?" (For Jews do not associate with Samaritans.[c])

[10] Jesus answered her, "If you knew the gift of God and who it is that asks you for a drink, you would have asked him and he would have given you living water."

[11] "Sir," the woman said, "you have nothing to draw with and the well is deep. Where can you get this living water? [12] Are you greater than our father Jacob, who gave us the well and drank from it himself, as did also his sons and his livestock?"

[13] Jesus answered, "Everyone who drinks this water will be thirsty again, [14] but whoever drinks the water I give them will never thirst. Indeed, the water I give them will become in them a spring of water welling up to eternal life."

[15] The woman said to him, "Sir, give me this water so that I won't get thirsty and have to keep coming here to draw water."

[16] He told her, "Go, call your husband and come back."

---

[a] 30 Some interpreters end the quotation with verse 36.   [b] 34 Greek *he*   [c] 9 Or *do not use dishes Samaritans have used*

> My school has students of different races and religions. I have been taught to treat people of all races with respect. I get that totally. But what about people who believe in other religions? I hear so many different things about that. Should we avoid them? >> Kevin

Dear Jordan

Dear Kevin,

John 4 shows how Jesus treated a Samaritan woman. Samaritans were looked down on by the Jewish people. But Jesus asked her for a drink at a well. She was surprised he would even speak to her. He was respectful and told her about salvation. She was led to faith and brought many people from her town to Jesus as well.

It may surprise you to know that many people think Christians are judgmental and mean to people who believe differently than they do. Jesus teaches us to treat others as we would like to be treated. Sometimes when we are kind to people, we later get the chance to share our faith with them. Even if we don't, we have shown kindness to another person. Respect and kindness show good manners and show the world that Christians are caring, not judgmental.

Jordan

17 "I have no husband," she replied.

Jesus said to her, "You are right when you say you have no husband. 18 The fact is, you have had five husbands, and the man you now have is not your husband. What you have just said is quite true."

19 "Sir," the woman said, "I can see that you are a prophet. 20 Our ancestors worshiped on this mountain, but you Jews claim that the place where we must worship is in Jerusalem."

21 "Woman," Jesus replied, "believe me, a time is coming when you will worship the Father neither on this mountain nor in Jerusalem. 22 You Samaritans worship what you do not know; we worship what we do know, for salvation is from the Jews. 23 Yet a time is coming and has now come when the true worshipers will worship the Father in the Spirit and in truth, for they are the kind of worshipers the Father seeks. 24 God is spirit, and his worshipers must worship in the Spirit and in truth."

25 The woman said, "I know that Messiah" (called Christ) "is coming. When he comes, he will explain everything to us."

26 Then Jesus declared, "I, the one speaking to you—I am he."

The Disciples Rejoin Jesus

27 Just then his disciples returned and were surprised to find him talking with a woman. But no one asked, "What do you want?" or "Why are you talking with her?"

28 Then, leaving her water jar, the woman went back to the town and said to the people, 29 "Come, see a man who told me everything I ever did. Could this be the Messiah?" 30 They came out of the town and made their way toward him.

31 Meanwhile his disciples urged him, "Rabbi, eat something."

32 But he said to them, "I have food to eat that you know nothing about."

33 Then his disciples said to each other, "Could someone have brought him food?"

34 "My food," said Jesus, "is to do the will of him who sent me and to finish his work. 35 Don't you have a saying, 'It's still four months until harvest'? I tell you, open your eyes and look at the fields!

They are ripe for harvest. 36 Even now the one who reaps draws a wage and harvests a crop for eternal life, so that the sower and the reaper may be glad together. 37 Thus the saying 'One sows and another reaps' is true. 38 I sent you to reap what you have not worked for. Others have done the hard work, and you have reaped the benefits of their labor."

Many Samaritans Believe

39 Many of the Samaritans from that town believed in him because of the woman's testimony, "He told me everything I ever did." 40 So when the Samaritans came to him, they urged him to stay with them, and he stayed two days. 41 And because of his words many more became believers.

42 They said to the woman, "We no longer believe just because of what you said; now we have heard for ourselves, and we know that this man really is the Savior of the world."

Jesus Heals an Official's Son

43 After the two days he left for Galilee. 44 (Now Jesus himself had pointed out that a prophet has no honor in his own country.) 45 When he arrived in Galilee, the Galileans welcomed him. They had seen all that he had done in Jerusalem at the Passover Festival, for they also had been there.

46 Once more he visited Cana in Galilee, where he had turned the water into wine. And there was a certain royal official whose son lay sick at Capernaum. 47 When this man heard that Jesus had arrived in Galilee from Judea, he went to him and begged him to come and heal his son, who was close to death.

48 "Unless you people see signs and wonders," Jesus told him, "you will never believe."

49 The royal official said, "Sir, come down before my child dies."

50 "Go," Jesus replied, "your son will live."

The man took Jesus at his word and departed. 51 While he was still on the way, his servants met him with the news that his boy was living. 52When he inquired as to the time when his son got better, they said to him, "Yesterday, at one in the afternoon, the fever left him."

53Then the father realized that this was the exact time at which Jesus had said to him, "Your son will live." So he and his whole household believed.

54This was the second sign Jesus performed after coming from Judea to Galilee.

The Healing at the Pool

5 Some time later, Jesus went up to Jerusalem for one of the Jewish festivals. 2Now there is in Jerusalem near the Sheep Gate a pool, which in Aramaic is called Bethesda[a] and which is surrounded by five covered colonnades. 3Here a great number of disabled people used to lie—the blind, the lame, the paralyzed. [4]b 5One who was there had been an invalid for thirty-eight years. 6When Jesus saw him lying there and learned that he had been in this condition for a long time, he asked him, "Do you want to get well?"

7"Sir," the invalid replied, "I have no one to help me into the pool when the water is stirred. While I am trying to get in, someone else goes down ahead of me."

8Then Jesus said to him, "Get up! Pick up your mat and walk." 9At once the man was cured; he picked up his mat and walked.

The day on which this took place was a Sabbath, 10and so the Jewish leaders said to the man who had been healed, "It is the Sabbath; the law forbids you to carry your mat."

11But he replied, "The man who made me well said to me, 'Pick up your mat and walk.'"

12So they asked him, "Who is this fellow who told you to pick it up and walk?"

13The man who was healed had no idea who it was, for Jesus had slipped away into the crowd that was there.

14Later Jesus found him at the temple and said to him, "See, you are well again.

>> INSTANT ACCESS

Do you want to get well?" (John 5:6). That's the question Jesus asked a man who was paralyzed for 38 years. Why that question? Maybe because he didn't want to get well. For 38 years he lived by begging. Healed, he'd have to go to work and support himself. How about your prayers? God can answer them. Did you ask God to help you pass that test? If so, you'll have to study. Did you tell God you want to witness? Then you'll have to speak up. God can answer your prayers, but you'll have to do your part too.

{John 5:1–13}

Stop sinning or something worse may happen to you." 15The man went away and told the Jewish leaders that it was Jesus who had made him well.

The Authority of the Son

16So, because Jesus was doing these things on the Sabbath, the Jewish leaders began to persecute him. 17In his defense Jesus said to them, "My Father is always at his work to this very day, and I too am working." 18For this reason they tried all the more to kill him; not only was he breaking the Sabbath, but he was even calling God his own Father, making himself equal with God.

a 2 Some manuscripts Bethzatha; other manuscripts Bethsaida   b 3,4 Some manuscripts include here, wholly or in part, paralyzed—and they waited for the moving of the waters. 4From time to time an angel of the Lord would come down and stir up the waters. The first one into the pool after each such disturbance would be cured of whatever disease they had.

¹⁹Jesus gave them this answer: "Very truly I tell you, the Son can do nothing by himself; he can do only what he sees his Father doing, because whatever the Father does the Son also does. ²⁰For the Father loves the Son and shows him all he does. Yes, and he will show him even greater works than these, so that you will be amazed. ²¹For just as the Father raises the dead and gives them life, even so the Son gives life to whom he is pleased to give it. ²²Moreover, the Father judges no one, but has entrusted all judgment to the Son, ²³that all may honor the Son just as they honor the Father. Whoever does not honor the Son does not honor the Father, who sent him.

²⁴"Very truly I tell you, whoever hears my word and believes him who sent me has eternal life and will not be judged but has crossed over from death to life. ²⁵Very truly I tell you, a time is coming and has now come when the dead will hear the voice of the Son of God and those who hear will live. ²⁶For as the Father has life in himself, so he has granted the Son also to have life in himself. ²⁷And he has given him authority to judge because he is the Son of Man.

²⁸"Do not be amazed at this, for a time is coming when all who are in their graves will hear his voice ²⁹and come out—those who have done what is good will rise to live, and those who have done what is evil will rise to be condemned. ³⁰By myself I can do nothing; I judge only as I hear, and my judgment is just, for I seek not to please myself but him who sent me.

Testimonies About Jesus

³¹"If I testify about myself, my testimony is not true. ³²There is another who testifies in my favor, and I know that his testimony about me is true.

³³"You have sent to John and he has testified to the truth. ³⁴Not that I accept human testimony; but I mention it that you may be saved. ³⁵John was a lamp that burned and gave light, and you chose for a time to enjoy his light.

³⁶"I have testimony weightier than that of John. For the works that the Father has given me to finish—the very works that I am doing—testify that the Father has sent me. ³⁷And the Father who sent me has himself testified concerning me. You have never heard his voice nor seen his form, ³⁸nor does his word dwell in you, for you do not believe the one he sent. ³⁹You study*a* the Scriptures diligently because you think that in them you have eternal life. These are the very Scriptures that testify about me, ⁴⁰yet you refuse to come to me to have life.

⁴¹"I do not accept glory from human beings, ⁴²but I know you. I know that you do not have the love of God in your hearts. ⁴³I have come in my Father's name, and you do not accept me; but if someone else comes in his own name, you will accept him. ⁴⁴How can you believe since you accept glory from one another but do not seek the glory that comes from the only God*b*?

⁴⁵"But do not think I will accuse you before the Father. Your accuser is Moses, on whom your hopes are set. ⁴⁶If you believed Moses, you would believe me, for he wrote about me. ⁴⁷But since you do not believe what he wrote, how are you going to believe what I say?"

Jesus Feeds the Five Thousand

6 Some time after this, Jesus crossed to the far shore of the Sea of Galilee (that is, the Sea of Tiberias), ²and a great crowd of people followed him because they saw the signs he had performed by healing the sick. ³Then Jesus went up on a mountainside and sat down with his disciples. ⁴The Jewish Passover Festival was near.

⁵When Jesus looked up and saw a great crowd coming toward him, he said to Philip, "Where shall we buy bread for these people to eat?" ⁶He asked this only to test him, for he already had in mind what he was going to do.

⁷Philip answered him, "It would take more than half a year's wages*c* to buy enough bread for each one to have a bite!"

---

a 39 Or ³⁹*Study*   *b* 44 Some early manuscripts *the Only One*   *c* 7 Greek *take two hundred denarii*

8Another of his disciples, Andrew, Simon Peter's brother, spoke up, 9"Here is a boy with five small barley loaves and two small fish, but how far will they go among so many?"

10Jesus said, "Have the people sit down." There was plenty of grass in that place, and they sat down (about five thousand men were there). 11Jesus then took the loaves, gave thanks, and distributed to those who were seated as much as they wanted. He did the same with the fish.

12When they had all had enough to eat, he said to his disciples, "Gather the pieces that are left over. Let nothing be wasted." 13So they gathered them and filled twelve baskets with the pieces of the five barley loaves left over by those who had eaten.

14After the people saw the sign Jesus performed, they began to say, "Surely this is the Prophet who is to come into the world." 15Jesus, knowing that they intended to come and make him king by force, withdrew again to a mountain by himself.

Jesus Walks on the Water

16When evening came, his disciples went down to the lake, 17where they got into a boat and set off across the lake for Capernaum. By now it was dark, and Jesus had not yet joined them. 18A strong wind was blowing and the waters grew rough. 19When they had rowed about three or four miles,ᵃ they saw Jesus approaching the boat, walking on the water; and they were frightened. 20But he said to them, "It is I; don't be afraid." 21Then they were willing to take him into the boat, and immediately the boat reached the shore where they were heading.

22The next day the crowd that had stayed on the opposite shore of the lake realized that only one boat had been there, and that Jesus had not entered it with his disciples, but that they had gone away alone. 23Then some boats from Tiberias landed near the place where the people had eaten the bread after the Lord had given thanks. 24Once the crowd realized that neither Jesus nor his disciples were there, they got into the boats and went to Capernaum in search of Jesus.

Jesus the Bread of Life

25When they found him on the other side of the lake, they asked him, "Rabbi, when did you get here?"

26Jesus answered, "Very truly I tell you, you are looking for me, not because you saw the signs I performed but because you ate the loaves and had your fill. 27Do not work for food that spoils, but for food that endures to eternal life, which the Son of Man will give you. For on him God the Father has placed his seal of approval."

28Then they asked him, "What must we do to do the works God requires?"

29Jesus answered, "The work of God is this: to believe in the one he has sent."

30So they asked him, "What sign then will you give that we may see it and believe you? What will you do? 31Our ancestors ate the manna in the wilderness; as it is written: 'He gave them bread from heaven to eat.'ᵇ"

32Jesus said to them, "Very truly I tell you, it is not Moses who has given you the bread from heaven, but it is my Father who gives you the true bread from heaven. 33For the bread of God is the bread that comes down from heaven and gives life to the world."

34"Sir," they said, "always give us this bread."

35Then Jesus declared, "I am the bread of life. Whoever comes to me will never go hungry, and whoever believes in me will never be thirsty. 36But as I told you, you have seen me and still you do not believe. 37All those the Father gives me will come to me, and whoever comes to me I will never drive away. 38For I have come down from heaven not to do my will but to do the will of him who sent me. 39And this is the will of him who sent me, that I shall lose none of all those he has given me, but raise them up at the last day. 40For my Father's will is that everyone who looks to the Son and believes in

---

ᵃ 19 Or about 5 or 6 kilometers   ᵇ 31 Exodus 16:4; Neh. 9:15; Psalm 78:24,25

him shall have eternal life, and I will raise them up at the last day."

41 At this the Jews there began to grumble about him because he said, "I am the bread that came down from heaven." 42 They said, "Is this not Jesus, the son of Joseph, whose father and mother we know? How can he now say, 'I came down from heaven'?"

43 "Stop grumbling among yourselves," Jesus answered. 44 "No one can come to me unless the Father who sent me draws them, and I will raise them up at the last day. 45 It is written in the Prophets: 'They will all be taught by God.'[a] Everyone who has heard the Father and learned from him comes to me. 46 No one has seen the Father except the one who is from God; only he has seen the Father. 47 Very truly I tell you, the one who believes has eternal life. 48 I am the bread of life. 49 Your ancestors ate the manna in the wilderness, yet they died. 50 But here is the bread that comes down from heaven, which anyone may eat and not die. 51 I am the living bread that came down from heaven. Whoever eats this bread will live forever. This bread is my flesh, which I will give for the life of the world."

52 Then the Jews began to argue sharply among themselves, "How can this man give us his flesh to eat?"

53 Jesus said to them, "Very truly I tell you, unless you eat the flesh of the Son of Man and drink his blood, you have no life in you. 54 Whoever eats my flesh and drinks my blood has eternal life, and I will raise them up at the last day. 55 For my flesh is real food and my blood is real drink. 56 Whoever eats my flesh and drinks my blood remains in me, and I in them. 57 Just as the living Father sent me and I live because of the Father, so the one who feeds on me will live because of me. 58 This is the bread that came down from heaven. Your ancestors ate manna and died, but whoever feeds on this bread will live forever." 59 He said this while teaching in the synagogue in Capernaum.

Many Disciples Desert Jesus

60 On hearing it, many of his disciples said, "This is a hard teaching. Who can accept it?"

61 Aware that his disciples were grumbling about this, Jesus said to them, "Does this offend you? 62 Then what if you see the Son of Man ascend to where he was before! 63 The Spirit gives life; the flesh counts for nothing. The words I have spoken to you—they are full of the Spirit[b] and life. 64 Yet there are some of you who do not believe." For Jesus had known from the beginning which of them did not believe and who would betray him. 65 He went on to say, "This is why I told you that no one can come to me unless the Father has enabled them."

66 From this time many of his disciples turned back and no longer followed him.

67 "You do not want to leave too, do you?" Jesus asked the Twelve.

68 Simon Peter answered him, "Lord, to whom shall we go? You have the words of eternal life. 69 We have come to believe and to know that you are the Holy One of God."

70 Then Jesus replied, "Have I not chosen you, the Twelve? Yet one of you is a devil!" 71 (He meant Judas, the son of Simon Iscariot, who, though one of the Twelve, was later to betray him.)

Jesus Goes to the Festival of Tabernacles

7 After this, Jesus went around in Galilee. He did not want[c] to go about in Judea because the Jewish leaders there were looking for a way to kill him. 2 But

> My Father's will is that everyone who looks to the Son and believes in him shall have eternal life.
> John 6:40

---

[a] 45 Isaiah 54:13   [b] 63 Or *are Spirit*; or *are spirit*   [c] 1 Some manuscripts *not have authority*

when the Jewish Festival of Tabernacles was near, ³Jesus' brothers said to him, "Leave Galilee and go to Judea, so that your disciples there may see the works you do. ⁴No one who wants to become a public figure acts in secret. Since you are doing these things, show yourself to the world." ⁵For even his own brothers did not believe in him.

⁶Therefore Jesus told them, "My time is not yet here; for you any time will do. ⁷The world cannot hate you, but it hates me because I testify that its works are evil. ⁸You go to the festival. I am not*ᵃ going up to this festival, because my time has not yet fully come." ⁹After he had said this, he stayed in Galilee.

¹⁰However, after his brothers had left for the festival, he went also, not publicly, but in secret. ¹¹Now at the festival the Jewish leaders were watching for Jesus and asking, "Where is he?"

¹²Among the crowds there was widespread whispering about him. Some said, "He is a good man."

Others replied, "No, he deceives the people." ¹³But no one would say anything publicly about him for fear of the leaders.

Jesus Teaches at the Festival

¹⁴Not until halfway through the festival did Jesus go up to the temple courts and begin to teach. ¹⁵The Jews there were amazed and asked, "How did this man get such learning without having been taught?"

¹⁶Jesus answered, "My teaching is not my own. It comes from the one who sent me. ¹⁷Anyone who chooses to do the will of God will find out whether my teaching comes from God or whether I speak on my own. ¹⁸Whoever speaks on their own does so to gain personal glory, but he who seeks the glory of the one who sent him is a man of truth; there is nothing false about him. ¹⁹Has not Moses given you the law? Yet not one of you keeps the law. Why are you trying to kill me?"

²⁰"You are demon-possessed," the crowd answered. "Who is trying to kill you?"

>> INSTANT ACCESS

Where did God come from? Why doesn't the Bible say anything about dinosaurs? How could Jesus be born without a human father? There are no easy answers to questions like these. No one created God; he always existed. We don't know where dinosaurs fit in. And Mary was a virgin when Jesus was conceived. We can't explain everything we believe. So what do we do when we don't understand some teaching of the Bible? Stop following Jesus, like the disciples in this story? No way! Like the Twelve we say, "We have come to believe and to know that you are the Holy One of God" (John 6:69). Our hard questions will be answered when Jesus comes again.

{John 6:60–69}

²¹Jesus said to them, "I did one miracle, and you are all amazed. ²²Yet, because Moses gave you circumcision (though actually it did not come from Moses, but from the patriarchs), you circumcise a boy on the Sabbath. ²³Now if a boy can be circumcised on the Sabbath so that the law of Moses may not be broken, why are you angry with me for healing a man's whole body on the Sabbath?

ᵃ 8 Some manuscripts *not yet*

24 Stop judging by mere appearances, but instead judge correctly."

Division Over Who Jesus Is

25 At that point some of the people of Jerusalem began to ask, "Isn't this the man they are trying to kill? 26 Here he is, speaking publicly, and they are not saying a word to him. Have the authorities really concluded that he is the Messiah? 27 But we know where this man is from; when the Messiah comes, no one will know where he is from."

28 Then Jesus, still teaching in the temple courts, cried out, "Yes, you know me, and you know where I am from. I am not here on my own authority, but he who sent me is true. You do not know him, 29 but I know him because I am from him and he sent me."

30 At this they tried to seize him, but no one laid a hand on him, because his hour had not yet come. 31 Still, many in the crowd believed in him. They said, "When the Messiah comes, will he perform more signs than this man?"

32 The Pharisees heard the crowd whispering such things about him. Then the chief priests and the Pharisees sent temple guards to arrest him.

33 Jesus said, "I am with you for only a short time, and then I am going to the one who sent me. 34 You will look for me, but you will not find me; and where I am, you cannot come."

35 The Jews said to one another, "Where does this man intend to go that we cannot find him? Will he go where our people live scattered among the Greeks, and teach the Greeks? 36 What did he mean when he said, 'You will look for me, but you will not find me,' and 'Where I am, you cannot come'?"

37 On the last and greatest day of the festival, Jesus stood and said in a loud voice, "Let anyone who is thirsty come to me and drink. 38 Whoever believes in me, as Scripture has said, rivers of living water will flow from within them."[a] 39 By this he meant the Spirit, whom those who believed in him were later to receive. Up to that time the Spirit had not been given, since Jesus had not yet been glorified.

40 On hearing his words, some of the people said, "Surely this man is the Prophet."

41 Others said, "He is the Messiah."

Still others asked, "How can the Messiah come from Galilee? 42 Does not Scripture say that the Messiah will come from David's descendants and from Bethlehem, the town where David lived?" 43 Thus the people were divided because of Jesus. 44 Some wanted to seize him, but no one laid a hand on him.

Unbelief of the Jewish Leaders

45 Finally the temple guards went back to the chief priests and the Pharisees, who asked them, "Why didn't you bring him in?"

46 "No one ever spoke the way this man does," the guards replied.

47 "You mean he has deceived you also?" the Pharisees retorted. 48 "Have any of the rulers or of the Pharisees believed in him? 49 No! But this mob that knows nothing of the law—there is a curse on them."

50 Nicodemus, who had gone to Jesus earlier and who was one of their own number, asked, 51 "Does our law condemn a man without first hearing him to find out what he has been doing?"

52 They replied, "Are you from Galilee, too? Look into it, and you will find that a prophet does not come out of Galilee."

[The earliest manuscripts and many other ancient witnesses do not have John 7:53—8:11. A few manuscripts include these verses, wholly or in part, after John 7:36, John 21:25, Luke 21:38 or Luke 24:53.]

8 53 Then they all went home, 1 but Jesus went to the Mount of Olives.

2 At dawn he appeared again in the temple courts, where all the people gathered around him, and he sat down to teach them. 3 The teachers of the law and the Pharisees brought

---

a 37,38 Or me. And let anyone drink 38 who believes in me." As Scripture has said, "Out of him (or them) will flow rivers of living water."

in a woman caught in adultery. They made her stand before the group [4] and said to Jesus, "Teacher, this woman was caught in the act of adultery. [5] In the Law Moses commanded us to stone such women. Now what do you say?" [6] They were using this question as a trap, in order to have a basis for accusing him.

But Jesus bent down and started to write on the ground with his finger. [7] When they kept on questioning him, he straightened up and said to them, "Let any one of you who is without sin be the first to throw a stone at her." [8] Again he stooped down and wrote on the ground.

[9] At this, those who heard began to go away one at a time, the older ones first, until only Jesus was left, with the woman still standing there. [10] Jesus straightened up and asked her, "Woman, where are they? Has no one condemned you?"

[11] "No one, sir," she said.

"Then neither do I condemn you," Jesus declared. "Go now and leave your life of sin."

Dispute Over Jesus' Testimony

[12] When Jesus spoke again to the people, he said, "I am the light of the world. Whoever follows me will never walk in darkness, but will have the light of life."

[13] The Pharisees challenged him, "Here you are, appearing as your own witness; your testimony is not valid."

[14] Jesus answered, "Even if I testify on my own behalf, my testimony is valid, for I know where I came from and where I am going. But you have no idea where I come from or where I am going. [15] You judge by human standards; I pass judgment on no one. [16] But if I do judge, my decisions are true, because I am not alone. I stand with the Father, who sent me. [17] In your own Law it is written that the testimony of two witnesses is true. [18] I am one who testifies for myself; my other witness is the Father, who sent me."

[19] Then they asked him, "Where is your father?"

"You do not know me or my Father," Jesus replied. "If you knew me, you would know my Father also." [20] He spoke these words while teaching in the temple courts near the place where the offerings were put. Yet no one seized him, because his hour had not yet come.

Dispute Over Who Jesus Is

[21] Once more Jesus said to them, "I am going away, and you will look for me, and you will die in your sin. Where I go, you cannot come."

[22] This made the Jews ask, "Will he kill himself? Is that why he says, 'Where I go, you cannot come'?"

[23] But he continued, "You are from below; I am from above. You are of this world; I am not of this world. [24] I told you that you would die in your sins; if you do not believe that I am he, you will indeed die in your sins."

[25] "Who are you?" they asked.

"Just what I have been telling you from the beginning," Jesus replied. [26] "I have much to say in judgment of you. But he who sent me is trustworthy, and what I have heard from him I tell the world."

[27] They did not understand that he was telling them about his Father. [28] So Jesus said, "When you have lifted up[a] the Son of Man, then you will know that I am he and that I do nothing on my own but speak just what the Father has taught

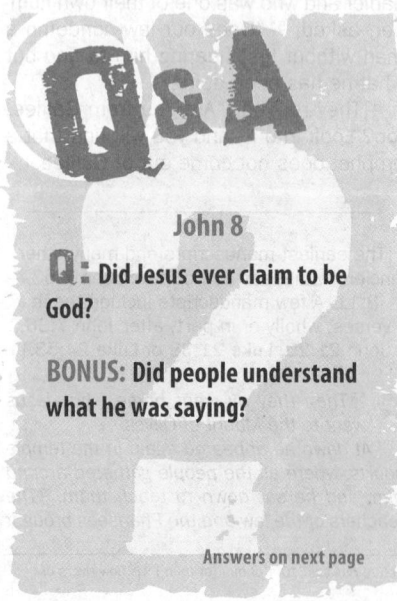

John 8

Q: Did Jesus ever claim to be God?

BONUS: Did people understand what he was saying?

Answers on next page

---

[a] 28 The Greek for *lifted up* also means *exalted*.

me. ²⁹The one who sent me is with me; he has not left me alone, for I always do what pleases him." ³⁰Even as he spoke, many believed in him.

Dispute Over Whose Children Jesus' Opponents Are

³¹To the Jews who had believed him, Jesus said, "If you hold to my teaching, you are really my disciples. ³²Then you will know the truth, and the truth will set you free."

³³They answered him, "We are Abraham's descendants and have never been slaves of anyone. How can you say that we shall be set free?"

³⁴Jesus replied, "Very truly I tell you, everyone who sins is a slave to sin. ³⁵Now a slave has no permanent place in the family, but a son belongs to it forever. ³⁶So if the Son sets you free, you will be free indeed. ³⁷I know that you are Abraham's descendants. Yet you are looking for a way to kill me, because you have no room for my word. ³⁸I am telling you what I have seen in the Father's presence, and you are doing what you have heard from your father.ᵃ"

³⁹"Abraham is our father," they answered.

"If you were Abraham's children," said Jesus, "then you wouldᵇ do what Abraham did. ⁴⁰As it is, you are looking for a way to kill me, a man who has told you the truth that I heard from God. Abraham did not do such things. ⁴¹You are doing the works of your own father."

"We are not illegitimate children," they protested. "The only Father we have is God himself."

⁴²Jesus said to them, "If God were your Father, you would love me, for I have come here from God. I have not come on my own; God sent me. ⁴³Why is my language not clear to you? Because you are unable to hear what I say. ⁴⁴You belong to your father, the devil, and you want to carry out your father's desires. He was a murderer from the beginning, not holding to the truth, for there is no truth in him.

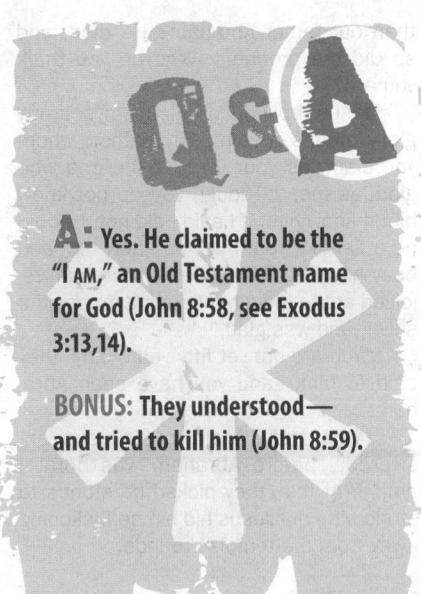

A: Yes. He claimed to be the "I AM," an Old Testament name for God (John 8:58, see Exodus 3:13,14).

BONUS: They understood— and tried to kill him (John 8:59).

When he lies, he speaks his native language, for he is a liar and the father of lies. ⁴⁵Yet because I tell the truth, you do not believe me! ⁴⁶Can any of you prove me guilty of sin? If I am telling the truth, why don't you believe me? ⁴⁷Whoever belongs to God hears what God says. The reason you do not hear is that you do not belong to God."

Jesus' Claims About Himself

⁴⁸The Jews answered him, "Aren't we right in saying that you are a Samaritan and demon-possessed?"

⁴⁹"I am not possessed by a demon," said Jesus, "but I honor my Father and you dishonor me. ⁵⁰I am not seeking glory for myself; but there is one who seeks it, and he is the judge. ⁵¹Very truly I tell you, whoever obeys my word will never see death."

⁵²At this they exclaimed, "Now we know that you are demon-possessed! Abraham died and so did the prophets, yet you say that whoever obeys your word will never taste death. ⁵³Are you greater

---

ᵃ 38 Or *presence. Therefore do what you have heard from the Father.* ᵇ 39 Some early manuscripts *"If you are Abraham's children," said Jesus, "then*

than our father Abraham? He died, and so did the prophets. Who do you think you are?"

⁵⁴Jesus replied, "If I glorify myself, my glory means nothing. My Father, whom you claim as your God, is the one who glorifies me. ⁵⁵Though you do not know him, I know him. If I said I did not, I would be a liar like you, but I do know him and obey his word. ⁵⁶Your father Abraham rejoiced at the thought of seeing my day; he saw it and was glad."

⁵⁷"You are not yet fifty years old," they said to him, "and you have seen Abraham!"

⁵⁸"Very truly I tell you," Jesus answered, "before Abraham was born, I am!" ⁵⁹At this, they picked up stones to stone him, but Jesus hid himself, slipping away from the temple grounds.

Jesus Heals a Man Born Blind

9 As he went along, he saw a man blind from birth. ²His disciples asked him, "Rabbi, who sinned, this man or his parents, that he was born blind?"

³"Neither this man nor his parents sinned," said Jesus, "but this happened so that the works of God might be displayed in him. ⁴As long as it is day, we must do the works of him who sent me. Night is coming, when no one can work. ⁵While I am in the world, I am the light of the world."

⁶After saying this, he spit on the ground, made some mud with the saliva, and put it on the man's eyes. ⁷"Go," he told him, "wash in the Pool of Siloam" (this word means "Sent"). So the man went and washed, and came home seeing.

⁸His neighbors and those who had formerly seen him begging asked, "Isn't this the same man who used to sit and beg?" ⁹Some claimed that he was.

Others said, "No, he only looks like him."

But he himself insisted, "I am the man."

¹⁰"How then were your eyes opened?" they asked.

¹¹He replied, "The man they call Jesus made some mud and put it on my eyes. He told me to go to Siloam and wash. So I went and washed, and then I could see."

¹²"Where is this man?" they asked him.

"I don't know," he said.

The Pharisees Investigate the Healing

¹³They brought to the Pharisees the man who had been blind. ¹⁴Now the day on which Jesus had made the mud and opened the man's eyes was a Sabbath. ¹⁵Therefore the Pharisees also asked him how he had received his sight. "He put mud on my eyes," the man replied, "and I washed, and now I see."

¹⁶Some of the Pharisees said, "This man is not from God, for he does not keep the Sabbath."

But others asked, "How can a sinner perform such signs?" So they were divided.

¹⁷Then they turned again to the blind man, "What have you to say about him? It was your eyes he opened."

The man replied, "He is a prophet."

¹⁸They still did not believe that he had been blind and had received his sight until they sent for the man's parents. ¹⁹"Is this your son?" they asked. "Is this the one you say was born blind? How is it that now he can see?"

²⁰"We know he is our son," the parents answered, "and we know he was born blind. ²¹But how he can see now, or who opened his eyes, we don't know. Ask him. He is of age; he will speak for himself." ²²His parents said this because they were afraid of the Jewish leaders, who already had decided that anyone who acknowledged that Jesus was the Messiah would be put out of the synagogue. ²³That was why his parents said, "He is of age; ask him."

²⁴A second time they summoned the man who had been blind. "Give glory to God by telling the truth," they said. "We know this man is a sinner."

²⁵He replied, "Whether he is a sinner or not, I don't know. One thing I do know. I was blind but now I see!"

26 Then they asked him, "What did he do to you? How did he open your eyes?"

27 He answered, "I have told you already and you did not listen. Why do you want to hear it again? Do you want to become his disciples too?"

28 Then they hurled insults at him and said, "You are this fellow's disciple! We are disciples of Moses! 29 We know that God spoke to Moses, but as for this fellow, we don't even know where he comes from."

30 The man answered, "Now that is remarkable! You don't know where he comes from, yet he opened my eyes. 31 We know that God does not listen to sinners. He listens to the godly person who does his will. 32 Nobody has ever heard of opening the eyes of a man born blind. 33 If this man were not from God, he could do nothing."

34 To this they replied, "You were steeped in sin at birth; how dare you lecture us!" And they threw him out.

Spiritual Blindness

35 Jesus heard that they had thrown him out, and when he found him, he said, "Do you believe in the Son of Man?"

36 "Who is he, sir?" the man asked. "Tell me so that I may believe in him."

37 Jesus said, "You have now seen him; in fact, he is the one speaking with you."

38 Then the man said, "Lord, I believe," and he worshiped him.

39 Jesus said,[a] "For judgment I have come into this world, so that the blind will see and those who see will become blind."

40 Some Pharisees who were with him heard him say this and asked, "What? Are we blind too?"

41 Jesus said, "If you were blind, you would not be guilty of sin; but now that you claim you can see, your guilt remains.

The Good Shepherd and His Sheep

10 "Very truly I tell you Pharisees, anyone who does not enter the sheep pen by the gate, but climbs in by some other way, is a thief and a robber. 2 The one who enters by the gate is the shepherd of the sheep. 3 The gatekeeper opens the gate for him, and the sheep listen to his voice. He calls his own sheep by name and leads them out. 4 When he has brought out all his own, he goes on ahead of them, and his sheep follow him because they know his voice. 5 But they will never follow a stranger; in fact, they will run away from him because they do not recognize a stranger's voice." 6 Jesus used this figure of speech, but the Pharisees did not understand what he was telling them.

7 Therefore Jesus said again, "Very truly I tell you, I am the gate for the sheep. 8 All who have come before me are thieves and robbers, but the sheep have not listened to them. 9 I am the gate; whoever enters through me will be saved.[b] They will come in and go out, and find pasture. 10 The thief comes only to steal and kill and destroy; I have come that they may have life, and have it to the full.

11 "I am the good shepherd. The good shepherd lays down his life for the sheep. 12 The hired hand is not the shepherd and does not own the sheep. So when he sees the wolf coming, he abandons the sheep and runs away. Then the wolf attacks the flock and scatters it. 13 The man runs away because he is a hired hand and cares nothing for the sheep.

14 "I am the good shepherd; I know my sheep and my sheep know me— 15 just as the Father knows me and I know the Father—and I lay down my life for the sheep. 16 I have other sheep that are not of this sheep pen. I must bring them also. They too will listen to my voice, and there shall be one flock and one shepherd. 17 The reason my Father loves me is that I lay down my life—only to take it up again. 18 No one takes it from me, but I lay it down of my own accord. I have authority to lay it down and authority to take it up again. This command I received from my Father."

---

a 38,39 Some early manuscripts do not have *Then the man said . . . 39 Jesus said.*   *b* 9 Or *kept safe*

¹⁹The Jews who heard these words were again divided. ²⁰Many of them said, "He is demon-possessed and raving mad. Why listen to him?"

²¹But others said, "These are not the sayings of a man possessed by a demon. Can a demon open the eyes of the blind?"

Further Conflict Over Jesus' Claims

²²Then came the Festival of Dedication*a* at Jerusalem. It was winter, ²³and Jesus was in the temple courts walking in Solomon's Colonnade. ²⁴The Jews who were there gathered around him, saying, "How long will you keep us in suspense? If you are the Messiah, tell us plainly."

²⁵Jesus answered, "I did tell you, but you do not believe. The works I do in my Father's name testify about me, ²⁶but you do not believe because you are not my sheep. ²⁷My sheep listen to my voice; I know them, and they follow me. ²⁸I give them eternal life, and they shall never perish; no one will snatch them out of my hand. ²⁹My Father, who has given them to me, is greater than all*b*; no one can snatch them out of my Father's hand. ³⁰I and the Father are one."

³¹Again his Jewish opponents picked up stones to stone him, ³²but Jesus said to them, "I have shown you many good works from the Father. For which of these do you stone me?"

³³"We are not stoning you for any good work," they replied, "but for blasphemy, because you, a mere man, claim to be God."

³⁴Jesus answered them, "Is it not written in your Law, 'I have said you are "gods"'*c*? ³⁵If he called them 'gods,' to whom the word of God came—and Scripture cannot be set aside— ³⁶what about the one whom the Father set apart as his very own and sent into the world? Why then do you accuse me of blasphemy because I said, 'I am God's Son'? ³⁷Do not believe me unless I do the works of my Father. ³⁸But if I do them, even though you do not believe me, believe the works,

that you may know and understand that the Father is in me, and I in the Father." ³⁹Again they tried to seize him, but he escaped their grasp.

⁴⁰Then Jesus went back across the Jordan to the place where John had been baptizing in the early days. There he stayed, ⁴¹and many people came to him. They said, "Though John never performed a sign, all that John said about this man

INSTANT ACCESS

Oops. Here it is again. Another one of those stories for little kids. Sheep? And shepherds? How cute, right? Wrong. Little kids see sheep as furry, cuddly things. But in Jesus' day people saw sheep as wealth. A shepherd often risked his life to protect the sheep under his care. Think about this passage that way, and sheep and shepherds aren't just for little kids. When Jesus says, "I am the good shepherd," he's telling you how valuable you are to God. And he proved that claim by dying for you. Check this passage out. What else do you see that tells you you're really important to the Lord?

{John 10:1–21}

---

a 22 That is, Hanukkah   *b 29* Many early manuscripts *What my Father has given me is greater than all*
c 34 Psalm 82:6

was true." 42And in that place many believed in Jesus.

The Death of Lazarus

11 Now a man named Lazarus was sick. He was from Bethany, the village of Mary and her sister Martha. 2(This Mary, whose brother Lazarus now lay sick, was the same one who poured perfume on the Lord and wiped his feet with her hair.) 3So the sisters sent word to Jesus, "Lord, the one you love is sick."

4When he heard this, Jesus said, "This sickness will not end in death. No, it is for God's glory so that God's Son may be glorified through it." 5Now Jesus loved Martha and her sister and Lazarus. 6So when he heard that Lazarus was sick, he stayed where he was two more days, 7and then he said to his disciples, "Let us go back to Judea."

8"But Rabbi," they said, "a short while ago the Jews there tried to stone you, and yet you are going back?"

9Jesus answered, "Are there not twelve hours of daylight? Anyone who walks in the daytime will not stumble, for they see by this world's light. 10It is when a person walks at night that they stumble, for they have no light."

11After he had said this, he went on to tell them, "Our friend Lazarus has fallen asleep; but I am going there to wake him up."

12His disciples replied, "Lord, if he sleeps, he will get better." 13Jesus had been speaking of his death, but his disciples thought he meant natural sleep.

14So then he told them plainly, "Lazarus is dead, 15and for your sake I am glad I was not there, so that you may believe. But let us go to him."

16Then Thomas (also known as Didymus[a]) said to the rest of the disciples, "Let us also go, that we may die with him."

Jesus Comforts the Sisters of Lazarus

17On his arrival, Jesus found that Lazarus had already been in the tomb for four days. 18Now Bethany was less than two miles[b] from Jerusalem, 19and many Jews had come to Martha and Mary to comfort them in the loss of their brother. 20When Martha heard that Jesus was coming, she went out to meet him, but Mary stayed at home.

21"Lord," Martha said to Jesus, "if you had been here, my brother would not have died. 22But I know that even now God will give you whatever you ask."

23Jesus said to her, "Your brother will rise again."

24Martha answered, "I know he will rise again in the resurrection at the last day."

25Jesus said to her, "I am the resurrection and the life. The one who believes in me will live, even though they die; 26and whoever lives by believing in me will never die. Do you believe this?"

27"Yes, Lord," she replied, "I believe that you are the Messiah, the Son of God, who is to come into the world."

28After she had said this, she went back and called her sister Mary aside. "The Teacher is here," she said, "and is asking for you." 29When Mary heard this, she got up quickly and went to him. 30Now Jesus had not yet entered the village, but was still at the place where Martha had met him. 31When the Jews who had been with Mary in the house, comforting her, noticed how quickly she got up and went out, they followed her, supposing she was going to the tomb to mourn there.

32When Mary reached the place where Jesus was and saw him, she fell at his feet and said, "Lord, if you had been here, my brother would not have died."

33When Jesus saw her weeping, and the Jews who had come along with her also weeping, he was deeply moved in spirit and troubled. 34"Where have you laid him?" he asked.

"Come and see, Lord," they replied.

35Jesus wept.

36Then the Jews said, "See how he loved him!"

37But some of them said, "Could not he who opened the eyes of the blind man have kept this man from dying?"

---

a 16 *Thomas* (Aramaic) and *Didymus* (Greek) both mean *twin*.   b 18 Or about 3 kilometers

Jesus Raises Lazarus From the Dead

³⁸ Jesus, once more deeply moved, came to the tomb. It was a cave with a stone laid across the entrance. ³⁹ "Take away the stone," he said.

"But, Lord," said Martha, the sister of the dead man, "by this time there is a bad odor, for he has been there four days."

⁴⁰ Then Jesus said, "Did I not tell you that if you believe, you will see the glory of God?"

⁴¹ So they took away the stone. Then Jesus looked up and said, "Father, I thank you that you have heard me. ⁴² I knew that you always hear me, but I said this for the benefit of the people standing here, that they may believe that you sent me."

⁴³ When he had said this, Jesus called in a loud voice, "Lazarus, come out!" ⁴⁴ The dead man came out, his hands and feet wrapped with strips of linen, and a cloth around his face.

Jesus said to them, "Take off the grave clothes and let him go."

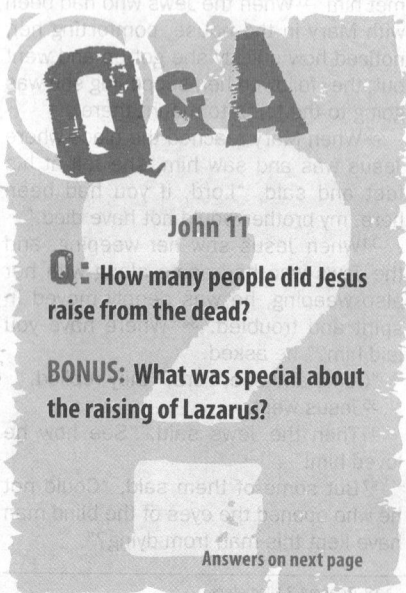

John 11

Q: How many people did Jesus raise from the dead?

BONUS: What was special about the raising of Lazarus?

Answers on next page

The Plot to Kill Jesus

⁴⁵ Therefore many of the Jews who had come to visit Mary, and had seen what Jesus did, believed in him. ⁴⁶ But some of them went to the Pharisees and told them what Jesus had done. ⁴⁷ Then the chief priests and the Pharisees called a meeting of the Sanhedrin.

"What are we accomplishing?" they asked. "Here is this man performing many signs. ⁴⁸ If we let him go on like this, everyone will believe in him, and then the Romans will come and take away both our temple and our nation."

⁴⁹ Then one of them, named Caiaphas, who was high priest that year, spoke up, "You know nothing at all! ⁵⁰ You do not realize that it is better for you that one man die for the people than that the whole nation perish."

⁵¹ He did not say this on his own, but as high priest that year he prophesied that Jesus would die for the Jewish nation, ⁵² and not only for that nation but also for the scattered children of God, to bring them together and make them one. ⁵³ So from that day on they plotted to take his life.

⁵⁴ Therefore Jesus no longer moved about publicly among the people of Judea. Instead he withdrew to a region near the wilderness, to a village called Ephraim, where he stayed with his disciples.

⁵⁵ When it was almost time for the Jewish Passover, many went up from the country to Jerusalem for their ceremonial cleansing before the Passover. ⁵⁶ They kept looking for Jesus, and as they stood in the temple courts they asked one another, "What do you think? Isn't he coming to the festival at all?" ⁵⁷ But the chief priests and the Pharisees had given orders that anyone who found out where Jesus was should report it so that they might arrest him.

Jesus Anointed at Bethany

12 Six days before the Passover, Jesus came to Bethany, where Lazarus lived, whom Jesus had raised from the dead. ² Here a dinner was given in Jesus' honor. Martha served, while

Lazarus was among those reclining at the table with him. [3] Then Mary took about a pint[a] of pure nard, an expensive perfume; she poured it on Jesus' feet and wiped his feet with her hair. And the house was filled with the fragrance of the perfume.

[4] But one of his disciples, Judas Iscariot, who was later to betray him, objected, [5] "Why wasn't this perfume sold and the money given to the poor? It was worth a year's wages.[b]" [6] He did not say this because he cared about the poor but because he was a thief; as keeper of the money bag, he used to help himself to what was put into it.

[7] "Leave her alone," Jesus replied. "It was intended that she should save this perfume for the day of my burial. [8] You will always have the poor among you,[c] but you will not always have me."

[9] Meanwhile a large crowd of Jews found out that Jesus was there and came, not only because of him but also to see Lazarus, whom he had raised from the dead. [10] So the chief priests made plans to kill Lazarus as well, [11] for on account of him many of the Jews were going over to Jesus and believing in him.

Jesus Comes to Jerusalem as King

[12] The next day the great crowd that had come for the festival heard that Jesus was on his way to Jerusalem. [13] They took palm branches and went out to meet him, shouting,

"Hosanna![d]"

"Blessed is he who comes in the name of the Lord!"[e]

"Blessed is the king of Israel!"

[14] Jesus found a young donkey and sat on it, as it is written:

[15] "Do not be afraid, Daughter Zion;
  see, your king is coming,
    seated on a donkey's colt."[f]

[16] At first his disciples did not understand all this. Only after Jesus was glorified did they realize that these things had

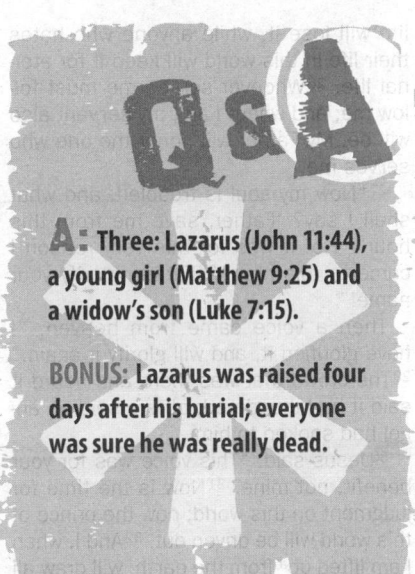

A: Three: Lazarus (John 11:44), a young girl (Matthew 9:25) and a widow's son (Luke 7:15).

BONUS: Lazarus was raised four days after his burial; everyone was sure he was really dead.

been written about him and that these things had been done to him.

[17] Now the crowd that was with him when he called Lazarus from the tomb and raised him from the dead continued to spread the word. [18] Many people, because they had heard that he had performed this sign, went out to meet him. [19] So the Pharisees said to one another, "See, this is getting us nowhere. Look how the whole world has gone after him!"

Jesus Predicts His Death

[20] Now there were some Greeks among those who went up to worship at the festival. [21] They came to Philip, who was from Bethsaida in Galilee, with a request. "Sir," they said, "we would like to see Jesus." [22] Philip went to tell Andrew; Andrew and Philip in turn told Jesus.

[23] Jesus replied, "The hour has come for the Son of Man to be glorified. [24] Very truly I tell you, unless a kernel of wheat falls to the ground and dies, it remains only a single seed. But if it dies, it produces many seeds. [25] Anyone who loves their

---

[a] 3 Or about 0.5 liter   [b] 5 Greek *three hundred denarii*   [c] 8 See Deut. 15:11.   [d] 13 A Hebrew expression meaning "Save!" which became an exclamation of praise   [e] 13 Psalm 118:25,26   [f] 15 Zech. 9:9

life will lose it, while anyone who hates their life in this world will keep it for eternal life. 26 Whoever serves me must follow me; and where I am, my servant also will be. My Father will honor the one who serves me.

27 "Now my soul is troubled, and what shall I say? 'Father, save me from this hour'? No, it was for this very reason I came to this hour. 28 Father, glorify your name!"

Then a voice came from heaven, "I have glorified it, and will glorify it again." 29 The crowd that was there and heard it said it had thundered; others said an angel had spoken to him.

30 Jesus said, "This voice was for your benefit, not mine. 31 Now is the time for judgment on this world; now the prince of this world will be driven out. 32 And I, when I am lifted up[a] from the earth, will draw all people to myself." 33 He said this to show the kind of death he was going to die.

34 The crowd spoke up, "We have heard from the Law that the Messiah will remain forever, so how can you say, 'The Son of Man must be lifted up'? Who is this 'Son of Man'?"

35 Then Jesus told them, "You are going to have the light just a little while longer. Walk while you have the light, before darkness overtakes you. Whoever walks in the dark does not know where they are going. 36 Believe in the light while you have the light, so that you may become children of light." When he had finished speaking, Jesus left and hid himself from them.

Belief and Unbelief Among the Jews

37 Even after Jesus had performed so many signs in their presence, they still would not believe in him. 38 This was to fulfill the word of Isaiah the prophet:

"Lord, who has believed our message
and to whom has the arm of the Lord been revealed?"[b]

39 For this reason they could not believe, because, as Isaiah says elsewhere:

INSTANT ACCESS

These verses identify three groups of people. Some would not believe even after Jesus "performed so many signs in their presence" (John 12:37). Some believed but didn't want to tell anyone. Some, like the disciples, believed and were eager to say they were followers of Jesus. Which group do you fit into?

- Unbeliever
- Secret believer
- Open believer

In a way, both unbelievers and open believers are being honest. The secret believer, who doesn't want anyone to know he or she is a Christian, isn't being honest. It is great to be an open believer, who cares more about what God thinks than about what people think.

{John 12:37–44}

40 "He has blinded their eyes
and hardened their hearts,
so they can neither see with their eyes,
nor understand with their hearts,
nor turn—and I would heal them."[c]

41 Isaiah said this because he saw Jesus' glory and spoke about him.

---

[a] 32 The Greek for *lifted up* also means *exalted*.   [b] 38 Isaiah 53:1   [c] 40 Isaiah 6:10

42 Yet at the same time many even among the leaders believed in him. But because of the Pharisees they would not openly acknowledge their faith for fear they would be put out of the synagogue; 43 for they loved human praise more than praise from God.

44 Then Jesus cried out, "Whoever believes in me does not believe in me only, but in the one who sent me. 45 The one who looks at me is seeing the one who sent me. 46 I have come into the world as a light, so that no one who believes in me should stay in darkness.

47 "If anyone hears my words but does not keep them, I do not judge that person. For I did not come to judge the world, but to save the world. 48 There is a judge for the one who rejects me and does not accept my words; the very words I have spoken will condemn them at the last day. 49 For I did not speak on my own, but the Father who sent me commanded me to say all that I have spoken. 50 I know that his command leads to eternal life. So whatever I say is just what the Father has told me to say."

Jesus Washes His Disciples' Feet

13 It was just before the Passover Festival. Jesus knew that the hour had come for him to leave this world and go to the Father. Having loved his own who were in the world, he loved them to the end.

2 The evening meal was in progress, and the devil had already prompted Judas, the son of Simon Iscariot, to betray Jesus. 3 Jesus knew that the Father had put all things under his power, and that he had come from God and was returning to God; 4 so he got up from the meal, took off his outer clothing, and wrapped a towel around his waist. 5 After that, he poured water into a basin and began to wash his disciples' feet, drying them with the towel that was wrapped around him.

6 He came to Simon Peter, who said to him, "Lord, are you going to wash my feet?"

7 Jesus replied, "You do not realize now what I am doing, but later you will understand."

8 "No," said Peter, "you shall never wash my feet."

Jesus answered, "Unless I wash you, you have no part with me."

9 "Then, Lord," Simon Peter replied, "not just my feet but my hands and my head as well!"

10 Jesus answered, "Those who have had a bath need only to wash their feet; their whole body is clean. And you are clean, though not every one of you." 11 For he knew who was going to betray him, and that was why he said not every one was clean.

12 When he had finished washing their feet, he put on his clothes and returned to his place. "Do you understand what I have done for you?" he asked them. 13 "You call me 'Teacher' and 'Lord,' and rightly so, for that is what I am. 14 Now that I, your Lord and Teacher, have washed your feet, you also should wash one another's feet. 15 I have set you an example that you should do as I have done for you. 16 Very truly I tell you, no servant is greater than his master, nor is a messenger greater than the one who sent him. 17 Now that you know these things, you will be blessed if you do them.

Jesus Predicts His Betrayal

18 "I am not referring to all of you; I know those I have chosen. But this is to fulfill this passage of Scripture: 'He who shared my bread has turned*a* against me.'*b*

19 "I am telling you now before it happens, so that when it does happen you will believe that I am who I am. 20 Very truly I tell you, whoever accepts anyone I send accepts me; and whoever accepts me accepts the one who sent me."

21 After he had said this, Jesus was troubled in spirit and testified, "Very truly I tell you, one of you is going to betray me."

22 His disciples stared at one another, at a loss to know which of them he meant. 23 One of them, the disciple whom Jesus loved, was reclining next to him.

---

a 18 Greek has *lifted up his heel*   *b* 18 Psalm 41:9

24 Simon Peter motioned to this disciple and said, "Ask him which one he means."
25 Leaning back against Jesus, he asked him, "Lord, who is it?"
26 Jesus answered, "It is the one to whom I will give this piece of bread when I have dipped it in the dish." Then, dipping the piece of bread, he gave it to Judas, the son of Simon Iscariot. 27 As soon as Judas took the bread, Satan entered into him.

So Jesus told him, "What you are about to do, do quickly." 28 But no one at the meal understood why Jesus said this to him. 29 Since Judas had charge of the money, some thought Jesus was telling him to buy what was needed for the festival, or to give something to the poor. 30 As soon as Judas had taken the bread, he went out. And it was night.

Jesus Predicts Peter's Denial

31 When he was gone, Jesus said, "Now the Son of Man is glorified and God is glorified in him. 32 If God is glorified in him,[a] God will glorify the Son in himself, and will glorify him at once.

33 "My children, I will be with you only a little longer. You will look for me, and just as I told the Jews, so I tell you now: Where I am going, you cannot come.

34 "A new command I give you: Love one another. As I have loved you, so you must love one another. 35 By this everyone will know that you are my disciples, if you love one another."

---

a 32 Many early manuscripts do not have *If God is glorified in him.*

TO THE POINT

Love One Another

The night before he was crucified, Jesus issued a "new command" that his disciples love one another (John 13:34).

The call to love others isn't new (Leviticus 19:18,34). What then is "new" about this commandment?

+ A new relationship—Christians are family, not just neighbors.

+ A new standard—Christians love as Jesus loved.

+ A new outcome—when Christians love each other, people who are not yet believers realize these are Jesus' followers.

Love isn't optional for Christians. They are to be people who love. When they love each other in the self-sacrificing way that Jesus loves, non-Christians see how real Jesus is by the difference he makes in their lives.

[36]Simon Peter asked him, "Lord, where are you going?"

Jesus replied, "Where I am going, you cannot follow now, but you will follow later."

[37]Peter asked, "Lord, why can't I follow you now? I will lay down my life for you."

[38]Then Jesus answered, "Will you really lay down your life for me? Very truly I tell you, before the rooster crows, you will disown me three times!

Jesus Comforts His Disciples

14 "Do not let your hearts be troubled. You believe in God[a]; believe also in me. [2]My Father's house has many rooms; if that were not so, would I have told you that I am going there to prepare a place for you? [3]And if I go and prepare a place for you, I will come back and take you to be with me that you also may be where I am. [4]You know the way to the place where I am going."

Jesus the Way to the Father

[5]Thomas said to him, "Lord, we don't know where you are going, so how can we know the way?"

[6]Jesus answered, "I am the way and the truth and the life. No one comes to the Father except through me. [7]If you really know me, you will know[b] my Father as well. From now on, you do know him and have seen him."

[8]Philip said, "Lord, show us the Father and that will be enough for us."

[9]Jesus answered: "Don't you know me, Philip, even after I have been among you such a long time? Anyone who has seen me has seen the Father. How can you say, 'Show us the Father'? [10]Don't you believe that I am in the Father, and that the Father is in me? The words I say to you I do not speak on my own authority. Rather, it is the Father, living in me, who is doing his work. [11]Believe me when I say that I am in the Father and the Father is in me; or at least believe on the evidence of the works themselves. [12]Very truly I tell you, whoever believes in me will do the works I have been doing, and they will do even greater things than these, because I am going to the Father. [13]And I will do whatever you ask in my name, so that the Father may be glorified in the Son. [14]You may ask me for anything in my name, and I will do it.

Jesus Promises the Holy Spirit

[15]"If you love me, keep my commands. [16]And I will ask the Father, and he will give you another advocate to help you and be with you forever— [17]the Spirit of truth. The world cannot accept him, because it neither sees him nor knows him. But you know him, for he lives with you and will be[c] in you. [18]I will not leave you as orphans; I will come to you. [19]Before long, the world will not see me anymore, but you will see me. Because I live, you also will live. [20]On that day you will realize that I am in my Father, and you are in me, and I am in you. [21]Whoever has my commands and keeps them is the one who loves me. The one who loves me will be loved by my Father, and I too will love them and show myself to them."

[22]Then Judas (not Judas Iscariot) said, "But, Lord, why do you intend to show yourself to us and not to the world?"

[23]Jesus replied, "Anyone who loves me will obey my teaching. My Father will love them, and we will come to them and make our home with them. [24]Anyone who does not love me will not obey my teaching. These words you hear are not my own; they belong to the Father who sent me.

[25]"All this I have spoken while still with you. [26]But the Advocate, the Holy Spirit, whom the Father will send in my name, will teach you all things and will remind you of everything I have said to you. [27]Peace I leave with you; my peace I give you. I do not give to you as the world gives. Do not let your hearts be troubled and do not be afraid.

[28]"You heard me say, 'I am going away and I am coming back to you.' If you loved me, you would be glad that I am going to the Father, for the Father is greater than I. [29]I have told you now before it happens,

---

[a] 1 Or *Believe in God*   [b] 7 Some manuscripts *If you really knew me, you would know*   [c] 17 Some early manuscripts *and is*

so that when it does happen you will believe. [30]I will not say much more to you, for the prince of this world is coming. He has no hold over me, [31]but he comes so that the world may learn that I love the Father and do exactly what my Father has commanded me.

"Come now; let us leave.

The Vine and the Branches

15 "I am the true vine, and my Father is the gardener. [2]He cuts off every branch in me that bears no fruit, while every branch that does bear fruit he prunes[a] so that it will be even more fruitful. [3]You are already clean because of the word I have spoken to you. [4]Remain in me, as I also remain in you. No branch can bear fruit by itself; it must remain in the vine. Neither can you bear fruit unless you remain in me.

[5]"I am the vine; you are the branches. If you remain in me and I in you, you will bear much fruit; apart from me you can do nothing. [6]If you do not remain in me, you are like a branch that is thrown away and withers; such branches are picked up, thrown into the fire and burned. [7]If you remain in me and my words remain in you, ask whatever you wish, and it will be done for you. [8]This is to my Father's glory, that you bear much fruit, showing yourselves to be my disciples.

[9]"As the Father has loved me, so have I loved you. Now remain in my love. [10]If you keep my commands, you will remain in my love, just as I have kept my Father's commands and remain in his love. [11]I have told you this so that my joy may be in you and that your joy may be complete. [12]My command is this: Love each other as I have loved you. [13]Greater love has no one than this: to lay down one's life for one's friends. [14]You are my friends if you do what I command. [15]I no longer call you servants, because a servant does not know his master's business. Instead, I have called you friends, for everything that I learned from my Father I have made known to you. [16]You did not choose me, but I chose you and appointed you so that you might go and bear fruit—fruit that will last—and so that whatever you ask in my name the Father will give you. [17]This is my command: Love each other.

The World Hates the Disciples

[18]"If the world hates you, keep in mind that it hated me first. [19]If you belonged to the world, it would love you as its own. As it is, you do not belong to the world, but I have chosen you out of the world. That is why the world hates you. [20]Remember what I told you: 'A servant is not greater than his master.'[b] If they persecuted me, they will persecute you also. If they

---

[a] 2 The Greek for *he prunes* also means *he cleans*.   [b] 20 John 13:16

PANORAMA

God?

Is Jesus really God? Yes, he is the Son of God, who loved you enough to come to earth to be with you and to save you from your sins.

{JOHN}

> I'm an honor student, athlete, beautiful inside and out, and have a ton of friends. But some of my friends think I'm conceited. How can I make them understand that I feel good about myself because I'm just naturally good at almost everything? Why should I get down on myself if others can't keep up with me? >> Maya

Dear Jordan

Dear Maya,

It's terrific to feel good about yourself. But I think your reasons show a lack of understanding in why we should have good self-esteem. In Genesis 1 God said, "Let us make mankind in our image, in our likeness ..." (verse 26). Our value as human beings is not measured by what we succeed in. Instead, when we are born we are given special value because we alone are made in the image and likeness of God.

You said you are naturally good at almost everything. Where did these talents or gifts come from? According to King David, "For [God] created my inmost being; [he] knit me together in my mother's womb" (Psalm 139:13). God gave each of us different abilities. So you are correct that these things are natural for you.

"Apart from me you can do nothing" Jesus said in John 15:5. He goes on to say that it "is to my Father's glory, that you bear much fruit" (verse 8). In the future when someone says you're good at something, try saying, "I'm trying to use the abilities God gave me." Then perhaps people will think you are godly instead of conceited.

Jordan

obeyed my teaching, they will obey yours also. 21They will treat you this way because of my name, for they do not know the one who sent me. 22If I had not come and spoken to them, they would not be guilty of sin; but now they have no excuse for their sin. 23Whoever hates me hates my Father as well. 24If I had not done among them the works no one else did, they would not be guilty of sin. As it is, they have seen, and yet they have hated both me and my Father. 25But this is to fulfill what is written in their Law: 'They hated me without reason.'*a*

The Work of the Holy Spirit

26"When the Advocate comes, whom I will send to you from the Father—the Spirit of truth who goes out from the Father—he will testify about me. 27And you also must testify, for you have been with me from the beginning.

16 "All this I have told you so that you will not fall away. 2They will put you out of the synagogue; in fact, the time is coming when anyone who kills you will think they are offering a service to God. 3They will do such things because they have not known the Father or me. 4I have told you this, so that when their time comes you will remember that I warned you about them. I did not tell you this from the beginning because I was with you, 5but now I am going to him who sent me. None of you asks me, 'Where are you going?' 6Rather, you are filled with grief because I have said these things. 7But very truly I tell you, it is for your good that I am going away. Unless I go away, the Advocate will not come to you; but if I go, I will send him to you. 8When he comes, he will prove the world to be in the wrong about sin and righteousness and judgment: 9about sin, because people do not believe in me; 10about righteousness, because I am going to the Father, where you can see me no longer; 11and about judgment, because the prince of this world now stands condemned.

12"I have much more to say to you, more than you can now bear. 13But when he, the Spirit of truth, comes, he will guide you into all the truth. He will not speak on his own; he will speak only what he hears, and he will tell you what is yet to come. 14He will glorify me because it is from me that he will receive what he will make known to you. 15All that belongs to the Father is mine. That is why I said the Spirit will receive from me what he will make known to you."

The Disciples' Grief Will Turn to Joy

16Jesus went on to say, "In a little while you will see me no more, and then after a little while you will see me."

17At this, some of his disciples said to one another, "What does he mean by saying, 'In a little while you will see me no more, and then after a little while you will see me,' and 'Because I am going to the Father'?" 18They kept asking, "What does he mean by 'a little while'? We don't understand what he is saying."

19Jesus saw that they wanted to ask him about this, so he said to them, "Are you asking one another what I meant when I said, 'In a little while you will see me no more, and then after a little while you will see me'? 20Very truly I tell you, you will weep and mourn while the world rejoices. You will grieve, but your grief will turn to joy. 21A woman giving birth to a child has pain because her time has come; but when her baby is born she forgets the anguish because of her joy that a child is born into the world. 22So with you: Now is your time of grief, but I will see you again and you will rejoice, and no one will take away your joy. 23In that day you will no longer ask me anything. Very truly I tell you, my Father will give you whatever you ask in my name. 24Until now you have not asked for anything in my name. Ask and you will receive, and your joy will be complete.

25"Though I have been speaking figuratively, a time is coming when I will no longer use this kind of language but will tell you plainly about my Father. 26In that day you will ask in my name. I am not saying that I will ask the Father on your

---

a 25 Psalms 35:19; 69:4

Is Jesus' promise in John 16:23, "My Father will give you whatever you ask in my name," sort of like a blank check? You get whatever you want? What will you ask for? First you need to understand the "in my name" part. In Bible times a name wasn't just a label. Names reflected character. Asking "in Jesus' name" doesn't mean tacking those words on at the end of your prayers. It means asking for the kind of thing Jesus himself would ask for. Jesus' promise means that when you want to glorify God as he did and serve others as he served them, God will gladly answer those prayers!

{John 16:23–24}

behalf. 27 No, the Father himself loves you because you have loved me and have believed that I came from God. 28 I came from the Father and entered the world; now I am leaving the world and going back to the Father."

29 Then Jesus' disciples said, "Now you are speaking clearly and without figures of speech. 30 Now we can see that you know all things and that you do not even need to have anyone ask you questions. This makes us believe that you came from God."

31 "Do you now believe?" Jesus replied. 32 "A time is coming and in fact has come when you will be scattered, each to your own home. You will leave me all alone. Yet I am not alone, for my Father is with me.

33 "I have told you these things, so that in me you may have peace. In this world you will have trouble. But take heart! I have overcome the world."

Jesus Prays to Be Glorified

17 After Jesus said this, he looked toward heaven and prayed:

"Father, the hour has come. Glorify your Son, that your Son may glorify you. 2 For you granted him authority over all people that he might give eternal life to all those you have given him. 3 Now this is eternal life: that they know you, the only true God, and Jesus Christ, whom you have sent. 4 I have brought you glory on earth by finishing the work you gave me to do. 5 And now, Father, glorify me in your presence with the glory I had with you before the world began.

Jesus Prays for His Disciples

6 "I have revealed you[a] to those whom you gave me out of the world. They were yours; you gave them to me and they have obeyed your word. 7 Now they know that everything you have given me comes from you. 8 For I gave them the words you gave me and they accepted them. They knew with certainty that I came from you, and they believed that you sent me. 9 I pray for them. I am not praying for the world, but for those you have given me, for they are yours. 10 All I have is yours, and all you have is mine. And glory has come to me through them. 11 I will remain in the world no longer, but they are still in the world, and I am coming to you. Holy Father, protect them by the power of[b] your name, the name you gave me, so that they may be one as we are one.

a 6 Greek your name   b 11 Or Father, keep them faithful to

Dear Jordan

My friend's father died last week. I gave her a big hug and said how depressed she must be. She told me she was very sad and grieving but not depressed. She said she felt joyful her father was with Jesus and no longer suffering. I'm confused. How can someone be sad and grieving but not depressed?   >> Victoria

Dear Victoria,

Grief and sadness are feelings people have when they have lost someone or something close to their heart. Depression is sadness that doesn't go away for a long time. It could come after someone dies if grieving continues and the person can't function. Depression can be feeling down or sad and crying. It's often a feeling of hopelessness which may not have a known cause. Depression is serious and needs to be treated by a doctor.

It's normal to feel sad when someone we love has died. We will always remember that person and sometimes we may cry when we think of him or her. But normally our deep sadness begins to pass.

Your friend said she felt joy that her father was no longer suffering. That's what John 16:20, 22 tells us: "You will grieve, but your grief will turn to joy … and no one will take away your joy." The joy of the Lord is a feeling of deep well-being and happiness that comes from God even when we may feel sad or troubled. Because it comes from God, no one else can take it away.

Jordan

INSTANT ACCESS

Jesus prayed that believers would "be one" and "be brought to complete unity." Ha! That's one prayer that wasn't answered! Right? Look at all the different denominations! But read carefully. What Jesus asked was that believers be one with him, be united to him and the Father. This isn't about denominations at all. And this prayer has been answered: Every Christian is united to Jesus when he or she believes (see Romans 6:1–14).

{John 17:20–23}

12While I was with them, I protected them and kept them safe by[a] that name you gave me. None has been lost except the one doomed to destruction so that Scripture would be fulfilled.

13"I am coming to you now, but I say these things while I am still in the world, so that they may have the full measure of my joy within them. 14I have given them your word and the world has hated them, for they are not of the world any more than I am of the world. 15My prayer is not that you take them out of the world but that you protect them from the evil one. 16They are not of the world, even as I am not of it. 17Sanctify them by[b] the truth; your word is truth. 18As you sent me into the world, I have sent them into the

world. 19For them I sanctify myself, that they too may be truly sanctified.

Jesus Prays for All Believers

20"My prayer is not for them alone. I pray also for those who will believe in me through their message, 21that all of them may be one, Father, just as you are in me and I am in you. May they also be in us so that the world may believe that you have sent me. 22I have given them the glory that you gave me, that they may be one as we are one— 23I in them and you in me—so that they may be brought to complete unity. Then the world will know that you sent me and have loved them even as you have loved me.

24"Father, I want those you have given me to be with me where I am, and to see my glory, the glory you have given me because you loved me before the creation of the world.

25"Righteous Father, though the world does not know you, I know you, and they know that you have sent me. 26I have made you[c] known to them, and will continue to make you known in order that the love you have for me may be in them and that I myself may be in them."

Jesus Arrested

18 When he had finished praying, Jesus left with his disciples and crossed the Kidron Valley. On the other side there was a garden, and he and his disciples went into it.

2Now Judas, who betrayed him, knew the place, because Jesus had often met there with his disciples. 3So Judas came to the garden, guiding a detachment of soldiers and some officials from the chief priests and the Pharisees. They were carrying torches, lanterns and weapons.

4Jesus, knowing all that was going to happen to him, went out and asked them, "Who is it you want?"

5"Jesus of Nazareth," they replied.

"I am he," Jesus said. (And Judas the

---

[a] 12 Or kept them faithful to   [b] 17 Or them to live in accordance with   [c] 26 Greek your name

traitor was standing there with them.) ⁶When Jesus said, "I am he," they drew back and fell to the ground.

⁷Again he asked them, "Who is it you want?"

"Jesus of Nazareth," they said.

⁸Jesus answered, "I told you that I am he. If you are looking for me, then let these men go." ⁹This happened so that the words he had spoken would be fulfilled: "I have not lost one of those you gave me."ᵃ

¹⁰Then Simon Peter, who had a sword, drew it and struck the high priest's servant, cutting off his right ear. (The servant's name was Malchus.)

¹¹Jesus commanded Peter, "Put your sword away! Shall I not drink the cup the Father has given me?"

¹²Then the detachment of soldiers with its commander and the Jewish officials arrested Jesus. They bound him ¹³and brought him first to Annas, who was the father-in-law of Caiaphas, the high priest that year. ¹⁴Caiaphas was the one who had advised the Jewish leaders that it would be good if one man died for the people.

Peter's First Denial

¹⁵Simon Peter and another disciple were following Jesus. Because this disciple was known to the high priest, he went with Jesus into the high priest's courtyard, ¹⁶but Peter had to wait outside at the door. The other disciple, who was known to the high priest, came back, spoke to the servant girl on duty there and brought Peter in.

¹⁷"You aren't one of this man's disciples too, are you?" she asked Peter.

He replied, "I am not."

¹⁸It was cold, and the servants and officials stood around a fire they had made to keep warm. Peter also was standing with them, warming himself.

The High Priest Questions Jesus

¹⁹Meanwhile, the high priest questioned Jesus about his disciples and his teaching.

²⁰"I have spoken openly to the world," Jesus replied. "I always taught in synagogues or at the temple, where all the Jews come together. I said nothing in secret. ²¹Why question me? Ask those who heard me. Surely they know what I said."

²²When Jesus said this, one of the officials nearby slapped him in the face. "Is this the way you answer the high priest?" he demanded.

²³"If I said something wrong," Jesus replied, "testify as to what is wrong. But if I spoke the truth, why did you strike me?" ²⁴Then Annas sent him bound to Caiaphas the high priest.

Peter's Second and Third Denials

²⁵Meanwhile, Simon Peter was still standing there, warming himself. So they asked him, "You aren't one of his disciples too, are you?"

He denied it, saying, "I am not."

²⁶One of the high priest's servants, a relative of the man whose ear Peter had cut off, challenged him, "Didn't I see you with him in the garden?" ²⁷Again Peter denied it, and at that moment a rooster began to crow.

Jesus Before Pilate

²⁸Then the Jewish leaders took Jesus from Caiaphas to the palace of the Roman governor. By now it was early morning, and to avoid ceremonial uncleanness they did not enter the palace, because they wanted to be able to eat the Passover. ²⁹So Pilate came out to them and asked, "What charges are you bringing against this man?"

³⁰"If he were not a criminal," they replied, "we would not have handed him over to you."

³¹Pilate said, "Take him yourselves and judge him by your own law."

"But we have no right to execute anyone," they objected. ³²This took place to fulfill what Jesus had said about the kind of death he was going to die.

³³Pilate then went back inside the palace, summoned Jesus and asked him, "Are you the king of the Jews?"

ᵃ 9 John 6:39

34 "Is that your own idea," Jesus asked, "or did others talk to you about me?"

35 "Am I a Jew?" Pilate replied. "Your own people and chief priests handed you over to me. What is it you have done?"

36 Jesus said, "My kingdom is not of this world. If it were, my servants would fight to prevent my arrest by the Jewish leaders. But now my kingdom is from another place."

37 "You are a king, then!" said Pilate.

Jesus answered, "You say that I am a king. In fact, the reason I was born and came into the world is to testify to the truth. Everyone on the side of truth listens to me."

38 "What is truth?" retorted Pilate. With this he went out again to the Jews gathered there and said, "I find no basis for a charge against him. 39 But it is your custom for me to release to you one prisoner at the time of the Passover. Do you want me to release 'the king of the Jews'?"

40 They shouted back, "No, not him! Give us Barabbas!" Now Barabbas had taken part in an uprising.

Jesus Sentenced to Be Crucified

19 Then Pilate took Jesus and had him flogged. 2 The soldiers twisted together a crown of thorns and put it on his head. They clothed him in a purple robe 3 and went up to him again and again, saying, "Hail, king of the Jews!" And they slapped him in the face.

4 Once more Pilate came out and said to the Jews gathered there, "Look, I am bringing him out to you to let you know that I find no basis for a charge against him." 5 When Jesus came out wearing the crown of thorns and the purple robe, Pilate said to them, "Here is the man!"

6 As soon as the chief priests and their officials saw him, they shouted, "Crucify! Crucify!"

But Pilate answered, "You take him and crucify him. As for me, I find no basis for a charge against him."

7 The Jewish leaders insisted, "We have a law, and according to that law he must die, because he claimed to be the Son of God."

8 When Pilate heard this, he was even more afraid, 9 and he went back inside the palace. "Where do you come from?" he asked Jesus, but Jesus gave him no answer. 10 "Do you refuse to speak to me?" Pilate said. "Don't you realize I have power either to free you or to crucify you?"

11 Jesus answered, "You would have no power over me if it were not given to you from above. Therefore the one who handed me over to you is guilty of a greater sin."

12 From then on, Pilate tried to set Jesus free, but the Jewish leaders kept shouting, "If you let this man go, you are no friend of Caesar. Anyone who claims to be a king opposes Caesar."

13 When Pilate heard this, he brought Jesus out and sat down on the judge's seat at a place known as the Stone Pavement (which in Aramaic is Gabbatha). 14 It was the day of Preparation of the Passover; it was about noon.

"Here is your king," Pilate said to the Jews.

15 But they shouted, "Take him away! Take him away! Crucify him!"

"Shall I crucify your king?" Pilate asked.

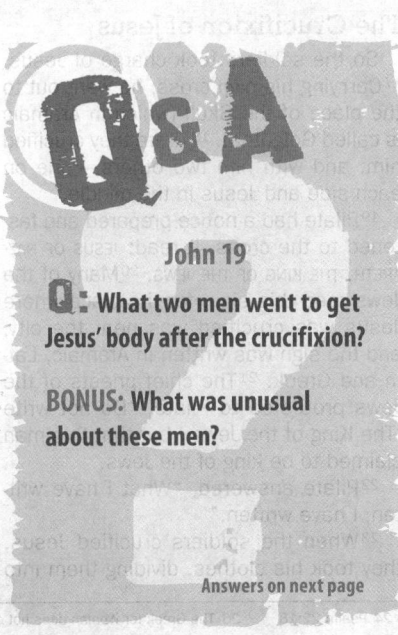

John 19

Q: What two men went to get Jesus' body after the crucifixion?

BONUS: What was unusual about these men?

Answers on next page

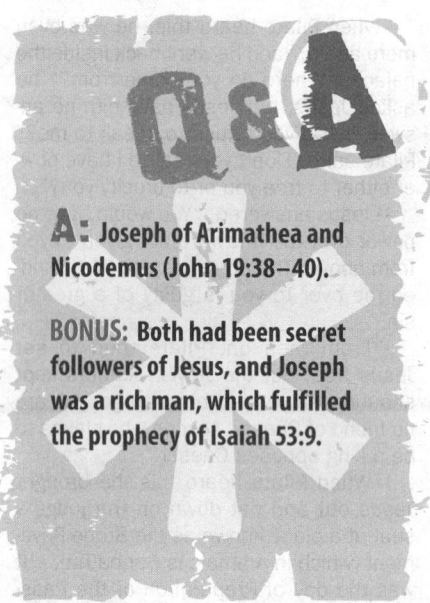

A: Joseph of Arimathea and Nicodemus (John 19:38–40).

BONUS: Both had been secret followers of Jesus, and Joseph was a rich man, which fulfilled the prophecy of Isaiah 53:9.

"We have no king but Caesar," the chief priests answered.

¹⁶Finally Pilate handed him over to them to be crucified.

The Crucifixion of Jesus

So the soldiers took charge of Jesus. ¹⁷Carrying his own cross, he went out to the place of the Skull (which in Aramaic is called Golgotha). ¹⁸There they crucified him, and with him two others—one on each side and Jesus in the middle.

¹⁹Pilate had a notice prepared and fastened to the cross. It read: JESUS OF NAZARETH, THE KING OF THE JEWS. ²⁰Many of the Jews read this sign, for the place where Jesus was crucified was near the city, and the sign was written in Aramaic, Latin and Greek. ²¹The chief priests of the Jews protested to Pilate, "Do not write 'The King of the Jews,' but that this man claimed to be king of the Jews."

²²Pilate answered, "What I have written, I have written."

²³When the soldiers crucified Jesus, they took his clothes, dividing them into four shares, one for each of them, with the undergarment remaining. This garment was seamless, woven in one piece from top to bottom.

²⁴"Let's not tear it," they said to one another. "Let's decide by lot who will get it."

This happened that the scripture might be fulfilled that said,

"They divided my clothes among them
   and cast lots for my garment."[a]

So this is what the soldiers did.

²⁵Near the cross of Jesus stood his mother, his mother's sister, Mary the wife of Clopas, and Mary Magdalene. ²⁶When Jesus saw his mother there, and the disciple whom he loved standing nearby, he said to her, "Woman,[b] here is your son," ²⁷and to the disciple, "Here is your mother." From that time on, this disciple took her into his home.

The Death of Jesus

²⁸Later, knowing that everything had now been finished, and so that Scripture would be fulfilled, Jesus said, "I am thirsty." ²⁹A jar of wine vinegar was there, so they soaked a sponge in it, put the sponge on a stalk of the hyssop plant, and lifted it to Jesus' lips. ³⁰When he had received the drink, Jesus said, "It is finished." With that, he bowed his head and gave up his spirit.

³¹Now it was the day of Preparation, and the next day was to be a special Sabbath. Because the Jewish leaders did not want the bodies left on the crosses during the Sabbath, they asked Pilate to have the legs broken and the bodies taken down. ³²The soldiers therefore came and broke the legs of the first man who had been crucified with Jesus, and then those of the other. ³³But when they came to Jesus and found that he was already dead, they did not break his legs. ³⁴Instead, one of the soldiers pierced Jesus' side with a spear, bringing a sudden flow of blood and water. ³⁵The man who saw it has given testimony, and his testimony is true. He knows that he tells the truth,

---

^a 24 Psalm 22:18   ^b 26 The Greek for *Woman* does not denote any disrespect.

and he testifies so that you also may believe. 36These things happened so that the scripture would be fulfilled: "Not one of his bones will be broken,"a 37and, as another scripture says, "They will look on the one they have pierced."b

The Burial of Jesus

38Later, Joseph of Arimathea asked Pilate for the body of Jesus. Now Joseph was a disciple of Jesus, but secretly because he feared the Jewish leaders. With Pilate's permission, he came and took the body away. 39He was accompanied by Nicodemus, the man who earlier had visited Jesus at night. Nicodemus brought a mixture of myrrh and aloes, about seventy-five pounds.c 40Taking Jesus' body, the two of them wrapped it, with the spices, in strips of linen. This was in accordance with Jewish burial customs. 41At the place where Jesus was crucified, there was a garden, and in the garden a new tomb, in which no one had ever been laid. 42Because it was the Jewish day of Preparation and since the tomb was nearby, they laid Jesus there.

The Empty Tomb

20 Early on the first day of the week, while it was still dark, Mary Magdalene went to the tomb and saw that the stone had been removed from the entrance. 2So she came running to Simon Peter and the other disciple, the one Jesus loved, and said, "They have taken the Lord out of the tomb, and we don't know where they have put him!"

3So Peter and the other disciple started for the tomb. 4Both were running, but the other disciple outran Peter and reached the tomb first. 5He bent over and looked in at the strips of linen lying there but did not go in. 6Then Simon Peter came along behind him and went straight into the tomb. He saw the strips of linen lying there, 7as well as the cloth that had been wrapped around Jesus' head. The cloth was still lying in its place, separate from the linen. 8Finally the other disciple, who had reached the tomb first, also went in-

side. He saw and believed. 9(They still did not understand from Scripture that Jesus had to rise from the dead.) 10Then the disciples went back to where they were staying.

Jesus Appears to Mary Magdalene

11Now Mary stood outside the tomb crying. As she wept, she bent over to look into the tomb 12and saw two angels in white, seated where Jesus' body had been, one at the head and the other at the foot.

13They asked her, "Woman, why are you crying?"

"They have taken my Lord away," she said, "and I don't know where they have put him." 14At this, she turned around and saw Jesus standing there, but she did not realize that it was Jesus.

15He asked her, "Woman, why are you crying? Who is it you are looking for?"

Thinking he was the gardener, she said, "Sir, if you have carried him away, tell me where you have put him, and I will get him."

16Jesus said to her, "Mary."

She turned toward him and cried out in Aramaic, "Rabboni!" (which means "Teacher").

17Jesus said, "Do not hold on to me, for I have not yet ascended to the Father. Go instead to my brothers and tell them, 'I am ascending to my Father and your Father, to my God and your God.'"

18Mary Magdalene went to the disciples with the news: "I have seen the Lord!" And she told them that he had said these things to her.

Jesus Appears to His Disciples

19On the evening of that first day of the week, when the disciples were together, with the doors locked for fear of the Jewish leaders, Jesus came and stood among them and said, "Peace be with you!" 20After he said this, he showed them his hands and side. The disciples were overjoyed when they saw the Lord.

---

a 36 Exodus 12:46; Num. 9:12; Psalm 34:20   b 37 Zech. 12:10   c 39 Or about 34 kilograms

21 Again Jesus said, "Peace be with you! As the Father has sent me, I am sending you." 22 And with that he breathed on them and said, "Receive the Holy Spirit. 23 If you forgive anyone's sins, their sins are forgiven; if you do not forgive them, they are not forgiven."

Jesus Appears to Thomas

24 Now Thomas (also known as Didymus*a*), one of the Twelve, was not with the disciples when Jesus came. 25 So the other disciples told him, "We have seen the Lord!"

But he said to them, "Unless I see the nail marks in his hands and put my finger where the nails were, and put my hand into his side, I will not believe."

26 A week later his disciples were in the house again, and Thomas was with them. Though the doors were locked, Jesus came and stood among them and said, "Peace be with you!" 27 Then he said to Thomas, "Put your finger here; see my hands. Reach out your hand and put it into my side. Stop doubting and believe."

28 Thomas said to him, "My Lord and my God!"

29 Then Jesus told him, "Because you have seen me, you have believed; blessed are those who have not seen and yet have believed."

The Purpose of John's Gospel

30 Jesus performed many other signs in the presence of his disciples, which are not recorded in this book. 31 But these are written that you may believe*b* that Jesus is the Messiah, the Son of God, and that by believing you may have life in his name.

Jesus and the Miraculous Catch of Fish

21 Afterward Jesus appeared again to his disciples, by the Sea of Galilee.*c* It happened this way: 2 Simon Peter, Thomas (also known as Didymus*a*), Nathanael from Cana in Galilee, the sons of Zebedee, and two other disciples were together. 3 "I'm going out to fish," Simon Pe-

ter told them, and they said, "We'll go with you." So they went out and got into the boat, but that night they caught nothing.

4 Early in the morning, Jesus stood on the shore, but the disciples did not realize that it was Jesus.

5 He called out to them, "Friends, haven't you any fish?"

"No," they answered.

6 He said, "Throw your net on the right side of the boat and you will find some." When they did, they were unable to haul the net in because of the large number of fish.

7 Then the disciple whom Jesus loved said to Peter, "It is the Lord!" As soon as Simon Peter heard him say, "It is the Lord," he wrapped his outer garment around him (for he had taken it off) and jumped into the water. 8 The other disciples followed in the boat, towing the net full of fish, for they were not far from shore, about a hundred yards.*d* 9 When they landed, they saw a fire of burning coals there with fish on it, and some bread.

10 Jesus said to them, "Bring some of the fish you have just caught." 11 So Simon Peter climbed back into the boat and dragged the net ashore. It was full of large fish, 153, but even with so many the net was not torn. 12 Jesus said to them, "Come and have breakfast." None of the disciples dared ask him, "Who are you?" They knew it was the Lord. 13 Jesus came, took the bread and gave it to them, and did the same with the fish. 14 This was now the third time Jesus appeared to his disciples after he was raised from the dead.

Jesus Reinstates Peter

15 When they had finished eating, Jesus said to Simon Peter, "Simon son of John, do you love me more than these?"

"Yes, Lord," he said, "you know that I love you."

Jesus said, "Feed my lambs."

16 Again Jesus said, "Simon son of John, do you love me?"

He answered, "Yes, Lord, you know that I love you."

Jesus said, "Take care of my sheep."

---

a 24,2 *Thomas* (Aramaic) and *Didymus* (Greek) both mean twin.   *b* 31 Or *may continue to believe*   *c* 1 Greek *Tiberias*
d 8 Or *about 90 meters*

Have you ever made a bad choice and felt like you let your parents and God down? Something like Peter's choice to deny that he knew Jesus (John 18:15–27)? When you make that kind of choice, it's natural to wonder if the Lord still loves you. The next time Jesus saw Peter he asked him, "Do you love me?" (John 21:15). Peter felt embarrassed and ashamed, but he answered, "Yes, Lord, you know that I love you" (John 21:15). A mistake, even a terribly wrong choice, doesn't mean that the bond of love you have with Jesus has been broken. If you should make one of those bad choices, picture Christ asking you, "Do you love me?" Then answer yes.

{John 21:15–19}

>> INSTANT ACCESS

[17] The third time he said to him, "Simon son of John, do you love me?"

Peter was hurt because Jesus asked him the third time, "Do you love me?" He said, "Lord, you know all things; you know that I love you."

Jesus said, "Feed my sheep. [18] Very truly I tell you, when you were younger you dressed yourself and went where you wanted; but when you are old you will stretch out your hands, and someone else will dress you and lead you where you do not want to go." [19] Jesus said this to indicate the kind of death by which Peter would glorify God. Then he said to him, "Follow me!"

[20] Peter turned and saw that the disciple whom Jesus loved was following them. (This was the one who had leaned back against Jesus at the supper and had said, "Lord, who is going to betray you?") [21] When Peter saw him, he asked, "Lord, what about him?"

[22] Jesus answered, "If I want him to remain alive until I return, what is that to you? You must follow me." [23] Because of this, the rumor spread among the believers that this disciple would not die. But Jesus did not say that he would not die; he only said, "If I want him to remain alive until I return, what is that to you?"

[24] This is the disciple who testifies to these things and who wrote them down. We know that his testimony is true.

[25] Jesus did many other things as well. If every one of them were written down, I suppose that even the whole world would not have room for the books that would be written.

ACTS

preview

Luke, the author of the Gospel of Luke, wrote Acts.

The mission trips reported here take place between 36 and 66 A.D.

You Belong.

You are a member of a very special group: the church of Jesus Christ. The people in this group care about you. They will support you when you're down and help you when doing right seems hard. They love you, and you love them. You're family.

The book of Acts tells how this family began and grew. Some people think "church" is just a building where people go to worship. In fact, for nearly 300 years there were no church buildings! In the book of Acts you'll learn the truth. The church is people, people who love Jesus and care about each other.

>>**WIND AND FIRE MARK BIRTHDAY**
   For a first-hand report, see Acts 2:1–13

>>**A WARM WELCOME HERE**
   Like a family, suggests Acts 2:42–47

>>**DEACONS SETTLE CHURCH DISPUTE**
   Story in Acts 6:1–7

>>**COUNCIL WELCOMES GENTILES**
   Jewish Christians reject prejudice. See Acts 15

>>**PRISONER APPEAL TO ROYALS: ONLY BELIEVE**
   King "almost" a Christian. Story in Acts 25

As missionaries spread the good news about Jesus, the Greek merchant Hippolus reaches the coast of India. The Emperor Claudius conquers Britain. Smallpox first appears in China. Two Vietnamese sisters take 65 Chinese fortresses, proclaim themselves queens.

Jesus Taken Up Into Heaven

1 In my former book, Theophilus, I wrote about all that Jesus began to do and to teach [2] until the day he was taken up to heaven, after giving instructions through the Holy Spirit to the apostles he had chosen. [3] After his suffering, he presented himself to them and gave many convincing proofs that he was alive. He appeared to them over a period of forty days and spoke about the kingdom of God. [4] On one occasion, while he was eating with them, he gave them this command: "Do not leave Jerusalem, but wait for the gift my Father promised, which you have heard me speak about. [5] For John baptized with[a] water, but in a few days you will be baptized with[a] the Holy Spirit."

[6] Then they gathered around him and asked him, "Lord, are you at this time going to restore the kingdom to Israel?"

[7] He said to them: "It is not for you to know the times or dates the Father has set by his own authority. [8] But you will receive power when the Holy Spirit comes on you; and you will be my witnesses in Jerusalem, and in all Judea and Samaria, and to the ends of the earth."

[9] After he said this, he was taken up before their very eyes, and a cloud hid him from their sight.

[10] They were looking intently up into the sky as he was going, when suddenly two men dressed in white stood beside them. [11] "Men of Galilee," they said, "why do you stand here looking into the sky? This same Jesus, who has been taken from you into heaven, will come back in the same way you have seen him go into heaven."

Matthias Chosen to Replace Judas

[12] Then the apostles returned to Jerusalem from the hill called the Mount of Olives, a Sabbath day's walk[b] from the city. [13] When they arrived, they went upstairs to the room where they were staying. Those present were Peter, John, James and Andrew; Philip and Thomas, Bartholomew and Matthew; James son of Alphaeus and Simon the Zealot, and Judas son of James. [14] They all joined together constantly in prayer, along with the women and Mary the mother of Jesus, and with his brothers.

[15] In those days Peter stood up among the believers (a group numbering about a hundred and twenty) [16] and said, "Brothers and sisters,[c] the Scripture had to be fulfilled in which the Holy Spirit spoke long ago through David concerning Judas, who served as guide for those who arrested Jesus. [17] He was one of our number and shared in our ministry."

[18] (With the payment he received for his wickedness, Judas bought a field; there he fell headlong, his body burst open and all his intestines spilled out. [19] Everyone in Jerusalem heard about this, so they called that field in their language Akeldama, that is, Field of Blood.)

[20] "For," said Peter, "it is written in the Book of Psalms:

" 'May his place be deserted;
    let there be no one to dwell in it,'[d]

and,

" 'May another take his place of
    leadership.'[e]

[21] Therefore it is necessary to choose one of the men who have been with us the whole time the Lord Jesus was living among us, [22] beginning from John's baptism to the time when Jesus was taken up from us. For one of these must become a witness with us of his resurrection."

> *You will receive power when the Holy Spirit comes on you; and you will be my witnesses.*
> **Acts 1:8**

---

[a] 5 Or *in*   [b] 12 That is, about 5/8 mile or about 1 kilometer   [c] 16 The Greek word for *brothers and sisters* (*adelphoi*) refers here to believers, both men and women, as part of God's family; also in 6:3; 11:29; 12:17; 16:40; 18:18, 27; 21:7, 17; 28:14, 15.   [d] 20 Psalm 69:25   [e] 20 Psalm 109:8

²³So they nominated two men: Joseph called Barsabbas (also known as Justus) and Matthias. ²⁴Then they prayed, "Lord, you know everyone's heart. Show us which of these two you have chosen ²⁵to take over this apostolic ministry, which Judas left to go where he belongs." ²⁶Then they cast lots, and the lot fell to Matthias; so he was added to the eleven apostles.

The Holy Spirit Comes at Pentecost

2 When the day of Pentecost came, they were all together in one place. ²Suddenly a sound like the blowing of a violent wind came from heaven and filled the whole house where they were sitting. ³They saw what seemed to be tongues of fire that separated and came to rest on each of them. ⁴All of them were filled with the Holy Spirit and began to speak in other tongues[a] as the Spirit enabled them.

⁵Now there were staying in Jerusalem God-fearing Jews from every nation under heaven. ⁶When they heard this sound, a crowd came together in bewilderment, because each one heard their own language being spoken. ⁷Utterly amazed, they asked: "Aren't all these who are speaking Galileans? ⁸Then how is it that each of us hears them in our native language? ⁹Parthians, Medes and Elamites; residents of Mesopotamia, Judea and Cappadocia, Pontus and Asia,[b] ¹⁰Phrygia and Pamphylia, Egypt and the parts of Libya near Cyrene; visitors from Rome ¹¹(both Jews and converts to Judaism); Cretans and Arabs—we hear them declaring the wonders of God in our own tongues!" ¹²Amazed and perplexed, they asked one another, "What does this mean?"

¹³Some, however, made fun of them and said, "They have had too much wine."

Peter Addresses the Crowd

¹⁴Then Peter stood up with the Eleven, raised his voice and addressed the crowd: "Fellow Jews and all of you who live in Jerusalem, let me explain this to you; listen carefully to what I say. ¹⁵These people are not drunk, as you suppose. It's only nine in the morning! ¹⁶No, this is what was spoken by the prophet Joel:

¹⁷ " 'In the last days, God says,
  I will pour out my Spirit on all people.
Your sons and daughters will prophesy,
  your young men will see visions,
  your old men will dream dreams.
¹⁸Even on my servants, both men and women,
  I will pour out my Spirit in those days,
  and they will prophesy.
¹⁹I will show wonders in the heavens above
  and signs on the earth below,
  blood and fire and billows of smoke.
²⁰The sun will be turned to darkness
  and the moon to blood
  before the coming of the great and glorious day of the Lord.
²¹And everyone who calls
  on the name of the Lord will be saved.'[c]

²²"Fellow Israelites, listen to this: Jesus of Nazareth was a man accredited by God to you by miracles, wonders and signs, which God did among you through him, as you yourselves know. ²³This man was handed over to you by God's deliberate plan and foreknowledge; and you, with the help of wicked men,[d] put him to death by nailing him to the cross. ²⁴But God raised him from the dead, freeing him from the agony of death, because it was impossible for death to keep its hold on him. ²⁵David said about him:

" 'I saw the Lord always before me.
  Because he is at my right hand,
  I will not be shaken.
²⁶Therefore my heart is glad and my tongue rejoices;
  my body also will rest in hope,

---

a 4 Or languages; also in verse 11   *b 9 That is, the Roman province by that name*   *c 21 Joel 2:28-32*   *d 23 Or of those not having the law (that is, Gentiles)*

We Believe...

"in the Holy Spirit"

+ What happened on the day of Pentecost? Peter said it was the day the Holy Spirit was poured out on the followers of Jesus (Acts 2:17). Jesus had told his disciples that the Spirit was "with" them and one day soon would be "in" them (John 14:17). Pentecost was the day the Holy Spirit came to live within those who trust Jesus.

Who is the Holy Spirit? The Holy Spirit, like the Father and the Son, is God. Can you imagine how special it is to have God living in you? Here are just a few things the Holy Spirit will do for you:

* When you pray, the Holy Spirit will pray with and for you (Romans 8:26).

* When you face temptation, the Holy Spirit will give you the strength to do what's right (Romans 8:9–11).

* As you live a Christian life, the Holy Spirit will give you joy, peace, and many other blessings (Galatians 5:22–23).

* As you keep on living the Christian life, the Holy Spirit will transform you so that you become more and more like Christ (2 Corinthians 3:18).

What do you have to do? Simply step out in faith to do what you know is right, trusting the Holy Spirit to give you the strength and the wisdom you need.

Oh yes. We believe in the Holy Spirit. We believe that God himself is with us and within us. And we count on him to enable us as we live to please Jesus.

Go to page 1536 for the next We Believe

27 because you will not abandon me to
the realm of the dead,
  you will not let your holy one see
  decay.
28 You have made known to me the
paths of life;
  you will fill me with joy in your
  presence.'*a*

29 "Fellow Israelites, I can tell you confidently that the patriarch David died and was buried, and his tomb is here to this day. 30 But he was a prophet and knew that God had promised him on oath that he would place one of his descendants on his throne. 31 Seeing what was to come, he spoke of the resurrection of the Messiah, that he was not abandoned to the realm of the dead, nor did his body see decay. 32 God has raised this Jesus to life, and we are all witnesses of it. 33 Exalted to the right hand of God, he has received from the Father the promised Holy Spirit and has poured out what you now see and hear. 34 For David did not ascend to heaven, and yet he said,

" 'The Lord said to my Lord:
  "Sit at my right hand
35 until I make your enemies
  a footstool for your feet." ' *b*

36 "Therefore let all Israel be assured of this: God has made this Jesus, whom you crucified, both Lord and Messiah."

37 When the people heard this, they were cut to the heart and said to Peter and the other apostles, "Brothers, what shall we do?"

38 Peter replied, "Repent and be baptized, every one of you, in the name of Jesus Christ for the forgiveness of your sins. And you will receive the gift of the Holy Spirit. 39 The promise is for you and your children and for all who are far off— for all whom the Lord our God will call."

40 With many other words he warned them; and he pleaded with them, "Save yourselves from this corrupt generation." 41 Those who accepted his message were baptized, and about three thousand were added to their number that day.

The Fellowship of the Believers

42 They devoted themselves to the apostles' teaching and to fellowship, to the breaking of bread and to prayer. 43 Everyone was filled with awe at the many wonders and signs performed by the apostles. 44 All the believers were together and had everything in common. 45 They sold property and possessions to give to anyone who had need. 46 Every day they continued to meet together in the temple courts. They broke bread in their homes and ate together with glad and sincere hearts, 47 praising God and enjoying the favor of all the people. And the Lord added to their number daily those who were being saved.

Peter Heals a Lame Beggar

3 One day Peter and John were going up to the temple at the time of prayer—at three in the afternoon. 2 Now a man who was lame from birth was being carried to the temple gate called Beautiful, where he was put every day to beg from those going into the temple courts. 3 When he saw Peter and John about to enter, he asked them for money. 4 Peter looked straight at him, as did John. Then Peter said, "Look at us!" 5 So the man gave them his attention, expecting to get something from them.

6 Then Peter said, "Silver or gold I do not have, but what I do have I give you. In the name of Jesus Christ of Nazareth, walk." 7 Taking him by the right hand, he helped him up, and instantly the man's feet and ankles became strong. 8 He jumped to his feet and began to walk. Then he went with them into the temple courts, walking and jumping, and praising God. 9 When all the people saw him walking and praising God, 10 they recognized him as the same man who used to sit begging at the temple gate called Beautiful, and they were filled with wonder and amazement at what had happened to him.

Peter Speaks to the Onlookers

11 While the man held on to Peter and John, all the people were astonished and

---

a 28 Psalm 16:8-11 (see Septuagint)   *b* 35 Psalm 110:1

came running to them in the place called Solomon's Colonnade. ¹²When Peter saw this, he said to them: "Fellow Israelites, why does this surprise you? Why do you stare at us as if by our own power or godliness we had made this man walk? ¹³The God of Abraham, Isaac and Jacob, the God of our fathers, has glorified his servant Jesus. You handed him over to be killed, and you disowned him before Pilate, though he had decided to let him go. ¹⁴You disowned the Holy and Righteous One and asked that a murderer be released to you. ¹⁵You killed the author of life, but God raised him from the dead. We are witnesses of this. ¹⁶By faith in the name of Jesus, this man whom you see and know was made strong. It is Jesus' name and the faith that comes through him that has completely healed him, as you can all see.

¹⁷"Now, fellow Israelites, I know that you acted in ignorance, as did your leaders. ¹⁸But this is how God fulfilled what he had foretold through all the prophets, saying that his Messiah would suffer. ¹⁹Repent, then, and turn to God, so that your sins may be wiped out, that times of refreshing may come from the Lord, ²⁰and that he may send the Messiah, who has been appointed for you—even Jesus. ²¹Heaven must receive him until the time comes for God to restore everything, as he promised long ago through his holy prophets. ²²For Moses said, 'The Lord your God will raise up for you a prophet like me from among your own people; you must listen to everything he tells you. ²³Anyone who does not listen to him will be completely cut off from their people.'ᵃ

²⁴"Indeed, beginning with Samuel, all the prophets who have spoken have foretold these days. ²⁵And you are heirs of the prophets and of the covenant God made with your fathers. He said to Abraham, 'Through your offspring all peoples on earth will be blessed.'ᵇ ²⁶When God raised up his servant, he sent him first to you to bless you by turning each of you from your wicked ways."

Peter and John Before the Sanhedrin

4 The priests and the captain of the temple guard and the Sadducees came up to Peter and John while they were speaking to the people. ²They were greatly disturbed because the apostles were teaching the people, proclaiming in Jesus the resurrection of the dead. ³They seized Peter and John and, because it was evening, they put them in jail until the next day. ⁴But many who heard the message believed; so the number of men who believed grew to about five thousand.

⁵The next day the rulers, the elders and the teachers of the law met in Jerusalem. ⁶Annas the high priest was there, and so were Caiaphas, John, Alexander and others of the high priest's family. ⁷They had Peter and John brought before them and began to question them: "By what power or what name did you do this?"

⁸Then Peter, filled with the Holy Spirit, said to them: "Rulers and elders of the people! ⁹If we are being called to account today for an act of kindness shown to a man who was lame and are being asked how he was healed, ¹⁰then know this, you and all the people of Israel: It is by the name of Jesus Christ of Nazareth, whom you crucified but whom God raised from the dead, that this man stands before you healed. ¹¹Jesus is

" 'the stone you builders rejected,
    which has become the
        cornerstone.'ᶜ

¹²Salvation is found in no one else, for there is no other name under heaven given to mankind by which we must be saved."

¹³When they saw the courage of Peter and John and realized that they were unschooled, ordinary men, they were astonished and they took note that these men had been with Jesus. ¹⁴But since they could see the man who had been healed standing there with them, there was nothing they could say. ¹⁵So they ordered them to withdraw from the Sanhedrin and

---

ᵃ 23 Deut. 18:15,18,19   ᵇ 25 Gen. 22:18; 26:4   ᶜ 11 Psalm 118:22

then conferred together. [16]"What are we going to do with these men?" they asked. "Everyone living in Jerusalem knows they have performed a notable sign, and we cannot deny it. [17]But to stop this thing from spreading any further among the people, we must warn them to speak no longer to anyone in this name."

[18]Then they called them in again and commanded them not to speak or teach at all in the name of Jesus. [19]But Peter and John replied, "Which is right in God's eyes: to listen to you, or to him? You be the judges! [20]As for us, we cannot help speaking about what we have seen and heard."

[21]After further threats they let them go. They could not decide how to punish them, because all the people were praising God for what had happened. [22]For the man who was miraculously healed was over forty years old.

The Believers Pray

[23]On their release, Peter and John went back to their own people and reported all that the chief priests and the elders had said to them. [24]When they heard this, they raised their voices together in prayer to God. "Sovereign Lord," they said, "you made the heavens and the earth and the sea, and everything in them. [25]You spoke by the Holy Spirit through the mouth of your servant, our father David:

" 'Why do the nations rage
    and the peoples plot in vain?
[26]The kings of the earth rise up
    and the rulers band together
against the Lord
    and against his anointed one.[a' b]

[27]Indeed Herod and Pontius Pilate met together with the Gentiles and the people of Israel in this city to conspire against your holy servant Jesus, whom you anointed. [28]They did what your power and will had decided beforehand should happen. [29]Now, Lord, consider their threats and enable your servants to speak your word with great boldness. [30]Stretch out your hand to heal and perform signs and

wonders through the name of your holy servant Jesus."

[31]After they prayed, the place where they were meeting was shaken. And they were all filled with the Holy Spirit and spoke the word of God boldly.

The Believers Share Their Possessions

[32]All the believers were one in heart and mind. No one claimed that any of their possessions was their own, but they shared everything they had. [33]With great power the apostles continued to testify to the resurrection of the Lord Jesus. And God's grace was so powerfully at work in them all [34]that there were no needy persons among them. For from time to time those who owned land or houses sold them, brought the money from the sales [35]and put it at the apostles' feet, and it was distributed to anyone who had need.

[36]Joseph, a Levite from Cyprus, whom the apostles called Barnabas (which means "son of encouragement"), [37]sold a field he owned and brought the money and put it at the apostles' feet.

Ananias and Sapphira

5 Now a man named Ananias, together with his wife Sapphira, also sold a piece of property. [2]With his wife's full knowledge he kept back part of the money for himself, but brought the rest and put it at the apostles' feet.

[3]Then Peter said, "Ananias, how is it that Satan has so filled your heart that you have lied to the Holy Spirit and have kept for yourself some of the money you received for the land? [4]Didn't it belong to you before it was sold? And after it was sold, wasn't the money at your disposal? What made you think of doing such a thing? You have not lied just to human beings but to God."

[5]When Ananias heard this, he fell down and died. And great fear seized all who heard what had happened. [6]Then some young men came forward, wrapped up his body, and carried him out and buried him.

---

[a] 26 That is, Messiah or Christ   [b] 26 Psalm 2:1,2

How much does God care about your money? Actually, not much. He can get along without the dollars or cents you put in the offering plate. He could get along without the money of Ananias and Sapphira too. So why did he strike them dead when they held back some of the money? Because they lied, not just before other people, but before God. They acted as if God wasn't real and didn't know what they were doing. As Peter said, the property belonged to them before it was sold, and the money was theirs to use as they saw fit. Giving is a privilege for Christians, not a duty. What's important is to remember that God is real. Don't behave as if he isn't.

{Acts 5:1-11}

>> INSTANT ACCESS

7About three hours later his wife came in, not knowing what had happened. 8Peter asked her, "Tell me, is this the price you and Ananias got for the land?"

"Yes," she said, "that is the price."

9Peter said to her, "How could you conspire to test the Spirit of the Lord? Listen! The feet of the men who buried your husband are at the door, and they will carry you out also."

10At that moment she fell down at his feet and died. Then the young men came in and, finding her dead, carried her out and buried her beside her husband. 11Great fear seized the whole church and all who heard about these events.

The Apostles Heal Many

12The apostles performed many signs and wonders among the people. And all the believers used to meet together in Solomon's Colonnade. 13No one else dared join them, even though they were highly regarded by the people. 14Nevertheless, more and more men and women believed in the Lord and were added to their number. 15As a result, people brought the sick into the streets and laid them on beds and mats so that at least Peter's shadow might fall on some of them as he passed by. 16Crowds gathered also from the towns around Jerusalem, bringing their sick and those tormented by impure spirits, and all of them were healed.

The Apostles Persecuted

17Then the high priest and all his associates, who were members of the party of the Sadducees, were filled with jealousy. 18They arrested the apostles and put them in the public jail. 19But during the night an angel of the Lord opened the doors of the jail and brought them out. 20"Go, stand in the temple courts," he said, "and tell the people all about this new life."

21At daybreak they entered the temple courts, as they had been told, and began to teach the people.

When the high priest and his associates arrived, they called together the Sanhedrin—the full assembly of the elders of Israel—and sent to the jail for the apostles. 22But on arriving at the jail, the officers did not find them there. So they went back and reported, 23"We found the jail securely locked, with the guards standing at the doors; but when we opened them, we found no one inside." 24On hearing this report, the captain of the temple guard and the chief priests were at a loss, wondering what this might lead to.

25Then someone came and said, "Look! The men you put in jail are standing in the temple courts teaching the people." 26At that, the captain went with his officers and brought the apostles. They did not use force, because they feared that the people would stone them.

27The apostles were brought in and made to appear before the Sanhedrin to be questioned by the high priest. 28"We gave you strict orders not to teach in this name," he said. "Yet you have filled Jerusalem with your teaching and are determined to make us guilty of this man's blood."

29Peter and the other apostles replied: "We must obey God rather than human beings! 30The God of our ancestors raised Jesus from the dead—whom you killed by hanging him on a cross. 31God exalted him to his own right hand as Prince and Savior that he might bring Israel to repentance and forgive their sins. 32We are witnesses of these things, and so is the Holy Spirit, whom God has given to those who obey him."

33When they heard this, they were furious and wanted to put them to death. 34But a Pharisee named Gamaliel, a teacher of the law, who was honored by all the people, stood up in the Sanhedrin and ordered that the men be put outside for a little while. 35Then he addressed the Sanhedrin: "Men of Israel, consider carefully what you intend to do to these men. 36Some time ago Theudas appeared, claiming to be somebody, and about four hundred men rallied to him. He was killed, all his followers were dispersed, and it all came to nothing. 37After him, Judas the Galilean appeared in the days of the census and led a band of people in revolt. He too was killed, and all his followers were scattered. 38Therefore, in the present case I advise you: Leave these men alone! Let them go! For if their purpose or activity is of human origin, it will fail. 39But if it is from God, you will not be able to stop these men; you will only find yourselves fighting against God."

40His speech persuaded them. They called the apostles in and had them flogged. Then they ordered them not to speak in the name of Jesus, and let them go.

41The apostles left the Sanhedrin, rejoicing because they had been counted worthy of suffering disgrace for the Name. 42Day after day, in the temple courts and from house to house, they never stopped teaching and proclaiming the good news that Jesus is the Messiah.

The Choosing of the Seven

6 In those days when the number of disciples was increasing, the Hellenistic Jews[a] among them complained against the Hebraic Jews because their widows were being overlooked in the daily distribution of food. 2So the Twelve gathered all the disciples together and said, "It would not be right for us to neglect the ministry of the word of God in order to wait on tables. 3Brothers and sisters, choose seven men from among you who are known to be full of the Spirit and wisdom. We will turn this responsibility over to them 4and will give our attention to prayer and the ministry of the word."

5This proposal pleased the whole group. They chose Stephen, a man full of faith and of the Holy Spirit; also Philip, Procorus, Nicanor, Timon, Parmenas, and Nicolas from Antioch, a convert to Judaism. 6They presented these men to the apostles, who prayed and laid their hands on them.

7So the word of God spread. The number of disciples in Jerusalem increased rapidly, and a large number of priests became obedient to the faith.

Stephen Seized

8Now Stephen, a man full of God's grace and power, performed great wonders and signs among the people. 9Opposition arose, however, from members of the Synagogue of the Freedmen (as it was called)—Jews of Cyrene and Alexandria as well as the provinces of Cilicia and

---

a 1 That is, Jews who had adopted the Greek language and culture

Asia—who began to argue with Stephen. ¹⁰But they could not stand up against the wisdom the Spirit gave him as he spoke.

¹¹Then they secretly persuaded some men to say, "We have heard Stephen speak blasphemous words against Moses and against God."

¹²So they stirred up the people and the elders and the teachers of the law. They seized Stephen and brought him before the Sanhedrin. ¹³They produced false witnesses, who testified, "This fellow never stops speaking against this holy place and against the law. ¹⁴For we have heard him say that this Jesus of Nazareth will destroy this place and change the customs Moses handed down to us."

¹⁵All who were sitting in the Sanhedrin looked intently at Stephen, and they saw that his face was like the face of an angel.

Stephen's Speech to the Sanhedrin

7 Then the high priest asked Stephen, "Are these charges true?"

²To this he replied: "Brothers and fathers, listen to me! The God of glory appeared to our father Abraham while he was still in Mesopotamia, before he lived in Harran. ³'Leave your country and your people,' God said, 'and go to the land I will show you.'ᵃ

⁴"So he left the land of the Chaldeans and settled in Harran. After the death of his father, God sent him to this land where you are now living. ⁵He gave him no inheritance here, not even enough ground to set his foot on. But God promised him that he and his descendants after him would possess the land, even though at that time Abraham had no child. ⁶God spoke to him in this way: 'For four hundred years your descendants will be strangers in a country not their own, and they will be enslaved and mistreated. ⁷But I will punish the nation they serve as slaves,' God said, 'and afterward they will come out of that country and worship me in this place.'ᵇ ⁸Then he gave Abraham the covenant of circumcision.

And Abraham became the father of Isaac and circumcised him eight days after his birth. Later Isaac became the father of Jacob, and Jacob became the father of the twelve patriarchs.

⁹"Because the patriarchs were jealous of Joseph, they sold him as a slave into Egypt. But God was with him ¹⁰and rescued him from all his troubles. He gave Joseph wisdom and enabled him to gain the goodwill of Pharaoh king of Egypt. So Pharaoh made him ruler over Egypt and all his palace.

¹¹"Then a famine struck all Egypt and Canaan, bringing great suffering, and our ancestors could not find food. ¹²When Jacob heard that there was grain in Egypt, he sent our forefathers on their first visit. ¹³On their second visit, Joseph told his brothers who he was, and Pharaoh learned about Joseph's family. ¹⁴After this, Joseph sent for his father Jacob and his whole family, seventy-five in all. ¹⁵Then Jacob went down to Egypt, where he and our ancestors died. ¹⁶Their bodies were brought back to Shechem and placed in the tomb that Abraham had bought from the sons of Hamor at Shechem for a certain sum of money.

¹⁷"As the time drew near for God to fulfill his promise to Abraham, the number of our people in Egypt had greatly increased. ¹⁸Then 'a new king, to whom Joseph meant nothing, came to power in Egypt.'ᶜ ¹⁹He dealt treacherously with our people and oppressed our ancestors by forcing them to throw out their newborn babies so that they would die.

²⁰"At that time Moses was born, and he was no ordinary child.ᵈ For three months he was cared for by his family. ²¹When he was placed outside, Pharaoh's daughter took him and brought him up as her own son. ²²Moses was educated in all the wisdom of the Egyptians and was powerful in speech and action.

²³"When Moses was forty years old, he decided to visit his own people, the Israelites. ²⁴He saw one of them being mistreated by an Egyptian, so he went to his defense and avenged him by killing

---

ᵃ 3 Gen. 12:1   ᵇ 7 Gen. 15:13,14   ᶜ 18 Exodus 1:8   ᵈ 20 Or *was fair in the sight of God*

the Egyptian. 25 Moses thought that his own people would realize that God was using him to rescue them, but they did not. 26 The next day Moses came upon two Israelites who were fighting. He tried to reconcile them by saying, 'Men, you are brothers; why do you want to hurt each other?'

27 "But the man who was mistreating the other pushed Moses aside and said, 'Who made you ruler and judge over us? 28 Are you thinking of killing me as you killed the Egyptian yesterday?' *a* 29 When Moses heard this, he fled to Midian, where he settled as a foreigner and had two sons.

30 "After forty years had passed, an angel appeared to Moses in the flames of a burning bush in the desert near Mount Sinai. 31 When he saw this, he was amazed at the sight. As he went over to get a closer look, he heard the Lord say: 32 'I am the God of your fathers, the God of Abraham, Isaac and Jacob.' *b* Moses trembled with fear and did not dare to look.

33 "Then the Lord said to him, 'Take off your sandals, for the place where you are standing is holy ground. 34 I have indeed seen the oppression of my people in Egypt. I have heard their groaning and have come down to set them free. Now come, I will send you back to Egypt.' *c*

35 "This is the same Moses they had rejected with the words, 'Who made you ruler and judge?' He was sent to be their ruler and deliverer by God himself, through the angel who appeared to him in the bush. 36 He led them out of Egypt and performed wonders and signs in Egypt, at the Red Sea and for forty years in the wilderness.

37 "This is the Moses who told the Israelites, 'God will raise up for you a prophet like me from your own people.' *d* 38 He was in the assembly in the wilderness, with the angel who spoke to him on Mount Sinai, and with our ancestors; and he received living words to pass on to us.

39 "But our ancestors refused to obey him. Instead, they rejected him and in their hearts turned back to Egypt. 40 They told Aaron, 'Make us gods who will go before us. As for this fellow Moses who led us out of Egypt—we don't know what has happened to him!' *e* 41 That was the time they made an idol in the form of a calf. They brought sacrifices to it and reveled in what their own hands had made. 42 But God turned away from them and gave them over to the worship of the sun, moon and stars. This agrees with what is written in the book of the prophets:

" 'Did you bring me sacrifices and
offerings
forty years in the wilderness,
people of Israel?
43 You have taken up the tabernacle of
Molek
and the star of your god Rephan,
the idols you made to worship.
Therefore I will send you into exile' *f*
beyond Babylon.

44 "Our ancestors had the tabernacle of the covenant law with them in the wilderness. It had been made as God directed Moses, according to the pattern he had seen. 45 After receiving the tabernacle, our ancestors under Joshua brought it with them when they took the land from the nations God drove out before them. It remained in the land until the time of David, 46 who enjoyed God's favor and asked that he might provide a dwelling place for the God of Jacob. *g* 47 But it was Solomon who built a house for him.

48 "However, the Most High does not live in houses made by human hands. As the prophet says:

49 " 'Heaven is my throne,
and the earth is my footstool.
What kind of house will you build for
me?
says the Lord.
Or where will my resting place be?
50 Has not my hand made all these
things?' *h*

51 "You stiff-necked people! Your hearts and ears are still uncircumcised. You are just like your ancestors: You always resist

---

a 28 Exodus 2:14   *b* 32 Exodus 3:6   *c* 34 Exodus 3:5,7,8,10   *d* 37 Deut. 18:15   *e* 40 Exodus 32:1
f 43 Amos 5:25-27 (see Septuagint)   *g* 46 Some early manuscripts *the house of Jacob*   *h* 50 Isaiah 66:1,2

the Holy Spirit! [52]Was there ever a prophet your ancestors did not persecute? They even killed those who predicted the coming of the Righteous One. And now you have betrayed and murdered him— [53]you who have received the law that was given through angels but have not obeyed it."

The Stoning of Stephen

[54]When the members of the Sanhedrin heard this, they were furious and gnashed their teeth at him. [55]But Stephen, full of the Holy Spirit, looked up to heaven and saw the glory of God, and Jesus standing at the right hand of God. [56]"Look," he said, "I see heaven open and the Son of Man standing at the right hand of God."

[57]At this they covered their ears and, yelling at the top of their voices, they all rushed at him, [58]dragged him out of the city and began to stone him. Meanwhile, the witnesses laid their coats at the feet of a young man named Saul.

[59]While they were stoning him, Stephen prayed, "Lord Jesus, receive my spirit." [60]Then he fell on his knees and cried out, "Lord, do not hold this sin against them." When he had said this, he fell asleep.

8 And Saul approved of their killing him.

The Church Persecuted and Scattered

On that day a great persecution broke out against the church in Jerusalem, and all except the apostles were scattered throughout Judea and Samaria. [2]Godly men buried Stephen and mourned deeply for him. [3]But Saul began to destroy the church. Going from house to house, he dragged off both men and women and put them in prison.

Philip in Samaria

[4]Those who had been scattered preached the word wherever they went. [5]Philip went down to a city in Samaria and proclaimed the Messiah there. [6]When the crowds heard Philip and saw the signs he performed, they all paid close attention to what he said. [7]For with shrieks, impure spirits came out of many, and many who were paralyzed or lame were healed. [8]So there was great joy in that city.

Simon the Sorcerer

[9]Now for some time a man named Simon had practiced sorcery in the city and amazed all the people of Samaria. He boasted that he was someone great, [10]and all the people, both high and low, gave him their attention and exclaimed, "This man is rightly called the Great Power of God." [11]They followed him because he had amazed them for a long time with his sorcery. [12]But when they believed Philip as he proclaimed the good news of the kingdom of God and the name of Jesus Christ, they were baptized, both men and women. [13]Simon himself believed and was baptized. And he followed Philip everywhere, astonished by the great signs and miracles he saw.

[14]When the apostles in Jerusalem heard that Samaria had accepted the word of God, they sent Peter and John to Samaria. [15]When they arrived, they prayed for the new believers there that they might receive the Holy Spirit, [16]because the Holy Spirit had not yet come on any of them; they had simply been baptized in the name of the Lord Jesus. [17]Then Peter and John placed their hands on them, and they received the Holy Spirit.

[18]When Simon saw that the Spirit was given at the laying on of the apostles' hands, he offered them money [19]and said, "Give me also this ability so that everyone on whom I lay my hands may receive the Holy Spirit."

[20]Peter answered: "May your money perish with you, because you thought you could buy the gift of God with money! [21]You have no part or share in this ministry, because your heart is not right before God. [22]Repent of this wickedness and pray to the Lord in the hope that he may forgive you for having such a thought in your heart. [23]For I see that you are full of bitterness and captive to sin."

[24]Then Simon answered, "Pray to the Lord for me so that nothing you have said may happen to me."

25 After they had further proclaimed the word of the Lord and testified about Jesus, Peter and John returned to Jerusalem, preaching the gospel in many Samaritan villages.

Philip and the Ethiopian

26 Now an angel of the Lord said to Philip, "Go south to the road—the desert road—that goes down from Jerusalem to Gaza." 27 So he started out, and on his way he met an Ethiopian[a] eunuch, an important official in charge of all the treasury of the Kandake (which means "queen of the Ethiopians"). This man had gone to Jerusalem to worship, 28 and on his way home was sitting in his chariot reading the Book of Isaiah the prophet. 29 The Spirit told Philip, "Go to that chariot and stay near it."

30 Then Philip ran up to the chariot and heard the man reading Isaiah the prophet. "Do you understand what you are reading?" Philip asked.

31 "How can I," he said, "unless someone explains it to me?" So he invited Philip to come up and sit with him.

32 This is the passage of Scripture the eunuch was reading:

"He was led like a sheep to the
        slaughter,
    and as a lamb before its shearer is
        silent,
    so he did not open his mouth.
33 In his humiliation he was deprived of
        justice.
    Who can speak of his descendants?
    For his life was taken from the
        earth."[b]

34 The eunuch asked Philip, "Tell me, please, who is the prophet talking about, himself or someone else?" 35 Then Philip began with that very passage of Scripture and told him the good news about Jesus.

36 As they traveled along the road, they came to some water and the eunuch said, "Look, here is water. What can stand in the way of my being baptized?" [37][c] 38 And he gave orders to stop the chariot. Then both Philip and the eunuch went down into the water and Philip baptized him. 39 When they came up out of the water, the Spirit of the Lord suddenly took Philip away, and the eunuch did not see him again, but went on his way rejoicing. 40 Philip, however, appeared at Azotus and traveled about, preaching the gospel in all the towns until he reached Caesarea.

INSTANT ACCESS

Does the thought of giving a presentation in school terrify you? Would you rather give away your favorite pair of jeans than sing a solo in church? Lots of people feel that way. Everyone has a different comfort level when it comes to speaking up with others around. Some are comfortable with a thousand. Some are OK if a group isn't over twenty. For some the comfort level is two or three, or even one. And that's all right. In fact, God took Philip away from a ministry to crowds (Acts 8:6) to send him to just one person. If your comfort level is one or two, don't be down on yourself. That's you. And God can use you the way you are.

{Acts 8:26–40}

---

[a] 27 That is, from the southern Nile region   [b] 33 Isaiah 53:7,8 (see Septuagint)   [c] 37 Some manuscripts include here Philip said, "If you believe with all your heart, you may." The eunuch answered, "I believe that Jesus Christ is the Son of God."

Saul's Conversion

9 Meanwhile, Saul was still breathing out murderous threats against the Lord's disciples. He went to the high priest 2 and asked him for letters to the synagogues in Damascus, so that if he found any there who belonged to the Way, whether men or women, he might take them as prisoners to Jerusalem. 3 As he neared Damascus on his journey, suddenly a light from heaven flashed around him. 4 He fell to the ground and heard a voice say to him, "Saul, Saul, why do you persecute me?"

5 "Who are you, Lord?" Saul asked.

"I am Jesus, whom you are persecuting," he replied. 6 "Now get up and go into the city, and you will be told what you must do."

7 The men traveling with Saul stood there speechless; they heard the sound but did not see anyone. 8 Saul got up from the ground, but when he opened his eyes he could see nothing. So they led him by the hand into Damascus. 9 For three days he was blind, and did not eat or drink anything.

10 In Damascus there was a disciple named Ananias. The Lord called to him in a vision, "Ananias!"

"Yes, Lord," he answered.

11 The Lord told him, "Go to the house of Judas on Straight Street and ask for a man from Tarsus named Saul, for he is praying. 12 In a vision he has seen a man named Ananias come and place his hands on him to restore his sight."

13 "Lord," Ananias answered, "I have heard many reports about this man and all the harm he has done to your holy people in Jerusalem. 14 And he has come here with authority from the chief priests to arrest all who call on your name."

15 But the Lord said to Ananias, "Go! This man is my chosen instrument to proclaim my name to the Gentiles and their kings and to the people of Israel. 16 I will show him how much he must suffer for my name."

17 Then Ananias went to the house and entered it. Placing his hands on Saul, he said, "Brother Saul, the Lord—Jesus, who appeared to you on the road as you were coming here—has sent me so that you may see again and be filled with the Holy Spirit." 18 Immediately, something like scales fell from Saul's eyes, and he could see again. He got up and was baptized, 19 and after taking some food, he regained his strength.

Saul in Damascus and Jerusalem

Saul spent several days with the disciples in Damascus. 20 At once he began to preach in the synagogues that Jesus is the Son of God. 21 All those who heard him were astonished and asked, "Isn't he the man who raised havoc in Jerusalem among those who call on this name? And hasn't he come here to take them as prisoners to the chief priests?" 22 Yet Saul grew more and more powerful and baffled the Jews living in Damascus by proving that Jesus is the Messiah.

23 After many days had gone by, there was a conspiracy among the Jews to kill him, 24 but Saul learned of their plan. Day and night they kept close watch on the city gates in order to kill him. 25 But his followers took him by night and lowered him in a basket through an opening in the wall.

26 When he came to Jerusalem, he tried to join the disciples, but they were all afraid of him, not believing that he really was a disciple. 27 But Barnabas took him and brought him to the apostles. He told them how Saul on his journey had seen the Lord and that the Lord had spoken to him, and how in Damascus he had preached fearlessly in the name of Jesus. 28 So Saul stayed with them and moved about freely in Jerusalem, speaking boldly in the name of the Lord. 29 He talked and debated with the Hellenistic Jews,*a* but they tried to kill him. 30 When the believers learned of this, they took him down to Caesarea and sent him off to Tarsus.

31 Then the church throughout Judea, Galilee and Samaria enjoyed a time of peace and was strengthened. Living in

---

a 29 That is, Jews who had adopted the Greek language and culture

the fear of the Lord and encouraged by the Holy Spirit, it increased in numbers.

Aeneas and Dorcas

32 As Peter traveled about the country, he went to visit the Lord's people who lived in Lydda. 33 There he found a man named Aeneas, who was paralyzed and had been bedridden for eight years. 34 "Aeneas," Peter said to him, "Jesus Christ heals you. Get up and roll up your mat." Immediately Aeneas got up. 35 All those who lived in Lydda and Sharon saw him and turned to the Lord.

36 In Joppa there was a disciple named Tabitha (in Greek her name is Dorcas); she was always doing good and helping the poor. 37 About that time she became sick and died, and her body was washed and placed in an upstairs room. 38 Lydda was near Joppa; so when the disciples heard that Peter was in Lydda, they sent two men to him and urged him, "Please come at once!"

39 Peter went with them, and when he arrived he was taken upstairs to the room. All the widows stood around him, crying and showing him the robes and other clothing that Dorcas had made while she was still with them.

40 Peter sent them all out of the room; then he got down on his knees and prayed. Turning toward the dead woman, he said, "Tabitha, get up." She opened her eyes, and seeing Peter she sat up. 41 He took her by the hand and helped her to her feet. Then he called for the believers, especially the widows, and presented her to them alive. 42 This became known all over Joppa, and many people believed in the Lord. 43 Peter stayed in Joppa for some time with a tanner named Simon.

Cornelius Calls for Peter

10 At Caesarea there was a man named Cornelius, a centurion in what was known as the Italian Regiment. 2 He and all his family were devout and God-fearing; he gave generously to those in need and prayed to God regularly. 3 One day at about three in the afternoon he had a vision. He distinctly saw an angel of God, who came to him and said, "Cornelius!"

>> INSTANT ACCESS

When Paul came to Jerusalem he was more than an outsider. He'd been an enemy, and everyone was suspicious of him. Only Barnabas was willing to risk being a friend to Paul, bringing this outsider in. It's especially important for Christians to reach out and welcome others. Introduce yourself to the newcomer. Invite him or her to the next youth group activity. You'll not only do a good deed, you may also help start someone out on an exciting spiritual journey.

{Acts 9:26–30}

4 Cornelius stared at him in fear. "What is it, Lord?" he asked.

The angel answered, "Your prayers and gifts to the poor have come up as a memorial offering before God. 5 Now send men to Joppa to bring back a man named Simon who is called Peter. 6 He is staying with Simon the tanner, whose house is by the sea."

7 When the angel who spoke to him had gone, Cornelius called two of his servants and a devout soldier who was one of his attendants. 8 He told them everything that had happened and sent them to Joppa.

Peter's Vision

9 About noon the following day as they were on their journey and approaching the city, Peter went up on the roof to pray. 10 He became hungry and wanted something to eat, and while the meal was being

prepared, he fell into a trance. ¹¹He saw heaven opened and something like a large sheet being let down to earth by its four corners. ¹²It contained all kinds of four-footed animals, as well as reptiles and birds. ¹³Then a voice told him, "Get up, Peter. Kill and eat."

¹⁴"Surely not, Lord!" Peter replied. "I have never eaten anything impure or unclean."

¹⁵The voice spoke to him a second time, "Do not call anything impure that God has made clean."

¹⁶This happened three times, and immediately the sheet was taken back to heaven.

¹⁷While Peter was wondering about the meaning of the vision, the men sent by Cornelius found out where Simon's house was and stopped at the gate. ¹⁸They called out, asking if Simon who was known as Peter was staying there.

¹⁹While Peter was still thinking about the vision, the Spirit said to him, "Simon, three*a* men are looking for you. ²⁰So get up and go downstairs. Do not hesitate to go with them, for I have sent them."

²¹Peter went down and said to the men, "I'm the one you're looking for. Why have you come?"

²²The men replied, "We have come from Cornelius the centurion. He is a righteous and God-fearing man, who is respected by all the Jewish people. A holy angel told him to ask you to come to his house so that he could hear what you have to say." ²³Then Peter invited the men into the house to be his guests.

Peter at Cornelius's House

The next day Peter started out with them, and some of the believers from Joppa went along. ²⁴The following day he arrived in Caesarea. Cornelius was expecting them and had called together his relatives and close friends. ²⁵As Peter entered the house, Cornelius met him and fell at his feet in reverence. ²⁶But Peter made him get up. "Stand up," he said, "I am only a man myself."

²⁷While talking with him, Peter went inside and found a large gathering of people. ²⁸He said to them: "You are well aware that it is against our law for a Jew to associate with or visit a Gentile. But God has shown me that I should not call anyone impure or unclean. ²⁹So when I was sent for, I came without raising any objection. May I ask why you sent for me?"

³⁰Cornelius answered: "Three days ago I was in my house praying at this hour, at three in the afternoon. Suddenly a man in shining clothes stood before me ³¹and said, 'Cornelius, God has heard your prayer and remembered your gifts to the poor. ³²Send to Joppa for Simon who is called Peter. He is a guest in the home of Simon the tanner, who lives by the sea.' ³³So I sent for you immediately, and it was good of you to come. Now we are all here in the presence of God to listen to everything the Lord has commanded you to tell us."

³⁴Then Peter began to speak: "I now realize how true it is that God does not show favoritism ³⁵but accepts from every nation the one who fears him and does what is right. ³⁶You know the message God sent to the people of Israel, announcing the good news of peace through Jesus Christ, who is Lord of all. ³⁷You know what has happened throughout the province of Judea, beginning in Galilee after the baptism that John preached— ³⁸how God anointed Jesus of Nazareth with the Holy Spirit and power, and how he went around doing good and healing all who were under the power of the devil, because God was with him.

³⁹"We are witnesses of everything he did in the country of the Jews and in Jerusalem. They killed him by hanging him on a cross, ⁴⁰but God raised him from the dead on the third day and caused him to be seen. ⁴¹He was not seen by all the people, but by witnesses whom God had already chosen—by us who ate and drank with him after he rose from the dead. ⁴²He commanded us to preach to the people and to testify that he is the one whom God appointed as judge of the

---

a 19 One early manuscript *two*; other manuscripts do not have the number.

living and the dead. ⁴³All the prophets testify about him that everyone who believes in him receives forgiveness of sins through his name."

⁴⁴While Peter was still speaking these words, the Holy Spirit came on all who heard the message. ⁴⁵The circumcised believers who had come with Peter were astonished that the gift of the Holy Spirit had been poured out even on Gentiles. ⁴⁶For they heard them speaking in tongues*ᵃ* and praising God.

Then Peter said, ⁴⁷"Surely no one can stand in the way of their being baptized with water. They have received the Holy Spirit just as we have." ⁴⁸So he ordered that they be baptized in the name of Jesus Christ. Then they asked Peter to stay with them for a few days.

Peter Explains His Actions

11 The apostles and the believers throughout Judea heard that the Gentiles also had received the word of God. ²So when Peter went up to Jerusalem, the circumcised believers criticized him ³and said, "You went into the house of uncircumcised men and ate with them."

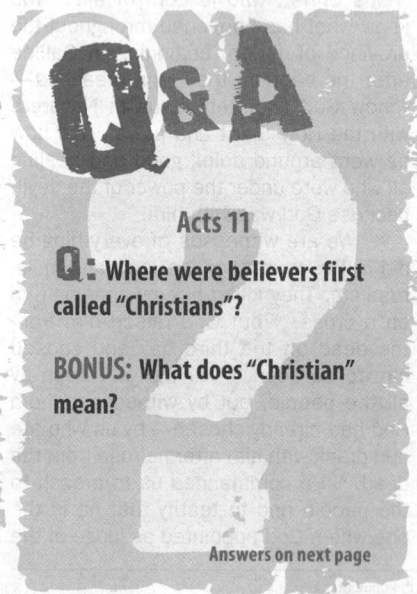

Acts 11

Q: Where were believers first called "Christians"?

BONUS: What does "Christian" mean?

Answers on next page

⁴Starting from the beginning, Peter told them the whole story: ⁵"I was in the city of Joppa praying, and in a trance I saw a vision. I saw something like a large sheet being let down from heaven by its four corners, and it came down to where I was. ⁶I looked into it and saw four-footed animals of the earth, wild beasts, reptiles and birds. ⁷Then I heard a voice telling me, 'Get up, Peter. Kill and eat.'

⁸"I replied, 'Surely not, Lord! Nothing impure or unclean has ever entered my mouth.'

⁹"The voice spoke from heaven a second time, 'Do not call anything impure that God has made clean.' ¹⁰This happened three times, and then it was all pulled up to heaven again.

¹¹"Right then three men who had been sent to me from Caesarea stopped at the house where I was staying. ¹²The Spirit told me to have no hesitation about going with them. These six brothers also went with me, and we entered the man's house. ¹³He told us how he had seen an angel appear in his house and say, 'Send to Joppa for Simon who is called Peter. ¹⁴He will bring you a message through which you and all your household will be saved.'

¹⁵"As I began to speak, the Holy Spirit came on them as he had come on us at the beginning. ¹⁶Then I remembered what the Lord had said: 'John baptized with*ᵇ* water, but you will be baptized with*ᵇ* the Holy Spirit.' ¹⁷So if God gave them the same gift he gave us who believed in the Lord Jesus Christ, who was I to think that I could stand in God's way?"

¹⁸When they heard this, they had no further objections and praised God, saying, "So then, even to Gentiles God has granted repentance that leads to life."

The Church in Antioch

¹⁹Now those who had been scattered by the persecution that broke out when Stephen was killed traveled as far as Phoenicia, Cyprus and Antioch, spreading the word only among Jews. ²⁰Some of them, however, men from Cyprus and

---

ᵃ 46 Or other languages   *ᵇ* 16 Or in

Cyrene, went to Antioch and began to speak to Greeks also, telling them the good news about the Lord Jesus. ²¹The Lord's hand was with them, and a great number of people believed and turned to the Lord.

²²News of this reached the church in Jerusalem, and they sent Barnabas to Antioch. ²³When he arrived and saw what the grace of God had done, he was glad and encouraged them all to remain true to the Lord with all their hearts. ²⁴He was a good man, full of the Holy Spirit and faith, and a great number of people were brought to the Lord.

²⁵Then Barnabas went to Tarsus to look for Saul, ²⁶and when he found him, he brought him to Antioch. So for a whole year Barnabas and Saul met with the church and taught great numbers of people. The disciples were called Christians first at Antioch.

²⁷During this time some prophets came down from Jerusalem to Antioch. ²⁸One of them, named Agabus, stood up and through the Spirit predicted that a severe famine would spread over the entire Roman world. (This happened during the reign of Claudius.) ²⁹The disciples, as each one was able, decided to provide help for the brothers and sisters living in Judea. ³⁰This they did, sending their gift to the elders by Barnabas and Saul.

Peter's Miraculous Escape From Prison

12 It was about this time that King Herod arrested some who belonged to the church, intending to persecute them. ²He had James, the brother of John, put to death with the sword. ³When he saw that this met with approval among the Jews, he proceeded to seize Peter also. This happened during the Festival of Unleavened Bread. ⁴After arresting him, he put him in prison, handing him over to be guarded by four squads of four soldiers each. Herod intended to bring him out for public trial after the Passover.

⁵So Peter was kept in prison, but the church was earnestly praying to God for him.

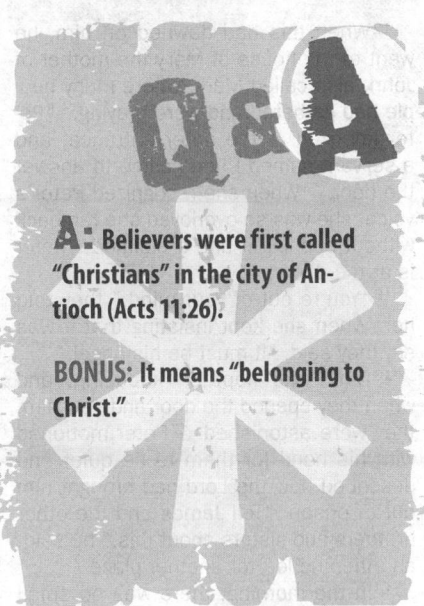

A: Believers were first called "Christians" in the city of Antioch (Acts 11:26).

BONUS: It means "belonging to Christ."

⁶The night before Herod was to bring him to trial, Peter was sleeping between two soldiers, bound with two chains, and sentries stood guard at the entrance. ⁷Suddenly an angel of the Lord appeared and a light shone in the cell. He struck Peter on the side and woke him up. "Quick, get up!" he said, and the chains fell off Peter's wrists.

⁸Then the angel said to him, "Put on your clothes and sandals." And Peter did so. "Wrap your cloak around you and follow me," the angel told him. ⁹Peter followed him out of the prison, but he had no idea that what the angel was doing was really happening; he thought he was seeing a vision. ¹⁰They passed the first and second guards and came to the iron gate leading to the city. It opened for them by itself, and they went through it. When they had walked the length of one street, suddenly the angel left him.

¹¹Then Peter came to himself and said, "Now I know without a doubt that the Lord has sent his angel and rescued me from Herod's clutches and from everything the Jewish people were hoping would happen."

1364 | Acts 12

12When this had dawned on him, he went to the house of Mary the mother of John, also called Mark, where many people had gathered and were praying. 13Peter knocked at the outer entrance, and a servant named Rhoda came to answer the door. 14When she recognized Peter's voice, she was so overjoyed she ran back without opening it and exclaimed, "Peter is at the door!"

15"You're out of your mind," they told her. When she kept insisting that it was so, they said, "It must be his angel."

16But Peter kept on knocking, and when they opened the door and saw him, they were astonished. 17Peter motioned with his hand for them to be quiet and described how the Lord had brought him out of prison. "Tell James and the other brothers and sisters about this," he said, and then he left for another place.

18In the morning, there was no small commotion among the soldiers as to what had become of Peter. 19After Herod had a thorough search made for him and did not find him, he cross-examined the guards and ordered that they be executed.

Herod's Death

Then Herod went from Judea to Caesarea and stayed there. 20He had been quarreling with the people of Tyre and Sidon; they now joined together and sought an audience with him. After securing the support of Blastus, a trusted personal servant of the king, they asked for peace, because they depended on the king's country for their food supply.

21On the appointed day Herod, wearing his royal robes, sat on his throne and delivered a public address to the people. 22They shouted, "This is the voice of a god, not of a man." 23Immediately, because Herod did not give praise to God, an angel of the Lord struck him down, and he was eaten by worms and died.

24But the word of God continued to spread and flourish.

Barnabas and Saul Sent Off

25When Barnabas and Saul had fin-

ished their mission, they returned from[a] Jerusalem, taking with them John, also called Mark. 13 1Now in the church at Antioch there were prophets and teachers: Barnabas, Simeon called Niger, Lucius of Cyrene, Manaen (who had been brought up with Herod the tetrarch) and Saul. 2While they were worshiping the Lord and fasting, the Holy Spirit said, "Set apart for me Barnabas and Saul for the work to which I have called them." 3So after they had fasted and prayed, they placed their hands on them and sent them off.

On Cyprus

4The two of them, sent on their way by the Holy Spirit, went down to Seleucia and sailed from there to Cyprus. 5When they arrived at Salamis, they proclaimed the word of God in the Jewish synagogues. John was with them as their helper.

6They traveled through the whole island until they came to Paphos. There they met a Jewish sorcerer and false prophet named Bar-Jesus, 7who was an attendant of the proconsul, Sergius Paulus. The proconsul, an intelligent man, sent for Barnabas and Saul because he wanted to hear the word of God. 8But Elymas the sorcerer (for that is what his name means) opposed them and tried to turn the proconsul from the faith. 9Then Saul, who was also called Paul, filled with the Holy Spirit, looked straight at Elymas and said, 10"You are a child of the devil and an enemy of everything that is right! You are full of all kinds of deceit and trickery. Will you never stop perverting the right ways of the Lord? 11Now the hand of the Lord is against you. You are going to be blind for a time, not even able to see the light of the sun."

Immediately mist and darkness came over him, and he groped about, seeking someone to lead him by the hand. 12When the proconsul saw what had happened, he believed, for he was amazed at the teaching about the Lord.

In Pisidian Antioch

13From Paphos, Paul and his companions sailed to Perga in Pamphylia, where

a 25 Some manuscripts *to*

John left them to return to Jerusalem.
¹⁴From Perga they went on to Pisidian
Antioch. On the Sabbath they entered
the synagogue and sat down. ¹⁵After the
reading from the Law and the Prophets,
the leaders of the synagogue sent word
to them, saying, "Brothers, if you have a
word of exhortation for the people, please
speak."

¹⁶Standing up, Paul motioned with his
hand and said: "Fellow Israelites and you
Gentiles who worship God, listen to me!
¹⁷The God of the people of Israel chose
our ancestors; he made the people prosper during their stay in Egypt; with mighty
power he led them out of that country;
¹⁸for about forty years he endured their
conduct^a in the wilderness; ¹⁹and he
overthrew seven nations in Canaan, giv-
ing their land to his people as their inheritance. ²⁰All this took about 450 years.

"After this, God gave them judges until
the time of Samuel the prophet. ²¹Then
the people asked for a king, and he gave
them Saul son of Kish, of the tribe of Benjamin, who ruled forty years. ²²After removing Saul, he made David their king.
God testified concerning him: 'I have
found David son of Jesse, a man after my
own heart; he will do everything I want
him to do.'

²³"From this man's descendants God
has brought to Israel the Savior Jesus,
as he promised. ²⁴Before the coming of
Jesus, John preached repentance and
baptism to all the people of Israel. ²⁵As
John was completing his work, he said:
'Who do you suppose I am? I am not the
one you are looking for. But there is one
coming after me whose sandals I am not
worthy to untie.'

²⁶"Fellow children of Abraham and you
God-fearing Gentiles, it is to us that this
message of salvation has been sent.
²⁷The people of Jerusalem and their rul-
ers did not recognize Jesus, yet in condemning him they fulfilled the words of
the prophets that are read every Sabbath. ²⁸Though they found no proper
ground for a death sentence, they asked

Pilate to have him executed. ²⁹When they
had carried out all that was written about
him, they took him down from the cross
and laid him in a tomb. ³⁰But God raised
him from the dead, ³¹and for many days
he was seen by those who had traveled
with him from Galilee to Jerusalem. They
are now his witnesses to our people.

³²"We tell you the good news: What
God promised our ancestors ³³he has
fulfilled for us, their children, by raising
up Jesus. As it is written in the second
Psalm:

" 'You are my son;
    today I have become your
        father.'^b

³⁴God raised him from the dead so that
he will never be subject to decay. As God
has said,

" 'I will give you the holy and sure
    blessings promised to David.'^c

³⁵So it is also stated elsewhere:

" 'You will not let your holy one see
    decay.'^d

³⁶"Now when David had served God's
purpose in his own generation, he fell
asleep; he was buried with his ances-
tors and his body decayed. ³⁷But the one
whom God raised from the dead did not
see decay.

³⁸"Therefore, my friends, I want you to
know that through Jesus the forgiveness
of sins is proclaimed to you. ³⁹Through
him everyone who believes is set free
from every sin, a justification you were
not able to obtain under the law of Moses. ⁴⁰Take care that what the prophets
have said does not happen to you:

⁴¹" 'Look, you scoffers,
    wonder and perish,
for I am going to do something in your
        days
    that you would never believe,
        even if someone told you.'^e"

⁴²As Paul and Barnabas were leaving
the synagogue, the people invited them

---

^a 18 Some manuscripts *he cared for them*   ^b 33 Psalm 2:7   ^c 34 Isaiah 55:3   ^d 35 Psalm 16:10 (see Septuagint)
^e 41 Hab. 1:5

to speak further about these things on the next Sabbath. ⁴³When the congregation was dismissed, many of the Jews and devout converts to Judaism followed Paul and Barnabas, who talked with them and urged them to continue in the grace of God.

⁴⁴On the next Sabbath almost the whole city gathered to hear the word of the Lord. ⁴⁵When the Jews saw the crowds, they were filled with jealousy. They began to contradict what Paul was saying and heaped abuse on him.

⁴⁶Then Paul and Barnabas answered them boldly: "We had to speak the word of God to you first. Since you reject it and do not consider yourselves worthy of eternal life, we now turn to the Gentiles. ⁴⁷For this is what the Lord has commanded us:

" 'I have made you[a] a light for the
     Gentiles,
   that you[a] may bring salvation to the
     ends of the earth.'[b]"

⁴⁸When the Gentiles heard this, they were glad and honored the word of the Lord; and all who were appointed for eternal life believed.

⁴⁹The word of the Lord spread through the whole region. ⁵⁰But the Jewish leaders incited the God-fearing women of high standing and the leading men of the city. They stirred up persecution against Paul and Barnabas, and expelled them from their region. ⁵¹So they shook the dust off their feet as a warning to them and went to Iconium. ⁵²And the disciples were filled with joy and with the Holy Spirit.

In Iconium

14 At Iconium Paul and Barnabas went as usual into the Jewish synagogue. There they spoke so effectively that a great number of Jews and Greeks believed. ²But the Jews who refused to believe stirred up the other Gentiles and poisoned their minds against the brothers. ³So Paul and Barnabas spent considerable time there, speaking boldly for the Lord, who confirmed the message of his grace by enabling them to perform

signs and wonders. ⁴The people of the city were divided; some sided with the Jews, others with the apostles. ⁵There was a plot afoot among both Gentiles and Jews, together with their leaders, to mistreat them and stone them. ⁶But they found out about it and fled to the Lycaonian cities of Lystra and Derbe and to the surrounding country, ⁷where they continued to preach the gospel.

INSTANT ACCESS

The devil doesn't bother some Christians. Like believers who go along with the crowd or who keep quiet about their relationship with Jesus. The person who doesn't go along with the crowd and who shares his or her faith is the one who gets persecuted. It happened in Acts. Persecution was stirred up when "the word of the Lord spread" (Acts 13:49). So if you start a morning prayer group or if a couple of people become Christians through your witness, don't be surprised if you face opposition. It's not much fun, but if persecution does come, it tells you that you're getting to Satan and becoming a spiritual success!

{Acts 13:46-52}

---

a 47 The Greek is singular.   *b 47* Isaiah 49:6

In Lystra and Derbe

8In Lystra there sat a man who was lame. He had been that way from birth and had never walked. 9He listened to Paul as he was speaking. Paul looked directly at him, saw that he had faith to be healed 10and called out, "Stand up on your feet!" At that, the man jumped up and began to walk.

11When the crowd saw what Paul had done, they shouted in the Lycaonian language, "The gods have come down to us in human form!" 12Barnabas they called Zeus, and Paul they called Hermes because he was the chief speaker. 13The priest of Zeus, whose temple was just outside the city, brought bulls and wreaths to the city gates because he and the crowd wanted to offer sacrifices to them.

14But when the apostles Barnabas and Paul heard of this, they tore their clothes and rushed out into the crowd, shouting: 15"Friends, why are you doing this? We too are only human, like you. We are bringing you good news, telling you to turn from these worthless things to the living God, who made the heavens and the earth and the sea and everything in them. 16In the past, he let all nations go their own way. 17Yet he has not left himself without testimony: He has shown kindness by giving you rain from heaven and crops in their seasons; he provides you with plenty of food and fills your hearts with joy." 18Even with these words, they had difficulty keeping the crowd from sacrificing to them.

19Then some Jews came from Antioch and Iconium and won the crowd over. They stoned Paul and dragged him outside the city, thinking he was dead. 20But after the disciples had gathered around him, he got up and went back into the city. The next day he and Barnabas left for Derbe.

The Return to Antioch in Syria

21They preached the gospel in that city and won a large number of disciples. Then they returned to Lystra, Iconium and Antioch, 22strengthening the disciples and encouraging them to remain true to the faith. "We must go through many hardships to enter the kingdom of God," they said. 23Paul and Barnabas appointed elders[a] for them in each church and, with prayer and fasting, committed them to the Lord, in whom they had put their trust. 24After going through Pisidia, they came into Pamphylia, 25and when they had preached the word in Perga, they went down to Attalia.

26From Attalia they sailed back to Antioch, where they had been committed to the grace of God for the work they had now completed. 27On arriving there, they gathered the church together and reported all that God had done through them and how he had opened a door of faith to the Gentiles. 28And they stayed there a long time with the disciples.

The Council at Jerusalem

15 Certain people came down from Judea to Antioch and were teaching the believers: "Unless you are circumcised, according to the custom taught by Moses, you cannot be saved." 2This

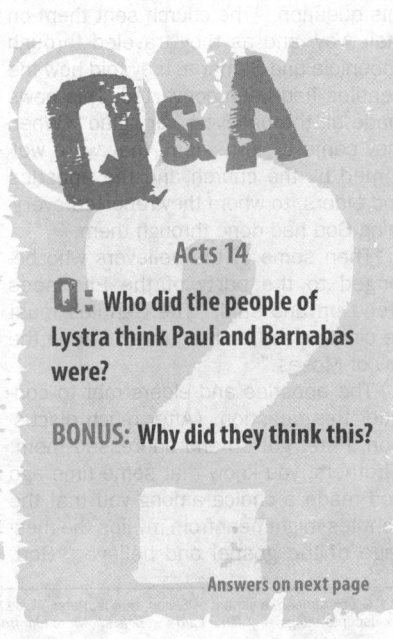

Acts 14

Q: Who did the people of Lystra think Paul and Barnabas were?

BONUS: Why did they think this?

Answers on next page

---

a 23 Or Barnabas ordained elders; or Barnabas had elders elected

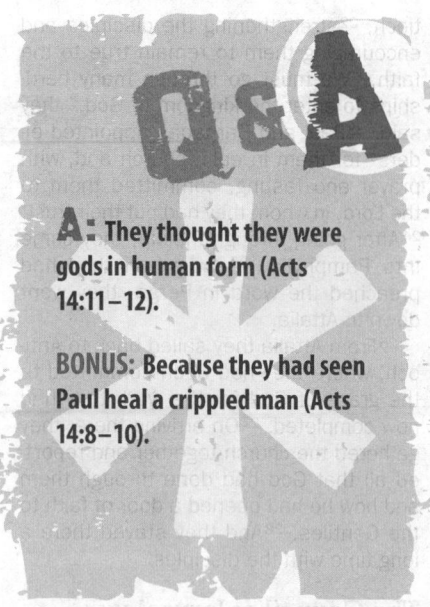

A: They thought they were gods in human form (Acts 14:11–12).

BONUS: Because they had seen Paul heal a crippled man (Acts 14:8–10).

brought Paul and Barnabas into sharp dispute and debate with them. So Paul and Barnabas were appointed, along with some other believers, to go up to Jerusalem to see the apostles and elders about this question. ³The church sent them on their way, and as they traveled through Phoenicia and Samaria, they told how the Gentiles had been converted. This news made all the believers very glad. ⁴When they came to Jerusalem, they were welcomed by the church and the apostles and elders, to whom they reported everything God had done through them.

⁵Then some of the believers who belonged to the party of the Pharisees stood up and said, "The Gentiles must be circumcised and required to keep the law of Moses."

⁶The apostles and elders met to consider this question. ⁷After much discussion, Peter got up and addressed them: "Brothers, you know that some time ago God made a choice among you that the Gentiles might hear from my lips the message of the gospel and believe. ⁸God,

who knows the heart, showed that he accepted them by giving the Holy Spirit to them, just as he did to us. ⁹He did not discriminate between us and them, for he purified their hearts by faith. ¹⁰Now then, why do you try to test God by putting on the necks of Gentiles a yoke that neither we nor our ancestors have been able to bear? ¹¹No! We believe it is through the grace of our Lord Jesus that we are saved, just as they are."

¹²The whole assembly became silent as they listened to Barnabas and Paul telling about the signs and wonders God had done among the Gentiles through them. ¹³When they finished, James spoke up. "Brothers," he said, "listen to me. ¹⁴Simon[a] has described to us how God first intervened to choose a people for his name from the Gentiles. ¹⁵The words of the prophets are in agreement with this, as it is written:

¹⁶ " 'After this I will return
and rebuild David's fallen
tent.
Its ruins I will rebuild,
and I will restore it,
¹⁷that the rest of mankind may seek the
Lord,
even all the Gentiles who bear my
name,
says the Lord, who does these
things'[b]—
¹⁸ things known from long ago.[c]

¹⁹"It is my judgment, therefore, that we should not make it difficult for the Gentiles who are turning to God. ²⁰Instead we should write to them, telling them to abstain from food polluted by idols, from sexual immorality, from the meat of strangled animals and from blood. ²¹For the law of Moses has been preached in every city from the earliest times and is read in the synagogues on every Sabbath."

The Council's Letter to Gentile Believers

²²Then the apostles and elders, with the whole church, decided to choose

---

[a] 14 Greek *Simeon*, a variant of *Simon*; that is, Peter   [b] 17 Amos 9:11,12 (see Septuagint)   [c] 17,18 Some manuscripts *things'— / ¹⁸the Lord's work is known to him from long ago*

I t would be nice if all arguments could be quickly settled. On TV maybe it happens. But in real life? Even in Christian families hostility can develop between brothers and sisters and husbands and wives. Take Paul and Barnabas. They'd been friends, and both were working together as dedicated Christians. But they had a "sharp disagreement" that drove them apart. The beauty is that the split caused each to go his own way, providing for two missionary endeavors instead of one. This is proof that God can use even our disagreements to accomplish his good!

{Acts 15:36–40}

》》INSTANT ACCESS

24 We have heard that some went out from us without our authorization and disturbed you, troubling your minds by what they said. 25 So we all agreed to choose some men and send them to you with our dear friends Barnabas and Paul— 26 men who have risked their lives for the name of our Lord Jesus Christ. 27 Therefore we are sending Judas and Silas to confirm by word of mouth what we are writing. 28 It seemed good to the Holy Spirit and to us not to burden you with anything beyond the following requirements: 29 You are to abstain from food sacrificed to idols, from blood, from the meat of strangled animals and from sexual immorality. You will do well to avoid these things.

Farewell.

30 So the men were sent off and went down to Antioch, where they gathered the church together and delivered the letter. 31 The people read it and were glad for its encouraging message. 32 Judas and Silas, who themselves were prophets, said much to encourage and strengthen the believers. 33 After spending some time there, they were sent off by the believers with the blessing of peace to return to those who had sent them. [34]a 35 But Paul and Barnabas remained in Antioch, where they and many others taught and preached the word of the Lord.

Disagreement Between Paul and Barnabas

36 Some time later Paul said to Barnabas, "Let us go back and visit the believers in all the towns where we preached the word of the Lord and see how they are doing." 37 Barnabas wanted to take John, also called Mark, with them, 38 but Paul did not think it wise to take him, because he had deserted them in Pamphylia and had not continued with them in the work. 39 They had such a sharp disagreement that they parted company. Barnabas took Mark and sailed for Cyprus, 40 but Paul

some of their own men and send them to Antioch with Paul and Barnabas. They chose Judas (called Barsabbas) and Silas, men who were leaders among the believers. 23 With them they sent the following letter:

The apostles and elders, your brothers,

To the Gentile believers in Antioch, Syria and Cilicia:

Greetings.

a 34 Some manuscripts include here *But Silas decided to remain there.*

chose Silas and left, commended by the believers to the grace of the Lord. [41]He went through Syria and Cilicia, strengthening the churches.

Timothy Joins Paul and Silas

16 Paul came to Derbe and then to Lystra, where a disciple named Timothy lived, whose mother was Jewish and a believer but whose father was a Greek. [2]The believers at Lystra and Iconium spoke well of him. [3]Paul wanted to take him along on the journey, so he circumcised him because of the Jews who lived in that area, for they all knew that his father was a Greek. [4]As they traveled from town to town, they delivered the decisions reached by the apostles and elders in Jerusalem for the people to obey. [5]So the churches were strengthened in the faith and grew daily in numbers.

Paul's Vision of the Man of Macedonia

[6]Paul and his companions traveled throughout the region of Phrygia and Galatia, having been kept by the Holy Spirit from preaching the word in the province of Asia. [7]When they came to the border of Mysia, they tried to enter Bithynia, but the Spirit of Jesus would not allow them to. [8]So they passed by Mysia and went down to Troas. [9]During the night Paul had a vision of a man of Macedonia standing and begging him, "Come over to Macedonia and help us." [10]After Paul had seen the vision, we got ready at once to leave for Macedonia, concluding that God had called us to preach the gospel to them.

Lydia's Conversion in Philippi

[11]From Troas we put out to sea and sailed straight for Samothrace, and the next day we went on to Neapolis. [12]From there we traveled to Philippi, a Roman colony and the leading city of that district[a] of Macedonia. And we stayed there several days.

[13]On the Sabbath we went outside the city gate to the river, where we expected to find a place of prayer. We sat down and began to speak to the women who had gathered there. [14]One of those listening was a woman from the city of Thyatira named Lydia, a dealer in purple cloth. She was a worshiper of God. The Lord opened her heart to respond to Paul's message. [15]When she and the members of her household were baptized, she invited us to her home. "If you consider me a believer in the Lord," she said, "come and stay at my house." And she persuaded us.

Paul and Silas in Prison

[16]Once when we were going to the place of prayer, we were met by a female slave who had a spirit by which she predicted the future. She earned a great deal of money for her owners by fortune-telling. [17]She followed Paul and the rest of us, shouting, "These men are servants of the Most High God, who are telling you the way to be saved." [18]She kept this up for many days. Finally Paul became so annoyed that he turned around and said to the spirit, "In the name of Jesus Christ I command you to come out of her!" At that moment the spirit left her.

Q&A

Acts 16

Q: What did Paul and Silas do while they were in prison in Philippi?

BONUS: What exciting events happened that night?

Answers on next page

---

[a] 12 The text and meaning of the Greek for *the leading city of that district* are uncertain.

19When her owners realized that their hope of making money was gone, they seized Paul and Silas and dragged them into the marketplace to face the authorities. 20They brought them before the magistrates and said, "These men are Jews, and are throwing our city into an uproar 21by advocating customs unlawful for us Romans to accept or practice."

22The crowd joined in the attack against Paul and Silas, and the magistrates ordered them to be stripped and beaten with rods. 23After they had been severely flogged, they were thrown into prison, and the jailer was commanded to guard them carefully. 24When he received these orders, he put them in the inner cell and fastened their feet in the stocks.

25About midnight Paul and Silas were praying and singing hymns to God, and the other prisoners were listening to them. 26Suddenly there was such a violent earthquake that the foundations of the prison were shaken. At once all the prison doors flew open, and everyone's chains came loose. 27The jailer woke up, and when he saw the prison doors open, he drew his sword and was about to kill himself because he thought the prisoners had escaped. 28But Paul shouted, "Don't harm yourself! We are all here!"

29The jailer called for lights, rushed in and fell trembling before Paul and Silas. 30He then brought them out and asked, "Sirs, what must I do to be saved?"

31They replied, "Believe in the Lord Jesus, and you will be saved—you and your household." 32Then they spoke the word of the Lord to him and to all the others in his house. 33At that hour of the night the jailer took them and washed their wounds; then immediately he and all his household were baptized. 34The jailer brought them into his house and set a meal before them; he was filled with joy because he had come to believe in God—he and his whole household.

35When it was daylight, the magistrates sent their officers to the jailer with the order: "Release those men." 36The jailer told Paul, "The magistrates have ordered that you and Silas be released. Now you can leave. Go in peace."

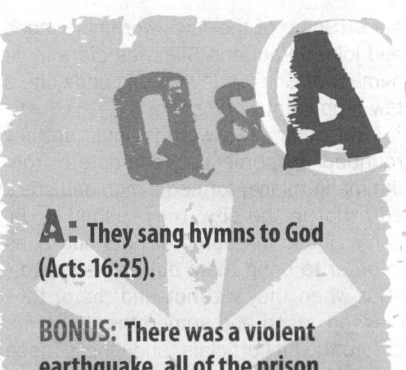

A: They sang hymns to God (Acts 16:25).

BONUS: There was a violent earthquake, all of the prison doors fell open, and the jailer became a believer in Jesus (Acts 16:26–34).

37But Paul said to the officers: "They beat us publicly without a trial, even though we are Roman citizens, and threw us into prison. And now do they want to get rid of us quietly? No! Let them come themselves and escort us out."

38The officers reported this to the magistrates, and when they heard that Paul and Silas were Roman citizens, they were alarmed. 39They came to appease them and escorted them from the prison, requesting them to leave the city. 40After Paul and Silas came out of the prison, they went to Lydia's house, where they met with the brothers and sisters and encouraged them. Then they left.

In Thessalonica

17 When Paul and his companions had passed through Amphipolis and Apollonia, they came to Thessalonica, where there was a Jewish synagogue. 2As was his custom, Paul went into the synagogue, and on three Sabbath days he reasoned with them from the Scriptures, 3explaining and proving that the Messiah had to suffer and rise from the dead. "This Jesus I am proclaiming to you is the Messiah," he said. [4] Some of the Jews were persuaded and joined Paul and Silas, as did a large number of God-fearing Greeks and quite a few prominent women.

[5] But other Jews were jealous; so they rounded up some bad characters from the marketplace, formed a mob and started a riot in the city. They rushed to Jason's house in search of Paul and Silas in order to bring them out to the crowd.[a] [6] But when they did not find them, they dragged Jason and some other believers before the city officials, shouting: "These men who have caused trouble all over the world have now come here, [7] and Jason has welcomed them into his house. They are all defying Caesar's decrees, saying that there is another king, one called Jesus." [8] When they heard this, the crowd and the city officials were thrown into turmoil. [9] Then they made Jason and the others post bond and let them go.

In Berea

[10] As soon as it was night, the believers sent Paul and Silas away to Berea. On arriving there, they went to the Jewish synagogue. [11] Now the Berean Jews were of more noble character than those in Thessalonica, for they received the message with great eagerness and examined the Scriptures every day to see if what Paul said was true. [12] As a result, many of them believed, as did also a number of prominent Greek women and many Greek men.

[13] But when the Jews in Thessalonica learned that Paul was preaching the word of God at Berea, some of them went there too, agitating the crowds and stirring them up. [14] The believers immediately sent Paul to the coast, but Silas and Timothy stayed at Berea. [15] Those who escorted Paul brought him to Athens and then left with instructions for Silas and Timothy to join him as soon as possible.

In Athens

[16] While Paul was waiting for them in Athens, he was greatly distressed to see that the city was full of idols. [17] So he rea-

soned in the synagogue with both Jews and God-fearing Greeks, as well as in the marketplace day by day with those who happened to be there. [18] A group of Epicurean and Stoic philosophers began to debate with him. Some of them asked; "What is this babbler trying to say?" Others remarked, "He seems to be advocating foreign gods." They said this because Paul was preaching the good news about Jesus and the resurrection. [19] Then they took him and brought him to a meeting of the Areopagus, where they said to him, "May we know what this new teaching is that you are presenting? [20] You are bringing some strange ideas to our ears, and we would like to know what they mean." [21] (All the Athenians and the foreigners who lived there spent their time doing nothing but talking about and listening to the latest ideas.)

[22] Paul then stood up in the meeting of the Areopagus and said: "People of Athens! I see that in every way you are very religious. [23] For as I walked around and looked carefully at your objects of worship, I even found an altar with this inscription: TO AN UNKNOWN GOD. So you are ignorant of the very thing you worship—and this is what I am going to proclaim to you.

[24] "The God who made the world and everything in it is the Lord of heaven and earth and does not live in temples built by human hands. [25] And he is not served by human hands, as if he needed anything. Rather, he himself gives everyone life and breath and everything else. [26] From one man he made all the nations, that they should inhabit the whole earth; and he marked out their appointed times in history and the boundaries of their lands. [27] God did this so that they would seek him and perhaps reach out for him and find him, though he is not far from any one of us. [28] 'For in him we live and move and have our being.'[b] As some of your own poets have said, 'We are his offspring.'[c]

[29] "Therefore since we are God's offspring, we should not think that the divine being is like gold or silver or stone—

---

[a] 5 Or the assembly of the people   [b] 28 From the Cretan philosopher Epimenides   [c] 28 From the Cilician Stoic philosopher Aratus

an image made by human design and skill. ³⁰In the past God overlooked such ignorance, but now he commands all people everywhere to repent. ³¹For he has set a day when he will judge the world with justice by the man he has appointed. He has given proof of this to everyone by raising him from the dead."

³²When they heard about the resurrection of the dead, some of them sneered, but others said, "We want to hear you again on this subject." ³³At that, Paul left the Council. ³⁴Some of the people became followers of Paul and believed. Among them was Dionysius, a member of the Areopagus, also a woman named Damaris, and a number of others.

In Corinth

18 After this, Paul left Athens and went to Corinth. ²There he met a Jew named Aquila, a native of Pontus, who had recently come from Italy with his wife Priscilla, because Claudius had ordered all Jews to leave Rome. Paul went to see them, ³and because he was a tentmaker as they were, he stayed and worked with them. ⁴Every Sabbath he reasoned in the synagogue, trying to persuade Jews and Greeks.

⁵When Silas and Timothy came from Macedonia, Paul devoted himself exclusively to preaching, testifying to the Jews that Jesus was the Messiah. ⁶But when they opposed Paul and became abusive,

he shook out his clothes in protest and said to them, "Your blood be on your own heads! I am innocent of it. From now on I will go to the Gentiles."

⁷Then Paul left the synagogue and went next door to the house of Titius Justus, a worshiper of God. ⁸Crispus, the synagogue leader, and his entire household believed in the Lord; and many of the Corinthians who heard Paul believed and were baptized.

⁹One night the Lord spoke to Paul in a vision: "Do not be afraid; keep on speaking, do not be silent. ¹⁰For I am with you, and no one is going to attack and harm you, because I have many people in this city." ¹¹So Paul stayed in Corinth for a year and a half, teaching them the word of God.

¹²While Gallio was proconsul of Achaia, the Jews of Corinth made a united attack on Paul and brought him to the place of judgment. ¹³"This man," they charged, "is persuading the people to worship God in ways contrary to the law."

¹⁴Just as Paul was about to speak, Gallio said to them, "If you Jews were making a complaint about some misdemeanor or serious crime, it would be reasonable for me to listen to you. ¹⁵But since it involves questions about words and names and your own law—settle the matter yourselves. I will not be a judge of such things." ¹⁶So he drove them off. ¹⁷Then the crowd there turned on Sosthenes the synagogue leader and beat him in front

PANORAMA

You Belong.

You are a member of the church of Jesus Christ. This book tells how the church family began and grew.

{ACTS}

of the proconsul; and Gallio showed no concern whatever.

Priscilla, Aquila and Apollos

[18]Paul stayed on in Corinth for some time. Then he left the brothers and sisters and sailed for Syria, accompanied by Priscilla and Aquila. Before he sailed, he had his hair cut off at Cenchreae because of a vow he had taken. [19]They arrived at Ephesus, where Paul left Priscilla and Aquila. He himself went into the synagogue and reasoned with the Jews. [20]When they asked him to spend more time with them, he declined. [21]But as he left, he promised, "I will come back if it is God's will." Then he set sail from Ephesus. [22]When he landed at Caesarea, he went up to Jerusalem and greeted the church and then went down to Antioch.

[23]After spending some time in Antioch, Paul set out from there and traveled from place to place throughout the region of Galatia and Phrygia, strengthening all the disciples.

[24]Meanwhile a Jew named Apollos, a native of Alexandria, came to Ephesus. He was a learned man, with a thorough knowledge of the Scriptures. [25]He had been instructed in the way of the Lord, and he spoke with great fervor[a] and taught about Jesus accurately, though he knew only the baptism of John. [26]He began to speak boldly in the synagogue. When Priscilla and Aquila heard him, they invited him to their home and explained to him the way of God more adequately.

[27]When Apollos wanted to go to Achaia, the brothers and sisters encouraged him and wrote to the disciples there to welcome him. When he arrived, he was a great help to those who by grace had believed. [28]For he vigorously refuted his Jewish opponents in public debate, proving from the Scriptures that Jesus was the Messiah.

Paul in Ephesus

19 While Apollos was at Corinth, Paul took the road through the interior and arrived at Ephesus. There he found some disciples [2]and asked them, "Did you receive the Holy Spirit when[b] you believed?"

They answered, "No, we have not even heard that there is a Holy Spirit."

[3]So Paul asked, "Then what baptism did you receive?"

"John's baptism," they replied.

[4]Paul said, "John's baptism was a baptism of repentance. He told the people to believe in the one coming after him, that is, in Jesus." [5]On hearing this, they were baptized in the name of the Lord Jesus. [6]When Paul placed his hands on them, the Holy Spirit came on them, and they spoke in tongues[c] and prophesied. [7]There were about twelve men in all.

[8]Paul entered the synagogue and spoke boldly there for three months, arguing persuasively about the kingdom of God. [9]But some of them became obstinate; they refused to believe and publicly maligned the Way. So Paul left them. He took the disciples with him and had discussions daily in the lecture hall of Tyrannus. [10]This went on for two years, so that all the Jews and Greeks who lived in the province of Asia heard the word of the Lord.

[11]God did extraordinary miracles through Paul, [12]so that even handkerchiefs and aprons that had touched him were taken to the sick, and their illnesses were cured and the evil spirits left them.

[13]Some Jews who went around driving out evil spirits tried to invoke the name of the Lord Jesus over those who were demon-possessed. They would say, "In the name of the Jesus whom Paul preaches, I command you to come out." [14]Seven sons of Sceva, a Jewish chief priest, were doing this. [15]One day the evil spirit answered them, "Jesus I know, and Paul I know about, but who are you?" [16]Then the man who had the evil spirit jumped on them and overpowered them all. He gave them such a beating that they ran out of the house naked and bleeding.

[17]When this became known to the Jews and Greeks living in Ephesus, they were all seized with fear, and the name of the Lord Jesus was held in high honor. [18]Many of

---

[a] 25 Or *with fervor in the Spirit*   [b] 2 Or *after*   [c] 6 Or *other languages*

those who believed now came and openly confessed what they had done. ¹⁹A number who had practiced sorcery brought their scrolls together and burned them publicly. When they calculated the value of the scrolls, the total came to fifty thousand drachmas.ᵃ ²⁰In this way the word of the Lord spread widely and grew in power.

²¹After all this had happened, Paul decidedᵇ to go to Jerusalem, passing through Macedonia and Achaia. "After I have been there," he said, "I must visit Rome also." ²²He sent two of his helpers, Timothy and Erastus, to Macedonia, while he stayed in the province of Asia a little longer.

The Riot in Ephesus

²³About that time there arose a great disturbance about the Way. ²⁴A silver-smith named Demetrius, who made silver shrines of Artemis, brought in a lot of business for the craftsmen there. ²⁵He called them together, along with the workers in related trades, and said: "You know, my friends, that we receive a good income from this business. ²⁶And you see and hear how this fellow Paul has convinced and led astray large numbers of people here in Ephesus and in practically the whole province of Asia. He says that gods made by human hands are no gods at all. ²⁷There is danger not only that our trade will lose its good name, but also that the temple of the great goddess Artemis will be discredited; and the goddess herself, who is worshiped throughout the province of Asia and the world, will be robbed of her divine majesty."

ᵃ 19 A drachma was a silver coin worth about a day's wages.   ᵇ 21 Or *decided in the Spirit*

TO THE POINT

Magic, No

Today's magicians pull rabbits out of hats and do other tricks to make people or even elephants seem to disappear. But that's not real magic. Real magic involves the use of charms, spells or rituals to influence people or events. Much magic in Bible times was an attempt to control demons and other supernatural beings. To some extent, all occult practices involve the use of real magic.

People often turn to magic because they want more control over what happens to them. They're afraid, and they don't trust God's control of the events of their lives.

When many people in Ephesus became Christians, they realized the evil in real magic. They burned their books of magic (Acts 19:18–20). People who know that God loves them don't have to be afraid of the future. God is in control, and he will take care of them always.

28When they heard this, they were furious and began shouting: "Great is Artemis of the Ephesians!" 29Soon the whole city was in an uproar. The people seized Gaius and Aristarchus, Paul's traveling companions from Macedonia, and all of them rushed into the theater together. 30Paul wanted to appear before the crowd, but the disciples would not let him. 31Even some of the officials of the province, friends of Paul, sent him a message begging him not to venture into the theater.

32The assembly was in confusion: Some were shouting one thing, some another. Most of the people did not even know why they were there. 33The Jews in the crowd pushed Alexander to the front, and they shouted instructions to him. He motioned for silence in order to make a defense before the people. 34But when they realized he was a Jew, they all shouted in unison for about two hours: "Great is Artemis of the Ephesians!"

35The city clerk quieted the crowd and said: "Fellow Ephesians, doesn't all the world know that the city of Ephesus is the guardian of the temple of the great Artemis and of her image, which fell from heaven? 36Therefore, since these facts are undeniable, you ought to calm down and not do anything rash. 37You have brought these men here, though they have neither robbed temples nor blasphemed our goddess. 38If, then, Demetrius and his fellow craftsmen have a grievance against anybody, the courts are open and there are proconsuls. They can press charges. 39If there is anything further you want to bring up, it must be settled in a legal assembly. 40As it is, we are in danger of being charged with rioting because of what happened today. In that case we would not be able to account for this commotion, since there is no reason for it." 41After he had said this, he dismissed the assembly.

Through Macedonia and Greece

20 When the uproar had ended, Paul sent for the disciples and, after encouraging them, said goodbye and set out for Macedonia. 2He traveled through that area, speaking many words of encouragement to the people, and finally arrived in Greece, 3where he stayed three months. Because some Jews had plotted against him just as he was about to sail for Syria, he decided to go back through Macedonia. 4He was accompanied by Sopater son of Pyrrhus from Berea, Aristarchus and Secundus from Thessalonica, Gaius from Derbe, Timothy also, and Tychicus and Trophimus from the province of Asia. 5These men went on ahead and waited for us at Troas. 6But we sailed from Philippi after the Festival of Unleavened Bread, and five days later joined the others at Troas, where we stayed seven days.

Eutychus Raised From the Dead at Troas

7On the first day of the week we came together to break bread. Paul spoke to the people and, because he intended to leave the next day, kept on talking until midnight. 8There were many lamps in the upstairs room where we were meeting. 9Seated in a window was a young man named Eutychus, who was sinking into a deep sleep as Paul talked on and on. When he was sound asleep, he fell to the ground from the third story and was picked up dead. 10Paul went down, threw himself on the young man and put his arms around him. "Don't be alarmed," he said. "He's alive!" 11Then he went upstairs again and broke bread and ate. After talking until daylight, he left. 12The people took the young man home alive and were greatly comforted.

Paul's Farewell to the Ephesian Elders

13We went on ahead to the ship and sailed for Assos, where we were going to take Paul aboard. He had made this arrangement because he was going there on foot. 14When he met us at Assos, we took him aboard and went on to Mitylene. 15The next day we set sail from there and arrived off Chios. The day after that we crossed over to Samos, and on the following day arrived at Miletus. 16Paul had

Want to build a good self-image? Take on a tough task and see it through. After going out for football, don't quit after the first sweaty training session. Don't drop geometry the first week. Don't decide to read your Bible every morning and then hit the snooze button when you skipped it twice in two days. Take a look at Paul. He was warned that he faced prison and hardship in Jerusalem. But he said, "I am going" (Acts 20:22). Paul had confidence, not only that God was sending him, but also that he'd be able to see hard times through. There's only one way to develop that kind of confidence in yourself. Don't quit.

{Acts 20:22–24}

decided to sail past Ephesus to avoid spending time in the province of Asia, for he was in a hurry to reach Jerusalem, if possible, by the day of Pentecost.

[17] From Miletus, Paul sent to Ephesus for the elders of the church. [18] When they arrived, he said to them: "You know how I lived the whole time I was with you, from the first day I came into the province of Asia. [19] I served the Lord with great humility and with tears and in the midst of severe testing by the plots of my Jewish opponents. [20] You know that I have not hesitated to preach anything that would be helpful to you but have taught you publicly and from house to house. [21] I have declared to both Jews and Greeks that they must turn to God in repentance and have faith in our Lord Jesus.

[22] "And now, compelled by the Spirit, I am going to Jerusalem, not knowing what will happen to me there. [23] I only know that in every city the Holy Spirit warns me that prison and hardships are facing me. [24] However, I consider my life worth nothing to me; my only aim is to finish the race and complete the task the Lord Jesus has given me—the task of testifying to the good news of God's grace.

[25] "Now I know that none of you among whom I have gone about preaching the kingdom will ever see me again. [26] Therefore, I declare to you today that I am innocent of the blood of any of you. [27] For I have not hesitated to proclaim to you the whole will of God. [28] Keep watch over yourselves and all the flock of which the Holy Spirit has made you overseers. Be shepherds of the church of God,[a] which he bought with his own blood.[b] [29] I know that after I leave, savage wolves will come in among you and will not spare the flock. [30] Even from your own number men will arise and distort the truth in order to draw away disciples after them. [31] So be on your guard! Remember that for three years I never stopped warning each of you night and day with tears.

[32] "Now I commit you to God and to the word of his grace, which can build you up and give you an inheritance among all those who are sanctified. [33] I have not coveted anyone's silver or gold or clothing. [34] You yourselves know that these hands of mine have supplied my own needs and the needs of my companions. [35] In everything I did, I showed you that by this kind of hard work we must help the weak, remembering the words the Lord Jesus himself said: 'It is more blessed to give than to receive.' "

[36] When Paul had finished speaking, he knelt down with all of them and prayed.

a 28 Many manuscripts of the Lord   b 28 Or with the blood of his own Son.

37 They all wept as they embraced him and kissed him. 38 What grieved them most was his statement that they would never see his face again. Then they accompanied him to the ship.

On to Jerusalem

21 After we had torn ourselves away from them, we put out to sea and sailed straight to Kos. The next day we went to Rhodes and from there to Patara. 2 We found a ship crossing over to Phoenicia, went on board and set sail. 3 After sighting Cyprus and passing to the south of it, we sailed on to Syria. We landed at Tyre, where our ship was to unload its cargo. 4 We sought out the disciples there and stayed with them seven days. Through the Spirit they urged Paul not to go on to Jerusalem. 5 When it was time to leave, we left and continued on our way. All of them, including wives and children, accompanied us out of the city, and there on the beach we knelt to pray. 6 After saying goodbye to each other, we went aboard the ship, and they returned home.

7 We continued our voyage from Tyre and landed at Ptolemais, where we greeted the brothers and sisters and stayed with them for a day. 8 Leaving the next day, we reached Caesarea and stayed at the house of Philip the evangelist, one of the Seven. 9 He had four unmarried daughters who prophesied.

10 After we had been there a number of days, a prophet named Agabus came down from Judea. 11 Coming over to us, he took Paul's belt, tied his own hands and feet with it and said, "The Holy Spirit says, 'In this way the Jewish leaders in Jerusalem will bind the owner of this belt and will hand him over to the Gentiles.'"

12 When we heard this, we and the people there pleaded with Paul not to go up to Jerusalem. 13 Then Paul answered, "Why are you weeping and breaking my heart? I am ready not only to be bound, but also to die in Jerusalem for the name of the Lord Jesus." 14 When he would not be dissuaded, we gave up and said, "The Lord's will be done."

15 After this, we started on our way up to Jerusalem. 16 Some of the disciples from Caesarea accompanied us and brought us to the home of Mnason, where we were to stay. He was a man from Cyprus and one of the early disciples.

Paul's Arrival at Jerusalem

17 When we arrived at Jerusalem, the brothers and sisters received us warmly. 18 The next day Paul and the rest of us went to see James, and all the elders were present. 19 Paul greeted them and reported in detail what God had done among the Gentiles through his ministry.

20 When they heard this, they praised God. Then they said to Paul: "You see, brother, how many thousands of Jews have believed, and all of them are zealous for the law. 21 They have been informed that you teach all the Jews who live among the Gentiles to turn away from Moses, telling them not to circumcise their children or live according to our customs. 22 What shall we do? They will certainly hear that you have come, 23 so do what we tell you. There are four men with us who have made a vow. 24 Take these men, join in their purification rites and pay their expenses, so that they can have their heads shaved. Then everyone will know there is no truth in these reports about you, but that you yourself are living in obedience to the law. 25 As for the Gentile believers, we have written to them our decision that they should abstain from food sacrificed to idols, from blood, from the meat of strangled animals and from sexual immorality."

26 The next day Paul took the men and purified himself along with them. Then he went to the temple to give notice of the date when the days of purification would end and the offering would be made for each of them.

Paul Arrested

27 When the seven days were nearly over, some Jews from the province of Asia saw Paul at the temple. They stirred up the whole crowd and seized him, 28 shouting, "Fellow Israelites, help us! This is the man who teaches everyone everywhere against our people and our law and this place. And besides, he

Lots of teens wonder why they have to dress up for church. The answer? You don't. But picture yourself getting ready for a special date. Do you wear your oldest, dirtiest sweatpants? Of course not. Church is pretty much the same thing. You dress appropriately. When Paul went to Jerusalem, he followed some rules that he didn't think were necessary. He didn't have to, but he was sensitive to the convictions of others. Dressing appropriately for church falls into this category. It shows those around you that you are sensitive to their opinions and that you love and respect the God you both serve.

{Acts 21:17–26}

INSTANT ACCESS

has brought Greeks into the temple and defiled this holy place." 29(They had previously seen Trophimus the Ephesian in the city with Paul and assumed that Paul had brought him into the temple.)

30The whole city was aroused, and the people came running from all directions. Seizing Paul, they dragged him from the temple, and immediately the gates were shut. 31While they were trying to kill him, news reached the commander of the Roman troops that the whole city of Jerusalem was in an uproar. 32He at once

took some officers and soldiers and ran down to the crowd. When the rioters saw the commander and his soldiers, they stopped beating Paul.

33The commander came up and arrested him and ordered him to be bound with two chains. Then he asked who he was and what he had done. 34Some in the crowd shouted one thing and some another, and since the commander could not get at the truth because of the uproar, he ordered that Paul be taken into the barracks. 35When Paul reached the steps, the violence of the mob was so great he had to be carried by the soldiers. 36The crowd that followed kept shouting, "Get rid of him!"

Paul Speaks to the Crowd

37As the soldiers were about to take Paul into the barracks, he asked the commander, "May I say something to you?"

"Do you speak Greek?" he replied. 38"Aren't you the Egyptian who started a revolt and led four thousand terrorists out into the wilderness some time ago?"

39Paul answered, "I am a Jew, from Tarsus in Cilicia, a citizen of no ordinary city. Please let me speak to the people."

40After receiving the commander's permission, Paul stood on the steps and motioned to the crowd. When they were all silent, he said to them in Arama-

22 ic[a]: 1"Brothers and fathers, listen now to my defense."

2When they heard him speak to them in Aramaic, they became very quiet.

Then Paul said: 3"I am a Jew, born in Tarsus of Cilicia, but brought up in this city. I studied under Gamaliel and was thoroughly trained in the law of our ancestors. I was just as zealous for God as any of you are today. 4I persecuted the followers of this Way to their death, arresting both men and women and throwing them into prison, 5as the high priest and all the Council can themselves testify. I even obtained letters from them to their associates in Damascus, and went there to bring these people as prisoners to Jerusalem to be punished.

a 40 Or possibly *Hebrew*; also in 22:2

6 "About noon as I came near Damascus, suddenly a bright light from heaven flashed around me. 7 I fell to the ground and heard a voice say to me, 'Saul! Saul! Why do you persecute me?'

8 " 'Who are you, Lord?' I asked.

" 'I am Jesus of Nazareth, whom you are persecuting,' he replied. 9 My companions saw the light, but they did not understand the voice of him who was speaking to me.

10 " 'What shall I do, Lord?' I asked.

" 'Get up,' the Lord said, 'and go into Damascus. There you will be told all that you have been assigned to do.' 11 My companions led me by the hand into Damascus, because the brilliance of the light had blinded me.

12 "A man named Ananias came to see me. He was a devout observer of the law and highly respected by all the Jews living there. 13 He stood beside me and said, 'Brother Saul, receive your sight!' And at that very moment I was able to see him.

14 "Then he said: 'The God of our ancestors has chosen you to know his will and to see the Righteous One and to hear words from his mouth. 15 You will be his witness to all people of what you have seen and heard. 16 And now what are you waiting for? Get up, be baptized and wash your sins away, calling on his name.'

17 "When I returned to Jerusalem and was praying at the temple, I fell into a trance 18 and saw the Lord speaking to me. 'Quick!' he said. 'Leave Jerusalem immediately, because the people here will not accept your testimony about me.'

19 " 'Lord,' I replied, 'these people know that I went from one synagogue to another to imprison and beat those who believe in you. 20 And when the blood of your martyr[a] Stephen was shed, I stood there giving my approval and guarding the clothes of those who were killing him.'

21 "Then the Lord said to me, 'Go; I will send you far away to the Gentiles.' "

Paul the Roman Citizen

22 The crowd listened to Paul until he said this. Then they raised their voices and shouted, "Rid the earth of him! He's not fit to live!"

23 As they were shouting and throwing off their cloaks and flinging dust into the air, 24 the commander ordered that Paul be taken into the barracks. He directed that he be flogged and interrogated in order to find out why the people were shouting at him like this. 25 As they stretched him out to flog him, Paul said to the centurion standing there, "Is it legal for you to flog a Roman citizen who hasn't even been found guilty?"

26 When the centurion heard this, he went to the commander and reported it. "What are you going to do?" he asked. "This man is a Roman citizen."

27 The commander went to Paul and asked, "Tell me, are you a Roman citizen?"

"Yes, I am," he answered.

28 Then the commander said, "I had to pay a lot of money for my citizenship."

"But I was born a citizen," Paul replied.

29 Those who were about to interrogate him withdrew immediately. The commander himself was alarmed when he realized that he had put Paul, a Roman citizen, in chains.

Paul Before the Sanhedrin

30 The commander wanted to find out exactly why Paul was being accused by the Jews. So the next day he released him and ordered the chief priests and all the members of the Sanhedrin to assemble. Then he brought Paul and had him stand before them.

23 Paul looked straight at the Sanhedrin and said, "My brothers, I have fulfilled my duty to God in all good conscience to this day." 2 At this the high priest Ananias ordered those standing near Paul to strike him on the mouth. 3 Then Paul said to him, "God will strike you, you whitewashed wall! You sit there to judge me according to the law, yet you yourself violate the law by commanding that I be struck!"

4 Those who were standing near Paul said, "How dare you insult God's high priest!"

---

[a] 20 Or *witness*

⁵Paul replied, "Brothers, I did not realize that he was the high priest; for it is written: 'Do not speak evil about the ruler of your people.'ᵃ"

⁶Then Paul, knowing that some of them were Sadducees and the others Pharisees, called out in the Sanhedrin, "My brothers, I am a Pharisee, descended from Pharisees. I stand on trial because of the hope of the resurrection of the dead." ⁷When he said this, a dispute broke out between the Pharisees and the Sadducees, and the assembly was divided. ⁸(The Sadducees say that there is no resurrection, and that there are neither angels nor spirits, but the Pharisees believe all these things.)

⁹There was a great uproar, and some of the teachers of the law who were Pharisees stood up and argued vigorously. "We find nothing wrong with this man," they said. "What if a spirit or an angel has spoken to him?" ¹⁰The dispute became so violent that the commander was afraid Paul would be torn to pieces by them. He ordered the troops to go down and take him away from them by force and bring him into the barracks.

¹¹The following night the Lord stood near Paul and said, "Take courage! As you have testified about me in Jerusalem, so you must also testify in Rome."

The Plot to Kill Paul

¹²The next morning some Jews formed a conspiracy and bound themselves with an oath not to eat or drink until they had killed Paul. ¹³More than forty men were involved in this plot. ¹⁴They went to the chief priests and the elders and said, "We have taken a solemn oath not to eat anything until we have killed Paul. ¹⁵Now then, you and the Sanhedrin petition the commander to bring him before you on the pretext of wanting more accurate information about his case. We are ready to kill him before he gets here."

¹⁶But when the son of Paul's sister heard of this plot, he went into the barracks and told Paul.

¹⁷Then Paul called one of the centuri-

ons and said, "Take this young man to the commander; he has something to tell him." ¹⁸So he took him to the commander.

The centurion said, "Paul, the prisoner, sent for me and asked me to bring this young man to you because he has something to tell you."

¹⁹The commander took the young man by the hand, drew him aside and asked, "What is it you want to tell me?"

²⁰He said: "Some Jews have agreed to ask you to bring Paul before the Sanhedrin tomorrow on the pretext of wanting more accurate information about him. ²¹Don't give in to them, because more than forty of them are waiting in ambush for him. They have taken an oath not to eat or drink until they have killed him. They are ready now, waiting for your consent to their request."

²²The commander dismissed the young man with this warning: "Don't tell anyone that you have reported this to me."

Paul Transferred to Caesarea

²³Then he called two of his centurions and ordered them, "Get ready a detachment of two hundred soldiers, seventy horsemen and two hundred spearmenᵇ to go to Caesarea at nine tonight. ²⁴Provide horses for Paul so that he may be taken safely to Governor Felix."

²⁵He wrote a letter as follows:

²⁶Claudius Lysias,

To His Excellency, Governor Felix:

Greetings.

²⁷This man was seized by the Jews and they were about to kill him, but I came with my troops and rescued him, for I had learned that he is a Roman citizen. ²⁸I wanted to know why they were accusing him, so I brought him to their Sanhedrin. ²⁹I found that the accusation had to do with questions about their law, but there was no charge against him that deserved death or imprisonment. ³⁰When I was informed of

---

ᵃ 5 Exodus 22:28   ᵇ 23 The meaning of the Greek for this word is uncertain.

a plot to be carried out against the man, I sent him to you at once. I also ordered his accusers to present to you their case against him.

31 So the soldiers, carrying out their orders, took Paul with them during the night and brought him as far as Antipatris. 32 The next day they let the cavalry go on with him, while they returned to the barracks. 33 When the cavalry arrived in Caesarea, they delivered the letter to the governor and handed Paul over to him. 34 The governor read the letter and asked what province he was from. Learning that he was from Cilicia, 35 he said, "I will hear your case when your accusers get here." Then he ordered that Paul be kept under guard in Herod's palace.

Paul's Trial Before Felix

24 Five days later the high priest Ananias went down to Caesarea with some of the elders and a lawyer named Tertullus, and they brought their charges against Paul before the governor. 2 When Paul was called in, Tertullus presented his case before Felix: "We have enjoyed a long period of peace under you, and your foresight has brought about reforms in this nation. 3 Everywhere and in every way, most excellent Felix, we acknowledge this with profound gratitude. 4 But in order not to weary you further, I would request that you be kind enough to hear us briefly.

5 "We have found this man to be a troublemaker, stirring up riots among the Jews all over the world. He is a ringleader of the Nazarene sect 6 and even tried to desecrate the temple; so we seized him. [7]a 8 By examining him yourself you will be able to learn the truth about all these charges we are bringing against him."

9 The other Jews joined in the accusation, asserting that these things were true.

10 When the governor motioned for him to speak, Paul replied: "I know that for a number of years you have been a judge over this nation; so I gladly make my defense. 11 You can easily verify that no more than twelve days ago I went up to Jerusalem to worship. 12 My accusers did not find me arguing with anyone at the temple, or stirring up a crowd in the synagogues or anywhere else in the city. 13 And they cannot prove to you the charges they are now making against me. 14 However, I admit that I worship the God of our ancestors as a follower of the Way, which they call a sect. I believe everything that is in accordance with the Law and that is written in the Prophets, 15 and I have the same hope in God as these men themselves have, that there will be a resurrection of both the righteous and the wicked. 16 So I strive always to keep my conscience clear before God and man.

17 "After an absence of several years, I came to Jerusalem to bring my people gifts for the poor and to present offerings. 18 I was ceremonially clean when they found me in the temple courts doing this. There was no crowd with me, nor was I involved in any disturbance. 19 But there are some Jews from the province of Asia, who ought to be here before you and bring charges if they have anything against me. 20 Or these who are here should state what crime they found in me when I stood before the Sanhedrin— 21 unless it was this one thing I shouted as I stood in their presence: 'It is concerning the resurrection of the dead that I am on trial before you today.' "

22 Then Felix, who was well acquainted with the Way, adjourned the proceedings. "When Lysias the commander comes," he said, "I will decide your case." 23 He ordered the centurion to keep Paul under guard but to give him some freedom and permit his friends to take care of his needs.

24 Several days later Felix came with his wife Drusilla, who was Jewish. He sent for Paul and listened to him as he spoke about faith in Christ Jesus. 25 As Paul talked about righteousness, self-control and the judgment to come, Felix was

---

a 6-8 Some manuscripts include here *him, and we would have judged him in accordance with our law.* 7*But the commander Lysias came and took him from us with much violence,* 8*ordering his accusers to come before you.*

afraid and said, "That's enough for now! You may leave. When I find it convenient, I will send for you." ²⁶At the same time he was hoping that Paul would offer him a bribe, so he sent for him frequently and talked with him.

²⁷When two years had passed, Felix was succeeded by Porcius Festus, but because Felix wanted to grant a favor to the Jews, he left Paul in prison.

Paul's Trial Before Festus

25 Three days after arriving in the province, Festus went up from Caesarea to Jerusalem, ²where the chief priests and the Jewish leaders appeared before him and presented the charges against Paul. ³They requested Festus, as a favor to them, to have Paul transferred to Jerusalem, for they were preparing an ambush to kill him along the way. ⁴Festus answered, "Paul is being held at Caesarea, and I myself am going there soon. ⁵Let some of your leaders come with me, and if the man has done anything wrong, they can press charges against him there."

⁶After spending eight or ten days with them, Festus went down to Caesarea. The next day he convened the court and ordered that Paul be brought before him. ⁷When Paul came in, the Jews who had come down from Jerusalem stood around him. They brought many serious charges against him, but they could not prove them.

⁸Then Paul made his defense: "I have done nothing wrong against the Jewish law or against the temple or against Caesar."

TO THE POINT

Guilty?

Your conscience is that inner voice that tells you when you've done something wrong or warns you that what you want to do isn't right.

Here are some things the Bible says about the conscience:

+ The conscience can be weak (1 Corinthians 8:12).

+ The conscience can be corrupted (Titus 1:15).

+ The conscience can be cleansed (Hebrews 10:22).

It's wonderful to know that God forgives you and will cleanse your conscience. But it's even better to keep your conscience clear. Paul said, "I strive always to keep my conscience clear before God and man" (Acts 24:16). Live the way God wants you to live, and your conscience won't nag at you about what you've done wrong.

9Festus, wishing to do the Jews a favor, said to Paul, "Are you willing to go up to Jerusalem and stand trial before me there on these charges?"

10Paul answered: "I am now standing before Caesar's court, where I ought to be tried. I have not done any wrong to the Jews, as you yourself know very well. 11If, however, I am guilty of doing anything deserving death, I do not refuse to die. But if the charges brought against me by these Jews are not true, no one has the right to hand me over to them. I appeal to Caesar!"

12After Festus had conferred with his council, he declared: "You have appealed to Caesar. To Caesar you will go!"

Festus Consults King Agrippa

13A few days later King Agrippa and Bernice arrived at Caesarea to pay their respects to Festus. 14Since they were spending many days there, Festus discussed Paul's case with the king. He said: "There is a man here whom Felix left as a prisoner. 15When I went to Jerusalem, the chief priests and the elders of the Jews brought charges against him and asked that he be condemned.

16"I told them that it is not the Roman custom to hand over anyone before they have faced their accusers and have had an opportunity to defend themselves against the charges. 17When they came here with me, I did not delay the case, but convened the court the next day and ordered the man to be brought in. 18When his accusers got up to speak, they did not charge him with any of the crimes I had expected. 19Instead, they had some points of dispute with him about their own religion and about a dead man named Jesus who Paul claimed was alive. 20I was at a loss how to investigate such matters; so I asked if he would be willing to go to Jerusalem and stand trial there on these charges. 21But when Paul made his appeal to be held over for the Emperor's decision, I ordered him held until I could send him to Caesar."

22Then Agrippa said to Festus, "I would like to hear this man myself."

He replied, "Tomorrow you will hear him."

Paul Before Agrippa

23The next day Agrippa and Bernice came with great pomp and entered the audience room with the high-ranking military officers and the prominent men of the city. At the command of Festus, Paul was brought in. 24Festus said: "King Agrippa, and all who are present with us, you see this man! The whole Jewish community has petitioned me about him in Jerusalem and here in Caesarea, shouting that he ought not to live any longer. 25I found he had done nothing deserving of death, but because he made his appeal to the Emperor I decided to send him to Rome. 26But I have nothing definite to write to His Majesty about him. Therefore I have brought him before all of you, and especially before you, King Agrippa, so that as a result of this investigation I may have something to write. 27For I think it is unreasonable to send a prisoner on to Rome without specifying the charges against him."

26 Then Agrippa said to Paul, "You have permission to speak for yourself."

So Paul motioned with his hand and began his defense: 2"King Agrippa, I consider myself fortunate to stand before you today as I make my defense against all the accusations of the Jews, 3and especially so because you are well acquainted with all the Jewish customs and controversies. Therefore, I beg you to listen to me patiently.

4"The Jewish people all know the way I have lived ever since I was a child, from the beginning of my life in my own country, and also in Jerusalem. 5They have known me for a long time and can testify, if they are willing, that I conformed to the strictest sect of our religion, living as a Pharisee. 6And now it is because of my hope in what God has promised our ancestors that I am on trial today. 7This is the promise our twelve tribes are hoping to see fulfilled as they earnestly serve God day and night. King Agrippa, it is because of this hope that these Jews are accusing me. 8Why should any of you consider it incredible that God raises the dead?

I t may be hard to believe, but a lot of teens know next to nothing about Christianity. Only one student in a certain eleventh-grade class knew what Good Friday and Easter celebrate. Others had never heard that Jesus had no human father but was the Son of God. Often the people who give you the hardest time about your beliefs don't have any idea what the Bible teaches! So if someone pulls a Festus and says, "You are out of your mind" (Acts 26:24), don't back down. Give him Paul's answer: "What I am saying is true and reasonable" (Acts 26:25). And be ready to tell how Jesus has changed your life.

{Acts 26:24–25}

9 "I too was convinced that I ought to do all that was possible to oppose the name of Jesus of Nazareth. 10 And that is just what I did in Jerusalem. On the authority of the chief priests I put many of the Lord's people in prison, and when they were put to death, I cast my vote against them. 11 Many a time I went from one synagogue to another to have them punished, and I tried to force them to blaspheme. I was so obsessed with persecuting them that I even hunted them down in foreign cities.

12 "On one of these journeys I was going to Damascus with the authority and commission of the chief priests. 13 About noon, King Agrippa, as I was on the road, I saw a light from heaven, brighter than the sun, blazing around me and my companions. 14 We all fell to the ground, and I heard a voice saying to me in Aramaic,[a] 'Saul, Saul, why do you persecute me? It is hard for you to kick against the goads.'

15 "Then I asked, 'Who are you, Lord?'

" 'I am Jesus, whom you are persecuting,' the Lord replied. 16 'Now get up and stand on your feet. I have appeared to you to appoint you as a servant and as a witness of what you have seen and will see of me. 17 I will rescue you from your own people and from the Gentiles. I am sending you to them 18 to open their eyes and turn them from darkness to light, and from the power of Satan to God, so that they may receive forgiveness of sins and a place among those who are sanctified by faith in me.'

19 "So then, King Agrippa, I was not disobedient to the vision from heaven. 20 First to those in Damascus, then to those in Jerusalem and in all Judea, and then to the Gentiles, I preached that they should repent and turn to God and demonstrate their repentance by their deeds. 21 That is why some Jews seized me in the temple courts and tried to kill me. 22 But God has helped me to this very day; so I stand here and testify to small and great alike. I am saying nothing beyond what the prophets and Moses said would happen— 23 that the Messiah would suffer and, as the first to rise from the dead, would bring the message of light to his own people and to the Gentiles."

24 At this point Festus interrupted Paul's defense. "You are out of your mind, Paul!" he shouted. "Your great learning is driving you insane."

25 "I am not insane, most excellent Festus," Paul replied. "What I am saying is true and reasonable. 26 The king is familiar with these things, and I can speak freely to him. I am convinced that none of this has escaped his notice, because it was

not done in a corner. 27 King Agrippa, do you believe the prophets? I know you do."

28 Then Agrippa said to Paul, "Do you think that in such a short time you can persuade me to be a Christian?"

29 Paul replied, "Short time or long—I pray to God that not only you but all who are listening to me today may become what I am, except for these chains."

30 The king rose, and with him the governor and Bernice and those sitting with them. 31 After they left the room, they began saying to one another, "This man is not doing anything that deserves death or imprisonment."

32 Agrippa said to Festus, "This man could have been set free if he had not appealed to Caesar."

Paul Sails for Rome

27 When it was decided that we would sail for Italy, Paul and some other prisoners were handed over to a centurion named Julius, who belonged to the Imperial Regiment. 2 We boarded a ship from Adramyttium about to sail for ports along the coast of the province of Asia, and we put out to sea. Aristarchus, a Macedonian from Thessalonica, was with us.

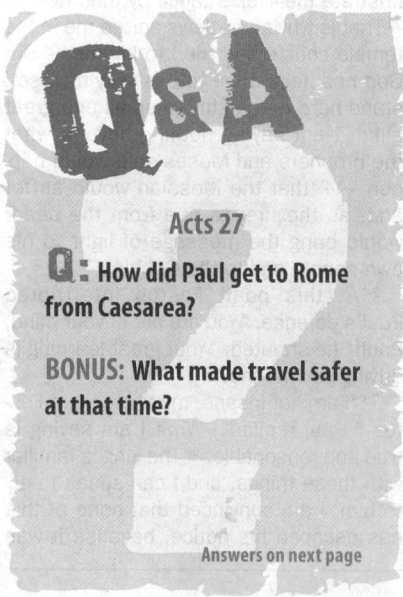

Acts 27

Q: How did Paul get to Rome from Caesarea?

BONUS: What made travel safer at that time?

Answers on next page

3 The next day we landed at Sidon; and Julius, in kindness to Paul, allowed him to go to his friends so they might provide for his needs. 4 From there we put out to sea again and passed to the lee of Cyprus because the winds were against us. 5 When we had sailed across the open sea off the coast of Cilicia and Pamphylia, we landed at Myra in Lycia. 6 There the centurion found an Alexandrian ship sailing for Italy and put us on board. 7 We made slow headway for many days and had difficulty arriving off Cnidus. When the wind did not allow us to hold our course, we sailed to the lee of Crete, opposite Salmone. 8 We moved along the coast with difficulty and came to a place called Fair Havens, near the town of Lasea.

9 Much time had been lost, and sailing had already become dangerous because by now it was after the Day of Atonement.[a] So Paul warned them, 10 "Men, I can see that our voyage is going to be disastrous and bring great loss to ship and cargo, and to our own lives also." 11 But the centurion, instead of listening to what Paul said, followed the advice of the pilot and of the owner of the ship. 12 Since the harbor was unsuitable to winter in, the majority decided that we should sail on, hoping to reach Phoenix and winter there. This was a harbor in Crete, facing both southwest and northwest.

The Storm

13 When a gentle south wind began to blow, they saw their opportunity; so they weighed anchor and sailed along the shore of Crete. 14 Before very long, a wind of hurricane force, called the Northeaster, swept down from the island. 15 The ship was caught by the storm and could not head into the wind; so we gave way to it and were driven along. 16 As we passed to the lee of a small island called Cauda, we were hardly able to make the lifeboat secure, 17 so the men hoisted it aboard. Then they passed ropes under the ship itself to hold it together. Because they were afraid they would run aground on the sandbars of Syrtis, they lowered the

---

[a] 9 That is, Yom Kippur

sea anchor[a] and let the ship be driven along. [18]We took such a violent battering from the storm that the next day they began to throw the cargo overboard. [19]On the third day, they threw the ship's tackle overboard with their own hands. [20]When neither sun nor stars appeared for many days and the storm continued raging, we finally gave up all hope of being saved.

[21]After they had gone a long time without food, Paul stood up before them and said: "Men, you should have taken my advice not to sail from Crete; then you would have spared yourselves this damage and loss. [22]But now I urge you to keep up your courage, because not one of you will be lost; only the ship will be destroyed. [23]Last night an angel of the God to whom I belong and whom I serve stood beside me [24]and said, 'Do not be afraid, Paul. You must stand trial before Caesar; and God has graciously given you the lives of all who sail with you.' [25]So keep up your courage, men, for I have faith in God that it will happen just as he told me. [26]Nevertheless, we must run aground on some island."

The Shipwreck

[27]On the fourteenth night we were still being driven across the Adriatic[b] Sea, when about midnight the sailors sensed they were approaching land. [28]They took soundings and found that the water was a hundred and twenty feet[c] deep. A short time later they took soundings again and found it was ninety feet[d] deep. [29]Fearing that we would be dashed against the rocks, they dropped four anchors from the stern and prayed for daylight. [30]In an attempt to escape from the ship, the sailors let the lifeboat down into the sea, pretending they were going to lower some anchors from the bow. [31]Then Paul said to the centurion and the soldiers, "Unless these men stay with the ship, you cannot be saved." [32]So the soldiers cut the ropes that held the lifeboat and let it drift away.

[33]Just before dawn Paul urged them

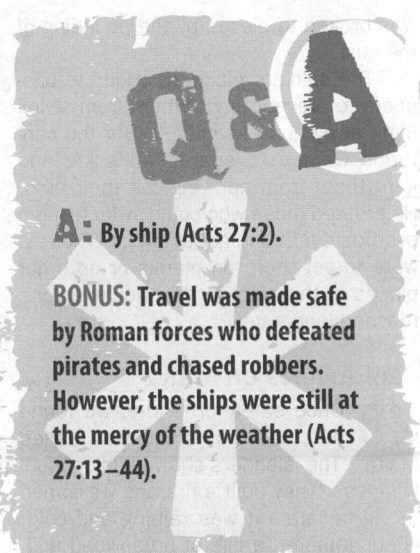

A: By ship (Acts 27:2).

BONUS: Travel was made safe by Roman forces who defeated pirates and chased robbers. However, the ships were still at the mercy of the weather (Acts 27:13–44).

all to eat. "For the last fourteen days," he said, "you have been in constant suspense and have gone without food—you haven't eaten anything. [34]Now I urge you to take some food. You need it to survive. Not one of you will lose a single hair from his head." [35]After he said this, he took some bread and gave thanks to God in front of them all. Then he broke it and began to eat. [36]They were all encouraged and ate some food themselves. [37]Altogether there were 276 of us on board. [38]When they had eaten as much as they wanted, they lightened the ship by throwing the grain into the sea.

[39]When daylight came, they did not recognize the land, but they saw a bay with a sandy beach, where they decided to run the ship aground if they could. [40]Cutting loose the anchors, they left them in the sea and at the same time untied the ropes that held the rudders. Then they hoisted the foresail to the wind and made for the beach. [41]But the ship struck a sandbar and ran aground. The bow stuck fast and would not move, and the stern

---

[a] 17 Or the sails   [b] 27 In ancient times the name referred to an area extending well south of Italy.   [c] 28 Or about 37 meters   [d] 28 Or about 27 meters

was broken to pieces by the pounding of the surf.

42 The soldiers planned to kill the prisoners to prevent any of them from swimming away and escaping. 43 But the centurion wanted to spare Paul's life and kept them from carrying out their plan. He ordered those who could swim to jump overboard first and get to land. 44 The rest were to get there on planks or on other pieces of the ship. In this way everyone reached land safely.

Paul Ashore on Malta

28 Once safely on shore, we found out that the island was called Malta. 2 The islanders showed us unusual kindness. They built a fire and welcomed us all because it was raining and cold. 3 Paul gathered a pile of brushwood and, as he put it on the fire, a viper, driven out by the heat, fastened itself on his hand. 4 When the islanders saw the snake hanging from his hand, they said to each other, "This man must be a murderer; for though he escaped from the sea, the goddess Justice has not allowed him to live." 5 But Paul shook the snake off into the fire and suffered no ill effects. 6 The people expected him to swell up or suddenly fall dead; but after waiting a long time and seeing nothing unusual happen to him, they changed their minds and said he was a god.

7 There was an estate nearby that belonged to Publius, the chief official of the island. He welcomed us to his home and showed us generous hospitality for three days. 8 His father was sick in bed, suffering from fever and dysentery. Paul went in to see him and, after prayer, placed his hands on him and healed him. 9 When this had happened, the rest of the sick on the island came and were cured. 10 They honored us in many ways; and when we were ready to sail, they furnished us with the supplies we needed.

Paul's Arrival at Rome

11 After three months we put out to sea in a ship that had wintered in the island—it was an Alexandrian ship with the figurehead of the twin gods Castor and Pollux. 12 We put in at Syracuse and stayed there three days. 13 From there we set sail and arrived at Rhegium. The next day the south wind came up, and on the following day we reached Puteoli. 14 There we found some brothers and sisters who invited us to spend a week with them. And so we came to Rome. 15 The brothers and sisters there had heard that we were coming, and they traveled as far as the Forum of Appius and the Three Taverns to meet us. At the sight of these people Paul thanked God and was encouraged. 16 When we got to Rome, Paul was allowed to live by himself, with a soldier to guard him.

Paul Preaches at Rome Under Guard

17 Three days later he called together the local Jewish leaders. When they had assembled, Paul said to them: "My brothers, although I have done nothing against our people or against the customs of our ancestors, I was arrested in Jerusalem and handed over to the Romans. 18 They examined me and wanted to release me, because I was not guilty of any crime deserving death. 19 The Jews objected, so I was compelled to make an appeal to Caesar. I certainly did not intend to bring any charge against my own people. 20 For this reason I have asked to see you and talk with you. It is because of the hope of Israel that I am bound with this chain."

21 They replied, "We have not received any letters from Judea concerning you, and none of our people who have come from there has reported or said anything bad about you. 22 But we want to hear what your views are, for we know that people everywhere are talking against this sect."

23 They arranged to meet Paul on a certain day, and came in even larger numbers to the place where he was staying. He witnessed to them from morning till evening, explaining about the kingdom of God, and from the Law of Moses and from the Prophets he tried to persuade them about Jesus. 24 Some were convinced by what he said, but others would

not believe. ²⁵They disagreed among themselves and began to leave after Paul had made this final statement: "The Holy Spirit spoke the truth to your ancestors when he said through Isaiah the prophet:

²⁶ " 'Go to this people and say,
"You will be ever hearing but never understanding;
you will be ever seeing but never perceiving."
²⁷ For this people's heart has become calloused;
they hardly hear with their ears,
and they have closed their eyes.

Otherwise they might see with their eyes,
hear with their ears,
understand with their hearts
and turn, and I would heal them.'[a]

²⁸"Therefore I want you to know that God's salvation has been sent to the Gentiles, and they will listen!" [29][b]

³⁰For two whole years Paul stayed there in his own rented house and welcomed all who came to see him. ³¹He proclaimed the kingdom of God and taught about the Lord Jesus Christ—with all boldness and without hindrance!

---

[a] 27 Isaiah 6:9,10 (see Septuagint)   [b] 29 Some manuscripts include here *After he said this, the Jews left, arguing vigorously among themselves.*

ROMANS

preview

Rome is the capital of the Roman Empire. One million of the empire's 54 million people live in Rome.

Many Jews live in Rome at this time.

Paul writes this letter about 57 A.D. while he is in Corinth.

A Good Person.

That's what most of you probably want to be. But everyone falls short. Oh, maybe you do better than many others. Compared to some, you may be doing great. But compared to God or compared to what you know you ought to be, well, you know none of us quite measure up.

Romans tells you what God has done for "not quite good enough" people. Instead of insisting that you be perfect, God invites you to trust in him. Then he gives you the Holy Spirit so you can live a holy life. God doesn't want you to fail. He intends to help you be all you can be.

>>**GOOD NEWS FOR THE NOT-GOOD-ENOUGH**
   Bible quote settles issue. See Romans 3:9–26

>>**NOT "HOW MUCH," BUT "WHO"?**
   Secret of faith revealed in Romans 4

>>**WE CAN'T, BUT HE CAN**
   Paul teaches "rely, not try." See Romans 8:1–11

>>**WE NEED YOU IN GOD'S FAMILY**
   You're important, apostle says. See Romans 12:1–8

As Paul writes, Ming-Ti, the new emperor, introduces Buddhism in China. An ambassador from Japan arrives in China.

1 Paul, a servant of Christ Jesus, called to be an apostle and set apart for the gospel of God— ²the gospel he promised beforehand through his prophets in the Holy Scriptures ³regarding his Son, who as to his earthly life[a] was a descendant of David, ⁴and who through the Spirit of holiness was appointed the Son of God in power[b] by his resurrection from the dead: Jesus Christ our Lord. ⁵Through him we received grace and apostleship to call all the Gentiles to the obedience that comes from[c] faith for his name's sake. ⁶And you also are among those Gentiles who are called to belong to Jesus Christ.

⁷To all in Rome who are loved by God and called to be his holy people:

Grace and peace to you from God our Father and from the Lord Jesus Christ.

Paul's Longing to Visit Rome

⁸First, I thank my God through Jesus Christ for all of you, because your faith is being reported all over the world. ⁹God, whom I serve in my spirit in preaching the gospel of his Son, is my witness how constantly I remember you ¹⁰in my prayers at all times; and I pray that now at last by God's will the way may be opened for me to come to you.

¹¹I long to see you so that I may impart to you some spiritual gift to make you strong— ¹²that is, that you and I may be mutually encouraged by each other's faith. ¹³I do not want you to be unaware, brothers and sisters,[d] that I planned many times to come to you (but have been prevented from doing so until now) in order that I might have a harvest among you, just as I have had among the other Gentiles.

¹⁴I am obligated both to Greeks and non-Greeks, both to the wise and the foolish. ¹⁵That is why I am so eager to preach the gospel also to you who are in Rome.

¹⁶For I am not ashamed of the gospel, because it is the power of God that brings salvation to everyone who believes: first to the Jew, then to the Gentile. ¹⁷For in the gospel the righteousness of God is revealed—a righteousness that is by faith from first to last,[e] just as it is written: "The righteous will live by faith."[f]

God's Wrath Against Sinful Humanity

¹⁸The wrath of God is being revealed from heaven against all the godlessness and wickedness of people, who suppress the truth by their wickedness, ¹⁹since what may be known about God is plain to them, because God has made it plain to them. ²⁰For since the creation of the world God's invisible qualities—his eternal power and divine nature—have been clearly seen, being understood from what has been made, so that people are without excuse.

²¹For although they knew God, they neither glorified him as God nor gave thanks to him, but their thinking became futile and their foolish hearts were darkened. ²²Although they claimed to be wise, they became fools ²³and exchanged the glory of the immortal God for images made to look like a mortal human being and birds and animals and reptiles.

²⁴Therefore God gave them over in the sinful desires of their hearts to sexual impurity for the degrading of their bodies with one another. ²⁵They exchanged the truth about God for a lie, and worshiped and served created things rather than the Creator—who is forever praised. Amen.

²⁶Because of this, God gave them over to shameful lusts. Even their women exchanged natural sexual relations for unnatural ones. ²⁷In the same way the men also abandoned natural relations with women and were inflamed with lust for one another. Men committed shameful acts with other men, and received in themselves the due penalty for their error.

²⁸Furthermore, just as they did not think it worthwhile to retain the knowledge of God, so God gave them over to a depraved mind, so that they do what ought not to be done. ²⁹They have become filled with every kind of wickedness, evil, greed and

depravity. They are full of envy, murder, strife, deceit and malice. They are gossips, [30]slanderers, God-haters, insolent, arrogant and boastful; they invent ways of doing evil; they disobey their parents; [31]they have no understanding, no fidelity, no love, no mercy. [32]Although they know God's righteous decree that those who do such things deserve death, they not only continue to do these very things but also approve of those who practice them.

God's Righteous Judgment

2 You, therefore, have no excuse, you who pass judgment on someone else, for at whatever point you judge another, you are condemning yourself, because you who pass judgment do the same things. [2]Now we know that God's judgment against those who do such things is based on truth. [3]So when you, a mere human being, pass judgment on them and yet do the same things, do you think you will escape God's judgment? [4]Or do you show contempt for the riches of his kindness, forbearance and patience, not realizing that God's kindness is intended to lead you to repentance?

[5]But because of your stubbornness and your unrepentant heart, you are storing up wrath against yourself for the day of God's wrath, when his righteous judgment will be revealed. [6]God "will repay each person according to what they have done."[a] [7]To those who by persistence in doing good seek glory, honor and

[a] 6 Psalm 62:12; Prov. 24:12

TO THE POINT

All Know God Exists

Creation is like God's radio station, sending out the message that God exists and that he is all-powerful. When the Bible says, "What may be known about God is plain" (Romans 1:19), it means that God has created human beings with an internal radio, tuned to his station. The message that God exists is sent and received!

Does that mean everyone will be saved? Not at all. Some people do not worship God (Romans 1:21). Or instead of responding to God, they turn away from him.

Just knowing that God exists isn't enough. Having faith in him, loving him, accepting his love for you—that is what makes the difference.

immortality, he will give eternal life. [8]But for those who are self-seeking and who reject the truth and follow evil, there will be wrath and anger. [9]There will be trouble and distress for every human being who does evil: first for the Jew, then for the Gentile; [10]but glory, honor and peace for everyone who does good: first for the Jew, then for the Gentile. [11]For God does not show favoritism.

[12]All who sin apart from the law will also perish apart from the law, and all who sin under the law will be judged by the law. [13]For it is not those who hear the law who are righteous in God's sight, but it is those who obey the law who will be declared righteous. [14](Indeed, when Gentiles, who do not have the law, do by nature things required by the law, they are a law for themselves, even though they do not have the law. [15]They show that the requirements of the law are written on their hearts, their consciences also bearing witness, and their thoughts sometimes accusing them and at other times even defending them.) [16]This will take place on the day when God judges people's secrets through Jesus Christ, as my gospel declares.

The Jews and the Law

[17]Now you, if you call yourself a Jew; if you rely on the law and boast in God; [18]if you know his will and approve of what is superior because you are instructed by the law; [19]if you are convinced that you are a guide for the blind, a light for those who are in the dark, [20]an instructor of the foolish, a teacher of little children, because you have in the law the embodiment of knowledge and truth— [21]you, then, who teach others, do you not teach yourself? You who preach against stealing, do you steal? [22]You who say that people should not commit adultery, do you commit adultery? You who abhor idols, do you rob temples? [23]You who boast in the law, do you dishonor God by breaking the law? [24]As it is written: "God's name is blasphemed among the Gentiles because of you."[a]

[25]Circumcision has value if you observe the law, but if you break the law, you have become as though you had not been circumcised. [26]So then, if those who are not circumcised keep the law's requirements, will they not be regarded as though they were circumcised? [27]The one who is not circumcised physically and yet obeys the law will condemn you who, even though you have the[b] written code and circumcision, are a lawbreaker.

[28]A person is not a Jew who is one only outwardly, nor is circumcision merely outward and physical. [29]No, a person is a Jew who is one inwardly; and circumcision is circumcision of the heart, by the Spirit, not by the written code. Such a person's praise is not from other people, but from God.

God's Faithfulness

3 What advantage, then, is there in being a Jew, or what value is there in circumcision? [2]Much in every way! First of all, the Jews have been entrusted with the very words of God.

[3]What if some were unfaithful? Will their unfaithfulness nullify God's faithfulness? [4]Not at all! Let God be true, and every human being a liar. As it is written:

"So that you may be proved right
    when you speak
and prevail when you judge."[c]

[5]But if our unrighteousness brings out God's righteousness more clearly, what shall we say? That God is unjust in bringing his wrath on us? (I am using a human argument.) [6]Certainly not! If that were so, how could God judge the world? [7]Someone might argue, "If my falsehood enhances God's truthfulness and so increases his glory, why am I still condemned as a sinner?" [8]Why not say—as some slanderously claim that we say— "Let us do evil that good may result"? Their condemnation is just!

No One Is Righteous

[9]What shall we conclude then? Do we have any advantage? Not at all! For we have already made the charge that Jews and Gentiles alike are all under the power of sin. [10]As it is written:

---

[a] 24 Isaiah 52:5 (see Septuagint); Ezek. 36:20,22   [b] 27 Or who, by means of a   [c] 4 Psalm 51:4

"There is no one righteous, not even
one;
11   there is no one who understands;
     there is no one who seeks God.
12 All have turned away,
     they have together become
        worthless;
     there is no one who does good,
        not even one."[a]
13 "Their throats are open graves;
     their tongues practice deceit."[b]
   "The poison of vipers is on their lips."[c]
14   "Their mouths are full of cursing
        and bitterness."[d]
15 "Their feet are swift to shed blood;
16   ruin and misery mark their ways,
17 and the way of peace they do not
        know."[e]
18   "There is no fear of God before
        their eyes."[f]

19 Now we know that whatever the law
says, it says to those who are under the
law, so that every mouth may be silenced
and the whole world held accountable to
God. 20 Therefore no one will be declared
righteous in God's sight by the works of
the law; rather, through the law we become conscious of our sin.

Righteousness Through Faith

21 But now apart from the law the righteousness of God has been made known,
to which the Law and the Prophets testify. 22 This righteousness is given through
faith in[g] Jesus Christ to all who believe.
There is no difference between Jew and
Gentile, 23 for all have sinned and fall
short of the glory of God, 24 and all are
justified freely by his grace through the
redemption that came by Christ Jesus.
25 God presented Christ as a sacrifice of
atonement,[h] through the shedding of his
blood—to be received by faith. He did
this to demonstrate his righteousness,
because in his forbearance he had left
the sins committed beforehand unpunished— 26 he did it to demonstrate his
righteousness at the present time, so as
to be just and the one who justifies those
who have faith in Jesus.

27 Where, then, is boasting? It is excluded. Because of what law? The law that
requires works? No, because of the law
that requires faith. 28 For we maintain that
a person is justified by faith apart from
the works of the law. 29 Or is God the God
of Jews only? Is he not the God of Gentiles too? Yes, of Gentiles too, 30 since
there is only one God, who will justify the
circumcised by faith and the uncircumcised through that same faith. 31 Do we,
then, nullify the law by this faith? Not at
all! Rather, we uphold the law.

Abraham Justified by Faith

4 What then shall we say that Abraham, our forefather according to the
flesh, discovered in this matter? 2 If, in
fact, Abraham was justified by works, he
had something to boast about—but not
before God. 3 What does Scripture say?
"Abraham believed God, and it was credited to him as righteousness."[i]

4 Now to the one who works, wages are
not credited as a gift but as an obligation. 5 However, to the one who does not
work but trusts God who justifies the ungodly, their faith is credited as righteousness. 6 David says the same thing when
he speaks of the blessedness of the one
to whom God credits righteousness apart
from works:

7 "Blessed are those
     whose transgressions are forgiven,
     whose sins are covered.
8 Blessed is the one
     whose sin the Lord will never count
        against them."[j]

9 Is this blessedness only for the circumcised, or also for the uncircumcised?
We have been saying that Abraham's
faith was credited to him as righteousness. 10 Under what circumstances was
it credited? Was it after he was circumcised, or before? It was not after, but before! 11 And he received circumcision as a
sign, a seal of the righteousness that he
had by faith while he was still uncircumcised. So then, he is the father of all who

---

[a] 12 Psalms 14:1-3; 53:1-3; Eccles. 7:20   [b] 13 Psalm 5:9   [c] 13 Psalm 140:3   [d] 14 Psalm 10:7 (see Septuagint)
[e] 17 Isaiah 59:7,8   [f] 18 Psalm 36:1   [g] 22 Or through the faithfulness of   [h] 25 The Greek for sacrifice of atonement
refers to the atonement cover on the ark of the covenant (see Lev. 16:15,16).   [i] 3 Gen. 15:6; also in verse 22
[j] 8 Psalm 32:1,2

How can Abraham be praised for his faith even though he lied twice and said his wife Sarah was his sister? Or how can David be praised even though he sinned with Bathsheba? For that matter, how can you be on your way to heaven? You haven't been perfect either. This passage explains: God didn't just say, "Oh forget it. Sin isn't all that bad." Instead God said, "Sin is so terrible it must be punished." And Jesus took that punishment for you so that God could do the right thing—punish sin—and still forgive.

{Romans 4:1–8}

INSTANT ACCESS

believe but have not been circumcised, in order that righteousness might be credited to them. [12]And he is then also the father of the circumcised who not only are circumcised but who also follow in the footsteps of the faith that our father Abraham had before he was circumcised.

[13]It was not through the law that Abraham and his offspring received the promise that he would be heir of the world, but through the righteousness that comes by faith. [14]For if those who depend on the law are heirs, faith means nothing and the promise is worthless, [15]because the law brings wrath. And where there is no law there is no transgression.

[16]Therefore, the promise comes by faith, so that it may be by grace and may be guaranteed to all Abraham's offspring—not only to those who are of the law but also to those who have the faith of Abraham. He is the father of us all. [17]As it is written: "I have made you a father of many nations."[a] He is our father in the sight of God, in whom he believed—the God who gives life to the dead and calls into being things that were not.

[18]Against all hope, Abraham in hope believed and so became the father of many nations, just as it had been said to him, "So shall your offspring be."[b] [19]Without weakening in his faith, he faced the fact that his body was as good as dead—since he was about a hundred years old—and that Sarah's womb was also dead. [20]Yet he did not waver through unbelief regarding the promise of God, but was strengthened in his faith and gave glory to God, [21]being fully persuaded that God had power to do what he had promised. [22]This is why "it was credited to him as righteousness." [23]The words "it was credited to him" were written not for him alone, [24]but also for us, to whom God will credit righteousness—for us who believe in him who raised Jesus our Lord from the dead. [25]He was delivered over to death for our sins and was raised to life for our justification.

Peace and Hope

5 Therefore, since we have been justified through faith, we[c] have peace with God through our Lord Jesus Christ, [2]through whom we have gained access by faith into this grace in which we now stand. And we[d] boast in the hope of the glory of God. [3]Not only so, but we[d] also glory in our sufferings, because we know that suffering produces perseverance; [4]perseverance, character; and character, hope. [5]And hope does not put us to shame, because God's love has been poured out into our hearts through the Holy Spirit, who has been given to us.

[6]You see, at just the right time, when we were still powerless, Christ died for the ungodly. [7]Very rarely will anyone die for a righteous person, though for a good person someone might possibly dare to die.

[a] 17 Gen. 17:5   [b] 18 Gen. 15:5   [c] 1 Many manuscripts let us   [d] 2,3 Or let us

[8]But God demonstrates his own love for us in this: While we were still sinners, Christ died for us.

[9]Since we have now been justified by his blood, how much more shall we be saved from God's wrath through him! [10]For if, while we were God's enemies, we were reconciled to him through the death of his Son, how much more, having been reconciled, shall we be saved through his life! [11]Not only is this so, but we also boast in God through our Lord Jesus Christ, through whom we have now received reconciliation.

Death Through Adam, Life Through Christ

[12]Therefore, just as sin entered the world through one man, and death through sin, and in this way death came to all people, because all sinned—

[13]To be sure, sin was in the world before the law was given, but sin is not charged against anyone's account where there is no law. [14]Nevertheless, death reigned from the time of Adam to the time of Moses, even over those who did not sin by breaking a command, as did Adam, who is a pattern of the one to come.

[15]But the gift is not like the trespass. For if the many died by the trespass of the one man, how much more did God's grace and the gift that came by the grace of the one man, Jesus Christ, overflow to the many! [16]Nor can the gift of God be compared with the result of one man's sin: The judgment followed one sin and brought condemnation, but the gift followed many trespasses and brought justification. [17]For if, by the trespass of the one man, death reigned through that one man, how much more will those who receive God's abundant provision of grace and of the gift of righteousness reign in life through the one man, Jesus Christ!

[18]Consequently, just as one trespass resulted in condemnation for all people, so also one righteous act resulted in justification and life for all people. [19]For just as through the disobedience of the one man the many were made sinners, so also through the obedience of the one man the many will be made righteous.

INSTANT ACCESS

What's the difference between wishful thinking and faith? Wishful thinking says, "Maybe we'll win a sweepstakes so I can go to college." Faith says, "If I don't get a scholarship, I'll work to put myself through." Wishful thinking is unrealistic. Faith looks at things honestly and squarely, and believes. That's what Abraham did. He knew he and Sarah were too old to have children. But when God said they would have a son, Abraham chose to believe. Some people think faith is wishful thinking. It isn't. The wishful thinker is kidding himself or herself. The person with faith sees the difficulties but also clearly sees God.

{Romans 4:18-25}

[20]The law was brought in so that the trespass might increase. But where sin increased, grace increased all the more, [21]so that, just as sin reigned in death, so also grace might reign through righteousness to bring eternal life through Jesus Christ our Lord.

Dead to Sin, Alive in Christ

6 What shall we say, then? Shall we go on sinning so that grace may increase? [2]By no means! We are those who have died to sin; how can we live in it any longer? [3]Or don't you know that all of us who were baptized into Christ Jesus were baptized into his death? [4]We were therefore buried with him through baptism into death in order that, just as Christ was raised from the dead through the glory of the Father, we too may live a new life.

[5]For if we have been united with him in a death like his, we will certainly also be united with him in a resurrection like his. [6]For we know that our old self was crucified with him so that the body ruled by sin might be done away with,[a] that we should no longer be slaves to sin— [7]because anyone who has died has been set free from sin.

[8]Now if we died with Christ, we believe that we will also live with him. [9]For we know that since Christ was raised from the dead, he cannot die again; death no longer has mastery over him. [10]The death he died, he died to sin once for all; but the life he lives, he lives to God.

[11]In the same way, count yourselves dead to sin but alive to God in Christ Jesus. [12]Therefore do not let sin reign in your mortal body so that you obey its evil desires. [13]Do not offer any part of yourself to sin as an instrument of wickedness, but rather offer yourselves to God as those who have been brought from death to life; and offer every part of yourself to him as an instrument of righteousness. [14]For sin shall no longer be your master, because you are not under the law, but under grace.

Slaves to Righteousness

[15]What then? Shall we sin because we are not under the law but under grace? By no means! [16]Don't you know that when you offer yourselves to someone as obedient slaves, you are slaves of the one you obey—whether you are slaves to sin, which leads to death, or to obedience, which leads to righteousness? [17]But thanks be to God that, though you used

to be slaves to sin, you have come to obey from your heart the pattern of teaching that has now claimed your allegiance. [18]You have been set free from sin and have become slaves to righteousness.

[19]I am using an example from everyday life because of your human limitations. Just as you used to offer yourselves as slaves to impurity and to ever-increasing wickedness, so now offer yourselves as slaves to righteousness leading to holiness. [20]When you were slaves to sin, you were free from the control of righteousness. [21]What benefit did you reap at that time from the things you are now ashamed of? Those things result in death! [22]But now that you have been set free from sin and have become slaves of God, the benefit you reap leads to holiness, and the result is eternal life. [23]For the wages of sin is death, but the gift of God is eternal life in[b] Christ Jesus our Lord.

Released From the Law, Bound to Christ

7 Do you not know, brothers and sisters—for I am speaking to those who know the law—that the law has authority over someone only as long as that person lives? [2]For example, by law a married woman is bound to her husband as long as he is alive, but if her husband dies, she is released from the law that binds her to him. [3]So then, if she has sexual relations with another man while her husband is still alive, she is called an adulteress. But if her husband dies, she is released from that law and is not an adulteress if she marries another man.

[4]So, my brothers and sisters, you also died to the law through the body of Christ, that you might belong to another, to him who was raised from the dead, in order that we might bear fruit for God. [5]For when we were in the realm of the flesh,[c] the

> *Now if we died with Christ, we believe that we will also live with him.*
> Romans 6:8

---

[a] 6 Or *be rendered powerless*   [b] 23 Or *through*   [c] 5 In contexts like this, the Greek word for *flesh* (*sarx*) refers to the sinful state of human beings, often presented as a power in opposition to the Spirit.

sinful passions aroused by the law were at work in us, so that we bore fruit for death. [6]But now, by dying to what once bound us, we have been released from the law so that we serve in the new way of the Spirit, and not in the old way of the written code.

The Law and Sin

[7]What shall we say, then? Is the law sinful? Certainly not! Nevertheless, I would not have known what sin was had it not been for the law. For I would not have known what coveting really was if the law had not said, "You shall not covet."[a] [8]But sin, seizing the opportunity afforded by the commandment, produced in me every kind of coveting. For apart from the law, sin was dead. [9]Once I was alive apart from the law; but when the commandment came, sin sprang to life and I died. [10]I found that the very commandment that was intended to bring life actually brought death. [11]For sin, seizing the opportunity afforded by the commandment, deceived me, and through the commandment put me to death. [12]So then, the law is holy, and the commandment is holy, righteous and good.

[13]Did that which is good, then, become death to me? By no means! Nevertheless, in order that sin might be recognized as sin, it used what is good to bring about my death, so that through the commandment sin might become utterly sinful.

[14]We know that the law is spiritual; but I am unspiritual, sold as a slave to sin. [15]I do not understand what I do. For what I want to do I do not do, but what I hate I do. [16]And if I do what I do not want to do, I agree that the law is good. [17]As it is, it is no longer I myself who do it, but it is sin living in me. [18]For I know that good itself does not dwell in me, that is, in my sinful nature.[b] For I have the desire to do what is good, but I cannot carry it out. [19]For I do not do the good I want to do, but the evil I do not want to do—this I keep on doing. [20]Now if I do what I do not want to do, it is no longer I who do it, but it is sin living in me that does it.

[21]So I find this law at work: Although I want to do good, evil is right there with

me. [22]For in my inner being I delight in God's law; [23]but I see another law at work in me, waging war against the law of my mind and making me a prisoner of the law of sin at work within me. [24]What a wretched man I am! Who will rescue me from this body that is subject to death? [25]Thanks be to God, who delivers me through Jesus Christ our Lord!

So then, I myself in my mind am a slave to God's law, but in my sinful nature[c] a slave to the law of sin.

Life Through the Spirit

8 Therefore, there is now no condemnation for those who are in Christ Jesus, [2]because through Christ Jesus the law of the Spirit who gives life has set

---

[a] 7 Exodus 20:17; Deut. 5:21   [b] 18 Or *my flesh*   [c] 25 Or *in the flesh*

you[a] free from the law of sin and death. [3]For what the law was powerless to do because it was weakened by the flesh,[b] God did by sending his own Son in the likeness of sinful flesh to be a sin offering.[c] And so he condemned sin in the flesh, [4]in order that the righteous requirement of the law might be fully met in us, who do not live according to the flesh but according to the Spirit.

[5]Those who live according to the flesh have their minds set on what the flesh desires; but those who live in accordance with the Spirit have their minds set on what the Spirit desires. [6]The mind governed by the flesh is death, but the mind governed by the Spirit is life and peace. [7]The mind governed by the flesh is hostile to God; it does not submit to God's law, nor can it do so. [8]Those who are in the realm of the flesh cannot please God.

[9]You, however, are not in the realm of the flesh but are in the realm of the Spirit, if indeed the Spirit of God lives in you. And if anyone does not have the Spirit of Christ, they do not belong to Christ. [10]But if Christ is in you, then even though your body is subject to death because of sin, the Spirit gives life[d] because of righteousness. [11]And if the Spirit of him who raised Jesus from the dead is living in you, he who raised Christ from the dead will also give life to your mortal bodies because of[e] his Spirit who lives in you.

[12]Therefore, brothers and sisters, we have an obligation—but it is not to the flesh, to live according to it. [13]For if you live according to the flesh, you will die; but if by the Spirit you put to death the misdeeds of the body, you will live.

[14]For those who are led by the Spirit of God are the children of God. [15]The Spirit you received does not make you slaves, so that you live in fear again; rather, the Spirit you received brought about your adoption to sonship.[f] And by him we cry, "Abba,[g] Father." [16]The Spirit himself testifies with our spirit that we are God's children. [17]Now if we are children, then we are heirs—heirs of God and co-heirs with Christ, if indeed we share in his sufferings in order that we may also share in his glory.

Present Suffering and Future Glory

[18]I consider that our present sufferings are not worth comparing with the glory that will be revealed in us. [19]For the creation waits in eager expectation for the children of God to be revealed. [20]For the creation was subjected to frustration, not by its own choice, but by the will of the one who subjected it, in hope [21]that[h] the creation itself will be liberated from its bondage to decay and brought into the freedom and glory of the children of God.

[22]We know that the whole creation has been groaning as in the pains of childbirth right up to the present time. [23]Not only so, but we ourselves, who have the firstfruits of the Spirit, groan inwardly as we wait eagerly for our adoption to sonship, the redemption of our bodies. [24]For in this hope we were saved. But hope that is seen is no hope at all. Who hopes for what they already have? [25]But if we hope for what we do not yet have, we wait for it patiently.

[26]In the same way, the Spirit helps us in our weakness. We do not know what we ought to pray for, but the Spirit himself intercedes for us through wordless groans. [27]And he who searches our hearts knows the mind of the Spirit, because the Spirit intercedes for God's people in accordance with the will of God.

[28]And we know that in all things God works for the good of those who love him,

> **In all things God works for the good of those who love him.**
>
> Romans 8:28

---

[a] 2 The Greek is singular; some manuscripts *me*   [b] 3 In contexts like this, the Greek word for *flesh* (*sarx*) refers to the sinful state of human beings, often presented as a power in opposition to the Spirit; also in verses 4-13.   [c] 3 Or *flesh, for sin*   [d] 10 Or *you, your body is dead because of sin, yet your spirit is alive*   [e] 11 Some manuscripts *bodies through*   [f] 15 The Greek word for *adoption to sonship* is a term referring to the full legal standing of an adopted male heir in Roman culture; also in verse 23.   [g] 15 Aramaic for *father*   [h] 20,21 Or *subjected it in hope. 21For*

who[a] have been called according to his purpose. [29]For those God foreknew he also predestined to be conformed to the image of his Son, that he might be the firstborn among many brothers and sisters. [30]And those he predestined, he also called; those he called, he also justified; those he justified, he also glorified.

More Than Conquerors

[31]What, then, shall we say in response to these things? If God is for us, who can be against us? [32]He who did not spare his own Son, but gave him up for us all—how will he not also, along with him, graciously give us all things? [33]Who will bring any charge against those whom God has chosen? It is God who justifies. [34]Who then is the one who condemns? No one. Christ Jesus who died—more than that, who was raised to life—is at the right hand of God and is also interceding for us. [35]Who shall separate us from the love of Christ? Shall trouble or hardship or persecution or famine or nakedness or danger or sword? [36]As it is written:

"For your sake we face death all day long;
     we are considered as sheep to be slaughtered."[b]

[37]No, in all these things we are more than conquerors through him who loved us. [38]For I am convinced that neither death nor life, neither angels nor demons,[c] neither the present nor the future, nor any powers, [39]neither height nor depth, nor anything else in all creation, will be able to separate us from the love of God that is in Christ Jesus our Lord.

Paul's Anguish Over Israel

9 I speak the truth in Christ—I am not lying, my conscience confirms it through the Holy Spirit— [2]I have great sorrow and unceasing anguish in my heart. [3]For I could wish that I myself were cursed and cut off from Christ for the sake of my people, those of my own race, [4]the people of Israel. Theirs is the adoption to

---

INSTANT ACCESS

Paul explains in this passage that because of Jesus you're not condemned to keep on sinning. Jesus died so you would be able to live a good life—the good life that law describes but can't help anyone achieve. What's the secret? The Holy Spirit. Through the Holy Spirit Jesus himself lives in you. The Spirit's power is here right now to help you do what's right in spite of the pull that sin still has on you (see Romans 7:7–25). How do you do it? You don't. You just fix your thoughts on what the Spirit desires, choose to respond and let God's Spirit give you the strength to obey.

{Romans 8:1–11}

---

sonship; theirs the divine glory, the covenants, the receiving of the law, the temple worship and the promises. [5]Theirs are the patriarchs, and from them is traced the human ancestry of the Messiah, who is God over all, forever praised![d] Amen.

God's Sovereign Choice

[6]It is not as though God's word had failed. For not all who are descended from Israel are Israel. [7]Nor because they are his descendants are they all Abraham's children. On the contrary, "It is through Isaac that your offspring will be

---

[a] 28 Or that all things work together for good to those who love God, who; or that in all things God works together with those who love him to bring about what is good—with those who   [b] 36 Psalm 44:22   [c] 38 Or nor heavenly rulers   [d] 5 Or Messiah, who is over all. God be forever praised! Or Messiah. God who is over all be forever praised!

reckoned."[a] [8]In other words, it is not the children by physical descent who are God's children, but it is the children of the promise who are regarded as Abraham's offspring. [9]For this was how the promise was stated: "At the appointed time I will return, and Sarah will have a son."[b]

[10]Not only that, but Rebekah's children were conceived at the same time by our father Isaac. [11]Yet, before the twins were born or had done anything good or bad—in order that God's purpose in election might stand: [12]not by works but by him who calls—she was told, "The older will serve the younger."[c] [13]Just as it is written: "Jacob I loved, but Esau I hated."[d]

[14]What then shall we say? Is God unjust? Not at all! [15]For he says to Moses,

"I will have mercy on whom I have mercy,
and I will have compassion on whom I have compassion."[e]

[16]It does not, therefore, depend on human desire or effort, but on God's mercy. [17]For Scripture says to Pharaoh: "I raised you up for this very purpose, that I might display my power in you and that my name might be proclaimed in all the earth."[f] [18]Therefore God has mercy on whom he wants to have mercy, and he hardens whom he wants to harden.

[19]One of you will say to me: "Then why does God still blame us? For who is able to resist his will?" [20]But who are you, a human being, to talk back to God? "Shall what is formed say to the one who formed

---

[a] 7 Gen. 21:12   [b] 9 Gen. 18:10,14   [c] 12 Gen. 25:23   [d] 13 Mal. 1:2,3   [e] 15 Exodus 33:19
[f] 17 Exodus 9:16

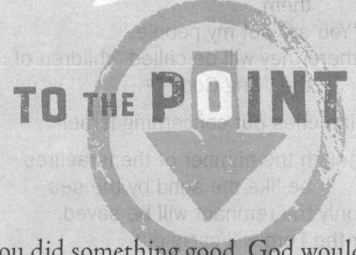

God Chooses

Did you ever think that if you did something good, God would *have* to reward you? Like, if you gave all your money to starving children, God would have to make sure you got that new outfit? In Romans 9 Paul shows from Bible history that people can't "make" God do anything. God is free to choose.

+ God chose Isaac, not Ishmael (Romans 9:7–9).

+ God chose Jacob rather than Esau (Romans 9:10–13).

+ God let Pharaoh follow his own heart (Romans 9:14–18).

Paul isn't saying that God chooses to send some people to hell. He is saying that God doesn't "depend on human desire or effort" (Romans 9:16). He depends on his own free choice to have mercy. No one deserves any reward from God. Everyone deserves to be punished. It's a good thing that God is free to choose—because God chooses to have mercy.

it, 'Why did you make me like this?' "ᵃ
²¹ Does not the potter have the right to make out of the same lump of clay some pottery for special purposes and some for common use?

²² What if God, although choosing to show his wrath and make his power known, bore with great patience the objects of his wrath—prepared for destruction? ²³ What if he did this to make the riches of his glory known to the objects of his mercy, whom he prepared in advance for glory— ²⁴ even us, whom he also called, not only from the Jews but also from the Gentiles? ²⁵ As he says in Hosea:

"I will call them 'my people' who are
      not my people;
and I will call her 'my loved one'
      who is not my loved one,"ᵇ

²⁶ and,

"In the very place where it was said to
      them,
      'You are not my people,'
there they will be called 'children of
      the living God.' "ᶜ

²⁷ Isaiah cries out concerning Israel:

"Though the number of the Israelites
      be like the sand by the sea,
only the remnant will be saved.
²⁸ For the Lord will carry out
      his sentence on earth with speed
      and finality."ᵈ

²⁹ It is just as Isaiah said previously:

"Unless the Lord Almighty
      had left us descendants,
we would have become like Sodom,
we would have been like
      Gomorrah."ᵉ

Israel's Unbelief

³⁰ What then shall we say? That the Gentiles, who did not pursue righteousness, have obtained it, a righteousness that is by faith; ³¹ but the people of Israel, who pursued the law as the way of righteousness, have not attained their goal. ³² Why not? Because they pursued it not by faith but as if it were by works. They stumbled over the stumbling stone. ³³ As it is written:

"See, I lay in Zion a stone that causes
      people to stumble
and a rock that makes them fall,
and the one who believes in him will
      never be put to shame."ᶠ

10 Brothers and sisters, my heart's desire and prayer to God for the Israelites is that they may be saved. ² For I can testify about them that they are zealous for God, but their zeal is not based on knowledge. ³ Since they did not know the righteousness of God and sought to establish their own, they did not submit to God's righteousness. ⁴ Christ is the culmination of the law so that there may be righteousness for everyone who believes.

⁵ Moses writes this about the righteousness that is by the law: "The person who does these things will live by them."ᵍ ⁶ But the righteousness that is by faith says: "Do not say in your heart, 'Who will ascend into heaven?' "ʰ (that is, to bring Christ down) ⁷ "or 'Who will descend into the deep?' "ⁱ (that is, to bring Christ up from the dead). ⁸ But what does it say? "The word is near you; it is in your mouth and in your heart,"ʲ that is, the message concerning faith that we proclaim: ⁹ If you declare with your mouth, "Jesus is Lord," and believe in your heart that God raised him from the dead, you will be saved. ¹⁰ For it is with your heart that you believe and are justified, and it is with your mouth that you profess your faith and are saved. ¹¹ As Scripture says, "Anyone who believes in him will never be put to shame."ᵏ ¹² For there is no difference between Jew and Gentile—the same Lord is Lord of all and richly blesses all who call on him, ¹³ for, "Everyone who calls on the name of the Lord will be saved."ˡ

¹⁴ How, then, can they call on the one they have not believed in? And how can they believe in the one of whom they have not heard? And how can they hear without someone preaching to them? ¹⁵ And

---

ᵃ *20* Isaiah 29:16; 45:9   ᵇ *25* Hosea 2:23   ᶜ *26* Hosea 1:10   ᵈ *28* Isaiah 10:22,23 (see Septuagint)
ᵉ *29* Isaiah 1:9   ᶠ *33* Isaiah 8:14; 28:16   ᵍ *5* Lev. 18:5   ʰ *6* Deut. 30:12   ⁱ *7* Deut. 30:13   ʲ *8* Deut. 30:14
ᵏ *11* Isaiah 28:16 (see Septuagint)   ˡ *13* Joel 2:32

The best-looking feet don't belong to a famous model or a basketball superstar. The really beautiful feet belong to people who bring others the Good News. These verses raise questions every Christian needs to ask. How can unbelievers call on Jesus if they don't believe? And how can they believe if they've never heard of him? And how can they hear if no one tells them? When some people use "Jesus" as a swear word, it doesn't mean they know about him. In fact, it shows they don't know enough! They can't believe until they hear. And they can't hear unless someone (you?) tells them. Check out your feet. Beautiful? You bet!

{Romans 10:12–15}

INSTANT ACCESS

"Their voice has gone out into all the earth,
their words to the ends of the world."[c]

¹⁹Again I ask: Did Israel not understand? First, Moses says,

"I will make you envious by those who are not a nation;
I will make you angry by a nation that has no understanding."[d]

²⁰And Isaiah boldly says,

"I was found by those who did not seek me;
I revealed myself to those who did not ask for me."[e]

²¹But concerning Israel he says,

"All day long I have held out my hands to a disobedient and obstinate people."[f]

The Remnant of Israel

11 I ask then: Did God reject his people? By no means! I am an Israelite myself, a descendant of Abraham, from the tribe of Benjamin. ²God did not reject his people, whom he foreknew. Don't you know what Scripture says in the passage about Elijah—how he appealed to God against Israel: ³"Lord, they have killed your prophets and torn down your altars; I am the only one left, and they are trying to kill me"[g]? ⁴And what was God's answer to him? "I have reserved for myself seven thousand who have not bowed the knee to Baal."[h] ⁵So too, at the present time there is a remnant chosen by grace. ⁶And if by grace, then it cannot be based on works; if it were, grace would no longer be grace.

⁷What then? What the people of Israel sought so earnestly they did not obtain. The elect among them did, but the others were hardened, ⁸as it is written:

"God gave them a spirit of stupor,
eyes that could not see
and ears that could not hear,
to this very day."[i]

how can anyone preach unless they are sent? As it is written: "How beautiful are the feet of those who bring good news!"[a]

¹⁶But not all the Israelites accepted the good news. For Isaiah says, "Lord, who has believed our message?"[b] ¹⁷Consequently, faith comes from hearing the message, and the message is heard through the word about Christ. ¹⁸But I ask: Did they not hear? Of course they did:

ᵃ 15 Isaiah 52:7   ᵇ 16 Isaiah 53:1   ᶜ 18 Psalm 19:4   ᵈ 19 Deut. 32:21   ᵉ 20 Isaiah 65:1   ᶠ 21 Isaiah 65:2
ᵍ 3 1 Kings 19:10,14   ʰ 4 1 Kings 19:18   ⁱ 8 Deut. 29:4; Isaiah 29:10

⁹And David says:

"May their table become a snare and
a trap,
a stumbling block and a retribution
for them.
¹⁰May their eyes be darkened so they
cannot see,
and their backs be bent forever."ᵃ

Ingrafted Branches

¹¹Again I ask: Did they stumble so as
to fall beyond recovery? Not at all! Rather,
because of their transgression, salvation
has come to the Gentiles to make Israel envious. ¹²But if their transgression
means riches for the world, and their loss
means riches for the Gentiles, how much
greater riches will their full inclusion bring!

¹³I am talking to you Gentiles. Inasmuch as I am the apostle to the Gentiles,
I take pride in my ministry ¹⁴in the hope
that I may somehow arouse my own people to envy and save some of them. ¹⁵For
if their rejection brought reconciliation to
the world, what will their acceptance be
but life from the dead? ¹⁶If the part of the
dough offered as firstfruits is holy, then
the whole batch is holy; if the root is holy,
so are the branches.

¹⁷If some of the branches have been
broken off, and you, though a wild olive
shoot, have been grafted in among the
others and now share in the nourishing
sap from the olive root, ¹⁸do not consider yourself to be superior to those other
branches. If you do, consider this: You do
not support the root, but the root supports you. ¹⁹You will say then, "Branches
were broken off so that I could be grafted in." ²⁰Granted. But they were broken
off because of unbelief, and you stand
by faith. Do not be arrogant, but tremble. ²¹For if God did not spare the natural
branches, he will not spare you either.

²²Consider therefore the kindness and
sternness of God: sternness to those
who fell, but kindness to you, provided
that you continue in his kindness. Otherwise, you also will be cut off. ²³And if

they do not persist in unbelief, they will
be grafted in, for God is able to graft them
in again. ²⁴After all, if you were cut out of
an olive tree that is wild by nature, and
contrary to nature were grafted into a cultivated olive tree, how much more readily
will these, the natural branches, be grafted into their own olive tree!

All Israel Will Be Saved

²⁵I do not want you to be ignorant of
this mystery, brothers and sisters, so
that you may not be conceited: Israel has
experienced a hardening in part until the
full number of the Gentiles has come in,
²⁶and in this wayᵇ all Israel will be saved.
As it is written:

"The deliverer will come from Zion;
he will turn godlessness away from
Jacob.
²⁷And this isᶜ my covenant with them
when I take away their sins."ᵈ

²⁸As far as the gospel is concerned,
they are enemies for your sake; but as far
as election is concerned, they are loved
on account of the patriarchs, ²⁹for God's
gifts and his call are irrevocable. ³⁰Just
as you who were at one time disobedient
to God have now received mercy as a result of their disobedience, ³¹so they too
have now become disobedient in order
that they too may nowᵉ receive mercy as
a result of God's mercy to you. ³²For God
has bound everyone over to disobedience
so that he may have mercy on them all.

Doxology

³³Oh, the depth of the riches of the
wisdom andᶠ knowledge of God!
How unsearchable his judgments,
and his paths beyond tracing out!
³⁴"Who has known the mind of the Lord?
Or who has been his counselor?"ᵍ
³⁵"Who has ever given to God,
that God should repay them?"ʰ
³⁶For from him and through him and for
him are all things.
To him be the glory forever! Amen.

ᵃ 10 Psalm 69:22,23   ᵇ 26 Or and so   ᶜ 27 Or will be   ᵈ 27 Isaiah 59:20,21; 27:9 (see Septuagint); Jer. 31:33,34
ᵉ 31 Some manuscripts do not have now.   ᶠ 33 Or riches and the wisdom and the   ᵍ 34 Isaiah 40:13
ʰ 35 Job 41:11

> My parents are old-fashioned. I want to do so many things that they claim "real" Christians don't do. I want to have fun and do the things that other young people do. Of course I also want to do what's right. How can I get my parents to change? >> Paige

Dear Jordan

Dear Paige,

It's natural to want to have fun and make your own choices. Unfortunately, it is also human nature to desire to do things that are sinful. It's possible that some of the things you'd like to do could lead you down paths that could be very harmful to you.

Look at Romans 12:2. God wants you to be "transformed by the renewing of your mind." That means allowing God to change the way your mind thinks. He can change the direction of your desires away from sin and toward godliness. He doesn't want you to follow in "the pattern of this world." It is safer to stay away from fire than to see how close you can get to it without getting burned.

Talk things over openly with your parents. You must obey them, but perhaps there are some activities they will negotiate with you. Your parents want you to have fun, but it is also their duty to protect you until you are an adult on your own. It's not easy to grow up, but it's not easy to be a good parent either.

Jordan

A Living Sacrifice

12 Therefore, I urge you, brothers and sisters, in view of God's mercy, to offer your bodies as a living sacrifice, holy and pleasing to God—this is your true and proper worship. [2] Do not conform to the pattern of this world, but be transformed by the renewing of your mind. Then you will be able to test and approve what God's will is—his good, pleasing and perfect will.

Humble Service in the Body of Christ

[3] For by the grace given me I say to every one of you: Do not think of yourself more highly than you ought, but rather think of yourself with sober judgment, in accordance with the faith God has distributed to each of you. [4] For just as each of us has one body with many members, and these members do not all have the same function, [5] so in Christ we, though many, form one body, and each member belongs to all the others. [6] We have different gifts, according to the grace given to each of us. If your gift is prophesying, then prophesy in accordance with your[a] faith; [7] if it is serving, then serve; if it is teaching, then teach; [8] if it is to encourage, then give encouragement; if it is giving, then give generously; if it is to lead,[b] do it diligently; if it is to show mercy, do it cheerfully.

Love in Action

[9] Love must be sincere. Hate what is evil; cling to what is good. [10] Be devoted to one another in love. Honor one another above yourselves. [11] Never be lacking in zeal, but keep your spiritual fervor, serving the Lord. [12] Be joyful in hope, patient in affliction, faithful in prayer. [13] Share with the Lord's people who are in need. Practice hospitality.

[14] Bless those who persecute you; bless and do not curse. [15] Rejoice with those who rejoice; mourn with those who mourn. [16] Live in harmony with one another. Do not be proud, but be willing to associate with people of low position.[c] Do not be conceited.

[17] Do not repay anyone evil for evil. Be careful to do what is right in the eyes of everyone. [18] If it is possible, as far as it depends on you, live at peace with everyone. [19] Do not take revenge, my dear friends, but leave room for God's wrath, for it is written: "It is mine to avenge; I will repay,"[d] says the Lord. [20] On the contrary:

> "If your enemy is hungry, feed him;
>   if he is thirsty, give him something
>   to drink.
> In doing this, you will heap burning
>   coals on his head."[e]

[21] Do not be overcome by evil, but overcome evil with good.

---

[a] 6 Or the   [b] 8 Or to provide for others   [c] 16 Or willing to do menial work   [d] 19 Deut. 32:35   [e] 20 Prov. 25:21,22

PANORAMA

A Good Person.

Instead of insisting that you be perfect, God invites you to trust him. Then he gives you the Holy Spirit so you can live a holy life. God wants you to be all you can be.

{ROMANS}

Submission to Governing Authorities

13 Let everyone be subject to the governing authorities, for there is no authority except that which God has established. The authorities that exist have been established by God. ²Consequently, whoever rebels against the authority is rebelling against what God has instituted, and those who do so will bring judgment on themselves. ³For rulers hold no terror for those who do right, but for those who do wrong. Do you want to be free from fear of the one in authority? Then do what is right and you will be commended. ⁴For the one in authority is God's servant for your good. But if you do wrong, be afraid, for rulers do not bear the sword for no reason. They are God's servants, agents of wrath to bring punishment on the wrongdoer. ⁵Therefore, it is necessary to submit to the authorities, not only because of possible punishment but also as a matter of conscience.

⁶This is also why you pay taxes, for the authorities are God's servants, who give their full time to governing. ⁷Give to everyone what you owe them: If you owe taxes, pay taxes; if revenue, then revenue; if respect, then respect; if honor, then honor.

Love Fulfills the Law

⁸Let no debt remain outstanding, except the continuing debt to love one another, for whoever loves others has fulfilled the law. ⁹The commandments, "You shall not commit adultery," "You shall not murder," "You shall not steal," "You shall not covet,"ᵃ and whatever other command there may be, are summed up in this one command: "Love your neighbor as yourself."ᵇ ¹⁰Love does no harm to a neighbor. Therefore love is the fulfillment of the law.

The Day Is Near

¹¹And do this, understanding the present time: The hour has already come for you to wake up from your slumber, because our salvation is nearer now than when we first believed. ¹²The night is nearly over; the day is almost here. So let us put aside the deeds of darkness and put on the armor of light. ¹³Let us behave decently, as in the daytime, not in carousing and drunkenness, not in sexual immorality and debauchery, not in dissension and jealousy. ¹⁴Rather, clothe yourselves with the Lord Jesus Christ, and do not think about how to gratify the desires of the flesh.ᶜ

The Weak and the Strong

14 Accept the one whose faith is weak, without quarreling over disputable matters. ²One person's faith allows them to eat anything, but another, whose faith is weak, eats only vegetables. ³The one who eats everything must not treat with contempt the one who does not, and the one who does not eat everything must not judge the one who does, for God has accepted them. ⁴Who are you to judge someone else's servant? To their own master, servants stand or fall. And they will stand, for the Lord is able to make them stand.

⁵One person considers one day more sacred than another; another considers every day alike. Each of them should be fully convinced in their own mind. ⁶Whoever regards one day as special does so to the Lord. Whoever eats meat does so to the Lord, for they give thanks to God; and whoever abstains does so to the Lord and gives thanks to God. ⁷For none of us lives for ourselves alone, and none of us dies for ourselves alone. ⁸If we live, we live for the Lord; and if we die, we die for the Lord. So, whether we live or die, we belong to the Lord. ⁹For this very reason, Christ died and returned to life so that he might be the Lord of both the dead and the living.

¹⁰You, then, why do you judge your brother or sisterᵈ? Or why do you treat them with contempt? For we will all stand before God's judgment seat. ¹¹It is written:

ᵃ 9 Exodus 20:13-15,17; Deut. 5:17-19,21   ᵇ 9 Lev. 19:18   ᶜ 14 In contexts like this, the Greek word for *flesh* (*sarx*) refers to the sinful state of human beings, often presented as a power in opposition to the Spirit.   ᵈ 10 The Greek word for *brother or sister* (*adelphos*) refers here to a believer, whether man or woman, as part of God's family; also in verses 13, 15 and 21.

We Believe...

Jesus is "Our Lord"

✝ Who's in charge here? It's a good question, and the Bible has a good answer: Jesus. When the first Christians said, "Jesus Christ is Lord" (Philippians 2:11), they meant several things. They meant that

* Jesus has *universal* authority. He is seated at God's right hand, "far above all rule and authority, power and dominion" (Ephesians 1:21).

* Jesus has *complete* authority, for all "angels, authorities and powers in submission to him" (1 Peter 3:22).

* Jesus has *personal* authority; Christ "died and returned to life so that he might be the Lord of both the dead and the living" (Romans 14:9).

Today when Christians recite, "We believe ... in Jesus Christ his only Son, our Lord," the focus is on Christ's personal authority. We're saying that we acknowledge Jesus' authority over our daily lives, and that we pledge to live our lives as he wants us to live them.

It's a tremendous relief to have Jesus as Lord of our lives. We don't have to go to teens at school to tell us what to do. We don't have to look to the rich and famous. We don't have to let money or possessions or sex control our choices. When we say Jesus is our Lord, we're saying that we've turned control of our lives over to Jesus. We pledge to do what pleases him.

Go to page 1258 for the next We Believe

" 'As surely as I live,' says the Lord,
'every knee will bow before me;
    every tongue will acknowledge
        God.' "[a]

[12]So then, each of us will give an account of ourselves to God.

[13]Therefore let us stop passing judgment on one another. Instead, make up your mind not to put any stumbling block or obstacle in the way of a brother or sister. [14]I am convinced, being fully persuaded in the Lord Jesus, that nothing is unclean in itself. But if anyone regards something as unclean, then for that person it is unclean. [15]If your brother or sister is distressed because of what you eat, you are no longer acting in love. Do not by your eating destroy someone for whom Christ died. [16]Therefore do not let what you know is good be spoken of as evil. [17]For the kingdom of God is not a matter of eating and drinking, but of righteousness, peace and joy in the Holy Spirit, [18]because anyone who serves Christ in this way is pleasing to God and receives human approval.

[19]Let us therefore make every effort to do what leads to peace and to mutual edification. [20]Do not destroy the work of God for the sake of food. All food is clean, but it is wrong for a person to eat anything that causes someone else to stumble. [21]It is better not to eat meat or drink wine or to do anything else that will cause your brother or sister to fall.

[22]So whatever you believe about these things keep between yourself and God. Blessed is the one who does not condemn himself by what he approves. [23]But whoever has doubts is condemned if they eat, because their eating is not from faith; and everything that does not come from faith is sin.[b]

15 We who are strong ought to bear with the failings of the weak and not to please ourselves. [2]Each of us should please our neighbors for their good, to build them up. [3]For even Christ did not please himself but, as it is written: "The insults of those who insult you have fallen on me."[c] [4]For everything that was written in the past was written to teach us, so that through the endurance taught in the Scriptures and the encouragement they provide we might have hope.

[5]May the God who gives endurance and encouragement give you the same attitude of mind toward each other that Christ Jesus had, [6]so that with one mind and one voice you may glorify the God and Father of our Lord Jesus Christ.

[7]Accept one another, then, just as Christ accepted you, in order to bring praise to God. [8]For I tell you that Christ has become a servant of the Jews[d] on behalf of God's truth, so that the promises made to the patriarchs might be confirmed [9]and, moreover, that the Gentiles might glorify God for his mercy. As it is written:

"Therefore I will praise you among the
        Gentiles;
    I will sing the praises of your name."[e]

[10]Again, it says,

"Rejoice, you Gentiles, with his
        people."[f]

[11]And again,

"Praise the Lord, all you Gentiles;
    let all the peoples extol him."[g]

[12]And again, Isaiah says,

"The Root of Jesse will spring up,
    one who will arise to rule over the
        nations;
    in him the Gentiles will hope."[h]

[13]May the God of hope fill you with all joy and peace as you trust in him, so that you may overflow with hope by the power of the Holy Spirit.

Accept one another, then, just as Christ accepted you, in order to bring praise to God.

Romans 15:7

---

a 11 Isaiah 45:23   *b 23* Some manuscripts place 16:25-27 here; others after 15:33.   *c 3* Psalm 69:9   *d 8* Greek *circumcision*   *e 9* 2 Samuel 22:50; Psalm 18:49   *f 10* Deut. 32:43   *g 11* Psalm 117:1   *h 12* Isaiah 11:10 (see Septuagint)

Paul the Minister to the Gentiles

14 I myself am convinced, my brothers and sisters, that you yourselves are full of goodness, filled with knowledge and competent to instruct one another. 15 Yet I have written you quite boldly on some points to remind you of them again, because of the grace God gave me 16 to be a minister of Christ Jesus to the Gentiles. He gave me the priestly duty of proclaiming the gospel of God, so that the Gentiles might become an offering acceptable to God, sanctified by the Holy Spirit.

17 Therefore I glory in Christ Jesus in my service to God. 18 I will not venture to speak of anything except what Christ has accomplished through me in leading the Gentiles to obey God by what I have said and done— 19 by the power of signs and wonders, through the power of the Spirit of God. So from Jerusalem all the way around to Illyricum, I have fully proclaimed the gospel of Christ. 20 It has always been my ambition to preach the gospel where Christ was not known, so that I would not be building on someone else's foundation. 21 Rather, as it is written:

"Those who were not told about him
    will see,
and those who have not heard will
    understand."[a]

22 This is why I have often been hindered from coming to you.

Paul's Plan to Visit Rome

23 But now that there is no more place for me to work in these regions, and since I have been longing for many years to visit you, 24 I plan to do so when I go to Spain. I hope to see you while passing through and to have you assist me on my journey there, after I have enjoyed your company for a while. 25 Now, however, I am on my way to Jerusalem in the service of the Lord's people there. 26 For Macedonia and Achaia were pleased to make a contribution for the poor among the Lord's people in Jerusalem. 27 They were pleased to do it, and indeed they owe it to them. For if the Gentiles have shared in the Jews' spiritual blessings, they owe it to the Jews to share with them their material blessings. 28 So after I have completed this task and have made sure that they have received this contribution, I will go to Spain and visit you on the way. 29 I know that when I come to you, I will come in the full measure of the blessing of Christ.

30 I urge you, brothers and sisters, by our Lord Jesus Christ and by the love of the Spirit, to join me in my struggle by praying to God for me. 31 Pray that I may be kept safe from the unbelievers in

INSTANT ACCESS

In Rome all sorts of people belonged to the church. Romans 16 points out some of the variety. Some names here are Roman and some are Greek. Women are mentioned often and are praised as dedicated Christian workers. The mention of Aristobulus's "household" (Romans 16:10) is a reminder that some early Christians were rich while others were slaves. But they all knew Jesus and that made them members of God's family. The differences didn't count. They don't count at your church or youth group either. Since every Christian belongs to God's family, make sure all believers are welcome in your group.

{Romans 16:1–18}

[a] 21 Isaiah 52:15 (see Septuagint)

Judea and that the contribution I take to Jerusalem may be favorably received by the Lord's people there, ³²so that I may come to you with joy, by God's will, and in your company be refreshed. ³³The God of peace be with you all. Amen.

Personal Greetings

16 I commend to you our sister Phoebe, a deacon^{a,b} of the church in Cenchreae. ²I ask you to receive her in the Lord in a way worthy of his people and to give her any help she may need from you, for she has been the benefactor of many people, including me.

³Greet Priscilla^c and Aquila, my co-workers in Christ Jesus. ⁴They risked their lives for me. Not only I but all the churches of the Gentiles are grateful to them.

⁵Greet also the church that meets at their house.

Greet my dear friend Epenetus, who was the first convert to Christ in the province of Asia.

⁶Greet Mary, who worked very hard for you.

⁷Greet Andronicus and Junia, my fellow Jews who have been in prison with me. They are outstanding among^d the apostles, and they were in Christ before I was.

⁸Greet Ampliatus, my dear friend in the Lord.

⁹Greet Urbanus, our co-worker in Christ, and my dear friend Stachys.

¹⁰Greet Apelles, whose fidelity to Christ has stood the test.

Greet those who belong to the household of Aristobulus.

¹¹Greet Herodion, my fellow Jew.

Greet those in the household of Narcissus who are in the Lord.

¹²Greet Tryphena and Tryphosa, those women who work hard in the Lord.

Greet my dear friend Persis, another woman who has worked very hard in the Lord.

¹³Greet Rufus, chosen in the Lord, and

his mother, who has been a mother to me, too.

¹⁴Greet Asyncritus, Phlegon, Hermes, Patrobas, Hermas and the other brothers and sisters with them.

¹⁵Greet Philologus, Julia, Nereus and his sister, and Olympas and all the Lord's people who are with them.

¹⁶Greet one another with a holy kiss.

All the churches of Christ send greetings.

¹⁷I urge you, brothers and sisters, to watch out for those who cause divisions and put obstacles in your way that are contrary to the teaching you have learned. Keep away from them. ¹⁸For such people are not serving our Lord Christ, but their own appetites. By smooth talk and flattery they deceive the minds of naive people. ¹⁹Everyone has heard about your obedience, so I rejoice because of you; but I want you to be wise about what is good, and innocent about what is evil.

²⁰The God of peace will soon crush Satan under your feet.

The grace of our Lord Jesus be with you.

²¹Timothy, my co-worker, sends his greetings to you, as do Lucius, Jason and Sosipater, my fellow Jews.

²²I, Tertius, who wrote down this letter, greet you in the Lord.

²³Gaius, whose hospitality I and the whole church here enjoy, sends you his greetings.

Erastus, who is the city's director of public works, and our brother Quartus send you their greetings. [24]^e

²⁵Now to him who is able to establish you in accordance with my gospel, the message I proclaim about Jesus Christ, in keeping with the revelation of the mystery hidden for long ages past, ²⁶but now revealed and made known through the prophetic writings by the command of the eternal God, so that all the Gentiles might come to the obedience that comes from^f faith — ²⁷to the only wise God be glory forever through Jesus Christ! Amen.

---

^a 1 Or *servant*   ^b 1 The word *deacon* refers here to a Christian designated to serve with the overseers/elders of the church in a variety of ways; similarly in Phil. 1:1 and 1 Tim. 3:8,12.   ^c 3 Greek *Prisca*, a variant of *Priscilla*   ^d 7 Or *are esteemed by*   ^e 24 Some manuscripts include here *May the grace of our Lord Jesus Christ be with all of you. Amen.*
^f 26 Or *that is*

1 CORINTHIANS

Problems.

Who helps you with your problems? Good friends with whom you talk things over. A mom and dad who listen and give good advice. A youth leader at church. Everyone needs help sometimes to think through difficult issues.

When the church at Corinth had problems, Paul helped. What if little groups of close friends won't let outsiders in? What do you do about a Christian friend who's living an immoral life? Why do some people have such strict convictions? Paul answers these and many other practical questions in this practical New Testament book.

>>**CHURCH IGNORES SEX SINS**
  "Don't," says apostle. See 1 Corinthians 5:1–13

>>**APOSTLE CHOOSES TO FORGO RIGHTS**
  Paul sets an example. Report in 1 Corinthians 9:7–23

>>**WHAT MAKES YOU SPECIAL?**
  Answers in 1 Corinthians 12:1–26

>>**GETTING SPIRITUAL?**
  Surprising answer given in 1 Corinthians 13

As the Corinthians struggle with problems, the city of London is founded in Britain. In Rome the Emperor Nero plots the murder of his mother. The Roman poet Juvenal is born. In China the Emperor Zuhang begins a 75-year reign.

1 Paul, called to be an apostle of Christ Jesus by the will of God, and our brother Sosthenes,

2 To the church of God in Corinth, to those sanctified in Christ Jesus and called to be his holy people, together with all those everywhere who call on the name of our Lord Jesus Christ—their Lord and ours:

3 Grace and peace to you from God our Father and the Lord Jesus Christ.

Thanksgiving

4 I always thank my God for you because of his grace given you in Christ Jesus. 5 For in him you have been enriched in every way—with all kinds of speech and with all knowledge— 6 God thus confirming our testimony about Christ among you. 7 Therefore you do not lack any spiritual gift as you eagerly wait for our Lord Jesus Christ to be revealed. 8 He will also keep you firm to the end, so that you will be blameless on the day of our Lord Jesus Christ. 9 God is faithful, who has called you into fellowship with his Son, Jesus Christ our Lord.

A Church Divided Over Leaders

10 I appeal to you, brothers and sisters,[a] in the name of our Lord Jesus Christ, that all of you agree with one another in what you say and that there be no divisions among you, but that you be perfectly united in mind and thought. 11 My brothers and sisters, some from Chloe's household have informed me that there are quarrels among you. 12 What I mean is this: One of you says, "I follow Paul"; another, "I follow Apollos"; another, "I follow Cephas[b]"; still another, "I follow Christ."

13 Is Christ divided? Was Paul crucified for you? Were you baptized in the name of Paul? 14 I thank God that I did not baptize any of you except Crispus and Gaius, 15 so no one can say that you were baptized in my name. 16 (Yes, I also baptized the household of Stephanas; beyond that, I don't remember if I baptized anyone else.) 17 For Christ did not send me to baptize, but to preach the gospel—not with wisdom and eloquence, lest the cross of Christ be emptied of its power.

Christ Crucified Is God's Power and Wisdom

18 For the message of the cross is foolishness to those who are perishing, but to us who are being saved it is the power of God. 19 For it is written:

"I will destroy the wisdom of the wise;
    the intelligence of the intelligent I
        will frustrate."[c]

20 Where is the wise person? Where is the teacher of the law? Where is the philosopher of this age? Has not God made foolish the wisdom of the world? 21 For since in the wisdom of God the world through its wisdom did not know him, God was pleased through the foolishness of what was preached to save those who believe. 22 Jews demand signs and Greeks look for wisdom, 23 but we preach Christ crucified: a stumbling block to Jews and foolishness to Gentiles, 24 but to those whom God has called, both Jews and Greeks, Christ the power of God and the wisdom of God. 25 For the foolishness of God is wiser than human wisdom, and the weakness of God is stronger than human strength.

26 Brothers and sisters, think of what you were when you were called. Not many of you were wise by human standards; not many were influential; not many were of noble birth. 27 But God chose the foolish things of the world to shame the wise; God chose the weak things of the world to shame the strong. 28 God chose the lowly things of this world and the despised things—and the things that are not—to nullify the things that are, 29 so that no one may boast before him. 30 It is because of him that you are in Christ Jesus, who has become for us wisdom from God—that is, our righteousness, holiness and redemption. 31 Therefore, as it is written: "Let the one who boasts boast in the Lord."[d]

2 And so it was with me, brothers and sisters. When I came to you, I did

---

[a] 10 The Greek word for *brothers and sisters* (*adelphoi*) refers here to believers, both men and women, as part of God's family; also in verses 11 and 26; and in 2:1; 3:1; 4:6; 6:8; 7:24, 29; 10:1; 11:33; 12:1; 14:6, 20, 26, 39; 15:1, 6, 50, 58; 16:15, 20.   [b] 12 That is, Peter   [c] 19 Isaiah 29:14   [d] 31 Jer. 9:24

not come with eloquence or human wisdom as I proclaimed to you the testimony about God.[a] [2]For I resolved to know nothing while I was with you except Jesus Christ and him crucified. [3]I came to you in weakness with great fear and trembling. [4]My message and my preaching were not with wise and persuasive words, but with a demonstration of the Spirit's power, [5]so that your faith might not rest on human wisdom, but on God's power.

God's Wisdom Revealed by the Spirit

[6]We do, however, speak a message of wisdom among the mature, but not the wisdom of this age or of the rulers of this age, who are coming to nothing. [7]No, we declare God's wisdom, a mystery that has been hidden and that God destined for our glory before time began. [8]None of the rulers of this age understood it, for if they had, they would not have crucified the Lord of glory. [9]However, as it is written:

"What no eye has seen,
    what no ear has heard,
and what no human mind has
        conceived"[b]—
    the things God has prepared for
        those who love him—

[10]these are the things God has revealed to us by his Spirit.

The Spirit searches all things, even the deep things of God. [11]For who knows a person's thoughts except their own spirit within them? In the same way no one knows the thoughts of God except the Spirit of God. [12]What we have received is not the spirit of the world, but the Spirit who is from God, so that we may understand what God has freely given us. [13]This is what we speak, not in words taught us by human wisdom but in words taught by the Spirit, explaining spiritual realities with Spirit-taught words.[c] [14]The person without the Spirit does not accept the things that come from the Spirit of God but considers them foolishness, and cannot understand them because they are discerned only through the Spirit. [15]The person with the

Spirit makes judgments about all things, but such a person is not subject to merely human judgments, [16]for,

"Who has known the mind of the Lord
    so as to instruct him?"[d]

But we have the mind of Christ.

The Church and Its Leaders

3 Brothers and sisters, I could not address you as people who live by the Spirit but as people who are still world-

---

INSTANT ACCESS

You want to speak up when your biology teacher jokes about the creation theory. Or when the class brain says he can prove God doesn't exist. But you don't know enough biology to argue. And you're not half as smart as the class brain. So what do you do? You might do what the apostle Paul did. Paul was an educated man. But instead of relying on his superior knowledge, Paul "resolved to know nothing while I was with you except Jesus Christ and him crucified." Witnessing isn't trying to persuade others. It's telling them about Jesus and counting on the Holy Spirit's power to bring the message home.

{1 Corinthians 2:2–5}

---

[a] 1 Some manuscripts *proclaimed to you God's mystery*   [b] 9 Isaiah 64:4   [c] 13 Or *Spirit, interpreting spiritual truths to those who are spiritual*   [d] 16 Isaiah 40:13

Do you ever feel like you just can't do anything totally right? You get four A's and Dad zeroes in on the one B. You clean the basement, and Mom finds two cobwebs you missed. These verses in 1 Corinthians may sound like God is going to do the same thing: examine the bad you've done and ignore the good. But take a look at verse 14. It speaks of reward. God won't ignore the A's or the parts of the basement you did clean. It can be tough not to be appreciated when you try so hard. But remember: God appreciates what you do and who you are. From him you'll get praise and a reward.

{1 Corinthians 3:10–15}

INSTANT ACCESS

making it grow. [7] So neither the one who plants nor the one who waters is anything, but only God, who makes things grow. [8] The one who plants and the one who waters have one purpose, and they will each be rewarded according to their own labor. [9] For we are co-workers in God's service; you are God's field, God's building.

[10] By the grace God has given me, I laid a foundation as a wise builder, and someone else is building on it. But each one should build with care. [11] For no one can lay any foundation other than the one already laid, which is Jesus Christ. [12] If anyone builds on this foundation using gold, silver, costly stones, wood, hay or straw, [13] their work will be shown for what it is, because the Day will bring it to light. It will be revealed with fire, and the fire will test the quality of each person's work. [14] If what has been built survives, the builder will receive a reward. [15] If it is burned up, the builder will suffer loss but yet will be saved—even though only as one escaping through the flames.

[16] Don't you know that you yourselves are God's temple and that God's Spirit dwells in your midst? [17] If anyone destroys God's temple, God will destroy that person; for God's temple is sacred, and you together are that temple.

[18] Do not deceive yourselves. If any of you think you are wise by the standards of this age, you should become "fools" so that you may become wise. [19] For the wisdom of this world is foolishness in God's sight. As it is written: "He catches the wise in their craftiness"[a]; [20] and again, "The Lord knows that the thoughts of the wise are futile."[b] [21] So then, no more boasting about human leaders! All things are yours, [22] whether Paul or Apollos or Cephas[c] or the world or life or death or the present or the future—all are yours, [23] and you are of Christ, and Christ is of God.

The Nature of True Apostleship

4 This, then, is how you ought to regard us: as servants of Christ and as those entrusted with the mysteries God has revealed. [2] Now it is required

ly—mere infants in Christ. [2] I gave you milk, not solid food, for you were not yet ready for it. Indeed, you are still not ready. [3] You are still worldly. For since there is jealousy and quarreling among you, are you not worldly? Are you not acting like mere humans? [4] For when one says, "I follow Paul," and another, "I follow Apollos," are you not mere human beings?

[5] What, after all, is Apollos? And what is Paul? Only servants, through whom you came to believe—as the Lord has assigned to each his task. [6] I planted the seed, Apollos watered it, but God has been

---

[a] 19 Job 5:13   [b] 20 Psalm 94:11   [c] 22 That is, Peter

There are so many gangs at my school it makes me sick. Why can't everybody just get along with everybody else?

>> Trinity

Dear Jordan

Dear Trinity,

Gangs give lots of power to a few people in charge. This requires other gang members to give up control of which people, things, clothes and activities they like or dislike and instead conform. They have people to talk to before and after school and during passing periods. They have people to eat lunch with.

It feels good to belong and to have the support of friends. But some of the other things that come with "belonging" aren't so nice. Like when a member of your gang has a problem with someone you like and now you're expected to be nasty to a friend. That feels sickening. But the consequences are no one to talk to, eating alone and the gang turning against you.

Paul talks about some early Christians who were basically forming gangs, or cliques. Some insisted they follow Paul, others, Apollos. But Paul reminds them "… you are of Christ" (1 Corinthians 3:23). One way to avoid getting trapped in a gang is to "Be kind and compassionate to one another" (Ephesians 4:32). "Do nothing out of selfish ambition or vain conceit. Rather, in humility value others above yourselves, not looking to your own interests but each of you to the interests of the others" (Philippians 2:3–4). Don't limit your circle of friends. Be friends with people in many circles.

Jordan

that those who have been given a trust must prove faithful. ³I care very little if I am judged by you or by any human court; indeed, I do not even judge myself. ⁴My conscience is clear, but that does not make me innocent. It is the Lord who judges me. ⁵Therefore judge nothing before the appointed time; wait until the Lord comes. He will bring to light what is hidden in darkness and will expose the motives of the heart. At that time each will receive their praise from God.

⁶Now, brothers and sisters, I have applied these things to myself and Apollos for your benefit, so that you may learn from us the meaning of the saying, "Do not go beyond what is written." Then you will not be puffed up in being a follower of one of us over against the other. ⁷For who makes you different from anyone else? What do you have that you did not receive? And if you did receive it, why do you boast as though you did not?

⁸Already you have all you want! Already you have become rich! You have begun to reign—and that without us! How I wish that you really had begun to reign so that we also might reign with you! ⁹For it seems to me that God has put us apostles on display at the end of the procession, like those condemned to die in the arena. We have been made a spectacle to the whole universe, to angels as well as to human beings. ¹⁰We are fools for Christ, but you are so wise in Christ! We are weak, but you are strong! You are honored, we are dishonored! ¹¹To this very hour we go hungry and thirsty, we are in rags, we are brutally treated, we are homeless. ¹²We work hard with our own hands. When we are cursed, we bless; when we are persecuted, we endure it; ¹³when we are slandered, we answer kindly. We have become the scum of the earth, the garbage of the world—right up to this moment.

Paul's Appeal and Warning

¹⁴I am writing this not to shame you but to warn you as my dear children. ¹⁵Even if you had ten thousand guardians in Christ, you do not have many fathers, for in Christ Jesus I became your father through the gospel. ¹⁶Therefore I urge you to imitate me. ¹⁷For this reason I have sent to you Timothy, my son whom I love, who is faithful in the Lord. He will remind you of my way of life in Christ Jesus, which agrees with what I teach everywhere in every church.

¹⁸Some of you have become arrogant, as if I were not coming to you. ¹⁹But I will come to you very soon, if the Lord is willing, and then I will find out not only how these arrogant people are talking, but what power they have. ²⁰For the kingdom of God is not a matter of talk but of power. ²¹What do you prefer? Shall I come to you with a rod of discipline, or shall I come in love and with a gentle spirit?

Dealing With a Case of Incest

5 It is actually reported that there is sexual immorality among you, and of a kind that even pagans do not tolerate: A man is sleeping with his father's wife. ²And you are proud! Shouldn't you rather have gone into mourning and have put out of your fellowship the man who has been doing this? ³For my part, even though I am not physically present, I am with you in spirit. As one who is present with you in this way, I have already passed judgment in the name of our Lord Jesus on the one who has been doing this. ⁴So when you are assembled and I am with you in spirit, and the power of our Lord Jesus is present, ⁵hand this man over to Satan for the destruction of the flesh,ᵃ,ᵇ so that his spirit may be saved on the day of the Lord.

⁶Your boasting is not good. Don't you know that a little yeast leavens the whole batch of dough? ⁷Get rid of the old yeast, so that you may be a new unleavened batch—as you really are. For Christ, our Passover lamb, has been sacrificed. ⁸Therefore let us keep the Festival, not with the old bread leavened with malice and wickedness, but with the unleavened bread of sincerity and truth.

⁹I wrote to you in my letter not to associate with sexually immoral people— ¹⁰not at all meaning the people of this world who

---

ᵃ 5 In contexts like this, the Greek word for *flesh* (*sarx*) refers to the sinful state of human beings, often presented as a power in opposition to the Spirit.   ᵇ 5 Or *of his body*

are immoral, or the greedy and swindlers, or idolaters. In that case you would have to leave this world. ¹¹But now I am writing to you that you must not associate with anyone who claims to be a brother or sister[a] but is sexually immoral or greedy, an idolater or slanderer, a drunkard or swindler. Do not even eat with such people.

¹²What business is it of mine to judge those outside the church? Are you not to judge those inside? ¹³God will judge those outside. "Expel the wicked person from among you."[b]

Lawsuits Among Believers

6 If any of you has a dispute with another, do you dare to take it before the ungodly for judgment instead of before the Lord's people? ²Or do you not know that the Lord's people will judge the world? And if you are to judge the world, are you not competent to judge trivial cases? ³Do you not know that we will judge angels? How much more the things of this life! ⁴Therefore, if you have disputes about such matters, do you ask for a ruling from those whose way of life is scorned in the church? ⁵I say this to shame you. Is it possible that there is nobody among you wise enough to judge a dispute between believers? ⁶But instead, one brother takes another to court—and this in front of unbelievers!

⁷The very fact that you have lawsuits among you means you have been completely defeated already. Why not rather be wronged? Why not rather be cheated?

---

[a] 11 The Greek word for *brother or sister* (*adelphos*) refers here to a believer, whether man or woman, as part of God's family; also in 8:11, 13.   [b] 13 Deut. 13:5; 17:7; 19:19; 21:21; 22:21,24; 24:7

TO THE POINT

Don't Judge

Sometimes it's confusing. Paul tells you not to judge (Romans 14:1); he says he doesn't even judge himself (1 Corinthians 4:3). And then he says he has "already passed judgment" and tells the church to expel a sinning believer (1 Corinthians 5:3–5)! Actually, it's not so confusing if you look carefully at each Bible passage:

+ Don't judge others' personal convictions (Romans 14:1–8).

+ Don't judge others' motives or service (1 Corinthians 4:3).

+ Do judge others who do what the Bible says is sin (1 Corinthians 5).

When a fellow Christian makes a habit of doing something God says is sin, you can agree with God and say, "That's wrong!" Don't criticize others or gossip about them. But if a friend makes a habit of sinning, urge him or her to stop.

[8]Instead, you yourselves cheat and do wrong, and you do this to your brothers and sisters. [9]Or do you not know that wrongdoers will not inherit the kingdom of God? Do not be deceived: Neither the sexually immoral nor idolaters nor adulterers nor men who have sex with men[a] [10]nor thieves nor the greedy nor drunkards nor slanderers nor swindlers will inherit the kingdom of God. [11]And that is what some of you were. But you were washed, you were sanctified, you were justified in the name of the Lord Jesus Christ and by the Spirit of our God.

Sexual Immorality

[12]"I have the right to do anything," you say—but not everything is beneficial. "I have the right to do anything"—but I will not be mastered by anything. [13]You say, "Food for the stomach and the stomach for food, and God will destroy them both." The body, however, is not meant for sexual immorality but for the Lord, and the Lord for the body. [14]By his power God raised the Lord from the dead, and he will raise us also. [15]Do you not know that your bodies are members of Christ himself? Shall I then take the members of Christ and unite them with a prostitute? Never! [16]Do you not know that he who unites himself with a prostitute is one with her in body? For it is said, "The two will become one flesh."[b] [17]But whoever is united with the Lord is one with him in spirit.[c]

[18]Flee from sexual immorality. All other sins a person commits are outside the body, but whoever sins sexually, sins against their own body. [19]Do you not know that your bodies are temples of the Holy Spirit, who is in you, whom you have received from God? You are not your own; [20]you were bought at a price. Therefore honor God with your bodies.

Concerning Married Life

7 Now for the matters you wrote about: "It is good for a man not to have sexual relations with a woman." [2]But since sexual immorality is occurring, each man should have sexual relations with his own wife, and each woman with her own husband. [3]The husband should fulfill his marital duty to his wife, and likewise the wife to her husband. [4]The wife does not have authority over her own body but yields it to her husband. In the same way, the husband does not have authority over his own body but yields it to his wife. [5]Do not deprive each other except perhaps by mutual consent and for a time, so that you may devote yourselves to prayer. Then come together again so that Satan will not tempt you because of your lack of self-control. [6]I say this as a concession, not as a command. [7]I wish that all of you were as I am. But each of you has your own gift from God; one has this gift, another has that.

[8]Now to the unmarried[d] and the widows I say: It is good for them to stay unmarried, as I do. [9]But if they cannot control themselves, they should marry, for it is better to marry than to burn with passion.

[10]To the married I give this command (not I, but the Lord): A wife must not separate from her husband. [11]But if she does, she must remain unmarried or else be reconciled to her husband. And a husband must not divorce his wife.

[12]To the rest I say this (I, not the Lord): If any brother has a wife who is not a believer and she is willing to live with him, he must not divorce her. [13]And if a woman has a husband who is not a believer and he is willing to live with her, she must not divorce him. [14]For the unbelieving husband has been sanctified through his wife, and the unbelieving wife has been sanctified through her believing husband.

Your bodies are temples of the Holy Spirit, who is in you, whom you have received from God.

1 Corinthians 6:19

---

[a] 9 The words *men who have sex with men* translate two Greek words that refer to the passive and active participants in homosexual acts. [b] 16 Gen. 2:24 [c] 17 Or *in the Spirit* [d] 8 Or *widowers*

> I heard that pot was less damaging to your body than tobacco. Why shouldn't we smoke it?
>
> >> Jayden

Dear Jordan

Dear Jayden,

I have read many letters asking a variety of questions on drugs, alcohol, eating disorders, fight clubs … the list goes on. While each one could be given a more specific answer, space here is limited. So I'm going to give you a verse which will be meaningful to your question and to many others such as those listed above.

"Do you not know that your bodies are temples of the Holy Spirit, who is in you, whom you have received from God? You are not your own; you were bought at a price. Therefore honor God with your bodies" (1 Corinthians 6:19–20).

The price paid for you is the blood of Christ. The Holy Spirit lives in you if you have accepted Christ's sacrifice. That's why your body is a temple of the Holy Spirit.

Think for a moment. God the Holy Spirit lives in you. That makes your body a sacred place. Do you think God wants you to put anything harmful in that sacred place? Do you think he wants you to mistreat this place he lives in with you by starving it, having it beaten, polluting it with any drug including alcohol? Or that he wants you doing any number of sexual things with another person?

Honor God with your body. End of story.

Jordan

More than likely there are things about yourself you would like to change. Maybe it's your looks or your financial situation. Whatever it is, it isn't easy to hear Paul's words, "Don't let it trouble you" (1 Corinthians 7:21). And Paul said this to slaves. Seems like it was probably easy for Paul to say—he wasn't a slave. He had full Roman citizenship. But what Paul is saying here is that you are important to God. Your identity as a child of God doesn't depend on being handsome or beautiful or smart. The you inside is important. And Paul's "Don't let it trouble you" makes a lot of sense.

{1 Corinthians 7:19–24}

» INSTANT ACCESS

He should not become uncircumcised. Was a man uncircumcised when he was called? He should not be circumcised. 19 Circumcision is nothing and uncircumcision is nothing. Keeping God's commands is what counts. 20 Each person should remain in the situation they were in when God called them.

21 Were you a slave when you were called? Don't let it trouble you—although if you can gain your freedom, do so. 22 For the one who was a slave when called to faith in the Lord is the Lord's freed person; similarly, the one who was free when called is Christ's slave. 23 You were bought at a price; do not become slaves of human beings. 24 Brothers and sisters, each person, as responsible to God, should remain in the situation they were in when God called them.

Concerning the Unmarried

25 Now about virgins: I have no command from the Lord, but I give a judgment as one who by the Lord's mercy is trustworthy. 26 Because of the present crisis, I think that it is good for a man to remain as he is. 27 Are you pledged to a woman? Do not seek to be released. Are you free from such a commitment? Do not look for a wife. 28 But if you do marry, you have not sinned; and if a virgin marries, she has not sinned. But those who marry will face many troubles in this life, and I want to spare you this.

29 What I mean, brothers and sisters, is that the time is short. From now on those who have wives should live as if they do not; 30 those who mourn, as if they did not; those who are happy, as if they were not; those who buy something, as if it were not theirs to keep; 31 those who use the things of the world, as if not engrossed in them. For this world in its present form is passing away.

32 I would like you to be free from concern. An unmarried man is concerned about the Lord's affairs—how he can please the Lord. 33 But a married man is concerned about the affairs of this world— how he can please his wife— 34 and his interests are divided. An unmarried woman or virgin is concerned about the Lord's affairs: Her aim is to be devoted to the Lord

Otherwise your children would be unclean, but as it is, they are holy.

15 But if the unbeliever leaves, let it be so. The brother or the sister is not bound in such circumstances; God has called us to live in peace. 16 How do you know, wife, whether you will save your husband? Or, how do you know, husband, whether you will save your wife?

Concerning Change of Status

17 Nevertheless, each person should live as a believer in whatever situation the Lord has assigned to them, just as God has called them. This is the rule I lay down in all the churches. 18 Was a man already circumcised when he was called?

in both body and spirit. But a married woman is concerned about the affairs of this world—how she can please her husband. ³⁵I am saying this for your own good, not to restrict you, but that you may live in a right way in undivided devotion to the Lord.

³⁶If anyone is worried that he might not be acting honorably toward the virgin he is engaged to, and if his passions are too strong[a] and he feels he ought to marry, he should do as he wants. He is not sinning. They should get married. ³⁷But the man who has settled the matter in his own mind, who is under no compulsion but has control over his own will, and who has made up his mind not to marry the virgin—this man also does the right thing. ³⁸So then, he who marries the virgin does right, but he who does not marry her does better.[b]

³⁹A woman is bound to her husband as long as he lives. But if her husband dies, she is free to marry anyone she wishes, but he must belong to the Lord. ⁴⁰In my judgment, she is happier if she stays as she is—and I think that I too have the Spirit of God.

Concerning Food Sacrificed to Idols

8 Now about food sacrificed to idols: We know that "We all possess knowledge." But knowledge puffs up while love builds up. ²Those who think they know something do not yet know as they ought to know. ³But whoever loves God is known by God.[c]

⁴So then, about eating food sacrificed to idols: We know that "An idol is nothing at all in the world" and that "There is no God but one." ⁵For even if there are so-called gods, whether in heaven or on earth (as indeed there are many "gods" and many "lords"), ⁶yet for us there is but one God, the Father, from whom all things came and for whom we live; and there is but one Lord, Jesus Christ, through whom all things came and through whom we live.

⁷But not everyone possesses this knowledge. Some people are still so accustomed to idols that when they eat sacrificial food they think of it as having been sacrificed to a god, and since their conscience is weak, it is defiled. ⁸But food does not bring us near to God; we are no worse if we do not eat, and no better if we do.

⁹Be careful, however, that the exercise of your rights does not become a stumbling block to the weak. ¹⁰For if someone with a weak conscience sees you, with all your knowledge, eating in an idol's temple, won't that person be emboldened to eat what is sacrificed to idols? ¹¹So this weak brother or sister, for whom Christ died, is destroyed by your knowledge. ¹²When you sin against them in this way and wound their weak conscience, you sin against Christ. ¹³Therefore, if what I eat causes my brother or sister to fall into sin, I will never eat meat again, so that I will not cause them to fall.

Paul's Rights as an Apostle

9 Am I not free? Am I not an apostle? Have I not seen Jesus our Lord? Are you not the result of my work in the Lord? ²Even though I may not be an apostle to others, surely I am to you! For you are the seal of my apostleship in the Lord.

³This is my defense to those who sit in judgment on me. ⁴Don't we have the right to food and drink? ⁵Don't we have the right to take a believing wife along with us, as do the other apostles and the Lord's brothers and Cephas[d]? ⁶Or is it only I and Barnabas who lack the right to not work for a living?

⁷Who serves as a soldier at his own expense? Who plants a vineyard and does not eat its grapes? Who tends a flock and does not drink the milk? ⁸Do I say this merely on human authority? Doesn't the Law say the same thing? ⁹For it is written in the Law of Moses: "Do not muzzle an ox while it is treading out the grain."[e] Is it about oxen that God is concerned?

---

[a] 36 Or if she is getting beyond the usual age for marriage   [b] 36-38 Or ³⁶If anyone thinks he is not treating his daughter properly, and if she is getting along in years (or if her passions are too strong), and he feels she ought to marry, he should do as he wants. He is not sinning. He should let her get married. ³⁷But the man who has settled the matter in his own mind, who is under no compulsion but has control over his own will, and who has made up his mind to keep the virgin unmarried—this man also does the right thing. ³⁸So then, he who gives his virgin in marriage does right, but he who does not give her in marriage does better.   [c] 2,3 An early manuscript and another ancient witness think they have knowledge do not yet know as they ought to know. ³But whoever loves truly knows.   [d] 5 That is, Peter   [e] 9 Deut. 25:4

How different is a Christian supposed to be? Should you carry a big Bible with your books? Or preach in the street near your school? If you want to be persecuted, maybe. But if you're serious about sharing Christ, you'd do a lot better trying to fit in. That's what Paul says here. Instead of emphasizing his differences from the people he was with, Paul made a real effort to fit in with them. Of course, Paul didn't take part in any of their sins, but he knew if he was accepted, they would be much more likely to listen to him. So go out and get involved. And don't be afraid to make friends with those who aren't Christians.

{1 Corinthians 9:19–23}

》》INSTANT ACCESS

share in what is offered on the altar? 14 In the same way, the Lord has commanded that those who preach the gospel should receive their living from the gospel.

15 But I have not used any of these rights. And I am not writing this in the hope that you will do such things for me, for I would rather die than allow anyone to deprive me of this boast. 16 For when I preach the gospel, I cannot boast, since I am compelled to preach. Woe to me if I do not preach the gospel! 17 If I preach voluntarily, I have a reward; if not voluntarily, I am simply discharging the trust committed to me. 18 What then is my reward? Just this: that in preaching the gospel I may offer it free of charge, and so not make full use of my rights as a preacher of the gospel.

Paul's Use of His Freedom

19 Though I am free and belong to no one, I have made myself a slave to everyone, to win as many as possible. 20 To the Jews I became like a Jew, to win the Jews. To those under the law I became like one under the law (though I myself am not under the law), so as to win those under the law. 21 To those not having the law I became like one not having the law (though I am not free from God's law but am under Christ's law), so as to win those not having the law. 22 To the weak I became weak, to win the weak. I have become all things to all people so that by all possible means I might save some. 23 I do all this for the sake of the gospel, that I may share in its blessings.

The Need for Self-Discipline

24 Do you not know that in a race all the runners run, but only one gets the prize? Run in such a way as to get the prize. 25 Everyone who competes in the games goes into strict training. They do it to get a crown that will not last, but we do it to get a crown that will last forever. 26 Therefore I do not run like someone running aimlessly; I do not fight like a boxer beating the air. 27 No, I strike a blow to my body and make it my slave so that after I have preached to others, I myself will not be disqualified for the prize.

10 Surely he says this for us, doesn't he? Yes, this was written for us, because whoever plows and threshes should be able to do so in the hope of sharing in the harvest. 11 If we have sown spiritual seed among you, is it too much if we reap a material harvest from you? 12 If others have this right of support from you, shouldn't we have it all the more?

But we did not use this right. On the contrary, we put up with anything rather than hinder the gospel of Christ.

13 Don't you know that those who serve in the temple get their food from the temple, and that those who serve at the altar

Warnings From Israel's History

10 For I do not want you to be ignorant of the fact, brothers and sisters, that our ancestors were all under the cloud and that they all passed through the sea. [2] They were all baptized into Moses in the cloud and in the sea. [3] They all ate the same spiritual food [4] and drank the same spiritual drink; for they drank from the spiritual rock that accompanied them, and that rock was Christ. [5] Nevertheless, God was not pleased with most of them; their bodies were scattered in the wilderness.

[6] Now these things occurred as examples to keep us from setting our hearts on evil things as they did. [7] Do not be idolaters, as some of them were; as it is written: "The people sat down to eat and drink and got up to indulge in revelry."[a] [8] We should not commit sexual immorality, as some of them did—and in one day twenty-three thousand of them died. [9] We should not test Christ,[b] as some of them did—and were killed by snakes. [10] And do not grumble, as some of them did—and were killed by the destroying angel.

[11] These things happened to them as examples and were written down as warnings for us, on whom the culmination of the ages has come. [12] So, if you think you are standing firm, be careful that you don't fall! [13] No temptation[c] has overtaken you except what is common to mankind. And God is faithful; he will not let you be tempted[c] beyond what you can bear. But when you are tempted,[c] he will also provide a way out so that you can endure it.

Idol Feasts and the Lord's Supper

[14] Therefore, my dear friends, flee from idolatry. [15] I speak to sensible people; judge for yourselves what I say. [16] Is not the cup of thanksgiving for which we give thanks a participation in the blood of Christ? And is not the bread that we break a participation in the body of Christ? [17] Because there is one loaf, we, who are many, are one body, for we all share the one loaf.

[18] Consider the people of Israel: Do not

Would you like a simple way to overcome temptation? One that always works? It's laid out right here in this verse. With every temptation, God provides a way out. Now think about those words: "a way out." Let's say that some friends are gossiping about a person you know, and you have something juicy to add. What a temptation. So you get up and leave! Or some guys are looking at a trashy magazine. You just turn around and leave. The best way out of temptation is to get out of situations where you feel tempted. And stay out!

» INSTANT ACCESS

{1 Corinthians 10:13}

those who eat the sacrifices participate in the altar? [19] Do I mean then that food sacrificed to an idol is anything, or that an idol is anything? [20] No, but the sacrifices of pagans are offered to demons, not to God, and I do not want you to be participants with demons. [21] You cannot drink the cup of the Lord and the cup of demons too; you cannot have a part in both the Lord's table and the table of demons. [22] Are we trying to arouse the Lord's jealousy? Are we stronger than he?

The Believer's Freedom

[23] "I have the right to do anything," you say—but not everything is beneficial. "I have the right to do anything"—but not everything is constructive. [24] No one

---

[a] 7 Exodus 32:6   [b] 9 Some manuscripts *test the Lord testing* and *tested*.   [c] 13 The Greek for *temptation* and *tempted* can also mean *testing* and *tested*.

should seek their own good, but the good of others.

25 Eat anything sold in the meat market without raising questions of conscience, 26 for, "The earth is the Lord's, and everything in it."[a]

27 If an unbeliever invites you to a meal and you want to go, eat whatever is put before you without raising questions of conscience. 28 But if someone says to you, "This has been offered in sacrifice," then do not eat it, both for the sake of the one who told you and for the sake of conscience. 29 I am referring to the other person's conscience, not yours. For why is my freedom being judged by another's conscience? 30 If I take part in the meal with thankfulness, why am I denounced because of something I thank God for?

31 So whether you eat or drink or whatever you do, do it all for the glory of God. 32 Do not cause anyone to stumble, whether Jews, Greeks or the church of God— 33 even as I try to please everyone in every way. For I am not seeking my own good but the good of many, so that they may be saved. 1 Follow my example, as I follow the example of Christ.

On Covering the Head in Worship

2 I praise you for remembering me in everything and for holding to the traditions just as I passed them on to you. 3 But I want you to realize that the head of every man is Christ, and the head of the woman is man,[b] and the head of Christ is God. 4 Every man who prays or prophesies with his head covered dishonors his head. 5 But every woman who prays or prophesies with her head uncovered dishonors her head—it is the same as having her head shaved. 6 For if a woman does not cover her head, she might as well have her hair cut off; but if it is a disgrace for a woman to have her hair cut off or her head shaved, then she should cover her head.

7 A man ought not to cover his head,[c] since he is the image and glory of God; but woman is the glory of man. 8 For man did not come from woman, but woman from man; 9 neither was man created for woman, but woman for man. 10 It is for this reason that a woman ought to have authority over her own[d] head, because of the angels. 11 Nevertheless, in the Lord woman is not independent of man, nor is man independent of woman. 12 For as woman came from man, so also man is born of woman. But everything comes from God.

13 Judge for yourselves: Is it proper for a woman to pray to God with her head uncovered? 14 Does not the very nature of things teach you that if a man has long hair, it is a disgrace to him, 15 but that if a

---

[a] 26 Psalm 24:1   [b] 3 Or of the wife is her husband   [c] 4-7 Or 4Every man who prays or prophesies with long hair dishonors his head. 5But every woman who prays or prophesies with no covering of hair dishonors her head—she is just like one of the "shorn women." 6If a woman has no covering, let her be for now with short hair; but since it is a disgrace for a woman to have her hair shorn or shaved, she should grow it again. 7A man ought not to have long hair   [d] 10 Or have a sign of authority on her

PANORAMA

Problems.

When the church at Corinth had problems, Paul helped. He gave them a lot of practical answers.

{1 CORINTHIANS}

woman has long hair, it is her glory? For long hair is given to her as a covering. 16 If anyone wants to be contentious about this, we have no other practice—nor do the churches of God.

Correcting an Abuse of the Lord's Supper

17 In the following directives I have no praise for you, for your meetings do more harm than good. 18 In the first place, I hear that when you come together as a church, there are divisions among you, and to some extent I believe it. 19 No doubt there have to be differences among you to show which of you have God's approval. 20 So then, when you come together, it is not the Lord's Supper you eat, 21 for when you are eating, some of you go ahead with your own private suppers. As a result, one person remains hungry and another gets drunk. 22 Don't you have homes to eat and drink in? Or do you despise the church of God by humiliating those who have nothing? What shall I say to you? Shall I praise you? Certainly not in this matter!

23 For I received from the Lord what I also passed on to you: The Lord Jesus, on the night he was betrayed, took bread, 24 and when he had given thanks, he broke it and said, "This is my body, which is for you; do this in remembrance of me." 25 In the same way, after supper he took the cup, saying, "This cup is the new covenant in my blood; do this, whenever you drink it, in remembrance of me." 26 For whenever you eat this bread and drink this cup, you proclaim the Lord's death until he comes.

27 So then, whoever eats the bread or drinks the cup of the Lord in an unworthy manner will be guilty of sinning against the body and blood of the Lord. 28 Everyone ought to examine themselves before they eat of the bread and drink from the cup. 29 For those who eat and drink without discerning the body of Christ eat and drink judgment on themselves. 30 That is why many among you are weak and sick, and a number of you have fallen asleep. 31 But if we were more discerning with regard to ourselves, we would not come under such judgment. 32 Nevertheless, when we are judged in this way by the Lord, we are being disciplined so that we will not be finally condemned with the world.

33 So then, my brothers and sisters, when you gather to eat, you should all eat together. 34 Anyone who is hungry should eat something at home, so that when you meet together it may not result in judgment.

And when I come I will give further directions.

Concerning Spiritual Gifts

12 Now about the gifts of the Spirit, brothers and sisters, I do not want you to be uninformed. 2 You know that when you were pagans, somehow or other you were influenced and led astray to mute idols. 3 Therefore I want you to know that no one who is speaking by the Spirit of God says, "Jesus be cursed," and no one can say, "Jesus is Lord," except by the Holy Spirit.

4 There are different kinds of gifts, but the same Spirit distributes them. 5 There are different kinds of service, but the same Lord. 6 There are different kinds of working, but in all of them and in everyone it is the same God at work.

7 Now to each one the manifestation of the Spirit is given for the common good. 8 To one there is given through the Spirit a message of wisdom, to another a message of knowledge by means of the same Spirit, 9 to another faith by the same Spirit, to another gifts of healing by that one Spirit, 10 to another miraculous powers, to another prophecy, to another distinguishing between spirits, to another speaking in different kinds of tongues,[a] and to still another the interpretation of tongues.[a] 11 All these are the work of one and the same Spirit, and he distributes them to each one, just as he determines.

Unity and Diversity in the Body

12 Just as a body, though one, has many parts, but all its many parts form one body, so it is with Christ. 13 For we were all baptized by[b] one Spirit so as to form one body—whether Jews or Gentiles, slave or free—and we were all given the one Spirit

---

a 10 Or languages; also in verse 28   b 13 Or with; or in

to drink. ¹⁴Even so the body is not made up of one part but of many.

¹⁵Now if the foot should say, "Because I am not a hand, I do not belong to the body," it would not for that reason stop being part of the body. ¹⁶And if the ear should say, "Because I am not an eye, I do not belong to the body," it would not for that reason stop being part of the body. ¹⁷If the whole body were an eye, where would the sense of hearing be? If the whole body were an ear, where would the sense of smell be? ¹⁸But in fact God has placed the parts in the body, every one of them, just as he wanted them to be. ¹⁹If they were all one part, where would the body be? ²⁰As it is, there are many parts, but one body.

²¹The eye cannot say to the hand, "I don't need you!" And the head cannot say to the feet, "I don't need you!" ²²On the contrary, those parts of the body that seem to be weaker are indispensable, ²³and the parts that we think are less honorable we treat with special honor. And the parts that are unpresentable are treated with special modesty, ²⁴while our presentable parts need no special treatment. But God has put the body together, giving greater honor to the parts that lacked it, ²⁵so that there should be no division in the body, but that its parts should have equal concern for each other. ²⁶If one part suffers, every part suffers with it; if one part is honored, every part rejoices with it.

²⁷Now you are the body of Christ, and each one of you is a part of it. ²⁸And God has placed in the church first of all apostles, second prophets, third teachers, then miracles, then gifts of healing,

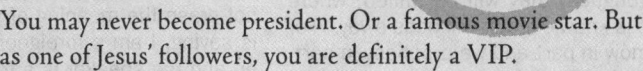

TO THE POINT

You Count

You may never become president. Or a famous movie star. But as one of Jesus' followers, you are definitely a VIP.

The church is like a body, and each member is like a body part (1 Corinthians 12). And God has given you a "spiritual gift," a special way the Holy Spirit will work through you to help others grow in the Lord. How do you find your gift and use it?

◆ Remember there are many different kinds of gifts (1 Corinthians 12:4–6).

◆ Remember all gifts are intended to help others (1 Corinthians 12:7).

Get involved with other Christian young people and look for ways to help. God will use you, and as he does, you'll discover what your spiritual gift is.

of helping, of guidance, and of different kinds of tongues. ²⁹Are all apostles? Are all prophets? Are all teachers? Do all work miracles? ³⁰Do all have gifts of healing? Do all speak in tongues*ᵃ*? Do all interpret? ³¹Now eagerly desire the greater gifts.

Love Is Indispensable

And yet I will show you the most excellent way.

13 If I speak in the tongues*ᵇ* of men or of angels, but do not have love, I am only a resounding gong or a clanging cymbal. ²If I have the gift of prophecy and can fathom all mysteries and all knowledge, and if I have a faith that can move mountains, but do not have love, I am nothing. ³If I give all I possess to the poor and give over my body to hardship that I may boast,*ᶜ* but do not have love, I gain nothing.

⁴Love is patient, love is kind. It does not envy, it does not boast, it is not proud. ⁵It does not dishonor others, it is not self-seeking, it is not easily angered, it keeps no record of wrongs. ⁶Love does not delight in evil but rejoices with the truth. ⁷It always protects, always trusts, always hopes, always perseveres.

⁸Love never fails. But where there are prophecies, they will cease; where there are tongues, they will be stilled; where there is knowledge, it will pass away. ⁹For we know in part and we prophesy in part, ¹⁰but when completeness comes, what is in part disappears. ¹¹When I was a child, I talked like a child, I thought like a child, I reasoned like a child. When I became a man, I put the ways of childhood behind me. ¹²For now we see only a reflection as in a mirror; then we shall see face to face. Now I know in part; then I shall know fully, even as I am fully known.

¹³And now these three remain: faith, hope and love. But the greatest of these is love.

Intelligibility in Worship

14 Follow the way of love and eagerly desire gifts of the Spirit, especially prophecy. ²For anyone who speaks in a tongue*ᵈ* does not speak to people but to God. Indeed, no one understands them; they utter mysteries by the Spirit. ³But the one who prophesies speaks to people for their strengthening, encouraging and comfort. ⁴Anyone who speaks in a tongue edifies themselves, but the one who prophesies edifies the church. ⁵I would like every one of you to speak in tongues,*ᵉ* but I would rather have you prophesy. The one who prophesies is greater than the one who speaks in tongues,*ᵉ* unless someone interprets, so that the church may be edified.

⁶Now, brothers and sisters, if I come to you and speak in tongues, what good will I be to you, unless I bring you some revelation or knowledge or prophecy or word of instruction? ⁷Even in the case of lifeless things that make sounds, such as the pipe or harp, how will anyone know what tune is being played unless there is a distinction in the notes? ⁸Again, if the trumpet does not sound a clear call, who will get ready for battle? ⁹So it is with you. Unless you speak intelligible words with your tongue, how will anyone know what you are saying? You will just be speaking into the air. ¹⁰Undoubtedly there are all sorts of languages in the world, yet none of them is without meaning. ¹¹If then I do not grasp the meaning of what someone is saying, I am a foreigner to the speaker, and the speaker is a foreigner to me. ¹²So it is with you. Since you are eager for gifts of the Spirit, try to excel in those that build up the church.

¹³For this reason the one who speaks in a tongue should pray that they may interpret what they say. ¹⁴For if I pray in a tongue, my spirit prays, but my mind is unfruitful. ¹⁵So what shall I do? I will pray with my spirit, but I will also pray with my understanding; I will sing with my spirit, but I will also sing with my understanding. ¹⁶Otherwise when you are praising God in the Spirit, how can someone else, who is now put in the position of an inquirer,*ᶠ* say "Amen" to your thanksgiving, since they do not know what you are saying?

ᵃ 30 Or other languages   *ᵇ 1 Or languages*   *ᶜ 3 Some manuscripts body to the flames*   *ᵈ 2 Or in another language; also in verses 4, 13, 14, 19, 26 and 27*   *ᵉ 5 Or in other languages; also in verses 6, 18, 22, 23 and 39*   *ᶠ 16 The Greek word for inquirer is a technical term for someone not fully initiated into a religion; also in verses 23 and 24.*

My parents and I have a big argument almost every day about my messy room. I like my room the way it is. Can't I have a little space of my own? Can't I have control over anything in my life?   >> Savannah

Dear Jordan

Dear Savannah,

This is a classic problem. I can see your point about wanting to have some space to call your own. But I also understand that damp bath towels thrown in heaps of clothes can grow mold and mildew. Library books get lost and the fines get expensive. Food left on plates attracts bugs and turns fuzzy like a science project.

Being a teenager is hard because you're not really ready to put aside all of your childish ways, yet you're not happy to be treated like a child (1 Corinthians 13). Perhaps you can do some negotiating with your parents so you both can have your way at least part of the time.

Are you allowed to put up posters? Can you select a new color for your walls? Can you choose how you want your furniture arranged? How often and how much do your parents want your room cleaned up? Sit down and talk to your parents. Be respectful. It will get you further than losing your temper. Remember to live up to your part of the agreement if you can reach one. This will help if you want to get changes in other areas in the future.

Jordan

[17] You are giving thanks well enough, but no one else is edified.

[18] I thank God that I speak in tongues more than all of you. [19] But in the church I would rather speak five intelligible words to instruct others than ten thousand words in a tongue.

[20] Brothers and sisters, stop thinking like children. In regard to evil be infants, but in your thinking be adults. [21] In the Law it is written:

> "With other tongues
>   and through the lips of foreigners
> I will speak to this people,
>   but even then they will not listen
>   to me,
>   says the Lord."[a]

[22] Tongues, then, are a sign, not for believers but for unbelievers; prophecy, however, is not for unbelievers but for believers. [23] So if the whole church comes together and everyone speaks in tongues, and inquirers or unbelievers come in, will they not say that you are out of your mind? [24] But if an unbeliever or an inquirer comes in while everyone is prophesying, they are convicted of sin and are brought under judgment by all, [25] as the secrets of their hearts are laid bare. So they will fall down and worship God, exclaiming, "God is really among you!"

Good Order in Worship

[26] What then shall we say, brothers and sisters? When you come together, each of you has a hymn, or a word of instruction, a revelation, a tongue or an interpretation. Everything must be done so that the church may be built up. [27] If anyone speaks in a tongue, two—or at the most three—should speak, one at a time, and someone must interpret. [28] If there is no interpreter, the speaker should keep quiet in the church and speak to himself and to God.

[29] Two or three prophets should speak, and the others should weigh carefully what is said. [30] And if a revelation comes to someone who is sitting down, the first speaker should stop. [31] For you can all prophesy in turn so that everyone may be instructed and encouraged. [32] The spirits of prophets are subject to the control of prophets. [33] For God is not a God of disorder but of peace—as in all the congregations of the Lord's people.

[34] Women[b] should remain silent in the churches. They are not allowed to speak, but must be in submission, as the law says. [35] If they want to inquire about something, they should ask their own husbands at home; for it is disgraceful for a woman to speak in the church.[c]

[36] Or did the word of God originate with you? Or are you the only people it has reached? [37] If anyone thinks they are a prophet or otherwise gifted by the Spirit, let them acknowledge that what I am writing to you is the Lord's command. [38] But if anyone ignores this, they will themselves be ignored.[d]

[39] Therefore, my brothers and sisters, be eager to prophesy, and do not forbid speaking in tongues. [40] But everything should be done in a fitting and orderly way.

The Resurrection of Christ

15 Now, brothers and sisters, I want to remind you of the gospel I preached to you, which you received and on which you have taken your stand. [2] By this gospel you are saved, if you hold firmly to the word I preached to you. Otherwise, you have believed in vain.

[3] For what I received I passed on to you as of first importance[e]: that Christ died for our sins according to the Scriptures, [4] that he was buried, that he was raised on the third day according to the Scriptures, [5] and that he appeared to Cephas,[f] and then to the Twelve. [6] After that, he appeared to more than five hundred of the brothers and sisters at the same time, most of whom are still living, though some have fallen asleep. [7] Then he appeared to James, then to all the apostles, [8] and last of all he appeared to me also, as to one abnormally born.

[9] For I am the least of the apostles and do not even deserve to be called an apostle, because I persecuted the church of God. [10] But by the grace of God I am what

---

a 21 Isaiah 28:11,12   *b* 33,34 Or *peace. As in all the congregations of the Lord's people,* 34*women*   *c* 34,35 In a few manuscripts these verses come after verse 40.   *d* 38 Some manuscripts *But anyone who is ignorant of this will be ignorant*   *e* 3 Or *you at the first*   *f* 5 That is, Peter

Death isn't scary for Christians. Yes, it hurts if a loved one dies. But for you, personally, what lies beyond can be exciting. Like this new body you'll have. First John 3:2 says that when Jesus comes you'll be like him. After his resurrection Jesus could pass through walls and enter a locked room (John 20:19). There's no telling just what your resurrection life will be like. But from hints in the Bible, you can be sure it's going to be great! Yes, God wants you to enjoy a long and active life here. But he also wants to be sure you don't fear dying. You have good years ahead of you. And after that, a great eternity.

{1 Corinthians 15:35–49}

INSTANT ACCESS

has been raised. [14] And if Christ has not been raised, our preaching is useless and so is your faith. [15] More than that, we are then found to be false witnesses about God, for we have testified about God that he raised Christ from the dead. But he did not raise him if in fact the dead are not raised. [16] For if the dead are not raised, then Christ has not been raised either. [17] And if Christ has not been raised, your faith is futile; you are still in your sins. [18] Then those also who have fallen asleep in Christ are lost. [19] If only for this life we have hope in Christ, we are of all people most to be pitied.

[20] But Christ has indeed been raised from the dead, the firstfruits of those who have fallen asleep. [21] For since death came through a man, the resurrection of the dead comes also through a man. [22] For as in Adam all die, so in Christ all will be made alive. [23] But each in turn: Christ, the firstfruits; then, when he comes, those who belong to him. [24] Then the end will come, when he hands over the kingdom to God the Father after he has destroyed all dominion, authority and power. [25] For he must reign until he has put all his enemies under his feet. [26] The last enemy to be destroyed is death. [27] For he "has put everything under his feet."[a] Now when it says that "everything" has been put under him, it is clear that this does not include God himself, who put everything under Christ. [28] When he has done this, then the Son himself will be made subject to him who put everything under him, so that God may be all in all.

[29] Now if there is no resurrection, what will those do who are baptized for the dead? If the dead are not raised at all, why are people baptized for them? [30] And as for us, why do we endanger ourselves every hour? [31] I face death every day— yes, just as surely as I boast about you in Christ Jesus our Lord. [32] If I fought wild beasts in Ephesus with no more than human hopes, what have I gained? If the dead are not raised,

"Let us eat and drink,
 for tomorrow we die."[b]

I am, and his grace to me was not without effect. No, I worked harder than all of them—yet not I, but the grace of God that was with me. [11] Whether, then, it is I or they, this is what we preach, and this is what you believed.

The Resurrection of the Dead

[12] But if it is preached that Christ has been raised from the dead, how can some of you say that there is no resurrection of the dead? [13] If there is no resurrection of the dead, then not even Christ

---

a 27 Psalm 8:6   b 32 Isaiah 22:13

[33] Do not be misled: "Bad company corrupts good character."[a] [34] Come back to your senses as you ought, and stop sinning; for there are some who are ignorant of God—I say this to your shame.

The Resurrection Body

[35] But someone will ask, "How are the dead raised? With what kind of body will they come?" [36] How foolish! What you sow does not come to life unless it dies. [37] When you sow, you do not plant the body that will be, but just a seed, perhaps of wheat or of something else. [38] But God gives it a body as he has determined, and to each kind of seed he gives its own body. [39] Not all flesh is the same: People have one kind of flesh, animals have another, birds another and fish another. [40] There are also heavenly bodies and there are earthly bodies; but the splendor of the heavenly bodies is one kind, and the splendor of the earthly bodies is another. [41] The sun has one kind of splendor, the moon another and the stars another; and star differs from star in splendor.

[42] So will it be with the resurrection of the dead. The body that is sown is perishable, it is raised imperishable; [43] it is sown in dishonor, it is raised in glory; it is sown in weakness, it is raised in power; [44] it is sown a natural body, it is raised a spiritual body.

If there is a natural body, there is also a spiritual body. [45] So it is written: "The first man Adam became a living being"[b]; the last Adam, a life-giving spirit. [46] The spiritual did not come first, but the natural, and after that the spiritual. [47] The first man was of the dust of the earth; the second man is of heaven. [48] As was the earthly man, so are those who are of the earth; and as is the heavenly man, so also are those who are of heaven. [49] And just as we have borne the image of the earthly man, so shall we[c] bear the image of the heavenly man.

[50] I declare to you, brothers and sisters, that flesh and blood cannot inherit the kingdom of God, nor does the perishable inherit the imperishable. [51] Listen, I tell you a mystery: We will not all sleep, but we will all be changed— [52] in a flash, in the twinkling of an eye, at the last trumpet. For the trumpet will sound, the dead will be raised imperishable, and we will be changed. [53] For the perishable must clothe itself with the imperishable, and the mortal with immortality. [54] When the perishable has been clothed with the imperishable, and the mortal with immortality, then the saying that is written will come true: "Death has been swallowed up in victory."[d]

[55] "Where, O death, is your victory?
Where, O death, is your sting?"[e]

[56] The sting of death is sin, and the power of sin is the law. [57] But thanks be to God! He gives us the victory through our Lord Jesus Christ.

[58] Therefore, my dear brothers and sisters, stand firm. Let nothing move you. Always give yourselves fully to the work of the Lord, because you know that your labor in the Lord is not in vain.

The Collection for the Lord's People

16 Now about the collection for the Lord's people: Do what I told the Galatian churches to do. [2] On the first day of every week, each one of you should set aside a sum of money in keeping with your income, saving it up, so that when I come no collections will have to be made. [3] Then, when I arrive, I will give letters of introduction to the men you approve and send them with your gift to Jerusalem. [4] If it seems advisable for me to go also, they will accompany me.

> *We will not all sleep, but we will all be changed . . . For the trumpet will sound, [and] the dead will be raised.*
>
> **1 Corinthians 15:51–52**

---

[a] 33 From the Greek poet Menander   [b] 45 Gen. 2:7   [c] 49 Some early manuscripts so *let us*   [d] 54 Isaiah 25:8   [e] 55 Hosea 13:14

You're tired of being a 98-pound weakling? Then you should eat healthy foods, lift weights and exercise. You'll do it because you don't want to stay a weakling all your life. How do you rate yourself spiritually? Are you strong? Or are you a spiritual weakling? You can become strong spiritually the same way you become strong physically: by exercising your faith! How? Be on your guard (against evil). Stand firm (in your convictions). Be a person of courage (speak out for what's right). Be strong (don't quit under pressure). Exercise your faith in these ways, and watch yourself grow!

{1 Corinthians 16:13}

INSTANT ACCESS

permits. ⁸But I will stay on at Ephesus until Pentecost, ⁹because a great door for effective work has opened to me, and there are many who oppose me.

¹⁰When Timothy comes, see to it that he has nothing to fear while he is with you, for he is carrying on the work of the Lord, just as I am. ¹¹No one, then, should treat him with contempt. Send him on his way in peace so that he may return to me. I am expecting him along with the brothers.

¹²Now about our brother Apollos: I strongly urged him to go to you with the brothers. He was quite unwilling to go now, but he will go when he has the opportunity.

¹³Be on your guard; stand firm in the faith; be courageous; be strong. ¹⁴Do everything in love.

¹⁵You know that the household of Stephanas were the first converts in Achaia, and they have devoted themselves to the service of the Lord's people. I urge you, brothers and sisters, ¹⁶to submit to such people and to everyone who joins in the work and labors at it. ¹⁷I was glad when Stephanas, Fortunatus and Achaicus arrived, because they have supplied what was lacking from you. ¹⁸For they refreshed my spirit and yours also. Such men deserve recognition.

Final Greetings

¹⁹The churches in the province of Asia send you greetings. Aquila and Priscilla*a* greet you warmly in the Lord, and so does the church that meets at their house. ²⁰All the brothers and sisters here send you greetings. Greet one another with a holy kiss.

²¹I, Paul, write this greeting in my own hand.

²²If anyone does not love the Lord, let that person be cursed! Come, Lord*b*!

²³The grace of the Lord Jesus be with you.

²⁴My love to all of you in Christ Jesus. Amen.*c*

Personal Requests

⁵After I go through Macedonia, I will come to you—for I will be going through Macedonia. ⁶Perhaps I will stay with you for a while, or even spend the winter, so that you can help me on my journey, wherever I go. ⁷For I do not want to see you now and make only a passing visit; I hope to spend some time with you, if the Lord

---

a 19 Greek *Prisca*, a variant of *Priscilla*   *b* 22 The Greek for *Come, Lord* reproduces an Aramaic expression (*Marana tha*) used by early Christians.   *c* 24 Some manuscripts do not have *Amen*.

2 CORINTHIANS

preview

Paul writes this letter after hearing that most in Corinth followed the instructions in his first letter.

In this letter Paul explains how he ministers to others — and how we can too.

Love Them?

Why should you? Why should you love those "friends" who are now saying they don't like you? They're trying to turn others against you? What can you do? Tell them off? Start talking about them like they're talking about you? What can a person do, anyway?

Most people in Corinth followed the advice Paul gave in his first letter. But some kept talking against Paul. Instead of getting mad, Paul wrote this letter. In it he shares how he feels and tells why he acts as he does. Paul loves the Corinthians. If you care about others, people who criticize or lie about you won't get very far.

>> **HAVE TROUBLES? THEN YOU CAN HELP**
Explanation in 2 Corinthians 1:3–7

>> **CAN'T BE MORE GENEROUS THAN GOD!**
Reminder encourages giving. See 2 Corinthians 9:6–15

>> **SOMETIMES BEING GOD'S PERSON IS HARD**
Example found in 2 Corinthians 11:16–29

>> **NO WEAK JESUS THESE DAYS**
"Watch out," warns Paul. Check out 2 Corinthians 13:1–4

As Paul writes about 58 A.D. from Macedonia, Judean terrorists called Sicarii (knifemen) carry daggers to assassinate any Jews favorable to Rome.

1 Paul, an apostle of Christ Jesus by the will of God, and Timothy our brother,

To the church of God in Corinth, together with all his holy people throughout Achaia:

[2] Grace and peace to you from God our Father and the Lord Jesus Christ.

Praise to the God of All Comfort

[3] Praise be to the God and Father of our Lord Jesus Christ, the Father of compassion and the God of all comfort, [4] who comforts us in all our troubles, so that we can comfort those in any trouble with the comfort we ourselves receive from God. [5] For just as we share abundantly in the sufferings of Christ, so also our comfort abounds through Christ. [6] If we are distressed, it is for your comfort and salvation; if we are comforted, it is for your comfort, which produces in you patient endurance of the same sufferings we suffer. [7] And our hope for you is firm, because we know that just as you share in our sufferings, so also you share in our comfort.

[8] We do not want you to be uninformed, brothers and sisters,[a] about the troubles we experienced in the province of Asia. We were under great pressure, far beyond our ability to endure, so that we despaired of life itself. [9] Indeed, we felt we had received the sentence of death. But this happened that we might not rely on ourselves but on God, who raises the dead. [10] He has delivered us from such a deadly peril, and he will deliver us again. On him we have set our hope that he will continue to deliver us, [11] as you help us by your prayers. Then many will give thanks on our behalf for the gracious favor granted us in answer to the prayers of many.

Paul's Change of Plans

[12] Now this is our boast: Our conscience testifies that we have conducted ourselves in the world, and especially in our relations with you, with integrity[b] and godly sincerity. We have done so, relying not on worldly wisdom but on God's grace. [13] For we do not write you anything you cannot read or understand. And I hope that, [14] as you have understood us in part, you will come to understand fully that you can boast of us just as we will boast of you in the day of the Lord Jesus.

[15] Because I was confident of this, I wanted to visit you first so that you might benefit twice. [16] I wanted to visit you on my way to Macedonia and to come back to you from Macedonia, and then to have you send me on my way to Judea. [17] Was I fickle when I intended to do this? Or do I make my plans in a worldly manner so that in the same breath I say both "Yes, yes" and "No, no"?

[18] But as surely as God is faithful, our message to you is not "Yes" and "No." [19] For the Son of God, Jesus Christ, who was preached among you by us—by me and Silas[c] and Timothy—was not "Yes" and "No," but in him it has always been "Yes." [20] For no matter how many promises God has made, they are "Yes" in Christ. And so through him the "Amen" is spoken by us to the glory of God. [21] Now it is God who makes both us and you stand firm in Christ. He anointed us, [22] set his seal of ownership on us, and put his Spirit in our hearts as a deposit, guaranteeing what is to come.

[23] I call God as my witness—and I stake my life on it—that it was in order to spare you that I did not return to Corinth. [24] Not that we lord it over your faith, but we work with you for your joy, because it is by faith you stand firm. **2** [1] So I made up my mind that I would not make another painful visit to you. [2] For if I grieve you, who is left to make me glad but you whom I have grieved? [3] I wrote as I did, so that when I came I would not be distressed by those who should have made me rejoice. I had confidence in all of you, that you would all share my joy. [4] For I wrote you out of great distress and anguish of heart and with many tears, not to grieve you but to let you know the depth of my love for you.

---

[a] 8 The Greek word for *brothers and sisters* (*adelphoi*) refers here to believers, both men and women, as part of God's family; also in 8:1; 13:11.   [b] 12 Many manuscripts *holiness*   [c] 19 Greek *Silvanus*, a variant of *Silas*

Forgiveness for the Offender

5 If anyone has caused grief, he has not so much grieved me as he has grieved all of you to some extent—not to put it too severely. 6 The punishment inflicted on him by the majority is sufficient. 7 Now instead, you ought to forgive and comfort him, so that he will not be overwhelmed by excessive sorrow. 8 I urge you, therefore, to reaffirm your love for him. 9 Another reason I wrote you was to see if you would stand the test and be obedient in everything. 10 Anyone you forgive, I also forgive. And what I have forgiven—if there was anything to forgive—I have forgiven in the sight of Christ for your sake, 11 in order that Satan might not outwit us. For we are not unaware of his schemes.

Ministers of the New Covenant

12 Now when I went to Troas to preach the gospel of Christ and found that the Lord had opened a door for me, 13 I still had no peace of mind, because I did not find my brother Titus there. So I said goodbye to them and went on to Macedonia.

14 But thanks be to God, who always leads us as captives in Christ's triumphal procession and uses us to spread the aroma of the knowledge of him everywhere. 15 For we are to God the pleasing aroma of Christ among those who are being saved and those who are perishing. 16 To the one we are an aroma that brings death; to the other, an aroma that brings life. And who is equal to such a task? 17 Unlike so many, we do not peddle the word of God for profit. On the contrary, in Christ we speak before God with sincerity, as those sent from God.

3 Are we beginning to commend ourselves again? Or do we need, like some people, letters of recommendation to you or from you? 2 You yourselves are our letter, written on our hearts, known and read by everyone. 3 You show that you are a letter from Christ, the result of our ministry, written not with ink but with the Spirit of the living God, not on tablets of stone but on tablets of human hearts.

4 Such confidence we have through Christ before God. 5 Not that we are competent in ourselves to claim anything for ourselves, but our competence comes from God. 6 He has made us competent as ministers of a new covenant—not of the letter but of the Spirit; for the letter kills, but the Spirit gives life.

The Greater Glory of the New Covenant

7 Now if the ministry that brought death, which was engraved in letters on stone, came with glory, so that the Israelites could not look steadily at the face of Mo-

>> INSTANT ACCESS

Mike asks you to the movies and then says he can't go. Mom says she'll take you to the mall and then decides she has to go to Grandma's instead. Do you have a right to be angry and call them both liars? The apostle Paul was accused of going back on a promise to visit the Corinthian church. Paul explained that when he told them his plan to visit, he didn't do it lightly (2 Corinthians 1:17). He meant what he said. But at times things beyond people's control cause them to change their plans. Of course, if someone lets you down again and again, he or she probably does promise lightly. But as for others? Hey, give them a break.

{2 Corinthians 1:15–21}

ses because of its glory, transitory though it was, [8]will not the ministry of the Spirit be even more glorious? [9]If the ministry that brought condemnation was glorious, how much more glorious is the ministry that brings righteousness! [10]For what was glorious has no glory now in comparison with the surpassing glory. [11]And if what was transitory came with glory, how much greater is the glory of that which lasts!

[12]Therefore, since we have such a hope, we are very bold. [13]We are not like Moses, who would put a veil over his face to prevent the Israelites from seeing the end of what was passing away. [14]But their minds were made dull, for to this day the same veil remains when the old covenant is read. It has not been removed, because only in Christ is it taken away. [15]Even to this day when Moses is read, a veil covers their hearts. [16]But whenever anyone turns to the Lord, the veil is taken away. [17]Now the Lord is the Spirit, and where the Spirit of the Lord is, there is freedom. [18]And we all, who with unveiled faces contemplate[a] the Lord's glory, are being transformed into his image with ever-increasing glory, which comes from the Lord, who is the Spirit.

Where the Spirit of the Lord is, there is freedom.
2 Corinthians 3:17

Present Weakness and Resurrection Life

4 Therefore, since through God's mercy we have this ministry, we do not lose heart. [2]Rather, we have renounced secret and shameful ways; we do not use deception, nor do we distort the word of God. On the contrary, by setting forth the truth plainly we commend ourselves to everyone's conscience in the sight of God. [3]And even if our gospel is veiled, it is veiled to those who are perishing. [4]The god of this age has blinded the minds of unbelievers, so that they cannot see the light of the gospel that displays the glory of Christ, who is the image of God. [5]For what we preach is not ourselves, but Jesus Christ as Lord, and ourselves as your servants for Jesus' sake. [6]For God, who said, "Let light shine out of darkness,"[b] made his light shine in our hearts to give us the light of the knowledge of God's glory displayed in the face of Christ.

[7]But we have this treasure in jars of clay to show that this all-surpassing power is from God and not from us. [8]We are hard pressed on every side, but not crushed; perplexed, but not in despair; [9]persecuted, but not abandoned; struck down, but not destroyed. [10]We always carry around in our body the death of Jesus, so that the life of Jesus may also be revealed in our body. [11]For we who are alive are always being given over to death for Jesus' sake, so that his life may also be revealed in our mortal body. [12]So then, death is at work in us, but life is at work in you.

[13]It is written: "I believed; therefore I have spoken."[c] Since we have that same spirit of[d] faith, we also believe and therefore speak, [14]because we know that the one who raised the Lord Jesus from the dead will also raise us with Jesus and present us with you to himself. [15]All this is for your benefit, so that the grace that is reaching more and more people may cause thanksgiving to overflow to the glory of God.

[16]Therefore we do not lose heart. Though outwardly we are wasting away, yet inwardly we are being renewed day by day. [17]For our light and momentary troubles are achieving for us an eternal glory that far outweighs them all. [18]So we fix our eyes not on what is seen, but on what is unseen, since what is seen is temporary, but what is unseen is eternal.

Awaiting the New Body

5 For we know that if the earthly tent we live in is destroyed, we have a building from God, an eternal house in heaven,

---

[a] 18 Or *reflect*   [b] 6 Gen. 1:3   [c] 13 Psalm 116:10 (see Septuagint)   [d] 13 Or *Spirit-given*

not built by human hands. ²Meanwhile we groan, longing to be clothed instead with our heavenly dwelling, ³because when we are clothed, we will not be found naked. ⁴For while we are in this tent, we groan and are burdened, because we do not wish to be unclothed but to be clothed instead with our heavenly dwelling, so that what is mortal may be swallowed up by life. ⁵Now the one who has fashioned us for this very purpose is God, who has given us the Spirit as a deposit, guaranteeing what is to come.

⁶Therefore we are always confident and know that as long as we are at home in the body we are away from the Lord. ⁷For we live by faith, not by sight. ⁸We are confident, I say, and would prefer to be away from the body and at home with the Lord. ⁹So we make it our goal to please him, whether we are at home in the body or away from it. ¹⁰For we must all appear before the judgment seat of Christ, so that each of us may receive what is due us for the things done while in the body, whether good or bad.

The Ministry of Reconciliation

¹¹Since, then, we know what it is to fear the Lord, we try to persuade others. What we are is plain to God, and I hope it is also plain to your conscience. ¹²We are not trying to commend ourselves to you again, but are giving you an opportunity to take pride in us, so that you can answer those who take pride in what is seen rather than in what is in the heart. ¹³If we are "out of our mind," as some say, it is for God; if we are in our right mind, it is for you. ¹⁴For Christ's love compels us, because we are convinced that one died for all, and therefore all died. ¹⁵And he died for all, that those who live should no longer live for themselves but for him who died for them and was raised again.

¹⁶So from now on we regard no one from a worldly point of view. Though we once regarded Christ in this way, we do so no longer. ¹⁷Therefore, if anyone is in Christ, the new creation has come:ᵃ The old has gone, the new is here! ¹⁸All this

is from God, who reconciled us to himself through Christ and gave us the ministry of reconciliation: ¹⁹that God was reconciling the world to himself in Christ, not counting people's sins against them. And he has committed to us the message of reconciliation. ²⁰We are therefore Christ's ambassadors, as though God were making his appeal through us. We implore you on Christ's behalf: Be reconciled to God. ²¹God made him who had no sin to be sinᵇ for us, so that in him we might become the righteousness of God.

6 As God's co-workers we urge you not to receive God's grace in vain. ²For he says,

"In the time of my favor I heard you,
    and in the day of salvation I helped you."ᶜ

I tell you, now is the time of God's favor, now is the day of salvation.

Paul's Hardships

³We put no stumbling block in anyone's path, so that our ministry will not be discredited. ⁴Rather, as servants of God we commend ourselves in every way: in great endurance; in troubles, hardships and distresses; ⁵in beatings, imprisonments and riots; in hard work, sleepless nights and hunger; ⁶in purity, understanding, patience and kindness; in the Holy Spirit and in sincere love; ⁷in truthful speech and in the power of God; with weapons of righteousness in the right hand and in the left; ⁸through glory and dishonor, bad report and good report; genuine, yet regarded as impostors; ⁹known, yet regarded as unknown; dying, and yet we live on; beaten, and yet not killed; ¹⁰sorrowful, yet always rejoicing; poor, yet making many rich; having nothing, and yet possessing everything.

¹¹We have spoken freely to you, Corinthians, and opened wide our hearts to you. ¹²We are not withholding our affection from you, but you are withholding yours from us. ¹³As a fair exchange—I speak as to my children—open wide your hearts also.

ᵃ 17 Or Christ, that person is a new creation.   ᵇ 21 Or be a sin offering   ᶜ 2 Isaiah 49:8

> Can you give me some facts on how to live like
> a Christian and live like a person of faith? I've
> made some bad choices already and I don't
> know if I can get back like I used to be.
>
> **>> Olivia**

Dear Jordan

Dear Olivia,

You probably know more about how to live like a Christian than you realize, with things like being kind, respecting your parents, telling the truth, obeying God.

Sometimes when we make bad choices we continue on that path. But did you know that when you are in Christ you are a new creation? That's what 2 Corinthians 5:17–19 tells us.

We all sin. But if we ask for forgiveness, Jesus' sacrifice takes away our sin. Then we are made clean. And that means we can get a fresh start. We can make better choices today than we may have made yesterday. We don't have to continue down a wrong path forever because of a past bad choice. Things may feel a little rocky when we start on the right path. It's not always easy. But starting each day fresh and making good choices help us feel better about ourselves. And when we feel better about ourselves, we are encouraged in what we do. And then we can encourage others too.

Jordan

Warning Against Idolatry

¹⁴Do not be yoked together with unbelievers. For what do righteousness and wickedness have in common? Or what fellowship can light have with darkness? ¹⁵What harmony is there between Christ and Belial[a]? Or what does a believer have in common with an unbeliever? ¹⁶What agreement is there between the temple of God and idols? For we are the temple of the living God. As God has said:

"I will live with them
    and walk among them,
and I will be their God,
    and they will be my people."[b]

¹⁷Therefore,

"Come out from them
    and be separate,
                    says the Lord.
Touch no unclean thing,
    and I will receive you."[c]

¹⁸And,

"I will be a Father to you,
    and you will be my sons and
        daughters,
            says the Lord Almighty."[d]

7 Therefore, since we have these promises, dear friends, let us purify ourselves from everything that contaminates body and spirit, perfecting holiness out of reverence for God.

Paul's Joy Over the Church's Repentance

²Make room for us in your hearts. We have wronged no one, we have corrupted no one, we have exploited no one. ³I do not say this to condemn you; I have said before that you have such a place in our hearts that we would live or die with you. ⁴I have spoken to you with great frankness; I take great pride in you. I am greatly encouraged; in all our troubles my joy knows no bounds.

⁵For when we came into Macedonia, we had no rest, but we were harassed at every turn—conflicts on the outside, fears within. ⁶But God, who comforts the

downcast, comforted us by the coming of Titus, ⁷and not only by his coming but also by the comfort you had given him. He told us about your longing for me, your deep sorrow, your ardent concern for me, so that my joy was greater than ever.

⁸Even if I caused you sorrow by my letter, I do not regret it. Though I did regret it—I see that my letter hurt you, but only for a little while— ⁹yet now I am happy,

>> INSTANT ACCESS

Is it good or bad to be friends with non-Christians? Should a Christian date a non-Christian? Many just say, "Do not be yoked together with unbelievers." But what does that mean? Does it mean that you must not be friends with non-Christians? But how will they hear about Jesus if Christians don't befriend them? The best thing is to understand "yoked" as a partnership, a relationship involving commitment. Don't be partners with non-Christians because when it comes to values and commitments you have nothing in common. Marry someone who isn't a Christian? Definitely no. Date or hang around? You decide whether any commitment is involved.

{2 Corinthians 6:14–18}

a 15 Greek *Beliar*, a variant of *Belial*   b 16 Lev. 26:12; Jer. 32:38; Ezek. 37:27   c 17 Isaiah 52:11; Ezek. 20:34,41   d 18 2 Samuel 7:14; 7:8

not because you were made sorry, but because your sorrow led you to repentance. For you became sorrowful as God intended and so were not harmed in any way by us. ¹⁰Godly sorrow brings repentance that leads to salvation and leaves no regret, but worldly sorrow brings death. ¹¹See what this godly sorrow has produced in you: what earnestness, what eagerness to clear yourselves, what indignation, what alarm, what longing, what concern, what readiness to see justice done. At every point you have proved yourselves to be innocent in this matter. ¹²So even though I wrote to you, it was neither on account of the one who did the wrong nor on account of the injured party, but rather that before God you could see for yourselves how devoted to us you are. ¹³By all this we are encouraged.

In addition to our own encouragement, we were especially delighted to see how happy Titus was, because his spirit has been refreshed by all of you. ¹⁴I had boasted to him about you, and you have not embarrassed me. But just as everything we said to you was true, so our boasting about you to Titus has proved to be true as well. ¹⁵And his affection for you is all the greater when he remembers that you were all obedient, receiving him with fear and trembling. ¹⁶I am glad I can have complete confidence in you.

The Collection for the Lord's People

8 And now, brothers and sisters, we want you to know about the grace that God has given the Macedonian churches. ²In the midst of a very severe trial, their overflowing joy and their extreme poverty welled up in rich generosity. ³For I testify that they gave as much as they were able, and even beyond their ability. Entirely on their own, ⁴they urgently pleaded with us for the privilege of sharing in this service to the Lord's people. ⁵And they exceeded our expectations: They gave themselves first of all to the Lord, and then by the will of God also to us. ⁶So we urged Titus, just as he had earlier made a beginning, to bring also to completion this act of grace on your part. ⁷But since you excel in everything—in faith, in speech, in knowledge, in complete earnestness and in the love we have kindled in you[a]—see that you also excel in this grace of giving.

⁸I am not commanding you, but I want to test the sincerity of your love by comparing it with the earnestness of others. ⁹For you know the grace of our Lord Jesus Christ, that though he was rich, yet for your sake he became poor, so that you through his poverty might become rich.

¹⁰And here is my judgment about what is best for you in this matter. Last year

---

ᵃ 7 Some manuscripts *and in your love for us*

PANORAMA

Love Them?

Why should you love those "friends" who are now saying they don't like you? In this letter, Paul shares his feelings and tells why he does what he does. He loves the Corinthians, even if they put him down.

{2 CORINTHIANS}

you were the first not only to give but also to have the desire to do so. ¹¹Now finish the work, so that your eager willingness to do it may be matched by your completion of it, according to your means. ¹²For if the willingness is there, the gift is acceptable according to what one has, not according to what one does not have.

¹³Our desire is not that others might be relieved while you are hard pressed, but that there might be equality. ¹⁴At the present time your plenty will supply what they need, so that in turn their plenty will supply what you need. The goal is equality, ¹⁵as it is written: "The one who gathered much did not have too much, and the one who gathered little did not have too little."ᵃ

ᵃ 15 Exodus 16:18

Titus Sent to Receive the Collection

¹⁶Thanks be to God, who put into the heart of Titus the same concern I have for you. ¹⁷For Titus not only welcomed our appeal, but he is coming to you with much enthusiasm and on his own initiative. ¹⁸And we are sending along with him the brother who is praised by all the churches for his service to the gospel. ¹⁹What is more, he was chosen by the churches to accompany us as we carry the offering, which we administer in order to honor the Lord himself and to show our eagerness to help. ²⁰We want to avoid any criticism of the way we administer this liberal gift. ²¹For we are taking pains to do what is

TO THE POINT

Give Until it Feels Good

The Israelites were commanded to tithe, to give 10 percent of their income to God. The New Testament does not repeat that command, but it does teach these principles:

+ Giving is a privilege (2 Corinthians 8:4).

+ Jesus set an excellent example of giving (2 Corinthians 8:9).

+ Give generously, and you will reap generously (2 Corinthians 9:6).

+ You are free to decide how much to give (2 Corinthians 9:7).

+ Give cheerfully (2 Corinthians 9:7).

+ Trust God to supply your needs (2 Corinthians 9:10–11).

Now is a good time to get into the habit of giving. Don't think, "I don't have much now, but I'll give when I get a job." God measures your giving by what you have, not by what you don't have (2 Corinthians 8:12).

right, not only in the eyes of the Lord but also in the eyes of man.

22 In addition, we are sending with them our brother who has often proved to us in many ways that he is zealous, and now even more so because of his great confidence in you. 23 As for Titus, he is my partner and co-worker among you; as for our brothers, they are representatives of the churches and an honor to Christ. 24 Therefore show these men the proof of your love and the reason for our pride in you, so that the churches can see it.

9 There is no need for me to write to you about this service to the Lord's people. 2 For I know your eagerness to help, and I have been boasting about it to the Macedonians, telling them that since last year you in Achaia were ready to give; and your enthusiasm has stirred most of them to action. 3 But I am sending the brothers in order that our boasting about you in this matter should not prove hollow, but that you may be ready, as I said you would be. 4 For if any Macedonians come with me and find you unprepared, we—not to say anything about you—would be ashamed of having been so confident. 5 So I thought it necessary to urge the brothers to visit you in advance and finish the arrangements for the generous gift you had promised. Then it will be ready as a generous gift, not as one grudgingly given.

Generosity Encouraged

6 Remember this: Whoever sows sparingly will also reap sparingly, and whoever sows generously will also reap generously. 7 Each of you should give what you have decided in your heart to give, not reluctantly or under compulsion, for God loves a cheerful giver. 8 And God is able to bless you abundantly, so that in all things at all times, having all that you need, you will abound in every good work. 9 As it is written:

"They have freely scattered their gifts
    to the poor;
  their righteousness endures
    forever."ᵃ

10 Now he who supplies seed to the sower and bread for food will also supply and increase your store of seed and will enlarge the harvest of your righteousness. 11 You will be enriched in every way so that you can be generous on every occasion, and through us your generosity will result in thanksgiving to God.

12 This service that you perform is not only supplying the needs of the Lord's people but is also overflowing in many expressions of thanks to God. 13 Because of the service by which you have proved yourselves, others will praise God for the obedience that accompanies your confession of the gospel of Christ, and for your generosity in sharing with them and with everyone else. 14 And in their prayers for you their hearts will go out to you, because of the surpassing grace God has given you. 15 Thanks be to God for his indescribable gift!

Paul's Defense of His Ministry

10 By the humility and gentleness of Christ, I appeal to you—I, Paul, who am "timid" when face to face with you, but "bold" toward you when away! 2 I beg you that when I come I may not have to be as bold as I expect to be toward some people who think that we live by the standards of this world. 3 For though we live in the world, we do not wage war as the world does. 4 The weapons we fight with are not the weapons of the world. On the contrary, they have divine power to demolish strongholds. 5 We demolish arguments and every pretension that sets itself up against the knowledge of God, and we take captive every thought to make it obedient to Christ. 6 And we will be ready to punish every act of disobedience, once your obedience is complete.

7 You are judging by appearances.ᵇ If anyone is confident that they belong to Christ, they should consider again that we belong to Christ just as much as they do. 8 So even if I boast somewhat freely about the authority the Lord gave us for building you up rather than tearing you down, I will not be ashamed of it. 9 I do not want to

---

ᵃ 9 Psalm 112:9   ᵇ 7 Or *Look at the obvious facts*

seem to be trying to frighten you with my letters. [10]For some say, "His letters are weighty and forceful, but in person he is unimpressive and his speaking amounts to nothing." [11]Such people should realize that what we are in our letters when we are absent, we will be in our actions when we are present.

[12]We do not dare to classify or compare ourselves with some who commend themselves. When they measure themselves by themselves and compare themselves with themselves, they are not wise. [13]We, however, will not boast beyond proper limits, but will confine our boasting to the sphere of service God himself has assigned to us, a sphere that also includes you. [14]We are not going too far in our boasting, as would be the case if we had not come to you, for we did get as far as you with the gospel of Christ. [15]Neither do we go beyond our limits by boasting of work done by others. Our hope is that, as your faith continues to grow, our sphere of activity among you will greatly expand, [16]so that we can preach the gospel in the regions beyond you. For we do not want to boast about work already done in someone else's territory. [17]But, "Let the one who boasts boast in the Lord."[a] [18]For it is not the one who commends himself who is approved, but the one whom the Lord commends.

Paul and the False Apostles

11 I hope you will put up with me in a little foolishness. Yes, please put up with me! [2]I am jealous for you with a godly jealousy. I promised you to one husband, to Christ, so that I might present you as a pure virgin to him. [3]But I am afraid that just as Eve was deceived by the serpent's cunning, your minds may somehow be led astray from your sincere and pure devotion to Christ. [4]For if someone comes to you and preaches a Jesus other than the Jesus we preached, or if you receive a different spirit from the Spirit you received, or a different gospel from the one you accepted, you put up with it easily enough.

[5]I do not think I am in the least inferior to those "super-apostles."[b] [6]I may indeed be untrained as a speaker, but I do have knowledge. We have made this perfectly clear to you in every way. [7]Was it a sin for me to lower myself in order to elevate you by preaching the gospel of God to you free of charge? [8]I robbed other churches by receiving support from them so as to serve you. [9]And when I was with you and needed something, I was not a burden to anyone, for the brothers who came from Macedonia supplied what I needed. I have kept myself from being a burden to you in any way, and will continue to do so. [10]As surely as the truth of Christ is in me, nobody in the regions of Achaia will stop

---

INSTANT ACCESS

Shelby has nicer clothes. Jason is smarter. Ryan can dunk a basketball. Heather has thick, wavy hair. Dan makes friends easily. And there you are. Discount store clothes. Mostly C's. Straight hair. And shy. Even if this isn't you, to measure yourself by others, as Paul says, is "not wise." So to whom do you compare yourself? No one. Learn to see yourself as God made you, with your own strengths and weaknesses. And work hard to develop strengths and overcome weaknesses. When you become the best "you" that you can be, you'll be a success.

{2 Corinthians 10:12}

---

this boasting of mine. [11]Why? Because I do not love you? God knows I do!

[12]And I will keep on doing what I am doing in order to cut the ground from under those who want an opportunity to be considered equal with us in the things they boast about. [13]For such people are false apostles, deceitful workers, masquerading as apostles of Christ. [14]And no wonder, for Satan himself masquerades as an angel of light. [15]It is not surprising, then, if his servants also masquerade as servants of righteousness. Their end will be what their actions deserve.

Paul Boasts About His Sufferings

[16]I repeat: Let no one take me for a fool. But if you do, then tolerate me just as you would a fool, so that I may do a little boasting. [17]In this self-confident boasting I am not talking as the Lord would, but as a fool. [18]Since many are boasting the way the world does, I too will boast. [19]You gladly put up with fools since you are so wise! [20]In fact, you even put up with anyone who enslaves you or exploits you or takes advantage of you or puts on airs or slaps you in the face. [21]To my shame I admit that we were too weak for that!

Whatever anyone else dares to boast about—I am speaking as a fool—I also dare to boast about. [22]Are they Hebrews? So am I. Are they Israelites? So am I. Are they Abraham's descendants? So am I. [23]Are they servants of Christ? (I am out of my mind to talk like this.) I am more. I have worked much harder, been in prison more frequently, been flogged more severely, and been exposed to death again and again. [24]Five times I received from the Jews the forty lashes minus one. [25]Three times I was beaten with rods, once I was pelted with stones, three times I was shipwrecked, I spent a night and a day in the open sea, [26]I have been constantly on the move. I have been in danger from rivers, in danger from bandits, in danger from my fellow Jews, in danger from Gentiles; in danger in the city, in danger in the country, in danger at sea; and in danger from false believers. [27]I have labored and toiled and have often gone without sleep;

I have known hunger and thirst and have often gone without food; I have been cold and naked. [28]Besides everything else, I face daily the pressure of my concern for all the churches. [29]Who is weak, and I do not feel weak? Who is led into sin, and I do not inwardly burn?

[30]If I must boast, I will boast of the things that show my weakness. [31]The God and Father of the Lord Jesus, who is to be praised forever, knows that I am not lying. [32]In Damascus the governor under King Aretas had the city of the Damascenes guarded in order to arrest me. [33]But I was lowered in a basket from a window in the wall and slipped through his hands.

Paul's Vision and His Thorn

12 I must go on boasting. Although there is nothing to be gained, I will go on to visions and revelations from the Lord. [2]I know a man in Christ who fourteen years ago was caught up to the third heaven. Whether it was in the body or out of the body I do not know—God knows. [3]And I know that this man—whether in the body or apart from the body I do not know, but God knows— [4]was caught up to paradise and heard inexpressible things, things that no one is permitted to tell. [5]I will boast about a man like that, but I will not boast about myself, except about my weaknesses. [6]Even if I should choose to boast, I would not be a fool, because I would be speaking the truth. But I refrain, so no one will think more of me than is warranted by what I do or say, [7]or because of these surpassingly great revelations. Therefore, in order to keep me from becoming conceited, I was given a thorn in my flesh, a messenger of Satan, to torment me. [8]Three times I pleaded with the Lord to take it away from me. [9]But he said to me, "My grace is sufficient for you, for my power is made perfect in weakness." Therefore I will boast all the more gladly about my weaknesses, so that Christ's power may rest on me. [10]That is why, for Christ's sake, I delight in weaknesses, in insults, in hardships, in persecutions, in difficulties. For when I am weak, then I am strong.

Paul's Concern for the Corinthians

11 I have made a fool of myself, but you drove me to it. I ought to have been commended by you, for I am not in the least inferior to the "super-apostles,"[a] even though I am nothing. 12 I persevered in demonstrating among you the marks of a true apostle, including signs, wonders and miracles. 13 How were you inferior to the other churches, except that I was never a burden to you? Forgive me this wrong!

14 Now I am ready to visit you for the third time, and I will not be a burden to you, because what I want is not your possessions but you. After all, children should not have to save up for their parents, but parents for their children. 15 So I will very gladly spend for you everything I have and expend myself as well. If I love you more, will you love me less? 16 Be that as it may, I have not been a burden to you. Yet, crafty fellow that I am, I caught you by trickery! 17 Did I exploit you through any of the men I sent to you? 18 I urged Titus to go to you and I sent our brother with him. Titus did not exploit you, did he? Did we not walk in the same footsteps by the same Spirit?

19 Have you been thinking all along that we have been defending ourselves to you? We have been speaking in the sight of God as those in Christ; and everything we do, dear friends, is for your strengthening. 20 For I am afraid that when I come I may not find you as I want you to be, and you may not find me as you want me to be. I fear that there may be discord, jealousy, fits of rage, selfish ambition, slander, gossip, arrogance and disorder. 21 I am afraid that when I come again my God will humble me before you, and I will be grieved over many who have sinned earlier and have not repented of the impurity, sexual sin and debauchery in which they have indulged.

Final Warnings

13 This will be my third visit to you. "Every matter must be established

---

INSTANT ACCESS

Stay out too late? You get grounded. Get in a fight at school? Suspended! Someone is always there to punish you when you mess up. However, your parents and other adults can't follow you around all the time. You know there are lots of things you could do that Mom and Dad would probably never find out about. So why not go ahead? Some Corinthians figured that since Paul wasn't around they could do whatever they wanted. Paul didn't threaten, but he did warn them: "Christ . . . is not weak in dealing with you" (2 Corinthians 13:3). Remember that God will know what you've done, and he doesn't let Christians get away with practicing sin.

{2 Corinthians 13:1–4}

---

by the testimony of two or three witnesses."[b] 2 I already gave you a warning when I was with you the second time. I now repeat it while absent: On my return I will not spare those who sinned earlier or any of the others, 3 since you are demanding proof that Christ is speaking through me. He is not weak in dealing with you, but is powerful among you. 4 For to be sure, he was crucified in weakness, yet he lives

---

[a] 11 Or *the most eminent apostles*   [b] 1 Deut. 19:15

by God's power. Likewise, we are weak in him, yet by God's power we will live with him in our dealing with you.

⁵Examine yourselves to see whether you are in the faith; test yourselves. Do you not realize that Christ Jesus is in you—unless, of course, you fail the test? ⁶And I trust that you will discover that we have not failed the test. ⁷Now we pray to God that you will not do anything wrong— not so that people will see that we have stood the test but so that you will do what is right even though we may seem to have failed. ⁸For we cannot do anything against the truth, but only for the truth. ⁹We are glad whenever we are weak but you are strong; and our prayer is that you may be fully restored. ¹⁰This is why I write these

things when I am absent, that when I come I may not have to be harsh in my use of authority—the authority the Lord gave me for building you up, not for tearing you down.

Final Greetings

¹¹Finally, brothers and sisters, rejoice! Strive for full restoration, encourage one another, be of one mind, live in peace. And the God of love and peace will be with you.

¹²Greet one another with a holy kiss. ¹³All God's people here send their greetings.

¹⁴May the grace of the Lord Jesus Christ, and the love of God, and the fellowship of the Holy Spirit be with you all.

GALATIANS

Those Rules Again.

Do you ever feel like it's hard to be a Christian? That Christians have to obey all sort of rules other people ignore? Not that you don't want to be a good Christian, it's just hard sometimes.

In New Testament times false teachers visited some of the churches founded by Paul. They told the new Christians they had to follow all the Old Testament rules. In this letter to the Galatians Paul explains that being a Christian means trusting Jesus completely and letting the Holy Spirit change you as a person from within. It's not trying to change by keeping somebody's rules.

>>**PETER CAVES IN TO PRESSURE**
Apostles' clash reported in Galatians 2:11–21

>>**THOSE RULES AREN'T FOR CHRISTIANS**
Something better, says letter writer in Galatians 3:11–25

>>**FREEDOM TO DO WHAT?**
Paul explains. See Galatians 5:1–12

>>**LOVE, JOY AND PEACE BEAT SIN**
Benefits listed in Galatians 5:16–26

As Paul writes, noblemen from Gaul are accepted in the Roman Senate. China regains control of Mongolia.

1 Paul, an apostle—sent not from men nor by a man, but by Jesus Christ and God the Father, who raised him from the dead— ²and all the brothers and sisters*ᵃ* with me,

To the churches in Galatia:

³Grace and peace to you from God our Father and the Lord Jesus Christ, ⁴who gave himself for our sins to rescue us from the present evil age, according to the will of our God and Father, ⁵to whom be glory for ever and ever. Amen.

No Other Gospel

⁶I am astonished that you are so quickly deserting the one who called you to live in the grace of Christ and are turning to a different gospel— ⁷which is really no gospel at all. Evidently some people are throwing you into confusion and are trying to pervert the gospel of Christ. ⁸But even if we or an angel from heaven should preach a gospel other than the one we preached to you, let them be under God's curse! ⁹As we have already said, so now I say again: If anybody is preaching to you a gospel other than what you accepted, let them be under God's curse!

¹⁰Am I now trying to win the approval of human beings, or of God? Or am I trying to please people? If I were still trying to please people, I would not be a servant of Christ.

Paul Called by God

¹¹I want you to know, brothers and sisters, that the gospel I preached is not of human origin. ¹²I did not receive it from any man, nor was I taught it; rather, I received it by revelation from Jesus Christ.

¹³For you have heard of my previous way of life in Judaism, how intensely I persecuted the church of God and tried to destroy it. ¹⁴I was advancing in Judaism beyond many of my own age among my people and was extremely zealous for the traditions of my fathers. ¹⁵But when God, who set me apart from my mother's womb and called me by his grace, was pleased ¹⁶to reveal his Son in me so that I might preach him among the Gentiles, my immediate response was not to consult any human being. ¹⁷I did not go up to Jerusalem to see those who were apostles before I was, but I went into Arabia. Later I returned to Damascus.

¹⁸Then after three years, I went up to Jerusalem to get acquainted with Cephas*ᵇ* and stayed with him fifteen days. ¹⁹I saw none of the other apostles— only James, the Lord's brother. ²⁰I assure you before God that what I am writing you is no lie. ²¹Then I went to Syria and Cilicia. ²²I was personally unknown to the churches of Judea that are in Christ. ²³They only heard the report: "The man who formerly persecuted us is now preaching the faith he once tried to destroy." ²⁴And they praised God because of me.

Paul Accepted by the Apostles

2 Then after fourteen years, I went up again to Jerusalem, this time with Barnabas. I took Titus along also. ²I went in response to a revelation and, meeting privately with those esteemed as leaders, I presented to them the gospel that I preach among the Gentiles. I wanted to be sure I was not running and had not been running my race in vain. ³Yet not even Titus, who was with me, was compelled to be circumcised, even though he was a Greek. ⁴This matter arose because some false believers had infiltrated our ranks to spy on the freedom we have in Christ Jesus and to make us slaves. ⁵We did not give in to them for a moment, so that the truth of the gospel might be preserved for you.

⁶As for those who were held in high esteem—whatever they were makes no

> The Lord Jesus Christ . . . gave himself for our sins to rescue us from the present evil age.
>
> Galatians 1:3–4

ᵃ 2 The Greek word for *brothers and sisters* (*adelphoi*) refers here to believers, both men and women, as part of God's family; also in verse 11; and in 3:15; 4:12, 28, 31; 5:11, 13; 6:1, 18.   *ᵇ* 18 That is, Peter

difference to me; God does not show favoritism—they added nothing to my message. ⁷On the contrary, they recognized that I had been entrusted with the task of preaching the gospel to the uncircumcised,ᵃ just as Peter had been to the circumcised.ᵇ ⁸For God, who was at work in Peter as an apostle to the circumcised, was also at work in me as an apostle to the Gentiles. ⁹James, Cephasᶜ and John, those esteemed as pillars, gave me and Barnabas the right hand of fellowship when they recognized the grace given to me. They agreed that we should go to the Gentiles, and they to the circumcised. ¹⁰All they asked was that we should continue to remember the poor, the very thing I had been eager to do all along.

Paul Opposes Cephas

¹¹When Cephas came to Antioch, I opposed him to his face, because he stood condemned. ¹²For before certain men came from James, he used to eat with the Gentiles. But when they arrived, he began to draw back and separate himself from the Gentiles because he was afraid of those who belonged to the circumcision group. ¹³The other Jews joined him in his hypocrisy, so that by their hypocrisy even Barnabas was led astray.

¹⁴When I saw that they were not acting in line with the truth of the gospel, I said to Cephas in front of them all, "You are a Jew, yet you live like a Gentile and not like a Jew. How is it, then, that you force Gentiles to follow Jewish customs?

¹⁵"We who are Jews by birth and not sinful Gentiles ¹⁶know that a person is not justified by the works of the law, but by faith in Jesus Christ. So we, too, have put our faith in Christ Jesus that we may be justified by faith inᵈ Christ and not by the works of the law, because by the works of the law no one will be justified.

¹⁷"But if, in seeking to be justified in Christ, we Jews find ourselves also among the sinners, doesn't that mean that Christ promotes sin? Absolutely not! ¹⁸If I rebuild what I destroyed, then I really would be a lawbreaker.

¹⁹"For through the law I died to the law so that I might live for God. ²⁰I have been crucified with Christ and I no longer live, but Christ lives in me. The life I now live in the body, I live by faith in the Son of God, who loved me and gave himself for me. ²¹I do not set aside the grace of God, for if righteousness could be gained through the law, Christ died for nothing!"ᵉ

Faith or Works of the Law

3 You foolish Galatians! Who has bewitched you? Before your very eyes Jesus Christ was clearly portrayed as crucified. ²I would like to learn just one thing from you: Did you receive the Spirit by the works of the law, or by believing what you heard? ³Are you so foolish? After beginning by means of the Spirit, are you now trying to finish by means of the flesh?ᶠ ⁴Have you experiencedᵍ so much in vain—if it really was in vain? ⁵So again I ask, does God give you his Spirit and work miracles among you by the works of the law, or by your believing what you heard? ⁶So also Abraham "believed God, and it was credited to him as righteousness."ʰ

⁷Understand, then, that those who have faith are children of Abraham. ⁸Scripture foresaw that God would justify the Gentiles by faith, and announced the gospel in advance to Abraham: "All nations will be blessed through you."ⁱ ⁹So those who rely on faith are blessed along with Abraham, the man of faith.

¹⁰For all who rely on the works of the law are under a curse, as it is written: "Cursed is everyone who does not continue to do everything written in the Book of the Law."ʲ ¹¹Clearly no one who relies on the law is justified before God, because "the righteous will live by faith."ᵏ ¹²The law is not based on faith; on the contrary, it says, "The person who does these things will live by them."ˡ ¹³Christ redeemed us from the curse of the law by becoming a curse for us, for it is written: "Cursed is

---

ᵃ 7 That is, Gentiles   ᵇ 7 That is, Jews; also in verses 8 and 9   ᶜ 9 That is, Peter; also in verses 11 and 14
ᵈ 16 Or but through the faithfulness of . . . justified on the basis of the faithfulness of   ᵉ 21 Some interpreters end the quotation after verse 14.   ᶠ 3 In contexts like this, the Greek word for flesh (sarx) refers to the sinful state of human beings, often presented as a power in opposition to the Spirit.   ᵍ 4 Or suffered   ʰ 6 Gen. 15:6   ⁱ 8 Gen. 12:3; 18:18; 22:18   ʲ 10 Deut. 27:26   ᵏ 11 Hab. 2:4   ˡ 12 Lev. 18:5

everyone who is hung on a pole."ᵃ ¹⁴He redeemed us in order that the blessing given to Abraham might come to the Gentiles through Christ Jesus, so that by faith we might receive the promise of the Spirit.

The Law and the Promise

¹⁵Brothers and sisters, let me take an example from everyday life. Just as no one can set aside or add to a human covenant that has been duly established, so it is in this case. ¹⁶The promises were spoken to Abraham and to his seed. Scripture does not say "and to seeds," meaning many people, but "and to your seed,"ᵇ meaning one person, who is Christ. ¹⁷What I mean is this: The law, introduced 430 years later, does not set aside the covenant previously established by God and thus do away with the promise. ¹⁸For if the inheritance depends on the law, then it no longer depends on

the promise; but God in his grace gave it to Abraham through a promise.

¹⁹Why, then, was the law given at all? It was added because of transgressions until the Seed to whom the promise referred had come. The law was given through angels and entrusted to a mediator. ²⁰A mediator, however, implies more than one party; but God is one.

²¹Is the law, therefore, opposed to the promises of God? Absolutely not! For if a law had been given that could impart life, then righteousness would certainly have come by the law. ²²But Scripture has locked up everything under the control of sin, so that what was promised, being given through faith in Jesus Christ, might be given to those who believe.

Children of God

²³Before the coming of this faith,ᶜ we were held in custody under the law, locked

ᵃ 13 Deut. 21:23   ᵇ 16 Gen. 12:7; 13:15; 24:7   ᶜ 22,23 Or through the faithfulness of Jesus . . . ²³Before faith came

TO THE POINT

Don't Try—Rely

Try as hard as you can, you can't earn heaven and you can't become a stronger Christian by trying to keep God's law. The important word here is *try*. To try is to attempt to do something on your own. You've done that, and you know how easy it is to fail. Try harder, and you still fail. In fact, that's what the law is best at: showing you how you fail no matter how hard you try (Galatians 3:19–22).

The Bible says to rely, not try. Your relationship with God is based on faith, not on trying to keep his law (Galatians 3:6–9). That means you trust God so much you step out and do what's right. Not by extra effort. Not by depending on yourself. But by relying on the Lord and discovering that he really will help you succeed, not fail.

up until the faith that was to come would be revealed. [24]So the law was our guardian until Christ came that we might be justified by faith. [25]Now that this faith has come, we are no longer under a guardian.

[26]So in Christ Jesus you are all children of God through faith, [27]for all of you who were baptized into Christ have clothed yourselves with Christ. [28]There is neither Jew nor Gentile, neither slave nor free, nor is there male and female, for you are all one in Christ Jesus. [29]If you belong to Christ, then you are Abraham's seed, and heirs according to the promise.

4 What I am saying is that as long as an heir is underage, he is no different from a slave, although he owns the whole estate. [2]The heir is subject to guardians and trustees until the time set by his father. [3]So also, when we were underage, we were in slavery under the elemental spiritual forces[a] of the world. [4]But when the set time had fully come, God sent his Son, born of a woman, born under the law, [5]to redeem those under the law, that we might receive adoption to sonship.[b] [6]Because you are his sons, God sent the Spirit of his Son into our hearts, the Spirit who calls out, *"Abba,[c] Father."* [7]So you are no longer a slave, but God's child; and since you are his child, God has made you also an heir.

Paul's Concern for the Galatians

[8]Formerly, when you did not know God, you were slaves to those who by nature are not gods. [9]But now that you know God— or rather are known by God—how is it that you are turning back to those weak and miserable forces[d]? Do you wish to be enslaved by them all over again? [10]You are observing special days and months and seasons and years! [11]I fear for you, that somehow I have wasted my efforts on you.

[12]I plead with you, brothers and sisters, become like me, for I became like you. You did me no wrong. [13]As you know, it was because of an illness that I first preached the gospel to you, [14]and even though my illness was a trial to you, you did not treat me with contempt or scorn. Instead, you welcomed me as if I were an angel of God, as if I were Christ Jesus himself. [15]Where, then, is your blessing of me now? I can testify that, if you could have done so, you would have torn out your eyes and given them to me. [16]Have I now become your enemy by telling you the truth?

[17]Those people are zealous to win you over, but for no good. What they want is to alienate you from us, so that you may have zeal for them. [18]It is fine to be zealous, provided the purpose is good, and to be so always, not just when I am with you. [19]My dear children, for whom I am again in the pains of childbirth until Christ is formed in you, [20]how I wish I could be with you now and change my tone, because I am perplexed about you!

---

[a] 3 Or *under the basic principles*   [b] 5 The Greek word for *adoption to sonship* is a legal term referring to the full legal standing of an adopted male heir in Roman culture.   [c] 6 Aramaic for *Father*   [d] 9 Or *principles*

Hagar and Sarah

21 Tell me, you who want to be under the law, are you not aware of what the law says? 22 For it is written that Abraham had two sons, one by the slave woman and the other by the free woman. 23 His son by the slave woman was born according to the flesh, but his son by the free woman was born as the result of a divine promise.

24 These things are being taken figuratively: The women represent two covenants. One covenant is from Mount Sinai and bears children who are to be slaves: This is Hagar. 25 Now Hagar stands for Mount Sinai in Arabia and corresponds to the present city of Jerusalem, because she is in slavery with her children. 26 But the Jerusalem that is above is free, and she is our mother. 27 For it is written:

"Be glad, barren woman,
    you who never bore a child;
shout for joy and cry aloud,
    you who were never in labor;
because more are the children of the
        desolate woman
    than of her who has a husband."[a]

28 Now you, brothers and sisters, like Isaac, are children of promise. 29 At that time the son born according to the flesh persecuted the son born by the power of the Spirit. It is the same now. 30 But what does Scripture say? "Get rid of the slave woman and her son, for the slave woman's son will never share in the inheritance with the free woman's son."[b] 31 Therefore, brothers and sisters, we are not children of the slave woman, but of the free woman.

Freedom in Christ

5 It is for freedom that Christ has set us free. Stand firm, then, and do not let yourselves be burdened again by a yoke of slavery.

2 Mark my words! I, Paul, tell you that if you let yourselves be circumcised, Christ will be of no value to you at all. 3 Again I declare to every man who lets himself be circumcised that he is obligated to obey the whole law. 4 You who are trying to be justified by the law have been alienated from Christ; you have fallen away from grace. 5 For through the Spirit we eagerly await by faith the righteousness for which we hope. 6 For in Christ Jesus neither circumcision nor uncircumcision has any value. The only thing that counts is faith expressing itself through love.

7 You were running a good race. Who cut in on you to keep you from obeying the truth? 8 That kind of persuasion does not come from the one who calls you. 9 "A little yeast works through the whole batch of dough." 10 I am confident in the Lord that you will take no other view. The one who is throwing you into confusion, whoever that may be, will have to pay the penalty. 11 Brothers and sisters, if I am still preaching circumcision, why am I still being persecuted? In that case the offense of the cross has been abolished. 12 As for those agitators, I wish they would go the whole way and emasculate themselves!

Life by the Spirit

13 You, my brothers and sisters, were called to be free. But do not use your freedom to indulge the flesh[c]; rather, serve one another humbly in love. 14 For the entire law is fulfilled in keeping this one command: "Love your neighbor as yourself."[d] 15 If you bite and devour each other, watch out or you will be destroyed by each other.

16 So I say, walk by the Spirit, and you will not gratify the desires of the flesh. 17 For the flesh desires what is contrary to the Spirit, and the Spirit what is contrary to the flesh. They are in conflict with each other, so that you are not to do whatever[e] you want. 18 But if you are led by the Spirit, you are not under the law.

19 The acts of the flesh are obvious: sexual immorality, impurity and debauchery; 20 idolatry and witchcraft; hatred, discord, jealousy, fits of rage, selfish ambition, dissensions, factions 21 and envy; drunkenness, orgies, and the like. I warn you, as I did before, that those who live like this will not inherit the kingdom of God.

---

a 27 Isaiah 54:1   b 30 Gen. 21:10   c 13 In contexts like this, the Greek word for flesh (sarx) refers to the sinful state of human beings, often presented as a power in opposition to the Spirit; also in verses 16, 17, 19 and 24; and in 6:8.
d 14 Lev. 19:18   e 17 Or you do not do what

22 But the fruit of the Spirit is love, joy, peace, forbearance, kindness, goodness, faithfulness, 23 gentleness and self-control. Against such things there is no law. 24 Those who belong to Christ Jesus have crucified the flesh with its passions and desires. 25 Since we live by the Spirit, let us keep in step with the Spirit. 26 Let us not become conceited, provoking and envying each other.

Doing Good to All

6 Brothers and sisters, if someone is caught in a sin, you who live by the Spirit should restore that person gently. But watch yourselves, or you also may be tempted. 2 Carry each other's burdens, and in this way you will fulfill the law of Christ. 3 If anyone thinks they are something when they are not, they deceive themselves. 4 Each one should test their own actions. Then they can take pride in themselves alone, without comparing themselves to someone else, 5 for each one should carry their own load. 6 Nevertheless, the one who receives instruction in the word should share all good things with their instructor.

7 Do not be deceived: God cannot be mocked. A man reaps what he sows. 8 Whoever sows to please their flesh, from the flesh will reap destruction; whoever sows to please the Spirit, from the Spirit will reap eternal life. 9 Let us not become weary in doing good, for at the proper time we will reap a harvest if we do not give up. 10 Therefore, as we have opportunity, let us do good to all people, especially to those who belong to the family of believers.

Not Circumcision but the New Creation

11 See what large letters I use as I write to you with my own hand!

12 Those who want to impress people by means of the flesh are trying to compel you to be circumcised. The only reason they do this is to avoid being persecuted for the cross of Christ. 13 Not even those who are circumcised keep the law, yet they want you to be circumcised that they may boast about your circumcision in the flesh. 14 May I never boast except in the cross of our Lord Jesus Christ, through which[a] the world has been crucified to me, and I to the world. 15 Neither circumcision nor uncircumcision means anything; what counts is the new creation. 16 Peace and mercy to all who follow this rule—to[b] the Israel of God.

17 From now on, let no one cause me trouble, for I bear on my body the marks of Jesus.

18 The grace of our Lord Jesus Christ be with your spirit, brothers and sisters. Amen.

INSTANT ACCESS

What does God want from you? Does he want you to pray five hours a day? Or be a missionary? Or a preacher? Maybe. But there is something he wants. And not from you. *For* you. What God wants for you is a life filled with love, joy, peace, forbearance (patience), kindness, goodness, faithfulness, gentleness and self-control. To make sure you have that kind of life, he has given you the Holy Spirit. Sure, you can choose to follow your sinful impulses (Galatians 5:16–21). Or you can choose to follow those good impulses that the Holy Spirit gives you. Why not concentrate on what God wants for you? And enjoy!

{Galatians 5:22–25}

---

a 14 Or whom   b 16 Or rule and to

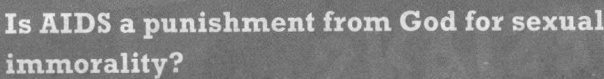

Is AIDS a punishment from God for sexual immorality?

Dear Noah,

I have heard this question debated more than once. Some people say yes. Others say that for many it is the consequence of sin. For instance, if you put your hand on a hot stove, it will get burned. If putting your hand on a hot stove were a sin, would getting burned be a punishment from God? Or would it be a consequence of your actions?

AIDS used to be thought of as a disease that only homosexuals or drug users contracted. Today we know that all people who have sex with an infected person are at risk. Often people who have AIDS infect others without even knowing they have the disease. Even nice healthy looking people get AIDS.

Galatians 6:7–8 warns us, "A man reaps what he sows. Whoever sows to please their flesh, from the flesh will reap destruction." If you don't want the possible consequences that come from sexual impurity, don't be sexually active outside of marriage.

Sometimes innocent people can also get AIDS. This could happen if someone were given infected blood, for instance. Or if a child's mom had it and he or she is born with it. This happens not as a consequence of that person's sin, but as a consequence of living in a sinful world.

Jordan

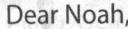

EPHESIANS

preview

Paul writes four letters while he awaits trial in Rome. Ephesians is one of them.

As Paul writes, Ephesus is the fourth largest city in the Roman Empire.

The temple of Artemis in Ephesus is longer than a football field. Thousands of pilgrims visit the temple every year.

Jesus' church isn't a marble building. It's people who love and obey him.

Lonely.

Chances are you'll feel lonely at some time or other. You will probably have times when you're sure no one cares about you. And most of you realize that you need other people in order to get by. Going it alone will only get you so far. That's why God invented the church—not the building, but people who are family for you.

That's what Ephesians is all about. Before you were born, God knew you would be a member of his church. He gave you new life and made a place for you in his family. Ephesians shows you how to combat loneliness and how to find love and support in the family of God.

>>**PICKED BY GOD, SAVED BY JESUS**
Divine acts described. See Ephesians 1:1–14

>>**NOT WHAT YOU WERE ... OR WILL BE**
Our past and future sketched in Ephesians 2:1–10

>>**YOU ARE DIFFERENT, SO BE DIFFERENT**
Exhortation reported in Ephesians 4:1–32

>>**THIS COMMAND CARRIES A PROMISE**
Something to think about found in Ephesians 6:1–3

As the apostle Paul wrote Ephesians from a Roman prison, the emperor Ming-Ti was introducing Buddhism in China. Nero has his wife Octavia killed and is about to launch his persecution of Christians in Rome.

1 Paul, an apostle of Christ Jesus by the will of God,

To God's holy people in Ephesus,[a] the faithful in Christ Jesus:

[2] Grace and peace to you from God our Father and the Lord Jesus Christ.

Praise for Spiritual Blessings in Christ

[3] Praise be to the God and Father of our Lord Jesus Christ, who has blessed us in the heavenly realms with every spiritual blessing in Christ. [4] For he chose us in him before the creation of the world to be holy and blameless in his sight. In love [5] he[b] predestined us for adoption to sonship[c] through Jesus Christ, in accordance with his pleasure and will— [6] to the praise of his glorious grace, which he has freely given us in the One he loves. [7] In him we have redemption through his blood, the forgiveness of sins, in accordance with the riches of God's grace [8] that he lavished on us. With all wisdom and understanding, [9] he[d] made known to us the mystery of his will according to his good pleasure, which he purposed in Christ, [10] to be put into effect when the times reach their fulfillment—to bring unity to all things in heaven and on earth under Christ.

[11] In him we were also chosen,[e] having been predestined according to the plan of him who works out everything in conformity with the purpose of his will, [12] in order that we, who were the first to put our hope in Christ, might be for the praise of his glory. [13] And you also were included in Christ when you heard the message of truth, the gospel of your salvation. When you believed, you were marked in him with a seal, the promised Holy Spirit, [14] who is a deposit guaranteeing our inheritance until the redemption of those who are God's possession—to the praise of his glory.

Thanksgiving and Prayer

[15] For this reason, ever since I heard about your faith in the Lord Jesus and your love for all God's people, [16] I have not stopped giving thanks for you, remembering you in my prayers. [17] I keep asking that the God of our Lord Jesus Christ, the glorious Father, may give you the Spirit[f] of wisdom and revelation, so that you may know him better. [18] I pray that the eyes of your heart may be enlightened in order that you may know the hope to which he has called you, the riches of his glorious inheritance in his holy people, [19] and his incomparably great power for us who believe. That power is the same as the mighty strength [20] he exerted when he raised Christ from the dead and seated him at his right hand in the heavenly realms, [21] far above all rule and authority, power and dominion, and every name that is invoked, not only in the present age but also in the one to come. [22] And God placed all things under his feet and appointed him to be head over everything for the church, [23] which is his body, the fullness of him who fills everything in every way.

Made Alive in Christ

2 As for you, you were dead in your transgressions and sins, [2] in which you used to live when you followed the ways of this world and of the ruler of the kingdom of the air, the spirit who is now at work in those who are disobedient. [3] All of us also lived among them at one time, gratifying the cravings of our flesh[g] and following its desires and thoughts. Like the rest, we were by nature deserving of wrath. [4] But because of his great love for us, God, who is rich in mercy, [5] made us alive with Christ even when we were dead in transgressions—it is by grace you have been saved. [6] And God raised us up with Christ and seated us with him in the heavenly realms in Christ Jesus, [7] in order that in the coming ages he might show the incomparable riches of his grace, expressed in his kindness to us in Christ Jesus. [8] For it is by grace you have been saved, through faith—and this is not from yourselves, it is the gift of God—

---

[a] 1 Some early manuscripts do not have *in Ephesus.*   [b] 4,5 Or *sight in love.* [5] *He*   [c] 5 The Greek word for *adoption to sonship* is a legal term referring to the full legal standing of an adopted male heir in Roman culture.   [d] 8,9 Or *us with all wisdom and understanding.* [9] *And he*   [e] 11 Or *were made heirs*   [f] 17 Or *a spirit*   [g] 3 In contexts like this, the Greek word for *flesh (sarx)* refers to the sinful state of human beings, often presented as a power in opposition to the Spirit.

We Believe...

"in the communion of the saints"

✝ Ever notice how we tend to define people by their differences? As in, he's a jock, she's a nerd. Or her parents are poor, his are rich. Or even, he's a Methodist, she's Baptist. In New Testament times, people did the same thing. She's a Hebrew Christian, he's a Gentile Christian.

Focusing on differences tends to divide people. When we define someone by their difference from us, we feel uncomfortable around them. Actually, defining by differences is society's way of creating distance. We don't want to get close to someone who's "not like us."

Paul takes on this approach to relationships in Ephesians 2:11–22. The differences are real, but for Jesus' followers they no longer matter. When Jesus died for our sins, he broke down the barriers that society puts up between groups of people. He did it by making all Christians "fellow citizens with God's people and also members of his household" (verse 19).

"The communion of the saints" means that we're now to emphasize what we have in common with other Christians, instead of following the world's approach of emphasizing differences. We no longer see a poor Methodist jock, or rich Baptist nerd. What we see is a brother or sister in Christ, someone to care about and to worship with, someone to draw close to and to be a friend.

This doesn't mean that it's easy to get over real differences. But it does mean that it's possible, and a goal true Christians work toward.

Go to page 963 for the next We Believe

⁹not by works, so that no one can boast. ¹⁰For we are God's handiwork, created in Christ Jesus to do good works, which God prepared in advance for us to do.

Jew and Gentile Reconciled Through Christ

¹¹Therefore, remember that formerly you who are Gentiles by birth and called "uncircumcised" by those who call themselves "the circumcision" (which is done in the body by human hands)— ¹²remember that at that time you were separate from Christ, excluded from citizenship in Israel and foreigners to the covenants of the promise, without hope and without God in the world. ¹³But now in Christ Jesus you who once were far away have been brought near by the blood of Christ.

¹⁴For he himself is our peace, who has made the two groups one and has destroyed the barrier, the dividing wall of hostility, ¹⁵by setting aside in his flesh the law with its commands and regulations. His purpose was to create in himself one new humanity out of the two, thus making peace, ¹⁶and in one body to reconcile both of them to God through the cross, by which he put to death their hostility. ¹⁷He came and preached peace to you who were far away and peace to those who were near. ¹⁸For through him we both have access to the Father by one Spirit.

¹⁹Consequently, you are no longer foreigners and strangers, but fellow citizens with God's people and also members of his household, ²⁰built on the foundation of the apostles and prophets, with Christ Jesus himself as the chief cornerstone. ²¹In him the whole building is joined together and rises to become a holy temple in the Lord. ²²And in him you too are being built together to become a dwelling in which God lives by his Spirit.

God's Marvelous Plan for the Gentiles

3 For this reason I, Paul, the prisoner of Christ Jesus for the sake of you Gentiles—

²Surely you have heard about the administration of God's grace that was given to me for you, ³that is, the mystery made known to me by revelation, as I have already written briefly. ⁴In reading this, then, you will be able to understand my insight into the mystery of Christ, ⁵which was not made known to people in other generations as it has now been revealed by the Spirit to God's holy apostles and prophets. ⁶This mystery is that through the gospel the Gentiles are heirs together with Israel, members together of one body, and sharers together in the promise in Christ Jesus.

⁷I became a servant of this gospel by the gift of God's grace given me through the working of his power. ⁸Although I am less than the least of all the Lord's people, this grace was given me: to preach to the Gentiles the boundless riches of Christ, ⁹and to make plain to everyone the administration of this mystery, which for ages past was kept hidden in God, who created all things. ¹⁰His intent was that now, through the church, the manifold wisdom of God should be made known to the rulers and authorities in the heavenly realms, ¹¹according to his eternal purpose that he accomplished in Christ Jesus our Lord. ¹²In him and through faith in him we may approach God with freedom and confidence. ¹³I ask you, therefore, not to be discouraged because of my sufferings for you, which are your glory.

A Prayer for the Ephesians

¹⁴For this reason I kneel before the Father, ¹⁵from whom every family[a] in heaven and on earth derives its name. ¹⁶I pray that out of his glorious riches he may strengthen you with power through his Spirit in your inner being, ¹⁷so that Christ may dwell in your hearts through faith. And I pray that you, being rooted and established in love, ¹⁸may have power, together with all the Lord's holy people, to grasp how wide and long and high and deep is the love of Christ, ¹⁹and to know this love that surpasses knowledge—that you may be filled to the measure of all the fullness of God.

---

[a] 15 The Greek for *family* (*patria*) is derived from the Greek for *father* (*pater*).

[20]Now to him who is able to do immeasurably more than all we ask or imagine, according to his power that is at work within us, [21]to him be glory in the church and in Christ Jesus throughout all generations, for ever and ever! Amen.

Unity and Maturity in the Body of Christ

4 As a prisoner for the Lord, then, I urge you to live a life worthy of the calling you have received. [2]Be completely humble and gentle; be patient, bearing with one another in love. [3]Make every effort to keep the unity of the Spirit through the bond of peace. [4]There is one body and one Spirit, just as you were called to one hope when you were called; [5]one Lord, one faith, one baptism; [6]one God and Father of all, who is over all and through all and in all.

[7]But to each one of us grace has been given as Christ apportioned it. [8]This is why it[a] says:

"When he ascended on high,
he took many captives
and gave gifts to his people."[b]

[9](What does "he ascended" mean except that he also descended to the lower, earthly regions[c]? [10]He who descended is the very one who ascended higher than all the heavens, in order to fill the whole universe.) [11]So Christ himself gave the apostles, the prophets, the evangelists, the pastors and teachers, [12]to equip his people for works of service, so that the body of Christ may be built up [13]until we all reach unity in the faith and in the knowledge of the Son of God and become mature, attaining to the whole measure of the fullness of Christ.

[14]Then we will no longer be infants, tossed back and forth by the waves, and blown here and there by every wind of teaching and by the cunning and craftiness of people in their deceitful scheming. [15]Instead, speaking the truth in love, we will grow to become in every respect the mature body of him who is the head, that is, Christ. [16]From him the whole body, joined and held together by every supporting ligament, grows and builds itself up in love, as each part does its work.

Instructions for Christian Living

[17]So I tell you this, and insist on it in the Lord, that you must no longer live as the Gentiles do, in the futility of their thinking. [18]They are darkened in their understanding and separated from the life of God because of the ignorance that is in them due to the hardening of their hearts. [19]Having lost all sensitivity, they have given themselves over to sensuality so as to indulge in every kind of impurity, and they are full of greed.

---

[a] 8 Or God   [b] 8 Psalm 68:18   [c] 9 Or the depths of the earth

---

D on't you hate it when someone says, "Be patient?" Hey, we want what we want now! The trouble is, for most things everyone has to wait. Farmers have to wait for crops to grow. Kids have to wait to get a driver's license. We can get all upset and impatient, but that won't change a thing. Crops will still grow as slowly. Our days will still pass 24 hours at a time. Maybe the best thing to do is to be patient and use today to prepare for tomorrow. After all, God probably had a good reason to build waiting time into the way the world works.

{Ephesians 4:2–3}

INSTANT ACCESS

²⁰That, however, is not the way of life you learned ²¹when you heard about Christ and were taught in him in accordance with the truth that is in Jesus. ²²You were taught, with regard to your former way of life, to put off your old self, which is being corrupted by its deceitful desires; ²³to be made new in the attitude of your minds; ²⁴and to put on the new self, created to be like God in true righteousness and holiness.

²⁵Therefore each of you must put off falsehood and speak truthfully to your neighbor, for we are all members of one body. ²⁶"In your anger do not sin"ᵃ: Do

not let the sun go down while you are still angry, ²⁷and do not give the devil a foothold. ²⁸Anyone who has been stealing must steal no longer, but must work, doing something useful with their own hands, that they may have something to share with those in need.

²⁹Do not let any unwholesome talk come out of your mouths, but only what is helpful for building others up according to their needs, that it may benefit those who listen. ³⁰And do not grieve the Holy Spirit of God, with whom you were sealed for the day of redemption. ³¹Get rid of all bitterness, rage and anger, brawling and slander, along with every form of malice. ³²Be kind and compassionate to one another, forgiving each other, just as in Christ God forgave you. ¹Follow God's example, therefore, as dearly loved children ²and walk in the way of love, just as Christ loved us and gave himself up for us as a fragrant offering and sacrifice to God.

³But among you there must not be even a hint of sexual immorality, or of any kind of impurity, or of greed, because these are improper for God's holy people. ⁴Nor should there be obscenity, foolish talk or coarse joking, which are out of place, but rather thanksgiving. ⁵For of this you can be sure: No immoral, impure or greedy person—such a person is an idolater—has any inheritance in the kingdom of Christ and of God.ᵇ ⁶Let no one deceive you with empty words, for because of such things God's wrath comes on those who are disobedient. ⁷Therefore do not be partners with them.

⁸For you were once darkness, but now you are light in the Lord. Live as children of light ⁹(for the fruit of the light consists in all goodness, righteousness and truth) ¹⁰and find out what pleases the Lord. ¹¹Have nothing to do with the fruitless deeds of darkness, but rather expose them. ¹²It is shameful even to mention what the disobedient do in secret. ¹³But everything exposed by the light becomes visible—and everything that is illuminated becomes a light. ¹⁴This is why it is said:

ᵃ 26 Psalm 4:4 (see Septuagint) ᵇ 5 Or kingdom of the Messiah and God

"Wake up, sleeper,
rise from the dead,
and Christ will shine on you."

[15] Be very careful, then, how you live—not as unwise but as wise, [16] making the most of every opportunity, because the days are evil. [17] Therefore do not be foolish, but understand what the Lord's will is. [18] Do not get drunk on wine, which leads to debauchery. Instead, be filled with the Spirit, [19] speaking to one another with psalms, hymns, and songs from the Spirit. Sing and make music from your heart to the Lord, [20] always giving thanks to God the Father for everything, in the name of our Lord Jesus Christ.

Instructions for Christian Households

[21] Submit to one another out of reverence for Christ.

[22] Wives, submit yourselves to your own husbands as you do to the Lord. [23] For the husband is the head of the wife as Christ is the head of the church, his body, of which he is the Savior. [24] Now as the church submits to Christ, so also wives should submit to their husbands in everything.

[25] Husbands, love your wives, just as Christ loved the church and gave himself up for her [26] to make her holy, cleansing[a] her by the washing with water through the word, [27] and to present her to himself as a radiant church, without stain or wrinkle or any other blemish, but holy and blameless. [28] In this same way, husbands ought to love their wives as their own bodies. He who loves his wife loves himself. [29] After all, no one ever hated their own body, but they feed and care for their body, just as Christ does the church— [30] for we are members of his body. [31] "For this reason a man will leave his father and mother and be united to his wife, and the two will become one flesh."[b] [32] This is a profound mystery—but I am talking about Christ and the church. [33] However, each one of you also must love his wife as he loves himself, and the wife must respect her husband.

>> INSTANT ACCESS

Debauchery. The sound of the word is almost as disgusting as its meaning: "orgies; extreme involvement in sensuality or sexual immorality." The Bible uses it only five times, four times in relation to sexual immorality and once, in this verse, in relation to drunkenness. Paul wants the Ephesian Christians to be filled with the Holy Spirit instead of wine. Sounds like good advice for today too. Drinking alcohol loosens inhibitions and leads to acts that you'd never consider when sober. Think about it. Is it worth the risk?

{Ephesians 5:17–20}

6 Children, obey your parents in the Lord, for this is right. [2] "Honor your father and mother"—which is the first commandment with a promise— [3] "so that it may go well with you and that you may enjoy long life on the earth."[c]

[4] Fathers,[d] do not exasperate your children; instead, bring them up in the training and instruction of the Lord.

[5] Slaves, obey your earthly masters with respect and fear, and with sincerity of heart, just as you would obey Christ. [6] Obey them not only to win their favor when their eye is on you, but as slaves of Christ, doing the will of God from your heart. [7] Serve wholeheartedly, as if you

---

[a] 26 Or having cleansed   [b] 31 Gen. 2:24   [c] 3 Deut. 5:16   [d] 4 Or Parents

were serving the Lord, not people, [8]because you know that the Lord will reward each one for whatever good they do, whether they are slave or free.

[9]And masters, treat your slaves in the same way. Do not threaten them, since you know that he who is both their Master and yours is in heaven, and there is no favoritism with him.

The Armor of God

[10]Finally, be strong in the Lord and in his mighty power. [11]Put on the full armor of God, so that you can take your stand against the devil's schemes. [12]For our struggle is not against flesh and blood, but against the rulers, against the authorities, against the powers of this dark world and against the spiritual forces of evil in the heavenly realms. [13]Therefore put on the full armor of God, so that when the day of evil comes, you may be able to stand your ground, and after you have done everything, to stand. [14]Stand firm then, with the belt of truth buckled around your waist, with the breastplate of righteousness in place, [15]and with your feet fitted with the readiness that comes from the gospel of peace. [16]In addition to all this, take up the shield of faith, with which you can extinguish all the flaming arrows of the evil one. [17]Take the helmet of salvation and the sword of the Spirit, which is the word of God.

[18]And pray in the Spirit on all occasions with all kinds of prayers and requests. With this in mind, be alert and always keep on praying for all the Lord's people. [19]Pray also for me, that whenever I speak, words may be given me so that I will fearlessly make known the mystery of the gospel, [20]for which I am an ambassador in chains. Pray that I may declare it fearlessly, as I should.

Final Greetings

[21]Tychicus, the dear brother and faithful servant in the Lord, will tell you everything, so that you also may know how I am and what I am doing. [22]I am sending him to you for this very purpose, that you may know how we are, and that he may encourage you.

[23]Peace to the brothers and sisters,[a] and love with faith from God the Father and the Lord Jesus Christ. [24]Grace to all who love our Lord Jesus Christ with an undying love.[b]

---

[a] 23 The Greek word for *brothers and sisters* (*adelphoi*) refers here to believers, both men and women, as part of God's family.   [b] 24 Or *Grace and immortality to all who love our Lord Jesus Christ.*

PHILIPPIANS

preview

Paul writes
four letters
while he awaits
trial in Rome.
Philippians is
one of them.

On Paul's first visit to
Philippi he was beaten
and put in prison.

Be Happy!

Most people want to have fun and be happy.
The trouble is all those emotional ups and
downs. You feel happy, and then something
goes wrong and you feel down.

In Philippians the key words are "joy" and "rejoice." Paul was in prison when he wrote this
letter. He didn't have any of the things people
today think will make them happy. But Paul
knew the secret of an inner joy that won't quit
when things go wrong. That's a secret worth
knowing!

>>**EXPECT AND HOPE FOR ... COURAGE**
    See Philippians 1:20,21

>>**JESUS' ATTITUDE KEY TO FRIENDSHIPS**
    Explanation in Philippians 2:2–11

>>**MATURE CHRISTIANS LOOK AHEAD**
    Where's your focus, Paul asks. See Philippians 3:12–15

>>**GOOD STUFF TO THINK ABOUT**
    Wise counsel found in Philippians 4:8

As Paul writes, many retired Roman soldiers live in Philippi. Rome is soon to be
destroyed by a great fire that will lead to persecution of Christians.

1 Paul and Timothy, servants of Christ Jesus,

To all God's holy people in Christ Jesus at Philippi, together with the overseers and deacons[a]:

[2] Grace and peace to you from God our Father and the Lord Jesus Christ.

Thanksgiving and Prayer

[3] I thank my God every time I remember you. [4] In all my prayers for all of you, I always pray with joy [5] because of your partnership in the gospel from the first day until now, [6] being confident of this, that he who began a good work in you will carry it on to completion until the day of Christ Jesus.

[7] It is right for me to feel this way about all of you, since I have you in my heart and, whether I am in chains or defending and confirming the gospel, all of you share in God's grace with me. [8] God can testify how I long for all of you with the affection of Christ Jesus.

[9] And this is my prayer: that your love may abound more and more in knowledge and depth of insight, [10] so that you may be able to discern what is best and may be pure and blameless for the day of Christ, [11] filled with the fruit of righteousness that comes through Jesus Christ—to the glory and praise of God.

Paul's Chains Advance the Gospel

[12] Now I want you to know, brothers and sisters,[b] that what has happened to me has actually served to advance the gospel. [13] As a result, it has become clear throughout the whole palace guard[c] and to everyone else that I am in chains for Christ. [14] And because of my chains, most of the brothers and sisters have become

confident in the Lord and dare all the more to proclaim the gospel without fear.

[15] It is true that some preach Christ out of envy and rivalry, but others out of goodwill. [16] The latter do so out of love, knowing that I am put here for the defense of the gospel. [17] The former preach Christ out of selfish ambition, not sincerely, supposing that they can stir up trouble for me while I am in chains. [18] But what does it matter? The important thing is that in every way, whether from false motives or true, Christ is preached. And because of this I rejoice.

Yes, and I will continue to rejoice, [19] for I know that through your prayers and God's provision of the Spirit of Jesus Christ what has happened to me will turn out for my deliverance.[d] [20] I eagerly expect and hope that I will in no way be ashamed, but will have sufficient courage so that now as always Christ will be exalted in my body, whether by life or by death. [21] For to me, to live is Christ and to die is gain. [22] If I am to go on living in the body, this will mean fruitful labor for me. Yet what shall I choose? I do not know! [23] I am torn between the two: I desire to depart and be with Christ, which is better by far; [24] but it is more necessary for you that I remain in the body. [25] Convinced of this, I know that I will remain, and I will continue with all of you for your progress and joy in the faith, [26] so that through my being with you again your boasting in Christ Jesus will abound on account of me.

Life Worthy of the Gospel

[27] Whatever happens, conduct yourselves in a manner worthy of the gospel of Christ. Then, whether I come and see you or only hear about you in my absence, I will know that you stand firm in the one Spirit,[e] striving together as one

He who began a good work in you will carry it on to completion until the day of Christ Jesus.
Philippians 1:6

for the faith of the gospel ²⁸without being frightened in any way by those who oppose you. This is a sign to them that they will be destroyed, but that you will be saved—and that by God. ²⁹For it has been granted to you on behalf of Christ not only to believe in him, but also to suffer for him, ³⁰since you are going through the same struggle you saw I had, and now hear that I still have.

Imitating Christ's Humility

2 Therefore if you have any encouragement from being united with Christ, if any comfort from his love, if any common sharing in the Spirit, if any tenderness and compassion, ²then make my joy complete by being like-minded, having the same love, being one in spirit and of one mind. ³Do nothing out of selfish ambition or vain conceit. Rather, in humility value others above yourselves, ⁴not looking to your own interests but each of you to the interests of the others.

⁵In your relationships with one another, have the same mindset as Christ Jesus:

⁶Who, being in very nature[a] God,
did not consider equality with God
something to be used to his
own advantage;
⁷rather, he made himself nothing
by taking the very nature[b] of a
servant,
being made in human likeness.
⁸And being found in appearance as a
man,
he humbled himself
by becoming obedient to death—
even death on a cross!

⁹Therefore God exalted him to the
highest place
and gave him the name that is
above every name,
¹⁰that at the name of Jesus every knee
should bow,
in heaven and on earth and under
the earth,
¹¹and every tongue acknowledge that
Jesus Christ is Lord,
to the glory of God the Father.

K now any complainers? Those who gripe about folding clothes or doing dishes? Who nag to go shopping when Mom's busy? Or complain about not spending more time online? It's about just such things that this passage says, "Do everything without grumbling or arguing" (Philippians 2:14). God is ready to work in your life. But a complaining attitude blocks what he is eager to do. So, if you're one of those negative types, now is a good time to change. A negative attitude makes life miserable for those around you. And it makes you miserable too.

{Philippians 2:12–18}

INSTANT ACCESS

Do Everything Without Grumbling

¹²Therefore, my dear friends, as you have always obeyed—not only in my presence, but now much more in my absence—continue to work out your salvation with fear and trembling, ¹³for it is God who works in you to will and to act in order to fulfill his good purpose.

¹⁴Do everything without grumbling or arguing, ¹⁵so that you may become blameless and pure, "children of God without fault in a warped and crooked generation."[c] Then you will shine among

---

a 6 Or *in the form of*   b 7 Or *the form*   c 15 Deut. 32:5

them like stars in the sky [16] as you hold firmly to the word of life. And then I will be able to boast on the day of Christ that I did not run or labor in vain. [17] But even if I am being poured out like a drink offering on the sacrifice and service coming from your faith, I am glad and rejoice with all of you. [18] So you too should be glad and rejoice with me.

Timothy and Epaphroditus

[19] I hope in the Lord Jesus to send Timothy to you soon, that I also may be cheered when I receive news about you. [20] I have no one else like him, who will show genuine concern for your welfare. [21] For everyone looks out for their own interests, not those of Jesus Christ. [22] But you know that Timothy has proved himself, because as a son with his father he has served with me in the work of the gospel. [23] I hope, therefore, to send him as soon as I see how things go with me. [24] And I am confident in the Lord that I myself will come soon.

[25] But I think it is necessary to send back to you Epaphroditus, my brother, co-worker and fellow soldier, who is also your messenger, whom you sent to take care of my needs. [26] For he longs for all of you and is distressed because you heard he was ill. [27] Indeed he was ill, and almost died. But God had mercy on him, and not on him only but also on me, to spare me sorrow upon sorrow. [28] Therefore I am all the more eager to send him, so that when you see him again you may be glad and I may have less anxiety. [29] So then, welcome him in the Lord with great joy, and honor people like him, [30] because he almost died for the work of Christ. He risked his life to make up for the help you yourselves could not give me.

No Confidence in the Flesh

3 Further, my brothers and sisters, rejoice in the Lord! It is no trouble for me to write the same things to you again, and it is a safeguard for you. [2] Watch out for those dogs, those evildoers, those mutilators of the flesh. [3] For it is we who are the circumcision, we who serve God by his Spirit, who boast in Christ Jesus, and who put no confidence in the flesh— [4] though I myself have reasons for such confidence.

If someone else thinks they have reasons to put confidence in the flesh, I have more: [5] circumcised on the eighth day, of the people of Israel, of the tribe of Benjamin, a Hebrew of Hebrews; in regard to the law, a Pharisee; [6] as for zeal, persecuting the church; as for righteousness based on the law, faultless.

[7] But whatever were gains to me I now consider loss for the sake of Christ. [8] What is more, I consider everything a loss because of the surpassing worth of knowing Christ Jesus my Lord, for whose sake I have lost all things. I consider them garbage, that I may gain Christ [9] and be

PANORAMA

{PHILIPPIANS}

Be Happy!

The key words in this book are "joy" and "rejoice." Paul was in prison when he wrote this letter. But he knew the secret of an inner joy that won't quit when things go wrong.

found in him, not having a righteousness of my own that comes from the law, but that which is through faith in^a Christ— the righteousness that comes from God on the basis of faith. ¹⁰I want to know Christ—yes, to know the power of his resurrection and participation in his sufferings, becoming like him in his death, ¹¹and so, somehow, attaining to the resurrection from the dead.

¹²Not that I have already obtained all this, or have already arrived at my goal, but I press on to take hold of that for which Christ Jesus took hold of me. ¹³Brothers and sisters, I do not consider myself yet to have taken hold of it. But one thing I do: Forgetting what is behind and straining toward what is ahead, ¹⁴I press on toward the goal to win the prize for which God has called me heavenward in Christ Jesus.

Following Paul's Example

¹⁵All of us, then, who are mature should take such a view of things. And if on some point you think differently, that too God will make clear to you. ¹⁶Only let us live up to what we have already attained.

¹⁷Join together in following my example, brothers and sisters, and just as you have us as a model, keep your eyes on those who live as we do. ¹⁸For, as I have often told you before and now tell you again even with tears, many live as enemies of the cross of Christ. ¹⁹Their destiny is destruction, their god is their stomach, and their glory is in their shame. Their mind is set on earthly things. ²⁰But our citizenship is in heaven. And we eagerly await a Savior from there, the Lord Jesus Christ, ²¹who, by the power that enables him to bring everything under his control, will transform our lowly bodies so that they will be like his glorious body.

Closing Appeal for Steadfastness and Unity

4 Therefore, my brothers and sisters, you whom I love and long for, my joy and crown, stand firm in the Lord in this way, dear friends!

»INSTANT ACCESS

When you're a little kid, the place you live determines who your friends are. When all you have for wheels is a tricycle, you pretty much have to play with kids who live on your block. When you become a teen, things change. Then you meet kids from all over, and you get to choose your friends. Of course, along with that privilege comes responsibility. You get to choose your friends, but you need to choose wisely. Paul's advice is to pay attention to the way others live. Note the way they talk about others. And pick as your friends teens who live according to the example God outlines in the Bible.

{Philippians 3:17–21}

²I plead with Euodia and I plead with Syntyche to be of the same mind in the Lord. ³Yes, and I ask you, my true companion, help these women since they have contended at my side in the cause of the gospel, along with Clement and the rest of my co-workers, whose names are in the book of life.

Final Exhortations

⁴Rejoice in the Lord always. I will say it again: Rejoice! ⁵Let your gentleness be evident to all. The Lord is near. ⁶Do not be

> What could the Bible possibly say about music videos, computer games, movies, blogs, cyber sex or modern music since none of them existed in Bible times?
>
> >> José

Dear José,

You're right. There is no verse that reads, "Thou shall not watch violent or explicit movies." But if you study God's Word, your answer is just as clear as if it did. Paul tells us what to focus our minds on. "Whatever is true, whatever is noble, whatever is right, whatever is pure, whatever is lovely, whatever is admirable—if anything is excellent or praiseworthy—think about such things" (Philippians 4:8). If what you want to entertain yourself with falls into these categories, enjoy!

But be very careful. Don't just pass it off and say, "The stuff I listen to isn't so bad." Examine what you see and hear very carefully. Do the words (or their meanings) fit the categories mentioned in the passage? You decide. But remember, you will be responsible directly to God for your choices, and your life will reflect what you're thinking about (Matthew 12:36–37).

Jordan

anxious about anything, but in every situation, by prayer and petition, with thanksgiving, present your requests to God. [7]And the peace of God, which transcends all understanding, will guard your hearts and your minds in Christ Jesus.

[8]Finally, brothers and sisters, whatever is true, whatever is noble, whatever is right, whatever is pure, whatever is lovely, whatever is admirable—if anything is excellent or praiseworthy—think about such things. [9]Whatever you have learned or received or heard from me, or seen in me—put it into practice. And the God of peace will be with you.

Thanks for Their Gifts

[10]I rejoiced greatly in the Lord that at last you renewed your concern for me. Indeed, you were concerned, but you had no opportunity to show it. [11]I am not saying this because I am in need, for I have learned to be content whatever the circumstances. [12]I know what it is to be in need, and I know what it is to have plenty. I have learned the secret of being content in any and every situation, whether well fed or hungry, whether living in plenty or in want. [13]I can do all this through him who gives me strength.

[14]Yet it was good of you to share in my troubles. [15]Moreover, as you Philippians know, in the early days of your acquaintance with the gospel, when I set out from Macedonia, not one church shared with me in the matter of giving and receiving, except you only; [16]for even when I was in Thessalonica, you sent me aid more than once when I was in need. [17]Not that I desire your gifts; what I desire is that more be credited to your account. [18]I have received full payment and have more than enough. I am amply supplied, now that I have received from Epaphroditus the gifts you sent. They are a fragrant offering, an acceptable sacrifice, pleasing to God. [19]And my God will meet all your needs according to the riches of his glory in Christ Jesus.

> ## INSTANT ACCESS
>
> You get a new bike, and then you want the trendy shoes. Get the shoes, and you want a car, right? Sometimes Mom or Dad try to make you feel guilty by saying things like, "I only had two dresses," or "I had to walk 23 miles to school in snow over my head." But that misses the point. When Paul talks about contentment, he's reminding you that the never-satisfied person is miserable. Why settle for misery? Enjoy that bike now. When the car comes, enjoy it too. Enjoy life's good gifts. It really isn't any fun being a "gotta-have-more" type.
>
> {Philippians 4:10–13}

[20]To our God and Father be glory for ever and ever. Amen.

Final Greetings

[21]Greet all God's people in Christ Jesus. The brothers and sisters who are with me send greetings. [22]All God's people here send you greetings, especially those who belong to Caesar's household.

[23]The grace of the Lord Jesus Christ be with your spirit. Amen.[a]

---

[a] 23 Some manuscripts do not have *Amen*.

COLOSSIANS

Horoscopes. Mediums. Palm Readers.

Ouija boards. Psychics. People who say they talk with a "friendly spirit." Past lives people claim to remember. All these ideas about what's real can be confusing.

The Colossians were confused too. Some of them believed they had to go through spirits to reach God. Some said Jesus was a spirit but not a very important one. Paul wrote Colossians to explain who Jesus is and how you can stay close to God. Anyone who understands what Colossians teaches won't be confused any longer!

>>**TAKE A LOOK AT THE REAL JESUS**
God the Son described, see Colossians 1:15–20

>>**WHAT "DON'T" MAKE SUPER-CHRISTIANS**
Warning registered in Colossians 2:20–23

>>**SUBTRACT THIS, ADD THAT**
Meet the new you. Check out Colossians 3:5–14

>>**THERE IT IS AGAIN!**
Discover why in Colossians 3:20

preview

Paul writes four letters as he awaits trial in Rome. Colossians is one of them.

In Colosse people called "Gnostics" teach that the body is evil. But Jesus came in a real body. "Good" and "evil" are about what we choose to do with our bodies.

As Paul writes, superstitious people throughout the Roman Empire look to horoscopes, magic and the occult for help. In Peru the Nazca create miles-long mystic lines and patterns in the desert.

1 Paul, an apostle of Christ Jesus by the will of God, and Timothy our brother,

[2] To God's holy people in Colossae, the faithful brothers and sisters[a] in Christ:

Grace and peace to you from God our Father.[b]

Thanksgiving and Prayer

[3] We always thank God, the Father of our Lord Jesus Christ, when we pray for you, [4] because we have heard of your faith in Christ Jesus and of the love you have for all God's people— [5] the faith and love that spring from the hope stored up for you in heaven and about which you have already heard in the true message of the gospel [6] that has come to you. In the same way, the gospel is bearing fruit and growing throughout the whole world—just as it has been doing among you since the day you heard it and truly understood God's grace. [7] You learned it from Epaphras, our dear fellow servant,[c] who is a faithful minister of Christ on our[d] behalf, [8] and who also told us of your love in the Spirit.

[9] For this reason, since the day we heard about you, we have not stopped praying for you. We continually ask God to fill you with the knowledge of his will through all the wisdom and understanding that the Spirit gives,[e] [10] so that you may live a life worthy of the Lord and please him in every way: bearing fruit in every good work, growing in the knowledge of God, [11] being strengthened with all power according to his glorious might so that you may have great endurance and patience, [12] and giving joyful thanks to the Father, who has qualified you[f] to share in the inheritance of his holy people in the kingdom of light. [13] For he has rescued us from the dominion of darkness and brought us into the kingdom of the Son he loves, [14] in whom we have redemption, the forgiveness of sins.

The Supremacy of the Son of God

[15] The Son is the image of the invisible God, the firstborn over all creation. [16] For in him all things were created: things in heaven and on earth, visible and invisible, whether thrones or powers or rulers or authorities; all things have been created through him and for him. [17] He is before all things, and in him all things hold together. [18] And he is the head of the body, the church; he is the beginning and the firstborn from among the dead, so that in everything he might have the supremacy. [19] For God was pleased to have all his fullness dwell in him, [20] and through him to reconcile to himself all things, whether things on earth or things in heaven, by making peace through his blood, shed on the cross.

[21] Once you were alienated from God and were enemies in your minds because of[g] your evil behavior. [22] But now he has reconciled you by Christ's physical body through death to present you holy in his sight, without blemish and free from accusation— [23] if you continue in your faith, established and firm, and do not move from the hope held out in the gospel. This is the gospel that you heard and that has been proclaimed to every creature under heaven, and of which I, Paul, have become a servant.

Paul's Labor for the Church

[24] Now I rejoice in what I am suffering for you, and I fill up in my flesh what is still lacking in regard to Christ's afflictions, for the sake of his body, which is the church. [25] I have become its servant by the commission God gave me to present to you the word of God in its fullness— [26] the mystery that has been kept hidden for ages and generations, but is now disclosed to the Lord's people. [27] To them God has chosen to make known among the Gentiles the glorious riches of this mystery, which is Christ in you, the hope of glory.

[28] He is the one we proclaim, admonishing and teaching everyone with all wisdom, so that we may present everyone fully mature in Christ. [29] To this end I strenuously contend with all the energy Christ so powerfully works in me.

---

[a] 2 The Greek word for *brothers and sisters* (*adelphoi*) refers here to believers, both men and women, as part of God's family; also in 4:15.   [b] 2 Some manuscripts *Father and the Lord Jesus Christ*   [c] 7 Or *slave*   [d] 7 Some manuscripts *your*   [e] 9 Or *all spiritual wisdom and understanding*   [f] 12 Some manuscripts *us*   [g] 21 Or *minds, as shown by*

We Believe...

"in Jesus Christ"

✠ Say the name, and you probably think of the baby born in a manger. Or of miracles, or maybe of Jesus' death and resurrection. Each of these images of Jesus is accurate. But the story of Jesus, and Jesus himself, didn't begin with his birth.

The Bible says that Jesus is God; that he was God from the beginning and that he created all things. Here are some of the ways the Bible describes Jesus Christ before his birth:

* In the very beginning Jesus [called "the Word" in this passage] "was with God [the Father] and the Word was God" (John 1:1).

* Jesus is "the radiance of God's [the Father's] glory and the exact representation of his being (Hebrews 1:3).

* Jesus is "in very nature God" (Philippians 2:6).

* Jesus created all things (Colossians 1:16).

* All God's fullness dwells in Jesus (Colossians 1:19).

* Jesus sustains "all things by his powerful word." Without Jesus the universe would dissolve (Hebrews 1:3).

After Jesus' resurrection he returned to heaven. When Jesus comes back everyone will "acknowledge that Jesus Christ is Lord" (Philippians 2:11)—whether they want to or not. Then all will see Jesus in his glory and be forced to admit that he really is God. But we don't have to be forced; we already believe he's God. And best of all, he's our Lord and Savior.

Go to page 1308 for the next We Believe

2 I want you to know how hard I am contending for you and for those at Laodicea, and for all who have not met me personally. ²My goal is that they may be encouraged in heart and united in love, so that they may have the full riches of complete understanding, in order that they may know the mystery of God, namely, Christ, ³in whom are hidden all the treasures of wisdom and knowledge. ⁴I tell you this so that no one may deceive you by fine-sounding arguments. ⁵For though I am absent from you in body, I am present with you in spirit and delight to see how disciplined you are and how firm your faith in Christ is.

Spiritual Fullness in Christ

⁶So then, just as you received Christ Jesus as Lord, continue to live your lives in him, ⁷rooted and built up in him, strengthened in the faith as you were taught, and overflowing with thankfulness.

⁸See to it that no one takes you captive through hollow and deceptive philosophy, which depends on human tradition and the elemental spiritual forces[a] of this world rather than on Christ.

⁹For in Christ all the fullness of the Deity lives in bodily form, ¹⁰and in Christ you have been brought to fullness. He is the head over every power and authority. ¹¹In him you were also circumcised with a circumcision not performed by human hands. Your whole self ruled by the flesh[b] was put off when you were circumcised by[c] Christ, ¹²having been buried with him in baptism, in which you were also raised with him through your faith in the working of God, who raised him from the dead.

¹³When you were dead in your sins and in the uncircumcision of your flesh, God made you[d] alive with Christ. He forgave us all our sins, ¹⁴having canceled the charge of our legal indebtedness, which stood against us and condemned us; he has taken it away, nailing it to the cross. ¹⁵And having disarmed the powers and authorities, he made a public spectacle of them, triumphing over them by the cross.[e]

≫ INSTANT ACCESS

Have you ever gone on a diet? Your stomach twists. You're starving. If you're suffering that much, you *must* be losing weight. Then you get on the scales and find you've lost a half pound! Some people take the same approach to spirituality. They figure if they cut out everything that's fun, they'll be more spiritual. Paul says such things "have an appearance of wisdom" but, like diets, "lack any value in restraining sensual indulgence" (Colossians 2:23). You feel spiritual without being spiritual. What's the true way to become a spiritual Christian? Check out Colossians 3:5–14.

{Colossians 2:20–23}

Freedom From Human Rules

¹⁶Therefore do not let anyone judge you by what you eat or drink, or with regard to a religious festival, a New Moon celebration or a Sabbath day. ¹⁷These are a shadow of the things that were to come; the reality, however, is found in Christ. ¹⁸Do not let anyone who delights in false humility and the worship of angels disqualify you. Such a person also goes into great detail about what they have seen; they are puffed up with idle notions by their unspiritual mind. ¹⁹They have lost

---

a 8 Or *the basic principles*; also in verse 20   *b* 11 In contexts like this, the Greek word for *flesh* (sarx) refers to the sinful state of human beings, often presented as a power in opposition to the Spirit; also in verse 13.   *c* 11 Or *put off in the circumcision of*   *d* 13 Some manuscripts *us*   *e* 15 Or *them in him*

connection with the head, from whom the whole body, supported and held together by its ligaments and sinews, grows as God causes it to grow.

20 Since you died with Christ to the elemental spiritual forces of this world, why, as though you still belonged to the world, do you submit to its rules: 21 "Do not handle! Do not taste! Do not touch!"? 22 These rules, which have to do with things that are all destined to perish with use, are based on merely human commands and teachings. 23 Such regulations indeed have an appearance of wisdom, with their self-imposed worship, their false humility and their harsh treatment of the body, but they lack any value in restraining sensual indulgence.

Forgive as the Lord forgave you.
Colossians 3:13

Living as Those Made Alive in Christ

3 Since, then, you have been raised with Christ, set your hearts on things above, where Christ is, seated at the right hand of God. 2 Set your minds on things above, not on earthly things. 3 For you died, and your life is now hidden with Christ in God. 4 When Christ, who is your[a] life, appears, then you also will appear with him in glory.

5 Put to death, therefore, whatever belongs to your earthly nature: sexual immorality, impurity, lust, evil desires and greed, which is idolatry. 6 Because of these, the wrath of God is coming.[b] 7 You used to walk in these ways, in the life you once lived. 8 But now you must also rid yourselves of all such things as these: anger, rage, malice, slander, and filthy language from your lips. 9 Do not lie to each other, since you have taken off your old self with its practices 10 and have put on the new self, which is being renewed in knowledge in the image of its Creator. 11 Here there is no Gentile or Jew, circumcised or uncircumcised, barbarian, Scythian, slave or free, but Christ is all, and is in all.

12 Therefore, as God's chosen people, holy and dearly loved, clothe yourselves with compassion, kindness, humility, gentleness and patience. 13 Bear with each other and forgive one another if any of you has a grievance against someone. Forgive as the Lord forgave you. 14 And

---

a 4 Some manuscripts *our*   *b* 6 Some early manuscripts *coming on those who are disobedient*

> Both my parents work so my brother, sister and I have assigned jobs to help out around the house. The trouble is, I get all the worst ones. Complaining doesn't help. What else can I do?
>
> >> Aiden

Dear Aiden,

Have you considered asking for a family meeting to discuss job assignments? Or if that can't be worked out, maybe you could write your parents a note. Explain that you feel you have the worst job assignments. Ask if one or more tasks could be done on a monthly rotation. Offer to make slips of paper with all the jobs. Each week all three children could draw out the same number of tasks. Once you start putting out some ideas other ideas may come up as well. Perhaps a compromise can be reached and you can get a break.

If the assignments can't be changed, here's a perspective you might want to adopt. God gave the Levites the task of transporting and setting up the ark of God (1 Chronicles 15:2). They were, in fact, the only ones allowed to touch the ark. God had prescribed exactly how these duties were to be carried out. The job was not glamorous and was at times difficult. Yet the Levites were the chosen ones.

So if you've been "chosen" and there's no way to get out of it, try to see your chores as necessary and important even if they're hard or gross. We're told, "Whatever you do, whether in word or deed, do it all in the name of the Lord Jesus, giving thanks to God the Father through him" (Colossians 3:17).

Jordan

Dear Jordan

So your parents are unfair. You do your work, and they still won't let you go out with your friends. Or you work hard at a grocery store, and the manager is crabby at you anyway. What do you do? Paul reminds you that if your boss or your parents are unfair, that doesn't mean you're released from your responsibility to them. How can you keep on being a good person when others are bad to you? Here's the secret: Remember that you are "working for the Lord," not for your unfair parent or boss. And because it is for the Lord, "you know that you will receive an inheritance" (Colossians 3:24). What you do right is appreciated. By God himself.

{Colossians 3:18—4:1}

» INSTANT ACCESS

whether in word or deed, do it all in the name of the Lord Jesus, giving thanks to God the Father through him.

Instructions for Christian Households

¹⁸Wives, submit yourselves to your husbands, as is fitting in the Lord.

¹⁹Husbands, love your wives and do not be harsh with them.

²⁰Children, obey your parents in everything, for this pleases the Lord.

²¹Fathers,ᵃ do not embitter your children, or they will become discouraged.

²²Slaves, obey your earthly masters in everything; and do it, not only when their eye is on you and to curry their favor, but with sincerity of heart and reverence for the Lord. ²³Whatever you do, work at it with all your heart, as working for the Lord, not for human masters, ²⁴since you know that you will receive an inheritance from the Lord as a reward. It is the Lord Christ you are serving. ²⁵Anyone who does wrong will be repaid for their wrongs, and there is no favoritism.

4 Masters, provide your slaves with what is right and fair, because you know that you also have a Master in heaven.

Further Instructions

²Devote yourselves to prayer, being watchful and thankful. ³And pray for us, too, that God may open a door for our message, so that we may proclaim the mystery of Christ, for which I am in chains. ⁴Pray that I may proclaim it clearly, as I should. ⁵Be wise in the way you act toward outsiders; make the most of every opportunity. ⁶Let your conversation be always full of grace, seasoned with salt, so that you may know how to answer everyone.

Final Greetings

⁷Tychicus will tell you all the news about me. He is a dear brother, a faithful minister and fellow servantᵇ in the Lord. ⁸I am sending him to you for the express purpose that you may know about ourᶜ circumstances and that he may encourage

over all these virtues put on love, which binds them all together in perfect unity.

¹⁵Let the peace of Christ rule in your hearts, since as members of one body you were called to peace. And be thankful. ¹⁶Let the message of Christ dwell among you richly as you teach and admonish one another with all wisdom through psalms, hymns, and songs from the Spirit, singing to God with gratitude in your hearts. ¹⁷And whatever you do,

---

ᵃ 21 Or *Parents*   ᵇ 7 Or *slave*; also in verse 12   ᶜ 8 Some manuscripts *that he may know about your*

your hearts. [9] He is coming with Onesimus, our faithful and dear brother, who is one of you. They will tell you everything that is happening here.

[10] My fellow prisoner Aristarchus sends you his greetings, as does Mark, the cousin of Barnabas. (You have received instructions about him; if he comes to you, welcome him.) [11] Jesus, who is called Justus, also sends greetings. These are the only Jews[a] among my co-workers for the kingdom of God, and they have proved a comfort to me. [12] Epaphras, who is one of you and a servant of Christ Jesus, sends greetings. He is always wrestling in prayer for you, that you may stand firm in all the will of God, mature and fully assured. [13] I

vouch for him that he is working hard for you and for those at Laodicea and Hierapolis. [14] Our dear friend Luke, the doctor, and Demas send greetings. [15] Give my greetings to the brothers and sisters at Laodicea, and to Nympha and the church in her house.

[16] After this letter has been read to you, see that it is also read in the church of the Laodiceans and that you in turn read the letter from Laodicea.

[17] Tell Archippus: "See to it that you complete the ministry you have received in the Lord."

[18] I, Paul, write this greeting in my own hand. Remember my chains. Grace be with you.

---

a 11 Greek *only ones of the circumcision group*

1 THESSALONIANS

Hard Times.

Some of you will face hard times while you're young. A friend may get killed in a car accident. A mom or grandma may get cancer. Someone you know may commit suicide. How can you stand it when suffering or death comes?

Paul wrote to the Thessalonian Christians to encourage them. They'd been true to God in spite of sufferings. But they were worried about Christians who had died. Paul let them know that death isn't the end. When Jesus comes, you'll be reunited with the people you love.

>> **TOUGH, BUT OH SO GENTLE**
See description, 1 Thessalonians 2:7–12

>> **SAFE SEX? CHECK THIS OUT**
Straight talk in 1 Thessalonians 4:1–8

>> **SOMEONE DIE? HERE'S GOOD NEWS**
Read it in 1 Thessalonians 4:13–18

>> **WIDE AWAKE, DAYTIME CHRISTIANS**
Biographies found in 1 Thessalonians 5:4–11

Paul visits Thessalonica for a few weeks on his first missionary journey. He leaves when anti-Paul riots threaten the new Christians there.

preview

As Paul writes, Thessalonica is the capital of Macedonia. The Romans have a naval base there. Roman armies battle to subdue Wales. Romans learn about soap from the people of Gaul.

1 Paul, Silas[a] and Timothy,

To the church of the Thessalonians in God the Father and the Lord Jesus Christ:

Grace and peace to you.

Thanksgiving for the Thessalonians' Faith

2 We always thank God for all of you and continually mention you in our prayers. 3 We remember before our God and Father your work produced by faith, your labor prompted by love, and your endurance inspired by hope in our Lord Jesus Christ.

4 For we know, brothers and sisters[b] loved by God, that he has chosen you, 5 because our gospel came to you not simply with words but also with power, with the Holy Spirit and deep conviction. You know how we lived among you for your sake. 6 You became imitators of us and of the Lord, for you welcomed the message in the midst of severe suffering with the joy given by the Holy Spirit. 7 And so you became a model to all the believers in Macedonia and Achaia. 8 The Lord's message rang out from you not only in Macedonia and Achaia—your faith in God has become known everywhere. Therefore we do not need to say anything about it, 9 for they themselves report what kind of reception you gave us. They tell how you turned to God from idols to serve the living and true God, 10 and to wait for his Son from heaven, whom he raised from the dead—Jesus, who rescues us from the coming wrath.

Paul's Ministry in Thessalonica

2 You know, brothers and sisters, that our visit to you was not without results. 2 We had previously suffered and been treated outrageously in Philippi, as you know, but with the help of our God we dared to tell you his gospel in the face of strong opposition. 3 For the appeal we make does not spring from error or impure motives, nor are we trying to trick you. 4 On the contrary, we speak as those approved by God to be entrusted with the gospel. We are not trying to please people but God, who tests our hearts. 5 You know we never used flattery, nor did we put on a mask to cover up greed—God is our witness. 6 We were not looking for praise from people, not from you or anyone else, even though as apostles of Christ we could

>> INSTANT ACCESS

Your friends are pretty important to you, aren't they? Oh yeah, Mom and Dad get upset at times because you're always on the phone. But, hey, they're important! Friends are so important that it's good to know how to make them and keep them. These verses tell how Paul made lasting friendships. He didn't flatter. He didn't say things just so others would like him better. He really cared about his friends. And he was willing to share personal things with them. You may not feel free to share with all the kids you know. But you can get close to a few if you treat them as Paul treated his friends.

{1 Thessalonians 2:5–12}

---

a 1 Greek *Silvanus*, a variant of *Silas*   b 4 The Greek word for *brothers and sisters* (*adelphoi*) refers here to believers, both men and women, as part of God's family; also in 2:1, 9, 14, 17; 3:7; 4:1, 10, 13; 5:1, 4, 12, 14, 25, 27.

have asserted our authority. [7] Instead, we were like young children[a] among you.

Just as a nursing mother cares for her children, [8] so we cared for you. Because we loved you so much, we were delighted to share with you not only the gospel of God but our lives as well. [9] Surely you remember, brothers and sisters, our toil and hardship; we worked night and day in order not to be a burden to anyone while we preached the gospel of God to you. [10] You are witnesses, and so is God, of how holy, righteous and blameless we were among you who believed. [11] For you know that we dealt with each of you as a father deals with his own children, [12] encouraging, comforting and urging you to live lives worthy of God, who calls you into his kingdom and glory.

[13] And we also thank God continually because, when you received the word of God, which you heard from us, you accepted it not as a human word, but as it actually is, the word of God, which is indeed at work in you who believe. [14] For you, brothers and sisters, became imitators of God's churches in Judea, which are in Christ Jesus: You suffered from your own people the same things those churches suffered from the Jews [15] who killed the Lord Jesus and the prophets and also drove us out. They displease God and are hostile to everyone [16] in their effort to keep us from speaking to the Gentiles so that they may be saved. In this way they always heap up their sins to the limit. The wrath of God has come upon them at last.[b]

Paul's Longing to See the Thessalonians

[17] But, brothers and sisters, when we were orphaned by being separated from you for a short time (in person, not in thought), out of our intense longing we made every effort to see you. [18] For we wanted to come to you—certainly I, Paul, did, again and again—but Satan blocked our way. [19] For what is our hope, our joy, or the crown in which we will glory in the presence of our Lord Jesus when he comes? Is it not you? [20] Indeed, you are our glory and joy.

3 So when we could stand it no longer, we thought it best to be left by ourselves in Athens. [2] We sent Timothy, who is our brother and co-worker in God's service in spreading the gospel of Christ, to strengthen and encourage you in your faith, [3] so that no one would be unsettled by these trials. For you know quite well that we are destined for them. [4] In fact, when we were with you, we kept telling you that we would be persecuted. And it turned out that way, as you well know. [5] For this reason, when I could stand it no longer, I sent to find out about your faith. I was afraid that in some way the tempter had tempted you and that our labors might have been in vain.

Timothy's Encouraging Report

[6] But Timothy has just now come to us from you and has brought good news about your faith and love. He has told us that you always have pleasant memories of us and that you long to see us, just as we also long to see you. [7] Therefore, brothers and sisters, in all our distress and persecution we were encouraged about you because of your faith. [8] For now we really live, since you are standing firm in the Lord. [9] How can we thank God enough for you in return for all the joy we have in the presence of our God because of you? [10] Night and day we pray most earnestly that we may see you again and supply what is lacking in your faith.

[11] Now may our God and Father himself and our Lord Jesus clear the way for us to come to you. [12] May the Lord make your love increase and overflow for each other and for everyone else, just as ours does for you. [13] May he strengthen your hearts so that you will be blameless and holy in the presence of our God and Father when our Lord Jesus comes with all his holy ones.

Living to Please God

4 As for other matters, brothers and sisters, we instructed you how to live

---

[a] 7 Some manuscripts *were gentle* [b] 16 Or *them fully*

in order to please God, as in fact you are living. Now we ask you and urge you in the Lord Jesus to do this more and more. ²For you know what instructions we gave you by the authority of the Lord Jesus.

³It is God's will that you should be sanctified: that you should avoid sexual immorality; ⁴that each of you should learn to control your own body[a] in a way that is holy and honorable, ⁵not in passionate lust like the pagans, who do not know God; ⁶and that in this matter no one should wrong or take advantage of a brother or sister.[b] The Lord will punish all those who commit such sins, as we told you and warned you before. ⁷For God did not call us to be impure, but to live a holy life. ⁸Therefore, anyone who rejects this instruction does not reject a human being but God, the very God who gives you his Holy Spirit.

⁹Now about your love for one another we do not need to write to you, for you yourselves have been taught by God to love each other. ¹⁰And in fact, you do love all of God's family throughout Macedonia. Yet we urge you, brothers and sisters, to do so more and more, ¹¹and to make it your ambition to lead a quiet life: You should mind your own business and work with your hands, just as we told you, ¹²so that your daily life may win the respect of outsiders and so that you will not be dependent on anybody.

---

a 4 Or *learn to live with your own wife; or learn to acquire a wife*   *b* 6 The Greek word for *brother or sister (adelphos)* refers here to a believer, whether man or woman, as part of God's family.

TO THE POINT

You'll See Them Again

It hurts when someone you love dies. You feel empty. You know things will never be the same again. Everybody grieves. But Paul says that Christians do not grieve "like the rest of mankind, who have no hope" (1 Thessalonians 4:13).

In the Bible hoping is not the same as wishing. It's not like hoping your parents will buy you a sports car. In the Bible hope is being sure about something for which you have to wait. You know that what you hope for will happen because God has promised it.

When Christians experience the death of someone they love, they also experience hope—hope that when Jesus returns he will bring that loved one with him. They will be caught up and reunited. They will "be with the Lord forever" (1 Thessalonians 4:17). Nothing will ever again separate them from those they love.

> Some of my friends and I have been disagree-ing on what activities are really "sex" and what is just messing around. Does the Bible make this clear?

>> Friends in a library

Dear Jordan

Dear Friends,

1 Thessalonians 4:3–8 tells us we're to live in order to please God: "You should avoid sexual immorality; that each of you should learn to control your own body in a way that is holy and honorable, not in passionate lust like the pagans, who do not know God."

God doesn't want his loved ones trying to find a weak spot in the debate, like this activity isn't "really" sex. If what you want to do isn't holy and honorable, don't do it! Live in order to please God. List the things you know aren't holy and pleasing to God. Make a commitment to avoid them. Don't go to parties where there will be alcohol or others do-ing the things on your list. This will help you succeed in your commitment.

Did you know that monkeys can't be potty-trained? But people learn to control those functions. People can also be in control of sexual urges. God says to learn to control your body. That pleases him. It will also keep your life sim-pler. I have met lots of young people who were sorry they did sexual things. But I have never met anyone who was sorry to have honored God.

Jordan

Believers Who Have Died

¹³Brothers and sisters, we do not want you to be uninformed about those who sleep in death, so that you do not grieve like the rest of mankind, who have no hope. ¹⁴For we believe that Jesus died and rose again, and so we believe that God will bring with Jesus those who have fallen asleep in him. ¹⁵According to the Lord's word, we tell you that we who are still alive, who are left until the coming of the Lord, will certainly not precede those who have fallen asleep. ¹⁶For the Lord himself will come down from heaven, with a loud command, with the voice of the archangel and with the trumpet call of God, and the dead in Christ will rise first. ¹⁷After that, we who are still alive and are left will be caught up together with them in the clouds to meet the Lord in the air. And so we will be with the Lord forever. ¹⁸Therefore encourage one another with these words.

The Day of the Lord

5 Now, brothers and sisters, about times and dates we do not need to write to you, ²for you know very well that the day of the Lord will come like a thief in the night. ³While people are saying, "Peace and safety," destruction will come on them suddenly, as labor pains on a pregnant woman, and they will not escape.

⁴But you, brothers and sisters, are not in darkness so that this day should surprise you like a thief. ⁵You are all children of the light and children of the day. We do not belong to the night or to the darkness. ⁶So then, let us not be like others, who are asleep, but let us be awake and sober. ⁷For those who sleep, sleep at night, and those who get drunk, get drunk at night. ⁸But since we belong to the day, let us be sober, putting on faith and love as a breastplate, and the hope of salvation as a helmet. ⁹For God did not appoint us to suffer wrath but to receive salvation through our Lord Jesus Christ. ¹⁰He died for us so that, whether we are awake or asleep, we may live together with him. ¹¹Therefore encourage one another and build each other up, just as in fact you are doing.

Final Instructions

¹²Now we ask you, brothers and sisters, to acknowledge those who work hard among you, who care for you in the Lord and who admonish you. ¹³Hold them in the highest regard in love because of their work. Live in peace with each other. ¹⁴And we urge you, brothers and sisters, warn those who are idle and disruptive, encourage the disheartened, help the weak, be patient with everyone. ¹⁵Make sure that nobody pays back wrong for wrong, but always strive to do what is good for each other and for everyone else.

PANORAMA

Hard Times.

{1 THESSALONIANS}

How can you stand it when suffering or death comes? Paul wrote to the Thessalonian Christians to encourage them. They were worried about Christians who had died. Paul let them know that death isn't the end. When Jesus comes, you'll be reunited with the people you love.

¹⁶Rejoice always, ¹⁷pray continually, ¹⁸give thanks in all circumstances; for this is God's will for you in Christ Jesus.

¹⁹Do not quench the Spirit. ²⁰Do not treat prophecies with contempt ²¹but test them all; hold on to what is good, ²²reject every kind of evil.

²³May God himself, the God of peace, sanctify you through and through. May your whole spirit, soul and body be kept blameless at the coming of our Lord Jesus Christ. ²⁴The one who calls you is faithful, and he will do it.

²⁵Brothers and sisters, pray for us. ²⁶Greet all God's people with a holy kiss. ²⁷I charge you before the Lord to have this letter read to all the brothers and sisters.

²⁸The grace of our Lord Jesus Christ be with you.

2 THESSALONIANS

Drugs. Killings.

Things do look pretty bad. Fighting all over the world. Terrorist attacks. Drug wars and school shootings. Maybe this is what the Bible talks about when it says things will get really bad just before Jesus comes back.

Paul wrote this letter to people who thought things couldn't get worse. He wrote that, yes, Satan is behind the terrible things that happen in our time. But the situation will get a lot worse when Satan really turns loose! So, how are you supposed to live in a world that's pretty bad already? You keep on loving God and hold tight to his Word.

>> **PERSECUTORS TO BE PUNISHED**
Take heart. See 2 Thessalonians 1:3–10

>> **DON'T BE FOOLED BY *THESE* MIRACLES**
Warning recorded in 2 Thessalonians 2:5–12

>> **THE LITTLE RED HEN WAS RIGHT**
Won't work? Then don't eat. 2 Thessalonians 3:6–13

As Paul writes, Agrippina is planning to murder her husband, the Emperor Claudius, and make her son Nero emperor. Later Nero will have his mother executed.

1 Paul, Silas[a] and Timothy,

To the church of the Thessalonians in God our Father and the Lord Jesus Christ:

[2] Grace and peace to you from God the Father and the Lord Jesus Christ.

Thanksgiving and Prayer

[3] We ought always to thank God for you, brothers and sisters,[b] and rightly so, because your faith is growing more and more, and the love all of you have for one another is increasing. [4] Therefore, among God's churches we boast about your perseverance and faith in all the persecutions and trials you are enduring.

[5] All this is evidence that God's judgment is right, and as a result you will be counted worthy of the kingdom of God, for which you are suffering. [6] God is just: He will pay back trouble to those who trouble you [7] and give relief to you who are troubled, and to us as well. This will happen when the Lord Jesus is revealed from heaven in blazing fire with his powerful angels. [8] He will punish those who do not know God and do not obey the gospel of our Lord Jesus. [9] They will be punished with everlasting destruction and shut out from the presence of the Lord and from the glory of his might [10] on the day he comes to be glorified in his holy people and to be marveled at among all those

---

[a] *1* Greek *Silvanus*, a variant of *Silas* [b] *3* The Greek word for *brothers and sisters* (*adelphoi*) refers here to believers, both men and women, as part of God's family; also in 2:1, 13, 15; 3:1, 6, 13.

TO THE POINT

God Plays Fair

So many things in life aren't fair. Untrue rumors ruin your reputation. A drunk driver smashes into a bus filled with kids. A terrorist bomb goes off in a park. A girl is date raped by a guy she trusted. Does it ever make you wonder: Where is God? Why doesn't he do something?

God does not cause terrible things like this. They're caused by people who choose to sin and in their sin hurt innocent people. God usually doesn't pay them back right away. But 2 Thessalonians 1:5–10 tells you that God surely will. It really isn't fair that people can sin against and hurt others. But they won't get away with it. Not in the end. When Jesus comes, "they will be punished ... and shut out from the presence of the Lord" (2 Thessalonians 1:9).

who have believed. This includes you, because you believed our testimony to you.

¹¹With this in mind, we constantly pray for you, that our God may make you worthy of his calling, and that by his power he may bring to fruition your every desire for goodness and your every deed prompted by faith. ¹²We pray this so that the name of our Lord Jesus may be glorified in you, and you in him, according to the grace of our God and the Lord Jesus Christ.ª

The Man of Lawlessness

2 Concerning the coming of our Lord Jesus Christ and our being gathered to him, we ask you, brothers and sisters, ²not to become easily unsettled or alarmed by the teaching allegedly from us—whether by a prophecy or by word of mouth or by letter—asserting that the day of the Lord has already come. ³Don't let anyone deceive you in any way, for that day will not come until the rebellion occurs and the man of lawlessnessᵇ is revealed, the man doomed to destruction. ⁴He will oppose and will exalt himself over everything that is called God or is worshiped, so that he sets himself up in God's temple, proclaiming himself to be God.

⁵Don't you remember that when I was with you I used to tell you these things? ⁶And now you know what is holding him back, so that he may be revealed at the proper time. ⁷For the secret power of lawlessness is already at work; but the one who now holds it back will continue to do so till he is taken out of the way. ⁸And then the lawless one will be revealed, whom the Lord Jesus will overthrow with the breath of his mouth and destroy by the splendor of his coming. ⁹The coming of the lawless one will be in accordance with how Satan works. He will use all sorts of displays of power through signs and wonders that serve the lie, ¹⁰and all the ways that wickedness deceives those who are perishing. They perish because they refused to love the truth and so be saved. ¹¹For this reason God sends them a powerful delusion so that they will believe the lie ¹²and so that all will be condemned who have not believed the truth but have delighted in wickedness.

Stand Firm

¹³But we ought always to thank God for you, brothers and sisters loved by the Lord, because God chose you as firstfruitsᶜ to be saved through the sanctifying work of the Spirit and through belief in the truth. ¹⁴He called you to this through our gospel, that you might share in the glory of our Lord Jesus Christ.

¹⁵So then, brothers and sisters, stand

ª 12 Or God and Lord, Jesus Christ   ᵇ 3 Some manuscripts sin   ᶜ 13 Some manuscripts because from the beginning God chose you

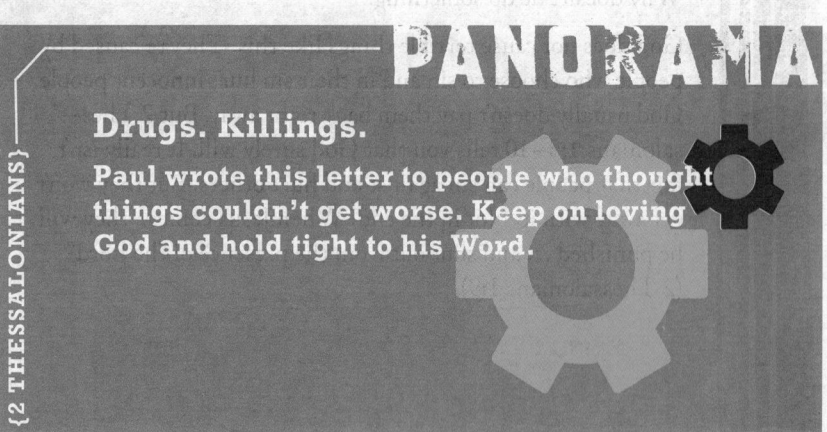

PANORAMA

Drugs. Killings.

Paul wrote this letter to people who thought things couldn't get worse. Keep on loving God and hold tight to his Word.

firm and hold fast to the teachings[a] we passed on to you, whether by word of mouth or by letter.

[16] May our Lord Jesus Christ himself and God our Father, who loved us and by his grace gave us eternal encouragement and good hope, [17] encourage your hearts and strengthen you in every good deed and word.

Request for Prayer

3 As for other matters, brothers and sisters, pray for us that the message of the Lord may spread rapidly and be honored, just as it was with you. [2] And pray that we may be delivered from wicked and evil people, for not everyone has faith. [3] But the Lord is faithful, and he will strengthen you and protect you from the evil one. [4] We have confidence in the Lord that you are doing and will continue to do the things we command. [5] May the Lord direct your hearts into God's love and Christ's perseverance.

The Lord is faithful, and he will strengthen you and protect you from the evil one.

2 Thessalonians 3:3

Warning Against Idleness

[6] In the name of the Lord Jesus Christ, we command you, brothers and sisters, to keep away from every believer who is idle and disruptive and does not live according to the teaching[b] you received from us. [7] For you yourselves know how you ought to follow our example. We were not idle when we were with you, [8] nor did we eat anyone's food without paying for it. On the contrary, we worked night and day, laboring and toiling so that we would not be a burden to any of you. [9] We did this, not because we do not have the right to such help, but in order to offer ourselves as a model for you to imitate. [10] For even when we were with you, we gave you this rule: "The one who is unwilling to work shall not eat."

[11] We hear that some among you are idle and disruptive. They are not busy; they are busybodies. [12] Such people we command and urge in the Lord Jesus Christ to settle down and earn the food they eat. [13] And as for you, brothers and sisters, never tire of doing what is good.

[14] Take special note of anyone who does not obey our instruction in this letter. Do not associate with them, in order that they may feel ashamed. [15] Yet do not regard them as an enemy, but warn them as you would a fellow believer.

Final Greetings

[16] Now may the Lord of peace himself give you peace at all times and in every way. The Lord be with all of you.

[17] I, Paul, write this greeting in my own hand, which is the distinguishing mark in all my letters. This is how I write.

[18] The grace of our Lord Jesus Christ be with you all.

---

[a] 15 Or *traditions*   [b] 6 Or *tradition*

1 TIMOTHY

preview

Paul writes this letter to Timothy near the end of his life, about 65 A.D.

Timothy travels with Paul on two missionary journeys. Even though Timothy is young, Paul sends him on important missions.

Teens.

Have you ever noticed how older people often look down on teens? Not all adults, of course. But many adults don't listen very closely to teenagers.

In this letter to a young follower, the apostle Paul tells him, "Don't let anyone look down on you because you are young" (1 Timothy 4:12). Better yet, Paul tells Timothy what to do to earn older people's respect! His words of wisdom may show you how to get more respect too!

》TRY THESE ON FOR SIZE
Check out 1 Timothy 2:9,10

》IT'S WHAT THEY DO
Read leader qualifications in 1 Timothy 3:1–10

》YOUNG FOLKS SET AN EXAMPLE TOO
Expect the best from yourself, says 1 Timothy 4:12–14

》RICHES BAIT TRAP SET FOR WANDERERS
Warning recorded in 1 Timothy 6:3–10

As Paul writes, Christians in Rome are persecuted, accused by Nero of starting a fire that devastated the city. Several important men who plot to kill Nero commit suicide. Buddhism is introduced in China.

1 Paul, an apostle of Christ Jesus by the command of God our Savior and of Christ Jesus our hope,

2 To Timothy my true son in the faith:

Grace, mercy and peace from God the Father and Christ Jesus our Lord.

Timothy Charged to Oppose False Teachers

3 As I urged you when I went into Macedonia, stay there in Ephesus so that you may command certain people not to teach false doctrines any longer 4 or to devote themselves to myths and endless genealogies. Such things promote controversial speculations rather than advancing God's work—which is by faith. 5 The goal of this command is love, which comes from a pure heart and a good conscience and a sincere faith. 6 Some have departed from these and have turned to meaningless talk. 7 They want to be teachers of the law, but they do not know what they are talking about or what they so confidently affirm.

8 We know that the law is good if one uses it properly. 9 We also know that the law is made not for the righteous but for lawbreakers and rebels, the ungodly and sinful, the unholy and irreligious, for those who kill their fathers or mothers, for murderers, 10 for the sexually immoral, for those practicing homosexuality, for slave traders and liars and perjurers—and for whatever else is contrary to the sound doctrine 11 that conforms to the gospel concerning the glory of the blessed God, which he entrusted to me.

The Lord's Grace to Paul

12 I thank Christ Jesus our Lord, who has given me strength, that he considered me trustworthy, appointing me to his service. 13 Even though I was once a blasphemer and a persecutor and a violent man, I was shown mercy because I acted in ignorance and unbelief. 14 The grace of our Lord was poured out on me abundantly, along with the faith and love that are in Christ Jesus.

15 Here is a trustworthy saying that deserves full acceptance: Christ Jesus came into the world to save sinners—of whom I am the worst. 16 But for that very reason I was shown mercy so that in me, the worst of sinners, Christ Jesus might display his immense patience as an example for those who would believe in him and receive eternal life. 17 Now to the King eternal, immortal, invisible, the only God, be honor and glory for ever and ever. Amen.

The Charge to Timothy Renewed

18 Timothy, my son, I am giving you this command in keeping with the prophecies once made about you, so that by recalling them you may fight the battle well, 19 holding on to faith and a good conscience, which some have rejected and so have suffered shipwreck with regard to the faith. 20 Among them are Hymenaeus and Alexander, whom I have handed over to Satan to be taught not to blaspheme.

Instructions on Worship

2 I urge, then, first of all, that petitions, prayers, intercession and thanksgiving be made for all people— 2 for kings and all those in authority, that we may live peaceful and quiet lives in all godliness and holiness. 3 This is good, and pleases God our Savior, 4 who wants all people to be saved and to come to a knowledge of the truth. 5 For there is one God and one mediator between God and mankind, the man Christ Jesus, 6 who gave himself as a ransom for all people. This has now been witnessed to at the proper time. 7 And for this purpose I was appointed a herald and an apostle—I am telling the truth, I am not lying—and a true and faithful teacher of the Gentiles.

8 Therefore I want the men everywhere to pray, lifting up holy hands without anger or disputing. 9 I also want the women to dress modestly, with decency and propriety, adorning themselves, not with elaborate hairstyles or gold or pearls or expensive clothes, 10 but with good deeds, appropriate for women who profess to worship God.

Dear Jordan

Dear Hailey,

You may find it interesting that the Apostle Paul said he was the worst of sinners (1 Timothy 1:15). One of his favorite activities before he accepted Christ as his Savior was persecuting Christians. But God spoke to Paul, and Paul had a change of heart. He realized Jesus is Lord, so he stopped doing wrong and asked for forgiveness. Paul knew if God could forgive him, God could forgive anyone, and that includes you too (1 Timothy 1:13–16).

You say you can't expect to be forgiven and you know you aren't because you don't feel it. If you believe that Christ died for your sins and you have asked for forgiveness, God in his grace has forgiven you whether you can feel it or not. Perhaps it will help if you will forgive yourself.

Let God help you experience the joy of your salvation (Psalm 51:12). Here are some verses to look up. Read and reread them until you can hear that "still, small voice" telling you that you are loved and forgiven: Psalm 85:2; Jeremiah 31:34; 1 John 1:9; Psalm 103:10–12.

Jordan

¹¹A woman*a* should learn in quietness and full submission. ¹²I do not permit a woman to teach or to assume authority over a man;*b* she must be quiet. ¹³For Adam was formed first, then Eve. ¹⁴And Adam was not the one deceived; it was the woman who was deceived and became a sinner. ¹⁵But women*c* will be saved through childbearing—if they continue in faith, love and holiness with propriety.

Qualifications for Overseers and Deacons

3 Here is a trustworthy saying: Whoever aspires to be an overseer desires a noble task. ²Now the overseer is to be above reproach, faithful to his wife, temperate, self-controlled, respectable, hospitable, able to teach, ³not given to drunkenness, not violent but gentle, not quarrelsome, not a lover of money. ⁴He must manage his own family well and see that his children obey him, and he must do so in a manner worthy of full*d* respect. ⁵(If anyone does not know how to manage his own family, how can he take care of God's church?) ⁶He must not be a recent convert, or he may become conceited and fall under the same judgment as the devil. ⁷He must also have a good reputation with outsiders, so that he will not fall into disgrace and into the devil's trap.

⁸In the same way, deacons*e* are to be

---

a 11 Or *wife*; also in verse 12   *b* 12 Or *over her husband*   *c* 15 Greek *she*   *d* 4 Or *him with proper*   *e* 8 The word *deacons* refers here to Christians designated to serve with the overseers/elders of the church in a variety of ways; similarly in verse 12; and in Romans 16:1 and Phil. 1:1.

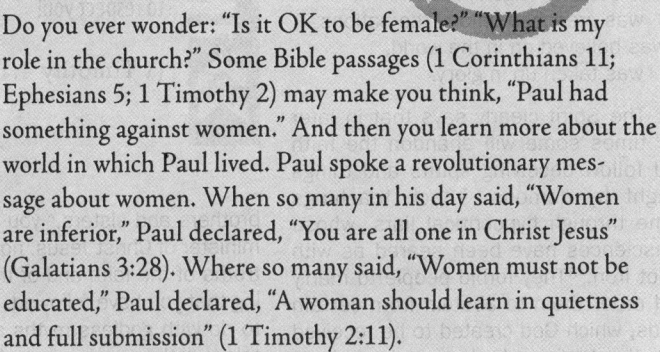

TO THE POINT

Gifted Women

Do you ever wonder: "Is it OK to be female?" "What is my role in the church?" Some Bible passages (1 Corinthians 11; Ephesians 5; 1 Timothy 2) may make you think, "Paul had something against women." And then you learn more about the world in which Paul lived. Paul spoke a revolutionary message about women. When so many in his day said, "Women are inferior," Paul declared, "You are all one in Christ Jesus" (Galatians 3:28). Where so many said, "Women must not be educated," Paul declared, "A woman should learn in quietness and full submission" (1 Timothy 2:11).

Though interpretations of this passage differ, Christians can agree on two conclusions: Women are spiritually gifted members (not inferior members) of the body of Christ, the church. All of us, men and women, must stand quietly before God, submitting to his Word and to each other in love.

worthy of respect, sincere, not indulging in much wine, and not pursuing dishonest gain. [9] They must keep hold of the deep truths of the faith with a clear conscience. [10] They must first be tested; and then if there is nothing against them, let them serve as deacons.

[11] In the same way, the women[a] are to be worthy of respect, not malicious talkers but temperate and trustworthy in everything.

[12] A deacon must be faithful to his wife and must manage his children and his household well. [13] Those who have served well gain an excellent standing and great assurance in their faith in Christ Jesus.

Reasons for Paul's Instructions

[14] Although I hope to come to you soon, I am writing you these instructions so that, [15] if I am delayed, you will know how people ought to conduct themselves in God's household, which is the church of the living God, the pillar and foundation of the truth. [16] Beyond all question, the mystery from which true godliness springs is great:

He appeared in the flesh,
    was vindicated by the Spirit,[b]
was seen by angels,
    was preached among the nations,
was believed on in the world,
    was taken up in glory.

4 The Spirit clearly says that in later times some will abandon the faith and follow deceiving spirits and things taught by demons. [2] Such teachings come through hypocritical liars, whose consciences have been seared as with a hot iron. [3] They forbid people to marry and order them to abstain from certain foods, which God created to be received with thanksgiving by those who believe and who know the truth. [4] For everything God created is good, and nothing is to be rejected if it is received with thanksgiving, [5] because it is consecrated by the word of God and prayer.

[6] If you point these things out to the

Old Mr. Bronson is always yelling at you for cutting through his yard. You haven't, but he won't believe you. You sit with your friends in church, and some of the old folks watch every move, ready to criticize you if you say something to each other. Some of this comes with the territory. Many older people figure today's teens are a lot worse than they were. But you don't have to stand for it. Paul says so in 1 Timothy 4:12: "Set an example for the believers in speech, in conduct, in love, in faith and in purity." Live the Christian life consistently, and in time everyone will learn to respect you!

{1 Timothy 4:11–16}

brothers and sisters,[c] you will be a good minister of Christ Jesus, nourished on the truths of the faith and of the good teaching that you have followed. [7] Have nothing to do with godless myths and old wives' tales; rather, train yourself to be godly. [8] For physical training is of some value, but godliness has value for all things, holding promise for both the present life and the life to come. [9] This is a trustworthy saying that deserves full acceptance. [10] That is why we labor and strive, because

---

[a] 11 Possibly deacons' wives or women who are deacons   [b] 16 Or *vindicated in spirit*   [c] 6 The Greek word for *brothers and sisters* (*adelphoi*) refers here to believers, both men and women, as part of God's family.

we have put our hope in the living God, who is the Savior of all people, and especially of those who believe.

¹¹Command and teach these things. ¹²Don't let anyone look down on you because you are young, but set an example for the believers in speech, in conduct, in love, in faith and in purity. ¹³Until I come, devote yourself to the public reading of Scripture, to preaching and to teaching. ¹⁴Do not neglect your gift, which was given you through prophecy when the body of elders laid their hands on you.

¹⁵Be diligent in these matters; give yourself wholly to them, so that everyone may see your progress. ¹⁶Watch your life and doctrine closely. Persevere in them, because if you do, you will save both yourself and your hearers.

Widows, Elders and Slaves

5 Do not rebuke an older man harshly, but exhort him as if he were your father. Treat younger men as brothers, ²older women as mothers, and younger women as sisters, with absolute purity.

³Give proper recognition to those widows who are really in need. ⁴But if a widow has children or grandchildren, these should learn first of all to put their religion into practice by caring for their own family and so repaying their parents and grandparents, for this is pleasing to God. ⁵The widow who is really in need and left all alone puts her hope in God and continues

night and day to pray and to ask God for help. ⁶But the widow who lives for pleasure is dead even while she lives. ⁷Give the people these instructions, so that no one may be open to blame. ⁸Anyone who does not provide for their relatives, and especially for their own household, has denied the faith and is worse than an unbeliever.

⁹No widow may be put on the list of widows unless she is over sixty, has been faithful to her husband, ¹⁰and is well known for her good deeds, such as bringing up children, showing hospitality, washing the feet of the Lord's people, helping those in trouble and devoting herself to all kinds of good deeds.

¹¹As for younger widows, do not put them on such a list. For when their sensual desires overcome their dedication to Christ, they want to marry. ¹²Thus they bring judgment on themselves, because they have broken their first pledge. ¹³Besides, they get into the habit of being idle and going about from house to house. And not only do they become idlers, but also busybodies who talk nonsense, saying things they ought not to. ¹⁴So I counsel younger widows to marry, to have children, to manage their homes and to give the enemy no opportunity for slander. ¹⁵Some have in fact already turned away to follow Satan.

¹⁶If any woman who is a believer has widows in her care, she should continue

---

PANORAMA

Teens.

Paul tells young Timothy, "Don't let anyone look down on you because you are young." This book tells you what to do to earn older people's respect.

{1 TIMOTHY}

to help them and not let the church be burdened with them, so that the church can help those widows who are really in need.

17 The elders who direct the affairs of the church well are worthy of double honor, especially those whose work is preaching and teaching. 18 For Scripture says, "Do not muzzle an ox while it is treading out the grain,"[a] and "The worker deserves his wages."[b] 19 Do not entertain an accusation against an elder unless it is brought by two or three witnesses. 20 But those elders who are sinning you are to reprove before everyone, so that the others may take warning. 21 I charge you, in the sight of God and Christ Jesus and the elect angels, to keep these instructions without partiality, and to do nothing out of favoritism.

22 Do not be hasty in the laying on of hands, and do not share in the sins of others. Keep yourself pure.

23 Stop drinking only water, and use a little wine because of your stomach and your frequent illnesses.

24 The sins of some are obvious, reaching the place of judgment ahead of them; the sins of others trail behind them. 25 In the same way, good deeds are obvious, and even those that are not obvious cannot remain hidden forever.

6 All who are under the yoke of slavery should consider their masters worthy of full respect, so that God's name and our teaching may not be slandered. 2 Those who have believing masters should not show them disrespect just because they are fellow believers. Instead, they should serve them even better because their masters are dear to them as fellow believers and are devoted to the welfare[c] of their slaves.

False Teachers and the Love of Money

These are the things you are to teach and insist on. 3 If anyone teaches otherwise and does not agree to the sound instruction of our Lord Jesus Christ and to godly teaching, 4 they are conceited

and understand nothing. They have an unhealthy interest in controversies and quarrels about words that result in envy, strife, malicious talk, evil suspicions 5 and constant friction between people of corrupt mind, who have been robbed of the truth and who think that godliness is a means to financial gain.

6 But godliness with contentment is great gain. 7 For we brought nothing into the world, and we can take nothing out

>> INSTANT ACCESS

If money a root of all kinds of evil, it must be that those without any money are better off than those with a lot. Right? Maybe. But the verse says "the *love* of money." Money itself isn't bad, but loving money can lead to making bad choices. A person who is poor and loves money may rob a store or sell drugs, yet refuse to buy medicine for a sick child. A person who is rich and loves money may be stingy and cheat others in business. It doesn't make any difference if you're rich or poor, young or old. Start loving money, and you'll make bad choices in life. Instead, use money, and use it wisely. But keep your love for God at the top of your priorities.

{1 Timothy 6:3–10}

---

[a] 18 Deut. 25:4   [b] 18 Luke 10:7   [c] 2 Or *and benefit from the service*

of it. [8]But if we have food and clothing, we will be content with that. [9]Those who want to get rich fall into temptation and a trap and into many foolish and harmful desires that plunge people into ruin and destruction. [10]For the love of money is a root of all kinds of evil. Some people, eager for money, have wandered from the faith and pierced themselves with many griefs.

Final Charge to Timothy

[11]But you, man of God, flee from all this, and pursue righteousness, godliness, faith, love, endurance and gentleness. [12]Fight the good fight of the faith. Take hold of the eternal life to which you were called when you made your good confession in the presence of many witnesses. [13]In the sight of God, who gives life to everything, and of Christ Jesus, who while testifying before Pontius Pilate made the good confession, I charge you [14]to keep this command without spot or blame until the appearing of our Lord Jesus Christ, [15]which God will bring about in his own time — God, the blessed and only Ruler, the King of kings and Lord of lords, [16]who alone is immortal and who lives in unapproachable light, whom no one has seen or can see. To him be honor and might forever. Amen.

[17]Command those who are rich in this present world not to be arrogant nor to put their hope in wealth, which is so uncertain, but to put their hope in God, who richly provides us with everything for our enjoyment. [18]Command them to do good, to be rich in good deeds, and to be generous and willing to share. [19]In this way they will lay up treasure for themselves as a firm foundation for the coming age, so that they may take hold of the life that is truly life.

[20]Timothy, guard what has been entrusted to your care. Turn away from godless chatter and the opposing ideas of what is falsely called knowledge, [21]which some have professed and in so doing have departed from the faith.

Grace be with you all.

2 TIMOTHY

preview

Paul writes this letter shortly before he is executed in Rome in 67 A.D.

After Paul's death, Timothy will become a leader in the church. Paul wants Timothy to understand what leadership involves.

Character.

You'll probably read about it sooner or later in school. Young Ben Franklin made a list of things to work on to develop his character. If you made such a list, what would you put on it? What would you work on first?

Paul knew he was about to be executed when he wrote this second letter to Timothy. It was the last letter he ever wrote, so he jotted down things he thought were important to encourage and guide his young friend. Paul's last words can help you keep on the right path too.

>>**SOLDIER? FARMER? ATHLETE?**
   Learn from them, says apostle in 2 Timothy 2:3–7

>>**WATCH OUT FOR HORMONES**
   See 2 Timothy 2:22–26

>>**ISN'T IT THE TRUTH!**
   Paul hits nail on the head. See 2 Timothy 3:1–5

>>**PERSONAL FITNESS TRAINER, FREE!**
   Sign up now. Read 2 Timothy 3:16,17

As Paul writes, Nero orders a canal dug through the Isthmus of Corinth. The Jews finally revolt against Rome. An army under Vespasian recovers Galilee, invades Judea.

1 Paul, an apostle of Christ Jesus by the will of God, in keeping with the promise of life that is in Christ Jesus,

2 To Timothy, my dear son:

Grace, mercy and peace from God the Father and Christ Jesus our Lord.

Thanksgiving

3 I thank God, whom I serve, as my ancestors did, with a clear conscience, as night and day I constantly remember you in my prayers. 4 Recalling your tears, I long to see you, so that I may be filled with joy. 5 I am reminded of your sincere faith, which first lived in your grandmother Lois and in your mother Eunice and, I am persuaded, now lives in you also.

Appeal for Loyalty to Paul and the Gospel

6 For this reason I remind you to fan into flame the gift of God, which is in you through the laying on of my hands. 7 For the Spirit God gave us does not make us timid, but gives us power, love and self-discipline. 8 So do not be ashamed of the testimony about our Lord or of me his prisoner. Rather, join with me in suffering for the gospel, by the power of God. 9 He has saved us and called us to a holy life—not because of anything we have done but because of his own purpose and grace. This grace was given us in Christ Jesus before the beginning of time, 10 but it has now been revealed through the appearing of our Savior, Christ Jesus, who has destroyed death and has brought life and immortality to light through the gospel. 11 And of this gospel I was appointed a herald and an apostle and a teacher. 12 That is why I am suffering as I am. Yet this is no cause for shame, because I know whom I have believed, and am convinced that he is able to guard what I have entrusted to him until that day. 13 What you heard from me, keep as the pattern of sound teaching, with faith and love in Christ Jesus. 14 Guard the good deposit that was entrusted to you—guard it with the help of the Holy Spirit who lives in us.

≫ INSTANT ACCESS

If you have a mom and grandmother like Timothy's, you're fortunate. They each had a sincere faith, and they passed it on to Timothy, and it became his personal faith. There was no way their faith could do Timothy any good. That's one of the first lessons any person who comes from a Christian home needs to learn. You can't get to heaven on your parents' faith any more than you can get there on a skateboard. If you have Christian parents or grandparents, make their faith your own. Tell Jesus you accept him as your personal Savior. You'll be glad you did.

{2 Timothy 1:5–7}

Examples of Disloyalty and Loyalty

15 You know that everyone in the province of Asia has deserted me, including Phygelus and Hermogenes.

16 May the Lord show mercy to the household of Onesiphorus, because he often refreshed me and was not ashamed of my chains. 17 On the contrary, when he was in Rome, he searched hard for me until he found me. 18 May the Lord grant that he will find mercy from the Lord on that day! You know very well in how many ways he helped me in Ephesus.

The Appeal Renewed

2 You then, my son, be strong in the grace that is in Christ Jesus. 2 And the things you have heard me say in the presence of many witnesses entrust to reliable people who will also be qualified to teach others. ³Join with me in suffering, like a good soldier of Christ Jesus. ⁴No one serving as a soldier gets entangled in civilian affairs, but rather tries to please his commanding officer. ⁵Similarly, anyone who competes as an athlete does not receive the victor's crown except by competing according to the rules. ⁶The hardworking farmer should be the first to receive a share of the crops. ⁷Reflect on what I am saying, for the Lord will give you insight into all this.

⁸Remember Jesus Christ, raised from the dead, descended from David. This is my gospel, ⁹for which I am suffering even to the point of being chained like a criminal. But God's word is not chained. ¹⁰Therefore I endure everything for the sake of the elect, that they too may obtain the salvation that is in Christ Jesus, with eternal glory.

¹¹Here is a trustworthy saying:

If we died with him,
  we will also live with him;
¹²if we endure,
  we will also reign with him.
If we disown him,
  he will also disown us;
¹³if we are faithless,
  he remains faithful,
  for he cannot disown himself.

Dealing With False Teachers

¹⁴Keep reminding God's people of these things. Warn them before God against quarreling about words; it is of no value, and only ruins those who listen. ¹⁵Do your best to present yourself to God as one approved, a worker who does not need to be ashamed and who correctly handles the word of truth. ¹⁶Avoid godless chatter, because those who indulge in it will become more and more ungodly. ¹⁷Their teaching will spread like gangrene. Among them are Hymenaeus and

Philetus, ¹⁸who have departed from the truth. They say that the resurrection has already taken place, and they destroy the faith of some. ¹⁹Nevertheless, God's solid foundation stands firm, sealed with this inscription: "The Lord knows those who are his," and, "Everyone who confesses the name of the Lord must turn away from wickedness."

The Lord knows those who are his.
2 Timothy 2:19

²⁰In a large house there are articles not only of gold and silver, but also of wood and clay; some are for special purposes and some for common use. ²¹Those who cleanse themselves from the latter will be instruments for special purposes, made holy, useful to the Master and prepared to do any good work.

²²Flee the evil desires of youth and pursue righteousness, faith, love and peace, along with those who call on the Lord out of a pure heart. ²³Don't have anything to do with foolish and stupid arguments, because you know they produce quarrels. ²⁴And the Lord's servant must not be quarrelsome but must be kind to everyone, able to teach, not resentful. ²⁵Opponents must be gently instructed, in the hope that God will grant them repentance leading them to a knowledge of the truth, ²⁶and that they will come to their senses and escape from the trap of the devil, who has taken them captive to do his will.

3 But mark this: There will be terrible times in the last days. ²People will be lovers of themselves, lovers of money, boastful, proud, abusive, disobedient to their parents, ungrateful, unholy, ³without love, unforgiving, slanderous, without self-control, brutal, not lovers of the good, ⁴treacherous, rash, conceited, lovers of pleasure rather than lovers of God— ⁵having a form of godliness but denying its power. Have nothing to do with such people.

⁶They are the kind who worm their way into homes and gain control over gullible women, who are loaded down with sins and are swayed by all kinds of evil desires,

7 always learning but never able to come to a knowledge of the truth. 8 Just as Jannes and Jambres opposed Moses, so also these teachers oppose the truth. They are men of depraved minds, who, as far as the faith is concerned, are rejected. 9 But they will not get very far because, as in the case of those men, their folly will be clear to everyone.

A Final Charge to Timothy

10 You, however, know all about my teaching, my way of life, my purpose, faith, patience, love, endurance, 11 persecutions, sufferings — what kinds of things happened to me in Antioch, Iconium and Lystra, the persecutions I endured. Yet the Lord rescued me from all of them.

12 In fact, everyone who wants to live a godly life in Christ Jesus will be persecuted, 13 while evildoers and impostors will go from bad to worse, deceiving and being deceived. 14 But as for you, continue in what you have learned and have become convinced of, because you know those from whom you learned it, 15 and how from infancy you have known the Holy Scriptures, which are able to make you wise for salvation through faith in Christ Jesus. 16 All Scripture is God-breathed and is useful for teaching, rebuking, correcting and training in righteousness, 17 so that the servant of God*a* may be thoroughly equipped for every good work.

4 In the presence of God and of Christ Jesus, who will judge the living and

a 17 Or that you, a man of God,

TO THE POINT

All Scripture Is Inspired

Everything in the Bible is not necessarily interesting or inspiring. But it is "inspired": God was at work making sure that what the writer put down was God's message.

Even if everything in the Bible may not seem interesting, it's there for a purpose. And when you read the Bible, you should look for these things (2 Timothy 3:16):

+ Teaching. What truths can you discover that will help you understand God and other people?

+ Rebuking. What have you been doing wrong that you need to change?

+ Correcting. What can you do to become more Christ-like?

+ Training. What can you discover that will equip you for good deeds?

the dead, and in view of his appearing and his kingdom, I give you this charge: [2]Preach the word; be prepared in season and out of season; correct, rebuke and encourage—with great patience and careful instruction. [3]For the time will come when people will not put up with sound doctrine. Instead, to suit their own desires, they will gather around them a great number of teachers to say what their itching ears want to hear. [4]They will turn their ears away from the truth and turn aside to myths. [5]But you, keep your head in all situations, endure hardship, do the work of an evangelist, discharge all the duties of your ministry.

[6]For I am already being poured out like a drink offering, and the time for my departure is near. [7]I have fought the good fight, I have finished the race, I have kept the faith. [8]Now there is in store for me the crown of righteousness, which the Lord, the righteous Judge, will award to me on that day—and not only to me, but also to all who have longed for his appearing.

Personal Remarks

[9]Do your best to come to me quickly, [10]for Demas, because he loved this world, has deserted me and has gone to Thessalonica. Crescens has gone to Galatia, and Titus to Dalmatia. [11]Only Luke is with me. Get Mark and bring him with you, because he is helpful to me in my ministry. [12]I sent Tychicus to Ephesus. [13]When you come, bring the cloak that I left with Carpus at Troas, and my scrolls, especially the parchments.

[14]Alexander the metalworker did me a great deal of harm. The Lord will repay him for what he has done. [15]You too should be on your guard against him, because he strongly opposed our message.

[16]At my first defense, no one came to my support, but everyone deserted me. May it not be held against them. [17]But the Lord stood at my side and gave me strength, so that through me the message might be fully proclaimed and all the Gentiles might hear it. And I was delivered from the lion's mouth. [18]The Lord will rescue me from every evil attack and will bring me safely to his heavenly kingdom. To him be glory for ever and ever. Amen.

Final Greetings

[19]Greet Priscilla[a] and Aquila and the household of Onesiphorus. [20]Erastus stayed in Corinth, and I left Trophimus sick in Miletus. [21]Do your best to get here before winter. Eubulus greets you, and so do Pudens, Linus, Claudia and all the brothers and sisters.[b]

[22]The Lord be with your spirit. Grace be with you all.

---

[a] 19 Greek *Prisca*, a variant of *Priscilla*   [b] 21 The Greek word for *brothers and sisters* (*adelphoi*) refers here to believers, both men and women, as part of God's family.

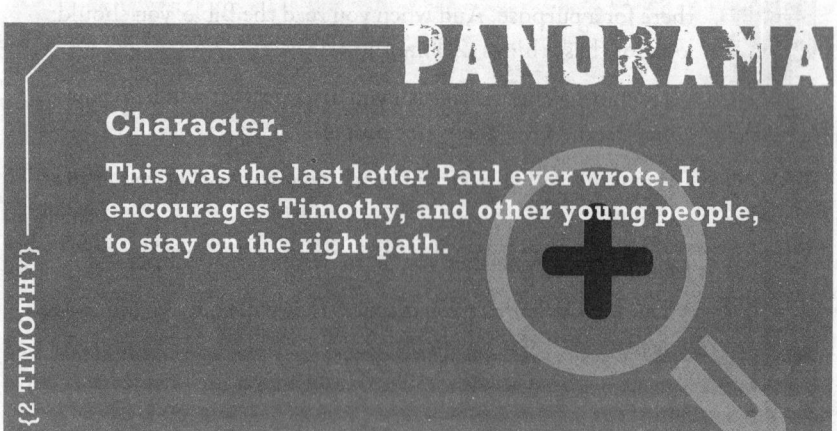

PANORAMA

Character.

This was the last letter Paul ever wrote. It encourages Timothy, and other young people, to stay on the right path.

{2 TIMOTHY}

TITUS

Leadership.

Are you a leader in your youth group? Do you ever get frustrated or feel like most of the other kids are lazy? And when you try to help, do they get angry at you? Well, this book of the New Testament may be just for you.

Paul wrote this short letter to Titus, a young leader he sent to Crete because of problems in that church. Paul reminds young Titus of the best way to influence others. Paul also reminds Titus that people who know Jesus should concentrate on doing good.

>>**LIP SERVICE YES, ACTIONS NO**
   See Titus 1:16

>>**BEST WAY TO SET AN EXAMPLE**
   See explanation in Titus 2:7

>>**TRUST, THEN DO GOOD**
   Faith produces works, says Titus 3:8

preview

Titus is a young leader in the church, on a mission to the island of Crete.

Paul's letter to Titus is filled with good advice for anyone wanting to be a leader.

Paul writes near the end of his life. The Jews have revolted against Rome. Within three years Jerusalem will fall and the temple will be burned. Captured Jewish General Josephus will write a "History of the Jewish Wars."

1 Paul, a servant of God and an apostle of Jesus Christ to further the faith of God's elect and their knowledge of the truth that leads to godliness— [2]in the hope of eternal life, which God, who does not lie, promised before the beginning of time, [3]and which now at his appointed season he has brought to light through the preaching entrusted to me by the command of God our Savior,

[4]To Titus, my true son in our common faith:

Grace and peace from God the Father and Christ Jesus our Savior.

Appointing Elders Who Love What Is Good

[5]The reason I left you in Crete was that you might put in order what was left unfinished and appoint[a] elders in every town, as I directed you. [6]An elder must be blameless, faithful to his wife, a man whose children believe[b] and are not open to the charge of being wild and disobedient. [7]Since an overseer manages God's household, he must be blameless—not overbearing, not quick-tempered, not given to drunkenness, not violent, not pursuing dishonest gain. [8]Rather, he must be hospitable, one who loves what is good, who is self-controlled, upright, holy and disciplined. [9]He must hold firmly to the trustworthy message as it has been taught, so that he can encourage others by sound doctrine and refute those who oppose it.

Rebuking Those Who Fail to Do Good

[10]For there are many rebellious people, full of meaningless talk and deception, especially those of the circumcision group. [11]They must be silenced, because they are disrupting whole households by teaching things they ought not to teach—

and that for the sake of dishonest gain. [12]One of Crete's own prophets has said it: "Cretans are always liars, evil brutes, lazy gluttons."[c] [13]This saying is true. Therefore rebuke them sharply, so that they will be sound in the faith [14]and will pay no attention to Jewish myths or to the merely human commands of those who reject the truth. [15]To the pure, all things are pure, but to those who are corrupted and do not believe, nothing is pure. In fact, both their minds and consciences are corrupted. [16]They claim to know God, but by their actions they deny him. They are detestable, disobedient and unfit for doing anything good.

Doing Good for the Sake of the Gospel

2 You, however, must teach what is appropriate to sound doctrine. [2]Teach the older men to be temperate, worthy of respect, self-controlled, and sound in faith, in love and in endurance.

[3]Likewise, teach the older women to be reverent in the way they live, not to be slanderers or addicted to much wine, but to teach what is good. [4]Then they can urge the younger women to love their husbands and children, [5]to be self-controlled and pure, to be busy at home, to be kind, and to be subject to their husbands, so that no one will malign the word of God.

[6]Similarly, encourage the young men to be self-controlled. [7]In everything set them an example by doing what is good. In your teaching show integrity, seriousness [8]and soundness of speech that cannot be condemned, so that those who oppose you may be ashamed because they have nothing bad to say about us.

[9]Teach slaves to be subject to their masters in everything, to try to please them, not to talk back to them, [10]and not to steal from them, but to show that they

> *We wait for the blessed hope—the appearing of the glory of our great God and Savior, Jesus Christ.*
> Titus 2:13

---

[a] 5 Or ordain   [b] 6 Or children are trustworthy   [c] 12 From the Cretan philosopher Epimenides

can be fully trusted, so that in every way they will make the teaching about God our Savior attractive.

¹¹For the grace of God has appeared that offers salvation to all people. ¹²It teaches us to say "No" to ungodliness and worldly passions, and to live self-controlled, upright and godly lives in this present age, ¹³while we wait for the blessed hope—the appearing of the glory of our great God and Savior, Jesus Christ, ¹⁴who gave himself for us to redeem us from all wickedness and to purify for himself a people that are his very own, eager to do what is good.

¹⁵These, then, are the things you should teach. Encourage and rebuke with all authority. Do not let anyone despise you.

Saved in Order to Do Good

3 Remind the people to be subject to rulers and authorities, to be obedient, to be ready to do whatever is good, ²to slander no one, to be peaceable and considerate, and always to be gentle toward everyone.

³At one time we too were foolish, disobedient, deceived and enslaved by all kinds of passions and pleasures. We lived in malice and envy, being hated and hating one another. ⁴But when the kindness and love of God our Savior appeared, ⁵he saved us, not because of righteous things we had done, but because of his mercy. He saved us through the washing of rebirth and renewal by the Holy Spirit, ⁶whom he poured out on us

TO THE POINT

Do Good

The Bible says you're not saved by doing good deeds (Ephesians 2:8–9). But it also says that people who are saved should "devote themselves to doing what is good" (Titus 3:14). The Greek word used here for *good* means "right and beneficial." Good deeds are actions you take to benefit others.

You don't have to look too far to find good deeds to do. You can help out at home. Help a friend study for a test. Volunteer at a hospital or retirement home. Give the clothes you outgrow to a thrift store. Help a neighbor with yard work or shopping. The opportunities are all around you. Be devoted to doing good, and the greatest blessing of all will be yours!

generously through Jesus Christ our Savior, [7]so that, having been justified by his grace, we might become heirs having the hope of eternal life. [8]This is a trustworthy saying. And I want you to stress these things, so that those who have trusted in God may be careful to devote themselves to doing what is good. These things are excellent and profitable for everyone.

[9]But avoid foolish controversies and genealogies and arguments and quarrels about the law, because these are unprofitable and useless. [10]Warn a divisive person once, and then warn them a second time. After that, have nothing to do with them. [11]You may be sure that such people are warped and sinful; they are self-condemned.

Final Remarks

[12]As soon as I send Artemas or Tychicus to you, do your best to come to me at Nicopolis, because I have decided to winter there. [13]Do everything you can to help Zenas the lawyer and Apollos on their way and see that they have everything they need. [14]Our people must learn to devote themselves to doing what is good, in order to provide for urgent needs and not live unproductive lives.

[15]Everyone with me sends you greetings. Greet those who love us in the faith. Grace be with you all.

PANORAMA

Leadership.

Paul wrote this short letter to Titus, a young leader in Crete. Paul tells him the best way to influence others. And Paul reminds him that people who know Jesus should concentrate on doing good.

{TITUS}

PHILEMON

Favors.

Have you ever asked someone for a favor? Maybe you felt someone owed you a favor? You'll be more likely to get what you want if you ask the right way.

Paul wanted a special favor from a Christian friend named Philemon. A slave of Philemon's named Onesimus had stolen Philemon's property and run away. Later Onesimus met Paul in prison and became a Christian. In this letter Paul asks Philemon to welcome back his returning slave as a Christian brother.

>>A GENTLE REMINDER WILL DO
See Philemon 8–11

>>STUNNING TRANSFORMATIONS HAPPEN
Slave becomes brother, reports Philemon 15–16

preview

Paul writes four letters while in prison in Rome. Philemon is one of them.

Onesimus is a runaway slave who has become a Christian.

Many slaves at this time have better food and housing than those who are free.

As Paul writes, half the population of most cities in the Roman Empire are slaves. So many owners free their slaves that the government levies a tax of five percent of each freed slave's value.

[1]Paul, a prisoner of Christ Jesus, and Timothy our brother,

To Philemon our dear friend and fellow worker— [2]also to Apphia our sister and Archippus our fellow soldier—and to the church that meets in your home:

[3]Grace and peace to you[a] from God our Father and the Lord Jesus Christ.

Thanksgiving and Prayer

[4]I always thank my God as I remember you in my prayers, [5]because I hear about your love for all his holy people and your faith in the Lord Jesus. [6]I pray that your partnership with us in the faith may be effective in deepening your understanding of every good thing we share for the sake of Christ. [7]Your love has given me great joy and encouragement, because you, brother, have refreshed the hearts of the Lord's people.

Paul's Plea for Onesimus

[8]Therefore, although in Christ I could be bold and order you to do what you ought to do, [9]yet I prefer to appeal to you on the basis of love. It is as none other than Paul—an old man and now also a prisoner of Christ Jesus— [10]that I appeal to you for my son Onesimus,[b] who became my son while I was in chains. [11]Formerly he was useless to you, but now he has become useful both to you and to me.

[12]I am sending him—who is my very heart—back to you. [13]I would have liked to keep him with me so that he could take your place in helping me while I am in chains for the gospel. [14]But I did not want to do anything without your consent, so that any favor you do would not seem forced but would be voluntary. [15]Perhaps the reason he was separated from you for a little while was that you might have him back forever— [16]no longer as a slave, but better than a slave, as a dear brother. He is very dear to me but even dearer to you, both as a fellow man and as a brother in the Lord.

[17]So if you consider me a partner, welcome him as you would welcome me. [18]If he has done you any wrong or owes you anything, charge it to me. [19]I, Paul, am writing this with my own hand. I will pay it back—not to mention that you owe me your very self. [20]I do wish, brother, that I may have some benefit from you in the Lord; refresh my heart in Christ. [21]Confident of your obedience, I write to you, knowing that you will do even more than I ask.

[22]And one thing more: Prepare a guest room for me, because I hope to be restored to you in answer to your prayers.

[23]Epaphras, my fellow prisoner in Christ Jesus, sends you greetings. [24]And so do Mark, Aristarchus, Demas and Luke, my fellow workers.

[25]The grace of the Lord Jesus Christ be with your spirit.

---

[a] 3 The Greek is plural; also in verses 22 and 25; elsewhere in this letter "you" is singular.   [b] 10 Onesimus means useful.

PANORAMA

{PHILEMON}

Favors.

Paul wanted a special favor from a Christian friend named Philemon—to welcome back Philemon's returning slave as a Christian brother.

HEBREWS

Churches.

There are lots of different Christian churches. Maybe you're a Lutheran Christian. Or a Baptist Christian. Or a Catholic Christian. You think your own church is special, and it probably is. But more important than the brand is that word *Christian*.

First-century Jews who accepted Jesus as their Savior saw themselves as Jewish Christians. As God's chosen people they felt special. Some began to think that "Jewish" was special enough without the "Christian"! The book of Hebrews is a reminder that what's so special about "Christian" is Jesus Christ himself.

>>**WHAT A BROTHER!**
Incarnation explained. See Hebrews 2:10–18

>>**MERCY AND HELP AVAILABLE NOW**
Prayer encouragement recorded in Hebrews 4:14–16

>>**NEW AND IMPROVED PROMISES**
Read them in Hebrews 8:7–13

>>**HE MADE IT ALL POSSIBLE**
Jesus' role explained. See Hebrews 10:11–14

preview

This letter is written to Jewish Christians living in the Holy Land and worshiping at the Jerusalem temple.

Soon after this letter is sent, the temple is destroyed by the Romans.

The general who leads the Roman army, Titus, becomes Emperor of Rome. Ten years after Jerusalem falls, Titus dedicates the Coliseum in Rome, which features carvings showing temple treasures carried off by Roman soldiers.

God's Final Word: His Son

1 In the past God spoke to our ancestors through the prophets at many times and in various ways, [2] but in these last days he has spoken to us by his Son, whom he appointed heir of all things, and through whom also he made the universe. [3] The Son is the radiance of God's glory and the exact representation of his being, sustaining all things by his powerful word. After he had provided purification for sins, he sat down at the right hand of the Majesty in heaven. [4] So he became as much superior to the angels as the name he has inherited is superior to theirs.

The Son Superior to Angels

[5] For to which of the angels did God ever say,

"You are my Son;
today I have become your Father"[a]?

Or again,

"I will be his Father,
and he will be my Son"[b]?

[6] And again, when God brings his firstborn into the world, he says,

"Let all God's angels worship him."[c]

[7] In speaking of the angels he says,

"He makes his angels spirits,
and his servants flames of fire."[d]

[8] But about the Son he says,

"Your throne, O God, will last for ever and ever;
a scepter of justice will be the scepter of your kingdom.
[9] You have loved righteousness and hated wickedness;
therefore God, your God, has set you above your companions
by anointing you with the oil of joy."[e]

[10] He also says,

"In the beginning, Lord, you laid the foundations of the earth,
and the heavens are the work of your hands.
[11] They will perish, but you remain;
they will all wear out like a garment.
[12] You will roll them up like a robe;
like a garment they will be changed.
But you remain the same,
and your years will never end."[f]

[13] To which of the angels did God ever say,

"Sit at my right hand
until I make your enemies
a footstool for your feet"[g]?

[14] Are not all angels ministering spirits sent to serve those who will inherit salvation?

Warning to Pay Attention

2 We must pay the most careful attention, therefore, to what we have heard, so that we do not drift away. [2] For since the message spoken through angels was binding, and every violation and disobedience received its just punishment, [3] how shall we escape if we ignore so great a salvation? This salvation, which was first announced by the Lord, was confirmed to us by those who heard him. [4] God also testified to it by signs, wonders and various miracles, and by gifts of the Holy Spirit distributed according to his will.

Jesus Made Fully Human

[5] It is not to angels that he has subjected the world to come, about which we are speaking. [6] But there is a place where someone has testified:

"What is mankind that you are mindful of them,
a son of man that you care for him?
[7] You made them a little[h] lower than the angels;
you crowned them with glory and honor
[8]   and put everything under their feet."[i,j]

In putting everything under them,[k] God left nothing that is not subject to them.[k]

---

[a] 5 Psalm 2:7   [b] 5 2 Samuel 7:14; 1 Chron. 17:13   [c] 6 Deut. 32:43 (see Dead Sea Scrolls and Septuagint)
[d] 7 Psalm 104:4   [e] 9 Psalm 45:6,7   [f] 12 Psalm 102:25-27   [g] 13 Psalm 110:1   [h] 7 Or them for a little while
[i] 6-8 Psalm 8:4-6   [j] 7,8 Or *You made him a little lower than the angels;/ you crowned him with glory and honor/ [8] and put everything under his feet."   [k] 8 Or him*

Who are these "angels" and where are they? They are "ministering spirits" whom God sends to serve you as one of "those who will inherit salvation." And they're right there beside and around you. That's comforting to know when you're facing some bully. Or wavering over a hard choice. You feel all alone, but remember—you're not! God doesn't say a lot about angels, but he does let you know that these powerful spiritual beings are with you. Whatever the situation, you're really not alone.

{Hebrews 1:14}

Yet at present we do not see everything subject to them.[a] 9But we do see Jesus, who was made lower than the angels for a little while, now crowned with glory and honor because he suffered death, so that by the grace of God he might taste death for everyone.

10In bringing many sons and daughters to glory, it was fitting that God, for whom and through whom everything exists, should make the pioneer of their salvation perfect through what he suffered. 11Both the one who makes people holy and those who are made holy are of the same family. So Jesus is not ashamed to call them brothers and sisters.[b] 12He says,

"I will declare your name to my brothers and sisters; in the assembly I will sing your praises."[c]

13And again,

"I will put my trust in him."[d]

And again he says,

"Here am I, and the children God has given me."[e]

14Since the children have flesh and blood, he too shared in their humanity so that by his death he might break the power of him who holds the power of death—that is, the devil— 15and free those who all their lives were held in slavery by their fear of death. 16For surely it is not angels he helps, but Abraham's descendants. 17For this reason he had to be made like them,[f] fully human in every way, in order that he might become a merciful and faithful high priest in service to God, and that he might make atonement for the sins of the people. 18Because he himself suffered when he was tempted, he is able to help those who are being tempted.

Jesus Greater Than Moses

3 Therefore, holy brothers and sisters, who share in the heavenly calling, fix your thoughts on Jesus, whom we acknowledge as our apostle and high priest. 2He was faithful to the one who appointed him, just as Moses was faithful in all God's house. 3Jesus has been found worthy of greater honor than Moses, just as the builder of a house has greater honor than the house itself. 4For every house is built by someone, but God is the builder of everything. 5"Moses was faithful as a servant in all God's house,"[g] bearing witness to what would be spoken by God in the future. 6But Christ is faithful as the Son over God's house. And we are his house, if indeed we hold firmly to our confidence and the hope in which we glory.

---

a 8 Or him   b 11 The Greek word for brothers and sisters (adelphoi) refers here to believers, both men and women, as part of God's family; also in verse 12; and in 3:1, 12; 10:19; 13:22.   c 12 Psalm 22:22   d 13 Isaiah 8:17   e 13 Isaiah 8:18   f 17 Or like his brothers   g 5 Num. 12:7

Warning Against Unbelief

[7] So, as the Holy Spirit says:

"Today, if you hear his voice,
[8] do not harden your hearts
as you did in the rebellion,
during the time of testing in the
wilderness,
[9] where your ancestors tested and tried
me,
though for forty years they saw what
I did.
[10] That is why I was angry with that
generation;
I said, 'Their hearts are always
going astray,
and they have not known my ways.'
[11] So I declared on oath in my anger,
'They shall never enter my rest.' "[a]

[12] See to it, brothers and sisters, that none of you has a sinful, unbelieving heart that turns away from the living God. [13] But encourage one another daily, as long as it is called "Today," so that none of you may be hardened by sin's deceitfulness. [14] We have come to share in Christ, if indeed we hold our original conviction firmly to the very end. [15] As has just been said:

"Today, if you hear his voice,
do not harden your hearts
as you did in the rebellion."[b]

[16] Who were they who heard and rebelled? Were they not all those Moses led out of Egypt? [17] And with whom was he angry for forty years? Was it not with those who sinned, whose bodies perished in the wilderness? [18] And to whom did God swear that they would never enter his rest if not to those who disobeyed? [19] So we see that they were not able to enter, because of their unbelief.

A Sabbath-Rest for the People of God

4 Therefore, since the promise of entering his rest still stands, let us be careful that none of you be found to have fallen short of it. [2] For we also have had the good news proclaimed to us, just as they did; but the message they heard was of no value to them, because they did not share the faith of those who obeyed.[c] [3] Now we who have believed enter that rest, just as God has said,

"So I declared on oath in my anger,
'They shall never enter my rest.' "[d]

And yet his works have been finished since the creation of the world. [4] For somewhere he has spoken about the seventh day in these words: "On the seventh day God rested from all his works."[e] [5] And again in the passage above he says, "They shall never enter my rest."

[6] Therefore since it still remains for some to enter that rest, and since those who formerly had the good news proclaimed to them did not go in because of their disobedience, [7] God again set a certain day, calling it "Today." This he did when a long time later he spoke through David, as in the passage already quoted:

"Today, if you hear his voice,
do not harden your hearts."[b]

[8] For if Joshua had given them rest, God would not have spoken later about another day. [9] There remains, then, a Sabbath-rest for the people of God; [10] for anyone who enters God's rest also rests from their works,[f] just as God did from his. [11] Let us, therefore, make every effort to enter that rest, so that no one will perish by following their example of disobedience.

[12] For the word of God is alive and active. Sharper than any double-edged sword, it penetrates even to dividing soul and spirit, joints and marrow; it judges the thoughts and attitudes of the heart. [13] Nothing in all creation is hidden from God's sight. Everything is uncovered and laid bare before the eyes of him to whom we must give account.

Jesus the Great High Priest

[14] Therefore, since we have a great high priest who has ascended into heaven,[g] Jesus the Son of God, let us hold firmly to the faith we profess. [15] For we do not have a high priest who is unable

---

[a] 11 Psalm 95:7-11   [b] 15,7 Psalm 95:7,8   [c] 2 Some manuscripts because those who heard did not combine it with faith   [d] 3 Psalm 95:11; also in verse 5   [e] 4 Gen. 2:2   [f] 10 Or labor   [g] 14 Greek has gone through the heavens

INSTANT ACCESS

Life is pretty tough at times, isn't it? There's pressure on every side to conform to what the world around you wants rather than to what God wants. There's pressure to wear the right thing, buy the right stuff, act the right way, go to the right places. Life is not easy. This verse says Jesus "has been tempted in every way, just as we are." Yeah. Sure. But he didn't live in this century. How could he know what it's like? Because Jesus was a true human being as well as God. He felt every pressure you feel. He knew disappointment and heartbreak. That's why you can bring everything to him. He does know what you're going through. And he cares.

{Hebrews 4:15}

who are ignorant and are going astray, since he himself is subject to weakness. [3]This is why he has to offer sacrifices for his own sins, as well as for the sins of the people. [4]And no one takes this honor on himself, but he receives it when called by God, just as Aaron was.

[5]In the same way, Christ did not take on himself the glory of becoming a high priest. But God said to him,

"You are my Son;
    today I have become your Father."[a]

[6]And he says in another place,

"You are a priest forever,
    in the order of Melchizedek."[b]

[7]During the days of Jesus' life on earth, he offered up prayers and petitions with fervent cries and tears to the one who could save him from death, and he was heard because of his reverent submission. [8]Son though he was, he learned obedience from what he suffered [9]and, once made perfect, he became the source of eternal salvation for all who obey him [10]and was designated by God to be high priest in the order of Melchizedek.

Warning Against Falling Away

[11]We have much to say about this, but it is hard to make it clear to you because you no longer try to understand. [12]In fact, though by this time you ought to be teachers, you need someone to teach you the elementary truths of God's word all over again. You need milk, not solid food! [13]Anyone who lives on milk, being still an infant, is not acquainted with the teaching about righteousness. [14]But solid food is for the mature, who by constant use have trained themselves to distinguish good from evil.

6 Therefore let us move beyond the elementary teachings about Christ and be taken forward to maturity, not laying again the foundation of repentance from acts that lead to death,[c] and of faith in God, [2]instruction about cleansing rites,[d] the laying on of hands, the resurrection of the dead, and eternal judgment. [3]And God permitting, we will do so.

to empathize with our weaknesses, but we have one who has been tempted in every way, just as we are—yet he did not sin. [16]Let us then approach God's throne of grace with confidence, so that we may receive mercy and find grace to help us in our time of need.

5 Every high priest is selected from among the people and is appointed to represent the people in matters related to God, to offer gifts and sacrifices for sins. [2]He is able to deal gently with those

---

[a] 5 Psalm 2:7   [b] 6 Psalm 110:4   [c] 1 Or from useless rituals   [d] 2 Or about baptisms

[4]It is impossible for those who have once been enlightened, who have tasted the heavenly gift, who have shared in the Holy Spirit, [5]who have tasted the goodness of the word of God and the powers of the coming age [6]and who have fallen[a] away, to be brought back to repentance. To their loss they are crucifying the Son of God all over again and subjecting him to public disgrace. [7]Land that drinks in the rain often falling on it and that produces a crop useful to those for whom it is farmed receives the blessing of God. [8]But land that produces thorns and thistles is worthless and is in danger of being cursed. In the end it will be burned.

[9]Even though we speak like this, dear friends, we are convinced of better things in your case—the things that have to do with salvation. [10]God is not unjust; he will not forget your work and the love you have shown him as you have helped his people and continue to help them. [11]We want each of you to show this same diligence to the very end, so that what you hope for may be fully realized. [12]We do not want you to become lazy, but to imitate those who through faith and patience inherit what has been promised.

The Certainty of God's Promise

[13]When God made his promise to Abraham, since there was no one greater for him to swear by, he swore by himself, [14]saying, "I will surely bless you and give you many descendants."[b] [15]And so after waiting patiently, Abraham received what was promised.

[16]People swear by someone greater than themselves, and the oath confirms what is said and puts an end to all argument. [17]Because God wanted to make the unchanging nature of his purpose very clear to the heirs of what was promised, he confirmed it with an oath. [18]God did this so that, by two unchangeable things in which it is impossible for God to lie, we who have fled to take hold of the hope set before us may be greatly encouraged. [19]We have this hope as an anchor for the

soul, firm and secure. It enters the inner sanctuary behind the curtain, [20]where our forerunner, Jesus, has entered on our behalf. He has become a high priest forever, in the order of Melchizedek.

Melchizedek the Priest

7 This Melchizedek was king of Salem and priest of God Most High. He met Abraham returning from the defeat of the kings and blessed him, [2]and Abraham gave him a tenth of everything. First, the name Melchizedek means "king of

> ## INSTANT ACCESS
>
> **M**ost teens want to grow up fast. If you're 13, you want to be 16. If you're 15, you want to be 18. Well, if you really want to grow up faster, this verse tells you how! It says that a person becomes mature by using the Bible's teachings to see the difference between good and evil. Here's how it works. Instead of taking your friend's word on whether something is right or wrong, good or bad, you follow God's direction. In other words, you learn to take responsibility for your decisions. And you make your decisions using God's Word as your guide. Show that kind of maturity, and you are truly grown up.
>
> {Hebrews 5:14}

---

[a] 6 Or age, [6]if they fall   [b] 14 Gen. 22:17

righteousness"; then also, "king of Salem" means "king of peace." ³Without father or mother, without genealogy, without beginning of days or end of life, resembling the Son of God, he remains a priest forever.

⁴Just think how great he was: Even the patriarch Abraham gave him a tenth of the plunder! ⁵Now the law requires the descendants of Levi who become priests to collect a tenth from the people—that is, from their fellow Israelites—even though they also are descended from Abraham. ⁶This man, however, did not trace his descent from Levi, yet he collected a tenth from Abraham and blessed him who had the promises. ⁷And without doubt the lesser is blessed by the greater. ⁸In the one case, the tenth is collected by people who die; but in the other case, by him who is declared to be living. ⁹One might even say that Levi, who collects the tenth, paid the tenth through Abraham, ¹⁰because when Melchizedek met Abraham, Levi was still in the body of his ancestor.

Jesus Like Melchizedek

¹¹If perfection could have been attained through the Levitical priesthood—and indeed the law given to the people established that priesthood—why was there still need for another priest to come, one in the order of Melchizedek, not in the order of Aaron? ¹²For when the priesthood is changed, the law must be changed also. ¹³He of whom these things are said belonged to a different tribe, and no one from that tribe has ever served at the altar. ¹⁴For it is clear that our Lord descended from Judah, and in regard to that tribe Moses said nothing about priests. ¹⁵And what we have said is even more clear if another priest like Melchizedek appears, ¹⁶one who has become a priest not on the basis of a regulation as to his ancestry but on the basis of the power of an indestructible life. ¹⁷For it is declared:

"You are a priest forever,
in the order of Melchizedek."[a]

¹⁸The former regulation is set aside because it was weak and useless ¹⁹(for the law made nothing perfect), and a better hope is introduced, by which we draw near to God.

²⁰And it was not without an oath! Others became priests without any oath, ²¹but he became a priest with an oath when God said to him:

"The Lord has sworn
and will not change his mind:
'You are a priest forever.'"[a]

²²Because of this oath, Jesus has become the guarantor of a better covenant.

²³Now there have been many of those priests, since death prevented them from continuing in office; ²⁴but because Jesus

---

[a] 17,21 Psalm 110:4

lives forever, he has a permanent priesthood. [25]Therefore he is able to save completely[a] those who come to God through him, because he always lives to intercede for them.

[26]Such a high priest truly meets our need—one who is holy, blameless, pure, set apart from sinners, exalted above the heavens. [27]Unlike the other high priests, he does not need to offer sacrifices day after day, first for his own sins, and then for the sins of the people. He sacrificed for their sins once for all when he offered himself. [28]For the law appoints as high priests men in all their weakness; but the oath, which came after the law, appointed the Son, who has been made perfect forever.

The High Priest of a New Covenant

8 Now the main point of what we are saying is this: We do have such a high priest, who sat down at the right hand of the throne of the Majesty in heaven, [2]and who serves in the sanctuary, the true tabernacle set up by the Lord, not by a mere human being.

[3]Every high priest is appointed to offer both gifts and sacrifices, and so it was necessary for this one also to have something to offer. [4]If he were on earth, he would not be a priest, for there are already priests who offer the gifts prescribed by the law. [5]They serve at a sanctuary that is a copy and shadow of what is in heaven. This is why Moses was warned when he was about to build the tabernacle: "See to it that you make everything according to the pattern shown you on the mountain."[b] [6]But in fact the ministry Jesus has received is as superior to theirs as the covenant of which he is mediator is superior to the old one, since the new covenant is established on better promises.

[7]For if there had been nothing wrong with that first covenant, no place would have been sought for another. [8]But God found fault with the people and said[c]:

"The days are coming, declares the Lord,
when I will make a new covenant
with the people of Israel
and with the people of Judah.
[9]It will not be like the covenant
I made with their ancestors
when I took them by the hand
to lead them out of Egypt,
because they did not remain faithful
to my covenant,
and I turned away from them,
declares the Lord.
[10]This is the covenant I will establish
with the people of Israel
after that time, declares the Lord.
I will put my laws in their minds
and write them on their hearts.
I will be their God,
and they will be my people.
[11]No longer will they teach their neighbor,
or say to one another, 'Know the
Lord,'
because they will all know me,
from the least of them to the
greatest.
[12]For I will forgive their wickedness
and will remember their sins no
more."[d]

[13]By calling this covenant "new," he has made the first one obsolete; and what is obsolete and outdated will soon disappear.

Worship in the Earthly Tabernacle

9 Now the first covenant had regulations for worship and also an earthly sanctuary. [2]A tabernacle was set up. In its first room were the lampstand and the table with its consecrated bread; this was called the Holy Place. [3]Behind the second curtain was a room called the Most Holy Place, [4]which had the golden altar of incense and the gold-covered ark of the covenant. This ark contained the gold jar of manna, Aaron's staff that had budded, and the stone tablets of the covenant. [5]Above the ark were the cherubim of

[a] 25 Or forever   [b] 5 Exodus 25:40   [c] 8 Some manuscripts may be translated fault and said to the people.
[d] 12 Jer. 31:31-34

the Glory, overshadowing the atonement cover. But we cannot discuss these things in detail now.

⁶When everything had been arranged like this, the priests entered regularly into the outer room to carry on their ministry. ⁷But only the high priest entered the inner room, and that only once a year, and never without blood, which he offered for himself and for the sins the people had committed in ignorance. ⁸The Holy Spirit was showing by this that the way into the Most Holy Place had not yet been disclosed as long as the first tabernacle was still functioning. ⁹This is an illustration for the present time, indicating that the gifts and sacrifices being offered were not able to clear the conscience of the worshiper. ¹⁰They are only a matter of food and drink and various ceremonial washings—external regulations applying until the time of the new order.

The Blood of Christ

¹¹But when Christ came as high priest of the good things that are now already here,ᵃ he went through the greater and more perfect tabernacle that is not made with human hands, that is to say, is not a part of this creation. ¹²He did not enter by means of the blood of goats and calves; but he entered the Most Holy Place once for all by his own blood, thus obtainingᵇ eternal redemption. ¹³The blood of goats and bulls and the ashes of a heifer sprinkled on those who are ceremonially unclean sanctify them so that they are outwardly clean. ¹⁴How much

ᵃ 11 Some early manuscripts are to come   ᵇ 12 Or blood, having obtained

TO THE POINT

New and Improved

The prophet Jeremiah announced that one day God would replace the law with a "new covenant" (Jeremiah 31:31–34). The law told people what good was, but the law couldn't *make* anyone good! A change from within was needed, not some command saying, "Do this!"

When Jesus died on the cross, the promised "new covenant" became a reality. God began to work in believers in a new way:

+ God writes his laws on your heart (Hebrews 8:10). Believers are changed from the inside to become more and more like Jesus.

+ God becomes yours and you become his (Hebrews 8:10–11). The Holy Spirit comes to live in you, bonding you to God forever.

+ God forgives you completely (Hebrews 8:12). Your sins are forgotten, and you can look ahead to a new, better life.

more, then, will the blood of Christ, who through the eternal Spirit offered himself unblemished to God, cleanse our consciences from acts that lead to death,[a] so that we may serve the living God!

[15]For this reason Christ is the mediator of a new covenant, that those who are called may receive the promised eternal inheritance—now that he has died as a ransom to set them free from the sins committed under the first covenant.

[16]In the case of a will,[b] it is necessary to prove the death of the one who made it, [17]because a will is in force only when somebody has died; it never takes effect while the one who made it is living. [18]This is why even the first covenant was not put into effect without blood. [19]When Moses had proclaimed every command of the law to all the people, he took the blood of calves, together with water, scarlet wool and branches of hyssop, and sprinkled the scroll and all the people. [20]He said, "This is the blood of the covenant, which God has commanded you to keep."[c] [21]In the same way, he sprinkled with the blood both the tabernacle and everything used in its ceremonies. [22]In fact, the law requires that nearly everything be cleansed with blood, and without the shedding of blood there is no forgiveness.

[23]It was necessary, then, for the copies of the heavenly things to be purified with these sacrifices, but the heavenly things themselves with better sacrifices than these. [24]For Christ did not enter a sanctuary made with human hands that was only a copy of the true one; he entered heaven itself, now to appear for us in God's presence. [25]Nor did he enter heaven to offer himself again and again, the way the high priest enters the Most Holy Place every year with blood that is not his own. [26]Otherwise Christ would have had to suffer many times since the creation of the world. But he has appeared once for all at the culmination of the ages to do away with sin by the sacrifice of himself. [27]Just as people are destined to die once, and after that to face judgment, [28]so Christ was sacrificed once to take away the sins

≫ INSTANT ACCESS

Some choices can have tragic results. You drink and drive, and a friend is injured. You have sex with your boyfriend, and you get pregnant or you get a disease. And your conscience constantly reminds you of your guilt and tells you you're useless. Well, it's true that bad choices often have tragic results. But you don't have to live with a guilty conscience. Hebrews 9:14 says that the blood of Christ cleanses. You see, you can't go back and undo your past mistakes. But you can be forgiven for them. Your guilt is gone, and God is with you to make your future bright.

{Hebrews 9:14}

of many; and he will appear a second time, not to bear sin, but to bring salvation to those who are waiting for him.

Christ's Sacrifice Once for All

10 The law is only a shadow of the good things that are coming—not the realities themselves. For this reason it can never, by the same sacrifices repeated endlessly year after year, make perfect those who draw near to worship. [2]Otherwise, would they not have stopped being offered? For the worshipers would have been cleansed once for all, and would no longer have felt guilty for their sins. [3]But

---

[a] 14 Or *from useless rituals*   [b] 16 Same Greek word as *covenant*; also in verse 17   [c] 20 Exodus 24:8

"he ascended into heaven and sits at the right hand of God"

✝ Some might have the impression that today Jesus is sort of sitting around waiting until it's time to return. Well, Jesus hasn't retired yet.

The New Testament says 19 times that Jesus, having returned to heaven, sits at God the Father's right hand. When something is repeated 19 times, it's important! But why? It's important because the Lord wants us to know that Jesus is God the Father's "right hand man"—he has authority and influence. And the Lord wants us to know that Jesus is there for us. Because Jesus is at the Father's right hand,

* He's there to answer our prayers for mercy and help in time of need (Hebrews 4:14–16).

* He's there to speak up in our defense when we sin (1 John 2:1).

* He's there to pray for us (Romans 8:34).

* He's there to ensure that we have the Holy Spirit to strengthen us (Acts 2:33,34).

Hebrews 9:24 sums it up: Jesus "entered heaven itself, now to appear for us in God's [the Father's] presence."

No, Jesus hasn't retired. He's there for us, guaranteeing forgiveness when we fail, providing the strength we need to overcome temptation, always ready to help when we call on him.

Go to page 1249 for the next We Believe

those sacrifices are an annual reminder of sins. [4] It is impossible for the blood of bulls and goats to take away sins.

[5] Therefore, when Christ came into the world, he said:

> "Sacrifice and offering you did not desire,
>   but a body you prepared for me;
> [6] with burnt offerings and sin offerings
>   you were not pleased.
> [7] Then I said, 'Here I am—it is written about me in the scroll—
>   I have come to do your will, my God.' "[a]

[8] First he said, "Sacrifices and offerings, burnt offerings and sin offerings you did not desire, nor were you pleased with them"—though they were offered in accordance with the law. [9] Then he said, "Here I am, I have come to do your will." He sets aside the first to establish the second. [10] And by that will, we have been made holy through the sacrifice of the body of Jesus Christ once for all.

[11] Day after day every priest stands and performs his religious duties; again and again he offers the same sacrifices, which can never take away sins. [12] But when this priest had offered for all time one sacrifice for sins, he sat down at the right hand of God, [13] and since that time he waits for his enemies to be made his footstool. [14] For by one sacrifice he has made perfect forever those who are being made holy.

[15] The Holy Spirit also testifies to us about this. First he says:

> [16] "This is the covenant I will make with them
>   after that time, says the Lord.
> I will put my laws in their hearts,
>   and I will write them on their minds."[b]

[17] Then he adds:

> "Their sins and lawless acts
>   I will remember no more."[c]

[18] And where these have been forgiven, sacrifice for sin is no longer necessary.

A Call to Persevere in Faith

[19] Therefore, brothers and sisters, since we have confidence to enter the Most Holy Place by the blood of Jesus, [20] by a new and living way opened for us through the curtain, that is, his body, [21] and since we have a great priest over the house of God, [22] let us draw near to God with a sincere heart and with the full assurance that faith brings, having our hearts sprinkled to cleanse us from a guilty conscience and having our bodies washed with pure water. [23] Let us hold unswervingly to the hope we profess, for he who promised is faithful. [24] And let us consider how we may spur one another on toward love and good deeds, [25] not giving up meeting together, as some are in the habit of doing, but encouraging one another—and all the more as you see the Day approaching.

[26] If we deliberately keep on sinning after we have received the knowledge of the truth, no sacrifice for sins is left, [27] but only a fearful expectation of judgment and of raging fire that will consume the enemies of God. [28] Anyone who rejected the law of Moses died without mercy on the testimony of two or three witnesses. [29] How much more severely do you think someone deserves to be punished who has trampled the Son of God underfoot, who has treated as an unholy thing the blood of the covenant that sanctified them, and who has insulted the Spirit of grace? [30] For we know him who said, "It is mine to avenge; I will repay,"[d] and again, "The Lord will judge his people."[e] [31] It is a dreadful thing to fall into the hands of the living God.

[32] Remember those earlier days after you had received the light, when you endured in a great conflict full of suffering. [33] Sometimes you were publicly exposed to insult and persecution; at other times you stood side by side with those who were so treated. [34] You suffered along with those in prison and joyfully accepted the confiscation of your property, because you knew that you yourselves had better and lasting possessions. [35] So do not throw away your confidence; it will be richly rewarded.

---

[a] 7 Psalm 40:6-8 (see Septuagint)   [b] 16 Jer. 31:33   [c] 17 Jer. 31:34   [d] 30 Deut. 32:35   [e] 30 Deut. 32:36; Psalm 135:14

Living a Christian life isn't easy. It can be really hard. That's when you need the support of Christian friends. But how do you get that support? First of all, make sure you get together regularly. Maybe at church. Maybe at an after-school club. Or maybe on your own with two or three Christian friends. What can you do when you get together? Talk about what's happening in your lives. Encourage each other. And "spur one another on toward love and good deeds" (Hebrews 10:24). It's a lot easier to stand firm in your Christian commitment if you know other teens are standing beside you.

{Hebrews 10:24–25}

>> INSTANT ACCESS

36 You need to persevere so that when you have done the will of God, you will receive what he has promised. 37 For,

"In just a little while,
 he who is coming will come
 and will not delay."[a]

38 And,

"But my righteous[b] one will live by faith.
 And I take no pleasure
 in the one who shrinks back."[c]

39 But we do not belong to those who shrink back and are destroyed, but to those who have faith and are saved.

Faith in Action

11 Now faith is confidence in what we hope for and assurance about what we do not see. 2 This is what the ancients were commended for.

3 By faith we understand that the universe was formed at God's command, so that what is seen was not made out of what was visible.

4 By faith Abel brought God a better offering than Cain did. By faith he was commended as righteous, when God spoke well of his offerings. And by faith Abel still speaks, even though he is dead.

5 By faith Enoch was taken from this life, so that he did not experience death: "He could not be found, because God had taken him away."[d] For before he was taken, he was commended as one who pleased God. 6 And without faith it is impossible to please God, because anyone who comes to him must believe that he exists and that he rewards those who earnestly seek him.

7 By faith Noah, when warned about things not yet seen, in holy fear built an ark to save his family. By his faith he condemned the world and became heir of the righteousness that is in keeping with faith.

8 By faith Abraham, when called to go to a place he would later receive as his inheritance, obeyed and went, even though he did not know where he was going. 9 By faith he made his home in the promised land like a stranger in a foreign country; he lived in tents, as did Isaac and Jacob, who were heirs with him of the same promise. 10 For he was looking forward to the city with foundations, whose architect and builder is God. 11 And by faith even Sarah, who was past childbearing age, was enabled to bear children because she[e] considered him faithful who had made the promise. 12 And so from this one man, and he as good as dead, came

---

a 37 Isaiah 26:20; Hab. 2:3   b 38 Some early manuscripts *But the righteous*   c 38 Hab. 2:4 (see Septuagint)
d 5 Gen. 5:24   e 11 Or *By faith Abraham, even though he was too old to have children—and Sarah herself was not able to conceive—was enabled to become a father because he*

descendants as numerous as the stars in the sky and as countless as the sand on the seashore.

13 All these people were still living by faith when they died. They did not receive the things promised; they only saw them and welcomed them from a distance, admitting that they were foreigners and strangers on earth. 14 People who say such things show that they are looking for a country of their own. 15 If they had been thinking of the country they had left, they would have had opportunity to return. 16 Instead, they were longing for a better country—a heavenly one. Therefore God is not ashamed to be called their God, for he has prepared a city for them.

17 By faith Abraham, when God tested him, offered Isaac as a sacrifice. He who had embraced the promises was about to sacrifice his one and only son, 18 even though God had said to him, "It is through Isaac that your offspring will be reckoned."[a] 19 Abraham reasoned that God could even raise the dead, and so in a manner of speaking he did receive Isaac back from death.

20 By faith Isaac blessed Jacob and Esau in regard to their future.

21 By faith Jacob, when he was dying, blessed each of Joseph's sons, and worshiped as he leaned on the top of his staff.

22 By faith Joseph, when his end was near, spoke about the exodus of the Israelites from Egypt and gave instructions concerning the burial of his bones.

23 By faith Moses' parents hid him for three months after he was born, because they saw he was no ordinary child, and they were not afraid of the king's edict.

24 By faith Moses, when he had grown up, refused to be known as the son of Pharaoh's daughter. 25 He chose to be mistreated along with the people of God rather than to enjoy the fleeting pleasures of sin. 26 He regarded disgrace for the sake of Christ as of greater value than the treasures of Egypt, because he was looking ahead to his reward. 27 By faith he left Egypt, not fearing the king's anger; he persevered because he saw him who is invisible. 28 By faith he kept the Passover and the application of blood, so that the destroyer of the firstborn would not touch the firstborn of Israel.

29 By faith the people passed through the Red Sea as on dry land; but when the Egyptians tried to do so, they were drowned.

30 By faith the walls of Jericho fell, after the army had marched around them for seven days.

31 By faith the prostitute Rahab, because she welcomed the spies, was not killed with those who were disobedient.[b]

32 And what more shall I say? I do not have time to tell about Gideon, Barak, Samson and Jephthah, about David and Samuel and the prophets, 33 who through faith conquered kingdoms, administered justice, and gained what was promised; who shut the mouths of lions, 34 quenched the fury of the flames, and escaped the edge of the sword; whose weakness was turned to strength; and who became powerful in battle and routed foreign armies. 35 Women received back their dead, raised to life again. There were others who were tortured, refusing to be released so that they might gain an even better resurrection. 36 Some faced jeers and flogging, and even chains and imprisonment. 37 They were put to death by stoning;[c] they were sawed in two; they were killed by the sword. They went about in sheepskins and goatskins, destitute, persecuted and mistreated— 38 the world was not worthy of them. They wandered in deserts and mountains, living in caves and in holes in the ground.

39 These were all commended for their faith, yet none of them received what had been promised, 40 since God had planned something better for us so that only together with us would they be made perfect.

12 Therefore, since we are surrounded by such a great cloud of witnesses, let us throw off everything that hinders and the sin that so easily entangles. And let us run with perseverance

---

a 18 Gen. 21:12   *b* 31 Or *unbelieving*   *c* 37 Some early manuscripts *stoning; they were put to the test;*

You break your leg a week before the big ski trip. Your mom gets sick just before you graduate. Hebrews 12 says to look at some of the painful things that happen to you as "God's discipline." No, not "God's punishment." Discipline means training, helping you grow up, preparing you to be strong. Some people fight any kind of discipline. Like crying babies, they want what they want, and they want it now. What a terrible way to live! Since you are not a baby anymore, sometimes God lets hard things happen to you. When they do, see them as God's discipline—and as a sign of his love for you.

{Hebrews 12:1–11}

» INSTANT ACCESS

your blood. [5] And have you completely forgotten this word of encouragement that addresses you as a father addresses his son? It says,

"My son, do not make light of the
    Lord's discipline,
and do not lose heart when he
    rebukes you,
[6] because the Lord disciplines the one
    he loves,
and he chastens everyone he
    accepts as his son." [a]

[7] Endure hardship as discipline; God is treating you as his children. For what children are not disciplined by their father? [8] If you are not disciplined—and everyone undergoes discipline—then you are not legitimate, not true sons and daughters at all. [9] Moreover, we have all had human fathers who disciplined us and we respected them for it. How much more should we submit to the Father of spirits and live! [10] They disciplined us for a little while as they thought best; but God disciplines us for our good, in order that we may share in his holiness. [11] No discipline seems pleasant at the time, but painful. Later on, however, it produces a harvest of righteousness and peace for those who have been trained by it.

[12] Therefore, strengthen your feeble arms and weak knees. [13] "Make level paths for your feet," [b] so that the lame may not be disabled, but rather healed.

Warning and Encouragement

[14] Make every effort to live in peace with everyone and to be holy; without holiness no one will see the Lord. [15] See to it that no one falls short of the grace of God and that no bitter root grows up to cause trouble and defile many. [16] See that no one is sexually immoral, or is godless like Esau, who for a single meal sold his inheritance rights as the oldest son. [17] Afterward, as you know, when he wanted to inherit this blessing, he was rejected. Even though he sought the blessing with tears, he could not change what he had done.

the race marked out for us, [2] fixing our eyes on Jesus, the pioneer and perfecter of faith. For the joy set before him he endured the cross, scorning its shame, and sat down at the right hand of the throne of God. [3] Consider him who endured such opposition from sinners, so that you will not grow weary and lose heart.

God Disciplines His Children

[4] In your struggle against sin, you have not yet resisted to the point of shedding

a 5,6 Prov. 3:11,12 (see Septuagint)   b 13 Prov. 4:26

The Mountain of Fear and the Mountain of Joy

¹⁸ You have not come to a mountain that can be touched and that is burning with fire; to darkness, gloom and storm; ¹⁹ to a trumpet blast or to such a voice speaking words that those who heard it begged that no further word be spoken to them, ²⁰ because they could not bear what was commanded: "If even an animal touches the mountain, it must be stoned to death."ᵃ ²¹ The sight was so terrifying that Moses said, "I am trembling with fear."ᵇ

²² But you have come to Mount Zion, to the city of the living God, the heavenly Jerusalem. You have come to thousands upon thousands of angels in joyful assembly, ²³ to the church of the firstborn, whose names are written in heaven. You have come to God, the Judge of all, to the spirits of the righteous made perfect, ²⁴ to Jesus the mediator of a new covenant, and to the sprinkled blood that speaks a better word than the blood of Abel.

²⁵ See to it that you do not refuse him who speaks. If they did not escape when they refused him who warned them on earth, how much less will we, if we turn away from him who warns us from heaven? ²⁶ At that time his voice shook the earth, but now he has promised, "Once more I will shake not only the earth but also the heavens."ᶜ ²⁷ The words "once more" indicate the removing of what can be shaken—that is, created things—so that what cannot be shaken may remain.

²⁸ Therefore, since we are receiving a kingdom that cannot be shaken, let us be thankful, and so worship God acceptably with reverence and awe, ²⁹ for our "God is a consuming fire."ᵈ

Concluding Exhortations

13 Keep on loving one another as brothers and sisters. ² Do not forget to show hospitality to strangers, for by so doing some people have shown hospitality to angels without knowing it. ³ Continue to remember those in prison as if you were together with them in prison, and those who are mistreated as if you yourselves were suffering.

⁴ Marriage should be honored by all, and the marriage bed kept pure, for God will judge the adulterer and all the sexually immoral. ⁵ Keep your lives free from the love of money and be content with what you have, because God has said,

"Never will I leave you;
    never will I forsake you."ᵉ

⁶ So we say with confidence,

"The Lord is my helper; I will not be
    afraid.
    What can mere mortals do to me?"ᶠ

⁷ Remember your leaders, who spoke the word of God to you. Consider the outcome of their way of life and imitate their faith. ⁸ Jesus Christ is the same yesterday and today and forever.

⁹ Do not be carried away by all kinds of strange teachings. It is good for our hearts to be strengthened by grace, not by eating ceremonial foods, which is of no benefit to those who do so. ¹⁰ We have an altar from which those who minister at the tabernacle have no right to eat.

¹¹ The high priest carries the blood of animals into the Most Holy Place as a sin offering, but the bodies are burned outside the camp. ¹² And so Jesus also suffered outside the city gate to make the people holy through his own blood. ¹³ Let us, then, go to him outside the camp, bearing the disgrace he bore. ¹⁴ For here we do not have an enduring city, but we are looking for the city that is to come.

¹⁵ Through Jesus, therefore, let us continually offer to God a sacrifice of

> *Jesus Christ is the same yesterday and today and forever.*
> Hebrews 13:8

ᵃ 20 Exodus 19:12,13   ᵇ 21 See Deut. 9:19.   ᶜ 26 Haggai 2:6   ᵈ 29 Deut. 4:24   ᵉ 5 Deut. 31:6
ᶠ 6 Psalm 118:6,7

> In 7 months I am having a baby. I'm 16. My parents and I do not believe in abortion, but I'm not sure what will be best for us and the baby. I'm scared and don't know what to do.
>
> >> Jenna

Dear Jordan

Dear Jenna,

You have already made some good choices in dealing with this difficult situation. You have told your parents which means you don't have to try to deal with this by yourself. Furthermore, you are respecting this child's life. I commend you on both of these decisions. Of course there are other important decisions that must be made as well. It's understandable that you have fears and things you're uncertain about.

There are pro-life counseling centers especially for pregnant teens that offer support and information which can be helpful to you and your family. I hope you will ask God to give you wisdom as you consider what to do. And remember to focus on the fact that God loves you and your unborn child too. He has promised never to leave you, never to forsake you (Hebrews 13:5). You can count on God every minute of every day. He will even use this painful experience for good in your life (Romans 8:28), which right now might seem hard to believe.

Jordan

praise—the fruit of lips that openly pro-fess his name. [16]And do not forget to do good and to share with others, for with such sacrifices God is pleased.

[17]Have confidence in your leaders and submit to their authority, because they keep watch over you as those who must give an account. Do this so that their work will be a joy, not a burden, for that would be of no benefit to you.

[18]Pray for us. We are sure that we have a clear conscience and desire to live hon-orably in every way. [19]I particularly urge you to pray so that I may be restored to you soon.

Benediction and Final Greetings

[20]Now may the God of peace, who through the blood of the eternal cov-enant brought back from the dead our Lord Jesus, that great Shepherd of the sheep, [21]equip you with everything good for doing his will, and may he work in us what is pleasing to him, through Jesus Christ, to whom be glory for ever and ever. Amen.

[22]Brothers and sisters, I urge you to bear with my word of exhortation, for in fact I have written to you quite briefly.

[23]I want you to know that our brother Timothy has been released. If he arrives soon, I will come with him to see you.

[24]Greet all your leaders and all the Lord's people. Those from Italy send you their greetings.

[25]Grace be with you all.

JAMES

As Is Christian.

Just saying so doesn't make you Christian. It's not just saying you believe the Bible. Or that you believe in Jesus. Being a real Christian will make a difference in the way you live. Not that you'll suddenly be perfect. Not at all.

James wrote this book to remind Christians to practice their faith. His letter is very practical. James talks about things like temptation, anger, showing favoritism, watching your mouth, fighting, boasting and patience. God doesn't expect you to be perfectly good. But he doesn't expect you to be perfectly awful either.

>>**I'M TEMPTED BECAUSE ...?**
Temptation analyzed. See James 1:13–15

>>**KING JESUS' "ROYAL LAW"**
Definition in James 2:1–9

>>**TAME THAT WILD TONGUE**
Take this to heart. See James 3:1–6

>>**DON'T ASK FOR THAT**
Unanswered prayer explained. See James 4:1–3

‹‹preview

The author, James, is Jesus' brother, the son of Mary and Joseph.

James leads the Jerusalem church until he's killed in 62 A.D.

This is probably the first book of the New Testament to be written.

As James writes in the mid-40's A.D., the city of London is founded in England. The Arawak people settle many West Indian islands.

1 James, a servant of God and of the Lord Jesus Christ,

To the twelve tribes scattered among the nations:

Greetings.

Trials and Temptations

[2] Consider it pure joy, my brothers and sisters,[a] whenever you face trials of many kinds, [3] because you know that the testing of your faith produces perseverance. [4] Let perseverance finish its work so that you may be mature and complete, not lacking anything. [5] If any of you lacks wisdom, you should ask God, who gives generously to all without finding fault, and it will be given to you. [6] But when you ask, you must believe and not doubt, because the one who doubts is like a wave of the sea, blown and tossed by the wind. [7] That person should not expect to receive anything from the Lord. [8] Such a person is double-minded and unstable in all they do.

[9] Believers in humble circumstances ought to take pride in their high position. [10] But the rich should take pride in their humiliation—since they will pass away like a wild flower. [11] For the sun rises with scorching heat and withers the plant; its blossom falls and its beauty is destroyed. In the same way, the rich will fade away even while they go about their business.

[12] Blessed is the one who perseveres under trial because, having stood the test, that person will receive the crown of

---

[a] 2 The Greek word for *brothers and sisters* (*adelphoi*) refers here to believers, both men and women, as part of God's family; also in verses 16 and 19; and in 2:1, 5, 14; 3:10, 12; 4:11; 5:7, 9, 10, 12, 19.

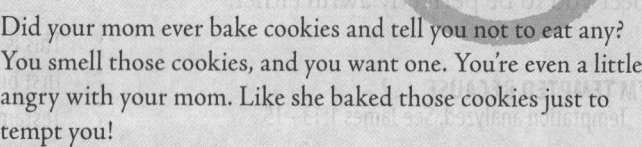
TO THE POINT

Don't Blame God

Did your mom ever bake cookies and tell you not to eat any? You smell those cookies, and you want one. You're even a little angry with your mom. Like she baked those cookies just to tempt you!

Some people feel the same way about God. They want something they know is wrong, and they wonder why God is tempting them. But God doesn't tempt anyone! Their own "evil desire" makes them want what is wrong (James 1:13–15). Like those cookies. If that were a spinach casserole, would you want any?

When you're tempted, it's because something inside you likes to do the wrong thing you know you shouldn't do. The problem is in you, not in the thing you want to do. God has made you new in Jesus. You may still like what you know is wrong—but you will like pleasing God better.

Have you ever heard anyone say, "I've just got a nasty temper"? They seem to think that having a "nasty temper" is a valid excuse for anything they do when angry. Well, it isn't. James says, "Everyone should be quick to listen, slow to speak and slow to become angry" (James 1:19). Anger isn't part of the "righteousness that God desires" (James 1:20). So how do you control a bad temper? You start by making sure you're living a good, moral life. Then you don't just listen to God's Word, you put it into practice. Put God first in your life, and your temper won't get the best of you. Or show you at your worst!

{James 1:19–25}

INSTANT ACCESS

life that the Lord has promised to those who love him.

¹³When tempted, no one should say, "God is tempting me." For God cannot be tempted by evil, nor does he tempt anyone; ¹⁴but each person is tempted when they are dragged away by their own evil desire and enticed. ¹⁵Then, after desire has conceived, it gives birth to sin; and sin, when it is full-grown, gives birth to death.

¹⁶Don't be deceived, my dear brothers and sisters. ¹⁷Every good and perfect gift is from above, coming down from the Father of the heavenly lights, who does not change like shifting shadows. ¹⁸He chose to give us birth through the word of truth, that we might be a kind of firstfruits of all he created.

Listening and Doing

¹⁹My dear brothers and sisters, take note of this: Everyone should be quick to listen, slow to speak and slow to become angry, ²⁰because human anger does not produce the righteousness that God desires. ²¹Therefore, get rid of all moral filth and the evil that is so prevalent and humbly accept the word planted in you, which can save you.

²²Do not merely listen to the word, and so deceive yourselves. Do what it says. ²³Anyone who listens to the word but does not do what it says is like someone who looks at his face in a mirror ²⁴and, after looking at himself, goes away and immediately forgets what he looks like. ²⁵But whoever looks intently into the perfect law that gives freedom, and continues in it—not forgetting what they have heard, but doing it—they will be blessed in what they do.

²⁶Those who consider themselves religious and yet do not keep a tight rein on their tongues deceive themselves, and their religion is worthless. ²⁷Religion that God our Father accepts as pure and faultless is this: to look after orphans and widows in their distress and to keep oneself from being polluted by the world.

Favoritism Forbidden

2 My brothers and sisters, believers in our glorious Lord Jesus Christ must not show favoritism. ²Suppose a man comes into your meeting wearing a gold ring and fine clothes, and a poor man in filthy old clothes also comes in. ³If you show special attention to the man wearing fine clothes and say, "Here's a good seat for you," but say to the poor man, "You stand there" or "Sit on the floor by my feet," ⁴have you not discriminated among yourselves and become judges with evil thoughts?

⁵Listen, my dear brothers and sisters: Has not God chosen those who are poor in the eyes of the world to be rich in faith and to inherit the kingdom he promised

those who love him? 6But you have dis-honored the poor. Is it not the rich who are exploiting you? Are they not the ones who are dragging you into court? 7Are they not the ones who are blaspheming the noble name of him to whom you belong?

8If you really keep the royal law found in Scripture, "Love your neighbor as your-self,"*a* you are doing right. 9But if you show favoritism, you sin and are convict-ed by the law as lawbreakers. 10For who-ever keeps the whole law and yet stum-bles at just one point is guilty of breaking all of it. 11For he who said, "You shall not commit adultery,"*b* also said, "You shall not murder."*c* If you do not commit adul-tery but do commit murder, you have be-come a lawbreaker.

12Speak and act as those who are going to be judged by the law that gives freedom, 13because judgment without mercy will be shown to anyone who has not been merciful. Mercy triumphs over judgment.

Faith and Deeds

14What good is it, my brothers and sisters, if someone claims to have faith but has no deeds? Can such faith save them? 15Suppose a brother or a sister is without clothes and daily food. 16If one of you says to them, "Go in peace; keep warm and well fed," but does nothing about their physical needs, what good is it? 17In the same way, faith by itself, if it is not accompanied by action, is dead.

18But someone will say, "You have faith; I have deeds."

Show me your faith without deeds, and I will show you my faith by my deeds. 19You believe that there is one God. Good! Even the demons believe that—and shudder.

20You foolish person, do you want ev-idence that faith without deeds is use-less*d*? 21Was not our father Abraham con-sidered righteous for what he did when he offered his son Isaac on the altar? 22You see that his faith and his actions were working together, and his faith was made complete by what he did. 23And the scrip-ture was fulfilled that says, "Abraham believed God, and it was credited to him as righteousness,"*e* and he was called God's friend. 24You see that a person is considered righteous by what they do and not by faith alone.

25In the same way, was not even Ra-hab the prostitute considered righteous for what she did when she gave lodging to the spies and sent them off in a different direction? 26As the body without the spirit is dead, so faith without deeds is dead.

Taming the Tongue

3 Not many of you should become teachers, my fellow believers,

---

a 8 Lev. 19:18   *b* 11 Exodus 20:14; Deut. 5:18   *c* 11 Exodus 20:13; Deut. 5:17   *d* 20 Some early manuscripts dead   *e* 23 Gen. 15:6

PANORAMA

Christian.

Being a real Christian will make a difference in the way you live. James wrote this book to remind Christians that God doesn't expect you to be perfect. But he expects you to try to make good choices and live a good life.

{JAMES}

Dear Jordan

Dear Dylan,

Take a look at James 3:3–12. James has some terrific insights about the power of the tongue. James points out in part of the passage that the tongue is like a tiny spark that can destroy a giant forest. While humans can control almost all wild animals, they still can't control their own tongues.

We are supposed to praise God and encourage those around us. But James says that praising and cursing from the same tongue is like fresh water and salt water coming from the same spring. It just can't happen.

You will find that if you start using bad language, soon that language will pop out even when you don't want it to. If you listen to and tell dirty jokes, soon those kinds of thoughts will fill your mind. What do you think God would rather you fill your mind with—praise and good thoughts, or bad language and dirty jokes?

Jordan

because you know that we who teach will be judged more strictly. ²We all stumble in many ways. Anyone who is never at fault in what they say is perfect, able to keep their whole body in check.

³When we put bits into the mouths of horses to make them obey us, we can turn the whole animal. ⁴Or take ships as an example. Although they are so large and are driven by strong winds, they are steered by a very small rudder wherever the pilot wants to go. ⁵Likewise, the tongue is a small part of the body, but it makes great boasts. Consider what a great forest is set on fire by a small spark. ⁶The tongue also is a fire, a world of evil among the parts of the body. It corrupts the whole body, sets the whole course of one's life on fire, and is itself set on fire by hell.

⁷All kinds of animals, birds, reptiles and sea creatures are being tamed and have been tamed by mankind, ⁸but no human being can tame the tongue. It is a restless evil, full of deadly poison.

⁹With the tongue we praise our Lord and Father, and with it we curse human beings, who have been made in God's likeness. ¹⁰Out of the same mouth come praise and cursing. My brothers and sisters, this should not be. ¹¹Can both fresh water and salt water flow from the same spring? ¹²My brothers and sisters, can a fig tree bear olives, or a grapevine bear figs? Neither can a salt spring produce fresh water.

Two Kinds of Wisdom

¹³Who is wise and understanding among you? Let them show it by their good life, by deeds done in the humility that comes from wisdom. ¹⁴But if you harbor bitter envy and selfish ambition in your hearts, do not boast about it or deny the truth. ¹⁵Such "wisdom" does not come down from heaven but is earthly, unspiritual, demonic. ¹⁶For where you have envy and selfish ambition, there you find disorder and every evil practice.

¹⁷But the wisdom that comes from heaven is first of all pure; then peace-loving, considerate, submissive, full of mercy and good fruit, impartial and sincere. ¹⁸Peacemakers who sow in peace reap a harvest of righteousness.

Submit Yourselves to God

4 What causes fights and quarrels among you? Don't they come from your desires that battle within you? ²You desire but do not have, so you kill. You covet but you cannot get what you want, so you quarrel and fight. You do not have because you do not ask God. ³When you ask, you do not receive, because you ask with wrong motives, that you may spend what you get on your pleasures.

⁴You adulterous people,ᵃ don't you know that friendship with the world means enmity against God? Therefore, anyone who chooses to be a friend of the world becomes an enemy of God. ⁵Or do you think Scripture says without reason that he jealously longs for the spirit he has caused to dwell in usᵇ? ⁶But he gives us more grace. That is why Scripture says:

> "God opposes the proud
> but shows favor to the humble."ᶜ

⁷Submit yourselves, then, to God. Resist the devil, and he will flee from you. ⁸Come near to God and he will come near to you. Wash your hands, you sinners, and purify your hearts, you double-minded. ⁹Grieve, mourn and wail. Change your laughter to mourning and your joy to gloom. ¹⁰Humble yourselves before the Lord, and he will lift you up.

¹¹Brothers and sisters, do not slander one another. Anyone who speaks against

> *Come near to God and he will come near to you.*
>
> **James 4:8**

ᵃ 4 An allusion to covenant unfaithfulness; see Hosea 3:1.   ᵇ 5 Or *that the spirit he caused to dwell in us envies intensely; or that the Spirit he caused to dwell in us longs jealously*   ᶜ 6 Prov. 3:34

a brother or sister[a] or judges them speaks against the law and judges it. When you judge the law, you are not keeping it, but sitting in judgment on it. [12]There is only one Lawgiver and Judge, the one who is able to save and destroy. But you—who are you to judge your neighbor?

Boasting About Tomorrow

[13]Now listen, you who say, "Today or tomorrow we will go to this or that city, spend a year there, carry on business and make money." [14]Why, you do not even know what will happen tomorrow. What is your life? You are a mist that appears for a little while and then vanishes. [15]Instead, you ought to say, "If it is the Lord's will, we will live and do this or that." [16]As it is, you boast in your arrogant schemes. All such boasting is evil. [17]If anyone, then, knows the good they ought to do and doesn't do it, it is sin for them.

Warning to Rich Oppressors

5 Now listen, you rich people, weep and wail because of the misery that is coming on you. [2]Your wealth has rotted, and moths have eaten your clothes. [3]Your gold and silver are corroded. Their corrosion will testify against you and eat your flesh like fire. You have hoarded wealth in the last days. [4]Look! The wages you failed to pay the workers who mowed your fields are crying out against you. The cries of the harvesters have reached the ears of the Lord Almighty. [5]You have lived on earth in luxury and self-indulgence. You have fattened yourselves in the day of slaughter.[b] [6]You have condemned and murdered the innocent one, who was not opposing you.

Patience in Suffering

[7]Be patient, then, brothers and sisters, until the Lord's coming. See how the farmer waits for the land to yield its valuable crop, patiently waiting for the autumn and spring rains. [8]You too, be patient and stand firm, because the Lord's coming is near. [9]Don't grumble against one another, brothers and sisters, or you will be judged. The Judge is standing at the door!

[10]Brothers and sisters, as an example of patience in the face of suffering, take the prophets who spoke in the name of the Lord. [11]As you know, we count as blessed those who have persevered. You have heard of Job's perseverance and have seen what the Lord finally brought about. The Lord is full of compassion and mercy.

[12]Above all, my brothers and sisters, do not swear—not by heaven or by earth or by anything else. All you need to say is a simple "Yes" or "No." Otherwise you will be condemned.

The Prayer of Faith

[13]Is anyone among you in trouble? Let them pray. Is anyone happy? Let them sing songs of praise. [14]Is anyone among you sick? Let them call the elders of the church to pray over them and anoint them with oil in the name of the Lord. [15]And the prayer offered in faith will make the sick person well; the Lord will raise them up. If they have sinned, they will be forgiven. [16]Therefore confess your sins to each other and pray for each other so that you may be healed. The prayer of a righteous person is powerful and effective.

[17]Elijah was a human being, even as we are. He prayed earnestly that it would not rain, and it did not rain on the land for three and a half years. [18]Again he prayed, and the heavens gave rain, and the earth produced its crops.

[19]My brothers and sisters, if one of you should wander from the truth and someone should bring that person back, [20]remember this: Whoever turns a sinner from the error of their way will save them from death and cover over a multitude of sins.

---

[a] 11 The Greek word for *brother or sister* (*adelphos*) refers here to a believer, whether man or woman, as part of God's family.   [b] 5 Or *yourselves as in a day of feasting*

1 PETER

preview

The writer is the apostle Peter, the leader of Jesus' twelve disciples.

Peter writes this letter around 64 A.D. to help Christians facing persecution.

It's Not Fair!

You do what's right, and still things turn out rotten. You help a friend who fell off his bike, miss the bus to the big game and get kicked off the team. Or you're accused of something you didn't do, and your parents ground you. How can that be fair?

Peter wrote this letter to Christians who were being treated unfairly. They were good citizens who obeyed the law, but they were being persecuted anyway. Some lost their jobs and homes, and some even lost their lives. Peter wrote to show them how to triumph when life is unfair.

>> **NO MORE LIVING IN IGNORANCE**
A new day, says 1 Peter 1:13–16

>> **NO CREDIT THIS TIME**
Troubles? Read 1 Peter 2:19–21

>> **FIVE STEPS FOR THE SUFFERER**
For Peter's list, go to 1 Peter 3:13–17

>> **NO SHAME IN PAINFUL TRIAL**
For an explanation, see 1 Peter 4:12–17

As Peter writes, Nero is emperor in Rome. Rome has been devastated by a fire Nero blames on Christians. In revenge, Nero burns many Christians alive. Christianity is now an illegal religion.

1 Peter, an apostle of Jesus Christ,

To God's elect, exiles scattered throughout the provinces of Pontus, Galatia, Cappadocia, Asia and Bithynia, [2]who have been chosen according to the foreknowledge of God the Father, through the sanctifying work of the Spirit, to be obedient to Jesus Christ and sprinkled with his blood:

Grace and peace be yours in abundance.

Praise to God for a Living Hope

[3]Praise be to the God and Father of our Lord Jesus Christ! In his great mercy he has given us new birth into a living hope through the resurrection of Jesus Christ from the dead, [4]and into an inheritance that can never perish, spoil or fade. This inheritance is kept in heaven for you, [5]who through faith are shielded by God's power until the coming of the salvation that is ready to be revealed in the last time. [6]In all this you greatly rejoice, though now for a little while you may have had to suffer grief in all kinds of trials. [7]These have come so that the proven genuineness of your faith—of greater worth than gold, which perishes even though refined by fire—may result in praise, glory and honor when Jesus Christ is revealed. [8]Though you have not seen him, you love him; and even though you do not see him now, you believe in him and are filled with an inexpressible and glorious joy, [9]for you are receiving the end result of your faith, the salvation of your souls.

[10]Concerning this salvation, the prophets, who spoke of the grace that was to come to you, searched intently and with the greatest care, [11]trying to find out the time and circumstances to which the Spirit of Christ in them was pointing when he predicted the sufferings of the Messiah and the glories that would follow. [12]It was revealed to them that they were not serving themselves but you, when they spoke of the things that have now been told you by those who have preached the gospel to you by the Holy Spirit sent from heaven. Even angels long to look into these things.

Be Holy

[13]Therefore, with minds that are alert and fully sober, set your hope on the grace to be brought to you when Jesus Christ is revealed at his coming. [14]As obedient children, do not conform to the evil desires you had when you lived in ignorance. [15]But just as he who called you is holy, so be holy in all you do; [16]for it is written: "Be holy, because I am holy."[a]

[17]Since you call on a Father who judges each person's work impartially, live out your time as foreigners here in reverent fear. [18]For you know that it was not with perishable things such as silver or gold that you were redeemed from the empty way of life handed down to you from your ancestors, [19]but with the precious blood of Christ, a lamb without blemish or defect. [20]He was chosen before the creation of the world, but was revealed in these last times for your sake. [21]Through him you believe in God, who raised him from the dead and glorified him, and so your faith and hope are in God.

[22]Now that you have purified yourselves by obeying the truth so that you have sincere love for each other, love one another deeply, from the heart.[b] [23]For you have been born again, not of perishable seed, but of imperishable, through the living and enduring word of God. [24]For,

> "All people are like grass,
>   and all their glory is like the flowers
>   of the field;

In his great mercy he has given us ... an inheritance that can never perish, spoil or fade.
1 Peter 1:3–4

---

[a] 16 Lev. 11:44,45; 19:2   [b] 22 Some early manuscripts *from a pure heart*

We Believe...

"in the holy Christian church"

✛ By now you know the "church" isn't a building you visit on Sunday. "The church" is the people who gather in the building. The church is us, the family of God, those who believe in Jesus and who gather to worship him.

In the Apostles' Creed and in the Bible we're called a "holy" people. That word *holy* can create some serious confusion. You see, *holy* doesn't mean that we're a perfect people. Just look around you on Sunday—or look in the mirror any day—and you know Christians are far from perfect. But *holy* doesn't mean "perfect." *Holy* means "to be set apart, to be different."

Peter tells us how we're to be different. We're not to conform to evil desires (1 Peter 1:14). We're to have a deep, sincere love for our Christian brothers and sisters (1 Peter 1:22). We're to rid ourselves of malice and deceit, of hypocrisy, envy and slander (1 Peter 2:1). And we're to "grow up" in our salvation (1 Peter 2:2).

That call to grow up, to mature, reminds us that God's church isn't perfect—that Jesus' church is made up of people who may be spiritual infants or children, as well as people who are closer to God's ideal. In fact, we can think of the church as people who are committed to love each other and to help each other mature and so become more holy. So don't be shocked if a Christian friend says something to hurt you, or does something that shows he or she is far from perfect. Like you, that friend has some growing to do. Concentrate on being different, being "holy," and respond with a sincere and deep love that will help your friend—and you—mature.

Go to page 1458 for the next We Believe

How are you different from those who aren't Christians? OK, so you don't have a third eye or six toes on each foot. And no one expects you to dress like your great-grandpa. Hey, it's all right to look and act like a teen. Still, Peter expects you to be different: "Now you are the people of God" (1 Peter 2:10). You belong to God. Being "different" as a Christian means making sure that everything you do reflects in a positive manner on God. Be a teen. And be a kind, thoughtful and honest person. Be a teen. And act toward your friends, both the guys and the girls, with integrity.

{1 Peter 2:9–10}

≫≫ INSTANT ACCESS

it you may grow up in your salvation, [3]now that you have tasted that the Lord is good.

The Living Stone and a Chosen People

[4]As you come to him, the living Stone—rejected by humans but chosen by God and precious to him— [5]you also, like living stones, are being built into a spiritual house[b] to be a holy priesthood, offering spiritual sacrifices acceptable to God through Jesus Christ. [6]For in Scripture it says:

"See, I lay a stone in Zion,
    a chosen and precious cornerstone,
and the one who trusts in him
    will never be put to shame."[c]

[7]Now to you who believe, this stone is precious. But to those who do not believe,

"The stone the builders rejected
    has become the cornerstone,"[d]

[8]and,

"A stone that causes people to
        stumble
    and a rock that makes them fall."[e]

They stumble because they disobey the message—which is also what they were destined for.

[9]But you are a chosen people, a royal priesthood, a holy nation, God's special possession, that you may declare the praises of him who called you out of darkness into his wonderful light. [10]Once you were not a people, but now you are the people of God; once you had not received mercy, but now you have received mercy.

Living Godly Lives in a Pagan Society

[11]Dear friends, I urge you, as foreigners and exiles, to abstain from sinful desires, which wage war against your soul. [12]Live such good lives among the pagans that, though they accuse you of doing wrong, they may see your good deeds and glorify God on the day he visits us.

the grass withers and the flowers fall,
[25]   but the word of the Lord endures
        forever."[a]

And this is the word that was preached to you.

2 Therefore, rid yourselves of all malice and all deceit, hypocrisy, envy, and slander of every kind. [2]Like newborn babies, crave pure spiritual milk, so that by

---

[a] 25 Isaiah 40:6-8 (see Septuagint)   [b] 5 Or *into a temple of the Spirit*   [c] 6 Isaiah 28:16   [d] 7 Psalm 118:22
[e] 8 Isaiah 8:14

> When someone at school says or does something wrong to me, I think about what I can do to get them back. My mom says it's not right to try to get back at someone. Why is revenge a bad thing? >> Dominic

Dear Jordan

Dear Dominic,

First Peter 3:8–12 is full of advice for living a godly life in spite of what others have done to you: "Be like-minded, be sympathetic, love one another…Do not repay evil with evil or insult with insult…turn from evil and do good…seek peace and pursue it."

In Romans 12:19–21 we're told not to take revenge because "It is mine to avenge; I will repay," says the Lord. The passage goes on to say if you show kindness to someone who has been unkind to you, "you will heap burning coals on his head." That's Christian revenge. It's kind of a "kill them with kindness" and they'll squirm knowing they don't deserve it. And you won't have to feel bad later because you returned kindness for evil.

Jordan

¹³Submit yourselves for the Lord's sake to every human authority: whether to the emperor, as the supreme authority, ¹⁴or to governors, who are sent by him to punish those who do wrong and to commend those who do right. ¹⁵For it is God's will that by doing good you should silence the ignorant talk of foolish people. ¹⁶Live as free people, but do not use your freedom as a cover-up for evil; live as God's slaves. ¹⁷Show proper respect to everyone, love the family of believers, fear God, honor the emperor.

¹⁸Slaves, in reverent fear of God submit yourselves to your masters, not only to those who are good and considerate, but also to those who are harsh. ¹⁹For it is commendable if someone bears up under the pain of unjust suffering because they are conscious of God. ²⁰But how is it to your credit if you receive a beating for doing wrong and endure it? But if you suffer for doing good and you endure it, this is commendable before God. ²¹To this you were called, because Christ suffered for you, leaving you an example, that you should follow in his steps.

²²"He committed no sin,
    and no deceit was found in his
        mouth."[a]

²³When they hurled their insults at him, he did not retaliate; when he suffered, he made no threats. Instead, he entrusted himself to him who judges justly. ²⁴"He himself bore our sins" in his body on the cross, so that we might die to sins and live for righteousness; "by his wounds you have been healed." ²⁵For "you were like sheep going astray,"[b] but now you have returned to the Shepherd and Overseer of your souls.

3 Wives, in the same way submit yourselves to your own husbands so that, if any of them do not believe the word, they may be won over without words by the behavior of their wives, ²when they see the purity and reverence of your lives. ³Your beauty should not come from outward adornment, such as elaborate hairstyles and the wearing of gold jewelry or fine clothes. ⁴Rather, it should be that of your inner self, the unfading beauty of a gentle and quiet spirit, which is of great worth in God's sight. ⁵For this is the way the holy women of the past who put their hope in God used to adorn themselves. They submitted themselves to their own husbands, ⁶like Sarah, who obeyed Abraham and called him her lord. You are her daughters if you do what is right and do not give way to fear.

⁷Husbands, in the same way be considerate as you live with your wives, and treat them with respect as the weaker partner and as heirs with you of the gracious gift of life, so that nothing will hinder your prayers.

---

[a] 22 Isaiah 53:9   [b] 24,25 Isaiah 53:4,5,6 (see Septuagint)

PANORAMA

It's Not Fair!

You do what's right and still things turn out rotten. Peter wrote this letter to Christians who were being treated unfairly. He showed them how to triumph when life is unfair.

{1 PETER}

Suffering for Doing Good

[8] Finally, all of you, be like-minded, be sympathetic, love one another, be compassionate and humble. [9] Do not repay evil with evil or insult with insult. On the contrary, repay evil with blessing, because to this you were called so that you may inherit a blessing. [10] For,

"Whoever would love life
   and see good days
must keep their tongue from evil
   and their lips from deceitful speech.
[11] They must turn from evil and do good;
   they must seek peace and pursue it.
[12] For the eyes of the Lord are on the
      righteous
   and his ears are attentive to their
      prayer,
but the face of the Lord is against
      those who do evil."[a]

[13] Who is going to harm you if you are eager to do good? [14] But even if you should suffer for what is right, you are blessed. "Do not fear their threats[b]; do not be frightened."[c] [15] But in your hearts revere Christ as Lord. Always be prepared to give an answer to everyone who asks you to give the reason for the hope that you have. But do this with gentleness and respect, [16] keeping a clear conscience, so that those who speak maliciously against your good behavior in Christ may be ashamed of their slander. [17] For it is better, if it is God's will, to suffer for doing good than for doing evil. [18] For Christ also suffered once for sins, the righteous for the unrighteous, to bring you to God. He was put to death in the body but made alive in the Spirit. [19] After being made alive,[d] he went and made proclamation to the imprisoned spirits— [20] to those who were disobedient long ago when God waited patiently in the days of Noah while the ark was being built. In it only a few people, eight in all, were saved through water, [21] and this water symbolizes baptism that now saves you also—not the removal of dirt from the body but the pledge of a clear conscience toward God.[e] It saves

you by the resurrection of Jesus Christ, [22] who has gone into heaven and is at God's right hand—with angels, authorities and powers in submission to him.

Living for God

4 Therefore, since Christ suffered in his body, arm yourselves also with the same attitude, because whoever suffers in the body is done with sin. [2] As a result, they do not live the rest of their

≫ INSTANT ACCESS

You "borrow" your mom's bracelet, lose it and when she asks if you've seen it, you say, "Bracelet? What bracelet?" Then your best friend walks in waving the bracelet and says, "Hey, Hillary, you left this in my locker." Oh, well. At least you suffer through your punishment without complaining. But don't expect to be praised for it. On the other hand, if you suffer because of your Christian commitment and accept it cheerfully, that merits praise. There's no reason to be ashamed if some teacher puts you down for what you believe or if some of the other teens call you a goody-goody. Don't be ashamed, be proud. You're being a follower of Jesus.

{1 Peter 4:12–19}

---

[a] 12 Psalm 34:12-16   [b] 14 Or fear what they fear   [c] 14 Isaiah 8:12   [d] 18,19 Or but made alive in the spirit, 19in which also   [e] 21 Or but an appeal to God for a clear conscience

Worrying isn't much fun. Test coming up? You get cramps and a cold sweat. Mom goes to visit Grandpa? You lie awake wondering if her plane crashed or if a hurricane will strike where she's visiting. Peter has a suggestion for worriers: Let God worry about it for you. "Cast all your anxiety on him because he cares for you" (1 Peter 5:7). Study for your test. But after that, let God do the worrying. Hug Mom and wave good-bye. Say a prayer, and let God take over. If you are peaceful, you'll do better on your test. And you'll sleep better at night too.

{1 Peter 5:7}

[7] The end of all things is near. Therefore be alert and of sober mind so that you may pray. [8] Above all, love each other deeply, because love covers over a multitude of sins. [9] Offer hospitality to one another without grumbling. [10] Each of you should use whatever gift you have received to serve others, as faithful stewards of God's grace in its various forms. [11] If anyone speaks, they should do so as one who speaks the very words of God. If anyone serves, they should do so with the strength God provides, so that in all things God may be praised through Jesus Christ. To him be the glory and the power for ever and ever. Amen.

Suffering for Being a Christian

[12] Dear friends, do not be surprised at the fiery ordeal that has come on you to test you, as though something strange were happening to you. [13] But rejoice inasmuch as you participate in the sufferings of Christ, so that you may be overjoyed when his glory is revealed. [14] If you are insulted because of the name of Christ, you are blessed, for the Spirit of glory and of God rests on you. [15] If you suffer, it should not be as a murderer or thief or any other kind of criminal, or even as a meddler. [16] However, if you suffer as a Christian, do not be ashamed, but praise God that you bear that name. [17] For it is time for judgment to begin with God's household; and if it begins with us, what will the outcome be for those who do not obey the gospel of God? [18] And,

> "If it is hard for the righteous to be saved,
> what will become of the ungodly and the sinner?"[a]

[19] So then, those who suffer according to God's will should commit themselves to their faithful Creator and continue to do good.

To the Elders and the Flock

5 To the elders among you, I appeal as a fellow elder and a witness of Christ's sufferings who also will share in

earthly lives for evil human desires, but rather for the will of God. [3] For you have spent enough time in the past doing what pagans choose to do—living in debauchery, lust, drunkenness, orgies, carousing and detestable idolatry. [4] They are surprised that you do not join them in their reckless, wild living, and they heap abuse on you. [5] But they will have to give account to him who is ready to judge the living and the dead. [6] For this is the reason the gospel was preached even to those who are now dead, so that they might be judged according to human standards in regard to the body, but live according to God in regard to the spirit.

---

[a] 18 Prov. 11:31 (see Septuagint)

the glory to be revealed: ²Be shepherds of God's flock that is under your care, watching over them—not because you must, but because you are willing, as God wants you to be; not pursuing dishonest gain, but eager to serve; ³not lording it over those entrusted to you, but being examples to the flock. ⁴And when the Chief Shepherd appears, you will receive the crown of glory that will never fade away.

⁵In the same way, you who are younger, submit yourselves to your elders. All of you, clothe yourselves with humility toward one another, because,

> "God opposes the proud
> but shows favor to the humble."ᵃ

⁶Humble yourselves, therefore, under God's mighty hand, that he may lift you up in due time. ⁷Cast all your anxiety on him because he cares for you.

⁸Be alert and of sober mind. Your enemy the devil prowls around like a roaring lion looking for someone to devour. ⁹Resist him, standing firm in the faith, because you know that the family of believers throughout the world is undergoing the same kind of sufferings.

¹⁰And the God of all grace, who called you to his eternal glory in Christ, after you have suffered a little while, will himself restore you and make you strong, firm and steadfast. ¹¹To him be the power for ever and ever. Amen.

Final Greetings

¹²With the help of Silas,ᵇ whom I regard as a faithful brother, I have written to you briefly, encouraging you and testifying that this is the true grace of God. Stand fast in it.

¹³She who is in Babylon, chosen together with you, sends you her greetings, and so does my son Mark. ¹⁴Greet one another with a kiss of love.

Peace to all of you who are in Christ.

ᵃ 5 Prov. 3:34   ᵇ 12 Greek *Silvanus*, a variant of *Silas*

2 PETER

Different Beliefs.

You know kids with beliefs that are different from yours. Some won't say the pledge of allegiance. Some won't go to doctors but say God will heal them. Sometimes these kids may try to convince you that what you believe is wrong. They can be convincing too—so convincing it may be hard to know who's right.

Peter's first letter was about persecution from non-Christians. This second letter is about danger from false teachers who claim to be believers. Peter shows you how to know what teachers and teachings are false.

>> **BLIND? CHECK YOUR "I" SIGHT**
Read 2 Peter 1:5–9

>> **PROMISE OF "FREEDOM"**
Be on guard, warns 2 Peter 2:17–21

>> **TALKING ABOUT MY SCIENCE TEACHER?**
A word about scoffers is found in 2 Peter 3:1–7

preview

Just before his execution in Rome, the apostle Peter writes this letter warning against false teachers.

Jude and 2 Timothy give similar warnings against heresy—teachings that contradict the Bible or promote sinful living.

As Peter writes, the Jews in Judea rebel against Rome.
Roman armies are on the march to put down the rebellion.

1 Simon Peter, a servant and apostle of Jesus Christ,

To those who through the righteousness of our God and Savior Jesus Christ have received a faith as precious as ours:

2 Grace and peace be yours in abundance through the knowledge of God and of Jesus our Lord.

Confirming One's Calling and Election

3 His divine power has given us everything we need for a godly life through our knowledge of him who called us by his own glory and goodness. 4 Through these he has given us his very great and precious promises, so that through them you may participate in the divine nature, having escaped the corruption in the world caused by evil desires.

5 For this very reason, make every effort to add to your faith goodness; and to goodness, knowledge; 6 and to knowledge, self-control; and to self-control, perseverance; and to perseverance, godliness; 7 and to godliness, mutual affection; and to mutual affection, love. 8 For if you possess these qualities in increasing measure, they will keep you from being ineffective and unproductive in your knowledge of our Lord Jesus Christ. 9 But whoever does not have them is nearsighted and blind, forgetting that they have been cleansed from their past sins.

10 Therefore, my brothers and sisters,[a] make every effort to confirm your calling and election. For if you do these things, you will never stumble, 11 and you will receive a rich welcome into the eternal kingdom of our Lord and Savior Jesus Christ.

Prophecy of Scripture

12 So I will always remind you of these things, even though you know them and are firmly established in the truth you now have. 13 I think it is right to refresh your memory as long as I live in the tent of this body, 14 because I know that I will soon put it aside, as our Lord Jesus Christ has made clear to me. 15 And I will make every effort to see that after my departure you will always be able to remember these things.

16 For we did not follow cleverly devised stories when we told you about the coming of our Lord Jesus Christ in power, but we were eyewitnesses of his majesty. 17 He received honor and glory from God the Father when the voice came to him from the Majestic Glory, saying, "This is my Son, whom I love; with him I am well pleased."[b] 18 We ourselves heard this voice that came from heaven when we were with him on the sacred mountain.

19 We also have the prophetic message as something completely reliable, and you will do well to pay attention to it, as to a light shining in a dark place, until the day dawns and the morning star rises in your hearts. 20 Above all, you must understand that no prophecy of Scripture came about by the prophet's own interpretation of things. 21 For prophecy never had its origin in the human will, but prophets, though human, spoke from God as they were carried along by the Holy Spirit.

False Teachers and Their Destruction

2 But there were also false prophets among the people, just as there will be false teachers among you. They will secretly introduce destructive heresies, even denying the sovereign Lord who bought them—bringing swift destruction on themselves. 2 Many will follow their depraved conduct and will bring the way of truth into disrepute. 3 In their greed these teachers will exploit you with fabricated stories. Their condemnation has long been hanging over them, and their destruction has not been sleeping.

4 For if God did not spare angels when they sinned, but sent them to hell,[c] putting them in chains of darkness[d] to be held for judgment; 5 if he did not spare the ancient world when he brought the flood on its ungodly people, but protected Noah, a preacher of righteousness, and

---

[a] 10 The Greek word for *brothers and sisters* (*adelphoi*) refers here to believers, both men and women, as part of God's family.   [b] 17 Matt. 17:5; Mark 9:7; Luke 9:35   [c] 4 Greek *Tartarus*   [d] 4 Some manuscripts *in gloomy dungeons*

seven others; [6] if he condemned the cities of Sodom and Gomorrah by burning them to ashes, and made them an example of what is going to happen to the ungodly; [7] and if he rescued Lot, a righteous man, who was distressed by the depraved conduct of the lawless [8] (for that righteous man, living among them day after day, was tormented in his righteous soul by the lawless deeds he saw and heard)— [9] if this is so, then the Lord knows how to rescue the godly from trials and to hold the unrighteous for punishment on the day of judgment. [10] This is especially true of those who follow the corrupt desire of the flesh[a] and despise authority.

Bold and arrogant, they are not afraid to heap abuse on celestial beings; [11] yet even angels, although they are stronger and more powerful, do not heap abuse on such beings when bringing judgment on them from[b] the Lord. [12] But these people blaspheme in matters they do not understand. They are like unreasoning animals, creatures of instinct, born only to be caught and destroyed, and like animals they too will perish.

[13] They will be paid back with harm for the harm they have done. Their idea of pleasure is to carouse in broad daylight. They are blots and blemishes, reveling in their pleasures while they feast with you.[c]

[14] With eyes full of adultery, they never stop sinning; they seduce the unstable; they are experts in greed—an accursed brood! [15] They have left the straight way and wandered off to follow the way of Balaam son of Bezer,[d] who loved the wages of wickedness. [16] But he was rebuked for his wrongdoing by a donkey—an animal without speech—who spoke with a human voice and restrained the prophet's madness.

[17] These people are springs without water and mists driven by a storm. Blackest darkness is reserved for them. [18] For they mouth empty, boastful words and, by appealing to the lustful desires of the flesh, they entice people who are just escaping from those who live in error. [19] They promise them freedom, while they themselves are slaves of depravity—for "people are slaves to whatever has mastered them." [20] If they have escaped the corruption of the world by knowing our Lord and Savior Jesus Christ and are again entangled in it and are overcome, they are worse off at the end than they were at the beginning. [21] It would have been better for them not to have known the way of righteousness, than to have known it and then to turn their backs on the sacred command that was passed on to them. [22] Of them the proverbs are true: "A dog returns to its

---

[a] 10 In contexts like this, the Greek word for *flesh* (*sarx*) refers to the sinful state of human beings, often presented as a power in opposition to the Spirit; also in verse 18. [b] 11 Many manuscripts *beings in the presence of* [c] 13 Some manuscripts *in their love feasts* [d] 15 Greek *Bosor*

PANORAMA

Different Beliefs.

You know people with different beliefs than yours. Sometimes it's hard to know who's right. Peter writes this letter to talk about danger from false teachers and shows you how to know what teachers and teachings are false.

{2 PETER}

vomit,"[a] and, "A sow that is washed returns to her wallowing in the mud."

The Day of the Lord

3 Dear friends, this is now my second letter to you. I have written both of them as reminders to stimulate you to wholesome thinking. [2]I want you to recall the words spoken in the past by the holy prophets and the command given by our Lord and Savior through your apostles.

[3]Above all, you must understand that in the last days scoffers will come, scoffing and following their own evil desires. [4]They will say, "Where is this 'coming' he promised? Ever since our ancestors died, everything goes on as it has since the beginning of creation." [5]But they deliberately forget that long ago by God's word the heavens came into being and the earth was formed out of water and by water. [6]By these waters also the world of that time was deluged and destroyed. [7]By the same word the present heavens and earth are reserved for fire, being kept for the day of judgment and destruction of the ungodly.

[8]But do not forget this one thing, dear friends: With the Lord a day is like a thousand years, and a thousand years are like a day. [9]The Lord is not slow in keeping his promise, as some understand slowness. Instead he is patient with you, not wanting anyone to perish, but everyone to come to repentance.

[10]But the day of the Lord will come like a thief. The heavens will disappear with a roar; the elements will be destroyed by fire, and the earth and everything done in it will be laid bare.[b]

[11]Since everything will be destroyed in this way, what kind of people ought you to be? You ought to live holy and godly lives [12]as you look forward to the day of God and speed its coming.[c] That day will bring about the destruction of the heavens by fire, and the elements will melt in the heat. [13]But in keeping with his promise we are looking forward to a new heaven and a new earth, where righteousness dwells.

INSTANT ACCESS

What's the latest theory on how the world will end? Global warming? A new ice age? A comet crashing into the earth? An ozone hole so wide we'll all be sunburned to death? And when will this happen? Fifty years? Fifty thousand years? Five million? Peter says Jesus *will* return. God will sweep away this earth to make room for a whole new creation. The Genesis flood is history's reminder that God does judge sin. Peter's vision helps to put lots of things into perspective. Never mind the doomsayers. But remember that this world is doomed, and don't get so involved in it that you forget to live for Jesus.

{2 Peter 3:10–16}

[14]So then, dear friends, since you are looking forward to this, make every effort to be found spotless, blameless and at peace with him. [15]Bear in mind that our Lord's patience means salvation, just as our dear brother Paul also wrote you with the wisdom that God gave him. [16]He writes the same way in all his letters, speaking in them of these matters. His letters contain some things that are hard to understand, which ignorant and unstable people

[a] 22 Prov. 26:11   [b] 10 Some manuscripts *be burned up*   [c] 12 Or *as you wait eagerly for the day of God to come*

distort, as they do the other Scriptures, to their own destruction.

[17] Therefore, dear friends, since you have been forewarned, be on your guard so that you may not be carried away by the error of the lawless and fall from your secure position. [18] But grow in the grace and knowledge of our Lord and Savior Jesus Christ. To him be glory both now and forever! Amen.

1 JOHN

preview

The apostle John writes this letter. John outlives the other twelve disciples.

John writes three letters that are in the New Testament. He writes in the early 90's A.D.

A Close Friend.

Wouldn't it be great to feel as close to God as you do to your best friend? Or maybe you feel that close already. If you do, you already understand the important things John has to say in this letter.

John's first letter is about fellowship. The word means "sharing": being close to God and other Christians. John says the keys to fellowship with God are love and obedience. If you love God, you'll stay close to him and pay attention to his Word. As you obey the Lord, you sense him near and learn to love him even more.

>> **SO YOU THINK YOU'RE PERFECT?**
Don't fool yourself, warns 1 John 1:5–10

>> **WANT EVERYTHING IN THE WORLD?**
Danger exposed. See 1 John 2:15–17

>> **LET'S NOT KID OURSELVES**
Take this test, found in 1 John 3:4–10

>> **LOVE GOD? THEN LOVE OTHERS**
It's all about love? Check out 1 John 4:16–21

As John writes, Domitian is emperor. His policy is to persecute Christians. Many believers are executed, others lose jobs and homes. In 96 A.D. Domitian will be assassinated.

The Incarnation of the Word of Life

1 That which was from the beginning, which we have heard, which we have seen with our eyes, which we have looked at and our hands have touched—this we proclaim concerning the Word of life. ²The life appeared; we have seen it and testify to it, and we proclaim to you the eternal life, which was with the Father and has appeared to us. ³We proclaim to you what we have seen and heard, so that you also may have fellowship with us. And our fellowship is with the Father and with his Son, Jesus Christ. ⁴We write this to make our[a] joy complete.

Light and Darkness, Sin and Forgiveness

⁵This is the message we have heard from him and declare to you: God is light; in him there is no darkness at all. ⁶If we claim to have fellowship with him and yet walk in the darkness, we lie and do not live out the truth. ⁷But if we walk in the light, as he is in the light, we have fellowship with one another, and the blood of Jesus, his Son, purifies us from all[b] sin.

⁸If we claim to be without sin, we deceive ourselves and the truth is not in us. ⁹If we confess our sins, he is faithful and just and will forgive us our sins and purify us from all unrighteousness. ¹⁰If we claim we have not sinned, we make him out to be a liar and his word is not in us.

2 My dear children, I write this to you so that you will not sin. But if anybody does sin, we have an advocate with the Father—Jesus Christ, the Righteous One. ²He is the atoning sacrifice for our sins, and not only for ours but also for the sins of the whole world.

Love and Hatred for Fellow Believers

³We know that we have come to know him if we keep his commands. ⁴Whoever says, "I know him," but does not do what he commands is a liar, and the truth is not in that person. ⁵But if anyone obeys

INSTANT ACCESS

John warns you to be honest about your faults. If you "claim to be without sin" (1 John 1:8), you don't fool others. But you will end up deceiving yourself. To stay close to God you have to be honest with yourself, even more than with others. You can't take your sister's sweater and then lie about it or say you're going one place and then go another. And then pretend it isn't wrong. If you find yourself doing things like this, face the fact that you are sinning. Confess your sin to God, and he will forgive you. He'll even cleanse you so you can start doing what's right. If you don't stop deceiving yourself, you'll never be really close to the Lord.

{1 John 1:5–10}

his word, love for God[c] is truly made complete in them. This is how we know we are in him: ⁶Whoever claims to live in him must live as Jesus did.

⁷Dear friends, I am not writing you a new command but an old one, which you have had since the beginning. This old command is the message you have heard. ⁸Yet I am writing you a new command; its truth is seen in him and in you,

---

[a] 4 Some manuscripts *your*   [b] 7 Or *every*   [c] 5 Or *word, God's love*

because the darkness is passing and the true light is already shining.

⁹Anyone who claims to be in the light but hates a brother or sister[a] is still in the darkness. ¹⁰Anyone who loves their brother and sister[b] lives in the light, and there is nothing in them to make them stumble. ¹¹But anyone who hates a brother or sister is in the darkness and walks around in the darkness. They do not know where they are going, because the darkness has blinded them.

Reasons for Writing

¹²I am writing to you, dear children,
   because your sins have been
      forgiven on account of his
      name.
¹³I am writing to you, fathers,
   because you know him who is from
      the beginning.
I am writing to you, young men,
   because you have overcome the evil
      one.
¹⁴I write to you, dear children,
   because you know the Father.
I write to you, fathers,
   because you know him who is from
      the beginning.
I write to you, young men,
   because you are strong,

and the word of God lives in you,
   and you have overcome the evil one.

On Not Loving the World

¹⁵Do not love the world or anything in the world. If anyone loves the world, love for the Father[c] is not in them. ¹⁶For everything in the world—the lust of the flesh, the lust of the eyes, and the pride of life—comes not from the Father but from the world. ¹⁷The world and its desires pass away, but whoever does the will of God lives forever.

Warnings Against Denying the Son

¹⁸Dear children, this is the last hour; and as you have heard that the antichrist is coming, even now many antichrists have come. This is how we know it is the last hour. ¹⁹They went out from us, but they did not really belong to us. For if they had belonged to us, they would have remained with us; but their going showed that none of them belonged to us.

²⁰But you have an anointing from the Holy One, and all of you know the truth.[d] ²¹I do not write to you because you do not know the truth, but because you do know it and because no lie comes from the truth. ²²Who is the liar? It is whoever

---

a 9 The Greek word for *brother or sister* (*adelphos*) refers here to a believer, whether man or woman, as part of God's family; also in verse 11; and in 3:15, 17; 4:20; 5:16.   *b* 10 The Greek word for *brother and sister* (*adelphos*) refers here to a believer, whether man or woman, as part of God's family; also in 3:10; 4:20, 21.   *c* 15 Or *world, the Father's love*   *d* 20 Some manuscripts *and you know all things*

PANORAMA

A Close Friend.

John's first letter is about "fellowship." The word means "sharing": being close to God and other Christians. The keys to fellowship with God are love and obedience. If you love God, you'll stay close to him and pay attention to his Word.

{1 JOHN}

denies that Jesus is the Christ. Such a person is the antichrist—denying the Father and the Son. 23No one who denies the Son has the Father; whoever acknowledges the Son has the Father also.

24As for you, see that what you have heard from the beginning remains in you. If it does, you also will remain in the Son and in the Father. 25And this is what he promised us—eternal life.

26I am writing these things to you about those who are trying to lead you astray. 27As for you, the anointing you received from him remains in you, and you do not need anyone to teach you. But as his anointing teaches you about all things and as that anointing is real, not counterfeit—just as it has taught you, remain in him.

God's Children and Sin

28And now, dear children, continue in him, so that when he appears we may be confident and unashamed before him at his coming.

29If you know that he is righteous, you know that everyone who does what is right has been born of him.

3 See what great love the Father has lavished on us, that we should be called children of God! And that is what we are! The reason the world does not know us is that it did not know him. 2Dear friends, now we are children of God, and what we will be has not yet been made known. But we know that when Christ appears,[a] we shall be like him, for we shall see him as he is. 3All who have this hope in him purify themselves, just as he is pure.

4Everyone who sins breaks the law; in fact, sin is lawlessness. 5But you know that he appeared so that he might take away our sins. And in him is no sin. 6No one who lives in him keeps on sinning. No one who continues to sin has either seen him or known him.

7Dear children, do not let anyone lead you astray. The one who does what is right is righteous, just as he is righteous. 8The one who does what is sinful is of the devil, because the devil has been sinning from the beginning. The reason the Son of God appeared was to destroy the devil's work. 9No one who is born of God will continue to sin, because God's seed remains in them; they cannot go on sinning, because they have been born of God. 10This is how we know who the children of God are and who the children of the devil are: Anyone who does not do what is right is not God's child, nor is anyone who does not love their brother and sister.

More on Love and Hatred

11For this is the message you heard from the beginning: We should love one another. 12Do not be like Cain, who belonged to the evil one and murdered his brother. And why did he murder him? Because his own actions were evil and his brother's were righteous. 13Do not be surprised, my brothers and sisters,[b] if the world hates you. 14We know that we have passed from death to life, because we love each other. Anyone who does not love remains in death. 15Anyone who hates a brother or sister is a murderer, and you know that no murderer has eternal life residing in him.

16This is how we know what love is: Jesus Christ laid down his life for us. And we ought to lay down our lives for our brothers and sisters. 17If anyone has material possessions and sees a brother or sister in need but has no pity on them, how can the love of God be in that person? 18Dear children, let us not love with words or speech but with actions and in truth.

19This is how we know that we belong to the truth and how we set our hearts at rest in his presence: 20If our hearts condemn

> *See what great love the Father has lavished on us, that we should be called children of God!*
> 1 John 3:1

---

a 2 Or *when it is made known*   b 13 The Greek word for *brothers and sisters* (adelphoi) refers here to believers, both men and women, as part of God's family; also in verse 16.

us, we know that God is greater than our hearts, and he knows everything. 21 Dear friends, if our hearts do not condemn us, we have confidence before God 22 and receive from him anything we ask, because we keep his commands and do what pleases him. 23 And this is his command: to believe in the name of his Son, Jesus Christ, and to love one another as he commanded us. 24 The one who keeps God's commands lives in him, and he in them. And this is how we know that he lives in us: We know it by the Spirit he gave us.

On Denying the Incarnation

4 Dear friends, do not believe every spirit, but test the spirits to see whether they are from God, because

many false prophets have gone out into the world. 2 This is how you can recognize the Spirit of God: Every spirit that acknowledges that Jesus Christ has come in the flesh is from God, 3 but every spirit that does not acknowledge Jesus is not from God. This is the spirit of the antichrist, which you have heard is coming and even now is already in the world.

4 You, dear children, are from God and have overcome them, because the one who is in you is greater than the one who is in the world. 5 They are from the world and therefore speak from the viewpoint of the world, and the world listens to them. 6 We are from God, and whoever knows God listens to us; but whoever is not from God does not listen to us. This is how we

TO THE POINT

God Is Love

Love is the key to understanding God and the life God wants you to live here on earth. One of the Bible's most beautiful passages about God's love (1 John 4:7–21) tells you:

+ Love motivates all God does (1 John 4:16).

+ Jesus proves God's love (1 John 4:9–10).

+ God's love changes you so that you love him (1 John 4:19).

+ God's love changes you so that you love others (1 John 4:20–21).

So don't let anyone tell you that Christianity is about lists of do's and don'ts that keep people from having fun. Christianity is all about love: God's love and your love for him and for others.

recognize the Spirit[a] of truth and the spirit of falsehood.

God's Love and Ours

[7] Dear friends, let us love one another, for love comes from God. Everyone who loves has been born of God and knows God. [8] Whoever does not love does not know God, because God is love. [9] This is how God showed his love among us: He sent his one and only Son into the world that we might live through him. [10] This is love: not that we loved God, but that he loved us and sent his Son as an atoning sacrifice for our sins. [11] Dear friends, since God so loved us, we also ought to love one another. [12] No one has ever seen God; but if we love one another, God lives in us and his love is made complete in us.

[13] This is how we know that we live in him and he in us: He has given us of his Spirit. [14] And we have seen and testify that the Father has sent his Son to be the Savior of the world. [15] If anyone acknowledges that Jesus is the Son of God, God lives in them and they in God. [16] And so we know and rely on the love God has for us.

God is love. Whoever lives in love lives in God, and God in them. [17] This is how love is made complete among us so that we will have confidence on the day of judgment: In this world we are like Jesus. [18] There is no fear in love. But perfect love drives out fear, because fear has to do with punishment. The one who fears is not made perfect in love.

[19] We love because he first loved us. [20] Whoever claims to love God yet hates a brother or sister is a liar. For whoever does not love their brother and sister, whom they have seen, cannot love God, whom they have not seen. [21] And he has given us this command: Anyone who loves God must also love their brother and sister.

Faith in the Incarnate Son of God

5 Everyone who believes that Jesus is the Christ is born of God, and everyone who loves the father loves his child as well. [2] This is how we know that we love the children of God: by loving God and carrying out his commands. [3] In fact, this is love for God: to keep his commands. And his commands are not burdensome, [4] for everyone born of God overcomes the world. This is the victory that has overcome the world, even our faith. [5] Who is it that overcomes the world? Only the one who believes that Jesus is the Son of God.

[6] This is the one who came by water and blood—Jesus Christ. He did not come by water only, but by water and blood. And it is the Spirit who testifies, because the Spirit is the truth. [7] For there are three that testify: [8] the[b] Spirit, the water and the blood; and the three are in agreement. [9] We accept human testimony, but God's testimony is greater because it is the testimony of God, which he has given about his Son. [10] Whoever believes in the Son of God accepts this testimony. Whoever does not believe God has made him out to be a liar, because they have not believed the testimony God has given about his Son. [11] And this is the testimony: God has given us eternal life, and this life is in his Son. [12] Whoever has the Son has life; whoever does not have the Son of God does not have life.

> **Whoever has the Son has life; whoever does not have the Son of God does not have life.**
> 1 John 5:12

Concluding Affirmations

[13] I write these things to you who believe in the name of the Son of God so that you may know that you have eternal life. [14] This is the confidence we have in approaching God: that if we ask anything according to his will, he hears us. [15] And if we know that he hears us—whatever

---

[a] 6 Or *spirit*   [b] 7,8 Late manuscripts of the Vulgate *testify in heaven: the Father, the Word and the Holy Spirit, and these three are one.* [8] *And there are three that testify on earth: the* (not found in any Greek manuscript before the fourteenth century)

we ask—we know that we have what we asked of him.

[16] If you see any brother or sister commit a sin that does not lead to death, you should pray and God will give them life. I refer to those whose sin does not lead to death. There is a sin that leads to death. I am not saying that you should pray about that. [17] All wrongdoing is sin, and there is sin that does not lead to death.

[18] We know that anyone born of God does not continue to sin; the One who was born of God keeps them safe, and the evil one cannot harm them. [19] We know that we are children of God, and that the whole world is under the control of the evil one. [20] We know also that the Son of God has come and has given us understanding, so that we may know him who is true. And we are in him who is true by being in his Son Jesus Christ. He is the true God and eternal life.

[21] Dear children, keep yourselves from idols.

2 JOHN

Notes.

Everyone likes to pass notes or send messages in school. They don't have to be long or even say anything exciting. It's just a way of staying close to friends.

John's second letter is really just a note. It doesn't reveal any startling new doctrine. It expresses John's love and concern for others. The kind of love God wants you to have for your friends.

>>**MAKE MOM AND DAD HAPPY**
How to help in 2 John 4

>>**LOVE? WHAT'S LOVE?**
See the simple definition in 2 John 6

preview

This brief letter is one of three in the New Testament written by the apostle John.

John is in his late 80's as he writes this letter.

He reminds us that what's important is loving one another and obeying God's commandments.

[1] The elder,

To the lady chosen by God and to her children, whom I love in the truth—and not I only, but also all who know the truth— [2] because of the truth, which lives in us and will be with us forever:

[3] Grace, mercy and peace from God the Father and from Jesus Christ, the Father's Son, will be with us in truth and love.

[4] It has given me great joy to find some of your children walking in the truth, just as the Father commanded us. [5] And now, dear lady, I am not writing you a new command but one we have had from the beginning. I ask that we love one another. [6] And this is love: that we walk in obedience to his commands. As you have heard from the beginning, his command is that you walk in love.

[7] I say this because many deceivers, who do not acknowledge Jesus Christ as coming in the flesh, have gone out into the world. Any such person is the deceiver and the antichrist. [8] Watch out that you do not lose what we[a] have worked for, but that you may be rewarded fully. [9] Anyone who runs ahead and does not continue in the teaching of Christ does not have God; whoever continues in the teaching has both the Father and the Son. [10] If anyone comes to you and does not bring this teaching, do not take them into your house or welcome them. [11] Anyone who welcomes them shares in their wicked work.

[12] I have much to write to you, but I do not want to use paper and ink. Instead, I hope to visit you and talk with you face to face, so that our joy may be complete.

[13] The children of your sister, who is chosen by God, send their greetings.

[a] 8 Some manuscripts *you*

>> INSTANT ACCESS

Let's see. What's a great Christmas gift for a Christian mom and dad? Or a birthday present that keeps on giving all year long? John gives you a clue to the very best gift of all when he writes, "It has given me great joy to find some of your children walking in the truth." Talk about joy! There's no greater gift you can give Christian parents than to live a life that shows you're following Jesus.

{2 John 4}

PANORAMA

Notes.

John's second letter is just a note, expressing love and concern for others. It's the kind of love God wants you to have for your friends.

{2 JOHN}

3 JOHN

More Notes.

You send a note to your friend across the room. She sends one back. You send hers back with more notes on it. It goes on and on. There's always more to tell each other!

The book of 3 John is a short note sent by John to Gaius, "my dear friend" (3 John 1). He writes to thank Gaius for his help, and he also wants to give him encouragement.

>>**IS GAIUS JUST LIKE ME?**
Check him out in 3 John 3

>>**OR AM I LIKE DIOTREPHES?**
Better hope not! See 3 John 9,10

This note is one of three letters in the New Testament written by the apostle John.

The common theme in all John's letters is love.

preview

As John writes, Christians are being persecuted. It's critical that believers not compete, but love and support each other.

¹The elder,

To my dear friend Gaius, whom I love in the truth.

²Dear friend, I pray that you may enjoy good health and that all may go well with you, even as your soul is getting along well. ³It gave me great joy when some believers came and testified about your faithfulness to the truth, telling how you continue to walk in it. ⁴I have no greater joy than to hear that my children are walking in the truth.

⁵Dear friend, you are faithful in what you are doing for the brothers and sisters,ᵃ even though they are strangers to you. ⁶They have told the church about your love. Please send them on their way in a manner that honors God. ⁷It was for the sake of the Name that they went out, receiving no help from the pagans. ⁸We ought therefore to show hospitality to such people so that we may work together for the truth.

> *Do not imitate what is evil but what is good.*
> 3 John 11

⁹I wrote to the church, but Diotrephes, who loves to be first, will not welcome us. ¹⁰So when I come, I will call attention to what he is doing, spreading malicious nonsense about us. Not satisfied with that, he even refuses to welcome other believers. He also stops those who want to do so and puts them out of the church.

¹¹Dear friend, do not imitate what is evil but what is good. Anyone who does what is good is from God. Anyone who does what is evil has not seen God. ¹²Demetrius is well spoken of by everyone—and even by the truth itself. We also speak well of him, and you know that our testimony is true.

¹³I have much to write you, but I do not want to do so with pen and ink. ¹⁴I hope to see you soon, and we will talk face to face.

Peace to you. The friends here send their greetings. Greet the friends there by name.

ᵃ 5 The Greek word for *brothers and sisters* (*adelphoi*) refers here to believers, both men and women, as part of God's family.

PANORAMA

More Notes.

This third "note" is sent from John to Gaius, a dear friend, thanking him for his help and encouraging him.

{3 JOHN}

Dear Jordan

> At school they make fun of me for being a virgin. I used to be proud of it. Now I feel embarrassed. I don't want to do something I'll be sorry for later. But I don't want to be the prude either.
>
> >> Isabel

Dear Isabel,

Many people today will tell you, "If it feels good, do it." But God has a different message. He tells you to save this special gift for marriage.

Today the results of promiscuous sex are obvious: AIDS, herpes, HPV (human papilloma virus), pregnancy, abortion, depression. Did you know that teens make up 10% of our population but they acquire 20–25% of all STD's (sexually transmitted diseases)? Or that one in five children over age 12 tests positive for herpes type 2 for which there is no cure?

God's laws aren't there to make life hard for you. They are there for a reason. In 3 John 11, John tells us, "Do not imitate what is evil but what is good." Fill your life with good things like friendships, fun activities, family, church and volunteering.

Chances are good that some of the people who make fun of you are already infected with things that can't be cured. They might even be passing these incurable diseases around without even knowing it. So feel good about your choice and try to hang around with others who share your values.

Jordan

JUDE

preview

Jude is the brother of James and of Jesus. He was Mary and Joseph's son.

Jude quotes Jewish writings that are not in the Bible (verses 9,14,15).

I'm Serious!

Have you ever noticed that when your parents are serious about something, they say it again and again. "Sarah, clean your room." Then five minutes later, "Sarah, clean your room." Hey, you just want to finish your email. But oh, no, five minutes later, and they're at it again. "Sarah, clean your room!"

Three New Testament books say, "Watch out for false teachers," "Watch out for false teachers," "Watch out for false teachers." God must be serious. Jude even says he planned to write a different kind of letter, but the Holy Spirit led him to write about false teachers instead. Maybe we'd better listen!

>>**CAN'T MISS THE FALSE TEACHER**
For a description, see Jude 4

>>**NASTY, NASTY!**
See Jude 16

>>**CAN WE PROTECT OURSELVES?**
For the good news, read Jude 20,21

As Jude writes, the city of Pompeii lies covered with lava from the recent eruption of Mt. Vesuvius.

¹Jude, a servant of Jesus Christ and a brother of James,

To those who have been called, who are loved in God the Father and kept for[a] Jesus Christ:

²Mercy, peace and love be yours in abundance.

The Sin and Doom of Ungodly People

³Dear friends, although I was very eager to write to you about the salvation we share, I felt compelled to write and urge you to contend for the faith that was once for all entrusted to God's holy people. ⁴For certain individuals whose condemnation was written about[b] long ago have secretly slipped in among you. They are ungodly people, who pervert the grace of our God into a license for immorality and deny Jesus Christ our only Sovereign and Lord.

⁵Though you already know all this, I want to remind you that the Lord[c] at one time delivered his people out of Egypt, but later destroyed those who did not believe. ⁶And the angels who did not keep their positions of authority but abandoned their proper dwelling—these he has kept in darkness, bound with everlasting chains for judgment on the great Day. ⁷In a similar way, Sodom and Gomorrah and the surrounding towns gave themselves up to sexual immorality and perversion. They serve as an example of those who suffer the punishment of eternal fire.

⁸In the very same way, on the strength of their dreams these ungodly people pollute their own bodies, reject authority and heap abuse on celestial beings. ⁹But even the archangel Michael, when he was disputing with the devil about the body of Moses, did not himself dare to condemn him for slander but said, "The Lord rebuke you!"[d] ¹⁰Yet these people slander whatever they do not understand, and the very things they do understand by instinct—as irrational animals do—will destroy them.

¹¹Woe to them! They have taken the way of Cain; they have rushed for profit into Balaam's error; they have been destroyed in Korah's rebellion.

¹²These people are blemishes at your love feasts, eating with you without the slightest qualm—shepherds who feed only themselves. They are clouds without rain, blown along by the wind; autumn trees, without fruit and uprooted—twice dead. ¹³They are wild waves of the sea, foaming up their shame; wandering stars, for whom blackest darkness has been reserved forever.

¹⁴Enoch, the seventh from Adam, prophesied about them: "See, the Lord is

---

[a] 1 Or by; or in   [b] 4 Or individuals who were marked out for condemnation   [c] 5 Some early manuscripts Jesus
[d] 9 Jude is alluding to the Jewish Testament of Moses (approximately the first century A.D.).

{JUDE}

PANORAMA

I'm Serious!

Watch out for false teachers! Three New Testament books have this same message, one worth repeating.

coming with thousands upon thousands of his holy ones [15] to judge everyone, and to convict all of them of all the ungodly acts they have committed in their ungodliness, and of all the defiant words ungodly sinners have spoken against him."[a] [16] These people are grumblers and faultfinders; they follow their own evil desires; they boast about themselves and flatter others for their own advantage.

A Call to Persevere

[17] But, dear friends, remember what the apostles of our Lord Jesus Christ foretold. [18] They said to you, "In the last times there will be scoffers who will follow their own ungodly desires." [19] These are the people who divide you, who follow mere natural instincts and do not have the Spirit.

[20] But you, dear friends, by building yourselves up in your most holy faith and praying in the Holy Spirit, [21] keep yourselves in God's love as you wait for the mercy of our Lord Jesus Christ to bring you to eternal life.

[22] Be merciful to those who doubt; [23] save others by snatching them from the fire; to others show mercy, mixed with fear—hating even the clothing stained by corrupted flesh.[b]

Doxology

[24] To him who is able to keep you from stumbling and to present you before his glorious presence without fault and with great joy— [25] to the only God our Savior be glory, majesty, power and authority, through Jesus Christ our Lord, before all ages, now and forevermore! Amen.

>> INSTANT ACCESS

According to Jude, a false teacher isn't the history teacher who promises you an essay test and then gives you multiple choice. False teachers are "ungodly people" (Jude 4) who look and sound religious but who lead you away instead of toward Jesus. Jude describes these false teachers and then gives instruction on how to avoid them (Jude 20–23):

- **Build your faith.** Count on what the Bible says, not on what false teachers teach.
- **Pray in the Spirit.** Let God's Spirit guide you.
- **Keep yourself in God's love.**

Stick to doing right while you're waiting for Jesus to come back. And be concerned about others. Do everything you can to help them get to know and love the Lord.

{Jude 3–23}

---

[a] 14,15 From the Jewish *First Book of Enoch* (approximately the first century B.C.)   [b] 22,23 The Greek manuscripts of these verses vary at several points.

REVELATION

Hard Words.

Sometimes when you don't understand a hard word, do you just ignore it and read on? Well, you can't ignore the hard words in this book of the Bible. There are just too many of them. And too many strange images: stars falling in the ocean and rivers turning to blood. What does it mean?

Even though Revelation uses difficult images and symbols, the message of the book is clear: This world will come to an end. Jesus will come back, and he'll punish evil. No matter how hard Satan and his forces struggle, Jesus will win. Then all will learn that both heaven and hell are real, for ever and ever.

>>**NO "GENTLE JESUS" NOW**
   John describes the risen Christ in Revelation 1:12–18

>>**LOTS OF JOY IN HEAVEN**
   The end is near. Revelation 5:6–14

>>**A WHOLE LOT OF MISERY ON EARTH**
   You'd think they'd believe now. But see Revelation 9:17–21

>>**HELL OR HEAVEN?**
   We'll live forever. The question is, where? See Revelation 20,21

preview

The apostle John is on the prison island of Patmos. He is over 90 years old.

Revelation records visions given to John. From chapter 4:1 on, the visions concern "what must take place after this."

As John sees visions the emperor Domitian is assassinated. The next emperor, Trajan, institutes liberal reforms. But for over 200 more years Christians are still persecuted in parts of the Roman empire.

Prologue

1 The revelation from Jesus Christ, which God gave him to show his servants what must soon take place. He made it known by sending his angel to his servant John, [2]who testifies to everything he saw—that is, the word of God and the testimony of Jesus Christ. [3]Blessed is the one who reads aloud the words of this prophecy, and blessed are those who hear it and take to heart what is written in it; because the time is near.

Greetings and Doxology

[4]John,

To the seven churches in the province of Asia:

Grace and peace to you from him who is, and who was, and who is to come, and from the seven spirits[a] before his throne, [5]and from Jesus Christ, who is the faithful witness, the firstborn from the dead, and the ruler of the kings of the earth.

To him who loves us and has freed us from our sins by his blood, [6]and has made us to be a kingdom and priests to serve his God and Father—to him be glory and power for ever and ever! Amen.

[7]"Look, he is coming with the clouds,"[b]
  and "every eye will see him,
  even those who pierced him";
  and all peoples on earth "will
  mourn because of him."[c]
      So shall it be! Amen.

[8]"I am the Alpha and the Omega," says the Lord God, "who is, and who was, and who is to come, the Almighty."

John's Vision of Christ

[9]I, John, your brother and companion in the suffering and kingdom and patient endurance that are ours in Jesus, was on the island of Patmos because of the word of God and the testimony of Jesus. [10]On the Lord's Day I was in the Spirit, and I heard behind me a loud voice like a trumpet, [11]which said: "Write on a scroll what

---

»> INSTANT ACCESS

When you were a little kid, did you think of Jesus as warm and friendly and walking around in a long white robe? Probably many adult Christians still have that image of "gentle Jesus, meek and mild." So it's kind of shocking to read these verses and see John, stunned, fall on his face before an overwhelmingly powerful revelation of Jesus as God the Son. John probably never forgot this later revelation. Jesus isn't weak. He's the most powerful person in the whole universe. And he's on your side!

{Revelation 1:9–18}

---

you see and send it to the seven churches: to Ephesus, Smyrna, Pergamum, Thyatira, Sardis, Philadelphia and Laodicea."

[12]I turned around to see the voice that was speaking to me. And when I turned I saw seven golden lampstands, [13]and among the lampstands was someone like a son of man,[d] dressed in a robe reaching down to his feet and with a golden sash around his chest. [14]The hair on his head was white like wool, as white as snow, and his eyes were like blazing fire. [15]His feet were like bronze glowing in a furnace, and his voice was like the sound of rushing waters. [16]In his right hand he

---

[a] 4 That is, the sevenfold Spirit   [b] 7 Daniel 7:13   [c] 7 Zech. 12:10   [d] 13 See Daniel 7:13.

held seven stars, and coming out of his mouth was a sharp, double-edged sword. His face was like the sun shining in all its brilliance.

17 When I saw him, I fell at his feet as though dead. Then he placed his right hand on me and said: "Do not be afraid. I am the First and the Last. 18 I am the Living One; I was dead, and now look, I am alive for ever and ever! And I hold the keys of death and Hades.

19 "Write, therefore, what you have seen, what is now and what will take place later. 20 The mystery of the seven stars that you saw in my right hand and of the seven golden lampstands is this: The seven stars are the angels[a] of the seven churches, and the seven lampstands are the seven churches.

To the Church in Ephesus

2 "To the angel[b] of the church in Ephesus write:

These are the words of him who holds the seven stars in his right hand and walks among the seven golden lampstands. 2 I know your deeds, your hard work and your perseverance. I know that you cannot tolerate wicked people, that you have tested those who claim to be apostles but are not, and have found them false. 3 You have persevered and have endured hardships for my name, and have not grown weary.

4 Yet I hold this against you: You have forsaken the love you had at first. 5 Consider how far you have fallen! Repent and do the things you did at first. If you do not repent, I will come to you and remove your lampstand from its place. 6 But you have this in your favor: You hate the practices of the Nicolaitans, which I also hate.

7 Whoever has ears, let them hear what the Spirit says to the churches. To the one who is victorious, I will give the right to eat from the tree of life, which is in the paradise of God.

To the Church in Smyrna

8 "To the angel of the church in Smyrna write:

These are the words of him who is the First and the Last, who died and came to life again. 9 I know your afflictions and your poverty—yet you are rich! I know about the slander of those who say they are Jews and are not, but are a synagogue of Satan. 10 Do not be afraid of what you are about to suffer. I tell you, the devil will put some of you in prison to test you, and you will suffer persecution for ten days. Be faithful, even to the point of death, and I will give you life as your victor's crown.

11 Whoever has ears, let them hear what the Spirit says to the churches. The one who is victorious will not be hurt at all by the second death.

To the Church in Pergamum

12 "To the angel of the church in Pergamum write:

These are the words of him who has the sharp, double-edged sword. 13 I know where you live—where Satan has his throne. Yet you remain true to my name. You did not renounce your faith in me, not even in the days of Antipas, my faithful witness, who was put to death in your city—where Satan lives.

14 Nevertheless, I have a few things against you: There are some among you who hold to the teaching of Balaam, who taught Balak to entice the Israelites to sin so that they ate food sacrificed to idols and committed sexual immorality. 15 Likewise, you also have those who hold to the teaching of the Nicolaitans. 16 Repent therefore! Otherwise, I will soon come to you and will fight against them with the sword of my mouth.

17 Whoever has ears, let them hear what the Spirit says to the churches. To the one who is victorious, I will give some of the hidden manna. I will

---

[a] 20 Or *messengers*   [b] 1 Or *messenger*; also in verses 8, 12 and 18

also give that person a white stone with a new name written on it, known only to the one who receives it.

To the Church in Thyatira

18 "To the angel of the church in Thyatira write:

These are the words of the Son of God, whose eyes are like blazing fire and whose feet are like burnished bronze. 19 I know your deeds, your love and faith, your service and perseverance, and that you are now doing more than you did at first.

20 Nevertheless, I have this against you: You tolerate that woman Jezebel, who calls herself a prophet. By her teaching she misleads my servants into sexual immorality and the eating of food sacrificed to idols. 21 I have given her time to repent of her immorality, but she is unwilling. 22 So I will cast her on a bed of suffering, and I will make those who commit adultery with her suffer intensely, unless they repent of her ways. 23 I will strike her children dead. Then all the churches will know that I am he who searches hearts and minds, and I will repay each of you according to your deeds.

24 Now I say to the rest of you in Thyatira, to you who do not hold to her teaching and have not learned Satan's so-called deep secrets, 'I will not impose any other burden on you, 25 except to hold on to what you have until I come.'

26 To the one who is victorious and does my will to the end, I will give authority over the nations— 27 that one 'will rule them with an iron scepter and will dash them to pieces like pottery'a—just as I have received authority from my Father. 28 I will also give that one the morning star. 29 Whoever has ears, let them hear what the Spirit says to the churches.

To the Church in Sardis

3 "To the angel b of the church in Sardis write:

These are the words of him who holds the seven spirits c of God and the seven stars. I know your deeds; you have a reputation of being alive, but you are dead. 2 Wake up! Strengthen what remains and is about to die, for I have found your deeds unfinished in the sight of my God. 3 Remember, therefore, what you have received and heard; hold it fast, and repent. But if you do not wake up, I will come like a thief, and you will not know at what time I will come to you.

4 Yet you have a few people in Sardis who have not soiled their clothes. They will walk with me, dressed in white, for they are worthy. 5 The one who is victorious will, like them, be dressed in white. I will never blot out the name of that person from the book of life, but will acknowledge that name before my Father and his angels. 6 Whoever has ears, let them hear what the Spirit says to the churches.

To the Church in Philadelphia

7 "To the angel of the church in Philadelphia write:

These are the words of him who is holy and true, who holds the key of David. What he opens no one can shut, and what he shuts no one can open. 8 I know your deeds. See, I have placed before you an open door that no one can shut. I know that you have little strength, yet you have kept my word and have not denied my name. 9 I will make those who are of the synagogue of Satan, who claim to be Jews though they are not, but are liars—I will make them come and fall down at your feet and acknowledge that I have loved you. 10 Since you have kept my command to endure patiently, I will also keep you from the hour of trial that is going to come on the whole world to test the inhabitants of the earth.

---

a 27 Psalm 2:9   b 1 Or messenger; also in verses 7 and 14   c 1 That is, the sevenfold Spirit

¹¹I am coming soon. Hold on to what you have, so that no one will take your crown. ¹²The one who is victorious I will make a pillar in the temple of my God. Never again will they leave it. I will write on them the name of my God and the name of the city of my God, the new Jerusalem, which is coming down out of heaven from my God; and I will also write on them my new name. ¹³Whoever has ears, let them hear what the Spirit says to the churches.

To the Church in Laodicea

¹⁴"To the angel of the church in Laodicea write:

These are the words of the Amen, the faithful and true witness, the ruler of God's creation. ¹⁵I know your deeds, that you are neither cold nor hot. I wish you were either one or the other! ¹⁶So, because you are lukewarm—neither hot nor cold—I am about to spit you out of my mouth. ¹⁷You say, 'I am rich; I have acquired wealth and do not need a thing.' But you do not realize that you are wretched, pitiful, poor, blind and naked. ¹⁸I counsel you to buy from me gold refined in the fire, so you can become rich; and white clothes to wear, so you can cover your shameful nakedness; and salve to put on your eyes, so you can see.

¹⁹Those whom I love I rebuke and discipline. So be earnest and repent. ²⁰Here I am! I stand at the door and knock. If anyone hears my voice and opens the door, I will come in and eat with that person, and they with me.

²¹To the one who is victorious, I will give the right to sit with me on my throne, just as I was victorious and sat down with my Father on his throne. ²²Whoever has ears, let them hear what the Spirit says to the churches."

The Throne in Heaven

4 After this I looked, and there before me was a door standing open in heaven. And the voice I had first heard speaking to me like a trumpet said, "Come up here, and I will show you what must take place after this." ²At once I was in the Spirit, and there before me was a throne in heaven with someone sitting on it. ³And the one who sat there had the appearance of jasper and ruby. A rainbow that shone like an emerald encircled the throne. ⁴Surrounding the throne were twenty-four other thrones, and seated on them were twenty-four elders. They were dressed in white and had crowns of gold on their heads. ⁵From the throne came flashes of lightning, rumblings and peals of thunder. In front of the throne, seven lamps were blazing. These are the seven spirits^a of God. ⁶Also in front of the throne there was what looked like a sea of glass, clear as crystal.

In the center, around the throne, were four living creatures, and they were covered with eyes, in front and in back. ⁷The first living creature was like a lion, the second was like an ox, the third had a face like a man, the fourth was like a flying eagle. ⁸Each of the four living creatures had six wings and was covered with eyes all around, even under its wings. Day and night they never stop saying:

" 'Holy, holy, holy
is the Lord God Almighty,'^{b}
who was, and is, and is to come."

⁹Whenever the living creatures give glory, honor and thanks to him who sits on the throne and who lives for ever and ever, ¹⁰the twenty-four elders fall down before him who sits on the throne and worship him who lives for ever and ever. They lay their crowns before the throne and say:

¹¹"You are worthy, our Lord and God,
to receive glory and honor and power,
for you created all things,
and by your will they were created
and have their being."

---

^{a} 5 That is, the sevenfold Spirit ^{b} 8 Isaiah 6:3

The Scroll and the Lamb

5 Then I saw in the right hand of him who sat on the throne a scroll with writing on both sides and sealed with seven seals. ²And I saw a mighty angel proclaiming in a loud voice, "Who is worthy to break the seals and open the scroll?" ³But no one in heaven or on earth or under the earth could open the scroll or even look inside it. ⁴I wept and wept because no one was found who was worthy to open the scroll or look inside. ⁵Then one of the elders said to me, "Do not weep! See, the Lion of the tribe of Judah, the Root of David, has triumphed. He is able to open the scroll and its seven seals."

⁶Then I saw a Lamb, looking as if it had been slain, standing at the center of the throne, encircled by the four living creatures and the elders. The Lamb had seven horns and seven eyes, which are the seven spirits[a] of God sent out into all the earth. ⁷He went and took the scroll from the right hand of him who sat on the throne. ⁸And when he had taken it, the four living creatures and the twenty-four elders fell down before the Lamb. Each one had a harp and they were holding golden bowls full of incense, which are the prayers of God's people. ⁹And they sang a new song, saying:

"You are worthy to take the scroll
    and to open its seals,

---

a 6 That is, the sevenfold Spirit

TO THE POINT

It's Special

The book of Revelation is hard to understand. It's full of images and symbols. Many of the things it describes are great and terrible: stars plunge into the seas, mountains tremble, mysterious beasts emerge to lead humans in war against God.

Some people see Revelation as a description of what lies ahead for our world. Others say that Revelation is speaking of an attack on the Roman Empire in the author's day.

What is the best way to study this special book? Read it without trying to figure out every image. Try to imagine the wonderful and terrible events it describes. Read it with a growing confidence that God is in charge and that he will triumph over evil at history's end.

because you were slain,
and with your blood you purchased
for God
persons from every tribe and
language and people and
nation.
10 You have made them to be a kingdom
and priests to serve our God,
and they will reign[a] on the earth."

11 Then I looked and heard the voice of many angels, numbering thousands upon thousands, and ten thousand times ten thousand. They encircled the throne and the living creatures and the elders. 12 In a loud voice they were saying:

"Worthy is the Lamb, who was slain,
to receive power and wealth and
wisdom and strength
and honor and glory and praise!"

13 Then I heard every creature in heaven and on earth and under the earth and on the sea, and all that is in them, saying:

"To him who sits on the throne and to
the Lamb
be praise and honor and glory and
power,
for ever and ever!"

14 The four living creatures said, "Amen," and the elders fell down and worshiped.

The Seals

6 I watched as the Lamb opened the first of the seven seals. Then I heard one of the four living creatures say in a voice like thunder, "Come!" 2 I looked, and there before me was a white horse! Its rider held a bow, and he was given a crown, and he rode out as a conqueror bent on conquest.

3 When the Lamb opened the second seal, I heard the second living creature say, "Come!" 4 Then another horse came out, a fiery red one. Its rider was given power to take peace from the earth and to make people kill each other. To him was given a large sword.

5 When the Lamb opened the third seal, I heard the third living creature say, "Come!" I looked, and there before me was a black horse! Its rider was holding a pair of scales in his hand. 6 Then I heard what sounded like a voice among the four living creatures, saying, "Two pounds[b] of wheat for a day's wages,[c] and six pounds[d] of barley for a day's wages,[c] and do not damage the oil and the wine!"

7 When the Lamb opened the fourth seal, I heard the voice of the fourth living creature say, "Come!" 8 I looked, and there before me was a pale horse! Its rider was named Death, and Hades was following close behind him. They were given power over a fourth of the earth to kill by sword, famine and plague, and by the wild beasts of the earth.

9 When he opened the fifth seal, I saw under the altar the souls of those who had been slain because of the word of God and the testimony they had maintained. 10 They called out in a loud voice, "How long, Sovereign Lord, holy and true, until you judge the inhabitants of the earth and avenge our blood?" 11 Then each of them was given a white robe, and they were told to wait a little longer, until the full number of their fellow servants,

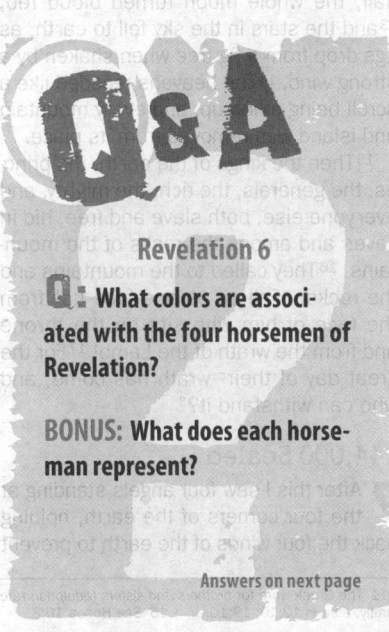

Revelation 6

Q: What colors are associated with the four horsemen of Revelation?

BONUS: What does each horseman represent?

Answers on next page

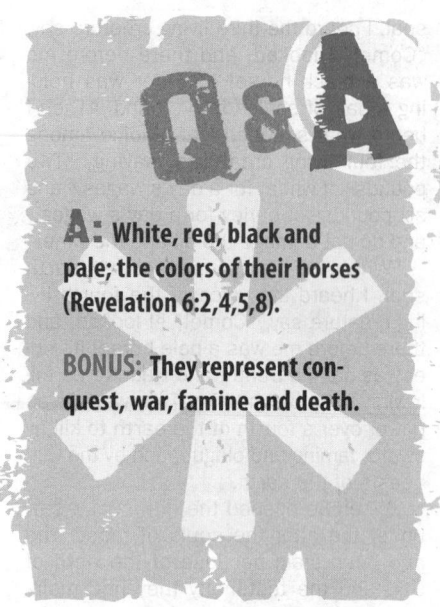

A: White, red, black and pale; the colors of their horses (Revelation 6:2,4,5,8).

BONUS: They represent conquest, war, famine and death.

their brothers and sisters,[a] were killed just as they had been.

[12] I watched as he opened the sixth seal. There was a great earthquake. The sun turned black like sackcloth made of goat hair, the whole moon turned blood red, [13] and the stars in the sky fell to earth, as figs drop from a fig tree when shaken by a strong wind. [14] The heavens receded like a scroll being rolled up, and every mountain and island was removed from its place.

[15] Then the kings of the earth, the princes, the generals, the rich, the mighty, and everyone else, both slave and free, hid in caves and among the rocks of the mountains. [16] They called to the mountains and the rocks, "Fall on us and hide us[b] from the face of him who sits on the throne and from the wrath of the Lamb! [17] For the great day of their[c] wrath has come, and who can withstand it?"

144,000 Sealed

7 After this I saw four angels standing at the four corners of the earth, holding back the four winds of the earth to prevent any wind from blowing on the land or on the sea or on any tree. [2] Then I saw another angel coming up from the east, having the seal of the living God. He called out in a loud voice to the four angels who had been given power to harm the land and the sea: [3] "Do not harm the land or the sea or the trees until we put a seal on the foreheads of the servants of our God." [4] Then I heard the number of those who were sealed: 144,000 from all the tribes of Israel.

[5] From the tribe of Judah 12,000 were sealed,
from the tribe of Reuben 12,000,
from the tribe of Gad 12,000,
[6] from the tribe of Asher 12,000,
from the tribe of Naphtali 12,000,
from the tribe of Manasseh 12,000,
[7] from the tribe of Simeon 12,000,
from the tribe of Levi 12,000,
from the tribe of Issachar 12,000,
[8] from the tribe of Zebulun 12,000,
from the tribe of Joseph 12,000,
from the tribe of Benjamin 12,000.

The Great Multitude in White Robes

[9] After this I looked, and there before me was a great multitude that no one could count, from every nation, tribe, people and language, standing before the throne and before the Lamb. They were wearing white robes and were holding palm branches in their hands. [10] And they cried out in a loud voice:

"Salvation belongs to our God,
who sits on the throne,
and to the Lamb."

[11] All the angels were standing around the throne and around the elders and the four living creatures. They fell down on their faces before the throne and worshiped God, [12] saying:

"Amen!
Praise and glory
and wisdom and thanks and honor
and power and strength
be to our God for ever and ever.
Amen!"

---

[a] 11 The Greek word for *brothers and sisters* (*adelphoi*) refers here to believers, both men and women, as part of God's family; also in 12:10; 19:10.   [b] 16 See Hosea 10:8.   [c] 17 Some manuscripts *his*

[13] Then one of the elders asked me, "These in white robes—who are they, and where did they come from?"

[14] I answered, "Sir, you know."

And he said, "These are they who have come out of the great tribulation; they have washed their robes and made them white in the blood of the Lamb. [15] Therefore,

"they are before the throne of God
and serve him day and night in his
temple;
and he who sits on the throne
will shelter them with his presence.
[16] 'Never again will they hunger;
never again will they thirst.
The sun will not beat down on them,'[a]
nor any scorching heat.
[17] For the Lamb at the center of the
throne
will be their shepherd;
'he will lead them to springs of living
water.'[a]
'And God will wipe away every tear
from their eyes.'[b]"

The Seventh Seal and the Golden Censer

8 When he opened the seventh seal, there was silence in heaven for about half an hour.

[2] And I saw the seven angels who stand before God, and seven trumpets were given to them.

[3] Another angel, who had a golden censer, came and stood at the altar. He was given much incense to offer, with the prayers of all God's people, on the golden altar in front of the throne. [4] The smoke of the incense, together with the prayers of God's people, went up before God from the angel's hand. [5] Then the angel took the censer, filled it with fire from the altar, and hurled it on the earth; and there came peals of thunder, rumblings, flashes of lightning and an earthquake.

The Trumpets

[6] Then the seven angels who had the seven trumpets prepared to sound them.

[7] The first angel sounded his trumpet, and there came hail and fire mixed with blood, and it was hurled down on the earth. A third of the earth was burned up, a third of the trees were burned up, and all the green grass was burned up.

[8] The second angel sounded his trumpet, and something like a huge mountain, all ablaze, was thrown into the sea. A third of the sea turned into blood, [9] a third of the living creatures in the sea died, and a third of the ships were destroyed.

[10] The third angel sounded his trumpet, and a great star, blazing like a torch, fell from the sky on a third of the rivers and on the springs of water— [11] the name of the star is Wormwood.[c] A third of the waters turned bitter, and many people died from the waters that had become bitter.

[12] The fourth angel sounded his trumpet, and a third of the sun was struck, a third of the moon, and a third of the stars, so that a third of them turned dark. A third of the day was without light, and also a third of the night.

[13] As I watched, I heard an eagle that was flying in midair call out in a loud voice: "Woe! Woe! Woe to the inhabitants of the earth, because of the trumpet blasts about to be sounded by the other three angels!"

9 The fifth angel sounded his trumpet, and I saw a star that had fallen from the sky to the earth. The star was given the key to the shaft of the Abyss. [2] When he opened the Abyss, smoke rose from it like the smoke from a gigantic furnace. The sun and sky were darkened by the smoke from the Abyss. [3] And out of the smoke locusts came down on the earth and were given power like that of scorpions of the earth. [4] They were told not to harm the grass of the earth or any plant or tree, but only those people who did not have the seal of God on their foreheads. [5] They were not allowed to kill them but only to torture them for five months. And the agony they suffered was like that of the sting of a scorpion when it strikes. [6] During those days people will seek death but will not find it; they will long to die, but death will elude them.

---

[a] 16,17 Isaiah 49:10   [b] 17 Isaiah 25:8   [c] 11 Wormwood is a bitter substance.

[7] The locusts looked like horses prepared for battle. On their heads they wore something like crowns of gold, and their faces resembled human faces. [8] Their hair was like women's hair, and their teeth were like lions' teeth. [9] They had breastplates like breastplates of iron, and the sound of their wings was like the thundering of many horses and chariots rushing into battle. [10] They had tails with stingers, like scorpions, and in their tails they had power to torment people for five months. [11] They had as king over them the angel of the Abyss, whose name in Hebrew is Abaddon and in Greek is Apollyon (that is, Destroyer).

[12] The first woe is past; two other woes are yet to come.

[13] The sixth angel sounded his trumpet, and I heard a voice coming from the four horns of the golden altar that is before God. [14] It said to the sixth angel who had the trumpet, "Release the four angels who are bound at the great river Euphrates." [15] And the four angels who had been kept ready for this very hour and day and month and year were released to kill a third of mankind. [16] The number of the mounted troops was twice ten thousand times ten thousand. I heard their number.

[17] The horses and riders I saw in my vision looked like this: Their breastplates were fiery red, dark blue, and yellow as sulfur. The heads of the horses resembled the heads of lions, and out of their mouths came fire, smoke and sulfur. [18] A third of mankind was killed by the three plagues of fire, smoke and sulfur that came out of their mouths. [19] The power of the horses was in their mouths and in their tails; for their tails were like snakes, having heads with which they inflict injury.

[20] The rest of mankind who were not killed by these plagues still did not repent of the work of their hands; they did not stop worshiping demons, and idols of gold, silver, bronze, stone and wood—idols that cannot see or hear or walk. [21] Nor did they repent of their murders, their magic arts, their sexual immorality or their thefts.

INSTANT ACCESS

Sometimes do you think that if God zapped people immediately, every time they did something wrong, they'd reform? Like if every time you told a lie, you got a pain in your left foot. That would work, wouldn't it? Well, it might keep you from lying, but it wouldn't change you inside. That's something you can learn from this picture of God's terrible future judgment of those who refuse to believe. Despite their terror, the survivors will not repent of their murders, magic, sexual immorality or thefts. The only chance people have to change is to hear and accept the gospel. Everyone has that chance today. When God's judgment day comes, it will be too late.

{Revelation 9:20–21}

The Angel and the Little Scroll

10 Then I saw another mighty angel coming down from heaven. He was robed in a cloud, with a rainbow above his head; his face was like the sun, and his legs were like fiery pillars. [2] He was holding a little scroll, which lay open in his hand. He planted his right foot on the sea and his left foot on the land, [3] and he gave a loud shout like the roar of a lion. When he shouted, the voices of the seven thunders spoke. [4] And when the seven thunders spoke, I was about to write; but I heard a voice from heaven say, "Seal up what the seven thunders have said and do not write it down."

[5] Then the angel I had seen standing on the sea and on the land raised his right hand to heaven. [6] And he swore by him who lives for ever and ever, who created the heavens and all that is in them, the earth and all that is in it, and the sea and all that is in it, and said, "There will be no more delay! [7] But in the days when the seventh angel is about to sound his trumpet, the mystery of God will be accomplished, just as he announced to his servants the prophets."

[8] Then the voice that I had heard from heaven spoke to me once more: "Go, take the scroll that lies open in the hand of the angel who is standing on the sea and on the land."

[9] So I went to the angel and asked him to give me the little scroll. He said to me, "Take it and eat it. It will turn your stomach sour, but 'in your mouth it will be as sweet as honey.'[a]" [10] I took the little scroll from the angel's hand and ate it. It tasted as sweet as honey in my mouth, but when I had eaten it, my stomach turned sour. [11] Then I was told, "You must prophesy again about many peoples, nations, languages and kings."

The Two Witnesses

11 I was given a reed like a measuring rod and was told, "Go and measure the temple of God and the altar, with its worshipers. [2] But exclude the outer court; do not measure it, because it has been given to the Gentiles. They will trample on the holy city for 42 months. [3] And I will appoint my two witnesses, and they will prophesy for 1,260 days, clothed in sackcloth." [4] They are "the two olive trees" and the two lampstands, and "they stand before the Lord of the earth."[b] [5] If anyone tries to harm them, fire comes from their mouths and devours their enemies. This is how anyone who wants to harm them must die. [6] They have power to shut up the heavens so that it will not rain during the time they are prophesying; and they have power to turn the waters into blood and to strike the earth with every kind of plague as often as they want.

[7] Now when they have finished their testimony, the beast that comes up from the Abyss will attack them, and overpower and kill them. [8] Their bodies will lie in the public square of the great city—which is figuratively called Sodom and Egypt—where also their Lord was crucified. [9] For three and a half days some from every people, tribe, language and nation will gaze on their bodies and refuse them burial. [10] The inhabitants of the earth will gloat over them and will celebrate by sending each other gifts, because these two prophets had tormented those who live on the earth.

[11] But after the three and a half days the breath[c] of life from God entered them, and they stood on their feet, and terror struck those who saw them. [12] Then they heard a loud voice from heaven saying to them, "Come up here." And they went up to heaven in a cloud, while their enemies looked on.

[13] At that very hour there was a severe earthquake and a tenth of the city collapsed. Seven thousand people were killed in the earthquake, and the survivors were terrified and gave glory to the God of heaven.

[14] The second woe has passed; the third woe is coming soon.

The Seventh Trumpet

[15] The seventh angel sounded his trumpet, and there were loud voices in heaven, which said:

"The kingdom of the world has
    become
    the kingdom of our Lord and of his
        Messiah,
    and he will reign for ever and ever."

[16] And the twenty-four elders, who were seated on their thrones before God, fell on their faces and worshiped God, [17] saying:

"We give thanks to you, Lord God
    Almighty,
    the One who is and who was,

---

[a] 9 Ezek. 3:3   [b] 4 See Zech. 4:3,11,14.   [c] 11 Or *Spirit* (see Ezek. 37:5,14)

because you have taken your
    great power
    and have begun to reign.
¹⁸ The nations were angry,
    and your wrath has come.
The time has come for judging the
    dead,
    and for rewarding your servants the
        prophets
    and your people who revere your name,
        both great and small—
    and for destroying those who destroy
        the earth."

¹⁹ Then God's temple in heaven was opened, and within his temple was seen the ark of his covenant. And there came flashes of lightning, rumblings, peals of thunder, an earthquake and a severe hailstorm.

The Woman and the Dragon

12 A great sign appeared in heaven: a woman clothed with the sun, with the moon under her feet and a crown of twelve stars on her head. ² She was pregnant and cried out in pain as she was about to give birth. ³ Then another sign appeared in heaven: an enormous red dragon with seven heads and ten horns and seven crowns on its heads. ⁴ Its tail swept a third of the stars out of the sky and flung them to the earth. The dragon stood in front of the woman who was about to give birth, so that it might devour her child the moment he was born. ⁵ She gave birth to a son, a male child, who "will rule all the nations with an iron scepter."ᵃ And her child was snatched up to God and to his throne. ⁶ The woman fled into the wilderness to a place prepared for her by God, where she might be taken care of for 1,260 days.

⁷ Then war broke out in heaven. Michael and his angels fought against the dragon, and the dragon and his angels fought back. ⁸ But he was not strong enough, and they lost their place in heaven. ⁹ The great dragon was hurled down—that ancient serpent called the devil, or Satan, who leads the whole world astray. He was hurled to the earth, and his angels with him.

¹⁰ Then I heard a loud voice in heaven say:

"Now have come the salvation and the
    power
    and the kingdom of our God,
    and the authority of his Messiah.
For the accuser of our brothers and
    sisters,
    who accuses them before our God
        day and night,
    has been hurled down.
¹¹ They triumphed over him
    by the blood of the Lamb
    and by the word of their testimony;
they did not love their lives so much
    as to shrink from death.
¹² Therefore rejoice, you heavens
    and you who dwell in them!
But woe to the earth and the sea,
    because the devil has gone down to
        you!
He is filled with fury,
    because he knows that his time is
        short."

¹³ When the dragon saw that he had been hurled to the earth, he pursued the woman who had given birth to the male child. ¹⁴ The woman was given the two wings of a great eagle, so that she might fly to the place prepared for her in the wilderness, where she would be taken care of for a time, times and half a time, out of the serpent's reach. ¹⁵ Then from his mouth the serpent spewed water like a river, to overtake the woman and sweep her away with the torrent. ¹⁶ But the earth helped the woman by opening its mouth and swallowing the river that the dragon had spewed out of his mouth. ¹⁷ Then the dragon was enraged at the woman and went off to wage war against the rest of her offspring—those who keep God's commands and hold fast their testimony about Jesus.

The Beast out of the Sea

13 The dragonᵇ stood on the shore of the sea. And I saw a beast coming out of the sea. It had ten horns and seven heads, with ten crowns on its horns,

---

ᵃ 5 Psalm 2:9   ᵇ 1 Some manuscripts And I

and on each head a blasphemous name. [2]The beast I saw resembled a leopard, but had feet like those of a bear and a mouth like that of a lion. The dragon gave the beast his power and his throne and great authority. [3]One of the heads of the beast seemed to have had a fatal wound, but the fatal wound had been healed. The whole world was filled with wonder and followed the beast. [4]People worshiped the dragon because he had given authority to the beast, and they also worshiped the beast and asked, "Who is like the beast? Who can wage war against it?"

[5]The beast was given a mouth to utter proud words and blasphemies and to exercise its authority for forty-two months. [6]It opened its mouth to blaspheme God, and to slander his name and his dwelling place and those who live in heaven. [7]It was given power to wage war against God's holy people and to conquer them. And it was given authority over every tribe, people, language and nation. [8]All inhabitants of the earth will worship the beast— all whose names have not been written in the Lamb's book of life, the Lamb who was slain from the creation of the world.[a]

[9]Whoever has ears, let them hear.

[10]"If anyone is to go into captivity,
    into captivity they will go.
If anyone is to be killed[b] with the
    sword,
    with the sword they will be killed."[c]

This calls for patient endurance and faithfulness on the part of God's people.

The Beast out of the Earth

[11]Then I saw a second beast, coming out of the earth. It had two horns like a lamb, but it spoke like a dragon. [12]It exercised all the authority of the first beast on its behalf, and made the earth and its inhabitants worship the first beast, whose fatal wound had been healed. [13]And it performed great signs, even causing fire to come down from heaven to the earth in full view of the people. [14]Because of the signs it was given power to perform on behalf of the first beast, it deceived the inhabitants of the earth. It ordered them to set up an image in honor of the beast who was wounded by the sword and yet lived. [15]The second beast was given power to give breath to the image of the first beast, so that the image could speak and cause all who refused to worship the image to be killed. [16]It also forced all people, great and small, rich and poor, free and slave, to receive a mark on their right hands or on their foreheads, [17]so that they could not buy or sell unless they had the mark, which is the name of the beast or the number of its name.

[18]This calls for wisdom. Let the person who has insight calculate the number of the beast, for it is the number of a man.[d] That number is 666.

The Lamb and the 144,000

14 Then I looked, and there before me was the Lamb, standing on Mount Zion, and with him 144,000 who had his name and his Father's name written on their foreheads. [2]And I heard a sound from heaven like the roar of rushing waters and like a loud peal of thunder. The sound I heard was like that of harpists playing their harps. [3]And they sang a new song before the throne and before the four living creatures and the elders. No one could learn the song except the 144,000 who had been redeemed from the earth. [4]These are those who did not defile themselves with women, for they remained virgins. They follow the Lamb wherever he goes. They were purchased from among mankind and offered as firstfruits to God and the Lamb. [5]No lie was found in their mouths; they are blameless.

The Three Angels

[6]Then I saw another angel flying in midair, and he had the eternal gospel to proclaim to those who live on the earth—to every nation, tribe, language and people. [7]He said in a loud voice, "Fear God and give him glory, because the hour of his judgment has come. Worship him who

---

[a] 8 Or written from the creation of the world in the book of life belonging to the Lamb who was slain   [b] 10 Some manuscripts anyone kills   [c] 10 Jer. 15:2   [d] 18 Or is humanity's number

made the heavens, the earth, the sea and the springs of water."

[8] A second angel followed and said, " 'Fallen! Fallen is Babylon the Great,'[a] which made all the nations drink the maddening wine of her adulteries."

[9] A third angel followed them and said in a loud voice: "If anyone worships the beast and its image and receives its mark on their forehead or on their hand, [10] they, too, will drink the wine of God's fury, which has been poured full strength into the cup of his wrath. They will be tormented with burning sulfur in the presence of the holy angels and of the Lamb. [11] And the smoke of their torment will rise for ever and ever. There will be no rest day or night for those who worship the beast and its image, or for anyone who receives the mark of its name." [12] This calls for patient endurance on the part of the people of God who keep his commands and remain faithful to Jesus.

[13] Then I heard a voice from heaven say, "Write this: Blessed are the dead who die in the Lord from now on."

"Yes," says the Spirit, "they will rest from their labor, for their deeds will follow them."

Harvesting the Earth and Trampling the Winepress

[14] I looked, and there before me was a white cloud, and seated on the cloud was one like a son of man[b] with a crown of gold on his head and a sharp sickle in his hand. [15] Then another angel came out of the temple and called in a loud voice to him who was sitting on the cloud, "Take your sickle and reap, because the time to reap has come, for the harvest of the earth is ripe." [16] So he who was seated on the cloud swung his sickle over the earth, and the earth was harvested.

[17] Another angel came out of the temple in heaven, and he too had a sharp sickle. [18] Still another angel, who had charge of the fire, came from the altar and called in a loud voice to him who had the sharp sickle, "Take your sharp sickle and gather the clusters of grapes from the earth's vine, because its grapes are ripe." [19] The angel swung his sickle on the earth, gathered its grapes and threw them into the great winepress of God's wrath. [20] They were trampled in the winepress outside the city, and blood flowed out of the press, rising as high as the horses' bridles for a distance of 1,600 stadia.[c]

Seven Angels With Seven Plagues

15 I saw in heaven another great and marvelous sign: seven angels with the seven last plagues—last, because with them God's wrath is completed. [2] And I saw what looked like a sea of glass glowing with fire and, standing beside the sea, those who had been victorious over the beast and its image and over the number of its name. They held harps given them by God [3] and sang the song of God's servant Moses and of the Lamb:

"Great and marvelous are your deeds,
    Lord God Almighty.
Just and true are your ways,
    King of the nations.[d]
[4] Who will not fear you, Lord,
    and bring glory to your name?
For you alone are holy.
All nations will come
    and worship before you,
for your righteous acts have been
    revealed."[e]

[5] After this I looked, and I saw in heaven the temple—that is, the tabernacle of the covenant law—and it was opened. [6] Out of the temple came the seven angels with the seven plagues. They were dressed in clean, shining linen and wore golden sashes around their chests. [7] Then one of the four living creatures gave to the seven angels seven golden bowls filled with the wrath of God, who lives for ever and ever. [8] And the temple was filled with smoke from the glory of God and from his power, and no one could enter the temple until the seven plagues of the seven angels were completed.

---

[a] 8 Isaiah 21:9   [b] 14 See Daniel 7:13.   [c] 20 That is, about 180 miles or about 300 kilometers   [d] 3 Some manuscripts ages   [e] 3,4 Phrases in this song are drawn from Psalm 111:2,3; Deut. 32:4; Jer. 10:7; Psalms 86:9; 98:2.

The Seven Bowls of God's Wrath

16 Then I heard a loud voice from the temple saying to the seven angels, "Go, pour out the seven bowls of God's wrath on the earth."

²The first angel went and poured out his bowl on the land, and ugly, festering sores broke out on the people who had the mark of the beast and worshiped its image.

³The second angel poured out his bowl on the sea, and it turned into blood like that of a dead person, and every living thing in the sea died.

⁴The third angel poured out his bowl on the rivers and springs of water, and they became blood. ⁵Then I heard the angel in charge of the waters say:

"You are just in these judgments,
  O Holy One,
you who are and who were;
⁶for they have shed the blood of your
    holy people and your prophets,
  and you have given them blood to
    drink as they deserve."

⁷And I heard the altar respond:

"Yes, Lord God Almighty,
  true and just are your judgments."

⁸The fourth angel poured out his bowl on the sun, and the sun was allowed to scorch people with fire. ⁹They were seared by the intense heat and they cursed the name of God, who had control over these plagues, but they refused to repent and glorify him.

¹⁰The fifth angel poured out his bowl on the throne of the beast, and its kingdom was plunged into darkness. People gnawed their tongues in agony ¹¹and cursed the God of heaven because of their pains and their sores, but they refused to repent of what they had done.

¹²The sixth angel poured out his bowl on the great river Euphrates, and its water was dried up to prepare the way for the kings from the East. ¹³Then I saw three impure spirits that looked like frogs; they came out of the mouth of the dragon, out of the mouth of the beast and out of the mouth of the false prophet. ¹⁴They are demonic spirits that perform signs, and they go out to the kings of the whole world, to gather them for the battle on the great day of God Almighty.

¹⁵"Look, I come like a thief! Blessed is the one who stays awake and remains clothed, so as not to go naked and be shamefully exposed."

¹⁶Then they gathered the kings together to the place that in Hebrew is called Armageddon.

¹⁷The seventh angel poured out his bowl into the air, and out of the temple came a loud voice from the throne, saying, "It is done!" ¹⁸Then there came flashes of lightning, rumblings, peals of thunder and a severe earthquake. No earthquake like it has ever occurred since mankind has been on earth, so tremendous was the quake. ¹⁹The great city split into three parts, and the cities of the nations collapsed. God remembered Babylon the Great and gave her the cup filled with the wine of the fury of his wrath. ²⁰Every island fled away and the mountains could not be found. ²¹From the sky huge hailstones, each weighing about a

Q&A

Revelation 16

Q: Where will history's last battle be fought?

BONUS: Where is this location?

Answers on next page

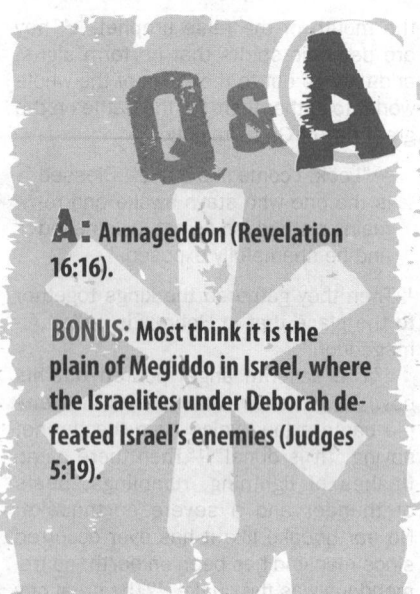

A: Armageddon (Revelation 16:16).

BONUS: Most think it is the plain of Megiddo in Israel, where the Israelites under Deborah defeated Israel's enemies (Judges 5:19).

hundred pounds,ᵃ fell on people. And they cursed God on account of the plague of hail, because the plague was so terrible.

Babylon, the Prostitute on the Beast

17 One of the seven angels who had the seven bowls came and said to me, "Come, I will show you the punishment of the great prostitute, who sits by many waters. ²With her the kings of the earth committed adultery, and the inhabitants of the earth were intoxicated with the wine of her adulteries."

³Then the angel carried me away in the Spirit into a wilderness. There I saw a woman sitting on a scarlet beast that was covered with blasphemous names and had seven heads and ten horns. ⁴The woman was dressed in purple and scarlet, and was glittering with gold, precious stones and pearls. She held a golden cup in her hand, filled with abominable things and the filth of her adulteries. ⁵The name written on her forehead was a mystery:

> BABYLON THE GREAT
> THE MOTHER OF PROSTITUTES
> AND OF THE ABOMINATIONS OF THE EARTH.

⁶I saw that the woman was drunk with the blood of God's holy people, the blood of those who bore testimony to Jesus.

When I saw her, I was greatly astonished. ⁷Then the angel said to me: "Why are you astonished? I will explain to you the mystery of the woman and of the beast she rides, which has the seven heads and ten horns. ⁸The beast, which you saw, once was, now is not, and yet will come up out of the Abyss and go to its destruction. The inhabitants of the earth whose names have not been written in the book of life from the creation of the world will be astonished when they see the beast, because it once was, now is not, and yet will come.

⁹"This calls for a mind with wisdom. The seven heads are seven hills on which the woman sits. ¹⁰They are also seven kings. Five have fallen, one is, the other has not yet come; but when he does come, he must remain for only a little while. ¹¹The beast who once was, and now is not, is an eighth king. He belongs to the seven and is going to his destruction.

¹²"The ten horns you saw are ten kings who have not yet received a kingdom, but who for one hour will receive authority as kings along with the beast. ¹³They have one purpose and will give their power and authority to the beast. ¹⁴They will wage war against the Lamb, but the Lamb will triumph over them because he is Lord of lords and King of kings—and with him will be his called, chosen and faithful followers."

¹⁵Then the angel said to me, "The waters you saw, where the prostitute sits, are peoples, multitudes, nations and languages. ¹⁶The beast and the ten horns you saw will hate the prostitute. They will bring her to ruin and leave her naked; they will eat her flesh and burn her with fire. ¹⁷For God has put it into their hearts to accomplish his purpose by agreeing to hand over to the beast their royal authority, until God's words are fulfilled. ¹⁸The woman you saw is the great city that rules over the kings of the earth."

ᵃ 21 Or about 45 kilograms

Lament Over Fallen Babylon

18 After this I saw another angel coming down from heaven. He had great authority, and the earth was illuminated by his splendor. ²With a mighty voice he shouted:

" 'Fallen! Fallen is Babylon the Great!'ᵃ
She has become a dwelling for demons
and a haunt for every impure spirit,
a haunt for every unclean bird,
a haunt for every unclean and detestable animal.
³For all the nations have drunk
the maddening wine of her adulteries.
The kings of the earth committed adultery with her,
and the merchants of the earth grew rich from her excessive luxuries."

Warning to Escape Babylon's Judgment

⁴Then I heard another voice from heaven say:

" 'Come out of her, my people,'ᵇ
so that you will not share in her sins,
so that you will not receive any of her plagues;

---

⁵for her sins are piled up to heaven,
and God has remembered her crimes.
⁶Give back to her as she has given;
pay her back double for what she has done.
Pour her a double portion from her own cup.
⁷Give her as much torment and grief
as the glory and luxury she gave herself.
In her heart she boasts,
'I sit enthroned as queen.
I am not a widow;ᶜ
I will never mourn.'
⁸Therefore in one day her plagues will overtake her:
death, mourning and famine.
She will be consumed by fire,
for mighty is the Lord God who judges her.

Threefold Woe Over Babylon's Fall

⁹"When the kings of the earth who committed adultery with her and shared her luxury see the smoke of her burning, they will weep and mourn over her. ¹⁰Terrified at her torment, they will stand far off and cry:

" 'Woe! Woe to you, great city,
you mighty city of Babylon!
In one hour your doom has come!'

ᵃ 2 Isaiah 21:9   ᵇ 4 Jer. 51:45   ᶜ 7 See Isaiah 47:7,8.

{REVELATION}

PANORAMA

Hard Words.

Even though Revelation uses difficult images and symbols, the message of the book is clear: This world will come to an end. Jesus will come back, and he will punish evil. Jesus will win.

11 "The merchants of the earth will weep and mourn over her because no one buys their cargoes anymore— 12 cargoes of gold, silver, precious stones and pearls; fine linen, purple, silk and scarlet cloth; every sort of citron wood, and articles of every kind made of ivory, costly wood, bronze, iron and marble; 13 cargoes of cinnamon and spice, of incense, myrrh and frankincense, of wine and olive oil, of fine flour and wheat; cattle and sheep; horses and carriages; and human beings sold as slaves.

14 "They will say, 'The fruit you longed for is gone from you. All your luxury and splendor have vanished, never to be recovered.' 15 The merchants who sold these things and gained their wealth from her will stand far off, terrified at her torment. They will weep and mourn 16 and cry out:

" 'Woe! Woe to you, great city,
    dressed in fine linen, purple and
        scarlet,
    and glittering with gold, precious
        stones and pearls!
17 In one hour such great wealth has
    been brought to ruin!'

"Every sea captain, and all who travel by ship, the sailors, and all who earn their living from the sea, will stand far off. 18 When they see the smoke of her burning, they will exclaim, 'Was there ever a city like this great city?' 19 They will throw dust on their heads, and with weeping and mourning cry out:

" 'Woe! Woe to you, great city,
    where all who had ships on the sea
        became rich through her wealth!
    In one hour she has been brought to
        ruin!'

20 "Rejoice over her, you heavens!
    Rejoice, you people of God!
    Rejoice, apostles and prophets!
    For God has judged her
        with the judgment she imposed on
            you."

The Finality of Babylon's Doom

21 Then a mighty angel picked up a boulder the size of a large millstone and threw it into the sea, and said:

"With such violence
    the great city of Babylon will be
        thrown down,
    never to be found again.
22 The music of harpists and musicians,
        pipers and trumpeters,
    will never be heard in you again.
No worker of any trade
    will ever be found in you again.
The sound of a millstone
    will never be heard in you again.
23 The light of a lamp
    will never shine in you again.
The voice of bridegroom and bride
    will never be heard in you again.
Your merchants were the world's
        important people.
    By your magic spell all the nations
        were led astray.
24 In her was found the blood of
        prophets and of God's holy
            people,
    of all who have been slaughtered on
        the earth."

Threefold Hallelujah Over Babylon's Fall

19 After this I heard what sounded like the roar of a great multitude in heaven shouting:

"Hallelujah!
Salvation and glory and power belong
    to our God,
2   for true and just are his
        judgments.
He has condemned the great
        prostitute
    who corrupted the earth by her
        adulteries.
He has avenged on her the blood of
        his servants."

3 And again they shouted:

"Hallelujah!
The smoke from her goes up for ever
    and ever."

4 The twenty-four elders and the four living creatures fell down and worshiped God, who was seated on the throne. And they cried:

"Amen, Hallelujah!"

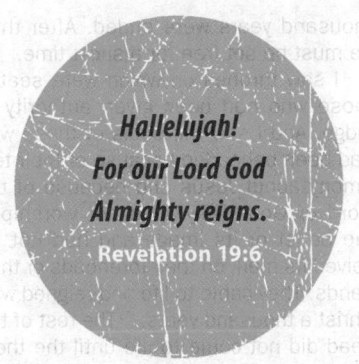

**Hallelujah!
For our Lord God
Almighty reigns.**
Revelation 19:6

The Heavenly Warrior Defeats the Beast

[11] I saw heaven standing open and there before me was a white horse, whose rider is called Faithful and True. With justice he judges and wages war. [12] His eyes are like blazing fire, and on his head are many crowns. He has a name written on him that no one knows but he himself. [13] He is dressed in a robe dipped in blood, and his name is the Word of God. [14] The armies of heaven were following him, riding on white horses and dressed in fine linen, white and clean. [15] Coming out of his mouth is a sharp sword with which to strike down the nations. "He will rule them with an iron scepter."[a] He treads the winepress of the fury of the wrath of God Almighty. [16] On his robe and on his thigh he has this name written:

KING OF KINGS AND LORD OF LORDS.

[17] And I saw an angel standing in the sun, who cried in a loud voice to all the birds flying in midair, "Come, gather together for the great supper of God, [18] so that you may eat the flesh of kings, generals, and the mighty, of horses and their

[5] Then a voice came from the throne, saying:

"Praise our God,
 all you his servants,
 you who fear him,
 both great and small!"

[6] Then I heard what sounded like a great multitude, like the roar of rushing waters and like loud peals of thunder, shouting:

"Hallelujah!
 For our Lord God Almighty reigns.
[7] Let us rejoice and be glad
 and give him glory!
 For the wedding of the Lamb has
 come,
 and his bride has made herself
 ready.
[8] Fine linen, bright and clean,
 was given her to wear."
(Fine linen stands for the righteous acts of God's holy people.)

[9] Then the angel said to me, "Write this: Blessed are those who are invited to the wedding supper of the Lamb!" And he added, "These are the true words of God."

[10] At this I fell at his feet to worship him. But he said to me, "Don't do that! I am a fellow servant with you and with your brothers and sisters who hold to the testimony of Jesus. Worship God! For it is the Spirit of prophecy who bears testimony to Jesus."

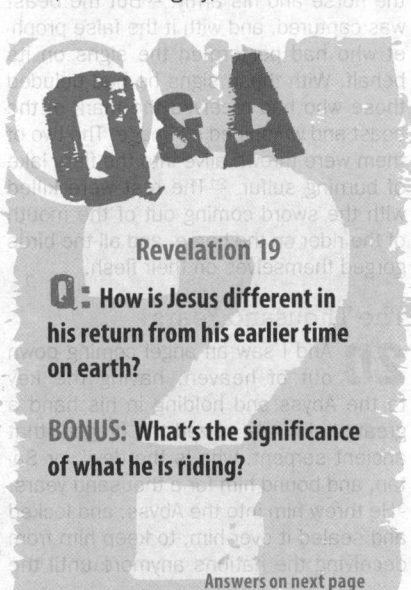

Revelation 19

Q: How is Jesus different in his return from his earlier time on earth?

BONUS: What's the significance of what he is riding?

Answers on next page

Q&A

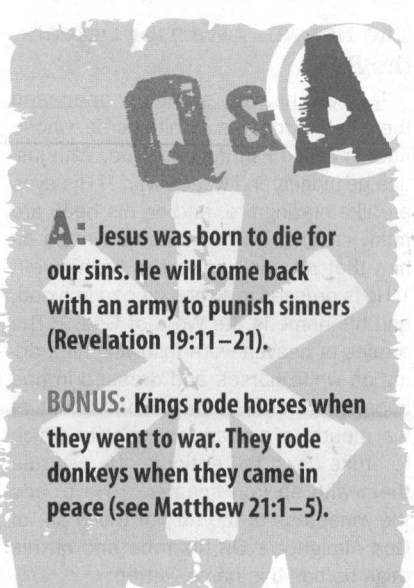

A: Jesus was born to die for our sins. He will come back with an army to punish sinners (Revelation 19:11–21).

BONUS: Kings rode horses when they went to war. They rode donkeys when they came in peace (see Matthew 21:1–5).

riders, and the flesh of all people, free
and slave, great and small."
19 Then I saw the beast and the kings
of the earth and their armies gathered together to wage war against the rider on
the horse and his army. 20 But the beast
was captured, and with it the false prophet who had performed the signs on its
behalf. With these signs he had deluded
those who had received the mark of the
beast and worshiped its image. The two of
them were thrown alive into the fiery lake
of burning sulfur. 21 The rest were killed
with the sword coming out of the mouth
of the rider on the horse, and all the birds
gorged themselves on their flesh.

The Thousand Years

20 And I saw an angel coming down
out of heaven, having the key
to the Abyss and holding in his hand a
great chain. 2 He seized the dragon, that
ancient serpent, who is the devil, or Satan, and bound him for a thousand years.
3 He threw him into the Abyss, and locked
and sealed it over him, to keep him from
deceiving the nations anymore until the
thousand years were ended. After that,
he must be set free for a short time.
4 I saw thrones on which were seated
those who had been given authority to
judge. And I saw the souls of those who
had been beheaded because of their testimony about Jesus and because of the
word of God. They[a] had not worshiped
the beast or its image and had not received its mark on their foreheads or their
hands. They came to life and reigned with
Christ a thousand years. 5 (The rest of the
dead did not come to life until the thousand years were ended.) This is the first
resurrection. 6 Blessed and holy are those
who share in the first resurrection. The
second death has no power over them,
but they will be priests of God and of
Christ and will reign with him for a thousand years.

The Judgment of Satan

7 When the thousand years are over,
Satan will be released from his prison
8 and will go out to deceive the nations in
the four corners of the earth—Gog and
Magog—and to gather them for battle. In
number they are like the sand on the seashore. 9 They marched across the breadth
of the earth and surrounded the camp of
God's people, the city he loves. But fire
came down from heaven and devoured
them. 10 And the devil, who deceived
them, was thrown into the lake of burning sulfur, where the beast and the false
prophet had been thrown. They will be tormented day and night for ever and ever.

The Judgment of the Dead

11 Then I saw a great white throne and
him who was seated on it. The earth and
the heavens fled from his presence, and
there was no place for them. 12 And I saw
the dead, great and small, standing before the throne, and books were opened.
Another book was opened, which is the
book of life. The dead were judged according to what they had done as recorded in
the books. 13 The sea gave up the dead
that were in it, and death and Hades gave
up the dead that were in them, and each

[a] 4 Or *God; I also saw those who*

"he's coming to judge"

✝ It's a frightening picture. God's sitting on a great white throne. Earth and even the stars are gone. The dead stand before the throne, about to be judged. Every sin is revealed, every mean thought and wicked act. No one passes that final test—everyone who hasn't trusted in Jesus as Savior is thrown into what appears to be a lake of fire.

In one of the earliest books of the Old Testament, God told Moses that, while he's compassionate and gracious, he "does not leave the guilty unpunished" (Exodus 34:7). God is the moral judge of the universe, and he will punish sin. So we shouldn't be surprised that the New Testament says when Jesus returns, he will "pay back trouble to those who trouble you" (2 Thessalonians 1:6). Nor should we be surprised that unbelievers "will be punished with everlasting destruction and shut out from the presence of the Lord" (2 Thessalonians 1:9).

But Jesus loved us so much that he went to the cross to personally pay the penalty for our sins. He took the judgment our sins and wicked acts deserve. That's why believers won't be standing in front of that great white throne, waiting to be judged. The sins of anyone who trusts Jesus as Savior have already been judged and punished, and they're gone.

What about those who haven't shown respect for Jesus' sacrifice by relying on his promise of forgiveness? They'll stand there on that great and final day. And they will be judged.

Go to page 1349 for the next We Believe

person was judged according to what they had done. [14] Then death and Hades were thrown into the lake of fire. The lake of fire is the second death. [15] Anyone whose name was not found written in the book of life was thrown into the lake of fire.

A New Heaven and a New Earth

21 Then I saw "a new heaven and a new earth,"[a] for the first heaven and the first earth had passed away, and there was no longer any sea. [2] I saw the Holy City, the new Jerusalem, coming down out of heaven from God, prepared as a bride beautifully dressed for her husband. [3] And I heard a loud voice from the throne saying, "Look! God's dwelling place is now among the people, and he will dwell with them. They will be his people, and God himself will be with them and be their God. [4] 'He will wipe every tear from their eyes. There will be no more death'[b] or mourning or crying or pain, for the old order of things has passed away."

[5] He who was seated on the throne said, "I am making everything new!" Then he said, "Write this down, for these words are trustworthy and true."

[6] He said to me: "It is done. I am the Alpha and the Omega, the Beginning and the End. To the thirsty I will give water without cost from the spring of the water of life. [7] Those who are victorious will inherit all this, and I will be their God and they will be my children. [8] But the cowardly, the unbelieving, the vile, the murderers, the sexually immoral, those who practice magic arts, the idolaters and all liars—they will be consigned to the fiery lake of burning sulfur. This is the second death."

The New Jerusalem, the Bride of the Lamb

[9] One of the seven angels who had the seven bowls full of the seven last plagues came and said to me, "Come, I will show you the bride, the wife of the Lamb." [10] And he carried me away in the Spirit to a mountain great and high, and showed me the Holy City, Jerusalem, coming down out of heaven from God. [11] It shone with the glory of God, and its brilliance was like that of a very precious jewel, like a jasper, clear as crystal. [12] It had a great, high wall with twelve gates, and with twelve angels at the gates. On the gates were written the names of the twelve tribes of Israel. [13] There were three gates on the east, three on the north, three on the south and three on the west. [14] The wall of the city had twelve foundations, and on them were the names of the twelve apostles of the Lamb.

[15] The angel who talked with me had a measuring rod of gold to measure the city, its gates and its walls. [16] The city was laid out like a square, as long as it was wide. He measured the city with the rod and found it to be 12,000 stadia[c] in length, and as wide and high as it is long. [17] The angel measured the wall using human measurement, and it was 144 cubits[d] thick.[e] [18] The wall was made of jasper, and the city of pure gold, as pure as glass. [19] The foundations of the city walls were decorated with every kind of precious stone. The first foundation was jasper, the second sapphire, the third agate, the fourth emerald, [20] the fifth onyx, the sixth ruby, the seventh chrysolite, the eighth beryl, the ninth topaz, the tenth turquoise, the eleventh jacinth, and the twelfth amethyst.[f] [21] The twelve gates were twelve pearls, each gate made of a single pearl. The great street of the city was of gold, as pure as transparent glass.

[22] I did not see a temple in the city, because the Lord God Almighty and the Lamb are its temple. [23] The city does not need the sun or the moon to shine on it, for the glory of God gives it light, and the Lamb is its lamp. [24] The nations will walk by its light, and the kings of the earth will bring their splendor into it. [25] On no day will its gates ever be shut, for there will

---

[a] *1* Isaiah 65:17   [b] *4* Isaiah 25:8   [c] *16* That is, about 1,400 miles or about 2,200 kilometers   [d] *17* That is, about 200 feet or about 65 meters   [e] *17* Or *high*   [f] *20* The precise identification of some of these precious stones is uncertain.

We Believe...

"in the life everlasting"

✝ It's hard to imagine. Life sometimes seems to go on and on and on, endlessly. We don't know a lot about the eternal life that we're promised in Jesus. What we do know is found here, in Revelation 21 and 22.

God will be there with us in a new heaven and earth he'll create. There will be no more death or mourning or pain. The new universe God creates will be spectacularly beautiful, and there will be no evil or sin. We'll serve God there. No one knows just how, but we won't be inactive or bored. We'll see God himself. And we will "reign for ever and ever" (Revelation 22:5).

The word "reign" is fascinating. It opens up all sorts of possibilities. Perhaps you'll be given a part of the new universe to rule on God's behalf. No one knows for sure. We do know everlasting life will be filled with more beauty, more excitement, more satisfying things to do, more love and fulfillment, than anyone finds in this life. And we know that the life God has planned for us to live will go on and on and on, forever.

To find the beginning of the Apostles' Creed turn to page 1312.

be no night there. 26 The glory and honor of the nations will be brought into it. 27 Nothing impure will ever enter it, nor will anyone who does what is shameful or deceitful, but only those whose names are written in the Lamb's book of life.

Eden Restored

22 Then the angel showed me the river of the water of life, as clear as crystal, flowing from the throne of God and of the Lamb 2 down the middle of the great street of the city. On each side of the river stood the tree of life, bearing twelve crops of fruit, yielding its fruit every month. And the leaves of the tree are for the healing of the nations. 3 No longer will there be any curse. The throne of God and of the Lamb will be in the city, and his servants will serve him. 4 They will see his face, and his name will be on their foreheads. 5 There will be no more night. They will not need the light of a lamp or the light of the sun, for the Lord God will give them light. And they will reign for ever and ever.

John and the Angel

6 The angel said to me, "These words are trustworthy and true. The Lord, the God who inspires the prophets, sent his angel to show his servants the things that must soon take place."

7 "Look, I am coming soon! Blessed is the one who keeps the words of the prophecy written in this scroll."

8 I, John, am the one who heard and saw these things. And when I had heard and seen them, I fell down to worship at the feet of the angel who had been showing them to me. 9 But he said to me, "Don't do that! I am a fellow servant with you and with your fellow prophets and with all who keep the words of this scroll. Worship God!"

10 Then he told me, "Do not seal up the words of the prophecy of this scroll, because the time is near. 11 Let the one who does wrong continue to do wrong; let the vile person continue to be vile; let the one who does right continue to do right; and let the holy person continue to be holy."

Epilogue: Invitation and Warning

12 "Look, I am coming soon! My reward is with me, and I will give to each person according to what they have done. 13 I am the Alpha and the Omega, the First and the Last, the Beginning and the End.

14 "Blessed are those who wash their robes, that they may have the right to the tree of life and may go through the gates into the city. 15 Outside are the dogs, those who practice magic arts, the sexually immoral, the murderers, the idolaters and everyone who loves and practices falsehood.

16 "I, Jesus, have sent my angel to give you[a] this testimony for the churches. I am the Root and the Offspring of David, and the bright Morning Star."

17 The Spirit and the bride say, "Come!" And let the one who hears say, "Come!" Let the one who is thirsty come; and let the one who wishes take the free gift of the water of life.

18 I warn everyone who hears the words of the prophecy of this scroll: If anyone adds anything to them, God will add to that person the plagues described in this scroll. 19 And if anyone takes words away from this scroll of prophecy, God will take away from that person any share in the tree of life and in the Holy City, which are described in this scroll.

20 He who testifies to these things says, "Yes, I am coming soon."

Amen. Come, Lord Jesus.

21 The grace of the Lord Jesus be with God's people. Amen.

---

a 16 The Greek is plural.

STUDY HELPS

STUDY HELPS

Weights and Measures

What Do I Read Today?

Bible Truth Index

Teen Life Index

Weights and MEASURES

	Biblical Unit	Approximate American Equivalent	Approximate Metric Equivalent
Weights	talent (60 minas)	75 pounds	34 kilograms
	mina (50 shekels)	1 1/4 pounds	560 grams
	shekel (2 bekas)	2/5 ounce	11.5 grams
	pim (2/3 shekel)	1/4 ounce	7.8 grams
	beka (10 gerahs)	1/5 ounce	5.7 grams
	gerah	1/50 ounce	0.6 gram
	daric	1/3 ounce	8.4 grams
Length	cubit	18 inches	45 centimeters
	span	9 inches	23 centimeters
	handbreadth	3 inches	7.5 centimeters
	stadion (pl. stadia)	600 feet	183 meters
Capacity *Dry Measure*	cor [homer] (10 ephahs)	6 bushels	220 liters
	lethek (5 ephahs)	3 bushels	110 liters
	ephah (10 omers)	3/5 bushel	22 liters
	seah (1/3 ephah)	7 quarts	7.5 liters
	omer (1/10 ephah)	2 quarts	2 liters
	cab (1/18 ephah)	1 quart	1 liter
Liquid Measure	bath (1 ephah)	6 gallons	22 liters
	hin (1/6 bath)	1 gallon	3.8 liters
	log (1/72 bath)	1/3 quart	0.3 liter

The figures of the table are calculated on the basis of a shekel equaling 11.5 grams, a cubit equaling 18 inches and an ephah equaling 22 liters. The quart referred to is either a dry quart (slightly larger than a liter) or a liquid quart (slightly smaller than a liter), whichever is applicable. The ton referred to in the footnotes is the American ton of 2,000 pounds. These weights are calculated relative to the particular commodity involved. Accordingly, the same measure of capacity in the text may be converted into different weights in the footnotes.

This table is based upon the best available information, but it is not intended to be mathematically precise; like the measurement equivalents in the footnotes, it merely gives approximate amounts and distances. Weights and measures differed somewhat at various times and places in the ancient world. There is uncertainty particularly about the ephah and the bath; further discoveries may shed more light on these units of capacity.

What Do I Read TODAY?

The Bible contains exciting action, characters with whom you can identify, and help for all the good and not-so-good situations in your life. All you have to do is read to find it all.

1. If you are reading the Bible for the first time:
   - Begin by reading the Gospel of Mark or the Gospel of John in the New Testament.
   - After reading one of these gospels, read the book of Acts or the book of Romans.
   - After reading Acts or Romans, pick an Old Testament book like Genesis or perhaps Psalms.
2. If you want to read through the entire Bible in one year:
   - Read three chapters each day, Monday through Saturday, and five chapters on Sunday.
3. If you want to read through the entire Bible in two years:
   - Read two chapters each day, Sunday through Saturday.

The following chart covers every book and chapter of the Bible. To keep track of what you have read, mark off each chapter as you complete it.

GENESIS ☐ 1 ☐ 2 ☐ 3 ☐ 4 ☐ 5 ☐ 6 ☐ 7 ☐ 8 ☐ 9 ☐ 10 ☐ 11 ☐ 12 ☐ 13 ☐ 14 ☐ 15 ☐ 16 ☐ 17 ☐ 18 ☐ 19 ☐ 20 ☐ 21 ☐ 22 ☐ 23 ☐ 24 ☐ 25 ☐ 26 ☐ 27 ☐ 28 ☐ 29 ☐ 30 ☐ 31 ☐ 32 ☐ 33 ☐ 34 ☐ 35 ☐ 36 ☐ 37 ☐ 38 ☐ 39 ☐ 40 ☐ 41 ☐ 42 ☐ 43 ☐ 44 ☐ 45 ☐ 46 ☐ 47 ☐ 48 ☐ 49 ☐ 50

EXODUS ☐ 1 ☐ 2 ☐ 3 ☐ 4 ☐ 5 ☐ 6 ☐ 7 ☐ 8 ☐ 9 ☐ 10 ☐ 11 ☐ 12 ☐ 13 ☐ 14 ☐ 15 ☐ 16 ☐ 17 ☐ 18 ☐ 19 ☐ 20 ☐ 21 ☐ 22 ☐ 23 ☐ 24 ☐ 25 ☐ 26 ☐ 27 ☐ 28 ☐ 29 ☐ 30 ☐ 31 ☐ 32 ☐ 33 ☐ 34 ☐ 35 ☐ 36 ☐ 37 ☐ 38 ☐ 39 ☐ 40

LEVITICUS ☐ 1 ☐ 2 ☐ 3 ☐ 4 ☐ 5 ☐ 6 ☐ 7 ☐ 8 ☐ 9 ☐ 10 ☐ 11 ☐ 12 ☐ 13 ☐ 14 ☐ 15 ☐ 16 ☐ 17 ☐ 18 ☐ 19 ☐ 20 ☐ 21 ☐ 22 ☐ 23 ☐ 24 ☐ 25 ☐ 26 ☐ 27

NUMBERS ☐ 1 ☐ 2 ☐ 3 ☐ 4 ☐ 5 ☐ 6 ☐ 7 ☐ 8 ☐ 9 ☐ 10 ☐ 11 ☐ 12 ☐ 13 ☐ 14 ☐ 15 ☐ 16 ☐ 17 ☐ 18 ☐ 19 ☐ 20 ☐ 21 ☐ 22 ☐ 23 ☐ 24 ☐ 25 ☐ 26 ☐ 27 ☐ 28 ☐ 29 ☐ 30 ☐ 31 ☐ 32 ☐ 33 ☐ 34 ☐ 35 ☐ 36

DEUTERONOMY ☐ 1 ☐ 2 ☐ 3 ☐ 4 ☐ 5 ☐ 6 ☐ 7 ☐ 8 ☐ 9 ☐ 10 ☐ 11 ☐ 12 ☐ 13 ☐ 14 ☐ 15 ☐ 16 ☐ 17 ☐ 18 ☐ 19 ☐ 20 ☐ 21 ☐ 22 ☐ 23 ☐ 24 ☐ 25 ☐ 26 ☐ 27 ☐ 28 ☐ 29 ☐ 30 ☐ 31 ☐ 32 ☐ 33 ☐ 34

JOSHUA ☐ 1 ☐ 2 ☐ 3 ☐ 4 ☐ 5 ☐ 6 ☐ 7 ☐ 8 ☐ 9 ☐ 10 ☐ 11 ☐ 12 ☐ 13 ☐ 14 ☐ 15 ☐ 16 ☐ 17 ☐ 18 ☐ 19 ☐ 20 ☐ 21 ☐ 22 ☐ 23 ☐ 24

JUDGES ☐ 1 ☐ 2 ☐ 3 ☐ 4 ☐ 5 ☐ 6 ☐ 7 ☐ 8 ☐ 9 ☐ 10 ☐ 11 ☐ 12 ☐ 13 ☐ 14 ☐ 15 ☐ 16 ☐ 17 ☐ 18 ☐ 19 ☐ 20 ☐ 21

RUTH ☐1 ☐2 ☐3 ☐4

1 SAMUEL ☐1 ☐2 ☐3 ☐4 ☐5
☐6 ☐7 ☐8 ☐9 ☐10 ☐11 ☐12
☐13 ☐14 ☐15 ☐16 ☐17 ☐18
☐19 ☐20 ☐21 ☐22 ☐23 ☐24
☐25 ☐26 ☐27 ☐28 ☐29 ☐30
☐31

2 SAMUEL ☐1 ☐2 ☐3 ☐4 ☐5
☐6 ☐7 ☐8 ☐9 ☐10 ☐11 ☐12
☐13 ☐14 ☐15 ☐16 ☐17 ☐18
☐19 ☐20 ☐21 ☐22 ☐23 ☐24

1 KINGS ☐1 ☐2 ☐3 ☐4 ☐5 ☐6
☐7 ☐8 ☐9 ☐10 ☐11 ☐12
☐13 ☐14 ☐15 ☐16 ☐17 ☐18
☐19 ☐20 ☐21 ☐22

2 KINGS ☐1 ☐2 ☐3 ☐4 ☐5 ☐6
☐7 ☐8 ☐9 ☐10 ☐11 ☐12
☐13 ☐14 ☐15 ☐16 ☐17 ☐18
☐19 ☐20 ☐21 ☐22 ☐23 ☐24
☐251

1 CHRONICLES ☐1 ☐2 ☐3 ☐4 ☐5
☐6 ☐7 ☐8 ☐9 ☐10 ☐11 ☐12
☐13 ☐14 ☐15 ☐16 ☐17 ☐18
☐19 ☐20 ☐21 ☐22 ☐23 ☐24
☐25 ☐26 ☐27 ☐28 ☐29

2 CHRONICLES ☐1 ☐2 ☐3 ☐4 ☐5
☐6 ☐7 ☐8 ☐9 ☐10 ☐11 ☐12
☐13 ☐14 ☐15 ☐16 ☐17 ☐18
☐19 ☐20 ☐21 ☐22 ☐23 ☐24
☐25 ☐26 ☐27 ☐28 ☐29 ☐30
☐31 ☐32 ☐33 ☐34 ☐35 ☐36

EZRA ☐1 ☐2 ☐3 ☐4 ☐5 ☐6
☐7 ☐8 ☐9 ☐10

NEHEMIAH ☐1 ☐2 ☐3 ☐4 ☐5
☐6 ☐7 ☐8 ☐9 ☐10 ☐11 ☐12
☐13

ESTHER ☐1 ☐2 ☐3 ☐4 ☐5 ☐6
☐7 ☐8 ☐9 ☐10

JOB ☐1 ☐2 ☐3 ☐4 ☐5 ☐6
☐7 ☐8 ☐9 ☐10 ☐11 ☐12
☐13 ☐14 ☐15 ☐16 ☐17 ☐18
☐19 ☐20 ☐21 ☐22 ☐23 ☐24
☐25 ☐26 ☐27 ☐28 ☐29 ☐30
☐31 ☐32 ☐33 ☐34 ☐35 ☐36
☐37 ☐38 ☐39 ☐40 ☐41 ☐42

PSALMS ☐1 ☐2 ☐3 ☐4 ☐5 ☐6
☐7 ☐8 ☐9 ☐10 ☐11 ☐12
☐13 ☐14 ☐15 ☐16 ☐17 ☐18
☐19 ☐20 ☐21 ☐22 ☐23 ☐24
☐25 ☐26 ☐27 ☐28 ☐29 ☐30
☐31 ☐32 ☐33 ☐34 ☐35 ☐36
☐37 ☐38 ☐39 ☐40 ☐41 ☐42
☐43 ☐44 ☐45 ☐46 ☐47 ☐48
☐49 ☐50 ☐51 ☐52 ☐53 ☐54
☐55 ☐56 ☐57 ☐58 ☐59 ☐60
☐61 ☐62 ☐63 ☐64 ☐65 ☐66
☐67 ☐68 ☐69 ☐70 ☐71 ☐72
☐73 ☐74 ☐75 ☐76 ☐77 ☐78
☐79 ☐80 ☐81 ☐82 ☐83 ☐84
☐85 ☐86 ☐87 ☐88 ☐89 ☐90
☐91 ☐92 ☐93 ☐94 ☐95 ☐96
☐97 ☐98 ☐99 ☐100 ☐101
☐102 ☐103 ☐104 ☐105 ☐106
☐107 ☐108 ☐109 ☐110 ☐111
☐112 ☐113 ☐114 ☐115 ☐116
☐117 ☐118 ☐119 ☐120 ☐121
☐122 ☐123 ☐124 ☐125 ☐126
☐127 ☐128 ☐129 ☐130 ☐131
☐132 ☐133 ☐134 ☐135 ☐136
☐137 ☐138 ☐139 ☐140 ☐141
☐142 ☐143 ☐144 ☐145 ☐146
☐147 ☐148 ☐149 ☐150

PROVERBS ☐1 ☐2 ☐3 ☐4 ☐5
☐6 ☐7 ☐8 ☐9 ☐10 ☐11 ☐12
☐13 ☐14 ☐15 ☐16 ☐17 ☐18
☐19 ☐20 ☐21 ☐22 ☐23 ☐24
☐25 ☐26 ☐27 ☐28 ☐29 ☐30
☐31

ECCLESIASTES ☐1 ☐2 ☐3 ☐4 ☐5
☐6 ☐7 ☐8 ☐9 ☐10 ☐11 ☐12

SONG OF SONGS ☐ 1 ☐ 2 ☐ 3 ☐ 4 ☐ 5 ☐ 6 ☐ 7 ☐ 8

ISAIAH ☐ 1 ☐ 2 ☐ 3 ☐ 4 ☐ 5 ☐ 6 ☐ 7 ☐ 8 ☐ 9 ☐ 10 ☐ 11 ☐ 12 ☐ 13 ☐ 14 ☐ 15 ☐ 16 ☐ 17 ☐ 18 ☐ 19 ☐ 20 ☐ 21 ☐ 22 ☐ 23 ☐ 24 ☐ 25 ☐ 26 ☐ 27 ☐ 28 ☐ 29 ☐ 30 ☐ 31 ☐ 32 ☐ 33 ☐ 34 ☐ 35 ☐ 36 ☐ 37 ☐ 38 ☐ 39 ☐ 40 ☐ 41 ☐ 42 ☐ 43 ☐ 44 ☐ 45 ☐ 46 ☐ 47 ☐ 48 ☐ 49 ☐ 50 ☐ 51 ☐ 52 ☐ 53 ☐ 54 ☐ 55 ☐ 56 ☐ 57 ☐ 58 ☐ 59 ☐ 60 ☐ 61 ☐ 62 ☐ 63 ☐ 64 ☐ 65 ☐ 66

JEREMIAH ☐ 1 ☐ 2 ☐ 3 ☐ 4 ☐ 5 ☐ 6 ☐ 7 ☐ 8 ☐ 9 ☐ 10 ☐ 11 ☐ 12 ☐ 13 ☐ 14 ☐ 15 ☐ 16 ☐ 17 ☐ 18 ☐ 19 ☐ 20 ☐ 21 ☐ 22 ☐ 23 ☐ 24 ☐ 25 ☐ 26 ☐ 27 ☐ 28 ☐ 29 ☐ 30 ☐ 31 ☐ 32 ☐ 33 ☐ 34 ☐ 35 ☐ 36 ☐ 37 ☐ 38 ☐ 39 ☐ 40 ☐ 41 ☐ 42 ☐ 43 ☐ 44 ☐ 45 ☐ 46 ☐ 47 ☐ 48 ☐ 49 ☐ 50 ☐ 51 ☐ 52

LAMENTATIONS ☐ 1 ☐ 2 ☐ 3 ☐ 4 ☐ 5

EZEKIEL ☐ 1 ☐ 2 ☐ 3 ☐ 4 ☐ 5 ☐ 6 ☐ 7 ☐ 8 ☐ 9 ☐ 10 ☐ 11 ☐ 12 ☐ 13 ☐ 14 ☐ 15 ☐ 16 ☐ 17 ☐ 18 ☐ 19 ☐ 20 ☐ 21 ☐ 22 ☐ 23 ☐ 24 ☐ 25 ☐ 26 ☐ 27 ☐ 28 ☐ 29 ☐ 30 ☐ 31 ☐ 32 ☐ 33 ☐ 34 ☐ 35 ☐ 36 ☐ 37 ☐ 38 ☐ 39 ☐ 40 ☐ 41 ☐ 42 ☐ 43 ☐ 44 ☐ 45 ☐ 46 ☐ 47 ☐ 48

DANIEL ☐ 1 ☐ 2 ☐ 3 ☐ 4 ☐ 5 ☐ 6 ☐ 7 ☐ 8 ☐ 9 ☐ 10 ☐ 11 ☐ 12

HOSEA ☐ 1 ☐ 2 ☐ 3 ☐ 4 ☐ 5 ☐ 6 ☐ 7 ☐ 8 ☐ 9 ☐ 10 ☐ 11 ☐ 12 ☐ 13 ☐ 14

JOEL ☐ 1 ☐ 2 ☐ 3

AMOS ☐ 1 ☐ 2 ☐ 3 ☐ 4 ☐ 5 ☐ 6 ☐ 7 ☐ 8 ☐ 9

OBADIAH ☐ Obadiah

JONAH ☐ 1 ☐ 2 ☐ 3 ☐ 4

MICAH ☐ 1 ☐ 2 ☐ 3 ☐ 4 ☐ 5 ☐ 6 ☐ 7

NAHUM ☐ 1 ☐ 2 ☐ 3

HABAKKUK ☐ 1 ☐ 2 ☐ 3

ZEPHANIAH ☐ 1 ☐ 2 ☐ 3

HAGGAI ☐ 1 ☐ 2

ZECHARIAH ☐ 1 ☐ 2 ☐ 3 ☐ 4 ☐ 5 ☐ 6 ☐ 7 ☐ 8 ☐ 9 ☐ 10 ☐ 11 ☐ 12 ☐ 13 ☐ 14

MALACHI ☐ 1 ☐ 2 ☐ 3 ☐ 4

MATTHEW ☐ 1 ☐ 2 ☐ 3 ☐ 4 ☐ 5 ☐ 6 ☐ 7 ☐ 8 ☐ 9 ☐ 10 ☐ 11 ☐ 12 ☐ 13 ☐ 14 ☐ 15 ☐ 16 ☐ 17 ☐ 18 ☐ 19 ☐ 20 ☐ 21 ☐ 22 ☐ 23 ☐ 24 ☐ 25 ☐ 26 ☐ 27 ☐ 28

MARK ☐ 1 ☐ 2 ☐ 3 ☐ 4 ☐ 5 ☐ 6 ☐ 7 ☐ 8 ☐ 9 ☐ 10 ☐ 11 ☐ 12 ☐ 13 ☐ 14 ☐ 15 ☐ 16

LUKE ☐ 1 ☐ 2 ☐ 3 ☐ 4 ☐ 5 ☐ 6 ☐ 7 ☐ 8 ☐ 9 ☐ 10 ☐ 11 ☐ 12 ☐ 13 ☐ 14 ☐ 15 ☐ 16 ☐ 17 ☐ 18 ☐ 19 ☐ 20 ☐ 21 ☐ 22 ☐ 23 ☐ 24

JOHN ☐ 1 ☐ 2 ☐ 3 ☐ 4 ☐ 5 ☐ 6 ☐ 7 ☐ 8 ☐ 9 ☐ 10 ☐ 11 ☐ 12 ☐ 13 ☐ 14 ☐ 15 ☐ 16 ☐ 17 ☐ 18 ☐ 19 ☐ 20 ☐ 21

ACTS ☐ 1 ☐ 2 ☐ 3 ☐ 4 ☐ 5 ☐ 6 ☐ 7 ☐ 8 ☐ 9 ☐ 10 ☐ 11 ☐ 12 ☐ 13 ☐ 14 ☐ 15 ☐ 16 ☐ 17 ☐ 18 ☐ 19 ☐ 20 ☐ 21 ☐ 22 ☐ 23 ☐ 24 ☐ 25 ☐ 26 ☐ 27 ☐ 28

ROMANS ☐ 1 ☐ 2 ☐ 3 ☐ 4 ☐ 5 ☐ 6

☐7 ☐8 ☐9 ☐10 ☐11 ☐12 ☐13 ☐14 ☐15 ☐16

1 CORINTHIANS ☐1 ☐2 ☐3 ☐4 ☐5 ☐6 ☐7 ☐8 ☐9 ☐10 ☐11 ☐12 ☐13 ☐14 ☐15 ☐16

2 CORINTHIANS ☐1 ☐2 ☐3 ☐4 ☐5 ☐6 ☐7 ☐8 ☐9 ☐10 ☐11 ☐12 ☐13

GALATIANS ☐1 ☐2 ☐3 ☐4 ☐5 ☐6

EPHESIANS ☐1 ☐2 ☐3 ☐4 ☐5 ☐6

PHILIPPIANS ☐1 ☐2 ☐3 ☐4

COLOSSIANS ☐1 ☐2 ☐3 ☐4

1 THESSALONIANS ☐1 ☐2 ☐3 ☐4 ☐5

2 THESSALONIANS ☐1 ☐2 ☐3

1 TIMOTHY ☐1 ☐2 ☐3 ☐4 ☐5 ☐6

2 TIMOTHY ☐1 ☐2 ☐3 ☐4

TITUS ☐1 ☐2 ☐3

PHILEMON ☐ Philemon

HEBREWS ☐1 ☐2 ☐3 ☐4 ☐5 ☐6 ☐7 ☐8 ☐9 ☐10 ☐11 ☐12 ☐13

JAMES ☐1 ☐2 ☐3 ☐4 ☐5

1 PETER ☐1 ☐2 ☐3 ☐4 ☐5

2 PETER ☐1 ☐2 ☐3

1 JOHN ☐1 ☐2 ☐3 ☐4 ☐5

2 JOHN ☐ 2 John

3 JOHN ☐ 3 John

JUDE ☐ Jude

REVELATION ☐1 ☐2 ☐3 ☐4 ☐5 ☐6 ☐7 ☐8 ☐9 ☐10 ☐11 ☐12 ☐13 ☐14 ☐15 ☐16 ☐17 ☐18 ☐19 ☐20 ☐21 ☐22

Bible Truth INDEX

This subject index will help you find just where you need to look to find information about a particular topic that relates to Bible Truths and theology. Look through the list, and you'll probably find something you want to look up and read. This index tracks the "To the Point" feature and the "We Believe" feature.

Teen Life INDEX

Ever wish you could get God on your cell phone? This **Teen Life Index** is the next best thing. Pick any topic. Go to the page indicated. Help is there, either in the "Instant Access" feature or in the "Dear Jordan" feature (which is indicated in **Bold**).

You're special
934

Youth group
203, 1521

Zits
4, **346**

NIV TEEN STUDY BIBLE

Project Management and Editorial: Carol Postma

Project Management and Editorial (first and second editions): Catherine DeVries

Project Art Direction and Cover Design: Sarah Molegraaf

Interior and Tip-In Page Design: Gayle Raymer

Typesetting Management and Typesetting: Nancy Wilson, Mark Sheeres

Typesetting: Sherri Hoffman, Katherine Lloyd, Matthew VanZomeren, Kirk Luttrell

Interior Proofreading: Peachtree Editorial and Proofreading Services, Peachtree City, GA

Production Management: Scott Hibbs

NIV TEEN STUDY BIBLE

Project Management and Editorial: Carol Postma

Project Management and Editorial (first and second editions): Catherine DeVries

Project Art Direction and Cover Design: Sarah Molegraaf

Interior and Tip-In Page Design: Gayle Raymer

Typesetting Management and Typesetting: Nancy Wilson
Mark Sheeres

Typesetting: Sherri Hoffman
Katherine Lloyd
Matthew VanZomeren
Kirk Luttrell

Interior Proofreading: Peachtree Editorial and
Proofreading Services,
Peachtree City, GA

Production Management: Scott Hibbs

Guarantee

Thank you for choosing a Zondervan product. We want to make sure you're satisfied with the quality of your purchase. We stand behind every product we make; that's why we guarantee each one for a lifetime against manufacturing defects. For more information on our quality guarantee and product care instructions, visit us at www.zondervan.com/guarantee.

WORLD OF THE PATRIARCHS

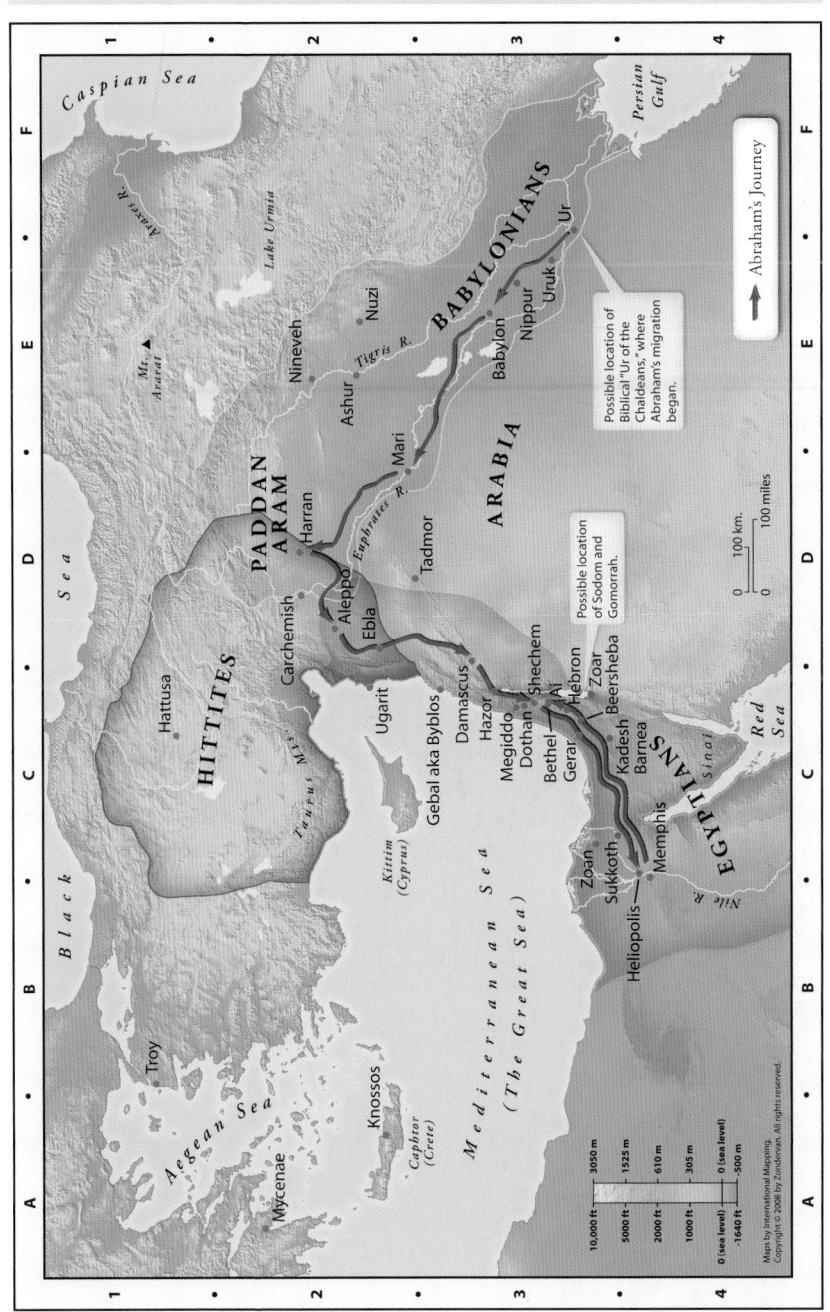

Possible location of Biblical "Ur of the Chaldeans," where Abraham's migration began.

Possible location of Sodom and Gomorrah.

→ Abraham's Journey

Caspian Sea

Persian Gulf

Araxes R.

Lake Urmia

Mt. Ararat

BABYLONIANS

Nineveh

Nuzi

Ashur

Tigris R.

Babylon

Nippur

Uruk

Ur

Mari

Euphrates R.

ARABIA

PADDAN ARAM

Harran

Tadmor

Black Sea

HITTITES

Hattusa

Taurus Mts.

Carchemish

Aleppo

Ebla

Ugarit

Kittim (Cyprus)

Damascus

Hazor

Megiddo

Dothan

Gebal aka Byblos

Shechem

Ai

Bethel

Hebron

Gerar

Zoar

Beersheba

Kadesh Barnea

Red Sea

Sinai

EGYPTIANS

Zoan

Sukkoth

Memphis

Heliopolis

Nile R.

Troy

Knossos

Caphtor (Crete)

Mycenae

Aegean Sea

Mediterranean Sea (The Great Sea)

100 km.
100 miles

0

10,000 ft — 3050 m
5000 ft — 1525 m
2000 ft — 610 m
1000 ft — 305 m
0 (sea level) — 0 (sea level)
-1640 ft — -500 m

Maps by International Mapping
Copyright © 2008 by Zondervan. All rights reserved.

EXODUS AND CONQUEST OF CANAAN

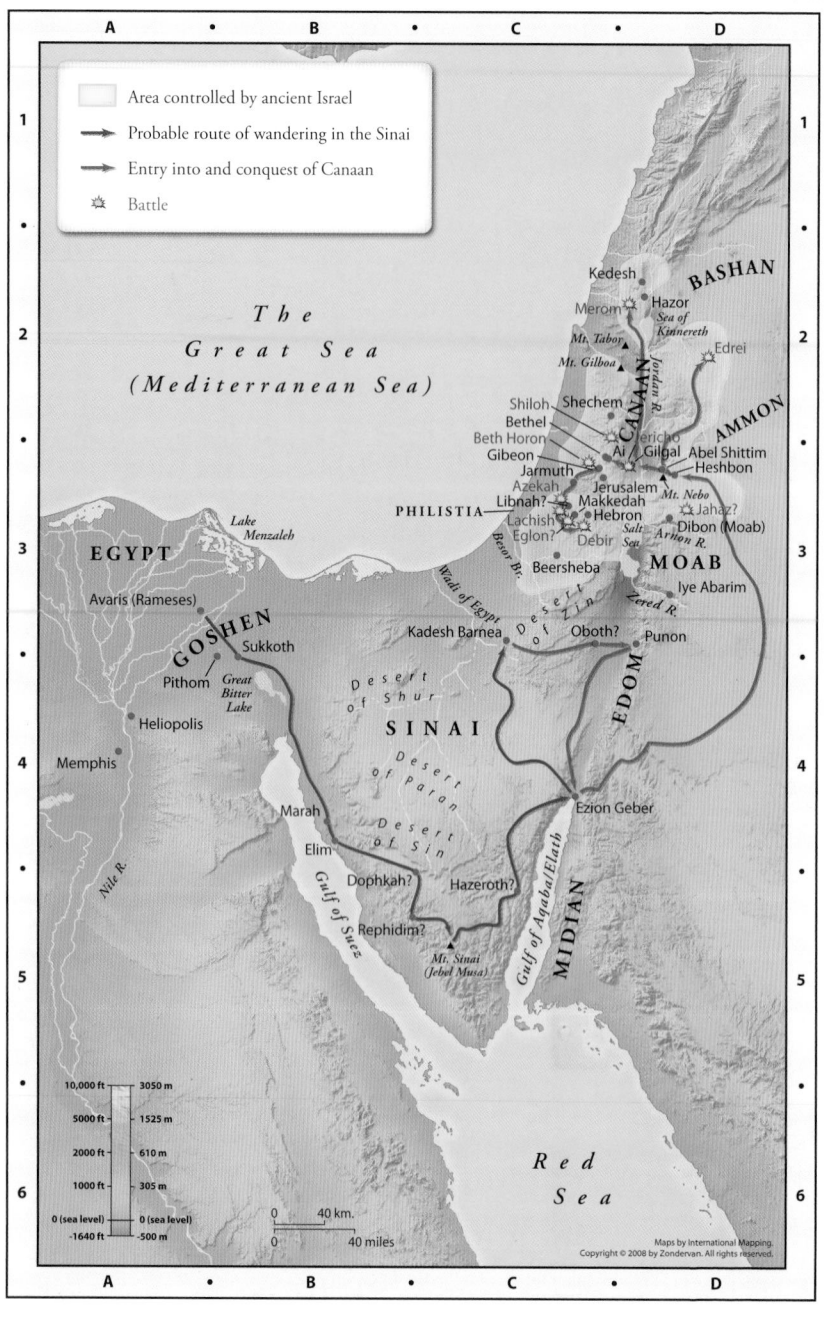

Area controlled by ancient Israel
Probable route of wandering in the Sinai
Entry into and conquest of Canaan
Battle

The Great Sea (Mediterranean Sea)

Kedesh
BASHAN
Merom
Hazor
Sea of Kinnereth
Edrei
Mt. Tabor
Mt. Gilboa
Jordan R.
CANAAN
AMMON
Shiloh
Shechem
Bethel
Beth Horon
Jericho
Gibeon
Ai
Gilgal
Abel Shittim
Heshbon
Jarmuth
Azekah
Jerusalem
Mt. Nebo
Libnah?
Makkedah
Jahaz?
PHILISTIA
Lachish
Hebron
Salt
Dibon (Moab)
Eglon?
Debir
Sea
Arnon R.
Besor Br.
Beersheba
MOAB
Iye Abarim
Zered R.
EGYPT
Lake Menzaleh
Wadi of Egypt
Desert of Zin
Avaris (Rameses)
Kadesh Barnea
Oboth?
Punon
GOSHEN
Sukkoth
EDOM
Pithom
Great Bitter Lake
Desert of Shur
Heliopolis
SINAI
Memphis
Desert of Paran
Marah
Ezion Geber
Desert of Sin
Elim
Nile R.
Dophkah?
Hazeroth?
Gulf of Suez
Rephidim?
MIDIAN
Gulf of Aqaba/Elath
Mt. Sinai (Jebel Musa)

Red Sea

10,000 ft — 3050 m
5000 ft — 1525 m
2000 ft — 610 m
1000 ft — 305 m
0 (sea level) — 0 (sea level)
-1640 ft — -500 m

0 — 40 km.
0 — 40 miles

LAND OF THE TWELVE TRIBES

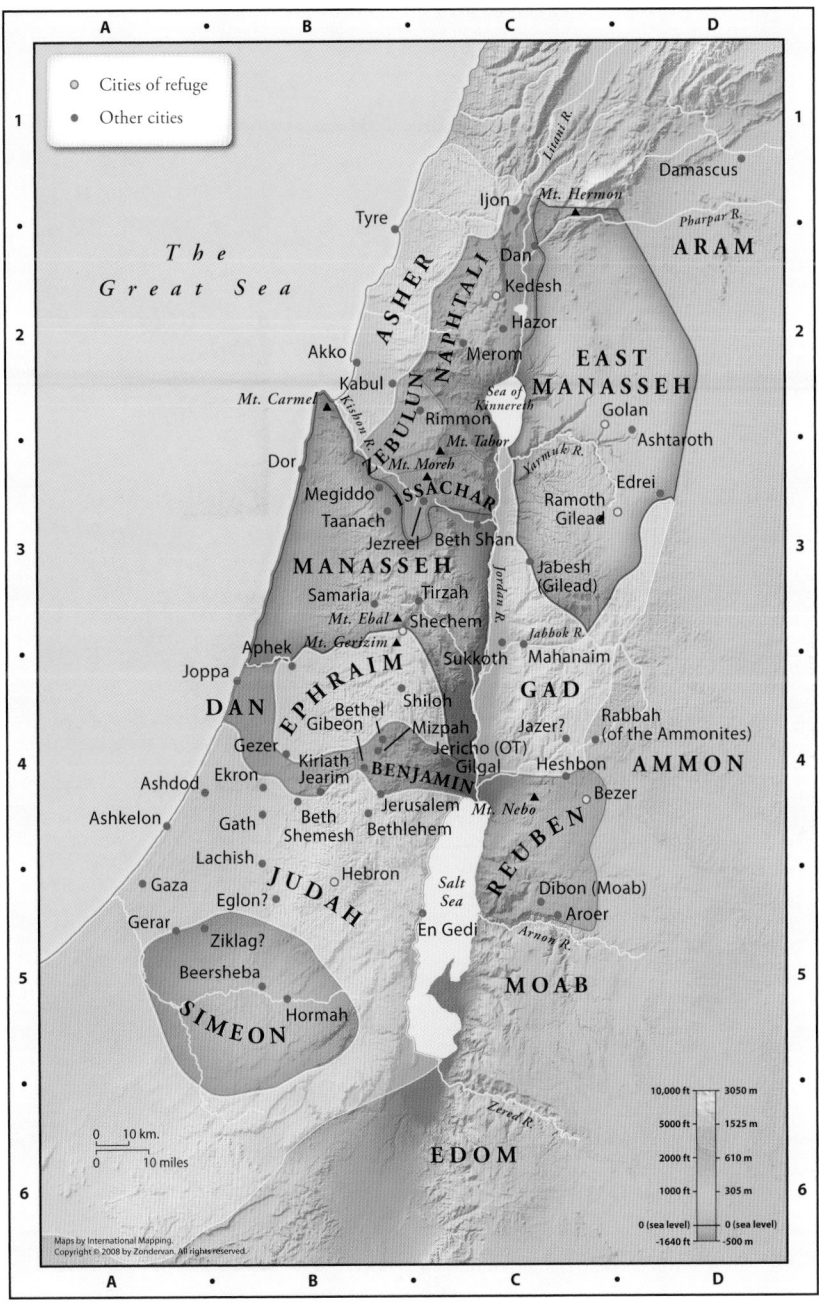

Cities of refuge

Other cities

Damascus

Litani R.

Tyre Ijon *Mt. Hermon* *Pharpar R.*

ARAM

The Great Sea

Dan

Kedesh

ASHER NAPHTALI Hazor

Akko Merom

Kabul **EAST**

Mt. Carmel *Kishon R.* ZEBULUN Rimmon **MANASSEH**

Sea of Kinnereth Golan

Dor *Mt. Tabor* *Mt. Moreh* Ashtaroth

ISSACHAR *Yarmuk R.*

Megiddo Edrei

Taanach Ramoth (Gilead)

Jezreel Beth Shan

MANASSEH *Jordan R.* Jabesh (Gilead)

Samaria Tirzah

Mt. Ebal Shechem *Jabbok R.*

Aphek *Mt. Gerizim* Sukkoth Mahanaim

Joppa EPHRAIM **GAD**

DAN Shiloh

Bethel Jazer? Rabbah (of the Ammonites)

Gezer Gibeon Mizpah

Kirlath Jericho (OT) Heshbon **AMMON**

Ashdod Ekron Jearim **BENJAMIN** Gilgal

Jerusalem *Mt. Nebo* Bezer

Ashkelon Gath Beth Bethlehem

Shemesh REUBEN

Lachish Dibon (Moab)

Gaza JUDAH Hebron *Salt Sea* Aroer

Eglon?

Gerar *Arnon R.*

Ziklag? En Gedi

Beersheba **MOAB**

SIMEON Hormah

Zered R.

0 10 km.
0 10 miles

10,000 ft	3050 m
5000 ft	1525 m
2000 ft	610 m
1000 ft	305 m
0 (sea level)	0 (sea level)
-1640 ft	-500 m

EDOM

KINGDOM OF DAVID AND SOLOMON

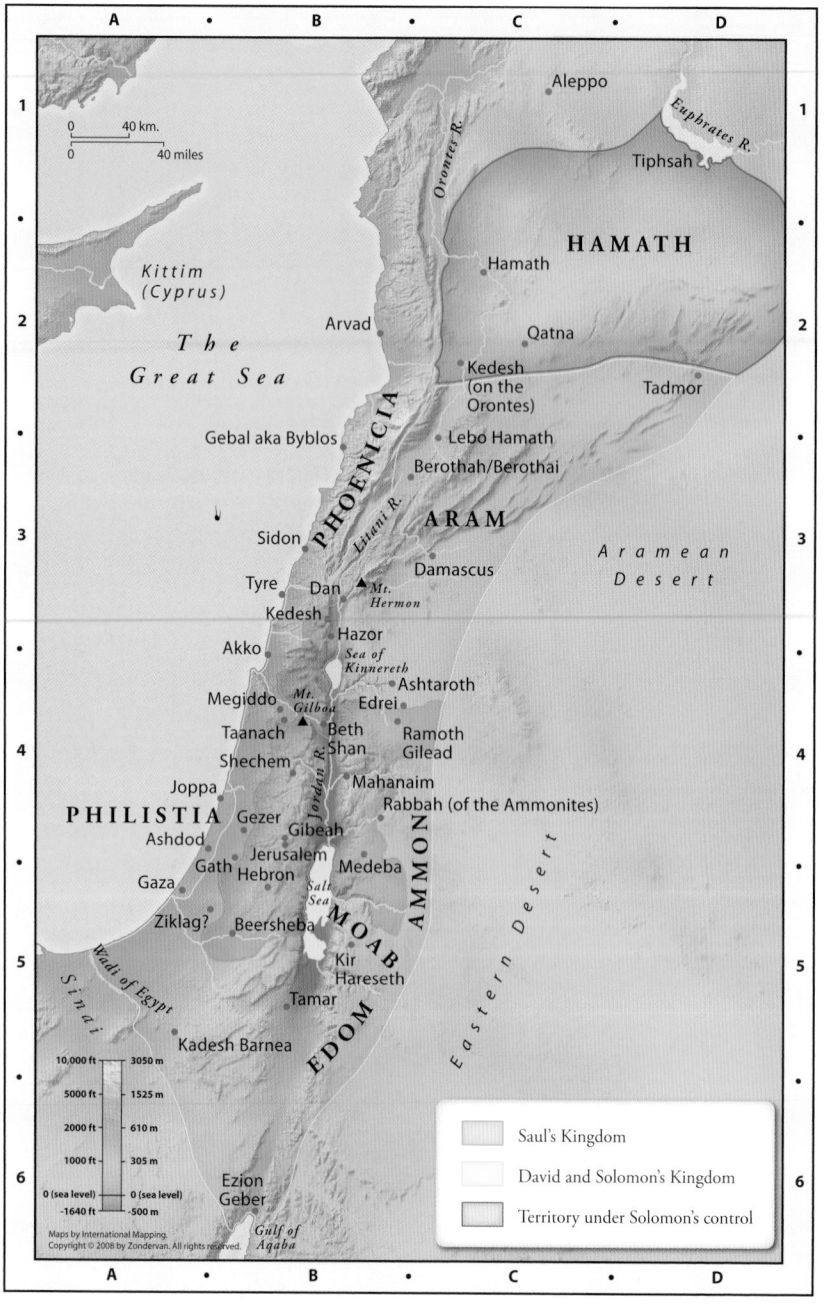

Aleppo

Euphrates R.

Orontes R.

Tiphsah

HAMATH

Hamath

Kittim
(Cyprus)

Arvad

Qatna

The
Great Sea

Kedesh
(on the
Orontes)

Tadmor

Gebal aka Byblos

Lebo Hamath

Berothah/Berothai

PHOENICIA

Litani R.

ARAM

Aramean
Desert

Sidon

Damascus

Tyre   Dan   Mt.
Hermon

Kedesh

Hazor

Akko

Sea of
Kinnereth

Ashtaroth

Megiddo   Mt.
Gilboa   Edrei

Taanach   Beth   Ramoth
Shan   Gilead

Shechem

Jordan R.

Joppa

Mahanaim

PHILISTIA   Gezer   Gibeah   Rabbah (of the Ammonites)

Ashdod

Jerusalem

Gath   Hebron   Medeba

Gaza

Salt
Sea

Eastern Desert

AMMON

Ziklag?   Beersheba

MOAB

Wadi of Egypt

Sinai

Kir
Hareseth

Tamar

EDOM

Kadesh Barnea

10,000 ft — 3050 m

5000 ft — 1525 m

2000 ft — 610 m

1000 ft — 305 m

0 (sea level) — 0 (sea level)

-1640 ft — -500 m

Ezion
Geber

Gulf of
Aqaba

0   40 km.
0   40 miles

Saul's Kingdom

David and Solomon's Kingdom

Territory under Solomon's control

JESUS' MINISTRY

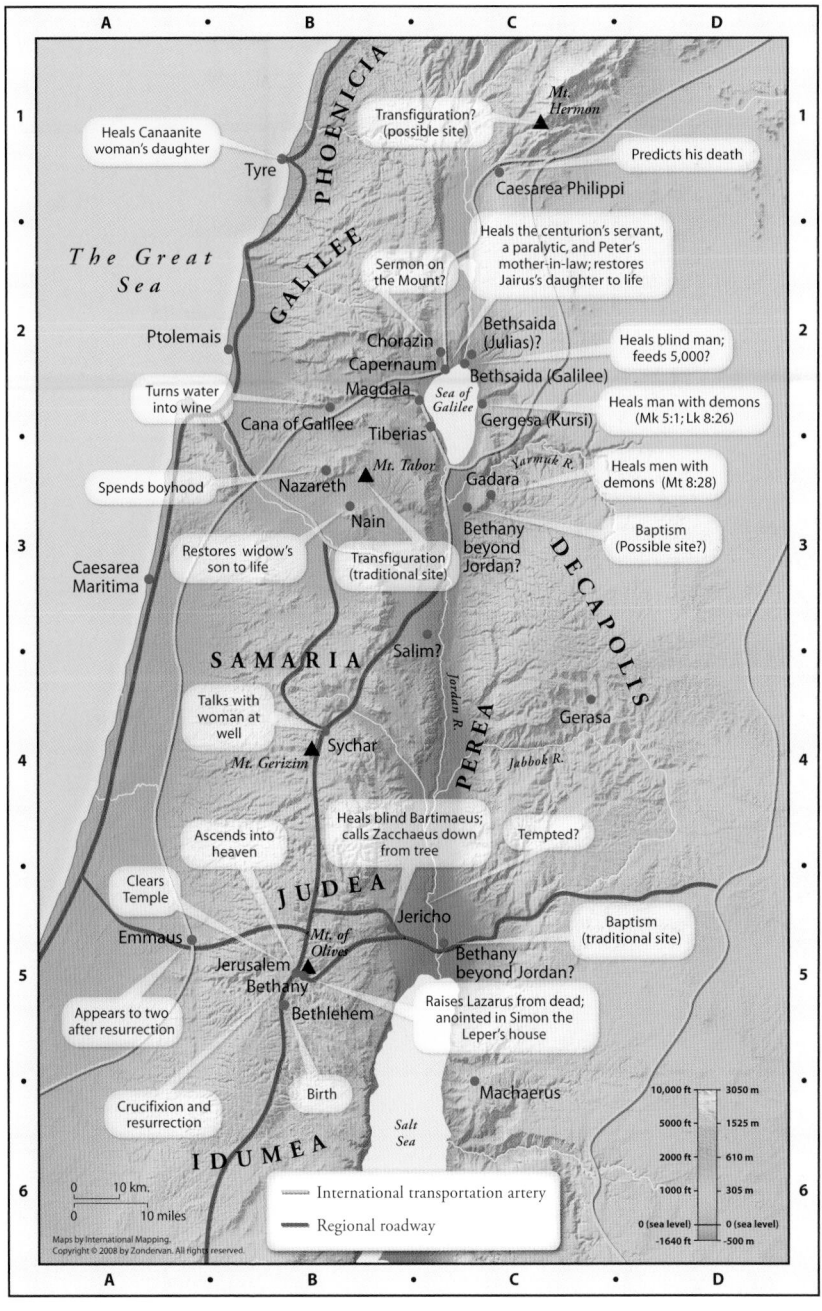

Heals Canaanite woman's daughter

Transfiguration? (possible site)

Mt. Hermon

Predicts his death

Tyre

PHOENICIA

Caesarea Philippi

The Great Sea

GALILEE

Sermon on the Mount?

Heals the centurion's servant, a paralytic, and Peter's mother-in-law; restores Jairus's daughter to life

Ptolemais

Chorazin

Bethsaida (Julias)?

Heals blind man; feeds 5,000?

Capernaum

Turns water into wine

Magdala

Bethsaida (Galilee)

Sea of Galilee

Heals man with demons (Mk 5:1; Lk 8:26)

Cana of Galilee

Tiberias

Gergesa (Kursi)

Yarmuk R.

Heals men with demons (Mt 8:28)

Spends boyhood

Nazareth

Mt. Tabor

Gadara

Nain

Baptism (Possible site?)

Restores widow's son to life

Transfiguration (traditional site)

Bethany beyond Jordan?

DECAPOLIS

Caesarea Maritima

SAMARIA

Salim?

Jordan R.

Talks with woman at well

Gerasa

PEREA

Mt. Gerizim

Sychar

Jabbok R.

Ascends into heaven

Heals blind Bartimaeus; calls Zacchaeus down from tree

Tempted?

Clears Temple

JUDEA

Emmaus

Jericho

Baptism (traditional site)

Mt. of Olives

Jerusalem

Bethany

Bethany beyond Jordan?

Appears to two after resurrection

Bethlehem

Raises Lazarus from dead; anointed in Simon the Leper's house

Crucifixion and resurrection

Birth

Salt Sea

Machaerus

10,000 ft — 3050 m

5000 ft — 1525 m

2000 ft — 610 m

IDUMEA

1000 ft — 305 m

0 (sea level) — 0 (sea level)

-1640 ft — -500 m

0   10 km.
0   10 miles

International transportation artery

Regional roadway

Maps by International Mapping.
Copyright © 2008 by Zondervan. All rights reserved.

PAUL'S MISSIONARY JOURNEYS

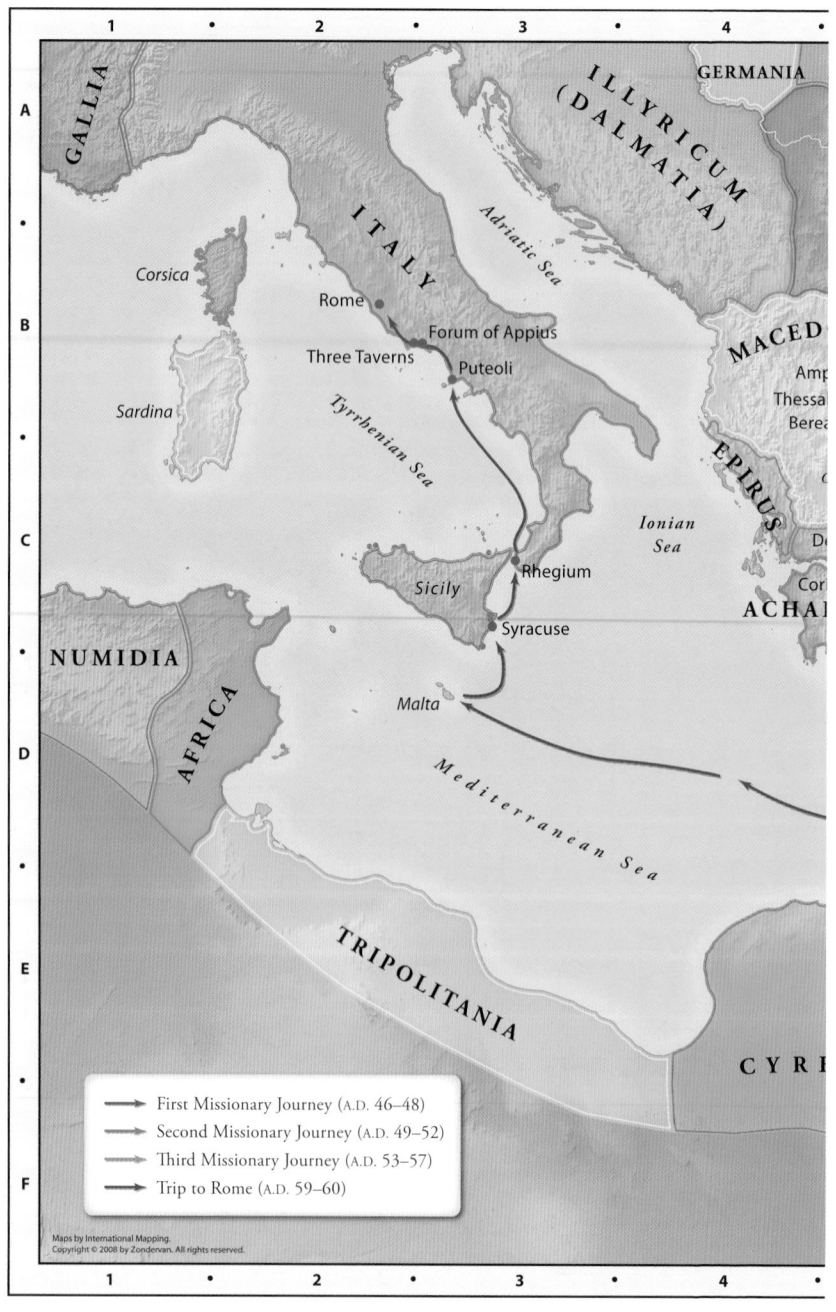

First Missionary Journey (A.D. 46–48)
Second Missionary Journey (A.D. 49–52)
Third Missionary Journey (A.D. 53–57)
Trip to Rome (A.D. 59–60)

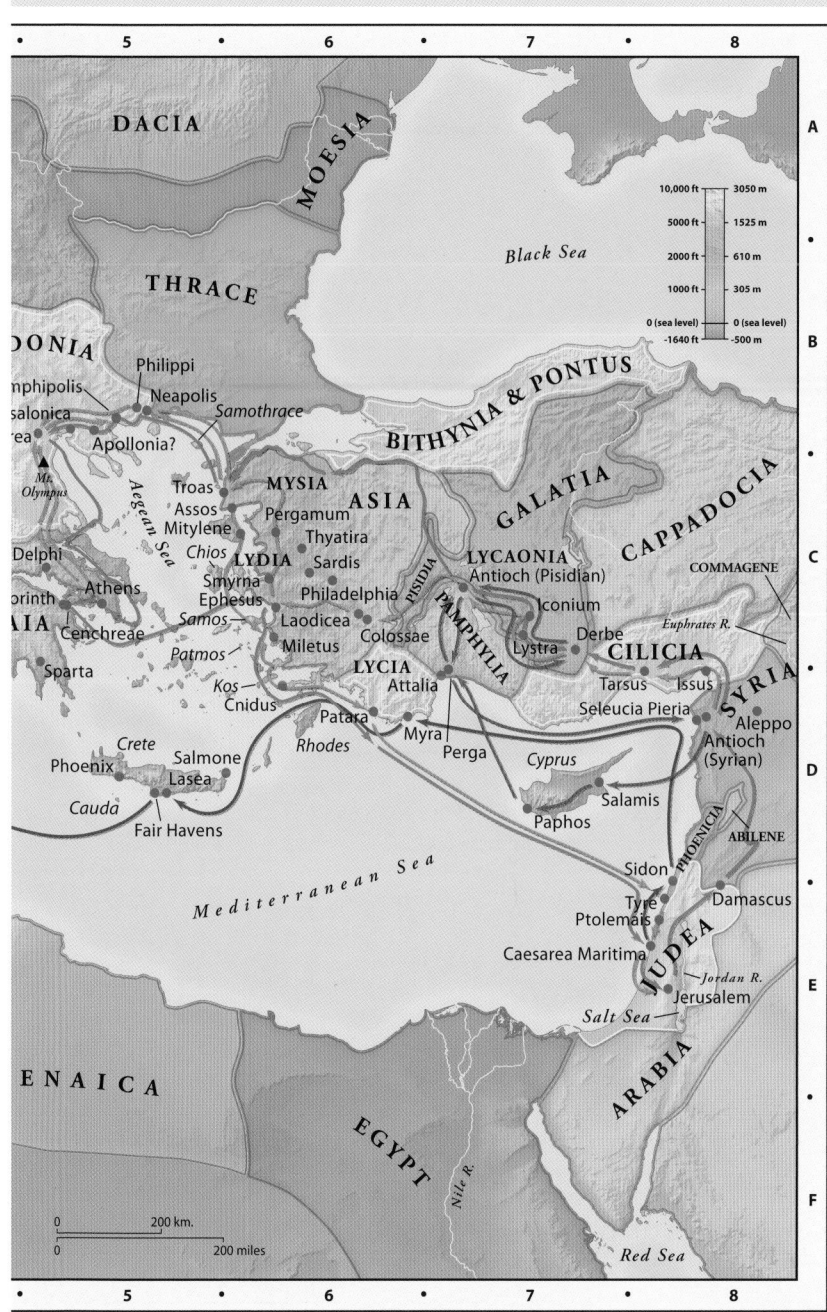

Column headers: 5, 6, 7, 8

Row labels: A, B, C, D, E, F

DACIA

MOESIA

THRACE

Black Sea

10,000 ft	3050 m
5000 ft	1525 m
2000 ft	610 m
1000 ft	305 m
0 (sea level)	0 (sea level)
-1640 ft	-500 m

BITHYNIA & PONTUS

...DONIA

...mphipolis

Philippi

...salonica

Neapolis

...rea

Samothrace

Apollonia?

Mt. Olympus

Troas

MYSIA

ASIA

GALATIA

CAPPADOCIA

Assos

Pergamum

Mitylene

Thyatira

COMMAGENE

Aegean Sea

Chios

LYDIA

Sardis

LYCAONIA

Delphi

Smyrna

Philadelphia

Antioch (Pisidian)

Athens

Ephesus

PISIDIA

Iconium

Euphrates R.

...rinth

Samos

Laodicea

Colossae

PAMPHYLIA

Lystra

Derbe

CILICIA

...IA

Cenchreae

Miletus

LYCIA

Tarsus

Issus

SYRIA

Sparta

Patmos

Attalia

Seleucia Pieria

Aleppo

Kos

Cnidus

Patara

Myra

Perga

Antioch (Syrian)

Crete

Rhodes

Cyprus

Phoenix

Salmone

PHOENICIA

ABILENE

Phoenix

Lasea

Cauda

Fair Havens

Salamis

Paphos

Sidon

Damascus

Mediterranean Sea

Tyre

Ptolemais

Caesarea Maritima

JUDEA

Jordan R.

...ENAICA

Jerusalem

Salt Sea

ARABIA

EGYPT

Nile R.

Red Sea

| 0 | 200 km. |
| 0 | 200 miles |

JERUSALEM IN THE TIME OF JESUS

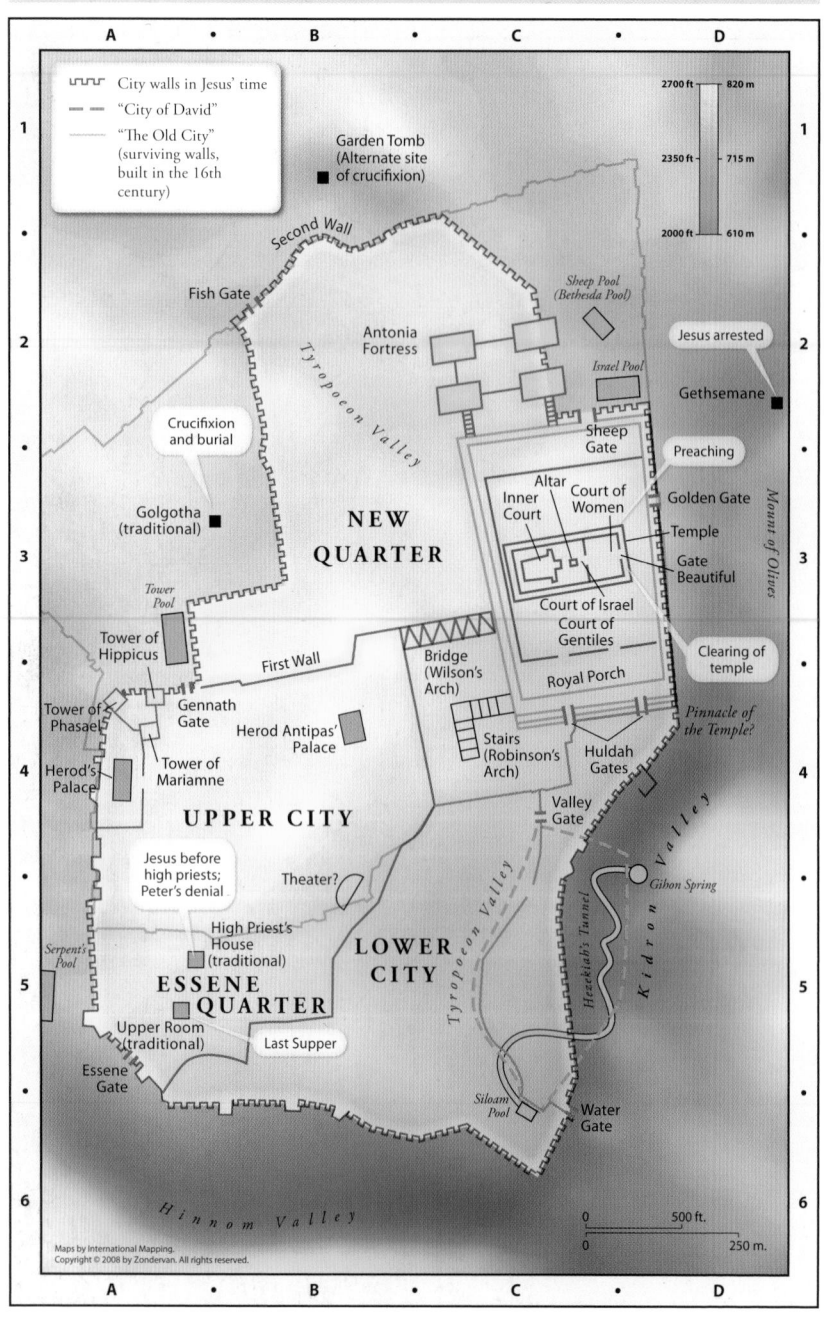

A • B • C • D

City walls in Jesus' time
"City of David"
"The Old City" (surviving walls, built in the 16th century)

Garden Tomb (Alternate site of crucifixion)

2700 ft — 820 m
2350 ft — 715 m
2000 ft — 610 m

Second Wall

Fish Gate

Sheep Pool (Bethesda Pool)

Antonia Fortress

Israel Pool

Jesus arrested

Gethsemane

Sheep Gate

Preaching

Crucifixion and burial

Altar
Inner Court
Court of Women

Golden Gate

Temple

Golgotha (traditional)

NEW QUARTER

Gate Beautiful

Court of Israel
Court of Gentiles

Mount of Olives

Tower Pool

Tower of Hippicus

First Wall

Bridge (Wilson's Arch)

Royal Porch

Clearing of temple

Tower of Phasael

Gennath Gate

Herod Antipas' Palace

Pinnacle of the Temple?

Stairs (Robinson's Arch)

Huldah Gates

Herod's Palace

Tower of Mariamne

UPPER CITY

Valley Gate

Jesus before high priests; Peter's denial

Theater?

Gihon Spring

Serpents' Pool

High Priest's House (traditional)

LOWER CITY

ESSENE QUARTER

Hezekiah's Tunnel

Kidron Valley

Upper Room (traditional)

Last Supper

Essene Gate

Siloam Pool

Water Gate

Tyropoeon Valley

Hinnom Valley

0   500 ft.
0   250 m.

Maps by International Mapping.
Copyright © 2008 by Zondervan. All rights reserved.

A • B • C • D